AMERICAN NATIONAL BIOGRAPHY

AMERICAN
NATIONAL BIOGRAPHY

Published under the auspices of the
AMERICAN COUNCIL OF LEARNED SOCIETIES

General Editors

John A. Garraty

Mark C. Carnes

VOLUME 12

OXFORD UNIVERSITY PRESS
New York   1999   Oxford

OXFORD UNIVERSITY PRESS

Oxford New York
Athens Auckland Bangkok Bogotá
Buenos Aires Calcutta Cape Town Chennai
Dar es Salaam Delhi Florence Hong Kong Istanbul
Karachi Kuala Lumpur Madrid Melbourne Mexico City
Mumbai Nairobi Paris São Paulo Singapore
Taipei Tokyo Toronto Warsaw
and associated companies in
Berlin Ibadan

Published by Oxford University Press, Inc.,
198 Madison Avenue, New York, New York 10016
http://www.oup-usa.org

Funding for this publication was provided in part by
the Andrew W. Mellon Foundation, the Rockefeller Foundation,
and the National Endowment for the Humanities,
a federal agency.

Library of Congress Cataloging-in-Publication Data

American national biography / general editors, John A. Garraty, Mark C. Carnes
p.   cm.
"Published under the auspices of the American Council of Learned Societies."
Includes bibliographical references and index.
1. United States—Biography—Dictionaries.   I. Garraty, John Arthur,
1920– .   II. Carnes, Mark C. (Mark Christopher), 1950– .
III. American Council of Learned Societies.
CT213.A68   1998   98-20826   920.073—dc21   CIP
ISBN 0-19-520635-5 (set)
ISBN 0-19-512791-9 (vol. 12)

Printing (last digit): 9 8 7 6 5 4 3 2 1

Printed in the United States of America
on acid-free paper

J

CONTINUED

JEREMIAH, Thomas (?–18 Aug. 1775), free black pilot and fisherman who was executed for allegedly fomenting a slave uprising, was born a slave to unknown parentage. Although his birthplace is unknown, Jeremiah lived his adult life in Charleston, South Carolina. By the middle of the eighteenth century, he had somehow secured his freedom. He married, but when and to whom are a mystery. There were no known children. At least by the early 1750s, Jeremiah worked as a harbor pilot. In 1755 a newspaper report attributed an accident to the "Carelessness of a Negro Pilot (Jerry)." But Jeremiah earned more respect for his skill and courage as a firefighter. Indeed, in 1768 he capitalized on his good reputation to establish himself as a fisherman, offering fresh fish daily to urban residents. He became a prosperous member of the Charleston community and perhaps one of the richest free blacks in prerevolutionary North America.

Even his occasional reverses were more notable for his ability to overcome them. Thus, in 1771 Jeremiah was convicted of assaulting a white ship captain—a bold act for a free black. Sentenced to one hour in the stocks and ten lashes, Jeremiah escaped punishment through an executive pardon. He obviously had influence in high places.

Jeremiah's continued economic success was remarkable. Lord William Campbell, who became governor of South Carolina in the summer of 1775, described him as a man "of considerable property, one of the most valuable and useful men in his way in this province." Even his detractors noted his economic standing. Henry Laurens, a prominent Charlestonian merchant and patriot, thought Jeremiah "a forward fellow, puffed up by prosperity, ruined by Luxury & debauchery & grown to an amazing pitch of vanity & ambition." By the time of his death, Jeremiah had apparently become a slaveholder and was reputed to be worth more than £1,000 sterling.

As the heated passions of the revolutionary crisis reached a fever pitch in the summer of 1775, Jeremiah became one of its victims. In early June a special committee of South Carolina's Provincial Congress held hearings to investigate reports of insurrectionary plots. Jeremiah was arrested and on 11 August faced trial in Charleston before a court of two justices of the peace and five freeholders on charges of plotting an insurrection and of offering assistance to the Royal Navy. There were at least three witnesses. Sambo, his main accuser, reported that Jeremiah predicted an imminent "great war" that would "help the poor negroes." Another witness, Jemmy, his brother-in-law, claimed that Jeremiah had asked him to convey guns to a runaway slave. Jemmy later retracted his testimony and declared "Jerry" innocent, but Sambo would not recant. Jeremiah was convicted, hanged, and burned.

Jeremiah's death sentence was controversial, as he became a pawn between patriots and Loyalists. He had many friends among free blacks, a number of whom tried to save him. Both the governor and his secretary, as well as Charleston's two Anglican clergymen, were his sympathizers. His supporters tried legal strategies, questioning the validity of a free black's trial under the Negro Act of 1740. On the other side, Laurens, president of the Council of Safety, was convinced of Jeremiah's guilt. Other whites predicted a racial war unless Jeremiah was executed.

Whether Jeremiah actually plotted an insurrection against the state is unclear. He protested his innocence to the last; many prominent whites, including the governor who futilely pardoned him, believed him; but there was damning black testimony and apparent perjury from Jeremiah himself. In a real sense, however, Jeremiah's fall can be attributed to his unusually elevated and precarious position in Charleston society. Either this induced him to envisage a role for blacks, one in which he would have as Jemmy claimed, "the Chief Command" in the imminent war between Britain and America, or it made him the best available scapegoat for patriot forces who wanted both to intimidate other black harbor pilots and to promote military preparedness. Either way, Jeremiah was a victim of his own success.

• The best account of Jeremiah's career can be found in Robert M. Weir, *Colonial South Carolina: A History* (1983). Jeremiah's place in the revolutionary crisis is explicated in Peter H. Wood, "'Taking Care of Business' in Revolutionary South Carolina: Republicanism and the Slave Society," in *The Southern Experience in the American Revolution*, ed. Jeffrey J. Crow and Larry E. Tise (1978), pp. 268–93, and Sylvia R. Frey, *Water from the Rock: Black Resistance in a Revolutionary Age* (1991). The urban context of Jeremiah's life is explored in Philip D. Morgan, "Black Life in Eighteenth-Century Charleston," *Perspectives in American History*, 1 (1984): 187–232.

PHILIP D. MORGAN

JERITZA, Maria (6 Oct. 1887–10 July 1982), operatic soprano, was born Marie Marcellina Jedlitzková in Brünn, Moravia; she became a naturalized American citizen in 1943. (Her parents' identities are unknown.) Jeritza began her serious vocal studies with Professor Auspitzer in Brünn at the age of fourteen. She gained stage experience singing in the chorus of the local opera company, and she later studied with the legendary Marcella Sembrich in New York City. Shortly after her marriage in 1907 to factory owner Fritz Wiener, she earned her first solo experience, singing operetta roles at the Münchner Künstlertheater (1908–1910).

Jeritza's official operatic debut was as Elsa in Wagner's *Lohengrin* at the Stadttheater Olmütz in 1910. In 1911 she appeared at the Volksoper in Vienna, where she received rave reviews for her portrayal of Stefana in Umberto Giordano's *Sibirien*, and she also participated in the world premiere of Wilhelm Kienzl's *Der Kuhreigen* in the role of Blanchefleur. She quickly became one of the most celebrated prima donnas of the era, and Max Reinhardt's Munich production of *La Belle Hélène* added to her growing reputation as a magnetic singer. Cast as Rosalinde in *Die Fledermaus* during the 1912 summer season at Bad Ischl, where the emperor had his summer residence, she caught the attention of Franz Josef and, apparently at his request, was contracted by the Imperial Opera in Vienna in 1912. Jeritza made her debut there in March 1912 as Chrysis in Max von Oberleithner's *Aphrodite*. Her selection as Imperial and Royal Chamber Singer to the Court was the last imperial appointment at the Court Opera before the last Habsburg emperor, Karl I, abdicated and Austria became a republic in 1918.

At Richard Strauss's request Jeritza appeared in the title role in the world premiere of his *Ariadne auf Naxos*, which was staged in Stuttgart in October 1912 under the direction of Max Reinhardt. In Vienna four years later she repeated the role in the revised version, with Lotte Lehmann cast as the Composer; both artists created a sensation. In October 1913, when Jeritza sang Minnie in the Vienna premiere of Giacomo Puccini's *La Fanciulla del West*, she became one of that composer's favorites. Puccini was so impressed that he personally staged her in the role of Giorgetta (*Il Tabarro*). Representatives from the Metropolitan Opera in New York heard her as Elisabeth in *Tannhäuser* in 1914 and would have invited her to America had World War I not prevented her from leaving Europe. In 1919, a year after starring in Strauss's *Salome*, she portrayed the Empress in the premiere of his *Die Frau ohne Schatten* in Vienna, which signaled the rebirth of the former Hofoper as the Staatsoper following the war. Also in 1919 Jeritza married again, this time to Leopold, Freiherr von Popper. She was the favorite singer of both Richard Strauss and his librettist Hugo von Hofmannsthal, and they had her in mind for a number of roles, including ones in *Die ägyptische Helena* and *Intermezzo*; but she declined both offers. She remained a principal artist with the Vienna Staatsoper until 1935. Her major guest appearances took place in Berlin, Budapest, London, Milan, Moscow, Paris, Prague, and Stockholm.

Between 1921 and 1932 she was also a principal artist with the Metropolitan Opera in New York, where she was the highest paid artist on the roster. A reigning diva after the early retirement of Geraldine Farrar in 1922, she shared top billing with the acclaimed Rosa Ponselle, and she was unquestionably one of the great singing actresses of the first half of the twentieth century. Critics called her "the Duse of opera." She made her Met debut on 19 November 1921 as Marietta in the first American production of Erich Wolfgang Korngold's *Die tote Stadt*, a role composed especially for her, which she had introduced in Vienna at the start of the year. Her Tosca several weeks later was a dramatic tour de force that had the critics recalling the stage magnetism of Sarah Bernhardt. The Metropolitan's general manager, Giulio Gatti-Casazza, wrote in his memoirs: "The theatre broke out in a demonstration the equal of which I can scarcely recall. The American public was completely conquered. For a good many years it was lavished all its favor on this artist."

In the intense competition for opening nights at the Met, Jeritza prevailed in the 1922 season as Tosca, the 1923 season as Thaïs, and the 1927 season as Princess Turandot, a role she had sung at the American premiere in November 1926. Her assignments at the Met ranged from the Wagnerian roles of Elisabeth, Elsa, Senta, and Sieglinde to Carmen, Santuzza, Octavian, and Thaïs. She also sang Jenůfa, a portrait that the composer, Leoš Janáček, considered his ideal; Turandot, a choice that was advocated by Puccini himself; and Helena in Strauss's *Die ägyptische Helena* in 1928. The range of her roles reflects the fact that Jeritza was one of the greatest box office draws in the 1920s. Appearing in a total of twenty different operas during her thirteen seasons at the Met, she sang 293 performances in New York and fifty-six on tour. Besides her great physical beauty and lovely voice, she brought a breath of realism to her portrayals. Her "farewell" appearance at age sixty-four as Rosalinde in *Die Fledermaus* was a benefit in support of Rudolf Bing's inaugural season as general manager.

In addition to her operatic and recital activities, for which she received the Austrian Order of Knighthood, first class (1935), she was actively involved in films during the 1930s. In 1935 she divorced her second husband and married motion picture executive Winfield R. Sheehan, who died in 1945. Her fourth marriage, in 1948, was to businessman Irving Patrick Seery, who died in 1966. Following World War II she was deeply involved in efforts to rebuild the Vienna Staatsoper, which reopened in 1955. She kept tight control of her professional and personal destiny, accepting engagements only when the terms were highly favorable. Throughout her career her performances elicited strong reactions, and critics were divided in their evaluations of her voice, her acting, and her artistic presence. Her voice did not record well, and, in her commitment to realistic character portrayals, her singing often lost precision. Her career was more akin to that of a movie star, and rumors of her many amorous adventures attracted widespread attention. A risqué novel by Dietrich Arndt, *Bagage: Reigen um eine Sängerin* (1931), was written about her. Much has been said about the personal stamp she gave to particular operatic scenes: her incredible use of the staircase in Turandot's riddle scene; Tosca's "Vissi d'arte," sung in a prone position; and Elisabeth's "Dich teure Halle, Grüß ich wieder," sung with her back to the audience. No one else of her generation could match her hypnotizing stage presence, and she was the favorite of her considerable public.

Jeritza died in Orange, New Jersey. In December 1984 the only known copy of the manuscript of Richard Strauss's last song, dated November 1948, was auctioned at Sotheby's in New York as a part of her estate. A setting of "Malven" by the Swiss poet Betty Knobel, the manuscript was inscribed by the composer "To beloved Maria—this last rose!"

• The most comprehensive bibliography can be found in Robert H. Cowden, *Concert and Opera Singers: A Bibliography of Biographical Materials* (1985), revised and expanded as *Singers of the World* (1994). Her autobiography, *Sunlight and Song: A Singer's Life* (1924; repr. 1977), is largely a public relations exercise of little factual importance. A valuable study of her career is Robert Werba, *Maria Jeritza Primadonna des Verismo* (1981). See also Rodolfo Celletti, *Le Grandi Voci* (1964, with discography by Steven Smolian); David Ewen, *Living Musicians* (1940); Jürgen Kesting, *Die Grossen Sänger* (1986); and Irving Kolodin, *The Metropolitan Opera 1883–1966: A Candid History* (1967). Important articles include a memorial piece by Gustl Breuer, *Opera News*, Sept. 1982, pp. 22, 24, 26, and 59. An obituary by John Rockwell is in the *New York Times*, 11 July 1982.

ROBERT H. COWDEN

JERMAIN, Louis Francis (10 Oct. 1867–24 July 1935), physician and medical educator, was born in Meeme, a rural community in Manitowoc County, Wisconsin, the son of George Jermain, a building contractor, and Laura Simon. He was educated in the public schools and the Oshkosh Normal School and taught for seven years, working as a carpenter in the summers, before pursuing his medical education. He received his M.D. from Northwestern University Medical School in 1894 and undertook postgraduate medical studies in Berlin and Vienna in 1910.

Jermain established a medical practice in Milwaukee in 1894 and became prominent as a consultant in internal medicine, especially pulmonary diseases. He founded the Jermain Clinic in 1920. He served as assistant commissioner of health for the city of Milwaukee from 1898 to 1910. He also taught at the two medical schools in Milwaukee, the Wisconsin College of Physicians and Surgeons and the Milwaukee Medical College. Beginning in 1904 increasingly rigorous academic standards were being imposed on the nation's medical schools largely through the efforts of the Council on Medical Education of the American Medical Association. These efforts to improve the quality of physician graduates posed a growing threat to the Milwaukee medical schools, which, by 1912, were about to lose accreditation. Jermain was a leader in the efforts to salvage the schools, and in 1913 they were merged to become the Marquette University School of Medicine. Jermain became dean, a position he held until 1926. He also served as professor and director of the Department of Medicine from 1913 to 1928.

Jermain led the school through a financial crisis that was resolved in 1919 by establishing an endowment fund of $1 million with local support and a gift from the Carnegie Foundation. The following year he guided the school through another crisis involving an ideological dispute over therapeutic abortion between the administration of the Jesuit university and some prominent members of the medical faculty, who considered the issue one of academic freedom and inappropriate interference with medical practice. The resignations of key faculty members threatened the survival of the medical school. Through the crisis "the imperturbable Doctor Jermain . . . stood out as a solid rock," replacing those who left (Zeit, p. 297). A man of firm convictions and respected by his colleagues, Jermain was not easily upset or distracted from his mission to advance the medical school.

Jermain's ideas about medical education were in part constrained by the standardized curriculum that had been imposed on the nation's medical schools. He firmly believed in laboratory and clinical investigation as essential to a science-based medical education, but he argued that the physician must also have a background in the arts and humanities. In his 1919 report to the board of trustees of the school he lamented the fact that students "must be trained intensively in science at the sacrifice of cultural subjects" and were "overburdened with the acquisition of facts and of technical skill." To relieve the overcrowded four-year medical curriculum he added a fifth year, the internship year, to the student's requirements for the medical degree. He advocated both basic and clinical research for faculty and students as a valuable tool of education, and he stressed the importance of the hospital as the major site of physician research and education. He warned graduates of 1914 that the education they had received so far was just the beginning and that a failure to continue that education would lead to "medical oblivion."

Active in many medical and fraternal organizations, Jermain served as president of the Milwaukee County Medical Society in 1910, the State Medical Society of Wisconsin during 1915–1916, and the Milwaukee Medical Society (now the Milwaukee Academy of Medicine) in 1915. He contributed many articles to the medical literature, including a chapter on pulmonary diseases in Frederick Tice's *Practice of Medicine*, a major medical reference text published as a multivolume work from 1920 to at least 1970. He also spoke frequently to both medical and lay groups. In his presidential address to the Wisconsin State Medical Society in 1916, Jermain reminded the members that "the most important function of the Society is education," including the difficult task of continuing education of physicians in practice. At the time several states were considering compulsory health insurance legislation, a move that he advocated, noting that only the very rich and the very poor received high quality medical care; however, he warned against the danger of "the despicable plane of competitive lodge practice," the capitation plan of remuneration, and he advised the medical profession to participate in formulating and administering any plan. As the incoming president of the society, he appointed a committee whose endorsement of a compulsory health insurance plan was quickly adopted by the society. Jermain firmly believed that physicians were public servants whose "ethics and morals must be of a higher, purer type" than those of ordinary business.

Jermain recognized the importance of preventive medicine, noting that "it is much easier to prevent impending disease than to cure existing disease." He defended what some considered to be the high cost of medical service by comparing it with the public's huge expenditures on items such as tobacco, cosmetics, and entertainment.

Jermain married Rose Barth in 1894. They had three children. A devout Catholic, he was invested as a Knight of the Order of St. Gregory the Great in 1925. He died in Milwaukee.

Jermain was a key figure in the early development of medical education in Wisconsin. As noted by Dean John S. Hirschboeck on the fiftieth anniversary of the establishment of the Marquette University School of Medicine (later the Medical College of Wisconsin), without the efforts of Jermain and a few others "Wisconsin would have been without a complete medical school for many years and a generation of physicians would never have come to be." Jermain's philosophy of medical education would have a major impact within the school well into the future.

• None of Jermain's personal papers is known to have survived. Jermain's presidential address to the Wisconsin State Medical Society was published in the *Wisconsin Medical Journal* 15 (Oct. 1916): 137–42. Other remarks by Jermain also were recorded in that journal: see "The High Cost of Medical Service," 30 (July 1931): 573–80, and "Periodic Health Examinations, Education of the Physician," 26 (May 1927): 253–54. See also his "The Educational Function of Hospitals," *Modern Hospital* 5 (1915): 104–7. Walter Zeit's reminiscences about the Marquette University School of Medicine, "The First Fifty Years," are in the *Wisconsin Medical Journal* 62 (July 1963): 295–302. John S. Hirschboeck's comments, "A Half Century of Service," appeared in the same issue, p. 293.

NORMAN H. ENGBRING

JERVIS, John Bloomfield (14 Dec. 1795–12 Jan. 1885), civil engineer, was born in Huntington, New York, the son of Timothy Jervis, a carpenter, and Phoebe Bloomfield. Jervis moved with his family to Fort Stanwix (later known as Rome) in upstate New York in 1798. His early schooling was rudimentary and geared to boys who were expected to engage in farming or perhaps take up a trade. He was, however, fortunate in having as his mentor a namesake uncle, John Bloomfield, who encouraged Jervis to devote himself to self-education. His uncle's strong Calvinistic faith also had a profound influence on all aspects of Jervis's life, particularly his engineering career, through his commitment to his profession, his work ethic, and his honesty and integrity.

Jervis's engineering training began when his father arranged for Jervis to be an apprentice to Benjamin Wright, the chief engineer of the Erie Canal. Jervis was not only a talented apprentice but was also known for his dedication to work and his eagerness to learn. He quickly advanced from a humble laborer employed in clearing brush for surveyors to the rank of resident engineer in 1819, at the age of twenty-two. In 1823 Wright made Jervis superintendent of a fifty-mile-long stretch of the canal.

After the completion and formal opening of the Erie Canal in 1825, Jervis accepted the position of principal assistant engineer under Wright to work on the Delaware and Hudson Canal. In 1827 Jervis was appointed chief engineer when Wright left for other projects. In his new role, Jervis oversaw the design and construction of the canal, which was strictly a coal-hauling line. He was also responsible for the design of the incline at the railway planes, which brought coal to the canal basin at Honesdale, and for the introduction of the first railway locomotive in America, as part of the connection between the mines and the canal basin.

In 1829 Jervis had imported a Stephenson locomotive from England, but it proved unsuccessful. He then set out to design his own locomotive with a swivel truck (i.e., bogie) that was much more suitable to the sharp curves, steep grades, and uneven track characteristic of most railways in America. The West Point Foundry built his locomotive, the *Experiment*, in 1832. An instant success, it achieved an unprecedented speed of eighty miles per hour. Jervis married Cynthia Brayton in 1834; she and their newborn daughter died in childbirth in 1839.

After serving as chief engineer with both the Mohawk and Hudson Railway and the Schenectady and Saratoga Railway Jervis became chief engineer of the Chenango Canal in upstate New York, a feeder canal connecting Binghamton, New York, with the Erie Canal at Utica. In building the canal, it was necessary to cross a watershed, which necessitated the design of a summit-level reservoir of sufficient capacity to supply water to the highest level of the canal. To meet this challenge, Jervis undertook a hydrological study of the drainage area of the proposed reservoir and determined the amount of water that could be collected. He accomplished this by designing and installing a series of rain gauges and control weirs to determine the amount of water available for the reservoir. Despite the misgivings of many, the reservoir was an unqualified success and enhanced Jervis's reputation.

While serving as chief engineer of the eastern section of the Erie Canal, Jervis accepted in 1836 the position of chief engineer of the Croton Aqueduct project. He replaced Daniel Douglass, who, as the first chief engineer of the project, had come into conflict with its board of directors over his progress on the project. This forty-mile-long aqueduct was designed on an unprecedented scale; when completed in 1842, it supplied New York City with a copious and wholesome supply of water. As chief engineer, Jervis was called on to display the many characteristics that made him one of the leading civil engineers in the antebellum period. His design and analysis were based on published works by hydraulic engineers in France and Germany.

Jervis showed his mastery of all of the available theories of hydraulics and successfully applied these design principles to the Croton Aqueduct. His earlier experience as chief engineer on various large-scale public works provided him with the background experience necessary to assume overall charge of this large project. His design for the Croton Dam, which included a totally new approach to the shape of the spillway, became standard practice in later designs by other engineers. The application of inverted siphons to cross valleys along the course of the aqueduct and the magnificent high bridge that carried the aqueduct across the East River earned for him worldwide acclaim and represented the high point of a distinguished career. Jervis married Eliza Ruthven Coates in 1841; they had no children.

In 1847 he accepted the position of chief engineer of the Hudson River Railroad at Poughkeepsie, New York. In 1850 he also became chief engineer for the Michigan Southern and Northern Indiana Railroad. In 1851 Jervis was appointed president of the Chicago and Rock Island Railway and served until it was completed in 1854. Thereafter, he served as a consultant at the company. During this time a steamboat crashed into the bridge and severely damaged it. Claiming the bridge a hazard, the boat owners sued the railway company. The litigation was brought to court, and attorney and future U.S. president Abraham Lincoln represented the railroad, with Jervis acting as consultant to Lincoln, in its successful suit against the river boat interests. Jervis died in Rome, New York.

Jervis was one of the leaders of his profession in a period during which great public works were undertaken in America and a transition occurred from a craft-oriented building technology to an engineering profession based on scientific principles.

• Jervis's papers and his entire library, including diaries, engineering designs, and plans, are in a special collection at his house in Rome, New York, which forms part of the Rome Public Library. Neal Fitzsimons, *The Reminiscences of John B. Jervis* (1971), is based on a series of autobiographical sketches titled "Facts and Circumstances in the Life of John B. Jervis by Himself." A more recent account of Jervis is F. Daniel Larkin, *John B. Jervis: An American Engineering Pioneer* (1990).

EMORY L. KEMP

JESSEL, George (3 Apr. 1898–24 May 1981), entertainer, was born George Albert Jessel in New York City, the son of Joseph Aaron Jessel, a playwright and traveling salesman, and Charlotte Schwartz. He began his singing career when he was nine years old by serenading customers in his maternal grandfather's tailor shop. Later that year, using the stage name "McKinley," he began singing baritone with the Imperial Trio at a Harlem theater where his mother worked as a ticket-taker and soon was appearing solo as Little Georgie Jessel. After his father died in 1908, he cut short his formal education after only six months to join Gus Edwards's School Boys and Girls, a traveling vaudeville troupe. He toured with a number of Edwards's shows

until 1914, when his voice changed and he lost his boyish appeal, whereupon he went to England to perform as a singer and comedian for the next three years.

Jessel returned to the United States in 1917 and for the next eight years made the rounds of the various vaudeville circuits in the country. His routine was an amalgam of wisecracks, patriotic and sentimental songs sung in a melodramatic fashion, and a comedy sketch called "Hello, Mama," during which he pretended to talk on the telephone with his mother, who, judging from his end of the conversation, was either deaf, daft, or both. It was an act that went over well in New York City but flopped miserably practically everywhere else. In 1919 he married Florence Courtney, a fellow vaudevillian; by 1922 they had divorced and remarried. In addition to his vaudeville performances, he appeared in several two-reel silent movies, wrote and produced a handful of vaudeville and Broadway productions, and dabbled with theatrical management.

The high point in Jessel's career as a performer came in 1925, when he appeared in the lead of the original Broadway stage version of *The Jazz Singer*. This was the first dramatic role of his career, and he performed it so brilliantly that the show ran for the next three seasons. In 1926 he became involved in talking motion pictures by appearing in *Talking to Mother* (a two-reel adaptation of his "Hello, Mama" routine) to demonstrate the potential of Vitaphone, or sound on disc, for the movie industry. Later that year he starred in *Private Izzy Murphy*, a sentimental tale about a Jewish boy who ends up in the trenches during World War I. The movie did well enough that Sam, Jack, and H. M. Warner, its producers, attempted to sign him for the lead in the movie version of *The Jazz Singer*. However, because the script had been changed dramatically to his utter dislike and because he had yet to be paid for his performance in *Private Izzy Murphy*, he declined the role. Had he not done so, then he and not Al Jolson would perhaps be remembered as the star of the first talking movie.

In 1927 Jessel created one of the most popular mixed drinks in American history. In an effort to settle his stomach after an all-night binge of drinking champagne, the notorious bon vivant mixed together vodka, tomato juice, lemon juice, and Worcestershire sauce early one morning in a Palm Beach, Florida, bar and offered a taste to Mary Brown Warburton, a Philadelphia socialite. She promptly spilled it down the front of her white evening gown, thereby christening both herself and the drink "Bloody Mary."

During the late 1920s Jessel continued to perform as a vaudevillian while also starring in a number of Broadway productions, silent and talking movies, and radio programs. In 1932 Jessel divorced Courtney for the second time; they had no children. In 1934 he married Norma Talmadge, the silent screen star, then divorced her in 1939; they also had no children. In 1940 he created a major publicity stir when he married Lois Andrews, a sixteen-year-old showgirl; they had one child and were divorced in 1942 (he was involved in another publicity flap in 1961 when he lost a paternity case after being sued by the actress Joan Tyler). In 1943 he moved to Hollywood, California, and for the next ten years produced a number of musicals for 20th Century–Fox. His most successful efforts were *I Wonder Who's Kissing Her Now* (1947), *Meet Me after the Show* (1951), *The Dolly Sisters* (1945), and *Wait till the Sun Shines, Nellie* (1952).

While in Hollywood Jessel began appearing as the master of ceremonies at a number of banquets and served in this capacity so well and so often that in 1948 President Harry S. Truman dubbed him toastmaster general of the United States. In 1950 he delivered a particularly moving eulogy at Jolson's funeral—they had been both rivals and partners throughout their careers—and he soon became the eulogist of choice at the funerals of the entertainment industry's biggest stars. In 1953 Jessel left the movie industry and embarked on a cross-country tour selling bonds for Israel during which he raised $60 million for that struggling new nation. Following this tour he began raising money for other charitable organizations, most notably the City of Hope Medical Center, and brought in an additional $5 million. He also toured extensively for the United Service Organization (USO), putting on shows for American servicemen overseas. Because of these charitable performances, in 1970 he was presented the Academy of Motion Picture Arts and Sciences' Jean Hersholt Humanitarian Award. He was a frequent guest on network television talk shows until 1971, when an interview was terminated after he implied none too subtly that the *Washington Post* and the *New York Times* had pro-Communist sympathies. He died in Los Angeles, California.

As an entertainer, Jessel was never able to rise above his big-city background and appeal to a broader, less urbane audience than the one he had grown up with in New York. He was somewhat more adept at writing and producing successful Broadway shows and Hollywood motion pictures. His most important contribution to American entertainment came in the role of banquet toastmaster, funeral eulogist, and charitable fundraiser.

• Jessel's papers have not been located. An autobiography is George Jessel, with John Austin, *The World I Lived In* (1975). Obituaries are in the *New York Times*, 26 May 1981, and *Newsweek* and *Time*, both 8 June 1981.

CHARLES W. CAREY, JR.

JESSOP, George H. (1850?–22 Mar. 1915), playwright and novelist, was born in Ireland to a family of the landed gentry. Biographical sources do not give his parents' names or specify the date or place of his birth. It is known that Jessop attended Trinity College, Dublin, and was awarded medals for literary essays. In a novel by Jessop that its preface identifies as a thinly fictionalized autobiography, *Gerald Ffrench's Friends* (1889), he tells of receiving a younger son's patrimony of £2,000 at the age of twenty-one and of spending it in extended travels across Europe and then the United States. In 1873, when the novel says he was twenty-three, he found himself in San Francisco with no other resources than a twenty-dollar gold piece.

Jessop found work as a journalist for the city's newspapers. By 1877 he was writing theater reviews for the *San Francisco Post*. His stay in San Francisco ended in 1878, and he went on to work as a theatrical journalist in New York City, then already becoming the great center of American theatrical enterprise. His career as a playwright began at this time with a comedy-drama written for a Jewish actor whose stage name was M. B. Curtis. The actor asked for a play about "a good Jew," not the unflattering comic or villainous stereotypes of Jews then seen in plays. Jessop wrote for him *Sam'l of Posen*, probably Jessop's most popular play. According to Jessop's friend and collaborator Brander Matthews, he wrote the piece "in less than a week and sold it for a small sum, only to see it performed all over the United States year after year to crowded houses."

With *Sam'l of Posen* as a playwriting credential, Jessop was next approached by J. B. Polk, another actor whose audience was in the hinterlands rather than New York. Polk wanted a play that would center around the figure of a bumptious American he had played successfully in another comedy's supporting role. For Polk, Jessop wrote *A Gentleman from Nevada*, where a rough diamond from the United States is comically abrasive to an upper-class English family. The play's crudities were deplored by the *New York Times* reviewer (28 Apr. 1880) when Polk presented the piece in New York; *Sam'l of Posen* was similarly panned (*New York Times*, 18 May 1881) when Curtis brought it to New York the next year. But Jessop was now established as a reliable crafter of pieces that would please "road" audiences.

Such historical significance as Jessop has lies in the way he successfully rode the tides of change coming to the American theater in the 1880s. He could produce works that were innovative and works that stuck to the tried and true. In collaboration with writer-actor William Gill, he put together several vehicles for popular comedians of the day, following established crowd-pleasing patterns. These included *In Paradise* (1883), *Facts; or, His Little Hatchet* (1883), and *A Bottle of Ink* (1885). A final work of japes and improbable plot situations, which Jessop wrote on his own, was *22, Second Floor* (1889). The more sophisticated New York theatergoers were not pleased with such vapid, incoherent fare. The *New York Times* reviewer of *22, Second Floor* spent two paragraphs blasting Jessop: "Truth and Wit are conspicuous by the absence; Vulgarity is on hand [and] that peculiar kind of exaggeration of commonplace ideas known as American humor is liberally employed; the time-worn mechanism of farce is worked over again with the old results" (5 Feb. 1889).

Yet one of the collaborations by Jessop and Gill, *Mam'zelle* (1884), is now seen as a harbinger of musical comedy in American theater. This work was done as a touring production for Marie Aimee, a Parisian star of opéra bouffe who had had a great success in the United States. In a day when there was no effective copyright law, the two authors simply "borrowed" the plot of an older comedy, *Betsy Baker*, but made the heroine a humble French milliner who longs to be a singer and finds success and stardom when, in a show-within-a-show, she sings various songs. Not only the use of songs as a story device moved the work toward being a musical; in the view of Gerald Bordman, "the plot foreshadowed the Cinderella yarns that would dominate American musical comedy forty-five years later."

In 1885 Jessop became associated with a new co-writer, Brander Matthews. The pair wrote for John T. Raymond another comedy where a homespun American collides with suave British aristocrats, *A Gold Mine*. But after a single performance in 1887, Raymond's death put the play on the shelf until comic Nat Goodwin took it on two years later and made it one of his great successes. Meanwhile, Jessop collaborated with Matthews on a novel, *Check and Counter-Check* (1888), and on his own began contributing short fiction to magazines. Venturing next into solo writing of novels, he produced *Judge Lynch; a Tale of the California Vineyards* and *Gerald Ffrench's Friends*, both published in 1889.

A new direction at this time was Jessop's writing of a stage work about Ireland. He had not previously tapped his Irish background for theatrical purposes. Now, with collaborator Horace Townsend, he wrote *Myles Aroon* for Irish singer-actor William J. Scanlan. A *New York Times* report on its Philadelphia opening noted it favorably as "a marked departure from the conventional Irish drama, [having] no political allusions, red-coats, or priests used . . . in the development of the plot" (25 Dec. 1888). It was a romantic evocation of the Ireland of a century ago, into which songs by Scanlan fitted naturally. The notice praised the work for good comedy writing and for some fresh plot situations. *Myles Aroon* had a successful engagement in New York and toured extensively.

Jessop and Matthews brought forth still another comedy about Americans in Europe in 1889: *On Probation*, written for comedian William H. Crane. After its Chicago opening, the *New York Times* reported the play "a hit beyond question" and said "Messrs. Matthews and Jessop have gauged Mr. Crane's abilities with nice judgment . . . " (17 Sept. 1889). A collaboration with Ben Teal, stage manager for E. L. Erlanger, resulted in *The Great Metropolis* (1889), a melodrama on conventional lines.

In 1891 Jessop and Townsend wrote another comedy with songs for Scanlan, *Mavourneen*. It was an even bigger hit. The same year, Jessop collaborated with writer-producer Augustus Pitou on *The Power of the Press*, a melodrama about a man wrongly condemned to Sing Sing. It ran for over fifty performances in New York and toured for years.

Another event in 1891 gave Jessop's life a dramatic turn. He inherited from a cousin the landed estate of Marlfield, a few miles from Dublin. After other legacies were paid, "the share of Mr. Jessop will not fall far short of . . . $250,000 in American money, from which an income of from $10,000 to $12,500 per annum will

be derived" (*New York Times*, 25 Sept. 1891). At that period, it was the income of a wealthy man. Following his years of uncertain earnings from the theater, this was a happy ending worthy of the footlights. "It is the intention of Mr. Jessop to reside permanently on the estate," the article said. "It is his purpose to continue his literary pursuits, but more in the way of recreation than . . . turning out what he denominates 'pot boilers.'"

The last heard of Jessop as a writer for the American theater was in 1894, when Pitou produced another comedy with songs he and Jessop had worked on together, *The Irish Artist*. Jessop's activity was thereafter in the British musical theater. In 1896 he wrote libretto and lyrics for a comic opera on an Irish theme, *Shamus O'Brien*. The *Times* (London) said: "The workmanship of the libretto is admirable, the dialogue being direct, concise and natural yet brimming over with genuine Irish humour, while the lyrics have plenty of point and charm . . ." (3 Mar. 1896). A New York production followed in 1897.

After some years as an estate owner, Jessop wrote the libretto and lyrics for *My Lady Molly* (1902), also a comic opera. It romanticized the Ireland of the eighteenth century and was an immense success: after touring the provinces for a year, the work opened in London in 1903 and achieved 342 performances there. Touring productions in South Africa and Australia were equally successful. Only on Broadway did *My Lady Molly* fail, closing after two weeks, largely because of the miscasting of the title role.

Jessop wrote no more for the stage after this triumph. He later published three novels in London: *Where the Shamrock Grows* (1911), *His American Wife* (1913), and *Desmond O'Connor.* (1914). The first of these was also published in the United States. He died at his London residence in Hampstead of undisclosed causes.

• A sample of Jessop's theatrical journalism and a review of Helena Modjeska from the *San Francisco Post* is in Donald Mullin, *Victorian Actors and Actresses in Review* (1983). The autobiography of Brander Matthews, *These Many Years: Recollections of a New Yorker* (1917), contains reminiscences of Jessop and a few further details are in John Sutherland, *The Stanford Companion to Victorian Fiction* (1989). Denis O'Donoghue in *Poets of Ireland* (1892) gives information on Jessop's early life. Gerald Bordman provides helpful summaries and commentary for Jessop's stage works in *American Theatre . . . 1869–1914* (1994) and *The American Musical Theatre: A Chronicle* (1978). His two British comic operas are extensively discussed in Kurt Gänzl, *British Musical Theatre*, vol. 1, *1865–1914* (1986). Obituaries are in the *Times* (London) and the *New York Times*, both 23 Mar. 1915.

WILLIAM STEPHENSON

JESSUP, Henry Harris (19 Apr. 1832–28 Apr. 1910), Presbyterian missionary, was born in Montrose, Pennsylvania, the son of William Jessup, a lawyer and judge, and Amanda Harris. Jessup's father had graduated from Yale, and he became an influential judge, a prominent lay Presbyterian leader, a temperance advocate, and the chair of the Platform Committee of the Republican convention that nominated Abraham Lincoln for the presidency in 1860. After a year at Cortland Academy in Homer, New York, Jessup began study at Yale at the age of fifteen. After graduating in 1851, he taught for a year in his hometown. At Yale Jessup became interested in foreign missions, especially as a result of a visit to the campus by David Stoddard, who was serving in Persia. In the summer of 1852, while appealing to the youth of his church in Montrose to support missions, Jessup felt called to become a missionary. During his three years at Union Theological Seminary in New York, he prepared for this vocation through his course work; his training in medical procedures, first aid, and practical dentistry with several physicians and dentists in New York; and his home missionary work in the asylums and slums of the city. Conversations during his seminary years with missionaries from the Middle East led him to decide to serve in Syria. Following his graduation from Union and his ordination to the Presbyterian ministry in 1855, he sailed for the Middle East, arriving in February 1856. Until 1860 he resided in Tripoli, where he learned Arabic, in which he eventually became an expert.

On a visit to the United States in 1857 Jessup married Caroline Bush, a teacher. He had hoped to marry her before going to the Middle East, but her poor health delayed their marriage. She died in 1864 while on a voyage with her husband and two of their three children. In 1868 Jessup married Harriet Elizabeth Dodge, with whom he had five children. Two years after her death in 1882, Jessup wed Theodosia Davenport Lockwood. They had no children.

Jessup originally went to Syria under the auspices of the American Board of Commissioners for Foreign Missions, an arm of the Congregational church. In 1870, however, the work in Syria was taken over by the Presbyterian Board of Foreign Missions, under whose direction Jessup labored for the rest of his career. While serving in Syria until his death, Jessup, along with other missionaries, endured many hardships, including Muslim intolerance of Christianity, rigid censorship of Christian literature, persecution, war, and financial problems. On one occasion he and his family narrowly escaped being killed by Turks. Jessup played a vital role in almost every aspect of the Presbyterian missionary enterprise in Syria. For thirty years he was the pastor of the Syrian Church in Beirut and the superintendent of its school. He helped to found the Syrian Protestant College (now the American University of Beirut) in 1866, edited an Arabic missionary journal, and served as secretary of a hospital for the insane. With his many skills, he significantly contributed to the mission's success in evangelism, education, translation, dissemination of literature, medical work, and church planning and growth. This work, along with his expertise in the literature and doctrine of Oriental religions, his numerous publications, and his many sermons and addresses given during seven visits to the United States, made him the most well known and revered Presbyterian missionary of the late nineteenth and early twentieth centuries. Political leaders in the Middle East and the United States frequently sought his advice. He was elected moderator of the general assembly of the Presbyterian church in 1879 and declined offers to teach at Union Theological Seminary, serve as pastor to several large Presbyterian congregations, direct the Presbyterian Board for Foreign Missions, and serve as the U.S. minister to Persia.

Jessup published books and articles to promote missions to the Moslem world. *The Women of the Arabs* (1873) and *Syrian Home-Life* (1874) described the oppressed state of women in the Moslem world, Islamic teaching about women, social and domestic practices, and the work of Protestant missionaries to improve economic and social conditions for Syrian women through educational and religious activities. In *The Mohammedan Missionary Problem* (1879), first preached as a sermon to the 1879 general assembly, Harris challenged Christians to increase their efforts to reach the world's 175 million Muslims. This endeavor, he insisted, would be successful only if it emphasized that Muslims must accept Jesus Christ as their savior and lord, as opposed to accepting only the ethical principles and social practices of Christianity. Jessup's *Fifty-three Years in Syria* (1910) is both an autobiography and a broader analysis of the Presbyterian missionary effort in Syria. Based on a diary Jessup kept for fifty-five years, voluminous correspondence, manuscripts, addresses, and articles, it is full of anecdotes; stories of individual converts; discussions of missionary policies, practices, and perils; and descriptions of civil and religious strife and of social customs and norms in a premodern nation undergoing considerable turmoil.

A tall, dignified man whose long beard reminded some of his contemporaries of the Old Testament prophets, Jessup possessed a deep, rich voice and skillfully used illustrations, humor, compelling arguments, and dramatic flair to move audiences in Syria and the United States. The political situation in the Muslim world led him to counsel missionaries to avoid taking sides on political questions and concentrate instead on preaching the Gospel, educating the young, caring for the sick and suffering, and publishing sound books. A theological conservative who believed in the infallibility of the Bible, the necessity of a new birth experience, the importance of evangelism, and fundamental Christian doctrines, Jessup sought during his long ministry in Syria to promote religious uplift, educational progress, and social morality. He died in Beirut.

Despite considerable opposition from Muslim authorities, Jessup and other Protestant missionaries planted numerous churches in Syria, won thousands of converts to Christianity, established many schools and one major college, provided a large amount of Christian literature, founded several hospitals and other humanitarian institutions, assisted the poor and victims of natural disasters, and helped elevate the status of women.

• Jessup's personal papers are at the Presbyterian Historical Society in Philadelphia. Also helpful are the records of the Board of Foreign Missions of the Presbyterian Church, 1870–1910, Presbyterian Historical Society, Philadelphia. In addition to the works cited in the text, Jessup wrote *The Greek Church and Protestant Missions* (1891) and *The Setting of the Crescent and the Rising of the Cross; or, Kamil Abdul Messiah, a Syrian Convert from Islam to Christianity* (1898). Jessup's *Fifty-three Years in Syria* (2 vols., 1910) includes a brief overview of his life before 1856 and a thorough discussion of his life beginning with that year. Also helpful are Arthur T. Pierson, "Henry Harris Jessup and the Syrian Pioneers," *Missionary Review of the World* 33 (July 1910): 487–92; Pierson, "The Syrian Mission and Its Pioneers; Second Period: 1870–1910," *Missionary Review of the World* 33 (Aug. 1910): 567–73; "The Death of a Great Missionary," *Assembly Herald* 10 (June 1910): 290–91; and James Smylie, "Henry Harris Jessup: Mission in the Land of the Bible," in *Go Therefore: 150 Years of Presbyterians in Global Mission,* ed. Smylie et al. (1987). *Historical Sketches of the Missions . . . of the Presbyterian Church, U.S.A.* (1897) and Robert E. Speer, *Presbyterian Foreign Missions* (1901), provide an account of Jessup's work in Syria. See also *A Memorial of Theodosia Davenport Jessup* (1908). An obituary is in the *Presbyterian Banner,* 5 May 1910.

GARY SCOTT SMITH

JESSUP, Philip C. (5 Jan. 1897–31 Jan. 1986), diplomat, professor, and member of the International Court of Justice, was born in New York City, the son of Henry Wynans Jessup, a law professor at New York University, and Mary Hay Stotesbury. Philip spent his early years in the city but was later sent to the Ridgefield School in Connecticut, the beginning of what would become a lifetime of scholarship. Following high school, Jessup enrolled at Hamilton College, receiving his bachelor's degree in 1919 after a brief stint in the U.S. Army during World War I. Despite his interest in academia, in 1919 Jessup began his professional career as a banker, working at the First National Bank in Utica, New York. In 1921 he married Lois Walcott Kellogg; the couple had one child.

For Jessup, a man who naturally gravitated toward the intellectually abstract, banking proved less than challenging, and in 1924 he simultaneously earned both an LL.B. from Yale University and a master's degree from Columbia. He was admitted to the bar in the District of Columbia in 1925 and served two years as assistant solicitor in the State Department. Jessup also received a doctorate from Columbia in 1927 after writing a thesis about maritime law, an obvious, though inchoate, indication of where his academic interests lay. Admitted to the New York bar that same year, Jessup worked at the law firm of Parker and Duryea until 1943. While in private practice, Jessup lectured on international law and served as an assistant, associate, and, finally, a full professor at Columbia. In 1946 he was named Hamilton Fish Professor of International Law and Diplomacy, a title and position he retained until 1961.

In addition to all of these academic honors and endeavors, from 1924 to 1953 Jessup acted as legal counsel to many federal officials, among them former secretary of state Dean Acheson. It was during the latter part of these years, while serving simultaneously as a U.S. representative to the United Nations General Assembly (1948–1952) and as U.S. ambassador at large (1949–1953), that Jessup earned a name for himself in the international community as the man who brought an end to the Berlin blockade. According to Acheson, Jessup's diplomatic abilities were put "to a most important and secret test" in 1949, when he was given the task of finding out the significance of an omission made by Soviet leader Joseph Stalin to a news correspondent.

The blockade, one of the most definitive crises of the Cold War, began in June 1948 when Stalin severed all overland communications between Berlin and West Germany in an effort to isolate Berlin economically and politically and thus prevent the creation of a stable West German government. Sepcifically, the Kremlin was upset over the Allied application of the new West German currency to West Berlin and in particular the use of Western currency by the United States. As Stalin perhaps predicted, the blockade forced the population of Berlin to choose between the East and the West. After the Allies began airlifting supplies to isolated Berliners, however, the inhabitants of the city became more secure in resisting Soviet pressure. Ironically, the blockade depleted Soviet power with regard to the West rather than increasing it as calculated, and ultimately, as a result of the failed military operation, West Germany secured a stable government. Perhaps a sign of the Soviets' growing lack of resolve, Stalin, when asked about his willingness to end the blockade in 1949, neglected to mention the monetary issues that were the initial cause of the conflict. Acheson, along with Jessup and others, felt that such an omission might implicitly mean that Stalin was willing to engage in a dialogue with the United States concerning halting a military campaign that had proven unprofitable for the Soviets.

Jessup handled his assignment paradoxically—with both a cautious and cavalier attitude. In a seemingly chance, although well-orchestrated meeting at the United Nations bar, Jessup casually asked Jacob Malik, the Soviet ambassador to the United Nations, whether or not Stalin's failure to mention the cause of the blockade was significant. Because Jessup claimed to be simply curious about the matter, Malik replied candidly that he did not know, but if he discovered the answer, he would remember Jessup's inquiry. A month later Malik informed Jessup that the omission was not an accident and that while economic matters involving the currency were important, they could be discussed at a meeting of the Council of Foreign Ministers. When Jessup asked whether or not the meeting would be considered before or after lifting the blockade, Malik again talked to Stalin and reported back to Jessup, explaining that if a definitive date were set for the meeting and if the United States would postpone plans for a West German government until after the council met, the blockade could be lifted before negotiations began. Although the following six weeks of meetings in Paris accomplished little, the blockade was lifted before the meeting, and Jessup was credited with ending a tense period in U.S.–Soviet relations. Quite remarkably, according to Acheson, no more than five individuals in the United States even knew of the talks, a remarkable feat for any diplomat in a country intent on knowing.

However, in the McCarthy era—a time riddled with Communist paranoia—any negotiations with the Soviets were considered highly suspicious, and despite Jessup's commitment to international peace and what Dwight D. Eisenhower described as a sincere "devotion to the principles of Americanism," he was criticized by the senator for what he deemed an "unusual affinity for Communist causes." Unwavering, Jessup continued to believe that diplomacy and international negotiations were the only way to establish a stable, rational world order, and, ignoring any criticisms, he spent the next thirty-three years of his life pursuing, both academically and practically, the use and application of international law.

Jessup eventually returned to Columbia for several years, where he taught international law in a way that engendered both "intellectual admiration and personal affection," according to several of his colleagues who edited a collection of essays in Jessup's honor titled *Transnational Law in a Changing Society* (1972). He remained, however, primarily an ambassador, a man who, according to Acheson, could "survive the longest and dullest meetings with their endless translations," with an "irrepressible humor" (Friedmann et al., eds., p. 6). Committed to the principles and the possibility of international law, Jessup remained on hand in both academia and the public sector, providing able diplomatic advice, and in November 1960 he was elected to the International Court of Justice, better known as the World Court, the primary judicial body of the United Nations. While there, Jessup fought tirelessly to establish a peaceful international community, crusading against what he believed were grave injustices. In 1966, when the World Court dismissed a complaint by Ethiopia and Liberia against the practice of apartheid in Namibia, Jessup wrote a violent dissent of the court's ruling that the plaintiff countries did not have sufficient evidence.

After retiring from the court in 1969, Jessup continued his career as a professor and writer. In characterizing Jessup in the introduction to the collection of essays in his honor, Acheson wrote, "Diplomatist, rather than diplomat, is the right word here. The latter took on a denigrating cast when we were young. . . . However, the rabble recognized here and there a man like Philip Jessup's hero, Elihu Root, who seemed to come of sterner stuff and to be worthy of respect. For these a syllable was added to their titles to indicate elevation to a peerage." Having chosen to toil in a field that was vast and at a job that was often thankless, Jessup refused to be daunted by the colossal and complicated task of forging a philosophy of international law that was capable of adapting to an ever changing world. Eric Stein, in an introduction to Jessup's *The Use of International Law* (1959), wrote, "We in 1958 are beholden to Philip C. Jessup for writing not only what practitioners, governments, national courts and international tribunals do but also what they ought to do." Jessup was a legal expert who believed in the fluidity of both national and international law, which he felt, "like the traveler, must be ready for the morrow. It must have a principle of growth." In addition to his optimistic hope for growth and peace, however, Jessup was a pragmatist, a man who according to Acheson saw trouble as "no occasion to pull a long face and push the panic button." Likewise, Jessup, always the diplomat, commented once about the World Court, saying, "When we have a case, the work is as hard as any I've ever done. Harder, perhaps, because we have to work our way through an immense amount of documentation" (*New York Times*, 1 Feb. 1986). Realizing that constructing the principles of international law was both difficult and time-consuming, Jessup remained patient, confident that success cannot be measured by its rapidity, but by its endurance. After suffering from Parkinson's disease for many years, Jessup died at his winter home in Newtown, Pennsylvania.

• Philip Jessup's books include *Elihu Root* (1938), a two-volume work about Jessup's legal hero; *A Modern Law of Nations* (1948); *Transnational Law* (1956); *The Price of International Justice* (1971); and *The Birth of Nations* (1974). For more information about Jessup's influence on his colleagues, see Wolfgang Friedmann et al., eds., *Transnational Law in a Changing Society: Essays in Honor of Philip C. Jessup* (1972). With regard to the circumstances surrounding the Berlin blockade, see W. Phillips Davison, *The Berlin Blockade* (1958). An obituary is in the *New York Times*, 1 Feb. 1986.

DONNA GREAR PARKER

JESSUP, Walter Albert (12 Aug. 1877–5 July 1944), educator, university and foundation president, was born in Richmond, Indiana, the only child of Albert Smiley Jessup and Anna Goodrich, farmers. Jessup's mother died when he was eleven. In 1890 his father married Gulia E. (Hunnicutt) Jones, a teacher, and the couple added two children to the family. Jessup attended Earlham College (Indiana), but he periodically withdrew to help his father on the farm and to teach in a nearby school. In 1898 he married Eleanor Hines; they later adopted two children. Jessup went from teacher to principal to superintendent during the next decade (Westfield Township, 1900–1907; Madison, Ind., 1907–1909) while earning a B.A. from Earlham College in 1903 and an M.A. from Hanover College in 1908. In 1909 Jessup left Indiana for New York City to enroll at Teachers College, Columbia University. He received his Ph.D. in 1911 and returned to Indiana as professor and dean of the School of Education at Indiana University. A year later Jessup was named professor and dean of the School of Education at the State University of Iowa in Iowa City.

As dean, Jessup was a key architect of the transformation of the School of Education into the College of Education in 1913. His blueprint established close ties between the liberal arts college and the College of Education, allowing pedagogical training only after subject-matter training. In addition, Jessup was involved in public education in the state, lecturing throughout Iowa and advising local school superintendents. He cultivated his national reputation through his work with the national educational honor society, Phi Delta Kappa, and through his collaborations with Lotus Delta Coffman, president of the University of Minnesota. In 1916 Jessup and Coffman completed a book, *The Supervision of Arithmetic*. In addition, Jessup directed a number of school surveys, including one of the Los Angeles public school system. In 1916 Jessup was named the fourteenth president of the University of Iowa.

At Iowa Jessup emerged as a highly respected educational leader. With the U.S. entry into World War I, Jessup mobilized the university to support the war effort, and much of the campus was given over to the training of officers. Following the war Jessup embarked on an aggressive building program to accommodate the university's growing enrollment. Although he became repeatedly involved in controversies with the state legislature over overlapping courses of study with Iowa State College (later University) at Ames, Jessup enjoyed general support for expansion.

Jessup was president of the University of Iowa for eighteen years and oversaw the university's unprecedented period of growth. During Jessup's tenure the campus expanded from 42 to 324 acres, enrollment increased from 3,500 to nearly 10,000, and the faculty grew from 273 to almost 500. Jessup embraced the progressive service orientation common to most state universities at the time. Extension programs, educational radio, correspondence courses, health services through hospitals and clinics, and counseling services all emerged during Jessup's administration. The university also added a comprehensive program for the study of child development, the Iowa Child Welfare Research Station. Within the College of Liberal Arts, schools of journalism, religion, fine arts, and letters were formed. In 1922 Jessup announced that the Rockefeller Foundation and the General Education Board had awarded $2.25 million to build a new medical college.

Arthur M. Schlesinger, Sr., whom Jessup had hired to head the history department, described Jessup in his autobiography as "a stocky, square-jawed man who looked and acted more like a business executive or banker than a university president" (*In Retrospect* [1963]). Indeed, Jessup's major accomplishment was to gather the necessary political and financial support for the rapid growth of the university. By all accounts, Jessup worked tirelessly to accomplish the expansion and change, meeting regularly with legislators, public figures, and citizens of the state to garner their support.

Jessup maintained tight control over the administration of the university while cultivating good relations with the university's board. He was actively involved in recruiting a strong faculty and was reasonably successful in doing so. He, nevertheless, expected his faculty to attend to matters of teaching and scholarship and cede the running of the institution to him.

Jessup's administrative style served him well throughout most of his career. He withstood two major controversies during his administration. In 1929 the university was suspended from the Big Ten for subsidizing athletes. At the end of the following year, the editor of the *Cedar Rapids Gazette-Republican*, Verne Marshall, launched a bitter and prolonged attack on Jessup and the university, charging fiscal mismanagement and fraud. The state legislature's joint investigating committee found no grounds for any of the substantive charges. More difficult for Jessup was the effect of the deepening depression on the university. Cuts in salaries and faculty positions began in 1930 and continued throughout the remainder of his administration. With increasing hostility from the governor toward Jessup's administration, the board, and the continuing fiscal crisis, Jessup welcomed the opportunity to return to New York City as president of the Carnegie Foundation for the Advancement of Teaching in 1934.

At the foundation Jessup acquired the funds from the Carnegie Corporation that were necessary to maintain commitments for teacher pensions during the depression. It was during his presidency that the foundation helped solidify the use of standardized test scores as criteria for selective college admission. He maintained close contact with many American college and university presidents, serving as both advocate and counselor. During World War II he expressed concern about the increasing centralization of scientific research in Washington, D.C. Jessup warned of the development of a system in which research grants were made directly to individuals and departments, thereby by-passing university presidents and undercutting their authority.

In 1941 Jessup took on additional responsibility as president of the Carnegie Corporation. Having replaced Frederick P. Keppel, who dominated the corporation for nearly twenty years, Jessup primarily oversaw the completion of Keppel's projects. He died in New York City.

Like such earlier well-known institution builders as Charles W. Eliot at Harvard, Nicholas Murray Butler at Columbia, or William R. Harper at Chicago, Jessup oversaw the rapid expansion of the University of Iowa. He is rightly credited with building the university into a modern institution of higher education and instilling the institution with a progressive service mission.

• The majority of Jessup's papers are in the University of Iowa Archives. Letters and papers relating to his term as president of the Carnegie Foundation for the Advancement of Teaching and the Carnegie Corporation are located in the Columbia University Archives. The best recent treatment of Jessup at the University of Iowa is Stow Persons, *The University of Iowa in the Twentieth Century: An Institutional History* (1990). See also John C. Gerber, *A Pictorial History of the University of Iowa* (1988); Frederick Gould Davies, "History of the State University of Iowa: The College of Liberal Arts, 1916–1934" (Ph.D. diss., State Univ. of Iowa, 1947); and *University of Iowa Extension Bulletin: Fifty Years of the College of Education of the University of Iowa* (1964). An obituary is in the *New York Times*, 8 July 1944.

DANIEL C. HUMPHREY

JESUP, Thomas Sidney (16 Dec. 1788–10 June 1860), army officer, was born in Berkeley County, Virginia, the son of James Edward Jesup and Ann O'Neill, farmers. Jesup's family moved to the Kentucky frontier in 1792, where his father rented a farm. The father died four years later, however, leaving his wife to raise her children in poverty and debt. As a young man, Jesup worked as a store clerk in Maysville, Kentucky, then procured a second lieutenant's commission in one of the infantry regiments added to the army in 1808 in response to the growing controversy with Great Britain.

Early in the War of 1812, Jesup served on the staff of Brigadier General William Hull, commander of the northwestern army, and he was captured when Hull surrendered Detroit in August 1812. Paroled soon afterward, Jesup distinguished himself as both a staff officer and a combat leader. As a 25-year-old major, he commanded a regiment in the bloody Niagara campaign of 1814, and he was wounded at the battle of Lundy's Lane. Late in the war, the War Department ordered him to Connecticut, ostensibly on recruiting duty but actually to keep the Madison administration informed on the deliberations of the Hartford Convention, a meeting of antiwar New England Federalists. Jesup was retained in the service when Congress reduced the army after the Peace of Ghent. While commanding at New Orleans in 1816, the ambitious young officer longed for a war with Spain and independently planned an attack on Cuba.

In 1818 Secretary of War John C. Calhoun appointed Jesup to the key staff office of quartermaster general of the army, a post that carried the rank of brigadier general and was charged with the procurement of light military equipment, the transportation of supplies of all sorts, and the construction of military roads, posts, and other buildings. During the years that followed, Jesup participated in a broad effort, coordinated by Calhoun, to renovate military management and introduce systematic administrative procedures—thereby avoiding a repetition of the breakdowns and confusion that had characterized the War of 1812 mobilization. He compiled a comprehensive set of departmental regulations that clearly specified each form of duty and established a strict system of property accountability, enforced through the regular submission of standardized reports and returns. He used his office as a training school to develop a cadre of competent young supply officers. Despite the logistical burdens imposed by an expanding frontier and the pressures of recurrent congressional retrenchment campaigns, Jesup brought an unprecedented degree of order and efficiency to quartermaster operations. Together with his counterparts in other army staff departments, he produced a pattern of administration and accountability that was adopted by both private companies and other government agencies and that helped lay the foundations of modern management in the United States. In 1822 he married Ann Heron Croghan, with whom he had eight children.

In May 1836 the War Department ordered Jesup to suspend his quartermaster duties and take a field command on the Georgia-Alabama border, where a faction of the Creek nation had rebelled against the Jackson administration's policy of American Indian removal. Acting under the orders of the theater commander, Brigadier General Winfield Scott, Jesup organized a force of Alabama militia as part of a planned two-pronged advance into the Creek country. Jesup decided to launch his offensive before Scott had completed his preparations, resulting in a quick suppression of the uprising but also in a politically charged quarrel between the two generals. President Andrew Jackson supported Jesup in this controversy, and late in 1836 he placed the quartermaster general in command of the regular and militia forces fighting the Second Seminole War in Florida, another outgrowth of the removal policy. This assignment proved to be the most frustrating of Jesup's career. Dispersed bands of American Indians, supported by escaped slaves and their descendants, tenaciously resisted removal, eluding the army in the Florida wilderness and fighting only when they held the advantage. Moreover, the conflict was controversial, and Jesup faced criticism from abolitionists, Whigs, and other opponents of the war. In October 1837 he ordered the seizure of the Seminole leader Osceola and a band of his followers after the American Indians had gathered for a council under a flag of truce—an action that tainted his reputation for the rest of his life. By early 1838 Jesup had grown disillusioned with the war, and he recommended allowing the remaining Seminoles to stay in a restricted part of Florida. The Van Buren administration held firmly to removal, however, and in April it replaced Jesup as Florida commander with Colonel Zachary Taylor.

Resuming his quartermaster duties in Washington, D.C., Jesup strove to meet the logistical demands of the seemingly interminable Seminole conflict. The end of that struggle in 1842 resulted in a reduction of the army and a congressional campaign to cut military expenses and sell off surplus equipment. Thus, the quartermaster service was hard-pressed in 1846, when the outbreak of war with Mexico brought a dramatic buildup of the army and required the support of operations on fronts as distant as the Rio Grande, California, and Central Mexico. Despite the inevitable grousing of field commanders about supply shortages, Jesup's administrative system responded remarkably well to the crisis. In sharp contrast to the War of 1812 experience, the army enjoyed a high level of logistical support as it conducted its first truly foreign war—a key factor in the overwhelming success of American arms. During the fall of 1846, the quartermaster general traveled to the Gulf of Mexico, where he personally directed forward supply operations, and he accompanied Scott's expedition against Veracruz during the following spring. Jesup continued to supervise his department throughout the 1850s, wrestling with difficult problems of transportation as the army dispersed across the Great Plains and Far West and engaged in almost constant campaigning against the American Indians. He died at his Washington home.

The "father" of the army Quartermaster Corps, Jesup was an important figure in the evolution of military management in the United States. His emphasis on uniform procedures and strict accountability helped make the army's supply system one of the most modern and efficient large organizations in the nineteenth-century United States.

• The largest collection of Jesup's personal papers is preserved at the Library of Congress; smaller collections are located at the Duke University library and the William L. Clements Library at the University of Michigan, Ann Arbor. The best biography is Chester L. Kiefer, *Maligned General: A Biography of Thomas S. Jesup* (1979). For Jesup's impact on military supply see also Erna Risch, *Quartermaster Support of the Army: A History of the Corps, 1775–1939* (1962). Other aspects of his career are considered in Jack A. Clarke, "Thomas Sidney Jesup: Military Observer at the Hartford Convention," *New England Quarterly* 29 (1956): 393–99; and John K. Mahon, *History of the Second Seminole War, 1835–1842* (1967).

WILLIAM B. SKELTON

JETER, Jeremiah Bell (18 July 1802–18 Feb. 1880), Southern Baptist minister and editor, was born in Bedford County, Virginia, the son of Pleasant Jeter and Jane Eke Hatcher, farmers. Jeter credited his mother with raising the family, and he remembered his father as a "thriftless dreamer." Jeter never attended college; he was educated in the rural schools of Bedford County.

Jeter was converted to the Christian faith at the age of nineteen. He later described his conversion in typically Calvinistic terms, emphasizing his sinfulness before God. He was baptized into the Baptist denomination in December 1821. Since Baptists did not insist on formal theological training for entrance into the ministry, one month after his baptism Jeter began preaching throughout Bedford and surrounding counties.

In 1823 Jeter and Daniel Whitt were appointed as the first missionaries of the new state organization for Virginia Baptists, the Baptist General Association of Virginia. They conducted preaching tours in western and eastern Virginia, covering about thirty counties. On 4 May 1824 Jeter was ordained to the gospel ministry.

Jeter began serving Baptist churches as pastor in 1826. He served the following churches, all but one of which were located in Virginia: Hill's Creek and Un-

ion Hill in Campbell County (1826–1827), Morattico Church in Lancaster County and Wicomico Church in Northumberland County (1827–1836), First Baptist Church of Richmond (1836–1849), Second Baptist Church in St. Louis, Missouri (1849–1852), and Grace Street Baptist Church of Richmond (1852–1870).

Jeter's pastoral ministry was highlighted by several events. In his nine-year ministry at the Morattico and Wicomico churches, Jeter baptized about 1,000 persons, about half of whom were white, and the other half were slaves. At First Baptist Church of Richmond, he also baptized approximately 1,000 converts, and the church's white membership doubled to 600 persons. In 1842 Jeter, amidst opposition from some whites in Richmond, encouraged and gave support to his black membership of 1,717 to separate and create their own First African Baptist Church of Richmond. The African Americans were given the old site of First Baptist, since in 1841 Jeter's congregation had built a new church building.

Jeter's sphere of influence extended to denominational affairs. He was active in the Baptist General Association of Virginia from its birth in 1823, serving as its president from 1854 to 1857. He attended meetings of the antebellum national body of Baptists, the Triennial Convention, and was a part of the Virginia delegation to the organizational meeting of the Southern Baptist Convention (SBC) in 1845. The SBC established a Foreign Mission Board, and Jeter served as president from 1845 to 1849.

Despite his limited formal education, Jeter promoted denominational schools. He was one of several Virginia Baptists who met in 1830 to establish the Virginia Baptist Seminary, which later became the University of Richmond. Until his death he served on the school's board of trustees and was its president twice (1868–1872, 1873–1880). At the time of his death, Jeter was also the president of the Board of Trustees of the Southern Baptist Theological Seminary, the Southern Baptists' only seminary at the time.

Jeter is best known for his work as editor of the influential Virginia Baptist paper, the *Religious Herald*. In 1865, while Jeter was still pastor of Grace Street Baptist Church of Richmond, he and Alfred Elijah Dickinson bought and revived the struggling paper. In 1870 Jeter resigned his church to be a full-time editor, writing two to four columns a week in the promotion and defense of Baptist causes. He was a loyal denominationalist, supporting the SBC against the independent and exclusivist spirit of landmarkism, a movement that suggested only Baptists were true Christians. Jeter also attacked Alexander Campbell's "Restoration movement," which made inroads into Baptist life, in his editorials and in a popular book, *Campbellism Examined* (1855). Campbell wanted to restore the "New Testament church," but Jeter and other Baptists accused Campbell of saying that baptism saves (a concept known as baptismal regeneration).

Jeter wrote several other books on a variety of topics, including *Life of Mrs. Henrietta Shuck* (1846), the first American female missionary to China who was converted under Jeter's ministry; *Life and Writings of the Reverend Andrew Broaddus* (1852), a prominent Virginia Baptist; and *Recollections of a Long Life* (1891), originally a series of articles published in the *Religious Herald*. Along with Richard Fuller, Jeter added a supplement to *The Psalmist* (1847), a Northern Baptist hymnal, but the work never gained wide use in the South.

As editor, Jeter expressed the predominant attitude of Southern Christians toward African Americans. While the editor claimed a personal aversion to slavery, he defended the institution on biblical grounds and had supported the Confederate cause during the Civil War. After slavery was abolished, Jeter argued for separate conventions of white and black Christians in order to maintain racial purity. According to Jeter, God had designed "an instinctive repugnance" between whites and blacks, which "no training and no philosophy can eradicate, and which divine grace does not." He feared that integrated worship would lead to calls for social equality and "the mongrelization of our noble Anglo-Saxon race" (Spain, p. 52).

During the nineteenth century, an era of rapid growth in American denominationalism, Jeter left a legacy of denominational activism on the state and national levels. Despite being regarded as just an average orator whose interpersonal skills were hampered by a poor memory, Jeter was a highly respected pastor throughout the SBC. Under his leadership, the *Religious Herald* became a dominant voice in Southern Baptist life. Jeter has been regarded as a dogmatic but amiable controversialist in the defense of Baptist views.

Jeter was married four times. His first wife, Margaret Waddy, died shortly after their marriage in 1826. In 1828 Jeter married Sarah Ann Gaskins. After Sarah's death in 1847, Jeter's third marriage was to Charlotte E. Wharton, from 1849 to her death in 1861. In 1863 Jeter married Mary Catherine Dabbs. Jeter had one child with his second wife, but the child died during infancy. Jeter died in Richmond, Virginia.

• The best source for Jeter's views are his editorials in the *Religious Herald*. Microfilm copies of the paper are at the Virginia Baptist Historical Society, located at the University of Richmond. Also at the Virginia Baptist Historical Society are *The Diaries of Jeremiah Bell Jeter, 1837–1874*, which are primarily sermon outlines and are also available there on microfilm. In addition to the books listed in the article, Jeter wrote *A Memoir of Reverend Abner W. Clopton* (1837), *The Mirror: A Delineation of Different Classes of Christians* (1855), *Campbellism Reexamined* (1856), and *The Seal of Heaven* (1871). A biography of Jeter is William E. Hatcher, *Life of J. B. Jeter* (1887). Important biographical material is also in George B. Taylor, *Virginia Baptist Preachers*, 3d ser. (1912). Jeter's influence in Baptist life is described in Garnett Ryland, *The Baptists of Virginia: 1699–1926* (1955). A good assessment of his racial views is in Rufus B. Spain, *At Ease in Zion: A Social History of Southern Baptists, 1865–1900* (1967). An obituary is in the *Richmond State*, 18 Feb. 1880.

C. DOUGLAS WEAVER

JEWELL, Marshall (20 Oct. 1825–10 Feb. 1883), businessman and politician, was born in Winchester, New Hampshire, the son of Pliny Jewell, a tanner, and Emily Alexander. As a young man Jewell, who lacked formal education, displayed great interest in the newly invented telegraph. In 1847 he helped erect the line from Louisville to New Orleans, and two years later he supervised connections between Boston and New York. While involved with these concerns, he rose from working in his father's tannery in Hartford, Connecticut, to become a partner in the family business, a belting factory, in 1850. During the next two decades he entered several businesses, including railroads and banking, and was part owner of the Hartford *Evening Post*. In 1852 he married Esther E. Dickinson; they had two children.

Jewell entered politics as a Republican in 1867, losing a bid for the Connecticut State Senate. The following year he secured the party's nomination for governor but lost to James English. In 1869 and 1871 he won election as governor, sandwiched around a defeat in 1870. His administrations were unremarkable. In 1873 Ulysses S. Grant appointed him minister to Russia, and the following year, on 3 July, the president, after struggling to find a replacement, named him postmaster general to succeed the retiring John A. J. Creswell.

Taking office on 2 September 1874, Jewell immediately demonstrated his commitment to the principles of civil service reform. In this endeavor Grant supported him. In contrast to Creswell, Jewell declined to use the powers of appointment and removal to promote Republican fortunes. However, the rate of turnover differed little from that during Creswell's tenure after 1872, in large part because Republicans already occupied the positions. Nevertheless, Jewell was concerned about Republican political prospects, especially after the Democrats secured control of the House of Representatives in 1874. He blamed talk of a third term for Grant as the cause for these setbacks and also worried about the success of the Democrats in the South. Thus, in his eyes, reform promoted the party's future as much as it promised efficient, business-like administration.

These political ambitions eventually estranged Jewell from Grant. The postmaster general supported the efforts of Treasury Secretary Benjamin H. Bristow to break up corruption in the revenue service, most notably in the collection of taxes on alcohol. At the same time, with the presidential contest of 1876 approaching, Grant and other Republicans sought to use post office patronage to strengthen the party's chances. Jewell rather brusquely rejected one of the president's requests, remarking, "Grant hasn't any influence in this department." Grant requested his resignation, and Jewell complied on 12 July 1876.

Jewell remained active in Republican politics as a member of that party's national committee. In 1876, after some people had spoken of him as a possible presidential candidate and he received some favorite son consideration, he worked for the election of Rutherford B. Hayes. He opposed the movement to nominate Grant for a third term in 1880. Afterward he chaired the national committee until his death in Hartford.

• Jewell left no papers. Dorothy G. Fowler, *The Cabinet Politician: The Postmasters General, 1829–1909* (1943), contains a brief treatment of his administration. See also William B. Hesseltine, *Ulysses S. Grant: Politician* (1935), and Allan Nevins, *Hamilton Fish: The Inner History of the Grant Administration* (1936).

BROOKS D. SIMPSON

JEWELL, Theodore Frelinghuysen (5 Aug. 1844–26 July 1932), naval officer, was born in Georgetown, District of Columbia, the son of Thomas Jewell and Eleanor Spencer. His parents' occupations are unknown. Appointed to the U.S. Naval Academy from Virginia in 1861, he graduated in 1864, having seen special duty at the Washington Navy Yard and with the Potomac Flotilla defending his native city during the Gettysburg campaign. After service with the European Squadron from 1865 to 1868, he was posted to the Hydrographic Office from 1868 to 1869 and the Naval Observatory from 1870 to 1871 in Washington. Jewell also served as instructor in physics and chemistry at the Naval Academy in Annapolis from 1871 to 1872 and from 1874 to 1878. He married Elizabeth Lindsay Poor in 1871; the couple had one son, Commander Charles T. Jewell.

While aboard the *Tuscarora* from 1872 to 1874, Jewell assisted in oceanic canal route surveys and northern Pacific soundings, which served as background for his professional article, "Deep Sea Soundings," in the U.S. Naval Institute *Proceedings* (1877). He also commanded shore parties that protected American lives and interests in Panama in 1873 and the following year in Hawaii. Later duty included coastal survey duty, 1878–1879, ship command on the Asiatic Station, 1886–1889, torpedo instruction at Newport, Rhode Island, in 1881–1886 and in 1889, and service on a board studying reorganization of the Navy Department in 1889 before returning to Torpedo Station duty at Newport as ordnance instructor.

Jewell's most impressive contribution may have been his superintendency of armaments fabrication at the naval gun factory in Washington from 1893 to 1896. Under his supervision, the factory provided the new American steel navy with superior guns, which would later be effective in the war with Spain. Charged with converting forgings and castings provided by the nation's steel industry into modern, rapid-fire, breechloading, rifled naval cannon, Jewell's factory in Washington speedily and efficiently provided the sinews of war for the fleet. Ordnance up to twelve and thirteen inches in diameter in addition to ammunition hoists, projectiles, electrical firing attachments, and even torpedo launching tubes proved their worth in the battles of Manila Bay and Santiago against the obsolete, outgunned Spanish vessels. Jewell's superintendency came at a crucial point in fleet modernization, as he declared in his 1893 report, "It has required

the utmost exertion to supply the guns, mounts, and equipments as rapidly as required by the new ships."

Jewell commanded the cruisers *Minneapolis* (during the Spanish-American War) and *Brooklyn* (from 1899 to 1900), and as rear admiral, he commanded the North Atlantic Squadron before his retirement on 22 November 1904. In the latter capacity, he again protected American interests during the tangled kidnapping of the elderly and wealthy American expatriate Ion Perdicaris by Moroccan brigand chief Mulai Ahmed el Raisuli. The affair led to President Theodore Roosevelt's dispatch of two squadrons of warships, including Jewell in the flagship *Olympia*, which engaged in gunboat diplomacy, becoming the subject of a 1975 movie, *The Wind and the Lion*, and secured Perdicaris's release. Jewell's squadron subsequently moved to Turkish waters to further demonstrate American sea power to protect American citizens and interests in the Mediterranean. Jewell retired to Washington, D.C., where he died.

• Jewell's annual reports as naval gun factory superintendent may be found in the secretary of the navy's *Annual Reports* (1893–1895). Standard biographical data may be found in William B. Cogar, *Dictionary of Admirals of the U.S. Navy*, vol. 2, *1901–1918* (1991); and the *Army and Navy Journal*, 30 July 1932. The 1904 Morocco affair can be followed in William J. Hourihan, "Marlinspike Diplomacy: The Navy in the Mediterranean, 1904," U.S. Naval Institute *Proceedings* 105 (Jan. 1979): 42–51.

B. FRANKLIN COOLING

JEWETT, Charles Coffin (12 Aug. 1816–9 Jan. 1868), librarian and bibliographer, was born in Lebanon, Maine, the son of Paul Jewett, a congregational minister, and Eleanor Masury Punchard. He grew up in Salem, Massachusetts, and graduated from the Latin School in 1831. He matriculated at Dartmouth College, but within a year he transferred to Brown University, from which he received a B.A. as the youngest member of his class. After two years of teaching at the Uxbridge (Mass.) Academy, feeling himself drawn to missionary work, he entered Andover Theological Seminary. His love of books attracted the attention of the librarian Oliver A. Taylor, who invited him to help prepare a catalog of the entire library. Already at Brown, Jewett and a fellow student had arranged and cataloged the more than 1,000 books of the Philermenian Society, the oldest and largest of the student libraries. Assisting Taylor on the alphabetical catalog introduced Jewett to library work, and after its publication in 1838 he was appointed acting librarian of the seminary. With his 1840 M.A. in hand, he booked passage on a ship for Palestine and Asia, in part for missionary purposes. Confirmation of its sailing reached him too late, having been incorrectly addressed. He resigned himself to this fateful turn of events and took the office of principal of Day's Academy in Wrentham, Massachusetts. In the fall of 1841 he joyfully accepted an offer to become the first full-time librarian of Brown University. A month after taking up his duties, he wrote on 12 November to his friend

David Greene Haskins, "I'm a real bibliomaniac & am always happy in a Library." In less than two years, busy every day of the week except Sunday, he produced a stout alphabetical and subject catalog of the library of Brown University, modeled on Taylor's 1838 volume that pointed the way to the modern dictionary catalog: author, title, and subject entries in alphabetical order. Simultaneously Jewett was named professor of modern languages and literature, a newly established department of the university. His standing with the administration, including President Francis Wayland, had been enhanced by a severe critique he had published—anonymously—of Dorr's Rebellion: *The Close of the Late Rebellion in Rhode Island: An Extract from a Letter by a Massachusetts Man Resident in Providence* (1842). To better fill his new office as librarian-professor, Jewett was granted a leave of absence to visit France, Germany, Italy, and England to look into what he termed "the science of libraries" and to purchase books for the library, many at the expense of John Carter Brown. After more than two years of visiting libraries, examining their methods, making the acquaintance of luminaries like Anthony Panizzi of the British Museum, and attending book auctions and sales galore, Jewett returned in December 1845 having increased the Brown University holdings almost two-fold (from 10,235 to almost 20,000). His book-buying expedition made its library an important academic research library and put Jewett among the top librarian-bibliographers of the day. Thus, respectful attention was given to his publicized opinion that Congress should not levy tariff duties on imported books in *Facts and Considerations Relative to Duties on Books: Addressed to the Library Committee of Brown University* (1846).

In 1846 Congress accepted the bequest of James Smithson, a British scientist, to establish an institution in Washington "for the increase and diffusion of knowledge among men," that would include a library, a museum, and an art gallery. The governing Board of Regents selected Joseph Henry, the renowned physicist of Princeton, as secretary and Henry chose Jewett, favored by several regents, as assistant secretary and librarian. On 11 February 1847 Jewett accepted the appointment on a part-time basis, for he had lingering doubts about the future distribution of the Smithsonian income, knowing full well that Henry was committed solely to scientific research and publication, while he championed the creation of a large library of works pertinent to all branches of knowledge. Living up to responsibilities in Providence and Washington was too draining. In March 1848 Jewett resigned from Brown. Later that year he married Rebecca Greene Haskins; they had three children. His tenure at the Smithsonian began on 1 January 1849.

Jewett envisioned the library of the Smithsonian as a great national library and the promoter of national cataloging, using stereotyped plates of entries owned by the institution. In 1850, as part of his annual report, he published a pioneering survey of more than 900 libraries, state by state, city by city: *Notices of Public Librar-*

ies in the United States. In 1852, while pushing a system of gifts and exchanges among libraries, assembling an unrivaled collection of catalogs and bibliographies as well as publications of learned societies throughout the world, he issued a small number of copies of *On the Construction of Catalogues of Libraries, and of a General Catalogue; and Their Publication by Means of Separate Stereotyped Titles. With Rules and Examples*. He had labored over the plates of Indiana clay during the summer "with the thermometer at 95° in the shade over a hot furnace from 9 in the morning till six in the evening without stopping to eat" (to Henry Stevens, 19 Dec. 1852; Yale). Shorthanded and with an overworked cataloger who nodded, Jewett was mortified at the errors in the titles that violated the thirty-nine rules he had himself derived from the reports of the royal commission hearings of 1848 and the famous rules of Panizzi. In 1853 he brought out a new edition of the publication, enlarged and corrected, which was widely distributed at home and abroad. All his dedicated and energetic endeavors now brought him a singular honor. The eighty-two librarians who gathered in September 1853 at New York University for the first American library conference unanimously elected him president. Before its conclusion they had approved the idea of a great national library at the Smithsonian, had endorsed Jewett's stereotyping scheme, and had named him a member of a commission to draft plans for the formation of a permanent librarians' association at a meeting in Washington, presumably when he so advised.

Jewett returned to a charged climate. The construction of the Smithsonian building was proceeding apace. Henry was more opposed than ever to the "library plan," which had lost at least one ardent supporter with the appointment of Regent George P. Marsh as minister to Turkey in 1847. The income-sharing arrangements for the future were being increasingly questioned and annual library allotments tended to diminish. Personal relations between Henry and Jewett had so deteriorated that they conducted most of their transactions in writing. In May 1854 a special committee of the regents, appointed more than a year previous, backed Henry. The compromise plan was dead. On 10 July Henry dismissed a stunned and incredulous Jewett. Leading newspapers and periodicals took up the cause, pro and con. A special House of Representatives investigation committee report of 3 March 1855, lost in a legislative shuffle, ended the matter. A furious Jewett, who needed to support himself and a family, returned to New England. Several offers had come to him, including a teaching position at Harvard and the presidency of a western college. On 14 June, as orator of the day, he attended a Jewett family gathering at Rowley, Massachusetts, planned together with his brother John, somewhat affluent after having published *Uncle Tom's Cabin*. A week later, 21 June, he accepted an offer from the trustees of the Boston Public Library to oversee its cataloging operations.

In March 1854 the city of Boston had opened a public library in two rooms of a schoolhouse to such popular success that that very year the city council authorized the construction of a permanent and spacious building in Boylston Street. Jewett soon also became an acquisitions librarian, using his expertise to select books that would constitute a reference (noncirculating) collection including many European titles, destined for the Upper Hall (later Bates Hall). He so satisfied the trustees that they appointed him superintendent of the library dedicated on 1 January 1858. It was a comforting vindication of his abilities. In ten years he made the Boston Public Library with its more than 140,000 volumes the second-largest library in the nation, the great exemplar of reference and circulation services under one roof. His constant concern with catalogs and cataloging resulted in two major publications: *Index to the Catalogue of a Portion of the Public Library of the City of Boston, Arranged in Lower Hall* (1858), and *Index to the Catalogue of Books in the Upper Hall of the Public Library of the City of Boston* (1861), which enjoyed a second edition (1865) for Bates Hall and a first supplement (1866). He sped up circulation of books by the use of call slips for recording loans rather than entries in ledgers.

He encouraged the exchanges of duplicate materials with other libraries and the sale of duplicate copies. And he advocated, ahead of his time, the establishment of branch libraries. But as a conservative Christian, and with a combativeness engendered by his Smithsonian troubles, he vigorously opposed opening the library on Sundays. Indeed the trustees had all they could do to keep him from resigning in 1865 when the Republican-dominated city council barely approved the annual reelection and salary of the outspoken Democratic superintendent. All told, he was the most prominent American librarian.

On the afternoon of 8 January 1868, while seated at his desk in the library, Jewett suffered a stroke of apoplexy. He died the next morning at his home in Braintree, Massachusetts.

• There is no considerable body of Jewett papers. Letters are scattered in northeastern archives and libraries: the American Antiquarian Society, Boston Public Library, Brown University, Dartmouth College (especially the Ralph Hastings Papers), Harvard University, New York Public Library, University of Vermont (notably the George Perkins Marsh and Henry Stevens Papers), and Yale University, as well as in the Library of Congress and the American Library Association Archives (the Seth Hastings Grant Papers). Despite the 1865 fire at the Smithsonian Institution that destroyed official records, many nuggets concerning the Henry-Jewett association will appear in the forthcoming volumes of *The Papers of Joseph Henry* under various editors, of which volume 6, *1844–1846*, ed. Marc Rothenberg (1992), brings Jewett into the picture. A biography of Jewett is Joseph A. Boromé, *Charles Coffin Jewett* (1951). Aspects of his works and career are found in George B. Utley, *The Librarians' Conference of 1853* (1951); Walter M. Whitehill, *The Boston Public Library: A Centennial History* (1956); David Lowenthal, *George Perkins Marsh: Versatile Vermonter* (1958); Jim Ranz, *The Printed Book Catalogue in American Libraries, 1723–1900* (1964); Michael H. Harris, ed., *The Age of Jewett: Charles Coffin Jewett and American Librarianship, 1841–1868* (1975); Maurice J. Freedman, *The Functions of the Catalog and the Main Entry as Found in the Work of Panizzi, Jewett, Cutter, and Lubetzky* (1983); and Kenneth Hafertepe, *America's Castle: The Evolution of the Smithsonian Building and Its Institution, 1840–1878* (1984). An obituary is in the *Providence (R.I.) Evening Press*, 10 Jan. 1868.

JOSEPH A. BOROMÉ

JEWETT, David (17 June 1772–26 July 1842), naval officer, was born in New London, Connecticut, the son of David Hibbard Jewett, a physician who served with state troops in the Revolution, and Patience Bulkley. Jewett's father arranged for him to read law with Governor John Griswold, but Jewett showed little interest. New London was a thriving port, and he instead shipped out to Spain. Seafaring agreed with him, and by the 1790s, during a time of considerable maritime expansion, Jewett was probably making regular voyages. He prospered as a merchant and a captain and, like so many of his neighbors, was a firm Federalist.

At the opening of the "Quasi-War" with France in 1798 Jewett volunteered for service. On 6 June 1799 he was commissioned a master commandant in the U.S. Navy and assigned to command the eighteen-gun sloop of war *Trumbull*, then being constructed by public subscription. *Trumbull* was completed late that year and subsequently ordered to New York. In mid-March 1800 Jewett received orders to convoy a store ship bound for Hispaniola with provisions for the American squadron there under the command of Silas Talbot. In the following months, *Trumbull* captured three French ships in the waters off Hispaniola—*Peggy* and *Vengeance*, both schooners, and *Tulipe*. After taking *Vengeance* back to New London to be libeled, Jewett returned to the West Indies in October, resuming his previous station at Hispaniola. Ordered to cruise off Puerto Rico, he remained there until early 1801 when, as a result of a peace agreement between the United States and France, he was recalled to New York. The new administration under Thomas Jefferson enacted the Peace Establishment Act, reducing the size of the navy and abolishing Jewett's rank of master commandant; he was discharged from the navy in June.

Jewett's activities during the next fourteen years are uncertain. He did not serve in the navy during the War of 1812, although it is possible that he might have gone privateering.

Whatever Jewett may have done during the War of 1812, he obviously enjoyed the life of a naval officer. With no possibility of serving in North America following the war, he traveled to Latin America, where struggles for national liberation were under way. In June 1815 he joined the navy of the United Provinces of the Río de la Plata, then fighting for autonomy. Jewett commanded the bark *Invincible*, cruising with effect against Spanish shipping. He later commanded another United Provinces vessel, *Heroina*. Forced to land in the Malvinas (Falkland) Islands in 1820, Jewett took the opportunity to claim them for the United

Provinces—despite the fact that Great Britain had established its own claim in 1592. Jewett's action, however, was not the primary basis for the later Argentine claim to the islands that precipitated the war with Britain in 1982.

After the United Provinces had secured independence from Spain, Jewett left their service in 1822. He traveled to Brazil, which had separated itself from Portugal in September of that year. Jewett joined the navy of the Brazilian emperor Dom Pedro I, which was under the command of Lord Thomas Cochrane, a former British navy captain. Jewett served with Cochrane at the siege of Salvador de Bahia. In a series of battles in 1823, Cochrane defeated the Portuguese and ended their power in the north of Brazil. Jewett distinguished himself in the campaign by capturing Portuguese vessels and helping to isolate their land forces. He also aided in the defeat of insurgent republican forces in Pernambuco.

In 1825 Brazil declared war on Argentina. Jewett was sent to New York to arrange for the construction of warships for the Brazilian navy. In 1827 he married a widow, Eliza McTiers, the daughter of alderman Augustine H. Lawrence. They had one child. By the time Jewett returned to Brazil the three-year war with Argentina had ended. Having been promoted to the rank of admiral commander in chief, Jewett spent the remainder of his career in the Brazilian navy. He died in Rio de Janeiro.

• Jewett's career in the American navy may be traced in the David Jewett "Z" file at the Naval Historical Center, Washington, D.C. On his family, see Frederic Clarke Jewett, *History and Genealogy of the Jewetts of America* (1908). For his service in Latin America, see Warren Tute, *Cochrane: A Life of Admiral the Earl of Dundonald* (1965); A. J. Carranza, *Campañas Navales de la República Argentina*, vol. 3 (1916); and T. M. da Silva, *Apontamentos para a Historia da Marinha de Guerra Brazileira*, vol. 2 (1882).

WILLIAM M. FOWLER, JR.

JEWETT, Frank Baldwin (5 Sept. 1879–18 Nov. 1949), engineer and industrial administrator, was born in Pasadena, California, the son of Stanley P. Jewett, an engineer, and Phebe C. Mead. The parents had shortly before moved from Ohio to a small community in California newly named Pasadena, where farmers and health-seekers planted a wide variety of fruit trees and grapevines. Jewett's grandmother had given the family a 25-acre parcel, but Jewett's father was more interested in engineering than in his apricot and orange trees. With two other men he organized and built the Los Angeles and San Gabriel Valley Railroad from Los Angeles to Pasadena. As a boy, Jewett became keenly interested in railroads and intended to make a career in that field.

When Jewett was about eight years old, the family moved five miles east of Pasadena to the community of Lamanda Park, where the boy attended a one-room school until he completed the eighth grade. he helped in the orchards, and he enjoyed hunting and fishing in the open country nearby. At some time in his early

years he had an infection that destroyed the use of one eye and impaired the other, but, while his vision was restricted, it did not prevent him from studying. Jewett attended the preparatory high school of Throop University (later the California Institute of Technology) in Pasadena. He matriculated at the university and received the A.B. in 1898.

Jewett, with his father's encouragement, intended to pursue graduate work at the Massachusetts Institute of Technology (MIT) in the fall of 1898 in electrical engineering. Jewett's mother died at that time, and he was unable to enter MIT immediately. His physics professor at Throop, on sabbatical leave at the University of Chicago, recommended that Jewett enter that college, and he was able to do so in the second term in January 1899. According to his college friend and later colleague John Mills: "Despite his youth Jewett was one of the most mature-minded of the graduate students at Chicago; and he associated on terms of congenial informality with professors and instructors as well as with his fellow students" (quoted in Buckley, p. 241). Among the instructors with whom he became acquainted was physicist Robert Andrews Millikan. Jewett organized a college group for studies in mathematical physics, he participated in a sociable group of graduate students who met for bimonthly symposia, and he was active in the Delta Upsilon fraternity. His adviser at the University of Chicago was Albert Abraham Michelson, for whom, as a research assistant, Jewett helped develop equipment for creating diffraction gratings for spectrographic analyses. At Michelson's suggestion, he carried out a study of the pressure and density relations of sodium vapor up to the boiling point of sodium and received the Ph.D. in physics in 1902.

Instead of returning to Pasadena, Jewett became an instructor in physics at MIT from 1902 to 1904. While there he met George Ashley Campbell of the engineering department of the American Telephone and Telegraph (AT&T) Company in Boston, who was very favorably impressed by Jewett's competence and personality, and so Campbell hired Jewett for AT&T as a transmission engineer in 1904. The telephone industry was in its juvenile stage, having been established by Alexander Graham Bell and financial associates in 1878 in Boston; long-distance telephoning existed from Boston and New York as far as Chicago and the company was intending to expand to greater distances. Jewett married Fannie C. Frisbie in 1905; they had three children, of whom one died in infancy.

Jewett became head of the AT&T electrical engineering department in 1906. He was recognized early by senior officials in the company as effective in recruiting highly qualified personnel. The entire engineering department, headed by John J. Carty, moved to New York City in 1907, where Jewett was responsible for transmission and production engineering. In the fall of 1908 Jewett was in a group of AT&T engineers who accompanied Carty to the west coast of the United States to determine the status of telephone service there. San Francisco, looking ahead to its recovery from its 1906 earthquake and fire, was planning a Panama-Pacific Exposition in 1914, and businessmen there hoped for transcontinental telephone service by the time of its opening. Carty turned the project over to Jewett.

Jewett recognized that the primary problem for transcontinental service was the need for an improved repeater, the device that received speech waves passed over a long telephone line and that amplified them for onward transmission. He visited Millikan at the University of Chicago for advice in the fall of 1910, commented to him that electronic discharges in a high vacuum, which was Millikan's field of study, might solve the problem, and asked for suggestions of physicists among Millikan's students whom he might hire. He urged a general study of telephone repeaters, with mathematical and laboratory investigations. Millikan recommended his student Harold DeForest Arnold, who in 1911 began working at Western Electric Company, which had been established in 1881 as the manufacturing branch of AT&T. Within a few years Arnold developed a high-vacuum electronic tube derived from the three-element tube first created by Lee de Forest in 1906, which proved to be satisfactory for long-distance communication.

Jewett was appointed assistant chief engineer of Western Electric in 1912, and from there he directed various aspects of the transcontinental telephone system, including necessary improvements in the open-wire lines and the circuit for the repeater. The line was completed in July 1914, before the delayed opening of the San Francisco exposition in 1915. Jewett advanced to chief engineer of Western Electric in New York City in 1916.

By then, events in Europe indicated a likelihood of U.S. involvement in war. Jewett supervised an increase in the manufacturing of vacuum tubes at Western Electric from 200 a week in March 1917 to 25,000 a week in November 1918, which were especially needed for military signaling. During World War I, he served as major in the Signal Officers' Reserve Corps, then as lieutenant colonel in the Signal Corps of the U.S. Army in 1917. He developed plans for a telephone system for the American Expeditionary Forces in France, carried out chiefly by his associate from Western Electric, Edwin Henry Colpitts, who was in that same military service. Jewett also organized a program to develop a wireless telephone for aircraft, which led to the first communication between the ground and an airplane in flight at Langley Field, Virginia, in June 1917.

This was followed within a few days by similar communication between airplanes in flight. Also during World War I Jewett was one of four advisory members of the Special Submarine Board of the U.S. Navy and a member of the Special Committee on Submarine Cables of the State Department.

In 1921 Jewett became vice president and director of Western Electric. Its engineering department worked closely with the engineering department of AT&T, where many of the theoretical studies were done. Company reorganization established Bell Telephone Laboratories from Western Electric in late 1924, and Jewett became its president. Simultaneously, he was appointed vice president of AT&T. All research and development facilities were incorporated into Bell Telephone Laboratories in 1934, under Jewett until 1940, when he became chairman of the board of directors of the laboratories. He retired in 1944. Jewett was considered an excellent administrator who found talented physicists and engineers for the company, which was expanding into worldwide communication. He advocated a strong role of nearly independent research in the engineering department, which was unusual in industry and contributed significantly to the success of his company.

Jewett was elected to the National Academy of Sciences in 1918. He became a member of the Committee on Scientific Aids to Learning of the National Research Council in 1923 and was chairman of its Division of Engineering and Industrial Research from 1923 to 1927. President Franklin D. Roosevelt appointed him to his Science Advisory Board in 1933, and he served on the board until 1935.

Jewett participated in both the National Academy of Sciences, a scientific organization that advised the federal government, and the National Research Council, a federation of government and educational and industrial agencies to promote scientific research, under the charter of the National Academy of Sciences. In 1939 he was elected president of the National Academy of Sciences and was the first engineering scientist to hold that position. Jewett's wide acquaintance among scientists and his ability to grasp concepts quickly in all disciplines contributed greatly to his accomplishments with the academy at a time when its services to the government were in demand. He reorganized its finances, especially its investment policy, and established a business office. He arranged for a rotating fund through the Carnegie Corporation so that projects could begin before government agencies had actually signed the contracts. He also ensured that the academy and the National Research Council worked together harmoniously. Readily elected for a second four-year term as president of the academy until 1947, Jewett's years spanned the preparation for war, then World War II itself, and the early postwar period. Recognizing its charter limitations on contracting research programs, Jewett and a few other scientists proposed the establishment of the National Defense Research Committee, which came into existence in 1940 under the chairmanship of Vannevar Bush, to act as a contract agency to the federal government for scientific programs. Jewett became chairman of its division (Section C) concerned with communication, transportation, and submarine warfare. When his former colleague Colpitts presented a subcommittee report in January 1941 urging that further research be done on the ocean environment for the requirements of the submarine fleet, Jewett strongly supported the recommendation, which led to considerable oceanographic research on sonar and other aspects of underwater sound by the U.S. Navy during the war.

As a separate wartime commitment, Jewett served as a member of the Coordination and Equipment Division of the Signal Corps from 1941 and as a consultant to the chief of ordnance from 1942 to 1945. He received the Medal for Merit in 1946 for his wartime services.

Probably through his involvement with the National Research Council, Jewett became interested in science programs in Japan, and at the time of a severe earthquake near Tokyo in 1923, he helped to arrange for relief assistance by the United States. In 1929 he participated in a World Engineering Conference in Tokyo, where he became acquainted with Japanese engineers and scientists. His involvement led to his receiving two awards from Japan. After World War II he arranged for two scientific missions to that country.

Jewett was cited by his colleague John Mills as having a "natural and unconscious ability to make friends rapidly" and "a character marked by frankness and sincerity" (quoted in Buckley, pp. 256–57). His contributions to AT&T were considerable, and his participation in the National Academy of Sciences greatly improved scientific and technical programs of the United States during a crucial period. He died in Summit, New Jersey.

• Archival material on Jewett is in the AT&T Archives in Warren, New Jersey. An account of Jewett at his retirement is John Mills, "The Career of Frank Baldwin Jewett," *Bell Laboratories Record* 22 (1944): 541–49. A biography is Oliver E. Buckley, National Academy of Sciences, *Biographical Memoirs* 27 (1952): 238–64, with bibliography. Leonard S. Reich, *The Making of American Industrial Research: Science and Business at GE and Bell, 1876–1926* (1985), has some discussion of Jewett's role. The technical side of the laboratory, with some mention of Jewett's activities, is in *A History of Engineering and Science in the Bell System* (7 vols., 1975). A somewhat closer look at Jewett as a person is offered in Maurice Holland, *Industrial Explorers* (1929). An obituary by Frank Gill is in *Nature* 164 (17 Dec. 1949): 1032, and another obituary is in the *New York Times*, 19 Nov. 1949.

ELIZABETH NOBLE SHOR

JEWETT, Hugh Judge (1 July 1817–6 Mar. 1898), lawyer, railroad president, and Democratic politician, was born at his family's homestead, "Landsdowne," in Deer Creek, Harford County, Maryland, the son of John Jewett and Susannah Judge, farmers. A graduate of Hopewell Academy in Chester County, Pennsylvania, Jewett attended Hiram (Ohio) College and studied law in the office of Colonel John C. Groome in Elkton, Maryland. In 1838 he was admitted to the Maryland bar and moved to St. Clairsville, Ohio. Jewett was married in 1841 to Sarah Jane Ellis of St. Clairsville, with whom he had four children. After briefly practicing law with Judge William Kennon, he removed to Zanesville, Muskingum County, in 1848. In Zanesville Jewett gained a reputation as an honest but astute lawyer with an ability to handle cases involving complex financial questions. Jewett's talent

for financial problem solving impressed local banking interests and led to his election as president of the Muskingum County branch of the State Bank of Ohio in 1852. After the death of his first wife, Sarah Jane, Jewett married Sarah Elizabeth (Guthrie) Kelly in 1853, with whom he had three children.

It was through his profitable legal and banking ventures that Jewett was introduced to the competitive world of Ohio politics. Like his father, Jewett became a staunch Democrat. He served as a presidential elector in 1852 and a year later was elected to the Ohio state senate. After two years as a state senator Jewett resigned to accept an appointment as U.S. district attorney for the Southern District of Ohio, a position that he held for one year. He also served as a delegate to the 1856 Democratic National Convention. In 1861 Jewett won the Ohio Democratic gubernatorial nomination. He ran on a platform that criticized the Lincoln administration and favored a negotiated settlement to the war, based on the compromise proposals of Senator John J. Crittenden of Kentucky; these included constitutional guarantees against congressional interference with slavery, rigid enforcement of the fugitive slave law, and the extension of the Missouri Compromise line to the Pacific, which would essentially allow slavery to expand. Jewett faced David Tod, a War Democrat who received the Union party nomination. The Union party was a nonpartisan coalition, composed of Republicans and Democrats who supported the war effort. Tod easily defeated Jewett by 206,997 votes to 151,774.

In order to finance the war effort, Congress passed the Legal Tender Act of 1862, authorizing the Treasury to issue $150 million (eventually $450 million) in paper money, popularly called "greenbacks" because of their distinctive color. Since this fiat currency was not backed by gold, it quickly depreciated in value and led to an inflationary price spiral during the postwar years. As a result hard money advocates wanted the greenbacks removed from circulation and the United States returned to the gold standard. By 1866 pressure from hard money advocates paid off, as the government began to gradually remove the greenbacks from circulation, thus making debts harder to pay.

One related issue was the payment of government bonds bought during the war. According to the Legal Tender Act of 1862, the interest on the bonds was to be paid in gold. Since government bonds were bought with greenbacks and the gold dollar was worth much more than the greenback, the act seemed unfair. Together with many western Democrats, Jewett found the currency problem of great concern. He questioned the validity of a policy that called for the redemption of government bonds in gold when greenbacks were accepted as legal tender for other exchanges. Jewett proposed a financial plan that gave bondholders two choices: acceptance of taxable, lower interest bonds in place of their present holdings or payment of the bonds they currently held in the same greenback currency with which they were purchased. Once the bondholders received their refunds a sinking fund could be set up by the government to pay off the national debt. He also suggested that the national banking system created in 1863 should be eliminated and greenbacks substituted for national banknotes. Jewett believed that under his plan the national debt could be paid off in eighteen years. Jewett's proposal, known as the "Ohio Idea," not only helped his election to the Ohio House of Representatives in 1868 but gained national attention after it was endorsed by fellow Ohioan George Hunt Pendleton, a leading candidate for the 1868 Democratic presidential nomination.

Meanwhile, Jewett had long been interested in the development of railroads. Partly through the efforts of his brother Thomas Lightfoot Jewett, who was involved with several Ohio railroads, but mainly because of his shrewdness as a financial manager, Jewett became an influential figure in Ohio railroad affairs. In 1855 he became a director of the Central Ohio Railroad Company, becoming its president two years later. Jewett held the presidency of the Central Ohio until it was sold to the Baltimore and Ohio Railroad in 1869, at which time he resigned to become president of the Little Miami, the Columbus and Xenia, and the Cincinnati and Muskingum Valley Railroads. In 1870 he and his brother Thomas succeeded in consolidating several smaller lines to form the Pittsburgh, Cincinnati, and St. Louis Railway (Panhandle Railroad), of which Jewett became vice president. The Panhandle was later leased by the Pennsylvania Railroad in 1871, and Jewett accepted the Pennsylvania's offer to become its general counsel. Jewett's involvement with greenbackism and his growing reputation as a practical railroad executive helped him win election to the U.S. House of Representatives, where he served from 1873 to 1874.

In 1874 Jewett resigned his congressional seat to accept the presidency of the financially troubled Erie Railway Company, earning an annual salary of $40,000 and a $150,000 advance on a ten-year contract. It was the largest salary paid to a railroad president up to that time. Jewett did not actively seek the Erie's presidency; in fact, he was the road's second choice after Colonel Thomas A. Scott, the successful first vice president of the Pennsylvania Railroad. However, Scott succeeded J. Edgar Thomson as president of the Pennsylvania when Thomson died unexpectedly. With Scott no longer available, the managers of the Erie searched for a new candidate. On Scott's recommendation, they contacted Jewett and offered him the road's presidency.

Jewett proved to be an outstanding choice. Years of financial exploitation by Jay Gould and Jim Fisk had left the Erie discredited and on the verge of bankruptcy. The Erie was owned almost entirely by English investors but was managed by an American board of directors, which followed a policy of distributing, as dividends, money that should have gone into improvements to the road. Jewett immediately worked to rid the road of any links to Jay Gould. He moved the Erie's headquarters out of the lavish Grand Opera House and back to its old headquarters at the corner of Duane and West streets in New York City. Try as he might, Jewett could not stop the Erie's impending bankruptcy and, thus, left its fate to the courts. The move was a success, as the New York Supreme Court appointed Jewett receiver of the bankrupt road. In 1875 it was sold under foreclosure for $6 million to the Erie Reconstruction Committee and reorganized as the New York, Lake Erie, and Western Railroad Company. Although a new board of directors was chosen, Jewett was retained as the road's president.

Instead of distributing the Erie's profits as dividends, Jewett used the money to improve its property. The entire road from New York to Buffalo was double-tracked, and outdated iron rails were replaced with steel. Jewett had air brakes and gas lights installed on passenger cars and improved the road's terminals, grain elevators, and connections with western rail lines. In 1883 he leased the New York, Pennsylvania, and Ohio Railroad (Atlantic and Great Western Railroad) and oversaw construction of the Chicago and Atlantic from Marion, Ohio, to Chicago, effectively developing a through line from the Atlantic Coast to Chicago. Under Jewett's direction, the Erie became one of the major broad gauge lines in the East to narrow its trackage. In 1880 the entire Erie line in New York State, from New York City to Buffalo, was converted from six-foot to standard gauge. Jewett saved the Erie from its desperate financial condition, and his policies brought needed improvements to the road, but its stockholders were not pleased with the lack of dividend payments, and in 1884 his contract was not renewed.

Jewett retired to his family homestead in Maryland, where he spent much of his time during the remainder of his life. His success in reviving the Erie Railroad earned Jewett token mention as a possible Democratic presidential candidate in 1884, but he made it known that he preferred a quiet retirement instead. He died in Augusta, Georgia.

• F. C. Jewett, *History and Genealogy of the Jewetts of America* (1908), is useful for tracing the history of the Jewett family. For a general view of Jewett's role in Ohio history, see Eugene H. Roseboom and Francis P. Weisenburger, *A History of Ohio* (1964). Jewett's attraction to greenbackism can be gleaned from Robert P. Sharkey, *Money, Class, and Party: An Economic Study of Civil War and Reconstruction* (1959), and Irwin Unger, *The Greenback Era: A Social and Political History of American Finance, 1865–1879* (1964). See also Chester M. Destler, "The Origin and Character of the Pendleton Plan," *Mississippi Valley Historical Review* 24 (1937): 171–84, and Max L. Shipley, "The Background and Legal Aspects of the Pendleton Plan," *Mississippi Valley Historical Review* 24 (1937): 329–40, for an extensive analysis of Jewett's financial plan. For a cursory treatment of Jewett's contributions to American railroad history, refer to John Moody, *The Railroad Builders* (1919), and John F. Stover, *The Life and Decline of the American Railroad* (1970). Perhaps the best account of Jewett's accomplishments as president of the Erie Railroad is Edward Hungerford, *Men of Erie: A Story of Human Effort* (1946). An obituary is in the *New York Times*, 7 Mar. 1898.

PHILIP PAPPAS

JEWETT, John Punchard (16 Aug. 1814–14 May 1884), publisher and antislavery activist, was born in Lebanon, Maine, the son of the Reverend Paul Jewett and Eleanor Masury Punchard. Jewett joined the American Anti-Slavery Society in 1835 during a period of volatile and often violent protest. He was an outspoken contributor to antislavery newspapers and counted among his friends antislavery luminaries such as Wendell Phillips, William Lloyd Garrison, and Charles Sumner. After selling books in Salem, Massachusetts, during the 1840s, he moved to Boston in 1847 and became both a bookseller and a publisher. Somewhat lacking in business skills himself, he shrewdly surrounded himself with advisers of probity, perception, and imagination. The success of his early career was commonly attributed to the acumen of his junior partner, Charles A. B. Shepard, who came to work for Jewett in Salem in 1845 when Shepard was fifteen years old. Shepard accompanied Jewett to Boston, where they established a bookstore on Publisher's Row. Buoyed by Shepard's "Algerish zeal" and willingness to work long hours, the firm flourished. Jewett's most spectacular success, however, was owing to the advice of his wife.

In 1837 Jewett married Harriette Cobb. They had five children, none of whom survived to maturity. Harriette Cobb Jewett's repeated loss of children surely contributed to her early death in 1860. It also primed her to respond powerfully to a serial published in 1851–1852 in the *National Era* called *Uncle Tom's Cabin; or, Life among the Lowly*, written by Harriet Beecher Stowe. Stowe had lost a baby in the cholera epidemic that swept through Cincinnati in 1849. "It was at *his* dying bed, and *his* grave," Stowe later wrote, "that I learnt what a poor slave mother may feel when her child is torn away from her." Drawing on powerful maternal feelings and writing in the wake of the Fugitive Slave Law, Stowe wrote a narrative that moved the nation. Publishers, however, were reluctant to invest in a first novel by a woman on a subject so controversial as slavery. Harriette Cobb Jewett stayed up all night reading and crying over the pages of the *National Era* and persuaded her husband that he must publish *Uncle Tom's Cabin*. Taking her advice, Jewett offered Stowe half the profits—if she were willing to assume half the costs. With a large family to support on the meager professorial salary of her husband, Calvin Stowe, and her sporadic literary earnings, Harriet Stowe could not afford such a risk. Calvin Stowe, acting as her agent, countered with a proposal for a 20 percent royalty. Promising to employ an army of agents to promote the book, Jewett persuaded him to accept 10 percent. Jewett was ingenious and innovative in his promotion of the book. He employed his friend John Greenleaf Whittier to write some verses about Little Eva, whose death in chapter twenty-six wrenched the hearts of readers. Set to music, these verses were the first of many spin-offs that spread the popularity of *Uncle Tom's Cabin*, from plates, spoons, wallpapers, and candlesticks to toys and games. The book, published in 1852, was an immediate sensation.

It sold 10,000 copies on the first day and more than 300,000 by the end of the first year. Stowe's first royalty check was for $10,000, but of course Jewett had the lion's share of the profits. Stowe conferred with businessmen at home and abroad and concluded that Jewett had taken advantage of her somewhat unworldly husband. When she wrote to him to ask him for confirmation of his theory that they would make more by agreeing to 10 percent instead of 20 percent, Jewett responded angrily and broke off communication. Stowe described him as "positive, overbearing, uneasy if crossed."

Jewett continued to be an important publisher of women writers. In 1853, on the advice of Whittier, he published Lucy Larcom's prose poems as *Similitudes*. With the hefty profits from *Uncle Tom's Cabin* Jewett opened a branch in Cleveland; by 1854 he was publishing there under the imprint Jewett, Proctor and Worthington. In 1854 he published another bestseller, Maria Cummins's *The Lamplighter*. Employing modern techniques of promotion such as noting "Thirty-Fifth Thousand" on the title page, Jewett drove Cummins's novel to a strong sale. In 1855 he brought out an edition of Margaret Fuller's *Woman in the Nineteenth Century*. Urged by his friends, he agreed to found a literary magazine that would be devoted to antislavery. Before this journal, which would eventually be born in 1857 under the title the *Atlantic Monthly*, could be realized, Jewett's business failed. It appears that in a dramatically expanded market, Jewett's business skills were not up to the challenge of managing two branches and the volume generated by booksellers. He was unable thereafter to establish himself. He reorganized his business, but Charles Shepard, his right-hand man, went his own way, leaving Jewett to weather the panic of 1857 by himself. That year he sold out to Crosby and Nichols, publishers of schoolbooks. He made several unsuccessful attempts to establish himself, first as a manufacturer of watches, then as a peddler of "Peruvian syrup," then as a seller of safety matches, then as a negotiator of patents. Around 1866 he made a final, unsuccessful attempt to reestablish himself as a bookseller, this time in New York. He did, however, succeed in his private life. In 1861 he married Helen Marie Crane, and together they had five children, all of whom survived to adulthood. He died in Orange, New Jersey.

• No collections of Jewett's papers exist; scattered letters can be found in various repositories, including the Connecticut Historical Society. The most complete account of Jewett's publishing career is in John Tebbell, *A History of Book Publishing in the United States*, vol. 1: *The Creation of an Industry, 1630–1865* (1972). For his dealings with Stowe, see Joan D. Hedrick, *Harriet Beecher Stowe: A Life* (1994). *The Letters of John Greenleaf Whittier*, vol. 2: *1846–1860*, ed. John B. Picard (1975), contains some correspondence regarding Jewett's publication of Lucy Larcom. An obituary is in the *Orange Chronicle*, 16 May 1884.

JOAN D. HEDRICK

JEWETT, Milo Parker (27 Apr. 1808–9 June 1882), educator, clergyman, and first president of Vassar Female College (later Vassar College), was born in St. Johnsbury, Vermont, the son of Calvin Jewett, a physician, and Sally Parker. After graduating with a bachelor of arts degree from Dartmouth College in 1828, Jewett served for a brief period as principal of Holmes Academy in New Hampshire while at the same time reading law. Subsequently he prepared himself for the ministry at Andover Theological Seminary, receiving a divinity degree in 1833. During this period he developed a keen interest in the emerging common school (public school) education movement and gave public lectures to popularize its growth. Jewett was married in 1833 to Jane Augusta Russell, also a New Englander. They were childless.

In 1834 Jewett was employed as one of the first professors at Marietta Collegiate Institute (later Marietta College) in Marietta, Ohio. He worked successfully to establish a common-school system in that state. Joining the Baptist church in 1839, Jewett left Marietta and opened Judson Female Institution, a Southern Baptist seminary in Marion, Alabama, where he also published a church periodical, *Alabama Baptist*. Judson prospered during his sixteen-year pre–Civil War administration. Anticipating the coming unrest, he resigned from his post in 1855 and moved to Poughkeepsie, New York, offering to have "such of his servants as accepted their freedom" accompany him to that northern city. There he purchased the Cottage Hill Seminary from the wealthy brewer and leading local citizen Matthew Vassar, whose deceased niece, Lydia Booth, had been the school's proprietor. This purchase would prove to be the most significant step of Jewett's career and would, indirectly, lead to the founding of Vassar Female College.

Cultivating Vassar's friendship in Poughkeepsie Baptist circles, Jewett learned that the brewer wished to leave for posterity an endowed institution "which would benefit mankind" and that he planned to establish a hospital. Jewett persuaded him instead to endow a college for women, which would be for them "what Yale and Harvard [were] for young men." Jewett wrote in a letter to Vassar in 1856, "If you will establish a real College for girls and endow it, you will build a monument for yourself more lasting than the Pyramids; you will perpetuate your name to the latest generations; it will be the pride and glory of Po'keepsie, an honor to the State and a blessing to the world." Vassar was convinced. Thereafter, Jewett took an aggressive lead in assisting Vassar, who had no background in education although he was an astute self-made businessman, to plan Vassar Female College, which was chartered in January 1861. Jewett was appointed the new college's president at the first meeting of the board of trustees on 26 February 1861.

Jewett aided Vassar in the gigantic task of formulating preliminary planning for the college. On 5 April 1862, in spite of the fact that his administrative work would fall on Vassar's shoulders, Jewett embarked for Great Britain and Europe to study foreign educational systems, libraries, and museums. His primary interest was in educating women in the liberal arts for their roles as wives, mothers, and especially teachers of young children, of whom he said there were in the 1860s "two million in the United States" with no provision for schooling. Both Jewett and Vassar believed that women's education should be as intellectually rigorous as that of men. They agreed to provide adequate apparatus and equipment as well as a demanding classical curriculum with excellent teaching, and they insisted firmly on oral discourse rather than rote memorization as pedagogic method.

Jewett lingered in Europe for eight months, improvidently long as it turned out. His absence at a critical time in the college's development seriously impaired his relations with the founder and certain important trustees, including Vassar's nephew Matthew Vassar, Jr., who disliked Jewett, distrusted his motives, and opposed both his presidency and his trip. Several factional issues erupted in the year following his return, culminating in a February 1864 dispute over the date for the college's opening. Favoring the following September, Jewett wrote an indiscreet letter to five trustees questioning Vassar's "fickle" behavior in desiring postponement until 1865. Once Jewett's betrayal was brought to Vassar's attention, he quickly sought his resignation, and the board appointed the Reverend John H. Raymond as Jewett's successor.

After leaving Vassar College, Jewett moved to Milwaukee, Wisconsin. There he continued his distinguished career as educator and public citizen while founding a business in coffees and spices. He served as chairman of the board of visitors of the Milwaukee Board of Health, trustee of Milwaukee College (later Milwaukee-Downer), of which he was chief officer of the board from 1877 to 1882, and president of the state Temperance Society. He died in Milwaukee while still very active.

There is no question that "without Jewett there would have been no Vassar Female College," claims Edward Linner, Matthew Vassar's biographer. Jewett did not bring to fruition his own incipient plans for a "university system" of education for women at Vassar College or chart in depth the college's early curricular development. His significance lay more broadly over those years in first stirring and then guiding Matthew Vassar's imagination to provide a serious educational opportunity for women.

• Jewett's papers are not very extensive and are found for the most part in the Vassar College library. His "Origin of Vassar College" was written in 1879 to clarify his relationship with Matthew Vassar and his influence on the founding of the college. It is included in Jewett's papers, as is an anonymous "Memorial of Milo P. Jewett," written in Milwaukee in 1882. Dartmouth College also has a collection of Jewett's papers. Jewett's influence on Vassar College is detailed in J. M. Taylor, *Before Vassar Opened* (1914), J. M. Taylor and Elizabeth H. Haight, *Vassar* (1915), and Edward R. Linner, *Vassar: The Remarkable Growth of a Man and His College, 1855–1865*, ed. Elizabeth A. Daniels (1984).

ELIZABETH A. DANIELS

JEWETT, Sarah Orne (3 Sept. 1849–24 June 1909), author, was born in South Berwick, Maine, the daughter of Theodore Herman Jewett, a doctor, and Caroline Frances Perry. As a child Jewett frequently accompanied her father on his medical rounds in the Maine countryside, sharpening her observational skills. In an 1888 letter to Emma Ellis, Jewett recalls her father's advice to "write about things *just as they are*." His advocacy of straightforward representation, along with Jewett's nostalgia for the disappearing rural Maine of her childhood, found expression in the voices that fill her sketches. After graduating from Berwick Academy in 1865, Jewett witnessed the gradual transformation of her quiet South Berwick community into a bustling retail district of post–Civil War New England. Jewett's response to the fading of rural Maine was to record the culture she cherished with optimistic realism.

The landscape surrounding her proved an influential tutor. Jewett was frequently sent outdoors as therapeutic treatment for her lifelong battle against rheumatoid arthritis, a condition that developed in early childhood. On her cross-country walks, she cultivated a love for flowers and herbs as she escaped the confines of the traditional classroom. Supplementing her education was an extensive family library, including not only traditional poets and novelists but also texts on history, philosophy, horticulture, medicine, theology, and the sciences. Jewett was never overtly religious, but her friendship with Harvard law professor Theophilus Parsons during the 1870s prompted interest in the teachings of Emanuel Swedenborg, an eighteenth-century Swedish scientist and theologian. Swedenborg held that nothing exists in isolation—the Divine is present in innumerable, joined forms—a concept underlying Jewett's belief in individual responsibility.

Published locally at age fourteen, the mature Jewett often neglected to mention her first regional publication, "Jenny Garrow's Lovers" (1868), a weak, conventional romance. She preferred to mark her literary debut with the 1869 *Atlantic Monthly* publication of "Mr. Bruce." Rejections of two stories followed as Jewett attempted to write conventional romances. In her 1871 correspondence with *Atlantic* editors James T. Fields and William Dean Howells, Jewett requested permission to develop "The Shore House" as a sketch rather than strengthening the plot as Howells had initially suggested. With Howells's editorial support, "The Shore House" (1873) became the first in an *Atlantic Monthly* series of Maine sketches that were collected in *Deephaven* (1877). These early works embody the descriptive style that Jewett continued to perfect throughout her literary career. She was influenced by the regional description and moral sensibility of Harriet Beecher Stowe's *Pearl of Orr's Island* (1862). Jewett later reflected that *Deephaven* was written as both a moral and a social education for her urban readers, validating the "grand, simple lives" of country people. In a letter to Jewett in 1875, Howells wrote, "You've got an uncommon feeling for *talk*—I *hear* your people."

While she loved her Berwick home, Jewett was readily welcomed in the social circles of Boston, as were her literary sketches. She began a round of visits to Boston, New York, Philadelphia, Concord, and Washington, D.C., during the 1870s, fostering important literary friendships. Jewett's friends included the families of Howells, Henry Wadsworth Longfellow, James Russell Lowell, Charles Eliot Norton, John Greenleaf Whittier, Julia Ward Howe, and Horace Elisha Scudder, editor of the *Riverside Magazine*. Following the shock of her father's death in 1878, Jewett found solace in further visits to these Bostonian friends. Distinctive among them was Annie Adams Fields, wife of publisher James T. Fields and hostess of one of Boston's most prominent literary salons. When James Fields died suddenly in 1881, the Jewett-Fields relationship flowered as the two women found friendship, humor, and literary encouragement in one another. Amiable traveling and living companions, the two women spent most of their following years in each other's company, visiting Europe and continuing to host American and European literati. Jewett never married.

In the following decade Jewett produced more than sixty articles and sketches, many of which were collected in *A White Heron and Other Stories* (1886). Her work also included three novels, *A Country Doctor* (1884), *A Marsh Island* (1885), and *Betty Leicester* (1890), as well as a history for young people, *The Story of the Normans* (1887). Like her short stories, Jewett's novels depict steadfast women in country settings and include moral reflection. *A Country Doctor* differs significantly in its feminist affirmation of the young heroine's self-reliance.

Jewett's revered work *The Country of the Pointed Firs* (1896) was first serialized in the *Atlantic*. Its publication was greeted warmly both at home and abroad; Rudyard Kipling wrote Jewett in 1897, saying, "It's immense—it is the very life." A twenty-sketch narrative of one woman's visit to Dunnet Landing, the work observes the joy and worth of the simple, isolated, and productive life. Jewett's characters gently reveal long-buried emotions: "I always liked Nathan," says Mrs. Todd, a widow. "But this pennyr'yal always reminded me, as I'd sit and gather it and hear him talkin'—it always reminded me of —the other one." Viewing her as "Antigone alone on the Theban plain," Jewett endows Mrs. Todd and other humble characters with mythic grandeur, celebrating the emotional complexity beneath their New England bluntness and humor.

The Country of the Pointed Firs secured a place for Jewett in the American literary canon. She was praised—and somewhat pigeon-holed—during her lifetime as a leader in the "local-color" movement of regional realism. Jewett's reputation was enhanced by her friend Willa Cather, whose preface to the 1925 edition of *Pointed Firs* aligns Jewett's text with Nathaniel Hawthorne's *The Scarlet Letter* and Mark Twain's *Huckleberry Finn*. Feminist critics have since championed her writing for its rich account of women's lives and voices. Jewett never abandoned her primary subject, the fruitful interdependence of community life. Counseling Cather in 1908 to write from her "own quiet centre of life," Jewett followed the success of *Pointed Firs* with further sketches and another novel, *The Tory Lover* (1901). Following a spinal concussion received from a carriage accident in 1902, Jewett's writing was limited to correspondence with friends. Three months after being paralyzed by a stroke, she died in South Berwick.

• The bulk of Jewett's letters is at Houghton Library, Harvard University; the Society for the Preservation of New England Antiquities; and Colby College, Waterville, Maine. Collections of her correspondence include *Letters of Sarah Orne Jewett* (1994); *Letters*, ed. Richard Cary (1956; rev. ed., 1967); and *Letters of Sarah Orne Jewett*, ed. Annie Fields (1911). For a listing of primary texts see Gwen L. Nagel and James Nagel, *Sarah Orne Jewett: A Reference Guide* (1978), as well as Clara C. Weber and Carl J. Weber, *A Bibliography of the Published Writings of Sarah Orne Jewett* (1949). Paula Blanchard, *Sarah Orne Jewett: Her World and Her Work* (1994), contains black and white plates of Jewett and her contemporaries. Earlier biographies include F. O. Matthiessen, *Sarah Orne Jewett* (1929), John Eldridge Frost, *Sarah Orne Jewett* (1960), and Josephine Donovan, *Sarah Orne Jewett* (1980). M. A. de Wolfe Howe, *Memories of a Hostess* (1922), depicts the Jewett-Fields friendship. Collected shorter criticism includes Cary, ed., *Appreciation of Sarah Orne Jewett* (1973); Gwen Nagel, ed., *Critical Essays on Sarah Orne Jewett* (1984); and June Howard, ed., *New Essays on "The Country of the Pointed Firs"* (1994). Selected readings of Jewett's work include Willa Cather, *Not under Forty* (1936); Sarah Way Sherman, *Sarah Orne Jewett: An American Persephone* (1989); and Margaret Roman, *Sarah Orne Jewett: Reconstructing Gender* (1992).

MARGARET A. AMSTUTZ

JEWETT, William (14 Jan. 1792–24 Mar. 1874), artist, was born in East Haddam, Connecticut, the son of Nathan Hibbard Jewett, a farmer, and Mary Griffin. There is little primary source material on Jewett. Most published accounts of his early life are based on William Dunlap's *A History of the Rise and Progress of the Arts of Design in the United States* (1834), and Dunlap acknowledges that his source was not Jewett himself. However, the fact that the two men were contemporaries and fellow artists in New York City gives his account some credibility.

Dunlap wrote that Jewett was employed at the age of sixteen by a New London (Conn.) coachmaker, perhaps a relative, to assist in the decoration of carriages. He was introduced to portrait painting when he met artist Samuel Lovett Waldo, who had come to New London seeking commissions. Intrigued with a form of art he believed to be superior to carriage decoration, Jewett offered to grind colors for Waldo in order to observe and learn as much as possible. Waldo accepted and, finding Jewett and his work agreeable, offered to give instruction to Jewett in return for assistance in his studio in New York. A short time later, Jewett arrived in New York and joined Waldo's household.

By 1817 Jewett had proved himself an apt pupil and a worthwhile assistant, and Waldo offered him a three-year contract to begin the following year. Jewett agreed to give his time and professional service to Waldo in exchange for a salary that would increase each year, along with board, lodging, and washing. Most importantly, Waldo allowed Jewett's name to be used with his own on all works they produced together. While artists' assistants were not uncommon at the time, it was unusual for masters to give public recognition to their assistants. The relationship between the two men appears to have been felicitous, lasting until Jewett's retirement in 1854.

Waldo and Jewett exhibited paintings at the American Academy of Fine Arts in New York for the first time as a partnership in 1818 and continually thereafter until 1833, the year of the academy's last exhibition. Jewett exhibited on his own only nine paintings, mainly still lifes, from 1816 to 1819. He became an associate of the academy in 1817 and an academician around 1824. At the National Academy of Design in New York, only portraits that he had painted with Waldo were exhibited. He became an associate member of that institution in 1848.

While works by Jewett and Waldo are in many major museums, there are only a few known to be by Jewett alone in institutions. Among them is *Portrait of a Man* (c. 1820s) at the Brooklyn Museum.

Jewett first appeared in New York City directories at an address other than Waldo's in 1826. He married Mary Lyon in 1830; they had one child. The fact that another artist with a name similar to Jewett's lived in New York contemporaneously has caused some confusion in attribution. William Smith Jewett, a portrait painter and landscapist, arrived in the city in the early 1830s as a student. He left in 1849 to spend the next twenty years in California. Jewett's son, William Samuel Lyon Jewett, was also an artist, known mainly for his engravings and sketches for *Harper's Weekly* and *Leslie's Illustrated Weekly*. In about 1840 Jewett moved to New Jersey, where he died, leaving a considerable estate.

• There are no private papers, diaries, or journals of William Jewett in public institutions. Secondary sources are faulty and should be used with caution. Dunlap's *History of the Rise and Progress of the Arts of Design in the United States* (1834) has been reprinted a number of times; see, for example, the 1965 reprint edited by Alexander Wyckoff. The artist's ancestry can be found in Frederic C. Jewett, *History and Genealogy of the Jewetts of America* (1908), but it is not reliable concerning the artist's professional history. The interest contract that began the partnership of Waldo and Jewett was published in Royal Cortissoz, "Waldo and Jewett," *New York Herald Tribune*, 17 Jan. 1943. Exhibition records for the American Academy of Fine Arts and National Academy of Design are the best sources for a chronology of the artist's professional life.

MARCIA GOLDBERG

JOFFREY, Robert (24 Dec. 1928–25 Mar. 1988), founder and artistic director of the Joffrey Ballet, was born Anver Joffrey in Seattle, Washington, the only child of Joseph (Dollha) Joffrey and Mary (Maria) Gallette, restaurant owners. He was also known as Anver Bey Abdullah Jaffa Khan. Joffrey was born with twisted feet that required him to wear casts. As a young boy he was bowlegged and severely asthmatic, and his family physician recommended that he participate in a regular exercise program. At nine he took boxing lessons. But Joffrey, who even in adulthood grew only to five feet four inches, was unsuited for the sport. He was subsequently enrolled in tap, ballroom, and theatrical dancing classes at a small studio above his parents' restaurant. His response was instantaneous and zealous. He envisioned "choreographing a snowflake ballet down a ramp" and told his teacher, Dorothy Culper, that he intended someday to direct his own ballet company.

Joffrey's formal ballet training began in 1939 with Ivan Novikoff, who was a Russian emigré and friend to many members of Sergei Denham's Ballet Russe de Monte Carlo. Over the next several years Joffrey performed small roles and served as a supernumerary in Ballet Russe productions of *The Nutcracker*, *Petrouchka*, and *Schéhérazade*.

In 1945 Joffrey met Gerald Arpino, with whom he would spend the rest of his life. Arpino was stationed with the U.S. Coast Guard in Seattle, and, although he became a charter member of the Joffrey Ballet in 1956 and chief choreographer by 1965, he had never taken a ballet class until introduced to it by Joffrey. They began studying exclusively with Mary Ann Wells. She offered instruction in Spanish, ballroom, preclassic, and modern dance (based on her training with Martha Graham and May O'Donnell). Her curriculum's core, however, was classical ballet. She took Joffrey's ambition to found a company seriously, cultivating his perfectionist's standards and taste. Throughout Joffrey's life, he credited Wells as his most profound influence.

In 1948 Joffrey choreographed his first works for a solo graduation program from Wells's school. The program was the formal start of his eclecticism. He synthesized modern technique with ballet in Hindemith's *Two Studies*—"grovelling around in bare feet looking for something lost," he recalled—and juxtaposed a suite of Schubert waltzes against Bartók's uncomforting Slavonic folk music in two separate, back-to-back dances. The idea of treating a ballet program as an opportunity to create a moving collage, a visual mix of stylistic contrasts, expressive of the discrete taste and broad-reaching eye of the director, became his hallmark.

In the summer of 1948 Joffrey and Arpino attended the School of American Ballet's summer program in New York City. They also studied modern dance with Gertrude Schurr and May O'Donnell, and Joffrey took private ballet lessons from Alexandra Fedorova. He became a soloist with Roland Petit's Les Ballets de Paris in October 1949, dancing in *Carmen*, *Le Rendezvous*, and *L'Oeuf à la Coque* for the company's fall season at New York's Winter Garden. After the engagement he rejected Petit's offer to continue on tour. With a penchant for teaching, he accepted a staff position at

the High School of Performing Arts, where he remained for five years.

From 1950 to 1953 Joffrey danced with May O'Donnell and Company, until a calf injury ended his performing career. But by this time he was securely established as an instructor and was beginning to make inroads as a choreographer. He taught at Ballet Theatre's school and in 1953 founded the American Ballet Center (also known as the Joffrey Ballet School) with Arpino in Greenwich Village, New York. In his classes he stressed placement and was one of the first instructors in New York to approach the body-in-motion scientifically, asking, how is the body built? Many flocked to him over the ensuing years, including Erik Bruhn, Eleanor D'Antuono, Sara Leland, Jillana, Lawrence Rhodes, Brunilda Ruiz, Paul Sutherland, Helgi Tomasson, and Jonathan Watts. His ideas about alignment changed the way his students approached the classical technique.

As a choreographer, Joffrey created most of his early works for High School of Performing Arts students. Although noted for providing well-crafted opportunities for dancers to shine, his ballets were largely assimilations of other choreographer's styles rather than articulations of an unyielding original voice. His first piece, *Persephone* (January 1952), reminded some critics of Balanchine's *Orpheus*. Storytelling also prevailed in his subsequent works *Scaramouche* (1952) and *Umpateedle* (1953). In the summers of 1952 and 1953, Ted Shawn invited Joffrey to Jacob's Pillow Dance Festival in Beckett, Massachusetts, to present his ballets.

In May 1954 Joffrey rented Kaufmann Auditorium at the Ninety-second Street Young Men's-Young Women's Hebrew Association (YM-YWHA) for a single evening event, the Robert Joffrey Ballet Concert. *Le Bal Masqué* and *Pas des Déesses* were given their premieres; the latter was a romantic pictorial ballet inspired by Chalon's famous lithograph of Taglioni, Cerrito, Grahn, and St. Léon in Jules Perrot's *The Judgement of Paris*. *Pas des Déesses* became Joffrey's signature work for more than a decade and was performed by his company, sometimes in excerpt, for forty years. It entered Ballet Theatre's repertory in 1956.

Drawing support from the establishment as one of the "most promising" young talents, Joffrey's choreographic output escalated in 1955. He presented an acclaimed "Evening of Original Ballets" in March at the Ninety-second Street Y. The following month, the legendary Marie Rambert asked Joffrey to stage *Pas des Déesses* and *Persephone* (revised) in London for Ballet Rambert's spring season. *Pas des Déesses* remained in Rambert's repertory until 1958, becoming the first American ballet to be performed behind the Iron Curtain when the company toured China.

Immediately upon Joffrey's return to New York, he formed the Robert Joffrey Theatre Dancers, his first professional ensemble. The troupe debuted on 2 October 1956 in Frostburg, Maryland, presented by Columbia Artists Management. Charter dancers Arpino, Dianne Consoer, Brunilda Ruiz, Glen Tetley, Beatrice Tompkins, and John Wilson traveled in a station wagon to ten southern states and managed the performances behind the scenes themselves. *Pas des Déesses* and Joffrey's new *Le Bal*, *Kaleidoscope*, and *Within Four Walls* constituted the repertory.

The Columbia Artist tours continued for the next eight years with the exception of 1963, covering over four hundred destinations in one-night stands. The Joffrey Ballet gained tremendous popularity and was sold out on most of the tours. By 1964 the troupe numbered thirty-five members, including a ten-piece orchestra. Joffrey said his intention was to make ballet more accessible. His dancers emphasized energy and spirit over form; their physiques, proportions, and lines were not usually in keeping with textbook ideals. "Dancers with perfect bodies don't have to work as hard," he said. He wanted rigorous performers committed to making dance seem fun; he wanted to bring ballet off the imperial pedestal, while maintaining high standards. From the beginning, he did not envision the company as a vehicle solely for his work; George Balanchine contributed four ballets during the touring years. Joffrey also presented Antony Tudor's *Soirée Musicale* and August Bournonville's pas de deux from *Flower Festival in Genzano*, neither of which had ever been danced by an American company.

To provide his company year-round employment and defray its costs, Joffrey created ballets for twenty-two New York City Opera productions under Julius Rudel between 1957 and 1968. He choreographed the NBC-TV Opera Theater production of *Griffelkin* (1955), the first of several television assignments, and frequently served as a guest instructor for ballet teachers' conventions and the National Association of Regional Ballet festivals.

In fall 1961 Joffrey received his first grant from an anonymous donor. He applied it toward a four-week choreographer's workshop, during which Arpino created *Sea Shadow*. Joffrey's fortunes turned dramatically because he had in Arpino a choreographer of considerable talent who was able to produce ballets rapidly (two in May 1961) and in almost whatever aesthetic vein Joffrey needed. Because many of Joffrey's dancers were, as he was himself, too short or oddly proportioned to become classical dancers in the strictest sense, he felt it was imperative to have works tailor-made for them that gave them a place in contemporary ballet.

In the summer of 1962 Joffrey secured financial backing from the Rebekah W. Harkness Foundation. His company spent twelve weeks at Rebekah Harkness Kean's estate in Watch Hill, Rhode Island, for another choreographers' workshop. There Joffrey created *Gamelan* (music by Lou Harrison), an ensemble piece inspired by Japanese haiku, and commissioned original works from Brian MacDonald (*Time Out of Mind*), Arpino (*Incubus*), Donald Saddler (*Dreams of Glory*), Fernand Nault (*Roundabout*), and the modern dance choreographer Alvin Ailey (*Feast of Ashes*). The American National Theatre and Academy (ANTA) selected the Robert Joffrey Ballet to perform a fifteen-week tour of the Near and Far East, sponsored by the U.S. State Department and the Rebekah Harkness Foundation. The tour began on 1 December 1962. The following year President John F. Kennedy invited the triumphant troupe to perform for Emperor Haile Selassie of Ethiopia at the White House only days before the company departed for a nine-week Russian tour on 17 October 1963, which was also underwritten by the Harkness Foundation.

In Russia, already strained relations between Joffrey and Kean reached the breaking point. An amateur composer, Kean had pressed Joffrey and Arpino into creating ballets to her music (*Dreams of Glory* and *The Palace*) and she had contested Joffrey's choice of repertory. When the company returned from Russia, Joffrey sent it out on the road for the final Columbia Artists national tour. Kean alerted him mid-tour that she was changing the company's name to Harkness Ballet, inviting him to stay on as artistic director. He said that "with only vague assurances about who would exercise final authority over the company's artistic policies" he could not accept her offer. The "company was not for sale," he added. On 14 March 1964 Joffrey severed his ties to Kean and the Harkness Foundation.

The dancers were still under contract to Kean, and most of the repertory was in her possession. Joffrey and Arpino were left with practically nothing. Girded by Alexander Ewing, Joffrey's stalwart executive director, he and Arpino reorganized. The triumvirate established the Foundation for American Dance, and a Ford Foundation grant of $155,000 was procured to reactivate the company and support the school.

In August 1965 the new Robert Joffrey Ballet made its official debut at Jacob's Pillow and a month later presented five world premieres at the Delacorte Theater in Central Park for a New York Shakespeare Festival series under Joseph Papp. "There is no doubt about it, the Robert Joffrey Ballet is a stunning company," wrote critic Allen Hughes in the *New York Times*, "bristling with talent, imagination and the courage to be daring and different" (11 Sept. 1965).

Joffrey was offered a free week of performances at City Center Fifty-fifth Street Theater from Morton Baum, the chairman and cofounder of City Center Music and Drama. But Ewing asked for a partnership instead: the Joffrey Ballet would perform one week in March and turn over 20 percent of the box office to Baum in exchange for an additional three weeks at City Center in the fall.

These kinds of novel and ingenious approaches defined the Joffrey's administrative style and even shaped the company's artistic profile. His dancers in the newly named City Center Joffrey Ballet were individual characters (*demi-caractères*), few by any stretch consummately classical. Their lasting impressions were made through drama and not, on the whole, in technical displays. Moreover, the repertory offered unparalleled opportunities to men, primarily in Arpino's works, in which they were treated with a confidence equal to women and not expected simply to transport ballerinas and anonymously support them.

The company reflected Joffrey's fascination with the counter culture. In March 1967 Joffrey exploded with a revival of Kurt Jooss's antiwar ballet *The Green Table* (1932), touching a nerve in audiences who were protesting the bitter realities of the Vietnam War. *The Green Table* initiated an ongoing association between Joffrey and Jooss. For the 1967 spring season Joffrey created his most famous ballet, *Astarte*, a psychedelic multimedia collaboration that was conceived by the film director Gardner Compton, using his films for a stage production overseen by Midge Mackenzie, who was responsible for *Astarte*'s overall design, which included live rock music by Crome Syrcus and sets by Thomas Skelton. *Astarte* conjured a chance sexual encounter between the Babylonian fertility goddess Astarte (Trinette Singleton) and an audience member (Maximiliano Zomosa). The ballet was the first ever to appear on the cover of *Time* magazine.

From 1969 to 1973 Joffrey's revivals of Léonide Massine's *Le Tricorne*, *Pulcinella*, *Le Beau Danube*, and *Parade* gave unprecedented insight into the Diaghilev period, spawned a small cadre of American dance historians, and lent credence to Joffrey's dichotomous philosophy that ballet can straddle many worlds. In 1969 he also introduced Frederick Ashton's *Façade* to the repertory and began a longtime association with the British choreographer. In 1970, aided by Massine and Yurek Lazowski, Joffrey reconstructed Michel Fokine's historic *Petrouchka*, and through the performances of Gary Chryst the company's national stature was better secured.

Then in 1973 Joffrey commissioned a choreographer who was mostly unknown to the New York mainstream audience, Twyla Tharp. Bringing her own modern-trained dancers with her to rehearse, create, and ultimately perform with Joffrey's dancers, Tharp created *Deunce Coupe*. Against a backdrop painted during the performance by self-anointed graffiti artists and accompanied by Beach Boys recordings, *Deuce Coupe* was a marriage of pop to classical form, one of the first times that high- and low-concept art were presented to the dancegoing public. It launched Tharp, and Joffrey was increasingly accepted as someone with a keen eye for the new direction, an artistic director of rare taste and aesthetic acumen.

In 1973 and 1980, respectively, he choreographed the last of his ballets, *Remembrances* (music by Richard Wagner) and *Postcards* (music by Erik Satie). After them he had little time for the studio. In 1979 the Joffrey Ballet closed down for six months. The Ford Foundation grants had dried up, and rising ticket prices had changed the audiences' essential composition from youths to mature, upwardly mobile professionals, who seemed more conservative. Joffrey responded, in part, by repositioning the company as a classical one. More or less chained to his desk, he hired dancers who were well suited to nineteenth-century full-lengths, and he put the repertoire into place that would provide the troupe a more grand and glamorous image. In 1982 he negotiated for a bicoastal residency between City Center in New York and the Music Cen-

ter of Los Angeles. The resourceful arrangement (which other artistic directors later copied in different cities) allowed the Joffrey Ballet a doubled fundraising base, which, in turn, helped provide for productions of John Cranko's *Romeo and Juliet*, Ashton's *La Fille Mal Gardée*, and Joffrey's *Nutcracker*.

In September 1987 at the Dorothy Chandler Pavilion in Los Angeles, Joffrey presented the premier of the reconstruction of Vaslav Nijinsky's *Le Sacre du Printemps*. A ballet that had practically no surviving links to the present was resurrected. It was a monumental achievement for Joffrey as the producer, assisting Millicent Hodson, a dance historian and choreographer, who for seventeen years had researched *Le Sacre* and had pieced the ballet together with Kenneth Archer, a British art historian responsible for the décor.

On 10 December 1987 Joffrey's production of *The Nutcracker* entered the repertory at Hancher Auditorium in Iowa City. Failing in health, Joffrey directed the staging from his sickbed, relying on Arpino, Scott Barnard, and George Verdak to choreograph and stage most of it. Joffrey reconceived the nineteenth-century classic with the designers Kermit Love, John David Ridge, and Oliver Smith in an American-Victorian setting that was inhabited by toys designed after many genuine articles from his own childhood collection.

Joffrey died in New York University Hospital. The company's press release stated that the cause of death was liver disease and renal and respiratory failure. Reports of Joffrey's affliction with the acquired immunodeficiency syndrome (AIDS) virus were widely circulated, and unofficial accounts by medical personnel and his personal colleagues confirm them. In his will, Joffrey requested that Arpino succeed him as artistic director. The Joffrey Foundation board carried out his plan, naming Arpino to direct the Joffrey Ballet of Chicago, as the troupe is called in recognition of its new home base since July 1995.

Joffrey was honored with the Dance Magazine Award (1963), the Capezio Award (1973), the Handel Medallion (1981), and the Distinguished Service Award of the Dance Notation Bureau (1985).

• Most of the papers of Robert Joffrey (including photographs, programs, newspaper clippings, and articles) are in the Dance Collection of the New York Public Library for the Performing Arts, Lincoln Center, and the Harvard Theater Collection at Harvard University. Videos of some of his ballets are also in the Dance Collection. Complete historical records of the Joffrey Ballet are available in the Joffrey Foundation and Joffrey Ballet School archives but are not open to the general public. Joffrey's life and the history of his company are chronicled in Sasha Anawalt, *The Joffrey Ballet: Robert Joffrey and the Making of an American Dance Company* (1996). Pegeen H. Albig, "A History of the Robert Joffrey Ballet" (Ph.D. diss., Florida State Univ., 1979), covers Joffrey's early training and the company's development through 1975. Joffrey's biography is in John Gruen, *The Private World of Ballet* (1975). See also the entries in Anatole Chuchoy and P. W. Manchester, *The Dance Encyclopedia* (rev. ed., 1967); Peter Brinson and Clement Crisp, *Ballet for All* (rev. ed., 1971); Walter Terry, *The Dance in America* (1971); and Richard Philp and Mary Whitney, *Danseur: The Male in Ballet* (1977). George Dorris, "The Choreography of Robert Joffrey: A Preliminary Checklist," *Dance Chronicle* 12, no. 1 (1989): 105–39, with additional material in *Dance Chronicle* 12, no. 3 (1989), provides essential reference material regarding Joffrey's work.

SASHA ANAWALT

JOGUES, Isaac (10 Jan. 1607–18 Oct. 1646), Jesuit missionary and martyr, was born in Orléans, France, the son of Laurent Jogues, a merchant, and Françoise de Saint-Mesmin. Isaac pursued a thoroughly Jesuit education. He entered the Jesuit college at Orléans in 1617, began his novitiate at Rouen under Father Louis Lalemant, the novice-master, in 1624, and studied philosophy from 1626 at the Collège de La Flèche, where the charismatic missionary to Port Royal (in present-day Nova Scotia), Énemond Massé, had been stationed. Jogues began theological studies at Clermont in 1634, but he curtailed them, taking ordination in January 1636 and embarking later that year for the Canadian missions. Jogues was accompanied on his voyage across the Atlantic by a substantial flotilla, including several Jesuits and Samuel de Champlain's successor, Charles Huault de Montmagny. After brief stops at Tadoussac, Quebec, and Trois-Rivières, Jogues went directly to the Huron mission, reaching Ihonatiria in September 1636, where he received the name "Ondessonk" (bird of prey) from his hosts.

Before September had ended Jogues and two other new arrivals, Charles Garnier and Pierre Chastelain, fell ill with influenza. Soon an outbreak spread among the Hurons, which led to a Huron council in which many laid responsibility for this and previous epidemics on the Jesuits' sorcery. Unable to deflect the animosity from the missionaries and realizing that all the Jesuits were in danger of execution, Jean de Brébeuf, superior of the Huron mission, boldly arranged for a Huron-style farewell feast at Ossossané, which successfully dissipated the hostilities. Before his first year among the Hurons was over, Jogues saw Huron support for the missionaries revive and witnessed the first baptism of a healthy adult male, Tsiouendaentaha.

In late summer of 1638 Jérôme Lalemant succeeded Brébeuf as superior of the Huron mission and put Jogues in charge of constructing a central Jesuit residence at Ste. Marie on the Wye River, in Ontario. Following the construction of the Jesuit residence, Jogues and Father Charles Garnier attempted to open a mission among the Khionontateronon (Petun nation) but were rejected, partly because Hurons, who were interested in protecting their control over trade between the French and Petuns, had accused the Jesuits of causing diseases and death. Later, Jogues and Father Charles Raymbaut traveled to Ojibwa country, reaching the Sault Ste. Marie area in 1641. While the second trip was more successful than the first, it was years before the Jesuits returned to maintain a residence there.

In June 1642 Jogues safely journeyed with a flotilla of Huron traders to Quebec. Mohawk warriors captured Jogues on his return trip the day after the group had left Three Rivers at the beginning of August. Captured along with Jogues were donnés René Goupil and Guillaume Couture and several Huron converts. In his account of the event, Jogues wrote that he could have easily escaped the Mohawks but decided he would rather stay and help his fellow Frenchmen and the Christian Hurons. All of the captives underwent customary tortures, including beating, forced marches, taunting, and mutilation; Goupil was killed, while Jogues and Couture were adopted into Mohawk families. Jogues's captivity ended with the help of Dutch officials; on 5 November 1643, he sailed out of New Amsterdam.

Jogues reached England at the end of December and the coast of Brittany on Christmas day. Worn from his captivity and travels, he was almost unrecognizable when he reached the Jesuit college in Rennes on 4 January 1644. After a brief stay in France, Jogues met the queen, Anne of Austria, and Cardinal Mazarin, as well as the Compagnie des Cent-Associés, and received a papal dispensation to celebrate mass despite the mutilation of his hands. By spring, Jogues was headed across the ocean to the Canadian mission again, reaching Quebec in July. His superior, Father Vimont, assigned him to the relatively peaceful Montreal. During this assignment Jogues recorded his captivity, described the death of Goupil, and reported on the geography of New York. Meanwhile the Mohawks were working to achieve peace with the French so they could retrieve prisoners. Both Couture and Father Bressani were released by the Mohawks during this peace initiative. In July 1645 Jogues appeared before a council meeting considering the peace at Three Rivers. In May 1646 Jogues shed the trappings of his office and traveled with Jean Bourdon to the Mohawks to finalize the peace treaty. On this diplomatic mission Jogues brought a box of clothes, articles for saying mass, and gifts. Following his successful diplomatic mission, he left the locked box with them because he expected to return shortly on his spiritual mission.

On returning to Quebec in early July, Jogues was denied permission by the superior general of the Jesuits in New France, Barthélemy Vincent, to return to the Mohawks because the French and the Mohawks were at war, but in late September he was permitted to join a Huron mission to the Mohawks. Before reaching their destination, the group learned that the peace with the Mohawks had ended. Having no reason to continue into Mohawk country, the Hurons retreated. Left alone except for a single Huron, Jogues and his companion, the donné Jean de la Lande, decided to continue. Mohawk warriors found them near Fort Richelieu in mid-October and treated them as captives because some considered Jogues's witchcraft to be responsible for the misfortune they had experienced since he had left the box with them the previous spring. The Frenchmen were taken to Ossernenon (now Auriesville, N.Y.). However, possibly because of the epidemic, drought, and famine that succeeded his summer embassy or possibly because some anti-French Mohawks of the Bear clan wanted to hinder a potential peace initiative, Jogues was unceremoniously executed on 18 October 1646, by a hatchet through the head. La Lande was probably killed the next day.

When the Jesuits finally learned of Jogues's death in June 1647, their sadness at losing one of their missionaries was tempered by their joy at his martyrdom. All had expected some martyrdoms since the mission had started, and Jogues was their first priest to die for his faith. He was beatified on 2 June 1925 by Pope Pius XI. On 29 June 1930 Jogues was canonized by the Roman Catholic church along with seven other martyrs of New France who, except for Goupil, were killed over the three years following his death.

• The oldest biographies and several samples of Jogues's writing are in R. G. Thwaites, ed., *The Jesuits Relations and Allied Documents: Travels and Explorations of the Jesuit Missionaries in New France 1610–1791* (73 vols., 1896–1901). See also Isaac Jogues, "The Jogues Paper," trans. and ed. John G. Shea, New York Historical Society, *Collections*, 2d ser., 3 (1857): 161–229. One of the more recent and complete biographies is Francis Talbot, *Saint among Savages: The Life of Isaac Jogues* (1935). His life is favorably recounted in many histories of New France, including François Du Creux, *The History of Canada or New France*, trans. P. J. Robinson, ed. James B. Conacher (1951–1952); P. F. X. de Charlevoix, *History and General Description of New France*, trans. and ed. John Gilmary Shea (6 vols., 1870); John G. Shea, *History of the Catholic Missions among the Indian Tribes of the United States, 1529–1854* (1854); Francis Parkman, *The Jesuits in North America in the 17th Century* (1867); Félix Martin, *Le R.P. Isaac Jogues de la Compagnie de Jésus, premier apôtre des Iroquois* (1873); and Camille De Rochemonteix, *Les Jésuites et la Nouvelle-France au XVII Siécle* (3 vols., 1895). For brief sketches, see Lucien Campeau, "Portrait de Saint Isaac Jogues," *Lettres du Bas-Canada* 4 (1952): 133–40, and John J. Wynne, *The Jesuit Martyrs of North America: Isaac Jogues, John De Brébeuf, Gabriel Lalemant, Noel Chabanel, Anthony Daniel, Charles Garnier, René Goupil, John Lalande* (1925).

SEAN O'NEILL

JOHNS, Clayton (24 Nov. 1857–5 Mar. 1932), composer, pianist, and teacher, was born in New Castle, Delaware, the son of James McCalmont Johns and Eliza Hopkins. Clayton received his early education at public and private schools in Delaware, including Rugby Academy in Wilmington. While his tradition-bound family envisioned for him a career in law or the clergy, he wished to pursue music. He compromised by studying architecture in Philadelphia (c. 1875–1879). He then moved to Boston to study at the Massachusetts Institute of Technology but after hearing the Boston Symphony Orchestra, decided on music after all. He studied composition at Harvard University with John Knowles Paine (1879–1881) and also studied piano privately with William H. Sherwood in 1879–1882.

In 1882 Johns went to England, where he and various traveling companions got "our first thrill of antiquity" (*Reminiscences of a Musician*, p. 11), moved on to Wagner's Bayreuth Festival for a performance of *Parsifal*, and then to Berlin, where he studied piano with Friedrich Grabau and Oskar Raif and counterpoint and composition with Friedrich Kiel, all three members of the faculty at the Hochschule für Musik. In July 1883 he briefly attended Franz Liszt's master class in Weimar. He also became friendly with the great violinist Joseph Joachim. In June 1884 he returned to Boston, establishing himself as a teacher of piano and composition, and publishing many of his songs and other works.

For twenty years he gave an annual recital featuring his latest songs, and he spent many summers in Europe, especially England, with old and new acquaintances. In the summer of 1895 he spent six weeks in London accompanying Nellie Melba, Emma Eames, David Bispham, and others as they performed his songs. Other singers who sang his songs during the course of his life included Julie Wyman, Marie Brema, Eliot Hubbard, Max Heinrich, John S. Codman, and Heinrich Meyn. His most loyal collaborator was the Boston soprano Lena Little. He confessed in *Reminiscences* that he "never got over a temperamental nervousness" in front of audiences but did enjoy playing chamber music. A notable series of performances in the 1880s, surveying the sonata literature for piano and violin with composer-violinist Charles Martin Loeffler, was held in the downtown Boston home of his friends John L. and Isabella Stewart Gardner. He taught piano at the New England Conservatory from 1912 to 1928.

Johns never married and judging from hints in his memoirs and in obituaries, may have been homosexual. "His home was in Brimmer Chambers, at Pinckney Street [an area popular with homosexuals] and the Esplanade," according to the obituary in the *Conservatory Bulletin*. He was a member of the Tavern Club (along with many other prominent musicians) and the Harvard Club and frequented the Church of the Advent. He died in Boston.

Johns's musical works include Introduction and Fugue for piano (1899), played by Josef Hoffmann; short pieces for violin and piano, for piano solo, and for string orchestra; and *The Mystery Play*, incidental music for a fourteenth-century miracle play performed at the Tavern Club in 1905. Of his more than 100 songs for solo voice and piano, many were published in sets (e.g., *Wonder Songs* [1895] and *French Songs* [1898]), some of them printed with unusual care for elegance and accuracy. Hughes and Elson reported that though several piano works held "well-earned popularity . . . his songs carry farthest with the public. One has yet to hear of a summer hotel in this broad country that has not echoed to 'I Cannot Help Loving Thee,' or 'I Love, And The World Is Mine'" (Hughes and Elson, pp. 551–52). Other Johns songs particularly appreciated in his lifetime were "The Scythe Song," "Were I a Prince Egyptian," "No Lotos Flower on Ganges Borne," and "Barefoot Boy with Cheek of Tan" (the latter was included in songbooks for use in public schools).

The songs are little heard today, but the best of them deserve revival for their melodiousness, grateful keyboard writing, and sensitivity to the well-chosen texts (e.g., by Arlo Bates, Emily Dickinson, Oliver

Herford, Robert Herrick, Andrew Lang, and Paul Verlaine). "While he is not at all revolutionary, he has a certain individuality of ease, and lyric quality without storm or stress of passion" (Hughes and Elson, p. 368).

Johns published three books, in addition to his travel-oriented *Reminiscences of a Musician* (1929), which includes eleven photographs. *The Essentials of Pianoforte-Playing* (1909) is notable for enriching the usual technical instruction with historical and music-theoretical guidelines to help the performer grasp the style and characteristic gestures of the various pieces (complete movements) reprinted and discussed. *From Bach to Chopin* (1911) prints passages from standard-repertoire works, with helpful commentary about how to play them with facility and musical sensitivity. *Do You Know That———?* (1926), was dedicated to the faculty and students of the New England Conservatory of Music and offers further words of wisdom and pet theories about musical style, form, performance, and aesthetics, including fascinating analogies between sonata form and both drama and architecture. For example, Johns views first theme, second theme, and confirmation of the new key as being like, respectively, the hero, heroine, and "other male character" in a play. Such hermeneutic tools, however simplistic in wording, are of interest to current musical scholarship for what they reveal about how gendered and other social meanings are encoded, or were once believed to be so, in the music itself.

• Letters from Johns to Isabella Stewart Gardner are in the Isabella Stewart Gardner Museum. Excerpts are cited and discussed in Louise Hall Tharp, *Mrs. Jack* (1965), which also contains a photograph of Johns with mustache; and in Ralph P. Locke, "Isabella Stewart Gardner: Music Patron and Music Lover," in *Cultivating Music in America: Women Patrons and Activists Since 1860*, ed. Locke and Cyrilla Barr (1997), pp. 90–121. The manuscript of *The Mystery Play* is in the New York Public Library. Johns's *Do You Know That———?* is discussed in Locke, "Comment and Chronicle [on Sonata Form]," *Nineteenth-Century Music* 16, no. 3 (Winter 1993): 304–5. Rupert Hughes and Arthur Elson's *American Composers* (1914), offers an evaluation of Johns's compositions. On the world of Pinckney Street, with discussions of Johns and various of his friends, see Douglas Shand-Tucci, *Boston Bohemia, 1881–1900*, vol. 1 of *Ralph Adams Cram: Life and Architecture* (1994). Obituaries are in the *Boston Evening Transcript*, 5 Mar. 1932; the *New York Times*, 6 Mar. 1932; *Musical Courier* 12 Mar. 1932; and the *New England Conservatory of Music Bulletin* 14, no. 3 (Winter 1993): 304–5.

RALPH P. LOCKE

JOHNS, Vernon Napoleon (22 Apr. 1892–10 June 1965), Baptist pastor and civil rights pioneer, was born in Darlington Heights, near Farmville, Prince Edward County, Virginia, the son of Willie Johns, a Baptist preacher and farmer, and Sallie Branch Price. At age three, according to family tradition, young Vernon began preaching "on the doorstep or on a stump." Two years later he went with his older sister Jessie to a one-room school four miles from the Johnses' home. At seven, Vernon was kicked in the face by a mule. The injury scarred his left cheek, damaged his eyesight, and caused his left eyelid to twitch throughout his life. Johns later compensated for his weak eyesight by committing long passages of poetry and scripture to memory.

For several years after 1902, Jessie and Vernon Johns attended the Boydton Institute, a Presbyterian mission school near Boydton, Virginia, but the death of their father in 1907 brought Johns back to the family farm. Two years later he was nearly killed by the horns of a bull. Shortly thereafter Johns left the family home to study at Virginia Theological Seminary and College in Lynchburg, where he received an A.B. in 1915. Admitted to the Oberlin School of Religion, Johns became the student pastor of a small Congregational church in Painesville, Ohio. While at Oberlin, Johns was offered a scholarship to Western Reserve Law School, but he felt that the ministry was his vocation. After giving the annual student oration at Oberlin's Memorial Arch in 1918, Johns received a B.D. from the Oberlin School of Religion and was ordained in the Baptist ministry.

In 1918 Vernon Johns began teaching homiletics and New Testament at Virginia Theological Seminary and became a graduate student in theology at the University of Chicago. Continuing to teach at the seminary, he became the pastor of Lynchburg's Court Street Baptist Church, where he served from 1920 to 1926. Economic self-help in African-American communities was a persistent theme in Johns's ministry, and, at Court Street Church, he persuaded the men's Bible class to launch a grocery store. In 1926 Vernon Johns preached for the first of many times at Howard University's Rankin Memorial Chapel, became the first African-American preacher to have a sermon, "Transfigured Moments," published in Joseph Fort Newton's *Best Sermons* series, and was named director of the Baptist Educational Center of New York City. A year later he married Altona Trent, the daughter of William Johnson Trent, the president of Livingstone College in Salisbury, North Carolina. Vernon and Altona Trent Johns became the parents of six children.

In 1929 Johns left New York to become president of Virginia Theological Seminary and College. In that capacity he founded an Institute for Rural Preachers of Virginia, which he conducted for ten years, and the Farm and City Club, which promoted economic ties between urban and rural African Americans. In 1933 Johns was pastor of Holy Trinity Baptist Church in Philadelphia, Pennsylvania. He retired from the college presidency in September 1934 to his farm in Prince Edward County, where he lived until 1937. During those years Johns farmed, cut and sold pulpwood, operated a grocery store in Darlington Heights, and traveled, lecturing and preaching on the black church and college circuits. He launched the struggle to get school buses for African-American students in Prince Edward County. Altona Trent Johns supplemented the family income by teaching public school in a one-room public school four miles from the family home.

In 1937 Johns became the pastor of First Baptist Church in Charleston, West Virginia. A former college president, the published pastor of an important African-American congregation, and son-in-law of a college president, Vernon Johns seemed bound to a secure position in the African-American elite. Yet he was rooted in the hard economic realities of Prince Edward County and grew contemptuous of the social pretense of the black bourgeoisie. As pastor of Charleston's First Baptist Church, he supplemented his income as a fishmonger. "I don't apologize for it," he later told students at Howard University, "because for every time I got one call about religion, I got forty calls about fish." It was a pattern of offense Johns would repeat. In 1941 he returned to Lynchburg as pastor of Court Street Baptist Church.

In January 1948, months after Altona Trent Johns joined the faculty of Alabama State College in Montgomery, Vernon Johns was called as the pastor of that city's Dexter Avenue Baptist Church. He renewed his credentials as the publishing pastor of a leading African-American congregation with an essay, "Civilized Interiors," in Herman Dreer's *American Literature by Negro Authors* in 1950, but he antagonized local white authorities with sermons such as "Segregation after Death," "It's Safe to Murder Negroes in Montgomery," and "When the Rapist Is White" and by summoning black passengers to join him in a protest of racial discrimination by walking off a bus in Montgomery.

In 1951, when his father-in-law became the first African-American appointed to the Salisbury, North Carolina, school board, Vernon Johns's sixteen-year-old niece, Barbara Johns, led African-American students at R.R. Moton High School in Farmville, Virginia, in a boycott to protest conditions in Prince Edward County's schools. A month later attorneys for the National Association for the Advancement of Colored People filed suit to desegregate the county schools. That summer Barbara Johns left Prince Edward County to live with her aunt and uncle and spend her senior year of high school in Montgomery, Alabama. By then, however, Vernon Johns was antagonizing his own congregation's bourgeois sensibilities with sermons such as "Mud Is Basic" and by hawking produce at church functions. After four stormy years at Dexter Avenue, the deacons accepted one of Vernon Johns's resignation threats in the summer of 1952. Altona Johns left Montgomery for a position at Virginia State College in Petersburg, but her husband thought the deacons would relent and sequestered himself in the parsonage. When the trustees cut off its electricity, gas, and water in December 1952, Johns finally left Montgomery.

Vernon Johns was never the pastor of a church again. From 1953 to 1955 he shuttled between his Prince Edward County farm, where he raised livestock, and his wife's home in Petersburg, where he became a mentor to Wyatt Tee Walker, the pastor of Gillfield Baptist Church. Between 1955 and 1960 Johns was director of the Maryland Baptist Center, but he was asked to resign after a public rebuke to white Baptist clergymen in Baltimore for their failure of nerve in race relations. Briefly in 1961 Johns edited and published *Second Century Magazine*. After preaching his last sermon, "The Romance of Death," in Howard University's Rankin Chapel, Vernon Johns died in Washington, D.C.

• In lieu of any collection of Vernon Johns's papers, researchers must rely on *Human Possibilities: A Vernon Johns Reader, Including an Unfinished Ms., Sermons, Essays, and Doggerel,* ed. Samuel L. Gandy (1977). Taylor Branch, *Parting the Waters: America in the King Years, 1954–63* (1988), and Vidmark Entertainment's videotape, *The Road to Freedom: The Vernon Johns Story* (1994), starring James Earl Jones in the title role, drew broad public attention to Johns. Other significant sources are Ralph David Abernathy, *And the Walls Came Tumbling Down: An Autobiography* (1989); Charles Emerson Boddie, *God's Bad Boys* (1972); Zelia S. Evans, with J. T. Alexander, eds., *Dexter Avenue Baptist Church, 1877–1977* (1977); Henry Mitchell, *Black Preaching: The Recovery of a Powerful Art* (1990); William Henry Rowland Powell, *Illustrations from a Supervised Life* (1968); Lester F. Russell, *Black Baptist Secondary Schools in Virginia, 1887–1957* (1981); Robert Collins Smith, *They Closed Their Schools: Prince Edward County, Virginia, 1951–1964* (1965); and Ethel L. Williams, ed., *Biographical Directory of Negro Ministers* (1970). A brief obituary is in *Jet,* 22 July 1965, p. 47.

RALPH E. LUKER

JOHNSON, Albert (5 Mar. 1869–17 Jan. 1957), journalist and congressman, was born in Springfield, Illinois, the son of Charles W. Johnson, an attorney, and Anna E. Ogden. He grew up in Hiawatha, Kansas, attending the public schools there and in nearby Atchison. After graduating from high school in 1888 Johnson embarked on a peripatetic career in journalism, working as a cub reporter on the *St. Louis Globe-Democrat.* He moved to the *Washington Morning Post* in 1892 or 1893, and in 1896 became managing editor of the *New Haven Register.* He returned to the *Morning Post* briefly in 1898 as news editor but soon agreed to edit the *Tacoma News,* a conservative Republican newspaper. This began a lifelong career in the state of Washington. In 1904 Johnson married Jennie S. Smith; they had one child.

From 1907 to 1909 Johnson worked on two Seattle newspapers, the *Morning Times* and the *Sunday Times.* In the latter year he moved to Hoquiam, a small lumbering center on the southern Washington coast, and purchased the *Grays Harbor Washingtonian,* which he published until his retirement twenty-five years later. From 1937 to 1939 he was a special writer for the *Wenatchee Daily World.*

Long associated with Republican politics, Johnson became a political leader in 1912 when he headed a citizens' committee that helped to break a timber workers' strike led by the Industrial Workers of the World (IWW). This was one of the early skirmishes in the war waged against the IWW in the Pacific Northwest that led to such events as the Everett massacre of 1916.

Also in 1912, benefiting from the split between Republicans and Progressives, he defeated a one-term incumbent congressman who ran as a Progressive. Johnson represented a largely rural and small town district in western Washington for twenty years in the House of Representatives until defeated in 1932. Without giving up his seat he secured a commission as a captain in the U.S. Army's Chemical Warfare Service during World War I; he served just ninety-one days, from 31 August to 29 November 1918.

Johnson's congressional career is notable chiefly for his work on immigration. He was a member of the Committee on Immigration and Naturalization throughout his House service and chaired it after Republicans assumed control in 1919. As an antiradical, antiforeign racist, he was fully attuned to the national climate of opinion in what researcher John Higham has labeled the "tribal twenties." According to Johnson's own highly imaginative account he had become a dedicated opponent of Japanese immigration in 1898 when he saw "hordes" of incoming Japanese taking the jobs of young Americans fighting in the Philippines.

In 1920 Johnson introduced and guided through the House a bill to suspend immigration entirely for two years; the bill was moderated by the Senate to become the 1921 quota act, vetoed by President Woodrow Wilson but repassed and signed by President Warren G. Harding. This act set annual quotas for each nationality group at 3 percent of the number of foreign-born persons of that nationality enumerated in the 1910 census. Johnson was the coauthor, with Senator David A. Reed (R.-Pa.), of the National Origins Act of 1924, which largely replicated the 1921 act, lowered the quotas to 2 percent, and moved the census base back to 1890, thus greatly reducing the number of eastern and southern Europeans eligible to enter the United States as well as the total number of entrants. Johnson was among those chiefly responsible for the inclusion in the act of the clause prohibiting the immigration of any "aliens ineligible to citizenship," i.e., Asians. The 1870 naturalization statute, as interpreted by the U.S. Supreme Court in *Ozawa v. U.S.* (1922) and *Third v. U.S.* (1923), provided only for the naturalization of whites and "persons of African descent." This abrogated the gentlemen's agreement of 1907–1908 with Japan, under which Japan—not the United States—inhibited the immigration of Japanese to America, and heightened tensions between the United States and Japan. The restrictive immigration policies thus established were not fully superseded until 1965. In 1927 Johnson defended the act as a defense "against a stream of alien blood, with all its inherited misconceptions respecting the relationships of the governing power to the governed." He proclaimed that "the myth of the melting pot has been discredited. . . . The United States is our land. . . . We intend to maintain it so. The day of unalloyed welcome to all peoples, the day of indiscriminate acceptance of all races, has definitely ended." After his defeat Johnson played no significant role in politics. He died in a Veterans Administration hospital outside of Tacoma.

• No corpus of Johnson papers exists; however, clippings by and about him are in the Hoquiam Public Library. A rambling reminiscence appeared in his newspaper between 7 Jan. and 9 Sept. 1934. Alfred J. Hillier, "Albert Johnson, Congressman," *Pacific Northwest Quarterly* (July 1945), is an uncritical biographical sketch. For accounts of his leadership in immigration matters, see John Higham, *Strangers in the Land Patterns of American Nativism, 1860–1925* (1955), and Roger Daniels, *The Politics of Prejudice: The Anti-Japanese Movement in California and the Struggle for Japanese Exclusion* (1962). An obituary is in the *New York Times*, 19 Jan. 1957.

ROGER DANIELS

JOHNSON, Albert Richard (1 Feb. 1910–21 Dec. 1967), scene designer, was born in LaCrosse, Wisconsin, the son of Albert Aaron Johnson, a college educator, and Anne Ellene Glenn, a newspaper reporter. Johnson began his show business career at age fifteen, painting scenery for the opera house in Farmingdale, Long Island. The following year, with his father's financial support, he became the manager of the Green Cove Springs Theatre in Florida, reportedly becoming the youngest motion picture exhibitor in the United States. At age seventeen Johnson went to New York City to study with Norman Bel Geddes, who exposed him to the theories of the New Stagecraft, which rejected the naturalistic for the abstract and the evocative.

For *The Criminal Code* (1929), Johnson's first Broadway commission, he created a grey unit set with a set of panels that moved vertically. To accommodate the several different settings in this melodrama about the penal system, the panels were raised and lowered for each scene; this device permitted quick scene changes and was praised for contributing to the play's oppressive and grim atmosphere. The ambitious theater artist was soon providing scenery for other Broadway shows, many of them musicals, including *Three's a Crowd* (1930), two Moss Hart-Irving Berlin creations, *Face the Music* (1932) and *As Thousands Cheer* (1933), and Ziegfeld's *Follies* of 1934. By his early twenties Johnson was recognized as a major theatrical designer, and several of his sketches were published in *Theatre Arts Monthly*. Bel Geddes's influence is evident in Johnson's designs with their utilization of large scale, minimal ornamentation, and architectural quality. In an early interview, Johnson explained that as a "visualizer" it was his task to establish harmony among a production's visual elements (which included the actors and costumes along with the scenery and lighting), and he criticized other designers for merely creating "more and more elaborate sets" without regard to the overall effect.

Johnson's "visualizations" for musicals were spectacular, utilizing grand, colorful scenery that balked at realistic conventions. Backdrops for the musical revue *As Thousands Cheer* were executed in a variety of styles and incorporated images from different periods in large collages. The playfully artificial settings in *Leave It to Me!* (1938) contrasted a bleak, dreary Paris train station with a brilliantly colored one in Russia, and Matisselike exteriors with overly angular interiors.

Johnson's musicals were notable for their inventive employment of stage machinery. For *The Band Wagon* (1931) Johnson used two large revolves, one set around the other like a ring. These turntables would rotate in similar or opposite directions, providing rapid, filmic scene shifts and a stunning spinning effect for the carousel scene. The ballroom finale for *The Great Waltz* (1934) was reportedly the largest and most expensive setting of the time. This scene, which some considered ostentatious, featured a platform of musicians slowly rising from the orchestra pit and rolling upstage as huge pillars simultaneously moved in from the side wings and enormous chandeliers descended from above. Johnson created this effect with director Hassard Short, with whom he also had worked on *The Band Wagon* and *Face the Music*.

Johnson's work outside the American theater included trips during the 1930s to Sweden and Russia, where he worked on stage and screen productions of the Moscow Art Theatre. During this period he also designed the Ballet Russes' *Union Pacific* (1934) and two films by Ben Hecht and Charles MacArthur, *Crime without Passion* (1934) and *The Scoundrel* (1935). With *Jumbo* (1935), Johnson went beyond scenery design, as he completely renovated the Hippodrome interior. For this musical, which was the beginning of a fruitful business relationship with impresario Billy Rose, Johnson removed the theater's legendary swimming tank, brought the stage forward like a circus ring, put in an extra bank of seats, and surrounded everything in a lavish red, blue, and gold interior. Johnson later provided the interior design for Rose's Diamond Horseshoe nightclub as well as the sets and costumes for its stage shows.

Between 1935 and 1937 Johnson served as the artistic director of Radio City Music Hall, where he created nearly thirty spectacles. His association with extravagant productions for large audiences eventually led Johnson to outdoor venues. He designed fairground expositions in Fort Worth (1936 and 1937) and Cleveland (1937). For the 1939 World's Fair in New York, he reproduced Billy Rose's *Aquacade* from the Cleveland Fair. For the swimming spectacular, which boasted hundreds of performers, Johnson set a 275-foot-long semicircular pool between two 75-foot-tall towers and provided an auditorium for 10,000 spectators. The stage featured a large staircase with the American flag, scene changes being executed by moving screens. Johnson served as a consultant and designer for the amusement zone for the World's Fair, and he produced *American Jubilee*, a patriotic musical pageant that he had written.

During the 1940s and 1950s Johnson continued to design for musicals, such as *Crazy with the Heat* (1941), *Sing Out Sweet Land* (1944), and revivals of *Shuffle Along* (1952) and *Of Thee I Sing* (1952). His dramas from this period include the premier production of *The Skin of Our Teeth* (1942) and Jose Ferrer's *The Chase* (1952). Other projects included producing spectacles at the Luna Park ice rink, experimenting with broadcasting techniques at a Philadelphia televi-

sion station, art direction for Ringling Bros., Barnum & Bailey Circus (1947), designs for the Canadian National Exhibition (1948 and 1949), and *Show Boat* at Jones Beach, New York (1956). By the mid-1950s the number of Johnson's theatrical projects had diminished as he focused on industrial exhibitions, such as automobile and trade shows. He never abandoned theater entirely, and months before his death he returned to Broadway with the settings for *What Did I Do Wrong?* (1967). During a career that lasted almost forty years, Johnson designed more than one hundred productions. Thanks to his penchant for popular entertainments in large venues, Johnson's creations were seen by millions of spectators.

Johnson had married Tilda Goetze, a dancer, in 1937; they were divorced the next year. In 1957 Johnson and Dianne Valvo, a cosmetics executive, were wed. Both marriages were childless. He died of a vascular ailment in New York City.

• A clipping file is available at the Billy Rose Collection of the New York Public Library for the Performing Arts at Lincoln Center. See also Orville Larson, *Scene Design in the American Theatre from 1915 to 1960* (1989), and articles in the *New York Times*, 6 Nov. 1932, and the *Magazine of Art*, May 1940. *The Biographical Encyclopedia and Who's Who of American Theatre* (1966) provides a very detailed listing of Johnson's productions. An obituary is in the *New York Times*, 22 Dec. 1967.

PHILIP A. ALEXANDER

JOHNSON, Alexander (2 Jan. 1847–17 May 1941), social worker, was born in Ashton-under-Lyne, Lancashire, England, the son of John Johnson, a prosperous merchant tailor, and Amelia Hill. Educated at private schools, the Mechanics' Institute, and Owens (later Victoria) College, Johnson left England for Canada in 1869, settling in Hamilton. There he found work in a tailoring factory and lived with his employer, William Johnston. In 1872 Johnson married Johnston's daughter, Eliza Ann, with whom he had seven children. Soon after their marriage the couple moved to Chicago, and around 1877 Johnson moved his family to Cincinnati, where he worked in the manufacturing department of a clothing company.

Johnson's first lessons in social work came from his mother, who in the 1850s covertly fed some of the starving children of striking cotton spinners and weavers who lived in houses his father owned, an act of charity she repeated with his father's knowledge in the 1860s during England's "cotton famine." Johnson later credited his entry into the field of social work to the man he called his "spiritual father," Rev. Charles W. Wendte, a Unitarian minister and ardent promoter of the Associated Charities of Cincinnati. Because his employers were Jewish, Johnson enjoyed Saturday off as well as Sunday, and in 1882 Wendte prevailed upon him to spend some of his free time as a "friendly visitor" to the poor for the Associated Charities. Soon elected to the Associated Charities board of trustees, Johnson was hired in 1884 as its general secretary. He expanded the reach of Cincinnati's charity organization society, persuading other relief groups to use the Associated Charities as the central investigative agency to certify relief cases. He also established a wood yard and organized fresh-air programs for children and their mothers. In 1886 Johnson returned to Chicago as general secretary of the Chicago Charity Organization Society, whose work was opposed by the established Chicago Relief and Aid Society.

Johnson was among the early proponents of a more organized and scientific charity. They believed that haphazard, indiscriminate charity prompted by sentiment alone, as practiced by individuals and well-meaning relief societies, tended both to "pauperize" the needy by making them dependent on such giving and to promote fraud. The new movement for organized charity distinguished between the worthy and unworthy poor by investigating individual cases to certify those whose circumstances warranted aid. By investigating qualifications and monitoring the progress of individual cases, scientific charity workers aimed to foster efforts toward work and self-sufficiency for both classes of the poor. As they gained experience in the field, many of these workers realized that not all of the needy poor required the same aid, and they began to differentiate among the various groups of the needy in order to provide appropriate care in the most proper setting. During the 1890s Johnson played an important role in developing the social welfare system in Indiana.

In 1889 Johnson moved from private charity to public welfare, accepting the position as secretary of Indiana's new State Board of Charities, with the responsibility of overseeing the welfare institutions maintained by the state and the counties. He developed a central registry for all institutional inmates and promoted the idea of specialized institutions to respond to the needs of different categories of inmates, such as the "feeble minded," or mentally retarded, who were a significant portion of the population in the state and local almshouses. In 1893 Johnson was appointed superintendent of the Indiana State School for the Feeble-minded at Fort Wayne. Johnson organized and operated the school along the lines that he elaborated in addresses such as "The Mother State and Her Weaker Children" (1897) and in his prescription for institutional management, *The Almshouse* (1911). He believed that needy, worthy inmates should receive "permanent maternal care" in comfortable institutions that were completely segregated by sex and that those who were able should receive training in a productive trade and help earn their own keep and that of their weaker colleagues. He also believed that the "matron" of each institution, responsible for the "comfort and order of the house," should be the wife of the superintendent, but his hiring of his wife as assistant superintendent and his brother-in-law, Edward R. Johnstone (he had added an "e" to his surname), as teacher and principal helped fuel charges of nepotism against him. In 1896–1897 a three-member panel from the Republican-dominated state senate investigated the charges against Johnson, a Democrat, and recommended no action against him,

but the investigation resulted in the dismissal of two employees, both of whom Johnson believed had been disloyal. Johnson fell into political disfavor again in 1901 after Republican Winfield Durbin was elected governor. Durbin favored county, rather than state, support of the feeble minded, according to Johnson, and believed "meticulous accuracy in financial transactions" to be more important than the welfare of the institution's inmates (*Adventures in Social Welfare*, p. 263). Faced with criticism over his financial management and disagreements with the institution's trustees, Johnson resigned in 1903.

Johnson's wide-ranging experience visiting a variety of institutions as head of the Indiana State Board of Charities and as an asylum administrator gave him a prominent position in the growing social work profession. During the 1890s he became an important officer of the National Conference of Charities and Correction (later the National Conference of Social Welfare), serving as its unpaid secretary from 1890 to 1893 and again in 1900 and as its president in 1897. In 1904 he became its paid secretary, moving to New York City, where from 1904 to 1906 he also became associate director of the New York School of Philanthropy, the first professional school for social work. As secretary of the National Conference, Johnson strengthened its finances, reorganized it to include individuals and organizations involved in a variety of progressive social reforms as well as those providing services, and edited and indexed the conference's *Proceedings* (33 vols., 1907). In growing demand as a lecturer and consultant, Johnson was recruited by the Russell Sage Foundation to visit Oklahoma in 1907 with other social policy experts to help draft the new state's social welfare legislation pertaining to compulsory education, the regulation of child labor, and the care and treatment of criminals and the mentally ill.

Johnson and his brother-in-law joined forces again in 1912 when Johnstone, principal of the Vineland (N.J.) Training School, hired Johnson as director of the school's extension department to promote the idea of occupational training for the mentally retarded. Johnson became the department's field secretary in 1915 when it was moved to Philadelphia under the auspices of the National Committee on Provision for the Feeble-Minded. There he continued to promote progressive legislation dealing with the treatment and care of the mentally retarded, emphasizing that they could be educated and that the source of their disability was genetic.

From 1918 until his retirement in 1922, Johnson worked for the American Red Cross's southern division. He worked first in its Home Service division, with soldiers and their families, and later served as a staff representative and lecturer. Even in retirement Johnson continued to work as a writer and consultant—such that one obituary dated his retirement at 1934. He died in Aurora, Illinois, at the home of his son Will. Despite once describing himself as "one of the untrained beginners" in social work, Johnson became a leading proponent of scientific social work and an expert in the care of the feeble minded.

• Material documenting Johnson's career is located in the Indiana State Archives' records from the State Board of Charities and the Fort Wayne Developmental Center, a successor to the school for the feeble minded; in the Edward Ransom Johnstone Papers in the Rutgers Universities Libraries, New Brunswick, N.J.; and in the Survey Associates Records in the Social Welfare History Archives at the University of Minnesota. Johnson's autobiography, *Adventures in Social Welfare; Being Reminiscences of Things, Thoughts, and Folks during Forty Years of Social Work* (1923), reviews his professional career. A significant biographical sketch of Johnson by Fred M. Cox appears in the *Biographical Dictionary of Social Welfare in America* (1986), pp. 424–25. Obituaries are in the *Social Service Review* 15 (Sept. 1941): 564–66, and the *New York Times*, 18 May 1941.

KENNETH ROSE

JOHNSON, Allan Chester (11 Aug. 1881–2 Mar. 1955), university teacher, was born in Loch Broom, Nova Scotia, Canada, the son of Leander Johnson and Hannah Creelman. His parents' occupations are unknown. Johnson took his A.B. in classics at Dalhousie University in Halifax in 1904, and his Ph.D. at the Johns Hopkins University in 1909, under the supervision of Basil Lanneau Gildersleeve. After two years of study at the American School of Classical Studies at Athens (1909–1911), followed by a year as lecturer at the University of Alberta (1911–1912), he was called to teach in the Department of Classics at Princeton University. He spent the remainder of his life at Princeton, rising through the academic ranks to become full professor in 1924, holding honorific chairs (Musgrave Professorship of Latin, 1933; West Professorship of Classics, 1943), and retiring in 1949. In these years he was also active abroad, on the managing committee of the American School of Classical Studies at Athens, and from 1932 as a trustee of the American Academy in Rome, where he was a visiting professor in 1933 and 1948.

The externals of his academic life are quickly sketched, but of the internal life little trace remains. At Princeton and elsewhere Johnson was universally remembered by his colleagues for his warm personality, inexhaustible patience, and quiet wit, a scholar happiest in the atmosphere of intensive learning to be found in advanced seminars, and one who avoided academic feuding. He had married Laura Williamson, a fellow Nova Scotian, in the year he came to Princeton, but the couple remained childless. Scholarship seems to have been the absorbing passion of his life.

As a student of Gildersleeve, Johnson was exposed to a Germanic tradition that demanded close reading of texts set against a background of deep erudition. Accordingly his highly technical doctoral dissertation compared the syntax of two Athenian orators of the fifth and fourth centuries B.C. with contemporary decrees of the popular assembly. After the First World War, he turned his attention to the tens of thousands of ancient papyri, written mostly in Greek, which turned up in the ruins and garbage dumps of Egypt. With scholars at Michigan, Cornell, and Columbia he vigorously sought to build up collections comparable to those begun in the nineteenth century at European universities and public archives. The manuscripts and fragments of long-lost or little-known works, transformed the study of classical literature. Johnson, however, unlike the classicists, did not wish to study or to acquire literary texts but rather documents, decrees, receipts, private letters, and the thousand other records of daily life that could cast light upon the social and economic history of Egypt under the Roman Empire from the first to the seventh centuries A.D. To that end he established and edited the series *Princeton University Studies in Papyrology*, which included three volumes that he coedited, *Papyri in the Princeton University Collections* (1931–1942).

Johnson's reputation rests on his contributions as a pioneer in the historical study of Roman Egypt based on a vast knowledge of documentary papyri. His major work, *Roman Egypt to the Reign of Diocletian* (1936), volume three of Tenney Frank's *An Economic Survey of Ancient Rome*, set out the economic history of the country over the first three centuries A.D. through a collection and analysis of mainly papyrological evidence, much of it presented in translation. *Byzantine Egypt: Economic Studies*, written with Lewis C. West (1949), attempted to do the same for the next three centuries up to the Arab conquest. Several of Johnson's other works shared the same approach, recreating the realities of ancient life—inflation, land tenure, taxation—through close readings of a wide range of documents.

Johnson was not a great historian. His books lack conclusions and ignore broad themes and economic theory. Despite these shortcomings he was an important scholar, the first in the English-speaking world to put in order, set into context, and lay before readers the complex evidence for the economic structures within which ordinary people led their lives in the Roman world. He died at Princeton.

• Material on Johnson including some correspondence, faculty record cards, memorials, and obituaries can be found in the Princeton University Archives. His other works include *Municipal Administration in the Roman Empire*, with Frank F. Abbott (1926); *Currency in Roman and Byzantine Egypt*, with Louis C. West (1944); *Egypt and the Roman Empire* (1951); and *Ancient Roman Statutes*, with Paul R. Coleman-Norton and Frank C. Bourne (1961).

EDWARD CHAMPLIN

JOHNSON, Allen (29 Jan. 1870–18 Jan. 1931), historian and editor, was born in Lowell, Massachusetts, the son of Moses Allen Johnson, manager of the Lowell Felting Mills, and Elmira J. Shattuck, a cultivated woman who had mastered New Testament Greek. Johnson attended the Lowell public schools and graduated as high school valedictorian in 1888. He then attended Amherst College, from which he received a B.A. in 1892. Johnson impressed both faculty and students at Amherst with his meticulous, orderly, and methodical scholarship. He was considered more mature than most college students and was always finely dressed, dignified, and cordial in his dealings with others.

Following graduation, Johnson became an instructor in history and English at the Lawrenceville School in Lawrenceville, New Jersey. In 1894 he was awarded the Roswell Dwight Hitchcock Fellowship at Amherst College, to which he returned to pursue specialized studies in philosophy and American history; he earned an M.A. in 1895. During the following two years, Johnson spent three semesters at the University of Leipzig under the tutelage of Karl Lamprecht, the renowned cultural historian, and a single semester at the École Libre des Sciences Politiques in Paris. Returning to the United States in 1897, he matriculated at Columbia University and received a Ph.D. from that institution in 1899. In the same year, he published his dissertation, *The Intendant as a Political Agent under Louis XIV.*

From 1898 to 1905, Johnson was a professor of history at Iowa College (now Grinnell College), where he excelled as a teacher and prepared the draft manuscript for a biographical interpretation of nineteenth-century statesman Stephen A. Douglas. *Stephen A. Douglas: A Study in American Politics* (1908) became the standard biography on Douglas. Retaining this rank throughout Johnson's life, the book greatly enhanced his prestige within the historical guild. It also broke new ground methodologically by treating biography not merely as the narrative of an individual life, but as a vehicle for illuminating broader cultural and political themes of American national history. In 1900 Johnson married Helen K. Ross; they had one child.

Johnson moved to Bowdoin College in 1905 to serve as professor of history and political science. He rose to national prominence as a historian while at Bowdoin, during which time he published his biography of Douglas and regularly attended meetings of the American Historical Association. In 1910 the AHA commissioned him to prepare a *Report on the Archives of Maine.* Bowdoin students described Johnson's lectures as knowledgeable, incisive, and lucid. As one of the first university teachers to introduce small, informal, undergraduate "discussion sections" as an adjunct to formal classroom lectures, Johnson received nationwide attention for his teaching skills.

In 1910 Yale University offered Johnson the Larned Chair of American History. Remaining at Yale until 1926, Johnson prepared two college textbooks, *Readings in American Constitutional History* (1912), and *Readings in Recent American Constitutional History, 1876–1926* (1927). After teaching a course on historical methods, he published *The Historian and Historical Evidence* (1926), which offered practical advice and guidance to American students, whom Johnson considered impatient with the subtleties of method and often careless in their scholarship. Johnson also published *Union and Democracy* (1915), the second volume of a popular four-volume series called the Riverside History of the United States. *Union and Democracy* was

highly regarded for its well-balanced narrative of American history from 1783 to 1829, an era that was then the subject of intense political controversy because of the significance assigned to it by scholars of Populist and Progressive sympathies. Johnson's most notable accomplishment during his tenure at Yale was his editorship of a fifty-volume series, The Chronicles of America (1918–1921), which was designed to be accessible to an educated lay audience while maintaining high standards of scholarship. Johnson's own contribution to the series, *Jefferson and His Colleagues* (1921), is considered exemplary in this regard.

Johnson's published works earned him a reputation as an impartial narrative historian, a readable author, and a skilled editor. Because of his success with the Chronicles of America series and his reputation as a fair-minded biographer, the American Council of Learned Societies invited Johnson in 1925 to edit its proposed *Dictionary of American Biography.* Johnson accepted and moved to Washington, D.C., where he spent the final years of his life. His accomplishments as editor of the *Dictionary* received international acclaim from scholars and learned societies, who recognized the immense effort involved in assembling a twenty-volume work that included 13,000 biographies by more than 1,100 contributors. Breaking with the past practice of giving biographical prominence exclusively to soldiers, statesmen, and clergymen, Johnson devoted a large proportion of the work to individuals who had made significant contributions in science, art, and industry. Six volumes of the *Dictionary* were published under his editorship (one posthumously), but the impact of Johnson's editorial decisions and his choice of contributors are evident throughout the entire collection. Johnson's life ended when he was struck by an automobile in Washington, D.C.

Johnson's careful and impartial scholarship as a biographer elevated the genre among professional historians who had previously regarded it as the province of unreliable amateurs and sycophants.

• Besides the Johnson entry in the *DAB*, vol. 10 (1932), the only other biographical sketch is Herbert P. Gallinger, "The Career of Allen Johnson," *Amherst Graduates' Quarterly* (Aug. 1931): 264–71. Johnson was widely eulogized with obituaries in the *New York Times*, 20 Jan. 1931, and 1 Feb. 1931; *American Historical Review* 36 (Apr. 1931): 660–61; *The Nation*, 28 Jan. 1931; *Christian Century*, 4 Feb. 1931; and Waldo G. Leland, "Historical Notes," *Michigan History* 15 (July 1931): 526–28.

CLYDE W. BARROW

JOHNSON, Alvin Saunders (18 Dec. 1874–7 June 1971), economist, educator, and journalist, was born near Homer, Dakota County, Nebraska, the son of John Johnson and Edel Maria Katrina Bille, farmers. Johnson's father emigrated from Denmark to the United States in 1849 with the name Jens Jensen Deyrup; the immigration officer gave him the name John Johnson. Johnson's mother emigrated from Denmark in 1867. By the time she arrived in Nebraska, John had fought in the Civil War and outlived two other wives, who had left him with five children. Johnson's parents subsequently had three more children.

Raised in an atmosphere of religious and political liberalism, Johnson received a meager education in the local school but a rich one at home. He studied classics and languages at the University of Nebraska (which he entered in 1891) and received an A.B. in 1897 and an M.A. in 1898. During the Spanish-American War he joined Company K of the Second Nebraska Regiment of the National Guard as a private; he spent from May to October of 1898 at Camp Thomas in Chickamauga, Georgia, where he survived a bout of typhoid fever.

In 1898 Johnson registered as a graduate student in the School of Political Science at Columbia University. He taught at Bryn Mawr in 1901–1902 and then received his Ph.D. in 1902, with a major in economics and a minor in sociology. Johnson's thesis, titled "Rent in Modern Economic Theory," was published in 1903. He taught economics at Columbia (1902–1906), the University of Nebraska (1906–1908), the University of Texas (1908–1910), the University of Chicago (1910–1911), Stanford University (1911–1912), and Cornell University (1912–1916).

Herbert Croly, the founder and editor of the influential *New Republic* magazine, invited Johnson to join the board of editors. Johnson did so, taking a leave from Cornell in 1915–1916 and moving to New York City. There he worked with an illustrious group of editors and writers that included Croly, Walter Lippmann, Randolph Bourne, and Walter Weyl.

Johnson relinquished his position at Cornell and returned to Stanford for the 1916–1917 academic year. But in the early spring of 1917 Croly persuaded him to return to the *New Republic*. He took a leave of absence and worked for the magazine for several months. Johnson joined the other editors in supporting U.S. entrance into World War I, and in June 1917 he went to Washington as a "dollar-a-year man" for the War Industries Board under the direction of Bernard Baruch. However, Johnson soon returned to the *New Republic*, for which he continued to write prolifically, mostly on economic and political subjects.

Johnson worked with Croly, historians Charles Beard and James Harvey Robinson, economist Thorstein Veblen, *New Republic* financial backer Dorothy Straight, and others to help found the New School for Social Research in 1919. Beard and Robinson had resigned from Columbia in protest over violations of academic freedom there. Occupying several Victorian buildings in the Chelsea section of New York, the New School was intended as a bastion of free inquiry on controversial issues. With such eminent lecturers (full-time and occasional) as Beard, Robinson, John Dewey, Thorstein Veblen, Wesley Mitchell, Harold Laski, Franz Boas, Lewis Mumford, and Morris Cohen, the school was for years the liveliest progressive institution in American adult and higher education.

Johnson was a charter member of the school's board of directors. When a struggle ensued between those who wanted the school to emphasize research (Croly,

Robert Bruère, Ordway Tead, and others) and those who preferred to concentrate on adult education (Robinson, Beard, and others), Johnson presented a plan that promised to maintain both in the long run. The board accepted his plan, and Johnson became director of the school in 1923 (the title was later changed to president). Croly, Robinson, and Beard resigned, leaving Johnson with a relatively free hand to develop the school as he and the board saw fit.

Johnson moved rapidly to find new sources of support, both among the families of the school's adult students and through foundations such as the Carnegie Corporation. He hired such lecturers as John Watson, Sandor Ferenczi, and Alfred Adler, who brought students, funds, and controversy to the school. In 1929 the property on which the New School stood had to be sold and a new location found. Johnson raised over half a million dollars and hired noted architect Joseph Urban to design an architecturally noteworthy modern building at 66 West Twelfth Street in Greenwich Village. The building was completed by January 1931.

With the move to the new building, the school broadened its curriculum to include more artistic and cultural subjects along with the social sciences. Through lectures, exhibits, and performances, the school presented new works by such talented modernists as artists Thomas Hart Benton and José Orozco, composer Aaron Copland, and choreographer Martha Graham.

Johnson found time to take on another massive project: *The Encyclopaedia of the Social Sciences*. During the 1920s anthropologist Alexander Goldenweiser, a faculty member of the New School, persuaded Edwin Seligman, a leading American economist, to help develop an encyclopedia of the social sciences. The Social Science Research Council appointed Seligman editor, and he persuaded Johnson to serve as associate editor. Johnson assembled a remarkably talented staff of fifty-five scholars, and between 1927 and 1935 the group produced the fifteen-volume *Encyclopaedia*, for decades a key source for social science researchers.

There was a symbiotic relationship between the *Encyclopaedia* and the New School. While working on the project Johnson made many contacts in the academic world and was able to hire as lecturers such distinguished scholars as philosophers Morris Cohen and Sidney Hook, historian Carlton Hayes, legal scholar Felix Frankfurter, and natural scientist Julian Huxley. Peter Rutkoff and William Scott, authors of *New School: A History of the New School for Social Research* (1986), write that "the *Encyclopaedia*, when completed, could be seen as an extension of the spirit and mission of Alvin Johnson and the New School. In many ways it stands as the crowning testament to the ideas which in 1917 had led to the formation of the New School" (P. 67).

During trips to Europe Johnson became deeply concerned about the growth of Nazism and Fascism and particularly about Jewish and liberal scholars who were being dismissed from their positions in German and Italian universities. He proposed a "University in

Exile" for such scholars, to be housed at the New School. With the help of New School and *Encyclopaedia* sponsors like Seligman, Johnson secured support for the proposal, raised funds, and began bringing distinguished scholars over from Germany, Italy, and Spain. The University in Exile can be seen as an expression of both Johnson's humanitarianism and his commitment to sustaining a worldwide community of scholars. Since many of the immigrant professors published significant scholarship, the university also helped Johnson to fulfill his 1923 commitment to develop the research component of the New School's original plan. In 1935 Johnson made the university a regular part of the New School under a new name, the Graduate Faculty of Political and Social Science.

As the German conquest of Europe expanded, Johnson became increasingly concerned about Jewish and liberal professors who fled to France and Belgium. He acquired funding from the Rockefeller Foundation and other sources to rescue many of these scholars and assisted their efforts to create what was called the "École Libre des Hautes Études." This was sponsored by the New School but was not integrated into its structure as was the University in Exile. Johnson helped many scholars from France and throughout Europe to find places in other American universities as well as at the New School.

Johnson was well known for his lifelong opposition to all forms of discrimination, and in 1943 newly elected New York governor Thomas Dewey appointed Johnson chairman of the War Council Committee against Discrimination in Employment. His service on the council led to his membership on the State Commission on Discrimination in Employment. Johnson worked with other members of the commission to draft and lobby for legislation barring discrimination in employment, which finally became law in 1949.

Johnson retired from the New School in 1945, leaving "an institution with a devoted board of trustees, a distinguished faculty, and a debt-free physical plant" (Rutkoff and Scott, p. 219). During his long retirement Johnson continued to write prolifically, publishing *The Clock of History* (1946), *Essays in Social Economics* (1955), *The Battle of the Wild Turkey* (1961), *A Touch of Color* (1963), and *Pioneer's Progress: An Autobiography* (1952).

Johnson was the recipient of many honors, including five honorary doctorates, during his long life. He was a member of Phi Beta Kappa, was decorated by the governments of West Germany, France, Denmark, and Belgium for his work with refugee scholars and other contributions, and was elected president of the American Economics Association in 1936 and of the American Association for Adult Education in 1939.

Johnson had been married to Margaret Edith Henry, a scholar who received her Ph.D. in philosophy from Columbia University, since 1904. They had seven children. Johnson died in Nyack, New York, where he and his family had lived since 1919.

• The most extensive collections of letters and other materials are the Alvin Saunders Johnson Collection, Sterling Memorial Library, Yale University; New School Archives; and the Alvin Johnson Papers, Felicia Deyrup Collection, Nyack, N.Y. During his active life Johnson wrote, in addition to nearly a thousand articles and his other books, a textbook entitled *Introduction to Economics* (1909); *John Stuyvesant, Ancestor*, a collection of essays (1919); *Deliver Us from Dogma* (1934); and *The Public Library: A People's University* (1938). He also wrote novels, including *The Professor and the Petticoat* (1914) and *Spring Storm* (1936). The most complete published source of information on Johnson's life is his autobiography, *Pioneer's Progress*. Max Lerner's appreciative review of the book, "Dominant Themes in Microcosm," *American Scholar* 22 (1952–1953): 120–25, provides perspective on Johnson's life and influence. The extensive notes to Peter Rutkoff and William Scott, *New School*, include frequent references to material about and by Johnson. See also *The Reminiscences of Alvin Johnson* (1972), from the Columbia University Oral History Collection. James M. Wallace has transcribed notes on an interview with Johnson, conducted on 17 Nov. 1965, primarily about Johnson's work with the *New Republic*. An obituary is in the *New York Times*, 9 June 1971.

JAMES M. WALLACE

JOHNSON, Andrew (29 Dec. 1808–31 July 1875), seventeenth president of the United States, was born in Raleigh, North Carolina, the son of the bank porter Jacob Johnson and the seamstress Mary McDonough. He lost his father at an early age and was apprenticed to the tailor James J. Selby. Like many poor whites, he never went to school but apparently learned to read and write at the tailor shop. At the age of fifteen he engaged in some youthful prank and ran away, causing Selby to post a reward of $10 for his apprehension. He returned in 1826 to settle his affairs with his employer but was unable to do so. He left on foot for Tennessee, then worked at his trade in Columbia, only to come back after six months to help his family. Together with his mother and stepfather, he set out once more for Tennessee, this time reaching the village of Greeneville, where he made his permanent home.

In Greeneville Johnson met Eliza McCardle, a shoemaker's daughter, whom he married in nearby Warrensburg in 1827. The attractive brunette and the swarthy, carefully groomed, black-haired newcomer had five children.

Johnson soon prospered. Talented and adept at business, he also frequented a local debating society, where he displayed a gift for public speaking. In 1829 he was elected alderman on a mechanics' ticket. He remained in village government for the next eight years, serving as mayor in 1834 and again in 1837. In 1835 he was elected to the Tennessee legislature, where he stood out as an advocate of economy and an enemy of railroads. He was defeated for reelection in 1837 but regained his seat in 1839.

By that time Johnson, whose political affiliation had not been too clearly determined, had become a Democrat of the strictest sort. Taking Andrew Jackson as his model, he combined Jacksonian notions of the rule of the common man with Jeffersonian concepts of agrarianism—principles from which he never swerved afterward. His oratorical gifts and organizational talents enabled him to build up a firm following in his home county of Greene, and in 1841 he moved to the state senate. There he stood out as one of the leaders of the so-called "immortal thirteen," a group of Democrats who prevented the election of a U.S. senator by refusing to go into joint session with the Whig assembly.

In 1843 he was elected to the U.S. House of Representatives, where he remained for the next ten years. Making a name for himself as an advocate of extreme economy, he was also the sponsor of a homestead act, a measure to enable every head of a family to enter sixty acres of public land free of charge. These policies estranged him from more conservative members of the Democratic party, including President James K. Polk, although he strongly supported the war with Mexico. They also alienated him from such southern spokesmen as Jefferson Davis because they would not benefit slaveholders. That he was an orthodox defender of slavery (he himself acquired some eight or nine slaves) and firmly insisted on the superiority of the white race made no difference: many southern leaders considered him unreliable.

During the biennial campaigns for his seat, Johnson was subjected to fierce attacks, particularly from "Parson" William G. Brownlow, who ran against him in 1845. He replied in kind and made enemies not only among Whigs but also among Democrats, particularly the "Nashville clique," which resented his populist appeals to the common man. Finally, in 1853, his opponents succeeded in so gerrymandering his district as to make his reelection impossible.

Johnson turned the tables on his antagonists. Securing the nomination for governor when he could no longer hope to win in his home district, he defeated Gustavus A. Henry, the author of the redistricting bill, and was elected governor in spite of opposition within his own party. He emphasized his populism in a sensational inaugural address in which he declared that Christianity and democracy proceeded in converging lines, but because of the limited powers of Tennessee governors, the chief executives were unable to accomplish much. He did, however, use his office as a forum for his ideas, and in 1855 he was reelected after a bitter campaign against the Know-Nothing candidate, Meredith P. Gentry, whose intolerance he had effectively denounced.

Johnson had always viewed the governorship as a stepping stone to higher office, and in 1857 he realized his ambition. Chosen U.S. senator, he advanced there the same causes he had espoused in the House. Still opposing federal expenditures, he voted against many internal improvement projects and resumed his advocacy of the homestead bill. Endlessly agitating for the measure, he finally succeeded in obtaining its passage on 19 July 1860, only to have it vetoed by President James Buchanan two days later.

Johnson had hopes of winning the Democratic presidential nomination in 1860. His quest was in vain, and the split in the party led him reluctantly to endorse the proslavery ticket of John C. Breckinridge and Joseph Lane. In spite of his spirited defense of the "peculiar institution," however, he opposed secession. Like the majority of the citizens of East Tennessee, he was an unconditional Unionist.

The election of Abraham Lincoln and the subsequent secession crisis confronted Johnson with a difficult choice. Should he, like other Tennessee Democrats, uphold southern pretentions, or should he declare his Unionism, a position more popular among the opposition in East Tennessee than among his own party associates? Johnson never hesitated; fully convinced that the Union must be preserved and knowing that there would be no future for him in a southern Confederacy dominated by men like Jefferson Davis, whom he had fought for years, he defied the southern mainstream. After introducing constitutional amendments calling for the direct election of presidents, limitation of the terms of Supreme Court justices, and the division of the remaining territories between free and slave states, on 18–19 December 1860, in a ringing Senate speech in support of these amendments, he called secession treason and demanded that the government enforce the Constitution and the laws. Although he never said that states could be coerced—he wanted individuals to be held to their obedience—he was denounced as a traitor throughout the South. But in the North he became a hero, and his reputation was not diminished by two more antisecession speeches on 5–6 February and 2 March 1861.

One of the results of Johnson's militant addresses was that Unionists in Tennessee defeated the call for a convention and elected loyal delegates. After the firing upon Fort Sumter, however, not even Johnson's campaigning in company with his erstwhile opponent, the Whig Thomas A. R. Nelson, could overcome secessionist sentiment in a second election, although East Tennessee remained Unionist. The senator had to flee to the North, where he was lionized as the only member of the upper house of Congress from a seceding state who remained loyal.

After a number of addresses in midwestern cities, Johnson returned to Washington to take part in the special session of Congress, which opened on July fourth. He vigorously supported all measures to further the war effort and cosponsored the Johnson-Crittenden Resolutions declaring that the war was not being prosecuted for the purpose "of overthrowing or interfering with the rights or established institutions" of the insurgent states "but to defend and maintain the supremacy of the Constitution" and that as soon as these objects were accomplished the conflict ought to cease.

Johnson also sought to obtain help for East Tennessee, then occupied by the Confederates. He implored the administration and traveled to Ohio and Kentucky to gain the support of generals in command but made little headway. When in December he returned for the regular session of Congress, he became a member of the Joint Committee on the Conduct of the War, which sought to spur on laggard generals.

On 3 March 1862, shortly after the fall of Nashville, Lincoln appointed Johnson military governor of Tennessee. Hoping to lead his fellow citizens back to their allegiance to the United States, the governor established at Nashville a vigorous regime seeking to discourage Confederate sympathizers. He kept order, disallowed the election of disloyal candidates, and sought to strengthen the defenses of the city. But because of the continued southern occupation of East Tennessee until 1863 and frequent hostile raids elsewhere in the state, he was unable to organize the new government the president desired. Although he collaborated with conservatives to secure the exemption of Tennessee from the Emancipation Proclamation, by the summer of 1863 he came to the conclusion that slavery should go. This put him at odds with conservative Unionists, a rift that was deepened when he imposed more stringent oaths for voters than had Lincoln. He demanded a declaration of a desire for the success of the Union, whereas the president had merely demanded a pledge of allegiance. Not until January 1865 did he finally succeed in inaugurating steps leading to the formation of a Unionist government.

Because of the need to attract "war Democrats" to the Lincoln ticket, Johnson was nominated vice president at the 1864 Baltimore National Union Party Convention. During the subsequent campaign, he promised blacks that he would be their "Moses," leading them out of bondage. Still, he never abandoned his racist prejudices. In November 1864 he was elected vice president, and on 4 March 1865 he took the oath of office. Already weakened by illness, he sought to steady himself with whiskey before the ceremony. He was obviously inebriated and delivered a painful harangue.

On 14 April Johnson urged Lincoln to punish leading insurgents swiftly. That night, Johnson was awakened by the news of Lincoln's assassination. Taking the oath on the morning of 15 April at the Kirkwood House, he made a few dignified remarks and announced his intention to keep Lincoln's cabinet.

Shortly after his assumption of the presidency, Johnson conferred with his former colleagues on the Committee on the Conduct of the War, whom he reassured about his attitude. "Treason must be made infamous and traitors must be impoverished," he said. Charles Sumner and Salmon P. Chase even thought he favored black suffrage. In reality, however, he had no such ideas. Firmly believing in the illegality of secession, he was convinced that the seceded states were still members of the Union. Therefore the federal government had no right to dictate suffrage qualifications to them. Accordingly, after recognizing the Restored Government of Virginia, on 29 May 1865 he issued a proclamation of amnesty to all former insurgents who were willing to take an oath of loyalty. Only fourteen exempted classes, including all persons worth more than $20,000, were excluded. At the same time, in a proclamation later extended to other states, he unfolded the so-called Presidential Plan of Reconstruction by appointing William W. Holden provisional governor

of North Carolina and inviting the legal voters of 1861 to set up a loyal government. He suggested that they ratify the Thirteenth Amendment, nullify the secession ordinances, and repudiate the Confederate debt, but he did not insist upon extending suffrage to the freedmen; neither did he insist upon these conditions. Although he urged Mississippi to enfranchise those blacks who could read and write or who owned property, he made it clear that he was doing so only because of political considerations, and the state failed to take his advice.

The result of these policies was a resurgence of conservative power in the South. Not one of the restored states enfranchised a single freedman; on the contrary, they enacted stringent black codes, remanding the freedmen to a status close to slavery. They elected former Confederate officers, including Vice President Alexander H. Stephens, to Congress. At the same time, Johnson ordered General Oliver O. Howard, the head of the Freedmen's Bureau, to restore lands already cultivated by blacks to their former white owners.

When Congress met again in December 1865, all the states except Texas had been organized in accordance with the president's plan. Both for ideological and political reasons, the indiscriminate readmission of southern Democrats did not suit the Republican majority. The radicals, led by Thaddeus Stevens, prevailed upon their colleagues to set up a Joint Committee on Reconstruction, to which all matters pertaining to the South were to be referred. In addition, on opening day, 4 December, the clerk of the House refused to include a single southern member-elect in his roll call.

Johnson's conciliatory message, written by George Bancroft, was well received, but a favorable report on conditions in the South composed by General Ulysses S. Grant conflicted with one submitted by Carl Schurz, who had also toured the section at the president's request. Schurz had found the situation so bad that he incurred the president's anger and was coldly received.

A complete break between the president and the Republicans in Congress followed. In February 1866 Johnson vetoed the Freedmen's Bureau Bill extending the life and powers of the organization, and in March he vetoed the subsequent Civil Rights Act granting citizenship and equal protection of the laws to freedmen. When on Washington's Birthday he bitterly attacked leading radicals, it was clear that the president and Congress could no longer cooperate. The Freedmen's Bureau Bill veto was upheld, but the veto of the Civil Rights Act was overridden. From then on a two-thirds majority was available to override all of the president's objections, and a new Freedmen's Bureau Bill was passed on 16 July 1866. And much as he disliked the Fourteenth Amendment, passed in June 1866, he did not have the power to veto it, although he sought to prevent its ratification in the states. His assertions that all was well in the South were contradicted by a riot in Memphis in May and a massacre of black and white Unionists in New Orleans in July, and that month his policies caused three members of his cabinet to resign.

The election of 1866 was a test of popular opinion of the president and Congress. Johnson, eager to organize a new party of conservative Republicans and moderate Democrats, called a National Union convention in Philadelphia in August; the Republicans countered with a Southern Loyalists' meeting, and two opposing Soldiers' and Sailors' conventions also met. Late in August the president embarked upon an ill-advised "swing around the circle," a campaign tour to Chicago, but his speeches were so crass that they did him more harm than good. The fall elections further strengthened the radicals. Johnson might well have compromised, but pugnacious as ever he refused to budge. Animated by his devotion to what he considered the correct interpretation of the Constitution and by his racial prejudices, he persisted in his opposition to the Fourteenth Amendment and counseled southern states to refuse to ratify it.

This intransigence led to restrictions on his powers and more stringent Reconstruction measures. After arranging for a meeting of the Fortieth Congress immediately after the expiration of the Thirty-ninth, on 2 March 1867 the Republicans enacted the Tenure of Office Act, requiring senatorial approval of dismissals of presidential appointees, and a military appropriations act mandating that orders of the president be issued through the commanding general of the army. In addition, they passed the Reconstruction Acts remanding southern states to military rule and requiring black suffrage and the ratification of the Fourteenth Amendment prior to readmission to the Union. Johnson's vetoes, as usual, were overridden.

In the meantime, a movement to impeach the president had been inaugurated. Upon the motion of James M. Ashley, an investigation was started to see whether Johnson was guilty of high crimes and misdemeanors. Johnson did not make things easier for himself by allowing his attorney general to so construct the Reconstruction Acts as to lessen greatly their impact. Congress passed another measure specifically reversing these interpretations.

Johnson, however, remained as determined as before. Aware of Secretary of War Edwin M. Stanton's collaboration with the radicals, on 12 August 1867 the president dismissed him and appointed General Grant secretary ad interim. He also replaced the more radical commanding generals in the South, first Philip H. Sheridan and Daniel E. Sickles, then John Pope.

When Congress reconvened in December, the judiciary committee brought in a resolution of impeachment. Because the charges were not based on any specific criminal acts, on 7 December they were easily defeated. But in January 1868, in accordance with the Tenure of Office Act, the Senate, refusing to concur in Stanton's suspension, ordered his reinstatement.

Johnson was now determined to rid himself of his troublesome subordinate once and for all. After first trying to induce General Grant to cooperate with him in denying the secretary access to the war office—an effort that not only failed but brought about a complete break between the president and the general—he sought to persuade General William T. Sherman or John Potts, the clerk of the War Department, to take over. Unsuccessful in these attempts, he appointed Lorenzo Thomas, the adjutant general, secretary ad interim. Amid scenes of great excitement, the House impeached Johnson on 24 February. It framed eleven tenuous charges, concerning mainly the alleged violation of the Tenure of Office Act by the dismissal of Stanton and the appointment of Thomas but also including an accusation that the president had disregarded the command of the army provisions of the appropriations act and that he had delivered speeches tending to bring Congress into disrepute. The eleventh article, drawn up by Thaddeus Stevens, combined most of these accusations as well as an allegation that he had failed to carry out the Reconstruction Acts.

The trial that followed was dramatic. The chief justice presided; the prosecution, called the managers, included Stevens and Benjamin F. Butler as well as the moderate John A. Bingham. Johnson's defense team boasted of such luminaries as former justice Benjamin R. Curtis, future secretary of state William M. Evarts, and former attorney general Henry Stanbery. To keep Thomas out, Stanton barricaded himself in the War Department. On 13 March Johnson's counsel asked for a delay of forty days; ten were granted, and on 30 March the formal trial opened with a flamboyant speech by Butler. The president made a number of deals with doubtful senators, assuring James W. Grimes that he would no longer obstruct the Reconstruction Acts, appointing John M. Schofield secretary of war, and promising patronage to Edmund G. Ross of Kansas. When on 16 May a ballot was taken on the eleventh article of impeachment, seven Republicans deserted their party to acquit Johnson by one vote, with the same result on 26 May when the Senate considered the second and third articles.

Thus the impeachment failed, partially because of concern about the constitutional implications of a conviction for the separation of powers, partially because of the weakness of the case, and partially because of fear of the legally mandated succession of Benjamin F. Wade, the president pro tem of the Senate, who was unorthodox on financial matters as well as an advocate of feminist and workers' causes. The presidential system of government was thus preserved, and conservative southerners were greatly encouraged.

During Johnson's remaining months in office he had little real power. His effort to obtain the Democratic nomination for president failed. Encouraged by the purchase of Alaska negotiated by Secretary of State William H. Seward in 1867, he tried to settle outstanding differences with Great Britain, particularly those arising from the *Alabama* claims, but the Senate rejected the convention negotiated by his envoy, Reverdy Johnson, and the Earl of Clarendon. A temporary peace with Indian nations capped his western policy, and a sweeping amnesty on Christmas 1868 included even Jefferson Davis. In February 1869 Johnson also pardoned the surviving members of the Lincoln assassination conspiracy, including Dr. Samuel A. Mudd.

On 4 March 1869, Johnson left office. Returning to Greeneville, he was anxious for vindication. In the fall he sought unsuccessfully to win reelection as senator from Tennessee. He made another unsuccessful effort in 1872, when he contested the seat for congressman-at-large. Finally, in 1875, overcoming almost incredible odds, he was returned to the Senate. One last speech in the special session called by President Grant betrayed Johnson's animus against Grant. He died a few months later near Carter's Station, Tennessee.

A skillful politician in his home state, Andrew Johnson was confronted with an unfamiliar milieu when he became president. His term, on the surface, was a failure; in reality, however, he so undermined Reconstruction efforts that in the end the congressional policy did not succeed. For another three generations the South remained a "white man's country," just as he had desired.

• The papers of Andrew Johnson are in the Library of Congress and are being published in an annotated and extended form by LeRoy P. Graf, Ralph W. Haskins, and Paul H. Bergeron, eds., *The Papers of Andrew Johnson* (1967–). Each volume contains a valuable introduction. The most modern biographies are Hans L. Trefousse, *Andrew Johnson: A Biography* (1989), and the shorter James E. Sefton, *Andrew Johnson and the Uses of Constitutional Power* (1980). Older treatments include Lately Thomas, *The First President Johnson: The Three Lives of the Seventeenth President of the United States of America* (1968); George Fort Milton, *The Age of Hate: Andrew Johnson and the Radicals* (1930); Lloyd Paul Stryker, *Andrew Johnson: A Study in Courage* (1929); and Robert Winston, *Andrew Johnson: Plebeian and Patriot* (1928). The presidential period has been well covered in Albert Castel, *The Presidency of Andrew Johnson* (1979), and in part in Eric L. McKitrick, *Andrew Johnson and Reconstruction* (1960). The impeachment is treated in Michael Les Benedict, *The Impeachment and Trial of Andrew Johnson* (1973), and in Hans L. Trefousse, *Impeachment of a President: Andrew Johnson, the Blacks, and Reconstruction* (1975), as well as in the pioneering but dated David Miller DeWitt, *The Impeachment and Trial of Andrew Johnson* (1903).

HANS L. TREFOUSSE

JOHNSON, Andrew N. (Apr. 1865–c. 1922), newspaper editor, businessman, and politician, was born in Marion, Alabama. Nothing is known of his parents. He was sent to a primary school, and he later attended the state normal school in his home town and Talladega College in Talladega, Alabama. At age twenty he married Lillie A. Jones of Marion, and they had two children. At age twenty-six he became editor of the *Mobile State Republican*, and between 1894 and 1907 he edited the *Mobile Weekly Press*, described by Booker T. Washington as a "thoughtful Negro journal."

In his editorials, Johnson attempted to put the best cast on racial conditions and outwardly expressed optimism about the future for African Americans in the South. At other times, however, as when the Alabama Constitutional Convention of 1901 disfranchised blacks, he was less optimistic. Whites, he said then, had made a mockery of popular democracy. His editorials also opposed the "lily-white" faction in the Republican party.

In business Johnson was a remarkable success. In 1896, while an editor, he opened a funeral home in Mobile for blacks. It took him a few years to build up his enterprise, but it became very profitable. In 1904 Johnson boasted that he had "the most remarkable record in business of any young man, in my line in Alabama, White or Colored." Despite his bluster, the statement held truth.

As an editor and successful businessman, Johnson was a natural to enter politics. He was a member of the Republican state committee and was a delegate to the Republican National Conventions in 1896, 1900, and 1904. In his struggles with the "lily whites" in 1902 and 1904, he had already shown himself to be an adept politician. The "black and tans," as the Johnson Republicans were called, had effectively silenced the opposing faction, and in 1904 Johnson was selected as a state-delegate-at-large to the Republican National Convention. However, in 1905 Johnson lost his fight with William Frye Tebbetts for the collectorship of the port of Mobile, an important and powerful patronage position. At Booker T. Washington's urging, President Theodore Roosevelt received Johnson at the White House for an interview about the position. "I have just left the President," he wrote in 1905, "and I was never more sincerely or cordially greeted in my life." In the end, however, Roosevelt reappointed Tebbetts and further outraged Johnson by failing to speak to a black audience when he visited Mobile later that year.

The next year Mobile was the setting of a racial crisis when two black men were accused of raping a white woman. At first Johnson remained silent, but at the urging of others he spoke out asserting that the men were guilty and had received their just punishment—they were lynched—but that "the white man makes and executes the law in the way that suits him." Unlike Atlanta in the same year, Mobile avoided a race riot, but in the aftermath of the episode rumors spread that Johnson was marked for assassination by blacks. Johnson thought that he was so marked because several of his enemies wanted to take over his prosperous undertaking business. Whatever the reality, he feared for his life and decided to leave Mobile.

In 1906 Johnson sold his business and moved to Nashville, Tennessee, the next year opening an undertaking establishment there. It quickly became a financial success, and in 1909 Johnson was elected president of the black Embalmers and Undertakers Association of Tennessee. "I am very busy and my business is even more a brilliant success than Mobile," he wrote Emmett Scott, Washington's private secretary. By 1913 Johnson had become the director of Nashville's black Board of Trade; a member of various black fraternal organizations, including Odd Fellows and Knights of Pythias; a Congregationalist church member; and he continued to participate actively in the National Negro Business League, an organization founded in 1900 by Washington.

Johnson had even reinvested in his old Mobile undertaking business, which had fallen on hard times, becoming a full partner in 1912 and sending his son Lorenzo back there to become the company's secretary. His one business failure was in 1912, when he opened the Majestic Theater in Nashville's black business district. Described as a magnificent playhouse, it drew few customers, in large measure because of the exorbitant $1 ticket price.

By the 1910s Johnson had moved away from politics, although he continued to offer advice on Republican patronage positions and was selected a delegate from Tennessee in 1916 to the Republican National Convention in Chicago. The location and cause of his death are unknown. Described as affable, polite, courteous, and refined, Johnson was a strikingly handsome man. Despite his political disappointments and his unfounded optimism about the possibilities for blacks in the South, his own life had made a mockery of racial stereotypes of lazy, docile, and ignorant black men. Active, energetic, and intelligent, Johnson struggled and prospered in an era of extreme racial bitterness, hostility, and conflict. Like others of the black middle class, he espoused black self-help, solidarity, and civic betterment, but he also acquired a comfortable estate by taking advantage of the separation of the races.

• There is no known repository of Johnson papers. Biographical information, sometimes marred by inaccuracies, is in W. N. Hartshorn, ed., *An Era of Progress and Promise, 1863–1910* (1910), and Frank Lincoln Mather, ed., *Who's Who of the Colored Race: A General Biographical Dictionary of Men and Women of African Descent* (1915). Also see David E. Alsobrook, "Mobile's Forgotten Progressive—A. N. Johnson, Editor and Entrepreneur," *Alabama Review* 32 (July 1979): 188–202; and Louis R. Harlan and Raymond W. Smock, eds., *The Booker T. Washington Papers* (14 vols., 1972–1989), especially vol. 1, p. 192; vol. 3, pp. 566–67; vol. 6, pp. 154, 360; and vol. 9, pp. 29–30.

LOREN SCHWENINGER

JOHNSON, Ban (6 Jan. 1863–28 Mar. 1931), sportswriter and baseball executive, was born Byron Bancroft Johnson in Avondale, Ohio, the son of Albert B. Johnson, a teacher and school administrator, and Eunice C. Fox. Johnson attended Oberlin and Marietta Colleges, paying more attention to athletics than to his studies and graduating from neither institution. After two years at the University of Cincinnati law school, he became a reporter for the Cincinnati *Commercial-Gazette*, taking over as its sports editor by 1887. Four years later he married Sara Jane Laymon; they had no children.

In Cincinnati, Johnson gained a thorough familiarity with the ill-governed, rowdy, often financially precarious professional baseball of the day. In 1893 he himself moved into baseball administration by accepting the presidency of the Western League, a top-level minor circuit based in eight midwestern cities.

Under Johnson's leadership, the Western League gained widespread praise as a model baseball organization. Freely meting out fines and suspensions, John-son was able to quell much of the abuse of umpires by players and managers that was commonplace in the 1890s. While he made a lifelong enemy in John T. Brush, owner of both the Western League's Indianapolis entry and the Cincinnati Reds of the National League (NL), he formed strong alliances with Charles Comiskey and Connie Mack, who headed the St. Paul and Milwaukee franchises, respectively.

After the 1899 season the NL dropped four of its twelve franchises, and Johnson grabbed the opportunity to move toward the creation of a second major league. Renaming his circuit the American League (AL) and relocating Comiskey's team to Chicago, Johnson announced that for 1900 the AL would abide by the existing National Agreement, under which the NL reigned as the sole "major league," but that unless the NL accepted the AL as an equal in 1901, his organization would ignore the National Agreement and sign the best players it could find—in the NL or anywhere else.

Snubbed by the NL club owners, Johnson and his associates launched a full-scale "baseball war," establishing the AL in Washington, Cleveland, and Baltimore (all recently vacated by the NL); challenging the NL head-on in Philadelphia (where Mack became manager), Chicago, and Boston; and luring NL players with substantially more money to join Johnson's league. Of the 182 men who appeared in the AL in 1901, 111 were former National Leaguers and 87 had been on NL rosters the previous year. The AL's catches included such stellar performers as Napoleon Lajoie, Cy Young, Joe McGinnity, Fielder Jones, Jimmy Collins, and Clark Griffith. Although Johnson put quite a lot of his own money into various franchises, the AL's principal financial angel was Charles Somers, the wealthy young owner of the Cleveland ball club.

Offering first-class baseball, the AL was a success from the outset. Much overweight but seemingly inexhaustible, Ban Johnson governed his circuit with a degree of authority unheard of in the NL. In 1902, when the Pennsylvania supreme court enjoined Lajoie from playing for any team other than the NL's Philadelphia Phillies (his former team), Johnson simply transferred Lajoie's contract to Cleveland, thereby keeping the AL's top performer and aiding Somers's weak franchise. Later that same season, John McGraw, Baltimore's pugnacious young manager, conspired with Andrew Freedman, owner of the NL's New York Giants, to destroy Baltimore's franchise while McGraw and four of his players jumped to the Giants. From then on, Johnson and McGraw were the bitterest of enemies.

The AL's president quickly reconstituted the Baltimore roster from other AL teams so that the Orioles could finish the season. He then transferred the franchise to New York, as he had long intended to do. (Meanwhile Brush, a partner in the Freedman-McGraw conspiracy, sold his interests in the Cincinnati Reds and purchased control of the Giants from Freedman.)

The AL's movement into New York solidified Johnson's circuit, which had already surpassed the NL in overall attendance. As a result the NL owners were finally ready to make peace and end the costly bidding for players, and in 1903 the two leagues formed a new National Agreement that established the dual major-league setup that remained in place (in drastically altered form) nearly a century later. The agreement also created the National Commission, which consisted of the AL and NL presidents and a chairman elected by the owners; the commission would function as the overall governing body for "Organized Baseball" (the AL and NL as well as officially recognized "minor leagues").

Because of his dominant presence in the AL, his friendship with National Commission chairman August "Garry" Herrmann (president of the Cincinnati Reds), and the sheer force of his personality, Johnson emerged as the most powerful single figure in baseball and became known as the "Czar of Baseball." Tirelessly promoting what he nearly always referred to as the "Great American League," he gloried in the victory of the Boston AL champions over Pittsburgh in the first "modern" World Series in 1903, and was outraged when Brush and McGraw refused to meet the Boston Americans the next year. (Under formally agreed-upon procedures, the Series resumed in 1905, McGraw's Giants defeating Mack's Athletics.)

While the NL owners continued to quarrel among themselves and change presidents frequently, Johnson remained the AL's unchallenged chief through repeated crises and controversies—the foremost of which were the 1914–1915 struggle against the Federal League (an unsuccessful effort to promote a third major circuit) and the troubles brought on by U.S. entry into the First World War.

By 1920, however, Johnson found his power slipping away. Following a series of rulings adverse to the NL over rights to various players, the NL president left the National Commission in disgust, Garry Herrmann was forced out, and the commission became virtually moribund. Meanwhile, besides sustaining a long-running feud with his onetime comrade-in-arms Comiskey, Johnson had alienated the owners of two other AL franchises by trying (unsuccessfully) to block the sale of pitcher Carl Mays by Boston to New York.

Late in 1920, following an arcane power struggle, the AL owners joined with their NL counterparts to scrap the National Commission, submit to governance by a single commissioner of baseball, and induce Kenesaw Mountain Landis, the bombastic, high-handed federal judge for the northern district of Illinois, to assume the post. Conceded supreme authority by the club owners, Landis banished from Organized Baseball about twenty players implicated in various gambling schemes, most notably eight Chicago White Sox players accused (but eventually acquitted) of taking bribes to lose the 1919 World Series. Thus, Landis received the credit for cleaning up the "Black Sox Scandal," despite the fact that without Johnson's dogged

pursuit of evidence against the players, they would never have been brought to trial.

In the 1920s Johnson helped promote youth baseball programs in the U.S. and made several visits to Mexico to boost the sport in that country, but it was a generally unhappy time for the onetime baseball overlord. The prideful Johnson never became reconciled to his subordinate status, and Landis treated him with barely concealed contempt.

A succession of setbacks in clashes between Johnson and Landis culminated during the winter of 1926–1927. Acting on allegations that Ty Cobb and Tris Speaker had been parties to a fixed ball game in 1919, Johnson pressured the two superstars into resigning as player-managers in Detroit and Cleveland, respectively, and ostensibly eased them out of baseball. But then Landis, after much delay, restored both Cobb and Speaker to good standing and, as a final affront to Johnson, decreed that they must both continue their careers in the AL.

Following the Cobb-Speaker affair, the AL owners "furloughed" Johnson for several months. Little more than a figurehead and in poor health, he returned in the spring and stayed on until October 1927, when he called the club owners to his offices in Chicago to tender his resignation. His contract with the AL, which still had eight years to run, was worth $320,000 (at $40,000 per year), but Johnson refused to take any additional compensation from the men whose organization he had built and led for twenty-eight years.

The Johnsons made Spencer, Indiana, Sara Laymon Johnson's hometown, their retirement base. For a couple of years they continued to travel extensively, but Johnson's health steadily worsened. He died in a St. Louis hospital.

In 1937 the Base Ball Writers Association of America elected him to the first class of inductees to the National Baseball Hall of Fame, which opened two years later.

• Considerable correspondence between Johnson and Garry Herrmann is in the Herrmann Collection at the National Baseball Library, Cooperstown, N.Y., which also holds the Ban Johnson file. The standard biography is Eugene C. Murdock, *Ban Johnson: Czar of Baseball* (1982), although readers should also consult Harold Seymour, *Baseball: The Golden Age* (1971); David Quentin Voigt, *American Baseball*, vols. 1–2 (3 vols., 1970–1984); Lee Allen, *The American League Story* (1962); Glenn Dickey, *The History of American League Baseball since 1901* (1980); J. G. Taylor Spink, *Judge Landis and Twenty-five Years of Baseball* (repr., 1974); and Charles C. Alexander, *Ty Cobb* (1984) and *John McGraw* (1988).

CHARLES C. ALEXANDER

JOHNSON, Bill (10 Aug. 1872 or 1874–3 Dec. 1972), jazz bassist and banjoist, was born William Manuel Johnson in Talladega, Alabama. Nothing is known of his parents, but of his five brothers, Dink Johnson played drums, piano, and clarinet, and his sister, Anita Gonzalez, was an early paramour of pianist and composer Jelly Roll Morton. At some point in the 1870s or 1880s the family moved to New Orleans, where Johnson started playing guitar at age fifteen. In 1900 he began doubling on bass and worked in a string trio at Tom Anderson's Annex in Storyville. Between 1901 and 1908 he played bass with the Peerless Orchestra and trombonist Frankie Dusen's Eagle Band, doubling on tuba for work with the Excelsior and other marching bands.

After touring the Southwest with a trio in 1908, Johnson, cornetist Ernest "Nenny" Coycault, and their trombonist, one H. Pattio (or Paddio), settled in Los Angeles in 1909. In 1913 the bassman added other New Orleanians to the group: violinist and saxophonist Jimmy Palao, guitarist Norwood "Giggy" Williams, and his brother Dink on piano and drums. But when he received an offer for a national tour on the flourishing Pantages circuit, Johnson sent to New Orleans for more skilled players—cornetist Freddie Keppard, trombonist Eddie Vincent, and clarinetist George Baquet—and with them he formed the Original Creole Band, although he may have used that name for the earlier group as well. Dink, however, chose to remain in Los Angeles when the band went on tour, and for some unknown reason a substitute was neither sought nor found.

Between 1914 and 1917 the now six-piece band of three horns and three strings toured extensively on the Pantages, Loew, and Orpheum vaudeville circuits, early on appearing regularly at the Grand Theater on Chicago's South State Street and the North American Restaurant on the Loop, thus making it the first jazz band of any sort to play for both black *and* white audiences in Chicago. In New York the band performed its "novelty" act—as jazz bands were billed in vaudeville houses—at the Winter Garden, Columbia Theater, American Theater, Loew's Orpheum, Lexington Opera House, and the prestigious Palace Theater, all exclusively white venues. Legend has it that in 1916, when offered an opportunity to record for the Victor Talking Machine Company, then the leading producer of the new sound medium, Keppard turned it down in the belief that recordings would enable other musicians, particularly northerners, to steal his band's style, a product unique to New Orleans and one of which he was justifiably proud. After disbanding briefly in Boston in the spring of 1917, Keppard reassembled the group in the fall, replacing Vincent and Baquet with trombonist George Filhe and clarinetist Jimmie Noone. After a residency at the Logan Square Theater in Chicago and a long tour with the *Tan Town Topics*, a vaudeville revue, the group disbanded in April 1918.

After the band's breakup, Johnson settled in Chicago, where he was asked to assemble a band of New Orleans musicians for the opening of the Royal Gardens. Using pianist Lottie Taylor and drummer Paul Barbarin, who were already living in Chicago, Johnson sent to New Orleans for cornetist Joe "King" Oliver, Vincent, and Noone to join him. However, another Original Creole Band, then under the leadership of clarinetist Lawrence Duhé, was also working in Chicago and seeking to hire Oliver. The newly arrived cornetist quickly settled the problem by working with both bands, typically on the same night. At some point in late 1918 Johnson left for New York to form the Seven Kings of Ragtime for an Orpheum circuit tour, but he returned to the Royal Gardens in 1919 to rejoin the band he had since turned over to Oliver. During his four-year stay with Oliver's Creole Jazz Band, the personnel consisted of trombonist Honoré Dutrey, clarinetist Johnny Dodds, pianist Lil Hardin (with Bertha Gonsoulin an occasional replacement), and drummer Baby Dodds. Louis Armstrong was added as second cornetist in August 1922, more than a year after the club had been renamed the Lincoln Gardens.

Johnson most likely concentrated on bass when the Oliver band played for dancing at the Gardens, but because the limited recording technology of the period was not yet able to reproduce the lower frequencies of the instrument without distortion, when the Creole Jazz Band recorded its first session for Gennett on 6 April 1923, Johnson had to play banjo, but even on that instrument his presence is barely discernible. He did, however, have the opportunity to utter the first jazz vocal break on record when he shouted the high-pitched, exhortatory "Oh, play that thing!" following Oliver's three solo choruses on "Dipper Mouth Blues." To all indications Johnson remained with Oliver through mid-1924, but his role in the recording ensemble ended with the first session. On subsequent dates in June and October 1923, his place was taken by banjoists Bud Scott and Johnny St. Cyr, respectively. When the Oliver band broke up in June 1924, Johnson, along with the Dodds brothers and Dutrey, joined Keppard and pianist Charlie Alexander at Kelly's Stables. Throughout the remainder of the decade, Johnson worked with Johnny Dodds at Kelly's Stables, led his own small groups at various South Side clubs, and worked with bandleaders Jimmy Wade and Clifford "Klarinet" King.

As a seminal New Orleans jazzman, Johnson was probably one of the first bassmen in history to alternate pizzicato rhythmic playing with conventional bowed techniques when playing dance music, whether traditional jigs, reels, and waltzes, or the then new syncopated styles of ragtime and early jazz. Unfortunately, however, no recorded documentation exists of the music played in New Orleans during the formative 1890–1915 period. Similarly, because of Keppard's decision not to record in 1916, we have no proof of the actual Original Creole Band sound, but later evidence, for example, the 1920s recordings of Keppard, suggests that the group probably played with a greater emphasis on blues intonation and a looser approach to ragtime rhythm than did the Original Dixieland Jass (later, Jazz) Band, the white New Orleans band that in 1917 became the first to record the new music.

Because the sound of Johnson's full-toned, resonant bass can be heard only on the records he made in 1928 and 1929, there are but a handful of citations, most notably Johnny Dodds's "Blue Piano Stomp," "Bull Fiddle Blues," "Blue Washboard Stomp," "Goober Dance," "Too Tight," and "Indigo Stomp." However, he was also present on some less well-known recordings by Jimmy Blythe, Junie Cobb, Frankie "Half Pint" Jaxon, his own Louisiana Jug Band, Banjo Ikey Robinson, the State Street Ramblers, Tampa Red, and Sippie Wallace. Although Johnson pioneered in creating the highly rhythmic style known as "slap bass," his contributions have been overshadowed by the more prominent work of other, younger, and more widely recorded New Orleans bassists such as Pops Foster, Wellman Braud, Steve Brown, John Lindsey, and Al Morgan. However, Johnson is still credited for his early influence on Milt Hinton, a renowned Swing Era bassist some forty years his junior. Nothing is known of Johnson's career during the 1930s except that he led his own small bands in Chicago and worked in a group called the Snizer Trio. His last known performances were in 1947, when he played in concerts with New Orleans—styled bands featuring trumpeters Bunk Johnson and Lee Collins. In the 1950s Johnson retired from music and moved to Texas, where he died in New Braunfels, near San Antonio.

• The only references to Johnson in jazz history books are limited to his connections with the Original Creole Band and King Oliver's Creole Jazz Band. See Alan Lomax, *Mr. Jelly Roll* (1950), for contradictory allusions to Johnson's status as Morton's brother-in-law. More accurate accounts of his activities are in Paul Eduard Miller and George Hoefer, "Chicago Jazz History," *Esquire Jazz Book*, ed. Miller (1946); William Russell and Stephen W. Smith, "New Orleans Music," and Frederic Ramsey, Jr., "King Oliver and His Creole Jazz Band," in *Jazzmen*, ed. Ramsey and Charles Edward Smith (1939); Samuel B. Charters and Leonard Kunstadt, *Jazz: A History of the New York Scene* (1962); and Walter C. Allen and Brian Rust, *"King" Oliver*, rev. ed. Laurie Wright (1987). Passing references to Johnson are in Samuel B. Charters, *Jazz New Orleans: 1885–1963* (1963), and Al Rose and Edmond Souchon, *New Orleans Jazz: A Family Album* (1978). Complete discographical listings are in Brian Rust, *Jazz Records, 1897–1942* (1982).

JACK SOHMER

JOHNSON, Blind Willie (1900?–1949?), gospel singer and guitarist, was born near Marlin, Texas, the son of George Johnson, a farmer, and a mother (name unknown) who died when Willie was quite young. Information about Johnson's life is very sketchy and based largely on brief interviews with his two wives and a few friends and fellow musicians, who sometimes gave vague and contradictory information. The only tangible documents of his life are the thirty recordings that he made between 1927 and 1930.

When Willie was about five years old, his father remarried. About the age of seven he was blinded, according to one report by his stepmother throwing lye water in his face after an argument with his father and in other reports by wearing defective glasses or watching an eclipse of the sun through a piece of glass. Like many poor African Americans of the time, he took up music as a profession, learning initially on a cigar box guitar made by his father and modeling his singing on that of another local blind man named Madkin Butler. He soon graduated to a regular guitar, and his father

would take him to Marlin and other nearby towns to play on the streets for tips. As far as is known, his repertoire consisted entirely of religious songs. In the 1920s he began to perform in Waco and Dallas on the streets as well as in church programs and revivals.

Johnson was first recorded by a mobile field unit of Columbia Records in Dallas on 3 December 1927, performing six songs alone with his guitar. On 5 December 1928 he recorded four more songs in Dallas for Columbia, this time with the help of female singer Willie B. Harris, who was from Marlin and a member of the pentecostal Church of God in Christ; she claimed to have married Johnson around 1926 or 1927. By June 1929, or possibly a year or two earlier, Johnson had married another woman in Dallas named Angeline, who was of the Baptist faith. They moved briefly to Waco and Temple but soon settled in Beaumont, where they remained until Johnson's death about twenty years later. On 10–11 December 1929 Johnson recorded ten songs for Columbia in New Orleans, accompanied on some by a local female singer whose identity is unknown. Johnson's final ten recordings were made for Columbia in Atlanta on 20 April 1930, with Willie B. Harris assisting in the singing.

Johnson's travels before his initial recording session appear to have been confined to the territory between Marlin and Dallas. The popularity of his recordings created a wider demand for his music, and in the late 1920s he apparently toured throughout much of East Texas and perhaps farther afield. His recording sessions in New Orleans and Atlanta provided him opportunities to remain in those cities and to perform for up to a month. Atlanta musician Blind Willie McTell claimed to have traveled with Johnson "from Maine to the Mobile Bay," probably following the 1930 session in Atlanta where both musicians recorded. McTell stated that he left Johnson in Union, Missouri, and later encountered him in Little Rock, Arkansas. Angeline Johnson, however, stated that her husband generally stayed close to their Beaumont home, particularly after she began having children. Johnson performed at church programs and conventions, sometimes with Angeline helping in the singing. They lived well in what were described as "fine homes," and Johnson bought a car and hired a driver. When his car was stolen at a Baptist convention in Houston, the delegates took up a collection and bought him another. Around 1949 in the winter Johnson's house caught fire. Although the family escaped and the flames were extinguished, Johnson caught pneumonia from sleeping on a damp mattress. He was refused admittance to a hospital for some reason connected to his blindness, and he died a few days later.

Johnson's recordings are a rich cross section of African-American religious music, including older spirituals and hymns and newer gospel songs. Several recounted stories from the Bible, whereas others detailed recent historical events, such as the sinking of the Titanic, World War I, and the influenza epidemic of 1918. Although Johnson was raised a Baptist and worked mostly in Baptist circles following his marriage to Angeline, several of his songs contain references to doctrines of the then emerging pentecostal denominations, such as the Church of God in Christ. This influence is probably attributable to the period he spent with Willie B. Harris and in general to the encouragement of instrumental music by pentecostal sects. Although the Baptists of the 1920s and 1930s were less tolerant of instrumental music, they too probably would have encouraged a blind performer who could make a living no other way. The themes of several of Johnson's songs likely had special meaning for him in respect to his blindness, the loss of his mother, and general feelings of helplessness. Among these songs are "Mother's Children Have a Hard Time," "If I Had My Way I'd Tear the Building Down," "Let Your Light Shine on Me," "Bye and Bye I'm Going to See the King," "Take Your Burden to the Lord and Leave It There," and "Everybody Ought to Treat a Stranger Right." Frequently using a growling false bass voice derived from folk preaching technique, Johnson sang with a passion and sense of command seldom matched by other gospel singers of his day. On his duets a contrasting female voice, sweeter and higher pitched, was heard in an antiphonal or heterophonic relationship to Johnson's rough singing. On some of his pieces he played a simple repeated rhythmic phrase on the guitar, and on a few others he outlined rudimentary harmonic changes. On about half of his recordings, however, he used a metal ring on his finger or a pocket knife to play the guitar in a slide technique, outlining the song's melody up and down one of the guitar strings while at the same time creating a driving rhythm. Johnson is generally regarded as one of the masters of this folk guitar technique, which eerily recalls the human voice in its tonal and textural flexibility. His singing and playing style and his repertoire were enormously influential on other gospel singers. Even many blues singers and guitarists performed versions of his songs. Eight of his recordings were reissued in 1935, and further reissues have occurred since the 1950s, with his entire recorded work remaining in print since the 1970s. His "Dark Was the Night—Cold Was the Ground" has been used as background music in films, and popular recording artists since the 1960s have performed pieces from his repertoire.

• Johnson's complete recordings are available on *The Complete Blind Willie Johnson*, Columbia/Legacy C2K 52835 (1993), which contains a discography as well as biographical information and commentary by Samuel Charters, who was the first to conduct research on Johnson's life. Charters published information earlier in his notes to *Blind Willie Johnson*, Folkways FG 3585 (1957), and in his book *The Country Blues* (1959), pp. 156–65. Additional information and commentary are contained in the notes by Steve Calt to *Praise God I'm Satisfied*, Yazoo 1058 (1989), and by David Evans to *Sweeter As the Years Go By*, Yazoo 1078 (1990), which together also contain Johnson's complete recordings. For a discussion of Johnson in the context of other "guitar evangelists" see Paul Oliver, *Songsters and Saints* (1984), pp. 199–228.

DAVID EVANS

JOHNSON, Bob (4 Mar. 1931–26 Nov. 1991), ice hockey coach, was born Robert Johnson in Minneapolis, Minnesota, the son of a Swedish immigrant who adopted his American surname in place of Olars; no other family information is available. He demonstrated his aptitude for ice hockey at an early age, winning the city ice skating championship when he was thirteen. After military service during the Korean War, he played collegiate ice hockey at the University of Minnesota for two years, leading the team in goal scoring; he had earlier played at the University of North Dakota. He married Martha (maiden name unknown); the couple had five children.

Johnson also excelled at baseball, earning a contract from the Chicago White Sox; however, he rejected life as a minor league baseball player in favor of coaching ice hockey. In 1956 he coached at Warroad High School in Warroad, Minnesota, after which he spent six years at Roosevelt High School in Minneapolis, where he led the hockey team to four city championships. In 1963 Colorado College hired him as its hockey coach; three years later Johnson became the first head coach of the University of Wisconsin hockey team. In the following fifteen years he led the Badgers to a record of 367 wins, 175 losses, and 23 ties, winning NCAA championships in 1973, 1977, and 1981. In 1977 he was named NCAA Coach of the Year; he also earned the nickname of "Badger Bob," a play on the Wisconsin mascot. At the same time Johnson promoted hockey in the United States, serving as coach of the national team in 1973–1975 and 1981. He coached the U.S. Olympic hockey team in 1976, guiding it to a fourth-place finish.

In 1982 Johnson became head coach for the Calgary Flames of the National Hockey League (NHL). In five seasons he fashioned a record of 193 wins, 155 losses, and 52 ties, highlighted by the team's upset triumph over the defending league champions, the Edmonton Oilers, during the 1986 playoffs—although the Flames lost the Stanley Cup finals that year to the Montreal Canadiens. In 1987 he left the Flames to become executive director of USA Hockey, overseeing amateur hockey in the United States.

The general manager of the NHL's Pittsburgh Penguins, Craig Patrick, hired Johnson as the team's head coach in 1990. Although the Penguins possessed one of the game's top forwards in center Mario Lemieux, an excellent offensive defenseman in Paul Coffey, and a group of talented young forwards, the franchise had made only one playoff appearance since 1982. Together Patrick and Johnson worked to remedy that, first by acquiring veteran forwards Bryan Trottier and Joe Mullen—two players with significant playoff experience and a total of five Stanley Cup championship rings—during the off-season. Johnson worked hard to eradicate the team's lackadaisical attitude toward defense, but the absence of Lemieux for most of the 1990–1991 regular season due to injury limited the club's overall improvement. The acquisition of center Ron Francis and defensemen Ulf Samuelsson and Larry Murphy helped the team finish strong, as it won its first division championship despite compiling a record of only 41 wins, 33 losses, and six ties. With Lemieux back for the playoffs, however, the Penguins put together an improbable series of victories and won the Stanley Cup by defeating the Minnesota North Stars 8–0 on 25 May 1991, winning the final series four games to two. It was the first league championship in the team's history. Many players credited Johnson's relentless optimism and drive as essential to the result. He was only the second American-born coach of a Stanley Cup champion.

Johnson never got to defend his title. In August 1991 hospital tests revealed that he had a cancerous brain tumor. The illness forced him to relinquish his coaching duties, first for Team USA in the 1991 Canada Cup international hockey tournament, and then for the Penguins. Veteran coach Scotty Bowman replaced him on an interim basis behind the Pittsburgh bench. Efforts at treatment of the cancer proved unsuccessful, and he died in Colorado Springs, Colorado, six weeks into the 1991–1992 season. The Penguins marked his passing with an on-ice ceremony, commemorative patches on their uniforms, and Johnson's favorite phrase—"It's a great day for hockey"—emblazoned on the ice surface. They dedicated the remainder of the season to him; some six months later, they honored his memory most appropriately by repeating as Stanley Cup champions.

Johnson played a pivotal role in the development of ice hockey in the United States. His combination of expertise—he was one of the first American coaches to study European and Russian styles of play and strategies—and enthusiasm inspired professionals as well as collegiate players. Awarded the Lester Patrick Trophy in 1988 for service to hockey in the United States, he was inducted into the U.S. Hockey Hall of Fame in Eveleth, Minnesota (1991), and the Hockey Hall of Fame in Toronto, Ontario, Canada (1992), in recognition of his efforts to promote American ice hockey.

• For Johnson's career with the Penguins, see Dave Molinari, *Best in the Game: The Turbulent Story of the Pittsburgh Penguins' Rise to Stanley Cup Champions* (1993). Obituaries are in the *Colorado Springs Gazette Telegraph* and the *New York Times*, both 27 Nov. 1991.

BROOKS D. SIMPSON

JOHNSON, Budd (14 Dec. 1910–20 Oct. 1984), jazz saxophonist and arranger, was born Albert J. Johnson in Dallas, Texas, the son of Albert Johnson, an automobile mechanic, cornetist, and church organist. His mother's name is not known. His older brother Frederick H. "Keg" Johnson studied trombone with his father and also became a career professional. After having taught himself cornet by ear, at age eight Johnson started taking piano lessons, but he soon switched to drums, which he played in the Moonlight Melody Six, a band formed by his brother Keg, pianist Jesse Stone, and other school friends. In 1923 or 1924, when a better drummer joined the band, Johnson started teaching himself saxophone. Renaming their group the

Blue Moon Chasers, in 1925 the boys traveled with the Gonzel White Show to Tulsa, but after becoming stranded they returned home. Around 1926 Budd and Keg Johnson joined William Holloway's Music Makers (or Syncopators), in which traveling group Budd learned to read music from Holloway and saxman Ben Smith, who in 1927 became the group's leader. In 1928 Johnson left Smith and joined Eugene Coy's Happy Black Aces in Oklahoma, staying with them until early 1929, when he joined Terrence Holder's Twelve Clouds of Joy in Dallas. It was while with Coy in Amarillo that Johnson chanced to give silent movie pianist Ben Webster his first lessons on the saxophone. After Holder was ousted for stealing his sidemen's money, the band, now under the name of Jesse Stone's Blue Serenaders, worked in St. Joseph, Missouri; Kansas City, Missouri; and Iowa. When this group disbanded, Johnson and Stone joined George E. Lee's Orchestra in Kansas City, where they made their rather undistinguished debut recordings in November 1929.

In January 1932, on his brother's urging, Johnson moved to Chicago, where he found work in the bands of Ed Carry, Irene (Mrs. Teddy) Wilson, Cassino Simpson, and Clarence Moore. Later that year Johnson and his brother played in Eddie Mallory's band before joining Louis Armstrong's newly formed orchestra in January 1933. Johnson played promising solos on Armstrong's "Some Sweet Day," "Mahogany Hall Stomp," "Dusky Stevedore," "Mighty River," and "St. Louis Blues," and on "Sweet Sue, Just You," he sang an amusing scat chorus in duet with Armstrong. When Armstrong disbanded his orchestra in July, Johnson played briefly with Jimmie Noone at the Lido, worked for a while with Jesse Stone, and in 1934 began substituting regularly for tenor saxophonist and arranger Cecil Irwin in Earl Hines's band at the Grand Terrace Ballroom. When Irwin was killed in a bus accident in May 1935, Johnson took his place. In 1936 tenor saxophonist and arranger Jimmy Mundy left Hines to join Benny Goodman's writing staff, at which time Johnson began turning out new arrangements of such older numbers as "Deep Forest," "Blue Because of You," and "Rosetta." Over the next six years he wrote scores on numbers such as "Grand Terrace Shuffle," "Father Steps In," "Piano Man," "Riff Medley," "XYZ," "Number 19," and "You Can Depend on Me," as well as perhaps dozens of others that were not recorded. With Hines's approval, in 1936 Johnson took some time off to join the writing staff of Gus Arnheim's revamped swing band for an opening at the Hotel New Yorker. When Arnheim disbanded the group, Johnson rejoined Hines in Chicago, recording four sessions with him between February 1937 and March 1938, out of which his Chu Berry–influenced solo on "I Can't Believe That You're in Love with Me" was particularly notable. During a layoff from the Hines band, in May 1938 Johnson accepted a job with Fletcher Henderson as a replacement for lead altoist Hilton Jefferson, leaving him in late July to remain in

Chicago and work with his brother Horace Henderson's band through October, when he rejoined Hines.

In October 1938 and again in February 1940, Johnson recorded two of his most fully realized solos to date on Lionel Hampton's "Rock Hill Special" and "Till Tom Special," and these, along with the Hines recordings from July 1939 on, exemplify his by now thorough conversion to Lester Young's style, as is evidenced in his higher pitched, alto-like tone; even, eighth-note phrasing; and occasional use of offbeat rhythmic accents. He is heard to increasing advantage on Hines's "Grand Terrace Shuffle," "Father Steps In," "Riff Medley," "XYZ," "Gator Swing," "Call Me Happy," "Easy Rhythm," "In Swamp Lands," "Windy City Jive," "Yellow Fire," "I Never Dreamt," "Skylark," and "Second Balcony Jump." Johnson seems to have left Hines briefly in early 1940 to work for Johnny Long, probably as an arranger, but he returned in the spring and remained through December 1942, when he quit following an argument over salary. After leaving Hines, Johnson moved to New York, where he worked briefly in Don Redman's orchestra and with Al Sears's band at the Renaissance Ballroom in Harlem, later touring with a Sears-led USO band that also included Lester Young.

In 1943 Johnson became staff arranger for Georgie Auld's band and later freelanced as a writer for the modern big bands of Woody Herman, Buddy Rich, Gene Krupa, Charlie Barnet, and Boyd Raeburn. In February 1944 he replaced tenor saxophonist Don Byas in Dizzy Gillespie's bebop quintet at the Onyx Club on Fifty-second Street in New York, later writing for and occasionally playing in Gillespie's various big bands from 1946 through 1949. He also led his own modern jazz combo at the Three Deuces, as well as organizing, writing for, and playing on two Coleman Hawkins record dates, one in February 1944 and the other in December 1947, on which he played a remarkably bop-tinged alto solo on "Jumping for Jane." Although primarily a swing-era musician whose playing rarely deviated from the mainstream, Johnson was also one of the first arrangers to transcribe the sometimes convoluted, multinoted melodic themes, rhythmic accents, and altered harmonies of bebop, thereby making this then unconventional music more accessible to others. Beginning in April 1944 he served as Billy Eckstine's musical director and chief arranger and was instrumental in organizing for him a bop-styled big band that between 1944 and 1947 included in its shifting personnel Dizzy Gillespie, Fats Navarro, Miles Davis, Charlie Parker, Sonny Stitt, Gene Ammons, Dexter Gordon, Wardell Gray, Lucky Thompson, and Art Blakey.

In early 1945 Johnson worked for three months in John Kirby's sextet, playing alongside swing veterans Emmett Berry, Buster Bailey, and Russell Procope, and in 1946 he was with J. C. Heard's sextet at Café Society Downtown in New York City on an engagement that also featured former Hines and Eckstine vocalist Sarah Vaughan. In the mid-1940s Johnson was very active on the freelance jazz combo recording

scene as well, appearing on sessions led by Cozy Cole, Clyde Hart, Coleman Hawkins, J. C. Heard, Pete Johnson, Jimmy Jones, Walter "Foots" Thomas, and Dicky Wells. From 1947 through the early 1950s he worked in the bands of Sy Oliver, Machito, Bennie Green, Snub Moseley, and Cab Calloway in addition to leading his own groups, establishing a music publishing company, and continuing his busy career as freelance arranger and recording session saxman. Between February 1956 and spring 1957 he played tenor sax with Benny Goodman's new band, most importantly on a tour of the Far East, and from the mid-1950s through the early 1970s he participated in countless recording dates, including ones led by Count Basie, Ray Brown, Buck Clayton, Bill Coleman, Roy Eldridge, Gil Evans, Dizzy Gillespie, Illinois Jacquet, Quincy Jones, Charlie Shavers, Clark Terry, Ben Webster, and many others. Starting in the mid-1940s, Johnson also appeared on recordings by such jazz, R & B, and pop singers as Mildred Bailey, La Vern Baker, Big Maybelle, Ruth Brown, Ray Charles, Billy Eckstine, Billie Holiday, Frankie Laine, Carmen McRae, Anita O'Day, Carrie Smith, Dakota Staton, Joe Turner, Sarah Vaughan, and at least three dozen others.

In 1960 he worked with Quincy Jones, and from mid-1961 through early 1962 he toured and recorded with Count Basie, later leading his own group at the Half Note in New York. He reunited with Hines for the latter's comeback in March 1964 and continued to record with him in small-band contexts through the 1960s, his last dates being in 1977 and 1982. After working briefly in New York with Gerald Wilson's Big Band in early 1966, Johnson visited Russia in the summer with Hines's septet, later playing with the Tommy Dorsey Orchestra under the direction of Urbie Green. In the spring of 1967, as a member of the Hines-led concert package called Jazz from a Swinging Era, Johnson toured Europe, also returning later that year as a featured soloist. After another European tour with Hines in 1968, he formed the JPJ Quartet in the summer of 1969, following that with a February 1970 European tour with Charlie Shavers. In 1974 he was appointed musical director of the New York Jazz Repertory Company's *Musical Life of Charlie Parker*. After disbanding the JPJ Quartet in 1975, he spent his later years freelancing as a soloist at festivals and recording with Benny Carter, Buck Clayton, Roy Eldridge, and Milt Hinton. He also appeared in the documentary film *Last of the Blue Devils* (1979). Johnson recorded his first leader date in June 1947 and after more than three prolific decades in the studio taped his last album in February 1984. He died in Kansas City, Missouri.

Although much has been made of the role that Johnson played as an arranger in the early years of bop, his contributions as an improvising jazzman appear to have been underrated. A technically fluent, strong-toned, inventive, and swinging soloist, Johnson played in a style that, though rooted in the swing era, came to reflect and in turn influence the work of such younger tenormen as Gene Ammons and Sonny Stitt, and through them thousands of others.

• The most thorough coverage of Budd Johnson's career is in Stanley Dance, *The World of Earl Hines* (1977), while that author's *The World of Swing* (1974) is also helpful but in more general ways. Discussions of his recorded work in the 1930s and early 1940s are in Max Jones and John Chilton, *Louis: The Louis Armstrong Story* (1971), and Gunther Schuller, *The Swing Era* (1989). His contributions to modern jazz as saxophonist, arranger, and musical director are treated in Ira Gitler, *Swing to Bop* (1985), and Dizzy Gillespie, *To Be or Not to Bop* (1979). Some oral-history materials relating to Johnson are at Rutgers University. The vast number of recordings he made between 1929 and 1984 are listed in Walter Bruyninckx, *Swing Discography, 1920–1988* (12 vols.), *Modern Jazz Discography* (6 vols.), *Modern Big Band Discography* (2 vols.), and *Vocalists Discography* (4 vols.). However, a handier listing of his earlier recordings is Brian Rust, *Jazz Records, 1897–1942* (1982). An obituary is in *Down Beat*, Jan. 1985.

JACK SOHMER

JOHNSON, Bunk (27 Dec. 1889?–7 July 1949), trumpeter, was born William Geary Johnson in New Orleans, Louisiana, the son of William Johnson and Theresa (maiden name unknown), a cook, both former slaves. Though his early life remains shrouded in obscurity, Johnson claimed that he learned to play the cornet from Professor Wallace Cutchey, a music teacher at New Orleans University. His mother bought him an inexpensive cornet when he was about fourteen, and he played his first job with Adam Olivier's band in 1904 or 1905. Johnson also claimed that he played with Buddy Bolden during this period, but this seems unlikely. He did play with the popular Eagle Band in parades, and in 1908 Pops Foster heard him playing with the Superior Orchestra, a ragtime band.

Johnson's tenure with the Superior Orchestra was cut short by the excessive drinking habits that plagued him his entire life. Over the next few years he played with several groups in New Orleans, and he may even have taught or influenced a very young Louis Armstrong. He was recognized as one of the best players in New Orleans during this decade, praised for his beautiful tone and evocative blues playing. But Johnson left the city sometime around 1915, apparently burned out. He wandered around the region for several years, playing in sporting houses and similar venues in small towns west of New Orleans, including New Iberia. He seems to have spent some time in 1918 touring with circuses and minstrel shows, a common enough course for musicians at the time. In 1922 he was in Texas with a traveling carnival show. Sometime in the early 1920s he established his base in New Iberia and married Maude Fontenette, his second wife (there are no extant details concerning his first marriage, and he apparently had no children). During the 1920s he often played with a territory group called the Banner Band and traveled as a soloist as far afield as Houston, Texas, and, in 1931, Kansas City. He also played regularly with the Black Eagles, and he was present when the

Eagles' leader was stabbed to death at a dance. In the melee that followed, Johnson's horn was destroyed. Already in some discomfort because of missing teeth, he put his musical career on the back burner, playing only occasional gigs with the Banner Band and retiring in 1932 to the life of a farmer in New Iberia.

For the next several years, Johnson essentially abandoned the jazz world. He occasionally taught children music under the auspices of the Works Progress Administration program and appeared as a whistler at local carnivals, but for the most part he worked as a laborer and truck driver. Then, in 1938 Frederic Ramsey, Jr., and Bill Russell, interviewing Chicago and New York musicians for a book on early jazz, "discovered" Johnson. They paid dentist Leonard Bechet (Sidney's brother) to make him a new set of teeth, and the members of the revivalist Lu Watters Band raised enough money for him to buy a used trumpet and cornet.

In February 1942 an RCA employee interviewed Johnson and recorded him playing solo on a portable disc recorder. After Eugene Williams, record producer and editor of a new magazine called *Jazz Information*, heard the recordings, he and some enthusiasts from Los Angeles arranged to record Johnson in New Orleans for the Jazz Man label. These June 1942 sessions were the trumpeter's first commercial recordings; he was to make over 100 others during the next three years. Johnson played with apparently undiminished skill and authority in a group that included the legendary, but then relatively unknown clarinetist George Lewis. On various blues and tunes like "Moose March," Johnson's "lead is splendid in its supple invention of variations, his attack is direct and full of urgency" (Hillman, p. 51). Essential for their historic value, the sessions also show that Johnson was no New Orleans purist; he always preferred to play a wide variety of tunes, including popular songs.

Johnson recorded again in October, this time at the San Jacinto Hall in New Orleans; the session included ragtime numbers, a Hawaiian song, a piece by Louis Armstrong, and traditional blues and spirituals. These sides were picked up and distributed by Commodore records. But though these recordings made him an instant celebrity among the rising number of jazz revivalists, Johnson returned to New Iberia, unaware of his growing fame.

In early 1943 jazz historian Rudi Blesh gave a series of lectures on New Orleans jazz at the Museum of Art in San Francisco, and he arranged for Johnson to illustrate his talks. While there, Johnson made a series of recordings in May with pianist Bertha Gonsoulin, later released on the American Music label. In pieces like "Pallet on the Floor," he revealed his continued mastery of the trumpet, with clean attacks and "a formal, almost precise, sense of variation" in his playing (Harrison, p. 36). Later in the year, prompted by the San Francisco Hot Jazz Society, he played a series of dates with Lu Watters's Yerba Buena Jazz Band, one of the best known of the many groups promoting traditional jazz. From the beginning, Johnson's own musical diversity and difficult personality created considerable tension among the players; his drinking habits caused him frequently to miss dates. However, he did record with members of the group in early 1944, playing with freshness and intensity on pieces like "Careless Love." He also recorded some traditional hymns in duets with gospel singer Sister Lottie Peavey. By the middle of the year he had his fill of life in the big city and returned to New Iberia, stopping off in Los Angeles to record some pieces for the World Transcription Service with a band that included Red Callender on bass and Lee Young on drums; he also played superlatively in a broadcast session with the Kid Ory band.

In late July Johnson traveled again to New Orleans to take part in a week-long recording session at the San Jacinto Hall. These have become known as the "American Music" recordings (after the company that first released them on LP), and they are some of the very best music of the revival years. A three-horn front line (including Lewis) produced astonishingly flexible ensemble playing, the lead shifting constantly and unpredictably. Johnson shines, both in the ensembles and in solos, in pieces like "Careless Love" and "Sugarfoot Stomp."

In January 1945 Johnson was back in New Orleans, playing in a concert at New Orleans Municipal Auditorium in a group headed by Armstrong that included Sidney Bechet, J. C. Higginbotham, James P. Johnson, and other luminaries. Johnson played well enough to arouse Bechet's interest, and before they left, the two agreed to play together in an engagement at the Savoy Cafe in Boston. After another less satisfying session with the "American Music" group, Johnson went first to New York City, recording a session for Blue Note Records with Bechet. The subsequent Boston meeting was, however, a failure, undermined by Johnson's drinking and uneven playing.

After returning to New Iberia he traveled again to New Orleans in May 1945 to make a series of recordings over three nights at George Lewis's house. He also recorded a session with a nine-piece band that produced a reasonable facsimile of a New Orleans marching band.

Meanwhile, in New York City Eugene Williams had decided to promote Johnson with a hand-picked band. The group included Lewis on clarinet and Baby Dodds on drums. The engagement began less than propitiously; Johnson arrived a day late, and tension existed between him and the other musicians from the beginning. As always, he favored a wide variety of songs, while Lewis and the others played a more limited range of New Orleans traditional standards. At their first public session, on a Friday night in September 1945 at the Stuyvesant Casino, the hall was filled with 400 fans, many of them musicians who subsequently told others of the exciting, "pure" New Orleans jazz they had heard. While the style was hardly pure, the impact of the music was indeed dramatic; few had ever heard such music played by its original practitioners. Record companies were just as interested, and the group recorded four sides for Decca and

eight for Victor. Though the results were uneven, the performances on tunes like "One Sweet Letter" and "Franklin Street Blues" were excellent. The band was also featured in a New Year's Day concert at Town Hall, part of a celebration emceed by Orson Welles. They made their final appearance at the Casino on 12 January. A second New York engagement in May, with somewhat different personnel, was less productive. Lewis and the others were frustrated by Johnson's condescending attitude and lack of professionalism, and only a single recording session came from this later stay.

Johnson's day on center stage was all but over, and he returned to New Iberia. He appeared in a 1946 concert at Orchestra Hall in Chicago in a group that included guitarist Lonnie Johnson, but he played poorly. A concert at the University of Minnesota in the summer of 1947 was recorded, with Johnson playing strongly, and he subsequently toured the Midwest and played at a variety of dances and concerts. In September 1947 he played at the opening concert of the New York Jazz Club in New York City, with a group that included Edmond Hall, Omer Simeon, and Dannie Barker. While there, he returned to the Stuyvesant Casino with a small group that included Barker, and the recorded results show Johnson playing with drive and confidence, for once satisfied with the skills of his fellow band members. But the dances attracted little attention and were dropped after five shows. Johnson recorded only once more, at Carnegie Recital Hall in December 1947. Shortly thereafter he returned to New Iberia. He tried to get gigs in the North for the remainder of his life without success. He apparently died of a stroke in New Iberia.

Johnson was by all accounts a difficult person, opportunistic and often professionally irresponsible. Musically, his last recordings are perhaps the best representation of his art. They are not as adventurous or as sophisticated as the American Music efforts, but they clearly present him as a transitional figure, rooted in turn-of-the-century styles but willing to experiment with form and approach. His playing may have lacked the emotional magnetism of the early jazz stars, but he was an impressive, confident stylist and was more adventurous than most in incorporating a variety of tunes and styles in his repertoire. In the end, he remains most important as the central figure in the revival of New Orleans style jazz during the 1940s and early 1950s.

• Christopher Hillman, *Bunk Johnson* (1988), does an excellent job of sorting out the confusing details of Johnson's early life and of perceptively assessing the quality of his later career. Max Harrison et al., *The Essential Jazz Records*, vol. 1, *Ragtime to Swing* (1984), has numerous perceptive comments on Johnson's recordings. Two texts have excellent, brief overviews of his significance: Frank Tirro, *Jazz: A History* (1993), and Lewis Porter and Michael Ullman, with Edward Hazell, *Jazz: From Its Origins to the Present* (1993). Also see A. M. Sonnier, Jr., *William Geary "Bunk" Johnson: The New Iberia Years* (1977). An obituary is in the *New York Times*, 9 July 1949.

RONALD P. DUFOUR

JOHNSON, Bushrod Rust (7 Oct. 1817–12 Sept. 1880), soldier and educator, was born on a farm near Morristown, Ohio, the son of Noah Johnson, a blacksmith and farmer, and Rachel Spencer. Apparently Johnson received little formal education except for a brief attendance at Marietta Academy in Marietta, Ohio. Although raised in an antislavery Quaker family, he decided to pursue a military education as a means of rising above his social status. His affiliation with the Quaker religion seems not to have been as strong as that of his parents and other relatives. In 1836 Johnson entered the U.S. Military Academy. He graduated twenty-third in a class of forty-two in 1840 and received a commission as a second lieutenant of infantry. He joined the Third U.S. Infantry Regiment at Fort Brooke, Florida, late in 1840 and served at various posts in that state during the next year. On 1 February 1844 he was promoted to first lieutenant. The Third Infantry joined General Zachary Taylor's army at Corpus Christi on the eve of the Mexican War. Johnson fought in the battles of Palo Alto, Resaca de la Palma, and Monterrey before his regiment was transferred to General Winfield Scott's army at Veracruz. On 10 March 1847 he assumed the duties of acting assistant commissary for the army and "offered a vague bribe" (Cummings, p. 115) to a superior officer on 1 July. In a letter to the chief commissary at New Orleans, he proposed the shipment of merchandise disguised as commissary property. These goods would be sold at a profit, which Johnson would share with his superior. That officer asked for a court of inquiry after receiving Johnson's letter. The court was appointed to establish Johnson's authorship of the letter and did this after a brief hearing. Johnson resigned his commission in a letter dated 21 October 1847 rather than risk dismissal.

In early 1848 Johnson became an instructor at the Western Military Institute, located in Georgetown, Kentucky. He assumed charge of the cadets early the next year. The school moved to Blue Lick Springs (now Blue Licks), Kentucky, in 1850, and Johnson became its acting superintendent that September. Early in 1852 he assumed the duties of president and superintendent. He married Mary E. Hatch in 1852; they had one child. The institute moved to Nashville, Tennessee, in 1854 and became the Collegiate Department of the University of Nashville with Johnson as superintendent and professor of civil engineering. He also held the rank of colonel in the state militia.

Johnson cast his lot with the South when the Civil War began. By that time he owned considerable property in Nashville and had become close friends with many states' rights advocates. Johnson undoubtedly still resented being forced to resign from the U.S. Army and probably felt that he could not rejoin it even if inclined to do so. Governor Isham G. Harris commissioned Johnson as major of engineers on his staff on 28 May 1861. The following month, Johnson was promoted to colonel of engineers in the Provisional Army of Tennessee. In this capacity, he approved the sites for Fort Henry and Fort Donelson. Johnson as-

sumed command of a training camp during the summer of 1861 and transferred to the state adjutant general's office in December. He received a commission as brigadier general in the Confederate army on 24 January 1862 and was sent to the garrison at Fort Donelson. He was assigned to command the left flank of the entrenchments during the attack on the fort by Brigadier General Ulysses S. Grant's Union army. Rather than face imprisonment, Johnson and one of his captains walked away from Donelson during the confusion surrounding the surrender of the garrison. He made his way from there to Nashville. Johnson received command of a Tennessee infantry brigade in Major General Benjamin F. Cheatham's division in March. At the battle of Shiloh, an enemy artillery shell killed Johnson's horse and wounded Johnson slightly. He did not return to duty until May.

During the Kentucky campaign in the summer of 1862, Johnson's brigade came under the command of Brigadier General Simon B. Buckner (1823–1914). Johnson's men helped break a portion of the Union line in the battle of Perryville on 8 October, and he had five horses shot from under him. Under Major General Patrick R. Cleburne, Johnson led his brigade at the battle of Murfreesboro. Though his men retreated unexpectedly in the engagement, Johnson personally performed well. The following June his brigade fought in several skirmishes with the enemy at Hoover's Gap. He assumed command of a provisional infantry division of the Army of Tennessee during the Chickamauga campaign in September 1863. During the fighting on 20 September, he led his men in the breakthrough of the Union center, receiving praise from his superiors for his actions.

The Army of Tennessee besieged Union forces in Chattanooga immediately after the battle of Chickamauga. Johnson was given command of a new division during those operations. On 22 November General Braxton Bragg ordered him to take his division to reinforce the army of Lieutenant General James Longstreet at Knoxville. Johnson's men played only a supporting role during Longstreet's assault on Fort Sanders on 28 November. They were heavily engaged at Bean's Station on 14 December. Johnson's division wintered in East Tennessee then moved to Abingdon, Virginia, in late April 1864. Shortly afterward he was ordered to take a brigade to Richmond to help defend that city. In the battle of Port Walthall Junction on 7 May, his troops repulsed a Union attack and protected a vital railroad from receiving serious damage. The brigade joined Major General Robert F. Hoke's division and participated in several engagements with the Federals near Petersburg.

General Pierre G. T. Beauregard assigned Johnson to the command of a division, and the Confederate Senate confirmed his promotion to major general on 21 May. Union troops exploded a mine under the entrenchments held by one of Johnson's brigades on 30 July. For reasons yet unexplained, Johnson remained at his headquarters to direct his men during the ensuing battle of the Crater, allowing Brigadier General

William Mahone to lead the Confederate counterattack. Mahone thus gained the credit for stopping the threatened Federal breakthrough. After the battle of Five Forks, 1 April 1865, Johnson's men moved to the army's right flank and participated in the retreat from the Petersburg lines the next day. Federal troops overran the division along with other troops during the battle of Sayler's Creek on 6 April. Johnson, two other major generals, and five brigadiers fled the field after failing to stop the rout. General Robert E. Lee relieved him and Major Generals George E. Pickett and Richard H. Anderson of their commands, ordering them to their homes on 8 April. No one has explained satisfactorily why Lee did this, since none of the generals had exhibited any cowardice in the battle. Johnson remained with the army, however, and received his parole at Appomattox Court House on 9 April.

Johnson returned to Nashville and went into the real estate business. In 1870 he assisted Edmund Kirby-Smith in reestablishing the University of Nashville, which had disappeared during the Civil War, and took charge of the Collegiate Department. The school dissolved in 1874, and Johnson moved briefly to St. Louis, Missouri, to enter the commission business. In January 1875 he moved to Brighton, Illinois, and began farming. He died at his home in Brighton.

Except for his actions in several battles, Johnson's performance as a general was less than spectacular. According to his biographer, Johnson "reached his military zenith" (Cummings, p. 268) in the battle of Chickamauga. Thereafter, bad luck and his own character flaws hampered him as a commander. He had an "impassive temperament" (Cummings, p. 164), was an introvert, was unduly cautious at times, and seems to have been insecure, even when his actions did not merit censure.

• Record Group 109 in the National Archives contains some of Johnson's official correspondence. The definitive biography of Johnson is Charles M. Cummings, *Yankee Quaker, Confederate General: The Curious Career of Bushrod Rust Johnson* (1971). A shorter treatment of the general's career is in Tracy M. Kegley, "Bushrod Rust Johnson: Soldier and Teacher," *Tennessee Historical Quarterly* 7 (1948): 249–58.

ARTHUR W. BERGERON, JR.

JOHNSON, Cave (11 Jan. 1793–23 Nov. 1866), politician, was born in Robertson County, Tennessee, the son of Thomas Johnson and Mary Noel, farmers. In his early years Johnson attended George Martin's Academy, located about two miles east of Nashville, and in 1807 he went to Mount Pleasant Academy in Sumner County. From 1808 through 1811 he attended Cumberland College in Nashville. While at Cumberland, he organized a student volunteer company that offered its services for Andrew Jackson's march to Mississippi in 1811. Jackson declined to accept the company and advised the students to continue their studies, but Johnson later served as deputy brigade quartermaster in Jackson's campaign against the Creek Nation in 1813 and 1814. By that time Johnson

had been expelled from college for refusing to follow Cumberland's heavily classical curriculum, and he had begun reading law with state supreme court justice William W. Cooke. Upon returning from military service, Johnson continued his legal studies with P. W. Humphreys and Robert West. After receiving his license in 1815, Johnson moved to Clarksville and established a successful law practice that included his election in 1817 as solicitor general. At the same time he combined his legal business with profitable investments in tobacco planting. The 1860 census showed him owning sixty-seven slaves and over $113,000 in real estate and personal property.

In 1829 Johnson was elected to Congress, where he served four terms until his defeat for reelection in 1837. A year later he married Elizabeth Dortch Brunson. They had three sons before her death in 1851. In 1839 he regained his seat and remained in Congress until 1845. Although he voted against the Force Bill in 1833, Johnson otherwise loyally supported President Jackson and the Democratic party. He became especially known for his tenacious challenge to proposed increases in government expenditures. One fellow congressman referred to Johnson as the "Cerberus of the treasury," while another, John Quincy Adams, labeled him "the nuisance of the House." While in Congress Johnson developed a close friendship with another Tennessee representative, James K. Polk. Charles Sellers, Polk's biographer, concluded that Johnson "was likely the only man for whom Polk felt deep affection" (*James K. Polk: Continentalist*, p. 183). Together with Senator Felix Grundy, Johnson and Polk during the 1830s assumed leadership of the Democratic party in Tennessee. In the early 1840s Johnson promoted Polk's claims for higher office, and he played a major role in the negotiations at the 1844 Democratic National Convention that nominated Polk for the presidency. After Polk's election, Johnson acted as one of the president-elect's agents in Washington, responsible for contacting potential cabinet members. Polk rewarded his friend for his services by naming Johnson to the cabinet as postmaster general.

As postmaster general, Johnson enjoyed a reputation for honesty and efficiency. During his tenure, the Post Office Department began experimenting with using prepaid postage stamps and with urban pickup and delivery service. It also dramatically reduced its budget deficit while opening nearly 2,000 new offices and expanding its service into Texas, Oregon, and the territory acquired in the Mexican War. Johnson acted as one of President Polk's principal advisers. He attended more than 90 percent of the meetings of the cabinet, advised Polk on prominent political issues, and "emerged as the president's man to see about practically all patronage concerns" (Bergeron, p. 149). He favored a policy of avoiding factionalism within his own party by leaving incumbent Democrats in their offices while removing members of the rival Whig party. Within his own department, Johnson replaced about 1,600 local postmasters, which constituted about 14% of the offices at his disposal.

After the expiration of Polk's term, Johnson returned to Clarksville. Through the 1850s, he remained active in national Democratic party affairs by promoting the presidential prospects of fellow cabinet member James Buchanan. In 1853 Governor Andrew Johnson appointed him to the presidency of the Bank of Tennessee, in which office Cave Johnson served from January 1854 until 1860. Later that year President Buchanan appointed him U.S. commissioner for the settlement of claims against the government of Paraguay by the American-owned Paraguay Navigation Company. With the secession of the Lower South states in 1861, Johnson became one of Tennessee's most prominent Union Democrats and was elected as a Unionist delegate to a proposed state convention. A popular referendum rejected the convention, but after the conflict at Fort Sumter opened the Civil War, Johnson joined most other Tennesseans to advocate membership in the Confederate States of America. He remained in Clarksville during the Union occupation of the town. President Andrew Johnson pardoned him in August 1865, and in the following April he was elected to fill a vacant seat in the state senate. A Republican majority disqualified him, however, because "his weight of character and influence was given in behalf of the rebellion." In his last political act, Johnson protested his disqualification in a public address. He died in Clarksville, Tennessee.

Jackson reputedly referred to Johnson as a "hollow fellow," but for the most part his reputation in his lifetime was one of an honest and dedicated Democratic partisan. Sellers described Johnson as "unambitious and unpretentious—one of the few balding politicians who scorned to camouflage a gleaming plate" and who "repeatedly sacrificed his own interests and incurred renewed rheumatic pains in order to serve his friend [Polk] on the stump and in caucus" (*James K. Polk: Continentalist*, pp. 4–5). Johnson stands as a prototype of a Jacksonian politician, devoted to limited government and faithful to the Union until the Civil War forced him to choose sides.

• The most extensive collections of Johnson's personal papers are his letters in the James K. Polk Papers, Library of Congress, many of which are published in *Correspondence of James K. Polk*, ed. Herbert Weaver and Wayne Cutler (1969–); and in the James Buchanan Papers, Historical Society of Pennsylvania. William P. Titus, *Picturesque Clarksville, Past and Present: A History of the City of the Hills* (1887; repr. 1973), contains a biographical sketch and several personal papers, including an autobiographical letter by Johnson to his children. Several congressional speeches are recorded in the *Congressional Globe*, 21st through 24th Cong. (1829–1837) and 26th through 28th Cong. (1839–1845). An extended biography of Johnson is Clement L. Grant, "The Public Career of Cave Johnson" (Ph.D. diss., Vanderbilt Univ., 1951), from which Grant derived three articles, "The Public Career of Cave Johnson," *Tennessee Historical Quarterly* 10 (Sept. 1951): 195–223; "Cave Johnson and the Presidential Campaign of 1844," *East Tennessee Historical Society's Publications* 25 (1953): 54–73; and "Cave Johnson: Postmaster General," *Tennessee Historical Quarterly* 20 (Dec. 1961): 323–49. On Johnson's relationship with Polk and his service as postmaster general, see Allan Nevins, ed., *Polk: The Diary of a President, 1845–49* (1929); Charles G. Sellers, *James K. Polk: Jacksonian, 1795–1843* (1957); Sellers, *James K. Polk: Continentalist, 1843–1846* (1966); and Paul H. Bergeron, *The Presidency of James K. Polk* (1987). Obituaries are in the *Clarksville Weekly Chronicle*, 30 Nov. 1866, and the *Nashville Union and Dispatch*, 27 Nov. 1866.

JONATHAN M. ATKINS

JOHNSON, Charles Spurgeon (24 July 1893–27 Oct. 1956), sociologist and educator, was born in Bristol, Virginia, the son of Reverend Charles Henry Johnson, a minister in the black Baptist church, and Winifred Branch. Bristol, a small city in the state's far southwest corner, had the usual pattern of racial segregation, and it is where Charles received his primary education. He was then sent to Richmond to a private Baptist academy linked to Virginia Union University, a leading black institution, where he completed his undergraduate degree with honors in 1916. Working part time in the Richmond ghetto, he was shocked by the racial discrimination and economic deprivation marking southern Negro life. That led him to decide on graduate work in sociology, to concentrate on race relations, and to focus in particular on conditions in the urban-industrial North in the setting of the Great Migration, the northward movement of thousands of southern blacks.

At the University of Chicago Johnson earned a Ph.B. degree in sociology in 1918, working primarily with Robert E. Park, one of the founders of the "Chicago School," which emphasized the need to integrate sociological theory with direct empirical experience in the urban community. That same year Park, president of the Chicago Urban League, helped Johnson obtain his first professional job as the league's research director. After a year in France during World War I as a sergeant-major in combat, Johnson returned to Chicago in 1919 in the midst of a devastating race riot. Appointed associate director of the investigating commission, he did most of the research and wrote the bulk of the report that became *The Negro in Chicago* (1922), a study now widely accepted as a classic depiction of the deep roots of race riots, including racial discrimination.

In 1921 Johnson left Chicago to become research director of the National Urban League in New York. (The year before he had married Marie Antoinette Burgette; they had four children.) Between 1921 and 1928 Johnson directed many research projects, which defined the racial barriers impeding Negro economic and social opportunity. In founding and editing the league's journal, *Opportunity*, in 1923, he hoped as well to develop black creativity in the arts. Thus he became the "entrepreneur of the Harlem Renaissance," the central figure in gaining acceptance in mainstream publishing for talented young black writers and artists such as Langston Hughes, Zora Neale Hurston, and Countee Cullen. The Harlem Renaissance, the creative surge of the "New Negro," declined during the Great Depression, but it left a permanent imprint on black creative expression.

Johnson always wanted to return to the South to analyze more fully the racial system as an integral part of the southern socioeconomic structure. In 1928 he accepted a position as professor of sociology and director of the social sciences department at Fisk University in Nashville, Tennessee. In that capacity he established his national reputation in the field of race relations, not only carrying out or directing countless research projects but in the process training a whole new generation of black social scientists. Further, he expanded his familiar bridging role, carried over from Harlem Renaissance days. With foundation funding, from the Rosenwald Fund and the American Missionary Association in particular, he brought white philanthropic support to black social science research and black community programs. All this was accomplished in the face of southern white hostility or indifference. For eighteen years the work went on, rivaling that of the only other comparable research center in the South, at the University of North Carolina. Even after being named president of Fisk in 1946—the first black president of that historic black institution—he continued, for example, to sponsor the annual Race Relations Institutes at Fisk begun in 1944. Scholars, activists, and national political figures concerned with human rights convened on an interracial basis, a striking innovation in the closed society of the South. However, the presidency (1946–1956) did mean a gradual diminishing of his dynamic research and bridging roles. In the last years he served more as a leading sociological authority on race relations and as a prominent member of the national black leadership.

Of the many books and scores of articles Johnson published during this period, three research studies in particular have enduring value. *Shadow of the Plantation* (1934), Johnson's best-known work, is a quietly powerful indictment of the fading, nearly feudal farm tenancy system as seen in the lives of black families in one cotton county in Alabama. *Growing up in the Black Belt* (1941), a six-county study, analyzes incisively how the socialization of Negro youth a half-century ago meant adaptation to both the "warping" influence of racism and the normal stages of the life cycle. *Patterns of Negro Segregation* (1943) catalogs the endless ways in which a racial quasi-caste system functioned in the South until recently to constrict and demean the lives of black Americans. All three books also make an important and distinctive contribution to methodology; personality profiles, often in the form of moving, eloquent commentaries by ordinary black people, are threaded into the quantitative survey data, providing a needed qualitative depth.

Over and above the research and bridging roles, Johnson engaged in a lifetime of racial justice advocacy and activism at the international, national, and regional level. In 1930 he investigated forced labor in Liberia for the League of Nations, although his report, *Bitter Canaan*, was not published until 1987. He was a member of a great many national commissions on such problems as public housing, farm tenancy, and racial violence. President Truman appointed him to the first American delegation to UNESCO in Paris in 1946 and to the commission for reorganizing education in postwar Japan. In advocacy, as in his other roles, Johnson followed a lifelong credo: comprehensive social science research as an indispensable prelude to vigorous action to combat racial discrimination and advance the cause of equality of opportunity. W. E. B. Du Bois and other outspoken black leaders found Johnson's position to be insufficiently militant and excessively accommodationist in its dependency on support from the white establishment philanthropically and on white liberalism politically. ("If not reactionary, certainly very cautious," Du Bois observed.) Such a view does Johnson an injustice. He yielded to no one in expressing his anger and indignation over racial injustice. But his particular strategy for overcoming racial oppression must be seen in the context of the thirties and forties. With faith in the power of social science to demonstrate the scope and depth of racism, with the conviction that incremental social change was inevitable in a democratic society, he held to his last, he did what he could, under constricting conditions during what was a far more racist era. His favorite aphorism, from the African experience, was: "If you know well the beginning, the end will not trouble you much." Massive resistance to the landmark Supreme Court decision in 1954, *Brown v. Board of Education*, declaring public school segregation unconstitutional, produced an uncharacteristic pessimism about race relations in his last published writing, but he remained convinced that "full American citizenship" would ultimately prevail for all black Americans. He died while changing trains in Louisville, Kentucky; he was on his way to a meeting in New York City with the Fisk board of trustees.

Johnson, together with Du Bois and E. Franklin Frazier, is considered a "founding father" among black sociologists for his work in the sociology of race relations. In its annual Du Bois-Frazier-Johnson Award for distinguished scholarship in sociology by a black sociologist, the American Sociological Association honors their achievements.

• Johnson's papers, including book and article manuscripts and bound volumes of speeches, are in the Special Collections Department, Fisk University Library, Nashville. The library also holds taped interviews with many of Johnson's associates and students, and it has published George L. Gardner, *A Bibliography of Charles S. Johnson's Published Writings* (1960). Additional works by Johnson not mentioned in the text are *The Negro in American Civilization* (1930); *Race Relations*, written with Willis D. Weatherford (1934); *The Collapse of Cotton Tenancy*, with Edwin R. Embree and Will Alexander (1935); *To Stem This Tide* (1943); *Into the Mainstream* (1947); and *Education and the Cultural Crisis* (1951). The last piece Johnson ever wrote, which expressed a tempered optimism about race relations, is "A Southern Negro's View of the South," *New York Times Magazine*, 26 Sept. 1956. A comprehensive assessment is Patrick J. Gilpin, "Charles S. Johnson" (Ph.D. diss., Vanderbilt Univ., 1973).

See also Embree, "Charles S. Johnson, Scholar and Gentleman," in his *Thirteen against the Odds* (1944); Ernest W. Burgess, "Charles S. Johnson, Social Scientist, Editor, and Educational Statesman," *Phylon* 17 (1956): 317–21; and Lewis W. Jones, "The Sociology of Charles S. Johnson" (draft notes, n.d.), Special Collections, Fisk University Library. A more recent interpretation is Richard Robbins, "Charles S. Johnson," in *Black Sociologists*, ed. James Blackwell and Morris Janowitz (1974).

RICHARD ROBBINS

JOHNSON, Chic. *See* Olsen, Ole, and Chic Johnson.

JOHNSON, Cornelius Cooper (21 Aug. 1913–15 Feb. 1946), track and field athlete, was born in Los Angeles, California, the son of Shadreak Johnson, a plasterer; his mother's name is not known. The elder Johnson had moved from Raleigh, North Carolina, to California in 1893 for better economic and social opportunities. Johnson first competed in organized track and field events at Berendo Junior High School in Los Angeles. He achieved greater athletic success as a student at Los Angeles High School, competing statewide in the sprints and the high jump. His skill as a high jumper earned him a position on the 1932 U.S. Olympic team. While only a junior in high school, Johnson tied veteran performers Robert van Osdel and George Spitz for first place at a height of 6′6⅝″ at the 1932 Amateur Athletic Union (AAU) Championship, which also served as the Olympic trials.

One of four African Americans representing the United States in track and field in the 1932 Summer Olympic Games, Johnson performed admirably before a hometown crowd in Los Angeles, finishing in a four-way tie for first place at 6′5½″ with van Osdel, Duncan McNaughton of Canada, and Simeon Toribo of the Philippines. Since all four athletes had failed to clear 6′6¾″ in regular competition, a jump-off was held to determine the gold, silver, and bronze medalists. As a result of the jump-off, Johnson finished in fourth place, as McNaughton won the gold, van Osdel the silver, and Toribo the bronze.

In 1933 Johnson graduated from high school and entered Compton Junior College in Pasadena, California. That same year he captured the outdoor AAU high jump title, equaling the meet record of 6′7″. In 1934 he shared the outdoor AAU championship with Walter Marty, as both athletes topped a new meet record of 6′8⅝″. The following year he soared above all American high jumpers, winning both the indoor and outdoor AAU titles with a mark of 6′7″. In 1936 Johnson finished second in a jump-off against Ed Burke in the indoor AAU championship, after both performers completed regular competition at 6′8¹⁵⁄₁₆″. In the outdoor AAU championship, which also served as the 1936 Olympic trials, both Johnson and Dave Albritton of Ohio State University set a world record with jumps of 6′9¾″.

Berlin, Germany, then the capital of the National Socialist (Nazi) Third Reich, hosted the 1936 Summer Olympic Games. By that time anti-Semitic public policies had systematically removed Jews from nearly every aspect of German life. American participation in the "Nazi Olympics" was hotly debated in the United States; African Americans in particular were divided over sending athletes to Germany. While some maintained that a boycott of African-American athletes would illuminate the racially discriminatory practices of the United States, others argued that a triumphant demonstration of African-American athletic prowess would powerfully undermine both American and German racial insolence. The United States sent to the 1936 Olympics nineteen African Americans—twelve track and field performers, including two women; five boxers; and two weightlifters. Johnson won the gold medal in the high jump, setting an Olympic record performance of 6′8″ and leading an American sweep of the medals. Other African-American trackmen, led by Jesse Owens's quadruple gold medal feat, won every running event from the 100 to the 800 meters, the 400-meter relay, and the long jump. By capturing silver and bronze medals in many of the same events, they discredited Nazi racial theories but accomplished little in dispiriting American racism. Johnson, rather than Owens, was the victim of Adolf Hitler's most pointed snub. After honoring German and Finnish medal winners, in accordance with his belief in Aryan superiority, the Nazi leader left the stadium before the conclusion of the high jump and did not congratulate the African-American medalists.

After the 1936 Olympics Johnson's dominance over the high jump diminished rapidly. In 1937 he finished fourth in the 1937 indoor AAU championships, won by Ed Burke, and he lost to Albritton in the outdoor AAU contest. Johnson, who later competed for the New York City Grand Street Boys Association, tied with Lloyd Thompson for the 1938 indoor AAU title at 6′6″. After retiring from the high jump, he became a letter carrier for the U.S. Post Office in Los Angeles, and in 1945 he joined the U.S. Merchant Marine and served as a baker on the *Santa Cruz*. The following year Johnson developed bronchial pneumonia aboard ship; he died before the ship reached the San Francisco harbor.

Although other aspects of his life may have been affected by discrimination and prejudice, Johnson was not denied opportunities to compete in track and field—except for the Nazi Olympics—because of his race. Unlike major league baseball and professional football, track and field had afforded African-American performers the opportunity to participate since the late nineteenth century. Although African Americans were denied membership in exclusive amateur athletic organizations, such as the New York Athletic Club, they either formed their own athletic clubs—such as the New York City Grand Street Boys Association—or competed on the teams of predominately white colleges and universities in the North, Midwest, and West. Only in the South, where the AAU recognized and upheld the region's discriminatory practices, were African Americans denied participation in track and field meets. Johnson and fellow African-American trackmen made their first significant impact on the sport internationally in the 1936 Olympics, and African Americans have remained the mainstay of American track and field superiority.

• A recent biographical account is Bob Oates, "If Anybody Was Snubbed by Hitler, It Was Cornelius Johnson," *Los Angeles Times*, 22 July 1984. Statistical information on Johnson's AAU national championship performances is in Frank G. Menke, *The Encyclopedia of Sports*, 4th rev. ed. (1969); his Olympic achievements are chronicled in David Wallechinsky, *The Complete Book of the Summer Olympics* (1996). For Johnson's place in the history of track and field, consult Roberto L. Quercetani, *A World History of Track and Field Athletics* (1964). The best English-language account of the 1936 Olympic Games, which discusses Johnson's gold medal performance, is Richard D. Mandell, *The Nazi Olympics* (1971). David K. Wiggins examined the debate among African Americans over participation in the 1936 Olympic Games in "The 1936 Olympic Games in Berlin: The Response of America's Black Press," *Research Quarterly for Exercise and Sport* 54 (1983): 279–82. For the impact of racism and inopportunity on Johnson, as well as those of many of the African-American trackmen of the late 1920s and 1930s, see William J. Baker, *Jesse Owens: An American Life* (1986). A general survey of African-American track and field athletes is Arthur R. Ashe, Jr., *A Hard Road to Glory—Track and Field: The African-American Athlete in Track and Field* (1988, 1993). Obituaries include the *Baltimore Afro-American* and the *Chicago Defender*, both 23 Feb. 1946.

ADAM R. HORNBUCKLE

JOHNSON, Crockett (20 Oct. 1906–11 July 1975), cartoonist, illustrator, and writer of children's books, was born David Johnson Leisk in New York City, the son of David Leisk, a writer, and Mary Burg. Crockett Johnson (as he was known from the beginning of his career as a cartoonist) grew up in Elmhurst, Long Island, and attended art school at Cooper Union and New York University, where he studied typography. For a time he played professional football. He also carted ice while trying to make a living as a freelance artist. In the mid-1920s he began his career in art in the advertising department of Macy's Department Store. After a short stay—he later reported that he quit over the store's requirement that he wear stiff collars at work—he found a job with the McGraw-Hill Publishing Company, where he worked as an art director for five trade journals and contributed to several others. While with McGraw-Hill from 1927 to 1940, he supplemented his meager wage with occasional freelance sales of advertising art and gag cartoons to local and national periodicals.

In March 1938 Johnson achieved national recognition with the first of a series of minimally drawn cartoons in *Collier's* showing a man reacting to an event by tiny changes of expression in his eyes. Never titled but generally known as "The Little Man with the Eyes," the feature appeared irregularly until 1942. In 1940 he married Ruth Krauss, a poet and children's book writer. The couple had no children. For two years Johnson attempted to sell a sophisticated comic strip named *Barnaby* but had no luck with either *Collier's* or King Features Syndicate. The strip was at last accepted by the liberal New York newspaper *PM*, which introduced it on 20 April 1942. The next year it was bought by the Chicago Sun-Times Syndicate, but it had so little mass market appeal that by 1944 only seven other newspapers had taken it on.

Barnaby was a literate fantasy-satire about a clear-headed five-year-old and his verbose and generally ineffectual fairy godfather J. J. O'Malley, a plump cigar-smoking pixie whose inflated prose recalled that of a carnival huckster and whose superb self-confidence was undiminished by the failure of his spells to work quite right. Drawn in an economical style of considerable graphic elegance, composed entirely of lines and areas of solid black with no shading, only the merest suggestion of background, and with the text of its speeches set in type and printed, the feature won immediate success with a small but enthusiastic audience. Although the circulation of *Barnaby* never exceeded fifty-two newspapers in the United States and twelve abroad, collections of the strip appeared in book form in 1942 and 1943, and it generated a quarterly magazine, a stage play, a radio series, a television special, a popular song, and an animated cartoon, which won first place in its category at the 1967 Venice Film Festival. Among the fans who wrote glowing comments for the dust jacket of the first *Barnaby* volume were Rockwell Kent, William Rose Benét, and Louis Untermeyer, who called the strip "the funniest high comedy since Aristophanes and Thurber." Collections of the strip were reprinted frequently after it ended in the newspapers, and it was considered a classic in the field, described in 1995 as "one of the century's undisputed comic-strip masterpieces" (Goulart, *The Funnies*, p. 164).

Johnson found the demands of daily creation difficult, and in 1945 he called on neighbors Jack Morley and Ted Ferro to take over the job of producing the strip, retaining supervision of the story line. *Barnaby* began to lose papers, however, and in 1952 Johnson resumed it to compose the concluding story. The Hall Syndicate persuaded him to revive *Barnaby* in 1962, but the strip ran only briefly before being abandoned for good. During the 1950s Johnson returned to freelancing gag cartoons and produced a series interpreting the meanings of a dog's bark. A collection, *Barkis*, appeared in 1956. He also drew advertising art and illustrated eight children's books, including four by his wife from 1945 (*The Carrot Seed*) to 1967 (*The Happy Egg*).

Johnson found a more lucrative career in writing and illustrating his own children's books, beginning with *Who's Upside Down* in 1952. Drawn in a simple style similar to that of *Barnaby*, his stories were aimed at younger readers than his comic strip but contained the same spirit of off-beat, slightly ironic fantasy and delight in word play. Of the twenty juvenile titles he produced, his greatest success was *Harold and the Purple Crayon* (1955), about a child who draws his own adventures and enters into them with the same composure as Barnaby, whom he much resembles. Six other

Harold books, concluding with *Harold's ABC* (1963), followed.

After the publication of his last children's book, *The Emperor's Gifts* (1965), Johnson turned to abstract painting, producing a number of well-regarded geometric oils and acrylics based on mathematical formulas. He had solo exhibitions at the Glezer Gallery in New York City in 1967 and the IBM International Resources Center in Yorktown Heights, New York, in 1975, and examples of his work were acquired by General Electric. His painting *A Construction for the Heptagon* was placed on permanent exhibit in the Hall of Mathematics of the Smithsonian Institution in Washington, D.C., in 1975. He wrote articles on his art and the mathematical theories underlying it for *Leonardo* and *Mathematical Gazette*.

Johnson had a precise, inventive mind and enjoyed devising labor-saving devices for the home. He designed his own drawing table, and he received a patent for an adjustable mattress in 1955. A bronzed six-footer devoted to sailing, he spent his last years in Westport, Connecticut. By the time of his death in Norwalk, Connecticut, he had almost forgotten the comic strip that made him famous and dismissed it as the work of a brief interlude in his life. However, even though his children's books have been warmly received and frequently reprinted, and his paintings have won critical respect, it is for *Barnaby* that Johnson earned a unique place as a creative artist.

• Johnson's work is discussed in numerous histories of cartoons, notably in Thomas Craven, *Cartoon Cavalcade* (1943), Coulton Waugh, *The Comics* (1947), Stephen Becker, *Comic Art in America* (1959), Jerry Robinson, *The Comics* (1974), and Ron Goulart, *The Funnies* (1995). Entries on the man and his strip are included in such reference books as Maurice Horn, ed., *World Encyclopedia of Comics* (1976), Goulart, *Encyclopedia of American Comics* (1990), and Horn, ed., *100 Years of American Newspaper Comics* (1996). Chapters on Johnson that pay special attention to his work as a children's author and illustrator are in Bertha Miller, *Illustrators of Children's Books, 1946–1956* (1958), and Lee Bennett Hopkins, *Books Are by People* (1969). See also *Newsweek*, 4 Oct. 1943, pp. 102, 104; and *Editor & Publisher*, 16 July 1960, p. 52. An obituary is in the *New York Times*, 13 July 1975.

DENNIS WEPMAN

JOHNSON, David (10 May 1827–30 Jan. 1908), artist, was born in New York City, the son of David Johnson, a native of Dorchester, Massachusetts, and Eliza (maiden name unknown), a native of Philadelphia. Very little has been discovered about his parents or ancestry but an entry in the 1904 edition of *Lamb's Biographical Dictionary* states that the elder Johnson built the first mail coaches in the United States. Young David was educated in the New York public schools. Records of the National Academy of Design indicate that he studied there from 1845 to 1847. His older brother, Joseph Hoffman Johnson, was also an artist, but what influence he had on his younger brother is not known.

In 1850 David Johnson studied landscape painting with the noted Hudson River school artist Jasper Francis Cropsey, but he was already a skilled painter who had exhibited at the National Academy of Design the previous year. His earliest surviving landscape, from 1849, depicts a view of Haines Falls in the Catskill Mountains of New York. Johnson wrote on the back: "My first Study from Nature—made in company with J. F. Kensett & J. W. Casilear." Kensett and Casilear later became, like Johnson, well-known painters of the Hudson River school. Even in this very early work, the hallmarks of Johnson's mature style are evident. He was fascinated by rock formations and painted them repeatedly throughout his career. His depiction of Haines Falls is not a monumental, panoramic view but a small, intimate image of the falls themselves and the rocks immediately surrounding them. Most of his paintings were small-scale, with few larger than two by three feet. His careful delineation of rocks, vegetation, and water may be indebted in part to the writings of the British art critic John Ruskin, whose book *Modern Painters* appeared in America in 1847, the year Johnson completed his studies at the National Academy of Design. Ruskin argued that painting must be "true to nature" and his theories led eventually to the founding of the Society for the Advancement of Truth in Painting and of the Pre-Raphaelite Brotherhood. Johnson, however, cannot be classified as a Pre-Raphaelite. Although his landscapes are painted with a fine brush stroke and are highly detailed, they do not have the bright, almost garish high-key colors characteristic of Pre-Raphaelite painting. Johnson preferred more subdued colors that more accurately captured nature.

Although based in New York City, Johnson traveled widely. He painted in the Catskill and Adirondack mountains of New York State and in New York's Mohawk Valley and Genesee region; in the White Mountains of New Hampshire; in Maine, Vermont, and Virginia; and in the rural sections of the New York metropolitan area. An 1865 painting, *Mountain Landscape*, appears to depict a Colorado locale, but it has not been determined whether Johnson actually visited the Rocky Mountains or based his picture on photographs.

All of Johnson's eastern landscapes were based on firsthand knowledge of the places depicted. His earliest landscapes show only natural settings, without figures, but he began adding people to his landscapes in the early 1850s. He also began to paint panoramic views during this time. Among the more notable pictures from the early part of his career are *North Conway, New Hampshire* (1852, Museum of Fine Arts, Boston); *A Study, Bash Bish Falls*, painted in western Massachusetts in 1856; and *Near Squam Lake, New Hampshire* (1856, Metropolitan Museum of Art, New York), exhibited at the National Academy of Design that same year. Johnson did some of the best work of his career in the White Mountains. *Chocorua Peak, New Hampshire*, painted in 1856, has the clarity and brilliance that came to characterize his painting, but it also has, as art historian John I. H. Baur remarked, "a new, almost Constable-like feeling for the movement of the land" (Baur, p. 44). Three years later, Johnson painted *Conway Valley, New Hampshire*, a very small painting (only five by eight inches), but one featuring a technique quite unlike that used in miniature painting. It is loosely painted with "sweeping brushstrokes . . . [that] give the picture a dramatic force" reminiscent of the work of John Constable (Baur, p. 48).

Johnson produced several paintings of both natural and man-made bridges in 1860. He traveled to Virginia, where he painted views of the Natural Bridge, a limestone arch over two hundred feet high that was once owned by Thomas Jefferson. He painted a fine close-up of the bridge reminiscent of Frederic Edwin Church's well-known 1852 depiction. He also captured a panoramic view in which the bridge appears almost subdued by the surrounding vegetation and the rolling hills in the background (Reynolda House Museum of American Art, Winston-Salem, N.C.). Both paintings rank among Johnson's very finest work. In the same year he produced two small paintings of New York's Harlem River Aqueduct, also known as the High Bridge, built between 1839 and 1842 as part of the system bringing water from upstate to New York City.

While he continued to paint the small, intimate depictions of nature he had produced from the beginning of his career, Johnson painted more panoramic landscapes, mostly small in size. One larger work is *Buck Mountain, Lake George*, painted circa 1867. Equally beautiful is *Study at Lancaster, New Hampshire*, also painted in 1867. Here the different elements are rendered in characteristic minute detail, with the composition held together by brilliant sunlight. *Franconia Mountains from West Compton, New Hampshire* (Wadsworth Athenaeum, Hartford, Conn.) also dates from around this time.

In 1869 Johnson married Maria Louise West. They lived at 106 West 20th Street in New York City until 1876, when they moved to 103 Lexington Avenue. Johnson maintained his studio at 626 Broadway from 1861 to 1871, then at 52 East 23rd Street from 1872 to 1894. In 1873 he painted *Brook Study at Warwick [New York]* (Munson-Williams-Proctor Institute, Utica, N.Y.), and in 1876 he executed one of his largest paintings, *Old Man of the Mountains* (State of New Hampshire). Measuring about five by four feet, it was commissioned by the owner of the Profile House Hotel, Richard Taft. The painting depicts the rock profile whose nickname is the painting's title and which has for many years been one of New Hampshire's best-known scenic attractions. The artist included several tourists at lower left gazing up at it. Both paintings were displayed at the Centennial Exposition in Philadelphia in 1876, where they attracted much favorable attention from the critics and Johnson received a medal for his contributions to art. He subsequently sold *Brook Study at Warwick* for $1,000, describing it as "an out door study, painted entirely on the spot and is, as far as I was able to make it so, a literal portrait of the place" (quoted in Owens, p. 15). Another painting, *Scenery on the Housatonic*, was also shown in Philadelphia in 1876 and at the Paris Salon the following year. Whether Johnson went to France then is unknown; in fact, it is unclear whether he ever traveled to Europe. No contemporary evidence indicates that he did so and no European landscapes by him are known, but he did own a number of paintings by European artists. According to a friend of his wife, these had been "purchased abroad."

Johnson's output appears to have decreased after 1880, although with no decline in quality. *On the Unadilla, New York* (1884), *Bayside, New Rochelle, New York* (1886) (both Metropolitan Museum of Art, New York), and *Passing Shower* (circa 1885, Amherst College, Amherst, Mass.) are as accomplished as any of his earlier works.

Although he mainly painted landscapes, Johnson also produced a few portraits throughout his career. These are well executed but, curiously, not painted from life. His earliest-known portrait, a likeness of his fellow artist William Sidney Mount (1850, Pennsylvania Academy of the Fine Arts, Philadelphia), is an excellent copy of an earlier portrait by Charles Loring Elliott. In 1861 he painted a portrait of General Winfield Scott (Pennsylvania Academy of the Fine Arts, Philadelphia), copied from a photograph by Mathew Brady. Despite its derivative origin, it is a strong depiction of the gruff old soldier. In 1871 he painted the actor Edwin Forrest (National Gallery of Art, Washington, D.C.). Despite the fact that the two men evidently were friends, Johnson appears to have based the likeness on a photograph by Napoleon Sarony. Johnson painted at least two self-portraits, one in 1860 and the other in 1894 (National Academy of Design, New York). He was elected an associate of the National Academy of Design in 1860 and became a full academician the following year.

Johnson also painted a few still lifes but apparently did not exhibit them. Perhaps the finest is *Phlox* (1886, Reynolda House Museum of American Art), produced late in his career. He also made many landscape drawings throughout his life; all seem to have been created as studies for his paintings rather than as independent works of art.

In February 1890 Johnson held a two-day auction in New York of a number of his paintings. He gave up his studio in New York but continued to live in the city until 1904, when he and his wife moved to Walden, New York, where he died.

Johnson earned a comfortable living as an artist but never received much attention from the critics. Yet his work is of uniformly high quality. The evidence of his paintings and the testimony of his artistic colleagues reveal him as one who took art seriously and was determined to depict the American landscape as skillfully as possible. As his fellow artist Benjamin Champney observed, "He has shown . . . what such conscientious study may lead to as he has quietly and modestly attained to a very high rank as one of the leading landscapists of New York" (quoted in Baur, p. 39).

• In addition to Johnson's two self-portraits, there is a portrait of him by his older brother, Joseph Hoffman Johnson, in the collection of the National Academy of Design, New York City. The best accounts of Johnson's life and career are Gwendolyn Owens, *Nature Transcribed: The Landscapes and Still Lifes of David Johnson (1827–1908)* (1988), a catalog of a traveling exhibition organized by the Herbert F. Johnson Museum of Art, Cornell University, Ithaca, N.Y.; John I. H. Baur, "'. . . the exact brushwork of Mr. David Johnson,' An American Landscape Painter, 1827–1908," *American Art Journal* 12, no. 4 (Autumn 1980): 32–65; and Johnson's entry in *Lamb's Biographical Dictionary of the United States* (1904).

DAVID MESCHUTT

JOHNSON, Douglas Wilson (30 Nov. 1878–24 Feb. 1944), geomorphologist, was born in Parkersburg, West Virginia, the son of Isaac Hollenback Johnson, a lawyer and editor of a prohibition newspaper, and Jane Amanda Wilson, chairwoman of the West Virginia Woman's Christian Temperance Union. Douglas's father died when he was twelve years old, and for the next six years he helped his mother, who was dying from tuberculosis, and an older brother in the family's job-printing office while completing his secondary education. He showed no interest in a scientific career as a youth; instead, because of the influence of his parents and his own success in declamation and oratorical contests, he seemed destined for a career in politics. In 1897 Johnson matriculated at Denison University, but he transferred two years later to the University of New Mexico, where he hoped the climate might help him avoid lung disease. He supported himself by working as a field assistant with the University Geological Survey under the guidance of Charles Luther Herrick, president of the university and a former professor at Denison. As a result of this experience, he determined on a career in science and received his B.S. in 1901. After graduation he taught high school in Albuquerque, New Mexico, for a year before entering Columbia University, where he received his Ph.D. in geology in 1903.

That same year Johnson married Alice Adkins; none of their five children survived infancy. He also obtained a position as an instructor in geology at the Massachusetts Institute of Technology (MIT) and began studying at Harvard University, where he came under the influence of William Morris Davis, the "father of physical geography," who regarded the development of topographical features in much the same way that an embryologist regards the development of a living organism. Johnson was promoted to assistant professor in 1905 but left MIT two years later to become an assistant professor of geology at Harvard and to edit Davis's *Geographical Essays* (1909). In 1911 he became interested in shoreline subsidence and organized and supervised the Shaler Memorial Expedition, a detailed investigation of changes to the North American Atlantic shoreline. In addition to studying the coast from Prince Edward Island to the Florida Keys, the expedition examined for comparative purposes parts of the shorelines of England, Germany, Holland, Scotland, and Sweden. Johnson published the results of this study in *Shore Processes and Shoreline Development* (1919), a discussion of the fundamental principles that govern the evolution and classification of shoreline.

In 1912 Johnson accepted an appointment as associate professor of physiography at Columbia. Shortly thereafter he became concerned with what he called "the perils of Prussianism," and in 1916 he was elected chairman of the executive committee of the American Rights League, an organization that favored the active participation of the United States in World War I on the side of the Allies. In 1917 he published *Topography and Strategy in the War*, his first attempt to understand how landforms affected twentieth-century warfare, and the next year he joined the U.S. Army as a major in the Intelligence Division. After the armistice he served as chief of the division of boundary geography of the American Commission to Negotiate Peace. In 1919 he was discharged from the army and returned to Columbia as a full professor. He was also appointed a geological adviser to the U.S. State Department and served as a special adviser to President Woodrow Wilson on territorial problems in southeastern Europe, particularly Yugoslavia. These experiences led him to write *Battlefields of the World War* (1921), an investigation of how topography influenced military planning and affected operations in Belgium, France, Italy, and the Balkans.

Johnson's most important contribution to geomorphological theory was *Stream Sculpture on the Atlantic Slope* (1931). In this work, considered a masterpiece of denudation chronology, he developed the most convincing explanation at that time of the theoretical history of the geomorphology of Appalachia. He rejected the existing views that Appalachia was of uniform age and that it had once been drained by rivers running toward the west; instead, he postulated that the coastal plain came into existence much later than the summit peneplain to the west and that as the seas receded from the coastal plain, the eastward-flowing riverbeds were cut into the underlying formations. Of less importance, but a significant contribution nonetheless, was his theory that pediments—flat bedrock surfaces normally found in arid basin-and-range regions—evolved from rock fans, fan-shaped bedrock surfaces at the foot of a mountain that usually underlie a stream flowing onto a piedmont slope.

Johnson was appointed executive officer of the Columbia Department of Geology in 1937 and Newberry Professor of Geology in 1943. His first wife had died five years earlier, and in 1943 he married Edith Sanford Caldwell, with whom he had no children.

Johnson served as president of the Association of American Geographers (1928) and of the Geological Society of America (1942). He was also president of the Paris International Geographical Congress's Section on Physiography and Geography (1931) and of the International Geographical Union's Terrace Commission (1934–1938). He received the Boston Society of Natural History's Walker Memorial Prize (1906), the Paris Geographical Society's Janssen Medal

(1920), the Geographical Society of Philadelphia's Elisha Kent Kane Gold Medal (1922), the University of Nancy (France) Medal (1924), the New York Academy of Science's A. Cressy Morrison Prize (1924 and 1930), the Society of Commercial Geography of Paris's Gaudy Medal (1925), and the Geographical Society of Belgrade's Cvijic Medal and the American Geographical Society's Cullum Medal (both 1935). He was decorated a chevalier in the French Legion of Honor, elected to the National Academy of Sciences, and awarded Yugoslavia's Order of St. Sava. He died while vacationing in Sebring, Florida.

Johnson was a pioneer in the field of geomorphology. Although he continued to expostulate many of Davis's methods after they had outlived their usefulness, Johnson's work led to an increased appreciation and understanding of the many factors concerning the development of specific geographical features and, to a certain extent, their effect on human behavior.

• A biography, with a bibliography, is Walter H. Bucher, "Douglas Wilson Johnson," National Academy of Sciences, *Biographical Memoirs* 24 (1947): 197–230. An obituary is in the *New York Times*, 12 Mar. 1944.

CHARLES W. CAREY, JR.

JOHNSON, Eastman (29 July 1824–5 Apr. 1906), genre and portrait painter, was born Jonathan Eastman Johnson in Lovell, Maine, the son of Philip C. Johnson, a government official, and Mary Chandler. Information about Johnson's youth and early education is sketchy. In 1827–1828 the family (Johnson was the third of eight siblings) moved to Fryeburg, Maine, and in 1834–1835 to Augusta, Maine, where Philip Johnson held various posts in the state government. According to a family-owned manuscript autobiography by Johnson's younger brother, Philip C. Johnson, Jr., Eastman lived for a time in Concord, New Hampshire, and then worked in a brother-in-law's dry goods store in Augusta, "where he manifested a natural taste for drawing and painting." Art historian John I. H. Baur found evidence that Johnson's father placed the budding artist in a lithographer's shop in Boston but that Johnson soon returned to Augusta, where he began to draw portraits in crayon of his family and neighbors.

In 1844 or 1845 Johnson moved to Washington, D.C., and began to draw crayon portraits, a career boosted when his family moved to the nation's capital following his father's appointment to a high-level post in the Navy Department. Johnson drew skilled portraits of, among others, John Quincy Adams (National Portrait Gallery, Washington, D.C.), and Dolley Madison (Fogg Art Museum, Harvard University). In 1846 Henry Wadsworth Longfellow invited Johnson to Cambridge, Massachusetts, to draw portraits of his family and friends. For the next three years Johnson maintained studios in Amory Hall and Tremont Temple while he drew such notables as Longfellow, Ralph Waldo Emerson, Nathaniel Hawthorne, and Charles

Sumner (all at the Longfellow National Historic Site, Cambridge, Mass.).

Ambitious to make his mark as a painter, Johnson knew he needed European training. Encouraged by the New York–based American Art-Union, the most influential patron of the arts during the 1840s, in 1849 he moved to Düsseldorf, then a popular art center for Americans. While there he took classes at the Royal Academy, and in January 1851 he entered the Düsseldorf studio of the celebrated German-born American history painter Emanuel Leutze. After a brief trip to Holland and London in the summer of 1851, Johnson relocated to The Hague in order to study Rembrandt and the Dutch masters firsthand. August Belmont, American minister to the Netherlands, helped Johnson secure portrait commissions, and Johnson remained there until August 1855, when he moved to Paris to study with Thomas Couture, another teacher popular with the Americans.

Johnson had to cut short his Paris stay and return to Washington, D.C., in October 1855, following news of his mother's death. For the next four years he searched out what would be considered typically "American" subjects—slave life in Virginia and the Ojibwa in Superior, Wisconsin, near where a sister was homesteading. Although he regularly sent his paintings to the National Academy of Design, in this period he supported himself by painting portraits, taking a studio in Cincinnati during the late winter and early spring of 1857–1858. He settled permanently in New York City in 1858.

Fame came in 1859 when Johnson exhibited *Negro Life at the South* (New-York Historical Society) at the National Academy of Design. For the setting, Johnson drew on his observations of slave quarters in the Georgetown section of Washington, D.C. Groups of slaves animate the composition by dancing, courting, and playing the banjo at the rear of the run-down building, while at the edge a white mistress steps through a fence to view the revelry in her back yard. A reviewer of that year's annual exhibition of the National Academy of Design, writing in the June 1859 issue of *The Crayon*, offered characteristic praise: "One of the best pictures in respect to Art and the most popular, because presenting familiar aspects of life, is E. Johnson's 'Negro Life at the South.' . . . Although a very humble subject, this picture is a very instructive one in relation to Art. It is conscientiously studied and painted, and full of ideas. Notwithstanding the general ugliness of the forms and objects, we recognize that its sentiment is one of beauty, for imitation and expression are vitalized by conveying to our mind the enjoyment of human beings in new and vivid aspects" (p. 191).

Because of its ambivalent message, *Negro Life at the South* seems to have pleased all viewers. To southerners, the depiction of happy, well-fed slaves served as an apologia for slavery; to abolitionists, the crumbling architecture had significance. One such critic was quoted in Henry Theodore Tuckerman's *Book of the Artists* (1867): "How fitly do the dilapidated and decaying negro quarters typify the approaching destruction of the 'system' that they serve to illustrate! And, in the picture before us, we have an illustration also of the 'rose-water' side of the institution. Here all is fun and freedom. We behold the very reality that the enthusiastic devotees of slavery have so often painted with high-sounding words. And yet this dilapidation, unheeded and unchecked, tells us that the end is near" (p. 468).

Elected as an associate of the prestigious National Academy of Design in 1859 and as a full academician the following year, Johnson continued to paint African Americans with a dignity that makes evident his Republican sympathies. During the Civil War years, however, he also painted genre scenes of the homefront that had popular appeal, such as *News from the Front* (1861, unlocated), *Knitting for the Soldiers* (1861, unlocated), *Woman Sewing—Work for the Fair* (1862, unlocated), and *Writing to Father* (1863, Museum of Fine Arts, Boston). Like other artists he traveled with the Union troops on military campaigns in search of fitting genre subjects, which he later completed as finished paintings: *The Wounded Drummer Boy* (1871, Union League Club, New York) and *The Field Hospital* (1867, Museum of Fine Arts, Boston). *The Ride for Liberty—The Fugitive Slaves* (1863, versions at the Virginia Museum of Fine Arts and the Brooklyn Museum) depicts an event he witnessed on 23 March 1862 as he accompanied General George B. McClellan's troops advancing toward Manassas. The picture depicts a slave family of four as agents of their own freedom—not just passive recipients of white benevolence; they sit astride a single horse, galloping toward the Union lines in the early dawn hours. In 1866, when sympathy for freed slaves ran high among northern artists, Johnson painted *Fiddling His Way* (Chrysler Museum, Norfolk, Va.), a representation of a recently freed slave earning his livelihood entertaining a white rustic family who listen respectfully to the handsome young African American. By the end of the 1860s Johnson was indisputedly the most praised genre painter in America. Russell Sturges, Jr., one of the new breed of professional art critics, in reviewing the 1867 annual exhibition of the National Academy of Design for the June issue of *The Galaxy*, praised Johnson's entry, *The Pension Claim Agent* (Fine Arts Museums of San Francisco) and then added: "A collection of Mr. Johnson's pictures would probably be more interesting to visit than one of any other American painter. His work, taken together, is more truly representative of his countrymen. . . . There is no painter, not even among the younger men who are just coming into sight from behind the horizon, who get on faster, or who leave the past of a year or two back more decidedly and forever behind" (p. 230).

New England continued to be a source of subjects for Johnson's brush. Even during the war years he returned to Maine in the early spring months and painted studies of farm families gathering sap from sugar maples, bringing buckets to forest camps, where huge kettles boiled down the sap into syrup, and dancing and conversing at the camp sites. He and his wife, Elizabeth Buckley of Troy, New York, whom he married in 1869 and with whom he would have one child, began to summer on Nantucket in 1870. The island provided a range of new subjects. He bought property there in 1871 and for the rest of his painting career spent long summer months on the island, where he painted *The Old Stage Coach* (1871, Milwaukee Art Center), *Hollyhocks* (1876, New Britain Museum of American Art, Conn.), *Cornhusking Bee* (1876, Art Institute of Chicago), and many studies of the cranberry harvest, culminating in his major picture *The Cranberry Harvest, Island of Nantucket* (1880, Timkin Gallery, San Diego). He also painted many pictures of the retired sea captains who reminisced around pot-bellied stoves, such as *The Nantucket School of Philosophy* (1887, Walters Art Gallery, Baltimore). Visits during 1877 and 1878 to his sister's family in Kennebunkport, Maine, resulted in a series of barn interiors featuring energetic children climbing on the beams. Not surprisingly, by 1880 critics began to identify him as a genre painter of a rural American way of life that was quickly disappearing as the nation became more urban, industrial, and cosmopolitan.

By the early 1880s, however, Johnson was turning away from genre painting and devoting himself to commissioned portraits. Throughout his career he painted friends, family, and, increasingly, wealthy art patrons who were fellow club members at the Union League Club and the Century Club. Along with many of these wealthy business and social leaders Johnson founded the Metropolitan Museum of Art in 1870. In the late 1860s and early 1870s he painted small "conversation pieces," such as *The Brown Family* (1869, versions at the National Gallery of Art, Washington D.C., and the Fine Arts Museums of San Francisco) and *The Hatch Family* (1871, Metropolitan Museum of Art, New York); however, he usually painted lifesized portraits. He was particularly skilled and successful at painting men, and his works constitute a pantheon of the great public figures of the time: Bishop Henry C. Potter, Frederick A. P. Barnard, William Evarts, George M. Pullman, William H. Vanderbilt, John D. Rockefeller, Jay Gould, and Presidents Grover Cleveland and Benjamin Harrison.

Even with the shift in taste from genre painting to realism and then impressionism, Johnson continued to be admired, both by the older academicians who served with him on committees at the National Academy of Design and by the younger artists who invited him to show his work at the annual exhibitions of the Society of American Artists, a group organized in 1878 to showcase the recent styles from Europe. The modernist critic Sadakichi Hartmann assessed Johnson's career two years after his death in New York City: "Although he typifies best the period of the sixties and seventies, the years previous to the general exodus of young American painters to Munich and Paris, he managed to hold his own even at a time when [William Merritt] Chase, [Julian Alden] Weir, [Walter] Shirlaw, [and Thomas] Eakins, became the brilliant exponents of a new, more technically perfect style of painting" (p. 108).

Johnson's achievement was to bring more sophisticated techniques to the United States, to extend the range of "American" subject matter, and to insist on a more dignified and democratic content to genre painting. He spoke to and for his own generation, and he greatly influenced a number of genre painters as they made their transition from genre painting to art-for-art's sake modernism. He could produce anecdotal and sentimental pictures while simultaneously experimenting with a lighter palette, looser brushwork, and summary treatment of forms. Seen in the broader context of American art, Johnson's work forges the strongest link between the genre painting of the pre–Civil War years and the realism of the late nineteenth century.

• Original letters are held by the Archives of American Art in Washington, D.C. Self-portraits are at the National Portrait Gallery, the Hirshhorn Museum and Sculpture Garden, the Museum of Fine Arts, Boston, and the National Academy of Design, to name a few. Like almost all of his contemporaries, Johnson had no major biography written during his lifetime, but he was included in all the major contemporary surveys of American art. His death, however, coincided with an efflorescence of art writing, and hence several long essays appeared on him in and after 1906: William Walton, "Eastman Johnson, Painter," *Scribner's Magazine*, Sept. 1906, pp. 263–74; Edgar P. French, "An American Portrait Painter of Three Historical Epochs," *World's Work*, Dec. 1906, pp. 8307–23; Mark Selby, "An American Painter: Eastman Johnson," *Putnam's Monthly*, Aug. 1907, pp. 533–42; and Sadakichi Hartmann, "Eastman Johnson: American Genre Painter," *International Studio* 34 (Apr. 1908): 106–11. The estate sale of Johnson's work held at Anderson Art Galleries in 1907 provided descriptions of the 150 pictures sold. In 1940 John I. H. Baur curated a major show of Johnson's work for the Brooklyn Museum; the accompanying catalog includes his assessment of Johnson's life and art and a checklist of almost 300 oil paintings and 180 drawings. For the Whitney Museum of American Art in 1972, Patricia Hills organized another major exhibition with a catalog; she also wrote "The Genre Painting of Eastman Johnson: The Sources and Development of His Style and Themes" (Ph.D. diss., New York Univ., 1973). The catalog of a focused exhibition for the Timken Art Gallery, San Diego, Calif., is Marc Simpson et al., *Eastman Johnson: The Cranberry Harvest, Island of Nantucket* (1990). Tributes by fellow artists Will H. Low, Carroll Beckwith, Samuel Isham, and Frank Fowler were published in *Scribner's Magazine*, Aug. 1906, pp. 253–56.

PATRICIA HILLS

JOHNSON, Edward (Sept. 1599–23 Apr. 1672), historian, was born in the county of Kent, near Canterbury, the son of William Johnson, the clerk of St. George's Parish, Canterbury, and Susan Porredge. Little else is known of his life in England, except that in 1618 he married Susan Munnter, with whom he had seven children. In 1630 he emigrated to New England with John Winthrop (1588–1649) aboard the Massachusetts Bay Colony's *Arbella*, where he heard Winthrop deliver "A Modell of Christian Charity," the sermon that inspired the early settlers to conceive of their journey as an "errand into the wilderness" to establish a "city upon a hill," or the New Jerusalem.

After journeying back to England to bring his family to the New World, Johnson became a leader of the Massachusetts Bay Colony, living first in Charlestown and then helping to found the town of Woburn. For most of his active life, he kept busy with governmental and practical affairs, apparently valuing politics more than the work of a historian, which he pursued only part time. He was a deputy to the General Court and sometime captain of the Charlestown militia. As a printer, he was responsible for making up the 1648 document known as the Cambridge Platform, a system of laws for the young colony. He also dabbled in surveying and mapmaking.

It was as a Puritan historian, however, that Johnson made a place for himself in the record of the Bay Colony. Like the histories by John Winthrop and Plymouth governor William Bradford (1590–1657), Johnson's narrative bears the mark of his involvement in governmental and practical affairs. His *A History of New England from the English Planting in the Yeere 1628, until the Yeere 1652* (1653) joined with Winthrop's *Journal* and Bradford's *History of Plimmouth Plantation* in establishing a methodology for the composition of historical narratives of the early colony. These works share a common mythology of early Massachusetts Bay, which assumes that the settlers recapitulated the experience of the ancient Israelites, leaving Egypt/England for a divinely ordained migration across the Atlantic wilderness to settle in the promised land of the New World and to build the New Jerusalem in America.

Johnson, like the other historians, sought to prove that the New England experience was a divine drama, produced, directed, and prompted by God, and that the settlers were actors in a scripted plot with a purposeful teleology. Just as Puritan biography tended toward hagiography in creating many collections of "saints' lives," Johnson's narrative treats the chronological experience of settlement as a providential moment in history, one that advanced the history of what Jonathan Edwards (1703–1758) would later call the work of redemption. Unlike Winthrop and Bradford, however, who told their story by way of the lives of eminent men, Johnson treated the narrative of the entire group, and his book's subtitle, *Wonder-Working Providence of Sion's Saviour in New England*, reflects this emphasis on the experience of the Puritan tribe. Although the work is written in prose, often turgid and dense, there are verses throughout used as epigraphs or division headings. Johnson's reputation as a literary figure rests entirely on this single document.

Together with Winthrop's and Bradford's narratives, Johnson's *History* greatly influenced the mightiest of the seventeenth-century Puritan histories, Cotton Mather's *Magnalia Christi Americana* (1702), which draws upon the methodologies and tropes set forth in the earlier works. Johnson's chronicle both typifies the Puritan historiographical method and reflects the sense of divine mission shared by these early colonists in their effort to define the errand into the wilderness.

Johnson died in Woburn.

• The authoritative primary text of Johnson's history is *Wonder-Working Providence of Sion's Savior in New England*, ed. William Poole (1867). The most important interpretative essay on Johnson's *History* by a modern scholar is Sacvan Bercovitch, "The Historiography of Johnson's Wonder-Working Providence," *Essex Institute Historical Collections* 104 (1968): 139–61. See also Ursula Brumm, "Edward Johnson's *Wonder-Working Providence* and the Puritan Conception of History," *Jahrbuch für Amerikastudien* 14 (1969): 140–51, and Edward Gallagher, "Johnson's *Wonder-Working Providence*," *Early American Literature* 5 (1971): 40–59. A seminal essay by one of the early teachers of Johnson's history, whose seminars at Harvard helped to establish the validity of Puritan literature, is Kenneth Murdock, "Clio in the Wilderness," *Church History* 24 (1955): 221–38. Perry Miller, *The New England Mind: The Seventeenth Century* (1954), contextualizes the author and his work. Mason I. Lowance, Jr., *The Language of Canaan: Metaphor and Symbol in New England from the Puritans to the Transcendentalists* (1980), a study of symbol and metaphor in the construction of myth in Puritan New England, treats Johnson's history in relation to Cotton Mather's *Magnalia Christi Americana*.

MASON I. LOWANCE, JR.

JOHNSON, Edward (16 Apr. 1816–2 Mar. 1873), Confederate general, was born in Chesterfield County, Virginia, the son of Edward Johnson, a medical doctor, and Caroline Turpin. Johnson graduated from West Point in 1838 in the lower third of his class and embarked on a varied and successful career in the U.S. Army. Participating extensively and with distinction in the Mexican War, he later fought against the Seminoles in Florida. During his more than two decades in the army before the Civil War, Johnson also saw duty in Kansas, New York, California, and the Dakota Territory. In 1861 he resigned from the army with brevet rank of major. In July of the same year Johnson assumed command of the Twelfth Georgia Infantry and turned that unit into one of the best regiments in Confederate service. That fall, as colonel of the Twelfth, he marched west from the Shenandoah Valley, taking up a position on a ridge of the Alleghany (Allegheny) Mountains. There on 13 December Johnson won a tough fight that made his reputation, earning him the wreath and three stars of a brigadier general and the fond nickname "Old Alleghany" Johnson.

The new general swore often and with real creative skill. He encouraged his men in battle with a combination of oaths and such inducements as "a stout cane," a club, or even a fence rail, with which he belabored both skulking Confederates and enemy soldiers who were slow to flee. After suffering a severe ankle wound at the battle of McDowell in May 1862, Johnson needed a cane for the rest of his life. Traces of Johnson's personality have survived in the diaries of Mary Boykin Chesnut, who knew him during his recuperation after McDowell. She described him vividly as "a different part of speech"; "red as a turkey cock in the face"; having a head shaped "like a cone, an old fashioned beehive"; and so hopelessly maladroit in his attempts at courting that he "roared with anguish and disappointment over his failures." Johnson never married, and Mrs. Chesnut was fond of the lovelorn general, as were most of his men, to whom his eccentricities supplied entertaining diversion.

When Johnson returned to duty in the spring of 1863, now with the rank of major general, he took command of the division that had once been Stonewall Jackson's. Leading his new command to a major success at the second battle of Winchester, he then commanded it in the bitter fighting on Culp's Hill at Gettysburg. In November Johnson personally headed an infantry charge at Mine Run and had his horse shot from under him in the process. "Alleghany" Johnson's career with Lee's army ended at Spotsylvania Court House on 12 May 1864, when a massive Federal assault captured much of his division and the general himself. One of Johnson's captors observed what must have been the most noticeable of the general's peculiar traits, an unconscious tic that a friend called "a state of incessant winking as soon as he was . . . agitated." When Johnson returned to the Confederacy as an exchanged prisoner of war, he was assigned to the Army of Tennessee, where he held division command in the corps led by Stephen Dill Lee. Johnson fell into Federal hands again at Nashville in December and was not paroled until July 1865. He took up farming in Chesterfield County, Virginia, and died in Richmond.

• Johnson's letters are in the Kentucky Historical Society. No sizable biographical sketch of the general exists. For a basic outline of his life and career see Clement A. Evans, ed., *Confederate Military History*, vol. 3 (1899). See also Johnson's Compiled Service Record in National Archives Microcopy M331, Roll 141; *Register of the Officers and Cadets of the U.S. Military Academy* (1838); and C. Vann Woodward, ed., *Mary Chesnut's Civil War* (1981).

ROBERT K. KRICK

JOHNSON, Edward (22 Aug. 1878–20 Apr. 1959), tenor and opera impresario, was born in Guelph, Ontario, Canada, the son of James Evans Johnson, a grain merchant, and Margaret O'Connel. His parents encouraged his musical development and he was singing solos in church by age seven. Ten years later he had become the leading oratorio and concert tenor in Ontario.

Broadening his horizons, in 1899 Johnson went to study music in New York City, where his early musical influences included the vocal teacher Madame Feilitsch and Henry Wolfson, head of New York's leading concert bureau. By 1902 he played the male lead in Reginald De Koven's *Maid Marian* in Boston and in 1908 he had a starring role in the operetta *A Waltz Dream* by Oscar Strauss, which opened in New York. Johnson's weekly salary of $700 made him the highest paid tenor on Broadway at that time.

About that time Enrico Caruso heard Johnson sing and recommended that he study with the great tenor's own teacher, Vincenzo Lombardi. Johnson left for Italy in the summer of 1908 for study with Lombardi and by 1912 began his career as an operatic tenor in Italy under the name of Edoardo di Giovanni, debuting in *Andrea Chenier* at Padua. He sang many leading roles in Italy during the next few years, including the title role in *Parsifal* in Italian for his La Scala debut in 1914.

While in Europe Johson wed the Countess Beatrice d'Anerio in Paris in 1909. The Countess died in 1919, leaving Johnson with a daughter.

In that same year Johnson returned to the United States with his daughter and became (under his own name) the leading tenor for the Chicago Grand Opera, making his debut in Giordano's *Fedora*. A few years later he and his daughter moved to New York City, where Johnson made his debut with the Metropolitan Opera in 1922 as Avito in *L'ammore dei tre re* by Montemezzi.

During his singing years with the Metropolitan, Johnson created the title role in Deems Taylor's *Peter Ibbetson* and became a great favorite in the roles of Romeo and Pelleas. His good looks, excellent voice, wide range, and ability to project a character assured him a highly successful career. Johnson sang twenty-three roles in 208 performances with the Metropolitan over a span of thirteen years. During his first season there, he sang ten different operas in less than three months.

In 1935, while still in his prime as a singer, circumstances led Johnson into another career connected with the Metropolitan Opera. The current general manager of the company, Giulio Gatti-Casazza, had retired and his successor, Herbert Witherspoon, a friend of Johnson's, died suddenly before assuming the position. In the face of this crisis, the Metropolitan's board of directors prevailed upon Johnson to accept the post.

Johnson's tenure as general manager of the Metropolitan Opera opened in the middle of the Great Depression, with the organization fighting to survive financially. Facing this challenge, Johnson steered a course that kept the Metropolitan's high musical standards and developed new financial resources for its fiscal salvation. During his years as the Metropolitan's general manager, he initiated nationwide broadcasts of operas, founded the Metropolitan Opera Auditions of the Air, raised funds for the Metropolitan Opera Association to buy the Metropolitan Opera House from its stockholders, took part in the inception of the Metropolitan Opera Guild, and perhaps most important, hired American singers for his productions.

Those American singers whose careers Johnson assisted and who sang at the Metropolitan while he was general manager included Risë Stevens, Dorothy Kirsten, Jerome Hines, and Richard Tucker. Among the European singers whose careers flourished during Johnson's management of the Metropolitan were the Wagnerian artists Kirsten Flagstad and Lauritz Melchoir. The conductors Johnson hired included Sir Thomas Beecham, Bruno Walter, George Szell, and Fritz Reiner. Johnson produced seventy-two operas during his managerial tenure, reviving Verdi's *Falstaff*

and *Otello* and greatly increasing the popularity of Mozart's *The Marriage of Figaro* and *Don Giovanni*.

Johnson's retirement as general manager of the Metropolitan Opera in 1950 was marked by a gala benefit at the Opera House. Following this festive occasion, Johnson returned to Canada and his hometown of Guelph. Johnson donated $25,000 of his own money (pledged at $5,000 a year) to promote a music program in the Guelph schools. Other ties also bound Johnson to Canada. His daughter had married George Drew, who became the premier of Ontario in 1943, and in 1945 Johnson was appointed chairman of the Board of Governors of the Royal Conservatory of Music in Toronto. Johnson's remaining years in Guelph, where he died, were punctuated by trips to Toronto and New York City to keep up with his duties at the conservatory and to maintain old ties with the Metropolitan.

Johnson was highly successful both as a singer and as general manager of the Metropolitan Opera. His good humor and lack of pretentions endeared him to his singers there, and he brought the organization through the perilous times of the Great Depression and World War II in a prosperous and renewed fashion.

• The New York Public Library for the Performing Arts, Lincoln Center, houses some archival material concerning Johnson. A comprehensive source for information about him is the biography by Ruby Mercer, *The Tenor of His Time* (1976), which also contains a discography of his work. *Musical America* followed his career avidly with articles and notes. Other information concerning Johnson is in various journal articles. R. A. Simon, "Profile: General Director," the *New Yorker*, 14 Dec. 1935, p. 30, describes Johnson's singing career and his status at taking on the Metropolitan's directorship. Additional material about Johnson's recordings is in H. P. Court, "Edward Johnson Discography," *Record News* 2 (1957–1958): 19. A Canadian perspective on Johnson is in J. Baur, "Edward Johnson: General Manager of the Metropolitan Opera Company," *Canadian Review of Music and Art* 3, nos. 7–8 (1944): 14; and E. Benson, "Edward Johnson," *Opera Canada* 9, no. 2 (1968): 18. An obituary is in the *New York Times*, 21 Apr. 1959.

JOHN W. WAGNER

JOHNSON, Edward Austin (23 Nov. 1860–24 July 1944), educator, lawyer, and politician, was born near Raleigh, North Carolina, the son of Columbus Johnson and Eliza A. Smith, slaves. He was taught to read and write by Nancy Walton, a free African American, and later attended the Washington School, an establishment founded by philanthropic northerners in Raleigh. There he was introduced to the Congregational church and became a lifelong member. Johnson completed his education at Atlanta University in Georgia, graduating in 1883. To pay his way through college, he worked as a barber and taught in the summers. After graduation he worked as a teacher and principal, first in Atlanta at the Mitchell Street Public School (1883–1885) and then in Raleigh at the Washington School (1885–1891). While teaching in Raleigh he studied at Shaw University, obtaining a law degree in 1891. He joined the faculty shortly after graduation and became dean of the law school at Shaw two years later. He acquired a reputation as a highly capable lawyer, successfully arguing many cases before the North Carolina Supreme Court.

Johnson was concerned that African-American history was not being taught in schools, so he wrote *A School History of the Negro Race in America from 1619 to 1890* (1891). This account, which sought to inform African-American schoolchildren of the "many brave deeds and noble characters of their own race," was the first textbook by an African-American author approved by the North Carolina State Board of Education for use in public schools. In 1894 Johnson married Lena Allen Kennedy; they had one child.

While dean at Shaw, Johnson became involved in Raleigh city politics. He chaired the Republican party in the Fourth Congressional District and was a delegate at the 1892, 1896, and 1900 Republican National conventions. He served on the Raleigh Board of Aldermen for two years, and he was the assistant to the U.S. attorney for the Eastern District of North Carolina from 1899 to 1907. He helped found the National Negro Business League in 1900 and helped organize the National Bar Association in 1903. He experimented with several business ventures and was vice president and later president of the Coleman Manufacturing Company, a cotton mill jointly owned by African-American investors. With six others he founded the North Carolina Mutual and Provident Association, which became the largest African-American owned insurance company in the world. By 1902 Johnson was one of only two African-American citizens of Raleigh with an income large enough to necessitate paying the state income tax. His novel *Light Ahead for the Negro* (1904), set in the year 2006, portrays an ideal society, free from racial discrimination.

Racial prejudice and a continuing lack of opportunities for African Americans in the South prompted Johnson to leave North Carolina in 1907 and settle in New York City, where he set up a law practice. He continued his political and civic involvement on the Republican committee for the Nineteenth Assembly District and as a member of the Harlem Board of Trade and Commerce and the Upper Harlem Taxpayers Association. In 1917 Johnson became the first African American to win a seat in the New York legislature. While in office he advocated bills to create free state employment bureaus and prevent racial discrimination in public hospitals. He also voted for an amendment to the Levy Civil Rights Act that outlawed racial or ethnic discrimination in public employment or public facilities. Largely because of a reorganization of political districts, Johnson was not reelected for a second term, so he returned to his law practice. In 1925 he became legally blind, although he retained some sight for at least ten years. He ran again in 1928 as the Republican candidate for the U.S. House of Representatives in the predominantly white and Democratic Twenty-first District. His candidacy, he later acknowledged, was not a serious bid to win office but a tool to encourage African Americans to register and vote. Johnson's final book, *Adam vs. Ape-Man in Ethiopia* (1931), contends that the first civilization emerged in Ethiopia at a time when Europe "had yet to emerge from the reindeer age and the apeman type." He also maintained that Egyptian culture, created by black Africans, had been corrupted and finally destroyed by the invasion of white "injustice and greed." Johnson died in New York City.

Johnson was one of the first African Americans to rise to social and political importance despite the climate of continuing racism and racial disfranchisement following the Civil War. He was a successful businessman, a Raleigh politician, an author of an early African-American history text, and mostly notably, the first African-American legislator in the New York House. Owing to the range of his achievements, Johnson provided an early model of African-American success.

• Johnson wrote two autobiographical articles, "A Student at Atlanta University," *Phylon* 3 (Second Quarter 1942), and "A Congressional Campaign," *Crisis* 40 (Apr. 1929), and the book *History of Negro Soldiers in the Spanish-American War* (1899). See also John A. Morsell, "The Political Behavior of Negroes in New York City" (Ph.D. diss., Columbia Univ., 1950). An excellent article on Johnson by Edwin R. Lawson is in the *Dictionary of North Carolina Biography* (1988). An obituary is in the *New York Times*, 25 July 1944.

ELIZABETH ZOE VICARY

JOHNSON, Eldridge Reeves (6 Feb. 1867–14 Nov. 1945), inventor and business leader, was born in Wilmington, Delaware, the son of Asa S. Johnson, a carpenter, and Caroline Reeves. Johnson spent the first three years of his life in Dover, Delaware. After the death of his mother in 1870, his father sent him to live on a relative's farm in Collins Landing, Delaware. He returned to Dover at the age of ten, when his father married Frances Smith.

Although Johnson hoped to attend college, his teachers at the Dover Academy recommended that he learn a skilled trade. As a result, his stepmother arranged an apprenticeship in the Philadelphia machine shop of William F. Lodge in 1883. Johnson took mechanical-drawing courses after work at the Spring Garden Institute to supplement his technical training. Within five years he became shop foreman, supervising a crew of fifteen machinists. Because of a wage dispute, Johnson left the Lodge shop in 1888 to become a supervisor in the Camden, New Jersey, machine shop of Andrew Scull. Scull hired Johnson to finish a bookbinding machine left uncompleted by his son, a mechanical engineer who had died suddenly.

In 1890 Johnson resigned from the Scull shop to take what he called "a general scouting expedition through the west" (Johnson papers, Johnson Victrola Museum). He worked in Washington state for about a year but returned to Philadelphia in 1891, dissatisfied with conditions in the West. Upon his return, Scull, who had failed to market the bookbinding machine, asked Johnson to become his business partner. Johnson improved the machine, for which he received his first patent in 1893. He organized the New Jersey Wire Stitching Company to market the device. The Scull and Johnson shop, unfortunately, lost money on its contract to manufacture the new machines, forcing Johnson to buy out his partner in October 1894 and open a machine shop under his own name.

As a skilled machinist, Johnson often helped other inventors perfect their machines. It was through this work that he became involved in the emerging talking-machine business during the late 1890s. In March 1896 Johnson began designing a spring motor for the gramophone, a hand-cranked, disc talking machine invented by Emile Berliner in 1887. Three months later he introduced a spring motor that turned the gramophone record at a steady, uniform speed. Johnson's machine shop obtained a contract to produce the spring motors for the Berliner Gramophone Company and eventually began manufacturing complete gramophones. Within two years, Johnson was supplying Berliner with more than 600 machines a week. Johnson married a distant cousin, Elsie Reeves Fenimore, in 1897. They had one son.

During the summer of 1896 Johnson had turned his attention toward perfecting other components of the gramophone. As he later recalled, "I conceived at that time that if the gramophone were really brought up to the high standards to which it was capable of being developed, there would be a great demand for such goods" (statement to D. E. Wolff, 25 Oct. 1910, Johnson papers, Johnson Victrola Museum). Working with Alfred C. Clark, Johnson invented a new sound box, which improved the gramophone's articulation. He also began a series of experiments that resulted, in January 1898, in the development of an improved disc-recording process. The spring motor, sound box, and recording process were the first of many improvements Johnson made in sound-recording technology. By the time he retired in 1927, Johnson had received more than seventy U.S. talking-machine patents.

Johnson originally planned to allow the Berliner company to market the records produced by his new recording process, while his shop continued to manufacture the machines. A series of complicated patent suits, however, temporarily restrained Berliner from selling its products. At Emile Berliner's suggestion, Johnson began selling gramophones under his own name in 1900. In October 1901 Johnson organized the Victor Talking Machine Company, which obtained a controlling interest in Berliner's gramophone patents.

Under Johnson's leadership, gramophone record and machine sales increased dramatically. In 1901 Victor sold approximately 7,600 machines. By 1907 it had sold more than 98,000 machines. In 1916 the value of Victor's sales was more than three times that of Thomas Edison, his principal competitor. Johnson's success can be attributed to several technical and design changes in his machines, as well as a highly effective marketing strategy. In 1903 Johnson developed a new tone arm, which improved the acoustic quality of the gramophone. In 1906 he unveiled the Victrola, a disc machine with an enclosed speaker horn. Elimina-tion of the exposed horn, a prominent feature of earlier talking machines, enabled Johnson to encase the gramophone in attractive wood cabinets.

Johnson relied heavily on mass-circulation newspaper and magazine advertisements to promote his products. Many of these ads featured one of the most recognized trademarks of the period, Francis Barraud's painting *His Master's Voice*. Johnson also developed a close relationship with his dealers, giving them valuable support. In return, Victor expected its dealers to generate minimum annual sales of $300. By signing long-term contracts with well-known artists such as Adelina Patti and Enrico Caruso, Johnson satisfied consumer demand for celebrity recordings.

From the beginning Victor played an active role in international markets. In 1901 Johnson agreed to supply the Gramophone Company Ltd., a British firm organized in 1898, with at least 50 percent of his factory's capacity. The Gramophone Company distributed Victor goods throughout the British empire except Canada, which was served by the Berliner Gramophone Company of Montreal. In 1903 Johnson organized the Victor Distributing & Export Company of New York to market his products in other parts of the world, including South America, Africa, and Asia. By the 1920s Victor had established subsidiaries in Argentina, Brazil, Japan, and other countries.

Johnson was never completely comfortable with the success of his company. As he wrote in the early 1920s, "I never felt that I was cut out for a man of large business responsibility temperamentally" (letter to Maurice Bower Saul, 28 Sept. 1922, Johnson papers, Johnson Victrola Museum). During his business career he suffered from depression and experienced several nervous breakdowns. With his health failing, Johnson sold his interest in the Victor company for $40 million and retired from business in 1927. He devoted the remaining years of his life to travel and charitable, civic, and scientific causes. In 1927 Johnson donated $800,000 to the University of Pennsylvania for the endowment of the Eldridge R. Johnson Foundation for Research in Medical Physics, established to study the physical treatment of diseases. In 1931 he constructed a 285-foot yacht, christened the *Caroline*, which Johnson used for personal travel and scientific research. A team of Smithsonian Institution scientists used the yacht in 1933 to study marine life in the Caribbean. Johnson died at his home in Moorestown, New Jersey.

Johnson played an important role in the development of the sound-recording industry in the early twentieth century. His technical improvements led to the introduction of a practical, affordable disc talking machine, and his marketing innovations brought high-quality music to millions of consumers.

• The American Heritage Center in Laramie, Wyo., contains a collection of Johnson's personal and business papers. A duplicate set of these papers, along with a collection of Victor phonographs, records, and memorabilia, is at the Johnson Victrola Museum, part of the Delaware State Museum, in

Dover. A biography by his son, Eldridge R. Fenimore Johnson, *His Master's Voice Was Eldridge R. Johnson* (1974), and an anonymously written pamphlet, *Eldridge Reeves Johnson: Industrial Pioneer* (1951), contain useful information. Robert W. Baumbach's *Look for the Dog* (1981) has detailed technical information about the Victor talking machines. For the history of the Victor Talking Machine Company, consult B. L. Aldridge, *The Victor Talking Machine Company* (1964), and the richly illustrated study by Frederick O. Barnum III, *"His Master's Voice" in America* (1991). Studies that place Johnson and the Victor company within the context of the sound-recording industry include Roland Gelatt, *The Fabulous Phonograph*, rev. ed. (1977); Walter L. Welch and Leah Burt, *From Tinfoil to Stereo* (1994); and Andre Millard, *America on Record: A History of Recorded Sound* (1995).

LEONARD DE GRAAF

JOHNSON, Eliza McCardle (4 Oct. 1810–15 Jan. 1876), wife of President Andrew Johnson, was born in Greeneville, Tennessee, the daughter of John McCardle, a shoemaker, and Sarah Phillips. Attending local schools up to the sixth grade, Eliza was unusually well educated for a woman in early East Tennessee and seems to have been exceptionally intelligent. After her father's death, she assisted her mother in making quilts.

An attractive young woman, Eliza met Andrew Johnson when he arrived in Greeneville in 1826. According to the commonly accepted story in town, when she saw him Eliza told her mother, "There goes the man I am going to marry." According to another version, she told some of her girlfriends, "There goes my beau, girls." These tales are probably apocryphal, but Eliza and Andrew undoubtedly were attracted to one another, and when Andrew Johnson went on to Rutledge, Tennessee, he often thought of the girl he had left behind. He wrote to her frequently, and in the spring of 1827 he returned to Greeneville, probably because of Eliza, and they married. The civil ceremony was performed by Mordecai Lincoln, a distant cousin of Abraham Lincoln, in nearby Warrensburg, where the bride's father had briefly kept a tavern. They had five children.

Andrew Johnson, an apprentice tailor, had run away from his employer in Raleigh in 1824. In 1827 he established a tailor's shop in Greeneville. He prospered, bought real estate, and by 1829 was elected alderman. He rose to mayor in 1834 and the next year won a seat in the state legislature. With one interruption, he was the local representative until 1843, when he was elected to Congress. During his absences in Nashville, Eliza Johnson stayed at home to care for the house and their children. The often-told story that she taught her husband how to read and write is not true, because he had a rudimentary knowledge of both before he was married, but she probably did improve his spelling and reading. Unlike his wife, Andrew Johnson had never gone to school.

When Andrew Johnson was elected to Congress in 1843, Eliza Johnson again remained in Greeneville, and she did not accompany him to Nashville when he was elected governor in 1853. Even when he went to Washington to represent the state in the Senate, she preferred to stay at home, although she did visit him briefly in the capital in 1860. These separations did not mean that Andrew Johnson was unmindful of her; he treasured her advice and in his 1853 campaign for governor made references to her efforts to improve his education.

The most trying time for Eliza Johnson came in 1861 with the outbreak of the Civil War. Left behind in Tennessee after her husband, the only loyal senator from a secessionist state to continue to serve in the U.S. Senate, fled, she was evicted from her house and sought refuge with her daughter Mary Stover in Carter County. In April 1862 Confederate general Edmund Kirby Smith told her to leave the state, but Johnson asked for a delay because she was too ill to comply. Finally in September she requested passports and with her children traveled to Murfreesboro, where she hoped to cross into the Union-occupied portion of the state to join her husband, who had been appointed military governor of Tennessee and was living in Nashville. Confederate general Nathan Bedford Forrest refused to allow her to cross his lines, insisting not even Jesus Christ would be allowed to pass. Only the interference of Confederate governor Isham G. Harris made it possible for her to go on. Although he loathed Andrew Johnson, Harris gave orders to let her cross the next morning. Joyously welcomed by her husband, Johnson moved into headquarters. Since she was not safe in Nashville due to rebel attacks, some weeks later she moved to Cincinnati and then to Vevay, Indiana, only to return to Nashville in May 1863.

In 1864 Andrew Johnson was nominated for vice president as Lincoln's running mate on the Republican ticket. Elected to office, he left for Washington, but Eliza Johnson again failed to accompany him. Thus she missed the embarrassing scene during his swearing in, when he was inebriated, as well as the dramatic events of the assassination of Lincoln and her husband's inauguration as president. Not until June 1865 did Eliza Johnson and other members of the family join Andrew Johnson and move into the White House.

Afflicted with "consumption," Johnson left most of the usual chores of the first lady to her daughters, especially to Martha, the wife of Judge David T. Patterson, later a senator. "My dears, I am an invalid," Johnson said and spent most of her time on the second floor of the mansion, where the living rooms were located. Sitting in her rocking chair, she busied herself with needlework and reading serious works. Yet in the words of White House guard William H. Crook, she was a "person of strong, forceful character. . . . Despite her afflictions . . . a woman of far more than the usual power—but hers was the power of the spirit and the mind rather than the body." Believing that throughout her husband's life she exercised great influence upon him, Crook pointed out that, like Andrew Johnson, she was absolutely inflexible when it came to a matter of principle. On the rare occasions when she received visitors, Johnson dressed in excellent taste and made a favorable impression upon them. Rarely seen in public, egg rolling at Easter and her grandchildren's birthday parties brought her out of her retirement.

Andrew Johnson's tenure was not easy, either for himself or his wife, especially when, as a result of his differences with Congress about Reconstruction, he was impeached. Eliza Johnson impatiently awaited the outcome of the trial, although she stated afterward she had always been convinced that he would be acquitted. Having already had the misfortune of witnessing the deaths of two of her sons (one in 1863 and another in 1869) and plagued as she was by ill health, the experience was an ordeal for her.

After her husband's term was up, Johnson returned with him to Greeneville. Retiring as ever, she did not accompany him on his political campaigns but was greatly cheered when in 1875 he was elected once again to the U.S. Senate. It was a vindication the whole family had eagerly sought. The ex-president, however, died shortly thereafter. Too ill to attend his funeral, Johnson died half a year later at her daughter Martha's in Home Depot, Tennessee.

Never seeking publicity and remaining in the background, Johnson has always been a somewhat enigmatic figure. She apparently helped her husband overcome some of his shortcomings and loyally supported him throughout their married life.

• Most of the material on Eliza Johnson may be found in the Andrew Johnson Papers at the University of Tennessee, especially in the Margaret G. Blanton Collection. It is, however, of limited extent. Much of the documentation is contained in LeRoy P. Graf and Ralph W. Haskins, eds., *The Papers of Andrew Johnson* (9 vols., 1967–1991). There are sketches of Johnson in Laura C. Holloway, *The Ladies of the White House* (1886), Carole Chandler Waldrup, *Presidents' Wives* (1989), and Carl S. Anthony, *First Ladies* (2 vols., 1990). Additional information may be found in Hans L. Trefousse, *Andrew Johnson* (1989). Also of interest is William Henry Crook, *Memories of the White House* (1911).

HANS L. TREFOUSSE

JOHNSON, George Francis (14 Oct. 1857–28 Nov. 1948), shoe manufacturer and philanthropist, was born in Milford, Massachusetts, the son of Francis A. Johnson, seaman and shoe worker, and Sarah Jane Aldrich. Johnson's childhood was spent in a series of New England villages as his father moved about in search of better work. He left school at age thirteen to go to work in a boot factory.

In 1881, when the superintendent of the Lester Brothers factory in Binghamton, New York, offered Johnson's father a job supervising the treeing room, Johnson seized the opportunity, convinced the superintendent of his worth, and was hired. He initiated a number of innovative changes, and his role in the Lester factory steadily expanded. In 1890 Lester's largest creditor, Henry B. Endicott, bought Lester's interest. In spite of Johnson's relative youth, Endicott took Lester's advice and made him superintendent of the enterprise.

Johnson, an advocate of industrial democracy and welfare capitalism, believed labor and management should function as a partnership. Johnson said:

I believed that we could build up a great enterprise by making our workers comfortable, free of worry, whether in the factory or in their homes; by thinking of them and treating them as human beings, not machines to be run till they broke down and had to be scrapped; to make them as contented as we could within reason. Men everywhere respond to that kind of treatment. It is decent; it is common sense—and it pays too; pays everybody in the enterprise and the whole community.

Johnson's vision was typical of early twentieth-century welfare capitalism, defined as a system offering "any service provided for the comfort or improvement of employees which was neither a necessity of the industry nor required by law" (Stuart D. Brandes, *American Welfare Capitalism, 1880–1940* [1976]). It was a solution to the difficulties of labor-management relations in an emerging industrial society that, for a variety of reasons, would ultimately prove unacceptable to labor.

In 1899 Endicott lent Johnson $150,000 to purchase a half interest in the business, which now became the Endicott-Johnson Company (EJ). In 1919 EJ changed from a partnership to a corporation, and when Henry Endicott died in 1920, Johnson succeeded him as president.

Johnson had a vision of a peaceful industrial countryside, where contented workers made fair wages, owned their own homes, worked hard, and prospered with the company. He believed that hourly wages benefited less productive workers and insisted that pay for piece work motivated workers more and resulted in higher wages. In fact, Endicott-Johnson workers usually had the highest wages in the industry. In 1919 Johnson established a profit-sharing plan for all employees that distributed shares solely according to time worked in the prior year. While he thought labor unions good in principle, he objected to unions at EJ. His faith in a partnership between labor and capital was upheld in 1940 when workers rejected unions by an overwhelming majority.

When business growth required construction of new factories, EJ bought land in the area that would become the city of Endicott. As more factory buildings arose, the company built homes in the area for EJ workers, an enterprise that would continue for the next fifty years. In 1936 Johnson wrote President Roosevelt that the company had by then built more than 2,500 houses, sold to EJ workers for just the cost of land and construction.

As a boy Johnson had enjoyed sports and games and thought that recreation made for better, happier workers. He insisted that there be playgrounds near the factories for workers and their families. He endowed parks throughout the area and even built a golf course and country club for employees, to prove that golf was not just for the rich. To help ensure productive workers, EJ maintained restaurants where workers could obtain nutritious meals at minimal cost (free during the 1930's depression) and operated stores where families could purchase food at reasonable prices. Endicott-Johnson was a pioneer in providing comprehensive health care for its employees. The company employed dozens of health professionals, and Johnson built or endowed three hospitals in Endicott, Johnson City, and Binghamton.

Politically, Johnson was an independent. He supported Franklin Roosevelt, both as governor and president, but at the same time he was an admirer of Father Coughlin, the radical Detroit priest. Johnson freely shared his beliefs through frequent communications to EJ employees and in a widespread correspondence. Johnson persuaded IBM president Thomas Watson to build factories in Endicott. Watson became an advocate of Johnson's management principles.

Johnson married Lucy Anna Willis of Braintree, Massachusetts in 1876. They had five children. According to Richard Saul, that marriage ended in divorce. He married Mary Ann McGlone in 1897; they had one daughter. In 1930 Johnson became chairman of the board of the company and his son George W. Johnson succeeded him as president. After a heart attack, he retired in 1939. He died in his home in Endicott, New York.

• The papers of George F. Johnson are deposited with Syracuse University and are the primary source for his ideas and business practices. Richard S. Saul, "An American Entrepreneur: George F. Johnson" (Ph.D. diss., Syracuse Univ., 1966), used these papers extensively but provides little information on his personal life. William Inglis, *George F. Johnson and His Industrial Democracy* (1935), was commissioned by Johnson and is uncritical. An obituary is in the *New York Times*, 29 Nov. 1948.

LEONARD F. RALSTON

JOHNSON, Georgia Douglas (10 Sept. 18?–14 May 1966), poet and dramatist, was born Georgia Blanche Douglas Camp in Atlanta, Georgia, the daughter of George Camp and Laura Jackson, a maid. Traditionally, her birth date has been recorded as 10 September 1886. However, recent biographies—based on obituary notices and school sources—alternatively list her year of birth as 1880 or 1877. Georgia Camp's paternal grandfather was a wealthy Englishman, her maternal grandmother was a Native American, and her maternal grandfather was an African American. Her early years were spent in Rome, Georgia, and she graduated from Atlanta University's Normal School in 1893. In 1902–1903 she continued her schooling at Oberlin Conservatory of Music, where she studied piano, violin, harmony, and voice. Her interest in music is reflected in her literary work.

She taught school in Marietta, Georgia, and later became an assistant principal in Atlanta. In September 1903 she married Henry Lincoln "Link" Johnson, an Atlanta lawyer and Georgia delegate-at-large to the Republican National Convention since 1896. They had two children. In 1910 the family moved to Washington, D.C., and in 1912 Link was appointed recorder of deeds by President William Howard Taft.

Johnson's first poems, "Omnipresence" and "Beautiful Eyes," were published in the Atlanta-based *Voice of the Negro* (June 1905). After the move to Washington, W. E. B. Du Bois selected three of her poems, "Gossamer," "Fame," and "My Little One," for the *Crisis* (1916). Her first volume of poetry was *The Heart of a Woman and Other Poems* (1918). Characteristic of Johnson's verse, it contains short, introspective lyrics written in traditional forms. It was criticized in some quarters because it did not contain enough "racially conscious" poems.

Perhaps in response to such criticism, her next book, *Bronze: A Book of Verse* (1922), is much concerned with issues of race as well as gender. In his foreword Du Bois noted somewhat condescendingly that Johnson's "word is simple, sometimes trite, but it is sincere and true." Alice Dunbar-Nelson, in her review in the *Messenger* (May 1923), called *Bronze* "a contribution to the poetry of America as well as to the race, that is well worth while."

In 1925 Link Johnson died. In appreciation of his services to the Republican party, Georgia Johnson was appointed commissioner of conciliation in the Department of Labor by Calvin Coolidge. Often beleaguered by professional, financial, and family pressures, Johnson lamented the lack of time to pursue her writing. She said, "If I might ask of some fairy godmother special favors, one would sure be for a clearing space, elbow room in which to think and write and live beyond the reach of the Wolf's fingers" (*Opportunity*, July 1927).

Despite these demands, in 1928 Johnson published *An Autumn Love Cycle*. The book contains what may be her most famous poem, "I Want to Die While You Love Me," later set to music by Johnson and sung by Henry T. Burleigh. The poems, like much of Johnson's verse, were in the "genteel" tradition of "raceless" literature advocated by fellow African-American writers like William Stanley Braithwaite and Countee Cullen. However, when reread from a feminist perspective, the volume contains some of Johnson's best work.

In addition to her poetry, Johnson wrote over thirty one-act plays. Only about a dozen have survived, and few have been produced. The focus of her plays, more than her poetry, is on racial issues. Plays such as *Blue Blood* (1926), *Safe* (193?), and *Blue-Eyed Black Boy* (193?) discuss such subjects as lynching and miscegenation. *Frederick Douglass* (1935) and *William and Ellen Craft* (1935) treat black heroes. Her folk drama *Plumes*, which deals with the plight of a mother who must decide between spending fifty dollars on a dubious operation or a splendid funeral for her daughter, won first prize in a 1927 *Opportunity* competition. *A Sunday Morning in the South* (c. 1925) concerns an innocent African-American male who is lynched for the rape of a white woman. The use of hymns ironically adds to the chilling horror that unfolds throughout the work. Johnson submitted several plays to the Federal

Theatre Project, but all were rejected by the readers, some of whom undoubtedly felt uncomfortable with her themes.

The need for money became an increasing burden in Johnson's life. She applied for many awards but was invariably rejected. However, her poems were published in scores of periodicals, and she wrote a column of practical advice called "Homely Philosophy," which was carried in many newspapers from 1926 to 1932. She also published several short stories under the pseudonym Paul Tremaine.

Over the years, Johnson became increasingly important as a literary hostess. She called her house at 1461 S Street in Northwest Washington "Half-Way House" because "I'm half-way between everybody and everything and I bring them together." Johnson's home was a popular haven for such writers as Jessie Fauset, Langston Hughes, Countee Cullen, and Jean Toomer.

Johnson published her final book of poetry, *Share My World*, in 1962. This slim volume contains many previously published poems. The work is reflective, generally optimistic, and displays her belief in the common bond of humanity. In 1965 Johnson was awarded an honorary doctorate of literature degree from Atlanta University. She died in Washington, D.C.

During her long life Johnson was frequently praised. James Weldon Johnson said that "[s]he was the first colored woman after Frances Harper to gain general recognition as a poet." Du Bois described her as being "the leading colored woman in poetry and one of our leading poets." Only late in the twentieth century did she begin to receive more critical attention, and several of her surviving plays were published for the first time.

• It is generally believed that a vast amount of Johnson's unpublished work (including a novel, a biography of her husband, and many poems, stories, and essays) were discarded when she died. A "Catalog of Writings" by her lists many works that now seem lost. Manuscript material is scattered in various locations, including the Schomburg Center for Research in Black Culture (New York Public Library), the Moorland-Spingarn Research Center at Howard University, the Federal Theatre Project Research Division at George Mason University, and the Robert W. Woodruff Library at Clark Atlanta University.

Gloria T. Hull, *Color, Sex, and Poetry: Three Women Writers of the Harlem Renaissance* (1987), is a critical and biographical study. See also Winona Fletcher, "Gloria Douglas Johnson," in *Afro-American Writers from the Harlem Renaissance to 1940*, ed. Trudier Harris (1987), vol. 51 of the *Dictionary of Literary Biography*; Lorraine Elena Roses and Ruth Elizabeth Randolph, *Harlem Renaissance and Beyond: Literary Biographies of 100 Black Women Writers, 1900–1945* (1990); Ann Allen Shockley, *Afro-American Women Writers 1746–1933* (1988); and Ann Trapasso, in *Notable Black American Women* (1992).

LOUIS J. PARASCANDOLA

JOHNSON, Guy (c. 1740–5 Mar. 1788), agent for Indian affairs, was born in County Meath, Ireland, the son of John Johnson. Guy's father managed the family es-

tates in Warrenstown, County Meath, Ireland, bound to Sir Peter Warren until Sir Peter's death. The bond was then released. Guy's mother's name is unknown. On 16 April 1756 he arrived in Boston, and by 10 June he had made his way to Fort Johnson, his uncle Sir William Johnson's home in the Mohawk Valley. Sir William found work for Guy immediately, placing him as an assistant with American Indian proceedings as early as 29 July 1756. Hugh Wallace, a friend of William Johnson's, described Guy as a "sensible modest worthy Young Gentleman & one who will yet make a figure" (*Sir William Johnson Papers*, vol. 2, pp. 478–79).

Guy Johnson settled into his uncle's household, where he served as secretary, friend, and artist/draftsman, producing a 1758 sketch of Fort Johnson that was reproduced in London in the Royal Magazine.

Sir William assisted Guy Johnson in his pursuit of a military career, recommending him to Lord Loudon in July 1757. Guy Johnson led the militia to Stone Arabia, New York, in April 1758 as lieutenant and in 1759 distinguished himself in the Niagara campaign, afterward receiving a lieutenant's commission in the New York regiment on 2 December 1759. Johnson was then stationed in the Mohawk Valley, where he served as his uncle's personal secretary on the Niagara expedition. Informal secretarial arrangements continued through 1761. Soon, all Indian department documents began to appear in his handwriting, and Sir William created situations that kept Guy Johnson away from his military responsibilities in order to serve the Indian department. His commanding officer, Sir Jeffrey Amherst, insisted that Lieutenant Johnson could no longer be absent from his company. Sir William convinced him to resign his commission and on 10 October 1762 appointed him "Deputy Agent for that District of the Mississagas and the other Dependent Tribes in their Neighborhood," a position Johnson held with the Six Nations with increasing responsibility.

Johnson produced a number of useful maps and charts during this time, the most notable surviving one being his "Map of the Country of the VI Nations, 1771." He made two maps of the western lands, one depicting the Fort Stanwix line of 1768, the other the Ohio country, after a survey by Thomas Hutchins.

In March 1763 Guy Johnson married Mary "Polly" Johnson, Sir William's daughter. Sir William gave them a square mile of property along the flatlands of the Mohawk River as a wedding present. Guy Johnson named the estate "Guy Park." His first house was destroyed by fire in 1773; the second, built of limestone, is still standing with nineteenth-century modifications. The couple had four children, only two surviving into adulthood.

In 1767 Sir William had influenced Governor Sir Henry Moore to reorganize the Albany County militia with himself as commanding officer. Guy Johnson was appointed colonel of the militia on 17 February 1768. He also held civil office, drawing up the boundaries for the new Tryon County on 12 March 1772 and becoming judge of the common pleas on 29 May 1772 for Tryon County. In July 1772 Sir William petitioned Governor William Tryon for two representatives to the provincial assembly, resulting in the naming of Guy Johnson and Hendrick Frey as the sole candidates in a special assembly election.

In July 1774 Sir William died in the midst of an Iroquois conference at Johnson Hall. Guy Johnson succeeded him immediately as superintendent of Indian affairs and resumed the conference the following day. He attempted to "Calm the public fears & once more restore Tranquility" (*Documents Relative to the Colonial History of New York*, vol. 5, pp. 474–80). In several letters he stressed Sir William's support of his appointment because of his "long and intimate knowledge of Indian Affairs & of the Duties of his department." He was finally confirmed in this office in 1776.

After the First Continental Congress met in August 1774 to adopt the Suffolk Resolves, condemning the Boston Port Act, Johnson's Tryon Court of Quarter Sessions issued a grand jury declaration against the work of the Congress. This caused the Tryon County committee of safety to attack the declaration, calling it a "disapprobation of the just opposition made by the colonies of the oppressive & arbitrary acts of the British Parliament." To diminish Johnson's influence with the Indians, the committee required a loyalty oath of certain persons so they would give no aid to "Coll Guy Johnson or any other person in his department with provisions or any other Necessarys nor . . . forward any dispatches of Intelligence whatsoever." In late April and early May 1775 Johnson and his brother-in-law John Johnson broke up several committee assemblies with armed force. They organized 500 militiamen, mostly tenants, and took control of all roads in and out of Tryon County.

After Ethan Allen captured the British garrison at Ticonderoga in May 1775, Johnson received a dispatch warning him that he was Allen's next victim. Rumors of seizure abounded and probably inspired an oath of association that the Johnsons circulated for signature among tenants and friends, but the local committee of safety confiscated the oath after it had received only three signatures.

Johnson left Guy Park for Oswego and then left for Montreal in July 1775, arriving there on 17 July. He met with the Canadian Indians on 26 July. When presented with the danger of losing their lands and hunting grounds, the Canadian Indians agreed to help against the rebels. They set up camps at St. John's near the American border, where they delayed the American advance into Canada. By November 1775 Johnson sailed for England to gain recognition as superintendent and to confer with European authorities. On his return he remained in New York City, where he managed the John Street Theater (called Clinton's Thespians at that time) and also performed in a play in September 1778. He then took a ship for Canada. After spending the winter in Halifax, he went on to Quebec, where he and General Frederick Haldimand were involved in a conference with the Iroquois.

Johnson was present at the battles of Chemung and Newtown in western New York in 1779, and in that year he established his headquarters at Fort Niagara, from which he directed Indian and Loyalist raids into the Mohawk Valley. He has been credited with cementing the alliance between the British Crown and the Iroquois. There were thousands of Indian refugees at Fort Niagara and severe shortages of food and other supplies. Johnson tried to convince some of the Indians to go to Carleton Island, but they felt they needed to stay together for protection and would not separate from their fellows. Johnson's property in the Mohawk Valley was confiscated by the New York government and, after the war, sold at public auction. (British commissioners later gave $34,000 to Johnson for his losses.) He remained in charge of the Indians at Fort Niagara until the end of the war. After the peace treaty Johnson went to England. He died at his residence in the Haymarket, London.

• James Sullivan et al., eds., *The Papers of Sir William Johnson* (14 vols., 1921–1965), is available in many libraries and at Johnson Hall State Historic Site. Original copies of letters can be found at the New York State Library. Also available is E. B. O'Callaghan and B. Fernow, eds., *Documents Relative to the Colonial History of the State of New York* (15 vols., 1853–1887), an excellent source for Johnson's years after Sir William Johnson's death. Some references also appear in O'Callaghan, ed., *The Documentary History of the State of New York* (4 vols., 1851). Manuscript collections with Johnson material are available in the New York State Library, the New-York Historical Society, and the Public Archives of Canada in Ottawa, Ontario, Canada. The original Haldimand papers, the Claus papers, and the Loyalist Claims are available at the Public Archives of Canada. Arthur S. Wolcott, ed., *Daniel Claus' Narrative of His Relations with Sir William Johnson and Experiences in the Lake George Fight* (1904), provides some material on Johnson and his appointment in the Indian affairs department. Barbara Graymont includes information on Johnson in *The Iroquois in the American Revolution* (1972).

WANDA BURCH

JOHNSON, Hall (12 Mar. 1888–30 Apr. 1970), composer, arranger, and choral conductor, was born Francis Hall Johnson in Athens, Georgia, the son of William Decker Johnson, an AME minister, and Alice (maiden name unknown). Music was an important part of Hall Johnson's childhood. He heard the singing of his grandmother and other former slaves as they sang the old spirituals in his father's Methodist church. This grounding in the original performance of Negro spirituals was to represent a significant influence on his later life. Johnson, exhibiting an early interest in music, received solfeggio lessons from his father and piano lessons from an older sister. As a teenager he developed an interest in the violin and taught himself to play.

Johnson was educated in the South at the Knox Institute, at Atlanta University, and at Allen University in Columbia, South Carolina, where his father was president. Frustrated by his inability to find a violin instructor in the segregated South, Hall Johnson left his southern roots and went to the Hahn School of Music in Philadelphia where he could study his instrument. In 1910 he transferred to the University of Pennsylvania, where he received a bachelor of music degree in composition and won the Simon Haessler Prize for outstanding composition.

Johnson married Polly Copening in 1914, and the young couple settled in New York City, where he opened a violin studio. He taught during the day and freelanced at night in various dance and theater orchestras, playing violin or viola. He played with Will Marion Cook's Southern Syncopated Orchestra in 1918 and with Vernon Castle's Orchestra in the 1921 Negro musical *Shuffle Along*. In 1923 he organized the Negro String Quartet, which included violinists Arthur Boyd and Felix Weir, cellist Marion Cumbo, and himself as violist.

From 1923 to 1924 Hall Johnson did graduate study at the New York Institute of Musical Arts (later combined with the Juilliard School of Music). He studied music theory, violin, and composition with his favorite teacher, Percy W. Goetschius. During his three-year stint as pit musician for *Shuffle Along*, Johnson became disenchanted with the manner in which a quartet sang spirituals. The barbershop treatment of Negro spirituals seemed a mockery of the rich choral style sung by ex-slaves during his childhood. In an article for *The Crisis* (Nov. 1966) Charles Hobson writes about Johnson's feelings toward the spiritual and quotes him as saying, " . . . it is serious music and should be performed seriously in the spirit of its original conception" (p. 483).

This experience served as a catalyst for Hall Johnson's true contribution to America's musical history. Johnson became a man with a mission. He resolved to forsake his instrumental career and devote his life to the preservation of an authentic performance style for Negro spirituals. Though his musical background was strictly instrumental, he decided to organize a choir that would realize his dream. In September 1925 he organized the Hall Johnson Choir—the first professional Negro choir to earn international acclaim. The choir was started with only eight members, but by the time of its debut in February 1926, its size had increased to twenty members because Johnson realized that he needed more singers to achieve the traditional stylistic effect.

Johnson achieved worldwide fame for his arrangements of spirituals and for his original spirituals. During his career he composed and arranged over forty choral selections and twenty solo spirituals—all with authentic Negro dialect and accurate rhythmic patterns. He arranged and directed music for Marc Connelly's production of *Green Pastures* (featuring the Hall Johnson Choir), which premiered on Broadway in 1930. Johnson received the 1931 Harmon Award for his role in the tremendous success of this Pulitzer Prize–winning musical.

In 1933 Johnson's own *Run Little Chillun*, a Negro folk drama, was produced on Broadway for a run of 126 performances. He wrote both the lyrics and the music (twenty-five spirituals) for this successful production, which was his first dramatic attempt.

Johnson took his choir to Hollywood in 1936 to film *Green Pastures*. He made Hollywood his base over the next eight years as he wrote musical scores and conducted choirs for nine films. They included *Dimples* with Shirley Temple; *Lost Horizons*, which won two Academy Awards; *Swanee River* with Al Jolson; and *Cabin in the Sky* with Lena Horne, Ethel Waters, Louis Armstrong, and Duke Ellington. He also organized a 200-voice Festival Negro Chorus in Los Angeles whose performances provided scholarships for talented students. While in Los Angeles, Johnson's *Run Little Chillun* was staged as a WPA Negro Theatre Project. Its Broadway success was matched in Los Angeles and later in San Francisco as the show played to many enthusiastic audiences.

Johnson returned to New York in 1943 for a revival of *Run Little Chillun*. His *Son of Man*, an Easter cantata (never published), was performed by the 300-voice Festival Negro Chorus at the New York City Center in April 1946. It was presented again at Carnegie Hall on Good Friday of 1948. Johnson inaugurated an annual concert series titled "New Artists" to give visibility to young Negro performers such as Kermit Moore, a cellist, and Robert McFerrin, a baritone singer.

In 1951 the Hall Johnson Choir was selected by the U.S. State Department to represent the nation at the International Festival of Fine Arts in Berlin. The choir won international acclaim as it toured Germany and other European countries. After the European tour Johnson alternated his career between Los Angeles and New York. A stroke in 1962 slowed his pace, but he soon recovered and resumed an active schedule of composing, teaching, and conducting. During that same year he was presented a citation by New York Mayor Robert F. Wagner for thirty-five years of significant contributions to the world of music.

In 1965 Johnson was asked by Marian Anderson to arrange some solo spirituals for an RCA album that she was doing. He also collaborated with Anderson and the Metropolitan Opera orchestra in arranging music for a concert production. He was honored again in March 1970 by Mayor John Lindsay, who presented him with New York's most prestigious citation—the George Frederic Handel Award.

Just over a month later Hall Johnson died of smoke inhalation from a fire in his New York apartment. Marian Anderson, in a *New York Times* tribute (1 May 1970), wrote, "Hall Johnson's music was a gift of inestimable value that brought to all people a greater understanding of the depth of the Negro spiritual." His outstanding legacy to the world lives on in his collections of spirituals that were published, in the few recordings that are still extant, and in his memoirs, which are housed at Glassboro State College in New Jersey.

• Hall Johnson's papers are at Glassboro State College, Glassboro, N.J. An interesting commentary on Johnson's life and work is found in Charles Hobson's "Hall Johnson: Preserver of the Negro Spiritual," *The Crisis*, Nov. 1966, pp. 480–85. Verna Arvey writes about "Hall Johnson and His Choir" in *Opportunity: Journal of Negro Life* (May 1941): 151, 158–59. Johnson provides his own insights and philosophy regarding the origin and importance of the Negro spiritual in "Notes on the Negro Spiritual," in *Readings in Black American Music*, ed. Eileen Southern (1983). Other sources with biographical notes on Johnson include John Lovell's *Black Song: The Forge and the Flame* (1972) and Hildred Roach's *Black American Music: Past and Present* (1985). Samuel A. Floyd's *Black Music in the Harlem Renaissance* (1990) lists a bibliography of Johnson's spirituals that includes publishers, publishing dates, voicings, libraries where located, recordings, and artists/conductors. A detailed description of the Los Angeles WPA production of *Run Little Chillun* is found in John O'Connor and Lorraine Brown's *Free, Adult, Uncensored: The Living History of the Federal Theatre Project* (1978). William Warfield's memorial, "A Tribute to Hall Johnson," is in the Carl Fischer Newsletter, *The Choral Consultant* (Fall 1970). Other obituaries are in the *New York Times* and the *New York Post*, both 1 May 1970, and *Jet Magazine*, 21 May 1970.

MARY FRANCES EARLY

JOHNSON, Halle Tanner Dillon (17 Oct. 1864–26 Apr. 1901), physician, was born in Pittsburgh, Pennsylvania, the daughter of Benjamin Tucker Tanner, a successful minister and bishop in the African Methodist Episcopal (AME) church and editor of the *Christian Recorder*, and Sarah Elizabeth Miller. Among the nine Tanner children was Henry Ossawa Tanner, the first African-American artist to be celebrated internationally.

Halle Tanner married Charles E. Dillon of Trenton, New Jersey, in 1886, and the next year their only child was born. While the circumstances and date of Dillon's death are unknown, afterward Halle returned to the Tanner family home in Philadelphia with her daughter, and then, at age twenty-four, she enrolled in the Woman's Medical College of Pennsylvania, the only black student in her class, and graduated with an M.D. in a class of thirty-six on 7 May 1891, with high honors.

Halle Tanner Dillon responded to Booker T. Washington's letter to the dean of the Woman's Medical College in search of a black woman to become resident physician at his Tuskegee Institute in Alabama. Although local white physicians had provided satisfactory school health services, Washington was determined to hire a black physician for the rural, black institution; he had led an unsuccessful four-year search. Washington wrote to Dillon on 16 April 1891 and described the town as one with 3,000 residents, half of whom were black. He said that the school was a "little colony" in the town, where 450 students were enrolled and thirty administrators and faculty were employed. Since the institution was supported by charity, Washington expected those who joined the staff to have "a broad missionary spirit" and to accept the modest salary that the school offered.

Dillon accepted Washington's offer as resident physician, arriving in Tuskegee on 3 August 1891. She received a salary of $600 for twelve months plus board

and one month's vacation. She agreed to teach two classes a day, head the health department, and compound medicine for the school's needs.

As Dillon knew, physicians were required to pass either a local or state examination before practicing in Alabama. She left Tuskegee for Montgomery on 8 August and took temporary quarters in a quiet place so that she might study for the examinations. Washington did what he could to ease Bishop Tanner's anxiety over the gender and racial bias that his daughter might encounter in the examinations. To aid in the preparation, Washington arranged for study sessions with Cornelius Nathaniel Dorsette, a black physician practicing in Montgomery and the first black physician to pass the Alabama medical examinations. But racial discrimination was an established practice in Alabama. Anna M. Longshore, a white woman physician, was permitted to practice after failing the examination earlier.

On 17 August Washington accompanied Dillon to the capitol building—the examination site—and introduced her to the supervisor. Both the supervisor and a white male candidate for the examination were startled. They told Dillon that they had never seen "a woman doctor before or a diploma from a Woman's Medical College" (Halle Dillon to Clara Marshall, 3 Oct. 1891, in Sterling). That she was a black woman probably aroused their curiosity even more. The ten-day testing period occurred without incident, with each day devoted to a different medical subject. The local press watched the event curiously and questioned what Dillon looked like and why she dared sit for the test. At the end the board supervisor complimented Dillon on the neatness and cleanliness of her work, but she was to return to Tuskegee and wait nearly three weeks before receiving the examination results.

Dillon passed the examination with an average of 78.81—a score lower than she expected. But she did not dismiss the possibility of racial and gender bias, noting that "the critical medical pen has been too rigorously applied" (*Atlanta University Bulletin*, n.p.). She described the examination in a letter to her former dean at the Women's Medical College of Pennsylvania: "Taking the examination as a whole is rather hard because there were so many questions, or rather a few questions which were technical in character. One question in Hygiene occurs to me now & it certainly was to my mind incomprehensible, 'Discuss the *hygiene* of the reproductive organs of the female' (3 Oct. 1891, in Sterling). By this time, too, the major newspapers had lauded her achievement.

Dillon became the first woman of any race to pass the medical examination and to practice medicine in Alabama with a license. She was resident physician at Tuskegee Institute from 1891 to 1894. In addition to the duties that Washington defined for her initially, she established a Nurses Training School and the Lafayette Dispensary.

In 1894 she married John Quincy Johnson, an African Methodist Episcopal minister who taught mathematics at Tuskegee in the 1893–1894 school year. The next year he became president of Allen University, an AME college in Columbia, South Carolina. The Johnsons lived in Princeton, New Jersey, while John Quincy did postgraduate work at Princeton Theological Seminary. Then they moved to Nashville, Tennessee, where he pastored Saint Paul AME Church, and Halle Johnson became the mother of their three sons. No additional information on her professional life is known. She died at home, 1010 South Cherry Street, during childbirth complicated by dysentery.

While Halle Tanner Dillon Johnson was born into prominence, she achieved it later in her own right. She overcame the racial and gender bias of the period in which she lived to become a physician. In her work as resident physician at the Tuskegee Institute and as founder of a nurses training program, she contributed to the health of rural black residents in Alabama and to the training of those who would later become health care professionals.

• Johnson's papers are in the University of Pennsylvania archives and the Archives and Special Collections on Women in Medicine, Black Women Physicians Project, the Medical College of Pennsylvania. Some items are in the Booker T. Washington Papers in the Library of Congress, published in *The Booker T. Washington Papers*, vol. 3 (1889–1899). Her death certificate is in the Tennessee State Library and Archives. The most complete assessments of Halle Tanner Dillon Johnson are Jessie Carney Smith's articles in *Notable Black American Women* (1992) and *Black Women in America* (1993). See also "Color and Sex No Barrier," Atlanta University *Bulletin* (Nov. 1891), and Dorothy Sterling, ed., *We Are Your Sisters* (1984).

JESSIE CARNEY SMITH

JOHNSON, Harold Keith (22 Feb. 1912–24 Sept. 1983), army officer, was born in Bowesmont, North Dakota, the son of Harold Johnson, a lumberman, and Edna Thompson. Upon his graduation from the U.S. Military Academy in 1933, Johnson was commissioned a second lieutenant in the infantry and assigned to the Third Infantry Regiment at Fort Snelling, Minnesota. In 1935 he married Dorothy Rennix; they had three children. Promoted to first lieutenant on 13 June 1936, he was from 1937 to 1938 a student at the Infantry School at Fort Benning, Georgia, and from 1938 to 1940 he served with the Twenty-eighth Infantry Regiment at Fort Niagara, New York. In the summer of 1940 Johnson, who was promoted to captain later that year, was assigned to the Fifty-seventh Infantry Regiment, which was stationed at Fort William McKinley in the Philippine Islands and consisted of U.S. officers and Filipino enlisted men.

After the Japanese invaded the Philippines in December 1941, Johnson, with the rank of major and then lieutenant colonel, served as the Fifty-seventh Infantry's operations officer and later as a battalion commander in the defense of the Bataan Peninsula and participated in the Bataan "Death March" after the beleaguered garrison surrendered in April 1942. During the remainder of World War II he was imprisoned at camps in the Philippines, Japan, and Korea. When he

was liberated on 8 September 1945, he weighed barely ninety pounds. Following his recuperation from malnutrition, Johnson was from 1946 to 1950 a student and instructor at the Command and General Staff College at Fort Leavenworth, Kansas, a student at the Armed Forces Staff College at Norfolk, Virginia, and a line officer with the Seventh Infantry Regiment at Fort Devens, Massachusetts.

When North Korea invaded South Korea in the summer of 1950, Johnson took a provisional battalion to Korea, where it was attached to the Eighth Cavalry Regiment and saw heavy combat in the defense of the Pusan Perimeter. During the fighting Johnson impressed his superiors as a strong and intelligent troop leader and a skilled tactician. At the end of October 1950 he was given temporary command of the Fifth Cavalry Regiment, and a month later he was given command of the Eighth Cavalry. As a regimental commander Johnson, who then held the rank of colonel, added to his stellar combat record in the bloody encounters with the Chinese Communists in the winter of 1950–1951. In February 1951 he was appointed operations officer for I Corps, a post he held until he returned to the United States in the fall of 1951.

During the next thirteen years Johnson rose to the rank of full general while holding a variety of assignments. These included attendance at the National War College, assistant commander of the Eighth Division, chief of staff of the Seventh Army Headquarters, assistant chief of staff of the U.S. Army in Europe, chief of staff of the Central Army Group at the North Atlantic Treaty Organization (NATO) headquarters, commandant of the Command and General Staff College, and deputy chief of staff for military operations. In these assignments Johnson earned a reputation as a tough-minded thinker with a readiness to challenge easy solutions, leading to his appointment as army chief of staff in July 1964 over forty-three generals with greater seniority.

As chief of staff, the head army adviser to the president and the secretary of defense, and the army's uniformed commander, Johnson worked to improve the army's mobility, flexibility, combat staying power, and morale through measures such as the acquisition of more helicopters, the expansion of reserve forces, and higher pay for soldiers. His primary concern, however, was the Vietnam War. Initially he was skeptical about U.S. involvement, fearing that the war might be a repeat of the Korean War with the Americans unwilling to utilize all of their power. As President Lyndon Johnson escalated America's effort in 1964–1965, Harold Johnson endorsed Operation Rolling Thunder, an air offensive launched against North Vietnam, and recommended the use of U.S. ground troops to combat the Communist threat in South Vietnam. Emphasizing that the United States should either commit itself totally to the defense of South Vietnam or get out completely, Johnson called for the rapid deployment of a large force, to demonstrate to North Vietnam and the Vietcong that they could not win the war, and a full military mobilization based on a call-up of the reserves. To General Johnson's dismay, President Johnson chose to build up U.S. forces in Vietnam gradually without a mobilization of the reserves.

As the war progressed Johnson increasingly disagreed with General William Westmoreland, commander of U.S. forces in Vietnam, and the nation's civilian leadership over its conduct. In his opinion, Westmoreland's strategy of seeking out and destroying North Vietnamese and Vietcong main-force units in large battles of attrition was needlessly bleeding U.S. forces while leaving the Vietcong infrastructure in South Vietnam largely intact. Through 1966 and 1967 Johnson prodded Westmoreland, with little success, to focus more on small-unit engagements, territorial security, and pacification and to have the South Vietnamese carry more of the fighting burden. He was able to have General Creighton Abrams, whose views on the war more closely reflected his own, named Westmoreland's deputy and heir apparent.

At the same time General Johnson criticized President Johnson's policy of "gradualism." Hard-pressed to come up with trained troops for Vietnam without dangerously stripping U.S. forces in Europe and convinced that Rolling Thunder was being undermined by presidential restrictions, General Johnson pressed for a call-up of the reserves and told a Senate subcommittee in 1967 that the United States should hit North Vietnam with "as heavy a blow as possible over as short a period of time as possible." President Johnson, however, refused to take those steps, prompting General Johnson to complain that the military was being blamed for a prolonged war over which it had no control. He urged the joint chiefs of staff to resign in protest against President Johnson's war policies. When he retired in July 1968 at the expiration of his term as chief of staff, Harold Johnson believed that victory was still possible but only if the United States expanded the ground war into Laos and Cambodia, activated the reserves, intensified the bombing of North Vietnam, and gave South Vietnam all of the help it needed.

After his retirement Johnson served for a time as president and chief executive officer of Financial General Bankshares, Inc., and was active with the Freedoms Foundation. A devoutly religious man who was highly regarded by his contemporaries for his iron will and integrity, Johnson died in Washington, D.C.

• Johnson's papers and an oral history are in the U.S. Military Institute, Carlisle Barracks, Pa. Other oral histories are in the U.S. Army Center of Military History, Washington, D.C., and the William E. Brougher Collection at Mississippi State University. References to Johnson's experiences in the Philippines are in John W. Whitman, *Bataan, Our Last Ditch: The Bataan Campaign, 1942* (1990). For Johnson's service in the Korean War see Roy E. Appleman, *South to the Naktong, North to the Yalu* (1961), and Clair Blair, *The Forgotten War: America in Korea, 1950–1953* (1987). For Johnson's tenure as chief of staff see Robert Buzzanco, *Masters of War: Military Dissent and Politics in the Vietnam Era* (1996); Andrew F. Krepinevich, Jr., *The Army and Vietnam* (1986); Mark Perry, *Four Stars* (1989); Lewis Sorley, *Thunderbolt:*

General Creighton Abrams and the Army of His Times (1992); and Samuel Zaffiri, *Westmoreland: A Biography of General William C. Westmoreland* (1994). An obituary is in the *New York Times*, 26 Sept. 1983.

JOHN KENNEDY OHL

JOHNSON, Herschel Vespasian (18 Sept. 1812–16 Aug. 1880), Georgia governor, U.S. and Confederate senator, and vice presidential candidate, was born in Burke County, Georgia, the son of Moses Johnson, a planter, and Nancy Palmer. He studied at local schools before entering Monaghan Academy near Warrenton at fourteen. Attending the University of Georgia, he became a friend of Alexander H. Stephens and graduated in the class of 1834 with Howell Cobb and Henry L. Benning. In 1833 Johnson married Ann F. Polk Walker, with whom he had nine children.

While completing college, Johnson began studying law with Judge William T. Gould in Augusta and passed the bar in 1834. He began his practice in 1835 in Augusta. In 1839 he relocated to Louisville, Georgia, and to Milledgeville, then the state capital, five years later. He entered politics as a Democrat in 1840, campaigning for Martin Van Buren. His diligence impressed state Democratic leaders, who nearly nominated Johnson for Congress in 1841. In 1843 he was nominated for Congress, but he lost the election. In 1844 he served as a presidential elector for his wife's uncle, James K. Polk.

Mentioned as a gubernatorial possibility in 1845, Johnson lost the nomination to George W. Towns two years later. Johnson campaigned for Towns and was rewarded with appointment to a vacated U.S. Senate seat, serving in 1848–1849. While in Washington he took great interest in what would be done with the lands acquired during the Mexican War, particularly concerning slavery. "In the deliberations of this body, the question of slavery should never be touched," Johnson declared. "By the Constitution, Congress has no jurisdiction whatever over the subject. . . . It belongs to the people of the territory." He believed, "If all parties would stand upon that platform, no note of discord, in relation to this delicate question, would ever disturb the harmony of our deliberations" (Flippin, *Herschel V. Johnson of Georgia*, p. 8).

Johnson returned to Georgia in 1849, and that November the legislature elected him to the judgeship of the Ocmulgee Circuit. Although he intended to keep himself "entirely aloof" from political questions, he joined the intense debate that led to the Compromise of 1850, which he initially opposed. He disagreed more passionately with disunion, however, and reluctantly threw his support to a later version of the compromise measures when he saw them as the only way to keep the Union intact.

Finding "much that is unpleasant" in his judicial duties, Johnson accepted his party's gubernatorial nomination in 1853 and narrowly defeated Whig candidate Charles J. Jenkins, 47,638 to 47,128. The moderation that had appeared in Johnson's rhetoric during the latter stages of the compromise debate continued during his two terms as governor (1853–1857). Long an advocate of popular sovereignty, he supported the 1854 Kansas-Nebraska Act and deplored the violence in the former territory. Mentioned as a possible vice presidential nominee with James Buchanan in 1856, Johnson was growing "weary of [the] turmoil" of public life and in retrospect was glad that the second spot went to John C. Breckinridge. A year later Johnson retired to his 3,600-acre "Sandy Grove" plantation near Louisville "with but little desire and less expectation of mingling again in political affairs."

The election of 1860 drew Johnson back into the fray. After southern Democrats bolted the Charleston convention, Johnson, who had come to believe that "the only hope of the Union, was in the integrity and ascendency of the National Democracy" and that slavery "was safer in than out of the Union," sided with the northern wing of the party and was the only Georgian to attend their convention in Baltimore. When Benjamin Fitzpatrick of Alabama declined the vice presidential nomination on the ticket with Stephen A. Douglas, Johnson reluctantly accepted. Douglas, who "grappled with vexed questions, more like a true Statesman than any public man of his day" (Flippin, ed., "From the Autobiography of Herschel V. Johnson," p. 318), actually had been Johnson's first choice in the two previous elections, but Johnson knew that his decision would not be popular at home. Nevertheless, he campaigned extensively in Georgia as well as in the Northeast and the Midwest.

With Abraham Lincoln's election, Johnson urged his state not to follow South Carolina out of the Union. As he later wrote, "I believed . . . that the State of Georgia had the right to secede, although I deplored the policy of exercising it and anticipated the worst of consequences" (Flippin, ed., "From the Autobiography of Herschel V. Johnson," p. 328). At the state convention he put forward a resolution calling for delegates from the southern states to gather in Atlanta in February and compose a list of terms to be presented to the Lincoln administration. It was narrowly defeated by the motion for immediate secession. Johnson pledged to support the course chosen by his state, even though he considered it "the most stupendous blunder ever made by rational men."

Johnson declined to seek a seat in the Provisional Congress but was pleased with its redesign of the Constitution and with the selection of Jefferson Davis and Alexander Stephens for the top positions in the new government. "At home in retirement without the expectation of any active participation in the struggle" (Flippin, ed., "From the Autobiography of Herschel V. Johnson," p. 330), Johnson once again answered his state's call in November 1862, when the legislature, without his even expressing interest in the position, selected him to fill the Confederate Senate seat vacated by John W. Lewis. Johnson was elected to a full term the following autumn and served in the Confederate Congress for the remainder of the war. Although he differed with Davis "in several particulars," Johnson continued to support him and chastised Stephens and other Georgians for their open criticisms. As a legislator, Johnson's voting record was consistent with states' rights doctrine, opposing conscription, a supreme court, and suspension of the writ of habeas corpus.

A postwar retirement from politics was short-lived as Johnson was chosen president of the October 1865 state constitutional convention. The legislature that convened the following January elected Johnson and Stephens to the U.S. Senate, but both were denied their seats. Elected again in 1867, Johnson was again rebuffed. "Ruined by the war," he reestablished his law practice in order to make a living. Despite declining health, financial concerns led him to accept Governor James M. Smith's 1873 offer of the Middle Circuit judgeship, a position he held until his death at Sandy Grove.

Johnson is best remembered as Douglas's running mate in 1860 and as one of the few southern voices calling for moderation during a radical time in the country's history. With this same levelheaded approach, he provided nearly four decades of distinguished public service for his native state.

• Johnson's papers are at Duke University. Johnson wrote an insightful autobiography in 1867, but it lay unpublished until Percy Scott Flippin edited and issued the latter half in "From the Autobiography of Herschel V. Johnson, 1856–1867," *American Historical Review* 30 (Jan. 1925). Flippin made good use of Johnson's papers in his excellent biography, *Herschel V. Johnson of Georgia: State Rights Unionist* (1931). Various aspects of his career are examined in Ethel Morris, "Herschel V. Johnson as Governor of Georgia, 1853–1857" (M.A. thesis, Univ. of Georgia, 1940); Elizabeth D. Greeman, "Stephen A. Douglas and Herschel V. Johnson: Examples of National Men in the Sectional Crisis of 1860" (Ph.D. diss., Duke Univ., 1974); and Willis Morrison, "The Confederate Career of Herschel V. Johnson: An Application of State Rights Doctrine" (M.A. thesis, Emory Univ., 1959). Johnson plays a major role in Michael P. Johnson, *Toward a Patriarchal Republic: The Secession of Georgia* (1977). John C. Inscoe's article on Johnson's career in the *Encyclopedia of the Confederacy* (1993) is also noteworthy. Obituaries are in the *Atlanta Constitution* and the *Savannah Morning News*, 18 Aug. 1880.

KENNETH H. WILLIAMS

JOHNSON, Hiram Warren (2 Sept. 1866–6 Aug. 1945), governor of California and U.S. senator, was born in Sacramento, California, the son of Grove L. Johnson, a lawyer and politician, and Ann Williamson de Montfredy. The Johnsons arrived in Sacramento from upstate New York in 1865. A Republican, Grove Johnson staunchly supported the political interests of the Southern Pacific Railroad, the state's most powerful corporation. Hiram Johnson entered the University of California at Berkeley in 1884 but dropped out in 1887 to marry Minerva "Minnie" McNeal. They had two sons.

After studying law in his father's office, Johnson was admitted to the bar in 1888. He later called himself "a natural rebel," and he first rebelled against his father. For a time, he and his brother Albert practiced law with their father and helped run his political campaigns. They opened their own law office in 1897, however, and soon broke with their father politically, too. In 1902, they moved their practice to San Francisco. Albert, an alcoholic, died in 1907, but Hiram quickly emerged as a prominent litigator.

In 1906 and 1907, Johnson served as an assistant district attorney in the San Francisco graft prosecution, aiding special prosecutor Francis Heney in trying bribery cases involving city officials elected by the Union Labor party. In 1908, when Heney was shot, Johnson took over as chief prosecutor, securing the conviction of Abraham Ruef, *éminence grise* of the Union Labor party, on charges of bribing members of the city's board of supervisors.

Johnson's work in the graft prosecution attracted the state's Lincoln-Roosevelt League (progressive Republicans), who convinced him to seek the Republican nomination for governor in 1910. An accomplished orator, Johnson conducted a vigorous statewide campaign, vowing to "kick the Southern Pacific out of politics." He led the reformers to victory and then set out to enact their platform.

As governor, Johnson established a record of reform unmatched in the state's history. A leading journalist called it a "political revolution." In 1911 and 1913, he and the legislature approved regulation of railroads and other public utility corporations; conservation measures; the initiative, referendum, and recall; woman suffrage; nonpartisan election of judicial officials, school officials, and local officials through the county level; administrative reorganization; employer's liability and workman's compensation laws; a child-labor law; the eight-hour day for women workers; creation of state commissions on industrial welfare, industrial accidents, and immigration and housing; local option on the sale of alcohol; and restrictions on gambling and brothels. The 1911 legislature created a state Board of Control, and Johnson's appointees to it launched a vigorous campaign to eliminate graft, inefficiency, and favoritism from state agencies.

These accomplishments attracted national attention. An early supporter of Theodore Roosevelt (1858–1919) for the 1912 Republican presidential nomination, Johnson bolted when William Howard Taft was nominated. He helped to create the Progressive party as a vehicle for Roosevelt to seek the presidency, and the new party nominated him for vice president. He waged a spirited campaign, but his combative personality brought him close to resigning his nomination over a logistical dispute with the campaign staff. In California, Johnson's allies took over the Republican party and denied Taft a place on the ballot; Roosevelt carried the state by a narrow margin.

The failure of Roosevelt's campaign nationally produced several repercussions in California. Reasoning that Roosevelt had lost some support in California for appearing insufficiently hostile to Asian immigration, Johnson and his supporters strengthened their own anti-Asian credentials by approving a 1913 law designed to prevent Asian immigrants from owning land. Johnson also faced a decision regarding his future party affiliation. The 1913 legislature amended the primary law to permit cross-filing, allowing candidates to seek the nomination of more than one party. Johnson, however, ran for reelection in 1914 only as a Progressive. Against both Democratic and Republican opponents, he won by a comfortable margin, due partly to solid labor support.

With the collapse of the national Progressive party in 1916, Johnson returned to the Republican party to run for the U.S. Senate. In the face of opposition from conservative Republicans, he won both the Progressive and Republican primaries. As before, he characterized the campaign as a struggle that pitted "rotten big business and crooked politics against the very essence of democracy." Johnson won by more than two to one, but Charles Evans Hughes, the Republican and Progressive presidential candidate, narrowly lost California to Woodrow Wilson. Some charged that Johnson abandoned Hughes, but the crucial support for both Johnson and Wilson seems to have come from organized labor.

Johnson cast his first Senate vote in favor of declaring war on Germany, but he became increasingly critical of Wilson's policies. He staked out positions well to the left of most members of Congress, favoring government ownership of the railroads and steeply graduated income taxes and opposing efforts to limit dissent, especially the Sedition Act of 1918. Johnson also criticized Wilson's war aims, especially the boundary changes endorsed in the Fourteen Points. Early in 1919, he nearly secured a resolution to withdraw American troops from Russia.

In 1919 Johnson took a prominent place among the "irreconcilables"—those senators who opposed the League of Nations in any form. In September 1919, when Wilson set out on a cross-country speaking tour in support of the league, Johnson followed him from city to city denouncing it. League membership, he argued, would permit American soldiers to be sent into combat without the consent of Congress and would "pledge your sons and your sons' sons to maintain and preserve for all time the present governments of the little nations we are setting up in Europe and the present governments and boundaries of the British and the Japanese Empires." Through the rest of his life, Johnson remained identified as a staunch isolationist. He resented that label, however, and insisted that he wanted only to separate the United States from "Europe's politics" and "Europe's wars."

In 1920 Johnson sought the Republican presidential nomination, but his campaign suffered from disorganization and lack of funds. Proclaiming himself the only progressive in the race, he attacked the other candidates as tools of bosses or moneyed interests. He focused on the relatively few presidential primaries, entered twelve, won seven, and collected far more popular votes than any of his rivals. A poll of *Literary Digest* readers shortly before the convention put him second in popularity behind Leonard Wood. Johnson placed third in initial balloting, but his attacks on party conservatives made him unacceptable as a compromise candidate when the convention deadlocked. Several other candidates offered him the vice presidential nomination, but he refused.

Throughout the 1920s, Johnson made little impact on national policy. He focused on foreign policy, where he continued to oppose the League of Nations, tried to defeat most of the results of the Washington Conference of 1921 (especially the Four Power Treaty, which he feared as committing the United States to an alliance with Britain, Japan, and France), and repeatedly attacked American participation in the World Court. In 1922 he made certain that California's agricultural products were well protected by the Fordney-McCumber Tariff, and he kept them protected in the Smoot-Hawley Tariff in 1930. He proposed a national presidential primary, gave tepid support to proposals by other Senate progressives, opposed the confirmations as chief justice of William Howard Taft in 1921 and Charles Evans Hughes in 1930, and despaired privately that Washington lacked leaders of vision or courage.

In 1922, when Johnson ran for reelection to the Senate, he confronted a strong opponent in the Republican primary and lost some previous progressive supporters who now opposed his relentless isolationism. Nevertheless, a speaking tour brought him victory in the Republican primary and a large majority in the general election. The death of President Warren G. Harding encouraged him to seek the Republican presidential nomination in 1924, but his badly organized campaign presented few issues beyond his own integrity and isolationism. He won only one primary and even lost California. He sat out the general election, supporting neither Republican Calvin Coolidge nor Progressive Robert La Follette (1855–1925).

Johnson could count only one significant legislative accomplishment during his first twelve years in the Senate. In the early 1920s he joined with Congressman Philip Swing in proposing to dam the Colorado River at Boulder Canyon as a means of preventing flood damage, generating cheap, publicly owned electrical power, and extending irrigation. Opposition came especially from electrical power companies (he called them the "Power Trust") and, Johnson thought, from Commerce Secretary Herbert Hoover (1874–1964). Success finally came in 1928, and Boulder Dam (later renamed Hoover Dam) became a prototype for similar projects during the New Deal.

From 1920 onward, Johnson considered Hoover as his major political opponent in California. In 1928, Hoover was the Republican presidential nominee when Johnson came up for reelection; the two agreed, through an intermediary, not to interfere in each other's campaign. The next year, however, with Hoover in the White House and the nation entering a major depression, Johnson unleashed his vitriol on his fellow Californian. Urged by Republican progressives and prominent isolationists to seek the Republican nomination against Hoover in 1932, he refused, announced his support for Franklin D. Roosevelt in late October, and undertook a speaking tour on his behalf.

Roosevelt, grateful for Johnson's support, asked him to serve as secretary of the interior. Johnson declined, preferring to keep the "absolute freedom of action" that the Senate permitted him, but he supported nearly all early New Deal measures. He and Minnie were also regular social visitors at the White House, and Roosevelt consulted him on policy. When Johnson came up for reelection in 1934, he received Roosevelt's endorsement and easily won both the Republican and Democratic nominations.

As events in Europe began to suggest the possibility of conflict there, Johnson found additional support for his isolationism. In 1934 he secured passage of the Johnson Act, prohibiting loans to any nation that had defaulted on its World War I debt to the United States. Despite misgivings, Roosevelt signed the measure. In 1935 Johnson led the successful fight against an administration proposal to join the World Court. He also supported legislation later in the 1930s designed to maintain neutrality.

The 1934 election proved the high point in relations between Johnson and Roosevelt. Concerned about the growth of both federal expenditures and presidential power, Johnson nonetheless continued to support New Deal measures through 1935. In June 1936 he suffered a severe stroke that required long recuperation. Anxious about Roosevelt's foreign policy but still supportive of his domestic policy, Johnson used his health as reason to stay out of the campaign. He did vote for Roosevelt. Roosevelt's proposal in 1937 to increase the size of the Supreme Court crystallized all Johnson's doubts: he called it a "sinister grasp of power." Increasingly embittered, he opposed all subsequent New Deal proposals.

When war threatened in Europe in 1939, Roosevelt asked Congress to repeal the arms embargo provisions in the Neutrality Act of 1937. Johnson joined William Borah in leading the Senate opposition. Initially successful, they confronted a more difficult task when war actually erupted and Roosevelt repeated his request. The Neutrality Act of 1939 repealed the arms embargo, but Senate isolationists, including Johnson, loaded the measure with other provisions intended to keep the nation out of war. He supported military and naval expenditures but opposed conscription in 1940.

Johnson sought a fifth term in 1940. Although his health limited his usual campaign activities, he easily won both Republican and Democratic nominations. Critical of the foreign policy positions of Wendell Willkie, the Republican presidential candidate, he nonetheless made a national radio address on Willkie's behalf, in which he emphasized the dangers to democracy posed by a third term for Roosevelt.

In 1941, as ranking Republican on the Foreign Relations Committee, Johnson organized the unsuccessful opposition to Roosevelt's lend-lease proposal. Thereafter Johnson had no significant role in the Senate. He voted for war after the Japanese attacked Pearl Harbor, but his declining health limited his activities.

After a second stroke in 1943, he never returned to full participation in the Senate. In 1945 he cast his final Senate vote, in committee, against American participation in the United Nations. He died soon after in Bethesda Naval Hospital, Bethesda, Maryland.

The political career of Hiram Johnson spanned the two most significant eras of political change during the first half of the twentieth century—progressivism and the New Deal. Throughout his long political career, Johnson always proclaimed himself to be the champion of the people, standing tenaciously against political corruption and big business. As governor, he led the California legislature in two of its most productive sessions; his support for organized labor and for extreme restrictions on political parties moved him well beyond the regulatory programs and efficiency efforts characteristic of most who called themselves progressive. As a U.S. senator, however, he seemed temperamentally incapable of joining any bloc of like-minded legislators and increasingly became a crusty loner. Throughout his Senate career he fought against American participation in any multilateral international endeavor, which he often equated with protection of the interests of bankers or of British and Japanese imperialism. Johnson's early support for the New Deal turned to opposition because of his concern over centralization of power and foreign policy issues. In this, he was characteristic of a number of progressives.

• The Hiram W. Johnson Papers are at the Bancroft Library, University of California, Berkeley. The most important are published in facsimile as Robert E. Burke, ed., *The Diary Letters of Hiram Johnson, 1917–1945* (7 vols., 1983). The most complete treatment of Johnson's career is Richard Coke Lower, *A Bloc of One: The Political Career of Hiram W. Johnson* (1993). There is also an interesting psychobiography, John James Fitzpatrick III, "Senator Hiram W. Johnson: A Life History, 1866–1945" (Ph.D. diss., Univ. of Calif., Berkeley, 1975). No thorough published biography is available, but short treatments are in Michael A. Weatherson and Hal Bochin, *Hiram Johnson: A Bio-Bibliography* (1988), and in the introductory volume to Burke, ed., *Diary Letters*. For Johnson's governorship, see Spencer C. Olin, Jr., *California's Prodigal Sons: Hiram Johnson and the Progressives, 1911–1917* (1968), and George E. Mowry, *The California Progressives* (1951). For Johnson's later Senate career, see Ronald L. Feinman, *Twilight of Progressivism: The Western Republican Senators and the New Deal* (1981). Weatherson and Bochin's work includes the most complete list of Johnson's writings and speeches and works about Johnson.

ROBERT W. CHERNY

JOHNSON, Howard Dearing (2 Feb. 1896–20 June 1972), restaurateur and franchise pioneer, was born in Boston, Massachusetts, the son of John Hayes Johnson, a cigar wholesaler, and Olive Bell Wright. In 1902 the family moved to the village of Wollaston (now part of Boston) to enjoy the amenities of suburban life. Johnson's parents were indulgent but demanding. His father, a firm advocate of an independent and ultravigorous lifestyle and fearful that his only son was being coddled by his mother and three sisters, took a strong hand in shaping his son's childhood.

Sometimes the results were unexpected, such as when young Johnson asserted his independence and refused to continue his formal education beyond grammar school.

Johnson worked full time in the family business from age sixteen, when he left school, to 1917, when the United States entered World War I. Johnson enlisted in the Twenty-sixth (Yankee) Division and served in France. After the war he returned to the cigar business. Later in life Johnson reminisced fondly about his carefree days spent working the East Coast out of his bright yellow Stutz Bearcat. Those days came to an end with the sudden death of his father in 1922 and Johnson's discovery that the business was deeply in debt.

For the next three years Johnson struggled to restore the business to prosperity, all the while becoming more convinced that the shift in public tastes toward cigarettes and the growth of cigar company chain stores had doomed independent wholesalers to gradual extinction. Accordingly, Johnson began looking for a business with better prospects. He found it in 1925 when he purchased the local drugstore/newsstand where he had been moonlighting. The store was debt-bound, but Johnson believed it held promise because of its location near the train station and the newspaper delivery franchise it controlled. After some bargaining the owner agreed to sell the store for its debts and loan Johnson $2,000 to help him get established.

Under Johnson's near-constant coaxing the store quickly became profitable, raising Johnson's net worth to roughly $30,000 by the mid-1920s. Despite this, Johnson was intermittently uneasy about his future. Recalling the fragility of his father's success and how he had been hurt by suppliers who were unwilling to maintain the quality of the cigars sold under the Johnson name, he was determined to gain as much control as practical over the quality of goods sold from his store.

Johnson began with the ice cream sold at his soda fountain. First, he bought the recipe of the most popular ice cream vendor in town. The secret was an exceptionally high butterfat content. Next he bought a second-hand freezer and hired an ice cream maker from Boston to teach him how to make his ice cream in volume. By the end of summer Johnson was starting to get a reputation beyond Wollaston. Reportedly on the advice of his accountant, who informed him that ice cream was the most profitable part of his business, Johnson began to expand. Over the next few summers he sold ice cream and soda out of seaside shacks to tourists. By 1928 his gross income was nearly a quarter of a million dollars. In 1929 he opened his first full-service restaurant, which lost nearly $50,000 in its first year because of the combined effects of Johnson's inexperience and the start of the Great Depression.

By the mid-1930s, however, the restaurant was profitable, the ice cream business was still growing, and Johnson was ready for a major expansion. The only thing he lacked was adequate capital. The depression had made bankers reluctant to loan to restaurants, which traditionally experienced exceptionally high failure rates, so Johnson was forced to look elsewhere.

Johnson found his solution in franchising. In 1935 a friend approached him about building another Howard Johnson's Restaurant (Johnson then had more than a dozen outlets, mostly seaside ice cream and hot-dog stands) in Orleans, a little village catering to the tourist business. Johnson liked the location but lacked the funds to build. Instead, he suggested that the friend, Reginald Sprague, open a Howard Johnson's Restaurant himself, with Johnson providing his name and design, along with full training and assistance. In exchange Johnson received the exclusive right to supply Sprague's restaurant and set standards. The restaurant was an immediate success, and the profits it and other franchisees provided allowed Johnson to expand his own operations. By 1939 there were 107 Howard Johnson's, most owned by franchisees, operating along the highways of the East Coast.

The key to Johnson's success in the 1930s was his ability to maintain strict control over the quality of goods sold through his stores. He did this by producing virtually everything needed in his restaurants. This, in turn, enabled him to create nearly identical outlets—serving nearly identical meals—far more effectively than his less well organized competitors. This also meant that when a franchisee joined Howard Johnson's they got not only a well-known name but aid in finding a site and designing their building as well as complete training and supply assistance. From the customers' point of view this meant that as they traveled the East Coast they could be assured of a uniform product in familiar surroundings. Johnson credited his decision to pioneer on the highway rather than staying downtown to his years spent traveling for his father.

Johnson had barely established a national reputation when the United States entered World War II. The accompanying travel restrictions nearly destroyed the business. It recovered and in fact continued to grow by shifting to catering, particularly at military training centers and war plants. After the war this left Johnson, with his expanded food-processing facilities, well placed to shift back to the highway. Driven by the growth of leisure and travel, Johnson's expansion kept pace with the rapidly burgeoning highway system during the postwar years.

In 1959, when Johnson retired, more than 550 Howard Johnson Restaurants and Motor Lodges, with their trademark "28 Flavors of Ice Cream," distinctive orange-and-blue color scheme, and reputation for catering to the middle-class family traveler, had made Johnson nationally famous as the "Host of the Highways." Although officially retired, he remained active in the business until his death. Johnson had married four times. He married his third wife, Bernice Manley, in the 1920s. They divorced in the 1930s. He married Marjorie Smith in the 1940s. Johnson had two children. He died in New York City.

• Johnson's personal and business papers no longer exist. For good, brief treatments of Johnson's life, see "The Howard Johnson Restaurants," *Fortune*, Sept. 1940, pp. 82, 84, 86, 94, 96, 99; Jessie Rainsford Sprague, "He Had an Idea," *Saturday Evening Post*, 2 Nov. 1940, pp. 34, 70–72, 74; Gordon Gaskill, "That Wild Johnson Boy," *American Magazine*, Mar. 1941, pp. 34–35, 127–28; Jack Alexander, "Host of the Highways," *Saturday Evening Post*, 19 July 1958, pp. 16–17, 48–50; the editors of *Nation's Business*, *Lessons of Leadership* (1968); and Theresa Howard, "Howard Johnson," *Nation's Restaurant News*, Feb. 1996, pp. 85, 88. An obituary is in the *New York Times*, 21 June 1972.

THOMAS S. DICKE

JOHNSON, Hugh Samuel (5 Aug. 1882–15 Apr. 1942), army officer and government administrator, was born in Fort Scott, Kansas, the son of Samuel L. Johnson (originally Johnston), a lawyer and rancher, and Elizabeth Mead. Seeking better economic opportunities, his family moved successively to Greenburg, Emporia, Greenwich, and Wichita, Kansas, before finally settling in 1893 in Alva, Oklahoma, in the newly opened Cherokee Strip. There Johnson grew up on the "frontier," attended Northwestern Normal School (1897–1899), and in 1899 won admission to West Point.

Commissioned in 1903, Johnson served with the First Cavalry in a variety of assignments, including disaster relief following the San Francisco earthquake, a tour in the Philippines (1907–1909), and national park duty in Yosemite and Sequoia. While in service, he also wrote and published two boys' adventure books (*Williams of West Point* in 1908 and *Williams on Service* in 1910) and some thirty short stories about military life. The latter appeared in popular magazines such as *Century*, *Collier's*, *Everybody's*, *Scribners*, and *Sunset* and for a time earned Johnson substantial financial rewards. In 1914 he was selected for legal training at the University of California Law School and, following his graduation in 1916, served briefly with the John J. Pershing expedition to Mexico before being transferred to the legal staff of the Bureau of Insular Affairs. In 1904 he married Helen Leslie Kilbourne; they had one child.

During World War I Johnson rose to the rank of brigadier general and became an important figure in war mobilization. In 1917 he worked with General Enoch Crowder to develop and implement the Selective Service System, taking credit particularly for the decisions to involve local voting precincts in a mass registration process and to establish broad classifications concerning availability for induction. For these contributions he later received the Distinguished Service Medal. In 1918, as army representative on the War Industries Board (WIB) and head of a new Purchase and Supply Branch, he helped to organize the institutional network coordinating military procurement with WIB operations. In this regard, he was particularly responsible for regularized consultation and increasingly efficient interaction between the WIB's commodity sections and the army's newly established commodity committees, an arrangement that not only epitomized the war-induced intertwining of the military and industrial sectors but also pointed toward the kind of corporatist economic planning that Johnson would espouse later.

In 1919 Johnson resigned from the army and became an executive with the Moline Plow Company. Subsequently, he also worked with George Peek to develop and promote the McNary-Haugen scheme of agricultural relief, under which farm surpluses were to be dumped abroad to guarantee American farmers fair or "parity" prices in domestic markets. A law to implement the scheme was blocked by presidential vetoes in 1927 and 1928. In 1927 Johnson became Bernard Baruch's economic investigator and assistant, a position that he held in 1932 when he became the "Baruch man" on Franklin D. Roosevelt's brain trust.

In 1933 Johnson helped to write the National Industrial Recovery Act and was chosen by Roosevelt to administer the system of fair-trade codes to be developed under the law. In part, the program was an attempt to resurrect the system of business-government cooperation once administered by the WIB, utilizing it in particular to curb the "destructive competition" thought to be undercutting business profitability and mass purchasing power. In the economic and political conditions of 1933–1934, the resurrected system worked badly and tended in practice to produce market restrictions that delayed recovery rather than promoted it.

Of the New Deal's top administrators, Johnson was one of the most colorful. Powerfully built, brusque in demeanor, skilled in vituperative invective, and given to fits of "demonic activity," he tried to invoke the war spirit of 1917 and project the image of a tough-minded troubleshooter cutting through the "guff" to get things done. Yet "Old Iron Pants" was also capable of imaginative theorizing, emotional evangelism, and maudlin sentimentality. Baruch had warned that Johnson was too "dangerous and unstable" to be a "number-one man," and this proved prophetic. As administrator of the National Recovery Administration (NRA), charged with resolving its confusing contradictions and policy conflicts, he swung from excitement to despair to escape into alcohol, all the while demonstrating a striking incapacity to sustain decisions or develop coherent policies. On minimum price fixing, for example, he endorsed directives seeking to eliminate it as bad policy but then ruled that codes already containing such a provision were exempt from the directives. On labor policy, he vacillated between support for collective bargaining and support for a labor-management partnership implemented through company unions. In September 1934, as criticism of the new code system mounted and disillusionment with its brand of "industrial self-government" became widespread, Roosevelt eased Johnson out, replacing him with an administrative board.

Following his departure from the NRA, Johnson wrote his memoirs, served briefly as head of the Works Progress Administration in New York City, and began a new career as a syndicated columnist and radio commentator. Initially he supported Roosevelt, but he was not happy with the policy changes of 1935 and 1936, especially with the revival of an antitrust approach, the mounting federal deficit, the resort to "made-work," and the restriction of agricultural production. These policies, he believed, were misguided departures from the New Deal as originally conceived. After mid-1937 his "Hugh Johnson Says" became increasingly critical of the president, the "dictatorship" he was allegedly trying to establish, and his "entanglement" of the United States in foreign affairs. In 1940 Johnson worked to elect Wendell Willkie and helped to launch the America First Committee, and as war approached Roosevelt saw to it that Johnson's reserve commission was not renewed. Johnson's death came shortly thereafter. Ill with pneumonia, he died in his apartment at the Wardman Park Hotel in Washington, D.C.

In histories of the New Deal, Johnson is remembered chiefly for his colorful invective, personal peccadilloes, and an administrative performance that helped to discredit the ideas of industrial self-government and business-government partnership. Seen in longer perspective, his career also reflected the emergence of an American corporatism, which, by consigning social duties to business organizations and helping them to cooperate for public purposes, could allegedly combine the virtues of free enterprise and national planning. From 1917 through 1934 he participated in both the successes and failures of this project and thus helped to shape what would become a new but unsettled component of U.S. political economy.

• The bulk of Johnson's personal papers was destroyed by a storm, and those surviving are privately held. His memoirs, useful but sometimes misleading, were published under the title *The Blue Eagle from Egg to Earth* (1935). A competent, full-scale biography is John Kennedy Ohl, *Hugh S. Johnson and the New Deal* (1985). See in addition the character sketches in Unofficial Observer, pseud. (John F. Carter), *The New Dealers* (1934), and Arthur M. Schlesinger, Jr., *The Coming of the New Deal* (1959); the appraisal by Matthew Josephson, "The General," *New Yorker*, 18 Aug. 1934, pp. 21–25; 25 Aug. 1934, pp. 23–28; and 1 Sept. 1934, pp. 22–28; and Ohl, "General Hugh S. Johnson and the War Industries Board," *Military Review* 55 (May 1975): 35–48. An obituary is in the *New York Times*, 16 Apr. 1942.

ELLIS W. HAWLEY

JOHNSON, Jack (31 Mar. 1878–10 June 1946), the first African-American world heavyweight boxing champion, was born Arthur John Johnson in Galveston, Texas, the son of Henry Johnson, a janitor and former slave, and Tiny (maiden name unknown). Johnson's parents were poor, churchgoing people. He received five or six years of elementary schooling and apparently left home several times during his youth. However, he always returned to live with his parents in Galveston, where he worked on the docks. His first known boxing experience was in "battle royals," in which several black youths were placed in the ring simultaneously and flailed away until only one remained. By

1899 he had engaged in a number of orthodox, but obscure, professional matches and was gaining a local reputation as a boxer.

In 1899 Johnson went to Chicago, where he was beaten by a local heavyweight called Klondike. Hungry and unable to get fights, he returned to Galveston, gaining a series of triumphs there in 1900. After victories in Hot Springs, Arkansas, and Memphis, Tennessee, including a defeat of Klondike, he went back to Galveston. There, on 25 February 1901, he had his first important fight, with the famous white boxer Joe Choynski. Choynski knocked him out in three rounds, after which both men were arrested for illegal prizefighting and held in jail for twenty-four days. As a result of this experience, Johnson afterward fought entirely outside his native state.

Fighting in the western United States from 1901 to 1903, Johnson took on better opponents and grew to his adult dimensions of 6′1″ and about 200 pounds. He knocked out Jack Jeffries, the brother of reigning heavyweight champion Jim Jeffries; defeated Frank Childs, George Gardner, and Mexican Pete Everett; and won the so-called black heavyweight title by outpointing Denver Ed Martin in Los Angeles in twenty rounds on 3 February 1903. After successfully defending his title against Sam McVea in Los Angeles, he traveled east and won one fight in Boston and two in Philadelphia. Johnson soon returned to California, where he successfully defended his title against Martin and twice against McVea.

Johnson's string of victories ended with a loss on points to Marvin Hart in San Francisco on 28 March 1905. Except for a loss on disqualification to Joe Jeannette in November 1905, he would not be defeated again for another ten years. From 1905 to 1908 he won many fights, mostly in the East, also scoring two knockouts in Australia and knocking out Jim Flynn in San Francisco on 2 November 1907. As early as 1905 he was a recognized contender for the heavyweight championship of the world, but his attempts to engage in a title fight were unsuccessful despite wins over Sam Langford, Jeannette, Jim Jeffords, and the aged former champion Bob Fitzsimmons.

Between 1902 and 1908 Johnson's fighting style became fully developed. He was extremely agile afoot, and his unusual ability to avoid punches, or to stop them with his gloves, made him one of the best defensive fighters in boxing history. Usually he did not attack, being content to counter effectively with left jabs and right uppercuts. If struck with an effective blow, he would respond with slashing punches, punishing his opponent badly or knocking him out. Often he seemed lazy, and he was content to win on points when he could have scored a knockout. During this period Johnson began to exhibit a controversial personality. His attire, both on the street and in the ring, was flamboyant. He taunted his opponents while he fought them and engaged in repartee with spectators. He showed a preference for the company of white women and traveled openly with them. Despite his lack of education, he was imaginative, read widely, and spoke with wit.

Johnson was determined to force heavyweight champion Tommy Burns, a Canadian, into a title fight. To this end he acquired a skillful manager, Sam Fitzpatrick, and followed Burns to England and then to Australia. Finally Burns met him for the championship in Sydney on 26 December 1908. Johnson proved to be superior in every way to his much shorter opponent and won by a knockout in fourteen rounds after inflicting severe punishment, thereby gaining general recognition as world heavyweight champion.

In 1909 Johnson had two minor six-round fights in which no official decision was given, showing poor form because he was overweight and had not trained. On 8 September he easily defeated Al Kaufman on points in ten rounds, the title being at stake. On 16 October he fought middleweight champion Stanley Ketchel in Colma, California, a suburb of San Francisco, easily outpointing his much smaller opponent until the twelfth round. Suddenly Ketchel landed a powerful right behind Johnson's ear, knocking him down. When Johnson arose, Ketchel attacked impetuously, only to be met with a terrific right uppercut that knocked him out.

The heavyweight championship has always been regarded as the ultimate prize of pugilism, carrying with it prestige not accorded to the championships of the lighter divisions. During this time many white persons regarded it as a threat to their supposed racial superiority for the titleholder to be a black man. The former heavyweight champion James J. Jeffries, who had retired undefeated in 1905 but was still regarded by many whites as the rightful champion, was persuaded to come out of retirement at the age of thirty-five and challenge Johnson. They met in Reno, Nevada, on 4 July 1910 in a fight promoted by Tex Rickard. Johnson completely dominated the fight and scored a knockout in the fifteenth round. In the aftermath, serious interracial disturbances occurred, especially in the South, mostly caused by the attacks of whites on black persons.

Johnson's victory over Jeffries instantly made him a hero to the black community. Many blacks celebrated his victory openly, which often led to conflict with whites. Although Booker T. Washington tried to persuade Johnson to behave circumspectly, the heavyweight champion persisted in doing just as he pleased, and in a manner that only upset whites even more.

Johnson's defeat of Jeffries initiated the next stage of "the White Hope Era" in boxing. Promoters sought to discover white heavyweights who might successfully challenge Johnson. However, worthy opponents could not simply be produced on demand; it typically took years to develop a good fighter. Because of the lack of suitable contenders, Johnson did not defend his title in 1911 and made only one defense in 1912, defeating Jim Flynn by disqualification after being fouled in the ninth round in Las Vegas, New Mexico, on 4 July.

After his win over Jeffries, Johnson, who had settled in Chicago, broke with Sam Fitzpatrick and began conducting his own affairs. He continued to receive much unfavorable publicity in connection with his personal life. He developed a fondness for fast automobiles and reckless driving, and he was frequently in trouble with the law on this account. He continued to travel and live with white women, and in January 1911 he married one of them, Etta Terry Duryea. Their unhappy marriage ended with Etta's suicide in the living quarters of Johnson's Chicago saloon, the Café de Champion, on 11 September 1912.

Johnson's activities led to the passage of laws by the white establishment that were clearly directed against him or other blacks who might wish to emulate him. A federal law passed in 1912 barred the interstate transportation of fight films, the intended result being to restrict the showing of movies in which Johnson defeated white boxers. Ten states passed new laws against miscegenation. However, it was the Mann Act, passed by Congress in 1910, that proved to be Johnson's downfall. The Mann Act forbade the transportation of women across state or national borders "for the purpose of prostitution, debauchery, or for any other immoral purpose." On 18 October 1912 Johnson was charged with having abducted Lucille Cameron, a white woman who worked as his secretary and was involved with him sexually, in violation of the Mann Act. Cameron refused to testify against Johnson and soon married him. A second Mann Act case was brought against Johnson; the key witness was Belle Schreiber, who had traveled with him as his companion for several years and had suffered ill treatment at his hands. At the trial, held in May 1913, Johnson was found guilty and sentenced to a year in jail. With bond posted, he appealed, but soon afterward left the United States for England to avoid serving his sentence.

In exile in Paris, Johnson defended his title twice. On 13 December 1913 he fought Battling Jim Johnson, another black man, and was held to a ten-round draw in a very poor fight. He then won a twenty-round decision from Frank Moran, a "white hope," on 27 June 1914, but it was apparent from these two fights that Johnson's abilities were declining. Johnson left Europe after the outbreak of World War I and briefly went to Argentina and Mexico. Promoter Jack Curley arranged a 45-round championship fight between Johnson and Jess Willard in Havana, Cuba, on 5 April 1915. Johnson outboxed his much bigger opponent for many rounds, but he could not hurt him and his strength waned. In the twenty-sixth round Willard scored a knockout. Johnson later claimed to have thrown the fight, but his assertion was not widely credited.

Johnson remained in exile for five more years. He lived in Spain from late 1915 to 1919, having a few inconsequential fights and gradually descending into poverty. Then he went to Mexico, where he gained the protection of President Venustiano Carranza. In Mexico he fought more frequently and successfully, living comfortably in Tijuana, where he opened a saloon. When Carranza was murdered in 1920, Johnson's saloon was closed and he was declared persona non grata. In May he returned to the United States, surrendered to the authorities, and served his one-year sentence for violation of the Mann Act.

After being released from prison in Leavenworth, Kansas, in 1921, Johnson fought occasionally, becoming more and more inept. In his last two appearances, in April and May 1928, he was knocked out by Bearcat Wright in Topeka, Kansas, and by Bill Hartwell in Kansas City. In 1924 he divorced Lucille Cameron and married his third white wife, Irene Pineau. In his remaining years he made his living by managing and training boxers, performing bit parts in plays and operas, and making personal appearances such as lecturing at Herbert's Museum in Manhattan. Still fond of driving automobiles recklessly, he died near Raleigh, North Carolina, from injuries suffered after losing control of his car.

The egocentric Johnson always seemed to believe that his money and championship placed him beyond the law. He treated his numerous female companions as property and sometimes beat and humiliated them. At times he assumed a British accent and other affectations. On the other hand, he suffered greatly from the extreme racial prejudice of his day. Much of his behavior can be interpreted as a rebellion against the social restrictions to which he was subjected. Although white antagonism toward Johnson made it difficult for other blacks to compete for boxing titles until the 1930s, he was undoubtedly an important folk hero to African Americans. However, Johnson's concern was always with his personal right to equality with whites, and he never translated his attitude into a general concern for racial equality.

Johnson was rated by some boxing authorities, including the knowledgeable Nat Fleischer as late as 1968, as the best heavyweight champion in history. He had 107 known fights, losing only ten times, and he was elected to the International Boxing Hall of Fame in 1990.

• Johnson's record is in Herbert G. Goldman, ed., *The Ring Record Book and Boxing Encyclopedia*, 1986–1987 ed. (1987). The most authoritative biography is Randy Roberts, *Papa Jack: Jack Johnson and the Era of White Hopes* (1983), which also provides a good bibliography. Johnson's autobiography, *Jack Johnson—in the Ring and Out* (1927), was reprinted in 1969 under the title *Jack Johnson Is a Dandy*. The autobiography, although notorious for its factual unreliability, was clearly an important source for other biographies, notably Finis Farr, *Black Champion: The Life and Times of Jack Johnson* (1964), and Denzil Batchelor, *Jack Johnson and His Times* (1956). An obituary is in the *New York Times*, 11 June 1946.

LUCKETT V. DAVIS

JOHNSON, James (1 Jan. 1774–13 Aug. 1826), soldier, entrepreneur, and political leader, was born in Orange County, Virginia, the son of Robert Johnson, a frontier planter and political leader, and Jemima Suggett. Emigrating to Kentucky, the family experienced the dangers of frontier life. According to Leland W. Meyer's description, during a battle with American Indians at Bryant's Station (Lexington) in 1782, eight-year-old James extinguished fire arrows on cabin roofs while his mother led a group of women to resupply the station with water.

In 1783 the Johnson family established a settlement at Great Crossings, in Scott County, Kentucky. There Johnson married Nancy Payne of Lexington, and in 1797 they began a family that would include twelve children. The extended Johnson family farmed the rich bluegrass land and created businesses that brought family wealth and a prosperous community. As a young adult, James Johnson participated in local militia action against marauding American Indians and fought in the War of 1812. Though overshadowed in publicity by his brother Richard M. Johnson, he was one of the most successful leaders of volunteers in the War of 1812. A lieutenant colonel in a company of mounted riflemen raised by his brother, James Johnson led the main American force against General Henry Procter's British troops at the battle of the Thames. While Richard won fame for his alleged killing of the American Indian chief Tecumseh, James's troops won the battle and performed the less-romantic task of caring for the wounded and arranging their transportation back to Kentucky.

With the end of the war, James Johnson turned his hard-driving frontier spirit to entrepreneurship. Quick to see an opportunity, he carried on a myriad of businesses, many of them in partnership with his brother Richard, while also running one of the largest plantations in Kentucky. He developed paper, grist-, and gunpowder mills and served as a director of the first bank in his community. Johnson was one of the principal figures in the transportation industry in central Kentucky, and in 1817 he established a stagecoach company to connect Kentucky to Washington, D.C. His son Edward P. Johnson expanded the company's operations to several other frontier states. James Johnson also operated a steamboat line that carried passengers and produce between central Kentucky and the markets of Memphis and New Orleans. During the War of 1812, he had developed major business interests with the military, becoming a supplier for military posts in the West and provisioning Andrew Jackson's army at New Orleans. By 1818 Johnson was outfitting western military garrisons with nearly $200,000 worth of provisions per year.

In his role as a military supplier, Johnson's reputation became tainted by scandal as a result of the Yellowstone Expedition. In 1818 Richard Johnson used his political influence to secure for the Johnson brothers a contract with the Department of War to carry men and supplies to forts west of St. Louis. The Yellowstone Expedition became a fiasco as low water levels delayed the steamboats, stores spoiled, and other goods were seized by the courts because of unrelated lawsuits. The Johnsons, who had borrowed heavily to finance the expedition, were nearly bankrupted. Richard Johnson again used his political influence with Secretary of War John C. Calhoun and former president James Madison (1751–1836) to secure government advances to cover the debts. The expedition eventually cost the government nearly $250,000.

Political enemies of the Johnsons seized on this episode to accuse James Johnson of corruption, citing the letting of contracts without public notice and Richard Johnson's extensive use of political influence for private gain. Though employing practices that were certainly illegal by modern standards, the Yellowstone Expedition involved no theft of public funds, and the Johnson brothers suffered serious financial losses as a result of the episode. County records indicate that both brothers were forced to sell large tracts of land to cover debts claimed by the Bank of the United States. In 1822 a federal court indirectly relieved Johnson of charges that he had misused public funds by ordering the federal government to reimburse him for some charges that the government had earlier denied. Despite criticism in the East, the expedition was highly popular in the West. The newspaper *Argus of Western America* (Frankfort, Ky.) argued that the project helped redistribute much-needed currency to the West. Johnson's government contracts also meant additional revenue for many struggling businesses west of the Allegheny Mountains.

Johnson served his community in political positions and encouraged the growth of education and culture. Actively involved in the Baptist denomination, he encouraged missionary work among the American Indians and, along with his brother, developed a school at Great Crossings, the Choctaw Indian Academy. He supported societies that promoted agricultural innovation, industrial development, and western migration. Johnson also supported an early version of Henry Clay's American System. From 1803 to 1811 Johnson served in Kentucky's state senate, and in 1816 he was a candidate for governor before withdrawing for reasons that remain unclear. Starting his political career as a passionate Jeffersonian Republican, Johnson once challenged a Federalist journalist to a duel for making insulting remarks about Thomas Jefferson. In the political crisis brought on by the panic of 1819, Johnson broke with the Kentucky elite by demanding state aid to debtors. The "relief" issue and his ongoing business disputes with the Bank of the United States undoubtedly moved Johnson and his brother Richard toward the political circles of Jackson. James Johnson also helped establish and maintain the political alliances at home that were necessary to his brother's political career in Washington, D.C. He himself served one term in the U.S. House of Representatives, from 4 March 1825 until his death in Washington.

While James Johnson has often been overshadowed by his brother Richard, in actuality the two brothers were partners in military, business, and political matters. Intent on carving a fortune and a civilization out of the frontier, Johnson was a motivating force in the development of the first American West.

• Johnson's activities can be traced in the Fayette County (Ky.) deed books; the Scott County (Ky.) deed books; and *The Johnson Family: A Genealogy* in the Kentucky Room,

Scott County Public Library. See also Leland W. Meyer, *The Life and Times of Colonel Richard M. Johnson of Kentucky* (1932), and J. Winston Coleman, Jr., *Stage-Coach Days in the Bluegrass* (1935).

LINDSEY APPLE

JOHNSON, James Price (1 Feb. 1894–17 Nov. 1955), jazz and popular pianist, composer, and songwriter, was born in New Brunswick, New Jersey, the son of William H. Johnson, a store helper and mechanic, and Josephine Harrison, a maid. Johnson's mother sang in the Methodist church choir and was a self-taught pianist. He later cited popular songs and African-American ring-shout dances at home and local brass bands in the streets as early influences. When his mother's piano was sold to help pay for their move to Jersey City in 1902, Johnson turned to singing, dancing, and playing the guitar but played piano whenever possible. In 1908 the family moved to Manhattan, at which point he enrolled at P.S. 69, and in 1911 the family moved uptown.

Johnson got his first job as a pianist in Far Rockaway, New York, in the summer of 1912. He so enjoyed the work that he decided not to return to school, and in the fall he got other engagements in Jersey City and then in Manhattan. He studied the European piano tradition with Bruto Giannini from about 1913 to 1916 while also absorbing the skills of the finest ragtime pianists, among whom he singled out Abba Labba (Richard McLean), Luckey Roberts, and—in the summer of 1914—Eubie Blake, who recalled Johnson's ability to play "Troublesome Ivories" perfectly after hearing it twice. Johnson was also composing rags that helped him win a piano contest in Egg Harbor, New Jersey, and he may have already developed a version of "Carolina Shout." He had certain advantages over his rivals, as he recalled in an interview with Tom Davin:

I was born with absolute pitch. . . . I played rags very accurately and brilliantly. . . . I did . . . glissandos in sixths and double tremolos. These would run other ticklers out of the place at cutting sessions. They wouldn't play after me. . . . To develop clear touch and the feel of the piano, I'd put a bed sheet over the keyboard and play difficult pieces through it. . . . I was considered one of the best in New York—if not the best.

In the fall of 1914, while performing in Newark with singer and dancer Lillie Mae Wright, he met Willie "the Lion" Smith. Both were formidable pianists and shared the belief that entertainers must be elegantly attired and have a dramatic stage presence. They became best friends; their personalities were complementary, Johnson as deferential as Smith was outspoken. That same year Johnson formed a songwriting and publishing partnership with William Farrell, who taught him to write music. He began touring and writing for shows and dances.

From 1916 to 1927 he made piano rolls, initially documenting many of his own ragtime compositions.

He punched an as-yet-unperfected "Carolina Shout" for a roll issued in February 1918. Johnson married Wright in 1917; later in life they had two children and adopted a third, but initially Wright continued her career as an entertainer. In 1918 they toured in the *Smart Set Revue*. While performing in a nightclub in Toledo, Ohio, he studied composition at the local conservatory of music. He returned to New York late in 1919. Further piano rolls included a polished version of "Carolina Shout," issued in May 1921, and in September and October he made the definitive early recordings in the stride piano style: "The Harlem Strut," "Keep Off the Grass," and, again, "Carolina Shout."

Stride piano has often been described as an orchestral style and indeed, in contrast to boogie-woogie blues piano playing, it requires a fabulous conceptual independence (as if the individual player were an orchestra), the left hand differentiating bass and mid-range lines while the right supplies melodic lines. Nevertheless, the overriding characteristic of Johnson's playing was his percussive attack. For all his harmonic subtlety and melodic invention, and for all his aspirations to become an arty orchestral composer, he was at his finest when he attacked the piano as if it were a drum set. By comparison with classic ragtime piano, Johnson's stride playing on these early recordings was vigorously faster, far more abrasive melodically, leaning rhythmically toward the uneven and propulsive feeling that later came to be called "swing," denser and purposefully irregular in the left-hand patterns that would "stride" between wide intervals in the piano's bass range and chords in the mid-range, more dissonant harmonically (especially when he "crushed" adjacent notes), and open to improvisation.

"Carolina Shout" became the test piece for aspiring pianists in the stride style. Those who copied it included Smith, Duke Ellington, Cliff Jackson, Joe Turner, Claude Hopkins, and Fats Waller, who became Johnson's student after learning "Carolina Shout" from the piano roll. Smith and Waller subsequently were Johnson's closest colleagues and rivals as pianists at the rent parties that Harlem featured through the 1920s. By many accounts Johnson won the majority of these informal contests on the strength of his originality and keyboard technique, but surviving recordings give the honors to Waller.

Toward the end of 1922 Johnson became the musical director for the revue *Plantation Days*, a little-known touring show that took him to England from March to June 1923. In the summer he and lyricist Cecil Mack wrote the hit revue *Runnin' Wild*, which ran for more than five years on tour and on Broadway. *Runnin' Wild* presented Johnson's "Old Fashioned Love" and "Charleston," the latter perhaps *the* defining song of America in the 1920s.

In 1926 he wrote "If I Could Be with You (One Hour Tonight)" with lyricist Henry Creamer; it became a hit song in 1930. From late 1927 into 1928 he collaborated with Fats Waller, lyricists Andy Razaf and Creamer, and others in the creation of the revue *Keep Shufflin'*, for which he coauthored the song "'Sippi," directed the pit orchestra, and served as intermission pianist in duets with Waller. With Razaf in 1930 he wrote "A Porter's Love Song to a Chambermaid" for the *Kitchen Mechanic's Revue* at Smalls' Paradise in Harlem.

During this period Johnson recorded regularly in jazz bands and as a soloist. The latter activity yielded interpretations of his compositions "Riffs" (1929), "You've Got to Be Modernistic" (1930), and "Jingles" (1930), all carrying his playing to a new level of frenetically syncopated zaniness. He also accompanied recordings by singers as diverse as Ethel Waters ("Guess Who's in Town," 1928) and Bessie Smith. On "Preachin' the Blues" and "Backwater Blues" from his first session with Smith in 1927, Johnson somewhat toned down his busy pianistic style to conform to the musical aesthetics of the blues. On "Backwater Blues" he discarded the jagged and fast-changing oompahs of stride playing in favor of a loping, repeated boogie-woogie bass pattern. He is the pianist on the soundtrack and onscreen in Bessie Smith's movie *St. Louis Blues*, made in late June 1929.

Johnson also sought to create an African-American version of European classical music, which proved to be the least successful of his many endeavors. Like most popular and jazz musicians of his era, he was a miniaturist whose great talent lay in the subtle manipulation of nuances of surface detail, not in the construction of grand architectural schemes characteristic of European classical masterpieces. *Yamekraw: Negro Rhapsody*, composed in 1927, was performed at Carnegie Hall for a 1928 concert organized by W. C. Handy, but Johnson's commitment as music director of *Keep Shufflin'* prevented him from participating. Portions of the rhapsody were recorded and in 1930 made into a movie short, again without Johnson's participation.

Although careless living and hard drinking began to catch up with him in the 1930s, Johnson continued working in all these areas. Unfortunately, like Jelly Roll Morton, Johnson was so rigidly tied to early jazz and popular styles that he could not adapt when the swing era arrived, and many of his efforts were unpopular. Johnson wrote for musical revues as the genre grew stale, and he composed largely forgotten pieces whose titles used words testifying to his European classical aspirations: symphony, concerto, ballet, opera. Many scores have been lost.

With the revival of interest in traditional jazz that began in the late 1930s, Johnson was sought out once again. He figured prominently in the "Spirituals to Swing" concerts that John Hammond produced and recorded at Carnegie Hall in December 1938 and December 1939. He also recorded in a trio with clarinetist Pee Wee Russell and drummer Zutty Singleton in 1938, for trumpeter Frankie Newton's mixed swing and Dixieland group in January 1939, and with his own group, including trumpeter Henry "Red" Allen and trombonist J. C. Higginbotham, in March. On a few titles from these sessions, and particularly on "Blueberry Rhyme," recorded in June, Johnson plays with a lyricism and introspection quite different from his norm. In 1940 he led a band briefly, but in August he suffered the first of eight strokes.

Johnson's return to activity began in 1942, when the Brooklyn Civic Orchestra gave a concert of his "serious" works. He resumed playing in 1943, initially as a member of trumpeter Wild Bill Davison's band in Boston and New York and then as a freelance bandleader and pianist. After Waller's death in December 1943, Johnson joined guitarist Eddie Condon at Town Hall to perform Waller's tunes and his own music in a series of concerts extending into 1944. From August 1944 he engaged in stride piano contests with Willie "the Lion" Smith at the Pied Piper in Greenwich Village, but in December Johnson's ill health ended this now-legendary association.

He recorded prolifically during 1942–1944, and discs such as "Arkansaw Blues," "Carolina Balmoral," and "Mule Walk—Stomp" (all from late 1943) give no indication that the stroke affected his playing. He also recorded as a bandleader and as a sideman, including beautifully melodic performances on Waller's song "Squeeze Me" and the slow blues "Too Many Times," both from trumpeter Yank Lawson's session of December 1943.

In 1945 Johnson performed with Louis Armstrong, and he heard performances of his concert works at Carnegie Hall and Town Hall. He worked occasionally the next year but became chronically ill. In 1947 he became a regular on Rudi Blesh's radio show "This Is Jazz," which was broadcast nationally and recorded. He held assorted freelance jobs, including participation in Friday night jam sessions at Stuyvesant Casino and Central Plaza in downtown Manhattan from June 1948 to February 1949. Johnson suffered a massive stroke in 1951. Paralyzed, he survived financially on songwriting royalties. He died in New York City.

Apart from his tremendously important contributions to American stage and song of the 1920s via *Runnin' Wild* and "Charleston," Johnson's significance lies in his stature as the creator of a jazz piano style, stride, and as one of the greatest practitioners and composers in that style. In his lifetime, Johnson's stride piano style was further developed along original and highly personalized paths by Waller, Art Tatum, and Thelonious Monk, and it made its way into the jazz mainstream in, for example, numerous moments of stride playing that pianists and bandleaders Duke Ellington and Count Basie introduced into their performances.

• The most important source consists of two works published and bound together: a biography, Scott E. Brown, *James P. Johnson: A Case of Mistaken Identity*, and a catalog of recordings, Robert Hilbert, *A James P. Johnson Discography, 1917–1950* (1986). Brown supplies full listings of Johnson's known participation in stage productions and his output as a composer as well as an exhaustive bibliography of primary sources and material for further reading. Among these last items, Tom Davin's interview is particularly informative: "Conversations with James P. Johnson," *Jazz Review*, 2, no. 5 (1959): 14–17; 2, no. 6 (1959): 10–13; 2, no. 7 (1959): 13–15;

2, no. 8 (1959): 26–27; and 3, no. 3 (1960): 10–13, repr. in John Hasse, ed., *Ragtime: Its History, Composers, and Music* (1985), pp. 166–77. See also Frank Kappler's fine biography in the pamphlet accompanying the Time-Life boxed LP set *Giants of Jazz: James P. Johnson* (1981). Johnson's friend Willie "the Lion" Smith offered oft-quoted reminiscences in his book with George Hoefer, *Music on My Mind* (1964; repr. 1975). For detailed and informed description of Johnson's music, see Gunther Schuller, *Early Jazz: Its Roots and Musical Development* (1968), pp. 214–23; see also notes by Dick Wellstood with Willa Rouder, following Kappler's essay in the aforementioned LP set. Howard Rye extends Brown's research into Johnson's visit to England in "Visiting Fireman 13: 'The Plantation Revues,'" *Storyville* 133 (1988): 4–14. Obituaries are in *Down Beat*, 28 Dec. 1955, p. 12; and the *New York Times*, 18 Nov. 1955.

BARRY KERNFELD

JOHNSON, James Weldon (17 June 1871–26 June 1938), civil-rights leader, poet, and novelist, was born in Jacksonville, Florida, the son of James Johnson, a resort hotel headwaiter, and Helen Dillet, a schoolteacher. He grew up in a secure, middle-class home in an era, Johnson recalled in *Along This Way* (1933), when "Jacksonville was known far and wide as a good town for Negroes" because of the jobs provided by its winter resorts. After completing the eighth grade at Stanton Grammar School, the only school open to African Americans in his hometown, Johnson attended the preparatory school and then the college division of Atlanta University, where he developed skills as a writer and a public speaker. Following his graduation in 1894 Johnson returned to his hometown and became principal of Stanton School.

School teaching, however, did not satisfy his ambitions. While continuing as principal Johnson started a short-lived newspaper and then read law in a local attorney's office well enough to pass the exam for admission to the Florida state bar. He also continued to write poetry, a practice he had started in college. In early 1900 he and his brother Rosamond, an accomplished musician, collaborated on "Lift Every Voice and Sing," an anthem commemorating Abraham Lincoln's birthday. African-American groups around the country found the song inspirational, and within fifteen years it had acquired a subtitle: "The Negro National Anthem."

"Lift Every Voice and Sing" was not the only song on which the brothers collaborated. In 1899 the two spent the summer in New York City, where they sold their first popular song, "Louisiana Lize." In 1902 they left Jacksonville to join Bob Cole, a young songwriter they had met early on in New York, in the quickly successful Broadway songwriting team of Cole and Johnson Brothers. Over the next few years Johnson was largely responsible for the lyrics of such hit songs as "Nobody's Lookin' but de Owl and de Moon" (1901), "Under the Bamboo Tree" (1902), and "Congo Love Song" (1903).

In 1906 Johnson's life took another turn when, through the influence of Booker T. Washington, Theodore Roosevelt appointed him U.S. consul to Puerto Cabello, Venezuela. In 1909 he moved to a more significant post as consul in Corinto, Nicaragua. A year later he returned to the United States for a brief stay in New York City, where he married Grace Nail, a member of a well-established African-American family. They did not have children. In 1912 revolution broke out in Nicaragua. Johnson's role in aiding U.S. Marines in defeating the rebels drew high praise from Washington. He left the Consular Service in 1913; there would be, he felt, little opportunity for an African American in the newly elected Democratic administration of Woodrow Wilson.

Johnson maintained his literary efforts during this period. Several of his poems (including "Fifty Years," commemorating the anniversary of the Emancipation Proclamation) appeared in nationally circulated publications. In 1912 he published *The Autobiography of an Ex-Colored Man*, a novel whose central character, unlike Johnson, was light enough to "pass" as a white man; the book explores the young man's struggles to find his place in American society. Johnson returned to New York City in 1914, and he soon began a weekly column on current affairs for the *New York Age*, a widely distributed African-American newspaper.

In 1917 Johnson joined the staff of the interracial National Association for the Advancement of Colored People (NAACP). He worked as field secretary, largely responsible for establishing local branches throughout the South and for increasing overall membership from 10,000 to 44,000 by the end of 1918. In 1920 Johnson became the NAACP's first African-American secretary (its chief operating officer), a position he held throughout the 1920s.

Johnson was deeply committed to exposing the injustice and brutality imposed on African Americans throughout the United States, especially in the Jim Crow South. He labored with considerable success to put the NAACP on secure financial ground. He spent much time in Washington unsuccessfully lobbying to have Congress pass the Dyer Anti-Lynching Bill, legislation that would have made lynching a federal crime. Finally, Johnson was a key figure in making the NAACP a clearinghouse for civil-rights court cases; he collaborated closely with such noted attorneys as Moorfield Storey, Louis Marshall, and Arthur Garfield Hayes in a series of cases defending African-American civil rights and attacking the legal structure of segregation. In all these efforts he worked closely with Walter White, whom he brought into the NAACP as his assistant and who succeeded him as secretary, and W. E. B. Du Bois, the editor of *Crisis*, the NAACP monthly journal.

Johnson was probably better known in the 1920s for his literary efforts than for his leadership of the NAACP. He played an active role, as an author and as a supporter of young talent, in what has come to be called the Harlem Renaissance. Johnson urged writers and other artists to draw on everyday life in African-American communities for their creative inspiration. He played the role of a father figure to a number of young writers, including Claude McKay and Langston Hughes, whose often blunt prose and poetry drew condemnation from more genteel critics.

His own work during this period included a widely praised anthology, *The Book of American Negro Poetry* (1922), a volume that helped to give an identity to the "New Negro" movement. His continued interest in the African-American musical tradition found expression in two collections of spirituals that he and Rosamond brought out: *The Book of American Negro Spirituals* in 1925 and *The Second Book of American Negro Spirituals* in 1926. A year later Johnson published his poetic interpretation of African-American religion in *God's Trombones: Seven Negro Sermons in Verse*, a theme he first developed in "O Black and Unknown Bards" (1908). The year 1927 also saw the reissuing of *The Autobiography of an Ex-Colored Man*. Finally, Johnson published *Black Manhattan* (1930), the first history of African Americans in New York City.

In 1931 Johnson stepped down as secretary of the NAACP (though he remained on the association's board of directors) to become a professor at Fisk University. For the remainder of his life he spent the winter and spring terms in Nashville teaching creative writing and classes in American and African-American literature. The rest of the year the Johnsons largely spent in New York City. He remained active as a writer, publishing *Along This Way*, his autobiography, in 1933 and *Negro Americans, What Now?*, a work of social criticism, a year later. Johnson's unexpected death was the result of an automobile accident near Wiscasset, Maine.

Johnson took deserved pride in his accomplishments across a wide variety of careers: teacher, Broadway lyricist, poet, diplomat, novelist, and civil-rights leader. Though he suffered most of the indignities forced on African Americans during the Jim Crow era, Johnson retained his sense of self-worth; he proclaimed forcefully in *Negro Americans, What Now?* that "My inner life is mine, and I shall defend and maintain its integrity against all the powers of hell." The defense of his "inner life" did not mean withdrawal, but active engagement. Thus Johnson was a key figure, perhaps the key figure, in making the NAACP a truly national organization capable of mounting the attack that eventually led to the dismantling of the system of segregation by law.

Maintaining his "inner life" also led Johnson to write both prose and poetry that has endured over the decades. "Lift Every Voice and Sing," written a century ago, can still be heard at African-American gatherings, and the title phrase appears on the U.S. postage stamp issued in 1988 to honor Johnson. *The Autobiography of an Ex-Colored Man* has remained in print since its reissue in the 1920s, and it holds a significant place in the history of African-American fiction. *Along This Way*, also still in print after more than sixty years, is acknowledged as a classic American autobiography. Finally, *God's Trombones*, Johnson's celebration of the creativity found in African-American religion, has been adapted for the stage several times, most notably by Vinnette Carroll (as *Trumpets of the Lord*) in 1963.

• The James Weldon Johnson Papers in the Beinecke Library, Yale University is the single most important primary source for the study of Johnson's life. Two other important manuscript collections are the NAACP Collection and the Booker T. Washington Papers, both in the Library of Congress. The standard biography is Eugene Levy, *James Weldon Johnson: Black Leader, Black Voice* (1973). A briefer biography is Robert E. Fleming, *James Weldon Johnson* (1987). Sondra K. Wilson has edited a two-volume collection, *The Selected Writings of James Weldon Johnson* (2 vols., 1995), making available much of his newspaper and magazine work.

EUGENE LEVY

JOHNSON, John (5 Nov. 1741–4 Jan. 1830), New York Loyalist, was born near Amsterdam, New York, the son of Sir William Johnson, a British Indian agent, and Catherine Weisenberg, a runaway servant. As John Johnson's parents never married, he was illegitimate, but because of his father's great importance to the colony and the empire, both New Yorkers and royal officials ignored that fact, and John became William Johnson's heir. John attended school in Philadelphia for awhile, but his formal education ended in 1760. During a journey through America, Lord Adam Gordon met the Johnsons and offered to take John to England, introduce him to people of note, and otherwise widen his outlook. Sir William agreed to this chance to soften his son's rustic background. The trip resulted in a knighthood—secured by his father's influence—for John in November 1765 and much flattering attention from the nobility. Sir John Johnson returned to America in September 1767.

After his return to the Mohawk Valley, Johnson cohabited with Clarissa Putman. Although they had two children, Johnson's father refused to accept her as his son's legal wife because she came from a common background. Obeying his father, Johnson wed the aristocratic Mary Watts, one of "the Princesses of America" (Sullivan, vol. 7, p. 1144), on 29 June 1773; they would have fourteen children.

Johnson received some local appointive offices, as was appropriate for a man with his status. He commanded a mounted unit in the militia and in 1770 became a magistrate, but he showed no desire to take over Indian relations from his father. After Sir William's death in 1774, his nephew and son-in-law, Guy Johnson, handled most of that job. By all appearances, Sir John preferred a "retired life" (Sullivan, vol. 11, p. 980) and would have lived out his days as a country gentleman who merely dabbled in politics if the American Revolution had not intervened.

By 5 January 1776 Johnson had volunteered his services to New York's royal governor, William Tryon. Distressed by revolutionary activity along the Mohawk, Johnson offered to raise a Loyalist regiment. Indeed, he had both eager officers and soldiers at hand; his tenants included Scottish Highlanders, who were British army veterans, and recent immigrants from Scotland and Ireland of the Roman Catholic faith, who also threw in their lot with the king. Johnson knew they needed funds and supplies before they could act, and although Tryon was enthused by his offer, the situation changed before anything could be done.

Attempting to neutralize Johnson, Continental army general Philip Schuyler confronted him with military force. On 17 January 1776 Johnson agreed to surrender his and his tenants' weapons, to remain near his home, and to stay neutral. By May 1776 Schuyler, suspicious of Johnson, had decided to seize him, but Johnson moved faster than the patriots. On 19 May Johnson deserted his property in Tryon County and fled to Canada.

During June 1776 Canada's governor, General Guy Carleton, made Johnson a lieutenant colonel, and he began trying to raise men for his "King's Royal Regiment of New York." Beyond his tenants, however, he found recruitment difficult. He even resorted to taking prisoners of war as recruits. On 10 February 1780 Carleton's successor, General Frederick Haldimand, commented that Johnson, despite his vigorous activity, had still experienced a recruiting failure. Nevertheless, Johnson commanded British forces during their victory at Oriskany (6 Aug. 1777).

Although Haldimand was not impressed by the military prowess of the "Royal Yorkers," as Johnson's men were sometimes called, a military objective was discovered at which they did excel—the destruction of Tryon County. During May 1780 Johnson led his troops in a devastating raid, destroying Caughnawaga and Johnstown and depriving the patriots of much food and other essentials. Many rescued Tories bolstered Johnson's ranks. In October 1780 Johnson reappeared to attack his old haunts, destroying Schoharie, Fort Hunter, and Stone Arabia and defeating patriot militia at Klock's Field (19 Oct. 1780). His terrifying partisan campaigns were very successful.

After journeying to Britain, in 1782 Johnson was commissioned a brigadier general. Finally fulfilling his father's hope, in 1782 he was placed in charge of Indian relations, because Guy Johnson had become enmeshed in financial irregularities. Sir John Johnson handled the task until his death.

Following the American Revolution, Johnson lived in Montreal and helped to settle exiled Loyalists at Cataraqui (now Kingston) in 1784. Named to the Council of Quebec (Lower Canada) in 1786, he tried to serve the interests of the exiles. During 1790 Johnson failed to obtain the lieutenant governorship of Ontario (Upper Canada), which went instead to John Graves Simcoe. Johnson died in Montreal.

• The Public Archives of Canada, Ottawa, has many Johnson letters, especially in the Frederick Haldimand Papers and Daniel Claus Papers. Copies of some of this material are at the Library of Congress, Washington, D.C., in its Claus papers and in the British Library's Haldimand papers. The Library of Congress also has transcripts of the John Blackburn Papers (British Library Additional Manuscript 24323), which include Johnson letters. James Sullivan et al., eds., *The Papers of Sir William Johnson* (14 vols., 1921–1965), and E. B. O'Callaghan, ed., *Documents Relative to the Colonial History of the State of New York*, vols. 7–8 (1856–1857), have letters by Johnson and referring to him. A biography is Earle Thomas, *Sir John Johnson: Loyalist Baronet* (1986). An obituary is in the *Montreal Gazette*, 7 Jan. 1830.

PHILIP RANLET

JOHNSON, John Albert (28 July 1861–21 Sept. 1909), newspaper editor and governor of Minnesota, was born in a log cabin near St. Peter on Minnesota's agricultural frontier, the son of Swedish immigrant parents Gustav Johnson, a farmer and blacksmith, and Caroline Christine Hedén. Because of his father's alcoholism and shiftlessness after the family had moved into the town of St. Peter, his mother supported the family by taking in washing. Johnson and his older brother Edward assisted her by delivering laundry to customers. Years later, after he had entered politics, his humble beginnings and youthful poverty worked to his advantage; his boosters freely likened his past to that of Abraham Lincoln.

When he was only thirteen years old Johnson quit school to work in a St. Peter grocery store. For the next twelve years he labored in various St. Peter businesses, including a general merchandise store and a drugstore. In the early 1880s he became a registered pharmacist and the sole supporter of his mother and younger siblings. Despite his heavy work schedule he read voraciously and participated in the town's debating society. In 1886 he moved to Decorah, Iowa, to work in a drugstore but soon returned to St. Peter as a clerk for a railroad construction company. His reputation for hard work, intelligence, and honesty attracted the attention of Henry Essler, the publisher of the *St. Peter Herald*, the town's only Democratic newspaper. With money advanced by family friends and community leaders, Johnson bought an interest in the paper and became its editor on 1 February 1887, abandoning his nominal Republicanism to accommodate the *Herald*'s editorial policy.

Through the newspaper Johnson became well known in his home community and beyond. An ardent civic booster, he joined the Knights of Pythias, helped organize programs at the St. Peter opera house, served as secretary of the Nicollet County Fair, assisted in his Presbyterian church's Sunday school programs, joined the local unit of the Minnesota National Guard, and spoke frequently to local groups and organizations. His membership in the NEYB (Nineteen Eligible Young Bachelors) ended when he married Elinor M. Preston, a parochial school teacher in St. Peter, in 1894. They had no children. Through his participation in the Minnesota Editors' and Publishers' Association he became acquainted with numerous editors who were invariably impressed by his talent as a speaker. In 1891 they chose him as the organization's secretary and two years later made him president.

Politically conservative, Johnson usually supported the policies of President Grover Cleveland. He thought the Democrats erred on two counts in 1896—running William Jennings Bryan and demanding free and unlimited coinage of silver. In 1898 Johnson was elected to the state senate and four years later was narrowly defeated for reelection in his predominantly Republican district. This defeat proved to be a blessing in disguise because it left him free to become the Democratic gubernatorial candidate in 1904. His backers, including many friendly country editors, promoted his nomination by acclamation at the Democratic state convention. The Democrats, who had won the governorship only twice in the 46-year history of the state, saw his charismatic personality and Scandinavian heritage as assets in an election where a bitter schism divided Republicans.

Johnson toured the state on a hectic speaking schedule, which entailed two to three speeches daily during the six-week campaign. Tall, handsome, and gentlemanly, he impressed listeners with his modesty, sense of humor, and common sense. An effort by some opponents, who interjected his family's background into the campaign, backfired. When asked what he had to say about reports of his father's drunkenness, he responded: "Nothing—it is true." In blunting the story that his mother had taken in washing, he said: "Took in washing? Yes, she did—until I was old enough to go out and earn something. But she never took in any washing after that" (Christianson, vol. 2, p. 291).

Benefiting from the Scandinavian vote and his opponent's abrasive personality, Johnson was elected by a margin of nearly 8,000 votes out of a total of 288,000, after a rigorous campaign devoid of major issues. It was clearly a personal rather than a party victory. The Republicans won every other elective state office, and Theodore Roosevelt, the Republican presidential candidate, carried the state by 160,000 votes. Johnson was easily reelected in 1906 and again in 1908. As governor he typified the mild reformism of the early Progressive Era. He proposed the election of nonpartisan judges, a state income tax, additional railroad regulation, and a workmen's compensation law. After instituting policies to curb fraudulent practices of insurance companies, he attracted national attention by chairing a conference formed by a number of states to consider the adoption of uniform insurance laws. As part of his insurance-reform effort he became involved with the International Policyholders' Committee based in Boston. Through this group he became a nationally recognized speaker and was first suggested as a presidential possibility by Thomas Lawson, the committee's leader. His national stature was enhanced in 1907 as a result of addresses in Philadelphia and Washington, D.C.

Various southern and eastern conservative party regulars and journalists urged Johnson to challenge Bryan for the presidential nomination in 1908. Although he refused to campaign actively, Johnson was nominated by the Minnesota delegation at the national convention. He attracted a scattering of support from other states, and after Bryan's defeat in the general election many Democrats nationally regarded him as their party's likely candidate in 1912. His sudden death in Rochester, Minnesota, as a result of his fourth intestinal surgery shocked the state and the nation because his long-standing health problems were not generally known. Thousands of mourners flocked to St. Peter for the funeral of the most popular state politician they had ever known.

• The Minnesota Historical Society, St. Paul, has the archival records of Johnson's governorship and a scrapbook of clippings on John Albert Johnson, comp. Fredrik Larsson. The standard scholarly biography is Winifred G. Helmes, *John A. Johnson, the People's Governor: A Political Biography* (1949). His personal secretary, Frank A. Day, collaborated with Theodore M. Knappen to write *Life of John Albert Johnson* (1910). For coverage of his career and gubernatorial administration in general Minnesota histories, see Theodore Christianson, *Minnesota: The Land of Sky-Tinted Waters* (5 vols., 1935), and William Watts Folwell, *A History of Minnesota* (4 vols., 1921–1930). For an analysis of Johnson's role in Progressive reforms, see Carl H. Chrislock, *The Progressive Era in Minnesota 1899–1918* (1971). A lengthy biographical sketch is in James H. Baker, *Lives of the Governors of Minnesota*, vol. 13: *Collections of the Minnesota Historical Society* (1908). Obituaries and related stories are in the *Minneapolis Tribune* and the *St. Paul Pioneer Press*, both 21, 22 Sept. 1909.

WILLIAM E. LASS

JOHNSON, Joseph French (24 Aug. 1853–22 Jan. 1925), educator and author, was born in Hardwick, Massachusetts, the son of Gardner Nye Johnson, a storekeeper, and Eliza French. When Johnson was seven his family moved to Illinois and settled in Aurora. There Johnson received his early schooling, including two years of high school, before matriculating at Clark Seminary, a local Methodist academy. Active in student activities, he graduated from Clark in 1872 and taught for a year at the Rockport (Illinois) Female Collegiate Institute. He entered Northwestern University in 1873 but transferred the following year to Harvard University, from which he graduated with an A.B. in 1878. While attending Harvard, Johnson spent the 1875–1876 academic year at the University of Halle in Germany, where he studied political economy and history in the company of fellow Harvard undergraduate and future college president Edmund J. James.

Johnson returned to the Midwest following graduation and took a teaching position at the Harvard School of Chicago. After three years there, he became a tutor for the son of noted Chicago retailer Marshall Field. After returning from a trip to Europe in the company of the younger Field, Johnson decided to embark on a career in journalism. He worked at the *Springfield Republican* (under Samuel Bowles) from 1881 until 1884, when he interrupted his latest career to spend a year as the superintendent of schools in Yazoo City, Mississippi. That same year he married Caroline Temperance Stolp of Aurora; they had two children. Johnson also worked for a period in Chicago with the Investors Agency, a firm that specialized in providing accurate financial data on various companies to potential investors. While at the agency, he employed fellow Auroran and future City National (Citibank) president Frank Vanderslip.

Johnson returned to journalism in 1887, becoming the financial editor of the *Chicago Tribune*. Still restless, he moved in 1890 to Spokane, Washington, where he founded the *Spokane Spokesman* with $5,000 in borrowed funds. After three years, he sold his fledgling enterprise and returned to academia. Having finally settled on his life's work, he was appointed associate professor of business practice at the University of Pennsylvania's Wharton School. Johnson developed financial courses that were practical in orientation during his tenure at the nation's first collegiate business school, and from 1895 to 1901 he also taught journalism. Johnson also found time to lecture on finance at Columbian (now George Washington) University in Washington, D.C., from 1900 to 1903.

In 1901 Johnson joined the faculty of the newly created (1900) School of Commerce, Accounts, and Finance at New York University. Serving initially as professor of political economy and school secretary, Johnson became dean of the school in 1903, following the 1902 death of the original dean, Charles Waldo Haskins. In his role as dean, circumstances served Johnson well. New York University was poised for rapid growth, and the increasing demand for academic instruction in business skills ensured that the School of Commerce would fully share in that growth. An initial enrollment of sixty-seven students, all of whom were enrolled in evening classes, grew within ten years to more than a thousand. By the time of Johnson's death, there were more than 5,000 students.

Forced by the necessity of the school's pioneer status to develop the curriculum from scratch, Johnson made sure that his program's offerings were broad in scope and content. Coursework in journalism appeared in 1910, with Johnson himself providing lectures during the 1910–1911 academic year. Instruction in politics began in 1912, the same year in which the day student division made its modest debut with sixty students. Faculty and guest lecturers included figures such as Vanderslip and poet and journalist Joyce Kilmer, all hand-picked by Johnson from among the elite of New York's business community. Johnson's belief that effective business instruction required involvement in both academia and the "real world" on the part of his instructors often made faculty recruitment difficult, and the school, along with the rest of the university, struggled with limited resources to meet the demands of NYU's rapid growth.

Despite these obstacles, Johnson managed to consistently raise his program's graduation standards. The school had originally offered evening students a three-year course leading to a bachelor of commercial science degree, but by 1917 that degree required four years for completion, and in 1926 the day division followed suit. Johnson's efforts reached their culmination in 1926, a year after his death, when the school began to grant the B.S. and moved into its own building on Washington Square.

In addition to fulfilling the demands of his NYU duties, Johnson honored a multitude of outside commitments. Active in the movement for financial reform, he served as secretary of the special currency committee of the New York Chamber of Commerce in 1906. Appointed in 1909 by Senator Nelson W. Aldrich's National Monetary Commission to investigate the Canadian banking system, Johnson undertook extensive field work in the spring of that year that resulted in the publication of *The Canadian Banking System* (1910). In 1912 he served on the Mayor's Commission on New Sources of Revenue for New York City and in the following year was a member of the Van Tuyl Commission to Revise the Banking Law of the State of New York.

Johnson was an organizer of the Alexander Hamilton Institute, which had as its goal the education of students in business and finance. He served as president of the institute from 1909 until his death and also edited its publications. He also served as an early editor of the *Journal of Accountancy* and was the author of *Syllabus of Money and Banking* (1899), *Money and Currency* (1906), *Business and the Man* (1917), *Organized Business Knowledge* (1923), and *We and Our Work* (1923). Johnson died at an inn in Newfoundland, New Jersey. His administration of the NYU School of Commerce during the period of its greatest growth is his greatest legacy, but his efforts on behalf of the overall development of academic business instruction are notable as well.

• No organized collection of Johnson papers appears to have survived, but the New York University archives does hold a scrapbook and some miscellaneous correspondence relating to his career. The best source of information on his career at NYU remains Theodore Francis Jones, *New York University, 1832–1932* (1933). A brief, unattributed remembrance is in the *Journal of Accountancy* 39 (Mar. 1925): 197. Obituaries are in the *New York Herald Tribune* and the *New York Times*, both 23 Jan. 1925.

EDWARD L. LACH, JR.

JOHNSON, Joshua (fl. 1795–1824), painter, was probably born in the West Indies. It is now generally believed by scholars of American art and history that Johnson was black and may have come to this country as a young man, probably as a slave. Johnson might be identified as the "negro boy" mentioned in the 1777 will of Captain Robert Polk of Maryland. This boy is thought to have been purchased by Polk's brother-in-law, the noted artist Charles Willson Peale. Stylistic resemblances between the work of Charles Willson Peale and Joshua Johnson are apparent. Unfortunately, very little documentation on Johnson exists and identification of his works is accomplished through provenance (mostly oral family tradition), and connoisseurship—observation of technique, subject matter, iconography, and style.

Johnson's artistic career spanned nearly thirty years, during which he worked only in Baltimore, painting portraits of many of its citizens. Like many artists of the period he more than likely also worked in a related field, such as sign painting or carriage painting, in order to make a living. It is likely that for most of his professional life he was a free man. If he had ever been a slave, he was evidently free by 19 December 1798, when he placed an advertisement for his services as a portrait artist in the *Baltimore Intelligencer*. A slave could not usually have advertised for clients in this manner, and in the advertisement he alluded to the difficulties of his life: "As a *self-taught genius*, deriving from nature and industry his knowledge of the Art; and having experienced many insufferable obstacles in the pursuit of his studies, it is highly gratifying to him to make assurances of his ability to execute all commands, with an effect, and in a style, which must give satisfaction." He is listed as a "Free Householder of Coulour" in the 1816–1817 Baltimore city directory, and an 1810 census lists a Josa. Johnston as a "free negro." "Johnson" was on occasion spelled with a "t," and there is some disagreement among scholars as to whether "Johnson" is the correct form of the artist's last name. The only signed painting attributed to him (*Sarah Ogden Gustin*, National Gallery of Art, Washington, D.C.) shows it as "Johnson," while his advertisement spells his name as "Johnston," as does his signature on a 1798 petition for the paving of German Lane, where he lived.

Johnson was able to earn portrait commissions because of the growing wealth of Baltimore's citizenry. Colonial Baltimore attracted major capital investors in the 1780s; along with this growth came a certain cosmopolitan atmosphere. By 1800 a fifth of Baltimore's population was black, and nearly half of those persons were free, a very high percentage for the American South. The increasing popularity of Quakerism and Methodism in Maryland, both with strong anti-slavery stances, encouraged manumissions. Unfortunately, kidnapping for resale into slavery was a constant and real possibility, but safety in numbers helped somewhat, and Johnson, like many free blacks, initially chose to live in the poorer Fells Point area. However, he subsequently moved near the intersection of German and Hanover Streets, a wealthier neighborhood that boasted a number of abolitionists and no doubt provided many more clients. All but two of his approximately eighty known portraits are of white subjects.

Johnson spent his entire career in Baltimore, the only artist of the first quarter of the nineteenth century to do so. He is listed as a limner at eight different Baltimore addresses between 1796 and 1824, apparently never moving to other cities or towns in search of new clients. This consistency may in part be attributable to the difficulties he faced as a free black in a slave-owning society. Johnson often painted likenesses of his near neighbors. The majority of his late images are of working and middle-class Baltimoreans, while his early subjects reflect more upper-class individuals—members of prominent families, many of whom were also clients of the Peales (once again indicating an early connection to the Peale family).

Johnson probably did not maintain a painting studio, but like many artists of this period, he worked in his sitters' homes. Children constitute a particularly large percentage of his portrait subjects. He often posed them standing, and he used such decorative devices as fruit, books, and even butterflies. A painting of an unidentified girl shows the young subject holding a flower in one hand while she stands in front of greenery (Baltimore Museum of Art). Just under her other hand, an over-large butterfly sits on a bush. In another painting of a child, a young girl stands on a marble floor near a window with drapery pulled aside to reveal a hint of an exterior garden scene. (*Emma Van Name*, Whitney Museum of American Art, New York). Emma holds a strawberry in one hand and gestures to a wine glass nearly as big as she is filled with berries next to her. Johnson modeled the forms of the figure to indicate depth and created spatial relationships by using overlapping forms that moved back within the composition. His linear approach with thinly applied paint reflects knowledge of, if not training by, Charles Willson Peale and indicates some awareness of European styles, though Johnson's works remain within the American folk tradition.

There are only two known portraits by Johnson of black sitters. These probably depict Abner (Bowdoin College Museum of Art, Brunswick, Maine) and Daniel Coker (American Museum in Britain, Bath, England), two dignitaries of the African Methodist Episcopal Church. The Daniel Coker identification is based on a comparison with a known portrait of him, while the identification of Abner Coker rests on its apparent pairing in size and composition with the other portrait and the professional relationship of the two men. There are few extant images of African-Americans from this period, and these two portraits are respectful and dignified likenesses. A portrait of the Most Reverend John Carroll, first Archbishop of Baltimore in 1808–1815, reflects Johnson's ties to the Catholic church, supported by baptismal and death records for his children. Stylistically the elongated eyes, thin paint, and crossed hands with book are all characteristic of Johnson's style.

Johnson's technical approach to painting was distinctive, helping with the identification of his works. Johnson stretched his canvases onto strainers with fixed corners using plain weave fabric that was tightly woven and quite textured. He apparently liked a colored ground, which ranged from gray to buff, and he painted with thin paint, making very few revisions. He would apply small areas of intense color that contrasted with the surrounding, more limited palette. His subjects, always portraits of individuals, place him squarely within the colonial tradition of American Art. Johnson's career parallels the development of painting in the colonies and he is significant within both African-American history and the tradition of American art. The date of Johnson's death is unknown; he last appears in the Baltimore City Directory in 1824, in which he is listed as "Johnson, Joshua, portrait painter, Sleigh's Lane, S side E of Spring."

• Very little archival documentation on Johnson exists, but both the Maryland Historical Society and the Abby Aldrich Rockefeller Folk Art Center have taken an interest in the artist. The first scholar to study and write about Johnson was Dr. J. Hall Pleasants of the Maryland Historical Society, whose publications include "Joshua Johnston: The First American Negro Portrait Painter," *Maryland Historical Magazine* 37, no. 2 (June 1942): 121–49, and *Catalogue: An Exhibition of Portraits by Joshua Johnston* (Municipal Museum of the City of Baltimore, January 1948). Studies include the exhibition catalog by Carolyn J. Weekley et al., *Joshua Johnson: Freeman and Early American Portrait Painter* (1987), and a chapter in Romare Bearden and Harry Henderson, *A History of African-American Artists From 1792–Present* (1993).

J. SUSAN ISAACS

JOHNSON, Judy (26 Oct. 1899–15 June 1989), Negro League baseball player and manager, was born William Julius Johnson in Snow Hill, Maryland, the son of William Henry Johnson, a seaman, and Annie Lane. In 1907 the family moved to Wilmington, Delaware, where the father was athletic director of the Negro Settlement House and provided William with opportunities to participate in boxing, football, and baseball programs. Johnson first played organized baseball with Rosedale in the Wilmington city league. In 1924 he married the team captain's sister, Anita Irons, a schoolteacher. They adopted one daughter.

Johnson left Howard High School in Wilmington after one year to stevedore in Deep Water Point, New Jersey, working through World War I to help support his family. Meanwhile, he began a baseball career in 1917 with the Chester, Pennsylvania, Stars. In 1918 Johnson earned five dollars a day playing for the Philadelphia Hilldale team of Darby, Pennsylvania, on Thursdays and Saturdays, and for the Bacharach Giants in Atlantic City, New Jersey, on Sundays. ("Same club, just different suits on," Johnson later explained.) In 1919 and 1920 Johnson established his niche as a slick-fielding third baseman with the Philadelphia Madison Stars, acquiring the nickname "Judy" because of his strong facial resemblance to previous Stars player Judy Gans. In 1920 Hilldale owner Ed Bolden acquired Johnson's contract from Madison for $100; in 1922 the 5'11" right-hander became Hilldale's regular third baseman, earning $135 per month.

Most African-American teams of the time, changing rosters often, conducted informal barnstorming tours against local white semiprofessional squads and other black teams. Hilldale traveled twice a month to Brooklyn to play the Bushwicks, a white semipro team that at times outdrew the hometown Dodgers. As a result, personal batting averages and team statistics have been often lost or difficult to substantiate.

In 1923 Bolden formed a six-team Eastern Colored League. His squad was the first league champion, with Johnson batting .391. The season was followed by a nine-game exhibition series against major league players of which Hilldale won seven. In the winter of 1923–1924 Johnson played in Cuba and batted .345. In 1924 Hilldale, with Johnson hitting .324, again emerged as eastern champions and lost five games to four in the first "blackball world series" against the Kansas City Monarchs of the Negro National League. Johnson led all series hitters, batting .364 and slugging

.614. In 1925 Hilldale and the Monarchs repeated as pennant winners, but in the championship series Philadelphia prevailed four games to one. Johnson, who had reportedly hit .392 during the season, batted .300 during the series. Afterward he played winter ball in Florida, where rival hotels hired black ballplayers to wait tables and entertain the hotel clientele.

In 1926 Johnson hit .302, and Hilldale lost the league title to the Bacharachs. However, in a four-game postseason series against major league all-stars, Hilldale won three, twice besting future Hall of Famer Lefty Grove. Johnson recalled that "the best was beating Lefty Grove. He just hated us. It was nigger this and nigger that. I never wanted a hit so bad in my life . . . I hit the first pitch he threw me right back at him. It took the cap right off his head . . . I couldn't have been happier." Such emotion was uncharacteristic of Johnson, who was often described as one of the game's true gentlemen. Johnson was the ultimate team player, dependable, heady, and smart. Connie Mack, the owner and manager of the Philadelphia Athletics, declared, "If Judy were only white, he could name his own price."

From 1926 through 1929 Johnson's career with Hilldale continued with sketchy statistics indicating that he batted .327 in 1926, .268 in 1927, .224 in 1928, and .406, his career best, in 1929. His disappointing 1927 and 1928 results may have been the aftereffects of a beaning in August 1926, though he batted well the following winter in Cuba. When the Eastern Colored League folded after the 1929 campaign, Johnson joined Cumberland Posey's barnstorming Homestead Grays as player-manager earning $500 per month, his career high. For the 1930 season, Johnson batted .288 while guiding the team—which included Hall of Famers Cool Papa Bell, Oscar Charleston, and Johnson's protégé Josh Gibson—to a record of 99 wins and 36 losses. In the 1930 Negro League championship series the Grays defeated the Lincoln Giants six games to four, with Johnson batting .286. In 1931 he returned to the Hilldale team, which had been renamed the Darby Daisies, as player-manager, but the Great Depression forced the team to forgo salaries. For the 1932 season Johnson and many others jumped to Gus Greenlee's Pittsburgh Crawfords, managed by Charleston and including Bell, Gibson, Buck Leonard, Satchel Paige, and John Henry Lloyd. For what may have been the best "blackball" team ever, Greenlee built a 7,500-seat stadium and outfitted a special touring team bus for four months of barnstorming in the South. In postseason exhibitions they defeated a team of major league all-stars managed by Casey Stengel in five of seven contests. In 1933 Johnson was selected by fans to play in the first Negro League East-West all-star game. In 1934 Johnson reportedly batted .333 for the year and helped the Crawfords sweep a three-game exhibition series against an all-star team led by Dizzy Dean and his brother Paul. Hitting .367 in 1935, Johnson assisted the Crawfords' victory in the Negro National League pennant race, and subsequent conquest, four games to three, of the New York Cubans in the "blackball" championship series. In 1936 Johnson was again voted to the Negro League all-star game roster, but his season average fell to .282. Facing financial difficulties, Greenlee sold Johnson to the Homestead Grays in 1937. Rather than return to the Grays, however, Johnson chose to retire after a 17-year career and an unconfirmed lifetime batting average of .309.

In retirement Johnson returned to Wilmington, served as a shipping platform supervisor for the Continental Can Company, and in 1940 joined his younger brother in running an ill-fated general store that closed after several years. In 1951 he returned to baseball as a scout for the Philadelphia Athletics and three years later became the first African-American coach in the major leagues, charged with aiding the transition of black players to the majors. In 1956 Johnson became a scout for the Milwaukee Braves and helped sign Billy Bruton, his future son-in-law. As a scout for the Philadelphia Phillies from 1959 to 1973, Johnson signed Richie Allen. Following his 1973 retirement Johnson lived the balance of his life in Marshallton, Delaware, but a stroke forced him to a Wilmington care facility, where he died. As a member of the National Baseball Hall of Fame Committee on the Negro Baseball Leagues, he aided the selection of Negro League standouts into the Hall. However, Johnson withdrew from the committee before the honor was bestowed on him in 1975 when he became the sixth Negro League star enshrined.

• A file of Johnson material is located in the National Baseball Library, Cooperstown, N.Y. Short personal profiles appear in Martin Appel and Burt Goldblatt, *Baseball's Best: The Hall of Fame Gallery* (1977); James Bankes, *The Pittsburgh Crawfords* (1991); Al Harvin, "Recognize Me Now!" *Black Sports* 3 (June 1933): 32–33, 55, 57; Dick Clark and Larry Lester, eds., *The Negro League Book* (1994); John Holway, *Blackball Stars: Negro League Pioneers* (1988); and James A. Riley, *The Biographical Encyclopedia of the Negro Baseball Leagues* (1994). An obituary is in the *Wilmington (Del.) News Journal*, 16 June 1989.

DAVID BERNSTEIN

JOHNSON, Lonnie (8 Feb. 1889?–16 June 1970), singer and guitarist, was born Alonzo Johnson in New Orleans, Louisiana. His parents' names are not known. His father was a string-band musician. Johnson first learned to play the fiddle, then the six- and twelve-string guitars, mandolin, banjo, string bass, piano, and harmonium. Dropping out of school around 1902, Johnson performed regularly around New Orleans in the Storyville Red Light district with his father, with his brother James "Steady Roll" Johnson, and with Punch Miller. In 1917 he sailed to London with a (now unidentified) musical revue, returning in 1919 to find most of his family wiped out by the influenza epidemic of 1918. From 1920 to 1922 Johnson was based in St. Louis, during which time he appeared with Charlie Creath's Jazz-O-Maniacs aboard the Mississippi riverboat SS *St. Paul* and with Fate Marable's band on the SS *Capitol*. In 1922–1924 Johnson performed solo or

with comedic dancers Clenn and Jenkins on the TOBA/RKO theater circuits in the South, but he worked outside music in 1924–1925 save for some performances with brother James in East St. Louis. In 1925 Johnson married blues singer Mary Smith, with whom he had six children before their marriage ended in 1932.

By this time the blues "craze" of the 1920s had reached its peak, and the as-yet unrecorded but remarkably original and versatile Johnson entered a blues singing contest at the Booker T. Washington Theatre in St. Louis as a means of securing a recording contract. Eight weeks later Johnson emerged victorious, signing with OKeh Records, but amused to be cast as a blues singer since he had only sung a blues song because the contest called for it. On 2 November 1925 he sang and played fiddle on "Won't Don't Blues" with Creath's band, two days later recording his first sides under his own name and exposing his prodigious guitar technique on record for the first time.

Johnson recorded more than 200 sides between 1925 and 1932, most of them under his own name and released on the OKeh, Gennett, and Columbia labels, including his groundbreaking and highly influential guitar duets with Eddie Lang and the Hokum recordings with Spencer Williams. In addition, Johnson answered OKeh's call to accompany a wide variety of performers, among them field holler-style vocalist Alger "Texas" Alexander, vaudeville blues singers Bertha "Chippie" Hill, Clara Smith, and Victoria Spivey, and pop performer Martha Raye, as well as jazz artists Louis Armstrong, Duke Ellington, and the Chocolate Dandies. During this time Johnson traveled around the country, playing dates in Chicago, New York, Dallas, and Philadelphia, coming in second in a blues contest to Lillian Glinn in Dallas, and touring with Bessie Smith in the Midnight Steppers Revue in 1929. After performing in the Lonnie Johnson, Recording Guitarist show in New York for about a year, he did some recordings for OKeh and his first for Victor from 1930 through 1932. However, by 1932 the depression and "talkies" helped dry up opportunities for live theater shows, so Johnson relocated to Cleveland and returned to factory work, appearing occasionally with Putney Dandridge in clubs and on the radio.

A Decca recording contract in 1937 helped revive Johnson's career, precipitating club dates in Chicago and, following his signing with the Bluebird label in 1939, around the country. By this time Johnson was featuring fewer guitar pyrotechnics on recordings, generating a duet or small-band sound that was distinctive yet within the parameters of Lester Melrose's streamlined design, with Josh Altheimer, Lil Armstrong, and Blind John Davis providing stellar accompaniment.

Following recordings for Disc in New York City in 1946 and Aladdin in Chicago in 1947, Johnson reemerged as a rhythm and blues star in 1947 as he began a five-year association with Cincinnati's King Records, scoring with pop hits "Tomorrow Night" and

"Pleasing You" and mixing intimate small-group blues and ballads with blasting larger-band blues. Still, Johnson mixed performing dates at the Apollo Theatre and Carnegie Hall (the latter with Kid Ory) in New York and in England during the "Trad" jazz craze in 1952 with periods of working outside of music while he resided in Cincinnati in the late 1940s and early 1950s. Recordings for the Rama label, probably in New York City in 1956, signaled the end of this phase of Johnson's career.

In the late 1950s Johnson worked as a janitor at the Ben Franklin Hotel in Philadelphia, his co-workers apparently unaware of his career as a musician. With help from jazz aficionado Chris Albertson, Johnson made yet another comeback, this time as part of the burgeoning folk music scene. A series of albums for Prestige-Bluesville, recorded in 1960–1962, sparked club dates across the country and with the American Folk Blues Festival in Europe, where he recorded for Fontana in Germany and Storyville in Denmark in 1963. He finished out his career recording for Spivey in New York (1963, 1965), King in Cincinnati (1964), HES in Canada (1965), and Folkways in New York (1967). Johnson settled around 1965–1966 in Toronto, Canada, owning and working at the Home of the Blues club and playing dates. After being struck by an automobile in 1969, he died in Toronto of a related stroke.

As a singer, Johnson was a notable exponent of the urbane city blues style, influenced by the vaudeville blues singers but providing a smoother, more relaxed delivery. As a guitarist, his influence on blues, rock, and jazz has been incalculable. His recordings influenced blues musicians performing a wide variety of styles: Chicago's Big Bill Broonzy, Mississippi's Robert Johnson, Georgia's Willie McTell, and Texas's Ramblin' Thomas, as well as post–World War II stylists T-Bone Walker; B. B. King, Albert King, and Freddy King; and Johnny Shines. Through the recordings of Walker and the three Kings, Johnson's melismatic single-string playing influenced virtually every modern blues and rock guitarist. In jazz, seminal guitarists Eddie Lang, Django Reinhardt, and Charlie Christian all acknowledged their debt to Johnson, as later through them would many a modern jazz guitarist. During five decades of recording activity Johnson provided some of the most breathtaking, imaginative, and sensitive performances and compositions of the twentieth century.

• The best sources of information concerning Johnson's life are Chris Albertson, "Chased by the Blues," in *Bluesland*, ed. Pete Welding and Toby Byron (1991); the entry concerning Lonnie Johnson in Sheldon Harris, *Blues Who's Who* (1979); the liner notes by Lawrence Cohn to the LP *Woke Up This Morning, Blues in My Fingers*, Origin OJL-23; and the liner notes by Per Notini to *The Originator of the Modern Guitar Blues*, Blues Boy RBD-300, which also presents some Disc, Aladdin, and King sides. Discographical information concerning Johnson's recordings is available in R. M. W. Dixon and John Godrich, *Blues and Gospel Records, 1902–1943* (1982), and Mike Leadbitter and Neil Slaven, *Blues Records, 1943–1970* (1987). Document CDs 5063–5069 collect John-

son's recordings from 1925 to 1932, while *Steppin' on the Blues*, Columbia CK46221, presents a strong overview of that period. *He's a Jelly Roll Baker*, RCA 66064-2, surveys Johnson's Bluebird recordings; *Me and My Crazy Self*, Charly CD 266, offers more King recordings; OBC has reissued some of Johnson's Prestige recordings; and *Stompin' at the Penny*, Columbia CD CK 57829, features six recordings with Jim McHarg's Metro Stompers. His last recordings are on *The Complete Folkways Recordings*, Smithsonian Folkways SF 40067.

STEVEN C. TRACY

JOHNSON, Louis Arthur (10 Jan. 1891–24 Apr. 1966), attorney and secretary of defense, was born in Roanoke, Virginia, the son of Marcellus A. Johnson, a grocer, and Katherine Leftwich Arthur. After earning an LL.B. from the University of Virginia in 1912, he practiced law in Clarksburg, West Virginia. He served in the West Virginia House of Delegates from 1917 to 1924, a tenure interrupted by World War I. When the war started, Johnson enlisted in the army. He earned a commission through officers' candidate school, served in France as an infantry captain, and returned at the war's end as a major. After the war he continued his law practice. In 1920 he married Ruth Frances Maxwell; they had two children. In 1924 he was selected as a delegate to the Democratic National Convention. He helped organize the American Legion and became its national commander in 1932–1933.

Johnson chaired the Veterans' Advisory Committee of the Democratic National Committee during President Franklin D. Roosevelt's 1936 reelection campaign and held the post until 1940. As assistant secretary of war from 1937 to 1940, he was a staunch proponent of preparedness, sometimes against the isolationist inclinations of his boss, Secretary Harry H. Woodring. In 1942 Johnson served as the president's personal representative in India and chaired the U.S. Advisory Commission to India. After the war he expanded his law practice and developed a reputation as a successful lawyer.

Johnson again chaired the Democratic National Finance Committee in 1948. By raising $1.5 million, he helped secure President Harry Truman's stunning reelection victory and won consideration for a high-level appointment. After the resignation of James Forrestal, Truman nominated Johnson on 23 March 1949 to be secretary of defense.

Johnson's eighteen-month tenure as secretary of defense was filled with controversy. When he took the helm, the Department of Defense faced two principal challenges, implementation of armed forces unification and reduction of defense expenditures. Both goals provoked interservice competition as roles changed and budgets shrank. Johnson was ill suited by temperament to deal with these vexing issues, and his actions exacerbated strained relations between the navy and the air force. Described as a bull who carried his own china shop with him, Johnson was a large, heavyset man who preferred bluster to diplomacy and whose unrestrained ambition included presidential aspirations.

Only weeks after taking office, Johnson tangled with the navy. The National Security Act of 1947 established the air force as a new branch on an equal footing with the army and the navy. The navy had the right to retain naval aviation, however, and had just laid the keel for a new 65,000-ton supercarrier, the USS *United States*. The air force argued that the carrier would infringe on its prerogatives, because the new ship could provide a platform for B-29s and thus could deliver the atomic bomb. Johnson, already suspected of antinavy inclinations, canceled construction of the supercarrier. Secretary of the Navy John L. Sullivan resigned immediately, and Johnson appointed Franklin P. Matthews, a Nebraskan who claimed he had never been on a vessel larger than a rowboat. Top-ranking navy officers joined Sullivan's criticism of Johnson, initiating a protest that swelled by the fall.

The "revolt of the admirals" reflected the competition for scarce funds, contrasting theories of military strategy, and the navy's conviction that Secretary Johnson intended to abolish naval aviation. The chief of naval operations, Admiral Louis Denfeld, and other high-ranking navy officers testified before the House Armed Services Committee in the fall of 1949, attacking the approval of appropriations for B-36 bombers on strategic and financial grounds. Secretary Matthews removed Denfeld by reassigning him, but Denfeld retired rather than accepting his dismissal. The issue exposed the raw nerves between the services, damaged Matthews, and confirmed the navy's conviction that Johnson was no friend.

Johnson differed frequently with the more refined Secretary of State Dean Acheson, particularly on China policy. The communist victory in China and the unwillingness of the administration to continue to provide aid to Chiang Kai-shek left Acheson vulnerable to Republican criticism. Johnson joined the chorus of critics, hoping to gain influence in the cabinet at Acheson's expense. Johnson and Acheson agreed, however, in their recommendation as participants in the three-member committee considering development of a hydrogen bomb, called the "super." They recommended development, and the third committee member, David Lilienthal, concurred despite serious reservations.

Johnson's problems increased in the spring and summer of 1950. Truman sought to hold defense spending to $14.4 billion in fiscal year 1950, and, with the cooperation of the Bureau of the Budget, Johnson made significant progress toward meeting the president's goals. The armed services bridled under the limits, however, and in April 1950 the National Security Council produced NSC-68 (under the direction of Acheson and Paul Nitze), which called for massive increases in defense spending. Thus, when the Korean War began in June 1950, critics claimed that Johnson's reductions had left the armed services ill prepared. Johnson also began to lose the confidence of the president. Although defense cuts were presidential policy, Johnson executed them with bombast that in-

creased rancor among the services. When Truman nominated New York lawyer Thomas K. Finletter to be secretary of the air force, Johnson threatened to resign. Finletter, an easterner and as persistent an advocate of a large air force as his predecessor Stuart Symington, was too independent for Johnson. But Truman called Johnson's bluff, and Johnson backed down. Feuding with Acheson continued; Averell Harriman reported that Johnson had praised Republican senator Robert A. Taft's call for Acheson's resignation. The White House staff heard rumors that Johnson had let Republican friends know that he might be interested in seeking their party's nomination for the presidency.

Matters came to a head in August. General Douglas MacArthur sent a message to the Veterans of Foreign Wars criticizing administration policy in Formosa (Taiwan). Truman directed Johnson to demand that MacArthur withdraw his statement. Johnson, who believed such an order would embarrass MacArthur, lacked the will to discipline the general. When he vacillated, the president read him a firm statement over the telephone and told him to relay it to the general. Again Johnson hesitated before sending the message. An exasperated Truman asked for Johnson's resignation on 11 September. Johnson left office when the Senate confirmed General George C. Marshall as his successor on 20 September. Historian Donald McCoy attributed the dismissal to Johnson's "conflicts with other officials, his verbal indiscretions, his chumminess with Republicans, and his slowness in conforming to new policies during a war" (McCoy, p. 236). Johnson remained in Washington as a senior partner in his old law firm, Steptoe and Johnson. He died in Washington.

Johnson's tenure as secretary of defense must be judged a failure. During an eighteen-month interlude between the terms of men of great stature, Forrestal and Marshall, Johnson was one of the least effective members of Truman's cabinet. Leading the Department of Defense at a critical juncture, Johnson became embroiled in politics and failed to manage effectively either the implementation of unification or the beginning of the Korean War.

• A collection of Johnson papers is at the University of Virginia. Among the more comprehensive accounts of Johnson's tenure as secretary of defense are Robert J. Donovan, *The Tumultuous Years* (1982), and Donald R. McCoy, *The Presidency of Harry S. Truman* (1984). Articles in Eleanora W. Schoenebaum, ed., *Political Profiles: The Truman Years* (1978), and Richard S. Kirkendall, ed., *The Harry S. Truman Encyclopedia* (1989), assess Johnson's career. *Truman in the White House: The Diary of Eben A. Ayers*, ed. Robert H. Ferrell (1991), provides the insider perspective of a member of Truman's staff. An obituary is in the *New York Times*, 25 Apr. 1966.

ANDREW J. DUNAR

JOHNSON, Lyndon Baines (27 Aug. 1908–22 Jan. 1973), thirty-sixth president of the United States, was born near Stonewall, Texas, the son of Sam Ealy Johnson, Jr., a farmer and politician, and Rebekah Baines, a sometime teacher. Sam Ealy eked out a modest living and served as a state legislator for several years. Lyndon was the couple's first child and by all accounts the favorite of Rebekah, who was determined that her son should have a proper education. From grade school on, Lyndon demonstrated a keen interest in politics, particularly his father's Populist orientation, passing out campaign literature and eagerly listening to political discussions when Sam Ealy's cronies visited the Johnson household.

Although he had done well in high school, Lyndon failed the entrance exams for Southwest Texas State Teachers College in San Marcos. Disappointed, he and several friends set out for California to make their fortunes, but he returned soon. Working as a day laborer building roads near Johnson City convinced him to try for college again. With Rebekah's tutoring and several preparatory courses, he barely passed the entrance exams to Southwest Texas State and was accepted in 1927.

At San Marcos Johnson dabbled in campus politics while studying to be a teacher—a common path at that time for aspirants to political careers, including one of Johnson's lifelong mentors in politics, fellow Texan Sam Rayburn. Several permanent traits emerged from Johnson's early years. One was a knack for getting along with elders through attention and flattery, which later served Johnson well during his early years in politics and during his tenure as Senate majority leader. Another was his penchant for exaggeration, especially concerning his family's supposedly desperate circumstances during his youth. Accompanied by reporters on one trip to his Texas ranch in the 1950s, for example, he pointed to a tiny shedlike building, declaring that he was born there. Fortunately, his mother was there to set the story straight.

Johnson's stories had a parablelike quality about them, suited to Texas politics of the day. They also revealed something about the man. For instance, he liked to repeat the story of an applicant for a teaching position in rural Texas during the depression who, when asked how he would teach about the earth, said he could teach it either way—round or flat.

Johnson left San Marcos in 1930 to begin a high-school teaching career. As a teacher, Johnson observed the plight of poor Mexican-American pupils, which reinforced his Populist views. In November 1931, Sam Ealy recommended his son for a position in the office of Richard Kleberg, a newly elected member of the U.S. House of Representatives. Impressed with Lyndon, Kleberg hired him as his secretary. Johnson arrived in Washington, where he remained until he returned to his ranch at the end of his presidency.

A wealthy rancher, Kleberg preferred golf to the wearisome duties of a congressional representative and left the running of his office to Johnson and one other assistant. For Johnson these were his real "school years," during which he learned and polished the skills necessary to be a successful politician. He soon established himself outside of Kleberg's limited domain as a leader in the so-called Little Congress, made up of congressional assistants from the representatives' offices.

In September 1934, he met Claudia Alta Taylor, a recent University of Texas graduate, and twenty-four hours later he asked her to marry him. They were married in November. Henceforward, she was known by her childhood nickname, Lady Bird. Their daughters, Lynda Bird and Luci Baines, would add two more "LBJs" to the family.

In 1935, at the behest of Sam Rayburn and two Texas congressional leaders, President Franklin D. Roosevelt appointed Johnson to head the state branch of the National Youth Administration. Part of the original New Deal package, the NYA sought to provide unemployed youth with education and training for gainful employment. Johnson's dedication and accomplishments soon dispelled any doubts about his ability to take charge of a major program. He gained recognition for his skills as a manager as well as for developing programs that served the educational and employment needs of blacks and Mexican-Americans as well as whites.

Having vowed that he would return to Washington as an elected representative to Congress, Johnson did just that in 1938, identifying himself closely with Roosevelt despite the growing anti–New Deal sentiment of Democratic conservatives across the South. Roosevelt was taken with this self-appointed protégé, predicting to aides that the next generation would see a power shift to the South and West, "and this boy could well be the first Southern President."

Throughout his life, Johnson brooded about his lack of impressive academic credentials. He suspected that the "Harvards" around Roosevelt held men like himself in contempt. During his presidency, he often told White House visitors that he had inherited the brainiest cabinet any president ever had, filled with Ivy League Ph.D.'s—and they all worked for *him*. When problems occurred during his presidency, he was prone to blame the "intellectuals," who he believed had never liked or understood him.

Johnson displayed his political prowess and determination almost immediately upon entering Congress. Determined to obtain federal aid for projects on the lower Colorado River to bring electricity to the Texas hill country, Representative Johnson lobbied effectively for his goals. He established early a "can-do" pattern that justified his reputation as a man who could make Washington work for his constituents, first the residents of the Texas hill country, then his wealthy backers atop the rapidly developing economy of the Southwest, and, finally, all the beneficiaries of the Great Society programs.

Johnson always identified himself with the Texas hill country and its people, even after he became the owner of an Austin radio and television station (1943) and other enterprises. The acquisition of this valuable property, which Johnson had purchased with money that Lady Bird had inherited, became the basis for a personal fortune that eventually grew to several million dollars. It also brought Johnson under sharp criticism for alleged manipulations to obtain the necessary licenses from the Federal Communications Commission.

As his ambitions widened to include the possibility of a seat in the U.S. Senate, Johnson downplayed his support of New Deal policies, without, however, deserting Roosevelt. In 1941 an opportunity arose to run for a Senate seat in a special election, without giving up his House seat. Balancing his old-style Populist/New Deal attacks on the rich with assaults on "isms" and labor unions, Johnson ran a strong campaign, the most expensive in Texas history up to that point. Even so, he lost a very close election to W. Lee O'Daniel. Strong evidence of vote fraud existed, but Johnson opted not to pursue the issue lest an investigation turn up irregularities on his side as well. Instead, he vowed not to be outmaneuvered ever again.

When it appeared that the United States might become involved in the Second World War, Johnson obtained a commission in the navy reserves. A few days after Pearl Harbor, he wrote Roosevelt, asking to be assigned to active duty. He was commissioned a lieutenant commander and sent to the Pacific on a presidential fact-finding mission to investigate conditions at General Douglas MacArthur's headquarters. Johnson's active duty tour lasted only a few months and included only one combat experience, when he tagged along on a bombing raid over Japanese-held territory. The mission came under heavy fire, and Johnson was awarded a Silver Star for bravery.

On 1 July 1942, President Roosevelt recalled all legislators to their duties in Washington, including a restless Lyndon Johnson. By 1947 he had served for a decade in the House and felt distant from the centers of power. Determined to rescue himself from early obscurity, Johnson decided to run again for the Senate. The incumbent, O'Daniel, had decided not to seek reelection in 1948, so Johnson faced off against the conservative Governor Coke Stevenson in the Democratic primary.

Postwar politics in Texas had continued to shift to the right, and Johnson kept pace. He stressed Cold War themes and declared his support for the Republican-sponsored Taft-Hartley Act that had sharply restricted the powers of labor unions. He also opposed the national Democratic party's stand on civil rights and federal ownership of offshore oil.

Johnson gained much attention during the campaign by using helicopters to get around the state quickly, but this innovation did not produce a clear-cut victory. Instead, the result looked like a dead heat. Charges and countercharges of vote fraud went to the U.S. Supreme Court, with Johnson finally prevailing—by eighty-seven votes. Thereafter he was sarcastically nicknamed "Landslide" Lyndon.

Johnson's Senate career prospered. With the powerful support of such figures as Georgia's Richard Russell, he was chosen Senate minority leader in 1953 and, after the Democrats regained control two years later, majority leader. He was seen by Russell and other southerners as a potential candidate for the White House. Johnson liked assuming the role of "centrist," often citing the biblical phrase, "Come let us reason together," as his credo. He liked to boast that he was more help to Dwight Eisenhower than most members of the president's own party.

Johnson's biggest senatorial challenge came with the Civil Rights Bill of 1957. In his previous years in the House and Senate, Johnson had always opposed civil rights legislation. However, although he attacked the original Republican version of the 1957 bill, he warned the southern bloc that some sort of civil rights bill was necessary to preserve national unity. Johnson attached key amendments that softened the bill's impact on southern segregationist practices, including a provision that required jury trials for those accused of certain civil rights violations. He was able to convince southern leaders to vote for closure to avoid facing a more radical civil rights bill; he convinced liberals, on the other hand, that the bill was the best package they could get without doing irreparable damage to the Democratic party. A major legislative accomplishment for Johnson, the 1957 Civil Rights Act was the first such legislation since Reconstruction. Acclaimed in some quarters as the greatest majority leader of all time, Johnson took credit for bringing about this multilayered compromise. The energy Johnson displayed in this campaign undercut concerns about a massive heart attack he had suffered in 1955.

When the Soviet Union launched the world's first space satellite, *Sputnik*, in October 1957, the nation's attention shifted again to national security concerns. Johnson was there to take the lead. Chairing a special Senate Preparedness Subcommittee, he held a series of hearings on the issue that brought daily newspaper headlines and prompted discussion about his availability as a presidential candidate in 1960. Yet Johnson seemed strangely unconcerned about the nominating process, perhaps unsure of his chances for success. His likely opponent, Massachusetts senator John F. Kennedy, actively pursued a vigorous primary campaign in several states, while Johnson stayed in Washington, counting on the support of fellow senators for his nomination. In any event, Kennedy won the nomination on the first ballot.

To the shock of many liberal supporters, Kennedy asked Johnson to accept second place on the ticket; to the dismay of many Johnson supporters, he agreed. Kennedy's motive was obvious. A liberal Catholic from the North, Kennedy needed Johnson, a conservative Protestant from the South, to bring Texas and perhaps other Deep South states into the Democratic column. However, why Johnson accepted remains a mystery. Although most of his supporters at least initially advised against it, House Speaker Sam Rayburn, who hated the thought of Richard Nixon becoming president, eventually urged Lyndon to accept. Despite being both feared and looked down upon as "Senator Cornpone" by Kennedy's inner circle, and despite many signs that his place in the New Frontier would be at the rear, Johnson finally agreed.

Serving as vice president quickly became an ordeal for the man who had, more or less, shared power with President Eisenhower. Excluded from both deliberations and decisions, Johnson suffered many humiliations, some self-inflicted, as he searched for a meaningful role in the Kennedy administration. When Kennedy was assassinated on 22 November 1963, however, Johnson moved into the Oval Office with a sure-handed grasp of the requirements of the moment and with a vision for the future. On the day after the assassination, Johnson told a close Kennedy aide that he knew he lacked the late president's education, culture, and learning, but that he would try his best. "But don't expect me to absorb things as fast as you're used to." More surprising, he told another aide that the talk about his being a conservative was wide of the mark. "As a matter of fact," he said, "to tell the truth, John F. Kennedy was a little too conservative to suit my taste."

The transition between the two administrations was not without difficulties. Johnson both resented and depended on the Ivy League "intellectuals" he inherited from Kennedy—a bad combination that perhaps explains why he often tested subordinates' loyalty by subjecting them to humiliating or embarrassing situations. Moreover, Kennedy had displayed an almost instinctive understanding of how to use television to his advantage. He had an easy style and, when confronted with difficult or hostile questions, a ready wit. Johnson, however, was stiff and overly formal in front of the camera. He also had a tendency to speak too loudly, as if he were trying to project to the furthest row in the back of the Grange Hall.

In his first State of the Union message the following January, Johnson nevertheless struck exactly the right note of commitment for a nation still recovering from the shock of the assassination. He vowed, "Let us continue." Various pieces of New Frontier legislation had been stalled in congressional committees. Johnson, who had watched White House aides mishandle Congress, hoped to break the deadlock with a dramatic announcement that his administration would declare unconditional war on poverty. For ammunition to fight this war, Johnson backed an unprecedented series of bills to extend the federal government's responsibility for and assistance to the poor, especially in the inner city.

After fully exploiting the controversial conservative positions of his Republican adversary, Senator Barry Goldwater of Arizona, Johnson won the 1964 election with a record plurality of more than 61 percent of the popular vote. He cautioned his advisers and aides, however, that the victory was not permanent. Every week that passed, he warned, would see the support erode, just as Roosevelt had seen his 1936 triumph melt away in the House and Senate within two years. After the 1964 Civil Rights Bill passed, he predicted to aides, "I think we just gave the South to the Republicans."

Nevertheless, Johnson pressed ahead, notching each legislative victory on pieces of paper that he carried around to display to White House visitors. His goal was to achieve what lay beyond the New Frontier in the Great Society. Johnson's strategy in fighting the war on poverty reflected a commonly held belief in that decade that no matter how deep-seated the problem was, it would ultimately yield to successful management techniques. Rejecting a massive federal public works program as too reminiscent of New Deal "welfarism," Johnson created the Office of Economic Opportunity as the principal agency to coordinate the various programs. The office encountered difficulties from the start. The administration sponsored bills calling for Community Action programs that would establish job-training centers along with more controversial bills that would grant funds to groups organized to challenge local bureaucracies. Big-city mayors welcomed federal funds but opposed what appeared to them to be federal sponsorship of alternative centers of authority. Headstart programs to provide impoverished inner-city children with preschool training, on the other hand, proved successful. Other legislation granted over a billion dollars to local school districts to fund efforts to equalize educational opportunities for poor children. The establishment of Medicare and Medicaid eased the burden of medical expenses for the elderly. The administration also backed legislation dealing with environmental concerns.

Johnson took charge of civil rights bills that had been stalled from the early days of the Kennedy administration. The high point of his public effort on behalf of the 1965 Voting Rights Bill came when he quoted Martin Luther King, Jr., to a joint session of Congress, vowing, "We shall overcome." Linking civil rights and the war on poverty, Johnson told a Howard University audience, "We must seek not just freedom but opportunity."

While happily surprised liberals and Democrats believed that the Goldwater "debacle" had left the opposition in disarray, Johnson continued to protect his right flank, sometimes justifying his actions after 1965 in escalating the Vietnam War as protection for his Great Society programs. He knew, however, that the war threatened to undo everything he had accomplished. During various discussions of the war, he compared himself to a man in a pilotless plane, a man about to jump into a deep pool, and a man in a car without a steering wheel. Neither these forebodings, nor the advice of some of his oldest friends, prevented him from ordering a massive troop buildup beginning in the summer of 1965 that would eventually extend U.S. troop commitments to a total of half a million men.

At each escalation, whether the 1964 retaliation against North Vietnamese PT-boat bases, the start of the bombing campaign in early 1965, or the fateful 28 July 1965 decision to send 100,000 troops to Vietnam, Johnson insisted that he was only following the lead of his three predecessors, each of whom had made Cold War commitments to the conflict in Vietnam. At the time of Kennedy's assassination, there were 16,000 American "advisers" in Vietnam. Holdover Kennedy appointees assured the new president that the United States had the capability to defend South Vietnam against its internal and external enemies, as well as the moral obligation to do so. They were convinced that North Vietnam would eventually realize it simply could not defy the United States, but only if Johnson did not falter at the crucial moment, which always seemed close at hand. So Johnson sent troops, then bombs, then more troops and more bombs. However, by 1968, another election year, Johnson's strategies had produced neither military security for South Vietnam nor political security at home for the Great Society.

The Tet Offensive at the end of January shattered hopes that the war could be won within a reasonable period of time—if ever—and broke open the cracks in the Democratic coalition. The war on poverty had also gone on the defensive. It had never received the huge amounts of resources the military was granted to fight the war in Vietnam; its appropriations were a few billion, compared with $100 billion spent to try to save South Vietnam from communism. Riots in several large U.S. cities and protests on college campuses denouncing what was becoming known as "Mr. Johnson's War" gave Johnson's opponents, on both the left and the right, ammunition for their complaints.

On 31 March 1968 Johnson addressed the nation, announcing a bombing halt over most of North Vietnam in hopes that peace negotiations could begin and ending with a surprise statement that, in order to devote his full energies to the search for peace, he would neither seek nor accept renomination.

Johnson left office scorned as the author of the most unpopular war in the nation's history. He has been called an American Lear, brought down by his own stubbornness and insecurities. His Great Society programs also came under attack for seemingly promising too much and for creating an atmosphere of lawlessness, resulting in an upsurge of urban race riots in Los Angeles, Newark, and Detroit. His principal legacy, critics charged, was black outrage and white backlash. However, Johnson's tragic flaw was not the hubris of Greek drama. It lay in the contradictions that made up this complex man who so often undermined his accomplishments by trying to run the country the way he had run the Senate—by cornering and cajoling wavering individuals to get the votes he needed—and, paradoxically, by failing to trust his best instincts, taking advice instead from experts.

Johnson spent his last remaining years at his ranch, near his birthplace. At one of his last public appearances, sustained by heart medications, the former president called upon conferees at a meeting on civil rights in Austin to put aside their arguments to work for the future. He died after suffering a heart attack at his ranch.

Ultimately, Johnson's responsibility for the Vietnam War will be weighed against his efforts to ensure economic and political rights for the disenfranchised. The Great Society was full of promises, but it was also a vision that called upon Americans to live up to their responsibilities to one another. Lyndon Johnson will continue to command our attention as we look at the American past and to its future.

• Johnson's papers are housed in the Lyndon Baines Johnson Presidential Library in Austin, Texas. Johnson's biographers, not surprisingly, take very strong views about their subject. Robert Caro, *The Years of Lyndon Johnson: The Path to Power* (1982) and *The Years of Lyndon Johnson: Means of Ascent* (1990), is critical of Johnson, while Robert Dallek, *Lone Star Rising: Lyndon Johnson and His Times, 1908–1960* (1991), is sympathetic. A shorter account is Paul Conklin, *Big Daddy from the Pedernales: Lyndon Baines Johnson* (1986). Ronnie Dugger, *The Politician: The Life and Times of Lyndon Johnson* (1982), combines research with knowing insight but is unremittingly harsh in its final judgments. To understand Johnson, one must also look at the interpretations offered in Doris Kearns, *Lyndon Johnson and the American Dream* (1976), and Harry McPherson, *A Political Education* (1972).

LLOYD GARDNER

JOHNSON, Marmaduke (c. 1629–25 Dec. 1674), printer and stationer, was born into an English printing and bookselling family in London, of whom the best known member was his elder brother Thomas. His parents' names are unknown. Marmaduke apparently married at an early age and had a son, but his wife left him to live with a married man. Before a divorce could be arranged, his wife died on a ship bound for Barbados. A second wife, Ruth Cane of Cambridge, Massachusetts, whom Johnson married in 1670 and with whom he had a daughter, survived him.

Personal problems as well as professional advancement may have encouraged Johnson to accept a three-year contract offered by the London Corporation for New England. The contract specified that he was to go to Massachusetts as a printer for a projected Bible in the American Indian language translated by John Eliot. The Proceedings of the London Corporation dated 21 April 1660 report that the treasurer:

hath treated with the printer Marmaduke Johnson about going into N.E. [New England] to print the Bible in the Indian language and reports the printer is willing to go and be employed in that service at the salary of 40 pounds per annum besides diet, lodging, and washing and a quarter's salary in advance and his time to be there for three years and more if the Corporation or Commissioners for the United Colonies please to command from the time of his going on shipboard and the Corporation to pay his passage thither. (quoted in Littlefield, pp. 212–13)

A master printer was needed because Samuel Green, with a press in Cambridge, was the only printer in Massachusetts. Johnson sailed from Gravesend on 14 May 1660 aboard the *Prudent Mary* and arrived in Massachusetts in early summer. He and Samuel Green worked together on the Bible until its completion in 1663.

There were problems in Johnson's relationship with Green. Before the death of his first wife, Johnson paid court to Green's daughter Elizabeth, who apparently encouraged him until her father brought suit to keep

Johnson away from Elizabeth. The commissioners of the United Colonies, in a letter dated 10 September 1662, complained to the London Corporation that Johnson "hath proved very idle and nought and absented himself from the work [on the Indian Bible] more than half a year at one time" (quoted in Thomas, pp. 72–73). He had been fined five pounds for the offense to Green and later was fined twenty pounds "for threatening the life of any man who should pay his addresses to Green's daughter" (Thomas, p. 73). The matter was resolved, probably by the death of Johnson's wife and by Johnson's renouncing his pursuit of Elizabeth Green. A letter from the governor of the London Corporation, dated 9 April 1663, cites John Eliot's assurances that Johnson was back to work on the Bible and that his brother Thomas "gives us great assurance of his brother's Reformation and following his business diligently for the time to come" (Thomas, p. 74).

With the help of his loyal supporters Johnson had his contract extended for a fourth year and continued working in Green's print shop. He returned to England in late 1664. On his return to Massachusetts in May 1665, he brought a new press and fonts of his own, hoping to establish an independent press in Boston. This being denied by the General Court of Massachusetts, he continued printing in Cambridge until he was finally permitted to start a press in Boston in 1674, shortly before his death. The imprint *Printed by S. G. and M. J.* appears frequently after 1670, showing, as George Littlefield noted, "that the relations between the rival offices were now amicable, and the Corporation press operated jointly. They, however, conducted separate offices, and on books printed on the College [Cambridge] press the imprint contained only the name of Samuel Green. On books printed on Johnson's press only the name Marmaduke Johnson appeared" (pp. 255–56).

Summing up Johnson's career in Massachusetts, Littlefield credited him with establishing both the first colonial press owned by a printer and the first printing office in Boston as well as being "the first person to open an independent printing office where any one could have a book or pamphlet printed subject only to the licensers of the press" (p. 269). Littlefield characterized Johnson as having been "active, industrious, prudent, successful in business, and respected in the community" (p. 269). George Parker Winship, in his history of the Cambridge Press, was less charitable, referring to Johnson's "temperamental lack of judgment" (p. 281). Winship expressed concern about the substantial estate left by Johnson at his death, given that "the work he is known to have done would not account for this, if he told the truth about his financial condition when he went to London in 1665, but he may have received an inheritance from England or have speculated luckily in America" (p. 329).

In dispute is Johnson's possible authorship of political pamphlets. A pamphlet about Ludgate prison, written in 1659, has sometimes been attributed to Marmaduke Johnson but more likely was the work of his brother Thomas. The seven-stanza poem "A Postscript to the Reader" is signed M. J. and appended to *Daily Meditations* by Philip Pain, printed by Johnson in 1668. The last stanza pays tribute to Pain, "this Pilot young," who had drowned in a shipwreck and was memorialized in the sixteen-page booklet of verses:

> Let the Example of this Pilot young,
> (So skill'd in Spiritual Sailing) thee inform
> To steer thy Course through Baca's Vale, along
> To this fair Haven, (fear nor Winds nor Storm)
> Till thou arrive with him, in whom did dwell
> Some good thing toward the God of Israel.
> (facsimile in Littlefield, facing p. 249)

Littlefield concluded that "the printer was gifted with a poetic nature, and possessed some literary talent" (p. 247).

• A detailed account of Marmaduke Johnson's career in Massachusetts is provided by George Parker Winship in *The Cambridge Press, 1638–1692* (1945). Isaiah Thomas, *The History of Printing in America* (1874; repr. 1970), includes a section on Johnson, pp. 71–78. George Emery Littlefield, *The Early Massachusetts Press, 1638–1711*, vols. 1 and 2 (1907; repr. 1969), covers Johnson's life and career, pp. 209–69.

DORA JEAN ASHE

JOHNSON, Mordecai Wyatt (12 Jan. 1890–10 Sept. 1976), university president and clergyman, was born in Paris, Henry County, Tennessee, the son of the Reverend Wyatt Johnson, a stationary engine operator in a mill, and Caroline Freeman. Johnson received his grammar school education in Paris, but in 1903 he enrolled in the Academy of the Roger Williams University in Nashville, Tennessee. The school burned in 1905, so Johnson finished the semester at the Howe Institute in Memphis. In the fall of that year, he moved to Atlanta to finish high school in the preparatory department of Atlanta Baptist College (renamed Morehouse College in 1913). There he completed a bachelor's degree in 1911. While at Atlanta Baptist, Johnson played varsity football and tennis, sang in various groups, and began his long career as a public speaker on the debating team.

After graduating, Johnson became an English instructor at his alma mater. For the 1912–1913 school year, he taught economics and history and served as acting dean of the college. During the summers, he earned a second bachelor's degree in the social sciences from the University of Chicago (1913). Johnson decided that he wanted to be a minister and enrolled in Rochester Theological Seminary. In seminary he was greatly influenced by Walter Rauschenbusch's theory of the Social Gospel, in which Christianity was responsible for economic and social change. While studying at Rochester he was a student pastor at the Second Baptist Church in Mumford, New York. He was granted a bachelor's of divinity degree in 1921 with a thesis titled "The Rise of the Knights Templars."

In December 1916 Johnson married Anna Ethelyn Gardner of Augusta, Georgia; they had five children. That year Johnson worked as a Student Secretary of the Young Men's Christian Association (YMCA). He traveled for one year in the Southwest, studying predominately black schools and colleges. This effort resulted in the formation of the Southwestern Annual Student Conference.

Johnson was ordained in 1916 and received an assignment in 1917 to be the pastor of the First Baptist Church in Charleston, West Virginia. In his nine years in West Virginia, Johnson was responsible for organizing the Commercial Cooperative Society, the Rochdale Cooperative Cash Grocery, and the Charleston branch of the National Association for the Advancement of Colored People (NAACP). Under his leadership, the membership of the local branch of the NAACP increased to 1,000 in nine years. He also became active in the Negro Baptist Convention. By the time he left in 1926, Johnson was well known as a community activist and speaker. In 1921 he took a year of absence while he studied at Harvard. The following year, Johnson received a master's degree in sacred theology and gave the commencement address on postwar racism, titled "The Faith of the American Negro."

On 30 June 1926 Johnson was elected the thirteenth president of Howard University in Washington, D.C. Howard was chartered in 1867 out of the Freedmen's Bureau and was originally intended to be a theological seminary for African Americans and a normal school. By 1917 Howard and Fisk University were considered the only traditionally black schools offering a college-level education. When Johnson assumed the presidency of Howard on 1 September 1926, he had a broad vision for improvements to the university.

Johnson was the first African American to hold the presidency of Howard and came to office at a time when all other presidents of traditionally black colleges were white. Further, Howard was currently undergoing a time of controversy: Johnson's predecessor had been asked to resign, and the administration and the faculty sharply disagreed on a number of issues. Johnson sought to elevate the position of the professors by raising their salaries and providing tenure and security. During his tenure, he brought in professors with national reputations and a large number of African Americans with Ph.D.s.

Johnson's priorities for improvements were explained in his Twenty-Year Plan, which called for educational and physical development. In 1926 the only two accredited schools at Howard were dentistry and liberal arts. During his years at Howard, Johnson doubled the number of faculty members, doubled the library resources, tripled the amount of laboratory equipment, and constructed twenty new buildings. Under Johnson, all of the schools and colleges became fully accredited. In addition, the university enrollment increased by 250 percent and the budget grew from $700,000 to $8 million.

Johnson's most important contribution to Howard was fundraising. He was not only successful at securing private donations and grants, but he also persuaded Congress to amend the charter of the university to provide annual appropriations on 13 December 1928.

Between 1946 and 1960, Howard received an average of more than $1 million annually. This added funding gave Howard an advantage over similar schools. For his work to gain Howard annual federal funds, Johnson received the Spingarn Medal for public service in 1929. (The Spingarn Medal is the highest award given by the NAACP.)

Johnson retired in June 1960 and became president emeritus. Howard had been remade in his 34-year tenure. The school had students from more than ninety countries. The professional schools in particular were impressive. Howard's medical school was producing half of the nation's African-American doctors, and the law school was in the vanguard of civil rights, providing 96 percent of the African-American lawyers.

After leaving Howard, Johnson served on the District of Columbia's Board of Education in 1962. In his three-year tenure, he was a vocal critic of the disparity between funding of predominately white schools and black schools in the district. Johnson was also a member of several charitable organizations. He was on the National Council of the United Negro College Fund; vice chairman of the National Council for the Prevention of War; director of the American Youth Committee; a member of the Advisory Council for the National Youth Administration; a member of the National Advisory Council on Education; a member of the National Religion and Labor Board; and director of the National Conference of Christians and Jews. In addition, he was a strong advocate for nations under colonial control by countries such as Great Britain and France, and he was a member of the advisory council for the Virgin Islands. He was an early proponent of India's independence from Great Britain and often spoke on the topic. In one such lecture, he spoke at Martin Luther King, Jr.'s seminary, Crozer Theological Seminary in Philadelphia.

In 1969 Johnson's wife died. In April 1970 he married Alice Clinton Taylor King; they had no children. Howard University honored Johnson in 1973 by naming the administration building after him. His service was also recognized internationally: Ethiopia, Haiti, Liberia, and Panama all gave him awards for his achievements. Johnson died in Washington, D.C.

Johnson has been recognized for his excellent administrative skills and as "one of the great platform orators of his day." His involvement in civil rights and religious causes gained him notoriety. His organization and development of Howard University is remarkable. Johnson insisted on a quality faculty, high-caliber students, adequate funding, and sufficient facilities and laboratory equipment. These factors put Howard onto a path for success. Johnson's contributions to Howard and his other causes have assured his legacy of improved educational opportunities for all.

• Johnson's papers concerning Howard University are in the Moorland-Spingarn Research Center at Howard. Richard I. McKinney, *Mordecai—The Man and His Message: The Story of Mordecai Wyatt Johnson* (1998), includes a biographical sketch as well as six sermons and seven addresses by Johnson. See also Walter Dyson, *Howard University: The Capstone of Negro Education* (1941); Edwin R. Embree, *Thirteen against the Odds* (1944); Rayford W. Logan, *Howard University: The First Hundred Years, 1867–1967* (1969); and Michael R. Winston, ed., *Education for Freedom* (1976). A bibliography appears in James P. Johnson et al., eds., *Mordecai Wyatt Johnson: A Bibliography of His Years at Howard, 1926–1960* (1976). Obituaries are in the *New York Times* and the *Washington Post*, both 11 Sept. 1976.

SARA GRAVES WHEELER

JOHNSON, Nathaniel (4 Apr. 1644–1713), colonial governor, was born in Kibblesworth, Durham County, England, the son of William Johnson, one time mayor of Newcastle-upon-Tyne, and Margaret Sherwood. He likely attended New College, Oxford, in 1657. As a young man Johnson sailed to Barbados and was deputy treasurer of the island during the governorship of William Willoughby. Johnson returned to England and in 1673 became a freeman of the city of Newcastle. There he held city commissions, including coal carriage and assessments, and was captain of the local militia. As had his father, Nathaniel Johnson served as mayor (1681–1682) and alderman (1682–1688) of Newcastle-upon-Tyne. He also represented the city in the House of Commons during the Oxford Parliament (1680–1681) and James II's brief 1685 Parliament. Johnson was knighted on 28 December 1680 and had an income as a farmer–tax collector of the hearth tax for Durham and other northern counties.

In August 1686 Johnson was commissioned governor of the Leeward Islands, which included St. Christopher, Nevis, Antigua, and Montserrat. His administration was preoccupied with defending the colony from French naval forces, but he improved toleration of Roman Catholic settlers at Montserrat and regularized the islands' court system and legal administration. In April 1689 Governor Johnson learned of William of Orange's invasion of England and of James's flight from the country. The governor immediately offered to return to England to support James Stuart in England or to follow him to France. A month later he resigned his governor's commission because he refused to swear allegiance to William and Mary. Johnson appointed Christopher Codrington to be deputy governor and planned to settle in Carolina where, in 1686, he had obtained extensive land grants from the Carolina proprietors. Johnson left for Charles Town in July 1689. The previous month he had sent his wife and children to England, but the family was captured at sea by the French and imprisoned under harsh conditions for nearly a year. Johnson's wife died as a result of her treatment, but his three children eventually returned to England, and two of them then came to South Carolina.

Sir Nathaniel Johnson lived privately from 1689 until 1702, when he was appointed governor of South Carolina. In 1696 he obtained a grant for "Silk Hope," a plantation he had previously settled on the Cooper River. There he conducted botanical experiments and successfully produced silk. An Anglican and a newcomer to the province, he became a leader of the political party in Carolina known as the "Goose Creek men." Named for their residence near Goose Creek on the Cooper River, this party opposed the Dissenter majority in the Commons House of Assembly and obstructed the policies of the Lords Proprietors. In 1700 the Goose Creek men wrested control of the Governor's Council from the Dissenters, and two years later, on 18 June 1702, Johnson was appointed governor of South Carolina. His appointment was achieved by the accession of a High Church Anglican, Sir John Granville, to the post of palatine, or chairman, of the proprietary board. Struck by a paralyzing illness, Johnson did not take active control of the province until early 1703.

Johnson governed with a strong hand. As leader of the High Church Anglican party, he used his influence to consolidate Anglican domination of the province. In 1704 he and his party enacted a law to exclude Nonconformists from membership in the Commons House of Assembly. They also passed the Establishment Act, which made the Church of England the official religion of the province. The Carolina government undertook to pay the salaries of Anglican clergymen and to construct and maintain Anglican church buildings. Anglican parishes became units of civil as well as church governance.

Johnson's 1704 laws outraged Dissenters in Carolina and London, who successfully complained to Crown authorities and to Parliament and had the acts disallowed for "repugnancy to laws of England." Johnson's autocratic sponsorship of the Establishment Act was later cited as a reason for his removal from the governorship. Despite disallowance of the 1704 laws, Johnson and his party were still in power. In 1706 they drafted a new Establishment Act that did not contain the objectionable features of the earlier act. That act became a cornerstone of South Carolina's religious and civil government.

Governor during Queen Anne's War (1702–1713), Johnson advocated construction of colonial fortifications and a strong militia. His martial labors were vindicated in August 1706 when he commanded provincial troops and successfully defended Charles Town against a combined French and Spanish amphibious attack. During his administration the Commons House of Assembly also sought to reform the colony's Indian trade policies. Johnson, with his son-in-law Thomas Broughton, was active in the Indian trade and, as a perquisite of the governor's office, was entitled to gifts and tribute from Indian tribes in the region. In 1708 the Commons House introduced a bill to regulate the Indian trade and to require licensing of traders. Johnson initially opposed the bill but signed it into law when it was amended to pay the governor a stipend in lieu of his Indian tribute.

As governor, Johnson made numerous political enemies in South Carolina because of his autocratic manner, his rigid High Church principles, and his loyalty to the Stuart family. After the death of his patron, Lord Granville, Johnson was removed from the Carolina governorship. In December 1708 he was replaced by Edward Tynte but held the office until Tynte's arrival in November 1709. Johnson retired to Silk Hope, where he died. His wife was Joanna Overton, daughter of Robert Overton and Anne Gardiner. Their children were Robert Johnson (1677–1735), the last proprietary and second royal governor of South Carolina; William Johnson (d. 1701); and Anne Johnson (d. 1733), who married Thomas Broughton at Charles Town.

Sir Nathaniel Johnson left his mark upon proprietary South Carolina. His sponsorship of the Anglican establishment was a key element in improving the religious and educational culture of the province and in shaping its political character. Governor and captain general during Queen Anne's War, Johnson defended the English province from rival European powers and led local campaigns against England's enemies in Florida and Louisiana. Imperious in personality, Johnson attempted to rule South Carolina rather than to govern it. He deemed political opponents to be personal enemies and avidly sought their destruction and defeat. In this regard Johnson's tenure as South Carolina governor was chaotic and helped consolidate opposition to his and the proprietors' government.

• Some of Johnson's official correspondence as governor of the Leeward Islands and South Carolina is found in *Calendar of State Papers, 1685–1688, 1689–1692, 1693–1696, 1702, 1708–1709* (1899, 1901–1903, 1912, 1922). Biographical sketches include Mabel Webber, "Sir Nathaniel Johnson and His Son Robert, Governors of South Carolina," *South Carolina Historical Magazine* 38 (Oct. 1937): 109–15, and Gillian Hampson, "Nathaniel Johnson (c. 1645–1713)," in *The House of Commons, 1660–1690*, ed. Basil Duke Henning, vol. 3 (1983), pp. 655–56. Richard P. Sherman, *Robert Johnson, Proprietary & Royal Governor of South Carolina* (1966), pp. 4–7, also contains biographical information. Henry A. M. Smith, "Seewee Barony," *South Carolina Historical Magazine* 9 (1911): 109–17, describes Johnson's planting activities at Silk Hope; Philip M. Brown, "Early Indian Trade in the Development of South Carolina: Politics, Economics, and Social Mobility during the Proprietary Era," *South Carolina Historical Magazine* 76 (July 1977): 118–28, depicts Johnson as an Indian trader. M. Eugene Sirmans, *Colonial South Carolina, a Political History, 1663–1763* (1966), contains a good history of South Carolina during Johnson's governorship. A portrait of Sir Nathaniel Johnson (c. 1705) by an unknown artist is among the collections of the Gibbes Art Museum in Charleston, S.C. See Francis W. Bilodeau et al., *South Carolina Art 1670–1970*, vol. 1 (1970), p. 31, for a reproduction and discussion of its provenance.

ALEXANDER MOORE

JOHNSON, Nunnally (5 Dec. 1897–25 Mar. 1977), screenwriter, was born in Columbus, Georgia, the son of James Johnson, a railroad coppersmith, and Johnny Pearl. Johnson's father eventually became a shop superintendent for the railroad, enabling the family to live a middle-class life. Middle-class values permeate Johnson's screenplays, one of the reasons for his success.

After graduating from high school in 1915, Johnson wrote for the Columbus newspaper, the *Enquirer-Sun*. He served a brief time in the army at the end of World War I, then moved to New York, where he found work as a reporter on the *New York Tribune*. In 1919 he took a reporting job with the *Brooklyn Eagle*, but his writing gifts were more suited to a humor column, which he wrote first for the *Eagle* in 1922, then for the *New York Herald Tribune*. Both his first wife, Alice Mason, whom he married in 1919, and his second wife, Marion Byrnes, whom he married in 1927, worked for the *Eagle*. He had one daughter with each wife, and both marriages ended in divorce.

In the early twenties Johnson also began writing short stories, which appeared in such different publications as the sophisticated *Smart Set* and the more middle-class *Saturday Evening Post*. During the depression magazines bought fewer stories from writers, and in 1932 Johnson, who had done some movie writing in New York, moved to Los Angeles to work as a screenwriter. He was convinced he could match or do better than the writers currently employed in Hollywood, and he was right.

Johnson began at Paramount, writing films in the same light comedy vein as his short stories. Paramount let him go after a year, but he was hired by producer Darryl F. Zanuck, who was establishing a company called 20th Century Pictures. Unlike the producers at Paramount, Zanuck respected scripts and screenwriters. He spent much time and effort on getting the script right and then insisting that the director shoot the film as written. Zanuck also emphasized narrative films, as opposed to the star vehicles of other studios. Johnson's talent for storytelling, scene construction, and dialogue developed and flourished under Zanuck, and Johnson later said, "When I'm working on a picture, he's a part of me, [and] he's a part of it."

The first pictures Johnson wrote for 20th Century were again light comedies, but then Zanuck asked him to write *The House of Rothschild* (1934), a historical film about the banking firm. Although Johnson told Zanuck that he wrote comedy and was liable to have characters falling into flour barrels, Zanuck encouraged him to try the serious script; the film was a success.

In 1935 20th Century was merged with the much larger Fox company to form 20th Century-Fox. Zanuck then asked Johnson to produce the films he was writing as well as others. Johnson tried to tell other writers how to write, but he discovered himself unable to do it, so he continued to produce only the films that he wrote. His greatest commercial success of this period was *Jesse James* (1939), a rousing, action-packed if highly romanticized view of the nineteenth-century outlaw. Johnson's script was filled with vivid characters and folksy humor.

Johnson is best remembered for his 1940 adaptation of John Steinbeck's novel *The Grapes of Wrath*, which tells the story of an Okie family's journey to California during the depression. Johnson found what he called "the spine" of the story, reduced the book's number of scenes with secondary family members, and gave the last half of the story more of a rising emotional arc. He also created the film's final scene, which was not in the novel but which used dialogue from two different chapters in a scene now played in the cab of the Joad truck. The screenplay was nominated for an Academy Award but did not win. Johnson also was nominated for an Oscar three years later (and lost again) for *Holy Matrimony*, an adaptation of the Arnold Bennett novel *Buried Alive*.

In February 1940 Johnson married Dorris Bowden, the actress who played Rosasharon in *The Grapes of Wrath*, and three years later she appeared in Johnson's adaptation of another Steinbeck novel, *The Moon Is Down*. She subsequently retired from acting, and the Johnsons had three children. Johnson continued to write and produce comedies as well as dramas, most notably *Roxie Hart* (1942) and *Holy Matrimony* (1943), and was a well-known Hollywood wit. When he wrote the screenplay for *Tobacco Road* (1941) he was asked if he came from such a poor part of Georgia. Johnson replied, "Where I come from, Tobacco Road is known as the country club set."

In 1943 Johnson left Fox and formed International Pictures, which later merged with Universal. His most notable film for International was the dark thriller *Woman in the Window* (1944). His 1947 political satire *The Senator Was Indiscreet* had the misfortune of being released in the midst of congressional investigations of communism in Hollywood, and the film had trouble finding theaters that would play it, although Johnson was not a Communist and was never called before the House Committee on Un-American Activities. When asked years later if the film had caused him any personal difficulties, Johnson replied, "In Hollywood a personal difficulty is if you make two pictures in a row that are unsuccessful."

Because the pictures he produced at International had not been big financial successes, Johnson returned to Fox in 1948. There he produced and wrote the final draft of the screenplay of the classic western *The Gunfighter* (1950); however, he refused screen credit as writer because he felt he was simply filling out details of a shorter-than-needed original script. In 1951 he wrote and produced *The Desert Fox*, a superb examination of Field Marshal Erwin Rommel's involvement with the plot to assassinate Hitler.

In 1952 Johnson began directing as well as writing and producing. He directed eight films, the best known of which are *The Man in the Gray Flannel Suit* (1956) and *The Three Faces of Eve* (1957), the latter a true story about a woman with multiple personalities; Joanne Woodward won an Academy Award for her performance under Johnson's direction.

In the early sixties Johnson returned to writing only. His last two produced scripts are two of his best. *The World of Henry Orient* (1964) is a witty, sophisticated adaptation of his daughter Nora's novel about her life as a child of divorce. *The Dirty Dozen* (1967) is a vigorous, violent World War II action film that suffers from changes made to Johnson's screenplay by another writer. No longer were there strong producers like Zanuck to protect the quality of a script.

Johnson retired in 1970. At the memorial service after his death, fellow screenwriter George Seaton said Johnson once told him that poorly constructed recent films with unbelievable characters made him feel like "a saddle maker in the age of Detroit." Seaton added, "If we only had more saddle makers like Johnson," an opinion shared by a growing number of film critics and historians as well as many screenwriters who admire Johnson's craft.

• Johnson's papers are in the Mugar Memorial Library at Boston University. An extensive oral history interview with Johnson was conducted in 1968–1969 as part of the UCLA Oral History of the Motion Pictures project, and the transcript is available at UCLA, the University of California at Berkeley, and at the American Film Institute's Center for Advanced Studies in Los Angeles. A collection of Johnson's short stories, *There Ought to Be a Law*, was published in 1931. Johnson's letters have been published in Dorris Johnson and Ellen Leventhal, eds., *The Letters of Nunnally Johnson* (1981). Nora Johnson, *Flashback* (1979), is a combination memoir/biography of her father and deals with both his personal and professional life. Tom Stempel, *Screenwriter: The Life and Times of Nunnally Johnson* (1980), focuses primarily on Johnson's work as a screenwriter.

TOM STEMPEL

JOHNSON, Oliver (27 Dec. 1809–10 Dec. 1889), reformer and journalist, was born in Peacham, Vermont, the son of Ziba Johnson and Sally Lincoln, farmers. After an elementary school education, Johnson apprenticed as a printer in the office of the Montpelier *Vermont Watchman*, edited by Ezekiel P. Walton.

As early as 1828, Johnson began publicly speaking out against slavery on behalf of the American Colonization Society. In 1831 he moved to Boston to edit his own newspaper, the *Christian Soldier*, which sought to discredit the tenets of Universalism. Johnson's paper shared the printing press of William Lloyd Garrison's *Liberator*, and the two young editors established a friendship based on common support for reform movements. Johnson later recalled of this intimate association, "Mr. Garrison did more and better for me than any college or theological seminary could have done." In 1832 Johnson joined Garrison in founding the New England Anti-Slavery Society, a pioneer abolitionist organization. He worked as a traveling lecturer for that society while filling in for Garrison as the *Liberator*'s editor when the latter was ill or traveling abroad.

From 1837 to 1839 Johnson was general agent of the Rhode Island Anti-Slavery Society and lectured throughout that state, once narrowly escaping a tarring-and-feathering in Greenville. During the late 1830s Johnson sided with Garrison in the growing quarrels among abolitionists over issues of women's rights and pacifism that ultimately divided the movement. Abolitionist principles eventually led Johnson to sever all ties with the Congregational church and to affiliate with a reformist sect, the Progressive Friends.

In the 1840s Johnson worked as an assistant to Horace Greeley on the *New York Tribune* and then briefly edited first the *Republic*, an antislavery newspaper in Philadelphia, and then the *Practical Christian* for the Hopedale Community, a utopian settlement at Milford, Massachusetts. He returned to abolitionist journalism as editor of the Salem, Ohio, *Anti-Slavery Bugle* (1849–1851) and the Philadelphia *Pennsylvania Freeman* (1851–1853). In 1853 he became the assistant to Sydney Howard Gay as editor of the American Anti-Slavery Society's official newspaper, the New York *National Anti-Slavery Standard*. Five years later he succeeded Gay and guided the *Standard* through the secession crisis and the Civil War. Like his mentor, Garrison, Johnson was editorially critical of the Republican party while still able to declare in 1860 that "I regard its success as the beginning of a new and better era." While privately feeling misgivings over coercive means used to abolish slavery, he editorially applauded Abraham Lincoln's Emancipation Proclamation and reelection.

When the Civil War ended, Johnson joined Garrison in supporting the dissolution of the American Anti-Slavery Society, declaring "Anti-Slavery Societies now are an anachronism—relics of the age of Slavery, now happily passed away." When the majority of other abolitionists rejected that position, Johnson resigned as editor of the *Standard*. Soon after, he became the managing editor of the *New York Independent* (1865–1870), where he promoted the causes of freedmen's rights and woman suffrage. Johnson then worked as editor of the *New York Weekly Tribune* (1870–1872). While there, he wrote a campaign biography to support Greeley's 1872 presidential race. Following Greeley's death, Johnson worked as managing editor for Henry Ward Beecher's *Christian Union* (1872–1876) and then published the *Orange (N.J.) Journal* (1876–1879). In 1880 Johnson wrote a biography of his mentor in the abolitionist movement, *William Lloyd Garrison and His Times*. This book was surprisingly conciliatory toward the other abolitionist factions, which Johnson had editorially battled for more than two decades. He spent his last years as an associate editor of the *New York Evening Post*. In a tribute to Johnson in 1884, Henry Ward Beecher wrote "All his life long he has subordinated ease, gain and reputation to the great duty of this age. Closely associated with Garrison and Phillips, he was a worthy member of the triad—for, if he was in speech less able, by his pen he was more able than they" (*New York Herald*, 11 Dec. 1889).

Johnson's first wife was Mary Anne White, assistant matron of the female state prison at Sing Sing and a lecturer on physiology. They were married in 1832 and had no children; she died in 1872. The following year Johnson married Jane Abbott, with whom he had one child. Johnson died in Brooklyn, New York.

• Among Johnson's other publications are *Consider This, Ye That Forget God* (1831), *Correspondence between Oliver Johnson and George F. White* (1841), *What I Know of Horace Gree-* ley (1872), and *The Abolitionists Vindicated in a Review of Eli Thayer's Paper on the New England Emigrant Aid Company* (1887). Considerable biographical information on Johnson can be found in Wendell Phillips Garrison and Francis Jackson Garrison, *William Lloyd Garrison, 1805–1879: The Story of His Life Told by His Children* (4 vols., 1885–1889). Helpful obituaries are in the *New York Herald*, 11 Dec. 1889, and *New York Independent*, 19 Dec. 1889.

JOHN R. McKIVIGAN

JOHNSON, Osa (14 Mar. 1894–7 Jan. 1953), author, lecturer, and film producer, was born Osa Helen Leighty in Chanute, Kansas, the daughter of William Sherman Leighty, a railroad engineer, and Ruby Isabel Holman. In 1910 she left high school to marry Martin Johnson, whom she had met eleven years earlier when he visited Chanute as an eighteen-year-old itinerant photographer. In the meantime he had visited Europe alone and traveled with Jack London on a 25,000-mile sailing trip. They had no children.

Johnson's husband had taken pictures of natives in the South Seas and was attempting to finance a photographic expedition of his own by showing slides and a one-reel motion picture made during his voyage with London. She accompanied his illustrated lecture tour for two years in small vaudeville houses, demonstrating Hawaiian songs and dances, until an engagement at Martin Beck's Palace Theater in New York brought them enough money for a trip to the New Hebrides Islands. There they were seized by the Malekula tribe and narrowly escaped. Back in the United States they exhibited the one-reel film *Captured by Cannibals* that they had made during their adventure. With the money they earned they were able to buy better equipment and return to the New Hebrides in 1914. There they made friends with their former captors and extended their photographic records, the first ever made of the people of the island.

In 1917 the Johnsons went to North Borneo, where they photographed the native tribes and wildlife. They returned for a lecture tour and prepared for an expedition to Africa, which was to become their principal area of work. They made their first trip there in 1921, and Osa managed the camp while Martin filmed. She also hunted but only to provide meat: "I did most of the marketing with a gun," she reported to S. J. Wolf in 1940, "but unless we were compelled to kill to save our lives we never shot an animal except for food." The two made a total of twelve expeditions, returning to the United States after each to lecture and raise money for future trips. Traveling in amphibian airplanes, which they were both licensed to fly, they visited the Nile Valley, the Belgian Congo, and Uganda on three trips between 1923 and 1934; they returned to North Borneo in 1935 and 1936, gathering material for museums and for their own lectures. In Africa they discovered Lake Paradise in Uganda, where they established a camp visited by George Eastman and the duke and duchess of York. They also worked with an expedition from the American Museum of Natural History to secure elephants for its permanent exhibit.

Together the Johnsons made about thirty-five one-reel motion pictures, as well as eight lecture films and ten full-length features, including the sound films *Simba* (1928), *Across the World with Mr. and Mrs. Martin Johnson* (1930), *Congorilla* (1932), *Baboona* (1935), and *Borneo* (1937), which were shown theatrically with great success. They also collaborated on six books: *Cannibal Land* (1922), *Camera Trails in Africa* (1924), *Lion* (1929), *Congorilla* (1931), *Over African Jungles* (1935), and *Borneo* (1935). Osa Johnson was president of Martin Johnson Pictures, Inc., and later of Osa Johnson, Inc. Her husband died in an airplane crash near Los Angeles in 1937. Although injured in the crash, Osa continued to travel and write. She led an expedition in 1937 for the 20th Century–Fox Film Corp., acting as technical adviser and shooting background footage for the 1939 feature *Stanley and Livingstone*.

With the guidance of her business manager, Clark Hallan Getts, Johnson succeeded in establishing a public image of her own after her husband's death. She made appearances in support of wildlife conservation, and in 1939 she gave her name to a line of leather gloves and women's and children's sportswear labeled "Osa Johnson," with an African motif and made from a fabric trademarked "Osafari." She also designed a collection of eight animal toys marketed as "Osa Johnson's Pets," each sold with a booklet describing the animal represented. The novelty was voted the most original plush toy of the year by the National Toy Show in 1939 and was endorsed by the National Wildlife Federation as a teaching tool.

Under her own name she published ten children's books and three adult books, as well as more than forty magazine articles. Her autobiography, *I Married Adventure*, ghostwritten by Winifred Dunn, was at the top of the *New York Times* bestseller list for many weeks in 1940 and was the June Book-of-the-Month Club selection, selling more than a half million copies in its first year. It was made into a successful motion picture, incorporating clips from the Johnsons' films. In 1941 Getts, still managing her public image, arranged for her to receive an honorary D.Sc. from Rollins College in Florida and to be appointed honorary chair of National Wildlife Restoration Week by the National Wildlife Federation. She married Getts secretly in 1940 and again in a highly publicized ceremony, conducted by Mayor Fiorello La Guardia at City Hall in New York City, the following year. They were divorced in 1949.

Johnson remained a popular lecturer and a symbol of self-reliant womanhood. Known for her smart wardrobe—she was voted one of the twelve best-dressed women in America in 1939 and claimed to have worn royal blue satin pajamas at the end of the day in the jungle—she was one of the most glamorous women of her time. But by the mid-1940s her high style of life and increasing problem with alcohol had ruined her financially, and she was forced to auction off her personal effects. She was reported to be planning another expedition to Africa when she died in New York City. Although the Johnsons' films became badly dated, and her books fell out of favor for their superficial and racially insensitive treatment of the native people she described, Osa and Martin Johnson made an important contribution to the accurate photographic record of wildlife in its native state and, in the words of their biographers Pascal and Eleanor Imperato, "shaped, for better and for worse, America's vision of Africa."

• Photographs, memorabilia, and documents of the Johnsons are collected in the Martin and Osa Johnson Safari Museum, Chanute, Kans., and the Clark H. Getts Collection in the American Heritage Center at the University of Wyoming, Laramie. In addition to Osa Johnson's autobiography, a detailed account of her life is in Pascal James Imperato and Eleanor M. Imperato, *They Married Adventure: The Wandering Lives of Martin and Osa Johnson* (1992). Bibliographies of the Johnsons' writings are in Gene DeGruson, *Kansas Authors of Best Sellers* (1970), and Evelyn V. Alden, "A Bibliography of Books Written by Osa Johnson," *Johnson Wait-a-Bit News* (1985). See also the *Christian Science Monitor*, 9 Feb. and 23 Mar. 1940; S. J. Wolf, "A Quarter Century of Jungle Adventure," *New York Times Magazine*, 21 Apr. 1940; and the *New York Times*, 23 May 1940. An obituary is in the *New York Times*, 8 Jan. 1953.

DENNIS WEPMAN

JOHNSON, Owen McMahon (27 Aug. 1878–27 Jan. 1952), fiction writer, was born in New York City, the son of Robert Underwood Johnson, a writer and later a distinguished editor and then ambassador to Italy, and Katherine McMahon. When he was six, Johnson sold a short story to *St. Nicholas Magazine* for a dollar. At twelve, he helped edit a two-issue publication to raise funds for the Washington Memorial Arch in New York. For four years he attended the Lawrenceville School, the distinguished preparatory academy in New Jersey near Princeton, and he remained for a fifth year to found and edit its literary magazine, the *Lawrenceville Lit*. He made numerous friends at the school, many of whom served as models for characters in his later school-days fiction. He entered Yale in 1896 but disliked its snobbery at several levels, its fraternities and secret senior societies, and its antiquated curriculum. At the same time, he made friends with several young men from influential families and was editor of the *Yale Literary Magazine*. When not yet twenty-three, Johnson published his first novel, *Arrows of the Almighty* (1901). This historical romance, set before and during the Civil War, is significant in Johnson's development mainly because of its depiction of life at Yale in the 1850s.

Johnson was married five times. He married Mary Galt Stockly, a Cleveland financier's daughter, in 1901. The couple, who had three children, went to Paris, where Johnson wrote *In the Name of Liberty: A Story of the Terror* (1905), a novel about the French Revolution. Back in the United States, he visited New York police courts, learned about work by unprincipled lawyers, and wrote *Max Fargus* (1906), a complex novel about sleazy revenge. The versatile Johnson then wrote *The Comet*, a play that enjoyed a two-year run on Broadway, beginning in 1907. Johnson assembled his stories about life in prep school and college, some of which had first appeared in *McClure's Magazine*, added to them, and published *The Eternal Boy: Being the Story of the Prodigious Hickey* (1909; republished as *The Prodigious Hickey* [1910]); *The Humming Bird* (1910); *The Varmint* (1910; republished as *The Varmint: A Lawrenceville Story* [1921]); and *The Tennessee Shad, Chronicling the Rise and Fall of the Firm of Doc Macnooder and the Tennessee Shad* (1911). *The Varmint* introduces John Humperdink Stover, Johnson's most famous fictional character. Other of Johnson's school lads, who indulged in juvenile high jinks and had study problems, include Barker Smith, Flash Condit, Great Big Man, Gutter Pup, Hungry Smeed, Lovely Mead, Turkey Reiter, and Uncooked Beefsteak—all based on Johnson's school chums. His wife died in 1910. He published his second play, *A Comedy for Wives*, in 1911.

Johnson capitalized on the popularity of his school and college fiction with *Stover at Yale* (1911), his most memorable novel, in which Dink Stover, of Lawrenceville, becomes a football star at Yale. Mainly, the novel satirizes the fraternity system, other social pressures forcing students to conform, and outmoded professorial demands and attitudes. Johnson also wrote "The Social Usurpation of Our Colleges" (*Collier's*, 18 and 25 May, 8, 15, and 22 June 1912), which comprises five serious articles also criticizing most phases of campus activity and suggesting social, political, and curricular reforms. He especially deplored snobbery and the elective system and recommended common dining facilities, democratic socializing, and rewards for sensible achievement.

Johnson married the San Francisco socialite Esther Ellen Cobb in 1912. The two, who had no children, traveled extensively in Europe. Johnson spoke French and Italian well and came to revere the French. His novel *The Salamander* (1913) concerns amoral young bohemian women in Manhattan, and in Doré "Dodo" Baxter Johnson presents an early example of the American flapper. (This novel was adapted for the stage in 1914.) Next came *The Spirit of France* (1916), in praise of the French love of peace, moral strength, sense of responsibility, and heroism, in contrast to German material strength and mechanical prowess and British moral and economic poverty. Johnson and his second wife were divorced in 1917. (She later married William A. Wright and as Cobina Wright became an actress and writer.) Johnson married Cecile Denise de la Garde, a Frenchwoman, later in 1917; they had a child before she died in 1918. Two works developed, separately, from *The Salamander* and *The Spirit of France*. *The Woman Gives: A Story of Regeneration* (1916) features more female bohemians in New York but also a selfless woman who puts one man back on his feet then goes to aid another. *The Wasted Generation* (1921) is a romantic, sentimental, and bitter novel in the form of the diary of an American who joins the French Foreign Legion and fights in the trenches in World War I. In 1919 the French government named Johnson a chevalier of the Legion of Honor.

For some decades after the war, Johnson lived in Stockbridge, Massachusetts. He married Catherine Sayre Burton in 1921. They had one child. Catherine Johnson died in 1923. Three years later, he married Gertrude Bovee Le Boutillier (the widow of John A. Le Boutillier). They had no children. Johnson continued to write until 1931, though less effectively. *Skippy Bedelle: His Sentimental Progress from Urchin to the Complete Man of the World* (1922) fails to recapture the bubbling brilliance of his earlier school novels. *Children of Divorce* (1927) and *Sacrifice* (1929) dramatize the problems of disastrous marriages. *The Coming of the Amazons: A Satiristic Speculation on the Scientific Future of Civilization* (1931) ludicrously depicts a world ruled by women. Johnson switched political parties in 1932 from Republican to Democrat to support Franklin D. Roosevelt and was himself an unsuccessful Democratic candidate for Congress, First Massachusetts District, in 1936 and again in 1938. In poor health, he moved with his wife in 1947 to Vineyard Haven, Massachusetts, where he died.

Johnson had a brilliant, restless, humor-loving mind and was quite prolific but perhaps too versatile for his own good. He is properly revered, however, for his stories and novels about school days and college life, especially the influential, standard-setting, and enduring *Stover at Yale*.

• Most of Johnson's scattered correspondence and other papers are at the American Academy of Arts and Letters in New York City; Butler Library, Columbia; and Houghton Library, Harvard. Robert McAlmon, *Being Geniuses Together, 1920–1930* (1938), credits Johnson for writing the first "flapper and . . . jazz age" fiction and calls him as good as F. Scott Fitzgerald. Cobina Wright, Johnson's second wife, reminisces in *I Never Grew Up* (1952). John O. Lyons, *The College Novel in America* (1962), praises *Stover at Yale* in detail for its criticism of campus pretentiousness. David Lamoreaux, "*Stover at Yale* and the Gridiron Metaphor," *Journal of Popular Culture* 11 (Fall 1977): 330–44, theorizes that Johnson used the gridiron as a metaphor to express the hope that team play in America would generate more responsible social and business leaders. Christian K. Messenger, *Sport and the Spirit of Play in American Fiction: Hawthorne to Faulkner* (1981), cites *Stover at Yale* to develop his theory that sport and play are central to America's social pattern. Alice Payne Hackett, *60 Years of Best Sellers* (1956), lists *The Salamander* as a bestseller in 1914, in competition with novels by Winston Churchill (the American), George Barr McCutcheon, Booth Tarkington, and Harold Bell Wright. An obituary is in the *New York Times*, 28 Jan. 1952.

ROBERT L. GALE

JOHNSON, Paul Emanuel (19 Feb. 1898–1 Sept. 1974), theological educator and psychologist, was born in Niantic, Connecticut, the son of John Edward Johnson, a Methodist clergyman, and Martha Cadwallander. He attended schools in Waterloo, Iowa, and in 1920 received his A.B. degree from Cornell College in Mt. Vernon, Iowa. In 1921 he was awarded an A.M. degree from the University of Chicago. He received a professional theological degree, the S.T.B., from the Boston University School of Theology in 1923 and in 1928 earned a Ph.D. in philosophy of religion from Boston University. In 1922 he married Evelyn Grant, who provided him with intellectual and emotional support throughout his career; they had two children.

Johnson was ordained a deacon in the Methodist Episcopal church in 1923 and an elder in 1925. He was received on trial in the denomination's New England Southern Conference in 1925 and was admitted in full connection in 1927. From 1925 until 1927 he served as a Methodist missionary teacher at West China Union University in Chentu, West China. After returning from China, Johnson served several churches and completed his Ph.D. From 1936 through 1941 he taught philosophy, religion, and psychology at Morningside College in Sioux City, Iowa, and served as that institution's academic dean. In 1941 he was called to Boston University School of Theology, where he began his distinguished career as a professor of psychology and pastoral counseling and where his scholarly accomplishments projected him into national and international forums within the broad arena of the pastoral arts and sciences. In 1963, after becoming a Boston University emeritus professor, Johnson continued as a theological educator at the Christian Theological Seminary in Indianapolis, Indiana, where he was instrumental in establishing a pastoral counseling center. He died in Centerville, Massachusetts.

When Johnson arrived at Boston University, he joined an academic tradition that was already familiar to him, philosophical personalism, a philosophical school characterized by the conviction that persons provide the most revealing clues to what is real. He had completed his dissertation under the American personalist philosopher Edgar Sheffield Brightman on the topic of Josiah Royce's philosophical idealism, the philosophical doctrine running counter to materialism and realism and claiming that the objects of external perceptions ultimately consist of ideas. Johnson tried to combine the tradition of personalist thought with that of dynamic psychology, a psychology concerned with mental forces or mental energy stressing such areas as motivation, will, affects, and the unconscious, which was beginning to be taught in theological schools and seminaries, primarily because of the growing popularity of clinical pastoral education, the training of theological students to provide pastoral care in hospitals and institutional settings. It was within this mix of theological, philosophical, and psychosocial notions and clinical practices that Johnson formulated his major intellectual contribution. Dynamic interpersonalism, as it came to be called, holds that persons-in-relationship provide the most revealing clues to the nature of reality, including ultimate reality; this was a synthesis of Brightman's philosophical personalism, Harry Stack Sullivan's interpersonal psychiatry, the individual psychology of Harvard professor Gordon W. Allport, and the liberal theology of Paul Tillich.

Johnson's dean at Boston University, Walter G. Muelder, encouraged him to concentrate his research on the emerging field of the psychology of religion, a discipline that had been given impetus by the publication of William James's *Varieties of Religious Experience* (1902) and offers observations and explications of religious experience and behavior using the terminologies and methodologies of psychological science. The topic was beginning to find a home in the more liberal schools of theology, and in 1945 Johnson published *Psychology of Religion* (rev. ed., 1959), which served for nearly two decades as a major textbook in the discipline.

By midcentury the psychology of religion had gained a tenuous place in theological school curricula, but it was viewed primarily as an academic discipline, whereas clinical pastoral education was approached as a means of relating ideas and notions of pastoral care in the context of actual human suffering. In New England, Johnson became a leader in introducing this training/education method into theological education, particularly by helping in 1952 to establish at the Boston University School of Theology the Institute of Pastoral Care, an organization that provided internships at mental and general hospitals to ministerial students.

Gradually Johnson's efforts shifted away from the psychology of religion and toward the establishment of clinical pastoral education and pastoral counseling as integral parts of theological curricula. In the ensuing dialogues, conflicts and differences with those theologians rooted in the "classical" theological disciplines such as biblical studies and church history were common, and Johnson is viewed by some historians as having been a mediator and synthesizer, both in the New England area as well as nationwide. Johnson emphasized the necessity of grounding clinical work in solid scholarship that was rooted in interdisciplinary studies, as opposed to some enthusiasts in the clinical end who resisted the academic and theoretical. This tendency was never embraced by Johnson, as illustrated by his strong leadership in establishing a doctoral program in pastoral psychology and counseling at Boston University, a program that for several decades educated a stream of men and women who assumed leadership roles in what came to be known as the pastoral care and counseling movement. His leadership in this field was evident also in Johnson's later publications, which included *Christian Love* (1951), *Psychology of Pastoral Care* (1953), *Personality and Religion* (1957), and *Person and Counselor* (1967), volumes rooted as much in psychological theories as in theological positions, with an implicit theological liberalism.

In his attempt to combine the academic and the clinical, Johnson worked to establish an institute that would provide clinical experiences for advanced doctoral students. His association with Albert V. Danielsen, a prominent Boston entrepreneur and philanthropist, led to a significant endowment to establish at Boston University both a professorial chair and a clinical facility, the Albert V. Danielsen Institute, which integrates theology and the behavioral sciences in the education, training, and supervision of pastoral counselors and pastoral psychotherapists.

Johnson influenced the development of the psychology of religion as an academic discipline, but his major contribution was to theological education, particularly to the fields of pastoral care and counseling, pastoral theology and psychology, and clinical pastoral education. Both his academic and clinical endeavors found expression in his system of dynamic interpersonalism, a comprehensive theory of personality that is capable of undergirding a variety of Christian as well as interfaith ministries.

• Johnson's papers, including a lengthy unpublished autobiography, are in the Archives of the Boston University School of Theology Library. A partial bibliography of his works may be found in the Jan. 1969 issue of *Pastoral Psychology*. A festschrift, *Dynamic Interpersonalism for Ministry: Essays in Honor of Paul E. Johnson* (1973), ed. Orlo Strunk, Jr., is a good source regarding his many contributions. Several historians of theological education have noted Johnson's contributions, including Edward E. Thornton, *Professional Education for Ministry: A History of Clinical Pastoral Education* (1970); E. Brooks Holifield, *A History of Pastoral Care in America: From Salvation to Self-Realization* (1983); and Charles E. Hall, *Head and Heart: The Story of the Clinical Pastoral Education Movement* (1992). The brief essays "Dynamic Interpersonalism" and "Personalism and Pastoral Care," which appear in Rodney J. Hunter, ed., *Dictionary of Pastoral Care and Counseling* (1990), also are relevant sources.

ORLO STRUNK, JR.

JOHNSON, Pete (24 Mar. 1904–23 Mar. 1967), blues and jazz pianist, was born in Kansas City, Missouri. His day of birth is given as 25 March in an interview with Johnny Simmen, but the date is corrected to 24 March in the reprint of Simmen's article in Hans Mauerer's book and repeated as 24 March in Mauerer's reprint of a 1962 article by Johnson's wife; the *New York Times* obituary concurs, giving 24 March. His full given name is probably Kermit Holden Johnson. The names of his parents are unknown.

Johnson was raised by his mother alone, who worked as a domestic to support him. She placed him in an orphanage for a time because she could not care for him adequately, but she took him back home when she learned that he was being ill treated. As a child Johnson played homemade drums, and in ward school he first played a real drum. He also learned piano from local players, most significantly his uncle Charles Johnson, who taught him a fast rag, "Nickels and Dimes." Johnson started school late and dropped out of the fifth grade, at age twelve or thirteen, to work mainly as a laborer. He worked as a drummer from about 1922 to 1926, when he switched to piano permanently.

The chronology of Johnson's activities in Kansas City nightclubs from the late 1920s through the mid-1930s is unclear. Around 1927, while performing at the Backbiter's Club, he accompanied singer Joe Turner and thereby initiated one of the best-matched partnerships in jazz and blues. At the Hole in the Wall he accompanied singer Edna Taylor, whom he then followed to Jazzland for better pay. He also worked, often with Turner, at the Hawaiian Gardens in a small band led by Abie Price, the Black and Tan Club, El Trocadore, the Yellow Front, the Peacock Inn, the Grey Goose, and the Spinning Wheel with Herman Walder's Rockette Swing Unit.

In 1933 or 1935 Johnson began working at the Sunset Crystal Palace in a duo with drummer Murl Johnson that gradually expanded to become a seven- or eight-piece band, plus singers Turner and Henry Lawson. The group also broadcast on radio. Johnson and Turner were discovered by jazz impressario John Hammond, who brought them to New York City for a performance at the Apollo Theater in Harlem in 1936. Singing a pop song instead of their strength, the blues, the duo was quickly pulled off the stage. They are also reported to have performed at the Famous Door, but it may be that this event happened two years later. They returned home, and Johnson resumed his job at the Sunset, from which he made nightly broadcasts in 1938. In May of that year Hammond introduced the duo on Benny Goodman's NBC radio show "Camel Caravan." Their breakthrough to success, however, began on 23 December 1938, when Hammond presented them at his "From Spirituals to Swing" concert at Carnegie Hall, where they performed the blues "It's All Right Baby." This concert also marked the formation of a boogie-woogie piano trio with Johnson, Albert Ammons, and Meade "Lux" Lewis, whose performances received considerable acclaim. (Recordings from this concert were first issued in 1958.) The next week Turner and Johnson recorded the blues classic "Roll 'em, Pete."

In 1939 the piano trio worked with Turner as their singer at Café Society in New York and the Hotel Sherman in Chicago and broadcast nationally, from the latter. In New York, Johnson broadcast with Turner from the Chamber Music Society of Lower Basin Street (Aug. 1940). He worked in a piano duo with Ammons at the uptown location of Café Society to 1942, when the two men began touring. Johnson's recordings from this period include "Pete's Blues" and "Let 'em Jump" as an unaccompanied pianist (Apr. 1939), "Cherry Red" and "Baby, Look at You" with his Boogie Woogie Boys (June 1939), and "Vine Street Bustle" and "Some Day Blues" with his Blues Trio (Dec. 1939). He also recorded "Piney Brown Blues" with a five-piece group that included trumpeter Hot Lips Page, under Turner's nominal leadership (Nov. 1940); "627 Stomp" from that same session of 1940, but with an eight-piece group and without Turner; and "Just for You" (1941), with his trio. He performed in the film short *Boogie Woogie Dream* (1941).

In the mid-1940s Johnson toured in duos with Ammons, Lewis, and Turner. He and Turner opened their own Blue Room Club in Los Angeles in 1945, and Johnson regularly appeared on Turner's recordings, including "Old Piney Brown Is Gone" (1948). From 1947 to 1948 Johnson worked in California both as a soloist and in duos with Ammons at the Streets of Paris in Hollywood or with Turner in Los Angeles and San Francisco. He then toured the Northeast.

From late 1948 onward Johnson's career declined severely. For over a decade he had been pigeonholed as a boogie-woogie pianist, a label that raised expectations of relentlessly repetitious piano bass patterns, and he had difficulty finding work within this restricted and by now rather worn-out blues style, even though he was actually a versatile pianist fluent not only in other blues styles, but in jazz and popular song as well.

In 1949 Johnson first played in Buffalo and met Margery (maiden name unknown). They married and had one daughter. Johnson decided to settle in Buffalo in 1950 but came to regret that decision because few places there offered him work. He toured the Northeast and Midwest in the Piano Parade with Erroll Garner, Lewis, and Art Tatum in 1952. That same year he worked with Lewis in Providence, Rhode Island, and Detroit, and he occasionally found jobs playing at little-known venues, but for most of the decade he worked by day, often doing heavy labor.

In 1955 Johnson recorded the album *Listen to the Blues* with singer Jimmy Rushing. The album *Joe Turner Sings Kansas City Jazz* (reissued as *Boss of the Blues*) included Johnson and a number of Count Basie's sidemen and presented pop songs and reprises of Turner and Johnson's early blues recordings (1956). In 1958 Johnson joined Turner on tour with Jazz at the Philharmonic in Europe, at the Newport Jazz Festival, where he also accompanied singer Big Maybelle and singer-guitarist Chuck Berry, and at the Great South Bay Jazz Festival. Johnson had a heart condition and diabetes, and this same year, 1958, he suffered a stroke that left him partially paralyzed, ending his musical career. He died in Buffalo after suffering another stroke.

Wertheim said, "Pete Johnson was a complete jazz musician who could handle an extensive variety of music and pianistic technique. The only link[s] Pete Johnson had with the piano style of the 'primitive' [are] that he did not read music too well, although he knew chords, and his fast boogie woogie solos generated the same wild excitement" (quoted in Mauerer, p. 37). By way of example, Turner's "Roll 'em Pete" offers Johnson's definitive boogie-woogie playing. The "627 Stomp" (1940) finds Johnson comfortably settled into a jazz band; this piece is a blues done in the style of Kansas City swing, and here a boogie-woogie bass line comes in only at the end, for climactic effect. On "Just for You" (1941), Johnson has the support of bassist Al Hall and drummer A. G. Godley, and he plays a relaxed, quiet, and elegant bass and chord pattern in the stride piano tradition while concentrating on the melody, ornamented by trills and cascading lines. "Pete's Lonesome Blues" (1946) finds him applying this elegant stride style to the unaccompanied blues, and in this setting his approach in its earthiness surpasses the work of the more famous practitioners of Harlem stride piano. On "Piney Brown Blues" and the duo "Little Bittie Gal's Blues" (1944), Johnson's focus is on trembly trills floating rhythmically across the beat; this sort of tuneful interplay between tinkling piano melodies and Turner's full-bodied voice, of which there are numerous additional examples, perhaps represents Johnson's finest work.

• The essential source is Hans J. Mauerer, comp. and ed., *The Pete Johnson Story* (1965). See also Sharon Pease, "Swing Piano Styles: Pete Johnson Got His Start Shining Shoes in Kaycee," *Down Beat* 6 (15 Dec. 1939): 22, which includes a notated example of his solo on "Let 'em Jump"; Virginia Irwin, "Kings of Boogie Woogie," *St. Louis Post-Dispatch*, 20 June 1943; Johnny Simmen, "My Life, My Music," *Jazz Journal* 12 (Aug. 1959): 8–11; H. A. Woodfin, "Pete Johnson: Jazz Pianist," *Jazz Monthly* 8 (Sept. 1962): 2–4; and James F. Wertheim, "Pete Johnson: To-Day," *Blues Unlimited* 8 (Jan. 1964): 8–10. For assessments of his playing, see Wertheim, in Mauerer, and Max Harrison, "Boogie Woogie," in *Jazz*, ed. Nat Hentoff and Albert J. McCarthy (1959), pp. 105–35, which is critical of Johnson's boogie-woogie style. Also helpful is Gunther Schuller, *The Swing Era: The Development of Jazz, 1930–1945* (1989), pp. 796–98. Obituaries are in the *New York Times*, 24 Mar. 1967, and *Down Beat* 34 (4 May 1967): 12.

BARRY KERNFELD

JOHNSON, Peter August (17 June 1851–1 Jan. 1914), physician, was born near Eatontown, New Jersey, the son of Joseph Johnson and Martha A. Frazier. Before moving to New York, where he would spend his entire professional career, Peter attended Roger Smith High School in Newport, Rhode Island. After completing additional studies at Clark's Collegiate Institute in New York, Johnson enrolled at the Long Island College Hospital (a precursor to the College of Medicine of the State University of New York Health Science Center of Brooklyn), a reputable private institution. On his graduation from the Brooklyn medical school in 1882, Johnson became the fifth black graduate of the institution, forty-five years after the first African-American M.D., James McCune Smith, had earned his degree in Scotland. Johnson initially practiced medicine in New York under the guidance of David K. McDonough, a physician who had been born a slave, and Edward J. Messener, a former mentor from medical school. Messener invited the young medical graduate to work with him at New York's Mount Sinai Hospital, where Johnson would spend seven years, four of which he also spent at the People's Dispensary. Johnson married Mary Elizabeth Whittle in 1882; they had two children.

Throughout his medical career, Johnson fought the discrimination and racism that constrained educational and clinical training opportunities for black physicians, who constituted less than 1 percent of all physicians when he graduated from medical school. Black Americans who aspired to enter medicine in the late nineteenth and early twentieth centuries commonly found that racism—and, in the case of black women, sexism as well—categorically excluded them from many medical schools. Even when some black applicants gained entrance and later graduated from medical school, they would confront, as graduates, discrimination and hostility while searching for training opportunities in hospitals and clinics. Prominent early twentieth-century black public figures, such as Booker T. Washington, told friends and colleagues that Johnson and other black physicians wrote to him about their difficulty in securing places for themselves on hospital staffs or rooms for their patients in some institutions. As cofounder of McDonough Memorial Hospital (named for his former colleague and friend), a voluntary institution that opened in 1898 at 439 West Forty-second Street, Johnson became active in this initiative to bring high quality medical services to the urban poor in New York City. McDonough's admission policy disallowed discrimination against patients on the basis of race, ethnicity, or religious affiliation. Johnson served as the chief of attending staff and chief surgeon during a five-year affiliation with the facility.

Johnson spent the remainder of his career with the New York Milk Committee for the Prevention and Cure of Infant Diseases and as a staff member in the Division of Tuberculosis Prevention and Control at the New York City Board of Health. A board member of the Committee for Improving the Industrial Condition of Negroes in New York and the National League on Urban Conditions Among Negroes (later organized as the National Urban League), Johnson's concern for social reform extended beyond his medical practice environment in New York City. In 1909 Johnson was elected to serve as the tenth president of the National Medical Association, an organization founded in 1895 to redress the exclusion of black physicians from the American Medical Association and to address the unique challenges facing their members. Johnson also remained an active member of the Medico-Chirurgical Society of Greater New York, the New York County Medical Society, and the New York State Medical Society. He died in New York City.

• A biographical account is "P. A. Johnson, M.D.," *Journal of the National Medical Association* 6 (Jan.–Mar. 1914): 61. See also *The Booker T. Washington Papers*, vol. 12, 1912–1914, ed. Louis R. Harlan and Reginald W. Smock (1982). Secondary sources include John A. Kenney, *The Negro in Medicine* (1912); Herbert M. Morais, *The History of the Negro in Medicine*, 2d ed. (1968); Joseph Howard Raymond, *History of the Long Island College Hospital and Its Graduates Together with the Hoagland Laboratory and the Polhemus Memorial Clinic* (1899); and Todd L. Savitt, "Entering a White Profession: Black Physicians in the New South, 1880–1920," *Bulletin of the History of Medicine* 61 (1987): 507–40.

GERARD FERGERSON

JOHNSON, Philip Gustav (5 Nov. 1894–14 Sept. 1944), aviation industrialist, was born in Seattle, Washington, the son of recent Swedish immigrants Charles S. Johnson, a laundry owner, and Hanna Gustavson. In 1913, rebuffing pressure to join the family laundry business, Johnson began studying mechanical engineering at the University of Washington. He was recruited in 1917 while still a student to work in William Boeing's one-year-old aircraft business. He had no aviation experience, but during high school he had chosen jobs in machine shops, whose work and organization had been similar to what he found in the early airplane factory.

After a few months in the engineering bay, Johnson was reassigned temporarily to help the factory foremen read drawings. In the factory his superior understanding of manufacturing processes was soon evident and particularly his ability to rise above details. The drawing board was permanently behind him. He introduced numerous improvements, such as arc-welded steel airframes, and his factory soon became known for its sound practices. In 1918–1919 he became factory superintendent and so began a rise remarkable even for a field used to rapid promotion.

Contemporaries were especially impressed by his swift reasoning and ability to act decisively. Boeing pegged him for promotion. Johnson became vice president and general manager over several hundred employees in 1922 and president of a front-rank aircraft company at the age of thirty-one in 1926. Johnson always acknowledged that he owed his success to William Boeing's trust. He, like other supervisors, was rewarded with stock of indeterminate value in lieu of pay. He liked joking that he had been too dumb to sell it, but later it made him rich.

In 1927 the Boeing enterprise started an entirely new kind of business, the 1,800-mile airmail route from Chicago to San Francisco. It was the first commercial transcontinental line Johnson would build and also the first in the United States. Johnson was simultaneously president of both the transport and the aircraft companies, and upon his decision to add passenger seats, the route also became the first transcontinental airline. Boeing acquired other airlines and merged with the Pratt & Whitney engine interests in 1929. In 1933 Johnson became president of America's most successful integrated array of airlines and manufacturers.

An airplane usually described as the first modern airliner, the Boeing 247, grew out of the mergers and was heavily influenced by Johnson. The all-metal monoplane introduced the era of streamlined propeller-driven airliners. However, further technical advances and broader marketing by competitors resulted in them capturing and holding the airliner market.

During the Great Depression, air industry executives attracted the ire of the Franklin D. Roosevelt administration and congressional Democrats. They charged the executives, including Johnson, with price collusion and limiting competition at a "spoils conference" with Herbert Hoover's postmaster in 1930. Johnson was formally blacklisted in 1934 although legally exonerated in the 1940s. Driven out of aviation, Johnson returned to Seattle and in 1936 set to straightening out Kenworth, a troubled motor truck manufacturer.

In 1937 he moved to Montreal, setting up operations for Trans-Canada, a national air carrier. This was his second transcontinental airline and with its early completion he again became president of the

Boeing aircraft firm, now nearly bankrupt. It was September 1939, exactly the start of war in Europe.

The size and complication of airplane manufacturing programs result in an unusual number of failures. However, Johnson's programs were always successful even though they involved very large, unusually complicated four-engine bombers. By 1944 as many Boeing bombers were being built per day as had been built annually when Johnson returned. Assembly lines, modular construction, labor-saving machines, swarms of tooling, and the division of labor made it possible to ultimately roll out an astonishing 10,000 B-17s and B-29s. The latter program is sometimes considered the second largest weapon program after the atom bomb.

Back during World War I, the Boeing crowd had been mostly bachelors and lived aviation day and night together. Along with the others Johnson became a family man, marrying in 1925 Catherine Foley, with whom he had two children. He continued to informally mix business and military guests as before with his private life. His enthusiasm waned after he was blacklisted, and he died of a cerebral hemorrhage during a wartime trip to the B-29 plant in Wichita.

Johnson usually worked with a corps of trusted lieutenants to whom he gave wide range. Much of his success came from firsthand knowledge of the tasks involved. To mechanics, no less than the chairman, he was known as P. G. or Phil, but he remained known to few outside the industry. Unlike so many attracted to aviation, he cared little about being well known. He was a social, soft-spoken leader and regarded as one of aviation's most successful.

Johnson rose from the position of draftsman to help create and later direct the world's largest aviation corporation. He headed companies that today are Boeing, United Airlines, United Technologies, Air Canada, and Kenworth Truck.

• A family scrapbook of clippings is kept at Seattle's Museum of History and Industry. W. L. White wrote a very sympathetic portrait, "Out of the Doghouse," *Saturday Evening Post*, 15 Nov. 1941, and Johnson is described in a *Fortune* article, Aug. 1940.

PAUL G. SPITZER

JOHNSON, Rachel Harris (11 Dec. 1887–8 Aug. 1983), founding president of the Girls Clubs of America, Inc., was born in Worcester, Massachusetts, the daughter of Henry Francis Harris, a lawyer and businessman, and Emma Dearborn, a choir director. Johnson traced her American roots to Thomas Dudley, the second governor of the Massachusetts Bay Colony. She grew up in an affluent neighborhood in the industrial city that would always be her home. Her parents were socially prominent and active in the local community. In 1909 Johnson received a bachelor of arts degree from Smith College.

Reflecting a popular concern over the plight of the low-wage-earning woman, Johnson volunteered in 1910 to help a friend start a club to provide inexpensive recreation for women between the ages of sixteen and thirty, "industrial girls," who worked in the local factories. Members met regularly for a few years until the club failed because of inadequate financial support and facilities.

In October 1912 Rachel married James Herbert Johnson, a salesman with Norton Company, the Worcester-based abrasives manufacturer, where his stepfather, George I. Alden, a founder of the company, was president. The Johnsons had two daughters. Her husband died in 1949.

In 1912 Johnson joined several women to start the Worcester Equal Franchise Club to work for woman suffrage. At the club's first meeting, she was elected corresponding secretary. During World War I she participated in door-to-door petition drives organized by the club to press for ratification of the constitutional amendment allowing women to vote. In 1920 this club became the Worcester League of Women Voters. Johnson was also affiliated with the Girls Welfare Society, the National Social Welfare Assembly, and the Worcester Smith College Club.

After Johnson's father died in 1915, her mother resurrected the idea of a recreation club for young female factory workers and decided to convert her home to a permanent facility for a girls' club. In 1916 twenty prominent women founded the Worcester Girls Clubhouse Corporation. Johnson's mother served as treasurer for ten years. Although Johnson had been a member of the initial fundraising committee in 1915, her active involvement with this club really began in 1919.

After World War I factory workers showed less interest in the club, but Johnson's interest in it soon became a passion. A Saturday program for younger school-aged girls, initiated on an experimental basis in 1922, met with immediate and overwhelming popularity. Club leaders felt they had uncovered a real need. They believed that these girls, growing up in overcrowded working-class neighborhoods, were the forgotten sisters who did not have access to the community-sponsored recreation programs that were available to boys.

Girls' club leadership became Johnson's life's work. She was annually elected secretary of the board of directors from 1921 to 1929. From 1931 to 1935 she was first vice president, and from 1936 to 1941 she served as president. She retired from the board in 1956. She was then named honorary president every year until her death.

Beginning in the early 1920s the club offered school-aged girls a variety of activities intended to foster self-confidence and promote healthy habits. When the depression hit in the early 1930s, financial support for after-school recreation programs for girls became increasingly difficult to attract. Recognizing that boys' clubs still received greater support, Johnson insisted that "girls are important," and she devoted much creative thought to promoting the girls' club concept.

Shortly after Johnson became president, Worcester leaders initiated plans to organize all existing clubs interested in maximizing publicity about the needs of girls. Johnson spearheaded a public relations effort based on the premise that motherhood was an "all-important job." The brilliantly successful campaign linked girls with their futures as mothers in order to persuade communities to support programs that prepared disadvantaged girls for responsible citizenship and motherhood. In 1941 Johnson wrote "The Girl's Bill of Rights," a series of nine statements articulating society's obligation to provide for the basic well-being of all girls. For the next three years, Johnson published a news bulletin for participating clubs. In 1943 seventeen clubs formed the Eastern Association of Girls Clubs of America, an informal association consisting of a public relations committee chaired by Johnson, in order to promote "Girls Club Week" slated to begin on Mother's Day 1944. Johnson's handbook, *Thirty Years of Girls' Club Experience* (1945), written with Dora E. Dodge, was based on the studied success of the Worcester club and provided some history, some philosophy, and some practical knowledge about popular programs.

When the Girls Clubs of America was founded in 1945 by nineteen charter clubs to set standards for clubs and encourage the formation of new clubs, Johnson was elected its first president. From 1945 to 1947 the national office was located in her Worcester home. As president, Johnson, said to be soft-spoken, traveled around the country gathering support for the organization. She was reelected president every year until she retired in 1952. In 1950 Paul Dever, the governor of Massachusetts, appointed Johnson to the state's committee for the Midcentury White House Conference on Children and Youth.

In 1951 there were thirty-two girls' clubs in thirteen states serving 25,000 girls. That year, Johnson was given the Isaiah Thomas Award for distinguished service to the Worcester community. Dorothy Lewis, of United States Radio, speaking at the awards banquet, described Johnson as "a founder" because she possessed "the driving urge, the clear knowledge of a need, the power to inspire others to a labor of love, the skill to handle personalities and problems, and that rare self-effacement of allowing others to take credit" (*Worcester Daily Telegram*, 29 Mar. 1951).

Johnson worked throughout her life to improve the social and legal status of women and girls. The Girls Clubs of America, Inc., the national organization created to enrich the lives of girls and developed largely as a result of Johnson's leadership, was continuing, after nearly four decades, when she died in Worcester.

• Johnson's manuscript, "A Little History," written in 1958 about her family, is at the Worcester Historical Museum. No known collection of her personal papers exists. Information on her family is in Charles Nutt, *History of Worcester and Its People*, vol. 3 (1919); for some information on her early club work, see vols. 1 and 2. Published and unpublished materials, including the manuscript, "History of Girls Clubs of America," the text of a speech Johnson delivered in 1965, are at Girls Incorporated of Worcester (the name of the organization was changed in 1991). A collection of newspaper clippings from 1915 on is at the Worcester Historical Museum; it provides some information about Johnson's work. See also Dora E. Dodge, *This Proud House* (1960), on the origins of the Worcester Girls Club. Obituaries are in the *Worcester Telegram*, 9 Aug. 1983, and the *New York Times*, 10 Aug. 1983.

LISA CONNELLY COOK

JOHNSON, Reverdy (21 May 1796–10 Feb. 1876), lawyer, U.S. attorney general, and U.S. senator, was born in Annapolis, Maryland, the son of John Johnson, a lawyer and Maryland legislator, and Deborah Ghieselen. A member of a distinguished Maryland legal family (John Johnson served as a judge of the Maryland Court of Appeals, chancellor, and attorney general), Johnson was educated at St. John's College in Annapolis. After graduating in 1811 and serving briefly as a private in the War of 1812, he began his legal training under his father and entered the bar in 1816. He established his law practice in Baltimore in 1817 and remained active in the Baltimore bar for the next sixty years. He married Mary Mackall Bowie in 1819, with whom he had fifteen children.

Johnson's first political service was as a state senator from Baltimore between 1821 and 1828. He resigned in the latter year to devote full time to his burgeoning legal business, having quickly made a name for himself as an accomplished trial lawyer in civil actions. He prepared thoroughly for his cases, was unrivaled at cross-examinations, and had a tremendous memory. A colleague from the Baltimore bar recalled, "His power of analysis and his reasoning faculties, supported by robustness of expression, commanded attention and carried conviction." In 1827 he began to acquire a national reputation as a constitutional lawyer when he argued his first case, *Brown v. Maryland*, in the U.S. Supreme Court.

Retained as a legal counsel by the Baltimore and Ohio Railroad in the late 1820s, Johnson soon amassed great wealth through his corporate practice. His annual income of $11,000 by the early 1830s made him one of the richest men in Baltimore. Indeed, he became a symbol of the uncaring rich when the Bank of Maryland failed in 1834. As a director of the bank, Johnson was instrumental in the legal maneuverings that blocked the bank from promptly paying the accounts of its small depositors. An infuriated mob destroyed his house in August 1835 during the Baltimore bank riot.

Johnson's wealth, conservative instincts, and broad view of the Constitution all inclined him to join the Whig party. In 1845 he was elected to the U.S. Senate as a Whig from Maryland. He broke with his party to support the Democratic president, James K. Polk, in going to war against Mexico in 1846. However, he strongly criticized Polk when it appeared that the war was being fought to acquire more territory. Johnson feared that any territorial additions would inevitably reopen the issue of slavery and lead to a sectional crisis that would "cause the Union to totter to its very foundations." Although he believed that "slavery is a great affliction to any country where it prevails" and had emancipated the slaves he had inherited from his father, he was bitterly opposed both to the abolitionists and to any federal interference with the institution of slavery. Like most Whigs from the Upper South, he tried to steer a middle course. He was against the expansion of slavery but also held that the individual states had the sole constitutional authority to deal with the institution. As for the status of slavery in the territories, he was willing to abide by any decision rendered by the Supreme Court.

In 1849 Johnson left the Senate to join the cabinet of President Zachary Taylor as attorney general. His service was brief and unrewarding. Since the Department of Justice had not yet been created, nearly all the legal work, including the writing of briefs, fell on Johnson. He soon handed down a decision on the longstanding Galphin Claim, which brought him under heavy criticism. The Galphin Claim concerned a prerevolutionary grant of American Indian land to one George Galphin. The land was eventually taken over by the state of Georgia and ceded to the federal government. The Galphin heirs sought payment for the land from the U.S. government. After the Polk administration agreed to make a principal payment of $43,518, Attorney General Johnson ruled in early 1850 that the heirs were also entitled to $191,352 in back interest since 1776. Nearly half of this sum, a considerable fortune in 1850 dollars, went to Secretary of War George Crawford, Johnson's fellow cabinet member and the Galphins' legal agent. Johnson claimed ignorance of Crawford's involvement in the case, but this did not prevent a major political scandal from erupting. Johnson was cleared of any improprieties by a House investigating committee. Soon after, he resigned, along with the rest of the cabinet, when Taylor died in the summer of 1850.

The Galphin scandal did not tarnish Johnson's sterling reputation as a constitutional lawyer. He continued to be sought after in major cases and in 1854 won a decision in the Supreme Court that validated the patent for the McCormick reaper. He was involved in the celebrated *Dred Scott* case of 1857. As one of the defense counsels, he was credited with presenting the constitutional argument that influenced the Court to rule that Congress had no power to prohibit slavery in the territories. Johnson's long and close friendship with Chief Justice Roger Taney of Maryland might also have been a factor in the Court's decision.

After the collapse of the Whig party in 1854, Johnson drifted somewhat reluctantly into the Democratic party. He continued to take a moderate position on sectional controversies and was particularly attracted to the popular sovereignty doctrine of Stephen A. Douglas as a means of resolving the vexing issue of slavery in the territories. He campaigned as a Douglas Democrat in 1860 in the belief that the Democratic party was the only national political organization. During the secession crisis that followed the election of Abraham Lincoln, Johnson took a strong stand in favor of the Union. He denounced the secessionists as "rebels and traitors" and insisted that the "offending citizen cannot rely, as a defence, on State power. His responsibility is to the United States alone." He played

a key role in keeping Maryland in the Union, delivering the keynote address at a large Unionist meeting at the Maryland Institute in Baltimore in January 1861, but failed in his efforts at sectional reconciliation as a member of the Washington Peace Conference in February 1861.

Johnson served briefly in the Maryland House of Delegates in 1861 before being reelected to the U.S. Senate in 1862. Sent to New Orleans by Lincoln to investigate complaints against the military rule of General Benjamin Franklin Butler (1818–1893), Johnson did not take his Senate seat until March 1863. A sharp and effective critic of the constitutional positions of Republicans in the Thirty-eighth Senate, Johnson combined his support of the war effort with a scrupulous regard for the constitutional protection of individual and property rights. Thus, he backed the enlistment of slaves as soldiers but held that their freedom should be linked to monetary compensation for loyal owners. He opposed the Emancipation Proclamation as an unconstitutional exercise of the executive's war powers but supported the Thirteenth Amendment freeing the slaves. Although he sided with Lincoln in the suspension of the writ of habeas corpus, he was relentless in criticizing federal interference with elections in the loyal border states of Kentucky and Maryland.

After the war, Johnson initially supported President Andrew Johnson in his Reconstruction program. He agreed with the president that the former rebel states had never left the Union and hence should be represented in Congress once they had reestablished their state governments. When Congress blocked the president's program, Reverdy Johnson, a member of the Committee on Reconstruction, broke with the president as a question of practicality. Dreading the constitutional consequences of a prolonged military occupation of the South, he backed the key demands of the congressional Republicans: the Fourteenth Amendment, black male suffrage, and the Military Reconstruction Act of 1867. Although he admitted that his position was inconsistent, he justified it by citing the majority power of the North in Congress. He opposed the Civil Rights Act of 1866 as an unconstitutional use of congressional power. Johnson was influential in swaying Senate Republicans to acquit the president during his impeachment trial and was then appointed minister to Great Britain in 1868, where he negotiated the Johnson-Clarendon Treaty. Although rejected by the Senate largely on partisan grounds, this treaty laid the basis for the subsequent settlement of the "Alabama claims" brought by the U.S. government for damages inflicted by Confederate naval raiders built in Britain.

Upon returning from England in 1869, Johnson resumed his law practice. In addition to his corporate litigation, he was defense counsel in several civil rights cases. He defended members of the Ku Klux Klan indicted in South Carolina for violating the Enforcement Act of 1870. His most significant case was *United States v. Cruikshank* in 1875. The case stemmed from the chronic electoral violence and fraud in postwar Louisiana. Arguing that the enforcement clause of the Fourteenth Amendment applied only to the actions of states and not individuals, the Supreme Court acquitted Johnson's client of the charge of conspiring to deprive blacks of their civil rights. Professionally active to the end of his life, Johnson died from a crushed skull, the result of an accidental fall in Annapolis.

Known throughout his career for his good sense and urbane manners, Johnson embodied the sectional moderation and reverence for the Union and the Constitution that were the distinguishing characteristics of the old Whig party in the Upper South. A brilliant lawyer, he was recognized following the death of Daniel Webster as the nation's preeminent constitutional authority in cases before the Supreme Court based on the consistency of his constitutional arguments and the extreme thoroughness with which he prepared his cases.

• The Library of Congress holds the largest collection of Johnson's papers. Other collections are at the Maryland Historical Society and Dickinson College. Bernard C. Steiner, *The Life of Reverdy Johnson* (1914), remains the only biography. Useful, brief accounts of his legal career can be found in W. D. Lewis, *Great American Lawyers*, vol. 4 (1908), Charles Warren, *A History of the American Bar* (1911), and Philip B. Perlman, "Some Maryland Lawyers in Supreme Court History," *Maryland Historical Magazine* 43 (1948): 180–96. An obituary is in the *Baltimore Sun*, 11 Feb. 1876.

WILLIAM L. BARNEY

JOHNSON, Richard Mentor (1780–19 Nov. 1850), U.S. congressman and vice president, was born at the frontier settlement of Beargrass, now part of Louisville, Kentucky, the son of Robert Johnson and Jemima Suggett, recent arrivals from Virginia. Soon after his birth the family moved to Bryant's Station, near Lexington, and in 1783 settled permanently at Great Crossings in Scott County. Johnson's father became active politically and served for a time in the Kentucky legislature. His work as a surveyor enabled him to locate and purchase some of the most valuable land in the county, and he managed to acquire a considerable estate.

Although the Johnsons were better off than most area families, the Kentucky frontier offered few opportunities to acquire a formal education. It is not known what schools Johnson attended, but he managed to learn Latin and later studied law under George Nicholas and James Brown. After being admitted to the bar in 1802, Johnson began to represent poor farmers whose land titles were challenged by absentee claimants from Virginia. Such disputes were common at the time because land titles granted under Virginia law often did not correspond with those granted by Kentucky. Johnson's early identification with the problems of ordinary people helped to shape the agenda of his later political career.

In 1804 Johnson became the first native Kentuckian elected to the state legislature. As a legislator he served on various committees and again worked to protect Kentucky farmers against out-of-state challenges to land titles. In 1806 he was elected to the U.S. House of Representatives, becoming in 1807 the first native Kentuckian to serve in Congress. Johnson entered national politics as a Jeffersonian Republican, and he faithfully followed the party line on all major issues, including President Thomas Jefferson's embargo policy in 1807. In 1811 Johnson opposed renewing the charter of the Bank of the United States, which he regarded as an unconstitutional monopoly that served the interests of the moneyed elite. His position on the bank, one of the fixed points on his political agenda, was important because the bill to recharter stalled in the House by a single vote. In foreign policy debates, Johnson advocated strong measures in defense of American neutral rights on the high seas, and in 1812 he voted for the declaration of war against Great Britain.

After the vote, Johnson left Washington to take an active part in the war. Returning to Kentucky, he organized and became the colonel of a regiment of mounted riflemen, which he skillfully led to significant advantage. Instead of deploying his troops for scouting or as an adjunct to infantry, he proposed that they be used as a striking force to deliver a blow at a point made vulnerable by their own mobility. Serving under William Henry Harrison during the Canadian campaign at the battle of the Thames in October 1813, he first pinned down the British and their Indian allies by harrying their baggage train and then led his mounted troops in a bold assault that broke the enemy front. Johnson was in the thick of the fighting, during which he killed an Indian chief, later said to have been the great Shawnee leader Tecumseh. Struck by five bullets during the engagement, he suffered wounds from which he never fully recovered. His personal courage and daring leadership made him something of a national hero.

As soon as he was physically able, Johnson returned to Congress, where he became chairman of the House Committee on Military Affairs—a position he used to secure pensions for veterans and benefits for the widows and children of military personnel killed in the war. In 1816 he opposed the second Bank of the United States on the same grounds that he had opposed the first. That same year he guided to passage a compensation bill granting congressmen an annual salary of $1,500 instead of the $6 per diem allowance they received when Congress was in session. His aim was to end the foot dragging and procrastination that per diem compensation encouraged; but public reaction to fixed salaries turned out to be unexpectedly hostile, and many of the bill's supporters were drummed out in the fall elections. Johnson, instead of defending the merits of the reform, avoided the backlash by pledging to work for the repeal of his own measure. He justified his reversal by arguing that representatives should reflect the popular will, but lack of political stamina may have been closer to the truth.

Johnson was a leading proponent of the protective tariff and internal improvements, measures favored by his Kentucky constituents. In February 1817 he voted for Congressman John C. Calhoun's bill earmarking for internal improvements the bonus paid by the Bank of the United States for its charter. After President James Madison vetoed the bill, Johnson was among those who voted unsuccessfully to override the veto. In 1819, during hearings before the House Military Affairs Committee about General Andrew Jackson's punitive expedition against the Seminoles in 1818, Johnson opposed the critical report filed by his committee, which censured Jackson for seizing Pensacola and executing two British subjects. Johnson vigorously defended the general in the House debate, which pitted him against fellow Kentuckian Henry Clay. Johnson emerged the clear winner after the House voted to accept his minority report vindicating Jackson.

In response to the panic of 1819, Johnson resigned his House seat in order to serve in the Kentucky legislature, where he helped pass legislation abolishing imprisonment for debt and providing relief for debtors generally. In December 1819 the state legislature returned him to Congress, electing him to fill the Senate seat left vacant by the resignation of John J. Crittenden. During the 1820s Johnson was the most consistent advocate of the common man in Congress, supporting legislation against imprisonment for debt and defending the right of settlers to public lands. In 1824 he initially favored Clay's presidential bid, but after the House Speaker was eliminated from contention, Johnson threw his support to Jackson. The split among Republicans that characterized the 1824 election marked the reemergence of two-party politics; Johnson aligned himself with the Jackson wing of the party, which after the election became known as the Democratic Republicans. Although Jackson carried Kentucky in winning the presidency in 1828, the state legislature failed to return Johnson to the Senate. The following year, however, he was again elected to the House of Representatives, where he backed the administration without reservation. In 1830, after Jackson vetoed the Maysville Road Bill, which authorized federal expenditures to build a turnpike in Kentucky, Johnson abstained from voting to override the veto despite his previous support for internal improvements and his strong support for the bill. In 1832 he signed a committee report condemning the Bank of the United States simply because that was the position of the administration. The following year he modified his support for the protective tariff by voting for the compromise tariff of 1833, also favored by the administration. Johnson's loyalty to Jackson, with whom he had close personal ties, never wavered, even when supporting the administration meant reversing himself on important issues. Being at the center of power more than offset the political costs of these reversals.

Jackson rewarded Johnson's loyalty at the Democratic National Convention in 1836, when he forced reluctant delegates to nominate Johnson for vice president on the ticket headed by Martin Van Buren. Johnson did not strengthen the ticket in the West as had been expected, and in fact he probably lost votes for the party in the South and East. Van Buren won the necessary electoral majority, but the refusal of some Democratic electors to vote for Johnson threw the choice of vice president to the Senate. Elected on the first ballot, Johnson became the first vice president ever chosen by that body. Some of the opposition to Johnson came from religious groups offended by his reports to Congress rejecting their petitions to close post offices and halt the transportation of mail on Sunday. His argument that the government could not show deference to any religion without violating the constitutional separation of church and state outraged political Sabbatarians everywhere. The most serious and damaging opposition, however, sprang from his unconventional domestic arrangements. Johnson, who never married, had a long-term relationship with Julia Chinn, a mulatto he inherited from his father's estate. Johnson made no attempt to conceal the relationship; their two daughters were raised and educated as his children, and on several occasions he insisted on their being recognized in society. After Chinn died, he had other mulatto mistresses, thus providing his political enemies with a steady supply of ammunition to use against him. Johnson's tenure as vice president was uneventful, and he returned to Kentucky after Van Buren's defeat in 1840. Although he nursed fatuous presidential ambitions, Johnson's national political career had effectively ended. Elected to the state legislature in 1850, he died a few weeks later at Frankfort while attending a legislative session.

Among all the political figures of the 1820s, Johnson seemed poised to play a leading role in the rapidly unfolding era of democratic reform. He became the chief spokesman of the common man in Congress and by 1830 was more popular among average Americans than any individual in political life. He also had standing as a military hero—no small advantage in any political era. Yet his star faded rapidly after 1830, and by the time he was vice president, Johnson was already a spent political force. That his career fell short of its bright early promise can be attributed in part to defects of character and judgment. His personal life undoubtedly worked against him, but a lack of political stamina was another serious liability. A willingness to sacrifice principle to expediency recurs repeatedly throughout his political career. Johnson showed great courage leading men into battle, yet he lacked the determination and commitment needed to be an effective political leader. His readiness to compromise for the sake of expediency kept him from standing for something long enough to have it passed along as a political legacy. Johnson fell so easily and completely into the role of Jackson's political satellite in part because his own gravitational force was insufficient to maintain an independent orbit. History has properly accorded him a place as an important but secondary figure of the Jackson era.

• A fully documented account of Johnson's life and career, as well as a bibliography listing the collections containing his scattered papers and correspondence, is in Leland W. Meyer,

The Life and Times of Colonel Richard M. Johnson of Kentucky (1932). William Emmons, *Authentic Biography of Col. Richard M. Johnson of Kentucky* (1833), which was prepared to promote Johnson's presidential ambitions, is useful for its contemporary perspective. Other useful sources are Henry Adams, *History of the United States During the Administrations of James Madison*, ed. Earl N. Harbert (2 vols., 1986); Adams, *The War of 1812*, ed. H. A. De Weerd (1944); Irving Brant, *James Madison* (6 vols., 1941–1961); Julius W. Pratt, *The Expansionists of 1812* (1957); Arthur M. Schlesinger, Jr., *The Age of Jackson* (1945); Glynden G. Van Deusen, *The Jacksonian Era, 1824–1848* (1959); Robert V. Remini, *Andrew Jackson and the Course of American Empire, Freedom, Democracy, 1767–1845* (3 vols., 1977–1984); Remini, *Henry Clay* (1991); Albert D. Kirwan, *John J. Crittenden* (1962); and Chase C. Mooney, *William H. Crawford, 1772–1834* (1974). For Johnson as a military leader and tactician, see Fletcher Pratt, "Richard Mentor Johnson: The Father of American Cavalry," *Cavalry Journal* 43 (May–June 1934): 5–9. A sampling of contemporary reactions to Johnson's death can be found in the *Louisville Weekly Courier* and the *Kentucky Statesman*, 23 Nov. 1850.

EDGAR J. MCMANUS

JOHNSON, Richard W. (27 Feb. 1827–21 Apr. 1897), soldier, educator, and author, was born near Smithland, Livingston County, Kentucky, the son of James L. Johnson, a physician, and Jane Leeper, both natives of Virginia. In 1844 an older brother, John Milton Johnson, who later became a Confederate surgeon, procured him an appointment to West Point, from which he graduated in 1849. He thereupon served until 1861 with both infantry and cavalry units at frontier outposts in Minnesota Territory, Texas, and the Indian Territory, participating in two skirmishes with the Comanches while in Texas and rising to the rank of captain. In 1855, while stationed at Fort Snelling, Minnesota, he married Rachael Elizabeth Steele. They had three children. Following the outbreak of the Civil War, he remained, despite his southern antecedents, loyal to the Union. In accordance with Abraham Lincoln's policy of encouraging Unionism in Kentucky, he became a brigadier general of volunteers on 11 October 1861.

Johnson's active career as a general began most inauspiciously. First, on 21 August 1862 he was defeated and captured, along with a large portion of his command, near Gallatin, Tennessee, by a smaller force headed by the Confederate raider John Hunt Morgan. Johnson had boasted that he would seize Morgan and put him "into a band box." Then, after being exchanged in December 1862, Johnson returned to duty just in time to take part in the battle of Stones River, Tennessee (31 Dec. 1862–1–2 Jan. 1863), during which the division he was commanding was, owing in large part to his carelessness, routed by the Confederates. Even so, he remained in command of his division and at the battles of Chickamauga (19–20 Sept. 1863) and Chattanooga (23–25 Nov. 1863) he performed adequately, contributing to Major General George H. Thomas's army-saving stand in the former engagement and to Thomas's successful assault on Missionary Ridge in the second.

Johnson's role in the Atlanta campaign was much less commendable. At the battle of Pickett's Mill, Georgia (27 May 1864), he failed to attack in a prompt and vigorous fashion, thereby helping turn a potential Union victory into a bloody defeat. Moreover, toward the end of the fighting he received a glancing blow in the side that put him out of action until mid-July. On 7 August 1864, as a consequence of the resignation of its commander, he assumed command, being its senior brigadier, of the XIV Corps of the Army of the Cumberland. He did not, however, retain this post long. Considering him deficient in skill and enterprise, William T. Sherman on 19 August appointed Johnson chief of cavalry of the Military Division of the Mississippi (essentially an administrative assignment) and sent him to Nashville to open the way for placing Brigadier General Jefferson C. Davis at the head of the XIV Corps.

Johnson's tenure in this new post likewise was brief, for in October 1864 Major General James H. Wilson superseded him. He reverted once more to the command of a division, this time of cavalry. In that capacity he performed creditably, albeit inconspicuously, in the defeat and pursuit of Confederate General John B. Hood's army in Tennessee in December 1864. This campaign ended his military career insofar as active service was concerned. On 12 October 1867, having been brevetted a major general in both the volunteer and regular services, he retired from the army to become a professor of military science at the University of Missouri and later at the University of Minnesota. Apart from an unsuccessful bid as the Democratic candidate for the governorship of Minnesota in 1881, he devoted the rest of his life to teaching and writing. His chief published works are *A Memoir of Maj. Gen. George H. Thomas* (1881) and an autobiography. In 1894 he married Julia Ann McFarland, herself a prominent educator; they had one child. He died in St. Paul, Minnesota.

The best commentary on Johnson's military character can be found in an exchange between Sherman and Thomas on 6 August 1864, when Johnson's seniority in rank put him in line to command, as he briefly did, the XIV Corps. Sherman wrote, "General Johnson has not the ability or vigor necessary to so large a command." While courageous and highly intelligent, Johnson simply lacked the temperament and force of personality to be a good combat leader. During the Civil War he would have been better suited to an administrative or staff assignment, and after it he found his proper niche in life as a college professor.

• Johnson's autobiography, *A Soldier's Reminiscences in Peace and War* (1886), is a dull, pedestrian work that contains little information and few insights of historical value, but it is the best and most readily available source on his postwar career. Far more revealing, in so far as his Civil War career is concerned, are his military reports and correspondence as published in *The War of the Rebellion: A Compilation of the Official Records of the Union and Confederate Armies* (128 vols., 1880–1901). Additional and more objective information about his war record, as well as citations of primary sources pertaining to it, may be found in Peter Cozzens, *No Better Place to Die: The Battle of Stones River* (1990); Cozzens, *This Terrible Sound: The Battle of Chickamauga* (1992); and Albert Castel, *Decision in the West: The Atlanta Campaign of 1864* (1992).

ALBERT CASTEL

JOHNSON, Robert (1676?–3 May 1735), governor of South Carolina, was born in England, the son of Nathaniel Johnson, a member of Parliament, and Margaret (maiden name unknown). Nathaniel, knighted in 1680, mayor of Newcastle-upon-Tyne and member of Parliament, obtained an appointment as governor of the Leeward Islands when Robert was ten. Subsequently Nathaniel moved without his family to South Carolina, secured a gubernatorial commission in 1702, and amassed an extensive landed estate. Robert Johnson in the meantime became a freeman of Newcastle-upon-Tyne and was a merchant adventurer and mercer in that port. Robert served as a surety for his father upon the latter's appointment as governor of South Carolina. Inheriting considerable property in South Carolina upon his father's death in 1713, Robert Johnson displayed an immediate interest in the governorship of that province.

In 1717 Johnson received a commission from the Proprietors naming him governor of the part of Carolina that lay south and west of Cape Fear, a nebulous description that fueled a protracted boundary dispute between South and North Carolina. Upon his arrival in South Carolina that year, Johnson encountered the usual unruly provincial legislature; the colony was also weakened by the Yamassee Indian War, menaced by pirates, and angry at the failure of the Proprietors to come to their assistance.

Johnson worked with the South Carolina General Assembly to restore the colony's finances by reissuing old bills of credit upon the promise to sink them within two years and by increasing provincial taxes. He also participated in an expedition that captured the pirate Stede Bonnet. Yet previous proprietary neglect of South Carolina during the Yamassee Indian War and subsequent proprietary vetoes of several laws passed by the General Assembly led to a rebellion in 1719 that overthrew proprietary government and sought royal control of South Carolina. Johnson refused an offer by the rebels to take command of the province, thus forfeiting his gubernatorial office in 1719. In 1723 he left for England, where he lobbied for the removal of rice from the enumerated articles list and for the reinstatement of the bounty on naval stores. Johnson also helped to facilitate negotiations between Proprietors and Crown that resulted in the royal purchase of both Carolinas in 1729.

Backed by his patron, the duke of Newcastle, Johnson secured an appointment in 1729 as the first royal governor of South Carolina. When he returned to the province in 1731, Johnson faced two overarching conflicts: the merchant/planter division and the royal prerogative/general assembly privilege clash. The governor's mercantile background and planting interests

helped him to bridge the first conflict by serving as an intermediary between the two; in the second conflict, his principled yet conciliatory attitude allowed him to represent the Crown without unduly antagonizing the legislature. Johnson achieved his greatest success through his township plan to settle the frontier of South Carolina. He proposed that the province establish ten townships in the west and people them with poor Protestants from Europe. Not only did his plan help to provide protection against Indian attacks from the west, but it also encouraged white immigration, which he thought was needed to offset the increasing proportion of blacks in the South Carolina population. Johnson also helped establish Georgia, which served as a buffer between Spanish Florida and South Carolina.

Johnson had married Margaret (maiden name possibly Bonner but not confirmed), who died in 1732, having borne six children. Following a long illness Johnson died in Charles Town (Charleston) and was buried at St. Philip's Church in the town, an indication of his family's long affiliation with the Church of England.

• In the absence of extant personal papers, Johnson's voluminous official and semi-official correspondence, found among numerous British agencies concerned with the colonies and lodged in the British Public Record Office, London, must suffice to reveal the man and his administrations. Also helpful are colonial records of South Carolina, including the *Journal of the Commons House of Assembly* and the *Journal of the Council*, found in the South Carolina Archives, Columbia. Richard P. Sherman, *Robert Johnson: Proprietary and Royal Governor of South Carolina* (1966), is the only biography. See also M. Eugene Sirmans, *Colonial South Carolina: A Political History* (1966); Robert L. Meriwether, *The Expansion of South Carolina, 1729–1765* (1940); and Mabel L. Webber, "Sir Nathaniel Johnson and His Son Robert," *South Carolina Historical Magazine* 38 (1937): 109–115.

ALAN D. WATSON

JOHNSON, Robert (8 May 1911–16 Aug. 1938), musician, was born Robert Leroy Johnson in Hazelhurst, Mississippi, the son of Noah Johnson and Julia Major Dodds (occupations unknown). His mother was married at the time to another man, Charles Dodds, Jr., who, because of an acquaintance's personal vendetta against him, had been forced to flee Mississippi for Memphis in 1907, changing his name to Charles Spencer. After his mother eked out a living for two years working in migrant labor camps supporting Robert and his sister Carrie, she and her children joined Spencer, his mistress, and their children in Memphis in 1914. Eventually Julia left her children. Around 1918 Robert, an unruly, strong-willed child, also left Memphis, joining his mother and new stepfather, Willie "Dusty" Willis, in Robinsonville, Mississippi. Although Robert went to the Indian Lake School at Commerce, Mississippi, through the mid-1920s, eyesight problems both plagued him and provided him with an excuse to quit school. Johnson's favored instruments of his early teen years, Jew's harp and harmonica, were supplanted around 1929 by an interest in what became his primary instrument, the guitar, though he continued to play harmonica in a neck rack.

Johnson next began absorbing the sounds of other guitarists, developing his technique by listening in houses and juke joints to little-known locals like Harvey "Hard Rock" Glenn, Myles Robson, and Ernest "Whiskey Red" Brown, as well as now-legendary bluesmen Charley Patton and Willie Brown. After Johnson's marriage to Virginia Travis in 1929 ended in tragedy—both she and their baby died in childbirth in April 1930—he intensified his musical efforts, benefiting from the arrival of Eddie "Son" House in June 1930. House had recorded with Patton and Louise Johnson for Paramount Records, and it was House's furiously emotional performances that helped inspire some of Robert Johnson's best recordings. At the time, though, House and Brown often ran off the younger Johnson, an inexperienced neophyte who House claimed "made such a mess outta everything he played" (Calt and Wardlow, p. 43).

When Johnson left behind sharecropping and Robinsonville in search of his birth father and a musical vocation, he returned around 1931 to Hazelhurst, performing with mentor Ike Zinnerman in juke joints, writing down and practicing his songs in isolation in the woods, and playing on the courthouse steps during the day on Saturdays. In May 1931 Johnson married Calletta Craft, a woman ten years his senior, who showered him with attention, making his stay in southern Mississippi personally and musically fruitful, spurring a newly confident Johnson to seek greener musical pastures. Deserting his family a short time later in Clarksdale, he headed back to Robinsonville to visit his mother and kin as well as to astonish House and Brown with his progress. After a couple of months he left this farming community for a performing base centered around Helena, Arkansas, though he traveled widely, playing in joints and levee camps in Mississippi, Arkansas, Tennessee, New York, and even in Canada. While around Helena, Johnson not only met Estella Coleman, who became his common-law wife, but also became a primary musical influence on her son, future recording artist Robert Lockwood, Jr. In this period he also played with and inspired some of the Delta's greatest blues musicians, Sonny Boy Williamson II, Howlin' Wolf (Chester Burnett), Robert Nighthawk, and Elmore James among them.

By the middle 1930s Johnson was a popular Delta musician, albeit one with a reputation for drinking and womanizing. He was also ambitious, anxious to record as his old teachers Brown, Patton, and House had done. He auditioned for Jackson, Mississippi, music store owner and talent scout H. C. Speir, who passed Johnson's name on to ARC record label salesman/talent scout Ernie Oertle. Oertle took Johnson to radio station KONO facilities at the Blue Bonnet hotel in San Antonio, Texas, in 1936, recording two takes each of sixteen different songs on 23, 26, and 27 November. The success of Robert's "Terraplane Blues," the title of which refers to a make of automobile, for the Voca-

lion label led to another session, in Dallas, where he recorded multiple takes of thirteen songs on 19 and 20 June 1937.

Riding the higher profile that "Terraplane Blues" brought him across the country, Johnson left the Delta with guitarists Calvin Frazier and Johnny Shines. They followed Highway 51 to St. Louis, Chicago, and Detroit and even played briefly in New York and New Jersey. Johnson proved to be an influential but elusive traveling partner, however, frequently departing unannounced, so the trio split, Frazier making a name for himself in Detroit, Shines, in Chicago. When Johnson produced no follow-up hits, ARC let his contract expire in June 1938 without recalling him to the studio. On 13 August 1938, at a club where Johnson was performing outside Greenwood, Mississippi, called Three Forks, he drank some whiskey reputedly poisoned at the direction of a husband jealous of the attention that his wife and Johnson were paying to each other. Three days later Johnson died of pneumonia, just months before talent scout John Hammond intended to bring him to Carnegie Hall and probable acclaim at the Spirituals to Swing Concert in New York.

Johnson is a pivotal musician in the development of the blues. In many ways his work is a culmination of the work of Mississippi blues artists who preceded him and is a startling transformation of that material into a personal vision and style that defined the direction of post–World War II Chicago blues. The distinctive boogie figure that became his trademark, the famous bottleneck guitar intro to "I Believe I'll Dust My Broom," and the striking imagery of compositions such as "Cross Road Blues," "Sweet Home Chicago," "Love in Vain Blues," and "Hellbound on My Trail" influenced Williamson, Wolf, Nighthawk, James, and especially the young Muddy Waters (McKinley Morganfield), cementing his position as primary fountainhead of inspiration for artists whose work would lead blues and rock musicians like Jimi Hendrix and the Rolling Stones back to Johnson's mesmerizing work. The sketchy nature of Johnson's biography before 1970 led to a good deal of mythologizing and misinformation, but his music has continued to startle listeners with its force and beauty. Chicago blues pioneer Muddy Waters called Johnson "one of the greatest there's ever been" (Welding and Byron, p. 139). British blues-rock performer Eric Clapton added reverently, "I have never found anything more deeply soulful than Robert Johnson. His music remains the most powerful cry that I think you can find in the human voice, really" (*Robert Johnson: The Complete Recordings*, p. 23). Longtime researcher Mack McCormack heard in Johnson's lyrics "a chilling confrontation with aspects of American consciousness. He is a visionary artist with a terrible kind of information about his time and place and personal experience" (Harris, p. 289). While Stephen Calt and Gayle Wardlow allow that among his contemporaries he was "conspicuous for his seediness, facial disfigurement . . . black derby," asserting that "only in his music did Johnson project anything but a prosaic figure," it is clear that, for many, Peter Guralnick's encomium—that Johnson was "certainly the most influential of all bluesmen"—is true (*Feel Like Going Home*, p. 54). He is a member of both the Rock and Roll Hall of Fame and the W. C. Handy Awards Blues Hall of Fame.

• Robert Johnson's complete extant recordings are available on the Grammy-winning *Robert Johnson: The Complete Recordings*, Columbia C2K 46222, which includes a booklet with authoritative notes by Stephen C. LaVere, tributes by musicians Keith Richards and Eric Clapton, and transcriptions of song lyrics. Stephen Calt and Gayle Dean Wardlow, "Robert Johnson," *78 Quarterly* 1, no. 4 (1989): 40–51 is based on exhaustive firsthand field research; Samuel B. Charter, *Robert Johnson* (1973), has been largely superseded by the work drawing on the research of LaVere and Mack McCormack, which informs Peter Guralnick, *Searching for Robert Johnson* (1988). Sheldon Harris, *Blues Who's Who* (1979), provides an outline of Johnson's career and influence, and chapters on Johnson and Muddy Waters in Pete Welding and Toby Byron, eds., *Bluesland* (1991), and on Muddy Waters in Guralnick, *Feel Like Going Home* (1971), also provide useful commentary.

STEVEN TRACY

JOHNSON, Robert Lee (26 Nov. 1906–6 July 1982), baseball player and manager, was born in Pryor, Oklahoma, the brother of outfielder Roy Cleveland Johnson. Little is known about either his parents or his early life. Johnson was given the nickname "Indian Bob" because his copper-toned complexion resembled that of his mother, who was half Cherokee.

Johnson left school in the fifth grade when his family moved to Tacoma, Washington. Almost by accident he turned from soccer, his favorite childhood sport, to baseball. Roy Johnson had been playing baseball semiprofessionally in Los Angeles for the Miner Building Company when Bob, only 15 years of age, ran away from home to join him. Bob worked at various low-paying jobs in Los Angeles and teamed with Roy on the Miner squad. When Roy joined the San Francisco Seals of the Pacific Coast League (PCL), Bob in 1928 joined the Glendale Fire Department and became a pump engineer. Roy quickly ascended from San Francisco to the Detroit Tigers, where he was sold for "important money," motivating Bob to follow him. "When I saw him getting away with it," confided Bob years later, "I said to myself, 'Hell, how long's this been going on?' I was always a better player than my brother and that decided it for me" (5 Mar. 1931 article, National Baseball Library).

After initially failing tryouts with San Francisco, Hollywood, and Los Angeles, all PCL teams, Johnson was signed by Art Griggs of Wichita, Kansas, in the Western League for 1929. After Johnson arrived in Wichita, however, Griggs was forced to loan him to the Pueblo, Colorado, team for a short time because Wichita had already met its quota of three outfielders. An injury to outfielder Woody Jensen allowed Johnson's entry into the Wichita lineup. Johnson promptly hit 16 home runs in a three-week span, batted .273

over 66 games, and showed sufficient promise to have his contract purchased by Tom Turner of Portland, Oregon, in the PCL for $12,000.

After finishing the 1929 campaign by batting .254 in 81 games at Portland, Johnson in 1930 hit .265 in 157 games, earning him a major league tryout the following spring. Johnson's 1931 spring debut with the Philadelphia Athletics did not go well, however, because in his own words, he "wasn't ready." He proved unable to master a major league curveball. Manager Connie Mack, possessing at that time an abundance of outfielders, returned Johnson to Portland for more seasoning.

After posting impressive numbers at Portland the next two seasons, Johnson returned to Philadelphia, rejoining the A's in 1933. A year later, Johnson and A's teammate Jimmie Foxx combined to hit 78 home runs: Foxx 44 and Johnson 34. The same season Johnson had a 26-game hitting streak and on 16 June against the Chicago White Sox went for an incredible six hits for six at bats, with two homers and two doubles, in an 11-inning contest. On 29 August 1937 his six RBIs in one inning tied a major league record. On 12 June 1938, against the St. Louis Browns, he set an American League record by driving in all eight runs scored by his team.

"One of Connie Mack's last great finds for the Philadelphia Athletics," Johnson became a stalwart on the "tall tactician's" depression-era clubs, driving in 100 or more runs in seven of his first nine seasons. He remained with the A's until a contract dispute and disagreement regarding the relative strength of the club forced Mack to trade him to the Washington Senators in March 1943.

Johnson suffered his worst season at Washington in 1943, batting .265 with only seven home runs. He rebounded the following year with the Boston Red Sox, scoring 106 runs, driving in 106 runs, and batting .234. Released after the 1945 season, Johnson finished his career in the minor leagues with Milwaukee (American Association) in 1946, Seattle (PCL) in 1948, and Tacoma (WIL) as player-manager in 1949. Johnson, who injured his knee in 1948, played one last season in 1951, in a comeback attempt with Tijuana, Mexico.

Batting "flatfooted" from the right side, the powerfully built, six-foot, 180-pound Johnson belted 288 career home runs, including nine grand slams; averaged 150 hits per season; never batted under .265; and maintained a .296 lifetime batting average with 2,051 hits, 396 doubles, and 1,283 runs batted in. Particularly dangerous in the clutch, Johnson spoiled no-hitters on three separate occasions. He also played in seven All-Star games, but he never participated in a World Series.

Despite his offensive skills, Johnson was known throughout his career for his defensive skills. In Portland, Tom Turner wisely moved Johnson from left field to center field and gave him, as Johnson put it, "the room to go get 'em." Johnson positioned himself at a very shallow depth, drawing comparisons with

Tris Speaker. Observers noted that Johnson threw "like a bullet" with accuracy. In 1931 he discussed his preference for playing defense, commenting that he "got a bigger kick out of running down a long fly or racing to catch a line drive" than out of hitting a home run. "I love to shag 'em," he explained.

Johnson married Caroline Stout in December 1924; they had two daughters. In September 1950 he married Elizabeth Pastore. After leaving baseball, Johnson worked for a brewery company and in the Glendale Fire Department as an engineer before retiring to Tacoma, where he died.

• The best collection of information on Johnson's career is his file at the National Baseball Library, Cooperstown, N.Y. The file contains helpful correspondence, interviews, multiple newspaper clippings from his playing days and retirement, and statistical data and analysis. An obituary is in the *Sporting News*, 26 July 1982.

WES SINGLETARY

JOHNSON, Robert Ward (22 July 1814–26 July 1879), Arkansas political leader and member of both the U.S. Congress and the Confederate Congress, was born in Scott County, Kentucky, the son of Benjamin Johnson and Matilda Williams. Young Johnson was named for his paternal grandfather, who headed a powerful political family in Kentucky. Two of his uncles won election to the U.S. House of Representatives, while another, Richard Mentor Johnson, served in both the House and Senate and became the ninth vice president of the United States.

A state judge in Kentucky, Benjamin Johnson won an appointment to the Arkansas Territorial Superior Court in 1821. In 1836, President Andrew Jackson appointed him the first federal district judge for the new state of Arkansas. Through politics and marriage Judge Johnson became associated with Arkansas's emerging Democratic leadership. One of his daughters married Ambrose H. Sevier, head of the state Democratic party and one of the state's first U.S. senators. Sevier was a cousin of the Conway family, whose members included two governors. Together, the Conways, Seviers, and Johnsons created a political triumvirate that dominated the Democratic party and controlled Arkansas's government from 1833 to 1860. Its enemies commonly referred to this coalition as the "dynasty" or the "family."

Robert W. "Bob" Johnson was educated at common schools in Kentucky. He graduated from St. Joseph's College in Bardstown, Kentucky, in 1833 and earned a law degree from Yale two years later. In 1836, Johnson married Sarah S. Smith of Louisville. The couple had six children, only three of whom lived to adulthood. When Sarah died in 1862, Johnson married her younger sister Laura; this union yielded no offspring. Johnson moved to Little Rock in 1835 and became Pulaski County's prosecuting attorney by 1840. Two years later, he was state attorney general, and in 1846 he won election as Arkansas's only member of the U.S. House of Representatives.

Entering Congress in 1847, he opposed the antislavery Wilmot Proviso and, initially, the Compromise of 1850, voting only for the new Fugitive Slave Act. His Whig opposition labeled him a disunionist and attempted to use this charge against him in 1851, but Johnson tempered his association with southern radicalism enough to win another congressional term. In Congress, he fought hard to ensure that the federal government would award millions of acres of swampland for farm reclamation, providing land to those who would drain the swamps or build levees. Such grants were especially beneficial to wealthy planters and to many of Johnson's political supporters. In 1853, Governor Elias N. Conway appointed Johnson to the U.S. Senate when a position was made vacant by the resignation of Solon Borland. Johnson won election to a full term the following year and served in the Senate until 1861.

As a senator, Johnson worked to secure federal land grants for railroad construction in his home state, yet his efforts yielded few results. He voted for the Kansas-Nebraska Act of 1854 and supported efforts to pass a homestead act until the Kansas question became prominent. After 1854, Johnson opposed all homestead bills, as he believed such legislation had come to be "tinctured" with abolitionism.

With Sevier's death in 1848, Johnson and Governor Conway reigned as the leaders of Arkansas's Democratic party during the 1850s. Johnson was one of the wealthiest lawyers/planters in Arkansas. His estate in Jefferson County, some fifty miles southeast of Little Rock, was assessed to be worth more than $800,000 in 1860, and he owned 193 slaves. Politically, Johnson had the loyal support of his brother Richard H. Johnson, who edited the "family's" main newspaper in Little Rock, the *True Democrat*.

By 1860, however, the political dominance of the Johnsons and their allies appeared to be at an end. That year the "dynasty" attempted to rotate leadership, giving Governor Conway the U.S. Senate seat that Johnson was vacating, while putting Richard H. Johnson in the governor's office. Such maneuvering prompted a revolt of former "family" members, who fielded an insurgent ticket that swept the state. The "dynasty" lost control of the governor's office and both seats in the U.S. House (the second seat was added after the 1850 census). Governor Conway did not fill Johnson's Senate seat, but it was won by another candidate backed by the Conway-Johnson faction.

Southern secession gave new life to Johnson's political fortunes. Working with some of the insurgent leaders, Johnson successfully carried Arkansas into the Confederacy, though only after fighting began at Fort Sumter. Although not a member of the Secession Convention, he was one of the five men chosen by that body to serve in the Provisional Confederate Congress in May 1861. When the Provisional Congress became a bicameral assembly, the Arkansas legislature selected Johnson as one of the state's two Confederate senators.

Johnson was the seventh wealthiest man in the Confederate Congress and the richest representative from the Upper South. He supported the Davis administration and served on the powerful Military Affairs Committee while chairing the Committee on Indian Affairs. He was reelected in 1862, but by the time of the Confederate Congress's final session (Nov. 1864–Mar. 1865), he did not even go to Richmond to represent his state's interests, sensing perhaps that southern separatism, a cause he had long championed, was now lost.

The South's defeat cost Johnson his fortune as well as his political career. At war's end, he fled to Galveston, Texas, intending to leave the country. He changed his mind, however, and traveled to Washington, D.C., to receive a pardon from President Andrew Johnson. He then returned to Little Rock to practice law with Albert Pike, an old political enemy and former Confederate general. Johnson attempted to regain a U.S. Senate seat in 1878 but lost to fellow Democrat James D. Walker. He died in Little Rock.

Known for his courtly manner and political ability, Johnson vigorously defended slavery and his section while he and his relatives maintained their dominance in Arkansas politics from statehood through the Civil War.

• Johnson left no papers, and much of the material on his life comes from public sources (newspapers, the *Congressional Globe*, etc.), which can be found in the archives of the Arkansas History Commission in Little Rock. On his early life and career, especially his family background, see John Hallum, *Biographical and Pictorial History of Arkansas* (1889); Fay Hempstead, *A History of Arkansas from the Earliest Times to 1890* (1890); Josiah Shinn, *Pioneers and Makers of Arkansas* (1908). On Johnson's antebellum and Confederate political career, as well as the role of the "family" in Arkansas government, see James M. Woods, *Rebellion and Realignment: Arkansas's Road to Secession* (1987); Elsie Mae Lewis, "Robert Ward Johnson: Militant Spokesman of the Old South-West," *Arkansas Historical Quarterly* 13 (1954): 16–30; Dewey Allen Stokes, "Public Affairs in Arkansas, 1836–1849" (Ph.D. diss., Univ. of Tex., 1966); Elsie Mae Lewis, "From Nationalism to Disunion: A Study of the Secession Movement in Arkansas, 1849–1861" (Ph.D. diss., Univ. of Chicago, 1947); Michael B. Dougan, *Confederate Arkansas: The People and Policies of a Frontier State in Wartime* (1976). For a look at Johnson in comparison with the state's other Confederate congressmen, see James M. Woods, "Devotees and Dissenters: Arkansans in the Confederate Congress, 1861–1865," *Arkansas Historical Quarterly* 38 (1979): 227–47. For a contemporary obituary, see the Little Rock *Arkansas Gazette*, 27 July 1879.

JAMES M. WOODS

JOHNSON, Samuel (14 Oct. 1696–6 Jan. 1772), Anglican priest-missionary, philosopher, and college president, was born in Guilford, Connecticut, the son of Samuel Johnson, a fuller, and Mary Sage. Samuel was devoted to books and learning even as a small boy. At fourteen he entered the Collegiate School (later Yale College). Adept in Latin, Greek, and Hebrew, he began a lifetime of intellectual activity by composing "A Synopsis of Natural Philosophy," which he expanded into "An Encyclopedia of Philosophy." Even before graduation in 1714, Johnson began teaching school at Guilford, and in 1716 he was made a tutor of the Collegiate School. Johnson expanded his intellectual horizons by voluminous reading in the library collected by Jeremiah Dummer and in discussions with Yale friends and fellow tutors, among them the new rector of the college, Timothy Cutler. Because of a student upheaval, Johnson resigned as tutor in 1719.

Despite considerable doubts about the validity of presbyterial-congregational polity, Johnson was ordained in Connecticut's "Standing Order" as pastor of West Haven on 20 March 1720. This position allowed Johnson to continue and expand his education. Increasingly, however, he questioned the validity of the "Congregational Way." In 1722, after conversations with the Anglican missionary George Pigot and debates with the Yale trustees about the issue, Johnson, Cutler, Daniel Browne (a Yale tutor), and James Wetmore (a fellow congregational minister) sailed to England to seek holy orders (the defection one critic called a "dark day" for Puritan New England). In 1723, after conditional baptism and confirmation, Johnson was ordained deacon and priest and appointed as missionary to Stratford, Connecticut, by the Society for the Propagation of the Gospel (SPG). Returning to the colonies, he took over a small Anglican congregation at Stratford. On Christmas Day 1724 its long-projected church was opened for worship according to the *Book of Common Prayer*, the first such church in Connecticut.

As a devoted sacramentalist and high churchman, Johnson introduced monthly celebrations of the Holy Communion, a notable variant from the general quarterly celebrations. His parish flourished. Johnson's marriage to Charity Floyd in 1725 allied him to some of New York's most prominent families and made him stepfather to two sons and a daughter. Charity also bore two sons by Johnson. Johnson soon opened a rectory school, to which New Yorkers often sent their children, and he helped found parishes in several towns in Connecticut, Rhode Island, and New York. Johnson filled his correspondence with the SPG and English bishops with advice on the placement of clergy and the opportunities for expanding missionary work. In the absence of a seminary, he undertook the instruction of men preparing for holy orders and produced a steady flow of men into the ministry. Among them were Samuel Seabury and his son Samuel, who became the first Anglican bishop in America. Despite much opposition, the Anglican movement made remarkable headway in New England, owing in substantial measure to Johnson's influence, courage, and tact. His overarching interest was to promote "the best of churches." At the time of Johnson's death, Connecticut had forty-three Anglican congregations with sixteen priests, many trained by Johnson.

Between 1732 and 1737 Johnson published a series of irenic defenses of Anglican doctrine, polity, and liturgy. Johnson was also largely responsible for spreading the idealistic philosophy of George Berkeley (the dean of Derry), to which he was converted before Berkeley settled in Rhode Island in 1729. Johnson's *An Introduction to Philosophy* (1731; rev. ed., 1744) was expanded into *Ethices Elementa; or, The First Principles of Moral Philosophy* (1746) and reprinted in expanded form by Benjamin Franklin (with a new title) in 1752. The latter was used as a textbook at the College of Philadelphia and at King's College (now Columbia University) during Johnson's presidency of King's from 1754 to 1763. In addition, Johnson published *A Letter from Aristocles to Authades* (1745), concerning the sovereignty of God (an attack on predestination and a defense of the Catholic doctrine of free will), and *A New System of Morality* (1746). In his doctrines of the self-activity of the mind and the mind as a creative cause, Johnson anticipated the thought of Immanuel Kant, and he "added to Descartes' first principle: not *I perceive*, but I *perceive and act*, therefore I am" (emphasis added).

From the time of his ordination as priest, Johnson campaigned for an American episcopate. Without bishops, the church in America lacked convenient access to the essentials of its polity and sacramental life: confirmation for the laity and ordination for the clergy. Johnson not only enlisted the support of fellow priests whose regional meetings he had begun in 1725 but also induced Thomas Bradbury Chandler, a protégé, to pamphleteer for the cause. At Johnson's urging in 1767, Chandler published a pamphlet, *Appeal to the Public, Concerning the Reasonableness, Usefulness, and Necessity of an American Episcopate*. This publication opened a battle of pamphlets and newspaper essays that raged until 1771, eliciting diatribes from Charles Chauncey and William Livingston. The controversy and parallel debates in New York coincided with colonial opposition to the Townshend Acts. American resistance discouraged the British government from risking more trouble by action in ecclesiastical matters. Not until after Johnson's death and the winning of independence were Anglicans able to obtain an American bishop (consecrated in 1784).

Johnson also made a considerable mark as an educator. After having declined the headship of the new College of Philadelphia, he accepted the presidency of King's College (1754–1763), perhaps because of his New York connections and the opportunity of making King's a part of the Anglican advance in the northern colonies. As an educational reformer, he combined standard classical studies with a considerable amount of science, history, "experimental philosophy," principles of law, government, and even "vocational studies" such as agriculture and merchandising. Despite the vigorous opposition of William Livingston to linking the college with any particular denomination or sectarian influence, Johnson prevailed in using much of the Anglican liturgy for chapel services and in teaching general principles of Christian religion and morality without imposing "the peculiar tenets of any particular sect of Christians." Johnson's presidency was not his

greatest accomplishment, and he failed to persuade the board of governors to begin a preparatory school and, on occasion, to add more faculty. But he "made King's College possible" and was recognized for his wisdom and abilities in educational matters.

Having lost his son William, who died of smallpox in London after being ordained in 1756, Johnson suffered more losses with the death of his wife in 1758 and two of his stepchildren in 1759 and 1760. Johnson sought the companionship of a second wife; after overtures to Anne Watts failed in 1759, he married Sarah Beach, the widowed mother of his daughter-in-law, in 1761.

With increasing age and straitened finances, Johnson prepared for retirement. After his second wife's death from smallpox early in 1763, he lived with William Samuel and his family in Stratford. There he arranged to resume the rectorship of Christ Church, produced English and Hebrew grammars, fostered the establishment of a new church at Milford, wrote his autobiography, and reviewed his "former studies in almost all parts of learning," a final testimony to his "impatient curiosity to know" which had begun in childhood. He died in Stratford.

• Johnson's papers are in the Columbia University Library, the New-York Historical Society, and scattered in the Fulham Palace manuscripts, collections of the Society for the Propagation of the Gospel, and manuscript parish records of Christ Church, Stratford, Conn. Published papers are in Herbert Schneider and Carol Schneider, eds., *Samuel Johnson, President of King's College: His Career and Writings* (4 vols., 1929), and in Francis L. Hawks and William Stevens Perry, eds., *Documentary History of the Protestant Episcopal Church in the United States of America, Containing Numerous Hitherto Unpublished Documents Concerning the Church in Connecticut* (2 vols., 1863–1864). Biographical studies include Thomas Bradbury Chandler, *The Life of Samuel Johnson, D.D.* (1805); E. Edwards Beardsley, *Life and Correspondence of Samuel Johnson, D.D.* (1874); Joseph J. Ellis, *The New England Mind in Transition: Samuel Johnson of Connecticut, 1696–1772* (1973), a work mostly devoted to intellectual history and neglectful of Johnson's major work as priest, missionary, and advocate of an American episcopate; and Peter N. Carroll, *The Other Samuel Johnson: A Psychohistory of Early New England* (1978). For Johnson's major activities as priest and educator, see George E. DeMille, "One Man Seminary," *Historical Magazine of the Protestant Episcopal Church* 38 (1969): 373–79; Don R. Gerlach, "Champions of an American Episcopate: Thomas Secker of Canterbury and Samuel Johnson of Connecticut," *Historical Magazine of the Protestant Episcopal Church* 41 (1972): 381–414; and Don R. Gerlach and George E. DeMille, "Samuel Johnson and the Founding of King's College, 1751–1755" and "Samuel Johnson: *Praeses Collegii Regis*, 1755–1763," *Historical Magazine of the Protestant Episcopal Church* 44 (1975): 335–52, 417–36.

DON R. GERLACH

JOHNSON, Samuel William (3 July 1830–21 July 1909), agricultural chemist, was born in Kingsboro, New York, the son of Abner Adolphus Johnson, a prosperous merchant, and Annah Wells Gilbert. Upon his father's retirement a few years later to a farm in Deer River, New York, young Johnson attended the nearby Lowville Academy. After developing an interest in chemistry in his final year there, a teacher, David Mayhew, gave him a copy of a recent chemical text translated from German. Johnson quickly became so adept at chemical analysis that a year later he published his first article, "On Fixing Ammonia," in the prominent farm journal *The Cultivator*, to which his father subscribed. Upon graduation in 1846, he taught school in New York State for three years before entering Yale College in January 1850. There he studied with John Pitkin Norton for about a year. In 1851–1853 Johnson spent a term teaching at the New York State Normal School at Albany, took a six-month water cure for "dyspepsia" at Glen Haven, New York, and then returned to Yale to study and to assist the now-ill Professor Norton with his agricultural writings. Finally, in May 1853, Johnson and classmate Mason Weld embarked for two years of study in Germany. While at Otto Erdmann's laboratory at Leipzig, Johnson and fellow American Evan Pugh (later president of Pennsylvania Agricultural College, since renamed Pennsylvania State University), took a walking tour in February 1854 to nearby Möckern, site of the world's first agricultural experiment station. Impressed by an institution that had a staff of several chemists and facilities for both laboratory and field tests, the two vowed to create similar institutions in the United States on their return. Johnson publicized (and was paid for) his views in many letters to the editor, Luther Tucker, appearing in the *Country Gentleman*, successor of the journal *The Cultivator*. After a year at Justus Liebig's laboratory in Munich and two months in Edward Frankland's in Manchester, Johnson returned home in 1855 ready to convince American farmers of the need for experiment stations of their own. The crusade, however, was to consume twenty years.

Johnson's return coincided with plans for a new "scientific school" at Yale and a substantial donation by Joseph Sheffield, a New Haven railroad magnate. Yale hired Johnson in 1855 as an assistant in chemistry, and in 1856 he was promoted to professor of analytical chemistry. He spent the rest of his career at Yale, rather than in New York State, teaching students, performing research (especially after the completion of the new Sheffield Laboratory in 1860) on analytical tests for various chemical elements, and writing two influential textbooks, *How Crops Grow* (1868) and *How Crops Feed* (1870); both were widely used in the emerging land-grant colleges of the time and were translated into several foreign languages. But mostly Johnson campaigned vigorously for an experiment station in Connecticut. To this end he accepted an appointment as chemist of the Connecticut State Agricultural Society in 1856 and for several years thereafter dramatized farmers' vulnerability to fraudulent fertilizers by publicizing both the calculated cost of commercial products, based on their chemical composition and market values, and the usually much higher selling price. The farm press reprinted his reports as well as the denials and rebuttals from manufacturers. Yet Connecticut farmers long resisted John-

son's recommendation that the state should pay for a station. In 1866 the legislature did, however, create a board of agriculture, to which Johnson was appointed, and then in 1869 passed one of the earliest state consumer protection laws, allowing the state chemist to inspect fertilizer labels for accuracy. Finally in 1875, with the aid of Orange Judd, publisher of Johnson's textbooks as well as the *American Agriculturalist* and a trustee of Wesleyan University, the Connecticut legislature did establish the first experiment station in the nation, with the proviso, quite upsetting to Johnson at the time, that the station be in Middletown (in Judd Hall at Wesleyan, which donated the space) and the director be Johnson's student W. O. Atwater on the faculty there. Two years later, however, in 1877, the state voted to support it fully, move it to New Haven, and install Johnson as the director. He continued in the dual appointment until retiring from Yale in 1896. He retired from the station in 1899.

Johnson's twenty-two years in office seemed, by contrast, anticlimactic. While struggling to run a station whose regulatory duties multiplied faster than its staff or appropriation, he was active in supporting similar movements in other states, where some of his students became leaders. Johnson, frail since his youth, took little direct role in the battles of the 1880s and 1890s, such as that for the passage of the Hatch Act of 1887. He may also have been hampered by the nebulous status of Yale as a land-grant institution. He was elected to the National Academy of Sciences in 1866, shortly after its formation, and served as the third president of the American Chemical Society in 1878. He also headed the American Association of Analytical Chemists, which he helped to found, in 1885, and the Association of Colleges and Experiment Stations in 1896. He died at home in New Haven, survived by his wife, the former Elizabeth Erwin Blinn of Essex, New York, whom he had married in 1858, and their daughter Elizabeth, who married Yale chemist and Johnson's former student Thomas Osborne. In 1913 Elizabeth Osborne published a biography and a selection of her father's correspondence titled *From the Letter-Files of Samuel W. Johnson*. He can be classed as an important leader of the first stage of the movement to bring agricultural experiment stations to the United States and the trainer of many of the movement's subsequent leaders.

• Many of Johnson's letters and letterbooks are still in the library of the Connecticut Experiment Station in New Haven. A portrait and a lengthy bibliography of his publications are in Thomas B. Osborne, "Samuel W. Johnson, 1830–1909," *Biographical Memoirs* (National Academy of Sciences) 7 (1911–1913): 203–22, which also lists several other obituaries. More recent treatments are Peter R. Day, ed., *"How Crops Grow," A Century Later*, Connecticut Agricultural Experiment Station (New Haven) Bulletin 708 (1969), and portions of Margaret W. Rossiter, *The Emergence of Agricultural Science, Justus Liebig and the Americans, 1840–1880* (1975), and Alan I. Marcus, *Agricultural Science and the Quest for Legitimacy* (1985).

MARGARET W. ROSSITER

JOHNSON, Sargent Claude (7 Oct. 1887–10 Oct. 1967), artist, was born in Boston, Massachusetts, the son of Anderson Johnson and Lizzie Jackson. When Johnson was ten years old, his father died of an unknown cause. Because his mother battled tuberculosis the children were sent to relatives. Johnson lived with his maternal uncle, Sherman William Jackson, and his wife, the sculptor May Howard Jackson, for several years in Washington, D.C. Then he and his siblings stayed briefly with their maternal grandparents in Alexandria, Virginia. When their mother died in 1902, the girls went to a Catholic school in Pennsylvania and the boys were sent to a Sisters of Charity Orphanage in Worcester, Massachusetts. Johnson attended public school and worked in the Sisters of Charity Hospital. He began painting as an adolescent while recovering from a long illness. After Johnson studied singing briefly at a music school in Boston, he lived with relatives in Chicago. Despite his tragic childhood Johnson was a cheerful man. His friend, the painter Clay Spohn, described him as "perenialy happy, joyous, exuberant in living."

In the early 1910s Johnson moved to San Francisco, where he married Pearl Lawson in 1915; the two had one child, then separated in 1936. Lawson was hospitalized for mental illness in 1947 and remained at the Stockton State Hospital until her death in 1964. Johnson worked as a fitter for Schlusser Bros. from 1917 until about 1920, as a photographic retouch artist for Willard E. Worden in 1920, and as a framer for Valdespino Framers from about 1921 until 1931.

Johnson began studying drawing and painting at the A. W. Best School of Art and then at the California School of Fine Arts (1919–1923 and again in 1940–1942) under sculptors Robert Stackpole and Beniamino Bufano. He won first prize for his work there in 1921 and 1922. Much later, he studied metal sculpture with Claire Falkenstein. Upon leaving school, Johnson made his primary living as a framer. From 1925 to 1933 Johnson worked in wood, ceramics, oils, watercolors, and graphics in a backyard studio in Berkeley. In 1928 he won the Harmon Foundation's Otto Kahn prize for *Sammy*, a terra cotta head. Two years later he won the foundation's bronze award for fine arts, and in 1933 he received the Robert C. Ogden prize for the most outstanding combination of materials for *Pearl*, a porcelain bust of his daughter, and two drawings, *Mother and Child* and *Defiant*. The sculptor also exhibited several pieces with the institution's traveling exhibitions, and thousands saw them in the Oakland Municipal Art Gallery in 1931 and 1933. Already recognized in the San Francisco Bay area, Johnson was the only Californian in these national shows. *Chester* (1931), a terra cotta portrait head of an African-American boy resting his cheek in his right hand, was purchased by the German minister to Italy.

In 1935 the Harmon Foundation presented Johnson in a three-man exhibition at the Delphic Studios in New York. Included was a lacquered, redwood, polychrome sculpture of a woman, *Forever Free*. Incised on the skirt of her tubular body are two children playing under their mother's protective care. Covered with several coats of gesso and fine linen and highlighted in black and white paint, this is Sargent's best-known piece. "It is the pure American Negro I am concerned with," he said, "aiming to show the natural beauty and dignity . . . in that characteristic hair, bearing and manner; and I wish to show that beauty not so much to the White man as to the Negro himself" (*San Francisco Chronicle*, 6 Oct. 1935). Johnson, whose mother was of Cherokee and black ancestry, identified himself as African American. Among his memorable sculpture of the 1930s is a series of stylized bronze and copper heads and masks on art deco-like wooden bases. The stoic faces borrow certain qualities from West African, Pre-Columbian (Mayan and Aztec), and cubist art.

In the mid-1930s Johnson was employed by the Federal Art Project of the Works Progress Administration as artist, senior sculptor, assistant supervisor, assistant state supervisor, and unit supervisor. He produced several large-scale works including an enormous carved redwood organ screen for the California School for the Blind (1937) and semi-abstract carvings of marine life in green Vermont slate and a tile mural for San Francisco's Maritime Museum at Aquatic Park (c. 1938). He also completed statues at the Golden Gate International Exposition in San Francisco: two Incas—one a rich man, the other an intellectual—seated on llamas for the South American front of the Court of Pacifica, and three works symbolizing Industry, Home Life, and Agriculture for the Alameda-Contra Costa County Fair Building (1939). In 1939 he also created a series of six animals in green and gray cast terrazzo for a child-care center playground in San Francisco.

Johnson had been elected to the San Francisco Art Association in May 1932 and to its council board in 1934. He served on the organization's annual juries (1936, 1938, 1940, 1942, 1947, and 1948) and received awards from the group in 1925 (for *Pearl*), 1931 (*Chester*, a terra cotta head), 1935 (*Forever Free*), and 1938 (*Black and White*, a lithograph). At the same time, local museums acquired Johnson's work; in the mid-1930s the San Francisco Museum of Art received the collection of local philanthropist Albert M. Bender, which included several of the sculptor's pieces (such as *Forever Free*), and in 1939 the San Diego Fine Arts Gallery purchased *Esther* (a terra cotta head). Various museums and collectors purchased a number of the 150 copies of the lithograph *Singing Saint* in 1940. The semi-abstract work of two women, one playing a guitar, was widely reproduced in the 1940s.

A contract for a piece from the San Francisco Art Commission in 1940 ended a long friendship between Johnson and Bufano, his principal mentor, after an extended public competition because Bufano wanted the work. Johnson's best-known large-scale decorative work is a tremendous cast-stone frieze, which covers the entire retaining wall across the back of the George Washington High School Athletic Field (1942). It depicts young men and women diving, rowing, wrestling, and playing football, basketball, baseball, and tennis.

Travel provided Johnson with much artistic inspiration. An unknown benefactor and two Abraham Rosenberg Scholarships (1944 and 1949) helped finance numerous trips between 1945 and 1965 to Mexico, where he visited renowned archeological sites and studied ancient art and Chelula polychrome pottery. Working with black clay found outside Oaxaca in the manner of Zapotec Indians and Mexicans, he produced many small, hollow forms, including representation of a do-nothing politician (a type that annoyed Johnson during the Great Depression). Johnson's anonymous patron also sponsored a seven-month trip to Japan in 1958. There Johnson visited Shinto shrines and studied Japanese art. An avid reader and guitarist, Johnson also taught art to several private students in his studio over several years and offered classes for the Junior Workshop program of the San Francisco Housing Authority and Mills College in 1947.

From 1947 to 1967 Johnson produced about 100 abstract, surrealist, and impressionist porcelain enamel panels and plates on steel, a technique he learned at the Paine-Mahoney Company, which produced enameled signs on steel plates. The company invited Johnson to create aesthetic porcelain plates on steel in his spare time. He shaped the metal in his studio or at the Architectural Porcelain Company, exploring religious, multiracial, antiwar, and mother and child themes. Johnson produced several commissions in this medium, including a semi-abstract mural of pots and pans for Nathan Dohrmann & Company, a crockery and glass shop (1948), and a decorative map of Richmond, California, for its City Hall Chambers (1949). In 1949 Paine-Mahoney Company hired Johnson to complete the details of a commission of an enamel mural for Harold's Club in Reno, Nevada. Reportedly the largest mural in the United States ever created by that method, it is thirty-eight feet high and seventy-eight feet long and depicts wagon-train pioneers crossing the Sierras. Johnson finished a similar mural (twenty-five feet long by fifty feet high) for the West Club Casino in Las Vegas.

Johnson continued large-scale works in other media, as well. The Matson Navigation Company of Honolulu commissioned two works for pleasure ships: a large mahogany panel depicting Hawaiian leaders and warriors for the SS *Lurline* (1948), and two ceramic tile walls for the SS *Monterey* (1956). Two years after Johnson moved to San Francisco in 1948, he began to bring color back to his sculpture, affirming his earlier artistic statement,

The slogan for the Negro artist should be 'Go south, young man!' Too many Negro artists go to Europe and come back imitators of Cézanne, Matisse or Picasso, and this attitude is not only a weakness of the artists, but of their racial public. In all artistic circles I hear too much talking and too much theorizing. All their theories do not help me any, and I have but one technical hobby to ride: I am interested in applying color to

sculpture as the Egyptian, Greek, and other ancient people did. (*San Francisco Chronicle*, 6 Oct. 1935)

In the late 1950s and 1960s the sculptor produced polychrome wood pieces with universal themes influenced by Asian, Northwest Native American, and ancient Egyptian and Greek art. He also executed works in diorite rock, cast bronze, and forged enameled forms, and he collaborated with ceramist John Magnani on glazes and clay bodies. During the 1960s Johnson also worked for the Flax Framing and Art Supply Company. Johnson died in San Francisco. Although somewhat isolated as one of the few African-American artists consistently active in California from the 1920s through the 1960s, Johnson was nationally known for his stylistic pluralism, versatility, and daring innovation.

• The whereabouts of Johnson's papers is not known. The Archives of American Art has a 33-page transcription of an oral history interview (1964). The most useful publications on the artist are Evangeline J. Montgomery, *Sargent Johnson: Retrospective* (Oakland Museum, 1971) and "Sargent Johnson," *International Review of African American Art* 6, no. 2 (1984), and a chapter in Romare Bearden and Harry Henderson, *A History of African-American Artists from 1792 to the Present* (1993). Johnson's obituary is in the *Oakland Tribune*, 12 Oct. 1967.

THERESA LEININGER-MILLER

JOHNSON, Theodore Elliott (9 Sept. 1931–20 Apr. 1986), librarian, scholar, and Shaker brother, was born in Boston, Massachusetts, the son of Elmer Carl Johnson, a purchasing agent, and Ruth D. Collins Johnson. In 1953 he graduated from Colby College in Waterville, Maine, with a B.A. in Latin. Johnson, who never married, spent the next year studying medieval Latin literature in Strasbourg, France, on a Fulbright fellowship, and in 1955 he received an M.A. in the teaching of classics from Harvard University School of Education. Then, from 1955 to 1957 he studied at Harvard Divinity School. As a member of the Episcopal church, Johnson attended a parish administered by the Cowley Fathers of the Society of Saint John the Evangelist, and both scholarship and religion remained the central interests of his life.

According to Johnson's recollections, he probably would have entered an Anglican religious community had he not discovered Shakerism in October 1957 when he visited the Shaker village at Hancock, Massachusetts. There he spoke with elderly Believers who urged him to contact the community at Sabbathday Lake, Maine. The latter visit ultimately changed his life and led to his conversion to Shakerism. Johnson soon found employment as a librarian at the Waterville Public Library, a location that allowed him to spend time with his Shaker friends at Sabbathday Lake. In the late 1950s he also assisted with the organization of the Shaker library there.

By 1960 Johnson was spending an increasing amount of time at Sabbathday Lake even though he was still employed in Waterville. Johnson officially entered the community on 28 May 1960, and soon he was playing an increasingly prominent role in the life of the small village. He was appointed the first director of the Shaker Library, and in 1961 he founded the *Shaker Quarterly*, a periodical devoted to the history, theology, and community life of the Shakers, and served as its editor. In 1963 he also became the director of the museum at Sabbathday Lake. These positions allowed him to use his scholarly training and religious interests on behalf of Shakerism and the Maine community.

These years were transitional ones for Shakerism. In 1961 Delmar Wilson, the last Shaker brother, had died. Johnson, who spent long hours with Wilson during his illness, stepped into that vacuum and began to assert leadership, especially in the public meetings. In 1965 the Shaker ministry decided to close the society to new members, a decision that divided Believers at the two remaining villages, Sabbathday Lake and Canterbury, New Hampshire. Canterbury favored closing the society to new Believers, while Sabbathday Lake welcomed newcomers. Gertrude Soule, the ranking Believer in Maine and a member of the ministry, ultimately left Sabbathday Lake for Canterbury. The remaining Shakers in Maine did not agree with the ministry, in part because that decision had implications for Johnson's status. Johnson had become an able spokesperson for Shakerism and a member of the Sabbathday Lake community. The rupture between the two villages became open and bitter. The Maine Believers defied a ministry directive to eject Johnson from the community. Although cautious in public statements about the controversy, the Shakers moved close to formal schism. At the heart of the conflict were contrasting views of the society's future.

Over the next fifteen years Johnson emerged as the leader of the Maine community. The strength of his convictions and his deep commitment to community life moved him to the center of the family's existence. He became the first president of the Shaker corporation, the United Society, founded in 1972. He lectured widely outside the community on both the history and contemporary situation of the Shakers. Johnson also attracted other new Believers to Shakerism. He used the pages of the *Shaker Quarterly* as the principal forum for the publication of his scholarship. He was also the founder and director of the Institute for Shaker Studies, which was established in 1974.

But Johnson never escaped the controversy surrounding his prominence in the Shaker community. Critics charged him with misrepresentation and ulterior motives while admirers spoke favorably of his fervor and dedication. The Believers in Maine loved and admired him, and he carried out many of the functions traditionally assigned to a Shaker elder without ever holding that position. Although Johnson experienced intermittent periods of ill health, his sudden and unexpected death at Sabbathday Lake shocked the small Shaker family in Maine.

Arguably, Johnson may have been the most significant Shaker in the twentieth century. His presence at Sabbathday Lake contributed instrumentally to the survival of the Shaker movement. It is possible that without his presence and the controversy surrounding him, the Maine Believers might have succumbed to the pressures to close the order. The determination to resist that option centered on their support of Johnson.

Johnson was a significant interpreter of Shaker tradition. His publications, especially the historical texts he edited, raised the level of appreciation for the past. He also influenced the direction of Shakerism at the end of the twentieth century, opening it to other religious influences and movements. He brought to it an ecumenical spirit and new appreciation for other expressions of Christian asceticism.

Johnson articulated a powerful and appealing contemporary formulation of Shaker theology. He identified the "indwelling presence of Christ" as the center of Shaker teaching and the basis for the community's commitment to unity and simplicity. He described the distinctive idea of God held by Believers as incorporating "male characteristics of strength and power" and "female characteristics of compassion and mercy." He also rejected the notion that the founder of the Shakers, Ann Lee, was the Christ; rather, he contended, the "second appearing of Christ" was in the church. He also emphasized the spiritual nature of all Shaker life, including the life of worship. Johnson was influential in attracting an expanding circle of patrons and friends for the Shakers, and his years of activity were a time of renewed interest in Shakerism.

• The library at Sabbathday Lake contains Johnson's papers, sermons, and lectures, as well as oral history materials. Johnson's career as a Shaker is documented in the issues of the *Shaker Quarterly*, which he edited. He published numerous essays in it, including "Shakerism for Today," *Shaker Quarterly* 3, no. 1 (1963): 3–6; "The 'Millennial Laws' of 1821," *Shaker Quarterly* 7, no. 2 (1967): 33–58; "Life in the Christ Spirit: Observations on Shaker Theology," *Shaker Quarterly* 8, no. 3 (1968): 67–76; and "Biographical Account of the Life, Character & Ministry of Father Joseph Meacham the Primary Leader in Establishing the United Order of Millennial Church by Calvin Green 1827," *Shaker Quarterly* 10, no. 1 (1970): 20–32; 10, no. 2 (1970): 51–68; 10, no. 3 (1970): 92–102. His activities within the community are recorded in the pages of the "Home Notes" published in each issue. The most instructive view of community life at Sabbathday Lake during Johnson's years is Gerard C. Wertkin, *The Four Seasons of Shaker Life: An Intimate Portrait of the Community at Sabbathday Lake, Maine* (1986). For further background on Shakerism in the period of Johnson's involvement, see Stephen J. Stein, *The Shaker Experience in America: A History of the United Society of Believers* (1992). R. Mildred Barker's obituary for Johnson is in the *Shaker Quarterly* 15, no. 1 (1987): 5–6.

STEPHEN STEIN

JOHNSON, Thomas (4 Nov. 1732–26 Oct. 1819), politician and jurist, was born on his parents' farm in Calvert County, Maryland, the son of Thomas Johnson and Dorcas Sedgwick. Educated at home, Johnson began his legal studies in Annapolis, where he read law with Stephen Bordley, one of the foremost lawyers in the province, and by working as a scrivener in the office of the clerk of the Maryland Provincial Court. First admitted to the bar of the Annapolis Mayor's Court in 1756, Johnson gained admission by 1760 to the bars of Frederick and Baltimore counties, the Charles County Court, and the provincial court. While pursuing advancement as an attorney, he became interested in public office and in 1762 was elected to represent Anne Arundel County in the lower house of assembly. He continued to serve in that position through 1774. In 1766 he married Ann Jennings; they had eight children.

As a delegate to the assembly, Johnson became known as an ardent defender of American rights and, when difficulties with England grew, was elected to the Annapolis Committee of Correspondence and to the First and Second Continental Congresses. Although at first a moderate, Johnson soon joined forces with those who favored independence. But shortly before Congress adopted the Declaration of Independence in 1776, he returned to Maryland to raise money and munitions for George Washington's army (it was Johnson who had nominated Washington to be commander in chief) and thus never signed the Declaration.

Back in Maryland, Johnson served in a variety of offices during the Revolution: commander of the militia, first governor of the state of Maryland (three one-year terms from 1777 to 1780), and member of the Maryland House of Delegates from 1780 to 1782. Once the war was won, however, Johnson retired from public office and used his legal skills in a private capacity, although for a number of public purposes. He served on a Maryland state committee that prepared legislation that dealt with the jurisdiction of the state court of admiralty, and in 1785 the Confederation Congress chose Johnson to be the judge between Massachusetts and New York in a dispute that concerned territory west of the Genesee River.

But most important to Johnson, he joined with Washington and several other men in 1785 to create the Potomac Company to further navigation on the Potomac River. Developing the Potomac region had been a lifelong interest of Johnson's, and he served on the company's board of directors and succeeded Washington as its president.

In 1786 Johnson returned to public office as Frederick County's representative in the house of delegates and also represented that county in the state ratifying convention, where he urged the adoption of the federal Constitution. Maryland's governor appointed Johnson chief judge of the Maryland General Court in April 1790. Although his tenure on the state bench was brief, he heard important cases in which the court upheld the supremacy of federal law over state law. He resigned from the state bench after accepting a recess appointment to the U.S. Supreme Court on 5 August 1791. That same year President Washington appointed Johnson a commissioner for the new capital on the Potomac, a position he held until 1794.

President Washington had already shown his respect for Johnson's legal ability by nominating him in 1789 U.S. district judge for the state of Maryland. Confirmed by the Senate on 26 September 1789, Johnson declined the appointment. Before nominating him for a second, higher post, the president wrote to Johnson to determine if he would be receptive to becoming an associate justice. Johnson responded that he had reservations about accepting the appointment because of his poor health and the burdensome circuit-riding duties that the office required. Overcoming his reluctance, he accepted the temporary commission in August and the Senate confirmed him to a permanent position on 7 November 1791.

It did not take Johnson long to discover that his duties were in fact too onerous for him. After holding a circuit court in Virginia in the fall of 1791, attending the Supreme Court in August 1792, and riding the southern circuit in the fall of 1792, he resigned on 16 January 1793. Though present for only one term of the Supreme Court, he participated in two significant rulings. In *Hayburn's Case* (1792), the Court divided equally in its opinion as to whether the attorney general had authority *ex officio*, without specific permission from the president, to move for a mandamus to the U.S. Circuit Court for the District of Pennsylvania that would compel it to hear the petition of William Hayburn; because the vote was a tie, the motion was denied. Johnson, however, belonged to the half of the Court that believed the attorney general should be allowed to proceed on his own. Had Johnson's view been in the majority, the case-or-controversy requirement to bring a suit into federal court might never have prevailed. In the initial hearing before the Supreme Court in the case of *Georgia v. Brailsford* (1792), which involved the legality of a Georgia statute authorizing the sequestration of British property during the Revolution, Johnson, in dissent, voiced the opinion that the state of Georgia did not need an injunction, because her "right to the debt in question . . . may be enforced at common law." The justices in the majority voted to issue the injunction so that the interests of all parties could be brought before the Supreme Court for adjudication. Although the justices voted only on a procedural matter at this stage of the litigation, the result enabled the suit to proceed before the Supreme Court. A jury trial, held in 1794 to settle the claims of the parties, led to a decision that supported the supremacy of federal treaties over state law, but by that time Johnson had departed.

After leaving the Court, Johnson retired to his estate in Frederick, Maryland, and declined further opportunities to serve the public. He refused appointments both as secretary of state in 1795 and as chief judge of the Circuit Court of the District of Columbia in 1801. He died at home.

Johnson was recognized in his own time for contributing to the success of the Revolution and the commencement of government under the Constitution. According to his contemporary John Adams (1735–1826), "Johnson of Maryland has a clear and a cool

Head, an extensive Knowledge of Trade, as well as Law. He is a deliberating Man, but not a shining orator" (*Diary of John Adams*, 10 Oct. 1774).

• No major collection of Johnson papers survives. A small number of documents can be found at the C. Burr Artz Library, Frederick, Md.; in the Washington papers at the Library of Congress; and in Record Group 59 at the National Archives. Some of his letters are published in Maeva Marcus, ed., *The Documentary History of the Supreme Court of the United States, 1789–1800* (1985–). Edward S. Delaplaine, *The Life of Thomas Johnson* (1927), remains the only full-length biography. An interesting short essay about Johnson, written by Herbert Alan Johnson, is in *The Justices of the United States Supreme Court 1789–1969: Their Lives and Major Opinions*, ed. Leon Friedman and Fred L. Israel, vol. 1 (1969).

MAEVA MARCUS

JOHNSON, Tom Loftin (18 July 1854–10 Apr. 1911), street railway magnate and municipal reformer, was born near Georgetown, Kentucky, the son of Albert William Johnson and Helen Loftin. His father was a slaveholding planter who served as a colonel in the Confederate army. Impoverished by the Civil War, in 1868 the family settled outside of Louisville, Kentucky, near supportive friends and relatives. Before Tom was fifteen he secured an office job with a Louisville street railway company that had recently been purchased by close family friends Alfred V. and A. B. du Pont. This was the beginning of Johnson's long business relationship with members of the wealthy family of explosive manufacturers. In 1873 Tom Johnson became superintendent of the streetcar company after having already patented the first coin fare box for streetcars. During his lifetime, the inventive Johnson was to obtain thirty-one patents.

Johnson, however, was not satisfied with a life of quiet prosperity in Louisville. Instead, in 1876 with a loan from the du Ponts he purchased control of an Indianapolis streetcar company, and three years later he bought his first street railway line in Cleveland. At this time he came into conflict with the plutocratic Republican leader Marcus A. Hanna, who controlled a competing transit line. Hanna and Johnson remained archrivals for the rest of their lives. Meanwhile, Johnson had married his distant cousin Margaret Johnson in 1874, and in 1883 she and the couple's two children settled in Cleveland. Though Tom Johnson continued to commute among his scattered business interests, henceforth the Ohio city was his permanent address.

In 1883 Johnson began reading the works of Henry George, and he soon became a disciple and close friend of the reformer, embracing his belief that the only necessary tax was a levy on the unearned increment on land values. According to George, profits from land speculation should enter the public till rather than enriching private investors. Like George, Johnson also opposed protective tariffs and monopolies. While serving in Congress as a Democrat from 1891 to 1895, Johnson expressed his support for George's ideas, but his two terms in Washington were on the whole unremarkable.

During the late 1880s and the 1890s Johnson continued his business exploits, some of which raised doubts among subsequent observers about the depth and sincerity of his devotion to George's message. Exploiting his patent monopoly and benefiting from ever-helpful du Pont money, Johnson embarked on the manufacture of streetcar rails in Johnstown, Pennsylvania, eventually building a rolling mill there. Moreover, he and his partners bought the acreage surrounding their mill site in the hope of profiting from the increase in land values once the mill was in operation. In the 1890s Johnson expanded his steel business, locating a mill in Lorain, Ohio. His syndicate purchased seven square miles at this site, again planning to profit from land speculation. Meanwhile, in 1895 he became president of the Citizens' Street Railway Company of Detroit, which was engaged in a heated battle with that city's reform mayor Hazen Pingree. By supporting a rival line charging only a three cent fare, Pingree sought to force the Citizens' Company to abandon its five cent rate. In the course of the fight Johnson became a symbol for Detroiters of the powerful and unscrupulous streetcar interests, and a local newspaper said of the Citizens' Company president: "His business methods are treacherous and his political methods are shady."

From his Detroit experience Johnson learned the popular appeal of the three cent fare among voters, and on his return to Cleveland he was ready to switch from friend to foe of the streetcar companies. In 1901 he ran successfully for mayor of Cleveland on the Democratic ticket; he was to win reelection three times, serving almost nine years as the city's executive. Like Pingree, as mayor he sponsored a new transit company to force the existing franchise holder to lower its fares, and he sought ultimately to overcome a state prohibition of municipal ownership of streetcar lines. Johnson battled Cleveland's streetcar magnates as vigorously as he had vied with Pingree and was eventually able to achieve lower fares. Yet municipal ownership eluded him, and in 1909 Cleveland's voters expressed their exasperation with continual transit wars and defeated Johnson's bid for yet another term.

During his tenure in city hall Johnson fought for other reforms as well. He sought to implement a fairer system of taxation through revision of property assessments, claiming that existing assessments favored big business at the expense of the ordinary citizen. His director of charitable and correctional institutions believed that criminals were victims of society and refused to send unruly prisoners to solitary confinement in dark cells; instead he assigned them to the "thinking tower" where the rooms were flooded with sunshine and fresh air. Johnson also built public bathhouses for the poor and tore down the "Keep Off the Grass" signs in public parks, allowing the masses to enjoy more fully these open spaces. Moreover, the reform mayor sponsored the construction of a civic center and imported to the city architect-planner Daniel Burnham to lead a design team for this project. The resulting plan earned plaudits throughout the United States and spawned similar projects in other cities.

Because of all of this Johnson won a nationwide reputation and became a reform idol. In some minds Cleveland under Johnson was a bastion of radicalism, and his rival Hanna labeled the mayor a "socialist-anarchist-nihilist." More sympathetic observers claimed that Johnson was "the best mayor of the best-governed city in the United States." Viewing his life as a whole, Johnson appears to be a paradox. He was both robber baron and radical. He was simultaneously a devoted follower of Henry George and a lifelong partner of the du Ponts. In Detroit he assumed the role of cutthroat business tycoon; a few years later in Cleveland he played the part of defender of the people. Johnson was, however, best remembered for this latter role, and after he died in Cleveland, he was buried next to Henry George.

• For additional information see Tom L. Johnson, *My Story* (1911); Carl Lorenz, *Tom L. Johnson* (1911); Lincoln Steffens, "Ohio: A Tale of Two Cities," *McClure's Magazine*, July 1905, pp. 293–311; Paul Leland Haworth, "Mayor Johnson of Cleveland: A Study of Mismanaged Political Reform," *Outlook*, 23 Oct. 1909, pp. 469–74; and Robert H. Bremner, "Tom L. Johnson," *Ohio State Archaeological and Historical Quarterly* 59 (Jan. 1950): 1–13. Also see a series of articles on Johnson by Eugene C. Murdock in *Ohio Historical Quarterly* 62 (Oct. 1953): 323–33, 63 (Oct. 1954): 319–35, 65 (Jan. 1956): 28–43, 66 (Oct. 1957): 375–90, and 67 (Jan. 1958): 35–49. Also helpful are Melvin G. Holli, *Reform in Detroit: Hazen S. Pingree and Urban Politics* (1969); Michael P. McCarthy, "'Suburban Power': A Footnote on Cleveland in the Tom Johnson Years," *Northwest Ohio Quarterly* 45 (Winter 1972–1973): 21–25; Michael Massouh, "Technological and Managerial Innovation: The Johnson Company, 1883–1898," *Business History Review* 50 (Spring 1976): 46–68; Massouh, "Innovations in Street Railways before Electric Traction: Tom L. Johnson's Contributions," *Technology and Culture* 18 (Apr. 1977): 202–17; and Eugene C. Murdock, "A Couple of Giants: Mark Hanna and Tom Johnson" in *Ohio's Western Reserve: A Regional Reader*, ed. Harry F. Lupold and Gladys Haddad (1988). An obituary is in the *New York Times*, 11 Apr. 1911.

JON C. TEAFORD

JOHNSON, Tommy (1896?–1 Nov. 1956), blues artist, was born in Hinds County, Mississippi, between the towns of Terry and Crystal Springs, the son of Idell Johnson and Mary Ella Wilson, farmers. One of thirteen children, he spent his early years on the George Miller plantation near his birthplace. One early musical influence could have been an uncle who supposedly played guitar and harmonica. Around 1910 Johnson moved to Crystal Springs and began learning guitar from an older brother, Ledell. Around 1912–1913 he ran away from home, took up with an older woman, and traveled north to the cotton-growing Delta region of the state. There he broadened his musical education, learning blues from Delta musicians, possibly including Charley Patton, later to be revered as one of the blues tradition's father figures. Johnson returned to Crystal Springs after a few years but soon moved back to the Delta to work on the Tom Sander plantation in Drew, where he came under the influence of Patton, Willie Brown, Dick Bankston, and other Delta artists. Mastering local blues styles, he began to perform regularly at juke joints and parties.

Around 1914 or 1915 he married Maggie Bidwell and continued to move back and forth between Crystal Springs and the Delta, where he played with Patton in the early 1920s. His marriage ended in 1917, and in the early 1920s he married again, this time to Ella Hill, and began to combine seasonal farming with hoboing trips to Arkansas and Louisiana, where he played music for handouts. In the mid- to late 1920s he performed around Jackson, Mississippi, working with such guitarists as Charley McCoy, Walter Vinson, and Ishman Bracey. Through Bracey he was introduced to Jackson music-store owner and talent scout H. C. Speir, who arranged a recording session with RCA Victor. In Memphis, Tennessee, on 3 and 4 Feb. 1928 Johnson recorded four sides, with McCoy backing him on three of them. All four sides are now considered classics: "Cool Drink of Water Blues," "Big Road Blues," "Maggie Campbell Blues," and the only solo, "Bye-Bye Blues." The following August, Johnson returned to Memphis for a follow-up session. It produced two influential tracks: "Canned Heat Blues" and "Big Fat Mama Blues." Based solely on these initial six sides for Victor, Johnson's future reputation was already assured.

His recordings were not huge sellers, however, and Johnson continued to join his brothers in seasonal farm work in the Delta. David "Honeyboy" Edwards recalled them coming to Greenwood around 1929: "They come up picking cotton—pick cotton all through the day; and at night they'd sit around and play the guitars. . . . They were cotton pickers, day hands—they pick cotton, make a little money, go back to the hills later in the fall." Edwards could remember Tommy, Clarence, and Mager Johnson working and playing together, and Tommy playing "Canned Heat Blues," "Big Road Blues," and "Bye and Bye."

With the Depression under way in early 1930, Johnson traveled to Grafton, Wisconsin, along with Ishman Bracey to record for Paramount. The session yielded six sides, including one with a small jazz combo, the New Orleans Nehi Boys, but the recordings failed to match the artistic excellence of Johnson's Victor sides. In the early 1930s Johnson supposedly ran a small café in Jackson. In the mid-1930s he and Bracey worked for Doctor Simpson's Medicine Show.

After his marriage to Ella Hill ended, around 1935 Johnson married Rosa Youngblood, and their marriage lasted about four years. In the 1940s he married his fourth wife, Emma Downes of New Orleans. Throughout this time he played at house parties or worked as a street musician from Jackson south to Tylertown to New Orleans and other Louisiana venues. His protégés included Roosevelt Holts and K. C. Douglas, as well as Jackson-born "Boogie Bill" Webb, whose mother regularly employed Johnson for her New Orleans house parties. By Webb's account, Johnson would take the train from Jackson to play all night for "six dollars and train fare." Webb said Johnson relied mainly on his most familiar recorded blues: "That's all he could play . . . but that was enough at that time. And he had an acoustic guitar, not electric, but good gracious, how loud it sounded at that time."

Considering Johnson's alcoholism and penchant for consuming toxic beverages such as canned heat and shoe polish, it is remarkable that he lived to be sixty. Supposedly he died of a heart attack probably in Jackson after playing an all-night house party celebrating a niece's birthday.

Due largely to the research of biographer David Evans, a good deal is known about Johnson's artistry and influence. Evans traced Johnson's role in transporting blues from the Delta to the southern part of Mississippi, noting that his influence in the southern half of the state was nearly as great as Patton's in the Delta. Stylistically, Johnson was distinguished by his use of falsetto, derived from the field holler tradition, and his competent guitar playing. His instrumental work with Charley McCoy was especially fine.

Blues artists ranging from Otis Spann to Johnny Temple to Howlin' Wolf acknowledged the influence of Johnson. So too did the numerous blues revival performers who included Johnson classics in their repertoires from the 1960s on. The rock band Canned Heat took its name from the Johnson blues and included the signature verse from his "Big Road Blues" in one of its hit tunes. All told, a remarkable number of Johnson's compositions entered tradition and were performed by countless artists.

Johnson became an intriguing curiosity in the history of the blues in part because of stories about his drinking and a tall tale that he obtained his musical talent in a trade with the devil. But any notoriety he gained from such accounts was unnecessary. He was a highly influential artist whose role in blues history may be second in importance only to that of Patton.

Johnson was inducted into the Blues Foundation's Hall of Fame in 1987.

• For discographical information, see Robert M. W. Dixon and John Godrich, *Blues and Gospel Records: 1902–1943* (1982). For more detailed biographical information, see David Evans, *Tommy Johnson* (1971), and Sheldon Harris, *Blues Who's Who: A Biographical Dictionary of Blues Singers* (1989). For more on Johnson's influence, see David Evans, *Big Road Blues: Tradition and Creativity in the Folk Blues* (1987). To hear Johnson's recorded music, try *Tommy Johnson: Complete Recorded Works in Chronological Order* (Document DocD5001).

BILL MCCULLOCH
BARRY PEARSON

JOHNSON, Treat Baldwin (29 Mar. 1875–28 July 1947), organic chemist, was born in Bethany, Connecticut, the son of Dwight Lauren Johnson and Harriet Adeline Baldwin, farmers. After attending a local ungraded school, Johnson, in 1890, entered the high school in nearby Ansonia. In 1894 he enrolled in the Sheffield Scientific School of Yale University, begin-

ning a five-decade association with Yale. Following a bachelor's degree in chemistry in 1898 and a doctorate in 1901, Johnson became an instructor of organic chemistry and rose through the professorial ranks to become the Sterling Professor of Chemistry in 1928. He married Emma Estelle Amerman in 1904; they had no children. In 1918 he was director of a Chemical Warfare Service laboratory at Yale.

Johnson was a student of Henry Wheeler, with whom he collaborated in research from his undergraduate years to Wheeler's death in 1914. Wheeler's investigations concerned the synthesis and properties of nitrogen heterocycles, structures containing carbon and nitrogen in a ring, and concentrated particularly on the pyrimidines. Wheeler and Johnson produced a long series of papers on pyrimidines and Johnson continued this research into the 1940s.

The pyrimidine studies began at the time of major discoveries about nucleic acids by the German chemist Albrecht Kossel. By 1900 Kossel revealed that the chemical composition of these cellular materials consisted of purine and pyrimidine bases, a carbohydrate, and phosphate groups. Kossel found that the purine bases in nucleic acids were adenine and guanine, and the pyrimidines were cytosine and thymine. A third pyrimidine base, uracil, was discovered by one of Kossel's associates in 1900. Wheeler and Johnson made noteworthy advances in this field. By 1903 Wheeler developed a new synthetic method for pyrimidines and reported the preparation of thymine and uracil and, with Johnson, the synthesis of cytosine. Although Kossel's group had discovered these compounds, Kossel could only propose possible structures for them. Structural determination depended on their synthesis, and Wheeler and Johnson established the correct structures. They also synthesized and determined the structures of all the then known naturally occurring pyrimidines.

Johnson continued to make useful contributions to pyrimidine chemistry after Wheeler's death. In 1907 Wheeler and Johnson studied orotic acid, a pyrimidine in milk that they believed to be a uracil carboxylic acid. Wheeler prepared uracil-4-carboxylic acid and with Johnson prepared uracil-5-carboxylic acid. When neither substance seemed to be orotic acid, they terminated their study. However, in 1930 Italian chemists reported a new synthesis of uracil-4-carboxylic acid and claimed that it was identical to orotic acid. In 1931 Johnson greatly improved the new synthesis, confirmed the substance's identity with orotic acid, and elaborated many of its reactions and properties. This pyrimidine was later found to be the key intermediate in the synthesis in living cells of all the pyrimidine bases in nucleic acids.

In the 1920s his research was supported by the National Tuberculosis Association. He determined the composition of the nucleic acids of the tubercle bacillus, discovering in 1925 with R. D. Coghill a new pyrimidine, 5-methylcytosine. With the development of chromatography in the 1940s, it proved to be present in the nucleic acid molecules of several plants and bacteria. He also devised new synthetic methods to pre-pare pyrimidines that had not been prepared by known methods. In 1931 he and Guido Hilbert, a for-mer doctoral student of Johnson, prepared a uracil glycoside that resembled natural nucleosides (the base-carbohydrate part of nucleic acids). Their meth-od proved to be a general procedure, and in 1937 Hil-bert achieved the first synthesis of a natural nucle-oside. Over the years Johnson built up an extensive literature on the pyrimidines to the benefit of chemists who found his work useful. Robert R. Williams, for example, in 1935 and 1936 adopted Johnson's meth-ods to synthesize and establish the structure of the vi-tamin thiamine, aided by Johnson's having already prepared the chemical relatives of the pyrimidine-con-taining vitamin.

Johnson was important in another area of research. During the 1930s he studied various drugs, including germicides. He found that alkyl-substituted phenols had pronounced antiseptic properties and then synthe-sized a series of alkyl resorcinols, determining and comparing their antiseptic strength. He found that hexyl resorcinol had the maximum antiseptic value. This research resulted in fifteen patents and the com-mercial production of hexyl resorcinol by the Johnson & Johnson Company to the considerable profit of Johnson. The drug research was done largely with paid assistants in a private laboratory that he founded in 1932. Johnson also profited from his consultantship with the A. C. Gilbert Company of New Haven. From 1915 to his death he designed toy chemistry sets for the company. These were among the first educational toys marketed.

Johnson retired in 1943. He lived his entire life in either New Haven or Bethany. At Yale he lived a quiet life in a New Haven apartment until the early 1920s when he built a summer cottage on his father's farm. He then built a home on the estate and moved perma-nently to Bethany in 1928. He was intimately involved in community affairs. He was the organizer and presi-dent of the Bethany Library Association from 1930 and founded the Bethany Library and its endowment fund. He was chairman of the committee to build a new school. Active in church affairs, he headed the Ecclesiastical Society of the Congregational Church in Bethany and in 1936 donated his mother's house as a parsonage. However, he engendered some dislike in the community because he insisted on being in charge and usually would not serve on a committee unless he could be chairman. To the dislike was added envy in his later years as he became very wealthy through pat-ent royalties. At the time of his death—in Bethany—he was a millionaire. Among his honors were election to the National Academy of Sciences in 1919 and membership on the executive committee of the board of trustees of the Sheffield Scientific School from 1921 to 1941.

Johnson's research on the pyrimidines was funda-mental to the chemistry of nucleic acids and nucleo-tides, the base-carbohydrate-phosphate subunits of nucleic acids. Biochemists many years later used his

work when it became possible to establish the struc-ture of DNA and RNA in terms of the nucleotide com-ponents. His work also proved valuable following the discovery of a diversity of nucleotide-containing coen-zymes.

• Johnson wrote two major reviews. "Pyrimidines: Their Amino and Aminoöxy Derivatives," *Chemical Reviews* 13 (1933): 193–303, written with Dorothy Hahn, was the first detailed, systematic review of the subject. "The Chemistry of Pyrimidines, Purines, and Nucleic Acids," *Organic Chemis-try*, ed. Henry Gilman (2 vols., 1938), was a broader survey and a collaborative work of great value to both students and research workers. Hubert Vickery wrote the biography of Johnson for the National Academy of Sciences, *Biographical Memoirs* 27 (1952): 83–119, with a list of his publications and his patents. Russell Chittenden, *The Development of Physio-logical Chemistry in the United States* (1930), describes John-son's early researches with Wheeler and his studies of the tubercle bacillus. Will H. Shearon, Jr., "Chemistry and the Toymaker," *Chemical and Engineering News* 30 (15 Dec. 1952): 5236–39, considers Johnson's consultantship with A. C. Gilbert. An obituary is in the *New York Times*, 29 July 1947.

ALBERT B. COSTA

JOHNSON, Walter (6 Nov. 1887–10 Dec. 1946), base-ball player and manager, was born Walter Perry John-son in Humboldt, Kansas, the son of Frank Edwin Johnson and Minnie Perry, farmers. In 1901, attracted by the southern California oil boom, the family moved to Olinda, near Los Angeles, where Johnson's father became a teamster for an oil-well equipment company. Johnson played his first baseball at fifteen as a catcher for the Olinda Wells, one of many local semipro teams. He soon was switched to the mound, where his pow-erful arm could be put to better use than throwing out base runners. At Fullerton Union High School in 1905 he absorbed a 21–0 loss in his first outing, then pitched a spectacular 15-inning scoreless game in the course of which he struck out 27.

He left high school after his freshman year, and in the spring of 1906 he had unsuccessful tryouts with professional teams. The Los Angeles Angels (Pacific Coast League) were unimpressed; the Tacoma, Wash-ington, Tigers of the Northwestern League pitched him in an exhibition game to raise money for victims of the San Francisco earthquake, but the club did not sign him. Johnson joined the Weiser, Idaho, Kids of the semipro Idaho State League, where he won at least six games and lost none. In 1907, now nineteen, he was brilliant, winning 14 for the Kids while losing only two, fanning 211, and hurling 65 consecutive scoreless innings.

His acquisition by Washington in midseason is a fa-miliar baseball legend. Someone—an umpire, a scout, a liquor salesman, depending on the version—wrote the Senators describing Johnson as faster than Amos Rusie and with better control than Christy Mathew-son, comparisons with nonpareils. In truth, four ma-jor league teams knew of Johnson, but only lowly Washington acted on the tip. Manager "Pongo Joe" Cantillon sent an injured catcher west on one of the all-time great scouting trips. At Wichita, en route to Weiser, he corraled the splendid outfielder Clyde "Deerfoot" Milan, who became Johnson's road roommate for fourteen years. Johnson was wary about signing and insisted on round-trip train fare in case he failed to make good. He settled for $350 a month.

Johnson was not an immediate sensation. Although everyone was impressed with his speed and the whiplash of his long right arm as it swung, scythelike, to deliver the ball, he was slow afoot and awkward at fielding. Not until 1910 did he become "the Big Train." The phenomenal Johnson of later years would compile winning records regardless of where the Senators finished. His first major league game, however, was a loss to Detroit, and he had a 5–9 won-lost record for his freshman season. After a late start in 1908 owing to an operation for mastoiditis, an affliction prevalent in an era before antibiotics, he won 14 and lost 14. In 1909 he and the team had their worst season ever—13 wins and 25 losses for him, 42–110 for the Senators.

Over the next decade he won 265 games, while losing 143, a percentage of .649. He never had fewer than 20 wins, twice had more than 30. Washington's fortunes improved; it twice finished second, but it also came in seventh four times. Up or down, Johnson serenely continued his outstanding performances. By the end of a 21-year career, he had achieved 417 victories, second only to Cy Young's 511 in major league history. (Johnson also stands high on the list in career losses with 279.) He was dominant in almost every pitching category, leading his league in wins and complete games six times, earned run average and innings pitched five times, shutouts seven times, and strikeouts twelve. His 110 career shutouts established a long-standing record. He ranks among the top pitchers in innings pitched, complete games, ERA, and strikeouts. His 3,508 strikeouts have been exceeded by a half-dozen pitchers, but his were achieved against hitters of an era far less susceptible to fanning. If his winning percentage of .599 is not outstanding, it must be measured against the Washington team's .492 during the same period. In only ten of Johnson's years did the Senators play better than .500 baseball.

Perhaps his greatest season was 1913, when he won a league-leading 36 games while losing only seven, and he also led in winning percentage, ERA (at 1.09 one of the best marks ever achieved), complete games, innings pitched, strikeouts, and shutouts. During that season he had winning streaks of seven, 10, and 14 games, threw five one-hitters, and had one stretch of 55⅔ scoreless innings. The Chalmers company awarded him one of its automobiles as the American League's most valuable player.

In 1912 Johnson's streak of 16 wins—an American League record accomplished in 51 days—was broken by Smokey Joe Wood, whose 1–0 triumph before an overflow crowd at Boston was his fourteenth consecutive win. (Wood matched Johnson's 16 a week later at St. Louis.) There were 27 matches between these arch rivals, Johnson winning 16 of them. One-run games were a Johnson specialty; he won 38 and lost 26, an-

other pair of long-standing records. Overall, 65 of his 279 losses were shutouts—a comment on the Senators' weak hitting.

His career is studded with uniquely Johnsonian deeds: 14 opening-day games pitched at Washington, including the first at which a U.S. president threw out the first ball; three shutouts of the Yankees in four days (1908); losses to Babe Ruth and George Sisler, two famous rookies making their debuts as pitchers (1915); retiring 28 consecutive Yankees in a 12-inning 0–0 tie and fanning three A's on nine pitches in a 1–0 victory (1919). And despite Ty Cobb's .335 career average against him, Johnson beat Detroit 66 times, the record for any pitcher against one team. Two unusual achievements are 40 wins and 30 losses in relief, large numbers for a starter, and a .433 batting average in 1925, long the highest for a pitcher.

The man who performed these prodigies was fairly big for his era: 6'1" and about 200 pounds. Contemporaries remarked that his arms seemed to reach to his knees, although that is not borne out by photographs. Probably the wrist and hand extending beyond the three-quarter sleeve of those older uniforms did create an illusion of unusual length, particularly as the ball flew toward the batter at the end of his sweeping, side-arm motion. No way was devised to clock pitches in Johnson's day, but he is one of several always named when the unanswerable question arises, "Who was fastest?" Old-timers recalled him with awe. Sam Crawford of the Tigers said the motion was deceptively easy: a minimal windup, then *swoosh*—the ball was in the catcher's mitt. The melodramatic Cobb thought the ball "hissed with danger" and said any batter's worst prospect was facing Johnson on a dark day in Washington. Even the nicknames he earned were redolent of speed: "Barney," after the noted auto racer, Barney Oldfield, and, in a highballing railroad era, "the Big Train." While he developed a curve in later years, the fastball was always his bread-and-butter pitch.

Curiously, there was nothing aggressive or overpowering in Johnson's personality. He was mild-mannered, imperturbable. His face was bland, his bearing modest. Perhaps the most frequently stated fact about him was his refusal to throw at batters. Cobb admitted crowding the plate to cut down the strike zone, knowing Johnson would never risk injuring him with a brushback pitch. Less well known is Johnson's lifetime record of 206 hit batsmen (and a one-season mark of 21 wild pitches), although no one would say he threw with malice aforethought. Like all the great ones, he had excellent control. In 802 games he averaged one walk every 4⅓ innings. In the paramount season of 1913 he walked only 38 batters in 346 innings.

He never argued with umpires and never berated teammates for errors that cost him games. Well ahead in a late inning with a struggling batter at the plate, he was even known to ease up. "Walter likes you today," the catcher might say, as Johnson, his blue eyes alight with friendliness, grooved one for a gift hit.

He rarely smoked, drank, or cussed, but he found ice cream irresistible. "Sir Walter" and "the White Knight" were sportswriters' tributes to what they saw as his chivalrous nature. In time his forebearance, his decency, his gentlemanly composure in what was still a roughneck game came to be seen as an embodiment of basic American values almost Lincolnesque in their simplicity. He was a devoted family man, the husband of Hazel Lee Roberts, daughter of a Nevada congressman, and father of six children. Walter, Jr., the eldest, pitched briefly in the minor leagues.

Johnson's even temper was not docility. In 1914 he shocked the baseball establishment by signing with the Chicago Whales of the insurgent Federal League for three years at $17,500, plus a bonus of $6,000. The Senators had paid him $10,000 and turned down his bid for a three-year contract at $18,000. But Clark Griffith, the club's manager and part-owner, persuaded his star to renege on the Chicago deal and rejoin Washington for $12,500, plus a bonus that Griffith allegedly induced Charles Comiskey to pay for being spared Johnson's presence as a crosstown rival of his White Sox.

During spring training in 1920, Johnson's arm went. He had pitched more than 300 innings for nine straight seasons, plus 290 in the tenth, while playing off-season with various semipro and "All-Star" teams in southern California. He endured a miserable season (8–10), yet accomplished a three-hit shutout of the A's that required only 69 pitches, and downed the Red Sox, 1–0, in the only no-hitter of his career.

In 1924, with Johnson contributing 23 victories and earning his second Most Valuable Player award, Washington won its first pennant. After years of toil in the lower depths, he was in a World Series. Against John J. McGraw's scrappy New York Giants, however, Johnson lost the first and fifth games, 4–3 in a 12-inning duel, and 6–2 as the Giants mauled him for 13 hits. In the seventh game he retrieved himself, entering the ninth inning with the score tied, 3–3, and winning in the twelfth when—as Washington fans always believed—fate bounced an errant grounder over the head of the Giants' third baseman, permitting the deciding run to score.

Against Pittsburgh in the 1925 World Series the situation was reversed. Johnson won the first and fourth games, 4–1 and 4–0, but lost the seventh. Not up to form, he was pounded for 15 hits and, as a rainstorm drenched the field, gave up five runs in the final innings to lose, 9–7.

He pitched his last opening-day game—a shutout, his seventh on such occasions—in 1926 and earned his 400th victory as the season progressed. In 1927 a line drive fractured his leg in spring training, and his record dwindled to 5–6. His final appearance was as a pinch hitter in the game made famous by Babe Ruth's sixtieth home run. Johnson managed Newark (International League) to a seventh-place finish in 1928 and then was manager of the Senators from 1929 to 1932 and of Cleveland from mid-1933 to mid-1935. Although his teams usually finished in the first division,

Johnson seemed temperamentally unsuited to managing.

In retirement on his 552-acre Maryland dairy farm he enjoyed his prize cattle, his hunting dogs, and his children. People never lost interest in him; he always was a celebrity, always "the Big Train." A Republican, he was elected as one of three commissioners in a strongly Democratic county; he also ran unsuccessfully for Congress. He threw a silver dollar across Virginia's Rappahanock River, thereby confirming that George Washington's legendary toss was credible. In 1936 he was among the five players first elected to the Baseball Hall of Fame at Cooperstown, New York. He died in Washington, D.C.

• The National Baseball Library in Cooperstown, N.Y., has a Johnson file. Shirley Povich, *The Washington Senators* (1954), and Franklin Lewis, *The Cleveland Indians* (1949), cover his career as player and manager. A good summary account of his life is in Bob Broeg, *Super Stars of Baseball* (1971). A. D. Suehsdorf, "Too Much Johnson," *Baseball History* 2, no. 4 (1987–1988): 32–51, concerns Johnson's life before he joined the Senators. For additional details of his career, see Charles C. Alexander, *Ty Cobb* (1984); Lawrence Ritter's oral-history interviews with Sam Crawford and Davy Jones in *The Glory of Their Times* (1966); and Red Smith, "The Big Train, Westbound," in his *Out of the Red* (1950). Johnson's own article, "Why I Signed with the Federal League," *Baseball Magazine*, Apr. 1915, pp. 53–62, provides insight into a star player's view of salaries at that time. Henry W. Thomas, one of Johnson's grandsons, generously provided information used in the preparation of the article published here. Johnson's statistics are compiled in *The Baseball Encyclopedia*, 9th ed. (1993); John Thorn and Pete Palmer, eds., *Total Baseball*, 3d ed. (1993); and Richard M. Cohen et al., *The World Series* (1979). An obituary by Frederick G. Lieb is in the *Sporting News*, 18 Dec. 1946.

A. D. SUEHSDORF

JOHNSON, Wendell Andrew Leroy (16 Apr. 1906–29 Aug. 1965), speech pathologist and psychologist, was born in Roxbury, Kansas, the son of Andrew Robert Johnson and Mary Helena Tarnstrom, farmers. Johnson began to stutter at an early age, a fact that had a profound impact on his personal and professional development. To compensate for his speech problem, Johnson filled his childhood by reading books from his father's library and by excelling in academics and athletics. He acquired a strong desire to express himself through writing.

At the age of eighteen Johnson enrolled at McPherson College in Kansas. He stayed at McPherson for two years; at the urging of one of his professors he then transferred to the University of Iowa to continue his studies and to seek treatment for his stuttering at the university's speech clinic under the direction of Lee Edward Travis. The treatment of Johnson's stuttering, which was unsuccessful, was based on the then-predominant theory that stuttering was the result of mixed cerebral dominance that was best treated through retraining of the cerebral hemispheres. In Johnson's case, this required him to try to learn to become left-handed. He received a B.A. in English in

1928. He continued studying at Iowa, researching stuttering as a graduate student in psychology under Travis. He received his M.A. in psychology in 1929 and his Ph.D. in psychology in 1931. He married Edna Amanda Bockwoldt in 1929; they had two children.

Graduate work provided Johnson with an opportunity to express in writing his personal experiences with stuttering. His master's thesis, "A Stutterer's Psychological Study of His Own Case," was published in 1930 with the title *Because I Stutter*. In the opening lines, Johnson relates the impact that stuttering had had on his life until that point: "I am a stutterer. I am not like other people. I must think differently, act differently, live differently—because I stutter. Like other stutterers, like other exiles, I have known all my life a great sorrow and a great hope together, and they have made of me the kind of person that I am." His graduate years also allowed him to establish a program of original research on the psychosocial aspects of stuttering, of which his dissertation, *The Influence of Stuttering on the Personality* (1932), was representative. He concluded that there were no significant personality differences between stutterers and fluent speakers.

Johnson remained at the speech clinic as a research associate until 1937, when he became an assistant professor of psychology, speech, and child welfare. In 1939 he was promoted to associate professor, and he attained the rank of full professor in speech pathology and psychology in 1945. Johnson was active in research, writing, and administrative duties during this period and no longer suffered from severe stuttering. He was appointed as director of the speech clinic in 1943, holding that position until a heart attack caused him to relinquish it in 1955. His program of research focused on four main areas, including the relationship between stuttering and personality, the conditions associated with the onset and development of stuttering, the efficacy of treatment, and the conditions associated with variations in the severity and amount of stuttering. Johnson's work was published in both academic journals and the popular press. Increasingly, Johnson expanded his views of stuttering to include issues of general semantics, and his 1946 book *People in Quandaries: The Semantics of Personal Adjustment* earned him widespread recognition in the field of general semantics. Another book on the topic, *Your Most Enchanted Listener* (1956), would appear a decade later.

Johnson's *Stuttering in Children and Adults: Thirty Years of Research at the University of Iowa* (1955) presented a comprehensive review of the research he and his colleagues performed concerning the causes of stuttering and its treatment. Contrary to the views of his mentor Travis, who emphasized neurophysiological mechanisms in stuttering, Johnson came to see the development of stuttering in children as the result of adult (usually parental) reactions to child speech. According to Johnson, most children who stutter had normal speech but developed anxiety in speaking when early attempts at speaking were met with adult disapproval. Johnson wrote that "the problem of stuttering, then, would seem to start, not in the speaker's mouth, but in the listener's ear." Based on an interpersonal communication model, Johnson advised parents to accept responsibility for their negative communication behavior and to work with their child to overcome his or her stuttering. His theory received mixed reviews from his colleagues.

Johnson went on to write, edit, and coauthor numerous volumes devoted to the understanding and treatment of speech problems, including *Speech Handicapped School Children* (1946; rev. eds. 1956, 1957), *Diagnostic Manual in Speech Correction: A Professional Training Workbook* (1952), *The Onset of Stuttering: Research Findings and Implications* (1959), *Stuttering and What You Can Do about It* (1961), and *Diagnostic Methods in Speech Pathology* (1963). He also served on the editorial boards of several professional publications.

Johnson was instrumental in the development of speech pathology and audiology at the University of Iowa. The clinic grew and expanded under his leadership, and when the clinic moved into a new building in 1967 it was named the Wendell Johnson Speech and Hearing Clinic. Throughout the 1950s and 1960s Johnson advanced the profession of speech pathology and audiology, raising awareness of the needs of individuals with speech and hearing problems through service to national professional organizations and government agencies. He was appointed Louis W. Hill Research Professor in 1963. Johnson died in Iowa City from heart disease.

Wendell Johnson traveled a fascinating road from being a boy in rural Kansas with a severe stutter to being an eloquent speaker on issues of the uses and dysfunctions of language. He combined clinical psychology, speech pathology, and general semantics in a unique way that emphasized the power and importance of communication in shaping and maintaining human behavior. His work on stuttering was both personal and professional, as was his means of communicating his findings. His collected works on stuttering rank among the most important and influential on the topic in the twentieth century.

• Johnson's papers are at the University of Iowa library. Dorothy Moeller, *Living With Change* (1972), is a posthumous publication of talks given by Johnson. See also Joseph L. Stewart, "Wendell Johnson: A Memoir," *Etc.: A Review of General Semantics* 49 (Winter 1992–1993): 424–32, and Dean Williams, "Remembering Wendell Johnson," *Etc.: A Review of General Semantics* 49 (Winter 1992–1993): 433–35. An obituary is in the *New York Times*, 31 Aug. 1965.

DAVID B. BAKER

JOHNSON, Sir William (c. 1715–11 July 1774), merchant, land speculator, and royal official among the Iroquois Indians, was born in County Meath, Ireland, the son of Christopher Johnson and Anne Warren, members of the gentry. William's mother provided the family connections that started her son on the way to fortune. Her brother, Vice Admiral Sir Peter Warren, acquired an estate on the Mohawk River, and in about 1738 Johnson came to Albany, New York, to supervise the property. The estate lay in the midst of the Mohawk nation of Iroquois Six Nations, and Johnson quickly learned of the wealth to be gained from trading with the Indians for furs. He must have brought personal capital with him, because almost immediately he bought an estate on the north bank of the river and established a trading post.

Johnson's importance rested largely on his business and influence with the Mohawks. He gained advantage by learning the Mohawk language and customs, but there is no truth in wild stories that he slept with innumerable Mohawk women. Equally absurd are the romanticisms about his adopting Mohawk culture. He did nothing of the sort. He sat in on tribal councils and joined war dances, but always as a superior being, a lord, and the Mohawks tolerated that pretension because he was useful to them in several ways: as an intermediary to New York's governor and the British Crown, and through that connection, as a sanction for Mohawk preeminence among the Iroquois Six Nations, much resented by their Iroquois rivals.

In 1739 Johnson began living with Catherine Weisenberg, a German who fled from indentured servitude. Though he never formalized the marriage, Johnson called her his wife, which indeed she was by the common law. The couple had three children. Catherine died in 1759, at which time Johnson took as his "housekeeper" a young woman named Mary (Molly) Brant, who belonged to one of the most important Mohawk families. The connection served Johnson well in relations with the Mohawks. Johnson's will distinguished plainly between his first three children as his legitimate heirs, and the eight children he had with Mary.

Johnson built several mansions, and he maintained grand style and hospitality for visitors. He imported hundreds of European tenants for his estate. As a merchant, Johnson used his connections in New York politics, especially with Governor George Clinton (1686–1761), to expand his business to the province's outpost at Oswego, and he acted as New York's agent in Indian affairs. Combining his office with opportunities in trade, Johnson quickly made a large fortune. His whole career was directed at amassing wealth and creating a feudal estate embracing both European tenants and a retinue of Iroquois warriors. Thus, his ambitions ran opposite to the imperatives of tribal cultures that stressed leaders' responsibilities to their people and the sharing of wealth. Johnson acknowledged responsibility only to the British Crown and demanded obedience from Iroquois people. The obedience was more cosmetic than real, but when reported in England it made good public relations. He gave lavish presents to the Indians, but always at the government's expense, while his own riches multiplied. Far from "going native" as an Indian, Johnson set himself in the image of a clan chieftain of seventeenth-century Ireland.

After war resumed between France and Britain in 1744, Johnson prevailed upon the Mohawks to attack the French, although the Iroquois refused to break from their policy of neutrality. The Mohawks were ambushed and suffered heavy casualties. Their primacy among the Iroquois suffered and Johnson's prestige plummeted for the time being.

Despite these setbacks, Johnson became colonel of the New York frontier militia and of the Albany militia in 1748. He resigned his responsibility for Indian affairs in 1751 and concentrated on making money, but during the Albany Congress of 1754, when deputies of the Iroquois met colonial representatives, Johnson cultivated the patronage of Thomas Pownall, the direct agent of the British Crown's Lords of Trade and Plantations. Consequently when Major General Edward Braddock arrived in Virginia in 1755 to oust the French from Britain's claimed lands, he brought a commission awarding Johnson "sole Management & direction of the Affairs of the Six Nations of Indians & their Allies," and warning all persons to "cease & forbear acting or intermeddling therein."

Johnson was ordered to capture the French fort of St. Frédéric at Crown Point (Lake Champlain) and commissioned major general of provincial troops by both Massachusetts and New York. The competition for Indian recruits between Johnson and Massachusetts Governor William Shirley, who planned a campaign against Fort Niagara, confused the Iroquois and contributed to their failure to send warriors in support of Braddock's advance upon Fort Duquesne (Pittsburgh). They might have prevented Braddock's defeat when French-allied Indians attacked his army in July 1755. Johnson himself was luckier. His mixed provincial-Indian force campaigning against Fort St. Frédéric were counterattacked on 8 September 1755 at Lake George by French and Indians. Johnson was wounded, but the French were repulsed, and their commander, Baron Dieskau, was both wounded and captured. The battle was a draw, but that was enough to certify Johnson a hero in a year when the British public was starved for good news. Parliament voted him £5000, and he also received a baronetcy from the Crown by purchase.

Boosted by his skill at self-advertisement, Johnson's stature grew, and in 1756 he was commissioned superintendent of Indian affairs for the Northern Department, independent of all provincial authority. However, despite lavish presents to the Iroquois from funds previously provided by Braddock, he could not bring those Indians to commit themselves to either side during the Seven Years' War or prevent them from playing along with both sides to their own advantage. In 1758 Major General James Abercromby instructed Johnson to furnish Iroquois for an assault on French Fort Carillon (Ticonderoga). With much effort he recruited a small force, but it observed rather than participated in Abercromby's defeat. In July 1759 Johnson served as second-in-command during the British siege of Fort Niagara. He took over when the commander was killed and received the surrender of the garrison after a French relief force had been repulsed by forces under Johnson's rival, the senior regular army officer Colonel Eyre Massey. By omitting Massey from his dispatches, Johnson exaggerated his own share in the successful outcome.

During the war Johnson tried to stop the Delaware attacks upon Pennsylvania by urging the Iroquois to pacify them. The Iroquois settled instead for an accommodation by which the eastern Delawares managed their own affairs under Teedyuscung. Western Delawares of the "Ohio country" governed themselves independently. Teedyuscung gained patronage from Pennsylvania's Quaker pacifists, who offered to redress Delaware grievances created by the land swindles of the province's lord proprietary, Thomas Penn. Fearing Quaker intrusion on his monopoly of Indian affairs and responding to Penn's offer of a bribe, Johnson severely traduced both the Quakers and Teedyuscung to London. He tried to oust Teedyuscung from chieftainship by "recognizing" another leader instead, but was unsuccessful. Brigadier General John Forbes (1710–1759), whose assignment was to capture Fort Duquesne, cooperated with Quaker leader Israel Pemberton, Jr., to win over the Delawares from the French. Forbes therefore overruled obstructions created by Johnson and others, and in 1758 peace was negotiated. The Indians withdrew from the French, who abandoned Fort Duquesne.

The condition for peace was the establishment of a boundary between Indians and colonials, but the line was forgotten by the British authorities as soon as the French had been defeated. Johnson's memory lapsed with others, and he tried to defuse Indian resentment by encouraging intertribal jealousies. As he wrote to General Thomas Gage, "fomenting a Coolness between them [the tribes] and Jealousy of each others power will be the surest means of preventing a Rupture [with us], dividing them in their Councils and rendering an union impracticable which cannot be too much guarded against." The violation of the promise of an Indian boundary, with other postwar grievances, contributed to Seneca and Delaware involvement in the Indian uprising of 1763 and 1764, which Johnson helped actively to suppress.

Sophisticated politicians in London realized that the way to an enduring peace with the Indians was to give them their promised boundary, and this was done, albeit equivocally, by the Royal Proclamation Line of 1763. As superintendent of Indian affairs for the Northern Department, Johnson continued to be involved in treaty negotiations adjusting the Indian boundary, notably the Treaty of Fort Stanwix in 1768. In the course of his dealings with the Indians he personally acquired millions of acres. Always the Crown's man, Johnson was spared the turmoils of the approaching American Revolution. He died at his estate near Johnstown, New York, in the midst of a treaty with the Iroquois.

• Johnson's multitudinous papers are scattered through several publications that also provide background material: James Sullivan et al., eds., *The Papers of Sir William Johnson* (14 vols., 1921–1965); Edmund B. O'Callaghan and Berthold Fernow, eds., *Documents Relative to the Colonial History of the State of New York* (15 vols., 1856–1887); O'Callaghan, ed., *Documentary History of the State of New York* (4 vols., 1849–1851). All have indexes. They do not duplicate each other's documents, but the index vol. 14 of *The Papers* points to locations in the other sets. Richard E. Day, comp., *Calendar of Sir William Johnson Manuscripts in the New York State Library* (1909), itemizes many documents that were destroyed by the Albany fire of 1911. The main biographies are William L. Stone, *The Life and Times of Sir William Johnson, Bart.* (2 vols., 1865); Arthur Pound and R. E. Day, *Johnson of the Mohawks* (1930); James Thomas Flexner, *Mohawk Baronet: Sir William Johnson of New York* (1959); and Milton W. Hamilton, *Sir William Johnson: Colonial American, 1715–1763* (1976). None is satisfactory, suffering from romanticism and inadequate knowledge of Indian peoples. Stone especially is factually unreliable. Flexner's ten-foot-tall Johnson is a creation of imagination unrestrained by research. Hamilton is more sober and better grounded in fact but is confined to Johnson's early career and also overshadowed by the romance of the hero living among the wild men. For corrections of concepts and data, see Francis Jennings, *The Ambiguous Iroquois Empire* (1984), and Jennings, *Empire of Fortune* (1988).

FRANCIS JENNINGS

JOHNSON, William (17 Dec. 1769–25 June 1848), law reporter, was born in Middletown, Connecticut, the son of Asahel Johnson and Eunice Wetmore, whose forebears numbered among Connecticut's earliest settlers. Born into comfortable circumstances, William Johnson attended Yale College, where he associated closely with later famous Connecticutans Noah Webster, Oliver Wolcott, Uriah Tracy, and Elihu Hubbard Smith. In 1788 Johnson graduated from Yale and subsequently embarked on the study of law. During the early 1790s he moved to New York City.

Johnson soon emerged as a prominent figure in New York's intellectual community. After moving in with Smith, a fellow bachelor, Johnson established his law practice and in 1796 helped revise the constitution of the New York Manumission Society, a charitable organization devoted to maintaining a school for the children of slaves. In 1793 Johnson and Smith's home became the headquarters of the New York Friendly Club, one of the most famous of the late eighteenth-century American literary societies. This small group of young men, generally Federalist in political orientation but diverse in their moral and religious outlooks, met weekly during several months of the year to discuss politics, history, and the latest works of literature. The group slowly dissolved during the end of the 1790s, particularly after Smith's untimely death in 1798. Johnson nevertheless continued his efforts on behalf of learning over the next decade. In 1805 Johnson assisted in founding the New-York Historical Society and later helped create the New York public school system and served as a trustee of Columbia College. In 1809 Johnson married Maria Templeton; the couple had four children.

During his years in the Friendly Society, Johnson met James Kent, a fellow lawyer and member of the society. Appointed judge of the New York Supreme

Court in 1798, Kent thought many English legal precedents inapplicable in the United States and hoped to establish a body of distinctly American law at a time when none existed. The first step in this process, he believed, was to record and disseminate his court's opinions. In 1806 Kent selected Johnson as the court's reporter, and the two thus began a long-standing personal and professional relationship. When Kent became chancellor in 1814, he made Johnson reporter of equity decisions as well.

In addition to publishing all of Kent's judicial work from 1806 to 1823, Johnson, when possible, gathered and reported earlier opinions of the New York courts. Once described as "a master of the art of written expression," Johnson exhibited superb skills as a recorder, compiler, and editor of his state's decisions and brought fame to both Kent and himself. By 1821 a delegate to the New York constitutional convention could observe without exaggeration that Johnson's reports were quoted "from Maine to New Orleans." Working together, Kent and Johnson had made important strides toward creating an American body of judicial precedents, and when Johnson announced his retirement in 1823, just before Kent's, the aging chancellor humbly wrote to his friend, "If my name is to live in judicial annals, it will be in association with yours." In 1826 Kent even dedicated his famous *Commentaries on American Law* to Johnson.

Kent's commendations aside, the chancellor far overshadowed Johnson, who never earned the degree of recognition that he probably deserved. Still, Johnson's devotion to legal learning and contributions to his state and nation spanned a lifetime. He earned doctor of laws degrees from Hamilton College in Clinton, New York, in 1819 and from the College of New Jersey (later Princeton University) in 1820. In addition to his famous reports, Johnson published *The Maritime Law of Europe* (1806), a translation of the French treatise by M. D. A. Azuni, and later compiled a *Digest of Cases in the Supreme Court of New York* in two volumes in 1825. Ten years later, he republished the *Digest* in three volumes. Johnson died in New York City.

Johnson played a key role in the formative era of American law. His reports not only disseminated the judicial writings of one of America's greatest legal thinkers, but they also established a standard for other reporters throughout the nation. At a time when written legal authorities were scarce or nonexistent in much of the country, Johnson's reports were a reliable source of welcome information and an important step in the establishment of a distinctly American jurisprudence.

• Johnson's reports include *Reports of Cases Argued and Determined in the Supreme Court of Judicature and in the Court for Trial of Impeachments and Corrections of Errors, 1806–1823*; *Cases Argued and Determined in the Court for the Trial of Impeachments and the Correction of Errors, 1799–1803*; and *Cases of the State Court of Chancery, 1814–1823*. Little biographical information about Johnson exists, except for scattered mentions in various diaries and letters of contemporary associates. Johnson's name appears throughout the writings of

Friendly Club members Elihu Hubbard Smith and William Dunlap, but there is little substantive biographical data in either. See James E. Cronin, ed., *The Diary of Elihu Hubbard Smith* (1973), pp. 3, 13–14, 44, 167–168, and *Diary of William Dunlap (1766–1839)* (1930), p. 336. See also Cronin, "Elihu Hubbard Smith and the New York Friendly Club, 1795–1798," *Publications of the Modern Language Association* 64 (1949): 471–79, and Thomas Bender, *New York Intellect: A History of Intellectual Life in New York City* (1987), pp. 27–34. A general biographical sketch of Johnson can be found in F. B. Dexter, *Biographical Sketches of the Graduates of Yale College, 1778–1792*, vol. 4 (1907). For comments on Johnson's skills as a reporter, see Henry W. Taft, *A Century and Half at the New York Bar* (1938), p. 109; Nathaniel H. Carter and William L. Stone, *Reports of the Proceedings and Debates of the Convention of 1821*, p. 616; and William Kent, ed., *Memoirs and Letters of James Kent* (1898), pp. 124–29.

TIMOTHY S. HUEBNER

JOHNSON, William (27 Dec. 1771–4 Aug. 1834), justice of the U.S. Supreme Court, was born in Charleston, South Carolina, the son of William Johnson, a blacksmith and revolutionary war leader, and Sarah Nightingale. Johnson graduated with honors from Princeton University in 1790 and returned to Charleston to read law with Federalist leader Charles Cotesworth Pinckney. He became a member of the South Carolina Bar in 1793 and in 1794 married Sarah Bennett, the sister of a political associate and later governor of South Carolina. Although only two of their eight children survived childhood, they adopted two refugee children who had fled the island of St. Domingue during the slave revolt.

Johnson's property holdings, which included several slaves, qualified him to run for the state house of representatives. He chose to stand for election as a Republican, allying himself with Charles Pinckney, the young cousin of the Federalist leader. After his election in 1794, he served three consecutive two-year terms; during the last term he was Speaker of the South Carolina House. In 1798 the legislature elected him to the Court of Common Pleas (South Carolina's highest court), where he continued to serve until 1804 when President Thomas Jefferson chose him as his first appointment to the Supreme Court. Loyalty to the Republican party was one of Jefferson's main considerations; the appointment was part of an ongoing political struggle between the Federalists and the Republicans for control of the judiciary. One of President John Adams's (1735–1826) last acts had been to appoint staunch Federalist John Marshall as chief justice of the Supreme Court. President Jefferson viewed Marshall's insistence on unanimous decisions as an alarming restriction of freedom of judicial expression; before Marshall became chief justice nearly one-fifth of the decisions contained seriatim opinions. Between Marshall's advent and Johnson's appointment, every decision was unanimous. One of Johnson's most important contributions to the court was that, although he often agreed with Marshall, he resisted the chief justice's attempt to impose unanimity, thereby establishing the expression of dissents as a regular practice of the Court.

His first controversial case was a circuit decision, *Gilchrist v. Collector of Charleston* (1808). Jefferson had chosen Johnson for his independence and for his strong convictions, although Johnson's tenacity was not always to Jefferson's liking. *Gilchrist* defended individual rights from executive encroachment. In this case Jefferson's Embargo Act caused a ship owned by Adam Gilchrist to be detained in Charleston. Gilchrist appealed to Johnson, who allegedly boarded the ship himself and issued sailing orders. In doing so, he reasoned that Congress had not authorized detention of vessels in such cases and that detention could not be effected by presidential order. Jefferson's attorney general, Caesar A. Rodney, published an opinion rebutting Johnson's argument, attacking Johnson's lack of jurisdiction to order the vessel to sail, a power not granted by the Constitution. Johnson wrote a lengthy reply, resting his argument on the judiciary's role as a protector of individual rights. Although Johnson conceded in an 1813 Supreme Court decision, *M'Intire v. Wood*, that he had erred in taking jurisdiction in *Gilchrist*, the decision came to strengthen the concept of executive responsibility to the law and helped to establish the court as a protector of individual rights. As a result of *Gilchrist*, the Jefferson administration secured new legislation clearly establishing the power of the president to order detentions and defined the rights of citizens to appeal to district courts for relief. Although Jefferson was initially dismayed at the *Gilchrist* decision, a rebuff from his own appointee, he and Johnson remained friends.

Anderson v. Dunn (1821) also dealt with important constitutional issues. *Anderson*, a decision of the Supreme Court, involved the implied powers of Congress, specifically whether Congress had the right to arrest nonmembers for contempt. In this case Colonel John Anderson had offered a congressman a "gift" of $500 to use his influence to secure favorable action on certain claims. After being reprimanded by the House of Representatives, Anderson sued the House's sergeant-at-arms, Thomas Dunn, for assault and battery and false imprisonment. The legitimization of the power to exercise legislative discretion to prevent nonmembers from interfering with the workings of Congress was essential to the effective functioning of the national legislature. Johnson, writing for a unanimous Court, upheld the contempt power in Congress, holding that the interests of people required the ultimate control of government and that legislatures needed access to a variety of measures to exercise that control.

Perhaps his most famous decision, *Elkison v. Delieselline* (1823), was made on circuit. In the decision Johnson held that a South Carolina act requiring free black sailors to be jailed while docked in South Carolina ports violated federal power over commerce, which he considered "paramount and exclusive." Johnson argued in *Elkison* that if states could each pass such restrictive laws on commerce, the Union would be but "a rope of sand." Although South Carolina ignored John-

son's decision and continued to incarcerate free black seamen, Johnson defended his views in a set of letters published in the Charleston newspapers under the name of "Philonimus." Johnson's nationalism made him unpopular in the South.

Johnson fancied himself a historian, and in 1822 he published, at his own expense, *Sketches of the Life and Correspondence of Nathanael Greene*, a two-volume tome of over one thousand pages. Although it contained excellent analyses of military campaigns, the book attracted criticism for its style and unflattering portrayals of some revolutionary war leaders. For example, Johnson asserted that Count Casimir Pulaski had fallen asleep during the battle of Germantown, causing George Washington's defeat, and that former Supreme Court justice James Wilson (1742–1798) had participated in the Conway Cabal, a plot to remove Washington from command of the American army. In 1826 he also published a *Eulogy of Thomas Jefferson*.

Johnson's staunch faith in the rightness of his convictions was not always appreciated by his contemporaries. A South Carolina attorney, Charles J. Ingersoll, called him "bold, independent, eccentric, and sometimes harsh." John Quincy Adams (1767–1848) commented that he was "a man of considerable talents and law knowledge, but a restless, turbulent, hotheaded, politician caballing Judge." When Johnson criticized Thomas Cooper, the president of South Carolina College, for his secessionist views, Cooper called him "a conceited man without talents."

Johnson was outspoken in his criticism of proposals in his home state to nullify the Tariff of 1828, first anonymously under the pseudonym "Hamilton," and then in a signed eight-point rebuttal to proposals to nullify the Tariff of 1828. Warning of civil war, he wrote, "every thing that makes this country worth a wise man's love, is bound up in the Union of these States." As for nullification, he termed it "a silly and wicked delusion." Johnson's views made him unpopular in his home state. In 1834 he moved to Philadelphia in order to avoid discussion of nullification, as he believed that his position required his silence on the issue. The same year he contracted "bilious remittent fever" (dengue fever) and died in Brooklyn, after thirty years of service to the Court.

Although Johnson's strong views sometimes enraged his critics, he was a man of integrity and courage. His insistence on the right of free expression meant that dissenting opinions became an established Court practice. Although his impetuosity sometimes enmeshed him in controversies that diminished his effectiveness as a judge, his strong support of the Constitution and the national government never wavered, and his views on congressional power, the limits of executive power, and state-federal relations foreshadowed later constitutional developments.

• No collection of Johnson's papers exists, but his letters may be found in more than a dozen libraries and collections. In addition, Johnson was the author of several pamphlets: *An*

Oration Delivered in St. Philip's Church (1813), *Nugae Georgicae* (1815), *To the Public of Charleston* (1822), *Remarks Critical and Historical* (1825), and *Review of a Late Pamphlet under the Signature of "Brutus"* (1828). The only biography of Johnson is Donald G. Morgan, *Justice William Johnson, the First Dissenter: The Career and Constitutional Philosophy of a Jeffersonian Judge* (1954). Several articles concerning Johnson and his jurisprudence include Donald G. Morgan, "Mr. Justice William Johnson and the Constitution," *Harvard Law Review* 57 (Jan. 1944): 328–61; Oliver Schroeder, Jr., "Life and Judicial Work of Justice William Johnson, Jr.," *University of Pennsylvania Law Review* 95 (Dec. 1946): 164–201, 344–86; Donald Morgan, "Justice William Johnson and the Treaty-Making Power," *George Washington Law Review* 22 (Oct. 1953): 187–215; Donald Morgan, "The Origin of Supreme Court Dissent," *William and Mary Quarterly* 10 (July 1953): 353–77; and Irwin F. Greenberg, "Justice William Johnson: South Carolina Unionist, 1823–1830," *Pennsylvania History* 36 (July 1969): 307–34.

JUDITH K. SCHAFER

JOHNSON, William (1809–17 June 1851), diarist and entrepreneur, was born in Natchez, Mississippi, the son of William Johnson, a slaveholder, and Amy Johnson, a slave. When William was five years old his mother was emancipated and established her household in Natchez. In 1820 the eleven-year-old William was freed by the Mississippi legislature at the request of his owner. Once emancipated, he apprenticed with his brother-in-law, James Miller, in his barber business in Natchez. Johnson became proprietor of the business—reportedly the most popular barber shop in Natchez—when Miller moved to New Orleans in 1830. Johnson and his African-American staff ran the shop, which served a predominantly white clientele. Johnson's barbers not only offered haircuts and shaves, they also fitted wigs, sold fancy soaps and oils, and, beginning in 1834, operated a bathhouse at the Main Street location.

Between 1830 and 1835 Johnson frequently traveled to New Orleans and to St. Francisville, Louisiana, as well as to other towns in Mississippi, to vacation and to court potential marriage partners. Johnson traveled less after 1835, the year he married twenty-year-old Ann Battles of Natchez, a free black woman. They had ten children together.

Also in 1835 Johnson began to keep a diary, writing journal entries almost daily until his death. The initial purpose of the diary was to record business transactions, purchases he made, and debts paid to him, but in addition, Johnson recorded town gossip, described events, and reported local political election results. Johnson's diary thus tells the unusual story of a free African American who lived in the antebellum South and successfully pushed the limits of his status. The barbering business was Johnson's primary source of revenue, but he was a true entrepreneur, acquiring additional income through money lending, property rentals, and agricultural endeavors. His other enterprises included a small toy shop, wallpaper sales, and buggy-and-cart rentals for the transportation of goods to the Natchez market. Johnson purchased and built

several buildings, homes as well as commercial structures, and at the time of his death he owned more than 350 acres of land, purchasing land toward the development of a small farm or plantation. He hired a white overseer and owned, at the most, fifteen African-American slaves, some of whom he periodically hired out for additional income. A few of his slaves became apprentices in his barbering business.

It is known that Johnson competed against both blacks and whites in sports such as hunting, fishing, and horse racing and that he participated in lotteries and raffles and played cards, shuffleboard, and checkers because he recorded his wins and losses in his diary. Johnson spent time reading each week, either the books he owned or the several newspapers and magazines to which he subscribed. Johnson contributed to philanthropic organizations and was a theater goer. He also attended church but did not continuously belong to one religious denomination.

Although the law prohibited him from voting, Johnson was actively interested in politics and expressed sympathy for the Democratic party. He was in favor of universal suffrage and education and opposed imprisonment for debt. In general, Johnson had unusual relationships with whites, renting property to them, loaning them money, suing them in court, and even employing them as workers on his farm. Indeed, the level of Johnson's participation in commerce, politics, and social events was rare for free blacks in the antebellum South. For the most part, he was able to conduct business and financial matters on an equal basis with whites, but despite his status as one of the most respected members of Natchez society, Johnson was subject to segregation as it applied to all African Americans in his community. Thus he sat in the balcony at the theater and stood outside of white churches in order to hear ministers speak. Exceptions were sometimes made for Johnson, but as the years passed, he became less satisfied with—and somewhat embittered by—the limitations placed on him because of his race.

At the age of forty-two Johnson was murdered in Natchez over a land dispute. His killer, Baylor Winn, was arrested but after two years of public trials was released from custody. The prosecution ultimately abandoned its case, in part because Winn was presumed to be white and the three witnesses were African American and, according to Mississippi law, were forbidden to testify against Winn. Johnson's diary, which was preserved by his children and published a century after his death, totals 2,000 pages and comprises fourteen volumes. It is an important and unique account of antebellum southern life, race relations, economic and social conditions, and political affairs.

• In 1938 the Johnson family donated Johnson's diary as well as 1,310 other items in his collection to the Department of Archives at Louisiana State University in Baton Rouge. The published version of the diary, edited by William Ransom Hogan and Edwin Adams Davis, is *William Johnson's Natchez: The Ante-Bellum Diary of a Free Negro* (1951). The *Barber of Natchez* (1954), by Davis and Hogan, is a biography of Johnson based on his diary. Johnson is cited in Ira Berlin,

Slaves without Masters: The Free Negro in the Antebellum South (1975), mainly in chap. 8, "The Sources of Free Negro Identity."

DEVORAH LISSEK

JOHNSON, William Samuel (7 Oct. 1727–14 Nov. 1819), lawyer and politician, was born in Stratford, Connecticut, the son of the Reverend Samuel Johnson, an Anglican clergyman, and Charity Floyd Nicholl, the widow of a wealthy Long Island lawyer. With a younger brother and three stepsiblings from his mother's first marriage, Johnson grew up in a convivial, intellectually stimulating home made comfortable by his mother's inherited wealth. His father's success in making Anglicanism a respectable alternative to Congregationalism fostered amicable relations between Anglican and Puritan acquaintances. A philosopher as well as a churchman, Samuel Johnson taught—in opposition to Puritan childrearing practice—"indulgence" to children's "intellectual curiosity, . . . candor, patience, and care" in moral and intellectual training. The recipient of this kind of nurture, William Samuel was also shaped by Connecticut's culture of "steady habits" and by Anglican decorum.

He entered Yale in 1740, just as Thomas Clap became rector and introduced Enlightenment rationalism while still stressing Congregational piety. "The Rector and tutors," Samuel Johnson noted, "indulge him as much as they are able [tolerating his Anglicanism and Arminian theology] without hazarding the resentment of the government which supports them." The Great Awakening disrupted Yale during William Samuel's first two years of study before Clap restored a regime of piety and dispassionate inquiry.

Though Johnson studied theology with his father after graduation in 1744, the contentiousness of Anglican-Congregationalist relations offended Johnson. His Yale classmate, William Smith, Jr. (1728–1793), of New York, urged him to study law. After yearning briefly for a military career and then wrestling with his family heritage, Johnson decided that a legal career offered opportunities for service and leadership. He read law in 1748 and opened his practice the following year as the first lawyer in the colony to support himself entirely at the bar.

His marriage the same year to Ann Beach complicated his new career. His "fiery-tempered" wife objected to the long absences from home that legal work and public service entailed, and the aggressive Anglicanism of the Beach family—stronger and more polemical than his father's—complicated relations with Congregationalist clients and judges.

The Stamp Act crisis brought the young lawyer and newly elected assemblyman political prominence. A delegate to the Stamp Act Congress in 1765, Johnson composed an eleven-page statement on colonial rights that conceded "due subordination of the colonies to the Crown and Parliament" but with the reservation that "this subordination and dependency is sufficiently secured . . . by the general superintending power and authority of the whole Empire [and] is . . . admitted

here so far as . . . is consistent with . . . our essential rights as freemen and British subjects." When the delegates rejected this conciliatory formula, Johnson acquiesced in a more forthright statement on colonial rights on the grounds that "our people will never submit to these fatal acts [Sugar and Stamp Acts]," and he predicted "ruin, destruction, and desolation, . . . should the ministry . . . be so infatuated as to insist upon them."

From 1767 to 1771 Johnson served in London assisting Connecticut's agent, Richard Jackson, in presenting a case to the Privy Council—a land dispute between the colony and the Mason family. It was a frustrating but formative experience for Johnson. Because the Townshend Acts had already enflamed colonial opinion, making a controversial ruling hazardous, the Privy Council dragged its feet. Connecticut's allowance for Johnson's expenses was inadequate, so he tried to redeem the situation by lobbying, unsuccessfully, for the imminent vacancy as chief justice of New York. He became disgusted with the Grafton ministry (1678–1770) for its opportunism and lack of purpose, and he saw the restrictive colonial policy of the 1760s as the poisonous product of amoral ministerial politics. He even condemned—privately and painfully in a letter to his father—Samuel's cherished goal of an American episcopate as a disruptive British intrusion into colonial affairs. And he watched from the vantage point of London another land dispute in Connecticut, the efforts of the Susquehanna Company of speculators to gain control of the Wyoming Valley in Pennsylvania. The company's claim that the 1661 Connecticut Charter granted sea-to-sea boundaries, Johnson warned, might well provoke the Crown to suspend the colony's chartered autonomy. He returned home before either dispute was settled.

Like his friend, the New York lawyer William Smith, Jr., Johnson agonized in 1774–1775 over both the unwillingness of the British to display "a little wisdom and a little shrewdness" in dealing with colonial restiveness and the colonists' "dangerous and unnecessary" demand for categorical acknowledgment of their rights. After independence, Johnson withdrew from politics, pleading that "I could not join in war against England and much less . . . against my own country."

He was jailed briefly in 1779 when his attempt to mediate between a British raiding party and his frightened Stratford neighbors was deemed treasonous. When he appeared before the Governor's Council and the Connecticut Committee of Safety on 28 July 1779, he saw only four familiar faces and nine newcomers to political power. Two weeks later he complied with the committee's demand that he swear allegiance to the new state government.

His political exile ended, Johnson was named one of three Connecticut agents to argue the state's case in a hearing of the Susquehanna land dispute with Pennsylvania before a special tribunal, agreed to by both sides, in New Jersey. After lengthy hearings, the tribunal ruled in favor of Pennsylvania, but Johnson's reputation did not suffer. Supporters of a moderate policy toward former Loyalists narrowly returned to power in Connecticut in 1783. In 1784 he was elected to the Continental Congress, and in 1787 he was named a delegate to the Constitutional Convention.

Johnson twice intervened decisively in the deliberations of the convention. On 29 June he provided the rationale for the "great compromise" over representation by suggesting that creating a new government for the states "in their political capacity as well as for the individuals composing them" would combine into a single structure ideas of national identity and indestructable statehood that had seemed mutually inimical. Then on 29 August he pushed through a taxation compromise in which importation of slaves could not be banned until 1808, a duty would be placed on imported slaves until that date, a simple majority could enact import duties, and no tax on exports would be permitted.

Elected to the first Senate in 1788, Johnson strongly supported Alexander Hamilton's (1755–1804) calls for assumption of state debts and his promotion of a pro-British foreign policy. He resigned from the Senate in 1791 to devote full time to his duties as president of Columbia University. The expansion and revitalization of the institution during the 1790s was the work of its vigorous and possessive board of trustees. Johnson was, however, popular with students at a time when the presidents of Harvard, Yale, and the College of New Jersey in Princeton faced student rebellions. Ill and saddened by his wife's death in 1796, Johnson resigned the post in 1800. On 11 December 1800, his health and spirits revived, Johnson married Mary Beach, his first wife's sister-in-law. In 1812 the superior court in Fairfield honored Johnson for his contributions to legal professionalism in Connecticut. He died in Stratford.

• Johnson's many papers are in the Connecticut Historical Society, and his Stamp Act Congress papers are in the Library of Congress. Elizabeth P. McCaughey, *From Loyalist to Founding Father: The Political Odyssey of William Samuel Johnson* (1980), is a superb biography that replaces George C. Groce, *William Samuel Johnson, a Maker of the Constitution* (1937). For Johnson's role in the Stamp Act crisis, see Edmund S. Morgan and Helen M. Morgan, *The Stamp Act Crisis: Prologue to Revolution* (1953); on his service in London as special colonial agent, see Michael Kammen, *A Rope of Sand* (1968); and as a framer of the Constitution, see Clinton Rossiter, *1787: The Grand Convention* (1966).

ROBERT M. CALHOON

JOHNSON, William Woolsey (23 June 1841–14 May 1927), mathematician, was born near Owego, New York, the son of Charles Frederick Johnson, a lawyer and landowner, and Sarah Dwight Woolsey. His family had been prominent in American higher education for a century and a half. Their forebears included the Puritan minister/educator, Jonathan Edwards (1703–1758); Samuel Johnson (1696–1772), the first President of King's College (now Columbia University); and Samuel's son, William Samuel Johnson (1727–1819), who was the first president of the reorganized

Columbia College (1787) and one of the framers of the U.S. Constitution. Johnson received his A.B. from Yale in 1862, and from 1862 to 1864 he worked at the U.S. Nautical Almanac Office in Cambridge, Massachusetts. From 1864 to 1870 he served as assistant professor at the U.S. Naval Academy (initially at Newport, Rhode Island, and later at Annapolis, Maryland). He was awarded an A.M. from Yale in 1868. He married Susannah Batcheller of Annapolis the following year; the couple had two sons.

During the periods 1870–1872 and 1872–1881, Johnson was employed as a professor of mathematics at Kenyon College in Gambier, Ohio, and St. John's College in Annapolis, respectively. In 1881 he became a professor of mathematics at the U.S. Naval Academy at Annapolis, remaining there until his retirement in 1921. By a special act of Congress in March 1913, he received a navy commission as a lieutenant, with the title of professor of mathematics in the navy; on his retirement, he was given the rank of commodore.

Johnson was one of the early members of the American Mathematical Society and served on its council from 1892 to 1893. Although primarily a textbook writer, he was also a frequent contributor of papers to various journals, including the *Analyst* (later replaced by *Annals of Mathematics*), the *American Journal of Mathematics*, the *Messenger of Mathematics*, and the *Proceedings of the London Mathematical Society*. In 1894 he wrote one of the first papers to appear in the newly founded *Bulletin of the American Mathematical Society*. Most of his work dealt with relatively elementary material drawn from analytic geometry (the geometry of linkages, strophoids, circular coordinate systems, and groups of circles and spheres), approximation rules, determinants, differential equations, elliptic functions, prime factorization tables, and quaternions. In particular, his work on Taylor's Theorem (1873), singular solutions of differential equations (1877), and the theory of generalized strophoids (1880) brought him to the attention of British and European mathematicians, because few Americans were publishing abroad.

However, Johnson's reputation rests not on such papers but on his seemingly tireless production of high-quality collegiate mathematics textbooks. Here he was in a class by himself—one of the first great American writers of mathematics texts. These included *An Elementary Treatise on Analytical Geometry* (1869), *An Elementary Treatise on the Differential Calculus*, coauthored with John M. Rice (1877), *An Elementary Treatise on the Integral Calculus* (1881), *Curve Tracing in Cartesian Coordinates* (1884), *A Treatise on Ordinary and Partial Differential Equations* (1889), *The Theory of Errors and Method of Least Squares* (1890), *Theoretical Mechanics* (1901), *Treatise on Differential Calculus* (1904), *Differential Equations* (1906), *Treatise on the Integral Calculus* (1907), and *An Elementary Treatise on the Differential Calculus* (1908). Each was well written and organized, with numerous examples and problems, and all were deservedly popular. Most of them went through several editions and were in print and widespread use until Johnson's death.

Johnson was respected as a mathematician and well known in the mathematical community, both in the United States and abroad. He was elected a member of the London Mathematical Society and the British Association for the Advancement of Sciences. After his retirement his health failed, and following a six-week illness he died in his Baltimore home.

• Some personal recollections of Johnson are in the biographical sketch of his brother, Charles Frederick Johnson, which appeared in the volume *Papers in Honor of Charles Frederick Johnson* (1926). Obituaries appear in the *New York Times*, 16 May 1927; the Annapolis *Evening Capital*, 16 May 1927; and the Baltimore *Evening Sun*, 15 May 1927.

JOSEPH D. ZUND

JOHNSTON, Albert Sidney (2 Feb. 1803–6 Apr. 1862), Confederate general, was born in Washington, Kentucky, the son of John Johnston, a physician, and Abigail Harris. Raised by a stepmother following the death of his mother when he was three, Johnston aspired to follow in his father's footsteps. He studied medicine at Transylvania University in Lexington, Kentucky, where he became a close friend of Jefferson Davis. In 1822 he entered the U.S. Military Academy at West Point, New York, through the nomination of his half brother, Congressman Josiah Stoddard Johnston. He graduated eighth in his class in 1826.

Johnston was assigned to duty near St. Louis, Missouri. In 1829 he married Henrietta Preston, of Louisville, Kentucky. Three children were born to the marriage. After participating in the Black Hawk War of 1832, Lieutenant Johnston resigned in April 1834 because his wife contracted tuberculosis. Following her death in August 1835 Johnston was attracted to the Texas Revolution of 1836. He became adjutant general of the Texas Republic and, in December 1836, senior brigadier general of the Texas army. Challenged to a duel by Felix Huston, Johnston was severely wounded in the right hip in February 1837. Later named Texas's secretary of war, he conducted the successful Cherokee campaigns of 1839.

Johnston resigned from the Texas army in March 1840 and spent the majority of the next ten years in varied civilian pursuits. His October 1843 marriage to Eliza Griffin, a cousin of his first wife, eventually resulted in the birth of six children. Volunteering for service in the Mexican War with Texas troops, Johnston was elected colonel and served with distinction during the battle of Monterey in September 1846. Shortly thereafter, Johnston returned to his plantation, "China Grove," near Galveston, Texas. In 1849 financial failure led Johnston to accept a position as paymaster in the U.S. Army. Five years later he was appointed colonel of the newly formed Second U.S. Cavalry Regiment. Subsequent service against the Comanche Indians heightened Johnston's reputation.

In mid-1857 Johnston commanded an expedition against insurgent Mormons in Utah. His campaign began that fall but was delayed until the following spring by severe weather. Following a series of negotiations, Johnston's army marched unopposed into Salt Lake City in June 1858. Promoted to brevet brigadier general that year, he remained in Utah until February 1860. Following his reassignment as commander of the department of California, Johnston reluctantly decided to resign from the U.S. Army in April 1861 when he learned that Texas had seceded. After a difficult three-month overland journey from Los Angeles to Richmond, Virginia, Johnston was appointed a full Confederate general, with rank second only to Adjutant General Samuel Cooper, and placed in command of the vast territory stretching from the Appalachian Mountains to Indian territory.

Instructed by President Jefferson Davis to defend this entire expanse, Johnston was unable to concentrate his troops. But by bluffing an offensive with his outnumbered and ill-supplied army, he was able to keep the Federal troops in central Kentucky largely idle. Yet early in 1862 Union columns advanced on both of his weakened flanks and defeated Confederate forces at Mill Springs, Kentucky, and Fort Henry, on the Tennessee River. Forced to withdraw from his advanced lines at Bowling Green, Kentucky, Johnston intended to hold Fort Donelson on the lower Cumberland River until his troops were safely south of Nashville. As a result of the failure of several key subordinates the fort surrendered on 16 February to Major General Ulysses S. Grant, and Johnston was compelled to retreat hastily into northern Alabama.

Johnston next concentrated his forces with those under General P. G. T. Beauregard at Corinth, Mississippi, for defense of the Mississippi Valley. After reaching Corinth in mid-March, Johnston determined to strike the Federal landing site at Pittsburg Landing, Tennessee, before Union troops under Major General Don Carlos Buell could reinforce Grant's column. On the morning of 6 April 1862 Johnston's troops burst from the woods and overran the outlying Union camps near Shiloh Church. In attempting to overcome an enemy line in the vicinity of the Peach Orchard, Johnston personally led a successful assault. Yet during the attack Johnston was struck by a stray rifle ball at the bend of his right leg and bled to death from a severed artery. Despite the enormously successful surprise attack, confusion and delay cost the Confederate army any chance for a major victory, and it withdrew to Corinth the following day.

After the war Johnston's remains were removed to Austin, Texas. Johnston's death came too early in the war to demonstrate his ultimate military talents; nevertheless, it proved to be a staggering blow to the southern Confederacy.

• The major portion of Johnston's papers are held in the Mrs. Mason Barret Collection at the Howard-Tilton Memorial Library, Tulane University, New Orleans, La. Principal biographies are William Preston Johnston, *The Life of Gen. Albert Sidney Johnston* (1879), and Charles P. Roland, *Albert Sidney Johnston: Soldier of Three Republics* (1964).

WILEY SWORD

JOHNSTON, Ella Bond (19 Nov. 1860–24 Apr. 1951), art administrator and educator, was born near Webster, Indiana, the daughter of Simon H. Bond and Susan Harris, farmers. After attending the Friends School in Webster and then Richmond High School for two years, she became a teacher at Culbertson School, a one-room schoolhouse for pupils in grades one through twelve. Among her students was the future inventor, Orville Wright. Ella then studied for two years at Earlham College in Richmond. In 1885 she accepted a position at the Richmond Public Grammar School, where she taught until 1890. She studied drawing and painting privately with the school's Boston-trained art superintendent, May E. Johnson, leading to her lifelong interest in art education. In 1889 she married Melville F. Johnston, a physician; they had one child.

The success of an art exhibition held in Richmond in 1897 led the community's art supporters to found the Richmond Art Association in June of the following year. Ella served as vice president the first year, then as president from 1899 through 1915. Under her leadership, the association advanced considerably. Backed by donations and membership fees, the group sponsored an annual art exhibition at the public school of paintings, sculpture, pottery, prints, graphics, textiles, and bronze medals produced in the region. Later, the show attracted works from across the United States and around the world for the edification of the local citizenry. Lectures, concerts, and other special cultural festivities marked the free June event.

The city prided itself on promoting widespread access to the arts and was particularly proud of the development of artistic awareness in its schoolchildren. "Bad taste is ignorance," Johnston wrote, and she cataloged the number of Richmond children who grew up to establish careers in art, architecture, and design, including her son, who became an Indianapolis landscape designer. A permanent town art collection grew with the purchase of one work each year by a local artist. When the town built Morton High School in 1910, the plans included skylit art galleries to show off the collection to advantage and to facilitate regular art education for the students. Johnston traveled to New York City, Washington, D.C., Boston, Philadelphia, and Europe to meet artists and arrange for the loan of exhibitions for display in Richmond. She worked to encourage learning about the arts by everyone by teaching art appreciation at Earlham College, offering Saturday morning classes for children and evening classes for adults, writing a column, "Gallery Notes," for Richmond's *Palladium-Item*, and organizing several trips to Europe to study art. By 1915 she had earned sufficient esteem in the art world that Chicago sculptor Lorado Taft nominated her to serve as senior docent in San Francisco at the Panama-Pacific Exposition's International Art Exhibition. She left Indiana for nearly a year to fulfill her duties, resigning the presidency of the Richmond Art Association. Upon her return, she assumed the association's unpaid directorship, a post she held until her death.

Johnston also expanded her constituency beyond Richmond, managing the Indiana Circuit Exhibition of Paintings by American Artists (1911–1927), traveled to several Indiana cities and towns. She chaired the Indiana Federation of Art Clubs (1908–1912) and the Art Department of the General Federation of Women's Clubs (1912–1916). As chair of the women's clubs art department, she delivered 200 lectures to clubwomen in 17 states, published 80 articles encouraging the creation of community art programs, supervised the circulation of 23 art collections to 125,000 viewers in 192 cities, surveyed community art, corresponded widely, and supervised the sale of American paintings and pottery.

Johnston's national reputation and activities never diverted her commitment to shaping Richmond into a model community for art appreciation. After the city outgrew its high school in 1941, she saw that the new plans included the construction of McGuire Hall, a fine arts building attached to the new school. The building offered improved exhibition space for the town's ever-growing collection of art by Indiana artists and is still in use today. The gallery displays a solid collection of work by significant American artists, including an oil painting by William Merritt Chase, a bronze sculpture by Janet Scudder, bronze medals by Paul Manship and Frederick MacMonnies, and pieces from the studios of Overbeck Pottery and Rookwood Pottery.

Johnston died in Richmond after a long life devoted to the advancement of art education and appreciation.

• Johnston's papers are at the Art Association of Richmond offices at the Richmond Art Museum. Johnston describes her own work in *A History of the Art Association of Richmond, Indiana* (1937); "Art in Indiana," *Outlook*, 24 June 1911, pp. 433–40; "The High School at the Art Centre of the Community," in *The Modern High School*, ed. Charles Hughes Johnston (1914); and "An Art Association for the People," *Outlook*, 27 Apr. 1911. See also Mary Q. Burnet, *Art and Artists of Indiana* (1921), and the obituary in the *Richmond Palladium-Item*, 26 Apr. 1951.

KAREN J. BLAIR

JOHNSTON, Eric Allen (21 Dec. 1896–22 Aug. 1963), president of the National Chamber of Commerce and the Motion Picture Association of America, was born in Washington, D.C., the son of Bertram Allen Johnston, a pharmacist, and Ida Fazio Ballinger, an office worker. Johnston's family moved to Montana and then to Spokane, Washington, where his father died from tuberculosis, leaving the family in straitened circumstances. Johnston graduated with an LL.B. from the University of Washington in 1917 and joined the U.S. Marine Corps, serving in the Far East. After suffering an injury in 1921, he returned to Spokane. He married Ina Harriet Hughes in 1922; they had two children.

Following the wedding, Johnston purchased a small electrical firm. Within ten years the firm had become so successful that he was able to divide it into the Brown-Johnston Company, specializing in electrical contracting, and the Columbia Electrical and Manufacturing Company, specializing in electrical manufacturing. The companies were industry leaders in the Pacific Northwest. Meanwhile, Johnston stayed involved with business associations taking shape in the Northwest, serving as president of the Inland Manufacturers Association (1929) and the Spokane Chamber of Commerce (1931). In 1933 he joined the Committee on Taxation of the national Chamber of Commerce. He became a vice president of the Chamber in 1941 after running unsuccessfully as a Republican for the U.S. Senate in 1940. Progressive industrialists saw Johnston as an alternative to the established leaders of the Chamber, who had isolated themselves from the government, from organized labor, and even from business outside the Northeast.

In 1942 the Chamber of Commerce elected Johnston president. In his first months, he conducted conferences with President Franklin D. Roosevelt, the American Federation of Labor (AFL) and the Congress of Industrial Organizations (CIO), and agricultural interests. These conferences helped build support from organized labor for a "no-strike pledge" and from business for what was later called the "maintenance-of-membership plan." According to the plan, workers would automatically become members of a plant union unless they quit the union within a specified number of days. By 1943 this type of agreement had divided much of the rank and file, who participated in wildcat strikes for higher wages, from union leaders, who struggled to enforce the wartime agreement.

Johnston gained recognition as a dynamic statesman. In 1943 President Roosevelt appointed him to chair a commission planning for postwar trade in South America. During the spring of 1944 Johnston visited Russia, and Joseph Stalin led him through a Siberian industrial development. Johnston converted the Chamber into an active political force, centralizing authority under the general manager and the board of directors and creating Department of Economic Research (to strengthen the Chamber's economic expertise) and of Governmental Affairs (to lobby Congress with the proposals the experts had helped to develop). The Chamber also established 800 local committees to mobilize public opinion and build electoral pressure regarding particular issues.

In addition to organizational change, Johnston promoted a political ideology within the Chamber, blending the ideas of welfare capitalism and New Deal liberalism. In doing so, Johnston emerged as a leading exponent of the ideology that historians call "corporate liberalism." Rooted in the progressive era, corporate liberal business leaders accepted the federal government and organized labor as essential to stabilizing corporate capitalism. Although he defended the profit system, Johnston wanted business to provide high wages and job security. He proposed limited government intervention for situations in which private capital failed to meet the population's needs. In his widely publicized book *America Unlimited* (1944), Johnston

championed a "people's capitalism." The book advocated various federal policies, including welfare for the deserving poor, agencies to defend workers' rights, tax incentives and economic assistance to strengthen fragile industries, wage and price controls to restrain inflation, and continued regulation of the stock market. Johnston described "responsible" unions as integral to harmonious industrial relations, urging colleagues to accept collective bargaining. Finally, he rejected economists who claimed the economy had reached its maximum potential. Johnston believed that through active fiscal policy—namely, the manipulation of taxation and spending—the government could stimulate higher levels of productivity, consumer demand, and economic growth. "We must preserve and even deepen the virtues of the profit system, but we must round it out with new kinds of co-operation between many groups and conflicting interests," Johnston wrote. "The alternative is chaos, or worse—total organization by a tyrannical state" (p. 34). At the same time *America Unlimited* cautioned labor to avoid its own "sins," including the closed shop and the disruption of production. Regarding politics, Johnston warned that should politicians expand the government too much, business would take over and use the government solely for its own interest.

During the debates over converting from a wartime to a peacetime economy in March 1945, Johnston designed the "Charter for Labor and Management" with William Green (AFL) and Phillip Murray (CIO). The document embodied corporate liberalism by calling for a high-wage and high-employment economy in exchange for a union promise to accept managerial prerogatives over the operations of private enterprise. "Arbitration," Johnston announced, "is the civilized way of settling disputes and grievances which may crop out under a collective bargaining contract" (*New York Times*, 19 Nov. 1945). Within his own companies, Johnston instituted the "labor dividend," a program that distributed a percentage of the net operating profit among all employees, and the "multimanagement plan," which created junior boards of directors comprised of shop floor employees.

When World War II ended, Johnston discovered the strengths and limitations of corporate liberalism. Within the federal government, corporate liberal business leaders encountered politicians who were receptive to their ideas, which included the use of countercyclical fiscal policy, the expansion of contributory social insurance, and the enforcement of collective bargaining agreements. Within the factories, however, the spirit of cooperation seemed fragile. Millions of workers participated in violent strikes despite the continued no-strike pledge of their leaders. Moreover, led by the National Association of Manufacturers, much of the business community mobilized to weaken the power and rights that unions had obtained during the New Deal. In the end, the Chamber's conservative majority grew intolerant of Johnston's views. They were happy when he left office in 1945 to succeed William Hays as president of the Motion Picture Association of America (MPAA).

During his tenure with the MPAA, Johnston stepped into several controversies involving censorship, Communism, independent producers, labor relations, and competition. First, Johnston successfully defended the industry's self-censorship board from attack by government officials, who sought to impose a stricter code of morality, as well as from attack by creative producers, who wanted to liberalize the boundaries of film. Several court decisions bolstered Johnston's efforts by guaranteeing movies the constitutional right to free speech. Second, Johnston faced the U.S. House Committee on Un-American Activities as it attempted to purge Communists from the movie industry. Throughout the hearings, Johnston pleaded with the committee to avoid unproven accusations and to use legal procedures in its investigations. "Too often, individuals and institutions have been condemned without a hearing or a chance to speak in self-defense, slandered and libeled by hostile witnesses not subject to cross-examination and immune from subsequent suit of prosecution" (*New York Times*, 26 Oct. 1947). Despite his reservations, Johnston cooperated with the investigation and reluctantly accepted the blacklisting of accused Communists from the movie industry. Third, Johnston mediated the struggle between independent companies and the "Big Five" (Paramount, Loew's, 20th Century–Fox, Warner Bros. and RKO). Through the antitrust laws, the independents won some important victories over Johnston and the MPAA. U.S. Supreme Court decisions in 1948 and 1956 restricted the monopolistic practices of the major companies. These decisions separated production-distribution and exhibition operations into distinct companies; thus, the "Big Five" lost control over the exhibition of movies in theaters. Fourth, Johnston attempted to resolve ongoing labor disputes within the movie industry. He negotiated an end to an interunion jurisdictional dispute that had stifled production for thirty-three weeks and even caused bloodshed. He also mediated a strike by the Screen Actors Guild and the Writers Guild of America against the movie studios. Although Johnston found temporary solutions to these disputes, labor relations within the movie industry remained volatile throughout his tenure.

As president of the MPAA, Johnston guided the industry through troubled economic times. Between 1946 and 1956 movies suffered as the television industry blossomed. This competition caused a sharp decline in earnings, production, and attendance. Johnston's most successful response to this problem involved the increased distribution of American films in international markets. Using his political connections, Johnston reduced the formal barriers to overseas markets that had limited the distribution of American films. For instance, he helped pressure the British government into repealing a tax on the earnings of imported films. In addition to opening new markets, Johnston led the industry through several initiatives to distinguish movies as superior to television. These efforts revitalized the film industry through the development of the large-scale movie extravaganza, technological innovations that enhanced the visual and audio experience of attending a movie, and on-location filming in exotic areas.

Throughout his career Johnston remained active in the world of policymaking. In January 1951 he took a leave of absence to head the Economic Stabilization Agency, where, for President Harry S. Truman, he oversaw a freeze of wages and prices. As a special envoy to the Middle East under President Dwight D. Eisenhower, Johnston designed a plan for the United Nations to help local groups develop hydroelectric power and water irrigation; the plan fell through because of the distrust between Arab states and Israel. Under Truman and Eisenhower, Johnston also encouraged a link between movies and foreign policy. Based on meetings with the Department of State, Johnston urged the studios to portray American society in a manner that would convey positive images abroad. He reminded them that American films helped dispel the "myths" of negative Communist propaganda about capitalism.

Johnston died in Washington, D.C., while he was still president of the MPAA. Johnston was one of a group of prominent industrialists, including Edward Filene, Henry Kaiser, Ralph Flanders, and Paul Hoffman, nurtured by institutions such as the Chamber of Commerce, the Business Advisory Council, and the Committee for Economic Development, who helped shape the federal government and attempted to reach an accommodation with organized labor. These business leaders represented a numerical minority within the corporate world, yet they were influential in national politics and played an important role in building the American state. Although they were less successful inside the factories, they nonetheless helped construct a collective bargaining system that produced rising wages, generous pensions, job security, and relative stability to unionized workers.

• The best primary material on Johnston's political activities is in the Chamber of Commerce Papers, Hagley Museum and Library, Wilmington, Del. For Johnston's role in the Middle East under Eisenhower, see his "Report to the President on Near East Mission," 17 Nov. 1953, Dwight D. Eisenhower Library, Ann Whitman File, Administration Series, Box 22. Johnston's extensive writings, including *We're All in It* (1948) and his articles "'An End to Reaction'—A Charter for Business," *New York Times*, 22 Aug. 1943, and "How America Can Avoid Socialism," *Fortune*, Feb. 1949, provide the most complete guide to his ideology. For an excellent analysis of Johnston's role within the Chamber, see Robert Collins, *The Business Response to Keynes* (1981). Useful obituaries are in the *New York Times* and *Washington Post*, both 23 Aug. 1963.

JULIAN E. ZELIZER

JOHNSTON, Gabriel (c. 1698–17 July 1752), second royal governor of North Carolina, was born in the Scottish Lowlands at Southdean, the son of the Reverend Samuel Johnston, a Church of Scotland minister, and Isobel Hall. Gabriel was baptized on 28 February 1698. Johnston attended the University of Edinburgh and the University of St. Andrews. In 1720 he received an M.A. from the latter institution. His intellectual interests included classical and Oriental languages, philosophy, and theology. Thereafter he studied medicine at the University of Leiden but never practiced. For several years after 1722, he taught Oriental languages at St. Andrews. About 1727 he resettled in London and lived for several years in the household of Spencer Compton, Lord Wilmington. Johnston became interested in liberal politics and wrote articles for the *Craftsman*, an anti-Walpole publication. He moved in elevated London circles and met the leading men of the day.

Although his financial resources were limited, Johnston was an engaging young man with influential friends. In March 1733 he was appointed royal governor of North Carolina and was sworn in that August. However, he did not reach Brunswick Town, North Carolina, until October 1734.

Johnston was warmly received, but he found the colony in turmoil. After over fifty years of proprietary rule, North Carolina had been royalized in 1729. The first royal governor, George Burrington, had enjoyed little success in implementing his instructions and had been driven from the colony. Suave, sophisticated, and well educated, Governor Johnston compared most favorably with his predecessor. However, after a halcyon period of a few months, the new governor faced the same problems that had plagued Burrington. The colonists had long experienced lenient government and low taxes. Moreover, the lower house of the colonial assembly claimed broad powers, including the right to determine taxes and pass the budget. This body was little interested in the king's plans for North Carolina.

As governor, Johnston encountered factionalism, sectionalism, and resistance to royal authority. Early in his tenure he noted that the "people seem here to be persuaded that they may do what they please and that they are below the notice of the King and his ministers which makes them highly insolent" (Saunders, vol. 4, p. 298). Quitrents caused years of controversy. In the proprietary period, these levies had been modest and were payable in commodities locally. Also, collectors had been lax. Royal governors sought to regularize collection procedures by designating four places to which citizens would come to pay their quitrents in specie. Governor Johnston also sought to establish accurate rent rolls in hopes of more revenue. Since his salary and the expenses of his administration depended on the collection of quitrents, he considered these matters very important.

Another troublesome legacy of the proprietary period was the circulation of blank land patents. Agents had sold patents without the name, location, description, or extent of the property in question filled in. These items were to be completed by purchasers, who sometimes failed to register their claims. Some 150,000 acres were involved, and most had not been registered on the tax rolls.

Complicating the resolution of questions involving quitrents and blank patents was the persistent problem of sectional rivalries within the colony. The Outer Banks prevented regular settlement patterns because only one major waterway, the Cape Fear River, flowed directly to the sea. Nature determined that the Albemarle region would be settled from Virginia and the Cape Fear region would be developed initially by South Carolinians. These northeastern and southeastern settlements were separated by forests and streams that rendered communication, commerce, and government difficult. In the older Albemarle Sound area, which had been settled first, each county had five representatives in the lower house of the assembly, while the new counties had only two. Sectionalism within the colony became worse as the backcountry population increased. Bitter political contests occurred over the organization of western counties and inequable representation.

Stymied for years by an uncooperative legislature, Governor Johnston adopted "political management" as a means of capitalizing on sectional rivalries. In 1739 he settled the conundrum of quitrents and blank patents by compromise. The governor agreed to confirm questionable land titles backed by reasonable documentation, and the legislature agreed to a compilation of rent rolls and the designation of collection points. Johnston agreed further to accept as payment certain commodities and provincial currency as well as specie. Within a year this major accomplishment was negated by the Privy Council. The governor's influence declined, and the collection of quitrents virtually ended. Johnston's salary was unpaid for thirteen years of his eighteen-year tenure.

Playing sharp politics in the matter, Governor Johnston sided with the Cape Fear settlements in their controversy with those in the Albemarle region. In 1741 he called the assembly to meet in Wilmington, thinking the Albemarle delegates would not come. Enough came to frustrate the governor's plan of manipulating the legislature. The next three unproductive sessions were held in New Bern, a location more central than Wilmington or Edenton, the usual seat of government, but Johnston persisted. In 1746 a legislature dominated by southeasterners met in Wilmington. Because of bad weather or by tacit agreement to frustrate Johnston's renewed efforts to secure enactment of a quitrent law, none of the Albemarle delegates attended, certain that no business could transpire without a quorum. The governor redefined what constituted a quorum, and, in imitation of the Rump Parliament, fifteen members acted for the colony. Two important laws were enacted. One declared that each county would have two representatives and each borough town one and subsequently fourteen delegates and the Speaker would constitute a quorum. The other law designated New Bern as the seat of government. The Albemarle counties refused to submit, and that area was unrepresented in the assembly for seven years.

From 1746 to 1754 virtual anarchy held sway. After Johnston's death, the Privy Council repealed the 1746 laws on constitutional grounds.

Despite numerous policy failures, Governor Johnston's administration was not a failure. The commercial and political problems he faced would defy solution for at least a century. Also, several reforms and notable achievements were accomplished. He encouraged immigration, and the colony's population increased from 30,000 to 90,000 during his tenure. He was particularly successful in bringing Scots and the Scotch-Irish to North Carolina. He installed a printer in the colony, and the laws were codified and printed. He built coastal fortifications as protection against foreign incursion, and eventually he obtained a workable property listing. Finally, although his efforts to promote public education and the Anglican church were unsuccessful, Johnston anticipated what his successors would do.

Even without his salary, Johnston prospered in North Carolina. About 1740 he married Penelope Gollard, the previously thrice-wed stepdaughter of Governor Charles Eden and one of the colony's wealthiest women. After his marriage he moved from Bladen County to "Eden House," his wife's home in Bertie County. One daughter was born to this union. After Penelope Johnston's death in 1741, he married Frances Burton, a widow. Johnston accumulated a large estate, especially in land. He died in Chowan County, and his remains were interred in Bertie County. Formed in 1746, Johnston County was named for him. He was the uncle of Samuel Johnston (1733–1816), North Carolina revolutionary leader, governor, and U.S. senator.

Although many of his contemporaries despised him and criticized him as tactless and uncompromising, historians have been kinder. One concluded: "Constantly confronted with opposition from the colonists, the uncooperative attitude of the British government, and sectional jealousies, Governor Johnston was hard pressed to keep any semblance of order or government in the colony. In spite of these obstacles, however, the colony grew and prospered, and the governor must be credited with advocating and encouraging this positive development. . . . Gabriel Johnston must be given a place among the most outstanding colonial governors of North Carolina, and America" (Cunningham, pp. 302–3).

• For Johnston's personal papers, see the Hayes collection, the Southern Historical Collection, University of North Carolina at Chapel Hill. Johnston's will is included in the Charles Johnston Collection, N.C. State Archives, Raleigh. The official documents relating to Johnston's governorship are in William Saunders, ed., *Colonial Records of North Carolina*, vols. 4 and 5 (1886–1887). See also the following secondary accounts: C. L. Raper, *North Carolina: A Study in English Colonial Government* (1940); H. T. Lefler and W. S. Powell, *Colonial North Carolina* (1973); James K. Huhta, "Government by Instruction: North Carolina, 1731–1776" (Ph.D. diss., Univ. of North Carolina at Chapel Hill, 1965); and

M. S. R. Cunningham, "Gabriel Johnston, Governor of North Carolina" (M.A. thesis, Univ. of North Carolina at Chapel Hill, 1944).

MAX R. WILLIAMS

JOHNSTON, Harriet Lane (9 May 1830–3 July 1903), first lady for President James Buchanan, was born Harriet Rebecca Lane in Mercersburg, Pennsylvania, the daughter of Elliott Tole Lane, a merchant, and Jane Buchanan. Nine years old when her mother died, she lived temporarily with her uncle, the Reverend Edward Y. Buchanan. When her father died in 1841, Harriet asked that her favorite bachelor uncle, James Buchanan, a U.S. senator, be made her guardian. He accepted the responsibility and sent her to a boarding school in Charleston, Virginia (now West Virginia). A good student, she demonstrated sharp intelligence and spirited independence that at times caused disciplinary problems, especially for her boarding school directors.

Harriet Lane enjoyed visiting her uncle, then secretary of state, in Washington, D.C. She particularly liked politics. Buchanan allowed her to attend conferences and discussed current events, literature, and history with her. Concerned about her finishing social education and believing she needed closer supervision, Buchanan enrolled her in the nearby Academy of the Visitation Convent at Georgetown, District of Columbia, in 1844. Here she displayed a special interest in history, astronomy, and mythology, became an accomplished pianist, and excelled in horsemanship. She also won high scholastic honors, which greatly pleased her uncle. Although she did not become a Roman Catholic, she experienced spiritual growth that led to humanitarian interests. The plight of the American Indians became her special concern, and she began to study and collect Indian art.

In 1849, when Buchanan's term as secretary of state ended, he purchased a country estate, "Wheatland," near Lancaster, Pennsylvania. He and Harriet lived there until 1853, when Buchanan became minister to Great Britain. By then Buchanan recognized Harriet's grasp of current affairs, listened to her advice, and acted on her opinions. He asked her to be his hostess overseas, and they set sail in April 1854.

Harriet Lane's good looks, lively sense of humor, horsemanship, and knowledge of politics and literature endeared her to the British as well as to Queen Victoria and the royal family. With a fondness for social life, she attended fashionable weddings, parties, and state dinners and made many friends. During her stay in England, she skillfully represented American interests, always speaking of her homeland in positive terms. She also introduced arts and crafts of American Indians to the British, who previously knew little about the works of Native Americans. Harriet fell in love with a wealthy British jurist and attorney general, Sir Fitzroy Kelly, but Buchanan opposed the marriage because Kelly was about forty years her senior. Buchanan also was considering running for the presidency in 1856 and needed her personal and political support. Harriet resigned herself to Buchanan's wishes, broke the engagement, and accepted whatever role she might have in her uncle's career.

Buchanan was elected president of the United States in 1856, and Harriet Lane became the first lady upon his inauguration. At age twenty-six, she added youth and grace to the White House and the capital cultural scene. She tried to imitate the standards she had experienced in Europe. Artists were always welcomed at the White House, and Harriet encouraged and supported their efforts to establish a national gallery of art. The president greeted a number of distinguished visitors to Washington, including Edward Albert, prince of Wales, in 1860. Harriet entertained him with dinners, receptions, dances, tours to patriotic sites, such as George Washington's tomb and home, and an excursion aboard the cutter *Harriet Lane*, named in honor of the president's niece. Many years later, when the prince became Edward VII, he invited Harriet to his coronation.

While in the White House, Harriet Lane also worked on behalf of the Indians, seeking to improve their educational and medical facilities. She used her influence to stop illegal liquor sales on the reservations and sought to curb government expulsion of missionaries working with the Indians. For her efforts, the Chippewa called her "great mother of the Indians." She also associated with and encouraged the efforts of social reform leaders. While she did not approve of slavery, she feared emancipation would increase poverty and disease among blacks. She hoped compromise could avoid civil war. The coming war dampened the social spirits of Washington and divided the nation and Buchanan's Democratic party. Some called the president a traitor as the country split between the North and South. Harriet retired with her uncle to Wheatland during the years of bitter warfare.

In retirement Buchanan became concerned about Harriet Lane's future and encouraged her to find a serious beau. She hated to leave her uncle, now in declining health, and the political life she had shared with him. She agreed to a quiet wedding in 1866, at Wheatland, to Henry Elliot Johnston, a Baltimore banker whom she had known many years. They had two sons. Henry Johnston encouraged Harriet's interest in art, and she began seriously collecting mementos, historical objects, and paintings. In her Baltimore home she provided a gathering place for artists and social leaders, and she contributed financially to their needs and causes.

In 1868 Harriet Johnston's uncle died. Grieving deeply, she determined to restore Buchanan's reputation, which had been tarnished by his failure in conciliation that led to the Civil War. She had inherited Wheatland, and she spent her summers there arranging Buchanan's papers for future publication. She hoped that through such a work the public might see his life and accomplishments and understand his actions during his many years of public service.

Tragedy struck when the Johnstons' older son became seriously ill with rheumatic fever and died on 25 March 1881. The second son developed similar symptoms. Although the family took him to a warmer climate in France, he also died, 30 October 1882.

To reconcile her loss, Johnston sought to advance medical research in children's diseases. In December 1883 the Johnstons incorporated Harriet Lane Home, which later formed the pediatrics unit of Johns Hopkins School of Medicine. It became the first medical center for pediatrics.

Her husband's sudden death on 5 May 1884 shattered Johnston. She sold Wheatland and her home in Baltimore and moved to Washington, D.C., where she devoted the remainder of her life to needy causes. To advance education, she established a scholarship fund at Johns Hopkins to encourage graduate research in the liberal arts and sciences. Johnston traveled frequently to Europe, where she added to her growing art collection. Upon her death, she left her collection to the Corcoran Gallery with the understanding that it would become part of the national gallery. In 1906 the Smithsonian Institution established the National Gallery of Art, where her collection found a permanent home. Johnston's other philanthropies included memorials to President Buchanan and his family and contributions to St. Albans and the Cathedral Choir School in Washington, D.C. She died at Narragansett Pier, Rhode Island.

Johnston served graciously as Buchanan's official White House hostess and became his confidant and adviser in political life. She used her resources to collect works of art, the gift of which led to the establishment of the National Gallery of Art, and she contributed to many philanthropic efforts, particularly in medical research for children.

• The primary resource for the study of Johnston is the James Buchanan–Harriet Lane Johnston Papers in the Library of Congress, Washington, D.C. She is featured in Lloyd C. Taylor, Jr., "Harriet Lane—Mirror of an Age," *Pennsylvania History* 30 (Apr. 1963): 212–25; and Thomas M. Beggs, "Harriet Lane Johnston and the National Collection of Fine Arts," in *Smithsonian Institution Annual Report* (1954). Biographies of Buchanan also contain a great deal of information about Johnston, such as Philip Shriver Klein, *President James Buchanan, a Biography* (1962), and the two-volume work by George Ticknor Curtis, *Life of James Buchanan, Fifteenth President of the United States* (1883).

MARY K. DAINS

JOHNSTON, Henrietta de Beaulieu Dering (c. 1674–Mar. 1729), artist, was born in France or England of Huguenot parents. No details of her life before 1694 are known. That year in London she married her first husband Robert Dering, a member of a wealthy Anglo-Irish family. The marriage application describes her as a resident of the parish of St. Martin-in-the-Fields, about twenty years old, the daughter of Susannah de Beaulieu, a widow. She and her husband moved to Dublin and had two daughters before his death sometime between 1698 and 1702.

Henrietta Dering made her first portraits in Dublin in 1704 and 1705. Nothing is known about her training as an artist, an unusual education for a woman at that time. The ten extant drawings of this period belong to a style of portraiture in pastel or colored crayon that was introduced into England and Ireland in the second half of the seventeenth century by artists from continental Europe. The waist-length portraits are skillfully rendered on paper about fourteen by ten inches in size. Nine of the portraits (private collection) represent members of her husband's family and their friends. Inscriptions on the original backing boards, when they survive, consist of her name, the place the portrait was made, the date, and in some cases the sitter's name. The subjects of these portraits include her husband's nephew, Sir John Percival, a baronet and member of the Irish House of Commons and Privy Council, who was created first earl of Egmont in 1733. It was perhaps through his patronage that Henrietta's daughter Mary Dering was later appointed dresser of the royal princesses, the daughters of George II.

In 1705 Henrietta Dering married Gideon Johnston, an Anglican clergyman who was a graduate of Trinity College, Dublin. Although one of her Irish drawings is signed Henrietta Johnston, her married name, she soon stopped making portraits. None are known for the years from 1706 to 1708. In 1707 Gideon Johnston was appointed commissary, or representative, of the bishop of London in North and South Carolina and the Bahama Islands, and minister of St. Philip's Church, Charleston. In the spring of 1708 the Johnstons arrived in Charleston, where almost immediately their lives were made difficult by illness, a lack of money and supplies, and distance from England. Henrietta Johnston drew portraits to provide income for the household, which included her daughters and her husband's two sons from his earlier marriage. Gideon Johnston wrote his English sponsor, Gilbert Burnet, the bishop of Salisbury, in 1709: "Were it not for the Assistance my wife gives me by drawing of Pictures (which can last but a little time in a place so ill peopled) I should not have been able to live" (Klingberg, p. 31). In 1710, to John Chamberlayne, secretary of the Society for the Propagation of the Gospel in Foreign Parts, he described the obstacles Henrietta encountered, including difficulties in obtaining drawing supplies from England: "My wife who greatly helped me, by drawing pictures, has long ago made an end to her materials, and to add to the misfortune, God has been pleased to visit her with a long and tedious Sickness" (Klingberg, p. 35).

Henrietta Johnston made more than forty portraits between 1708 and 1726, continuing the practice of inscribing them on the backing boards, many of which survive. Her American portraits are less carefully drawn and show less of the figure than her earlier works. The sitters were South Carolina landowners and merchants and their families, including Mary DuBose (Mrs. Samuel Wragg) (Gibbes Museum of Art, Charleston, S.C.), Peter and Mary Anne Bacot (Metropolitan Museum of Art, N.Y.), Samuel and Mary Magdalen Gendron Prioleau (Museum of Early Southern Decorative Arts, Winston-Salem, N.C.),

and Thomas Broughton (private collection). Many sitters, like the artist, were of Huguenot ancestry, which suggests that Johnston's relationship with them was also social. In 1711–1712 she returned to England, where she obtained for her husband an additional appointment as missionary of the Society for the Propagation of the Gospel. During that year she also visited her stepsons, who were at school in England.

After returning to Charleston, Henrietta Johnston continued to draw portraits until 1726. Gideon Johnston died in a boat accident in Charleston in 1716. Except for a trip to New York in 1725, she lived in Charleston for the rest of her life. Nothing is known of the trip north except for the five portraits that she made of Colonel John Moore (c. 1659–1732), his wife, and two children, and Elizabeth Colden, daughter of Cadwallader Colden (1688–1776). Moore and Colden were members of the provincial council of New York. Moore was born in South Carolina, where his father had been secretary of the province. The portraits of Moore's son Thomas (Virginia Museum of Fine Arts, Richmond) and Elizabeth Colden (private collection) are Johnston's only portraits of small children. Johnston died in Charleston.

Johnston was the first woman artist to work in colonial America. Although her modest drawings had no significant influence on other colonial artists, they are eloquent reminders of the value placed on portraits by those living in the American colonies at the beginning of the eighteenth century.

• Early publications on Johnston include Eola Willis, "The First Woman Painter in America," *International Studio* 87 (July 1927): 13–20, 84, and Anna Wells Rutledge, "Who Was Henrietta Johnston," *Antiques* 51 (Mar. 1947): 183–85. The first monograph is Margaret Simons Middleton, *Henrietta Johnston of Charles Town, South Carolina, America's First Pastellist* (1966). Her Irish work is discussed by Anne Crookshank and Desmond Fitz-Gerald, the Knight of Glin in *The Painters of Ireland, c. 1660–1920*, 2d ed. (1979), p. 71. About her second husband and their years in South Carolina, see Frank J. Klingberg, ed., *Carolina Chronicle: The Papers of Commissary Gideon Johnston, 1707–1716* (1946). Additional research and examination of the portraits for the exhibition of her work at the Museum of Early Southern Decorative Arts, Winston-Salem, N.C., is discussed in the catalog *Henrietta Johnston, "Who Greatly Helped . . . by Drawing Pictures"* (1991), which includes a biography and study of the artist's work by Whaley Batson.

ELLEN G. MILES

JOHNSTON, Henry Phelps (19 Apr. 1842–28 Feb. 1923), historian, was born in Trebizond, Turkey, the son of the Reverend Thomas Pinckney Johnston, a clergyman, and Marianne Cassandra Howe. His parents were serving as missionaries in Turkey at the time of his birth. His family returned to the United States, and Henry completed preparatory school at the Hopkins Grammar School in New Haven, Connecticut. He entered Yale University and in his sophomore year received awards for English composition and declamation. He received his B.A. in 1862. During his final years at Yale, he was uncertain of what he wanted to do after completing his degree. He considered continuing his schooling. In 1861 his brother William Johnston, who was studying at a seminary in Danville, Kentucky, encouraged him to become a minister.

Johnston decided not to return to school immediately, and in August 1862 he enlisted in the Fifteenth Connecticut Volunteers. His war participation was primarily in Virginia and North Carolina. He entered as a private but soon was promoted to orderly sergeant and, later, to second lieutenant. He took part in the battle of Fredericksburg in 1862, was at the siege of Suffolk in 1863, and was in the battle near Kinston, North Carolina, in 1865. Near the end of the war, he was transferred to the U.S. Signal Corps and was discharged in July 1865.

Johnston's family, like many others throughout the country, suffered loss and division during the war. His brother William had joined the Union forces as a chaplain but died in camp in December 1862, devastating Henry. A man of strong religious beliefs, Johnston wrote home shortly after entering the war that he wished that he had brought his Bible, and that he was attending prayer meetings in camp. His faith helped him to get through the loss of William. His other brother, Frontis Johnston, who was a preacher in North Carolina, had remained in the South throughout the war, as had their father.

After the war Johnston again was unsure of what he wanted to do with his life. He contemplated studying theology at Yale. This would have seemed a logical choice, given his strong religious beliefs and considering that his father was a clergyman, as was Frontis. One of Johnston's first acts after the end of the war was to visit Frontis and to hear him preach. Their father discouraged Johnston from studying theology at Yale, because of its reputation for less than orthodox theology, and encouraged him to study at the seminary in Danville, Kentucky, where William had studied.

Instead of studying theology, Johnston attended law school at Yale from 1865 until 1867. Following this he went to New York City, where he was admitted to the bar. After a brief period of independent law practice and a brief teaching experience at a school at Washington Heights in New York City that ended in 1868, he spent several years in newspaper work with the *Sun*, the *New York Times*, the *Christian Union*, and the *New York Observer*. He also spent time reading and studying American history, and in 1878 his first book, *The Campaign of 1776 around New York and Brooklyn*, was published as volume three of the Memoirs of the Long Island Historical Society. This work served to establish his reputation as an author and helped him secure a position as an instructor at the College of the City of New York, beginning 1 January 1879. He was made head of the Department of History in 1883, a position he held until 1916, when he retired from active teaching and became professor emeritus. Under his direction the department rapidly grew. In addition to being history department head, Johnston was the founder of the museum of the College of the City of New York and its curator from 1902 to 1916. During that time the museum acquired a large collection of manuscripts, maps, and other items.

During his years teaching at the College of the City of New York, Johnston wrote other books in addition to articles in publications such as *Harper's Magazine* and the *Magazine of American History*. Most of these publications involved colonial America or the American Revolution. His interest in Yale showed in his publications: *Yale and Her Honor-Role in the American Revolution, 1775–1783* (1888), and *Nathan Hale, 1776: Biography and Memorials* (1914).

Johnston married Elizabeth Kirtland Holmes, of Lebanon, Connecticut, in 1871 in Cleveland, Ohio. They had four sons. After his retirement from teaching, Johnston moved to Middletown, Connecticut, in 1917, where he died.

Johnston's historical research was considered to be quite good. He was thorough, accurate, and interesting. The primary mark of his publications was that they were based on original documents, many of which he included in the works, generally as appendixes. He took great pains to gather all of the available documents on a subject. In his *Battle of Harlem Heights, September 16, 1776* (1897), he included American, English, and Hessian authorities. His publications included maps, frequently prepared for that work, and illustrations of people and places. Reviews of his publications were almost always outstanding. A review of *The Yorktown Campaign and the Surrender of Cornwallis* (1881) says of his book, "Into the military details of the Yorktown siege . . . the reader can enter with the assurance of fullest detail by perusing Mr. Johnston's interesting monograph. Never before has the story been so well told" (*Nation*, 13 Oct. 1881, p. 297). Some of Johnston's books have been reprinted several times, decades after their initial publication, testifying to their popularity. The reviews of the later reprints also praise Johnston's work. Johnston's own words testify to the importance of his work. In the preface to *The Yorktown Campaign*, Johnston said, "The preservation of their history, in some form or other, seems to be one of the first duties of a people." By his work Johnston helped to preserve some of America's history.

• A collection of Johnston's papers is at the Sterling Memorial Library at Yale University. The papers consist primarily of correspondence to and from his mother and sisters during his military service in the Civil War. Other major works by Johnston include *Observations on Judge Jones' Loyalist History of the American Revolution* (1880), *The Storming of Stony Point on the Hudson, Midnight, July 15, 1779* (1900), and *The Correspondence and Public Papers of John Jay* (4 vols., 1890). Brief biographies may be found in Yale Class of 1862 reunion books, particularly the *Triennial Meeting of the Class of 1862, Yale University* (1865), *The Twenty Years' Record of the Yale University Class of 1862* (1884), and the *Fifty Years' Meeting of the Yale Class of 1862* (1914). A picture may be found in *Class of 1862 Yale Portraits and Sketches* (1899). An excerpt from N. P. Mead, "Henry Phelps Johnston," *City College Quarterly*, Mar. 1917, may be found in Yale Class of 1862, *Class*

Items, 1914–1917 (1917). An obituary is in *Yale University Obituary Record of Graduates Deceased during the Year Ending July 1, 1923* (1923).

CONNIE L. PHELPS

JOHNSTON, John Taylor (8 Apr. 1820–24 Mar. 1893), railroad president and art patron, was born in New York City, the son of John Johnston, a banker, and Margaret Taylor. His parents, who had come from Scotland, took Johnston on one of their periodic visits to their homeland; he studied briefly at Edinburgh High School and was named "dux" (top pupil) of his class. He graduated from the University of the City of New York (now New York University) in 1839 and proceeded to study law, first at the Yale College law school (1839–1841) and then in the New York office of Daniel Lord. Admitted to the New York bar in 1843, Johnston soon found that the profession did not engage his interests fully. He traveled abroad for two years, before returning to the United States and commencing his career in the field of railroad development.

In 1848 Johnston became president of a small railroad that connected Somerville and Elizabethtown, New Jersey. He gave all his energy to expanding from this start, and he soon succeeded in extending the line westward to Easton, Pennsylvania. Up to this point, he had been moderately successful. In 1850 he also became married. His union with Frances Colles resulted in five children, four of whom were to survive their father.

It was his acquisition of the Lehigh and Susquehanna Railroad, with its direct access from the anthracite coal fields of Pennsylvania to the seacoast, that gave true momentum to Johnston's career. Foreseeing a continuing demand for transport in this area, he acquired a right of way across the Jersey flats and built a rail connection from Elizabeth, New Jersey, across Newark Bay and into New York City. By the time the Civil War had ended, Johnston had propelled his railroad from its modest beginnings into the Central Railroad of New Jersey, one of the most important transport lines in the Northeast.

In his work as president of the railroad, Johnston sought to emphasize both safety and convenience. Following a trip to England, he introduced the use of uniforms for trainmen; he also took a keen interest in technical details such as grades, alignment, and grade crossings.

During the same time that he was energetically pushing forward the Central Railroad, Johnston was acquiring a collection of paintings in his home in New York City, a collection that had no private rival in North America. Desirous of sharing his interest in art with the public, he built two galleries that were attached to his house (at 8 Fifth Avenue) and opened the galleries to the public one day a week. Because of financial setbacks, he was forced to sell the bulk of his collection; the auction, conducted in December 1876, was the first large-scale art sale in the history of the city. It was therefore not surprising that in 1880 when a group of art enthusiasts combined to develop a museum of art in New York City, they elected as their president Johnston, who was out of the country at the time. On hearing of his election while he was on the Nile River in Egypt, he immediately cabled his acceptance.

The New York state legislature granted an act of incorporation (13 Apr. 1870) to the project and work began in earnest. Johnston was by no means a disinterested bystander in the process of the creation of the Metropolitan Museum of Art. Reelected president annually between 1870 and 1889, Johnston worked with great energy and diligence to bring the art museum into form. In early 1871 he gave $10,000 to the project, making him the single largest subscriber in that year's fund drive. In March 1871 Johnston and his fellow trustee William T. Blodgett collaborated in a coup; they each laid down $116,000 (the money was later reimbursed) for a collection of paintings from Europe, mainly Dutch and Flemish, that became the essential nucleus on which the museum's reputation would be built. The museum moved into the Dodworth building at 681 Fifth Avenue in 1872 and remained there for one year; during this time, the gallery was open to the public on the virtually free basis that has since remained a cornerstone of the museum's policy. In 1873 Johnston scored a second coup; for $60,000 he bought the collection of Cypriot antiquities that had been brought together by General Louis Palma di Cesnola (an Italian by birth, a U.S. citizen by choice). The museum moved to the Douglas mansion (1873–1879), and Cesnola became first the secretary (1877) and then the director (1879) of the museum.

On 30 March 1880 the museum was opened to the public for the first time in its Central Park location; Johnston gave a reception and luncheon at his home prior to the 3:30 P.M. ceremony, the last of his triumphs in the art world. As the decade advanced, he experienced failing health, and in February 1889 the trustees accepted his resignation, while at the same time making him honorary president for life. Johnston was succeeded in the presidency by Henry G. Marquand. Before his death (in New York City), Johnston made a bequest for monies that would later be used to cover the costs of the Italian Renaissance casts for the museum; due to his generosity (and later that of his family members), the John Taylor Johnston Collection became a permanent part of the museum.

Neither Johnston's life nor his career falls under a neat category. Fortunate in the wealth of his parents and in the education he received, Johnston appeared to be both a man of his times and to indulge a truly Victorian approach to art and antiquities. Shielded by wealth and privilege from the great convulsions of the time (the Mexican War, Civil War, and Industrial Revolution), he was free to follow his own star. If there was indeed an American Victorian era, then Johnston was one of its salient representatives. He was interested in and furthered the development of business, took a strong interest in artistic and cultural ventures, and looked to antiquity to provide the inspiration for his century. Much more a Lorenzo de Medici than a Michelangelo, Johnston was important in the development of an environment that supported the growth of the arts in late nineteenth-century Manhattan.

• Few sources exist for a study of Johnston. See Winifred E. Howe, *A History of the Metropolitan Museum of Art* (1913); Joshua L. Chamberlain, *Universities and Their Sons: New York University* (1901); and "The Old New Jersey Central," *Railroad Employee*, Mar. 1905. Obituaries are in the *New York Evening Post*, 24 Mar. 1893, and the *New York Times*, 25 Mar. 1893.

SAMUEL WILLARD CROMPTON

JOHNSTON, Joseph Eggleston (3 Feb. 1807–21 Mar. 1891), Confederate general, was born near Farmville, Virginia, the son of Peter Johnston, a circuit court judge, and Mary Wood Valentine. He grew to manhood in Abingdon, in the western toe of Virginia, and attended the local private academy. In 1825 he received an appointment to West Point, where he was a classmate of Robert E. Lee. Johnston graduated thirteenth out of a class of forty-six in 1829 and was commissioned a second lieutenant of artillery.

In January 1836 Johnston was appointed to the staff of Winfield Scott, who commanded U.S. forces en route to Florida to crush the Seminole uprising. Like many officers of his generation, Johnston found the war against the Seminoles disspiriting and the slow rate of promotion frustrating. In May 1837, with the war apparently winding down, he submitted his resignation. The panic of 1837 ruined his prospects for employment as a civilian engineer, and the best job he could find was that of civilian topographical engineer on an army-navy expedition to map the Florida coast. In that capacity he returned to the scene of the Seminole wars, and in January 1838 he participated in a skirmish with a band of Seminoles, winning official praise for his coolness under fire. That experience led Johnston to conclude that his future lay with the military after all, and he reentered the army in July. He married Lydia Mulligan Sims McLane, daughter of Louis McLane, president of the B&O Railroad and a former secretary of state, on 10 July 1845 in Baltimore; they had no children.

Johnston's next important service was in Mexico. Again appointed to the staff of Winfield Scott, Johnston was present at the siege of Vera Cruz (10–25 Mar. 1847) and was wounded (12 Apr.) while scouting the Mexican positions before the battle of Cerro Gordo (18 Apr.). Johnston recuperated in the mountain village of Jalapa, and when reinforcements arrived in June he was breveted to lieutenant colonel and appointed second in command, under Colonel Timothy Andrews, of the Voltigeurs regiment. Johnston fought in the battle of Contreras (19 Aug.), at the battle of Churubusco (20 Aug.), and, most notably, at Chapultepec (13 Sept.), where the men of his battalion were among the first to scale the walls of the citadel and plant the American flag on the ramparts. For his role in this action, Johnston was breveted to colonel, though he had

difficulty during the ensuing decade in getting the War Department to acknowledge his promotion.

During the 1850s Johnston helped map a southern route for a transcontinental railroad, served as second in command of the First Cavalry regiment during the troubles in "bleeding Kansas," and flirted with the idea of organizing a filibustering expedition into Mexico. At the end of the decade, Secretary of War John B. Floyd finally approved his brevet promotion to colonel and almost immediately thereafter appointed him quartermaster general of the army, a job that carried with it an automatic promotion to brigadier general. Johnston was the first West Point graduate to pin on the stars of a brigadier general in the regular army.

When Virginia seceded from the Union in April 1861, Johnston resigned his commission. After brief service organizing the defense of Richmond, he accepted a brigadier general's commission from the Confederate government at Montgomery and assumed command of Confederate forces at Harpers Ferry, Virginia, on 23 May 1861. Unhappy with the weak defensive position of Harpers Ferry, Johnston evacuated the town on 14 June and fell back to Winchester in the Shenandoah Valley. From there he led his forces to Manassas Junction to join with those of P. G. T. Beauregard in time to defeat the Federal army of Irvin McDowell at the first battle of Manassas (21 July 1861).

Soon afterward, Johnston had a falling-out with Confederate president Jefferson Davis. On 31 August 1861 Davis sent the names of five men to the Confederate Congress to be confirmed as full generals. Davis ranked Johnston fourth, despite legislation mandating that officers should retain the same relative seniority they had enjoyed in the old army. Johnston's angry letter of protest triggered a terse and dismissive response from the president, and the exchange marked the beginning of a bitter feud between president and general that lasted the rest of their lives.

In the spring of 1862 Johnston assumed command of the Confederate forces defending the Yorktown Peninsula to contest the advance of Federal major general George B. McClellan (1826–1885). Johnston delayed McClellan for most of a month at Yorktown before evacuating that position and then fought a rear guard action at Williamsburg, but by the end of May he had backed himself up to the outskirts of Richmond. Finally, on 31 May, he launched a poorly coordinated counterattack at Seven Pines (Fair Oaks), in which he was wounded. Robert E. Lee assumed command of the army and soon thereafter inaugurated the Seven Days' campaign that drove McClellan from the gates of the city.

Johnston recuperated from his wounds in the Richmond home of Texas senator Louis T. Wigfall, who was Jefferson Davis's most persistent and vitriolic critic in the Confederate Congress. Johnston's liaison with Wigfall had political overtones and exacerbated his increasingly bitter relationship with Davis.

Johnston returned to active service in November 1862, and Davis appointed him commander of the western theater, which encompassed all the area between the Appalachian Mountains and the Mississippi River. Johnston believed that the command arrangement was unworkable, and he carried on a long-distance dispute about it with Davis until May 1863, when the president ordered him to oversee the defense of Vicksburg. By the time Johnston arrived in Mississippi, however, Ulysses S. Grant had already maneuvered his army between Johnston's small relief force and John C. Pemberton's Army of Mississippi. Johnston urged Pemberton to keep his army free to maneuver, but Pemberton believed the defense of Vicksburg was essential, and after his defeat in the battle of Champion Hill (Baker's Creek, 16 May) he withdrew into the city. Johnston was unable to accumulate a force strong enough to relieve him, and after a long siege Pemberton surrendered on 4 July 1863.

Davis blamed Johnston for the fall of Vicksburg and reduced his command authority. For four months Johnston was relegated to a minor command in Alabama. But after the humiliating Confederate defeat at Missionary Ridge near Chattanooga in November 1863, Davis realized that the Army of Tennessee needed new leadership. Against his better judgment he yielded to demands that Johnston be made its commander. Johnston assumed command on 27 December 1863, and although Davis urged him to initiate a winter offensive he spent the winter months reorganizing the army and improving its morale.

Johnston's defense of North Georgia in the spring and summer of 1864 is the most controversial aspect of his career. Because Johnston was heavily outnumbered by the three armies of Major General William Tecumseh Sherman (who had 100,000 men to Johnston's 60,000), Sherman was able to maneuver him out of position after position: from Rocky Face Ridge in North Georgia, to Resaca, to Allatoona, and to Kennesaw Mountain west of Marietta. Each time, Sherman was able to hold Johnston's army in position with superior forces and send a flanking column to threaten the Confederate left. Each time, Johnston responded by abandoning his position and hurrying southward to interpose his forces once again in front of Sherman—but of course he had to surrender territory to do so. Engagements were fought at Resaca (13–15 May), New Hope Church (26–28 May), and Kennesaw Mountain (27 June). Though Johnston held his own in each, he was unable to inflict the kind of defeat that would drive Sherman from Georgia.

In Richmond, Davis grew increasingly concerned that Johnston was giving up so much territory. As a result of his retrograde movements, the Yankees had occupied Rome, Georgia, an important industrial town, and Johnston seemed unwilling to launch a serious counterattack. By the second week of July, Davis sent Braxton Bragg to Atlanta to inquire about Johnston's future plans. Unsatisfied with Johnston's response, Davis ordered him relieved and appointed John Bell Hood to command the army (17 July 1864).

For more than six months Johnston was out of the war. Meanwhile, Confederate fortunes worsened, and in January 1865 the Confederate Congress passed a resolution urging Johnston's reappointment to command. Believing that Johnston's name might at least raise troop morale, Lee, too, joined the chorus of his supporters, and in February Davis reluctantly made the appointment.

Johnston took command of the scattered elements of Confederate forces in the Carolinas that were trying to slow the inexorable advance of Sherman's armies. He sent reinforcements to Bragg so that he could fight and win the battle of Kinston, North Carolina (8 Mar. 1865), and then gathered his forces together for an assault on one of the advancing Federal columns in the battle of Bentonville (19 Mar.). Though it began well for the Confederates, the battle was indecisive, and Johnston had to retreat when the Federals brought up reinforcements.

After learning of Lee's surrender at Appomattox, Johnston believed the war was effectively over. Davis wanted to continue the fight, but Johnston convinced him to open negotiations for a settlement. Davis gave his approval, and Johnston met with Sherman near Durham, North Carolina, to write a comprehensive agreement to end the war. That agreement was disavowed by the U.S. executive, however, and Johnston met with Sherman again to surrender his army (26 Apr.) on the same terms Grant had given to Lee. Davis never forgave Johnston for surrendering when he was not surrounded or defeated.

In the years after the war, Johnston prospered as an insurance executive and a one-term congressman from Virginia and in the 1880s as U.S. Railroad Commissioner. He also engaged in an unseemly "battle of the books" with those who had criticized his leadership during the war. In particular, he attacked Davis, Bragg, and Hood in magazine articles and in his memoir, *A Narrative of Military Operations* (1874). Johnston died in his home in Washington, D.C., having contracted pneumonia while serving as a pallbearer at the funeral of William T. Sherman.

• Johnston's papers are scattered in small collections in several libraries and archives across the country. The most important of these are in the Swem Library at the College of William and Mary, the Henry E. Huntington Library in San Marino, Calif., and the Maryland Historical Society (the McLane-Fisher Family Papers) in Baltimore. Johnston's *A Narrative of Military Operations* is tainted by his vendetta against Davis, as are his several articles in *Battles and Leaders of the Civil War*. The two modern biographies of Johnston are Gilbert Govan and James W. Livingood, *A Different Valor: The Story of General Joseph E. Johnston, C.S.A.* (1956), and Craig L. Symonds, *Joseph E. Johnston: A Civil War Biography* (1992). Jeffrey Lash blames Johnston for poor handling of southern railroad assets in *Destroyer of the Iron Horse: General Joseph E. Johnston and Confederate Rail Transport* (1991).

CRAIG L. SYMONDS

JOHNSTON, Josiah Stoddard (24 Nov. 1784–19 May 1833), judge, congressman, and U.S. senator, was born in Salisbury, Connecticut, the son of John Johnston, a physician, and Mary Stoddard. The family moved west in 1788 and settled on the Kentucky frontier in Mason County. In 1796 Johnston's father returned to Connecticut to enroll his son in school in New Haven. After completing preparatory studies, Johnston entered Transylvania University in Lexington, Kentucky. Upon graduation in 1802, Johnston read the law under the tutelage of the famous George Nicholas.

After completing his legal studies, Johnston emigrated to the newly established Territory of Orleans (now Louisiana) in 1805. Settling in the small frontier hamlet of Alexandria on the Red River, he immediately set up a law practice. The rough and turbulent circumstances typical of a frontier area proved ideally suited for a talented and ambitious young attorney. Johnston quickly elicited professional and personal respect accompanied by handsome remunerations from his neighbors. He refused to become entangled in the heated divisions that raged in the raw riverfront hamlet; his polished and judicious manner earned him the appellation of "peacemaker" as well as election to the first territorial legislature in 1805.

Johnston's quiescent temperament was well suited to the quarrelsome and divisive nature of the territorial legislature, in which every issue fell victim to the acrimonious ethnic struggle between the American and Ancient populations. Fledgling American strength centered in the Red River Valley, and Johnston quickly became an acknowledged leader of the American faction. Still, Johnston's sagacious and amiable manner won respect, and at times support, among many of the Gallic legislators. He focused his attention upon issues that most concerned the territory: clear land titles, the administration of justice, and early statehood. Johnston served his community in the territorial legislature until 1812; he then became a district judge under the new state constitution, a position he maintained until 1821.

Johnston soon acquired land, slaves, and a plantation. His household served as a haven for his brothers, who sought and received advice, money, and influence to secure their futures. In 1814 Johnston married Eliza Sibley, the daughter of John Sibley, a physician in Natchitoches, Louisiana. The match was one of genuine affection. A pretty, intelligent woman, Eliza proved a gracious and charming hostess whether on the Red River frontier or in the salons of Philadelphia. The Johnstons had two sons. Shortly after his marriage, Johnston raised a regiment of volunteers for the defense of New Orleans, but they reached the city too late to participate in the battle on 8 January 1815.

Johnston was elected to Congress in 1821, but in 1823 William Brent defeated him for reelection in a vicious and highly personal campaign. In the same year Senator James Brown received an appointment as American ambassador to France, and Johnston and Edward Livingston contended for his vacant seat. The full weight of the American forces in the Louisiana legislature turned to Johnson as well as some French country representatives who refused to vote for Livingston, a "city man," even though he was an influential leader of the Gallic faction.

Immediately upon securing the Senate seat, Johnston assumed a key position in Henry Clay's campaign for the presidency in 1824. Ideologically, Johnston had long championed Clay's American System. His friendship with Martin Duralde, Clay's son-in-law, provided an entree into the Kentuckian's inner circle while Johnston served in the House. Johnston's sound judgment and even temperament made him a valuable ally to Clay, and by 1824 their relationship had grown into a firm personal friendship. Clay selected him as his second in his notorious duel with John Randolph. Johnston's political gifts, especially his ability to maintain friendships among men bitterly opposed to one another, clearly emerged during the campaign. He moved back and forth between Philadelphia and New York drumming up allies in these two pro-tariff cities. He secured needed newspaper support and even engaged the crafty Thurlow Weed in a prospective deal.

While the nation awaited the decision of the House on the presidential election, Johnston and Livingston again contended in the 1825 contest for a full-term Senate seat. The issues turned on familiar racial and personal animosities, and legislators again selected Johnston. Many of the National Republicans urged Johnston to run for the governorship in 1826, but he preferred the larger national stage and refused. Johnston and his wife moved in the most favored circles of President John Quincy Adams, but he continued to plan and to promote Clay's presidential candidacy.

Johnston deplored Andrew Jackson's election to the presidency in 1828, and he soon began scouring the eastern seaboard for allies who would rally to Clay's standard in 1832. His own reelection caused some concern, but the racial and economic peculiarities of Louisiana politics tipped the scales in his favor. When the doctrinaire Florida Parish Jacksonians insisted that Johnson's pro-tariff record must constitute the main issue in the Senate election of 1831, sugar area legislators and many of his personal friends among the Jacksonians hastened to Johnston's defense, and Johnston again won reelection to the Senate.

In addition to the obvious skill and enthusiasm that he brought to the political world, Johnston established a sound reputation as a statesman among both friends and foes. His prodigious memory frequently made him seem dogmatic, but those who knew him quickly learned that he had the necessary flexibility to achieve his objectives. He concerned himself primarily with economic questions in Congress, and his attention to the interests of Louisiana in tariff affairs won support that crossed ethnic and geographical lines.

While in the Senate Johnston served on both the finance and commerce committees, and he was chairman of the latter committee. A consistent champion of softening the rules of maritime warfare, he insisted that neutral vessels had the obligation of protecting their cargoes regardless of who owned them, and that contraband lists should be restricted. He also authored an able report on the British colonial trade question as well as several pamphlets on the effects of the repeal of the duty on sugar. In addition, Johnston supported and encouraged measures that gave the federal government an active role in promoting manufacturing and improving communication and transportation facilities. Louisianians had little patience with abstractions about the power of the central government regarding internal improvements. The great financial and commercial interests of New Orleans assured Johnston of constituents who approved his support of the national bank and projects designed to improve navigation, whether national or international. Johnston's opposition to nullification and his able arguments that such a doctrine would lead to disunion received widespread support in Louisiana.

Johnston was killed when the steamer *Lioness* exploded on the Red River near Alexandria. He was eulogized in the Senate by both friend and foe.

• Johnston's extensive papers are at the Historical Society of Pennsylvania. Joseph Tregle, Jr.'s classic study of Louisiana politics in the early national period, *Louisiana in the Age of Jackson: A Study in Ego-Politics* (1976), is essential to understanding Johnston's career. Critical information is provided in *The Papers of Henry Clay*, vols. 3, 6, and 8, ed. James F. Hopkins (1959–1992). Information on Johnston's early life is found in two biographies of Johnston's half-brother Albert S. Johnston: William P. Johnston, *The Life of Gen. Albert Sidney Johnston* (1878), and Charles P. Roland, *Albert Sidney Johnston, Soldier of Three Republics* (1964). William P. Johnston, *The Johnstons of Salisbury* (1897), gives some information on Johnston's family.

CAROLYN E. DE LATTE

JOHNSTON, Mary (21 Nov. 1870–9 May 1936), author and suffragette, was born in Buchanan, Botetourt County, Virginia, the daughter of John William Johnston, a major in the Confederate army who, following the Civil War, became president of Georgia Pacific Railway, and Elizabeth Dixon Alexander. Her mother died in 1889, leaving the role of family caretaker to Mary, who acted as surrogate mother to her siblings. Her father's career necessitated temporary residency, for varying periods of time, in Birmingham, New York City, and Richmond. In 1898 Johnston began her long publishing career, motivated in part by an 1895 reversal of family fortune.

Despite the difficulties of southern life during Reconstruction, Johnston was reared in the comforts and conventions of the genteel tradition. Because of frail health, however, she completed only three months in an Atlanta school for girls, becoming, by default, self-taught for the remainder of her life. Early accounts of her life, moreover, suggest that poor health led her to introspection and intensive reading, particularly American history, the Scottish ballads, and the works of Edmund Spenser, Percy Bysshe Shelley, John Keats, Charles Dickens, and Robert Browning. Reading, shyness, and withdrawal characterized her life, and a strong historical interest and a vivid imagination became her hallmark. Living in virtual isolation in the mountains of Virginia, she developed a romantic closeness to nature and a strong mystical response to life. Because of her father's experiences in the Civil War and her family's importance throughout Virginia history, she developed an intense pride in the roots of history as fact, code, and myth.

Her pride in southern history led her inevitably to a vivid, nearly symbolic portrayal of landscape. Johnston's romances of adventure not only brought her a national reading audience and her fortune; they created her place in literary history. Romances such as *Prisoners of Hope* (1898); *To Have and to Hold* (1900), which was the number one bestseller for 1900 and which was subsequently made into a motion picture; *Audrey* (1902); and *Sir Mortimer* (1904) focus on heroic action as the consequence of quest. Set in the past, her best-known romances focus on Virginia history. Her historical settings and costume descriptions offered a verisimilitude that endeared her to her readers.

Three works comprise Johnston's historical period: *Lewis Rand* (1908), set in Jeffersonian Virginia; *The Long Roll* (1911); and *Cease Firing* (1912). The latter two novels were set in Civil War Virginia, which she knew intimately from her readings and from her father's accounts of his role in the conflict. Avoiding Thomas Nelson Page's tendency to eulogize the Lost Cause, she attained an unusual realism within the body of Lost Cause literature because of her deep understanding of military traditions and maneuvers and her keen observation of detail.

Johnston wrote four novels of cause, *The Witch* (1914), *The Fortunes of Garin* (1915), *The Wanderers* (1917), and *Hagar* (1913). Of these, *Hagar*, written at the request of her friend Wisconsin suffragette Fola La Follette, became her major feminist tract. Early reviewers of the feminist novel saw it as a polemic and argued that Johnston's talent was not for the "problem novel" but for the romance, a judgment shared by many of her most loyal readers.

Johnston's later years were marked by an increasing emphasis on socialism and mysticism, including reincarnation, evolution, and theosophy. *Foes* (1918), set in eighteenth-century Scotland; *Michael Forth* (1919), set in the post-Civil War South; and *Sweet Rocket* (1920) are so rooted in mysticism that many readers lost interest altogether in her fiction.

Johnston spent the last decade and a half of her career trying, in part, to regain the reading audience alienated by her increased mysticism. *Silver Cross* (1922), *1492* (1922), *Croatan* (1923), *The Slave Ship* (1924), *The Great Valley* (1926), and *The Exile* (1927) suggest the pressure to return to historical settings to draw back her readers. *The Slave Ship* expresses a racial tolerance and understanding unusual for fiction of the day. *The Great Valley*, however, focuses on the kind of subject matter her readers loved, middle-class Scottish dissenters who pioneered the Virginia valley. Three novels—*Hunting Shirt* (1931), *Miss Delicia Allen* (1933), and *Drury Randall* (1934)—were motivated by Johnston's attempt to meet heavy maintenance expenses at her sumptuous home Three Hills. *Hunting Shirt* emphasizes quest, *Miss Delicia Allen* emphasizes character at the expense of plot, and *Drury Randall* explores issues of secession and slavery.

Johnston is remembered for her intense interest in history, her overpowering love of setting, her heavy emphasis on costume, her compassionate devotion to causes like feminism and racial relations, and, in her declining years, an odd, nearly incoherent mysticism. By and large, as the *Independent* for 20 November 1902 noted, she succeeded in making a "romantic rainbow of colonial civilization in Virginia." She died in Warm Springs, Virginia.

• The major source of Johnston papers is the Mary Johnston Collection (accession no. 3588), Manuscripts Department, Alderman Library, University of Virginia, Charlottesville. The extensive Johnston collection is comprised of diaries, clippings, letters, and a helpful, unpublished biography of the author by her sister Elizabeth Johnston. The major Johnston bibliography is George C. Longest, *Three Virginia Writers: Mary Johnston, Thomas Nelson Page, and Amelie Rives Troubetzkoy* (1978). The major biography is C. Ronald Cella, *Mary Johnston* (1981). Other helpful biographical treatments include E. S. Boddington, "Mary Johnston in Birmingham, Alabama," in *Women Authors of Our Day in Their Homes*, ed. Francis Whiting Halsey (1903); Anne Goodwyn Jones, *"Tomorrow Is Another Day": The Woman Writer in the South, 1859–1936* (1981); Grant Martin Overton, *The Women Who Make Our Novels* (1928); and Marjorie Spruill Wheeler, "Mary Johnston, Suffragist," *Virginia Magazine* 100, no. 1 (1992): 79–118. The most sympathetic critical estimation is Laurence G. Nelson, "Mary Johnston and the Historical Imagination," in *Southern Writers: Appraisals in Our Time*, ed. R. C. Simonini (1964). A helpful feminist view is Lynn Veach Sadler, "Women and Freedom in Selected Novels of Mary Johnston and Frances Gaither," *Jack London Newsletter* 16, no. 3 (1983): 115–24.

GEORGE C. LONGEST

JOHNSTON, Neil (4 Feb. 1929–27 Sept. 1978), basketball player, was born Donald Neil Johnston in Chillicothe, Ohio, the son of Alex Johnston, a railroad worker. His mother's name is unknown. Called by his middle name throughout his life, Johnston played baseball, football, and basketball in high school, and he was a high jumper on the track team. After being selected to the all-state basketball team in his senior year, he declined several scholarship offers in order to matriculate at Ohio State University.

In lieu of a scholarship, Johnston had a job in the athletic department supply room at Ohio State. He played creditably for coach William "Tippy" Dye, but he gave up his eligibility after only two seasons because he had trouble meeting his expenses. In the summer of 1948 Johnston signed a contract to play baseball with the Philadelphia Phillies organization. The small bonus he received enabled him to pay his bills and to buy a car. Besides, he recalled, his father had always wanted him to play major league baseball.

No longer an amateur, the 6'8" Johnston played industrial league basketball in the winter and honed his skills in occasional games against traveling pro teams. He joined the Phillies for spring training in 1949 and was assigned to pitch for Terre Haute, Indiana, in the Class B Three-I League. After two mediocre seasons he was promoted to the Wilmington, Delaware, Blue Rocks in the Class B Inter-State League, but his performance did not improve. Midway through the 1951 season, Johnston confided to Wilmington business manager Jim Ward that he had lost his confidence and wanted to try professional basketball instead.

Ward arranged for Eddie Gottlieb, owner and coach of the Philadelphia Warriors of the National Basketball Association (NBA), to give Johnston a tryout in the fall of 1951. A few days after joining the Warriors at their Hershey, Pennsylvania, training camp, Johnston returned to Chillicothe to marry Phyllis Wilson; they had five children. He made the team as a backup center and averaged 6.0 points per game in his rookie season.

Johnston gave baseball one last chance in 1952, but he injured his arm after just three decisions and then left the game for good. That fall he earned a starting spot with the Warriors and quickly became one of the best players in the league. Philadelphia was the NBA's worst team, winning only 12 of 69 games, but Johnston won the scoring title (22.3 points per game), led the league in field-goal percentage (.4524), and finished second in rebounds (13.9 per game). He played in the All-Star Game as a reserve and scored 11 points.

Johnston was a thin, ungainly player at first, but he developed a smooth, deceptive style near the basket. "He's the most effective awkward guy I've ever seen," said New York Knickerbockers coach Joe Lapchick. "He has real good moves." His best shot was a hook shot from close range, but he also learned how to pump in one-handers efficiently from 20 feet. "There isn't a good scorer in the league who shoots less than he does," said Gottlieb. Johnston drew a lot of fouls and led the NBA in free throws made three times, shooting underhanded.

In the 1953–1954 season Johnston averaged 24.4 points per game to win the scoring title again. He outdistanced runner-up Bob Cousy by more than five points per game, finished third in field-goal percentage and sixth in rebounding. "All they got to do is get the ball into him and Johnston will score," said Lapchick, against whose team Johnston scored 41 points one night. He won a third straight scoring title in 1954–1955 and led the league in rebounds. His single-game highs, 45 points against the Rochester Royals and 39 rebounds against the Syracuse Nationals, were the top NBA performances of that season.

For the 1955–1956 season the Warriors added All-American Tom Gola to their lineup to complement Johnston and star forward Paul Arizin. Philadelphia finished with the best record in the league and won the NBA championship. Johnston captured the field goal percentage title again and finished third in scoring. He won a third field goal crown in 1956–1957, but the Warriors, with Gola in the military, could not hold off the emerging Boston Celtics.

After one more strong season, Johnston suffered a leg injury that severely limited his playing time and his performance. He played in only 28 games during the

1958–1959 season, averaging only 6.3 points and 5.0 rebounds per game. He retired after the season, having scored 10,023 points (19.4 per game) and snared 5,856 rebounds (11.3 per game) and having played in six All-Star games. He then coached the Warriors for two seasons and saw his replacement at center, Wilt Chamberlain, win the scoring and rebounding titles both years.

For 1961–1962 Johnston signed as player-coach with the Pittsburgh Rens of the new American Basketball League (later American Basketball Association). He played in only five games but directed his team to second place in its division. Twenty-two games into the following season, he resigned. He then coached Wilmington in the minor-league Eastern Basketball League for two seasons, after which he worked for six years in industry. Johnston returned to basketball as an assistant coach at Wake Forest University and later with the Portland Trail Blazers of the NBA. After a short stint as head coach at Chemeketa Community College in Salem, Oregon, he became head coach and athletic director at North Lake Community College in Irving, Texas, in 1977. Johnston suffered a fatal heart attack while playing basketball in nearby Bedford, Texas, and in 1990 he was inducted posthumously into the Naismith Memorial Basketball Hall of Fame.

• There is no collection of papers. Clipping files are in the Naismith Memorial Basketball Hall of Fame, Springfield, Mass., and in the archives of the *Sporting News*, St. Louis, Mo. An obituary is in the *Sporting News*, 14 Oct. 1978.

STEVEN P. GIETSCHIER

JOHNSTON, Olin DeWitt Talmadge (18 Nov. 1896–18 Apr. 1965), politician, was born near Honea Path, South Carolina, the son of Ed Andrew Johnston, a tenant farmer and textile worker, and Leila Webb. Johnston attended local schools but gained another sort of education by working in a local textile mill. Before the outbreak of World War I he attended the Fruitland Institute in Hendersonville, North Carolina, and then the Textile Industrial Institute and Wofford College, both in Spartanburg, South Carolina. During World War I Johnston enlisted in the U.S. Army and served in France with the 117th Engineer Regiment of the Forty-second or Rainbow Division. He gained the rank of sergeant and received a citation for bravery.

After military service, Johnston resumed studies at Wofford and graduated in 1921, after which he entered the University of South Carolina Law School in Columbia. In 1922, while still studying for the bar, Johnston was elected as a Democrat from Anderson County to a term in the South Carolina house of the general assembly. He received a master's degree in 1923 and an LL.B. degree in 1924, specializing in workmen's compensation cases. He married Gladys Elizabeth Atkinson in 1924 in Macon, Georgia; they had three children. In 1927 and again in 1929 Johnston served in the South Carolina House of Representatives from Spartanburg County as a champion of the white working class serving on the judiciary committee. In 1930 he lost his party's gubernatorial nomination by a thousand votes. He was convinced that vote fraud in Charleston County cost him the election. Johnston returned to the practice of law, awaiting another political opportunity.

Four years later Johnston ran for governor and won in the party primary and the general election. Inaugurated as governor in January 1935, at the height of the Great Depression, his four-year term was beset with controversy and confrontation. His decision to order the National Guard to take charge of the state's highway department, which he regarded as graft-filled and opposed to the public's interest in efficient and effective administration, was an inflammatory issue with lasting political repercussions. Although elected as a friend of the upstate working class (the "lintheads"), Johnston found it necessary to call out the National Guard to quell labor/management unrest in the Pelzer community textile mills. His role in suppressing a riot at the state prison in Columbia also alienated many supporters, who believed that he overreacted. However, the enactment of the initial South Carolina Workmen's Compensation Acts was a principal legislative success in Johnston's first term. In addition, as part of the "Little New Deals" implemented nationwide, laws were passed promoting soil conservation, rural electrification, a forty-hour workweek for textile workers, and social security. Johnston's role in nominating President Franklin D. Roosevelt for a second term at the 1936 Democratic convention in Philadelphia demonstrated his support for the administration.

Traditionally, the South Carolina governor's suite is a favorite route to the U.S. Congress. Roosevelt's proverbial coattails were not long enough, however, to enable Johnston to fulfill his aspirations of becoming a U.S. senator. In August 1938 Johnston was defeated in the senatorial primary by veteran incumbent Ellison D. "Cotton Ed" Smith, in spite of Roosevelt's alleged desire to "purge" congressmen unsympathetic to the New Deal. On 16 September 1941 Johnston was defeated by Burnet R. Maybank for the state's other Senate seat made vacant by the appointment of James F. Byrnes to the U.S. Supreme Court. Undaunted, Johnston adjusted his timetable by returning to the governor's mansion. Even though there was a constitutional prohibition against reelection to the office, the language was construed only to prohibit successive terms. Johnston defeated Wyndham M. Manning on 25 August 1942. Johnston's second gubernatorial term was more conciliatory, in the spirit of winning the war abroad and resolving differences among personalities within the party, most notably those involving the state house "Barnwell ring" headed by state senator Edgar A. Brown and house Speaker Solomon Blatt. The most noteworthy legislative event in Johnston's truncated term was a special session to preserve the whites-only primary within the Democratic party. Johnston's constructive actions over the next two years, including his support for the Fair Labor Standards Act, provided the platform for his successful challenge to Cotton Ed Smith in the 25 July 1944 senatorial primary. When Johnston stood for reelection in 1950, he defeated J. Strom Thurmond in the latter's first attempt to enter the Senate. In 1956 Johnston ran virtually unopposed, and in 1962 he ran successfully against Ernest F. "Fritz" Hollings in the primary and against Republican William Workman in the November election.

Despite the length of Johnston's tenure in the U.S. Senate, and even though he served as chairman of the Post Office and Civil Service Committee when there were Democratic majorities, no legislation bears his name. Nevertheless, he had impact as a loyal proponent and oftentimes a constructive critic of measures primarily concerned with economic growth for the New South. In the immediate postwar years Johnston supported President Harry S. Truman's domestic policies, especially those favorable to labor. He opposed foreign aid proposals, such as the Marshall Plan, and proposals favorable to civil rights. Although a critic of the Eisenhower years, especially the civil rights and desegregation orders of the Supreme Court, Johnston did not join his colleague Thurmond's efforts to filibuster the legislative consequences of the Court actions. Except for civil rights measures, the liberal features of Kennedy's "New Frontier" and Johnson's "Great Society" met with Johnston's approval. The Charleston *News and Courier* (12 July 1944) described Johnston as a "Jim Crow New Dealer" for his straddling of liberal and conservative positions on national social issues relating to race relations. He died in Columbia.

As a strong-willed spokesperson for the white blue-collar worker over a forty-year period, Johnston supported many of the economic and social advances spawned by the New Deal era. However, his continual reliance on race baiting as a vehicle to gain and retain political power showed the limits of his reformism. Like many southern liberals of his era, Johnston failed to promote a more enlightened climate for race relations.

• Johnston's papers are in the Caroliniana Collection at the University of South Carolina in Columbia. See a sympathetic campaign biography by John E. Huss, *Senator for the South: A Biography of Olin D. Johnston* (1961); Jo Ann Deakin Carpenter, "Olin D. Johnston, The New Deal and the Politics of Class in South Carolina, 1934–1938" (Ph.D. diss., Emory Univ., 1987); and Anthony Barry Miller, "Palmetto Politician: The Early Political Career of Olin D. Johnston, 1896–1945" (Ph.D. diss., Univ. of North Carolina at Chapel Hill, 1976). Contemporary articles include Henry Steele Commager, "A South Carolina Dictator," *Current History* 43 (Mar. 1936): 568–72, on Johnston and the Highway Commission crisis; and Jasper B. Shannon, "Presidential Politics in the South: 1938," *Journal of Politics* 1 (Aug. 1939): 286–90, on Johnston's South Carolina senatorial campaign. For historical treatment, consult Jay Bender, "Olin D. Johnston and the Highway Controversy," South Carolina Historical Association, *Proceedings* (1972), pp. 39–54; John E. Borsos, "Support for the National Democratic Party in South Carolina during the Dixiecrat Revolt of 1948," *Southern Historian* 9 (1988): 7–21; Roger P. Leemhuis, "Olin Johnston Runs for the Senate, 1938 to 1962," South Carolina Historical Associa-

tion, *Proceedings* (1986), pp. 57–69; and Bryant Simon, "When Votes Don't Add Up: Labor Politics and South Carolina Workman's Compensation Acts, 1934–1938," South Carolina Historical Association, *Proceedings* (1991), pp. 69–74. Also deserving attention are Marvin Leigh Cann, "Burnet Rhett Maybank and the New Deal, 1933–1941" (Ph.D. diss., Univ. of North Carolina, 1969); John K. Cauthen, *Speaker Blatt: His Challenges Were Greater* (1965); Daniel W. Hollis, "'Cotton Ed' Smith—Showman or Statesman?," *South Carolina Historical Magazine* 71 (Oct. 1970): 235–56; and William D. Workman, *The Bishop from Barnwell, The Political Life and Times of Senator Edgar Allen Brown* (1963). See also Howard H. Quint, *Profile in Black and White: A Frank Portrait of South Carolina* (1958). An obituary is in the *New York Times*, 19 Apr. 1965.

ROBERT A. WALLER

JOHNSTON, Peter (6 Jan. 1763–8 Dec. 1831), jurist, legislator, and soldier, was born at Osborne's Landing on the James River, Virginia, the son of Peter Johnston, a merchant and farmer, and Martha Rogers. At two years of age Johnston moved with his parents to a large farm in Prince Edward County, Virginia, where he was educated by tutors before enrolling in Hampden-Sydney College (established on land donated by Johnston's father). In late 1779, in a decision that displeased his Loyalist father, Johnston quit college to join the cavalry legion of Lieutenant Colonel Henry Lee. Exhibiting great courage and a taste for battle, Johnston distinguished himself at the battles of Wright's Bluff, Guilford Court House, Eutaw Springs, and Ninety-Six. In 1782 he left Lee's legion to become adjutant and captain of the Light Corps, which had been established by General Nathanael Greene. At the conclusion of the war, the Virginia legislature commissioned him brigadier general of the militia, a confirmation of his great talents as a soldier. Johnston served actively in the Virginia chapter of the Society of the Cincinnati, a postwar organization of former officers of the American revolutionary army.

At war's end Johnston began the study of law, a decision that helped reconcile him with his father. Upon the completion of his studies he established a successful law practice in Prince Edward County and its environs. He also became an active politician, joining the Republican party and serving in the state legislature almost continuously from 1792 to 1811. As a legislator, in 1798 he helped lead the fight against the Alien and Sedition Acts and ardently championed the Virginia Resolutions that denounced the acts as a violation of the Constitution. He also served as Speaker of the state house of delegates from 1805 to 1807. In 1802 he was one of three Virginians on the joint commission to settle a boundary dispute with Tennessee.

In 1811 Johnston resigned from the legislature after that body elected him a judge of the General Court of Virginia, on which he served until a few months before his death. Comprised of fifteen judges, the general court was the court of last resort for appeals from criminal convictions and heard suits against public creditors, served as a probate court, tried impeachments, and ruled on certain questions of civil law. Each member also served as a judge of one of the circuit courts, the principal trial courts of Virginia. Johnston's circuit encompassed the southwestern corner of the commonwealth. None of Johnston's circuit court opinions has been preserved, and those few published decisions of the general court in which he participated involve only routine cases.

In 1788 Johnston married Mary Wood, a niece of Patrick Henry; they had ten children, the most celebrated of whom was Joseph Eggleston Johnston, a leading general in the Confederate army. Mary Wood died in 1825, and in 1828 he married Anne Bernard. They had no children. Johnston inherited his father's farm in Prince Edward County but shortly after his judicial appointment moved to the outskirts of Abingdon, where he had purchased a large estate. He died at his home.

• No biography of Johnston or corpus of his papers exists. Edgar Erskine Hume, "Peter Johnston, Junior: Virginia Soldier and Jurist," *Southern Sketches*, no. 4 (1935), is the most complete account of his life. Gilbert E. Govan and James W. Livingood's *A Different Valor: The Story of General Joseph E. Johnston, C.S.A.* (1956), pp. 12–14, provides a useful sketch, and discussion of some of Johnston's military exploits may be found in Alexander Garden's *Anecdotes of the Revolutionary War in America* (1822). The *Virginia Reports Annotated* contain some of the cases decided by the General Court of Virginia during Johnston's tenure and a sketch (vol. 2, pp. 101–6) of the jurisdiction of the court. An obituary is in the *Richmond Enquirer*, 20 Dec. 1831.

ROBERT M. IRELAND

JOHNSTON, Richard Malcolm (8 Mar. 1822–23 Sept. 1898), educator and writer, was born near Powelton, in Hancock County, Georgia, the son of Malcolm Johnston, a planter and preacher, and Catherine Smith Davenport. A member of the first graduating class of Mercer University (1841), Johnston conducted a rural school in Mt. Zion before studying law under prominent attorneys in Augusta. He was admitted to the Georgia bar in 1843 and, returning to Hancock County, alternated between the occupations of schoolmaster and lawyer. In 1844 he married Mary Frances Mansfield of Sparta, Georgia. Their marriage, which produced twelve children, ended with her death in 1897.

In 1857 Johnston was almost simultaneously offered three positions: an initial executive appointment with assured legislative election as a circuit judge; the presidency of Mercer University by that institution's board of trustees; and the state college's new professorship of belles lettres and oratory by the University of Georgia board of trustees. He accepted the professorship, an appointment he held for four years, during which he pioneered the college teaching of English literature and wrote a nationally distributed textbook, *The English Classics* (1860). He returned to Hancock County in 1861 to open Rockby, a select boarding school for boys. The school gained a high reputation in the state because of Johnston's gentlemanly, and comparatively very liberal and humane, system of instruction and discipline. Ultimately appointed a staff member to

Governor Joseph Emerson Brown during the Civil War, Johnston saw no actual military service; indeed, he may have run his greatest risks after the war when he helped friends who were former Confederate government officials conceal themselves and escape. In 1867, leaving Reconstruction Georgia and moving near Baltimore, Maryland, he established another school, Pen Lucy, which operated until 1883.

Always a thoughtful, religious person—he was raised a Baptist and later joined the Episcopal Church—Johnston shocked many of his acquaintances when, following his wife's lead, he became a Roman Catholic in 1875. Partly because this conversion resulted in reduced school revenues, he began writing fiction for money and from the early 1880s until the mid-1890s enjoyed considerable success as a national literary figure. Although he had published his first story in 1857 and had his short fiction collected in three earlier volumes—*Georgia Sketches* (1864) and *Dukesborough Tales* (1871 and 1874)—Johnston was widely believed to be a promising new young writer when Harper & Brothers brought out another *Dukesborough Tales* collection in 1883. All depicting the Middle Georgia characters and community life he knew so well, Johnston's "local color" stories appeared first in such national magazines as *Scribner's*, *Harper's*, and *Century* and then were collected in books: *Mr. Absalom Billingslea and Other Georgia Folk* (1888), *The Primes and Their Neighbors* (1891), *Dukesborough Tales: The Chronicles of Mr. Bill Williams* (1892), *Mr. Billy Downs and His Likes* (1892), *Mr. Fortner's Marital Claims and Other Stories* (1892), *Little Ike Templin and Other Stories* (1894), and *Old Times in Middle Georgia* (1897). Four novels and several works of nonfiction, also published during this period, were less successful. The stories in the *Dukesborough* collections were Johnston's most popular and are generally regarded as both typical and the best of his literary work.

Considering himself serious and scholarly, Johnston came to lament his extensive reputation as a humorous storyteller. Seen by family and friends as the charming embodiment of the Old South plantation gentleman, he is viewed by literary historians as a revealing transitional figure between earlier realistic "Old Southwest humor" and the more romantic, local-color humorous fiction of the late nineteenth century. Although his range was limited and he sometimes wrote over-fondly about the past, Johnston was able through his characters to re-create a culture and way of life that readers may still find informative, entertaining, and sometimes moving.

"I did not like the idea," Johnston wrote in his *Autobiography* (1900), "of continuing at story telling down to the very grave." Finding himself in demand for public appearances after he was sixty years old, he read from his own works and lectured on world literature. Later, beginning in 1895, he secured federal government appointments in Washington, D.C., working first in the Labor Department and then in the U.S. Bureau of Education. He died in Baltimore.

• The three largest, most important collections of Johnston papers are the R. M. Johnston collections at the Enoch Pratt Free Library in Baltimore and the Georgia Historical Society in Savannah, and the Alexander H. Stephens Papers in the Library of Congress. Other materials, primarily letters, may be found in manuscript holdings at Duke University, Emory University, Trinity College, Columbia University, Indiana University, and the New York Public Library. Johnston published four novels: *Old Mark Langston* (1884), *Ogeechee Cross-Firings* (1889), *Widow Guthrie* (1890), and *Pearce Amerson's Will* (1898). His nonfiction books include (with William Hand Browne) *Life of Alexander H. Stephens* (1878), *Two Gray Tourists* (1885), *Studies, Literary and Social* (1891, 1892), *Lectures on Literature* (1897), and *Autobiography of Colonel Richard Malcolm Johnston* (1900). A biographical-critical study of Johnston and his writings is Bert Hitchcock, *Richard Malcolm Johnston* (1978).

BERT HITCHCOCK

JOHNSTON, Samuel (15 Dec. 1733–17 Aug. 1816), North Carolina governor and U.S. senator, was born in Dundee, Scotland, the son of Samuel Johnston and Helen Scrymsoure (occupations unknown). He was the nephew of Gabriel Johnston, royal governor of North Carolina (1734–1752), and it was under the auspices of his uncle that Johnston's family emigrated to the colony in 1735, settling in Onslow County. The younger Johnston attended Yale and completed his education after moving to Edenton in 1753 by reading law with attorney Thomas Barker. A nearly half century of public service began with his appointment as clerk of court for the Edenton district in 1755. He received his attorney's license the following year. Elected to the lower house of the general assembly from Chowan County in 1759, he served continuously until 1775 when the Revolution intervened. He also served as Deputy Naval Officer of the Port of Edenton 1770–1775.

As his public stature increased he purchased a plantation, which he named "Hayes," in 1765 on the outskirts of Edenton. In 1770 Johnston married Frances Cathcart; they had nine children, of whom four survived childhood. A member of the Anglican church, Johnston served on the vestry of St. Paul's parish (1767–1776) and was church warden (1768–1770).

Johnston was involved from the outset in the revolutionary movement, which he saw as defending constitutional rights being usurped by the Crown and Parliament. Yet he consistently opposed radical measures that overstepped law in the name of liberty. In North Carolina's War of the Regulation (1765–1771), a back-country rebellion against eastern political domination and corrupt local government, Johnston viewed the Regulators as illegally challenging government authority, but he simultaneously sought redress of their grievances through legislative reform. Although Johnston sponsored the draconian "Bloody Riot Act" or "Johnston Act," which required the death penalty for illegal assembly, obstruction of justice, destruction of property, and refusal to answer a court summons, he also worked to secure laws establishing fees for public

officials and regulating the corruption-ridden county sheriffs.

Within two years he was swept into the revolutionary movement by his appointment to the general assembly's Committee of Correspondence, which included the core of the future revolutionary leadership. As royal authority crumbled throughout the province, local government was represented by town and county committees of safety, and the general assembly was superseded by Provincial Congresses. The royal governor's flight resulted in the appointment of a Provincial Council. Elected to the First and Second Provincial Congresses in 1774 and 1775, Johnston brought experience and status, which were recognized by his designation to convene another congress if the ailing moderator, John Harvey, was unable to do so. Following Harvey's death in May 1775, Johnston called a third congress in August 1775 and was elected its president. This congress named Johnston the treasurer of the province's northern district, and he was elected to the Provincial Council, which assumed the executive authority of the province. For several months in 1775 Johnston, as president of the congress and in the absence of the royal governor, had been the chief executive of the province. He again presided at the Fourth Provincial Congress in April 1776, which approved the Halifax Resolves, setting North Carolina firmly on the road toward independence.

While Johnston's "dignified appearance and Olympian attitude" satisfied his aristocratic peers, he was too remote for the more radical element in the revolutionary leadership who defeated him when he sought reelection to the fifth congress in the fall of 1776. In his capacity as provincial treasurer of the northern district, he attended the congress and was consulted by the committee that drafted the new state's constitution. His rejection by the electorate led to his temporary retirement from public life, but in 1779 he was elected state senator from Chowan County. In April 1780 he was chosen as a delegate to the Continental Congress, although ill health prevented him from traveling to Philadelphia until the end of the year. A few days after his reelection to Congress in June 1781 he was chosen to be president of the Continental Congress, but he declined, citing his health, family, and business affairs. At home in 1782 he was again elected to the state senate, serving 1783–1784. The contacts made in Congress led to his appointment in 1785 to the commission to settle the boundary between New York and Massachusetts.

In the crucial period of the consideration and ratification of the U.S. Constitution, Johnston was elected to three terms as governor (1787–1789). He also became North Carolina's first Masonic Grand Master (1787) and was in 1789 named a trustee of the newly chartered state university. Despite the fact that the first convention in Hillsborough in 1788 was dominated by the anti-Federalists, Johnston, a Federalist, was chosen to preside; he again presided over the second convention in Fayetteville in 1789 that ratified the Constitution. Throughout the ratification controversy,

Johnston was committed to the Constitution, which to him represented the stability of a strong central government that the country needed to survive. After ratification Johnston was elected one of the first U.S. senators of the new state and had to resign as governor. He drew the short term 1789–1793, after which he retired from the Senate. In the Senate Johnston generally favored Hamilton's fiscal program except for the assumption of state debts. His enthusiasm for the Bank of the United States led to his appointment to the first board of directors when the bank was chartered. His last public service was as a Superior Court judge from 1800 to 1813. His remaining years were taken up with his family, especially after the death of his wife in 1801, and with the management of his various plantations. He resided some years at the "Hermitage" in Martin County and died at Hayes in Chowan County.

Johnston was a dominant political figure of the revolutionary and early republican eras, ably filling virtually every civilian office the state could bestow. An earlier biographer, Griffith J. McRee, wrote of him that he "commanded the respect and admiration but not the love of the people." He was a staunch defender of constitutional liberty both as an English colonial and as an American, following his conscience and never seeking popular approval.

• The correspondence of Samuel Johnston is located primarily in the extensive Hayes collection, Southern Historical Collection, University of North Carolina Library, Chapel Hill. Additional letters are found in the Charles E. Johnston Collection and the Samuel Johnston Papers in the North Carolina State Archives, Raleigh; and in the James Iredell Collection, Duke University Library. Letters and papers of Johnston have been published in William L. Saunders, ed., *The Colonial Records of North Carolina*, vols. 6–10 (1888–1890); Walter J. Clark, ed., *The State Records of North Carolina*, vols. 11–25 (1895–1906); Don Higginbotham, ed., *The Papers of James Iredell* (2 vols., 1976); and Griffith J. McRee, ed., *Life and Correspondence of James Iredell* (2 vols., 1857). Biographical and background information is in Samuel A. Ashe, ed., *Biographical History of North Carolina*, vol. 4 (1906); Robert D. W. Conner, *Revolutionary Leaders of North Carolina* (1916); and Robert L. Ganyard, *The Emergence of North Carolina's Revolutionary State Government* (1978).

LINDLEY S. BUTLER

JOHNSTON, Thomas (1708?–8 May 1767), was a prominent engraver, organ builder, and decorative painter. His parentage and place of birth are unknown. Several artists and artisans named Thomas Johnston (or the variant Johnson) were active in eighteenth-century America and England, and early references sometimes confuse them. Nevertheless, his is one of the better-documented careers among craftsmen of colonial Boston.

Johnston's first appearance in documents shows he joined Boston's Brattle Street Church (Puritan) on 5 June 1726 and that on 22 June 1730 he married Rachel Thwing, with whom he had eight children; five survived. In 1742 he purchased property on the west side of Brattle Street and moved his commercial engraving and decorative painting business to a shop behind the house. His wife died about 1746, and on 7 August 1747 he married her cousin Bathsheba Thwing, with whom he had three more children.

The earliest certain documentation of Johnston's professional activity is a 1728 map of Boston, after William Burgis, bearing the indication "Engraven by Thos. Iohnson Boston N.E." His activity as an engraver continued throughout the remainder of his career, and some three dozen works have been proven to be his or confidently attributed to him. These include nearly every type of printing that could not be readily done in movable type, such as music, bookplates, and certificates. Best known and most prized are the maps. Notable in addition to the 1728 map of Boston are the large *Chart of Canada River from ye Island of Anticosty as Far Up as Quebeck* (1746), a map of the Kennebec River titled *A True Coppy from an Ancient Plan of E. Hutchinson's* (1753), the *Plan of Kennebeck & Sagadahock Rivers, and Country Adjacent* (1754), Timothy Clement's *Plan of Hudson River from Albany to Fort Edward* (1756), and *Quebec, the Capital of New-France* (1759). Particularly important then and now is Johnston's engraving of Samuel Blodgett's *A Prospective Plan of the Battle Fought near Lake George*, issued 22 December 1755. Both a map and a pictorial representation of the great clash earlier that year, it has been called America's first historical print. Some of these maps he continued to stock and sell well after their initial publication.

Johnston's music printing business was particularly lucrative. In 1753 the Brattle Street Church undertook a revision of its text-only metrical psalter, and Johnston served on the committee created for that purpose. To any such psalm book, such as Nicholas Brady and Nahum Tate's *A New Version of the Psalms of David*, could be and was appended Johnston's sixteen-page collection of tunes. In three or four vocal parts, the songs were introduced by a one-page summary of the fundamentals of music beginning with "To Learn to Sing, Observe these Rules" (often taken as a title for the entire collection). This publication was sufficiently popular to be reengraved by Johnston at least four times, and he was careful to will the plates to his wife. In 1760 and 1764 he republished Thomas Walter's *The Grounds and Rules of Musick Explained*, and in 1766 he issued his new engraving of Daniel Bayley's *A New and Compleat Introduction to the Grounds and Rules of Musick*. Johnston was not just a printer of music; he was also a performer. Records show that he was a paid singer at the Brattle Street Church in 1739 and at King's Chapel (Anglican) in 1754 and 1756.

His craft skills and knowledge of church music led him to undertake the maintenance, and in 1752 the rebuilding, of the organ at Christ (Old North) Church. Soon he was asked to replace it with a new instrument. Influenced by the new English organ at King's Chapel, Johnston's organ was completed in 1759 and was in use until 1821, when a new instrument was installed in the old case. He also built an organ for St. Peter's Church, Salem, which was later moved to St. Michael's at Marblehead; its nameboard had an ivory plaque (lost c. 1889) inscribed "Thomas Johnston Fecit, Boston: Nov-Anglorum 1754." At about the same time, he provided an instrument for the Deblois's Concert Hall in Boston; in 1771 it was transferred to King's (now St. John's) Church, Providence, where it served until 1851. An organ of his manufacture seems to have been in use in Queen's Chapel (now St. John's Church), Portsmouth, New Hampshire, until 1805. Unfinished organs were listed in the inventory of his estate at the time of his death. His instruments were modest in size and ordinary in specification but important as products of the first professional organ builder of Boston.

Attesting to Johnston's work as a decorative painter is his trade card of 1732, which offers "Coach, Chaise, or Sighn [sic] Painting at Reasonable Rates" as well as "Japan Work of All Sorts." Boston was very much the center of japanning in colonial America, and Johnston was unusual in being a financially successful practitioner of this popular art of decorating furniture with pseudo-Asian motifs on black paint and varnish meant to imitate lacquer. Such works were typically not signed, and no document links Johnston with any specific surviving example. Despite the lack of work known to be from his shop, he is considered to be the principal japanner of Boston during his lifetime, and fine works such as the suite of high chest of drawers, dressing table, and mirror at the Metropolitan Museum of Art have been cited as possible examples of his decorative painting.

The records of several lawsuits and the inventory of his estate reflect the diverse nature of Johnston's business. He died of apoplexy in Boston and was buried in the King's Chapel churchyard, suggesting he had joined the Anglican church. Aside from his own works, his legacy includes the training of several persons who were active variously in music, engraving, painting, and the decorative arts. They include sons Thomas, Jr., William, Benjamin, John, and Samuel; son-in-law Daniel Rea, Jr.; and apprentice John Greenwood.

• An overall summary of Johnston's life is Frederick Coburn, "The Johnstons of Boston: Part One: Thomas Johnston," *Art in America* 21 (Dec. 1932): 27–36. Several valuable publications deal with specific facets of his career. On engraving, see Sinclair Hitchings, "Thomas Johnston," in *Publications of the Colonial Society of Massachusetts*, vol. 46: *Boston Prints and Printmakers 1670–1775* (1973); and Richard Wolfe, *Early American Music Engraving and Printing* (1980). Information about his organ building is in Barbara Owen, *The Organ in New England* (1979). Johnston's japanning is discussed in Morrison Heckscher et al., "Boston Japanned furniture in the Metropolitan Museum of Art," *Antiques* 129 (May 1986): 1046–61; Hitchings, "Boston's Colonial Japanners: The Documentary Record," in *Publications of the Colonial Society of Massachusetts*, vol. 48: *Boston Furniture of the Eighteenth Century* (1974); Esther Brazer, "The Early Boston Japanners," *Antiques* 43 (May 1943): 208–11; and Joseph Downs, "American Japanned Furniture," *Bulletin of the Metropolitan Museum of Art* 28 (Mar. 1933): 42–48.

RONALD D. RARICK

JOHNSTON, Wayne Andrew (19 Nov. 1897–5 Dec. 1967), railroad executive, was born in Philo, Illinois, the son of Harry W. Johnston, a farmer and grain elevator operator, and DeEtta Bird Boomer. His father died when Wayne was two years old, and his mother returned to teaching school to support her family. After attending grade school in Philo and high school in Champaign, Illinois, Johnston studied railway administration at the University of Illinois. He worked his way through college by waiting tables, washing dishes, and being a janitor at a sorority. Receiving his B.S. in 1918, Johnston learned he was disqualified for military service in World War I for physical reasons.

Johnston went to work for the Illinois Central Railroad (IC) in October 1919 as an accountant in the office of the division superintendent at Champaign. A year later he moved to company headquarters in Chicago as assistant chief clerk to the general superintendent of northern lines. In 1922 Johnston married Blanche Lawson, a former fellow worker at Champaign. The couple settled in a Chicago residential community, where they raised a son and a daughter.

Johnston had diversified experience as he progressed in the Chicago headquarters of the IC. He was correspondent clerk to the vice president and general manager from 1925 to 1934. In 1934 Johnston transferred to the traffic department as office manager to the vice president. Later he became general agent for mail, baggage, express, and merchandise traffic. He returned to the operating department in 1935 as assistant to the vice president and general manager. In 1940 Johnston was acting superintendent of the Kentucky Division; he became assistant general manager in 1942. During the war he directed a program training sixteen- and seventeen-year-old boys for railroad jobs. In September 1944 Johnston was made general manager of the Illinois Central. Even though located in Chicago, some years saw Johnston out on the road 200 days. He knew hundreds of key people in the IC system.

Johnston became president of the Illinois Central in February 1945, shortly after the sudden death of IC president John L. Beven. He was the first Illinois native to become president and several years younger than his six top subordinates. Johnston was a great believer in team effort, and his first concern was the welfare of the "Illinois Central family." Johnston inherited a strong railroad from his predecessors. The Great Depression had brought the IC to the brink of receivership, with big declines in both revenue and workforce. But the years 1939 to 1944 had seen big gains in freight and passenger traffic. War prosperity had allowed Beven to cut the funded debt by $100 million. Johnston continued this debt reduction program, cutting the IC funded debt from $282 million in 1945 to $206 million by the end of 1951. During the same years Johnston simplified the debt structure and reduced the average interest rates.

With the war over, the Illinois Central and other major railroads celebrated by holding the Chicago Railroad Fair in the summers of 1948 and 1949. Postwar optimism was in the air. Illinois Central shareholders also had much to celebrate when Johnston resumed dividends on the preferred stock in 1948 and paid a three dollar dividend to common shareholders in 1950, the first dividend since 1931. In 1951 Johnston led the IC celebration of the centennial of the road's founding in 1851. Special events were held in all thirteen operating divisions in fourteen states. At the formal banquet at the Chicago Palmer House, observers recalled how Johnston was able to greet almost every guest using his first name. A major centennial project was the completion of a new $6 million bridge to span the Ohio River at Cairo, Illinois.

During Johnston's presidency only 100 miles were added to the 6,500-mile system. In the same years, Johnston directed the spending of over $500 million on capital improvements—nearly $200 million on fixed property and over $300 million on new equipment. Fixed-property improvements included new bridges, heavier and often welded rail, additional sidings, and new or enlarged freight yards in Chicago, East St. Louis, Memphis, and New Orleans. Improved signals, centralized traffic control (CTC), and new radio communication systems were added in all divisions. But the president spent far more on new equipment, much of it financed by equipment trusts rather than bonds. (Expensive equipment was often paid off in equal annual payments over a period of years to holders of equipment trusts.) Not long after the war ended the IC spent several million dollars for new streamliners for long-distance passenger runs. In 1946 Johnston ordered 1,900 new freight cars, in 1955 longer flat cars for the new piggyback service were acquired, and in the 1960s new rack cars were secured for new automobile delivery. A major share of the new equipment money went for new diesels, which cost from $150,000 to $250,000 per unit. When Johnston became president, steam engines made up 96 percent of the motive power roster. By 1961 the shift to diesel power was completed, a somewhat later date than for most railroads because nearly half of IC freight tonnage was coal.

The many improvements allowed a reduction in the labor force from 41,000 to 22,000 during Johnston's years. Also during this period the average annual wage rose from $2,500 to $7,000, an increase well above the inflation rate. In the same years the share of IC revenue going to labor climbed from 42 percent to 56 percent. Johnston joined other railroad presidents in arguing against excessive regulation, train crew featherbedding (padding wages based on out-of-date work rules), and the use of (unnecessary) firemen in freight diesels. Johnston pointed out that the fireman's shovel was an "expensive antique." By the 1960s all railroads were in a desperate fight for traffic with truckers, pipelines, barges, buses, airliners, and private automobiles. Some railroads sought a solution through mergers while others turned to diversification. In 1963 the IC became a leader in diversification when it created a holding company, Illinois Central Industries, which owned not only the IC Railroad but also lakefront air

rights in Chicago and a St. Louis electric company. Johnston resigned the presidency of Illinois Central Industries early in 1966, after being elected board chairman. His long service in IC leadership were years of extensive debt retirement and dieselization, of resumed dividends, and the introduction of diversification.

Wayne Johnston had a leading role in many nonrailroad activities. Both he and Blanche Johnston were active in the religious life of Chicago. Johnston also was busy with the Chicago Boy Scout Council and received every adult service award. In Chicago he supported the Young Men's Christian Association, the Child Care Society, and the Old People's Home. He was a member of the board of trustees of the University of Illinois and De Pauw University. In 1963 he was awarded the Horatio Alger Award of the American Schools and Colleges Association. Johnston died suddenly in his home in suburban Flossmoor only a week after retiring as chairman of the board.

• The early years of Johnston's career with the Illinois Central are reviewed in Carlton J. Corliss, *Main Line of Mid-America: The Story of the Illinois Central* (1950). George M. Crowson, *A Lifetime of Service: Wayne Johnston and the Illinois Central Railroad* (1968), is a brief biography written shortly after Johnston's death. For a review of Johnston's railroad years see John F. Stover, *History of the Illinois Central Railroad* (1975). Obituaries are in the *Illinois Central Magazine*, Dec. 1967, and the *New York Times*, 6 Dec. 1967.

JOHN F. STOVER

JOHNSTON, William Hugh (30 Dec. 1874–26 Mar. 1937), labor leader, was born in Westville, Nova Scotia, the son of Adam Johnston, a carpenter, and Jane Murray. Johnston moved with his family to Rhode Island in 1885. At age fourteen he entered an apprenticeship as a machinist at the Rhode Island Locomotive Works. He worked for the company for about a year after completing his training and then pursued his trade with a number of other New England firms, including the Builders Iron Foundry and the New York, Providence, and Boston Railroad. While employed at the Jencks Manufacturing Company in Pawtucket, Rhode Island, in 1895–1897 he helped to develop an improved automatic knitting machine.

When he first started working, Johnston joined the Knights of Labor, a reform-oriented union that welcomed workers of every trade and skill level. In 1895 he helped to organize a local of the International Association of Machinists (IAM) at Jencks. A few years later, while working at the Rhode Island Locomotive Company in Providence, he was offered a promotion to foreman, but he declined the offer because it would have required him to give up his union membership. Johnston was elected president of his local in 1901 and served three terms as business agent between 1906 and 1909. During these years he became more active in IAM affairs, representing his local at the national convention in 1905, being elected president of the New England district that year, and in 1909 being elected president and general organizer of District 44, a unit covering all machinists who worked for the federal government. He also joined the Socialist party, though the precise date is not known. He married Harriet L. Lunn in 1907; they had no children.

Johnston's rise within the IAM climaxed in 1911 when he defeated incumbent James O'Connell for the union presidency. The election of Johnston, a socialist, represented a victory for the IAM progressives, who had long opposed O'Connell's conservative policies. Their cause had been strengthened by the collapse in 1901 of the Murray Hill Agreement that O'Connell had negotiated with the leading employers association, but Johnston and his allies had broader complaints. They rejected the whole philosophy of apolitical "pure and simple unionism" espoused by O'Connell and by the American Federation of Labor (AFL) head Samuel Gompers. Instead, they argued that unions should act politically as well as economically and should encourage government action on behalf of workers. Further defying established labor policies, Johnston spoke out vigorously at AFL conventions on behalf of industrial unionism, maintaining that workers should be organized by industry, including both the skilled and unskilled, rather than limiting each union to the skilled members of one craft. In 1912, at the peak of socialist influence within the AFL, Johnston ran a creditable race against O'Connell for third vice president of the AFL, receiving about 6,000 votes to O'Connell's 10,000. He did less well in 1913, however, and in 1914 he himself nominated O'Connell for reelection.

In the bitter division among socialists over the entry of the United States into World War I, Johnston sided with those supporting the country's involvement. He even joined his old opponent Gompers in helping to suppress a munitions workers' strike in 1915. He also served on the National War Labor Board (1917–1919) and traveled to Europe with Gompers and other labor leaders in 1918 to rally workers there to the Allied cause. Johnston maintained his progressive political orientation, however, and in 1919 played a leading role in the American Labor Alliance for Trade Relations with Russia. He also tried to move the United States closer to public ownership of utilities by helping to organize the Plumb Plan League. This group urged that the federal government, which had taken over the nation's railroads during the war, buy the original owners out and operate the roads itself through a committee of railroad officials and employee representatives. Johnston also joined labor leaders from all points on the political spectrum in petitioning for the release of persons imprisoned during the war under the Espionage Act.

Johnston's long interest in political action by labor bore fruit when his formidable support helped pave the way for the organization in 1922 of the Conference for Progressive Political Action (CPPA), a coalition of agrarians, socialists, and progressive labor leaders. Though Johnston was one of only two socialists on the CPPA executive committee, he was chosen as its chair. The CPPA initially opposed creating a third party, but

after successful campaigns on behalf of several candidates in 1922, some members went on to establish the Progressive party in 1924. Johnston officiated at the new party's convention, where Senator Robert M. La Follette was nominated for president. The AFL endorsed La Follette, but it provided him with only modest support. He won 17 percent of the popular vote, carrying only one state.

In the years after World War I Johnston fought vigorously against radical groups like the Industrial Workers of the World, which he saw as divisive and undisciplined. Those who sympathized with such organizations, he said, had "no place" in the IAM; under his leadership several lodges purged their radical members. Ironically, Johnston's continuing effort to win AFL approval for industrial unions led him to be accused by one official of trying to "bring Russia over here." But in fact he was working hard to defeat radical—and particularly communist—influence in the labor movement. By the mid-1920s these positions had turned many IAM radicals against him, while other members blamed him for the union's declining membership, for the failure of a number of union business ventures, and for an unpopular plan to involve workers in cost-saving efforts by the Baltimore & Ohio Railroad. Johnston managed to win reelection in 1925 after a hard fight, but the following year he suffered a stroke that forced him to resign. He served for a time as vice president of the Mount Vernon Savings Bank, and he worked in the IAM headquarters 1933–1936, but he held no more elective offices. He died at his home in Washington, D.C.

Johnston's career illuminates the strengths and weaknesses of the moderate left in the American labor movement during the generation before the New Deal. His union broke little new ground, and he achieved hardly any of his reform goals for the AFL, but he remained a progressive voice within the mainstream, persistently keeping alive the ideas of industrial unionism, social legislation, and political action—ideas that would catch fire in the 1930s.

• For information on Johnston's life and career see Gary Fink, *Labor Unions* (1977); Mark Perlman, *The Machinists: A New Study in American Trade Unionism* (1961); John H. M. Laslett, *Labor and the Left: A Study of Socialism and Radical Influences in the American Labor Movement, 1881–1924* (1970); Bernard Mandel, *Samuel Gompers: A Biography* (1963); David Shannon, *The Socialist Party of America* (1955); Ira Kipnis, *The American Socialist Movement, 1897–1912* (1952); David Montgomery, *The Fall of the House of Labor* (1987); and Marc Karson, *American Labor Unions and Politics, 1900–1918* (1958). An obituary is in the *New York Times*, 28 Mar. 1937.

SANDRA OPDYCKE

JOHNSTON, William M. (2 Nov. 1894–1 May 1946), tennis player, was born in San Francisco, California, the son of Robert Johnston, an electric plant mechanic, and Margaret Burns. Johnston disliked his French-sounding middle name and never revealed it publicly. He played tennis first in 1905; when schools remained shut for several months following the San Francisco earthquake of 1906, he played constantly. For the next few years Johnston, Johnny Strachan, Roland Roberts, Ely Fottrell, Clarence "Peck" Griffin, and other talented juniors improved their tennis skills and were coached by nationally famous players Maurice McLoughlin and Mel Long on asphalt courts at Golden Gate Park. Johnston played in schoolboy tournaments while attending Crocker Grammar School, San Francisco Polytechnic High School, and Lowell High School, from which he graduated in 1913. He gained attention by taking a set from McLoughlin before losing to him at the 1911 Pacific Coast championship.

In 1912 Johnston won five tournaments, including the state titles of California, Oregon, and Washington. That same year he ranked third among Pacific Coast players behind McLoughlin and Long, and he won four doubles events with Fottrell. He scored his first major triumph by defeating Roberts, Strachan, and Fottrell to capture the 1913 Pacific Coast title, which prompted the California Lawn Tennis Association to send him as its representative to take part in eastern grass court tournaments. In 1913 he won the prestigious Longwood Bowl meeting. He played well elsewhere, reaching the fourth round of U.S. title play at Newport, Rhode Island, before losing a spirited match to Dick Williams, the ultimate champion. He became fourth-ranked nationally. Although he won several tournaments in 1914, he again lost to Williams at the nationals, and his ranking dropped to sixth.

Throughout his tennis career Johnston entered several West Coast tournaments on cement and asphalt courts through June each year, then journeyed to play in important eastern grass court competitions. He followed this schedule in 1915 with modestly successful results until the nationals at Forest Hills, New York, where, even with the unseeded draw randomly stacked against him, he prevailed over Harold Hackett, Karl Behr, Griffin, Williams, and McLoughlin to secure his first U.S. title. Williams took the championship back in 1916, reducing Johnston almost to exhaustion by the end of the five-set final. Johnston enlisted in the U.S. Navy in mid-1917 and served during World War I as an ensign, then as a lieutenant. He married Eleanor Irene Norman, also a competitive tennis player, in late 1917. They had no children.

Johnston in 1919 won five tournaments, including his second U.S. singles title. He defeated Gerald Patterson, Lindley Murray, Wallace Johnson, and, in the final, Bill Tilden, a rising star. Johnston mainly attacked Tilden's vulnerable backhand. Ranked first and second, Johnston and Tilden led the 1920 U.S. Davis Cup team to victories over France and Great Britain in England during July and over Australasia in New Zealand at year's end. They went undefeated in doubles and singles, with Johnston besting André Gobert, Cecil Parke (who defeated him at Wimbledon in the All England championship), Algy Kingscote, Patterson, and Norman Brookes. On meeting during September in the U.S. nationals final, "Big Bill" Tilden displayed a much-improved backhand and subdued "Little Bill" Johnston after five grueling sets.

Johnston and Tilden defended the Davis Cup against Japan in 1921 and Australasia in 1922, Johnston turning back Ichiya Kumagae, Zenzo Shimizu, Jim Anderson, and Patterson. Johnston won seven major tournaments during those years, but Tilden outplayed him at the U.S. nationals in both of their meetings. Johnston traveled to Europe in 1923 and scored major triumphs there. At Paris, on clay, he won the World Hard Court title, vanquishing René Lacoste and Jan Washer. At Wimbledon, on grass, he captured the All England championship, registering straight-set wins over Vinnie Richards, Babe Norton, and Frank Hunter. Back home, he helped the United States retain the Davis Cup, 4–1, against Australasia, defeating Jack Hawkes (although he lost to Anderson). At the U.S. championships he beat Howard Kinsey, Anderson, and Hunter before Tilden demolished him in the final.

His job as a stockbroker in San Francisco kept Johnston from entering many early season tournaments in 1924, but later that year he won the Newport Invitation. At the nationals he routed Lacoste and Patterson; once again, however, Tilden dismissed him in a straight-set final. The next year Johnston repeated his Newport victory, and in the Davis Cup challenge tie he defeated Lacoste and Jean Borotra. At the nationals he advanced to the final by disposing of George Lott, Manuel Alonso, and Williams, but Tilden narrowly defeated him in the five-set finals. Johnston competed less in 1926, but he still scored easy Davis Cup wins against Lacoste and Borotra; however, he lost to Borotra in a five-set quarterfinal at the U.S. championship.

Johnston's last year of competition came in 1927. He won the Pacific Coast championship for the tenth time during May. He delayed his trip to the East, arriving just before the Davis Cup challenge round versus France without playing in any of the grass court tournaments. His one-sided loss to Lacoste in the opening match of the tie painfully revealed a player bereft of his nimble court coverage and aggressive shotmaking. Cochet also bested him as France won the cup, 3–2. At the nationals, Johnston reached the semifinals before Lacoste dispatched him in four sets.

Subsequently, Johnston engaged in stock brokerage and real estate businesses, and he served a term as president of the California LTA. During the 1930s he suffered a chronic lung congestion illness. He died of heart disease in San Francisco.

In 1947 the U.S. Lawn Tennis Association honored him by posthumously establishing the William M. Johnston Trophy. To be awarded annually "to that male player, who by character, sportsmanship, manners, spirit of cooperation and contribution to the growth of the game ranks first," the award emphasized attributes shown by Johnston throughout his career. He was elected in 1958 to the National Lawn Tennis (later, International Tennis) Hall of Fame.

Quiet, unassuming, and of impeccable deportment, Johnston strictly observed the rules of amateurism, unlike Tilden. He refused offers to turn professional late in his career, and he was highly respected and popular with opponents, officials, and spectators. His mechanically sound, aggressive, all-court style featured a slightly topped forehand, acknowledged as the hardest-hit and best of his time. A right-hander, he used a western grip and met the ball with the same racket face on both flanks. His slightly undercut backhand carried less pace than his forehand, but it proved unusually accurate and steady. He followed his walloping forehands and his well-placed sliced first serves to the net where his excellent volleys and sure overheads generally prevailed. Endowed with an indomitable will to win, he attempted to overwhelm top opponents before his energetic methods spent his stamina and exhausted his slender, 5′8½″, 120-pound body. An outstanding doubles player, Johnston combined with Griffin to capture more than thirty doubles titles, including the 1915, 1916, and 1920 U.S. championships. He won more than twenty other doubles titles with Fottrell, Strachan, and others.

• William M. Johnston, "Speed through Timing," in *Fifty Years of Lawn Tennis in the United States* (1931, a USLTA publication), pp. 168–72, provides a self-description of his style and strategy of tennis. William T. Tilden 2nd, *My Story* (1948), pp. 34–42, furnishes Tilden's assessment of Johnston as a rival. Arthur Voss, *Tilden and Tennis in the Twenties* (1985), covers Johnston's play from 1919 until 1927. Stephen Wallis Merrihew, *The Quest of the Davis Cup* (1928), describes Johnston's Davis Cup career. Four articles in *American Lawn Tennis* provide detailed descriptions of his early tennis years and supply much biographical information: Merrihew, "William Johnston of California," 1 Aug. 1913, pp. 203–4; J. Parmly Paret, "Sound Game of the New Champion," 1 Sept. 1915, pp. 389–90, and "About the New Champion," 1 Sept. 1919, p. 356; and L. B. Rice and Merrihew, "William M. Johnston, Champion 1915–1919," 15 June 1922, pp. 109–10. Obituaries appear in *American Lawn Tennis*, 1 July 1946, pp. 5–7; the *New York Herald Tribune*, 3 May 1946; and the *New York Times*, 2 May 1946.

FRANK V. PHELPS

JOHNSTON, William Preston (5 Jan. 1831–16 July 1899), soldier and educator, was born in Louisville, Kentucky, the son of Albert Sidney Johnston, an army officer, and Henrietta Preston. Johnston's mother died when he was four and his father was stationed in Texas shortly afterward, so the boy was left in the care of his mother's relatives. He was educated first in public schools in Louisville and later at the S. V. Womack Academy in Shelbyville, Kentucky. He attended Centre College in Danville, Kentucky, for a brief time in 1846 and then matriculated with the first class of the Western Military Institute in Georgetown, Kentucky. An excellent student, Johnston was chosen by his classmates at WMI to give the address at the school celebration of Washington's birthday. Admitted to Yale as a junior in May 1851, he graduated the following year, earning the Townsend Prize for English composition and the Clark Prize for an essay titled "Political Abstractionists." He then entered law school at the University of Louisville, graduating in 1853.

In 1853 Johnston married Rosa Elizabeth Duncan; they had six children. The couple lived primarily in Louisville until the outbreak of the Civil War. Johnston then enlisted in the Confederate army and was appointed major in the Second Kentucky Regiment. He soon advanced to the rank of lieutenant colonel in the First Kentucky Regiment. In May 1862, his health failing and his regiment disbanded, Johnston accepted the position of aide-de-camp to Confederate president Jefferson Davis. He was simultaneously advanced to the rank of colonel. In this position he worked as the inspector general and as a confidential liaison between Davis and his generals in the field. He saw action at the battles of Seven Pines, Cold Harbor, Sheridan's Raid, and Petersburg. Captured with Davis in Georgia at the end of the war, Johnston was kept in solitary confinement for three months at Fort Delaware. After his release, Johnston spent a year in voluntary exile in Canada before returning to his law practice in Louisville.

In 1867 the president of Washington College (later Washington and Lee University), General Robert E. Lee, hired Johnston as chair of the department of history and English literature. Under his leadership, the department expanded its limited and sporadic class offerings into a broad and well-structured course of study. Johnston also instituted departmental entrance requirements and rigorous exams and began offering a graduate class. While teaching, he wrote a biography of his father, *The Life of Gen. Albert Sidney Johnston Embracing His Services in the Armies of the United States, the Republic of Texas, and the Confederate States* (1878), which details the accomplishments of Jefferson Davis's second-in-command, the man primarily responsible for leading the Confederate army in the western theater.

In 1880 Johnston left Washington College to become president of Louisiana State University at Baton Rouge. His job was a difficult one; the school was suffering from acute financial shortages and divisive internal political squabbling. Only thirty-nine students were enrolled and only eight instructors, Johnston included, were on the staff. Under his leadership, the school expanded quickly and secured state and private funding.

In 1883 the trustees of the Tulane Educational Fund asked Johnston to help plan and create Tulane University. He accepted and the following year the newly formed school, operating under his direction, merged with the University of Louisiana at New Orleans to become the Tulane University of Louisiana, with Johnston as president. The university, with its departments of medicine and law, and its women's and teachers' college, soon gained significant academic stature in the South. His first wife died in 1885, and in 1888 he married Margaret Henshaw Avery; they had no children.

Johnston's later life was devoted to writing. His only academic text, *Prototype of Hamlet and Other Shakespearean Problems* (1890), a collection of seven lectures, argues that the character of Hamlet is based on James VI of Scotland (who later became James I of

England) and the play's plot is drawn from events surrounding the murder of Lord Henry Darnley, James VI's father, and the beheading of Mary, Queen of Scots. He also wrote three books of poetry: *My Garden Walk* (1894), *Pictures of Patriarchs and Other Poems* (1895), and *Seekers after God: Sonnets* (1898). The latter two are deeply religious works, much influenced by John Milton. *Pictures of Patriarchs* has three sections: the first a collection of five poems narrating an event in the life of a Jewish leader, the second a rewriting of the Psalms, and the third a collection of "devotional verse." *Seekers after God* contains fifty-one sonnets in sections dealing with poetry, man's qualities, philosophers, the apostles, and other historical and contemporary religious figures, and one final poem, highly personal, which explains the writer's own close relationship with God. Johnston died in Lexington, Virginia.

• For further information, see Arthur Marvin Shaw, *William Preston Johnston: A Transitional Figure of the Confederacy* (1943). Articles on Johnston appear in the *Dictionary of American Biography* (1964) and the *National Cyclopedia of American Biography* (1930). Obituaries appear in the *New York Times, Washington Evening Star,* and *New Orleans Daily Picayune,* all 17 July 1899.

ELIZABETH ZOE VICARY

JOHNSTONE, George (1730–24 May 1787), naval officer and first governor of British West Florida, was born in Dumfriesshire, Scotland, the son of Sir James Johnstone, Laird of Westerhall, and Barbara Murray. After entering the Royal Navy in 1743, Johnstone fought in King George's War before his promotion to lieutenant in 1749. Johnstone was undoubtedly brave but also, wrote a superior, "incapable of subordination." He faced two courts-martial and fought at least one duel during the French and Indian War.

During that war, while commanding a sloop, Johnstone took many prizes. In 1761, before the Spanish in the Caribbean knew of it, he warned his friend Admiral George Rodney, who was also there, that Britain had declared war on Spain. Johnstone's initiative contributed to the subsequent British conquest of Havana.

Back in England in 1762, Johnstone achieved the long-desired security of a post-captaincy. This promotion would have meant more if peace talks had not been under way. Of greater importance was his promotion to a colonial governorship, the result of having an influential patron. It was Johnstone's friendship with the dramatist John Home, secretary to the earl of Bute (who became the king's first minister in 1761), that secured for Johnstone the office of governor of West Florida, which stretched along the Gulf Coast from the Florida peninsula to the Mississippi River.

In 1763 Spain ceded that colony, one of four new provinces acquired by a victorious Britain. Bute, a Scot, endured public vilification for appointing Scottish governors to all four, but the choice of Johnstone was defensible. He was experienced in combat and

could subdue possible discontent among the French inhabitants of Mobile and Indian hostilities resulting from Pontiac's War.

Johnstone showed considerable skill in placating local tribes in conferences at Mobile and Pensacola in 1765, convincing suspicious headmen that British intentions were peaceful and persuading them both to cede land for British settlement and also to allow royal officials to live in their villages. He also dealt cleverly with colonists' demands for constitutional rights. Overriding their complaints, he enforced the Stamp Act but accepted their demands for an elected assembly, even though it would give his critics a forum. He ordered an uncommonly wide franchise, allowing both householders and freeholders to vote for assemblymen of the lower house, and approved payment of its members. The assembly met first in 1766.

Under its energetic governor, within two years West Florida acquired roads, a mail service, self-sufficiency in food, and an expanding population. Johnstone cannot be faulted for not developing the colony's commerce with Mexico. Although West Florida was the nearest British colony to Mexico, merchants who migrated to Pensacola to satisfy the known Mexican demand for British manufactors were thwarted, thanks largely to the inflexible customs regulations of Spain and Britain. More culpably, Johnstone failed to work harmoniously with its military officers. The culmination of his bitter rivalry with these officers came with their refusal to back a punitive campaign against the Creeks that Johnstone and his council wanted.

Even before this deadlock, a new secretary of state, the earl of Shelburne, had decided that Johnstone's penchant for creating division in his colony was intolerable. Johnstone was on dueling terms with his lieutenant governor and had suspended West Florida's chief justice and attorney general. A colonists' petition to Shelburne complained of the governor's "unjustifiable, arbitrary and tyrannical principles." Shelburne sent the governor permission, which was in fact a command, to take a six-month leave of absence in Britain.

Johnstone returned to England in 1767. In 1768, thanks to the patronage of Sir James Lowther, he entered Parliament as member for Cockermouth. In the House of Commons he often spoke for the rights of Americans, denouncing the Tea Act of 1773 as "criminally absurd," insisting, correctly, that the Boston Port Bill of 1774 would unite the colonies in forcible resistance to Britain, and recommending "generous, just, pacific measures" toward America, rather than a war, from which he predicted no possible good for Britain.

In 1774 Johnstone became member for Appleby, another of Lowther's pocket boroughs. In 1778 the North administration, which Johnstone had consistently criticized, appointed him to the Carlisle Peace Commission. Johnstone sailed to America, convinced that concessions offering all but complete independence could bring peace. That he mentioned specific bribes to Americans has never been proved, but that he wrote to former acquaintances generally of rewards, if a conciliation were effected, is certain. An outraged Continental Congress refused to deal with the commission while he belonged to it.

Johnstone resigned his commissionership, returned to England and, for the first time, made hawkish speeches. In 1779 he accepted a commodoreship from the administration he had once excoriated. His squadron took many prizes off the coast of Portugal before he commanded an expedition in 1781 to seize the Cape of Good Hope from Britain's new Dutch enemies. The squadron of French admiral Pierre Suffren followed Johnstone's and attacked it at anchor in a harbor in the Cape Verde Islands. The damage Suffren inflicted caused a delay for repairs that enabled the French to reach the cape before Johnstone. Thwarted, the Scottish commodore sought, surprised, and captured a fleet of loaded Dutch East India ships hiding in nearby Saldanha Bay. However, this brilliant feat did not begin to match, strategically, the importance of taking Cape Town.

Johnstone went back to England by way of Lisbon, where in 1782 he married Charlotte Dee, with whom he had one child. He resumed a parliamentary seat, this time for Lostwithiel, to which he had been nominated in 1781. In 1784 he secured election to the directorate of the East India Company, in which he had long been active. With help from a local magnate he gained a parliamentary seat for Ilchester in 1785. Johnstone died at the Hot Wells, Bristol.

Johnstone's career shows some of the flaws in Britain's imperial system prior to the American Revolution, but his was not purely a case of promotion irrespective of merit. Although ambition rather than dedication to principle characterized him, he had virtues. Among them were energy, eloquence, and courage. His political gift, fully exercised in the East India Company's Court of Proprietors and in the House of Commons, was for attack rather than compromise, for creating division rather than harmony. Johnstone, like his friends Isaac Barré, John Wilkes, and the earl of Chatham, did much with his speeches to encourage American resistance to British pretensions. He was commonly called Governor Johnstone for the final twenty-three years of his life, and getting the colony of West Florida off to a good start was the achievement of which he was probably most proud.

• A centralized collection of Johnstone's papers does not exist, but manuscripts relating to his naval career may be found in the Admiralty series in the Public Record Office, Kew, England. There too are the official papers concerning his governorship, in the Colonial Office 5 series. A selection of these gubernatorial papers was printed in Dunbar Rowland, *Mississippi Provincial Archives, 1763–1766: English Dominion* (1911), to which a useful supplement is Robert R. Rea and Milo B. Howard, *Minutes, Journals and Acts of the General Assembly of British West Florida* (1979). Some of Johnstone's private letters are in the Laing manuscripts in the Edinburgh University Library, while others, to his brother, are housed in the Huntington Library, San Marino, Calif. Johnstone's speeches in Parliament are in relevant volumes of William Cobbett's *Parliamentary History* (1806–

1820). His speeches in East India House may be gleaned, invariably in truncated form, from the London newspapers of his era. The best primary source for his work on the peace commission is Benjamin F. Stevens, *Facsimiles of Manuscripts in European Archives* (1889–1895). The best secondary source is Carl Van Doren, *Secret History of the American Revolution* (1941). Vincent T. Harlow, *Founding of the Second British Empire, 1763–1793*, vol. 1 (1952), has a good account of Johnstone's clash with Suffren.

Considerations of Johnstone's governorship are included in Cecil Johnson, *British West Florida, 1763–1783* (1943); Clinton N. Howard, *The British Development of West Florida, 1763–1769* (1947); and J. Barton Starr, *Tories, Dons & Rebels* (1976). His entire life is considered in Robin F. A. Fabel, *Bombast and Broadsides* (1987).

ROBIN F. A. FABEL

JOLAS, Maria (Jan. 1893–4 Mar. 1987), cofounder of the Paris literary review *transition*, founder of the Ecole Bilingue in Neuilly, and translator and editor, was born Maria McDonald in Louisville, Kentucky, the daughter of Elizabeth (maiden name unknown) and Donald McDonald. The McDonalds, a wealthy family originally from Virginia, educated their daughter in New York boarding schools but derided her scholarship to the University of Chicago, which she turned down. She was, however, permitted to study voice in Berlin (1913–1914).

After the First World War, when she held a secretarial job at Charles Scribner's Sons in Manhattan, Maria McDonald followed her New York singing teacher to Paris, where she met poet-critic Eugene Jolas, an American reared in France then writing a weekly literary column for the European edition of the *Chicago Tribune*. Married to Jolas in 1926 in New York, she moved with him to a house (later bought by Charles de Gaulle) outside Paris in Colombey-Les-Deux-Eglises, had two children, and gave up her professional singing career. She and her husband began working on the journal *transition*, a longtime ambition of Eugene's, which the couple cofounded in 1926 with the income from Maria's father's estate.

Calling itself a "laboratory for poetic experiment," *transition* encouraged writing in "a fantastic, dreamlike, apocalyptic trend" and printed the work of many of the period's most distinguished authors, including Gertrude Stein, William Carlos Williams, H. D., Samuel Beckett, Kay Boyle, Ernest Hemingway, Hart Crane, and Katherine Anne Porter. Coedited by Eugene and Elliot Paul, former literary editor of the Paris edition of the *Chicago Tribune*, it also published photographs of artworks by Juan Gris, Kurt Schwitters, Hans Arp, and Pablo Picasso and in 1927 began to feature installments of James Joyce's *Work in Progress* (later *Finnegan's Wake*).

Although Maria Jolas's contribution to the journal was largely administrative, the 1928 *transition*, number 10, included her essay "Black Thoughts," the only article of hers ever to appear in a regular issue of the magazine. Arguing against the exploitation of African-American spirituals by those who knew nothing about them, she urged African Americans to "sink their roots even deeper into the rich black loam that is their heritage." The Jolases were at the time translating and editing a collection of traditional African songs, *Le Nègre Qui Chante*, published in Paris that year. Jolas published another piece in 1933 in the supplement to *transition* (the only supplement ever published by the magazine), called "Testimony against Gertrude Stein," which also included articles by Henri Matisse, Georges Braque, André Salmon, and Tristan Tzara, who refuted many of the claims made by Stein in her *Autobiography of Alice B. Tolkas*. Jolas denied Stein's assertion that Paul had founded *transition* and that Stein was its most significant writer.

After several years of sporadic publication and a reorganization of its staff, *transition* ceased publication with the tenth-anniversary issue, which did not appear until 1939. During the years of its publication, although Jolas wrote editorial and business letters, corrected proofs, and translated articles, she was not listed on the masthead of the magazine ("as a rule in our circle the men did the creative work and the women kept house," she recalled in 1970). Having corrected the proofs of *Finnegan's Wake*, she also performed countless other chores for Joyce, including caring for his schizophrenic daughter and, after his death, rescuing his papers from a Montparnasse attic. In 1949 she helped organize the first Joyce exhibition in Paris and edited the scholarly significant *A James Joyce Yearbook*.

From 1932 until the outbreak of the Second World War in 1939, Jolas also organized and ran a school, the Ecole Bilingue in Neuilly, where she used the standard French curriculum but had the children instructed in French and English as well as in song and dance. Although her husband returned to the United States in 1935 for a year to work for the French news service, Havas, Jolas stayed in Europe with their two daughters to run her school. During the invasion of France, she evacuated the children still remaining at the school to a château in south central France, where the Joyces eventually joined them before taking refuge in Switzerland. The Jolases then went back to New York, where they worked for the Office of War Information.

Returning to France in 1946 as public relations officer for the American Aid to France (a private organization), Jolas contributed several translations to *Transition Forty-Eight*, edited by French critic Georges Duthuit, but neither she nor her husband considered reviving *transition*. One of the founders and first members of the James Joyce Society in America, she arranged the sale of original Joyce manuscripts to the University of Buffalo after they had been offered without success to approximately thirty major American universities. She also began translating the experimental prose of Nathalie Sarraute, as well as that of other contemporary French authors, although she was quoted as saying that translation is essentially for lazy people: "Someone else has done the thinking, and you accompany him like a pianist accompanying the singer, self-effacing if essential."

After her husband died in 1952, Jolas stayed on in Paris, spending weekends and summers at their small house in Chérence, a village about an hour from Paris first introduced to them by Sarraute. Active in the Paris American Committee to Stop War, an organization of American citizens protesting U.S. involvement in Vietnam, she translated a sympathetic report of the student uprisings in Paris in 1968. In 1970 she won the Scott-Moncrieff prize for translation. She died in Paris at the age of ninety-four.

• Information on Maria Jolas, Eugene Jolas, and the magazine *transition* can be found in the Jolas papers at the Beinecke Rare Book and Manuscript Library, Yale University. Writings by Maria Jolas include "Joyce's Friend Jolas," *A James Joyce Miscellany*, ed. Marvin Magalaner (1957), and "A Bloomlein for Sam," in *Beckett at 60: A Festschrift* (1967). See also Eilis Dillon, "The Innocent Muse: An Interview with Maria Jolas," *James Joyce Quarterly*, Fall 1982, pp. 33–66, and Herbert R. Lottman, "One of the Quiet Ones," the *New York Times Book Review*, 22 Mar. 1970. Much useful information is contained in Richard Ellmann, *James Joyce* (1959); Dougald McMillan, *transition 1927–1938: The History of a Literary Era* (1976); and Deirdre Bair, *Samuel Beckett* (1978). An obituary is in the *New York Times*, 7 Mar. 1987.

BRENDA WINEAPPLE

JOLSON, Al (26 May 1886–23 Oct. 1950), singer and entertainer, was born Asa Yoelson in Seredzius, Lithuania, the son of Moses Reuben Yoelson, a rabbi and cantor, and Naomi Cantor. Brought to the United States in 1894, Jolson was educated at the Jefferson Public School in Washington, D.C., before entering the theatrical profession in 1900 as a singer with the Victoria Burlesquers. Jolson subsequently teamed with Fred E. Moore in a singing act featuring stereopticon slides, but his career as a "boy tenor" ended when his voice changed. He and his elder brother, Harry, performed together as "The Hebrew and the Cadet" prior to joining Joe Palmer as Jolson, Palmer and Jolson in "A Little of Everything," an act that toured the major vaudeville circuits beginning in late 1904. Jolson first performed in blackface at this time.

Harry left the team in November 1905, the act continuing as Palmer and Jolson until June 1906 when Al began his career as a single entertainer on the Sullivan & Considine Circuit. Jolson's sly but exuberant sense of comedy, electric presence, and dynamic singing style found a home in San Francisco, a major vaudeville center then recovering from the ravages of a major earthquake and fire. He married Henrietta Keller, the daughter of Danish immigrants, in Oakland, California, in September 1907. The couple did not have any children.

Jolson signed with Dockstader's Minstrels, one of the largest and most famous blackface minstrel organizations, in 1908. Appearing in a featured solo spot, he received favorable notice when the show played the Grand Opera House in New York in February 1909, and he scored a huge success in vaudeville at New York's Fifth Avenue Theatre the following July.

Further vaudeville successes at Hammerstein's Victoria and other theaters preceded Jolson's Broadway show debut in *La Belle Paree* at the new Winter Garden Theatre on 20 March 1911, where he became a leading favorite. Further success in *Vera Violetta* (1911) led to a cofeatured role in *The Whirl of Society* (1912), where Jolson's blackface character acquired the name "Gus." *The Honeymoon Express* (1913) firmly established him as one of the country's leading musical comedy performers; in it he probably used his trademark finale, falling to one knee with both arms extended.

Jolson's frequent touring in these Winter Garden shows made him known throughout the country, and his popularity increased in shows like *Dancing Around* (1914), *Robinson Crusoe, Jr.* (1916), in which he was first billed above the title, and *Sinbad* (1918), for which his name was spelled out in four-foot electric lights on Broadway. It was in *Sinbad* that he introduced his version of George Gershwin's "Swanee" (1919) and "My Mammy" (1921), the song with which he remained most identified.

Jolson's interests, centered on show business and the sports world, left him little room for married life, and Henrietta divorced him in 1919. Following his great success in *Bombo* (1921), in which he first sang "April Showers," at a theater named for him, Jolson married Broadway showgirl Ethel Delmar in 1922. They were divorced four years later.

In 1927, following three seasons as the star of the musical comedy *Big Boy*, Jolson starred in *The Jazz Singer* (Warner Bros.), America's first part-talking feature-length motion picture. The success of that film led to a starring role in *The Singing Fool* (Warner Bros., 1928), another part-"talker" in which he introduced the smash hit ballad, "Sonny Boy." Jolson married dancer Ruby Keeler in September of that year. The couple adopted one child.

Jolson's career declined in a series of unsuccessful films beginning with *Say It with Songs* in 1929. He returned to the Broadway stage in *The Wonder Bar* (1931), and he launched *Presenting Al Jolson*, his first starring radio series in November 1932. The 1933 release of *Hallelujah, I'm a Bum*, an attempt to enlarge on the use of "rhythmic dialogue," was greeted with disdain by critics and was a box office failure. Jolson returned to Warner Bros., costarring in *Wonder Bar* (1934) and *Go into Your Dance* (1935). *The Singing Kid* (1936) was his last starring movie vehicle.

Jolson continued on radio until 1939, the year he accepted featured billing in *Rose of Washington Square* and *Swanee River* at Twentieth Century–Fox. Keeler divorced him in the same year. In 1940 he returned to Broadway as the star of *Hold Onto Your Hats*, a show he toured in a year later.

World War II provided Jolson with new purpose, and the summer of 1942 saw him entertain U.S. servicemen in Alaska, the Caribbean, England, Scotland, and Ireland. He starred in "The Al Jolson Show" on CBS from October 1942 through June 1943, after which he entertained GIs in South America, Africa,

and Italy. Jolson contracted malaria in the Mediterranean and collapsed on his return to the United States.

The success of *Yankee Doodle Dandy* (1942), Warners' film biography of George M. Cohan, led newspaper columnist Sidney Skolsky to promote the idea of a similar film on Jolson. Temporarily recovered from malaria Jolson toured hospitals to perform for wounded servicemen in 1944, but recurrence of malaria forced him to undergo emergency surgery on his left lung in January 1945. Jolson married Erle Galbraith, a young X-ray technician he had met at the Eastman Annex in Hot Springs, Arkansas, in March of the same year.

Skolsky sold his film idea to Columbia Pictures, and Larry Parks, a B-picture actor at Columbia, played the title role in *The Jolson Story* (1946). Jolson, however, sang the songs for Parks on the soundtrack, and the picture's overwhelming success reestablished him as a major star. Jolson starred on the "Kraft Music Hall" for NBC radio for two seasons and did the singing for Parks in *Jolson Sings Again*, a sequel to *The Jolson Story*, released in August 1949.

Jolson was the first celebrity performer to entertain frontline soldiers during the Korean war, giving seven shows a day for six straight days despite his deteriorating health. He died of a heart attack in San Francisco, where he had gone to tape a guest appearance on "The Bing Crosby Show."

Jolson was lionized by many of his contemporaries, and he remained a show business hero for some years after his death. His reputation has suffered since the mid-1960s owing to the fact that he performed in blackface and belonged to a generation of musical comedy stars who were not captured well on film. His blackface performances, especially, may have prejudiced modern critics and led many to exaggerate the negative aspects of Jolson's personality. Insecure and frequently a braggart, he was not immensely popular with fellow artists, who nonetheless acknowledged his great talent. He was the quintessential entertainer.

• Harry Jolson's memoir, *Mistah Jolson* (1951), is a prime source of firsthand information about Al Jolson's life to the end of 1905. *The Immortal Jolson* by Pearl Sieben (1962), though fictional in style and extremely unreliable regarding specifics, provides an interesting look at the private individual. Herbert G. Goldman's *Jolson: The Legend Comes to Life* (1988) was the result of many interviews with Jolson's few remaining colleagues and innumerable hours of combing through reports in contemporary theatrical trade newspapers and other first hand sources. The book also includes booking schedules for Jolson's stage shows and vaudeville, minstrel, and early burlesque stage appearances. The Shubert Archive, located in the Lyceum Theatre building in New York, contains the papers of Jolson's theatrical producers during the years of his greatest stage success, including many letters, notes, and telegrams exchanged between Jolson and J. J. Shubert. The Billy Rose Theatre Collection of the New York Public Library, located in Lincoln Center, contains scrapbooks and innumerable loose clippings kept on Jolson by Robinson Locke, the Chamberlain and Lyman Brown Agency, and others. Tapes of radio shows on which Jolson was heard, especially those of post–World War II vintage, may be obtained from a number of private dealers. All his feature sound films are extant, as are the records made for Victor, Columbia, Brunswick, and Decca at various intervals from 1911 through 1950.

HERBERT G. GOLDMAN

JONES, Abner (28 Apr. 1772–29 May 1841), evangelist, founder and leader of the Christian Connection, was born on a farm in Royalston, Massachusetts, the son of Deacon Asa Jones and Dorcas Wade, both devout Separate Calvinist Baptists. In 1780 the family was among the first to inhabit the vicinity of Bridgewater, Vermont, a virtual wilderness in the upper Connecticut valley. Abner's religious upbringing, the influence of itinerating Baptist revivalists, and the harsh, uncertain conditions of the frontier occasioned periodic bouts of gloom and spiritual torment. In his *Memoirs* (1807) Jones likened his mental condition to that of his environs: "uncultivated, and inhabited by the wild beasts of prey; dreary and melancholy" (p. 7). He saw the judgment of God in every misfortune: the plunder of property and capture of white settlers by Indians, a death by accidental shooting, or the destruction of crops by worm infestation.

At age ten, Jones experienced some relief from his own spiritual anxiety when he was converted after attending a Separate Baptist meeting. He postponed baptism, however, for it signaled complete obedience to God—a commitment he felt unable to make. Consequently, Jones's teenage years were marked by a continued spiritual struggle. He grew "careless" in his faith, embraced the universal religious views of his older brother, pursued pleasure, and coveted wealth. At the same time, he was plagued with remorse and suffered God's judgment for his transgressions. His father died of consumption when Abner was fourteen; illness, accidents, and a meager formal education (limited to six weeks) dashed his hopes of becoming prosperous. Jones's prospects brightened at age nineteen when he went to work for a clothier in Granville, New York. When business fell off, his employer helped Jones get a teaching job, but when Jones became ill, he lost his position and had to return to Bridgewater. Chastened once again, Jones attended a Separatist revival in nearby Woodstock. There he resolved his conflicted condition and was baptized on 9 June 1793 by Elisha Ransom, a Separatist Baptist revivalist. In the following weeks Jones toured in the company of Baptist itinerants before returning to Bridgewater and teaching school at nearby Hartland.

In his spare time Jones immersed himself in the study of the Bible and medicine. Through his examination of scripture Jones gradually rejected the primary tenets of his inherited Calvinism: God's decrees, election, and reprobation. In casting off these dogmas and modifying traditional views of the Trinity and the atonement, Jones exemplified those religious radicals who in the tumultuous period following the American and French revolutions believed that ordinary people had the right to interpret the Bible for themselves. As Americans in the political realm threw off the accre-

tions of old-world political corruption to begin anew, so Jones and other populists embraced a primitivist, democratic religion originating, so they believed, in the first century. Jones thus eschewed any vestiges of hierarchy and preferential treatment by human or divine fiat, taking as his only creed "what I found required in the Bible, and no more" (*Memoirs*, p. 59). Yet at the time of these initial insights he feared being called a heretic, and so for five years, "I hid my light under the bed of Calvinism" (*Memoirs*, p. 66).

In 1796 Jones settled in the northeastern Vermont frontier village of Lyndon as a medical practitioner. He established a respectable practice, married Damaris Pryor (who died in 1836), and succeeded financially. He also continued his quest for the true gospel by regularly attending religious services in the community. During a revival in nearby Billymead in December 1800, Jones became convinced of his true calling to the gospel ministry. He thus began preaching and eventually abandoned his medical practice to become a full-time evangelist.

By 1801 Jones's successful preaching resulted in the formation of a nondenominational, independent "free Christian church" in Lyndon. Known simply as "Christians," the congregation represented a classical expression of a sectarian movement. Convinced that the parent Baptist church had abandoned its religious fervor and strict discipline in favor of increased members and respectability, the Christians stood for an unadulterated faith community that looked to the primitive church and the Bible as the only source of authority. Jones soon attracted other audiences among the hardscrabble, democratically minded frontier folk of northern New England. By the fall of 1802 he formed another church without "party name" or confession of faith in Hanover, New Hampshire, and that winter a third church was established in Piermont.

Because as a strict biblicist Jones recognized the validity and necessity of ordination into the ministry, in November 1802 he was ordained by a council of Free Will Baptists. Though it is not clear whether Jones officially affiliated with this group, he did recognize them as cobelligerents in their rejection of Calvinist teaching on election. Following ordination, Jones began a ministry that primarily covered the frontier regions of New England and New York. Between 1803 and 1840 he established and pastored churches in Boston, Bradford, Salem, Assonet, and Upton, Massachusetts; Lebanon, Portsmouth, Stratham, and Hopkinton, New Hampshire; and Milan, New York. During the height of Jones's evangelistic zeal (c. 1804–1806), his monthly labors included preaching twenty-five to thirty times, baptizing ten to fifty converts, and traveling 200 miles on horseback. Financial hardship (he was solely dependent on free will offerings) sometimes made it necessary that he return to teaching and medical practice. The dearth of time and money, however, did not dim Jones's enthusiasm for knowledge; he became proficient in reading Latin, Greek, and Hebrew and was an avid reader of history and biography. In addition, Jones was a zealous Mason until the outbreak of anti-Masonic fervor in the early 1820s. He withdrew from membership less out of conviction and more from expediency, concluding that his association with the society would damage his ministry.

In establishing the church at Portsmouth, New Hampshire, in 1803, Jones became reacquainted with Elias Smith, whom he had met on his tour with Baptist itinerants in 1793. The two men shared similar backgrounds, and both reached similar though independent conclusions about the Separate Baptists and the need to restore primitive Christianity. They labored together, although Smith, a prolific writer, was clearly superior in propagating the restorationist message. Their meeting at Portsmouth led to the creation of independent "Christian" churches throughout New England in the first decade of the nineteenth century and to an associational structure known as the Christian Connection. To spread the primitivist message, Jones and Smith collaborated in compiling a hymnal, *Hymns, Original and Selected, for the Use of Christians* (1804). The publication of seven editions by 1815 attests not only to the growing popularity of the Christian movement but also to the use of hymns and spiritual songs as a powerful medium of communication. Jones and Smith thus led the New England phase of a nationwide restorationist movement associated elsewhere with James O'Kelly in Virginia and North Carolina and Barton Stone in Kentucky.

Jones's retirement to Exeter, New Hampshire, in April 1840, following his marriage in 1839 to Nancy F. Clark of Nantucket, was short-lived. He died in Exeter.

• Jones's *Memoirs of the Life and Experience, Travels and Preaching of Abner Jones* (1807) and A. D. Jones (Abner's son), *Memoirs of Elder Abner Jones* (1842), remain the primary biographical sources, although A. H. Morrill's profile of Jones in J. Pressley Barett, ed., *The Centennial of Religious Journalism* (1908), pp. 285–96, is also useful. Apart from compiling hymnals, Jones published only a sermon, *The Vision Made Plain* (1809). In addition to his work with Smith, his compiled hymnals include *The Melody of the Heart* (1804), *Harmonia Sacra* (1831), *Melodies of the Church* (1832), *Church Melodies* (1833), and *Evening Melodies* (1834). Jones's relationship to Elias Smith and his role in founding the Christian Connection is discussed in Timothy E. Fulop, "Elias Smith and the Quest for Gospel Liberty: Popular Religion and Democratic Radicalism in Early Nineteenth-Century New England" (Ph.D. diss., Princeton Univ. 1992). On the rise and impact of democratic folk religion, see Nathan O. Hatch, "The Christian Movement and the Demand for a Theology of the People," *Journal of American History* 67 (1980): 545–67; and Hatch, *The Democratization of American Christianity* (1989).

DAVID KLING

JONES, Absalom (6 Nov. 1746–13 Feb. 1818), first black Protestant Episcopal priest, was born in Sussex, Delaware, the son of slave parents. He was a small child when his master took him from the fields to wait on him in the house. Jones was very fond of learning and was very careful to save the pennies that were given to him by ladies and gentlemen from time to time.

He soon bought a primer and would beg people to teach him how to read. Before long he was able to purchase a spelling book, and as his funds increased he began to buy books, including a copy of the New Testament. "Fondness for books gave me little or no time for amusements that took up the leisure hours of my companions" (Bragg, *The Story of the First of the Blacks*, p. 3).

When Jones was sixteen, his mother, five brothers and a sister were sold, and he was taken to Philadelphia by his master. There he worked in his master's store, where he would pack and carry out to customers' carriages goods that had been purchased. Gradually he learned to write and was soon able to write to his brothers and mother "with my own hand." In 1766 he began attending a Quaker-operated night school for blacks. When he was twenty-four, he married Mary (maiden name unknown), a slave woman. Shortly after the marriage, he arranged to purchase his wife's freedom. His wife's mistress agreed to a price of forty pounds, and Jones borrowed thirty pounds and the mistress forgave the remaining ten pounds. For the next eight years Jones worked almost every night until twelve or one o'clock to raise money to repay what he had borrowed.

By 1778 he had purchased his wife's freedom and made application to his owner to purchase his own freedom with some additional money that he had saved. This was not granted. Jones then bought a lot with a sizable house and continued to work and save his money. Again he applied to his master to purchase his freedom, and on 1 October 1784 he was granted manumission.

At this time the city of Philadelphia was alive with the spirit of the Revolution and the ideal of universal freedom. In 1780 a law was passed that called for the gradual emancipation of the slave population. Also at this time a new religious movement was developing in the emerging United States. The Methodists were evangelicals within the Church of England who met in small groups to enhance their religious life. They were particularly strong in New York, Baltimore, and Philadelphia. On 24–25 December 1784, under the leadership of Thomas Coke and Francis Asbury, members of these Methodist societies met at Lovely Lane Chapel in Baltimore and organized the Methodist Episcopal church as a new denomination separate from the Church of England. In the three large cities previously mentioned, numerous blacks joined the Methodist church. Many of the free blacks of Philadelphia attended the mostly white St. George's Methodist Episcopal Church, as did Jones. Also among them was Richard Allen, who became the founder and first bishop of the African Methodist Episcopal church. For a while the blacks and whites got along well at St. George's Church. As Methodism spread among the whites, the space occupied by black Methodists in the church building was more and more in demand by the increasing number of white congregants. The blacks were moved from place to place in the building as circumstances required. One Sunday morning in

1787 a number of blacks were seated together and had knelt for prayer. Jones, the leader of the group, was pulled from his knees, and the blacks were told to move to another place in the building. The entire group of blacks arose and walked out of the church never to return. This unpleasant episode was the occasion that prompted the first organization among free blacks of which there is any record.

On 12 April 1787 some of these black Methodists met in a home in Philadelphia and organized the Free African Society. Jones was the leader of the group, and Allen was one of the overseers. It was a benevolent and social reform organization at first. Episcopal bishop William White of Pennsylvania was a leader in the encouragement and support of the Free African Society. Gradually the Free African Society transformed itself into an "African Church" with no denominational ties. At a meeting held 21 July 1792, a resolution was adopted that appropriated money to purchase property on which to erect "a place of worship for this Society." The society erected a church building that was dedicated on 17 July 1794. Later in the year an election was held to determine with which denomination to unite. "There were two in favor of the Methodists, Absalom Jones and Richard Allen; and a large majority in favor of the Church of England. This majority carried" (Bragg, *The Story of the First of the Blacks*, p. 9). Jones went with the majority, but Allen did not. On 12 August 1794 the African Church became St. Thomas Episcopal Church, the first black Episcopal church in the United States. It was formally received into the diocese of Pennsylvania on 12 October 1794.

At that October diocesan convention Jones was received as a candidate for holy orders in the Episcopal church and was licensed as a lay reader. On 21 October 1794 he formally accepted the position of pastor of St. Thomas Church. At the diocesan convention on 2 June 1795, it was stipulated that St. Thomas Church was not entitled to send a clergyman or any lay deputies to the convention, nor was it "to interfere with the general government of the Episcopal Church." Jones was ordained a deacon on 23 August 1795 and then priest on September 1804, the first black to become a deacon or a priest in the Episcopal church. From 1795 until his death, Jones baptized 268 black adults and 927 black infants. His ministry among blacks was so significant that he was called the "Black Bishop of the Episcopal Church." Jones died in Philadelphia.

• The few extant Jones papers are in the Archives of the Episcopal Church, Austin, Texas. One of his sermons, "A Thanksgiving Sermon," is in John M. Burgess, ed., *Black Gospel/White Church* (1982). The earliest study of his life, which has quotations from him, is George F. Bragg, *The Story of the First of the Blacks, the Pathfinder, Absalom Jones, 1746–1818* (1929). A major study is Ann C. Lammers, "The Rev. Absalom Jones and the Episcopal Church: Christian Theology and Black Consciousness in a New Alliance," *Historical Magazine of the Protestant Episcopal Church* (1982): 159–84. Briefer studies are Anne B. Allen, "A Voice Counter to Public Opinion: Absalom Jones, 1746–1818," *Living Church* (11 Feb. 1990): 8–9. Jones's work is also noted in three other works by George F. Bragg: *Afro-American Church Work and Workers* (1904), *History of the Afro-American Group of the Episcopal Church* (1922), and "The Episcopal Church and the Negro Race," *Historical Magazine of the Protestant Episcopal Church* 4 (1935): 47–52. The latest study that treats Jones is Harold T. Lewis, *Yet with a Steady Beat: The African American Struggle for Recognition in the Episcopal Church* (1996).

DONALD S. ARMENTROUT

JONES, Allen (24 Dec. 1739–14 Nov. 1807), planter, revolutionary patriot, and Federalist, was born in Surry County, Virginia, the son of Robert "Robin" Jones, a planter, and Sarah Cobb. The family moved to Northampton County, North Carolina, in the early 1750s. There, Robin Jones served as Lord Granville's land agent and as the Crown-appointed attorney general for North Carolina, posts that enabled him to become one of the largest landowners in the Roanoke River valley. He sent his sons to England's Eton College, his alma mater, to be educated. The dates of their attendance are uncertain. Both were destined to become aristocratic planters, revolutionary leaders, members of the Continental Congress, and important state officials.

Before the Revolution Allen Jones manifested his interest in public affairs, acting both as clerk of the Halifax District Superior Court and as Northampton County representative in the colonial assembly (1773–1775). During these years, he became an implacable opponent of British taxes, contending that Americans should enjoy fully the rights of Englishmen. He moved easily into the patriot ranks. He was a member of the Halifax Committee of Safety and represented Northampton in five Provincial Congresses (1774–1776), where he supported the formation of a Continental army and activation of the state militia. He favored independence and a state constitution. In 1776, despite his protestation of inexperience, he was promoted from colonel to brigadier general of militia for the Halifax District.

Jones's military service in the two Carolinas was sporadic and inconspicuous, but he continued to serve ably in the civil government. He was successively a state senator (1777–1779; Speaker in the 1778 and 1779 sessions); a delegate to the Continental Congress (1779–1780); a member of the North Carolina Council Extraordinary (1781); and a councilor of state (1782). Jones was ever confident of American victory, and few men were more constant in promoting the patriot cause than he.

After the Revolution Jones was elected state senator three times, representing Northampton County in the general assemblies of 1783, 1784–1785, and 1787. During the 1780s, he feared that democratization threatened property rights, and he became staunchly conservative in outlook. He opposed the proscription of Loyalists seeking to recover their property. Convinced that a stronger central government was essential to order and stability, Jones favored the U.S. Constitution of 1787 but was twice defeated in the election of delegates to the North Carolina ratifying conventions. His position was diametrically opposed to that of his better-known brother Willie (pronounced Wiley) Jones, who became the leader of the state's anti-Federalist faction. Allen Jones was a Federalist as political parties developed in the 1790s, but his active political career was over. Nothing animated him as the independence movement of his youth had.

Jones settled into the life of a planter with his seat at "Mount Gallant" on the north bank of the Roanoke River. In 1790 he owned 177 slaves and several thousand acres. He held 218 slaves in 1800. He was married three times. In 1762 he married Mary Haynes, with whom he had three daughters, one of whom married William R. Davie. After the death of his first wife, Jones married Rebecca Edwards in 1768. This union produced one daughter. Later he married Mary Eaton (date unknown); they had no children. Jones died at his home in Northampton County, North Carolina.

Jones was regarded as a man of impeccable integrity. At his death, friends wrote: "Our revolution found him a man, and during the whole course of its rise and progress, he acted in a manly and conspicuous part on the side of his country. That spirit of freedom and independence which then guided his conduct never forsook him" (Raleigh *Minerva*, 26 Nov. 1807).

• For factual information about Jones see Francis B. Heitman, comp., *Historical Register of Officers of the Continental Army . . .* (1903; repr. 1967); John L. Cheney, Jr., *North Carolina Government* (1975); William L. Saunders, ed., *The Colonial Records of North Carolina* (10 vols., 1886–1890); Walter Clark, ed., *The State Records of North Carolina* (16 vols., 1895–1905); Stephen B. Weeks, comp. and ed., *Index to the Colonial and State Records of North Carolina* (4 vols., 1909–1914); Heads of Household Census, 1790; and U.S. Census, 1800. See also William C. Allen, *History of Halifax County* (1918); Cadwallader Jones, *A Genealogical History . . .* (1900); Samuel A. Ashe, *Biographical History of North Carolina*, vol. 4 (1906); and Blackwell P. Robinson, "Willie Jones of Halifax, North Carolina" (M.A. thesis, Duke Univ., 1939).

MAX R. WILLIAMS

JONES, Amanda Theodosia (19 Oct. 1835–31 Mar. 1914), inventor, poet, and Spiritualist, was born in East Bloomfield, New York, the daughter of Henry Jones, a master weaver, and Mary Alma Mott, a woman noted for her powers of memory and "splendid intellect." Her family, though of modest means, considered books "more necessary than daily bread," and Amanda, like her brothers and sisters, was reading the New Testament by age seven. In 1845 the family moved to Black Rock, New York, near Buffalo, where Amanda attended classes at the East Aurora (N.Y.) Academy (then the Normal School at East Aurora). She graduated by 1850 and at age fifteen began teaching at a country school, attending Buffalo High School during the summers. In 1854, exhausted from her rigorous schedule and encouraged by her father to become a poet, she abandoned teaching when her first poems were accepted by the *Methodist Ladies' Repository*.

Jones's father died soon afterward, and she fell ill with tuberculosis, necessitating the first of many stays at the Clifton Springs (N.Y.) Water Cure, where she took the "Compressed Air-Cure." Throughout her life she remained in precarious health, periodically resorting to popular treatments and to the Air-Cure whenever possible for rest and rejuvenation.

Although raised as a Methodist, by 1854 Jones had embraced the new Spiritualist movement (which originated in 1848 in nearby Wayne County, N.Y.), and she considered herself a medium. Beginning in her childhood, she claimed, she had occasionally been aware of events and actions before they happened, including the death of her own father. A welcome house-guest, she traveled widely in Spiritualist circles throughout western New York, "channeling" spirits at her leisure and writing. Her first book, *Ulah and Other Poems*, was published in 1861, and a second book, *Poems*, appeared in 1867. During the Civil War she published a series of patriotic pieces in *Frank Leslie's Illustrated Weekly*. In 1869, prompted by a psychic vision brought through a spirit she believed to be a physician, "Dr. [Jonathan] Andrews," she conceived the philanthropic goal that motivated her life's work—the establishment of a "rescue home" for abandoned women and a house of reform for young girls. Jones was determined "not to rescue fallen women only, but to prevent the fall." Impoverished, she nonetheless moved to Chicago, where, awaiting further inspiration, she edited a succession of small periodicals.

In 1872 the financial groundwork was laid for her philanthropic venture by a new spirit, "Mr. [J. R.] Evelyn," a lawyer from whose evening lectures she reportedly "learned respect for bargainers—little admired before." Convinced by this spirit that a profitable business was a worthy goal, Jones then envisioned a means of achieving her goal: a patent for a vacuum method for canning. "Air exhaustion coupled with fluid substitution" was Jones's own description of the process. Experimenting with various fruits, vegetables, meats, desserts, and oysters, she perfected methods for putting up these perishable and seasonal foods without cooking them, which greatly improved their quality in comparison with early canned goods then on the market. Participating in the great boon in commercial canning during the latter decades of the nineteenth century, the Jones Preserving Process depended on apparatus worked out with her brother-in-law LeRoy C. Cooley of Albany, New York. Together, Cooley and Jones controlled seven patents over the process. In 1873 Cooley obtained a patent (no. 139,547) for the fruit-preserving apparatus ("a simple set of tubes") and assigned the patent to Jones. A second patent (no. 139,581) covering the preservation method was issued the same day and went jointly to Jones and Cooley. Cooley procured an additional patent for the apparatus that took the place of vacuum pumps in the process, making it "more efficient" and "cheaper," and Jones received two more patents (nos. 139,580 and 140,508) for fruit jars "made to suit the tubes."

Although she credited spirits with guiding her into new avenues of interest, Jones vehemently denied that they played any role in the invention process for her patents or her writings. Instead, she admitted that both required much "hard work and anxious thought" while only modestly claiming that "it seems I had some natural aptitude for mechanism, or rather for adapting means to ends." In her *Psychic Autobiography*, published in 1910, Jones attributed her success to her flexibility, observing that "men, who are striving to invent, will take an obstacle, as though it were a hurdle; leap it if they can, or otherwise declare the race impossible. But I had dodged a dozen obstacles already and slipped around them rather prettily—being a simple woman. Better to be adroit than risk a broken neck."

Jones refused several partnership offers from men who wished to put her canning process patents to work. In 1879 she formed her own company, the U.S. Women's Pure Food Vacuum Preserving Company. But she remained dedicated to achieving her full vision: women building the factories and managing them "with righteousness" while sending out "perfect foods" and reaping "the golden profits." In her continued quest to raise the capital for her ambitious enterprise made up of "none but women, first and last," she was led in 1880 to patent what she termed an Automatic Safety Burner (no. 225,839), which provided a cost-efficient means of burning crude petroleum in furnaces. Three additional but related patents were granted to her in 1904, 1912, and 1914. The burner did not pay off immediately, however, and it was not until 1890 that she was finally able to incorporate the Woman's Canning and Preserving Company in Chicago. The company's stockholders were women, and all of the officers and employees, save one man who fired the boiler, and Cooley, who operated the patented preserving apparatus, were women. Internal divisions within the company, however, soon left her disillusioned, and she left Chicago around 1893 to settle near Junction City, Kansas, living with her closest sister, Mrs. [C. H.] Manley. Continuing her canning work, she received four more patents for canning methods between 1903 and 1906. The Woman's Canning and Preserving Company went bankrupt in 1921.

One of the most prolific female inventors in the late nineteenth and early twentieth centuries, Jones was not often recognized as such, perhaps because of her Spiritualism and perhaps because, in spite of her feminist reforms, she took no part in feminist reform movements, including the woman suffrage movement. Jones never married. She died in Brooklyn, New York.

• Amanda Jones's own *A Psychic Autobiography* (1910) is a key to linking the events of her life, attributing them, as she does, to psychic inspiration. In recent years, more attention has been paid to her numerous patents and contributions as an inventor. See Anne L. Macdonald, *Feminine Ingenuity: Women and Invention in America* (1992), and Autumn Stanley, *Mothers and Daughters of Invention: Notes for a Revised History of Technology* (1993). For assessments of her literary career, see Nettie Garmer Barker, *Kansas Women in Literature* (1915); Frank H. Severance, "Random Notes on the Authors of Buffalo," Buffalo Historical Society, *Publications* 4 (1896). Information on her patents can be found in *Specifications and Drawings of Patents Issued from the U.S. Patent Office*, June, July 1873, Mar. 1880. Scant information on her company can be found in "A Business Run by Women," *Chicago Daily News*, 15 Feb. 1892. An obituary is in the *Junction City (Kans.) Union*, 1 Apr. 1914.

SUZANNE WHITE JUNOD

JONES, Benjamin Franklin (8 Aug. 1824–19 May 1903), steel manufacturer, was born in Claysville, Washington County, Pennsylvania, the son of Jacob Aik Jones, a farmer and merchant, and Elizabeth Goshorn. Jones moved with his family to New Brighton, Pennsylvania, when he was fourteen, acquiring a good liberal education at the New Brighton Academy. At eighteen Jones moved to Pittsburgh, where he would become a prominent force in the young city's development during the next half-century.

In Pittsburgh Jones became a clerk in a transportation company owned by Samuel M. Kier, another pioneer in the economic development of western Pennsylvania. In 1847 Jones was offered an equal partnership in Kier's Mechanic's Line, a transportation system that consisted of canal boats and railroad facilities. Within a short time, however, this firm was forced out of business by the expansion of the Pennsylvania Railroad, and Jones and Kier decided to get involved in the fledgling iron industry.

In 1847 Kier and Jones purchased an iron furnace and forge near Armaugh, Pennsylvania. Jones, although he had no practical iron making experience, became the operating head of the company, and through his organizational genius and hard work the firm operated successfully for a number of years. It did, however, suffer from locational disadvantages that resulted in high transportation costs. Jones, therefore, wanted to find a mill in Pittsburgh, which was emerging as the center of the iron industry in western Pennsylvania and had vastly better transportation facilities and access to raw materials. The target of Jones's interest was a recently organized venture, American Iron Works. It had been set up by Bernard and John Lauth, who had purchased land on the south bank of the Monongahela River and established an ironworks there. The mill began operation in September 1853 and in December of that year was reorganized with capitalization of $20,000 in a partnership of Jones, Kier, and the Lauth brothers. A few years before, in 1850, Jones had married Mary McMasters of Allegheny County. The couple had four children.

The Lauths had charge of production in the new venture, while Jones handled the warehouse, accounts, and finances. Kier took no active role in the enterprise. The firm expanded rapidly during the 1850s, and in 1856 the company was again reorganized, as Kier and John Lauth left the partnership and the financier and merchant James Laughlin became the new partner. In 1861 Bernard Lauth left the enterprise, and it was reorganized as Jones & Laughlin, Ltd., with Jones, James Laughlin, and Laughlin's brother and two sons. At the same time, the firm erected two blast furnaces in Pittsburgh, initiating a drive toward vertical integration.

Jones was recognized by his contemporaries as one of the most farsighted and influential men in the early iron and steel industry. His most important early contribution was in vertical integration. In addition to erecting his own blast furnaces, Jones early also began to acquire control of a supply of raw materials. He was one of the first manufacturers to purchase Lake Superior iron ore lands as well as coal from around Connellsville. He also set up warehouse facilities for his product in Chicago to further integrate operations. Perhaps his most significant contribution was the sliding scale of wages, by which mill workers were paid at a stated rate per unit based on the selling price of the product. Created by Jones in 1865 to solve an industrywide labor impasse, the scale became the standard means of determining wages in the industry for the rest of the century and was termed by John Jarrett, president of the Amalgamated Association of Iron and Steel Workers, as the union's greatest achievement.

Jones also engaged in important technological innovations at his plant during these years, making the transition to mass production of steel. In 1886 Jones installed two seven-ton Bessemer converters in his plant, with a third Bessemer unit added in 1890. This brought J & L into the vast Bessemer market of the time. In 1896 there was a further important transformation in plant equipment as the vast array of puddling furnaces were replaced with open hearth furnaces. By the time of Jones's death, J & L was one of the largest independent steel producers in the country, with capacity for more than one million tons of Bessemer and open hearth steel, steel bars, sheet piling, rolled steel, shafting, and a variety of other products. Jones did not sell his firm to U.S. Steel or other consolidations at the turn of the century. It remained under family management throughout the first third of the twentieth century. As his last organizational act, Jones set up the Jones and Laughlin Steel Corporation in 1902, placing it under the management of his eldest son, B. F. Jones, Jr.

Jones was also important as a trade association official and political figure. For many years he was a major contributor to the Republican party in Pittsburgh, and in 1884 he was named chairman of the Republican National Committee, from which he directed the unsuccessful presidential campaign of James G. Blaine. One of Jones's major concerns in national politics was retention of a high protective tariff on iron and steel products. His strong defense of the tariff elevated him to president of the American Iron and Steel Association in 1885, and he served in that position until his death. In 1888 Jones published an article in the *North American Review* that contained a major statement defending the tariff, rejecting the contention that it was a special benefit for trusts and asserting instead that it

was the source of high wages for laborers in the industry. After his death in Pittsburgh, Jones was lauded as "the most highly respected man in the iron trade" in *Iron Age*, and the *Pittsburgh Gazette* published several pages of tributes to Jones from his workers and fellow steel masters. Jones was a figure of great importance in the transformation of the nation's iron and steel industry. If less significant than Andrew Carnegie, he more closely represented the profound transformation from small scale puddled iron production to large batch mass production of steel.

• Jones's diary is held at the Archives for Industrial Society at the University of Pittsburgh, as are some J & L Steel Corporation Papers. Jones's article, "Iron and Steel," is in *North American Review* 146 (1888): 437–39. The best short biographical treatment is John A. Heitmann, "Benjamin Franklin Jones," in *Encyclopedia of American Business History and Biography*, ed. Paul Paskoff (1989). See also Ben Moreell, *"J & L": The Growth of an American Business (1853–1953)* (1953), and John N. Ingham, *Making Iron and Steel: The Independent Iron and Steel Mills of Pittsburgh* (1991). Obituaries are in *Iron Age*, 21 May 1903, and the *New York Times* and *Pittsburgh Gazette*, 20 May 1903.

JOHN N. INGHAM

JONES, Bob (30 Oct. 1883–16 Jan. 1968), Protestant evangelist and college founder, was born Robert Reynolds Davis Jones in Skipperville, Alabama, the son of William Alexander Jones and Georgia Creel, peanut farmers. Jones, the eleventh of twelve children, grew up in the Reconstruction South, working hard on the family farm that barely supported the large family. He was named after his father's Civil War comrade Robert Reynolds and southern hero Jefferson Davis, though his parents dropped the second middle name "Davis" when he was very young.

Exhibiting excellent speaking ability at an early age, Jones was memorizing lengthy pieces of poetry and prose at age five and reciting them to family supper guests. By the age of twelve he had traveled throughout his county and preached in homes, schoolhouses, rural churches, and outdoor settings. His first recorded public speech was in defense of the Populist party. His first revival was held at the Mount Olive Methodist Church in Brannon's Stand, Alabama, where he had been elected Sunday school superintendent at age twelve. He recorded sixty conversions during the one-week meeting. Known locally as the "boy preacher," he had a commanding presence, not only because of his speaking ability but because of his physical presence. At age thirteen he was rotund and weighed 150 pounds.

At age fifteen, having founded his first church of fifty-four members two years earlier, Jones was licensed to preach by the Methodist Episcopal Church, South. The next year he became a circuit rider and served five churches on the Headland circuit of the Mariana district of the Alabama Conference of the Methodist church. During his first few years as a circuit preacher more than 400 people made confessions of faith in response to his preaching. His reputation as a preacher and evangelist began to spread, and by the age of sixteen he was preaching all over southeastern Alabama.

Jones's mother died when he was fourteen, his father when he was seventeen. In 1901, having received his high school diploma from Kinsey High School in 1899, he enrolled in Southern University in Greensboro, Alabama (now Birmingham Southern University). He supported himself on funds he earned as pastor of a few small country churches and as an occasional revivalist preacher. He was a diligent but average student, much of his time being dedicated to weekend revival meetings during the school year and week-long campaigns in the summers. He completed three years of coursework but never received a bachelor's degree (the often given title "Dr." is the result of several honorary doctorates given to Jones throughout his career). He married Bernice Sheffield, a student at nearby Judson College in Marion, Alabama, in October 1905. Ten months later she died of tuberculosis; they had no children.

From 1905 through the mid-1920s Jones traveled the nation and the globe as a full-time evangelist. On one of his evangelistic tours in Uniontown, Alabama, he met his second wife, Mary Gaston Stollenwerck. They were married in June 1908 and moved to Birmingham, Alabama; they had one son. As Jones preached he received increased notoriety, and by 1914 he had preached all over the southern states and was known as the "Billy Sunday of the South." Jones conducted his evangelistic campaigns in churches, outdoor canvas tents, and specially constructed tabernacles, often preaching to crowds as large as 15,000. His frequent citywide campaigns sparked extensive newspaper coverage, and as his name began to spread invitations came in from all over the United States.

Jones's message was not only one of the need for personal conversion. He also preached against social ills, such as liquor consumption, gambling, dancing, Hollywood movies, and casual mixing of the sexes. As a fundamentalist, he opposed modernism in all its forms. He opposed teaching evolution in the public schools and rejected Protestant liberalism with its acceptance of biblical higher criticism. Later in his career, he would oppose popular evangelist Billy Graham (who had attended Bob Jones College for one year) because he cooperated with liberal Protestants in his evangelistic campaigns. Politically, he was a friend of William Jennings Bryan, a Democrat. He did, however, oppose Roman Catholic Alfred E. Smith, the Democratic presidential nominee in 1928, and delivered more than 100 public speeches for Smith's Republican opponent, Herbert Hoover.

By the time Jones was forty years old, he had preached in hundreds of cities throughout thirty states and several foreign countries. In his first twenty-five years of ministry, he had preached more than 12,000 sermons to crowds exceeding 15 million total and witnessed over 300,000 conversions to the Christian faith. He was a convincing preacher because of his speaking style. He spoke directly and simply, communicating a practical gospel message with animation and clarity.

Although he is mostly known for his evangelistic crusades, he also maintained a ministry to Christian lay people and pastors by speaking at the nation's leading Bible conferences, such as the Winona Lake Bible Conference. Because of his popularity and his cultural influence, he was, except for Billy Sunday, the most significant American evangelist in the period between Dwight Moody and Billy Graham.

During the early decades of the twentieth century, many fundamentalists sensed a secularizing trend in higher education. During his travels Jones heard scores of stories from parents about young people who had left home to attend a college or university and returned with their faith shattered and their morals corrupted. Sensing an "atheistic drift" in America's institutions of higher learning, he decided to open a Christian college that would protect youth from the scourge of modernism. The school would provide an education in "the arts and sciences, giving special emphasis to the Christian religion and the ethics revealed in the Holy Scriptures."

He founded Bob Jones College in St. Andrews, Florida, in 1926, and students began taking classes in the fall of 1927. Because of financial pressures brought on by the Great Depression as well as the need for a more central location, Jones moved the school to Cleveland, Tennessee, in 1933 (now the site of Lee College, denominational school of the Church of God, Cleveland). In 1947, needing more land and facilities, he again moved the school, now Bob Jones University (BJU), to its present location in Greenville, South Carolina. In addition to running and promoting the university, he continued to preach at evangelistic crusades and Bible camps. He remained president of BJU until 1964, but by the mid-1950s his son, Bob Jones, Jr., had taken over much of the school's internal management.

Because Jones desired to protect Christian students from rampant secularism, he refused to take any government money or to submit his school to the official accreditation process. To this day, Bob Jones University remains an unaccredited institution. In addition to his rejection of governmental intrusion, Jones is also known for his affirmation of racial segregation on biblical grounds. By official policy Bob Jones University remained racially segregated until 1971, when Bob Jones III became president; and interracial dating was forbidden until 1983, when the Supreme Court forced the school to change its rules (*Bob Jones University v. the United States*).

Throughout its existence Bob Jones University has prepared students for a life of Christian ministry. Although many who attend the school plan to become pastors or evangelists, the university also offers a wide variety of majors in the arts, the sciences, and business. Bob Jones University, the nation's premier fundamentalist institution of higher learning, has fostered a commitment to the arts, maintaining an impressive art collection, sponsoring an artist series, and developing excellent drama and music programs. Jones died in Greenville.

• Jones's papers and other archival materials are in Bob Jones University, Greenville, S.C. Books written by him include *Comments on the Here and Hereafter* (1942) and *Things I Have Learned: Chapel Talks at Bob Jones College* (1944). For a complete biography with extensive information on his evangelistic campaigns, see R. K. Johnson, *Builder of Bridges: A Biography of Dr. Bob Jones, Sr.* (1982). For a general sketch of his life with more details regarding his role in founding and running Bob Jones University, see Melton Wright, *Fortress Of Faith: The Story of Bob Jones University*, 3d ed. (1984); this is an institutional history that also includes extensive biographical information on Jones, Bob Jones, Jr., and Bob Jones III. The works of Johnson and Wright are both in-house histories; hence, they are partisan in nature and largely uncritical of Jones and the university. They do, however, provide the basic historical details. For general information on North American Protestant fundamentalism, see Nancy T. Ammerman, "North American Protestant Fundamentalism," in *Fundamentalisms Observed*, ed. Martin E. Marty and R. Scott Appleby (1991). For a more lengthy and detailed account of fundamentalism and its role in American culture, see George M. Marsden, *Fundamentalism and American Culture: The Shaping of Twentieth-century Evangelicalism, 1870–1925* (1980). For a more popular account, see Marsden, *Understanding Fundamentalism and Evangelicalism* (1991).

KURT W. PETERSON

JONES, Bobby (17 Mar. 1902–18 Dec. 1971), amateur golfer, was born Robert Tyre Jones, Jr., in Atlanta, Georgia, the son of Robert P. Jones, an attorney, and Clara Thomas. Jones received degrees in mechanical engineering from Georgia School (now Institute) of Technology in 1922 and from Harvard University in English literature in 1924. Within a month of his Harvard graduation, he married his high school sweetheart, Mary Malone; they had three children. After two years spent selling Florida real estate, he attended Emory University Law School in 1926–1927. He passed the state bar exams in 1927, and the following year he joined his father's law firm.

Jones became a prominent Atlanta corporate lawyer and businessman, but he was best known as golf's premier amateur. He began playing at the age of six while following his parents around Atlanta's East Lake Country Club. At nine, he won the junior championship of the Atlanta Athletic Club; at eleven, he shot his first 80; at thirteen, he was the club champion of East Lake (beating his father in the finals) and of Druid Hills; and at fourteen, he won tournaments in Birmingham, Alabama, and Knoxville, Tennessee, and became the first Georgia State Amateur champion.

In golfing circles Jones's early exploits made him a national celebrity. A chunky 5'4" and 165 pounds, and still new to long pants, Jones astounded the golfing world in 1916 by leading the qualifying field after the first round at the U.S. Amateur Championship at the Merion Cricket Club in Philadelphia. He fell in the quarterfinals of match play at Merion, but he continued to make headlines, both from his exhibition of skill and his club-throwing tantrums. A series of matches during World War I with fellow prodigies Perry Adair, Alexa Stirling, and Elaine Rosenthal raised $150,000 for the Red Cross. Jones later won

three of his four matches in War Relief exhibitions against leading professionals. He also won several regional tournaments, but until 1923, during what his confidant, Atlanta newspaperman O. B. Keeler, called "the seven lean years," Jones failed to win a national championship. In the National Amateur he lost in the finals in 1919, the semifinals in 1920, the quarter-finals in 1921, and the semifinals in 1922. In the U.S. Open, a medal (or stroke) play championship, he was eighth in 1920, fifth in 1921, and second in 1922.

Then, from 1923 through 1930 Jones dominated the sport to an unmatched degree—"Jones against the field" was a common refrain. Competing eight times in the U.S. Open and three times in the British Open, "The Emperor Jones" (like "Bobby," a nickname he disliked) finished first or second all but once, including one-shot playoff losses in the 1925 and 1928 U.S. opens. During that period, except on one occasion, Jones finished ahead of both Gene Sarazen and Walter Hagen, the era's two best professionals. His feats made him one of the best-known sports figures in the world, and, helped by his ease with words and what Charles Price termed his "boyish good looks and apple pie personality," he was also among the most popular. He was especially beloved in St. Andrews, Scotland, the birthplace of golf.

Jones's greatest year, 1930, saw one of the most memorable single-season performances of any athlete in history. After finishing second (by a stroke) and first (by thirteen strokes) in two American tournaments against professionals, he set a record for a 36-hole event in Britain, and in May, while captaining the visiting American side against Britain in the Walker Cup matches at Royal St. George's, he won both of his matches. On 31 May, after several tough matches, he won his first British Amateur title, and on 20 June at the British Open at Royal Liverpool Golf Club (Hoylake) he added the British Open to his laurels. Jones returned home to a reception that included an unprecedented second ticker-tape parade down New York's Broadway—his first had come after winning the British Open in 1926. On 10–12 July, Jones shot a 287 (71-73-68-75) to capture the U.S. Open by two strokes. Then, in almost an anticlimax to everyone but himself, he won the medal in the qualifying round of the U.S. Amateur at Merion on 22–23 September and, after four lopsided victories, defeated Eugene V. Homans in the final, 8 and 7. Jones was the first man to win all four national championships in the same year, what O. B. Keeler dubbed "The Grand Slam" and another journalist, George Trevor, called the "Impregnable Quadrilateral of Golf." Fourteen years later, the Associated Press voted Jones's Grand Slam the outstanding sports achievement up to that time.

That autumn, Jones, at the age of twenty-eight, announced his retirement from tournament golf, which had left him physically and mentally drained. He wanted to place golf "in its proper place, a means of obtaining recreation and enjoyment." The timing of Jones's retirement and the reasons for it help explain why his acclaim and popularity extended well beyond the championships he won. He had always been only a part-time golfer and an amateur when nearly all other leading golfers were full-time professionals. Often months went by without his touching a golf club. From 1923 through 1930 he averaged less than four tournaments a year, and in some years he played in only two. "My wife and children came first, then my profession," Jones said. "Finally, and never in a life by itself, came golf." By learning not to expect perfection and to control his fiery temper, Jones became celebrated during his playing days and long after for his good sportsmanship. Although a ferocious competitor, after 1921 Jones was always a gentleman on the course. He even called penalties on himself for minor breaches of the rules in four national championships. His dedication to "amateurism" was so strong that he gave his concern about violating the amateur code as the reason for declining the gift of $50,000 offered in 1928 by Atlanta admirers to help him buy a house. Jones, who invariably attributed his victories to "luck," or "destiny," also was justly celebrated for his modesty and generosity toward opponents.

Yet, despite his larger-than-life image, Jones was neither aloof nor priggish, and he was surprisingly well liked by those he so regularly beat. He was adored by sportswriters. He loved opera and classical literature, but he was always ready to curse, smoke, or drink alcohol during Prohibition.

Jones's life in retirement embellished his reputation. His law firm of Jones, Bird, and Howell prospered with clients that included Coca-Cola (he owned several American and foreign bottling plants), and he was active in Atlanta business and civic affairs. He served as a director and then vice president of A. G. Spalding Co., for which he designed the first matched set of steel-shafted clubs with flanged soles on the backs of the irons. Over 2 million clubs from the "Robt. T. Jones, Jr." autograph line were sold from 1932 until 1973. His original twelve instructional films produced in 1931 were followed by a six-film series, *How to Break Ninety*; both series were successful in theaters and enjoyed good sales after being reissued on videotape in the 1980s. Jones wrote articles for *The American Golfer*, the script for the Spalding promotional film *The Keystone of Golf*, hosted a less-than-successful half-hour radio show in 1931, and between 1927 and 1935 wrote two columns a week for the Bell Syndicate. He also published a second, self-effacing autobiography, *Golf Is My Game* (1960), to go with his earlier *Down the Fairway* (with O. B. Keeler) (1927) and two collections of his articles, *Bobby Jones on Golf* (1966) and *Bobby Jones on the Basic Golf Swing* (1969).

Jones also influenced the development of American golf course architecture. He and architect Robert Trent Jones, Sr. (no relation), designed for him and his Atlanta friends the widely copied Peachtree Golf Club, which opened in 1948. Even more significant was the Augusta National Club in Augusta, Georgia, that Jones codesigned with Alister Mackenzie. Officially opened in January 1933 with an exclusive corporate membership, it hosted the first Augusta National

Invitational in 1934, a tournament that annually brought together Jones's former professional and amateur competitors. Thanks to the Jones aura, the organizing skill of financier Clifford Roberts, the strikingly beautiful setting that established a new standard for course design and maintenance, and, beginning in 1956, the adroit use of television, The Masters, as the tournament was officially named in 1938, soon joined the U.S. and British opens and the Professional Golfers' Association championship as one of the four "majors" in professional golf. Although Jones's views on race are unknown, he tolerated a selection process enforced by his openly racist associate Roberts that kept out black golfers until 1975, long after racial barriers had come down in other tournaments.

Aside from an occasional exhibition match for charity, Jones after retirement made his only competitive appearance each year in The Masters. The tournament was not held during World War II when, after playing in some relief-related exhibitions, Jones served in England and Normandy as an intelligence officer in the U.S. Army Air Corps, achieving the rank of lieutenant colonel in 1944. Jones's appearances in The Masters ended after 1948 when he experienced the first symptoms of a life-threatening spinal cord disease that was finally diagnosed in 1956 as syringomyelia, a rare, nonhereditary disease that victims are born with but that does not manifest itself until later in life. Jones's physical condition steadily deteriorated until he was confined to a wheelchair; at his death he weighed less than sixty pounds. Yet his mind remained sharp, and he refused to succumb to self-pity or publicly confirm the seriousness of his disease. Despite constant pain, the onset of heart and circulation problems in 1952, and gnarled fingers and withered limbs that made the simplest tasks impossible, Jones continued to attend The Masters until 1969 and went into his Atlanta office daily until a year before his death. Jones's courageous struggle against such adversity reinforced his public image. His friend, golf writer Herbert Warren Wind, wrote shortly after Jones died in Atlanta: "He had incredible strength of character. As a young man, he was able to stand up to just about the best that life can offer, which is not easy, and later he stood up with equal grace to just about the worst."

Jones left an enduring legacy of athletic prowess and exemplary personal characteristics. No one is likely to break his records of thirteen U.S. and British national championships, and four in one year (he won the U.S. Open a total of four times, the U.S. Amateur five times, the British Open three times, and the British Amateur one time), especially now that the best amateur golfers quickly become professionals; The Masters seems to have a secure place in the pantheon of golf; and the name Bobby Jones will continue to represent the highest standards of amateurism, sportsmanship, and self-mastery.

• The Robert T. Jones Papers, a mixture of selected personal correspondence, family and business records, and writings about golf, are available on microfilm at Golf House, the headquarters of the U.S. Golf Association in Far Hills, New Jersey. Golf House, the Atlantic Athletic Club, and the Augusta National Golf Club also have large collections of Jones golf memorabilia. Jones's four books, cited above, written without the aid of ghostwriters are the best introduction to his life and thoughts. See also *The Bobby Jones Story: From the Writings of O. B. Keeler*, ed. Grantland Rice (1953), a typically adulatory but often inaccurate account by Jones's Boswell; Clifford Roberts, *The Story of the Augusta National Golf Club* (1976), an alternately revealing and dissembling chronicle of the club and The Masters and Jones's role in establishing both; Herbert Warren Wind, "The Sporting Scene: Rule 38, Paragraph 3," *New Yorker*, 18 May 1968, pp. 125–39, on Jones's continuing involvement in The Masters, and "The Sporting Scene: Mainly about Jones," *New Yorker*, 29 Apr. 1972, pp. 114–28, a moving and illuminating farewell by the dean of American golf writers; Charles Price, *A Golf Story: Bobby Jones, Augusta National, and the Masters Tournament* (1986), an "authorized account" that settles some old scores with Roberts and sums up golf writer Price's thoughts about his longtime friend; also of interest is Price's even more personal "The Last Days of Bobby Jones," *Golf Digest*, Apr. 1991, pp. 184–88. The most dispassionate account, and the only full-scale biography, is Dick Miller, *Triumphant Journey: The Saga of Bobby Jones and the Grand Slam of Golf* (1980); although marred by idiosyncratic organization and a number of factual errors, Miller's book is especially useful for Jones's family life and business activities. Howard Rabinowitz, "Bob Jones' First Retirement," *Golf Journal*, May 1993, pp. 31–33, demonstrates the difficulty in establishing the basic facts about Jones's career. For golf's "Age of Jones," see Herbert Warren Wind, *The Story of American Golf*, 2d ed. (1956). For the charge against The Masters of racial discrimination and Roberts's responsibility for it, see Charlie Sifford (with James Gullo), *"Just Let Me Play": The Story of Charlie Sifford the First Black PGA Golfer* (1992). Jones's obituary is in the *New York Times*, 19 Dec. 1971.

HOWARD N. RABINOWITZ

JONES, Buffalo (Jan. 1844–1 Oct. 1919), frontiersman, rancher, and conservationist, was born Charles Jesse Jones in Tazewell County, Illinois, the son of Noah Nicholas Jones and Jane Munden; the exact date of his birth is unclear. His father often served as an election judge and reportedly once hired Abraham Lincoln as an attorney. Charles, the second of twelve children, grew up a backwoods farm boy on Money Creek, in McLean County near Springfield, Illinois. From an early age he developed a passion for wild creatures and often kept several as pets. Although he studied for two years at Wesleyan University in Bloomington, a bout with typhoid fever cut short his college education. Subsequently, "itchy feet" prompted Jones to move west, and in 1866 he settled at Troy, in Doniphan County, Kansas. There he set up a fruit tree nursery and married Martha J. Walton. They had four children, two of whom died from a severe blight when they were young.

Despite some moderate success with his fruit orchard and grape vineyard, the lure of the wilderness spurred him onward. By 1869 Jones had sold his Troy interests and moved his growing family to what would later become Osborne County, Kansas, where he built a sod house. There he began hunting buffalo, initially for his own family's needs and later to market the hides. These early hunting exploits eventually took him into West Texas, where he became acquainted with Pat Garrett and John R. Cook. He also had his share of encounters with Indians. According to some accounts, Jones was a participant in the battle of Yellowhouse (or Thompson's) Canyon against Black Horse's recalcitrant Comanches near present-day Lubbock, Texas, on 18 March 1877. His hunting prowess soon earned him the sobriquet "Buffalo" Jones. Even as he was hunting bison, on occasion he captured and tamed several buffalo calves, selling them for $7.50 a head or exhibiting them at county fairs.

In 1878, along with the brothers J. R. and W. D. Fulton and others, Jones laid out the town of Garden City, Kansas, and was elected its first mayor. In that capacity he came to know such legends as Wyatt Earp and "Buffalo Bill" Cody. He also became involved in real estate and occasionally drove a team of buffalo calves through the streets of Garden City as a promotional stunt.

Increasingly concerned with the threat of extinction of the buffalo, Jones set out from Kendall, Kansas, in April 1886 toward the Texas Panhandle to see if any were left in that area. On finding several, he lassoed eighteen calves and took them back alive. That and similar such feats brought him increased publicity, particularly from writers like Emerson Hough. Having apparently learned of pioneer rancher Charles Goodnight's success at raising buffalo, Jones established a ranch across the Arkansas River from Garden City. There he experimented at crossing buffalo with cattle to produce the cattalo, a sturdy breed with good qualities but too often sterile. Between 1886 and 1889 Jones accumulated over fifty head, including the buffalo herd he purchased in 1888 from Sam I. Bedson of Winnipeg, Manitoba, and shipped them with some difficulty to Garden City. From this herd Jones began selling a few choice animals to zoos, parks, and other ranchers interested in preserving the bison. Once he personally delivered ten buffalo to a purchaser in Liverpool, England, who paid him $10,000 for his efforts. However, financial difficulties brought on by the panic of 1893 and compounded by the failure of a second ranch in Nebraska forced him by 1895 to sell off his herd to ranchers in Montana and California.

In 1897 Jones and several companions journeyed to the Canadian arctic to capture the musk oxen, an animal then seen by few Americans. Despite opposition from local Indians, who considered the oxen sacred, the party wintered in a cabin they had built near the Great Slave Lake until February 1898, when Jones figured the icy weather had driven the oxen south. Eventually he and John R. Rea roped five calves, but these were killed by superstitious Indians and afterward devoured by wolves. Jones returned to Kansas via Alaska and the Aleutian Islands, and while he realized little profit from that venture, his feats as a game catcher had extended his fame worldwide. In 1899 he captured a bighorn sheep for the National Zoological Park in Washington, D.C., and, with Henry Inman, published an autobiography, *Buffalo Jones' Forty Years of Adventure*. Jones's story of how he and his party shot and fended off a hungry wolf pack near the Great Slave Lake was verified in 1907 by Ernest Thompson Seton and Edward A. Preble when they discovered the wolves' remains around the abandoned cabin.

On hearing of the proposed buffalo herd at Yellowstone National Park, Jones offered his services to President Theodore Roosevelt and in 1902 was made a park game warden. (The story of how he roped an unruly bear to a tree and spanked its behind "to teach it some manners" added another dimension to the Jones legend.) But while he successfully developed the Yellowstone buffalo herd from Texas and Montana imports, his strict rules against drinking, smoking, and gambling led to dissension with the men working under him, and by 1906 he was discharged.

Undaunted, Jones next started a new buffalo preserve and experimental ranch on the Kaibab Plateau, north of Arizona's Grand Canyon, bringing in animals by rail from Montana and California to Lund, Utah, and trailing them to the new site in June 1906. These became the nucleus of the herd now maintained in the House Rock Valley, east of the Kaibab. In the summer of 1907 Jones led the aspiring writer Zane Grey on a hunting trip in which he roped mountain lions and captured wild mustangs. Grey subsequently launched his writing career by publishing his impressions of Jones in *The Last of the Plainsmen* (1908). Jones also engaged in nationwide lecture tours, which increased after his wife's death in October 1907. Eastern audiences, particularly those of the Camp Fire Club and other conservation groups, eagerly absorbed his colorful narratives, which he sometimes embellished.

Late in 1909 Jones persuaded industrialist Charles S. Bird of Willapah, Massachusetts, to finance a game-catching expedition to East Africa. With two cowboys, Marshall Loveless and Ambrose Means, plus twelve cow ponies and several hounds, Jones arrived at Nairobi, Kenya, on 3 March 1910. In the Kenyan savannahs they managed to rope warthogs, elands, zebras, a rhino, and a lioness (which lived at the New York Zoo until 1921). Then in 1913, in company with Means, Dallas McDaniel, and Ohio business magnate William Moguey and his wife, Jones traveled to the Belgian Congo (now Zaire) to capture gorillas, but that effort was less successful; finances ran out, and the expedition broke up in disarray, resulting in bad feelings between Jones and his sponsors. Weakened after contracting "jungle fever" on that escapade, Jones died of a heart attack in Topeka, Kansas, at the home of a daughter. He was interred in the Valley View Cemetery in Garden City, next to his wife and sons. Flamboyant in personality, Buffalo Jones was a true pioneer in the establishment of America's game preserves and wildlife refuges.

• Most of Jones's surviving papers may be found in the files of the Yellowstone Park Headquarters and the Kansas State Historical Society in Topeka as well as in the collection of the Finney County Historical Society of Garden City, where his home is maintained as a museum. See also Ralph T. Kersey, *Buffalo Jones: A True Biography* (1958); Robert Easton and Mackenzie Brown, *Lord of Beasts: The Saga of Buffalo Jones* (1961); and *Encyclopedia of Frontier Biography*, vol. 2 (1990). Obituaries are in the *Topeka Capital* and the *New York Times*, both 2 Oct. 1919.

H. ALLEN ANDERSON

JONES, Calvin (2 Apr. 1775–20 Sept. 1846), physician and militia leader, was born near Sheffield, Massachusetts, the son of Ebenezer Jones, a soldier of the Army of the Revolution, and Susannah Blackman. Little is known of his early schooling, though he probably acquired learning in local schools and by reading avidly throughout his life. To learn medicine, he apprenticed with a local Berkshire physician and was certified to practice by the United Medical Society shortly after his seventeenth birthday. By 1793 he was practicing medicine in Freehold, New York, and the following year published *A Treatise on the Scarlatina Anginosa; or, What Is Vulgarly Called the Scarlet Fever; or Canker Rash*, a collection of his clinical observations of the disease. By 1795 Jones had moved to Smithfield, North Carolina, drawn to the South by an "ambitious vein," according to his father. At least two brothers and one sister either preceded or followed him southward.

Jones established a medical practice and soon came to be regarded as one of the outstanding physicians in the area. He was the first in the state to promote Edward Jenner's new vaccination to fight small pox. In 1801 Jones argued that cow vaccine was both milder and less contagious than inoculation, which persuaded many North Carolinians of the efficacy of the treatment. In 1799 he became a founder of the North Carolina Medical Association and served as its corresponding secretary for the five years of the association's existence. He hoped that the organization would upgrade the state medical profession by licensing doctors, a practice that had fallen into some disfavor. In later years Jones became proficient as a surgeon and performed a number of delicate eye operations, especially on cataracts. Overall, he practiced heroic medicine, employing the popular concepts of bleeding and purging.

Military concerns absorbed Jones for more than two decades. He organized a volunteer regiment in 1807 and was appointed adjutant general of the North Carolina Militia from 1808 to 1813. He played an important role in the War of 1812, leading a defense to protect the North Carolina coast from a threatened British invasion in 1813. So widespread was his fame that a military march was composed in his honor, and many addressed him as "General" throughout his lifetime. One of his ongoing concerns was the lack of discipline among the troops, and he repeatedly sought means to create a more efficient army.

Jones moved to Raleigh in 1803 and pursued an active and varied public career. He was a member of the North Carolina House of Commons for the 1799,

1802, and 1807 terms. He also served as Intendent of Police (or mayor) of Raleigh. From 1808 until 1815 he joined with editor Thomas Henderson, Jr. (1787–1835), to publish and edit the state's third newspaper, the Raleigh *Star*. The paper promised its readers no gossip or trivia, but only honest reporting, with an emphasis on important political and scientific matters. Jones often advised government officials on public issues, such as a rumored slave insurrection in 1830. After a visit to Richmond, he presented the architectural design that he felt best suited the state's proposed governor's residence. He became involved in the Neuse River Navigation Company's ambitious but unsuccessful efforts to make that river navigable from New Bern to Raleigh. Jones was concerned about his adopted state's image and proud of the role that he could play in determining its future.

Jones was active in the Freemasons and advanced from master of his lodge in 1805 to grand master of North Carolina in 1817 and 1819. In 1819 he became a member of the American Colonization Society, whose principal efforts were to send free blacks to Africa. He worked to ensure fairer trials for slaves but believed that whites should act as caretakers for the "unhappy race." Devoted to education, he served as a trustee of the Raleigh Academy and of the University of North Carolina from 1802 until 1832. His collection of books and "artifical and natural curiosities" became the foundation for the university's museum. In 1819 he married Temperance Boddie Williams Jones, a widow. In addition to a son by her first marriage, the couple had several children, only three of whom survived to adulthood.

In 1821 Jones purchased 615 acres north of Raleigh and built a plantation home, which he named "Wake Forest." He conducted a variety of agricultural experiments and sought to use the most modern scientific methods. He sold his plantation in 1832 to the Baptist State Convention, and the denomination formed a school from his estate, which became Wake Forest College. Seized by the desire for greater fortune in the West, in 1819 Jones gradually began to purchase acreage in western Tennessee, which included land grants awarded to revolutionary war soldiers. He undertook annual trips to that state to inspect soil conditions and crops, and he kept detailed records of his travels and encounters with Native-American tribes. In 1832 Jones and his family moved to Bolivar, Tennessee, where he spent the last fourteen years of his life. The family lived on a substantial plantation named "Pontine." Jones gave up his active medical practice, though many still sought his advice. He maintained an interest in politics and attended the 1844 Whig Convention that nominated Henry Clay as its presidential candidate.

Jones was a distinguished citizen of early North Carolina. He made his mark in a variety of fields, was a respected physician, and had enormous impact on the state's development. He died at "Pontine" and was buried in Polk Cemetery in Bolivar. His personal writings reveal a man with enormous powers of observation, who was fascinated by the world around him. Jones possessed great self-discipline and ambition, was successful, independent, caring of his family, and was devoted to his adopted region.

• The private writings and letter books of Calvin Jones can be found in the Southern Historical Collection at the University of North Carolina, Chapel Hill, and the Tennessee State Archives and Library in Nashville. Two useful biographical articles are S. R. Breusch, "Calvin Jones (1775–1846): Some of His Contributions to Medical Practice in New York, North Carolina, and Tennessee," *Bulletin of the History of Medicine* 31 (1957): 246–59, and Thomas B. Jones, "Calvin Jones, M.D.: A Case Study in the Practice of Early American Medicine," *North Carolina Historical Review* 49 (1972): 56–71. Older, laudatory accounts include Marshall DeLancey Haywood, *Calvin Jones: Physician, Soldier and Freemason, 1775–1846, Being an Account of His Career in North Carolina and Tennessee* (repr. 1919), and Edgar M. Timberlake, "Calvin Jones, Ninth Grand Master of Masons of North Carolina," in *Nocalore: Being the Transactions of the North Carolina Lodge of Research*, no. 666 A.F. and A.M., ed. John Raymond Shute, vols. 12–19, 1942–1949 (1949). A brief account that reveals Jones's broad interests is Catherine W. Bishir and Marshall Bullock, "Mr Jones Goes to Richmond: A Note on the Influence of Alexander Parris' Wickham House," *Journal of the Society of Architectural Historians* 43 (1984): 71–74.

SALLY G. McMILLEN

JONES, Catesby ap Roger (15 Apr. 1821–20 June 1877), naval officer, was born in Fairfield, Virginia, the son of Roger Jones, an army officer who became army adjutant general, and Mary Anne Mason Page. Catesby Jones was appointed a midshipman in the U.S. Navy on 18 June 1836. His decision to join the navy was strongly influenced by an uncle, Captain Thomas ap Catesby Jones, USN, under whose command young Jones experienced his first cruise. Almost constantly at sea for the next fifteen years, Jones qualified as passed midshipman in 1842 and lieutenant in 1849. While visiting Paris on extended leave in 1851, he was seriously injured when struck by a shot fired during a street disturbance. Following his recovery, Jones was assigned to the Washington Navy Yard, where for the next three years he worked with Lieutenant John A. Dahlgren, USN, in developing the powerful Dahlgren naval cannon. Because of Jones's familiarity with this new smoothbore shellgun, he was assigned to the USS *Merrimac* as ordnance officer (Feb. 1856).

Following the secession of Virginia, Jones resigned his commission and joined the Virginia navy as a captain. Two months later, as a newly commissioned lieutenant in the Confederate States Navy, he commanded the batteries on Jamestown Island. Jones was then ordered to Norfolk, where he worked with Lieutenant John M. Brooke, CSN, in rebuilding the hull of the *Merrimac* and converting it into the ironclad *Virginia*. Jones hoped to command the vessel with which he was so familiar, but command instead went to Captain Franklin Buchanan, CSN, with Jones as first lieutenant and executive officer.

On 8 March 1862 the *Virginia* engaged the Federal blockaders off Hampton Roads, sinking two of the enemy vessels and damaging another. After Buchanan was wounded, Jones assumed command of the ironclad. The next day the *Virginia* fought the Federal ironclad *Monitor* to a standoff before the two vessels finally broke off the contest. The *Virginia* then returned to Norfolk, Jones having played a major role in the historic engagement that would determine the future of naval warfare. That single contest made wooden warships obsolete.

Two months after the engagement off Hampton Roads, the *Virginia* was blown up by the Confederates to prevent its capture. Jones next saw action commanding a land battery at Drewry's Bluff, 15 May 1862. His promotion to commander the following year was attributed to Jones's "gallant and meritorious conduct" aboard the *Virginia* and at Drewry's Bluff. In July 1862 he briefly commanded the steamer *Chattahoochee* while it was being completed near Columbus, Georgia. However, Jones's recognized background in ordnance was too valuable not to utilize, and he was sent to the Naval Ordnance Works at Charlotte, North Carolina. In May 1863 he received orders to take charge of the Selma, Alabama, Iron Works, which became the Confederate Foundry and Ordnance Works. While Jones was in command of the foundry, some 200 heavy cannon were manufactured there for military use. Jones personally supervised the casting of every cannon and added his initials to each on completion. On one occasion he was miraculously spared when an explosion and fire burned his hat and clothing but left him uninjured. Jones took a special interest in the Selma-built ironclad *Tennessee*, which he hoped to command. Secretary of the Navy Stephen R. Mallory refused Jones the command he so coveted, assuring him that his service at the foundry was "more important . . . than any which you could otherwise perform in the Navy."

In March 1865 Jones married Gertrude T. Tartt; they had six children. That same month, with Federal capture of the foundry imminent, Jones had its machinery dismantled and transferred to steamboats and railroad cars. He and his wife escaped by steamer to Gainsville. He continued on alone to Mobile, where he surrendered and was paroled, 9 May 1865.

After the war Jones formed a partnership with ex-Confederate naval officers Brooke and Robert D. Minor. Acting as private citizens, the trio engaged in securing and selling U.S.–made arms to foreign governments. In 1866, while in Lima, Peru, negotiating a sale of arms to that nation, which was then engaged in war with Spain, Jones was offered command of the Peruvian and Chilean navy; however, he declined the offer. After the business partnership was dissolved, Jones settled in Selma with his family. He died there after being fatally shot by a neighbor as a result of a quarrel between their children.

Jones was an experienced officer and an expert on ordnance, whose resignation from the U.S. Navy in 1861 was a serious loss to the North. His work, together with that of his colleague Brooke, made it possible for the South to manufacture its own heavy cannon even late in the war. Ironically, it was Jones's expertise in ordnance that prevented him from obtaining what he desired most—command of a warship.

• Official Civil War correspondence of Jones is found in *The Official Records of the Union and Confederate Navies in the War of the Rebellion* (30 vols., 1894–1922). Additional Jones correspondence from the war years appears in George Mercer Brooke, Jr., *John M. Brooke: Naval Scientist and Educator* (1980). See also Catesby ap R. Jones Folder, BZ File, Naval History Division, Department of the Navy, National Archives. For Jones's own published writings, see Jones, "The First Confederate Iron-Clad 'the *Virginia*,' formerly the U.S. Steam Frigate '*Merrimac*,'" *Southern Messenger* 15 (Dec. 1874): 200–207, and "Services of the *Virginia*," *Southern Historical Society Papers* 11 (Jan. 1883): 65–75. A brief biography of Jones is W. S. Mabry, *Brief Sketch of Capt. Catesby ap R. Jones* (1912). An obituary is in the *Selma Times*, 20 and 21 June 1877.

NORMAN C. DELANEY

JONES, Charles Colcock (20 Dec. 1804–16 Mar. 1863), Presbyterian clergyman, professor, and missionary to African-American slaves, was born at Liberty Hall plantation in Liberty County, Georgia, the son of John Jones, a wealthy planter, and Susannah Hyrne Girardeau. Jones attended Sunbury Academy, in Sunbury, Georgia (1811–1819); Phillips Academy, in Andover, Massachusetts (1825–1827); Andover Theological Seminary (1827–1829); and Princeton Theological Seminary (1829–1830). After graduating from Princeton, he returned to Georgia and married his first cousin Mary Jones. They had three children. Ordained by the Georgia Presbytery, in May 1831 he accepted a call to be pastor of the First Presbyterian Church, Savannah. Eighteen months later he resigned his pastorate, returned to a family plantation in Liberty County, and began his work as a missionary to the African-American slaves of the region.

A wealthy planter, Jones was best known during his lifetime as a tireless worker for the evangelization of African-American slaves. In 1833 he overcame local white suspicions of such work by enlisting the support of influential neighbors and relatives and organized the Liberty County Association for the Religious Instruction of Negroes. The annual reports of the association, written by Jones, became widely read pleas not only for religious instruction but also for the humane treatment of slaves. In 1837 he published his *Catechism of Scripture Doctrine and Practice* for the oral instruction of slaves. In it he made an evangelical presentation of the Christian faith and advocated a paternalistic social order. His *Religious Instruction of the Negroes in the United States* (1842) was a careful history of the subject and a call for whites to accept their religious responsibilities to their "servants." Many slaves heard Jones preach, and hundreds joined one of his Liberty County churches. He was frequently asked to perform slave weddings and funerals. Though he was frequently sought out for advice and counsel, slaves never forgot that Jones was a slaveholder and their response was always filtered through that reality.

From 1836 to 1838 Jones served as professor of ecclesiastical history and church polity at Columbia Theological Seminary in Columbia, South Carolina. In 1838 he returned to Liberty County and resumed his missionary work, becoming known as the "Apostle to the Negro Slaves." Returning to his old position at Columbia in 1848, he served two years before accepting a call to Philadelphia to become the secretary of the Board of Domestic Missions, Presbyterian Church, U.S.A. Ill health forced his resignation in 1853, and he returned once again to Liberty County. Although he served the remainder of his years as the stated supply (a minister appointed by a presbytery to perform the functions of a pastor for a specified period of time in a congregation not seeking an installed pastor) of the Presbyterian Church, Pleasant Grove, Georgia, his primary work was devoted to writing *The History of the Church of God during the Period of Revelation* (1867).

As a young man in the North, Jones had written his fiancée that slavery was "a violation of all the laws of God and man at once. A complete annihilation of justice." Deeply troubled by what course he should follow in regard to slavery, his decision to become a missionary represented what appeared to him to be the most faithful choice available to him. He took a reformist position on slavery, advocating for slaves good housing, adequate clothing and food, some free time, and, above all, religious instruction in the Christian faith, but he did not call for an end to slavery. Jones died at "Arcadia," his plantation, of "wasting palsy."

• Letters and papers of Jones and his family are in the Jones collection, Tulane University; University of Georgia, Athens; Duke University, Durham, N.C.; and in private hands. Some 1,200 letters (out of a total of approximately 6,000), centered around life on Liberty County plantations from 1854 to 1868, were printed in Robert Manson Myers, *Children of Pride: A True Story of Georgia and the Civil War* (1972). See also James Stacy, *History of the Midway Congregational Church, Liberty County, Georgia*, rev. ed. (1903); R. Q. Mallard, *Montevideo-Maybank: Some Memoirs of a Southern Christian Household in the Olden Time; or, The Family Life of the Rev. Charles Colcock Jones, D.D., of Liberty County, Ga.* (1898); Mallard, *Plantation Life before Emancipation* (1892); Eduard N. Loring, "Charles C. Jones: Missionary to Plantation Slaves, 1831–1847" (Ph.D. diss., Vanderbilt Univ., 1976); and Erskine Clarke, *Wrestlin' Jacob: A Portrait of Religion in the Old South* (1979).

T. ERSKINE CLARKE

JONES, Charles Colcock, Jr. (28 Oct. 1831–19 July 1893), lawyer, archaeologist, and historian, was born in Savannah, Georgia, the son of Charles Colcock Jones, a Presbyterian clergyman, professor, and wealthy plantation owner, and Mary Jones. His youth was spent in Liberty County, Georgia, moving by season among the three plantations of his parents ("Arcadia," "Montevideo," and "Maybank") while his father worked as a missionary to slaves on surrounding plantations, and in Columbia, South Carolina, where his father served two terms (1837–1838 and 1848–1850) as a professor of church history and polity at Columbia Theological Seminary.

Jones's early education was with private tutors on his parents' plantations and under the rigorous discipline of his parents. Liberty County, on the Georgia seaboard, had a population in 1845 of 5,493 slaves, twenty-four free blacks, and 1,854 whites. The large African-American population that surrounded Jones in his youth was composed primarily of Gullah-speaking people whose folkways and folklore provided Jones with resources for some of his later published materials. The white population was composed largely of descendants of New England Puritans who had moved first to South Carolina in the 1690s and then to Liberty County in the 1750s. By the 1840s this white community, centered in the Midway Congregational Church, had provided Georgia with some of its most distinguished families. The interaction of these two distinct populations—one African American and one white—provided the context for Jones's childhood and youth and shaped much of his later interests.

When Jones's family moved to Columbia in 1848 he enrolled in South Carolina College. When his father accepted the position of corresponding secretary of the Board of Domestic Missions of the Presbyterian Church, U.S.A., he moved with his family to Philadelphia and shortly thereafter enrolled at the College of New Jersey (later Princeton). He graduated in 1852 and read law for a year in the office of Samuel H. Perkins of Philadelphia. In 1853 he entered the Dane Law School at Harvard University. He graduated in 1855 and for the next six years practiced law in Savannah with John Elliot Ward. In 1858 Jones married Ruth Berrien Whitehead; they had two children. He was elected a city alderman, and in 1860–1861 he served as mayor of Savannah.

Jones was a vigorous supporter of secession. During the Civil War he was a lieutenant colonel of artillery and served in Savannah as chief of artillery for the military district of Georgia. During the siege of Savannah (December 1864) he was chief of artillery. Because of the economic devastation of the South, he moved to New York City and practiced law there (1866–1877) with Ward, wrote extensively on the history of Georgia, and gave numerous speeches on historical and archaeological subjects. In 1877 he moved to Augusta, Georgia, bought an antebellum mansion ("Montrose") in the suburb of Summerville, practiced law, and continued to write about the history of his native state. He organized and directed the Confederate Survivors' Association of Augusta until his death. He delivered annual addresses to this association; included among them were some of his most notable published speeches.

In 1863, two years after his wife died of puerperal fever, Jones married her first cousin Eva Berrien Eve; they had one son. Jones's extensive and influential family connections were extended through his marriages to a bewildering web of relations throughout the South.

Jones is best known for his writings on the history of Georgia and for his studies of Native-American antiquities, a subject of interest to him from childhood. His published works include *Indian Remains in Southern Georgia* (1859); *The Monumental Remains of Georgia* (1861); *Historical Sketch of the Chatham Artillery* (1867); *Antiquities of the Southern Indians* (1873); *The Siege of Savannah in December 1864* (1874); *The Dead Towns of Georgia* (1878); *The History of Georgia* (2 vols., 1883); and *Negro Myths from the Georgia Coast* (1888). Jones was a meticulous scholar whose concern for details often limited the scope of his studies. His *History of Savannah, Ga.* (1890), and *Memorial History of Augusta, Ga.* (1890), for example, cover only the eighteenth century, while his two-volume *History of Georgia* is a history of the state only through the American Revolution. Yet his books were popular and appreciated by other historians. George Bancroft thought that Jones's *The History of Georgia* was the best state history he knew and called Jones "the Macaulay of the South." Jones died in Augusta.

• Letters and papers of the Jones family are in the Jones collection at Tulane University, New Orleans; the University of Georgia, Athens; Duke University, Durham, N.C.; and in the private possession of the Waller family in Augusta, Ga. The post–Civil War papers of Jones are concentrated at Duke. Some 1,200 Jones family letters (out of a total of approximately 6,000) are published in Robert Manson Myers, *The Children of Pride: A True Story of Georgia and the Civil War* (1972). Included are numerous letters to and from Jones. Myers also presents a graphic picture of Jones's family relations and personal life. An article that contains an extensive bibliography of Jones's work is by his son, C. E. Jones, *Gulf States Historical Magazine*, Mar. 1903. R. Q. Mallard, *Plantation Life before Emancipation* (1892), provides a retrospective view of the Jones family during the antebellum period. See also C. E. Jones, *In Memoriam: Col. Charles C. Jones, Jr.* (1893); James Stacy, *History of the Midway Congregational Church, Liberty County, Ga.* (1899); and *American Anthropologist* (Oct. 1893). An obituary is in the *Atlanta Constitution*, 20 July 1893.

T. ERSKINE CLARKE

JONES, Clarence Wesley (15 Dec. 1900–29 Apr. 1986), pioneer missionary broadcaster, was born in Sherrard, Illinois, the son of George Jones, a Salvation Army captain and part-time coal miner, and Emma Detbrenner, a Salvation Army captain. In 1907 the family moved to Chicago, where Jones's father managed an apartment building and worked for the Salvation Army. In 1918 Clarence entered the Moody Bible Institute in Chicago, an evangelical training center known as the "West Point of Christian service." He graduated in 1921 as valedictorian. Jones was a gifted trombonist, and his brother Howard played trumpet. Together they became well known performing and recording artists. Their recordings were released on 78 rpm discs, the most famous of which include "Christ Arose" and "Onward Christian Soldiers." While traveling as an evangelistic musician Jones met Katherine

Welty, a minister's daughter, in Lima, Ohio, in 1924. They were married the same year and had four children who survived to adulthood.

After his graduation from Moody, Jones assisted minister Paul Rader with a radio program originating from the interdenominational Chicago Gospel Tabernacle. Under the auspices of the Scandinavian Alliance Mission, he traveled in 1928 to Venezuela and Ecuador with hopes of founding a missionary radio station. In 1930 radio station HCJB broadcast test programs in Ecuador. The call letters stood for *Hoy Christo Jesus Bendice* (Today Christ Jesus Blesses) and "Heralding Christ Jesus' Blessings." On 9 March 1931 Jones established the World Radio Missionary Fellowship in Lima, Ohio. On Christmas Day of that year he aired the first regular broadcast of HCJB. As one of several innovations in religious broadcasting he created a University of the Air that disseminated agricultural information to the farmers of Ecuador and surrounding countries. By 1940 HCJB had increased its power to 10,000 watts by erecting a transmitter in Quito, Ecuador. The construction and operation of the radio station was funded by donations from North American churches and individuals. The format of broadcasting included morning talk shows, classical music programs, children's broadcasts, and an ample number of preaching programs. The evangelical, premillennial doctrinal basis of Moody Bible Institute gave theological parameters to the religious broadcasting.

During World War II Jones was appointed by the U.S. embassy to head the Committee of Coordination, a group that conducted propaganda on behalf of the United States as a military and economic power against the propaganda from the German embassy. Jones also devised an evacuation plan for American expatriots in Quito in the event that Germany invaded South America. At the same time the National Broadcasting Company (NBC) designated HCJB as home of "The Voice of Democracy" in South America. NBC sent programs on seventeen-inch records for broadcast throughout South America. In effect, HCJB became a noncommercial affiliate of NBC in the war effort. NBC even sponsored a gala honoring HCJB's twelfth anniversary, on which occasion NBC funded the erection of a new building. HCJB eventually expanded its programming to include short-wave broadcasting to Russia and Sweden, as well as broadcasts in German, Portuguese, Japanese, French, and Quichua. The World Radio Missionary Fellowship opened a sister station, HOXO, in Panama City, Panama. WVMV, a Spanish-language station in McAllen, Texas, also joined the HCJB network.

Jones found time for other work in education and social service. He taught at the national conservatory of music in Quito, and in 1946 he launched the Summer School of Christian Radio, which had teaching centers in Providence, Rhode Island, Chicago, and Los Angeles. He also helped to organize an international gathering in 1944 that led to the formation of the World Conference on Missionary Radio, the precursor of International Christian Broadcasters. In order to fulfill the social mission of HCJB, Jones helped to found a hospital in Quito in 1949. He later helped to establish a second hospital in Shell Mera, Ecuador, and he promoted mobile clinics. Moreover, HCJB established a regional medical center to serve much of Ecuador.

Jones officially retired from HCJB in 1961, but he subsequently visited HCJB listeners in Europe, Africa, and Asia, areas covered by the short-wave broadcasts. Within thirty years after his retirement HCJB was broadcasting from a 500,000-watt transmitter. It maintained a printing press and a color television station. Jones retired to Largo, Florida, where he died.

Jones was widely honored for his religious broadcasting. He was named "Alumnus of the Year" by Moody Bible Institute in 1957, and in 1975 he became the first inductee to the Religious Broadcasting Hall of Fame, sponsored by the National Religious Broadcasters. In 1975 the Graduate School of Wheaton College in Illinois established the Clarence Jones Lectureship in Christian Communications as the first chair in missionary broadcasting in an American college. Jones summarized his mission with one sentence: "In this struggle for the minds of men, the air is the last great missionary frontier." He led the way in utilizing electronic communication, namely radio and television, insisting on excellence and integrity. He has been called "the dean of international Christian broadcasters."

• Jones wrote *Radio: The New Missionary* (1946). A biography is Lois Neely, *Come up to This Mountain: The Miracle of Clarence W. Jones and HCJB* (1980). See also "Clarence W. Jones and HCJB," a chapter in Ruth A. Tucker, *From Jerusalem to Irian Jaya* (1983).

WAYNE A. DETZLER

JONES, Donald Forsha (16 Apr. 1890–19 June 1963), plant breeder and first to develop hybrid corn on a commercial scale, was born near Hutchinson, Kansas, the son of Oliver Winslow Jones, a teacher and school principal, and Minnie Wilcox Bush, a teacher. Jones grew up on a small farm with responsibilities for tending the family garden that gave him the agricultural background that led to his career in plant genetics, with an emphasis on corn (maize) breeding. After obtaining his undergraduate degree in agriculture in 1911 from Kansas State College (now Kansas State University), Jones worked on alfalfa breeding for two years at the Arizona Agricultural Experiment Station, doing what he wryly called "taking the place of the bumblebee" (Mangelsdorf, p. 143). He then taught horticulture at Syracuse University (1913–1914), where he also received a master of science degree in 1916. His doctorate was earned at Harvard University in 1918 under Edward Murray East, a renowned geneticist. Jones's dissertation, "The Effects of Inbreeding and Crossbreeding upon Development," published in 1918 as Bulletin 207 of the Connecticut Agricultural Experiment Station (CAES), was clearly influenced by East, who had initiated a corn inbreed-

ing and crossbreeding program at the CAES in 1905. Jones, who would spend the rest of his professional career at CAES, was in charge of the breeding program in 1915. In December 1915 he married Eleanor March of Manhattan, Kansas, with whom he had two children.

Jones followed East's plan initially but also recognized the value of corn-breeding experiments carried out by George Harrison Shull on Long Island in the first decade of the twentieth century. Jones saw that neither East nor Shull had tried to find a practical, commercial use of their studies. He believed that the phenomenon of heterosis, or hybrid vigor, "an accumulation of favorable dominant effects" (Jones [1958], p. 325) could be used to increase yields and improve disease resistance of corn. Inbred varieties of most plants were puny, disease prone, and poor yielders of seed. The crossing of two such inbreds often resulted in a plant that was vigorous, disease resistant, and high yielding. However, this first, or single, cross was too expensive to use in commercial practice because it demanded too much seed from low-yielding inbreds. Jones thought that a second cross, one between two single crosses, might be commercially viable while maintaining the robustness and disease resistance of the single cross.

In 1917 Jones demonstrated in experimental plots the successful application of this procedure, which he called the "double-cross" method of producing hybrid seed corn. By 1922 he showed that hybrid corn obtained from double crosses was vigorous and productive in some parts of Connecticut. Although not all inbreds proved to be worthwhile, with time and practice selected varieties turned out to be extraordinarily valuable when used in the double-cross procedure. By the late 1920s Jones's method was shown to be remarkably useful in the midwestern corn belt of the United States. Thus was born the modern hybrid seed corn industry, which today supplies seed to produce nearly 100 percent of all corn grown in the United States and more than 75 percent of the rest of the world's corn crops.

Jones discovered, however, a serious drawback in his procedure. Selective crossing required manual detasseling (emasculation) of the seed parent, an expensive, tedious, and sometimes damaging process that he spent more than thirty years searching for a way to avoid. The discovery of cytoplasmic male sterility (CMS) in corn by Marcus Rhoades in the early 1930s gave impetus to experiment station researchers and commercial seedsmen to incorporate CMS into corn breeding to eliminate the manual detasseling operation. But, where others tried and failed, Jones finally succeeded. Using a variety of CMS corn found in Texas, he hybridized this strain into other varieties; by the late 1940s he had demonstrated its usefulness in avoiding about two-thirds of the detasseling. In addition, Jones recognized the usefulness of fertility-restoring genes in an elegant synthesis of rendering the seed parent sterile with CMS and then crossing this parent with a restored, male-fertile parent to produce fertile seed without manual detasseling.

In 1948 and again in 1950 Jones applied for U.S. patents on the two methods used to produce hybrid seed corn without detasseling. Only the second application, using CMS and fertility-restoring genes, was issued as a patent in 1956, the first patent to incorporate a genetic process in its claims. The patent was assigned to Research Corporation, a nonprofit patent management company that attempted to license the process to seed-corn producers who were rapidly adopting the method. However, the producers refused to pay royalties, and attempts to collect royalties were met with anger and hostility. Those who had applauded Jones in 1948 for his pioneering work with hybrid corn condemned him for attempting to profit from his work. Some of his critics believed that Jones, an employee of the state of Connecticut, should not profit financially from his efforts, but even in this contentious area he was an innovator. Nearly all universities, experiment stations, and seed companies have since developed patent policies for employee researchers. Research Corporation, unable to collect royalties from hybrid seed-corn producers, took the matter in 1963 to civil court, where it finally was resolved in 1970, after his death, in favor of Jones and the company. The income from royalty payments went principally to the CAES, Harvard University, and Research Corporation to further research in theoretical and applied genetics and plant breeding.

Although more than half of Jones's publications were on corn improvement, he had a wide interest in both plant and animal sciences. His interest in eugenics, for example, led him to the belief that animals, including humans, could be "improved" through selective breeding in a manner analogous to the improvement in corn. More important, as it turned out, Jones's expertise in horticulture helped to educate a large audience in the applied aspects of genetics. By speaking to garden clubs, giving radio talks on vegetable growing during World War II, and responding to readers' questions as an associate editor of the *Rural New Yorker*, Jones resolved horticultural problems for home gardeners. He also was managing editor of *Genetics* from 1925 to 1935 and secretary of various international meetings and symposiums. He was a member of numerous scientific societies, including the American Association for the Advancement of Science, the Botanical Society of America, the American Society of Naturalists, and the National Academy of Sciences. In addition, Jones was a mentor to individuals who became distinguished in their own right, such as W. Ralph Singleton, a sweet corn breeder, and Paul C. Mangelsdorf, a geneticist and historian of corn.

Jones retired from the CAES in 1960. He died at his home in Hamden, Connecticut. He had been a major contributor to the growth of agriculture in the United States and abroad, helping to make hybrid corn a larger component of the world's food supply. By extending the principle of hybrid vigor to the double-cross method of producing seed corn he demonstrated a clear relationship between theoretical and applied genetics. Jones's later work with CMS and fertility-restoring genes paved the way for even greater yields and for introducing the patent system into plant breeding.

• Some of Jones's papers together with microfilm copies of portions of papers, notebooks, correspondence, and documents related to the patent on hybrid seed corn are at the Connecticut Agricultural Experiment Station, New Haven. Significant publications by Jones include "Dominance of Linked Factors as a Means of Accounting for Heterosis," *Genetics* 2 (1917): 466–79, "Selection in Self-Fertilized Lines as the Basis for Corn Improvement," *Journal of the American Society of Agronomy* 12 (1920): 77–100, "Like Father, Like Son-in-Law," *Scientific Monthly* 26 (1928): 557–60, "The Production of Hybrid Seed Corn without Detasseling," written with Mangelsdorf, *Bulletin 550, Connecticut Agricultural Experiment Station* (1951): 1–21, and "Heterosis and Homeostasis in Evolution and in Applied Genetics," *American Naturalist* 92 (1958): 321–28. The most informative biographical sketch is Paul C. Mangelsdorf, "Donald Forsha Jones, April 16, 1890–June 19, 1963," National Academy of Sciences, *Biographical Memoirs* 46 (1975): 134–55. Additional biographical data can be found in Stanley L. Becker, "Donald F. Jones and Hybrid Corn," *Bulletin 763, Connecticut Agricultural Experiment Station* (1976): 1–9, and A. Richard Crabb, *The Hybrid-Corn Makers: Prophets of Plenty* (1947). Also see W. Ralph Singleton's enlightening obituary in *Genetics* 50, supplement (1965): 13–14.

STANLEY L. BECKER

JONES, Edward (1808?–14 May 1865), African-American Episcopal priest and missionary, was born in Charleston, South Carolina, the son of Jehu Jones, proprietor of a prestigious hotel, and Abigail (maiden name unknown). Little is known of his early education. In 1822 he attended Amherst College in Amherst, Massachusetts. When Jones graduated in 1826, he was one of the first African-American college graduates in the nation.

Although not noted as a particularly spiritual individual while at Amherst, Jones decided to pursue religious study a couple of years after graduation. He attended Andover Theological Seminary from 1828 to 1830, followed by study at the African Mission School in Hartford, Connecticut. He received an honorary M.A. from Trinity College in 1830. That same year, on 6 August, he was ordained a deacon, and on 15 September he was ordained an Episcopal priest, both times by Bishop Thomas Church Brownell at Christ Church, Hartford.

Jones chose work abroad, and in 1831 he went to Freetown, Sierra Leone, as a missionary for the Domestic and Foreign Missionary Society of the Episcopal Church. He then worked as a schoolmaster in Kent village on the southwestern tip of Freetown peninsula, and from there schoolmaster on the Banana Islands further south. On 23 May 1838 he wrote a letter to the Reverend Dr. Thomas Staughton Savage, another Episcopal missionary, and it was published in *The Spirit of Missions*. In the letter he described the conditions in Sierra Leone and noted that "the heathen around us are entirely unprovided for. They have none to teach them the way of salvation, are without God, know not his son Jesus Christ, and therefore have no hope."

In 1840 Jones became a missionary in Sierra Leone with the British Church Missionary Society (CMS), founded in 1799 by the Church of England Evangelicals. Known at first as the Society for Missions in Africa and the East, the name was changed to the Church Missionary Society in 1813. It was the most effective Anglican missionary society among the non-Christians. Jones traveled to England frequently on their behalf to raise funds and oversaw the construction in Sierra Leone of essential new buildings.

When the CMS could not attract English people to the mission field, it turned to German Lutherans trained in Berlin. It was because of this that Jones was able to meet and marry Hannah Nylander, the daughter of German missionary pastor Gustav R. Nylander, in 1838. She died shortly afterward; however, it is believed he had several children with her.

In Freetown, the Church Missionary Society had established a school called the Christian Institution, sometimes known as the African Institution. It was founded by the Reverend Leopold Butscher, another German Lutheran missionary, who had come to Sierra Leone with Nylander in 1806. The Christian Institution was a training school for recaptive children; that is, children who had been captured and enslaved by the Muslims and then recaptured by the Christians. One of the most famous persons to attend the Christian Institution was Samuel Ajayi Crowther, later a leader of the Niger Mission and Bishop of the Niger Territories, the first non-European bishop of the Anglican Communion.

In 1827 the Christian Institution was transformed into the Fourah Bay College, and in 1840 Jones became the principal, a position he held for over twenty years. He was "the Principal who succeeded in carrying it on longest without interruption" (Stock, vol. 1, p. 336). In the nineteenth century Fourah Bay College educated the majority of the African clergy and many of the leading laity. In 1845 Jones opened the Grammar School and later established a Girl's Boarding School, afterwards known as the Annie Walsh Female Institution. That same year Dr. William Ferguson, the first governor of Sierra Leone of African descent, laid the cornerstone of a new building, which opened on 1 November 1848.

In 1853 the Church Missionary Society asked Jones and three Ibo companions to lead an expedition to visit the Niger and report on the prospects for emigrants there. The Ibos were among the liberated Africans in Sierra Leone, and they wanted to return to their native land and have a Christian mission established among their people. Jones and his companions were to survey the situation and make a report to the CMS. A mail boat took them to Fernando Po, and from there they visited the Cross River. There Jones became convinced that it would not be possible for them to ascend the Niger and reach Aboh, unless in a steamer. They went to Calabar, where they found the Scottish Presbyterians already established.

On his return to Sierra Leone, Jones began work as a pastor and newspaperman. He helped to edit the *African and Sierra Leone Weekly Advertiser*, a missionary sponsored paper, and in 1861 he was editor of the *Sierra Leone Weekly Times and West African*. He was relieved of his duties by the latter after backing the bishop in his dispute with Governor Stephen John Hill.

Jones remarried twice, first in 1845 to a woman whose last name was Wilkins, with whom he would have at least two children, and then in 1862 to Elizabeth Shuff, a CMS missionary. The date of Wilkins's death is unknown.

In 1864 the family settled in England, and Jones died at New Brompton, Chatham, Kent. Jones was a successful African American, an ordained Episcopal missionary and an outstanding educator. He was a leader in taking Christianity to Sierra Leone.

• Very little information is available about Jones. The only three documents of his that have been located are *Journal of a Mission to the Niger* (1853), another account of the trip in *The Church Missionary Intelligencer* (1853), pp. 33–34, and the 23 May 1838 letter published in *The Spirit of Missions* (Dec. 1838): 392–94. Eugene Stock, *The History of the Church Missionary Society, Its Environment, Its Men and Its Work* (3 vols., 1899), has scattered references to Jones and Fourah Bay College. Jones's work is noted briefly in Lamin Sanneh, *West African Christianity: The Religious Impact* (1983).

DONALD S. ARMENTROUT

JONES, Eli Stanley (3 Jan. 1884–25 Jan. 1973), Methodist missionary to India, was born in Clarksville, Maryland, the son of Albin Davis Jones, a tollkeeper, and Sarah Alice Peddicord. His early years featured the training of a strict mother and the religious discipline of Methodist churches. He began to study law while working as a clerk in the Baltimore County law library. After his Christian conversion at the age of seventeen, he turned to the ministry. Meanwhile his father lost his political job, forcing Stanley to delay his college matriculation for one year during which time he worked as an insurance agent.

Jones enrolled in Asbury College (Kentucky) because he wanted to learn to preach like its promoter and future president, Henry Clay Morrison, one of the most prominent southern evangelists at the turn of the century. The college represented the Holiness wing of Methodism and was widely known for producing ministers, missionaries, and intense campus revivals. Jones participated fully in the religious life at Asbury, and through his involvement in the Student Volunteer Movement he began to prepare himself for missionary service. Upon graduation in 1906 he declined an invitation from the college to return as an instructor and also rejected the advice of a trusted friend who suggested that he pursue evangelistic work in the United States. Instead he accepted an invitation from the Methodist Episcopal Church North to become a missionary to India. In 1907 Jones began an 8½-year term in India, serving as the minister of the Lal Bagh

Church in Lucknow. This city was the center of Indian Methodism, and many of the denominational leaders—both Anglo and Indian—worshiped in this congregation. Lucknow was also the location for the first Asian college for women, Isabella Thoburn College, and in 1911 Jones married one of its instructors, Mabel Lossing, who was of Iowa Quaker origin. That same year the couple moved fifty miles to Sitapur—which was to be their base for the next forty years—where Stanley worked mostly with the outcastes and Mabel was head of a school for boys. Here they raised their only child.

The middle 1910s were a period of crisis for Jones. Offered a demanding ministry with the Indian intellectual elite, and feeling both his emotional stamina and physical health weakening (he suffered nearly simultaneous bouts with a ruptured appendix and tetanus), Jones undertook an intense reevaluation of the basis of his spiritual resources. The result was renewed vigor and an enlarged vision for what he called "the greatest adventure of my life." He adopted a radical Christocentric message and highly innovative methods in his new work with the Indian leadership class. His only task, he decided, was to boldly and joyously introduce Christ. He need not—indeed he must not—introduce Western civilization, the Old Testament culture, or even institutional Christianity. Indians must be free to adapt the incarnation message to their own personal and cultural settings. As the Hindus and other non-Christians would not naturally visit Christian churches, which they associated with Western imperialism, Jones met them in neutral places, such as public assembly halls, where he gave lectures and participated empathically in open dialogue. Jones sought to present to India "the disentangled Christ." "We are not out to replace the cultures of the East with Western culture. The only thing we have to give is Christ, a gift to us, so a gift to you. If you can build up around Christ a better culture and civilization than we have been able to do, we will sit at your feet."

In the 1920s Jones began introducing meeting formats that were distinctly Indian. Throughout India he held round-table conferences involving cordial but frank discussions among Hindu, Christian, and other religious leaders, each seeking to learn from the religious experiences of the others. By 1930 Jones had founded the first Christian ashram, or retreat center, at Sat Tal in the lower Himalayas, where British and Indians of all types could come together for an intense period of inquiry into the personal and social meaning of the Christian faith. Later he exported the ashram idea to the United States and Europe, especially during the early 1940s when British authorities temporarily blocked his return to India because of his known sympathy with the Indian independence movement and his close friendship with Mohandas (Mahatma) Gandhi.

While on furlough in the United States in 1925, Jones received a request from a church executive to write about his missionary views and experiences. These recollections became known as *The Christ of the Indian Road*, a bestselling book that contributed to his growing reputation in this country and abroad. In 1928 the Methodist church offered him a bishopric; however, he resigned before the consecration ceremony, suggesting that he preferred to continue his work as an evangelist. After 1930 his missionary appointment was "evangelist-at-large for India and the world" in recognition of his wide travels and influence. He then redefined the goals of his evangelistic work, expressing his desire "to strengthen and convert the church—to try to Christianize un-Christian Christianity wherever found—and to win the educated non-Christian to an allegiance to Christ."

In the course of his life, Jones preached approximately 60,000 sermons and published twenty-eight books, including a devotional guide, *Abundant Living* (1942), which sold nearly one million copies and appeared in thirty languages. He was a friend and confidant of many world leaders. He worked actively for racial understanding, human peace and reconciliation, and Christian unity. For example, he attempted to mediate between Japan and the United States in late 1941, and after 1935 he promoted a plan for uniting the Protestant churches of the United States, emphasizing spiritual rather than organizational unity. In 1961 he was nominated for the Nobel Prize, and two years later he was awarded the Gandhi Peace Prize. He died in Bareilly, India.

• The main body of Jones papers is in the possession of his daughter, Eunice Mathews. The best institutional collection is at Asbury Theological Seminary. The best introduction to Jones is his own *Song of Ascents* (1968), an autobiographical revelation of his mind and spirit no less than his experiences. An especially insightful summary of his career in India is Richard W. Taylor, "The Legacy of E. Stanley Jones," *International Bulletin of Missionary Research* 6 (July 1982): 102–6. Also see Martin Ross Johnson, "The Christian Vision of E. Stanley Jones: Missionary, Evangelist, Prophet, and Statesman" (Ph.D. diss., Florida State Univ. 1978). Obituaries are in the *New York Times*, 26 Jan. 1973; the *Christian Century*, 14 Feb. 1973; and *World Vision*, Apr. 1973.

WILLIAM C. RINGENBERG

JONES, George (16 Aug. 1811–12 Aug. 1891), newspaper publisher and financial manager, was born in Poultney, Vermont, the son of John Jones, a manufacturer of woolens, and Barbara Davis. Orphaned at thirteen with only a country-school education, Jones supported himself by working in a general store operated by Amos Bliss, publisher of the *Northern Spectator* newspaper. He became friends with Horace Greeley, also from Poultney, who began an apprenticeship at the newspaper in 1824.

Jones found work in a dry-goods store when he moved to New York City in 1833. In 1836 he married Sarah M. Gilbert of Troy, New York, with whom he had four children. Greeley invited Jones to become his partner in founding the *New York Tribune* in 1841, but having no funds to do so Jones instead took a job in the *Tribune* business office. There he became friends with fellow *Tribune* employee Henry J. Raymond. The two talked occasionally of starting their own newspaper but lacked the money.

In 1843 Jones moved to Albany, where he ran a news agency and then went into business as a banker. He accumulated some capital, as did Raymond, and their interest in owning a newspaper was revived. When a deal for them to purchase the *Albany Evening Journal* from Whig politician Thurlow Weed collapsed in 1848, the success of Greeley and others in New York attracted them there. On 18 September 1851 they launched the *New York Times* with Jones as publisher and financial manager and Raymond as editor. The paper was Republican politically, and it became profitable in its second year. Its stock rose from $1,000 to $11,000 a share by the time Raymond died on 19 June 1869.

Jones took charge of both the business and editorial departments of the newspaper following Raymond's death even though Raymond's heirs were the majority shareholders. He rebuffed Greeley's offer to buy the *Times* with the comment that he never would sell as long as he "was on the top of the ground." Jones significantly shaped the journalistic development of the newspaper by hiring and supporting gifted editors. Further, he insisted that there could be no business-office interference with editorial policymaking, one of the first publishers to enforce this major tenet of modern American journalism.

In September 1870 Jones launched the *Times*'s most daring venture of its nineteenth-century history by attacking the powerful and corrupt Democratic political machine of Tammany boss William Marcy Tweed. The Tammany plunder of public coffers was well known, but other city newspapers shrank from confrontation with Tweed. Instead, they were silent or, as in the case of the *New York World* and the *New York Sun*, critical of the *Times* for its attacks. Newspapers did not want to risk the loss of city advertising doled out by Tweed and his associates; the *Times* alone rejected city advertising. *Harper's Weekly*, whose cartoonist Thomas Nast depicted Tammany as a voracious tiger, was supportive of the *Times* campaign, but *Harper's* joined in only after the *Times* had attacked Tweed for more than a year. Advertisers large and small deserted the *Times*, and Tweed's Wall Street cronies exerted other financial pressures on the paper.

Jones stood the losses. He seldom wrote, but he allowed editor Louis J. Jennings and reporter John Foord, highly capable Britons who had worked in London, full rein in developing and interpreting the facts. In 1870 Jones, Jennings, and Foord took on as well a group of prominent city businessmen, among them John Jacob Astor, Moses Taylor, and George K. Sistare. The *Times* accused them and others of falsely certifying that city financial records, carefully abridged by the Tweed-directed city controller, were in perfect order. As the newspaper gradually uncovered more support for its charges, Tweed operatives sought to gain control of the *Times* for $5 million, pointing out to Jones that he could live like a prince. "All true," he replied. "But I should know that while I lived like a prince, that I was a rascal. I cannot consider your offer—or any offer. The Times will continue to publish the facts" (Berger, p. 48).

Jones's determination eventually prevailed, abetted by the honesty of some low-level government employees who at considerable risk fed to the *Times* irrefutable evidence of millions being diverted into the hands of Tweed and his cohorts. Jones's persistence was remarkable given the power of his adversary, the lack of public interest in Tammany's plunder, and the fact that all the other newspapers turned their backs. When the evidence could no longer be ignored, wished, or rationalized out of existence, interest in the *Times*'s exposures grew and their accuracy was accepted. The estimate of Tammany graft between early 1869 and the autumn of 1871, when Tweed controlled both city and state government, ranged from $50 million to $150 million. This was mostly in the form of diverting the bulk of grossly inflated collections for government building projects to Tweed and friends. Boss Tweed died in jail, and the Tammany ring was defeated.

In 1876 Jones solidified the newspaper's independence by becoming its majority stockholder. Although a staunch Republican himself, Jones would not countenance an attempt by editor Jennings that year to allow the *Times* to become a Republican party organ. He dismissed Jennings, and in 1884 did not object when the new editor took the unprecedented step of giving the paper's presidential endorsement to Grover Cleveland, a Democrat. Bolting the party the paper always had supported lost it a substantial volume of advertising, which was never recovered during Jones's tenure. Even so, he again deferred to the editors in endorsing Cleveland in 1888 even though he personally preferred Republican Benjamin Harrison, who won.

In the last decade of Jones's life, the *Times* distinguished itself in two crusades. The first, in 1881, revealed how mail route contractors, with the collusion of some U.S. senators, were defrauding the government of millions by falsely padding the sizes of their routes. Though no convictions resulted, newspapers nationwide took up the cause, raising the *Times*'s prestige. The second, shortly before Jones's death, exposed abuses by officers who operated the New York Life Insurance Company; this exposé resulted in reforms. Jones died in South Poland, Maine.

The financial drains of erecting a new building in 1888, one-cent competition, and outdated business practices led Jones's heirs to sell the *Times* to a group of buyers in 1893 for $1 million. The buyers suffered losses and in 1896 sold to Adolph S. Ochs, who rebuilt the paper to national prestige. *Times* historian Elmer Davis wrote of Jones: "His true monument . . . is to be found in a better informed public opinion, a higher standard of public morality" (p. 166).

• Jones's papers are in the New York Public Library. His career and contributions to journalism are described in Elmer Davis, *History of the New York Times 1851–1921* (1921), and Meyer Berger, *The Story of the New York Times 1851–1951*

(1951). Other sources are Francis Brown, *Raymond of the Times* (1951), which covers the founding of the newspaper and the relationship between the two men and also contains a useful bibliographical essay, and Leo Hershkowitz, *Tweed's New York* (1977), on the newspaper's exposure of the Tweed "ring." Obituaries appear in the *New York Times* and the *New York Herald*, 13 Aug. 1891. See also the editorial commentaries published in the *Times*, 13 and 16 Aug. 1891.

DANIEL W. PFAFF

JONES, George Heber (14 Aug. 1867–11 May 1919), Methodist missionary and student of Korean culture, was born in Mohawk, New York, the son of Charles Edward Jones and Susan Cosser. Educated in the public schools of Utica, New York, he left for the Korean mission field at the age of twenty in 1887, less than three years after the Methodist church had begun its work there. American Methodists William B. Scranton and Henry Gerhardt Appenzeller had reached Seoul, Korea, early in 1885 and realized the daunting obstacles they faced, principally profound cultural differences and local suspicions. But they persevered and in 1886 called for two new men to augment their work. In 1887 Jones accompanied Franklin Ollinger, a veteran missionary, to Seoul. Two years later other Methodist missionaries arrived, notably women. This small staff endured continual hardships, including disease and political turmoil, in establishing an enduring Methodist presence in Korea.

Jones's contribution to the mission began modestly. For the first five years he taught at the Pai Chai school and college in Seoul. In 1892 he received a correspondent bachelor's degree from the American University at Harriman, Tennessee. In May 1893 he married Margaret Josephine Bengel. Together they worked at Chemulpo, where no missionaries previously had been. For ten years Jones was in charge of missionary endeavors there, overseeing the creation of forty-four churches and baptizing nearly 3,000 people. Leading businessmen of the area became converts, indicating the advance of Christianity among more influential groups. Jones hoped to utilize Methodism's influential niche as a basis for exerting a beneficial social influence, a common vision for Western missionaries of the time. As a result of his successes Jones's stature in the Methodist church grew, and he later served two terms as superintendent of the Methodist mission in Korea (1897–1899 and 1907–1909).

Given his interest not merely in evangelism but in social development, Jones was a student of Korean culture. He served from 1902 to 1905 as a member of the group translating the Bible into Korean. He also edited the *Korean Repository* from 1895 to 1898 and founded and edited a Korean theological journal. His books about Korea, *Korea: The Land, People, and Customs* (1907) and *The Korean Revival* (1910), reveal both a longing for missionary success and a discerning eye for social patterns. *The Korean Revival* noted that by 1907 a powerful expansion of Christianity was underway, led largely by students. The nature of this grassroots religious movement required ecumenical

missionary cooperation. But the results could be seen in both a deepened understanding between Koreans and foreigners, and an improved social morality and stability. Though the manner of such writing and analysis became antiquated, in their day the works enhanced popular understanding. Jones also wrote brief works on the Old Testament and church history in Korean, produced a Korean Methodist hymnbook, and a Korean dictionary of scientific terms. For a time he was the Korean correspondent for the *Times* (London). In addition, during Japanese occupation of Korea, Jones helped organize a plan for Korean immigration to Hawaii between 1903 and 1905, with Korean government support.

Jones occasionally visited the United States, lecturing at Morningside College, De Pauw University, and Boston University. In 1909 he returned permanently to the United States. From 1913 to 1919 he served as editorial secretary and associate secretary of the Methodist Board of Foreign Missions. He died in Miami, Florida.

• Jones's extensive missionary journals have not been published. His published works are available in research libraries and missionary archives, such as the Day Missions Collection at Yale Divinity School, which also houses his unpublished works. Brief references to him can be found among essays in *Korean Mission Field*, a missionary magazine, including biographical sketches in 1928 and 1929. L. G. Paik's *The History of Protestant Missions in Korea* (1929) includes references to Jones. An obituary is in the *New York Times*, 13 May 1919.

WILLIAM L. SACHS

JONES, George Wallace (12 Apr. 1804–22 July 1896), miner, merchant, and political leader, was born in Vincennes, Indiana Territory, the son of John Rice Jones, a lawyer and jurist, and Mary Barger. After studying at the Catholic College in St. Louis, Jones, armed with letters of introduction, entered Transylvania University in Lexington, Kentucky. He met a host of then and future political leaders and "formed a warm friendship" with Jefferson Davis, a fellow student. Graduating in 1825, Jones briefly practiced law, but ill health caused him to take up an outdoor occupation, which he found in operating lead mines at Sinsinawa Mound, Michigan Territory (now in Wisconsin), and in smelting. He also kept a store. Together with Daniel Webster, he engaged in profitable land speculation. For a time he served as clerk of the U.S. district court based in St. Louis.

In 1829 he married Josephine Grégoire, member of an old French family. They had five children. Not until 1831 did she move to Sinsinawa Mound with seven slaves in defiance of the Missouri Compromise prohibition. (In 1837 Jones owned ten or twelve slaves.) During the Black Hawk War Jones served as aid-decamp to a family friend, General Henry Dodge (1782–1867), one of many family connections that promoted Jones's rise in politics. In a four-cornered contest in 1835, Jones was elected territorial delegate to Congress for Michigan, soon to be a state. Taking up duties "far more arduous than I had any idea of," he claimed major credit for a law establishing the territory of Wisconsin, divided from Michigan. With the organization of the new territory, he was elected its congressional delegate.

Though without a vote, Jones proved to be an effective representative of the rising Northwest; in 1838 he saw to fruition a law establishing the territory of Iowa. His unwise participation as a second in a sensational duel between two congressmen, Jonathan Cilley and William Jordan Graves, cost him reelection as a delegate in 1838 and appointment as territorial governor of Iowa.

During the next several years Jones twice (1840–1841 and 1845–1848) served as surveyor general for Wisconsin and Iowa, and in 1843 he was clerk of the supreme court of Wisconsin. He moved to Mineral Point, Wisconsin, with his family in 1842, and three years later he settled in Dubuque, his home for the rest of his life. The Iowa legislature in 1848 elected him one of the new state's first senators. An experienced shaper of laws, Jones quickly put through an amendment to the Illinois Central Railroad Bill that extended the line to Dubuque. In 1856 he succeeded in securing a federal land grant to run four rail lines across the state, linking the Mississippi and Missouri rivers.

Iowa's first settlers migrated from Missouri and border states, giving the young state a Democratic majority and a prosouthern outlook. Confronted with the great sectional crisis of 1850, Jones reflected his constituents' views as well as his own "residence of several years in slave States," as he stated it. Saying he was opposed to slavery but unwilling to interfere with it where the Constitution and laws had placed it, he ardently supported the Compromise of 1850, hoping it would "settle this negro question."

Reelected in 1852, Jones fully supported the Kansas-Nebraska Bill introduced by his colleague Augustus Caesar Dodge and attacked in debate an amendment intended to restrict suffrage and officeholding to citizens of the United States. Passage of the Kansas-Nebraska Bill, repealing the Missouri Compromise ban on slavery in the northern part of the Louisiana Purchase, prompted the rise of a northern antislavery party and a swift change in sentiment in Iowa that failed to sway Jones's thinking. His colleague Dodge was replaced by the anti-Nebraska Whig candidate James Harlan (1820–1899). A loyal administration Democrat enjoying distribution of the patronage under Franklin Pierce, Jones in 1856 made an unwontedly long speech in the Senate excoriating Harlan for his views favoring congressional intervention in the territories and African-American equality. Heedless of fissures in the Democratic party and mounting northern antislavery and antiforeign sentiment, Jones denounced the notion of racial equality, supported by Harlan, and defended both popular sovereignty and participation of foreign-born whites in government.

Jones refused to obey the Iowa legislature's instructions to vote for admission of Kansas as a free state. Saying he believed the only way to solve the slavery question was to admit Kansas as a slave state and Minnesota as a free state, he cast his vote for admission of Kansas under the proslavery Lecompton constitution. His stand helped split the Democratic party in Iowa and assured his own failure to be renominated as U.S. senator by his party. He left office in 1859 and accepted appointment as minister to New Granada (now Colombia). For two years he immersed himself in controversies connected with transit rights over the Isthmus of Panama.

Replaced as minister by President Abraham Lincoln, on his return to the United States Jones was clapped into jail for indiscreet letters he had written to Davis. Among other matters, Jones acknowledged his sympathy for the Confederate cause, hoped Lincoln would repudiate abolitionism, and told Davis he had "more confidence in your opinion than in that of any living man." He spent two months in jail but was never prosecuted. In a public letter he defended himself, saying he had opposed secession and had urged Davis to fight for his rights under the Constitution.

His public life finished, Jones spent his remaining thirty-five years in Dubuque, his raven black hair turning white and his prosouthern sympathies being forgotten by his fellow citizens. He wrote his autobiography, though his memory at times was confused, and the state legislature recognized his ninetieth birthday with resolutions of gratitude and friendship. He died in Dubuque, having served the nation well as territorial delegate and advocate for internal improvements in Iowa.

• Jones's papers are in the State Historical Library of Iowa, Des Moines. John Carl Parish, *George Wallace Jones* (1912), comprises a short biography and autobiography with helpful editorial notes and corrections. *Annals of Iowa*, 3d ser., vol. 3 (1863–), contains many letters by Henry Dodge to Jones. Clarence Carter, ed., later John P. Bloom, ed., *The Territorial Papers of the United States*, vols. 12, 27, and 28 (28 vols., 1934–1969), have much material on Jones's work as territorial delegate. The *Congressional Globe* (1849–1859) details Jones's activity as U.S. senator. William R. Manning, ed., *Diplomatic Correspondence; Inter-American Affairs*, vol. 5 (12 vols., 1932–1939), publishes many letters by Jones as minister to New Granada. For Jones's arrest and letters to Davis, see *The War of the Rebellion: A Compilation of the Official Records of the Union and Confederate Armies*, ser. 2, vol. 2 (128 vols., 1880–1901).

JAMES A. RAWLEY

JONES, Hamilton C. (23 Aug. 1798–10 Sept. 1868), humorist, lawyer, and journalist, was born Hamilton Chamberlain Jones in Greenville County, Virginia, the son of William Jones and Martha Loftin. His father, about whom little is known, died while Jones was still an infant, soon after the family's move to Stokes County, North Carolina. His mother then married Colonel James Martin, a wealthy and politically influential landowner and brother to Alexander Martin, North Carolina's former governor and senator. Growing up in the Martin family, "Ham," as he was known by family and friends, gained many valuable political and business connections and was educated at Chapel

Hill Academy for boys. In 1818 Jones earned his B.A. from the University of North Carolina, finishing fourth in the same class as future president James K. Polk. After graduation, Jones remained at the university for an additional year as a Greek tutor, before studying law with prominent attorney William Gaston in New Bern.

In 1820 Jones obtained his license to practice law, married Ann Eliza Henderson, Colonel Martin's granddaughter, and moved to Salisbury, North Carolina, to establish himself in the legal profession. In Salisbury he acquired a successful practice, a plantation called "Como," and a growing family of ten children, six of whom survived infancy. In 1827 he began his long public career when he was elected to represent Rowan County in the state House of Commons, an office to which he was reelected in 1828, 1838, and 1840. Influenced by the Martins' conservative political views, Jones was a strong Federalist at the university and later supported the Whig cause. In the House of Commons he was a vocal opponent of nullification. Because Salisbury's only newspaper was the anti-Federalist and anti-Whig *Western Carolinian*, Jones founded his own newspaper, the *Carolina Watchman*, as a voice of opposition. The first edition, published on 28 July 1832, announced that the paper was intended both "to instruct and to please." To accomplish these goals, Jones included many humorous sketches and tales among the serious discussions of national and local affairs. Though he used much material exchanged from other papers, he wrote a large portion of the news and sketches published in the *Watchman* himself, while continuing to maintain both his law practice and his political career.

Already well known for his humorous storytelling while at the university and even during speeches on the floor of the legislature, Jones's reputation became widespread as he published his favorite tales, many of which he had heard from clients and fellow attorneys. His first known work, upon which his fame would rest, "Cousin Sally Dilliard," appeared in *Atkinson's Saturday Evening Post* in 1831. The tale portrays a frustrated country lawyer trying to elicit worthwhile testimony from a stubborn and inept backwoods witness who repeats his tale's beginning over and over: "Captain Rice, he gin a treat, and cousin Sally Dilliard, she came over to our house and axed me if my wife, she mought'nt go." After giving only irrelevant testimony, the witness shocks the lawyer by confessing "that's the height of what I know about it." The sketch quickly became popular as it was picked up by national papers, including William T. Porter's influential *Spirit of the Times*, where it was reprinted four times before being included in Porter's 1845 anthology, *The Big Bear of Arkansas and Other Tales*.

A series of dialect sketches about frontier characters soon followed, including, "The Sandy Creek Literary Society," "The Lost Breeches," and "McAlpin's Trip to Charleston," which was anthologized in Porter's *A Quarter Race in Kentucky and Other Sketches* (1847). Though Jones wrote and published these and numerous other tales in both his own paper and Porter's, he continued to be known as merely "The Author of 'Cousin Sally Dilliard.'" This sketch had great influence on the future of southern humor because it was often imitated and retold, and its rambling pattern became a formula for later humorists. It was among Abraham Lincoln's favorite stories for entertaining listeners, and Porter suggested that it may have provided the inspiration for Augustus Baldwin Longstreet's *Georgia Scenes*, long considered the early masterpiece of frontier humor.

The demands of public service allowed Jones little time for writing. After selling the *Watchman* in 1839, he served as solicitor for North Carolina's Sixth Judicial District from 1842 to 1848 and became the reporter of the state supreme court in 1853. His time-consuming duties, including publishing the annual reports of the supreme court, even led him to abandon his law practice. At the state's 1861 convention considering secession, Jones signed the state's Ordinance of Secession. He spent the duration of the Civil War as many parents did, worrying about his three soldier sons. He maintained his position as court reporter but resigned in 1863. Though he seems to have had no professional activity following this resignation, there is also no record of further writing in the last years of his life, which he spent in Reconstruction Salisbury with his wife, helping his son establish his own legal practice. Following the death of his wife two months before, Jones died at his daughter's home in Morganton, North Carolina.

Though Jones's contributions to southwestern frontier humor have been all but forgotten, his work, especially "Cousin Sally Dilliard," was an early success in the genre that became the domain primarily of Longstreet, George Washington Harris, and Mark Twain. The prominent status of his trademark story in its time is illustrated in Jones's *Daily Sentinel* obituary, which claimed that "as a humorous writer he was known the whole country over, and his 'Cousin Sally Dilliard' has had a reputation in that line equal to Longstreet's best." Furthermore, the story's significant inclusion in Porter's anthologies, William Evans Burton's *The Cyclopaedia of Wit* (1858), Henry Watterson's *Oddities in Southern Life and Character* (1880), and Franklin Meine's *Tall Tales of the Southwest* (1930) positions it as part of the foundation of a movement that has been integral to southern literature for well over a century.

• All of Jones's known extant works have been collected in *Ham Jones, Ante-bellum Southern Humorist* (1990), which includes an informative introduction by George Hendrick and Willene Hendrick. Further information can be found in Jones's obituaries in the *Raleigh Daily Sentinel*, 16 Sept. 1868, and in *Watchman & Old North State*, 17 Sept. 1868. See also Richard Walser, "Ham Jones: Southern Folk Humorist," *Journal of American Folklore* 78 (1965): 295–316; Steven Gale, *Encyclopedia of American Humorists* (1988); and William Powell, ed., *Dictionary of North Carolina Biography*, vol. 3 (1988).

PAUL CHRISTIAN JONES

JONES, Harry Clary (11 Nov. 1865–9 Apr. 1916), professor of chemistry and physical chemist, was born in New London, Maryland, the son of William Jones and Johanna Clary, prosperous farmers. He was raised in his grandfather's house and received his early education in a small country schoolhouse near his home. His studies continued with one year under Edward Reisler, principal of the high school in Union Bridge, Maryland, and approximately another year at Western Maryland College, which he left for reasons of poor health. After three years of home study, Jones applied for admission to Johns Hopkins University, noting his interests as German, French, chemistry, physics, and mathematics. His previous readings included John Porter's *Chemistry*, Edward Olney's *Trigonometry*, James Dana's *Geology*, and several works in physical science by John Tyndall. Admitted to Hopkins in 1885 as a special student, he worked hard and received his bachelor of Arts degree in 1889. His earliest research studies were carried out on cadmium under the direction of Professor Harmon N. Morse. Jones's dissertation on the atomic weight of cadmium resulted in his receipt of a Ph.D. in chemistry from Johns Hopkins in June 1892.

Despite the fact that a number of chemists at the time had been involved in studies on selective physical properties such as boiling and melting points, solubility, viscosity, and optical activity, descriptive chemistry, and especially descriptive organic chemistry, dominated chemical research studies. In the 1880s a new field of chemistry, physical chemistry, the study of physical properties and chemical constitution, began to clearly emerge aided by the 1887 founding of a new journal by Wilhelm Ostwald, the *Zeitschrift für physikalische Chemie*, which was dedicated to physical chemistry. Jones became aware of these developments and went to Europe to visit and work in the laboratories of the most important practitioners of this new field, Ostwald at Leipzig, J. H. van't Hoff at Amsterdam, and Svante Arrhenius at Stockholm. While working with Arrhenius he began his studies on hydrates in solution as he carried out a research project on the hydrates of sulfuric acid. He returned to Johns Hopkins in 1894, having been designated there a Fellow by Courtesy, a strictly honorary appointment that let him devote nearly all of his time to research. In 1895 he was appointed an instructor in physical chemistry and then rose through the ranks, being appointed associate in 1898, associate professor in 1900, and finally professor of physical chemistry in 1903. His tenure at Hopkins extended until his death. He married Harriett Brooks in 1902; they had no children.

Jones's research work had begun on selected cadmium compounds; the determination of the atomic masses of cadmium, lanthanum, yttrium, praseodymium, and neodymium; the design of a new boiling point apparatus; and the value of certain quantitative analytical reagents. In 1893 it advanced into the nature of solutions; the research he had begun with the hydrates of sulfuric acid developed into a detailed study of the physical characteristics of concentrated versus dilute solutions. Jones's studies on freezing point depression, boiling point elevation, conductivity, and other physical characteristics showed deviations from predicted values based on the generally held view of electrolytic dissociation in highly concentrated solutions. For example, his freezing point data indicated an unusually large lowering of the freezing point of solutions compared to predictions based on data obtained in dilute solutions.

To explain these discrepancies, Jones developed in 1900 his hydrate theory, first published that year in the *American Chemical Journal*, which maintained that a number of water molecules would combine with various ions in a particular ratio to form a new unit known as a hydrate. Reflecting on the theory's development, Jones recalled in *The Nature of Solution* (1917), "If a part of the water present is combined with the dissolved substance, there would be less water acting as solvent and of the dissolved substance, the less solvent present, the greater the lowering of its freezing point."

Jones further developed his ideas into a more general solvation theory published in 1904 in the *American Chemical Journal*, the result of similar work with other solvent systems. He continued to attempt to determine the quantitative nature of a wide variety of hydrates. While his theory received much recognition, it was also criticized on several fronts. Some critics conceded that solvation might be a factor but questioned whether it was the most significant factor. Louis Kahlenberg doubted the existence of hydrates, while Wilhelm Boettger believed that Jones ignored the laws of mass action in his explanation. Indeed the hydrate solution theory has been disregarded in explaining the colligative properties of solutions even though hydrates have been isolated as real entities. Jones's reluctance to modify or surrender his basic position on this theory damaged his reputation. Nevertheless he continued his work, focusing later on the theory of electrolytic dissociation, the absorption spectra of solutions, and physical organic chemistry.

Despite some criticism mentioned above, Jones's research and publications and hence the ability of the program to attract students had made his department at Johns Hopkins one of the leaders in physical chemistry, and his influence was furthur advanced by the publication of his popular physical chemistry textbooks. Besides Jones's numerous articles and his popular textbook *The Elements of Physical Chemistry* (1902), published in four American editions and also in Italian and Russian translations, he wrote another eleven books, including *The Modern Theory of Solution* (1899) in two editions, *Outlines of Electrochemistry* (1901), and *A New Era in Chemistry* (1913), which contains Jones's commentaries concerning important chemists of that period, including August Kekule, J. W. Gibbs, Dimitri Mendeleev, Arrhenius, and William Ramsay. The Carnegie Institution of Washington, D.C., published ten monographs coauthored by Jones between 1907 and 1915. These monographs focused on his varied researches, especially in hydrates, absorption spectroscopy, viscosity and conductivity of solutions, and other physical properties of solutions. While some critics such as A. W. C. Menzies criticized Jones for making numerous errors and leaving out important details, most were supportive of his work. *Elements of Physical Chemistry* was described as an excellent introduction to physical chemistry by Julius Stieglitz, while *Elements of Inorganic Chemistry* (1903) was characterized as a brief but exceptionally clear introduction to the new theories by G. B. Frankforter.

Jones's contemporaries gave him mixed reviews. Ostwald described him as a devoted scholar who had contributed a large number of investigations and researches. Arrhenius stated that Jones had contributed much important data and had conclusively shown that solvents may combine with dissolved substances. John Nef of the University of Chicago described him as a hard worker but as not having any originality. Theodore Richards stated that Jones's enthusiasm had caused him to carry out his work too fast.

Jones held memberships in many scientific societies, including the American Chemical Society, the Franklin Institute, the American Philosophical Society, and the Washington Academy of Science. His responsibilities included service as associate editor of the *Zeitschrift für physikalische Chemie*, the *Journal de chimie physique*, and the *Journal of the Franklin Institute*.

Jones's nonscientific interests extended to music, art, and his farm, but his main interest in life remained his active and extensive research program. Although over the years his health had deteriorated, and he was described as being close to a nervous breakdown, he refused to take time off from his work. After his sudden death at his Baltimore home, the autopsy concluded that death had been caused by the suicidal ingestion of potassium cyanide under a condition of mild depression.

Jones was responsible for helping to make Johns Hopkins a major center for graduate study and research in physical chemistry between 1894 and 1916. He ran a laboratory with high scholarly output, contributing to the fact that from its inception to 1919 more American Ph.D.s in physical chemistry, seventeen, were awarded by Hopkins than by any other American university. His students included Atherton Seidell, who wrote several volumes on the solubilities of organic compounds; Eugene C. Bingham, a pioneer in plastics; Frederick Getman, author of the popular textbook *Outline of Theoretical Chemistry*; and William Reed Veazey. Overall Jones's books were well received, and about 20,000 copies have been sold. Jones is remembered as an important chemist who helped to establish the field of physical chemistry in the United States as a distinctive specialty and as a scientist who provided significant information and insights on the properties of solutions.

• Documents concerning Jones, while not extensive, may be found in the Archives and Special Collections of the main library of Johns Hopkins University. Biographical accounts are by Ira Remsen, "Harry Clary Jones," *Proceedings of the American Chemical Society* 38 (July 1916): 94–96, and a more comprehensive one by E. Emmet Reid that appeared as a preface in Jones's book, *The Nature of Solution* (1917). This book also contains a complete list of all of Jones's publications. Jones's views on the chemists of his time are examined in W. B. Jensen, "Harry Jones Meets the Famous," *Bulletin for the History of Chemistry* 7 (Fall 1990): 26–33. The development of physical chemistry and Jones's role are critically described by John W. Servos, *Physical Chemistry from Ostwald to Pauling* (1990). Information concerning his controversial death may be found in obituaries in the *Baltimore American* and the *Baltimore Sun*, both 10 Apr. 1916, and his death certificate prepared in Baltimore on 12 Apr. 1916 can be found in the Maryland Hall of Records in Annapolis.

ROBERT H. GOLDSMITH

JONES, Hilary Pollard (14 Nov. 1863–1 Jan. 1938), admiral in the U.S. Navy, was born at Hanover Academy, near Doswell, Hanover County, Virginia, the son of Hilary P. Jones, Sr., the headmaster of the academy, and Claudia H. Marshall. Jones graduated seventeenth in his class from the U.S. Naval Academy in 1884 and received his commission as an ensign two years later. As a lieutenant (jg), Jones served in the gunboat *Dorothea* during the Spanish-American War. Subsequent duties included command of the cruisers *Birmingham* and *Tennessee* (1911) and the battleships *Rhode Island* (1911–1912) and *Florida* (1914–1916). Jones was also commandant of the Washington Navy Yard and superintendent of the Naval Gun Factory (1913–1914). Promoted to rear admiral in 1917, he commanded a cruiser division with the Atlantic Fleet during World War I. He married Virginia Lippincott in 1917; they had no children.

After the war, Jones was assigned to duty as commander in chief, Atlantic Fleet. In this capacity, he had responsibility for conducting the aerial bombing experiments off the Virginia capes in July 1921. Army planes sank a number of captured German warships. The experiment gave Jones an appreciation for the potential value of aircraft at sea, but it also caused General William "Billy" Mitchell (1879–1936) to launch an intensive propaganda campaign for the creation of an independent air force.

Promoted to commander in chief, U.S. Fleet with the rank of full admiral in 1922, Jones used his authority to employ airplanes in fleet exercises and dispatched elements of the Atlantic Fleet air divisions on long overseas patrol missions. His assignment to the navy's General Board in 1923 enabled him to take part in important planning and policy decisions. Much of the board's work was concentrated on integrating the new technologies of aviation and submarines into the fleet and dealing with naval arms limitation. Jones and other members of the board were acutely aware of the need to build a balanced fleet within the terms of the Washington Treaty and to plan for the extension of the treaty's tonnage restrictions on battleships and aircraft carriers to other naval vessels.

Jones spent the remainder of his career immersed in the diplomacy of naval arms limitation. In 1926, he served as a technical adviser at the League of Nations Preparatory Commission for the Disarmament Conference in Geneva. Jones also participated in the Geneva Naval Conference (20 June–4 Aug. 1927) as a codelegate. The conference bogged down over British insistence on a large number of small cruisers for defense of the empire and the American desire for smaller numbers of larger 10,000-ton cruisers needed for long-range operations in the Pacific. Last-minute attempts to reach a compromise collapsed, and the conference broke up. Despite the failure at Geneva, Jones remained committed to the limitation of armaments as a means of achieving parity with Great Britain and superiority over Japan in all ship types. He retired in 1929 but a few months later returned to active duty to attend the London Naval Conference (1930) as a technical adviser. He died at his home in Washington, D.C.

A hardheaded professional officer, Jones was steeped in the traditions of the old navy. He was strongly nationalistic and distrusted both the British and the Japanese. Yet he realized that in the political and economic climate of the 1920s it was unlikely the United States would outbuild its potential naval rivals. Reluctantly, Jones accepted diplomacy and international arms agreements as the best means of ensuring the nation's maritime security in an uncertain world.

• Biographical material on Jones is in the Admiral Hilary P. Jones Papers, Naval Historical Foundation Collection, Library of Congress Manuscript Division, Washington, D.C. See also William F. Trimble, "Admiral Hilary P. Jones and the 1927 Geneva Naval Conference," *Military Affairs* 43 (Feb. 1979): 1–4. Additional references to Jones and his participation in naval arms limitation conferences appear in Raymond G. O'Connor, *Perilous Equilibrium: The United States and the London Naval Conference of 1930* (1962); Stephen Roskill, *Naval Policy between the Wars*, vol. 1, *The Period of Anglo-American Antagonism, 1919–1929* (1968); and Gerald E. Wheeler, *Prelude to Pearl Harbor: The United States Navy and the Far East, 1921–1931* (1963). An obituary is in the *New York Times*, 2 Jan. 1938.

WILLIAM F. TRIMBLE

JONES, Howard Mumford (16 Apr. 1892–11 May 1980), educator and author, was born in Saganaw, Michigan, the son of Frank Alexander Jones, a salesman and businessman, and Josephine Whitman Miles, a hairdresser and masseuse. The family moved to Milwaukee and then to La Crosse, Wisconsin, where Jones's father died in 1906. While in high school, Jones debated, was a newspaper carrier, and took dictation on a typewriter from author Hamlin Garland. After graduating from high school in 1910, Jones studied at the La Crosse Normal School for two years, enrolled as a junior in 1912 at the University of Wisconsin, obtained a B.A. there in 1914, and earned his M.A. in English literature at the University of Chicago in 1915. He quit the graduate program there short of the Ph.D. after arguing with the dean over credit requirements. A year later he published his thesis as *Heine's Poem 'The North Sea'* (a translation, with introduction). He never received the doctoral degree.

For the next two decades, continuing to read widely and developing an incredible memory, Jones taught English, American, and comparative literature at several universities: he was adjunct professor at the University of Texas (1916–1917); assistant professor, Montana State University (1917–1919); associate professor and department head back at Texas (1919–1924); associate professor and then professor, University of North Carolina (1925–1930); and professor, University of Michigan (1930–1936). While in Texas he was involved in school play production and in public speaking. He described his time at Chapel Hill, North Carolina, as "blessed." He published with astonishing frequency, including articles, reviews, and five books. *The King in "Hamlet"* (1918) praises the political acumen of Hamlet's uncle. *A Bibliography of the Works and Manuscripts of Byron* (1924), with coauthor, identifies university library locations of Byroniana. *America and French Culture, 1750–1848* (1927), mostly prepared in Chicago during a 1924–1925 leave of absence, was a prize-winning study of French influence on American life and thought. In 1933 he issued *The Life of Moses Coit Tyler*, an urbane, well-documented biography of the pioneering Americanist, and also lectured at the University of Bristol. *The Harp That Once—: A Chronicle of the Life of Thomas Moore* (1937) concerns Byron's poet friend, was based partly on research in Dublin and London supported by a 1932–1933 Guggenheim Fellowship, was praised for its detail and vigorous style, and remained Jones's favorite among his own books. Jones was also leading an eventful private life. In 1918 he married Clara McLure in Montana. The couple had one child before they divorced in 1925. In 1927 he married Bessie Judith Zaban, a brilliant Chicago student; they had no children.

In 1936 Jones received an honorary doctoral degree from Harvard, accepted a professorship there, and continued a spectacular career formally ending with his retirement in 1962. He lectured histrionically on English and American literature to huge undergraduate classes, impressing them with facts, reciting poetry, singing songs, covering the blackboard with dates, and demanding that his students find answers to his questions. He conducted graduate seminars in American literature by a combination of mentoring and bullying, in the process honing the research, writing, and teaching techniques of many future scholar-teachers, including Albert Guérard, Mark Schorer, and Henry Nash Smith. Beginning in the late 1930s he developed an American Civilization Program at the doctoral level that emphasized non-European influences in higher education and a more cosmopolitan and interdisciplinary approach. As dean of the Graduate School of Arts and Sciences in 1943–1944, he tried to demand reforms but was restrained by bureaucrats. His legendary impatience and abrasive ways did not serve him well at this time—or ever. He explained his aim in *Education and World Tragedy* (1946), which was to encourage pragmatic research, especially at the graduate level, into cultures of other nations. He was a guest professor at Cornell in 1948 and at Munich's American Institute in 1950.

In the 1950s, while teaching was his main occupation, Jones published numerous short items and seven books, some of which were collections of lectures. They include a useful *Guide to American Literature and Its Backgrounds since 1890* (1953; rev. ed., 1972); *The Pursuit of Happiness* (1953), on changing concepts of happiness in America, from Puritan restrictions to recent psychological emphases; *The Frontier in American Fiction: Four Lectures on the Relation of Landscape to Literature* (1956), stressing the frontier's fecundity and terror; and *One Great Society: Humane Learning in the United States* (1959), urging businesspeople and financiers to become more aware of the interdependence of science and the liberal arts. Through the 1960s Jones was often away from Harvard as a visiting professor: at York University (1962), the Massachusetts Institute of Technology (1962–1963), the University of Wisconsin (1963), the Hebrew University of Jerusalem (1964), the Hebrew Union College (1967), and Middlebury College (1967). He continued to publish. Among other titles is his *O Strange New World: American Culture: The Formative Years* (1964). The recipient of a Pulitzer Prize and perhaps his finest work, it analyzes the interplay of Old and New World civilizations and the resulting effect on the "atmosphere and quality" of American cultural life from the fifteenth century to the nineteenth. Smaller items followed before Jones's next major work, *The Age of Energy: Varieties of American Experience, 1865–1915* (1971), a discussion of the uses, exploitation, and expressions of energy in American education, entertainment, literature, politics, technology, and theology.

With *Revolution and Romanticism* (1974), which explores the relationship between democratic revolutions in America and France and the roughly concomitant romantic espousal of freedom in thought and action, Jones completed his "trilogy" on American cultural history, the other parts being *O Strange New World* and *The Age of Energy*. In 1975 he lectured at the University of Arkansas. Though seemingly never tired, Jones thought it appropriate to compose *Howard Mumford Jones: An Autobiography* (1979). In it are asides about colleagues and comments about his work in humanistic studies but especially welcome are dozens of sparkling anecdotes about his more private actions.

In general, his peers, critics, and reviewers marveled at and commended Jones for his profound knowledge of American cultural history, his commitment to improving education both in and out of universities, and his uncompromising liberalism. Twice he declined visiting professorships at universities requiring the loyalty oath. Some complained that his parading in his autobiography of exemplary details and minutiae, perhaps inevitable given the nature of his mind, distorted his perspective and thinned the cohesiveness of his analyses. This minor criticism, however, amounts to little in the face of Jones's enormous accomplishments.

Lack of space permits only brief mention of the fact that Jones also was an editor, wrote introductions to reprints of many standard books, addressed several learned societies, was a published poet and a short-story writer, wrote a few plays, and was a translator. When he died in Cambridge, Massachusetts, the world of scholarship mourned the loss of a prolific, wide-ranging, and sagacious American cultural and intellectual historian.

• The bulk of Jones's papers are at Harvard in the archives, Houghton Library, and the Law School Library; in the Manuscript Division of the Library of Congress; and in libraries at Columbia University, the University of Michigan, the University of South Carolina, the University of Texas, and the University of Virginia. Bibliographies of his voluminous work are in Richard M. Ludwig, ed., *Aspects of American Poetry: Essays Presented to Howard Mumford Jones* (1962), and Peter Brier, *Howard Mumford Jones and the Dynamics of Liberal Humanism* (1994). Especially important titles by Jones not mentioned above are *They Say the Forties* (1937), a collection of poems; *Primer of Intellectual Freedom* (1949); *The Theory of American Literature* (1949); *The Bright Medusa* (1952), which is about youth; *American Humanism* (1957); *Reflections on Learning* (1958); *Jeffersonianism and the American Novel* (1966); and *The Literature of Virginia in the Seventeenth Century* (1968). Brier's book contains a balanced discussion of Jones's career, works, and professional beliefs. Kermit Vanderbilt, *American Literature and the Academy: The Roots, Growth and Maturity of a Profession* (1986), details some of Jones's academic contributions. Obituaries are in the *Chicago Tribune*, the *New York Times*, and the *Washington Post*, all 13 May 1980.

ROBERT L. GALE

JONES, Hugh Bolton (20 Oct. 1848–24 Sept. 1927), landscape painter, was born in Baltimore, Maryland, the son of Hugh Burgess Jones, a wealthy businessman, and Laura Eliza Bolton. After showing an early interest in drawing, Jones, while still in his teens, began studies at the Maryland Institute of Art, most likely with the portraitist David Acheson Woodward. Jones's earliest works were paintings of the countryside of his native Baltimore, and he first exhibited his work at the Maryland Institute Fair in 1860. Though he maintained a residence in Baltimore, beginning in 1865 Jones began to spend an increasing amount of time in New York City. There Jones studied briefly with landscape painter and Baltimore native Horace W. Robbins and with Carey Smith.

Jones first exhibited at the National Academy of Design in 1867. His first entries were *Summer* and *Saw-Mill*. He continued to show at the academy every year until his death. He was elected an associate of the academy in 1881 and a national academician in 1883. An active member, Jones served on many of the institution's committees over the years. Though he spent much of his time in New York City, Jones got inspiration from the Maryland countryside for many subjects, including *Morning on the Severn River, Maryland* and *Near Union Bridge, Maryland* (both 1873, Peabody Institute).

Jones had briefly toured Europe in 1870 with members of his family. He made a longer visit to France in 1876 with his younger brother Francis Coates Jones, a figure painter. It is said by family tradition that the two studied at the Académie Julian. The brothers spent about a year in the artists' colony near Pont-Aven in Brittany, where they joined painter Thomas Hovenden, with whom Jones is said to have shared a studio in Baltimore previous to Hovenden's departure for France in 1874. In 1877 Jones painted and exhibited one of his Breton landscapes, *A Deeply Cut Road in Brittany* (exhibited as *Un chemin creux, en Bretagne*), at the Salon; he continued to exhibit there regularly for the next three years. In 1878 he showed another of his works from Brittany, *A Heath in Bloom, Brittany* (c. 1877–1878; exhibited as *Un lande de Bretagne, en Fleurs*), and the next year *La fin du jour*.

After briefly returning to the United States, Jones again crossed the Atlantic for a tour of Spain in 1879. He completed a number of works there, including *Spanish Court Yard* (1879), which was shown at the Peabody Art Loan Exhibition in Baltimore in 1879. That same year, after a brief visit to the United States, Jones traveled to Morocco. This trip resulted in, among other works, *Près de Tanger, Maroc*. In 1881, his final year exhibiting at the Salon, he showed *L'Hiver à New York*. Jones was also a regular exhibitor at the Royal Academy in London between 1873 and 1883, showing *When Drop the Leaves from Branches Sear* in 1880.

Returning to the United States in 1881, Jones settled in New York City and shared a studio with his brother Francis. Jones made frequent sketching and painting trips to the surrounding countryside of New Jersey and north to New England. One of his favorite spots was South Egremont, Massachusetts, a popular destination for artists. Among the works he completed at this time was *Near Annisquam, Massachusetts Coast* (1883). Becoming an active participant in the New York art establishment, he joined the Society of American Artists in 1881 and was a member of other art associations and social clubs, including the Century Club, the Salmagundi Club, the Lotus Club, and the McDowell Club.

Jones was a regular and successful exhibitor at the numerous expositions and world's fairs in the late nineteenth and early twentieth centuries. *Ferry Inn* (1874) was shown at the Centennial Exposition in Philadelphia in 1876. He won medals at the Exposition Universalle in Paris in both 1893 and 1900, at the St. Louis Exposition in 1904, and at the Panama-Pacific Exposition in 1915 in San Francisco. In 1891 Jones made a foray into illustration when he traveled to California. His illustrations include depictions of Pasadena, Santa Barbara, and Yosemite for Charles Dudley Warner's *Our Italy* (1891). He also created illustrations of the 1893 World's Columbian Exposition in Chicago for the Columbian Memorial Publishing Society. Jones served as secretary of the New York painting jury for the Chicago exposition and also won a medal for his painting. In 1902 he received a medal for landscape painting from the Society of American Artists and the same year saw a solo exhibition of his work at the Noé Art Gallery in New York City. Among the works exhibited, all on subjects reflecting his trips outside New York, were *In New Hampshire*, *Meadows near Chadd's Ford*, and *Spring on the Brandywine* (all c. 1902).

Jones's landscapes were a favorite with collectors in the nineteenth and early twentieth centuries. Particularly fond of the brilliant colors nature provided during spring and autumn, Jones depicted these seasons with the meticulous accuracy learned during his stay in France and from his contact with the French plein-air school. His work was represented in the collections of William T. Walters of Baltimore and the Corcoran Gallery of Art in Washington, D.C. Five of Jones's works were in the noted collection of Thomas B. Clarke.

During the First World War Jones—like a number of artists—painted in support of the war effort. Among his works in this genre are *Wheat for the Allies* and *Finger of the Hun* (National Museum of American History, Division of Military History, Smithsonian Institution).

Jones's academic style had become increasingly unfashionable after the turn of the century, particularly after the Armory Show of 1913, which introduced European modernism to America. In a review of the art of the Panama-Pacific Exposition, Christian Beinton in *International Studio* (Aug. 1915, pp. xxvi–xxxi) classed Jones among those whose work "reveals few departures and no surprises" in contrast to the work of more "modern" painters such as Childe Hassam. Others noted that his work had become repetitive in subject and composition. He was, however, a versatile painter who in his later work developed an American landscape style removed from the Hudson River school and more closely aligned in the Barbizon tradition of French painter Charles-François Daubigny. Joan Zeizel has noted that "his simple, sensitive, and delicate landscapes reflect deep understanding of nature and a finely developed ability to portray its changing moods" (p. 5). Jones, called Bolton by friends and family, was termed by acquaintances a shy, dignified, and reserved man. He never married and shared a large apartment with his brother and widowed sister in New York City, where he died.

• Much of Jones's work is unlocated or in private collections. Some of his paintings are at the Metropolitan Museum of Art; the Corcoran Gallery of Art, Washington, D.C.; the Pennsylvania Academy of the Fine Arts, Philadelphia; the National Academy of Design, New York City; the West Point Museum, U.S. Military Academy, West Point, N.Y.; and the Museum of Fine Art, Boston. See "H. Bolton Jones" in *American Paintings in the Metropolitan Museum of Art*, ed. Doreen Bolger Burke, vol. 3 (1980), pp. 70–73. "American Painters: Hugh Bolton Jones," *Art Journal* (Feb. 1880): 53–4, is a brief article discussing his career. Jones is mentioned in David Sellin, *Americans in Brittany and Normandy, 1860–1910* (1982). Joan Hanson Zeizel, "Hugh Bolton Jones, American Landscape Painter" (master's thesis, George Washington Univ.,

1972), is the longest work on Jones. See also *American Painters on the French Scene 1874–1914* (1996), the catalog to the exhibition at the Beacon Hill Fine Art Gallery, with text by Sellin. Obituaries are in the *New York Times*, 25 Sept. 1927, and *Art Digest*, 1 Oct. 1927.

MARTIN R. KALFATOVIC

JONES, Jacob (Mar. 1768–3 Aug. 1850), naval officer, was born near Smyrna, Kent County, Delaware, the son of Jacob Jones, a prosperous farmer. His mother, whose name is unknown, died in Jones's infancy and was followed soon after by his father. He was raised by Penelope Holt, daughter of the chief justice of the Three Lower Counties. Jones attended the Lewes Academy and subsequently studied medicine under James Sykes of Dover. He took classes at the University of Pennsylvania in 1792, then established a small medical practice in Dover. Discouraged, he abandoned medicine in favor of appointment as clerk of the Delaware Supreme Court. Following the death of his first wife, the youngest sister of Dr. Sykes, Jones married Janet Moore of Newport, Rhode Island, in 1796. The couple had two children. Dissatisfied with employment prospects, Jones joined the navy on 10 April 1799 as a midshipman. He was twice the age of others his rank, but ability sustained him. Jones spent the Quasi-War with France under Captain John Barry of the frigate *United States* and rose to lieutenant on 22 February 1801. Two years later he participated in the Tripolitan War aboard William Bainbridge's frigate *Philadelphia*. When that vessel grounded in Tripoli harbor, Jones was captured and remained a prisoner for twenty months. Released in 1805, he resumed shipboard activities on the frigates *President* and *Adams* before rising to master commandant on 20 April 1810. Shortly after, Jones assumed command of the eighteen-gun sloop *Wasp* and spent several months relaying diplomatic dispatches to Europe.

Renewed war with England found Jones cruising southern waters in search of British merchant vessels. The *Wasp* lost her jib boom in a gale on 15 October 1812, but three days later she engaged a convoy escorted by the 22-gun brig *Frolic*. Jones masterfully sailed his injured ship and defeated the slightly larger enemy vessel in a running fight of forty-five minutes. He took advantage of heavy seas, firing his broadsides as the *Wasp* rolled down into the wave troughs while *Frolic* fired as it rolled up. Consequently, the British aimed too high while Jones's fire was deadly and culminated in the most lopsided naval victory of the war. The *Frolic* lost 90 men out of 107 while the *Wasp* sustained only five killed and five wounded. Both ships were badly damaged, however, and being unable to sail were recaptured by the ship-of-the-line *Poictiers*. Jones and his crew were taken to Bermuda and exchanged several weeks later. His victory, the third consecutive naval triumph after those of Isaac Hull and Stephen Decatur, was a cause for national celebration. Jones was feted and received a gold medal from Congress, while $25,000 was divided among his crew.

On 3 March 1813 Jones received promotion to captain and took post with the frigate *Macedonian* as part of Decatur's squadron at New York. The British heavily blockaded both ends of Long Island Sound and kept the Americans in port for nearly a year. During the interim, Jones served on a commission studying the plans for Robert Fulton's steam battery *Demologos*. In April 1814 Jones was ordered to Sackets Harbor, New York, as part of Commodore Isaac Chauncey's Lake Ontario Squadron. There he took command of the frigate *Mohawk* and completed several uneventful lake cruises before the war ended.

In June 1815 Jones returned to the *Macedonian* and sailed with Decatur's squadron during the brief war with Algiers. He subsequently commanded the frigate *Guerriere* between 1816 and 1818 and served as commodore of the Mediterranean Squadron from 1821 to 1823. After the end of his second marriage, in 1821 he married Ruth Lusby of Cecil County, Maryland, with whom he had four children. He also gained appointment as a navy commissioner until 1826, when he took command of the Pacific Squadron. Jones concluded his seafaring career in 1829 and accepted numerous duties ashore. These included commanding the Baltimore Navy Yard, 1829–1839, being port captain of New York, 1842–1845, and finally serving as director of the Philadelphia Naval Asylum in 1847. Jones held this position for three years before his death there.

Jones enjoyed an active and enterprising naval career. His success is even more surprising considering that he joined the navy at thirty-one and, in fifty-two years of service, compiled more sea duty than many younger colleagues. His victory over the *Frolic* was murderously effective and a major contribution to the growing naval tradition. In an age of martinets, he remained a genial, fatherly figure who guarded the welfare of his crew and was also an outspoken proponent of temperance.

• Jones's official correspondence is in RG 45, Captains' Letters, National Archives. A large collection of personal papers is at the Historical Society of Pennsylvania, with smaller caches in the Preble Collection, Manuscript Division, Library of Congress, and the New-York Historical Society. See also William S. Dudley, ed., *The Naval War of 1812* (3 vols., 1985–). Panegyrical sketches include "Biography of Captain Jacob Jones," *Analectic Magazine* 2 (1813): 70–78; Mark M. Cleaver, *The Life, Character and Public Services of Commodore Jacob Jones* (1906); and Ronald Ringwalt, *Commodore Jacob Jones* (1906). A modern treatment is J. Worth Estes, "Commodore Jacob Jones: A Doctor Goes to Sea," *Delaware History* 24 (1990): 109–22. Background on his famous seafight is in James Henderson, *Sloops and Brigs* (1972), and James M. Perry, "The U.S. Sloop of War *Wasp*," U.S. Naval Institute, *Proceedings* 87 (Feb. 1961): 84–93.

JOHN C. FREDRIKSEN

JONES, James (6 Nov. 1921–9 May 1977), author, was born James Ramon Jones in Robinson, Illinois, the son of Ramon Jones, a dentist, and Ada Blessing. The discovery of oil on his farm made Jones's paternal grandfather wealthy, but the crash of 1929 wiped out the man's investments. Jones's father ruined his dental practice by excessive drinking. Jones's mother suffered from diabetes and became obese. Growing up in a family of diminished finances and emotional violence, Jones graduated from high school in June 1939 and enlisted in the U.S. Army, at Chanute Field, Illinois, that November. He went to Fort Slocum, New York, then by troopship via Puerto Rico, the Panama Canal, and California to Hawaii. He was stationed in the army air corps there, at Hickham Field and then Wheeler Field. He became a welterweight boxer while at Pearl Harbor. In March 1941 his mother died. In September Jones transferred to the infantry and to Schofield Barracks, near Honolulu. He frequently visited the Hotel Street strip of that city and participated wholeheartedly in the drinking and whoring life of many enlisted men of that time.

Jones was at Schofield when the Japanese attacked Pearl Harbor on 7 December 1941. That morning he ran messages at headquarters and later that day helped build and man pillboxes at Makapuu Point. In March 1942 his father committed suicide. In May, Jones was promoted to corporal. While awaiting orders to go to the South Pacific, he attended a few classes in English composition and American literature at the University of Hawaii, at Manoa. In December his unit, the Twenty-fifth Infantry Division, shipped out for Guadalcanal in the Solomon Islands, east of New Guinea and northeast of Australia. His and other units landed at Guadalcanal on 1 January 1943. His outfit, F Company of the Twenty-seventh Infantry Regiment, went into combat on 11 January. Jones killed a Japanese soldier in hand-to-hand fighting, was wounded in the head by mortar fragments on 12 January, was hospitalized, and returned to duty a week later. He then participated in the capture of the village of Kokumbona on 23 January, badly injured his right ankle, required surgery at a naval hospital in the New Hebrides, and was returned home to San Francisco, California, and to Memphis, Tennessee, where he arrived in May. Following his release from the hospital there, he requested limited duty instead of a discharge but was assigned to full infantry duty instead. Still denied a leave, he went AWOL in November. While back in Robinson, he met Harry E. Handy, an oil-company administrator, and Handy's wife, Lowney Handy, an unpublished writer, occultist, and faddist who befriended misfits and regarded Jones as someone to help. In December 1943 he was demoted to private and became a latrine orderly, but in March 1944 he was promoted to sergeant. In June he became a patient in the psychiatric ward of the army hospital at Camp Campbell, Kentucky. It was determined that he was suffering from psychoneurosis, and he was given an honorable discharge a month later. After receiving a small pension, he moved in with the Handys and became Lowney Handy's lover. Both were indiscreet, but evidently her promiscuous husband knew and did not mind.

Long before his release from military duty, Jones had been interested in a writing career. His older brother George W. Jones had taken courses in journalism at Northwestern University, and the two kept in touch during Jones's military career—and later. Jones read Thomas Wolfe's *Look Homeward, Angel* while at Hickham Field, was inspired by Wolfe's style and approach to life, and expressed the fear that he might be killed during the war and never realize his literary potential. In January 1945 he left the Handys for a while, moved to New York City, attended classes at New York University until June, lived and wrote in Maggie, North Carolina, until August, and then returned to Illinois and the Handys. In January 1946 he sent Scribner's a draft of war fiction he called "They Shall Inherit the Laughter," which Maxwell Perkins, Scribner's brilliant editor, rejected. He offered careful encouragement, however, and gave Jones a $500 option for a novel that Jones had described and that became *From Here to Eternity*. When Perkins died in 1947, Burroughs Mitchell of Scribner's became Jones's editor, and options were renewed. Jones published "Temper of Steel," his first short story (*Atlantic Monthly*, Mar. 1948), received in 1950 a $2,000 advance on his second novel—*Some Came Running*—and saw *From Here to Eternity* into print in 1951. Film rights immediately gained him $82,000 even as book sales steadily climbed to more than 4 million copies. His novel was given the National Book Award in 1952, winning over J. D. Salinger's *The Catcher in the Rye*. The stunning 1953 movie, starring Montgomery Clift, Deborah Kerr, Burt Lancaster, Donna Reed, and Frank Sinatra, won eight Academy Awards. (The novel was published in England in 1952 and was also translated into eleven foreign languages.)

Jones was now spectacularly launched. With his ample earnings, he built a lavish $85,000 house for himself in Marshall, Illinois, near Robinson, and, with the Handys, generously funded the Handy Colony for writers in Marshall. In 1957 he was paid $250,000 for film rights to *Some Came Running*. It became obvious to Jones that Lowney Handy was foolish in demanding that writers-in-training copy literary masterpieces verbatim so as to absorb their style; it was also obvious that she was attempting to dominate him. Through the novelist Budd Schulberg in New York, he met Gloria Patricia Mosolino, a beautiful actress and a bright, unpublished writer. Within weeks, in 1957, they were married in Haiti, where they honeymooned for three months. Soon after the two visited the Handys in Illinois, Lowney attacked Gloria with a knife; Jones, who broke up the ensuing fight, had to tell his wife about his previously concealed relationship. Prolonged arguing ensued, but then the Joneses were able to establish and maintain a strong, lasting marriage.

After living and working for a year in New York, Jones published *Some Came Running* in 1958 and was happy to see it on the bestseller charts and to view the movie based on it later that year. This dreadfully long novel, which sold well but was adversely reviewed, dramatizes a soldier's attempt to understand the narrow-minded materialism of his hometown, a composite of Robinson and Marshall, Illinois, in the three years immediately after the war. Jones moved with his wife to London for four months in mid-1958, and then they established their residence in Paris—for the next sixteen years. Their decision was based on tax benefits, cheaper living, and easier use of substantial foreign royalties. The Joneses had two children, both born in Paris.

Jones published *The Pistol* (1959), a short novel about a soldier clinging fiercely to his .45, as to a talisman, immediately after the bombing of Pearl Harbor. In 1960 Jones sold his house in Illinois for half what it cost. He was a well-paid but hardly competent consultant-writer for Darryl Zanuck's war movie *The Longest Day* in 1961, and in 1962 he published *The Thin Red Line*. This novel became the second part of Jones's massive war trilogy, which began with *From Here to Eternity* and concluded with *Whistle* (posthumously published in 1978). The Joneses celebrated the publication of *The Thin Red Line* by taking a prolonged vacation in Jamaica, where Jones enjoyed skin diving.

Always short of money and ridiculously hospitable and generous, Jones was encouraged by novelist Irwin Shaw to seek better guarantees for future work than Scribner's was ever willing to offer. He reluctantly broke with his original publisher and negotiated a contract with Delacorte Press to provide three novels for $750,000, plus substantial perks. The novels turned out to be *Go to the Widow-Maker* (1967), *The Merry Month of May* (1971), and *Whistle*. *Go to the Widow-Maker* concerns skin diving and male uncertainties about sexual prowess. *The Merry Month of May* features a 1968 rebellion of American expatriate students in Paris. Amid all of this writing, Jones was otherwise busy. Delacorte published his *The Ice-Cream Headache and Other Stories* (1968); these thirteen stories, some published earlier in periodicals, concern either small-town life or war and demonstrate Jones's skill in composing short fiction. For $250,000, Doubleday bought his mystery novel *A Touch of Danger* (1973); it features a cynical American private eye, aged fifty, confronting murder, drugs, and hippies on a Greek island. From 26 February to 28 March 1973 Jones was in South Vietnam as a special reporter for the *New York Times Magazine*. His vivid *Viet Journal* (1974) makes it clear that he opposed American involvement in Southeast Asia, despised the corruption of leaders in South Vietnam, admired the ordinary American enlisted man, and disliked North Vietnamese duplicitous cunning and Viet Cong savagery.

In 1974 Jones and his family left Paris permanently. He never really liked France or came to understand the French. He taught at Florida International University in Miami for the 1974–1975 academic year. In 1975 he and his wife bought a farmhouse in Sagaponack, on Long Island, New York, and sold their Parisian apartment for $449,000. He wrote the text for *WWII: A Chronicle of Soldiering* (1975), a book featuring war art. In it Jones combines terse history, casualty figures, and personal reminiscence. Hospitalized on occasion for chronic congestive heart failure, Jones worked hard to complete *Whistle*. Toward the end, weakened by bronchitis, he dictated parts of the book. The last three and a half chapters (of thirty-four) were assembled by his close friend Willie Morris, a writer. Jones died in Southampton, Long Island.

Jones, who was understandably obsessed by war, is significant in the development of American literature because of his three major war novels, all of which closely reflect his military experiences. *From Here to Eternity* features men in the regular army in Hawaii just before Pearl Harbor. The two main characters are Private Robert E. Lee Prewitt, who is idealistic, and First Sergeant Milton Anthony Warden, who is cynical. Prewitt, a skillful boxer, refuses to join his regimental boxing squad because he once blinded a friend in the ring. He temporarily loves Alma Schmidt, a prostitute with her own rigid code of conduct. Warden, like Prewitt a career soldier, is transiently in love with Karen Holmes, the wife of the company captain. Both Prewitt and Warden love their army but hate it too. Jones graphically portrays the enlisted man's inevitable misery in an institution full of rank consciousness, individuality-defacing discipline, favoritism, and moral and physical corruption. Evil at the top, with the commanding general, seeps down not only to Captain Holmes but also to Fatso, a sadistic stockade sergeant, and Maggio, a lovable private who feigns insanity to get a medical discharge. The brutal plot involves degradation, mayhem, torture, and murder and is rendered bitterly real by obscene language—credible but tiresome. *The Thin Red Line* carries C-for-Charlie Company, an infantry unit, into combat on Guadalcanal, during which soldiers are systematically dehumanized so that the outfit, a relentless machine with replaceable parts, can grind on at all costs. Jones creates more than eighty characters, several of whom are continuations—with different names—of persons appearing in *From Here to Eternity*. *The Thin Red Line*, shorter than its predecessor, is perhaps Jones's masterpiece. It is a relentless picture of a world so deterministic that heroism and cowardice are alike meaningless. *Whistle* begins on a hospital ship in 1943 and concentrates on four wounded infantrymen who survived the action in *From Here to Eternity* and *The Thin Red Line*. When home again, they feel guilty for still being alive, apprehensive about their future duty, uncertain of friendships, troubled by women, and disgusted at stateside civilians with good jobs and easy lives. Three recuperating soldiers are continuations—again with different names—from the two earlier volumes. One sergeant—named Stark and then Storm earlier, and Strange in *Whistle*—cannot face being shipped to Europe to participate in more slaughter and unceremoniously slips into the cold ocean on the way across. He had seen enough.

Jones's brutal war fiction is traditional rather than innovative in technique. Typically, he depicts a multitude of characters in the male-dominated world of war, where bureaucracy is demeaning and women a risky distraction. Jones's unsophisticated, naturalistic conclusion is that the individual is hopelessly lost in a world of chance. Despite his later experiments, particularly in short fiction, it is probable that Jones's first book, like those of many other American authors, will always be regarded as his most representative and personally revealing.

• Jones's voluminous papers are at the University of Illinois, Urbana; Princeton University; the Sangamon State University Library, Springfield, Ill.; the University of Texas, Austin; and Yale University. *To Reach Eternity: The Letters of James Jones*, ed. George Hendrick (1989), includes Hendrick's informative introduction and a valuable foreword by Jones's close friend, novelist William Styron. A bibliography is John R. Hopkins, *James Jones: A Checklist* (1974). Snide but sometimes valuable remarks concerning Jones are in Norman Mailer, *Advertisements for Myself* (1959) and *Cannibals and Christians* (1966). A superb short essay is Edmund L. Volpe, "James Jones—Norman Mailer," in *Contemporary American Novelists*, ed. Harry T. Moore (1964). Critical and biographical works are Willie Morris, *James Jones: A Friendship* (1978); James R. Giles, *James Jones* (1981); George Garrett, *James Jones* (1984); and Frank MacShane, *Into Eternity: The Life of James Jones, American Writer* (1985). Robert La Guardia, *Monty: A Biography of Montgomery Clift* (1977), and La Guardia and Patricia Bosworth, *Montgomery Clift: A Biography* (1978), describe Jones's long friendship with Clift. In "Back to Eternity," *Travel Holiday*, Mar. 1990, pp. 42–51, 136–37, Kaylie Jones, Jones's daughter and a novelist herself, poignantly reports her visit to Hawaii to observe places important to her father. An obituary is in the *New York Times*, 10 May 1977.

ROBERT L. GALE

JONES, James Athearn (17 Oct. 1791–7 July 1854), novelist, poet, and folklorist, was born in Tisbury, on Martha's Vineyard, Massachusetts, the son of Ebenezer Jones, a farmer, and Susanna Athearn, the daughter of a county probate judge in Tisbury. Several bands of Gay Head Indians lived within a few miles of the Joneses. Young Jones's grandfather had a lonely coastal farm, where the boy was born and lived, where Indians were employed as field hands, and where an Indian nurse cared for him until he was fifteen. Her stories about fabulous Indians inspired his lifelong fascination with Native-American folklore. Denied formal schooling by the remoteness of his home, he read voraciously and studied under ministers at Tisbury and nearby Edgartown. He visited the West Indies on a few occasions and also sold or bartered food and other items with sailors anchored off Martha's Vineyard. Jones has been described as tall, slender, a little vain and quarrelsome, and in later years slightly deaf.

Jones published several juvenile pieces in the *United States Literary Gazette*, the *Atlantic Souvenir*, and the *Token*. More substantial, however, is his *Hardenbrass and Haverhill; or, The Secret of the Castle, a Novel*. Its subtitle hints sufficiently at its Gothic contents: *Containing a Madman and No Madman, Who Walks, Deeds of Darkness, Remarkable Characters, Incidents, Adventures, &c., &c. Instructive and Entertaining* (4 vols., 1817). Later the same year came his *Reft Rob; or, the Witch of Scot-Muir, Commonly Called Madge the Snoo-*

ver. *A Scottish Tale* . . . . His *Bonaparte; with the Storm at Sea, Madaline, and Other Poems* (1820) begins with a blank-verse poem, "Bonaparte," in which the young bard praises Napoleon, laments his exile, admits his oppressiveness, but calls him "a saint, compared / With those who rule the European States, / So lately leagu'd." Jones adds some pretentious informational notes. In "The Storm at Sea," the narrator confesses to a misspent youth despite good parents, going to sea under a severe captain and with a "motley" crew, surviving a "fearful storm," and vowing to return to his studies. "Madaline, A Fragment of a Swiss Tale" is an old-fashioned ballad about an Alpine "goatherd" offering comfort to a wandering, insane maiden, who laments that she has killed all members of her noble family because they murdered her true love. Four short poems round out the collection: "Egbert and Matilda. 1814," "Fly, Edwin, Fly," "Christ Calming the Tempest," and "Revelations, Ch. 1." These and other poems by Jones were praised by contemporary critics and editors.

After traveling through the Carolinas to New Orleans and Ohio, Jones married his cousin Avis Ahearn in 1817. The couple had no children. Jones read for and practiced law in New York City (by 1822), and also found time to teach school and do some journalistic work (to 1827). A piece indicative of his legal erudition is "A Digest of All the Criminal Cases, Which Have Been Decided in the Supreme Circuit, and District Courts of the United States, and in the Supreme Courts of the Several States, with a Few Decisions of the Court of Sessions for New York City." This work was appended to *A Digested Index of the Crown Law . . .* by Harold Nuttall Tomlins (1823). Then came Jones's *The Refugee: A Romance*, published as though written by Captain Matthew Murgatroyd (2 vols., 1825) and concerning—as its title page explains—the derring-do of Murgatroyd of the Ninth Continentals during the American Revolution. This mostly wooden novel is livened by descriptions of vigorous action in and around New York City in the 1770s. Next, Jones saw fit to issue a 43-page pamphlet rebuking the British titled *A Letter to an English Gentleman, on the Libels and Calumnies on America by British Writers and Reviewers* (1826). After editing the daily *National Palladium* in Philadelphia for a few months in 1827, Jones went to England and undertook literary work there. It was said that he became mentally unstable while abroad. Returning home in 1829, Jones capitalized on the success of his *Hardenbrass and Haverhill*. His novel *Haverhill; or, Memoirs of an Officer in the Army of Wolfe* (2 vols., 1831) presents the derring-do of Ensign Lynn Haverhill during General James Wolfe's campaign against Quebec, all of which, however, is followed by some inferior melodrama in the West Indies. This disunified novel merits praise mainly for its New England local-color details and accurately recorded dialogue of speakers from different backgrounds.

The only work by which Jones is renowned today is his *Tales of an Indian Camp*, which he saw into print while in England (3 vols., 1829). It was reissued as

Traditions of the North American Indians: Being a Second and Revised Edition of "Tales of an Indian Camp" (1830). Although soon translated into German as *Sagen der nordamerikanischen Indianer . . .* (1837), this solid work was never published in the United States. It has been said that *Tales of an Indian Camp* represents the first effort of any length by an American to preserve the folklore of Native Americans. In a long, pseudohistorical introduction, Jones tells how a learned Frenchman named Philippe Verdier went to North America in 1697, lived for years with different Indian tribes from New England to the Midwest, earned their admiration and trust, was allowed to assemble many spokesmen for an intertribal meeting in 1703, observed their colorful festivities, and heard and recorded some fifty-six of their "traditions." These legends concern the creation, religious worship, spirits and ghosts, fabulous animals, activities of celebrated persons at home and faraway, death and funerals, and the "Happy Hunting-Grounds." Jones annotates about half of these legends to explain Indian characteristics, living habits, and activities in war and peace and cites several published authorities in the process.

From 1829 or so, Jones lived and farmed at the Tisbury farm he inherited from his grandfather, moved to West Tisbury and built a house and store there, wrote biographical memoirs of two Martha's Vineyard residents—Ichabod Norton and Captain Elisha Dexter—in the 1840s, and did editorial work in Buffalo, New York, in 1850. Sometime after 1851 he moved to Brooklyn, New York, where he died of cholera.

James Athearn Jones goes entirely unmentioned in modern surveys of American fiction and poetry, but he is deservedly remembered for his valuable and engaging *Traditions of the North American Indians*.

• Jones's very few extant papers are at the Boston Public Library, the Newberry Library in Chicago, the Historical Society of Pennsylvania, and the libraries of the University of Illinois, Indiana University, the University of Texas, and the University of Virginia. Two biographical sketches and critical evaluations of Jones are Richard L. Pease, "James Athearn Jones," *Memorial Biographies of the New England Historic Genealogical Society* 2 (1881): 204–22, and John T. Flanagan, "A Pioneer in Indian Folklore: James Athearn Jones," *New England Quarterly* 12 (1939): 443–53. William S. Simmons, *Spirit of the New England Tribes: Indian History and Folklore, 1620–1984* (1986), shows that Jones, though of value as an amateur ethnologist, unfortunately used the unprofessional method of combining and then rewriting material from unspecified oral sources and from published sources to create his "Indian tales."

ROBERT L. GALE

JONES, Jane Elizabeth (13 Mar. 1813–13 Jan. 1896), antislavery and women's rights lecturer, was born Jane Elizabeth Hitchcock at Vernon, Oneida County, New York, the daughter of Reuben Hitchcock and Electa Spaulding. Although there is little record of her early years, accounts suggest that the family was financially comfortable and that she had a "pampered and protected" childhood.

Hitchcock was thirty years old when she met abolitionist Abby Kelley, who later married Stephen Foster. Preparing for a lengthy antislavery lecturing tour, Kelley needed a woman traveling companion and thought Hitchcock would be a good candidate as she "had shown a talent for public speaking." Hitchcock's brother opposed his sister leaving because he had planned to enter Oneida, a utopian community, and expected her to come with him. She had no intention of entering Oneida and decided to join Kelley to speak out against slavery despite opposition. She declared that she could not "fail to do what . . . [it] be my duty to do."

In December 1844 the two women set out on their lecture tour, taking three days by rail and boat to reach Philadelphia. In the months that followed they traveled through Pennsylvania and New York with an entourage of men and women abolitionists. Hitchcock, whom Kelley nicknamed Lizzie, began addressing audiences to give Kelley an occasional rest. Hitchcock's own speaking style matured, and she soon captured the attention of audiences. In 1845 William Lloyd Garrison, a radical abolitionist, introduced her in one of her first speeches. Addressing the American Anti-Slavery Society in New York, she attacked the Constitution as the cause of slavery. Garrison was quite impressed with Hitchcock and noted the "clearness and cogency of her reasoning." Hitchcock and Kelley traveled to Ohio to attend that state's antislavery society's annual meeting, intending to speak throughout the state at conventions of the Western Anti-Slavery Society during the summer. Daily meetings drew large crowds, and in order to gain publicity and spread the news of the abolitionists further west Kelley suggested that they start a newspaper. The *Anti-Slavery Bugle*, headquartered in Salem, Ohio, began operations but needed an editor.

Hitchcock and Benjamin Smith Jones, a Philadelphia Quaker, were convinced to temporarily take charge of the paper in September 1845. This union cemented the relationship the pair had already begun while on the lecture circuit. In January 1846 they married in New Brighton, Pennsylvania. After a simple ceremony they returned to Salem, where they set up their household on the meager annual salary of $400 that he received for editing the *Bugle*. She continued to act as coeditor without pay until 1849. The family lived in poverty, and before their only child was born in 1848 Benjamin Jones considered returning to his original trade of cabinetmaker. In order to supplement the family income Jane Jones returned to the antislavery lecture circuit and published *The Young Abolitionists* (1848), an informative book for children about slavery. Although she had come from a comfortable family, she chose privation for the good of abolitionism.

Women's rights activism was often a natural extension for women active in the antislavery movement, and Jones was no exception. In early issues of the *Bugle*, she had published feminist articles, and despite the small circulation of the paper she gave the feminist cause a forum. While lecturing she was sometimes harassed by males in the audience for having stepped out of the bounds of the "woman's sphere." In one editorial she wrote that "sphere" was not a good choice of words. "Circle," she claimed, was a much better word to indicate a woman's position "for it is round, round, round, like a blind horse on a mill wheel." Jones spoke out against the injustice of inequality and stated that woman was man's equal, "his partner, his co-laborer; not his toy and drudge."

Ohio women called for a convention on 19 April 1850 similar to the historic Seneca Falls Convention in New York, where Elizabeth Cady Stanton and others had asserted their "inalienable right to the elective franchise." The call went out in the *Bugle* for the women of Ohio to attend, and Jones became one of the thirty-five signers that demanded suffrage and equal rights. Men were allowed to attend the two-day meeting but could not speak or vote. Jones addressed the group on the legal rights of women to own property, and she continued to use the theme of women's rights after the convention in her antislavery lectures.

In addition to her roles as an antislavery lecturer and feminist, Jones became an important component of a new movement in the nineteenth century. After having studied anatomy and physiology she traveled as a "science lecturer" during the 1850s. She provided women with information about their health and the best treatments available, which were not always understood by male doctors. Attracting large female audiences in Ohio and surrounding states, Jones used mannequins and engravings to demonstrate her points.

Jones continued to speak out on the moral issues of slavery. She also focused on women's property rights and the custodial rights of children. She took part in the New York women's rights campaign of 1859–1860, and in the following year, acting as general agent of the Ohio Woman's Rights Association, she testified before a joint legislative committee. Following the passage of the married woman's property law, her *Address to the Woman's Rights Committee of the Ohio Legislature* was published in 1861. The last issue of the *Bugle* was printed that same year. After her husband's death in 1862 Jones and her daughter returned to Vernon, New York, where she died.

Willing to sacrifice the comforts of a better life in the East, Jones settled in Ohio, a place she thought primitive and where people were "mere half-abolitionists" but where she felt she was needed. Strong-willed, energetic, and duty-driven, she was a true forerunner in the abolitionist-feminist movement.

• Some of Jones's letters can be found in the Abby Kelley–Stephen Foster Papers, American Antiquarian Society, Worcester, Mass., and in the Blackwell Family Papers, Manuscript Division, Library of Congress. Other sources of information on Jones are Elizabeth C. Stanton et al., *History of Woman Suffrage*, vol. 1 (6 vols., 1881–1922); Wendell P. Garrison and Francis J. Garrison, *William Lloyd Garrison*, vols. 3 and 4 (1889); Lillian O'Connor, *Pioneer Women Orators: Rhetoric in the Ante-Bellum Reform Movement* (1954);

Alma Lutz, *Crusade for Freedom: Women of the Antislavery Movement* (1968); Blanche Glassman Hersh, *The Slavery of Sex: Feminist-Abolitionists in America* (1978); *Friends and Sisters: Letters between Lucy Stone and Antoinette Brown Blackwell, 1846–93*, ed. Carol Lasser and Marlene Deahl Merrill (1987); and Dorothy Sterling, *Ahead of Her Time: Abby Kelley and the Politics of Antislavery* (1991).

MARILYN ELIZABETH PERRY

JONES, Jenkin Lloyd (14 Nov. 1843–12 Sept. 1918), clergyman, was born in Cardiganshire, Wales, the son of Richard Lloyd Jones and Mallie Thomas James, farmers. The family emigrated to the United States in 1844, eventually settling near Spring Green, Wisconsin. Jones served in the Civil War from 1862 to 1865 as a private in the Sixth Wisconsin Artillery Battery. In 1866, following a family tradition, he entered Meadville Theological School, a Unitarian seminary in Meadville, Pennsylvania. Upon graduation and ordination in 1870, he married Susan Charlotte Barber; the couple had two children.

Jones served briefly as pastor in Winnetka, Illinois, and as missionary for the Wisconsin Unitarian Conference before accepting a call to All Souls' Church of Janesville, Wisconsin, in 1872. The congregation prospered; he and his wife developed *The Sunday School*, a pioneering curriculum centering on moral education and using material from nature and non-Christian religions. They introduced the adult study program of poetry, novels, and philosophy that was widely adopted by Unitarian congregations as "Unity Club." The success at Janesville and Jones's vigorous promotion of autonomy for Western Unitarian institutions led to his appointment in 1875 as missionary for the Western Unitarian Conference. As the conference prospered, this position evolved in 1880 into the full-time office of executive secretary. Jones accepted this position and moved to Chicago, which became his permanent home.

First as missionary secretary and later as executive secretary, Jones led the conference to its most successful years, starting many new churches, opening a permanent headquarters, and establishing a strong publishing program. Jones was largely responsible for opening up the Unitarian ministry to women, many of whom he located in the Western Conference. He was popular for his strong leadership, common touch, and genial optimism. In 1878 Jones and others founded *Unity*, the semiofficial conference newspaper. Jones became its editor once he moved to Chicago, and throughout the rest of his life, *Unity* was "his" paper.

Jones resigned as executive secretary of the Western Unitarian Conference in 1884 to become pastor of All Souls' Church on the South Side of Chicago. He had reopened under the new name the old Fourth Unitarian Church, which had been inactive since its building was sold in 1880. As pastor he set about to realize his ideal church, which was open to all earnest persons, ready to hear all new ideas, and committed to the practical service of its community and world. In 1886 he built a striking homelike church building for All

Souls', which was widely copied. At the same time he saw to the building of a family chapel near Spring Green, Wisconsin. In 1890 the chapel became the anchor for the Tower Hill Summer School of Literature and Religion on a nearby bluff overlooking the Wisconsin River. The school boasted many important religious liberals as teachers over the years. It also served as a vacation resort for clergy and church members from Illinois and Wisconsin.

Shortly after his resignation as secretary, a schism arose in the conference over the question of an explicit Christian basis for the conference. Jones's leadership of the conference had developed the principle that its unity lay in a common commitment to human betterment, not in Christian—or even theistic—beliefs. A large part of the conference had become enthusiastic supporters of this "ethical basis," but a significant part had not. The controversy divided the conference, generated bitterness, and had repercussions in the American Unitarian Association. "The Issue in the West," as the schism was called, was settled by compromises in the conference in 1892 and in the National Unitarian Conference meeting of 1894. Verbal formulae were arrived at that incorporated the "Christian basis" in the Western Conference and toned down the Christian basis of the National Conference. Jones understood these to be a watering down of the principles he stood for and took them for a personal rejection. He ceased activity in the Unitarian church and led All Souls' to nondenominational status in 1898.

The climax of Jones's early career was his involvement in the World's Parliament of Religions, which was part of the World's Columbian Exposition in Chicago in 1893. He was one of the original promoters of the event and was the secretary of the general committee. Before and during the parliament, Jones's work in planning, arranging programs, and executing the actual event was second in importance only to that of John Henry Barrows, supervisor of the parliament. Inspired by the ideals of the parliament and resentful of his "rejection" by the Unitarians, Jones organized the American Congress of Liberal Religious Societies in 1894, embracing liberal-minded Christians and Jews and open in principle to all others. *Unity*, which he had earlier founded, became *New Unity*, the official organ of the congress. The organization changed its name several times before disappearing completely by 1911. With the end of the congress, *Unity* regained its old name.

The Spanish-American War (1898) awakened a latent pacifism in Jones, and for the rest of his life following the war he was an ardent crusader for peace, joining all of the American peace organizations and even cofounding some, including the Chicago Peace Society, the National Arbitration and Peace Congress, and the Church Peace Union. He based his position on human unity and his belief that the human race was evolving away from a reliance on force. Jones, who had been an advocate of temperance since childhood, also supported prohibition, a cause second only to peace. His concerns were not limited to peace and pro-

hibition, however; he worked for all the reform causes of his time—race relations, industrial peace, humane treatment of animals, conservation, better roads, and many others. He became nationally popular as a lecturer and served on many local, state, and national commissions involved in addressing such issues as penal reform, labor arbitration, and civic government.

In 1905, after many years of planning, the congregation of All Souls' Church undertook the construction of Abraham Lincoln Center, honoring Jones's lifelong hero. This seven-story building became a center for educational, recreational, and social service work as well as for worship. With its construction, Jones realized his dream of a church for all seven days of the week, not just Sunday. It came as close to his ideal as could be expected.

Jones's first wife died in 1911, and in 1915 he married Edith Lackersteen. With the outbreak of World War I, Jones remained a staunch pacifist. He sailed with the Ford Peace Ship Mission to attempt to negotiate an end to the European war in 1915 and was a member of the Committee on Administration, which assumed leadership of the mission when Henry Ford returned to the United States. Over the Abraham Lincoln Center he flew the American flag with a white border to symbolize peace. His pacifist position as editor of *Unity* led to the banning of the newspaper from the mails. Jones died just before the war's end at his cottage in Tower Hill, Wisconsin.

• The major collection of Jones's papers is at Meadville/Lombard Library in Chicago, and a smaller, select collection is at the Joseph Regenstein Library in Chicago. All of Jones's published books were collections of his sermons. These include *The Faith That Makes Faithful*, with William Channing Gannett (1886), *Religions of the World* (1893), and *Jess, Bits of a Wayside Gospel* (1899). The few biographical sources include Richard Thomas, "Jenkin Lloyd Jones: Lincoln's Soldier of Civic Righteousness" (Ph.D. diss., Rutgers Univ., 1967); Charles Lyttle, *Freedom Moves West*, pt. 3 (1952); and Thomas Graham, "The Making of a Secretary" and "Jenkin Lloyd Jones and the Western Unitarian Conference," both in the *Proceedings of the Unitarian Universalist Historical Society* (1982–1983, 1989). Throughout Sept., Oct., and Nov. 1918, *Unity* printed lengthy obituary tributes.

THOMAS E. GRAHAM

JONES, Jesse Holman (5 Apr. 1874–1 June 1956), businessman, federal agency head, and cabinet member, was born in Robertson County, Tennessee, the son of William Hasque Jones and Anne Holman, farmers and merchants. Jones's mother died when he was six. In 1883 the family moved to Dallas, Texas, where his father helped manage the expanding lumber business of his brother M. T. Jones. In 1886 the family returned to north central Tennessee, where his father purchased a 600-acre farm and resumed an active interest in the tobacco business. Despite the family's modest wealth and comfortable home life, at age fourteen Jones left school and began grading, buying, and selling tobacco for his father and uncles. His father offered to send him to college, but Jones was anxious to make money. When his father died in 1894, Jones became the Dallas branch manager for M. T. Jones Lumber Company. When M. T. Jones died in 1898, Jones moved to Houston to become general manager of the company and an executor of the $1 million estate.

Soon after moving to Houston, Jones borrowed from Dallas and Houston bankers familiar with his family's good name and began business on his own. Although he became a famous banker, Jones always thought of himself as a borrower, not a lender. During the panic of 1907 he borrowed from New York bankers according to prearranged agreements and bought when others sold at depressed prices. By 1912 Jones held a half interest in the Houston *Chronicle*, and owned a major Houston hotel, substantial bank stock, a mortgage company, a large number of office buildings, and his own lumber company.

Houston's rapid growth enhanced Jones's wealth, but he was not merely a passive beneficiary of location and circumstance. From the late 1890s on, Jones, together with other members of the business elite, built their city. Jones led the campaign to sell ship channel bonds, purchased struggling banks and merged them with healthier ones, and convinced the company that became Texaco to locate its headquarters in Houston.

Jones, however, could be remarkably petty and avaricious in his business dealings and was obsessed with controlling everything in which he took part. In 1917 the other major stockholder in Union National Bank accused Jones of billing the bank for the electricity used by an adjacent building that Jones owned. Infuriated by the charge, Jones sold his stock in Union National and soon purchased a majority interest in the rival National Bank of Commerce, which he delighted in building into the city's largest.

Later in 1917, at the urging of President Woodrow Wilson, Jones accepted the position of director general of military relief for the Red Cross. During World War I he developed a deep commitment to Wilson and at the close of the war accompanied him to the Paris Peace Conference.

Despite increased exposure to the distant world, Jones remained a citizen of Houston with the habits of its traditional elite. In 1920 he married Mary Gibbs, and the couple, although childless, headed up their extended families. Jones also considered himself the patriarch of another family, his "business family." He shared the intense anticolonialism of Houstonians, and in building up Houston he hoped to set it free from Wall Street. Thus he remained loyal to Wilson's Democratic party, an institution more prone to challenge Wall Street and more open to traditional southern folkways.

Besides, the Democrats rewarded Jones and Houston. Jones served as the finance chairman for John W. Davis's ill-fated 1924 presidential campaign. Although Davis lost badly, Jones raised the money to pay off the Democratic debt. Out of gratitude, the party agreed to hold its 1928 convention in Houston, and four years later, when Herbert Hoover searched for a Democrat

to name to the board of the Reconstruction Finance Corporation, Democratic congressional leaders suggested Jones. Hoover complied, appointing Jones one of the original members of the RFC in January 1932.

In 1931 Jones had warmed up for his later activities by leading the successful effort of the local elite to rescue two Houston banks on the verge of failure. No banks failed in his hometown during the depression.

When Franklin D. Roosevelt became president in 1933, he named Jones to chair the RFC and quickly used the agency to help stabilize the banking industry and expand the availability of credit. In some ways Jones advocated a more aggressive role for the federal government than did Roosevelt. He was an early and important advocate of federal deposit insurance and after some initial reluctance effectively championed the purchase of preferred stock in banks by the RFC. He hoped that this action, by increasing the capitalization of banks, would stimulate lending. He also cheerfully expanded the power of the RFC by funding such agencies as the Commodities Credit Corporation. He opposed balancing the federal budget at the cost of reducing RFC lending. After 1937, although he was less willing than some New Dealers to lend directly to individuals and particularly to small businesses, he led the RFC toward the gradual expansion of direct federal lending. On occasion Jones even insisted that a company's management be changed before a loan was approved. Until the outbreak of World War II, however, he refused to lend without expectation of being repaid.

By February 1939 Congress had authorized in excess of $13 billion for the RFC. Some $3 billion had been spent at the direct instruction of Congress, and the other $10 billion, Jones happily reported, was returning a profit. Jones's character had become that of the RFC: shaped by total personal control based on familial loyalty, with the mind-set of a borrower but obsessed with profit, and deeply distrustful of Wall Street.

Later in 1939 Jones turned over the chair of the RFC to Emil Schram, one of his "RFC family," and became federal loan administrator. As such he controlled not only the RFC but a burgeoning array of government sources of credit, among them the Home Owners Loan Corporation. In 1940 Jones became secretary of commerce and by a special act of Congress retained the post of federal loan administrator. Such support was commonplace for Jones, who used kinship, friendship, and close attention to pet projects to exert influence on Congress unrivaled by any member of the executive branch except the president.

With the advent of World War II, Jones's responsibilities and the RFC's expenditures increased. He designed a host of entities to supply crucial war material, the most famous perhaps being the Rubber Reserve Company, which purchased scarce supplies of natural rubber before the Japanese occupation of Southeast Asia. It later pioneered the development of synthetic rubber.

Jones had long feuded with Henry A. Wallace, the vice president during Roosevelt's third term. In 1943 a particularly bitter quarrel over purchases of strategic raw materials led to the abolition of the Wallace-headed Board of Economic Warfare. After Harry S. Truman became vice president in Roosevelt's fourth term, the president asked Jones to step aside as secretary of commerce so that the position might be given to Wallace. Jones angrily resigned all his federal offices and, despite efforts by Roosevelt to placate him, left Washington a bitter man determined to make the Democrats pay for their disloyalty. He opposed Truman's reelection in 1948 and supported Dwight D. Eisenhower in 1952.

After leaving government service Jones returned to Houston, where he died. He and his wife spent most of their last years giving away their substantial wealth through the Houston Endowment. Until the end Jones remained of two worlds. He did business with bankers, businessmen, and government leaders around the world. Yet he remained a Houstonian with a pronounced bias against Wall Street. During the New Deal and World War II his power rested not just on Roosevelt's need for the flexibility of the RFC and Jones's technical competence. It rested as well on the carefully nurtured personal loyalties of the Texas delegation and other members of Congress and on the unswerving devotion of his RFC family. Jones helped to create the modern age by vastly increasing the role of government in business.

• Early and personal papers are in the Jesse H. Jones Papers, Barker Texas History Center, University of Texas, Austin. Materials from his years in government service are in the Jesse H. Jones Papers, Manuscript Division, Library of Congress. His autobiography, with Edward Angly, is *Fifty Billion Dollars: My Thirteen Years with the RFC, 1932–1945* (1951). See also Jesse H. Jones, *Reconstruction Finance Corporation: Seven Year Report* (1939). Bascom N. Timmons, *Jesse H. Jones: The Man and the Statesman* (1956), is an uncritical and undocumented biography. See also Walter L. Buenger, "Between Community and Corporation: The Southern Roots of Jesse H. Jones and the Reconstruction Finance Corporation," *Journal of Southern History* 56 (Aug. 1990): 481–510, and James S. Olson, *Saving Capitalism: The Reconstruction Finance Corporation and the New Deal, 1933–1940* (1988). For a description of Jones when appointed to the RFC, see the *Washington Post*, 26 Jan. 1932. An obituary is in the *New York Times*, 2 June 1956.

WALTER L. BUENGER

JONES, Jim (13 May 1931–18 Nov. 1978), religious cult leader, was born James Warren Jones in Crete, Indiana, the son of James Thurman Jones, a road construction worker, and Lynetta Putnam. While still a teenager Jones developed a vaguely focused social conscience and a wish to help the needy through volunteer work. By 1947 he was serving as a hospital orderly in Richmond, Indiana, where he met Marceline Baldwin, a student nurse. They married in 1949, and for the next three years Jones studied at Indiana University in Bloomington. By 1952 the couple had moved to Indianapolis, where Jones pursued his humanitarian goals as a student pastor of the Somerset Methodist Church. Though earlier he had been highly critical of organized religion, the Methodist social creed of 1952 changed his mind. His ministry in a poor section of town helped bring his views on racism and poverty to maturity. As an advocate of racial integration and community sharing, he organized an independent congregation, which he named "Community Unity" in 1954, "Wings of Deliverance" in 1956, and sometime thereafter "Peoples Temple." Jones had been something of an outsider while growing up, and he entreated those on the margins of society to seek psychological acceptance, physical welfare, and spiritual improvement on common ground in the Peoples Temple. He also began displaying eclectic religious tastes by adding Pentecostal emphases to his social gospel.

The practice of speaking in tongues might initially have seemed incongruous in a church that was affiliated with the Disciples of Christ after 1960, but Jones had acquired an interest in this and other less restricted aspects of religious experience. Without much formal education, and no theological training at all, he was always prone to read his own ideas into biblical texts. Moreover, his sermons were often extended monologues of his own reaction to news events, and he frequently shocked listeners by contradicting Scripture or rejecting standard interpretations if they contravened his own social and religious expectations. Speaking in tongues, or glossolalia, enhanced his authority and gave him greater freedom to assert his own ideas. It also enabled him to recruit new members for the Peoples Temple from among those fascinated by this medium of spiritual communication. Jones's congregation was actually a loose coalition of revivalists, Pentecostals, and social reformers, and his growing success was due in part to his ability to satisfy the needs of each of these groups. To this he added a proclivity for spiritualism and communing with spirits that evolved into his claims to be a prophet. Jones would often identify strangers in the church, describe what was in their pockets, and tell about their pasts. Acting as more than a clairvoyant, he also made bold predictions about congregants, thrilling many with a sense of mystic power and inside knowledge. Beginning in 1953, first at special meetings in Columbus, Indiana, and Detroit, Michigan, Jones also acted as if he had a gift of healing. Scores of people asserted that they had been healed of various "cancers" through Jones's wondrous influence. These apparent miracles, together with charismatic prophecies and untrammeled spiritualism, caused the various segments of his constituency to grow.

Some people were attracted because they sought the miraculous; others joined because they shared the ideal of gradual social reform with church groups leading by example. In 1959 Jones traveled to Philadelphia, where he visited Father Divine, an aging religious cult leader who also emphasized egalitarianism and human services within his following. This meeting confirmed many of Jones's ideas and may have encouraged him to think of himself as successor to Father Divine's leadership, including the eventual claim that he was God. The tangible benefits of Peoples

Temple were proving an unqualified success. Jones urged his people to love each other and share their possessions. The resulting communalism provided shelter, soup kitchens, and nursing homes for the lonely and indigent. The church distributed canned goods, heating fuel, and clothing. Jones and his wife had one son, but they exemplified the church's ideals by adopting other children including blacks and Koreans to form an extended "rainbow family." Many others voluntarily participated in the cooperative routines that blended church members into a divinely inspired commune. People of different ethnic, economic, and educational backgrounds devoted years of labor, their life savings, and their children to this closed community because they shared a mutual appreciation of each other in unified pursuit of a common cause.

In 1965 Jones moved the Peoples Temple to Ukiah, California, and many of his followers went with him. Using the same socioreligious appeals as before, he attracted more supporters, claiming without proof a following of many thousands. He soon established auxiliary temples in San Francisco and Los Angeles. But as his power grew, so did increasingly obvious signs of a disturbed personality. The prophet, healer, and provider made more blatant assertions that he was divine. He developed manipulative techniques in order to dominate and control the lives of everyone around him. Through persistence and repetition, deprivation and reward, threats and cajolery, he wore down resistance and fashioned cadres of pliant disciples. Rumors of enforcement squads circulated, reinforcing the idea of Jones's total power and the cultists' absolute dependence on him—or the futility of escape. Apparently Jones also felt that he had transcended customary sexual restraints, and he fathered at least one more son in a series of extramarital affairs.

Just as Jones was domineering to those under him, he was unjustifiably paranoid about the prospect of conspiracy and persecution from the outside. He had long been obsessed with what he perceived as increased governmental interference in private lives and institutional exploitation of the poor and the socially disadvantaged. These fears led him in the early 1970s to contemplate emigration. Agents secured property in the South American country of Guyana and began clearing jungle for what would be called Jonestown. In 1977 Jones himself joined a population of approximately 1,000 followers who hoped to create a socialistic Eden in a new land. Most of them acquiesced to primitive living conditions, inadequate food, and harshly enforced discipline. Some, however, became disgruntled and added their voices to critics who remained in the United States. The protests of defectors and relatives of young converts who had gone to Guyana became louder and more persistent. Finally, on 15 November 1978, Congressman Leo Ryan of California visited Jonestown and made assurances that he would see that anyone who wished to leave could do so. On 18 November Jonestown guards murdered Ryan, one defector, and three newsmen. Sensing that the end had come, Jones induced his followers to commit mass suicide, as they had already pretended to do several times. This time, more than 900 people obediently swallowed a grape-flavored drink laced with potassium cyanide. Jones was found dead, shot in the left temple apparently by an aide, who then turned the gun on herself.

• The *New York Times* carried several lengthy articles on Jones and the Peoples Temple in Guyana shortly after the incidents of November 1978. Books of divergent quality rapidly appeared, some of the better ones being Stephen C. Rose, *Jesus and Jim Jones* (1979); Shiva Naipaul, *Black and White* (1980); James Reston, Jr., *Our Father Who Art in Hell* (1981); and Ethan Feinsod, *Awake in a Nightmare, Jonestown: The Only Eyewitness Account* (1981). All of these studies have now been superseded by Tim Reiterman, with John Jacobs, *Raven: The Untold Story of the Rev. Jim Jones and His People* (1982), which is by far the most thorough and balanced treatment.

HENRY WARNER BOWDEN

JONES, Jo (17 Oct. 1911–3 Sept. 1985), jazz drummer, was born Jonathan David Samuel Jones in Chicago, the son of Samuel Jones, an artificer, and Elizabeth (maiden name unknown). Jones suffered severe burns as a young child, and in his long convalescence he turned to music. He was raised by relatives in Alabama, mainly in the Birmingham area. His aunt bought a snare drum for him when he was ten. Two or three years later, he studied with drummer Wilson Driver at the Famous Theater in Birmingham. He also played trumpet, saxophone, and piano, and he danced, sang, and acted, all of those talents put to use when he toured in shows and carnivals as a teenager. When not wrapped up in practice and performance, Jones attended the Tuggle Institute and in 1926 Lincoln Junior High School, both in Birmingham, and Alabama A&M near Huntsville.

By the late 1920s Jones was working as a drummer. In Omaha he joined Lloyd Hunter's Serenaders. He played with Hunter from 1931 to 1933, but also worked with Grant Moore in Milwaukee during some portion of this same period. Hunter's group recorded in Kansas City in 1931. In 1933 Jones worked as a pianist and vibraphonist with reed player Tommy Douglas in Joplin, Missouri, and Kansas City. The following year marked the beginning of his association with Count Basie, again as a drummer. After holding jobs with lesser-known bands in Minneapolis and Kansas City, he rejoined Basie in Topeka in late 1935, played briefly alongside Walter Page with the Jeter-Pillars band in St. Louis in 1936, and then followed Page back into Basie's band at the Reno Club in Kansas City late that year. When in March 1937 guitarist Freddie Green joined pianist Basie, bassist Page, and drummer Jones in Basie's big band, the finest rhythm section of the swing era was in place. Jones's career paralleled Basie's until August 1948, apart from freelance recordings (including sessions with Teddy Wilson and Billie Holiday), absences because of illness, a feature role in the film short *Jammin' the Blues* (1944), a period of drafted army service (mid-Sept. 1944–Jan.

1946), a tour with Norman Granz's Jazz at the Philharmonic (1947), and another feature in the movie *The Unsuspected* (1947).

Jones joined tenor saxophonist Illinois Jacquet (1948–1950), and in 1948 he led his own trio. He worked with Lester Young at Birdland in New York in 1950, rejoined Jazz at the Philharmonic (1951), and then became a member of pianist Joe Bushkin's quartet for two years. He led groups and recorded a session for the Vanguard label in 1955. For a few days in December 1957 he was reunited with Basie for the making of the television show "The Sound of Jazz." He accompanied pianists Teddy Wilson, Claude Hopkins, Ray Bryant, and Bushkin, among others. By this time he was sometimes called Papa Jo, and he was chagrined to be confused with the younger drummer Philly Joe Jones, a fiery and flamboyant hard bop musician whose work with Miles Davis had perhaps made him more famous than Papa Jo in these years. Jones again toured with Jazz at the Philharmonic, and in 1969 he worked in Europe with pianist-organist Milt Buckner. He figured prominently in the documentary films *Born to Swing* (1973) and *The Last of the Blue Devils* (c. 1979). After a long bout with cancer, he died in New York. His wife, Vivian, had died in 1946; details of the marriage are unknown. They had four children.

Jones exemplified the highest standards in responsibility and musicianship. He demanded the same and was rarely satisfied outside Basie's sphere, an attitude made legendary by his act of throwing a cymbal at the then-incompetent Charlie Parker at a jam session in Kansas City in 1937. Alternately sweet or abusive, he was outspoken on music and race, and perhaps he was excessively aware of his stature as one of the most important jazz drummers.

Jones may be heard as a soloist on "Shoe Shine Boy," recorded by a small group from Basie's band under the name Jones-Smith, Inc. (1936); "I Know That You Know," with a few of Basie's sidemen as the Kansas City Five (1938); and "Swingin' the Blues," with Basie's orchestra (also 1938). These solos emphasize drums rather than cymbals to heighten the contrast with his regular accompanying style. He was an innovator in developing a crisp technique for wire brushes (rather than wooden sticks), as heard on "I Know That You Know."

Jones's great contribution was as an accompanist playing swing rhythms. He softened the role of the bass drum. He played the hi-hat cymbals in a gentle manner, with the opposing cymbals struck while slightly open, so that a sizzling sound replaced the abrupt click or chomp of earlier drumming styles. He achieved extraordinary gradations in the tone and duration of cymbal sounds by varying the position and manner of striking with sticks, brushes, or mallets; he later demonstrated these techniques in detail on his album *The Drum* (1973). "Jo Jones discovered he could play the *flow* of the rhythm and not its demarcation. And he perceived that the rhythmic lead was passing to the [string] bass, which he could complement with his cymbals," jazz critic Martin Williams wrote. Any

of Basie's classic recordings—"One O'Clock Jump," "Jumpin' at the Woodside," etc.—demonstrate his achievement.

• Interviews of Jones are held in the oral history collections at Yale University and the Institute of Jazz Studies, Newark, N.J. The finest survey is by Burt Korall, *Drummin' Men: The Heartbeat of Jazz: The Swing Years* (1990), pp. 117–62. Lewis K. McMillan describes Jones's character in "Jo Jones: Percussion Patriarch," *Down Beat*, 18 Mar. 1971, pp. 16–17, 38. Jones's reminiscences form an integral part of Nat Shapiro and Nat Hentoff, eds., *Hear Me Talkin' to Ya: The Story of Jazz as Told by the Men Who Made It* (1955). Other interviews focus, at Jones's insistence, on attitudes rather than biographical detail: Dan Morgenstern, "Jo Jones: Taking Care of Business," *Down Beat*, 25 Mar. 1965, pp. 15, 35; Max Jones: "Keep-fit Drum Giant," *Melody Maker*, 7 June 1969, p. 12; Graham Columbé, "Jo Jones Speaks Out," *Jazz Journal*, Dec. 1972, pp. 6–8; Richard Brown, "Ain't He Sweet?: Jo Jones," *Down Beat*, 8 Feb. 1979, pp. 18–19, 45–46; Stanley Dance, *The World of Count Basie* (1980), pp. 47–59, with additional stories of Jones elsewhere in the book; Chip Stern, "Papa Jo," *Modern Drummer*, Jan. 1984, pp. 8–13ff.

An account of his activities in the early 1930s appears in Nathan W. Pearson, Jr., *Goin' to Kansas City* (1988), p. 139. Chris Sheridan, *Count Basie: A Bio-Discography* (1986), details his years with the Basie band. Jones's musical contributions are described by Whitney Balliett, *Dinosaurs in the Morning: 41 Pieces on Jazz* (1962), pp. 61–67, who places his drumming achievements in relation to his contemporaries; Martin Williams, *The Jazz Tradition* (1970); and Ross Russell, *Jazz Style in Kansas City and the Southwest* (1971). More precise analyses are by Theodore Dennis Brown, "A History and Analysis of Jazz Drumming to 1942" (Ph.D. diss., Univ. of Michigan, 1976), pp. 443–67, and Gunther Schuller, *The Swing Era: The Development of Jazz, 1930–1945* (1989). Obituaries appear in the *New York Times*, 5 Sept. 1985, and the London *Times*, 6 Sept. 1985.

BARRY KERNFELD

JONES, John (10 May 1729–23 June 1791), physician and surgeon, was born in Jamaica, Long Island, New York, the son of Quaker parents, Evan Jones, a physician, and Mary Stephenson. He studied medicine, first with his father, then with his cousin Thomas Cadwalader of Philadelphia. To the latter, he wrote afterward, he owed "both in physic and morals . . . the best and earliest lessons of my life." In 1750 Jones went to London, where he attended the lectures of the anatomist William Hunter and the practice of the surgeons Colin Mackenzie and Percivall Pott at St. Bartholomew's Hospital. In Paris he visited the Hôtel-Dieu and attended the practice of Claude-Nicolas Le Cat and of Henri-François Le Dran, a famous lithotomist (or surgeon who operates to remove stones in the bladder). He received his M.D. from the University of Rheims in 1751.

After establishing a practice in New York in the winter of 1752–1753, Jones served a time as a surgeon with the provincial troops in the French and Indian War, during which he won fame for treating the French general Baron Dieskau, who had been wounded and captured by the British at the battle of Lake George (1755). Acquiring a favorable reputation, especially as a lithotomist, Jones was praised in a Philadelphia newspaper for "dexterity . . . and judgement in manual operation." In 1767, with his colleagues Peter Middleton, Samuel Bard, Samuel Clossy, and James Smith, he petitioned the trustees of King's College (now Columbia University) for the establishment of a medical department and was elected its first professor of surgery. Jones was also an organizer of the New York Hospital and one of its first attending physicians (1774). Rejecting the notion that surgery was "a low mechanic art, which may be taught a butchers boy in a fortnight," Jones stressed that surgeons should be "thoroughly acquainted with all those branches of medicine, which are requisite to form, the most accomplished Physician. . . . An operation alone," he insisted, "is but a single point in the cure of diseases" ("Introductory Lecture").

With the outbreak of the revolutionary war, Jones was frequently called on to examine candidates for military surgeon and surgeons' mate. For the instruction of young surgeons he prepared a manual of *Plain, Concise, Practical Remarks on the Treatment of Wounds and Fractures* (1775). It included suggestions for the construction and organization of hospitals and hints for the preservation of health, such as the maintenance of proper ventilation in tents and barracks. When the British army occupied New York in the fall of 1776, Jones received assurances that, despite his Whig sympathies, he would not be molested. Nonetheless, he withdrew from the city, attended the army wounded at New Windsor, New York, and other places, and was elected to the New York Assembly in 1776. Committees of Congress sought his advice on reorganizing the medical department of the Continental army, and in December 1777 Benjamin Rush, at that time physician-general to the Hospital of the Middle Department of the army, recommended that he be made inspector general, but the post was never created.

Jones's exile from New York caused his practice and income to decline. His library, papers, and anatomical collection were lost through the carelessness or perfidy of the friend into whose custody he put them. For these reasons, and for his health's sake, Jones moved to Philadelphia in 1779. There his reputation, his Philadelphia family connections, and his unquestioned abilities brought him at once to the front of the profession. He was elected a physician of the Pennsylvania Hospital in 1780, president of the Humane Society (for the rescue of persons from death by drowning and similar accidents) in the same year, and was made a consulting physician of the Philadelphia Dispensary in 1786. A member of the American Philosophical Society since 1769, he was now able to attend its meetings and was chosen a member of its council in 1786. He was an original Fellow and the first vice president of the College of Physicians of Philadelphia (1787). Among his patients was Benjamin Franklin (1706–1790), whom he attended in the latter's final illness in 1790. A few weeks later he was summoned to New York to assist in an operation on President George Washington for the removal of a carbuncle.

Although he was the author of the first surgical text to be published in the American colonies, Jones published little. With the astronomer David Rittenhouse he wrote a description of a lightning strike on some houses in Philadelphia that was printed in the Philosophical Society's *Transactions* (1793), and he was author of a paper on anthrax in the *Transactions of the College of Physicians* (1793). Brief observations by him on climate and diseases in New York were included in William Currie's *Historical Account of the Climate and Diseases of the United States of America* (1792). He appears to have taken no part in the acrimonious disputes that sometimes vexed the medical profession of his day. Although a birthright Quaker who never separated himself from the Society of Friends, he was thought, Benjamin Rush noted, to be something of a deist at the end of his life. According to Rush, Jones never married, but he named a daughter in his will. Jones died in Philadelphia. "He was," Rush wrote, "without a rival in Surgery in the United States" (*Autobiography*, ed. G. W. Corner [1948], pp. 200–201).

• Few of Jones's letters or other papers survive, but useful information may be gleaned from the Papers of the Continental Congress (National Archives) and the correspondence of such contemporaries as Cadwallader Colden, George Clinton, Benjamin Rush, Benjamin Franklin, and George Washington. His ideas on the relation of surgery to medicine are expressed in "John Jones' Introductory Lecture to his Course in Surgery (1769), Kings' College . . . ," ed. W. B. McDaniel 2d, College of Physicians of Philadelphia, *Transactions and Studies*, 4th ser., 8 (1940–1941): 180–189. Biographical sketches of Jones all derive from James Mease's introduction to *Surgical Works of the late John Jones, M.D.*, 3d ed. (1795), pp. 1–48. See also "Account of the Life and Character of the Late John Jones, M.D." *American Medical and Philosophical Register* 3 (1813): 325–37. Obituaries are in the Philadelphia *Federal Gazette*, 27 June 1791, and the *Pennsylvania Gazette*, 29 June 1791.

WHITFIELD J. BELL, JR.

JONES, John (3 Nov. 1816–21 May 1879), civil rights activist and Chicago county commissioner, was born on a plantation in Greene County, North Carolina, the son of John Bromfield (occupation unknown), of German ancestry, and a free mulatto mother, whose last name was Jones (first name unknown). Due to the ancestry of his parents, John Jones was considered a free black. His mother, fearing that his father might attempt to reduce Jones to slavery, apprenticed Jones to learn a trade. It was in Tennessee that he received training as a tailor.

In 1841, while working for a tailor in Memphis, Jones fell in love with Mary Jane Richardson, the daughter of a free blacksmith. The Richardsons moved to Alton, Illinois, and Jones remained in Memphis to complete his apprenticeship. At age twenty-seven, after saving approximately $100, he went north to Alton and married Richardson in 1844. Little is known of their life in Alton, but both Jones and his wife were compelled in 1844 to obtain certificates of freedom in accordance with Illinois law, which required all free blacks or mulattos to file a certificate of freedom, with bond, so that they would not become a charge of the county in which they resided.

Their freedom certified, the Jones family, including their only child, journeyed to Chicago in March 1845. Jones opened a downtown tailoring shop that was one of the first black business establishments in Chicago. Located at his home at 119 Dearborn, "J. Jones, Clothes Dresser and Repairer" became a thriving business. During the earliest days of Jones's residency in Chicago, the prominent Chicago abolitionist Lemanuel C. Paine Freer taught Jones the fundamentals of reading and writing. Not having any formal schooling because of his race, Jones realized that a knowledge of such basic rudiments was essential to the operation of his business.

Jones worked actively with the abolitionist movement. His home became the major center of the Underground Railroad and the rendezvous site for escaped slaves. He frequently played host to abolitionists such as Frederick Douglass, John Brown (1800–1859), and Wendell Phillips.

Jones particularly distinguished himself in the black convention movement and in his long but ultimately successful campaign for the repeal of the Illinois Black Laws. According to laws passed by the first general assembly of Illinois in 1819, blacks had no legal rights. They could not sue or be sued, nor could they testify against whites. They had no right to an education; their oath was not binding; and they could not make a contract (*Laws of Illinois*, pp. 143, 354–61). Jones's first attempt to repeal the Black Laws began in the heated debate surrounding the constitutional convention of 1847. In a series of articles in Chicago's *Western Citizen* (21 Sept. 1847, p. 2; 28 Sept. 1847, p. 2), Jones defended the rights of blacks. He stated that the enlightenment of the nineteenth century, the standards of republican government, and the record of blacks during the American Revolution were sufficient reasons for recognizing black citizenship. He insisted that blacks were entitled to equal representation and equality before the law.

On 7 August 1848, black Chicagoans meeting at the Baptist Church selected Jones, who was already achieving a reputation as a spokesperson for black rights, and the Reverend Abraham T. Hall as delegates to the Colored National Convention of black free men to be held on 6 September in Cleveland, Ohio. Frederick Douglass, already prominent nationally, was named president, and Jones became vice president. The Cleveland delegates were primarily interested in improving the status of blacks in the United States. Jones believed that equality of persons could be achieved only by equality of attainments. For example, he felt mechanical trades, business, farming, and the learned professions were honorable occupations that should be pursued by blacks. Jones demeaned menial labor, calling on delegates to "deem it our bounden duty to discountenance such pursuits, except where necessity compels the person to resort thereto as a means of livelihood" (*Liberator*, 20 Oct. 1848, p. 2).

After Jones returned to Chicago, he concentrated on the repeal of the Illinois Black Laws. On 11 September 1848, Jones and other prominent Chicago blacks, notably Henry O. Wagoner, William Johnson, and Rev. Abraham T. Hall, established a correspondence committee that had two functions: ascertaining the feasibility of circulating a petition for the repeal of the Black Laws, and canvassing the Fourth Congressional District (including Chicago) for the names of blacks. Their efforts provided a model for the establishment of repeal associations and petition drives throughout the state. In spite of Jones's efforts at repeal, the Illinois legislature passed a measure in 1853 banning the immigration of free blacks into the state.

The severity of the Fugitive Slave Act and the intensity of discrimination against blacks promoted the revival of the black national convention movement. Jones denounced the Fugitive Slave Act as "not only unconstitutional but also inconsistent with the view that all men are created equal; it was a measure dictated by the vested interests of the South, ignoring the rights of every party save those of the master" (*Western Citizen*, 24 Dec. 1850, p. 2). At the Rochester, New York, Black Convention of 6 July 1853 and as elected president of the first Black Illinois State Convention in Chicago on 6–8 October, Jones denounced any schemes for colonizing blacks. Jones was chairman of the colonization committee, and the delegates enthusiastically adopted his report that "we regard all schemes for colonizing the free people of color of the U.S. in Africa . . . as directly calculated to increase pro slavery prejudice, to depress moral energies, and to unsettle all our plans for improvement" (*Chicago Tribune*, 11 Oct. 1853, p. 3). As president of the convention, Jones was lauded for presiding "both with dignity and with truly surprising parliamentary accuracy" (*Chicago Tribune*, 11 Oct. 1853, p. 3).

On 4 November 1864, Jones published *The Black Laws of Illinois and a Few Reasons Why They Should Be Repealed*, a sixteen-page pamphlet he himself financed. Basing his arguments on moral, economic, legal, and constitutional principles, Jones directed his comments to the people of Illinois and to newly elected members of the legislature. Addressing individuals who did not consider blacks as citizens, Jones argued, "If being natives and born in the soil of parents belonging to no other nation or tribe, does not constitute a citizen in this country, under the theory and genius of our government, I am at a loss to know in what manner citizenship is acquired by birth." Jones's publication generally received favorable treatment in the press. An editorial in the *Chicago Tribune* (27 Nov. 1864, p. 2) urged the public to become informed about the Black Laws by reading Jones's pamphlet; the editorial insisted on repeal of the laws as well. The *Chicago Evening Journal* (19 Nov. 1864, p. 4) also praised Jones for his efforts. Jones did not rely solely on his rhetoric. He continued to circulate petitions and to organize correspondence committees and repeal associations.

The climate generated by the Civil War and the ratification of the Thirteenth Amendment by Congress were additional factors that aided Jones in his fight for repeal. He supported wartime emancipation and black enlistment. The performance of black soldiers in battle earned the gratitude and respect of many midwesterners who had previously questioned the capabilities of blacks in battle. This war spirit began to break down some of the barriers against the blacks. With the arrival of the news of congressional adoption of the Thirteenth Amendment to the U.S. Constitution, the Illinois General Assembly on 1 February 1865 ratified it, being the first state to approve the abolition of slavery. As a proper corollary toward black freedom, the Illinois legislature acted to repeal the Black Laws. The repeal became law on 7 February 1865.

Jones continued his civil rights work when he went to Washington in 1866 with a committee headed by Frederick Douglass to urge President Andrew Johnson to grant suffrage to the freed slaves. In 1869, when blacks were eligible for political office, Governor John M. Palmer appointed Jones as the state's first black notary public. Ratification of the Fifteenth Amendment on 30 March 1870 allowed blacks to participate for the first time in Illinois elections. In 1871 when the Republican and Democratic central committees selected fifteen Cook County commissioners to run on the Fire-Proof ticket, Jones was nominated by the Republicans and was unanimously accepted by the Democrats. He was elected for a one-year term, practically without opposition, and was the first black man elected to public office in Chicago. In 1872 he was renominated by the Republicans and was reelected for a three-year term. His election was politically unique since there was neither a separate black political organization nor a black community large enough to serve as a base for electoral support. In 1875 he was defeated with the other Republican candidates.

After a lengthy illness, Jones died in Chicago. Chicago's most prominent black citizen left an estate valued at $60,000.

• The John Jones Papers are on file in the Chicago Historical Society, including his significant work, *The Black Laws of Illinois and a Few Reasons Why They Should Be Repealed*. See also Paul Angle, ed., "The Illinois Black Laws," *Chicago History* 8 (Spring 1967): 65–74; Howard F. Bell, "Chicago Negroes in the Reform Movement, 1847–1853," *Negro History Bulletin* 21 (Apr. 1958): 153–55; Charles Branham, "Black Chicago: Accommodationist Politics before the Great Migration," in *The Ethic Frontier*, eds. Melvin G. Holli and Peter d'A. Jones (1977); John W. Cromwell, *The Early Negro Convention Movement* (1904); Charles A. Gliozzo, "John Jones and the Black Convention Movement, 1848–1856," *Journal of Black Studies* 3 (1972): 227–36; "John Jones and the Repeal of the Illinois Black Laws," University of Minnesota, Duluth, Social Science Research Publications (1975); "John Jones: A Study of a Black Chicagoan," *Illinois Historical Journal* 80 (Autumn 1987): 177–88; and Harold F. Gosnell, *Negro Politicians* (1935). For a brief biography and portrait, see "John Jones and His Portrait," *Chicago History* 3 (Winter 1951–1952): 59–63. Significant information on Jones appears in the following newspapers: *Anti-Slavery Bugle* (1848), *Chicago Evening Journal* (1864–1865), *Chicago Times* (1864–1865), *Chicago Tribune* (1853, 1864–1865, 1875, 1879), *Gem of the Prairie* (1848), *Illinois State Journal* (1865), *Liberator* (1848), and *Western Citizen* (1847–1848, 1850, 1853). An obituary is in the *Chicago Tribune*, 22 May 1879.

CHARLES A. GLIOZZO

JONES, John B. (22 Dec. 1834–19 July 1881), Texas Ranger, was born in Fairfield County, South Carolina, the son of Henry Jones, a farmer and stock raiser, and Nancy Robertson. In 1838 the family migrated across the South, eventually reaching Texas and settling at Corsicana, Navarro County. Jones attended local schools but returned to Mount Zion College in Winnsboro, South Carolina, for higher education. Like his father, Jones devoted himself to stock raising and had his own spread near Frost, about twenty miles west of Corsicana. After Texas seceded in March 1861, he considered his options, finally choosing that summer to enlist as a private in the Eighth Texas Cavalry Regiment (unofficially known as Terry's Texas Rangers). Later Jones transferred to the Fifteenth Texas Infantry Regiment, becoming its adjutant. He served in the Trans-Mississippi theater and finished the war with the rank of captain as adjutant of the infantry brigade commanded by General Camille A. J. M. de Polignac.

After Jones returned home in 1865, fellow former Confederates implored him to seek out a haven for them, perhaps in Mexico. He reconnoitered spots to colonize in Mexico and also in Brazil but concluded that there was no place better than Texas. Running as a Democrat in 1869, Jones sought and won a seat in the Texas House of Representatives, where he would have represented Navarro, Hill, Kaufman, and Ellis counties. Instead, due to controversies over vote fraud, the Republican returning board decided the election in favor of Jones's opponent.

Jones attended to his ranch until May 1874, when Governor Richard Coke (a Democrat) offered him the rank of major and command of one of two battalions in the reorganized Texas Rangers. Although Jones stood 5'8" tall and weighed 135 pounds, many contemporaries agreed that he had a commanding presence. Like other superlative riders, Jones cut an impressive figure on horseback. He fixed everyone with piercing dark eyes. His dark bushy mustache, with points brushed well below his mouth, complemented carefully combed black hair. In contrast to many men of his generation, Jones neither took tobacco in any form nor drank alcoholic beverages.

Impressed by Jones's qualities, Governor Coke ordered him to raise six companies, each with seventy-five rangers, for the Frontier Battalion to operate in the vast area comprising the western half of the state. His first duty would be to defend the region against American Indian raiders. In two months Jones recruited his rangers and took steps to institute exceptional discipline, exceptional at least for an organization noted for its freewheeling use of violence and lack of regimentation. Setting a rigorous personal example, Jones conducted inspections of ranger camps and equipment, kept careful records on subordinates and units under his command, and limited furloughs. Nevertheless, Jones's companies would never be mistaken for the Prussian army: the rangers had no required uniform or standardized weapons. Only a silver badge distinguished them from civilians.

The Frontier Battalion fought fifteen skirmishes with American Indians during 1874. One of the most important occurred in July west of Jacksboro, Jack County, between a detachment of twenty-eight rangers led by Jones and a force of perhaps one hundred Kiowas and other American Indians led by Lone Wolf. The fighting lasted several hours; the American Indians trapped the rangers overnight in an isolated place called Lost Valley, killing two and wounding two others. Twelve of the rangers' horses were killed, dismounting nearly half of the detachment. Maintaining a good defensive position and unit morale, Jones sent a rider to seek help. By the time troopers of the U.S. Army's Tenth Cavalry Regiment arrived, the American Indians had withdrawn. Later that year an army column under Colonel Ranald S. Mackenzie inflicted a crushing defeat on the Comanches in West Texas at Palo Duro Canyon (27 Sept. 1874), greatly undermining American Indian strength in the state.

Gradually the threat of American Indian raids receded, and Jones turned his energies toward pacifying civil unrest and apprehending bandits. In 1875 he settled the "Mason County War" between former Confederates and ethnic German settlers, some of whom had been Unionists during the Civil War. In 1877 he entered Kimble County, a stronghold for stock thieves and other criminals. Jones and ranger patrols arrested forty-one men on various felony charges and obtained twenty-five indictments without the loss of a single ranger. That summer Jones's cool-headedness ended the contentious cattle rustling that provoked the Horrell-Higgins feud in Lampasas County by incarcerating the principals on both sides. In three years he had built a remarkable reputation as a law enforcement officer.

That reputation was tarnished by the El Paso Salt War. Antagonisms grew between two groups, Mexican nationals and Hispanic-Americans on one hand, and Anglo-Americans on the other, rivals for the use and control of salt-producing lands outside El Paso. Mexicans had relied upon the area for salt, which had been available to anyone for the taking. In 1877 Charles Howard, an Anglo politician and businessman, laid claim to the salt and planned to monopolize its sale. Confrontations between the two sides produced violence, in which Louis Cardis, the Italian-born leader of the Hispanics, and others were killed. Jones arrived alone on 7 November and, without waiting for reinforcements, sought to end the crisis. He faced down an angry crowd of Hispanics and ordered them to disperse. Believing that the crisis had ended, on 22 November he departed, leaving a newly commissioned lieutenant with a freshly recruited company of rangers to keep the peace. Despite this precaution, the violence reignited and the inexperienced rangers failed to maintain order. Several more persons were killed, including Howard. It was a rare instance of Jones miscalculating. He had underestimated the depth of feelings among Hispanics and overrated the presence of rangers to awe them. Governor Richard B. Hubbard named Jones as the Texas representative on a federal commission to investigate the El Paso disturbances; the other two commissioners were U.S. Army officers. The commission issued its report on 16 March 1878 and recommended stronger federal military presence in the area, prompting the reestablishment of Fort Bliss as a permanent army post.

After completing his role in the Salt War investigation, Jones took up pursuit of Sam Bass, the notorious train robber. Cooperating with federal marshals and local sheriffs, Jones and other rangers hunted for Bass across Central Texas. Relying on information from a member of Bass's gang, Jones arranged to capture the outlaw at the town of Round Rock, north of Austin, where the gang planned to rob a bank. Jones and three rangers went ahead, and he directed a detachment to join them. On 19 July 1878, before the detachment arrived, Bass and two henchmen rode into town. Local deputies challenged Bass, and a hail of gunfire erupted. Jones and his rangers joined in the melee, killing one bandit and mortally wounding Bass. The third outlaw escaped.

The fight at Round Rock was Jones's last significant field assignment for the Texas Rangers. In January 1879 he accepted Governor Oran M. Roberts's appointment as state adjutant general, effectively making Jones commander of the rangers. Jones settled in Austin and married Ann Halliday Anderson, a widow, in 1879; they had no children. Jones died in Austin, evidently of suppurative hepatitis.

Although not known by name to most Americans, Jones in fact virtually matches the legendary image of a Texas Ranger. He was taciturn, calm, brave, fearless against the odds, and with the exception of the El Paso Salt War, successful at all of his assignments. Jones's leadership helped to establish the rangers' reputation for hardiness and persistence. His actions in the field fueled the favorable publicity that further enhanced the rangers' reputation (at least among most Anglo-Texans) as an outstanding law enforcement organization, a notion that survived into the twentieth century.

• Jones's ranger personnel file and reports as adjutant general of Texas are in the Texas State Archives, Austin. An important federal government document is *El Paso Troubles in Texas*, 45th Cong., 2d sess., 1878, H. Doc. 93, Serial 1809. Secondary treatments can be found in Walter P. Webb, *The Texas Rangers* (1935); Wayne Gard, *Sam Bass* (1936); and C. L. Sonnichsen, *Ten Texas Feuds* (1957), which covers the Salt War. An obituary is in the Austin *Daily Statesman*, 20 July 1881.

JOSEPH G. DAWSON III

JONES, John Beauchamp (6 Mar. 1810–4 Feb. 1866), author and journalist, was born in Baltimore, Maryland. The names and circumstances of his parents are unknown. Jones's early days in Baltimore and his childhood on the frontier in Kentucky and Missouri are blank pages from an early life that is obscure at best. Evidently he received a basic education in local schools, for journalism and literature became his livelihood. In 1841 he edited the Baltimore *Saturday Visitor*, in which he serialized the first and most popular of his ten novels, *Wild Western Scenes* (1841), a story of Daniel Boone and frontier life in Kentucky. This book was reprinted at various times from the 1840s to the 1880s, selling 100,000 copies. From 1842 to 1845 he edited the Washington, D.C., *Madisonian*, the primary Whig party newspaper serving the interests of President John Tyler (1790–1862). During the remainder of the antebellum years Jones wrote nine other novels in an effort to support his family, which included his wife, Frances T. Curtis, of Virginia, whom he married in 1840, and four children. However, none of Jones's other books equaled the popularity of *Wild Western Scenes*, and he turned again to journalism.

In 1857 Jones began a four-year stint as editor of the *Southern Monitor*, based in Philadelphia, Pennsylvania. He and his family resided in nearby Burlington, New Jersey. The *Monitor* probably started up in response to the presidential campaign of Republican John C. Frémont in 1856. Jones used the newspaper to promote the brand of Unionism favored by conservative Democrats. On its masthead the *Monitor* carried the motto, "The Union as it was, the Constitution as it is." The newspaper also favorably reflected on the South's institutions, especially "the institution of African slavery, upon which the welfare and existence of the Southern people seem to depend" (Jones, *Diary*, vol. 1, p. 13). In 1859 Jones published his tenth novel, *Wild Southern Scenes*, an obvious attempt to play off the title of his best-known book. This novel warned of the violence and social upheavals (including the destruction of slavery) that disunion would bring, but it found few readers. He unsuccessfully reissued it with a new title, *Secession, Coercion, and Civil War*, in 1861 (in Philadelphia) and 1863 (in Richmond).

Anticipating the firing on Fort Sumter, in April 1861 Jones fled southward to Montgomery, Alabama, to seek a post in the new Confederate government. His family soon followed him south, and eventually they ended up in Richmond, where Jones found an office as a clerk in the Confederate War Department, a job akin to a modern senior administrative staff assistant. He intentionally set out to "write and preserve a Diary of the revolution," with the prospect of retiring on the profits. His record of the war years was eventually published as *A Rebel War Clerk's Diary* (1866). Offered a desk at the Treasury Department, he had declined it, saying that "the Treasury would not answer so well for my Diary" as a place "to preserve interesting facts for future publication." Jones kept up with many duties, including drafting and answering correspondence and filing documents. He was a bureaucrat in the burgeoning Confederate War Department, which at its height employed more than 57,000 civilians across the South.

One of the most significant contributions of Jones's *Diary* is the image that emerges of Jefferson Davis. Jones calculated that Davis was "probably not equal to the rôle he is now called upon to play. He has not the broad intellect requisite for the gigantic measures needed in such a crisis, nor the health and physique for the labors devolving upon him. Besides he is too much of a politician to discard his old prejudices." In two sentences Jones encapsulated Davis's personality and the physical flaws that numerous historians have used to paint a negative picture of the Confederate president. According to Jones, Davis diverted his attention from strategic decisions to spend time on relatively inconsequential administrative details. These included "many little matters, such as solicitations for passports to leave the country." Jones's *Diary* also is one of the best sources on the topic of Davis's health during the war. Davis suffered from neuralgia, insomnia, loss of eyesight, and headaches—maladies that sometimes combined to leave him bedridden and undoubtedly affected his ability to carry out presidential duties.

From his vantage at the war office, Jones observed many other top Confederate officials. He noted his opinions of their personalities and actions. Historians have relied on Jones for pen portraits of leading Confederates, among them Secretaries of War George Wythe Randolph, Leroy P. Walker, James A. Seddon, and Judah P. Benjamin, Secretary of State Robert Toombs, and Governors Zebulon Vance of North Carolina and Joseph Emerson Brown of Georgia.

Among many other features of Jones's *Diary*, two warrant attention. Jones's low pay meant that he barely scraped by; reportedly, he lost twenty pounds during the war. Therefore he became fascinated with the rising prices and shortages of goods and food in Richmond. Also, in several places in his *Diary* Jones revealed a virulent anti-Semitism. In Jones's view, Jews "injured the [Confederate] cause more than the armies of Lincoln." His negativism toward Jews is perhaps best summed up in his statement, "Having no nationality, all wars are harvests for them."

Totaling nearly nine hundred printed pages in two volumes, Jones's *Diary* touches on a kaleidoscope of issues, events, and people. Recounting a purported conversation with Jefferson Davis, Jones claimed that Davis doubted northerners' ability to wage a hard and costly war. Having resided among northerners, Jones wrote, "I know them better. And it will be found that they will learn how to fight and will not be afraid to fight." This entry, among others, could have been added after the war to give an impression of Jones's foresight and analytical ability. Some modern critics have suspected that Jones may have doctored passages in his journal before publication, such as anticipating success for General Thomas J. Jackson, a little-known professor at the Virginia Military Institute. Even if Jones made such changes, *A Rebel War Clerk's Diary* remains one of the best published primary accounts of the Confederacy written by a civilian, standing alongside such works as Mary Boykin Chesnut's famous *Diary from Dixie* and *Inside the Confederate Government: The Diary of Robert Garlick Hill Kean.*

Although an ardent supporter of southern rights, Jones returned to Burlington, New Jersey, after the Civil War, where he died before the publication of his noteworthy diary.

• A durable article on Jones and his *Diary* is Gamaliel Bradford, "A Confederate Pepys," *American Mercury* 6 (1925): 470–78. Valuable for its analysis is Howard Swiggett's "Introduction" to the reprinting of the *Diary* (1935), which included a helpful index, something missing from the original work. Rembert Patrick, *Jefferson Davis and His Cabinet* (1944), mentions Jones numerous times. Jones's anti-Semitism is referenced in Bertram W. Korn, *American Jewry in the Civil War* (1951). See also E. Merton Coulter, *The Confederate States of America* (1950), and Paul D. Escott, *After Secession: Jefferson Davis and the Failure of Confederate Nationalism* (1978).

JOSEPH G. DAWSON III

JONES, John Paul (6 July 1747–18 July 1792), revolutionary war naval officer and hero, was born John Paul in Kirkbean, Kirkcudbrightshire, on the southwestern coast of Scotland, the son of John Paul, a gardener, and Jean MacDuff. After attending the local Presbyterian school, he apprenticed at age thirteen to a shipowner at the nearby port of Whitehaven. His first ship made several voyages that carried provisions to Barbados, thence rum and sugar to Virginia, and returned to Whitehaven with tobacco. The postwar economic slump ended his apprenticeship and sent him briefly into the slave trade, which he called "abominable." At twenty-one Paul was master and supercargo of a ship sailing out of Kirkcudbright to the West Indies. Returning to Scotland from Tobago, he was briefly jailed in 1770 on a charge of murder, for having flogged a sailor who later died. Exonerated, Paul became the master of a large West Indies trader out of London. Again he found trouble in Tobago: during a mutiny he killed a sailor in what he claimed was self-defense. Perhaps in fear for his life, he fled to Virginia in October 1773 and became "Mr. John Jones."

A small, slim, but strongly built man, Jones was tough, impatient, self-absorbed, aggressive, and charming. Determined to advance economically and socially, he had become a Freemason in Scotland and was on the verge of success and affluence when he fled Tobago. His Scottish and Masonic connections probably account for his appearance in Philadelphia in the summer of 1775, looking for a job in the new American navy. His political convictions seem to have been as nebulous as his interest in religion; he later described himself as a "Citizen of the World" committed to "universal philanthropy." Through the Masonic friendship of Dr. John Read of Virginia, and the help of the North Carolina delegate Joseph Hewes, who served on the Marine Committee of Congress, "John Paul Jones Esq." became a first lieutenant in the U.S. Navy.

Unlike the army, there was nothing resembling a colonial structure for a navy, which meant that American seapower relied totally on improvization. Every plan, promotion, and ship assignment required congressional support. Robert Morris, whom Jones met through Hewes in 1776, and Benjamin Franklin, whom he met later in France, supported him at critical points, but their support would entangle him later in serious political trouble, making the faction led by Samuel Adams of Massachusetts and the Lees of Virginia his natural enemy.

In early 1776 he sailed to the Bahamas on the flagship of a small fleet of converted merchantmen. Returning from Nassau to Rhode Island with captured munitions, the fleet met the twenty-gun HMS *Glasgow*. The American ships badly damaged the *Glasgow*, but, unschooled in fleet maneuvers, they let it escape. In the congressional inquiry and courts-martial that followed, Jones, who had served capably under his commodore, got a captaincy and command of the sloop *Providence*. Operating out of Narragansett Bay, he dodged British blockaders in his fast, agile little ship, escorting troopships carrying soldiers to Washington's doomed army while it awaited attack on Long Island. When he reached Philadelphia in August 1776, Jones received orders from the Marine Committee to cruise against the enemy. In seven weeks, he took several prizes near Bermuda, then sailed north to Nova Scotia, where he took several more prizes and, eluding stronger British warships, returned safely.

A second voyage north in late 1776, this time in command of the much larger square-rigged *Alfred*, had comparable success. Despite serious problems of manning and discipline, Jones captured numerous prizes, including a large British munitions ship, which brought badly needed supplies to Washington's army in New Jersey. While most of his seniors were inept or unlucky, Jones had a good record in 1776 and was picked to lead a more ambitious naval campaign in European waters. Faced with the overwhelming strength of the British navy and the futility of raiding British commerce, Morris and Jones shared the idea that "to attack the enemies' defenceless places" was the best use of meager American seapower.

In late 1777, after the American victory at Saratoga, Jones got the eighteen-gun sloop *Ranger* ready to sail out of Portsmouth to the French port of Nantes. Weeks spent in Paris dealing with the American commissioners, Benjamin Franklin and Arthur Lee, lobbying for a bigger ship and more help from French officials, and seducing Madame de Chaumont, wife of the wealthy merchant who handled clandestine French aid to the Americans, delayed *Ranger*'s departure until early spring 1778. Jones then sailed into the Irish Sea, took a few prizes, and headed for the familiar waters of Solway Firth. Landing at his old port of Whitehaven, which was packed with more than 200 ships, he spiked the guns of the battery, but aroused townspeople forced him to flee after burning only one ship. He then sailed up the Firth, intending to take the Earl of Selkirk hostage and use the minor aristocrat in bargaining with the British government. He missed Lord Selkirk, who was away, but got the family silver. Near the Irish coast *Ranger* met and captured HMS *Drake*, a more lightly armed British warship, in an hour's hot fight. Jones returned to Brest, having done little of military importance but creating a sensation in the British opposition press, who cast him as a piratical Robin Hood, embarrassing the British navy for its failure to protect the homeland.

Jones, with help from Franklin, used his new glamour to lobby in Paris for a bigger enterprise. In the summer of 1779 he took command of a 900-ton French East Indiaman, armed and renamed *Bonhomme Richard* as a compliment to his patron, Franklin. With a motley squadron, he set out on a diversionary raid on north Britain while a large French and Spanish force was to invade England. An outbreak of disease in the French fleet wrecked the invasion, but on 14 August Jones and his squadron headed for the North Sea, sailing west around Ireland, under orders to disrupt Britain's vital Baltic trade. His own crew included many experienced seamen as well as an unusually large force of French marines. After sowing brief panic at Leith (Edinburgh's port), he then sailed down the east coast of England, where on 23 September, off Flamborough Head in Yorkshire, he sighted a large Baltic convoy escorted by two warships. Unable to engage the British escort until near sunset, Jones tried to form a line of battle with his squadron, but in the confusion and fading light *Bonhomme Richard* alone tackled the much stronger HMS *Serapis*.

The heavier guns of the *Serapis* smashed the *Richard* during the first half hour, but Jones seized a moment when *Serapis* lost way in a failing breeze to close in. By 9:00 P.M., both ships were ablaze. The American ship *Alliance*, under the eccentric French Captain Landais, appeared and fired several broadsides, doing more damage to *Richard* than to *Serapis*—deliberately so, in the opinion of Jones's chief biographer. But when hand grenades thrown from *Richard* ignited powder cartridges on the British gundeck, killing or wounding about fifty seamen, the British captain surrendered. About half of each crew had been killed or wounded. Transferring his flag to the crippled *Serapis* from the sinking *Richard*, Jones and his squadron limped to The Texel, Amsterdam's port, as his orders dictated. His presence there compromised Dutch neutrality, but in Amsterdam he was a popular hero, as he was in Paris, where he returned in April 1780. Upon his return to America, however, he never received the public recognition that he and many others thought his record deserved.

In 1783, with no more war to fight, Congress sent Jones back to France to collect prize money owed to his officers and men. Helped by Franklin and the new American minister, Thomas Jefferson, he navigated the financial and political complexities of the task, at some personal profit. He also resumed his strenuous sex life, never marrying. After a brief visit to New York in 1787, Jones returned to Europe and accepted a rear admiral's commission offered by Catherine II of Russia, who had just gone to war against Ottoman Turkey. Jones served capably in the Black Sea campaign of 1788, but without a Morris or a Franklin to protect him, he foundered on the rocks of Russian court politics. He was arrested in St. Petersburg in April 1789 for the alleged rape of a ten-year-old girl. Whether he was guilty, or framed by his enemies, remains unclear. Allowed by Catherine to return to Paris in July, he showed no interest in the French Revolution and lived simply on the rue de Tournon, writing letters, visiting friends, and badgering the American minister until he died, probably of nephritis and jaundice complicated by pneumonia. More than a century later, his remains were identified and removed to the U.S. Naval Academy, where they lie in a tomb resembling that of Napoleon in the Invalides.

In a moment of candor Jones concluded that the Continental navy had "upon the whole done nothing" to win the American Revolution. As a judgment on his own naval career as well as on the role of American seapower from 1775 to 1783, his verdict is harsh but fair. But the spectacular, well-publicized exploits of this courageous sailor helped to give the Revolution credibility at a time when international support was crucial. His popularity in France made it easier for Louis XVI to support a colonial rebellion, and his notoriety in Britain undercut public support for an increasingly unpopular war. His ideas on strategy, naval organization, and professional education were sensible and forcefully expressed. He would have been pleased to know that his fate was to become the central mythic figure of the modern U.S. Navy.

• Jones's papers as well as copies of relevant documents from the French and British archives are in the Library of Congress, which has published his autobiography, John Paul Jones *Memoir of the American Revolution Presented to King XVI of France*, ed. and trans. G. W. Gawalt (1979). There is also important published evidence in *The Papers of Benjamin Franklin*, ed. L. Labaree et al. (1959–), vols. 24–28, and in *Naval Documents of the American Revolution*, ed. W. B. Clark et al. (1964–). Samuel Eliot Morison, *John Paul Jones* (1959), is especially valuable for its critical treatment of both evidence and Jones biographers. Older works of value are Alexander Slidell Mackenzie, *The Life of John Paul Jones* (1841), written by a professional naval officer, and Lincoln Lorenz, *John Paul Jones* (1943). Two highly technical works are William Gilkerson, *The Ships of John Paul Jones* (1987), and Jean Boudriot, *John Paul Jones and the Bonhomme Richard* (1987).

JOHN SHY

JONES, John Percival (27 Jan. 1829–27 Nov. 1912), U.S. senator, was born at Herefordshire, England, the son of Thomas Jones, a farmer and laborer, and Mary Pugh. Shortly after his birth, Jones's Welsh parents immigrated to Cleveland, Ohio, where he attended the city's public schools and also received private tutoring. Jones worked for a time in a marble yard. Succumbing to the pioneer spirit of adventure, he journeyed in 1849 to California. There he engaged in farming and mining, served as sheriff and justice of the peace, represented Trinity County in the state senate from 1863 to 1867, and tried unsuccessfully to become lieutenant governor. In 1861 Jones married Hanna Cornelia Conger Greathouse, the daughter of Judge Thomas Conger of Sacramento. They had one child before her death later that decade.

In 1867 Jones relocated to western Nevada and entered silver mining. With the assistance of friends, he became superintendent of the Kentuck mine in Gold Hill and later advanced to the superintendency of the Yellow Jacket and Crown Point mines. His investments in Crown Point's stock made him a millionaire, allowing him to build an icehouse in New Orleans, start a railroad from Santa Monica to Salt Lake City, and exert influence on the political life of the new state. This wealth contributed to his quick rise in Nevada politics. State legislators in 1873 elected Jones, a Republican, to the U.S. Senate to succeed James W. Nye, a Carson City Republican. Jones served in the upper chamber continuously until 1903. Also in 1873 Jones married Georgina Frances Sullivan. He had five children with his second wife.

Jones's senatorial career revolved primarily around the issue of free silver and mining legislation. A member of the Senate Committee on Mines and Mining, he chaired a congressional monetary commission in New York City in 1876. His report contained a thorough examination of the silver question. Jones also traveled to European nations to ascertain their views on international bimetallism. In addition to silver coinage, he supported protective tariffs, favored antitrust legislation, and endorsed Republican foreign policy during his legislative career. Jones chaired the Committee to Audit and Control the Contingent Expense and the Committee on Epidemic Diseases in several congresses and also served on the Committee on Post Offices and Post Roads, among others.

When President Grover Cleveland asked Congress in 1893 to repeal the Sherman Silver Purchase Act, Jones participated in a lengthy Senate filibuster against rescission. His speech, encompassing more than 100 pages in the *Congressional Record*, topped 450 pages when printed the next year. Silverites immediately hailed the published work as a compendium on the subject. "If the people of this country . . . do not destroy the gold standard," Jones warned, "it will destroy them." To Jones, free coinage of silver promised better times, more employment, increased farm prices, reduced indebtedness, and, particularly important for a mining state, government purchases of the white metal. He believed silver was not only a panacea to remedy the nation's economic troubles but was also a sacred dogma and symbol of protest against eastern gold barons and Wall Street.

A turning point in Jones's career occurred in 1894 when he renounced his allegiance to the Republicans and joined the Populists. Placing silver ahead of other issues and looking toward his own reelection in 1896, he abandoned a party that seemed committed to sound money. "A change of party affiliations is not to be either advised or commended except in obedience to the imperative demands of principle," he wrote to Enoch Strother, chairman of the Republican State Central Committee of Nevada. The letter was published in the *Washington Evening Star* on 5 September 1894. Jones gave freely of his time and talents, traveling the country to address various groups as a recognized representative of free silver. To oppose free silver at that time was tantamount to political suicide in Nevada, where Silver Republicans and free coinage Democrats dominated the state.

In 1896 Jones endorsed the fusion of Populists and Silver Republicans with Democrats under the leadership of the Democratic presidential nominee, William Jennings Bryan. He campaigned vigorously for the free coinage platform and for Bryan, whom he thought was a "wonderfully clever man." He believed that Bryanism heralded the first steps toward a golden age of political peace, economic recovery, and social justice. During the campaign he wrote an article, "What the Remonetization of Silver Would Do for the Republic," which appeared in the October 1896 issue of *The Arena*. "The demonetization of silver has checked our advancement as a nation, and brought us under tribute to thieves; but if we succeed in securing its remonetization, the wheels of progress will turn again," Jones predicted (pp. 736–42).

Nevada fusionists (Silver and Democratic parties) endorsed Jones for reelection in 1896. Although George Nixon, a powerful leader of the Silver party, challenged Jones belatedly, he stood no chance of defeating the venerable senator, who won easily. The Republican presidential triumph that year profoundly disappointed Jones. An age of prosperity and prodigious new gold discoveries occurred during President William McKinley's years in office. Congress passed the Gold Standard Act in 1900, the year of Bryan's second defeat for the presidency. When the money debate ceased to be a major political issue after the presidential election of 1900, Jones returned to the Republican party. Tired of political battles, however, he declined to be a candidate for reelection in 1902, thereby bringing to a close thirty years of service as a legislator.

After retiring from the Senate, Jones resumed his former business activities and took care of his mining investments. He retired to his large home in Santa Monica, California, a city that had figured prominently in his early land speculations. He died in Los Angeles.

Jones was a competent and dedicated public servant and a leading western spokesman for free coinage. His colleagues on Capitol Hill were cognizant of his loyalty to silver, his important role on the Finance Committee, and his strengths as a politician. James G. Blaine, former Speaker of the House of Representatives and unsuccessful Republican presidential nominee, recorded in his memoirs, *Twenty Years of Congress* (1886), that Jones was "a rare and somewhat remarkable character" who was "a close observer of men" and "a genial companion" possessing "an enthusiastic faith in silver" (pp. 540, 606). Like others, Blaine recognized Jones's intellectual power and his insistence on formulating his own conclusions.

• The Jones papers are divided among four manuscript collections at different repositories: the Henry E. Huntington Library and Art Museum at San Marino, Calif.; the Nevada Historical Society at Reno; the Society of California Pioneers at San Francisco; and the Department of Special Collections of the University of California Library at Los Angeles. The UCLA holding is the largest, most valuable, and most accessible collection of correspondence, writings, scrapbooks, clippings, and photographs. Jones letters are also in the manuscript collections of many of his contemporaries, including Benjamin Harrison and William E. Chandler (Library of Congress), William M. Stewart (Nevada Historical Society), and Tasker L. Oddie (Huntington Library). In addition to their publication in the *Congressional Record*, Jones's speeches appear in a collection of pamphlets in the New York Public Library. Two of Jones's own works dealing with the currency issue are *Resumption and the Double Standard* (1876) and *The Money Question* (1894). A complete study of Jones is Leonard Schlup, "Nevada's Doctrinaire Senator: John P. Jones and the Politics of Silver in the Gilded Age," *Nevada Historical Society Quarterly* 36 (1993): 246–62. Jones's early California experiences are detailed in John E. Baur, "Early Days and California Years of John Percival Jones, 1849–1867," *Southern California Quarterly* 44 (1962): 97–131. A useful book on this period in Nevada history is Mary Ellen Glass, *Silver and Politics in Nevada, 1892–1902* (1969). Valuable material on the silver movement is contained in the papers of Henry M. Teller and Edward O. Wolcott at the Colorado Historical Society in Denver. Excellent insights on Jones may be gleaned from Lucy Scheid, "An Interview with David Toll," Oral History Program, Special Collections Department, University Archives, University of Nevada, Reno. Obituaries are in the *Los Angeles Times*, 28 Nov. 1912, and the *New York Times*, 29 Nov. 1912.

LEONARD SCHLUP

JONES, John William (25 Sept. 1836–17 Mar. 1909), minister and author, was born at Louisa Court House, Virginia, the son of Colonel Francis William Jones and Ann Pendleton Ashby. As a young man Jones underwent a conversion experience that led to his decision to enter the Baptist ministry. After attending preparatory academies in Louisa and Orange counties, he enrolled at the University of Virginia, where he was active in a number of religious activities, including serving as treasurer of the Young Men's Christian Association and teaching Sunday school. After graduation in 1859, he became a member of the first class at the Southern Baptist Theological Seminary in Greenville, South Carolina. Jones graduated from the seminary and was ordained in 1860. Although he was approved by his denomination for missionary work in China, the political turmoil in the United States delayed his departure, and he returned to Louisa County, Virginia, to become the pastor of the Little River Baptist Church. He married Judith Page Helm in December 1860; they had five children.

With Virginia's secession from the Union in 1861, Jones enlisted in the Confederate army as a private in the Thirteenth Virginia Regiment. Known as "the fighting parson," he remained in the ranks for a year and then assumed the chaplain's position of his regiment. In November 1863 the Baptist Home Mission Board appointed him missionary chaplain in the army

corps under A. P. Hill's command, an assignment he held until the war ended. Jones was also instrumental in the formation of the Chaplains' Association of the Army of Northern Virginia, in which he worked closely with Generals Robert E. Lee and Thomas J. "Stonewall" Jackson in attending to the spiritual needs of the Confederate troops. During the winter of 1862–1863, when Lee's army was encamped near Fredericksburg, Virginia, Jones helped organize revival meetings, preached to the soldiers, and baptized several hundred converts. On one occasion, he even cut a hole in the ice on a frozen pond in order to baptize a group of men by immersion.

In the fall of 1865, Jones assumed the pastor's position at the Baptist Church in Lexington, Virginia. In the same period, he served as a chaplain at nearby Washington College (now Washington and Lee), where Robert E. Lee was president. He left the church in Lexington to become an agent of the Southern Baptist Theological Seminary (then in Louisville, Kentucky) in 1871, and in 1873 he became superintendent of the Virginia Baptist Sunday School and Bible Board in Richmond, Virginia. Although Jones held a number of church positions over the next thirty-five years, including pastorates at Ashland, Virginia, and Chapel Hill, North Carolina, college chaplaincies at the University of Virginia (1893–1895) and the University of North Carolina (late 1890s to 1903), and an administrative post at the Home Mission Board of the Southern Baptist Convention (1887–1893), his most notable achievement was as secretary of the Southern Historical Society between 1875 and 1887. During that period, he was responsible for the publication and editing of the first fourteen volumes of the *Southern Historical Society Papers*, an important, albeit highly partisan, collection of source materials about the history of the Confederacy. Jones also served as chaplain general of the United Confederate Veterans for the last nineteen years of his life. He died in Columbus, Georgia.

In addition to his career as a Baptist minister and publicist of the Southern Historical Society, Jones wrote and lectured extensively on his wartime experiences. He drew on his acquaintance with Lee to publish two widely read biographies: *Personal Reminiscences, Anecdotes, and Letters of Gen. Robert E. Lee* (1874) and *Life and Letters of Robert Edward Lee, Soldier and Man* (1906). After the death of Jefferson Davis, the only president of the Confederate States of America, Jones edited a tribute approved by the Davis family, *The Davis Memorial Volume* (1890). He also composed a textbook, *School History of the United States* (1896), in which he sought to demonstrate the central role of the South in American history. Jones's most significant and creative work was *Christ in the Camp* (1887; new ed., 1904). This book contains a collection of inspiring stories about the significance of religious revivals in the Confederate armies and the ways in which Christian belief enabled white southern men to transcend the temporal consequences of military defeat. Jones argued that throughout history no army had displayed more piety and devotion to spiritual concerns than Lee's Army of Northern Virginia.

Jones's most important contributions were as a writer, collector of historical documents, and apologist for the "Lost Cause." He played a significant role in keeping alive the memory of the Civil War and giving shape to the process of self-justification of white southerners during the last decades of the nineteenth century. Throughout the postwar period Jones proclaimed that, notwithstanding the defeat of the Confederacy, the South's cultural and religious ideals were worthy ones that all Americans ought to celebrate.

• Useful descriptions of Jones's career are in his obituary notice in *Confederate Veteran* 17 (May 1909): 239, and in George Braxton Taylor, *Virginia Baptist Ministers*, 5th ser. (1915). An excellent assessment of Jones's work is found in Charles Reagan Wilson, *Baptized in Blood: The Religion of the Lost Cause, 1865–1920* (1980).

GARDINER H. SHATTUCK, JR.

JONES, Joseph (6 Sept. 1833–17 Feb. 1896), physician and scientist, was born in Liberty County, Georgia, the son of Charles Colcock Jones, a major planter and prominent minister to the slaves, and his first cousin, Mary Sharpe Jones. Joseph Jones was educated at South Carolina College (now the University of South Carolina), Princeton College (now University, B.A., 1853), and the University of Pennsylvania (M.D., 1856). Jones developed a lifelong interest in scientific research during his college years and chose teaching over private practice in order to have time for his original investigations. Between 1856 and 1861 he taught chemistry at the Savannah Medical College, natural sciences at the University of Georgia, and medical chemistry and pharmacy at the Medical College of Georgia. Jones's reputation as a leading student of health conditions in the nineteenth-century South was launched during these years. In 1859 he married Caroline Smelt Davis, of Augusta, Georgia. The couple had three children.

The Civil War interrupted Jones's budding scientific career. After six month's service with a local militia unit, he accepted a Confederate surgeon's commission. But Jones was a most unusual medical officer. Viewing the hostilities as an immense laboratory from which to learn valuable medical lessons, he prevailed upon Surgeon General Samuel P. Moore to allow him to investigate health conditions in the Confederacy's principal armies, hospitals, and prisons. He presented his findings to Moore in masterful reports; those on gangrene and Andersonville Prison are the best known.

Jones returned to the Medical College of Georgia in the fall of 1865. The following spring he was elected to the chair of physiology and pathology at the University of Nashville. The excavation of some pre-Columbian Indian mounds along the Cumberland River, in which he found convincing signs of syphilis, was the high point of his stay in Tennessee. In 1868 Jones moved to New Orleans to accept the chair of chemistry and clin-

ical medicine in the medical department of the University of Louisiana (now Tulane University) and to become a visiting physician at Charity Hospital. He was to spend the rest of his life here. Jones's first wife died in 1868, and in 1870 he wed Susan Rayner Polk, of New Orleans, daughter of Episcopalian bishop and Confederate general Leonidas Polk. This union also produced three children.

Conditions in New Orleans—an elevated rate of morbidity and a large public hospital that offered easy access to patients and records—made it ideal for the study of disease, and Jones's career blossomed there. He was increasingly recognized as an authority on southern diseases, but it is for his work in public health that he is most remembered. The sickly image of New Orleans inexorably interested him in sanitary reform. Good health was thought in that era to depend upon sanitary precautions against pathogenic environmental factors and the battle against epidemic disease. Jones campaigned for a thorough cleansing of New Orleans and for sanitary reform. The most lethal epidemic disease was yellow fever. This historic scourge of the South slowly subsided in the region after the Civil War, with the only major visitations occurring in 1867 and 1878. The latter, however, was one of the most widespread and virulent in the nation's history. While Jones had first encountered this much-feared killer as early as the 1850s in the wards of the Savannah marine hospital, it was in New Orleans that he was introduced to epidemic yellow fever. By the great outbreak of 1878 he had become a yellow fever expert. Jones, like most of his contemporaries, erroneously attributed the disease to a specific poison of undetermined origin and called for preventive measures, mainly civic hygiene and a limited quarantine.

Jones's growing reputation as a sanitarian earned him an appointment to the Louisiana State Board of Health in 1877. Three years later he was named president. Founded in 1855, this was the nation's oldest permanent state board of health. Under Jones's guidance it promoted health reform in New Orleans and the Mississippi Valley with an unprecedented zeal. Although opposed to quarantine as a single defense, Jones vigorously endorsed it as a crucial weapon in the struggle against imported pestilence. The board of health repaired, updated, and expanded the state's network of quarantine stations and rigidly enforced all sanitary and quarantine laws and ordinances. By the end of his administration, Jones had demonstrated that through a rigidly enforced quarantine yellow fever could be excluded from New Orleans and the Mississippi Valley. To pay for the quarantine system, Jones fought for and won the right to collect fees from ships entering the Mississippi. In 1881 the powerful Morgan Company took the board of health to court, arguing that the fees violated the commerce clause of the U.S. Constitution. The district court ruled in the company's favor, but on appeal first the Louisiana Supreme Court (1884) and then the U.S. Supreme Court (1886) upheld the quarantine fees as a legitimate exercise of the state's police power to protect the health of its citizens.

Jones's tenure as president of the Louisiana State Board of Health was marred by a bitter conflict with the National Board of Health. Congress established this organization on 3 March 1879 in response to the demands for a national quarantine law and a central agency to administer it in the wake of the devastating yellow fever epidemic of 1878. From the outset there was strong opposition to the National Board of Health from those who saw it as federal interference in state health and quarantine policy. Jones, an ardent believer in states' rights, was its boldest opponent, loudly resisting the national agency's attempts to play a role in administering the quarantine along the Gulf Coast. The controversy lasted until the summer of 1882, when Congress slashed funding for the National Board of Health and drastically curtailed its functions.

Jones's retreat from public life the next year did not slacken his interest in health reform. He enthusiastically returned to teaching and research. Jones was a prolific writer and during his long career published over 100 papers on a wide range of medical and scientific topics in the best journals of the day. He is chiefly remembered for his *Medical and Surgical Memoirs*. Consisting of four massive volumes, which appeared between 1876 and 1890, this work was a compilation of a lifetime of investigation of disease and observations on the practice of medicine. Jones died at his New Orleans home.

• Two collections of Jones's papers, an extensive one at Tulane University and a smaller one at Louisiana State University in Baton Rouge, are indispensable. Of comparable value are the papers of his father, Charles Colcock Jones, at Tulane University, a large portion of which is readily available in Robert Manson Myers, *The Children of Pride* (1972). Also useful are collections of the papers of Charles Colcock Jones, Jr., Jones's brother, at the University of Georgia and Duke University. There is no full-scale biography. Stanhope Bayne-Jones, *Joseph Jones, 1833–1896* (1957?), is a biographical sketch and is uncritical. James O. Breeden, *Joseph Jones, M.D.: Scientist of the Old South* (1975), surveys and analyzes Jones's life and career only through the Civil War.

JAMES O. BREEDEN

JONES, Lewis Ralph (5 Dec. 1864–31 Mar. 1945), plant pathologist, was born in Brandon, Wisconsin, the son of Lucy Knapp and David Jones, farmers. After early education at Brandon, he attended Ripon College (a Congregational school). In 1886 he entered the University of Michigan, planning to study medicine, but like another professor, Erwin F. Smith, he was influenced by Professor Volney M. Spalding, and after attending E. F. Smith's doctoral examination on peach yellows, on which Smith had made a detailed investigation, he decided to take up research in plant pathology. During 1887–1888, between his junior and senior years, Jones spent three terms as instructor in natural science at the Mount Morris Academy, Illinois. After receiving the Ph.B. degree in 1889 (the Ph.D. followed in 1904), he was appointed to the University of Vermont. There he served as botanist to the Agricultural Experiment Station (1889–1910) and became in turn instructor in natural history (1889–1891), assistant professor (1891–1892), associate professor (1892–1893), and finally professor of botany (1893–1910).

During the twenty years Jones spent at Vermont he investigated a wide variety of diseases, trained many students who subsequently became prominent, and gradually gained recognition as a leading American plant pathologist. He first studied potato blight, which was causing serious losses and did much to popularize Bordeaux Mixture, which had recently been introduced to control blight. In 1904 he went on a trip to Europe to study potato blight and to collect resistant varieties. He visited many leading laboratories and returned with ninety potato varieties, which were tested at Vermont by Professor W. Stewart. These studies culminated in Jones's classic paper, written with N. J. Giddings and B. F. Lutman, entitled "Investigations on the Potato Fungus *Phytophthora infestans*" (*U.S. Department of Agriculture, Bureau of Plant Industries Bulletin* 245 [1912]).

Another important event during the Vermont years was the six-month period in 1899 during which Jones was seconded to Erwin F. Smith's laboratory at Washington, where he was allocated the problem of soft rot. Jones isolated the causal bacterium, which he named *Bacillus carotovorus* [*Erwina carotovora*], and demonstrated that the organism disintegrated tissue by producing a pectinase enzyme that dissolves the middle lamella of the host cells. Jones also investigated diseases of orchard fruit, cereals, forest trees (the L. R. Jones State Forest of Vermont was named in his honor), and other topics such as lightning injury.

In 1909 Jones was invited by the University of Wisconsin to start a plant pathology department, and he took up his duties in February 1910. In Jones's own words, the decision to leave Vermont was easy, "since we could by returning to Wisconsin personally renew our early home associations and professionally meet the increasingly evident responsibilities of opening thus, a larger university particularly strong in botanical traditions and associations, opportunities for the training of younger men and women beyond those which had been possible to us of the older generation" (*Phytopathology* 35 [1946]: 5). Jones integrated his new department with both the U.S. Department of Agriculture and with other departments of the university, particularly the Department of Botany, then chaired by Professor Robert A. Harper. Students came to the Department of Plant Pathology from all over the world, and during that period some 145 students majored in plant pathology or were awarded the Wisconsin University Ph.D.

Early work on plant pathology had concentrated on the pathogen, then on the effects of the pathogen on the host. Jones's innovation, for which he will be remembered, is host-pathogen interaction. With the help of such able colleagues as James G. Dickson, James Johnson (the virologist), G. W. Keitt, and John C. Walker he set standards for such investigations throughout the world. One innovation that was widely adopted (or adapted) was the "Wisconsin soil tank" by which soil temperature could be controlled, and later Keitt and Jones used a primitive inoculation chamber devised by Johnson and Dickson to study epidemiology and control of apple scab. It was essentially such a chamber, combined with a "Wisconsin soil tank," that was subsequently used by R. H. Stoughton at the Rothamsted Experimental Station for his study of black arm of cotton.

Jones received many honors. He was one of the founding members of the American Phytopathological Society and its first president (1909). He became the first editor in chief of *Phytopathology* (1911–1914); played a leading role in establishing the Botanical Society of America, which he served as vice president (1910) and president (1913); and was twice a member of the editorial committee of the *American Journal of Botany* (1914–1916, 1919–1921). He was also one of the founders of the Tropical Plant Research Foundation (president, 1924–1943) and a life member of its board. Jones was a member of many scientific societies both American and foreign. He was a Mason and a Rotarian and was a member of the Republican party, the University Heights Poetry Club, and the Madison City Literary Club. One honor that particularly pleased him was the presentation to him of his portrait for the University of Wisconsin at a dinner on 19 August 1926 during the International Congress of Plant Science at Ithaca, New York, when a range of speakers paid tribute to Jones and his achievements.

Jones was one of the outstanding teachers of plant pathology in America during the first twenty-five years of the twentieth century, and during his time at Madison students from all over the world came to his university to study under him. He will long be remembered as a key figure in the development of the teaching of plant pathology in North America and for his own researches in many aspects of this field.

Jones married twice. In 1890 he married May I. Bennett, who had been a classmate at Ripon College. After her death in 1926, he married in 1929 Anna M. Clark, a former student at Vermont, who had become a professor of biology at Hunter College, New York City. After retirement, Jones and his second wife traveled widely. There were no children of either marriage. Jones died at Orlando, Florida.

• Smith's research on the bacterium causing soft rot is reported in *New York (Geneva) Agricultural Experiment Station Technical Bulletin* 11, part 2 (1909): 289–368. For information on the "Wisconsin soil tank," see his "Experimental Work on the Relation of Soil Temperature to Disease in Plants," *Transactions of the Wisconsin Academy of Sciences, Arts, and Letters* 20 (1922): 433–59. His work with Johnson and Dickson's inoculation chamber is in G. W. Keitt and L. R. Jones, "Studies on the Epidemiology and Control of Apple Scab," *Research Bulletin of the Wisconsin Agricultural Experiment Station* 71 (1926). For biographical information, see J. C. Walker and A. J. Riker, National Academy of Sciences, *Biographical Memoirs* 31 (1958): 156–79, which has a complete bibliography, and J. C. Walker, *Annual Review of*

Phytopathology 17 (1979): 13–20, with a portrait. The most important obituary notice is G. W. Keitt and F. V. Rand, *Phytopathology* 36 (1946): 1–17, with a portrait and a bibliography.

G. C. AINSWORTH

JONES, Lynds (5 Jan. 1865–11 Feb. 1951), ornithologist and college professor, was born in Jefferson, Ohio, the son of Publius Virgilius Jones, an impecunious millwright, and Lavinia Burton. When the boy was several months old, the family moved to a farm near Grinnell, Iowa, where the father struggled to make ends meet. When not helping his father with farm chores, Jones attended the local country schools. A neighbor who sold eggs for a living employed the teenaged Jones to collect them, and this job piqued a lifelong interest in birds. Jones also learned to hunt, a skill that helped him to augment the family income and taught him much about nature and wildlife. Shortly afterwards one of Jones's teachers, George W. Tallmon, got some of the local youngsters together to form a chapter of the Louis Agassiz Association, a national organization for children interested in natural history, which was sponsored by *St. Nicholas Magazine*. Through his membership in this group, Jones decided to expand his interest in birds, and in doing so, soon became acquainted with some other young ornithologists in his area.

As his schedule permitted, Jones took high school classes through the academic program of Iowa College (now Grinnell University). Graduating at age twenty-three, he began the college course there but decided to seek a school with a more scientifically oriented curriculum. In 1890 he transferred to Oberlin College in Oberlin, Ohio, and in 1892 he completed his undergraduate coursework there. Jones was then appointed a laboratory assistant in geology and ornithology at Oberlin, where he also taught private classes in ornithology while concurrently completing his graduate coursework. When he obtained his M.A. in 1895, his ornithology classes became part of the regular curriculum at Oberlin, the first time this had happened at any American college or university. Jones was appointed an instructor at Oberlin in 1899, and after further study at the University of Chicago, wrote his dissertation, titled "The Development of Nestling Feathers," and received his Ph.D. in 1905.

In 1888, prior to Jones's departure for Oberlin, he and several of his fellow ornithologists formed the Wilson Ornithological Club, named for the early nineteenth-century Scottish-American naturalist Alexander Wilson. These young men founded the club in part because the *Auk*, journal of the recently organized American Ornithologists' Union (AOU), would not publish their research. Jones was selected to edit the club's fledgling journal, which was named the *Wilson Bulletin* in 1894. He contributed the majority of his own articles to this publication between 1892 and 1930 and served as its editor until 1900, when he began his coursework at Chicago, and again from 1902 to 1924. He also served as president of the club and acted in various other capacities on its behalf. At the same time Jones became a member of the AOU, being selected as a fellow in 1905.

Following the completion of his doctorate, Jones returned to Oberlin and was promoted to associate professor. His plans to teach courses in ecology were briefly blocked because the zoology department chair wanted to discontinue all fieldwork for students, including Jones's own course in ornithology. The chairman stepped aside when Jones's plans received strong approval from the zoology faculty. In 1908 Jones was named to head a subdepartment of animal ecology, and in 1922 he was promoted to full professor. His ornithology classes were popular—approximately 150 students signed up each year—and he offered a field ecology class in 1910 and a major in that field in 1915. By 1926 a master's level program in ecology had been organized and was well under way. For fifteen years (1915–1930), except for the World War I years and 1927, Jones led well-subscribed field trips to the Pacific Northwest. Jones's summer classes in both ornithology and ecology, offered at Oberlin and elsewhere along the shore of Lake Erie, were also extremely popular.

Jones extended his fieldwork emphasis to include bird migration. He maintained records on all arriving and departing birds in the region for four decades. He called for counts of local birds on a daily basis and proposed the use of census-taking techniques for that purpose, both of which presaged the Christmas bird counts later promoted by the magazine *Bird Lore* (subsequently renamed *Audubon* magazine). Field work continued as the focus of Jones's teaching and research for nearly fifty years until his retirement in 1930. The ornithology and ecology programs that Jones established were terminated following his retirement, however; the Animal Ecology Department, which had been created as an administrative unit for his classes in 1922, ceased operations soon after 1930.

Jones's major publications included *A Revised Catalog of the Birds of Ohio* and *Birds of Ohio* (both 1903), completed with the aid of his former student William Dawson. Most of Jones's other shorter articles completed between 1887 and 1935 appeared in *Curlew*, *Bird Lore*, under his own private auspices, or in the *Oberlin College Laboratory Bulletin*. Jones was later described by a former student as "very quiet, modest, retiring, but effective," both as a man and as a teacher. His contributions to Ohio and Midwest regional ornithology from the 1890s through the mid-1930s was considerable. He married Clara Mabelle Tallmon, the daughter of his former teacher in Iowa, in September 1892, and the couple had five children. Jones died in Oberlin.

• Useful source material includes an unpublished biographical sketch written by Jones's son George at Oberlin College. Published appreciations include one by H. J. Taylor in *Wilson Bulletin* 50 (1938); another in the *Ohio Journal of Science*, July 1951; and an obituary by S. Charles Kendeigh in *Auk*, July 1952, to which is appended a bibliography of Jones's publications. A brief obituary is in the *New York Times*, 13 Feb. 1951.

KEIR B. STERLING

JONES, Margo (12 Dec. 1911–24 July 1955), originator and inspirer of America's professional regional theater movement, was born Margaret Virginia Jones in Livingston, Texas, the daughter of Richard Harper Jones, a lawyer, and Martha Pearl Collins, a teacher. In the Drama Club at Girls' Industrial College (later Texas Women's University), she was the only student interested in directing. In 1931, after experiencing what she called "something wonderful" at her first professional production, Walter Hampden's touring *Cyrano de Bergerac*, she devoured the library's issues of *Theatre Arts*, absorbing its artistic idealism, and began her habit of reading at least one play every day.

Jones's energy and dedication attracted the notice of influential *Dallas Morning News* critic John Rosenfield, who became her mentor and lifelong ally. On the day she graduated (B.A., 1932; M.S., 1933), Jones enrolled at Dallas's Southwestern School of Theatre, paying her way by, according to one of the school's owners, "pretty much running things" after answering the office phone during her first interview. She attended Pasadena Playhouse's summer school in 1934, then, as secretary/companion to a wealthy widow she met there, toured the world's theater capitals in 1935, ending in New York, where she found the Group Theatre inspiring.

Back in Texas, Jones was hired as assistant director of the Houston Federal Theatre project. When that collapsed, she was elected the Texas Centennial's delegate to the Fourth Moscow Art Theatre Festival in 1936, charming the *Houston Chronicle*'s editor into publishing her articles about it. Brooks Atkinson long remembered her bold self-introduction in Moscow: "You don't know me, but someday you will."

That fall, Jones accepted a recreation department position teaching Houston's playground directors to put on plays with children. Convincing her employers to give her a building where she could direct adults on her own time, Jones organized the Houston Community Players and produced a four-month season of four plays. She then persuaded the department to pay her salary and production costs from box-office receipts and to free her from teaching duties. She became a full-time director and producer at twenty-six. Her all-volunteer theater lasted six seasons, growing from nine to six hundred members, buying $15,000 worth of equipment, and producing sixty plays with no public subsidy other than the free use of the building.

Having attracted national attention, Jones was named director of the South by the Confederacy of American Community Theatres and elected to the executive council of the National Theatre Conference in 1939. After seeing arena staging demonstrated, she produced three summer seasons of in-the-round productions in Houston hotel ballrooms. Pictured in *Stage* in December 1939 as one of twelve outstanding little-theater directors outside New York, Jones was the only woman.

Volunteer community theater declined during World War II, and Jones left Houston in 1942 to teach at the University of Texas. In November, after reading Tennessee Williams's *Battle of Angels*, given her by Broadway agent Audrey Wood, Jones went to New York for the National Theatre Conference and to meet this new playwright. In the summer of 1943, teaching at the Pasadena Playhouse, she promoted Williams's talent to Hollywood and to her friends all over the country. She worked with Williams on *You Touched Me*, obtaining a leave from the University of Texas to direct the play at the Cleveland Playhouse (the first woman to direct there) and later at the Pasadena Playhouse.

In 1944, dreaming of a network of fully professional resident theaters outside of New York, Jones returned to Texas determined to create a European-style noncommercial, nonprofit municipal theater, a low-priced theater for the people. Suggesting Dallas as her site, John Rosenfield helped Jones apply for a Rockefeller Foundation grant to study theaters around the country. In her grant proposal, she wrote, "I believe passionately in Art as a form of Salvation, and that the things art brings—beauty and spiritual growth—are the most important things in human life."

Before receiving the grant, she directed *The Purification*, which Tennessee Williams dedicated to her, at the Pasadena Playhouse. Then she toured theaters searching out talent for a Dallas theater she said she wanted to be not merely good, but great. Meanwhile, Rosenfield built enthusiasm among Dallas's wealthy elite and published articles on Jones and her work.

On reading *The Glass Menagerie*, Jones interrupted her travels and persuaded actor/producer Eddie Dowling to hire her as assistant director of the Broadway premiere. Quickly becoming Dowling's codirector, Jones nursed Williams's play to its 1945 success. In Dallas, Jones's Theatre '45 was stalled by lack of a suitable space. She returned to New York in 1946 to direct Canada Lee in *On Whitman Avenue*. Then, directing Ingrid Bergman in a star-troubled production of *Joan of Lorraine*, in the midst of a complex situation, she was fired by Maxwell Anderson just before the opening.

Finally, Jones was given free use of an exhibition building in Dallas's Fair Park, which Broadway designer Jo Mielziner helped convert into a 198-seat theater-in-the-round. The new Theatre '47 would ceremonially change its name each New Year's eve, but Dallas theatergoers just called it "Margo's."

Theatre '47 opened with William Inge's first play *Farther Off from Heaven* (later retitled *The Dark at the Top of the Stairs*); Tennessee Williams's *Summer and Smoke* was the last of the ten-week season's five plays. From her community theater days, Jones had sought out new playwrights; now her firm policy was new plays or classics only. Rehearsing three plays at once, working nine to twelve hours a day, Jones produced thirteen plays within less than a year, nine of them world premieres.

Some plays that succeeded in Jones's intimate, scenery-less arena got lost in New York's proscenium-arch playhouses. Produced and directed on Broadway by Jones in 1948, *Summer and Smoke* failed, chilling her relations with Tennessee Williams and Audrey Wood. Ironically, the play was a historic off-Broadway success in 1952, when José Quintero's revival at Circle in the Square's intimate arena recaptured its original effect.

Jones was elected vice president of the American National Theatre and Academy (ANTA) in 1949. The next year, Sean O'Casey gave her *Cock-a-Doodle Dandy* to premiere at Theatre '50; she wrote her influential book *Theatre in the Round* with Ted Apstein and inspired Zelda Fichandler to found the Arena Stage in Washington, D.C.

Theatre '54 had grown into a year-round, 45-week operation. In 1955 Jones staged the world premiere of *Inherit the Wind*, expecting it to be dangerously controversial. It broke all Dallas attendance records. Its Broadway production was the sixth and most successful play brought by Jones from Dallas to Broadway.

Professionally, Jones was triumphant, but her private life had grown increasingly unhappy. Often lonely, she kept friends up late drinking with her. The aftermath of one such night caused her sudden accidental death in Dallas; reading scripts on the floor, she fell asleep and was poisoned by fumes from recently cleaned carpeting.

Theatre '55, renamed the Margo Jones Theatre, became mired in power struggles between the board and artistic management. It closed in December 1959 after four years of steady decline.

Over the years, other theaters and awards were named in honor of Margo Jones. She did not live to see the national flowering of the movement she inspired. Her early followers founded theaters and went to others as directors. Among hundreds of regional theater directors, few can rival her record of discovering and supporting new playwrights. As one Dallas supporter mourned, "If you want another Margo Jones Theatre, you need another Margo Jones" (quoted in Sheehy, p. 267).

• Margo Jones's own *Theatre-in-the-Round* (1951) is a good retelling of her Dallas theater story. Clipping files are in the Harvard Theatre Collection and the Billy Rose Theatre Collection of the New York Public Library for the Performing Arts. Helen Sheehy's well-researched biography *Margo: The Life and Theatre of Margo Jones* (1989) is the best single source on Jones's active professional and sometimes troubled private life; it also contains the most comprehensive listing of available source materials. Also useful is Don B. Wilmeth, "A History of the Margo Jones Theatre" (Ph.D. diss., Univ. of Illinois, Urbana, 1964). Periodicals (*Dallas Morning News, New York Times, Theatre Arts*) offer detailed information on Jones's Broadway activities and those of Theatre '47–'56. Sections devoted to Margo Jones in J. W. Ziegler, *Regional Theatre: The Revolutionary Stage* (1973), and Donald Spoto, *The Kindness of Strangers: The Life of Tennessee Williams*

(1985), should be read with awareness of the authors' own agendas and biases, not as objective reports. Obituaries are in the *New York Times*, 25 July 1955, *Time*, 8 Aug. 1955, and *Theatre Arts*, July 1955.

DANIEL S. KREMPEL

JONES, Mary Amanda Dixon (17 Feb. 1828–1908), physician and surgeon, was born in Dorchester County, Maryland, the daughter of Noah Dixon and Sarah Turner, middle-class shipbuilders. Mary Dixon graduated from Wesleyan Female College in Wilmington, Delaware, in 1845. She taught physiology and literature, first at her alma mater and then at the Baltimore Female College. Later she became principal of a girls' seminary in southern Maryland. In the 1840s she read medicine with two local physicians, Henry F. Askew and Thomas E. Bond.

In 1854 Mary Dixon married John Quincy Adams Jones, a lawyer and the cousin of Isaac Dashiell Jones, a two-term Whig member of the House of Representatives in the 1840s and Maryland's attorney general in 1867. For a time, the couple went west, first to Rockford, Illinois, and then to Madison, Wisconsin. During that period Jones gave birth to three children. The westward venture must have failed, however, because by 1860 the couple had returned to Baltimore. There John resumed the practice of law with his cousin.

In 1862 Jones left her family in Maryland to study medicine in New York. She received her degree that year from the Hygeio-Therapeutic College, a water-cure institution teaching a therapeutic system that used water in a variety of curative ways, and a hotbed of reform and women's rights. In 1865 she and her children settled in Brooklyn, leaving her husband behind. Although he lived with his family on occasion in New York, the record suggests that Jones's husband maintained an active law practice in Maryland and, by the end of the 1870s, had disappeared from their lives.

For a decade Jones lived as other sectarian women physicians did, lecturing to ladies on the "laws of health" and advertising in the radical women's rights journal, *The Revolution*. In 1872, however, she made a decision that eventually altered her therapeutic world view and management of patient care: she returned to medical school for a second, orthodox medical degree, matriculating for three years at the Woman's Medical College of Pennsylvania. Here she developed an interest in surgery and pathology. She studied microscopy under the direction of professor John Gibbons Hunt, a skilled technician who was aware of the exciting laboratory work being done in Germany. She also engaged professor of surgery Benjamin B. Wilson as a private tutor.

Returning to Brooklyn to reopen her practice in 1876, Jones gradually devoted herself exclusively to surgery and the diseases of women. In addition, she continued her pathology work under the direction of the Hungarian-born Charles Heitzman, an accomplished microscopist with degrees from Pesth, Hungary, and Vienna, Austria. For Jones and most nineteenth-century surgeons, surgical skills were acquired through a loose system of apprenticeship, intellectual exchange, and mutual observation. Realizing that, as a woman, the informal networks open to her were somewhat circumscribed, she enrolled in 1881 in the newly established post-graduate medical school for an advanced course on gynecology and surgery. The course was taught by Benjamin Franklin Dawson, the founding editor of the *American Journal of Obstetrics and Diseases of Women and Children*, who later assisted her at her first abdominal operation.

In 1882 Jones took an appointment as chief medical officer with the Women's Dispensary and Hospital of the city of Brooklyn. When she quarreled about a range of policy issues with its board of lady managers a year later, all agreed to disband the first hospital, and Jones incorporated a second institution with the same name five months later. Running her own hospital provided her with the clinical opportunities to pursue her interest in gynecological surgery.

In 1883 Jones performed her first laparotomy, removing the ovaries and fallopian tubes from a woman whom she had diagnosed as suffering from hysterical symptoms brought on by diseased organs. In the next decade, like many male gynecological surgeons testing out new operative techniques, she performed between 100 and 300 similar operations. From 1884 until her death she promoted her work through the publication of case studies and pathology reports in various leading medical journals. In 1886 she took a trip to Europe with her son Charles, also a physician, to observe and assist at operations performed by the international surgical elite in England, France, and Germany. During the late 1880s she corresponded with the world-renowned surgeon and ovariotomist Lawson Tait.

In 1889 the *Brooklyn Eagle* newspaper published a series of unflattering articles about Jones, accusing her of performing aggressive surgery on improperly informed female patients and of financial mismanagement of her hospital. Although some financial improprieties having to do with the receipt of public funds were found to exist, Jones's surgical practices were probably no more aggressive than those of the male colleagues she admired. But in some ways the *Eagle*'s accusations represented the public's suspicion of the new specialty. In 1892 Jones sued the newspaper for libel and lost. Soon afterward, her hospital was closed, and she and her son Charles moved to New York City. There she ceased to perform surgery and concentrated for the next fifteen years on publishing articles on pathology, using specimens gleaned from her operations. She died in New York City.

Jones was probably the only woman surgeon of her generation whose operative technique and contributions to the cellular pathology of the female reproductive system were discussed and taken seriously by male colleagues in the United States and abroad. She is credited with the first complete hysterectomy for uterine myoma performed in the United States.

• Jones's publications include "A Case of Tait's Operation," *American Journal of Obstetrics and Diseases of Women and*

Children 17 (Nov. 1884): 1155–61; "Personal Experiences in Laparotomy," *Medical Record* 52 (Aug. 1897): 182–92; and "The Opinions of Different Surgeons and Pathologists as to the Origin and Cause of Fibroid Tumors," *Medical Record* 62 (Aug. 1902): 323–31. Biographical information is in trial testimony reprinted in the *Brooklyn Eagle*, 4 and 5 Feb. 1892; Irving A. Watson, *Physicians and Surgeons of America* (1896), pp. 808–10; and *Catalogue of the Officers and Students of the Wesleyan Female Collegiate Institute, of Wilmington, Delaware, 1838–1849* (1848), pp. 1, 13, 17, 23, and 26. See the *Brooklyn Eagle*, 24 Apr. to 31 May 1889, for articles on Jones.

REGINA MORANTZ-SANCHEZ

JONES, Mary Elizabeth Cover (1 Sept. 1896–22 July 1987), developmental psychologist, was born in Johnstown, Pennsylvania, the daughter of Charles Blair Cover, a businessman, and Carrie Louise Higson. Neither parent was educated beyond high school, yet both encouraged their children to attend college. In 1915 Mary went to Vassar College, where she majored in economics, having also taken elective courses in psychology taught by Margaret Floy Washburn. She then went to Columbia University in part because her brother was there studying economics, but she decided to specialize in psychology. Soon after her arrival she met Harold E. Jones, then a graduate student at Columbia under Robert S. Woodworth, and they were married in 1920. She obtained her doctorate in psychology in 1926, having in the meantime become the mother of two children.

In 1919, while a student at Vassar, Mary met John B. Watson, then a professor of psychology at Johns Hopkins University. Impressed by his elucidation of behaviorism, she managed as a graduate student to work with him as mentor although, by then, Watson had left academia. Their collaboration culminated in the publication in 1924 of "The Elimination of Children's Fears" in the *Journal of Experimental Psychology* and "A Laboratory Study of Fear: The Case of Peter" in *Pedagogical Seminary*. Although their study of the "deconditioning" of a behavioral characteristic would become a classic, it was not considered acceptable for Mary's doctoral thesis because only a single subject was involved. To satisfy the requirements of Columbia University, she therefore also investigated the development of behavior patterns in more than three hundred children from well-baby clinics in New York City and compared her findings with those of earlier "baby biographers."

In 1925 Jones was awarded a two-year Laura Spelman Rockefeller fellowship in child development. During this time her husband, originally an experimental psychologist, also became active in the developmental field. In 1927 he was offered an appointment as director of research at the Institute of Child Welfare, now the Institute of Human Development, at the University of California in Berkeley, one of six developmental institutes recently established by the Laura Spelman Rockefeller Foundation. He accepted, and the Jones family moved to California.

At the Berkeley institute, which was directed by Herbert Stolz, Jones worked as a part-time research associate. Initially, she was involved in setting up the institute nursery school and in parent education. In 1931 she assisted her husband and Stolz in organizing a longitudinal study of adolescent development, which is still ongoing and is now known as the Oakland Growth Study. This investigation was intended to complement a child guidance study directed by Jean Macfarlane and a growth study directed by Nancy Bayley, both of which were initiated in 1928. (Now all three longitudinal studies are combined as the Intergenerational Study.) The adolescent study used ten-year-old children attending Oakland schools as subjects and was originally expected to last six or seven years. Instead, thanks to the skills of the investigators and the long-term loyalty of many subjects, it became a study of their entire lifespan.

Jones's work with the subjects of the Oakland Growth Study was the source of about fifty papers on adolescent development published during the 1930s, 1940s, and 1950s. Particularly original and notable were her investigations of early and late physical maturation and its long-term consequences in both sexes. During this period she was sometimes paid out of Rockefeller grant funds and sometimes worked without salary. Because her husband was a professor of psychology, she could not receive an academic appointment in the Department of Psychology; such an appointment would have flouted the regulation against "nepotism" then extant at the University of California. Ultimately, in 1952, she was appointed an assistant professor in the Department of Education. She became a full professor in 1959.

In 1960 Jones and her husband both retired. They went abroad on a vacation, which was soon curtailed by her husband's death from a heart attack on 7 June 1960. To help cope with her grief, she returned to work as a research associate with Nevitt Sanford at the Institute for the Study of Human Problems at Stanford University. She stayed for four years, during which she began what would again prove to be long-term research on the problem of alcoholism. Using now-adult subjects from the Oakland Growth Study, she sought to establish the antecedents, as expressed in personality, of current drinking behavior. Jones continued these investigations when she returned to the University of California in 1969 as a consultant to the Intergenerational Study at the Institute of Human Development. She remained actively associated with the Berkeley longitudinal studies until a few months before her death in Santa Barbara, California.

In addition to her academic work, Jones gave freely of her time to public service. During World War II she was a member of the Committee on Children, organized by the Berkeley Civilian Defense. In 1949 she was chairman of the Committee on Nursery School Standards set up by the California Department of Education. She also acted as an adviser on research and practice in adoption to many public organizations. In recognition of her contributions to the field of child development, she received many awards. In 1960 she was president of the Division of Developmental Psychology of the American Psychological Association, which gave her the G. Stanley Hall Award in 1968.

Jones was profoundly concerned with the ethics of child study. As a graduate student working on the classic case of Peter, she had chosen to try to reduce fear rather than induce it. Her respect for the welfare and rights of subjects influenced the design of later longitudinal studies that were not strictly objective. Rather than remain an aloof observer, Jones became the friend of the children she studied and of their families. No other course would have long suited Jones's generous and sociable nature.

• Jones's papers are at the Bancroft Library, University of California, Berkeley. Some material is also in the Archives of the History of American Psychology, University of Akron. For a complete listing of her publications and presentations, see "Harold E. Jones and Mary C. Jones, Partners in Longitudinal Studies," an oral history conducted with Mary Cover Jones in 1981–1982 by Susan D. Riess, Bancroft Library, University of California, Berkeley. This oral history discusses the personal, social, and academic aspects of her life. The transcript of Milton Senn's interview with Jones is in the Milton J. E. Senn Oral History Collection in Child Development, History of Medicine Division, National Library of Medicine, Bethesda, Md. In addition to her classic study with John B. Watson on children's fear, her best-known papers on physical maturation are "The Later Careers of Boys Who Were Early- or Late-Maturing," *Child Development* 28 (1957): 113–28, and "Psychological Correlates of Somatic Development," *Child Development* 36 (1965): 899–912. Her publications on alcohol consumption include "Personality Antecedents and Correlates of Drinking Patterns in Adult Males," *Journal of Consulting and Clinical Psychology* 32, no. 1 (1968): 2–12, and "Personality Antecedents and Correlates of Drinking Patterns in Women," *Journal of Consulting and Clinical Psychology* 36, no. 1 (1971): 61–69. On Jones's contributions to developmental psychology, see Deana Dorman Logan, "Mary Cover Jones: Feminine as Asset," *Psychology of Women Quarterly* 5 (1980): 103–14. An obituary is in the *New York Times*, 21 Aug. 1987.

ELIZABETH M. R. LOMAX

JONES, Mother (c. 1 Aug. 1837–30 Nov. 1930), labor organizer, was born Mary Harris in Cork, Ireland, the daughter of Ellen Cotter and Richard Harris, a laborer. In her 1925 autobiography, Jones claimed to have been born on May Day, 1830, but this was part of her habit of exaggerating her longevity in the labor movement. Late in the 1840s her father fled the potato famine, and around 1852 the family joined him in Toronto, Canada, where he had gone to work on railroad construction. She often declared that before they migrated, her people had been active in the Irish resistance against England. Thus hard physical labor, exploitation, class consciousness, and political dissent were part of Mary Harris's heritage.

Mary Harris attained a common-school education, attended normal school for two terms, and then began a career as a teacher, working in a convent school in Monroe, Michigan, in 1860. She also learned the seamstress trade and worked briefly as a dressmaker in Chicago. Just before the Civil War she moved to Memphis, Tennessee. There in 1861 she met and married George Jones, an iron molder and a member of the iron molders union. They had four children, all of whom, along with her husband, died of yellow fever in 1867. Mary Jones moved back to Chicago, where she opened a small seamstress shop with a partner but was burned out in the Chicago fire of 1871. The next quarter century of her life was spent mostly in Chicago, a center of rapid industrial growth, union organizing, and radical ferment.

Jones became a bit player in the labor movement. According to her own reminiscences, she joined the Knights of Labor in the 1870s and began a lifelong friendship with Master Workman Terence Powderly. She also claimed to have been in California for the Workingmen's Movement in the 1870s, in Pittsburgh during the great railroad strike of 1877, in Chicago for the Haymarket riot of 1886, and in Washington with James S. Coxey's army in 1894. Her work with textile operatives in Cottondale and Birmingham, Alabama, in 1894 had impassioned her against child labor, and by the late 1890s she was helping to organize miners in Pennsylvania. Also during the 1890s, she made the acquaintance of Eugene V. Debs, helped organize the Socialist party, and tirelessly distributed Julius Wayland's new socialist newspaper, the *Appeal to Reason*.

Mary Jones burst on the American scene around 1900, when she became known as "Mother Jones." She published articles in the *International Socialist Review* under that moniker; she also signed herself as "Mother" in personal correspondence to Eugene Debs, Secretary of Labor William Wilson, United Mine Workers president John Mitchell, and other labor leaders, who, in turn, addressed her as such. Workingmen too called her "Mother," and she called them her boys. The image she cultivated did not represent motherhood victimized and docile, however, but motherhood aroused. In speeches and articles, she elaborated her image as a woman who faced down old age and gun-toting thugs for the family of labor, and she invoked her own history in the labor movement to enhance her venerability. *Mother* Jones implicitly rejected the self-celebratory ideology of triumphant capitalism—the ideal of every man for himself—in favor of the rhetoric of brotherhood, or, more precisely, of labor as a family. She did not invent the symbolism of brotherhood and family, but she dramatized these staples of worker consciousness. A fiercely proletarian political radical, Mother Jones imposed her presence on the national consciousness.

Before the turn of the century Jones had become a paid organizer for the United Mine Workers, an on-again, off-again relationship that lasted for thirty years. In 1899 she organized anthracite miners in Pennsylvania but attracted special attention by organizing the miners' wives into broom and mop brigades who routed strikebreakers. In 1903 she organized a children's crusade of under-age textile workers in a march on the home of President Theodore Roosevelt in Oyster Bay, New York. She traveled from town to town in the bituminous regions of West Virginia and Colorado in 1902 and 1903, talking to the miners and giving speeches, always organizing despite the threat of company guards and court injunctions. She also found time to support striking machinists on the Southern Pacific Railroad in 1904, to cofound the Industrial Workers of the World in 1905, to aid Mexican revolutionaries in 1907, to help organize New York shirtwaist workers in 1909, and to assist the militant Western Federation of Miners in shutting down the copper pits of Arizona in 1910.

Perhaps the most dramatic episodes in Jones's life occurred in the years before World War I, again in the coalfields. Unionization in West Virginia culminated in an intense strike in 1912–1913. In the midst of her organizing efforts, violence broke out between miners and the private detectives hired by the owners. Seeing her as a rabble-rouser, a military court charged Mother Jones with conspiracy to commit murder, placed her under arrest, and sentenced her to twenty years in prison. The newly elected governor commuted her sentence but not before a tremendous outcry arose nationwide against her incarceration. No sooner was Jones freed than she headed to Colorado, where miners had struck John D. Rockefeller's Colorado Fuel and Iron Company. Three times she was locked up, then deported from the state, and three times she snuck back in and continued to organize. Her charges of brutality were borne out when the Colorado militia machine-gunned and torched the miners' tent colony at Ludlow, Colorado, on 20 April 1914, killing twenty women and children. Jones moved audiences to tears with her accounts of the massacre; she also testified before Congress, and for years thereafter Ludlow became a byword for the oppression of miners, the greed of operators, and the courage of Mother Jones.

Even as Jones entered her ninth decade, her efforts did not slacken. She helped organize New York City streetcar and garment workers just before World War I and rallied steel workers after it ended. In 1921 she went to Mexico for the Pan-American Federation of Labor meeting (she had supported the Mexican Revolution and the rights of Mexican nationals held in American prisons) and even continued to organize West Virginia miners. While the old revolutionary fervor continued to show itself, Mother Jones's loyalties grew increasingly erratic. Never overly consistent in her ideological commitments, she now veered from calling herself a bolshevik to supporting Calvin Coolidge. Poor health slowed her down, and she also took time out to write her autobiography, working on it in Chicago with the help of social worker and magazine writer Mary Field Parton. She spent the last year of her life as a guest at the home of her friends Walter and Lillie May Burgess in Silver Spring, Maryland. A grand hundredth birthday party was given for her there on 1 May 1930, but before the year was over Mother Jones was dead. She had insisted on being buried with some of her "boys," the victims of the Virden (Ill.) Massacre, in the Union Miners' Cemetery in Mount Olive, Illinois.

While her commitment to organizing workers was unwavering, Jones frequently became entangled in sectarian troubles and personality disputes, which sometimes revealed a streak of pettiness. More fundamentally, her gift for on-site organizing did not include much patience for long-term union-building. For example, she was a founding member of the Industrial Workers of the World but abandoned that organization soon after its opening days. Also, although she organized women in various industries and brought the wives of working men into the labor movement, she repudiated the suffrage movement as a bourgeois diversion from the real issue, class struggle. In good Victorian fashion, Jones believed that women should educate, support, and elevate their men—but for rebellion, not for middle-class respectability.

Mary Harris "Mother" Jones was one of the best-known American women of her day. In terms of organizations built, strikes won, or industries unionized she was not notably successful; and, measured by her intellectual contribution, the history of American radicalism would scarcely have been altered if she had never lived. Nonetheless, for roughly a quarter century Mother Jones embodied the spirit of the American Left. It was the image of this willful old woman—telling miners to "pray for the dead, and fight like hell for the living," organizing sites where no one else would venture, and articulating an ideal of justice not just for the workers but for working-class families—that helped energize her popular critique of capitalism and gave working people the sense that she was one with them.

• A small collection of Mother Jones's personal correspondence is located in the archives of Catholic University in Washington, D.C. Her words are most readily found in *Mother Jones Speaks: Collected Writings and Speeches*, ed. Philip S. Foner (1983), and *The Correspondence of Mother Jones*, ed. Edward M. Steel (1988). Also important is *The Autobiography of Mother Jones*, ed. Mary Field Parton (1925). Dale Fetherling, *Mother Jones: The Miners' Angel* (1974), is a complete biography. Obituaries are in the *New York Times*, 1 Dec. 1930, and the *United Mine Workers Journal*, 15 Dec. 1930.

ELLIOTT J. GORN

JONES, Noble (1702–2 Nov. 1775), carpenter, doctor, and political official, was born in Lambeth, County Surrey, England. The names of his parents are unknown. Jones married Sarah Hack before 1723. They had four children, one of whom died in infancy. The extent of Jones's education remains unknown, but he acquired some skills as a physician, carpenter, architect, and surveyor by the early 1730s. He came to Georgia in 1733 as one of its first settlers. He worked diligently to succeed at his venture, and his many skills provided opportunities for profit and prominence. Jones helped construct the first buildings in Savannah, Georgia's colonial capital. He assumed greater responsibilities upon the death of the colony's two leading carpenters and physician in the summer of 1733. From 1748 to 1755 Jones formed a medical partnership with his eldest son, Noble Wimberly Jones.

Above all, Jones sought wealth in land. He received a town lot in Savannah from the trustees who organized the colony. In the 1730s he obtained a 500-acre tract on the Isle of Hope and named it "Wormsloe." The site strategically bordered a coastal waterway, Skidaway Narrows, which made the plantation a popular gathering place and a convenient stop for travelers. Jones preferred to raise fruits, vegetables, experimental crops, and exotic plants at Wormsloe, and his efforts attracted the attention of naturalist John Bartram, who visited in 1765. Jones accumulated five town lots and over 5,500 acres during the trustee and royal periods, becoming one of the largest landowners in the colony.

Jones probably knew James Oglethorpe, Georgia's founder, before he left England, since the two men lived in Surrey County. Oglethorpe demonstrated his friendship and patronage toward Jones by assigning him numerous civil and military positions in Georgia. Oglethorpe respected Jones's opinion about conditions in Georgia and often supported his protégé when others criticized him. Because of his association with Oglethorpe and in appreciation of the lands and responsibilities bestowed upon him by the trustees, he generally supported their strict regulations prohibiting slavery, rum, and female land inheritance.

During the early 1740s a group of dissatisfied settlers, known as the Malcontents, openly criticized trustee policies and their insistence that colonists produce silk, wine, and exotic crops. Some Malcontents claimed that Jones agreed with their complaints. Even William Stephens, trustee secretary, questioned his loyalty. In 1742 Jones quieted those fears by signing Stephens's pamphlet, *A State of the Province of Georgia*, which upheld Trustee policies, but joined a 1749 protest urging the trustees to permit slavery. When the trustees lifted their restriction that year, Jones quickly acquired seven slaves, accumulating up to fifty-three during his lifetime.

The trustees appointed Jones a conservator of the peace, or small-claims justice, before he left England. Soon after arriving in Georgia Jones acquired additional positions, including constable, spokesman for the neighboring Yamacraw natives, surveyor, and prohibition officer against rum. While generally conscientious, Jones may have let ambition overrule good sense. He could not devote full attention to his many responsibilities and lost his appointment as conservator and surveyor in 1738. In spite of these difficulties, Jones continued to provide information about land conditions and distribution when called upon by the trustees, colonists, and royal officials. In 1750 he served as register and surveyor of roads for lands southeast of Savannah.

Jones fared better in military affairs. During the 1730s he began service as a ranger to patrol the coastal regions. When Britain and Spain went to war (1739–1748), Jones fought under Oglethorpe during the unsuccessful siege of St. Augustine in 1740. When he returned, Jones became lieutenant then captain lieutenant of the Northern Company of Marines, commanding veteran scout troops who were to protect the area between Savannah and Fort Frederica. He operated a fort on his property to defend Skidaway Narrows. When the Spanish briefly attacked St. Simons Island in 1742, Jones was stationed there and with his rangers captured a small number of Spanish soldiers. In 1751 Georgians feared a Cherokee uprising on the northern frontier, and Jones was appointed cavalry captain to protect Savannah. During the last years of the French and Indian War, he supervised construction of a powder magazine in the town and strengthened the design of surrounding forts.

When James Oglethorpe left Georgia in 1743, the trustees created the offices of president and assistants to govern the colony. Jones became an assistant in 1750. More mature and experienced by that time, he took his duties seriously and attended required meetings. During the royal period from 1752 to 1776, Jones acted as elder statesman and served in almost every capacity of public service available. He helped construct a legislative house, a courthouse, and suitable buildings for the royal governor and improved the public market in Savannah. He also served on a commission to oversee the first printing of Georgia laws and was a vestryman of Christ Church parish.

Jones received an appointment to the Governor's Council in 1754, frequently presiding over its meetings. He served as judge of the General Court, Court of Appeals, and Court of Oyer and Terminer, occasionally acting as chief justice. Although uneducated in law, most contemporaries considered him a fair dispenser of justice. In 1760 he also became treasurer of the colony. He retained these offices until his death except for a brief suspension from the council between 1755 and 1758, because of his opposition to the unethical practices of Governor John Reynold's secretary and favorite, William Little.

As Georgians protested new tax laws from Parliament and prerogatives the British government claimed over the colonies, beginning in 1763, Noble Jones remained a supporter of the mother country and of Georgia's third royal governor, Sir James Wright. He could not accept a Georgia colony defiant toward the British Empire. During his final years in office Jones worked to reduce the influence of Whig opposition in Georgia. His opinions clashed with those of his son, Noble Wimberly Jones, who served in the Commons House and who supported American rights and the authority of colonial legislatures. Noble Jones passed away at Wormsloe, less than a year before American colonists proclaimed their independence. Georgia lost a dedicated public servant, a knowledgeable physician, and one of its first citizens.

• Some of the letters written by Noble Jones and his family are printed in John Eddins Simpson, ed., *The Jones Family Papers, 1760–1810, Collections of the Georgia Historical Society*, vol. 17 (1976). Other sources that contain letters about Jones are found in E. Merton Coulter, ed., *The Journal of William Stephens 1741–1743* (2 vols., 1958), and Mills Lane, ed., *General Oglethorpe's Georgia: Colonial Letters 1733–1743* (2 vols., 1975). One of the most complete accounts of Noble

Jones is E. Merton Coulter's biography of the Jones clan in *Wormsloe: Two Centuries of a Georgia Family* (1955). Other narratives include William M. Kelso, *Captain Jones's Wormsloe* (1979), and Sarah B. Gober Temple and Kenneth Coleman, *Georgia Journeys* (1961). For general accounts of colonial and revolutionary Georgia that make reference to Noble Jones, see two works by Kenneth Coleman, *Colonial Georgia: A History* (1976) and *The American Revolution in Georgia: 1763–1789* (1958); Larry E. Ivers, *British Drums on the Southern Frontier* (1974); and Harold E. Davis, *Fledgling Province* (1976).

CAROL S. EBEL

JONES, Noble Wimberly (1723?–9 Jan. 1805), revolutionary era patriot, was born in Lambeth, England, the son of Noble Jones and Sarah Hack. He came to Georgia as a young man, accompanying his family aboard the *Anne* as one of the original settlers who founded the colony in 1733. His father was a carpenter, surveyor, and physician whose friendship with James Oglethorpe quickly elevated him to a position of prominence in the colony; indeed, the elder Jones ably served the trustees and, after Georgia fell under royal control in 1754, the Crown as a councillor, justice of the general court, and treasurer of the colony. Not surprisingly, then, Noble Wimberly's adolescence included military service under Oglethorpe in the struggle to secure Georgia from Spanish and Indian threats. While he apparently received no formal schooling, he studied medicine with his father—who also lacked formal education in medicine. In 1755 Jones married Sarah Davis; they had fourteen children.

Given his father's connection with Oglethorpe, it was almost inevitable that Jones would also develop a political career of some significance. Elected to Georgia's initial Commons House of Assembly in 1755, he served in every session until it went out of existence in 1775. While his father remained steadfastly loyal to Great Britain until his death in 1775, Jones followed a different path. In 1765 he was "a distinguished opposer of the stamp act," as his obituary noted, who soon "began to enjoy the honour of being hateful to tyrants." Jones was in the forefront during a dispute with the governor and council over who should serve as Georgia's colonial agent in England, a dispute that ultimately replaced William Knox (considered too sympathetic to Parliamentary authority by Georgia's Whigs) with Benjamin Franklin. Elected Speaker in 1768, he led the Georgia lower house in protesting the Townshend Acts and in approving letters received from the lower houses in Massachusetts and Virginia, which did the same, though the king had ordered the dissolution of Georgia's assembly should the Massachusetts letter be considered.

When a new assembly was elected in 1769, however, Jones was again chosen Speaker, though he had become increasingly unacceptable to Governor James Wright. When the 1771 assembly met and the commons house again made Jones its Speaker, Wright used the authority granted him by his royal instructions to reject the choice and required the house to make another selection. Although the Georgia lower house then elected Archibald Bulloch, it praised Jones for his devotion to the public welfare and denounced Wright's action as a "high Breach of the Privilege of the House" which tended to "subvert the most valuable Rights and Liberties of the People." Wright then dissolved the assembly. Following new elections, however, the next house proved no more compliant, again electing Jones as its Speaker. Wright had temporarily returned to England, but acting governor James Habersham informed the house that England had instructed him to uphold the royal prerogative and veto the initial selection of Speaker. When the Georgia house elected Jones a second time, Habersham again vetoed the selection. Unwilling to yield, the house elected Jones a third time. Jones now declined the office and Bulloch was elected, but when the house refused to strike notice of its third vote from its journal it was dissolved by Habersham. At the next session the house again elected Jones as its Speaker, but further confrontation was avoided when he declined to serve and William Young, another Whig, was elected in his place.

Passage of the Intolerable Acts, England's response to the Boston Tea Party, stirred more active resistance in the thirteen colonies. But Georgia moved slowly, still relatively dependent on England and hampered by ideological and sectional differences within the colony and by personal rivalries among some Whig leaders. From start to finish, though, Jones remained one of the most important and most steadfast Whig leaders. Along with Bulloch, John Houstoun, and George Walton, Jones issued a public appeal that led to a protest meeting in Savannah on 27 July 1774. When those present reconvened at Tondee Tavern on 10 August, they were joined by representatives from other parishes and issued a series of resolutions protesting British policy. Still, division within the colony remained serious enough to prevent Georgia from sending delegates to the First Continental Congress. Georgia's first provincial congress met in January 1775 and elected Jones, Bulloch, and Houstoun as delegates to the Second Continental Congress. They refused to attend, however, as Whig sentiment had still not won effective control of the colony.

In Georgia, as elsewhere, news of the battles at Lexington and Concord rapidly moved the colony to open rebellion. As British authority waned, several prominent Whigs joined Jones in raiding the colony's powder magazine; according to legend, American troops used some of this powder at the battle of Bunker Hill. A second provincial congress met, this one more broadly representative and more confident than the first, and again elected representatives to attend the Second Continental Congress. Jones, one of the five delegates selected, was unable to serve due to the illness of his father, whose subsequent death removed one of the king's most loyal servants. Jones, however, remained an active member of the Whig leadership, which seized control of the colony and governed it as an independent state.

The successful invasion of Savannah, however, restored British authority in 1778 and caused Jones and his family to move to Charleston, South Carolina. When that city fell in 1780, he was captured and ultimately imprisoned in St. Augustine. In a 1781 prisoner exchange he was taken to Philadelphia, where he became friends with Dr. Benjamin Rush and resumed practicing medicine. Georgia's assembly then quickly returned him to the political arena by electing him to Congress. He served briefly before returning to Georgia when British forces finally left Savannah at the war's end.

Now in his sixties, Jones played a less conspicuous role in Georgia's political life after the Revolution. He was elected to the 1783 session of the assembly and again served as Speaker. But the turmoil and dissension of the revolutionary period had not fully dissipated, and Jones was injured while attempting to calm an angry mob. Shortly thereafter he returned to Charleston and did not move back to Georgia until 1788. Although he served as president of the convention called in 1795 to consider amending the state constitution, he avoided any significant involvement in politics for the remainder of his life. He died at his home in Savannah.

Jones obviously derived considerable personal satisfaction from his other career as a physician. He never had any formal training in medicine, but he learned from other practitioners such as Rush, from reading, and most of all from experience. He helped found, and was elected first president of, the Georgia Medical Society.

Jones was also a planter. He had property outside of Savannah where farming operations were conducted, and at the time of his death he had sixty-five slaves.

Others were more significant than Jones in founding the colony and in securing its independence once the Revolution began. But in the decade prior to independence, he easily ranked among the handful of most important citizens in the colony. His active participation in that crucial period was vital to the Whig cause.

• Only a few of Jones's papers survived the British occupation of Savannah and a 1796 fire at his home. The Georgia Historical Society in Savannah has holdings in three collections—the Jones Family Papers, the Noble Wimberly Jones Papers, and the John Grimes Papers. The latter collection includes an eighteen-page letter from George Jones (son of Noble Wimberly) to John Grimes, providing the most detailed original account available concerning the life of Noble Wimberly Jones. Most of these papers have been published in John Eddins Simpson, ed., *The Jones Family Papers: 1760–1810* Georgia Historical Society, *Collections*, vol. 17 (1976). The University of Georgia has the De Renne Family Papers, the Noble Jones-Noble Wymberley Jones-George Jones Papers, and the Coulter Historical Manuscripts, all containing a few relevant items. Duke University also has a small collection of Noble Wimberly Jones Papers.

Jones's public career can be easily followed in the standard published sources, including Allen D. Candler et al., eds., *The Colonial Records of the State of Georgia* (39 vols., 1904–), and Allen D. Candler, ed., *The Revolutionary Records of the State of Georgia* (3 vols., 1908). The most significant secondary account of Jones's life is in E. Merton Coulter, *Wormsloe: Two Centuries of a Georgia Family* (1955). See also Charles C. Jones, Jr., *Biographical Sketches of the Delegates from Georgia to the Continental Congress* (1891), and Kenneth Coleman, *The American Revolution in Georgia* (1958). Gerald L. Cates, "A Medical History of Georgia, 1733–1833" (Ph.D. diss., Univ. of Georgia, 1976), includes useful information relating to Jones's medical career. An obituary is in the *Georgia Republican and State Intelligencer*, 14 Jan. 1805. Also worthwhile is John Grimes, "Eulogy on the Life and Character of Dr. Noble Wymberley Jones," *Georgia Historical Quarterly* 4 (1920): 17–32, 141–58.

RAYMOND C. BAILEY

JONES, Philly Joe (15 July 1923–30 Aug. 1985), jazz drummer, was born Joseph Rudolph Jones in Philadelphia, Pennsylvania, the son of Amelia J. Abbott, a piano teacher and church organist. His father, whose name is unknown, died shortly after he was born. During his early childhood Jones was featured as a tap dancer on a local Philadelphia radio program, "The Kiddie Show." Interestingly, several other important jazz drummers, including Jo Jones and Buddy Rich, were also tap dancers. Jones's sisters studied violin and piano, and his first organized musical experience began in grade school, where he played drums. In 1941 Jones left high school and enlisted in the U.S. Army, where he served as a military policeman until his release in 1943. His wife's name was Eloise (maiden name and marriage date unknown), with whom he had one child.

After he was discharged Jones played in local Philadelphia bands before moving in 1947 to New York City, where he came in contact with a number of important bebop musicians, including Dizzy Gillespie, Dexter Gordon, and Charlie Parker. In the late 1940s he worked with Ben Webster in Washington, D.C., and toured with a rhythm-and-blues band led by trumpeter Joe Morris. This ensemble at one time included tenor saxophonist Johnny Griffin, pianist Elmo Hope, trombonist Matthew Gee, and string bassist Percy Heath, all of whom later became established bop musicians. After brief appearances with Tiny Grimes and Lionel Hampton, Jones returned in 1952 to New York, where he worked with Zoot Sims, Lee Konitz, Tony Scott, and Miles Davis before playing and recording with Tadd Dameron's band in 1953.

In 1955 Jones became a member (along with Paul Chambers, Red Garland, and John Coltrane) of one of the most artistically successful Miles Davis ensembles. This association gave him and the other members of the group popular recognition as the definitive bop ensemble of the 1950s. Jones worked in Davis-led small groups in 1958 and 1962 and was drummer on the memorable jazz orchestra recordings Davis made with pianist Gil Evans in 1957. He shared the drumming position with Jimmy Cobb in later Davis groups while appearing and recording with other well-known jazz figures in New York City, including Duke Ellington, Coltrane, Jimmy Oliver, and Billie Holiday. Jones left Davis (along with Coltrane) when the trumpeter decided Jones's substance abuse interfered with the success of the ensemble.

Jones led his own jazz groups starting in 1958 and toured from 1959 to 1962, during which time he played briefly with Gil Evans's band. In 1967 he joined pianist Bill Evans before moving to London, where he taught percussion until 1969 and then moved to Paris. In Paris, Jones played in local jazz clubs, toured, and taught drums with expatriate and bop drummer Kenny Clarke. He returned to Philadelphia in 1972, later forming (with Byard Lancaster) a jazz/rock group called Le Grand Prix (1975). In the late 1970s Jones worked again with pianists Evans and Garland and in 1981 formed Dameronia, a nine-piece ensemble dedicated to playing the music of the late Tadd Dameron. He fronted this group until 1985, when he replaced Clarke as drummer with Pieces of Time. He died in Philadelphia.

Jones was primarily a self-taught drummer but credited Cozy Cole, Charlie Wilcox, and James "Coatesville" Harris among his earliest teachers. Although anchored in swing drumming traditions, he displays a unique style of playing that at times can be subtle (especially in his use of brushes) but is more often clean, precise, forceful, and commanding. He evolved a bop drumming style in which straight eighth-note patterns formed the basis for his solos and fills combining unusual phrase lengths, tight, controlled rhythmic patterns, and creative use of silence. A small-group player, he favored musicality and imaginative rhythmic patterns over technique. This is demonstrated in his frequent use of cross-rhythmic solo and accompaniment patterns. He had few imitators in jazz but perhaps because of his affinity to even-note patterns so commonly found in rock, several rock drummers (including Blood, Sweat, and Tears drummer Bobby Colomby) incorporated Jones's concepts into their playing.

• Insights into Jones's excellent brush technique can be found in a manual he wrote titled *Brush Artistry* (n.d.). Informative articles on him include "The Return of Dracula," *Down Beat* 27, no. 5 (Mar. 1959): 22; Ralph Gleason, "The Forming of Philly Joe," *Down Beat* 27, no. 15 (3 Mar. 1960): 28–29; Sandy Davis, "Philly Joe Jones: Straight Ahead and Rarin' to Go," *Down Beat* 43, no. 15 (9 Sept. 1976): 18–21+; and Rick Mattingly's extensive interview, "Philly Joe Jones," *Modern Drummer* 6, no. 1 (Jan. 1982): 10–13+. See also Bill Crosby, "Bill Crosby Remembers Philly Joe," *Down Beat* 52, no. 1 (Dec. 1985): 13; and Art Taylor, *Notes and Tones: Musician to Musician Interviews* (1979). Transcriptions of his solo playing appear in *Modern Drummer*, including the upbeat "Lazy Bird," recorded with John Coltrane (Blue Note BLP-1577-815 77 [1957]) and written by Dan Tomlinson (*Modern Drummer* 8 no. 8 [Aug. 1984]), and "Monopoly," a 32-bar brush solo Jones recorded with Bud Powell (*Time Waits: The Amazing Bud Powell*, Blue Note St-81598, vol. 4 [1958]) and written by Glenn Davis (*Modern Drummer* 10, no. 4 [Mar. 1986]). His early playing can be heard on *Lou Donaldson with Clifford Brown* (Blue Note 5030 [1953], re-released on *The Complete Blue Note and Pacific Recordings of Clifford Brown*, Mosaic MR5-104 [1984]), and on recordings he made with his own band (*Blues for Dracula*, Riverside 12-282 [1958]).

His work with Coltrane is on *Blue Train* (Blue Note p1984 [1984]), recorded in 1957. However, his most important recordings date from his association with Miles Davis and include '*Round Midnight* (Columbia CL949 [1955–1956]), *Workin'* (Prestige 7166 [1956]), and *Milestones* (Columbia CL1193 [1958]). Jones allied himself with several major bop musicians during the 1960s and his style is well documented on *The Complete Prestige Recordings of Sonny Rollins* (Prestige Records p1992 [1992]) and also *The Complete Blue Note Recordings of the Tina Brooks Quintets* (Mosaic MR4-106 [1985]). Here, he demonstrates a mature bop drumming style that, in many cases, defines the genre during this era. Obituaries are in the *New York Times*, 3 Sept. 1985; *Jazz Journal* 38, no. 11 (Nov. 1985): 15; and *Down Beat* 52, no. 1 (Dec. 1985): 13.

T. DENNIS BROWN

JONES, Rebecca (8 July 1739–15 Apr. 1818), Quaker minister, was born in Philadelphia, Pennsylvania, the daughter of William Jones, a seaman, and Mary Porter, a school mistress. While Rebecca was still an infant her father died at sea, leaving her mother alone to raise her and her older brother Daniel. Mary Jones supported her family by keeping a school for young girls in her home where her daughter was educated. As a member of the Church of England, she raised her children in the Anglican tradition. Rebecca, however, showed interest in the Quaker religion. At age twelve, she asked to attend the Friends meetinghouse with the neighborhood children. Her mother assented, believing she was too young to make a serious decision about religion. Rebecca admired the "order and becoming deportment" of the Friends and attended as many meetings as possible, though she still admitted that she "loved vanity and folly" and kept "unprofitable company."

In 1754, at the age of sixteen, Jones heard Catherine Peyton, an English Quaker minister, preach at the Philadelphia meeting. Deeply affected, this marked the beginning of her conversion to the Quaker religion. From this point on she constantly attended meetings despite the growing objections of family and friends, who "with bitter invectives and hard speeches" ridiculed her interest in the Society of Friends. She not only attended the biweekly meetings but monthly and quarterly meetings as well. By 1758 Rebecca was a regular speaker at the Friends meetinghouse in Philadelphia. Two years later, her gift for preaching was acknowledged by the Meeting of Ministers and Elders and she became a minister. With such approbation, her mother relented in her opposition to her daughter becoming a Quaker.

In 1761, when her mother's health began to decline, Jones took over her school while also nursing her sick parent. After her mother's death, she asked Hannah Cathrall, a fellow Quaker minister, to join her as a teacher at the school. This began a close professional and personal relationship that would last many years. Jones and Cathrall taught girls and boys reading, writing, and arithmetic, and by 1764, the William Penn Charter School was subsidizing their efforts to educate Quaker children. Through the 1760s and 1770s, Jones continued teaching at the same time that she became more active as a minister, traveling to meetings in New York, New Jersey, and Virginia.

In 1783, after many years of contemplation, Jones felt called to labor among Friends in England and applied to the Philadelphia Monthly Meeting for a certificate as a traveling minister. She sailed for Europe with six other Quakers in 1784. Upon arrival, the American Friends attended the London Yearly Meeting. Jones, along with Rebecca Wright, Patience Brayton, and Mehetabel Jenkins, supported the efforts of English Quaker women to gain the right to hold a women's yearly meeting, and their intervention helped achieve this goal. As she later wrote, "My heart was made thankful in that the women's application carried the weighty evidence of Truth with it, and that men Friends were made so feelingly sensible thereof, that they yielded as brethren" (Journal of Rebecca Jones, 1788–1789).

From 1784 to 1788, Jones traveled in England, Ireland, Scotland, and Wales, often accompanied by the English Quaker, Christiana Hustler, who became a lifelong friend. During her journeys, she attended numerous monthly, preparative, and yearly meetings throughout the British Isles. Because of her interest in education, she also visited several schools in England, including Ackworth, a Quaker boarding school for girls and boys.

Jones returned to Philadelphia in 1788. Having previously closed her school, she opened a small shop where she sold material, thread, and other sundries. She continued her ministerial efforts in the Delaware valley and New England. In 1794 she began to make regular visits to families of the North District Meeting in Philadelphia and also attended meetings in Quaker households. Elizabeth Drinker recalled such a meeting at her home in February 1795, when Jones and four others preached and had "something to offer us, not in the terrific and threatning [sic] order, but rather the reverse" (The Diary of Elizabeth Drinker, vol. 1, p. 646). Although no longer teaching, Jones contributed to local educational efforts by Quakers in 1799 when she helped establish the Westtown Friends School, in Westtown, Pennsylvania.

Jones was part of a transatlantic community of Quakers and was close friends with leading ministers and prominent Friends of the day. Although she never married, she had particularly close relationships with other Quaker women, such as Hannah Cathrall ("my beloved companion"), Mary Brooks ("my little handmaiden"), and Bernice Chattin, who became her adopted daughter. In the 1790s Chattin went to live with Jones and to care for her household while the latter was away on ministerial journeys.

Jones fell ill with yellow fever during the epidemic of 1793. She lingered for many months but survived to resume her ministry. She also suffered from rheumatism and, in 1813, she contracted typhus fever from which she never completely recovered. Although sickly and unable to attend meeting, she was still consulted for her religious expertise. She remained an invalid until her death in Philadelphia.

Jones lived at a critical time in Quaker history. She witnessed the erosion of Quaker political power, the division among Friends over the revolutionary war, and the first signs of the Hicksite schism, a doctrinal split between liberal and conservative Quakers. Admired for her common sense and plain speaking, Jones took part in a movement to revitalize the Quaker religion. She endorsed the traditional plainness of the Friends while she rued the worldliness of late eighteenth-century Quakers who owned "pleasure carriages" and engaged in "formal visiting." She also combined her spiritual beliefs with educational contributions and philanthropic interests. Finally, as a role model and mentor to other women, Jones helped maintain a tradition of female preaching and leadership among American Quakers.

• The papers of Jones are in the Quaker Collection in the Magill Library at Haverford College, Haverford, Pa. These papers include letters, a journal, and several memorandum books. Jones was a prolific correspondent and her many friendships are evident in the papers of various Quaker families including the Allinson Family Papers, the Robert B. Haines III Collection, the Scattergood Family Papers, the Waln Family Papers, the George Vaux Papers, the Haddon-Estaugh-Hopkins Family Papers, and the Charles Evans Collection, all found at Haverford. Jones is also referred to in the James Thornton Papers and the Joshua Sharpless Papers housed at Swarthmore College, in Swarthmore, Pennsylvania. Jones was close friends with John and Hannah Pemberton and James Pemberton. Their letters are found in the Pemberton Papers in the Historical Society of Pennsylvania. Jones is also mentioned in the journal of Thomas Scattergood, a close friend and fellow minister. See *Journal of the Life and Labors of Thomas Scattergood* (1874). She is referred to several times in Elizabeth Drinker's diary as well. See Elaine Forman Crane, ed., *The Diary of Elizabeth Drinker* (3 vols., 1991). Jones's career as a teacher is evident in the accounts of the William Penn Charter School Archives at Haverford.

There are several biographical sketches of Jones. The most comprehensive was compiled by William T. Allinson, *Memorials of Rebecca Jones* (1849). Others include Nathan Kite, *Biographical Sketches and Anecdotes of Members of the Religious Society of Friends* (1871), pp. 80–126, and Ruth E. Chambers, "A Short Account of Rebecca Jones," *The Westonian* 13, no. 2 (1907): 24–28.

JANET MOORE LINDMAN

JONES, Robert Edmond (12 Dec. 1887–26 Nov. 1954), scene designer and director, was born in Milton, New Hampshire, the son of Fred Jones, a farmer, and Emma Cowell, a piano teacher. He attended public schools in Milton and in 1906 entered Harvard University, from which he graduated cum laude in 1910. While a student in liberal arts he studied music, art, and drama under George Pierce Baker, Harvard's first professor of dramatic literature. Jones played the violin in the Pierian Sodality Orchestra and staged amateur productions of plays such as *Salome* in his dormitory. He continued teaching drama on the Harvard faculty for two years and then worked in New York as a costume designer for the firm of Comstock and Gest.

In 1913 a group of his friends, headed by John Reed (1887–1920) and Kenneth MacGowan, established the "Robert Edmond Jones Transportation and Development Company" to collect funds to send him to Europe to study. His application for admission to the innovative art school headed by Edward Gordon Craig in Florence was rejected, but while there he created one of the first of his strikingly evocative designs, for Shelley's *The Cenci*. In Berlin he was accepted for a year of study with Max Reinhardt and the Deutsches Theater, where he was exposed to the revolutionary changes that would lead to the break with traditional realism in European design and staging. He was a leader in bringing the new style to the United States under the name of "the new stagecraft."

Back in New York in 1914, Jones was represented in an exhibit of theater art arranged by the Stage Society of New York. His first article on the interpretive power of stage lighting appeared in the *New York Times*, and he became involved with the leading experimental theater groups of the period. He designed Lord Dunsany's *The Glittering Gate* (1914) and Maurice Maeterlinck's *Interior* (1915), the first productions of the Washington Square Players (later the Theatre Guild), and in 1915 created the scenery for the first seasons of the Provincetown Players. Probably his best known design from this significant first year of the "new stagecraft" was his design for Arthur Hopkins's production of Anatole France's *The Man Who Married a Dumb Wife*, a striking but simple setting stressing artistic form, style, and simplicity that became almost an emblem of the new style. Jones's brilliant visual imagination made him an ideal designer for the lavish visual spectacles called "community masques" that Percy MacKaye and Joseph Urban were popularizing in America during the years of the First World War, the most lavish of which was *Caliban by the Yellow Sands* in Lewisohn Stadium, created to celebrate the New York City Shakespeare Tercentenary in 1916. He also began to create ballet designs, such as the sets for the Metropolitan Opera's production of Nijinsky's ballets *Til Eulenspiegel* (1916) and *Mephisto Waltz* (not produced). Hopkins began to employ Jones as a designer for Broadway productions, and over the next twenty years this body of work gave Jones a position of central importance in the major commercial theater. Among the forty Hopkins productions designed by Jones, most of them featuring leading actors of the period such as Alla Nazimova and members of the Barrymore family, were *The Wild Duck* and *Hedda Gabler* (1918), Sem Benelli's *The Jest* (1919), *Richard III* and *Macbeth* (1920), *Anna Christie* (1921), *Hamlet* and *Romeo and Juliet* (1922), and Sophie Treadwell's *Machinal* and Philip Barry's *Holiday* (1928).

In 1922 Jones and fellow stage designer MacGowan toured Europe collecting material for their book *Continental Stagecraft*, a major contribution to the new movement. In 1923 Jones married Margaret Huston Carrington, and in 1925 he mounted a one-man show of his designs in New York and published his *Drawings for the Theatre*. In the early 1920s he also became closely involved with the Experimental Theatre, an outgrowth of the Provincetown Playhouse headed by Jones, MacGowan, and Eugene O'Neill. Simultaneously, he became interested in directing as well as design. He began as designer and codirector with James Light on August Strindberg's *Spook Sonata*, Anna Mowatt's *Fashion*, and O'Neill's dramatization of *The Ancient Mariner* (all 1924). Subsequently, he directed on his own and designed *Hedda Gabler*, *Patience*, and *Desire under the Elms* (all 1924, as well), followed by William Congreve's *Love for Love* and O'Neill's *The Fountain* (1925), and then O'Neill's *The Great God Brown* (1926).

In 1932 Jones created the designs for the opening production of the Radio City Music Hall and provided a striking setting for Maxwell Anderson's *Night over Taos* for the recently formed Group Theatre. In 1934 he designed his first film, a short called *La Cucaracha*, followed by the Pioneer color films *Becky Sharp* (1934) and *The Dancing Pirate* (1936). During this decade and the next he was closely associated with the Theatre Guild, for which he designed, among others, *Mourning Becomes Electra* (1931), *Ah, Wilderness!* and *Mary of Scotland* (1933), *The Sea Gull* (1938), *The Philadelphia Story* (1939), *Othello* (directed by Margaret Webster with Paul Robeson in 1943), *The Iceman Cometh* (1946), and one of his most famous projects, Sidney Howard and Will Irwin's *The Lute Song* (1946). During the summers between 1932 and 1942 he worked at the opera house in Central City, Colorado, where he produced, designed, and directed Alexandre Dumas's *Camille* (1932), *Othello* (with Walter Huston in 1934), and Victor Hugo's *Ruy Blas* (1938). By 1941, when he published *The Dramatic Imagination*, Jones was among the best-known and most admired of American scenic designers, a stature confirmed by his triumphal tour that year to speak at many of the nation's leading universities. Although he continued to design until the early 1950s and published *Towards a New Theatre* in 1952, failing health steadily reduced his activity in his final years. He retired to his family home in New Hampshire in 1953, not long before his death. Leaders of the American theater attended a memorial service for him in New York at the Plymouth Theatre. Many tributes have been paid to him, but Jones's own writings probably best capture the excitement and vision he brought to the stage of his day: "Romance and glamor have always seemed to me to be the very foundation of the theatre," he wrote. "I believe that audiences naturally crave a theatre of poetry, mystery, and magic." As a result of his work, a new attention to beauty and romance entered American scene design, profoundly influencing other major designers such as Lee Simonson and Mordecai Gorelik.

• The Museum of Modern Art in New York holds important collections of Jones's designs. The most complete study of

Jones's career is Ralph Pendleton, ed., *The Theatre of Robert Edmond Jones* (1958), which includes a comprehensive chronology. An obituary is in the *New York Times*, 27 Nov. 1954.

MARVIN CARLSON

JONES, Rufus Matthew (25 Jan. 1863–16 June 1948), exemplar of mysticism and rebuilder of Quakerism, was born on his family's farm in South China, Maine, the son of Edwin Jones and Mary Hoxie. Despite the demands of the farm and financial need, as well as an almost fatal injury at age ten, Jones attended local day and Quaker boarding schools. The vitality of worship and loving guidance in his Quaker home were described in the first of his humorous, small autobiographical books, *Finding the Trail of Life* (1926; events retold in *A Small-Town Boy*, 1941), followed by *The Trail of Life in College* (1929) and *The Trail of Life in the Middle Years* (1934). His sister Alice and brothers Walter and Herbert lived on in central Maine, but he felt spiritually called, and encouraged by his aunt Peace and uncle and aunt Eli and Sybil Jones (the three were noted unpaid traveling Quaker ministers about whom he wrote his first book), to enroll in Friends School (later called Moses Brown) in Providence, Rhode Island, in 1879. The headmaster there, Jones's older cousin Augustine Jones, had written a pioneer summary of Quaker beliefs.

In 1882 Jones entered Haverford College (Haverford, Pa.), where he transferred his love of history and classics to philosophy and, guided by President Thomas Chase and his brother Pliny Earle Chase, completed a B.A. in 1885. In 1885–1886 he taught at the Quaker School in Union Springs, New York, and there became engaged to a keen fellow teacher, Sarah "Sallie" Coutant. In 1886 he was awarded a master's degree by Haverford College based on a thesis on mysticism he had written in his senior year there. Then, in 1886–1887, he studied in Germany and France, where a mystical experience called him to a lifework based on the writings of Meister Eckhart, Johannes Tauler, and Jakob Böhme.

In 1887 to 1889 Jones taught at the Friends School in Providence, and in 1888 he married Sallie Coutant. From 1889 to 1893 he and his wife were principals of the Friends' Oak Grove School in Maine. Their son, Lowell, who was born there, became even more precious to Jones after his wife died of tuberculosis in 1899. The boy's sudden death in 1903 was the occasion for Jones's second intense experience of God's love.

In 1893 Jones went to Pennsylvania to take a teaching position at Haverford and to edit the weekly *Friends Review*, which in 1894 merged with the evangelical *Christian Worker* to become the *American Friend*. Jones would live on the Haverford campus and summer in Maine for the rest of his life. He helped to bring Douglas Steere and Thomas Kelly to teach philosophy and religion at Haverford and Howard Brinton to direct the Pendle Hill study center nearby; all three men shared his vision of Quakers as mystics. Beginning in 1900, Jones studied for a year at Harvard

under philosophers George Herbert Palmer and Josiah Royce. In 1902 he married Elizabeth Cadbury; she became his constant editorial helper, and her brother, New Testament scholar Henry Cadbury, became his lifelong friend. The couple's only child, Mary Hoxie Jones, was born in 1904.

The ideas that underlay all of Jones's 550 articles and editorials and his 57 books—from *Social Law in the Spiritual World* (1904) through *Pathways to the Reality of God* (1931) and *The Eternal Gospel* (1938) to *A Call to What Is Vital* (1948)—became mainstays of liberal Protestantism. These include a belief in the immanence as well as the transcendence of God (in his writings Jones encapsulated this belief by popularizing George Fox's phrase "that of God in every man"); the direct experience of God's personal presence (which Jones conceived as affirmation or socially conscious mysticism in contrast to a mysticism of negation, that is, asceticism and the dissolution of the self into the timeless, divine Absolute); the unity of religious, historical, and scientific truth, even in the Bible; God's power in the perfect humanness of Jesus; and the call of the divine "Light within" to eternal ideals and values. Jones thus shared in and synthesized four distinct traditions. American Quakers, though they had been divided since 1827 over the doctrine of the Atonement, critical study of the Bible, and the means by which God's spirit works, nonetheless shared common "testimonies" on honesty, simplicity in life and worship, social equality, and the rejection of violence. Like Jones, most evangelical Protestants had come to hold an optimistic view of human progress achieved by foreign and home missions and social justice. The philosophers with whom Jones associated identified reality with ideas, beauty, and morality and located the potential for a mystical union with the eternal within the human mind. Finally, Jones did not think that faith was endangered by science, which as practiced by such psychologists as William James, depended on experiments and the observation of natural processes as well as of varieties of mystical experience.

Jones hoped that Quakers would be led by the *American Friend* to revitalize their role as "a movement, not a sect" within Christian American society. He kept his membership in the Yearly Meeting for Friends in New England and worked to unify it with the other regional bodies of the Christ-centered, or "Orthodox," Friends. Eli and Augustine Jones had been among the American and English Quaker leaders in 1887 at the first in a series of meetings that led to the formation of the body called Five Years (later Friends United) Meeting. Rufus Jones helped draft and re-edit the *Uniform Discipline* and the linked constitution of the Meeting and also led committees that coordinated Quaker foreign mission outreach. For his opposition to creedalism, he and the *American Friend*, the official organ of the Meeting and the conferences that formed it, were increasingly attacked by midwestern evangelical Quakers, who stressed revivals, the value of pastors, programmed worship, strict Protestant doctrines, and sudden experiences of conversion and holiness. Though he made many friendly visits to their homes, Jones did not win most evangelical Friends to his understanding of Quakerism.

British Quakers meanwhile had embraced peacemaking and the critical study of the Bible through the efforts of young men such as Rendel Harris, Henry Hodgkin, and John Wilhelm Rowntree, men who befriended Jones on his trip to England in 1897 and who worked with him on several projects afterward. The group produced a series of "summer schools" in England and at Haverford on the Bible, Quakerism, and modern society; these developed into the permanent study centers of Woodbrooke, located on the edge of Birmingham, England, and Pendle Hill, near Philadelphia. The group also agreed to write a detailed series of Quaker histories, for which Jones wrote the prefaces; the volumes on *Quakers in the American Colonies* (1911) and (with coauthors) *The Later Periods of Quakerism* (2 vols., 1921); and as prefatory works, *Studies in Mystical Religion* (1909) and *Spiritual Reformers in the Sixteenth and Seventeenth Centuries* (1914). He later wrote the well-researched histories *The Church's Debt to Heretics* (1924), *The Flowering of Mysticism: The Friends of God in the Fourteenth Century* (1939), *New Studies in Mystical Religion* (1927), and *Mysticism and Democracy in the English Commonwealth* (1932), the latter of which drew from his friend Theodor Sippell's work on "spiritual puritans." Jones wrote more popularly on George Fox and Quakerism.

The First World War and a concussion caused by a fall sent Jones into a depression, which he was brought out of by the organizing of a training program at Haverford for Quaker conscientious objectors and relief workers in France. From 1917 to 1944 he chaired the American Friends Service Committee (AFSC), set up to oversee those workers, who later organized the feeding of more than one million German children after the war ended. Relief programs were extended into Poland and Soviet Russia, and Jones had to coordinate AFSC efforts with those of the Red Cross and of U.S. Food Administrator Herbert Hoover's American Relief Administration. Later, in 1931, the suffering of the families of striking Pennsylvania miners confirmed the AFSC's decision to remain a permanent agency, which shared with British Friends the 1947 Nobel Prize for Peace.

In 1920 Quakers called the first All Friends Conference in Oxford and London, and this led Jones and others to set up the American Friends Fellowship Council, which was transformed after a second world Quaker gathering at Swarthmore College in 1937 and World War II into the Friends World Committee for Consultation. Efforts by the Five Years Meeting to share in the Forward Movement among Protestant churches to centralize fundraising and staff, and Jones's own multiple involvements that distanced him in perspective from midwestern Friends, led Kansas and Oregon Yearly Meetings, the most evangelical and evangelistic, to withdraw from Five Years Meeting, despite Jones's partial reconciliation with them in 1922

and the Meeting's acclamation of him as chairman in 1935.

In addition to the life-shaping impact he often had on his own students, Jones influenced a wider audience at American universities by delivering an annual sermon at Harvard University and by giving lecture series at Yale, Columbia, Vanderbilt, Southern California, Stanford, and Southern Methodist universities and at Oberlin and Rochester seminaries (most were later published) and by serving as chairman of the Bryn Mawr College Board and joining the board of Brown University. During each of his seventeen trips to England, Jones gave multiple lectures; he also studied while abroad, at Marburg in 1911 and at Oxford in 1923. He was invited to lecture in India in 1926, when he visited Gandhi; in China and Japan in 1932, when he was a key member of the Laymen's Missionary Inquiry in China and Japan; and in South Africa in 1938, when he spent two months there. In November 1938 Jones and Friends George Walton and Robert Yarnall made a famous but fairly fruitless visit to Gestapo headquarters in Berlin to try to arrange for the exit of persecuted Jews. Jones retired from teaching in 1934. He died at Haverford, Pennsylvania.

• Twelve archive boxes of letters by Jones, forty-seven boxes of letters to Jones, his lecture notes and book manuscripts, as well as his own collection of books by and about mystics, are in the Quaker Collection of the Haverford College Library. Biographies are David Hinshaw, *Rufus Jones, Master Quaker* (1951); the fuller and better Elizabeth Gray Vining, *Friend of Life* (1958); and a short book by his daughter, *Rufus M. Jones* (1955; U.S. ed., 1970), for British Friends. A careful topical anthology is Harry Emerson Fosdick, *Rufus Jones Speaks to Our Time* (1951; paperback ed., 1961). Vining and Fosdick include bibliographies of Jones's numerous works. Doctoral theses on Jones's ethics include those of Wilmer A. Cooper (Vanderbilt, 1956) and Floyd Moore (Boston Univ., 1960); on his theology, that of Glen T. Cain (Duke, 1963); on his mystical thought, those of William A. Alsobrook (Drew, 1954), Gordon Charles Atkins (Univ. of Southern California, 1962), Augustine J. Caffrey (Catholic Univ. of America, 1967), and Daniel E. Bassuk (Drew, 1974). Most of these present Jones's ideas accurately but assess them in relation to the convictions of each writer more than from the perspectives of Jones's contemporaries. Jones's understanding of Catholic and Quaker mystics in light of each other, as challenged by Lewis Benson's New Foundations tracts and Christopher Holdsworth's 1972 paper for Friends Historical Society, was the subject of articles by Donald Durnbaugh in *Quaker History* 62 (1973), by Stephen A. Kent in *Quaker History* 66 (1976), and by Melvin D. Endy in *Quaker History* 76 (1987). Diana Alten, in *Quaker History* 74 (1985), and John Oliver, in *Quaker History* 80 (1991), described the role of the *American Friend* in uniting Quakers.

HUGH BARBOUR

JONES, Sam (?–1867), leader of the Mikasuki Seminole during the war against removal from Florida, was born near present-day Tallahassee. His Indian name was Arpeika. Nothing is known of his parents or his early life. In 1827, when Fort King was established in Florida, Arpeika lived at Silver Springs, and he was first called Sam Jones by a soldier at the fort. Reputedly then over seventy years of age, he had white hair but was small and well formed and possessed great energy. His influence among the Indians depended heavily on his reputation as a holy man capable of invoking supernatural powers.

With fourteen other chiefs and subchiefs, Jones marked the Treaty of Payne's Landing on 9 May 1832. He was one of seven Florida Indians delegated, under the terms of the treaty, to inspect the land in Arkansas Territory that the U.S. government wanted the Seminoles to move to in the West, which they would share with the Creeks, who had already been moved there. He did not make the trip, however, and John Hicks (Tukose Emathla) made a mark for him on a treaty drawn up at Fort Gibson, Arkansas Territory, on 28 March 1833. The terms of the treaty required the Indians to leave Florida, but when the Indian agent, Wiley Thompson, demanded that the leaders agree to go to Arkansas Territory, Jones, with Micanopy, Jumper, Alligator, and Black Dirt, refused, considering no move out of Florida really acceptable and sharing land with the Creeks totally unacceptable. Thompson arbitrarily struck their names from the roster of leaders. Jones made no attempt to conceal his rage, stamping his feet and gnashing his teeth.

The Second Seminole War began on 28 December 1835 when the Indians wiped out all but three men of a U.S. troop detachment near what is now Bushnell, Florida. That same day Osceola ambushed and killed Thompson and three others outside Fort King near present-day Ocala. Jones was not present at the opening skirmishes of the war but led an attack at Fort Drane near Micanopy, Florida, on 11 August 1836. This was the only battle in which he stayed in the zone of fire. His usual practice was to excite young warriors to fighting pitch, fire the first shot, and then retire to the flanks to engage in incantations and to tend the wounded.

As fighting moved southward, Jones went with it. He instigated an attack on Fort Mellon in the vicinity of Micanopy in 1837 but left Wildcat (Coacoochee) in command. Later, officers detained Wildcat when he entered the fort for discussions and sent him as a prisoner to Fort Marion, the old Spanish fort at St. Augustine. Wildcat escaped on 29 November 1837, and on his way southward to join the fighters he met Jones going to a talk at Fort Mellon. Wildcat's experience convinced Jones to stay away from the fort and to prevent others from entering. Thereafter Jones refused to enter the enemy's strongholds or treat with their emissaries.

On Christmas Day 1837 Jones joined the Seminole defense just north of Lake Okeechobee. He, with the Prophet (Otulke Thlocko), controlled the right of the Indian position. Alligator later claimed that Jones fled at the first fire, implying cowardice, but Jones may simply have been following his customary battle practice. During part of 1838 Jones's bands inhabited the wetlands on the Gulf Coast. There he threatened to kill any Indian preparing to give up. His no-surrender strategy influenced all action in the Alachua and Suwannee areas.

Alexander Macomb, commanding general of the U.S. Army, traveled to Florida and summoned chiefs to meet him in a grand council at Fort King on 20 May 1839. Jones, unwilling to risk capture, sent Chitto Tustenuggee. Macomb chose to treat Chitto as Jones's replacement to head the Seminoles. The Indian leaders at the Grand Council agreed to retire into the southern tip of the peninsula, to end the war; but new hostilities erupted, and the agreement failed.

By 1841 the conflict had continued for six years. White men ascribed its wasteful duration to the stubbornness of Sam Jones: "Sam Jones, Sam Jones, thou great unwhipped / Thou makest a world of bother / Indeed we quite expect that thou art / One Davy Jones's brother" (Theopholis Rodenbough, *From Everglades to Canon with the Second Dragoons* [1875]). Alligator, who surrendered with several hundred followers in March 1838, said he would have given up earlier had not Jones's Mikasukis prevented it.

The free Indian bands were eventually pushed to the fringes of the Everglades. Jones met there with Billy Bowlegs (Holata Mico), the Prophet, Hospetarche, Fuze Hadjo, and Parsacke in August 1841. They decided to kill any Indian bearing communications from the enemy, but they lacked the power to carry out this threat. During that same month Jones met with Wildcat, who had been sent by the whites to bring in some of the holdouts. Jones, however, refused to migrate.

The Seminoles were worn down. Captives told white commanders that Jones was somewhere around the mouth of the Kissimmee River in June 1841 with only seventeen warriors and burdened by many women and children. In the fall he sent an emissary, with vague hints about surrender, into Fort Denaud, asking for food, whiskey, and tobacco. In December an army detachment destroyed one of his towns on a pine and cabbage island in the Everglades but did not catch him. His band was down to seven men, still with many women and children. The old man's ability to elude them rankled the U.S. officers. In February 1842 Lieutenant John T. McLaughlin of the U.S. Navy authorized his men "To use any measure of severity to compel them [captives] to lead you to the haunts of Jones." Finally tiring of the struggle, in August 1842 the United States declared the Second Seminole War ended. Jones with about 300 other Seminoles remained in Florida.

During the next thirteen years Jones and Billy Bowlegs cooperated with U.S. authorities enough to stay in Florida. For example, in October 1849, when U.S. authorities demanded that five Seminole youths charged with murder be delivered to them, the two had the renegades hunted down. They turned over four of them and the severed hand of the fifth, who had been killed.

When friction between Seminoles and the U.S. Army sparked the so-called Third Seminole War in 1855, Jones's band was instrumental in starting it. Jones himself was then said to be more than 100 years old. For unknown reasons, in 1856 the secretary of war authorized negotiations to permit Jones to remain in Florida. In 1858 Bowlegs, convinced that continued resistance was useless, surrendered with his band and was shipped to Indian Territory. Although ten of Jones's meager band also left, Jones stayed, along with seventeen warriors and several women and children. Captives said that he had become childlike, requiring constant care.

White impressions of Sam Jones were generally harsh. One observer thought him ferocious; others considered him remarkable for his obstinate ill nature. Surgeon Jacob Rhett Motte of the U.S. Army considered him a great rascal. It was noted that when Jones was over seventy, he had a young wife and that at all ages he had been a hard drinker. These judgments derived in part from recognition that Jones personified the will of the Florida Indians, especially the Mikasukis, to hold on to the land they believed to be theirs. Sam Jones died on a small island in the Big Cypress Swamp, supposed at the time to have been at least 111 years old.

• Sam Jones figures in the histories of the Seminole wars, principally in the contemporary John T. Sprague, *The Origin, Progress and Conclusion of the Florida War* (1848; repr. 1964), and the modern scholarly accounts by John K. Mahon, *History of the Second Seminole War, 1835–1842* (1967), and James W. Covington, *The Seminoles of Florida* (1993).

JOHN K. MAHON

JONES, Sam (12 Nov. 1924–15 Dec. 1981), jazz string bassist, was born Samuel Jones in Jacksonville, Florida. His parents' names are unknown. His father was a professional pianist. Jones was born with an infected kidney that led to a series of childhood illnesses, but by his adolescent years he was fully recovered. He was the only child of his mother's first marriage; he had eleven step-siblings from her second marriage, and evidently (his own accounts are contradictory) he was raised from age three in Tampa with his mother's sisters. This was a musical home, with a piano available.

One of Jones's uncles was a professional guitarist, and around age ten Jones taught himself to play that instrument. By the time he was in junior high school, he performed in church, and elsewhere he played blues. He joined the band at Middleton High School as a bass drummer, but when he heard string bassist Oscar Pettiford play a solo on a recording by rhythm-and-blues singer Wynonie Harris, Jones became fascinated by the sound and acquired his own instrument. He soon began to work professionally, and after graduating from Middleton in 1941 he toured Florida as a string bassist in popular groups. Around mid-decade he worked with pianist Ray Charles in the Honeydrippers, a rhythm-and-blues band. In Miami Beach he led a bop group that copied Dizzy Gillespie and Charlie Parker's recordings, with trumpeter Blue Mitchell taking Gillespie's role. Jones also worked in Florida with alto saxophonist Cannonball Adderley.

Jones continued working alongside Mitchell in Paul Williams's rhythm-and-blues group, with which he toured. In December 1951 he made his first recording. He recorded "Powder Puff" and "Ping Pong" with Tiny Bradshaw's rhythm-and-blues group in 1953 and toured with Bradshaw until 1955 on the strength of these hit recordings. He then became a member of trumpeter Kenny Dorham's Jazz Prophets (1956), modeled after Horace Silver and Art Blakey's Jazz Messengers. After working in Illinois Jacquet's band, Jones joined the Jazz Modes of tenor saxophonist Charlie Rouse and french horn player Julius Watkins. He played with Adderley from 1956 to 1957, and he may be heard as a soloist on "Tribute to Brownie" on Adderley's album *Sophisticated Swing* (1957).

While Adderley disbanded to work with Miles Davis, Jones joined the small groups of tenor saxophonist Stan Getz (1957–1958), trumpeter Gillespie (Jan. 1958–Feb. 1959), and pianist Thelonious Monk (Feb.–Oct. 1959). Among notable albums from this period with Jones as a performer are pianist Bill Evans's *Everybody Digs Bill Evans* (1958), including a solo on "Night and Day," and tenor saxophonist Johnny Griffin's album *The Little Giant*, including a solo on "63rd. Street Theme" (1959).

By this time, if not many years earlier, Jones's nickname was "Home." He explained to writer Chris Sheridan, "I used to call everyone that—and they called me 'Home' back. It just stuck." From November 1959 through 1965 Jones was a member of Adderley's group, for which he composed "Del Sasser," heard on *Them Dirty Blues* (1960), and "Unit 7," on *Nancy Wilson / Cannonball Adderley* (1962); "Unit 7" has a nicely crafted 44-bar structure, resulting from a fusion of blues and pop song forms. During this period Jones also recorded as a soloist on "Sam Sack" on *Bags Meets Wes*, a session co-led by vibraphonist Milt Jackson and guitarist Wes Montgomery (1961), and as both a string bass and a cello soloist on his own albums, including *The Soul Society* (1960).

In January 1966 Jones replaced Ray Brown in the trio of pianist Oscar Peterson, with whom he remained until 1970. In the early 1970s he held freelance jobs in New York, performing with pianists Bobby Timmons and Wynton Kelly and with the Thad Jones–Mel Lewis quintet, but his career was disrupted by emphysema. He had formed a trio with pianist Cedar Walton and drummer Billy Higgins by 1972, when they first recorded. The three men worked under the names of the Magic Triangle and Eastern Rebellion and toured Japan yearly. In 1978 they formed a quintet with trumpeter Art Farmer and alto saxophonist Jackie McLean. Jones also recorded further albums as a leader, including *Cello Again* (1976).

After performing regularly in Europe during the mid-1970s, Jones settled there temporarily. By 1978 he had returned to the United States, where he co-led groups with trumpeter Tom Harrell, with whom he recorded the album *Something New* in 1979. Incapacitated by lung cancer, Jones stopped playing in the early 1980s. Obituaries give his place of death as New Jersey (the city unidentified) or New York City.

Although Jones could improvise fine melodies, he seemed uninterested in becoming a great jazz string bass soloist in the tradition of Pettiford, Brown, Charles Mingus, and others. Except on his own albums, he was often content to play walking bass lines rather than to step into a melodic role. His special talent was as an accompanist, supplying an utterly reliable carpet of rhythm, harmony, and tone for a succession of notable instrumentalists.

• A tape and transcript of an Apr. 1980 interview by Larry Ridley are at the Institute of Jazz Studies in Newark, N.J. Jones discusses his life in Barbara Gardner, "Along Came Jones," *Down Beat* 33 (10 Mar. 1966): 14–15, 36, and string bass techniques in Kenny Baldock, "Sam Jones," *Crescendo* 4 (July 1966): 14–15, 26. A brief interview appears in Dizzy Gillespie with Al Fraser, *To Be, or Not . . . to Bop: Memoirs* (1979). Obituaries are in *Melody Maker*, 16 Jan. 1982; *Cadence* 8, no. 2 (Feb. 1982); *Down Beat* 49 (Mar. 1982); and by Chris Sheridan in *Jazz Journal International* 35 (Apr. 1982), which includes an annotated discography. (The *Jazz Journal International* obituary gives Jones's date of death as 14 Mar. 1981.)

BARRY KERNFELD

JONES, Samuel (26 July 1734–25 Nov. 1819), lawyer, was born in Fort Hill, Queens County, Long Island, New York, the son of William Jones, a prosperous farmer and landowner, and Phoebe Jackson. After some limited schooling in Hempstead on Long Island, Jones, whose paternal grandfather had been a notable English privateer, became a sailor and made several trips to Europe. Giving up the life of a mariner, apparently at the behest of his anxious mother, he served an apprenticeship in the 1750s with William Smith, Jr., a rising attorney in New York City. As a talented young lawyer, Jones developed an extensive practice and served as attorney for the New York City Common Council. He was among the founding members of "The Moot," the legal debating society that limited its membership to the most accomplished attorneys. Aspiring young men, among them DeWitt Clinton, prized the opportunity to serve their legal apprenticeship in his office.

In 1765, Jones married Eleanor Turk, who died shortly thereafter. They had no children. In 1768 Jones married Cornelia Haring or Herring; they had five sons. Cornelia's grandfather became a member of the Second Continental Congress, which voted for independence.

Much like his mentor Smith, Jones fit into the category that has been called Whig Loyalist. Opposed to parliamentary taxation, Jones was chosen to the Committee of One Hundred, the extralegal body that after April 1775 was charged with enforcing the Continental Association imposed by the First Continental Congress. But also like Smith, Jones did not want to break with the British empire, and in the summer of 1775 he left New York City. He spent most of his time at West Neck, Long Island, where he continued his practice.

"Every office shut up almost," wrote fellow lawyer John Morin Scott in November 1775, "but Sam Jones who will work for 6/ a day and live according" (Todd, p. 292). Jones wanted to remain neutral, but New York's provisional government disbarred him for Loyalist sympathies. When the British invaded Long Island in the summer of 1776, Queens County was placed under martial law, and Jones pretty much sat out the remainder of the war. He remained friends with many of the patriot leaders, however, and never lost his lands.

Following the War for Independence, Jones quickly regained his reputation as a leading lawyer. In 1782 the state government appointed Jones and Richard Varick to review and codify those laws of British New York that should remain in force under the New York State Constitution of 1777. The insight and erudition of this work demonstrated that Jones possessed great learning and established his reputation as the leading legal scholar in the state. Between 1789 and 1796 he served as the recorder of New York City, and in that capacity he revised the laws and ordinances of the municipality. In 1796 Governor John Jay asked Jones to draft legislation establishing the office of state comptroller, to which he was appointed and served from 1797 to 1800.

Jones was also quite active politically. From 1786 to 1790 he represented Queens County in the state assembly, and from 1791 to 1797 he served in the New York State Senate. Jones emerged as a "leading and strong man" among Governor George Clinton's inner circle of advisers, the only Loyalist in that group. His legal expertise was doubtlessly valuable to Governor Clinton. In the assembly, he labored to remove the legal penalties imposed on his fellow Tories. Although elected as an Antifederalist delegate, Jones played a major role in the Poughkeepsie convention in bringing about the ratification of the Constitution of 1787 with recommendations. In the mid-1790s Jones broke with the Clintonians and became a Federalist party leader. In 1806 and again in 1807 he tried without success to win election as a Federalist to the New York Senate.

During his old age, Jones took an avid interest in New York history. He sought to preserve its literary sources, and he spent considerable time and effort reviewing Smith's famous *History of the Province of New York* (1757) to correct what he believed were his mentor's errors. At his death, in West Neck, Jones was the acknowledged "father of the New York bar." In October 1853 a writer in the *New York Legal Observer* explained:

His learning was vast. His principles . . . were ultra conservative. . . . He was the man above all others to adapt the system of laws to the new condition of things, . . . and on every subject of that description the Legislature followed him implicitly, while upon any subject connected with politics, they were sure to be on the other side, with entire unanimity.

More judicious was the characterization of Jones made by Chancellor James Kent. "No one surpassed him in clearness of intellect, and in moderation and extreme simplicity of character, no one equaled him in his accurate knowledge of the technical rules and doctrines of real property, and in familiarity with the skillful and elaborate, but now obsolete and mysterious black letter learning of the common law" (Thompson, p. 531).

• Few of Jones's papers have survived. His active role in the Poughkeepsie ratifying convention is in Harold C. Syrett and Jacob E. Cooke, eds., *The Papers of Alexander Hamilton: June 1788–Nov. 1789*, vol. 5 (1962). Pertinent information about Jones is in J. H. Jones, *Jones Family of Long Island* (1907); B. F. Thompson, *History of Long Island* (1839); and C. B. Todd, *The Story of the City of New York* (1888). Conservative Whig ideology is discussed by William Allen Benton, *Whig-Loyalism: An Aspect of Political Ideology in the American Revolutionary Era* (1969). His role in the Poughkeepsie convention is discussed by E. Wilder Spaulding, *New York in the Critical Period, 1783–1789* (1932); Linda Grant DePaw, *The Eleventh Pillar: New York State and the Federal Constitution* (1966); and Alfred Young, *The Democratic Republicans of New York: The Origins, 1763–1797* (1967). Other useful assessments are Richard B. Morris, "John Jay and the Adoption of the Federal Constitution in New York: A New Reading of Persons and Events," *New York History* 63 (1982): 133–64; and several articles in Stephen L. Schechter, ed., *The Reluctant Pillar: New York and the Adoption of the Federal Constitution* (1987). His disagreements with his old mentor over the history of provincial New York are discussed in William Smith, Jr., *The History of the Province of New York*, ed. Michael Kammen (2 vols., 1972). An obituary is in the *New York Evening Post*, 26 Nov. 1819.

RONALD W. HOWARD

JONES, Samuel Milton (8 Aug. 1846–12 July 1904), manufacturer, mayor, reformer, nicknamed "Golden Rule," was born near Beddgelert, Caernarvonshire, Wales, the son of Hugh Samuel Jones, a stone mason and tenant farmer, and Margaret Williams. In 1849 the family immigrated to the United States, settling near Collinsville, New York. During his childhood the young Jones attended school for a total of only thirty months, never studying grammar nor advancing beyond fractions in arithmetic. At the age of fourteen he took a job in a sawmill, and soon after secured a position as wiper and greaser on a steamboat. In 1865 Jones moved to the Pennsylvania oilfields, where he remained for most of the next twenty-one years. Working as a driller, pumper, tool dresser, and pipe liner, he saved enough money to go into the oil business for himself. In 1875 the young oilman married Alma Bernice Curtiss of Pleasantville, Pennsylvania, and during the next ten years three children were born to the couple. In 1881 Jones's infant daughter died, and his wife's death followed four years later. Jones characterized these losses as "the greatest trial and severest shock" of his life.

Grief-stricken and depressed, in 1886 Jones decided to seek his fortune in the oil fields developing near Lima, Ohio. There he drilled the first major oil well in the region and was among the founders of the Ohio Oil Company, a successful enterprise which sold out to

Standard Oil Company in 1889. Three years later he married Helen Beach and moved to Toledo, where the couple had one son.

In Toledo Jones experimented with oil drilling equipment and in 1894 secured a patent for an iron pumping rod. To manufacture this and other drilling appliances, he founded the Acme Sucker Rod Company. At the company's plant Jones instituted labor policies based on his conception of the Golden Rule. In sharp contrast to other manufacturers of the period, he established an eight-hour work day, refused to employ child labor, used no time keepers or time clocks, granted each worker a week's vacation with pay, and offered a Christmas bonus amounting to five percent of the employee's annual salary. He also transformed a vacant lot into Golden Rule Park and Playground for the use of his workers, and maintained Golden Rule Hall at his factory for club meetings. Jones even urged his employees to join unions and marched beside them in Labor Day parades. The benevolent manufacturer's motto proclaimed: "The Business of this shop is to make men; the making of money is only an incidental detail." As a result of these policies, Jones won the nickname "Golden Rule."

In 1897 Toledo's Republican city convention was deadlocked until the sixth ballot, when the delegates finally agreed upon Jones as a compromise candidate for mayor. The idealistic manufacturer won the ensuing election by a narrow margin and embarked on a career in city government that brought him nationwide attention. As mayor he instituted the eight-hour day for municipal employees as well as fixing a minimum wage. He also sponsored the creation of playgrounds, public baths, and free kindergartens for Toledo's poorer residents. Moreover, he campaigned vigorously, but unsuccessfully, for the municipal ownership of public utilities. Jones firmly believed that the electric, gas, and streetcar companies should be city property, operating for the benefit of the general public rather than for the profit of a few privileged stockholders.

The crusading mayor's views on criminal justice earned him further notoriety. He ordered the police to exchange their billy clubs for light canes, thus limiting their ability to inflict bodily harm. In addition, Jones inveighed against arrests for suspicion and loitering, claiming that such arrests victimized the poor. As mayor he was able to serve as police judge, and he often released those who came before him, using the opportunity to deliver short sermons on the evils of society and the persecution of the downtrodden. In February 1902 he set a record for leniency, dismissing every case brought before him. Over his desk hung the motto: "Judge not that ye be not judged."

Jones's seeming laxity toward crime and vice, as well as his attacks on capitalism and his predilection for Christian socialism, earned him the enmity of many leading citizens. Consequently, in 1899 the Republican party refused to nominate him for reelection as mayor. Unwilling to submit to the party's decision, Jones ran as an independent and won the contest by a landslide, garnering more than twice the votes of the Republican and Democratic candidates combined. The reform mayor also won reelection as an independent in 1901 and 1903. In addition, he was an independent candidate for governor of Ohio in 1899, running behind his Republican and Democratic opponents but carrying Toledo's Lucas County and Cleveland's Cuyahoga County.

During his seven years as mayor, Jones not only sought to convince the people of Toledo to join in the building of a cooperative commonwealth; he also carried his message to people throughout the nation. In 1899 he made a speaking tour of the East Coast, addressing two thousand people at New York's Cooper Union. That same year he published *The New Right: A Plea for Fair Play through a More Just Social Order*, and in 1900–1901 he authored *Letters of Love and Labor*, a two-volume collection of letters to his factory employees. In 1900 he stumped on behalf of William Jennings Bryan, attacking the imperialist policies of the McKinley administration. Moreover, he spoke at numerous conferences and contributed to leading reform journals.

On the whole, Jones was a charismatic idealist who inspired many Americans troubled by the seeming injustices resulting from industrialization and rapid urban growth. His repeated triumphs at the polls proved that advocates of Christian egalitarianism could win votes in hardheaded manufacturing towns like Toledo. Yet he failed to achieve municipal ownership of public utilities, a battle he was still fighting at the time of his death in Toledo.

• The Samuel M. Jones Papers are in the Toledo–Lucas County Public Library, Toledo, Ohio. His autobiography is contained in *The New Right* (1899). See also James H. Rodabaugh, "Samuel M. Jones—Evangel of Equality," *Quarterly Bulletin Historical Society of Northwestern Ohio* 15, no. 1 (Jan. 1943): 17–46; Hoyt Landon Warner, *Progressivism in Ohio, 1897–1917* (1964); Donald E. Pitzer, "Revivalism and Politics in Toledo: 1899," *Northwest Ohio Quarterly* (1968–1969); Morgan J. Barclay, "Reform in Toledo: The Political Career of Samuel M. Jones," *Northwest Ohio Quarterly* 50, no. 3 (Summer 1978): 79–89; and Morgan J. Barclay and Jean W. Strong, *The Samuel Milton Jones Papers: An Inventory to the Microfilm Edition* (1978).

JON C. TEAFORD

JONES, Samuel Porter (16 Oct. 1847–15 Oct. 1906), evangelist, was born in Chambers County, Alabama, the son of John J. Jones, a successful lawyer and businessman, and Nancy Porter. His father's family had a long tradition of producing Methodist preachers. Both his great-grandfather and his grandfather had entered the ministry, and his father also felt called to the ministry but never was convinced that it offered enough financial security. Sam Jones's mother had an equally significant religious influence on him. "My mother was a painstaking, sweet-spirited, Christian woman," he later wrote. Jones's mother died when he was nine years old, and about four years later John Jones married Jennie Skinner of Cartersville, Georgia, and

moved the family there in 1859. Like Nancy Jones before her, the new stepmother also "did all she could in instilling the principles of virtue and right" in the hearts of Jones and his three siblings.

Jones's first schooling was in Chambers County, Alabama, where he came under the tutorship of Major W. F. Slaton, later superintendent of the Atlanta Public Schools. Although Professor Slaton gave Jones a solid elementary education, his studies were interrupted when the family moved to Georgia and his father joined the Army of Virginia in 1861. After his father returned home, before the conclusion of the Civil War, Jones resumed his studies at the school of future Congressman W. H. Felton and his wife, Rebecca, who later would become the first woman in the U.S. Senate.

After leaving the Feltons' private school, Jones entered high school in Euharlee, Georgia, where his health broke; the diagnosis was nervous dyspepsia. With his hopes for a college education in ruins, he decided to stay at home and read law. In 1868, after completing only one year of studying law, he was admitted to the Georgia bar. Shortly after beginning what seemed to be a promising career in the legal profession, he accepted the advice of a physician to take wine to alleviate the pain of his nervous condition. Though he had begun drinking five or so years before, in his efforts to "seek relief in the intoxicating cup" Jones developed a dependence on alcohol and began to drink heavily. His new bride, Laura McElwain, whom he had married a month after his admission to the bar, was a woman of deep religious faith. Both his early success as a lawyer and his marriage were seriously jeopardized by his alcoholism.

A series of events in 1872, however, resulted in his victory over the "intoxicating cup." In July, Beulah, the first of his seven children, died. Two weeks later, Laura Jones gave birth to their second daughter, Mary. In August, while sitting beside his father's deathbed, Jones promised to overcome his alcoholism. At the same time, he underwent a religious conversion, which enabled him to quit drinking, though for the rest of his life he periodically struggled with nervousness and depression.

Soon after his conversion, and with no formal training in theology or preaching, Jones initiated his 34-year ministry as a preacher and evangelist. Armed with a Bible, a volume of C. H. Spurgeon's sermons, and a book of sermon outlines, he rode off to assume the duties of the first of his three circuits—groups of small churches—of the North Georgia Conference of the Methodist Episcopal Church, South. Although he possessed a quick mind, Jones noted later that when he began to preach he realized that to be a great preacher he would have to be either a great thinker or a great worker. He chose the latter, having "serious doubts as to whether I could think above the plane where the masses stood." Successful preaching, he came to believe, was the result of "earnest exhortation" and not cleverly crafted sermons punctuated with the finest of theological arguments. "I have never made theology a study," he stated in his 1886 autobiography. He believed less in conversion as the result of an individual crisis than in salvation as a process. His formula for salvation was similar to that held by Charles Finney earlier in the nineteenth century. It was the result of both law and good works. "You do what God tells you to do, and then if God doesn't do what he said he would do, you have an issue that will bankrupt heaven in a minute."

In 1880, when Jones concluded his third preaching circuit, he was already spending half his time in revival meetings in Georgia. In the fall of 1881 he was appointed agent of the Decatur Orphans' Home, a work of the North Georgia Conference, in Decatur, Georgia. By then he had become weary of the demands of circuit-riding. He wanted more time at home with his wife and children. Revival preaching was in his blood, however, and for the next twenty years he traveled to cities throughout the North and South to decry the evils of urban America with its vices of drink and prostitution.

Jones attracted sizable crowds wherever he went. In Chicago he conducted his revivals in a renovated skating rink that held upwards of 7,000 people; the total attendance over a five-week period was estimated at more than a quarter million. For similar periods in other cities attendance figures were usually about 150,000. By his own estimate, for the one-year period from September 1885 to September 1886 he traveled 20,000 miles, preached 1,000 sermons to three million people, and was responsible for the addition of 70,000 to the membership rolls of the Methodist Episcopal Church, South. By the end of that year, scores of reporters from across the country were elbowing each other around the press tables to telegraph Jones's latest sermon back to their hometown paper. Jones estimated that every sermon he preached in Chicago during March 1886 was read by a million and a half people. His final six years were spent preaching in the South, from Mississippi to Texas to Louisiana to Arkansas.

Jones's flamboyant delivery and mannerisms were the keys to his widespread acceptance by traditionally rural Americans who felt threatened by the changes taking place in the cities. His homespun style of evangelism intermingled with an espousal of laissez-faire economic ethics. "God projected this world on the root-hog-or-die-poor principle," he wrote. He scorned the modernist religion of urban America. "We have been clamoring for forty years for a learned ministry, and we have got it today and the church is deader than it has been in history. Half of the literary preachers in this town are A.B.'s, Ph.D's D.D.'s, LL.D.'s, and A.S.S.'s."

The hectic pace he kept for more than thirty years of preaching perhaps contributed to his death on the day before his fifty-ninth birthday. With his wife at his side, Jones died in his sleep of undetermined causes while traveling by train from a revival in Oklahoma City to his home in Cartersville. His beloved Georgia honored him with a state funeral.

Because of his ability to hold sway over his audiences, Jones has been acclaimed as one of the nation's foremost public speakers in the late nineteenth century. Active at the same time as the northern evangelist Dwight L. Moody, Samuel Porter Jones came to be known by many as "the Moody of the South."

• The papers of Samuel Porter Jones are in the Emory University Library, Atlanta, Ga. His autobiography is *Sam Jones' Own Book: A Series of Sermons with an Autobiographical Sketch* (1887). Fellow Methodist preacher of the South George Rutledge Stuart wrote *Sam P. Jones, the Preacher* [n.d.], probably soon after Jones's death; it is a helpful account by someone who knew Jones well. The most complete biography of Jones was written by his son-in-law, Walt Holcomb: *Sam Jones: An Ambassador of the Almighty, Commemorating the Centennial Year of the Birth of Sam Jones* (1947). See also *The Life and Sayings of Sam P. Jones, a Minister of the Gospel* (1907), written by his wife with the assistance of Walt Holcomb. Numerous books of Jones's sermons are available, including *Sam Jones' Anecdotes and Illustrations* (1896), *Sam Jones' Revival Sermons* (1912), and *Rifle Shots at the King's Enemies, Being Sermons Delivered in Toronto* [n.d.]. An extensive, scholarly interpretation of Jones appears in William McLoughlin, *Modern Revivalism: Charles Grandison Finney to Billy Graham* (1959).

ROBERT R. MATHISEN

JONES, Scipio Africanus (1863–28 Mar. 1943), lawyer, was born in Dallas County, Arkansas, the son of a white father, whose identity remains uncertain, and Jemmima, a slave who belonged to Dr. Sanford Reamey, a physician and landowner. After emancipation, Jemmima and her freedman husband, Horace, became farmers and adopted the surname of Jones, in memory of Dr. Adolphus Jones, a previous owner. Scipio Jones attended rural black schools in Tulip, Arkansas, and moved to Little Rock in 1881 to pursue a college preparatory course at Bethel University. He then entered Shorter College, from which he graduated in 1885 with a bachelor's degree in education. When the University of Arkansas Law School denied him admission because of his race, he read law with several white attorneys in Little Rock and was admitted to the bar in 1889. His marriage to Carrie Edwards in 1896 ended in his wife's early death and left him with a daughter to raise. In 1917 he married Lillie M. Jackson of Pine Bluff, Arkansas.

By the turn of the century Jones had become the leading black practitioner in Little Rock. His clients, who were drawn exclusively from the African-American community, included several large, fraternal organizations, such as the Mosaic Templars of America. He also played an active role in Republican politics, supporting the efforts of the "Black and Tan" faction to wrest control of the state party from the "Lily Whites." In 1902 he promoted a slate of black Republicans to challenge the party regulars and the Democrats in a local election, and in 1920 he made an unsuccessful bid for the post of Republican national committeeman. The struggle to secure equal treatment for African Americans within the party lasted from the late 1880s to the 1930s and resulted in a compromise that guaranteed black representation on the Republican state central committee. As a sign of changing times, Jones was elected as a delegate to the Republican National Conventions of 1928 and 1940. Despite the existence of poll taxes that disfranchised most black voters, he also won election as a special judge of the Little Rock municipal court in 1915, at a time when few African Americans held judicial office anywhere in the country.

Jones's lifelong commitment to protecting the civil rights of blacks led to his involvement in the greatest legal battle of his career: the defense of twelve tenant farmers who were sentenced to death for alleged murders committed during the bloody Elaine, Arkansas, race riot of October 1919. The violence grew out of black efforts to establish a farmers' union and white fears that a dangerous conspiracy was being plotted at their secret meetings. When two white men were reportedly shot near a black church, the white community engaged in murderous reprisals that left more than 200 blacks and five whites dead. An all-white grand jury quickly indicted 122 blacks, and because most of the defendants were indigent, the court appointed defense counsel for them. These white lawyers did not interview their clients, request a change of venue, or object to all-white trial juries. The trials themselves lasted less than an hour, and it took juries only five or six minutes to return guilty verdicts. Several defendants and witnesses later claimed that they had been tortured, and an angry white mob surrounded the courthouse during the trials. Besides the twelve men who were sentenced to death, sixty-seven others received long prison terms.

The National Association for the Advancement of Colored People retained Jones and George W. Murphy, a white Little Rock attorney, to appeal the convictions. Jones became the senior defense counsel after Murphy died in October 1920, and he tirelessly pursued every avenue of relief under state law, risking his life on several occasions by his courtroom appearances in the hostile community of Helena. Jones's arguments impressed the Arkansas Supreme Court, which twice ordered new trials for six defendants. In the first instance Jones pointed to technical defects in the form of the verdicts. On the second appeal he contended that the trial judge's rejection of evidence pointing to racial discrimination in the selection of jurors had deprived his clients of their equal protection rights under the Fourteenth Amendment. To prevent the impending executions of the remaining six defendants, Jones turned to the federal courts. Arguing that the prisoners had been deprived of their constitutional right to a fair trial, he sought their release through a habeas corpus proceeding. Eventually the case reached the U.S. Supreme Court, where it resulted in a landmark decision, *Moore v. Dempsey* (1923). By looking behind the formal state record for the first time, the Court overturned the convictions and held that the defendants had been denied due process, since their original trial had been little more than a legalized lynching bee. Although Jones did not participate in the final argument

of the case, his strategy had guided the litigation process from the beginning. In the aftermath of *Moore v. Dempsey*, he secured an order from the Arkansas Supreme Court for the discharge of six prisoners in June 1923. He then negotiated with state authorities to secure commutation of sentences and parole for all of the remaining Elaine "rioters" by January 1925.

In his later years Jones continued to attack racially discriminatory laws and practices in Arkansas. He was instrumental in obtaining legislation that granted out-of-state tuition payments to black students who could not enter the state's all-white professional schools. He died in Little Rock. To commemorate his community leadership, the all-white school board of North Little Rock named the black high school in his memory.

• Letters from Jones are in the NAACP Papers in the Library of Congress and in the Republican Party State Central Committee Records in the University of Arkansas Library. The best biographical sketch is Tom Dillard, "Scipio A. Jones," *Arkansas Historical Quarterly* 31 (Autumn 1972): 201–19. Richard C. Cortner, *A Mob Intent on Death* (1988), provides a definitive account of the Elaine riot litigation and of Jones's role as defense counsel. See also Mary White Ovington, *Portraits in Color* (1927), and Arthur I. Waskow, *From Race Riot to Sit-In, 1919 and the 1960s* (1966).

MAXWELL BLOOMFIELD

JONES, Spike (14 Dec. 1911–1 May 1965), bandleader, was born Lindley Armstrong Jones in Long Beach, California, the son of Lindley Murray Jones, a depot agent for the Southern Pacific Railroad, and Ada Armstrong, a schoolteacher. Jones grew up in Calexico, California, and received his nickname at about age eleven when a telegrapher dubbed him "Spike" because he was always hanging around the railroad tracks. Jones developed an early love of music, which included an interest in playing the drums, and he received his first drum set for Christmas 1922.

Jones first attended Calipatria High School, but then transferred to Long Beach Polytechnic High School because of the high quality of its music program. Throughout his high school years, Jones played the drums with various local dance bands and orchestras. He also formed his own jazz combo, Spike Jones and His Five Tacks, which played for local events. He graduated from high school in June 1929 and immediately joined the Los Angeles chapter of the American Federation of Musicians, Local 47, to get occasional professional work as a drummer.

Jones enrolled in Chaffey Junior College in Ontario, California, in 1929 to further his education, but he became disenchanted and quit soon after. He then began to play drums with various dance bands in southern California and became thoroughly ingrained in the music scene, playing alongside greats such as Stan Kenton and Freddie Slack. In 1934 Jones formed his first novelty band (also called Spike Jones and His Five Tacks), a forerunner of the band for which he would eventually become famous. In 1934 Jones met Patricia Ann Middleton, who was a singer for Al Lyons's orchestra; they married in 1935 and had one child.

In the mid-1930s Jones began working as a freelance studio musician for recordings, radio, and motion pictures. During this time he also continued to perform with his own novelty band. Sometime between 1939 and 1941 Jones would rename his group Spike Jones and His City Slickers. Even at this stage he began to experiment with interspersing comic sound effects such as gunshots and breaking glass within some musical numbers, although these early arrangements were somewhat tamer than those that would later become Jones's signature pieces.

Although the exact genesis of the City Slickers is unclear, the band was definitely performing under that name by mid-1941. It made its radio debut in July of that year and entered the recording studio for the first time in August. The next year the City Slickers recorded the novelty song that made Jones widely known—"Der Fuehrer's Face"—in which the group gives Adolf Hitler "the razzberry." The song helped to raise the spirits of a war-weary United States and became a surprise hit that propelled the group to stardom. From then on Jones's popularity grew, a tribute both to his creativity as a bandleader and to his genius as a self-promoter. In 1943 *Down Beat* magazine dubbed Jones "The King of Corn," a title he held for the next ten years.

Jones's novelty music was a much-needed tension reliever for a country anxious over the escalating war overseas; Americans needed a laugh, and Jones provided it. In 1944 Jones recorded his signature piece, "Cocktails for Two," complete with honking horns, "glugs," and his famous gunshots. Just weeks after its release it was one of the country's hottest-selling records.

While Jones's career continued to climb, his home life faltered. In 1945 he separated from his wife, and they were divorced the next year. At the same time, however, Jones and the City Slickers were at the height of their popularity. They effected a new look—garish, brightly colored plaid suits—and recorded some of their most popular arrangements ("Chloe," "My Old Flame," "The William Tell Overture," "Laura"). In 1946 Jones launched his *Musical Depreciation Revue*, a madcap touring variety show featuring the City Slickers, complete with nonstop zany antics, slapstick humor, and vaudeville-inspired skits. The revue became a popular favorite and broke attendance records in many of the theaters in which it played. Jones's reputation as a master of comedy and novelty music continued to grow steadily, and in 1947 he and the band recorded another tune destined to become a classic, "All I Want for Christmas Is My Two Front Teeth." It was released for Christmas 1948 and sold 1.3 million copies in six weeks.

Also in 1948 Jones married singer Helen Grayco (née Greco), who had been touring with his band since 1945, and they moved to a mansion in Beverly Hills. The couple had three children.

Throughout the 1950s Jones divided his time between touring with the City Slickers (both in the United States and in Australia), making television appearances (including in 1954 his own short-lived series, "The Spike Jones Show"), making film appearances, and recording for various record labels. In 1951 the band made its debut in network television on "The Colgate Comedy Hour."

Jones and the City Slickers worked steadily throughout the 1950s, but their popularity waned during the decade. Undeterred, Jones continued to make recordings and plan projects. The albums *Spike Spoofs the Pops, Dinner Music for People Who Aren't Very Hungry*, and *Omnibust* were all recorded between 1956 and 1959.

Jones's years as a heavy cigarette smoker finally caught up with him. He was diagnosed with emphysema in 1960 but continued to work both onstage and in film. In 1962 he launched another tour with a revue titled *The Show of the Year*. His failing health began to hamper his ability to perform, however. During his final years he became dependent on an oxygen tank, and some performances were cut back or cancelled because of Jones's worsening condition. He died at his Beverly Hills home.

Jones regained popularity in the 1970s when disc jockey Dr. Demento (Barret Hansen) regularly featured his music on a weekly radio program and Jones's legacy continues in the work of musicians whom he inspired. Among those who have cited him as an influence in their career are Jimmy Buffett, George Carlin, Frank Zappa, Peter Schickele (also known as P. D. Q. Bach), and the members of the Monty Python comedy troupe. Jones is one of the few performers who has been honored with three separate stars on Hollywood's Walk of Fame: for records, for radio, and for television. He became associated with a style of performance that included crazy musical arrangements combined with various vaudeville gags, garish costumes, and slapstick comedy. His name is synonymous with a style of novelty music containing zany sound effects.

• A valuable assessment of Jones's life and career is Jordan R. Young, *Spike Jones Off the Record: The Man Who Murdered Music* (1994), previously published as *Spike Jones and His City Slickers* (1984), which contains a filmography, discography, videography, radiography, and a brief bibliography. See also Jack Mirtle, comp., *Thank You Music Lovers: A Biodiscography of Spike Jones and His City Slickers, 1941 to 1965* (1986), for a brief overview of Jones's life and a complete discography of his later career. An obituary is in the *New York Times*, 2 May 1965.

BETH A. KATTELMAN

JONES, Susan Charlotte Barber (15 May 1832–26 Oct. 1911), religious leader, was born in Rome, New York, the daughter of John Barber and Susan Cartwright, clerks and innkeepers. In her childhood her family moved to Meadville, Pennsylvania. Privately educated, she became private secretary to Jan Huidekoper and his son, Frederic, successive presidents of Meadville Theological School (Unitarian). She married a student at the school, Jenkin Lloyd Jones, in 1870; the couple had two children. Susan Jones was very accomplished in practical skills as well as in the arts and scholarship, all of which she put to good use as the partner of a young, ambitious, idealistic Unitarian minister in small midwestern churches. She was often as much tutor and secretary to her husband as she was wife. Indeed, much of his later special interest in art and literature can be traced to her coaching of him.

During her husband's term as mission secretary and secretary of the Western Unitarian Conference, especially in the early years from 1875 to 1880, Jones was seen by the conference to be equally important to her husband in carrying out the duties of the office, and she was so recognized in the conference minutes. From 1875 to 1885 the western conference was the most liberal and innovative branch of the Unitarian church, stretching both the traditional forms of the religion and the Unitarian identity as Christian. In addition to her contribution as administrative assistant to her husband, Jones developed significant roles of her own. She held office in most of the auxiliaries, wrote for the conference newspaper, *Unity*, and authored tracts. She also was one of the founders of the Western Women's Unitarian Conference in 1873.

The Western Unitarian Conference was a pioneer in recognizing women in leadership roles, and Jones's example led the way for many others to follow. From 1872 to 1880, she and her husband served All Souls Church in Janesville, Wisconsin. Whenever he was ill or away on conference business, she fulfilled all of the ministerial roles, including preaching. In all but name she was cominister and presaged the emergence of the "sisterhood" of women ministers in the western conference, which began with the ordination of Mary Safford in 1881.

For Jenkin Jones, the Janesville ministry was a time for finding new directions. During those years he developed an open theology and a missionary strategy, discovered the religious value of art and literature, reconceived religious education, and found a worship pattern that would serve as his lifelong framework. Undoubtedly his wife played a major role in all of these religious innovations, but, unfortunately, in most cases her particular contribution cannot be traced. One such role is her part in the development of the western conference Sunday school material. The *Sunday School*, a four-page weekly sheet distributed to church schools from "Uncle Jenk and Aunt Susan" as early as 1871, cut loose from the Bible study model and took its material from nature and history. It is impossible to separate Susan Jones's contributions from those of her husband, but her broader education and greater experience makes it likely that the *Sunday School* was more her work than his. During the next decade, this early weekly paper developed into the full, six-year Sunday school curriculum of the western conference.

One important innovation is clearly that of Susan Jones, though her husband is usually given the credit.

In 1875 she organized the young men and women of the Janesville church into a club that met to discuss literary topics, followed by a dance. Meetings of this Mutual Improvement Club (MIC) quickly became popular educational and social events in the church and in the town as a whole, and the club soon had to be divided into several sections, focusing on different topics, to accommodate all who wanted to attend. The idea caught the imagination of the Unitarian church nationwide, and soon many churches had Unity Clubs (the later name for the MIC), and a Unity Club Bureau was formed at the Boston headquarters in the 1880s.

In 1880, when Jenkin Jones moved to Chicago where he had an office and a staff, there was less opportunity, and less need, for Susan Jones to participate directly in his work. She did continue to write, and she helped design the innovative combination church-parsonage for All Souls, Chicago, but mostly she became a kind of superwife to her husband. By the early 1890s, she was increasingly afflicted by ill health, including blindingly painful headaches and hearing loss, and for the last decade and a half of her life she did little outside her home. She died in Madison, Wisconsin, during a visit to the home of her son.

Susan Charlotte Lloyd Jones (as she usually signed her name) was a pioneering figure for the entrance of women into leadership positions in the Unitarian church and an important, though undocumentable, source for the flowering of the church in the Midwest in the last quarter of the nineteenth century.

• The only extant writings by Susan Jones can be found in issues of *Unity*, between 1878 and 1892. Besides editorials, reports, book reviews, and moral tales for children, her most important contributions in *Unity* are "Historic Unitarianism in the West" (a four-part history of the Western Unitarian Conference) 17 (24 July 1886): 298–99, 17 (7 Aug. 1886): 322–24, 17 (21 Aug. 1886): 348–49, and 18 (4 Sept. 1886): 6–8; and two printed sermons, "The Co-education of Husband and Wife," 17 (24 Apr. 1886): 109–13, and "The Co-education of Parent and Child," 21 (12 May 1888): 144–49. No biographical work has been written, and the only treatment of her life is the 14 Nov. 1911 issue of *Unity*, which is mostly given to tributes to her and is not very useful. A brief death notice is in the Chicago *Daily Journal*, 27 Oct. 1911.

THOMAS E. GRAHAM

JONES, Sybil (28 Feb. 1808–4 Dec. 1873), Quaker minister, was born in Brunswick, Maine, the daughter of Ephraim Jones and Susanna Dudley, farmers. In her early life she was influenced by the evangelicalism of the Methodists but did not leave the Friends. In 1824–1825 she attended the Friends school in Providence, Rhode Island. She taught public school for eight years in various locations in Maine and on 26 June 1833 married Eli Jones, another Quaker school teacher who had grown up on a farm in Maine. They settled on a farm in Dirigo, Maine, where they had five children.

New England Yearly Meeting recognized Sybil, like her husband, as a minister. The Joneses remained Gurneyite Quakers, opposing both the Hicksites (followers of Elias Hicks, whose views on the Inner Light had led in 1827–1828 to a great schism between his adherents and the much smaller group referred to as Orthodox Friends) and Wilburite Friends (supporters of John Wilbur, leader of an Orthodox faction that in the 1840s and 1850s separated from the less conservative Orthodox Friends allied with Joseph John Gurney, whose theological views were increasingly influenced by those of English evangelicals). Sybil Jones's diaries reveal her to have been a quietist evangelical Friend, and she remained a supporter of silent or undirected Quaker meetings. Perhaps because she had experienced her first religious awakening among Methodists, during her missionary journeys Jones associated with other Protestants and occasionally showed sympathy to individual Roman Catholics and those of the Greek Orthodox faith.

Although the Joneses made their living as farmers and teachers, their primary vocation was as itinerant Quaker ministers. Beginning in 1840 they journeyed often, preaching evangelical religion, antislavery, temperance, and peace at Quaker meetings in Canada as well as in the eastern and southern United States. In 1851 Sybil Jones persuaded her husband that the Lord wanted them to sail to Liberia to preach to and to view the progress of free Africans. After two months in Liberia, they returned briefly to the United States, and then spent two years traveling in Ireland, England, Norway, Germany, and France, ministering either in Friends meetings or in gatherings of sympathizers. Both in her journeys and at home, Sybil Jones frequently experienced ill health; she believed that the Lord enabled her to conquer illness.

During the Civil War the Joneses' oldest son renounced his parents' pacifism so that he could fight to free slaves. Before and after his death in 1864 during a battle at Crystal Springs, the Joneses visited military camps and hospitals where they ministered to an estimated 30,000 soldiers. After the assassination of Abraham Lincoln, Sybil Jones met on two occasions with Mary Todd Lincoln and also met with President Andrew Johnson, providing religious counsel to both. In 1867 the Joneses traveled to Palestine and Syria and founded a school for girls in Ramallah (near Jerusalem), which, along with an already existing school for boys, was supported by British and American Friends. In Muslim countries she stressed the rights of women to education and even was allowed to preach in some harems.

Sybil Jones did not live to witness the full impact of the emerging holiness and pastoral emphases on middlewestern Quakers, but she did attend the Indiana Yearly Meeting in 1860 where one of the first Quaker revivals occurred, and she also participated in a series of general meetings in Maine shortly before her death in China, Maine. Sybil Jones saw the testimonies given at the general meetings as a sign of religious vitality. The emotional conversions and testimonies she witnessed were the forerunners of the revival/holiness emphases that came to prevail in the Midwest in the late nineteenth century.

• Sybil Jones's diaries and manuscripts are in the Quaker Collection at Haverford College. For additional information see the *Christian Worker* 4, no. 4 (1874): 49–52, and Rufus Jones, *Eli and Sybil Jones* (1889).

J. WILLIAM FROST

JONES, Thad (28 Mar. 1923–20 Aug. 1986), jazz horn player, composer, and bandleader, was born Thaddeus Joseph Jones in Pontiac, Michigan. The names of his parents and details of his early childhood are unknown. However, it would seem that his was a musical family: his uncle William was a bandleader, and two of his four brothers were musicians.

Jones was inspired to play music by his older brother, Hank, who was an accomplished jazz pianist; his brother gave him his first job, at age sixteen, playing cornet in his band. During the Second World War, he was employed as an entertainer with various Midwestern bands, playing United Service Organizations shows. After the war was over, he joined forces with his younger brother, drummer Elvin, working in a quintet led by Billy Mitchell in Detroit. Jones worked for a year from 1954–1955 with composer and jazz bassist Charles Mingus in his Jazz Composers' Workshop orchestra and then held a nine-year post with the Count Basie Orchestra.

Discouraged by the lack of opportunity for performing in and composing for big bands in the 1960s, Jones settled in New York City in the mid-1960s. He formed a rehearsal band with drummer Mel Lewis in 1965, specifically to highlight his own composing; the group had a regular, Monday night engagement at New York's Village Vanguard for the next thirteen years. With this band he primarily played flugelhorn, developing a melodic style in his playing, arrangements, and compositions that separated his work from his more bop-oriented recordings of the 1950s. While working with the band, Jones wrote in a variety of styles, exploring waltz tempo in "The Waltz You Swang for Me" (1968), bossa nova in "It Only Happens Every Time" (1970), and jazz-rock in "Greetings and Salutations" (1975–1976), as well as traditional swing and bop, although even in traditional styles he experimented with new tonalities, voicings, and especially meters. The band became so successful that it toured and recorded extensively, becoming one of the few big bands to achieve success in the 1960s and the early 1970s and redefining the big-band style for a new generation.

Jones left the band in 1979, when an injury to his hip led him to change to a new instrument, the valve trombone. (Lewis continued to lead the Monday-night group under his own name.) Jones moved to Europe that same year, settling in Denmark; formed his own orchestra, Thad Jones' Eclipse; taught jazz at the Royal Conservatory; and worked as the leader of the Danish Radio Orchestra. In 1985 he returned to the United States to take over the helm of the revitalized Count Basie Orchestra; a year later he left the post and, six months later, died. Jones was married twice, fathering son Bruce and daughter Thedia from his first marriage and a son from his second marriage to a Danish woman.

• Several articles have appeared about Jones and his brothers, including Nat Hentoff's early appreciation, "They're All Talking about the Jones Boys," *Down Beat* 22, no. 23 (1955); L. Tompkins offered a career overview through the early 1970s in "The Thad Jones Story," *Crescendo International* 10, nos. 10–11 (1972); and W. Royal Stokes documented Jones's return to the Basie orchestra in "Thad Jones: At the Helm of the Basie Band," *Jazz Times* (June 1985). The Jones and Lewis orchestra recorded prolifically from 1966 through 1977, on the Blue Note, Solid State, and A&M Horizon labels, although only a small portion of this material is available on CD. Obituaries are in the *New York Times*, 21 Aug. 1986, and *Down Beat* (Nov. 1986).

RICHARD CARLIN

JONES, Thomas (30 Apr. 1731–25 July 1792), lawyer and judge, was born in Fort Neck, Long Island, New York, the son of David Jones, a wealthy politician, lawyer and judge, and Anna Willet. He went to Yale College at age fifteen, graduated in 1750, and then studied law with both his father and Joseph Murray, a well-known New York City lawyer. He became an attorney in 1755; clerk of the court of common pleas for Queens County in 1757; recorder for New York City in 1769; and, upon the resignation of his father, a justice on the New York Supreme Court in 1773.

In 1762 Jones married Anne deLancey, the daughter of James De Lancey, chief justice and lieutenant governor of New York and one of the colony's leading politicians. The marriage produced no children, but it did connect Jones to many prominent wealthy New York families who became loyalists during the Revolution. Meantime, in the 1760s and early 1770s Jones prospered. He lived in an elegant house, "Mount Pitt," that he built on lower Manhattan's highest point, and he inherited an impressive country estate that his father developed in Fort Neck.

After 1774, family ties, appointment as a Crown official, and personal opposition to republicanism all contributed to making Jones a Tory whom patriots regarded with particularly deep suspicion. Like others who later became Loyalists, Jones objected both to taxation of Americans and the "rabble's" methods of opposition. He held fast to his position as a judge and presided at the last session held by the royal Supreme Court in New York in 1776. He maintained allegiance to the king, refused to take an oath of loyalty to New York, and, as a consequence, was arrested by the New York Committee of Safety. Released on parole, he was arrested again two months later when George Washington, facing British troops in New York City, ordered a sweep of Tories liable to aid the enemy. After spending several months in Connecticut, Jones was again paroled, and he returned to his home in Fort Neck.

In 1779, while hosting a party, Jones was taken by a patriot raiding party from Connecticut specifically looking for a prisoner of importance who could be exchanged for General Gold Selleck Silliman, an officer

previously kidnapped by Loyalists. Jones claimed his house was plundered and his wife robbed of her "wearing apparel," while he was forced to march sixty miles on foot "through woods, swamps, and morasses . . . without fire, victuals, or drink" except for " a little mouldy cheese and hard biscuit" (Jones, vol. 2, pp. 277–78). Lodged for the first few days of his captivity with Mrs. Silliman, Jones (according to her diary) was an "unsociable" and "sullen" guest. It was five months before the prisoner exchange was worked out, and then the ships carrying the two men unexpectedly met on Long Island Sound—exchanging their prisoners. Before proceeding, the two men, who thirty years earlier had been students at Yale together, shared a turkey Mrs. Silliman had sent along for her husband. The Sillimans' efforts at cordiality under difficult circumstances did nothing to alleviate Jones's bitter memories of the incident.

While held in Connecticut, Jones was included in the New York Act of Attainder that confiscated the property of fifty-nine Loyalists, an action that clearly added to his resentment. He also was injured in a sleighing accident that delayed the prisoner exchange, and led him to leave for England with his wife and niece in 1781 to seek relief in the waters at Bath. Anticipating a British victory, Jones wrote relatives of his intention to return; peace intervened, however, and Jones's trip became permanent exile. Opposed to independence, on the list of Attainder, he saw the peace treaty as a national and personal disaster—a "patched up . . . ignominious peace" which "dismembered the empire, disgraced the nation, and made Britain the laughing stock, the ridicule, the jest, of all Europe" (Jones, vol. 1, pp. 122, 299).

All of Jones's property not entailed by his father's will was confiscated. He filed claims for $63,000 and is listed as receiving about half that amount in compensation, about $28,000 [Flick, p. 212]. Because Jones had no children, the entailed property went to a nephew. Jones stayed in Bath for two years, and in 1783 he settled in Hoddesdon, in Hertfordshire, England, even though in 1790 a friend obtained permission for him to return to New York. He remained in Hoddesdon until his death there from a sudden illness; his wife remained there until her death in 1817.

Jones occupied much of his time from 1783 to 1788 writing *A History of New York during the Revolutionary War, and of the Leading Events in the Other Colonies at that Period*, a two-volume work in which, with a pen dipped in acid ink, he condemned both Americans and British alike for the war, treatment of Loyalists in general and his family in particular. This was kept by family members first in England and then America, until in 1879 Edward Floyd deLancey, a distant descendant, prepared it for publication by the New-York Historical Society.

Jones saw the source of the American Revolution in a conspiracy begun by the ambitious New York "triumvirate" of William Livingston, John Morin Scott, and William Smith, Jr., a group of Presbyterian lawyers, aided by the local "rabble." From the 1750s on, their objective was the establishment of a republic. Once the war started, Jones credited American victories to British "stupidity," seeing one general after another as incompetent "haughty, morose, churlish" or in his "dotage." The war was lengthened because quartermasters robbed the British treasury: "had there been as much pains taken to put an end to the rebellion as there was to plunder and rob the treasury, *two years* would have finished the war" (Jones, vol. 1, pp. 122, 164, 319). Both Americans and British preyed upon the Loyalists, himself included (always referred to in the third person and as a "gentleman of character"), subjecting them to "ill usage, bad treatment." His statement on George Washington illustrates his views—Parliament not Washington conquered America, while the reported virtues of the "rebel chief" provoked a "Curse on his virtues! they've undone his country" (Jones, vol. 2, p. 349).

Within a year of its publication the book produced a critical response that questioned his interpretations, biases, and supposed facts. Nearly one hundred years later Lawrence Henry Gipson summed up the problems when he observed that Jones wrote "in the white heat of resentment and for this reason" must "be used with caution." Yet Gipson concluded since his work "is not a mere fabrication" it "presents many valuable insights" (Gipson, vol. 13, p. 309).

Jones was a member of the group in colonial society most likely to become Loyalist—crown appointed officials. His allegiance, opposition to republicanism, and inability to accept independence and the peace settlement were all attitudes shared with other Tories. He refused to see the Revolution as justified until the day he died, for which he paid a heavy price. His bitterness is not surprising. However, his caustic comments apply to British officers and politicians as well as American. As a result his life, actions, and writings provide an important insight into how and why the British lost the American Revolution.

• For biographical information on Jones, see Lorenzo Sabine, *Biographical Sketches of Loyalists in the American Revolution*, vol. 1 (1864); Franklin Bowditch Dexter, *Biographical Sketches of the Graduates of Yale College*, vol. 2 (1896); and Edward Floyd deLancey's introduction to Jones, *History*. Material on Jones's treatment as a Loyalist appears in Alexander C. F. Flick, *Loyalism in New York During the American Revolution* (1901); for his capture and exchange in 1779–1780, see Joy Day Buel and Richard Buel, Jr., *The Way of Duty: A Woman and Her Family in Revolutionary America* (1984). For a discussion of his loyalist ideology and how it matched that of his contemporaries, see Janice Potter, *The Liberty We Seek: Loyalist Ideology in Colonial New York and Massachusetts* (1983); and Leopold S. Launitz-Schurer, Jr., *Loyal Whigs and Revolutionaries: The Making of the Revolution in New York, 1765–1776* (1980). For criticisms of Jones's *History*, see Henry P. Johnston, *Observations on Judge Jones' Loyalist History of the American Revolution: How Far Is It an Authority* (1880); and Lawrence Henry Gipson, *The British Empire before the American Revolution*, vol. 13 (1974), pp. 308–12.

MAXINE N. LURIE

JONES, Thomas ap Catesby (24 Apr. 1790–30 May 1858), naval officer, was born in Westmoreland County, Virginia, the son of Catesby Jones and Lettice Tuberville, farmers. After his father's death in September 1800, he entered the College of William and Mary. After spending a year there, he moved to Richmond, where his uncle secured him a midshipman's warrant in the navy. He was not commissioned until the *Chesapeake* incident of June 1807 enabled him to enter the gunboat service at Norfolk.

In January 1808 Jones was transferred to New Orleans and four years later was promoted to lieutenant. His most significant action took place during the War of 1812. In September 1814 Commodore Daniel Patterson and Colonel Robert Ross attacked the encampment of Baratarian pirates Jean Laffitte and Pierre Laffitte. During the melee, Jones distinguished himself by boarding a burning schooner and extinguishing the fire before the ship exploded. On Louisiana's Lake Borgne in late December, with five gunboats and 175 men, he confronted forty barges carrying over a thousand British troops commanded by Vice Admiral Alexander Cochrane. For over two hours Jones's gunboats fought a desperate contest before each succumbed to British superiority. During the battle he received a serious wound in his right shoulder, which affected him the remainder of his life.

In January 1816 Jones began a cruise of the Mediterranean and gained knowledge of and experience with capital ships. Three years later he accepted appointment to the Washington Naval Yard and inherited land in nearby Fairfax County, Virginia, where he built "Sharon," his permanent home. Soon thereafter he was promoted to master commandant and was later named inspector of ordnance for the Washington Navy Yard. In 1823 he married Mary Walker Carter; they had four children.

Early in 1826 Jones sailed to the Pacific, where he assumed command of the *Peacock* and proceeded to Hawaii to establish diplomatic relations. During his voyage he stopped at Tahiti, negotiating a friendship and commercial treaty. In Hawaii in December 1826 he negotiated a treaty to arrest American deserters and worked out a compromise for outstanding debts owed by the chiefs to trading companies. His crowning achievement, however, was arranging a trade agreement in 1827 between the United States and Hawaii that weakened the influence Great Britain had formerly exerted; this treaty, however, was never ratified by the U.S. Senate.

Jones was promoted to captain in March 1829, then named inspector of ordnance for the navy. This latter position allowed him to experiment with new types of ordnance. During 1833 he traveled to stations throughout the country to test every weapon the department owned.

At President Andrew Jackson's behest, in June 1836 Jones was appointed commander of the South Seas Surveying and Exploring Expedition. For months he worked to modify ships, acquire equipment, and train men for the voyage. Yet political intrigues involving

Lieutenant Charles Wilkes and Secretary of the Navy Mahlon Dickerson, combined with Jones's obstinacy and overwork, broke his spirit. In December 1837 the fleet surgeon recommended that Jones resign to save his health. Jones returned to Sharon, where he remained on leave of absence.

Jones was appointed commander of the Pacific Squadron in September 1841 and arrived at Callao, Peru, eight months later. During the summer, reports circulated of an impending war between the United States and Mexico. In early September the British fleet's mysterious departure convinced him that war had begun and that England intended to seize California. Using the Monroe Doctrine as justification, he proceeded to California to forestall British designs. He arrived at Monterey, California, on 19 October 1842 and demanded the town's surrender. The following morning, Mexican officials capitulated. Jones soon learned that no war existed and he had mistakenly seized the city. The Mexican flag was rehoisted, all seized property was returned, American troops reembarked, and a formal salute was fired to the Mexican government. Afterward he traveled to the Hawaiian Islands, where the fleet helped thwart British occupation of Hawaii. In October 1843 Jones returned to the United States to face censure for his actions, but he was not punished.

Jones again received command of the Pacific Squadron and arrived off California in October 1848. Although the Mexican War had ended, he found a chaotic situation. The gold rush stripped San Francisco of its civil government and most of its inhabitants. The navy was needed to maintain order, but it, too, quickly faced problems, including a shortage of supplies and desertion of seamen. To stop desertions, between February 1849 and July 1850 Jones resorted to courts-martial; one resulted in the execution of two seamen. Though California was not yet a U.S. territory, the use of courts-martial in what was considered "national waters," ordinarily convened only by the secretary of the navy, brought about his downfall. He also took interest in the California gold fields and tried to alleviate the region's lack of coinage by using public monies to buy gold dust, thereby interjecting specie into the economy. The Navy Department, charging that he had exceeded his authority, recalled him on 24 April and 10 May 1850; he transferred command to his successor on 1 July 1850.

In December 1850 Jones faced court-martial. He was charged with five counts: fraud against the United States for the misappropriation of government funds, attempting a fraud against the United States relating to false reports concerning money involved in the first charge, scandalous conduct tending to the destruction of good morals, neglect of duty, and oppression. In a curious verdict the court found him innocent of the first two charges yet guilty of the last three, whose specifications reiterated the previous charges. His punishment was a five-year suspension from the service, the first two and a half without pay.

Jones returned to his home a bitter civilian determined to exonerate himself, maintaining he did not violate the law. For the next two years he wrote letters of protest to newspapers, the secretary of the navy, congressmen, and the president pleading his innocence. In February 1853 the secretary of the navy restored him to service and offered command of the navy yard at Mare Island, California. Before he could accept the assignment, Jones was placed on the reserve list and forced to retire. He spent the rest of his life on his farm, a bitter and broken man, and died there.

While Jones is best known for his heroic defense of Lake Borgne in 1814 and his infamous seizure of Monterey, California, in 1842, his diplomatic activities in the Pacific are generally overlooked. During the 1820s and 1840s Jones worked to establish closer diplomatic relations with the Pacific islands, and in doing so he helped prevent England from economically dominating the area.

• The most thorough exposition on Jones is Udolpho Theodore Bradley, "The Contentious Commodore: Thomas ap Catesby Jones of the Old Navy, 1788–1858" (Ph.D. diss., Cornell Univ., 1933), although it contains errors. The Jones Family Papers in the Manuscript Division at the Library of Congress, Washington, D.C., provide information concerning his early life. His participation at the battle of New Orleans has been chronicled in several sources including Clericus, "Biographical Sketch of Thomas ap Catesby Jones," *Military and Naval Magazine of the United States* 3 (1834): 27–34. Frank W. Gapp, " 'The Kind-Eyed Chief': Forgotten Champion of Hawaii's Freedom," *Hawaiian Journal of History* 19 (1985): 101–21, examines his negotiations with Hawaii in the 1820s. The seizure of Monterey has produced several studies, including Hubert H. Bancroft, *History of California*, vol. 4 (1886); and Gene A. Smith, "The War That Wasn't: Thomas ap Catesby Jones's Seizure of Monterey," *California History* 66 (1987): 104–13, 155–57. His last service during the Gold Rush is briefly described in Dan O'Neil, "From Forecastle to Mother Lode: The U.S. Navy in the California Gold Fields," *Southern California Quarterly* 71 (1989): 69–88. Walter Jones et al., *Review of the Evidence, Findings, and Sentence of the Naval Court Martial in the Case of Comm. Thomas ap Catesby Jones* (1851), offers the causes, documents, and proceedings of his dismissal from service in 1852. An obituary is in the *Daily National Intelligencer* (Washington, D.C.), 1 June 1858.

GENE A. SMITH

JONES, Thomas P. (1774–11 Mar. 1848), science publisher and patent expert, was born in Herefordshire County, England, and trained as a physician. Little is known about his early life. As a young man he emigrated to the United States, possibly in company with Joseph Priestley, for he was a member of a small religious society founded in Philadelphia in 1796 as a result of Priestley's lectures there. In the early 1800s Jones became a popular science lecturer and traveled throughout the East, giving lectures in chemistry that included demonstrations of the effects of nitrous oxide or "exhilarating gas." By 1811 Jones was back in Philadelphia offering further lectures on chemistry, optics, pneumatics, electricity, and galvanism, and in 1813 he began to offer similar courses for boys and girls. In 1814 Jones was appointed professor of natural philosophy and chemistry at the College of William and Mary. In 1818 he returned again to Philadelphia, where he continued his lectures, sometimes at C. W. Peale's Museum, and engaged in experiments on steam engines.

In 1824 a group of prominent Philadelphians founded a society, named the Franklin Institute in honor of Benjamin Franklin, for the purpose of offering technical and vocational training to both men and women. One of the leaders was Peter A. Browne, chairman of the lecture committee and an acquaintance of Jones, who had spearheaded an early fight with the Patent Office for the right to use patent models for institute lectures. Browne also advocated the publishing of a journal by the institute. In early 1825 Browne urged the board to hire Jones as professor of mechanics at the institute, adding that Jones would be "a valuable acquisition as the Editor of a Mechanics' journal which he has both the capacity and desire to publish" (Sinclair, p. 53). Jones was offered the position and accepted in March 1825 but was unable to return to Philadelphia until the fall. Meanwhile, Jones had himself purchased the *American Mechanics' Magazine*, a journal published in New York and based on the *Mechanics' Magazine* of London. When the new institute journal was published in February 1826, it had the combined title of the *Franklin Journal and American Mechanics' Magazine* but shortly thereafter became known as the *Journal of the Franklin Institute*. It quickly became a clearinghouse of all kinds of mechanical, scientific, and technical information. One of the popular features of the *Journal* was a list of current patents filed in the government Patent Office. After a disastrous fire in the Patent Office on 16 December 1836 destroyed all the official records of patent applications and grants, the *Journal* suddenly became virtually the only source of information on early patent descriptions and illustrations. The institute was so pleased with the journal that in April 1828 Jones was appointed editor for life, a position he held for twenty years.

On 28 March 1828 Dr. William Thornton, the first chief of the Patent Office, died and Jones was appointed to replace him. He moved to Washington, D.C., and served as superintendent of the Patent Office (which was under the State Department) from 12 April 1828 to 10 June 1829. In 1829 Jones was transferred to an administrative position at the State Department's Bureau of Archives, Laws and Commissions and simultaneously filled the chair of chemistry at Columbian College. After the reorganization Act of 1836, Jones switched back to the Patent Office as an examiner, but he resigned the position in December 1838 to open an office as a patent solicitor, an occupation that did not exist before he created it. One of Jones's more prominent clients was Charles Goodyear.

For the remainder of his life Jones lived in Washington, continuing to edit the *Journal* and holding the chemistry chair at Columbian College Medical School,

which eventually became George Washington University Medical School. He also served as a trustee of that institution from 1840 until his death. He died in Washington, D.C., and is buried in the Congressional Cemetery. He was married and had two daughters. (His wife's name and the date of their marriage unknown.)

It has been said that Jones "was at home in almost every branch of mechanics, natural philosophy, chemistry and physics, and was also familiar to a remarkable degree with all the leading practical arts (Fowler, p. 5). It was Jones's lifelong efforts, however, of keeping the "intelligent mechanic" always in mind, in both his work and his writings, that greatly influenced early American attitudes toward technology and its contribution to industrial development in the United States. In the early days not much attention was paid to patents and patent rights. Jones was one of the first to recognize their value and document them. The Patent Act of 1836 opened the system for wider democratic use, and Jones did much to promote the system and use it.

• Correspondence and papers related to Jones's editorship of the *Franklin Journal* may be found in the Franklin Institute Archives, Philadelphia. Jones published two texts that a reviewer called "two of the best treatises on chemistry and mechanical philosophy which have appeared": *Conversations on Natural Philosophy, in Which the Elements of That Science Are Familiarly Explained* (1826) and *New Conversations on Chemistry, Adapted to the Present State of That Science: Wherein Its Elements Are Clearly and Familiarly Explained* (1831). Jones also published a small monograph, *Observations upon the Automation Chess Player . . . and upon Other Automata and Androides . . .* (1827), and edited the eighth edition of Oliver Evans, *The Young Mill-Wright and Miller's Guide* (1834). Articles by Jones appeared in the *Franklin Journal and American Mechanics' Magazine*, 1826–1827, and the *Journal of the Franklin Institute*, 1827–1847 (the title of the journal changed in 1827). The basic biographical sketch of Jones is Francis Fowler, "Memoir of Dr. Thomas P. Jones," *Journal of the Franklin Institute* 130 (July 1890): 1–7. Biographical information is also available in Wyndham D. Miles, *American Chemists and Chemical Engineers* (1976). The best description of Jones's contribution to the Franklin Institute, as well as additional information on his career, is found in Bruce Sinclair, *Philadelphia's Philosopher Mechanics: A History of the Franklin Institute, 1824–1865* (1974). An obituary and related article are in the *National Intelligencer*, 13 Mar. and 3 Apr. 1848.

ROBERT J. HAVLIK

JONES, Walter (7 Oct. 1776–14 Oct. 1861), lawyer, was born at "Hayfield," Northumberland County, Virginia, the son of Walter Jones, a physician and statesman, and Alice Flood. Schooled at home, Jones developed a love of classical literature from one of his teachers, the eminent if eccentric Scottish orator James Ogilvie. In the 1790s he studied law with Bushrod Washington in Richmond, Virginia, and reportedly secured his license before he reached the age of twenty-one. Shortly thereafter he launched his legal career in the local courts of Fairfax and Loudoun counties. He quickly and steadily advanced in the ranks of the Virginia legal profession and soon resettled in Washington, where in 1802 President Thomas Jefferson (an old friend of Jones's father) appointed him federal attorney for the District of the Potomac and two years later for the District of Columbia.

As district attorney, a post he held until 1821, Jones gained considerable experience and acclaim. He prosecuted two of Aaron Burr's alleged treason co-conspirators in 1807—a case he ultimately lost in the U.S. Supreme Court—but the attention generated by that and other successful efforts brought him much business. Allowed to pursue private practice in addition to his federal duties, Jones soon dominated practice before the Supreme Court, appearing in some of the most important and legally influential cases of the era alongside many prominent national attorneys.

Jones argued the appeals in *The Bank of the U.S. v. Deveaux* in 1810, a diversity of citizenship case that significantly affected the development of federal corporation law for a generation; in *Fairfax's Devisee v. Hunter's Lessee* (1810; a win for Jones) and later *Martin v. Hunter's Lessee*, concerning title to land in Virginia's Northern Neck Proprietary; and as one of the state of Maryland's counsel in *McCulloch v. Maryland* (1819; a loss for Jones's side). Among the most complex and extended appellate cases in which Jones represented clients in the Supreme Court were the well-known *Charles River Bridge Company v. Warren Bridge Company* (1831; he did not participate when the case was reargued and decided in 1837); *Vidal et al. v. Philadelphia* (1844; a loss for Jones), the famous Stephen Girard will case, in which Girard left a bequest to fund a college for poor white orphans in Philadelphia but stipulated that missionaries and ministers be excluded from holding office or visiting the school (Jones and Webster contended that these restrictions were anti-Christian and illegal); and *Groves v. Slaughter* (1841; a win for Jones), with Henry Clay and Daniel Webster, a pivotal appeal concerning the powers of state and federal governments to control the introduction of slaves within state borders.

Although a small man, Jones proved to be an imposing figure in the courtroom. He had a handsome—some said striking—countenance highlighted by "brilliant and expressive brown eyes," as his grandson remembered (quoted in Packard, p. 233). Although never known as a rousing orator, Jones possessed a voice that was rich and clear and could be heard distinctly throughout any courtroom. In eulogies, testimonials, newspaper articles, and personal letters, contemporaries, both within and outside of the legal profession, acknowledged his towering intellect and finely honed reasoning powers, his near encyclopedic knowledge of the law and clear articulation of legal principles, and his skill at bringing the perfect story, anecdote, or literary allusion to play at just the right moment in his arguments. His speeches were superior legal presentations, but because they were not designed to fascinate public audiences, they were not remembered like those of Webster and Clay. Contem-

poraries, however, considered Jones to be "fully their equal in legal ability" (Warren, vol. 2, p. 343).

Although associated in appellate practice with some of the great political figures of the day, and at the same time a strong supporter of the Jefferson Republicans and later the Whig party, Jones did not seek political office. As a young attorney he became a confidant of Jefferson during the latter's presidential administrations, and he was a close friend of James Madison (whom he admired greatly) and of Henry Clay. He wrote articles for local newspapers on issues of the day (most of them appearing anonymously) and supported movements he felt worthy of his commitment. He was a founding member (1817) of the American Colonization Society, for instance, and served as an officer of the Washington National Monument Society. His contemporary Washingtonians expressed particular regard for his involvement in a number of civic improvement and community development projects.

Jones was often referred to as "general" by his contemporaries because he served for many years as commander of the D.C. militia. For the most part, his duties were limited to leading the local forces in inaugural parades, funeral processions, and other ceremonies, although he was known for helping to avert or calm several riots in the turbulent antebellum era by his commanding presence and bravery. His one actual field experience, at the battle of Bladensburg, Maryland, during the War of 1812, proved disastrous (primarily because local troops could not stand up to British regulars), and he found himself defending his own actions and those of several federal officials for some years thereafter.

In 1808 Jones married Anne Lucinda Lee, daughter of Charles Lee, U.S. attorney general in George Washington's presidential administration. The couple had fourteen children, a dozen of whom survived into adulthood. Jones spent much time in his early legal career settling the complicated legal affairs of his father-in-law's estate; however, the marriage provided him with lands in Alexandria and elsewhere in Virginia and with numerous slaves. Although also a wise investor, Jones was not a good money manager, and gradually indebtedness forced him to sell his property in Essex and Fairfax counties, Virginia, and his lots in Alexandria and the District of Columbia. Eventually, he even lost his residence on Second and B streets, near the national capitol, and he and his wife and unmarried daughters were forced to live in the home of another daughter, Virginia, the wife of Dr. Thomas Miller, during the last fifteen years of Jones's life.

Jones remained active in his legal practice until nearly his final days. He was the consummate appellate attorney of his day and, much like his contemporary William Wirt, was capable of skillfully arguing either side of the cases in which he appeared. On his death, in Washington, D.C., the local bar honored his memory with extensive ceremonies.

• Modest collections of Jones's papers can be found at Duke University and at the Virginia Historical Society, Richmond (primarily in the Peyton family papers). Biographical sketches of Jones include Joseph Packard, "General Walter Jones," *Virginia Law Register* 7 (1901–1902): 233–38; Fanny Lee Jones, "Walter Jones and His Times," *Records of the Columbia Historical Society* 5 (1902): 139–50; and L. H. Jones, *Captain Roger Jones of London and Virginia* (1891), pp. 106–10. The best treatment of Jones's legal career is in Charles Warren, *The Supreme Court in United States History* (1923). See also Ludwell Lee Montague, "The Glebe of Fairfax Parish," *Arlington Historical Magazine* 4, no. 3 (1971): 3–10. Obituaries and tributes are in the (Washington, D.C.) *Daily National Intelligencer*, 15–18 Oct. 1861.

E. LEE SHEPARD

JONES, Wesley Livsey (9 Oct. 1863–19 Nov. 1932), U.S. senator, was born in Bethany, Illinois, the son of Wesley Jones and Phoebe McKay, farmers recently arrived from West Virginia. His father died in Union army service only days before Jones's birth; his mother later remarried. Jones grew up in Bethany and attended Southern Illinois College, a small Presbyterian academy at Enfield—a classmate was later Senate colleague William E. Borah—obtaining an A.B. degree in 1885. He read law and was admitted to the Illinois bar in 1886, practicing in nearby Decatur. That same year he married Minda Nelson of Enfield; they had two children. Periodically, he taught school and took part in Republican political campaigns.

During Washington's statehood year, 1889, the couple and Jones's brother moved to North Yakima, a newly established railroad town in a budding agricultural region. He briefly sold real estate before forming a law practice with two partners, and he entered Republican politics. His was the dominant party in Washington, but reform groups posed strong challenges, with Populists controlling state government for several years in the late 1890s. Conservative but pragmatic, Jones recognized the legitimacy of calls for reform and would later often associate with progressive factions in the party. During his first election campaign, however, Jones remained within the dominant faction headed by John L. Wilson, the conservative outgoing U.S. senator from Spokane. In 1898 Jones's successful campaign for congressman-at-large against colorful incumbent James Hamilton Lewis inaugurated his long congressional career. Among the issues affecting the campaign were the conduct of the Spanish-American War (Jones supported President William McKinley's conduct of the war, and Lewis criticized it), an improving state economy, and the apparent decline of enthusiasm for Populist issues, including free silver.

During ten years in the U.S. House of Representatives, Jones viewed himself as the "servant and errand boy" of his constituents, especially conservative business interests, such as forestry, agriculture, land settlement and use, and waterborne commerce. He established himself as a consensus builder and conciliator rather than as an innovator in drafting legislation. His committee assignments and the bills he introduced reflected issues important to his state and his enduring interests: public lands, the merchant marine, and fisheries.

In 1908 Jones defeated the reputedly corrupt Senator Levi Ankeny in a recently enacted preferential primary and was elected to the Senate by the state legislature. He returned to Washington, D.C., as a loyal follower of President William H. Taft, whom he supported even as other local Republicans moved toward Progressive insurgency. Jones maintained his interest in measures of regional importance such as a merchant marine, an Alaska railroad, and tariffs protective of lumber and agriculture, and he supported Interior Secretary Richard A. Ballinger, a Seattleite, in the celebrated dispute with Chief Forester Gifford Pinchot over conservation of public lands. Yet Jones, who regarded himself as "conservatively progressive," also supported many hallmark progressive proposals, including the federal reserve system; labor laws, including the Adamson Eight-hour Bill and a child labor law; the Federal Trade Commission Bill; and the Clayton Antitrust Act. In 1914 he won reelection easily and was among those who welcomed back into the Republican fold the 1912 defectors to the Progressive party. Neutral and even pacifistic at the outbreak of World War I, Jones opposed President Woodrow Wilson's request to arm American ships, but he enthusiastically supported war efforts after the United States entered. He favored the concept of the League of Nations but viewed the treaty as ambiguous and likely to restrict American interests, particularly in the Western Hemisphere. Ultimately he voted for the Lodge Reservations, which were designed to protect the United States from overcommitment in European affairs. Meanwhile he became alarmed by such radical labor groups as the Industrial Workers of the World. Meanwhile, Jones had moved his residence from Yakima to the larger population center of Seattle in 1918, a change some viewed as a matter of political expediency.

During the 1920s Jones became more clearly identified with certain policies and programs that he aggressively promoted. The needs of eastern Washington constituents had aroused an early interest in land reclamation; in the early 1900s Jones was responsible for the federal construction of irrigation canals in the Yakima Valley helping to transform that broad but barren valley into one rich with farms and orchards. Jones hit his stride advocating projects to make other western drylands productive and wealthy, and he formed alliances with directors of the Reclamation Service. Yet progress was delayed by rivalries between competing geographical regions, farmers disillusioned by earlier projects, and a personal distaste for federal paternalism.

As local agitation mounted, Jones became a major advocate of further irrigation and then hydroelectric projects throughout the Columbia River basin. Nevertheless, he maintained a neutral posture between proponents of a gravity-flow system diverting waters from the far northwest highlands of the state and those favoring a dam at the Grand Coulee of the Columbia. He eventually veered toward the latter and introduced the original legislation—destined to die in committee—that foreshadowed the construction of Grand Coulee Dam.

Similarly, Jones's long advocacy of a strong maritime service prompted him to steer through the Merchant Marine Act of 1920 that gave the U.S. Shipping Board a central role in developing a merchant marine and establishing shipping routes. U.S. vessels were to carry coastwise cargo. Over the next decade he continued efforts to reconcile private and governmental interests and to offset competition from foreign cargo carriers. He also took a moralistic stance favoring prohibition at federal, state, and local levels throughout his career. In line with his constituency, he increasingly supported "farm bloc" measures and worked to guarantee tariff protection for lumber-industry products.

With considerable Senate seniority, Jones chaired the Appropriations Committee from 1929 to 1932. He continued to support the increasingly unpopular President Herbert Hoover while the Great Depression mounted, and he seemed to lose touch with public opinion in his state, including local frustration with Prohibition. In the 1932 Democratic landslide, Jones lost his seat to a onetime Socialist and recent Republican, Homer T. Bone, garnering even fewer votes than Hoover in the state of Washington. Having suffered declining health for several years and exhausted from the recent political campaign, he was hospitalized the day after his defeat. Ten days later he died in Seattle of heart failure.

• The Wesley L. Jones Papers are held in the Manuscripts and Archives Division, University of Washington Libraries, Seattle. He is the subject of a Ph.D. dissertation by William Stuart Forth, "Wesley L. Jones: A Political Biography" (Univ. of Washington, 1962). Obituaries are in major Washington State newspapers, including the *Seattle Daily Times*, 19 Nov. 1932, the *Post-Intelligencer* (Seattle), 20 Nov. 1932, and the *Yakima Daily Herald*, 19 Nov. 1932.

CHARLES P. LEWARNE

JONES, William (1760–6 Sept. 1831), merchant and cabinet officer, was born in Philadelphia, Pennsylvania. Nothing is known about his family or his childhood, except that he was apprenticed at a shipyard in Bethlehem, Pennsylvania. When the revolutionary war broke out, he joined a company of volunteers at the age of sixteen and fought in the battles of Trenton and Princeton. Later in the war Jones served in the Continental navy. He was twice wounded and twice captured. By the war's end he had been promoted to first lieutenant for gallantry. He married Eleanor (maiden name and date of marriage unknown).

Little is known of his immediate postwar activity. In the early 1790s Jones was serving in the merchant marine, stationed in Charleston, South Carolina. He settled permanently in Philadelphia in 1793 and prospered as a merchant. He became involved in politics as a Jeffersonian Republican, and he was elected to the Seventh Congress (1801–1803). Jones's standing was such that President Thomas Jefferson offered him the position of secretary of the navy in 1801, but Jones declined. After one term, he returned to an active political, social, and economic life in Philadelphia. In 1805 he became a member of the American Philosophical Society. Jones sailed around the world between 1805 and 1807.

When Paul Hamilton resigned as secretary of the navy in December 1812, President James Madison offered the position to Jones, who accepted reluctantly. Jones was well aware of the difficulties that confronted him. The War of 1812 was well under way, and although the small American navy had won several surprising victories in 1812, they were unlikely to be repeated against the vastly larger British fleet. Jones opposed ship duels with the Royal Navy, and he moved quickly to stop such actions. Instead, in 1813 Jones issued specific orders to his naval commanders to go "on station," to undertake planned cruises to specific areas. Some splendid victories were won, but naval commanders objected to the limitations placed on their free hand to fight at will.

Jones was a vigorous and efficient secretary. Soon after taking office in late January 1813, he called for more ships in the fleet and for more personnel in his office. One of Jones's most important duties was obtaining naval building yards and naval depots on Lakes Erie, Ontario, and Champlain. With the assistance of Commodore Isaac Chauncey, a naval yard was established at Black Rock on the Niagara River, which was later removed to Erie, Pennsylvania. Ship carpenters, seamen, naval stores, and supplies were rushed to this point. Ships built there enabled Commodore Oliver Hazard Perry to win the critical battle of Lake Erie in 1813. On Lake Ontario a disappointing stalemate was achieved with each side achieving temporary naval supremacy with the floating of each new ship. Better results were obtained on Lake Champlain with Commodore Thomas Macdonough's victory over the British in September 1814. The construction, manning, and provisioning of these fleets were probably the most brilliant naval achievements of the War of 1812, and Jones deserves much of the credit for the success of these endeavors.

In addition to his responsibilities as secretary of the navy, Jones was also appointed acting secretary of the Treasury in May 1813, a position he held until February 1814. Because the government's credit was sinking, Jones recommended additional taxes, but his proposals were ignored, and the military forces remained underfunded. Jones's own personal finances worsened during his government service; by the end of the war he had fallen deeply in debt. On 11 September 1814 he submitted his resignation, effective 1 December.

Shortly before leaving office, Jones submitted to Congress a plan for the reorganization of the navy. He recommended the creation of a board of commissioners to supervise the construction of war ships as well as the procurement of naval stores and to advise the secretary of the navy on deployment of the fleet. He also called for the creation of a naval academy and a system of compulsory service to supply seamen for the navy. The latter two recommendations were not acted on at that time, but the Board of Commissioners was established early in 1815.

When the Republicans established the second Bank of the United States in July 1816, Jones was chosen by President Madison and Secretary of the Treasury Alexander James Dallas to become the president of the bank. Jones was an unfortunate choice. Although specie backing for bank notes was resumed in 1817, Jones encouraged the branch banks in the interior of the country to expand their loans to aid local businesses. Speculators in land took advantage of the loosening of available credit. Southern and western banks rarely had to redeem their bank notes, which were frequently redeemed in the eastern cities. This eventually had the effect of shifting capital and resources to the interior. The board of the Bank of the United States belatedly recognized the problem and moved to curtail southern and western loans and to force a transfer of funds to eastern banks. This halted the postwar expansion and precipitated a financial crisis. A House of Representatives investigation found evidence of mismanagement and even fraud in some banks. Although no direct charges were made against Jones, he was removed from office after the report was issued in January 1819.

Jones returned to mercantile activities and prospered in the steamship business. In 1822 he wrote a pamphlet, *Winter Navigation on the Delaware*. From 1827 to 1829 he served as the collector of the port of Philadelphia. Jones died in Bethlehem, Pennsylvania.

Jones's inept performance as president of the Bank of the United States has clouded his reputation, which would be better if based on his conduct as secretary of the navy alone. President Madison spoke highly of Jones, calling him "the fittest minister who had ever been charged with the Navy Department." That view has not been uniformly accepted by historians. While Jones was not one of the most outstanding cabinet officers, he served his country competently and at great personal sacrifice.

• A manuscript collection of Jones's papers is in the Historical Society of Pennsylvania. Further information about his career may be found in Edward K. Eckert, "William Jones: Mr. Madison's Secretary of the Navy," *Pennsylvania Magazine of History and Biography* (Apr. 1972): 167–82. See also Charles O. Paullin, *Paullin's History of Naval Administration, 1775–1911* (1968); Harold D. Langley, *Social Reform in the U.S. Navy, 1798–1862* (1967); Donald R. Hickey, *The War of 1812: A Forgotten Conflict* (1989); and Thomas Payne Govan, *Nicholas Biddle: Nationalist and Public Banker, 1786–1844* (1959).

C. EDWARD SKEEN

JONES, William (28 Mar. 1871–29 Mar. 1909), ethnologist, was born on the Sauk and Fox Indian Reservation, Kansas, the son of Henry Clay Jones, a blacksmith and farmer, and Sarah Penny. After his mother's death when he was a year old, Jones was raised by his paternal grandmother, Katiqwa, the daughter of a Fox chief. Jones had a traditional Fox

upbringing until the age of nine, when his grandmother died and he returned to his father's home. The eight years spent living with his grandmother had a strong influence on his personal interests and choice of career.

Jones was chosen to receive scholarships to both Hampton Institute and Phillips Andover Academy as a result of these institutions' attempts to recruit qualified Native American students. After graduation from Andover, Jones attended Harvard College, from which he received a bachelor's degree in ethnology in 1900. He entered Columbia University that fall to study Native American ethnology with Franz Boas, the leading scholar in the field. By 1904 Jones had received both an M.A. and a Ph.D. in anthropology from Columbia.

Jones's continued relationship with his Fox extended family instilled within him a deep interest in and commitment to the study of the Algonquian language and traditional culture. Living in a time of great change for Native American groups in the Midwest, he was committed to the goal, fundamental to American anthropology at the turn of the century, of recording the ancient ways of his people as these traditions slipped out of the hands of all but the oldest members of tribes.

Jones made important use of his knowledge of Sauk and Fox traditions and his intimacy with the Fox people during his years at Columbia. In 1901 and 1902 he undertook fieldwork among these tribes in Oklahoma and Iowa for the American Museum of Natural History and the Bureau of American Ethnology. Much of the excellent material on language and literature he collected from these expeditions appeared as *Fox Texts*, volume one of the Publications of the American Ethnological Society. Boas describes Jones's publication as

the first considerable body of Algonquian lore published in accurate and reliable form in the native tongue, with translation rendering faithfully the style and the contents of the original. In form, and so far as philological accuracy is concerned, these texts are probably among the best North American texts that have ever been published. (*American Anthropologist* 11 [1909]: 138)

In 1903, after completion of his fieldwork among the Sauk and Fox, Jones was appointed research assistant in the Carnegie Institution and began to investigate the language and culture of the Ojibwe, another Algonquian tribe, at Fort William and Grand River in the Great Lakes region. In 1904 he completed his dissertation, "Some Principles of Algonkian Word Formation," a grammar of the Fox language, at Columbia and resumed his studies of the Ojibwe.

Through 1905 Jones conducted intensive research among the Ojibwe tribes living in Bois Fort and Leech Lake in northern Minnesota, focusing primarily on their language, folklore, and cultural traditions. He developed a strong working knowledge of the Ojibwe language and was able to record a large amount of material in its original form. Jones's greatest contribution from this fieldwork, his large collection of traditional Ojibwe tales, were told to him by master storytellers within the various bands with which he worked. Committed to presenting the English translation of the texts along with the transcribed Ojibwe originals, Jones has, consequently, left a legacy of sound scholarship that fulfills his intent to preserve the traditional heritage as accurately as possible.

After 1905 Jones looked forward to continuing his research in North American ethnology and developing his knowledge and understanding of various Native American groups. While he had hoped to undertake research on the Naskapi Indians in Labrador, no positions were open at the time. In 1906 George Dorsey of the Field Museum of Natural History in Chicago offered Jones his choice of three locations for ethnological expeditions: Africa, the South Seas, or the Philippines. Disappointed not to continue with his Native American research but in need of employment, Jones chose the latter expedition. In September 1907 he left for the Philippines, where he undertook ethnological research and collection while working and living primarily with the Ilongot tribe. Artifacts collected from this expedition are now held in the Field Museum.

This period of Jones's life has been analyzed and discussed in several sources in an attempt to understand the circumstances leading to his murder by members of the Ilongot tribe. Many suspect that jealousies among tribes with which Jones worked precipitated his death. Others have suggested that Jones's growing impatience with, and cultural insensitivity toward, an Ilongot tribal elder led to his murder. Jones died at Dumabutu, Isbela Province, Luzon, Philippine Islands. He never married.

Jones was one of many early twentieth century American ethnologists who were devoted to the study and preservation of Native American language and culture. Without these scientists' careful research and their commitment to accuracy and detail, knowledge of many Native American groups who once thrived but have now dwindled or disappeared would be lost to us. Jones's role in this process of collection and preservation is significant because of the accuracy and detail of his work. His collections of Fox and Ojibwe texts provide an enduring glimpse into the traditional worldview and culture of these people, and his published texts will continue to play an important role in the study of Algonquian language and culture.

• Jones's diaries and other correspondence connected to his work in the Philippines are in the Field Museum of Natural History in Chicago. His Ojibwe linguistic and ethnographic field notes, including photographs, are in the American Philosophical Society in Philadelphia, which also holds his correspondence with Franz Boas concerning his fieldwork, preparation of manuscripts, and publication of his Fox texts. Jones's primary publications are "Episodes in the Culture-Hero Myth of the Sauks and Foxes," *Journal of American Folklore* 14 (1901): 225–39; "Some Principles of Algonquian Word Formation," *American Anthropologist* 6 (1904): 369–412; "The Algonkian Manitou," *Journal of American Folklore* 18 (1905): 183–90; "Central Algonquian," *Annual Archaeo-*

logical Report (1905), pp. 136–46; "An Algonquian Syllabary," in *Boas Anniversary Album*, ed. Gerthold Laufer (1906); "Mortuary Observances and the Adoption Rites of the Algonkin Foxes of Iowa," *Congrès International des Américanistes* 1 (1906): 263–77; *Fox Texts*, vol. 1, Publications of the American Ethnological Society (1907); "Notes on the Fox Indians," *Journal of American Anthropology* 24 (1911): 209–37; "Algonquian (Fox), an Illustrative Sketch," Bureau of American Ethnology Bulletin no. 40, pt. 1 (1911). Jones also collected and compiled *Kickapoo Texts*, trans. Truman Michelson (1915), and *Ojibwa Texts*, ed. Michelson (1917–1919), the unfinished texts of which were retrieved after Jones's death and returned to Boas, who passed them on to Michelson for completion. A biography of Jones by Henry Milner Rideout, *William Jones* (1912), uses Jones's diaries as a primary source of information. For a discussion of the events leading to Jones's death see Barbara Stoner, "Why Was William Jones Killed?" in Field Museum of Natural History Bulletin no. 42 (1971): 10–13. The most notable obituary is by Franz Boas in *American Anthropologist*, n.s. 11 (1909): 137–39.

RIDIE WILSON GHEZZI

JONES, William Palmer (17 Oct. 1819–25 Sept. 1897), psychiatrist, was born in Adair County, Kentucky. He was the great-grandson of David Jones, a Welsh immigrant who settled in Maryland. His father, William Jones, a native of Lincoln County, Kentucky, fought with Andrew Jackson at New Orleans and died at the age of forty-two. His mother, Mary Powell Jones, was the daughter of Virginia farmer Robert Powell, who held the rank of major during the Revolution. Left with nine children to raise when she was widowed, she cared for them until her death in 1851 at the age of forty-five. Jones spent his earliest years living on a farm and received little formal education. Deciding at a young age to pursue a medical career, he was tutored by Dr. T. Q. Walker for two years before attending Louisville Medical College. Subsequently he earned medical degrees from both the Medical College of Ohio and Memphis Medical College.

In 1840, at the age of twenty, Jones started a medical practice in Edmonton, Kentucky, but soon relocated to Bowling Green in the same state. He lived there until he moved to Nashville, Tennessee, where he was to reside with his wife, Elizabeth J. Currey (they married in Oct. 1851) and their nine children until his death in 1897. In 1858 Jones, along with a group of his colleagues, founded the Shelby Medical College. Here he held the position of professor of materia medica. He was a Union supporter during the Civil War and upon the arrival of Union troops in Nashville was appointed to supervise the Academy Hospital, the city's first federal hospital.

A dedicated physician, Jones devoted much of his life to the study and care of the mentally ill, and it is in this field where his primary contributions lie. From 1862 until 1869 he held the position of medical superintendent at the Tennessee Hospital for the Insane. Many nineteenth-century mental institutions were reluctant to racially integrate their facilities, and Jones, recognizing the void in the care for blacks, successfully lobbied for the creation of an adjacent facility. The

Central Hospital for the Insane was opened in 1868 and was one of the earliest American asylums founded exclusively to treat blacks suffering from insanity. In 1876 he was elected president of Nashville Medical College, where he was professor of psychology, medicine, and mental hygiene.

In addition to working actively as a physician, Jones wrote and edited a number of publications. In 1852 he established the *Parlor Visitor*, a popular journal that was published for a number of years. From 1853 to 1856 he was co-editor of the *Southern Journal of Medicine and Physical Sciences*, published in Nashville. In 1874 he became the associate editor of the *Tennessee School Journal*. His interest in procuring adequate treatment for the insane is reflected in his two final contributions to the medical journals, "Necessities of the Insane in Tennessee" and "Adequate and Impartial Provision for the Insane of the State." Actively participating in a number of organizations, Jones was a member of the American Medical Association, the Association of Medical Superintendents of American Institutions for the Insane, the American Medico-Psychological Association (a forerunner to the American Psychiatric Association), and the American Association for the Advancement of Science.

Besides playing an important role in health care, Jones wielded considerable influence in both local and state politics. He served as president of the Nashville city council and also was elected to the position of city postmaster. In 1873 he was elected to the state senate. As he did in his medical career, Jones continued in his efforts to fight racial discrimination, this time with regard to education. He introduced into the senate a bill that became known as the public school law, providing for "equal educational advantages for all the children of the state, without reference to race, color, or condition." He also continued to lobby on behalf of the mentally ill, and the senate approved the establishment of two additional facilities for the treatment of the insane. William Palmer Jones, through his many achievements in the fields of medicine and education, as well as his tireless struggle to end racial discrimination, undoubtedly influenced the lives of countless individuals.

• For brief accounts of the life of William Palmer Jones, see William B. Atkinson, M.D., ed., *The Physicians and Surgeons of the United States* (1878); Henry Hurd, ed., *The Institutional Care of the Insane in the United States and Canada*, vol. 3 (1916) and vol. 4 (1917); and Howard Kelly and Walter Burrage, eds., *Dictionary of American Medical Biography* (1928). Two books by Gerald N. Grob provide insight into the treatment of the mentally ill in the nineteenth century: *Mental Institutions in America: Social Policy to 1875* (1973) and *Mental Illness and American Society, 1875–1940* (1987). Obituaries are in the *Journal of the American Medical Association*, 2 Oct. 1897, and the *American Journal of Insanity*, 18 Apr. 1898.

CHRISTINE CLARK ZEMLA

JONES, Willie (25 May 1741–18 June 1801), statesman, was born in Northampton County, North Carolina, the son of Robert Jones, a colonial agent and colonial attorney general, and Sarah Cobb. He attended Eton in England, his father's alma mater, until 1758, when he left to take the "grand tour" of the Continent. Choosing agriculture as his vocation, tore down his ancestral home and settled in Halifax in an ornate abode of his own construction, apparently devoted to a life of celibacy, society, and—as the imperial crisis reached its peak—politics; his new residence, "The Groves," became a center of the North Carolina Whigs. Jones's first office was a seat in the lower house of the colonial assembly in 1767, in which he played a very inconspicuous part. He also had a seat in the assembly of 1771, and his political path to that point was marked by an aristocrat's association with the royal governors of the colony.

When Governor William Tryon put down the North Carolina Regulation in 1771, Jones was among the colonial forces. On 15 May 1771 he was appointed aide-de-camp to the governor with the rank of captain. On Tryon's departure of the colony for New York later that year, Jones was among those publicly lamenting his departure. Tryon's successor, Governor Josiah Martin, appointed him to the colonial council. However, Jones became one of the radical leaders of the North Carolina Whigs when friction with England began. He therefore refused to accept his place on the council, which had long been seen as one of the leading honorifics in the governors' gift.

In 1774 Jones was chairman of the Halifax Committee of Public Safety. As the crisis progressed, he served in the North Carolina Provincial Congress in 1774 and 1776. That Jones was a leader of the patriot cause was fairly predictable in light of the fact that he was immensely wealthy and had been powerful even in prerevolutionay days. Jones was elected president of the North Carolina Committee of Public Safety in 1776, and he became the first governor ex officio of independent North Carolina. Also in 1776 the Continental Congress asked him to be superintendent of Indian affairs for the southern colonies; his duties in this regard prevented him from attending the Provincial Congress, and he resigned his superintendency later that year. In these assemblies, as in all public activities, Jones was seldom heard, yet his presence was always felt. All agree that he was the dominant person in the North Carolina revolutionary movement, and his method seems to have been private persuasion rather than public oratory; a contemporary said, "He could draw a bill in better language than any other man of his day" (Robinson, p. 24). He also seems to have been averse to political grudges, earning a reputation as an even-handed, though steadfastly radical and democratic, statesman. Also in 1776 Jones, whose first name was pronounced "WHY-lee," gave up his avowed celibacy and married Mary Montfort. They had fifteen children, five of whom survived to adulthood.

Jones's land holdings were substantial, including 9,942.5 acres in Halifax County alone. Those lands contained at least one racetrack, and Jones had many fine racehorses. He owned approximately 120 slaves in the census of 1790, and he had a significant private library.

Jones was a member of the first North Carolina constitutional convention in 1776, and the state's constitution has often been held to be the product of his hand. He served in the North Carolina House of Commons from 1776 to 1778, and his state sent him to the Continental Congress in 1780 and 1781. Jones left Congress in 1781 on the basis that the war had ended, and so had the Congress's legitimate function; the only sovereignty he recognized was that of North Carolina. In 1783 Jones paid the price for standing up on behalf of Loyalist Carolinians' claims under the Treaty of Paris: he failed to secure election to the assembly. Although he had long opposed strengthening the Confederation government, Jones was elected a delegate to the Federal Convention in Philadelphia in 1787; he refused to attend.

Having been the leading figure in North Carolina politics since the onset of the Revolution, Jones was the dominant influence at the first North Carolina ratification convention in 1788. There, he led his fellow Carolinians to their rejection of the proposed constitution. Following Thomas Jefferson's suggestion, Jones intended for his state to hold out in favor of previous amendments; at Jones's behest, the convention proposed a set of twenty-six. When the political tide in his state shifted in favor of ratification, Jones voted against the move in the state senate to call a new convention; he then retired from public life to follow agricultural pursuits. Yet, by the time Jones's opposition to the new document abated, Congressman James Madison had already moved to amend the Constitution in Congress. His ongoing attitude toward the U.S. government is illustrated by the fact that when President George Washington, touring the South, came to Halifax, Jones said he could not greet him as the president of the United States, although he would be happy to meet him as a general and gentleman.

Known in his lifetime as "the Jefferson of North Carolina" (Robinson, p. 1), Jones served on the first board of trustees of the University of North Carolina after his political retirement, and he helped establish the state capital and capitol. He died at his summer home in Raleigh, North Carolina. At his request, his grave was left unmarked, and he supposedly had himself buried with his head to the South and his feet to the North to symbolize his disbelief in Christianity.

• The official records of Jones's career are in *Colonial Records of North Carolina*, vols. 9–10 (1886), and *State Records of North Carolina*, vols. 11–20 (1886). The *Biographical Directory of Members of Congress, 1774–1961* provides a bare outline of his career. Also of use is Robert Rutland, *The Ordeal of the Constitution: The Antifederalists and the Ratification Struggle of 1787–1788*, 2d ed. (1983), which shows Jones's role in North Carolina's initial rejection of the federal Constitution in its context. The same subject is treated, to even better effect, in "A Great Refusal: The North Carolina Ratification Convention of 1788," in M. E. Bradford, *Original Intentions: On the Making and Ratification of the United States Constitution* (1993), pp. 71–86. The closest thing to a biography is Blackwell P. Robinson's two-part article "Willie Jones of Halifax," *North Carolina Historical Review* 18 (Apr. 1941): 1–26, and (July 1941): 133–70. A few old histories of North Carolina in Jones's time feature him prominently; one in particular is John Wheeler, *Historical Sketches of North Carolina, from 1584 to 1851* (1851). Jones is also a central figure in William Allen, *History of Halifax County* (1918), a study of Jones's home county; and in Louise Trenholme, *The Ratification of the Federal Constitution in North Carolina* (1932).

K. R. CONSTANTINE GUTZMAN

JONSON, Raymond (18 July 1891–10 May 1982), painter and theater graphic designer, was born Carl Raymond Johnson near Chariton, Iowa, the son of the Reverend Gustav Johnson and Josephine Abrahamson. Jonson was home-schooled until 1899, when he attended his first school in Colorado Springs, Colorado, where the family lived for a brief period. In 1902 the family settled in Portland, Oregon. Jonson studied at the Portland Art Museum in 1909 with an instructor who had been a student of Arthur Wesley Dow. Jonson moved to Chicago in 1910 to study art at the Academy of Fine Arts. He later enrolled at the Art Institute of Chicago.

While at the academy in 1912, Jonson roomed with students J. Blanding Sloan and Carl Oscar Erikson and began an informal yet close teacher-student association with B. J. O. Nordfeldt, who served as Jonson's early mentor. Along with Nordfeldt, these three young artists were a significant part of the Jackson Park art colony and the artistic renaissance in Chicago. During this period Jonson had the opportunity to view the work of Arthur Dove in 1912 and the work of European modernists at the Armory Show in 1913. Jonson wrote his mother on 24 March 1913, "Such an exhibit. . . . The Cubists, Futurists, Extremists, etc. . . . There are no rules in art, . . . each man may paint as to express himself or to express . . . the way one feels. . . . Believe me there is some movement in art. . . . And to think . . . I am here where I can see, learn, and take part in the thing my system seems to be built with. Art. Such a word."

In 1913 Jonson, known then as C. Raymond Johnson, became the graphic art designer for the Chicago Little Theatre (CLT). The presentation of Euripides' *Trojan Women*, acclaimed for Jonson's inventive set design and lighting, became CLT's signature production. The Trojan wall, the single facade of the stage set and the focal point of stage activity, utilized a minimal aesthetic to create monumentality on a tiny stage. Expressive lighting created by Jonson's invention of a nine-switch dimmer board enhanced this effect. For his efforts Jonson achieved international recognition, and his innovations are still utilized today in American theater. In 1916 Jonson married Vera E. White, secretary and actress for the CLT. They had no children. He began teaching at the Chicago Academy of Fine Arts, and the CLT presented its final season in 1917.

After receiving a scholarship in 1919 to the MacDowell Colony at Peterborough, New Hampshire, Jonson taught stagecraft in 1921 at Grace Hickox Studios in Chicago. That same year in Chicago he met Russian mystic and artist Nicholas Roerich and helped him to establish Cor Ardens, an idealistic brotherhood of artists. A final important early theoretical development for Jonson also occurred in 1921 when he first viewed Wassily Kandinsky's paintings and later that year read Kandinsky's *The Art of Spiritual Harmony*, which introduced him to the analogy between art and music and the idea that there was a spiritual value within the inner, emotional content of art that could be pursued through color. He wrote in his diary, "It is the greatest book concerning art I have ever read. . . . To be able to live and actually work in the spiritual is of course a great ideal and one to hope and work for."

During Jonson's Chicago period, the development of his minimal aesthetic, his modernist perspective, his idealistic and spiritual purpose for art, and his application of color as emotional equivalents within his paintings set the course for his life's work.

Jonson moved to Santa Fe, New Mexico, in 1924 to make painting the center of his life. Before leaving Chicago, Jonson changed his name to reflect the Swedish spelling. He painted abstract landscapes, including the 1928 *Grand Canyon Trilogy*, believed to represent the first shaped canvas by an American painter. Works of this period and those of the 1930s established Jonson in the nonobjective arena of painting. In a 1928 letter to philosopher Charles Morris, Jonson wrote, "I feel that it is the inner significance of things that counts, and that is a quality that is abstract. . . . I believe all emotions, if pure enough, are abstract. Also, all forms exist to us because of an abstract rhythm and design. It is my aim to define them." Jonson's abstract works and promotion of modernist issues and images were a counterforce to the provincial, regional, and realistic paintings being done in New Mexico at that time. In his fight to keep abstraction before the objecting public, in 1927 he established the Modernist Wing at the Museum of New Mexico in Santa Fe, which held a total of thirty-two monthly exhibitions.

In the winter of 1931–1932 Jonson traveled to New York for his exhibition at the Delphic Studios and then to Chicago to renew former connections. After receiving a negative response to his exhibition, he returned to Santa Fe and became, as MaLin Wilson says, "increasingly proud of his outsider position, his purity and independence from the vagaries and degradations of the market" (p. 22). In 1934, with the support of the Works Progress Administration, he painted six large murals for the University of New Mexico's library and began to commute to Albuquerque to teach at the university's Department of Art and Art History.

In 1938 Jonson organized the Transcendental Painting Group (TPG), comprised of Jonson and nine other painters: Emil Bisttram, Stuart Walker, William Lumpkins, Agnes Pelton, Florence Miller Pierce, Horace Towner Pierce, Robert Gribbroek, Lawren Harris, and Ed Garman. These artists explained that their purpose was "the development and presentation of various types of non-representational painting; painting that finds its source in the creative imagination . . . to carry painting beyond the appearance of the physical world, through new concepts of space, color, light and design, to imaginative realms that are idealistic and spiritual." A transcendental painting often involves the use of unique and eccentric nonobjective shapes that may be geometric, biomorphic, or both, that are located within a created environment that is a nonreferential space, often perceived as an atmospheric field. The most important part of the painting is the artist's intention to transcend the materials and conventional understandings to establish a sense of idealism and the spiritual. Through the created art icon and the viewer's receptivity, the artist offers a perspective for the betterment of human society.

Jonson and Dane Rudhyar, composer-musician-astrologer, established the American Foundation for Transcendental Painting, an educational and supportive organization for transcendental painting. In 1939 the TPG exhibited at the Golden Gate International Exposition and the Guggenheim Museum. Because of the war the group broke apart in 1941, but the TPG remained one of America's important early indigenous art organizations.

Jonson established the Jonson Gallery on the UNM campus in 1950, presenting the university with works from his private collection to remain as the gallery's permanent collection. His gift included his own paintings, Chicago Little Theatre designs, works by other artists with whom he had been associated, among them Anthony Angarola, Jean Xceron, Elaine De Kooning, Joseph Albers, and TPG artists, and works by his students, such as Richard Diebenkorn, Joe H. Herrera, and Connie Fox. The gallery continues Jonson's commitment to support underrecognized or emerging artists, to provide the opportunity to view art works that would otherwise not be seen, and to regularly exhibit works by Jonson.

Jonson was at the center of an ongoing exchange of artists and ideas in Albuquerque during the 1950s. A mature group of art students enrolled at the university after World War II, many backed by the G.I. Bill. Jonson organized UNM exhibitions by artists such as Josef Albers, Arshile Gorky, and Xceron, giving these students direct experience with leading artists of the time. At Jonson Gallery he hung works by Olavi Sihvonen, Diebenkorn, Adja Yunkers, Enrique Montenegro, and many others. During the 1950s New Mexico became a major environment outside of New York City and Los Angeles in which American artists could create art. This active, receptive art community could not have happened without Raymond Jonson. For the foreword of Ed Garman's 1976 biography of Jonson, De Kooning wrote, "When I met Jonson [1957], I knew I had found the key—the force that created a climate that enabled art to endure in a desert."

Jonson retired from teaching in 1954 and served as professor emeritus. As his career came to a close, Jonson received in 1972 a grant from the National Endowment for the Arts, and in 1975 he was awarded the New Mexico Arts Commission Award for achievement and excellence in visual arts. Jonson's last painting, *Polymer No. 19*, was painted in 1978.

During his career as a pioneer modernist painter his most remarkable contributions were realized through the painted image and the promotion of abstract and nonobjective art. His work is represented in major museums throughout the United States such as the Museum of Modern Art, National Museum of American Art, Smithsonian Institution, San Francisco Museum of Modern Art, and the Art Institute of Chicago. He died in Albuquerque.

Jonson's seventy-year painting career included stylistic variations, yet each work was crafted with such precision and care that it too becomes an identifying characteristic of his body of work. Jonson moved from executing watercolor theater stage designs and radically painted oil portraits of actors and his wife, such as *Violet Light* (1918), in which he explored a new sense of color inspired by the European moderns, to the landscape as subject. Progressing from allegorical content, such as in *Winter (Season's Series)* (1922), to some of his most magnificent abstract works in the *Earth Rhythms* series (1923–1927) and the *Grand Canyon Trilogy* (1927–1928), Jonson began to understand that light, rhythm, form, texture, and color were his real subjects. His first steps toward nonobjective images began with works such as the alphabet series, *Variations on a Rhythm A–Z*. The pursuit to establish pure emotional experience and an inner environment on canvas developed with the *Growth Variant* series that he created in the early 1930s. In 1938 he began to use the airbrush, a tool that allowed him to use watercolors and casein tempera to create spontaneous, translucent form, light, and texture in paintings such as the transcendental work *Watercolor No. 9* (1938). Jonson began the use of polymer emulsions in 1957 and by 1960, with few exceptions, used only polymers (acrylics) because he believed polymer was the most perfect medium ever devised. His work ultimately achieved total nonobjectivity in form and met his earliest desire for his art to inspire a sense of the spiritual.

• Jonson's papers, including diaries, scrapbooks, and lectures, are at the Jonson Gallery on the University of New Mexico campus in Albuquerque. The Archives of American Art at the Smithsonian Institution contain documentation of the Jonson Gallery archive, including artists' files, through 1965. The only complete Jonson biography is Ed Garman, *Raymond Jonson Painter* (1976). References to Jonson's early painting career appears in Sheldon Cheney, *A Primer of Modern Art* (1924); Leo Katz, *Understanding Modern Art* (1939); Martha Candler Cheney, *Modern Art in America* (1939); and Sheldon Cheney, *The Story of Modern Art* (1941). Documentation of the New Mexico years in the context of American abstract painting is in essays by Charles C. Eldredge et al., *Art in New Mexico, 1900–1945: Paths to Taos and Santa Fe* (1986); Sharyn Rohlfsen Udall, *Modernist Painting in New Mexico 1913–1935* (1984); MaLin Wilson, "Cosmic Cityscapes: Desiring an Ideal," in *Cityscapes* (exhibition catalog, 1989); and Tiska Blankenship, *Geometrical Form in the Pursuit of a Unifying Principle* (exhibition catalog, 1990). Two dissertations that include extensive discussions of Jonson's Chicago Little Theatre years are Arthur Feinsod, "The Simple Stage—Its Origins in the Modern American Theater" (Trinity College, Hartford, Conn., 1992), and Bernard Frank Dukore, "Maurice Browne and the Chicago Little Theatre" (Univ. of Illinois, Urbana, 1957). Two other early theater viewpoints are Sheldon Cheney, *The Art Theatre* (1917), and Clarence Stratton, *Producing in Little Theaters* (1921). Discussions of the Transcendental Painting Group can be found in Garman, *Vision and Spirit: The Transcendental Painting Group* (exhibition catalog, 1997); Marianne Lorenz, "Kandinsky and American Abstraction," in *Theme and Improvisation: Kandinsky and the American Avant-Garde 1912–1950* (exhibition catalog, 1992); and Maurice Tuckman, "Hidden Meanings in Abstract Art," in *The Spiritual in Art: Abstract Painting 1890–1985* (exhibition catalog, 1986). A book discussing technical aspects of Jonson's painting is Russell O. Woody, Jr., *Painting with Synthetic Media* (1965).

TISKA BLANKENSHIP

JOPLIN, Janis (19 Jan. 1943–4 Oct. 1970), rock singer, was born Janis Lyn Joplin in Port Arthur, Texas, the daughter of Seth Joplin, an engineer, and Dorothy East, a businesswoman. A quiet and studious child, during her years at Thomas Jefferson High School Joplin began showing signs of the defiant and iconoclastic personality for which she later became famous. Overweight and uncomfortable with the conventions of feminine behavior for young southern ladies, Joplin increasingly adopted a coarseness of demeanor in an attempt to win the acceptance of her male cohorts. These efforts achieved limited success, and she was ostracized by the majority of her classmates. Withdrawing from their society, Joplin took refuge in painting (with which she had some modest success), poetry, and singing, having become enamored with the popular folk music that swept the nation in the late 1950s and early 1960s. Joplin's favorite artists were Leadbelly, the Kingston Trio, Jean Ritchie, and especially Odetta, whose expansive, demonstrative style she often imitated for her friends.

After graduating from high school in 1960, Joplin attended classes at both Lamar State College in Beaumont and Port Arthur Community College. During this time she would often travel to Houston, spending time at the coffeehouses and drinking heavily. In 1961 she traveled to Los Angeles to seek employment. She lived briefly in the Venice Beach area, becoming acquainted with its "beatnik" community, before returning to Port Arthur in 1962. Having adopted the vocal style of classic blues singer Bessie Smith, she began singing in public at coffeehouses in Beaumont and Houston. She earned a modest reputation for her efforts, even recording a local radio commercial.

In the spring of 1962 she returned briefly to Lamar State College before moving to Austin to attend the University of Texas. She joined a folk trio and continued to sing in the style of Jean Ritchie as well as Bessie Smith and country singer Rose Maddox. While she was recognized for her singing, she felt alienated from the college community and in early 1963 went to San Francisco, where she sang at various coffeehouses. In

San Francisco she continued her excessive drinking and became heavily involved with drugs. Committed to pursuing a career as a singer, she visited New York City in 1964, singing briefly at a club in the East Village. Failing to achieve major success in New York, she returned to San Francisco in the fall of 1964, supporting herself primarily as a drug dealer. Recognizing her need for help, she attempted unsuccessfully to commit herself to a hospital in San Francisco.

In the summer of 1965 she returned to Port Arthur. She registered again at Lamar State College as a sociology major and tried to shed her dependence on drugs. She began performing again in Austin in the fall of 1965, and in March 1966 she sang occasionally with a country and western group.

Joplin was convinced by the manager for the band Big Brother and the Holding Company to return to San Francisco in June 1966 to sing with the five-member group, which was known for its rough and spontaneous blues style. Working with Big Brother, Joplin developed a raucous, frenzied vocal delivery that was influenced not only by Bessie Smith but by rhythm and blues vocalists such as Willie Mae "Big Mama" Thornton and Tina Turner as well. Joplin's extroverted performances, hoarse gospel screams, and often raspy vocals were considered unique for a female rock singer and drew considerable media attention to the band.

In late 1966 she recorded an album with Big Brother on a small independent label and in June 1967 performed with the band at the Monterey Pop Festival to great critical acclaim, with her version of Big Mama Thornton's "Ball and Chain" drawing particular attention. Shortly thereafter Big Brother signed with well-known manager Albert Grossman and secured a lucrative recording contract with Columbia Records. Joplin's exuberant and highly charged performances became the focal point for the band and led to its significantly increased popularity. Her rapport with audience members—both male and female—was extraordinary, and she quickly emerged as one of the most charismatic performers on the late 1960s rock scene. While some other female singers in the late 1960s were also beginning to break free from the gender-related stereotypes established in the 1950s, Joplin was widely considered to be the model of the strong, assertive woman singer who demanded to be treated as an equal with the male rock stars of the day.

Joplin's offstage behavior was also remarkable. She assumed a brazen and often controversial posture with reporters and media representatives, projecting the image of a tough, worldly blues singer with a substantial appetite for sex and whiskey. And yet, despite her fame and financial success, she complained to her friends that she felt isolated and lonely.

Big Brother released their first album with Columbia, *Cheap Thrills*, in August 1968. Joplin's distinctive combination of toughness and vulnerability was demonstrated with particular effectiveness in "Piece of My Heart" and "Down on Me," while her intensely emotional and somewhat mannered style was apparent in her version of George Gershwin's "Summertime."

While the album sold well, quickly achieving "gold" status and eventually rising to number one on the album charts, Joplin and the band continued to be considered dynamic and spontaneous concert performers rather than disciplined or accomplished studio musicians. Increasingly dissatisfied with Big Brother's casual musicianship and encouraged by friends to strike out on her own, Joplin left the band and formed, in December 1968, the Kozmic Blues Band, which, in emulation of a late 1960s soul band, featured two saxophones and a trumpet along with the standard instrumentation of bass, guitar, drums, and keyboards. While Joplin's presence dominated her new band even more than it had Big Brother, the group's first concerts, including their inaugural public performance at the Fillmore East in February 1969, were not well received by audiences or critics. Joplin's European tour with the band was more successful, and her album with the new band, *I Got Dem Ol' Kozmic Blues Again Mama!*, recorded in June 1969, showed a new direction. With this album Joplin moved away from the frenzied, blues-influenced vocals she had pioneered with Big Brother and toward a style that was based heavily on the gospel mode as mediated by 1960s black soul singers such as Otis Redding and Aretha Franklin. This new trend was particularly notable in her recorded performances of songs such as "Try," "Work Me, Lord," and "Little Girl Blue." Her earlier, blues-influenced style continued to be represented on her performance of "One Good Man," composed by Joplin herself.

Given constant media attention because of her dramatic performances and her brash responses to the press, Joplin was in wide demand on the talk-show circuit. In the meantime, she once again fell prey to her sporadic heroin addiction, and her performances became erratic from time to time. Her performance at the 1969 Woodstock Festival was dubbed subpar by many critics, and in November Joplin was arrested for public profanity in Florida. Following that incident, some rock venues began to avoid her because of her reputation for provoking her audience to a near-frenzy. Nevertheless, her influence as a pop culture icon was at its highest in this period, and her taste for eclectic combinations of plumes, belts, satins, and dramatic headgear played a major role in defining the commercial hippie fashions of the day.

In 1970 she made a concerted effort to kick her heroin addiction, and after an unsuccessful attempt to revamp the Kozmic Blues Band she put together her third band, the Full-Tilt Boogie Band, a smaller group that eschewed the horn section of her previous band. At this point Joplin adopted a somewhat less raucous performance style, incorporating the blues and gospel–influenced shouts, growls, and vocal slurs more judiciously than before. Her voice, too, was darker and richer, and she experimented with a freer approach to phrasing.

Although attendance at her concerts began to fall off somewhat, she looked forward eagerly to her recording sessions for *Pearl*, her first album with the new band. Nevertheless, she suffered from periodic bouts with depression, and her intermittent problems with alcohol and heroin returned in her final months. While she commented frequently to friends regarding her mortality and even hinted at suicide after hearing of the drug-related death of rock guitarist Jimi Hendrix, she also spoke positively of her engagement and upcoming marriage to Seth Morgan, the son of affluent New Yorkers.

Before the conclusion of the recording sessions for *Pearl*, Joplin died from an accidental overdose of heroin in a Hollywood hotel. Following her death, "Me and Bobby McGee" (written by her former lover Kris Kristofferson), her single from the posthumous album, rose to number one on the charts. It was the only Joplin single release to enjoy great success and the most distinctive performance on the album in its combination of country and western and folk influences and its expression of vulnerability. Other performances from the album, such as "Cry Baby," were notable for their wide range of greater coloristic and timbral devices and for their combination of the 1960s soul style with more traditional blues mannerisms.

While Joplin has not been accorded the cult status of fellow rock musician Jimi Hendrix, who died in the same year, Joplin's recordings (particularly her posthumous "greatest hits" compilation) have sold steadily since her death, and there were signs of a resurgence of interest in her work in the 1990s. Her reputation as the leading white female interpreter of blues rock in the 1960s seems secure, while her often aggressive posturing has led a number of commentators to consider her an important precursor of the feminism that emerged in the 1970s.

• The most complete biography is Myra Friedman, *Buried Alive: The Biography of Janis Joplin* (1973). Also of interest is David Dalton, *Piece of My Heart: The Life, Times, and Legend of Janis Joplin* (1985), and Deborah Landau, *Janis Joplin: Her Life and Times* (1971). Among the most revealing interview articles on Joplin are Mark Wolf, "The Uninhibited Janis Joplin," *Downbeat*, 14 Nov. 1968, pp. 18–19, and T. Wilson, "Straight-talking, Hard-drinking and Sexy—That's Miss Janis Joplin," *Melodymaker*, 12 Apr. 1969, p. 19. See also "An Interview with Janis' Father," *Rolling Stone*, 12 Nov. 1970, pp. 18–19. An insightful analysis of Joplin's influence, including her "pre-Feminist consciousness," is in Ellen Willis's article on Joplin in *The Rolling Stone Illustrated History of Rock and Roll*, ed. Jim Miller, 2d ed. (1980). Obituaries are in the *New York Times*, 5 Oct. 1970, and in *Rolling Stone*, 29 Oct. 1970.

TERENCE J. O'GRADY

JOPLIN, Scott (1867 or 1868–1 Apr. 1917), composer, was born between July 1867 and April 1868 in East Texas, probably near Marshall, the son of Jiles Joplin, formerly a slave and then a laborer, and Florence Givens, a free-born African-American woman and a domestic. The frequently cited birthdate of 24 November 1868 for Joplin is incorrect.

Joplin spent his childhood in Texarkana, on both the Texas and Arkansas sides, where he had a secondary school education. At age seven he began practicing piano in the home of a white family where his mother cleaned house. Julius Weiss, a German immigrant musician who taught the children of a local wealthy white family, noticed Joplin's talents and gave him music instruction. He taught Joplin European classics and opera and imbued the youth with the understanding that music could be art as well as entertainment. In later years, Joplin maintained a correspondence with this teacher.

Scott Joplin's fame was as a composer of ragtime, a syncopated (or "ragged time") music of African-American origins that emerged in the early 1890s. Ragtime became America's popular music in the early 1900s and flourished until replaced by jazz in the late 1910s. Joplin was not the first ragtime composer, but he came on the scene early and set a standard of excellence and sophistication that few others matched. He wrote both vocal and instrumental ragtime, but it was with piano ragtime that he made his mark.

Joplin began his career while still a teenager, singing with vocal quartets and playing piano, violin, and cornet. He left home in the 1880s, going to Sedalia, Missouri, and to St. Louis. In the summer of 1891 he was back in Texarkana with a minstrel troupe; in 1893 he played cornet in a band at the World's Columbian Exposition in Chicago. It was at this world's fair that ragtime first attracted popular notice.

Joplin settled in Sedalia in 1894 and remained there until early 1901. It was a lively town of about fifteen thousand people and had many employment opportunities for musicians. He played first cornet with the town's black Queen City Cornet Band, led a small dance band (playing piano), and formed the Texas Medley Quartette, a vocal group. He toured with this quartet in late 1894 and early 1895, going as far east as Syracuse, New York. His performances in that city attracted the attention of two white businessmen who in 1895 issued his first two publications, both songs in the genteel parlor style, "Please Say You Will" and "A Picture of Her Face."

Sometime between 1895 and 1897 Joplin studied music at the George R. Smith College, a Methodist institution in Sedalia for African Americans. He became well known in town as a pianist and composer; because of his musicianship and his refined personal demeanor, he also gained the respect of the white population, which ordinarily treated blacks with disdain. Among the places in town were he performed regularly were two black social clubs—the Maple Leaf Club, of which he was a charter member, and the Black 400 Club. Joplin's interest in education led him to befriend and encourage several of the town's young pianists, two of whom, Arthur Marshall and Scott Hayden, became notable ragtimers.

In 1896 Joplin published two marches and a waltz, and early in 1899 he became a published composer of ragtime with "Original Rags." Later that year, in August, he contracted with John Stark, a small publisher in Sedalia, to issue "The Maple Leaf Rag." This work, on which he earned royalties, became the most famous and successful piano rag of the period. In the next ten years it sold approximately a half-million copies, a significant number for an instrumental piece. It made Joplin's reputation, earning him the title "King of Ragtime Writers," and provided him with a modest income, sufficient to change the course of his life.

While Joplin excelled as a composer of piano ragtime, he had a strong desire to write for the lyric stage. In November 1899, at Wood's Opera House in Sedalia, he presented his first stage work, *The Ragtime Dance*. This piece, for singing narrator and dancers, portrays a ball in a black social club. The performers included his students Marshall and Hayden, his brother William, possibly his brother Robert, and several members of the Black 400 Club. Because of the piece's length it was not published until 1902, but Joplin did publish six more pieces in the next two years, including "Swipesy Cakewalk" and "Sunflower Slow Drag," collaborations with Marshall and Hayden, respectively.

In 1901 Joplin moved to St. Louis, a center for black ragtime. He was not sufficiently skilled as a pianist to compete as a performer in this city of ragtime virtuosos, but he was highly regarded as a composer. Among his close colleagues were Tom Turpin, a pianist and composer who operated the Rosebud Saloon (a famed meeting place for ragtimers), and Louis Chauvin, billed as the "King of Ragtime Players" and "the Paderewski of Ragtime." Sometime in this period Joplin married Belle Jones, the widow of Scott Hayden's older brother, but the marriage (perhaps common-law) lasted less than three years. One child born to the Joplins died in infancy.

By 1903 Joplin had published twenty rags and other pieces but put most of his energy into another attempt at the lyric stage with his first ragtime opera, *A Guest of Honor*. He applied for a copyright in February 1903, indicated that the opera would be published by Stark, and formed the Scott Joplin Ragtime Opera Company to perform it. He opened in East St. Louis, Illinois, on 31 August 1903 and then took the opera on tour. Two days later, in Springfield, Illinois, someone connected with the company stole the box-office receipts and the tour may have ended there. However, it is possible that it continued for another two weeks, ending in Pittsburg, Kansas. The music was never published and is lost; it reportedly had been confiscated for nonpayment of a boardinghouse bill.

Early in 1904 Joplin visited relatives in Arkansas, where he met a young woman named Freddie Alexander, age nineteen. He dedicated to her one of his most lyrical piano rags, "Chrysanthemum: An Afro-American Intermezzo." He then went to the opening of the Louisiana Purchase Exposition in St. Louis, for which he composed "The Cascades," a rag that depicts the artificial waterfalls that were the centerpiece of that world's fair. He returned to Alexander's home in Little Rock in June, and they married. From there they traveled to Sedalia, stopping along the way for Joplin to give concerts. When they arrived in early July, Freddie Joplin was suffering from a bad cold; in mid-September she died of pneumonia.

The next two-and-a-half years were difficult for Joplin. He seems to have suffered severe financial setbacks, probably brought on by the failed opera tour. He composed some important works, such as the 1905 ragtime waltz "Bethena" (which has a cover photograph that might be Freddie Joplin), but many were issued by small, insignificant publishers. He lived mostly in St. Louis but also spent time in Chicago. While in Chicago, he and Chauvin collaborated on "Heliotrope Bouquet" (published in 1907), with Chauvin composing the first two strains and Joplin the next two. Though an extraordinary pianist, Chauvin was musically illiterate. Joplin, in notating his collaborator's sections, preserved the only sample we have of Chauvin's legendary ragtime style.

In the summer of 1907 Joplin went to New York to find backing for a second opera. That same year he also published with several new companies, including Jos. W. Stern, a major house. Seminary Music, a small firm that published eight of his piano pieces in 1908 and 1909, including such favorites as "Solace" and "Pine Apple Rag," brought him into contact with Irving Berlin, who was soon to become the most celebrated songwriter in the industry.

Joplin completed his second opera, *Treemonisha*, in mid-1910 and showed it to publishers and potential backers. When Berlin's hit song "Alexander's Ragtime Band" was published in March 1911, Joplin claimed that the verse had been stolen from "A Real Slow Drag," the concluding section of *Treemonisha*. Nothing developed from his claim, and he altered the section slightly before publishing the opera himself in May 1911. He considered the work not a ragtime opera, but a grand opera that simply includes a few ragtime sections. The opera, in three acts, has twenty-seven musical numbers, including solos, duets, and ensembles. Most of the music is stylistically conventional for the time, but a few sections suggest black rural music of the 1880s, and a few are in the then-modern ragtime. The libretto carries a serious message that he hoped would reach his racial peers: that African Americans are victimized by ignorance and superstition and can improve their lives through education. The work also celebrates rural black culture and contains autobiographical references that commemorate his mother and his deceased wife, Freddie.

The opera score received a glowing review in the *American Musician and Art Journal* (June 1911), in which the writer suggested that *Treemonisha* was the first American opera to express an indigenous character. Thereafter, Joplin directed his energies toward obtaining a stage production. He never succeeded in having the work staged, however; plans for productions in 1911 and 1913 floundered. An informal performance with piano accompaniment is reported to have occurred in 1915, but 1911 or 1913 are more likely dates. In 1915 Joplin heard "The Frolic of the Bears," a ballet section of the opera, performed by a student orchestra in New York City. He was never to hear an orchestral performance of any other part of the opera.

Joplin greatly diminished his ragtime output in his last years, but the quality of those few that were published is outstanding. In 1912 Stern issued "Scott Joplin's New Rag," a rollicking work that suggests new directions in ragtime. "Magnetic Rag" (1914) is similarly atypical and forward-looking. Joplin published this last work himself with a company he formed with Lottie Stokes, whom he married (probably common-law) between 1911 and 1913.

In his last year of life, Joplin developed dementia paralytica as a result of syphilis. He had periods of depression, rage, and paranoia and destroyed many of his still-unpublished works. He was admitted to a mental institution in New York City early in 1917 and died there several weeks later.

At the time of his death, Joplin had sixty-four published works: forty-one rags and other syncopated piano pieces (in addition, "Reflection Rag," composed around 1907–1908 was published a few months after his death, and "Silver Swan Rag," issued on piano roll in 1914, was published in 1971); one opera; twelve songs; five marches and unsyncopated two-steps; four unsyncopated waltzes; and one instructional work. Among his unpublished (and lost) works were a few piano rags, the opera *A Guest of Honor*, a vaudeville act called *Syncopated Jamboree*, a musical comedy titled *If*, several songs, and a symphony. Two of the rags, "Pretty Pansy Rag" and "Recitative Rag," and several other compositions and arrangements survived in manuscript until the 1960s but then disappeared.

By the time of Joplin's death, ragtime had faded as America's primary popular music. For the next two-and-a-half decades it remained mostly forgotten, except for the "Maple Leaf Rag." A renewed interest developed in the 1940s, accompanying the traditional jazz (or Dixieland) movement. Following the publication in 1950 of Rudi Blesh and Harriet Janis's *They All Played Ragtime*, a biography of Joplin and a social history of ragtime, ragtime fan clubs emerged, with Joplin as the main focus.

In the late 1960s and early 1970s several concert and academic musicians took an active interest in Joplin, and quite unexpectedly, their work led to another Scott Joplin revival. Joplin was brought to the attention of the classical music community in 1971 by a recording of musicologist Joshua Rifkin. Recording on the classical record label Nonesuch, Rifkin performed Joplin's rags not in the customary honky-tonk or jazz styles, but as classical music on a concert grand piano. The recording became the biggest-selling classical record of the year.

Later in 1971 the New York Public Library published a two-volume *Collected Works of Scott Joplin*, making the music widely available and giving Joplin the endorsement of one of America's leading institutions of intellectual life. This was followed early in 1972 with the first fully staged performance of *Treemonisha*, occurring in conjunction with a black music conference at Morehouse College in Atlanta. In 1973 Gunther Schuller, a major concert composer and president of the New England Conservatory of Music, conducted and recorded—again, on a classical label—a student ragtime ensemble of Joplin works in period band arrangements.

These events led in 1974 to the use of Joplin's music in the popular, award-winning film *The Sting*, which brought the composer to the attention of the wider American public. An explosion of interest followed. His 1902 rag "The Entertainer" became one of the most frequently heard pieces in 1974–1975, and recordings of his music rose to the top positions on the popular sales charts, alongside the most recent rock hits. At the same time, recordings on classical labels were receiving unprecedented acclaim. In 1976 Joplin was awarded a Pulitzer Prize, and in 1983 he was honored on a U.S. postage stamp. More than a half-century after his death, Scott Joplin achieved a most remarkable distinction: with the broad, American public, he was immensely popular; and from the worlds of concert music and music scholarship, he received the recognition that he was a serious and gifted artist.

• The most complete collection of Joplin's music (lacking only three song arrangements) is *The Complete Works of Scott Joplin* (1981; rev. ed. of *The Collected Works of Scott Joplin* [1971]). The three missing songs are included in Edward A. Berlin, *King of Ragtime: Scott Joplin and His Era* (1994), a biography that, with the introduction of an enormous number of new facts, is radically different from earlier accounts of Joplin's life. Rudi Blesh and Harriet Janis, *They All Played Ragtime* (1950; rev. ed., 1971), the first Joplin biography, contains important source material and is interesting to read but suffers from fictionalizing. James Haskins and Kathleen Benson, *Scott Joplin* (1978), is a good work that presents an African-American perspective. Katherine Preston, *Scott Joplin* (1988), is a sensible and nicely illustrated book designed for older children. Terry Waldo, *This Is Ragtime* (1976), is particularly strong on the ragtime-Joplin revival of the 1970s. Essential background information on ragtime is included in Berlin, *Ragtime: A Musical and Cultural History* (1980; rev. ed., 1984) and *Reflections and Research on Ragtime* (1987); David A. Jasen and Trebor Jay Tichenor, *Rags and Ragtime: A Musical History* (1978); and John Edward Hasse, ed., *Ragtime: Its History, Composers, and Music* (1985). Jasen, *Recorded Ragtime, 1897–1958* (1973), is a valuable discography of 78-rpm recordings. Important articles that treat Joplin's compositions are Peter Dickinson, "The Achievement of Ragtime: An Introductory Study with Some Implications for British Research in Popular Music," *Proceedings of the Royal Musical Association* (1978–1979), pp. 69–75, and James Bennighof, "*Heliotrope Bouquet* and the Critical Analysis of American Music," *American Music* (Winter 1992): 391–410.

EDWARD A. BERLIN

JORDAN, David Starr (19 Jan. 1851–19 Sept. 1931), naturalist and educator, was born in Gainesville, New York, the son of Hiram Jordan and Huldah Hawley, farmers. Jordan obtained his secondary education in the Gainesville Female Seminary (1865) and then briefly became a primary teacher (1868). A county scholarship permitted his belated entry to the initial class at Cornell University. To support himself, he became an instructor in biology in his junior year and completed sufficient work to be granted a master of science degree after less than four years of study (1872).

In 1872 Jordan was hired as professor of natural science at Lombard University in Galesburg, Illinois, where he taught at least eight subjects. The next year he became principal of a preparatory school in Appleton, Wisconsin, followed by a year of teaching high school science in Indianapolis. During this time, Jordan extended his training as a naturalist. He spent the summers of 1873 and 1874 at Penikese in Buzzard's Bay, Massachusetts, studying marine biology with Louis Agassiz of Harvard University, and the ensuing year, while teaching high school, he obtained an M.D. from the Indiana Medical College ("scarcely earned": Jordan, vol. 1, p. 146). In 1875 he married Susan Bowen; they had three children. That same year Jordan was named professor of natural history at North Western Christian University, later called Butler University. Four years later he was called to a similar post at Indiana University.

Jordan's rapid rise was due to his innate ability and dedication as a naturalist. He experienced some of the best scientific training that America had to offer—undergraduate study at Cornell, the premier land-grant institution, and summer study with Harvard biologists. He then undertook a succession of expeditions to gather and classify fish species. He became attached to the U.S. Fish Commission and published widely in ichthyology. These accomplishments made Jordan stand out in the Midwest, where the higher education system was still inchoate and research rare. After just five years at Indiana, Jordan was named president in 1885. That same year Jordan's wife of ten years passed away. He married Jessie Louise Knight in 1887. They had three children, only one of whom survived childhood.

In the mid-1880s the flagship university of Indiana had just 135 students in the college and another 150 in its preparatory department. Under Jordan's leadership, however, it climbed toward true university status. The preparatory department and old curriculum were jettisoned, and a "major subject" system similar to Cornell's was instituted. He built the faculty with young Indiana graduates, sending them to the East or Europe for advanced training. Jordan himself lectured throughout the state on the value of higher education, thereby acquiring a lifelong knack for public speaking. He expanded recruitment to the university and raised its standing with the state legislature.

Jordan became an adept administrator, even while determined not to abandon teaching and research. He was conscious of being not only the youngest university president in the country, but also the only president who was a practicing scientist. Presidents of this era still came almost exclusively from clerical backgrounds and bore special responsibility for teaching moral philosophy. Jordan transposed this role according to his own naturalistic outlook, tinged with biological determinism. At both Indiana and Stanford he taught a regular freshman course in "the Science of Bionomics . . . the philosophy of Biology beginning with the laws of organic life and leading up to Eugenics and Ethics" (Jordan, vol. 1, p. 298). Jordan remained an active scientist throughout his presidencies. The constants in his career were an idealistic commitment to natural science, energy and practicality as an administrator, and an active public life of travel and lecturing.

In March 1891, on the recommendation of Andrew Dickson White, Jordan was asked by Leland Stanford and his wife, Jane Lathrop Stanford, to assume the presidency of the university they had founded to honor their late son. Jordan quickly accepted. The new institution would be, at least on paper, the wealthiest university in the country. Its leader would have an incomparable opportunity to build the ideal American university. This institution was to meld the founders' desire for practical training with Jordan's commitment to cultivating the liberal arts, science, and faculty research—an amalgam clearly inspired by Cornell University.

In just six months Jordan recruited a faculty and prepared for the fall's opening class of more than 400 students. He chose faculty first from among scholars he respected at Cornell and Indiana. Almost all were younger than their youthful president. The new university offered an elective curriculum in which students chose their studies with guidance from a major-subject professor. The primitive physical conditions created a shared bond for all participants in this great adventure—a bond that was soon sorely tested.

After a promising beginning, the university experienced a series of fiscal, moral, and physical setbacks. The first was precipitated by the death of Leland Stanford in 1893. The estate he bequeathed to the university consisted of quite illiquid assets and was also challenged in court. For six years the university's funds were tied up. Charging no tuition, it maintained operations through personal contributions from Jane Stanford, the university's sole trustee for the decade after her husband's death. Jordan's scope of action was constrained both by the dearth of funds and by the strong-willed founder.

The second calamity was caused by the firing in 1900, at Jane Stanford's insistence, of an outspoken sociology professor, E. A. Ross. (Stanford considered Ross to be politically partisan for advocating free silver and opposing Japanese immigration.) The dismissal of Ross was an egregious breach of academic freedom—so much so that it contributed to the definition and acceptance of the concept in America. Had Jordan defied Stanford he might have endangered the financial base of the university, but the course he chose besmirched the reputation of the university and even more so that of its president.

It seems regrettable that David Starr Jordan is best known to posterity for having fired E. A. Ross, but this act was not out of character. Jordan was a paternalistic figure who kept authority over all campus matters in his own hands. University statutes accorded him full power to remove faculty at will, and Jordan used this power before and after the Ross affair, defending the practice against prevailing academic opinion. Harvard president Charles William Eliot explicitly warned him that top scholars would not come to Stanford under such conditions (Elliott, p. 490). Indeed, not only did several professors resign in protest over the Ross affair, but Jordan subsequently seems to have made little effort to recruit renowned scholars to Stanford.

The restoration of the Stanford endowment in 1899 was followed by a massive building campaign, almost all undone by the earthquake of 1906. Afterward, operating funds were again constricted in the interest of rebuilding shattered structures. These years were further clouded by prolonged conflict over the misbehavior of students. The most salient issue was student drinking, which Jordan opposed on biological as well as moral grounds. In the background, however, was the growing importance of the student extracurriculum (including fraternities and athletics), which chafed against Jordan's belief in an ascetic university ideal. In reaction, he advocated separating the freshman and sophomore classes from the university.

Beginning with the Spanish-American War, Jordan became increasingly identified with the cause of world peace. He based his opposition to war on eugenics, the supposed weakening of the races, claiming that modern warfare killed the "fittest" of the species; this subject became the chief topic of his numerous public addresses. In 1909 he became head of the World Peace Foundation, which claimed increasing amounts of his time.

At this juncture, a "modernizing" faction emerged within the Stanford Board of Trustees, led by Herbert Hoover, an alumnus of Stanford's initial class. They sought to expand the scope of the university, particularly by developing the medical school, and were more sympathetic than their president toward collegiate mores. In 1913 Hoover engineered a reorganization that removed Jordan from the presidency, making him the largely honorific chancellor. Thus, one of the most progressive university presidents of the late nineteenth century was perceived by the second decade of the twentieth as an obstacle to his university's advancement.

Nor were the times propitious for Jordan's new cause of international peace. He crusaded strenuously against American intervention in World War I, but he supported the war effort after the die was cast. In 1924 he won the Raphael Herman Prize for a peace plan titled "A Plan for Education to Develop International Justice and Friendship." He died at his home on the campus of Stanford University.

David Starr Jordan rightfully occupies a place in the pantheon of American university builders, but he was known to contemporaries even more by his writings and lectures. For a scientist, he had a rare ability and inclination "to write books and magazine articles in a popular style on timely topics" (Slosson, p. 113). His bibliography lists 645 separate books and articles. Yet all this effort left little intellectual legacy. Jordan was a clear but not a profound thinker. He often gave vigorous expression to conventional views, like the value of higher education. His stance on public issues was largely shaped by a facile social Darwinism. Even as a scientist, his contributions were taxonomic rather than theoretical.

As a university president, Jordan's leadership was exerted largely through personal example. He was accessible to students and faculty; bluntly honest, he also possessed a self-deprecating sense of humor. Physically vigorous (he climbed the Matterhorn in 1881) as well as being an accomplished scientist, Jordan also exhibited extraordinary energy in pursuing his manifold activities. He was capable of dominating those beneath him yet, ironically, was never able to control the overall direction of the university. This was determined above all by control of the purse strings—first by the founders, then by Jane Stanford alone, and after 1903 by the trustees. As a result, David Starr Jordan presided over the creation of a university of the first rank but, according to a contemporary, "did not create a university in his own image" (Slosson, p. 113). After 1913 Stanford evolved away from the distinctive features that Jordan had installed, especially the major-subject system, toward the pattern of the standard American university.

• The David Starr Jordan Papers are located in the Stanford University Archives. His autobiography, *The Days of a Man* (2 vols., 1921), details above all his extensive public life. An intellectual biography by Edward McNall Burns, *David Starr Jordan: Prophet of Freedom* (1953), is the only systematic account of his ideas. His Indiana years are covered in Thomas D. Clark, *Indiana University: Midwestern Pioneer*, vol. 1 (1970); the indispensable source for the Stanford years is Orrin L. Elliott, *Stanford University: The First Twenty-Five Years* (1937). Jordan's Stanford is placed in context in Laurence R. Veysey, *The Emergence of the American University* (1965), and Edwin E. Slosson, *The Great American Universities* (1910). An obituary is in *Science* 74 (2 Oct. 1931): 27–29.

ROGER L. GEIGER

JORDAN, Edwin Oakes (28 July 1866–2 Sept. 1936), bacteriologist, was born in Thomaston, Maine, the son of Joshua Lane Jordan, a ship captain, and Eliza D. Bugbee, a schoolteacher. Jordan's first three years were spent sailing with his parents to faraway ports-of-call. Then his father retired, resettled the family in Thomaston, Maine, and turned to banking. In 1881, desiring better educational opportunities for the children, the family moved to Auburndale, Massachusetts.

When Jordan entered the Massachusetts Institute of Technology (MIT) in 1884, biology was changing from a descriptive to an experimental science, and bacteriology was a dynamic new field on the American scene. Jordan earned his B.S. in biology in 1888 at MIT under William Thompson Sedgwick, whose biology department was the center for the new field of sanitary science. After graduation, Jordan spent two years as chief assistant biologist at the Massachusetts State Board of Health's new Lawrence Experiment Station for water and sewage treatment. There Jordan made extensive studies of bacteria in sewage-contaminated water supplies and, with Ellen Swallow Richards, did pioneering research on nitrifying bacteria. These early investigations placed Jordan among the first practitioners of bacteriology in the United States.

At the summer sessions of the Marine Biological Laboratory at Woods Hole on Cape Cod, which opened in 1888, Jordan met the leaders of American biology. Its director, Charles Otis Whitman, interested Jordan in experimental embryology and in 1890 offered him a research fellowship in zoology at Clark University, which had opened the previous year. Jordan received his Ph.D. from Clark in 1892. He followed Whitman to the University of Chicago, when it opened in 1892, to become an instructor in zoology.

Once in Chicago, Jordan's primary interest turned again to bacteriology. He played a central role in the professional development of bacteriology as cofounder, in 1899, of the Society of American Bacteriology and as its president in 1905. With his colleague Ludvig Hektoen he edited the *Journal of Infectious Disease*, founded in 1904. At the University of Chicago, he defined the curriculum in bacteriology and sanitary science, built the program into one of the finest in the country, and served as chairman of the Department of Hygiene and Bacteriology from its founding in 1913 until 1933. A modest and reserved man, he was admired by his students and known for his elegant scientific writing. His popular *Textbook of General Bacteriology*, published in 1908, appeared in its eleventh edition by 1935. Jordan remained at Chicago for his entire career, advancing to professor of bacteriology by 1906. In 1931, two years before his retirement, he was honored as Andrew McLeish Distinguished Service Professor of Bacteriology.

Throughout his career Jordan was active in the public health affairs of Chicago. His bacteriological assessment of the Chicago Drainage Canal's impact on the water quality of the Illinois River, conducted between 1899 and 1903, brought him national prominence as a sanitarian. His United States Supreme Court testimony on the self-purification of streams helped Chicago defend the Drainage Canal against charges that the sewage it diverted into the Mississippi River had contaminated the St. Louis water supply. As director of the Serum Division of the John McCormick Institute for Infectious Disease, which was founded at the University of Chicago in 1902, Jordan oversaw the production of serum therapies distributed by the Illinois State Board of Health. In 1915 he directed his attention to food poisoning and acted as an adviser to Chicago's meat-packing concerns. During World War I Jordan organized courses at the University of Chicago to train bacteriologists for army laboratories and served as director of the Lister, one of four U.S. railroad car laboratories sponsored by the American Red Cross.

Jordan investigated possible bacterial causes of the influenza epidemic of 1918–1919 as a member of a commission funded by the Metropolitan Life Insurance Company. Although the commission's results were inconclusive, Jordan's comprehensive review of the literature, *Epidemic Influenza* (1927), undertaken for the American Medical Association, served for years as the best guide to the subject.

Jordan's scientific work made him the foremost American authority on the typhoid-paratyphoid bacteria and an expert on the epidemiology of water-borne diseases. He served as a member of the International Health Board of the Rockefeller Foundation from 1920 to 1927, reporting on sanitary conditions in Argentina, Puerto Rico, Panama, and Jamaica. From 1930 to 1933 he was appointed to the Board of Scientific Directors of the Rockefeller Foundation's International Health Division. He also served for many years on the Medical Fellowship Board of the National Research Council and as a trustee of the McCormick Institute.

Jordan was married to Elsie Fay Pratt in 1893. They had three children. He died in Lewiston, Maine.

Jordan was among the most highly respected scientists in the second generation of American bacteriologists. Although he is remembered principally for his research in sanitary bacteriology, bacteriology for him was as much a biological science as a sanitary or medical science. This perspective informed his entire career and, through his writings and his students, influenced the development of bacteriology as a scientific discipline.

• A small collection of Jordan's papers is located in the Department of Special Collections of the University of Chicago Library. Jordan's complete bibliography is included in the biographical account by William Burrows in *Biographical Memoirs, National Academy of Sciences* 20 (1939): 197–228. See also the obituaries by N. Paul Hudson, *Journal of Bacteriology* 33 (1937): 243–48, and Ludvig Hektoen, *Science* 84 (6 Nov. 1936): 411–12.

Jordan's book-length works not mentioned above include a translation of *The Principles of Bacteriology* by Ferdinand Hueppe (1899), and *Food Poisoning* (1917). He coauthored *William Thompson Sedgwick: A Pioneer of Public Health* with S. C. Whipple and C.-E. A. Winslow. With I. S. Falk, he edited *The Newer Knowledge of Bacteriology and Immunology* (1928), in which eighty-three authors reviewed the state of research in those fields. In addition to the scores of scientific papers he wrote, from 1913 to 1936 he produced an anonymous report annually for the *Journal of the American Medical Association* on "Typhoid in the Large Cities of the United States," and from 1925 to 1936 he added a report on "Diphtheria Mortality in the Large Cities of the United States." Helpful accounts of Jordan's work and his university department include his article "University of Chicago, Division of Biological Sciences, Department of Hygiene and Bacteriology," in *Methods and Problems of Medical Education*, 19th series (1931); Stewart A. Koser, "Bacteriology at the University of Chicago," *Bios* 23 (1952): 175–91; and Paul F. Clark, *Pioneer Microbiologists of America* (1961).

PATRICIA PECK GOSSEL

JORDAN, Elizabeth Garver (9 May 1867–24 Feb. 1947), journalist, editor, and fiction writer, was born in Milwaukee, Wisconsin, the daughter of William Francis Jordan, a meat market manager and real estate broker, and Margaretta Garver. A Roman Catholic like her father, Jordan attended the Convent of Notre Dame in Milwaukee. She published a short story in the *Milwaukee Evening Wisconsin* at age fourteen and another a year later in *Texas Siftings* magazine. After graduating in 1884 as class valedictorian, she thought of becoming a concert pianist (as her Protestant mother wanted) and of being a nun. Her father persuaded her to try journalism for four years instead. Mastering shorthand, Jordan worked in Milwaukee for a year as editor of the women's page of a newspaper called *Peck's Sun*, as a secretary for another year for the superintendent of schools, and as a feature writer for the *Chicago Tribune* from 1888 to 1890. Then, momentously, she moved to New York City to work for the *New York World*.

Jordan slaved as a reporter for the *World* in 1890 and 1891 and then edited several of its departments, including the "Editorial Forum." She occasionally saw Joseph Pulitzer, the dynamic *World* owner, and worked with George Harvey, its managing editor. To gather material for its "True Stories of the News," she visited hospitals and morgues, police courts and prisons, the Chinese quarter and the underworld, and dark tenements. When promoted in 1897 to assistant editor of the *Sunday World*, she profited professionally by working with its editor, Arthur Brisbane. Three of her most notable writings were an exclusive interview in 1893 with Caroline Scott Harrison, the wife of President Benjamin Harrison; coverage of the murder trial of Lizzie Borden, also in 1893; and a series called "The Submerged Tenth" concerning New York's infamous tenements. Jordan also made journalistic capital out of ventures such as seeking out an eccentric preacher in the Tennessee mountains, interviewing aging eyewitnesses of John Brown's Harpers Ferry raid, and spending a night in a haunted house in Sea Cliff, New Jersey.

Jordan began to edit *Harper's Bazar* in 1900, hired by Harvey, by then president of Harper & Brothers; she soon changed the weekly magazine to a monthly. When it was sold in 1913 to William Randolph Hearst, she became the literary adviser for the Harpers until 1918. Jordan "discovered"—or at least helped in the process of discovering—authors who quickly achieved fame to various degrees. They included Dorothy Canfield Fisher, Zona Gale, and Sinclair Lewis; each appreciated her tough-minded editing. She also met and published many other writers, among them notable women such as Gertrude Atherton, Mary Austin, Frances Hodgson Burnett, Margaret Deland, Fannie Hurst, Kate Douglas Wiggin, and Ella Wheeler Wilcox. On one of her many working trips abroad, Jordan met Henry James, whom she later helped persuade to lecture during his 1904–1905 return to the United States. One of her most unusual publishing ventures was *The Whole Family: A Novel by Twelve Authors.*

Her friend William Dean Howells originally had the idea and offered a subject for the plot—how an engagement or a marriage affects and is affected by members of a family. He suggested that Jordan recruit contributors and wrote the first chapter himself. Jordan persuaded Mary E. Wilkins Freeman, John Kendrick Bangs, James, Elizabeth Stuart Phelps, and Henry Van Dyke, among others, to add an anonymous chapter each and contributed a chapter herself. She even asked for one from her friend Mark Twain, who declined. That she got so many well-known writers to agree hints at both her importance and her persuasiveness. The engaging mishmash was serialized in *Harper's Bazar* (Dec. 1907–Nov. 1908) and then published in book form, also in 1908. Although *The Whole Family* is probably the most interesting composite novel in American literature, it has been largely ignored by the critics. (In 1917 Jordan edited another such novel, *The Sturdy Oak*, by fourteen prosuffrage authors, including Fisher, Hurst, and Kathleen Norris.)

In 1918 Jordan became the editorial director for Goldwyn Pictures Incorporated for only three days of work a week at $25,000 a year. This sum made her one of the era's best-paid professional women. To accept this position, she resigned from *Harper's*, for which by this time she was also working only three days a week. The movie venture proved so unsatisfactory that she happily quit at the end of the year when Samuel Goldwyn moved his studios from New Jersey to California. Jordan continued providing the Hearst Syndicate three special editorials a week; more significantly, she was free to concentrate more fully on her creative writing. Over the years her short stories had appeared in the *Atlantic Monthly*, *Century*, *Harper's Magazine*, and *Scribner's Monthly*. In all she produced about thirty novels and collections of stories—always competent and clever, but usually ephemeral as well. Her first book, *Tales of the City Room* (1898), was a collection of ten stories evoking the atmosphere of the *World* city editor's office. Next came *Tales of the Cloister* (1901), with a convent background and introducing the character May Iverson. Jordan then wrote *The Lady from Oklahoma*, a four-act play that was produced in 1911. She assembled three collections of May Iverson yarns, of which *May Iverson's Career* (1914) is especially autobiographical—until the peppy, versatile heroine gets married, which Jordan never did. She also wrote romantic novels, for example, *Miss Blake's Husband* (1926), about a rich, homeless young woman traveling in search of a perfect husband, only to be challenged by mystery and choices. Jordan also wrote detective fiction, including *The Night Club Mystery* (1929), about a bank teller aiding an idolized old friend, a gambler framed by the police. She published her last novel, *Mrs. Warren's Son* (1944), when she was seventy-seven years old. Her fiction, no longer widely read, has verbal charm, ingenious plots, simplistic characters, and snappy endings.

Elizabeth Jordan was one of America's most perspicacious editors. She was also a forceful and gracious public speaker, was a generous director of the Big Sisters' Association of New York, and took a lively interest in action revolving around her home in Gramercy Park in New York City, where she died.

• In the Manuscript Division of the New York Public Library are a typescript of *The Sturdy Oak* and numerous letters to Jordan by literary figures and others. Her cocky autobiography, describing her work and her friends, is *Three Rousing Cheers* (1938). Alfred Bendixen's introduction to his edition of *The Whole Family* (1986) is informative, while Maggie Dunn and Ann Morris in *The Composite Novel: The Short Story Cycle in Transition* (1995) touch on both *The Whole Family* and *The Sturdy Oak*. Obituaries are in the *New York Times*, 25 Feb. 1947, and the *Catholic World*, Apr. 1947, p. 83.

ROBERT L. GALE

JORDAN, Jim (16 Nov. 1896–2 Apr. 1988), and **Marian Jordan** (16 Apr. 1898–7 Apr. 1961), radio entertainers, were born James Edward Jordan and Marian Driscoll in Peoria, Illinois. Jim was the son of James W. Jordan and Mary Tighe, farmers. Marian was the daughter of Daniel Driscoll, a coal miner, and Anna Carroll. Jim Jordan and Marian Driscoll met in a church choir and married in 1918. They had two children. In 1922, when a theatrical agent offered them the chance to tour professionally, they mortgaged their house, sold their car, borrowed money from family, left their baby daughter with Jim's parents, and jumped at the chance. Several other vaudeville tours and many other Peoria performances followed, with only minimal success. Their failure in vaudeville led the Jordans to radio at a time when most other entertainers still shunned the airwaves.

After hearing a mediocre singer over a Chicago radio station in 1925, the Jordans auditioned and quickly began daily broadcasts that featured the kind of song and piano duets they had performed in vaudeville. Two years later they changed stations and began to act in comedies and soap operas. Radio stations in the 1920s were desperate for performers but lacked money to pay professionals. Entertainers who, like the Jordans, were willing to work for low wages could expect to play many roles. Jim began perfecting a character who told tall tales in "Luke and Mirandi," while Marian worked on her understanding-Irish-wife role in "The Smith Family."

In 1931 the Jordans got work at WMAQ (a Chicago station famous for originating programs) starring in "Smackout," a show about country grocery store owners "smackout" of everything. Vaudeville comedians wrote, or at least polished, their own material, but the Jordans had no such experience and depended on the station's overworked writers for daily fifteen-minute scripts. The Jordans asked a struggling cartoonist, Don Quinn, for writing help and soon extended their own collaboration to include Quinn, a move that proved crucial to the success the trio later enjoyed. From Grand Rapids himself, Quinn came to write sophisticated wordplay that still allowed the characters portrayed by the Jordans to seem small-town, midwestern, and endearing. Beginning in the early 1930s

and continuing for the next twenty years, the Jordans and Quinn split all their earnings three ways.

After hearing "Smackout," an advertising executive suggested to Johnson's Wax that they sponsor a program featuring Jim and Marian Jordan. Broadcast from Chicago, "Fibber McGee and Molly" began on NBC's smaller Blue Network in April 1935. At first, Jim Jordan played a braggart and a liar whose character's name reflected his inclination. But Marian Jordan pushed to make the characters more realistic, like people she had known in Peoria, and more appealing. "Fibber McGee and Molly" was far from an overnight success, but a 1939 move to the Red Network's Tuesday comedy lineup, a move to Hollywood for the cast and crew, and better scripts brought the team more than a decade of high ratings.

Jim Jordan noted that "an effective comedy series . . . presents situations that actually happen to everyday folks. . . . we follow a policy of situation comedy, in which a sequence is built up, instead of relying on jokes." Situation comedies were not new to radio. "The Amos and Andy Show" and "The Rise of the Goldbergs" had been very popular shows but, beginning in 1932, the airwaves were taken over by vaudeville comedians, often Jewish, who told jokes within a variety format. "Fibber McGee and Molly," along with the programs of Fred Allen and Paul Rhymer's "Vic and Sade," brought back domestic comedies, this time with a midwestern, WASP (white Anglo-Saxon Protestant) flavor.

Each week "Fibber McGee and Molly" presented the McGees at home at 79 Wistful Vista with a stock company of actors (each of whom did several voices) serving as neighbors, interacting with the title characters, and responding to the week's situation. The aural nature of the program showed that Quinn understood the difference between writing for radio and working in cartoons or vaudeville. The contents of Fibber's hall closet overflowed with wonderful sound effects (ending with a tinkling bell) whenever he opened the door. Famous for his tongue-twisting alliterations, Fibber once boasted he was "Punch bowl McGee, pronounced by press and public the pugilistic pixie of the pedigreed paperweight pugs, pummelling pudgy palooka, pulverizing proboscises and paralyzing plug-uglies." Dialogue repeated from week to week, such as Molly's long-suffering "'Tain't funny, McGee" and "heavenly days" and Fibber's frustrated "dad-rat the dad-ratted," entered the national language. Two supporting characters, Hal Peary, as the pompous Throckmorton P. Gildersleeve, and Marlin Hurt, a white man who played the heavily stereotyped African-American maid Beulah, became so popular that they left for their own programs. Marian Jordan did several voices while Jim Jordan played only Fibber, but both contributed to the success of the formula. Each show revolved around Fibber, but Molly refereed all the fights and presented a warmer character to whom the audience could relate.

The program integrated commercials into the action, never stopping for Johnson's Wax advertisements. The announcer, Harlow Wilcox, simply visited and, despite Fibber's attempts to stop him, described the benefits of the sponsor's product. During World War II government programs became like a second sponsor, with Fibber, Molly, and their neighbors discussing the black market, rationing, and war-bond drives in their weekly conversations. Johnson's Wax dropped the program in 1950 because of low ratings, but different sponsors stepped in for the next three years. After 1953 the Jordans did a daily program and in the late 1950s five-minute spots on NBC's "Monitor." Marian Jordan died in Encino, California; Jim Jordan in Los Angeles.

The Jordans always wanted to be performers, and from their vaudeville beginnings to their success playing Fibber McGee and Molly, they devoted their lives to show business, despite family objections, the depression, and growing up in Peoria, a town known throughout vaudeville for its difficult audiences. Although network publicity always portrayed the Jordans as ordinary, small-town folks unconcerned with Hollywood glitter, their lives are of interest because they lived wholly in and for show business—they bombed in Peoria but played well in the rest of the country.

• Scripts for "Fibber McGee and Molly" are included in the collection of the Pacific Pioneer Broadcasters, Hollywood, Calif., and tapes of the broadcasts are available at the Recorded Sound Collection, Library of Congress, Washington, D.C., and the Museum of Television and Radio, New York City. The Jordans and their radio programs are given a chapter in Arthur Frank Wertheim, *Radio Comedy* (1979). Other useful discussions can be found in J. Fred MacDonald, *Don't Touch That Dial! Radio Programming in American Life, 1920–1960* (1979); Frank Buxton and Bill Owen, *The Big Broadcast, 1920–1950* (1972); and John Dunning, *Tune in Yesterday: The Ultimate Encyclopedia of Old-Time Radio, 1925–1976* (1976). A two-part article about the Jordans appeared at the height of their popularity in the *Saturday Evening Post*, 9 Apr., pp. 26–27, 80, 82, 84, 86, 89, and 16 Apr. 1949, pp. 36, 179–80, 182, while a comparison with an earlier article in *American Magazine*, Mar. 1942, pp. 46–48, 75–76, illustrates the continuity in the publicity surrounding the Jordans. Marian Jordan's obituary is in the *New York Times*, 8 Apr. 1961; Jim Jordan's is in the *New York Times*, 2 Apr. 1988, and *Variety*, 6 Apr. 1988.

SUSAN SMULYAN

JORDAN, John Woolf (14 Sept. 1840–11 June 1921), editor and antiquary, was born in Philadelphia, Pennsylvania, the son of Francis Jordan, a grocery and chemical merchant, and Emily Woolf. His uncle, John Jordan, a Philadelphia antiquarian and an active member of the Historical Society of Pennsylvania, was an important influence on his nephew's life and career. Jordan was educated in Philadelphia private schools and then at Nazareth Hall Military Academy near Bethlehem, Pennsylvania. He graduated in 1856 and went to work with his father in the family business. When Pennsylvania was invaded by the Confederate army in 1863, Jordan served as quartermaster sergeant in Starr's Battery, Thirty-second Regular Pennsylva-

nia Militia. After his military service he married Ann Page in 1883; they had three children. He became assistant librarian of the Historical Society of Pennsylvania in 1885 under Frederick D. Stone, first editor of the society's quarterly, *Pennsylvania Magazine of History and Biography*. Stone had started the classification of the society's manuscripts, engravings, and broadsides.

The Historical Society of Pennsylvania was incorporated in Philadelphia in 1826 and its library became one of the great historical research centers in the northeastern United States. Jordan was appointed its librarian in 1903 and remained in the position until his death. As librarian, Jordan continued Stone's classification project, but he accomplished his most important work as editor of the *Pennsylvania Magazine of History and Biography*, from 1887 until his death. In this position, Jordan became an authority on Pennsylvania history, especially of the American Revolution period. He edited important manuscript sources, including revolutionary orderly books, wrote historical articles, and edited the journals of Jacob Hiltzheimer (1893) and of Adam Hubley, Jr. (1909). Many were later reprinted as separate publications. He also edited William C. Reichel's *Friedensthal and Its Stockaded Mill, 1749–67* (1877); *A Red Rose from the Olden Time; or, A Ramble through the Annals of the Red Rose Inn and the Barony of Nazareth in the Days of the Province, 1752–1772* (1883); David Zeisberger's *Essay of an Onondaga Grammar* (1888); and the travel narratives of John Heckewelder to the Wabash (1877) and to Ohio (1886) and of Bishop Spangenburg to Onondaga (1877). Jordan was chief editor of *Historic Homes and Institutions and Genealogical and Personal Memorials of the Lehigh Valley, Pa.* (1905) and vols. 1–13 (1914–1921) of the *Encyclopedia of Pennsylvania Biography*. He contributed to *Colonial Families of Philadelphia* (2 vols., 1911) and *Colonial and Revolutionary Families of Pennsylvania* (3 vols., 1911). Jordan was also knowledgeable about Moravian settlements, contributed to *Moravian*, and compiled various genealogical histories of Pennsylvania regions. Although he was not well known outside his library, his knowledge of Pennsylvania history was valued by other researchers. His focus on the Philadelphia area and his subject specialties appealed to a limited audience. In addition to receiving an honorary L.L.D. degree from Lafayette College, he was a founder and member of several historical societies. He died in Philadelphia.

• The Historical Society of Pennsylvania has Jordan correspondence in the William J. Buck Papers, which have biographical sketches of Quakers in Pennsylvania and in adjoining territories and in the Civil War Papers with letters (1862–1864) between A. A. Jones of the Eighty-eighth Pennsylvania Volunteers and Jordan. The Joseph M. Toner Papers, Manuscript Division, Library of Congress, contain correspondence as well. The Harold G. Rugg Papers, Dartmouth University Archives, have letters (1899–1920). The John B. Reeves Papers, South Carolina Historical Society, have Jordan letters relating to letter books of Enos Reeves, a revolutionary war soldier. Walter Muir Whitehill, *Independent Historical Societies* (1962), has a good chapter on the Historical Society of Pennsylvania during Jordan's tenure as director but doesn't mention his name. Biographical listings are in *New England Historical and Geneological Register* (Apr. 1923, suppl.) and *Encyclopedia of Pennsylvania Biography* 2 (1914). An obituary is in the *Public Ledger and North American* (now the *Philadelphia Inquirer*), 13 June 1921.

MARTIN J. MANNING

JORDAN, Louis (8 July 1908–4 Feb. 1975), jazz musician, was born in Brinkley, Arkansas, the son of Jimmy Jordan, a bandleader and music teacher, and Lizzia Read. He was taught both clarinet and saxophone by his father and while still in high school, performed with his father's band, the Rabbit Foot Minstrels. Jordan's professional career began in 1929 with Jimmy Pryor's Imperial Serenaders. From 1930 to 1936 he performed with various bands, joining Chick Webb (1936–1938), playing alto and soprano saxophones and occasionally singing. While in Arkansas he also worked with Ruby Williams between 1930 and 1936.

Jordan moved to Philadelphia in 1932 and became a sideman in tuba player Jim Winters's band. Between 1933 and 1938 he performed with Charlie Gaines (1933–1935), Leroy Smith (1935–1936), and Chick Webb (1936–1938) and had brief stints with Fats Waller and Tyler Marshall before forming the Tympany Five in 1938. The Tympany Five appeared in several films, including *Follow the Boys* (1944), *Meet Miss Bobby Sox* (1944), *Beware* (1946), *Swing Parade of 1946* (1946), *Reet, Petite and Gone* (1947), and *Look Out Sister* (1948). The group, a combination of rhythm and blues and jazz, achieved immense popularity throughout the 1940s. Jordan's role included his swinging alto saxophone style, his blues-inflected vocal style, and his engaging sense of humor. On his wide-ranging vocals he would croon and scat sing with his lyrics occasionally focusing on problems confronting African Americans. The Tympany Five recorded with Decca from 1939 to 1955. During this tenure Jordan produced over two dozen recordings, many becoming hits, including "Five Guys Named Moe" (1943, Decca 8653); "Buzz Me" (1945, Decca 18734); "Caldonia" (1945, Decca 8670); *Louis Jordan and His Tympany Five* (1945, Cir [USA], CLP 53); "My Baby Said Yes" (1945), with Bing Crosby; "GI Jive" (1948); "Is You or Is You Ain't My Baby" (1943, V-disc 158), which sold over one million copies; "Beware" (1946, Decca 18818); "Choo, Choo Ch'Boogie" (1946, Decca 23610); "Ain't That Just Like a Woman" (1946, Decca 236669); "Let the Good Times Roll" (1946, Decca 23741); "Open the Door Richard" (1947); "Baby It's Cold Outside" (1948), with Ella Fitzgerald; and "Saturday Night Fish Fry" (1949, Decca 24725). Between 1942 and 1951 Jordan had fifty-seven singles released, fifty-five of which made the top ten on rhythm and blues charts. It was also during this period that he transformed African-American popular music by demonstrating that a big band could be paired down into a combo without losing its power.

After the breakup of the Tympany Five, Jordan signed as a soloist with Mercury. To capitalize on the fame that he achieved with Decca, Mercury had him rerecord some of his old hits, including "Caldonia," "I'm Gonna Move to the Outskirts of Town," "Is You or Is You Ain't My Baby," "Let the Good Times Roll," and "Choo Choo Ch'Boogie." To compensate for the end of the Tympany Five, Mercury hired Quincy Jones to do the arrangements and sidemen such as Jimmy Cleveland, Budd Johnson, Ernie Royal, and Sam "the Man" Taylor as accompanists. In 1951 Jordan organized a big band with which he recorded *Silver Star Series Presents Louis Jordan & His Orchestra* and toured for a couple of years. He also recorded with Louis Armstrong, Bing Crosby, and Fitzgerald during the 1950s. Jordan moved to Phoenix, Arizona, in the early 1950s because of health problems and then to Los Angeles. From the early 1960s to 1968 he toured England, recorded a single low-sale album with Tangerine Records in 1964, and toured Asia in both 1967 and 1968.

Jordan returned to the big band format in 1968, recording the album *Santa Claus, Santa Claus/Sakatumi* on his newly formed label, PZAZZ, with arranging and conducting by Teddy Edwards. He also recorded *Louis Jordan Swings* with the Chris Barber Band in the 1960s. His career experienced a revival with the help of a 1974 recording by British pop musician Joe Jackson. The album, *Great Rhythm and Blues Oldies, Vol. 1*, introduced a new music generation to Jordan's style. Jordan died in Los Angeles. This musical renaissance continued without Jordan, however, when Jackson recorded *Jumpin' Five* in 1981 in which he revived songs by artists such as Cab Calloway, King Pleasure, and Armstrong. Other groups, notably the Chevalier Brothers, Ian Stewart's Rocket 88, and the Big Town Playboys carried Jordan's influence into the 1980s with covers of his music. Jordan's compositions also were recorded by Chuck Berry, B. B. King, Ray Charles, Fats Domino, and Little Richard. Both Nat King Cole and Dizzy Gillespie admired Jordan for his inventiveness.

Jordan's style, though rooted in blues and jazz, featured strong rhythms that drew on ballads, boogie-woogie, calypso, jump blues instrumentals and vocals, and rhumbas. Comedy and showmanship were integral to the way in which he performed; satirical lyrics were even aimed at the social and political ills to which African Americans were vulnerable. Charles and Berry, among others, have noted his role as a pioneer of rock and roll, exemplified by the boogie beat on Bill Haley's "Rock around the Clock." Jordan was one of the most creative artists in the history of African-American popular music.

• A detailed treatment of Jordan's life and music, including discographical information, can be found in John Chilton, *Let the Good Times Roll: The Story of Louis Jordan and His Music* (1992). Additional general information on Jordan and his time can be found in A. Shaw, *Honkers and Shouters: The Golden Years of Rhythm and Blues* (1978). More specific information appears in Frank Driggs's entry on Jordan in *The New Grove Dictionary of Jazz*, vol. 1 (1988), and in the entry in *The Harmony Illustrated Encyclopedia of Jazz* (1986). Informative articles include D. Boyce, "Here Comes Mr. Jordan," *New Beat*, Jan. 1950, p. 12; Leonard Feather, "Let the Good Times Roll," *Down Beat* 36, no. 11 (1969): 16; and J. Otis, "The Otis Tapes, 1: Louis Jordan," *Blues Unlimited*, no. 106 (1974): 12. An obituary is in the *New York Times*, 6 Feb. 1975.

EDDIE S. MEADOWS

JORDAN, Marian. *See* Jordan, Jim, and Marian Jordan.

JORDAN, Mary Augusta (5 July 1855–14 April 1941), educator, was born in Ironton, Ohio, the daughter of Edward Jordan, a lawyer, and Augusta Woodbury Ricker. In 1861, when her father was appointed solicitor of the treasury by President-elect Abraham Lincoln, the family returned to the East. Always a lively storyteller, Jordan described the family move as "traveling by water for forty days and forty nights." In one of Jordan's childhood memories, President Lincoln held her in his arms to view the parade of troops on their way to Manassas. Family members later noted that since Jordan would have been seven years old at the time, they hoped for Lincoln's sake that it had been a very short parade.

In 1870 or 1871 Jordan's family relocated to Elizabeth, New Jersey. Shortly thereafter, Jordan entered Vassar College, one of the pioneering women's colleges. There she received her baccalaureate degree in English in 1876 and her master's degree in 1878. For three years she was the Vassar librarian, and she spent another three as an English tutor to Vassar undergraduates. In 1884 she received a call from Smith College president Clark Seelye to teach English.

Julia Ray, a former principal at Vassar and a friend of President Seelye, described Jordan at the time as "little, but fierce." She was a tiny woman, lithe and graceful, with darting eyes and constantly moving hands. She expressed her style in everything she did. She never shied away from controversy or admiration and was quite accustomed to both as she held court in her classroom and at Hatfield House, a student residence, for nearly forty years.

During her first semester at Smith, however, Jordan was scrutinized and openly challenged by the young women she was hired to teach. She embarked on her teaching career on a snowy January morning. Students had heard that the new teacher would be sitting in the front row at morning prayers. In an article written for the *Smith Alumnae Quarterly*, "Life and the Classroom: Thirty Seven Years of It" (1921), Jordan confided: "I was pathologically innocent to the point of ignorance. . . . [A]s the students filed past, it seemed as if they each, one and all reduced me . . . low, low down and very, very far away from human companionship, and still further from active usefulness." She describes the classes during those early years at Smith, when enrollment was still relatively low, as "social and academic units . . . with a keen sense of class reputation and . . . a haughty sense of class dignity." In fact, by the close of her first semester she had offended one class to the point that the elective she taught during the next term was boycotted and only four students registered for the course. With rows of empty seats greeting her each day, Jordan recalled the semester as an academic tragic comedy that was both painful and beneficial. Jordan soon began to transform herself into Smith's most vivacious, charismatic professor. Yet she did not grow immune to the vagaries of college opinion. Sometime in the 1880s, an entire senior class of twenty-four women shunned Jordan for a week over her "attitude."

Undaunted, Jordan continued to challenge, inspire, and chastise her students. She was feisty, demanding, and at times overwhelming. Colleagues and well-intentioned friends had advised her that in order to be successful in the classroom she should teach to the average student and not teach over the students' heads. Instead, she believed that the "classroom was a spiritual powerhouse, whose builder and maker and engineer was God." She was relatively unpublished, save for one book, *Correct Writing and Speaking* (1904), a few academic articles on education, and one pamphlet opposing suffrage for women. Instead, she made teaching and the classroom lecture her life's work. She not only taught literature and rules of grammar, but she insisted on the development of critical thinking and analytical skills. She mandated intellectual standards of excellence that became institutionalized at Smith. Her lectures were events, attended by her colleagues as well as her students. They were running commentaries on literary works and their authors, on college and town life, on society and the human condition, and on human nature. In 1902 Ethel Chase wrote:

You never knew where she would break out next
But you knew she would break; you went to her class
To learn how to read and write English, and you heard all
About current styles and the bolshevik movement
And post-impressionism and how to grow dahlias,
Or words to that effect; you couldn't sleep a
Minute in her class because you were afraid of
Missing something; and when you got out of class
Your brain was doing nose dives and tail spins
And looping the loop all at once and you loved it.

Jordan required that her students write daily, believing that if they were given the opportunity to express themselves their experiences would lead them to self-knowledge. Her students also hoped these exercises would lead to sophistication and fame. "Jordie," as she was affectionately called by many of her students, held individual appointments with her students on Wednesday and Saturday afternoons for the express purpose of discussing their work. These were anxious personal meetings and could be humbling experiences or exhilarating ones, depending upon Jordan's assessment of the young women's abilities. It was these meetings that kept Jordan fully involved in the lives of her students. She seemed to one incoming president to "dart about the campus, interested in everybody and everything, and taking a hand in most things that occurred."

Jordan retired from Smith College in 1921. Upon her death in New Haven, Connecticut, Smith College released a statement that it had lost "one of the most influential figures of the first half-century of its history." A quintessential teacher, Jordan stimulated her students to act. Many of them, including such artists and reformers as Olive Higgins Prouty, Anne Morrow Lindbergh, Elizabeth Cutter Morrow, Mary Van Kleeck, and Alice Morgan Wright, went on to lead distinguished lives.

• Jordan's letters, including her lecture notes, are located in the Sophia Smith Collection and College Archives at Smith College. Her Pamphlet, *Why Women Do Not Want the Vote* (1921), is a vital source for understanding her politics and philosophy.

KATHLEEN PERKINS

JORDAN, Sara Claudia Murray (20 Oct. 1884–21 Nov. 1959), gastroenterologist and cofounder of the Lahey Clinic, was born in Newton, Massachusetts, the daughter of Patrick Andrew Murray, the owner of a carriage repair shop, and Maria Stuart. The Murrays sent all seven of their children to the local public schools, where from an early age Sara excelled at academics. In 1901 she matriculated at Radcliffe College. There she majored in the classics under an accelerated program, receiving her diploma in three years instead of the customary four. She then entered a doctoral program in classical philology and archaeology at the University of Munich, where in just four years she finished a dissertation on two medieval interpretations of a tenth-century Greek text. This work was published two years later in Germany. She returned to the United States briefly to take a teaching job at Adelphi University but in 1913 returned to Germany to marry Sebastian Jordan; they had a daughter the following year.

At Jordan's father's insistence, Jordan returned to Massachusetts after the birth of her child. It is not clear whether her willingness to move back to the United States was a reflection of the state of her marriage, but international events certainly did not ease matters for the couple. World war broke out in 1914, further complicating Sara and Sebastian's relationship.

During this period in her life, Jordan decided, despite her father's objections, to become a doctor and in 1917, at the age of thirty-three, was accepted by Tufts College Medical School. Although the school had balked originally at admitting her full-time (causing Jordan to threaten to complain to the American Medical Association), Jordan quickly stood out in her medical school class as one of the best students. Prominent surgeon Frank Lahey noticed this unusual student in her second year and invited her to assist him in his research. Under Lahey's guidance, Jordan studied whether a basal metabolism test could serve as a barometer of thyroid function. In 1921 Jordan graduated

summa cum laude from Tufts and decided to specialize in gastroenterology. After a year-long internship at Worcester Memorial Hospital, Jordan went to Chicago to study gastroenterology with Bertram Sippy, a renowned specialist there.

When Lahey sent her an invitation to join him and two other doctors in opening a clinic in Boston, Jordan leapt at the chance to return to her native Boston. She also opened a general practice of her own in her Brookline home. But most of her best-known work was done in her capacity as the gastroenterologist for the Lahey Clinic. There she specialized in gastroenterological diseases that were brought on by stress, such as peptic ulcers. Her reputation drew wealthy patients, who appreciated her nonsurgical approach to most problems. Instead, she prescribed diet, exercise, and rest. She was known for the aphorism: "Every businessman over fifty should have a daily nap and nip—a short nap after lunch, and a relaxing highball before dinner."

Unlike many women of her generation who entered medicine, Jordan did not compromise her social life for her career. In 1935 she remarried, this time to a Boston stockbroker, Penfield Mower, who shared her love of golf. The two lived in Marblehead, on the coast north of Boston, and spent time enjoying Jordan's five grandchildren.

Very active in professional organizations, Jordan served as president of the American Gastroenterology Association from 1942 to 1944 and was an officer of the AMA's Section on Gastroenterology from 1941 to 1948. In 1948 she became the first woman elected to the Boston Chamber of Commerce, on which she served for three years. In 1957, two years before her death, she became vice president of the organization. She also served as a trustee of Tufts University, the New England Baptist Hospital, and the Boston Museum of Science.

Throughout her career Jordan had developed more than 500 special recipes and diets for her patients who suffered from digestive diseases. In the late 1940s *New Yorker* editor Harold Ross, one of her patients, suggested that she compile her recommendations into a book. Along with Sheila Hibbern, the magazine's food writer, Jordan wrote *Good Food for Bad Stomachs* (1951). This experience may have whetted her appetite for popular writing, for after she retired in 1958 she wrote a medical column that appeared in the *Boston American and Sunday Advertiser*.

In 1951 Jordan was awarded the Elizabeth Blackwell Teaching Award for her accomplishments throughout her career. While many female doctors of her generation complained about receiving prejudicial treatment on the basis of their gender, Jordan frequently argued that women doctors could pursue their professional careers without compromising their femininity and eventually asserted, in an article that appeared in a Radcliffe alumnae magazine in 1954, that such prejudice "no longer exists in medicine today." Certainly Jordan had managed to carve a unique path for herself on her terms. After diagnosing her own illness—cancer of the colon—Jordan died at the New England Baptist Hospital in Boston.

• A biographical account is in *Current Biography*, ed. Marjorie Dent Canda (1954). An obituary is in the *New York Times*, 22 Nov. 1959.

SHARI RUDAVSKY

JORGENSEN, Christine (30 May 1926–3 May 1989), who achieved fame by undergoing a surgical sex change, was born George William Jorgensen, Jr., in New York City, the son of George William Jorgensen, a carpenter and building contractor, and Florence Davis Hansen. Born in Manhattan and raised in the Bronx, where he attended local schools, Jorgensen was somewhat of a loner, particularly in high school, where he was sexually underdeveloped, less than five feet tall, and weighed less than 100 pounds. Underweight and probably underage, he was initially turned down for enlistment in the armed services after graduation. He worked briefly as a temporary photographer for Pathé News before being drafted into the U.S. Army in October 1945. After serving a little more than a year he was given an honorable discharge. Over the next several years he drifted from one failure to another. He tried unsuccessfully to get a studio job in Hollywood; failure led to his return to New York. For less than a semester, he attended Mohawk College in Utica, New York, on the G.I. Bill, after which he transferred to the Progressive School of Photography in New Haven, Connecticut. Still unemployed, in 1949 he entered the Manhattan Medical and Dental Assistant School, where he trained to become a lab technician.

During these years of drifting Jorgensen became increasingly worried about his lack of male physical development and wondered if he was meant to be a female. He sought out medical and psychiatric advice and after he returned to New York began on his own to take ethinyl estradiol, a female hormone. He finally found a physician, Joseph Angelo, the husband of a fellow student, in whom he could confide. Unable to receive in the United States the kind of medical help he wanted, on the advice of Angelo and others, Jorgensen set out for Sweden, where he believed such help might be available. On the way he stopped in Denmark, where he lived with relatives for a time. While there he was put in contact with Christian Hamburger, a physician who was conducting hormonal experiments and who consented to treat him free of charge. With special permission from the Danish minister of justice, Jorgensen had his testicles removed first and his still-undeveloped penis a year later. Though technically a eunuch, Jorgensen received massive doses of hormones, which led to changes in his body contours and fat distribution, and with help from the American ambassador had his passport changed to identify him as female and began life as a woman.

Jorgensen took the name Christine in recognition of Hamburger's importance to her. Much of her spare time in Copenhagen was spent making a documentary that she hoped to market in the United States. As news leaked out about the sex change in late November 1952, a media frenzy ensued. Jorgensen ultimately signed a contract with the Hearst newspapers paying $20,000 for an exclusive series to be published in the *American Weekly* on how she changed from a man to a woman. She was flown back to New York by the Hearst interests to generate publicity for the series. Capitalizing on her notoriety and needing money, she went on stage and became a celebrity performer. Her early performances, in which she presented a film of her life and commented on it, were not well received and attracted curiosity seekers, but she soon learned to present herself better, aided by her agent, Charlie Yates, who had her coached by entertainment professionals. Jorgensen's subsequent shows featured her with a partner and consisted of a 25-minute routine that included dance, music, and short dialogues.

In 1954, with the help of Dr. Angelo and her new medical adviser, Harry Benjamin, who popularized the word transsexual, Jorgensen underwent plastic surgery, this time in the United States. A vagina was constructed for her, and her external genitalia were made to look more feminine. She later wrote that only after this third round of surgery did she feel she had completed the full "transition to womanhood." For a time she even contemplated marriage with John Traub, a labor union statistician, but their request for a license was denied by authorities in New York, and while the ruling was being appealed each rethought the proposed marriage and decided not to proceed farther. In 1959 Jorgensen moved to Los Angeles, and the city served as her home from which she flew to other engagements. She also became increasingly selective of her appearances, in part because of trouble with the Internal Revenue Service and in part to live more normally. At the same time she broadened her roles by appearing as Madam Roszpettle in the Arthur Kopit play *Oh, Dad*, which opened at a summer theater on Long Island, and her success in this production was followed by other theatrical and movie ventures.

Jorgensen published her autobiography in 1967, and a film based on her life, *The Christine Jorgensen Story*, also appeared that year. The book opened up a career for her on the college lecture circuit, where she talked about gender matters and sex roles. Jorgensen's greatest accomplishment was widening the discussion of gender and sex-role problems. It was to describe her that the term transsexualism entered into medical and popular discourse. In his first discussion of the case in a medical journal, Hamburger referred to Jorgensen incorrectly as a transvestite; this article drew more than 400 letters from people requesting a sex change. Though Jorgensen was not the first to undergo sexual reassignment surgery, the massive publicity associated with her throughout her life led to increased research in the area. The major difference between her sex-change and previous sex alterations was the availability of commercially produced hormones that changed her appearance from a eunuch to a woman. The same commercial production of hormones also led to the development of chemical contraceptives such as the birth control pill. Perhaps the fact that she had to take hormones for the rest of her life was a factor in her death in San Clemente, California, from bladder and lung cancer.

• The best account of her life is *Christine Jorgensen: A Personal Autobiography* (1967). For a discussion of her importance in gender studies, see Vern L. Bullough and Bonnie Bullough, *Cross Dressing, Sex, and Gender* (1993). For a description of her case in a medical journal, see Christian Hamburger et al., "Transvestism: Hormonal, Psychiatric, and Surgical Treatment," *Journal of the American Medical Association* 152 (30 May 1953): 391–96. The first general discussion of the topic is Harry Benjamin, *The Transsexual Phenomenon* (1966). Benjamin did not coin the word transsexual; it first appeared in 1910 in the writings of Magnus Hirschfeld, but it was used little until Benjamin popularized it. An obituary is in the *New York Times*, 4 May 1989.

VERN L. BULLOUGH

JORY, Victor (23 Nov. 1902–11 Feb. 1982), screen and stage actor, was born in Dawson City, Yukon Territory, the son of Edwin Jory, a rancher, and Joanna Snyder. Jory went to school in Dawson City; Vancouver, British Columbia; and Pasadena, California. He graduated from high school in Pasadena and attended the University of California at Berkeley, ending his formal education after his freshman year.

During his late teens or early twenties, Jory became interested in pursuing an acting career. He joined a theatrical stock company in Vancouver, and, following a stint with the Canadian players, he was hired by other ensembles that toured from Denver to Cleveland to Los Angeles. Tall and physically strong, he usually was cast in youthful, athletic roles. As a sideline to acting, he competed as a boxer and wrestler, winning minor titles in both sports in British Columbia and California.

In 1929, when the motion picture studios only recently had converted from silent films to talkies, Jory was discovered by Hollywood. Gifted with an authoritative, resonant voice, he seemed an excellent candidate for the dramatically changed medium. His movie debut came in *Renegades* (1930). To earn a living, however, he continued with his stage work. In 1930 he finally reached New York City, where he had featured roles in five theater revivals. Then in 1933 and 1934 Jory achieved his Hollywood breakthrough, being cast in at least sixteen films. He took on romantic male leads in *The Devil's in Love* and *My Woman* (both 1933) and *I Believed in You* (1934). But in *Sailor's Luck* (1933) he took on a different type of role, giving—in the words of movie reviewer Leonard Maltin—"an insanely funny performance as Baron Bartolo," the lecherous villain.

The year 1935 saw a major career change for Jory after he played his final leading role in *Escape from Devil's Island*. By then, it was clear that studio producers looked on him primarily as a villain, a heavy, or a brooding eccentric. Without question, Jory's distinc-

tive facial features inspired such typecasting. His face was undoubtedly memorable, with piercing dark eyes, a long, flaring nose, and a seemingly cruel mouth that never creased in a smile. Film critics and historians have variously described him as "grim-faced," "menacing," "evil-eyed," "dour," "mesmerizing," "gloomy-visaged," and "saturnine." In all, he was a player that movie audiences of the day would dislike—even loathe—and fear.

Jory's new screen incarnation found its mark from the start. In the lavish Warner Bros. production of *A Mid-summer Night's Dream* (1935) he was called "very sinister." That descriptive phrase aptly captured the kind of parts that Jory assumed until the end of his motion picture career. From 1936 through 1939 Jory acted in supporting parts in a number of better-than-average pictures: *Meet Nero Wolfe* (1936), *First Lady* (1937), and *Dodge City* with Errol Flynn, *Each Dawn I Die* with James Cagney, and *Man of Conquest* (all 1939). But his two best roles from this period—and arguably the finest of his career—were as the "superbly villainous" Injun Joe in *The Adventures of Tom Sawyer* (1938) and as "Tara's" cruel overseer, Jonas Wilkerson, in *Gone with the Wind* (1939).

Following these lofty successes, Jory's film parts inexplicably went flat over the next two decades. During the 1940s he appeared in an average of three pictures a year, virtually all of them forgettable B movies. Rather than accepting this disappointment, Jory appeared to grasp it as an opportunity. In 1942 he returned to the stage with *Angel Street* in Chicago, and in August 1943 he made his starring debut on Broadway in *The Two Mrs. Carrolls*. New York critics scorned the play, but Jory received praise for his "good performance" in a weakly written part. He met with greater success the following year in *The Perfect Marriage* with costar Miriam Hopkins. In 1945 he played in *Therese* opposite Eva Le Gallienne and Dame May Whitty, and in 1946–1947, as a member of the American Repertory Theater, he costarred in *The Devil's Disciple*, *Androcles and the Lion*, *Henry VIII*, and other quality dramas.

At some point during his career Jory wrote two plays that received Broadway productions, *Bodies by Fisher* and *Five Who Went Mad*. In the late 1940s he also loaned his voice to radio dramas, most notably "Masterpiece Theater."

When Jory's motion picture roles dwindled to about twenty during the 1950s, he worked with theatrical touring companies in such productions as *Bell, Book and Candle* (1953), *My Three Angels* (1954), and Tennessee Williams's *Cat on a Hot Tin Roof* as Big Daddy (1957–1958). In 1959 his movie career received a prestige boost when he was cast with Marlon Brando and Anna Magnani in *The Fugitive Kind* (1960), an adaptation of Williams's *Orpheus Descending*. The film led to better parts for Jory in the 1960s, the best of them being a brief but effective portrayal of Helen Keller's father in *The Miracle Worker* (1962) and the role of a dignified Indian chief in John Ford's *Cheyenne Autumn* (1964).

Also in the 1960s, Jory focused more of his attention on television work. He starred in "Manhunt" for the full 1959–1960 season, and he made frequent appearances on such popular weekly series as "Ironside," "The Virginian," "Banacek," "Mannix," and "High Chaparral."

In addition to a handful of film roles during the 1970s, most notably *Papillon* (1973), Jory worked with several stock repertory troupes. He starred or co-starred in *Long Day's Journey into Night* (1973), *The Best Man* (1976), and *The Front Page* (1978). He also directed and starred in several plays with the Actors' Theater of Louisville, Kentucky.

The date of Jory's marriage to screen actress Jean Innes, who died in 1979, is unknown. The couple had two children, one of whom, Jon Jory, became involved in professional theater.

Victor Jory died in Santa Monica, California. Although he was of minor significance as a motion picture and stage actor, many movie lovers of all ages today can identify him by name on sight. In films, at least, Jory's villain's face was his fortune.

• No sources mention any collections of Jory's letters, diaries, or journals. Film historians markedly differ on the total number of his movie appearances. Leonard Maltin claims more than 150, and David Quinlan suggests 117. A check of the combined published filmographies of Jory turns up about 125. Reference works lack details of his life history, especially regarding his early years. Descriptive terms and phrases about Jory are culled from, among other sources, Maltin, *Leonard Maltin's Movie Encyclopedia* (1994); Ephraim Katz, *The Film Encyclopedia*, 2d ed. (1994); the *New York Times*; and Quinlan, *Quinlan's Illustrated Registry of Film Stars* (1991). Information about Jory can also be gleaned from James Robert Parish and William T. Leonard, *Hollywood Players: The Thirties* (1976), and Alfred E. Twomey, *The Versatiles: A Study of Supporting Character Actors and Actresses in the American Motion Picture, 1930–1955* (1969). An obituary is in the *New York Times*, 13 Feb. 1982.

ROBERT MIRANDON

JOSEPH (1840?–21 Sept. 1904), Nez Percé leader sometimes known as Young Joseph, was born in a cave near Joseph Creek in the Wallowa Valley, the son of Tueka-kas, or Old Joseph, a Cayuse, and Etoweenmy (Asenath), a Nez Percé. The names Joseph and Asenath were conferred on his parents by missionaries of the American Board of Commissioners for Foreign Missions, who had established themselves on Lapwai Creek, Idaho, in 1836. His Indian name, Hin-mut-too-uah-lat-kekht, in English means Thunder Rolling in the Mountains.

Joseph spent most of his boyhood in his ancestral home on the Grande Ronde River of southeastern Washington and the Wallowa country of northeastern Oregon. In a polygamous manner not unusual among the native aristocracy, Joseph married four times. Two of his wives, Wash-win-tip-yo-la-katsuh and Iah-to-win-not-mi, were widows of the Nez Percé chief Looking Glass, who was killed in 1877. Of the nine children whom Joseph fathered, all died in infancy or in youth except a daughter who reached adulthood, leaving no progeny.

Joseph's significance rested much on his opposition to U.S. government policy, which attempted to confine the Nez Percés, as other Indian peoples, to reservations. The original Nez Percé reservation, most of which encompassed present-day Idaho, included Joseph's homeland as mandated by the Walla Walla Treaty of 11 June 1855. A subsequent treaty of June 1863, however, reduced the size of the Nez Percé reservation and excluded Joseph's Grande Ronde/Wallowa territory from it. Old Joseph refused to sign the 1863 treaty or to receive annuities from it. After his death in 1871, his sons continued the policy of fierce independence, with young Joseph as the political head of the band, and Ollokot as its war chief. The encroachments of whites in their territory resulted in the brothers making common cause with other nontreaty bands of Nez Percés, such as White Bird's Salmon River band and Looking Glass's band on the forks of the Clearwater, both in present-day Idaho. Some whites intruding upon Nez Percé land seemed to have wanted to provoke the Indians so that U.S. troops would remove them to the reservation.

Joseph's protests led the United States to create another reservation in the Wallowa in June 1873, protecting a little over half of the band's territory, but pressure from settlers and developers had it rescinded after two years. Matters came to a head in the summer of 1876, when whites killed one of Joseph's people. Two councils conducted in July and November by the Nez Percé agent, J. B. Monteith, and the U.S. military revealed Joseph's determination to refuse to abandon his homeland for the diminished reservation. Rather than being forcibly removed to that confine, he preferred removal westerly to the Umatilla in northeastern Oregon among the Cayuse, with whom his people had close ties. One evidence of the cultural closeness of the Nez Percés and Cayuses was the latter's adoption of the Nez Percé Sahaptin language. Joseph also had kin among the Cayuses. Furthermore, Joseph evidenced a strong dislike of Nez Percé chief Lawyer who, with other so-called praying chiefs influenced by Christian missionaries, had signed away portions of Nez Percé land in 1863. Joseph's father, although an early Christian convert, had abandoned that faith after 1863 because of the attempts of the whites to take his lands and confine his people on the small reservation.

In May 1877 there followed a "show-down" council at Lapwai, in which Joseph and Ollokot were supported by Hush-hus-cute, chief of the Sahaptin-speaking Palouses who were also resisting confinement; by the Nez Percé prophet, Toohoolhoolsote; and by other nontreaty leaders. Toohoolhoolsote was the dominant Indian spokesman at the council, disrupting the proceedings and refusing to remove his people to the reservation. Joseph himself sought a peaceful settlement between the American Indians and the whites, while Looking Glass, perhaps as a stalling maneuver, feigned a willingness to look over lands on the reservation upon which he might settle. The council ended with the American Indians agreeing to assemble their stock and people for removal.

In the meantime the anger of the Nez Percés deepened at the prospect of removal. During preparations in June, a group of Nez Percé warriors, angry at previous outrages committed by whites against American Indians, killed several settlers in the Salmon River area. Joseph still urged the Indians not to provoke the United States, but unsure of the American reaction to the raids, many Nez Percés, including the bands of Joseph and White Bird, retired to White Bird Canyon near the Salmon River. There a United States detachment under Captain David Perry came upon them on 17 June; fighting broke out, and the troops were defeated. Joseph and White Bird then fought their way to the Clearwater, where they were joined by the bands of Looking Glass and Hahtalekin and on 11–12 July repulsed an attack made by a superior American force under General Oliver O. Howard of the Military Department of Columbia.

The extraordinary military performances of the Nez Percés led to Joseph being lauded by Americans as a master of war. In truth, the chief spent more time caring for the Indian noncombatants, and it was the head warriors such as Ollokot, Rainbow, and Five Wounds who directed most of the fighting. General strategy was determined in council, but it was Looking Glass, rather than Joseph, who was its most influential member and who advised a retreat to join the Crows of Montana. The Nez Percés fled across the Bitterroot Mountains over the Lolo Trail and turned southerly into Montana's Big Hole valley, where they successfully repulsed U.S. troops under Colonel John Gibbon on 9 August. Retreating south and west the Indians skirmished with troops again at Camas Meadows at the western entrance to Yellowstone Park on 20 August. The Crows refused to harbor the fleeing Nez Percés, and they turned northward toward Canada, skirmishing at Canyon Creek near Billings on 12 September and after crossing the Missouri River at Cow Island on 23 September.

Approaching from the east, Colonel Nelson Miles's force intercepted the Nez Percés on 30 September at Bear Paw Mountain, Montana, after the Indians had traveled 1,170 miles and come close to the Canadian border. After some of the Nez Percés, including Looking Glass and other chiefs, were killed, Joseph surrendered on 5 October. The speech he then made, with the famous words, "From where the sun now stands I will fight no more forever," has become perhaps the most quoted made by any American Indian.

The Nez Percé prisoners were taken from Montana and eventually to Oklahoma. They were transferred to Kansas in 1878, but after protesting, they were situated on the more suitable Oakland Reservation in Oklahoma. Despite this, many of the Indians continued to sicken, and Joseph campaigned for a return to the Northwest, visiting Washington and arousing much sympathy among the American public. His autobiography, denouncing his eviction from the Wallowa country, was published as "An Indian's View of Indi-

an Affairs" in the *North American Review* of April 1879. The exiled Nez Percés, reduced to but 268 souls, were finally allowed to leave in May 1885. Of this group 150, including Joseph, went on the Colville Reservation of north-central eastern Washington under the auspices of Columbia Sinkiuse peoples under Chief Moses, Joseph's longtime friend. On the Colville Joseph and even Moses were regarded by its native inhabitants as unwelcome guests, but threats on Joseph's life and warrants for his arrest precluded his return to the Wallowa. Although Joseph never abandoned his hope of moving to this homeland, he remained at Colville, resistant to the cultural changes advocated by American agents. He died at Colville and was buried immediately north of the town of Nespelem in the Nez Percé cemetery that in 1993 was declared a part of the Nez Percé National Historical Park. Joseph's reputation has grown with the years. He was not the military genius portrayed in early books and articles, but his integrity, his dignity in adversity, and his long and largely futile fight for justice have made him a powerful symbol of the tragic history of the American Indian.

• Joseph's autobiography was reprinted in Cyrus T. Brady, ed., *Northwestern Fights and Fighters* (1907). Biographies include O. O. Howard, *Nez Perce Joseph* (1881), and Helen Addison Howard, *Saga of Chief Joseph* (1965). Francis Haines, *The Nez Percés* (1955), and Alvin Josephy, *The Nez Perce Indians and the Opening of the Northwest* (1965), place Joseph's story within the context of tribal history. Grace Bartlett, *The Wallowa Country* (1984), deals with the period before 1877, but for the campaign of 1877 itself, see L. V. McWhorter, *Hear Me, My Chiefs!* (1952); Merrill D. Beal, *I Will Fight No More Forever* (1963); and Mark M. Brown, *The Flight of the Nez Perce* (1967). See also Robert H. Ruby, "Josiah Red Wolf Tells His Story," *Inland Empire Magazine Spokesman-Review*, 17 Sept. 1963, pp. 2–4; and Robert H. Ruby, "Return of the Nez Perce," *Idaho Yesterdays* 11 (Spring 1968): 12–15. Unfortunately, there is less research on Joseph's later career, but Mick Gidley, *Kopet: A Documentary Narrative of Chief Joseph's Last Years* (1981), and Robert H. Ruby and John A. Brown, *Half-Sun on the Columbia* (1965), should be consulted. See also Clifford E. Trafzer, *Yakima, Palouse, Cayuse, Umatilla, Walla Walla and Wanapum Indians* (1992).

ROBERT H. RUBY

JOSEPH, Jacob (1840 or 1841–29 July 1902), rabbi, was born in Krozsh (Kraziai), Lithuania. Little is known about his parents, wife, or children. Around the age of thirteen young Jacob Joseph went to study at the Volozhin Yeshiva, and soon after he went on to study under Rabbi Israel Salanter in Kovno (Kaunas), Lithuania. Salanter's influence on Joseph was quite significant. Joseph remained in Kovno until 1857.

Some sources claim that Joseph held his first rabbinic position in 1858; however, in 1861, or possibly earlier, he held a teaching position in at least one yeshiva. No later than 1870 Joseph was head of his own yeshiva, which was originally located in Vilon (Veliuona) and then relocated later to Jorburg (Jurbarkas) and New Zagher (Novy Zhagere). In 1883 Joseph was chosen to be a "Maggid Meisharim" (one of the official preachers) in Vilna, where he remained until 1888.

Sources relating to Joseph's East European career suggest that he was a well-respected rabbinical figure, even though he cannot be considered as one of the first-rate rabbis of East European Jewish Orthodoxy of the time. In Vilna, Joseph served as an arbitrator of several disputes pertaining to the collection of money for the Jewish communities who settled in Palestine. He endorsed many books, both in Eastern Europe and in the United States. In addition, Joseph was involved in promoting Zionist ideas, and in 1885 he was chosen as one of Vilna's representatives to a Zionist conference in Kattowitz.

Joseph's fame as a preacher in Vilna was the main reason he was nominated for the position of chief rabbi of New York's Orthodox Jews. After several years, beginning in the late 1870s, of discussions with different rabbis, the two final candidates were Joseph and Rabbi Zvi H. Rabinowitz, the son of Isaac E. Spektor, Kovno's famous rabbi. Although not the first choice of the Agudat Ha-Kehilot (consortium of Orthodox congregations), Joseph was elected to the position. Before Joseph left Vilna he insisted on receiving a six-year contract ($3,000 per annum), as well as additional funds to cover debts that he had accumulated in Eastern Europe. Only after these conditions were met did he agree to set sail for the United States. Joseph arrived on the shores of New Jersey on 7 July 1888, and his apartment was rented and furnished by the Orthodox congregations who hired him.

The nomination of Joseph by the Orthodox congregations in New York was the result of a "self-conscious attempt by East European Jewry at communal unity and united enterprise," in the words of Abraham J. Karp ("New York Chooses a Chief Rabbi," p. 182), and an attempt to raise the self-image of American Jewry. The New York Jewish community had great respect and high expectations of Joseph. Some 10,000 people attempted to enter the Beth Ha-Midrash Ha-Gadol synagogue to hear his first public sermon in the New World. However, his decline began shortly thereafter. This decline resulted in the Orthodox congregations ceasing payment of Joseph's salary in 1895, as well as in several attempts to replace him.

Many factors contributed to Joseph's failure as the chief rabbi of New York. First, he was not the community's first choice among the East European candidates for the position. Furthermore, Joseph's nomination and authority were not accepted by the Reform leadership, many of New York's uptown rabbis, several Orthodox congregations, and a number of Orthodox rabbis who resided in New York. Soon after his arrival, tensions increased between Joseph and the Orthodox congregations who hired him—mainly over issues pertaining to the supervision of slaughtering meat according to Jewish dietary laws. Finally, the rapid decline of Joseph's popularity mainly was due to the fact that he did not significantly change the style and content of his sermons as they were delivered in Eastern Europe.

Joseph did, however, succeed in establishing at least partial order and authority in the supervision over kosher meat. Furthermore, his decision to cross the ocean influenced several East European Orthodox rabbis to immigrate, including Israel Kaplan. In addition, Joseph was involved in finding rabbinical positions for rabbis who immigrated to the United States, such as Judah L. Levine, Zalman J. Friederman, and Abraham M. Shershevsky.

During the early 1890s Joseph began suffering from an unclear series of illnesses that were eventually diagnosed as paralysis. As a result, Joseph canceled more and more public appearances, and his handwriting deteriorated until it became virtually impossible for him to write. He died in New York City. The funeral procession passed by the R. H. Hoe and Company building on the way to the cemetery, where mourners were bombarded with stones, pieces of metal, and other objects. This incident started a riot that caused several injuries and was followed by a police investigation.

The death of Rabbi Joseph ended the first and last attempt to unite New York's Orthodox community behind one chief rabbi. The attempt failed in the eyes of most, if not all, of the parties involved. This evaluation of the events is agreed upon from a historical perspective as well.

• Rabbi Joseph's published writings include a collection of his sermons, *L'Beit Ya'akov*, published in four editions (Vilna 1888; Warsaw 1898; Warsaw 1900; Vilna 1912), some of which include sermons given in the United States. A number of Joseph's sermons appeared in the pamphlet *Toldot Ya'akov Yoseph B'New York* (1889). Two of his letters were published by H. R. Rabinowitz in *Talpiyot* 8, nos. 3–4 (1963): 569–73. Judah D. Eisenstein, "Toldot Agudat Ha-Kehilot B'Amerika," *Ner Ha-Ma'aravi* 1 (1895), pamphlets no. 11–13, and especially no. 12, pp. 41–47, are the first writings on Joseph's American experience (this series of articles was republished in Eisenstein's *Otzar Zichronotai* [1929]). Another noteworthy account of Joseph's American experience, written by a person who knew him, is A. Cahan, "The Late Rabbi Joseph, Hebrew Patriarch of New York," *American Monthly Review of Reviews* 26, no. 3 (Sept. 1902): 311–15; a shorter version was published in the *American Hebrew* 71, no. 16 (5 Sept. 1902): 426. See also Cahan's "A Back Number" in *Grandma Never Lived in America: The New Journalism of Abraham Cahan*, ed. M. Rischin (1985). The best account of Joseph's time in the United States remains Abraham J. Karp's remarkable article "New York Chooses a Chief Rabbi," *Publications of the American Jewish Historical Society* 44, no. 3 (1955): 129–99. By using rare source material Karp uncovers much of the background leading up to Joseph's appointment, arrival in New York, experience, decline, and funeral. In addition, Karp also discusses the possible reasons for his failure. L. Dinnerstein, "The Funeral of Rabbi Jacob Joseph," in *Anti-Semitism in American History*, ed. D. A. Gerber (1986), discusses the riots at Rabbi Joseph's funeral as well as the police investigation that followed the incident. Additional references to Joseph include K. Caplan, "Rabbi Jacob Joseph, New York's Chief Rabbi: New Perspectives," *Hebrew Union College Annual* 67 (1996): 1–43 (Hebrew paging); J. S. Gurock, "Resisters and Accommodators," *American Jewish Archives* 35, no. 2 (1983): 100–87; Karp, *Haven and Home* (1985); A. Rakeffet-Rothkoff, *The Silver Era in*

American Jewish Orthodoxy (1981); and M. D. Sherman, *Orthodox Judaism in America: A Biographical Dictionary and Sourcebook* (1996).

KIMMY CAPLAN

JOSEPHSON, Matthew (15 Feb. 1899–13 Mar. 1978), writer, was born in Brooklyn, New York, the son of Julius Josephson, a banker, and Sarah Kasindorf. A child of Jewish immigrants from Romania and Russia, Josephson graduated from Columbia University in 1920. That same year he married Hannah Geffen, a nineteen-year-old reporter for the *New York American* who had attended Hunter College and the Columbia School of Journalism. While a student, Josephson had frequented the bohemian cafés of Greenwich Village and developed a consuming passion to be a poet. In the Village he befriended the volatile young poet Hart Crane and played a key role in encouraging Crane's literary genius.

In October 1921 the Josephsons joined the wave of American writers headed for Paris. Josephson went to Europe primarily because he considered the United States to be a cultural backwater and because his literary idols were European. In Paris, Josephson aligned himself with the Dadaists and helped edit *Secession* and *Broom*, two short-lived but highly visible and contentious international journals devoted to artistic experimentalism. "We have decided to attach ourselves to the Dadaists," he reported to a friend, "of whom thrills may be wrested at the lowest cost."

In 1923 the Josephsons returned to New York, and several months later Josephson began work as a stockbroker on Wall Street as a means of paying the bills and supporting his literary efforts. But even though he found the financial world fascinating, its relentless pressures and material calculus eventually wore him down, and early in 1926 he resigned to devote his full attention to writing. "I have decided to be middle class," he reported to his close friend Kenneth Burke.

Josephson hoped to write a novel of distinction, but he floundered as a writer of fiction. His literary fortunes took an upturn when he was commissioned to write a biography of Émile Zola in 1926. While researching the book, Josephson fastened on a literary outlook and social philosophy that would shape the rest of his career. Until then, he had been largely unconcerned with issues of social injustice or political corruption. When he read about Zola and the Dreyfus Affair, however, he found that through the written word to gain public support for some important cause, a writer could become "heroic."

Josephson's biography of Zola, *Zola and His Time*, published in 1928, enjoyed brisk sales and received high praise from reviewers. Malcolm Cowley described it as "vigorous, absorbing, hastily written, superbly documented, and rich, amazingly rich." Josephson had discovered his genre. Realizing that his greatest talent was not for poetry or fiction, he felt confident with biography and history, making vivid characters and weaving the themes that made up great lives. Through biography, he believed, "I could communicate with my readers on a variety of ideas—on art and life, love and death, on human freedom and justice—and would feel myself in contact with a real public." He followed his study of Zola with an equally successful portrait of Jean-Jacques Rousseau (1931). As a popular biographer and prolific journalist, Josephson developed a steady income from his writing, earning enough to provide for his wife and two children and to maintain a New York apartment and a country home in Sherman, Connecticut.

During the 1930s Josephson put his aroused social conscience and new literary outlook into practice. He became active on the literary Left as a self-described "fellow traveler" of the Communist party (he claimed he "was not virtuous enough" to be a formal member), writing dozens of articles in the *New Republic*, *New Masses*, and other left-wing journals. He also participated in political rallies, writers' congresses, and labor protests. Determined to probe the roots of the Great Depression, Josephson during the thirties wrote *The Robber Barons* (1934), *The Politicos* (1938), and *The President Makers* (1940). *The Robber Barons*, written with the support of a Guggenheim Fellowship and dedicated to Josephson's friend and neighbor, the muckraking historian Charles Beard, vividly captured the buccaneering activities of Jay Gould, John D. Rockefeller, Andrew Carnegie, and other captains of industry and finance. The book was an immediate bestseller and exercised a powerful impact on popular understanding of America's first industrial giants.

Josephson wrote history with rage and partisanship, turning to the past out of a passionate concern for the present and future of American society. History, in his view, should be written by moralists rather than by pedants. It should move people, stir them to awakening, and thereby promote social improvement. Historical writing, he once asserted, cannot be accomplished well "by persons who are fish-blooded, without moral fibre, without any sense of human values, without human compassion or the capacity for 'noble indignation.' The game is to make history come alive, and impress us as true." Josephson at times, driven by his moral urgency and socioeconomic convictions, made villains of people who deserve greater understanding. But despite their subjectivity and their minor factual errors, his three historical studies surpassed all previous efforts to explain political and economic life in the half-century after the Civil War.

After Pearl Harbor, Josephson supported the Allied cause even though he shared Beard's suspicions that President Franklin Roosevelt had somehow engineered the Japanese attack. During the 1940s Josephson continued to make his living as a writer, producing well-received biographies of Victor Hugo and Stendhal and a series of profiles of prominent Americans for the *New Yorker* and *Saturday Evening Post*. He was elected to the National Academy of Arts and Letters in 1948.

Like so many other left-wing intellectuals, Josephson was stunned by the Nazi-Soviet Pact in 1939 and the revelations of Stalin's purge trials, but he never recanted his political activism of the 1930s or his radical sympathies. After 1945 Josephson doggedly maintained his militant stance, aligning himself with the *Nation* magazine and embracing its version of progressive liberalism. During the Cold War era Josephson used the pages of the magazine to support Henry Wallace, organized labor, social welfare legislation, arms control, and civil liberties. Although the target of an FBI investigation, he refused to be cowed by McCarthyism. Writing in the *Nation* in 1952, he charged that "federal and state loyalty boards, Congressional committees aiming at thought control, and our big Drummer Boy Joe in the Senate have created a veritable panic over the alleged internal danger offered by a few Communists—a panic that has particularly affected our less sophisticated citizenry."

Meanwhile, Josephson continued his career as biographer and historian. In 1960 he won the Francis Parkman Prize for his study of Thomas Edison. Nine years later he received the Van Wyck Brooks Prize for a lively biography of Al Smith, coauthored with his wife. Josephson also published two colorful volumes of memoirs during the 1960s—*Life among the Surrealists* (1962) and *Infidel in the Temple* (1967). When he died in Santa Cruz, California, he was at work on a redemptive biography of Alger Hiss.

Josephson was a fascinating, often paradoxical man, a combination of noble ideals and self-serving ambition. He was stubborn, temperamental, vain, disagreeable—and a good hater. Quick to detect errors in others, he was slow to discern his own faults. Late in life he admitted that he "was a rather indiscreet person. I made a lot of enemies. I offended many people. I have enjoyed that. I never pulled my punches. Some people liked me for that, others are down on it." Yet if Josephson was often arrogant and petulant in dealing with critics, he could be warm and convivial, witty and urbane, when among friends. He had an ironic sense of humor and a cosmopolitan charm that served to disarm much of his bluster. Cowley remembered him as a "delightful and stimulating companion with a sweep and swoop of imagination, more than any other of my friends."

Viewed in retrospect, Josephson's career followed the pattern of alienation, exile, return, and reintegration common to many middle-class writers of his literary generation. At heart, he always remained essentially a bourgeois intellectual with a strong sense of social concern and a disdain for corporate power. Hannah Josephson recognized that her husband was a split personality, torn between being a bohemian rebel and being a bourgeois social reformer. The tense relationship between politics and literature, journalism and art, rebellion and responsibility, provided the mainspring of his life and career.

• Letters to and from Josephson are in the Matthew and Hannah Josephson Papers, Beinecke Library, Yale University. Additional correspondence can be found in the Malcolm Cowley Papers, Newberry Library, Chicago, and the Kenneth Burke Papers in the Pennsylvania State University Library. The only biography of Josephson is David E. Shi, *Matthew Josephson, Bourgeois Bohemian* (1981). See also Malcolm Cowley, *Exile's Return* (1951); Daniel Aaron; *Writers on the Left* (1961); and Harold Loeb, *The Way It Was* (1959). An obituary is in the *New York Times*, 14 Mar. 1978.

DAVID E. SHI

JOSLIN, Elliott Proctor (6 June 1869–28 Jan. 1962), physician and medical educator, was born in Oxford, Massachusetts, the son of Allen L. Joslin, a shoe manufacturer, and Sara Emerson Proctor, a member of the prominent Salem, Massachusetts, family. His early schooling was at Leicester Academy and Yale College (1890). He studied chemistry at Yale's Sheffield Scientific School in 1891 under R. H. Chittenden, a pioneer in clinical chemistry. From 1891 to 1895 he attended Harvard Medical School in Boston, graduating as the valedictorian. In his second year of medical school, he won the Boylston (Honors) Society prize for a work later published as *The Pathology of Diabetes Mellitus* (1894). From 1895 to the start of his own practice of medicine in 1898, he trained at the Massachusetts General Hospital and studied twice in Germany and Austria with the leading investigators in the field of metabolism. He married Elizabeth Denny in 1902; they had three children.

Joslin practiced medicine in the Back Bay section of Boston at 81 Bay State Road, where his townhouse and an adjacent building were expanded over the next fifty years to accommodate his practice and staff. In 1956 he moved his office to a modern complex later named the Joslin Diabetes Center. He advanced his practice from the broad area of internal medicine (emphasizing diagnostic methods) to specializing in the treatment and study of diabetes.

Starting in 1908, Joslin collaborated with the physiologist Francis G. Benedict, the director of the Nutrition Laboratory of the Carnegie Institution in Boston, on metabolic balance studies (an extensive series of calorimetric determinations on fasting and variously fed diabetic patients with a spectrum of degrees of severity of diabetes). Desperation for an advancement in treating the increasing numbers of his private patients dying of diabetic ketoacidosis (a clinical condition, usually abrupt in onset, of nausea, vomitting, air hunger, and stupor called "coma" that inevitably signaled death) attracted him to the observations of Frederick Allen. Allen was a young, eccentric investigator who had determined the beneficial effects of carbohydrate-restricted diets in prolonging the lives of experimentally induced diabetic animals (Harvard) and later humans (Rockefeller Institute). Combining Benedict's balance study format with the Allen diets, Joslin was able to show to his satisfaction that "undernutrition" prolonged the lives of his patients. His patients were often near death from infection and acidosis when they were admitted to "cottage" units located on the grounds of the nearby New England Deaconess Hospital, often staying for weeks at a time. A partnership with the Deaconess School of Nursing developed; there the rigorous training program allowed him to employ well-disciplined nurses as allies for the measured-diets program.

When Joslin had collected 1,000 of his own cases, he felt that the new diet treatment had made enough of a difference. As he stated in the preface to his 1916 monograph titled *The Treatment of Diabetes Mellitus,* the "mortality of [his] patients was approximately 20 percent lower than for the previous year," a result of "the introduction of fasting and the emphasis on physical exercise." This textbook rapidly became the leading review on the subject and projected Joslin onto the world scene. It was revised ten times during his lifetime. Through this medium and countless articles and lectures, Joslin alerted other investigators, public health officials, and general practioners to this "silent epidemic."

Joslin maintained an epidemiological chronicle of his patients with diabetes by methodically recording the extensive data from their charts to large ledgers called by his staff the "Black Books." Joslin wrote in 1928 that his "private statistics [have] preceded public statistics." The Metropolitan Life Insurance Company contracted with Joslin to use his statistics for their actuarial tables. These records, today numbering more than 200,000, are the largest repository of clinical data on the subject in the world.

In 1918 Joslin published a companion volume to his previous textbook, titled *Diabetic Manual—for the Doctor and Patient.* This manual's preventive medicine advice translated to the patient agenda what he had previously required of nurses. It became a bestseller, forecasting the modern, medically sponsored "self-help" movement, and it served as the syllabus of preventive medicine for his mandatory classroom instruction. Educating patients about their condition so that they could take corrective action became the "Joslin" method. He expanded the role of his nurses in the community after the arrival of insulin, sending them forth with an instructional mandate on correct diet substitutions, exercise, foot care, and insulin adjustment. These so-called wandering diabetic nurses became the forerunners of later certified diabetes educators (C.D.E.) in the United States. Joslin's special nurses were also pioneers in the children's camp effort that started in New England in the decade after the availability of insulin.

With the commercial availability of insulin in 1923, Joslin's practice skyrocketed. His private group practice was gradually termed the Joslin Clinic, but this association was not legalized until 1952. Joslin expected his associates and consultants to administer to the patient as a team. Following a large benefaction in 1928 from George F. Baker, key collaborations were organized, including publications on limb salvage (involving surgeons, physicians, and podiatrists) and the pathology of diabetes complications. Early cesarean delivery for pregnant mothers with insulin-dependent diabetes emerged with the combined work of obstetricians and endocrinologists (principally Priscilla White, who created the international classification of pregnancy complicated by diabetes according to fetal

risk). The first hospital blood-glucose monitoring system of premeal testing, the forerunner of the home-monitoring revolution, emerged under his direction by 1940. The ophthalmologist of the Joslin group, William Beetham, was able to plan the landmark method of laser retinal treatment (1967) from his previous three-decade observations of the retinae of Joslin's clinic patients.

Joslin was a persistent fundraiser for Harvard Medical School and diabetes research. His "free care" camp and diabetes research laboratory funds were incorporated into the Diabetes Foundation, Inc. in 1953.

Joslin and his team became identified with the clinical position enumerated in Joslin's early writings, which proposed that strict control of blood-sugar levels through a restricted carbohydrate diet, frequent urine/blood-glucose testing to establish the correct insulin dosage, and a daily planned exercise regimen prevents complications of the eye, the kidney, and the arteries of the lower limbs. The evidence for this position was endlessly and often acrimoniously debated among investigators and endocrinologists across the country, especially from 1950 to 1975. The American Diabetes Association clearly was divided on this topic from its founding. Opposition to the Joslin thesis often led to stereotyping of Joslin's group as medical reactionaries. Eventually, increasing evidence of glucose-driven lesions in the retina capillaries and kidney glomerulus tempered the enthusiasm of opponents of "tight" blood-glucose control. This controversy was settled and Joslin's position supported by a ten-year national study, "The Diabetes Control and Complications Trial Report," published in the *New England Journal of Medicine* in 1993. This study showed that very good levels of glucose control delayed the onset of the new complications under investigation as well as delaying the progression of established vascular and neurological lesions. Joslin died in Brookline, Massachusetts.

• Joslin's papers, including his edited textbooks, notebooks, medical record tabulations, and correspondence with patients, are in the Joslin Diabetes Center Marble Library Special Collection Room and medical records vault. Anna C. Holt, *A Memoir* (1969), traces his life but does not include the impact or medical context of Joslin and his staff's work. The prefaces to his *The Treatment of Diabetes Mellitus* and *A Diabetic Manual* are important guides to his work. His work is also discussed at length in Chris Feudtner, "Bittersweet: The Transformation of Diabetes into a Chronic Illness in Twentieth-Century America" (Ph.D. diss., Univ. of Pennsylvania, 1995). A longer summary of Joslin's life is the tribute by his principal editor, Alexander Marble, "Elliott Proctor Joslin (1869–1962)," *Transactions of the Association of American Physicians* 75 (1962): 25–29. The glucose control controversy is outlined in the history of the American Diabetes Association, Dorothy Born, ed., *The Journey and the Dream* (1990). An overview of key topics in the history of diabetes is L. Krall et al., "The History of Diabetes" in *Joslin's Diabetes Mellitus,* 13th ed., ed. C. Ronald Kahn and Gordon Weir (1994).

DONALD M. BARNETT

JOSS, Addie (12 Apr. 1880–14 Apr. 1911), baseball player, was born Adrian Joss in Juneau, Wisconsin, the son of Jacob Joss and Theresa Staudenmeyer, farmers. Joss began his career as a teenager, playing semiprofessional baseball in Wisconsin. He then enrolled at the University of Wisconsin, where he pitched for the baseball team. His stellar pitching for the semipro team in Sheboygan, however, first attracted the attention of the professional leagues. Bob Gilks, manager of the Toledo team of the Inter-State League, hearing about the talented youngster, scouted and signed him to a Toledo contract in 1900. That season, Joss won 19 games and lost 16. Toledo joined the Western Association in 1901, and Joss accompanied them, winning 25 games and losing 15 and striking out a career-high 217 batters.

The right-handed thrower and batter became baseball's newest pitching phenomenon, attracting major league talent hunters. The Brooklyn Dodgers of the National League attempted to recruit him, but Bill Armour, manager of the Cleveland Indians of the American League, ultimately signed Joss. The signing of Joss gave the Cleveland fans reason to rejoice, as the 1901 Cleveland club, then known as the Bluebirds, had finished in seventh place in the first American League season. Joss made his first start in the major leagues on 26 April 1902 against the St. Louis Browns. The stunning debut for a rookie saw him one-hit the Browns, a feat few pitchers have accomplished in their initial game. Jesse Burkett of St. Louis, with two strikes, hit a sinking liner to right field. Some believe Erwin Harvey caught the ball inches off the ground, but umpire Robert L. Caruthers ruled that Harvey had trapped the ball.

Despite overpowering pitching by Joss and timely hitting by Napoleon Lajoie, the Cleveland club finished in fifth place. Joss, however, sparked renewed interest in the club, drawing record crowds while boasting a 17-win, 13-loss season. He married Lillian Shinivar in October 1902; they had two children. In 1903 Joss won 18 games and lost 13, leading the Cleveland Bluebirds into third place. His record fell to 14–10 in 1904, but during the next four seasons he won 20, 21, 27, and 24 games, respectively, leading the league with 27 wins in 1907.

Joss had a fine fastball and an exceptional curve. His pinwheel motion enabled him to hurl two no-hitters. His 2 October 1908 masterpiece was extraordinary, only the second perfect game in the relatively new league. It came in the last week of the season during an intense pennant race, in which Cleveland, the Chicago White Sox, and the Detroit Tigers were virtually tied. Detroit won the pennant on the last day of the season. Joss faced Chicago ace and future Hall of Famer "Big Ed" Walsh, who, having enjoyed an incredible season, was seeking his 41st win. Walsh, working on two days rest, pitched an excellent game, allowing only four hits, walking one, and striking out 15. Joss bettered Walsh's performance with a perfect game, winning 1–0 on a tainted run. It remains one of the classic pitching duels in baseball history and kept the Naps,

as the Cleveland team was then known, in the pennant chase. His second no-hitter, on 20 April 1910, also came against the White Sox. He walked two, and one batter reached base on an error, but only five balls were hit to the outfield.

During spring training in 1911, Joss fainted on the bench. Doctors ordered him home. The baseball world was stunned when the popular pitcher died of tubercular meningitis in Toledo, Ohio, two days after the 1911 season opened. His funeral, one of the largest in Toledo history, included all his teammates; the sermon was delivered by evangelist Billy Sunday. The top American League players formed an all-star team to play the Indians for the benefit of the Joss family. The National Baseball Hall of Fame bent its rules in 1978 to allow him to become a member, even though he had not pitched ten complete major league seasons. Altogether, Joss won 160 games and lost 97, remarkably completed 234 of 260 starts, and compiled a lifetime 1.88 ERA. Had he lived longer, the excellent pitcher might have become one of the all-time best.

• Biographical material appears in the Adrian "Addie" Joss File, National Baseball Hall of Fame Library, Cooperstown, N.Y. For biographical profiles, see Mike Shatzkin, ed., *The Ballplayers* (1990), and David L. Porter, ed., *Biographical Dictionary of American Sports: Baseball* (1987). Playing career statistics can be found in *Daguerreotypes*, 8th ed. (1990), and *Who's Who in Baseball, 1872–1990* (1990). For Joss's role in the Indians, see Franklin Lewis, *The Cleveland Indians* (1949). An obituary is in the *Cleveland Plain Dealer*, 15 Apr. 1911.

EDWARD H. WALTON

JOSSELYN, John (fl. 1630–1675), travel writer and naturalist, was born in Willingale-Doe (probably at Torrell's Hall), Essex, England, the son of Sir Thomas Josselyn, a gentleman landholder, and Theodora Cooke Bere of Kent. Josselyn's formal education is unknown, though one may well infer from his writings easy familiarity with the classics and English poets as well as extensive knowledge of medicine, botany, and natural history. It is likely that the young Josselyn accompanied his family in their move to the Isle of Ely sometime in the period 1614–1618 when financial reverses forced Sir Thomas's sale of Torrell's Hall. This decline in fortune was followed by others that resulted in the loss of most if not all of the family estate.

Josselyn's whereabouts prior to 1638 are unknown, but on 26 April of that year he sailed from England on board the ship *New Supply* for New England, arriving in Boston on 2 July. There he paid his respects to two of the colony's leading citizens, Governor John Winthrop and the Reverend John Cotton. To Cotton he presented a metrical version of the Psalms by the English poet Francis Quarles. From Boston Josselyn proceeded to Black Point (now Scarborough), Maine, where his elder brother, Henry, had been living since 1634 and was associated with the governing body of the province. He remained there until October 1639, when he returned to England, and thereafter for the next twenty-four years his life is unknown.

On 23 May 1663 Josselyn arrived in Gravesend and three days later sailed from England aboard the *Society*, a Massachusetts-owned vessel. On 28 July he landed in Boston, where he remained until 8 September, sailing up the coast with several stops until arriving on the fifteenth at Black Point again to visit his brother. Here, Josselyn recorded, "I resided eight years, and made it my business to discover all along the Natural, Physical, and Chyrugical Rarities of this New-found World." And so he did, exploring in detail the natural history of the country as well as sympathetically observing the culture and customs of the Native Americans in the area. The mores, motives, and social practices of the Puritans of New England also attracted his much less appreciative, indeed caustic, view. A royalist in sympathy and sentiment, Josselyn found little attractive in the Puritan divines and magistrates of Massachusetts Bay, and he was thrice, in 1665, 1667, and 1668, fined for lack of church attendance. On 28 August 1671 Josselyn left Black Point to return to Boston, where on 10 October he left New England for the last time, arriving in London on 1 December.

In the three years immediately following his return to England, Josselyn wrote the two works upon which his reputation rests. *New-Englands Rarities Discovered: In Birds, Beasts, Fishes, Serpents, and Plants of that Country* was published in 1672, sometime before 15 July, for it was noted in the *Philosophical Transactions* of the Royal Society on that date. Two years later *An Account of Two Voyages to New-England* appeared, dedicated to the Royal Society. No mention appeared in the *Transactions* this time, but the book was popular enough to warrant a second edition in 1675.

Both *New-Englands Rarities* and *An Account of Two Voyages* evoke a sense of wonder and infinite possibility in the presence of the New World's munificence. Josselyn is an early writer in a long succession to develop this theme in American literature. The prose in his inventories of beasts, birds, fish, and plants is often exuberant and occasionally lyrical and exhibits a heightened sensibility in which the marvelous coexists in understated tension with scientifically recorded observation. This creative tension springs from Josselyn's own double loyalty: to the new science of his own era and to the residual dream of a golden age in the brave new world of the American continent—an enduring legacy of the Renaissance.

Josselyn's organization and method typically reflect the desire of the Royal Academy for scientific observation as well as that of promoters of colonization for useful information, as in, for example, his description of "The *Soile* or *Sea Calf*, a Creature that brings forth her young ones upon dry land, but at other times keeps in the Sea preying upon Fish. . . . The Oyl of it is much used by the *Indians*, who eat of it with their Fish, and anoint their limbs therewith, and their Wounds and Sores." At other times keen observation and lore combine to lyrical effect, as in his account of

"The *Humming Bird*, the least of all Birds, little bigger than a *Dor*, of variable glittering Colours, they feed upon Honey, which they suck out of Blossoms and Flowers with their long Needle-like Bills; they sleep all Winter, and are not to be seen till the Spring, at which time they breed in little Nests made up like a bottom of soft Silk-like matter, their Eggs no bigger than white Pease, they hatch three or four at a time, and are proper to this Country."

In yet other descriptions Josselyn's sense of wonder and possibility is central: Sturgeon are "here in great plenty, and in some rivers so numerous, that it is hazardous for Canoes and the like small Vessels to pass to and again," and bears are never aggressive except "in rutting time, and then they walk the Country twenty, thirty, forty in a company making a hideous noise with roaring, which you may hear a mile or two before they come so near to endanger the Traveller." Josselyn's account of Native Americans most clearly reveals his vision of America as a rediscovered Eden, a classical world preserved in innocence by Nature. Here the lives of the inhabitants are reminiscent of classical models of pagan virtue and decorum. "Their Language is very significant, using but few words, every word having a diverse signification, which is express by gesture," and "Their Speeches in their Assemblies are very gravely delivered, commonly in perfect *Hexamiter* Verse, with great silence and attention, and answered again *ex tempore* after the same manner." Occasionally, however, the tension in Josselyn's prose between science and myth becomes self-conscious, as in his entry on rubies, and he releases it by ironic acknowledgment designed to bolster his own scientific credibility: "I have heard a story of an Indian, that found a stone, up in the Country, by a great Pond as big as an Egg, that in a dark Night would give light to read by; but I take it to be but a story."

Josselyn's work provides a wealth of information on the natural history of coastal Maine, New Hampshire, and northern Massachusetts in the seventeenth century. His historical, political, and social observations are of continuing interest to scholars, and his sharply etched satire and blunt criticism of the Puritans in *An Account of Two Voyages* is a valuable royalist counterpoint to the majority of New England writing of the period. In addition, Josselyn combines with his neoclassic vision of Native Americans a sensitivity and humane curiosity almost entirely lacking in the work of his Puritan contemporaries, and his detailed observations of native customs, manners, and behavior contain much valuable historical and anthropological information. Both volumes also contain verses. The smooth neoclassicism of "Verses . . . upon the Indian Squa" suggests an adaptation of an earlier poem, probably by another hand. In his version Josselyn turns the question of "Whether White or Black be best" to a sympathetic exploration of the naive sensuality of physical beauty in the natural state where "such perfection here appears / It neither Wind or Sun-shine fears." More original and more powerful is the stunningly good "And the bitter storm augments; the wild winds rage," Josselyn's taut, dramatic evocation of a sea storm he witnessed aboard ship in November 1639. There is a hard-edged Elizabethan tone to the lines, the images are compressed and jammed together, the cadence is rough, and paradox reigns in what is a nearly perfectly realized sea-deliverance poem:

And Heaven to Seas descended; no star shown;
Blind night in darkness, tempests, and her own
Dread terrours lost; yet this dire lightning turns
To more fear'd light; the Sea with lightning Burns.
The Pilot knew not what to chuse or fly,
Art stood amaz'd in Ambiguity.

Nothing is known of Josselyn's life after 1675, although there is an indication of royal patronage after his resettlement in England. In the course of *An Account of Two Voyages* he notes that "I am now return'd into my Native Countrey, and by the providence of the Almighty, and the bounty of my Royal Soveraigness am disposed to a holy quiet of study and meditation for the good of my soul." A tombstone has been located in Willingale Doe bearing his name and a death date of 1700; if it is his, he lived to a very ripe age.

• Edward Tuckerman edited *New-Englands Rarities* in *American Antiquarian Society Transactions and Proceedings* 4 (1860): 103–238, and the Massachusetts Historical Society produced a facsimile edition in 1972. *An Account of Two Voyages* is available in a scholarly edition with an excellent introduction and notes by Paul J. Lindholdt in *John Josselyn, Colonial Traveler* (1988). Josselyn's poetry is in Harrison T. Meserole, *Seventeenth-Century American Poetry* (1968). Additional biographical information and analysis is available in Horace P. Beck, *The Folklore of Maine* (1957); George Carey, "John Josselyn: Maine's First Folklorist," *Down East* 19 (1973): 20, 23–25, 27–28; Charles E. Clark, *Maine: A Bicentennial History* (1977); Beatrice H. Comas, "John Josselyn, 'Gent,' Maine's First Folklorist," *Early American Life* 15 (1984): 70–82; Karl Josef Hltgen, "Frances Quarles, John Josselyn, and the Bay Psalm Book," *Seventeenth-Century News* 34 (1976): 42–46; and Philip F. Gura, "Thoreau and John Josselyn," *New England Quarterly* 48 (1975): 505–18.

DONALD WHARTON

JOUETT, James Edward (7 Feb. 1826–30 Sept. 1902), naval officer, was born near Lexington, Kentucky, the son of Matthew Harris Jouett, a portrait painter, and Margaret Henderson Allen. He secured an appointment in the U.S. Navy as a midshipman at age fifteen and first saw action in 1843 in the "Berribee War" aboard the *Decatur* as a part of the African Squadron under the command of Captain Matthew Calbraith Perry. In this conflict, Perry punished a tribe that had been harassing and pillaging merchantmen and the former slave settlement in Liberia. During the war with Mexico, Jouett, on board the *John Adams*, was a part of the contingent that landed in defense of Port Isabel.

The navy sent Jouett in 1846 to the newly established U.S. Naval Academy at Annapolis for a year's instruction. In 1847 he graduated, becoming a passed midshipman, and drew duty aboard the *St. Lawrence* on a Mediterranean cruise. After his return, in 1852 he married Galena Stockett; they had one son. Jouett's next sea duty was in the Pacific, serving on both the *Lexington* and the *St. Mary's*. Promoted to lieutenant, he served aboard the steamer *M. W. Chapin* in the 1858–1859 Paraguayan expedition.

Jouett was stationed at Pensacola, Florida, when the Civil War broke out, and he was promptly captured by Confederate forces. However, he soon saw action against the southerners. The Confederates had released him, claiming the naval officer had given his parole not to bear arms against Florida. Jouett's story refuted that assertion, and he made his way north and was dispatched to the Union blockade of Galveston, Texas. Operating there aboard the *Santee*, he led a boat party in early November 1861 and, in spite of several wounds in the action, captured the southern armed schooner *Royal Yacht*. Jouett took the crew and set fire to the Confederate warship, earning the praise of his superiors. He was placed in command of the USS *Montgomery* in December 1861.

Jouett, known as "Fighting Jim," increased his reputation for battle prowess off the coast of Mobile. He was the skipper of the fast steamer *R. R. Cuyler*, and he and his crew were part of the Union blockade of Mobile Bay in April 1863. Catching the eye of Admiral David G. Farragut for his skill in ship handling in September, he was given command of the fastest gunboat in the blockading squadron, the sidewheeler *Metacomet*. In the August 1864 battle of Mobile Bay, the *Metacomet* and its skipper were given the mission of protecting Farragut and his flagship, the *Hartford*. The *Metacomet* was lashed to the *Hartford*, and they proceeded into the teeth of the Confederate defenses, at which time Farragut uttered his oft-quoted "Damn the torpedoes!" However, the full quote also included the command, "Jouett, full speed!" Once inside the bay, the *Metacomet* was cut away and sent after the Confederate gunboats *Selma* and *Gaines*. Again Jouett did not disappoint his commander. He threaded through unfamiliar shoals in fast pursuit of the southern warships, and he and his crew badly damaged the *Selma* and captured the *Gaines*. Since Jouett and his crew had already divided almost $100,000 in prize money from captured ships that had attempted to run the Union blockade off Mobile Bay, the successful Federal naval officer was not specially singled out for his brilliant performance during the battle of Mobile Bay.

Jouett's postwar reputation was somewhat tarnished among his contemporaries by a single incident. In 1880 he attempted to be advanced to the rank of rear admiral over the heads of sixteen officers senior to him, an act considered not in keeping with the better customs of the service. However, his overall career performance secured for him a special place among the naval officers of his times. Therefore, he was promoted to rear admiral, and he performed admirably as the commander of the North Atlantic Squadron. It is believed that in that position he established the lasting custom of the ship's crew saluting the flag as it was lowered or raised. His last notable service to the United States was in 1885, when he led an eight-ship expedition to Panama, where, at Colon, vital commerce and transport had been curtailed by an insurrection against the Colombian government. Upon his arrival off Panama, Jouett's aggressive actions resulted in the resumption of trans-isthmus rail traffic. He retired in 1890. In an unusual gesture of appreciation for long and faithful contributions to the United States, the Congress allowed Jouett to continue drawing his full active duty pay in his declining years. He died in Sandy Spring, Maryland.

• Descriptions of Jouett are in Alfred Pirtle, *United Service* (Dec. 1896 and Jan. 1897), and J. M. Morgan, "Jim Jouett," in *Prince and Boatswain*, ed. C. E. Clark (1915). See also articles in *Army and Naval Journal* (6, 13, 20, and 27 Mar. and 12 and 19 June 1880). Additional information about the admiral is in George Baber, *Kentucky State Historical Social Register* (May 1914), and Loyall Farragut, *The Life of David Glascow Farragut* (1879). Jouett's career highlights are traced in L. R. Hamersly, *The Records of Living Officers of the U.S. Navy and Marine Corps*, 4th ed. (1890). His Civil War service is in *The Official Records of the Union and Confederate Navies in the War of the Rebellion*, vol. 4, 16, and 21 (30 vols., 1894–1922). Obituaries are in the *Army and Naval Journal* (4 Oct. 1902), and the *New York Times*, 2 Oct. 1902.

ROD PASCHALL

JOUETT, Matthew Harris (22 Apr. 1788–10 Aug. 1827), portrait painter, was born near Harrodsburg in Mercer County, Kentucky, the son of Captain John "Jack" Jouett, a revolutionary war militia officer and farmer, and Sallie Robards. He showed artistic ability at a very early age and was able to create realistic likenesses without any formal training. One of his earliest subjects was an Indian chief drawn with a brush made from a turkey feather.

About 1793 the Jouett family moved to Woodford County, Kentucky, where Jouett spent his formative years. He showed outstanding precocity and was selected to attend Transylvania University in Lexington. His friend, William Leavy, recalled that he attended college from 1803 to 1807, while another account says he was there from 1804 until graduation with honors in 1808. On graduation he began to study law with Judge George M. Bibb, Chief Justice of the Appellate Court of Kentucky. After slightly more than a year under the tutelage of Judge Bibb, Jouett moved to Lexington and began to practice his profession while continuing to paint portraits on the side.

On 25 May 1812 Jouett married Margaret "Peggy" Henderson Allen of Fayette County, Kentucky. War with England was declared that same year, and Jouett entered the Third Mounted Regiment of Kentucky Volunteers. He later served as first lieutenant and paymaster of the Twenty-eighth U.S. Infantry, was appointed a captain on 13 July 1814, and resigned his commission on 20 January 1815. During his service the payrolls were lost in battle. Although he was not personally responsible for the loss, Jouett's sense of honor prompted him to assume the debt, which was not paid off until shortly before his death.

In 1815, on resigning from the army, Jouett decided to forego the practice of law and opened a studio in Lexington, Kentucky, for painting miniatures and portraits. His reputation as an artist was already established, for in addition to more formal portraits done previously, he had entertained his fellow War of 1812 officers by drawing their likenesses in charcoal on drum heads. He was often able to complete three portraits a week at twenty-five dollars each, thus earning a comfortable living. His preference for painting over law irritated his father, who remarked: "I sent Matthew to college to make a gentleman of him, and he has turned out to be nothing but a damned sign painter" (Price, p. 20).

In the early summer of 1816 Jouett's desire to obtain further instruction in painting took him to Boston and the studio of Gilbert Stuart. They established an immediate rapport, and soon the Kentuckian began studying under America's then most eminent portrait painter. Jouett was a methodical student who kept a notebook of his conversations on painting with Stuart. This small volume, kept during the four months of July through October 1816, is the most comprehensive primary account of the master's theory and practice of portrait painting. Jouett was greatly influenced by the straightforward, unadorned bust portraits that were characteristic of Stuart's style during the first and second decades of the nineteenth century. He followed his master's precepts in composition, color, and technique. Always called "Kentucky" by Stuart, Jouett was regarded as his teacher's best and favorite pupil by nineteenth-century artists such as George P. A. Healy, James Reid Lambdin, and John Neagle.

Jouett returned to Kentucky late in 1816, reestablished his studio in Lexington, and began to charge fifty dollars per portrait. In spite of considerable patronage at home, he made trips to the Deep South to paint the wealthy planter families of Louisiana and Mississippi when Kentucky was snowbound and travel was difficult. This continued from 1817 until his death. These extended painting trips were necessary to help support his ever-growing family, which eventually numbered nine children. In 1823 he wrote: "For years I have not known what it was to enjoy this life to the brim's full. . . . I go from home and locate for months. Then come increasing restless longings for the little home where are garnered up the priceless treasures of my heart" (Hart, "Jouett's Kentucky Children," p. 52).

Jouett painted many of the outstanding political, social, and military leaders of his day, including multiple likenesses of Henry Clay, Marquis de Lafayette, Governor Isaac Shelby, Senator John Brown, and Dr. Samuel Brown. His pictures of children were especially successful, but he was not a flatterer and did not glamorize his sitters. He often made replicas of his portraits for the general market as well as for the families who commissioned them. Copies of Gilbert Stuart's *Athenaeum* George Washington and *Edgehill* Thomas Jefferson were produced for the commercial market, and Jouett occasionally sponsored exhibitions of his own and other artists' works.

During his lifetime Jouett was admired for his social graces and his deep devotion to his family. An inveterate reader, he was especially fond of poetry; his engaging conversation and sparkling wit charmed everyone. He was a man of strong religious convictions, and he was also an accomplished performer on the flute and violin. His contemporary, James Reid Lambdin, remarked that "His well-stored mind, his astonishing powers of conversation and companionable disposition, caused his society to be constantly courted, and gave him an amount of employment never enjoyed by any other artist in the West" (Floyd, *Jouett-Bush-Frazer*, p. 81).

Jouett was struck down in the prime of life, being only thirty-nine when he died of bilious fever at his farm near Lexington. He was buried in the family graveyard of William Allen, his father-in-law, in Fayette County, but he was later reinterred beside his wife at Cave Hill Cemetery in Louisville.

Jouett was the foremost artist of Kentucky during the second and third decades of the nineteenth century, the favorite pupil of Gilbert Stuart, and one of the most significant portraitists of his era in New Orleans and Natchez. His reputation has never wavered, and his works are still prized by collectors and museums.

• The family Bible of Captain Jack Jouett, giving the artist's correct date of birth, is at the Filson Club, Louisville, Ky. The most comprehensive biography of Jouett is in William Barrow Floyd, *Jouett-Bush-Frazer: Early Kentucky Artists* (1968). It reprints in full Jouett's 1816 notebook. See also Floyd's exhibition catalog, *Matthew Harris Jouett, Portraitist of the Ante-Bellum South* (1980). Other sources are Samuel Woodson Price, *The Old Masters of the Bluegrass* (1902), which contains a list of 308 Jouett paintings that was assembled by Jouett's grandson; William Dunlap, *A History of the Rise and Progress of the Arts of Design in the United States* (2 vols., 1834); John Hill Morgan, *Gilbert Stuart and His Pupils* (1939); and Isaac M. Cline, *Art and Artists of New Orleans during the Last Century* (1922). Mrs. William H. Martin, *Catalogue of Paintings by Matthew Harris Jouett* (1939), is sometimes helpful, but approximately one-fourth of its 529 entries are misattributions. Two articles by a nineteenth-century art historian are significant: Charles Henry Hart, "Kentucky's Master Painter: Matthew Harris Jouett," *Harper's New Monthly Magazine*, May 1899, pp. 914–21, and "Jouett's Kentucky Children," *Harper's Monthly Magazine*, June 1900, pp. 51–56.

WILLIAM BARROW FLOYD

JOY, Alfred Harrison (23 Sept. 1882–18 Apr. 1973), astrophysicist, was born in Greenville, Illinois, the son of Frank Joy and Louise Maynard. He received a degree in Latin and science from Greenville College, a small Methodist institution, in 1903 and continued his studies in science at Oberlin College in Ohio, where he obtained an M.A. in physics in 1904. At Oberlin, Joy worked under Charles E. St. John, who would later become his colleague at the Mount Wilson Observatory.

Following graduation from Oberlin, Joy became an instructor in physics at the American University of Beirut (then called Syrian Protestant College). Joy's duties at Beirut included teaching astronomy, and his interest in the subject quickly grew. He took part in the University of California's Lick Observatory solar eclipse expedition to Egypt in 1905, observed a transit of Mercury at Beirut, and participated in the worldwide network of observations of Halley's Comet in 1910.

The period from 1909 to 1911 forged Joy into a professional astronomer. He spent the summer of 1909 in Oxford and Cambridge working on the *Carte du Ciel* project, which was initiated in 1887 to produce a photographic map of the sky and an accompanying catalog (the project was completed in 1964). He also assisted at the University of Chicago's Yerkes Observatory in Williams Bay, Wisconsin, in the summer of 1910. Joy then received a Thaw Fellowship to study astronomy at Princeton University during the academic year 1910–1911 under Henry Norris Russell.

Joy returned in 1911 to Beirut, where he was appointed director of the American University Observatory. In 1914 he continued his peripatetic studies by traveling to Potsdam, Germany, where he came into contact with two major astrophysicists, Karl Schwarzschild and Ejnar Hertzsprung. Prior to the start of World War I, Joy went back to Yerkes Observatory and assisted in their research on trigonometric stellar parallaxes. By the time he was ready to return to Beirut in 1915, the war made travel impracticable. Fortunately, Joy had come into contact with the former director of Yerkes, George Ellery Hale, who had founded the Carnegie Institution of Washington's Mount Wilson Observatory in California in 1904. Hale, who was on the lookout for young astronomers with experience in astrophysics, quickly offered Joy a job as assistant astronomer at Mount Wilson.

Working at first on solar observations with St. John, Joy was assigned in 1916 to work on stellar spectroscopy and worked closely with the senior Mount Wilson astronomer, Walter Sydney Adams. Earlier, Adams and Arnold Kohlschütter had learned how to accurately determine a star's spectral class and absolute luminosity by examining the absorption lines in its spectrum. Using this information it became possible for them to calculate the distance to the star, a quantity referred to as its "spectroscopic parallax." Joy worked at deciphering numerous stellar spectra until, in 1935, Joy and Adams had published a catalog of spectroscopic parallaxes of 4,179 stars.

Joy's personal research interest centered on stars that changed their brightness over a period of time, the so-called variable stars. Dividing up the variable stars with two other astronomers at Mount Wilson, Roscoe F. Sanford and Paul W. Merrill, Joy worked on the class of red semiregular variable stars. One exception was the remarkable long-period red variable, Mira (omicron Ceti). Joy had a fondness for this famous star, perhaps because of his spectroscopic discovery of its faint companion star in 1920. Noting the odd spectrum, Joy had written to Robert G. Aitken at the Lick Observatory to see if he could visually observe Mira's companion in Lick's large refracting telescope. Aitken soon saw the faint star, thus confirming Joy's discovery. Joy also amassed a great deal of information on the W Virginis (Population II) Cepheids and RR Lyrae variable stars, material that has led to a greater understanding of our galaxy.

Joy's work on variable stars led to many new results that increased astronomers' understanding of these peculiar objects. He showed in 1933 that the emission lines in RW Tauri's spectrum were due to a small Saturn-like ring around the brighter primary star. Joy identified many spectroscopic binaries and initiated spectroscopic studies of dwarf novae.

Another of Joy's important researches was his study of galactic rotation. From his earlier studies of the radial velocity of Cepheid variables, he collected a large sample of data, demonstrating that the Population I Cepheids constituted a low-velocity family of stars, and was able to calculate the coordinates of the galaxy's center.

Perhaps Joy's most important contribution was his work on the T Tauri stars, an outcome of his study of cool red (M-class) dwarf stars, with which he had become acquainted during his work with Adams. As Joy became interested in the M dwarfs' habit of "flaring," he was able to recognize common traits in a group of these stars: low luminosity associated with a bright or dark nebulosity. These stars, described by Joy as T Tauri variables (named after the prototype) in 1945, later proved to be the transition between interstellar clouds and main-sequence stars.

In 1919 Joy married Margherita O. Burns, a computer operator at the observatory; they had two children. The next year, he was appointed secretary of the observatory. In this new position, Joy was constantly in contact with the community and press regarding astronomical matters in general and happenings at the Mount Wilson Observatory in particular. Joy served as secretary, in addition to his other duties, until his retirement in 1948. He maintained an office at the observatory and continued to work up until the time of his death in Pasadena, California, on data he had collected in previous years.

Joy served in many capacities with the Astronomical Society of the Pacific, as a member of its board of directors, as president in 1931 and 1939, and as editor from 1945 to 1968 of the *Leaflets*, a monthly issuance of small eight-page reports for laymen and astronomers on new results in astronomy. In 1950 the society presented Joy with its highest award, the Bruce Gold Medal. Joy was active in other organizations as well, particularly the American Astronomical Society, serving as its president from 1949 to 1952. In 1944 Joy was elected to the National Academy of Sciences and in 1964 was named an associate of the Royal Astronomical Society.

Joy was well respected and well liked by his colleagues. His work on galactic rotation and T Tauri variables marks him as a seminal figure in the understanding of our galaxy and stellar formation.

• Joy's papers are at the Henry E. Huntington Library, San Marino, Calif., and form part of the Carnegie Observatories Collection. The best descriptions of Joy's life and work are found in the obituaries by Olin C. Wilson in National Academy of Sciences, Biographical Memoirs 47 (1975): 225–47, and George H. Herbig in *Quarterly Journal of the Royal Astronomical Society* 15 (1974): 526–31. The former also contains a complete bibliography of Joy's publications. Another useful obituary is by Helmut A. Abt in *Mercury* 2 (Sept.–Oct. 1973): 9–10. A contemporary account of Joy's life and work is Robert J. Trumpler, "The Award of the Bruce Gold Medal to Dr. Alfred Joy," *Publications of the Astronomical Society of the Pacific* 62 (1950): 33–36. J. B. Hearnshaw places Joy's work in a larger context in *The Analysis of Starlight: One Hundred and Fifty Years of Astronomical Spectroscopy* (1986).

RONALD BRASHEAR

JOY, Charles Turner (17 Feb. 1895–6 June 1956), naval officer and diplomat, was born in St. Louis, Missouri, the son of Duncan Joy, a cotton broker, and Lucy Barlow Turner. Educated at private schools in St. Louis, New York, and Pennsylvania, and appointed to the U.S. Naval Academy from Illinois's Twenty-second District in July 1912, Joy received his ensign's commission in June 1916.

After service in the battleship *Pennsylvania* (June 1916–Dec. 1920), during which he received temporary wartime promotions to lieutenant, junior grade, and lieutenant, he underwent ordnance instruction at a succession of locations—the postgraduate school at the Naval Academy, the University of Michigan (Ann Arbor), the Naval Proving Grounds (Indian Head, Md.), the Bureau of Ordnance (BuOrd) (Washington, D.C.), the Army Proving Ground (Aberdeen, Md.), and the Pittsburgh (Penn.) Experimental Station of the Bureau of Mines. He ultimately attained a master's degree in explosive engineering from the University of Michigan in 1922. Permanent promotions to lieutenant, junior grade, and lieutenant came during that time.

In November 1923 Joy became flag lieutenant for Rear Admiral Charles B. McVay, Jr., commander of the Yangtze Patrol. During that tour of duty he married Martha Ann Chess of Pittsburgh, in Hankow, China, in October 1924, a union that ultimately produced three children. Then, after serving as executive officer of the destroyer *Pope* (Oct. 1925–Apr. 1926), Joy returned to Washington, to BuOrd's aviation ordnance section (June 1926–June 1928), receiving his promotion to lieutenant commander during that tour. He subsequently returned to sea, as assistant gunnery officer of the battleship *California* (June 1928–May 1931), before he served as ordnance officer at the Naval Mine Depot, Yorktown, Virginia (June 1931–May 1933).

Joy's first sea command came in June 1933, when he assumed command of the destroyer *Litchfield*. He then served as gunnery and operations officer on the staff of Rear Admiral Clark H. Woodward, commander, Destroyers, Battle Force (Mar. 1935–June 1937), receiving promotion to commander during that tour. He then returned to the Naval Academy to serve as its executive officer and later headed its ordnance and gunnery department (June 1937–May 1940).

In June 1940 Joy became executive officer of the heavy cruiser *Indianapolis* and in February 1941 operations officer for Vice Admiral Wilson Brown, Jr., commander, Scouting Force. Promoted to captain eleven months later, Joy helped to plan carrier operations in the southwest Pacific—most notably those that took place off Bougainville in February 1942 and at Lae and Salamaua, New Guinea, in March—and earned the Bronze Star.

Detached from staff duty in July 1942, Joy assumed command of the heavy cruiser *Louisville* that September. Under his leadership (for which he earned his first Legion of Merit) *Louisville* supported the occupation of Adak (Sept.–Oct. 1942), fought in the battle of Rennell Island (Jan. 1943), helped secure Guadalcanal (Jan.–Feb. 1943), and supported the capture of Attu (Apr.–May 1943).

After heading the Pacific Plans Division in the Washington headquarters of Admiral Ernest J. King, commander in chief of the U.S. Fleet (Aug. 1943–Apr. 1944), Joy—promoted to rear admiral at the end of that tour—returned to sea to command Cruiser Division Six. His ships (heavy cruisers *Wichita*, *San Francisco*, *New Orleans*, and *Minneapolis*) screened fast carrier task forces and supported amphibious landings from the Marianas to Okinawa. He earned three more Legions of Merit: one for commanding the unit covering the retirement of the damaged cruisers *Canberra* and *Houston* off Formosa (Oct. 1944), one for his skillfully deploying his division to provide gunfire support off Iwo Jima (Feb. 1945), and one for handling multifaceted operations off Okinawa between March and May 1945. During the Okinawa operations he had skillfully carried out gunfire support while combating Japanese air attacks, simultaneously directing unloading operations and arranging rescue and salvage operations.

Detached in June 1945 to command Amphibious Group Two, Joy was training his group off Coronado, California, for the assault on the Japanese homeland when hostilities ceased in the Pacific in August 1945. Ordered to command Task Force Seventy-three, he journeyed to the Far East soon thereafter. Under Joy's direction, Task Force Seventy-three cleared the Yangtze River of mines and entered Shanghai, where he remained until January 1946. He then served as commander of Task Force Seventy-four at Hong Kong (Jan.–Apr. 1946).

Joy then commanded the Naval Proving Ground at Dahlgren, Virginia (June 1946–Aug. 1949), before he returned to the Orient to become commander of Naval Forces, Far East, with the rank of vice admiral. He was serving in that post when North Korean forces invaded South Korea in June 1950. Joy directed the complex mobilization of United Nations naval forces in Korean waters to perform reconnaissance, mine-sweeping, logistics, fire-support, and troop-lift. His previous service had prepared him well for the organizational aspects of the hazardous Inchon landings that succeeded with minimal loss to the attacking UN force and severed North Korean supply lines. In addition, he oversaw operations at Wonsan and Hungnam, in the former even embarking in a minesweeper to familiarize himself with the grave problems confronting his force as it sought to eliminate the extensive enemy minefield.

In July 1951 the UN command in Korea entered into armistice talks with the Communists. Admiral Joy represented the United Nations as its senior negotiator and exhibited, according to his Army Distinguished Service Medal citation, a "comprehensive grasp of far-reaching strategic and diplomatic implications" that proved valuable in the cease-fire negotiations though he could not win an acceptable armistice. He came away from the conferences convinced that the Korean War was one of the most important wars the United States had fought, since he believed it awakened the country to the dangers posed by Communism.

Detached from the thankless task of negotiating with the Communists in May 1952 and from serving as commander of Naval Forces, Far East, in June 1952, he became superintendent of the Naval Academy (with concurrent responsibility as commander, Severn River Naval Command) in August of that year and served in that capacity, universally popular with both midshipmen and faculty, until he retired on 1 July 1954. He was advanced to admiral on the retired list on the basis of his combat awards.

Reflecting on his experience in the truce negotiations, Joy wrote *How Communists Negotiate* (1955). In it he expressed his conviction that Communists would only "negotiate seriously" when confronted by "the imminent threat of application of military power." Joy believed that the U.S. failure to take "punitive action" against China after the Chinese entry into the conflict adversely influenced the outcome of the armistice negotiations. That failure, Joy contended, meant that the 1953 armistice represented a triumph for the Communist Chinese. He died at San Diego, California.

• An officer biography file on Admiral Joy is in the Operational Archives Branch of the Naval Historical Center, which also holds the war diaries and action reports for the *Louisville* and the ships of Cruiser Division Six. Biographical material, as well as papers relating to the naming of the destroyer *Turner Joy* in 1957, are held by the Ships' Histories Branch of the Naval Historical Center in its Ship Name and Sponsor files. Accounts of the battles in which Joy participated during World War II can be found in primary documents (war diaries and action reports) in the Operational Archives Branch and in secondary sources such as John B. Lundstrom, *First South Pacific Campaign* (1976) and *The First Team: Pacific Naval Air Combat from Pearl Harbor to Midway* (1984), and Samuel Eliot Morison, *History of United States Naval Operations in World War II* (15 vols., 1947–1962). On Joy's role during the Korean conflict, see Malcolm W. Cagle and Frank A. Manson, *The Sea War in Korea* (1957), and James A. Field, Jr., *History of United States Naval Operations, Korea* (1962). Joy's diary of the armistice negotiations has been published in Allan E. Goodman, ed., *Negotiating while Fighting: The Diary of Admiral C. Turner Joy at the Korean Armistice Conference* (1978). A brief account of his tour as superintendent of the Naval Academy is in Jack Sweetman, *The U.S. Naval Academy: An Illustrated History* (1979). Obituaries are in the *Washington Post and Times Herald* and the *Washington Star*, both 7 June 1956, and the *Navy Times*, 16 June 1956.

ROBERT JAMES CRESSMAN

JOY, James Frederick (2 Dec. 1810–24 Sept. 1896), lawyer and railroad builder, was born in Durham, New Hampshire, the son of James Joy, a manufacturer of farm implements, and Sarah Pickering. Joy attended the local schools before clerking in a store for several years. He graduated from Dartmouth College at the head of his class in 1833. Joy then entered Harvard Law School but left after a year to become the principal of an academy in Pittsfield, New Hampshire, and a tutor of Latin at Dartmouth College. He returned to Harvard, where he completed his law course in 1836, and was admitted to the bar. In the same year Joy moved west to Detroit and gained admission to the Michigan bar. In 1837 he entered into a law partnership with George F. Porter that lasted for nearly twenty-five years.

In 1837 Michigan became a state and at once embarked on an ambitious state system of railroad-building. In the early 1840s financial and construction problems brought the program to a virtual halt. Joy wrote a series of articles for Detroit newspapers advocating the sale of the Michigan Central Railroad to private investors. In association with John W. Brooks, a New York railroad engineer, Joy interested John Murray Forbes, a Boston merchant, in the Michigan railroad. In 1846 Forbes and a group of Boston and New York investors purchased the Michigan Central for $2 million. Forbes was president and Joy became counsel for the new company. The Michigan road was extended west to Michigan City, Indiana, by 1850 and two years later entered Chicago over the tracks of the Illinois Central. Joy was solicitor for the Illinois Central from 1852 to 1857. He became a director of the Michigan Central in 1852, and later he was president of the line from 1867 to 1877.

Once the Michigan Central reached Chicago, the next objective of the "Forbes Group" was to build or acquire an extension from Chicago west to the Mississippi River. Four short lines between Chicago and the Mississippi had been chartered between 1849 and 1852. Joy suggested to these struggling lines that Forbes and his associates might be willing to help meet their needs for fresh capital. By 1856 the four roads were merged into the Chicago, Burlington & Quincy, a 138-mile line from Chicago west to Burlington and Quincy on the Mississippi. Joy was president of the CB&Q from 1853 to 1857 and again from 1865 to 1871. In the late 1850s the CB&Q had annual gross revenues of over $1 million and was starting to pay dividends. During the Civil War the line's mileage doubled and revenue tripled; by 1865 its annual net income had reached $1.5 million.

Joy was a prime mover in railroad promotion in Illinois in the 1850s and 1860s. Rail mileage in Illinois grew from 111 miles to 2,790 miles in the 1850s. During the 1860s an additional 2,000 miles were added, and Illinois was first in rail mileage in the nation. Joy proved to be a master of "booster politics." His sharp mind and fine legal training gave him an advantage in the tasks of obtaining corporate charters, issuing securities, and condemning rights-of-way. When federal land grants were offered to Iowa and Missouri lines, Joy often outmaneuvered rival railroad lawyers. By the early 1850s Joy had become the major adviser and lieutenant to Forbes back in Boston. Forbes was the more conservative of the two men. He believed that railways should normally only be built to serve an existing population, while Joy was willing to project and build a railroad well ahead of the frontier line.

The Chicago, Burlington & Quincy was also interested in roads beyond the Mississippi. West of Burlington, Iowa, the CB&Q gained control of the Burlington & Missouri River Railroad when Joy purchased the line for a low figure in 1857. The Iowa road was built to Ottumwa by the eve of the Civil War, and Joy extended it west to Council Bluffs on the Missouri by 1869. Joy was a director of the Burlington & Missouri River from 1859 to 1871. The CB&Q also had had a major investment in the Hannibal & St. Joseph Railroad since the 1850s. This line in western Missouri made it natural for Joy to take a new interest in several lines serving Kansas City. The Forbes Group had investments in some but not all of these "southwestern" lines. Forbes complained that Joy seemed to favor the lines in Missouri over the CB&Q lines serving Iowa. When Jay Gould gained control of the Hannibal & St. Joseph in 1871, he ended Joy's dream of a "Joy System" in the Southwest. In 1875 Joy was dropped from the Forbes Group after Forbes discovered that Joy was a major figure in some questionable construction company contracts in the building of the "River Roads"—short CB&Q branch lines in eastern Iowa. Joy had been a director of the CB&Q since 1855.

Even though Joy was no longer a member of the Forbes Group after 1875, he retained an interest in several railroads. He continued as president of the Michigan Central until 1877. During his management of that line he added several branches and rebuilt much of the original line. Later he invested in the bankrupt Wabash, St. Louis & Pacific Railroad. As president of the Wabash from 1884 to 1887, he extended the line to Detroit. Joy also asked the Detroit city council for permission to construct a tunnel under the Detroit River to Canada to give his adopted hometown a better rail connection to the East. Work crews dug for two years but were forced to abandon the project because of gas deposits found in the bore. Between the 1850s and the 1890s Joy was a director of at least twenty different railroads. In the early 1890s he participated in the establishment of a railroad car-building plant in Detroit.

Joy was originally a Whig in politics, briefly a Free Soiler, and later an active Republican. He strongly supported Lincoln in the election of 1860. During 1861–1862 he served in the Michigan legislature and was floor leader in the house. Between 1881 and 1884 he was president of the Detroit *Post and Tribune*. For several years Joy was a director of the Detroit National Bank. Joy was married twice, first to Martha Alger Reed of Yarmouth, Massachusetts, in 1841. Before her death in 1850, the couple had four children. In 1860 he married Mary Bourne of Hartford, Connecticut, with whom he had three children. James Joy died at his home in Detroit.

• Archival materials are in the Burlington Archives (1851–1901) at the Newberry Library, Chicago. For additional information, see Richard C. Overton, *Burlington Route: A History of the Burlington Lines* (1965); John Lauritz Larson, *Bonds of Enterprise: John Murray Forbes and Western Development in America's Railway Age* (1984); Arthur M. Johnson and Barry E. Supple, *Boston Capitalists and Western Railroads* (1967); and Thomas C. Cochran, *Railroad Leaders, 1845–1890: The Business Mind in Action* (1953). Obituaries are in the *Detroit Free Press* and *Detroit Tribune*, 25 Sept. 1896.

JOHN F. STOVER

JUBA. *See* Lane, William Henry.

JUDAH, Samuel (10 July 1798–24 Apr. 1869), lawyer and politician, was born in New York City, the eldest son of Samuel Bernard Judah, a physician, and Catherine Hart. He attended the common schools of New York, after which he enrolled in Rutgers College, becoming in 1816 its first Jewish graduate. From 1 October 1816 to 1 October 1818, he was an apprentice in the law office of George Wood, an eminent New Brunswick attorney. Judah was admitted to the New Jersey bar immediately, but then moved to Indiana to start his own practice in 1819.

Settling first in Merom in Sullivan County, Judah was delighted with his new surroundings, particularly the "exceedingly good company" provided by, among others, a newspaper editor and two well-traveled "old sea captains." Following a three-month illness, Judah moved his law office to nearby Vincennes in Knox County, the former Indiana territorial capital. There Judah lived for the rest of his life. His classical education and his extraordinary abilities as an attorney provided the basis not only for an extensive legal practice within and without the state but also for a short and contentious political career. In 1825 he married Harriet Brandon, a former Vincennes resident whose family had moved to Corydon when the territorial government moved there in 1813. The Judahs had eleven children, only five of whom survived infancy.

Judah served six one-year terms in the Indiana House of Representatives, two terms as a Democrat between 1827 and 1829, and four terms, from 1837 to 1841, as a Whig, ultimately becoming speaker of the house (1840–1841). Although originally a Jacksonian, Judah supported the state's internal improvements programs, primarily the Wabash and Erie Canal and improvement of the lower Wabash River near Vincennes (a bill that Jackson vetoed). Immediately after his first election in October 1827, Judah used six columns of the local newspaper to spell out his support for internal improvements, greater educational opportunities for all children, and fundamental reform of the state's legal and economic systems. In this erudite and closely reasoned essay, he boldly advocated abandonment of the arcane common law system inherited from the English, calling it "a vast and confused mass of sayings and opinions and rules, scattered through a thousand heavy volumes," resulting in a law whose rules are "inconsistent," "without fixed principles," and "often contrary to justice and common honesty." In its place Judah proposed "the collection of all the laws by which we are governed," as Napoleon had done for France. He also recommended replacing the rule of "caveat emptor" with what he termed "caveat venditor" (let the seller beware of, or be responsible for, what he sells).

Unable to achieve these sweeping reforms during his first two terms in the legislature, Judah retired from the house, and in 1829 accepted a four-year appointment from President Andrew Jackson as U.S. attorney for the district of Indiana. During this time he added to his fame as an attorney and also received support for election to the U.S. Senate, but the Indiana General Assembly elected Democrat John Tipton of Logansport to complete the unexpired term of James Noble. In 1836 Judah lost his only bid for a seat in the Indiana Senate, but a year later he returned to the house, where he proved to be effective. Although "under the common size" and prematurely balding, he had piercing black eyes and a penetrating voice that could be "full of severity and sarcasm." An onlooker considered Judah "a good debater, a classical scholar, apt in his quotations, happy in his allusions," and one who did more good "by making officers watchful through a dread of him, than by any bold original measures." Such traits helped Judah reach the pinnacle of his profession. Constantly engaged during sessions of the court in Vincennes, he was said to have participated in every important litigation conducted in the Knox County Circuit Court during his years of practice.

His greatest achievement as an attorney involved the venerable Vincennes University, chartered in 1806. Judah laid foundations for the litigation in 1838 by getting a bill through the legislature that reconstituted the Board of Trustees of the nearly moribund university. Subsequently Judah became both a member of the board and its attorney. In 1842 the board authorized him to institute legal proceedings designed to recapture revenue from the sale of lands granted to the "state university" by Congress in 1804; these funds had fallen into the hands of the institution later known as Indiana University, established in 1820. As the Vincennes University attorney, Judah first took the personally risky step of filing ejectment suits against innocent purchasers of the Seminary Township lands. Undoubtedly the local outcry supported Judah's second step of obtaining legislation that permitted the state to be sued over the issue of which university was entitled to the proceeds of the land sales. Upon passage of the required law in 1846, Judah dropped all of his actions against individuals and pressed forward with the case of *Vincennes University v. State of Indiana*. He was initially successful, but the state won a reversal of the circuit court's ruling upon appeal to the Indiana Supreme Court. Judah then persuaded his fellow trustees to carry an appeal to the U.S. Supreme Court by personally assuming the expenses of the appeal. He was vindicated with a divided opinion upholding the university's position in 1854.

The next step involved passage of a statute authorizing payment of the land-sale proceeds from the state treasury rather than, as planned earlier, from Indiana University funds. In 1855 Judah obtained the required law and a payment of $66,585, from which he withheld $26,728 for his fees and expenses. His fellow trustees objected to this approach and to the fee, which they considered exorbitant, and sued Judah for an accounting. In the Indiana Supreme Court case that resulted, Judah explained that $4,500 of his expenses had gone to pay members of the legislature. The high court refused to condemn either Judah or the legislators for their actions, thereby validating the attorney's collection of his fee.

Judah was acclaimed for this "splendid victory." One Vincennes newspaper praised the lawyer's skill and perseverance in "literally carving" an ample endowment fund for the university "out of the mist of vanishing rights." Despite the time devoted to this singular case—from 1842 into the 1860s—but perhaps because of its notoriety, Judah's legal career flourished during these years. Learned in matters beyond the law, Judah pursued interests in history, politics, and culture. The Judahs lived in one of the finest homes in Vincennes, where they also maintained large and celebrated gardens and an orchard. Judah died in his adopted hometown.

• The Lilly Library at Indiana University, Bloomington, and the Smith Library of the Indiana Historical Society in Indianapolis hold small collections of Judah family papers, but no biographies have been published. Among the most useful secondary materials are Justin E. Walsh, *The Centennial History of the Indiana General Assembly, 1816–1978* (1987); Thomas D. Clark, *Indiana University, Midwestern Pioneer: Vol. I, The Early Years* (1970); and Matthew E. Welsh, "An Old Wound Finally Healed: Vincennes University's Struggle for Survival," *Indiana Magazine of History* 84 (1988): 217–36.
RALPH D. GRAY

JUDAH, Theodore Dehone (4 Mar. 1826–2 Nov. 1863), engineer and railroad promoter, was born in Bridgeport, Connecticut, the son of Henry R. Judah, an Episcopal clergyman (his mother's name and occupation are unknown). The family moved to Troy, New York, where Judah attended Rensselaer Polytechnic Institute. He went to work as a surveyor's assistant at thirteen and became a civil engineer by 1844. Judah erected a bridge at Vergennes, Vermont, and planned and built the Niagara Gorge Railroad, a task that amply demonstrated his ingenuity and skill. He married Anna Ferona Pierce of Greenfield, Massachusetts, in 1847; the couple apparently had no children who lived to adulthood.

In 1854 Colonel Charles Lincoln Wilson offered Judah the position of chief engineer for the first projected railway in California—the Sacramento Valley Railroad. Despite some misgivings on Anna Judah's part, the couple took a steamship to Panama, crossed the isthmus, and took another ship to San Francisco. Arriving at Sacramento, California, in mid-May 1854, Judah took up his duties with energy and vigor. He soon became enamored of the West Coast and spoke so often and so enthusiastically about the need for a transcontinental railroad that he became known as "Crazy Judah." Friendly with Lauren Upson, editor of the *Sacramento Union*, Judah submitted essays to the newspaper that promoted his dream of connecting the East and West coasts of the United States. In September 1859 Judah was selected as one of the delegates for the Pacific Railroad Convention in San Francisco. His knowledge and enthusiasm impressed his fellow delegates, and he was appointed as the convention's agent to present the case for a transcontinental railroad to the U.S. Congress.

Judah went to Washington, D.C., and lobbied intensively for the project. Disappointed when the measure was tabled in Congress, he and his wife returned to California by the now-familiar isthmus route. Judah surveyed in the Sierra Mountains, seeking to find a way over or through that great obstacle. In company with Daniel Strong, the pharmacist of Dutch Flat, California, Judah located a ridge between two deep river valleys (the south fork of the Yuba and Bear rivers and the north fork of the American River). Euphoric over his discovery, Judah laid out his plan for a railroad through Donner Pass and Dutch Flat in a pamphlet, *Central Pacific Railroad to California*, published in November 1860. Returning to Sacramento, Judah lobbied for financial support. Rebuffed at first by skeptical Californians who had heard of many railroad schemes, Judah found his backers in the men who would become known as the "Big Four": Charles Crocker, Mark Hopkins, Leland Stanford, and Collis Huntington (like Judah, they all came from either Connecticut or New York state and some of them had direct connections with Troy, New York).

The Central Pacific Railroad Company of California was incorporated on 28 June 1861. Judah again traveled to Washington to muster federal support. The timing of his proposal was fortuitous; the start of the Civil War had increased the likelihood that the government would fund a railroad to keep California in the Union. Judah became the secretary of the Senate committee and the clerk of the House committee on railroads; more than any other single individual he was responsible for the legislation that became the Pacific Railroad Act, signed by President Abraham Lincoln on 1 July 1862.

Judah returned to California in triumph. He found, however, that the Big Four were slowly squeezing him out of the decision-making process for the building of the railroad. The Big Four were anxious to build a wagon road to Dutch Flat to ensure that some profit came to them from the federal monies allocated for that part of the project, regardless of whether the railroad itself was ever completed. Judah entered into discussions with the Big Four, but he found to his dismay that he was treated more as an employee than as an equal; he was not given respect as the founder and developer of the concept and route of the transcontinental railroad. In July 1863 Judah received $91,000 in cash and stock and was granted an option by the Big Four to buy out each of them for the sum of $100,000 apiece.

Judah and his wife left California on 3 October 1863 determined to find financial backers on the East Coast and to recover control of the railroad project. Sadly, Judah contracted yellow fever while crossing the isthmus at Panama. Nursed by his wife they reached New York City on 26 October; he died a week later. His body was transported to his wife's home town of Greenfield, where he was buried. As the final spike was driven into the completed transcontinental railroad on 10 May 1869, Anna Judah spent the day near her husband's grave and recalled that she had been married to Judah on 10 May 1847, exactly twenty-two years earlier. Although she enjoyed a comfortable retirement, she received no further compensation from the Big Four.

Judah was a vigorous, bold, and practical individual. Both as a surveyor and as a promoter he had many talents. He did make numerous errors in underestimating the cost of the railroad, and had he lived to see its completion those errors might have damaged his reputation. As an engineer, pamphletist, and promoter, he fell to the mercy of his financial backers. Judah stands as an excellent example of the intrepid and practical man of vision who started a worthy project but was unable to control its development. As he wrote in a telegram sent just after President Lincoln signed the railroad bill, "We have drawn the elephant. Now let us see if we can harness him up." The harnessing, the building, the production, and the profits would fall to the Big Four and not to the idealistic and slightly fanatical engineer who had arrived on the West Coast in 1854.

• Judah's papers are in the Anna Judah Papers at the Bancroft Library, University of California at Berkeley. Primary sources include his *Practical Plan for Building the Pacific Railroad* (1857) and *The Central Pacific Railroad of California* (1860). The only full-length biography is Helen Hinckley Jones, *Rails from the West: A Biography of Theodore D. Judah* (1969). Other valuable sources are Oscar Lewis, *The Big Four* (1938); Theodore H. Hittell, *History of California*, vol. 4 (1879); and John Hoyt Williams, *A Great and Shining Road: The Epic Story of the Transcontinental Railroad* (1988).

SAMUEL WILLARD CROMPTON

JUDAY, Chancey (5 May 1871–29 Mar. 1944), limnologist, was born on his family's farm near Millersburg, Indiana, the son of Baltzer Juday and Elizabeth Heltzel, farmers. His parents had only modest education,

but Chancey nevertheless went to Indiana University and received a B.A. (1896) and an M.A. (1897). His interest in aquatic life may have predated his college experience. He studied under zoologist Carl Eigenmann, who in 1895 established a biological station on a lake near the Juday farm.

Juday taught school for two years and then accepted the position of biologist with the Wisconsin Geological and Natural History Survey in 1900, under the supervision of the zoology professor Edward A. Birge. After a year he had to withdraw because of tuberculosis. He then took advantage of his need to live in drier climates by serving on the biology faculties of the Universities of Colorado and California, and he studied fishes and other aquatic life in those states. In 1905 he returned to Madison, where he resumed work as biologist for the Wisconsin Survey. From October 1907 until June 1908 he visited universities and biological stations in England, France, Denmark, Sweden, Germany, Austria, Hungary, and Italy, meeting leading aquatic biologists. On Juday's return to Madison he was appointed lecturer in limnology, in the Department of Zoology at the University of Wisconsin. He held these two positions at the survey and university until 1931, when he became professor of limnology and resigned from the survey.

In September 1910 Juday married a Wisconsin native, Magdalen Evans. They had three children, one of whom, Richard, became a professor of chemistry at the University of Montana.

Birge was the senior partner in most of Juday's research, but, because Birge was a university administrator, the graduate students with whom they worked came under Juday's supervision. Although taciturn and lacking oratorical skills, Juday was devoted to limnology and was helpful to serious students. His awkward situation of supervising doctoral students while lacking a doctoral degree himself was alleviated in 1933 when his alma mater awarded him an honorary doctorate.

From 1900 until 1917 the Birge-Juday team concentrated on the chain of five lakes along the Yahara River. Three of these lakes border the university and the city of Madison. One of them, Mendota, became, because of the research momentum the team initiated, the most intensively studied lake in the world. They began by studying animal plankton, but soon the physical and chemical environment occupied more of their attention.

After 1919 they shifted most of their work beyond the Madison region, first to the very deep Green Lake, and then in 1924 to lakes in northern Wisconsin. The reason for doing so was that those lakes were both diverse and unpolluted. In June 1925 Birge and Juday established a summer biology station at Trout Lake, which would become headquarters for their surveys of northern lakes. Juday became director of this station until his retirement in 1942.

Although neither Birge nor Juday was ever to achieve a grand synthesis of their many researches, the numerous scientific monographs and shorter papers that their team continuously published brought them great prominence at a time when the sciences of limnology and ecology were still young.

Two of their most important publications illustrate the character of their work. In "The Inland Lakes of Wisconsin: The Dissolved Gases of the Water and Their Biological Significance" (1911) Birge and Juday documented the seasonal changes in the thermal structure of lakes and showed how these changes affect biological activity in photosynthetic and decomposer zones. In "The Inland Lakes of Wisconsin: The Plankton Quantity and Chemical Composition" (1922) they presented a detailed picture of the annual cycle of plankton species, biomass, and chemical constituents based on collections filtered from more than 2 million liters of water from Lake Mendota.

Juday served as president of the Ecological Society of America in 1927, and he also became the first president of the Limnological Society of America in 1935. Other honors that came to him were the Leidy Medal of the Academy of Natural Sciences in Philadelphia (1943), and, (posthumously) with Birge, the Einar Naumann Medal of the International Association of Limnology (1950).

Juday retired from teaching in 1937, but he had to remain a university research associate and director of the Trout Lake Laboratory until 1942 because Birge had neglected to arrange a retirement plan for him at the Wisconsin Geological and Natural History Survey. He died in Madison. (Magdalen Juday eventually expressed her annoyance at the survey for her husband's lack of pension by sending his private library to the Academy of Natural Sciences of Philadelphia.)

• Some of Juday's letters are in the archives of the Center for Limnology, University of Wisconsin-Madison. The two important monographs mentioned above, which Juday coauthored with Birge, are included in the reprint volume *Limnology in Wisconsin* (1977). David G. Frey, one of Juday's doctoral students, has described Juday's work and also published his bibliography in "Wisconsin: The Birge-Juday Era," in *Limnology in North America*, ed. Frey (1963). Lowell E. Noland, one of Juday's longtime colleagues at the University of Wisconsin, published a tribute, "Chancey Juday," in *Limnological Society of America Special Publications*, no. 16 (1945). Annamarie L. Beckel and Frank N. Egerton have drawn upon a wide historical background to place Juday and Birge's work in perspective in *Breaking New Waters: A Century of Limnology at the University of Wisconsin* (1987). An obituary is Paul S. Welch, "Chancey Juday (1871–1944)," *Ecology* 25 (July 1944): 270–72.

FRANK N. EGERTON

JUDD, Albert Francis (7 Jan. 1838–21 May 1900), attorney, and chief justice of the Supreme Court of the Hawaiian Kingdom and later of the Republic of Hawaii, was born in Honolulu, the son of Gerrit Parmele Judd, a medical missionary, and Laura Fish. Judd's parents had arrived in the islands in 1828 with the third company of American Protestant missionaries. Judd's father left the mission after fourteen years to become a government official and adviser to the king and to engage in private medical practice.

Judd's skill in the native tongue and understanding of island culture was to be of great advantage to him throughout his career on the bench. Most of the missionaries did not encourage their children to learn the Hawaiian language. Some went to extreme lengths to prevent contact between their children and the islanders. In spite of criticism from other missionaries, the Judd children learned Hawaiian along with English from earliest childhood. Judd's early education was received at Punahou School in Honolulu, a private school established in 1841 for the education, in English, of the children of the American Protestant missionaries stationed in the islands. Judd was also tutored privately by W. D. Alexander, a Yale graduate, in order to enter Yale University. On arriving in New Haven in 1860, he joined five other missionary sons from Hawaii, who referred to themselves as "the Cannibals." Much to the satisfaction of Alexander and himself, Judd was able to pass examinations that enabled him to enter the junior class. He obtained a B.A. in 1862. He then entered Harvard Law School and received an LL.B. in 1864.

Before returning to the islands, Judd traveled extensively and on a tour of Europe, met his future wife, Agnes Hall Boyd, an American who was studying music there at the time. Arriving back home late in 1864, Judd set up a private practice in Honolulu. In 1872 he returned to the mainland to marry, and the couple made their home in Honolulu, which was to become a social center and showcase for Agnes Judd's musical talent and training. They had nine children.

In 1873 Judd was appointed attorney general by King Lunalilo. After the king's death, Judd returned to private practice briefly before becoming a justice in 1874. In 1881 he was named chief justice by King Kalakaua and then served the king's successor, Queen Liliuokalani, Hawaii's last monarch. When the monarchy was overthrown in 1893, he remained in his position, serving the five-year provisional government of what now was called the Republic of Hawaii. A contemporary newspaper source described him as having "presided as Chief Justice during the revolutionary period 1886–1895 when the Supreme Court acted as the balance wheel which preserved the government from complete destruction by warring factions."

Judd remained true to the religion of his missionary parents. He was a deacon of Central Union Church (Congregational) in Honolulu and served many years on the Hawaiian Board of Missions of the Hawaiian Evangelical Association, which had taken over the mission work in the islands in 1864 when the American Board of Commissioners for Foreign Missions, based in Boston, discontinued its subsidy. The ABCFM, which needed the money for expansion elsewhere in the world, had informed the mission of its intent to withdraw when it sent the last company of missionaries in 1848. The mission to the islands was considered so successful that it could now become a self-supporting congregation.

Judd, along with other professionals and businessmen, invested in sugar stock after 1876. In the year of the U.S. centennial, the Pacific Mail Steamship Company's ship *City of San Francisco* entered Honolulu harbor draped in bunting, with the news that the Reciprocity Treaty, allowing Hawaiian sugar to enter the United States duty free, had been passed by the U.S. Senate. This proved the basis for a very profitable industry that was to dominate the island economy for the next eighty years. Judd noted in a letter of 1893 (the year of the overthrow of the monarchy) that his plantation stock was yielding 12 percent annually. Although Judd declared himself in favor of the overthrow and the change from what the revolutionary element considered a corrupt monarchy, his name is conspicuously absent from the lists of leaders of the revolutionary party, the most prominent of these leaders being sons and grandsons of missionaries, as was Judd. His command of the Hawaiian language made him valuable to both sides during this critical period of change in Hawaii's history, and he was one of the few who continued to serve his country in the transition from a monarchy to the Republic of Hawaii.

In 1894, six years before his death, Yale conferred on Judd an honorary LL.D. in recognition of his outstanding service to the Kingdom of Hawaii, which had been overthrown the previous year. In 1899, the twenty-fifth anniversary of Judd's appointment to the supreme court, the Hawaii Bar Association held a dinner in honor of Judd's many years of service to the kingdom and the republic. The highlight speech was by Sanford B. Dole, the president of the Republic of Hawaii, who was appointed first governor of the territory by President William McKinley. Judd was six years older than Dole, but they had much in common. Both were missionary sons who had attended Punahou School; both had "gone east" to obtain U.S. law degrees; both had married American wives whom they had met while absent from the islands; and both had returned home to spend their lives serving the changing governing bodies in the land of their birth. Judd still held the position of chief justice in 1898 when Hawaii was annexed as a territory of the United States, but his health was failing and he spent his last months traveling on the mainland hoping to restore his health. He returned to the islands in April 1900 but never left his home. He died the same year that the territorial government was fully organized.

Judd, like his parents and many of his descendants, was unique in his unconditional service to Hawaii and its people. His tenure as chief justice, uninterrupted even by political revolution, transcended the religious, racial, political, and economic factions that tore apart the bonds of community in this period of Hawaii's history. The large and extended Judd family is still a respected influence in the state of Hawaii. One son, A. F. Judd, Jr., followed his father in the practice of law and government service. Lawrence McCully Judd, another son, was appointed governor of the ter-

ritory by President Herbert Hoover in 1928. He was appointed again in 1932 and, although he was a Republican, continued to serve under Franklin D. Roosevelt. At the time of statehood in 1959, the Judd name could still be found in the roster of legislators.

• Judd family papers are in the Manuscript Collections of the Mission Houses Museum Library in Honolulu. For this essay extensive use was made of that part of the collection titled "Children of the Mission." Additional material regarding government service is in the Hawaii State Archives, also in Honolulu. All standard published histories of Hawaii have material about the Judd family in the islands. Most often cited are Gavan Daws, *Shoal of Time* (1968), and Ralph S. Kuykendall, *The Hawaiian Kingdom* (3 vols., 1938–1967).

LELA GOODELL

JUDD, Charles Hubbard (23 Feb. 1873–19 July 1946), psychologist and educator, was born in Bareilly, India, the son of Charles Wesley Judd, a Methodist missionary, and Sarah Annis Hubbard. Judd went to Binghamton, New York, at the age of six with his parents, who were returning home, because of poor health, from missionary service in India. Both parents died within five years, and he was cared for by an older sister. After graduation from Binghamton public schools, Judd entered Wesleyan University (1890–1894) with the intention of preparing for the ministry. Psychology classes at Wesleyan taught by Andrew C. Armstrong influenced Judd to change plans and dedicate himself to the study of psychology. While at Wesleyan Judd renounced all religion and replaced it with a lifelong allegiance to science. Throughout his life, however, he maintained a forceful evangelical speaking style that reflected his pietistic upbringing.

After graduation from Wesleyan with honors, Judd followed Armstrong's suggestion and went to Leipzig, Germany, to earn a doctorate in psychology from Wilhelm Wundt, founder of the first institutionally recognized psychology laboratory, which was then an international Mecca for the training of psychologists. Judd's dissertation concerned space perception, a phenomenon that figured highly in Wundt's arguments about the creativity of consciousness. Judd showed in his dissertation that the mental construction of the experience of space could be based as much on tactile (touch) stimulation as on visual or auditory stimulation. Judd developed a close relationship with Wundt, who considered him to be one of the best of many American students who studied psychology in Leipzig. Wundt granted Judd permission to translate his *Outlines of Psychology* (1896 and two subsequent editions) from German into English.

Judd returned to Wesleyan University in 1896 to begin his teaching career. In 1898 he married Ella LeCompte, who died in 1935. They had one child. In 1898 Judd accepted an appointment as professor of psychology at New York University, but he left after two years, unsuccessful in that position because of his overzealous effort to upgrade the educational standards of the school. In 1901–1902 Judd was professor of psychology and pedagogy at the University of Cincinnati; while there he published *Genetic Psychology for Teachers* (1903). "Genetic," as Judd uses it in this work, reflects his German training and refers to the genesis, or unfolding, of mental processes from primitive or diffuse mental processes observed developmentally to become more differentiated and structured with advancing maturity. In 1902 Judd was appointed an instructor at Yale University and became a full professor and director of the school's psychology laboratory in 1907. By then his interests were turning strongly toward experimental educational psychology.

The Yale psychology department at the time consisted of three Wundtian psychologists, Judd, Edward W. Scripture, and George T. Ladd, who fell into conflict over assuming authority in representing the new, German-imported, scientific psychology. That conflict reached a deadlock in 1909 that led Yale's president to close down the psychology activities there. In that same year Judd was elected president of the American Psychological Association, and he was appointed to replace John Dewey as director of the School of Education at the University of Chicago.

His departure from Yale signaled the end of Judd's activities as an experimentalist. During the previous ten years he had published numerous experimental investigations of perception and learning. The most-often cited of that research concerned a dispute between Judd and Edward L. Thorndike regarding transfer of training, a subject that received considerable attention at the turn of the century. It concerned the possibility that an act of learning could transfer so as to reduce the time or effort in learning new acts or material. Thorndike expressed the predominant view among American psychologists that transfer occurred only when two acts share some similar elements. It was supposedly those elements (subcomponents of the learning) that transferred from the old to the new. In a series of articles based on experimental data Judd disagreed and argued that transfer occurred because of a "cognitive grasp" of the situation—an understanding of general principals.

In his 1908 study Judd had two groups of subjects learn to throw darts at a target under water. To succeed, a correction had to be made for light refraction, caused by the water, that displaced the target's apparent position. One group received instruction in refraction theory; the other did not. Both groups practiced until they hit the target consistently. Then Judd moved the target to a different depth creating a different refraction and thus a different displacement of the apparent position of the target. The subjects who had had no instruction in refraction theory had to learn all over again to hit the target. Those who had learned of refraction, a general principle of the situation, quickly readjusted to hit the target. This appeared to illustrate that the grasp of a general principle facilitated transfer.

Judd remained a representative of Wundt's ideas, particularly in the area of social-cultural psychology. Those ideas had few followers in the United States because most of this part of Wundt's work reached completion around the years of the First World War when

an anti-German atmosphere was forming in the West and also when American psychology was moving in radically different directions, namely toward behaviorism.

In the Wundtian system consciousness, rather than external behavior or physical brain mechanisms, was the defining subject of psychology. Wundt argued that clues to the operation of human consciousness are to be found first in carefully controlled experimental studies (exploiting controlled reaction times, perceptual discriminations, and measurable emotional reactions). Clues to the workings of consciousness could be drawn, Wundt also argued, from the formal analysis of the social-cultural products of that consciousness. The study of the formal structure of language was, as Judd pointed out in his 1932 autobiography, Wundt's most successful use of the social-cultural approach.

The core explanatory principles in Wundt's mature psychological system (which came to be known as "voluntarism" and was carried forward by Judd) were the delineation of different types of volition and their effects on mental processes and also the description of automatic (involuntary) processes of creative synthesis. The principle of creative synthesis can be expressed as follows: When forms of experience (sensations, thoughts, emotions) become more complexly organized, new phenomena emerge that are different in kind, not merely in degree, from the earlier forms. This emphasis on creativity reflected the view that consciousness has the capacity for endlessly forming new experiences, perceptions, or thoughts, which emerge from earlier very different elements—as when water, with its quality of wetness, emerges from the combination of the substances oxygen and hydrogen.

Judd carried Wundtian psychology into the study of education in American schools, opposing practices that emphasized rote learning and a fixed set of mental abilities. He favored, instead, an emphasis on creatively self-controlled mental processes and on their interaction with social-cultural contexts that influence the course of that creativity. As a consequence of that orientation, Judd opposed the trends in early American learning theory that emphasized the study of elemental processes such as habits or instrumental responses as the building blocks of higher mental processes or behaviors. Judd argued that an educational psychology must begin with an emphasis on more general or global mental phenomena that guide and give meaning to the more easily observed elementary responses in acts of learning. At the beginning of the educational task the learner, according to Judd, must be guided toward general explanatory principals to make the learner's elemental actions meaningful.

The Chicago appointment, as director of the School of Education, was in response to Judd's interest in applying the methods of experimental psychology to educational problems. Another acknowledgment of that interest was his election, in 1911 and 1915, to the presidency of the National Society of College Teachers of Education. At Chicago Judd inherited the educational program that Dewey had founded there. As a Wundtian theorist, Judd stood in contrast to Dewey's pragmatic functionalism, which deemphasized the abstract mental processes that were central to Judd's approach.

Judd soon became identified with the scientific education movement that aimed to reform schools of education to make them primarily research centers rather than teacher-training centers. In this view, teachers were to come, instead, from general liberal arts programs and not from separate education schools or education departments.

As a nationally influential educational administrator, Judd argued in his speeches and writings that scientific findings about school practices could be gained through experimental and social-cultural analyses that could be applied in a way that would uplift the teaching profession in the United States to a status similar to that of medicine or engineering.

Judd had remained in his later years involved in academic psychology, chairing the University of Chicago psychology department from 1920 to 1925 and publishing *Psychology of Social Institutions* (1926). Books by Judd from this period that reflect his central educational interests include *Silent Reading* (1923), *Psychological Analysis of the Fundamentals of Arithmetic* (1927), and later *Educational Psychology* (1939).

After retirement from Chicago in 1938 Judd was a consultant for the National Youth Administration (1935–1940) and the War Department (1942–1943). Judd died at his retirement home in Santa Barbara, California, where, since 1944, he had served as a consultant on social studies to the city schools, expressing his concern that social studies teach the evolution of human civilization.

• Judd's personal papers are in the University of Chicago Archives. His chapter-length autobiography is in Carl A. Murchison, ed., *A History of Psychology in Autobiography*, vol. 2 (1932), pp. 207–35. For additional information on his career, see Mathew W. Clark, "Charles Hubbard Judd: Educational Leadership in American Secondary Education" (Ph.D. diss., Stanford Univ., 1960). For documentation of Wundt's preference and fondness for Judd among his many American students, see David K. Robinson, "Wilhelm Wundt and the Establishment of Experiential Psychology, 1875–1914" (Ph.D. diss., Univ. of California, Berkeley, 1989). For a review of Judd's major experimental research, which was confined to the earliest part of his career, see Robert S. Woodworth, *Experimental Psychology* (1938). For a review of Judd's later numerous leadership roles in education, and a list of his main books, see R. M. W. Travers, *How Research Has Changed American Schools: A History from 1840 to the Present* (1983). Two of the more prominent of the many obituaries of Judd were written by his former students at the University of Chicago: Guy T. Buswell in the *American Journal of Psychology* 60 (Jan. 1947): 135–37 and Frank N. Freeman in *Psychological Review* 54 (Mar. 1947): 59–65.

ARTHUR L. BLUMENTHAL

JUDD, Gerrit Parmele (23 Apr. 1803–12 July 1873), physician, medical missionary, and Hawaiian government official and adviser, was born in Paris, New York, the son of Elnathan Judd, Jr., a physician, and Betsey Hastings. Being the eldest son of a physician, Judd took an early interest in the medical profession and attended medical school in Fairfield, Herkimer County, where he received his M.D. in 1825. In 1826 Judd dedicated his life to the missionary cause as directed by the Boston-based Congregational American Board of Commissioners for Foreign Missions (ABCFM). At this time the board was recruiting missionaries for the third company to join the Sandwich Islands Mission in Hawaii in the fall of 1827.

The board required all male missionaries to marry before departing on the months-long voyage to the foreign islands. Judd chose Laura Fish, a schoolteacher whose education and strong character were to prove a wise choice. They were married in September 1827 in Clinton, New York. They had nine children.

The Judds arrived in Hawaii in March 1828 after a five-month voyage. Gerrit quickly mastered the native Hawaiian language and became an adviser and translator to the king and chiefs. Although he was to serve the mission for the next fourteen years, he became a controversial character within a short time. Judd was stationed in Honolulu at the central mission station on the island of Oahu and so was affiliated with the original mission church at Kawaiahao. As the mission physician he made frequent professional visits to the other mission stations on all islands throughout the kingdom. He also became a trustee of the mission-established Chiefs' Children's School so he could attend to the royal children who were being given a Christian education as future rulers of the kingdom.

The ABCFM forbade members of the mission to engage in any way in the affairs of the local government. However, the rulers frequently called on Judd for advice in dealing with an increasing foreign population, and they came to depend on his council and judgment. As he began spending more time on government affairs, he became the target of criticism by both other missionaries and elements of the foreign community. As mission physician Judd did not engage directly in the evangelization of the kingdom but brought his strong Christian principles to bear in all of his personal and professional dealings.

In 1835, at the request of the mission, Judd wrote a sixty-page medical textbook in Hawaiian titled *Anatomia* (Anatomy), which was illustrated at Lahainaluna Seminary with fifty-eight copperplate engravings prepared by the students and copied from a contemporary American textbook, *Class Book of Anatomy, Designed for Schools* (1834). A few copies of the edition of 500 still exist.

Judd was strong-minded and outspoken. He was determined to keep the kingdom of Hawaii as an independent nation in the face of growing Pacific colonialism by European powers. He possessed a firm conviction that he could accomplish this end while introducing Western business and government practices to the islands. For foreign traders and investors he was the key to the ear of King Kamehameha III.

In 1842 Judd separated himself from the mission during a crisis in government. Due to a combination of factors, including dwindling native population and British colonial designs, the island kingdom seemed in danger of losing its independence to Britain. So, beginning as a treasury board adviser, he served for the next ten years in various capacities. Due to the extent of his activities most historians have described him as prime minister in fact if not by title. From 1842 to 1845 he was minister of foreign affairs; from 1845 to 1846 he served as minister of the interior; and from 1846 to 1853 he was minister of finance. Before prospective traders were allowed to do business in the islands, Judd insisted that they take an oath of allegiance to the king.

The chiefs had complete confidence in him. He cared for them when they were sick, translated official documents, and advised them on policy. He also made enemies along the way. At one point a clerk of the Department of the Interior brought sixteen charges against him citing 175 specifications. Most of these charges resulted from Judd's insistence on strict adherence to the laws of the kingdom in litigation with foreigners, mostly American, one of whom charged him with "improper threats against American merchants."

In 1849 Judd traveled to the United States and Europe in attempts to negotiate treaties with other nations to gain recognition of Hawaiian sovereignty and to obtain reparations from France over an earlier dispute. In his care were two future Hawaiian kings, Kamehameha IV and his brother Kamehameha V, ages eighteen and fifteen. Although some progress was made in treaties, his efforts in France failed, and the princes resented his strict supervision of their activities and education.

They returned to a kingdom in upheaval. Judd represented Kamehameha III in forming a new and more liberal constitution, but in 1852 Judd's opponents forced him out of the government.

Though no longer in the inner circle, Judd gave good service to the government during the smallpox epidemic of 1853. He helped organize plans for general vaccination and for opening hospitals. He promoted a system for warning and inspecting ships entering the harbor. He was distressed by the rapid decline of the native population due to diseases introduced by European contact, as evidenced by his correspondence and later efforts in establishing a local medical school for native Hawaiians.

Judd returned to private practice but remained active in both the religious life of Honolulu and politics. He was a member of the 1858 legislature and the constitutional convention of 1864. When the ABCFM withdrew from the islands in 1864, its place was taken by the Hawaiian Evangelical Association (HEA). Judd was a charter board member and served the organization until his death. He joined the newly formed Fort Street Congregational Church, where one of his sons was a deacon.

In his last years Judd's interests widened. He was part of the pioneering of Western agricultural practice in the islands. He invested in sugar planting and ranching. He became an enthusiastic supporter of the Royal Hawaiian Agricultural Society, which had been formed in 1850 while he was abroad. He and Laura entered the annual exhibition held by the society and won many prizes. He imported and planted fruit trees from the Pacific Northwest.

In 1870 Judd used a grant from the Hawaiian legislature to establish a small medical school for ten select Hawaiians, to whom he presented "plain medical lectures." This was to be a two-year course after which the graduates would travel to the far reaches of the islands.

To the end his personal letters reflect concern for the islands and his willingness to admit to mistakes in judgment he had made during his more active years, always taking full responsibility for his actions and opinions. In 1872 his wife died, and Judd indicated his grief in a letter to the ABCFM board in Boston when he wrote in part, "I am still weak and without my usual buoyancy of mind and body." He died at his Nuuanu estate, "Sweet Home."

• Judd's letters are in several manuscript collections of the Mission Houses Museum in Honolulu. "Missionary Letters" in Honolulu and "ABCFM–Hawaii Papers, Houghton Library (Harvard), 1820–1900" at Harvard (copies are in Honolulu) are especially important. Additional papers, including those from Judd's government service, are located in the Hawaii State Archives in Honolulu. All standard histories of Hawaii contain material relating to the Judd family in the islands. Particularly useful are F. J. Halford, *Nine Doctors and Gold* (1954); Gerrit P. Judd 4th, *Dr. Judd, Hawaii's Friend* (1960); and Garan Daws, *Shoal of Time* (1968).

LELA GOODELL

JUDD, Laura Fish (2 Apr. 1804–2 Oct. 1872), missionary and historian, was born in Plainfield, New York, the daughter of Elias Fish, a carpenter and sailor, and Sybil Williams. After her mother's death in 1806, she and her six older brothers were raised by an elder sister. Laura was educated at a boarding school from the age of four and lived for a time in the home of her maternal grandfather. After her elder sister married, she lived with the couple in Watertown, New York. At the age of fourteen she accepted a position in the home of her schoolmaster, exchanging domestic service for her education. In 1819 she accepted a teaching position in Mexico, Oswego County, New York, where she lived with a brother.

A religious revival sweeping upstate New York influenced Laura Fish to enroll in Miss N. Boyce's Female Seminary, and after a failed engagement in 1826 she directed her energies toward becoming a missionary. She had read with interest the diary and journal of Sybil Bingham, published in the *Missionary Herald*, a publication of the American Board of Commissioners for Foreign Missions, and applied to the ABCFM for overseas duty. On 11 August 1827 she was offered a position as missionary to the Sandwich Islands (Hawaii) and was introduced to her future husband, Gerrit Parmele Judd, a physician and missionary also bound for the Sandwich Islands. Missionaries had to be married, and realizing the commonality of their desires, the couple were married on 20 September 1827 and prepared to leave almost immediately for Hawaii aboard the *Parthian*. The couple had nine children, all born in Hawaii.

They arrived in Owhyhee (Hawaii) on 30 March 1828 in the third company of Congregational missionaries to the Sandwich Islands. Laura Fish Judd founded a school for native Hawaiian women in collaboration with the kuhina nui (coruler) Kaahumanu. This school was for the alii (chiefly class) women and included Kaahumanu and other women interested in learning reading and writing as well as religious instruction. Judd recorded: "We have commenced a school for native women, which already numbers forty-five." She made the initial plans for a school for the alii's children, called the Chiefs' Children's School. Here Judd, who was fluent in both English and Hawaiian, taught reading, geography, and mathematics.

Judd began writing a historical narrative upon her arrival, recording with almost photographic detail the island environment and the activities and customs of the native Hawaiians. She described Honolulu as "a mass of brown huts, looking precisely like so many haystacks in the country; not one white cottage, no church spire, not a garden nor a tree to be seen save the grove of cocoanuts. . . . A host of living, moving beings are coming out of that long brown building; it must be Mr. Bingham's congregation just dismissed from morning service; they pour out like bees from a hive. I can see the draperies of brown, white, pink and yellow native tapa." For analysis and anecdote, "few writers about Hawaii in the 19th Century are her equal," wrote an admirer, and "rare is the book, on almost any phase of Hawaiian life between 1828 and 1861 that does not quote from her record." Judd's book, *Honolulu, Sketches of the Life, Social, Political and Religious, in the Hawaiian Islands from 1828–1861* (1880; rev. ed., 1928), describes not only the landscape, but also the men and women chiefs who ruled Hawaii and cooperated with the missionaries to oversee the dispensing of literacy and the gospel.

Her record painted authoritative portraits of high-ranking native women. Judd also recorded firsthand significant events in Hawaiian foreign relations, including the attempt by the French to capture Hawaii by force in 1839, the American mission of Commodore Charles Wilkes to explore and describe the islands from 1840 to 1841, and Lord George Paulet's efforts to claim the islands for Britain in 1843. Throughout these years, the missionaries supported Hawaiian leaders, who were committed to an independent Hawaii and a strong monarchy. Gerrit Judd severed his ties with the ABCFM in 1842 to serve the Hawaiian monarchy as recorder, translator, member of the treasury board, secretary for foreign affairs (1843), and minister of the interior (1845).

Laura Judd's manuscript, completed in 1861, was taken to New England by the Judds on a visit to relatives and was given to the ABCFM. The society never published the book. Upon the family's request that it be returned, it appeared in 1880 as a family commemorative. Laura Fish Judd died at the family home in Honolulu. Pioneer educator and historian, she played a significant part in the Christianization and modernization of Hawaii.

• The archives, papers, diaries, and journals of the Judds are located at the Hawaiian Mission Children's Society on the grounds of the original Mission House Museum in Honolulu and are collected under the title *Fragments: Family Record, House of Judd*, 5 vols. See also "Mrs. G. P. Judd, 1804–1872, a Suppressed Chapter of American History," *Hawaiian Historical Society Annual Report* (1902), pp. 7–14. Gerrit Parmele Judd III has offered a recent biographical portrait of his family in *Hawaii: An Informal History* (1961). Barbara Bennett Peterson, ed., *Notable Women of Hawaii* (1984), includes a biography of Laura Fish Judd that contains more information on her early life and details the careers of her children.

BARBARA BENNETT PETERSON

JUDD, Norman Buel (10 Jan. 1815–11 Nov. 1878), diplomat and congressman, was born in Rome, New York, the son of Norman Judd, a potter, and Catherine Van der Heyden. Norman finished high school in Rome, studied law, and in 1836 was admitted to the bar of New York. He moved west in 1836, settling in Chicago, where he drafted the first city charter based on the charter of Buffalo, New York. Incorporated as a city in 1837, Chicago would be home to Judd for the rest of his life, and he was elected to a succession of public offices there: first city attorney of Chicago (1837 and 1838), attorney for Cook County (1839), alderman (1842), and state senator (1844–1860). During his years as a public official, he was also a successful private attorney, representing a number of midwestern railroad corporations. He helped consolidate a number of these lines into the Rock Island Railway and became the first attorney for this organization. He also was a leading attorney for the Illinois Central Railroad. In 1844 he married Adeline Rossiter. Of their many children, only two survived to adulthood.

Judd was always active in party politics. Until 1854 he was a devoted Democrat, an affiliation perhaps born from the strength of the Democratic party in upstate New York, where he grew up, and reinforced by the Democratic inclinations of many of his fellow attorneys for the Illinois Central Railroad, such as Stephen A. Douglas. Judd broke with the Democrats in 1854 over the issue of the expansion of slavery into the territories. Always a firm believer that slavery should be prohibited in the territories, Judd opposed Douglas's Kansas-Nebraska Act, which would have allowed territorial residents to determine the status of slavery. Like many Democrats who opposed Douglas's bill, Judd was conservative on the race issue in the 1850s, believing that black Americans should ultimately be colonized outside of the United States. Also, although he opposed the specific form of Douglas's territorial bill, he was generally sympathetic to territorial acquisition—so long as slavery was not carried to the acquired areas—and advocated expansion into Mexico and Canada.

Judd and his faction of Independent Democrats in the Illinois State Senate held the balance of power in the election of a U.S. senator in 1855. He and three other Independent Democrats decided not to support Abraham Lincoln for the position, mostly because of Lincoln's Whig affiliation. When Lincoln saw that he might be defeated, he threw his support to the anti-Nebraska Democrat Lyman Trumbull, the ultimate victor and a friend of Judd's. By 1856 Judd had become a Republican. He attended the anti-Nebraska convention at Bloomington, Illinois, that created the state Republican organization, he was chairman of the Republican State Central Committee from 1856 to 1861, and during that same period he was a member of the Republican National Committee. However, because of his opposition to Lincoln in the 1855 election, Judd was always regarded with suspicion by former Whigs within the Illinois Republican party. He was nevertheless genuinely devoted to the Republican party and to Lincoln. In 1858 he helped arrange the Lincoln-Douglas debates, advised Lincoln throughout the contest for the senatorship, and helped manage the campaign in northern Illinois. When Lincoln lost the election, Judd received much of the blame. One of his leading critics was John Wentworth of Chicago, who privately circulated the opinion that Judd cared more about his own political advancement than he did about Lincoln's. The charge was a harmful exaggeration: Judd did wish to become governor of Illinois, but he was equally interested in Lincoln's election as senator. Judd denied Wentworth's accusations, and a feud ensued, known locally as the "War of the Roses." Despite Lincoln's public defense of Judd as a sincere ally, Wentworth, who in 1860 was elected mayor of Chicago, in that same year helped to block Judd's effort to become the Republican nominee for governor of Illinois.

The same state convention that denied the gubernatorial nomination to Judd also elected delegates to the Republican National Convention, and Judd helped ensure that these delegates were committed to Lincoln. Acting on Lincoln's advice, Judd then swayed the Republican National Committee to hold the national convention in Chicago, where Lincoln, the Illinois favorite, was bound to gain some advantage. Judd helped manipulate the convention for Lincoln by seating the Pennsylvania delegates, many of whom were uncommitted, between the Illinois and Indiana delegates, most of whom were pledged to Lincoln. During the balloting, many of the Pennsylvania delegates were swayed to Lincoln by the loud cries for him on either side of them. Following the convention, Judd campaigned assiduously for Lincoln's election. The president-elect initially planned to appoint Judd to a cabinet position, but former Illinois Whigs, most notably David Davis and Leonard Swett, opposed the appointment. Also, Mary Todd Lincoln despised Judd. What ultimately turned the tide against Judd, however, was Lincoln's recognition that, since one representative from Illinois occupied the White House, others from that state should not hold cabinet positions. Perhaps as

compensation, Lincoln had Judd join him on the train that transported the president-elect from Springfield to Washington, D.C. When they received reports from Allan Pinkerton of a plot to assassinate Lincoln, Judd and others advised Lincoln to enter Washington by a secret route through Baltimore. Immediately after Lincoln took office, Judd was appointed minister to Prussia.

Although Judd sent valuable dispatches to Washington regarding events and sentiments of the European continent, he was not satisfied in this position. He hated being away from politics and business in the United States, and he was annoyed by the Prussians treating his Berlin office as a recruiting station for would-be immigrants seeking enlistment in Union armies. In a conversation with Lincoln in November 1863, Judd asked for a position in the United States, but the president persuaded him to return to Berlin.

By this time Judd and Lincoln were good personal friends. In the late 1850s Lincoln had occasionally loaned Judd money, and one of these loans, which Judd had used to speculate in Iowa lands, returned a nice profit. Lincoln secured the appointment of Judd's son Frank Judd to West Point. Frank enlisted instead, and Lincoln twice had to pardon him for desertion. Judd expected to stay on in Berlin after Lincoln's re-election in 1864, but after the president's assassination, Wentworth, then serving in Congress, used his influence with President Andrew Johnson to oust Judd.

Judd returned to Chicago and, in 1866, took Wentworth's place in Congress. He was reelected in 1868 but declined to be a candidate in 1870. As a congressman, he was a member of the committee that brought articles of impeachment against President Johnson. He also introduced the bill allowing direct shipment of foreign goods to inland ports, a measure that helped commerce in the United States flourish. In 1872 President Ulysses S. Grant appointed him collector of the port of Chicago, where he remained until his resignation in 1876 because of failing health.

During Reconstruction, Judd continued to advocate expansion into Mexico and Canada, as he had during the 1850s. However, his views on race became far less conservative than they had been in the prewar era. He supported Lincoln's Emancipation Proclamation and the enlistment of black troops into the Union army, and he pushed for a speedy ratification of the Thirteenth Amendment abolishing slavery and the enactment of civil rights for African Americans. On financial issues, he supported a slight expansion of the monetary supply and a moderate tariff.

A successful businessman, Judd was somewhat artless in his political maneuvering. Thwarted at crucial moments in his political career by Wentworth, Judd never fully realized his ambitions for high office. Nevertheless, he retained a selfless commitment to public service until his death in Chicago, and he was fondly remembered as the man who helped to create the Republican party in Illinois and to make Lincoln a nationally renowned politician.

• A small collection of Judd's papers resides in the Illinois State Historical Library in Springfield. Many of Judd's original letters are in the Lyman Trumbull Papers at the Illinois State Historical Library and in the larger collection of Trumbull Papers at the Library of Congress. For details on Judd's ancestry, see Sylvester Judd, *Thomas Judd and His Descendants* (1856). For Judd's political career before 1866 and his association with Abraham Lincoln, see the article on him in Mark E. Neely, Jr., *The Abraham Lincoln Encyclopedia* (1982). Much detail on Judd's work in the Republican party leading to Lincoln's election in 1860 is in Arthur C. Cole, *The Era of the Civil War, 1848–1870* (1918); William Baringer, *Lincoln's Rise to Power* (1937); Reinhard H. Luthin, *The First Lincoln Campaign* (1944); Jay Monaghan, *The Man Who Elected Lincoln* (1956); Don E. Fehrenbacher, *Chicago Giant: A Biography of "Long John" Wentworth* (1957); and Willard L. King, *Lincoln's Manager, David Davis* (1960). Monaghan, *Diplomat in Carpet Slippers: Abraham Lincoln Deals with Foreign Affairs* (1945), offers a few details on Judd's career as a diplomat. An obituary is in the *Chicago Daily Tribune*, 12 Nov. 1878.

MICHAEL VORENBERG

JUDD, Sylvester (23 July 1813–26 Jan. 1853), novelist and Unitarian minister, was born in Westhampton, Massachusetts, the son of Apphia Hall and Sylvester Judd II, who in 1822 became proprietor of the one newspaper in nearby Northampton. Judd began preparing for the Congregational ministry at Yale College (1832–1836) but was converted to Unitarianism in 1837. At Harvard Divinity School (1837–1840) he came under the influence of Henry Ware, Jr. (1794–1843), Jones Very, and Ralph Waldo Emerson.

From 1840 until his death Judd served the Unitarian church of Augusta, Maine. In 1841 he married Jane Elizabeth Williams, the daughter of his wealthiest parishioner, U.S. Senator Reuel Williams. A few months later—after Judd commented at his church on the necessary evils of all wars, pointing out that civil liberties were curtailed during even the best of wars, the American Revolution—the Maine legislature dismissed him as one of its chaplains. This made him an instant martyr of the pacifist movement; Judd was noticed favorably, more often than not, by newspapers throughout New England.

Even at sixteen, Judd, an avid novel reader, entertained literary ambitions. His activities at Yale College were hardly those expected of a future minister. He dabbled in Byronic verse, and he wrote, produced, and acted in a poetic drama about seduction, which concluded with murder and lovers' suicides in a brothel. In a short story published in the *Yale Literary Magazine* (1836), Judd anticipated some aspects of his first major work, *Margaret, A Tale of the Real and Ideal* (1845).

Margaret is virtually the only novel of the Transcendentalist movement. Its lyricism reflects Judd's personality: a bit too sweet, despite some vinegar in the honey. William Dean Howells praised *Margaret's* "inexhaustible sweetness, quaintness, and tenderness." Margaret, at nine, is a child of nature, too far from town to learn its Calvinism. Unspoiled, immune to sin-mongering, she fills the Calvinist gloom with flowers. Margaret grows up, acquires religion from a Unitarian, marries him, inherits money, changes from town outcast to town leader, and creates a village utopia. That this nonconformist savior-figure is a woman does not escape our notice. *Margaret* was described by James Russell Lowell as "the most emphatically *American* book ever written." Nathaniel Hawthorne said it was "intensely" American. Margaret Fuller, to whom Judd sent a copy with a note saying that she had "one admirer in the State of Maine," thought this "a distinction of which I am not a little proud, now that I have read his book." She called *Margaret* "this one 'Yankee novel.'"

Judd's audience was distinguished, but his plots were too awkward and slow moving to draw the general reader along. After 1895 Judd was almost forgotten. In 1856 F. O. C. Darley's book of drawings based on *Margaret*, still considered significant by art historians, renewed interest in the novel. The 1851 revised version of *Margaret* was reprinted in 1857, 1871, 1874 (in England), 1882, 1891, and 1968. Reviewing the 1871 edition in the *Atlantic Monthly*, Howells spoke of "this beautiful old romance," "marvelously, almost matchlessly frank in dealing with . . . rude life." Indeed, *Margaret* is a hand-hewn book, rough, dawdling, poetic, folky. Judd, like Emerson, combines Transcendental idealism and earthiness: "In myself seems sometimes to reside an infant universe. . . . The spider builds his house from his own bowels." "Children that germinate with a plenty of mother earth about them, come out in the fairest hues." For both Judd and Emerson, vital language also germinated in mother earth. Some called this linguistic primitivism "vulgar," but in the 1851 revision, Judd cut only a few of his more earthy expressions, such as "Panguts!" and "Don't deary me with your dishcloth tongue."

Judd never admitted to being a Transcendentalist, and eventually he explicitly denied that he was one. He always emphasized Christ-centeredness. Despite the utopianism of his literary works, he was essentially more moderate than radical. His most abolitionist lecture, in 1838 to a large audience in Northampton, advocated personal conversion, not political action. An outspoken temperance man, Judd nevertheless opposed the Maine prohibition law of 1846 on the grounds that it would lead to public corruption, private concealment, and a collision "where force shall be repelled by force." Foreseeing civil war, he gradually moderated his antislavery stand. When antislavery and peace were the same cause during the Mexican War, Judd was uncompromising, but by the 1850s he cautioned against abusing slaveholders and spoke of loving them "into repentance and reformation." For Judd, peace and love were primary principles.

Judd's *Philo, An Evangeliad* (1850), a verse drama, is a Unitarian fantasia of universal reform. It culminates in the abolition—by divine love expressed in human choice—of war, slavery, imprisonment, and poverty. Compared with Judd's best rhythmic prose, *Philo's* verse is awkward; despite homely and interesting metaphors, it lacks *Margaret's* simultaneous earthiness and exaltedness. Yet Emerson liked *Philo*, and Judd's friend Edward Everett Hale at one time "seriously expected 'Philo' was to convert the world."

Richard Edney and the Governor's Family (1850), a novel about a young man's rise in the world through pluck, luck, virtue, and marriage to the governor's daughter, depicts the lovable antics of children and proposes YMCA-type solutions to urban social problems.

As Judd's books were child-centered, so was his church. His pet project was a "birthright church" with children as communicants. On his way to Boston to deliver his most important lecture on this subject, he was turned back by a sudden illness and died at home in Augusta, Maine, a few weeks later. According to family tradition, Judd's unspecified illness was caused by damp sheets in a cold hotel. Judd left his wife with three daughters, the third not yet born.

• Other works by Judd include *A Young Man's Account of His Conversion from Calvinism* (1838); *A Moral Review of the Revolutionary War, or Some of the Evils of That Event Considered* (1842); and *The Church: In a Series of Discourses* (1854). The Judd papers are at the Harvard University Library. Other source materials are in Arethusa Hall, *Life and Character of the Reverend Sylvester Judd* (1854). A critical biography is Richard D. Hathaway, *Sylvester Judd's New England* (1981). Francis B. Dedmond, *Sylvester Judd* (1980), summarizes Judd's works and the critical reaction.

RICHARD D. HATHAWAY

JUDGE, Thomas Augustine (23 Aug. 1868–23 Nov. 1933), Roman Catholic priest, was born in Boston, Massachusetts, the son of Thomas Judge, a laborer and painter, and Mary Donahue. Both parents were Irish immigrants. In 1890 Judge entered St. Vincent's Seminary in Germantown, Pennsylvania. In 1895 he professed vows as a member of the Congregation of the Mission, or Vincentians. He was ordained to the priesthood in 1899.

Light parish work in Emmitsburg, Maryland, and Germantown brought temporary recovery from chronic lung disease. Italian immigrants in Germantown sensitized him to the problem of Catholic immigrants leaving the church because of inadequate pastoral care. This began his characteristic concern for the "preservation of the faith." Judge was an excellent preacher. From 1903 to 1909 he traveled in northeastern cities as a member of the Vincentian Mission Band, a team of priests assigned to give parish missions or Catholic revivals.

Judge worked in the antimodernist climate that followed upon twin Vatican censures of "Americanism" (1899) and "modernism" (1907). As a member of the Mission Band, he guided the Holy Name Society and other devotional associations of the period. They encouraged personal piety and the support of parish activities. But Judge also shared the conviction of earlier progressive Catholics that the Holy Spirit moves within all who are baptized, urging them to "missionary" works. His sense of the lay apostolate, therefore, extended to areas that his more authoritarian contemporaries might have reserved to the clergy. He envisioned "working-class missionaries" as a vital presence in urban neighborhoods, addressing the spiritual needs of recent immigrants. Lay apostles, he believed, would "stand for their Church . . . zealous to reclaim the wayward, to strengthen the weak." Such work might be "done without offence and as quietly as God's angels pass through a crowd" (*Ecclesiastical Review*, pp. 277, 280).

Judge adapted a previous generation's emphasis on an active laity to the often antimodernist devotional world of the immigrant church. "Devotion to the Holy Ghost" was the distinguishing mark of his movement, which came to be called the "Missionary Cenacle." (Cenacle is a traditional name for the upper room where Jesus' disciples awaited the coming of the Holy Spirit and from which they went out as missionaries.) On 11 April 1909, in Brooklyn, New York, Judge gathered the five women who would formally begin the Missionary Cenacle. Between 1909 and 1915 the movement prospered. As he traveled with the Mission Band, Judge continued to form small groups of lay apostles. He kept in touch with them through "letter conferences." Three such groups opened neighborhood houses in Baltimore, Maryland; Bridgeport, Connecticut; and Orange, New Jersey. The Cenacle drew some criticism, notably from Cardinal William O'Connell of Boston. In 1915 Judge's Vincentian superiors ordered him to stop Cenacle work and transferred him to the East Alabama Mission at Opelika, where he shortly became the pastor.

With few Catholics and a traditional hostility to priests, Alabama struck Judge as perfect for lay apostles. With the approval of Bishop Edward Allen of Mobile, Judge invited some of the Cenacle women to come south as missionaries for two or three years. By the fall of 1916 Amy Croke, Ella Lonergan, Margaret Louise Keasey, and their companions had opened a modest school in Phenix City. They were soon joined by Andrew Philips and Eugene Brennan. By 1918 the Cenacle women were legally incorporated in Alabama, a fledgling religious community with eighty-five sisters and some 800 Cenacle associates. With Philips and Brennan as its nucleus, the men's group was similarly incorporated in 1921.

Between 1918 and 1926 Judge presided over the institutional consolidation and expansion of a movement that grew to include both religious and lay members, known respectively as the Inner and Outer Cenacles. In 1919 he appointed Keasey (who became Mother M. Boniface) to head the sisters' community. They collaborated closely over the next decade. Two old plantations Judge acquired in Cottonton, Alabama, became the Missionary Cenacle's "Jerusalem." From this center, known as Holy Trinity, their work expanded dramatically. In a daring decision, Judge also established the Cenacle in Puerto Rico. He saw the need to preserve the faith in the wake of the departure of Spanish clergy after the Spanish-American War of 1848.

After working for more than a decade to secure formal ecclesiastical approval, Judge lived to see the recognition in church law of the Missionary Servants of the Most Holy Trinity (men) in 1929 and the Missionary Servants of the Most Blessed Trinity (women) in 1932. But the last seven years of his life brought many setbacks. Bishop Allen, his closest episcopal ally, died in 1926. Allen's successor, Bishop Thomas Toolen, who had few priests and religious for pastoral work and who thought Judge should work exclusively in the South, took the Cenacle's expansion to be an abandonment of the South. Amid increasing financial strain from the Great Depression, Toolen criticized Judge's handling of finances. This conflict underscored the urgency of canonical recognition: without it, appeals of Toolen's decisions would likely not succeed. In January 1930 the sisters' six-year-old mother house at Holy Trinity burned to the ground. In November 1931 Mother Boniface died of typhoid. Shortly before Judge's death in Washington, D.C., both the women's and the men's communities moved their mother houses to the North. A two-year battle with Toolen ensued over the Cenacle's right, under church law, to remain at Holy Trinity.

Judge's enlistment of the laity in the work of preserving the faith signaled an important moment in Catholicism's creative adaptation to American culture and resulted in the founding of two religious communities. By continuing to encourage lay involvement in their work through the Missionary Cenacle apostolate, these communities have institutionalized Judge's vision. This vision of a "Cenacle family," in which women and men religious work together with lay men and women, is Judge's enduring contribution to American religious history. Puerto Rico indeed proved a gateway through which the Missionary Cenacle has spread to other parts of Latin America.

• Judge's papers, including correspondence, sermons, and letter conferences, are in the Archives of the Missionary Servants of the Most Blessed Trinity in Philadelphia, Pa., and the Archives of the Missionary Servants of the Most Holy Trinity in Silver Spring, Md. Many of Judge's previously unpublished writings, edited by Timothy Lynch, are now available in individual monographs published by Missionary Cenacle Press; see, for example, *Early and Final Days* (1983), *Father Judge Teaches Ministry* (1983), *Writings of Father Judge: Key Documents* (1984), *The Oracle of Our Founder* (1984), and *Father Judge and the Missionary Cenacle* (1985). Judge explains his vision of the lay apostolate in "The Lay Apostolate in the South," *Catholic Convert*, Sept. 1918, pp. 4–18, and "A Spiritual Militia: Another Phase of the Lay Apostolate," *Ecclesiastical Review* 61 (1919): 276–85. The best available studies are written by members of the religious communities Judge founded: Dennis Berry, *God's Valiant Warrior* (1992), and J. Miriam Blackwell, *Ecclesial People: A Study in the Life and Times of Thomas Augustine Judge, C.M.* (1984). See also James P. O'Bryan, *Awake the Giant: A History of the Missionary Cenacle Apostolate* (1986). An obituary is in the *Washington Post*, 24 Nov. 1933.

WILLIAM L. PORTIER

JUDGE, William Quan (13 Apr. 1851–21 Mar. 1896), Theosophist, was born in Dublin, Ireland, the son of Frederick H. Judge (occupation unknown) and Alice Mary Quan. In 1864 his father, now a widower, emigrated with his children to the United States, eventually settling in Brooklyn. Although the Judges faced hard times as immigrants, William was able to finish his schooling before settling into employment as a law clerk in New York City. Learning law on the job, he was admitted to the State Bar of New York in 1872, the same year he became a naturalized citizen. Two years later he married Ella M. Smith. Living in Brooklyn, the couple had a daughter who died of diphtheria in infancy.

Raised a strict Methodist, Judge from boyhood was nevertheless curious about occultism. Through Henry Steel Olcott, whose writings on Spiritualism he had read, he was invited in 1875 to visit the occultist Helena Petrovna Blavatsky in her New York residence. Thus began his loyal association with Blavatsky, who, in a letter of 1889, was to write that Judge was "*part of herself since several aeons*" (repr. in Eklund, vol. 1, p. xxxviii). Active in the inaugural meetings of the Theosophical Society in 1875, Judge was considered a cofounder of that organization along with Blavatsky and its president, Olcott. While propounding a broad, nonsectarian mysticism, the society emphasized Eastern spirituality, and in 1878 Blavatsky and Olcott moved to India to establish headquarters for the organization there. Judge had hoped to accompany them but felt it was his responsibility to care for his debts and stay in the United States with his wife. For the next few years the Theosophical Society in the United States was virtually inactive, and Judge, now the group's corresponding secretary, was often in Venezuela and Mexico where he had mining interests.

In 1882 local American branches of the Theosophical Society began to appear, and in the following year the New York Theosophists organized their own branch with Judge as president. Around 1885 Judge secured a position in the law firm of Olcott's brother. This helped to settle his financial difficulties and freed him to devote more time to the society. In 1886 the various U.S. branches organized themselves into the American Section and elected Judge as general secretary. Two years later Olcott honored him with an additional title, appointing him vice president of the international society. In 1893 Judge gave up law to devote himself fully to his Theosophical work, and he also moved from Brooklyn to New York City to be closer to the society's headquarters there.

Largely due to Judge, American interest in Theosophy resurged beginning in 1886, and new branches were established in many cities. His work to further the society included issuing a journal, *The Path* (started in 1886), and instituting a plan to mail out thousands of copies of tracts. In addition to many articles, he published several books, including *The Yoga Aphorisms of Patanjali* (1889) and *Echoes from the Orient* (1890). Because of its conciseness and clarity, his *The Ocean of Theosophy* (1893) became a standard introduction to Theosophical ideas. In it, he discussed such subjects as reincarnation, karma, psychic practices, and the cycles of cosmic evolution. In one particularly lyrical passage he elaborated on the nature of the soul:

That man possesses an immortal soul is the common belief of humanity; to this Theosophy adds that he is a soul; and further that all nature is sentient, that the vast array of objects and men are not mere collections of atoms fortuitously thrown together and thus without law evolving law, but down to the smallest atom all is soul and spirit ever evolving under the rule of law which is inherent in the whole. (P. 2)

Judge also lectured across the country, touring the West Coast, for example, in 1891. In September 1893 he was the chief representative of the Theosophical Society at the World Parliament of Religions held at the World's Columbian Exposition in Chicago. During the parliament the society held its own congress, which received much publicity and did much to promote the organization. Chairing the congress, Judge delivered several lectures in the course of its three days of meetings.

As he became increasingly active in the Theosophical movement, Judge attracted numerous followers, many of whom believed he was an advanced soul. By 1891 he was also promulgating the idea that he was actually an Indian Yogi living in a Westerner's body. It seems that Judge had been declared dead when he suffered a severe illness at the age of seven. It was at this point, he suggested, that the ego of a Hindu, seeking to help enlighten the West, had entered and revived the boy's body.

Judge was also known to produce, supposedly by supernatural means, letters from the mysterious Masters thought to guide the Theosophical Society. By 1892, however, rumors were circulating that Judge was forging these letters. The following year, prompted by Olcott, Annie Besant, a leading English Theosophist, formulated charges against Judge in this matter. She believed that Judge was in psychic communication with the Masters but thought it was inappropriate for him to assume their handwriting when transcribing their messages and then pass these letters off as having come directly from them. Besant's charges led to turmoil within the organization at a time when Judge was in line to assume the presidency of the international society. Matters came to a head at the annual convention of the American Section held in Boston on 28 and 29 April 1895. A majority of the American branches declared their loyalty to Judge and seceded from the parent society, forming an independent group, with Judge as its president. Judge, unfortunately, was not to hold this office for long; in the following year, at the age of forty-four, he died in New York City from tuberculosis.

Although he was sometimes abrupt, Judge was known for his generosity and friendliness. Through his hard work and strong leadership he promoted Theosophy in the United States and made this country an important center for it. Furthermore, the divisions created by the secession of 1895 determined the future course of the American movement, with Judge's own group forming several offshoots after his death.

• Judge's papers are held by the Archives of the Theosophical Society International, Pasadena, Calif., and the Archives of the Theosophical Society, Adyar, Madras, India. His collected articles, compiled by Dara Eklund, have been published as *Echoes of the Orient: The Writings of William Quan Judge* (4 vols., 1975–1993). Selections of his letters appear in *Letters That Have Helped Me*, comp. Jasper Niemand and Thomas Green (2 vols., 1891–1905), and *Practical Occultism*, ed. Arthur L. Conger (1951). *Echoes of the Orient* and *Letters That Have Helped Me* also contain biographical material on Judge, and in addition, the former reprints Sven Eek and Boris de Zirkoff, *William Quan Judge, 1851–1896: The Life of a Theosophical Pioneer* (1969), which presents a cursory overview of Judge's life. Additional information can be found in histories of the Theosophical movement, such as Josephine Ransom, *A Short History of the Theosophical Society, 1875–1937* (1938), and the anonymously written *The Theosophical Movement, 1875–1950* (1951). Judge is discussed also in biographies of other Theosophical leaders, such as Sylvia Cranston, *HPB: The Extraordinary Life and Influence of Helena Blavatsky, Founder of the Modern Theosophical Movement* (1993).

X. THEODORE BARBER

JUDSON, Adoniram (9 Aug. 1788–12 Apr. 1850), missionary, was born in Malden, Massachusetts, the son of Adoniram Judson, a Congregational minister, and Abigail Brown. He spent his childhood in Wenham, Braintree, and Plymouth, where his father held pastorates, and entered Brown University as a sophomore at the age of sixteen. After graduation in 1807, he spent a year teaching elementary school and then entered the new evangelical theological seminary at Andover, again as a second-year student. He graduated with the first class in 1810.

Raised an evangelical Congregationalist and imbued by his father with a strong sense of personal ambition, Judson had rejected his father's faith while in college. He entered seminary only in order to examine Christianity's claims more fully but soon experienced the conversion hoped for in his tradition. He became intrigued with the idea of carrying the Christian gospel to non-Christians overseas and, discovering he was not alone in that ambition, joined the secret student missionary society known as "the Brethren," brought to Andover from Williams College by founders Samuel J. Mills and James Richards.

Judson was one of four seminarians whose 1810 petition to the General Association of Massachusetts prodded that newly organized Congregational ministerial body to create the American Board of Commissioners for Foreign Missions, the first foreign mission organization in the United States. He was sent to London in 1811 (via a Bayonne prison after capture by a French privateer) to explore the possibility of a joint English-American missionary undertaking. When the British proved willing to accept the young Americans as missionaries but reluctant to cooperate with an American society, the American Board ordained Judson, Gordon Hall, Samuel Newell, Samuel Nott, Jr., and Luther Rice as its first missionaries, in Salem, Massachusetts, on 6 February 1812. Judson had married Ann Hasseltine of Bradford the day before, and the new couple sailed with the Newells from Salem for Calcutta on 19 February 1812. They had instructions to start a mission in Burma or elsewhere in Asia.

Shipboard Bible study led the Judsons to accept the Baptist view of baptism, and in Calcutta they had themselves baptized by immersion by British Baptist missionary William Ward in September 1812. This led to the conversion of Luther Rice as well, the immediate severance of the three from the American Board, and the creation in 1814 of the Triennial Convention and its Baptist Board of Foreign Missions by American Baptists. Rice returned to the United States to raise Baptist interest and funds while the Judsons remained in British India to open a mission. Their extended efforts to avoid deportation (the East India Company prohibited Christian missions in its territory, and war began between the United States and Great Britain in mid-1812) and to find a suitable location for evangelism took them to the Isle of France and Madras before they settled in Rangoon, Burma, in July 1813. Judson lived in Burma until his death, returning to the United States only once, for nine months in 1845–1846.

Judson was convinced throughout his life that the translation and publication of the Christian Scriptures in indigenous languages was the most effective and enduring form of evangelism. Learning Burmese and translating the Bible into that language in the face of illness, lack of local interest, and—eventually—government opposition and harassment, he completed a Burmese New Testament in 1823. It was published in 1832; the complete Bible, in 1834. Judson finished compiling a Burmese-English dictionary shortly before his death.

This pioneer scholarly work, along with his simultaneous efforts to make converts through preaching and to gather Burmese Christians into new churches, gained Judson a secure place in the leading ranks of early American Protestant foreign missionaries. But it was the suffering he and his successive wives, Ann Hasseltine (1812–1826), missionary widow Sarah Hall Boardman (1834–1845), and popular author Emily Chubbuck (1846–1850) endured—and the Christian fortitude with which they endured it—that made them revered religious figures.

Some of their hardships came from illnesses brought on by the rigors of missionary life in an unfamiliar climate. Judson suffered from eyestrain and headaches in 1816, cholera in 1822, various fevers over the years, a chronic throat ailment that made speaking difficult during his 1845 visit to the United States, and the dysentery and fever that weakened him until, accompanied only by another missionary on an ocean voyage for his health, he died at sea and was buried in the Indian Ocean. The Judsons also endured the death of Ann's three children and three of Sarah's eight children. Judson withdrew into seclusion, self-denial, and mystical religion for several years after

Ann's death, before immersing himself in translation and emerging from depression to enter his second marriage. He was survived by five of Sarah's children and Emily and her daughter.

Repression by the Burmese government also contributed to the Judsons' suffering. Inconsistent official attitudes toward the mission led Judson to make unsuccessful direct appeals to the king for religious tolerance in 1819 and 1822 and to move to the capital of Ava in 1823. When war began between Burma and Great Britain, Judson was imprisoned along with other Europeans. He was held in Ava and the nearby village of Oung-pen-la under brutal conditions from June 1824 to November 1825. Ann worked tirelessly to improve his care and secure his freedom. Before releasing him the Burmese used him as an interpreter in negotiations with the British. The Judsons then moved with the other American Baptist missionaries to the British settlements of Amherst and Moulmein. After Sarah's death Judson explored new mission fields in Burma before returning to Rangoon with Emily for part of 1847. Continued government intolerance, however, was one factor in their decision to retreat again to Moulmein.

Judson and "the Mrs. Judsons" were without a doubt the most widely known American foreign missionaries of the first two-thirds of the nineteenth century. "For more than thirty years his name had been a household word. . . . A whole generation had grown up, familiar with the story of his labors and sufferings, not one of whom had ever seen his face" (Conant, p. 470). Their exemplary efforts invigorated the young Protestant foreign mission movement and initiated the Baptist contribution to that movement (second in size only to the American Board). When they visited the United States, Ann in 1822–1823 and Adoniram in 1845–1846, they received widespread attention from the supporters of Baptist and other evangelical missions.

The Judsons' broader historical significance rests at least as much on the power and pervasiveness of the tradition of evangelical missionary devotion their deeds inspired as on the deeds themselves. "With the possible exception of the Beechers, no nineteenth-century American family was so closely tied in the public mind to the cause of evangelical Christianity" (Brumberg, p. xiv). The Judsons were inspirational role models for generations of Protestant missionaries, ministers, and their spouses—and for ordinary evangelical Christians as well. They demonstrated the power of personal faith, selfless service, and Christian family life; they embodied the expansion of both evangelical religion and American presence into the world. To the extent that popular Protestantism permeated American culture in the nineteenth century, the Judsons of Burma were famous and influential Americans.

• Few of Judson's papers or letters survived the nineteenth century; some are in the library of the Andover Newton Theological School, Newton Centre, Mass. Outside of his Burmese translations, Judson's publications consist primarily of letters printed in Baptist periodicals, such as the *Massachusetts Baptist Missionary Magazine* and the *American Baptist Magazine*, and in the posthumous biographies. See Edward Starr, *A Baptist Bibliography* (1947–1976).

Judson and his wives have been the subjects of numerous biographies and memorials since the early nineteenth century. The studies of Judson include Francis Wayland, *A Memoir of the Life and Labors of the Rev. Adoniram Judson* (1853), the formal "official" two-volume biography compiled by the prominent Baptist president of Brown University, with the help of Emily Chubbuck Judson; [Robert Middleditch], *Burmah's Great Missionary: Records of the Life of Adoniram Judson* (1854), a competing popular biography published despite Mrs. Judson's opposition; Hannah C. Conant, *The Earnest Man or the Character and Labors of Adoniram Judson* (1856); Edward Judson, *The Life of Adoniram Judson* (1883), by his son, a prominent New York City Baptist minister; and Stacy R. Warburton, *Eastward! The Story of Adoniram Judson* (1937). Courtney Anderson, *To the Golden Shore: The Life of Adoniram Judson* (1956), is a comprehensive modern biography of Judson, and Joan Jacobs Brumberg, *Mission for Life* (1980), analyzes the evangelical fascination with the Judsons and discusses family historiography; both contain extensive bibliographies.

ROBERT A. SCHNEIDER

JUDSON, Adoniram Brown (7 Apr. 1837–20 Sept. 1916), orthopedic surgeon, was born in Maulmain, Burma, the son of Adoniram Judson, a noted missionary, and his second wife, Sarah Hall Boardman. After graduation from Brown University in 1859 with his A.M., Judson attended lectures at the Harvard Medical School. In 1861, without having completed his medical education but having passed the necessary examination, Judson was commissioned as assistant surgeon in the U.S. Navy. He was promoted to passed assistant surgeon in 1864, and having pursued his medical studies while in service and having attained his medical degree from the Jefferson Medical College in Philadelphia in 1865, he was commissioned surgeon in 1866. Judson resigned his post in 1868 and took up the practice of medicine in New York. In the same year he obtained a second M.D., *ad eundem*, from the College of Physicians and Surgeons of New York. Judson married Anna Margaret Haughwout in 1868. They had no children.

In 1869 Judson became inspector on the New York City Board of Health and eventually held the office of assistant superintendent until resigning in 1877. He then served as pension examining surgeon of the city from 1877 to 1884 and again from 1901 to 1914 and as medical examiner for the New York State Civil Service Commission from 1901 to 1909.

Judson's career as an orthopedic surgeon began in 1875 after he had studied for a year under Charles Fayette Taylor. In that year he was lecturer at the women's medical school associated with the New York Infirmary. For twenty-five years, 1878–1903, he was orthopedic surgeon to the outpatient department of the New York Hospital. In 1887 Judson was active in the formation of the American Orthopaedic Association and was elected its vice president in September

1889 and its president a year later. He was particularly energetic in having association papers published in European as well as American journals and was thus instrumental in gaining recognition abroad for American orthopedics. His interest in the national association gave way to concentration on the section of orthopedics of the New York Academy of Medicine, of which he became chairman. Again he made a point of promoting widespread publication of the activities of the section, making it one of the most widely known throughout the medical world.

From 1886 until his death, Judson was also statistical secretary of the New York Academy of Medicine. He prepared memoirs of the fellows of the academy "with painstaking accuracy." Judson was also a member of the American Medical Association, a fellow of the American Academy of Medicine, and a fellow of the American College of Surgeons.

Although Judson's early publications showed his interest in public health, he contributed more than fifty papers, mainly original studies, to the literature of orthopedics. His studies of the lateral curvature of the spine were particularly of importance, and his "Practical Inferences from Clinician Observations in Lateral Curvature of the Spine," which appeared in the *Medical News* in 1896, was translated and published in French and German journals. Also translated was his article "Practical Points in the Treatment of Hip Disease," which appeared in the *Medical Record* in 1893. His "Mensuration of the Deformity of Hip Disease," published in the *Journal of the American Medical Association* in 1896, appeared in both German and Italian. Other publications appeared in European journals as well. He published only one modest book, *The Influence of Growth on Congenital and Acquired Deformities* (1905), which the *Journal of the American Medical Association* noted as presenting a "point of view [that was] new and instructive," and which it judged "an interesting and useful" book. According to the historian of New York medicine James J. Walsh, Judson deserved "to be looked upon as a leader in non-surgical orthopedics."

Judson maintained an interest in Brown University, his alma mater, where he had been a member of its first crew. In 1910 Judson took up his pen to protest the proposal to change the provision in the charter of the university that required that a majority of the governing bodies be Baptists. His letters to the *Baptist World* and the *Providence Journal*, for example, argued that the Baptist tradition of liberalism and democracy would fall victim to authoritarian religious domination if the restriction were removed. The charter was not revised at the time. Judson died in New York City, having been predeceased by his wife.

• Judson's publications are listed in the *Index-Catalogue of the Library of the Surgeon-General's Office, United States Army*, 1st ser., vol. 8 (1886), p. 305, and 2d ser., vol. 8 (1903), pp. 535–36; and in *The New York Academy of Medicine Author Catalogue of the Library*, vol. 20 (1969), pp. 769–72. The most complete biography is in H. A. Kelly and W. L. Burrage,

Dictionary of American Medical Biography (1928). Brief obituary notices are in the *New York Times*, 21 Sept. 1916, and the *New York Medical Journal*, 14 Oct. 1916.

DAVID L. COWEN

JUDSON, Ann Hasseltine (22 Dec. 1789–24 Oct. 1826), missionary, was born in Bradford, Massachusetts, the daughter of John Hasseltine and Rebecca Burton, farmers. She was educated at the Bradford Academy along with her friend Harriet Atwood and future mission administrator Rufus Anderson. In 1806 she experienced the personal conversion to Christian faith expected in her parents' evangelical Congregational tradition and encouraged by her teachers and joined the Congregational church in Bradford that September. She taught school in surrounding towns for several years after 1807.

Hasseltine was familiar with the missionary movement before she met Adoniram Judson in June 1810, when her father invited him to dinner. Judson was one of several Andover seminary students petitioning the Bradford meeting of the state association of Congregational ministers for support as foreign missionaries. The association's response was to form the American Board of Commissioners for Foreign Missions (ABCFM), the first Protestant foreign-mission organization in the United States. Judson soon proposed marriage to Hasseltine. Missionaries' wives had taken part in missions to American Indians and in British foreign missions, but as the first American woman to consider an overseas mission, Hasseltine found that the disapproval of friends and neighbors added to her own concerns about her readiness for both marriage and mission. She accepted the dual challenge, however, and by the autumn of 1810 agreed to marry Judson. Her decision no doubt influenced Atwood to accept missionary candidate Samuel Newell's proposal the following year.

When opportunities arose to send missionaries to South Asia, the ABCFM ordained Judson, Newell, Gordon Hall, Samuel Nott, Jr., and Luther Rice as missionaries on 6 February 1812. Judson and Hasseltine were married in Bradford the day before the ordination, Newell and Atwood and Nott and Rosanna Peck in the days after. The wives were appointed assistant missionaries, and the board began publicizing the justification of missionary wives that became pervasive throughout the American Protestant missionary movement: in addition to supporting and assisting their husbands, wives served the cause of missions by exemplifying the Christian family, educating non-Christian children, and evangelizing among non-Christian women. Within two weeks of their ordination, Hall, Rice, and the Notts sailed from the Philadelphia area and the Judsons and Newells from Salem, all bound for India. The Judsons and the Newells reached Calcutta in June.

Adoniram Judson's personal study of the Bible led first him, then Ann Judson, and finally Rice to abandon the Congregationalist practice of infant baptism and to adopt Baptist beliefs. In September 1812 the Judsons were baptized by the English missionaries of the Baptist Missionary Society in Serampore near Calcutta. News of their decision led the ABCFM to withdraw its support and American Baptists to organize to provide for their new missionaries. Seeking first to obtain permission to settle in India and then to avoid the deportation ordered by the East India Company, which was opposed to Christian missions in its territory and provoked by news of war between Great Britain and the United States, the Judsons left Calcutta for the Isle of France (Mauritius), Madras, and then Burma. At the Isle of France they learned of the death of Harriet Atwood Newell and her newborn infant. The Judsons' early chroniclers mention only that Judson was taken seriously ill between Madras and Burma, but according to twentieth-century biographers she barely survived the premature birth of her first child, who was stillborn.

In Rangoon from 1813 to 1821 and from 1823 to 1824, and in Ava in early 1824, Judson worked alongside her husband as a missionary. She learned the Burmese and Siamese languages, and she translated her catechism, Adoniram's tract on Christianity, and the Gospel of Matthew into the latter. She taught Burmese girls and explained Christianity to their mothers. The couple's evangelistic efforts finally led to the baptism of a Burmese convert in 1819. When Adoniram was absent, Judson managed the mission and dealt with both inconsistent local rulers and the recurrent crises among the small but changing group of American Baptist missionaries. She coped with her husband's and her own numerous illnesses, sailed alone to Madras for several months in 1815 to regain her health, gave birth to a son that September, and the following May nursed him through the fever that led to his death at the age of seven months. Her liver trouble led Adoniram to take her to Calcutta for part of 1820, and when it recurred a year later she returned there alone and then went on to England, Scotland, and the United States.

The Judsons' letters to friends and family, widely published in religious periodicals, had been instrumental in introducing American evangelicals to the new foreign mission enterprise. Although they spoke primarily to Baptists, the missionary couple continued to hold and act on the beliefs of New England Calvinism as expressed by Congregationalist Samuel Hopkins, which inspired the missionary outreach of both the ABCFM and the Baptist Triennial Convention created to support them. In Massachusetts, New York, Maryland, and Washington, D.C., from September 1822 to June 1823 Judson further promoted the cause of missions through personal appearances, addresses to women, attendance at the meeting of the Baptist convention, and the publication of her history of the mission in Burma. By the time she accompanied a new missionary couple to the mission in December 1823, both support for Baptist missions and the Judsons' status as religious celebrities were secure.

Judson resumed her missionary labors at the mission's new site in Ava, the royal capital. The outbreak of war between Great Britain and Burma led to Adoniram's arrest as a spy in June 1824. For the year and a half her husband was imprisoned at Ava and Oung-pen-la (Aungbinle), Judson managed her household with meager means in the face of constant harassment. She visited her husband, paid prison guards and local officials to ensure his care, and negotiated with the government for his release. In January 1825 she gave birth to a daughter.

Adoniram was released late in 1825, and the following spring the Baptist missionaries moved to Amherst, the new capital of British Burma. Judson and her daughter remained in Amherst while Adoniram returned to Rangoon and then Ava to negotiate a British commercial treaty. In the fall of 1826, weakened by years of illness and the stress and deprivations of the previous two years, Judson succumbed to yet another bout of tropical fever. Her daughter died the following April.

As an individual and as the first wife and co-worker of a famous missionary, Judson attracted widespread interest throughout the nineteenth and twentieth centuries and inspired a vast number of biographies, sermons, and poems, as well as a novel. She helped expand the traditional sphere of women's work even as she seemed to embody it. She demonstrated that women could function as effectively in the traditionally male roles into which their missionary commitment led them as they could in their own domestic capacities. As wife, mother, nurse, teacher, evangelist, writer, translator, and diplomat, she became a prominent model for activist American Protestant women.

• Judson's major publication in English is *A Particular Relation of the American Baptist Mission to the Burman Empire* (1823). James D. Knowles, *Memoir of Mrs. Ann H. Judson, Late Missionary to Burma* (1829), was reprinted throughout the nineteenth century, and, since no collection of Judson's papers survived, served as primary source material for all subsequent treatments of her. Widely read and long-lived biographies include Arabella Stuart Willson, *The Lives of Mrs. Ann H. Judson and Mrs. Sarah B. Judson, with a Biographical Sketch of Mrs. Emily C. Judson* (1851); Daniel C. Eddy, *Heroines of the Missionary Enterprise* (1850; later retitled *Daughters of the Cross*, 1855) and *The Three Mrs. Judsons and Other Daughters of the Cross* (1859); Cecil B. Hartley, *The Three Mrs. Judsons, the Celebrated Female Missionaries* (1863); Walter N. Wyeth, *Ann H. Judson: A Memorial* (1888); Ethel Daniels Hubbard, *Ann of Ava* (1913); and Gordon L. Hall [Dawn Langley Simmons], *Golden Boats from Burma* (1961). Honoré Willsie Morrow, *The Splendor of God* (1929), is a novel based on Judson's life. John Dowling, ed., *The Judson Offering* (1846), includes samples of the poetry written about the Judsons.

The best scholarly study of all the Judsons and their role in American religion and culture, which discusses Ann Judson at length and includes an extensive bibliography, is Joan Jacobs Brumberg, *Mission for Life* (1980). Dana L. Robert, *American Women in Mission* (1996), describes the context, nature, and influence of Judson's missionary thought and practice.

ROBERT A. SCHNEIDER

JUDSON, Edward Zane Carroll (20 Mar. 1823–16 July 1886), adventurer and writer known as "Ned Buntline," was born in Stamford, New York, the son of Levi Judson, a schoolmaster and, later, an attorney; his mother's name is unknown. After his father moved the family to Philadelphia, the adolescent Judson rebelled and ran away to sea as a cabin boy. He served for about five years on voyages to various Caribbean and South American ports. Judson's life and career—one might say lives and careers—epitomize a restlessness that made him thirst for adventures and misadventures in- and out-of-doors, and they show that he had a keen eye for the chance to promote himself as heroic in sensationally fictionalized accounts of his own adventures. The list of epithets he inspires is almost encyclopedic: sailor and U.S. Navy officer; soldier; magazine editor; writer of several hundred "shilling shockers," dime novels, and other "continuous" stories; temperance lecturer (and drunkard); superpatriot to those of Know Nothing (Buntlinite) persuasion, jingoist bigot to others; expert marksman and angler; bigamist; "discoverer" of Buffalo Bill; playwright; proselytizer; generic showman; and occasionally outright con artist. To these might be added still others.

At fourteen, Judson, impulsive and impetuous, enlisted in the U.S. Navy, hoping to be part of an Antarctic expedition. He had to settle for ships that took him, first, to the Mexican coast and, later, to Florida and the exciting prospect of the Seminole wars. Though he saw no actual combat, he mined imaginary battles for two decades in essentially trashy fiction. Resigning his midshipman commission in mid-1842, he remained unaccounted for until May 1844. His interests had turned inland and literary.

Two attempts to establish monthly literary journals, first in Pittsburgh and then in Cincinnati, failed. Almost immediately he resurrected his first journal as *Ned Buntline's Own*, a magazine he enriched with a continuing narrative of his own "actual" adventures and a pietistic guide for travelers about how to avoid a variety of confidence games. At the same time he had published in Lewis Gaylord Clark's *Knickerbocker* two stories and had an agreement with Clark for a serialized narrative of sea adventures, "Ned Buntline's Life-Yarn." His hankering for a literary career led him into publicity stunts. In a typical escapade he fabricated his single-handed capture of two of three murderers near Eddyville, Kentucky. Any notoriety seemed welcome, even that attached to real-life events. In Nashville, Judson was suspected of seducing a teenaged bride; when the husband came after him firing several shots, Judson shot him in the forehead. Falsely accused by the victim's friends of shooting the man in the back, Judson fled the courtroom with a serious chest wound when they opened fire. Trying to escape through a hotel's third-story window, he fell, as he later put it, "forty seven feet three inches, (measured), . . . and not a bone cracked!" He was in fact seriously crippled. Recaptured and taken to jail, that night he was put upon by a lynch mob and hanged in the public square; he was saved, he reported, when a friend cut the rope. A grand jury later accepted his plea of self-defense. Meanwhile, his wife Seberina, virtually abandoned, died in childbirth.

A year later, back in New York Judson became aware of the emergence of a new reading class of uneducated, relatively poor people engrossed in shilling shockers, the kind of melodramatic adventure trash he had earlier panned in his magazine reviews. Some writers, he learned, were turning out one and two dozen such volumes annually, and Judson took them as his models. The titles of his earliest narratives are typical of all of them: *The Last Days of Calleo; or, The Doomed City of Sin, The King of the Sea: A Tale of the Fearless and Free* (1847), and *The Queen of the Sea; or, Our Lady of the Ocean: A Tale of Love, Strife and Chivalry* (1848). His output in the next twenty years was prodigious; he once boasted that he had written a book of over 600 pages in just sixty-two hours. By the 1860s he was said to be earning $20,000 yearly. Though some of these shockers and dime novels sold in the hundreds of thousands, none is seen in twentieth-century literary histories. Judson himself, in his reformist zeal, put more stock in his *Mysteries and Miseries of New York: A Story of Real Life* (1848), a melodramatic exposé of gambling, prostitution, and various forms of gangsterism done up with a sociological air. By 1869, when he met William F. Cody near the North Platte and began creating the legend of Buffalo Bill in a series of dime novels and a play in which Judson himself took a role, Judson was a celebrity as one of the creators of the Beadle's and the Street and Smith genre.

Judson by no means had to cloister himself to write so many volumes. In 1849 he led a mob to New York's Astor Place Opera House to protest English actor William Macready's performance of *Macbeth*. Twenty-three people were killed, and Judson was tried, found guilty, and sentenced to a year in prison. Concurrently, Annie Bennett, whom he had married in 1848 and with whom he had one child, was divorcing him for infidelity and drunkenness while Judson was achieving further notoriety on the temperance lecture circuit and was reported by several scandal sheets as having six mistresses in the city. The next year found him in St. Louis, and by 1852 he was in jail there for leading a mob of enthusiasts of the "nativist"—America for Americans—movement. He jumped bail, only to be rearrested on the charges twenty years later when touring with Buffalo Bill in *The Scouts of the Plains* (1872). In 1853, while campaigning for his Know Nothing party, he married Lovanche Swart as well as a young actress, Josie Juda. He was charged with bigamy and again jailed.

After he was released by New York's governor, Judson lectured on temperance in Maine. He was charged with shooting and wounding a black man (thinking him to be a Greek) and was jailed and tried, but this time he was acquitted. The middle and late 1850s found him retreating to cabin life in the Adirondacks—hunting, fishing, and writing—while, around 1857, eschewing both Lovanche and Josie for another

teenaged bride, Eva Gardiner, who died in childbirth in early 1860. By the end of that year he had both entered into a clandestine relationship and married still another wife, Kate Myers.

The unhappiness of the match probably influenced Judson's decision to enlist in the Union army in late 1862. Because of his superb marksmanship he was quickly made sergeant, and he acted ably in one skirmish before being imprisoned for desertion when he overextended a furlough. Released, he was given an honorable discharge in late 1864 and returned home telling his readers he had served as "Chief of Scouts with the rank of a Colonel." He mythologized his war experiences in *Life in the Saddle; or, The Cavalry Scout*.

After the Civil War Judson concentrated on the Buffalo Bill legend and launched a successful tour of *The Scouts of the Plains*. In 1871 he married Anna Fuller, with whom he had two children. In 1884 Lovanche publicly accused him of bigamy again. On a second trip west, he traveled to Dodge City to present Wyatt Earp and Bat Masterson with "Buntline Specials," which Colt had made for him. He retired to "Eagle's Nest," a luxurious home in Stamford, New York, built with his considerable literary profits. There he lived as a family man, expert angler, and writer for numerous New York newspapers and magazines, especially *Turf, Field and Farm*. Ever the boyish patriot, he prided himself on the pyrotechnic displays he put on for July Fourth celebrations. He died in Stamford.

• A biography is F. E. Pond, *Life and Adventures of "Ned Buntline"* (1919). See also R. J. Walsh, *The Making of Buffalo Bill* (1928). An obituary is in the *New York Herald*, 18 July 1886.

J. DONALD CROWLEY

JUDSON, Emily Chubbuck (22 Aug. 1817–1 June 1854), author and missionary, was born in Eaton, New York, the daughter of Charles Chubbuck and Lavinia Richards. Judson's childhood and youth were impoverished, as her father failed at careers in farming, newspaper distribution, and stagecoach transportation. In addition to economic hardship, Judson suffered frail health. Owing to her poverty and health, Judson's formal education was sporadic. Nevertheless, the Chubbuck household contained books and newspapers, and Judson was able to borrow books from a lending library. Her educational opportunities improved in April 1831 when an academy opened in Morrisville, New York, where her family then resided. As an adolescent, Judson devised a career plan that would improve her social status if not her economic prospects. Rejecting her mother's suggestion that she become a milliner, Judson decided to become a teacher and earned her academy master's recommendation for a position in a local school. She supported herself and contributed to the family income from 1832 to 1840 by teaching in a succession of district schools. During these years Judson joined the Baptist church at Morrisville and launched her literary career by contributing anonymous poems and sketches to local newspapers. Many of her early poems were later collected in *An Olio of Domestic Verses* (1852).

In 1840 the Utica (N.Y.) Female Seminary offered Judson a one-year scholarship on the understanding that she would teach at the school after completing her studies. She accepted and in 1841 became a teacher of English composition, a position she retained until 1846. While at the seminary, Judson supplemented her family's income with earnings from her publications. Under her maiden name, Emily Chubbuck, she first gained literary recognition for a series of moralistic, nondoctrinal children's books entitled *Charles Linn; or, How to Observe the Golden Rule* (1841), *The Great Secret; or, How to Be Happy* (1842), *Allen Lucas: The Self-Made Man* (1843), and *John Frick; or, The Third Commandment Illustrated* (1844). Yet Judson was largely dissatisfied with her literary work and with her modest literary reputation.

Through a flamboyant act of self-promotion, Judson initiated a second and distinctly different phase of her literary career in June 1844 by writing a witty letter to the *Mirror*, a popular New York weekly edited by Nathaniel P. Willis and George P. Morris, in which she offered her services as a regular contributor. Willis and Morris found her letter signed "Fanny Forester" so "adroit and fanciful" that they accepted (Kendrick, p. 96). Judson received no financial remuneration for the sentimental and whimsical sketches she wrote for the *Mirror* as Fanny Forester, but her new literary persona gained her immediate recognition and wide success. *Graham's*, the *Columbian*, and other popular publications that were willing to pay contributors clamored for sketches. Depicting life in Alderbrook, a fictional village modeled on Judson's birthplace, the Fanny Forester sketches typically celebrate the simplicity and beauty of rural life, although negative aspects occasionally intrude. "Lucy Dutton" concerns seduction and betrayal, while "Angel's Pilgrimage" deals with greed and murder. The initial collections of Fanny Forester sketches were published as *Trippings in Author-Land* (1846) and *Lilias Fane, and Other Tales* (1846).

Judson's life abruptly changed direction in December 1845 when, at the height of her fame as Fanny Forester, she was introduced to Adoniram Judson, the legendary Baptist missionary to Burma whom she first read about and admired as a child of eleven. A widower with a grown stepson and five dependent children of his own, Adoniram Judson approached her with the idea of writing a memorial to his recently deceased second wife, Sarah Boardman Judson. Within a month of their first meeting, they became engaged, despite the misgivings of his missionary colleagues and her admirers. Letters to friends sympathetic to her choice of a husband indicate Judson's dissatisfaction with her writing career. To Horace Wallace, Judson complained, "Did you ever feel as though all the things that you were engaged in were so trivial, so aimless, that you fairly sickened of them, and longed to do something more worthy of your origin and destiny?"

(Kendrick, p. 159). Apparently even success in the literary societies of New York and Philadelphia could not satisfy Judson's energy, ambition, and desire for social approval. They were married 2 June 1846 in Hamilton, New York, and set sail for Burma on 11 July. Before leaving for Asia, Judson secured future income for her family by authorizing the Ticknor company to publish a two-volume collection of Fanny Forester sketches under the title *Alderbrook*, which includes some of the tales in *Lilias Fane*. *Alderbrook* eventually went through eleven editions.

In November 1846 the Judsons arrived in Moulmein, the center of British missionary activity in Burma. Here they remained until February, when they moved to Rangoon, leaving behind the few comforts British missionary society afforded. Judson adapted to missionary life in Rangoon as well as could be expected. She learned Burmese rapidly, became a fond mother to Adoniram's two surviving children in Burma, and even managed to joke about living in a bat-infested house. Nevertheless, her frequent illnesses and those of her children and husband greatly slowed work on her memorial of Sarah B. Judson. Her husband's work also met with disappointment, as local officials thwarted his efforts to make converts. Discouraged by illness and poor food and concerned about his wife's pregnancy, Adoniram Judson in September 1847 moved his family back to Moulmein, where they remained for the next three years. On 24 December Emily Judson gave birth to a daughter, Emily Frances. While in Moulmein she finished her *Memoir of Sarah B. Judson* (1848), assisted her husband in compiling a Burmese dictionary, conducted prayer meetings and spiritual exercises for women, and planned a Burmese translation of Bunyan's *Pilgrim's Progress*.

Judson's missionary life ended as a result of her husband's death in April 1850 during an ocean voyage intended to restore his failing health. When she learned of his death some months later, she resolved to leave Burma for the sake of the Judson children. She sailed from Moulmein in January 1851, arriving in Boston in early October, some five years after her departure from the United States.

Judson spent the remainder of her brief life in Hamilton, New York, promoting missionary activity, defending her husband's achievements, and supporting a family that included her parents, an unmarried sister, five stepchildren, and her daughter. To rebut criticisms leveled against her husband, Judson spent the winter of 1851–1852 in Providence, Rhode Island, assisting Francis Wayland (1796–1865) in the research, writing, and proofreading of his *Memoir of the Life and Labors of the Rev. Adoniram Judson* (2 vols., 1853); Wayland signed the copyright over to her. *The Kathayan Slave, and Other Papers Connected with Missionary Life* (1853) defends her husband's work as well as missionary activity in Burma and India more generally. She also wrote *My Two Sisters* (1854), a family memoir and spiritual biography of two older sisters whose even briefer lives profoundly influenced her own. Shortly thereafter Judson died of tuberculosis in Hamilton, where she is buried.

Emily Judson achieved much in her short life, attaining success as both an author and a missionary. Although she is little read today, her distinct literary personas—Emily Chubbuck, Fanny Forester, and Emily Judson—illustrate several of the literary roles open to American women in the mid-nineteenth century: children's didactic storyteller, fashionable magazine writer, religious polemicist, and spiritual biographer. Unfortunately, Judson felt torn between these roles, unable to satisfactorily reconcile her identity as the author of didactic tales and whimsical sketches that brought her financial security and literary renown with her identity as a missionary and serious spiritual writer. Judson's career nevertheless provides an early example of an important trend: the effort of evangelicals to win converts and raise funds through popular literature and communication media.

• Manuscripts of Judson's work are located in the Henry E. Huntington Library, San Marino, Calif., the Beinecke Rare Book and Manuscript Library of Yale University, the Schlesinger Library of Radcliffe College, the Houghton Library of Harvard University, the John Hay Library of Brown University, and the Alderman Library of the University of Virginia. The most important collection of letters by Judson is found in the Chubbuck Family Papers, File # 1837, State Historical Society of Wisconsin, Archives Division. For descriptions and locations of additional letters by and materials concerning Judson, see J. Albert Robbins, *American Literary Manuscripts* (1960; 2d ed., 1977).

Asahel Clark Kendrick, *The Life and Letters of Mrs. Emily C. Judson* (1860), is the standard biography. Walter N. Wyeth, *Emily C. Judson: A Memorial* (1890), is based on Kendrick. Joan Jacobs Brumberg sensitively analyzes the cultural significance of Judson's life and career in *Mission for Life: The Judson Family and American Evangelical Culture* (1980; repr. 1984). Ann Douglas discusses the clergy's disapproval of Judson's Fanny Forester stories in *The Feminization of American Culture* (1977; repr. 1988).

JEANNE M. MALLOY

JUDSON, Harry Pratt (20 Dec. 1849–4 Mar. 1927), educator and administrator, was born in Jamestown, New York, the son of the Reverend Lyman Parsons Judson and Abigail Cook Pratt. He attended the Classical and Union School in Geneva, New York, the Lansingburg Academy, and Williams College, graduating in 1870. He held his first job as teacher and principal of Troy High School in New York for fifteen years. In 1879 Judson married Rebecca Anna Gilbert; they had two daughters, one of whom died in infancy.

In 1885 he moved to Minneapolis to assume the post of professor of history at the University of Minnesota. Here he was liked and respected by his students, earning the nickname "Juddy." He was an exacting but popular teacher and was one of the first to develop the use of magazines and newspapers in studying contemporary history.

In 1892 he accepted the position of professor of political science and dean of the colleges at the University of Chicago. He remained with this institution for the rest of his career. He was promoted to head of the Department of Political Science and dean of the faculties of arts, literature, and science in 1894, acting president in 1906, and president in 1907. In 1923 he retired with the title of professor emeritus.

As an administrator, Judson was effective rather than imaginative. His first priority was to stabilize the university's financial position by increasing its income and ensuring that it operated within its means. His success was mainly due to the largesse of the university's founder, John D. Rockefeller, who donated both money (in excess of $20 million) and land to the university during his presidency. Judson also nearly tripled the size of the student body. As his successor, Ernest DeWitt Burton, commented in the *President's Report* for 1922–1923, Judson's achievements included:

a steady development of the work of research in various departments of the University; a marked development of the libraries . . . the conversion of the University Press from a burden on the financial resources of the University into a self-supporting institution . . . and a marked improvement in the University's provision for the physical and social welfare of the women students.

In addition to his administrative duties, Judson continued his academic career by writing a number of successful history textbooks, such as *Europe in the Nineteenth Century* (1894) and *The Growth of the American Nation* (1895). The latter provided a brief, well-organized summary of American history that was adopted as a Chautauqua text. Judson wrote more scholarly historical works, such as *Caesar's Army* (1885) and *The Government of Illinois* (1900). In addition he published *The Higher Education as a Training for Business* (1896). He also served as coeditor of the *American Historical Review* from 1895 to 1902.

Judson was concerned that the caliber of students at the university be maintained. He believed that higher education could serve the purposes of business by inculcating "industry, intelligence, acuteness and reliability" (*New York Times*, 21 Jan. 1911). However, he thought that too many people put faith in education for its own sake and failed to realize that it just provided an opportunity for learning that had to be grasped by the individual student. The result of this almost superstitious belief in education was that too many students were attending school who would have been better off going straight to work. The presence of these students harmed educational establishments that lowered their standards to accommodate them. Judson recommended that schools raise their standards to exclude the indolent and focus on teaching students morality and the effective application of their knowledge.

In addition to his academic work, Judson gained an international reputation, largely through his connection with Rockefeller. In 1914 Judson was part of a Rockefeller Foundation commission investigating the medical and surgical needs of the Chinese. The commission found a general distrust of Western-trained doctors. This report was the basis for later philanthropic spending in China, including the construction of the foundation's large medical center in Peking.

Judson was also active politically, using his position to promote U.S. involvement in World War I. During the war he served as chair of the Draft Appeals Board for northern Illinois. After the war he was appointed head of the American Committee for Relief in Persia. The purpose of the committee was to put the nearly $3 million collected nationwide to good use.

During his life he was awarded many honors. He was made an officer of the French Foreign Legion in 1910 and received the Royal Prussian Order of the Crown, First Class, in 1904, the Persian Order of the Lion and the Sun in 1918, and the Order of Sava of Jugoslavia in 1919. He was awarded the gold medal of the National Institute of Social Sciences in 1920. Judson died in Chicago.

• For personal background on Judson see Charles Barney Whittelesey, *The Ancestry and Descendants of John Pratt of Hartford, Conn.* (1900). For information on his career at the University of Chicago see *University of Chicago Magazine* (Apr. 1927); Thomas Wakefield Goodspeed, *The Story of the University of Chicago 1890–1925* (1925); Goodspeed, *A History of the University of Chicago: The First Quarter Century* (1916); William Michael Murphy and D. J. R. Bruckner, *The Idea of the University of Chicago: Selections from the Papers of the First Eight Chief Executives of the University of Chicago 1891 to 1975* (1976); and Richard J. Storr, *Harper's University: The Beginnings: A History of the University of Chicago* (1966). Other information on Judson can be obtained from numerous articles in the *New York Times*, including "Planning to Train Chinese as Doctors," 6 July 1914; "Most College Heads Favor Prohibition," 11 May 1922; and "University Union Re-elects Dr. Judson," 25 Nov. 1923. Judson's obituaries appear in the *New York Times* and the *Chicago Daily Tribune*, both 5 Mar. 1927.

CLAIRE STROM

JUDSON, Sarah Hall Boardman. *See* Boardman, Sarah Hall.

JUH (c. 1825–21 Sept. 1883), Nednhi Apache chief and war leader, also known by his tribal name, Tandinbilnojui (He Brings Many Things with Him), was the son of a leading man of the Nednhi or Southern Chiricahua Apaches, principally of Sonora. His parents' names are unknown. Juh's name, apparently a derivative of the last syllable of his tribal cognomen, was pronounced as an explosive "Who!" As an adult, wrote Colonel Orland Willcox, Juh became known as "a bad Indian." Another contemporary, Charles Lummis, reported him "a hard, merciless savage" whose "name was a terror all along the border," and anthropologist Morris Opler noted that he had been "consistently described as aggressive and cruel." At six feet, Juh weighed 225 pounds, was dark-skinned, wore his hair in two braids hanging below his shoulders, and when excited stuttered so badly that others had to speak for him. He was the only Apache of record who might fairly be said to have possessed a genuine military genius.

Juh was raised among the Bedonkohe Apaches near Clifton, Arizona, where in the 1840s he married Ish-keh (Ishton), with whom he had five children. Ish-keh was the granddaughter of the noted chief Mahko and first cousin of Geronimo, with whom Juh became closely associated. Juh took his wife to his people in Mexico, where he became war leader and eventually chief, remaining such until his death. In the mid-1850s his "brilliant generalship" was said to have won the Apaches a great victory over the Mexicans at Namiquipa, Chihuahua. Juh's fame spread north of the border as he participated in the Apache wars against the Americans after 1861. He was present on 14–15 July 1862 when the Indians ambushed white soldiers in Apache Pass, Arizona, and he apparently led the ambush in the Whetstone Mountains in May 1871 in which the noted lieutenant Howard B. Cushing was killed. Sergeant John Mott, a survivor, reported that "the Indians were well-handled by their chief, a thick, heavy set man. . . . They paid great attention to [him who] delivered his instructions by gestures." This is probably a description of Juh, who possessed exceptional discipline over his warriors.

In 1872 a reservation was established in Arizona for the Chiricahua Apaches. Following its breakup in 1876, Juh and Geronimo escaped into Sonora. Juh lived there quietly for several years, but when Victorio's band of Apaches bolted from a reservation in New Mexico in 1879, Juh, although no particular friend to Victorio, moved north to support him. Slashing into towns and ranches along the Rio Grande, Juh's party created enough confusion to enable Victorio and his people to slip safely into Chihuahua, a raid that suggested both strategic vision and military capacity. When Major Albert Morrow's force pursued Victorio into Mexico, Juh organized defenses against the advancing column and led the Indians in a moonlight engagement that turned the cavalry back, despite the normal Apache dislike for night operations. Under increasing pressure to sustain his independence, and late in the year, he and Geronimo voluntarily entered the San Carlos Reservation in Arizona.

Juh may have been involved in the celebrated Cibecue affair of August 1881, disturbances following the arrest of an Apache religious leader, for in September he and Geronimo led a flight to Mexico, en route fighting off elements of the First and Sixth Cavalry regiments in another night action, during which Juh directed his warriors in a remarkable charge against the soldier positions in order to allow his dependents to escape. In April 1882 the chief conducted what must be regarded as the most spectacular feat of Apache arms on record, extracting at gunpoint several hundred Indian residents of San Carlos and herding them to Mexico. He remained aloof when General George Crook's command penetrated the Sierra Madre in 1883 to persuade other Apaches to return to Arizona, and he died on the Rio Casas Grandes, Chihuahua. According to white versions, he toppled into the river while drunk and drowned; however, Juh's son Asa Daklugie, who was present at his father's death, said that Juh suffered a heart attack and died before help could arrive.

• Information about Juh is scattered throughout contemporary military reports, Indian Bureau documents, and newspaper dispatches, but until recently there was no connected biographical treatment of this important Apache chief. See Dan L. Thrapp, *Juh: An Incredible Indian* (1973); Gillett Griswold, comp., "The Fort Sill Apaches: Their Vital Statistics, Tribal Origins, Antecedents," an unpublished manuscript at the U.S. Army Field Artillery and Fort Sill Museum at Fort Sill, Okla. (see pp. 71–72); Eve Ball et al., *Indeh: An Apache Odyssey* (1980); Edwin R. Sweeney, *Cochise: Chiricahua Apache Chief* (1991); Keith Basso, ed., *Western Apache Raiding and Warfare* (1971); and John Mott's narrative of the Juh-Cushing fight in Thrapp, *Conquest of Apacheria* (1967).

DAN L. THRAPP

JUILLIARD, Augustus D. (19 Apr. 1836–25 Apr. 1919), industrialist and patron of the arts, was born at sea during the voyage that brought his parents, Jean Nicholas Juilliard, a farmer, and Anna Burlette, to the United States from Burgundy, France. Although he had been a shoemaker in France, Augustus's father believed that farming offered greater potential for success in America. He and his family settled near Canton, Ohio. Following Juilliard's schooling he worked in his brother-in-law's dry goods store in Bucyrus, Ohio. After making a number of buying trips to New York he decided to settle there. He eventually was employed by one of the leading textile commission houses, Hoyt, Spragues & Company. In 1873, when Hoyt, Spragues declared bankruptcy, Juilliard was appointed receiver. Sometime thereafter he formed his own successful textile commission house, A. D. Juilliard and Company, where he served as senior partner.

Juilliard's numerous and wide-ranging corporate connections illustrate his importance in the business world. He was on the board of directors of the National Bank of Commerce, the Chemical National Bank, the Bank of America, the Atchison, Topeka and Santa Fe Railroad, Realty Associates, and the North British and Mercantile Insurance Company. He served as a trustee of the Guaranty Trust Company, the Central Trust, the Title Guarantee and Trust Company, the New York Life Insurance and Trust Company, and the Mutual Life Insurance Company of New York. He was also a member of the board of governors of New York Hospital. Juilliard married Helen Marcelus Cossitt of New York City in 1877. They had no children.

Juilliard became prominently involved with the arts after a fire destroyed much of the interior of the Metropolitan Opera House in August 1892. On 26 September the property was sold to the newly created Metropolitan Opera and Real Estate Company. Many of the shareholders had been directors of the Metropolitan Opera's former holding company. With this reorganization Juilliard was invited to join the new company. Reconstruction of the house began in April 1893, and it reopened on 27 November 1893. From 1908 until the end of his life Juilliard was president of the new holding company. In addition, from 8 May 1898 until

his death Juilliard was a trustee of the American Museum of Natural History. He served on the finance committee (1903–1905), the auditing committee (1908), and the executive committee (1909–1919). He donated a collection of Nazca pottery and a series of Peruvian textiles to the museum and provided money for annual maintenance of the collections as well as support for exploration of the Congo.

Juilliard was a member of a number of other organizations, including the American Geographical Society, the American Fine Arts Society, the Ohio Geographical Society, the Metropolitan Museum of Art, the Union League, the New York Athletic Club, the Ohio Society of New York, and the Huguenot Society of America.

He died in New York City. In his will he left bequests to family members and various organizations and, perhaps most importantly, directed the creation of the Juilliard Foundation. One of its purposes, as stated in the will, was to "aid worthy students of music in securing a complete and adequate musical education, either at appropriate institutions now in existence or hereafter created." The foundation also was to arrange concerts and recitals for the general public and to aid the Metropolitan Opera Company in the production of opera "provided that arrangements can be made with such company that such gifts shall in no wise inure to its monetary profit." Responses to Juilliard's bequest were announced within days. Otto Kahn, president of the Metropolitan Opera Company, stated: "That so wise, cool-headed, conservative and universally respected a business man as A. D. Juilliard should have given such conspicuous and resounding testimony to his recognition of the place of art in American life, and of its civic value, is of auspicious significance and affords much ground for hope in its bearing as a precedent and example" (*New York Times*, 1 July 1919). Artur Bodanzky, conductor of the New Symphony Orchestra, provided the first suggestion to the foundation, recommending that "what America needs most is a great national conservatory of music, with a personnel of instructors selected from the best in the world" (*New York Times*, 7 July 1919). Josef Stransky, conductor of the Philharmonic Society, reacting kindly to previous proposals, said: "However, an idea does occur to me which has always seemed fraught with possibilities for America: and that is the plan which has been definitely worked out in Europe, of a sort of 'super-school' for the best pupils of other conservatories. The students at the super-school would receive the highest polish of education at this institution. Their presence there would be in the nature of a reward for their abilities" (*New York Times*, 10 Aug. 1919).

In 1924 the trustees of the foundation created a conservatory that provided free instruction to American citizens who could pass an entrance examination. In 1926 a merger between this institution, the Juilliard Graduate School, and the Institute of Musical Art, founded in 1905 by James Loeb and Frank Damrosch, was announced. The new institution was renamed the

Juilliard School of Music (known since 1968 as the Juilliard School), with each division retaining a separate identity. The institute continued as a conservatory with elementary and advanced students paying tuition and the graduate school providing fellowships to advanced students based on examination results. The two schools did not complete their merger until 1946.

The Juilliard name is synonymous with excellence in music training. Juilliard graduates grace concert halls and operatic stages throughout the world. Augustus Juilliard's greatest gift as a patron of the arts was the legacy that created a world-renowned institution.

• Materials related to Augustus Juilliard, including his will, are housed in the Juilliard School Archives. George Whitney Martin, *The Damrosch Dynasty* (1983), and John Erskine, "To the Glory of Music," *The Baton* 11, 1–2 (1931): 3–6, are important sources for information on the creation of the Juilliard School. See also Irving Kolodin, *The Metropolitan Opera, 1883–1939* (1940), on Juilliard's support of that institution. Robert Finn, "Recalling Juilliard's Ohio Years," *The Cleveland Plain Dealer*, 9 Jan. 1981, assesses Juilliard's youth and early business career. Obituaries are in the *New York Times* and the *New York Herald*, both 26 Apr. 1919.

DEBORAH GRIFFITH DAVIS

JULIAN, George Washington (5 May 1817–7 July 1899), reformer-politician, was born in Centerville, Indiana, the son of Isaac Julian, a county official, and Rebecca Hoover. The fourth of six children, Julian was raised by his devout Quaker mother after his father's death in 1823. At eighteen, he began teaching while also studying law. Julian's legal efforts were sporadic, for he was always more interested in politics. His political career began when he was elected as a Whig to the Indiana legislature in 1845. That same year he married Anne Elizabeth Finch, with whom he was to have three children.

Deeply religious, he found the writings of William Ellery Channing (1780–1842) especially helpful for both his personal faith and his conversion to the cause of antislavery reform. Channing's teachings concerning slavery as a moral evil and a restraint on the basic civil liberties of free thought and speech influenced Julian's opinions throughout his career.

Julian's conversion to the antislavery movement led him to break with the Whigs and join the Free Soil party. He attended the third party's Buffalo convention, which nominated Martin Van Buren for president in 1848. His strenuous efforts on Van Buren's behalf also revealed his growing interest in reform of all kinds, including homestead laws endorsed by the Free Soilers. With aid from Indiana Democrats, he was elected to Congress in 1849, where he joined the small group of third-party members who sought to force northern Democrats and Whigs to hear its antislavery demands. He became an outspoken opponent of the compromise measures of 1850, especially the Fugitive Slave Act, which led him to defend runaway slaves in the Indiana courts during the 1850s. He also won recognition as a land reformer with his endorsement of the homestead bill of 1851. The opposition to Julian's third-party candidacy by the Indiana Democratic party, under its leader, Oliver Morton, helped bring his brief congressional career to an end. Julian remained active in the Free Soil movement and was nominated for vice president in 1852. Despite a vigorous campaign effort by Julian and others, the third party saw its support cut in half in the procompromise spirit that brought Franklin Pierce to the White House.

Returning to his Indiana law practice, Julian played an active role in the Republican party's formation in Indiana in the mid 1850s. He worked to move the party toward a stronger antislavery stance and to purge it of nativist sentiment. Julian opposed the anti-Irish, anti-Catholic Know Nothing movement both because he believed such bigotry morally wrong and because it diverted attention from the crusade against slavery. He gradually overcame his own feelings against blacks, and his friendship with Frederick Douglass helped convince him of the "ridiculous and wicked prejudice against color which even most anti-slavery men were unable to overcome" (Julian's journal, 5 May 1852, quoted in Clarke, p. 123). In 1860 he campaigned for Abraham Lincoln and won the first of five consecutive terms in Congress on a strong antislavery platform that appealed to the Quaker element in his eastern Indiana district. Also in 1860 Julian's wife died. He was remarried in 1863, to Laura Giddings, the daughter of antislavery leader Joshua Giddings; they had two children.

During the Civil War, Julian used his growing influence to guide his party and president toward a stronger antislavery stance. Appointed to the powerful Joint Committee on the Conduct of the War, he worked for the removal of General George B. McClellan (1826–1885), who did not support Julian's insistence that abolition be a war goal. Dissatisfied at first that the president was not moving rapidly enough toward emancipation, Julian enthusiastically endorsed Lincoln's Emancipation Proclamation and continued to pressure him to arm the freedmen.

A keen desire of Julian's was to preserve the rural way of life and prevent land monopoly. He used his position as chair of the Committee on Public Lands to facilitate the passage of the Homestead Act of 1862. He then led the fight for confiscation of planters' lands with an eye toward providing poor southerners, including freedmen, with small land grants. Frustrated by Lincoln's policies of moderation on racial issues, he nonetheless supported the president's renomination and reelection in 1864.

Julian was among the more advanced radicals as the battle with Andrew Johnson developed over Reconstruction policies. Among the few Republicans seeking the confiscation of Confederate land and its distribution to freedmen, he endorsed the seizure and "sale of the real estate of traitors and their abettors" (Julian, *Speeches on Political Questions*, pp. 217–18). By 1864 he was an early advocate of black suffrage. A member of the House committee that drew up the impeachment charges against Johnson, he was deeply disappointed when the Senate acquitted the president. Nevertheless, he maintained his advocacy of a Reconstruction policy that sought (unsuccessfully) to reshape the South by fostering economic independence and land proprietorship among the former slaves. Julian was instrumental in the passage of the Southern Homestead Act of 1866, which made forty-six million acres of federal land available to poor southerners. His reform interests expanded to include a proposed constitutional amendment granting suffrage to women.

Defeated for renomination to Congress by the Oliver Morton machine, which opposed much of his Reconstruction policy, Julian joined the Liberal Republican movement in 1872 and supported Horace Greeley against Ulysses S. Grant. His fourth and final change of parties came in 1876 when, tired of the corruption of the administration and opposed to Republican economic policies, he joined the Democrats in support of Samuel J. Tilden. He spent much of the 1870s and early 1880s practicing law, writing, and lecturing. His second wife died in 1884.

Reportedly considered for high position in a Greeley or Tilden administration, Julian was finally rewarded by Grover Cleveland in 1885 with his appointment as surveyor general for New Mexico. There he used his influence to continue his crusade for land reform against railroad and other corporate interests that he charged controlled federal land policy at the expense of individual settlers. Never one to shirk a controversy, he became an outspoken opponent of inflationary or "cheap money" and a supporter of the Gold Democrats in the controversy over the coinage of silver during the 1890s. At seventy-five he published a biography of Joshua Giddings (1892). He died at his home in Irvington, Indiana.

• The major Julian manuscript collections are found in the Indiana State Library and the Giddings-Julian papers at the Library of Congress. Julian's own writings are best represented by his *Speeches on Political Questions* (1872) and *Political Recollections, 1840 to 1872* (1884), along with numerous articles in such journals as the *North American Review*. Portions of his journal and his unpublished autobiography were unfortunately destroyed by his daughter, Grace Julian Clarke. Her uncritical biography *George W. Julian* (1923) is useful, but the only scholarly and objective account is that of Patrick W. Riddleberger, *George Washington Julian, Radical Republican* (1966). For Julian's role in Indiana politics, see Kenneth M. Stampp, *Indiana Politics during the Civil War* (1949).

FREDERICK J. BLUE

JULIAN, Percy Lavon (11 Apr. 1899–19 Apr. 1975), chemist, was born in Montgomery, Alabama, the son of James Sumner Julian, a railway mail clerk, and Elizabeth Lena Adams, a teacher. He received his A.B. from DePauw University in 1920, and for the next two years he taught chemistry at Fisk University. In 1922 he was awarded Harvard University's Austin Fellowship in chemistry; he received his M.A. from that school in 1923. He remained at Harvard for three more years as a research assistant in biophysics and or-

ganic chemistry. In 1926 he joined the faculty at West Virginia State College, and in 1928 he became associate professor and head of the chemistry department at Howard University. The following year he was awarded a fellowship from the Rockefeller Foundation's General Education Board to pursue his doctorate at the University of Vienna in Austria, where he earned that degree in organic chemistry in 1931. After graduating he returned to Howard, but he left in 1932 to accept a position as chemistry professor and research fellow at DePauw.

Julian's first major discovery involved physostigmine, a drug made from Calabar beans that is used to treat glaucoma and myasthenia gravis. In 1934, while he was preparing to publish his findings concerning d, 1-eserethole, the penultimate step in synthesizing physostigmine, Sir Robert Robinson, the eminent Oxford chemist, made public the results of his work on the synthesis of eserethole. Much to Julian's surprise, the eserethole described in Robinson's paper bore no resemblance to the compound he had developed. Despite the professional stature of Robinson, Julian published his own findings and detailed the differences between his results and Robinson's. The next year, when Julian successfully synthesized physostigmine from his version of d, 1-eserethole, he clearly demonstrated that he, not Robinson, had been correct.

Julian's next project involved the extraction from soybean oil of stigmasterol, a sterol used in the production of sex hormones, which in turn were used to treat a variety of medical conditions. However, he abandoned this line of research in 1936 when he was invited to join the Glidden Company of Chicago, Illinois, as director of research of the soya products division. His first task was to oversee the completion of a modern plant for extracting oil from soybeans; his second was to develop uses for the oil that the plant would produce. He soon devised a method for extracting from the oil vegetable protein, which he then developed into an inexpensive coating for paper. After he learned how to adjust the size of the soya protein molecule, Julian was able to create soya derivatives for use in textiles, paints, livestock and poultry feed, candy, ink, cosmetics, food additives, and "Aero Foam," used by the U.S. Navy during World War II to put out oil and gasoline fires and known throughout the fleet as "bean soup." Serendipitously, in 1940, when a large tank of soybean oil became contaminated with water and turned into an oily paste, Julian discovered that the paste was an excellent source from which to extract inexpensively sterols such as stigmasterol. Soon Glidden was producing in bulk quantity the female hormone progesterone, used to prevent miscarriages and to treat certain menstrual complications, and the male hormone testosterone, used in the therapy of certain types of breast cancer. In 1949, Julian developed a method for synthesizing cortisone—used to treat rheumatoid arthritis—from sterols.

In 1954 Julian, having become more interested in steroid research than in soybeans, left Glidden to start Julian Laboratories in Oak Park, Illinois, with a factory and farms in Mexico. The Mexican branch of the operation harvested and processed the roots of *Dioscorea*, a wild Mexican yam, which Julian had discovered was an even better source than soybeans from which to synthesize cortisone and the sex hormones. In 1961 he sold the business to Smith, Kline and French, a pharmaceutical firm that was one of his best customers, but he remained as president until 1964, when he began the Julian Research Institute and Julian Associates, both in Franklin Park, Illinois. He continued to experiment with the production of synthetic drugs until his death.

Julian also played an active role in the civil rights movement. In 1956 he chaired the Council for Social Action of the Congregational Christian Churches, and in 1967 he became cochairman of a group of forty-seven prominent blacks recruited by the Legal Defense and Educational Fund of the National Association for the Advancement of Colored People (NAACP) to raise a million dollars for the purpose of financing lawsuits to enforce civil rights legislation.

In 1935 Julian married Anna Johnson; they had two children. Julian received a number of honors and awards, including the NAACP's Spingarn Medal (1947) and nineteen honorary doctoral degrees. He was elected to membership in the American Association for the Advancement of Science, the National Academy of Sciences, and the National Inventors Hall of Fame. Classroom buildings at MacMurray College, Coppin State College, and Illinois State University bear his name, as do elementary schools in Arizona and Louisiana and a high school in Chicago. He held ninety-four U.S. patents for methods of producing vegetable protein, sterols, and steroids and published his research in more than fifty scholarly articles. He died in Waukegan, Illinois.

Julian contributed to the advance of science in two ways. His pioneering research into the synthesization of hormones and other chemical substances made it possible for people of average means to obtain relief from such maladies as glaucoma and arthritis. His work with soybeans led to the development of a number of new and valuable products for industrial and agricultural applications.

• Julian's papers did not survive. A good biographical sketch of Julian appears in Bernhard Witkop, "Percy Lavon Julian," National Academy of Sciences, *Biographical Memoirs* 52 (1980): 223–66, which includes a complete bibliography of Julian's works and a complete list of his patents and honors. An obituary is in the *New York Times*, 21 Apr. 1975.

CHARLES W. CAREY, JR.

JUMEL, Eliza Bowen (1775–16 July 1865), second wife of Aaron Burr (1756–1836), was born in Providence, Rhode Island, the daughter of John Bowen, a sailor and vagrant who disappeared when Eliza was young, and Phebe Kelley, a prostitute. Her mother raised Eliza and three other children. Eliza Bowen, also known as Betsy, fabricated the story of her birth, and it was repeated in her obituary in the *New York Times*. This

account held that her mother, a Mrs. Capet, died at Eliza's birth aboard a French frigate and that the ship's captain placed her in the care of an elderly woman, a Mrs. Thompson, of Newport, Rhode Island, where she was reared in a good home. In fact, almost nothing is known about Eliza's early years or her education. She evidently followed her mother's profession and on 9 October 1794 gave birth to an illegitimate son whom she named George Washington Bowen before placing him with foster parents.

Eliza's *New York Times* obituary notes her marriage to a French sea captain, Jacques de la Croix, when she was about seventeen. The newspaper also recalls her intimate association with such important countrymen as George Washington, Benedict Arnold, Thomas Jefferson, Ben Franklin, Patrick Henry, and young Aaron Burr. Quite possibly, Eliza may have embellished this portion of her life story as well. She appears to have remained an outcast from society for most of her life.

Sometime before 1800, beautiful, blond, shapely Eliza met Stephen Jumel, a wealthy French wine merchant in New York City. They lived together for several years and were married in 1804. Six years later he purchased for his wife the large Roger Morris mansion overlooking the Hudson and East rivers in Washington Heights, New York. It had once been the headquarters of George Washington as well as the British army during the revolutionary war. Sometime after their marriage, the Jumels adopted Mary Eliza, the illegitimate daughter of Eliza's half sister, Polly Clarke.

Despite Eliza Jumel's beauty, new-found wealth, and lavish parties, she was not accepted by New York socialites. Because of her unhappiness in New York, the Jumels sailed for France, where they took up residence in June 1815. Eliza found life in Paris much more enjoyable, although her sympathy for deposed French emperor Napoleon Bonaparte sparked major criticism.

Her happiness proved short-lived, however, as the Jumels began to experience marital problems. In 1816 Eliza and her daughter returned to New York and resumed their life in the Jumel mansion. Five years later husband and wife reconciled their differences, and Eliza sailed back to her spouse in France.

Soon financial problems plagued the couple. Jumel's fortune dwindled, perhaps because of Eliza's elaborate style of living. This time with her husband's blessings, Eliza left France for America in 1826 with power of attorney to represent him in financial dealings. He had asked her to sell his property and forward the money to him. She followed his wishes and made substantial sales with good profits. Instead of sending the money overseas, however, she kept it for herself. Jumel arrived two years later with almost no money. He died in New York in 1832, leaving Eliza fully in control of his former estate. A thrifty woman in business if not in life-style, with a talent for management, she now owned shares in prosperous companies and had retained ownership of the New York mansion.

According to her *New York Times* obituary, while seeking some legal advice, Eliza again met Aaron Burr, now widowed and a successful New York lawyer. They renewed their acquaintance, and the 77-year-old former vice president married 58-year-old Eliza on 1 July 1833. After honeymooning in New England, they made their home in the Jumel mansion.

Problems soon arose. As Eliza's husband, Burr had legal rights to his wife's estate, and he began selling her stocks and making unwise investments. A year after their marriage she kicked him out of the house and began divorce proceedings. Ironically Eliza hired as her attorney Alexander Hamilton, Jr., whose father Burr had killed in a duel in 1804. Burr suffered several strokes in his last years and died the day his divorce from Eliza was granted on 14 September 1836.

Thereafter Eliza moved from place to place, spending time in her mansion, in the house of John Jacob Astor (1763–1848), and in her summer home in Saratoga. She became even more mysterious and eccentric as she grew older, and her mansion and grounds deteriorated. Eliza's adopted daughter, son-in-law Nelson Chase, and two grandchildren made up her family circle. After her daughter Mary Eliza died in 1843, quarrels soon caused Chase and his children to abandon the aging woman. A mentally unbalanced recluse, she lived in her mansion attended by some elderly servants. There she died. Eliza's illegitimate son, George Washington Bowen, and Nelson Chase and his children contested Eliza's will, which designated that her estate should go to charity. A legal battle for the remaining fortune continued over several years until it was awarded to the Chases. The city of New York purchased the Jumel mansion in 1903 and opened it as the Morris-Jumel Museum.

• Information about Eliza Bowen Jumel may be found in William H. Shelton, *The Jumel Mansion* (1916), and William C. Duncan, *The Amazing Madame Jumel* (1935). Mention is also made of Aaron Burr's second wife in various Burr biographies, such as Philip Vail, *The Great American Rascal: The Turbulent Life of Aaron Burr* (1973). A rather unreliable obituary is in the *New York Times*, 18 July 1865.

MARY K. DAINS

JUNE, Jennie. *See* Croly, Jane Cunningham.

JUNG, Leo (20 June 1892–19 Dec. 1987), rabbi, teacher, and author, was born in Ungarisch Brod in Moravia, the son of Meir Tzevi Jung, a rabbi, and Ernestine Silbermann. As a young man he was exposed to a number of diverse influences that combined to fashion his intellectual orientation. While yet a young lad, he attended traditional Hungarian talmudic academies in Eperjes and Galanta, and from 1911 to 1914 he continued his religious studies in the more enlightened environment of the famed Hildesheimer Rabbinical Seminary in Berlin. Beginning in 1910 he also devoted himself to pursuing a secular education, studying philosophy and classical languages at the University of Vienna (1910–1911); Arabic, Assyrian, the history of art,

English drama, German literature, and the philosophy of history at the University of Berlin (1912–1914); at the University of Marburg (1913–1914); at the University of Giessen (1914), where he received his first Ph.D.; at the University of London (1916–1918), from which he received a B.A. with honors in Hebrew, Aramaic, Syriac, and elementary Arabic; and at Cambridge University (1918–1919). His revised dissertation on "Legends of the Fall of Angels in Judaism and Other Religions" was approved in 1921, and the University of London awarded him a Ph.D. in 1922. While in England he received two rabbinic ordinations, one from Rabbi Mordecai Zevi Schwartz in 1915 and one from the future chief rabbi of Palestine, Rabbi Abraham Kook, in 1918. In 1920 he also received his third ordination from Rabbi David Z. Hoffmann, then rector of the Hildesheimer Rabbinical Seminary. Jung married Irma Rothschild of Zurich in February 1922. The couple had four daughters.

In combining a rigorous commitment to traditional Orthodoxy with a genuine openness to secular culture and learning, Jung was following in the footsteps of his illustrious father, one of Europe's most distinguished modern Orthodox rabbis in the late nineteenth and early twentieth centuries who, even more remarkably, joined these two worlds one generation earlier. "Moses and Hillel were at the core of his philosophy of life," wrote his son Leo. "Kant, Shakespeare, and Goethe were auxiliary sources of his personality."

After having previously served as rabbi of Cleveland's Knesset Israel congregation from 1920 to 1922, Jung brought his amalgamation of Orthodoxy and modern culture to the pulpit of the Jewish Center, a prominent Orthodox synagogue on Manhattan's Upper West Side, which he served until his death and from which emanated his significant influence on American and world Jewry.

For more than a half century, Jung devoted himself to bringing sophistication and dignity to American Orthodoxy, dedicating his efforts to merging the practices, passion, and piety of traditional Orthodoxy with the new intellectual and cultural worlds of the twentieth century, combining Torah and Tennyson, davening (prayer) and Dickens, Shabbos (Sabbath) and Shakespeare. In his spoken and written words, Jung argued for the compatibility of "Torah-true Judaism" with modern thought and through his teaching and personal example brought new respect to Orthodoxy in America.

Jung's influence was felt most directly within his synagogue, his "Jewish Center family," which he molded into a bastion of Americanized Orthodoxy, unusual with its vigorous insistence upon proper decorum and dignified attire during services, its "atmosphere of beauty and harmony," and its emphasis on congregational singing. In addition, he served as professor of Jewish ethics at Yeshiva College, later Yeshiva University, and Stern College from 1931 into the 1970s. Jung was often the featured speaker at many Orthodox synagogues and institutions across America.

Jung was also directly involved in other activities that strengthened his reputation as one of American Orthodoxy's most important leaders. In 1925 he founded the Rabbinical Council of the Union of Orthodox Jewish Congregations of America as a more modern alternative to the more traditional Agudath ha-Rabbanim (Union of Orthodox Rabbis of the United States and Canada), heading that body from 1925 to 1934. In 1935 the New York State Legislature established an Advisory Board on Kosher Law Enforcement to ensure compliance with its kashruth laws, and Jung was named its first chairman, a post he held for thirty years. Together with his wife, he founded the Rabbonim Aid Society in the 1930s, an organization designed to support indigent refugee rabbis and their widows in a dignified and respectful manner. During World War II Jung represented Orthodoxy on the Jewish Welfare Board's (JWB) Chaplaincy Commission and on the subcommittee on Jewish law of the Committee on Army and Navy Religious Activities. He served with Conservative rabbi Milton Steinberg and Reform rabbi Solomon B. Freehof on the JWB's Responsa Committee, responding to issues raised by Jewish soldiers and chaplains; he also collaborated on JWB's "interdenominational prayerbook" for Jewish soldiers in the U.S. armed forces. After the war the War Department invited Jung to tour areas of the Far Eastern Command to bring the spiritual message of Judaism to all Jewish soldiers, Orthodox and non-Orthodox alike. From 1950 to 1968, he served as vice president of the Jewish Conciliation Board of America, an institution founded in 1920 to settle disputes within the Jewish community. In the 1960s and 1970s he presided over the Brith Milah Board of New York, raising the standards for the training and certification of ritual circumcisers in that city and beyond.

Jung's interests also extended to world Jewry. In 1920 he became involved with the newly founded Beth Jacob schools in Eastern Europe, and five years later he raised the money to build the first strictly Orthodox Beth Jacob teacher's seminary in Cracow from the Sisterhood of Temple Emanuel, New York's leading Reform synagogue. In 1927 Jung established the American Beth Jacob Committee, which he headed for many decades. More significant was Jung's longtime involvement with the Joint Distribution Committee (JDC). He joined its leadership in 1926 and in 1941 became chairman of its Committee on Cultural and Religious Affairs. In this capacity Jung traveled extensively throughout North Africa, Asia, South America, and Europe in order to determine the needs of local Jewish communities and to disburse millions of dollars in assistance, much of it earmarked for Jewish education.

Through the JDC, Jung also became actively involved with the Jews of Palestine and later the state of Israel. Although at first affiliated with the non-Zionist Agudath Israel organization, Jung broke with it in 1929 and became one of the leaders of Poalei Agudath Israel. He devoted a great deal of effort, especially after his first trip to Palestine in 1933, to supporting Jewish education in Israel, with a special interest in traditional yeshivas of higher learning and vocational high schools. Also, during the Second World War he secured 1,176 affidavits, primarily signed by affluent members of his congregation, which enabled him to bring some 9,000 potential victims of Nazi Germany to safety in the United States.

Jung influenced American Jewry through the written word as well, publishing thirty-seven books and hundreds of articles, mostly of a popular nature, in which he elucidated the values to which he dedicated his life: commitment to Torah, openness to the world, and kindness to fellow human beings. Herman Wouk echoed the sentiments of many when he wrote, "It has been my lifelong endeavor to carry out lessons learned from you." Jung died in New York City.

• Jung's papers are in the Rabbi Dr. Leo Jung Collection in the Yeshiva University Archives, Mendel Gottesman Library, Yeshiva University. His autobiography, *The Path of a Pioneer* (1980), written late in his life, is not always factually correct but presents a very useful overall portrait of the man and his interests. The most comprehensive objective assessment of Jung's career, including a fairly complete bibliography of his writings, is Marc Lee Raphael, "Rabbi Leo Jung and the Americanization of Orthodox Judaism: A Bibliographical Essay," in *Reverence, Righteousness and Rahamanut: Essays in Memory of Rabbi Dr. Leo Jung*, ed. Jacob J. Schacter (1992). That volume also includes illuminating eulogies delivered in his memory. See also Schacter, "Rabbi Dr. Leo Jung: Reflections on the Centennial of His Birth," *Jewish Action* 53, no. 2 (Winter 1992–1993): 20–24; Menahem M. Kasher et al., eds., *The Leo Jung Jubilee Volume* (1962), especially the articles by Nima H. Adlerblum and Herman Wouk.

JACOB J. SCHACTER

JUNKIN, George (1 Nov. 1790–20 May 1868), Presbyterian clergyman and educator, was born near Kingston, Cumberland County, Pennsylvania, the son of Joseph Junkin, Jr., and Eleanor Cochran, farmers. After attending frontier schools, he accompanied his family as they relocated westward to Mercer County, Pennsylvania, in 1806. Junkin then worked in a variety of professions (farming, carpentry, lumbering, milling, and wool-carding) until 1809, when he entered the grammar school associated with Jefferson College (now Washington and Jefferson College) in Canonsburg, Pennsylvania, graduating in 1813 with a B.A. from the college itself. He then went to New York City, where he studied theology in a seminary (the forerunner of the Union Theological Seminary) established by the Reverend John Mitchell Mason. By September 1816 he had been licensed to preach by the Associate Reformed Presbytery of Monongahela, and he then engaged in missionary work in the region; he was formally ordained by the Associate Reformed Presbytery of Philadelphia on 29 June 1818. In 1819 he married Julia Rush Miller, the wealthy daughter of John and Margaret Miller of Philadelphia; the Junkins had two children.

Leaving missionary work, Junkin was installed as pastor of the Associate Reformed Church at Milton,

Pennsylvania, on 17 October 1819. For the next eleven years he devoted himself to the interests of religion and the temperance movement. His main interest, however, was in the field of education. Junkin was an avid proponent of the manual labor system of education, which had been invented and refined in Europe by the Swiss educators Johann Heinrich Pestalozzi and Phillipp Emanuel von Fellenberg. The system combined classical academic training and manual labor with the aim of developing well-rounded individuals. Junkin had worked to establish the Milton Academy, and through a former seminary classmate he learned of the vacancy in the president's office at the Manual Labor Academy of Pennsylvania at Germantown.

Joining the academy in July 1830, Junkin worked with dedication and zeal. The academy was filled to capacity with students; however, several problems developed, some of which were to be repeated throughout Junkin's career. When debt threatened the academy, Junkin advanced his own funds to help keep the school afloat. He also faced an apathetic board of trustees, a manual labor system that was difficult to administer (it was nearly impossible to be cost-competitive with Philadelphia artisans in the sale of products manufactured at the school), and Presbyterian doctrinal disputes. As a strong advocate of the "Old School" (old-line Calvinist) faction, Junkin managed to alienate his board of trustees, most of whom were "New School" adherents, that is, more open to innovation in the areas of missions and the training of new clergy. Junkin's most controversial act centered on the Reverend Albert Barnes, who had recently been installed as pastor of the First Presbyterian Church of Philadelphia. Junkin spared no effort in attacking Barnes for his so-called heresy, and the resulting strain in his relationship with the trustees left him receptive to new opportunities.

In January 1832 Junkin was invited to Easton, Pennsylvania, where he met with the trustees of Lafayette College. He agreed to accept the presidency of the college provided that the manual labor system was adopted. The college, although chartered in 1826, existed only on paper and was directed by a board of trustees, whose members varied widely in their dedication to the college. Accepting the presidency on 6 February 1832, Junkin agreed to assume the entire business risk of operation. The trustees were to provide land and buildings, but Junkin was responsible for collecting student fees; out of these funds all supplies, equipment, and salaries (including his own) were to be paid.

Lafayette College was initially located on sixty acres on the south bank of the Lehigh River, where temporary buildings were erected. The entire student body from the academy formed the core of the first classes (the academy closed for good in the process), and the college opened on 9 May 1832 with a first-year enrollment of sixty-seven students and two faculty members. The inadequacy of the physical plant became apparent almost immediately, and a new site located north of Easton was selected. Land was purchased late in 1832, and plans for a new college building were completed. Junkin and the students assisted in the construction of the first permanent structure at the college's new (and present) location, with Junkin also serving as a contractor in the construction; his former occupational skills were utilized in excavation work and carpentry trimming.

The new facility was completed in May 1834. Junkin established an innovative "model school," which represented one of the first opportunities for students to practice teaching within formal college coursework. Problems soon arose, however. Debt had accumulated, and Junkin once again advanced his own money to cover expenses. The manual labor system again proved unworkable and was abandoned in 1839. As at the academy, Junkin faced apathetic trustees, and when the son of the governor of Pennsylvania (who also happened to be the nephew of a leading board member) was expelled, the resulting controversy led to Junkin's resignation in December 1840.

Departing Easton with great fanfare, Junkin assumed the presidency of Miami University in Oxford, Ohio. His attempts to install higher academic standards and to enforce student discipline, combined with lingering tensions from Old School–New School controversy, soon made Junkin's stay at Miami an unhappy one.

The passage of time healed some of the wounds between Junkin and the trustees at Lafayette, and his successor had fallen into disfavor with the trustees as well. Junkin therefore returned to Lafayette in October 1844 and served as president until 1848, when new conflicts with the trustees arose over matters of patronage and finances. These new controversies led to Junkin's acceptance of the presidency of Washington College (now Washington and Lee University) in Lexington, Virginia. Loyal to the Union, Junkin felt compelled to resign this post as well in 1861. In the last three years of his life he served as emeritus professor of metaphysics and lecturer on political philosophy at Lafayette. He died in Easton, after making an emotional appearance at the commencement of 1867, in which it was apparent that his devotion to the college remained while the rancor and bitterness of the previous years appeared to have been forgotten.

The primary legacy of George Junkin is the development of three innovative institutions of higher learning, at which he served as president. Hardworking and zealous, yet stubborn and dogmatic, his life also reflects the tensions inherent in religious factionalism in antebellum America.

• The papers of George Junkin are scattered between the archives of Lafayette College, Miami University (Ohio), and Washington and Lee University. *The Reverend George Junkin, D.D., LL.D.: A Historical Biography* (1871) was written by his youngest brother, David X. Junkin. Although rich in detail, it is overly laudatory. The best source for information on his life and career is David Bishop Skillman, *The Biogra-*

phy of a College: Being the History of the First Century of the Life of Lafayette College, vol. 1 (1932). An obituary is in the *Philadelphia Public Ledger*, 21 May 1868.

EDWARD L. LACH, JR.

JUST, Ernest Everett (14 Aug. 1883–27 Oct. 1941), zoologist, was born in Charleston, South Carolina, the son of Charles Fraser Just, a carpenter and wharf-builder, and Mary Mathews Cooper. Following his father's death in 1887, his mother moved the family to James Island, off the South Carolina coast. There she labored in phosphate mines, opened a church and a school, and mobilized farmers into a moss-curing enterprise. A dynamic community leader, she was the prime mover behind the establishment of a township—Maryville—named in her honor. Maryville served as a model for all-black town governments elsewhere.

Ernest attended his mother's school, the Frederick Deming, Jr. Industrial School, until the age of twelve. Under her influence, he entered the teacher training program of the Colored Normal, Industrial, Agricultural and Mechanical College (now South Carolina State College) in Orangeburg, South Carolina, in 1896. After graduating in 1899, he attended Kimball Union Academy in Meriden, New Hampshire (1900–1903), before proceeding to Dartmouth College. At Dartmouth he majored in biology and minored in Greek and history. Under the guidance of two eminent zoologists, William Patten and John H. Gerould, he developed a passion for scientific research. Some of his work, on oral arches in frogs, was included in Patten's classic book *The Evolution of the Vertebrates and Their Kin* (1912). Ernest graduated magna cum laude from Dartmouth in 1907.

Essentially, there were two career options available at the time to an African American with Just's academic background: teaching in a black institution or preaching in a black church. Just chose the former, beginning his career in the fall of 1907 as instructor in English and rhetoric at Howard University. In 1909 he taught English and biology and a year later assumed a permanent full-time commitment in zoology as part of a general revitalization of the science curriculum at Howard. He also taught physiology in the medical school. A devoted teacher, he served as faculty adviser to a group that was trying to establish a nationwide fraternity of black students. The Alpha chapter of Omega Psi Phi was organized at Howard in 1911, and Just became its first honorary member. In 1912 he married a fellow Howard faculty member, Ethel Highwarden, with whom he later had three children.

Meanwhile, Just laid plans to pursue scientific research. Patten had placed him in touch with Frank Rattray Lillie, head of the zoology department at the University of Chicago and director of the Marine Biological Laboratory (MBL) at Woods Hole, Massachusetts. Although both Patten and Lillie considered it impractical for a black to seek a scientific career (in the face of overwhelming odds against finding suitable employment), Just's persistence and determination won them over. Lillie invited Just to the MBL as his research assistant in 1909. Their teacher-student relationship quickly blossomed into a full and equal scientific collaboration. By the time Just earned a Ph.D. in zoology at the University of Chicago in 1916, he had already coauthored a paper with Lillie and written several of his own.

The two worked on fertilization in marine animals. Just's first paper, "The Relation of the First Cleavage Plane to the Entrance Point of the Sperm," appeared in *Biological Bulletin* in 1912 and was cited frequently as a classic and authoritative study. Just went on to champion a theory—the fertilizin theory—first proposed by Lillie, who postulated the existence of a substance called fertilizin as the essential biochemical catalyst in the fertilization of the egg by the sperm. In 1915 Just was awarded the NAACP's first Spingarn Medal in recognition of his scientific contributions and "foremost service to his race."

As Patten and Lillie had predicted, no scientific positions opened up for Just. Science was for him a deeply felt avocation, an activity that he looked forward to doing each summer at the MBL as a welcome respite from his heavy teaching and administrative responsibilities at Howard. Under the circumstances, his productivity was extraordinary. Within ten years (1919–1928), he published thirty-five articles, mostly relating to his studies on fertilization. Though proud of his output, he yearned for a position or environment in which he could pursue his research full time.

The MBL, while serving in some respects as a haven of opportunity for Just, generated thinly disguised, occasionally overt racial tensions. Just was excluded from certain social gatherings and subjected to verbal slurs. A few of the more liberal scientists cultivated his acquaintance, protecting him at times from confrontations and embarrassment, but to Just this behavior seemed paternalistic. Further, while many MBL scientists relied on his technical expertise, some showed little regard for the intellectual or theoretical side of Just's work. Others, citing a special duty to his race, urged him to abandon science in favor of teaching and more practical pursuits.

In 1928 Just received a substantial grant from the Julius Rosenwald Fund, which allowed him a change of environment and longer stretches of time for his research. His first excursion, in 1929, took him to Italy, where he worked for seven months at the Stazione Zoologica in Naples. He traveled to Europe ten times over the course of the next decade, staying for periods ranging from three weeks to two years. He worked primarily at the Stazione Zoologica, the Kaiser-Wilhelm Institut für Biologie in Berlin, and the Station Biologique in Roscoff, France. As the political turmoil in Europe grew, Just remained relatively unaffected and continued to be productive in his research. That he felt more comfortable there amid the rise of nazism and fascism suggests how dismal his outlook on life in America had become.

In Europe, Just worked on what he considered his magnum opus: a book synthesizing many of the scientific theories, philosophical ideas, and experimental results of his career. The book was published in 1939 under the title *Biology of the Cell Surface*. Its thesis, that the ectoplasm or cell surface has a fundamental role in development, did not receive much attention at the time but later became a focus of serious scientific investigation. Just was assisted in this work by a German, Maid Hedwig Schnetzler, whom he married in 1939 after divorcing his first wife. Also in 1939, he published a compendium of experimental advice under the title *Basic Methods for Experiments on Eggs of Marine Animals*. In 1940 Just was interned briefly in France following the German invasion, then was released to return to America, where he died of pancreatic cancer a year later in Washington, D.C.

• A collection of Just's papers is preserved in the Manuscript Division of the Moorland-Spingarn Research Center, Howard University, Washington, D.C. The collection consists of correspondence, manuscripts, reprints, photographs, and other materials. The only full-length biography is Kenneth R. Manning, *Black Apollo of Science: The Life of Ernest Everett Just* (1983). For the significance of Just's scientific work, see Stephen Jay Gould, "Just in the Middle: A Solution to the Mechanist-Vitalist Controversy," *Natural History*, Jan. 1984, pp. 24–33; and Scott F. Gilbert, "Cellular Politics: Ernest Everett Just, Richard B. Goldschmidt, and the Attempt to Reconcile Embryology and Genetics," in *The American Development of Biology*, ed. Ronald Rainger, Keith R. Benson, and Jane Maienschein (1988). An obituary by Frank R. Lillie is in *Science* 95 (2 Jan. 1942): 10–11.

KENNETH R. MANNING

K

KAAHUMANU (17 Mar. 1768–5 June 1832), Hawaiian kuhina nui (premier or coruler), was born on the island of Maui, the daughter of Keeaumoku and Namahana. Keeaumoku was a trusted friend and counselor of Kamehameha the Great and fought in the king's wars to unify the islands. Namahana was of noble lineage and was the widow of the king of Maui. Although Kaahumanu's birth date is in dispute, various Hawaiian cultural societies, such as the Kaahumanu Society in Honolulu, cite the date as 17 March 1768.

Promised at birth to Kamehameha the Great, Kaahumanu married the king when she was thirteen or fourteen, joining the numerous wives he had already married. Beautiful and fiery tempered, she became his favorite wife and encouraged him in his wars to unite the islands. Hawaiian scholar Samuel M. Kamakau has described her as "six feet tall, straight and well formed, without blemish and comely." She attained the weight of 300 pounds, which was seen as attractive in her day. "Her arms were like the inside of a banana stalk, her fingers tapering, her palms pliable like kukuene grass, graceful in repose, her cheeks long in shape and pink as the bud of a banana stem . . . her hair dark, wavy, and fine, her skin very light."

After the death of Kamehameha the Great on 8 May 1819, Kaahumanu confronted the new 22-year-old king Kamehameha II (Liholiho) before an assembly of chiefs and stated that it was the wish of her husband that she should share in the rule of Hawaii. The assembly concurred and created the post of kuhina nui for her. The young king vacillated on decisions, but Kaahumanu was seen as a strong and resolute stabilizing force. As kuhina nui, Kaahumanu kept the islands of Hawaii united. Historian Ralph Kuykendall appraised her as, "next to Kamehameha I . . . certainly the most imposing figure among the native rulers of Hawaii. . . . Of high rank and autocratic temper, she governed her people, as a contemporary observer remarked, 'with a rod of iron.'"

One of her first political acts was to liberate Hawaiian women from taboos that restricted them from eating foods such as bananas, pork, coconuts, and certain fishes and that prevented them from eating in the presence of men. Kaahumanu conspired with Keopuolani, Kamehameha II's highest-ranking wife, to break the kapu or taboo system by persuading the young king to eat with the women, who then deliberately ate foods formerly forbidden to them. Other challenges to the old religious taboo system followed, and subsequently Kaahumanu and the king on 6 November 1819 ordered that all the heiaus or old temples of worship be destroyed, resulting in a total end to the former taboo system. Although there was some resistance, an insurrection was quelled at the battle of Kuamoo, and the edict to destroy all the heiaus was never again challenged. The act opened the way for the rapid conversion of the islands to Christianity after the arrival of Hiram Bingham (1789–1869) and the first missionaries sent by the American Board of Commissioners of Foreign Missions in Boston in 1820.

The only island never conquered by Kamehameha the Great, although it had sworn loyalty to him, was Kauai. Kaahumanu feared that now that the king was dead Kauai might attempt to break away, so she kidnapped and married Kaumualii, the king of Kauai, on 9 October 1821. She also married his son Kealiiahonui, whom she later released at the request of the missionaries. In 1822 Kaahumanu visited all of the islands as an illustration of her power and her ability to rule. In 1823 Kamehameha II journeyed to England with his wife and retinue, after empowering Kaahumanu as regent for his brother, the young Kauikeaouli, who was next in line for the throne. After the king died in London, Kauikeaouli became Kamehameha III. For the next nine years, Kaahumanu as regent and kuhina nui firmly ruled the unified islands of Hawaii.

Kaahumanu embraced Protestant Christianity in April 1824, after initially attempting to distance herself from the faith. She had readily seen the advantages of reading and writing, which she encouraged among all of her retainers. She employed a private tutor who taught her to read and write, and she passed an examination given by the missionaries. She was baptized on 5 December 1825 and zealously worked to spread Christianity throughout the islands. In gratitude she gave the Binghams a tract of land in the cooler uplands of Oahu, where the missionaries built a school for their own children, and she allotted other lands elsewhere throughout the islands for both schools and churches. She also disallowed any competing faith. When the Catholic Fathers Alexis Bachelot, Abraham Armand, and Patrick Short arrived in the islands on 7 July 1827, she ordered them to leave. Although they at first refused, in 1830 Kaahumanu forbade the teaching of the Catholic faith, and the priests were eventually deported.

In 1824 Kaahumanu proclaimed the first codified law in Hawaii, which was based on Christian ethics and decreed that every native Hawaiian should learn to read and write. Trial by jury and other Western judicial procedures were instituted a year later. Also in 1824 her second husband Kaumualii died, and she moved swiftly to successfully put down an insurrection against her rule on Kauai. She appointed an old friend and loyal retainer, Kaikioewa, to govern Kauai in her name.

Kaahumanu negotiated the first treaty, or "articles of agreement," between Hawaii and the United States in 1826. Captain Thomas ap Catesby Jones was sent by President John Quincy Adams to the islands to press American claims against Hawaiians who had purchased goods from American traders but never paid for them. Kaahumanu agreed that the Hawaiian government would assume responsibility for these debts and paid Captain Jones $150,000 in sandalwood as compensation. The treaty also provided that American ships be allowed to enter all Hawaiian ports for purposes of free and open trade, that Americans could sue for justice in Hawaiian courts, and that Americans would be protected at all times by Hawaiian laws.

Kaahumanu's health steadily declined after 1827. Shortly before her death the missionaries honored her by making a copy of the New Testament in Hawaiian with her name embossed on the cover. She died at her summer retreat in Manoa Valley. Hiram Bingham supervised the funeral at Kawaiahao Church, and she was buried at the Iolani Palace grounds. The coffin was later moved to Nuuanu Valley and placed in the Royal Mausoleum.

• Samuel M. Kamakau, *Ruling Chiefs of Hawaii* (1961), includes translations of various articles on Kaahumanu that were originally published in the Hawaiian newspaper *Nupepa Kuokoa* in 1866–1868. Ralph S. Kuykendall, *The Hawaiian Kingdom, 1778–1854* (1938), is the best secondary source in English. Other sources include Gwenfread E. Allen, "Kaahumanu: A Study," *The Friend*, June 1925, pp. 128–29, 135–40; July 1925, pp. 157–64; Aug. 1925, pp. 180, 182–85; Jane Silverman, *Kaahumanu, Molder of Change* (1987); Kathleen Mellen, *The Magnificent Matriarch* (1952); and "Kaahumanu," in *Notable Women of Hawaii*, ed. Barbara Bennett Peterson (1984).

BARBARA BENNETT PETERSON

KAC, Mark (16 Aug. 1914–25 Oct. 1984), mathematician, was born in Krzemieniec, Russia (later Poland), the son of Bencion Kac and Chana Rojchel. His mother came from a family of textile merchants. His father held advanced degrees from the University of Leipzig and the University of Moscow, but an official policy of anti-Semitism prevented him from teaching at the university. As a child, Kac discovered mathematics while listening to his father, who tutored the town's youths in Euclidean geometry for a living. Although he received little formal primary education, Kac attended the Lycée in Krzemieniec and wrote his first paper before he graduated (1930); it appeared in the journal *Mlody Matematyk* (The young mathematician). Although his family wanted him to become an engineer, Kac set his mind on studying mathematics. He went to the John Casimir University of Lwów, where he earned an M.Phil. in 1935 and a Ph.D. in mathematics in 1937. He was a personal assistant and collaborator to the renowned mathematician Hugo Steinhaus from 1935 to 1937. After obtaining his degree, he supported himself by working as an actuary while continually

trying to escape from his homeland. His whole family perished, along with most of the Jewish population of Krzemieniec, in the Nazi slaughter of 1943.

With the help of Steinhaus, Kac obtained a postdoctoral fellowship from the Parnas Foundation; the terms of the endowment (from a wealthy family of assimilated Polish Jews) stipulated that one of the two yearly awards must be given to a Jewish applicant. Thus, Kac came to the United States in 1938, at a time when great numbers of European immigrants were seeking asylum. He took up residence in 1938–1939 at Johns Hopkins University, where he worked with Egbertus R. van Kampen and Arthur Wintner. In 1939 Cornell University offered him a position in the mathematics department, at the rank of instructor, thus allowing him to stay in the United States. Kac spent the first twenty-two years of his career at Cornell. In 1942 he married Katherine Elizabeth Mayberry; they had two children. Kac became an assistant professor in 1943 and a full professor of mathematics in 1946. He took a sabbatical leave at the Institute for Advanced Study in Princeton (1951–1952) and another in Geneva (1955–1956).

In 1959 the Rockefeller Institute for Medical Research in New York, which was transforming itself into a graduate university in science, invited Kac and two of his closest scientific associates, George Uhlenbeck and Ted Berlin, to join its faculty. The trio embarked on what looked at the time like a promising academic venture; Kac was professor of mathematics at the Rockefeller from 1961, although he returned to Cornell, in the interim, as an Andrew-White Professor-at-Large from 1965 to 1972. Four years away from the mandatory retirement age, Kac left an impoverished Rockefeller University in 1981 for the University of Southern California and kept this affiliation until his death.

Kac enjoyed an international reputation. He was H. A. Lorentz Visiting Professor in Leiden, the Netherlands (1963); Nordita Visitor in Trondheim, Norway (1968); and Brasenose College Visiting Fellow and Visiting Lecturer at Oxford University (1969). He gave the Solvay lectures at the University of Brussels in 1971 and was the incumbent of the André-Aisenstadt chair in applied mathematics at the University of Montreal, where he lectured in 1974. In 1980 he was Fermi Lecturer at the Scuola Normale Superiore in Pisa, Italy; he was Hendrick Kramers Visiting Professor at the University of Utrecht; and he gave the first Marian Smoluchowski Lecture in Warsaw. He was elected a member of the American Academy of Arts and Sciences as well as of the Royal Netherlands Academy of Arts and Sciences and the Royal Norwegian Academy. He received the Alfred-Jurzykowski Foundation Award in science (1976) and the George D. Birkoff Prize, which the American Mathematical Society and the Society of Industrial and Applied Mathematics conferred jointly (1978).

The hallmark of Kac's work was his examination of mathematical problems in different areas from a probabilistic viewpoint. he started this original style of investigation in Lwów, when Steinhaus introduced him to his own "stochastically independent" functions. This led Kac to study "independent random quantities"—as defined by Andrei Markov—and to realize that probability theory might be a part of the theory of functions of a real variable then in vogue in Poland and France. When Andrei Kolmogorov published his work on the foundations of probability theory (1933), Steinhaus and Kac strove to give mathematical meaning to the probabilistic notion of independence of events. They related the law of errors to sums of independent quantities and showed that the normal law is present in mathematics in terms other than histograms and games of chance. Kac continued this line of investigation when, in 1939, he cooperated with wizard problem-solver Paul Erdös and introduced probabilistic methods in number theory. Kac and Erdös showed the way in which the function that gives the number of prime divisors of a given integer obeys the normal law (1940). Looking at primes as if they were playing a game of chance was novel to both probability and number theory, and not until the 1950s did mathematicians appreciate the full power of this approach. Kac reviewed much of this earlier work in *Statistical Independence in Probability, Analysis and Number Theory* (1959).

During World War II, Kac became consultant to the Fundamental Research Division that physicist George Uhlenbeck headed at Massachusetts Institute of Technology's Radiation Laboratory, the second largest and most important wartime research laboratory in the United States after Los Alamos. Kac worked on noise in radar detection that is caused by the thermal random motion of electrons in resistors. This research marked a turning point in his career as it led him to study stochastic functions in the context of the Brownian (or erratic) motion of a particle in a fluid. His MIT colleagues, William T. Martin and Robert H. Cameron, looked at a particular kind of process (discovered by Norbert Wiener) in the displacement of a free Brownian particle from the point of view of measure and integration of continuous functions. Applying the probabilistic approach enabled Kac to associate the Wiener measure of a certain set of Brownian paths to the distribution of the portion of time during which a player is winning at a game of "honest" coin tossing with independent tosses. This idea embodies the "invariance principle," which yielded useful theorems in probability theory and allowed the calculation of a special class of Wiener integrals. While seeking ways to apply this principle, Kac devised a formula that is close to what later became known as the Feynman-Kac formula. Kac's formula connected Wiener integrals with the solution of certain differential equations that are closely related to the Schrödinger equation in nonrelativistic quantum mechanics, while Richard Feynman's independently discovered formula connected the quantum mechanical concept of propagator to classical mechanics. The Feynman-Kac formula is present in much of quantum physics as well as in probability theory.

Kac's numerous contributions to statistical physics include a study of the hidden asymptotic behavior of eigenvalues of the Ehrenfest urn ("dog-flea") model. He published his solution in the expository article "Random Walk and the Theory of Brownian Motion" (*American Mathematical Monthly* 54 [1947]: 369–91), for which he won his first Chauvenet Prize from the Mathematical Association of America in 1950. He considered this result a footnote to the understanding of the statistical nature of the Second Law of Thermodynamics. Kac also developed a stochastic model of differential equations and applied it to study phase transitions in gas and in association with magnetism; he showed that there is no phase transition in one dimension nor in two dimensions, but that there is one in three (1952). Phase transitions remained one of Kac's preoccupations throughout his career.

Kac became known to a wide audience with the publication of "Can One Hear the Shape of a Drum?" (*American Mathematical Monthly* 73 [1966]: 1–23), for which he won a second Chauvenet Prize in 1968. He showed how one can determine the area, perimeter, and connectivity of a plane region, solely from the asymptotic behavior of the natural frequencies of a membrane fixed along the edge of that region. In his development of this principle, he appealed to a variety of subjects in statistical mechanics, diffusion theory, probability theory, and the theory of asymptotic expansions, all fields to which he had made original contributions.

Taking stock of his own mathematical accomplishments, Kac declared, in an interview conducted by physicist Mitchell Feigenbaum, that he had been mainly fascinated with the question of why only certain things observed in nature can happen in the space of a certain dimension and was content with having contributed to its answer (*Los Alamos Science* [Fall 1982]; repr. in *Journal of Statistical Physics* 39 [1985]: 455–76). Indeed, this focus might have kept him away from the gratuitous "games mathematicians like to play," which he had shunned as so many "dehydrated elephants" or useless modelization and applications ("On Applying Mathematics: Reflections and Examples," *Quarterly of Applied Mathematics* 30 [1972]: 17–29).

• Some of Kac's letters are found in the Theodore H. Berlin Collection at Rockefeller University Archives in Tarrytown, N.Y. A selection of fifty-two papers, *Mark Kac: Probability, Number Theory, and Statistical Physics* (1979), contains an insightful introduction and commentary by editors K. Baclawski and M. D. Donsker. After Kac's death, the *Annals of Probability* (14 [1986]: 1149–54) printed a complete list of his publications, including his collaborative work with Steinhaus in the 1930s. The results of his work with P. Erdös on probability in number theory are in "The Gaussian Law of Errors in the Theory of Additive Number Theoretic Functions," *American Journal of Mathematics* 62 (1940): 738–42. Kac's work related to the Feynman-Kac formula is found in "On the Average of a Certain Wiener Functional and a Related Limit Theorem in Calculus of Probability," *Transactions of the American Mathematical Society* 59 (1946): 401–14. On phase transitions Kac wrote a series of papers with G. E. Uhlenbeck and P. C. Hemmer: "On the van der Waals Theory of Vapor-Liquid Equilibrium," *Journal of Mathematical Physics* 4 (1963): 216–28 and 229–47; 5 (1964): 60–74. A group of more general discussions by Kac appeared in *Probability and Related Topics in Physical Sciences* (1959). Kac discussed the limits of research and applications in "Probability Theory: Its Role and Its Impact," *SIAM Review* 4 (1962): 1–11, and in "Dehydrated Elephants Revisited," *American Scientist* 70 (1982): 633–34. Most of Kac's mathematical publications were reviewed in *Mathematical Reviews*. Kac's autobiography is *Enigmas of Chance* (1985; repr. 1987). A short obituary is in *Letters in Mathematical Physics* 8 (1984): 453.

LILIANE BEAULIEU

KADAR, Jan (1 Apr. 1918–1 June 1979), film director, was born in Budapest, Hungary, and raised in Lucenec, a Slovak town occupied by Hungarians. His parents' names are unknown. He attended Charles University in Prague, where he studied law, but in 1938 he shifted to film studies at the Bratislava Film School in Slovakia. That same year his education was interrupted by the German invasion of Czechoslovakia. His parents and sister were sent to Auschwitz, where they died, and he was sent to a Nazi labor camp near Budapest.

After he was liberated in 1945, he returned to the Slovak capital of Bratislava, where, with the help of Prague technicians and directors, a few independent feature films began to appear. Later that same year he produced the appropriately titled documentary short *Life Is Rising from the Ruins*. Under the new nationalized cinema, committed to the Czechoslovak tradition that art and culture were public activities and were therefore to be subsidized with public funds, the self-confidence of Czech cinema was fortified. It was a "magnificent time of illusions," recalled Kadar, who, despite the loss of his entire family, felt as if he had been reborn. "I myself remained alive only thanks to coincidence," Kadar continued, "and I wouldn't permit myself to entertain any doubts about the road I had embarked upon." A quarter of a century later Kadar still marveled at the intensity of those illusions that enabled him to ignore the political realities of living under a repressive Communist regime. Out of his initial enthusiasm, he directed the comedy *Katka* (1950), a film that urged young people to leave the farm for industry. Kadar was "thunderstruck" when the film met with official rejection. The Communist party, which had extended its control of Czechoslovakia, denounced the film as lacking in folkloric qualities and "nationalism."

In 1950 Kadar left Slovakia and went to the Barandov Studios in Prague, the state film company that had escaped destruction and had become a functioning industry after the war. There he continued as a scriptwriter and assistant director and was given a helping hand by Elmar Klos—one of the authors of the proposal for nationalism—who belonged to an earlier film generation. Kadar's twenty-year collaboration with Klos, which began in 1952, was described by Kadar as "a little bit like a good marriage—it's a question of

confidence, of friendship, of respect." Kadar, who was responsible for shooting, also saw Klos, who did the editing, as the "ideal producer." Their first film, *Kidnapped* (1952), about a group of people unhappy with the post-1948 regime, was denounced as "bourgeois objectivism" and banned. The second collaboration of Kadar and Klos, *Music from Mars* (1955), a musical satiric comedy in color that critiqued bureaucratic stupidity, encountered sharp rejection for having "slandered public figures." "Posters," said Kadar, "were ripped from billboards overnight at the last moment." For their next venture, *House at the Terminus* (1957), Klos and Kadar left ideology alone for a while and avoided problems.

In 1958 Kadar and Klos filmed *Three Wishes*, a successful stage play that attacked social corruption, cowardice, and hypocrisy. They were immediately released from work, blacklisted, and fined. The cornerstone of the Communist party's argument against Czech film, *Three Wishes* was banned and withheld from the screen until 1963. Following their two years of enforced silence, they began work on *Death Is Called Engelchen*, the winner of the top prize at the 1962 Moscow Film Festival. Inspired by numerous other Czech films that used wartime experiences and the Nazi occupation as a disguise for more contemporary situations and themes, their film attacking war as an evil that caused destruction on all sides was widely perceived as libelous of the wartime resistance.

In 1963 Czech filmmakers openly broke with government imposed cultural orthodoxies. Between 1963 and 1969 filmmakers of all generations found it possible to make films as they wanted. This was the period of the Czechoslovak "film miracle." Buoyed on the crest of the "New Wave," Kadar and Klos began exploring contemporary problems in *The Defendant* (1964), their most political film—an open-ended vehicle that turns to viewers as the court of last resort. But it was *The Shop on Main Street* (1965) that won international acclaim and received the 1965 best foreign film Academy Award. In this film the story of an elderly, deaf Jewish woman who goes to a concentration camp through the indifference of others, Kadar and Klos address the problem of responsibility, as relevant in 1965 as it was in 1940. Kadar and Klos each received the title of "national artist."

But Czech freedom of expression was destined for new restraint. In August 1968 Kadar was in tension-filled Bratislava shooting *Adrift* when suddenly two Russian tanks rolled down the square. The Soviet intervention effectively ended the brief period of free expression in Czech film and literature. With the arrest of the Czechoslovak film manager, Kadar and other directors, including Milos Forman and Ivan Passer, immigrated to the United States. Thinking back to that day, Kadar admitted, "The greatest shock was the realization that we had never been free for an instant, that we had only been kidding ourselves for twenty years."

While Klos remained in the "tangle of confusion" that Prague had become, Kadar came to New York and plunged into work on *The Angel Levine*, a supernatural fantasy about a black angel named Levine who comes to the aid of troubled Morris Mishkin. Kadar faced many obstacles in *The Angel Levine*. He was working in a new country, from a script that was never completed, and with no knowledge of English or the complex cultural relations between American Jews and blacks. Nevertheless, the film was an artistic success. Kadar returned to Prague during the period of "normalization" to finish *Adrift*.

Following *The Angel Levine* in 1970 and *Adrift* in 1971, Kadar spent four years in Los Angeles with the American Film Institute. In 1975 he directed *Lies My Father Told Me*, a bittersweet film about a boy and his grandfather. In 1978 Kadar completed *Freedom Road*, a sprawling, slow-moving film for American television about a former slave who rose to become a U.S. senator during Reconstruction. The project was primarily a vehicle to launch the short-lived acting career of former heavyweight boxing champion Muhammad Ali. The expatriate Czech director died in Los Angeles. He was survived by his wife, Judith. A few years before his death, Kadar insisted, "I'm still a Czechoslovak. . . . If I cannot be a free citizen at home, I try to be a citizen of the world."

• There is an extensive interview by Antonin J. Liehm with Kadar and Klos in Liehm, *Closely Watched Films: The Czechoslovak Experience* (1974). An obituary is in the *New York Times*, 4 June 1979.

MARY HURD

KADUSHIN, Max (6 Dec. 1895–23 July 1980), rabbinic scholar, was born in Minsk, Russia, the son of Solomon Phineas Kadushin, a merchant, and Rebecca Mazel. Solomon Kadushin, the son of the lumber dealer and noted collector of Jewish books Joseph of Viasin, brought his wife and children to Seattle, Washington, in 1897, where he opened a shop outfitting lumberjacks and gold prospectors. Max, like his father, received a secular as well as a religious education. As a child, he obtained his formal Jewish training from rabbis and tutors who occasionally traveled to Seattle. In 1912 he enrolled in both New York University, where he majored in philosophy and English literature, and the Teacher's Institute of the Jewish Theological Seminary, where he studied under Mordecai Kaplan, head of the institute. After graduation from New York University in 1916, Kadushin enrolled in the Rabbinical School of the seminary. There, the noted scholar Louis Ginzberg introduced him to the historical-critical study of the Talmud and *midrash* (rabbinic scriptural interpretation), while Kaplan, the pragmatic reformer, guided his social scientific study of Judaism and his philosophic development as a spokesperson for Kaplan's new movement of Reconstructionism. In the 1920s Reconstructionism emerged as a naturalistic, more radically reformatory offshoot of the Jewish Theological Seminary's Conservative Judaism.

While studying at the seminary, Kadushin taught in the religious school of Kaplan's congregation, the Jewish Center. After his ordination in 1920, he served under Kaplan as instructor of Jewish history at the Teacher's Institute. The two worked together closely and also shared many personal characteristics: both were physically small, assertive, highly intellectual, and quick-tempered in defense of their beliefs. Starting in 1921, Kadushin also worked as a pulpit rabbi, for Temple B'nai Israel in New York City (1921–1926) and for the Humboldt Boulevard Temple in Chicago (1926–1931). In 1923 he married Evelyn Garfiel, an experimental psychologist who later taught at the Universities of Chicago and Wisconsin; they had two children. Garfield devoted most of her professional efforts to supporting Kadushin's work; her influence is most evident in Kadushin's uses of social science and psychology. She later published *The Service of the Heart: A Guide to the Jewish Prayer Book* (1958), a very readable illustration of their shared approach to the prayerbook.

In the decade after his ordination, Kadushin published his first articles promoting a reconstructionist reform of classical Judaism, but he also began to articulate a more pious pragmatism. As he later described it, he experienced a "religious turning" (*teshuvah*) in 1929–1930 while completing his seminary doctoral dissertation, "The Theology of *Seder Eliahu*." Critical scholars believed that the great collections of rabbinic Bible interpretations, or *midrash aggadah*, lacked logical coherence since they tolerated contradictions among individual interpretations. Studying each of the interpretations, or statements, in the collection *Seder Eliahu*, however, Kadushin discovered what he considered the collection's "principle of coherence." Describing his work years later in *The Rabbinic Mind* (1952), he explained that, while other scholars looked in vain "for an organizing principle which would systematize the many . . . rabbinic *statements*," he "went behind the statements to the *concepts* which the statements embodied, to the concepts which the Rabbis themselves had crystallized into single words. . . . We found that the concepts, not the statements, are elements of a great organismic complex, and that rabbinic thought . . . is completely coherent." Kadushin called this complex "the rabbinic mind," or the value system of rabbinic Judaism. He claimed that the individual concepts, which he called "value concepts," such as "God's justice" (*middat hadin*) or "compassion" (*rachamim*), had names derived from biblical roots. The value concepts were not precisely defined but offered a range of related meanings and a "drive to concretization" that stimulated people to embody them in actions or statements. For Kadushin, this meant that classical Judaism left room for change and reform in the varying ways that future generations might *embody* a fundamentally stable system of value concepts. He believed that the system allowed for more freedom of interpretation than Orthodox scholars acknowledged but needed less radical reconstruction than Kaplan urged. *The Theology of Seder Eliahu* was published in 1932, the same year that Kadushin received his doctor of Hebrew letters degree from the Jewish Theological Seminary.

In 1931 Kadushin accepted a position as director of the B'nai B'rith Hillel Foundation at the University of Wisconsin. There, he later completed his second book, *Organic Thinking: A Study in Rabbinic Thought* (1938), which the theologian Milton Steinberg considered a new approach to the whole of rabbinic literature, even "the answer to the riddle of perception, of the nature of personality, of culture and culture change" (review in the *Reconstructionist* 5 [1939]: 11). In the book, Kadushin described rabbinic theology as "but a special case of . . . the valuational life in general." His portrayal of rabbinic value concepts served as a prototype for a more general theory of the "organismic" variety of rationality that characterized religious and social systems, a variety that was irreducible to the mechanistic, atomistic, and hierarchical standards of rationality on which, in Kadushin's opinion, modern as well as medieval philosophies of religion and society were based. Here, Kadushin entered into dialogue with Gestalt psychologists and with the organismic social theories of his day, such as those of R. H. Wheeler and Alfred North Whitehead. Kadushin found that "many of [Whitehead's] metaphysical concepts can be taken as generalizations of the characteristics of rabbinic theology," but he also criticized Whitehead for failing to comprehend each social organism in its own terms. Kadushin argued—overzealously in his later work—that philosophic analysis in the modern tradition misrepresents the patterns of rationality that are indigenous to individual religious and social systems and to individual bodies of literature within those systems. He called his alternative method nonphilosophic, but in today's terms it may be called a pioneering form of postmodern or postcritical philosophy applied to the study of religious text traditions.

Although Kadushin thrived in the scholarly environment at Wisconsin, he failed to establish effective relations with the general student body and the local Jewish community. He was, by reputation, personable and warm as a teacher, but he was impatient with issues he felt were irrelevant to intellectual and religious life. His resulting conflicts with the National Hillel Foundation led to his resignation in 1942. He then accepted the invitation of Alexander Dushkin of the Jewish Education Committee of New York to become principal of the Hebrew High School of Greater New York, later known as the Marshaliah Hebrew High School. There, he was able successfully to embody his own value theories in daily educational practice and to share his method with a receptive faculty. He also wrote his third book, *The Rabbinic Mind* (1952), which brought his theory of organic thinking to its mature expression. Marshaliah prospered under Kadushin's leadership until Dushkin left the Jewish Education Committee in 1949. A series of factors, including the school's financial problems, its loss of students to the suburbs, and the new committee's lack of interest in Kadushin's scholarly work, led to Kadushin's resignation in 1952.

Between 1952 and 1960, Kadushin held a series of unsatisfying positions: as pulpit rabbi in New York congregations that failed to support his scholarly interests and as teacher and dean at the Academy for Higher Jewish Learning, a rabbinical school that failed to attract significant funding or enrollment. In 1960 he finally received the invitation he had long sought—to teach at the Jewish Theological Seminary. Remaining there until his death, he enjoyed his most productive period of teaching. In 1964 he published *Worship and Ethics: A Study in Rabbinic Judaism*, which explains how, through the agency of obligatory prayer, rabbinic Judaism socializes individual Jews in a way that nurtures both shared values and individual personhood. In *A Conceptual Approach to the Mekilta* (1969) and *A Conceptual Commentary on Midrash Leviticus Rabbah* (1987), he interpreted specific collections of rabbinic midrash as embodiments of the system of rabbinic value concepts. Kadushin died in New York City.

The density of Kadushin's writing and uniqueness of his approach precluded his having a popular following. Appointing him only as visiting professor (first in psychology of religion, then in ethics and rabbinic thought), the seminary faculty itself appeared hardpressed to find a category for him; he was neither a classical Talmudist, nor kabalist, nor historical-critical text scholar, nor modern philosophic theologian, nor institutional fundraiser. Kadushin's students only recently have found a place for him in the tradition of postmodernist Jewish thought that emerged in the work of Martin Buber and Franz Rosenzweig and that now, as anticipated in many of Kadushin's theories, interrelates a family of text scholars, social thinkers, and religious philosophers. Of interest now also to postcritical Christian theologians, Kadushin's work remains a prototype for the pragmatic and semiotic study of religious and value systems.

• Kadushin's papers are archived in the Rare Book Library of the Jewish Theological Seminary of America in New York City and cataloged in the seminary's Joseph and Miriam Ratner Center for the Study of Conservative Judaism. A principal biography and introduction is Theodore Steinberg, "Max Kadushin, Scholar of Rabbinic Judaism: A Study of His Life, Work, and Theory of Valuational Thought" (Ph.D. diss., New York Univ., 1979). An essay version of Steinberg's biography appears in *Understanding the Rabbinic Mind: Essays on the Hermeneutic of Max Kadushin*, ed. Peter Ochs (1990), along with a complete bibliography. This volume also includes reviews of Kadushin's theory of the value concept (Simon Greenberg), of his use of midrash (Richard Sarason and Alan Avery-Peck), of his *Worship and Ethics* (Martin Jaffee), of his significance for Christian theologians (George Lindbeck and Gary Comstock), of his pragmatism (Peter Ochs), and of his approach to rabbinics (Jacob Neusner). Pamela Nadell includes a brief biographical sketch of Kadushin in her *Conservative Judaism in America* (1988). The most complete introduction to Kadushin's work in Hebrew is Avraham Holtz, *Ba-olam Ha-Mahshabah shel Hazal Be-Ikbot M. Kadushin* (The conceptual world of the sages according to M. Kadushin) (1978–1979). Simon Greenberg has interpreted Kadushin's theories in *Foundations of Faith* (1967), *The Ethical in the Jewish and American Heritage* (1977), and *A*

Jewish Philosophy and Pattern of Life (1981). Among reviews of his rabbinic studies, see Jacob Agus, *Judaism* 2 (1953): 177–81; Louis Finkelstein, *Jewish Quarterly Review*, n.s., 25 (1934): 13–16; Marvin Fox, *Commentary* 38 (1964): 78–82; Judah Goldin, *Judaism* 5 (1956): 3–12; and Avraham Holtz, *Judaism* 13 (1964): 237–42. On his theories of rabbinics, see Ernst Simon, "The Halakhic Dimension: Law and Observance in Jewish Experience," in *Conservative Judaism and Jewish Law*, ed. Seymour Siegel (1977). On his thoughts on Jewish education, see Theodore Steinberg, "Max Kadushin's Study of Jewish Thought and Its Implications for Jewish Education," *Jewish Education* 48 (1980): 21–27. On his opinions on Jewish philosophy, see the following by Peter Ochs: *The Return to Scripture in Judaism and Christianity* (1993); "Rabbinic Semiotics," *American Journal of Semiotics* 10, no. 1 (1992): 35–66; "Rabbinic Text Process Theology," *Journal of Jewish Thought and Philosophy* 1 (1990): 141–77; and "A Rabbinic Pragmatism," in *Theology and Dialogue*, ed. Bruce Marshall (1990).

PETER OCHS
THEODORE STEINBERG

KAGEN, Sergius (22 Aug. 1908–1 Mar. 1964), pianist, pedagogue, and composer, was born in St. Petersburg, Russia, the son of Isaiah Kagen, a newspaperman, and Vera Lipshitz, a writer and educator. At age nine Sergius was sent to study piano with Glazunov at the Petersburg Conservatory. To escape the famine and destruction that accompanied the Russian Revolution, Kagen's family fled to Berlin in 1921 in a cattle car, a difficult journey of several months' duration. There Kagen was enrolled at the Hochschule für Musik and studied piano with Leonid Kreutzer. In 1922 the family began to emigrate to the United States, one member at a time. The fifteen-year-old Kagen, already a veteran of historical and personal turmoil, was the last to follow.

Once settled in New York, Kagen practiced piano many hours a day and kept house for his parents; he became an American citizen in 1930. He did not, however, find a teacher who inspired him until he encountered the playing of Carl Friedberg in 1930. When Kagen auditioned to study piano with Friedberg at the Juilliard Institute of Musical Art, he was prepared to play all forty-eight preludes and fugues of J. S. Bach's *Well-Tempered Clavier*, but he was accepted before he had finished playing the work. Kagen's years at Juilliard from 1930 to 1934 were difficult socially, owing largely to his independent and introverted nature. A clash with Frank Damrosch, the institute's director, in conducting class, led to Kagen's expulsion, and it was only through Friedberg's intervention that he was admitted to the Juilliard Graduate School to complete his diploma in piano.

More rewarding aspects of Kagen's Juilliard years were his friendships with Charles Naginski, the promising American composer who died in 1940 in a boating accident at age thirty-one, and Marcella Sembrich, the renowned singer and teacher who became Kagen's mentor in the study of vocal literature. Naginski witnessed Kagen's marriage to Genevieve Greer, a student of Sembrich, in 1937; their union produced two children.

After Sembrich's death in 1935, Kagen continued to work with many of Sembrich's students and, as a coach and accompanist of growing reputation, became one of the principal purveyors of the European opera and song tradition in the United States. In 1940 he attained full-time status on the Juilliard faculty; he initially served as a voice coach and an instructor of a lieder class for singers, and he eventually became a member on the voice faculty and participated in a training program for accompanists. Coincident with Kagen's teaching career was his life as a concert accompanist, and he was in demand for recitals both in New York and elsewhere with the finest singers of the time, notably Povla Frisch, Lucille Browning, Mack Harrell, and the Bach Aria Group.

After a decade on the Juilliard faculty, Kagen published two important books containing information on repertoire and technique, still widely in use by both students and teachers of voice: *Music for the Voice* (1949), an annotated listing of concert and teaching material, and *On Studying Singing* (1950), a distillation of his years of thinking about the art of vocal performance. Around the same time, he began to edit what became a landmark series of thirty-nine volumes of songs and arias in the principal European languages, with his own word-for-word translations of the texts, which is also widely in use today. Also during the 1950s, Kagen published a series of articles for the *Juilliard Review*, with subjects ranging from "The Teaching of Carl Friedberg" (1956–1957) and "Training Accompanists at Juilliard" (1959–1960) to "The American Concert Song" (1954), which Kagen considered "a stepchild of contemporary American music" because those available were either too "lightweight" or too wildly dissonant.

Convinced that serious concert songs had been given short shrift by American composers, Kagen, in response to his wife's challenge, began to compose his own songs in 1949; he set many texts by his favorite American poets, such as Carl Sandburg, Sara Teasdale, Walt Whitman, and Emily Dickinson. Over the next eight years Kagen wrote sixty-nine songs (seven remained unfinished), nineteen of which were published. He also composed two operas: *Hamlet*, which premiered in Baltimore in 1962 and received critical acclaim, and *The Suitor*, still unfinished at the time of his death. Kagen's command of vocal writing was praised by fellow composer William Flanagan, who commented that "he can set words with the best of them—one, indeed, looks in vain for prosody that is even dubious" ("Reviews of Songs," *Notes* 9 [Mar. 1952]: 333). Interestingly, despite Kagen's pianistic command, the accompaniments to his songs tend to be fairly sparse, but they unfailingly outline the singer's notes, which facilitates performance of his sometimes heavily chromatic style.

The frenetic pace of Kagen's life during the concert season found relief in peaceful Vermont summers, spent in a series of progressively less Spartan houses.

But the long years of struggle and achievement had taken their toll; Kagen developed a heart condition and died in New York. He was buried in Vermont. Kagen remains a towering figure of the mid-twentieth-century American musical scene. His publications are in virtually every singer's library, his songs are receiving renewed attention in concert and in studios, and his career is perceived as the initial impetus to the recent rapid growth of professional recognition in the United States of the coach-accompanist.

• The principal publishers of Kagen's songs are Mercury Music Corp., Leeds Music Corp., and Weintraub Music Co. More than thirty unpublished songs as well as his personal papers are held in manuscript by the Kagen family. For the most complete treatment of Kagen, see Billy Jon Woods, "Sergius Kagen: His Life and Works" (Ph.D. diss., George Peabody College for Teachers, 1969). For further discussion of his songs see Woods, "The Songs of Sergius Kagen," *NATS Bulletin* 27 (Feb.–Mar. 1974): 24–25, and Ruth C. Friedberg, *American Art Song and American Poetry*, vol. 2 (1984), p. 167. An obituary is in *Musical America*, Apr. 1964.

RUTH C. FRIEDBERG

KAHANAMOKU, Duke Paoa (24 Aug. 1890–22 Jan. 1968), Olympic swimming champion and world-recognized surfer, was born and raised in the old Kalia District of Honolulu near the present location of the Hawaiian Village Hotel, the son of Halapu Kahanamoku, a police officer, and Paakonia Lonokahikini Paoa, or Julia. He was named after his father, who had been christened "Duke" by Princess Bernice Pauahi in 1869 for Queen Victoria's second son, the duke of Edinburgh, who was visiting the islands. Kahanamoku and his friends grew up as beach boys in Waikiki. They would gather under a big hau tree near the Moana Hotel, and there, in 1911, they formed Hui Nalu (Surf Club), which is still active today. At the beach Kahanamoku developed the skills that would lead him to prominence as both a swimmer and a surfer.

While swimming was a competitive sport at that time, surfing was not. Those who surfed did so just for the pleasure and thrill of riding the waves. Even in Hawaii, recognized as the birthplace of modern surfing, the sport did not enjoy a large following because existing surfboards were very heavy and unmaneuverable. Through Kahanamoku, however, surfing gained widespread popularity, and although he never intended to be known as a missionary of surfing, that is what he became. He wanted to be able to surf even when he was away from Hawaii, so he made a surfboard of redwood, which was much smaller and lighter than those currently in use, and took it with him wherever he traveled to participate in swimming events. During a trip to Australia in 1915 he introduced the sport there. As his travels continued, word of his skill spread. England's prince of Wales heard of the young athlete's surfing ability, and during a visit to Hawaii in 1920 he asked to meet with "the much-heralded Duke Paoa Kahanamoku . . . to witness some of his fabulous surfing" (Brennan, *Father of Surfing*, p. 14). A close friendship developed between the two men, and before the prince left the islands, he knew how to surf.

Kahanamoku rode his board on both coasts of the mainland United States, and during a visit to Corona Del Mar, California, in 1925 he won national acclaim for himself and his surfing skill. A fishing boat capsized in a raging surf, and Kahanamoku, using his surfboard as a rescue vehicle, paddled twelve people to safety in repeated trips between the wreckage and shore. J. A. Porter, chief of police of Newport Beach, called Kahanamoku's feat "the most superhuman rescue act and the finest display of surfboard riding ever seen in the World" (Luis, p. B3).

It was considered a fair exchange that Kahanamoku introduced surfing to Australia, because it was from studying the swimming style of Australians visiting Hawaii that he developed his famous flutter kick. This style, which was a flexible-knee version of the stiff-legged "Australian Crawl," provided the extra speed needed to make him a champion. He called this modified Australian style the "Hawaiian Crawl," and later, when Kahanamoku had gained world recognition, it became known as the "American Crawl."

Kahanamoku's competitive swimming career was launched in 1911 during the first swimming meet of the newly formed Honolulu Amateur Athletic Union. In the meet, which took place in Honolulu Harbor's Alakea Slip, the 21-year-old Kahanamoku set a world record of 55.8 seconds in the 100-yard freestyle—although his time was not recognized by the AAU, possibly because the race was held on a temporary course rather than in the controlled setting of a regulation pool. He traveled to Chicago to try out for the U.S. Olympic team that would compete in the 1912 games in Sweden. He made the team on 14 March with an impressive 57-second record in the 100-yard freestyle event.

In July 1912 in Stockholm, Kahanamoku continued to excel, winning the gold medal in the 100-meter freestyle with a world-record time of 63.4 seconds. His performance brought attention to his American Crawl, which was soon imitated by swimmers the world over. King Gustaf of Sweden was so impressed with Kahanamoku that he motioned the new record holder to the royal box, where he addressed him in English, saying, "My heartiest congratulations," and presented him to the queen.

Eight years later, in 1920, Kahanamoku swam in his second Olympiad, in Antwerp, Belgium, and continued his mastery of the 100-meter freestyle. On 24 August he won the event in 61.4 seconds, another world-record time. The victory came under protest, however, so the race was rescheduled for six days later; he won again, in 60.4 seconds. Kahanamoku also swam on the four-man 800-meter relay team with Pua Kealoha, Perry McGillivray, and Norman Ross. They won the event in 10 minutes and 4.4 seconds, setting yet another world record.

Following his return home from the 1920 Olympics, Kahanamoku was approached with a $50,000 offer to turn professional. He did not accept, however, because he was planning to participate in the 1924 Paris games, and his acceptance of the offer would have conflicted with the Olympic policy regarding the amateur standing of athletes. Kahanamoku made the 1924 team but did not win a gold medal. Johnny Weismuller, another member of the American team, edged Kahanamoku in Indianapolis during the trials and again at the games in Paris. After his victory in the 100-meter event, Weismuller demonstrated his respect for Kahanamoku when he commented, "I beat a better man than I'll ever be." Kahanamoku won the silver medal with a time of 61.4 seconds, just 2.4 seconds short of Weismuller's new record.

Although he had been beaten by Weismuller, Kahanamoku was not ready to quit. In 1932 at the Olympiad in Los Angeles he participated once again. He failed to qualify for the swimming team, however, but competed as a member of the Los Angeles Athletic Club Water Polo team; they did not win. Thus ended a nearly impossible-to-equal Olympic swimming career.

When he was not participating in Olympic games and furthering his skills in water sports, Kahanamoku found a place in Hollywood following a path in acting similar to that of Buster Crabbe, another noted swimmer from Hawaii. Although he never became a star, he earned recognition as an accomplished character actor playing a variety of roles, among them a Hindu thief, a Sioux Indian chief, and even a native-born Hawaiian. His films included *Lord Jim* (1925) and *Wake of the Red Witch* (1948), in which he shared the screen with another "Duke," John Wayne.

In 1934 Kahanamoku came home to stay and entered the race for sheriff of Honolulu. The people of Honolulu elected him to this post for thirteen consecutive terms. While Kahanamoku was sheriff, the position took on a ceremonial focus, with his principal role becoming that of a promotional emissary for Hawaii. He left office in 1960 because the position of sheriff had been discontinued. In 1940 Kahanamoku married Nadine Alexander; the couple had no children.

Throughout his life as a four-time Olympic competitor, a surfer, an actor, and later the sheriff of Honolulu, Kahanamoku's warm personality, his courage, and his sense of fair play made him one of Hawaii's most beloved citizens. From the moment he left his native shores to become a swimming champion, he served as the islands' unofficial ambassador of goodwill. After his tenure as sheriff, that role took on a new meaning when he was appointed Hawaii's official "greeter," a post he held until his death in Honolulu. In 1965 Kahanamoku was inducted into the International Swimming Hall of Fame in Fort Lauderdale, Florida, along with Johnny Weismuller and Buster Crabbe, and in 1969 a bust of him was placed in the International Surfing Hall of Fame in Huntington Beach, California. A statue on Kuhio Beach, Waikiki, also commemorates this famed Hawaiian.

• The best biographical sources are Joe Brennan, *Duke Kahanamoku, Hawaii's Golden Man* (1974); Brennan, *Duke of Hawaii* (1968); Brennan, *The Father of Surfing: The Duke of Hawaii* (1968); Duke Kahanamoku, with Brennan, *Duke Kahanamoku's World of Surfing* (1968); and Sandra Kimberley Hall and Greg Ambrose, *Memories of Duke: The Legend Comes to Life* (1975). Robert W. Wheeler, *Jim Thorpe, World's Greatest Athlete* (1979), offers insight as to why Kahanamoku would not turn professional. Lord Killanin and John Rodda, eds., *The Olympic Games* (1976), pp. 210, 246, provides the record times achieved by Kahanamoku. Leevan Dasig, "The Bronze Duke of Waikiki" (unpublished paper, Univ. of Hawaii, 1992), and "Hawaii's Duke," *Paradise of the Pacific*, Sept. 1961, p. 12, provide overviews of his career. Charles Hogue, "A Day with Duke Kahanamoku," *Paradise of the Pacific*, Dec. 1950, pp. 16–17; Don Mayo, "Royal Hawaiian Champ of Champs: The Great Duke Kahanamoku," *Paradise of the Pacific*, June 1956, p. 27; "Mr. Ambassador," *Paradise of the Pacific*, May 1960, pp. 10–11; and Ann L. Moore, "The Living Waters of Oha," *Ka Wai Ola O Oha*, Aug. 1990, pp. 12–13, give magazine reviews of his life. Earl Albert Selle, *The Story of Duke Paoa Kahanamoku* (1959), written under the auspices of the Golden Man Foundation, is a commemorative tribute. *The Hawaiian Annual* (1913) records his early feats. "Duke's Own Story of Life," *Honolulu Star Bulletin*, 22 Jan. 1968, is an obituary. Cindy Luis, "Duke: A Century of Aloha," *Honolulu Star Bulletin*, 22 Aug. 1990, offers an adoring tribute.

ALAN M. YONAN

KAHN, Albert (21 Mar. 1869–8 Dec. 1942), architect, was born in Rhaunen, Germany, the son of Joseph Kahn, a rabbi, and Rosalie Cohn. His childhood was spent in Echternach, Luxembourg, about 100 miles from the emerging industrial heart of the Rhineland. The family immigrated to Detroit in 1880, and Albert, as the eldest of eight children, contributed to its support instead of continuing his education and developing his musical talent. Through the efforts of the sculptor Julius Melchers, he learned how to draw, and in 1884 he entered the architectural firm of Mason and Rice, where from 1888 he was in charge of residential work. His architectural education was enhanced in 1890 by a traveling scholarship granted by *American Architect and Building News* and by time spent abroad with the architect Henry Bacon. Upon his return, he became the chief designer in the office. In 1896 Kahn joined with colleagues to form the firm of Nettleton, Kahn and Trowbridge. That same year he married Ernestine Krolik, daughter of a Detroit client. Lydia Winston Malbin, one of their four children, became a renowned collector, specializing in futurist art. In 1902 Kahn established his own firm with associate Ernest Wilby (until 1918) and brother Julius as chief engineer. In 1910 his brother Louis joined the staff of forty in architecture and engineering.

Kahn's career as the leading American industrial architect began in 1903 when he became designer for the Packard Motor Car Co. in Detroit. Unlike the conventional nine buildings of slow-burning construction, Plant Number Ten (1905) was the first automobile factory to be built with a reinforced fireproof concrete frame. Other innovations followed. In the George N. Pierce Plant in Buffalo, New York (1906), Kahn introduced the "all under one roof" factory. This kind of factory, lit from above, proved ideal for making assembly line production possible (perfected 1912–1915) in the Ford Highland Park Plant in Highland Park, Michigan (begun 1909), where an enormous expanse of glass was bound by a concrete frame set in steel sash. Before Kahn, the New England textile mill was standard factory design. Often wood frame of brick or masonry construction, the multistoried building featured clerestory monitors. An adjoining tower containing stairs and services was crowned by a bell within a cupola, thereby constituting a distinct landmark of the industrial complex.

In Kahn, Henry Ford found his match. Their relationship lasted thirty-five years. Ford's vision of a free-flowing operation was fulfilled in Kahn's design for the River Rouge complex in Dearborn, Michigan (1917–1938), a gigantic plant encompassing all stages of the automobile manufacturing process from making steel to shipping the final product by rail and water. In the Ford Eagle Plant (1918) and the Motor Assembly Building (1924–1925), the assembly line received its manifest destiny—grand steel-frame open single-story structures, whose glass walls provided abundant air, light, and space.

The late 1920s witnessed remarkable advances in the production of Kahn's firm. Like Ford, Kahn was approached by the USSR to aid its industrialization by building an enormous tractor plant at Chelyabinsk. The success of this venture led to the establishment of a Moscow branch of Kahn's company, which between 1929 and 1932 set up 521 plants in twenty-five Soviet cities and was responsible for the training of more than 4,000 Soviet engineers. The year 1929 also marks the beginning of Kahn's designs for Glenn Martin's aircraft plants. In the Assembly Building in Middle River, Maryland (1937), Kahn used a truss common in bridges to create the longest flat-span trusses ever used in a building, thereby opening up a vast, column-free area 300 by 450 feet. Spurred on by the growing demands of the automotive and aircraft industries, Kahn produced some of his finest glass and steel sheds in the thirties, including the Chevrolet Commercial Body Plant, Indianapolis (1935), and the De Soto Press Shop on Wyoming Avenue in downtown Detroit (1936). Few works of industrial architecture rival Chrysler's Dodge Half-Ton Truck Plant and Export Building in Warren, Michigan (1937), for the sheer elegance of its pristine planar surfaces and cantilevered beams, the logic of its monitor system providing maximum light, and the clarity of its great central span.

No American architectural firm contributed more to military operations in World War II. If the United States became the "arsenal of democracy," it was Kahn who built the plants, and designed a majority of airfields and naval bases. Working with characteristic speed and efficiency under strict governmental regulations, Kahn's office was perfectly suited for such wartime projects as the Chrysler Tank Arsenal in Detroit (1941), the Amertop Corporation Torpedo Plant in Chicago (1942), and the world's largest production factory for the making of B-24s, the Willow Run Bomber Plant for the Ford Motor Company in Ypsi-

lanti, Michigan (1943). In the Curtis-Wright Corporation Airport Plant in Buffalo, New York (1941), Kahn introduced an underground corridor that connected all parts of the factory.

Remarkable as were his achievements in industrial architecture, Kahn must be recognized too for his prolific work in institutional, commercial, and residential building, in which he drew freely on historical styles. For the University of Michigan in Ann Arbor, he designed the Engineering Building (1903) and the Hill Auditorium (1910–1911), the latter known for its excellent acoustics. Kahn's own favorite was the William L. Clements Library (1920–1921) with its well-proportioned classical portico. For the Detroit Athletic Club (1913–1915), it was quite natural for Kahn to adopt a Renaissance palace type, similar to designs by McKim, Mead and White for comparable clients.

Downtown Detroit is marked by a dialogue between two Kahn office structures. In the massive General Motors Building (1917–1921), eight wings are attached to a central spine in a combination of Sullivanian and classical motifs. Dramatically situated, diagonally across West Grand Boulevard, the Fisher Building (1927–1929) shares the modern Gothic vocabulary of 1920s skyscrapers.

Kahn's domestic architecture is even more eclectic, as exemplified in his summer home at Walnut Lake outside Detroit (1914–1917), a baronial "farm" that pays homage to Frank Lloyd Wright. Houses built for industrial magnates in the Detroit suburbs speak in a distinctly romantic mode, none more than that for Edsel Ford in Grosse Pointe (1927), with its Cotswold-derived imagery, evident in the stone roof, carved panels, and Tudor manor hall.

Albert Kahn's dictum that "architecture is 90% business and 10% art or science" was confirmed by his organizational genius and direction of an adaptable and versatile office that could provide maximum amenities at minimum costs. His achievement, representing the ideal merger of architecture and engineering, was based on expert team work in which all interests were taken into account at the start of each operation. In his industrial architecture, Kahn always sought practical rather than formal or expressive solutions; hence, forms symbolizing the contents of industrial architecture emerged—the utilitarian designs of smokestacks, butterfly roofs, and trestles. Always, Kahn spoke the language of the engineer/architect in his advocacy of a straightforward and functional approach in which all nonessentials were eliminated. Not given to abstract speculation, he was in harmony with the exigencies of the times and the spirit of his adopted city. An American pragmatist, he was a contemporary of the leaders of the modern movement. As a man of action, Kahn practiced what the European architects preached; his industrial architecture, combining utility with beauty, reached the goals toward which they were striving.

At the time of Kahn's death in Detroit, the firm had attained its greatest expansion, with a staff of 600, largely engaged in war production. Considering the technological innovations and the enormous output of the firm (in 1937 the office was responsible for 19 percent of architecturally designed industrial buildings in the United States), Kahn's work has not generated the attention it merits. A pioneer of industrial design, he was, in the words of the American Institute of Architects Award (1942), "an exponent of organized efficiency, of disciplined energy, of broad visioned planning . . . a master of concrete and steel . . . a master of space and time." Paul Cret's tribute (*The Octagon*, Feb. 1943) cites his "good taste and clear judgment" and extols his experimentation with new materials and management, demonstrating "that the talent of the organizer, the clear vision of the business man on current problems, are not incompatible with the creative mind of the artist and with his persistent quest for beauty" (pp. 15–16). But it is Kahn himself in "The Approach to Design" (*Pencil Points*, May 1932) who best provides the key to his entire opus: "It is the day of the machine, the airplane, the automobile, and quantity production. That these must find expression in our architecture . . . is not to be disputed. But does this necessarily mean that modern architecture must be machine-like, or that the architecture of the past must be abandoned?" Kahn's concluding words to the young architect may well describe himself: "Let him be honest, sincere, conscientious and energetic. . . . Thus he will neither be carried away by the present nor unduly fettered by the past" (no. 5, pp. 299–301; Kahn's ideas are also encapsulated in his article "Industrial Architecture—An Opportunity and a Challenge," *Architectural Forum* 73 [Dec. 1940]: 501–3).

• Letters, notes, photos, drawings, European sketches, and other personal memorabilia were in the hands of Kahn's daughters. Some of these documents are now in collections at the University of Michigan and the Detroit Institute of Arts. Original drawings, papers, and photos of all projects are in the possession of Albert Kahn Associates, Inc., Detroit. The source for Kahn's major works is Grant Hildebrand, *Designing for Industry: The Architecture of Albert Kahn* (1974). A survey of Kahn's architecture is found in the catalog accompanying the exhibition by W. Hawkins Ferry, *The Legacy of Albert Kahn* (1970; see review by Naomi Miller, "The Legacy of Albert Kahn," *Art Quarterly* 34, no. 1 [1971]: 105–8). George Nelson, *Industrial Architecture of Albert Kahn* (1939; an expansion of his contribution in the issue devoted to Albert Kahn, *Architectural Forum*, Aug. 1938, special issue), focuses on the firm's work in the 1930s. See, too, three articles by Ada Louise Huxtable for *Progressive Architecture*: "Factory for Packard Motor Car Co.—1905," 38 (Oct. 1957): 121–22, "Factory for Ford Motor Company, Highland Park, Michigan—1909–1914," 38 (Dec. 1957): 184–85, and "River Rouge Plant for Ford Motor Company, Dearborn, Michigan—1917," 39 (Dec. 1958): 119–22; and Albert Kahn, "Architects of Defense," *Atlantic Monthly*, Jan.–June 1942, pp. 355–60. Biographies appear in Henry A. Whithey and Elsie Rathbone Whithey, *Biographical Dictionary of American Architects (Deceased)* (1970), pp. 329–31, and in the *Dictionary of American Biography* (1973). Testimony to Kahn's rising critical fortune is found in Federico Bucci, *L'architetto di Ford: Albert Kahn e il progetto della fabbrica moderna* (1991), published in translation as *Albert Kahn: Architect of Ford* (1993), and Joe Sherman, "Like the Factories He Designed, Albert Kahn Lived to Work," *Smithsonian*, Sept. 1994, pp. 48–59.

NAOMI MILLER

KAHN, Albert Eugene (11 May 1912–15 Sept. 1979), political activist, writer, and publisher, was born in London, England. The names of his parents cannot be ascertained. He attended Dartmouth College, where he served as class poet, was a member of the track and boxing teams, and earned a baccalaureate degree in 1934. In the same year he married Harriet Pillsbury Warner (known also as Riette), a sculptor, and they had three children.

From 1938 until 1941 Kahn worked as executive secretary of the American Council against Nazi Propaganda. Between 1940 and 1944 he also edited the *Hour*, a weekly newsletter focusing on Nazi espionage and addressed primarily to the communications industry. Beginning in 1948 he organized delegations to a series of international peace conferences held in Poland, France, and Sweden. Also in 1948 he was an unsuccessful Progressive party candidate for Congress from his district in the Bronx.

Kahn's attention to Nazi activities around the world led to his first books. In collaboration with Michael Sayers, he wrote *Sabotage! The Secret War against America* (1942). This volume intensified anti-Nazi sentiments by exposing schemes of Axis saboteurs within the United States. As examples of unwitting or deliberate psychological sabotage, Kahn focused on activities of the America First movement and antiwar speeches written by George Viereck for delivery by prominent politicians. As World War II ended, Kahn worked again with Sayers to write *The Plot against the Peace: A Warning to the Nation* (1945). Here they argued that Nazis were already attempting to provoke World War III. Kahn's third book written jointly with Sayers was *The Great Conspiracy: The Secret War against Soviet Russia* (1946), a defense of the Soviet Union against alleged misrepresentation by reactionary anti-Communists.

Although Kahn ended his collaboration with Sayers, he continued to write fervently about the evils of McCarthyism. In *High Treason: The Plot against the People* (1950) he argued that right-wing business leaders were using hysteria about Communism as a justification for repressive measures, especially against the labor movement. A *New Republic* reviewer criticized the book's exaggerations but saw in Kahn's "distorted painting much that is true." In *The Game of Death: Effects of the Cold War on Our Children* (1953) Kahn criticized atom-bomb drills, paranoid indoctrination of youth, and the prevalence of violence in popular entertainment.

Although Kahn's first three books had been issued by major trade publishers, the stridency of his later works (and occasional references to flying saucers) made them less attractive to commercial houses. To publish *The Game of Death* and also provide an outlet for other writers blacklisted during the McCarthy period, Kahn joined with Angus Cameron to establish the publishing company Cameron & Kahn. The most notable book released by this new press was Harvey Matusow's *False Witness* (1955). Matusow's manuscript contained admissions that he had lied as a government witness in identifying certain individuals as Communists. When Kahn defied a court order to surrender the manuscript before publication, he was sentenced to six months in prison. Kahn subsequently released significant portions of the manuscript to the press, and his sentence was rescinded.

Kahn's later works focused more on the arts than on political controversy. *Days with Ulanova: An Intimate Portrait of the Legendary Russian Ballerina* (1962) was a written and pictorial depiction of the ballet star. Over a two-year period Kahn collected anecdotes and took more than 5,000 photographs of Ulanova. The original photographs are now in the Library and Museum of the Performing Arts at Lincoln Center. In *Joys and Sorrows: Reflections by Pablo Casals* (1970) Kahn provided an intimate look at another famous artist. The book contains Casals's memoirs as told to Kahn, but Kahn supplied informative notes and graceful editing of the interviews.

Kahn's last book (with his sons Steven and Brian) was again highly political. *The Unholy Hymnal: Falsities and Delusions Rendered by President Richard M. Nixon and Others* (1971) offered an exposé of deceptive practices during the Lyndon B. Johnson and Nixon administrations.

Kahn died in Glen Ellen, California. He had described himself as "a Marxist without party affiliation" and "a radical in the tradition of Jack London." His advocacy of liberal political causes was fervent and consistent. Although some of his political writings were considered extreme and poorly supported, his works on Ulanova and Casals received uniform praise.

• There is no known collection of Kahn's personal papers. For basic biographical information, see Kahn's obituary in the *New York Times*, 19 Sept. 1979. An essay in *Contemporary Authors*, vol. 118, provides brief commentaries on his books.

ALBERT E. WILHELM

KAHN, Florence Prag (9 Nov. 1866–16 Nov. 1948), congresswoman, was born in Salt Lake City, Utah, the daughter of Conrad Prag, a businessman, and Mary Goldsmith. When Florence was three, her father's business failed, and her parents, both Polish Jewish immigrants who had migrated to California in the gold rush years, relocated in San Francisco. Mary Prag became a secondary school history teacher and the primary breadwinner. After graduating from Girls' High School, where her mother taught, Florence Prag entered the University of California at Berkeley in 1883 and earned her A.B. in 1887. Although she wanted to study law, financial necessity led her to accept a teaching position in the San Francisco public schools until March 1899, when she married Julius Kahn, a former Broadway actor, a former state legislator, and a first-term Republican congressman. While devoting her primary energies to raising their two children, Florence Kahn also served as confidante and unpaid secretary to her husband, who represented the Fourth Congressional District of California (with the exception of 1903–1905) until his death in December 1924.

Florence Kahn won the special election for her husband's seat in February 1925. Beginning her congressional career at fifty-eight, she was already well known as an accomplished, witty Washington hostess. In the decade of the flapper, she wore her hair in a knot on top of her head and "her appearance reflected no effort at compromise with the dictates of fashion" (Chamberlin, p. 49). A master of one-liners, Kahn attracted visitors to the House gallery whenever she spoke. Asked of her success in getting her bills passed, she retorted, "It's my sex appeal!" (*New York Times*, 17 Nov. 1948). For fun and also to make a statement, the stocky Kahn and a congresswoman colleague dressed as cigarette girls and crashed a stag gathering of seventy representatives in 1936. Although active in women's organizations, she did not describe herself as a feminist, explaining, "I am not specifically interested in so-called women's questions as all national positions are sexless" (Keyes, *Delineator*, July 1928, p. 16).

In her first term Kahn became a leader of the wet contingent in the House, believing from her experience in San Francisco that Prohibition could not be enforced. She worked to modify the Volstead Act to permit the manufacture and sale of light wines and beer. On most other issues she voted with the party leadership; a contemporary quip was, "You always know how Florence Kahn is going to vote (Republican), but only God has the slightest inkling of what she's going to say" (*San Francisco Chronicle*, 17 Nov. 1948). She challenged her first assignment to the Indian Affairs Committee, asserting, "The only Indians in my district are in front of cigar stores and I can't do anything for them" (Gilfond, p. 159).

Kahn was returned to Congress in the next four elections. In 1928 she became the first woman appointed to the Military Affairs Committee, which her husband had chaired. She was an ardent advocate for a strong defense. Speaking for army appropriations on 15 January 1927, she asserted, "Preparedness has never caused a war, nor has unpreparedness prevented one." She won pensions for army nurses and established the designation of Gold Star Mothers. She served her constituents by gaining authorization for San Francisco's Marine Hospital, improvements for the harbor and Presidio, and naval airbases for northern California. She was also a major factor in the legislation authorizing construction of the San Francisco–Oakland and Golden Gate bridges. As the first woman appointed to the Appropriations Committee and stung by the kidnapping of Charles A. Lindbergh's (1902–1974) baby, she sought to make that crime a federal offense. She fought so assiduously for funding for the Federal Bureau of Investigation (FBI) that Director J. Edgar Hoover named her the "Mother of the Federal Bureau of Investigation."

Though some San Francisco labor leaders supported her reelection in 1936, her "stalwart Republican" record combined with the landslide victory of Franklin D. Roosevelt in California led to her defeat (*Los Angeles Times*, 5 Nov. 1936). Kahn remained active in civic and charitable activities and was a prized guest at luncheons and dinners in San Francisco. At the Golden Gate Exposition in 1939, she was named one of the twelve outstanding women of California. Though stricken by a series of heart attacks in 1942, her intelligence and wit were undimmed, and her Nob Hill apartment remained a gathering place for San Francisco's leaders until her death in San Francisco.

Though she entered Congress through the widow's route followed by three other congresswomen in the 1920s, Kahn's posts on powerful committees, her rhetorical skill, and "her talent for jamming through legislation" won her reelection and national recognition on her own.

• A small collection of papers of Julius and Florence Kahn is at the Western Jewish History Center in Berkeley, Calif. Kahn recorded her positions on legislation in the *Congressional Record* at the end of each session; see 15 June 1926, 15 Jan. 1927, and 3 July 1930. Short biographies are in the *Biographical Directory of Congress* (1961); Hope Chamberlin, *A Minority of Members: Women in the U.S. Congress* (1973); Edith Walker Maddux, "The New Congresswoman," *Woman Citizen*, 7 Mar. 1925, pp. 10–11, 30; and Frances Parkinson Keyes, "Seven Successful Women," *Delineator*, July 1928, pp. 16, 82–83, and "The Lady from California, *Delineator*, Feb. 1931, p. 14. Aspects of her career are treated in Duff Gilfond, "Gentlewomen of the House," *American Mercury*, Oct. 1929, pp. 151–59; "Women in Legislative Halls," *Literary Digest*, 25 Jan. 1936, p. 29; "Beauty and the Feast," *Newsweek*, 29 Feb. 1936, p. 12; Alice Roosevelt Longworth, "What Are the Women Up To?" *Ladies' Home Journal*, Mar. 1934, pp. 9, 132; Willie S. Ethridge, "Another Washington Gadabout," *Good Housekeeping*, July 1928, pp. 50–51, 104–10; and Gertrude Atherton, *My San Francisco* (1946). Obituaries are in the *San Francisco Chronicle*, the *Los Angeles Times*, and the *New York Times*, 17 Nov. 1948.

DOROTHY M. BROWN

KAHN, Gus (6 Nov. 1886–8 Oct. 1941), lyricist, was born Gustav Gerson Kahn in Coblenz, Germany, the son of Isaac Kahn, a cattle rancher, and Theresa Mayer. He immigrated to the United States with his family in 1891. The family finally settled in Chicago, Illinois, where Kahn began writing songs while in high school. His first song, "My Dreamy China Lady" (music by Egbert Van Alstyne), was published when he was twenty-one. For a time Kahn contributed specialty lyrics to the material of several vaudevillians and worked at a hotel supply firm. He collaborated with Grace LeBoy on some songs that brought his first success. Their first major hit, "I Wish I Had a Girl," written in 1908, led to eventual collaborations with virtually every composer of popular music of the day. Kahn and LeBoy were married in August 1915, settled in New York City, and subsequently had a son and a daughter. That same year Kahn wrote the lyrics for "Memories," which had music by Van Alstyne. With

Van Alstyne and Tony Jackson, Kahn had another hit, "Pretty Baby," in 1916. Kahn also contributed lyrics to two Broadway shows, *Holka Polka* (1925) and *Kitty's Kisses* (1926), but neither produced any outstanding song.

It was in partnership with composer Walter Donaldson that Kahn produced some of his most popular and enduring songs. They wrote a series of popular "baby" songs, including "Yes Sir, That's My Baby," "There Ain't No Maybe in My Baby's Eyes," "My Baby Just Cares for Me," "I Wonder Where My Baby Is Tonight?" and "Sing Me a Baby Song." Kahn and Donaldson also had top-of-the-chart hits with "That Certain Party," "Carolina in the Morning," "My Buddy," and "Beside a Babbling Brook." The leading stage and recording stars of the day, including Al Jolson and Sophie Tucker, scored hits with Donaldson-Kahn songs. The team turned to writing a musical comedy with the 1928 show *Whoopee*, which starred Eddie Cantor and Ruth Etting in a lavish production supervised by Florenz Ziegfeld, Jr. The score was filled with songs that became popular standards, including "Makin' Whoopee," which Cantor used for the remainder of his career as his trademark song, "Love me or Leave Me," and "I'm Bringing a Red, Red Rose." The last two were introduced by Etting, with whom they became permanently associated ("Love Me or Leave Me" provided the title of Etting's screen biography in 1955). *Whoopee* also became an early musical film (with an exclamation point added to the title), featuring most of the Donaldson-Kahn score intact and including "My Baby Just Cares for Me," written specifically for the movie version of the show. The collaboration of Kahn and Donaldson was so natural that if a new idea for a song came up while they were dining in a restaurant, they would jot down their ideas on a tablecloth. After dinner they would take the tablecloth home and finish the song.

The partnership was troubled, however, because of Donaldson's drinking, and Kahn began working with other composers after *Whoopee*. In 1929 he contributed to another Ziegfeld musical, *Show Girl*, starring Ruby Keeler. In collaboration with George and Ira Gershwin, Kahn wrote the song "Liza" for the show. Legend has it that Keeler's husband, Al Jolson, rose from his seat in the audience to sing the song to Keeler while she danced on stage. Although the song had been written for Keeler, it forever after became a staple of Jolson's repertoire. Years earlier, with Ernie Erdman and Dan Russo, Kahn had written "Toot, Toot, Tootsie," which Jolson interpolated into his stage show *Bombo* (1922).

Turning to Hollywood in the early 1930s, Kahn worked with Vincent Youmans on songs for *Flying Down to Rio* (1933), the first Fred Astaire–Ginger Rogers film, including "The Carioca." Numerous films featured popular Kahn lyrics in this era, with the best including *Bottoms Up* ("Waiting at the Gate For Katy"; 1934), *Caravan* ("Ha-Cha-Cha"; 1934) *Hollywood Party* ("I've Had My Moments"; 1934), *Kid Millions* ("Okay, Toots," "When My Ship Comes In," and

"Your Head on My Shoulder"; 1934), *San Francisco* ("San Francisco"; 1936), *Rose Marie* ("Just for You" and "Pardon Me, Madame"; 1936), *A Day at the Races* ("All God's Chillun Got Rhythm"; 1937), *Three Smart Girls* ("Someone to Care for Me"; 1937), *Everybody Sing* ("The One I Love"; 1937), *Girl of the Golden West* ("Shadows on the Moon" and "Who Are We to Say"; 1938), and *Ziegfeld Girl* ("You Stepped Out of a Dream"; 1941).

Kahn wrote many successful songs not connected to any particular show or movie (although some were ultimately interpolated into musical shows or films) with numerous collaborators, including Isham Jones ("I'll See You in My Dreams," "The One I Love Belongs to Somebody Else," "Swingin' down the Lane," "It Had to Be You"), Richard Whiting ("Ukulele Lady"), Whiting and Ray Egan ("Ain't We Got Fun?"), Whiting and Harry Akst ("Guilty"), Ted Fio Rito ("I Never Knew," "Charley My Boy," "Sometime"), Wilbur Schwandt and Fabian Andre ("Dream a Little Dream of Me"), Charlie Rossoff ("When You and I Were Seventeen"), Carmen Lombardo and John Green ("Coquette"), Neil Moret ("Chloe"), Matty Malneck and Fud Livingston ("I'm Through with Love"), and Victor Schertzinger ("One Night of Love"). Kahn's last song, "Day Dreaming" (1941), fulfilled a lifelong dream of collaborating with composer Jerome Kern.

The lasting popularity of Kahn's songs is due in large measure to their simplicity and humor, as well as their sensitivity and sentimentality. As the lyricist for both comic tunes and intimate ballads, Kahn created songs that impressively span the available genres of American popular music. The success of his work is surpassed by very few lyricists, and only Irving Berlin produced more popular hits. Kahn explained the success of his songs by noting that they "express colloquially something that every young person has tried to say and somehow can't" (*American Songwriters*, p. 235).

Kahn was also significantly involved in various songwriters' organizations, most particularly ASCAP. He was a leader in an early struggle between ASCAP and the radio networks over royalties for songwriters and was often an outspoken voice on behalf of the writers in the protection of their work.

Kahn died unexpectedly of a heart attack in Beverly Hills, California. Over a decade later he was portrayed by Danny Thomas in a highly fictional biographical film, *I'll See You in My Dreams* (1952), costarring Doris Day as Kahn's wife, Grace. At the time of his death the *New York Times* noted that his monument was made up of "tunes which have been hummed and whistled by the young and old for many years."

• For information on Kahn, see J. Burton, *The Blue Book of Tin Pan Alley* (1950); W. Craig, *Sweet and Lowdown: America's Popular Song Writers* (1978); David Ewen, *American Songwriters* (1987); Ewen, *Popular American Composers* (1962); Peter Gammond, *Oxford Companion to Popular Music* (1991); and Kurt Gänzl, *The Encyclopedia of the Musical Theatre* (1994). An obituary is in the *New York Times*, 9 Oct. 1941.

JAMES FISHER

KAHN, Herman (15 Feb. 1922–7 July 1983), civilian military strategist and futurologist, was born in Bayonne, New Jersey, the son of Abraham Kahn, a tailor, and Yetta Koslowsky. His Polish Jewish parents divorced when he was ten years old, and Kahn and his two brothers moved to Los Angeles with their mother. The family remained poor, and Kahn worked throughout his school and college years. His youthful experience in his aunt's grocery had a lasting impact, shaping his ideas about economic decision making. In 1940 he enrolled at the University of Southern California and then transferred to the University of California at Los Angeles (UCLA) with a major in physics. He enlisted in the army in May 1943.

Upon his discharge from the Signal Corps in November 1945, Kahn completed his bachelor's degree in physics at UCLA. After graduating, he worked briefly as a mathematician for Douglas Aircraft Corporation. While working toward his master's degree at the California Institute of Technology, he was employed as a mathematician for Northrop Aviation. In October 1947 he was hired in the physics division at the newly established RAND Corporation. He earned his master's degree in 1948 and was then engaged as a senior physicist at RAND. (He did not attain his Ph.D.) In 1953 Kahn married Rosalie Jane Heilner, a junior mathematician who worked at RAND. The Kahns had two children.

Kahn worked at RAND from 1947 to 1961. RAND was established by the Air Force as a nonprofit research organization whose mission was to identify important near-future problems. Kahn worked in mathematical physics, applying Monte Carlo sampling, stochastic analyses, and game theory to problems in nuclear weapons design and war-fighting strategy. He was a junior member of the hydrogen bomb design team directed by Edward Teller at the Lawrence Livermore Laboratory. In 1956 he conducted a course on systems analysis for the RAND research staff. Systems analysis, which emerged from the successes of operations research during the war, was then being developed by RAND personnel for ascertaining the optimal strategic, tactical, operational, and weapons-system needs of the air force. During the late 1950s Kahn worked mainly on strategic rather than technical issues. He was particularly interested in problems of civil and passive defense.

Kahn spent 1958–1959 as a visiting researcher at the Center for International Studies at Princeton University, where he developed the material for his major book, *On Thermonuclear War* (1960), an exhaustive critique of Dwight D. Eisenhower's deterrence policy. Kahn argued that the doctrine of massive retaliation did not provide guidance for responding to Soviet actions against NATO countries or U.S. foreign bases. What was needed was the implementation of three types of deterrence, each of which would require different strategic capabilities: type 1 would deter the Soviets from a direct attack on the United States; type 2 would deter the Soviets from attacking Western Europe or other U.S. allies; type 3 would deter the Soviets from limited provocative actions by a graduated intensification of military and nonmilitary responses. Moreover, Kahn argued that unless the United States drew up plans to fight a "3–30 day war," bolstered air defense, and built a massive civil defense infrastructure, the resolve to commit U.S. forces to a nuclear war that lay behind the deterrent threat was barely credible. The book's eccentric style captured his readers' attention. To some it was rigorous and astute; to others its substance and tone were horrifying. For example, Kahn argued that the United States should develop a "credible first strike capability." That is, if the United States threatens to use nuclear weapons first in the event of a Soviet invasion of Western Europe, it must be willing to accept Soviet retaliation. Kahn concluded that the type 2 deterrent posture must be backed up by improved air and civil defense.

In *On Thermonuclear War* Kahn frequently employed scenarios. A "scenario" is an extrapolation from current trends or historical possibilities in the form of a story that changes one or more premises of strategic conventions. Kahn introduced the scenario of the "Doomsday Machine" in order to clarify the weaknesses in the official policy of immediate all-out retaliation. The Doomsday Machine describes a weapons system designed to destroy all life. It consists of a network of thermonuclear bombs connected to a computer that would detect explosions of a certain magnitude on U.S. territory. If it sensed five nuclear explosions, it would automatically be triggered to explode and annihilate the earth. While the device sounded gruesome (and was satirized in Stanley Kubrick's comic film about nuclear strategy, *Dr. Strangelove*, in 1964), Kahn pointed out that the scenario satisfied most of the requirements for a stable deterrent. The Doomsday Machine was "frightening, inexorable, persuasive, cheap, non–accident prone" (p. 146). However, it did not permit human intervention. In this book and others, Kahn stressed the importance of "intrawar deterrence" or "intrawar bargaining," that is, crisis management *during* a nuclear war. Even when a war has begun, it is possible to limit its scope by building thresholds between an initial strike and all-out war.

Kahn argued that decision makers must accept the possibility that deterrence might fail—that a nuclear war was a distinct possibility. He enumerated the different ways in which such a war might begin: through accident, technical error, miscalculation of the risks, the actions of a madman or a rogue commander, and, most important, through the rational calculation that in an extreme crisis it might be less risky to initiate war than not. Kahn determined the potential magnitudes of damage from a large and limited strike against the United States and concluded that even the large strike would not result in the annihilation of life. Although casualties might run from 20 to 60 million dead, American society would survive, recover, and recuperate. In the most famous passage from *On Thermonuclear War*, he asserted, "Despite a widespread belief to the contrary, objective studies indicate that even though the amount of human tragedy would be greatly increased in the postwar world, the increase would not preclude normal and happy lives for the majority of survivors and their descendants" (p. 21).

Given his conviction that a nuclear war was a realistic possibility and would not result in oblivion, Kahn insisted that the magnitude of damage was a direct consequence of prewar preparations. Therefore U.S. decision makers should accept the idea that early defensive preparations would mitigate the destructiveness of a Soviet first strike. The book is replete with concrete suggestions for preattack preparations, the most important of which are hardened, dispersed, or mobile retaliatory systems, hardened air defense, centralized command and control, and a massive civil-defense program including the establishment of industrial mobilization plans, disaster training, available fallout shelters, mass distribution of radiation dosimeters, warehoused medicine and foodstuffs, and basic industry located underground.

On Thermonuclear War enjoyed an unexpected popular success. The book was excerpted in some periodicals and was selected as the January 1961 main selection by two book clubs, the Aerospace Bookclub and the History Book Club. It was widely regarded as something that must be judged, condemned, praised, or justified. Critics attacked his scientific competence, political judgment, rationality, and morality. James R. Newman's famous book review remarked, "Is there really a Herman Kahn? It is hard to believe. . . . [N]o one could write like this; no one could think like this. Perhaps the whole thing is a . . . hoax in bad taste. . . . This is a moral tract on mass murder: how to plan it, how to commit it, how to get away with it, how to justify it" (*Scientific American*, Mar. 1961, p. 197). These charges framed the ensuing controversy. How could a man think the unthinkable? Was Kahn representative of some gross evil in American society? Many championed Kahn for his insight into the convolutions of deterrence, his commitment to civil defense, and his psychological resilience that gave him the courage to face the worst fearlessly. (In 1962 Kahn published the book *Thinking about the Unthinkable* in response to the charge of inhumanity.)

In 1961 Kahn left RAND and with two associates founded a new policy research organization, the Hudson Institute, in New York. At Hudson, Kahn began to conduct a series of studies, of the future with which he would be identified throughout his career. As illustrated by his *On Escalation: Metaphors and Scenarios* (1965), the typical Hudson method of futures research compiled a catalog of possible, plausible, and "not-im-plausible" future scenarios, with the aim of "stimulating and stretching the imagination" (p. xvi). By mid-1967 Kahn and an associate, Anthony Weiner, presented the first of many such studies, *The Year 2000: A Framework for Speculation on the Next Thirty-three Years*. He argued that by extrapolating from a combination of "emergent trends" in economics, society, and technology, one could validly project the most likely world of the future. Kahn justified this approach by asserting that "the pace at which the various technological, social, political, and economic changes are taking place has reduced the relevance of experience as a guide to public policy judgments" (*Daedalus*, Summer 1967, p. 705).

In 1972 the Club of Rome published the *Limits to Growth* report, which cautioned that the world economy should seek an equilibrium between its demands and its resources by the year 2000. Kahn spent much of the final decade of his life rebutting its thesis. He argued that the limit-to-growth thesis was a delusion, that on the contrary the market could sustain consistent growth for several centuries to come. In 1976 Kahn and two associates, William Brown and Leon Martel, issued *The Next Two Hundred Years*. They argued that the potentials of capitalism, science, technology, and human reason and self-discipline were boundless. The planet's resources set no limits to economic growth, rather, human beings will colonize the solar system everywhere they choose. He predicted that "200 years from now, we expect, almost everywhere [human beings] will be numerous, rich and in control of the forces of nature" (*The Next Two Hundred Years*, p. 1). The only checks to this scenario were short-term "dislocations and crises" among which were "regional overpopulation, . . . energy shortfalls, raw materials shortages, local famines, short-run but intense pollution, . . . and large scale thermonuclear war" (*New York Times*, 14 Apr. 1976).

In addition to his future studies at Hudson, Kahn continued to work on military affairs. From 1966 to 1968 he consulted with the Pentagon on the direction of the Vietnam war. He argued for the utility of coupling graduated escalations in force with bargaining. He argued that U.S. strategy erred "by constantly offering to negotiate" in Vietnam. He suggested "a sharp, potentially uncontrollable increase in threat, which might raise anxiety about points of no return" (*New York Times*, 10 Mar. 1967). Throughout his career Kahn consistently advocated the political benefits of rationally controlled use of violence. He also consistently urged the benefits of civil defense to the Gerald Ford administration in 1976 and the Ronald Reagan administration in 1982.

Herman Kahn died in his home in Chappaqua, New York. One of his final projects was a public school curriculum designed "to redress the imbalance of unrelenting negativism" about the future. His plan was to dispel dismal prognostications with "more accurate and therefore more optimistic data" about energy, pollution, resources, population, food supplies, economics, and technology (*New York Times*, 8 July 1983).

Given the collaborative organization of research at RAND and the Hudson Institute, Kahn's originality is difficult to assess. The uniqueness of his ideas was their dramatic cast, but his main arguments concerning flexible response, retaliation, limited war, vulnerability, and intrawar bargaining must be considered a synthesis of current ideas. Certainly, Kahn's remarkable imagination distinguished him from other policy analysts, yet his work had major failings. While he boasted that his combination of logic and imagination

engendered superlative insight, especially into future affairs, there were notable weaknesses in his reasoning and his grasp of American society. Commentators often remarked on his alternately brilliant and erroneous analyses. No matter what the topic, Kahn's much-vaunted fearless realism consistently expressed a patriotic worldview in which national survival justifies any military action, including the first use of nuclear weapons in extreme crises; a devotion to the merits of unregulated capitalism; perpetual optimism about humanity's infinite adaptability and inventiveness; and the belief that the future will be so radically different from the past that systems analysis, scenarios, models, and simulations must take the place of the traditional authority of history, political science, and sociology. In fact, Kahn demonstrated little understanding of history or political theory. While he ingeniously entertained fine distinctions between "not incredible" and "impossible" future possibilities, his interpretation of complex social and political realities was superficial and, at times, injudicious.

Kahn's application of systems analysis and scenarios to future studies significantly influenced the development of speculative policy analysis. More generally, the Hudson Institute's enthusiastic sponsorship of future studies lent it public legitimacy. Undoubtedly, Kahn's lasting contribution was to initiate public discussion about the reality of thermonuclear war, the ways in which such a war could start, be fought, and be survived. Critics asserted that his arguments about surviving a war made the deployment of nuclear weapons more likely, while others credit him with helping to foster superpower stability by contributing to the arguments that ultimately shifted official deterrence policy to the flexible response strategy of the 1970s, which was perceived to be a safer, more controllable alternative.

• While Kahn's papers dating from his tenure at RAND remain with his family, there is a sizable archive of his later papers, including correspondence, memoranda, and other unpublished materials, deposited in the Hudson Institute Papers at the National Defense University. There is no single comprehensive bibliography of Kahn's reports, articles, and books, but one can consult the publications catalogs of the RAND Corporation and the Hudson Institute. His major books, besides those mentioned in the text, include *Things to Come*, written with Barry Bruce-Briggs (1972); *World Economic Development: 1979 and Beyond* (1979); *The Coming Boom* (1982); and a collection of essays edited with Julian Simon, *The Resourceful Earth: A Response to Global 2000* (1984).

A great many profiles, interviews, and book chapters about Kahn have been published. Among them the most interesting portraits are Arthur Herzog, "Report on a Think Factory," *New York Times*, 10 Nov. 1963, and "Genghis Kahn," in Herzog, *The War-Peace Establishment* (1963); James C. Fleck, "Doctor Jekyll and Mr. Kahn," *Christian Century*, 25 Mar. 1966, pp. 680–83; Richard Kostelanetz, "One-Man Think Tank," *New York Times Sunday Magazine*, 1 Dec. 1968; Norman Moss, "The Strategist: The Intellect of Herman Kahn," in his *Men Who Play God* (1968); William McWhirter, "I Am One of the 10 Most Famous Obscure

Americans," *Life Magazine*, 6 Dec. 1968, pp. 110–26; G. R. Urban, "Herman Kahn Thinks about the Unthinkable," *New York Times Magazine*, 20 June 1971, pp. 12–24; J. N. Miller, "Unthinkable Thoughts of Herman Kahn," *Reader's Digest*, Apr. 1973; Subrata N. Chakravorty, "Thinking about the Unthinkable," *Forbes*, 22 Nov. 1982, pp. 106–13; and Fred Kaplan, "Dr. Strangelove," in his *The Wizards of Armageddon* (1983).

For views on his contributions to nuclear strategy, see Jeffrey D. Porro, "The Policy War: Brodie vs. Kahn," *Bulletin of Atomic Scientists*, June–July 1982, pp. 16–19; and John Garnett, "Herman Kahn," in *Makers of Nuclear Strategy*, ed. John Baylis and Garnett (1991). The most influential critiques of *On Thermonuclear War* are James Newman's review in *Scientific American*, Mar. 1961, pp. 197–204; Philip Green's lengthy chapter, "Systems Analysis and National Policy," in his *Deadly Logic: The Theory of Nuclear Deterrence* (1966); and Anatol Rapoport, *Strategy and Conscience* (1964), an attempt to rebut *On Thermonuclear War*.

SHARON GHAMARI-TABRIZI

KAHN, Julius (28 Feb. 1861–18 Dec. 1924), congressman, was born in Kuppenheim, Baden, Germany, the son of Jewish parents Herman Kahn and Jeanette Weil, farmers. He immigrated to the United States with his mother at the age of seven to join his father in Calaveras County, California. After several moves, the family settled in San Francisco, where Kahn attended the public schools until he was sixteen. At the age of eighteen he became a dramatic actor and played supporting roles across the country with such stars as Joseph Jefferson and Edwin Booth.

In 1890 Kahn took up the study of law, and he was admitted to the bar in 1894. While still a student, in 1892 he won election to the state assembly as a Republican and served one term. Genial and gregarious, Kahn also had a flair for oratory. Thus he was a suitable candidate for Congress in 1898 and was elected. The following year he married Florence Prag; they had two children. After two terms in Congress, Kahn lost in 1902. He regained his seat in 1904 and held it until his death.

In Congress, Kahn attended to local interests. His principal achievement in that connection was in leading the successful campaign to schedule the Panama-Pacific International Exposition for San Francisco in 1915, celebrating completion of the Panama Canal and discovery of the Pacific Ocean. An issue with national and international import that also had a local dimension was the question of exempting American ships from tolls in the soon to be opened Panama Canal. Kahn took a prominent role in securing tolls exemption in the 1912 Panama Canal Act, as recommended by President William Howard Taft. When Taft's successor, Woodrow Wilson, in 1914 sought repeal of the exemption, Kahn vigorously though vainly opposed him.

A member of the Military Affairs Committee starting in 1905, Kahn became a pioneering advocate of improving the army, navy, and National Guard and of universal military training. In 1913 he helped found the National Defense League and later served as its chairman.

Soon after World War I broke out in Europe in 1914, Americans began to debate the issue of military preparedness, especially when both Great Britain and Germany violated American neutral rights on the seas and in 1915 Germany began to take American lives with submarine warfare. Proponents, including Kahn, warned of unexpected attack and said the United States must be ready. Opponents feared involvement in the European war. The political parties reflected national division, though the Democrats were the more skeptical of preparedness, even after President Wilson, reversing himself, called for it in December 1915. At immediate issue was authorizing legislation for the armed forces, the National Defense Act of 1916, in which Kahn, as ranking Republican on the Military Affairs Committee, played a leading role. In committee he continued his longstanding campaign for preparedness, and partly owing to his efforts, the Democrats made some concessions. The bill that Chairman James Hay reported expanded the army from 100,000 to 140,000 men and federalized the National Guard. Not content with that, on the floor Kahn offered an amendment to authorize an army of 220,000 men and delivered a stirring speech. The amendment failed, 191–213, but succeeded in largely unifying Republicans. Kahn's position was essentially moderate, couched in terms of emergency, and that helped bind together Republicans. Party unification bore fruit with adoption of several Republican-sponsored amendments and, months later, approval of strong army and navy appropriations bills.

In April 1917 the United States declared war on Germany after suffering an all-out submarine campaign. Promptly, Kahn accomplished his greatest achievement. The Wilson administration proposed military conscription to raise the large army that it deemed necessary. But the president encountered strong opposition from leaders of his own party in the House, including Speaker Champ Clark, Majority Leader Claude Kitchin, and the new chairman of the Military Affairs Committee, S. Hubert Dent, Jr. They and many other Democrats, principally from the South and West, preferred to rely on volunteers, as was traditional, with the draft as a last resort. In committee Kahn led in support of the draft, but in vain. After conferring with Secretary of War Newton Baker, Kahn announced himself ready to lead the administration forces on the House floor. Thus, on the first and arguably most important piece of wartime legislation, it was a German-born Republican who championed the Democratic administration's cause, a widely remarked upon circumstance. In debate, Kahn eloquently argued that under Dent's bill "slackers" would get off while brave volunteers would die. He traced the failure of the volunteer system historically, most recently in Great Britain. In the voting, Kahn put party advantage aside and successfully opposed an amendment to permit former president Theodore Roosevelt, a potential 1920 Republican presidential nominee, to recruit and lead a volunteer division. The amendment, Kahn thought, was inconsistent with exclusive reliance on the draft. Following Kahn's lead, the House by a vote of 313–109 adopted the Kahn amendment eliminating the volunteer section of the Dent Bill and restoring exclusive reliance on the draft, as the administration proposed. The Selective Draft Bill became law and proved a great success. Kahn went on to repeatedly lead for other administration war measures in 1917 and 1918.

When in 1918 Republicans won control of the House, Kahn became chairman of the Military Affairs Committee. He capped his career by leading in development and adoption in the House of what became the National Defense Act of 1920, which reorganized and modernized the military establishment. Kahn was less active thereafter. He died in San Francisco, and his wife was elected to his seat in the House.

Kahn is not well remembered in history. In his day, however, he was widely recognized as the principal architect and spokesman for the Republican party on military matters in the House of Representatives. Although a strong partisan, he was an even stronger patriot, and he enjoyed the friendship and respect of colleagues in both parties.

• A modest collection of Kahn's papers and those of his wife are at the Western Jewish History Center in the Judah L. Magnus Memorial Museum at Berkeley, Calif. A fine short published summary of Kahn's life is Alan Boxerman, "Kahn of California," *California Historical Quarterly* 55 (Winter 1976): 340–51. Kahn's role in 1916 preparedness legislation, the 1917 draft act, and other congressional matters is described in Herbert F. Margulies, *Reconciliation and Revival: James R. Mann and the House Republicans in the Wilson Era* (1996). Obituaries are in the *San Francisco Chronicle* and the *New York Times*, 19 Dec. 1924.

HERBERT F. MARGULIES

KAHN, Louis I. (20 Feb. 1901–17 Mar. 1974), architect, was born in Kingisepp, Saaremaa, Estonia, the son of Leopold Kahn, a paymaster in the Russian army, and Bertha Mendelsohn. The family emigrated to Philadelphia in 1906, where he attended public schools and took additional courses in art and music for gifted children. Kahn graduated in architecture from the University of Pennsylvania in 1924, where the head of the design studio and Kahn's senior-year critic was the French-born Paul Philippe Cret, who conducted architectural education at Pennsylvania according to the model of the École des Beaux-Arts in Paris.

Kahn served as chief of design for the exhibition buildings erected in Philadelphia for the Sesquicentennial Exposition of 1926. In 1928–1929 he undertook an extended European tour, returning on the eve of the depression. He married Esther Israeli in 1930; they had one daughter. After brief stints in the offices of Cret and the firm of Zantzinger, Borie, and Medary, Kahn found himself unemployed, as he was to remain for most of the 1930s. It was during this time that he became interested in the modern architecture that would soon be christened the International Style.

Kahn was particularly concerned with the use of modern architecture as a tool for social change, and in collaboration with other young, unemployed architects he began to experiment with the design of public housing. He and his friends submitted several projects to the infant federal housing program, but none was funded. Kahn's developing stature as a housing expert did, however, lead to his employment in 1935–1937 by the Resettlement Administration as assistant principal architect (with Alfred Kastner) for Jersey Homesteads (now Roosevelt, N.J.). In 1939 two large Philadelphia projects of his design (in partial collaboration with Kenneth Day) were granted federal funding, but construction was blocked by local political opposition.

With the outbreak of World War II, Kahn's talents were at last fully employed. He spent most of 1941 and 1942 designing seven communities for wartime factory workers, five of which, totaling more than 2,200 units, were built. In this work Kahn was associated briefly with George Howe and, for a longer time, with Oscar Stonorov, who remained his partner until 1947. With work like Carver Court, near Coatesville, Pennsylvania (1941–1943), and the Lily Ponds Houses, Washington, D.C. (1942–1943), Kahn demonstrated his up-to-date awareness of the aesthetic and social issues of modern housing. But he felt increasingly confined by the functionalist and materialist themes of modernist ideology and he became disenchanted with centralized government control over architecture and city planning. Together with Stonorov, Kahn authored two pamphlets that called for a humane, client-oriented approach to postwar planning and architecture. Both *Why City Planning Is Your Responsibility* (1943) and *You and Your Neighborhood: A Primer for Neighborhood Planning* (1944) eschewed large-scale demolition of neighborhoods and exalted the concept of strong, local-level political activism. They attracted much attention during the last years of the war, as Americans began to contemplate the future.

Diminished government support for housing after the war meant that Kahn's larger scale ideas were deferred. He continued to serve his ideals in work for labor unions, for which he designed office buildings, summer camps, and clinics. But during the early postwar period, Kahn, like most architects of the time, found his principal employment in the booming suburbs. His house designs of the period, notably the Weiss House, East Norriton, Pennsylvania (1947–1950), and the Genel House, Wynnewood, Pennsylvania (1948–1951), combined rustic materials with the modernist jutting rooflines and clustered, "bi-nuclear" planning. They merit comparison with the contemporary work of Marcel Breuer and the most recent architecture graduates of Harvard, where the program had been overhauled by Breuer and Walter Gropius, the founder of the Bauhaus.

Kahn's reputation might have been pinned at this middling level if he had not been appointed to the architecture faculty at Yale in the fall of 1947. In his Yale classes, he began to grapple with the problem of designing monumental public buildings for postwar society. This was a preoccupation of many architects at this time and one about which Kahn, with his interest in public service, felt deeply. But Kahn's small-scale practice had not given him much chance to deal with public architecture. Yale not only afforded him the opportunity to explore the question of "monumentality," as he and others called it; in the commission for the Yale Art Gallery (1951–1953), the university also offered Kahn his first opportunity to build at a monumental scale.

In the design of the Yale Art Gallery, Kahn adopted the characteristic "open plan" of modernism, but rather than the chilly slices of universal space that were the norm for the day, he created galleries that were wrapped in powerful masonry and warmly textured by a rugged ceiling structure. The ceilings were contrived at once to resemble heroic space frames—although the building code required him to create this effect by disguising a more conventional system of tilted concrete beams—and to allude to the coffered ceilings of ancient architecture. R. Buckminster Fuller was the champion of such technological displays, and Kahn's associate Anne Tyng (with whom he had a daughter) had been experimenting along the same lines. Antiquity was newly alive in Kahn's imagination after his brief sojourn in the winter of 1950–1951 as resident architect at the American Academy in Rome, whence he had departed on a one-month tour of Greece and Egypt. The Yale Art Gallery's big-boned structure and historical allusion lifted it out of what was then mainstream modernist thinking, and provided one of the first clues about his idea of the course to be taken by postwar architecture. For a time, it seemed that Kahn's work could be subsumed within the broader movement called Brutalism, that muscular style of rough-textured concrete and exposed steel that flourished in the fifties and early sixties, but his individuality was soon made apparent.

The building that clearly separated Kahn from the other architects of the early 1950s was the diminutive Bath House (in fact, a swimming pool changing room) that he designed in 1955 for the Trenton Jewish Community Center in Ewing, New Jersey. Here he gathered four pyramid-roofed pavilions with perfect symmetry around a central courtyard. The four discrete spaces, each with its own supporting structure and distinct function (men's and women's shower rooms, a check room for clothing, and a sheltered stairway leading up to the pool), rejected the generalities of modernist open planning. Moreover, the fundamentally classical plan here abandoned relaxed, modernist asymmetries. Despite its tiny size, the Trenton Bath House seemed grave and serious.

In 1957 Kahn returned to his alma mater, the University of Pennsylvania, as a teacher, and also as the architect of the Richards Medical Research Building (1957–1965). In the Richards Building he revealed the fuller development of the thinking that lay behind the little Trenton design. Rather than universally useful spaces, Kahn created small laboratory studios, defined by his understanding that medical research was conducted by small teams, and stacked them in a group of brawnily structured towers that alluded to the picturesque hill towns of Italy. After it was too late, Kahn's clients realized that their research would have been better served by larger, easily rearrangeable laboratories, but contemporary architectural observers had no such reservations. For them, the Richards Building offered a stunning alternative to the slick steel and glass of the International style, especially as it had been commercialized in America. In 1961 the building was the subject of a one-building exhibition at the Museum of Modern Art in New York, in which it was hailed as the most significant design of the postwar period. *Progressive Architecture* (Apr. 1961) identified Kahn as the central figure of a new "Philadelphia School," whose other members included Robert Venturi, Romaldo Giurgola, and Robert Geddes.

Kahn's growing fame was not based solely on his still rather small architectural output. He had also established himself as a provocative teacher, who drew students from around the world to his Master's Studio at the University of Pennsylvania, and he was the most compelling theorist of his time. Kahn's philosophy had matured throughout the fifties, and in November 1960 he presented his thinking with special eloquence and clarity in a broadcast lecture for the Voice of America. Published by VOA as the booklet *Structure and Form* (1961) and widely republished in subsequent years, the 1960 lecture explained architecture in Platonist terms that emphasized the difficulty and seriousness of the architect's task. Kahn's argument distinguished between an immanent, generalized "form," strongly shaped by the architect's definition of the clients' needs (such as Kahn had created for the Richards Building), and the real-world "design," developed by the architect after taking into account such constraints as site, budget, and building material. This idealist argument reinvigorated modern architecture by attaching it to the similarly principled architecture of the past—notably the classical tradition that had survived into Kahn's own lifetime through the energy of the École des Beaux-Arts. While his intention was thus to broaden and strengthen modernist thinking, his open acceptance of the architecture and architectural thinking of the past also helped to inspire the more negative critique of twentieth-century architecture that came to be called Post Modernism.

The work of Kahn's office expanded dramatically in the early 1960s. Following the Richards Building came another laboratory project for the Salk Institute for Biological Studies in La Jolla, California (1959–1965), this one reconfigured as a horizontally oriented open plan and expanded to incorporate a small village of residences and a large meeting center. There was also Erdman Hall, a dormitory for Bryn Mawr College (1960–1965), and a synagogue for the Philadelphia congregation of Mikveh Israel (1961–1972, unbuilt). Kahn's international reputation brought him the two largest commissions of his career: an entire campus for the Indian Institute of Management in Ahmedabad (1962–1974) and a new capitol complex for East Pakistan at Dacca (1962–1983), christened Sher-e-Bangla Nagar after the declaration of Bangladeshi independence. All of these designs dealt with the challenge of defining architectural environments for what he considered to be the two archetypal human activities: the individual activity of study, research, or contemplation, and the congregant activity of learning, worship, and government. Each building created memorable spaces within powerful shapes, harkening unmistakably to the masonry architecture of antiquity and the middle ages.

Distinctive of all these buildings was Kahn's emphasis on planning. For Beaux-Arts and modern theorists alike, the plan was the only acceptable starting point for principled architectural design. Whereas modernism had embraced the freedom of the open plan, Kahn now reverted in his mature work to the orderliness of the Beaux-Arts style. Not that the order of his planning was always overt. Indeed, after experimenting with rigid symmetry in the Trenton Bath House, Kahn turned increasingly to patterns of clustering and oblique alignment that were powerful on paper, where the architect worked out his platonic ideas, but often almost undetectable to the casual visitor. Two unbuilt designs that were presented to their clients in 1966—St. Andrew's Priory in Valyermo, California (1961–1967), and the Dominican Motherhouse of St. Catherine de Ricci in Media, Pennsylvania (1965–1969)—pushed this seeming informality into the semblance of collage.

The work of Kahn's last years assumed the mien of a quiet classicism. In contained, symmetrical buildings like Phillips Exeter Academy Library (1965–1972), the Kimbell Art Museum in Fort Worth, Texas (1966–1972), and the Yale Center for British Art (1969–1974), Kahn's architecture achieved a magical kind of equipoise between light and structure—the simplest and yet most demanding elements of architectural expression. The most celebrated of these designs was the Kimbell Museum, whose multiple, barrel-vaulted bays were split along their crowns to admit a slice of the Texas sun—an alchemical weaving together of structure and that absence of structure through which light enters. Landscape design played an increasingly large role in Kahn's later work, as in the courtyard of the Salk Institute and the grounds of the Kimbell Museum. In this he often collaborated with Harriet Pattison, the mother of his third child.

Kahn's enduring fame rests on his success in restoring a sense of serious, almost spiritual, purpose to modern architecture as it passed the midpoint of the twentieth century—in making it once more a difficult, idealist endeavor. By creating simplicity out of the often intractable material of the real world, and by attaching the philosophy of modernism to its historical antecedents, he enlarged the challenge and increased the means for a new generation of architects.

Kahn died of a heart attack in Pennsylvania Station in New York City while returning home after a visit to Ahmedabad, India.

• Kahn's papers are the property of the Pennsylvania Historical and Museum Commission, on deposit in the Architectural Archives of the University of Pennsylvania. *The Louis I. Kahn Archive: Personal Drawings* (7 vols., 1987) reproduces the autograph drawings from that collection. The most thorough biography is David B. Brownlee and David G. De Long, *Louis I. Kahn: In the Realm of Architecture* (1991), which includes a complete list of works and a bibliography of Kahn's writings. The latter are anthologized in Alessandra Latour, ed., *Louis I. Kahn: Writings, Lectures, Interviews* (1991), and in Richard S. Wurman, ed., *What Will Be Has Always Been: The Words of Louis I. Kahn* (1986). Kahn's travel sketches and other nonarchitectural drawings and paintings are assembled in Jan Hochstim, *The Paintings and Sketches of Louis I. Kahn* (1991). Vincent Scully provides a prescient and compelling view of Kahn in *Louis I. Kahn* (1962). Similarly vivid are the several articles published by William Jordy. For them and the vast body of periodical literature, see Jack Perry Brown, *Louis I. Kahn: A Bibliography* (1987).

DAVID B. BROWNLEE

KAHN, Otto Herman (21 Feb. 1867–29 Mar. 1934), investment banker and patron of the fine arts, was born in Mannheim, Germany, the son of Bernhard Kahn, a banker, and Emma Eberstadt. Reared in a home with a rich cultural atmosphere and with valuable works of art, Otto was privately tutored and displayed a keen interest in music. He became familiar with banking and in 1883 began to work in a small bank in Karlsruhe.

At age twenty Kahn satisfied his military obligation, learning discipline serving in a regiment of Hussars, but he disliked militarism. He took a position in 1888 with the Deutsche Bank in Berlin and two years later went to work in its London office. He became a naturalized British citizen and continued to succeed as a banker.

In 1893 Kahn left London and worked in the New York City office of Speyer and Company for two years as an investment banker. On 6 January 1896 he married the sculptor Addie Wolff; they had four children. Her father, Abraham Wolff, had been a partner in the investment firm of Kuhn, Loeb and Company. In January 1897 Kahn joined this company as a partner and became an eminent leader in the field of railroad financing. In 1897 Kahn helped Edward H. Harriman to acquire control of the Union Pacific and in 1899 assisted him in raising capital to secure controlling interests in the Chicago and Alton Railway and in the Oregon Shortline. After Harriman bought out the Central and Southern Pacific Railroads in 1901, Kahn advanced his client's takeover attempts of James J. Hill's Northern Pacific Line; he played a major role in November of that year in creating the Northern Securities Company, which was the cornerstone of the settlement between Harriman and Hill, holding 96 percent of the stock in the Northern Pacific Line.

During the first decade of the twentieth century, Kahn became a director of railroad carriers such as the Missouri Pacific, the Denver and Rio Grande, and the Baltimore and Ohio. Between 1910 and 1912 Kahn also marketed securities of American Telephone and Telegraph, of Westinghouse, and of United States Rubber.

During this time Kahn became a major patron of the performing arts and of painting. His passionate devotion to music well explains why he decided in 1903 to invest in the Metropolitan Opera Company, owned by Heinrich Conried. When this company encountered financial problems and when Oscar Hammerstein established a competing company at the Manhattan Opera House, Kahn and William K. Vanderbilt, Sr., purchased (for $100,000 each) Conried's troubled company during the 1907–1908 season. The following year Kahn bought out Vanderbilt and hired two prominent individuals from La Scala in Milan: Giulio Gatti-Casazza as the Metropolitan's director and Arturo Toscanini as its chief conductor. To atone for his wealth, Kahn gave money to restore the Metropolitan's solvency and success, donating $350,000 to cover company losses between 1908 and 1910. Competition from Hammerstein ended in 1910, for Kahn paid him $1.2 million to suspend the operations of his Manhattan and Philadelphia Opera Companies. Kahn's funding and energetic leadership ensured the Metropolitan's success for more than twenty-five years; in 1911 he became its chairman and in 1918 its president. He occupied this position for the next thirteen years, and at his death he held 84 percent of its stock.

Like opera, drama also interested Kahn. Along with J. Pierpont Morgan, John Jacob Astor, and other wealthy financiers and industrialists, Kahn in 1905 contributed money to build the New Theatre in New York. Kahn lost money in this venture: the building, which was intended to house the best drama in America, encountered structural problems, had poor acoustics, and attracted only small audiences.

An eminent connoisseur of art, Kahn owned a home on Fifth Avenue in New York and a mansion at Cold Spring Harbor on Long Island that were compared to Medici palaces with their galleries of European masterpieces, including Franz Hals's "The Painter and His Family" which Kahn bought for $500,000; Lorenzo di Credi's "Florentine Girls"; and Giovanni Bellini's "Flight into Egypt." Kahn's other European treasures were either sold or given to museums in America.

Kahn was involved in important activities during World War I. He allowed an English manor he had acquired in 1913 to be used as a home for blinded soldiers; he spoke against German militarism; and he played a major role in securing aid for Britain and the Allies. In 1915 he helped to acquire an Anglo-French loan for $100,000 and personally purchased a piece of it. In 1916 he obtained a loan for Paris for $50 million and loans for Bordeaux, Lyons, and Marseilles amounting to $20 million for each city. When the United States entered the war in 1917, Kahn became a naturalized American citizen.

After the war he expressed disappointment about central provisions of the Paris Peace Treaties and about the diplomatic stance of the United States in the world. Kahn in 1919 thought that Woodrow Wilson's League of Nations would not be effective in settling European conflicts. Moreover, he believed that Germany would encounter major economic and financial problems in being required to make excessive reparations payments. In 1919 he also denounced Republican isolationists in the U.S. Senate for their failure to ratify the Paris Treaty. He believed that the United States was abdicating its international responsibilities.

During the war and the early 1920s, Kahn was acknowledged for his achievements. For bringing Diaghilev, the Nijinskys, and other Russian Ballet members to the United States for a tour in 1916, he was made an honorary member of the Moscow Art Theatre. In 1918 he became one of the founders of the Council on Foreign Relations and served on its board of directors for the rest of his life. Several European governments also paid tribute to him; Kahn in 1919 was named a member of both the Crown of Italy and the Order of the Belgian Crown. In 1921 he was received into the French Legion of Honor and into the Order of Charles II of Spain.

Kahn also contributed to many organizations. He endowed university art courses and made donations to art schools. He helped finance the restoration of the Parthenon in Athens. He also contributed to theatrical companies and during the 1920s gave money to the talented Paul Robeson and other black actors. He was a major promoter of the Chicago Opera Company, for a short time a director of the Boston Opera Company, and an honorary director of the Royal Opera in Covent Garden in London. He also was a trustee or a director of universities and numerous business and civic organizations.

As a result of the stock market crash of 1929, Kahn experienced large financial losses. After the election of Franklin Delano Roosevelt as president in 1932, Kahn, a liberal Republican, supported the New Deal, believing that government spending was required to bring the American economy out of the depression. At this time, he showed concern about the advent of Hitler and his anti-Semitic policies in 1933. Kahn, who had not been particularly religious, renounced his former homeland and called for support for German Jews. He died in New York City.

Kahn was recognized as one of the foremost investment bankers of his time; a fine dresser and a shrewd negotiator, he was known for financing transcontinental railroads and for reorganizing several major rail lines. Another significant achievement was his financial backing of the English and the French during World War I. After the war, Kahn acquired respect in some circles for his economic views, for he claimed correctly that terms of the Paris Treaties would culminate in damaging the European and U.S. economies. However, Kahn's most significant achievement was his support of the arts in the United States. Kahn has been perceived as an American Maecenas, generously funding operatic and other cultural institutions in this nation.

• Kahn's papers are in the William Seymour Theatre Collection at Princeton University's Firestone Library. Mary Jane Matz, *The Many Lives of Otto Kahn* (1963), presents a comprehensive survey of his life, emphasizing his role in investment banking. On the other hand, John Kobler, *Otto the Magnificent: The Life of Otto Kahn* (1988), devotes attention to his cultural achievements. Kuhn, Loeb, and Company, *A Century of Investment Banking* (1967), refers to Kahn's role in this firm. Vincent P. Carosso, *The Morgans: Private International Bankers, 1854–1913* (1987), describes Kahn's railroad transactions. Irving Kolodin, *The Metropolitan Opera, 1883–1939* (1940), assesses Kahn's leadership role in this institution. For Kahn's activities during World War I, consult Howard M. Sachar, *A History of the Jews in America* (1992), and Ron Chernow, *The Warburgs: The Twentieth-Century Odyssey of a Remarkable Jewish Family* (1993). Robert D. Schulzinger, *The Wise Men of Foreign Affairs: The History of the Council on Foreign Relations* (1984), alludes to Kann's involvement in this organization. Stephen Birmingham, *Our Crowd: The Great Jewish Families of New York* (1967), describes Kahn's support of German Jewry during his last years. Two lengthy works contain major addresses and writings by Kahn: *Our Economic and Other Problems: A Financier's Point of View* (1920) and *Of Many Things* (1926).

WILLIAM WEISBERGER

KAISER, Alois (10 Nov. 1840–5 Jan. 1908), cantor and composer of synagogue music, was born in Szobotist, Hungary (now Subotica, Yugoslavia), the son of David Loeb Kaiser. His mother's name and father's occupation are unknown. The evident talent of their son at the age of five convinced his parents to move to Vienna. Jews who wished to reside in the capital of the Austro-Hungarian Empire in 1845 had to secure permission from the authorities. At considerable cost, Kaiser's parents acquired permission, and the lad was enrolled in religious school as well as the secular Realschule. His precocity in music earned him admission to the Conservatory of Music and a place in the choir of Vienna's Temple, led by the outstanding cantor-composer of his day, Salomon Sulzer. At age fourteen Kaiser was the choir's leading soprano, and at age nineteen he secured the post of assistant cantor in suburban Funfhaus. Three years later he was chosen cantor of Prague's important Neusynagoge. He took advantage of that city's musical resources to broaden his education in voice and theory.

In 1866 the rabbi of the Neusynagoge, Adolph Huebsch, moved to the United States and was elected spiritual leader of New York City's Bohemian congregation, now Central Synagogue. Kaiser emigrated to the United States soon afterward and obtained the post of cantor and music director at Baltimore's Congregation Oheb Shalom, where he served for the remaining forty-two years of his life.

Trained Jewish musicians were a rarity in the nineteenth-century United States. The growing Reform movement, imitating the patterns of Protestant worship, replaced the unaccompanied chanting of liturgy with a mixed male and female choir and organ accompaniment. The role of the cantor became that of antiphonal soloist, selector of music, and director of the choir. Most choirs were composed of non-Jewish sing-

ers, and little four-part music for the synagogue was in print. Kaiser attempted to fill this need by arranging the great works of his teacher, Sulzer, and by enlisting fellow cantors in the United States to join him in composing and arranging synagogue music. Between 1871 and 1886 they produced four volumes of music for the Sabbath and various festivals entitled *Zimrath Yah* (Song of the Lord). Reform Judaism's substitution of a class confirmation for the bar mitzvah inspired Kaiser to publish *Confirmation Hymns* (1873). In 1879 he produced *Memorial Service for the Day of Atonement*. With Cantor William Sparger of New York City's Temple Emanu-El, he wrote *Cantata for Simhat Torah* (1890).

In 1893 Kaiser was commissioned to produce a souvenir volume of music for the Jewish Women's Congress held in connection with the Columbian Exposition in Chicago. Two years later he organized and served as president of the Society of American Cantors. His goal was to enhance the place of the cantor in the American synagogue. While the larger Jewish communities on the East and West coasts of the United States retained the services of cantors, those in the Midwest and South did not. The paucity of opportunities for the growing group of immigrants from Europe and the lack of training in Westernized music among many of those who sought positions as cantors made Kaiser's task a difficult one. His own talent and dedication earned him, in 1895, honorary membership in the recently organized Central Conference of American Rabbis, as well as a commission to create the first *Union Hymnal*, published by that organization in 1897.

Kaiser died in Baltimore, respected for his fine character, gentle dignity, and benevolent nature and admired for the religious fervor that inspired his singing. Few of his compositions survive, however. His compositions were largely in the Germanic style of Sulzer, whose published works included some contributed by Franz Schubert and other Viennese composers of his day. However, the pre–World War I period brought to the United States its largest Jewish immigration, Jews from czarist Russia, whose children and grandchildren came to dominate Reform Judaism. As a consequence, during the mid-twentieth century the Reform movement adopted music from the Eastern European tradition, and more recently from Israel; the legacy of composers of the Germanic, so-called "classic" period of American Reform has been very nearly obliterated. Of all Kaiser's output, only his setting of the liturgical text "May the words of my mouth" survives in occasional use in the synagogue.

• No collection of Kaiser's manuscripts survives. The *American Jewish Year Book, 1903–1904*, outlines his career. A brief biography appears in Louis F. Cahn, *The History of Oheb Shalom, 1853–1953*. Kaiser's labors for the Central Conference of American Rabbis are described in that organization's annual *Yearbook* between 1894 and 1905, with a special testimonial in the 1905 volume and a memorial in 1908. Further details can be found in articles in *The Jewish Encyclopedia* and *The Universal Jewish Encyclopedia*.

MALCOLM H. STERN

KAISER, Henry John (9 May 1882–24 Aug. 1967), industrialist, was born in Sprout Brook, New York, the son of German immigrants Frank Kaiser, a shoemaker, and Mary Yops. Henry and three older sisters were raised in modest circumstances. He quit school after the eighth grade and found a job as a dry goods clerk in nearby Utica. Between customers, Kaiser studied photography and moonlighted in that trade. From age sixteen through his mid-twenties, photography was Kaiser's career. In the late 1890s Eastman-Kodak marketed pioneering advances in photography, and Americans were captivated. By 1899 Kaiser was a photographic supplies salesman, well versed in technical phases of the business. In 1901 he acquired part of a studio in Lake Placid, New York; within a year he bought out partner W. W. Brownell.

In 1902 Lake Placid attracted visitors only during warm months. There was little winter business, so Kaiser followed "snowbirds" to Florida. By 1903 he had saved several thousand dollars, which he used to build a modest chain of photography shops in Florida. Kaiser diversified his services by making postcards, doing promotional shots for railroads, and producing portraits.

During a portrait sitting in 1906, Kaiser met Bess Fosburgh, daughter of a Virginia lumber magnate, and recent graduate of a Boston finishing school. A romance developed, but Bess's father, Edgar Fosburgh, considered photography a frivolous enterprise. If Kaiser wished to marry Bess, he had to find suitable employment. Kaiser accepted the challenge. He sold his studios, moved to Spokane, Washington, and entered the wholesale hardware business. He became a star salesman for McGowan Brothers, a major regional wholesale supplier. Kaiser's earnings soon convinced Fosburgh that he could provide a good home for Bess; they were married in 1907. The couple built a home in Spokane and had two sons.

Kaiser's business trips provided him an awareness of growing opportunities in public works. By 1910 Henry Ford was transforming the automobile into the working man's achievable dream; lacking were decent streets and roads. Kaiser left hardware and served a brief apprenticeship in construction with J. F. Hill, a Canadian-owned company. In December 1914 he founded his own company in Vancouver and quickly established himself in road construction. During and after World War I he rapidly expanded operations, building hundreds of miles of roads in Washington, Oregon, and California. In 1921 Kaiser established his headquarters in Oakland, California. High quality and fast work earned him the respect of leading construction men. In 1927 he overcame many difficulties while building a 200-mile section of a trans-Cuba highway that traversed many miles of swampland.

As the nation entered the Great Depression, the federal government commenced a program of public works. Kaiser joined a consortium named Six Companies, which won the bid to build Hoover Dam in 1931. The partners divided responsibilities; Kaiser had little to do with the actual construction of the dam. His main task was serving as liaison between the contractors and federal bureaucrats. Between 1931 and 1935, Kaiser spent many months in Washington, where he learned how bureaucrats worked, knowledge he used to great advantage throughout his career.

In the late 1930s, Six Companies won major portions of the Bonneville and Grand Coulee dam jobs, which lasted into World War II. Ironically, failure to land the Shasta Dam job in 1939 launched Kaiser into supplying construction materials, because he did win the contract to supply cement for the dam. Within months, Kaiser built a huge plant south of San Francisco. This Permanente Cement plant supplied much of the cement for military installations in the Pacific during World War II.

The war marked Kaiser's emergence as a national industrial hero. The outbreak of war in Europe led Kaiser to sense much earlier than most American businessmen the likelihood of the nation's participation. Analysts in many industries insisted that they had sufficient capacity to meet any increases in demand. Kaiser believed otherwise. Between 1939 and 1941 he urged immediate expansion in magnesium, steel, aluminum, and other producer goods.

Such concerns were partly a result of Kaiser's heavy involvement in shipbuilding. In 1940 he and two partners won a contract to build thirty cargo ships for the British. By spring 1941, Kaiser and his engineers had erected a huge shipyard in Richmond, California. The federal government provided a stream of contracts, mainly for cargo ships. By 1944 the Richmond yards employed nearly 100,000 workers, and Kaiser had developed a similar operation in the Portland/Vancouver region. During the war, his yards launched 1,490 vessels, including fifty small aircraft carriers and nearly one-third of the nation's cargo ships. Kaiser's feats won him profound admiration from journalists, who dubbed him the nation's "Miracle Man," and America's "Number One Industrial Hero." President Roosevelt was so impressed with Kaiser that he seriously considered him as his running mate in 1944.

Many rival entrepreneurs seethed at what they perceived as Kaiser's grandstanding. In their eyes, he had become a public hero only because of government work. Eastern steel men vigorously opposed his repeated efforts to build his own plant. Kaiser argued that he needed a western mill to supply steel to the shipyards. Throughout 1941 eastern steel men successfully blocked Kaiser. Pearl Harbor changed the situation overnight. Within weeks, Kaiser had government authorization, plus millions of dollars in loans from the Reconstruction Finance Corporation. He quickly built a large plant in Fontana, fifty miles east of Los Angeles.

In mid-July 1942, Kaiser suggested building a fleet of 5,000 large cargo planes, which could fly men and materials across the Atlantic to avoid the Axis submarines then wreaking havoc on Allied shipping. If the aircraft manufacturers could not do the job, he would. In fact, the aircraft industry was also performing miracles. Aircraft manufacturers sidetracked his initiative, and Kaiser's critics saw the episode as naked publicity-seeking.

As early as 4 December 1942, when most businessmen were still gearing up for war, Kaiser urged the country to start preparing for peace. The war years marked his emergence as a visionary; anticipating an unprecedented postwar economic boom, he dreamed of meeting an impressive variety of consumer needs. A primary goal was to produce a good, cheap automobile. Two weeks before V-J day, Kaiser and Joseph W. Frazer, an experienced automobile executive, formed Kaiser-Frazer Corporation. The ban on private automobile production, wartime rationing, and the surge of boom times had created millions of potential customers with hefty savings accounts. Kaiser and Frazer believed that if they could get new cars onto the market quickly they could mount a successful challenge to GM, Ford, and Chrysler. Kaiser wanted a vehicle in the $400 price range, but Frazer urged production of conventional, full-sized models. Realizing that Frazer's strategy promised significant numbers of cars more quickly, Kaiser bowed to his partner's experience. By September 1947 the partners were producing 15,000 cars each month. For a time the cars sold well. In 1947 and 1948, the company's heyday, they produced more than 300,000 automobiles and earned combined profits of $29 million. But by mid-1948 the company experienced trouble selling cars. The big three were catching up with demand, and consumers clearly preferred their products. Even more worrisome, the giants were spending tens of millions on research and design of new models. No independents could match those efforts. The company produced some good models in the early 1950s, but the end was inevitable. When Kaiser-Frazer suspended domestic operations in 1955, the company had lost $123 million.

Kaiser-Frazer collapsed while Kaiser's other enterprises were achieving record-level expansion and profits. Kaiser Steel became a key supplier for rapidly expanding western markets. Kaiser Aluminum, an outgrowth of Kaiser's magnesium production during the war, became a force in national and world markets. The Justice Department wanted to encourage competition for Alcoa and provided crucial concessions. In the 1950s Kaiser Aluminum gained more than one-fourth of the domestic market and challenged Reynolds Metals for the number two position.

The collapse of Kaiser-Frazer and the emergence of several publicly held corporations in Kaiser's industrial empire induced him to create a holding company, Kaiser Industries, in 1956. The consolidation facilitated access to financial markets. Kaiser-Frazer investors were allowed to exchange shares on a four-for-one basis for Kaiser Industries shares.

The 1950s marked important changes in Kaiser's business and personal life. His wife died in 1951 after a lengthy illness, and three weeks later he married her thirty-four-year-old nurse, Alyce Chester. This created a minor scandal. In 1954 Kaiser semiretired to Hawaii, where he launched yet another career, promoting air travel and building a large resort hotel and a cement plant. He spearheaded development of Hawaii Kai, a planned city on Oahu. He also entered radio and television, first underwriting and later sponsoring the highly successful series "Maverick."

In addition, Kaiser promoted the Kaiser Health plan and hospital program. Founded in 1938 as a prepaid plan for employees at Grand Coulee Dam by Dr. Sidney R. Garfield, the plan mushroomed during the war. Despite determined opposition from the American Medical Association, which labeled the plan "socialized medicine," the Kaiser organization opened the plan to the general public. By 1967 it was the nation's largest health maintenance organization, with 1.5 million members.

In 1962 Kaiser celebrated his eightieth birthday at the new high-rise headquarters building in Oakland. Having enjoyed good health until his last months, he died in Hawaii. As one of America's self-made men, Kaiser maintained throughout his life unbounded faith in the nation's economic future. In many respects, his death symbolized the end of a simpler, more optimistic era.

• The Henry J. Kaiser papers, Bancroft Library, Berkeley, California, contain 700 linear feet of material. Government collections, particularly those featuring materials from the 1930s through the 1960s, contain large amounts of material pertaining to Kaiser, his businesses, and his relations with federal agencies. At the National Archives these include the War Assets Administration papers, War Production Board papers, Fair Employment Practices Commission papers, and many other collections. Between the early 1930s and his death, Kaiser was the subject of hundreds of magazine articles, listed in the annual *Index to Periodicals*. Biographical works include Mark S. Foster, *Henry J. Kaiser: Builder in the Modern American West* (1989); Al Heiner, *Henry J. Kaiser, American Empire Builder: An Insider's View* (1989); and Richard M. Langworth, *Kaiser-Frazer: The Last Onslaught on Detroit* (1975). Although Kaiser and his activities have been treated in detail only by the few authors listed above, several other published works provide excellent context. See Alfred D. Chandler, Jr., *Strategy and Structure: Chapters in the History of American Industrial Enterprise* (1962); and Gerald D. Nash, *The American West in the Twentieth Century: A Short History of an Urban Oasis* (1973) and *The American West Transformed: The Impact of the Second World War* (1985).

MARK S. FOSTER

KALAKAUA, David Laamea (16 Nov. 1836–20 Jan. 1891), king of the Hawaiian Islands, was born in Honolulu, the son of the high chief Kahanu Kapaakea and the high chiefess Analea Keohokalole. The infant was adopted, according to Hawaiian custom, by the chiefess Haaheo Kaniu, who took him to the court of King Kamehameha III on the island of Maui. At age four Kalakaua returned to Honolulu and for the next nine years was educated at the Royal School, taught by American missionary teachers. His formal education ended when he was fourteen, but he continued to read widely and to receive tutoring in subjects designed to fit him to assume high office in the kingdom of Hawaii.

At sixteen Kalakaua took up the study of law and qualified in 1869 to practice in Hawaii. The delay in completing his legal training was due to his holding various government positions. In 1852 he was commissioned in the militia; by 1856 he was a major on the staff of King Kamehameha IV. In that position he met and talked with all of the prominent foreign visitors to the islands. Kalakaua had an abiding interest in military matters. He read military texts and when traveling abroad always took particular note of the organization and discipline of the armed forces of other countries.

In 1860 Kalakaua made his first trip abroad, accompanying Prince Lot (later Kamehameha V) to Victoria, British Columbia, and San Francisco. On their return Kalakaua was appointed to the House of Nobles, the senior house in the Hawaiian parliament. He had previously been a leader of a political group known as the Young Hawaiians and a strong proponent of the motto "Hawaii for the Hawaiians." He understood, however, that Americans dominated the economy of Hawaii and had a decisive voice in its politics, and he accepted the necessity of conciliating them, short of annexation. Charles Nordhoff, author of *Northern California, Oregon, and the Sandwich Islands* (1874), wrote, "Colonel Kalakaua is a man of education, . . . vigorous will, and a strong determination to maintain the independence of the Islands."

In addition to his military duties, Kalakaua served in the Department of the Interior and in 1863 was appointed postmaster general. He resigned from that position in 1865 to serve as secretary to the privy council and chamberlain under King Kamehameha V. Kalakaua was fluent in English as well as Hawaiian and was at ease with foreign dignitaries. This was of particular assistance to Kamehameha V, whose command of languages was not extensive.

In 1863 Kalakaua married Chiefess Kapiolani, granddaughter of Kaumualii, the last king of Kauai. They had no children. One of their greatest pleasures was music, and like many members of his family Kalakaua was a talented musician. He wrote the words to "Hawaii Ponoi," which became the Hawaiian national anthem and is now the state's, and the words and music to many other Hawaiian songs.

Kamehameha V died on 11 December 1872 without designating an heir. In the election held to determine a successor, Kalakaua was one of the chief candidates, but Prince William Charles Lunalilo was elected almost unanimously. Lunalilo died on 3 February 1874, also without naming a successor. This time Kalakaua was opposed by Dowager Queen Emma, the widow of Kamehameha IV. When the ballots were counted, the tally was Kalakaua 39, Queen Emma 6.

The Emmaites did not accept the result with equanimity. They marched on the Court House, where the election had taken place, and a riot erupted. When it became clear that the police were unable to handle the angry people, the king and his advisers turned to the diplomatic representatives of the British and U.S. governments resident in Hawaii, who approved the landing of men from their naval vessels. Order was restored by the mere presence of the disciplined foreign seamen.

On 13 February 1874 Kalakaua took the oath of office. Upon assuming the throne he was faced with the necessity of restoring the political and economic stability of the kingdom and of building the confidence of the people in the monarchy. He viewed elections for monarchs as a disruptive factor, and to avoid another such political upheaval he named his younger brother, Prince William Pitt Leleiohoku, as his successor. When that young man died, he chose his oldest sister, Princes Liliuokalani.

Kalakaua's next problem was the economy. A boom in Hawaiian sugar, created by the disruption of the production of sugar in the southern states during and just after the American Civil War, ended when the U.S. plantations resumed full operation. Hawaiian sugar, subject to duty in the U.S. market, could no longer compete. For twenty-five years the Hawaiian government had been attempting to negotiate a reciprocity treaty that would allow Hawaiian sugar into the United States without duty, but the U.S. Congress would not agree. King Kalakaua was determined to achieve a treaty that would give Hawaiian sugar an edge over other foreign sugars in the American market. In October 1874 he sent his chancellor, Chief Justice Elisha H. Allen, to Washington, D.C., to pave the way, and in December he himself went there.

Kalakaua conferred with President Ulysses S. Grant and prominent American politicians and officials, and during his short stay he engendered so much goodwill toward Hawaii that within a month after he left Washington Congress passed a reciprocity treaty. When the treaty went into effect in 1875 and Hawaiian sugar was allowed to enter the United States free of duty, land values in Hawaii skyrocketed as sugar production rose. The king had achieved a basis for economic stability for the islands.

Kalakaua then set out to enhance the government's prestige at home and abroad. He promoted public works; sponsored new technology such as artesian wells, telephones, and electricity; and improved education and public health facilities. He was also concerned about the decline of the native Hawaiian population and of many aspects of Hawaiian culture, particularly ancient forms of dance and music. He wrote *Legends and Myths of Hawaii* (1888) and fostered among his people the appreciation and enjoyment of the culture of their ancestors.

Kalakaua was the first reigning monarch to travel around the world. The king first visited Japan, where he was a guest of the emperor and was treated with royal deference. In China, his next stop, it was a different story; he went ashore in Shanghai and Tientsin, where he was entertained by the viceroy, but he was not invited to Peking (Beijing). From then on, however, it was a grand tour: Hong Kong, Siam (Thailand), Singapore, Malacca, Penang, Burma (Myanmar), India, Egypt, Italy, England, Belgium, Germany, Austria, Spain, France, and home via the United States.

Everywhere the king and his small party were entertained by kings, queens, princes, and government officials. He sent home long reports on world conditions, new ideas, and possible sources of desperately needed labor for the rapidly expanding sugar plantations. He tried to provide leadership among the other Pacific islands, and he entered into tentative discussions of a matrimonial alliance between Japanese prince Komatsu and his niece, Princess Kaiulani. These projects did not come to fruition, but they illustrate Kalakaua's view of Hawaii's expanding role in the world.

Kalakaua built a new palace in Honolulu after the old palace was discovered to be riddled with termites. In August 1882 Kalakaua held his first formal entertainment in the new Iolani Palace. From then until his death and throughout the reign of Queen Liliuokalani, Iolani Palace was the formal residence of the king and queen of Hawaii and the focal point of the political and social life of the kingdom.

On 12 February 1883, the ninth anniversary of his succession to the Hawaiian throne, Kalakaua held his coronation. The ceremony was a combination of traditional Hawaiian symbolism and Christian ritual during which the king placed the jeweled crown of Hawaii on his own head and a smaller crown on Queen Kapiolani's. The festivities lasted for two weeks, with parades, fireworks, a traditional Hawaiian feast, formal European-style receptions, and gun salutes.

According to David G. Adee, an officer of the U.S. State Department, Kalakaua "usually appears at evening entertainments in the modest dress of our American president. His Majesty's dignity of deportment, however, and unstudied courtesy and graciousness of address sufficiently serve to designate him from the other gentlemen of the company, while his kingly stature and manly countenance recall to mind the traditional demeanor of the stately Hapsburg line . . . soldierly, knightly and princely King Kalakaua" (*Honolulu Daily Bulletin*, 14 Mar. 1884).

Kalakaua had to propitiate an increasingly restive foreign or first-generation Hawaiian-born business community. Also, some of the king's advisers were not wise, some of his financial transactions were not prudent, and his effort to increase his own power met strong opposition, particularly from businessmen of American extraction. In 1887, in response to what they considered political and economic excesses, Kalakaua was forced to accept a new cabinet, handpicked by the Reform party, and a new constitution under which the powers of the king were greatly diminished. He could not dismiss cabinet members without legislative approval; the House of Nobles, whose members were previously appointed for life, was henceforth to be elected; and the franchise was accorded to all male residents of Hawaiian, European, or American birth who could meet certain literacy and property qualifications. This last provision denied the vote to Asians, of whom there was a rapidly increasing number, particularly on the plantations. Also, the majority of the native Hawaiians, who had been accorded universal suffrage without educational or property qualifications by King Lunalilo's amendment to the constitution of 1874, were precipitately disenfranchised by the property requirement. Known as the "Bayonet Constitution" for the manner in which it was imposed on the king, it was a highly unpopular measure.

In 1899 Robert W. Wilcox, a part-Hawaiian activist, led a short-lived revolution to overthrow the 1887 Bayonet Constitution and restore the royal powers. Aware that Wilcox was a close adviser to his sister, Princess Liliuokalani, Kalakaua was wary of his motives. Kalakaua not only did not participate in the rebellion, but he authorized the landing of foreign sailors, this time from the only naval vessel in Honolulu harbor, the USS *Adams*.

In 1890 the Hawaiian economy was dealt a severe blow when the McKinley Tariff was passed by the U.S. Congress. Under this act all foreign sugars were allowed to enter the American market on an equal basis. Forced to compete, Hawaii's economy faltered and the plantations experienced a severe recession. At this juncture, discussion of annexation of the Hawaiian Islands to the United States was renewed among American businessmen of Hawaii, a proposal to which the king was adamantly opposed.

In addition to his political and economic problems, Kalakaua was not well. In November 1890 he boarded the USS *Charleston* for a trip to California to recoup his failing health. While at the Palace Hotel in San Francisco, Kalakaua died.

• The government documents pertaining to Kalakaua, both as king and during his many years of government service, are held in the Archives of Hawaii. William N. Armstrong published *Around the World with a King* (1904), and Kalakaua published *The Legends and Myths of Hawaii: The Fables and Folk-Lore of a Strange People*, ed. and with an introduction by Hon. R. M. Daggett (1888). Among the many histories of Kalakaua and his reign, the best is Ralph S. Kuykendall, *The Hawaiian Kingdom, 1874–1893: The Kalakaua Dynasty*, vol. 3 (1967). Many pictures of the king and his associates have been gathered by Kristin Zambucka in *Kalakaua, Hawaii's Last King* (1983).

RHODA E. A. HACKLER

KALB, Johann (19 June 1721–19 Aug. 1780), soldier of fortune and revolutionary general, was born in Hüttendorf, Bavaria, the son of Johann Leonhard Kalb and Margarethe Seitz, peasants. Covetous of adventure and glory, he left home at age sixteen with only a modest education. Little is known of Kalb in the next few years, but in 1743 he surfaced as Jean de Kalb, an officer in the Loewendal Regiment, a German contingent of the French army. Apparently he realized that a title was essential for military advancement and simply assumed one. Even more curious is the question as to how he learned English and French and took on the manners of the nobility. He must have had an ear for languages and natural graces. During the war of the Austrian succession, he participated in several sieges in Flanders while serving his regiment as a captain and *officer de detail*, a post unique to the eighteenth-century French army. His duties were largely administrative and were crucial to the regiment. He held this post until 1756, when he was promoted to major. The Seven Year's War (1756–1763) brought opportunity and distinction to Kalb. He served in Europe throughout the war under the command of the comte de Broglie. In 1760 the Loewendal Regiment was disbanded and divided into two German regiments, and Kalb was appointed assistant quartermaster general in the Army of the Upper Rhine, a staff position he held throughout the war. He was promoted to lieutenant colonel in May 1761 and was awarded the Order of Military Merit in 1763.

In 1764 Kalb resigned from the army. That year he married Anna Elizabeth Emilie van Robais, heiress to a cloth manufacturing fortune, and settled into the comparatively dull life of a country gentleman. At the time of the marriage Kalb was forty-three, and his bride was sixteen. Three children were born to what proved to be a happy union.

In 1767 Kalb undertook a secret mission to America at the request of the duc de Choiseul, minister of France. Embittered by the French defeat in the Seven Years' War, Choiseul noted the dissatisfaction of the British North American colonists and hoped to enlist them in a war of revenge against the British. He needed to gain intelligence as to the mood of the colonists and the size and disposition of British forces in America. Choiseul chose Kalb for this purpose because he spoke English and could move easily among British military and civilian officers. For four months in early 1768 Kalb traveled from the Carolinas to New England gathering information and establishing a coterie of future correspondents. He admired the Americans, who protested British taxation, and empathized with their views; however, he saw no disposition of the colonists to ally with a foreign power. He concluded prophetically, "All people here are imbued with such a spirit of independence and even license, that if all the provinces can be united under a common representation, an independent state will certainly come forth in time" (Zucker, p. 75). Kalb's full and impartial reports were apparently intercepted by the British; all did not reach France.

Upon his return to France, Kalb discovered that Choiseul had lost interest in the Americas. A period of inactivity ensued, broken finally by the accession of Louis XVI and the return to influence of the duc de Broglie, Kalb's former commander and patron. In November 1776 Kalb was appointed brigadier general of French colonial troops in anticipation of a war with Great Britain, but by then he had determined to participate in the war in North America. Promised appointment as a major general by the American agent Silas Deane Kalb, along with the marquis de Lafayette and several other ambitious Europeans, reached the South Carolina coast in June 1777. Kalb was dismayed to discover that the American Congress was prepared to commission the young and inexperienced Lafayette as major general but declined to honor Deane's agreement with him. He protested bitterly and threatened

civil suit. On 5 September 1777, shortly before he planned to return to France, Kalb was appointed major general, a post he accepted with some misgivings because of his previous treatment. In November 1777 he joined George Washington in Pennsylvania just in time to encamp at Valley Forge. He was second in command to Lafayette in the aborted invasion of Canada in 1778, yet distinguished service eluded him.

Kalb's ambitions were partially fulfilled in the Carolinas when the British undertook a southern campaign (1779–1781). Ordered to relieve besieged Charleston, he and his Delaware and Maryland Continentals arrived too late but remained in North Carolina to contest the British. He had few men, scant rations, and little local assistance. To his dismay, Congress superseded him by naming Horatio Gates to command in the South. Kalb acquiesced gracefully but urged caution when Gates proposed a forced march through barren country to intercept General Charles Cornwallis, who was moving northwestward from Charleston. His advice was ignored, and the battle of Camden (16 Aug. 1780) proved disastrous. However, at Camden Kalb achieved immortality. Positioned on the American right, he and his regulars were exposed when the militia forces under Gates on the left and center collapsed and fled. Surrounded by superior forces, Kalb resisted stubbornly and mounted three assaults in an attempt to break the British lines. He sustained eleven wounds and died at Camden, having earned the apotheosis he sought. To a British officer who consoled him in his last hours, Kalb said, "I thank you for your generous sympathy, but I die the death I always prayed for—the death of a soldier fighting for the rights of man" (Zucker, p. 227).

Kalb was tall, physically powerful, good natured, and shrewd. His contemporaries recognized his bravery and nobility of character. Even the discredited Gates held him in high esteem. On 3 September 1780 Gates wrote to General Washington, "Too much honor cannot be paid by Congress to the memory of the Baron de Kalb; he was everything an excellent officer should be, and in the cause of the United States he sacrificed his life" (Zucker, p. 228). Kalb had come to America as a mercenary, but he died firmly committed to American independence.

• For Kalb letters see Papers of the Continental Congress, vol. 164, National Archives; and Paul G. Sifton, ed., "La Caroline Méridional: . . . Two Unpublished Letters of Baron de Kalb," *South Carolina Historical Magazine* 66 (1965): 102–8. The fullest treatments of Kalb are Friedrich Kapp, *The Life of John Kalb*, trans. from German by Charles Goepp (1884); A. E. Zucker, *General de Kalb, Lafayette's Mentor* (1966); and Ludovic de Colleville, *Les missions secrètes du Général-Major Baron de Kalb et son rôle dans la guerre de l'indépendance Américaine* (1885). For a good, brief description of the battle of Camden see Christopher War, *The War of Revolution* (2 vols., 1952), and Robert Middlekauff, *The Glorious Cause* (1982).

MAX R. WILLIAMS

KALICH, Bertha (1872–18 Apr. 1939), actress, was born Beylke Kalakh in Lemberg, Galicia, the daughter of small brush makers whose Americanized names may be Solomon Kalich and Babette Halber. Kalich started her theatrical career at the age of thirteen, when she sang in the chorus of *La Traviata*, produced by the local Polish theatre. At age fourteen she began to train seriously, taking voice, music, acting, and declamation lessons. Soon she was acting in the local Yiddish theater, first with a supporting singing part in Goldfaden's popular operetta *Shulamis*. At seventeen Kalich ventured outside her home town, traveling first to Budapest, Hungary, where she sang at the Cabaret Imperial, and then to Bucharest, Rumania. Her great talent was quickly recognized, and she was invited to join the Rumanian National (or Imperial) Theatre, an unprecedented opportunity for a Jewish actress. According to the story, anti-Semitic members of the audience, who had initially planned to stone her with onions, were overwhelmed by her stage performance and instead showered her with flowers. Nevertheless, her position was precarious, and when she was invited to star in the budding Yiddish theater in the United States, she accepted. In 1896 Kalich sailed to New York with her young husband, Leopold Spachner, whom she had married around 1890 and with whom she would have two children. Kalich's first American appearance was in late 1896 at the Thalia Theatre in the Bowery in *De Vilde Keynigin* (The wild queen). Staying at the Thalia, she performed in both singing and dramatic roles, notably cast as the female leads in *Shulamis*, *Othello*, and *Romeo and Juliet*. A good indication of her success was the rapid increase in her salary. During her first New York season she earned $35 per week. A year later at the same theater she was paid $150 per week.

Some of Kalich's more memorable musical and dramatic parts at the Thalia Theatre were in *La Belle Helene*, *The Gypsy Baron*, *A Doll's House*, *Fedora*, *Madame Sans Gene*, *Magda*, and *Die Varheit*. Her greatest triumphs, however, were in plays written for her by Jacob Gordin, the greatest Yiddish playwright of the time. Two parts that established her position as a superstar of the Yiddish stage and eventually led to a spectacular career on the English-language stage were the leads in Gordin's *Sappho* and *The Kreutzer Sonata*, first produced during the 1900–1901 season. Following these two phenomenal successes, the critics began to compare Kalich to the great Sarah Bernhardt and Eleonora Duse. In 1905 the Windsor Theatre was renamed the Kalich Theatre in recognition of her theatrical contributions.

Kalich made her English-language debut on 3 September 1906 in Pittsburgh, in the title role in Sardou's *Fedora*. Harrison Grey Fiske, one of Broadway's major producers, attended the modest production. Impressed with Kalich's distinctive form, striking intensity, and exquisite voice, he offered her an excellent long-term contract. Kalich worked closely with Minnie Maddern Fiske, a major actress of the American stage, on the elimination of her foreign accent. Kalich opened on Broadway in Fiske's production of Maeterlinck's *Monna Vanna*, followed by *Therese Raquin* (1906) and *The Kreutzer Sonata* (1907); her acting was applauded by critics and audiences. After 1910 Kalich played for producer Lee Shubert. Additional celebrated roles on the English-language stage were in *Sappho and Phaon* (1912), *Rachel* (1913), and *Magda* (1926).

In 1915 Kalich resumed her Yiddish career, appearing with David Kessler at the opening of the Second Avenue Theatre in New York. A major triumph came in 1921 when she performed at the Irving Place Theatre in the drama *One of the People* by Rosa Shomer and Miriam Shomer-Zunser, a production that Kalich took on tour across the United States in 1922. Critic Nathaniel Buchwald noted that when Kalich returned to the New York Yiddish stage in the late 1920s, it was not an altogether fortunate homecoming. She was already in her fifties but refused to age on stage and continued to play young parts. Buchwald also noted that by that time her fiery and romantic style had become outdated, no longer appealing to the younger generation.

Kalich, who excelled as a tragedienne, became a tragic figure herself: she developed a malignant eye tumor that led to virtual blindness during the last decade of her life. She valiantly continued to make stage appearances in between treatments. In 1930 it was reported that her husband, a theatrical producer, spent the family's entire fortune in efforts to cure his wife, and on 18 January 1931 Kalich's friends and admirers from the American theater community organized a benefit performance for her at the Majestic Theatre in New York in which they raised $12,000 to cover medical expenses. At a similar benefit on 23 February 1933, the nearly blind actress performed "Heinrich Heine's Death," a poem by Louis Untermeyer. In 1934 Kalich appeared for the last time in a regular production as Sara in Goldfaden's *The Sacrifice of Isaac*. Her pathos and beautiful singing voice moved the audience to tears. Kalich appeared on stage for the last time at a Yiddish-language benefit performance in her honor at the Parkway Theatre in Brooklyn on 15 December 1938. Four months later she died in New York City.

All told, Kalich played some 125 roles in seven different languages, a testimony to a spectacular talent that knew no linguistic or territorial boundaries. Steeped in literature, art, and music, she earned renown as the greatest dramatic actress of the Yiddish stage in the United States. Kalich excelled in roles in which she played grand European ladies, well-bred women of culture and style whose emotional experiences were far removed from the lackluster drudgery of her audience's everyday life, roles she played in the heightened emotional manner of the nineteenth century romantic theater. During her heyday Kalich was often compared to a high priestess or a Greek goddess, and her voice was said to have the range and richness of a symphonic orchestra. Critic Sholem Perlmutter wrote about her, "For her the stage was a sacred place until her very last living moment, and acting . . . a God's prayer to which she devoted all her nerves and senses, regardless of how large or small her audience was" (*Lexicon*, p. 2455; trans. Edna Nahshon). Kalich was not the only Yiddish performer to find a second home on the English-language stage, but no other Yiddish actress achieved similar prominence.

• The most comprehensive source on Kalich is in Yiddish in the *Lexicon fun yidishn teater*, vol. 4 (1963). Also helpful is B. Goren, *Di geshikte fun yidishn teater* (1923), and Yosef Rumshinsky, *Klangen fun mayn lebn* (1944). Sources in English are Nahma Sandrow, *Vagabond Stars: A World History of Yiddish Theater* (1977), David S. Lifson, *The Yiddish Theatre in America* (1963), and Irving Howe, *World of Our Fathers* (1975).

EDNA NAHSHON

KALLEN, Horace Meyer (11 Aug. 1882–16 Feb. 1974), philosopher and educator, was born in Berenstadt, Germany, the son of Jacob David Kallen, a rabbi and Hebrew scholar, and Esther Rebecca Glazier. Born in Latvia, his father brought the family to the United States in 1888. Kallen grew up in Boston, attended public schools, then worked in settlement houses while he studied at Harvard University, graduating in 1903 with a B.A. As a young man he suffered anxieties of identity and loyalty typical of immigrant intellectuals caught between parental provincialism and modern cosmopolitanism. Kallen was ready to jettison his Jewish identity when his English professor Barrett Wendell's enthusiasm for the Old Testament and "the role of Hebraic tradition in the development of the American character" changed his mind. A subsequent meeting with Solomon Schechter, head of the Jewish Theological Seminary, made the Hebraic tradition "come alive" (Horace M. Kallen, "Interview with Milton Konvitz and Dorothy Oko," cited in Toll, fn. 12, p. 165). Following his return to Harvard to study philosophy after two years spent teaching and studying English literature at Princeton, Kallen helped found the Menorah Society (1906), the first collegiate organization devoted to revitalizing Jewish culture and overcoming a "shameful ignorance of things Jewish" among Jewish students (Higham, p. 204).

Kallen received his Ph.D. in philosophy in 1908 and stayed at Harvard as a lecturer and assistant to his mentor William James. He also taught logic at Clark College in 1910. In 1911 he accepted a position as lecturer in psychology and philosophy at the University of Wisconsin, but was forced to resign in 1918 after he defended the rights of pacifists in World War I. *The Structure of Lasting Peace* (1918) articulates his defense of difference, the right to hold unpopular views and to live as a minority. "An Irishman is always an Irishman, a Jew is always a Jew," he wrote. "Irishman or Jew is born; citizen, lawyer, or church-member is made" (p. 31). Later Kallen complained that Wisconsin had been culturally backward, pro-German, illiberal, and anti-Semitic.

Like other liberal professors forced to resign due to political pressures of World War I, Kallen came to New York City in 1918 and immediately joined the weekly planning sessions to create a new school of adult education that would encourage free intellectual inquiry. When the New School for Social Research opened its doors in 1919, Kallen made an intellectual home in its mixed liberal, radical, egalitarian educational atmosphere and later served as dean of the graduate faculty (1944–1946). One of the school's founders, Kallen remained associated with it even during an active retirement, first as research professor of social philosophy (1952–1969) and then as emeritus (1969–1974). His presence at the New School—along with Morris R. Cohen and Sidney Hook—helped to make pragmatism its unofficial philosophy. As a pragmatist, Kallen tested ideas by their consequences and believed in scientific method. His critique of Zionism when it became insular and parochial reflected this pragmatism, as did his consistent efforts to demonstrate the viability of ethnic loyalty and humane pluralism. His embrace of secularism, urbanity, cosmopolitanism, and democracy was shared by his New School colleagues. Such an environment also gave Kallen the freedom to be a Jew, in contrast to his experience at Harvard. He favored political and academic structures that encouraged dissent and tolerated a wide diversity of opinions.

Kallen wrote extensively, preferring the essay form. An early two-part essay, "Democracy vs. the Melting Pot: A Study of American Nationality" (*Nation*, 18 and 25 Feb. 1915) argued that democracy guarantees individuals cultural rights, including the right to maintain ethnic languages, traditions, religion, and identity. Attacking the melting pot concept of immigrant assimilation in his book *Culture and Democracy in the United States* (1924), in which "Democracy vs. the Melting Pot" was reprinted, Kallen proposed cultural pluralism. He often compared his vision of cultural pluralism to an orchestra, with each ethnic group playing its own instruments yet contributing to the American symphony. The goal in a federation of nationalities like the United States was harmony, not unison or conformity. "Democracy," he wrote, "involves not the elimination of differences but the perfection and conservation of differences" (p. 61). An avowed secularist, he also wished to free individuals from religious constraints. A late volume, *Secularism Is the Will of God* (1954), expressed his convictions. Kallen rejected Judaism in favor of the secular philosophies of Hebraism and Zionism. He supported the American Jewish Congress movement in 1915 as a cultural process designed to teach second-generation Jews a new democratic political style that challenged ethnic leadership by a self-appointed elite. He remained a leader of the revived American Jewish Congress (1922) and was a member of the executive board of the World Jewish Congress (1935). In 1926 Kallen had married Rachel Oatman Van Arsdale; they had two children.

Kallen's involvement with Zionism led him to an early interest in consumer cooperatives. He rejected theories of economic determinism and rugged individualism in favor of organizing society through separate congresses of consumer and producer cooperatives. Cooperation, as he wrote in *The Decline and Rise of the*

Consumer: A Philosophy of Consumer Cooperation (1936), implemented the expression of individual tastes. Kallen discussed the relation between aesthetics and freedom in his two-volume *Art and Freedom* (1942), writing that "art is a new use of nature, or of other art, which liberates the spirit." Without art, he thought, human freedom could not exist, for artfulness was the essence of "liberal humanism."

As an active educator who believed in bringing the fruits of scholarship to the people, Kallen participated in many educational ventures. He chaired the academic council of the YIVO Institute for Jewish Research, helped found the Conference on Jewish Relations (1933) to educate the public on the international threat of anti-Semitism, and served on the Presidential Commission on Higher Education. He willingly lectured to popular audiences, often speaking under the auspices of the American Association for Jewish Education.

After World War II his ideas, as reflected in the anthology *Cultural Pluralism and the American Idea* (1956), reached a broad new audience. In this book Kallen emphasized an almost religious faith in "the American Idea." Change also overtook his understanding of Zionism. In *Utopians at Bay* (1958), he expressed his disillusionment at the betrayal of Zionist ideas in the establishment of the state of Israel because of the focus on state building rather than on creating a cooperative commonwealth. He remained a vigorous intellectual until he died while vacationing in Palm Beach, Florida.

Though Kallen belongs to the interwar period when pragmatism dominated American philosophy, he is remembered as the father of cultural pluralism, a philosophy of ethnic differences in democracy. Despite its connections to the tensions of World War I, cultural pluralism's affirmation of spiritual differences continues to intrigue those educators who seek to accommodate diverse Americans in a common society.

• Kallen's papers are collected at the American Jewish Archives, though some may be found at the YIVO Institute for Jewish Research. He was a prolific author. His first book, *William James and Henri Bergson: A Study in Contrasting Theories of Life* (1914), pays homage to his mentor, while his second, *The Book of Job as a Greek Tragedy* (1918), presents Job as a modern account for all people, a drama of the human will against arbitrary authority. Other volumes include *Zionism and World Politics* (1924), *Education, the Machine and the Worker* (1925), *Why Religion* (1927), and *Frontiers of Hope* (1929). During the depression years he published a critique of Judaism, *Judaism at Bay: Essays Toward the Adjustment of Judaism to Modernity* (1933), as well as two discussions of American society, *Individualism: An American Way of Life* (1933) and *A Free Society* (1934). In the years after World War II, he returned to similar themes in *Americanism and Its Makers* (1945), *The Liberal Spirit* (1948), *The Education of Free Men* (1949), *Patterns of Progress* (1950), and *Democracy's True Religion* (1951). A festschrift in honor of his sixty-fifth birthday, *Freedom and Experience* (1947), contains essays by many liberal thinkers.

In contrast to his own prolific writings, there is relatively little written on Kallen. Milton R. Konvitz published a brief tribute in the *American Jewish Year Book* (1974–1975). A longer essay discussing both his biography and thought is William Toll, "Ethnicity and Freedom in the Philosophy of Horace M. Kallen," in *The Jews of North America*, ed. Moses Rischin (1987). Konvitz edited a collection of essays on aspects of Kallen's thought, *The Legacy of Horace Kallen* (1987). John Higham includes Kallen in his essay "Ethnic Pluralism in Modern American Thought," in *Send These to Me* (1975), and Suzanne Klingenstein devotes a chapter to him in her *Jews in the American Academy, 1900–1940: The Dynamics of Intellectual Assimilation* (1991). James H. Powell, "The Concept of Cultural Pluralism in American Social Thought, 1915–1965" (Ph.D. diss., Notre Dame, 1971), and Sarah L. Schmidt, *Horace M. Kallen: Prophet of American Zionism* (1995), focus on different aspects of his philosophy. Obituaries are in the *American Jewish Archives* 28 (Apr. 1976) and in the *New York Times*, 17 Feb. 1974.

DEBORAH DASH MOORE

KALLET, Arthur (15 Dec. 1902–24 Feb. 1972), engineer, labor activist, and founder of the Consumers Union, was born in Syracuse, New York, the son of Barnett Kallet and Etta Kaplan. Kallet received a B.S. from the Massachusetts Institute of Technology in 1924 and then accepted a position with the New York Edison Company performing editorial work. Three years later Kallet married Opal Boston, with whom he had one child. The marriage lasted until her death in 1952. He remarried in 1954, to Mary R. Fitzpatrick, with whom he had two children.

From 1927 until 1934 Kallet edited and wrote for *Industrial Standardization*, published by the American Standards Association (later the American National Standards Institute). During this period he also did publicity work for the New York Regional Plan Association, a newly created organization of urban planners. Attracted to ideas about scientific management and industrial efficiency studies advanced by social conservatives such as Herbert Hoover and Frederick Taylor, Kallet applied them to the Progressive vision of a regulated workplace for laborers and a more rational marketplace for consumers.

In 1929 Kallet joined the board of directors of Consumers' Research. There he combined with Frederick J. Schlink, then its technical director, to conduct the first published ratings of products for consumers. Schlink and Kallet had worked together at the American Standards Association. Consumers' Research "aspired to offer consumers the impartial services of an economist, a scientist, an accountant, and goodness knows what more." In 1933, together with Schlink, Kallet published a groundbreaking book on consumer protection, *100,000 Guinea Pigs: Dangers in Everyday Foods, Drugs and Cosmetics*, which chronicles the dangers inherent in many consumer goods. By using congressional interviews, public testimony, and files kept by the organization, the book discusses and criticizes products such as Bromo-Seltzer, Pepsodent, Kelloggs' All-Bran, Crisco, Listerine, and Fleischmann's Yeast. Kallet and Schlink demanded the mandatory disclosure of additives and ingredients because weak laws "left a hundred million Americans . . . as unwitting test animals in a gigantic experiment with poisons, conducted by food, drug, and cosmetic manufacturers."

The book spawned an entire genre of "guinea pig" literature, including such notable works as M. C. Phillips, *Skin Deep* (1934); James Rorty, *Our Master's Voice: Advertising* (1934); J. B. Matthews, *Guinea Pigs No More* (1935); and Rachel Palmer and Isadore Alpher, *40,000,000 Guinea Pig Children* (1937). Remaining on the bestseller list for two years, *100,000 Guinea Pigs* sold more than 250,000 copies and reinforced public support for new amendments to the Pure Food and Drug Law.

In 1935 Kallet left Consumers' Research after a labor dispute at the organization in which he sided with the strikers against Schlink. That year he also wrote *Counterfeit: Not Your Money but What It Buys* (1935), another effort to ridicule advertising and to uncover the "true facts" about consumer products otherwise concealed from the public. In 1936 he helped start a new organization, Consumers Union, and a new magazine, *Consumer Union Reports* (renamed *Consumer Reports* after World War II). The new venture was designed to advance both the consumer movement and the labor movement through objective reports about consumer goods and the working conditions under which they were made.

Kallet's distaste for most advertising, his enthusiasm for radical causes, his belief in social planning, and, in particular, his leadership role during the strike at Consumers' Research made him a target for antisubversive investigations by congressional un-American activities committees before and after the Second World War. Subpoenaed on several occasions to appear before committee panels in Washington and faced with the dilemma of testifying or being listed as a Communist, he testified that he was not and never had been one, although he said he had "signed up for this and that," explaining, "I had a curiosity." Kallet and Consumers Union survived a period of blacklisting, and *Consumer Reports* flourished.

Kallet's scientific training and creativity as executive director of Consumers Union had helped build the organization into an internationally respected leader of the consumer movement during its first twenty years. In 1957 he left Consumers Union and, together with Dr. Harold Aaron, founded the *Medical Letter*, a fortnightly, nonprofit publication that evaluated new drugs and therapies. In 1961 Kallet founded the Buyers Laboratory to test office equipment, machinery, and maintenance supplies for industry, schools, and other institutions. He died in New York City.

Kallet's unusual mix of strengths as an engineer, administrator, writer, and innovator helped to shape the activist perspective and articulated the philosophy of the consumer movement of the 1930s, 1940s, and 1950s. On one hand devoted genuinely to providing pragmatic, objective advice about the competitive marketplace and on the other hand committed to changing more profoundly the way Americans did their consuming, Kallet, like the consumer movement of that era, hardly could contain its contradictory elements.

• Some of Kallet's manuscripts and correspondence are located at the Consumers Union Archives in Yonkers, N.Y. For a historical account of the consumer movement, see Norman I. Silber, *Test and Protest: The Influence of Consumers Union* (1983). See also Colston E. Warne and Richard L. D. Morse, *The Consumer Movement* (1993), which contains lectures by Warne, the first president of Consumers Union. J. B. Matthews, *The Odyssey of a Fellow Traveler* (1938), discusses the strike at Consumers' Research. An obituary is in the *New York Times*, 26 Feb. 1972.

NORMAN I. SILBER

KALM, Peter (6 Mar. 1716–16 Nov. 1779), botanist, was born in the province of Ångermanland, Sweden, the posthumous son of Gabriel Kalm, a clergyman from Osterbotten, Finland, and Catherina Ross. (His name was actually Pehr Kalm, but his given name was anglicized in the American colonies and England.) He was educated at the Gymnasium at Vasa (or Vaasa) and in 1735 entered the Åbo Academy in Åbo, Sweden (later Turku, Finland). Although he studied theology at the academy, he was encouraged to pursue his interest in the natural sciences by Bishop Johan Brovallius, who influenced Baron Sten Carl Bjelke to support Kalm. Bjelke introduced his protégé to his rich library of natural history on his estate at Lofstad, and for the next seven years Kalm was the superintendent of Bjelke's experimental plantation.

At Bjelke's behest, Kalm went on botanical expeditions to southern Sweden and Finland. Bjelke was also responsible for introducing Kalm to the great taxonomist Carl von Linné, whose published work appeared under the Latin version of his name, Carolus Linnaeus. (Linnaeus's classifications of flora and fauna became the standard means of scientifically identifying and naming genera and species.) In 1740 Kalm entered Uppsala University to study with Linnaeus. Trained as a practical botanist, Kalm specialized in medicinal, dye-yielding, and poisonous plants and their beneficial or harmful effects. He also sought to find new, potentially useful plants and seeds, which he then grew and observed in Linnaeus's botanical garden in Uppsala. He was elected to the Swedish Academy of Sciences in 1745 and was granted the title of docent in natural history and economy (the equivalent of practical husbandry or agriculture) in 1746. In 1747 he was appointed the first professor of natural history and economy at the Åbo Academy, a position that he would retain until his death.

Almost immediately, however, Kalm was given leave to undertake a scientific expedition to North America sponsored by the Swedish Academy of Sciences. He was specifically charged with finding a species of mulberry that could survive in Sweden and provide a basis for an independent silk industry. In addition, he was expected to collect other plants and seeds of plants that could perhaps be grown in Sweden. Having spent several months in England en route to North America, Kalm, accompanied by a gardener,

Lars Jungström, landed in Philadelphia in September 1748. There he associated himself with Benjamin Franklin and two botanical correspondents of Linnaeus, John Bartram and Cadwallader Colden, both of whom were significant naturalists in their own right. In May 1749 Kalm embarked on a trip to New York, Albany, Lake Champlain, and Canada, seeking plants and seeds. After returning to Philadelphia in October, he again traveled to Canada in 1750. He provided one of the first descriptions of Niagara Falls in a letter to Franklin dated 2 September 1750, which was reprinted in Bartram's *Travels in Pensilvania and Canada* (1751; repr., 1966). Kalm resided for some time among the Swedish residents in Raccoon (now Swedesboro), New Jersey, and reported on the community's history and customs. In 1750 he married one of the residents, Anna Margaretha Sjöman, the widow of a pastor.

Kalm went back to Sweden in 1751, arriving in June. While he resumed his academic responsibilities, he tended to his American plants in his own garden in Åbo and prepared his American diary for publication. *En Resa til Norra America* (1753–1761), published in English as *Travels into North America* (1770–1771), is a wide-ranging account of the natural history, social conditions, politics, and history of colonial Pennsylvania, New Jersey, New York, and southern Canada. It was also translated into Dutch, German, and French. Although Kalm was not the first to publish a descriptive account of travels in eastern North America, he was the first professional scientist to gather data in the field in a systematic manner and the first to publish an extensive, genuinely scientific report of his observations. As he said in his letter to Franklin concerning Niagara Falls, "You must excuse me if you find in my account no extravagant wonders. I cannot make nature otherwise than I find it. I would rather it should be said of me in time to come, that I related things as they were."

Until 1778 Kalm also published numerous articles on his American travels in the transactions of the Swedish Academy of Science, seventeen in all. Although he largely failed to bring horticulturally and agriculturally significant plants to Sweden, Kalm did return with about ninety plants new to Europe. One of these, the mountain laurel, *Kalmia latifolia*, was named for him by Linnaeus. He died in Åbo, Sweden.

• Sets of Kalm's North American plants can be found in herbaria at the Linnaean Society of London and the Museum of Natural History at Uppsala. A modern edition of Kalm's book appears under the title *The America of 1750: Peter Kalm's Travels in North America* (2 vols., 1964) and includes a short biographical sketch. Kalm's contribution to North American botany is summarized in H. O. Juel and John W. Harshberger, "New Light on the Collection of North American Plants Made by Peter Kalm," *Proceedings of the Philadelphia Academy* 81 (1929): 297–303. Joseph Kastner, *World of Naturalists* (1978), includes a chapter describing Kalm's relationship to Linnaeus and his association with American natu-

ralists. Mardi Kerkkonen, *Peter Kalm's North American Journey: Its Ideological Background and Results* (1959), summarizes the importance of his trip.

RALPH L. LANGENHEIM, JR.

KALMAR, Bert (16 Feb. 1884–18 Sept. 1947), vaudeville entertainer, lyricist, and writer for the musical stage and films, was born in New York City. Nothing is known of his parents. Born into a poor community on the Lower East Side of Manhattan, as a child Kalmar became known as "the marvel of the neighborhood" for parlor stunts, hat juggling, and sleight-of-hand tricks. He ran away from home at the age of ten and entered the world of entertainment in tent shows, initially as a magician. Kalmar created and performed good-natured parodies of the popular songs of the day, the high point of many comic acts. His professional breakthrough occurred when he was hired by Mortimer Theise to imitate George M. Cohan in *Wine, Women and Song*. Kalmar quickly achieved recognition as both a comedian and a song-and-dance man on the Orpheum and Keith circuits and as a writer of vaudeville skits. Kalmar created "Nurseryland," the principal variety act of the team Kalmar and Brown, in partnership with Jessie Brown, whom he married (they had two children). The act's plot, gags, and songs (both lyrics and music) were written by Kalmar. Together the couple reportedly earned as much as $1,000 a week.

Forced to retire because of a knee injury sustained during a backstage accident in Washington, D.C., Kalmar formed with another vaudevillian, Harry Puck, the music publishing firm Kalmar and Puck, financed by his vaudeville earnings. At that time he began to concentrate his efforts on writing song lyrics. His earliest publication, "In the Land of Harmony" (music by Ted Snyder), dates from 1911. Kalmar soon teamed up with his own employee, accompanist Harry Ruby, to write songs, initially for singer Belle Baker. Their professional partnership, although not an exclusive one, lasted for more than three decades—from 1916 until Kalmer's death—and yielded a series of notable songs, written primarily after 1918 for the Broadway stage and after 1930 for the Hollywood screen. The prominent publishing house of Waterson, Berlin, and Snyder invited Kalmar and Ruby to join its staff. They were among the first Tin Pan Alley insiders to travel to California to work in the movie studios after the invention of "talkies." Their friendship with the Marx Brothers resulted in the use of Kalmar and Ruby songs in the film comedies *Animal Crackers* (1930), *Horse Feathers* (1932), and *Duck Soup* (1933), assuring the duo of certain immortality as contributors to American popular culture. Their last hit, "A Kiss to Build a Dream On" from the film *The Strip*, achieved popularity with the movie's release in 1951. Kalmar and Ruby's songwriting collaboration was the subject of the film biography *Three Little Words* (1950), starring Fred Astaire and Red Skelton. During the course of his long career Kalmar also provided lyrics for composers Irving Berlin, Oscar Hammerstein II, Jerome

Kern, Herbert Stothart, Harry Tierney, Harry Akst, Con Conrad, Edgar Leslie, Fred Ahlert, and Pete Wendling. He also wrote several screenplays, most notably *The Kid from Spain* (1932), *Bright Lights* (1935), *Horse Feathers*, *Duck Soup*, and *Look for the Silver Lining* (1949).

A number of the bestselling songs by Kalmar and Ruby acquired special distinction because of celebrated interpreters. On the vaudeville stage, "He Sits Around" (1916) became one of Belle Baker's signature songs, and "I'm a Vamp from East Broadway," with music by Irving Berlin, was a showstopper for Fanny Brice in the Ziegfeld *Follies* of 1920. On the New York stage, "My Sunny Tennessee" was popularized by Eddie Cantor in *The Midnight Rounders* (1921), and "I Wanna Be Loved by You" became closely identified with "boop-a-doop" girl Helen Kane in *Good Boy* (1928). Two of Kalmar and Ruby's most memorable and popular hits were generated by Fox film projects: "Three Little Words," which became a favorite of singer Rudy Vallee, was crooned by Bing Crosby to a background provided by Duke Ellington and His Orchestra in the Amos 'n' Andy feature *Check and Double Check* (1930); and "Nevertheless," from *I'm So Afraid of You* (1931), was recorded by both Crosby and Vallee. "Hooray for Captain Spaulding" from the 1928 stage production of *Animal Crackers* was later adopted by Groucho Marx as the theme for his radio and television shows. A revival of "Who's Sorry Now?" (1923), with lyrics by Kalmar and Ruby and music by Snyder, launched the career of singer Connie Francis in 1957. *The Kalmar and Ruby Song Book*, published by Random House in 1936, contains eleven songs and witty tributes to Kalmar and Ruby by luminaries such as Ben Hecht, Groucho Marx, Moss Hart, Irving Berlin, and Nunnally Johnson.

Broadway stage shows not already mentioned for which Kalmar contributed to the score include *Ladies First* (1918); *Broadway Brevities of 1920*; *Greenwich Village Follies of 1922*; Kalmar and Ruby's first full-length Broadway musical, *Helen of Troy, New York* (1923); *No Other Girl* (1924); *Puzzles of 1925*; *The Ramblers* (1926); *Twinkle, Twinkle* (1926); *The Five O'clock Girl* (1927); *Lucky* (1927); *Top Speed* (1929); and *High Kickers* (1941). His Hollywood musical credits not discussed earlier include *The Cuckoos* (1930); *Top Speed* (1930); *Hips Hips Hooray* (1934); *Kentucky Kernels* (1935); *Thanks a Million* (1935); and *Story of Vernon and Irene Castle* (1939).

It is clear from Kalmar's record of associations, opportunities, and achievements that he was a versatile, well-respected, and dedicated participant in the popular entertainment industry of his time. Remembered by his partner as a kind and gentle man, he was a facile writer and rhymester and a master of theatrical gags. Respecting the trends of the day, Kalmar worked with a variety of celebrated figures over a long career marked by collaborative efforts of both enduring value and passing interest. A life member of the American Society of Magicians, Kalmar maintained an interest in magic throughout his career. He was also an influ-

ential member of the American Society of Composers, Authors and Publishers (ASCAP) after 1920. He died in Los Angeles, California. Kalmar was posthumously inducted into the National Academy of Popular Music's Songwriters' Hall of Fame. An obituary in the *New York Times* identifies him as "one of the nation's foremost lyric writers" (19 Sept. 1947).

• Though there are no known repositories of Kalmar papers, Ruby collections are at the library of the University of Southern California, Los Angeles; the State Historical Society of Wisconsin, Madison; and the American Heritage Center, University of Wyoming, Laramie. Accounts of Kalmar's career are in "More or Less in the Spotlight: The Rise of Kalmar and Ruby," *New York Times*, 17 Oct. 1926; David Ewen, *All the Years of American Popular Music* (1977); Arnold Shaw, *The Jazz Age: Popular Music in the 1920s* (1987); Gerald Bordman, *American Musical Theatre: A Chronicle*, 2d ed. (1992); and Kurt Gänzl, *The Encyclopedia of the Musical Theatre* (2 vols., 1994). Kalmar's entry in the *ASCAP Biographical Dictionary*, 4th ed. (1980), with information presumably supplied by the subject, lists his principal songs and scores. A chronology of similar information appears in Roger D. Kinkle, *The Complete Encyclopedia of Popular Music and Jazz, 1900–1950* (1974). Twenty-nine songs by Kalmar are documented as standards in Nat Shapiro and Bruce Pollack, eds., *Popular Music, 1920–1979*, rev. ed. (1985). Philip Furia, *The Poets of Tin Pan Alley*, 2d ed. (1992), suggests the general importance of Kalmar's contributions but treats his work only in passing.

MICHAEL J. BUDDS

KALMUS, Herbert Thomas (9 Nov. 1881–11 July 1963), physicist and inventor, and **Natalie Mabelle Dunfee Kalmus** (1883–15 Nov. 1965), cinematographer, were born, respectively, in Chelsea, Massachusetts, and Norfolk, Virginia. Herbert was the son of Benjamin G. Kalmus and Ada Isabella Gurney, musicians. Natalie was the daughter of George Kayser Dunfee (wife's name unknown). Herbert attended schools in Boston and intended to become a concert pianist, but he gave up the idea when he injured his fingers playing baseball. He attended the Massachusetts Institute of Technology (MIT), where he received a B.S. in physics in 1904. He married Natalie in 1902; they had no children. When very young Natalie had moved with her parents to Boston. She attended Stetson University in Florida, the Boston School of Art, and the Curry School of Expressionism in Boston.

In 1904 Herbert became principal and part owner of the University School in San Francisco. Upon receiving a fellowship from MIT to study abroad in 1905, he went to the University of Berlin and the University of Zurich. Natalie studied art in Zurich. Herbert received a Ph.D. from the University of Zurich in 1906 with a dissertation titled "Electrical Conductivity and Viscosity of Some Fused Electrolytes."

In 1906 Kalmus became a research associate in physics at MIT, and from 1907 to 1910 he was an instructor there. From 1910 to 1912 he was an assistant professor of physics at Queens University (Kingston, Ontario, Canada) and advanced to professor of electrochemistry and metallurgy in 1915. He published articles on the destructive effect of electrical discharges on bacteria, the determination of electromotive forces in humans from emotions, and the nature of the metal cobalt. Separately he directed a Canadian government research laboratory from 1913 to 1915. He developed industrial uses for cobalt in the production of extremely durable abrasives, for which he obtained patents. In 1914 Kalmus set up a company, Exolon, to manufacture these abrasives; he served as vice president, then treasurer, and finally president during the years 1915 to 1925.

Simultaneously Kalmus formed a consulting firm in engineering in 1912 with Daniel Comstock, a former MIT classmate, and W. Burton Westcott, an expert in mechanical techniques. Around 1914 this firm was asked by William H. Coolidge of the U.S. Shoe Machinery Company to advise on a machine to remove the flicker in motion pictures. Kalmus suggested that a more useful machine would be one that could make motion pictures in color.

At the turn of the twentieth century, color motion pictures had sometimes been created by hand tinting the film frame by frame. In 1906 British film producer and promoter Charles Urban and inventor George Albert Smith developed Kinemacolor, in which process red and green filters were passed in front of the lens during photographing and again during projection. Color accuracy was imperfect because it was limited to two tones, and the process trailed behind objects in motion. Urban produced feature-length films of scenes in India and nature studies that were shown widely in the United States and Europe. His company and a British competitor, Bicolour, went out of business in 1914 when World War I began.

In 1915 Kalmus founded a corporation consisting of his consulting firm, Coolidge, and C. A. Hight, the president of the U.S. Smelting Company. The purpose of the firm was to develop and control a method of producing movies in color. Kalmus proposed the name based on his alma mater MIT: Technicolor Motion Picture Corporation. He became the corporation's president and general manager.

The company outfitted a laboratory in a railway car in Boston and at first used a new technique that involved color-sensitive emulsion and a prism that split the light beam as it entered the camera into two parts—red and green. The two bands of film were developed separately and printed; they were then passed through dyes and laminated together.

The railway car was moved to Jacksonville, Florida, where in 1917 the company produced *The Gulf Between*, the first feature motion picture in color. The process of filming was complex, and showing the film necessitated special attachments on the projector and additional light in the booth. Kalmus concluded that it required "an operator who was a cross between a college professor and an acrobat" (Kalmus, p. 107). Everything about the process was expensive, and the first investors withdrew. Kalmus found financial support of more than $1 million through an offering of stock

and through the assistance of William Travers Jerome, a former district attorney of New York City who drew in movie magnates Marcus Loew and Joseph Nicholas Schenck and other businessmen. Retaining a half interest himself, Kalmus employed an efficient group of engineers and photographic experimenters to improve the entire filming and developing process. In 1922 he founded Technicolor, Inc., under which the original company became a wholly owned subsidiary with Kalmus as president and general manager of both.

In 1922 the company produced *The Toll of the Sea*, and in the next few years Technicolor was used in some scenes of *The Ten Commandments*, *The Phantom of the Opera*, and *Ben Hur*. In 1926 the silent film *The Black Pirate*, made in Technicolor under a contract with Douglas Fairbanks, was a moderate box-office success, although it was imperfect in the color process. Kalmus moved his business to Hollywood, California, in 1927, and there produced *On with the Show* in 1929, the first talking movie in Technicolor.

Natalie Kalmus was the adviser on color. In 1921 the Kalmuses divorced secretly, but they continued to work together for many years. From 1928 she was employed by Technicolor and put in charge of all aspects of color in film production, including sets, lighting, actor makeup, and final editing. Her name appeared on Technicolor productions until 1948. The first woman cinematographer, she described her contribution as "playing ringmaster to the rainbow."

Demand for the new technique increased, but the colors were imperfect and the Technicolor laboratories could not always provide clear color prints in a timely manner. By the early 1930s Kalmus was experimenting with an improved process that added blue color. His engineers invented a three-strip camera, a new type of film, and a dye-transfer method for producing prints. This appealed to Walt Disney for his animated cartoons: his *Flowers and Trees* in 1932 was the first to use the three-color technique. Disney's cartoons *The Three Little Pigs* and *The Big Bad Wolf* followed in 1933 and 1934, and in 1933 came the short *La Cucaracha*, the first live-action film that used the three color components. Pioneer Pictures contracted for eight movies with Technicolor and in 1935 produced the first of them, *Becky Sharp*, an adaptation of William M. Thackeray's *Vanity Fair*. The quality of its color was excellent.

From then on, Kalmus's companies prospered, and the success of Technicolor was assured with the box-office receipts of *Snow White and the Seven Dwarfs* (Disney, 1937) and *Gone with the Wind* (Turner Entertainment Co., 1939). Kalmus received the Progress Award of the Society of Motion Picture Engineers in 1938. His only competition for color films was Cinecolor, which used a two-color process chiefly for shorts and westerns.

During World War II the activities of the companies were reduced by shortages of materials and personnel. Kalmus spent some time in the Office of Scientific Research and Development under Vannevar Bush, for which he received a citation in 1945. He was also on the Technical Advisory Committee of William Donovan of the Office of Strategic Services.

The Technicolor companies expanded after the war, when color films were the industry's answer to black-and-white television. Kalmus operated about thirty cameras in the United States and England, never selling any. His prices were high, and he was noted for maintaining control over his equipment, establishing the set lighting, and sometimes interfering with the script. His company joined with Eastman Kodak Company in research, and in 1947 the federal government brought suit against the two companies on the basis that they were monopolizing the industry. No final resolution was made. The Technicolor companies began using Kodak film in the 1960s.

In 1948 Natalie sued in California for half of her former husband's assets, and the next year in Massachusetts she attempted to have the 1921 divorce vacated. Both initiatives were unsuccessful, and Kalmus ended her association with his companies. For them Natalie had traveled a great deal in the United States and Europe to supervise staging and filming, to advise art directors and technicians, and to adjudicate contracts with the studios. She had lived in a separate apartment in the house in Los Angeles long after their unpublicized divorce. After the first lawsuit she moved to the East Coast. She died in Boston, Massachusetts.

In 1949 Kalmus married Eleanore King, a newspaper columnist; they had no children. After retiring from Technicolor in 1959, he enjoyed entertaining with private screenings of new films. Because he disliked publicity, he hired a press agent to keep his name out of the news. He was on the board of directors of the Stanford Research Institute from 1953 until his death. His inventive nature went into developing an ultraviolet lamp to treat tubercular growths and designing a galvanometer to measure stress in humans. He died in West Los Angeles, California.

• Herbert T. Kalmus summarized his company's early history in "Technicolor," *Tech Engineering News* 19 (1938): 107–9, 122. A detailed summary of both Kalmuses is by Jack J. Cardoso in the *Dictionary of American Biography*, supp. 7 (1981). Obituaries of Herbert are in *Physics Today* 16 (1963): 107, and the *New York Times*, 12 July 1963. An obituary of Natalie is in the *New York Times*, 18 Nov. 1965.

ELIZABETH NOBLE SHOR

KALTENBORN, H. V. (9 July 1878–14 June 1965), radio newscaster, was born Hans von Kaltenborn in Milwaukee, Wisconsin, the son of Rudolf von Kaltenborn, a former Hessian Guards officer from a noble German family who left Hesse in protest over its absorption into Germany by Prussia, and Betty Wessels. The family soon moved to the small town of Merrill, Wisconsin, where Rudolf opened a building supply business and where Hans grew up.

Kaltenborn ran away from home after one year at Merrill High School to work in a lumber camp but returned home to spend five years, from 1893 to 1898, working for his father for three dollars a week. In addition, he published articles in the *Merrill Advocate*. When the Spanish-American War erupted, Kaltenborn enlisted in Company F, Fourth Wisconsin Volunteer Infantry. He was nineteen at the time. Although his unit sat out the war in Alabama, never leaving the United States, Kaltenborn made good use of his time there by continuing his journalistic efforts, writing feature articles in both German and English about army camp life. After leaving active service, he returned to Merrill, where he served as city editor of the *Advocate* for a year.

By this time Kaltenborn had acquired a taste for travel that was to last a lifetime. Leaving Merrill, in 1900 he sailed to France where he spent two years learning about the country while supporting himself by selling stereoscopes. When he returned to the United States, he became a reporter for the *Brooklyn Eagle*, a larger and more prestigious newspaper than the *Merrill Advocate*. After three years working for the newspaper, Kaltenborn decided to remedy his lack of formal education and applied to Harvard. He passed the entrance exams after much independent study, although he was later only able to show his competence in algebra. He entered Harvard in 1905 at the age of twenty-seven.

Kaltenborn was an excellent and motivated student who was elected to Phi Beta Kappa and who graduated cum laude in 1909 despite interrupting his studies to act as secretary for a Harvard–Berlin exchange professor in Berlin in the academic year 1907–1908. Upon his graduation, the Astor family hired him as a tutor; he sailed with the Astors aboard their yacht the *Naurmahal* as it cruised the Caribbean. The ship lost contact with the United States for several days, and Kaltenborn was thought to be dead. The *Brooklyn Eagle* ran a laudatory obituary for him. After leaving the Astors and journeying to Berlin to marry Baroness Olga von Nordenflycht in 1910, Kaltenborn used the newspaper's professed high opinion of him to regain his old position there.

Kaltenborn remained at the *Brooklyn Eagle* until 1930 when other commitments made it impossible to continue. During that time, he and his wife had two children. In April 1922 he made his first appearance as a news analyst on the radio, beginning a 33-year career in that medium. Meanwhile, he acted as a foreign correspondent for the *Eagle* in Russia and the Far East in 1926–1927. In 1930 he joined CBS, then a new radio network.

As a radio analyst for CBS, Kaltenborn first covered the Republican and Democratic national conventions in 1932, a practice he continued until his retirement. He also commented on international events. In 1933 he broadcast news on the London Economic Conference and in 1936 on the Spanish Civil War. The latter attracted much attention since he was close enough to the front for battle sounds to be heard in his reports.

The high point of Kaltenborn's international broadcasting, according to his autobiography *Fifty Fabulous Years* (1950), was his coverage from Munich during the 1938 crisis. Kaltenborn never left his office for eighteen straight days, sleeping on a cot and subsisting on sandwiches and coffee. During that time, he made 102 broadcasts ranging in duration from two minutes to two hours.

These overseas broadcasts earned Kaltenborn considerable fame as well as criticism of such isolationist groups as America First. Kaltenborn, an avowed internationalist, was not a neutral observer. He did not spare his listeners his opinion, nor did he hesitate to make predictions. At the same time, he promoted radio broadcasting and helped found the Association of Radio News Analysts and the Radio Pioneers.

In 1940 Kaltenborn switched networks to NBC, for which he ranged widely during World War II, reporting from the British Isles, Italy, France, Germany, West Africa, Latin America, and the Southwest Pacific. Following the war, he returned to analysis of domestic politics. As he grew older, he became more opinionated and conservative, leaving himself open to attack as a reactionary by those on the left. He continued to make predictions and sometimes allowed his hopes to overpower his judgment. This wishful thinking led to his most famous gaffe. In the election of 1948, he predicted a Thomas Dewey victory; as returns showed Harry Truman leading, Kaltenborn clung stubbornly to his original prediction. His error made him the butt of Truman's jokes.

Kaltenborn's radio style, which was arrogant and opinionated, and the rise of television gradually diminished his popularity. When he retired in September 1955, his audience had shrunk. He died in New York City.

Kaltenborn is perhaps the leading figure in the first generation of radio commentators who made the transition from print journalism to broadcasting. His roots in the latter ran deep; he wrote seven books, most of which were descriptive of his work as a correspondent and newscaster. His two later books, *Fifty Fabulous Years* (1950) and *It Seems Like Yesterday* (1956), give a good sense of the confidence of the man.

• Biographical material on Kaltenborn is quite sparse. Kaltenborn himself wrote several books that appear on the surface to be autobiographical, including *Fifty Fabulous Years, 1900–1950: A Personal Review* (1950) and *It Seems Like Yesterday* (1956), which largely consist, however, of material drawn from his broadcasts interspersed with personal comments. In 1940 *Current Biography* and the *New Yorker*, 27 Apr., published profiles of him. For his later years, the best source is "The Reminiscences of H. V. Kaltenborn," interviews done in 1950 by Frank Ernest Hill for the Oral History Research Office of Columbia University, which the Microfilm Corporation of America made available on microfiche in 1972. An obituary is in the *New York Times*, 15 June 1965.

DWIGHT HOOVER

KAMEHAMEHA I (1758–5 May 1819), unifier of the Hawaiian Islands, was born in Kohala, Hawaii. His lineage is disputed, with three men listed as his possible father: Kalani-Kupu-A-Keoua, Keouakalani, and Kahekili, the king of Maui. Although Kekuiapoiwa was his mother, he probably was adopted at birth by Naeole, who is credited with caring for him during the first five years of his life. Shortly before the birth of Kamehameha, a comet had appeared in the sky in 1758, which was interpreted by the kahunas (priests) to mean that the mightiest ruler of Hawaii was about to be born. Seeing this as a threat to his power, King Alapai, uncle of Kekuiapoiwa, ordered that her child be killed at birth. For this reason she had entrusted her newborn son, Kamehameha, to chief Naeole, who, with his sister Kakunuialaimoku, raised Kamehameha in secret until Alapai relented and allowed the child to be brought back to court. Kamehameha, whose name means the Lonely One, was not in line to inherit the kingdom in Kohala. As Kamehameha was growing up, the islands were divided into four kingdoms, each ruled by an alii-aimoku (ruling chief). The most significant of these chiefs were Kalaniopuu, of Hawaii (the largest island in the Hawaiian chain), who was the uncle of Kamehameha; and Kahekili. Kamehameha grew up in the court of his uncle Kalaniopuu. When Kalaniopuu died in 1782, his power was divided between Kamehameha, who was given guardianship of the war god Kukailimoku, and Kalaniopuu's natural son Kiwalao, who inherited the kingship.

The relationship of Kamehameha and Kiwalao had been poisoned by a serious breech of decorum committed by Kamehameha, who had picked up the body of a slain rebel chief and presented it to the gods at the heiau (a religious temple) rather than allowing the honor to Kiwalao, who was politically his senior. After the death of Kalaniopuu, this breech culminated in a series of bloody civil wars, first on the island of Hawaii and then throughout the island chain. The civil wars originated in the customary redistribution of land that occurred after the death of an important ruler. Fearing an unfair division of the land, five chiefs in the Kona district on the island of Hawaii formed a cabal and invited Kamehameha to be their leader, precipitating the civil wars on that island. Through these wars Kamehameha rose to power. He defeated Kiwalao at the battle of Mokuohai, in which Kiwalao was killed; the island of Hawaii was divided into three kingdoms, with Kamehameha in control of Kohala, Kona, and Hamakua; soon he took overall control of the entire island.

During the ten years of war that followed, Kamehameha vanquished Keawemauhili of Puna; Keoua, brother of Kiwalao, of Kau; and Kahekili, king of the island of Maui. During the raid on Puna, Kamehameha, after attacking some unarmed fishermen, slipped and caught his foot in a crevice of lava. Seeing him fall, one of the fleeing fishermen boldly returned and beat him on the head with a canoe paddle until it broke. From this incident Kamehameha proclaimed the "Law of the Splintered Paddle," or Mamalahoe Kanawai, giving protection to unarmed noncombatants in war. "Let the aged, men and women, and little children lie down safely in the road," the law decreed.

Keawemauhili, the defeated king of Puna, now allied with Kamehameha, was slain by Keoua, who attacked him after Kamehameha had left Hawaii to invade Maui and Oahu. Keoua took advantage of Kamehameha's absence and attacked the Hilo district, ravaging the Waipio and Waimea regions. Returning, Kamehameha chased Keoua's forces back toward the Kau region past the volcano Kilauea, which erupted, destroying a third of Keoua's fleeing army (1790). This timely eruption was considered a sign that Pele, the fire goddess, sided with Kamehameha.

Keoua had not been killed by the volcano, however, and still controlled half of the island of Hawaii. Uncertain what his next step should be, Kamehameha consulted a famous oracle on the island of Kauai. The oracle told him that if he wished to conquer all the island of Hawaii he must construct an enormous heiau at Puukohola, Kawaihae. After building the heiau, Kamehameha invited Keoua to visit it in 1791. During his visit, Keoua was speared by Keeaumoku, one of Kamehameha's allies, and most of Keoua's chiefs and warriors also were killed and sacrificed at the heiau.

Having gained control of his homeland, the island of Hawaii, Kamehameha turned to the other islands. He planned another invasion of Maui to subdue Kahekili, who also controlled the islands of Molokai, Lanai, Oahu, and Kauai. In preparation for the invasion, Kamehameha purchased weapons from American and European ships trading with Hawaii. John Kendrick, captain of the American ship *Lady Washington*, sold guns and ammunition to Kamehameha, and two Englishmen, Isaac Davis and John Young, instructed him on how to use these weapons. Davis, who had arrived on the *Fair American*, barely escaped death when its crew was killed by Hawaiians retaliating for the Olowalu Massacre perpetrated by the captain of the *Eleanora*, who had fired on Hawaiians seeking to trade. The boatswain of the *Eleanora*, Young had been left behind when his ship fled the island.

Fortune again favored Kamehameha. In the summer of 1794 Kahekili died on Maui, and his domain was divided between his brother Kaeo Kaeokulani and his son Kalanikupule. Helped by the trading vessels *Jackall* and *Prince Lee Boo*, Kalanikupule's forces were victorious in the civil war after Kahekili's death. Viewing the war's destruction on Maui and Oahu, Kamehameha decided the time was opportune for an invasion. He raised an enormous fleet of war canoes, conquered Maui and Molokai, and turned on Oahu. His canoes landed at Waikiki, and his warriors pursued Kalanikupule's army up the Nuuanu Valley. During the final battle at Pali precipice, hundreds of defending warriors were killed, many being driven over the precipice and dashed to pieces on the rocks below. Having captured Oahu, Kamehameha planned an invasion of Kauai, but it was necessary for him first to crush a rebellion on the island of Hawaii in the autumn of 1796.

In 1804 a severe plague killed many of the former chiefs who had supported Kamehameha, and he himself barely survived the disease. When Kaumualii, the king of Kauai, tried to remain semiautonomous, Kamehameha between 1796 and 1809 planned a massive invasion of Kauai. With the help of many foreigners in his service, he constructed an enormous fleet (the *peleleu* fleet) of war canoes over several years, and Kaumualii, realizing he faced certain defeat, came to Honolulu in 1810 to pledge his loyalty. Kamehameha allowed him to remain governor of Kauai as long as he paid taxes and tribute.

Kamehameha promulgated laws common to all the newly unified islands in approximately 1810, the year the civil wars ended in Hawaii. Continuing the feudal system of landholding, Kamehameha redistributed the land to his loyal chiefs. They, in turn, divided their land into smaller parcels, which they gave to their retainers as a reward for their services. Trusted allies were given governorships on the various islands; Keeaumoku was made governor of Maui, and John Young for a time was the governor of the island of Hawaii. Kalanimoku, a young and reliable chief, was appointed prime minister and treasurer.

Moving quickly to restore the economy of the islands, long devastated by civil wars, Kamehameha first collected taxes in food and later in sandalwood. The sale of sandalwood proved an important source of revenue for him, and he cultivated the friendship of overseas traders interested in purchasing that wood. The seat of Kamehameha's power was Kailua-Kona, on the island of Hawaii.

When Kamehameha died, he had laid the foundation for a strong monarchical tradition. To the end he remained a believer in the Hawaiian gods, who had apparently supported his wars of unification. After his death, Kaahumanu, his favorite wife, who ruled with Kamehameha's son Kamehameha II, and Keopuolani, Kamehameha's highest-ranking widow, destroyed the kapu system of religious taboos and burned the heiaus. But the enduring legacy of Kamehameha the Great was the unification of the Hawaiian chain of islands, which remained independent, despite the threat of imperialism throughout the nineteenth century, until annexed by the United States in 1898.

• The best source is Gavan Daws, *The Shoal of Time: A History of the Hawaiian Islands* (1968); early Hawaiian scholar Samuel Kamakau, in *Ruling Chiefs of Hawaii* (repr. 1961), offers an authentic native Hawaiian view; Ralph Kuykendall, *Hawaiian Kingdom* (3 vols., 1938–1967), offers an additional excellent secondary perspective; Maude W. Makemson, "The Legend of Kokoiki and the Birthdate of Kamehameha I," *Hawaiian Historical Society Reports* 44 (1935): 44–50, resolves some significant questions about the proper date of Kamehameha's birth.

BARBARA BENNETT PETERSON

KAMEHAMEHA II (Nov. 1797–14 July 1824), second king in the Kamehameha line, was born Liholiho in Hilo, Hawaii, the son of Kamehameha the Great, king of the Hawaiian (or Sandwich) Islands, and Keopuolani, the king's highest-ranking wife. Liholiho was brought up in his father's court on the island of Hawaii. When the boy was five, his father declared him his successor, and from then on Liholiho was schooled in the traditional religious and political forms of Hawaiian rule. At nineteen he was described by several foreign visitors and sketched by Louis Choris, an artist aboard the Russian ship *Rurick*. Liholiho appears tall, corpulent, and highly tattooed.

In May 1819 Kamehameha I died. As tradition dictated, Liholiho went to the mountains during the mourning period so that he would not be contaminated by the death. On his return to his father's home in Kailua, Hawaii, he was met by the Council of Chiefs, who included his own mother and his father's favorite wife, Kaahumanu. As was their prerogative, they laid down the conditions under which the young man could succeed. Liholiho was to assume only his father's ceremonial role; the administrative power was to be vested in Kaahumanu and in the *kalaimoku*, or prime minister, the former king's chief adviser. Furthermore, the chiefs demanded security in the possession of their lands, which had traditionally been reallocated on the succession of a new chief, and an end to the king's monopoly on trade with the foreigners. In insisting on these conditions the chiefs asserted that they were carrying out the will of Kamehameha I, which may or may not have been accurate; but the chiefs were united, and Liholiho had to accept their dictates, which left him with little or no power.

Six months after Liholiho became Kamehameha II, in November 1819, the religious and secular laws and regulations, collectively called the *kapu* (taboo) system, were abolished. That momentous change did not come overnight but appears to have been the culmination of six months of discussion and intrigue among the chiefs and priests (*kahuna*) and probably many years of growing restiveness and dissatisfaction with the *kapu* system. The king is generally credited with the dissolution of the traditional laws, but he seems to have merely acquiesced, for he was without any governmental authority. Kamehameha II's concurrence appears to have been essential to the Hawaiian people and has been woven into history.

For the chiefs and the common people the abolition of the *kapu* meant a welcome relief from a whole set of confining rules, but it also meant bewilderment, because for some years nothing was put in the place of the *kapu* system. The Hawaiian people, formerly strictly governed by detailed rules and regulations with severe punishments for infractions, were suddenly cast adrift with no immediate controls over their behavior and no guides to their conduct.

During his brief reign, Liholiho carried out two efforts to complete negotiations initiated by his father with a view to ensuring the independence of the kingdom. The first took place in 1821 when he traveled to the island of Kauai, where he received the submission of its king. This action completed the unification of all the Hawaiian islands. At about that time the Reverend Charles Stewart, an American Protestant missionary, described Kamehameha II. "There is nothing particularly striking in his countenance, but his figure is noble, perhaps more so than that of any other chief; his manners polite and easy, and his whole deportment that of a gentleman" (Stewart, p. 108).

The other pending matter was with the British. In 1793 Captain George Vancouver of the Royal Navy had drawn up a deed of alliance with Kamehameha I aimed at protecting the Hawaiian kingdom from foreigners, but the agreement was never acknowledged by the British government. In November 1823 Liholiho sailed to England to endeavor to complete his father's negotiations with King George IV. He took with him on his voyage to England his favorite wife, Kamamalu. They reached Portsmouth in late May 1824 and traveled immediately to London, where although their arrival was completely unexpected, they were accorded respectful treatment by the British government. All arrangements were made for their comfort and entertainment. They were shown the sights of the city and taken to the Theatre Royal. Unfortunately, before Kamehameha II's scheduled audience with King George IV, both he and his queen caught measles, a disease to which, like many Polynesians, they had no immunity. On 8 July 1824 Queen Kamamalu died, and six days later the king passed away. Their bodies were placed in splendid coffins; put aboard the HMS *Blonde*, whose captain was the Right Honorable Lord Byron; and returned to their homeland, arriving in May 1825.

Liholiho reigned for only five years, during which time he never escaped the domination of the chiefs or of his stepmother, Kaahumanu. History has depicted him rather disparagingly in comparison with Kamehameha I, a strong leader, and Kamehameha III, his younger brother, who, during a long reign, developed into a wise and prudent ruler. In his negotiations with the kings of Kauai and England, Liholiho attempted to break out of the ceremonial role to which he had been relegated by the chiefs, but his best efforts were cut short by his early death.

• Ralph S. Kuykendall, *The Hawaiian Kingdom*, vol. 1, *1778–1854* (1968), chaps. 4–7, provides an overview and analysis of the life and times of Kamehameha II. A series of newspaper articles written in the 1860s and 1870s by the Hawaiian historian S. M. Kamakau gives an insight into the history of Kamehameha II from the Hawaiian point of view. The articles have been translated by Mary Kawena Pukui et al. and published in *Ruling Chiefs of Hawaii*, ed. Pukui and Martha W. Beckwith (1961). A description of Kamehameha II in 1816 and a portrait from life are in Otto Von Kotzebue, *A Voyage of Discovery in the South Seas and to the Behring's Straits, 1815–1818*, pt. 1 (1821). Other descriptions of Kamehameha II are, in 1815, Captain Peter Corney, *Early Voyages in the North Pacific, 1813–1818* (1896; repr. 1965), and, in 1823–1825, Charles Samuel Stewart, *Journal of a Residence in the Sandwich Islands* (1828; 3rd ed., 1830; repr. 1970).

RHODA E. A. HACKLER

KAMEHAMEHA III (17 Mar. 1813–15 Dec. 1854), third king in the Kamehameha line, was born Kauikeaouli at Keauhou, North Kona, the son of Kamehameha the Great, king of the Hawaiian (or Sandwich) Islands, and Keopuolani, the king's highest-ranking wife. He was the younger brother of Kamehameha II. Kauikeaouli received the traditional instruction and training of a Hawaiian chief, combined with Western education, which he received from the American Protestant missionaries who began to arrive in the islands in 1820. He was still a minor when his older brother, Kamehameha II, died in England in 1824, and he assumed the title of Kamehameha III in 1825.

For the first seven years of the reign of Kamehameha III, Kaahumanu, the prime minister who had dominated the Hawaiian government during Kamehameha II's entire reign, continued her rule. The young king was educated and allowed to carry out traditional Hawaiian ceremonial functions and to travel about the islands and meet the chiefs and people.

When Kaahumanu died in 1832 and Kamehameha III was finally able to take over the government, he was faced with the necessity of formulating new laws to replace the traditional legal and religious rules and regulations, the *kapu* (taboo), which had governed the Hawaiian people since their settlement on the islands over a thousand years earlier but had been abolished by Kamehameha II in 1819. A new code of behavior was vital not only to control the Hawaiian people and the many foreigners who had come to settle in the islands but to demonstrate to the world that the Hawaiian kingdom was a legally constituted and sovereign nation.

When the first new laws were promulgated, many of the chiefs and most of the resident foreigners, particularly the merchants and seamen, made it clear to the king and his advisers that they liked their present freedom and did not want to be bound by any new restrictions. Also, the *makaainana* (the people), who were beginning to absorb ideas of freedom and equality from the foreigners, were not anxious to return to the *kapu* system that had severely restricted their lives for so many years, even in a new guise.

The king, however, was persuaded by his advisers, both Hawaiian and foreign, that some laws were necessary, and by 1840 he had approved a succession of them. The first formal constitution of the Hawaiian kingdom was then written. The devising of this constitution had two objectives: to clarify the lines of authority within the kingdom among the king, the chiefs, and the people; and to set up the kingdom as a nation with a modern constitutional government that would be respected by the other nations of the world. This first Hawaiian constitution lasted for twelve years. Toward the end of his reign, in 1852, Kamehameha III signed a new constitution that was subsequently revised in 1864 and 1887.

Most foreign visitors to Hawaii in the late 1830s and the 1840s commented on the king's height, which at 5′7″ or 5′8″ was below average for a Hawaiian chief, and on his meticulous attention to dress. Dr. William S. W. Ruschenberger, who was in Honolulu in 1836, reported that the king

has recently come out of his minority, a stoutly limbed young man. . . . He is fond of athletic exercises, plays skillfully both at billiards and bowls; rides well, hunts well, and readily joins his lowest subjects in the severest toils. He is of a cold temperament and not easily excited; but whatever he undertakes, he executes with enthusiasm. . . . He was dressed in white drilling pantaloons, without suspenders, and a white jacket, wearing a neatly plaited parti-coloured straw hat, set knowingly on one side of his head. (Ruschenberger, vol. 2, pp. 327–28)

In the 1840s there hung over the kingdom the vexing problem of how to regulate the land. After the secular laws were set, the land question was partially adjusted by the *Mahele* of 1848, the great division of land between the king and chiefs. This issue was of great importance to the king. He personally conferred with each chief in turn, reached an agreement as to the proper allocation of all the lands in the islands, and oversaw that division as it was recorded on opposite pages of the *Mahele Book*, the king's portion listed on one page and the chief's on the opposite. Two years later provision was made for the king and the chiefs to give some portion of their lands to the *makaainana* and eventually to foreigners.

The 1840s were a period of foreign imperialism in the Pacific. The British took over New Zealand (they already had Australia), and the French took Tahiti and the Marquesas. The Hawaiian government was aware of these actions against other Polynesian kingdoms and was wisely apprehensive of foreign incursions. In 1842 French and British naval vessels visited Hawaii, demanding equal status for their nationals. The French insisted that French priests and French wine be allowed into Hawaii. The British wanted some questionable land claims by British subjects settled in their favor. On 10 February 1843 Lord Paulet of the Royal Navy sailed into Honolulu harbor and captured the town. During the weeks that followed, the king and his advisers conferred personally with Paulet and the acting British consul, Alexander Simpson, but the British were adamant in their demands. On 25 February 1843 the king was forced to sign a provisional cession of his kingdom to the British. Meanwhile, the king had sent protests to England and to Paulet's superior, Admiral Richard D. Thomas. Summoned by frantic appeals from the Hawaiian government, the admiral sailed from Valparaiso directly to Honolulu. He consulted with Kamehameha III and repudiated Lord Paulet, and on 31 July 1843, a day which is still remembered in Hawaii as a state holiday, the Hawaiian flag was raised, symbolizing the restoration of Hawaiian sovereignty. Years later Admiral Thomas, at the request of Kamehameha III, sent his portrait to Hawaii, where it still hangs in Iolani Palace. To forestall any more warlike incursions, the Hawaiian foreign minister then negotiated a series of treaties with Western nations in an effort to preserve the independence of the kingdom and to meet the demands of the foreigners.

Although Kamehameha III never espoused Christianity, in 1837, when he married Kalama, he was the first Hawaiian king to be wedded in a Christian ceremony. They had two children, but both died in infancy. Before the king died in Honolulu, in the thirtieth year of his reign, he designated as his successor his adopted son and nephew, Alexander Liholiho, who reigned as Kamehameha IV.

Kamehameha III lived in a more complicated world than had his predecessors. During his reign the government of the Hawaiian kingdom was established on a Western model. He gave his people a new set of laws and two constitutions, each one giving them a small additional measure of recognition and power. Kamehameha III also survived the onslaughts of foreign naval officers, and from foreign governments he gained recognition of the Hawaiian kingdom as an independent nation governed by modern laws and of himself as a respected constitutional monarch.

• Ralph S. Kuykendall in vol. 1 of *The Hawaiian Kingdom* (1968) provides a detailed account of the life and times of Kamehameha III. S. M. Kamakau, a Hawaiian historian writing for Hawaiian language newspapers in the 1860s and 1870s, gives valuable insight into the events of the king's reign in *Ruling Chiefs of Hawaii* (1992), which is a collection and translation of his newspaper articles. Descriptions of Kamehameha III are included in Charles S. Stewart, *A Visit to the South Seas . . . 1829 and 1830* (1831), in W. S. W. Ruschenberger, *Narrative of a Voyage Round the World during the years 1835, 36 and 37* (1838), and in Francis A. Olmsted, *Incidents of a Whaling Voyage* (1841).

RHODA E. A. HACKLER

KAMEHAMEHA IV (9 Feb. 1834–30 Nov. 1863), fourth king of the Hawaiian Islands in the Kamehameha line, was born Alexander Liholiho in Honolulu, Hawaii, the son of Mataio Kekuanaoa, the governor of Oahu, and Kinau, the second *kuhina nui* or prime minister of the kingdom. He was the grandson of Kamehameha the Great and the adopted son and heir of his uncle, King Kamehameha III.

Alexander was educated by American Protestant missionaries at the Hawaiian chiefs' children's or Royal School in Honolulu. When almost fifteen, Alexander and his eighteen-year-old brother Lot, who later succeeded him as King Kamehameha V, were taken out of school so they could expand their education through travel. They sailed to San Francisco in September 1849, then to the East Coast of the United States via Panama and Jamaica. After a short time in New York and Washington, D.C., they went on to Europe, where they visited a number of countries under the stern supervision of their guardian, Dr. Gerrit P. Judd. In May 1850 they left England for a more extensive visit to the United States, returning to Honolulu in September.

Back in Honolulu, King Kamehameha III appointed Alexander his heir and began his administrative education by giving him a position in his cabinet. The young prince settled down to train for his future royal role. He was intelligent and strong-willed, good at languages, and at ease in both Hawaiian and European society.

Alexander was about a month shy of his twenty-first birthday when, upon the death of Kamehameha III, he became king of the Hawaiian Islands on 11 January 1855. Charles de Varigny, the secretary of the French consulate in Honolulu (later minister of finance and foreign affairs in the Hawaiian government), described the young king at the time he came to the throne.

Like all the nobles he was tall, but obesity . . . did not disfigure his slender, athletic frame. His features were regular, his forehead high, his smile delightful. Lively, intelligent eyes lent brightness and animation to his very sympathetic facial expression. His manners were those of an English gentleman of aristocratic birth; he gladly adopted a similar style of grooming and dress. . . . His most prominent quality was his imagination: he caught on to an idea very quickly, but he was easily put off and discouraged, and his volatile imagination detracted from his ability and from his firmness in carrying out his plans. (Varigny, pp. 57–58)

In 1856 Kamehameha IV married Emma Rooke. They had one child who died at the age of four. Emma was a significant influence on her husband, and much has been made of their supposed pro-British leanings. She was both a Hawaiian chief, a great-grandniece of Kamehameha the Great, and part English, a granddaughter of John Young, that king's English adviser and companion. In infancy Emma was adopted by her aunt, Grace Kamaikui Young Rooke, whose husband was a British doctor, and the young girl grew up in a home where she was surrounded by English books, furnishings, and artifacts and was educated partially by an English governess.

The young king disliked the all too evident economic and political influences he saw exerted on his kingdom by its American residents because he feared that eventually the United States might take over his nation. He sought a balance of power and found it, he thought, in the British. In Hawaii, at the time, trade with England could not match that with the United States, but the young king strove to ally his monarchy in other ways with the powerful British empire. He corresponded with Queen Victoria; cultivated the British in the islands; attempted to blend elements of British civilization and usage, styles of dress, and manner of entertaining into the fabric of Hawaiian society; adopted British royal court ritual; patterned the lives of the Hawaiian royal family on what he knew of the conduct of the English royal family; and welcomed the Anglican church into the islands.

All these actions can be interpreted as pro-British, but they were probably more a wise apprehension of America's domineering attitude toward his country. During the reign of Kamehameha IV the people of Hawaii began to realize how closely they were bound to the economy of the United States and the consequent threat to their independence. Their king's solution was to advocate fewer and less confining political and economic ties with the United States and to promote those with Great Britain and other powers, but the nine years of his rule were not sufficient for him to achieve his goals. The problem of how to lessen Hawaiian dependence on the United States was not resolved by his successors either and, in 1898, resulted in the annexation of the kingdom to the United States.

Kamehameha IV and his wife dedicated themselves to the promotion of education and public health. Low birth rates and serious epidemics, prevalent since the arrival of foreigners in 1778, had decimated the native Hawaiian population. In his first message to the legislature as Kamehameha IV, in 1855, he laid out a plan for public hospitals to care for the sick and elderly of the islands. Throughout his short reign, however, the king was hampered with restraints put on his power to rule by the constitution of 1852, passed during the last days of his predecessor. In his first plea to the legislature he met with their refusal to act. The royal couple then took matters into their own hands and, going from business house to business house in downtown Honolulu, personally solicited funds for a new hospital in Honolulu that was designed primarily for Hawaiians. (The Queen's Hospital is still the major hospital in Honolulu, open to the sick of all races.) They also recognized the need for special care and quarantine for the victims of *mai pake* or leprosy, now known as Hansen's Disease, and provided a separate facility that later was moved to the island of Maui.

Kamehameha IV was also concerned about the education of all the children of the Hawaiian Islands. At his insistence the system of instruction in the schools of Hawaii was expanded so that every child had access not only to an elementary education in the Hawaiian language but also to higher education in Hawaiian and English.

Kamehameha IV died of complications of chronic asthma. His short reign was one of beginnings rather than conclusions. He understood the dire consequences of his country's too close political and economic ties to the United States and made an effort to mitigate the problem. He realized his people's need for more education and better health care and took steps to enhance the system of instruction and medical treatment. Because of his premature death, however, these issues were left to his successors.

• For a description of the life and reign of Kamehameha IV, the best source is Ralph S. Kuykendall, *The Hawaiian Kingdom*, vol. 2 (1966). Jacob Adler has edited *The Journal of Prince Alexander Liholiho* (1967). Laura Fish Judd alludes to Kamehameha IV as prince and king in *Honolulu, 1828–1861* (1861), and Charles de Varigny, *Fourteen Years in the Sandwich Islands, 1855–1868* (1981), discusses the king's reign with which he was intimately involved.

RHODA E. A. HACKLER

KAMEHAMEHA V (11 Dec. 1830–11 Dec. 1872), king of Hawaii, was born Lot, the third son of Kinau, a daughter of Kamehameha the Great, and Mataio Kekuanaoa. Kinau was the half sister of Kamehameha II (Liholiho) and Kamehameha III (Kauikeaouli). When the two children of Kamehameha III died in infancy, he adopted the children of Kinau as his heirs;

Kamehameha IV (Alexander Liholiho), Kinau's youngest son, ruled from 1855 until 1863 and was followed by his eldest surviving brother, Lot, who ruled as Kamehameha V. Lot was educated at court and at the Chief's Childrens' School, established by American missionaries for royal children, and was polished in manners and etiquette by Kalama, wife of Kamehameha III. In 1849–1850 Dr. Gerrit P. Judd, an American missionary who had become an adviser to the king, took Lot and his brother Alexander Liholiho on a tour of the United States and Europe. The entourage visited New York; Washington, D.C.; London; and Paris, and Lot became aware of the politics and diplomacy behind amicable foreign relations. Judd had been instructed by Kamehameha III to visit the United States, Britain, and France to demand protection for the independence of the islands.

Following the death of his brother Alexander Liholiho in 1863, Lot was named king by order of the cabinet, the privy council, and the *kuhina nui* (coruler or premier), Princess Victoria Kamamalu. Previously he had served as minister of interior and headed the finance department in his brother's government (1854–1863). As king, Kamehameha V selected ministers and court advisers that mirrored his opinions and policies, becoming "the last great chief of the olden type" (Kuykendall, p. 125). He ruled more forcefully than his brother but believed his policies more in keeping with the traditions of his grandfather Kamehameha the Great, whom he resembled both physically and spiritually. His firm grasp on the reigns of power was complemented by his concern for Hawaiians' welfare. When he was asked to sign a bill removing the ban on selling liquor to Hawaiian natives, he replied, "I will never sign the death warrant of my people," believing the bill was injurious to their health. Kamehameha V was deeply concerned about the decimation of the native Hawaiians and was determined to protect them. He encouraged immigration from other Pacific islands to repopulate the Hawaiian Islands, to supply labor for the developing plantations that contributed to the revenues of the monarchy, and to protect the islands from foreign annexation or domination by building up a strong indigenous population. Bolstering independence further, Kamehameha V, like his brother, encouraged a reciprocity treaty that would allow Hawaii and the United States to import each other's commodities free of duty so that both could prosper. Kamehameha V continued his brother's policy of seeking, through Robert C. Wyllie, Hawaii's minister of foreign affairs, a treaty guaranteeing Hawaii's sovereignty, but following Wyllie's death in 1865 this policy ended because Kamehameha V felt the islands could protect themselves under his leadership and diplomacy. However, a treaty between Hawaii and Japan, allowing trade, was signed in 1871 and was a measure of Hawaii's fierce desire under Kamehameha V's kingship to retain its economic integrity and independence. Fearing complete Westernization, Kamehameha V also worked to preserve Hawaiian culture and customs, a prospect that appeared to some of his Western advisers as unrefined, cantankerous, and even boorish.

Kamehameha V never married and was reputed to have been in love with Bernice Pauahi, who married Charles Reed Bishop, founder of Hawaii's first bank, Bishop and Co. (later First Hawaiian Bank), and also with the widowed Queen Emma, his deceased brother's wife.

When Kamehameha V became king, he viewed the constitution of 1852 as too restrictive of the king's powers and prerogatives. He refused to take an oath to uphold this constitution and promised to create a new one. He viewed universal manhood suffrage in elections for the house of representatives (as provided for in the 1852 constitution) as too liberal and too advanced. Kamehameha V desired to restrict the vote to those whose education and property qualified them, and this would eliminate most native Hawaiian voters. In the past, votes of native Hawaiians had been bought with gifts or promises of free liquor, and Kamehameha V believed this crude manipulation was unsafe, as too much democracy might lead to a republic and thence to annexation. Kamehameha V set about to draft a new constitution or to modify the constitution of 1852, cognizant that "Hawaii has scarcely emerged from a feudal state, and already the American influence pushes us toward a republic" (Kuykendall and Day, p. 112). Wyllie agreed with the king's posture on republicanism, writing it could be "less so, & still free" (Daws, p. 184). The king wanted restrictions placed on voters for the lower house of representatives, while keeping the legislative upper house, the nobles, and the cabinet appointive.

Kamehameha V issued a proclamation on 5 May 1864 calling for a constitutional convention of representatives elected by the people to meet and confer with the nobles and the king for the purpose of revising the existing constitution. The king's proclamation violated the 1852 constitution's amendment provisions. To offset criticism the King toured the islands, speaking on behalf of his proposal. When the constitutional convention met on 7 July 1864, most delegates opposed the king's plan. And the king's cabinet, Robert C. Wyllie, minister of foreign affairs; C. G. Hopkins, minister of the interior; Charles de Varigny, minister of finance; C. C. Harris, attorney general; and Elisha Allen, chancellor and chief justice, split over the issue whether to propose a new constitution or to simply amend the 1852 constitution. Kamehameha V decided to put forth a new constitution that introduced property qualifications and a literacy test for voters. The convention delegates rejected the restrictions on universal manhood suffrage, believing the king asked them to disfranchise themselves; the king believed unrestricted suffrage would destroy the power of the monarchy. Both sides held firm, and the king proclaimed: "As we do not agree it is useless to prolong the session, and . . . on the part of the Sovereignty of the Hawaiian Islands I make known today that the Constitution of 1852 is abrogated. I will give you a Constitution" (Kuykendall and Day, p. 113). Kamehameha V issued his new constitution 20 August 1864, which gave the king more power, abolished the position of the *kuhina nui*, and enfranchised literate resident males who possessed property valued at $150, paid lease-rent of $25 per year, or earned an annual income of $75. The king's prerogative was now felt everywhere in government, and Kamehameha V's 1864 constitution remained for twenty-three years.

Kamehameha IV had issued a proclamation of neutrality in 1861 toward the American Civil War, and Kamehameha V continued this policy. Taking advantage of the rise in sugar prices during the Civil War, he dispatched Elisha Allen to negotiate a reciprocity treaty with Washington, D.C. Although the U.S. government turned this offer down, warm relations were established between the two countries, and James McBride remained as an American minister resident in Honolulu. Kamehameha V's reciprocity idea received encouragement from General Edward M. McCook, who followed McBride as American minister to Hawaii. In 1867 McCook received instructions from Secretary of State William Seward to negotiate such a treaty. Under Kamehameha V's direction, a treaty agreement was worked out between McCook and C. C. Harris in May 1867. Kamehameha V's government affirmed the treaty, but in 1870 the U.S. Congress defeated it during acrimonious debates over Reconstruction.

Kamehameha V claimed to have sought both the constitutional changes and the reciprocity treaties to protect Hawaii and Hawaiians, viewing both measures as a means for self-strengthening politically, socially, and economically. Toward this same end, he attempted to diversify the Hawaiian economy, noting the inevitable end to the whaling era, and as a member of the Grazier's Association, promoting the cattle industry. In 1863 Kamehameha V constructed the Royal Mausoleum, the resting place for past rulers, and introduced Kamehameha Day, 11 June, as an annual celebration of ancient times when Kamehameha the Great had ruled Hawaii without foreign interference. He sold the island of Niihau to the Sinclair-Gay-Robinson family with the idea that the Hawaiian culture and language would be maintained there. He established Kalaupapa on Molokai as a segregated leper colony to protect uninfected native Hawaiians.

Failing health, diagnosed as an "internal abscess" or "fatty tissue around the heart," by 1872 forced Kamehameha V to offer the throne to Bernice Pauahi Bishop on his deathbed. She refused, however, saying the throne should pass to Princess Ruth, who like Kamehameha V sought to preserve native Hawaiian culture. Kamehameha V refused to name an heir, and following his death the kingship became elective. Kamehameha V ruled as a real king who stood up to growing American influence in the islands, refusing to be intimidated, and with a certain grace and dignity honored native culture and maintained independence.

• Kamehameha V's governmental papers are located in the Archives of Hawaii, Honolulu. Excellent general references that deal with Kamehameha V's kingship include Ralph S. Kuykendall, *The Hawaiian Kingdom*, vol. 2 (1966); Gavan Daws, *The Shoal of Time: A History of the Hawaiian Islands* (1968; repr. 1974); Helen Wong and Ann Rayson, *Hawaii's Royal History* (1987); and Kuykendall and A. Grove Day, *Hawaii: A History from Polynesian Kingdom to American State* (1948; rev. eds., 1961, 1976). Short biographies are found in Day, *History Makers of Hawaii* (1984), and Paul Bailey, *Those Kings and Queens of Old Hawaii* (1975). A description of Kamehameha V's final illness and death appear in the *Third Annual Report* of the Hawaiian Historical Society (1895), pp. 12–19.

BARBARA BENNETT PETERSON

KAMIAKIN (c. 1800–1877), war chief of the Shahaptian-speaking Yakima tribe, was born near Starbuck in present-day Washington State, the son of Si-Yi, a Palouse, and Kah Mash Ni, a Yakima. Around 1805 his mother fled the Palouse country with him and two younger sons after her husband decided to bring a new wife into his household. The refugees found a new home with Kah Mash Ni's family to the west in the Yakima Valley. Several circumstances accounted for Kamiakin's rise to leadership among the Yakimas and other Shahaptian tribes. His maternal grandfather belonged to the powerful Weowitch family, conferring upon Kamiakin credentials that eventually enabled him to usurp power from an uncle. His diplomacy and sense of fair play also drew others to him for counsel. Important also in his rise were his four marriages, the first to his niece San Chlow, daughter of Upper Yakima chief Teias, which gave him important social ties. Such connections subsequently helped him create local alliances to resist U.S. expansion into the Pacific Northwest.

Kamiakin spent much of his time in Medicine Valley and along Ahtanum Creek, a tributary of the Yakima River, on the present-day Yakima Reservation. He was possibly the first to introduce agriculture to his people by establishing a garden watershed along the creek, although this has been credited to the Roman Catholic priest Charles Pandosy, whom Kamiakin brought to the Yakimas. Nevertheless, Kamiakin was certainly enterprising: he purchased cattle from the Hudson's Bay Company at Fort Vancouver on the lower Columbia River and from immigrants in the Grande Ronde Valley of northeastern Oregon and at the Dalles of the Columbia; and the large band of horses he accumulated gave him wealth and influence, especially among the Yakimas.

After whites began settling in the Pacific Northwest in the 1840s, Kamiakin became increasingly concerned for the sovereignty of his people, a concern also articulated by Indian prophets. When neighboring Cayuses, irritated by the Immigrant Road (or Oregon Trail) traversing their lands, clashed with Oregon volunteer troops, however, Kamiakin offered the Cayuses no assistance. Nevertheless, Shahaptians soon joined with Salish speakers to the north to form a loose confederation under Kamiakin to prevent further settler encroachment. Aware that southwestern Oregon tribes were already at war with whites, warriors of a number of interior Sahaptin and Salish tribes assembled in the Grande Ronde Valley in the summer of 1854, seeking to bring western Washington tribes into their confederacy. Kamiakin emerged in a leadership role at this council.

Before the confederacy could formulate its plan of action, the U.S. government convened a meeting of local tribes near present-day Walla Walla to negotiate government purchase of their lands and the establishment of reservations. Despite their opposition to the treaty, the Indians were induced to sign it. Adding his signature on 9 June 1855, Kamiakin thus consented to confining Yakimas on a reservation in the Yakima Valley and in a much smaller area on the Wenatchee River to the north. He refused federal officials' offer of gifts. Reportedly biting his lip so hard that it drew blood during the signing of the treaty, Kamiakin later sought to persuade other tribesmen to join him in an attempt to undo the treaty. However, that fall the murder of Indian subagent A. J. Bolon precipitated the Yakimas into what became known as the Yakima War.

In September 1855 Kamiakin directed an unsuccessful skirmish against Washington territorial governor Isaac I. Stevens's party en route to a second Walla Walla treaty council. In October U.S. troops that had rushed into southern Yakima territory were defeated by Yakimas under Kamiakin's command on the Toppenish plain. Encouraged by his success, Kamiakin sent envoys westward across the Cascade Mountains to prevent troops from coastal areas from invading Yakima territory. In early November troops from the south headed toward Yakima country and defeated Kamiakin's warriors at the battle of Union Gap near present-day Yakima. Kamiakin fled to the east and in the winter of 1856 directed skirmishes against whites in the Walla Walla Valley. He also planned the battle of the Cascades of the Columbia River, an important communications center along the route of troops moving up the Columbia River into the interior. His forces were defeated, however, and two months later Colonel George Wright moved into Yakima country to suppress the volatile Yakimas.

Kamiakin then worked to consolidate Palouses, other Shahaptians, Cayuses, and Salish-speaking tribesmen, seeking victory in all-out combat against their foe. The coalition defeated Colonel Edward J. Steptoe in May 1858. Although it has not been established that Kamiakin was present at this battle, he did take part in the major engagement of the Yakima War along with other leaders of the Yakimas, Palouses, Spokanes, Coeur D'Alenes, and others against Wright at Four Lakes and Spokane Plains near present-day Spokane. Wright's troops used rifles superior to those used by Steptoe, however, and the Indians were soundly defeated. Having broken the resistance, Wright rounded up and executed the Indian leaders except for Kamiakin, who escaped to Canada.

After returning to Rock Lake, south of Spokane, in the lands of his Palouse father, in 1860 Kamiakin refused an offer of a $500 annuity to serve as Yakima chief. Kamiakin died at his home on Rock Lake a day after he was baptized a Catholic and given the name Matthew.

• For further information, see Robert Ignatius Burns, S.J., *The Jesuits and the Indian Wars of the Northwest* (1966); Click Relander, ed., *Treaty Centennial, 1855–1955: The Yakimas* (1955); Robert H. Ruby and John A. Brown, *Indians of the Pacific Northwest: A History* (1981); Helen H. Schuster, *The Yakimas* (1982); A. J. Splawn, *Ka-mi-akin*, 2d ed. (1944); Clifford E. Trafzer, *Yakima, Palouse, Cayuse, Umatilla, Walla Walla, and Wanapum Indians: An Historical Bibliography* (1992); and Trafzer and Richard D. Scheuerman, *Renegade Tribe: The Palouse Indians and the Invasion of the Inland Northwest* (1986).

ROBERT H. RUBY

KAMINSKA, Ida (4 Sept. 1899–21 May 1980), actress, director, and producer, was born in Odessa, Russia, the daughter of Avram Izhak (Abraham Isaac) Kaminski and Ester Rachel Halpern. Her father was an actor, director, and producer at the family's Yiddish theater in Warsaw, and her mother was a famous Yiddish actress known as "the Jewish Eleonora Duse." Ida Kaminska made her stage debut at the age of five in her father's production of David Pinski's *The Mother*. Thereafter, she performed regularly with her mother, playing children's roles in the plays of Abraham Goldfaden and Jacob Gordin. After graduating from the Gymnasium Francke in 1916, Kaminska applied for admission to university, but her success in a leading role in Goldfaden's historic operetta, *The Binding of Isaac*, led her to choose a theatrical career. By the time she was eighteen, her theatrical activities had broadened to include directing and translating plays.

From 1916 to 1921 Kaminska performed at the Kaminsky Theatre in Warsaw and toured dozens of towns and villages in czarist Russia. During this time she met and married Zygmunt Turkow, an actor with the company, and in 1919 she gave birth to a daughter, Ruth. In 1923 Kaminska and Turkow founded the Warsaw Yiddish Art Theatre (Varshaver Yiddisher Kunst Teater), which for eight years presented such works as Romain Rolland's *The Wolves*, a dramatization of Dostoevsky's *The Brothers Karamazov*, and Goldfaden's *The Tenth Commandment*. The troupe toured regularly to European cities such as Brussels and Paris. The couple divorced in 1931, and Kaminska organized her own theater ensemble. It included her second husband, Meir Melman, whom she married in 1936; they had one child.

In 1939, when the Germans invaded Poland and restrictions were imposed on the Yiddish theater, Kaminska and her family moved to Lvov in the western Ukraine, where she managed the Jewish State Theatre. In 1941 the advance of the Nazis forced her to flee to the Soviet Kirghiz Republic in Central Asia, where she appeared in Yiddish productions. In 1944 Kaminska and Melman went to Moscow, where they both broadcast radio propaganda for the Polish Patriots Organization.

In 1946 Kaminska and her family returned to Warsaw. The Jewish community had been reduced to a tiny fraction of its prewar numbers, but Kaminska and Melman commenced to reestablish a Yiddish theater, in part as a monument to the victims of the Holocaust. In 1949 the Polish government designated Kaminska's theater the Jewish State Theater of Poland and subsidized it. For the next twenty-one years, under the Communist regime in Poland, Kaminska remained apolitical and dedicated her life to her work in the theater. In addition to the staples of Yiddish drama, its repertory included works by Ibsen, Brecht, Miller, Dürrenmatt, and Chayefsky. Kaminska taught Yiddish to a generation of young actors and actresses, adapted scores of Jewish stories, and translated many contemporary plays into Yiddish.

Kaminska's rise to international stature came with her role in a Czechoslovakian film, *The Shop on Main Street* (1965), directed by Jan Kadar. Her performance—as an aged and widowed Jewish shopkeeper whose store was being appropriated by the Nazis—won her an award from the Cannes Film Festival in 1965 and a nomination for the best actress award from the Academy of Motion Picture Arts and Sciences in 1966. Her triumph in the film established her reputation outside the Yiddish-speaking world and helped to persuade the Polish authorities to grant expenses for an eight-week engagement in New York for the actress and her troupe. On 19 October 1967 the Jewish State Theatre made its first appearance in the United States at the Billy Rose Theatre, performing Gordin's *Mirele Efros* and Kaminska's own Yiddish translation of Brecht's *Mother Courage and Her Children*. In both productions Kaminska played the title roles. Her distinct stage personality impressed critics; a writer for the *New York Times* (1980) later observed, "She did not thunder in the declamatory tradition so often associated with Yiddish drama. She often spoke in a firm voice, very low, so low as to make the audience lean forward in unaccustomed silence to catch the power of her words. . . . She could wheedle and coax on stage with a charm that attested to a rare stage presence."

One year after her American debut, in the wake of the 1967 Arab-Israeli war that kindled an anti-Zionist campaign in Poland, Kaminska decided to make her home in New York. She also spent time in Israel, where she and her second husband tried unsuccessfully to establish a Yiddish repertory theater. During the late 1960s and 1970s she presided over a Yiddish theater workshop in Queens and appeared in several stage productions with her family, including her own version of *The Trees Die Standing*, by Alejandro Casona. In 1970 she costarred with Harry Belafonte and Zero Mostel in a film, *The Angel Levine*, again directed by Jan Kadar, who had also emigrated.

Kaminska was honored by tributes presented at Madison Square Garden and at Queens College; in 1969 she received a citation from the National Council on Jewish Audio-Visual Materials for her contribution to Yiddish language and theater. She wrote two original plays—*Once There Was a King* (1928) and *Close the Bunkers* (1964)—and an autobiography, *My Life, My Theatre* (1973). One month before her death, she appeared in a production of Peter Weiss's *The Investigation*.

• The most comprehensive account of Ida Kaminska's career is found in her autobiography. Other valuable sources include Adolf Rudnicki, *Théâtre, théâtre!* (1989), and William Berkowitz, *Conversations with . . .* (1975). Additional information is in the *New York Times*, 24 Sept. 1961, and the *New York Post*, 7 Dec. 1968. An obituary is in the *New York Times*, 22 May 1980.

LORIEN A. CORBELLETTI

KANDER, Lizzie Black (28 May 1858–24 July 1940), settlement founder and cookbook author, was born in Milwaukee, Wisconsin, the daughter of John Black, an owner of a dry goods store, and Mary Pereles, a native of Austria. Lizzie was raised within a Jewish Reform tradition of service to the poor. She graduated from Milwaukee High School in 1878 and married Simon Kander, a clothing salesman, on 17 May 1881. The couple had no children.

Strong family ties combined with her personal conviction that women who had economic means should not be idle led Lizzie Kander to take up social service work. She joined the newly formed Ladies Relief Sewing Society in 1879 and was assigned to the South Side Truancy Committee. She helped society members gather up cast-off clothing, then washed and mended it for needy families, mainly Orthodox Jewish immigrants from Russia who were arriving in large numbers. Like other Jewish residents of Milwaukee, most of whom were German, Kander worried that the poverty of the Russian Jewish newcomers might create anti-Semitic feelings.

Underlying all of Kander's work was her belief that a woman was the center of the family. Although she felt it her duty to rescue immigrants from poverty and introduce them to American ways, she strove to do so without undermining poor women's roles within their own homes. Realizing that poor women might have to work outside the home, Kander stressed that they be trained in the domestic arts of sewing and cooking to prepare them for work in garment and food-processing factories. In turn these jobs, she argued, would reinforce their homemaking responsibilities.

During her term as president of the society in 1894–1895, Kander began to realize that the best way to help needy immigrants was to establish a personal relationship between individual volunteers and poor families. A closer relationship, she concluded, would enable immigrants to learn English more easily, become more accustomed to American practices, and assimilate into the culture more readily. Her efforts to bring people together resulted in her establishment of the Keep Clean Mission in 1895. Operating the mission from a small room at the back of a synagogue, volunteers conducted weekly lectures on cleanliness and education for the children of immigrants. The didactic classes failed to impress the children, and in 1896 the mission was renamed the Milwaukee Jewish Mission. The organization now offered classes in cooking, sewing, and industrial education along with job training to help immigrants gain the necessary skills to work their way out of poverty.

In 1900 Kander helped merge the mission with a similar agency, the Sisterhood of Personal Service, to establish Milwaukee's first settlement house, called simply "The Settlement." An able leader and organizer, Kander attracted both financial and volunteer support from Milwaukee's Federated Jewish Charities, community leaders, businesses, and teachers. During her tenure as president from 1900 to 1918, educational programs expanded to include night classes in English and history for adults, music and literary clubs, a lending library, a savings bank, instruction in Hebrew and manual training, public baths, and a gymnasium. By emphasizing the common Jewish heritage of both workers and immigrants, the Settlement encouraged a community spirit that bridged nationalities and classes.

In keeping with her sentiment that a woman's ultimate career was in the home, Kander taught cooking and sewing classes at the Settlement. The only school outside New York City to keep a kosher kitchen for Orthodox Jewish students, the Settlement prepared food that was simple, nutritious, and American. The students, mainly of high school age, spent hours copying recipes for use at home. Recognizing that it would be more efficient to provide printed recipes, Kander appealed unsuccessfully to the Settlement's board for $18 to print a cookbook. With the help of other women, she solicited advertising to partially defray the costs and found a printer who offered his services gratis. *The Settlement Cook Book: The Way to a Man's Heart* was published in 1901. The collection consisted of nearly two hundred pages divided into two sections, one with simple classroom recipes and another with heirloom recipes. Copies were distributed to students and also sold locally for fifty cents a copy. The first one thousand copies were either distributed or sold by 1903. Eventually more than two million copies were sold. From 1914 until her death, Kander edited and revised editions of the cookbook, adding new recipes from around the world. Profits enabled the cookbook committee to purchase land to build a new settlement house. Subsequent proceeds from Kander's Settlement Cook Book Company helped to fund the new Settlement, which was built in 1911 and renamed the Abraham Lincoln House and later the Jewish Community Center in 1931. Kander died in Milwaukee.

Kander's strength and abilities earned her the nickname "the Jane Addams of Milwaukee." She is remembered not only for her cookbook and settlement work but for her far-reaching service to the community. A member of the Milwaukee Board of Education from 1907 to 1919, she worked to keep young girls away from prostitution by advocating the establishment of the Girls' Trade School in 1909. She crusaded for better housing, cleaner streets, and playgrounds and utilized her growing influence to improve the lives of the needy. Cognizant of women's important role in the family and community, Lizzie Kander dedicated her life to ensuring that women made the most of their abilities in the modern world.

• Some of Kander's papers and correspondence are located at the State Historical Society of Wisconsin, Madison, and the University of Wisconsin–Milwaukee Library Area Research Center. Papers on the Settlement and *The Settlement Cook Book* are in the Wisconsin Jewish Archives at the State Historical Society of Wisconsin. Biographical material is in Ann Shirley Waligorski, "Social Action and Women: The Experience of Lizzie Black Kander" (M.A. thesis, Univ. of Wisconsin–Madison, 1969); David Paul Thelan, *The New Citizenship: Origins of Progressivism in Wisconsin, 1885–1900* (1972); Victoria Brown, *Uncommon Lives of Common Women: The Missing Half of Wisconsin History* (1975); and Charles Pierce, ed., *The New Settlement Cookbook* (1991). See also the *Milwaukee Sentinel*, 12 May 1901; the *Milwaukee Free Press*, 27 Nov. 1910; and the *New York Times*, 5 Sept. 1965. Obituaries are in the *New York Times*, 26 July 1940; the *Milwaukee Journal*, 24 and 26 July 1940; and the *Milwaukee Jewish Chronicle*, 26 July 1940.

MARILYN ELIZABETH PERRY

KANE, Elisha Kent (3 Feb. 1820–16 Feb. 1857), physician and Arctic explorer, was born in Philadelphia, Pennsylvania, the son of John Kintzing Kane, a federal judge, and Jane Duval Leiper. The Kane family was prominent in Philadelphia and Washington, D.C., through Judge Kane's association with President Andrew Jackson. Elisha's younger brother Thomas Leiper Kane would become a general in the Union army and a hero in Mormon history. As a boy, Kane had a strong interest in natural sciences. While a teenager, rheumatic fever seriously damaged his heart. After a long convalescence, Kane expected to live for only a short time, but his father suggested that he "die in the harness" rather than spend his life moping in despondency. Young Kane embarked on a life of adventure.

Overcoming his ill health, Kane obtained a medical degree from the University of Pennsylvania in 1842. His research thesis, "Experiments on Keisteine with Remarks on its Application to the Diagnosis of Pregnancy" (published in *American Journal of Medical Sciences*, n.s., 4 [1842]: 13–37), was a remarkable pioneering study about using urine samples to determine pregnancy and became the leading research study in the field during the next two decades.

The Kane family believed that Elisha could not endure the rigors of a normal medical practice, so Judge Kane secured his appointment as surgeon in the U.S. Navy. In 1844, while awaiting his commission, he joined Caleb Cushing on the first U.S. diplomatic mission to China. During his time in the Far East, he initiated bold adventures, including a descent into a Philippine volcano. In 1846 he officially began his naval duties with a cruise to Africa.

When Kane returned home in 1847, during the Mexican War, President James Polk sent him as a special courier to General Winfield Scott in Mexico City. Polk suspected Scott of insubordination and ordered Kane to cross enemy-infested territory to deliver his dispatch. Traveling with an allied group of Mexican partisans, Kane fought a bloody battle with the Mexican army. After the battle, the partisans seriously wounded Kane when he prevented their slaughter of the captured Mexican general Antonio Gaona. Kane's original mission proved futile because the president had already removed Scott from command. Kane's wounds left him near death, but General Gaona and his family nursed Kane back to health. Kane returned home as a war hero.

In 1850, after naval duty in the Mediterranean and South America, Kane joined an American expedition to search for the lost British explorer Sir John Franklin. The Franklin expedition had entered the Canadian Arctic in 1845 with two ships and 129 men, seeking the Northwest Passage, and had vanished in the Arctic. British, French, and American groups mounted an international rescue mission to find the missing explorers. Whaling magnate Henry Grinnell donated two ships for the American expedition while the U.S. Navy furnished personnel and supplies.

Lieutenant Edwin De Haven commanded the brig *Advance*, with Kane as surgeon and official historian. The *Advance* and a sister ship joined forces with the rescue fleet in Lancaster Sound, north of Hudson Bay. Kane quickly impressed British explorers with his intelligence and traveling experience. In August 1850 the fleet located Franklin's first winter base on Beechey Island, along with the graves of three of Franklin's men. Further searches by the *Advance* failed to locate Franklin's expedition. The *Advance* returned to the United States in September 1851.

Kane's belief that Franklin might have gone further north persuaded Grinnell and the U.S. Navy to support a second expedition to search for the lost explorers. Kane led this new expedition in the *Advance* to seek a more northerly route near Greenland. During the preparations for the voyage, 32-year-old Kane fell in love with a teenaged spiritualist, Margaret Fox. Margaret and her sister were the famous "spirit rapping" team that performed seances for mid-nineteenth-century celebrities. Both the Kane and the Fox families opposed the relationship between the socially prominent physician and the scandalous girl who supposedly communicated with the dead. Before departing on his polar expedition, Kane and his aunt placed Margaret in a private home for tutoring. When he returned from his expedition, Kane believed that Margaret would complete her transformation into a socially accomplished young lady.

Kane's expedition departed in 1853, traveling northward along the Greenland coast. As the ship entered Smith Sound, the channel separating Greenland from Ellesmere Island, Canada, heavy ice stopped its progress. Rather than retreat to the south, Kane elected to keep his ship in Smith Sound. The ice soon froze around the ship, trapping Kane and his men in the high Arctic for the winter. When spring arrived, Kane sent exploring parties to the north along Smith Sound. One of his men, William Morton, discovered a broad expanse of open water, which he thought was an ocean. Morton's report led Kane to the erroneous conclusion that there was an open polar sea. Kane did chart many new discoveries in what later became known as "the American route to the pole."

The 1854 summer thaw failed to release the ship from the ice. Some of Kane's men, fearing that they would not survive another winter in the Arctic, demanded to go south to reach the Greenland settlements. Kane, unable to quell the mutiny, refused to abandon the ship and his sick men. The dissenters, who included Isaac Hayes, then insisted that Kane supply food and equipment for their escape. Kane reluctantly complied.

Kane and his remaining men faced a second bleak winter in the Arctic. While strong men wilted, Kane, the invalid, became a pillar of strength. The innovative doctor traded with the local Inuit for food. He also used the bountiful supply of the ship's rats for food and as a remedy for scurvy. When Kane learned that the deserters were starving, he sent them food and assisted their return to the ship.

During the summer of 1855 Kane successfully led his men south to the Greenland settlements. He quickly became the United States' first Arctic hero. Reports to Congress and lectures seriously disrupted Kane's happy reunion with Fox. His parents continued to oppose the marriage of their son to the notorious spirit rapper. Seeking to become financially independent from his family, Kane labored to complete his book. He juggled a few brief interludes with Fox while struggling against publication deadlines.

From across the Atlantic, Franklin's wife implored Kane to come to England to organize a new search for her husband. The British government and the prestigious Royal Geographical Society also wished to honor the American hero. In October 1856 Kane reluctantly sailed to England, where his health rapidly deteriorated. Seeking a warmer climate, Kane sailed to Havana, Cuba, in December 1856, but his physical condition worsened. Kane died in Havana. Margaret Fox never obtained a widow's share of his estate. When Kane's remains arrived in the United States, thousands gathered in each city, from New Orleans to Philadelphia, to express their grief. In American history, only the funeral processions of Abraham Lincoln and Robert Kennedy have approached the public tribute given to America's first Arctic hero.

During his short life, Kane experienced travel and adventures that rivaled Marco Polo. His extensive travels on five continents yielded major contributions to medical research, Arctic exploration, and international understanding. He inspired and blazed the trail for future American explorers such as Charles Hall, General A. W. Greely, Admiral Robert Peary, and Dr. Frederick Cook. Even more remarkable was the high esteem he earned from the people and nations around the world.

• Kane's original expedition journal is at the Stanford University Library, and part of the ship's log is at the Pennsylvania Historical Society. His account of his first polar trip was *The U.S. Grinnell Expedition in Search of Sir John Franklin* (1853). His book about his second expedition was *Arctic Ex-*plorations: The Second Grinnell Expedition in Search of Sir John Franklin, 1853, '54, '55 (1856). He also published articles in journals of the American Geographical Society, American Philosophical Society, and other institutions. The Smithsonian Institution published scientific results from his astronomical, magnetic, meteorological, and tidal observations. Other accounts of his second expedition include Isaac I. Hayes, *An Arctic Boat Journey in the Autumn of 1854* (1860); William C. Godfrey, *Narrative of the Last Grinnell Arctic Exploring Expedition in Search of Sir John Franklin, 1853–4–5, with a Biography of Dr. Elisha Kent Kane, from the Cradle to the Grave* (1857); and Oscar M. Villarejo, *Dr. Kane's Voyage to the Polar Lands* (1965). Biographies include William Elder, *Biography of Elisha Kent Kane* (1858); Samuel M. Smucker, *The Life of Dr. Elisha Kent Kane, and of Other Distinguished American Explorers* (1858); Jeannette Mirsky, *Elisha Kent Kane and the Seafaring Frontier* (1954); and George W. Corner, *Dr. Kane of the Arctic Seas* (1972). Margaret Fox wrote *The Love Life of Dr. Kane* (1866). Jay Walz and Audrey Walz wrote a well-researched novel about the Kane-Fox romance, *The Undiscovered Country* (1958).

TED HECKATHORN

KANE, John Kintzing (16 May 1795–21 Feb. 1858), jurist, was born in Albany, New York, the son of Elisha Kane, a merchant, and Alida Van Rensselaer. The Kane family removed to Philadelphia in 1801, following the death of Mrs. Kane, and in 1807 Elisha Kane married Elizabeth Kintzing of Philadelphia. A fondness for his father's bride, and a desire to distinguish himself from several cousins bearing the same name, prompted John Kane to adopt his stepmother's maiden name as part of his own.

Kane received his early education at boarding schools outside Philadelphia. In October 1809 he traveled to New Haven to prepare for admission to Yale College, which he entered the following year. Graduating from college in 1814, Kane returned to Philadelphia. Resolute from childhood to practice law, he entered the law office of Joseph Hopkinson as a student in the spring of 1815. On 8 April 1817 Kane was admitted to the bar and commenced practicing in Philadelphia. In April 1819 he married the elegant Jane Duval Leiper of Philadelphia; among their seven children was the celebrated Arctic explorer, Elisha Kent Kane.

Kane campaigned for the Pennsylvania legislature in 1824 and took his seat as a Federalist. He returned to Philadelphia the following year, however, devoting much of his time to the Chesapeake and Delaware Canal Company as attorney and board member. As a Federalist representative in the party's final days, he was a Democrat in all but name. Put off by what he considered to be John Quincy Adams's "ancient apostacy, and the libels under which he sought to mask it" (Autobiography, p. 22), he supported Andrew Jackson for president in 1828. By raising money, coordinating meetings, and writing the nationally circulated *Candid View of the Presidential Question*, Kane helped secure the General's election. He later wrote in support of Jackson's position against the Second Bank of the United States, creating enmity between himself and fellow Philadelphian and Bank president, Nicholas Biddle.

During the elections of 1828 Kane contributed to the successful campaign of Philadelphia's Democratic mayoral candidate. For his efforts he was named solicitor of the city, a position he held until 1830. Kane resumed the office in January 1832, only to resign in July of that year when President Jackson appointed him to a commission on spoliation claims established pursuant to the 1831 Convention of Indemnity with France. In 1836 he published the substance of the Commission's work in *Notes on Some of the Questions Decided by the Board of Commissioners under the Convention with France, on 4th July, 1831.*

The commission concluded its work in 1836, and Kane returned to Philadelphia. Having inherited a considerable estate, however, he was willing to devote only as much time to his practice as his many social endeavors would allow. Kane was involved principally with the Presbyterian Church, serving as a board member of the denomination's General Assembly. In 1837 he and other Old School board members severed ties that existed with the New School synods from the Great Awakening (the pervasive evangelical, revivalist movement), thus dividing the denomination. Presiding over the board of trustees of Philadelphia's Second Presbyterian Church, Kane, who had an interest in architectural design, involved himself with nearly every facet of operation in the erection of that facility.

Kane also devoted his time to the American Philosophical Society, which he joined in 1825, serving as secretary from 1828 to 1848, vice president from 1849 to 1857, and president from 1857 until his death. Kane involved himself as well with the Musical Fund Society, a philanthropic organization that he cofounded in 1820 to raise money through public concerts. Additionally, he served on the board of the Academy of Fine Arts, as vice president of the Institution for the Instruction of the Blind, as a trustee of Girard College, and as vice provost for the Law Academy of Philadelphia.

Kane remained a key figure in politics, and in December 1838 he helped lead the Democratic effort to unseat two illegally elected Whig state senators, a political struggle known as the Buckshot War. He labored in the state and national elections of 1844 as well, writing pamphlets, delivering speeches, and organizing the Democratic party in Pennsylvania. For his contributions to a successful gubernatorial campaign, Kane was appointed Attorney General of Pennsylvania in January 1845. He held the position until June 1846, when President James K. Polk appointed him to a judgeship on the United States District Court for the Eastern District of Pennsylvania, an office he held for the remainder of his life.

Like other facets of his career, Kane's judicial tenure was not without controversy. One Philadelphian noted he had been "unscrupulous as a politician, and was a demagogue even on the bench." In 1856 in his most controversial action, Judge Kane sentenced a Philadelphia Quaker to jail for refusing to produce for the court a fugitive female slave and her two children.

The ordeal exacerbated the volatile controversy surrounding the Fugitive Slave Act.

Although not broadly published, Kane wrote on various subjects and, by his own admission, "in almost every assignable degree of ignorance." *A Discourse Pronounced Before the Law Academy of Philadelphia* (1831) and *Autobiography of the Honorable John K. Kane* (1949) are his most notable works. The latter is a privately published edition of Kane's manuscript "Myself from 1795–1849," which he wrote for his family. In addition to his political writings and reports, Kane wrote bulletins for several organizations, compiled reports on transportation and manufactures, and edited a psalm book and medical treatise. Additionally, he served as a newspaper editor, bringing, in his words, "the Philadelphia Gazette from its ancient Federal repose to be the active supporter on Jackson's first election" (*Autobiography*, p. 67).

Kane is best remembered as a federal judge, but his most influential role was that of political strategist and writer. It was this office that won him the confidence, respect, and gratitude of two presidents and a host of Pennsylvania officeholders, but it also earned him a reputation as a ruthless politician. He was remembered by some as a man of "ability, acuteness, some learning, [and] plausibility, but . . . without moral principle." His political machinations notwithstanding, Kane's abiding commitment to the public welfare moved him to labor diligently on behalf of the Presbyterian Church, the blind, and for the furtherance of science, the arts, and education. He died in Philadelphia.

• The correspondence of John Kintzing Kane is gathered at the Historical Society of Pennsylvania. Select correspondence is reprinted in Wayne Cutler, ed., *Correspondence of James K. Polk*, vol. 7 (1989), and vol. 8 (1993). A useful biographical sketch appears in Franklin B. Dexter, *Biographical Sketches of the Graduates of Yale College* (1912). Other sources are J. T. Scharff and Thompson Westcott, *History of Philadelphia*, vols. 1 and 2 (1884); E. P. Oberholtzer, *Philadelphia, A History of the City and Its People*, vols. 2 and 3 (n.d.); J. H. Martin, *Martin's Bench and Bar of Philadelphia* (1883); Henry Simpson, *The Lives of Eminent Philadelphians* (1859); Nathaniel Burt, *The Perennial Philadelphians, The Anatomy of the American Aristocracy* (1963; repr., 1975); Nicholas B. Wainwright, ed., *A Philadelphia Perspective: The Diary of Sidney George Fisher Covering the Years 1834–1871* (1967); John S. Bassett, ed., *Correspondence of Andrew Jackson*, vol. 6 (1933); *Proceedings of the American Philosophical Society*, vol. 6 (1859); and L. V. Briggs, *Genealogies of the Different Families Bearing the Name of Kent* (1898). Articles include Ralph L. Eckert, "Antislavery Martyrdom: The Ordeal of Passmore Williamson," *Pennsylvania Magazine of History and Biography*, 100 (Oct. 1976); Julius Yanuck, "The Force Act in Pennsylvania," *Pennsylvania Magazine of History and Biography*, 92 (July 1968). Obituaries are in the Philadelphia *Daily News* and the *Philadelphian*, both 23 Feb. 1858.

KEVIN R. CHANEY

KANE, Thomas Leiper (27 Jan. 1822–26 Dec. 1883), lawyer, soldier, philanthropist, entrepreneur, and defender of the Mormons, was born in Philadelphia, the son of John Kintzing Kane, a jurist, and Jane Duval Leiper. He attended school in Philadelphia and from 1839 to 1844 traveled in England and France, studying and visiting relatives. While in Paris he served for a time as an attaché of the American legation. Small in stature and never robust, he would spend most of his life struggling with ill health. In Paris he met Auguste Comte and others who surely encouraged his social conscience, which would be manifested later in his concern for philanthropic causes. In 1844 Kane returned to Philadelphia, where he studied law with his father. Although he was admitted to the bar in 1846 and clerked briefly for his father, who was a federal judge, his interests and activities generally moved in other directions.

One of Kane's most important associations began in 1846 when he read Philadelphia newspaper accounts of the forced exodus of members of the Church of Jesus Christ of Latter-day Saints (commonly called Mormons) across Iowa from their Illinois homes. Kane sought out local Mormon leaders, learned more of their western hegira, and—after obtaining letters of introduction to Brigham Young—headed west to the Mormon encampments on the Missouri River near present-day Omaha, Nebraska. Moved by earlier Mormon requests for federal aid, Kane's father used his influence to obtain help for the Mormons from the Polk administration, which came in the form of government assistance (advance pay and equipment) in return for Mormon men enlisting to fight for the United States in the Mexican War. Kane himself delivered the president's instructions to the military officials at Fort Leavenworth and then helped to recruit the individuals who would eventually make up the Mormon Battalion. He assisted the Mormons in getting a post office established for their settlements, and in 1848, in tribute to his work on their behalf, they named their main settlement on the east side of the Missouri River, located within Iowa Territory, Kanesville (which was changed in 1853 to Council Bluffs).

Kane, who was made a U.S. district commissioner for the eastern district of Pennsylvania, remained a powerful advocate for social justice. An active supporter of the abolitionist cause, he was appointed chairman of the Pennsylvania Free Soil State Central Committee in 1848. In 1849 he advised Brigham Young to apply for statehood for Utah (proposed as "Deseret") rather than for territorial status, but Utah's future became caught up in the Compromise of 1850 and entered the Union as a territory. In March 1850 Kane, although very ill, delivered an address to the Historical Society of Pennsylvania titled "The Mormons." In printed form it was widely distributed and helped to modify public opinion about the Latter-day Saints. Kane's close friendship with newspapermen like Horace Greeley also helped in shaping more positive public perceptions of the Mormons.

In 1850 Kane resigned as a U.S. district commissioner in protest of the Fugitive Slave Law. His father ordered him jailed for contempt of court, but he was soon released by a Supreme Court ruling. He joined the Free Soil Movement in the 1850s and worked with the underground railroad. Despite his departure from public office, he maintained an influential presence in the U.S. government; when President Millard Fillmore was being politically attacked in 1851 for his policies toward the Mormons, Kane wrote several important letters to Fillmore supporting the Mormons.

In the winter of 1852–1853 Kane traveled to the West Indies to observe the progress of slave emancipation there. Returning to Pennsylvania in April, he married his sixteen-year-old second cousin Elizabeth Dennistoun Wood, who later attended the Women's Medical College of Philadelphia and became a doctor (graduating in 1883). They had four children.

In 1854 Kane rejected Brigham Young's offer to be the territorial delegate in the U.S. Congress from Utah. A grave crisis arose in 1857–1858, however, and he again went west to assist Young. President James Buchanan, acting on various reports claiming various kinds of illegal behavior by the Mormons and their leaders, had dispatched a federal military expedition to Utah and appointed a new governor to replace Young. Kane, who managed to moderate Buchanan's views, obtained presidential support for an unofficial attempt at peace-making, helped soften Mormon defensiveness, won the confidence of the new governor, Alfred Cumming, and thus helped to bring a peaceful end to a potentially bloody confrontation. His personal travel to Utah, and then to the winter encampment of the army in Wyoming, and his moderating approach to all major parties revealed his communication skills at their best.

When the Civil War began in 1861, Kane organized a volunteer regiment, the 13th Pennsylvania Reserves (also known as the Kane Rifles or "Bucktails"), for the Union army. Commissioned a lieutenant colonel in June 1861, Kane took part in engagements in mid-December at Dranesville, Virginia, and then at Harrisonburg in the Shenandoah Valley, after which he was taken prisoner in June 1862. Released a short time later as part of a prisoner exchange, he fought at Chancellorsville in May 1863 and at Gettysburg in July 1863. He authored in 1862 a military manual, "Instructions for Skirmishers," which he planned to be the first volume of a series on tactics. But wounds and continued ill health led to his resignation in November 1863; before the end of the war in 1865, he was brevetted a major general for his gallantry at Gettysburg.

Following the Civil War, Kane returned to his involvement in the McKean and Elk Land Improvement Company, of which he was a principal organizer. As early as 1856 he had been involved in land development in western Pennsylvania, especially in the area around the town of Kane. Now he opened roads, encouraged railroad construction, and worked to generally improve the area. Kane also remained active in public life. He was the first president of the Pennsylvania Board of State Charities, was a member of the American Philosophical Society, and was an organizer of the New York, Lake Erie, and Western Coal Railroad Company. He was also the moving force for the building of what was once considered the largest railroad bridge in the world, the 2,053-foot Kinzua viaduct that spans the 301-foot-deep Kinzua Creek Valley near the town of Kane.

In 1869 Kane lobbied the Grant administration unsuccessfully for appointment as governor of the Utah Territory, even though the president spent part of that summer as a guest at Kane's house. Still a close friend of Brigham Young, Kane took his family to southern Utah for a sojourn during the winter of 1872–1873. Elizabeth Kane's account of this journey, *Twelve Mormon Homes Visited in Succession on a Journey through Utah to Arizona* (1874), remains a classic description of Mormon social and religious history. At the time of the family's visit, Kane and Young discussed expanding Mormon settlements into Mexico, a project that both actively pursued: Kane by trying to get a Mexican land grant and Young by dispatching a Mormon colony into Arizona. Kane's pamphlet *Coahuila*, concerning the Mexican province of that name, was a byproduct of these efforts. He continued to encourage Mormon expansion in the West. Kane also provided direction for the preparation of Young's will and counseled him to separate his personal property from that of the church. In addition, Kane helped Young in the founding of several colleges in Utah: Brigham Young College in Logan, Young University in Salt Lake City, and—the only one to survive—the Brigham Young Academy in Provo (now Brigham Young University). In spite of his close association with the Mormons, Kane never joined the LDS church.

When Young died in 1877, Kane traveled to Utah to offer his condolences to the Mormon people and to reassure church leaders of his own continued support of their cause. He continued to meet and correspond with various leaders of the Mormon church. He died in 1883 at his home in Philadelphia. Even though he had requested that his heart be buried in Salt Lake City, he was interred near the family chapel in Kane, Pennsylvania.

• The largest group of Thomas L. Kane papers is housed in the Special Collections and Manuscripts, Harold B. Lee Library, Brigham Young University, Provo, Utah. Thomas L. Kane papers can also be found in the library of Stanford University, the Beineke Library at Yale University, and at the American Philosophical Society in Philadelphia. The Church of Jesus Christ of Latter-day Saints in Salt Lake City also has a significant collection of Kane papers, as well as the research collection of Israel Frank Evans on Thomas L. Kane. Some of the material at Stanford was published in *The Private Papers and Diary of Thomas Leiper Kane: A Friend of the Mormons*, ed. Oscar O. Winther (1937). In addition to *Coahuila* (1877), Kane published two privately printed books, *The Mormons: A Historical Discourse* (1850) and *Alaska and the Polar Regions* (1868). Elizabeth Kane's diary after their arrival in southern Utah was published as *A Gentile Account of Life in Utah's Dixie, 1872–73: Elizabeth Kane's St. George Journal*, ed. Norman Bowan (1995).

A book-length study is Albert L. Zobell, Jr., *Sentinel in the East: A Biography of Thomas L. Kane* (1965), based on a master's thesis (Univ. of Utah, 1944); the source citations are omitted from the published volume. See also Leonard J. Arrington, " 'In Honorable Remembrance': Thomas L. Kane's Services to the Mormons," *Brigham Young University Studies* 21 (Fall 1981): 389–402, which includes a useful bibliography; and Richard D. Poll, *Quixotic Mediator: Thomas L. Kane and the Utah War*, Dello G. Drayton Memorial Lecture, Weber State College, 25 Apr. 1984 (1984). Kane's Civil War regiment is the subject of O. R. Howard Thomson and William H. Ranch, *History of the "Bucktails"* (1906), and Edwin A. Glover, *Bucktailed Wildcats, a Regiment of Civil War Volunteers* (1960). Obituaries appear in the *Deseret News*, 2 Jan. 1884; *Juvenile Instructor* (Salt Lake City) 19 (15 Jan. 1884): 24–25; and *The Press* (Philadelphia), 27 Dec. 1883.

DAVID J. WHITTAKER

KANTOR, Jacob Robert (8 Aug. 1888–2 Feb. 1984), psychologist, was born in Harrisburg, Pennsylvania, the son of Russian immigrants Julius Kantor and Mary Slocum. He earned both the Ph.B. (1914) and Ph.D. (1917) from the University of Chicago. In 1916, while an instructor at the University of Minnesota (1915–1917), he married Helen Rich, who served as his collaborator until her death in 1956. After three years as instructor at the University of Chicago (1917–1920) Kantor joined the Indiana University faculty as assistant professor. Promoted to associate professor in 1921 and professor of psychology in 1923, he remained there until retiring in 1959. He then went to live with his only child, Helene J. Kantor, professor of Near Eastern Languages and Civilizations at the University of Chicago, who effectively replaced her mother as his collaborator. Kantor's scholarly productivity and impassioned advocacy for scientific psychology continued unabated during his later years. Following a full workday he was fatally stricken and died two days later in Chicago in the fifth month of his ninety-sixth year.

When Kantor began his career as a psychologist, the new science was seeking to objectively measure behavior by reducing it to simple reflexes. In contrast, Kantor declared that behavior arises from the interaction of multiple factors in the present event field, which is composed of living beings whose potential to behave results from biological evolution of the organism, the stimulational situation, and their prior individual histories. Kantor's vision of analyzing this complex event field began to be realized with the development of sophisticated recording devices and computerized statistical analyses after World War II.

Between 1918 and 1924 Kantor published thirty-two papers devoted to concepts and terminology for a naturalistic (i.e., nonmentalistic) science of psychology. His two-volume *Principles of Psychology* (1924, 1926) grew out of these papers and introduced what he called at first "organismic psychology," later renamed "interbehavioral psychology." Kantor described all classes of psychological events then accepted as the subject matter of psychology without invoking any psychic factors as explanatory components. Neither were psychological events reduced to biology. Major concepts utilized to describe interbehavior were the behavior segment (contact of organism with stimulus object), the coordinate response function, and the stimulus function, the last two being used to describe functions developed during a temporal series of behavior segments. Interbehaviors in which the stimulus object was not immediately present were described in terms of a substitute stimulus, which could be either another object or a response. Through this means, thinking was described naturalistically.

Kantor used these objective concepts in separate full-length works covering cultural (*An Outline of Social Psychology* [1929]) and linguistic (*An Objective Psychology of Grammar* [1935]) interbehaviors. His *Problems of Physiological Psychology* (1947) listed the deficiencies of biological reductionism and argued for a broad interbehavioral field. He used extensive historical analysis to introduce his rationale for interbehavioral psychology.

The two-volume *Psychology and Logic* (1945, 1950) signified Kantor's shift toward historical and logical analysis of psychology and a more general interest in the philosophy of science. In this work he presented a logic of specificity (arguing that logic deals with specific events rather than universal and transcendent systems), and he provided an analysis of the psychological dimension of logic in actual practice. In his closely related *The Logic of Modern Science* (1953), Kantor indicated the value for actual scientific investigations of the eight postulates from *Psychology and Logic* and distinguished between actual events and the constructs developed by scientists to describe events. *Interbehavioral Psychology* (1957; 2d ed., 1959) elucidated a comprehensive psychological system of definitions and postulates and included data subsystems for, among others, physiological psychology, cultural psychology, zoopsychology, and abnormal psychology. Kantor's aim was to provide a logic of scientific psychology based on observation of the complete range of human experience. He was reacting against those who based their theories on (1) psychic faculties, (2) simple physiological correlation, (3) elimination of all but the simplest forms of human behavior such as rote memorization, or (4) solely on the study of infrahuman animals.

Kantor's first major work following his retirement was the two-volume *The Scientific Evolution of Psychology* (1963, 1969). Here he traced the historical career of the sciences in general, and psychology in particular, from the earliest documented Hellenic systems to the mid-twentieth century. He demonstrated with a detailed analysis of historical figures that all scientific work is dependent on specific cultural conditions. Kantor distinguished between observation of events and cultural assumptions and impositions (which he called "patinas"). He also emphasized the coordination of postulate sets with actual events and investigations and highlighted the struggle of modern philosophers and scientists to eliminate psychic postulates, which cannot by their very nature be coordinated with concrete events.

Kantor completed four additional works in succeeding years. *Psychological Linguistics* (1977) continued the emphasis of his *An Objective Psychology of Grammar* on the adjustmental aspects of uniquely human language interbehaviors. He returned to social psychology as a specific psychological domain in *Cultural Psychology* (1982), which presented a refined and completely naturalistic treatment of the manifold events of human societies. His *Interbehavioral Philosophy* (1983) departed radically from the transcendental thinking of traditional philosophers and demonstrated that his logic of specificity allowed a scientific analysis of topics such as ethics, aesthetics, and religion, which had by default remained largely the domain of speculative philosophers. Unique for a man of his years was *Tragedy and the Event Continuum* (1983). His analysis of the events of human existence was completely original. His broad sweep of the literature of tragedy from Hellenic times to the present day analyzed the failure to realize potential and made clear his intellectual debt to Aristotle. Again, Kantor's treatment remained free of all mystical principles as had been his hallmark.

Founder in 1937 of the *Psychological Record*, the first journal to actively seek behaviorally oriented articles, Kantor served on the editorial board until his death. He also was a charter member of the editorial board of *Behaviorism*. After his death Kantor's followers actively continued to develop his concepts in such diverse areas as child psychology, physiological psychology, behavior modification, and the history of psychology.

When an authentic natural science of psychology has fully evolved, Kantor's followers believe he will be evaluated as one of the towering contributors. His work falls into two major areas. First, he demonstrated that all psychological events, even the most subtle, could be described without recourse to psychic fictions. Second, he developed a comprehensive logic of science to serve the orientational, evaluative, and critical functions necessary for the successful prosecution of any natural science, but with special orientation toward psychology as an objective science. His lasting legacy is the complimentary assumptions that all reality is composed of observable events and that all these events are amenable to scientific analysis.

• Kantor's papers, including his personal library, are in the archives of the History of American Psychology, University of Akron. Most of Kantor's articles, including many of his nearly 150 book reviews, are in the *Psychological Record* and the *Mexican Journal of Behavior Analysis*. Selected collections of papers are available in his *The Aim and Progress of Psychology and Other Sciences* (1971), *Psychological Comments and Queries* (1984), and *Selected Writings* (1984). Noel W. Smith, *Greek and Interbehavioral Psychology* (1990), contains a complete bibliography of works by Kantor plus some selected publications about him. Evaluative essays are collected in Smith et al., eds., *Reassessment in Psychology* (1983). Extensions of interbehaviorism to clinical practice constitute Douglas H. Rubin and Dennis J. Delprato, eds., *New Ideas in Therapy* (1987). Eliot Hearst and James H. Capshew summarized Kantor's career in its academic context in *Psychology at Indiana University: A Centennial Review and Compendium* (1988). Files of *The Interbehaviorist: A Newsletter of Interbehavioral Psychology* should be consulted for developments among participants within the system. See also the obituary by Paul T. Mountjoy and Jay D. Hansor in *American Psychologist* 41, no. 11 (1986): 1296–97.

PAUL T. MOUNTJOY

KANTOR, MacKinlay (4 Feb. 1904–11 Oct. 1977), novelist and short-story writer, was born Benjamin McKinlay Kantor in Webster City, Iowa, the son of John Martin Kantor and Effie Rachel McKinlay, a clerk, a nurse, and later a newspaper editor. An unstable man who could not hold jobs, John Kantor deserted his pregnant wife, who divorced him soon after her son's birth. (The father, later an international con man who spent time in prison, distressed the family by periodic reappearances.) Kantor dropped his first name and added a second "a" to his middle name. After attending public schools in Iowa and Illinois, he entered the field of journalism. He worked with his mother as a reporter on the *Webster City Daily News* (1921–1925). His winning $50 in 1922 as first prize in a short-story contest sponsored by the *Des Moines Register* confirmed his desire to be an author. He placed stories in *Outdoor America* in 1924 and *Iowa Magazine* in 1925 but was paid for neither. Meanwhile, he worked in a Chicago department store and published detective stories in pulp magazines (1925–1926). While he was a member of a small theater company in Chicago, he met Irene Layne, a painter, and they were married in 1926, although both were poverty-stricken. They had two children. Kantor was a reporter again and also a freelance writer for the *Cedar Rapids Republican* in Cedar Rapids, Iowa (1927), and a columnist for the *Des Moines Tribune* (1930–1931). His first three novels appeared in 1928–1932. He moved with his family to New York City in 1932.

After years of financial struggle, Kantor achieved popular success with *Long Remember* (1934), his first historical novel. In that same year he went to Hollywood to write scenarios for Paramount Productions, Metro-Goldwyn-Mayer, 20th Century Fox, and Samuel Goldwyn. In the late 1930s a stream of books followed, including the immensely popular *Voice of Bugle Ann* (1935), which he claimed to have written in four days. During the years of World War II, Kantor published seven books, including *Gentle Annie: A Western Novel* (1942) and *Glory for Me* (1945). As a war correspondent for the *Saturday Evening Post* and *Esquire*, he covered the British Royal Air Force and the U.S. Army Air Force (1943, 1945) and wrote about flying several American combat missions over Germany with the famous U.S. Eighth Air Force. These missions were technically illegal, since he was a civilian. In 1947 he published *But Look, the Morn: The Story of a Childhood*, in which he praised his mother and criticized his father.

The ever-restless Kantor joined the uniformed division of the New York City police (1948–1950), wrote *Signal Thirty-Two* (1950) based on his experiences, and served as a war correspondent for the U.S. Air Force during part of the Korean War (1950), again flying combat missions. His military expertise made him

of value as a technical consultant for the Air Force (1951–1953). His *Lee and Grant at Appomattox* (1950), for juvenile readers, indicated a continued interest in the Civil War. Steadily following were *Gettysburg* (1952), his masterwork *Andersonville* (1955), *Silent Grow the Guns, and Other Tales of the Civil War* (1958), and the captivating "If the South Had Won the Civil War" (*Look* paid $25,000 for serial rights and published it on 22 Nov. 1960). In this hypothetical history, Grant is killed, the Confederates seize Washington, and the United States is divided into three countries, which "Consolidationists" ultimately begin to reunite in 1960 to deter the Soviets. In 1963 Kantor studied military operations at Mediterranean bases of Italian and Greek air forces. He helped General Curtis E. LeMay write *Mission with LeMay* (1965), in which the general suggests that North Vietnam be atom-bombed into retreat and good behavior. Among Kantor's final fiction, two historical novels stand out—*Spirit Lake* (1962) and *Valley Forge* (1975).

Much acclaim and many honors came to Kantor. "Silent Grow the Guns" won the O. Henry Award as the best short story of 1935. Several movies based on his fiction were made. His *Glory for Me*, a critical failure in often monotonous verse, was adapted by Robert E. Sherwood, became *The Best Years of Our Lives*, and won thirteen Academy Awards in 1946. *Andersonville* won a Pulitzer Prize in 1956. Kantor received five honorary doctorates (1957–1961) and was appointed a consultant to the Library of Congress (1967–1973). Kantor died in Sarasota, Florida, where he had lived since 1936.

Although Kantor was too prolific and wide-ranging to be regarded as a literary artist of enduring importance, he did win praise from notable critics of his time. Allen Tate, the distinguished southern writer and critic, said of *Long Remember* that "no book ever written . . . creates so well . . . the look and smell of battle, the gathering of two armies, the clash, and the sullen separation" (*Books*, 8 Apr. 1934). *Andersonville*, which the historian Bruce Catton called "[t]he best Civil War novel I have ever read" (*Chicago Sunday Tribune*, 30 Oct. 1955), is based on the hell-hole in which Confederate soldiers stockaded Union prisoners of war in Georgia. In unsparing, massive detail, Kantor presents the whole spectrum of human emotions, from courage and tenderness to brutality, perversion, and cowardice. Its excruciating horrors are lightened by a well-integrated and idealistic love story involving the daughter of a decent farmer on whose land the prison was built. Kantor's penultimate novel, *Spirit Lake*, is a panoramic drama of too many characters, a prolix combination of well-researched facts, fiction, folksy dialogue, and occasionally poetic prose. The historian Paul Engle described it as a model "novel-in-depth about the Midwestern frontier" (*New York Times Book Review*, 22 Oct. 1961). *Valley Forge*, Kantor's last novel, combines historical and fictional figures in a dramatic enough way; but overall, it marks a decline in the author's powers.

MacKinlay Kantor led too varied a life to enable him to focus singlemindedly on true greatness. He wrote far too much and often mistook length for profundity. But he deserves to be remembered as immensely popular and entertaining and—above all—as the writer of the enduring *Andersonville*.

• Most of Kantor's papers and manuscripts are at the Library of Congress and in the library of the University of Iowa. Ben Hibbs, one of Kantor's many editors, in a preface to *Story Teller* (1967), which collects twenty-three stories published by Kantor in sixteen different magazines, provides a delightful personality sketch of the writer. Tim Kantor, *My Father's Voice: MacKinlay Kantor Long Remembered* (1988), may be too sentimental and verbose in spots, but he also frankly presents Kantor as a vital, noisy, dominating, amoral personality. An obituary is in the *New York Times*, 12 Oct. 1977.

ROBERT L. GALE

KAPER, Bronislaw (5 Feb. 1902–25 Apr. 1983), composer (first name also spelled Bronislau), was born in Warsaw, Poland, where he began playing the piano at age seven. His parents' names are unknown. He attended the Warsaw Conservatory, and during the 1920s and early 1930s he worked as a composer and a pianist in the cultural capitals of Europe, including Vienna, London, Paris, and Berlin, where he also worked as a cabaret pianist.

In 1930 Kaper began his career as a screen composer for German films, usually working in collaboration with Walter Jurman. His German movie credits included *Der Korvettenkapitän* (1930), *Die grosse Attraktion* (1931), *Melodie der Liebe* (1932), *Es wird schon wieder besser* (1932), *Ein toller Einfall* (1932), *Hochzeitsreise zu Dritt* (1932), *Ein Lied für Dich* (1933), *Heut' kommt's drauf an* (1933), *Madame wünscht keine Kinder* (1933), and *On a volé un homme* (1934), directed by Max Ophuls. Kaper's German career was cut short by the rise of the Nazis. He fled Germany in 1933, stopping first in France for a time before immigrating to the United States. He came to America at the behest of Metro-Goldwyn-Mayer's studio head, Louis B. Mayer, who was impressed with Kaper's popular song "Ninon," which he heard repeatedly on the radio while visiting Paris. Kaper settled permanently in Hollywood, where he would provide scores for more than one hundred motion pictures over the next thirty-three years as one of the movies' most sought-after and respected composers. One of the reasons may be that Kaper seemed to have an innate understanding of the task of film composing. He himself did not believe that so-called serious musicians understood the demands of writing for the screen. In an April 1968 interview in the *Music Journal*, he stated,

The music for films deals with the particular problems inherent in writing around sound effects and dialogue. Motion picture music is a bridge, a dramatic bridge if you will, connecting together a dramatic narrative told in terms of visual images. Always there are the pragmatic limitations of the medium itself to be dealt with, and always I am confronted with my arch enemies—the crickets, the crinolines, and those eternally crackling fireplaces—those ever-present sound effects so necessary for dramatic reality, but so destructive to our work. Sometimes I think all film music should be written by John Cage or, better still, by those crickets themselves! (P. 71)

For the first five years of his Hollywood career, Kaper worked mostly on writing songs, usually in partnership with lyricist Gus Kahn, and arranging musicals. Kaper and Kahn provided songs for two Marx Brothers films, *A Night at the Opera* (1935) and *A Day at the Races* (1937), as well as songs for 20th Century–Fox's *Lillian Russell* (1940). In the same era, Kaper collaborated with Walter Jurman on the hit title song of MGM's screen blockbuster *San Francisco* (1936), and Kaper worked on musical arrangements for such MGM classics as *Mutiny on the Bounty* (1935) and *The Mortal Storm* (1940). In 1940 Kaper began a long-term contract with MGM. With his scoring for the Spencer Tracy–Hedy Lamarr romantic comedy *I Take This Woman* (1940), Kaper moved into the area of composing film scores almost exclusively. He was associated with MGM until 1962, although he also scored a number of non-MGM films on loan-outs to other studios.

Kaper was most frequently thought of as a composer of romantic films, musicals, and comedies, although he did some of his finest work for serious dramas like *Keeper of the Flame* (1942), *Gaslight* (1944), *Green Dolphin Street* (1947), *Act of Violence* (1948), *The Red Badge of Courage* (1951), and *Them!* (1954). More typically, his scores could be heard in movies like *The Chocolate Soldier* (1941), for which he and collaborator Herbert Stothart were nominated for an Academy Award for best score (and wrote "While My Lady Sleeps" for the film's star, Nelson Eddy), *A Yank at Eton* (1942), *Without Love* (1945), *Courage of Lassie* (1946), *Key to the City* (1949), *Her Twelve Men* (1953), *Forever Darling* (1955), and *The Swan* (1956). Kaper scored *The Stranger* (1946), and one of its stars, Edward G. Robinson, told the composer: "My acting became so much better after they added your music."

Kaper finally won an Oscar (for best scoring of a dramatic or comedy picture) for *Lili* (1953), a lavish MGM musical starring Leslie Caron. *Lili*'s bittersweet love story, fantasy, and carnival setting provided Kaper a definitive opportunity to compose in the romantic vein, an area in which he was an acknowledged master. Of this experience, Kaper told interviewer Tony Thomas: "I like pictures like *Lili*, and another one with Leslie [Caron], *The Glass Slipper*, because they contain songs and dances that are part of the story line, and they have to shoot to your music. This way you aren't carrying the burden of someone else's mistakes. Usually, you come to a film that is finished, and it's like inheriting cancer" (*Music for the Movies*, p. 88). Kaper later received two Academy Award nominations, for best song (with lyrics by Paul Francis Webster) and best score, for the 1962 remake of *Mutiny on the Bounty*. Coincidentally, he had made musical arrangements for the original in his first days at MGM, and *Mutiny on the Bounty* would be his last film in his 26-year career at MGM.

The best of Kaper's later work was heard in *Auntie Mame* (1958), of which he noted that he attempted to accentuate Mame's "deeper nature" rather than her gaiety: "With *Mame* the first temptation is to comment musically on her gay, vivacious manner, but you *see* that on the screen, you don't have to say it again. What I did was try and show that beneath her frivolity was a woman of deep sentiment, that she was genuinely concerned about her nephew" (Thomas, *Music for the Movies*, p. 90). Other late Kaper scores were heard in *Lord Jim* (1965), *Tobruk* (1967), and *A Flea in Her Ear* (1968), and he also composed the popular theme for the television series "The F.B.I." His last screen assignment was for *The Salzburg Connection* (1972), but it was replaced at the last minute with a score by Lionel Newman by order of the movie's director, Lee H. Katzin, much to Kaper's disappointment. The film was not a success.

Many of Kaper's scores survive on soundtrack recordings (including those for *The Swan*, *Auntie Mame*, *Lili*, *Green Dolphin Street*, and *Mutiny on the Bounty*), and bits of others are heard on a variety of compilations of film music. Newman, who had replaced Kaper as composer of *The Salzburg Connection* score, conducted a tribute recording called *Filmusic of Kaper* (20th Century–Fox S4200).

Well known for his charming personality, as well as his skill at the keyboard (although he never performed in public), Kaper involved himself fully in the musical life of Los Angeles. He served as a member of the board of directors of the Los Angeles Philharmonic Orchestra and was known for encouraging young composers. Before his death at the age of eighty-one in Los Angeles, California, Kaper was asked if film scores had run their course. He replied, "No, if you're excited by something, you'll come up with new ideas. How many women have you known in your life? Then along comes another and you love her. It's the same with film. All you need are a few little things and off you go again. If I were bothered by the clichés of the past, I couldn't live. Not just music. Life is also full of clichés. Don't fall for them" (Thomas, *Music for the Movies*, p. 91).

• Transcripts of Irene Kahn Atkins's interviews with Bronislaw Kaper, 14 July–14 Oct. 1975, are part of the *American Film Institute/Louis B. Mayer Foundation Oral History Program* (microfilm, 1975). For further information on Kaper, see Elmer Bernstein, "Bronislau Kaper Interview," *Film Music Notebook* 4, no. 2 (1978): 12–28; "Biography of Bronislau Kaper," *Film Music Notes* 4, no. 2 (Nov. 1944): 19–20; Page Cook, "The Sound Track," *Films in Review* 16, no. 5 (May 1965): 303–4; Cook, "The Sound Track," *Films in Review* 34, no. 6 (June–July 1983): 375–78; Cook, "The Sound Track," *Films in Review* 35, no. 3 (Mar. 1984): 184–86; *Films in Review* (Jan. 1989); Charles Matthew, *Oscar A to Z* (1995); Stanlie McConnell, "Teaching Possibilities in Current Films: 'Song of Love,'" *Film Music Notes* 7, no. 1 (Sept.–Oct. 1947): 5–13; Joel Reisner, "Cinema Music: Kaper's Film Capers," *Music Journal* 26, no. 4 (Apr. 1968): 71, 77; Lillian Ross,

"Piccolos under Your Name, Strings under Mine," in her *Picture* (1952); Tony Thomas, ed., *Film Score* (1979); and Thomas, *Music for the Movies* (1973). Obituaries are in *New Zealand Film Music Bulletin* (Aug. 1983); *Variety*, 4 May 1983, p. 541; and the *Los Angeles Times*, 27 Apr. 1983.

JAMES FISHER

KAPLAN, Henry Seymour (24 Apr. 1918–4 Feb. 1984), radiologist, was born in Chicago, Illinois, the son of Nathan Kaplan, a dentist, and Sarah Brillant, a pharmacist. He earned his undergraduate degree from the University of Chicago in 1938 and his medical degree from Rush Medical College just two years later. In 1942 he married Leah Hope Lebenson, a psychiatric social worker; they had two children.

Having watched his father die at a young age from lung cancer, Kaplan resolved to specialize in cancer research and therapy. He interned in radiology at Michael Reese Hospital in Chicago, spent a year as a research fellow at the University of Minnesota, and then joined the faculty of the Yale Medical School in 1945.

Kaplan left Yale in 1948 to become chair of the radiology department at the Stanford Medical School, then situated in San Francisco. Compared with Yale or the National Cancer Institute, where he had been a visiting researcher in 1947, Kaplan considered Stanford's radiology program second-rate, with outdated equipment and a faculty more interested in routine diagnosis and treatment than in research. "The only thing being called research for diagnostic radiologists," he later scoffed, "was to sit on their butts in front of a viewing box and look at films and perhaps collect one or two cases of some rare malformation" ("A Conversation with Henry Kaplan," Dept. of Special Collections, Stanford). Kaplan led by example, continuing his own laboratory studies while carrying a full share of the clinical load, even when that meant long hours and seven-day work weeks.

Convinced that improved radiation treatment would ultimately depend on a more detailed understanding of cancer on the cellular and molecular level, Kaplan encouraged closer collaboration between basic and clinical researchers. His own early studies focused on how X rays triggered thymic lymphomas in mice. Working with a purebred colony (the C57BL strain) that he had brought from Yale, Kaplan demonstrated that radiation did not induce malignancy directly. Instead, it seemed to activate some sort of latent virus, which in 1959 Kaplan isolated and identified as an oncogenic virus, specifically causing radiation leukemia. He also discovered that shielding the bone marrow from the X rays or replacing the bone marrow up to a week after radiation could prevent the onset of this type of leukemia. Kaplan and his collaborators later extended these studies to humans, exploring how radiation or chemicals suppressed the normal immune system (increasing the body's susceptibility to oncogenic viruses) and how such biological countermeasures as monoclonal antibodies could strengthen resistance.

Kaplan simultaneously sought to improve radiation therapy. Intrigued by rumors of a new atom smasher being built at Stanford's main campus in Palo Alto, he arranged a luncheon meeting in 1951 to discuss possible medical applications with Edward Ginzton, its designer. Ginzton's Microwave Laboratory had earned an international reputation for its high-power linear electron accelerators and had recently begun planning the two-mile-long Stanford Linear Accelerator Center. Kaplan knew that an electron accelerator could provide a ready source of high energy X rays for cancer treatment, and he was hoping to persuade Ginzton to design a version small and flexible enough for the clinic. Such an accelerator could offer higher energies and more penetrating power than either radioactive cobalt therapy or existing X-ray machines. Ginzton, as a founder and board member of Varian Associates (organized in 1948 by a group of Stanford faculty to commercialize scientific ideas), was always looking for new markets for microwave tubes. Together, they recognized a promising medical and business opportunity.

With financial support from the Office of Naval Research and the Irvine Foundation, Kaplan and Ginzton collaborated in designing and building an experimental five-million-electron-volt medical accelerator suitable for clinical trials. As impressed by its precision as by its power, Kaplan liked to say, "This is like a rifle. Whereas the past machines have been like shotguns" ("A Conversation with Henry Kaplan"). Installed at the Stanford Hospital in 1955, the medical accelerator proved particularly effective in treating small, inaccessible tumors, beginning with the successful treatment of a seven-month-old baby with retinoblastoma, a cancer of the eye. Gaining experience, Kaplan put his medical accelerator to work against cervical, testicular, ovarian, prostate, and other cancers, with considerable success. For Varian Associates, Kaplan's machine provided a prototype for a profitable and widely imitated line of clinical accelerators.

Kaplan's medical accelerator helped to revolutionize the treatment of Hodgkin's disease, an often-fatal cancer of the lymph system. To make the most of their new clinical tool, Kaplan and his longtime collaborator Saul Rosenberg undertook an intensive study of the natural history of the disease. They discovered that, contrary to accepted doctrine, Hodgkin's disease spread directly through the lymphatic channels. Armed with this insight, they devised what they called "total lymphoid irradiation" for treating advanced cases, with gratifying results. With a combination of radiation and chemotherapy, Kaplan's patients had a ten-year survival rate of 70 percent, compared with 23 percent for conventional treatments. Kaplan's *Hodgkin's Disease* (1972) was the first comprehensive text on the subject since the 1940s.

Convinced by his experiences with radiation therapy that "the medical school could not flourish unless it was located in proximity to the scientific departments of the main university" ("A Conversation with Henry Kaplan"), Kaplan campaigned vigorously to move the medical school from San Francisco to Palo Alto, over fierce opposition from the clinical departments. He won that academic battle, as he did most others, and the medical school came to the campus in 1960. To strengthen the university's academic departments, he helped to recruit outstanding scientists such as biochemist Arthur Kornberg and geneticist Joshua Lederberg, both future Nobel laureates. Kaplan's forcefulness, including repeated threats to go elsewhere unless the university met his demands, may have earned him a reputation as a "dean killer," but it undoubtedly contributed to Stanford's rise to the top ranks of American medical research and educational institutions.

Kaplan took an equally active role in promoting radiology as a medical specialty. He helped to organize the Association of University Radiologists, the Radiation Research Society, and the American Society of Therapeutic Radiologists, serving terms in each as president. He was a member of several national advisory committee studies on radiation and chaired the committee to set standards for clinical training in radiotherapy. Among other major honors, he won the Atoms for Peace Award (1969), election to the National Academy of Sciences (1972), and the inaugural Charles Kettering Prize (1979). He headed Stanford's radiology department until 1972; he remained an active researcher until—ironically—lung cancer cut short the career of one of the country's great cancer fighters. He died in Palo Alto, California.

• Kaplan's papers, including professional and administrative correspondence, research notebooks, clinical abstracts, and an unusually frank oral history interview, are held by Stanford University's Department of Special Collections. Kaplan, *Hodgkin's Disease* (1972), and Kaplan and Saul Joel Robinson, *Congenital Heart Disease: An Illustrated Diagnostic Approach* (1954), are classics. Zvi Fuks and Michael Feldman, "Henry S. Kaplan, 1918–1984: A Physician, a Scientist, a Friend," *Cancer Surveys* 4 (1985): 295–311, offers a technically informed account of Kaplan's career by two former colleagues and includes an extensive bibliography. A special issue of *International Journal of Radiation Oncology, Biology, and Physics* 11 (1985), dedicated to Kaplan, has a short biographical sketch of him by Malcom Bagshaw and Robert Kallman and technical articles by other former Kaplan students and collaborators. Edward Ginzton, Kenneth Mallory, and Kaplan, "The Stanford Medical Linear Accelerator," *Stanford Medical Bulletin* 15 (1957): 123–51, provides a contemporary description of the clinical accelerator, while Ginzton and Craig Nunan, "History of Microwave Electron Linear Accelerators for Radiotherapy," *International Journal of Radiation Oncology, Biology, and Physics* 11 (1985): 205–16, is a retrospective assessment. An obituary is in the *New York Times*, 6 Feb. 1984.

STUART W. LESLIE

KAPLAN, Mordecai Menahem (11 June 1881–8 Nov. 1983), rabbi and founder of Reconstructionism, was born in Sventzian, Lithuania, the son of Israel Kaplan, a rabbi and prominent talmudic scholar, and Haya Nehama Kovarsky, who managed the family store. At the age of eight, he emigrated to the United States with his family, and they settled in New York City. He received a traditional education mostly from his father, which gave him a solid grounding in classical rabbinic texts. Kaplan attended City College of New York (B.A., 1900) and Columbia University (M.A., 1902) and received rabbinical ordination from the Jewish Theological Seminary (1902).

Because he had both a traditional and a secular education, spoke English without an accent, and was able to relate to young people well, Kaplan was engaged as a rabbi in 1903 by the "modern" New York Orthodox congregation Kehilath Jeshurun. Although the congregation was happy with his work, the young rabbi was tortured with doubts as his graduate studies in sociology began to undermine his belief in the absolute truth and divine origin of his own tradition. In 1908 he met and married Lena Rubin, daughter of a prominent family in the congregation; they had four children. The next year Solomon Schechter, the head of the Jewish Theological Seminary, invited Kaplan to become principal of the seminary's newly created Teachers' Institute, and Kaplan enthusiastically accepted.

Kaplan remained at the Jewish Theological Seminary, the center of the Conservative Jewish movement, training rabbis and teachers, until he retired in 1963. As the first director of the Teachers' Institute, he laid the foundations for Jewish education in the United States. Working closely with Samson Benderly, the director of the Board of Jewish Education in New York City, he helped train the educational leaders of the next generation.

Kaplan had a strong personality and was a demanding teacher. For many years he taught homiletics and Midrash (classical rabbinic homilies) to rabbinical students at the seminary in addition to the "Philosophies of Judaism." Critical of his colleagues who seemed to be concerned only with scholarly issues, Kaplan addressed the central religious questions that troubled his students. His own graduate studies in sociology led him to formulate a religious ideology that emphasized the link between religion and experience. Because experience changes, religion must change, Kaplan believed, and one must find ways in which beliefs and rituals can function in the modern era as they did in the past. This process might involve changing a ritual, replacing it, or dropping it completely. Heavily influenced by the Utilitarians and by William James, Kaplan called himself a functionalist. He was determined to pursue the path most likely to make religion and particularly Judaism functional in the American setting.

Religion's goal of the perfection of the individual, Kaplan believed, could only be achieved within the context of a community. He held that Jews must have more in common than their religion for Judaism to survive in the secular culture of the modern era. Throughout the ages, Judaism as the evolving religious civilization of the Jewish people had bound them together into a vital organic entity. However, a vigorous Jewish life in the United States could be brought into being, he maintained, only with the creation of new institutions appropriate to a democratic techno-logically advanced society. Kaplan saw the expanded synagogue as the vehicle for the survival of Jewish civilization. In 1918 the Jewish Center on 86th Street in Manhattan, a magnificent building with many recreational facilities in addition to a synagogue was dedicated, with Kaplan serving as rabbi. It quickly became the prototype for many other synagogue-centers in the United States and Canada.

Kaplan's increasingly radical views led to his departure from the Orthodox Jewish Center in 1922 with a large group of supporters in order to organize the Society for the Advancement of Judaism, also in New York City. He attempted to establish his ideology, which he called Reconstructionism, as a school of thought within the Jewish community rather than as a separate denomination to avoid furthering the fragmentation of American Jewry. Reconstructionism defined Judaism as an evolving religious civilization and stressed Judaism's efforts to achieve social justice in addition to individual salvation or fulfillment as the primary values of Jewish life.

In 1934 Kaplan published his magnum opus, *Judaism as a Civilization*, which became the landmark for second-generation American Jewish leaders desperately seeking a way to live as both Jews and Americans. He held that Jews could live in two civilizations (Jewish and American) without any sense of tension or contradiction because the two cultures were absolutely compatible. His major thrust was to set the Jewish people, their past experience, and their present welfare at the center of his conception of Judaism. The revelation of the Torah and God were explained in terms relating to Jewish peoplehood. Because he did not see Judaism as a system of dogmas or a set of laws, his ideas helped even the most skeptical of modern Jews to relate to Jewish civilization. He also maintained that Jewish laws were in reality customs of the Jewish community that had retained enduring value. He encouraged Jews to observe as much religious ritual as possible rather than considering Jewish ritual as a set of laws that were either kept or broken. These guidelines for observance were spelled out in *A Guide to Jewish Ritual* later published (1962) by the Reconstructionist movement.

In the following years, Kaplan produced a series of works that spelled out his philosophy. Of particular importance are *The Meaning of God in Modern Jewish Religion* (1937), his primary theological work, and *The Future of the American Jew* (1948), in which he applied his philosophy.

Kaplan's literary productivity was overwhelming considering that many of his books were written when he was in his seventies and eighties, with his final work appearing in his early nineties. In addition to his published works, he was a prodigious diarist, ultimately producing a journal amounting to twenty-seven volumes. An intense and serious person, he maintained a very full schedule including his duties at the Jewish Theological Seminary, writing, and lecturing throughout the country at synagogues and colleges. In addition, he served as a full-time rabbi at the Jewish

Center (1917–1922) and later at the Society for the Advancement of Judaism (SAJ).

Kaplan used his position as rabbi at the SAJ to explore new rituals, reformulate liturgies, and experiment with new prayers. In 1922 he inaugurated the first bat mitzvah with a ceremony for his daughter. *The New Haggadah* (for the Passover seder service), which he published in 1941, and *The Sabbath Prayer Book*, which appeared in 1945, shocked and outraged many traditional Jews because some of the original Hebrew prayers were changed or omitted. Following the publication of the prayer book, he was excommunicated (a *herem* or ban was issued) by the Union of Orthodox Rabbis of the United States and Canada, and according to the *New York Times* report of the incident, his prayer book was publicly burned during the *herem* ceremony. Because Kaplan had no contact with Orthodox Jews except on a personal level, the excommunication did not affect him in other ways.

Kaplan's radicalism had caused problems at the Jewish Theological Seminary from the beginning of his tenure. He was the first at the seminary to openly support biblical criticism, a textual methodology that maintained that the Pentateuch was not written by Moses but was authored by many hands. Seminary president Solomon Schechter labeled biblical criticism a form of "higher anti-Semitism." Kaplan, on the other hand, asserted that the significance of the Torah was not determined by its origin but by the function it performed in Jewish life. It had been central and could be again, but only if it were reinterpreted so that it was functional for contemporary American Jews.

Kaplan had never felt completely comfortable with his colleagues at the seminary, who often opposed his ideology and his innovation. Having often considered leaving the seminary, in 1927 he resigned in order to take a position at the more liberal Jewish Institute of Religion that Stephen Wise had organized in 1922. However, at the persistent urging of his students and many seminary alumni, Kaplan returned to his position at the seminary within a few months. His remaining at the Jewish Theological Seminary in effect prevented Reconstructionism from becoming a separate denomination with its own rabbinical seminary.

Kaplan was a lifelong Zionist, believing that Jewish civilization required the natural setting of its own land in order to flourish and grow. Rabbi Isaac Jacob Reines, the founder of the religious Zionist group Mizrachi, had been the rabbi in Kaplan's hometown of Sventzian and was a close family friend. Also deeply influenced by the cultural Zionist Ahad Ha'am, Kaplan later stated that this Zionist thinker had revealed to him "the spiritual reality of the Jewish people." At the same time, Kaplan found Ahad Ha'am deficient in that his approach to Jewish life was "wanting in a basic appreciation of Religion."

Kaplan attended a number of international Zionist congresses and for a brief period served in an administrative capacity with the Zionist Organization of America. Chaim Weizmann, the World Zionist Organization leader, a regular visitor to the Kaplan household, considered Kaplan a close friend and on a number of occasions invited him to assume positions of responsibility in the Jewish community in Palestine. Upon the opening of the Hebrew University of Jerusalem in 1925, Kaplan was asked to give a lecture and to represent the Zionist Organization of America. In his address, he stated his belief that the university would help in solving Israel's adjustment to the modern world by "assimilating the method of science and the spirit of democracy without surrendering Israel's unique character." It would become the prime mover in creating a Judaism synonymous with humanism, Kaplan maintained, and in reawakening the spiritual urges of the Jewish people.

Kaplan's lifelong Zionism and his devotion to the Jewish people existed alongside a profound commitment to American culture and its ideals. He believed not only that the values of Jews and Americans were mutually supportive, but also that Jewish culture (or any subculture) must be the vehicle for transmitting the democratic values of American society. His metaphor for American ethnic life was not the melting pot, in which differences disappeared, but, like the philosopher Horace Kallen who advocated an ideology of cultural pluralism, the orchestra, in which the various voices blended together in perfect harmony. In addition, Kaplan believed that the Jewish community in the United States must be hospitable to all expressions of Jewish commitment and that the synagogue must be a place of democracy where Jews choose, under the guidance of their rabbi, their own ways to express their values and beliefs. According to Kaplan, in a modern democratic society tradition and Jewish law have a "vote but not a veto" over the group policies and individual behavior of Jews.

Kaplan was criticized by many groups throughout his career. Traditional Jews considered him heretical because he altered the liturgy and rejected the belief in a supernatural deity who performed miracles and intervened in the historical process. Secular universalists saw his nationalism as regressive, and some liberal religious thinkers believed that he reduced Jewish life to community values, completely omitting the spiritual element of Jewish civilization.

Although Kaplan rejected traditional theism in favor of process theology, he affirmed the belief that the divine is experienced in the positive forces of the universe that aid human beings individually and collectively in their search for salvation (e.g., life abundant). Kaplan was no atheist, and the quest for the divine was invariably part of his religious life. His belief in group life as the vehicle for the spiritual quest was present throughout his career, but he stated emphatically that although religion could not exist without a community to legitimate it, matters of the spirit were not reducible to the group life.

Mordecai Kaplan was vigorous and productive well into his nineties. He died in New York City at age 102, having lived through the entire saga of the American Jew in the twentieth century. As rabbi, teacher, writer, and lecturer, he spearheaded the founding of new institutions and stimulated the reconsideration of long-held assumptions. He is remembered primarily as the principal theologian of the cultural integration of the American Jewish community and as the founder of Reconstructionism.

• The majority of Kaplan's private papers can be found in the Kaplan Archive at the Reconstructionist Rabbinical College in Wyncote, Pa. Works by Kaplan other than those mentioned above include *The Greater Judaism in the Making* (1960) and *A New Zionism* (1955). The most comprehensive bibliography of Kaplan's published works is in Emanuel S. Goldsmith, Mel Scult, and Robert M. Seltzer, eds., *The American Judaism of Mordecai M. Kaplan* (1990). The primary biographical work on Kaplan is Mel Scult, *Judaism Faces the Twentieth Century: A Biography of Mordecai M. Kaplan* (1993).

MEL SCULT

KAPP, Jack (15 June 1901–25 Mar. 1949), record producer and executive, was born in Chicago, Illinois, the son of Meyer Kapp, a salesman for Columbia Records, and Minnie Leader. Both parents had emigrated from Russia. The elder Kapp was known in his profession as a "hit forecaster" and encouraged his three sons to follow him into the swiftly growing phonograph business.

Jack Kapp began working in Columbia's Chicago office as a part-time shipping clerk when he was only fourteen, and he took a full-time position in the order department upon graduating from high school in 1918. In 1921 he and his brother Dave, who also stayed in the record business, opened a Columbia record store on the West Side, a few blocks from the second largest African-American neighborhood in Chicago. There they sold race and hillbilly records, both marketing categories for rural southern customers, and also developed a mail-order business. Kapp married Frieda Lutz in 1922; they had two children.

In 1925 Kapp became head of sales in the Chicago office of Columbia Records, and one year later he accepted the position of head of the Vocalion Race Record Division of the Brunswick-Balke-Collender Co. in Chicago. His career in the race-record business did not flower; the greater number of his recording artists were undistinguished. His main contribution was recording a new blend of religious and secular music performed by guitar-playing evangelists such as "Blind Joe" Taggert and Edward W. Clayborn. The mixing of musical genres would become one of his trademarks as a record producer.

Kapp's big career break came in 1928 when he produced for the Brunswick label a double-hit record of Al Jolson's "Sonny Boy," backed by "There's a Rainbow 'Round My Shoulder." The record sold an estimated 2 million copies worldwide. This triumph earned Kapp a promotion to sales and recording director of the Vocalion label, and he soon took over the same position for Brunswick.

Kapp's career was interrupted by the depression, which hit the phonograph industry in the United States particularly hard. From 1929 to 1933 little re-

cording took place, but Kapp played a key role in the revival of the shattered industry beginning in 1934, when he succeeded in securing an initial investment of $250,000 from E. R. Lewis, head of the Decca Record Company, Ltd., of Great Britain. Kapp became president and Lewis chairman of the board of a new Decca Record Company in the United States. With repeated injections of capital from Lewis, Kapp led American Decca to great success by marketing cheaply priced records of such top popular artists as Bing Crosby and Guy Lombardo. By 1939 Decca had become the second largest producer of records in the country, putting out 18 million of the 50 million records produced in the United States that year. By 1943 Decca had made more than $1 million net consolidated profit.

Kapp's success came from his uncanny ability to anticipate which records would appeal to the very large numbers of people (particularly young people) in the United States who had neither musical training nor any particularly developed musical tastes. Early in his Chicago days Kapp had concluded that the majority of customers entering his record store had "no idea as to what records to get and either say we want a dance record or a song, leaving the rest to the dealer's judgment." Kapp believed that such customers were in the majority and that they would prefer to hear gently reassuring vocal and dance band music with a firmly emphasized melody (his first Decca release featured Lombardo's dance band playing "Down by the Old Mill Stream"). Kapp is reported to have had mounted on his recording studio walls several large posters of an Indian maiden beseeching, "Where is the melody?" He relied on radio and movies to further attract the public's attention to his latest records.

Kapp's success is often attributed to his introduction of top talent on 35-cent records (or three for a dollar). While he did do this, English Decca had specialized in inexpensive popular records since World War I. Perhaps as important as his pricing policy was American Decca's domination of the jukebox market. The repeal of Prohibition in 1933 in the midst of the depression stimulated the rise of jukeboxes, and by 1936 at least 40 percent of all records produced went into them. Kapp lowered his prices to jukebox operators and still made a profit by cutting the costs of production and vastly increasing sales volume.

Kapp directed the recording careers of a wide variety of top popular music stars, including the Dorsey Brothers, the Mills Brothers, the Andrews Sisters, Woody Herman, Count Basie, and for a time Louis Armstrong. In addition to getting all of his artists to highlight the melody, Kapp often mixed genres with great success. He convinced Crosby to record "White Christmas," "Silent Night," and "Adeste Fidelis." "Crooning," the sound of a rich but untrained baritone voice sliding through a revered hymn in a warmly intimate manner, provided a distinctly American sound. The Andrews Sisters made such hit records as "Bei mir bist du schoen" and "Beer Barrel Polka," crossing over from Polish to English. Kapp consistently recorded traditional American folk music in a slick, commercialized manner. Novel combinations of distinct sounds accounted for many of his greatest hits.

Kapp delegated the recording of folk music, particularly rural southern materials, to his brother Dave, who developed a series of country records from 1934 to 1945. Decca also pioneered long playing 33⅓ RPM albums of the complete musical scores of Broadway plays. The Kapps brought the ears of the public into their recording studio, anticipating what would please the average citizen. At the time of his premature death from a cerebral hemorrhage, Kapp was setting up a pressing plant in Israel and launching a new label called Coral Records in order to invade the British market, from which contractual arrangements barred American Decca.

From 1934 to 1949 Kapp was the nation's leading popular record producer and, as such, a highly controversial figure. He championed popular music in an industry that had prided itself on its operatic and symphonic recordings. The press tended to portray him as a flamboyant vulgarian. At the same time, jazz writers and critics found his records "corny." Yet *Life* magazine and the *Congressional Record* praised Kapp as "the boy Horatio Alger wrote about" and a "symbol of the American answer to Communism."

• For further insight into Kapp's career see his article "Reasons for Popularity of Certain Selections and Their Effect on Sales," *Talking Machine World* 19, no. 3 (1923). Also see "Interview with Dave Kapp," Nov. 1959, transcript, Oral History Research Office, Columbia University. E. R. Lewis, *No C.I.C.* (1956); Lester Velie, "Vocal Boy Makes Good," *Collier's*, 13 Dec. 1947, pp. 24–25, 122–25; and Howard Whitman, "Profiles: 'Pulse on the Public,'" *New Yorker*, 24 Aug. 1940, pp. 22–26, also discuss Kapp. Obituaries are in the *New York Times*, 26 Mar. 1949, and *Variety*, 30 Mar. 1949.

WILLIAM HOWLAND KENNEY

KAPPEL, Philip (10 Feb. 1901–17 Mar. 1981), artist, author, and illustrator, was born in Hartford, Connecticut, the son of Morris Kappel, who had come from Russia on business, and Anna Superior. While a student at Hartford High School, Kappel's artistic ability was sufficiently developed to secure his employment as a staff artist for the *Hartford Courant* and admission to Pratt Institute in Brooklyn, from which he graduated in 1924. Summer employment assisting artist Henry B. Snell at Boothbay Harbor, Maine, during his years at Pratt brought Kappel into contact with Philip Little, an artist from Salem, Massachusetts, who welcomed Kappel into his studio and introduced him to a number of fellow artists and friends. Among them was Lawrence W. Jenkins, then curator of the Peabody Museum of Salem, who introduced Kappel to Chinese porcelain, Japanese prints, and American antiques, areas in which Kappel acquired considerable expertise, developed significant collections of his own, and served as consultant to other collectors.

In Salem Kappel was captivated by sailing vessels and the sea, which became his principal subject for the rest of his career. *Repairs*, a drypoint from his early days in Salem, earned him his first significant honor,

the Nathan I. Bijur Prize of the Brooklyn Society of Etchers in 1926. In 1928 he sailed on a steamship from New York for the West Indies, where he spent a year making drypoints of waterfront activities. When he returned to New York, the prints attracted favorable notice, sold well, and brought him commissions from several steamship lines. Kappel continued to follow the sea, in sail aboard the full-rigged ship *Tusitala* and the bark *Aloha*, and aboard ships of the Columbian Steamship and Cuba Mail lines. Through these experiences Kappel acquired a thorough technical knowledge of ships and thereby the ability to produce pictures that satisfied the sailor as well as the art critic. Many of his works—such as *The Hay Boat, Ipswich Marsh*—have become significant historical documents.

After only five years' work, Kappel was chosen as the subject of volume 4 in the *American Etchers* series of monographs, published in 1929. By then he had made almost ninety prints, and two years later he was given an exhibition at the Corcoran Gallery of Art in Washington, D.C.

Earning a living selling etchings during the depression in New York was not an easy task, but Kappel had some other skills. He designed and illustrated a number of books for Minton, Balch, & Co., including John P. Marquand's *Lord Timothy Dexter*. The steamship companies gave him steady employment designing promotional material and printed ephemera, and he further supplemented his income by providing consulting services to museums and collectors.

To escape the cost of city dwelling, in the early 1930s Kappel bought an eighteenth-century farmhouse in New Milford, Connecticut, which he repaired over a number of years with the help of his wife, Theresa M. Pentz, whom he married in 1935. The couple had no children. The house came to be very much the mirror of its owner: meticulously maintained, well ordered, and tastefully furnished with his collections of Chinese porcelain, Japanese and old master prints, American antiques, and nautical artifacts.

In 1950 Kappel's first book, *Louisiana Gallery*, was published. It contained seventy-four drawings of scenes in Louisiana, from the picturesque streets of New Orleans to grand plantation houses accompanied by historical, anecdotal, or descriptive text. This volume was cited for excellence by the American Institute of Graphic Arts, and he used the same format again in two subsequent books, *Jamaica Gallery* (1960) and *New England Gallery* (1966).

Kappel's contribution to art went considerably beyond the more than 360 prints he made and the books he wrote. Mindful of the fact that his career had advanced the way it did not only because of his own hard work but also because his elders had taken an interest in him and had helped him along, he was ever ready to participate in the artistic affairs of his community, take an active part in various artists' organizations, and help younger aspirants. In 1966 he was appointed to the Connecticut Commission on the Arts, on which he remained for more than a decade. In 1967 he was awarded the Alumni Medal for Distinguished Service by Pratt Institute in recognition of the honor brought to his alma mater by his "exemplary professional achievements." In 1979 the Salmagundi Club of New York awarded Kappel their Honor Medal for his "many contributions to the arts as one of the outstanding etchers in this country."

Kappel's productivity was greatly reduced by chronic poor health during the last fifteen years of his life. His wife had died about 1963 after a long illness, and in 1968 he moved to a smaller house in Roxbury, Connecticut. He died at New Milford Hospital.

• Kappel's papers are in the Archives of American Art. His art work may be found in the print departments of most major art museums in the United States. The Peabody Museum of Salem, Mass., has a large collection of his marine subjects. Wesleyan University has a particularly fine collection of early drypoints. Trinity College has a large collection of his prints, the original drawings for *New England Gallery*, and his Japanese print collection. The last major exhibition of his work was at the Davison Art Center, Wesleyan University, of which a catalog by Richard S. Field, including a checklist of all known prints, was published in 1979.

ELTON W. HALL

KARDINER, Abram (17 Aug. 1891–20 July 1981), psychiatrist and psychoanalyst, was born Abraham Elionais Kardiner in New York City, the son of Isaac Kardiner, a tailor, and Mildred Wolff. Growing up in severe poverty in New York's Lower East Side, the three-year-old Kardiner lost his mother to tuberculosis. His father soon remarried, and Kardiner was raised largely by a stern yet kindly stepmother. He attended City College in New York City, graduating with a B.A. in 1912.

Attending Cornell University Medical College in New York City, first in 1911–1912 and then in 1914–1917, Kardiner excelled in surgery and neurology. He found the psychiatrist Horace Westlake Frink's lectures on the theories of Sigmund Freud particularly intriguing. In 1913–1914, during a brief hiatus from his medical studies, Kardiner also studied anthropology at Columbia University under the famed anthropologist Franz Boas—an experience that broadened his understanding of psychology in the context of culture. Resolving to specialize in psychiatry, Kardiner was awarded his M.D. in 1917, after which he spent a two-year internship (1917–1919) at Mount Sinai Hospital and a psychiatric residency (1919–1921) at Manhattan State Hospital, both in New York City. Fascinated by the new science of psychoanalysis, Kardiner joined the fledgling New York Psychoanalytic Society, a small circle of Freudian psychoanalysts practicing in New York City that included Frink and A. A. Brill. In September 1921, with three other members of the society Kardiner made the pilgrimage to Vienna where he embarked on a six-month training analysis with Freud himself.

Returning to New York in 1922, Kardiner began three years of clinical psychiatric study and treatment of the "war neuroses" at the U.S. Veterans Hospital in the Bronx. His research on the symptoms induced by shell shock during the First World War yielded new theoretical insights on the adaptive maneuvers of the ego in response to traumatic stress. Years later, Kardiner summarized his findings in *The Traumatic Neuroses of War* (1941); after World War II additional case studies were included in an updated edition retitled *War Stress and Neurotic Illness* (1947).

In the late 1920s, as a member of the New York Psychoanalytic Society, Kardiner played an important role in the planning of the New York Psychoanalytic Institute, established in 1931 as the first psychoanalytic training school in the United States. As he developed his private practice of psychoanalysis, Kardiner also shared teaching duties at the Institute with A. A. Brill, Sandor Rado, Karen Horney, and others. In 1933 he introduced a course on applications of psychoanalysis in the social sciences; within a few years participants in this continuing seminar included leading anthropologists such as Ruth Benedict and Edward Sapir.

Students found Kardiner to be a compelling and effective teacher with a remarkable ability to synthesize Freudian psychology with social and cultural theories. In the late 1930s and early 1940s, working with the anthropologists Ralph Linton and Cora Du Bois, Kardiner investigated the impact of varying cultural practices on the development of the ego. Like the neo-Freudian psychoanalysts Karen Horney and Erich Fromm, Kardiner criticized the biological assumptions of orthodox Freudians and emphasized the importance of cultural factors in personality formation.

In his interdisciplinary seminars, which were held in the anthropology department of Columbia University from 1939 to 1947, Kardiner developed a psychocultural model for tracing the relationship between childrearing dynamics (as patterned by family and economic organization) and the formation of basic personality structure in different societies. Thus, as an early psychoanalytic contributor to the new field of ego psychology, Kardiner was also a major influence on the emergence of the "culture and personality" field in anthropology. His interdisciplinary research design set a precedent for subsequent collaborations between anthropologists and psychiatrists investigating the cultural context of personality adaptation. Kardiner reported his findings and theoretical conclusions in two important volumes: *The Individual and His Society* (1939) and *The Psychological Frontiers of Society* (1945). Kardiner's work in the field of culture and personality has been increasingly recognized as a formative influence on the postwar development of psychological anthropology and crosscultural studies of socialization and personality.

In the aftermath of factional rivalries at the New York Psychoanalytic Institute, Kardiner left the faculty in 1944 to join his colleagues Sandor Rado, David Levy, and George Daniels in the founding of the Columbia University Psychoanalytic Clinic (later, the

Center for Psychoanalytic Training and Research), where he became a clinical professor of psychiatry. In 1948 he married Ethel D. Rabinowitz; they had one child.

Kardiner continued his interest in the social implications of Freudian theory and presented case studies in the psychodynamics of racial discrimination in his important 1951 study *The Mark of Oppression*, which was coauthored with the psychiatrist Lionel Ovesey. Intrigued by changing sexual mores and the impact of the influential Kinsey Reports in American society, Kardiner also published his *Sex and Morality* in 1954. After briefly serving as the director of the Columbia Psychoanalytic Center (1955–1957), Kardiner held an appointment for several years as research professor of psychiatry at Emory University. His last major work, a brief autobiographical study, *My Analysis with Freud* (1977), recounted not only his experiences in Vienna but also his later discoveries in the application of Freudian psychoanalysis to the social sciences.

In addition to his broad interests in anthropology, sociology, and other fields, Kardiner retained throughout his life an enthusiasm for classical music, especially the work of Richard Wagner. In his final years, Kardiner continued his psychoanalytic treatment of patients until a few months before his death at his summer home in Easton, Connecticut.

• An unpublished transcript, "The Reminiscences of Abram Kardiner" (1965), is in the Columbia University Oral History Collection. Kardiner's major works also include *They Studied Man* (1961; coauthored with Edward Preble). The most complete assessment is William Manson, *The Psychodynamics of Culture: Abram Kardiner and Neo-Freudian Anthropology* (1988).

WILLIAM MANSON

KARLOFF, Boris (23 Nov. 1887–2 Feb. 1969), actor, was born William Henry Pratt in Camberwell, England, the youngest son of Edward John Pratt, a civil servant in India, and Eliza Sarah Millard. Within a year of William's birth, his father left the family and a legal separation followed.

Karloff once told a friend that his mother, while returning to England from India, had had an affair with an Egyptian in Suez and implied that he was the result of that encounter. This incident could explain Edward Pratt's departure, the boy's dark skin tone and later isolation from his family, and his future ability as an actor to empathize with social outcasts.

Following the early death of his mother, William was raised in Enfield by a half sister. Several of his brothers had entered the consular service, and during their infrequent visits, they urged the boy to follow the same path. However, as a youth, William enjoyed performing in local stage productions and was drawn to a brother who had once been a professional actor. William took courses at King's College of the University of London but found himself more interested in the theater than in education or the consular service.

In 1909 a small inheritance from his half sister permitted him to emigrate to Canada. On his arrival there, he worked for several months on a farm in Hamilton, Ontario, before making his way to Vancouver, where he dug ditches and shoveled coal. Around 1910 he joined the Jean Russell Stock Company (also known as the Ray Brandon Players), in Kamloops, British Columbia. During his trip from Vancouver to Kamloops, he decided upon a stage name, selecting "Karloff" from his mother's background and adding "Boris" because it seemed to fit. With no professional stage experience, he learned his craft acting in the company's repertory of eighteen plays until, in 1912, a cyclone caused the company to disband in Regina, Saskatchewan. Later that year, after working again briefly as a laborer, he joined another touring company, the Harry St. Clair Players, in Prince Albert, Saskatchewan, and toured with them until 1916. In 1913 he was admitted into the United States when the touring company went to North Dakota to give a performance. He reportedly attempted to enlist in the British army in 1914 but was turned down because of a heart murmur.

A 1917 tour in *The Virginian* brought Karloff to California, where he joined a series of stock companies. Finally, stranded in Los Angeles, he sought work as an extra in films. Some sources list *The Dumb Girl of Portici* (1916) as his first film, and others mention an unknown picture directed by Frank Borzage, but Karloff's first screen appearance was probably as part of a gang of spies in *His Majesty, the American* (1919), starring Douglas Fairbanks. He soon moved up to identifiable bit parts, and because of his dark complexion, he was cast mainly as Arab, Hindu, Mexican, and half-breed villains.

In 1923, rather than returning to work as an extra, he spent the next year and a half working as a laborer and truck driver for a building materials company. The risk to his acting career paid off, and in 1925 Karloff again found significant supporting roles. He received featured billing in *Forbidden Cargo* (1925), in which his character tries to pour molten lead into the eyes of the hero, and his performance as a cocaine addict and murderer in *Her Honor the Governor* (1926) received critical praise. He played opposite Lionel Barrymore in *The Bells* (1926) as a mysterious carnival hypnotist. His first appearance in a sound film was in *Behind That Curtain* (1929).

Records of Karloff's early marriages are elusive. Actress Olive de Wilton claimed to have been his wife in the early 1910s, but this marriage has not been documented. He married Montana Laurena Williams in 1920; no divorce date is known. In 1924 Karloff married Helen Vivian Soule, a dancer also known as "Pauline" and "Polly," whom he divorced around 1929. In 1930 he married Dorothy Stine, with whom he had a daughter, born in 1938. Immediately after divorcing Stine in 1946, he married Evelyn Hope Helmore.

A major turning point in Karloff's career came in 1930, when he was cast as Galloway, a prison trusty who kills a squealer, in the Los Angeles stage production of *The Criminal Code*. His re-creation of the role in the 1931 film version attracted attention, and he appeared in sixteen films released that year. In one of these films, *Frankenstein*, he portrays the Monster with an unexpectedly sensitive combination of menace and pathos. Karloff and the film were so successful that he was quickly cast in other horror pictures: *The Old Dark House* (in which he received star billing for the first time), *The Mask of Fu Manchu*, and *The Mummy*, all of which appeared in 1932.

Karloff's harsh but distinguished features, his lean, bowlegged form, and his lisping British accent made him difficult to cast in conventional roles. In *Scarface* (1932), for example, he plays a rather unlikely Chicago gangster. Also, a tendency to exaggerate his articulation and facial expressions sometimes led to overacting in such parts. Because of his unusual, larger-than-life aura, Karloff's best early performances were as eccentrics, such as the poetry-quoting friend of the hero in *The Public Defender* (1931) and the sleazy fake clergyman in *Five Star Final* (1931). Horror films proved ideal for Karloff because in them his extraordinary demeanor did not throw the final effect off-balance.

In 1933 Karloff returned to England to make *The Ghoul*. He also helped found the Screen Actors Guild in 1933, remaining on the guild's board through 1950. In 1934 he enhanced his position as a major character actor by appearing in the nonhorror films *The Lost Patrol* and *The House of Rothschild*. He followed these with the classic horror films *The Black Cat* (1934), *Bride of Frankenstein* (1935), *The Raven* (1935), and *The Invisible Ray* (1936). Following his appearances in this cycle of horror films, he played a murderer in *Charlie Chan at the Opera* (1937) and the detective Mr. Wong in a series of low-budget films.

Karloff helped define the horror film by portraying two general types: the dangerous but innocent brute who is as much victim as victimizer, and the intelligent, sardonic sadist. In a category by itself is *The Mummy*, in which he creates a reserved, sophisticated figure with an aura of tragic solitude. In *The Black Room* (1935) he portrays both a crude, corrupt aristocrat and the aristocrat's gentle, kindly twin brother, adding subtle variations to his dual portrayal when in the film the former disguises himself as the latter.

In 1939 Karloff made *Son of Frankenstein*, playing the Monster for his third and final time in film. He also began a series of movies that year about idealistic scientists whose experiments go awry and propel them into villainy. In 1941 he returned to the stage, making his Broadway debut in the comedy *Arsenic and Old Lace*. He played the tailor-made part of Jonathan Brewster, a multiple murderer who resents the fact that he looks "like Boris Karloff," for more than fourteen hundred performances, and later he toured with the play, joined a GI production of it in the South Pacific, and appeared in two separate television versions (1955, 1962). Karloff also starred in three subtle and literate films for producer Val Lewton; the first, *The Body Snatcher* (1945), was one of the best of his career.

Karloff acted in relatively few films during the 1940s and 1950s. He either supported the leads in major productions such as Cecil B. DeMille's *Unconquered* (1947) or starred in minor works such as *Abbott and Costello Meet Dr. Jekyll and Mr. Hyde* (1953). Only the British-made *The Haunted Strangler* (1957) and *Corridors of Blood* (1958) offered him any kind of acting challenge. Karloff found greater satisfaction acting on Broadway, with short runs but good reviews in *The Linden Tree* (1948) and *The Shop at Sly Corner* (1949). He had longer runs as Mr. Darling and Captain Hook in a musical version of *Peter Pan* (1950) and as Bishop Cauchon in Jean Anouilh's *The Lark* (1955), repeating the latter role on television in 1957. In 1959 Karloff and his wife settled permanently in England, dividing their time between their home in London and their Hampshire cottage.

The release of Karloff's old films to television in 1957 brought him new fame. In the 1960s he costarred with Vincent Price and Peter Lorre in the comedy *The Raven* (1963), appeared as a Russian vampire in one segment of *Black Sabbath* (Italy, 1964), and played an elderly hypnotist who controls the actions of a young man in *The Sorcerers* (England, 1967). He capped his career with *Targets* (1968), portraying a disillusioned movie star modeled on Karloff himself. His final film work consisted of four low-budget horror films shot in 1968 for a Mexican producer.

During the 1930s and 1940s, Karloff made frequent appearances on radio. He performed in dramas, guested on variety shows, and joined the "Information Please" quiz panel. He made his television debut in 1949. In television, in addition to making many guest appearances on variety and quiz shows, he acted in *Uncle Vanya* (1950), played the title role in *Don Quixote* (1952), sang in his role as King Arthur in a musical version of *A Connecticut Yankee* (1955), and portrayed Kurtz in *Heart of Darkness* (1958). He revived the Frankenstein monster for an episode of "Route 66" (1962) and played a villainous woman in "The Girl from UNCLE" (1966).

In 1949 he had his first television series, "Starring Boris Karloff." This was followed by the British-made "Colonel March of Scotland Yard" (1952) and the American-made "Thriller" (1960), with Karloff appearing as host and occasional star of the latter. Among his last appearances in television were guest bits in 1968 with Red Skelton and Jonathan Winters. Over the years, Karloff also made numerous recordings, including fairy tales, stories by Rudyard Kipling, and the narration to Prokofiev's *Peter and the Wolf*. He edited and annotated two short-story collections, *Tales of Terror* (1943) and *And the Darkness Falls* (1946).

Perhaps because Karloff did not become famous and financially secure until the age of forty-four, he never disdained being typecast, nor did he condescend to horror fans. He worked hard to bring sincerity and individuality to his roles. On the personal level, he was cultured but not intellectual, friendly but private, reliable yet eccentric. He loved children, although he remained a distant figure to his own daughter. He inspired affectionate respect in nearly all of his co-workers and friends. Crippled and suffering from emphysema in his later years, Karloff still remained in demand and continued to work until his death in Midhurst, Sussex.

• Karloff recounts his life in "Memoirs of a Monster," *Saturday Evening Post*, 3 Nov. 1962. Cynthia Lindsay, *Dear Boris* (1975), discusses Karloff's life from the point of view of a family friend. Richard Bojarski and Kenneth Beale, *The Films of Boris Karloff* (1974), offers a detailed, annotated filmography. Paul M. Jensen, *Boris Karloff and His Films* (1974), and Scott Allen Nollen, *Boris Karloff: A Critical Account of His Screen, Stage, Radio, Television, and Recording Work* (1991), analyze Karloff's films in some detail. Newly researched information appears in Gregory William Mank, *Karloff and Lugosi: The Story of a Haunting Collaboration* (1990). An obituary is in the *New York Times*, 4 Feb. 1969.

PAUL M. JENSEN

KÁRMÁN, Theodore von (11 May 1881–7 May 1963), aeronautical engineer, was born in Budapest, Hungary, the son of Maurice (Mór in Hungarian) Kármán, a professor, and Helen Kohn. In Hungarian the boy's name was von Sköllöskislaki Kármán Todor. For a few years he was tutored at home by a former student of his father, and through his school years he was almost totally dominated by his father's strictures. When Kármán was six, his older brothers found that he could multiply large numbers in his head, but his father considered this a show-off ability only and forbade all mathematics for several years, and instead encouraged him in geography, history, and literature.

In 1890 Kármán entered the Minta Gymnasium, established by his father for elite students. In his final year there, 1897, Kármán won a national contest, the Eötvös prize for the most outstanding student in science or mathematics. Kármán's father had a nervous breakdown at that time, and so, as he had intended, Kármán entered the Palatine Joseph Polytechnic in Budapest, a technical school. There, at his father's urging, he chose the engineering course instead of science or mathematics. Encouraged by a professor of engineering and hydraulics, Donat Banki, Kármán investigated the problem of clatter in engine valves and predicted the necessary mechanical modifications to prevent it.

Kármán received a B.S. degree in mechanical engineering in 1902, with a thesis "The Motion of a Heavy Rod Supported on Its Rounded End by a Horizontal Plane" (actually a child's toy). After a year of compulsory military service in the Austro-Hungarian artillery, he became assistant professor of hydraulics at Palatine Joseph Polytechnic. He also joined Banki as a consultant for Ganz and Company in Germany, a manufacturer of locomotive engines. He pursued research in combustion, fluid motion, and compression. Widely noted by engineers was his 1906 paper, "The Theory of Buckling and Compression Tests on Long Slender Columns," which was applicable in machinery, bridges, buildings, and aircraft.

In 1906 Kármán received a fellowship from the Hungarian Academy of Sciences and chose to study at the University of Göttingen in Germany, where his professors included Felix Klein in applied mechanics, Ludwig Prandtl in fluid mechanics, and mathematician David Hilbert. Using a large hydraulic press donated by arms manufacturer Alfried Krupp, Kármán determined the nature of buckling in columns of large structures and derived the associated mathematical equations. He received a Ph.D. in engineering in 1908, with a dissertation on this subject.

While visiting Paris in March 1908, Kármán observed a short flight by Henry Farman in a test airplane (five years after the Wright brothers' flight in the United States), and his curiosity was drawn to the physical principles of flying machines, which led to his lifetime involvement in aerodynamics. He accepted a position in the fall of 1908 as laboratory assistant at the University of Göttingen, where an airship wind tunnel was under construction for the Zeppelin Company, directed by Prandtl. Kármán analyzed the flow of fluid past a cylindrical obstacle at right angle and determined that the wake separated into two rows that create vibrations, as in aircraft wing flutter and a bridge in high wind. The concept, presented by him in several papers in 1911 and 1912, came to be called Kármán vortex street or Kármán vortices. It led to the redesign of many structures to withstand oscillations and to modifications in the design of ships and aircraft to a streamlined shape. Also at Göttingen with physicist Max Born in 1912 he devised a three-dimensional mathematical model of vibrating atoms, which came to be accepted as illustrating atomic structure in solid matter and was later useful in studies of materials at very low temperatures.

Believing that he could not advance to a senior position at Göttingen, in 1912 Kármán became professor of applied mechanics at the College of Mining Engineering in Selmeszbánya, Hungary, but he found it lacking in equipment and scholarly ability, and so he left it after a few weeks. In February 1913 he became professor of aeronautics and mechanics at the Technical University in Aachen, Germany, and director of the Aachen Aerodynamics Institute. He promptly began improving the institute's facilities, including the wind tunnel for testing aircraft, and he enlarged the teaching staff, which already included inventor and industrialist Hugo Junkers as professor of engines. Kármán began researches on aircraft design that led to changes in wing shape. His approach to engineering problems was through mathematical calculations, which were then tested in a laboratory, often by his students, for he was not mechanically adept.

During World War I Kármán was called into military service in 1914 as a first lieutenant in the Austro-Hungarian Army and director of research in its aviation corps, for which he developed improvements in airplanes for military use and designed a helicopter with two counter-rotating propellers. At the end of the war, back in Hungary, he tried briefly to revise the country's curriculum in the sciences, but he abandoned the effort because of political upheaval there and returned to his former position in Aachen in 1919. He obtained financial support for research from airplane manufacturer Hugo Junkers and from the von Zeppelin Company. With colleagues he carried out studies especially on the frictional resistance of fluids, including laminar flow and turbulence, as related to the shape and lift of airplanes. His institute became internationally known through its many publications and Kármán's extensive lecturing in various countries, and it drew students from many places. With Johannes Martinue Burgers he published *General Aerodynamic Theory* (two volumes) in 1924. Kármán called for the first International Congress on Aerodynamics and Hydrodynamics in 1922 in Austria and the first International Congress of Applied Mechanics in 1924 in Holland.

At the Holland meeting Kármán first met the head of the California Institute of Technology (Caltech), Robert Andrews Millikan, who in 1926 invited him to the United States for consultation on the design of a wind tunnel. Kármán recommended a closed air-circulation system, and the construction was supervised by Clark Millikan and Arthur L. Klein. The next year Millikan asked Kármán to head the newly established aeronautical laboratory at Caltech in Pasadena, California. After devoting some months to advising the Kawanishi Machinery Company in Kobe, Japan, on that country's first wind tunnel, and other delays, from 1928 to 1929 Kármán spent half his time at Aachen and the other half at Pasadena. In 1930 he became full-time director of the Daniel Guggenheim Aeronautical Laboratory of Caltech. His decision to leave Germany was based partly on increased Nazi sentiment and anti-Jewish attitude there. His mother and his sister accompanied him to the United States. He became a U.S. citizen in 1936.

According to Kármán's biographer, Michael H. Gorn: "Millikan made clear to him just what Cal Tech expected from the Guggenheim Laboratory—a vehicle to draw the U.S. aviation industry to Southern California and to bring to the campus national preeminence in aeronautics" (*The Universal Man*, p. 56). The graduate department in aeronautics soon reached a high stature, in large part because of Kármán's insistence on the use of mathematics in engineering problems and his personal involvement with each student's project. Half a dozen West Coast aircraft companies availed themselves of the wind tunnel for testing models, aided by students. Among the results was the successful design of the Douglas commercial airplanes for passengers: the DC-1, DC-2, and the highly satisfactory DC-3, which began commercial service in 1935. Kármán contributed to the design, working with Arthur Klein, by determining that a fairing at the joining of the fuselage and upper wing reduced turbulence and that sheet metal with appropriate stiffening was a satisfactory replacement for the wood and fabric that had been commonly used in airplanes.

Work on rockets began at the Caltech laboratory with graduate student Frank J. Malina in 1935, at first encouraged only slightly by Kármán, who was not certain that such a technology could be devised. Malina's efforts in developing propulsion with liquid propellant had some successes and a few disasters, and the small group moved along to solid propellants. Kármán suggested the term jet propulsion, to avoid a general antipathy to rockets, which at the time were considered impossible. In 1938 the research group continued under the financial support of the U.S. Air Corps, strongly supported in its goals by General Henry H. Arnold. Kármán became closely involved in the physics and mathematics of the program, which in 1940 was called the Air Corps Jet Propulsion Research Project and was located (for safety from explosions) in a remote canyon outside Pasadena. In 1942 Kármán and five of the other scientists in the program formed Aerojet Engineering Corporation, to accept contracts for building jet engines. In 1943 General Tire and Rubber Company purchased half the stock in Aerojet, and Kármán continued as an adviser to the company.

Other studies on rocket research continued at Caltech's aeronautical laboratory under Kármán. After reports that German scientists might have successfully designed rockets for military use that flew as far as one hundred miles, U.S. Army Ordnance offered a $3 million contract to Caltech for one year to produce a projectile. The result was the establishment of the Jet Propulsion Laboratory by Caltech in November 1944, with Kármán as its director. Under the National Aeronautics and Space Administration since the late 1950s, it has continued as a major contributor to scientific work on rockets, supersonic flight, and the space program.

In 1944 Kármán accepted a request from General Arnold to review the future air power of the United States as it would relate to rockets, guided missiles, and jet propulsion. He led U.S. scientists on two trips to Europe in February and April 1945 to inspect aircraft construction facilities and to interview the scientists who advised them in locations where fighting of World War II was over. The report by the group, *Where We Stand*, concluded that the supersonic aircraft could be built, that unmanned aerial devices and target-seeking missiles would come into use, and that pilots would have aerial communications that function under any conditions of visibility and weather. Kármán warned that atomic weapons that could be delivered over long distances would revolutionize future aerial warfare. He noted that jet engines would soon come into use for aircraft and that radar would have a much greater role in flight and in warfare. After a second trip to Europe with other scientists, Kármán wrote *Science, the Key to Air Supremacy* in 1945 for General Arnold, as one of the group's eleven volumes under the title *Toward New Horizons*. Concerned with military needs, he spent most of his time in Washington, D.C., until 1951 and continued on the U.S. Air Force Scientific Advisory Board until 1954. In 1949 he resigned from the Guggenheim Aeronautical Laboratory and the Jet Propulsion Laboratory and became professor emeritus at Caltech. During the summers of

1957 and 1958, in Woods Hole, Massachusetts, he led a group of scientists in conferences to advise the air force on its future direction.

Keenly interested in international exchange of scientific ideas, in 1951 Kármán organized a meeting of the North Atlantic Treaty Organization on means of strengthening common defense. This led to establishing the Advisory Group for Aeronautical Research and Development (AGARD), in Paris, of which Kármán was chairman until his death. Through its auspices he founded the Training Center for Experimental Aerodynamics (later named the Von Kármán Center). He helped found the International Council of the Aeronautical Sciences in 1958, which sponsors international congresses in that field. He was among those who created the Advanced Research Projects Agency of the Department of Defense.

With M. A. Biot, Kármán wrote *Mathematical Methods in Engineering* (1940). His other books were *Aerodynamics: Selected Topics in Light of Their Historical Development* (1954) and, with Shih I. Pai, *From Low-Speed Aerodynamics to Astronautics* (1963). He wrote almost 200 articles.

Among many honors, Kármán received the Medal for Merit in 1946 and the Franklin Gold Medal in 1948, and he was the first recipient of the National Medal of Science in 1963. Kármán never married. With his sister Josephine as his hostess for many years, he vastly enjoyed entertaining students, colleagues, and visitors. He died in Aachen, Germany, where he had gone to seek improved health in the hot springs.

• Many of Kármán's records are in the archives of the California Institute of Technology; others are in the archives of the Jet Propulsion Laboratory in Pasadena, Calif.; some material on World War II is in the Office of Air Force History in Washington, D.C. His technical papers to 1956 other than books were gathered into *Collected Works of Dr. Theodore von Kármán* (4 vols., 1956). He presented many reminiscences to journalist Lee Edson, but Kármán died before the manuscript was completed; Edson completed it as *The Wind and Beyond: Theodore von Kármán, Pioneer in Aviation and Pathfinder in Space* (1967). It includes a bibliography but does not discuss Kármán's scientific work in detail. A biography is Hugh L. Dryden, National Academy of Sciences, *Biographical Memoirs* 38 (1965): 344–84, with a selected bibliography. A longer biography is Michael H. Gorn, *The Universal Man: Theodore von Kármán's Life in Aeronautics* (1992), with information on other sources and a caveat on the accuracy of Edson's book. A summary of Kármán's years at Caltech is in Judith R. Goodstein, *Millikan's School* (1991). See also S. Goldstein, Fellows of the Royal Society, *Biographical Memoirs* 12 (1966): 335–65. An obituary is in the *New York Times*, 8 May 1963.

ELIZABETH NOBLE SHOR

KAROLIK, Maxim (1893–20 Dec. 1963), art collector and philanthropist, was born in Bessarabia, Russia (now Rumania), the son of Orthodox Jewish parents. He was trained as an operatic tenor at the Academy in St. Petersburg and performed with the Petrograd Grand Opera Company as well as in opera houses in England and Italy. Karolik came to the United States about 1922 and made his New York debut in 1924 in a recital at Aeolian Hall. He performed to moderate acclaim until the early 1930s, when unspecified health problems caused him to abandon his singing career.

In 1927 Karolik gave a private recital at the Washington, D.C., home of Martha Codman (1858–1948), a member of a prominent family. A romance ensued, and in 1928 they were married despite the opposition of her family, who resented the difference in their social status and their ages: Karolik was thirty-five, and Codman was nearly seventy when they married. The couple settled in Codman's Newport, Rhode Island, home on fashionable Bellevue Avenue.

At the time of Karolik's marriage, Codman had already achieved distinction as a collector of American antiques—she was particularly interested in works of art that had been made for her ancestors—and as a benefactor of New England cultural institutions. She had been encouraged in these endeavors by her cousin, the architect and designer Ogden Codman, Jr., who had helped her decorate her mansion with family heirlooms such as a chest of drawers by distinguished colonial cabinetmaker Thomas Seymour and portraits by John Singleton Copley, New England's greatest eighteenth-century painter. Maxim became involved in Martha's collecting activities; his enthusiasm for the art of his adopted country soon surpassed his wife's. Together they began collecting works of great quality in order to assemble the most significant pieces of silver, furniture, paintings, and prints produced in eighteenth-century New England and the mid-Atlantic states. In 1938 the Karoliks gave this collection of some 300 objects to the Museum of Fine Arts, Boston, where it forms the nucleus of that institution's great holdings in American art of the colonial and federal periods.

The eighteenth-century collection was the first of three assembled by the Karoliks for the Museum of Fine Arts. It consisted of objects that were almost uniformly high style, made of the finest materials by well-known masters, and intended for upper-class urban patrons. The collection reflected Martha's patrician heritage as well as the widespread interest in art and architecture of the colonial era that flourished in the 1920s and 1930s. Shortly after that collection was presented to the Museum of Fine Arts, the Karoliks began assembling a second collection that would be more innovative than the first and that would reflect Maxim's taste and heritage in its populist character. Working in partnership with the museum, the Karoliks put together a collection of American paintings created between 1815 and 1865. With some irony, Karolik termed this era "the barren period," because it had been overlooked by scholars and connoisseurs despite the many talented artists who worked during the age, among them Frederic Edwin Church, George Caleb Bingham, Fitz Hugh Lane, and William Sidney Mount. The paintings—landscapes, portraits, still lifes, and scenes of everyday life—that Karolik sought were for the most part modest in scale, created by self-taught artists whose names were seldom well known.

Created not for the elite but for the new industrial and merchant classes of the nineteenth century, the pictures portray a seemingly egalitarian society. They emphasize the beauty of America's scenery, the fortitude of its citizens, and the charms of provincial life—themes that appealed greatly to Karolik, who had an immigrant's love and gratitude for American democracy. He claimed that the collection was nothing less than a representation of the American way of life: "The beauty of the collection springs from the roots of this nation . . . it contains its own national characteristics; . . . it expresses its own idiom, which is definitely American. In that idiom, I believe, lies the reason for its universal appeal" (Baur, p. xi).

Karolik began buying this material for the Museum of Fine Arts around 1943. Among his first major purchases was a dramatic thunderstorm scene by Martin Johnson Heade. Heade had been all but forgotten since his death in 1904; he became a favorite of Karolik's, who would eventually acquire some fifty paintings by the artist, as well as many other works by Jasper Cropsey, Thomas Cole, Albert Bierstadt, John Frederick Kensett, and others now considered the major figures of the Hudson River School of landscape painting. Karolik's enthusiasm for these painters was instrumental in their rediscovery; the 1949 gift of 232 early and mid-nineteenth-century American paintings made the Museum of Fine Arts the principal repository of the art of this period and resurrected a whole chapter in the history of American art.

Martha Codman Karolik died in 1948. From that point Maxim Karolik spent a great deal of his time at the Museum of Fine Arts, encouraging the cataloging of their collection. The book that resulted, *M. and M. Karolik Collection of American Paintings, 1815 to 1865* (1949), was probably the first scholarly study of American art of this period.

Karolik also continued to buy works of art. He had always envisioned the Karolik Collection as a trilogy, and in 1962 he donated to the Museum of Fine Arts the third collection, consisting of more than 3,000 drawings, watercolors, and folk sculpture by American artists, both academic and self-taught, who worked between about 1800 and 1875. That collection was accompanied by a landmark catalog, the first to treat folk art and American works on paper in a serious, scholarly fashion. Karolik died while on a business trip to New York City.

Neither modest nor retiring, Karolik was given to self-promotion and to proselytizing on behalf of the artists of the barren period. If his exuberance and wit sometimes were even more daring, rescuing from oblivion many artists whose works have since come to dominate American art installations and exhibitions. As eminent critic and connoisseur James Thrall Soby noted shortly after the second Karolik collection was presented to the Museum of Fine Arts, "From now on no one can study seriously nineteenth-century American paintings without knowing this collection" (quoted in Rossiter, p. 16).

• The Karolik collections have been cataloged in the following volumes, which also contain statements by Maxim Karolik concerning his philosophy of collection and his assessment of the artists and schools he championed: Edwin J. Hipkiss, *Eighteenth-century American Arts: The M. and M. Karolik Collection of Paintings, Drawings, Engravings, Furniture, Silver, Needlework, and Incidental Objects Gathered to Illustrate the Achievements of American Artists and Craftsmen of the Period from 1720 to 1820* (1941); John I. H. Baur's introduction to *M. and M. Karolik Collection of American Paintings, 1815 to 1865* (1949); and Henry P. Rossiter, *M. and M. Karolik Collection of American Water Colors and Drawings, 1800–1875* (2 vols., 1962). For profiles of Maxim Karolik and analyses of the Karolik collections, see Brian O'Doherty, "Maxim Karolik," *Art in America* 50, no. 4 (1962): 62–67, and Carol Troyen, "The Incomparable Max: Maxim Karolik and the Taste for American Art," *American Art* 7 (Summer 1993): 64–87. An obituary is in the *New York Times*, 21 Dec. 1963.

CAROL TROYEN

KARZHAVIN, Fedor Vasil'evich (20 Jan. 1745–28 Mar. 1812), Russian traveler and man of letters, was born in St. Petersburg, Russia, the son of Vasilii Nikitich Karzhavin, a merchant, and Anna Isaevna. He was educated in Paris, where he was exposed to the French Enlightenment. Returning to Russia in 1765, Karzhavin taught the French language in seminary (church college) in 1767–1768 and beginning in 1768 worked as an assistant in the architectural office of V. I. Bazhenov.

In 1773 Karzhavin again went to Western Europe. Once more in Paris in the beginning of 1774 he "thought to soften the severity of his fate by marriage" to Charlotte Rembour, a poor orphan. Her correspondence suggests that she was capricious, and Karzhavin did not find peace in the marital state. They had no children.

An early misunderstanding with his wife and financial problems led Karzhavin to seek happiness across the ocean. In September 1776 he went to the island of Martinique, where he was connected with the American-French side.

Karzhavin visited America initially at the climax of the revolutionary war (May 1777–25 Jan. 1780), then while he was living aboard a Spanish ship in New York (12 May–11 June 1782), and again after the end of military operations (4 Sept. 1784–Apr. 1787).

On the first occasion Karzhavin arrived in Virginia in May 1777 aboard the brigantine *Le Gentil* with a cargo of gunpowder, arms, and salt. On 15 June he sent a letter to the president of the Continental Congress, John Hancock, offering him his services "for the translating and interpreting Russian," but he did not receive an answer (Bashkina et al., pp. 45–46). It was clear that no Russian soldiers would be sent to America, and his knowledge of Russian in America was useless. Karzhavin found himself in hard circumstances on this sojourn. He occupied himself trying to make a living in commerce, and he nursed sick men, but he achieved no financial success.

More fruitful was Karzhavin's stay in Virginia after the revolutionary war when he lived in Smithfield and Williamsburg. Within the circle of Karzhavin's friends and colleagues in Virginia were Carlo Bellini, George Wythe, Bishop James Madison, and other professors at the College of William and Mary. Especially close to Karzhavin was the prominent linguist Bellini, with whom he continued to correspond even after his return to Russia in 1788, and he dedicated one of his books to Bellini, asking him to accept it "as a sign of the close connection, existing between true-believers [literally, *vrais-croyans*] in spite of the boundless seas dividing them." (They both were Masons.)

Karzhavin's American impressions are partly preserved in the archives of St. Petersburg and Moscow in letters and diaries that deserve more careful study. On his return to Russia, Karzhavin translated and published a number of books, one of which he signed "Russian American."

Having lived for such a long time in Western Europe and America, Karzhavin was suspect in feudal Russia. It becomes understandable why this clever and educated man did not find a place in Russia. His application to the College of Foreign Affairs for "service in foreign lands" was not acted on, and until his death he never ceased to struggle with life's misfortunes. He worked as an interpreter in the College of Admiralty and got by on casual earnings.

Karzhavin died in St. Petersburg. He is remembered first as the only person of Russian origin who spent a number of years in America during the Revolution. It seems also fully justified that, as a representative of the Russian "third estate," Karzhavin found himself allied to the American-French side.

• Karzhavin's papers are preserved in the Pushkin House in the P. Ia. Dashkov Collection at the Institute of History in St. Petersburg; in the N. P. Likhachev Collection at the National Library in St. Petersburg (fond 1000—the manuscripts of his diary and works); and various other places. Among the most important biographies are N. P. Durov, "Fedor Vasil'evich Karzhavin (1745–1812)," *Russkaia starina* 12 (1875): 272–97, 655–59; A. I. Startsev, "F. V. Karzhavin i ego amerikanskoe puteshestvie" (F. V. Karzhavin and his American voyage), *Istoriia SSSR* 3 (1960); Nikolai N. Bolkhovitinov, *Russia and the American Revolution* (1976); S. P. Dolgova, *Tvorcheskii put' F. V. Karzhavina* (The creative way of F. V. Karzhavin, 1984); "Ob oshibkakh v osvetshenii zhizni i deiatelnosti F. V. Karzhavina. Sm.: dickussiiu na stranitsakh zhurnala *Voprosy istorii*" (The mistakes in the elucidation of life and activity of F. V. Karzhavin. See: the discussion in the magazine *Voprosy istorii*, 1986), N 4: 200–202; (1987), N 12: 159–68. Some new documents on Karzhavin are included in Nina N. Bashkina et al., eds., *The United States and Russia: The Beginning of Relations, 1765–1815* (1980).

N. N. BOLKHOVITINOV

KÄSEBIER, Gertrude Stanton (18 May 1852–13 Oct. 1934), photographer, was born in Fort Des Moines, Iowa, the daughter of John W. Stanton, a mining entrepreneur, and Gertrude Muncy Shaw, a boardinghouse operator. As a child of eight, Gertrude crossed the plains by wagon with her mother, brother, aunt, and uncle, to Colorado Territory to join her father, who had preceded them in 1859 to search for gold and set up a processing mill in Eureka Gulch, near Central City. Then, around 1864 the Stanton family moved east to Brooklyn, New York. During 1868–1870 Gertrude stayed with her grandmother in Bethlehem, Pennsylvania, while attending the Moravian Seminary for Women. In 1874 she married Eduard Käsebier, an immigrant shellac importer from Wiesbaden, Germany, whom she had met at her mother's boardinghouse in Brooklyn. The couple had three children.

In 1889 Käsebier, at age thirty-seven, enrolled in art courses at Pratt Institute in Brooklyn. She graduated in 1893 with training in portrait painting, but by that time she had learned to use a camera and had accumulated several years of experience recording her growing children. The invention of the dry-plate negative and the hand camera in the late 1880s had simplified picture taking, and many women like Käsebier were taking it up as a hobby. Although her teachers at Pratt tried to discourage her, she ultimately chose photography over painting.

She began publishing and exhibiting her photographs around 1894, receiving a $50 prize from the *Quarterly Illustrator* for her picture of a woman posing in Greek costume. Using photographs she took while chaperoning art students in Paris, she wrote and illustrated two articles about French country life, "Peasant Life in Normandy" and "An Art Village" (*Monthly Illustrator*, Mar. and Apr. 1895). To improve her technical skills, she studied in Germany in 1893–1894 with a chemist who knew photography.

In 1896 Käsebier decided to turn professional. She apprenticed with Samuel Lifshey, a Brooklyn portrait photographer, then opened her first commercial studio around 1897 on East Thirtieth Street in Manhattan. Using her art school training, she was instrumental in revitalizing what had become a stale, standardized commercial-portrait tradition. The photographer Joseph T. Keiley wrote in *Photography* that, due to her influence, "[t]he retouched, unreal, unatmospheric, stiff-posed, head-rested abominations have almost completely disappeared from the showcases of the leading professional workers throughout the country. In their places have appeared tastefully mounted, nicely lighted, naturally posed studies, showing shadow, atmosphere, and often good pictorial composition" (Mar. 1904).

Käsebier's work drew the admiration of Alfred Stieglitz (whom she had met and befriended in 1898) and his circle of pictorial photographers. She became one of the founding members of the Photo-Secession (organized 1902), and Stieglitz honored her as the featured photographer in the first issue of his *Camera Work* magazine (Jan. 1903).

She made portraits of many turn-of-the-century notables, including Mark Twain; Booker T. Washington; the architect Stanford White; the Ashcan School painters Robert Henri, William Glackens, Everett Shinn, and John Sloan; and her colleagues Clarence H. White, Edward Steichen, Baron Adolf de Meyer, and Stieglitz. Inspired by memories of her youthful encounters with American Indians in Colorado, Käsebier convinced Sioux performers from Buffalo Bill's Wild West Troupe to pose for her in her New York studio. An extensive article featuring the American Indian portraits was published in *Everybody's Magazine* (Jan. 1901). Käsebier's photographs of Auguste Rodin at work in his studio, taken around 1905 on one of her trips to Europe, remain some of the most admired images of the famous French sculptor.

One of Käsebier's most fascinating portraits, the provocative *Miss N.* (1902), displays Evelyn Nesbit, the showgirl mistress of Stanford White, wearing a shoulder-baring, empire-style gown and leaning her comely young face seductively toward the viewer. Nesbit grasps a small china pitcher in one hand, recalling *The Broken Pitcher*, J. B. Greuze's eighteenth-century painting of lost innocence. In a more sentimental vein, Käsebier made photographic studies that emphasize the spiritual and emotional bonds between mothers and children. Her friends and family posed for works such as *Blessed Art Thou among Women* (1899), which showed a mother and daughter framed in an open doorway anticipating the growing girl's emergence from her childhood home into the world; *The Picture Book* (1903), depicting a woman and child sharing a storybook in the shade of a tree; and the nativity-like scene, *The Manger* (1899), a print of which sold in its time for a record $100. In contrast, in a visual pun on marriage titled *Yoked and Muzzled—Marriage* (c. 1915), a young girl and boy stand holding hands and dourly contemplating two muzzled oxen bound together by a double yoke.

Käsebier achieved her pictorial affects—the atmospheric massings of light and shade and suppression of detail—through methods common to pictorial photographers. These included long exposure times, during which any movement by the subject blurred outlines and softened forms, and the use of printing papers prepared with platinum salts or gum bichromate, materials that can be manipulated during the printing process to achieve painterly effects. Käsebier also rephotographed prints on which she had drawn or painted. When Stieglitz and other photographers eventually abandoned pictorialism for sharper-focused and more abstract photography, Käsebier did not follow suit. Instead, with Clarence White and Alvin Langdon Coburn, she founded the Pictorial Photographers of America in 1916 and continued the pictorial practices that were quickly becoming outmoded.

Käsebier was one of the few professional women photographers in turn-of-the-century America. In addition to her practice and promotion at pictorial photography, she was acclaimed for her innovative commercial portraits and studies of intimate mother-child relationships. During her career, Käsebier's photographs appeared in many popular and photographic magazines and were accepted for exhibition in dozens of influential American and European venues. She won the grand prize at the Turin Exhibition of Artistic Photography in 1902 and the Gold Medal in the professional photography class at the International Photographic Exposition in Dresden in 1909. The last major exhibition of her works in her lifetime was held in 1929 at the Brooklyn Institute of Arts and Sciences. Käsebier actively encouraged women to take up professional photography, hiring female apprentices and serving in 1910 as president of the Women's Federation of the Professional Photographers of America. Her daughter, Hermine Turner, took over her mother's business after she retired in 1927. She died at home in New York City. Renewed and favorable critical appreciation of Käsebier's work came with two major retrospective exhibitions, one in 1979 that originated at the Delaware Art Museum and traveled to the Brooklyn Museum, and the other in 1991 at the Museum of Modern Art in New York.

• Collections of Käsebier's photographs are in the Museum of Modern Art, New York; the Alfred Stieglitz Collection, Metropolitan Museum of Art, New York; the Library of Congress, Washington, D.C.; the National Museum of American History, Smithsonian Institution, Washington, D.C.; the International Museum of Photography at the George Eastman House, Rochester, N.Y.; the Delaware Art Museum, Wilmington; the Virginia Museum, Richmond; and the Spencer Museum of Art, University of Kansas, Lawrence. Biographical information and personal papers can be found at the University of Delaware Library, Newark; the New York Public Library Manuscript Division; the Library of Congress Manuscript Division; the Alfred Stieglitz Archive, Yale University, Beinecke Rare Book and Manuscript Library, New Haven, Conn.; and the Amon Carter Museum of Western Art, Fort Worth, Tex. Käsebier describes her own work in "Picture Making: A Talk to the Department of Photography, Brooklyn Institute," *American Photography* 9 (Apr. 1915): 224, 226. Monographs on Käsebier include Barbara L. Michaels, *Gertrude Käsebier: The Photographer and Her Photographs* (1992), and William Innes Homer, *A Pictorial Heritage: The Photographs of Gertrude Käsebier* (1979). Her contributions to photography are discussed by her contemporaries in Charles H. Caffin, "Mrs. Käsebier and the Artistic-Commercial Portrait," *Everybody's Magazine*, May 1901, pp. 480–95; and Giles Edgerton (pseud. Mary Fanton Roberts), "Photography as an Emotional Art: A Study of the Work of Gertrude Käsebier," *Craftsman* 12 (Apr. 1907): 80–93. An obituary is in the *New York Times*, 14 Oct. 1934.

PATRICIA A. FAIRCHILD

KASNER, Edward (2 Apr. 1878–7 Jan. 1955), mathematician, was born in New York City, the son of Bernard Kasner and Fanny Ritterman. At age thirteen, he entered the College of the City of New York to pursue a five-year course of study that combined the then standard high school and undergraduate curricula. Kasner completed this program on schedule to earn his B.S. in 1896. He followed this with graduate work at Columbia University, where he studied principally under the Göttingen-trained American mathematician Frank Nelson Cole. Kasner took his Columbia A.M. and Ph.D. in mathematics in 1897 and 1899, respectively. He next proceeded, like his professor as well as so many other American mathematical aspirants in the closing quarter of the nineteenth century, to Göttingen for additional postgraduate training. Kasner spent the

1899–1900 academic year abroad, principally in the lecture rooms of two of the German mathematical standard-bearers, Felix Klein and David Hilbert.

Kasner returned to New York in time to take up his new post as tutor in mathematics at Barnard College in the fall of 1900. He remained in that position for five years, receiving a promotion to the rank of instructor in 1905 and to that of adjunct professor one year later. In all, Kasner spent ten years officially on the faculty at Barnard, and during that time he established a reputation as not only a notable teacher but also as an influential member of the American mathematical research community. His undergraduate teaching aimed not so much to produce future mathematicians as to instill an appreciation of the subject in his students. To this end, he instituted the "mathematics bulletin board" on which he regularly posted students' work of special interest or merit. It became a recognized, though unofficial, honor for students to find their work so displayed. Relative to the broader mathematical community, Kasner participated in the monthly meetings (held in New York City) of the American Mathematical Society (AMS), frequently presenting talks on his latest research work in the field of differential geometry. His contributions won important recognition as early as 1904 when he was asked to give a keynote address on geometry at the International Congress of Arts and Sciences associated with the St. Louis World's Fair. On this occasion, he chose as his topic "Present Problems of Geometry," and he shared the platform with the noted French mathematician Henri Poincaré. Kasner's stature in the scientific community was also made manifest through his election, in 1906, to the vice presidency of the American Association for the Advancement of Science (AAAS) and to the chair of the AAAS's Section on Mathematics and Astronomy and to the vice presidency of the AMS in 1908. His research accomplishments were further acknowledged when the AMS selected him to deliver the prestigious Colloquium Lectures of the AMS in the summer of 1909. He spoke on his then recent work in the trajectories of dynamics, and his lectures came out in book form in 1913 as *Differential Geometric Aspects of Dynamics* (repr. 1934).

Kasner shifted his position permanently from Barnard to Columbia in 1910, when the Columbia trustees offered him a full professorship. He remained on the Columbia faculty for the rest of a career that found him engaged in essentially four related areas of mathematical research: differential geometry applied to dynamics (through roughly 1920), the geometrical aspects of Einsteinian relativity (1920–1927), the analysis of so-called polygenic functions of a complex variable (1927–1940), and the geometrical analysis of horn angles (1940–1955). As early as 1917 his contributions to differential geometry won him election to the National Academy of Sciences.

In addition to his research work at Columbia, Kasner also devoted himself to the training of graduate students, regularly running his "Seminar in Differential Geometry." Among the students who fell under

his influence there, Joseph F. Ritt, Philip Franklin, and Jesse Douglas may be singled out for their subsequent contributions to mathematics. As Douglas has described it, "Kasner's mode of presentation was ideal for those seeking fruitful research problems. The theme of his advanced teaching, in any mathematical situation under discussion, was this: 'Have we a problem here? Is there something still incomplete, something of significance or interest left to be investigated? Is there a property stated which is not characteristic?—then find a characteristic property'" (Douglas, p. 187). Kasner thus challenged his auditors to do mathematics actively by critically questioning and examining—not merely accepting—the mathematics received.

Kasner's ability to communicate effectively about mathematics was, moreover, not limited to the context of the graduate seminar. He often was asked to give mathematical presentations in kindergartens and private schools, building his lectures on such occasions around common and easily understood questions like "How many pennies can you place on the floor touching one penny?" With apparent ease, he would proceed to give the children in his audience an intuitive appreciation of deep problems in mathematics, such as the three-dimensional analog of this question, namely, sphere-packing. Kasner also offered, through New York's New School of Social Research, a popular evening course, "Fundamental Concepts of Mathematics," that aimed to introduce adult students to some of the key concepts of basic mathematics. In what was perhaps his most successful effort in taking mathematics to a broader public, however, Kasner coauthored, with his student James Newman, the widely read book *Mathematics and the Imagination* (1940). There he popularized two terms he had challenged his young nephews to invent in the course of his ongoing mathematical discussions with them, namely, googol for 10^{100} and googolplex or 10^{googol}.

Kasner assumed the Robert Adrain Professorship in mathematics at Columbia in 1937. From this point on, he conducted much of his research in collaboration with his student John De Cicco. Kasner retired as Adrain Professor Emeritus in 1949. Never married, he died in New York City.

An able mathematician and a committed teacher at all levels, Kasner played an influential role in establishing, maintaining, and fostering a research-level program in mathematics at Columbia during what has been characterized as a period of consolidation and growth of mathematics at the advanced level in the United States.

• There is no major archival collection of Kasner's papers. Among his most important works not mentioned above are "The Present Problems of Geometry," *Bulletin of the American Mathematical Society* 11 (1905): 283–314; and "The Theorem of Thomson and Tait and Natural Families of Trajectories," *Transactions of the American Mathematical Society* 11 (1910): 121–40. On Kasner's life, consult Jesse Douglas, "Edward Kasner: April 2, 1878–January 7, 1955," National Academy of Sciences, *Biographical Memoirs* 31 (1958): 179–

209, which includes a photograph, a technical discussion of Kasner's mathematical achievements, and a complete bibliography of his works. For a sense of Kasner's place in the American mathematical community, consult Della Dumbaugh Fenster and Karen Hunger Parshall, "A Profile of the American Mathematical Research Community: 1891–1906," in *The History of Modern Mathematics*, vol. 3 (1994), pp. 179–227. An obituary is in the *New York Times* 8 Jan. 1955.

KAREN HUNGER PARSHALL

KASSON, John Adam (11 Jan. 1822–18 May 1910), diplomat, congressman, and postal official, was born in Charlotte, Vermont, the son of John Steele Kasson and Nancy Blackman, farmers. His father died a few years after Kasson's birth, and his mother managed the farm. He was educated in the common schools, Burlington Academy, and the University of Vermont, where he received an A.B. in 1842. Kasson tutored for a season in a slaveholding family near Charlottesville, Virginia. He then spent three months in his brother's law office in Burlington, Vermont, before moving to Worcester, Massachusetts, to read intensively under Emory Washburn, later a professor of law at Harvard. Kasson was admitted to the bar in 1844. Although he was only mildly antislavery, he attended the Free Soil Convention of 1848 in Buffalo. In 1850, after practicing law for six years in New Bedford, Massachusetts, he reestablished himself in St. Louis. That year he married Catherine Eliot; they had no children.

Handsome in appearance and impressive in bearing, Kasson was intelligent, articulate, and unusually observant. He also was witty and, by middle age, somewhat crotchety. Although he was farsighted on international matters, conflict between his idealistic and opportunistic strains often compromised his stand on domestic issues. In 1857 ambition prompted him to settle in Des Moines, Iowa, where he soon became state chairman of the Republican party. Three years later Kasson marshaled support for Abraham Lincoln at the national convention. He also exercized a moderating influence on the party platform. Appointed assistant postmaster general in 1861, he was soon recognized for his administrative skill. He played a key role at the Paris Postal Conference of 1863, the first of nine diplomatic missions on which he served.

Kasson's control of patronage in Iowa helped him win election to Congress in 1862 for the first of six terms spread over twenty-two years. He supported Lincoln's military, emancipation, and Reconstruction programs, and he remained loyal to Andrew Johnson, though he voted for the Civil Rights Act of 1866. Privately Kasson disapproved of the vengefulness of Radical Republicans and scorned conservative Democrats who wanted no Reconstruction at all. Publicly he went along with the Radicals on some issues and avoided confrontation on others by not voting. On balance, he apparently restrained the Radicals somewhat. They retaliated by using publicity over his 1866 divorce to thwart his nomination for a third term that year. Elected to the Iowa state legislature in 1867, Kasson led the movement to build a state capitol in Des Moines.

Kasson returned to Congress in 1873 to reemerge as an expedient moderate with a larger public vision than most of his colleagues. Yet he had no solution to the refusal of militant white southerners to observe federal law; even though he supported the second Civil Rights Bill in 1875, he voted against the Force Bills of 1874 and 1875. When an 1876 libel suit against his more malicious critics resulted in a hung verdict, he declined to run for a third consecutive term. He made rankly partisan speeches for Rutherford B. Hayes in the presidential campaign that fall, then involved himself indirectly in the arrangements leading to Hayes's disputed designation as president.

As Hayes's minister to Austria-Hungary in 1877, Kasson gave special attention to the newly created Balkan countries. He succeeded, for example, in drawing up commercial treaties with Serbia and Romania that were signed after he left Vienna. On the other hand, he failed to interest Secretary of State William M. Evarts in proposing that the Berlin Congress of 1879 provide religious and political freedom to Jews in Romania. Yet his repeated calls for commercial expansion and its concomitants—marine and naval expansion and an American-controlled isthmian canal—helped build the intellectual foundations for the expansionist nineties.

Elected again to Congress in 1880 for the first of two final terms, Kasson lost a bid for the Speakership but emerged as the leader of the House on foreign affairs. He piloted through committee a measure to foster a flexible tariff system, which eventuated instead in the "Mongrel Tariff" of 1883. He resisted a bill to exclude Chinese immigration for twenty years but was forced to accept a ten-year exclusion. He convinced the Foreign Affairs Committee, though not the entire House, to align behind federal incorporation of a private company to construct a canal across Nicaragua. He supported funding the Civil Service Commission under the Pendleton Act, even as he continued to support aspects of the patronage system. He voted enthusiastically for the Naval Appropriation Bill of 1884.

Kasson left Congress in the summer of 1884 to become minister to Germany. As head of the American delegation to an international conference on Central Africa presided over by Otto von Bismarck, he championed a host of enlightened policies ranging from neutralization of the Congo to free trade within it. His proposals to extend the "rights" of natives were rejected, as was his resolution to prohibit the liquor trade. He won approval of a strong resolution outlawing the slave trade, but the United States failed to ratify the Congo Treaty.

Kasson continued to serve the American government into his eightieth year. He performed notably as president of the Centennial Commission of 1887 and less successfully as commissioner to the Berlin Conference on Samoa in 1889, partly because of the obstructionism of President Benjamin Harrison and Secretary of State James G. Blaine. He was one of six American members of the British-American Joint High Commission that made an inconclusive effort in 1898–1899 to settle a Canadian-American boundary dispute in Alaska. From 1897 to 1901 Kasson served as President William McKinley's minister plenipotentiary to negotiate tariff reciprocity treaties. He negotiated numerous treaties, some on very favorable terms for the United States, that languished in the Senate unratified.

Kasson was a secondary figure of substantially more than average merit. By defining terms, crystallizing problems, fostering international arbitration, and pushing tariff reciprocity, he advanced many important programs incrementally. As his biographer appropriately concluded, Kasson's reputation "rests firmly upon his cumulative record as a constructive conservative" (Younger, p. 383). Kasson died in Washington, D.C.

• The most important collection of Kasson's papers is in the Iowa State Department of History and Archives, Des Moines. The Grenville M. Dodge and Samuel J. Kirkwood Collections are housed there, as is part of the James S. Clarkson Collection. Another part of the Clarkson collection is in the Manuscripts Division of the Library of Congress. Kasson's letters as a tutor in Virginia are in the Alderman Library, University of Virginia. The Department of State Archives contain Kasson's diplomatic dispatches. Other useful Department of State series include the John A. Kasson Samoan Conference Papers, 1889; the John A. Kasson Reciprocity Papers, 1897–1901; and the *Post Office Department: Journal and Letterbooks of the Postmaster General* (n.d.). Two autobiographical statements by Kasson are in the *Annals of Iowa* 4 (Jan. 1910) and 12 (July 1920). Edward Younger, *John A. Kasson: Politics and Diplmacy from Lincoln to McKinley* (1955), is a full, authoritative, and well-written biography. Obituaries are in the *New York Times* and the *Washington Post*, both 19 May 1910.

WILLIAM H. HARBAUGH

KATCHEN, Julius (15 Aug. 1926–29 Apr. 1969), concert pianist, born in Long Branch, New Jersey, the son of Ira J. Katchen, an attorney, and Lucille Svet, a pianist and arts patron. Evincing the talents of a child prodigy, Julius was homeschooled until the age of fifteen, so that his keyboard gifts could be developed fully under the tutelage of his maternal grandmother, Mrs. Mandel Svet, who served on the faculty of the Warsaw Conservatory prior to immigrating to the United States early in the twentieth century. She was his only piano teacher during his formative years, which saw his official public debut at the age of eleven with the Philadelphia Orchestra under the direction of Eugene Ormandy. With his highly acclaimed performance of Mozart's Concerto in D Minor, K. 466 on 21 October 1937, Katchen became the youngest solo performer to appear on a Philadelphia Orchestra subscription concert up to that time. His solo recital debut occurred slightly over a year later, on 13 November 1938, in one of New York's most prestigious venues—Town Hall. Performing works by "the three Bs"—Johann Sebastian Bach, Ludwig van Beethoven, and Johannes Brahms—as well as compositions by Frederic Chopin and Robert Schumann, Katchen demonstrated at twelve years of age many of the hallmarks that were to permeate his mature playing style—most notably, a firm command of technique and an athletic sense of execution that many critics believed evaded a large number of senior keyboard artists. He was subsequently invited by the New York Philharmonic Orchestra to perform at its summer concert series held outdoors at Lewisohn Stadium for thousands of music lovers and secured yet another triumph with his performance of Schumann's Concerto in A Minor, op. 54 on 6 July 1939. Complementing these engagements were various recitals wherein Katchen was often paired with other talented performers of his generation. His collaborations with the violinist Patricia Travers and others laid much of the foundation for his later reputation as a chamber musician.

As if realizing that there was more to life than that which could be experienced on the child prodigy circuit, Katchen's parents withdrew him from performances so that he might complete his formal education. His piano studies, however, continued privately under the direction of David Saperton, a member of the Curtis Institute of Music faculty in Philadelphia. He eventually matriculated at Haveford College and studied foreign languages, English literature, and philosophy, graduating with honors in 1946. This led to a fellowship awarded by the French government for further studies abroad. While living and studying in Paris, Katchen was invited to perform for the delegates attending the first International United Nations Educational, Scientific, and Cultural Organization Festival. This concert met with such success that he resumed his public performing career. Such was the success Katchen enjoyed in Europe that he settled there permanently, only returning to the United States for intermittent concert tours and visits with his family, which came to include his French-born wife, Arlette Patoux, whom he had married in 1956. They had one son.

That he did not consider himself an expatriate in the strictest sense of the word is borne out by statements Katchen made during a *New York Times* interview on 18 November 1962, to the effect that his European residency was determined primarily by the number of performance opportunities there, as opposed to those in the United States. No less valid was the choice of repertory Europe allowed Katchen to cultivate: he was one of the few artists of his generation to revive the virtuoso keyboard works of the nineteenth-century Russian school, including the original version of *Pictures at an Exhibition* by Modest Moussorgsky and *Islamey* by Mili Balakireff. He also championed modern composers, in particular the Americans Lukas Foss and Ned Rorem, both of whom had works premiered by Katchen. In between, he played virtually the entire spectrum of acknowledged masters—from the music of Bach in the baroque era through the Viennese classical composers Franz Joseph Haydn and Wolfgang Amadeus Mozart and culminating with the mainstream romantics Beethoven, Schumann, and Franz Liszt. Yet, it is the keyboard works of Brahms with which the name of Julius Katchen will forever be associated. He was the first pianist to perform the entire solo keyboard output of Brahms (in a series of four recitals in New York during the 1966–1967 concert season), and he often performed both of the composer's massive piano concertos during the same evening. His approach to these works stripped away much of the rhetoric usually found in less than sincere readings and emphasized the lyricism and warmth of the music without sacrificing any of the virtuosity and technique that is also inherent. Katchen recorded the complete Brahms solo keyboard music (as well as the concertos) for the Decca/London label, and as a complete entity, which has since been re-released on compact disc, it has yet to be equalled—let alone surpassed—by contemporary artists. He was the first pianist to record a solo LP (of Brahms's F-minor Sonata, op. 5) in the United Kingdom, and his recording of Sergei Rachmaninoff's Concerto in C Minor, op. 18 was the first LP made of a piano concerto anywhere. Katchen's collaborations with the violinist Josef Suk and the cellist Janos Starker in the piano trio music of Brahms indicated a new path he might have pursued with others, had he not been mortally stricken with the lung cancer from which he died prematurely in Paris, France. His legacy of superb recordings has remained, however, to remind one of his unique approach to the keyboard—lyrical yet powerful, serene and full of bravura—often at the same time.

• Katchen described his life as a concert pianist in "The Wand'ring Minstrel," *Concert Goer's Annual* (1957). Biographical information may be found in *Baker's Biographical Dictionary of Musicians* (1991) and the *New Grove Dictionary of Music and Musicians* (1980), while a retrospective of his recording career is published in *Gramophone* 1057 (1969): 21. See also C. B. Rees, "Impressions: Julius Katchen," *Musical Events*, Apr. 1965. An obituary is in the *New York Times*, 30 Apr. 1969.

LEIGH DAVIS SOUFAS

KATONA, George (6 Nov. 1901–18 June 1981), behavioral economist, was born in Budapest, Hungary, the son of Sigmund Katona, operator of the city's largest grain mill, and Olga Wittman. Katona grew up in a prosperous Jewish family in Budapest. He entered the University of Budapest in 1918 in order to study law, but a 1919 Communist putsch led by Bela Kun forced the closure of the university and led Katona to study under Georg Elias Müller at the Psychological Institute of the University of Göttingen, from which he received his Ph.D. in experimental psychology in 1921. Inflation in Germany in 1922–1923 made him abandon his plans to become a privatdocent at the University of Frankfurt. Instead, he accepted a position in the research department of a Frankfurt bank, where he studied the psychology of inflation. In 1923 he went to Berlin to continue his education in Gestalt psychology under Max Wertheimer and Kurt Lewin. He also focused on economic issues as he worked on the staff of German publications and traveled to the United States from the fall of 1925 until the summer of 1926. In 1926 the politician, publicist, and author Gustav Stolper of-

fered him a position as an associate editor of the weekly magazine *Der Deutsche Volkswirt*, a position he held from 1926 to 1933 and where he wrote appreciatively of the role of consumption in the American economy. During these years he continued to do experimental work at the Berlin Psychological Institute. In November 1929 he married Marian Beck; they had no children. He served as a German correspondent for the *Wall Street Journal* from 1930 to 1933. After Adolf Hitler came to power and the Nazis banned the *Volkswirt*, Katona came to the United States in the summer of 1933, becoming an American citizen in 1939. Central to his life as an émigré was an eagerness to understand how America might escape the fate that befell Weimar and Nazi Germany.

From 1933 to 1936 he worked at an investment advisory firm in New York that Stolper established. In 1936 tuberculosis forced Katona to give up this job and resume his psychological research and academic career. With the help of Wertheimer, he secured a grant (1938–1940) from the Carnegie Corporation, which he used to write *Organizing and Memorizing: Studies in the Psychology of Learning and Teaching* (1940), a book that argued for the transferability of material that was meaningfully learned, a process that facilitated its application under different circumstances. From 1940 to 1942 Katona used a Guggenheim Fellowship to integrate his work in economics and psychology, with the results appearing in courses he taught at the New School for Social Research from 1940 to 1942 and in *War without Inflation: The Psychological Approach to Problems of War Economy* (1942). He argued that it was possible to achieve prosperity without inflation, largely through the reasonableness of consumers' decisions, a position that shaped his later work. At the invitation of Jacob Marschak, whom he had known in Germany, Katona directed a study from 1942 to 1944 on price controls under the auspices of the Cowles Commission for Research in Economics at the University of Chicago and the National Bureau of Economic Research. This work resulted in *Price Control and Business* (1945), in which he first used survey methods, developed in other disciplines, to study the economy. In 1944 Katona accepted Rensis Likert's offer of a position at the U.S. Department of Agriculture's Division of Program Surveys, where he and Eleanor Maccoby carried out research, funded by the Federal Reserve Board, on the psychological and economic factors that might influence what Americans would do with the personal savings accumulated during World War II. In 1945 the Federal Reserve Board began to sponsor the Survey of Consumer Finances, which Katona directed, first at the Department of Agriculture and later at the University of Michigan. After 1959, when support from the Federal Reserve Board ended, Katona secured funds from foundations, the university, government agencies, and corporations.

In 1946 Katona joined colleagues from the Division of Program Surveys in a move to the University of Michigan, where from 1946 to 1972 he was a professor of economics and psychology and directed the university's Economic Behavior Program at the Survey Research Center, which he helped launch and which later became part of the university's Institute for Social Research. He studied both the research strategies and theoretical issues involved in using data on consumers' attitudes to forecast shifts in economic activity. In this endeavor he worked with others to establish, in 1952, an index of consumer sentiment.

Central to his position was the argument that levels of consumer confidence predicted levels of consumers' discretionary purchases of durable goods and, in turn, of economic activity. "His pioneering work was the development of a new body of knowledge bridging the gap between economics and psychology. . . . His great methodological innovation in behavioral economics was to explain changes in the economic system by analyzing actions and predispositions to action on the individual level and applying micro-data to macro-economic analysis and prediction" (*American Psychologist*, p. 69). He urged economists to expand the data they used in forecasting to include consumer attitudes and in the process expanded the use of survey research in economics. Katona's work was interdisciplinary: exploring the relationships between economics and psychology, he helped develop the field of psychological or behavioral economics. He argued for the centrality of middle-class consumers in the economy, seeing them as heroic people whose aspirations and rationality, by helping to moderate inflation and promote prosperity, helped make the United States a stable society. He emphasized the way cognition and learning influenced the gestalt of consumers—their attitudes, aspirations, values, and frames of reference. The procedures he developed provided the basis for examinations of consumer expectations carried out in the United States, Europe, Japan, Australia, and Canada. Although events of the early 1970s began to shake his confidence and that of the people he surveyed, during his life in his adopted homeland he sustained a confidence in the power of a consumer-driven economy to prevent the United States from experiencing the turmoil he had witnessed in Germany earlier in his life.

Katona retired in 1972, after which he stayed in Ann Arbor and served as a consultant to the Economic Behavior Program. Recognition came from numerous sources. He taught at the Massachusetts Institute of Technology (1961) and New York University (1964), received the first Hegemann Prize in Düsseldorf, Germany (1963), earned membership in the American Academy of Arts and Sciences, served as president of the Consumer Psychology section of the American Psychological Association (1966–1967), and received the Distinguished Professional Contribution Award of the APA (1977). Katona died in West Berlin, the day after he had received an honorary doctorate in economics from the Free University of Berlin.

Many regarded Katona as the dean of behavioral economics. Based on extensive empirical data and making advances in survey techniques, his studies provided pioneering explorations of the relationship between consumer expectations and national economic activity.

• Katona's papers, consisting mostly of reprints, reports, speeches, and reviews, are in the Bentley Historical Library at the University of Michigan. Katona's recollections can be found in *Psychological Economics* (1975); "Reminiscences" in *Human Behavior in Economic Affairs: Essays in Honor of George Katona*, ed. Burkhard Strumpel et al. (1972); and *Ehrenpromotion von Prof. Dr. George Katona, Ann Arbor, Michigan am 15. June 1981*. The most complete discussion of Katona's life and assessment of his career is Richard Curtin, "Curtin on Katona," *Contemporary Economists in Perspective*, ed. Henry W. Spiegel and Warren J. Samuels (1984), which also contains a list of Katona's publications. Useful information can also be found in "George Katona," *American Psychologist* 33 (Jan. 1978): 69–74, and Toni Stolper, *Ein Leben in Brennpunkten Unserer Zeit: Wien, Berlin, New York; Gustav Stolper, 1888–1947* (1960). Katona presented his findings in reports of the surveys he directed, in economics and psychology journals, and in a series of books. *Consumer Attitudes and Demand, 1950–1952* (with Eva Mueller, 1953); *Consumer Expectations, 1953–1956* (with Mueller, 1956); *Private Pensions and Individual Saving* (1965); and *Consumer Response to Income Increases* (with Mueller, 1968) presented conclusions from specific studies. In *Psychological Analysis of Economic Behavior* (1951) and *Psychological Economics*, Katona developed his theories of a behavioral economics. *The Powerful Consumer: Psychological Studies of the American Economy* (1960) and *The Mass Consumption Society* (1964) presented his findings to an audience of nonspecialists. In *Aspirations and Affluence: Comparative Studies in the United States and Western Europe* (1971), Katona, Strumpel, and Ernest Zahn explored the consumer economy in Western Europe and America. In *A New Economic Era* (1978), Katona and Strumpel explored the consequences of an economic environment shaped by stagflation, threats to the environment, and lessened consumer confidence. *Essays on Behavioral Economics* (1980) summarized a life's work in economics and psychology. Obituaries are in the *Ann Arbor News*, 18 June 1981; the *New York Times*, 19 June 1981; and *ISR Newsletter*, Autumn 1981.

DANIEL HOROWITZ

KATZER, Frederick Xavier (7 Feb. 1844–20 July 1903), third Roman Catholic archbishop of Milwaukee, Wisconsin, was born in Ebensee, Austria, the son of Carl Katzer and Barbara Schwarzenbrunner (occupations unknown). In 1857 he entered the preparatory seminary at Freinberg near Linz operated by the Jesuits. During the course of his studies an emissary of the Leopoldine Mission Society, Father Francis Pierz, encouraged the young man to go to the United States for priestly ministry in Minnesota. However, upon arriving in the United States in May 1864, Katzer was informed that his services were not needed, and he accepted a request from a fellow countryman, Father Joseph Salzmann, to come to St. Francis Seminary in Milwaukee. He was ordained to the priesthood there in December 1866 by Bishop John Martin Henni and immediately began a career as a seminary professor, teaching mathematics, philosophy, and dogma. He also founded a literary and dramatic society for the

German seminarians and in 1873 wrote a play, *Der Kampf der Gegenwart*, which was a paean to his Jesuit instructors and a diagnosis of Europe's social ills.

In 1875 he accompanied newly appointed Bishop Francis X. Krautbauer to the diocese of Green Bay. There he served as the bishop's secretary and in 1878 was named vicar general of the diocese. When Krautbauer died in 1885, Katzer administrated diocesan affairs until he was appointed bishop of Green Bay in 1886. He was consecrated a bishop on 21 September 1886 by Archbishop Michael Heiss of Milwaukee. Katzer spent four more years in Green Bay, distinguishing himself by his strenuous opposition to the Bennett Law of 1889, which made the teaching of English compulsory in all Wisconsin schools. He viewed public schools with alarm. Of the Bennett Law he said to the Wisconsin branch of the Central Verein: "It is a step by which the state has transgressed the limits of its powers and arrogated rights which . . . belong solely to parents. . . . It is a step by which Antichrist is trying to promote its attacks on the Church and accomplish its oppression by the state." As a result of a vigorous campaign waged by the unlikely alliance of German Catholics and Lutherans, Governor William Hoard, who signed the law, and the members of the legislature who voted for it were driven from office. A new administration under Governor George Wilbur Peck succeeded in repealing the law in 1890.

In January 1891 Katzer succeeded Heiss and became the third archbishop of Milwaukee despite considerable opposition from prelates such as Cardinal James Gibbons of Baltimore and Archbishop John Ireland (1838–1918) of St. Paul. The latter characterized him as "thoroughly German and thoroughly unfit to be an archbishop." Katzer was indeed closely associated with the "Germanizing" faction of the American hierarchy and believed with them that the survival of German Catholicism in the United States was inextricably linked to the preservation of their distinctive ethnic traits, especially language. When Pope Leo XIII indirectly rebuked the so-called "Americanists" like Gibbons and Ireland in his 1899 encyclical, *Testem Benevolentiae*, for too readily adapting Catholicism to American ways, Katzer publicly thanked the pontiff.

In his administration of archdiocesan affairs, Katzer liberally allowed the creation of national parishes, thereby encouraging the ethnic diversity of the archdiocese. His regime dovetailed with some of the heaviest Polish immigration to Wisconsin, and Polish immigrants made their presence felt in Milwaukee and other cities of the archdiocese by the creation of a number of parishes. Katzer's benevolence toward the Poles raised their hopes that one day an auxiliary bishop of their nationality would be appointed to Milwaukee. These expectations later raised serious difficulties for his successor, Sebastian G. Messmer, a German-speaking Swiss.

Katzer viewed American society and culture with a skewed eye and saw little to be gained for the church by an overeager acceptance of American values and political institutions. As a result, he was quick to condemn popular fraternal organizations, which he considered forbidden secret societies. Moreover, he felt uncomfortable with the egalitarian tenets of the Populist movement and publicly repudiated the candidacy of William Jennings Bryan in the 1896 presidential election.

Katzer died unexpectedly of natural causes in Fond du Lac, Wisconsin, on the very day of Pope Leo XIII's death.

• There is no general biography of Katzer. The few of his papers that are extant are in the Archives of the Archdiocese of Milwaukee and the Diocese of Green Bay. See Benjamin Blied, *Three Archbishops of Milwaukee* (1955); Anthony Kuzniewski, *Faith and Fatherland: The Polish Church War in Milwaukee* (1980); and K. Gerald Marsden, "Father Marquette and the A.P.A.: An Incident in American Nativism," *Catholic Historical Review* 46 (Apr. 1960): 1–21.

STEVEN M. AVELLA

KAUFMAN, Bob (18 Apr. 1925–12 Jan. 1986), poet, was born in New Orleans, Louisiana, the son of Joseph Kaufman, a Pullman porter, and Lillian Vigne, a former schoolteacher. His home was a mix of ethnic and religious traditions. His father was part black and Jewish; his mother, from a Martinique family, was a black Roman Catholic. Kaufman's early formal education did not go much beyond elementary school, but his mother collected books, and young Kaufman was an avid reader. He was also exposed to the rhythms, melodies, and themes of New Orleans jazz.

As a teenager, Kaufman joined the merchant marine. A shipmate introduced him to the poetry of Federico García Lorca, Hart Crane, T. S. Eliot, and Walt Whitman and the political economy of Marx and Lenin. On land, Kaufman divided his time between New York City and the West Coast, usually San Francisco. In New York, he sought the acquaintance of jazz musicians, including Charlie Parker and Miles Davis. In the late 1940s he took classes at the New School for Social Research, his only formal college education. In 1948 Kaufman worked in Appalachia as an organizer for Henry Wallace's presidential campaign. In the 1940s and 1950s Kaufman also worked as a union organizer among merchant mariners on the West Coast.

In May 1958 Kaufman met Eileen Singhe in San Francisco. They were married in June and had two children. The couple separated in 1964, reconciled, and then separated again in the 1980s. Eileen Kaufman encouraged her husband to write down the oral, improvisational poetry that he had begun to develop. Kaufman's first published poems were three broadsides issued by Beat poet and promoter Lawrence Ferlinghetti's City Lights Books. The first broadside, *Abomunist Manifesto* (1959), was a satire, reflecting the disdain of the avant garde for organized political and religious movements. The other broadsides, *Second April* (1959) and *Does the Secret Mind Whisper* (1960), presented a series of jazz-inspired stream of consciousness images.

Kaufman left the sea and settled in San Francisco's North Beach, where he became a fixture at the Coexistence Bagel Shop. He recited his poetry there, as well as in the street and from the roofs of parked cars. The police were hostile to the North Beach avant-garde community, and Kaufman, a black man married to a white woman, became a special target. The police repeatedly responded to Kaufman's poetry performances by arresting him for disorderly conduct.

In the spring of 1959 Kaufman joined John Kelly, William Margolis, and Allen Ginsberg to edit the little magazine *Beatitude*. This became a publishing vehicle for work by Beats and other West Coast vanguardists, including Ferlinghetti, Ginsberg, Jack Kerouac, Gregory Corso, Peter Orlovsky, Philip Lamantia, Michael McClure, Philip Whalen, and Richard Brautigan. Kaufman wanted to present unpublished writers and use the mimeographed magazine as the center of a community that integrated art with life.

In the spring of 1960, when Kaufman's poem "Bagel Shop Jazz" was nominated for the British Guinness Poetry Award, he was invited to read at Harvard University. Kaufman jumped at the chance to move east and escape the surveillance of the San Francisco police. After settling in New York's Greenwich Village, he wrote and read poetry in coffeehouses and bars. But these were also years of poverty and growing addiction to alcohol and other drugs. Another argument with police in 1963 led the authorities to inter him in Bellevue Hospital and force him to undergo electric shock therapy. He returned to San Francisco; on 22 November he was so moved by the news of the assassination of President John F. Kennedy that he took a Buddhist vow of silence.

In 1965 the East Coast champion of vanguardism, James Laughlin of New Directions Press, published Kaufman's first book, *Solitudes Crowded with Loneliness*, which included work written from 1958 to 1963. In 1967 City Lights Books published his second volume, *Golden Sardine*, the poems taken from a bundle of old manuscripts. Kaufman's poetry in these books ranged from long-lined pieces reminiscent of Whitman, to shorter, more lyrical poems. Through surrealist juxtapositions of imagery he presented a comic, tragic, and usually ironic depiction of relationships, poetry, and contemporary American society. Kaufman, like other avant gardists of his time, explored how modern technocratic society, symbolized especially by the atomic bomb, created a dehumanized world. Through bebop jazz and the poetry it inspired, he searched for a new consciousness that could integrate art and life and create a more humane world.

After the signing of the treaty ending the war in Vietnam in February 1973, Kaufman surprised the audience at a Palo Alto gallery and broke his silence. He recited a speech from Eliot's *Murder in the Cathedral* and a new poem by himself, "All Those Ships That Never Sailed," announcing his return to literature and expressing hope in the midst of tragedy.

In 1975 *Solitudes* was translated into French. The work created a sensation, and Kaufman became known as the American Rimbaud. Because skilled translators championed Kaufman, he became more widely known in France than in the United States during his lifetime.

Kaufman's last poems were collected in *The Ancient Rain*, published by New Directions in 1981. By then he had earned a reputation as a burned-out case. He wandered around North Beach, his face ravaged by tics, barely able to talk. Although in 1981 the National Endowment for the Arts awarded him a creative writing grant, he spent it mostly on vodka. Yet, at a 1982 tribute in San Francisco, he recited poetry by Crane in a clear, strong voice. He died in San Francisco. His friends gave him a New Orleans–style funeral procession down Grant Avenue.

Through his use of jazz, Kaufman created an American surrealist idiom. More than most poets of the Beat movement, Kaufman explored the black experience of alienation. He presented hope for an end to that alienation, yet his often elegiac tone and the addictions in his life suggest a sense of tragedy that often proved overwhelming.

• Kaufman's papers are in the library of the Sorbonne University, Paris. *Cranial Guitar: Selected Poems by Bob Kaufman*, ed. Gerald Nicosia (1996), includes previously unpublished poetry, a biographical essay, and a bibliography of other biographical sources. Mel Clay, *Jazz—Jail and God: Bob Kaufman; an Impressionistic Biography* (1987), has a detailed bibliography. Kaufman is discussed in relation to other black poets in Eugene B. Redmond, *Drumvoices: The Mission of Afro-American Poetry* (1976). An obituary is in the *San Francisco Chronicle*, 13 Jan. 1986.

STUART D. HOBBS

KAUFMAN, George S. (16 Nov. 1889–2 June 1961), playwright and stage director, was born in Pittsburgh, Pennsylvania, the son of Joseph Kaufman, a small-businessman, and Henrietta Myers. Raised in a middle-class Jewish family, Kaufman attended public schools and immersed himself in plays and books—particularly those by Mark Twain. After high school, he moved near New York in 1909 and supported himself by working in a hatband factory while attending the theater and contributing small pieces of verse to Franklin P. Adams's widely read column in the *New York Evening Mail*.

Recognizing his talent, Adams got him a job on the *Washington Times* in 1912, then, in 1917, on the *New York Tribune* as a drama desk reporter. With Adams's encouragement, Kaufman began to get some notice as a humorist, and later in the year he moved to the *New York Times* as a drama reporter, soon becoming the paper's drama editor, a post he held until 1930. In March 1917 he married Beatrice Bakrow of Rochester, New York; they adopted one child.

Kaufman's reputation as a playwright began inauspiciously in 1918 with the Broadway premiere of a heavily doctored comedy about safecracking, *Someone in the House*, which Kaufman revised extensively. Its quick failure did not unsettle his equanimity; he suggested as an advertising slogan for the show, which played during the 1918 influenza epidemic: "Avoid crowds. See *Someone in the House.*"

Kaufman was at the center of the theatrical and literary world of New York in the 1920s. Usually he had lunch at the Algonquin Hotel, where the Algonquin Round Table, an informal group of New York literati, traded luncheon entrées and verbal sorties right up until the stock market crash. The group's leader was the drama critic and radio personality Alexander Woollcott. Joining him were Kaufman, writers Dorothy Parker and Robert Benchley, playwright Robert E. Sherwood, critic Heywood Broun, comedian Harpo Marx, composer Irving Berlin, and others. The impact of the Round Table's participants on American culture is impossible to determine, but their blend of cleverness, insouciance, and arrogance made them fitting representatives of their age. Their anecdotes and witticisms alone, to which Kaufman added many, significantly contributed to American humor.

Another drama columnist at the Algonquin was Marc Connelly. Although he and Kaufman were different in temperament, they enjoyed each other's company and collaborated on writing plays. *Dulcy* (1921), their first effort, was inspired by the well-meaning but banal heroine of Franklin P. Adams's column; a great success, it made a star of actress Lynn Fontanne and set a pattern for future Kaufman-Connelly stories of good-natured dolts who outwit their more sophisticated rivals. Kaufman and Connelly wrote seven more plays over the next three years, the highlights of which were *To The Ladies* (1922) with Helen Hayes; *Merton of the Movies* (1922), Kaufman's first satire on Hollywood; and *Beggar On Horseback* (1924), a satire on business, written—uncharacteristically for Kaufman—in the Expressionistic style then fashionable.

Kaufman and Connelly then went their separate ways, and in 1924 Kaufman approached novelist Edna Ferber, whose interest lay in dynastic dramas of American families, to adapt her novel *Old Man Minick* for the stage. Initially cautious, Ferber agreed, and the resulting play was a success. Kaufman wrote five more plays with Ferber in the next twenty-four years. These collaborations are among his least frenetically comic works, but several have become popular classics. *The Royal Family* (1927) was a veiled encomium to the Barrymore acting clan; *Dinner at Eight* (1932) was a poignant and precise portrait of upper-middle-class manners during the depression; and *Stage Door* (1936) showed the tribulations of a group of aspiring young actresses. Each play was a huge success, and each was made into a successful motion picture, particularly *Dinner at Eight* in 1933.

By the middle of the 1920s vaudeville was dying out, and one of the medium's best acts, the Marx Brothers, looked to make a transition to the legitimate stage. The producer Sam H. Harris brought Kaufman together with Irving Berlin to craft a major musical for the Marxes. The result, *The Cocoanuts* (1925), was extremely popular and launched several projects for which Kaufman worked with the wildly anarchic comedy team. Another musical, *Animal Crackers* (1928), followed, this time with a score by Bert Kalmar and Harry Ruby. Kaufman wrote the book to this show

with Morrie Ryskind, a journalist and satirist who contributed some work to *The Cocoanuts*. These two musicals became the Marx Brothers' first two films, and Kaufman and Ryskind later wrote the screenplay for *A Night at the Opera* (1935), perhaps the brothers' best picture. Although his ability to ad lib appeared to be effortless, Groucho Marx's best lines in the early projects were written by Kaufman, and the comedian always gave the playwright credit for helping to create his enduring comic persona. However, the explosive spontaneity of the Marxes was a thorn in the side of the perfectionist Kaufman; once, in the back of the theater during a Marx musical, he interrupted a conversation with a companion, saying, "Excuse me, I thought I heard one of my original lines."

The second half of the 1920s brought a number of unusual projects. Kaufman's only completely solo effort, *The Butter and Egg Man*, another spoof on theater, was produced in 1925. In 1929 he wrote *June Moon*, which was his only collaboration with humorist Ring Lardner. The comedy combined Lardner's acidulous wit with Kaufman's penchant for wry wisecracks in an unusually bitter look at tunemaking on Tin Pan Alley.

Kaufman turned to Tin Pan Alley himself for a highly ambitious project with composer George Gershwin and lyricist Ira Gershwin. The show, *Strike Up the Band*, was an aggressive political satire on American government with a strong antiwar sentiment. It closed out of town in 1927, prompting Kaufman's remark that "satire is what closes on Saturday night." In 1930, with Kaufman's blessing, Ryskind softened the book's tone and changed much of its structure, and the revision gave the Gershwins the Broadway hit that had eluded them three years earlier. *Strike Up the Band* set the tone for the four collaborators' next musical, a groundbreaking masterpiece in American theater history. *Of Thee I Sing* put presidential politics center stage, spoofing the electoral process and the tenuous tenets of American governance. Candidate John P. Wintergreen, having no real issues to endorse, runs on the "Love" platform and is catapulted to the presidency. The integration of the libretto and score was more seamless and sophisticated than had been seen before on the Broadway stage, a fact recognized when the show received the 1931 Pulitzer Prize. The team's next attempt, a sequel entitled *Let 'Em Eat Cake* (1933), brought the characters of *Of Thee I Sing* face to face with the implications of international fascism with a shrillness that intimidated audiences. Unlike its predecessor, it was not a hit and has never had a successful revival.

When the 1930s began, however, Kaufman's spirits were generally high. He was relatively unaffected by the stock market crash. He remained devoted to his wife, although they had gone their separate ways sexually (which caused Kaufman acute embarrassment when film actress Mary Astor's diary detailing their relationship became public in 1936). And he was much in demand as a director after helming Ben Hecht and

Charles MacArthur's 1928 hit, *The Front Page*, as well as being well regarded for his talent as a play doctor.

But the decade's most significant event for Kaufman actually occurred in 1929, when Moss Hart sought him as a collaborator for a comedy Hart had written about the introduction of talkies to a panicked Hollywood. Kaufman's partnership with the 25-year-old Hart led to eight plays during the 1930s, some among his best and certainly among his most successful. *Once in a Lifetime*, a Hollywood spoof, with Kaufman directing and playing the supporting role of a Broadway playwright, was a leading hit of the 1930 season. Hart's taste for pageantry led to their 1934 play, *Merrily We Roll Along*, which traced a Broadway playwright's fall and rise through the century by telling his story in reverse chronological order. The play was not successful.

That show's failure was made up for by *You Can't Take It with You* in 1936. Kaufman's (and Hart's) greatest financial success, it is among Broadway's most popular, highly regarded, and specifically American plays. A young man from a wealthy Wall Street family and a young woman from an anarchically unconventional family fall in love despite the culture clash between the clans. The show delighted audiences, ran for 837 performances, and earned Kaufman his second Pulitzer Prize.

After writing the book for a provocative musical portrait of President Franklin D. Roosevelt in *I'd Rather Be Right* (1937), with a score by Richard Rodgers and Lorenz Hart, the team's next major creation, *The Man Who Came to Dinner* (1939), used the character of their friend Alexander Woollcott as the basis for a play about an egomaniacal celebrity and raconteur who invades the domain of a quiet midwestern family. Kaufman and Hart's final collaboration, *George Washington Slept Here* (1940), was an unambitious tale of the inconveniences of country life. Like Connelly before him, Hart parted with Kaufman amicably, to pursue his own career.

From the advent of World War II until the end of his career, Kaufman rarely reached the heights he attained in the 1920s and 1930s. He was a begrudging visitor to Hollywood, preferring to let others adapt his work for the screen (fourteen of his plays were made into films) and only occasionally, as with *A Night at the Opera*, writing original screenplays. As a playwright, he had few successes in his final twenty years: *The Late George Apley* (1944), adapted with John P. Marquand from Marquand's bestselling novel; *The Solid Gold Cadillac* (1953), a fable about the corporate world written with Howard Teichmann; and *Silk Stockings* (1955), a musical version of the film *Ninotchka* (1939), written with his second wife, Leueen MacGrath, whom he married in 1949. (His first wife had died in 1944 of a cerebral hemorrhage.) Kaufman enjoyed a greater reputation as a stage director during this period, particularly with the comedy *My Sister Eileen* (1940) and the highly successful musical *Guys And Dolls* (1950), and as a witty raconteur on television's "This Is Show Business."

But these were lesser triumphs compared to those of the 1930s. Although still lionized as a Broadway master when he died in New York City, Kaufman had little interest or hope that his plays would be treated well by posterity. He would have been surprised by the large number of revivals of his work on Broadway and in regional theaters that began in the late 1960s and still continues.

Although it is easy to chart Kaufman's successes, his influence on American playwriting is harder to define. If Eugene O'Neill represents the tragic mask of American drama, Kaufman can lay claim to its comedic counterpart. The successful American stage comedies before World War I are naive, sentimental, and closer to European manners and morals than to American ones. Kaufman added a distinctly American touch to his comedy, bringing the brashness of the postwar era to the Broadway stage.

Kaufman's insight into the American character was nearly as biting and witty as Mark Twain's. The two dueling families of *You Can't Take It with You* represent the conflict between the moral absolute of American capitalism and the idiosyncratic individualism of American democracy, and Kaufman sympathized with the latter. Although little of his Jewish ancestry was evident in his plays, Kaufman drew heavily on the value system of immigration and American assimilation. His heroes are invariably without lineage, money, or breeding, but they have industry, intelligence, and wit in large supply; usually they win out over exclusion, avarice, and stupidity.

No American playwright has been more respected for the kind of solid craftsmanship and economy that Kaufman brought to his works. His plays have served as models of comic construction for the stage, films, and television. In addition, his expert use of the wisecrack—the sly, sharp line that bolsters the speaker's ego or deflates his opponent's—has earned him a reputation as an American wit, and the wisecrack has become a staple of popular comedy in every medium. To attempt to classify Kaufman's comedies is fruitless. The Marx Brothers comedies were undeniably farces, while *Dinner at Eight* was an elegant comedy of manners, but for the most part the plays are simply comedies with three particular characteristics: outstanding parts for talented actors, tremendous physical and verbal energy, and a keen satirical outlook on timeless American preoccupations and institutions. In ironic contrast to Kaufman's remark about satire, there has not been a Saturday night since 1925 when a George S. Kaufman comedy has not been playing somewhere in America.

• Few of Kaufman's letters or papers give much insight into his work. These can be found largely in the New York Public Library Theater Collection, Lincoln Center, and the Wisconsin Center for Theater Research, Madison. Several of Kaufman's first drafts, which reveal more about his methods, are located in the Manuscript Division, Library of Congress. Kaufman's plays are largely out of print; Random House published most of them, including *Six Plays by Kaufman and Hart* (1941). Most of the plays can be read in acting editions published by Samuel French. The major biography is Malcolm Goldstein's *George S. Kaufman: His Life, His Theater* (1979). Howard S. Teichmann's *George S. Kaufman: An Intimate Portrait* (1972) is entertaining but filled with inaccuracies. A superior memoir of a briefer period of Kaufman's life is Moss Hart's *Act One* (1959). The best article on Kaufman's modus operandi as writer and director is "*The Man Who Came to Dinner*," by Morton Eustis, *Theatre Arts* 23 (Nov. 1939): 789–98. An obituary is in the *New York Times*, 3 June 1961.

LAURENCE MASLON

KAUFMAN, Joseph William (27 Mar. 1899–13 Feb. 1981), lawyer and judge, was born in New York City, the son of Samuel Kaufman and Adelaide Brenner. During World War I he served in the U.S. Army. Kaufman received an A.B. from Columbia University in 1920. Continuing his education there, he was awarded an LL.B. in 1923 and a J.D. in 1969. After his studies in law he clerked for New York U.S. district judge John C. Knox for one year. He entered private law practice immediately thereafter, working in both New York City and Washington, D.C.

Kaufman frequently served as counsel to state and federal agencies and legislative committees. From 1939 to 1941 he was a special trial examiner for the New York Labor Relations Board. During World War II he served as the general counsel for the Smaller War Plants Corporation of the Department of Commerce.

After the war, Kaufman made his most distinctive mark as a prosecutor in the Nuremberg war crime trials. He functioned as a deputy chief counsel overall and as chief prosecutor at the trial of Alfried Krupp and eleven other executives of the Krupp armaments industries. The Krupp trial, held in the Palace of Justice in Nuremberg, lasted eleven months and resulted in the conviction of the defendants for the crimes of plunder and using slave labor. They were found not guilty of the charge of waging aggressive war. Kaufman was praised by contemporaries for his handling of the difficult and detailed case.

Returning to the United States and private practice at the conclusion of the Nuremberg proceedings, Kaufman accepted the post of chief counsel to the House of Representatives Small Business Committee, serving from 1949 to 1950. His next government-related position was as chief referee of claims and appeals for the Social Security Administration, from 1956 to 1961.

From 1961 to 1969 Kaufman was chiefly occupied as an administrative law judge for the Federal Trade Commission. Thereafter he occasionally held special master assignments for the U.S. Court of Appeals.

Kaufman was a member of the American Bar Association, federal bar associations, the Association of the Bar of the City of New York, and the Federal Administrative Law Judges Conference. He also held membership in the American Arbitration Association and on the panel of the National Mediation Board.

Kaufman died in Washington, D.C. He never married.

• Kaufman's service in the Nuremberg trials is noted in full-length accounts of the events. In particular, his work as deputy chief counsel for the prosecution in the Krupp trial is chronicled in the U.S. government's account, published as *Trials of War Criminals before the Nuernberg Military Tribunals*, vol. 9 (1950). An obituary is in the *New York Times*, 17 Feb. 1981.

BARRY RYAN

KAUFMANN, Edgar Jonas, Sr. (1 Nov. 1885–14 Apr. 1955), retailer and patron of architecture, was born in Pittsburgh, Pennsylvania, the son of Morris Kaufmann, a merchant, and Betty Wolf. Kaufmann's grandfather was a horse trader in the Rhineland town of Viernheim, Germany. Two of his uncles left Germany in 1868 for Pittsburgh, where they were first peddlers and then tailors. In 1872 the two brothers were joined by Kaufmann's father and another uncle. In 1877 the four Kaufmann brothers opened a department store in downtown Pittsburgh, doors away from the cast-iron Mellon Bank. In 1905 Edgar Kaufmann attended the Sheffield Scientific School of Yale University, after which he spent two years as an apprentice at the Marshall Field store in Chicago, at Les Galeries Lafayette in Paris, and at the Karstadt store in Hamburg. He returned from Europe in 1908, and by 1913 he held or controlled a majority interest in the family store. In 1909 he married his cousin Lilianne Kaufmann; they had one child.

Like his father, Kaufmann had an excellent feel for the uses of architecture in advancing a commercial or social agenda. Although he had no professional connection with real estate, he involved himself with more than two dozen buildings and projects. Kaufmann exploited the artistic potential of the family store for its beneficial public image as the heart of Pittsburgh's Golden Triangle. He expanded the store in 1913 and in 1922 and then had the ground floor unified in 1930 in modern style, with a full set of murals by the prominent artist Boardman Robinson. Kaufmann's store supposedly had the world's most sophisticated air conditioning and lighting. *Harper's Monthly Magazine* (Oct. 1930) declared: "Edgar Kaufmann, son of a Jewish peddler, has just completed what is perhaps the most beautiful department store in the United States, if not in the world."

Kaufmann purchased or rented four or five houses and commissioned a half-dozen more between 1920 and 1950: one in Pittsburgh, two in the woods of southwestern Pennsylvania, and one each in upstate New York, Ontario, and California. Three of these were simple structures, but his 1928 Pittsburgh house, "La Tourelle," was a picturesque Anglo-Norman composition designed by the local architect Benno Janssen. The house's conservative design resisted the ahistoricism, abstraction, severity, and industrial patina that had become the main tenets of modern architecture.

It was therefore surprising that Kaufmann, seemingly an artistic conservative, financed one of architect Frank Lloyd Wright's most audacious conceptions. In

1934 he commissioned Wright to design "Fallingwater," Kaufmann's weekend house seventy-one miles southeast of Pittsburgh. Kaufmann's role in the project has been made to sound casual or capricious, but it was neither. Credit for the invitation to Wright is typically assigned to Kaufmann's son, Edgar J. Kaufmann, Jr., but it was the senior Kaufmann who invited Wright to bid on a project of a tunnel, multiple bridges, highways, and riverfront improvements for Pittsburgh. These and other aborted commissions eventually led to the commissioning of Fallingwater and a private office for Kaufmann in his store (the latter on view today at London's Victoria and Albert Museum).

The house, over a waterfall, was designed in the fall of 1935, constructed in 1936 and 1937, and opened to worldwide acclaim in 1938. Along with traditional Japanese architecture, Fallingwater is often singled out for its delicate synthesis of nature and the built environment. The house is also a synthesis of the romantic and technological traits of modern architecture, and it did much to convince skeptical Americans of the livability of the new style.

After Fallingwater, Kaufmann went on to commission two other notable structures. One is the winter home built for him in 1948 in Palm Springs, California, by Richard Neutra, which is also an important icon of modern architecture. The other is Pittsburgh's Civic Arena (opened in 1962), a distinguished example of postwar engineering. Other commissions followed for Wright as well: five were public projects for downtown Pittsburgh, including a vast megastructure for the confluence of the Allegheny, Monongahela, and Ohio rivers. All were abandoned before execution, as was the case with numerous other projects that Wright and Kaufmann had planned together. Kaufmann died in 1955 at his home in Palm Springs.

The three roles Kaufmann played—civic leader, retailer, patron of architecture—were closely related, since he made the Kaufmann store into a major force in the cultural and artistic life of Pittsburgh. Though the construction of Fallingwater occupied just a few years of his life, Kaufmann's renown as a patron of architecture was neither accidental nor unmerited: building the radical house was another example of Kaufmann's ability to identify the emerging social as well as economic trends of his customers.

• Kaufmann's letters to Wright are now at the Frank Lloyd Wright Foundation in Arizona. Selected letters are reprinted in Frank Lloyd Wright, *Letters to Clients* (1986). See "Seller's Market: In War Kaufmann's of Pittsburgh, like All U.S. Department Stores, Has Sold Everything It Could Buy. It Expects Soon to Buy More," *Fortune*, Nov. 1944, for an insightful portrait of Kaufmann as businessman. Leon Harris, *Merchant Princes* (1979), paints a vivid though one-sided portrait of Kaufmann as a social creature. Franklin Toker, *Pittsburgh: An Urban Portrait* (1994), establishes the context for Kaufmann in Pittsburgh; Donald Hoffman, *Frank Lloyd Wright's Fallingwater: The House and Its History* (1993), is the best single source on the house. Christopher Wilk, *Frank Lloyd Wright: The Kaufmann Office* (1993), documents Kaufmann's other executed commission from Wright. Robert Alberts, *The Shaping of the Point* (1980), and Richard Cleary, "Edgar J. Kaufmann, Frank Lloyd Wright and the 'Pittsburgh Point Park Coney Island in Automobile Scale,'" *Journal of the Society of Architectural Historians* 52 (1993): 139–58, document many of the aborted Kaufmann-Wright projects.

FRANKLIN K. TOKER

KAUFMANN, Peter (3 Oct. 1800–27 July 1869), publisher and social reformer, was born in Münstermaifeld near Koblenz, Germany, the illegitimate son of Johann Kaufmann, a cavalry officer and civil official, and Hulda (last name unknown). After graduation from the Gymnasium and two years at the University of Berlin attending Hegel's lectures, Kaufmann emigrated to the United States around 1820. In spite of financial difficulties with his trade as tobacconist in Philadelphia, he married Catherine Wiltz in 1822 and fathered seven surviving children. He studied for the ministry part time but was never ordained. In that study he was particularly impressed by the ideas of Johannes Tauler, who emphasized the unity of man and God through love and Jesus's sharing of poverty with the simple folk of his time. Kaufmann met Robert Owen a few times in Philadelphia and helped to establish a Labor-for-Labor store such as Owen had organized in Scotland. The store exchanged needed commodities for certificates of labor time. (Later Kaufmann wrote that well before the publicity of Owen, St. Simon, and Fourier he had been committed to the emancipation of mankind by the "Idea of Christian Social Life" inspired by Tauler and early Christianity.)

While Kaufmann was engaged in the Labor-for-Labor store, he wrote a book, *Betrachtung über den Menschen* (1825), elaborating Alexander Pope's maxim that "the proper study of mankind is man." There he contrasted the kingdom of Jesus with the present kingdom of Mammon; insisted that education as development of the human spirit toward godliness must be spread to all classes of society; saw in man's physical aspect, the nervous system, his "link to the cosmos [*Weltall*]"; and found in man's political aspect a natural sociality and the road to his full development under a republican constitution, a variant of democracy. The development of man's unique aspect, his spiritual and moral existence, Kaufmann further held, involves progress to become "perfect as our father in heaven is perfect." As a whole, *Betrachtung über den Menschen* was short on philosophical argument and long on homiletical exhortation. But its fundamental pantheism derived from Tauler, and its emphasis on unifying, perfecting process predisposed Kaufmann to accept what he later found in Hegel.

For a time Kaufmann taught languages, in which he was highly competent, at the Rappite "Harmony Society" near Pittsburgh. There he was pleased to find a band of sincere souls trying to practice the Christian love they preached. Arriving in Ohio around 1827, he helped to found the Society of United Germans at Teutonia near Petersburg in Columbiana County. The society took the welfare and salvation of all humanity as its aim, followed early Christianity in the sharing of goods and labor, and committed itself to freeing slaves and spreading "the holy doctrine of the Cross." The society was successful enough to last four years, longer than the Kendal Community of Massillon, Ohio, for which Robert Owen had held high hopes. Kaufmann also visited Zoar, Ohio, the long-lasting community of German Pietists, and drafted its history from 1817 to 1832. He presented his Christian perfectionism to members of the Trumbull Phalanx, a Fourierist Association near Warren, Ohio. There he found some dissatisfaction with its religious toleration. One member said that "this Babylon" particularly needs "your works of Love." Kaufmann drafted and published the call for "A Convention of Reformers" as "Messengers of Christ." The convention met at the Trumbull Phalanx in 1847 and further weakened Associationism. Most of these communalist movements took the U.S. Constitution as their political premise. All were strongly antislavery. Otherwise they were largely indifferent to national political movements and parties. Many of the Germans were, at least nominally, Jacksonian Democrats until the late 1850s, but there were also Whigs and independents among them.

In 1831 Kaufmann settled in Canton, Ohio, and six years later headed a national committee seeking the right to use German in school instruction as well as the English required by law. The committee established a seminary in Pennsylvania to train teachers to use both languages. Kaufmann's activities on the committee came to the attention of President Martin Van Buren and led to his appointment as postmaster of Canton in 1837. The committee disseminated Kaufmann's *Treatise on American Popular Education* (1839), which viewed education as the means to happiness, prosperity, and welfare in "the whole life of man." Language is particularly important as the mark of mankind's reason, its special distinction. Facility in both German and English, Kaufmann held, would promote national unity, be advantageous to business, and provide a bridge to the literary treasure of three great nations. Above all, it is essential for "free or republican institutions," the guardians against national degradation and tyranny.

While editing in Canton *Der Vaterlandsfreund*, a weekly Jacksonian newspaper with two later changes of name, Kaufmann became a highly successful publisher of almanacs in German and English. They were a means, one biographer has noted, of spreading his "Hegelian philosophy" in popular form. The fullest expression of his philosophical and social views came with *The Temple of Truth or the Science of Ever-Progressive Knowledge*, published in German and English in 1858. There he used Hegel's view of logic and dialectic as a foundation for his peculiarly American perfectionism expressing his passion for social reform, a perfectionism not to be identified with that of John Humphrey Noyes's Oneida community.

The Temple of Truth was first concerned with the elements and test of "absolute and unassailable truth." It sought a theory of knowledge that might serve as an Archimedean fulcrum for enduring progress of the human mind. Kaufmann's method was a combination of analysis and synthesis, inseparable because the part-whole relationship is one of the "permanent features of being and existence." There were two collateral aspects of the method to which Kaufmann gave special attention. First, it was inseparable from language. With his special knowledge of Greek, Latin, and French as well as German and English he emphasized the interpenetration of language and thought. Like recent linguistic philosophers and semanticists he saw how misuse of words can mislead understanding and developed rules for precise use of language. Second, he saw his method of analysis-synthesis as fusing data of sense with the classifying generality of reflection. This would show that multiplicity coexists in and with unity as Hegel held in his notion of a "concrete universal."

With his discussion of logic and dialectic Kaufmann made his debt to Hegel explicit. He viewed the mind's knowledge of itself and of nature through sense as adequate "to authenticate the facts of the case." But logic and dialectic are indispensable to the organization of thought. Logic is primarily concerned with the form of thought and its use. To explain the proper form of thought Kaufmann went to Kant's table of categories from which he derived the "laws of thinking" in syllogisms, proper combinations of judgments. The form of judgments indicates that language itself is logical in scope, so millions use logic who never heard of syllogisms. Dialectic is quite distinct from logic and goes further. It is concerned not with the form of knowledge but "the matter or substance of truth itself." Here Kaufmann followed Hegel's distinction between the externality of formal, Aristotelian logic and the concreteness of dialectic moving through opposition and conflict to synthesis and unity, thus expressing the very movement of actuality.

As Kaufmann developed his view of dialectic, his kinship with Hegel became more remote. The world, he thought, must be viewed as "a trinal disclosure of the Being and attributes of the infinite Author of all things"—as Nature revealed by the senses in science, Reason involving the whole of mankind in thought, and Religion relating the race to its ineffable Cause. On this basis he claimed to have taken the road to the "final ruling philosophy" defining the supreme end of man as "all-sided perfection" involving the harmony of all mankind. This, in Kaufmann's view, was the core teaching of Jesus whose disciples lived as brothers and sisters with all things in common. If it were put into practice, there would arise a true community of pleasant homes, education, and healthy labor lightened by machinery instead of existing compulsion and greed. The United States, Kaufmann believed, is especially able to realize such a community and become "a Saviour-nation" leading to a United States of the Earth.

Kaufmann's development of dialectic as applied to man's social perfection reflected, it would appear, more of his early communalism than adherence to Hegel. To be sure, it contained reference to the trinal disclosure of "all-embracing Being" vaguely paralleling Hegel's system. Beyond that Kaufmann's ideas were his own. Hence one biographer referred to his Hegelianism as "undigested." *The Temple of Truth* often relied on invective for argument, was needlessly repetitious in its twenty-six long chapters of fine print, and failed to make cogent transitions from one major position to another. Yet it had considerable recognition and influence. In reviews from ten Ohio newspapers it was called "profound" and "the book of the age." It was the occasion of correspondence and meetings with Ralph Waldo Emerson, whom Kaufmann intensely revered. Emerson praised the way it "marches with method, and, best of all, to a moral determination."

In 1861 Kaufmann became chairman of the Stark County Workingmen's Union devoted to extending the principles of the republic into the organization and improvement of labor. No specific data are available on the history of this union, but like many others of its type, its purpose survived, in varying degrees, in the later National Labor Union, Knights of Labor, and particularly the American Federation of Labor, which was independent of any specific political party.

Though Kaufmann had held a commission in the Ohio militia for some years before the Civil War, he was too old to join the Union army, the side he ardently supported and for which one of his sons died in battle on the western front. In turn he was well supported by the Republicans of Canton though he had been a delegate to three Democratic conventions and had been appointed Canton's postmaster by President Van Buren. Adhering to the policies of President Andrew Johnson in 1866, he was drawn back into the Democratic party as were many Germans after the Civil War in reaction against "Grantism." Then support for the successor to *Der Vaterlandsfreund* dwindled until it expired. Kaufmann closely followed the fortunes of battle in the Civil War and particularly the brilliant exploits of his fellow Germans in the Ninth Ohio Volunteers, trained by August Willich and commanded by Robert McCook, who wrote to Kaufmann that he was very proud of his all-German regiment and "you should be proud of them" too.

Peter Kaufmann died in the large brick house near the center of Canton that had served as his home and workplace for some thirty years.

• Kaufmann's surviving papers with a biographical sketch by Ernest Wesson and a typescript biography of his father are in the Ohio State Historical Society library. H. A. Rattermann, "Der Deutsch-Amerikanische Journalismus und seine Verbreitung von 1800," *Deutsch-Amerikanische Geschichtsblätter* 12 (1912): 291–97, contains a biography but neglects the content of Kaufmann's books noted in the preceding text. Loyd Easton, *Hegel's First American Followers* (1966), has biographical details on Kaufmann, some corrected here, and details on the content of his books, including key sections of *The Temple of Truth* in an appendix, pp. 278–98. Gustav Körner, *Das Deutsche Element* (1884), pp. 228–29, has some biographical data and perceptive remarks on Kaufmann's thought.

LOYD D. EASTON

KAUFMANN, Walter Arnold (1 July 1921–4 Sept. 1980), philosopher, was born in Freiburg, Germany, the son of Bruno Kaufmann, a lawyer, and Edith Seligsohn. His family soon moved to Berlin, where he received his primary and secondary education. Raised as a Lutheran, Kaufmann, who found himself unable to accept the doctrines of the Trinity or of the divinity of Jesus, converted to Judaism at the age of eleven. He learned only a little later that all of his grandparents had been born Jewish. This fact, and not the conversion to Christianity by his father's parents, was to determine the treatment of the family by the National Socialist regime in the 1930s. After completing his studies at the Grunewald Gymnasium in 1938, Kaufmann visited Palestine and then began studying Jewish history and the Talmud at the Institute for the Study of Judaism in Berlin.

Early in 1939, amid the worsening persecution of Jews in Germany, Kaufmann left for the United States. He enrolled at Williams College, where he studied philosophy and religion, graduating in two years with highest honors and Phi Beta Kappa. In the course of this study, he came gradually to give up his religious beliefs and affiliation, though not his abiding interest in religion, adopting instead a more rational and humanistic approach to the question religion addresses. In 1941 he moved from Williams to Harvard for graduate work in philosophy. The following year he completed his preliminary examinations for the Ph.D., received his master's degree, and married Hazel Dennis; they had two children.

Kaufmann's graduate studies were interrupted by military service in the U.S. Army Air Corps and then in Military Intelligence, which brought him to Austria and Germany in 1944–1946. Back in Berlin, Kaufmann purchased a copy of the Musarion edition of the complete works of the German philosopher Friedrich Nietzsche, whom he had read and admired. He decided to write his doctoral dissertation on Nietzsche, whom he believed had been willfully misrepresented as propounding ideas congenial to Nazism by Nazi ideologues, who wanted to appropriate his stirring texts for their cause. Kaufmann was able to enlist C. I. Lewis, perhaps the brightest light in the Harvard department, as his adviser.

Having written the dissertation in a little over a year, Kaufmann was awarded the Ph.D. in 1947 and joined the Department of Philosophy at Princeton University, where he worked for the rest of his life. Appointed as an instructor, he was promoted to assistant professor in 1950, associate professor in 1954, and professor in 1962, and he became the Stuart Professor of Philosophy in 1979.

After reworking his dissertation, Kaufmann published *Nietzsche: Philosopher, Psychologist, Antichrist* (1950). It was praised by some of the most respected interpreters of Nietzsche as the best work ever to have been written on the philosopher. Thomas Mann called it "a work of great superiority to everything previously achieved in Nietzsche criticism and interpretation." Kaufmann showed that Nietzsche, despite his highly literary and aphoristic style, had constructed and maintained with some consistency philosophic positions for which he gave arguments—even if these arguments were presented elliptically, or in bits and pieces, discontinuously across the body of his work.

Kaufmann's book helped greatly to rehabilitate Nietzsche both politically and philosophically; it became one of the major sources of the renewed interest in Nietzsche's work in the mid-twentieth century. He also translated many of Nietzsche's works into English, far superseding the previously available translations in accuracy and style.

Kaufmann was also instrumental in bringing European existentialism to America. In 1956 he published *Existentialism: From Dostoevsky to Sartre*, a collection of existentialist writings. His selection of texts, which included works of imaginative literature as well as essays, along with his introduction and notes to the volume, contributed to a better understanding of existentialism. The book, a huge success, went through seven printings in less than two years.

Kaufmann's abiding interest in religion and in its relation to philosophy gave rise to *Critique of Religion and Philosophy* (1958) and *The Faith of a Heretic* (1961). Although his own voice, sensibility, and views had been unmistakably present in his presentation and evaluations of other philosophers, in these books he developed a philosophic position of his own. The *Critique*, as its title indicates, is notable for its trenchant criticisms of many traditional religious and philosophic views. Kaufmann was particularly critical of the tendency to maintain one's affiliation with traditional religions, when one's beliefs and commitments were so attenuated as to render the affiliation almost meaningless. He became a prominent proponent of a critical, rational humanism and an implacable critic of what he saw as retrograde, conformist, and sometimes opportunistic attempts to hang on to religious doctrines and affiliations.

In *The Faith of a Heretic* Kaufmann developed these themes further, arguing that what essentially defines our philosophical tradition, and makes it valuable, is its critical or "heretical" character:

In medieval philosophy, apologetics triumphed over criticism. In modern philosophy, critical thinking re-emerges. Both tendencies are prominent in the great modern thinkers. But as we examine their progression, we discover that their rationalizations have proven less enduring than their criticism. And instead of seeing the history of philosophy as an accumulation of fantastic systems, one may view it as the gradual analysis of, and liberation from, one illusion after an another, a stripping away of fantasies, a slow destruction of once hallowed truths that are found to be errors. (P. 32)

In the 1960s Kaufmann became involved in the rehabilitation of another German thinker, G. W. F. Hegel, who had enjoyed considerable influence in the English-speaking world during the nineteenth and early twentieth centuries. But, because of the prolixity and obscurity of his thought, he had come to be re-garded as a notorious paradigm of the sort of murky metaphysical speculation that the then dominant neo-empiricist and neo-positivist, analytic philosophy was intent upon rejecting.

Kaufmann's *Hegel: A Reinterpretation* (1965) was an attempt to combat many of the current misunderstandings and misrepresentations of Hegel and recover some sense of his worth as a philosopher. While calling attention to Hegel's great flaws, particularly his obscure style, Kaufmann still insisted on Hegel's considerable contributions. His book was well received and contributed significantly to a revival of interest in Hegel in the 1960s and 1970s. Kaufmann also accompanied his reinterpretation with a translation of one the most important and difficult of Hegel's texts, the "Preface" to the *Phenomenology of the Spirit* (1807), whose accuracy and helpful commentary in the form of explanatory notes made Hegel's philosophy more accessible.

Kaufmann's interests, erudition, and publication were not limited to the discipline of philosophy as it is usually conceived. He acquired a remarkable knowledge of world religions, literature, and the visual arts, and he integrated this knowledge into his work. In 1961 he published a translation of Goethe's *Faust* and, in 1962, a book of his own poetry, *Cain and Other Poems*, as well as a collection of German poetry, *20 German Poets: A Bilingual Collection*. In *Tragedy and Philosophy* (1968) he examined Greek philosophers and tragedians and modern thinkers like Sartre and Brecht. In *Religion in Four Dimensions: Existential, Aesthetic, Historical, Comparative* (1976) Kaufmann returned to religion to illuminate, with both pen and camera, how various religions had affected and enriched human life, contrary to his previous dismissal of religious doctrines and practices. *Man's Lot: A Trilogy, Photographs and Text* (1978), whose three parts are titled *Life at the Limits*, *Time Is an Artist*, and *What Is Man?*, contains 400 of his photographs.

Kaufmann's last work, *Discovering the Mind* (1980), was his final reconsideration of the intellectual tradition that was the abiding source and focus of his teaching and writing, that of European, and particularly German, letters since the Enlightenment. He defined the subject of this work, however, not historically, but as the human enterprise of "discovering the mind," one's own mind, the minds of others, and how the mind works in general. Though his avowed "central aim throughout" was "to contribute to the discovery of the mind," he also claimed, "It should be one of the compensations of this study that it leads to a new and better understanding of a good deal of the intellectual history of the last two hundred years." Each of the work's three volumes deals with three major figures: volume 1 with Goethe, Kant, and Hegel; volume 2 with Nietzsche, Heidegger, and Buber; and volume 3 with Freud, Adler, and Jung.

Kaufmann's list of subjects reveals that he viewed the enterprise of discovering the mind to have had its center of gravity for the last two centuries in the world of German letters. Goethe, Nietzsche, and Freud are championed as admirable human beings who greatly contributed to the discovery of the mind. Kant, Hegel, and Buber receive decidedly mixed reviews, as having both helped and hindered our understanding. Heidegger, Adler, and Jung are severely criticized as reprehensible human beings who not only contributed little to the discovery of the mind but also impeded it. Kaufmann's work presents an intellectual landscape in which what is not a help is usually a hindrance, in which an author's character is usually relevant to his contribution, and in which intellectual interventions are rarely impersonal.

Kaufmann focused with obvious favor on a tradition in which boundaries between disciplines, which more and more characterize intellectual life, were less pronounced and did not interfere with fruitful interchange among thinkers from what are now considered divergent disciplines. Kaufmann's advocacy of this tradition was an attempt to encourage a reintegration of what he saw as the fragmented state of our current culture.

Kaufmann was a visiting professor at numerous institutions, including Cornell, the University of Heidelberg, the New School for Social Research, and the Hebrew University in Jerusalem. He won the International Leo Baeck Prize in 1961. At Princeton he was named Witherspoon Lecturer, a distinction bestowed upon outstanding faculty by the undergraduates (1962), and acting director of the prestigious Gauss Seminars in Criticism (1967–1968, 1972, 1975–1976).

Kaufmann was one of the most influential interpreters in the last half of the twentieth century in America of an intellectual tradition that derives principally from continental Europe, particularly from texts written in German. He studied philosophy, literature, psychology, and religion in an attempt to understand the human condition.

• Kaufmann's *The Portable Nietzsche* (1954) includes translations of *Thus Spake Zarathustra, The Antichrist,* and *Twilight of the Idols.* He also published translations of Nietzsche's *Beyond Good and Evil* (1966), *The Birth of Tragedy, The Case Wagner, On the Genealogy of Morals, Ecce Homo, The Will to Power,* with R. J. Hollingdale (1967), and *The Gay Science* (1974). He translated *Judaism and Christianity: Essays by Leo Baeck* (1958) and Martin Buber's *I and Thou* (1970). In *From Shakespeare to Existentialism* (1959) he collected twenty of his essays on various topics, including Shakespeare, Goethe, Hegel, Kierkegaard, Nietzsche, Freud, Heidegger, and Toynbee. A second collection of his essays, *Existentialism, Religion, and Death,* appeared in 1976. He edited and introduced the collections *Philosophic Classics* (2 vols., 1961), *Religion from Tolstoy to Camus* (1961), and *Hegel's Political Philosophy* (1970). In *Without Guilt and Justice* (1973), which he considered one of his most important works, Kaufmann argued for abandoning these two central concepts of our social and ethical thinking. In *The Future of the Humanities* (1977) he proposed changes that would make the humanities more relevant to our concerns as human beings.

IVAN SOLL

KAUSER, Alice (1872–9 Sept. 1945), playbroker and playwright's agent, was born in the American consulate in Budapest, Hungary, where her father Joseph Kauser was consul. Her mother was Berta Gerster, a well-known Hungarian opera singer with many connections to the European world of the arts. Alice Kauser, the goddaughter of Franz Liszt, was educated in Europe to be multilingual and well grounded in music, literature, and the theater.

Joseph Kauser eventually relocated to Pensacola, Florida, to resume his profession of engineering. His daughter sought work in New York. About 1895 she became a stenographer for the first woman to become a Broadway playbroker, Elizabeth Marbury. After learning the business, Kauser soon struck out on her own as a playbroker, placing Broadway plays with managers of stock companies. By 1905 her office had more than a dozen employees and 100,000 scripts on hand, new ones for the New York theaters, older ones for road and stock companies. Her office "probably handles more plays than any other two agents together" (*Theatre Magazine,* July 1905). An employee of hers, Crosby Gaige, recalled her in *Footlights and Highlights* as having "more driving energy than most men" (p. 54).

Kauser made a specialty of representing Continental playwrights, bringing their works to the American stage. She went to European theatrical centers—London, Paris, Berlin, and Vienna—regularly every year to seek out plays offered there that might suit American tastes. Her interest was not only in commercial possibilities but also in elevating the nation's taste for high dramatic art. She was especially interested in serious drama for intelligent adults. During her career she represented many European playwrights of distinction, including Sir Arthur Wing Pinero, Henry Arthur Jones, Victorien Sardou, Anatole France, Hermann Sudermann, Gerhardt Hauptmann, Arthur Schnitzler, and Maurice Maeterlinck. She worked for three years to get Maeterlinck's *The Blue Bird* produced in New York and brought about New York's first productions of Ibsen's plays.

Kauser also went on to champion American playwrights with new ideas. Among these were Langdon Mitchell, Edward Knoblock, Edward Sheldon, Rupert Hughes, Channing Pollock, and Edward Childs Carpenter. What she did as playwright's agent to launch 23-year-old Edward Sheldon is a good example of how far she would go for a writer in whom she believed. He sent her the script of a play he had written in a Harvard playwriting class, which she read and thought promising but in some ways too similar to a play already on Broadway. She asked him for other ideas and sent him away to write a play about the one she liked best. When he returned with *Salvation Nell,* she showed it to various actresses until she interested a close friend, Minnie Maddern Fiske, in starring in it. The play was a huge success in 1909, and Sheldon remained Kauser's client and friend for the rest of his life. She was described as "Sheldon's stage mother . . . [though] there was little to suggest the maternal in Alice Kauser's Valkyrie-like physique and temperament. But . . . no mother ever watched with more careful eyes . . . than did Alice Kauser as she guided Sheldon to success" (Barnes, p. 40).

Kauser's method of working was to read every script sent to her office and to write a report of its stage possibilities—both commercial and artistic—for her file. As a playbroker, she might present a particular play to a particular star for whom it would be suitable. More often, she let managers and stars come and tell her what sort of plays they wanted for the next season. Kauser might propose some work she had on hand or, lacking one, might suggest which playwright she represented was most likely to come up with such a play by the time it was needed. The play might be sold just on the basis of a scenario outline. She mediated between writer and producer when revisions were called for. As a playwright's agent, she arranged advances and the percentage of the play's profits the writer would receive (getting 10 percent of that amount for herself). She represented absent European playwrights at rehearsals and out-of-town openings. Several times she sued theater people who tried to present her foreign playwrights' work without paying, either stopping the production or getting royalties.

Kauser was variously described as having "an active brain and level head" with "strong purpose in her gray, girlish eyes" (*Theatre Magazine*, July 1905) and as being a "shrewd, matter-of-fact, often callous-seeming woman of the world" (Barnes, p. 40). Never married, she maintained an office for fifty years until her death. Her final years, during World War II, "proved a heavy drain on her, bringing personal losses and the destruction of the whole world of her youth in Europe. Before its close, she was an exhausted, broken old woman. She wrote [Sheldon] to say how feeble and ineffectual she now felt herself" (Barnes, p. 343). A short time later, she died in New York City after an emergency operation. Kauser's place in theatrical history is that of a pioneer playbroker, a co-creator, with Elizabeth Marbury, of the first field where women could succeed in the business side of the theater.

• Materials on Kauser are in the Billy Rose Theatre Collection at the New York Public Library for the Performing Arts, Lincoln Center. Substantial reminiscences of her are in Crosby Gaige, *Footlights and Highlights* (1948), and in a biography of Edward Sheldon by Eric Wollencott Barnes, *The Man Who Lived Twice* (1956). Informative articles are Henry T. Stewart, "The Playbrokers of New York," *Theatre Magazine*, July 1905; Alice Kauser, "From the Agent's Point of View," *New York Dramatic Mirrors*, 24 Aug. 1911; "The Playbroker Alice Kauser Describes Parts She Plays in Theatrical Season," *New York Tribune*, 25 Feb. 1912); and "A Placer of Plays, Miss Alice Kauser, Woman Dramatist's Agent, Tells of Her Work," *New York Dramatic News*, 25 Dec. 1913. Portraits of Kauser accompany the Stewart article. An obituary is in the *New York Times*, 10 Sept. 1945.

WILLIAM STEPHENSON

KAUTZ, August Valentine (5 Jan. 1828–4 Sept. 1895), soldier and author, was born in Ispringen, Baden (now Germany), the son of George Kautz and Doratha Lalwing. The family immigrated to the United States

the year of August's birth and settled in Brown County, Ohio. His younger brother Albert Kautz joined the U.S. Navy and rose to the rank of admiral. August attended school and joined the First Ohio Infantry at age eighteen, participating in the Mexican War. On his return, he secured an appointment to the U.S. Military Academy at West Point in 1848 and graduated with the class of 1852. He then joined the Fourth Infantry, stationed at Vancouver Barracks in the Pacific Northwest. With his regiment, he saw regular campaigning against the Puget Sound Indians, and he was wounded in the Rogue River expedition on 25 October 1855. During another campaign along the White River on 1 March of the next year, he was again wounded. While with the Fourth Infantry, August was promoted to first lieutenant.

During the Civil War, Kautz switched branches, becoming a captain in the Sixth Cavalry, and participated in operations on both sides of the Alleghenies for the entire length of the conflict. He first began action in Major General George B. McClellan's 1862 Peninsula campaign, mostly leading the Sixth Cavalry Regiment. On 10 September, after the campaign had ended, he was promoted to colonel and given command of the Second Ohio Cavalry. After service for several months as commander of Camp Chase, Ohio, he was placed in command of the First Cavalry Brigade, and he led the unit in battle at Monticello, Kentucky, on 9 June 1863. Following this action, Kautz attained some notoriety when he and his unit ran the Confederate cavalry raider Brigadier John Hunt Morgan to ground and assisted in Morgan's capture. Also at about this time his first quasi-official text, *The Company Clerk* (1863), was published. The book describes the proper conduct of duties by a soldier assigned to be a company clerk, an administrative position.

Kautz was elevated to chief of cavalry of the XXIII Army Corps. In this position, he participated in the East Tennessee campaign and was involved in the Federal siege of Knoxville. During this period he published a second text, *Customs of the Service for Non-Commissioned Officers* (1864), which lists the duties of a noncommissioned officer and advises on how to properly perform them. Kautz was then sent back to the eastern theater of operations, where in April he was given command of a cavalry division with the Army of the James. This duty was temporarily interrupted on 7 May 1864, when he briefly held the position of chief of cavalry for the Department of Virginia. However, he returned to his command duties, taking part in the operations against the Petersburg & Weldon rail line and the Petersburg & Lynchburg Railroad. He and his division conducted a probe at Petersburg on 9 June 1864. The division then joined Brigadier General James Harrison Wilson's raid to the south of the Confederate capital, fighting at Roanoke Bridge on 25 June and at Ream's Station on 29 June. Kautz's division was subjected to high losses on 7 October, when it protected the left flank of the Army of the James near Darbytown. On 3 April 1865 Kautz, now a brevet major general and leading the First Division of the XXV Corps, a black corps, entered the Confederate capital in the last few days of the war.

In the postwar era, Kautz resumed his regular army rank, performed judicial duties, married, wrote, and fought Indians. In the period May–June 1865 he was a member of the military court that tried and convicted those connected with the assassination of President Abraham Lincoln. In September he married Charlotte Tod, the daughter of the governor of Ohio, David Tod. In January 1866 Kautz was deprived of his rank in the volunteer service and reverted to his regular army rank of lieutenant colonel. He was also no longer in the cavalry, his initial assignment being with the Thirty-fourth Infantry. In that year he published his third text, *Customs of the Service for Officers of the Army.* In 1869 he was with the Fifteenth Infantry in the southwestern part of the United States, where he was involved in one of several operations returning Mescalero Apaches to their reservation. In 1872 he married Fannie Markbreit; they had a son and two daughters. The fate of his first wife is unknown. He was promoted to colonel on 7 June 1874 and was given command of the Eighth Infantry. In the 1880s he chiefly served in the West and Southwest, and during this time he published "The Operations South of the James River," in *Battles and Leaders of the Civil War,* volume 4, edited by Robert U. Johnson and Clarence C. Buel. On 20 April 1891 he was promoted to brigadier general and placed in command of the Department of the Columbia, where he served until his retirement on 5 January 1892. He died in Seattle, Washington.

Kautz made a contribution to the United States by representing the nation on its battlefields and in its uniform for almost fifty years. His service was marked by bravery, a talent for leadership, and an ability to influence his fellow soldiers and officers through writing.

• Excerpts from Kautz's diary are published in "The Diary of General A. V. Kautz," *Washington Historian* (Apr.–Oct. 1900). References to the Kautz family are in Josiah Morrow, *The History of Brown County, Ohio* (1883). Kautz's battle record is detailed in numerous citations throughout relevant volumes of *The War of the Rebellion: A Compilation of the Official Records of the Union and Confederate Armies* (128 vols., 1880–1901) and in U.S. Congress, *Report of the Joint Committee on the Conduct of the War,* 38th Cong., 2d sess. (3 vols., 1865). The highlights of Kautz's entire military career are detailed in George W. Cullum, *Biographical Register of the Officers and Graduates of the U.S. Military Academy,* 3d ed., vol. 2 (1891). His service and life in the Pacific Northwest are mentioned in C. A. Snowden, *History of Washington,* vols. 3 and 4 (1909). His obituary is in *Army and Navy Journal,* 7 Sept. 1895; *Annual Association of Graduates of the United States Military Academy Bulletin* (1896); and the *Seattle Post-Intelligencer,* 5 Sept. 1895.

ROD PASCHALL

KAVANAGH, Edward (27 Apr. 1795–21 Jan. 1844), politician and diplomat, was born in Damariscotta Mills, in what was then the District of Maine, part of Massachusetts. His father, James Kavanagh, a pio-

neering lumberman and prosperous merchant, emigrated from Ireland in 1784; his mother was Sarah Jackson of Boston. Edward grew up in a staunchly Catholic household. His mother was a convert to Catholicism in Boston before he was born. His father was a major donor for the construction costs of the brick St. Patrick's Church in Newcastle built in 1808, the oldest standing Catholic church in New England. The family played a role similar to other middle-class Catholics in Ireland and Maine, "consolidating the community" and "maintaining cultural continuity" (McCarron, p. 285).

Edward had a privileged childhood and a thoroughly Catholic education. At age eleven, he was sent away to school in Montreal for four years, then to Georgetown for one year, and finally to St. Mary's College in Baltimore for two years. Seriously thinking of becoming a priest, he spent a year in Boston in religious and philosophical study. However, Edward came home to assist when his father's business experienced problems brought on by the Napoleonic Wars. In 1815 he sailed on his father's ship to the West Indies, then to England; he toured England, Ireland, and France. It was on this trip that he acquired that "extensive knowledge of the languages spoken all over Europe and his acquaintance with their manners and customs" written about in a letter of recommendation for a diplomatic post fourteen years later (Portland Diocesan Archives).

In the years between 1816 and 1824 he studied law and begun a practice, still assisting his father in business. His experience in presenting claims and dealing with property transactions suggest Kavanagh's specialty was property law.

As a Catholic with political aspirations, it was fortunate that Kavanagh lived in Maine, which, unlike Massachusetts, had no test oath for public office. His long career took him from local to state politics, and then to the national level and back. Starting in 1824 he served for four years as a selectman of Newcastle. He was elected to the Maine House of Representatives in 1826 and to the state senate in 1827. After his father died in June 1828, Kavanagh did not seek reelection but did, unsuccessfully, seek a diplomatic post.

In 1830 he won a seat in the U.S. House of Representatives. Before actually entering Congress, Kavanagh had his first experience with the issue of the northeastern boundary of the United States between New Brunswick and Maine. Because of his fluent French and his religious background, he was appointed to travel up to the Madawaska region to ascertain the political loyalties of the largely Catholic Acadian settlers. The Treaty of Paris of 1783 had not been sufficiently clear about the boundary, and the dispute simmered on. Kavanagh's personal journal reveals that he had a keen eye for grand views and for small details, as well as for the character of people.

In Congress, Kavanagh voted against the rechartering and for the sale of government shares of stock in the Second Bank of the United States, as did other Jacksonian Democrats. However, he supported the tariff bills of 1832–1833. On the internal improvements issue, he supported Clay's bill to appropriate the proceeds from the sale of public lands for such. He contributed substantially to the defeat of a questionable proposal by agents to the Passamaquoddy Indians of Maine to sell off assets. Kavanagh was his own man but perhaps at a cost, for he was not reelected in 1834.

Kavanagh's desire to gain a diplomatic post proved successful in 1835 when he was appointed chargé d'affaires in Lisbon, Portugal. His two major tasks were to seek settlement of claims and to arrange a commercial treaty. Most of the American claims had been settled and paid for by the summer of 1839, but the commercial treaty still eluded him. His draft dispatches to Washington on both tasks reveal that he was put off again and again by excuses, change of ministers, and the turbulence associated with developing representative government. Finally, exasperated and not in the best of health, in the spring of 1840 Kavanagh asked permission of his government to return to the United States, at the same time pushing for approval of the treaty he had first presented in 1836. These tactics resulted in the achievement of his goal in late August 1840. The most significant treaty provision established a "most favored nation" relationship between the two powers.

In his last years, Kavanagh did not enjoy good health; nevertheless, he continued his activities as legislator and diplomat. In August 1841 he was elected to the Maine Senate and returned to the boundary issue. This time he was appointed one of four commissioners to negotiate along with Secretary of State Daniel Webster in Washington on the terms of the proposed treaty with England. The negotiations occurred in June–July 1842. Webster and the British representative, Lord Ashburton, settled upon terms which established the present boundaries of Maine and New Brunswick. The Maine delegation was not pleased with the treaty, but they agreed in order to avoid war, with Kavanagh playing an important role in gaining the assent of the other commissioners to the terms.

Reelected to the Maine Senate, Kavanagh became presiding officer and lieutenant governor in January 1843. When Governor John Fairfield was chosen to take a vacated seat in the U.S. Senate in March, Kavanagh became thirteenth governor of the state, serving for almost ten months. The border issue returned one last time when the secretary of war ordered federal troops withdrawn from the Maine-New Brunswick border, even though conditions were unsettled. Kavanagh vigorously but unsuccessfully protested against the troop withdrawal. In ill health, he resigned his position as governor effective 1 January 1844. Three weeks later he passed away at home in Damariscotta Mills, never having married.

"Urbanity" was the key word that emerged in recommendations of Kavanagh for diplomatic posts and in the tribute to his work as governor. Ashburton, after meeting with him one evening in 1842, described him simply as "a sensible, liberal man" (Lucey, p. 179). Kavanagh was the first Catholic in Maine to play successful political roles. His early training as a lawyer fitted him to deal with property issues on an international level. As a diplomat he brought his experience to bear successfully in commercial relations with Catholic Portugal and the difficult question of the border of Maine and New Brunswick.

• The Archives of the Catholic Diocese of Portland, Maine, hold the most substantial collection of letters, drafts of diplomatic dispatches, and other documents by and to Kavanagh. William Leo Lucey drew on this collection extensively and on others for his biography, *Edward Kavanagh, Catholic, Statesman, Diplomat from Maine 1795–1855* (1946). Edward Thomas McCarron, "The World of Kavanagh and Cottrill: A Portrait of Irish Emigration, Entrepreneurship and Ethnic Diversity in Mid-Maine, 1760–1820" (Ph.D. diss., Univ. of New Hampshire, 1992), places the work of Edward's father and the family's position in context. Kavanagh's personal record of the journey to the northeast frontier area in 1831 appears in "Wilderness Journey: A 19th Century Journal," *Maine History News* 16, no. 2 and 4 (1980); the manuscript is in the Maine State Archives. Along with many deed records for the period 1825–1846, his will and inventory in the Lincoln County Court House in Wiscasett cast additional light on Edward's activities. See also George Dow, "Nobleboro History," *Lincoln County News*, 28 Apr., 12 May, 19 May 1977 and 1 May 1980; Arthur J. Gerrier, "Nicholas Codd" in looseleaf series, *A Biographical Dictionary of Architects in Maine*, ed. Earle Shettleworth, vol. 6 (1991).

EDWARD L. HAWES

KAWANANAKOA, Abigail Wahiikaahuula Campbell (1 Jan. 1882–12 Apr. 1945), politician, was born in Honolulu, Hawaii, the daughter of James Campbell, a millionaire financier, landowner, and businessman, and Abigail Kuaihelani Maipinepine Bright. Her mother was a member of a part-native Hawaiian family from Lahaina, Maui, Hawaii. Her father was an immigrant from Derry, Ireland. Kawananakoa was educated at private schools in Honolulu. She then went to San Jose, California, where her father had business interests. Kawananakoa attended San Jose's College of Notre Dame, a Roman Catholic convent, from which she graduated in 1900.

In 1902 Kawananakoa married Prince David Laamea Kahalepouli Kawananakoa Piikoi in San Francisco. Kawananakoa received the courtesy title of princess through her marriage. During their marriage Kawananakoa and Prince David had three children. Prince David died of pneumonia in San Francisco on 2 June 1908, only forty-one years old.

After the death of her brother-in-law, Prince Kuhio, in 1922, Kawananakoa effectively became the leader of the native Hawaiian community and took an increasingly active part in territorial politics. She was not a Democrat like her husband but, rather, a Republican like Prince Kuhio and her stepfather, Colonel Samuel Parker. She was an enthusiastic party worker from the early days after the party's foundation in Hawaii in 1900. For twelve years from 1924 she served as the Republican national committeewoman for Hawaii and on several occasions attended sessions of the national party organization on the mainland. She did not seek reelection in 1936, as she had been offered a government position.

She first registered as a voter on 8 February 1922, and her example influenced thousands of other women to become voters. Kawananakoa was one of the earliest campaigners for women's rights in Hawaii and sponsored legislation for the welfare of women and children. She advocated jury service for women and often argued for its inclusion as an item in the platform of the Territorial Republicans.

As a native Hawaiian leader Kawananakoa was particularly angered by the way the territory's Euroamerican leadership handled the notorious Massie Case during the early 1930s. She believed that the native Hawaiians were cruelly and outrageously misrepresented. In May 1932 she opposed Governor L. M. Judd's commutation from ten years to one hour of the sentences of the four convicted Euroamerican murderers (actually convicted of manslaughter), Lieutenant Thomas Hedges Massie, USN, Grace Fortescue (Massie's mother-in-law), Machinist's Mate Albert O. Jones, and Fireman First Class Edward J. Lord. They had murdered a native Hawaiian man, Joe Kahahawai, one of the five native Hawaiian and Japanese-American alleged rapists of Massie's wife. Kawananakoa declared, "Are we to infer from the governor's act that there are two sets of laws in Hawaii, one for the favored few and another for the people in general?" She also resisted the Euroamerican backlash against the participation by native Hawaiians in the territorial public service and local politics. Kawananakoa opposed the abolition of the five-year residency proviso for the Honolulu chief of police and supported the Democrats in opposing her own party's Euroamerican leadership's effort to abandon the direct primary in Hawaii.

As a result of her steadfast position supporting the defendants' rights to a fair trial during the Massie Case, Kawananakoa gained a reputation for nonpartisanship by following her conscience rather than the positions taken by her party. Hence in July 1935 twelve U.S. senators from both the Republican and Democratic parties, including Senator M. E. Tydings, chairman of the Committee on Territorial and Insular Affairs, recommended that she be appointed to the reorganized Hawaiian Homes Commission (HHC). However, her appointment was opposed by some of the territory's Euroamerican politicians, and it was not confirmed until March 1936. The HHC, which had been established by the U.S. Congress in 1921, sought to rehabilitate the native Hawaiian community by returning it to the land. Kawananakoa had taken an active interest in the HHC for many years. In October 1931 she had been appointed chairperson of a special committee by Governor Judd to investigate complaints made by some of the homesteaders against the HHC. The committee's report, presented on 31 December 1931, found in favor of the complainants. As chairman of the HHC, Judd ignored the report's recommendations and introduced a paternalistic regime that controlled every aspect of the homesteaders' agricultural ventures, which Kawananakoa condemned.

As a member of the HHC, Kawananakoa was responsible for the establishment of a finance committee and, as its first chairperson, put the commission's finances in order. She also initiated a new rehabilitation project, an additional houselot area at Keaukaha on the island of Hawaii. She did not always have a high opinion of her fellow commissioners. In April 1937 Kawananakoa wrote that she had "never met such a helpless group of people in my life, they are either ignorant, too lazy or too busy." She resigned prematurely at the end of 1938, refusing to comment on rumors of friction in the HHC. The Keaukaha project was not completed until spring 1940.

During World War II Kawananakoa became a "mother" to the American servicemen and -women in Hawaii. In February 1942 she loaned her Malaekahana beach house to the United Service Organization (USO) for use as a recreation center for the U.S. armed forces. In December 1944 she also leased her Pensacola Street home in Honolulu to the USO to be a Service Women's Club. She died in Honolulu. Her treasured collection of Royal Hawaiian artifacts was bequeathed to the Smithsonian Institution in Washington, D.C.

Kawananakoa was one of the earliest feminists in Hawaii. Furthermore, as a political, social, and cultural leader of the native Hawaiian community, she also fought fearlessly for its rights against the territory's Euroamerican political leaders, in particular fellow Republicans. She believed, "It is high time that we became a[g]gressive enough to fight for the rights of the Hawaiian people in any [of] their *pilikias* [troubles]." She gave much of her time to the native Hawaiian societies, especially the Hale o na Alii, which was devoted to the preservation of the traditions and obligations of the Hawaiian chiefs and of which she was regent. Kawananakoa completely reorganized this ancient society and put it on a sound financial basis.

• Further information about Kawananakoa's family can be found in *James Campbell Esq., 1826–1900* (1978). Personal correspondence relating to Kawananakoa's membership in the HHC (Feb.–Aug. 1937) can be found in Sam Wilder King, "Hawaiian Homes Commission 1935–June 1942," Hawaii State Archives, Delegate's File. Her bequest to the Smithsonian Institution is fully documented in the catalog records of the National Museum of Natural History. Biographies are in George F. Nellist, ed., *Women of Hawaii* (1929), and Barbara Bennett Peterson, ed., *Notable Women of Hawaii* (1984). Obituaries are in the *Honolulu Star-Bulletin* and *Honolulu Advertiser*, both 13 Apr. 1945.

RICHARD A. HAWKINS

KAY, Hershy (17 Nov. 1919–2 Dec. 1981), arranger and composer, was born in Philadelphia, Pennsylvania, the son of Louis H. Kay, a printer, and Ida Aisen, both Russian immigrants. There is no evidence that his parents or other close relatives were musical, but as a child Kay was encouraged to study the cello. At age sixteen he was awarded a scholarship to study cello with Felix Salmond at the prestigious Curtis Institute of Music in Philadelphia. At about the same time he became fascinated with the art of arranging and orchestrating. His study of the cello began to suffer, and on two different occasions he was asked to leave the institute for lack of suitable progress. Kay remained, however, and from 1936 to 1940 he studied orchestration with Randall Thompson, under whose guidance he flourished.

At the age of twenty he left Curtis and went to New York City, where he supported himself by playing the cello in pit orchestras on Broadway. This activity afforded him the opportunity to witness firsthand the workings of the theater and to understand the role of the arranger in Broadway musicals. He circulated his own arrangements among musical colleagues and friends.

Kay's first major commission came in 1940 when Brazilian soprano Elsie Houston hired him to arrange the music for her Rainbow Room performances. His success continued when a former Curtis classmate, Leonard Bernstein, asked him to do the orchestrations for *On the Town* (1944), a musical comedy about the adventures of a group of sailors on leave in New York City. The show was a critical and financial success; it ran for more than 450 performances and brought both Bernstein and Kay significant critical acclaim. The two men collaborated on other works: *Peter Pan* (1951); *Candide* (1956), an adaptation of Voltaire's 1758 novella, which, though short-lived, garnered high praise for Kay; Bernstein's *Mass* (1971), a piece written for the opening of the John F. Kennedy Center for the Performing Arts in Washington, D.C., that featured a text drawn from the Catholic liturgy; and *1600 Pennsylvania Avenue* (1976), a musical about the problems of housekeeping.

In all, Kay was the arranger/orchestrator of twenty-one Broadway shows (including the aforementioned Bernstein works), among the most famous of which are *The Golden Apple* (1954), which retells the story of Helen of Troy; *Once upon a Mattress* (1958); *The Happiest Girl in the World* (1961), based on Aristophanes's *Lysistrata*; *Milk and Honey* (1961), set in modern Israel; *110 in the Shade* (1963); *Coco* (1969); *A Chorus Line* (1975); and *Evita* (1979). In 1981 his orchestrations were still being heard in three Broadway productions, *Evita*, *A Chorus Line*, and *Barnum* (1980).

Kay composed music for six Hollywood films, including *Man with the Gun* (1955), *The King and Four Queens* (1956), and *Girl of the Night* (1960). Kay also wrote arrangements for television and radio shows. His only foray into the genre of opera was to complete Robert Kurka's *The Good Soldier Schweik* (1959), based on the comic novel by Jaroslav Hašek, which was still unfinished at the time of the composer's death.

Kay had a special gift for dance composition. A few of his dance works were his own original music, but the majority consisted of reshaping and orchestrating preexisting material. His association with the dance world began in 1947 when he arranged some scores for Martha Graham's company. George Balanchine commissioned him to do several scores for the New York City Ballet, the first of which was *The Thief Who Loved a Ghost* (1950), based on music by Carl Maria von Weber. *Cakewalk* (1951) was derived from music by Louis Moreau Gottschalk, a nineteenth-century New Orleans composer. *Western Symphony* (1954), which showcases American ballads and cowboy songs in a formal symphonic framework, was performed by the New York City Ballet at a time when their funding was so tight as to make elaborate costumes or sets impossible. The female ballerinas performed in tights and sweaters and the men in dungarees. Despite the lack of pageantry, the show was a huge commercial success, and although critics' reviews were mixed, most were positive. *The Concert* (1956), built on the music of Frédéric Chopin, is an illustration of the images that pass through the mind when listening to Chopin's music. *Stars and Stripes* (1958), arrangements of John Philip Sousa's march music, was described by critic Walter Terry as "gorgeous, corny, affectionate, ebullient, humorous, and tastefully vulgar" (*New York Herald Tribune*, 26 Jan. 1958). *Who Cares?* (1970) was based on sixteen George Gershwin songs written between 1924 and 1931, including "I Got Rhythm," "My One and Only," and "The Man I Love." In 1968 Kay wrote an original twelve-tone work, *The Clowns*, for the Joffrey Ballet. In 1971 he produced *Grand Tour*, based on music by Noël Coward for the Royal Ballet Company of England. The last work he orchestrated was Bernstein's "Olympic Hymn," which was performed for the opening of the Olympic Congress in Baden-Baden, West Germany, in October 1981.

Kay joined the faculty at Columbia University in 1972, briefly serving as a teacher of orchestration. He died at his home in Danbury, Connecticut, survived by his wife Maria Lawrenz, whom he had married in 1973. They had no children.

Kay was one of the leading American arrangers and orchestrators of the 1950s and 1960s. His work includes numerous Broadway musicals, several Hollywood feature films, documentaries for the U.S. Department of State, and music for the dance companies of Martha Graham, George Balanchine, and other prominent ballet figures. Kay described the job of orchestrator as "crawling into a composer's mind," in order to reshape and then realize the abstract ideas of a composer into a tangible, performance-ready score. Stylistically, Kay's work, while often playful and witty, remains elegant. He was especially talented at translating obscure or difficult works into popular, whistleable tunes. Kay was known to be consistently professional, rarely slipping from his high musical standards and impervious to the pressure and tight deadlines that arranging music for productions demanded.

• Some of Kay's manuscripts and a collection of clippings are at the New York Public Library for the Performing Arts. Michael Sonino, "Hershy Kay," *Musical America*, Oct. 1961, and *Time*, 18 Aug. 1961, are useful sources on Kay's career.

See also the biographies in *Current Biography* (1962) and *Annual Obituary* (1981). An obituary is in the *New York Times*, 4 Dec. 1981.

RON BYRNSIDE

KAYE, Danny (18 Jan. 1913–3 Mar. 1987), entertainer, was born David Daniel Kaminski in Brooklyn, New York, the son of Jacob Kaminski, a tailor, and Clara Nemerovsky. He dropped out of high school during his sophomore year and hitchhiked with a friend to Miami Beach, Florida, to become professional song-and-dance men. After returning to Brooklyn two weeks later, he worked as a soda jerk, office clerk, and insurance appraiser by day and performed at private parties by night. In 1929 he went to work at White Roe Lake House in New York's Catskill Mountains as a tummler, an entertainer who amused the guests during their every waking hour. For the next four summers he performed at White Roe as Danny Kaye and unsuccessfully sought work on Broadway during the winter.

Kaye's first break came in 1933 when he joined a comedy and dance act called the Three Terpsichoreans. This act led to a tour of the Orient between 1934 and 1936 during which he developed many of the routines and techniques that became his trademarks. Because most of his audiences did not understand English, he relied on exaggerated facial expressions, wildly kinetic pantomimes and dance routines, and "scat" singing, whereby he would chant long strings of nonsensical syllables occasionally punctuated, to the audience's delight, by a word in the native language. During one performance in Osaka, Japan, the lights went out in the middle of a typhoon, and he calmed the audience by sitting on the edge of the stage and singing without accompaniment for hours while illuminating himself with a flashlight. After returning to the United States he accepted bookings wherever he could get them, including a disastrous eight-week stint in England.

Kaye's next break, and the one that ultimately made his career, came in 1939 while performing at Camp Tamiment, a summer resort in the Pennsylvania hills. He began working with Sylvia Fine, the camp's pianist and songwriter, whose sophisticated satire meshed perfectly with his singing style. This collaboration led directly to his Broadway debut that fall when he appeared in ten scenes of *The Straw Hat Revue*, a showcase of Fine's best compositions. It also led to their marriage in 1940; they had one child. Henceforth, she wrote virtually all of his original material and served as his unofficial manager. Her ability to write the type of songs that worked best for him and his ability to deliver what was right for a particular audience at any given moment combined to create a persona that made him an international star.

Kaye returned to Broadway later that year as a headliner in *Lady in the Dark*. His rendition in thirty-eight seconds of "Tschaikovsky," a string of names of fifty Russian composers, was the hit of the show. He soon became the darling of New York's theatergoers and in 1941 appeared as the star of *Let's Face It*, a musical comedy featuring several tunes written by Fine. He tried to enlist during World War II but was rejected because of a bad back, so he contributed to the war effort by performing at bond rallies and entertaining servicemen in the South Pacific and Europe. In 1943 he changed his name legally to Danny Kaye and the next year made his motion picture debut in *Up in Arms*, a big-budget army comedy. In 1945, after a disappointing engagement as the star of his own radio program, he appeared in *Wonder Man*, the first of many movies in which he played multiple characters. Altogether he starred in eighteen movies, usually as a mild-mannered victim of circumstance who somehow ended up a winner. His most critically acclaimed and popular movie performances came in the 1940s, particularly in *The Secret Life of Walter Mitty* (1947) and *The Inspector General* (1949), in which he played seven and four different roles, respectively. With the exception of *The Court Jester* (1956), his subsequent films were assailed by critics as poorly conceived, dispirited efforts, although several of them, most notably *White Christmas* (1954), did exceptionally well at the box office.

Despite his success as a movie actor, Kaye was at his best while on stage. He was a dapper and charming entertainer who easily transcended the barrier between audience and performer. In the middle of a performance he would often sit on the stage with his legs dangling into the orchestra pit and chat nonchalantly with the audience while smoking a borrowed cigarette before resuming his madcap routine. In 1948 he toured extensively in Great Britain and proved to be so popular that he returned to packed houses each of the next four years. During this trip he met the English actor Sir Laurence Olivier; over the years these two uniquely talented entertainers developed a close personal friendship.

In 1954 Kaye was appointed ambassador at large for the United Nations International Children's Emergency Fund (UNICEF) and appeared in *Assignment: Children*, a short documentary film of his global travels on behalf of the agency. Later that year the film was shown in movie theaters around the world as part of a highly successful international fundraising promotion. In addition to raising money, the promotion helped to boost the image of the fledgling United Nations, considered by many to be a stooge of international communism, by identifying it with the cause of needy children; it also earned him a special award at the 1955 Academy Awards. From 1963 to 1967 he starred in "The Danny Kaye Show," an Emmy Award–winning television program that featured dancing, singing, and comedy routines.

Kaye's career began to wane after his television show was cancelled, although he continued to tour for UNICEF until 1975. He devoted himself increasingly to his hobbies, which included cooking Chinese food in the restaurant-quality kitchen in his home, flying his own Lear jet, and owning part of the Seattle Mariners professional baseball franchise. In 1982 he received the Academy of Motion Picture Arts and Sciences' Jean Hersholt Humanitarian Award as well as Denmark's Knight's Cross of the First Class of the Order of Danneborg for his portrayal of the Danish national hero in *Hans Christian Andersen* (1952). He died in Los Angeles, California.

Kaye's ability to combine childlike enthusiasm with sophisticated charm made him one of the most unique and beloved entertainers in the United States. His movie antics inspired a rash of imitators, including the comic genius Jerry Lewis. As a live entertainer he possessed the rare ability to singlehandedly enthrall an audience for over an hour. As Mr. Unicef he raised millions of dollars for needy children.

• Kaye's papers have not been located. Biographies include Martin Gottfried, *Nobody's Fool: The Lives of Danny Kaye* (1994); Kurt D. Singer, *The Danny Kaye Story* (1958); and D. Richards, *The Life Story of Danny Kaye* (1949). Kaye's film career is briefly but astutely assessed in David Shipman, *The Great Movie Stars: The International Years* (1972). Obituaries are in the *New York Times*, 4 Mar. 1987, and in *Newsweek* and *Time*, both 16 Mar. 1987.

CHARLES W. CAREY, JR.

KAYE, Nora (17 Jan. 1920–28 Feb. 1987), ballerina, was born Nora Koreff in New York City, the daughter of Russian immigrants Gregory Koreff, a theater employee, and Lisa (maiden name unknown), a milliner. Her father, once an actor in the Moscow Art Theater, wanted her trained for a theater career; her mother preferred ballet and started her in dance classes before she was five. Kaye began serious study by the age of eight with choreographer Michel Fokine and at the Metropolitan Opera Ballet School with Margaret Curtis. She performed as a child in the Met's opera ballets and in Fokine's concert group and signed her first professional contract with the American Ballet, directed by George Balanchine, when the group was engaged as resident company at the Met in 1935. Soon she began to audition for Broadway and found work in three musicals, including *Stars in Your Eyes*, with Jimmy Durante and Ethel Merman. She also danced briefly in the corps de ballet at Radio City Music Hall. During these years, when ballet was generally considered a Russian art, Nora Koreff changed her own Russian name to become Nora Kaye because "an American dancer ought to have an American name."

In fall 1939 a new ballet company called Ballet Theatre began preparations for its first season. Kaye was hired for the corps de ballet and established an immediate rapport with the choreographer Antony Tudor. In the first season (1940) she performed a small role in his *Lilac Garden* and the following year was given a larger role in *Gala Performance*. Tudor began rehearsals for a new ballet in 1941 with his principal collaborator, Hugh Laing, and with Kaye in the central female role. This was Tudor's first original work for Ballet Theatre, and its premiere, on 8 April 1942, proved fateful for both Tudor and Kaye. *Pillar of Fire* was applauded with more than twenty curtain calls. The reviewers called it a masterpiece and hailed Nora

Kaye as a new star. After that momentous evening she was assigned leading roles in other Tudor ballets, particularly *Dark Elegies* and as Caroline in *Lilac Garden*, and the rest of the company repertory. The following year, Tudor created a major role for her in his new *Dim Lustre*. She was a central figure in the close-knit "Tudor group" of dancers within Ballet Theatre. Kaye later said, "Tudor changed my whole life—the way I moved and the way I thought. He told me what to think and what to read, even what to wear and what to eat. We were inseparable."

In 1943 Kaye married Michael M. van Beuren II, scion of a socially prominent family, but the marriage was annulled a few months later. In 1947 Agnes de Mille created the next ballet that became indelibly associated with Kaye. In *Fall River Legend* she danced the murderous heroine Lizzie Borden. Kaye was recovering from several months' illness when the ballet was prepared, and she did not dance the opening night. Her friend Maria Karnilova later described this period as "a kind of nervous breakdown," and it coincided with rearrangements of Tudor's inner circle. The next season in autumn 1948, when Kaye resumed regular performances in *Fall River Legend*, Lizzie Borden became exclusively her role. At the same time she announced a change in her personal life with her marriage to concert violinist Isaac Stern. In de Mille's book *Lizzie Borden* (1968, p. 166), she provides an acute description of Kaye: "She was a dark, spare, New York Jewess, with wry New York wit, a flat Bronx voice, a hard, driving plastique, great force and brilliance, and a beauty of phrasing, an ability to suggest more with sparser means than anyone in our time."

In 1950 Kaye and Stern were divorced. In 1951, after ten years with Ballet Theatre and at a time when the company's continued financing seemed doubtful, Kaye joined Tudor, Laing, Diana Adams, and Jerome Robbins in transferring to Balanchine's New York City Ballet. Kaye knew that she was not physically or temperamentally suited to be an ideal Balanchine dancer, but she was cast in several works, including *Symphony in C*, and she continued to dance the Tudor repertory, which entered the New York City Ballet. Robbins also chose Kaye for his ballets, including *Age of Anxiety*. When he premiered *The Cage* in June 1951, with Kaye dancing the central role of the Novice, they created a sensation. *The Cage* also became permanently identified with her. Robbins and Kaye had known each other since adolescence, and during this period they were romantic partners as well. Kaye made a brief return to Broadway in 1952 in *Two's Company* with choreography by Robbins. In 1952 and 1953 she continued on a limited schedule with New York City Ballet, including a European tour, and danced for several months in Japan as a guest artist with the Komaki Ballet.

In 1954 Kaye returned to Ballet Theatre. She was the company's reigning ballerina until 1960, headlining seasons in New York and major American cities, a South American tour in 1955, and European tours in

1956 and 1958. Many considered Kaye the quintessential American ballerina of the 1940s and 1950s and certainly one of this century's great dramatic dancers. In a *New York Times* review of 15 May 1949, the critic John Martin described her qualities: "The body is superbly placed, its line firm and straight, its arms and head and torso free, its feet strong as steel on points yet flexible and alive in movement. There are no dead spots between movements: the phrasing is easy and flowing, and its dynamic color is rich and varied." Kaye performed a wide repertory, but she remained unequaled as an interpreter of Tudor's ballets.

Kaye married the dancer and choreographer Herbert Ross in 1959, and the following year they formed a new small company, Ballet of Two Worlds, with which they toured Europe. The couple decided not to continue the group a second season, and Kaye felt it was time to give up her performing career. She tossed her ballet slippers out the window of their car one afternoon as they were driving through the Black Forest in Germany. This marriage proved to be an enduring personal and professional partnership. Kaye devoted herself to assisting Ross's burgeoning Broadway and Hollywood career. She also kept up an association with Ballet Theatre, by then named American Ballet Theatre, where she was appointed assistant director in 1965 and was associate director with Mikhail Baryshnikov from 1977 to 1983.

Ross and Kaye shared credits on films including *The Seven Percent Solution* (1977), *Nijinsky* (1980), *The Secret of My Success* (1987), and *Pennies from Heaven* (1981). *The Turning Point* (1977) presented Baryshnikov in his first popular starring screen role and co-starred Kaye's goddaughter, Leslie Browne. Many dance-world insiders considered the story of the rivalrous friendship portrayed by Anne Bancroft and Shirley MacLaine to be a composite of Kaye's competitive relationships in Ballet Theatre, although she denied it. Certainly it was Herb Ross's and Nora Kaye's most personal film project. During the last months of her life Kaye worked on the production of another Ross film starring Baryshnikov, which was released under the title *Dancers*. Kaye died in Los Angeles.

• Kaye was interviewed frequently, and her performances were reviewed regularly; the primary sources on her are her collected clippings, photographs, films, and scrapbooks in the Dance Collection of the New York Public Library for the Performing Arts. Interviews by Saul Goodman in *Dance Magazine* (Feb. 1965, pp. 36–43; Mar. 1965, pp. 54–58) and by Selma Jeanne Cohen, on the work with Tudor, in the *Proceedings* (1985, pp. 84–90) of the Society of Dance History Scholars, provide important details. Agnes de Mille, *Lizzie Borden: A Dance of Death* (1968), draws a portrait of Kaye in *Pillar of Fire*. Books on Antony Tudor by Judith Chazin-Bennahum and Donna Perlmutter and a television documentary by Gerd Andersson and Viola Aberlé describe Kaye's influence in his work. Obituaries are "Remembering Nora Kaye," *Dance Magazine*, May 1987, pp. 24–25, and John Taras, "Nora Kaye: A Tribute," *Ballet Review* 14, no. 4 (Winter 1987): 36–48.

MONICA MOSELEY

KAYE, Sammy (13 Mar. 1910–2 June 1987), bandleader, was born Samuel Zarnocay, Jr., in Lakewood, Ohio, the son of Samuel Zarnocay, a laborer, and Mary Sukenik. The son of Czech immigrants, he spoke Czech before he learned English and was raised in the neighboring Cleveland suburb of Rocky River. There he organized his first band, Sammy's Hot Peppers. He attended Ohio University on a track scholarship and, under the Americanized name of Sammy Kaye, continued to play band engagements on campus and during vacations around Cleveland.

Though earning a bachelor's degree in engineering in 1933, Kaye kept his band intact after graduation, opening the Varsity Inn on the Ohio University campus in Athens. He played clarinet and alto saxophone himself, but his featured soloists tended to be vocalists such as Don Cornell, Tommy Ryan, Clyde Burke, Nancy Norman, and Tony Alamo. During a Cleveland engagement in the mid-1930s, he adopted the slogan "Swing and Sway with Sammy Kaye." According to Stephen Holden in the *New York Times*, his signature sound "had more sway than swing" and was stylistically related to the smooth ensemble tones of Guy Lombardo and Kay Kyser.

Kaye first gained national attention in 1935 as the result of a broadcast over the NBC radio network from a Cleveland area country club. Recording for RCA Victor, he had his first major hit in the title song from the movie version of *Rosalie* in 1937. After his New York debut at the Commodore Hotel in 1938, his band was known as one of the top "sweet bands" of the big band era. He was featured on the NBC radio show "Sunday Serenade" for twelve years. He married Ruth Knox Elden in March 1940.

It was during Kaye's "Sunday Serenade" broadcast of 7 December 1941 that announcer Ben Grauer cut in to inform the nationwide radio audience of Japan's attack on Pearl Harbor. Following the show Kaye went home and wrote the song "Remember Pearl Harbor," which he completed with Don Reid. Recorded by Kaye and released only eight days later, it was described by Kaye's publicist as the "first American war song of World War II." Kaye turned his composer's royalties from the more than one million copies sold over to the Navy Relief Society. Other hits recorded by his band during the war included "The White Cliffs of Dover," "There Goes That Song Again," "My Buddy," and "Harbor Lights." In 1942 Kaye appeared with the band in the Sonja Henie film *Iceland*, in which they received top marquee billing over the skating star on Broadway. They appeared in a second film, *Song of the Open Road*, in 1944.

Kaye's big band was one of the few to survive in the postwar era, thanks largely to the leader's business acumen. Known for his astuteness in drawing up a contract, he also controlled three music publishing houses and a recording company. Heard nationally on 400 radio stations in 1949, he broke into television with "The Sammy Kaye Show" on CBS in 1951. He moved to NBC briefly in 1953 and then to ABC in 1958–1959. (Kaye once joked that he might have been as big on television as Lawrence Welk if he hadn't taken elocution lessons to suppress his Czech accent.) In 1954 ABC turned one of his stage gimmicks into a game show, "So You Want to Lead a Band," in which audience members were invited to compete for prizes by conducting.

Some of Kaye's biggest recording hits were "Love Walked In," "Penny Serenade," "That's My Desire," "Serenade of the Bells," "Careless Hands," "Room Full of Roses," and "It Isn't Fair." His later recordings appeared on the Columbia label. During the 1950s actor Hal Linden played saxophone in the Sammy Kaye band.

A personal friend of President Richard Nixon, Kaye played at the Republican's inauguration and occasionally golfed with him. Though investments in publishing and bowling alleys made him wealthy, he continued to conduct until 1986, when he turned his band over to Roger Thorpe. Divorced since 1956, he had no children. He died in Ridgewood, New Jersey.

Kaye was never considered a musical innovator of the big band era but was noted instead for his ability to pace his song sets and maintain danceable tempos. In the words of swing historian George T. Simon, he was adept at "supplying satisfying sounds for those unable to appreciate and/or comprehend what the more musical bands were playing."

• Kaye was the subject of a short essay in Richard Lamparski, *Whatever Became Of . . . ?*, 9th ser. (1985). A descriptive account of Kaye's "So You Want to Lead a Band" routine appeared in *Time*, 15 July 1940, pp. 32–33. "Sammy Kaye" in George T. Simon's *The Big Bands*, 4th ed. (1981), includes personal reminiscences. Obituaries are in the *New York Times* and *Cleveland Plain Dealer*, both 4 June 1987, and *Variety*, 10 June 1987.

JOHN VACHA

KAZANJIAN, Varaztad (18 Mar. 1879–19 Oct. 1974), plastic surgeon, was born Varaztad Hovannes Kazanjian in Erzinga, Turkish Armenia, the son of Hovannes Kazanjian, a coppersmith, and Anna Sironian. When he was a child his family moved to Sivas, Armenia, where he attended a French Jesuit missionary school. In 1895, at the age of sixteen, he immigrated to the United States. For most of the next seven years he lived, worked, and studied in Worcester, Massachusetts. After laboring all day as a wire-drawer in a large local mill, he took English classes at night and correspondence courses. In 1900 he became a U.S. citizen and determined to pursue the profession of dentistry.

By 1902 Kazanjian had successfully completed the examination required to gain entrance to Harvard Dental School. He became very interested in prosthetic dentistry and the treatment of jaw fractures during his years as a dental student. He graduated in 1905, receiving his D.M.D., and was appointed assistant in prosthetic dentistry at Harvard. Before the advent of antibiotics, surgery had often led to postoperative infection and other complications. As a result, hospital facilities and surgical techniques for the treatment of jaw fractures or facial deformities were limited. Patients with congenital deformities such as cleft palate, or those caused by facial injury, instead chose to go to dental clinics like the one at Harvard, where Kazanjian used his exceptional manual skill and intelligence to build innovative prosthetic devices. He was the first in the United States to adopt intermaxillary wiring to join broken jaw fragments. By 1912 he had become department head and had treated more than four hundred cases of jaw fracture. That year he married Sophie Cuendet.

In 1915 Kazanjian's expertise was recognized with his appointment as dental chief of the First Harvard Unit, which served in France with the British Expeditionary Forces during World War I. Kazanjian established the first organized dental clinic under the canvas hospital tents at General Hospital No. 22 in Camiers, France. He extended his stay in France at the request of the British War Office. His wife joined him in France through the remainder of the war. From 1915 to 1919, Kazanjian and his colleagues treated more than three thousand cases of facial wounds in an enlarged clinic transferred to Hospital No. 20 in the same area. Gunshot and shrapnel caused facial injuries characterized by a degree of shattering and bone loss far more extensive than the less serious civilian injuries Kazanjian had treated in Boston; an upper-jaw fracture, in particular, was a rare injury outside the battlefield. Kazanjian distinguished himself as a leader in plastic surgery by combining his formidable prosthetic dental skills with the invention of new oral and plastic reconstructive surgical techniques to treat the dreadfully wounded faces of World War I soldiers. His accomplishments became so well known throughout the British Army that he was referred to as "the miracle man of the Western Front." Before his return to the United States in 1919, King George V recognized Kazanjian's achievement by investing him as a Companion of the Order of St. Michael and St. George in a ceremony at Buckingham Palace.

Harvard University also recognized Kazanjian's accomplishments by appointing him professor of military oral surgery. On his return Kazanjian enrolled as a student at Harvard Medical School, seeking to advance and formalize his medical training to further the pioneering surgical work he had begun during the war. His wife died in 1919, leaving him with a daughter. Kazanjian went on to earn his M.D. in 1921. In 1922 Harvard named him professor of clinical oral surgery. The following year he married Marion V. Hanford, with whom he later had two children.

Kazanjian maintained a long career as a surgeon as well as a teacher at Harvard. He saw patients from all over the world and held staff appointments at all the major hospitals in Boston. In 1941 he was named Harvard's first professor of plastic surgery, holding this position until he became professor emeritus in 1947. He wrote more than 150 scholarly articles on plastic and reconstructive surgery, and with a colleague and former student, John Marquis Converse, he authored the classic text, *The Surgical Treatment of Facial Injuries* (1949).

Over the years Kazanjian held positions of professional leadership, including serving one-year terms as president of the American Association of Plastic Surgeons (1940) and the American Academy of Dental Science (1937), and was granted numerous honors and awards from surgical and dental societies in the United States and Europe, including a special honorary citation from the American Society of Plastic and Reconstructive Surgery, a society award from the American Society of Oral Surgeons, and honorary membership in the Royal College of Physicians and Surgeons, Glasgow, Scotland. He was also a diplomat and member of the Founders Group, American Board of Plastic Surgery. In 1962 New York University School of Medicine established the V. H. Kazanjian Visiting Professorship in Plastic Surgery. He died at his home in Belmont, Massachusetts.

• All of Kazanjian's papers and records are in the Countway Library at Harvard Medical School. An autobiographical retrospective is V. H. Kazanjian, "Remembrance of Things Past," *Plastic and Reconstructive Surgery* 35 (1965): 5–13. See also Martin Hagop Deranian, "With a Passion for Humanity: The Story of Dr. Varaztad Kazanjian," *Ararat* (Autumn 1978): 2–12. An obituary is in the *New York Times*, 23 Oct. 1974, and a faculty of medicine memorial is in the *Harvard Gazette*, 2 May 1975.

BARBARA KAZANJIAN MCGOLDRICK

KAZEE, Buell (29 Aug. 1900–Aug. 1976), folk singer, banjo player, and minister, was born at the head of Burton Fork in Magoffin County, east of Richmond in eastern Kentucky, the son of Frank Kazee and Abijane Conley Helton, farmers. Kazee learned old hymns and songs from both parents, who "just sang by nature." By the time he was five, Kazee had received his first banjo, and within a few years he was playing at the rural mountain "frolics" (dances) in the area. Up through his teenage years, Kazee led a lifestyle typical of many mountain musicians of the day. This changed, however, when he decided to prepare for the ministry; he went on to complete high school and attend Georgetown College in central Kentucky.

At Georgetown College Kazee majored in nonmusical subjects like English, Latin, and Greek, and he discovered that some of the old English ballads in his literature books were similar to the old songs that he had learned back home, which fascinated him. Sensing that this older music was more important than he had thought, he added music to his studies. At first his teachers urged him to abandon the high, keening mountain singing style for a more formal, European way of singing—a more cultured sound. For a time he was taken with the idea of performing the authentic old ballads in a "proper" and acceptable musical setting, and in 1925, after he had graduated from Georgetown, he presented a concert of folk music at the University of Kentucky, replete with the singer appearing in coat and tails and singing to carefully crafted piano accompaniment. This presentation proved so successful that he followed it with other similar concerts as he continued to develop his career as a minister.

In 1927 Kazee traveled to New York City to record for the Brunswick Record Company. He began his audition by singing in the formal style of his concerts, but the record executives remained uninterested until, as an afterthought, he unpacked his banjo and sang a couple of mountain songs in his old style. The first country record had been made only four years earlier, in 1923, and Brunswick was eager to tap into this new market. They did not need any more formal, well-trained singers; they were desperate for ones who sang in authentic, down-home accents. Kazee thus had to unlearn his vocal style and return to the old high lonesome sound, done with a "tight throat." He later recalled, "I had to make the record seven or eight times to get it bad enough to sell." He also produced classic performances of "John Hardy," "Roll on, John," "Lady Gay," "East Virginia Blues," and "The Orphan Child." From 1927 to 1929 he would record more than fifty songs for Brunswick, an impressive canon that would remain popular and partially in print up to the 1990s.

Friends and neighbors assumed Kazee was making huge amounts of money with his records, but in fact he, like many early recording artists, received no royalties, only a flat fee per record. And though *Billboard*, the music trade publication, praised his singing and predicted big things, Kazee was reluctant to do the kind of touring and intensive radio work that would have developed his music career. Instead he became a minister, serving one church in Morehead, Kentucky, for some twenty-two years. In later years he often sang at revival meetings and composed a number of formal musical pieces, including a cantata based on an old piece from the shape-note songbook *Sacred Harp*, "The White Pilgrim," and an operetta titled "The Wagoner Lad." He also authored three books on religion, a book about banjo playing, and a partial autobiography. He was rediscovered by the folk revival movement of the 1960s and coaxed back into performing on stage. A couple of new albums were recorded and released in the 1970s, and many of his old 1920s records were reissued on LPs and eventually on compact discs.

Kazee was married twice. In 1929 he married Lucille Jones; they had two sons. After Kazee's first marriage ended, in about 1954 he wed Jennie Turnmyer; they had no children together. Kazee died in Winchester, Kentucky.

Kazee was certainly one of the most complex, demanding, and multifaceted of Kentucky's traditional musicians, and his career as a composer and interpreter of folk songs has yet to be properly evaluated. His various banjo styles and arrangements remain very influential on young banjo players around the nation. His son Phil Kazee was active in maintaining the tradition in the 1980s and 1990s.

• A useful source is Charles K. Wolfe, *Kentucky Country: Folk and Country Music of Kentucky*, rev. ed. (1996).

CHARLES K. WOLFE

KEALOHA, Warren Daniels (3 Mar. 1904–8 Sept. 1972), Olympic gold medal swimmer, was born in Honolulu, Hawaii, then a territory of the United States, and was adopted by Kaio and Kaai Kealoha, who were relatives of his Hawaiian mother. His father was a foreigner or "haole," surnamed Daniels. Kealoha attended St. Louis and Punahou Schools and learned to swim in a pond known as "Blue Pool." Some biographies have erroneously referred to him as the brother of Pua Kealoha, also a gold medal swimmer from Hawaii in the 1920 Olympic Games, but the two were not related.

As a member of the Hui Makani Swim Club, Kealoha unofficially broke the world record for the 100-meter backstroke in his first attempt at the distance. Kealoha was one of ten Hawaii swimmers representing the United States in the 1920 Olympic Games in Antwerp, Belgium. In order to qualify for the U.S. team, the Hawaii contingent, captained by the now legendary Duke Kahanamoku, had to travel by ship to California, then best all challengers on the West Coast. They then had to overcome competitors in Chicago, and finally in New York City. On the ship to Antwerp, the swimmers had only a small canvas pool with sea water and a harness in which they could take turns training while swimming in place. The sixteen-year-old Kealoha officially broke the world record of 1 minute 15.6 seconds, set by Germany's Otto Farh eight years earlier, while recording 1:14.8 in winning his Olympic preliminary round on 22 August. He then won the gold medal with a 1:15.2 the following day. Kealoha finished a full second ahead of silver medalist Ray Kegeris, also representing the United States, and nearly four seconds ahead of the bronze medalist from the host country. There was some controversy among the officials following Kealoha's victory as he used an unorthodox stroke. The European officials were familiar with a style in which the swimmer thrust both arms together and used the leg scissors motion. Kealoha used a style common in Hawaii, alternating his arms and kicking his legs. After some deliberation, the judges allowed Kealoha's stroke, concluding that the only requirement was that a swimmer be flat on his back.

On 17 October 1922, in Honolulu, Kealoha lowered his world record to 1:12.6; he further reduced that to 1:12.4 on 13 April 1924, also in a Honolulu meet. On 8 July at the 1924 Paris Olympic Games he again won the gold medal in his specialty while setting an Olympic record of 1:13.2, defeating silver medalist Paul Wyatt of the United States by 2.2 seconds, a long-standing record for the largest winning margin in the Olympic 100-meter backstroke. On 19 June 1926 Kealoha broke the world record for the fourth time with a time of 1:11.4 in a Honolulu meet. In 1923 he also set a world record (time unknown), besting Johnny Weissmuller's record, for the 150-yard backstroke, an event since discontinued. The record sparked much technical discussion relative to form, since Kealoha used a straight-arm stroke and Weissmuller a bent-arm stroke. Kealoha was undefeated in the backstroke until 1926, when Weissmuller was declared the winner in a near dead heat with Kealoha in a meet at Honolulu's Punahou School. After that meet, Kealoha traveled to Japan and won his specialty in the All-Japan meet. He retired soon afterward, having held four world records and won two Olympic medals. Proficient as a freestyler as well as in the backstroke, Kealoha also won two U.S. freestyle championships and defeated both Weissmuller and Kahanamoku in the event.

Following his retirement from swimming, Kealoha worked with the U.S. Prohibition Administration to implement the Eighteenth Amendment. Kealoha and six others were indicted in 1928 and charged with conspiring to set up a still; lack of evidence led to the charges being dropped. In 1944 he entered politics as a Republican but failed in his attempt to win election to the Territorial House. He then operated two taverns in Honolulu for approximately twenty years before taking charge of the federal government evaporation plant on Johnston Island, located in the Pacific east of Hawaii. After retirement, he became active in the Honolulu Masonic lodge. In 1922 Kealoha had married Eleanor Ribeiro, with whom he had three sons. They later divorced and Kealoha married Dora Kim, with whom he had one daughter.

Kealoha was inducted into the International Swimming Hall of Fame in 1968. Always shy and unpretentious, he was unable to provide photographs or clippings to the Hall of Fame. During the induction ceremonies, friends good-naturedly pushed the 64-year-old Kealoha into the pool. He sank to the bottom and remained there seemingly lifeless until his fully clothed friends jumped in to "rescue" him. Kealoha had the last laugh, claiming he had been holding his breath and only feigning unconsciousness. Kealoha died in Honolulu.

• The library files of the *Honolulu Advertiser* include a number of articles about Kealoha. Additional information, including records and times, is in Pat Besford, *Encyclopedia of Swimming* (1971); Lord Killian and John Rodda, *The Olympic Games* (1976); and David Wallechinsky, *The Complete Book of the Olympics* (1984). Obituaries are in the *Honolulu Advertiser* and the *Honolulu Star-Bulletin*, 9 Sept. 1972.

MICHAEL TYMN

KEAN, Jefferson Randolph (27 June 1860–4 Sept. 1950), U.S. Army medical officer, was born in Lynchburg, Virginia, the son of Robert Garlick Kean, a lawyer, and Jane Nicholas Randolph, a great-granddaughter of Thomas Jefferson. Entering the University of Virginia in 1879, he was withdrawn for a year because of inadequate progress in his studies. His father required him to teach school for a year before allowing him to return to the university, where Kean received his M.D. in 1883. After graduate study at New York's Polyclinic Hospital and Medical College, he passed the required entrance examinations for the Army Medical Department and in December 1884 was commissioned first lieutenant.

Kean was assistant post surgeon at two western forts and was promoted to captain in 1889. In October 1890 he accompanied a cavalry battalion to Pine Ridge, South Dakota, where he cared for casualties from the battle of Wounded Knee. In the spring of 1892 he was assigned to a Florida post. He married Louise Hurlbut Young in 1894; they had two children.

In 1897 Kean was ordered to a post in Boston Harbor. When war was declared against Spain in the spring of 1898, he conducted physical examinations for volunteers in Vermont before being commissioned major and brigade surgeon of the volunteers at the request of Major General Fitzhugh Lee, commander of the VII Army Corps. Kean served the corps's Second Division in Jacksonville, Florida, initially as medical inspector and then as commanding officer of the division hospital, where he was responsible for the care of hundreds of victims of the typhoid epidemic sweeping army camps.

After the war Kean accompanied the VII Corps's First Division to Cuba in December 1898 and served the army of occupation in roles of increasing responsibility, rising to the rank of lieutenant colonel in the volunteers. Ironically, although he urged the use of mosquito netting before Walter Reed proved that yellow fever was mosquito-borne, he contracted yellow fever himself in 1900, the first case of the disease Reed had ever seen. In February 1901, having been promoted to major in the Regular Army, Kean left the volunteers but continued to serve the army of occupation. He returned to the United States in May 1902 at the end of the occupation.

During the following four years Kean served in the Surgeon General's Office as executive officer and head of the Supply Division. He contributed significantly to the success of the Medical Department's campaign for a medical reserve corps, which became the army's first reserve corps in 1908. Returning to Cuba as the sanitary officer of the Army of Pacification in 1906, he drafted laws to maintain high standards of sanitation. He was promoted to lieutenant colonel on leaving the island when the second occupation ended in 1909.

Returning to the United States, Kean became chief of the Sanitary Division of the Surgeon General's Office, traveling briefly to Puerto Rico in 1909 to assess the threat posed by bubonic plague, which had broken out in San Juan. In 1913 he requested the position of post surgeon at Fort Leavenworth, Kansas, where many complaints had arisen about the medical service. While there he was promoted to colonel and was chosen to serve for a year as president of the Association of Military Surgeons. Tragedy struck in 1915 with the death of his wife.

In 1916 Kean was detailed as director of military relief for the American Red Cross. During his initial four-month assignment, he began organizing the staffs of prominent medical schools and hospitals into Red Cross base hospitals capable of being called to active duty with the army on short notice. During World War I these units gave vital support to both the Allies and the American Expeditionary Force (AEF). In the course of his successful attempt to have his period of service with the Red Cross lengthened he appealed to President Woodrow Wilson over the head of Secretary of War Newton D. Baker, thereby earning the secretary's lasting enmity.

Relieved of his assignment with the Red Cross because of his successful opposition to efforts to create a more influential role for that organization in its wartime relationship to the Medical Department, in 1917 Kean was sent to France as chief of the U.S. Ambulance Service, which was supporting the French army. In February 1918 he was assigned to Tours as chief surgeon of the AEF's Line of Communications, and he later became deputy chief surgeon of the AEF. Although Kean was commissioned brigadier general of the National Army while in France, this promotion did not affect his rank in the Regular Army, where he remained a colonel. On 24 March 1919, while still in France, he married Cornelia Knox; they had no children.

Upon his return to the United States in 1919, Kean was assigned to serve as First Corps area surgeon in Boston, Massachusetts, a position he retained until his retirement on 27 June 1924. He then moved to Washington, D.C., where he continued to play an active role supporting numerous organizations. In retirement he was secretary of the Association of Military Surgeons of the United States and editor of the association's publication, *Military Surgeon*, from 1924 to 1935. At the request of President Franklin D. Roosevelt he also served on both the commission for the construction of the National Expansion Memorial at St. Louis and the commission that created the Jefferson Memorial in Washington, D.C. He died in Washington, D.C., having retained a vigorous mind until the end.

An army colleague, Percy M. Ashburn, described Kean as "one of the far-seeing and long-planning men of the Corps, to whose foresight and plans, more than to those of any other man, we are indebted for the Medical Reserve Corps, the close liaison with the Red Cross, and the Red Cross Hospital Units of the World War." Nevertheless, Kean's alienation of Secretary Baker during World War I severely crippled his subsequent career in the Medical Department. Despite his considerable administrative skills, his many contributions both to the army and to public health in the Caribbean and the United States, and the many friends he formed throughout his life, he was never promoted beyond the rank of colonel.

• The principal repository for Kean's papers is the University of Virginia Library in Charlottesville, where they form part of the Kean family papers and cover a wide range of topics and correspondents. The most valuable single document for the biographer is Kean's unpublished autobiography written in 1924, a copy of which is part of a small collection of Kean's papers held by the National Library of Medicine in Bethesda, Md. Also among the items held by the National Library of Medicine are a somewhat terse diary of his work in World War I, a transcript of an interview he gave shortly before his death, a few letters from colleagues concerning his work as a medical officer, and a memorandum prepared by Kean urging the creation of a medical reserve corps. Kean's life and work are discussed in Edgar Erskine Hume, *The Golden Jubilee of the Association of Military Surgeons of the United States* (1941). Walter Muir Whitehill's article on Kean in the *Dictionary of American Biography*, supp. 4, is especially valuable because Whitehill was able to interview Kean personally. Kean's work is also briefly mentioned in the first volume of the Office of the Surgeon General's massive *Medical Department of the United States Army in the World War* (1923) and Percy M. Ashburn, *A History of the Medical Department of the United States Army* (1929). An obituary is in *Military Surgeon* 107 (1950): 427–28.

MARY C. GILLETT

KEANE, James John (26 Aug. 1857–2 Aug. 1929), Roman Catholic archbishop, was born in Joliet, Illinois, the son of John Keane and Margaret O'Connor, Irish immigrants. Keane (pronounced "cane") grew up on a farm near Rochester, Minnesota. He attended St. John's Seminary in Collegeville, Minnesota; the College of St. Francis Xavier in New York City; and the Grand Seminary in Montreal, Canada, where he was ordained a priest in 1882. He then served in parishes in St. Paul, Minnesota, until 1885, when he was appointed as an instructor at and the bursar of St. Thomas College in St. Paul. He became its rector in 1888. From 1892 to 1901 he was the pastor of Immaculate Conception Church in Minneapolis. As pastor, Keane took an active part in local community affairs. He participated in one of the major building projects of Archbishop John Ireland by actively raising funds for the construction of the huge St. Mary's Basilica in Minneapolis.

In 1902 Keane was appointed third bishop of Cheyenne, Wyoming, where he presided over a small flock scattered over a large area. In 1911 Keane was appointed third archbishop of Dubuque, Iowa, succeeding the aging Archbishop John Joseph Keane (no relation). The two Keanes were a study in contrasts. The elder Keane—the affable, scholarly, polished, and nationally known former rector of the Catholic University of America—was known in Dubuque Catholic circles as "Sugar Cane," while the younger Keane was a strict disciplinarian who came to be known locally as "Hickory Cane." Unlike his predecessor, Keane had few intellectual interests.

Keane's reputation as a churchman rests on his careful attention to archdiocesan administration. He kept a close watch over pastors and parishes by requiring thorough financial reports. During his administration, each parish property was separately incorporated with a board consisting of the archbishop, the vicar general, the pastor, and two lay trustees. The archdiocese's St. Joseph's College (now Loras College in Dubuque) was likewise reincorporated, with control resting in a self-perpetuating board, the members of which were predominately lay. Keane kept the college in the forefront of his flock's attention with appeals for funds for new buildings. He likewise supported the interests of Clarke College, a women's college in Dubuque that was owned by the Sisters of Charity of the Blessed Virgin Mary.

To raise the standards of education in the many parish schools of his largely rural archdiocese, Keane established an Office of Catholic Education in 1922. He supported Dubuque's Catholic daily newspaper, the *Daily American Tribune*, and in 1921 he established an archdiocesan weekly, *The Witness*.

Keane's interests as a churchman reflect the values of an era in which episcopal leaders worked to maintain the Catholic community's separate subculture. His name was not attached to any national Catholic causes, and he was scarcely known outside the areas in which he served. After a period of declining health, he died in Dubuque.

• Keane's papers are in the Archives of the Archdiocese of Dubuque. Mathias Hoffman, ed., *Centennial History of the Archdiocese of Dubuque* (1938), includes an account of his administration. David L. Salvaterra, "Deep Are the Roots," in *Seed/Harvest: A History of the Archdiocese of Dubuque*, ed. Mary Kevin Gallagher (1987), is the most extensive published account of Keane's life and activities in Dubuque. Other sources include Paul T. Steinmel, "A Sketch of the Life of James J. Keane: Priest and Archbishop, 1856–1929" (M.A. thesis, St. Paul Seminary, 1952), and Mary Rosina O'Neill, "A Sketch of the Life of the Most Reverend James J. Keane, Third Archbishop of Dubuque, 1856–1929" (M.A. thesis, Catholic Univ. of America, 1947).

JOSEPH M. WHITE

KEANE, John Joseph (12 Sept. 1839–22 June 1918), Roman Catholic clergyman, was born in Ballyshannon, County Donegal, Ireland, the son of Hugh Keane, a tailor, and Fannie Connolly. In December 1848 the family moved to Baltimore, Maryland. During the late 1850s, Keane sold books and dry goods before entering St. Charles' College, Ellicott City, Maryland, in September 1859. He finished the usual six-year curriculum within three years. In the fall of 1862 he began studies at St. Mary's Seminary, Baltimore, graduating with a baccalaureate in theology three years later. He was ordained a priest on 2 July 1866.

From 1866 to 1878 Keane served as assistant pastor of St. Patrick's Church, Washington, D.C. During his years at St. Patrick's, Keane came under the influence of pastor Joseph Ambrose Walter and Isaac Hecker, founder and superior general of the Missionary Society of St. Paul the Apostle (Paulists). While at St. Patrick's he offered vigorous support to the Catholic temperance movement, an interest he displayed throughout his career.

On 25 August 1878 Keane was consecrated bishop of Richmond, Virginia, and administrator of the vicariate of North Carolina. In addition to his activities on behalf of temperance, he took the lead in inviting African Americans into the Roman Catholic church. He played a prominent role at the Third Plenary Council of Baltimore in 1884, especially promoting the establishment of a national Catholic university in the United States.

From 1889 to the mid-1890s Keane served as the first rector of the Catholic University of America in Washington, D.C. Along with fundraising and recruiting both faculty and students for the infant institution, he continued his efforts in the temperance movement. In company with James Cardinal Gibbons of Baltimore and Archbishop John Ireland of St. Paul, Minnesota, he provided strong leadership for the so-called Americanists within the Catholic church. Charles E. Eliot, president of Harvard, invited Keane to deliver the prestigious Dudleian Lecture in October 1890, and Keane participated in the World's Parliament of Religions in September 1893 in Chicago, Illinois. However, these activities generated suspicion and hostility among some conservative Roman Catholics.

In a letter of 15 September 1896, Pope Leo XIII removed Keane from the rectorship of Catholic University, thereby delivering a major setback to the Americanist movement. During the next three years Keane served in Rome as consulter to the Congregations of the Propaganda and of Studies. He also received a titular archbishopric and was appointed a canon at St. John Lateran and assistant at the pontifical throne. While in Rome, he attracted considerable attention, both positive and negative, for his preaching and lecturing. In the meantime, he was seen as a leader of the Americanists.

Keane and other Americanists sought a positive relationship between the Roman Catholic church and American culture. They praised American institutions, including democracy, separation of church and state, and religious freedom. Without yielding commitment to Roman Catholic theological doctrines, they strove for harmonious relations with non–Roman Catholics. Furthermore, they tended to celebrate the experience of the Roman Catholic church in America, thereby earning the enmity of some Catholics both in the United States and in Europe who were suspicious of American politics and culture. Opposition to the Americanists came from Michael A. Corrigan, archbishop of New York, and Bishop Bernard McQuaid of Rochester, New York.

Pope Leo XIII ended the controversy in a carefully phrased encyclical, *Testem benevolentiae*, released in February 1899. The pontiff condemned a variety of errors without accusing any American Roman Catholics of holding disreputable beliefs such as seeking to adapt the Roman Catholic faith to non-Catholics and muting the distinctive aspects of Catholicism. The prominent Americanists submitted to the encyclical but tended to deny that American Catholics held the condemned tenets. Leading conservatives, however, hailed the encyclical as a solid defeat for their opponents.

Late in 1899 Keane returned to the United States to raise funds for Catholic University. Then from 1900 to 1911 he served as the second archbishop of Dubuque, Iowa. He helped St. Joseph's College (now Loras College) in Dubuque, expanded the parochial school system, and promoted charitable activities and the temperance movement.

Encountering major cardiac difficulties, Keane requested a coadjutor, but officials at the Vatican refused, thereby effectively forcing him to resign as archbishop in 1911. His successor, James John Keane, former bishop of Cheyenne, generously invited the ailing prelate to live in the cathedral rectory, an offer that Keane accepted. He spent his remaining years in Dubuque, where he died.

Keane helped the Roman Catholic church adjust to late nineteenth- and early twentieth-century American society, despite strong opposition from some of his coreligionists in the United States and in Rome. According to his biographer, Patrick Henry Ahern, he "showed his generation how to love God, the Church, and America."

• Virtually all of Keane's papers, both official and personal, apparently were destroyed. Patrick Henry Ahern wrote a comprehensive biography, *The Life of John J. Keane: Educator and Archbishop, 1839–1918* (1955). For useful treatments of Keane and Americanism, consult Robert D. Cross, *The Emergence of Liberal Catholicism in America* (1958); Andrew M. Greeley, *The Catholic Experience: An Interpretation of the History of American Catholicism* (1967); Winthrop S. Hudson and John Corrigan, *Religion in America: An Historical Account of the Development of American Religious Life*, 5th ed. (1992); and Thomas T. McAvoy, *The Great Crisis in American Catholic History, 1895–1900* (1957).

CHARLES E. QUIRK

KEARNEY, Belle (6 Mar. 1863–27 Feb. 1939), temperance advocate, suffragist, and legislator, was born Carrie Belle Kearney in Madison County, Mississippi, the daughter of Walter Gunston Kearney, a planter, lawyer, and politician, and Susannah Owens. Kearney was educated consecutively by a governess, public school, and the Canton Young Ladies' Academy until the family could no longer afford the tuition. Between the ages of sixteen and nineteen, she led the life of an impoverished "belle": her autobiographical account describes taking in sewing for former slaves as well as dancing at the governor's inaugural ball.

Reared by parents who regarded the use of alcoholic beverages as sinful, Kearney grew contemptuous of her intemperate friends. At age nineteen she defied convention and opened a small school at her parents' home in Vernon Heights, Mississippi. The next year she secured a position as a public school teacher and continued to teach for four years, investing her earnings during summer vacations in self-education that included a visit to the southern chautauqua (a lecture program for adults) at Monteagle, Tennessee. Religious doubts had led her to resign from the Methodist church at age fifteen, but following a spiritual awakening in 1887 she felt called to serve God as a reformer.

Inspired by Frances Willard, the president of the Woman's Christian Temperance Union (WCTU), Kearney accepted a position directing the Mississippi WCTU's youth programs. Her work quickly attracted the attention of national WCTU leaders including Willard, who encouraged her to develop her already impressive oratorical skills. In 1891 Kearney was invited to become a lecturer and organizer for the national WCTU. At first she spoke primarily in the South, urging women into temperance work even though women's political activism defied southern tradition, but later she lectured throughout the nation and abroad. In 1895 she was one of the WCTU representatives who presented the "Polyglot Petition" to President Grover Cleveland and Queen Victoria. The petition, containing millions of signatures in fifty languages, sought government aid to curtail trade in alcohol and opium. During this period Kearney was also affiliated with the Prohibition party.

In 1898 Kearney gave up her position with the WCTU to become a professional lecturer and writer. In 1900 she published an autobiography, *A Slaveholder's Daughter*, which went into ten editions; it contained her thoughts on education, reform, race relations, the role of women, and other aspects of life in the postwar South. For many years thereafter she traveled extensively as a speaker at chautauquas and lyceums, where she addressed a wide range of social and political issues. In 1904–1905 Kearney attended the International Congress of Women at Berlin, organized WCTU chapters in Athens and Jerusalem, and spoke in China, Singapore, Hong Kong, and Japan. She studied the social conditions in the countries she visited and sent back articles to newspapers. Promoted by her agents as "the foremost woman orator in America," she was particularly proud of her lectures on the South in which she "defended southern ideals" and promoted sectional reconciliation. Whatever the topic, she seized the opportunity to promote temperance and woman suffrage.

As a young woman Kearney was dismayed by the restrictions she faced as a woman and the fact that her brothers could vote when she could not, and she was encouraged in her nascent feminism by Lucy Stone, Susan B. Anthony, and Laura Clay as well as her mentor Willard. As early as 1894 she attempted to create a state suffrage organization in Mississippi. When organizers for the National American Woman Suffrage Association (NAWSA) succeeded in organizing a state suffrage organization in Mississippi in 1897, Kearney was selected to serve as a vice president. In 1906 she organized a convention of southern suffragists that met in Memphis and established the short-lived Southern Woman Suffrage Conference; the conference led, however, to the renewal of suffrage activity in Tennessee and in Mississippi, where Kearney was elected president of the Mississippi Woman Suffrage Association.

A white supremacist, Kearney was receptive to a plan devised by Henry Blackwell, a founder with his wife, Lucy Stone, and others of the American Woman Suffragist Association, to promote woman suffrage in the South, with literacy or property restrictions as a means of countering the black vote. In her autobiography and in suffrage speeches, including her highly publicized keynote speech at the 1903 NAWSA convention in New Orleans, Kearney praised "qualified" woman suffrage as the means of ensuring "immediate and durable white supremacy, honestly attained." In 1911 she was appointed to the NAWSA Congressional Committee. She joined the Southern States Woman Suffrage Conference but objected forcefully to leader Kate Gordon's demand that southern suffragists seek enfranchisement by state action only. Aware that the pleas of southern suffragists for state suffrage amendments were falling on deaf ears, Kearney recognized that a federal amendment might prove necessary, and she lobbied for the proposed Nineteenth Amendment in Congress and then supported ratification. Though state, regional, and national suffrage leaders admired Kearney's oratorical skills, many regarded her as flamboyant, impetuous, and egotistical.

Kearney was also a supporter of the social purity movement and in 1907 served as a field secretary of the World's Purity Federation. An advocate of "sex hygiene instruction" in schools and of legislation to reduce the incidence of venereal disease, in 1921 she published a novel, *Conqueror or Conquered*, that depicted "the tragic results of ignorance surrounding the mysteries of sex." She argued that drinking promoted venereal disease and that men should be held to the same high standards of "purity" as women. From 1912 to 1920 Kearney lived between travels in Washington, D.C., where she lobbied extensively for prohibition and woman suffrage. A strong supporter of American involvement in World War I, in 1917 and 1918 she lectured at military camps in the United States under the auspices of the Young Men's Christian Association and promoted the war effort in the Midwest, where, in her words, "the German element was so strong."

In December 1920 Kearney returned to Mississippi and declared her candidacy for the U.S. Senate, embarking on an unsuccessful two-year campaign. In the Democratic primary of 1922 she received 18,303 votes, a respectable showing in a state that had been so hostile to woman suffrage. In 1923 she ran successfully for the Mississippi senate, making her the first woman in the South to serve as a state senator, and she sponsored a number of progressive bills including an unsuccessful antilynching bill. She was a delegate to the Democratic National Convention in 1924. She fought vigorously for the enforcement of prohibition and against its repeal, serving as a first vice president of the National Woman's Democratic Law Enforcement League. She broke with the Democratic party to support Herbert Hoover against Al Smith in 1928. She rejoined the Methodist church in 1938, delighted by the reconciliation of its northern and southern branches. She died in Jackson. On the day of her funeral, her body lay in state in the capitol and state offices were closed in tribute.

Kearney believed that her educational work was largely responsible for Mississippi's early adoption of prohibition and its position as the first state to ratify the Eighteenth Amendment. Though she failed to persuade her state to endorse state or federal woman suffrage measures, she convinced many to broaden their view of the role of women and played a pioneering role in the politics of her state and region.

• Kearney's papers are housed at the Mississippi Department of Archives and History (MDAH), Jackson. Important information on Kearney is in the Lily Wilkinson Thompson Papers at both the MDAH and the University of Mississippi Library; the Woman's Christian Temperance Union Collection at the MDAH; and the Somerville-Howorth Family Papers at the Schlesinger Library at Radcliffe College (portions of these are on microfilm at the MDAH as the Nellie Nugent Somerville Papers). See also Nancy Carol Tipton, " 'It Is My Duty': The Public Career of Belle Kearney" (M.A. thesis, Univ. of Mississippi, 1975), a well-researched and thorough if somewhat hagiographical monograph. On Kearney's role in the suffrage movement, see Marjorie Spruill Wheeler, *New Women of the New South: The Leaders of the Woman Suffrage Movement in the Southern States* (1993), which discusses Kearney as one of eleven prominent regional leaders; Anne Firor Scott, *The Southern Lady: From Pedestal to Politics, 1830–1930* (1970; repr. 1995); and A. Elizabeth Taylor, "The Woman Suffrage Movement in Mississippi," *Journal of Mississippi History* 30 (Feb. 1968): 1–34.

MARJORIE SPRUILL WHEELER

KEARNEY, Denis (1 Feb. 1847–24 Apr. 1907), labor leader, was born in Oakmount, County Cork, Ireland. His parents' names are unknown. Orphaned at an early age, Kearney went to sea as a cabin boy at the age of eleven. For the next decade he sailed on both English and American vessels, and by the time he arrived in San Francisco on the clipper ship *Shooting Star* in 1868, he had risen to the rank of chief mate. He then began working on steamers out of San Francisco. In 1870 he married Mary Ann Leary; they had four children. With his savings he bought a draying business in the city in 1872, and four years later he became an American citizen.

During these years Kearney tended to act more like a businessman than an advocate for labor. When he spoke up at the local Lyceum for Self Culture, it was generally to praise self-made men like himself and denounce lazy workingmen; he even joined the "merchants' militia" that helped put down a workers' riot in 1877. Kearney's interests broadened, however, partly because of his wide reading in history, philosophy, and economics, and partly because he was politically ambitious. He began attending the boisterous outdoor meetings of workers at a location then known as the "sandlot" (later the site of the San Francisco Civic Center), and within weeks he developed a reputation as a rousing orator on labor's behalf.

San Francisco's working class had significant grievances during this period, including widespread unemployment, corrupt banking, unequal taxation, political graft, and the domination of corporate monopolies like the railroad. Kearney assailed all these enemies, but the speeches that evoked the most dramatic response were his diatribes against the Chinese. The importation of "coolie" laborers who would work for starvation wages, he told his enthusiastic audiences, deprived "Americans" of their rightful employment; this immigration must be stopped. The Chinese issue also fed Kearney's broader critique, since he blamed the wealthy industrialists and their political stooges for bringing in the Chinese workers.

In October 1877 Kearney called for the formation of a new Workingmen's party: "The rich have ruled us until they have ruined us. We will now take our own affairs into our own hands. The republic must and shall be preserved, and only workingmen will do it" (Saxton, p. 118). Kearney became the president of the new party and began editing a party organ, the *Open Letter*, to publicize its activities. He addressed workers' meetings almost every night, convening some rallies right on Nob Hill, opposite the headquarters of the city's leading importer of Chinese labor, the Central Pacific Railroad. "Are you ready to march down to the wharf and stop the leprous Chinamen from landing?" Kearney shouted to one crowd. On another occasion, he advised every one of his listeners to obtain a musket and a hundred rounds of ammunition. It was essential to maintain "the dignity of labor," he asserted, "even if we have to kill every wretch that opposes it" (Saxton, p. 118).

The Workingmen's flamboyant language cast a pall of fear over the city's Chinese community, although few actual violent incidents occurred. The party's blistering attacks on the city's financial and political leaders were mostly rhetorical, too, but these evoked a strong official response. The city police force was expanded, the governor was given additional funds to combat insurgency, and the state legislature passed a "gag law," making it a felony to "suggest or advise or encourage" riots. Kearney and the other party leaders were repeatedly arrested, released on bail, and arrested again. Kearney's political standing soared with the publicity. One of his releases from prison was celebrated by a procession of more than 7,000 workingmen representing unions, ethnic associations, and political ward clubs.

By 1878 the Workingmen's party had become a significant political force in the state. It won a string of victories in local elections and seemed poised to send a decisive number of delegates to the state's upcoming constitutional convention. Alarmed sufficiently by this prospect to bury their differences, the Democrats and Republicans together backed an opposing nonpartisan slate. After Kearney quashed a rebellion within his own ranks (during which he himself was almost killed), the Workingmen's party went on to win nearly one-third of the seats at the convention, including every seat from San Francisco.

The Workingmen made their presence felt at the convention in two ways. First, their votes helped pass the package of regulatory reform proposals known as the "Granger program." Second, they took the lead in enacting a set of harsh anti-Chinese constitutional clauses, including denying them the vote, forbidding their employment on any state or local public works, and encouraging the passage of further restrictions in state and local laws. Beyond this, however, few measures of interest to labor were even introduced. The reformer Henry George, who attended the convention as a Democrat, blamed the Workingmen's lack of impact on their policy of electing delegates who were "utterly ignorant and inexperienced." Others pointed out, however, that the party members caucused regularly and voted in a disciplined manner. The larger problem apparently was that they had not organized around any shared program beyond their common venom toward the wealthy and the Chinese. Kearney had built a movement, but he had not given it a goal toward which to march.

The Workingmen's party won a number of victories in 1879, electing the San Francisco mayor, the supreme court justice, and two dozen state legislators. But the party fell apart rapidly thereafter, and Kearney soon returned to private business, explaining later that he had had to make money to support his "helpless family." He died in Alameda, California.

Kearney's success in building the Workingmen's party so quickly suggests the potential of labor politics in late nineteenth-century America. At the same time, the party's rapid demise reflects the problems that bedeviled many such movements: domination by a single charismatic leader, intraparty bickering, opposition to virtually every established institution, and—illustrated most dramatically in the Workingmen's party—ethnic hatreds that divided the working class instead of united it. Kearney later maintained that his party was a major factor in the passage of the anti-Chinese federal Exclusion Act of 1882. The claim was probably exaggerated, but the fact that Kearney would identify this act as his party's major legacy says much about the limitations of the movement he led.

• Correspondence with Kearney appears in the papers of Horace Gray in the Library of Congress and in those of Richard S. Floyd in the Bancroft Library at the University of California at Berkeley. Contemporary accounts of Kearney's career are in Henry George, "The Kearney Agitation in California," *Popular Science Monthly* (Aug. 1880); in a pamphlet by two party members, J. C. Stedman and R. A. Leonard, *The Workingmen's Party of California* (1878); and in Hubert Howe Bancroft, *History of California*, vol. 7 (1890) and *Popular Tribunals*, vol. 2 (1887). See also Alexander Saxton, *The Indispensable Enemy: Labor and the Anti-Chinese Movement in California* (1971); Walton Bean, *California: An Interpretative History*, 2d ed. (1973); R. A. Burchell, *The San Francisco Irish, 1848–1880* (1980); and William Issel and Robert W. Cherny, *San Francisco, 1865–1932* (1986). An obituary is in the *New York Times*, 26 Apr. 1907.

SANDRA OPDYCKE

KEARNS, Jack (17 Aug. 1882–7 July 1963), boxing manager and promoter, was born John Leo McKernan on a farm in Waterloo, Michigan, the son of John Philip McKernan and Frances Hoff. Until the age of seven he lived on a ranch in North Dakota. With his father as a scout, he then traveled with his family by wagon train to North Yakima, Washington. They later settled in Seattle, Washington, where his father ran a wholesale grocery business.

In 1896 Kearns left home to participate in the Klondike gold rush, stowing away on a freighter bound for Alaska. There he began boxing, first with bareknuck-les and then progressing to gloved bouts. He was soon fighting professionally in northwestern U.S. towns under the name of "Young Kid Kearns." While in San Francisco at the turn of the century, he met Dal Hawkins, a top featherweight who taught Kearns how to box more effectively. Kearns continued traveling throughout the West, boxing for $10–$300 per bout. In 1904 after a street brawl in Seattle he was sent to prison in Walla Walla, Washington, for one year. Released after serving eight months of his sentence, he headed for Portland, Oregon, intending to return to the ring. While there he met Maude Harper, a nightclub entertainer whom he married; however his constant traveling brought a quick end to the marriage.

Kearns opened a boxing club in Spokane, Washington, and began promoting fights and managing boxers. On a trip to Los Angeles he met William A. Brady, the theatrical entrepreneur and manager of heavyweight champions Jim Corbett and Jim Jeffries. Brady taught Kearns that to succeed he must be first and foremost a showman, and Kearns never forgot that lesson. His growing stable of fighters included Harry Wills, Eddie McGoorty, Jimmy Clabby, Billy Murray, Red Watson, and Joe Bonds. In 1915 Kearns took McGoorty, Murray, and Clabby to Australia for bouts with middleweight champion Les Darcy. In less than three months, Darcy defeated all three of them in championship bouts.

Back in San Francisco in 1917, Kearns met Jack Dempsey, then fighting as "Kid Blackie" or "Young Dempsey." Becoming Dempsey's manager, he arranged for Dempsey to fight every few weeks (25 bouts, 21 knockouts, 16 first-round knockouts in 14 months) and soon had Dempsey established as the top contender for Jess Willard's heavyweight title. Kearns convinced promoter Tex Rickard to offer Willard $100,000 to fight Dempsey. On 4 July 1919 in Toledo, Dempsey easily defeated Willard, knocking him down seven times in the first round before the bout was stopped at the end of the third round.

With the help of Rickard's promotion, Kearns achieved his greatest feat when he arranged a fight between Dempsey and Frenchman Georges Carpentier, the world light heavyweight champion. Kearns played up Carpentier's boxing ability, good looks, and war hero status against Dempsey's knockout punch, scowling countenance, and draft dodger reputation. The 2 July 1921 bout, easily won by Dempsey with a fourth-round knockout, drew 80,083 people and produced receipts of $1,789,238, the first time that a boxing match produced $1 million in revenue. Kearns demanded $300,000 for Dempsey's share but under the table arranged for 50 percent of everything over $1,000,000.

For Dempsey's next title defense, Kearns persuaded the citizens of Shelby, Montana—a town of 500 people that had just become rich from local oil reserves—to guarantee Dempsey $300,000 for a bout against Tommy Gibbons. The 4 July 1923 fight, won by Dempsey in a dull 15-round contest, did not draw the anticipated crowds and with Kearns insisting on his guarantee, Gibbons and the promoters received nothing for their efforts. On 14 September 1923 Rickard and Kearns collaborated in boxing's second million-dollar gate when Dempsey knocked out the Argentinian Luis Angel Firpo in the second round of an exciting bout.

In 1925, at Dempsey's recommendation, Kearns became the manager of welterweight champion Mickey Walker. Shortly afterward Dempsey and Kearns parted ways after Dempsey married actress Estelle Taylor against the advice of Kearns. Financial disputes also contributed to the separation, resulting in a number of lawsuits filed between Kearns and Dempsey before the disputes were settled. Afterward Kearns devoted his efforts toward Walker and helped him win the middleweight title in 1926. His promotional skills and ability to create champions enabled him to continue to attract first-class fighters. In 1929 he became the manager of Jackie Fields, the 1924 Olympic gold medalist, and led him to the world welterweight title. He also managed former lightweight champion Benny Leonard during Leonard's comeback attempt in 1931–1932.

In 1931 Kearns married Lillian Kansler of Lexington, Kentucky, a manicurist in a Chicago barber shop. They had two sons before they divorced in 1948. After his world champions retired in the mid-1930s, Kearns continued to manage boxers, in the process always insisting on receiving 50 percent of the profits. His fighters during this time included heavyweights Enzo Fiermonte, Roscoe Toles, Jimmy Adamick, and Lorenzo Pack—all contenders, but none of championship caliber. During this time Kearns engaged in other business ventures that met with little success. He bought a restaurant in Detroit but only lasted four months in that business before filing for bankruptcy. He then bought into a fire extinguisher business, which resulted in a fraudulent stock scheme. In 1945 he was indicted and tried for mail fraud and violations of the Securities Exchange Act but was found not guilty in federal court.

In 1946 Kearns returned to the boxing business as the manager of light-hitting light heavyweight Joey Maxim, and he guided Maxim to the world title in 1950. Maxim held the title until 17 December 1952, when he was defeated by Archie Moore. An agreement made prior to that bout was that Kearns would receive a share of Moore's contract if Moore was victorious. With Kearns as his new manager, Moore retained his title until 1962. Kearns remained a boxing manager, overseeing such fighters as lightweight Kenny Lane and heavyweight Jefferson Davis, until his death at his son's home in Miami Beach, Florida.

Jack Kearns's promotional and managerial skills spanned six decades of boxing and provided the sport with some of its most memorable moments as well as one of its most memorable characters. He was elected as a charter member to the International Boxing Hall of Fame in 1990.

• The most complete source for anecdotes about Kearns's intriguing life is his autobiography as told to Oscar Fraley, *The Million Dollar Gate* (1966). Complete records of the champions he managed, Dempsey, Walker, Fields, Leonard, Maxim, and Moore, are in Herbert G. Goldman, ed., *The Ring 1986–87 Record Book and Boxing Encyclopedia* (1986). A number of biographies of Jack Dempsey detail the relationship between Dempsey and Kearns. Among the best is Randy Roberts, *Jack Dempsey, The Manassa Mauler* (1979). Obituaries include the *New York Times*, 8 July 1963; Harold Rosenthal, "The Last Bell," *New York Herald Tribune*, 8 July 1963, included in Edward Ehre and Irving T. Marsh, eds., *Best Sports Stories 1964* (1965); and Nat Fleischer, "Kearns, Ballyhoo King," *The Ring* 42 (Sept. 1963): 28–30, 47.

JOHN GRASSO

KEARNY, Lawrence (30 Nov. 1789–29 Nov. 1868), naval officer, was born in Perth Amboy, New Jersey, the son of Michael Kearny, a merchant, and Elizabeth Lawrence, a poet. A member of a distinguished family, he was imbued from childhood with high aspirations. His mother's half-brother, Captain James Lawrence, who later achieved fame as a naval hero of the War of 1812, was his namesake. After an education at home, Kearny entered the U.S. Navy as a midshipman in 1807. During the years of the embargo and nonintercourse acts, he served on gunboats and the frigates *Constitution* and *President*. In 1810 he was transferred to the *Enterprise*, where he was at the beginning of the War of 1812. In 1813 he was promoted to lieutenant. During the war he commanded the schooners *Caroline*, *Ferret*, and *Nonsuch* and later a small flotilla, defending America's southern coast. He proved himself a fighting sailor in 1815 by capturing a British tender, and he emerged from the war with a distinguished reputation and a promising future.

Rewarded in the postwar navy with command of the *Enterprise*, Kearny carried out a successful expedition in 1821 against pirate strongholds on Cuba's southern coast. Four years later, promoted to master commandant, he was given command of the *Warren* and sent to the eastern Mediterranean to fight Greek pirates, who were preying on international shipping. There he attacked pirate strongholds and ships, often seizing several vessels a day, and captured much stolen booty and many prisoners. The British Parliament congratulated him for single-handedly doing more to suppress piracy in the eastern Mediterranean than all other nations' naval officers combined. In 1832 he was promoted to captain and spent the next few years on shore duty, then was given command of the *Potomac*. During that time, in 1834, he married Josephine C. Hall, with whom he had two children. In 1840 he was given command of the *Constellation* and dispatched to Buenos Aires on official service. While there, he received word from James K. Paulding, secretary of the navy, that he was appointed commander of the East India Squadron, consisting of his ship and the *Boston*, and ordered to China to defend American mercantile interests during the Opium War.

Kearny sailed first to Macao then to Canton, where he arrived in March 1842, half a year before the war came to an end. He established relations with British officials and Chinese authorities, studied the situation as it affected the United States, particularly the loss of trade, and favorably impressed the Chinese by declaring that his country was opposed to illegal opium smuggling. Discovering that American mercantile houses had suffered extensive damage from mobs, he secured substantial reparations but placated Chinese officials by not making excessive claims. In the meantime, he vigorously pursued his main diplomatic mission: demanding that American merchants be given the same postwar trading privileges accorded other nations under most favored nation status. Learning that China had negotiated a treaty with Britain that opened five ports to English merchants, he sent dispatches to his government encouraging the United States to attempt to secure similar treaty concessions. On his own authority, he requested of the governor of Canton in October that American traders be given equal trade status with the English; ten months later he learned that this concession had been granted. Thus Kearny established the principle of the Open Door in China, which would later be a cornerstone of American Asian policy, and he laid the groundwork for U.S. envoy Caleb Cushing in 1844 to negotiate the first Sino-American treaty.

His mission in China completed, Kearny sailed for home in April 1843. Following Paulding's instructions regarding his return voyage, he sailed along the Australian coast and to New Zealand, showing the flag in protection of American whalers' rights. Then he proceeded to the Sandwich (now Hawaiian) Islands, where he discovered that Lord George Paulet, an imperious British naval officer, had just browbeaten Prince Timoleo Haolilio into signing a treaty that ceded his kingdom to England. Realizing that such a measure was inimical to American Pacific interests, Kearny protested Paulet's takeover but remained calm until the British Pacific commander, Rear Admiral Richard Thomas, arrived and rescinded the cession.

For the remainder of his career Kearny held a number of shore appointments, including the presidency of a board to examine officers (1846), membership in the lighthouse board, command of Norfolk Navy Yard (1847), superintendent of Atlantic mail ships (1852), and command of New York Navy Yard (1857). Continuing close ties with his hometown of Perth Amboy, he was elected mayor for one term in 1848. He retired from the navy in 1861 and was promoted to commodore on the retired list in 1867. That same year he was appointed to the New Jersey Board of Pilot Commissioners. He died in the same house in which he was born.

• Kearny's official correspondence is in the Office of Naval Records, Navy Department, and the State Department Archives. Some documents are published in *Papers Relating to the Foreign Relations of the United States . . . 1894*, app. 2 (1895). Carroll Storr Alden, *Lawrence Kearny: Sailor Diplomat* (1936), is a good biography. Analyses of Kearny's role in formulating Asian policy are Thomas Kearny, "Commodore Lawrence Kearny and the Open Door and Most Favored Na-

tion Policy in China in 1842 to 1843," New Jersey Historical Society, *Proceedings* 50 (1932): 162–90; John W. Foster, *American Diplomacy in the Orient* (1903); and Charles Oscar Paullin, *Diplomatic Negotiations of American Naval Officers, 1778–1883* (1912). Background information is in Gardner Allen, *Our Navy and the West Indian Pirates* (1929); John H. Schroeder, *Shaping a Maritime Empire: The Commercial and Diplomatic Role of the American Navy, 1829–1861* (1985); and Kenneth J. Hagan, *This People's Navy: The Making of American Sea Power* (1991).

PAUL DAVID NELSON

KEARNY, Philip (1 June 1814–1 Sept. 1862), soldier, was born in New York City, the son of Philip Kearny, a businessman, and Susan Watts. He attended Highland Academy and Columbia College, from which he graduated in 1833. His grandfather's bequest of $1 million in 1836 relieved Kearny of financial concerns and allowed him (despite the objections of his grandparents) to pursue his passion: soldiering. In 1837 he received a second lieutenant's commission in the First U.S. Dragoons. Two years later he was sent by the secretary of war to France to study cavalry tactics. Kearny did more than study; he distinguished himself in several battles. The French awarded him the Cross of the Legion of Honor for "services to France . . . above the call of duty." He returned to the United States to write a book—published in 1844 as *Service with the French Troops in Africa*—and to serve on the staff of the U.S. Army's commander in chief, Winfield Scott.

In 1846 his wife of five years, Diana Moore Bullitt (with whom he had five children), convinced him to resign his commission, but the respite lasted only a month. Kearny rode to Mexico as a captain, commander of a company in the First Dragoons. He led his troops in a bold, bloody, but ultimately unsuccessful attack against the defenses of Mexico City on 20 August 1847. During the assault, Kearny's arm was shattered; it was amputated just above the elbow. In 1851, after several years of duty as a recruiter, Kearny rejoined his regiment and participated in the campaign against the Rogue River Indians in California. Without prospects for promotion, however, later that year he resigned his commission. A trip to Europe followed—his second—and there he met young Agnes Maxwell, with whom he embarked on an illicit romance. Though his wife would refuse to grant Kearny a divorce until 1857, in 1854 Agnes moved in with him on his New Jersey estate, "Bellegrove." They married in Paris in 1858 and had three children. The following year Kearny succumbed to the lure of the battlefield again and joined the French chasseurs in the campaign of Napoleon III against Austria. This adventurous service was cut short by the outbreak of civil war in the United States.

In 1861 few if any men in America could boast more combat experience than Kearny. He received a commission as brigadier general in August 1861 and assumed command of a brigade of New Jersey regiments. By the time he saw combat during the 1862

Peninsula campaign, he had risen to command of a division. At the battle of Williamsburg in May, he and his division arrived on the field just as the Union line started to crumble; Kearny helped stave off disaster. Likewise at Fair Oaks on 31 May 1862, Kearny found himself faced with fleeing Union troops. He personally led his troops into the fight—at one point ordering his own men to fire on fleeing Union soldiers—and by dint of personal bravery and skilled maneuver helped slow the Confederate advance. Kearny and his division also bore a heavy part of the fighting at Glendale on 30 June, where his efforts were instrumental in preserving the Union retreat route to Harrison's Landing. By the end of the Peninsula campaign, perhaps only George B. McClellan exceeded Kearny in popularity within the army. Of him one man wrote, "A good deal has been said abt [sic] brave men in the late fight. I saw some but none like Gen. Kearney [sic]. It was not rashness. No one would call it so. It was cool, deliberate, well timed bravery."

Detached from McClellan (whom he despised) in August 1862, Kearny and his division joined John Pope's army in northern Virginia. On 29 August 1862, at Second Manassas, Kearny led the most successful Union attack of the battle. His efforts notwithstanding, the Union army was defeated the next day. During the Union retreat toward Washington, Kearny's men met the Confederates again in a driving rainstorm near Chantilly. At the height of the battle, impatient with the failure of a regiment to advance promptly, Kearny galloped beyond Union lines and inadvertently rode into a regiment of Confederates. His dash to escape ended in a fatal hail of bullets.

Kearny ended his career as one of the most colorful soldiers of his era. The sight of the one-armed Kearny—reins in his teeth, cape blowing, and sword upraised—exhorting or excoriating his men on the battlefield became one of the enduring (and oft-noted) images of the war. Though ambitious, impatient, and brave to deadly fault, he was anything but rash in his practice of the military art. His controlled aggressiveness on many battlefields served the Army of the Potomac well; at his death, he was one of the best division commanders in the Union army. Scott called him "the bravest man I ever knew." Kearny, New Jersey, is named in his honor.

• Kearny's personal papers are at the New Jersey Historical Society. His Civil War letters, along with much contemporary commentary, are published in William B. Styple, ed., *Letters from the Peninsula: The Civil War Letters of General Philip Kearny* (1988). John Watts De Peyster, *Personal and Military History of Philip Kearny* (1870), contains much important information. The only modern biography of Kearny is Irving Werstein, *Kearny the Magnificent* (1962). See also Cortlandt Parker, *Philip Kearny* (1868). *The War of the Rebellion: A Compilation of the Official Records of the Union and Confederate Armies* (128 vols., 1880–1901) also includes much material pertinent to Kearny's battlefield performance. For modern commentary on Kearny's Civil War service see Ste-phen W. Sears, *To the Gates of Richmond: The Peninsula Campaign* (1992), and John Hennessy, *Return to Bull Run: The Campaign and Battle of Second Manassas* (1993).

JOHN HENNESSY

KEARNY, Stephen Watts (30 Aug. 1794–31 Oct. 1848), army officer, was born in Newark, New Jersey, the son of Philip Kearny, a landowner and wine merchant, and Susanna Watts. He attended common schools in Newark, and in 1808 he was admitted to Columbia College. Following two years of study, Kearny quit school to join the New York militia as an ensign on 24 April 1810. The impending war with England induced him to seek a regular army commission, and on 12 March 1812 the rank of first lieutenant, Thirteenth U.S. Infantry, was conferred. In this capacity he fought bravely on 13 October 1812 at Queenston Heights, where he was wounded and taken prisoner. Kearny spent several months in captivity before being paroled, but on 1 April 1813 he received promotion to captain. Later in the war Kearny served at Plattsburgh and Sackets Harbor, New York, but saw no additional combat. He was retained in the peacetime establishment as part of the Second Infantry, and he concluded several years of garrison duty in Missouri.

In 1819 Kearny accompanied Colonel Henry Atkinson's noted Yellowstone Expedition, initiating a thirty-year frontier career. On 1 April 1823 he was breveted major for ten years in grade and the following year participated in the Second Yellowstone Expedition. Kearny fulfilled an important task by helping establish the Jefferson Barracks, St. Louis, Missouri, in 1826; he subsequently commanded numerous frontier posts, including Fort Crawford, Wisconsin Territory, through 1830. That year he married Mary Radford, the stepdaughter of army general and explorer William Clark. When the First Dragoon Regiment was created in 1833, Kearny became lieutenant colonel as of 4 March. He rode in General Henry Leavenworth's ill-fated Southern Plains Expedition of 1834 and succeeded him as colonel on 4 June 1836. From his headquarters at Fort Leavenworth, he composed a noted tract, *Carbine Manual; or, Rules for the Exercise and Maneuvers for the U.S. Dragoons* (1837). Kearny was also active in peace and treaty negotiations with various Indian tribes, and in 1842 he was rewarded with command of the Third Military District, encompassing most of the Great Plains region. Among his final peacetime activities was conducting a major expedition along the Oregon Trail to South Pass in 1845 and establishing Fort Kearny (Nebr.) the following year.

Shortly after the commencement of war with Mexico, Kearny was elevated to brigadier general on 30 June 1846 and appointed commander of the Army of the West. He departed Fort Leavenworth that month with 1,660 men and orders to subdue Sante Fe, New Mexico. This was bloodlessly accomplished on 10 August 1846, and Kearny quickly established a territorial constitution and a civil government. His next task, the subjugation of California, proved more difficult. He arrived outside of Los Angeles with 100 dragoons on 2

December 1846 and four days later was nearly defeated at the battle of San Pascual. Assisted by naval reinforcements under Commodore Robert Field Stockton, U.S. forces captured San Diego on 10 December and Los Angeles on 9 January 1847. Their success was marred by a struggle for power between Kearny and Stockton over control of the territory. When Stockton appointed army officer and explorer John Charles Frémont to act as governor, Frémont summarily refused to obey Kearny's orders. Kearny had Frémont arrested and court-martialed, eventually resulting in Frémont's resignation. The general then commenced operations against Baja California before returning to Fort Leavenworth. Kearny traveled south and served as temporary governor-general of both Veracruz and Mexico City. In August 1848 he was ordered back north to receive promotion to brevet major general, which was awarded over the objections of Frémont's influential father-in-law, Senator Jesse Hart Benton. Kearny died at Jefferson Barracks in consequence of maladies contracted while at Veracruz.

Kearny was an archetypal frontier officer: gruff, inflexible, and blunt to the point of tactlessness. His treatment of Frémont, however justified, was vindictive and besmirched his reputation. Fortunately, Kearny effectively served three decades in a variety of military and diplomatic capacities. Next to Henry Atkinson, he was perhaps the most effective frontier officer of the antebellum West.

• Kearny's official correspondence is in RG 59, California Governor's Letters; RG 94, Records of the Adjutant General's Office; and RG 98, Record of the Tenth Military Department, National Archives. Manuscript collections are in the Stephen W. Kearny Papers, Missouri Historical Society; the Bancroft Library, University of California, Berkeley; the James Clyman Papers, Huntington Library, San Marino, Calif.; and the Arthur H. Clarke Company Papers, Barker Historical Center, University of Texas, Austin. See also Valentine M. Porter, ed., "The 1820 Journal of Stephen Watts Kearny," *Missouri Historical Society Collections* 3 (1908): 8–29, 99–131; and Stephen W. Kearny, "A Group of Kearny Letters," *New Mexico Historical Review* 5 (1930): 17–37. Detailed studies include Dwight L. Clarke, *Stephen Watts Kearny: Soldier of the West* (1962); Willis B. Hughes, "The Army and Stephen Watts Kearny in the West, 1819–1846" (Ph.D. diss., Univ. of Minnesota, 1955); and Mendel L. Taylor, "The Western Services of Stephen Watts Kearny" (Ph.D. diss., Univ. of Oklahoma, 1944). His wartime activities are amply covered in K. Jack Bauer, *The Mexican War, 1846–1848* (1974); and Thomas Kearny, "The Mexican War and the Conquest of California," *California Historical Quarterly* 8 (Sept. 1929): 251–61.

JOHN C. FREDRIKSEN

KEARSLEY, John (1684–11 Jan. 1772), physician, politician, and philanthropist, was baptized in the village of Greatham, County Durham, England. His father was John Kearsley, an Anglican minister; his mother's name is unknown. Kearsley's father provided two of his sons with a medical education; young John studied in London without earning a degree. For a time he practiced medicine in England, but in 1711 he emigrated and settled in Philadelphia.

Like most colonial physicians, Kearsley practiced both medicine and surgery. During his early career he treated artisans and tradesmen, but he soon developed a clientele of prominent figures such as Edward Shippen, Israel Pemberton, and James Logan. He trained many apprentices, including John Bard, Lloyd Zachary, and John Redman. Although historian William S. Middleton quoted one student as complaining that Kearsley had "a morose and churlish temper, which banished all cheerfulness and social converse from his pupils, and rendered him an unpleasant companion," he trained many outstanding physicians.

Kearsley played an important role in promoting and discussing public health. He claimed to be the first Philadelphia physician to inoculate for small pox, and in 1737, with other physicians, he reported on 129 cases. In 1750, when physician Adam Thomson urged that patients to be inoculated be weakened by liberal use of mercury and antimony along with a mild diet of milk and vegetables, Kearsley and others forcefully dissented. In a 1751 pamphlet, Kearsley pointed out the folly of weakening a patient before inoculation, urged physicians to adapt measures to the patient's condition, and dismissed some of Thomson's suggestions as "Amusements of Ignorance, or Tricks of low Craft" designed to "draw Pence out of the Pockets of the unthinking Populace." Eventually, however, Thomson's method, which became known as the American method of inoculation, generally prevailed. Ten years later Kearsley again plunged into print in a public dispute involving a former mayor and fistula lachrymalis. Kearsley had opened a cyst and inserted a tent to drain it. When infection developed; the mayor consulted other physicians who prescribed another treatment without consulting Kearsley.

Natural history interested Kearsley, who for about fifteen years corresponded with Peter Collinson of the Royal Society of London, sometimes sending him specimens. Kearsley tested ginseng and other American plants to determine if they might cure American illnesses. He observed a comet in February 1737 and sent a report and calculations to Collinson, who later read Kearsley's report to the Royal Society, as printed in the *Philosophical Transactions* (1741). In 1768 Kearsley was elected to the American Philosophical Society.

Kearsley ran successfully for election to the Pennsylvania Assembly as a representative for Philadelphia in 1722. Voters reelected him every year through 1740. He was appointed to the Committee of Accounts and subsequently regularly served on house committees that drafted important legislation. He usually represented the assembly in conferences with the governor.

Kearsley played a leading role in the 1728 controversy that followed Sir William Keith's removal as governor. Following that humiliation, Keith won election to the house. Instead of taking his seat, however, he departed for England and informed the Speaker that he would be absent for a year. The Philadelphia contingent considered his seat vacant and formally requested an election to fill it, but a majority in the assembly rejected the petition. The Philadelphia delegates boycotted assembly meetings to bring the issue to a head, and their absence created doubts that the assembly could conduct business without a quorum. The question was not officially decided, and new elections centered on it. Kearsley wrote some of the pamphlets used in the political skirmish. He and his associates won reelection and returned to the house in October 1728. For his courage on this issue and others, the *Pennsylvania Gazette* eulogized him as having "been born from the Assembly to his own House on the Shoulders of the People" (16 Jan. 1772).

Following that triumph, Kearsley was named, with Speaker Andrew Hamilton and Thomas Lawrence, to purchase land and to contract for the building of a structure to house provincial governmental bodies. By 1731 Kearsley had drafted a plan and elevation for the building. Hamilton, however, made his own plans and preferred construction on land owned by his son-in-law instead of the site Kearsley favored. Kearsley complained that the house had not approved that location, but the delegates upheld Hamilton.

Kearsley was a devoted member and regular communicant of Christ Church. He was elected to the vestry in 1719 and served until his death fifty-three years later. He was warden in 1743 and 1744. Christ Church is the most visible of Kearsley's philanthropic contributions. In 1720 Kearsley and Robert Assheton were appointed to collect money for a subscription "for the enlargement of the church, the building of a tower, and the purchasing of a set of bells." Not much happened until 1727, when the vestry again voted to enlarge the church. This time Kearsley offered to disburse his own money for work until subscriptions could be found. Funds trickled in, but not until 1744 was the church finished. Although Kearsley devoted much time, talent, energy, and money to the construction of the church, he received little praise and frequent criticism. He complained of this to the vestry, who replied with a formal statement of appreciation praising his diligence and asking him to continue his work. Two weeks later the *American Weekly Mercury* published "A Panegyrick," which described Kearsley as "a generous Benefactor, a zealous Promoter, . . . a prudent and skillful Manager and Contriver of the Building." The last verses of the poem praised his skill when dealing with any ill, for he could "almost raise the Dead."

Kearsley enjoyed the praise and continued to raise and contribute funds for church improvements. Upon the church's completion, the *Pennsylvania Gazette* announced that "in Point of Elegance and Taste, [it] surpasses every Thing of the Kind in America." In 1758 he accepted subscriptions to fund the erection of an Anglican church for the southern part of the city. Upon its completion in 1761, he served on the com-

mittee to prepare the plan for regulating and opening it.

Kearsley was married twice: first to Anne Magdalene Fauconnier Caillé, who died in August 1747, leaving one child who soon died; and second, in November 1748, to Margaret Bond (or Brand), with whom he had no children. He died in Philadelphia after a short illness.

The bulk of Kearsley's estate was bequeathed to the United Churches of Christ Church and St. Peter's to establish "an Infirmary or Alms House [for] Poor or Distressed Women of the Communion of the Church of England . . . (Preferring Clergymens Widows before others)." Christ Church Hospital, named as Kearsley required, soon opened. Following his widow's death in 1778, it received more of their property. The hospital remained a facility for the poor for more than two centuries.

• Manuscripts by Kearsley are held at the Historical Society of Pennsylvania and the Royal Society of London. See also the Philadelphia Register of Wills. Works by Kearsley include *A Letter to a Friend: Containing Remarks on a Discourse Proposing a Preparation of the Body for the Small-Pox* (1751), *A Defense of the Legislative Constitution of the Province of Pennsylvania* (1728), and *The Proceedings of Some Members of Assembly . . .* (1728). The best sketch of Kearsley is by Whitfield J. Bell, Jr., in his *Patriot-Improvers: Biographical Sketches of Members of the American Philosophical Society* (1998). Also useful is William S. Middleton, "The John Kearsleys," *Annals of Medical History* 3 (1921): 391–401. Contemporary assessments appear in the *Pennsylvania Gazette*, 16 Jan. 1772, and *American Weekly Mercury*, 8 Nov. 1744. See also Benjamin Dorr, *Historical Account of Christ Church, Philadelphia* (1841); and Deborah M. Gough, *Christ Church, Philadelphia* (1995).

RANDOLPH SHIPLEY KLEIN

KEATING, Kenneth Barnard (18 May 1900–5 May 1975), congressman, senator, ambassador, and judge, was born in Lima, New York, the son of Thomas Mosgrove Keating, a local businessman, and Louise Barnard, a schoolteacher. Much of Keating's early education was at Genesee Wesleyan Seminary in Lima, New York. He then attended the University of Rochester (N.Y.), from which he graduated in 1919, and Harvard Law School, which granted him an LL.B. in 1923. From that date until he entered the U.S. Congress in 1947 Keating was active in the law firm of Harris, Beach, Wilcox and Dale, earning a reputation as an adroit trial lawyer. In 1928 Keating married Louise Depuy; they had one daughter.

Keating was U.S. Army sergeant in World War I. He again entered the army during World War II and was commissioned a major on 15 April 1942. He rose to the rank of full colonel in early 1944. From 1943 to 1946 he served in the China-Burma-India theater of operations as executive assistant to Lieutenant General Raymond A. Wheeler, deputy supreme commander of the Southeast Asia Command. For his service in the war Keating was awarded the Legion of Merit and the

Order of the British Empire, both for superior administrative acumen.

In 1946 Keating was elected to Congress as a Republican representative from New York's Twentieth District on the east side of the Genesee River in Rochester. He served in the House of Representatives until 1958, when he was elected to the U.S. Senate. In 1959, in recognition of Keating's legislative service in the House of Representatives, the American Political Science Association awarded him their first Congressional Distinguished Service Award. Keating's active role in the House of Representatives was evidenced by his leadership in the passage of the Civil Rights Act of 1957. The legislation, contrary to the view of many liberal critics, was an important act that laid the groundwork for further civil rights legislation, especially with its establishment of a bipartisan civil rights investigative commission and a Civil Rights Division in the Justice Department. The latter provided for trying certain civil voting rights cases without juries to circumvent southern juries, which in the 1950s were almost always white in makeup. Neither Keating nor House Judiciary Committee chairman Emmanuel Celler could claim principal authorship of the act, however, for both Attorney General Herbert Brownell and President Dwight Eisenhower were heavily involved in a convoluted process that led to its final passage.

In the Senate Keating continued his specialization in judicial matters, again with regard to civil rights legislation. In particular, he persuaded some moderate and conservative Republican members to support further civil rights legislation and, especially, voting rights in the District of Columbia. He strongly advocated and introduced the Twenty-third Amendment to the U.S. Constitution, which gave the District of Columbia as many presidential electoral votes as a state with the same population. Keating also sponsored or coauthored legislation opposing hate bombings and subjecting organized interstate crime to federal law.

Keating gained almost singular national attention when, in late August 1962, he led a coterie of Republican senators who warned the nation that the Soviet Union was constructing intercontinental ballistic missiles in Cuba. Throughout September and early October he made numerous Senate speeches on the subject, charging the administration with not taking appropriate action to remove a massive threat to the nation's security. President John F. Kennedy adamantly refuted the charge and challenged Keating to reveal his sources. In fact, Keating and the administration shared many of the same sources about the missile buildup, including Cuban refugees and American intelligence sources, most importantly the latter. Senator Keating apparently felt honor bound not to reveal his intelligence sources. The administration refused to act hurriedly on the subject, evidently believing that Keating was either a political opportunist or a "Cassandra." In addition, the president wanted hard evidence of missiles in Cuba before taking any military action. In due course the administration confirmed Keating's findings and initiated its "quarantine" of So-

viet missiles in Cuba. Keating supported the president's action.

Keating's most challenging political effort was his 1964 campaign for reelection to the Senate against Robert Kennedy, the former attorney general and brother of the slain president. The race posed an uphill fight for Keating. He was frequently seen as a liberal who represented well New York's many ethnic constituencies, and most blacks considered him their principal representative in Congress. Senate patriarch Richard Russell of Georgia once disparagingly commented, as he witnessed Keating rise to address the Senate, "G'Amighty . . . here comes Keating." In many quarters of New York Keating was viewed favorably as a moderate to liberal. But his refusal to support Republican Barry Goldwater for president, as well as Kennedy's strength, especially with the aid of presidential candidate Lyndon Johnson's Democratic party coattails, spelled defeat for Keating.

Following his Senate defeat Keating headed various liberal causes, such as a national birth-curb drive. He also joined the prominent New York law firm Royall, Koegel and Rogers. In 1965 Keating was elected associate judge of the New York State Court of Appeals, one of the most prestigious of the nation's highest state courts. Perhaps his most significant actions on the court were his key votes in two 4–3 decisions, to uphold the state's legislation permitting school districts to loan books to private schools and to give "consortium" rights to women in cases where actions of third parties so injured husbands physically as to affect their sexual potency. Outside the court Keating frequently warned the nation against "irresponsible protest" by citizens in the 1960s era of demonstrations against the Vietnam War.

Keating resigned from the New York Court of Appeals in 1969, one year before he reached the mandatory retirement age. In the same year he was appointed ambassador to India. Keating had a love affair with India, and his behavior was viewed as charming although sometimes peculiar. For instance, he frequently called guests to dinner with a police whistle. Although relations between the United States and India were strained over the Richard Nixon administration's "tilt" to Pakistan in that country's dispute with India, most Indians generally thought of Keating kindly. He resigned in 1972 and returned to the United States to campaign for Nixon's reelection to the presidency. In 1973 Keating was appointed ambassador to Israel, where he served until his death. His first wife having died, in 1974 he married Mary P. Davis. His tenure in Israel was inauspicious. Some officials in the State Department questioned the quality of his reporting, and their judgment was apparently confirmed when he erred on the extent to which Israeli domestic policy would accept an interim agreement with Egypt over Israel relinquishing the Sinai Peninsula. Keating had a positive concept of the intellectual objectivity of Jews that stemmed from his many contacts with the Jews among his New York constituents. Presumably he thought Israel would yield the Sinai. Keating died in Rochester, New York, and was buried in Arlington National Cemetery.

• The Keating papers are in the Rush Rhee Library at the University of Rochester. For Keating's philosophy of the U.S. Congress see Keating, *Government of the People* (1964). On Keating and the Cuban missile crisis see Keating, "My Advance View of the Cuban Crisis," *Look*, 3 Nov. 1964; Robert A. Divine, ed., *The Cuban Missile Crisis* (1971); and Dino A. Brudioni, *The Inside Story of the Cuban Missile Crisis: Eyeball to Eyeball* (1990). For background on Keating's role in the passage of the Civil Rights Act of 1957 see J. W. Anderson, *Eisenhower, Brownell, and the Congress: The Tangled Origins of the Civil Rights Bill of 1956–1957* (1964). Regarding the 1964 Senate election see Meg Greenfield, "New York: The Keating Record," *Reporter*, 22 Oct. 1964, and Arthur Schlesinger, Jr., *Robert Kennedy and His Time* (1978). An obituary is in the *New York Times*, 6 May 1975.

MARTIN L. FAUSOLD

KEATING, William Hypolitus (11 Aug. 1799–17 May 1840), scientist, explorer, and lawyer, was born in Wilmington, Delaware, to Baron John Keating, a colonel in the Irish Brigade of the French army, and Eulalia Deschapelles. Keating's father settled initially in Delaware after resigning his commission. The family moved to Philadelphia, and Keating entered the University of Pennsylvania in 1813, receiving his bachelor's degree in 1816. His interest in mineralogy and mining took him to Europe for five years, where he studied at the Paris School of Mines and visited mines in various countries. He returned to the United States and summarized his studies in a monograph, *Considerations upon the Art of Mining* (1821), which was likely the first book on mining science published in the United States. Keating then undertook geological excursions in New Jersey and New York in 1821 and 1822. He married Elizabeth Bollman; they had one daughter.

In March 1822 Keating became a professor of mineralogy and chemistry as applied to agriculture and the arts at the University of Pennsylvania, serving in that position until 1828. The post was unsalaried, but Keating taught both lecture and laboratory courses, the student fees from which were his principal source of income. His laboratory course "in the various branches of Chemistry applied to the Arts, and to Analysis" was among the earliest such courses taught to undergraduate students in the United States.

In the spring of 1823 Keating was recruited as geologist and mineralogist for an expedition formed by the War Department and commanded by Major Stephen Long. The territory to be explored included the valleys of the Minnesota and Red rivers and the country between the Red River and Lake Superior (now known as Minnesota and lower Manitoba). The party included Samuel Seymour, an artist; J. Edward Calhoun, a topographer; and Thomas Say, an entomologist. After a six-month, 4,500-mile journey, Keating returned to Philadelphia in October 1823 and prepared the expedition's notes for publication. They appeared in the fall of 1824 as *Narrative of an Expedition to the Source of St. Peter's River*. This publication was widely read, and it was reprinted in London and translated into German. Although the geological observations were criticized as superficial because of the rapidity with which the party traveled, the descriptions of the Native Americans met by the group are of considerable interest.

After returning to Philadelphia, Keating and Samuel Merrick, a Philadelphia merchant and engineer who later became the first president of the Pennsylvania railroad, decided to found an institute where workingmen could learn science. A public meeting on this subject in early 1824 proved that such an institute was desired, and in March 1824 the Franklin Institute of the State of Pennsylvania for the Promotion of the Mechanic Arts was chartered by the state legislature. The institute sponsored lecture courses, supported a museum and a library, and encouraged invention. Keating taught its applied chemistry course from 1824 to 1826 using Jane Marcet's *Conversations on Chemistry* (1824) as the text. After an invitation to Mexico in the late 1820s, where he served for four years as director of operations of silver mines near Temascaltepec, Keating returned to Pennsylvania and was elected to the state house of representatives for a two-year term (1832–1834).

Keating studied law and was admitted to the state bar in 1834. His practice was focused primarily on the rapidly developing railroad industry. As counsel for the Reading Railroad he successfully lobbied the state legislature in 1838 for an extension of its routes. The railroad sent Keating to London, England, in 1840 to raise capital for its expansion; in the middle of these negotiations he died suddenly.

Keating is noteworthy for his versatility, his contribution to the exploration of the United States, and his efforts in science education, including laboratory instruction in chemistry and the founding of the Franklin Institute.

• A brief biography of Keating by Wyndham D. Miles is in *American Chemists and Chemical Engineers*, ed. Miles (1976). Two other articles by Miles expand on aspects of Keating's career: "A Versatile Explorer: A Sketch of William H. Keating," *Minnesota History* 36 (1959): 294–99, and "William H. Keating and the Beginning of Chemical Laboratory Instruction in America," University of Pennsylvania, *Library Chronicle* 19 (1952–1953): 1–34. Obituaries are in the *Times* (London), 20 May 1840, and the *Philadelphia Public Ledger*, 22 June 1840.

HAROLD GOLDWHITE

KEATON, Buster (4 Oct. 1895–1 Feb. 1966), actor and filmmaker, was born Joseph Francis Keaton in Piqua, Kansas, the son of Joseph Francis Keaton and Myra Edith Cutler, variety performers. Keaton's parents worked in traveling medicine shows in the rural Midwest, constantly on the verge of unemployment and poverty, until their New York debut in high-class vaudeville in 1899. They became headliners and achieved nationwide fame as "The Three Keatons" after 1901, when Keaton, who had occasionally appeared on stage since the age of three, was turned into the act's featured attraction. An accomplished singer, actor, mimic, and monologist, Keaton (known by then, as "Buster") attracted most attention for spectacular comic fights with his father.

In 1917, after the family act had lost much of its appeal, Keaton parted from his alcoholic father. A contract for a musical revue was canceled when, in March 1917, Keaton joined the Comique Film Company, which had been organized by Joseph Schenck to produce short comedies featuring and directed by the popular slapstick comedian Roscoe "Fatty" Arbuckle. By 1920 Keaton had costarred in, and occasionally co-directed, fourteen two-reelers. When Arbuckle was leased to Paramount, Keaton in 1920 took over his position at the Comique studio, which had relocated from New York to Los Angeles. A promotional campaign established Keaton as the "stone-faced comedian," creating a trademark as easily recognizable as Charlie Chaplin's tramp costume, Harold Lloyd's glasses, and Douglas Fairbanks's grin. Keaton costarred (with William H. Crane) in a full-length feature film, *The Saphead*, in 1920 and was both the star and the director of nineteen popular short comedies.

In 1921 Keaton's marriage to Natalie Talmadge, sister of film star Norma Talmadge (who was married to Joseph Schenck), bound him into one of the most powerful clans in the film business. After the birth of sons in 1922 and 1924, the marriage disintegrated. Following the Arbuckle scandal in September 1921, in which Arbuckle was charged with manslaughter following the death of Virginia Rappe, a young movie star who died a few days after Arbuckle allegedly sexually assaulted her (he later was acquitted), Comique was reorganized as Buster Keaton Productions, Inc. Generally careless in financial matters, Keaton never owned any shares of the corporation and was not involved in its management. However, he and his production staff enjoyed a fair amount of creative freedom.

Following the release in 1923 of *The Three Ages*, a full-length film made up of three shorts, Keaton directed and starred in nine features. These films integrated his characteristic dead-pan performance, acrobatic comedy, and intricate, often large-scale gag constructions into simple melodramatic stories that combined his character's romance, usually blocked by strong father figures, with spectacular adventures. The maritime comedy *The Navigator* (1924) and the boxing drama *Battling Butler* (1926) were considerable box office successes. However, after the commercial failure of the Civil War epic *The General* (1927), the Keaton studio lost its economic viability.

Keaton's critical reputation rests on these "independent" productions of the 1920s. Their full exploration of the resources of cinematic staging (large sets, location shooting, crowds, stunts, complex camerawork) qualifies Keaton as a major filmmaker. His nonsentimental, enigmatic portrayal of often displaced, yet highly adaptable and pragmatic characters has been applauded as evocative of the modern human condition, more so than Chaplin's Victorianism and Lloyd's blunt opportunism.

In 1928 Joseph Schenck transferred Keaton's contract to Metro-Goldwyn-Mayer, where he worked, without creative control, in a fairly stable production unit headed by director Edward Sedgwick and producer Lawrence Weingarten. His last two silent films, *The Cameraman* (1928) and *Spite Marriage* (1929), followed the established Keaton formula, albeit in a less spectacular and more romantic fashion. However, the seven MGM sound films following his brief appearance as a comic dancer in *The Hollywood Revue of 1929* were heavily influenced by the conventions of Broadway farce and musical comedy. These films were more successful commercially than his earlier features, but they are less popular with modern audiences. By MGM standards, they were low-budget productions with moderate returns. In 1932 Keaton's marital problems and alcoholism created unfavorable publicity, and Jimmy Durante briefly became his costar in several films. In February 1933 Keaton was fired by MGM, and in August he was divorced.

During the next fifteen years Keaton and his films of the 1920s and early 1930s disappeared from public view. In the mid-1930s he starred unsuccessfully in independent European features and then in two series of extremely low-budget short comedies produced by Educational Films (1934–1937) and Columbia Pictures (1939–1941). In 1937 he began to work as a gagman and technical adviser at MGM and, later, at 20th Century–Fox. Beginning with *Hollywood Cavalcade* (1939), he frequently played minor roles in feature films. He was married to Mae Scribbens (from 1933 to their divorce in 1936) and to Eleanor Norris (from 1940). Keaton enjoyed an extended stage revival at European circuses and variety shows from 1947 to 1954, performing a comic routine (taken from *Spite Marriage*) with his wife.

In 1949 Keaton regained a high public profile in the United States through his short-lived television show, "The Buster Keaton Comedy Show," which was followed by numerous appearances on many of the popular programs of the 1950s and 1960s, such as "The Ed Sullivan Show" and "The Twilight Zone," and in a wide range of American and European feature films, including Chaplin's *Limelight* (1952), as well as low-budget productions such as *How to Stuff a Wild Bikini* (1965). Always a compulsive worker, he also made commercials and promotional films and toured with theatrical companies.

James Agee's essay, "Comedy's Greatest Era," in *Life* magazine (Sept. 1949) revived interest in Keaton's silent films and established him as one of the four masters of silent comedy (together with Chaplin, Lloyd, and Harry Langdon). His critical reputation has been growing ever since, in many instances overtaking that of Chaplin. Raymond Rohauer rereleased his silent films in the early 1960s, and the standing ovation Keaton received for his performance in Samuel Beckett's *Film* at the Venice Film Festival in 1965 marked a late high point. He died in Woodland Hills, California.

• Keaton's films and business and personal papers are with the Raymond Rohauer estate in New York City. Kevin Brownlow and David Gill collected a wide range of material for their highly informative television program *Buster Keaton: A Hard Act to Follow* (1987). Myra Keaton's scrapbook of press clippings up to about 1910 is at the Charles K. Feldman Library of the American Film Institute in Beverly Hills, Calif. Keaton's autobiography, written with Charles Samuels, is *My Wonderful World of Slapstick* (1960). Biographies include Rudi Blesh, *Keaton* (1966), Tom Dardis, *Keaton, The Man Who Wouldn't Lie Down* (1979), and Marion Meade, *Buster Keaton: Cut to the Chase* (1995). Critical studies of Keaton's films of the 1920s include David Robinson, *Buster Keaton* (1969), and Daniel Moews, *Keaton: The Silent Features Close Up* (1977). George Wead and George Lellis's *The Film Career of Buster Keaton* (1977) contains an annotated bibliography. An obituary is in the *New York Times*, 2 Feb. 1966.

PETER KRÄMER

KECK, George Fred (17 May 1895–21 Nov. 1980), architect, was born in Watertown, Wisconsin, the son of Fred George Keck, a furniture manufacturer, and Amalie Henze, an amateur painter. He studied civil engineering at the University of Wisconsin-Madison in 1914–1915 and then architectural engineering at the University of Illinois at Urbana, receiving a Bachelor of Science degree in 1920. From 1917 to 1918 Keck served as a second lieutenant in the U.S. Coastal Artillery. He married Lucille Liebermann in 1921.

On graduating from college Keck had moved to Chicago, Illinois. Between the years 1920 and 1926 he worked as a designer in a number of well-known architectural offices, including D. H. Burnham and Company and Schmidt, Garden & Martin (later Schmidt, Garden & Erickson). He returned to the University of Illinois to teach design from 1923 to 1924. In 1926 Keck opened an office with Vale Faro, whom he had met while working at Schmidt, Garden & Martin. Although the partnership didn't last for more than a year, Keck was undoubtedly influenced by Faro's modernist approach, quite unlike his own Beaux-Arts education. In 1927 Keck opened his own practice in Chicago. His first important commission was the Cruger Apartments (1926–1927) in Elmhurst, Illinois, which reflected his enthusiasm for (but not yet a full understanding of) the principles of functional modern design. In seeming opposition to this was an early residential project of this period, the Newton B. Lauren House in Flossmoor, Illinois (1927). Although its sprawling country charm was probably a response to both region and client, it is notable that there is no superfluous ornamentation.

In 1929 Keck designed the Miralago Ballroom, located near Wilmette, Illinois. Its exterior inaugurated the use of the International Style in the area with an elegant art deco interior. In 1933 the Century of Progress International Exposition in Chicago gave Keck the chance to display his forward-looking approach to architecture; he was obviously influenced by the industrialized work of Le Corbusier and R. Buckminster Fuller. His "House of Tomorrow" was built around a central core that contained both the utilities and a staircase. The first floor housed, among other things, an airplane hangar and garage. The second and third floors were cantilevered off the central post, all encased by glass walls. Keck, who was throughout his career interested in prefabricated building and mass production, perceived future building possibilities in the House of Tomorrow. His impetus for this design came from his native Watertown through Orson Fowler's treatise *A Home for All* (1948), which presented the advantages of the octagonal home. In the second year of the exposition, Keck built the Crystal House (1934), designed to further his ideas on good housing through technology. An even clearer homage to European design, the Crystal House was one of the earliest domestic works constructed of steel and glass. Its interior furnishings were designed by Leland Atwood, capitalizing on designs by Mies van der Rohe and Marcel Breuer, with R. Buckminster Fuller's famous dymaxion car displayed in its garage.

It was during the exposition that Keck began formulating ideas on the use of passive solar heating with the help of his brother William, who was now just out of architecture school. The first house to incorporate the new solar ideas was the Wilde Residence in Watertown, Wisconsin (1935). That same year Keck designed the Bruning House in Wilmette, Illinois. Not only was the window design improved, with external blinds that could be raised out of sight if desired, but his modernist design of the helicoidal staircase demonstrated that Keck was interested in both function and aesthetics. In 1937 and 1939 respectively, Keck designed the Cahn House, in Lake Forest, Illinois, and the Kellett House in Menasha, Wisconsin. The improvements in both residences were the result of the Kecks' studies on solar paths. In 1940 thermopane windows were developed and became standard in all of the Kecks' designs. In 1937 the Keck-Gottschalk apartment house, a designated landmark, was designed as a residence for Keck, his brother William, and Dr. Louis Gottschalk in Hyde Park, Illinois. Using an altered and perhaps more humanistic example of the international style, Keck displayed his own personal preferences for residential living.

Keck's interest throughout the 1930s in technological and social issues was made manifest during the Second World War in the prefabricated homes that he designed in 1942 for the Green Company of Rockford, Illinois. After the war hundreds of Green's Ready-Built Homes were put up throughout the Midwest. It was in conjunction with these homes that radiant heating was developed and popularized. In 1946 William Keck joined his brother's firm and the name was changed to Keck and Keck. During the 1950s the Kecks designed a number of large residences, including the Kunstadter House (Highland Park, Ill., 1951), Blair House (Lake Bluff, Ill., 1953), and Payne House (Bucks County, Pa., 1959), which were all notable for their large "glass walls" of windows that made use of the homes' natural surroundings. During this same period they designed the Pioneer Co-op Apartments

(Chicago, 1949–1950), the Prairie Avenue Courts Apartments (Chicago, 1950), and the CHA Elderly Housing (Chicago, 1959).

From 1938 to 1944 George Fred Keck was the head of the department of architecture at the Institute of Design (now Illinois Institute of Technology), which he had helped found in 1938 with László Moholy-Nagy and Gyorgy Kepes. After teaching he devoted himself to his practice until his death in Chicago. He was awarded the first distinguished service award from the Chicago chapter of the AIA for his fifty years of dedication to the architectural profession the day before he died in Chicago. Amongst his many accomplishments, Keck was also a distinguished painter and exhibited his watercolors on numerous occasions. His architectural office was also an important training ground for numerous prominent architects of the twentieth century, including Ralph Rapson, Bertrand Goldberg, and Stanley Tigerman.

• Keck's papers are at the State Historical Society of Wisconsin along with a number of his drawings. Other drawings are in the Art Institute of Chicago's department of architecture. Articles of interest by Keck are "House of Tomorrow," *Architectural Record*, Jan. 1934; "Housing Standards," *Architectural Forum*, Sept. 1942; and "Three Houses for the Post-War World," *Architectural Record*, Dec. 1944. Two excellent sources about Keck are an exhibition catalog by Narciso G. Menocal, *Keck & Keck Architects* (1980), and Robert Piper Boyce, "George Fred Keck, 1895–1980: Midwest Architect" (Ph.D. diss., Univ. of Wisconsin, 1986). Other sources include "A Portfolio of Modern Houses: George Fred Keck, Architect," *Architectural Forum* (Aug. 1942); "Keck and Keck, Architects," *Inland Architect* (June 1965); Nory Miller, "Fred Keck at 81, A 'New' Hit," *Inland Architect*, May 1976; and "House of Tomorrow, Herbert Bruning House and B.J. Cahn House," *Architecture + Urbanism*, Sept. 1977. An obituary is in the *Chicago Sun-Times*, 23 Nov. 1980.

AMY L. GOLD

KECKLEY, Elizabeth Hobbs (1820?–26 May 1907), White House dressmaker during the Lincoln administration and author, was born in Dinwiddie Court House, Virginia, the daughter of George Pleasant and Agnes Hobbs, slaves. Her birth date is variously given from 1818 to 1824 based on different documents that report her age. The identity of her father is also uncertain; in later life Keckley reportedly claimed that her father was her master, Colonel A. Burwell. George Pleasant, who was owned by a different master, was allowed to visit only twice a year and was eventually taken west.

Elizabeth's life as a slave included harsh, arbitrary beatings "to subdue her stubborn pride," frequent moves to work for often poor family members, and being "persecuted for four years" by Alexander Kirkland, a white man, by whom she had a son. Her life improved when she was loaned to a Burwell daughter, Anne Garland, with whose family Keckley moved to St. Louis. There, her labor as a dressmaker was the sole support of the Garland household of seventeen members for more than two years. Because of her skill, engaging personality, and capacity for hard work, she developed a devoted clientele among the city's elite women. She persuaded the Garlands to set a price, $1,200, for her freedom and that of her son. In St. Louis (probably in 1852) she married James Keckley, a man who had told her he was free but was actually a "dissipated" slave. Because of the strain of supporting both her husband and the Garlands, she could not save the money needed to purchase her freedom. Her customers raised it among themselves, however, and the Deed of Emancipation was registered in 1855. With her labor now her own, she was soon able to repay the loan. In 1860 she separated from her husband and moved to Washington, D.C., where she set up a dressmaking establishment that trained dozens of young women over the years.

Keckley's clients were the wives of politically prominent men, such as Stephen Douglas and Jefferson Davis. In exchange for making a dress in an extremely short time, one of her customers recommended her to Mary Todd Lincoln, wife of the newly elected president, Abraham Lincoln. On 3 March 1861 a remarkable relationship began when Mary Lincoln hired Keckley as her dressmaker. Keckley was a woman of great presence and intelligence, tall (some say over six feet), with twinkling eyes, a radiant smile, light skin, straight black hair, and impeccable manners. Mary Lincoln not only liked the dresses designed to show off her neck and arms but also found Keckley an entertaining companion and soothing influence. Keckley was soon a confidante of the family, and her duties extended far beyond dressmaking.

Keckley's son, who had left Wilberforce University to enlist in the Union army (as a white man), was killed at the battle of Wilson's Creek, Missouri, in August 1861. Mary Lincoln described Keckley as heartbroken, commenting, "She is a very remarkable woman herself." At a client's urging, Keckley applied for the pension due the unsupported mother of an only son killed in the war and received $8, later $12, a month.

As the Civil War continued, black refugees, called contrabands, poured out of the South into the capital, where they lived in wretched conditions in makeshift camps. Keckley, who attended the Fifteenth Street Presbyterian Church, as did most of the other White House servants, organized forty women from that church into the Contraband Relief Association in August 1862. They raised money by sponsoring concerts and a festival, collected clothes that they repaired, and solicited donations of money, food, and blankets for the contrabands. In the fall, Keckley accompanied Mary Lincoln to New York City and Boston, where she took the opportunity to obtain donations from northern benevolent societies. Records show that "Mrs. President Lincoln" donated $200 and fifty comforters. The following year, Keckley and her associates changed the name of the association to the Freedmen and Soldiers' Relief Fund and received help from Frederick Douglass, who personally solicited contributions from antislavery societies in England and Scotland.

As Mary Lincoln's dresser, Keckley prepared her for every public occasion; as her confidante, she shared her anxieties; as her traveling companion, she went to the Gettysburg dedication and toured Richmond after the city fell; and, as her attendant, she cared for her after her son Willie's death and her husband's assassination. When Mary Lincoln left the White House in 1865, Keckley accompanied her to Chicago. After seeing the family settled, she returned to Washington, D.C., where she reopened her dressmaking business.

In the spring of 1867 she began to receive letters from Mary Lincoln, who wrote that she was impoverished and planned to sell her clothes and jewelry to raise money. After she begged Keckley to join her in New York City to help with the sale, Keckley closed her business and went. Newspapers had a field day with the "old clothes scandal," heaping scathing criticism on the president's widow for trying to augment her income in what was considered a vulgar manner. The clothes did not sell, however, and Mary Lincoln returned to Chicago. Keckley stayed in New York City to wind up affairs. She raised money within the black community to aid her former employer, but Mary Lincoln refused it. In 1868 Keckley published her autobiography, *Behind the Scenes; or, Thirty Years a Slave, and Four Years in the White House*, which she said she wrote to help Mary Lincoln financially as well as to counter what she considered unjust criticisms. Given her loyalty to Mary Lincoln, she must have had a strong motive to violate the code of confidentiality.

Lincoln scholars rely heavily on Keckley's autobiography for details of the Lincoln household, domestic anecdotes about the president, and Mary Lincoln's opinions and actions from 1861 through 1867. The initial chapters also provide a vivid slave narrative. Whether Keckley wrote *Behind the Scenes* by herself is questionable. That it was essentially an oral history is supported by the account of a witness to the process who recalled many years later that writer James Redpath, who had frequented the Lincoln White House, came to Keckley's boarding house every day for months, transcribed what Keckley told him, and brought back a written version, which they went over together. The book's basic authenticity is in no doubt, since almost all the documentable facts have proven accurate. Because Keckley was a sparkling raconteur, there is reason to believe that most of the lively anecdotes were directly recorded. Keckley was to claim later that she had lent her numerous letters from Mary Lincoln that formed the appendix to the person helping her, who promised to edit out any harmful passages. The publication of the unedited letters and the intimate portrait of the Lincoln family enraged Mary Lincoln's son Robert, who had the book suppressed. The two women never met again.

In 1892 Keckley joined the Domestic Arts Department at Wilberforce University, where she became a popular teacher of dressmaking. Ill health following a stroke forced her resignation after only a year. She spent some time in Philadelphia before returning to Washington, D.C. Little is known of her final years. At the end of her life, she lived in a small basement room in the home maintained by the National Association for Destitute Colored Women and Children, a venerable Washington, D.C., institution directly descended from the Contraband Relief Association she had founded. She died in Washington, D.C.

• Papers relating to Keckley are in the Library of Congress, the Moorland-Spingarn Research Center at Howard University, and the National Archives. A gown that she designed for Mary Lincoln is in the Smithsonian Institution, and a replica is in the Black Fashion Museum in New York, which published a significant account of Keckley in its illustrated catalog for a 1988 exhibit, "Modiste Elizabeth Keckley: From Slavery to the White House." Extensive quotations from her autobiography have been used by many Lincoln biographers: for example, Carl Sandburg, *Abraham Lincoln: The War Years* (1939), and Philip B. Kunhardt, Jr., et al., *Lincoln: An Illustrated Biography* (1992). Biographies of Mary Lincoln that use her letters about Keckley and discuss the significance of their relationship are Ruth Randall, *Mary Lincoln: Biography of a Marriage* (1953); Justin G. Turner and Linda Lovitt Turner, *Mary Todd Lincoln: Her Life and Letters* (1972); and Jean H. Baker, *Mary Todd Lincoln: A Biography* (1987). A valuable biographical account, including memories of people who knew her and photographs, is in John E. Washington, *They Knew Lincoln* (1942). The Wilberforce days are covered in Hallie Quinn Brown, ed., *Homespun Heroines and Other Women of Distinction* (1971).

GERTRUDE WOODRUFF MARLOWE

KEEFE, Timothy John (1 Jan. 1857–23 Apr. 1933), professional baseball player, was born in Cambridge, Massachusetts, the son of Irish immigrants Patrick Keefe, a builder, and Mary Leary. Keefe took a keen early interest in baseball. In 1879 the 5'10½", 185-pound right-hander began his professional career, splitting the season with Utica and New Bedford, New York, in the National Association. He appeared in 24 games his first season, and the following year he pitched in 18 games with Albany, New York, in the National Association before being promoted to Troy, New York, in the National League. On the major league level over three seasons (1880–1882), he won 42 games and lost 59.

With the New York Metropolitans of the American Association in 1883 and 1884, Keefe enjoyed his first major success. In 1883 he won 41 games and led the league in innings pitched (619), strikeouts (361), and complete games (68). His 361 strikeouts places him eleventh on the all-time list for strikeouts in a season before 1900. On 4 July 1883 Keefe allowed just one hit in the morning game against Columbus, returned that afternoon to hurl a two-hitter, and won both games. The following season he recorded 37 wins in leading New York to the league title. The Mets played the National League champion Providence Grays in a postseason series that marked the birth of the present-day World Series. The Grays won the series three games to none, with Keefe suffering two of the losses.

Between 1885 and 1889 Keefe pitched for the New York Giants in the National League. In his second season he recorded a league-tying 42 victories and led the league in complete games (62) and innings pitched (540). He suffered a nervous breakdown in 1887 after one of his fastballs struck Boston's John Burdock in the head. But the following season Keefe returned to pace the league with 333 strikeouts, eight shutouts, and an earned run average of 1.74. He completed that season by winning four games in the World Series in which the Giants defeated the St. Louis Browns of the American Association. In 1888 and 1889 Keefe and his teammate Mickey Welsh won 118 games (Keefe 63, Welsh 55) and led the Giants to league championships. Keefe established a major league record in 1888 when he won 19 consecutive games. This record went unequaled until 1912 when it was matched by another Giants pitcher, Rube Marquard. The Giants defeated the Brooklyn Bridegrooms in the 1889 World Series, but Keefe was unable to gain a victory. Following that season, he received a $4,500 contract, making him the team's highest-salaried player.

During this time hostilities between players and owners reached their peak. In 1885 when the Brotherhood of Professional Base Ball Players was formed to attain collective action, Keefe was named an officer. The players felt that contract restrictions and lowered salaries denied them the rights to sell their services to the highest bidders. When negotiations with the owners broke down, the brotherhood moved to field a rival league in 1890. Keefe and many other stars joined the new Players' League. Keefe won 17 games and lost 11 for the New York entry, but because of financial losses the league folded after one season. Keefe returned to the Giants the following year, but he was traded to the Philadelphia Phillies in August 1891. He completed his career with the Phillies in 1893, winning 30 games over his final two seasons.

During his fourteen seasons Keefe recorded 344 victories and 225 losses, started 595 games, completed 558 games, and pitched 5,072 innings. He allowed 4,552 base hits and 2,468 runs, struck out 2,533 batters, and gave up 1,231 base on balls. He compiled at least 30 victories six times, 20 or more triumphs seven consecutive seasons, and 40 or more wins twice, and he pitched 40 shutouts. His career earned run average was 2.62. In three postseason performances (1884, 1888, 1889) he won four games and lost three.

Following his playing career, Keefe became a National League umpire for two seasons. Returning to Cambridge in 1896, he entered the real estate business. He married Clara A. Gibson in 1889. One of the first pitchers to use the change-of-pace to complement his fastball and curve, Keefe was considered a master tactician who knew how to pitch each batter. He died in Cambridge, and in 1964 he was elected to the National Baseball Hall of Fame.

• Keefe's life history and contributions are found in Gene Karst and Martin J. Jones, Jr., *Who's Who in Professional Baseball* (1973), and Lowell Reidenbaugh, *Cooperstown: Where Baseball's Legends Live Forever* (1983). For statistics, records, and teams of Keefe's era, the most important sources are Paul MacFarlane, ed., *The Sporting News: Daguerreotypes of Great Stars of Baseball* (1981); Joseph L. Reichler, *The Great All-Time Baseball Record Book* (1981); and John Thorn and Peter Palmer, eds., *Total Baseball* (1989).

JOHN L. EVERS

KEELER, Clyde Edgar (11 Apr. 1900–22 Apr. 1994), biologist, educator, and cultural historian, was born in Marion, Ohio, the son of Anthony Sylvester Keeler, a watchmaker and teacher, and Amanda Jane Dumm Keeler, a teacher. Growing up in Marion, with nearby farmlands, Keeler had early opportunities—on his milk and paper routes—to observe nature, and he attributed the launching of his biomedical career to childhood observations of field mice. Keeler graduated from Denison University (Granville, Ohio) in 1923 with a zoology major and enough credits for a master's degree; he lacked only the research component, which he completed in 1925 at Harvard. Cited as "the school artist" in the yearbook, he was Phi Beta Kappa, president of the Zoology Club, and captain of the cross country team. He was also a member of the Student Army Training Corps (for World War I) and, after the war, the Reserve Officers Training Corps; he eventually rose to the rank of major in the U.S. Army Officers Reserve Corps.

In 1920 Keeler had attended the summer program at Long Island Biological Laboratory, Cold Spring Harbor, New York. His work there led Charles Davenport, head of the program, to insist that Keeler apply for a Harvard University Graduate Fellowship following graduation from Denison and to commend Keeler to William Ernest Castle, a pioneer in Mendelian genetics. Castle became a close friend and major mentor to Keeler, although embryologist Samuel Randall Detwiler was Keeler's initial adviser. In Keeler's first year at Harvard's Bussey Institution of Applied Biology, he discovered mice whose retinas lacked the crucial visual layer of rods. He soon demonstrated that this form of blindness was inherited as a simple Mendelian recessive and that it provided an animal model for the human condition of retinitis pigmentosa (RP). Research on different aspects of that work yielded Keeler the master's degree from Denison, a second master's from Harvard, and the doctorate from Harvard. He was awarded a fellowship in 1926 for continued research in Paris and Berlin.

Keeler then became the first biomedical geneticist at Harvard Medical School, teaching medical genetics there from 1927 to 1939 while doing research at Howe Laboratory of Ophthalmology at Massachusetts General Hospital's Eye and Ear Infirmary. Keeler was fascinated with medical and psychological implications of genetics, and as early as October 1947 he proposed the possibility of gene therapy in *The Journal of Heredity*. He studied a variety of animals and published prolifically on different hereditary conditions. Keeler and his colleagues originated the Himalayan (formerly "Siamese-Persian") and Burmese cats, and he planned the crosses for creating the Ocicat. Keeler married Melvina Summers in 1931; after they divorced, he married

Johanna Abel in 1939. Each marriage produced one child.

Like his mentor Castle, Keeler rejected eugenic extremes, recalling in his 1984 self-published autobiography, *The Gene Hunter*, a "paucity of accurate knowledge" in the 1930s. Rather, Keeler asserted that individuals diagnosed with disabling, hereditary conditions would, upon being informed of the risks, choose voluntarily not to marry or beget children (who might inherit those conditions). Furthermore, Keeler maintained that, in general, diversity of a population could promote health through hybrid vigor.

In 1939 Keeler recognized that human blood-group tests were a scientific way to rule out paternity in cases of men wrongfully accused, and he wrote the first book on this subject for lawyers and judges, published by the Massachusetts Society for the Prevention of Cruelty to Children. That same year Keeler left Harvard for research at the Wistar Institute in Philadelphia. Here technician Ruth Meeser showed Keeler how rats with different coat colors naturally exhibited different behaviors, causing Keeler and colleague Helen Dean King to demonstrate scientifically a coat color–behavior relationship. Later, Keeler repeated these studies in mink and foxes, with similar results.

Because of wartime disruptions, from 1941 until 1945 Keeler took a succession of temporary teaching posts, finally accepting the position of professor of biology at Georgia State College for Women (now Georgia College and State University) in Milledgeville. A popular teacher, he remained there for the next sixteen years, promoting science throughout Georgia, judging and organizing high school science fairs, as well as lecturing. He began a 22-year study of the Cuna (Kuna) Indians of San Blas, Panama, because they had the highest-known rate of albinism; however, his studies of Cuna genetics soon broadened into a commitment to preserve their rapidly vanishing culture. He wrote books to document Cuna customs and religion, illustrated the first Cuna alphabet book, and helped produce the first primer to teach Cuna children their written language. The Cuna studies evolved into cross-cultural comparisons, and in Keeler's latter years he explored and published mainly in that field.

In 1961 Keeler was appointed medical geneticist at Georgia's Milledgeville State Hospital (now Central State Hospital). In 1963 he became the hospital's Director of Research, founding and editing its *Bulletin of Current Research* until he retired in 1975. At that institution, Keeler investigated the effects of newly developed tranquilizers by using red foxes, which he considered to exhibit naturally a nervous fear equivalent to that of some human psychoses.

Keeler was very artistic, illustrating books and articles with his drawings. He also made numerous ceramic models to communicate everything from coat color heredity to epigraphic findings. He designed and built his own house. After retirement, he continued to work at Central State Hospital, devising projects to inspire patients who were judged "criminally insane."

Keeler's awards include a "Proclamation/Commendation" by the Governor of Georgia and lifetime achievement recognitions from the RP Foundation Fighting Blindness, the Association for Research in Vision and Ophthalmology, and the Institute for the Study of American Cultures. Elected to Sigma Xi, to life membership in the Société Zoologique de France, as Guggenheim Fellow, and as Paul Harris Fellow of Rotary International, his research was funded by multiple grants, including the Rockefeller Foundation, Harvard, the National Institutes of Health, and the National Institute of Mental Health. He died in Milledgeville, Georgia.

Keeler's legacy as biologist was the macroscopic view of genetics: while other researchers probed the chemical nature of the gene, Keeler explored and publicized the commonality of this heredity-unit in different life forms and its particular implications for human medicine and psychology. His legacy as educator was popularization of science, and his legacy as cultural historian was preservation of cultural and religious heritages.

• Keeler's published and unpublished papers are at the Ina Dillard Russell Library of Georgia College and State University in Milledgeville; they include his hand-annotated, self-published autobiography, *The Gene Hunter: Excerpts from a Life in Bio-Science* (1984), a useful source of information about Keeler's life and times. His extensive Cuna Indian art collection is housed at the Burke Gallery of Denison University. Keeler's scientific works include *The Laboratory Mouse: Its Origin, Heredity, and Culture* (1931), a standard reference for early biomedical researchers, and *Blood Group Tests as Evidence of Non-Paternity in Illegitimacy Cases* (1939), a pioneer work in forensic science. His writings on the Cuna Indians are classics in cultural history: *Land of the Moon-Children* (1956), *Secrets of the Cuna Earthmother* (1960), *Apples of Immortality from the Cuna Tree of Life* (1961), and *Cuna Indian Art* (1969). In addition, Keeler authored or coauthored more than 250 articles (often in *The Journal of Heredity* or *Bulletin of the Georgia Academy of Science*), three small books of poetry, and several self-published books, including his autobiography and *Timeless Threads in the Fabric of Cuna Indian Culture* (1987). He illustrated his own books and those of other authors, such as Otto Plath's *Bumblebees and Their Ways* (1934) and W. E. Castle's *Mammalian Genetics* (1940). His first and last scientific contributions were published in *Proceedings of the National Academy of Sciences USA*, in 1924 and 1993, respectively. Three memorials emphasize different aspects of Keeler's contributions: Irmgard Keeler Howard, "Clyde Edgar Keeler (1900–1994); Geneticist, Artist, Cultural Historian," *Journal of Heredity* 86 (1995): 489–91; Steven J. Pittler et al., "In Memoriam Clyde Edgar Keeler (1900–1994)," *Experimental Eye Research* 60 (1995): 3–4; and John J. White III, "A Tribute to Clyde Edgar Keeler (1900–1994): Medical Geneticist and Cultural Historian," *Midwestern Epigraphic Journal* 8 (1994): 1–4.

IRMGARD KEELER HOWARD

KEELER, James Edward (10 Sept. 1857–12 Aug. 1900), astronomer, was born in La Salle, Illinois, the son of William F. Keeler, the owner and manager of a foundry and machinery business, and Anna Dutton. Soon after the Civil War, Keeler's family moved to Mayport, Florida, where Keeler was educated at home by his parents. Mechanically adept and interested in science from an early age, in 1877 he entered Johns Hopkins University, which was in only its second year. There he specialized in physics and studied under Charles S. Hastings, Simon Newcomb, and Henry Rowland.

In the summer of 1878 Keeler joined an expedition headed by astronomer Edward S. Holden, which observed the total solar eclipse of 29 July from Central City, Colorado. On his graduation from Johns Hopkins in 1881, Keeler went to work immediately as a scientific assistant to Samuel P. Langley, director of Allegheny Observatory, in Pittsburgh, Pennsylvania. That summer he accompanied Langley on his expedition to Mount Whitney, California, to measure the solar radiation and spectrum from its summit, at an elevation of 14,495 feet the highest peak in the continental (now lower-48) United States. As he had at Johns Hopkins and in Colorado, Keeler showed great self-reliance, technical skills, and drafting ability. After the completion of the expedition in September, Keeler continued as Langley's assistant at Allegheny until 1886, with the exception of 1883–1884, which he spent as a physics graduate student in Heidelberg and Berlin, Germany.

In April 1886 Keeler was hired as the first staff member of Lick Observatory, then still under construction on Mount Hamilton, California (near San Jose). The observatory, with its "monster" 36-inch refracting telescope, the largest in the world, was being built by the Lick Trust, established by James Lick and headed by Richard S. Floyd, a wealthy gentleman of leisure. On completion it was to be operated by the University of California. Keeler acted as Floyd's astronomical expert on the mountain and reported regularly on progress to Holden, who had been named the observatory's first director, but now marked time in Berkeley as president of the university.

On 7 January 1888, the first night that the new telescope could be used effectively, Keeler discovered a narrow, dark gap in the outer part of the rings of Saturn. By February he had installed the giant spectroscope that he had designed, built by John A. Brashear in Pittsburgh, on the 36-inch refractor. On 1 June control of the observatory passed to the state, Holden resigned the presidency and became observatory director, and Keeler became a University of California faculty member.

In his initial three years at Lick, Keeler specialized in visual observations of the planets and spectroscopy. His keen eyesight and drafting skills, coupled with the largest telescope in the world on a well-chosen site, made it possible for him to produce an excellent series of drawings of Mars, Jupiter, and Saturn. Far superior to any ground-based photographs, they were widely reproduced in astronomy books for years.

Keeler's main work was spectroscopy; he became a pioneering astrophysicist of planets, stars, and nebulae. During his first three years at Lick Keeler became familiar with the spectra of normal stars and began to

study such now well-known "peculiar" stars, with aberrant spectra, such as Beta Lyrae, P Cygni, and Wolf-Rayet stars, to understand their physical nature. He measured spectroscopically, with unprecedented accuracy, the radial ("line-of-sight") velocities of a few, very bright stars, particularly Alpha Bootis (Arcturus) and Alpha Orionis (Betelgeuse). Keeler's most important work in this period at Lick was his similarly accurate measurements of the wavelengths of the two strongest lines in the spectra of gaseous nebulae, in the green spectral region. The brighter of them had been identified with a feature in the spectrum of MgO by the pioneer English astrophysicist J. Norman Lockyer. Keeler's accurate measurements disproved this hypothesis and showed that the two green lines were not emitted by any known element under conditions known in terrestrial laboratories. While some contemporary astronomers thought of them as "nebulium" lines, emitted by a hypothetical nebular element, in later years they were correctly interpreted as "forbidden" lines of doubly ionized oxygen, which are strong only under the peculiar low-density, high-temperature conditions in nebulae.

In 1891 Keeler left Lick Observatory to succeed Langley, who had become the secretary of the Smithsonian Institution, as director of Allegheny Observatory in Pittsburgh. Keeler was now engaged to Cora Matthews and considered Mount Hamilton too isolated for family life. They married in 1891 and had two children. At Allegheny Observatory Keeler had only a 13-inch refractor, but he outfitted it with an efficient photographic spectrograph (all his spectroscopic work at Lick had been done visually) and continued his pioneering astrophysical research. He realized that his small telescope was best suited for nebular spectroscopy and for work on bright stars. He was soon recognized as the leading American expert in astronomical spectroscopy. Much of his work was concentrated on the helium lines, observed in emission in gaseous nebulae and in absorption in hot stars. His most spectacular result was his spectroscopic confirmation that Saturn's rings are not solid, circular sheets, as they appear, but actually are composed of myriads of solid particles, each in its individual circular orbit about the planet.

Keeler became a close friend, guide, and adviser of solar astrophysicist George Ellery Hale, who was building Yerkes Observatory, with a 40-inch refractor that would "lick the Lick" for the University of Chicago. In 1895 Hale, playing the lead role, and Keeler founded the *Astrophysical Journal*, which remains the leading research journal in the field. In 1897 Keeler gave the keynote address, "The Importance of Astrophysical Research, and the Relation of Astrophysics to Other Physical Sciences," at the dedication of Yerkes Observatory. In this forward-looking speech, Keeler accurately predicted the main problems of astrophysics for the next fifty years. Although Hale tried to hire Keeler as the head of stellar spectroscopy on Yerkes Observatory faculty, Keeler instead accepted the directorship of Lick Observatory, which had become vacant when Holden was forced out by a staff rebellion.

Back at Lick in 1898, Keeler began a program of direct photography of nebulae with the Crossley reflector, a poorly constructed 36-inch telescope. At that time most American astronomers distrusted reflecting telescopes, because they had seen only amateur or cheaply made examples of them. These were much less efficient for visual observing than the superbly constructed refractors of the Lick and Yerkes telescopes, which were the wonder of their age. Keeler and other advanced astronomical thinkers (like Holden and Hale) realized that for astrophysics, direct photography, and photographic spectroscopy, well-made reflectors would be far superior. He used his superb instrumental and technical skills to modify and improve the Crossley reflector. With it, over the next two years, he obtained an outstanding series of direct, large-scale photographs of nebulae. They showed, for the first time, the many complicated structures of gaseous nebulae. They also showed many previously unrecognized, faint spiral "nebulae." Keeler's photographs revealed that these spirals were similar, rotating, flattened objects, seen in different orientations on the sky and with different angular sizes because of their different distances from the sun. They ranged from the nearby Andromeda "nebula," larger in angular size than the moon, to the most distant, apparently smallest, faintest spirals. Estimating that there were over 100,000 of them within reach of the Crossley reflector, he had recognized "spiral nebulae" as an important constituent of the universe.

By 1900 Keeler had a small, efficient spectrograph constructed for the Crossley reflector in order to observe the spectra of these spiral "nebulae." Before he could begin this program, however, he died suddenly in San Francisco from a stroke. Despite his early death, Keeler in his lifetime convinced American astronomers that large reflecting telescopes were their tools for the future. He was a pioneer of observational astrophysics, stellar, nebular, and (as we now realize) galaxy research.

• Keeler's papers are in the Allegheny Observatory Papers in the Archives of Industrial Society, Hillman Library, University of Pittsburgh, and in the Mary Lea Shane Archives of the Lick Observatory, University Library, University of California, Santa Cruz. Many of his letters to Hale are also preserved in the Yerkes Observatory Archives, Williams Bay, Wisc., and in the Mount Wilson Observatory Collection, Huntington Library, San Marino, Calif. Donald E. Osterbrock, *James E. Keeler, Pioneer American Astrophysicist: And the Early Development of American Astrophysics* (1984), gives a biographical account and contains references to all of Keeler's published papers. The best obituaries are by his colleagues George Ellery Hale, "James Edward Keeler," *Science* 12 (1900): 353–57, and W. W. Campbell, "James Edward Keeler," *Publications of the Astronomical Society of the Pacific* 12 (1900): 139–46. A moving memorial biography is by his teacher Charles S. Hastings, "James Edward Keeler 1857–1900," *Biographical Memoirs of the National Academy of Sciences* 5 (1903): 231–46, which also contains a complete bibliography of his published papers and articles.

DONALD E. OSTERBROCK

KEELER, Ruby (25 Aug. 1910–28 Feb. 1993), actress and dancer, was born in Halifax, Nova Scotia, Canada, the daughter of Ralph Keeler and Elnora Lehy. When she was three years old, the family moved to New York City, where her father worked as a truck driver. Ruby attended a parochial grammar school where exercise and drill classes were a regular part of the curriculum. She loved to dance and soon became locally known for performing the Charleston and other popular social dances at neighborhood and community events. In the early 1920s she entered the Professional Children's School.

In 1923, at the age of thirteen, Keeler made her first professional appearance in the chorus of George M. Cohan's *The Rise of Rosie O'Reilly*. She also entered and won a dance contest, which led to a job at Texas Guinan's famous speakeasy, where she danced, chaperoned by her mother. Despite the slightly sordid surroundings, Keeler later called the experience a happy one.

By the mid-1920s Keeler was on Broadway, usually in the chorus but occasionally as a featured dancer. Her first number to be singled out for favorable mention by critics was "Tampico Tap" in *Bye Bye Bonnie* (1927); it was followed by the Charles Dillingham show *Lucky*, which closed after a few performances. It led, however, to a featured role for Keeler in a successful Dillingham show, *The Sidewalks of New York* (1927). Keeler began to be recognized by critics and audiences, and in 1928 Florenz Ziegfeld signed her as the specialty tap dancer for *Whoopee!* Before joining its company, Keeler spent several weeks in California performing in live motion picture prologues for Loew's and met Al Jolson. *Whoopee!* was a Broadway hit, but Keeler had already deserted the show in Pittsburgh in order to marry Jolson, more than twenty years her senior.

The marriage brought Keeler national publicity. Despite her dropping out of *Whoopee!*, Ziegfeld seemed to harbor no ill will and offered her an even larger part in his next Broadway show, George Gershwin's *Show Girl*. Keeler opened in it on 2 July 1929, and Jolson added a chapter to the lore of Broadway when he stood up in the audience to serenade Keeler.

Jolson insisted that Keeler leave *Show Girl* and her Broadway career to return with him to California after his own New York engagement ended. Keeler remained out of the spotlight for several years—film musicals had declined in popularity after the initial burst of activity sparked by *The Jazz Singer*—but in 1932 an earlier test she had done for a Jolson film came to the attention of an executive at Warner Bros. Keeler signed for the ingenue role of Peggy Sawyer in *42nd Street*, opposite Dick Powell.

That role made Keeler a star; her appeal extended both to critics and ordinary viewers. The *Los Angeles Times* critic declared that Keeler was "a far more effective and appealing personality in her screen debut than her husband." The accolades continued through her next three films, all Busby Berkeley vehicles and all opposite Powell: *Gold Diggers of 1933* (1933), *Footlight*

Parade (1933), and *Dames* (1934). In *Dames* she danced with thousands of girls made up and dressed to look just like her in "I Only Have Eyes for You." Berkeley's dazzling camera work and his geometrically choreographed displays of multitudes of near-naked chorus girls made the films classics. Keeler choreographed her own dancing, however, since Berkeley could not dance "a step."

Keeler and Powell's partnership endured through a change of studios, from Warner Bros. to First National, where they made *Flirtation Walk* (1934). This was followed by Keeler's only film with Jolson, *Go Into Your Dance* (1935), which did moderately well. Her last two films with Powell—*Shipmates Forever* (1935) and *Colleen* (1936, back at Warners)—were not successful at the box office, nor was *Ready, Willing, and Able* (1937), opposite Ross Alexander. In the last, however, Keeler performed what would remain her favorite screen number, tap-dancing with Lee Dixon atop the keys of a giant typewriter.

By the late 1930s backstage movie musicals were declining in popularity, and Keeler's star persona did not adapt well to nonmusical narrative films. For RKO she made *Mother Carey's Chickens* (1938), a role that had been turned down by most of RKO's stable of stars. After its failure she terminated her contract with RKO; she made *Sweetheart of the Campus*, her last film, for Columbia in 1941.

Keeler's popularity had depended not only on her precision tap-dancing but also on her air of youthful innocence. As the musical genre became increasingly sophisticated in the 1940s and 1950s, it turned to literate plots and ballet-based dancing. Keeler, at a 1965 retrospective of Berkeley's films, evaluated her performances: "It's amazing. I couldn't act. I had that terrible singing voice, and now I can see I wasn't the greatest tap dancer in the world either." But she was enormously likable, and in the late 1960s and the 1970s, when nostalgia for the 1930s soared, Keeler returned to the Broadway stage.

Divorced from Jolson in 1939, Keeler had married a California businessman, John Homer Lowe, in 1941 and settled down to raise five children, including a son she and Jolson had adopted in 1935. Except for occasional appearances on television from 1950 on, often with Powell, and a short tour in a revival of *Bell, Book and Candle* in 1968, she appeared to have left the spotlight forever. After Lowe's death in 1969, however, she appeared with a host of other golden-age stars in a low-budget movie, *The Phynx* (1970). Then Busby Berkeley, hired to supervise a Broadway revival of the 1925 Vincent Youmans musical *No, No, Nanette*, suggested Keeler for a role. With some trepidation, she accepted. Opening to ecstatic reviews in January 1971, *No, No, Nanette* became one of the season's biggest box-office successes. Critic Clive Barnes wrote that Keeler tap-danced "like a trouper," wearing "indomitability shyly like a badge of service." Keeler regained some fame, and the Catholic Actors Guild presented her with their George M. Cohan Award in 1971. Despite suffering a brain aneurysm in 1974, she remained a prominent participant in film festivals and Berkeley retrospectives. In 1991 the Second Palm Springs International Film Festival featured a tribute to Keeler's career. She also became a lecturer, talking about Berkeley films and her days in Hollywood on cruise ships. When she died in Palm Springs, California, the National Stroke Association, for which she had served as a spokeswoman, established the Ruby Keeler Fellowship Memorial.

• Entries on Ruby Keeler can be found in most encyclopedias of film and film actors. There are essays about her in David Shipman, *The Great Movie Stars: The Golden Years* (1970), and in *Current Biography* (1971). John Gruen interviewed her for his book *Close-Up* (1968). Obituaries are in the *New York Times*, 1 Mar. 1993, and *Variety*, 8 Mar. 1993.

ADRIENNE L. McLEAN

KEELER, Wee Willie (3 Mar. 1872–1 Jan. 1923), baseball player, was born William Henry Keeler, Jr., in Brooklyn, New York, the son of William Henry Keeler, a trolley company worker. His mother's name is unknown. A lifelong resident of Brooklyn, Keeler attended P.S. 26 at Gates and Putnam Avenue before quitting in 1888. A teacher with the same surname hastened his departure by berating him before the class for his obsessive interest in baseball, averring that he would never amount to much and that she was glad to be no relative of his. But with the encouragement of his father and older brother, Keeler pursued his goal of playing professional baseball. Over the next four years he played semipro ball with teams in Brooklyn and New Jersey, earning as much as two dollars a game.

During these years the diminutive Keeler, who stood 5'4" and weighed 140 pounds, played every position. A well-coordinated athlete, the left-handed Keeler was strong of arm, speedy afoot, and used his excellent eyesight to develop his remarkable bat control. Early in 1892 the Binghamton, New York, team of the Eastern League signed him to play third base for $90 a month. After batting .373 with that team, Keeler's contract was purchased by the National League New York Giants for $800. In his brief stint as a major leaguer in 1892, he batted .321. The following season he suffered a broken ankle, and Giants' manager John Ward sold him to Brooklyn for $800. Keeler played only a few games before he was returned to Binghamton to finish out the 1893 season.

Early in 1894 Keeler was traded to the Baltimore Orioles, which gave him the opportunity to play regularly as an outfielder instead of remaining a rare left-handed third baseman. A good hitter and fielder, during spring training he worked with teammates John McGraw, Hugh Jennings, and Joe Kelley in mastering a "scientific style" of play that stressed offensive teamwork and employed tactics such as bunting, the hit-and-run play, and coordinated base running and base stealing. With Keeler batting .371, the Orioles rebounded from an eighth-place finish in 1893 to capture the first of three consecutive National League pennants. Although the successful young Orioles became notorious for their aggressive, rowdy, umpire-baiting style, the even-tempered Keeler became one of the league's most popular and respected players.

In his five seasons with the Orioles, Keeler was one of the top three hitters in the National League. During these years Keeler used his 29-ounce, thick-handled bat with a choke-up grip that "seemed like he used only half of it" to average nearly .390 at bat, with more than 200 hits and 150 runs scored each season. He won consecutive batting championships in 1897 and 1898, and in 1897, his greatest season, he batted .432, scored 143 runs, with a league-leading 239 hits, and set a consecutive game hitting record (at the 60′6″ distance) by batting safely in 44 straight games, a record that endured until 1941. No batter in major league history averaged fewer strikeouts per season than he did.

With the Orioles, Keeler played on three league champions (1894, 1895, and 1896) and two postseason Temple Cup champions (1896 and 1897). In 1899 he joined the Brooklyn Superbas when the Baltimore owners acquired that team as part of a syndicate venture. At Brooklyn he led the club to consecutive pennants in 1899 and 1900, batting .377 and .368 and leading the NL in hits with 208 in 1900. Keeler remained with the Superbas through 1902, up to which point his ten-year record in the majors had him batting at a level that surpassed any other player. Popular with Brooklyn fans, he won enduring fame for his casual comment on the secret of his batting prowess: "Just tell that guy to keep his eye clear and hit 'em where they ain't." Reported by Brooklyn sportswriter Abe Yager, it became one of the most quoted quips in baseball history.

During his first ten seasons, owing to the National League owners' salary cap, Keeler never earned more than $3,000 a season. Although he once said that he would pay to play the game he loved, when the New York Highlanders of the rival American League offered him a $10,000 contract in 1903, he jumped to the new league. As a Highlander from 1903 through 1909, he batted above .300 his first four seasons. His best effort, .343 with 186 hits in 1904, led the Highlanders, losers of the pennant that year by a single game. After he batted .304 in 1906, his production fell off, and in 1909 he was released. The following year he played his last season in the majors as a pinch hitter for the New York Giants. Following a brief stint with Toronto of the Eastern League, the aging Keeler retired.

Although Keeler had been offered the opportunity to manage the Highlanders in 1908, he declined. From 1909 to 1913 he played some and coached some. In 1914 he coached the Brooklyn team of the Federal League, and in 1915 he was a scout for the Boston Braves. Having saved much of his estimated $100,000 earnings from baseball and a lifelong bachelor, he appeared to be well off in his retirement. However, unwise investments and loans impoverished him. Plagued by heart disease, in 1921 he was living in straitened circumstances when his friends in major

league baseball gave him a $5,500 gift. He died in Brooklyn of heart disease.

In nineteen major league seasons Keeler played in 2,124 games, amassed 2,962 hits (all but 426 were singles), scored 1,722 runs, stole 495 bases, fielded .957, and posted a .345 batting average, which remains one of the highest in major league history. In 1939 Keeler was elected to the Baseball Hall of Fame.

• The National Baseball Library at Cooperstown, N.Y., has an extensive file of newspaper clippings. The best biographical sketch is Leo Trachtenberg, "Wee Willie Keeler. Fame and Failure," *National Pastime*, no. 13 (1993). Career records can be found in John Thorn and Pete Palmer, eds., *Total Baseball*, 3d ed. (1993), and Joseph L. Reichler, ed., *The Baseball Encyclopedia*, 6th ed. (1985). Additional insights into Keeler's career can be found in Mrs. John J. McGraw and Arthur Mann, eds., *The Real McGraw* (1953); David R. Phillips, *That Old Ball Game* (1975); Jerry Lansche, *Glory Fades Away* (1991); Stanley Cohn, *Dodgers: The First 100 Years* (1990); and David Q. Voigt, *American Baseball*, vol. 2 (1983). An obituary is in the *Brooklyn Daily Eagle*, 2 Jan. 1923.

DAVID Q. VOIGT

KEELEY, Leslie Enraught (1832–21 Feb. 1900), physician and founder of a notorious inebriety cure, was born in Potsdam, New York, the son of Thomas H. Keeley, a physician, and Maria Enraught. Little is known of his early life, and Keeley himself was notably vague on his background. He moved west in the 1850s, settling for a time in Beardstown, Illinois, where he took up the study of medicine with a local physician. In 1860 he entered the Rush Medical College in Chicago, from which he earned his M.D. in early 1864. That February he joined the Union army, in which he served for several months as acting assistant surgeon at Benton Barracks, near St. Louis, Missouri, after which he transferred to the field hospital of the Army of the Cumberland.

During his commission in the army, Keeley gained minor notoriety for reporting the poor sanitary conditions and his concern over the drinking practices of the soldiers. He left the army in September 1864 and eventually established his practice in Dwight, Illinois, in 1866. A few years later, he became the resident surgeon for the Chicago and Alton Railroad.

Well known around town and notable for his strong bearing and authoritative manner, Keeley continued his investigation into drunkenness and the possibility of its cure. Concerned by the excessive drinking of a veterinarian friend, Keeley and a colleague, the minister and temperance lecturer Frederick B. Hargreaves, began to investigate the numerous opinions on the best way to treat and cure drunkenness. Unsatisfied by the general insistence of temperance advocates on the centrality of moral suasion in evoking a cure, Keeley and Hargreaves became interested in the assorted chemical preparations and patent medicines that claimed to cure inebriety. From experimentation, they, along with a young Irish pharmacist John R. Oughton, devised their own preparation, based on the mythical and possibly genuine healing properties of gold. Keeley announced his discovery to the residents of Dwight in 1879, and in 1880 he and Hargreaves began selling their "Double Chloride of Gold and Sodium" preparation in a mail-order business. Later that same year, they opened a small sanitarium in Dwight, where alcoholics and opium and tobacco users could receive a more thorough treatment. This included a vigorous physical regimen and careful diet, along with application of the medicine four times a day.

"The Keeley Cure" as it became known, met with rapid success. In June 1881 Keeley and Hargreaves added Oughton, Curtis J. Judd, and John Halpin as partners in the business. Despite a brief suspension of the treatment from December 1885 to June 1887, during which time Keeley investigated means of eliminating some of the side effects of his cure, for the next decade both the mail-order and sanitarium businesses boomed. By 1890 the sanitarium had such a large demand for spaces and treatment that Keeley opened the first franchised institution in Des Moines, Iowa, that June. The franchising of the business spread rapidly, with "Keeley Institutes" opening across the country, as well as in Canada, Mexico, Great Britain, Denmark, Finland, and Sweden. After 1890, with the franchise business growing and bringing in strong profits, Keeley and his partners preferred not to sell the mail-order medicine, urging interested patrons to visit one of the increasingly numerous institutions for more valuable treatment. By the end of 1893, 118 Keeley Institutes had opened across North America and in Europe.

Keeley based his treatment on a particular perception of the nature of inebriety. Alcoholism, he insisted, was a physical disease, not a vice. As such, it could be treated like any physical disease. He also challenged hereditarian arguments that insisted inebriety was inherited and hence essentially incurable. Keeley suggested that one might inherit a weak resistance, which might make one more susceptible to temptation, but not a diseased constitution. These ideas, which made a cure possible and more generally accessible, appealed to notions of self-help and independence, sentiments that also fueled the widespread patent medicine trade so derided by the medical profession. Many doctors and other commentators viewed the trade in patent and proprietary medicines, with their extravagant claims of a miracle cure and their dubious ingredients, as a dangerous and unscrupulous form of quackery.

Keeley was not immune to such derision. He refused to reveal the details of his remedy, and because such secrecy suggested elements of charlatanism, the increasingly powerful medical profession condemned the Keeley cure as ineffective and potentially dangerous. Early on in the business, the Illinois State Board of Health revoked Keeley's medical license. It was restored a decade later when Governor Joseph W. Fifer determined that the board's decision was arbitrary and did not follow proper procedures. Keeley was further distanced from the medical profession by the fact that he was trained as a homeopath, a practice not accepted by the regular or "allopathic" physicians, who made up the bulk of the medical profession at the time.

Such condemnation from physicians upset Keeley, who had desired professional recognition of his contribution to treating a notable social problem. Nevertheless, his business grew and spread. In 1891 the "Bi-Chloride of Gold" club was formed by a group of patients at the Dwight Institution. By 1893 the club was large enough to celebrate "Keeley Day" at the World Columbian Exhibition in Chicago, at which members of the "Keeley League" proselytized and celebrated their victory over the demon alcohol.

Throughout the 1890s, Keeley spent less time working at the institute, and more time traveling with his wife, Mary Elizabeth Dow, whom he had married in 1888; they had no children. In 1898 he built a house in Los Angeles, California, where the couple lived for about six months of every year. The lucrative franchise business, which boomed between 1892 and 1894, remained quite popular during the entire decade. Keeley himself reaped great financial rewards, which many of the former patients at the Keeley Institutes felt he deserved. When Keeley died of heart failure in Los Angeles, many newspapers reported not only on his death, but also on his considerable fortune, which was said to be as high as $1 million.

• Keeley's papers are at the Illinois State Historical Society, Springfield. Among his several works are *The Morphine Eater; or, From Bondage to Freedom* (1881); *A Popular Treatise on Drunkeness and the Opium Habit and Their Successful Treatment with Double Chloride of Gold, the Only Cure* (1890); and *The Non-Heredity of Inebriety* (1896), as well as a number of articles printed in journals sympathetic to his work. Much of Keeley's early life is open to speculation, fueled by the myths built up around him by the adherents to his cure (see *The Keeley Institutes of the U.S., Canada, and Other Countries* [1895]); nevertheless, scholars have rediscovered Keeley's contribution to the study of inebriety and addiction. Biographical material can be found in H. Wayne Morgan, "'No Thank You, I've Been to Dwight': Reflections on the Keeley Cure for Alcoholism," *Illinois Historical Journal* 82 (Autumn 1989): 147–66; George A. Barclay, "The Keeley League," *Journal of the Illinois State Historical Society* 57 (1964): 341–65; Ben Scott, Jr., *Keeleyism: A History of Dr. Leslie Keeley's Gold Cure for Alcoholism* (master's thesis, Illinois State Univ. 1974); and Paul C. Weitz, "The Keeley Treatment: A Description and Analysis" (master's paper, Governors State Univ., 1989). Obituaries are in the *Chicago Daily Tribune*, the *Los Angeles Times*, and the *New York Times*, 22 Feb. 1900.

DANIEL J. MALLECK

KEELY, Patrick Charles (9 Aug. 1816–11 Aug. 1896), architect, was born Patrick Charles Keily in Kilkenny, County Tipperary, Ireland, the son of John (or William) Keily, a builder and architect. (His mother's name is unknown.) His formal education was limited. He apprenticed in the building crafts and worked for his father, whose principal commissions were institutional buildings for the Catholic church. His training in building construction and design coincided with the introduction of the Gothic Revival in Ireland, and he undoubtedly knew of the early ecclesiastical work in Ireland of A. W. N. Pugin.

In 1841 Keely immigrated to the United States. He settled in the "Irish Town" area of Brooklyn, New York, adjacent to the Brooklyn Navy Yard. In 1846 he married Sarah Farmer, a native of Long Island; they had seventeen children, of whom eleven survived to adulthood. He worked in obscurity as a carpenter, until his ability to carve an elaborate altar for the pro-cathedral in Brooklyn brought him to the attention of the clergy. In 1847 the Reverend Sylvester Malone, an Irish-born priest, selected Keely to design a church (Sts. Peter and Paul, demolished) in the Williamsburgh section of Brooklyn. Completed in 1848, the church was the first Catholic edifice with Gothic features in the United States since the early nineteenth century, and the first patterned after the early Gothic Revival work of Richard Upjohn and Minard Lafever.

Keely's entrance into architecture occurred at a propitious time for an Irish-born Catholic. In the 1840s, as immigrants from Ireland and the German states swelled its numbers, the American church recast itself with the devotional piety and liturgical theater espoused by Pius IX and European Catholicism in general. Led by Irish-born prelates and missionaries, the church also engaged in a massive effort to reach the immigrant populations in metropolitan areas. Hundreds of new church buildings were needed for proselytizing, and Keely emerged as the favored architect to fill this need.

His first major commission, in 1848, was to design the Cathedral of the Immaculate Conception in Albany. Dedicated in 1852, the cathedral, with its masonry exterior, twin towers, ornate interior, and monumental scale, became a prototype for the designs of his twenty-one other cathedrals. By 1850, when Keely began work on St. Finbar's Cathedral (demolished) in Charleston, he had already designed twenty-two churches. His reputation within Catholic circles extended throughout the eastern United States and into Quebec and the Maritime Provinces. Much of his early work was in New England, where he designed churches for the missionaries James Fitton and Jeremiah O'Callaghan. The Dominican order and the Jesuit missions in Canada, New York, and New England were also major patrons of his work.

From the outset of his career, Keely collaborated with sculptors, metal and stained-glass artisans, and fresco painters from France, England, Italy, Austria, and Bavaria to achieve the decorative brilliance of his church interiors. Typically, he designed the tableaux of the main altar (as in the Church of the Holy Redeemer, Boston, 1855, and St. Joseph's, Albany, completed in 1860) and then commissioned sculptors in Munich to execute the design in marble. Keely also sketched the elaborate scenes for murals and ceiling medallions in two of his Jesuit churches (Le Gesú de Montréal, 1866, and St. Michael's, Buffalo, 1867) for the Bavarian church painter Daniel Muller. For churches designed with modest budgets he employed

American painters, such as Charles J. Schumacher of Portland, Maine, for St. John's, Bangor (1856). Keely also designed scenes for many of his stained glass windows, a number of which he also commissioned from Munich (e.g., St. Joseph's Church, New Orleans, 1871–1892).

Most of Keely's work was in the Gothic idiom. Although his early designs included a castellated Gothic church (St. Peter's, Memphis, 1852), he commonly explored variations of the English Gothic (notably in St. Peter's, Rutland, Vt., 1873) and, increasingly in the 1860s and 1870s, the French Gothic (Cathedral of the Holy Name, Chicago, 1875). His work also ranged into the Renaissance Revival (Church of the Immaculate Conception, Boston, 1861), Richardsonian Romanesque (Cathedral of Sts. Peter and Paul, Providence, completed in 1889), and Roman baroque (St. Francis Xavier, New York City, 1878). Keely's designs hewed to the traditional "preaching church" interiors: longitudinal aisles, an open floor plan, and elaborate pulpits with scrolled sounding boards. Typically, giant order columns (often in polished granite) lined the center aisle. Lofty ornate altars, set within recessed chancels, evoked images of the "Court of Heaven." Richly colored stained glass filled lancet and rose windows. Ceilings, usually timbered, were also barrel vaulted and coffered. Majestic twin spires and rugged masonry walls distinguished the exteriors. Often, too, his churches occupied visually commanding sites.

Keely's foremost achievements were designs for three enormous cathedrals: the Cathedral of the Holy Cross, Boston (1865–1875), "one of the largest Gothic cathedrals in the world" (D. S. Tucci, *Built in Boston* [1983], p. 35); St. Joseph's Cathedral, Hartford, Connecticut (1876–1892, destroyed by fire in 1956); and the Cathedral of the Immaculate Conception, Brooklyn (begun in 1868). Designed to surpass St. Patrick's Cathedral in size, the Brooklyn Cathedral, like the colossal Anglican cathedral in Liverpool designed by Edward Lutyens, was never completed. The unfinished building was demolished in 1931.

Throughout his long career, Keely perceived his work as a "religious obligation." He attended mass daily and collected only a nominal fee for his work (1 percent of the cost of construction). He lived and worked near the chancery of the Diocese of Brooklyn, and many of his associations were with the Catholic clergy. He limited his practice almost entirely to designing Catholic churches. In 1884 the University of Notre Dame, citing Keely's work on behalf of the church, awarded him the Laetare Medal.

Intensely private and unassuming in demeanor, Keely preferred to work in partnership with two of his sons and a brother-in-law, whom he often dispatched to act as supervising architects on construction sites. His ambition—late in life—to continue his practice ended in 1890 with the premature death of his eldest son. Disabled for five years following a stroke, Keely died in Brooklyn and was buried from the chapel of his unfinished cathedral. His final design was the Church of the Sacred Hearts, Malden, Massachusetts (completed in 1901).

The leading American Catholic architect of the nineteenth century, Keely, according to sources during his lifetime, was responsible for the designs of approximately six hundred churches. This feat is astonishing not only because Keely was "probably the busiest architect in the United States" (*American Architect and Building News*, 22 Aug. 1896), but also because he was self-taught, with no academic training and no study of the ecclesiastical architecture of continental Europe. A later generation of American church architects, including Ralph Adams Cram and the Irish-born Charles Donagh Maginnis, dismissed Keely's work as "monstrous," inartistic, and unarchaeological. Their judgments, however, overlooked Keely's influential role in transforming the pictorial aspects of Roman Catholic worship in the United States, in disseminating the Gothic Revival, and in cultivating—at an early date—an architectural practice that was national in scope.

• Few manuscripts and drawings survive from Keely's long career. He never published any known writings on architecture, and items from his office that passed to his family vanished within decades of his death, a loss that contributes to his omission from most studies of the Gothic Revival in the United States. Some drawings exist in archival collections of several dioceses (e.g., Boston) and the Generalate of the Society of Jesus in Rome. Richard J. Purcell, "P. C. Keely: Builder of Churches in the United States," *Records of the American Catholic Historical Society* 55 (1943): 208–27, draws from careful research in diocesan records, diocesan newspapers, and Catholic journals of the nineteenth century (e.g., *Catholic Review*). The first major study of Keely was Walter Albert Daly, "Patrick Charles Keely: Architect and Church Builder" (master's thesis, Catholic Univ., 1934), which includes reminiscences from relatives and friends of the architect. The most widely circulated biography—albeit with some inaccuracies—is F. W. Kervick, *Patrick Charles Keely, Architect: A Record of His Life and Work* (1953). More recent studies with original material and assessments include J. Philip McAleer, "Keely, the Irish Pugin of America," *Irish Arts Review* 4 (1987): 16–23, and "St. Mary's Halifax: An Early Example of the Use of Gothic Revival Forms in Canada," *Journal of the Society of Architectural Historians* 45 (June 1986): 134–47; Ginette Laroche, "Les Jésuites du Québec et la Diffusion de l'Art Chrétien," *Journal of Canadian Art History* 15 (1991): 6–27; and Robert T. Murphy, "Patrick C. Keely, 1816–1896," *Biographical Dictionary of Architects in Maine*, vol. 4, no. 7 (1987), pp. 1–6. Informative obituaries are in the *Brooklyn Daily Eagle*, 12 Aug. 1896, *American Architect and Building News* 53 (22 Aug. 1896): 58, and the *New York Times*, 13 Aug. 1896 (the only source attributing unspecified churches in Europe to Keely).

JEFFREY CRONIN

KEEN, William Williams (19 Jan. 1837–7 June 1932), surgeon, was born in Philadelphia, Pennsylvania, the son of William W. Keen, a merchant, and Susan Budd. Upon completion of his preliminary education at Saunders' Academy and the Central High School of Philadelphia, Keen attended Brown University, graduating as class valedictorian in 1859. He continued for another year at Brown to study chemistry and physics and then entered Jefferson Medical College, receiving his M.D. degree in 1862. Between 1864 and 1866, when he started practice in Philadelphia, Keen pursued postgraduate education in Paris, Berlin, and Vienna.

Keen's formal medical education was interrupted by the Civil War. As a student he spent two months in 1861 with the Fifth Massachusetts Regiment and participated as an assistant surgeon in the first battle of Bull Run. Two months after his graduation from medical school in 1862, he was commissioned as acting assistant surgeon in the U.S. Army. He was involved in considerable action, including the second battle of Bull Run, before being ordered to the Satterlee Hospital in Philadelphia. In 1863 Union soldiers with injuries and diseases of the nervous system were grouped together for treatment in Philadelphia, first in some of the wards in the Christian Street Hospital. Later in 1863 this neurological center was moved to the grounds of an old estate and was called Turner's Lane Hospital. S. Weir Mitchell and George R. Morehouse, the physicians in charge, also maintained private practices and homes in Philadelphia. They requested that Keen be transferred to their unit as resident surgeon, and he then lived in the hospital. Mitchell, one of the outstanding physicians of his time, served as an excellent role model for the young Keen. The three physicians studied their patients closely and kept voluminous notes. They defined and named causalgia, a painful syndrome related to partial nerve injury, and studied malingering. In 1864 they published an important book on gunshot wounds and other injuries of nerves. Many more works were planned, but their notes were accidentally destroyed in a fire.

In 1866 Keen began his practice in Philadelphia. He also conducted the Philadelphia School of Anatomy (1866–1875) and began a series of academic associations that included lecturer in pathological anatomy at Jefferson Medical College (1866–1875), professor of artistic anatomy at the Pennsylvania Academy of Fine Arts (1876–1889), professor of surgery at the Women's Medical College (1884–1889), and professor of surgery at Jefferson Medical College (1889–1907). During the period from 1866 to 1907 Keen became one of the world's most renowned surgeons and an equally acclaimed teacher of surgery and anatomy. He was one of the first in the world to begin using antiseptic and then aseptic surgical technique, which in part explains his surgical success. He also became a prolific author and editor, producing numerous journal articles and books on a variety of medical topics and also on spiritual, religious, and historical subjects. During his long life he published more than 650 writings, including articles in lay magazines and editorials.

In 1886 Keen's wife, Emma Corinna Borden Keen, whom he married in 1867, died despite his ministrations and those of her physician, William Osler. The Keens had four children. Keen's grief was severe; he was rescued from this period of despair by the remedy that he and Osler often prescribed for their patients—

work. His friend, the publisher Henry Lea, convinced him to undertake a revision of the American edition of Gray's *Anatomy*, which he completed for publication in 1887. In his revision Keen gave special attention to the section on the nervous system, and as he revived his practice, he developed a special interest in the surgical treatment of disorders of the nervous system (such as epilepsy and trigeminal neuralgia), a subspecialty of surgery that previously had been given little attention. In 1887 Keen became one of the first surgeons in history to successfully remove a brain tumor; his patient subsequently lived for more than thirty years. Keen did not limit his work to neurosurgery; he also pioneered in the removal of liver tumors and made significant contributions to many other areas of surgical practice.

In 1893 Keen assisted Joseph Bryant in the surgical removal of a malignant tumor from the upper jaw of President Grover Cleveland. The operation was performed in secret on the presidential yacht as it cruised in Long Island Sound from New York City to the president's summer home on Cape Cod. The procedure was carried out through the mouth, and there were no external incisions. Cleveland died fifteen years later without evidence of recurrence of this tumor, and the operation remained a secret until 1917.

Keen was a very productive author and editor. Among his articles was a paper published in March 1896, describing the first clinical application of Roentgen's X-rays in the United States. Among his books were *An American Text-book of Surgery*, edited with J. W. White and first published in 1892, which achieved a worldwide reputation and passed through four editions; and the acclaimed *Principles and Practice of Surgery*, edited by Keen and published in eight volumes between 1906 and 1921.

When the United States entered World War I, Keen once again entered military service, this time at the age of eighty and as a major in the U.S. Army Medical Corps. He edited and contributed to a book, *The Treatment of War Wounds* (1917, 2d ed. 1918).

Although he did not conduct research himself, Keen was a passionate supporter of animal experimentation. All told, he published thirteen papers, one book, and three pamphlets concerning the vital importance to medical progress of this type of research. Largely because his writings were factual and objective, they were well received and had a broad influence.

Keen's honors and distinctions were many. Honorary degrees were given him by twelve universities in six countries. He was an honorary fellow of three royal colleges of surgeons and a foreign corresponding member or foreign associate of many academies and surgical societies outside the United States. He served as president of the American Surgical Association (1899), the American Medical Association (1900), the American Philosophical Society (1907–1917), and the International Congress of Surgery held in Paris in 1920.

During his long and productive life Keen made many important contributions to surgery in general and to neurosurgery, which was still in its infancy. He made equally important contributions to medical education through his many oral presentations and writings, through his work in medical organizations and through his long personal associations and correspondence with prominent surgeons and physicians throughout the world. On his ninetieth birthday Keen said, "My only regret is that the days are so short when there is so much to be done." He died at his home in Philadelphia.

• Biographical articles about Keen include those by Franklin Martin, *Surgery, Gynecology and Obstetrics* 55 (1932): 120–23; Donald Geist, *Transactions and Studies of the College of Physicians of Philadelphia* 44 (1977): 182–93; John Green, *Barrow Neurological Institute Quarterly* 1, no. 4 (1985): 15–28; James Stone, *Neurosurgery* 17 (1985): 997–1010; and William Bingham, *Journal of Neurosurgery* 64 (1986): 705–12. See also William Middleton, "Turner's Lane Hospital," *Bulletin of the History of Medicine* 40 (1996): 14–42. An obituary is in the *Philadelphia Inquirer*, 9 June 1932.

ROBERT H. WILKINS

KEENAN, Frank (8 Apr. 1858–24 Feb. 1929), actor, was born James Francis Keenan in Dubuque, Iowa, the son of Owen Keenan, a businessman, and Frances Kelly. His father's failure in business and farming prompted the family to relocate more than once between Massachusetts and Iowa, and young Keenan recalled that his first serious labor came as a farmhand for his father when he was eleven. Once his parents settled in Boston, he received piecemeal education interrupted often when he was pressed to work in menial jobs to help support his struggling family. In later adolescence he was a traveling salesman for a time, and he set up his own cigar store, which failed in short order. Interspersed with these episodes, he matriculated at Boston College, where he began to act and perfect imitations of famous people. He left college before earning his degree, distracted by interruptions from part-time jobs and, eventually, by his entry into professional theater. This came in stages in 1880, first with his professional debut as Archibald Carlyle in the melodramatic staple *East Lynne*, made with an apparently short-lived stock company in Richmond, Maine, and then by a series of appearances with more stable commercial groups, including a number of supporting roles with the prestigious Boston Museum Stock Company.

Keenan began earning leading male roles in the early 1890s, occasionally playing in New York City and touring frequently, consistent with standard regimens for successful stage actors of his day. His stately presence and fine voice gained him recognition in the costume and historical melodramas in vogue around the turn of the century. In such fare he played Brother Paul in *The Christian* (1898), Jack Rance in *The Girl of the Golden West* (1905), and General Warren in *The Warrens of Virginia* (1907). His most noted role in Shakespeare came as Cassius in *Julius Caesar* (1912).

In addition to his dramatic roles, Keenan was also among the wave of legitimate actors forced into new venues as stock companies dwindled. He gained a reputation for challenging vaudeville's affinity for light, escapist material, performing *The Oath*, which was based on a theme from Spanish Golden Age playwright Lope de Vega. Keenan also performed an adaptation from Edgar Allan Poe titled *The System of Dr. Tarr and Professor Feather*. In *Vindication* he flaunted vaudeville's prohibition against strong language by uttering the word "goddamn" while defending his character's son. Surprisingly, he got away with it, probably because of the familial loyalty that had prompted the oath.

Keenan's first appearance came when director Thomas Ince paid him $1,000 a week to star in *The Coward* in 1915. Keenan then appeared in over thirty features, among them adaptations of two hoary stage melodramas, *The Bells* (1918) and *East Lynne* (1926), several decades after he had debuted in the latter play in stocks, as well as in the more topical *Todd of the Times* (1919), in which he played a harried newspaper editor. As a mature actor, he specialized in strong, authoritarian characters, many of them domineering fathers. He staged plays and directed films as well during his years in Hollywood. He also returned to the stage as an actor, playing the title characters in *John Ferguson* (1920), in which he toured the country, and *Peter Weston* (1923).

Having adjusted his acting first to the tabloid demands of vaudeville and later to the still more disjunct demands of silent films, Keenan predicted in 1923, just after the advent of radio, that within a relatively short time, technological advances would allow shows in one area to be transmitted to private viewing screens located in homes thousands of miles away. Nevertheless, Keenan maintained that such advances would not bring about the demise of the film industry but would instead force the motion picture to evolve in ways not currently imaginable. Keenan died in Hollywood, California, six years after anticipating what later became television.

Frank Keenan's career stands as a model of histrionic adaptability at a time when popular entertainments in America were burgeoning and opportunities for actors were diversifying. Schooled in a heavy diet of melodrama, with a seasoning of Shakespeare, Keenan worked permutations around a robust style that appealed for nearly a half century to traditionalists in the theater, as well as to those generally less sophisticated spectators who watched him in vaudeville and silent films.

Keenan's very adaptability, however, worked to compromise his standing as a serious actor. He often alternated between more prestigious stage engagements and more lucrative ones in vaudeville; he also essayed feature films at a time when they, too, were regarded as a less demanding, though often more lucrative form. He may have limited himself further still with his fondness for strong drink. He came to be known as a "furniture actor," in a phrase that captured bibulous performers' habit of finding things to lean on as they worked their way around the stage. This designation was quite consistent with Keenan's reputation for barroom collegiality and the dogged professionalism that he cultivated, along with many of the other leading actors of his generation. He was married three times: to Katherine Agnes Long, who left him a widower; to Margaret White, who divorced him; and to Hilda Sloan, who survived him. He had two daughters by his first wife.

• Details of Keenan's work onstage and in vaudeville can be found in Anthony Slide, *The Encyclopedia of Vaudeville* (1994); Channing Pollock, *The Footlights Fore and Aft* (1911); and George C. D. Odell, *Annals of the New York Stage*, vols. 13–15 (1942). The most complete listings of his films appear in John Stewart, comp., *Filmarama*, vols. 1–2 (1975, 1977). Keenan's views on the differences between the stock system and the film industry are quoted at length in Fritzi Remont, "Ideals and Idols—Past and Present," *Motion Picture Classic* 8, no. 6 (Aug. 1919). Anecdotal and less verifiable recollections of Keenan appear in the books written by his grandson and great-grandson, respectively, Keenan Wynn (as told to James Brough), *Ed Wynn's Son* (1959), and Ned Wynn, *We Will Always Live in Beverly Hills: Growing Up Crazy in Hollywood* (1990). See also *Theatre Magazine*, March 1908. Keenan's obituary in *Variety*, 27 Feb. 1929, includes more information about his personal life, although still very brief, than any other single source.

LEIGH WOODS

KEENE, Laura (1820?–4 Nov. 1873), actress, theatrical manager, and playwright, was born in London, England. Nothing is known of her parents or even of her birth name. Much of her early life remains mysterious because she and Joseph A. Donahoe, one of her biographers, made a concerted effort to conceal it. One source reports that at fifteen she began supporting herself tending bar in London and that in 1846, when she was fifteen or sixteen, she married a tavern keeper named John Taylor. After the birth of two daughters and the deportation of Taylor as a convicted criminal, Keene, then in her mid to late twenties, attempted to secure work in the theater. She eventually received an acting position in the company of the fabulous theatrical manager Madame Vestris.

In 1852 Keene was noticed by theatrical manager J. W. Wallack (1795–1864), who offered her a position in his company in New York City. She accepted his offer and made her debut on 30 September 1852; she immediately became the star of his company. Shortly after winning the heart of New York audiences, she took the occasion of Wallack's absence from town to break her contract and run away to Baltimore with a professional gambler named John Lutz, with whom she spent the rest of her life.

Keene's popularity is attributable to her youthful, classical features, her ringing voice, and her rare energy. She was eager to take risks in playing a variety of roles. Critic William Winter, who was not fond of Keene's acting style, described it as frenetic, nervous, even reckless. Her real triumphs were in comedies, and she was also known for her portrayal of Pauline in

The Lady of Lyons, Lydia Languish in Sheridan's *The Rivals*, and Becky Sharp in a dramatization of Thackeray's *Vanity Fair*.

In the early 1850s Keene embarked on a tour of the Far West. In California, she encountered the highly successful manager Catherine Sinclair. Keene's apprenticeship as a manager began in California. For two months she oversaw San Francisco's Union Theater and for four months managed that city's American Theater. Quite suddenly, however, she slipped out of town in great secrecy in 1854 and boarded a ship bound for Australia—a ship, coincidentally, carrying Edwin Booth and his acting company. Her motive for going to California and then to Australia seems to have been to find her husband, John Taylor, and to straighten out her marital situation. (There is no indication that she was able to do this in that she was unable to marry John Lutz when she returned.) She played in Booth's company in Australia and eventually found her husband on a chain gang there; she then headed back to the United States. Scandal erupted after it surfaced that the two young girls whom Keene had called her nieces were actually her daughters by John Taylor and that she was living with Lutz without benefit of matrimony.

In 1855, determined to have her own theater in New York, Keene secured the Metropolitan Theater, which was up for lease. She redecorated it and renamed it the Laura Keene Theater. The established managers, who were unaccustomed to having a female competitor in their midst—especially a newcomer who refused to defer to the theatrical establishment—did everything they could to discourage her. A running battle ensued. Undaunted, Keene began waging a public war with the managers in the newspapers, writing acrimonious letters to the editor and launching a spectacular advertising campaign, all of which were persistent hallmarks of her years in management.

Keene's theater was plagued by vandalism that was difficult to pin on her adversaries, and she was forced to postpone the planned opening. At the end of her first year as owner of the theater, the lease for the building was found to be legally insecure, and another manager appropriated the lease. But, as George C. D. Odell, noted historian of the New York theater, writes, "The brave lady had fought an uphill fight, and had won her public. The managers were against her, perhaps on the principle that so long kept votes from women. And when victory seemed assured, Miss Keene lost the theatre on a technical quibble. . . . Those opposed to Laura Keene found her indomitable." How she finally managed to open her theater in 1856 in a new building is as much a mystery as her past, but in all likelihood she had the help of Lutz and his powerful friends.

Keene's theater made theatrical history. In every area of theater she made important innovations. Her success as a manager stemmed from a shrewd business sense, an intimate knowledge of every aspect of theatrical work, and from her encouragement of American plays. As a businesswoman, for example, she could sense when it was advisable to demand money up front. She extravagantly and elaborately staged her productions, making every effort to produce grand effects for as little money as possible. It was said that Keene knew how to scrimp on costumes and sets and yet make them appear expensive. She possessed a keen sense of drama that would play well, and she took great pains to seek out young, promising playwrights. She was an exacting director and a skilled actress with the willingness and ability to play many parts and with experience as an actress in both resident and touring companies. She did not regard herself to be above sewing costumes if a seamstress were needed or picking up a paintbrush if necessary. She always played whatever role was uncast, be it small or large, male or female.

Keene managed and accompanied her company on extensive and successful tours. Part of her success is attributable to her aggressive promotional tactics, often designed to anger other managers. She was shameless in her advertising, often spreading her publicity over half a news page and placing numerous quips throughout the paper to draw attention to an upcoming production. She even staged elaborate fireworks displays in front of the theater.

Keene valiantly fought against an expensive and limiting star system that closed many stock companies; she paid her regular actors well, often wooing the best performers away from their companies by offering them better parts and more pay. Edward H. Sothern and Joseph Jefferson (1829–1905) were among those who graced her company for a time.

Not only was Keene committed to paying actors well, she also sought out and encouraged new playwrights. She had a keen sense of public taste and recognized which new plays ought to be encouraged and which old ones would bear refurbishing. In a particularly bad financial period, her adaptation of a new afterpiece called *The Elves* carried the company through its difficulties. During another time of financial hardship, a new play by Charles Gaylor called *The Love of a Prince* saved the season. When Keene's company faced sure financial ruin in the 1858–1859 season following the great panic of 1857, she slashed prices and hunted madly for a play that would keep the company going. She found a melodrama called *The Sea of Ice*, which played for weeks. She adapted another play called *The Seven Sisters* and saw it through 203 consecutive performances, the longest unbroken run in New York at the time. Keene's production of *Our American Cousin* became an even more successful event in theatrical history—only two plays in the century, George L. Aiken's dramatization of *Uncle Tom's Cabin* and P. T. Barnum's *The Drunkard*, had longer runs. Keene's policy of using her theater to introduce new American material led her to offer $1,000 prizes for original plays. The most important playwright she sponsored was probably the Irish-American writer Dion Boucicault. She did not, however, operate in a nationalistic vacuum. She was interested in contemporary European theater and became the first manager to hire scouts to apprise her of new plays and talent on the Continent and in England.

Not only was Keene's the most successful theater in New York just before the Civil War; it continued to survive when other theaters failed after the outbreak of the war. Nevertheless, she closed the theater to go on tour in 1863. Odell said of the closing, "A poem of epic proportions should have marked the exit." For the remainder of the war Keene toured with her company and for a time directed the Chestnut Street Theater in Philadelphia.

Shortly after Keene's touring began, she went to Washington to play one of her most popular roles, that of Florence Trenchard in *Our American Cousin.* And it was the tragedy that took place in the theater, the assassination of President Abraham Lincoln, that assured Keene a place in American history, even though her full role in that event and the toll it took on her life are rarely acknowledged. Keene quieted the audience, which was screaming "Kill the actors!" after the president had been shot, and she held Lincoln's head in her lap until he was moved across the street, where he died. Her ordeal was not over when she left the balcony, however, for in the hysteria of the tragic moment, the public's anger was focused on all actors, not just John Wilkes Booth. After she had left Washington to continue her scheduled tour, Keene's train was stopped, and she was arrested for conspiracy to murder the president. The events of that week did irreparable damage to her health and profession. She was thereafter tainted with suspicion, and her career steadily declined. Keene ended her managerial career in an abortive comeback in New York in 1871. Attempts to recover her acting career and to make money from various other projects to pay off the debts that Lutz had left her after his death came to naught. She unsuccessfully tried to launch a new magazine of the arts and tried valiantly but fruitlessly to continue her work as a writer. She died of consumption in Montclair, New Jersey.

Keene's stage presence was described by her contemporaries as "bird-like" and frenetic. There was a taut, nervous quality to her style, her movements and her speech being unusually rapid. She appeared, nevertheless, to be extremely delicate and feminine. Her tiny, fragile appearance on stage belied an iron will and steel-like toughness off stage. She was a person who inspired more awe and respect than affection. She seemed to have been almost impossible to get to know personally, being very demanding and often difficult to work with, sometimes even unscrupulous professionally and very distant and private personally. Despite her difficult personality, theater historian DeWitt Bodeen believed that Keene did more for the growth of American drama than any other single person in the nineteenth century.

• Sources on Keene's life of are not always accurate or complete. They include John Creahan, *The Life of Laura Keene* (1897); Joseph A. Donahoe, *Laura Keene* (1928), a laudatory but unreliable account; "Laura Keene's Early Career," *New York Daily Mirror,* 22 Jan. 1887, which discusses some of the facts about her first marriage; and George C. D. Odell, *Annals of the New York Stage* (1927–1949). Catherine Reignolds-Winslow, *Yesterdays with Actors* (1887), is a good source for stories about Keene's managerial style; see also William Winter, *Vagrant Memories* (1915). An obituary is in the *New York Times,* 7 Nov. 1873.

CLAUDIA DURST JOHNSON

KEENE, Thomas Wallace (26 Oct. 1840–1 June 1898), actor, was born Thomas R. Eagleson in New York City. Little is known of his early life. His father, known only as "Mr. Eagleson," was a journalist who died when Thomas was a small child. As a boy, Thomas became interested in acting through frequent attendance at the Bowery Theatre on the Lower East Side of New York City. He soon became well known to the actors and theater personnel, who hired him for bit parts. In his teens he became a professional actor and adopted the name Thomas Wallace Keene.

For nearly a decade Keene appeared in minor roles on the New York stage and with touring companies on the eastern seaboard. He assumed his first important role in 1862, when he was hired by a touring company headed by James Henry Hackett to play Henry VI in Shakespeare's historical trilogy. Keene reportedly memorized the lengthy role while traveling upstate to join the company in Albany, New York. Although he apparently gave commendable performances in Albany, he returned to New York City after the run to assume a series of minor roles with various theater troupes. In the early 1870s he was also a member of touring companies that performed in England and the American West. These companies included such famous acting contemporaries as Edwin Booth, Charlotte Cushman, and Clara Morris.

In 1875 Keene moved to San Francisco to join the well-known California Theatre Stock Company, and he remained there for five years. Returning to the East Coast in 1880, Keene played a major role in a production of *Drink* in Boston, and after his success there he was given the lead in a production of the same play in Chicago. Keene's acclaimed performances made him a star, and he went on to tour the country with a repertory ensemble, playing Shakespearean roles, as well as such figures as Cardinal Richelieu and Louis XI in historical dramas. The tour became an annual affair, and Keene appeared before enthusiastic and admiring audiences in popular theaters across the country for more than a decade.

Keene, best known for his portrayal of Richard III, never had the stature of Booth or other great tragedians of the late nineteenth century, nor did he play at the top-ranked houses. He was an actor whose performances—and their low prices—attracted a mass following at a time when theatergoing was a major pastime of the American public. Keene was reportedly as popular with his fellow actors as he was with audiences; the support of his touring companions was undoubtedly a major factor in his success.

Keene's acting was reportedly florid, emotional, and overtly demonstrative, verging on the melodramatic. By the mid-1890s more subtle dramatic methods began to enjoy favor, and his popularity in large cities soon waned, although he continued to receive adulation in smaller communities nationwide.

Keene was married in the 1860s to the former Margaret Creighton of New York City and is known to have had at least two children. The family made their home on Staten Island, where Keene reportedly owned a tavern. After being stricken with appendicitis while on a tour of Canada, Keene was brought home to Tompkinsville, Staten Island, where he died.

• The theater collections of Harvard University and the New York Public Library include programs from some of Keene's performances. Biographical information on Keene can be found in *Who Was Who*, Historical Volume (1963), and T. A. Brown, *A History of the New York Stage* (1903). An obituary is in the *New York Times*, 2 June 1898; other obituaries, which include biographical data, appear in the *New York Dramatic Mirror* and *New York Clipper*, both 11 June 1898.

ANN T. KEENE

KEENER, William Albert (10 Mar. 1856–23 Apr. 1913), legal scholar and teacher, was born in Augusta, Georgia, the son of Henry Keener and Isabella (maiden name unknown). Orphaned at a very early age, he was raised by his married sister. Apparently endowed with a strong intellect, Keener entered Emory College at the age of fourteen and received a degree with distinction four years later, in 1874. Within a few months of his graduation, he entered Harvard Law School—an institution caught up in the process of changes that would revolutionize American legal education.

With the vital support of Harvard President Charles W. Eliot, Christopher Columbus Langdell, the first dean of the law school, had introduced both a new conception in legal education and an innovative technique to teach it. Langdell believed that law was essentially a science that consisted of certain principles and doctrines, to be studied and taught like any science. Arguing that these principles could best be found in appellate opinions, he proposed that each law student study a collection of such cases in front of him. Langdell proposed to teach students to isolate and apply legal principles through intensive case examination and analysis of cases rather than formal lecture. Keener was one of the first students to be taught by this new "case method," and apparently he thrived in its "Socratic give and take." Although Keener received his law degree in 1877, he remained at the law school for another year. In 1878 he married Frances McLeod Smith; they had one child. In 1879 they moved to New York, where Keener began to practice law.

In 1883 Langdell invited his former student to return to Harvard Law School as a member of the faculty—an appointment that disturbed senior members of Eliot's administration. One wrote to the Harvard president that, by hiring Keener, Langdell sought to breed "professors of Law, not practitioners." Keener's appointment implied that the law school "commits itself to the theory of breeding within itself its Corps of instructors and thus severs itself from the great current of legal life which flows through the courts and the bar[;] . . . the gravest error of policy which it could adopt" (Sutherland, p. 188). Doubts notwithstanding, Eliot not only supported Keener's appointment but five years later approved his election to one of the most distinguished chairs at the law school, the Story Professorship. This action was followed by Keener's acceptance of a professorship at Columbia Law School in 1890 and his elevation to the deanship of that school one year later. He remained there for ten years, the most productive period of his career.

Keener's claim to distinction as a legal scholar rests on two factors. He was remembered by Roscoe Pound, later to become dean of Harvard Law School, as one of a few "great natural teachers," part of a rare breed that "couldn't help teaching. They were just built that way" (Sutherland, p. 201). As an instructor, Keener popularized and broadened Langdell's case method. He compared it to the new graduate seminars that also avoided lectures and textbooks in favor of source material and classroom discussion. On the other hand, like many proponents of Langdell's approach, he tended to overemphasize the role of legal process at the expense of "tracing the substantive principles of law" (Stevens, p. 55). Emphasis on process rather than substance made it possible for proponents of the "new legal education" not to feel in any way responsible for the substantive abuses in corporate business practices that characterized late nineteenth-century industrial change.

Keener's other claim to distinction rests on his preparation of materials to serve as the sources for the case method. Between 1890 and 1900 he produced no less than six major treatises as well as collections of cases in subjects as varied as contracts, equity jurisdiction, and jurisprudence and private corporations. Exhaustive in their citations, Keener's works made it much easier for the current law school curriculum to adopt the case method, which by the turn of the century virtually dominated American legal education.

For reasons that are not clear, Keener resigned his deanship in 1901 and the following year left Columbia Law School. In September 1901 he accepted an appointment to the New York Supreme Court to complete the unexpired term of a judge who had died. Although he was offered renomination for a full term, Keener was defeated for reelection. In 1903 he returned to the private practice of law, which he had abandoned twenty years before, in New York City. Perhaps he had been away from it too long; possibly the skills of a law professor were not those needed for the successful law practitioner. After a ten-year period with only indifferent recognition, he died in New York City.

Keener is best remembered as one of the most prominent partisans and practitioners of Langdell's case method. But if he welcomed its undoubted potential, he was slow to recognize its very real limitations. The tendency in legal education to separate substance from process has not yet been satisfactorily resolved, if it ever can be. Although the evolving nature of legal scholarship made it inevitable that Keener's works would be superseded, in the continuing history of American legal education his place remains secure.

• Keener's own ideas on the case method are summarized in his article "The Inductive Method in Legal Education," *American Law Review* 28 (1894): 709. Keener's major treatises are *A Selection of Cases on the Law of Quasi-Contracts* (1888–1889), *A Treatise on the Law of Quasi-Contracts* (1893), *A Selection of Cases on Equity Jurisdiction* (1894–1896), and *A Selection of Cases on the Law of Private Corporations* (1899). Three valuable studies of American legal education that discuss Keener's contributions to its development are Arthur Sutherland, *The Law at Harvard: A History of Ideas and Men* (1967); William Chase, *The American Law School and the Rise of Administrative Government* (1982); and Robert Stevens, *Law School: Legal Education in America from the 1850s to the 1980s* (1983). See also Jerold Auerbach, *Unequal Justice Lawyers and Social Change in Modern America* (1976).

JONATHAN LURIE

KEEP, Henry (22 June 1818–30 July 1869), New York financier and railroad president, was born in Adams, New York, the son of Heman Chandler Keep and Dorothy Kent, impoverished farmers. When Heman Keep died in 1835, his relatives proved unable to support his family, which was forced to take refuge in the Jefferson County poorhouse. Young Henry was bound out to a farmer who agreed to send him to a public school but then reneged on the obligation. The young man fled to Honeoye Falls, New York, where for an initial wage of seven dollars per month he became a drayman for a cooper named Tuler. He proved able to save money, which he devoted to speculation in bank notes depreciated in the panic of 1837. He proceeded into arbitrage in Canadian bank notes, buying them at a discount in upstate New York and redeeming them at par in Ontario. With the proceeds, he was able to return to his home area to establish a bank at Watertown. While there he married Emma Woodruff, daughter of a prominent citizen of the town. The couple had one daughter, also named Emma. Keep expanded his activities in the 1840s by establishing several country banks in his area.

About 1850 Keep shifted his financial base to New York City. He became a specialist in finance of the expanding railroad industry, operating mainly in securities of lines that eventually became parts of the New York Central system. He was habitually closed-mouthed about his operations, but he served as treasurer of the Michigan Southern & Northern Indiana from 1861 to 1863 and as a director of the Cleveland & Toledo, both of which became components of the New York Central main line. He was also a major shareholder in the New York Central itself at a time when the company had achieved only an east-west line across upstate New York. The railroad was being actively sought by Cornelius Vanderbilt, whose Hudson River Railroad had been completed between New York City and Albany. Keep allied himself with Hen-

ry H. Baxter, William G. Fargo, founder of both the American and Wells Fargo express companies, and Rufus Hatch in a faction that resisted Vanderbilt. Dean Richmond, the dominant figure in the New York Central's management, died on 26 August 1866, precipitating a struggle for control of the company. At the shareholders' meeting of 12 December 1866 the anti-Vanderbilt faction decisively won election. Keep was chosen president, but he reported that he had no ambition to hold the office for any long period. He resigned on 25 July 1867 and was replaced by Baxter. At the meeting of 11 December 1867 the pro-Vanderbilt faction won, with Vanderbilt replacing Baxter as president. Keep, recognizing the futility of further resistance to Vanderbilt, sold out his holdings to him at prices reported from $95 to $98 per share. The transactions proved most profitable to Keep, who had by now amassed an enviable fortune. Vanderbilt merged the two properties into the New York Central & Hudson River Railroad on 1 November 1869.

Meanwhile, Hatch had failed to gain control of the Chicago & North Western Railway shortly after the Civil War and was eager to try again. He enlisted Keep's assistance in forming a pool of some $25 million in the company's stock, of which Keep was said to have owned $1.5 million. Keep became president of the company on 4 June 1868 but once again manifested no eagerness for a long tenure. The railway was embroiled in an ambivalent relation with its principal geographical rival, the Chicago, Milwaukee & St. Paul, ranging from vigorous rivalry to efforts at local monopoly by means of interlocking directorates and joint management. In the course of this, Keep also became a director of the Chicago, Milwaukee & St. Paul. Although a slim man of medium height, Keep had suffered from heart disease since about 1857. Apparently in anticipation of death, he resigned the presidency of the Chicago & North Western on 11 July 1869. Shortly after returning to New York from Sharon Springs, New York, where he had gone in an effort to palliate his physical condition, he died at his mansion at 601 Fifth Avenue.

Keep's benefactions, like his business transactions, were carried on with minimal publicity, but he is known shortly before his death to have offered $1.5 million for establishment of a National Academy for the Advancement of Art. Because his widow remarried, becoming Mrs. William Schley, probate of her estate following her death in 1900 proved controversial. The publicity given the action provided some atypical light on Keep's finances, indicating that he had left an estate of over $4 million. This was a remarkable achievement for a man who began life in rural poverty, with formal educational attainments so meager that he described himself as having "graduated at the poorhouse."

• For additional information, see the entry on Keep in *America's Successful Men of Affairs: An Encyclopedia of Contemporaneous Biography*, vol. 1 (1895); William H. Stennett, *Yesterday and Today: A History of the Chicago & North Western*

Railway System (1910); Robert J. Casey and W. A. S. Douglas, *Pioneer Railroad: The Story of the Chicago and North Western System* (1948); and Edward Hungerford, *Men and Iron: The History of the New York Central* (1938). Obituaries are in the *New York Herald*, *Times*, Tribune, and *World*, all 31 July 1869.

GEORGE W. HILTON

KEEP, Nathan Cooley (23 Dec. 1800–11 Mar. 1875), dental scientist and educator, was born in Longmeadow, Massachusetts, the son of Samuel Keep and Anne Bliss, farmers. His early education at the local village school was relatively meager. His family was intensely religious, and several family members were active in the Congregational church. He shared his father's interest in and skill with the use of tools and appeared destined for a career as an artisan. When Keep was sixteen his father apprenticed him to John Taylor, a jeweler in Newark, New Jersey, even though young Nathan's first choice was to become a schoolteacher. As a dutiful son, he followed his father's wishes and stayed with his indentureship. However, a general business slump in 1821 forced Taylor to lay him off after only five years.

By this time Keep had switched his career interest and was determined to become a dentist. It was common at that time for artisans to practice dentistry as well as their trades. Returning to Boston, Keep studied with John Randall, who also practiced medicine. This was the only method of instruction for aspiring dentists, since the first dental school, the Baltimore College of Dental Surgery, would not be established for another nineteen years. Keep was well prepared, as he combined a jeweler's mechanical skills with a knowledge of medicine. After approximately a year as a preceptoral student, he opened an office in Boston for the practice of dentistry. An inventory of the instruments and supplies he purchased for this purpose, dated 12 August 1822, establishes when he entered professional practice and provides an idea of his investment, about $120.

Keep, in consonance with his belief that a dentist should have a medical background, enrolled in 1825 at the Harvard Medical School. While maintaining his private practice, he attended the regular course of lectures and was awarded the degree of doctor of medicine in 1827. After completing his medical education, he returned to solely practicing dentistry, which he continued for some forty years. In 1830 he married Susan Prentice Haskell; they had two sons and two daughters. One of his sons, Samuel Hamilton Keep, also became a dentist and joined his father in practice until his untimely death in 1861.

One of the fields in which Keep received early recognition was in the manufacture of porcelain teeth for artificial dentures. Porcelain teeth, which had been invented in 1807 by an Italian dentist, replaced the highly objectionable human teeth or animal teeth that had previously been the only substitutes available. However, these new teeth were unattractive, and Keep began

his own research and experimentation into improving them.

Porcelain teeth were introduced into the United States in 1817 by a French dentist, Antoine Plantou. In 1827 Plantou, having heard of Keep's work, wrote to him, offering to teach Keep his method of making artificial teeth for $600. It is not known if Keep accepted Plantou's offer. However, in 1833 Keep joined with another prominent Boston dentist, Josiah F. Flagg, to experiment in making porcelain teeth. Keep apparently went on his own after that and improved them so much that the Massachusetts Charitable Mechanic Association, at its exhibition of 1839, awarded him its gold medal "for superior mineral teeth."

Keep, who was always interested in teaching aspiring dentists, was preceptor to William T. G. Morton, who achieved renown as the first to successfully administer ether as an anesthetic. Scholars believe that the young Horace Wells, the discoverer of anesthesia, may also have been a preceptoral student in Keep's office. Wells's parents were of sufficient means that they could have provided their son with the best education possible. The Boston city directories for the years 1834 to 1836 list only four individuals as dentists, with Keep one of the four. Keep was considered an expert in anesthesia, and he administered ether to Henry Wadsworth Longfellow's wife the first time an anesthetic was used in childbirth.

Keep came to national attention as the result of a sensational murder case in 1850. John W. Webster, professor of chemistry at Harvard, stood accused of the murder of George Parkman, a physician on the faculty of Harvard's medical school. The prosecution charged that Webster bludgeoned Parkman to death, dismembered his body, and burnt it in the stove in his office. A number of human bones were recovered from the ashes as well as part of a lower partial denture. Since Keep had been Parkman's dentist, he was called on to testify. He brought to the courtroom the stone model on which he had fabricated the partial denture and in the presence of the jury demonstrated that the denture fit the model perfectly. Keep was moved to tears and exclaimed, "I should never see my old friend Parkman again." This testimony, which resulted in a conviction and death sentence for Webster, was the first instance of the use of dental evidence in a criminal trial in the United States.

Keep labored unselfishly for the advancement of his profession and was one of the organizers of the Massachusetts Dental Society. He was elected its first member on 4 April 1864, and on 16 May he became its first president. In 1865, in his presidential address, he called for a dental school to be established as part of Harvard University. His persistent efforts convinced the university's board of trustees to recommend the establishment of such a school, and in 1868 the first university-affiliated dental school was opened, with Keep as its dean. His happiness over this momentous event in his life was, however, marred by the death of his wife that year.

Keep was highly regarded by his colleagues. Unfortunately, ill health forced him to resign from his position as dean after only three years. He died in Boston, Massachusetts.

• Keep published only one paper, "Aluminum as a Base for Artificial Teeth," *Dental Register* 20 (1866): 410–12. Reports of his speeches and addresses include "The Aims and Duties of the Dental Profession," *Dental Cosmos* 7 (1865–1866): 57–62, and "Address of Welcome," *Transactions of the American Dental Association* (1866): 246–47. For further information on Keep see Richard Locke Hapgood, *History of the Harvard Dental School* (1930); Charles R. E. Koch and Burton L. Thorpe, eds., *History of Dentistry* (2 vols., 1909); and Malvin E. Ring, "The Early Life of Nathan Cooley Keep, Monumental Figure in American Dentistry," *Bulletin of the History of Dentistry* 38, no. 2 (Oct. 1990). For coverage of the Webster-Parkman murder trial see Robert Sullivan, *The Disappearance of Dr. Parkman* (1971), and W. F. Rehfuss, *A Treatise on Dental Jurisprudence for Dentists and Lawyers* (1892), pp. 22–23. An obituary is in the *Boston Daily Advertiser*, 12 Mar. 1875.

MALVIN E. RING

KEES, Weldon (24 Feb. 1914–18 July 1955?), poet, was born Harry Weldon Kees in Beatrice, Nebraska, the son of John Kees, the owner of a relatively prosperous hardware manufacturing business, and Sarah Green. Weldon (he never used his first name) attended Doane College in Crete, Nebraska, the University of Missouri, and the University of Nebraska, where in 1935 he received a B.A. in English. In 1939 he received a B.A. in library science from the University of Denver.

Kees began publishing short stories in little magazines like *Prairie Schooner* during his senior year in college. Although he was fairly successful in placing stories over the next five or six years, his efforts of that time now seem dated and fairly unimaginative. Perhaps the peak of his success in this form was reached in 1942 when a story about a repressed homosexual, anti-Semitic professor of English was reprinted in *Best Short Stories of 1941*. Academia was also the subject of Kees's novel *Fall Quarter*, thought too parochial in its satire by publishers at the time, which was finally published in 1990.

From 1935 until 1940 Kees worked first for the Federal Writers Project in Lincoln, Nebraska, then as a librarian in Denver. In October 1937 he married Ann Swan, whom he had met while they were students at the University of Nebraska. They stayed married but childless, separating in 1943, until her alcoholism and his growing depression led to a divorce in 1954.

Although Kees is mainly remembered for his poetry, the most remarkable aspect of his life is how many careers he managed to cram into it. From 1937 he worked in the Denver Public Library; in 1940 he became director of the Bibliographic Center for Research, Rocky Mountain region, a position he kept until 1943 when he moved to New York City. There, he soon found a job as a writer for *Time*. His position on the magazine lasted about six months, and in November 1943 he became a newsreel writer and editor for Paramount, a position he kept for four years, supervising the melding of film and soundtrack. During this period he also wrote book reviews for various publications (including the *New Republic, Time*, the *New York Times Book Review*, and *Partisan Review*), and in 1944 he began painting with oil on canvas. Eventually he became a relatively well-known abstract expressionist—regarded highly enough to have a one-man show at the Peridot Gallery in New York in 1948. In 1949–1950 he contributed reviews for six months as art critic of the *Nation*, and in 1950 he moved to San Francisco, where for the next four years he worked as a writer, filmmaker, and still photographer with Juergen Reusch, M.D., and the anthropologist Gregory Bateson. With Reusch he coauthored and supplied photographs for *Non-Verbal Communication* (1956), and with Bateson he made the film *Three Families*. On his own, he made a thirteen-minute experimental film *Hotel Apex*, and he composed a jazz score for experimental filmmaker James Broughton's *Adventures of Jimmy*. Kees's work in music, films, and painting is sometimes performed or exhibited, but no reevaluation has suggested that he was as gifted in any of those art forms as he was in poetry.

Kees began publishing verse in the late 1930s, and, from the beginning, the attenuated social protest and midwestern satire of his fiction was replaced by a far more cosmopolitan tone (often ironic, usually despairing), heavily influenced at times by T. S. Eliot and W. H. Auden. In all, Kees published three volumes of poetry during his lifetime: *The Last Man* (1943), *The Fall of the Magicians* (1947), and *Poems 1947–1954* (1954). His collected poems were edited posthumously by Donald Justice (1962; rev. ed. 1992).

Kees's syntax was usually that of prose, but his verbal economy, his rhythms, and his frequent use of expressionistic or surreal effects and complex verse forms made his a distinctive poetic voice. His best-known efforts include "For My Daughter" and the Robinson poems. The former is a catalog of horrors awaiting the speaker's daughter as she grows up; in the last line he admits, "I have no daughter. I desire none." Robinson is a representative modern man, socially and fashionably correct on the outside but possessed of a "sad and usual heart, dry as a winter leaf." Among Kees's longer poems, the most impressive is "The Hourglass," a series of reflections or meditations on the nature of time, held together by recurring images, motifs, and symbols. During his stay in New York Kees came to know many of the period's literary and artistic figures, including Edmund Wilson and Malcolm Cowley. These personal relationships guaranteed a discerning initial readership for his poems and some sympathetic reviews.

Although he was extremely witty and worldly wise in his correspondence, Kees's personality always had its dark side, and in 1954 it was evident to his friends that he was becoming increasingly depressed. For reasons not easily apparent, he thought often of suicide, and in July 1955 his car was found abandoned on an approach to the Golden Gate Bridge. He was never seen again.

• The bulk of Kees's letters, manuscripts, and papers can be found in the Bennett Martin Public Library, Lincoln, Nebr. Many of his short stories have been reprinted in *The Ceremony and Other Stories* (1984). His more important reviews and critical essays can be found in *Reviews and Essays, 1935–1955* (1988), and many of his extremely interesting letters are published in Robert Knoll, ed., *Weldon Kees and the Midcentury Generation* (1986). The most complete critical study is William T. Ross, *Weldon Kees* (1985). The best biographical source is Raymond Nelson, "The Fitful Life of Weldon Kees," *American Literary History* 1, no. 4 (1989): 816–52.

WILLIAM T. ROSS

KEETON, William Tinsley (3 Feb. 1933–17 Aug. 1980), biologist, was born in Roanoke, Virginia, the son of William Ivie Keeton, a telephone engineer, and Doris Hancock Tinsley. His family moved to Lynchburg, Virginia, while he was still a youngster, and he received his early education from that city's public schools. Keeton contracted rheumatic fever as a child and suffered the rest of his life from rheumatic heart disease. When he was nine years old, he and his parents began to raise and train homing pigeons, and his fascination with their natural ability to navigate greatly influenced his professional development. He did his undergraduate work at the University of Chicago and received his A.B. in 1952 and his S.B. in zoology in 1954. He studied entomology in graduate school, receiving his M.S. from Virginia Polytechnic Institute (VPI) in 1956 and his Ph.D. from Cornell University in 1958. That same year he married Barbara Sue Orcutt; they had three children.

Keeton began his teaching career while still in graduate school. During his last year at VPI he taught biology at nearby Radford College, and after completing his course work at Cornell he taught biology at VPI in 1958. Later that year he joined Cornell's biology department as an assistant professor of entomology. His early research involved the development, geographical distribution, and classification of millipedes, and much of his work in this regard was supported by grants from the National Science Foundation. In 1959 he began teaching freshman biology, and from 1961 to 1973 he served as a consultant to the New York State Education Department on such matters as advanced placement programs and achievement tests in biology. This involvement at the state level and the enthusiastic student response to his teaching led him to devote more of his time and attention to the textbook needs of biology students, especially after his promotion to associate professor in 1964. To this end he authored *Biological Science* (1967; 3d ed., 1980) and *Elements of Biological Science* (1968; 2d ed., 1973) and coauthored *Biology in the Laboratory* (1970). These textbooks were particularly useful to students because they incorporated modern evolutionary theory into the study of biology and dealt at length with up-to-date developments in photosynthesis, cellular structure, molecular genetics, and embryology.

In 1965 Keeton transferred within the biology department from the entomology section to the newly created section of Neurobiology and Behavior so that he could indulge his fascination with avian orientation. Conventional wisdom held that homing pigeons plotted their course by using the sun as their only reference point, but in 1969 Keeton demonstrated that trained pigeons can easily find their way home on a day that is heavily overcast. After noticing that the pigeons became disoriented over certain land areas regardless of the weather, he hypothesized that the birds' normally unfailing sense of direction was related in some way to the earth's magnetic field. Further support was lent to this theory in 1971 when he discovered that a small magnet mounted to a trained pigeon's body interferes with its initial departure bearings. Interestingly, these birds showed an ability to change bearings once in flight, suggesting that homing pigeons rely on a number of cue systems while navigating.

In 1974 Keeton showed that homing pigeons can detect polarized light as well as changes in atmospheric pressure and that normal fluctuations in the earth's magnetic field influence pigeon orientation. In 1977 he discovered that homing pigeons can hear frequencies lower than the human ear can detect. In 1979 he demonstrated that fluctuations in the moon's gravitational pull caused by its natural monthly cycle affect the bearings of the pigeons and that deflected winds at the home loft have an effect on orientation. At the time of his death, he was working to understand how the different cue systems upon which homing pigeons rely are arranged hierarchically and whether or not this hierarchy is affected by changes in geography, weather, climate, or age of the bird.

Keeton became a full professor in 1969 and chaired the Section of Neurobiology and Behavior from 1970 to 1976. In 1971 he was appointed to the board of Cornell's Ornithology Laboratory, a post he held until 1977, when he was made the Liberty Hyde Bailey Professor of Biology. He was a visiting professor at the Max Planck Institute of Physiology in Seewiesen, Germany (1972–1973), the University of Konstantz, Germany (1978–1979). He was a fellow of the American Association for the Advancement of Science and served on that body's governing council from 1963 to 1973. He was also a fellow of the Animal Behavior Society and a member of the New York Academy of Sciences. In 1980 he became a member of the Cornell Board of Trustees and was elected to fellowship in the American Ornithological Union. Although his health had never been good because of the rheumatic fever (he underwent open-heart surgery twice), he conducted a great deal of his research in the field and traveled around the world to discuss the results of his work. He died from heart failure in Ithaca, New York.

Keeton's major contribution to science consisted of his work in bird navigation and migration. As he noted in the introduction to *Animal Migration, Navigation, and Homing* (1978), which he coedited with Klaus Schmidt-Koenig, the 1970s witnessed an explosion of new data, evidence, ideas, and methods for unraveling the modes of animal navigation. What he did not note was that the publication of the results of his own investigations into the nature of the navigational abilities of homing pigeons contributed significantly to the development of a more nuanced approach to the understanding of animal navigation and migratory behavior.

• A good biography of Keeton, including a complete bibliography of his work, is Stephen T. Emlen, "In Memoriam: William T. Keeton," *Auk* 98 (Jan. 1981): 167–72. An obituary is in the *New York Times*, 21 Aug. 1980.

CHARLES W. CAREY, JR.

KEFAUVER, Estes (26 July 1903–10 Aug. 1963), U.S. senator, was born Carey Estes Kefauver in Madisonville, Tennessee, the son of Robert Cooke Kefauver, a hardware merchant, and Phredonia Bradford Estes. He attended the University of Tennessee from 1922 to 1924, receiving a bachelor of arts degree. After a year of teaching mathematics and coaching football at a Hot Springs, Arkansas, high school, he attended Yale University, from which he received an LL.B. cum laude in 1927. For the next dozen years Kefauver practiced law in Chattanooga, first with the firm of Cooke, Swaney & Cooke and later as a partner in Sizer, Chambliss & Kefauver. In 1935 he married Nancy Pigott of Glasgow, Scotland, eight years his junior, whom he had met during her visit to relatives in Chattanooga. They became parents of four children, one of them adopted.

Aroused by his role as attorney for the *Chattanooga News*, Kefauver became interested in local politics and sought election to the Tennessee Senate in 1938. He lost but in 1939 spent two months as newly elected governor Prentice Cooper's finance and taxation commissioner. When Congressman Sam McReynolds of Tennessee's Third District, which included Chattanooga, died in 1939, Kefauver was elected to succeed him in the House.

During a nine-year tenure in the House of Representatives, Kefauver generally supported President Franklin D. Roosevelt's policies but established a reputation as a congressional "lone wolf." He concentrated much of his legislative efforts on congressional reform and antimonopoly measures; however, he was best known for his successful support of the Tennessee Valley Authority in rebuffing the efforts of Tennessee senator K. D. McKellar to gain political control over the agency.

In 1948 Kefauver sought election to the Senate. On the campaign trail, Kefauver was not an eloquent speaker, often stumbling over his words and making ridiculous mistakes—such as introducing Sen. J. Howard McGrath, chairman of the Democratic National Committee and Harry Truman's campaign manager, as "J. Hoover McGuire." Little-known outside his own district, he resorted to a campaign pattern that would characterize all his subsequent political races, national as well as local; it was intensely personal, with Kefauver meeting voters, shaking hands, and

following up with further contacts. In the balloting, he defeated the long-entrenched statewide political machine of Memphis mayor Edward Hull Crump in the three-way Democratic senatorial primary. Crump, leveling a typical attack on Kefauver, compared him to a pet coon that diverts its master's attention while stealing from his pocket. In response, Kefauver donned a coonskin cap, an item that became a lasting campaign symbol.

Kefauver was unique in Tennessee politics in his outspoken liberal views, a stand that established a permanent bloc of opposition to him in the state. He was ambivalent on civil rights. He admitted later that he had difficulty adjusting to the idea of integration, and in 1960 he held out to the last in favor of permitting cross-examination of black complainants in voting rights cases. But he did support the civil rights program generally and was a consistent supporter of organized labor and other movements considered liberal in the South at that time. Kefauver's success despite his liberal views was predicated largely on his support by the *Nashville Tennessean*, a consistently liberal newspaper that served as a focus for anti-Crump sentiment in the state. His constituency included many prominent citizens whose views were considerably less liberal than his but who admired him for his integrity.

Much of the first half of Kefauver's fourteen years in the Senate was taken up with two unsuccessful races for president. His chairmanship of the Senate Crime Investigating Committee in 1950–1951 had brought him national exposure and underlay his quest in 1952 for the Democratic presidential nomination. Under Kefauver's direction, the Senate investigation paraded one big organized crime figure after another before the public on the relatively new medium of television. By the time the crime hearings ended, Kefauver had become, according to pollster Elmo Roper, one of the ten most admired men in the United States.

"Estes," said his friend and senatorial campaign manager, Charlie Neese, "you can't run for President like you did for the Senate." But Kefauver did. He was not only opposed by the Democratic party leadership (because the crime investigation tarnished the reputation of many prominent Democratic mayors), but despised by his southern colleagues for his support of liberal causes. Kefauver pinned his hopes on winning the few presidential preference primaries and depended largely on campaigning town-to-town and meeting voters. This strategy worked well in the small rural state of New Hampshire and in the agricultural Midwest. The American people "knew him when he walked down the streets of their cities and towns. They knew him as a friend," recalled Senator Abraham Ribicoff of Connecticut.

Kefauver won an electrifying victory over President Truman in the first-in-the-nation New Hampshire primary and subsequently swept through the rest of the primaries, losing only in Florida and the District of Columbia. Going into the national convention held in Chicago in July with half again as many delegate votes as his nearest competitor, Kefauver was nonetheless beaten for the Democratic nomination when President Truman and other national party leaders threw their support to Illinois governor Adlai E. Stevenson II. Kefauver tried again four years later but bowed out when Stevenson beat him at his own game in several key primaries. When Stevenson threw open the vice presidential nomination, Kefauver turned back challenges from Governor Frank Clement and Senator Albert Gore of his own state and Massachusetts senator John F. Kennedy to garner the nomination. Stevenson and Kefauver were resoundingly defeated by the immensely popular incumbent Republican president, Dwight D. Eisenhower.

During the interim between his two presidential races, in the middle of a campaign for reelection to the Senate, Kefauver took the most courageous stand of his career in 1954, casting the sole Senate vote against a politically inspired Communist control bill. Kefauver told William Benton, publisher of the *Encyclopaedia Britannica* it was "the case in my career in which I take the most satisfaction."

Kefauver's abandonment of presidential ambitions after 1956 led to his most productive years as a senator. While he largely faded from the public eye, he earned the respect of congressional colleagues from both parties for his independence and his sponsorship of a number of important foreign and domestic legislative measures.

One of Kefauver's hard-fought successes, which ultimately proved of limited importance, was his promotion of Atlantic Union, a proposed federal union of the western democracies. The plan would have organized fifteen Atlantic democracies along the lines of the original American federation of states, each nation controlling its internal affairs but delegating foreign policy and defense to a joint federal government. Kefauver's efforts helped with congressional approval of Atlantic Union, and he attended the Atlantic Convention in Paris in 1962. But the idea was forgotten a few years later when the United States plunged into the morass of Vietnam.

Kefauver's lasting reputation was built as a fighter against monopoly in his role as chairman of the Senate Antitrust and Monopoly Subcommittee. Several antitrust bills came out of the subcommittee's extensive investigations, the major one being the Kefauver-Harris Drug Control Act of 1962. The measure, as watered down by the Kennedy administration, did not carry the provisions against excessive pricing of prescription drugs that Kefauver wanted but did carry safety measures.

A heavy smoker and drinker, Kefauver was in the middle of another antimonopoly fight, against President Kennedy's communications satellite bill, when he collapsed on the Senate floor. He died at Bethesda, Maryland, of a heart aneurysm.

• Kefauver's collected papers and letters are in the library of the University of Tennessee, Knoxville. Kefauver's own books on different aspects of his legislative career are *Crime in America* (1951), *In a Few Hands: Monopoly Power in America*

(1965), and, with Jack Levin, *A 20th Century Congress* (1947). A general biography is Charles L. Fontenay, *Estes Kefauver: A Biography* (1980), and a résumé of Kefauver's political career is Joseph Bruce Gorman, *Kefauver: A Political Biography* (1971). A limited but flattering biography is Harvey Swados, *Standing Up for the People: The Life and Work of Estes Kefauver* (1972). Jack Anderson and Fred Blumenthal, *The Kefauver Story* (1956), is an informative campaign biography.

Kefauver's two presidential races are described in considerable detail in Paul T. David, Malcolm Moos, and Ralph M. Goldman, *Presidential Nominating Politics in 1952* (5 vols., 1954). Kefauver's late antitrust activities are depicted in detail in the 29-volume *Administered Prices: Report of the Committee on the Judiciary, United States Senate, Made by Its Subcommittee on Antitrust and Monopoly*, (1957–1963). Different aspects of Kefauver's antitrust fights are delineated in John Herling, *The Great Price Conspiracy: The Story of the Antitrust Violations in the Electrical Industry* (1962), and Aaron Wildavsky, *Dixon-Yates: A Study in Power Politics* (1962).

CHARLES L. FONTENAY

KEFAUVER, Grayson Neikirk (31 Aug. 1900–4 Jan. 1946), educator and administrator, was born in Middletown, Maryland, the son of Oliver Henry Kefauver and Lillie May Neikirk, farmers. He attended a one-room school, the Valley View School, in Middletown and graduated from Middletown High School, to which he drove a horse and buggy, at the age of sixteen. After attending Franklin and Marshall College in Lancaster, Pennsylvania, and Heidelberg College in Tiffin, Ohio, Kefauver transferred to the University of Texas and then, because of health problems, to the University of Arizona, where he received an A.B. in 1921. He received an M.A. in 1925 from the Leland Stanford Junior University and a Ph.D. in 1928 from the University of Minnesota.

In the intervals between his advanced studies, Kefauver learned his craft through practical experience. After graduating from the University of Arizona, he became a high school teacher and vice principal in Tucson, where he married Anna Elizabeth Skinner on 25 December 1922. They had three children. In 1923 they moved to Fresno, California, where he was an elementary school principal, vice principal of the senior high school, and director of research for the city schools while pursuing an M.A. at Stanford.

Kefauver accepted a position as instructor of education at the University of Minnesota in 1926, received his doctorate there, and was appointed assistant professor in 1928. Following three years (1929–1932) as associate professor of secondary education at Teacher's College, Columbia University, Kefauver returned to Stanford to become visiting professor of education in 1932 and professor of education and dean of the school of education in 1933.

Kefauver served as a member of the staff of the National Survey of Secondary Education from 1930 to 1932, specializing in school organization. From 1933 to 1939 he was a member of the National Occupation Conference. He served as vice president of the National Association of Colleges and Departments of Education in 1936–1937 was its secretary-treasurer from

1937 to 1940. He was vice chair of the American Council on Education in 1938–1939, vice president of the Progressive Education Association from 1939 to 1942, and president of the National Society for the Study of Education in 1942–1943.

In 1943 Kefauver took a leave of absence from Stanford and moved to Washington, D.C., where he participated as chair in the formation of a worldwide organization, the Liaison Committee for International Education. The primary product of this committee was a plan for a two international educational agencies, a temporary one to address problems immediately following the war and a permanent one concerned with cultural and educational development. In an address to the committee, Kefauver outlined the role of the permanent agency: "The international organization for education should adequately and justly represent, in the transitional period, all the United Nations and eventually all nations. It should conduct studies, give advisory service on request, promote the exchange of people and materials and facilitate international cooperation in educational, cultural, and intellectual fields."

In 1944 Kefauver was appointed as a U.S. delegate to the Conference of Allied Ministers of Education, held in London in April of that year. The delegation was authorized by the State Department to work with the conference to establish a United Nations educational organization to assist in the reconstruction of education in postwar Europe. Following the April meeting, Kefauver remained in London as the American liaison to the conference with the purpose of preparing for the establishment of the United Nations Educational, Scientific, and Cultural Organization (UNESCO).

The constitutional conference that created UNESCO was held in London, 1–16 November 1945. Kefauver served as spokesman for the American delegation to the conference and, at its conclusion, was named American representative to the commission to implement UNESCO. While on a speaking tour to promote public understanding and support for the UNESCO charter, Kefauver suffered a cerebral hemorrhage and died in Los Angeles.

The UNESCO charter was ratified by the US Senate and signed by President Harry Truman in June 1946. It was through the efforts of Kefauver, on behalf of the United States, that UNESCO came to be, and he demonstrated his ability, skill, and enthusiasm for working with committees in its establishment. Kefauver's unexpected death at an early age came at the very time when he had attained international prominence as an effective diplomat in educational policies and transinstitutional coordination. He represented a new generation of educational leaders whose approaches to administration and planning, which had been taught and advocated in American graduate schools of education and implemented in the municipal public school systems of the United States after World War I, had gained worldwide prominence and respect, thanks to Kefauver's influence in conferences and discussions.

The combination of structure and style in decision making that Kefauver brought to planning for popularization of formal education in the United States also became the model for policies and programs in the emerging strategies for rebuilding cultural institutions and creating new international educational programs at the end of World War II.

• Documents dealing with Kefauver's professional work on the faculty and as dean of the School of Education at Stanford are housed in the Stanford University archives. Kefauver was the author of *Appraising Guidance in Secondary Schools* (1941) as well as of a number of monographs and articles on the subjects of guidance counseling and school organization. He coauthored, with Walter V. Kaulfers and Holland D. Roberts, *Foreign Languages and Cultures in American Education* (1942) and *English for Social Living* (1943). For information on his career, see Harold Bienvenu, "The Educational Career of Grayson Neikirk Kefauver" (Ph.D. diss., Stanford Univ., 1956); and for information on the early years of UNESCO, see Walter H. C. Laves and Charles A. Thomson, *UNESCO: Purpose, Progress, Prospects* (1957). Kefauver's obituary is in the *New York Times*, 6 Jan. 1946.

JOHN R. THELIN
SHARON THELIN-BLACKBURN
DAVID CAMPAIGNE

KEHEW, Mary Morton Kimball (8 Sept. 1859–13 Feb. 1918), social reformer, was born Mary Morton Kimball, in Boston, Massachusetts, the daughter of Moses Day Kimball, a banker, and Susan Tillinghast. She received private schooling and studied in Europe for two years before marrying William Brown Kehew, an oil merchant, in 1880; they had no children. He supported her lifelong reform activism, although he did not himself participate in social reform.

In 1886 Kehew joined the Women's Educational and Industrial Union of Boston (WEIU). Founded in 1877, the organization helped girls from rural New England make a smooth and safe transition to the city. In 1892 she became president, a post she would hold until her death. As president, Kehew redirected the focus of the union, advocating an educational approach to solving the problems of working women in cities. As early as 1895, the union began to offer vocational education to young women in dressmaking, housekeeping, and sales, while also maintaining its employment counseling services and legal aid to young women. By 1910 the union had also established an Appointment Bureau to help college-educated women pursue professional careers. Under Kehew's leadership, the union further expanded its agenda to take on other progressive reforms in Boston: child care and hygiene, child labor, and services to the blind. Kehew was a founder of the Denison Settlement, which became an important meeting ground for labor organizers. She also founded the Woolson House for blind women and was active in both the State Commission for Industrial Education and the Massachusetts Child Labor Commission.

Believing that collective action was the key to social change, Kehew was also active in the labor movement.

In 1891 she, along with Mary Kenney O'Sullivan of the American Federation of Labor, helped found the Union for Industrial Progress (UIP) to organize unions for working women in the bookbinding, tobacco, laundry, and garment trades. Anticipating the strategy of the Women's Trade Union League (WTUL) after its founding in 1903, Kehew and O'Sullivan conducted informal meetings of working women, encouraging them to join trade unions as an important step toward improving their working conditions.

Kehew's activism in the UIP led to her election as the first national president of the WTUL, a post she held from 1903 until 1904. During her presidency, she established a research department to enable the WTUL to acquire statistics on women's working conditions and "to train women to secure the facts." The statistics they gathered brought to light the need for legislation to protect working people from economic hardship and health hazards at work. The WTUL's research department also aided in the creation of the Massachusetts Department of Labor and Industry. In 1905 she created a research department within the WEIU, which between 1907 and 1915 prepared a series of model reports on Boston's working women. Yet Kehew's fact-finding methods were only one aspect of her approach to social reform. She also cultivated grass roots support for social justice causes, diligently courting the support of working women, other social reformers, political bosses, and legislators. Sustained by these groups, and especially by the support of the unions she had helped to organize, Kehew led several successful legislative campaigns in Massachusetts. Between 1906 and 1918 she used the WTUL research findings to bolster arguments for reform legislation, including minimum wage, old-age pensions, factory inspections, and the regulation of the sale of milk. Like other leading women reformers of her generation, she pursued a four-part strategy: "investigate, educate, legislate, enforce." Having pioneered in investigations, she served on many of the agencies that enforced reform legislation.

Kehew was the archetype of the volunteer professional woman in the Progressive era. She was deeply admired by those with whom she worked. Her selfless pursuit of social justice and personal generosity inspired others to greater activism. The economist Emily Greene Balch wrote that Mary "believed *literally* in democracy and a fair deal for everyone. . . . She was not seeking credit, but *results* and if the credit went elsewhere so much the better" (*Improper Bostonian*, p. 115). Kehew died in her home in Boston.

• The papers of the Women's Educational and Industrial Union, Schlesinger Library, Radcliffe College, have a scrapbook devoted to Kehew. The papers also contain annual reports and a manuscript by S. Agnes Donham, *History of the Women's Educational and Industrial Union* (1955), which illuminate Kehew's career. For Kehew's family background, see Leonard A. Morrison and Stephen P. Sharples, *History of the Kimball Family in America* (1897), although her birthplace is incorrectly given as Lynn. The best treatment of Kehew's work can be found in Sarah Deutsch, "Learning to Talk More Like a Man: Boston Women's Class-Bridging Organizations, 1870–1940," *American Historical Review* 97 (Apr. 1992): 379–404. Kehew is vividly described in Mercedes M. Randall, *Improper Bostonian: Emily Greene Balch* (1964). She is mentioned in Kenneth L. Mark, *Delayed by Fire, Being the Early History of Simmons College* (1945); and Elizabeth Anne Payne, *Reform, Labor, and Feminism: Margaret Dreier Robins and the Women's Trade Union League* (1988). Obituaries are in the *Boston Transcript*, 13 Feb. 1918; the *Boston Herald and Journal*, 14 Feb. 1918; and *Life and Labor*, Apr. 1918.

KATHRYN KISH SKLAR

KEIFER, Joseph Warren (30 Jan. 1836–22 Apr. 1932), soldier, congressman, and Speaker of the U.S. House of Representatives, was born near Springfield, Ohio, the son of Joseph Keifer, a farmer and sometime surveyor, and Mary Smith. Keifer was educated at home and in the district school. He taught for one term (1852–1853), worked on the family's farm, and attended nearby Antioch College (1854–1855). In 1856, after studying some on his own, he began reading law with a Springfield firm and was admitted to the bar in January 1858. Following a two-month tour of various midwestern cities, evaluating them as possible sites for relocation, Keifer returned to practice law in Springfield, where he remained for the rest of his life.

Establishing himself in Springfield, Keifer joined a local fire company. In 1860 he married Eliza Stout, with whom he had four children. The outbreak of the Civil War was the defining experience of Keifer's life. An able and valorous soldier, he remained in the army throughout the war, despite being wounded four times. He enlisted on 19 April 1861 and was commissioned a major. He was subsequently promoted to lieutenant colonel and brevetted as a brigadier general in October 1864. After participating in the battles at Petersburg and Richmond, he was promoted to major general on 9 April 1865.

Mustered out of the army on 26 June 1865, Keifer resumed his legal career, but he also became active in veterans' affairs and in politics. He served the Grand Army of the Republic (GAR) as commander of the Department of Ohio, 1868–1870, and junior vice commander, 1871–1872. He also helped set up the Soldiers and Sailors' Orphans Home in Xenia, Ohio, in 1868 and was a trustee of this institution from 1870 to 1878 and again in 1903–1904. His political involvement began when he organized a "Bohemian Club" of fellow Republicans that for thirty years shaped public affairs in Clark County. Elected to the Ohio State Senate in 1867, he served in the 1868–1869 session as a member of the important Judiciary Committee. He supported the Fourteenth and Fifteenth amendments and defended the principles of universal suffrage and political equality.

An active stump speaker, Keifer served as a delegate to the GOP National Convention in 1876 and that year was elected to the first of his seven terms in the U.S. House of Representatives. His service on the Committee on Claims shaped his cautious approach to financial claims on the federal government, especially from southern states, and in 1879 he supported implementation of the plan to redeem greenbacks. His activities on the Elections Committee reinforced his belief that the franchise of blacks should be protected, even to the point of using federal troops. Black suffrage and southern unreliability remained the central issues of Keifer's career. These positions, combined with his continuing support for President Ulysses S. Grant and his strong association with the GAR, made him a determined member of the Stalwart faction of the Republican party. He criticized as duplicitous the Half-Breed leaders James G. Blaine and Thomas Reed, his rival in Congress and later successor as Speaker, and while noting the limitations of Stalwart leader Roscoe Conkling, he described him as a great man.

Keifer's prominence in Congress grew because of factional connections in the party as well as his increased seniority and experience. Thus, when Republicans held a majority in the House in 1881, Keifer was the Stalwart faction's choice for Speaker, and he won the support of the divided party caucus. His one term in that office was controversial and relatively unsuccessful. Democrats complained of his partisanship, especially in committee appointments, while Half-Breed Republicans, especially future Speaker Thomas Reed, were highly critical, even scornful. Keifer felt that his term was successful and later touted various legislative measures passed during the two years, but except for the civil service reform, none of the measures was especially notable.

More significant than legislation was Keifer's decision to prohibit dilatory legislative motions, which allowed the closing of debate in the House and increased legislative effectiveness in that chamber. He also considered the equally significant measure of counting as present all members actually in the chamber, including those not answering the quorum call, an attack on the "disappearing quorum" that was later a crucial part of "Reed's Rules." In his memoirs Keifer claimed that he had proposed this rule but that Reed's opposition had dissuaded him.

In 1883 Republicans were again in the minority. Although Keifer was the caucus's losing nominee for Speaker and served on the important Appropriations and Rules committees, Reed effectively supplanted him as party leader. In 1884 Keifer failed to win renomination and so left office.

Keifer returned to military service during the Spanish-American War, when President William McKinley appointed him major general on 9 June 1898. He commanded the Seventh Army Corps and the American forces that marched into Havana after Spanish forces withdrew on 1 January 1899. He returned to private life on 12 May. Keifer again became active in veterans' affairs, serving as the first commander in chief of the Spanish-American War Veterans from 1900 to 1901 and in 1903–1904 as the Ohio commander of the Loyal Legion.

In 1904 Keifer returned to Congress, where he remained until his defeat in 1910. He was also a delegate to the 1908 national convention. He championed some of the same issues that had concerned him before. In particular, he criticized southern states' disfranchisement of blacks and argued that they should, as a result, have their representation reduced. Like a number of Civil War veterans active in politics after 1900, Keifer was a strong advocate of peace. While celebrating the causes for which he had fought, he believed that war had grown too deadly and awful to be permitted any longer. In 1910 he addressed the Interparliamentary Union Conference on Universal Peace in Brussels, in 1913 he was president of the commission memorializing Commodore Oliver Hazard Perry's naval victory in the War of 1812 and touted the resultant neutralizing of the Great Lakes, and in 1914 he was in Berlin on his way to Stockholm for a peace conference when war began.

Following his final electoral defeat in 1910, Keifer returned to Springfield, continuing his legal practice with two of his three sons until 1923. He was president of the Lagonda National Bank of Springfield, which he had begun in 1873. He also maintained his role as trustee of Antioch College, serving from 1873 into the 1920s. A life member of the Ohio Archaeological and Historical Society, he was the author of various historical and literary studies. Keifer died in Springfield.

• Collections of Keifer's papers are at the Clark County Historical Society in Springfield, Ohio; the Library of Congress, concerning his war activities 1861–1865; and Syracuse University Library. In addition to numerous printed orations and campaign speeches, Keifer published several historical articles in the *Ohio Archaeological and Historical Quarterly*; two articles concerning the authorship of Shakespeare's plays in *Open Court* 18 (1904); "Power of Congress to Reduce Representation in Congress and in the Electoral College: A Reply," *North American Review* 187 (Feb. 1906); and an attempt to refute criticism of his Speakership, "Address of General J. Warren Keifer," *Ohio Archaeological and Historical Quarterly* 22 (1913): 435–54. His most important work is *Slavery and Four Years of War: A Political History of Slavery in the United States, Together with a Narrative of the Campaigns and Battles of the Civil War in Which the Author Took Part: 1861–1865* (1900), which provides a useful and relatively lengthy exposition of Keifer's views of the history of American slavery, the Civil War, and his congressional career along with his war memoirs. The most useful biographical sketches are in Charles B. Galbreath, *History of Ohio* (1925); Benjamin F. Prince, *Standard History of Springfield and Clark County, Ohio* (1922); Marshall T. Carrington, *A History of the Courts and Lawyers of Ohio* (1934); and "General J. Warren Keifer: Tribute of Clark County Bar Association," *Ohio Archaeological and Historical Quarterly* 41 (1932): 572–82. J. Warren McCall, *Thomas Brackett Reed* (1904), essentially provides Reed's critical perspective; and Ari Hoogenboom, *Outlawing the Spoils* (1961), claims that Keifer was hostile to this reform. H. B. Fuller, *Speakers of the House* (1909), is critical of Keifer. The most useful guide to Congress is Joel Silbey et al., *Encyclopedia of the American Legislative System* (1994).

PHILIP R. VANDERMEER

KEIMER, Samuel (11 Feb. 1688–1742?), printer and poet, was born in Southwark, England. His parents' names are unknown. He was admitted to the Merchant Taylors' School in 1699. In 1707 Keimer was apprenticed to Robert Tookey, a London printer and, with his mother and sister Mary, joined the French Prophets, or Camisards, a small but enthusiastic religious sect led by Sir Richard Bulkeley and John Lacy. After Keimer married in 1713, he opened in 1722 a printing shop, which prospered only briefly. Imprisoned for debts, he nevertheless managed to publish the *London Post*. During a subsequent imprisonment for writing seditous articles that appeared in the *Weekly Journal* in 1717, Keimer wrote the works for which he was best known in England: *A Brand Pluck'd from the Burning* (1718), an often self-pitying autobiographical work that provides the most thorough firsthand account of the Camisards in London; *A Search after Religion among the Many Modern Pretenders to It* (1718); and *The Platonick Courtship* (1718); a combination of the Song of Solomon, vulgar commentary, and doggerel verse.

In 1722 Keimer deserted his wife and home for Philadelphia, where he proposed a plan for the biblical education of male African Americans. According to Benjamin Franklin, who met Keimer in 1723, Keimer "was an odd fish; ignorant of common life, fond of rudely opposing receiv'd opinions, slovenly to extream dirtiness, enthusiastic in some points of religion, and a little knavish withal." Keimer so antagonized the Philadelphia Monthly Meeting of Friends, with whom he had attempted to establish religious and business connections, that they disowned him for publishing *A Parable* (1723).

Keimer, nonetheless, was a significant force in early American printing. Between 1722 and 1729 he published pirated editions of Jacob Taylor's and Titan Leeds's almanacs and reprinted Sir Richard Steele's *The Crisis*, William Penn's Charter of Privileges of 1701, an English dictionary, and two histories, one of Diodorus Siculus, and the other of the wars of Charles XII of Sweden. In addition, he issued Epictetus's *Morals*, the first translation of a Latin or Greek classic in America; printed William Sewel's *History of the Quakers*, with Franklin's assistance; and was largely responsible for introducing Daniel Defoe's works to Pennsylvania.

In December 1728 Keimer began publishing the *Universal Instructor in All Arts and Sciences; and Pennsylvania Gazette*, a response to Andrew Bradford's *American Weekly Mercury* and to Franklin's plans for a similar weekly. Keimer attempted to reprint in its entirety Ephraim Chambers's encyclopedia (from which he borrowed his title) in the weekly, as well as including an occasional poem of his own (one against drinking rum and several aimed at Franklin's "Busy Body") and limited news and advertisements. When he relinquished control of the paper to Franklin in October 1729, he was still printing, for the eleventh week in a row, sections from Chambers's entry on "Air."

Keimer's 1723 elegy to Aquila Rose is best remembered for Franklin's account of its composition—Keimer devised the poem as he set the type for its printing—and for its place as "perhaps the worst elegy ever written" (*Cambridge History of American Literature*):

> In Sable CHARACTERS the News is Read,
> Our Rose is wither'd and our Eagle's fled.
> In that our dear Aquila Rose is dead.
> Cropt in the Blooming of his precious Youth!
> Who can forbear to weep at such a Truth!

Despite various business schemes (including a lottery) and publications, financial losses forced Keimer to sell his press to his apprentice, David Harry, in 1729. He then sailed for Barbados, where he published "The Sorrowful Lamentation of Samuel Keimer," alluding to the relative prosperity of Andrew Bradford and his father William Bradford:

> In Penn's wooded country, type feels no disaster,
> Their printer is rich and is made their Post Master.
> His father, a printer, is paid for his work,
> And wallows in plenty just now at New York.
> Tho' quite past his labour, and old as my grannum,
> The government pays him pounds sixty per annum.

Keimer also issued the *Barbadoes Gazette*—the island's first newspaper (1731–1738) and apparently the first twice-weekly paper in the Americas. Keimer died in Bridgetown, Barbados.

• For more information on Keimer and his work, see Stephen Bloore, "Samuel Keimer: A Footnote to the Life of Franklin," *Pennsylvania Magazine of History and Biography* 54 (1930): 255–87; C. Lennart Carlson, "Samuel Keimer: A Study in the Transit of English Culture to Colonial Pennsylvania," *Pennsylvania Magazine of History and Biography* 61 (1937): 357–86; Benjamin Franklin, *The Autobiography of Benjamin Franklin*, ed. Leonard Labaree et al. (1964); Chester Jorgensen, "A Brand Flung at Colonial Orthodoxy: Samuel J. Keimer's 'Universal Instructor in All Arts and Sciences,'" *Journalism Quarterly* 12 (1935), 272–77; James Sappenfield, *A Sweet Instruction: Franklin's Journalism as a Literary Apprenticeship* (1973); and Charles E. Clark and Charles Wetherell, "The Measure of Maturity: The Pennsylvania Gazette, 1728–1765," *William and Mary Quarterly* 3, no. 46 (1989): 279–303.

TIMOTHY K. CONLEY

KEITH, Arthur (30 Sept. 1864–7 Feb. 1944), structural geologist and geologic mapper, was born in St. Louis, Missouri, the son of Harrison Alonzo Keith, a high school principal and city administrator, and Mary Elizabeth Richardson. Keith grew up in Quincy, Massachusetts, attended Harvard University, and, after graduating in 1885, investigated the local geology around his hometown. In connection with graduate work at Harvard, for which he received an A.M., he mapped for the Massachusetts Topographic Survey in 1886. In June 1887 Keith joined the U.S. Geological Survey as a field assistant to Bailey Willis in Alabama and began his career with that organization. The following year, he began geologic mapping on his own in eastern Tennessee, a region that was to concern him for decades.

One of the premier fieldmen of the USGS and second only to Nelson H. Darton in total contributions to the *Geologic Atlas of the United States*, Keith authored sixteen of the approximately 200 folios (maps of one degree latitude and longitude). He and Darton collaborated on the Washington, D.C., folio, and Keith published fifteen himself between 1894 and 1907. He is best known for his work in the southern Appalachians, where he mapped 22,000 square miles, but during his early career he also mapped in West Virginia and Maryland. Although he had an intimate knowledge of the mountain chain extending northward into Quebec, his southern work is more highly regarded than his later mapping in the complex terrain of western New England.

Keith's fieldwork in the South was greatly hampered by poor transportation, lack of roads, and difficult living conditions. Notwithstanding these limitations, Keith produced extremely accurate maps for his time by "pace and compass" traverses between control points established by using an alidade, essentially a telescope fitted with cross-hairs and a device to measure angles, or transits. In this work, the control points are determined by standard surveying method, and from these spots one takes a compass bearing and uses uniform paces to measure distance to a rock outcrop that is then plotted on the map.

Keith recorded prodigious amounts of data on his draft maps; his contemporaries described him as a field geologist of perseverance, efficiency, and, above all, extraordinary energy and endurance. The large folds and, far more significantly, the overthrusts, wherein masses of rock were moved great distances westward, were then hardly recognized. Keith patiently unraveled the complex structure and the succession of strata confused by repetition of beds resulting from faulting and thrusting. The concept of overthrusts, expounded in Switzerland and being applied to the Scottish Highlands, was a new notion in American geology, yet Keith was able to recognize and exploit the significance of this new approach to the three-dimensional interpretation of mountain structure.

This work on structure had implications for coal deposits and iron ores, both of which Keith studied in Tennessee. Perhaps his greatest stratigraphic problem dealt with the Ocoee Series, a thick sequence of rocks in the Blue Ridge and Great Smoky mountains. The Ocoee lies between the crystalline rocks of the Piedmont and the undoubted Paleozoic rocks in the folded Appalachians. Consensus on the precise geologic age of these old rocks had still not been reached by the 1990s.

In 1907 Keith succeeded Bailey Willis as head of the Section of Areal and Structural Geology of the USGS. This position entailed national responsibilities in mapping, but Keith spent most of his first field season in the job in Massachusetts and Vermont coordinating the work of several field geologists. Though known as a harsh critic of careless mapping, Keith devoted much of his effort to assisting younger men in office and field, thereby reducing his own research time. Apart from maps and their associated text, he produced few publications.

During a USGS reorganization in 1913, Keith was placed in charge of geologic mapping east of the Rocky Mountains. As part of the Geological Survey effort during World War I, he made geographical studies of the New England border and, more important, documented the sources of high-grade limestone for the nitrogen-fixing plant under construction at Muscle Shoals, Alabama. In 1916 he married Elizabeth Marye Smith; they had no children.

After a "sabbatical" year as professor of geology at the University of Texas, Keith retired from administration in 1924 to devote his last decade of USGS service to field mapping in the northern Appalachians. He also conducted field studies in 1933 as consultant for the Tennessee Valley Authority on the site for Norris Dam. Like many geologists of his generation, he retained an office and continued field studies for more than a decade after official retirement.

Keith's structural studies provided the background for special assignments. In 1925 he investigated a major earthquake in the St. Lawrence Valley, and two years later one in Maine, but he is best known in seismology for his work in connection with the effects of the Grand Banks 1928 earthquake and resulting tidal wave. He made a special study in 1926 of eastern Tennessee and western North Carolina in connection with the proposed Great Smoky Mountains National Park. In 1933 Keith began compilation of a geologic map of Maine.

Highly regarded by his colleagues, despite his sparse publication record, Keith was elected president of the Geological Society of America in 1927. His presidential address, "Structural Symmetry in North America," which challenged the concept of continental drift, reflected prevailing attitudes among the profession. In 1928 he was elected to the National Academy of Sciences and almost immediately was appointed chair of the National Research Council's Division of Geology and Geography, succeeding Waldemar Lindgren. Keith served simultaneously as treasurer of the National Academy and of the National Research Council from 1932 to 1940. He was also active in other organizations, particularly in a financial capacity. Keith died in Silver Spring, Maryland.

• Biographical accounts include memorials by Esper S. Larsen, Jr., in Geological Society of America, *Proceedings for 1944* (1945): 241–57, and by Chester R. Longwell, in National Academy of Sciences, *Biographical Memoirs* 29 (1956): 191–200. Both memorials include a portrait and bibliography. See also Arthur C. Swinnerton's memorial in the *Bulletin of the American Association of Petroleum Geologists* 28 (1944): 1553–56. Aspects of Keith's career are recounted in Eugene C. Robertson, ed., *Centennial History of the Geological Society of Washington* (1993), pp. 75–76, and Mary C. Rabbitt, *Minerals, Lands, and Geology for the Common Defence and General Welfare*, vol. 3: *1904–1939* (1986).

ELLIS L. YOCHELSON

KEITH, B. F. (26 Jan. 1846–26 Mar. 1914), theater owner and manager, was born Benjamin Franklin Keith in Hillsboro Bridge, New Hampshire, the son of

Samuel C. Keith (occupation unknown) and Rhoda Gerould. Sent to live at a western Massachusetts farm at age seven, Keith was educated in district schools there. Attracted by a country circus, in 1863 Keith left for New York, where he worked for Bunnell's and later Barnum's museums.

After serving as mess boy on a coastal steamer, Keith traveled with various circuses as a "grifter," a "long con" specialist selling, for 1,000 percent profit, useless items such as the "blood tester," two pressable, hollow glass balls connected by a curved, twisted glass tube containing pink liquid. In 1873 Keith married Mary Catherine Branley of Providence, Rhode Island. The Keiths had one child. Called by vaudevillian and memoirist Hartley Davis an "inspirational" Catholic churchwoman, Mrs. Keith was morally adamant: she "would tolerate no profanity, suggestive allusions, *doubles entendres*, off-color monkey business." She also would bring Keith the support of her church.

In 1876 Keith met another circus-struck New Englander, Edward F. Albee, an accomplished shill who would a decade later become Keith's right-hand man. Robert W. Snyder claims that Keith and Albee "were never showmen at heart, they were business men, kingmakers with national aspirations" (pp. 26–27). Keith toured his own circus without success, and in 1880 he began making and selling brooms in Providence. But in 1883 Keith tried combining entertainment genres. He rented a Boston store, in one room of which he created a Barnum-style museum featuring a baby midget and a mermaid, a chicken with a human face, and the "biggest hog in America." In the other room he staged variety entertainments.

Keith next became part owner of Boston's Gaiety Theatre, terming his programs "vaudeville." This elegant variant on the term "variety" became identified with Keith. In 1885 he began "continuous performance" (10 A.M. to 10 P.M.) vaudeville at Boston's Bijou Theatre. He wrote of this innovation's attractiveness, "The theatre is always occupied . . . the show in full swing . . . everything [is] bright, cheerful, inviting." Admission cost 10 cents—15 cents with a chair. A balding man with a large, forthright mustache and piercing eyes, Keith carried a hammer in his belt, puttered, improved things, seeking to make his theater "homelike." His wife, in apron and bandanna, went through the Bijou like a housekeeper.

Still, Keith's theater did not fill until he hired Albee, who added to the variety bill condensed versions of Gilbert and Sullivan's *Mikado*, at that time America's rage. They advertised: "Why pay $1.50 when you can see our show for 25 cents?" Keith now spoke widely of his dedication to raising variety's "coarse and vulgar" level. New York impresario Tony Pastor had also pioneered "family variety" as a paying improvement on the genre's honky-tonk past, but Keith's policy and church connections enabled him to borrow heavily and build quickly. By 1893 he owned large theaters in Providence, Philadelphia, and Boston and on New York's Union Square. Describing his cleanup (Albee hired bouncers who cleared the hecklers, foot-stomp-

ers, and cane-pounders from the gallery) as a public service, Keith boasted that his shows attracted the best society. In 1894 the Union Square managers junked the operettas. In response to Pastor's big-star policy, they hired stars of the legitimate stage, thus establishing the all-variety continuous performance policy that characterized vaudeville for four decades.

Keith made "clean and decent" vaudeville his territory. All Keith's houses—the "Sunday School Circuit"—bore this sign: "You are hereby warned that your act must be free from all vulgarity and suggestiveness in words, actions and costumes." Decades later comedian Fred Allen recalled being admonished not to say "slob" or "son of a gun" or "hully gee" if he did not "want to be cancelled peremptorily." Charles Stein noted as the policy's downside the "freak, polite and hammy legit acts that were to make anemic the vigourous, lusty, kick in the belly and lima beans vaudeville which, for all its grossness, was virile and forthright."

During a "robber baron" era in all industries, smaller theatrical forms such as minstrelsy withered and Vaudeville circuits evolved. By the mid-1890s there were three in the Northeast—Keith's, Sylvester A. Poli's, and Frederick F. Proctor's. Vaudeville became the nation's most popular entertainment genre; by 1896 (the same year in which Keith added rudimentary motion pictures to his programs) an estimated one million attended weekly. Higher salaries for performers resulted; their booking agents acquired new influence.

Keith and Albee attempted to reverse the latter trend in 1900 with the Association of Vaudeville Managers of the United States, which, according to their "prospectus," was "not a trust, but . . . [through] sound business principles . . . [would] regulate performers' salaries, create more compact rights and end damaging competition." Some performers organized into the White Rats (a "part union, part fraternal order" that developed a cooperative circuit) under the romantic George Fuller Golden and for a time blocked Keith-Albee from establishing their vaudeville monopoly.

In 1906 Keith absorbed Proctor's organization, forming America's largest variety conglomerate to date. In the same year, Keith and Albee established the United Booking Office of America, in Snyder's words, "regulating performers' access to theatres and theatres' access to performers." This interlocking of theater ownership and booking agency imitated the success of Klaw and Erlanger's "Syndicate," which had monopolized American legitimate theater since 1896. Thus performers could count on an average thirty-week year but labored under the threat of blacklisting. A subsidiary, the Vaudeville Collection Agency, withheld 10 percent from salaries—5 percent for UBO and 5 percent for the account of the performers' agents—half of which went to UBO anyway. Keith and Albee completed their conquest by forming the National Vaudeville Artists, a "company union." But in 1907 Klaw and Erlanger united with Jake and Lee

Shubert to form a competing circuit, the United States Amusement Company ("Shuberts' Advanced Vaudeville"). After further blacklisting, the Shuberts, Klaw, and Erlanger took $250,000 from Keith to stay out of vaudeville for ten years.

By 1909 Keith had left direct management to Albee. Keith's first wife died in 1910, and in 1913 he married Ethel Bird Chase, a Boston arts patron. They had no children. In 1912 Keith-Albee interlocked with Martin Beck's Orpheum theaters, dominant west of Chicago, creating the 700-theater Keith-Albee-Orpheum circuit. One house thus acquired was the New York Palace, on whose side was painted "the goal of every aspiring vaudevillian." The theater became so prestigious that acts might agree to play for 25–33 percent below their asking rate.

Keith died in Palm Beach, Florida. His circuit continued to expand under Albee (in 1924 acquiring the world's largest theater, New York's Hippodrome). In 1928 Joseph Kennedy merged his Radio Corporation of America with Keith-Orpheum, creating R-K-O Radio motion pictures.

Under Keith and Albee, vaudeville became a huge business, the acceptable family entertainment (later supplanted by talking movies as the nation's favorite). Even adversary George Fuller Golden admitted, "If credit were a thing to be spoken of, unquestionably to the late Tony Pastor and to Mr. B. F. Keith and his clever lieutenants should go the palms. . . . Mr. Keith . . . swept the mire and slush. . . . He worked hard to banish vulgarity, slang and profanity from [vaudeville's] stages and succeeded."

• The Keith/Albee Special Collections are located in the University of Iowa Library, Iowa City. Other papers and clippings are in the theater collection at the New York Public Library for the Performing Arts, Lincoln Center, and the theater collection at Harvard University. Keith is very prominent in such works as Dromio [George Fuller Golden], My Lady Vaudeville (1909); Douglas Gilbert, American Vaudeville (1940); Charles Stein, American Vaudeville as Seen by Its Contemporaries (1984), which includes some of Keith's own essays; and Robert Snyder, The Voice of the City: Vaudeville and Popular Culture in New York City (1989). Obituaries are in the New York Times and the Boston Transcript, both 27 Mar. 1914.

JAMES ROSS MOORE

KEITH, George (c. 1638–27 Mar. 1716), Quaker theologian, founder of the "Christian Quakers," and Anglican priest, was born in Peterhead Aberdeenshire, Scotland, to a family he later described as loyal to the Solemn League and Covenant and who disowned him after he became a Quaker. Nothing else is known of his parentage or early years. Keith attended Marischall College, Aberdeen (1654–1658), received an M.A., and prepared to be a Presbyterian minister. Later he referred to universities as "the stews of Anti-Christ," but he had nonetheless gained an extensive knowledge in mathematics, philosophy, and languages. Keith, who read Descartes, testified that he became a Quaker through reading the Cambridge Platonist Henry More. In 1662 he was imprisoned for six months for his beliefs and wrote Immediate Revelation . . . Not Ceased, which was published in 1668 and was one of the best early defenses of Friends' ideas. Keith soon emerged as a leading Scottish Quaker. In 1667 he spent ten months in solitary confinement and was imprisoned again for fourteen months, beginning in March 1676, with Robert Barclay.

Keith married Elizabeth Johnston, the daughter of a doctor from Aberdeen; they had three children. In 1677 she and Keith joined George Fox, Barclay, and William Penn in a missionary journey to Holland and Germany. After his return Keith founded a boarding school. In 1682 he was imprisoned again for his religious beliefs and convicted of praemunire.

Keith and his fellow Scotchman Barclay, both raised as Presbyterians and given a rigorous theological education, together provided the clearest systematic expositions of Quaker beliefs. Keith provided Barclay with two important concepts, which the latter used in Apology for the True Christian Divinity (1678). The first was the Vehiculum Dei as a description of the inward light of Christ that conveyed within a person a presence but not the fullness of God. The second was the story of Hai Ebn Yokdan, which allegedly proved that a child shipwrecked on an island with no contact with other humans could inwardly arrive at the truths of religion. Keith was more adventurous intellectually than Barclay or most other early Friends. He retained an interest in mathematics, read in the cabala, and corresponded with Cambridge Platonists. He discussed mysteries of faith with mystics such as Anne Viscountess Conway and Francis Mercurius van Helmont and considered as a postulate of reason reincarnation, or the transmigration of souls, as a means used by God to make salvation available to good heathens who could not know of Jesus.

Through extensive publications, theological debates with Puritan and Anglican ministers, and preaching while traveling in the ministry, Keith helped to organize Quakerism intellectually. Immediate Revelation . . . Not Ceased, The Universal Free Grace of the Gospell (1671), and The Way to the City of God Described (1678) remain his most accessible Quaker writings, but his detailed critiques of opponents were influential in his lifetime.

In 1684 Keith moved to New Jersey, where he became surveyor-general of East Jersey with responsibility for drawing the dividing lines between East and West Jersey and their border with southern New York. He acquired 1,000 acres of land in New Jersey and 500 acres in Pennsylvania. In 1689 he became headmaster of the Latin school in Philadelphia. Entrusting much of his teaching responsibilities to an usher, Keith spent his time in the service of Friends, either traveling in the ministry or writing religious books. His most significant journey was to Rhode Island, where he engaged in a public debate and wrote a searing attack against Puritanism, The Presbyterian and Independent Visible Churches in New England and Elsewhere Brought to the Test (1689). After his return to

Pennsylvania, Keith published a catechism and in 1690 proposed several reforms to the Philadelphia Yearly Meeting of Ministers.

Neither contemporaries nor historians have agreed on the reasons for Keith's rupture from the Pennsylvania Friends in 1691. After the split occurred, the majority Quaker party insisted that Keith's acerbic personality and his doctrinal innovations were the causes. Keith and his followers, called "Keithians" or "Christian Quakers," insisted that the Philadelphia Friends were distorting Christian and Quaker doctrines and that his preaching and reforms preserved a rigorous pure faith. The deaths of Barclay (1690) and Fox (1691) may have caused Keith to seek to become the recognized Quaker leader. The social and political cleavages in Pennsylvania clearly influenced the course of the separation but not necessarily its origins.

The controversy began in 1691 when William Stockdale, an elderly minister, accused Keith of preaching two Christs. Keith demanded vindication from the Meeting of Ministers, who condemned Stockdale but refused to endorse all of Keith's ideas. The next year Thomas Fitzwater accused Keith of denying the sufficiency of Christ within and brought as witness William Stockdale. The Meeting of Ministers' second attempt at mediation failed, and, after failure to agree on the contents of a confession of faith, Keith began to discern heresy among weighty Friends. In the early summer of 1692 the Philadelphia meetings for worship divided between supporters of Keith and the majority party, led by Samuel Jennings and Thomas Lloyd. William Bradford, the only printer in the colony, published several tracts by Keith recounting his grievances and the errors of the Philadelphia Friends. Bradford also offered to print the responses of the majority party, but Quakers had long held that internal divisions should not be exposed to the world. Keith's charge of fundamental doctrinal error was especially damaging when Friends were trying to persuade the English government that they were entitled to the benefits of the Act of Toleration. For the majority Quaker party, Keith's publications allowed the dispute to be portrayed as not over beliefs or piety but over following correct Friendly procedures. Virtually all the extant information about the early stages of the schism comes from Keith's pamphlets because the answers of Jennings and Caleb Pusey were published in London in 1694 and 1696. In late 1692 and 1693 Keith's tracts complained of the power of ministers, the too-close relationship between religious and political authority in Pennsylvania that led to compromises on the testimonies on oaths and pacifism, heresies among ministers and laity, and many Friends' lack of moral purity. In 1693 Keith published the first American antislavery tract.

The Philadelphia Meeting for Ministers and the Yearly Meeting in July 1692 declared Keith out of unity. Claiming that the magistrates (who were also Quaker ministers) had been libeled by Keith, the government of Pennsylvania seized Bradford's press and charged Keith, Bradford, and Thomas Budd with undermining legal authority. Keith's account of their trial and conviction reads like the Penn-Mead trial, only here the Quaker magistrates are the persecutors. Following the Glorious Revolution, the Crown seized control of Pennsylvania. Governor Benjamin Fletcher released Keith in 1693, and Keith returned to London seeking vindication. He left behind a following of Christian Quakers who had adopted his requirement of a confession of beliefs before membership.

Before and after Keith arrived, London Quakers tried to bring conciliation. When Keith realized he could not gain vindication because of his manner of proceeding, he began attacking the English Friends. The London Yearly Meeting disowned Keith in 1695. Keith preached against Quakers in a hired hall in London and during travels around England. He published an attack against Penn, terming him a deist, and a critique of Barclay's *Apology*. Keith began to appreciate the value of outward baptism and communion. In 1700 he took communion, joined the Church of England, and was ordained a priest. He played an active role in the Society for the Propagation of the Gospel (SPG) and returned to America in 1702 as a missionary seeking to win back dissenters to the Church of England. He attempted to preach in Quaker meetings, wrote pamphlets against the Friends, and sought to create new Anglican churches. During his two-year stay in America he converted a few Friends to Anglicanism and persuaded some of the Christian Quakers to follow their leader's example, but he could not prevail on others who had become Baptists or Mennonites. Keith's tactics, like other activities of the newly invigorated SPG, served to embitter relations between Quakers and Anglicans in many areas. Keith returned to England in 1704 and continued to make tours preaching against the Friends. He became rector of Edburton, Sussex, and died there.

The Keithian controversy destroyed the unified Quaker culture of early Pennsylvania and contributed to the instability in its government and religious bodies from the 1690s until the 1720s. Keith first raised fundamental issues that recurred in colonial Pennsylvania and Quaker history. Quaker reformers in the 1750s unknowingly followed Keith in opposing slavery, seeing Quaker control of government as compromising the testimony on peace and oaths and stressing the need for a purified life. Later ambiguities in Quakerism over a new evangelical emphasis on the outward atonement of Christ rather than sole reliance on the inward light helped precipitate the Hicksite-Orthodox separation in 1827.

• Joseph Smith's *Descriptive Catalogue of Friends' Books* (1867) has twenty-three pages of Keith's writings plus eight more devoted to the schism. J. William Frost, *The Keithian Controversy in Early Pennsylvania* (1980), reprints the most significant writings of the American schism. Keith's *A Journal of Travels from New-Hampshire to Caratuck, on the Continent of North America* (1706) recounts his work for the SPG in America. Ethyn Williams Kirby, *George Keith* (1942), is the best biography and contains a complete bibliography of Keith's writings and manuscripts and those of his opponents.

Contrasting views of the causes of the schism are in Jon Butler, "'Gospel Order Improved,' the Keithian Schism and the Exercise of Quaker Ministerial Authority in Pennsylvania," *William and Mary Quarterly*, 3d ser., 31 (July 1974): 431–52; Frost, "Unlikely Controversialists: Caleb Pusey and George Keith," *Quaker History* 64 (Spring 1975): 16–36; Edwin Bronner, *William Penn's Holy Experiment* (1962); and Gary Nash, *Quakers and Politics: Pennsylvania 1681–1726* (1968).

J. WILLIAM FROST

KEITH, Minor Cooper (19 Jan. 1848–14 June 1929), entrepreneur, was born in Brooklyn, New York, the son of Minor Hubbell Keith, a lumber merchant, and Emily Meiggs, sister of Henry Meiggs, who built railroads in Chile, Bolivia, and Peru. Keith was educated in private schools in Stamford, Connecticut. In 1883 he married Cristina Castro, daughter of José María Castro, who served twice as Costa Rican president. They had no children.

Keith had worked for seven years in various businesses—a New York City store, a lumberyard, and Texas ranches—before his older brother Henry Meiggs Keith called him to Costa Rica in 1871. Their uncle Henry Meiggs had acquired the Costa Rican railroad concession and then turned it over to Henry Keith. After Henry Keith died in 1874, Minor Keith became the head of the project. Two other brothers also died working on this project. In 1873, to supply freight for the railroad before it reached the coffee region of the central plateau, Minor Keith ordered the planting of bananas and shipped out the fruit on the returning railcars that had delivered men and supplies to the railhead. The ships bringing in the labor force and supplies, most commonly from New Orleans, carried the fruit back. In London, where he borrowed millions of pounds sterling to finance his railroad, shipping lines, and fruit operations, he organized the Tropical Trading and Transport Company.

This railroad project passed through such difficult, disease-infested terrain that it cost numerous lives and millions of dollars. It is commonly alleged that 4,000 laborers died during the construction of the first twenty-five miles of track. Initially workers were brought from New Orleans, but the death rate prompted labor unrest and flight to other parts of Central America. Subsequent workers from Italy, Ireland, Sweden, India, Egypt, and other countries proved little different. Keith had the most success with Jamaican laborers. He dealt with the problem of disease with various public works projects in and around Puerto Limón, the terminal for the railroad. He drained the swamps and had water and sewer systems built. The rail line was completed on 7 December 1890, and the contract called for the Costa Rican government to share management after the railroad was completed.

Keith's ability to traffic in railroad contracts and to offer bribes to the right people served to give him control of the Costa Rican and Guatemalan railroads. In 1893, when the Costa Rican Railway was not serving Puerto Limón and Keith's fruit operation well, he organized the Northern Railway, which threatened competition, until the Costa Rican Railway turned over its valuable 99-year lease to his new Costa Rican Northern Railway. In 1904 Keith directly bribed Guatemalan dictator Manuel Estrada Cabrera (with stock worth $50,000) and other key people to obtain control of the main Guatemalan railroads. Later, he organized a New Jersey corporation, the Guatemalan Railroad Company, with a capitalization of $8 million from these holdings.

In the 1890s Keith acquired two additional banana companies, the Colombian Land Company (a British company operating near Santa Marta) and the Snyder Banana Company (a New Jersey company operating in the Panama province of Colombia). Because of financial problems during the depression of the 1890s, in 1899 Keith joined his Tropical Trading and Transport Company with several large fruit and fruit-shipping firms in the Caribbean and Central America, in particular the holdings of Andrew W. Preston, president of Boston Fruit, and a score of smaller operations to create United Fruit, a New Jersey holding company. Keith received $4 million in stock, a 40 percent share of United Fruit. Preston became president and managed operations in Boston while Keith remained in Central America. It is estimated that United Fruit controlled 80 percent of the world banana trade. One of the chief agents for expanding power was its Fruit Despatch Company, which dominated the pricing and distribution of bananas. Keith remained first vice president of United Fruit until 1922.

Keith sought to control all the prime banana land wherever he operated. He expected to own either the land or the railroad and waterways necessary to bring the fruit to a port. He also expected to monopolize the oceanic shipping and marketing arrangements. His determination produced major conflicts with Herbert L. McConnell of American Fruit Company, the Hamburg-American-Passagier-Aktien-Gesellschaft (HAPAG, the giant German shipping firm), and Samuel Zemurray of Cuyamel Fruit Company. The struggle with McConnell began around 1905 and involved the Sixaola region on the Panama–Costa Rican Atlantic coast. The dispute led to armed conflict and a tense border situation until Costa Rica gained firm control of the contested region. A conflict with HAPAG, which began in 1905, involved the German firm's Atlas line, which hauled bananas. United Fruit ultimately acquired the company. The trouble with Cuyamel Fruit Company involved land near the Motagua River on the Honduran–Guatemalan border. It resulted in several decades of fighting and diplomatic conflict.

By 1904 Keith's activity was shifting from Costa Rica to Guatemala and his primary interest had returned to railroads from bananas. He planned to develop Guatemalan railroads and fruit operations. His vision included a line from the United States to Panama (part of the Panamerican railroad project, which aimed to link Argentina and Chile with the United States) and a second line connecting the two oceans. Keith and entrepreneurs William van Horne of London and Thomas Hubbard of New York acquired the

Guatemala Railway Company in 1904. This company owned the concession, initiated in the 1870s, to link Guatemala City and Guatemala's highlands with Puerto Barrios on the north coast. Keith and his associates completed the project in 1908 and, in the process he acquired the Guatemala Central Railroad, which had been built by Collis P. Huntington, Leland Stanford, and Charles Crocker, the builders of the Central Pacific Railroad.

In 1908 and 1909 Keith negotiated the concession to build El Salvador's main railroad and the right to connect the Salvadoran railroad system with a Guatemalan line. When it was completed in 1929, El Salvador had a direct rail tie to an Atlantic ocean port. While Keith completed a transisthmian line with Pacific outlets in both El Salvador and Guatemala, he did not realize his desire to construct the Central American section of the Panamerican railroad; rapid development of the automobile and a planned Panamerican highway seriously undermined that project.

Still, Keith had acquired control of Guatemalan and Salvadoran railroads and in 1911 his Guatemalan railroad holdings reached the Mexican border. In 1912 he organized his railroad empire into the International Railways of Central America (IRCA). Keith had negotiated a contract with Honduran president Manuel Bonilla for a railroad through Honduras, but Bonilla died before it was implemented. He also had a tentative agreement with Nicaragua to connect the Honduran line with the Nicaraguan line and the Nicaraguan line with the Costa Rican railroad, but these plans also collapsed. Keith remained president or chairman of the board of the IRCA until his death. In 1929 the IRCA was valued at $80 million and United Fruit was worth about $250 million.

Keith's business holdings were varied. They included timber and railroads near St. Andrew Bay in Florida; gold mines in Costa Rica and British Columbia; Brazilian railroads; Cuban sugar mills; and mining, real estate, coffee, cattle, and meatpacking in Colombia, Bolivia, and Paraguay. United Fruit operated in Guatemala, Honduras, Nicaragua, Costa Rica, Jamaica, Cuba, Panama, Mexico, Colombia, the Canary Islands, and Ecuador. International Railroads had interests in Guatemala, El Salvador, and Honduras. He also functioned in Europe; he raised capital frequently in Great Britain, and United Fruit marketed bananas on the Continent.

The operations of Keith's companies often posed problems for the U.S. government. In 1909 his railroad concession from El Salvador imposed a surcharge on Salvadoran imports to subsidize the railroad construction project. This concession was granted shortly after U.S. diplomats ended several decades of negotiations to obtain some modest tariff reductions on U.S. exports from California to El Salvador. The State Department was frustrated, but helpless, when confronted with the tariff surcharge. It pleaded with Keith to do as little damage to U.S. commerce as possible. Beginning in 1913, Keith encouraged U.S. financial intervention in Honduras, Guatemala, and Costa Rica.

He had considerable impact upon the debt refunding scheme in Costa Rica but less upon one in Guatemala, and he failed to persuade the Honduran government to accept a U.S. refunding project.

Keith supported the revolt of Federico Tinoco in 1917 that overthrew the Costa Rican president. During the revolt, the U.S. diplomats were denied use of Costa Rican wires, but Keith was able to inform President Woodrow Wilson of the revolt and to request U.S. recognition of the new regime. Wilson considered Keith's privileged access to the Costa Rican wire service, when the U.S. legation was denied use, a sign of improper power and suspected Keith and United Fruit of improper conduct thereafter. Wilson insisted that Keith had labored against his own government.

Later in life, Keith became an avid student and collector of pre-Columbian mesoamerican native culture and artifacts. His collection, encompassing about 15,000 items of Aztec gold images and ornaments and Central American pottery, was bequeathed to the Brooklyn Museum and the American Museum of Natural History in New York. A few pieces were donated to the National Museum in Washington, D.C. He was a trustee of the American Indian Heye Foundation and a fellow of the Royal Geographical Society of London. He died in New York City.

Keith's role in railroads, shipping, wireless communications, and bananas made him a powerful and pervasive influence on the isthmus for five decades.

• The standard biography of Keith is Watt Stewart's *Keith and Costa Rica: A Biographical Study of Minor Cooper Keith* (1964). Other studies of Keith and United Fruit are Frederick U. Adams, *Conquest of the Tropics* (1914); Charles David Kepner, Jr., and Jay Henry Soothill, *The Banana Empire: A Case Study of Economic Imperialism* (1935); Charles David Kepner, Jr., *Social Aspects of the Banana Industry* (1936); Charles Morrow Wilson, *Empire in Green and Gold: The Story of the American Banana Trade* (1947); Dana G. Munro, *Intervention and Dollar Diplomacy in the Caribbean, 1900–1921* (1964); Thomas Schoonover, *The United States in Central America, 1860–1911: Episodes of Social Imperialism and Imperial Rivalry in the World System* (1991); and Paul Dosal, *Doing Business with the Dictators: A Political History of United Fruit in Guatemala* (1993).

In addition to biographical sketches of Keith in the general reference dictionaries, see John E. Findling, ed., *Dictionary of American Diplomatic History* (1989), p. 279. Obituaries are in the *New York Times*, 15 June 1929, and the *Nation*, 3 July 1929.

THOMAS SCHOONOVER

KEITH, Reuel (26 June 1792–3 Sept. 1842), Episcopal educator and theologian, was born in Pittsford, Vermont, the son of Reuel Keith, the keeper of a public house, and Abigail Allen. During his boyhood he worked for a while as a clerk in a store in Troy, New York, where he first became acquainted with the Episcopal church. He entered Middlebury College in Vermont in 1811 and graduated with high honors in 1814. For health reasons he decided to move to the warmer South and went to Prince George County, Virginia, where he became a private tutor. While working as a tutor he served as lay reader in the parish and began his studies preparatory to entering the ministry of the Episcopal church. The report to the Virginia Convention states, "The spirit of religion is reviving under Mr. Keith, who has large congregations" (Packard, p. 94). He returned to Vermont and was a tutor for his alma mater from 1816 to 1817. He then entered systematically into a course of study under John Prentis Kewley Henshaw, rector of a church in Brooklyn and later the first bishop of Rhode Island, in preparation for the ministry "and later pursued his studies as a resident graduate of Andover" (Goodwin, *History of the Theological Seminary in Virginia*, vol. 1, p. 544). He went to Alexandria, Virginia, and was ordained deacon on 10 May 1817. In December 1817 he married Marietta Cleveland, and they had four children.

Immediately upon his ordination to the diaconate, Keith was invited to become the assistant to Walter D. Addison, the rector of St. John's Parish, Georgetown, District of Columbia. He went to Washington, D.C., to help Dr. Thomas Henderson, a layman, establish a school that they hoped would grow into a college. Keith was ordained a priest on 24 May 1818. His ministry at Georgetown resulted in the establishment of a new parish, Christ Church, of which Keith was rector from 19 November 1817 to 29 January 1820. He then moved to Williamsburg, Virginia, where he was professor of theology in the College of William and Mary and rector of Bruton Parish. After a short stay in Vermont, he returned to Virginia in 1823.

The experiment of establishing a theological professorship in the College of William and Mary was a complete failure, probably because of the reported skepticism and infidelity in that locality. During his two-year residence at William and Mary, only one student presented himself for the course in theology.

At this time, 1823, the Episcopal church had only one theological seminary, General Theological Seminary, New York City. Many Virginia churchmen believed that General was dominated by the "high church" bishop of New York, John Henry Hobart. Virginia churchmen were willing to support a general seminary as long as it was not dominated by New York churchmanship. The high churchmanship of Hobart stressed the doctrine, discipline, and worship of the Episcopal church, and the low churchmanship of Virginia stressed a personal relationship with Jesus Christ. Bishop William Meade of Virginia said, "Not knowing how soon we might have to rely on a general institution, we wished it placed under more favorable auspices for the promotion of what we believed to be sound views of the Gospel and the Church, than it would be in New York" (Meade, vol. 2, p. 373). In the midst of this dilemma, the diocese of Virginia founded the Protestant Episcopal Theological Seminary in Alexandria, Virginia, which opened in October 1823 with Keith as professor of Old Testament literature, biblical criticism, and evidences and professor of pulpit eloquence and pastoral theology. He remained in this position until 1840. Marietta Keith died in 1830,

and Keith married Elizabeth Sewall Higginson. They had no children.

Keith became deeply interested in the work, especially the Christology, of Ernst Wilhelm Hengstenberg, a German Lutheran exegete and an opponent of rationalism. Hengstenberg opposed those who denied the divinity of Jesus Christ and who paid undue worship to reason, and he defended the Scriptures as the word of God. During 1829–1835 he published the *Christologie des Alten Testaments*, and Keith learned the German language thoroughly in order to translate it. Keith published it as *Christology of the Old Testament, and a Commentary on the Predictions of the Messiah by the Prophets* (3 vols., 1836–1839), and it was described as "one of the most admirable translations ever made into the England language" (Goodwin, *History of the Theological Seminary in Virginia*, vol. 1, p. 545).

Keith brought with him to the Virginia Seminary the influence of Andover and a theological system colored by the Calvinism of New England. He was a decided Calvinist and "the lowest of the low Churchmen." He was "so smitten with the beauty and loveliness of Calvinism, that he could hardly preach about anything else" (Morrison, p. 1). When a student on one occasion, after Keith had lectured on the Calvinistic view of a subject, said to him, "When, Doctor Keith, are we to have the other side?" he answered, "There is no other side" (Packard, p. 95). His only book, *Lectures on Those Doctrines in Theology, Usually Called Calvinistic, Delivered to His Class in the Theological Seminary of Virginia* (1868), published posthumously, is a defense of the Calvinistic doctrines of predestination, election, and reprobation.

Keith's views of the sacramental side of Christianity were very low church. Over the years he engaged in a controversy with Bishop John Stark Ravenscroft of North Carolina, a high churchman, over the doctrine of the church. On one occasion Bishop Ravenscroft remarked, "If there is a man in the world who lives close to God, it is Reuel Keith, but he knows no more of the Church than my horse." The editor of the *Southern Churchman*, commenting on the controversy, remarked, "If the Bishop's horse knows as much of the Church as Professor Keith, he is an ecclesiastical prodigy, worthy of a choice stall in the Cathedral" (Goodwin, *History of the Theological Seminary in Virginia*, vol. 1, p. 548).

Keith was the first professor at the Virginia Theological Seminary and a successful parish priest. He was a fine preacher and a noted lecturer. Bishop Meade said, "He was a most eloquent preacher, and the most earnest one I have ever heard." Keith suffered from depression, and after the death of his second wife in 1841, he entered a depression from which he never recovered. He died in Sheldon, Vermont.

• Keith's papers have not been preserved. The most biographical information available is in William Archer Rutherford Goodwin, *History of the Theological Seminary in Virginia and Its Historical Background* (2 vols., 1923, 1924); Joseph Packard, *Recollections of a Long Life* (1902); and William B.

Sprague, *Annals of the American Pulpit*, vol. 5 (1859). Some information is also in Goodwin, *Historical Sketch of Bruton Church, Williamsburg, Virginia* (1903); William Meade, *Old Churches, Ministers, and Families of Virginia* (2 vols., 1857); Walter W. Williams, *History of Christ Church, Georgetown, D.C., Prepared from the Records of the Church* (1867) and *Read at the Semi-Centennial Celebration* (1869); and *General Catalogue of the Theological Seminary, Andover, Massachusetts, 1808–1908* (1909). An appreciation of him is J. H. Morrison, "Reminiscences of Dr. Reuel Keith," *Southern Churchman* 46 (19 Feb. 1880): 1.

DON S. ARMENTROUT

KEITH, William (1680–18 Nov. 1749), colonial governor, was baptized on 16 Feb. 1680, probably at Peterhead in Scotland, the son of Sir William Keith, a baronet, and Jean Smith. His family supported the House of Stuart, and so when the Stuart king, James II, was driven into exile in 1688, they moved to France, where William grew up. No details of his education in France are known, but he was probably educated primarily through reading and political conversation. Keith first came to public notice when, as a young man, he was involved in an effort to restore the Stuarts to the English throne and in 1704 spent some time in an English prison under a charge of treason. He was able to reconcile himself to the English establishment and to seek government employment, for although he inherited the baronetcy (he succeeded to his father's title and became Sir William in 1720), he had a large family and no money. Under the eighteenth-century system, he lived on expectations and borrowed money in the hope of attracting the notice of an important politician, who would reward him with a remunerative office.

In 1714 Keith was appointed surveyor-general of customs for the southern colonies and spent two years on a tour of inspection, which took him from Virginia to Pennsylvania, Jamaica, and the Carolinas. He seems to have charmed all who met him, and when the provincial leaders of Pennsylvania were looking for a new governor, they recommended Keith. He went to England, received the approbation of the aged and ailing William Penn, secured the appointment, and was sworn in as lieutenant governor of Pennsylvania and the Lower Counties (now Delaware) on 31 May 1717.

For five years, from 1717 to 1722, Keith was the most popular governor since the founding of the colony. He satisfied the local interests, particularly the wealthy Quaker merchants who controlled the Assembly. He gave them a paper currency, which enabled them to expand their trade in the midst of an economic slump, and he encouraged hardworking and peaceable Germans to settle the land. He went personally to the headquarters of the Six Nations in present New York State to make peace treaties with this formidable coalition of Native American tribes.

Keith's written reports to the royal government, which were published in 1740, helped shape royal policy well into the 1760s. The most notable was his "Report on the Progress of the French Nation" of 1719, which warned of French encirclement of the English colonies. His "discourse" of 1728, a report on colonial settlement, trade, and industry, proposed, among other things, the imposition of a stamp tax to support a standing army on the frontier and to pay the expenses of an imperial government in the colonies.

Keith was very popular in Philadelphia, but he badly miscalculated when he tried to base his power on the artisan class, rather than to the merchant oligarchy, which, in every British trading city in the early eighteenth century, represented real authority. He seemed to threaten the merchants directly when he not only supported the popular party in the 1726 elections, but condoned its victory procession, which culminated in the burning of the stocks and pillory—symbols of authority and social control. He was hastily replaced as governor by the more deferential Patrick Gordon, and although he was elected to the Assembly in 1726 and 1727, he was unable to unseat the speaker and was never able to regain power. In 1728 Keith sailed for England and never returned to America.

Most Americans know of Keith from an incident related by Benjamin Franklin in his *Autobiography*. Franklin, an autodidact like Keith, still in his teens and the most competent printer in Philadelphia, had the kind of magnetic personality that appealed to the governor. Keith sent him back to Boston with a letter to Franklin's father, asking him to set him up in business as a printer and promising that he would give Franklin all the government documents to print. Wisely, Franklin's father turned down the idea, on the grounds that eighteen-year-old Benjamin was too young for the responsibility, but he would reconsider when his son turned twenty-one. The governor, in his grandiose way, sent Franklin off to London on a trip to purchase the most up-to-date equipment, a venture that supposedly was backed by an official letter. Unfortunately, the letter never existed, and Franklin had to support himself as a printer for other men in London until he could raise the money to return to Philadelphia. He met Keith, by then a private citizen, in the street, but the former governor refused to recognize the boy whom he had disappointed so keenly.

For some years after his return to England Keith acted as an adviser to the Board of Trade, but as he had no regular source of income, he contracted large debts. Following the custom of the day, he was sent to debtors' prison in 1734. He never emerged and died in prison. Even while in prison he was able to keep his papers, and in 1740 most of the official reports that he had written as governor were published.

Keith married Anne Newbury (or Newberry), the widow of Robert Diggs. The date of their marriage is unknown. She had a daughter by her first husband, and she and Keith had five sons and a daughter who survived infancy.

Keith was among the most able of the colonial governors of the first half of the eighteenth century. His published collection of reports deserves study, as they are able summaries of the British colonial situation and shrewd predictors of the inevitable tension that would grow out of this situation. That the British government made no proper use of his talents for the final twenty years of his life is an example of the tragic mismanagement that was only too prevalent during the eighteenth century.

• Keith's personal papers have not survived. A few speeches and short government documents were published in Philadelphia during his term of office. He published his own reports as *Collection of Papers and Other Tracts Written Occasionally on Various Subjects* in London in 1740. Gary B. Nash, *Quakers and Politics, Pennsylvania 1681–1726* (1968), includes an able summary of his public career. There are many editions of Franklin's *Autobiography*; that edited by Max Farrand (1949) is generally available.

MARY RHINELANDER McCARL

KEITT, Laurence Massillon (4 Oct. 1824–5 June 1864), congressman and Confederate colonel, was born in Orangeburg District, South Carolina, the son of George Keitt, a planter, and Mary Magdalene Wannamaker. (His first name is usually given as "Lawrence," but Keitt preferred—and used—the spelling of Laurence.) Raised on a large plantation near St. Matthews, South Carolina, Keitt attended a local academy and graduated from the South Carolina College in 1843. After moving to Charleston and reading law under James L. Petigru, one of the state's most eminent attorneys, he passed his bar exam in 1844 and returned to Orangeburg to open a law practice. In 1848 he was elected to the South Carolina House of Representatives, where he quickly established himself as a radical firebrand on the sectional issues that were emerging over slavery. During the sectional crisis over the Compromise of 1850, he actively promoted the secession of his state. Convinced that the compromise measures of Congress failed to protect southern rights and honor, he argued, "Loyalty to the Union is treason to liberty."

Although the voters of South Carolina rejected secession in 1851, Keitt easily won election to Congress in 1852 as a radical states' rights Democrat representing the Third Congressional District. For the rest of the decade, barring a brief resignation in 1856, he served continuously in Congress as one of the South's most outspoken and defiant defenders. As a southern nationalist, Keitt believed that northerners and southerners were two different peoples with antagonistic interests and values. "We have now in interest," he insisted in 1855, "two Confederacies, with a debauched Constitution, and a tyrannical and irresponsible Congress." He viewed the Union as an artificial arrangement that would soon dissolve.

These political beliefs, combined with a highly romanticized notion of individualism that demanded a life of action and bold self-assertion, shaped Keitt's most controversial actions as a congressman. Having been told in advance of the intentions of Preston Brooks to punish Senator Charles Sumner of Massachusetts for his attack on the character of South Carolina senator Andrew P. Butler, Brooks's cousin, Keitt was present in the Senate chamber when Brooks caned Sumner in May 1856. Keitt approved of Brooks's actions as the necessary duty of a southern gentleman of honor, and he himself brandished a cane to warn off bystanders from coming to Sumner's assistance. Censured by the House of Representatives for his part in the affair, Keitt resigned from Congress on 16 July 1856. Shortly reelected to his seat in a special election, he returned to Congress convinced that his honor had been vindicated. In a more serious breach of self-control in February 1858, Keitt attacked Galusha Grow, a Republican representative from Pennsylvania, when Grow crossed over to the Democratic side of the House in the midst of a bitter debate over the admission of Kansas. Keitt did apologize to the House for his actions, but he refused to do so to Grow.

The passion that Keitt brought to politics spilled over to his personal life. Married in May 1859 to Susan Mandeville Sparks, with whom he had two daughters, he cut short their European honeymoon on hearing of John Brown's raid at Harpers Ferry. Keitt blamed the antislavery principles of the Republican party for inciting Brown's raid, and his fear for the safety of slaveholders was shockingly heightened in February 1860, when his brother, Dr. William J. Keitt, was killed by his slaves while ill in bed at his plantation in Florida. Keitt was deadly serious when he characterized the election of 1860 as a matter of "life or Death" for southerners.

With the election of Abraham Lincoln in November 1860, Keitt immediately called on his fellow South Carolinians to "shatter this accursed Union." He left Washington on 10 December 1860 and returned home, where he served as a delegate to the South Carolina secession convention. He was also a member of the provisional Confederate Congress that met in Montgomery, Alabama. Suspecting that Jefferson Davis was a reluctant secessionist who favored a reunion with the North, Keitt unsuccessfully backed Howell Cobb of Georgia for the presidency of the confederacy. Despite his disappointment, Keitt helped organize the new government and served on the Foreign Affairs and Indian Affairs committees of the provisional Congress.

Keitt very quickly lost whatever confidence he might have had in the Davis administration. In August 1861, he wrote: "We are building upon the most unsubstantial foundations. The Gov't will neither buy nor advance upon cotton and, if the war lasts, its financial policy, unless corrected, will land us in bankruptcy." Keitt believed the government had erred in not purchasing cotton and shipping it abroad for needed war supplies. Preferring military glory to a political role in Richmond, he recruited the Twentieth South Carolina Infantry and was elected its colonel in January 1862.

For most of the war Keitt was stationed with his regiment on Sullivan's Island in Charleston. The command saw little fighting, and Keitt was close enough to his plantation in Orangeburg to receive regular visits from his wife and to pass on orders for the supervision of his 115 slaves. Still, he yearned for action, and the opportunity came when his regiment was transferred to the Virginia theater in May 1864. For Keitt, war was always the supreme test of a gentleman's courage and his ability to shape destiny, and he welcomed this chance to prove himself worthy of the southern cause. His first and last battle was Cold Harbor on 1 June 1864. In a display of raw but foolish courage, what veteran onlookers recognized as "inexperience and want of self-control," Keitt led his men across an open field toward a fortified Union position. He was cut down almost instantly by the Union fire and died from his wounds four days later in a field hospital.

• The largest collection of Keitt's papers is in the William R. Perkins Library at Duke University. Useful letters on his political views can also be found in the William Porcher Miles Papers, Southern Historical Collection, University of North Carolina at Chapel Hill, and in the James Henry Hammond Papers, Library of Congress. Many of his papers were destroyed during the Civil War, and no full-length biography has been published. Eric H. Walther, *The Fire-Eaters* (1992), provides the best sketch of his career. Charles Edward Cauthen, *South Carolina Goes to War, 1861–1865* (1950), is useful for the war years. See also the obituary in the *Charleston Mercury*, 6 June 1864.

WILLIAM L. BARNEY

KEKEWEPELETHY (fl. 1776–1808), principal civil chief of the Ohio Shawnees, was also known as Captain Johnny; his Indian name means "Great or Tame Hawk." He rose as a war leader, probably of the Mekoche division of the Shawnees, and first appears on record as a member of a delegation visiting the new American authorities in Pittsburgh in 1776. During the early years of the American Revolution the Mekoches tried to keep the Shawnees neutral, and in 1778 Kekewepelethy and others of the peace faction joined the neutral Delawares at Coshocton. As the war progressed, however, pressure to join those Shawnees armed and encouraged by the British at Detroit increased, and about 1780 Kekewepelethy moved farther west, apparently to the town of Wakatomica on the upper Mad River (near present-day Zanesfield, Ohio), and threw in his lot with the king.

After the war, Kekewepelethy opened negotiations with the United States but rejected their claim to have defeated the Indians and their demand for Indian land north of the Ohio. He supported an Iroquois plan to unite Indian peoples to resist American pretensions, and in a speech on behalf of the Shawnees, Delawares, and Mingoes in 1785 he boasted, "The people of one color are united so that we make but one man that has but one heart and one mind." Yet American negotiators swiftly opened divisions among the Indians north of the Ohio, and at Fort Finney (Jan. 1786) demanded that the Shawnees cede those lands they occupied east of the Great Miami. Speaking for the tribe "in a very clear and masterly manner" Kekewepelethy resisted, rejecting the American presents: "You say you have goods for our women and children. You may keep your goods and give them to other nations. We will have none of them." The Shawnee leaders were forced to agree to the cession, but the treaty was soon repudiated by the Indians, and warfare broke out.

In October 1786 an army of Kentucky settlers destroyed the Shawnee villages that were grouped about the headwaters of the Great Miami and murdered the principal civil chief, Molunthe. The Shawnees withdrew to the upper Maumee, where Kekewepelethy eventually built a town near the mouth of the Auglaize. He succeeded Molunthe and in that capacity negotiated an exchange of prisoners with the whites at Limestone, Ohio, in the summer of 1787. After some Indians, although not the Shawnees, acknowledged American land claims in treaties at Fort Harmar (1789), Kekewepelethy tried to resuscitate resistance by reforming the intertribal confederacy the Iroquois had once led. The chief was planning a congress of Indian peoples during the winter of 1789–1790, but the only immediate effective partners were the Shawnees, Miamis, and Delawares at the head of the Maumee.

During the next few years the confederacy defeated the armies of Josiah Harmar (1790) and Arthur St. Clair (1791), established a new headquarters around Kekewepelethy's town at the junction of the Auglaize and the Maumee, and widened its support, drawing also on the Wyandots, Ottawas, Potawatomis, and Ojibwas about the Great Lakes. The confederacy was also provisioned by the British, who feared American expansion into the Northwest, and Kekewepelethy worked closely with the British agents at Detroit, particularly Alexander McKee, whose Shawnee wife may have been a relation of the chief's. There is no evidence that Kekewepelethy fought in the battles with American forces, and Blue Jacket was the most important military leader of the confederacy, but he coordinated major negotiations, including those connected with the abortive talks with U.S. peace commissioners in the summer of 1793.

Kekewepelethy and most Shawnees insisted on the restitution of Indian land north of the Ohio as a requisite for peace, but the confederacy was defeated at Fallen Timbers in August 1794, and in the ensuing winter many Indians sued for peace. Although Blue Jacket led some Shawnees to the treaty of Greenville (Aug. 1795), in which the Indians ceded southern and eastern Ohio, Kekewepelethy, with British support, kept most of them away. Indeed, far from accepting that the war had been lost, at the beginning of 1796 Kekewepelethy was sending runners north and south, urging the tribes to resume the conflict.

Ultimately, further resistance was futile, but Kekewepelethy stubbornly refused to treat with the Americans. In 1794 he had withdrawn to Swan Creek, at the mouth of the Maumee, and when the United States occupied that area in 1796 he moved to locations still controlled by the British, first Bois Blanc Island and then, in 1797, Grosse Isle, both in the Detroit River. By then most of the Shawnees had returned to Ohio, and although he continued to receive British supplies, Kekewepelethy followed them about 1800, evidently settling again on the Maumee. He was regarded as a reliable source of information by British officials as late as 1808 and may have been the "Captain John" who met the Shakers in 1807, "an able and likely man" who was then settled in present-day Logan County, Ohio. In later years Ohio settlers remembered Kekewepelethy as "King John" to distinguish him from a younger "Captain Johnny" who aided the Americans in the War of 1812. The latter was also a Shawnee, and perhaps a relation, but never enjoyed the standing of Kekewepelethy.

The date of Kekewepelethy's death is unknown. He was reported to have been "very ill" during his last visit to the British post at Amherstburg (Upper Canada) in March 1808, and records contain no references to him thereafter. One son was remembered: Othowakasica ("Yellow Feather"). Although not considered to be an influential man, he signed treaties with the United States in 1814 and 1817 and removed to Kansas with the Shawnees in the 1830s.

• Documents relating to Kekewepelethy, some of which misidentify him, are scattered throughout Record Group 10 (Indian Affairs) and the Claus papers (MG 19/Fl) of the Public Archives of Canada, Ottawa, and through the YY, BB, and U series of the Draper manuscripts at the State Historical Society of Wisconsin, Madison. Useful glimpses of him can be found in "Gen. Butler's Journal," in *The Olden Time*, ed. Neville B. Craig (1846–1848), vol. 2, pp. 481–525, 530–31; *The Kentucky Gazette*, 25 Aug. 1787; Milo M. Quaife, ed., "Henry Hay's Journal from Detroit to the Mississippi River," *Proceedings of the State Historical Society of Wisconsin* 62 (1915): 208–61; Logan Esarey, ed., *Messages and Letters of William Henry Harrison*, vol. 1 (1922), p. 287; and Ernest A. Cruikshank, ed., *The Correspondence of Lieutenant-Governor John Graves Simcoe* (5 vols., 1923–1931). Reginald Horsman, *Matthew Elliott, British Indian Agent* (1964), contains useful references to him under both his Indian name and "Captain Johnny." A sketch of the chief is included in Dan L. Thrapp, *Encyclopedia of Frontier Biography*, vol. 4, *Supplemental Volume* (1994).

JOHN SUGDEN

KELCEY, Herbert (10 Oct. 1856–10 July 1917), actor, was born in London, England, to parents whose identities have been lost, though one source says his father was a judge. Born Herbert Kelcey Lamb, he dropped the family name when he became an actor. He was "pushed" onto the stage, he told an interviewer, when his misadventures on the stock exchange left him penniless (*Green Book Album*, June 1909). His first appearance was in *Flirtation* (1877), in Brighton, England; his first London appearance was in *Bow Bells* (1880).

Kelcey, accompanied by his wife, actress Caroline Hill, was brought to America by manager Lester Wallack. The marriage date is not known; there were no children. He appeared at Wallack's Theatre in a series of plays in the 1882–1883 season, beginning with *Taken from Life* (1882). Over the next five years he played a series of parts in what were known as "parlor dramas" about polite society, both at Wallack's and at the Madison Square Theatre, two playhouses frequented by fashionable New York playgoers. Essentially he always played himself, a good-looking young English gentleman of breeding and manners. Quite often the name of his character was preceded by "Captain," "Major," "Colonel," or "Lord." In a revival of one of the period's greatest hits, *Diplomacy* (1885), he was Count Orloff.

In 1887 Kelcey moved to Daniel Frohman's stock company at the Lyceum Theatre, where he played leading roles both in comedy and drama. Most notably he appeared in *The Wife* (1887) and *The Charity Ball* (1889), both written by co-authors Henry C. DeMille and David Belasco; in Sir Arthur Wing Pinero's *The Amazons* (1894); and in Oscar Wilde's *An Ideal Husband* (1895). In *The Amazons*, the part of Lord Litterly "fitted him like a Pool coat; he was the confident, debonair exquisite of the London variety to the very life, with just enough of well-bred rakishness to top it off nicely" (*Illustrated American Magazine*).

The *New York Dramatic Mirror* gave a clear-eyed assessment of Kelcey's strengths and his limits:

Mr. Kelcey is the most popular man connected with the New York stock companies . . . the idol of the matinee girl, collectively considered. He is a handsome young man, whose speech and manners denote gentle breeding. It is due to his fitness for the atmosphere of society plays, rather than to any histrionic power, that Mr. Kelcey has succeeded in becoming a metropolitan favorite. His methods have shown improvement . . . with the Lyceum company, and he can be relied upon always to play a part satisfactorily that comes within the boundaries of his dramatic limitations. (2 May 1891)

Unlike some other matinee idols of the day, Kelcey was a perfect gentleman offstage as well as on. "He lives quietly," said the *Dramatic Mirror* article, "dresses like a 'swell,' is fond of his home, and pursues the even tenor of his professional way with dignity and decorum." Quietly during the Lyceum years, Kelcey's marriage ended with his wife's return to England. He entered into a personal and professional alliance with Effie Shannon, an actress in the Lyceum company, that would last the rest of his life. His obituaries named her as his wife, but biographical sources do not give a marriage date.

In 1896 Kelcey left the Lyceum stock company to go out on his own. He replaced the leading man in David Belasco's great success, *The Heart of Maryland*, for its second season. "The role of Allen Kendrick calls for no emotional expression that lies beyond Mr. Kelcey's scope," the *New York Times* reported. "He represents pictorially manly virtue in affliction, bearing up against persecution and misfortune with splendid heroism" (5 May 1896). In 1898 Kelcey and Shannon began their years as a costarring team with a solid success. Their vehicle, *The Moth and The Flame*, was a drama of worldliness, marriage, and divorce. Other vehicles followed, dramas of the kinds popular in the period. Kelcey smoothly made the transition to character roles as he aged, beginning with *Taps* (1904), in which he appeared as Shannon's father rather than the romantic interest he would have been in earlier plays. He played William De Burgh Cokane in a production of Shaw's *Widower's Houses* (1907), taking it on tour after a New York opening. In two seasons of touring with Shannon in a Broadway hit, *The Thief*, he played the deceived husband in 1908, then switched to the role of the anguished father in 1909. Though the couple were better received by "road" audiences than by New York theatergoers, they had another success in *Years of Discretion* (1912), which ran a season in New York.

In 1905, 1910, and 1916 Kelcey and Shannon toured vaudeville circuits in short dramatic sketches when no suitable plays were offered for the two of them. They realized at an early date that stage stars could appear in dramatic sketches on variety stages without losing prestige, and "were among the first to take advantage of the pleasant work and easy money to be found in the two-a-day theatres" (*New York Telegraph*, 15 Sept. 1910). They also appeared in two motion pictures during the period when stage stars were being hired as "name" attractions: *After the Ball* (1914) and *The Sphinx* (1916).

In 1916 Kelcey and Shannon had important supporting roles in one of the sentimental hits of the Broadway season, *Pollyanna*. It proved to be Kelcey's last appearance. He began to suffer from "intestinal trouble," as his obituaries said, and had to leave the cast in January 1917. He died at his summer home in Bayport, Long Island, with Shannon at his side.

The obituaries were frank about Kelcey's limitations as an actor. The *New York Post* spoke of his "lack of versatility" and "tendency to monotonous delivery" (11 July 1917). They also made clear what other qualities allowed him to sustain a career in the theater for forty years. As far as age allowed, he kept his looks. "In presence he was exceedingly attractive," said the *Post*. If not versatile in the range of parts he could play, he was at least versatile in adapting to character roles, to vaudeville, and to motion pictures. Managers knew him to be a reliable professional, free of temperament. Daniel Frohman praised Kelcey for "never missing a performance," and that, "while he may not have been one of the great actors, he always filled his roles to the perfect satisfaction of author and audience, chiefly because of his serious interest in his profession" (*New York World*, 11 July 1917). The *Post* obituary concurred: he "was never a great actor but . . . was an eminently good one." Though Kelcey began as a matinee idol whose success rested on good looks and charm, his long acting career was the result of professionalism and hard work.

• Materials on the life and career of Kelcey are in the Billy Rose Theatre Collection at the New York Public Library for the Performing Arts, Lincoln Center. For a list of his stage appearances, see *Who Was Who in the Theatre 1912–1976* (1978). Information on his motion picture roles is in the *American Film Institute Catalog*, vol. 1, 1911–1920 (1988). Portraits and production photographs are in Daniel C. Blum, *A Pictorial History of the American Theatre* (1960). William deWagstaff, "Chats with Players," *Theatre Magazine*, May 1902, is a joint interview with Kelcey and Shannon, interesting for the way it skirts the question of their being married.

Obituaries are in the *New York Times*, the *New York World*, and the *New York Post*, all 11 July 1917, and in the *New York Dramatic Mirror*, 21 July 1917.

WILLIAM STEPHENSON

KELL, John McIntosh (23 Jan. 1823–5 Oct. 1900), naval officer, was born near Darien, Georgia, the son of John Kell, a lawyer and planter, and Marjory Spalding Baillie. Born and raised on a cotton and rice plantation on the Georgia coast, Kell's boyhood dream of becoming a naval officer became a reality with his appointment as midshipman in the U.S. Navy in 1841. After a first cruise aboard the *Falmouth*, Kell sailed on the frigate *Savannah*, 1843 to 1847, participating ashore in the battle of Santa Clara in California during the Mexican War. Graduating from the newly established Navy School (later the U.S. Naval Academy) in 1848, Kell was commissioned a passed midshipman. There followed, however, the darkest period in Kell's naval career, when he and three other passed midshipmen were court-martialed, found guilty, and dismissed from the service for refusing to obey an order they considered both illegal and demeaning to their rank: lighting a candle to summon the relief lieutenant, a task usually performed by ordinary, not passed, midshipmen. Serving as their counsel was an officer sympathetic to the four junior officers, Lieutenant Raphael Semmes, USN. All four passed midshipmen succeeded in securing reinstatement in 1850.

From 1851 to 1855 Kell participated in the Perry expedition to Japan, which opened up trade between that nation and the United States. Promoted to lieutenant in 1855, he accompanied the Paraguay expedition three years later. In 1856 he married Julia Blanche Munroe; they had ten children, of whom seven survived to adulthood.

On 18 January 1861, the day that Georgia left the Union, Kell—then stationed at Pensacola, Florida—resigned his commission. Appointed commander in the Georgia navy, he briefly commanded the *Savannah*, a former passenger steamer, on coast patrol. In April 1861 Kell was appointed lieutenant in the Confederate navy and ordered to New Orleans. Commander Semmes, CSN, had requested Kell as his first lieutenant and executive officer aboard the CSS *Sumter*, the South's first commerce raider. Although unfit for long periods at sea, the *Sumter* succeeded in taking seventeen prizes during six months. After the *Sumter* ended its service as a raider at Gibraltar, Semmes and Kell were ordered to the *Alabama* (formerly *Enrica* or *290*), a superior English-built vessel specially designed as a commerce raider. During almost two years at sea, the *Alabama*—the most famous of the South's raiders—took over sixty prizes and even fought and sank a Union warship. As Semmes's trusted first officer, Kell once again demonstrated his ability and loyalty. Completely devoted to duty, he rarely left his ship for any reason. The very success of the *Alabama*, however, contributed to its notoriety. Its officers and sailors were condemned by Federal authorities as "pirates" outside the pale of civilized warfare. The *Alabama* became figuratively a "ghost ship," appearing to strike at a merchantman or whaling vessel, disappearing, then reappearing where least expected. Finding and destroying the raider became an obsession with U.S. navy secretary Gideon Welles.

Eventually, in June 1864, the *Alabama*, badly in need of repairs, ended its cruise at Cherbourg, France. The USS *Kearsarge* arrived soon afterward, and Semmes made the decision to risk his ship in combat, despite Kell's concern that much of the powder and fuses had deteriorated from months at sea. Although the men of the *Alabama* fought well—Kell himself conspicuous during the action—it took the *Kearsarge* only an hour and ten minutes to sink the raider. Both Semmes and Kell were among those rescued from the ocean by the crew of an English yacht and then taken to England.

Back in the Confederacy, Kell, who had been promoted to commander while the *Alabama* was at sea, was assigned command of the ironclad *Richmond* of the James River Squadron. On 23–24 January 1865 the squadron was involved in an unsuccessful attack on the Union fleet at Trent's Reach. Not long afterward Semmes, now an admiral, took command of the squadron, while Kell returned to Georgia on sick leave. He was there when the war ended, closing his 24-year naval career.

Kell did not return to McIntosh County after the war. Instead, he turned to farming at Sunnyside, Georgia, to support a growing family. (Two young children had died of diphtheria while Kell was at sea.) In 1886 former Confederate general and newly elected governor John Gordon appointed Kell adjutant general, principally for the political advantage of appointing a Confederate naval hero to a state position. Once in office, however, Kell was determined to make the position more than merely ceremonial, by becoming involved in Georgia military affairs (his predecessor only signed paychecks). He was reappointed as adjutant general by three succeeding governors. When Semmes died in 1877, Kell assumed the role of partisan defender of both his captain and the now legendary *Alabama*. He suffered a stroke in 1895, from which he never fully recovered. In ill health during his final years, he dictated his memoirs to his wife (also referring to letters and journals), which were published in 1900. He died at Sunnyside.

As executive officer aboard two Confederate raiders, Kell was responsible for the daily operation of those vessels. His duties included disposing of captured prizes plus disciplining and drilling his crew. Indeed, Semmes himself found Kell the perfect chief officer and credited him with making the *Alabama* the success it became. Although a strict disciplinarian, as Semmes desired of his lieutenant, Kell appears to have been respected, even regarded with affection, by most of the sailors he supervised. He in turn defended them after the war against charges of drunken and mutinous conduct while aboard the *Alabama*.

• Kell family papers, including an unpublished manuscript by Blanche Kell, "Life and Letters of John McIntosh Kell," are located at Duke University. Additional family correspondence can be found in the Eugenius Nisbett Papers, also at Duke. Kell's published writings include *Recollections of a Naval Life* (1900) and "Cruise and Combats of the *Alabama*," in *Battles and Leaders of the Civil War* (1887–1888), vol. 4. See also Norman C. Delaney, *John McIntosh Kell of the Raider Alabama* (1973) and "John McIntosh Kell: A Confederate Veteran in Politics," *Georgia Historical Quarterly* 57 (Fall 1973): 376–89. An obituary is in the *Atlanta Constitution*, 6 Oct. 1900.

NORMAN C. DELANEY

KELLAND, Clarence Budington (11 July 1881–18 Feb. 1964), journalist and author, was born in Portland, Michigan, the son of Thomas Kelland, an English weaver who came to the United States just before the Civil War, and Margaret Budington, a millinery shop proprietor. Growing up in the small town of Portland, Kelland was left with a firm belief in the value of industry, frugality, honesty, and a strong sense of community spirit that when combined contributed to an idealistic view of the American experiment he never lost. When he was ten, the family moved to Detroit, where Kelland attended private schools. He received an LL.B. degree from Detroit College of Law in 1902. After a brief try at law, he began working for the *Detroit News*, moving up from night police reporter to Sunday editor in his four years there. He married Betty Carolina Smith in 1907; they had two sons. Following a brief tenure as principal of the Sprague Correspondence School of Law, in 1907 he became editor of *The American Boy*, a magazine for boys, serving until 1915. He was a lecturer on juvenile literature and writing as a profession at the University of Michigan from 1913 to 1915. He shifted to full-time writing in 1915 and moved to the New York area. In 1918 he served as the overseas publicist for the YMCA, even visiting the trenches of the American Expeditionary Forces in France.

While editor of *The American Boy*, Kelland sold his first stories to national magazines. Harper and Brothers Publishing Co. printed his first full-length work in 1913, the boys' book *Mark Tidd*. The title character is perceptive and shrewd, a born leader of his teenage contemporaries. One of his comrades, Binney, narrates their escapades in the village and in the Michigan woods. The Mark Tidd series, stretching to nine volumes in all, reflect the Tom Sawyer–Huck Finn tradition of boyhood scrapes and high jinks, but Kelland's differ in two ways; his hero is inordinately fat and displays a remarkable grasp of microeconomics. At times Tidd performs more like a combination detective and acute entrepreneur than a young lad. And the perceptive Binney tells all in slang and with humor. These novels were followed by a shorter series centered on the character of Catty Atkins, whose resourcefulness tends even more to business angles than adventure and whose bosom buddy, Wee-Wee Moore, serves as narrator. Both series underscore the values of small-town life, uprightness and honesty, and the virtue of hard work—resulting in the realization of the American Dream of material prosperity (see "The Happiest Days of My Life," *Saturday Evening Post*, 14 Oct. 1950).

Kelland's first attempt at adult fiction, *Hidden Spring*, was published in 1915 first serially in *The Delineator* and in hardback the following year, a procedure Kelland followed most of his career. Set in a Michigan lumber town, *Hidden Spring* was a mediocre beginning for Kelland; "as exciting as it is improbable," one reviewer noted. In 1919 short stories centering on a new character called Scattergood Baines began appearing in the *American Magazine*. Kelland collected the stories in the episodic novel named for the hero in 1921. Baines, a heavyset, deceptively slow-moving and simple fellow, knew people and business inside and out, and once engaged in a problem he pursued it with considered ingenuity (usually removing his shoes and wiggling his toes to encourage his thinking processes) to surprising but satisfying ends. Besides the earlier creations of Mark Tidd and Catty Atkins, prototypes of Baines had appeared as Zaanen Frame, justice of the peace and general arbiter in *Sudden Jim*, published in 1916, and Efficiency Edgar in the 1920 novel of that name. Reviewers gave faint praise to *Scattergood Baines*, yet it sold well.

By the mid-twenties, Kelland had made a considerable amount of money from his writing. He invested heavily in a Long Island bank, and when the bank failed in the depression, he lost it all. Undaunted, he turned back to his formula of publishing short stories and serialized novels in the magazines, followed by book publication, and eventually paid off all his debts to the full dollar amount. One of his most ambitious undertakings was a trilogy in the early thirties—*Hard Money* (1930), *Gold* (1931), and *Jealous House* (1934)—about a Dutch financier, Jan Van Horn, who amassed a fortune in the first book, whose daughter became head of the banking firm in the second, and whose latter-day descendant took over in the third. Movie producers were after his stories as well in the thirties. The first adaptation was the serial novel *Footlights*, which in 1932 appeared in the *Saturday Evening Post*, was published in hardback as *Speak Easily*, and was made into a movie starring Buster Keaton. That was followed by eight films, *Mr. Deeds Goes to Town* and *Dreamland* in 1936, *The Great Crooner* (1937), *Arizona* (1940), *Scattergood Baines* and *Skin Deep* (1941), *Valley of the Sun* (1942), and his most popular, *Sugarfoot* in 1951.

Also in the thirties Kelland moved to Phoenix, Arizona, and delved into cattle ranching, newspaper publishing, and politics. A staunch Republican all his life, he became Arizona committeeman to the National Republican Committee in 1940 and served in that capacity until 1956. During the war he criticized the Roosevelt administration, presented his own "Zones of Safety" plan for the postwar period, and attacked the Truman administration in the postwar years. He was a strong supporter of Barry Goldwater's successful 1952 Senate bid.

During all of this he continued to write. From the boys' books and the melodramas of the early years he moved on to novels—of romance, the Wild West, and Arizona—and murder mysteries and fictionalized biographies. Over the years of his career (he published his last novel at age eighty-one) he published more than thirty novels in magazines, some fifty-six in hardback, and about 300 short stories, over 100 of which concerned his most enduring creation, Scattergood Baines. The height of his career was probably the early forties when *Scattergood Baines Returns* and *Sugarfoot* were both bestsellers.

As with his near contemporary, O. Henry (William Sydney Porter), his literary reputation never matched his production. In a 1954 review, *Time* magazine (Mar. 22), recalling earlier epithets, labeled him "slick" and "superficial," a writer of "adroit hokum" that was "hopelessly fast-moving." His own resolute comment was, "I have never rated as a 'literary' man and as I have no vanity of that kind I don't care. But I am a good story-teller" (*New York Times Book Review*, 27 Apr. 1941). Kelland died in Scottsdale, Arizona.

• Kelland manuscript material is held in the University of Michigan Historical Collections; the I. Robert Kriendler Collection of Typescripts, Manuscripts, and Autographed Volumes of Contemporary Authors, Alexander Library, Rutgers University; and the Collected Papers of George Horace Lorrimer in the Historical Society of Pennsylvania Collections. Obituaries are in the *New York Times* and the *Arizona Republic*, 19 Feb. 1964; *Publishers Weekly*, 2 March 1964; and *Saturday Evening Post*, 14 Mar. 1964.

RICHARD O. BOUDREAU

KELLAR, Harry (11 July 1849–10 Mar. 1922), magician, was born Heinrich Keller in Erie, Pennsylvania, the son of German immigrants. He had little formal schooling and worked at a young age to assist his family. At the age of ten he hopped a train and traveled about the country, eventually earning his living selling newspapers in Manhattan. Robert Harcourt, a British-born clergyman, took him under his wing, taking Kellar to Canandaigua, New York. He began his career after seeing a performance by I. H. Hughes, known as the Fakir of Ava. Soon afterward Kellar became Hughes's assistant at the age of eleven. When he was sixteen, he attempted to succeed with his own show but failed, returning to Hughes after a short period of time.

Two years later Kellar took his own show on the road again; however, he lacked money and equipment. After one show with particularly poor attendance, he sneaked out a back window, leaving his meager props behind. He attempted a series of unsuccessful solo shows before, penniless, he talked his way into a loan to pay for a hall and advertisements. With borrowed cards, ropes, bottles, and a kitten to produce, he almost filled Phoenix Hall in Waukegan, Illinois. Successful for a number of weeks, he soon was broke again.

After a number of years of limited success, in 1869 Kellar was hired by the Davenport Brothers and Fay, who presented a spiritualist show specializing in ghostly happenings. This act took him to England and Europe for four years. He was promoted by the Davenports first to the position of advance agent, organizing shows in advance of the arrival of the troupe, and then to business manager.

In 1873 Kellar and Bill Fay, another of the Davenport assistants, set out with their own production. They successfully toured Canada, Mexico, and South America, presenting a combination of magic, escapes, and "spirit which manifestations." Kellar's signature illusion, originated by British magician John Nevil Maskelyne, was the "Levitation of Princess Karnac." This effect, involving the flotation and subsequent disappearance of a woman above the stage, became a staple illusion for all future illusion shows. While on their way to England their steamship struck a rock in the Bay of Biscay. Two crewmen lost their lives, but the rest of the passengers made it to the Island of Moleno. But Kellar's fortune and, more importantly, the show's costumes and equipment were lost. Finding himself without resources, Kellar once again talked his way into a loan, rebuilt his show, and traveled to the West Indies as "The Royal Illusionist."

In 1878 Kellar returned to the United States after traveling the world for five years. After one of his shows in Melbourne, Australia, Eva Medley, an enamored fan, approached Kellar for his autograph. He continued corresponding with her throughout his world tour. They were married in Kalamazoo, Michigan, in 1887. They had no children. After a disappointing year in the United States, he returned to South America and again traveled the world performing on five continents.

In 1884 Kellar returned to New York City and developed a spectacular show to rival that of Alexander Herrmann, who was then the leading magician in the United States. He continued to perfect and refine every effect and every line of his routine until it was flawless. For a time the two magicians competed directly with one another to present the most spectacular illusions. Upon Herrmann's death in 1898, Kellar became the undisputed leading magician in the world. In the fall of 1907 he began his final U.S. tour, accompanied by Howard Thurston, whom he identified as his successor. After the final show he went to New York, where the Society of American Magicians made him their first dean. He then retired, relatively wealthy, to Los Angeles, California.

Kellar performed publicly one last time. In 1917 Harry Houdini convinced him to participate in a benefit performance of the Society of American Magicians for the families of the first American casualties of World War I. After his performance Houdini insisted that he return to the stage for a finale. Amid a profusion of flowers, twenty-four men and women, including the leading magicians in the world, carried him off stage in a sedan chair while the 6,000 spectators provided a standing ovation. Harry Houdini once said of him, "When Harry Kellar was on stage, he was not merely acting the part of a magician, he was a magi-

cian" (quoted in Vincent Gaddis, *The Wide World of Magic* [1967], p. 105).

• Kellar chronicled his life of magic around the world in *A Magician's Tour up and down and round about the Earth* (1886). More detailed information on his life is also contained in Milbourne Christopher, *The Illustrated History of Magic* (1973), and John Mulholland, *Quicker Than the Eye* (1927).

R. DOUGLAS WHITMAN

KELLER, Helen (27 June 1880–1 June 1968), author, reformer, and symbol of personal courage, was born Helen Adams Keller in Tuscumbia, Alabama, the daughter of former Confederate captain Arthur H. Keller, a publisher and business entrepreneur, and Kate Adams. She was an unexceptional child until struck in her nineteenth month by an illness that was, possibly, scarlet fever. The event, she later recalled, "closed my eyes and ears and plunged me into the unconsciousness of a newborn baby." Profoundly and permanently deaf and blind, she was to carve out a life that astonished nearly everyone.

Until she was almost seven, Keller was largely untutored, living a life of boredom and frustration and meeting parental efforts at instruction with fits, kicks, and screams. After reading of Samuel Gridley Howe's success in teaching the blind Laura Bridgman, Kate Keller sought help and was referred to a variety of sight and hearing specialists, including Alexander Graham Bell. All thought Helen educable, and Bell recommended the services of his son-in-law Michael Anagnos, director of the Perkins Institution in Boston. It was Anagnos who selected twenty-year-old Anne Mansfield Sullivan to live with, and teach, the girl. Keller later recalled the arrival of Sullivan as "the most important day I remember in all my life." Partially blind herself, Sullivan set to work trying to teach Helen through an innovative technique learned at Perkins and pioneered by Howe: an exhausting, no-nonsense insistence on discipline combined with the spelling of words in the student's hand. Improving on the Howe method, Sullivan spelled the words not in structured settings but in moments when routine was broken by circumstances of surprise. Sullivan responded in kind to Keller's initial slaps and screams, but the revelation to Keller that the mysterious palm scrawls represented startling phenomena (the feel of water, the touch of love) soon elicited cooperation and exceptional progress. Within three months, Keller learned the entire alphabet and rudimentary spelling techniques. "Something tells me," Sullivan then wrote to Anagnos, "that I am going to succeed beyond all my dreams."

Keller learned to read Braille while still at Perkins in 1888. Two years later, at the Horace Mann School in New York, she attempted both speaking and lip reading through the same method (covering the speaker's mouth with her fingers). The results electrified Keller, but the public was much more fascinated by the strides she made, and the controversies she courted, with her writing. When, at ten, she wrote a short story, "The Frost King," much hailed by Anagnos, a storm of criticism attended the revelation that whole sections had been lifted from another author's book. Shadowed by the incident, Keller had difficulty convincing critics of the authenticity and merit of the later writings of her youth, which were all on the subject of the educability of the handicapped. When she published her autobiography, *The Story of My Life* (1902), critics whispered (erroneously) that it was ghosted by Anne Sullivan and the editor John Macy. Others claimed that, because of her isolation from "normal" experiences, Keller's "observations" were of necessity secondhand, derivative, lacking in experiential wisdom, and therefore worthless. Much more quietly, she completed her education during these years, moving from the Wright-Humason School for the Deaf in 1894 to the Cambridge School for Young Ladies (1896–1897). She was admitted to Radcliffe in 1900. Keller's improbable success (she took the same entrance exams as all others and graduated in 1904 with honors in German and English) answered most of the critics. Her protean accomplishments caused Mark Twain to dub her "the greatest woman since Joan of Arc."

Keller's extraordinary intellectual independence and her total reliance on her translators, two factors seemingly at odds, often took the young woman to the same end: a life that continuously offended convention and shattered expectations. From her unconventional religion (Swedenborgianism), which she adopted in 1896 and never relinquished, to her fascination with radical political causes—including the Industrial Workers of the World (IWW) and socialism in general—she never wavered in the face of criticism. Similar to the Social Gospel, the missionary orientation of her faith merged well with her personal intentions.

Particularly when she was a child Keller's handlers peddled her as half-wunderkind and half-freak. She was brought to Niagara Falls and the New York World's Fair of 1893 in the company of Alexander Bell and soon introduced to President Grover Cleveland. As an adult (and until Anne Sullivan's death in 1936), Keller leaned heavily on the advice of Sullivan and that of Sullivan's husband, John Macy. Macy's radical political views strengthened Keller's own tendencies.

Between 1909 and 1924, when she turned her energies to campaign for the American Foundation for the Blind, Keller was in the forefront of the most advanced Progressives and very often of American radicals as well. In 1909 she joined the Socialist party, only to resign just before World War I to protest what she saw as its excessive caution. In 1918, after joining the IWW, she supported the 101 "Wobblies" on trial in Chicago for illegal, antiwar activities, explaining that "their cause is my cause." She militantly opposed American entry into World War I, calling it a "capitalistic war." She also campaigned for woman suffrage, regarding votes for women as a sure cure for war. Pacifism energized her the most. "Let no workingman join the army that is to be organized by order of Congress," she declared in 1915. She even quoted Marx and Eng-

els approvingly on occasion. Such words landed less famous Americans in jail after war began in April 1917, and Keller was less strident thereafter, but she still denounced militarism and refused to retract her earlier statements. Socialism, which called for aid to the most helpless and to the disadvantaged, appealed to her. Her support for radicalism was thus of a piece with her humanitarianism and her self-conscious crusade for the essential equality of the handicapped. Her radicalism only hardened in the wake of public criticism, which she took as a sign of prejudice toward those in her condition. "I do not object to harsh criticism," she explained, "so long as I am treated like a human being with a mind of her own."

After the war, and increasingly in the 1920s, Keller's popularity as an author became a casualty of her ideas and the conservative political climate. To make money for herself and the cause of the blind, she appeared in a movie of her life (*Deliverance*, 1919) and between 1920 and 1923 toured the vaudeville circuit with her mentor Sullivan. Alone on stage, Sullivan would explain her achievement for the bulk of the twenty-minute act. Then Helen would appear, speak, and use humor to good advantage for a few moments. The act (which she seems to have enjoyed) did much to teach her how to rehabilitate her image and introduced her to a widening circle of admiring celebrities and financial supporters. In 1924 the American Foundation for the Blind began sending Keller and Sullivan to fundraising gatherings using the same techniques as in the vaudeville act to raise money for the blind, the cause that would remain her single focus for the rest of her life.

Only once, in the late 1920s, did Keller interrupt her lecturing efforts on behalf of the foundation, and then only to return to her writing. Hitherto her books had been consciously didactic, designed to teach the public about the plight of the blind everywhere through lessons extrapolated from her own personal experience. *The World I Live In* (1908), one of her most critically acclaimed books, was intended to assist the Massachusetts Commission for the Blind, to which she had been appointed in 1906. Her books from the 1920s to the end of her life were more personal and popular; less consciously reformist, they perhaps ironically had more impact for good than her earlier writings. *My Religion* (1927) and *Midstream—My Later Life* (1929) brought her story to a new generation, but it was her final book, *Teacher* (1955), that had the widest circulation and most impact. The book was a meditation on the meaning of her life with Sullivan, a final return to the subject of education, which the public much preferred to her political views.

During the Great Depression, the American Foundation for the Blind established a trust to meet Keller's financial needs for the rest of her life. She continued to lecture and write. The publication of *Helen Keller's Journal: 1936–1937* (1938) showed no softening of her political views. But in an age of fascism, she was more in the mainstream than before. Her condemnation of racism and Hitlerism, like her praise of the sit-down strikes of the 1930s, caused little stir. She supported the American war effort in World War II as a necessary fight for freedom and campaigned for Franklin D. Roosevelt in the election of 1944.

To her disappointment, Keller never married. In 1916 she and Peter Fagan, a 29-year-old secretary on her staff, took out a marriage license. A newspaper account of the wedding plans alarmed Kate Keller, who successfully pressured her daughter to break the engagement. Bitter at the episode, Keller remarked in later years, "If I could see, I would marry first of all." In spite of at least one later proposal (from a man she never met), however, Keller never again seems to have seriously considered the possibility of marriage.

In her final two decades, Keller's experiences and achievements were widely circulated by two films, the Academy Award–winning documentary *The Unconquered* (1953) and the 1962 film *The Miracle Worker*. Based on a television drama by William Gibson in 1957, then a prize-winning theater production in 1959, *The Miracle Worker* focused on the triumphs of her earliest years under the tutelage of Sullivan (who won the title billing). In Keller's last years every living president met or honored her, Lyndon Johnson in 1964 conferring upon her the nation's most distinguished civilian honor, the Presidential Medal of Freedom.

Keller died at her home in Easton, Connecticut. Within a generation of her death, most Americans had come to agree that the severely handicapped, while entitled to special public and private considerations, were not in any other respects necessarily limited in their capacities. Such a notion would have been unthinkable in 1880. To a significant if immeasurable degree, Helen Keller's private ordeal and public career helps account for this transformation. Some regarded her as a shameless self-promoter and publicity seeker, while most saw her and her principal teacher as a symbol of human potential and the indomitability of the spirit. To borrow a title from one of her books, few Americans had ever had so far to come, or had come so far "out of the dark."

• Keller's papers are at the American Foundation of the Blind in New York City. Her books not mentioned above include *The Song of the Stone Wall* (1910), *Out of the Dark: Essays, Letters and Addresses on Physical and Social Vision* (1913), *Optimism: My Key of Life* (1926), *We Bereaved* (1929), *Our Great Responsibility* (1931?), *Peace at Eventide* (1932), *Helen Keller in Scotland* (1933), *American Foundation for the Blind, 1923–1938* (1938), *Let Us Have Faith* (1940), and *The Open Door* (1957). An important account is Joseph P. Lash, *Helen and Teacher: The Story of Helen Keller and Anne Sullivan Macy* (1980). On Keller's political radicalism, see Frederick C. Giffin, "The Radical Vision of Helen Keller," *International Social Science Review* 59, no. 4 (1984): 27–32. See also Catherine Owen Peare, *The Helen Keller Story* (1959), and Lois Nicholson, *Helen Keller: Humanitarian* (1996). An extended obituary is in the *New York Times*, 2 June 1968.

RICHARD A. REIMAN

KELLER, James G. (27 June 1900–7 Feb. 1977), Roman Catholic priest and author, was born in Oakland, California, the son of James Keller, a haberdasher, and Margaret Selby. He studied for the priesthood in Menlo Park, California, from 1914 until 1921 when he joined the Catholic Foreign Mission Society of America (Maryknoll) in Ossining, New York, and continued his education. In 1925 he received an M.A. in medieval history from the Catholic University of America and was ordained to the priesthood. Placed in charge of the Maryknoll house in San Francisco, he quickly became the young missionary society's most successful recruiter and fundraiser. His youthful appearance, warm personality, persistent energy, and skill in appealing to people's emotions undergirded his success. He spoke in many Catholic schools and parishes but also devoted much time and effort to making more informal contacts with wealthy Catholics. He systematized the society's promotion efforts and established a house in Los Angeles. Although he joined Maryknoll to become a foreign missioner, he was never stationed outside the United States.

In 1932 Keller took charge of the society's New York city office and coordinated promotion efforts throughout the Northeast. He resided in New York the rest of his life. From 1934 to 1937 he helped rehabilitate the New York office of the Society for the Propagation of the Faith, the Catholic mission organization. Always concerned with effective use of the media, he redesigned its magazine, *Catholic Mission*, to give it a more contemporary look and also edited Maryknoll's own journal, *The Field Afar*. In 1943 he coauthored with *New York Times* writer Meyer Berger the bestselling *Men of Maryknoll*.

While promoting Maryknoll, Keller developed a more expansive understanding of his vocation. He felt his primary task should be to encourage lay Catholics not simply to support Maryknoll missioners but rather to work consciously themselves as Christian missioners in their own communities. In a 1945 article, "What about the Hundred Million?" published in a journal for Catholic clergy (*American Ecclesiastical Review* 112 [May 1945]: 321–49), he referred to such people as "Christophers" (Greek for "Christ-bearers") because they brought Christ to people who did not know him or who were hostile to Christianity. He estimated that 100 million Americans had no formal ties to religion and argued that it was up to ordinary people, acting as Christophers, to reach them.

Keller linked Christianity and the American way of life. He believed that American civilization depended upon "great Christian ideals," including "the concept of a personal God, the divinity of Christ, the Ten Commandments, the sacredness of the individual, and the sanctity of marriage and home." Accordingly he regarded various types of "materialism" and "atheism" as the major threats to Christianity and American democracy. Chief among these was Communism. He charged that Communists had influence far beyond their numbers in America because they had an organized and active membership that involved itself in influential areas such as education, communication, organized labor, and government. He advanced a "positive approach" to this problem: Christians should actively seek to exert a godly influence in these fields. His stories and later publications were soon filled with stories illustrating the difference one person could make. He summarized his message with the Chinese proverb: "It is better to light one candle than to curse the darkness."

Keller felt that promoting the Christopher idea should be a natural part of Maryknoll's work. The society, however, would not support it. Maryknoll superior general Bishop James E. Walsh believed that the society should focus only on foreign mission, and, like other critics within the church, he judged major aspects of Keller's Christopher proposal "entirely naive, with no grasp of what a spiritual problem really involves" (quoted in Armstrong, p. 73). In 1946, however, the new superior general Bishop Raymond A. Lane, granted Keller permission to found the Christophers as an independent organization.

The Christophers met with considerable popular support. In 1948 Keller's book *You Can Change the World* sold 150,000 copies in its first five months of publication. Keller insisted that his organization maintain neither a membership roll nor local chapters. Instead the organization served simply to awaken in others "a sense of personal responsibility to work for the corporate good of all, no matter what the sacrifice." He and his staff promoted his ideas through motivational newsletters, books, and daily devotional guides. By 1954 the *Christopher News Notes* boasted a circulation of 800,000. Keller sought to address not only Catholics but all who would listen. In motivating people to take an active and faithful role in their society he saw no need to distinguish between Protestants and Catholics. When this was challenged by some within the church, Keller emphasized the missionary role of the organization. In *You Can Change the World* he explained that each person "is a child of God, at least through creation. Each, doing even one thing for Him, can start to be a Christopher, a Christ-bearer."

Some of Keller's most pioneering work was in television and film. In order to promote films in concert with Christian principles he established annual Christopher awards in 1949. In 1950 he moved into film himself, summoning an all-star cast including Loretta Young, Jack Benny, Bing Crosby, and Bob Hope for his short film, *You Can Change the World*. He began to produce fifteen-minute films for television in 1952. Most consisted of inspirational interviews with celebrities. By 1954 202 television stations carried the program. In 1964 the program expanded to a half-hour in length and began to be produced in color. In 1969 Keller retired because of Parkinson's disease, entrusting the television program and the organization to fellow Maryknoller Father Richard Armstrong. He resided at the Maryknoll residence in New York City until his death at New York Hospital.

The popularity of Keller's publications and message indicate that he represented an important strain in American popular religion. Some leaders within Maryknoll and the Roman Catholic Church were uncomfortable with his easy marriage of Catholic Christianity and American culture and his lack of emphasis on spiritual development and the institution of the church. His emphasis on the individual, while very American, was at odds with the more communal emphasis of Catholic social teaching. Yet, his ecumenical openness and his emphasis on the active engagement of laity in society as an intrinsic part of their Christian duty was dramatically reaffirmed by the Second Vatican Council (1963–1965). His de-emphasis of a uniquely Catholic identity in favor of a broader Christian and American identity helped to integrate Catholics more fully into American culture.

Although its prominence had lessened by the end of the twentieth century, the Christophers continued the weekly television show, annual awards, *News Notes*, and other publications begun by Keller. Many had been printed in Spanish as well as English and circulated beyond the United States. While its leadership remained Roman Catholic, the organization continued to present Keller's message of individual worth and "service to God and humanity" within a broad Judeo-Christian framework.

• The archives of the Christophers, including Keller's papers, are at the organization's office in New York City. In addition to the works mentioned above, Keller wrote *To Light a Candle: The Autobiography of James Keller, Founder of the Christophers* (1963). Richard Armstrong, *Out to Change the World: A Life of Father James Keller of the Christophers* (1984), gives the most complete account of Keller's life and work. Martin E. Marty discussed Keller's impact on the changing role of Catholicism in American society in *Under God, Indivisible, 1941–1960*, vol. 3 of *Modern American Religion* (1996). Joseph P. Chinnici, *Living Stones: The History and Structure of American Catholic Spirituality* (1989), is an important study of Keller's place in American Catholicism and a guide to Keller's own work.

DAVID R. BAINS

KELLER, Kaufman Thuma (27 Nov. 1885–21 Jan. 1966), automobile executive, was born in Mount Joy, Pennsylvania, the son of Zachariah W. Keller and Carrie B. Thuma, farmers. Keller, who throughout his life was known by his first and middle initials, "K. T.," was thirteen when he was employed in his first job as a drill press operator in a factory, working after school and on Saturdays. After graduating from high school in 1901 he attended Wade Business College in Lancaster, Pennsylvania, where he studied secretarial courses. In 1904 he began a two-year stint in the British Isles, working as a secretary to a Baptist minister and lecturer. Upon his return to the United States, Keller became a clerk in the Westinghouse Machine Company in East Pittsburgh, Pennsylvania. But Keller decided that clerical work was not his calling, and he took a significant cut in pay to sign on as an apprentice in a machine shop at Westinghouse. In

1909, a year after completing his apprenticeship, he was promoted to assistant to the superintendent of Westinghouse's automobile engine department.

In 1910 Keller came to Detroit as chief inspector for the Detroit Metal Products Company, a maker of automobile axles. Keller grew deeply interested in automobiles and determined to learn more about them, working for a number of different companies and accepting a new job whenever it presented an opportunity to learn a new phase of the industry. Over the next year he found work with the Metzger, Hudson, and Maxwell automobile companies. In 1911 Keller began work at the central office of General Motors (GM), working primarily on the production of Cadillac cars. In that same year he married Adelaide Taylor; the couple would have two sons. At General Motors he encountered Walter P. Chrysler in a serendipitous meeting that later allowed Keller to rise to the top of the corporation that Chrysler was to found. Although Keller left GM to work for the Cole Company, in 1915 he returned to GM as a master mechanic of Buick. This position allowed him to rekindle his friendship with Chrysler, who was president of Buick. In 1918 Keller joined the mechanical and engineering staff in the GM central office, and three years later he became vice president of Chevrolet in charge of manufacturing. In 1924 Keller moved to Oshawa, Ontario, to become general manager of GM's Canadian operations.

In the meantime, Walter P. Chrysler had left GM and had formed his own company. In 1926 Chrysler lured Keller from GM to join the Chrysler Corporation as vice president in charge of manufacturing. The following year he also became a director of the corporation. In 1928 Keller took charge of the Homeric project of combining the Dodge Brothers plants and operations, which Chrysler had purchased that year, with those of the Chrysler Corporation. The following year Keller was rewarded for his work when he became president of Dodge; he also retained his positions as vice president and director of the parent Chrysler Corporation. Within three months after assuming command at Dodge he had increased efficiency so much that only half of the previous floor space was needed, and he had also laid plans for a new line of cars.

In 1935 Keller became president of the Chrysler Corporation. Although as chairman of the board Walter P. Chrysler continued to run the corporation, Keller assumed increasing responsibilities during the late 1930s as Chrysler's health began to fail. After Chrysler's death in 1940, Keller was made chief executive officer of the corporation. He held this position until 1950, when the corporation's directors named him chairman of the board, at which time Keller was succeeded as Chrysler president by Lester Colbert. Keller presided over a phenomenal growth in the Chrysler Corporation, which by 1941 had become the second largest automaker in the country and had produced over ten million passenger cars and trucks since its inception in 1925, accounting for one out of every four cars sold in the United States. During every year since

Keller had become president, Chrysler's annual output of cars and trucks had surpassed the one million mark.

Keller presided over many engineering innovations that contributed to Chrysler's success. The corporation introduced the "Superfinish" manufacturing process, which gave internal engine parts and chassis components a smooth surface so as to minimize friction and wear. Chrysler engines also offered the "Powermatic shift," a vacuum-assisted transmission that allowed the driver to change gears with greater ease, and the semiautomatic "Fluid Drive," which provided for automatic shifting in certain gear ranges, important at a time when American motorists were growing weary of manual shifting. Other engineering advances that came during Keller's tenure at Chrysler included built-in window defrosters, one-piece steel roof construction, push-button starters on the dashboard (replacing foot pedals), and the Safety-Rim wheel, which prevented the tire from completely collapsing during a blowout.

During his years as head of the Chrysler Corporation, Keller played a vital role in directing the company's involvement in military production. During World War II he led Chrysler's quick adjustment to wartime production and was responsible for creating an arsenal in Center Line, Michigan, which turned out tanks as fast as most automobile plants turned out cars. Chrysler produced more than 23,000 of its most successful tank, the 25-ton M-3 medium tank. During the war Chrysler also produced 18,000 B-29 bomber engines; B-29 fuselage sections; 60,000 heavy antiaircraft cannons; submarine nets; gyrocompasses; and small arms ammunition. During the Korean War Chrysler produced army trucks as well as heavy and medium tanks.

Keller also served as a government consultant for American military defense. During World War II he served on the advisory staff of the U.S. Army's Chief of Ordnance. In 1946 President Harry S. Truman awarded Keller the Medal for Merit for his service to the country during the war. In 1950 Secretary of Defense George C. Marshall appointed Keller director of guided missiles, a position he held for three years. Keller was credited with bringing drive and direction to the country's languishing guided missile program and with accelerating it by as much as two years. In 1954 he received the U.S. Air Force Exceptional Service Award for the Chrysler Corporation's role in aircraft production during World War II.

In the postwar years Keller guided the Chrysler Corporation through a successful reconversion to passenger car production and through plant expansions and the introduction of many engineering advances in its cars. Between 1945 and 1954 the company constructed or purchased twenty-seven plants, bringing its total number of plants to fifty-four, and doubled its factory floor space. In 1954 the company also established the 4,000-acre Chrysler proving grounds near Chelsea, Michigan. Postwar innovations in Chrysler automobiles included power steering, the advanced

Oriflow shock absorbers, and the 180-horsepower V-8 "FirePower" engine, which at the time was the world's most powerful production passenger car engine. Keller took an active interest in automobile styling and resisted the postwar trend, embraced by GM and Ford, toward longer and wider cars. He preferred a boxcar look, believing that this style enhanced passenger comfort; as a result, Chrysler cars were higher and shorter than others on the road. Keller insisted that a five-gallon milk container should be able to fit upright into the luggage compartment of every Chrysler car. He also insisted that passengers should be able to wear a hat while sitting in the front or back seats, a requirement that he personally verified by visiting the studios and sitting in cars himself. One story, perhaps apocryphal, was that the stoutly built Keller checked cars to ensure that their designs allowed room for himself behind the driver's seat, thereby guaranteeing that there would be ample room for the average-sized driver.

Keller retired from Chrysler in 1956 and opened an office in the Fisher Building in downtown Detroit, involving himself in civic and social projects. He was especially proud of his work in enhancing Detroit's cultural life, and he served for twenty-one years on the city's arts commission. During his retirement he also continued to serve as an adviser to the Defense Department.

Keller lived in Palmer Woods, Michigan. His glamorous residence included architectural innovations as well as art objects and gardens. Ever the machinist, he kept a machine shop in the basement of his house. Keller also owned a home in Fort Lauderdale, Florida, where he spent winters.

Keller died in London, England, while on a study tour with a group representing Detroit's Institute of Arts Museum. A colorful leader—forceful, blunt, and at times profane—Keller belonged to a generation of automobile executives who grew up with the American automobile and who were well versed in the mechanics of the car. Throughout his transition from machinist to corporation executive, Keller retained a love for tools and machines and preferred to be on the factory floor rather than at his desk. Most importantly, he helped Chrysler develop into one of the world's foremost automobile companies; he was one of a select group of automobile executives whose leadership transformed the industry.

• The National Automotive History Collection and the Burton Historical Collection of the Detroit Public Library maintain files on Keller. Keller was featured in a cover story, "K. T. of Chrysler," in *Time*, 16 Oct. 1939, pp. 87–88. An article describing Keller's leadership of Chrysler's postwar business is "Chrysler Operation," *Fortune*, Oct. 1948, pp. 101–5. "Shifting Guided Missiles From Lab To Defense Line," *U.S. News and World Report*, 5 Feb. 1954, p. 50ff., contains effusive praise for Keller's leadership of the government's guided missile program. Another description of this program is B. S. Lee, "Missiles Super-Agency Fast Taking Shape," *Aviation Week*, 30 Oct. 1950, pp. 12–14. Obituaries are in the *Detroit Free Press* and the *New York Times*, 22 Jan. 1966.

YANEK MIECZKOWSKI

KELLERMAN, Annette (6 July 1887–5 Nov. 1975), swimming, vaudeville, and film star, was born in Sydney, Australia, the daughter of Frederick Kellerman, a musician, and Alice Charbonnet, a concert pianist. A weak child, Kellerman began swimming as physical therapy for a mild case of polio. Feeling more graceful in water than on land in her leg braces, swimming literally became her life. As the strength in her legs increased, she also learned to dive. In 1902 she won her first title as Swim Champion of New South Wales and set a world record of 78 seconds for 100 yards using the newly introduced racing technique of the double-over arm crawl and scissors kick. By her own admission, she also reigned as the champion girl diver of Australia the same year. The next year, she set a world record for the mile at 32:29 minutes, subsequently lowering it to 28:00 minutes. Her first of many record-setting distance swims covered 10 miles in Australia's Yarrow River. She began professional swimming and diving exhibitions in Sydney, then toured Melbourne and Adelaide.

In 1904 her father took her to England to promote her aquatic skills. Sponsored by the Harmsworth newspapers, she swam 17 miles down the Thames and attempted to be the first woman—and the first person in thirty-six years—to swim the English Channel. Her three attempts failed, but her covering of three-fourths of the distance in 10.5 hours remained a women's record for many years. After more swimming stunts—notably a 7-mile swim in the Seine through Paris and a 22-mile swim in the Danube from Tuln to Vienna—garnered her more publicity, she signed with Arthur Collins, the "Prince of Showmen," to star in his London music hall. Her swimming and diving act then toured Great Britain with great success.

Kellerman's arrival in the United States in 1907 erupted in scandal when she appeared on Boston's Revere Beach in a one-piece bathing suit, a style of racing suit she always wore even when she was not competing. Arrested for indecent exposure, her court case brought her instant fame as the progenitor of modern swimwear. Women began to abandon the cumbersome and heavy wool skirts, blouses, and stockings Victorian mores dictated they wear. After her charges were dismissed in Boston, she traveled to Chicago for her first American playdate at the White City Amusement Park, where she did fifty-five shows a week for seven weeks. B. F. Keith then engaged her as a headliner in his Keith/Orpheum vaudeville circuit for $1,250 a week. She remained with Keith for two years, performing fourteen shows a week. Her act consisted of singing, dancing, playing the violin, tightrope walking, diving, and swimming in a large glass cage. In 1910 she signed with William Morris to manage her vaudeville career (resulting in a lawsuit by Keith/Orpheum), and in 1912, when she married James Sullivan, she decided to let her new husband manage her career (requiring her to sue William Morris). Under Sullivan's management, they built a small fortune in vaudeville (including five world tours between 1914 and 1929 and numerous appearances at New York City's Hippodrome) and moved into filmmaking.

Kellerman had made her U.S. film debut in a Vitagraph short, *Diving Venus* (1909), for which she received the largest salary the studio had ever paid and her own glass tank. She demonstrated some exercises, dives, and swimming techniques. Her first feature film, *Neptune's Daughter* (Universal, 1914), won major acclaim. She played a mermaid granted legs so that she could seek out the humans who killed her younger sister. The film, shot on location in Bermuda, fully exploited her diving and swimming skills featuring a 45-foot solo dive, a 30-foot tandem dive, and much underwater swimming. She followed this success with *A Daughter of the Gods* (Fox, 1916). Shot on location in Jamaica, the film took nine months to shoot, featured a cast of 20,000, required the construction of two cities (one underwater), employed a camera in a diving bell, and cost over $1 million (a record budget). As before, the film functioned as a showcase for Kellerman's abilities; her greatest stunt was a 92-foot dive—for which she was bound hand and foot. She made three more feature films, *Queen of the Sea* (1918), *What Women Love* (1920), and *Venus of the South Seas* (1924). *What Women Love* won her the title of "the Douglas Fairbanks of the Screen Girls Athletic Association." Of these five films, only ten minutes from *Neptune's Daughter* seems to have survived.

In 1918 Kellerman published two books designed for women, *Physical Beauty* and *How to Swim. Physical Beauty* railed against the corset while extolling the virtues of exercise and diet (she was a vegetarian) to achieve proper posture, strength, and body tone. She demonstrated through illustration and direction how to achieve her world-renowned physical perfection. *How to Swim* followed the same tack, advocating swimming as an excellent form of exercise. These books were among the first to offer women a regimen of physical fitness.

After her last world tour ended in 1929, she limited her activities to the always popular "Swimologues" (physical fitness lecture tours featuring underwater films shot by her husband), running a health food store in Long Beach, California, and relaxing on Pandamus Island, an island inside Australia's Great Barrier Reef that she and her husband owned. During World War II she devoted her talents to charity benefits (as she had during World War I) and established and ran an Australian Red Cross theatrical unit. Her life came full circle in 1952 when MGM released *Million Dollar Mermaid*, starring Esther Williams. A fictionalized biography of Kellerman, she served as technical adviser on the film. *Million Dollar Mermaid* follows Kellerman's life from her early years as a crippled child to the spectacular Hippodrome shows to her severe accident when an 8,000-gallon glass tank broke during the filming of *Neptune's Daughter*.

After her husband died in 1953, she moved to Southport, Queensland, Australia, where she lived for more than twenty years, until her death there. In 1974 she was inducted into the International Swimming Hall of Fame in Fort Lauderdale, Florida, for "doing more to popularize swimming (especially for women) than any other person in the early years."

Kellerman's aquatic skills set numerous records and served as the basis for many years of a successful international vaudeville career—a career in which she helped introduce synchronized swimming with her Acquabelles and women's high diving. Her move into film stardom established the tradition of Hollywood's exploitation of successful athletes (for example, Johnny Weissmuller, Sonja Henie, Esther Williams, and Arnold Schwarzenegger) in films tailored to showcase their unique talents. The publicity surrounding her one-piece bathing suit altered the course of women's swimwear design toward the contemporary styles of the maillot, tank, and bikini. She was an athletic feminist, and her lectures, books, performances, and films encouraged and inspired women to break away from the antiathletic tradition of their gender to pursue health and beauty through exercise and diet. As "swimming's greatest saleswoman," Kellerman took an esoteric sport and moved it into popular culture.

• The most complete Hollywood biography of Annette Kellerman is DeWitt Bodeen and Larry Holland, "Neptune's Daughters," *Films in Review* 30 (Feb. 1979): 73–88. A full listing of her swimming accomplishments is in *The 1975 Yearbook of the International Swimming Hall of Fame*, ed. Buck Dawson. Other profiles and biographical sketches are in Caroline Caffin, *Vaudeville* (1914); Agnes Roger, *Women Are Here to Stay* (1949); Richard Lamparski, *Whatever Became of . . . ?* (1968); Philip Scheuer, "Annette Kellerman All for Esther Now," *Los Angeles Times*, 23 Mar. 1952; and Jack Pollard, *Swimming: Australian Style* (1963). Reviews of her first three films are in *Moving Picture World*, 6 Dec. 1909, and *Film Index*, 6 Dec. 1909, *Diving Venus*; *Variety*, 10 Apr. 1914, *Neptune's Daughter*; and *Variety*, 16 Nov. 1916, *A Daughter of the Gods*. Obituaries are in the *New York Times*, 6 Nov. 1975, and *Newsweek* and *Time*, both 17 Nov. 1975.

GREG S. FALLER

KELLETT, W. Wallace (20 Dec. 1891–22 July 1951), aircraft executive and manufacturer, was born William Wallace Kellett in Boston, Massachusetts, the son of William W. Kellett and Frances R. Flagler. His family was well off, but his father's occupation is not known. He graduated from Princeton University in 1913, but his field of study is not known beyond his graduating with a bachelor of letters. He served with the American Ambulance Field Service during World War I then became a fighter pilot in the French Air Force. This service kindled an interest in aviation that would last the rest of Kellett's life.

In 1919 he began working in the field of aircraft manufacturing, and in July 1929 he and three partners founded the Kellett Aircraft Corporation in Philadelphia, an expansion of an aircraft dealership begun in 1923 at the Pine Valley airport. From the start, the new corporation focused on the development of rotary-wing aircraft. The company's first design, a gyroplane with a large horizontal tail, was incapable of flight. In 1928 Kellett married Virginia Fink; they did not have children.

In 1931 Kellett obtained a license to construct a more conventional autogiro, a type of aircraft first practically developed in 1923 by Juan de la Cierva Codorniu of Spain. The autogiro was an essential precursor to the helicopter but different from it in that its rotor was not power-driven in flight. Rather, the aircraft's engine started the rotor spinning, after which a clutch transferred power to a propeller for horizontal thrust. While it was significantly slower than even contemporary conventional airplanes, it could take off and land on shorter fields and was incapable of stalling like a fixed-wing aircraft.

Kellett's corporation assumed the name Kellett Autogiro Corporation in 1932. Over the course of the next eleven years, it developed at least nine different models of autogiros. The original, the K-2 or KA-1, made its initial flight on 24 April 1931 and had a production run of twelve aircraft. The KD-1 followed, the first American direct-control autogiro, so-called because it achieved control entirely by the tilting of the rotor head. Kellett delivered the KD-1 in 1935, and it flew on 19 May 1939 with a load of mail from a Washington, D.C., street to Hoover Airport on the grounds of the Pentagon, a demonstration that helped Eastern Air Lines obtain a contract for regular mail service in Philadelphia. Using a later model, the KD-1B, Eastern operated five round trips per day between 6 July 1939 and 5 July 1940 from Camden Central Airport in New Jersey to the roof of Philadelphia's central post office—the first use of an autogiro for delivery of daily mail. Meanwhile, the KD-1A had made the first Arctic flights in a rotary-wing aircraft in 1937.

The YG-1/1A/1B, the military version of the KD-1/KD-1A, equipped the U.S. Army Air Corps Autogiro School formed at Patterson Field near Dayton, Ohio, in 1938. This school trained nine pilots and nine mechanics that year before service testing showed that the difficult flying characteristics and comparatively small payload capacity put the autogiro at a disadvantage to fixed-wing aircraft despite its shorter take-off and landing distances. The series nevertheless played an important role in aviation history because tests on the YG-1B by the National Advisory Committee for Aeronautics (NACA) at Langley Field contributed to knowledge about rotor blades that was applied to some of the first helicopters.

A later Kellett model, the XR-2, was also important in the development of rotary-wing aircraft. Destroyed by ground resonance (a potentially destructive vibration caused by the interaction of the blade motion of a rotary-wing aircraft that is still on the ground with its supporting structure), it provided a dramatic demonstration of a problem that had plagued the industry, prompting engineers at Kellett Corporation and the NACA independently to arrive at mathematical solutions that yielded a proper configuration.

The first successful helicopter models were developed in Europe in 1935–1936 and were produced by Igor Sikorsky in the United States beginning in 1940.

Seeing the handwriting on the wall, the Kellett Corporation changed the middle part of its name back to Aircraft from Autogiro in June 1943. Although important for its role in development, it had remained small, generating only some 40 autogiros—not an insignificant percentage of the roughly 90 made in the United States but a smaller proportion of the 500 or so built worldwide.

During World War II, the Kellett Corporation—like other defense industries—grew enormously. According to Kellett's obituaries, the firm had twelve separate plants and employed over 3,000 people at one point during the war. It primarily manufactured parts for military aircraft but also produced an early successful helicopter, the XR-8, that first flew on 7 August 1944.

Besides being president of his own firm, Kellett joined the Seversky Aircraft Corporation when it reorganized in 1931. He became a director of that firm in 1938 and its president the following year, when it assumed the name Republic Aviation Corp. He was named chairman of the board in 1943, but two years later he resigned to devote all of his time to his own firm.

Kellett was a trustee of Temple University, and in 1937 he became a member of the Pennsylvania State Aviation Council. In 1939 he was named chairman of the Juan de la Cierva Memorial Fellowship Committee, which sponsored research into rotary-wing aerodynamics at New York University. He was also the head of the Aeronautical Chamber of Commerce of America, president of the Aero Club of Pennsylvania, and a member of the Institute of Aeronautical Sciences. After a short illness he died in Philadelphia and was buried in Boston.

The helicopter figured prominently in rescue and communication work during the Korean War and became a major weapon during the Vietnamese conflict. Kellett was a significant participant in its development, even though his role was secondary to those of Cierva and Sikorsky.

• Biographical information about Kellett is mostly restricted to obituaries in the *New York Times* and the *Philadelphia Inquirer*, 23 July 1951, and *American Helicopter*, Aug. 1951, p. 21. Information about the aircraft he produced and about the general development of the autogiro and the helicopter is available in Peter W. Brooks, *Cierva Autogiros: The Development of Rotary-Wing Flight* (1988). See also in the latter connection Lynn Montross, *Cavalry of the Sky: The Story of U.S. Marine Combat Helicopters* (1954).

J. D. HUNLEY

KELLEY, Alfred (7 Nov. 1789–2 Dec. 1859), promoter of canal, railroad, banking, and taxation systems, was born in Middlefield, Connecticut, the son of Daniel Kelley, a large property owner, and Jemima Stow. When Kelley was nine years old he and his family moved to Lowville, New York. He later attended an academy at Fairfield and read law for three years in Whitesboro, both in that state. In 1810 he went on horseback with his uncle, Joshua Stow (who in 1796 had helped survey the Western Reserve), and a young medical student, Jared P. Kirtland, to Cleveland, Ohio, which consisted of three frame houses and five or six log ones. Kelley's parents would later join him there. The trio followed the route later selected for the Erie Canal (which had been advocated in Congress the previous winter), and everywhere they stopped Kelley defended the project so vehemently that Kirtland considered him "a monomaniac" (Bates, p. 4). That same year he was admitted to the bar, becoming Cleveland's first lawyer and Cuyahoga County's prosecuting attorney.

In 1814 Kelley became the youngest person in the state assembly (serving twelve sessions in it and the state senate, before retiring in 1857 as its oldest member). In 1817 he married Mary Seymour Welles; they had eleven children (five of whom died in infancy). In 1819 he presented to the legislature the first bill framed in the United States or in Europe to abolish imprisonment for debt and predicted accurately that he would live to see it become law (1838). Kelley early favored allowing blacks to testify in trials as fully as whites. He also wanted state educational funds to be apportioned to every child in the state in equal amounts. In 1830 his bill making the management of public schools part of the state government and insisting that these schools become "systemized and made efficient" became law (Bates, p. 94).

A "masterful promoter of internal improvements," Kelley played in Ohio the role that DeWitt Clinton had played in New York before going beyond him to master "the challenge of canal construction in the field" (Scheiber, p. 366). From the beginning of his legislative service, Kelley (who became more familiar with Ohio's streams and topography than any of his contemporaries) was its expert on canals. In early 1819 Governor Ethan Allen Brown pushed a Lake Erie–Ohio River canal, and despite the panic of that year Kelley helped keep the idea alive. When a bill providing for a canal commission was finally passed in February 1822, he was one of its members; and later, along with Micajah Williams, he was made an acting commissioner, responsible for the project's surveys.

"Equally gifted in . . . conceiving the large design and understanding the necessity for perfection and mastery of detail," Kelley learned from his on-site visits to the Erie Canal and from its senior engineers whom he employed in the Ohio surveys (Scheiber, pp. 369–70). When in 1825 the construction of the Ohio and Miami canals was approved by the legislature, Kelley and Williams were again made acting commissioners. This time they served for the eight years it took to complete the two canals (at the least expensive cost per mile on record). No "slides" occurred on these canals because they were "braced and strengthened by taking the dirt to the bottom, and packing and building up with it" (Yaple, p. 6). Kelley was so occupied with his canal work (for which he was paid $3 per day) that he abandoned his lucrative law practice and in 1830 moved his family to Columbus. Like the engineers and laborers he hired and supervised, he lived

near the canal and suffered from "canal malaria." Sometimes his wife and a younger child would accompany him. While living nearby with a Quaker family, his six-year-old daughter Charlotte became feverish and died. He himself was so sick that he could not travel to Akron, where his wife without a physician gave birth to their son Henry. When his wife could not be with him, he complained to her of his headache caused by "constant confinement leaning over a table" while "making out maps and plans of our Canal lines," but insisted it would "wear off as I become accustomed to it" (Cummings, p. 42). He hoped that "a trip from Lake Erie to the Ohio River on a canal," which he "had a large share in making," would repay his wife "for many a solitary night" (Scheiber, p. 366).

In Columbus Kelley designed for his family one of the largest and finest Greek revival homes built in the Northwest, which they first occupied in 1838. When opposing Democrats called him a proud nabob living in a marble house (it was built of Ohio sandstone), his fellow Whigs countered, "Kelley is well known here to be a man of plain dress and manners" (Cummings, pp. 8–9). As the head of the Whig State Central Committee, Kelley called on Ohio Whigs to assemble in Columbus in February 1840 "to rescue the ark of the Constitution, and save your beloved country" and invited Cleveland delegates to make his new home their headquarters (Bates, p. 98). When sixty of them showed up, a feather bed was "placed in the middle of a carpeted library and used as a pillow" by the sleeping delegates, whose feet pointed out from the center, forming a "star" (Cummings, p. 8).

Having failed to follow Kelley's prudent advice to go slowly in further canal building, Ohio in 1841 was in danger of defaulting on its interest payments. In the years before the panic of 1837 state legislators had voted to extend the Miami Canal, build the Wabash and Erie Canal, and construct numerous branch lines simultaneously. To help the state weather its financial crisis, Kelley was appointed in March 1841 a canal fund commissioner. While in New York, he worked tirelessly to raise money for the January 1842 interest payment to preserve his state's credit and put up his New York and Ohio real-estate holdings as interest collateral to get foreign investors to buy Ohio bonds. In the spring of 1842 at a time of economic collapse when many states were defaulting on their bonds, Kelley went to England and succeeded, largely because of personal business relationships, in raising $400,000 to cover the July 1842 and January 1843 interest payments.

Kelley's role in salvaging the state's finances inspired him to support private investment through legislation. In February 1845 the bank bill he had introduced in the state legislature was enacted. It incorporated a State Bank of Ohio (which through its branches provided banking capital in areas that needed it), strictly regulated the independent banks of the state, and became the model for the federal law governing the national banking system.

Also in 1845 Kelley comprehensively investigated the state's revenue system. In his report he showed the necessity of changing the old policy, which relied primarily on realty taxes, to a policy by which all property would bear a portion of the burden according to its true value. Small burdens, spread fairly and evenly, he showed, would bring in enough revenue for the state to discharge its liabilities. This report led the following year to revisions in Ohio tax law that lasted more than a hundred years.

In 1847 Kelley closed his important career as he had started it by providing Ohio with needed transportation facilities. Working this time in the private corporate sector, he became involved in railroads when the backers of the faltering Columbus & Xenia and the Cleveland, Columbus, & Cincinnati (CC&C) railroads pressed him to take over the presidencies of these roads. In 1851 he also became the president of the Cleveland, Painesville, & Ashtabula Railroad (carrying on a successful, prolonged legal battle to have it join eastern roads at Erie). In constructing these three railroads, Kelley was aided by a surge in Ohio's economy and the national revival from the earlier depression, but without him these roads would not have been successfully built. For he turned indifference to support in local areas and was so successful in securing financing that he was able to contract at one time for the entire length of the CC&C Railroad.

During four decades of "hectic change in the Ohio economy," Kelley "proved remarkably flexible and skilled in adapting himself to rapid economic development" (Scheiber, p. 392). Although Henry Clay's remark that "Kelley had too much cast-iron in his composition to be popular" was true for most of his career, by the time he died in Columbus, Kelley had accomplished so much for Ohio that he was the most popular man in the state (Bates, p. 210). Even Mathias Martin, one of his political adversaries, remarked: "At the outset of Mr. Kelley's career, Ohio was a rude, frontier State. . . . at his death it was firmly established as the third State in the Union, prosperous and flourishing; and in bringing about these changes and paving the way for them, Mr. Kelley showed a master mind" (Bates, pp. 207–8).

• Kelley papers, including an 1827 letter from DeWitt Clinton and a biographical sketch of Kelley in David H. Beardsley to John Barr, 30 Sept. 1858, are located at the Western Reserve Historical Society, Cleveland. The best evaluation of Kelley's career is Harry N. Scheiber, "Alfred Kelley and the Ohio Business Elite, 1822–1859," *Ohio History* 87 (1978): 365–92. Also important are the biography by Kelly's son-in-law, James L. Bates, *Alfred Kelley: His Life and Work* (1888), and Alfred Yaple, *Reminiscences of Alfred Kelley* (1875). The delightful story of Kelley's house, which remains standing, as well as some family material, can be found in Abbott Lowell Cummings, *The Alfred Kelley House of Columbus, Ohio: The Home of a Pioneer Statesman, with Mrs. Kelley's Recollections and Some Family Letters* (1953). See also James Henry Kennedy, "Alfred Kelley," *Magazine of Western History* 3 (1885–1886): 550–57; Walter Rumsey Marvin, "Alfred Kelley," *Museum Echoes* 33 (Feb. 1960): 11–14.

OLIVE HOOGENBOOM

KELLEY, Edgar Stillman (14 Apr. 1857–12 Nov. 1944), composer and teacher, was born in Sparta, Wisconsin, the son of Hiram Edgar Kelley, a merchant and later newspaper editor and federal revenue officer, and Mary Clarinda Bingham. After piano lessons from his mother, Kelley was inspired to become a musician through hearing pianist Blind Tom (Thomas Greene Bethune) and Theodore Thomas and the Chicago Symphony. His professional musical education began in Chicago between 1870 and 1876. Then, like most aspiring composers of his generation, Kelley traveled to Europe in 1876, studying at the Stuttgart Conservatory.

Upon returning to the United States in 1880, Kelley worked as an organist in San Francisco, where he developed an interest in the music of the local Chinese community. His first major performance was his *Macbeth* overture, performed by Theodore Thomas and the Chicago Symphony on 3 August 1883. Kelley married Jessie Gregg, a pianist and teacher, in 1891; they would have no children. She was later active in the National Federation of Music Clubs. Together they formed the Kelley Stillman Publishing Company, which published several of Kelley's scores. She was also director of music at Western College in Oxford, Ohio (1910–1934).

Between 1887 and 1892 Kelley was a conductor and teacher in New York, including the New York College of Music (1891–1892). From 1893 to 1895 he was the music critic for the *San Francisco Examiner*. He returned to New York in 1896 to take a position at the University Extension of New York University (1896–1897). Kelley was elected to the National Institute of Arts and Letters in 1898. During 1901–1902 he taught at Yale University and between 1902 and 1910 taught piano and theory in Berlin. In 1910 Kelley received a permanent fellowship in composition from Western College, which was followed a year later by his major academic appointment, dean of the composition department of the Cincinnati Conservatory, a position he held until 1934. During these years, Kelley wrote two books, *Chopin the Composer* (1913) and *Musical Instruments* (1925). His eightieth birthday was honored in April 1937 with a nationally broadcast radio performance of his *Gulliver* Symphony performed by Walter Damrosch and the NBC Symphony.

Kelley's works were often successful, and he was held by some to be the successor of MacDowell. A major emphasis of his composition was for the theater, and he wrote several scores as incidental music to plays, as well as operettas: his *Puritania* ran for a hundred performances in Boston in 1892 and also went on tour. Kelley's incidental music to *Ben Hur*, the best-selling novel, premiered in 1899 and was a popular favorite for many years. He also seems to have had some interest in music for film, as there is a never-used film score among his papers (*Corianton*, 1930).

Kelley's early compositions were largely based on nineteenth-century German models, symphonic and chamber music based on literary themes, with little overt Americanism. But in the 1890s he became an early proponent of an emerging American art music, distinct from that of Europe. This idea began to gain some prominence around the turn of the century, owing in part to composer Antonin Dvořák's comments on the subject during his years in New York in the mid-1890s, and later through the efforts of Arthur Farwell and his Wa Wan Press, which published several works by Kelley in the first decade of the twentieth century. Kelley was among the first American composers to examine and make sympathetic use of musical materials from American musical traditions outside of the mainstream European repertory, especially the spirituals of African Americans and the music of Native Americans recently transcribed by ethnographers. His use of this material was relatively conservative, placing the borrowed music in settings typical of many nineteenth-century arrangements of folk music. In addition to his music on American themes, he wrote articles that expressed his ideas. With the change of taste following World War I, Kelley's works have fallen into obscurity in the concert hall, although recent research into the musical culture of this period may revive his reputation. Kelley died in New York City.

• Kelley's papers are in the Western College Archives at Miami University, Oxford, Ohio. His major compositions include *Alladin: A Chinese Suite*, op. 10 (1887–1993); *Puritania*, op. 11 (operetta, words by C. M. S. McClellan, 1892); *Ben Hur*, op. 17 (incidental music, after Lew Wallace, 1899); Symphony No. 1, *Gulliver: His Voyage to Lilliput*, op. 15 (1900, rev. 1936); *O Captain, My Captain!* op. 19 (chorus and orchestra, words by Walt Whitman, n.d.); Piano quintet, op. 20 (1898–1901); String quartet, op. 25 (1907, rev. of op. 1); *Alice in Wonderland* (orchestral suite, after Lewis Carroll, 1919); *America's Creed*, op. 40 (chorus and orchestra, 1919); and *Pit and the Pendulum* (orchestral suite after Edgar Allan Poe, 1930).

Two early appreciations of Kelly are R. Hughes, "Edgar Stillman Kelley," *Music* 10 (1896): 279, and Arthur Farwell and W. D. Darby, *Music in America* (1915), p. 368. Maurice King's "Edgar Stillman Kelley: American Composer, Teacher and Author" (Ph.D. diss., Florida State Univ., 1970) is a full-length study of Kelley. His theater works are examined in Leonard L. Rivenburg, "Edgar Stillman Kelley and the American Musical Theater," in *Musical Theater in America* (1984), p. 111. An obituary is in the *New York Times*, 13 Nov. 1944.

RON WIECKI

KELLEY, Edith Summers (28 Apr. 1884–9 June 1956), writer, was born in Ontario, Canada, the daughter of Scottish immigrants George Summers, the owner of a shingle mill, and Isabella Johnstone. Edith graduated with honors in modern languages from the University of Toronto in 1903. She then moved to New York and began work on Funk and Wagnall's *Standard Dictionary*, a job that led to the eye strain from which she suffered periodically throughout her life.

In 1906 Edith became secretary to Upton Sinclair, first at Princeton and then at the Socialist colony Helicon Hall. There she met Sinclair Lewis, to whom she was engaged for a short time and who proved an enthusiastic supporter of her work. Their relationship ended in the spring of 1907 after Lewis wrote a long letter of proposal. In January 1908 Edith married Lewis's roommate and friend Allan Updegraff, an aspiring writer and editor with whom she later had two children. Living in Greenwich Village until 1914, she met a variety of radical thinkers, including Charlotte Perkins Gilman, Emma Goldman, and Floyd Dell. When Edith's husband lost his job, she resorted to writing magazine stories ("stuff that I am not proud of, frothy and inconsequential") and taught night school in the Hell's Kitchen district of Manhattan.

After separating from Updegraff after five years, she became the common-law wife of Claude Fred Kelley, a sculptor she had met in the Village; they had one son. Realizing that Edith could not make a living from writing, the Kelleys pursued several unsuccessful ventures. Longing "for freedom from routine, open country, sunshine, leisure and a sense of independence," as Edith wrote, the Kelleys moved in 1914 to Kentucky to manage a 700-acre tobacco farm. Living for two years in a sharecropper's shack, she gathered much of the detail for her finest work, *Weeds*. From 1916 to 1920 the Kelleys ran a boarding house on an unprofitable farm in New Jersey. Then they moved to California's Imperial Valley, where they tried alfalfa farming. This failed experiment provided Kelley with material for her second book, *The Devil's Hand*.

Moving to a chicken ranch north of San Diego in 1921 and living in miserable conditions, Kelley began her novel *Weeds*, finishing it in 1923. Drawing upon her Kentucky experiences, Kelley drafted the story of a young girl who, in spite of unusual vitality and aesthetic sense, succumbs to the economic and social restrictions that rule in tobacco country. Sinclair Lewis enthusiastically recommended *Weeds* to his publishers and even volunteered to edit the text. Knowing the Kelleys' financial situation, he appealed for "hard dollars which will make it possible for her to work." Although *Weeds* received mostly favorable reviews, it was not a commercial success, and profits did not even match the advance Kelley had received.

An unsentimental account of a woman's descent from youthful potentialities to resignation to a gender-prescribed life, *Weeds* is a realistic, if painful, social history and character study. Heroine Judith Blackford, superior physically and spiritually to the inbred families around her, asserts a man-like independence, preferring outdoor chores to "women's work." Unusual eagerness and vision draw her to nature, but her natural drives also victimize her. The story traces her gradual submission to economic and patriarchal forces as she marries and works in the fields until pregnancy and motherhood trap her inside her tenant shack and stifle her search for a more meaningful life. Unwilling to accept the role society assigns to her, Judith is a "poppy among weeds." In an attempt to find someone who shares her sense of personal freedom, Judy has a brief affair with an itinerant evangelist and becomes pregnant. She attempts to induce a miscarriage and, after losing the child, rejects her husband as a lover.

She retreats from this stance only when her daughter suffers a near-fatal illness. Judy finally tragically submits to the hardships of the soil and to the constraints of her sex. At the novel's close, Judith realizes "the uselessness of struggle" and acquiesces "before the things which had to be."

Encouraged by Upton Sinclair and supported by a grant from the American Civil Liberties Union, Kelley was, by late 1924, at work on *The Devil's Hand*, published posthumously from her unrevised manuscript. The novel traces the psychological journey of a young woman whose dreams of an independent life on the land fade before the realities of oppressive work, economic dependence, and sexual needs. Rhoda Malone leaves a clerical job in Philadelphia to join the unconventional and assertive Kate Baxter in raising alfalfa in the Imperial Valley. Rhoda soon tires of sharing Kate's unrealized dream, rejects the valley as a second Eden, and finds her vitality drained. She has a brief affair with her Hindu neighbor and later thinks she finds a soul mate in an idealistic wanderer. But, when both desert her, Rhoda cannot cope with the physical and spiritual demands of farm life and marries a wealthy but unimaginative real estate broker. Ultimately the "new woman" fails to achieve her goal, lapsing into the security of conventional marriage and caught in the "Devil's Hand." Unlike *Weeds*, this novel incorporates restrained political messages, valorizing a socialist martyr and satirizing white-collar prejudices, but it is not a protest novel in the style of Sinclair. Kelley admitted, "I can't write such direct propaganda." Instead, *The Devil's Hand* is a realistic sociological study of life as Kelley had experienced it in southern California during the 1920s.

After 1925 the Kelleys made several moves within California as successive business ventures failed. During the depression Kelley worked as a cleaning woman, and not until the last ten years of her life did she find financial stability. In 1946 she moved to Los Gatos, California, where she later died.

Kelley's works lapsed into obscurity until 1972, when Matthew J. Bruccoli recovered *Weeds* and convinced Southern Illinois University Press to publish it in its Lost American Fiction series. The same series released *The Devil's Hand* in 1974 after obtaining the only extant manuscript from Kelley's son. Because her novels probe without sentimentality or bitterness the natural and cultural constraints on women, especially rural women, they hold special interest for feminist scholars. Kelley's fiction also prompts reconsideration of her place among the naturalists in its exploration of biological, psychological, and economic forces.

• Edith Summers Kelley's papers are in the Special Collections of the Morris Library at Southern Illinois University; her letters to Upton Sinclair and from Sinclair Lewis are in the Lilly Library of Indiana University. Matthew J. Bruccoli's introduction to *Weeds* and his afterword to *The Devil's Hand* provide valuable information, as do Charlotte Goodman's substantial entry in the *Dictionary of Literary Biography* and her afterword to the Feminist Press edition of *Weeds*. Goodman has also recovered a lengthy section on childbirth that was expurgated from the original edition of *Weeds*, and this appears in the Feminist Press edition. A brief postscript to *The Devil's Hand* by Patrick Kelley (Edith Summers Kelley's son) provides insight on the author's personality and point of view.

Recent critical commentaries are Elizabeth Ammons, *Conflicting Stories: American Women Writers at the Turn into the Twentieth Century* (1992), and Fran Zaniello, "Witnessing the Buried Life in Rural Kentucky: Edith Summers Kelley and *Weeds*," *Kentucky Review* 8, no. 3 (1988): 64–72. Feminist readings of Kelley's work include Charlotte Goodman, "Widening Perspectives, Narrowing Possibilities: The Trapped Woman in Edith Summers Kelley's *Weeds*," *Regionalism and the Female Imagination: A Collection of Essays* (1985), Goodman, "Images of American Rural Women in the Novel," *Michigan Papers in Women's Studies* 1 (1975): 57–70; Barbara Lootens, "A Struggle for Survival: Edith Summers Kelley's *Weeds*," *Women's Studies* 13 (1986): 103–13; and John Earl Bassett, "Edith Summers Kelley: The Trapped Women of Her Novels," *Ball State University Forum* 23, no. 1 (1982): 2–11.

MARY R. RYDER

KELLEY, Florence (12 Sept. 1859–17 Feb. 1932), social reformer, was born into a patrician Quaker and Unitarian family in Philadelphia, Pennsylvania, the daughter of William Darrah Kelley, a leading politician, and Caroline Bartram Bonsall, a descendant of John Bartram, the Quaker botanist. Kelley's rural residence and a childhood plagued by illness meant that she attended school only sporadically. Although her brief enrollment in Quaker schools introduced her to the wider reform world beyond her family and taught her mental discipline, most of her intellectual development occurred as part of her relationship with her father and her mother's aunt, Sarah Pugh. William Kelley, an abolitionist, founding member of the Republican party, Radical Reconstructionist, and U.S. congressman from Philadelphia from 1860 until his death in 1890, became her chief mentor, teaching her to read and instructing her in politics. Sarah Pugh, head of the Philadelphia Female Antislavery Society, a close friend of Lucretia Mott, and correspondent of British reformers such as Richard Cobden and John Bright, exemplified the ability of single women to devote their lives to reform causes. Kelley often visited her grandparents' home, where Sarah Pugh lived, and heard about the women's rights activism of Pugh and Mott. For her Sarah Pugh became "conscience incarnate."

During six mostly unschooled years before she entered Cornell University, Kelley systematically read her father's library, imbibing the fiction of Dickens and Thackeray, Louisa May Alcott, and Horatio Alger, the poetry of Shakespeare, Milton, Byron, and Goldsmith, the writings of James Madison, the histories by Bancroft, Prescott, and Parkman, and the moral and political philosophy of Emerson, Channing, Burke, Carlyle, Godwin, and Spencer.

Kelley's childhood was shaped as well by her mother's permanent depression—caused by the death of five of her eight children before they had reached the age of six. Two brothers but no sisters survived. Caroline Kelley developed a "settled, gentle melancholy" that threatened to envelope her daughter so long as she lived at home.

At Cornell Kelley studied history and social science, graduating in 1882. She spent her senior year in Washington, D.C., where she lived with her father and researched her honors essay in the Library of Congress. That essay, "On Some Changes in the Legal Status of the Child since Blackstone," was published in 1882 in the *International Review*. Facing a very limited set of opportunities after college, and her application for graduate study having been rejected by the University of Pennsylvania on account of her sex, Kelley threw her energies into the New Century Working Women's Guild, an organization that fostered middle-class aid for self-supporting women. She helped found the guild, taught classes in history, and assembled the group's library. Most importantly, perhaps, she escaped her mother's melancholy by developing a rage against social injustice, which she first expressed in an 1882 article, "Need Our Working Women Despair?"

A dutiful daughter, in 1882 she accompanied her older brother when his doctor prescribed a winter of European travel to cure temporary blindness. In Europe she encountered M. Carey Thomas, a Cornell acquaintance, who had just completed a Ph.D. at the University of Zurich, the only European university that granted degrees to women. From 1883 to 1886 Kelley also studied there, initially accompanied by her mother and younger brother. Her focus on government and law brought her into contact with the vital group of Russian émigrés, and in 1884 she married Lazare Wischnewetzky, a Russian Jewish socialist medical student. The first of their three children, Nicholas, was born in July 1885.

Kelley also joined the German Social Democratic party. Outlawed in Germany, the party maintained its European headquarters in Zurich, and Kelley met many of its leaders. Abandoning her pursuit of a postgraduate degree, she instead translated into English a classic work by Friedrich Engels, *The Condition of the Working Class in England*, published in German in 1845. This project launched a close but troubled relationship with Engels that persisted until his death in 1895.

Kelley returned to the United States in the fall of 1886 with her husband and young son, taking up residence in New York City. Another child, Margaret, was born in 1886, and another son, John, in 1888. In New York she found it extremely difficult to continue the political commitments she had begun in Zurich. Her Philadelphia friend Rachel Foster Avery, then secretary of the National Woman Suffrage Association, financed the publication of her translation of Engels's *Condition* (the book listed Avery as the copyright holder), but Kelley's insistence on the importance of the writings of Marx and Engels led to her expulsion from the Socialist Labor party in 1887. Party leaders resented Engels's preface to the *Condition*, which, at Kelley's urging, chastised the German-speaking majority of the party for its isolation from the American labor movement.

Forced to pursue a new path, Kelley returned to her interest in child labor. She quickly became known as a sharp critic of state bureaus of labor statistics for their inadequate attention to child labor, and she published articles on child labor in popular magazines. Lazare, meanwhile, never found his footing in the United States. His medical practice dwindling to nonexistence, he began beating her. At the end of 1891 she fled with their children to Chicago, going first to the "Woman's Temple" headquarters of the Women's Christian Temperance Union, the WCTU having published her hard-hitting pamphlet, *Our Toiling Children* (1889). Her WCTU editor directed Kelley to Hull-House, the innovative social settlement founded by Jane Addams and Ellen Gates Starr in 1889. There she lived happily and productively until 1899.

Kelley exerted an immediate and dramatic influence on the generation of women reformers who clustered within the social settlement movement during the Progressive Era. Her understanding of the material basis of class conflict and her familiarity with American political institutions, combined with her spirited personality, placed her in the vanguard of a generation of reformers who sought to make American government more responsive to what they saw as the needs of working people. In this way they were critical components in the process by which American governments, state and national, shifted from liberal laissez-faire policies to positive regulatory programs. Kelley summarized her reform strategy in the phrase "investigate, educate, legislate, and enforce." These tactics drew on her talents as a social scientist, a publicist, a lobbyist, and an attorney. They also provided women reformers with a blueprint for revising the contours of government.

Soon after her arrival in Chicago Kelley resumed the law studies she had begun in Zurich, completing her degree at Northwestern Law School in 1895. First, however, Addams helped Kelley place her children in the comfortable home of Henry Demarest Lloyd and Jessie Bross Lloyd in nearby Winnetka. Then she aided Kelley's appointment as a special agent of the Illinois Bureau of Labor Statistics. In that capacity Kelley completed roughly one thousand forms by "sweaters victims" in the garment industry, first visiting them at work, then at home. Hearing of her reputation, Carroll Wright, head of the U.S. Department of Labor, hired her in the fall of 1892 to direct a cadre of "schedule men" who collected data from each house, tenement, and room in the Nineteenth Ward, where Hull-House was located. With the help of other Hull-House residents, she used this data to compile pathbreaking occupational and nationality maps later printed in *Hull House Maps and Papers* (1895). Sharing the podium with other civic leaders, including Henry Demarest Lloyd, Kelley often spoke at "monster meetings" called to protest sweatshop working conditions. In the fall of 1892 she authored a sweeping report on the sweatshop problem and how to end it. The essentials of her recommendations were adopted in a bill passed by the Illinois legislature in June 1893; it limited women's and children's working hours to eight a day, prohibited commercial production in tenement homes, and provided for enforcement through the creation of the Factory Inspector office with a staff of twelve, half of whom were required to be women. The state's reform-minded governor, John Peter Altgeld, promptly appointed Kelley chief factory inspector.

As chief factory inspector Kelley supervised manufacturing working conditions throughout the state. No other woman in the western world exercised equivalent power. She assembled a dedicated staff that included union organizers and socialists. Their vigorous enforcement of the law precipitated the formation of the Illinois Manufacturers Association, which in 1895 obtained in *Ritchie v. the People of Illinois* an Illinois Supreme Court ruling that found unconstitutional the portion of the law mandating an eight-hour day for women. Kelley lost her office when Altgeld failed in his reelection bid in 1896. For three years she worked part time at Crerar Library and paid her children's tuition bills by writing regularly for German social reform publications.

In 1899 Kelley agreed to serve as secretary of the newly formed National Consumers' League, a position she held until her death. This took her to New York, where between 1899 and 1926 she lived at the Henry Street Settlement, Lillian Wald's "nurses' settlement" on Manhattan's Lower East Side. Her children moved with her. Supported by aid from Jane Addams's life partner, Mary Rozet Smith, Nicholas Kelley graduated from Harvard in 1905 and then from Harvard Law School. Living in Manhattan, he became his mother's closest adviser. In a blow that caused her mother to spend the rest of the year in retirement in Maine, Margaret Kelley died of heart failure during her first week at Smith College in 1905. After this bereavement Kelley maintained a summer home on Penobscot Bay, Maine, where she retreated for periods of intense work with a secretary each summer. John Kelley never found a professional niche but remained close to his mother and joined her in Maine each summer.

Kelley made the National Consumers' League into the nation's leading promoter of protective labor legislation for women and children. Between 1900 and 1904 she built sixty-four local consumer leagues—one in nearly every large city outside the South. Through a demanding travel schedule, which required her to spend one day on the road for every day she worked at her desk, Kelley maintained close contact with local leagues, urging them to implement the national organization's agenda and inspiring them to greater action within their states and municipalities. Aiding the development of local leagues was the NCL's campaign to promote the adoption of the Consumers' White Label among local manufacturers. The NCL awarded its label to manufacturers who obeyed state factory laws, produced goods only on their own premises, did not require employees to work overtime, and did not employ children under sixteen years of age. In determining whether local factories qualified for the label, league members learned a great deal about local working conditions. This prepared them for the next stage of league work—the promotion of state laws limiting women's working day to ten hours. The NCL also promoted its agenda through alliances with the mainstream women's organizations; within the General Federation of Women's Clubs between 1900 and 1902, Kelley chaired its standing committee on the Industrial Problem as It Affects Women and Children, and in 1903 she chaired the child labor committees in both the National Congress of Mothers and the National American Woman Suffrage Association. In her 1905 book, *Some Ethical Gains through Legislation*, Kelley urged upon her readers the child's "right to childhood," the working woman's "right to leisure," "the right to leisure of workingmen," along with "the right of women to the ballot," and "the rights of purchasers."

The path for the NCL's legislative agenda on women's working hours was cleared in 1908, when the U.S. Supreme Court upheld an Oregon ten-hour day law for women. This case, *Muller v. Oregon*, pitted the NCL and its Oregon branch against a laundry owner who disputed the state's ability to regulate working hours in nonhazardous occupations. Louis D. Brandeis argued Oregon's case before the Supreme Court, based on research done by his sister-in-law, Josephine Goldmark, who was director of research at NCL. For what became known as the "Brandeis Brief" Goldmark collected sociological rather than legal evidence, citing medical and other authorities to demonstrate that working days longer than ten hours were hazardous to the health of women. In accepting and basing their ruling on this data, the Supreme Court for the first time validated the use of sociological evidence.

Kelley was deeply gratified by this ruling because it partially overturned the Court's 1906 ruling in *Lochner v. New York*, which had found any regulation of hours in nonhazardous occupation unconstitutional, and it definitely overturned the Illinois Supreme Court's 1895 *Ritchie* ruling against the regulation of women's hours. Based on the *Muller* decision, inspired by Kelley's leadership, and joining with other groups, local consumer leagues gained the passage in twenty states of the first law limiting women's working hours. In response to the *Muller* decision, nineteen other states revised their laws governing women's working hours.

The Court's 1908 opinion emphasized women's special legal (they did not possess the same contractual rights as men) and physiological (their health affected the health of their future children) circumstances, trying thereby to block the extension of such protections to men. Nevertheless, in 1917 Kelley and the NCL again cooperated successfully with the Oregon local in bringing a case before the U.S. Supreme Court, *Bunting v. Oregon*, in which the Court upheld the constitutionality of hours' laws for men in nonhazardous occupations. The *Bunting* case highlighted Kelley's commitment to labor legislation protecting men as well as women. She viewed laws for women as an entering wedge for achieving remedies for all working people.

After 1909 Kelley gave state minimum wage legislation a prominent place in the NCL agenda. Her goal was to prevent the downward spiraling of wages in some industries that paid workers less than what it cost to support themselves. Such workers then needed public relief, and such assistance seemed to her and other reformers to constitute an unfair public subsidy of employers who paid their workers poorly. Although new British minimum wage laws applied to all persons in certain poorly paid occupations, Kelley knew that the feasibility of wage regulations in the United States would have to be demonstrated first with regard to women and then extended to men. The NCL's campaign was remarkably successful; by 1919 fourteen states and the District of Columbia and Puerto Rico had enacted minimum wage statutes for women. Their momentum stalled in 1923 when the U.S. Supreme Court in *Adkins v. Children's Hospital* found Washington, D.C.'s wage law unconstitutional. Many state wage boards continued to function during the 1920s and 1930s, however, providing ample evidence of the benefits of the law and serving as a basis for the inclusion of minimum wages for both women and men within the Fair Labor Standards Law of 1938.

At Henry Street Kelley continued to benefit from the same consolidation of female reform talents that had sustained her efforts at Hull-House in Chicago. The creation of the U.S. Children's Bureau in 1912 sprang from an idea generated by Kelley and Wald at Henry Street. That bureau was the only agency within governments in industrial societies that was run by women. Kelley herself thought that her most important social contribution was the passage in 1921 of the Sheppard-Towner Maternity and Infancy Protection Act, which first allocated federal funds to health care in a program administered by the Children's Bureau to combat infant and maternal mortality. Kelley was instrumental in the creation of the coalition that backed the act's passage, the Women's Joint Congressional Committee, and in the coalition's successful campaign for the bill in Congress.

By 1923 Kelley's strategy of using gender-specific legislation as a surrogate for class legislation had generated opposition from a new quarter—women who did not themselves benefit from gendered laws and opposed it on principle for those who did. Thus the nineteenth-century commitment to differences between the sexes collided with the twentieth-century commitment to similarities between women and men as the basis of public policy. The National Woman's Party (NWP), formed in 1916 by the charismatic leadership of Alice Paul and funded almost entirely by philanthropic suffragist Alva Belmont, created a small coalition consisting primarily of professional women with some wage-earning women who worked in male-dominated occupations. Despite Kelley's strong objections over the damage they would do to gender-specific legislation, including the Sheppard-Towner Act, in 1921 the NWP proposed the Equal Rights Amendment to

the U.S. Constitution. Although mainstream organizations such as the General Federation of Women's Clubs and the League of Women Voters continued to support gender-specific legislation, the NWP's proposed amendment undercut the momentum of such gendered strategies. In some cases, as in their consultation with Justice George Sutherland, who wrote the brief in the *Adkins* case, NWP leaders directly torpedoed women's labor legislation.

Kelley spent the last decade of her life trying to repair the damage done by attacks on her agenda during the "red scare" of the 1920s, both from the NWP and from virulent right-wing groups who called her Mrs. Wischnewetzky and named her "Moscow's chief conspirator." Although she did not live to see it, many of her initiatives were incorporated into federal legislation in the 1930s under the leadership of her protégée, Frances Perkins, who, as the first woman cabinet member in the United States, served as secretary of labor. Kelley died in Germantown, Pennsylvania.

• Florence Kelley's personal papers are at the New York Public Library. The National Consumer League Papers are located at the Library of Congress. Other related collections include the Jane Addams Papers at Swarthmore College; the Lillian Wald Papers at the New York Public Library and at Columbia University; the Consumers' League of Massachusetts Papers at the Schlesinger Library; and the Henry Demarest Lloyd Papers at the State Historical Society of Wisconsin. Kelley's writings are voluminous. Her brief autobiography has been reprinted as *Notes of Sixty Years: The Autobiography of Florence Kelley*, ed. Kathryn Kish Sklar (1986). For the most complete account of Kelley's life before 1900 and for a bibliography of her writings before 1900 see Sklar, *Florence Kelley and the Nation's Work: The Rise of Women's Political Culture, 1830–1900* (1995). For the NCL's minimum wage work, see Sklar, "Two Political Cultures in the Progressive Era: The National Consumers' League and the American Association for Labor Legislation," in *U.S. History as Women's History: New Feminist Essays*, ed. Linda K. Kerber et al. (1995). See also Nicholas Kelley, "Early Days at Hull House," *Social Service Review* 28 (Dec. 1954): 424–29; Josephine Goldmark, *Impatient Crusader: Florence Kelley's Life Story* (1953); and Dorothy Rose Blumberg, "Dear 'Mr. Engels': Unpublished Letters, 1884–1894, of Florence Kelley (Wischnewetzky) to Friedrich Engels," *Labor History* 5 (Spring 1964): 103–33; Dorothy Rose Blumberg, *Florence Kelley: The Making of a Social Pioneer* (1966); and Louis Athey, "The Consumers' Leagues and Social Reform, 1890–1923," (Ph.D. diss., Univ. of Delaware, 1965). Obituaries are in the *New York Times* and the *Boston Evening Globe*, both 18 Feb. 1932.

KATHRYN KISH SKLAR

KELLEY, Hall Jackson (24 Feb. 1790–20 Jan. 1874), promoter of Oregon settlement, was born in Northwood, New Hampshire, the son of Benjamin Kelley, a physician, and Mary Gile. The pious youth began serious reading early and came to entertain visions of a "lonely, laborious, and eventful life." After studying at the academy in Gilmanton, where his family had moved, he went to Middlebury College in Vermont. He graduated in 1813, and seven years later both Middlebury and Harvard conferred master of arts degrees on him. In the interval he had gone to Boston, where in 1815 he married Mary Baldwin, procreated a son, and began teaching in the public schools. His wife died in 1816. He was also active in church and welfare work, but his primary interest was in education. In 1820 he published a textbook, *The American Instructor, First Book*, and followed it in 1825 with the *Second Book*. Both books were popular and profitable and went through a number of editions. He married Mary Perry in 1822 and had three more sons.

Kelley lost his position in the Boston schools in 1823, moved briefly to Charlestown, Massachusetts, and spent more time in his work as a land surveyor. When a textile mill in which he had invested heavily went bankrupt, he bought some land at the forced sale of the company's property and in 1829 moved with his family to this property in Three Rivers, Massachusetts, where he was to spend most of his remaining years.

By now he had become totally obsessed with the distant land of Oregon, which since 1818 had been jointly occupied by the United States and Great Britain. Periodically prominent writers and statesmen, including Thomas Hart Benton, had urged the United States to strengthen its claims through settlement. In 1824 Kelley announced to the world his intention to settle and propagate Christianity in Oregon; in 1828 he presented to Congress a "memorial of citizens" praying for a grant of land and aid; and by 1829 he had found enough men to join him in establishing the American Society for Encouraging the Settlement of Oregon. As publicity agent, he was "the body and brains, the fingers and tongue of it" (H. H. Bancroft, *History of the Northwest Coast*, vol. 2 [1886], p. 545). Although he had never been to Oregon, he published *A Geographical Sketch* of the country in 1830 and the next year outlined the details of a plan for emigrating there in *Manual of the Oregon Expedition*. More memorials went to Congress pleading for financial assistance, military escort for the overland emigrants, and power to extinguish the Indian title to lands. The society enrolled about 500 persons to go, but when Congress did not act on its petitions, the project was abandoned. One recruit, however, Nathaniel Wyeth, broke with Kelley, organized a small party of his own, and set out for Oregon in the spring of 1832. He returned the next year and in 1834 led out a second party, which included Methodist missionaries Jason Lee and Daniel Lee.

In November 1832 Kelley, at his personal expense, started for Oregon with a number of men whom he dismissed after they robbed him. His two-year, 6,000-mile route by land and water included such points as New Orleans, Vera Cruz, San Blas, La Paz, and San Diego. In California, after first being refused, he persuaded Ewing Young to escort him to Oregon. Unfortunately for both Kelley and Young, who was driving horses to sell in Oregon, a group of undesirable characters with stolen horses attached themselves to their party. Word of this had reached Dr. John McLoughlin, factor of the Hudson Bay Company, before Kelley and Young arrived at Fort Vancouver, and it

stained their reception. McLoughlin attended to the physical needs of Kelley, who was stricken with malaria, but the fur trader would have no business dealings with this prospective colonizer. Kelley's American countrymen also avoided him. He made a few explorations before returning to Boston, by way of the Sandwich Islands and Cape Horn, and announcing plans for another colonizing adventure.

This time Kelley proposed to establish a colony at New Dungeness on the Strait of Juan de Fuca, as it lay within the land bought from the Indians in 1791 by Captain John Kendrick, but nothing came of it. He submitted to Congress a map and a memoir on Oregon and Upper California. Thereafter, most of his work was designed to seek "recognition" from the public, and his numerous memorials to Congress prayed for a grant of land or money as reimbursement for his services and sacrifices on behalf of Oregon. In several publications Kelley told the public about his estrangement from his wife. When he had gone west, he had left his children and wife in the care of her aunt, who was also her foster mother. Mary Kelley, whose home had been disrupted by her husband's continued obsession with his Oregon vision of the 1820s, never returned to Three Rivers, where Kelley lived out his life, broken in spirit, nearly blind, and largely dependent on the charity of neighbors before his death there. On his headstone in Gilmanton, New Hampshire, might well be inscribed the words of Robert Louis Stevenson: "Here lies one who meant well, tried a little, failed much."

• Fred Wilbur Powell is the primary authority on Kelley. His "Bibliography of Hall J. Kelley," *Oregon Historical Society* 8 (1907): 375–86, is a list of titles by and about Kelley; *Hall Jackson Kelley—Prophet of Oregon* (1917) is a biography; and *Hall J. Kelley on Oregon* (1932) is a collection of five of Kelley's published works and a number of hitherto unpublished letters.

MARY LEE SPENCE

KELLEY, Joseph James (9 Dec. 1871–14 Aug. 1943), baseball player and manager, was born in Cambridge, Massachusetts. Almost nothing is known about his early years, his family, or his education. In his late teens he spent much of his time playing baseball and decided that his goal would be to pitch for a Boston team. At nineteen he signed a contract to pitch for Lowell of the New England League, where in 1891 he won 10 games and lost 3, batting .331 as a part-time outfielder. These records were good enough that Boston of the National League bought his contract, and he played in a dozen games at the end of that season. He spent part of 1892 in the minor leagues, then joined the Pittsburgh club, which in September sold him to Baltimore. By now his pitching career had ended; occasionally he played first base, but his best position was as an outfielder.

Kelley, who was 5′11″ and 190 pounds, played seven years for Baltimore. He joined the team during the era of manager Ned Hanlon, who surrounded himself with aggressive, tough players and made many permanent changes in the way the game was played (among his innovations were the hit-and-run and the squeeze play). Kelley's teammates included Willie Keeler, John McGraw, Wilbert Robinson, Hughie Jennings, and Kid Gleason; McGraw, Robinson, and Jennings were all highly successful managers. Hanlon drove Kelley hard, giving him individual attention in daily practices because of the potential he saw.

Soon Kelley became a fine fielder with an exceptional right throwing arm. As a right-handed batter, he was typical of the hard-hitting Orioles who won the National League pennant three years in a row (1894–1896) in spite of the team's average pitching. During six-plus seasons with Baltimore, Kelley had an overall batting mark of .351. In 1894, when teams played shorter schedules, he hit .393 with 199 hits and 107 walks in 129 games. In one September doubleheader that year he had nine hits in nine at bats.

In 1899 Hanlon acquired an interest in the Brooklyn team and took a nucleus of Orioles with him, including Kelley; Brooklyn won the pennant that year and in 1900. Kelley played part of the 1902 season, again with Baltimore, then left to become manager of the Cincinnati Reds. His managerial success did not match his hitting, and after four mediocre seasons he was replaced, finishing the 1906 season as a player. His major league career ended after the 1908 season when he served as player-manager of Boston of the National League. Overall, the teams he managed won 338 and lost 321 games (a .513 percentage).

Kelley managed Toronto at the highest minor league level from 1909 through 1914, playing in a few games in 1910. In later years he did some scouting, then retired after coaching for Brooklyn in 1926. While still a player, Kelley entered the drayage business in Baltimore, work that he continued after he left baseball.

Kelley married twice; his first wife was Olive Hardy. His second wife was Margaret Mahon, the daughter of John J. Mahon who briefly owned the Orioles. Kelley and his second wife had two children. When Kelley died in Baltimore, his obituary concluded that he played as well as any of the stars of his era, but he was the least well known of the famous Orioles because his managerial record fell short of those achieved by several of his former teammates. He did not lack for color, however. Umpires caught him smuggling extra baseballs to the outfield to trap unwary baserunners, and he often entertained the crowd between pitches by studying his generally recognized good looks in a small mirror he carried in his cap.

The statistics make Kelley's baseball skills clear. He also must be recognized for his role in modernizing the game. No one is likely to know who invented the hit-and-run, the squeeze play, the drag bunt, and more. But the Orioles of the 1890s introduced them, and Kelley and his teammates permanently put them into baseball's "book" as they moved into early managerial posts. The Veterans Committee elected Kelley to the National Baseball Hall of Fame in 1971.

• The National Baseball Hall of Fame, Cooperstown, N.Y., has some family material on Kelley. Some interesting anecdotes and personal information are recorded in Martin Appel and Burt Goldblatt, *Baseball's Best: The Hall of Fame Gallery* (1977). Most of the statistical information on Kelley and others comes from John Thorn and Pete Palmer, eds., *Total Baseball*, 3d ed. (1993). His obituary is in the *New York Times*, 15 Aug. 1943.

THOMAS L. KARNES

KELLEY, Oliver Hudson (7 Jan. 1826–20 Jan. 1913), farmer and organizer of agricultural societies, was born in Boston, Massachusetts, the son of William Robinson Kelley, a tailor, and Nancy Hancock. Educated at Chauncy Hall School in Boston, at the age of sixteen Kelley showed his precocious writing ability by composing, illustrating, and publishing a satirical book of cartoons published under the nom de plume Robert Tristee. He left Boston for Chicago on 3 May 1847. He spent six months in the city, where he briefly worked in a drug store and as a reporter for the *Chicago Tribune*. Later that year he departed for Peoria, Illinois, where he received training as a telegrapher, and in August 1848 he moved to Muscatine, Iowa, where he worked as a telegraph operator.

In 1849 Kelley married Lucy Earle. In June the newlyweds moved to the recently formed Territory of Minnesota. Kelley was appointed assistant secretary of the St. Paul Election Precinct, later elected messenger by the Minnesota House of Representatives, and served as sergeant at arms pro tempore, and as a clerk for the judiciary committee of the house in the first territorial session.

While serving as messenger between the house and senate, Kelley learned that several legislators had plans to remove the territorial capital from its temporary location in St. Paul to Itasca, a town site on the Mississippi River about thirty-five miles above St. Anthony Falls. Sensing an opportunity to profit, Kelley rushed to the vicinity of Itasca and staked a claim there. The motion to move the capital fell a few votes short, and the capital remained at St. Paul.

The Kelleys found themselves in an isolated frontier area. Itasca lingered for a few years as a post office and trading post for the Winnebago Indians. A little more than a year later, Lucy Kelley gave birth to their only child in January 1851. But the birth was difficult, and the mother died in April. The child died a few months later. The next summer Kelley married Temperance Baldwin Lane, a schoolteacher, and they had four children.

During the 1850s Kelley devoted himself to becoming a progressive farmer by reading everything he could on the subject. As a so-called book farmer, Kelley became enamored of the latest technological innovations, the most improved seed varieties, and farming methods. He became an implement sales agent for the William Plant Company of St. Louis, Missouri, and published several articles in newspapers and national farm journals about the benefits of progressive agriculture.

To spread the gospel of progressive farming and, later, to address inequities in the capitalist system, Kelley became deeply involved in organizing agricultural societies. In 1852 Kelley, his father, and other farmers founded the Benton County Agricultural Society (BCAS). The BCAS was initially devoted to the traditional social and educational goals of agricultural societies, but it quickly became a much more radical organization that reflected Kelley's belief that producer-farmers were pitted in an antagonistic struggle with speculating middlemen. In 1855 Kelley became the agricultural editor of the *Sauk Rapids Frontierman* and edited a regular column called "The Farmer."

As corresponding secretary of the BCAS, Kelley began using his columns to outline an ambitious and socially radical agenda. Imitating the tactics of commercial businessmen, Kelley proposed that the BCAS form an agricultural board of trade to regulate agricultural prices. To defeat the monopolistic practices of the Mississippi steamboats and other middlemen, he advocated using the BCAS to organize trade union stores where farmers would deal directly with manufacturers and consumers.

Just as the BCAS was reaching its rhetorical and radical peak, the society disbanded as members turned their attention to the real estate speculation common in the territory in the mid-1850s. Kelley turned his attention to founding a town he called Northwood, across the Mississippi River from his old farm. Northwood failed in the panic of 1857, and Kelley lost the thousands of dollars he had mortgaged his farm to obtain. His dismal financial fortunes did not abate his interest in agricultural societies, and in 1858 he formed the Northwood Farmers' Club to exchange seeds grown on a proposed experimental farm and to serve as a central marketing location where farmers could buy and sell goods and produce.

In the 1860s Kelley switched to market gardening and installed an irrigation system. He secured work in Washington, D.C., as a clerk in the new Department of Agriculture. The House of Representatives published his report on agriculture in Minnesota; he also worked as a correspondent for several eastern and western newspapers.

In January 1866, with the support of President Andrew Johnson, Kelley was assigned by Secretary of Agriculture Isaac Newton to tour the southern states and report to the Department of Agriculture on the status of agriculture there. When he returned to Minnesota, he helped found the Minnesota Fruit Growers' Association. In 1867 Kelley secured an appointment in the Post Office Department in Washington, D.C. In December, with the advice of his niece Caroline Hall, he and six other men, including William Saunders, an experimental gardener from the Department of Agriculture, formed the Order of the Patrons of Husbandry. The group created a rough ritual to attract members and tested it by staging meetings with themselves and their wives as the members of Potomac Grange. Kelley served as the National Grange secretary from the organization's inception until he resigned in 1878.

Kelley returned to Minnesota in 1868 to begin the difficult task of organizing the Grange. The Grange was a national farmers fraternity whose agricultural ritual was inspired by that of the Freemasons. But unlike the fraternal orders, the patrons admitted women as full and equal members. In addition to the rituals, regular meetings contained educational presentations by a lecturer. Often debates were held, and social events like picnics and dances were very important to the members. But it was the radical political position and the promise of cooperative purchasing and selling that Kelley and his fellow midwestern organizers emphasized in the late 1860s and early 1870s that caused farmers to flock to the organization, swelling its membership to more than 850,000 in early 1875.

As the Grange's popularity began to spread throughout the nation, Kelley moved his family to Washington, D.C. The Kelleys lost the old farmstead in a mortgage foreclosure, only to repurchase it a few years later. When the Grange moved its national headquarters to Louisville in 1875, the Kelley family followed. Soon after the move, Kelley began to lose interest in the Grange. He became entangled in a scandal that involved his New York City brother-in-law Robert Farley, whom he had endorsed as a supplier of Grange supplies, and he lost influence to William Saunders and a conservative executive committee. Battered and disappointed, his prestige within the Grange diminished.

In 1877 Kelley became deeply involved in real estate speculation in northwestern Florida. He founded a town he named Carrabelle, after his niece and assistant, Caroline Arrabella Hall, and moved his Grange secretary's office there. A year after his move to Florida, he resigned his office with the Grange and focused on his new city, trying to promote it as the biggest port between Tampa and Mobile. During the next two decades, he concentrated his efforts on developing Carrabelle and the surrounding area, serving as mayor and a leading businessman.

In 1890 he began to make special appearances at Grange meetings to be toasted as the founder. In 1901 the family sold the old farmstead in Minnesota and their Florida property and moved back to Washington, D.C. In 1905 when Kelley was seventy-nine years old, the Grange voted to provide him with a $1,200 annual pension. Kelley died at his home in Washington, D.C.

Kelley played a significant role in organizing farmers in the young territory and state of Minnesota. But more importantly, as he struggled to breathe life into the Grange during the late 1860s and early 1870s, Kelley and his associates articulated an ideology of radical revolt of farmers against merchant monopolists that would resonate in other farm protest movements throughout the late nineteenth and early twentieth centuries. This republican critique of American capitalism, expressed through the organizational rhetoric and actions of the early Grange, showed Kelley to be a significant ideological bridge between Jeffersonian-Republicans and Jacksonian entrepreneurs and radical farmers of the nineteenth century. The spirit of the early Grange—Kelley's spirit—is clearly visible in the Farmers' Alliance, the Populist party, and later farmer-labor alliances.

• An important collection of papers on Kelley and the early years of the Grange is the National Grange Collection at the National Grange Headquarters in Washington, D.C. Another valuable collection is the National Grange Records at Cornell Library, Ithaca, N.Y. A small collection of Kelley's papers are housed at the Minnesota Historical Society. The best secondary source on Kelley is Thomas A. Woods, *Knights of the Plow: Oliver H. Kelley and the Origins of the Grange in Republican Ideology* (1991). Other useful treatments are William D. Barns, "Oliver Hudson Kelley and the Genesis of the Grange: A Reappraisal," *Agricultural History* 41 (July 1967): 229–42; Rhoda R. Gilman and Patricia Smith, "Oliver Hudson Kelley: Minnesota Pioneer, 1849–1868," *Minnesota History* 40 (Fall 1967): 3–32; and D. Sven Nordin, *Rich Harvest: A History of the Grange, 1867–1900* (1974). A still essential book on Kelley and the Grange is Solon Justus Buck, *The Granger Movement: A Study of Agricultural Organization and Its Political, Economic, and Social Manifestations, 1870–1880* (1913; repr. 1963).

THOMAS A. WOODS

KELLEY, Robert Lloyd (2 June 1925–28 Aug. 1993), historian, was born in Santa Barbara, California, the son of Lloyd Amos Kelley, a carpenter and grocery store owner, and Berta Lee Winniford. Kelley spent his childhood years in Santa Barbara working as a bagger and stock boy at Kelley's Korner, the family store. He graduated from Santa Barbara High School in 1942 and began his undergraduate studies at Santa Barbara State College (later the University of California, Santa Barbara) the same year.

Kelley married Rosalie Wolfe in 1945; they had four children. He later divorced her and married Madge Hasken in 1972. He and Hasken raised his children and two children from her first marriage. An enthusiastic family man, he was active in the Boy Scouts of America and enjoyed a host of outdoor activities.

In 1943 Kelley was drafted and became a flying officer (bombardier) in the Army Air Corps during World War II. He returned to Santa Barbara in 1946, received his A.B. in history in 1948, and began graduate work at Stanford University that fall. His graduate studies were interrupted by the Korean War. In 1951 he was recalled into service by the U.S. Air Force, becoming an administrative officer, historical officer, and adjutant before being discharged as a captain in 1953. During this period he completed the requirements of his master's (1949) and doctoral (1953) degrees.

Kelley's connections and success in the military led to his first professional position in 1953; he taught history at the U.S. Air Force Academy in Colorado Springs, Colorado. The following year he resigned from the air force and became an instructor in history at Santa Barbara State College.

After the publication of his doctoral dissertation as *Gold vs. Grain: The Hydraulic Mining Controversy in California's Sacramento Valley* (1959), Kelley joined veteran textbook author Leland D. Baldwin of the University of Pittsburgh to update *The Stream of American History* (1965). Kelley contributed an introductory essay titled "The Craft of the Historian," which closely followed Carl Becker's philosophy of the historical trade.

After becoming a full professor of history in 1968, Kelley spent the next eight years synthesizing his own interpretation of U.S. history, published as *The Shaping of the American Past* in 1975. With this work he distinguished himself as a broad thinker who could conceptualize and tie together the many threads and themes of American history. In 1969 he continued his examination of history in *The Transatlantic Persuasion: The Liberal-Democratic Mind in the Age of Gladstone*, a comparative study grounded in the Richard Hofstadter school of history, which attempted to place historical events in a social and cultural context.

In *The Cultural Pattern in American Politics: The First Century* (1979), Kelley demonstrated the importance of ethnocultural concepts in American politics and history. At the 1976 annual meeting of the American Historical Association, he presented a paper titled "Ideology and Political Culture from Jefferson to Nixon."

In 1963 Kelley was asked to serve as consultant to the office of the California attorney general and the Department of Water Resources. For the next ten years he served as an expert witness in a series of water resource controversies, assisting in the preparation of testimony for seventeen cases. In 1989 he wrote *Battling the Inland Sea: American Political Culture, Public Policy, and the Sacramento Valley, 1850–1986*.

Kelley believed that historians had a role to play outside academic institutions. During the late 1970s he began to argue that his discipline offered a unique asset: the ability to add a historical perspective to the decision-making process. He advocated new models for the study of history, and in the fall of 1976 the University of California, Santa Barbara, admitted its first students to the Program of Public Historical Studies. Under Kelley's direction the program became a model for revamping history curriculums across the country. Kelley retired from teaching in January 1993, although he stayed active in academic affairs and planned to teach a graduate seminar course just prior to his death. He died in Santa Barbara.

Kelley was a renowned American political and intellectual scholar within the academic community. He also conceptualized and founded entirely new approaches to the historical discipline, most notably in his development of public history. A westerner by birth, his academic career was spent writing extensively on water issues in California. His intellect allowed him to rise to the top of his profession, while his creativity allowed him to alter the craft along the way.

• Kelley's papers relating to the founding of the Program in Public Historical Studies are in the University Archives, Davidson Library, at the University of California, Santa Barbara. The university also has a small clippings file on Kelley in the Public Affairs Office. See also his "Public History: Its Origins, Nature, and Prospects," *Public Historian* 1, no. 1 (Fall 1978): 16–28. Most of Kelley's writings relating to public history can be found in David F. Trask and Robert W. Pomeroy III, eds., *The Craft of Public History: An Annotated Select Bibliography* (1983). A study of his academic career is in John Higham, "An American Original: Robert Kelley, Historian of Political change," *Public Historian* 17, no. 3 (Summer 1995): 61–75. His importance to the public history movement is considered in Joseph Roddy, "Historians Go Public," *RF Illustrated* 4 (Sept. 1979): 18; and G. Wesley Johnson, Jr., "Editor's Preface," *Public Historian* 1, no. 1 (Fall 1978): 4–10.

JASON H. GART

KELLEY, Truman Lee (25 May 1884–2 May 1961), psychologist, was born in Whitehall, Muskegon County, Michigan, the son of Marshall Charles Kelley, a lawyer, and Mary Strong Smith, who studied music at the Oberlin Conservatory. Kelley graduated from the University of Illinois with an A.B. in mathematics in 1909. After teaching mathematics at the Georgia Institute of Technology from 1909 to 1910 he returned to Illinois to study statistics under Henry L. Reitz. He received an A.M. in psychology in 1911. That year he married Lura Osgood; they had no children and were divorced in 1934. During the next year Kelley taught high school mathematics in Fresno, California. His interest in both statistics and educational psychology led him to Columbia University to study with E. L. Thorndike, and he received his Ph.D. in 1914.

Kelley taught at the University of Texas from 1914 to 1917; he then left to begin a three-year appointment as an assistant professor at Teacher's College, Columbia University. It was during this tenure that Kelley became involved in the war effort as a consultant to the Committee on Classification of Personnel in the surgeon general's office. In 1920 Kelley accepted a temporary position as professor of education at Stanford University. In 1921 this position was made permanent, and Kelley remained at Stanford until 1930. In the spring of 1930 he accepted Harvard's offer to become a professor in the Graduate School of Education. He married Grace Winifred Cookney Madge in 1936; they had two children. He remained at Harvard until his retirement in 1950.

Although Kelley's greatest impact on psychology and education was to draw statistical methodology to the core of its research practices, he made important contributions to the field of psychometrics, a research area that is concerned with measurement assumptions that make the interpretation of test scores statistically and theoretically meaningful. Throughout his career Kelley's work reflected his interests in mental and achievement test development and statistics.

Kelley also facilitated the quick assimilation of statistical methods into the mainstream of educational and psychological research by publishing tables that made statistics easier to use. In 1916 he published *Tables to Facilitate the Calculation of Partial Coefficients of Correlation and Regression Equations*, and upon his failure to convince the Keuffel-Esser Company (manufacturers of scientific instruments) to produce what he called the "Biometricians' and Social Statisticians' slide-ruler," he reworked and republished his tables with Stanford University in 1921. The Kelley-Wood Tables—a simplified and reworked version of the Sheppard's Tables, which calculated the normal probability integral in terms of the standard deviation—added columns for the proportion of area in each tail of the normal distribution, an addition that became a standard inclusion in statistics textbooks. Kelley remained dedicated throughout his career to making statistics accessible to researchers. To this end he gathered together all his tables and published them as *The Kelley Statistical Tables* (1938; 2d ed., 1948).

Kelley was one of psychology's most eminent statisticians during the 1920s and 1930s. He clarified and developed True Score Theory, a statistical/interpretative model involving assumptions that describe a person's score on a test as being made up of errors of measurement and an individual's true ability on the task; and he was one of a small group of Americans who made significant contributions to the theory of factor analysis, a branch of multivariate statistics that attempts to account for patterns of correlations that exist between a series of psychological tests in terms of underlying factors that are common to all the tests, as well as factors that are specific to individual tests.

Kelley's early papers on reliability theory were highly influential and carried the discussion of reliability beyond the procedures of obtaining the statistic to considerations of its psychometric properties. Reliability theory focuses on those aspects of measurement theory that are concerned with "repeatability," or the fact that a person's ability as measured by a test should be relatively stable across different testing times if the measurement is reliable. Kelley acknowledged that although anyone can easily calculate a "test-retest" reliability (which is a simple correlation coefficient), one must recognize that there are psychometric limits on the interpretation of this coefficient. In fact the term "index of reliability" was first used by W. S. Monroe in *An Introduction to the Theory of Educational Measurements* (1923), and he claimed to have borrowed the term from Kelley. Kelley collected many of his early arguments concerning reliability and validity in measurement theory in *Interpretation of Educational Measurements* (1927), which became an exemplary textbook showing the important place of psychometric theory in test interpretation.

Kelley was instrumental in the development of the Stanford Achievement Test (SAT), first issued in 1923, serving principally as a consulting statistician to Lewis Terman and E. L. Thorndike—both leaders in the development of intelligence tests. In 1923 Kelley wrote a popular and widely respected statistics text, *Statistical Method*. Cyril Burt wrote to Kelley as late as 1944 commenting that even after twenty years *Statistical Method* was "still *the* book on the subject for every psychologist in every teaching department." There is little doubt that Kelley's text established the standard for all other statistics books in psychology and education.

Kelley's next book, *Crossroads in the Mind of Man: A Study of Differentiable Mental Abilities* (1928), provided a thorough statistical analysis that supported a multiple-factor interpretation of mental ability. This work challenged the popular two-factor theory supported by Charles Spearman, which proposed that the correlations among mental tests could be accounted for by a single unitary factor called "g" for general intelligence, and a factor unique to each test that Spearman called "s" for specific factors. Kelley suggested that Spearman's two factors were largely a result of a statistical decision, and therefore did not establish as fact that only two factors are necessary in order to account for mental ability. Rather, through analyzing mental test data from another statistical perspective, one could derive multiple factors of mental ability.

The impact of Kelley's *Crossroads*, and the extension and refinement of his arguments as they appeared in his 1935 publication *Essential Traits of Mental Life*, stand as classic depictions of the trend in North America toward multiple factorial theories of mind. Furthermore, through a revision of his statistical analysis used in *Crossroads*, Kelley's *Essential Traits* introduced psychologists to Harold Hotelling's elegant factor analytic solutions known as Principal Component Analysis (a technical branch of multivariate statistics used to maintain factors that are mathematically meaningful, if not so easily interpreted from a psychological perspective).

Kelley's next contribution to statistics was published in a pamphlet under the title *Talents and Tasks: Their Conjunction in a Democracy for Wholesome Living and National Defense* (1940). In this pamphlet, Kelley offered a solution to the problem of the correlation between two sets of variables, a solution that is recognized as a form of "canonical analysis." Simultaneously with Hotelling, Kelley was one of the architects of canonical correlation. Kelley referred to his method as one of determining the correlation between "consociated factors." His last major publication was *Fundamentals of Statistics* (1947), which emphasized the mathematical background of statistical theory.

Kelley was active in all aspects of the promotion of statistics as a research practice. He sat on the editorial committee that launched the *Journal of Educational Statistics* in 1920; he served on the executive board of the New York Society for the Experimental Study of Education (1919); he was a member of the National Research Council's Committee on the Mathematical Analysis of Statistics (a group formed in 1921 by H. L. Reitz); and he was a member of the unitary traits committee that was activated by the American Council of Education and chaired by E. L. Thorndike (1931). In 1924 Kelley was elected to the advisory council of the Eugenics Committee of the United States. The same year he became a fellow of the American Statistical Association and served as its vice president in 1926–1927. In 1928 Kelley was elected vice president of section Q of the American Association for the Advancement of Science. In 1938–1939 he served as the president of the Psychometric Society, and from 1946 to 1948 he was president of the Educational Research Corporation. Kelley cofounded Kappa Delta Pi, an honorary education society.

Although Kelley's contribution were not widely acknowledged at the end of the twentieth century, his influence on the assimilation of statistical and measurement practices into educational and psychological research was substantial. He died in Santa Barbara, California.

• The largest collection of Kelley's papers is held in the Pussey Library, Harvard University Archives. There is a smaller deposit of his letters in the Stanford University Archives. Two short biographical essays on Kelley are John C. Flanagan, "Truman Lee Kelley," *Psychometrika* 26 (1961): 343–45, and David V. Tiedeman, "Kelley, Truman L.," in *International Encyclopedia of Social Science* (1968). A perspective on Kelley's contributions to the history of statistics in American psychology can be found in Dale Stout, "Statistics in American Psychology: The Social Construction of Experimental and Correlational Psychology, 1900–1930" (Ph.D. thesis, Univ. of Edinburgh, Scotland, 1987); and Stout, "A Question of Statistical Inference: E. G. Boring, T. L. Kelley, and the Probable Error," *American Journal of Psychology* 102 (1989): 549–62. Kelley's work is reviewed in two classic publications on statistics in America: Helen M. Walker, *Studies in the History of Statistical Method* (1929), and Dael Wolfle, *Factor Analysis to 1940*, Psychometric Monographs, No. 3 (1940). An obituary is in the *New York Times*, 3 May 1961.

DALE STOUT

KELLEY, Walter Pearson (19 Feb. 1878–19 May 1965), soil chemist, was born in Franklin, Kentucky, the son of John William Kelley, a tobacco farmer, and Mary Eliza Mayes. Educated in Kentucky public elementary and private high schools, Kelley graduated with a B.S. in chemistry from the University of Kentucky in 1904. In 1907 he received his M.S. from Purdue University, and in 1912 he earned a Ph.D. in soil chemistry from the University of California at Berkeley.

An early interest in medicine ended when Kelley took a position as assistant chemist with the Purdue Agricultural Experiment Station in 1904. After finishing his master's degree at Purdue, he obtained a research appointment at the Hawaii Agricultural Experiment Station from the U.S. Department of Agriculture (USDA). Kelley directed research in agricultural chemistry in Hawaii from 1908 until 1911, when he returned to graduate school. At the University of California, Kelley's major professor was Eugene W. Hilgard. Kelley was fortunate to study in the agricultural chemistry department at a time when the foundations of soil science (pedology) were being formed. Hilgard, who is regarded as the American father of soil science, had an international reputation and drew students from all over the world. Kelley himself had already demonstrated his considerable abilities as a researcher at the Hawaii station. Chlorotic pineapples had led him to investigate the chemical composition of the soil producing the damaged fruit and to explain, in his first independent publication, that excess manganese caused the harmful effects. At Berkeley, the young researcher's natural affinity for problems with complex soils was further stimulated by Hilgard's work with the solonetz, a type of alkali soil prevalent in parts of the West.

After two more years at the Hawaii station, Kelley became head of the agricultural chemistry department of the Citrus Experiment Station and Graduate School in Riverside, California. He had married Sue Katherine Eubank in August 1913, and the couple moved to Riverside the next year, where they remained until 1939; they had no children. Kelley held professorial rank, but the appointment was for research; he never taught. At Riverside, research he helped conduct on irrigation salinity led to work in the areas where he would make his most significant contributions: alkali soils, cation exchange, and clay mineralogy.

Kelley and his colleagues at the Citrus Experiment Station (E. E. Thomas, S. M. Brown, and A. B. Cummins) surveyed irrigated orchards in the area to determine how citrus products were incurring salt damage. The survey allowed them to map patterns of alkalinity and led to classification of irrigation waters for their suitability with citrus. Also, salt residues observed at root levels drew Kelley's attention to the capillarity caused by too aggressive irrigation and seepage from unlined canals and laterals. He vigorously promoted the importance of drainage for prevention and reclamation of the troublesome alkalis. However, one type of soil, the black alkalis, proved especially resistant to management or reclamation. These soils remain virtually impermeable, even after the application of gypsum. The impermeability of the black alkalis led Kelley to his most important theoretical research with soils.

Subsequent laboratory studies on the chemical effects of salts on soils revealed black alkalis were "black" because they absorbed great amounts of sodium. This investigation, in which two different soils were treated with equivalent concentrations of chlorides of sodium, potassium, calcium, magnesium, and ammonium, demonstrated an exchange reaction in soils, which had been observed before but had not been understood for its importance in the formation of alkali soils. Cation exchange is one of the most important interactions between the solid phase of soil and the solution phase. In the process, positively charged ions (cations) in the soil solution leave the solution and attach themselves loosely to the solid phase, which has a net negative charge. At the same time cations on solids enter the solution. Cation exchange is important, because the exchangeable ions are available to plants and supplement the small quantity in solution. Also, they are retained in soils and not lost with leaching water. In the black alkalis, sodium salts reacting with clay components form sodium clays. The generation of sodium carbonate and the leaching away of its soluable salts explained the soil's tendency to be impermeable. Kelley, as he discovered shortly after publication of these findings, was not the first to recognize the role that the cation exchange plays in alkali soils, but by 1923 the independent research of Kelley and his associates had confirmed its importance. An assignment to reclaim salt-impregnated lands in a Fresno County vineyard provided an adequate laboratory. The remainder of Kelley's long career was largely devoted to increasing the knowledge and understanding of alkali soils and exchangeable constituents.

In 1930, at the Second International Congress of Soil Scientists in the Soviet Union, Kelley and W. H. Dore presented a paper on the chemical investigation and X-ray analysis of exchangeable base constituents. ("Exchangeable base" is a term soil scientists have applied to the exchangeable cations—calcium, magnesium, sodium, and potassium.) The paper described research that demonstrated the crystalline structure of the soil and soil colloid constituents. Kelley and Dore did not introduce these findings (a USDA scientist had submitted his results months ahead of the California team in 1929), but the work was no less valuable for the new science of the soil that was scarcely in its adolescence when Kelley entered the field. By the time Kelley left Riverside in 1940 to become chairman of the new Division of Soils at Berkeley, he had already produced a body of work remarkable for its thoroughness, clarity, practical consequences, and consolidation of current theories.

Kelley remained at the University of California until his retirement in 1948. He continued to work in his field, producing two monographs and eight articles. Three of the articles were published the year before he died. Kelley served during his retirement as a consultant for Gulf Research and Development of Pittsburgh from 1948 to 1955 and in the same capacity with the U.S. Bureau of Reclamation from 1948 to 1958.

Though he obviously preferred research to organizational activities, Kelley actively supported the growing professionalization of the sciences. He was a member of the American Chemical Society, the American Association for the Advancement of Science, the International Society of Soil Science, the Western Society of Soil Science (which he cofounded and served as president), the Soil Science Society of America, the American Society of Agronomy (of which he was elected president in 1930), the Western Society of Naturalists, the Geophysical Union, the American Mineralogical Society, and the National Academy of Sciences. Kelley also was an associate editor of both *Soil Science* and *Agrochimica*, an Italian publication. Kelley died in Berkeley, California.

• Kelley's collected papers are located in the archives of the University of California at Berkeley. The collection contains reprints of Kelley's work from 1909 to 1939 and a bibliography compiled by Katherine McCreery. His monographs, *Cation Exchange in Soils* (1948) and *Alkali Soils: Their Formation, Properties, and Reclamation* (1950), are classics in the field. For the paper delivered in the Soviet Union, see W. P. Kelley and W. H. Dore, "The Nature of the Base-Exchange Material of Soils and of the Bentonitic Clays as Revealed by Chemical Investigation and X-ray Analysis," *Proceedings and Papers of the Second International Congress of Soil Science:*

Commission II (1933), pp. 34–36. Kelley's role in pedological development is better understood with reference to the pioneering work of Eugene Hilgard, clearly explained in Hans Jenny, *E. W. Hilgard and the Birth of Modern Soil Science* (1961). An obituary is Homer D. Chapman, "Walter Pearson Kelley," National Academy of Sciences, *Biographical Memoirs* 40 (1969): 142–75, which also includes a bibliography of Kelley's extensive publications.

JOAN KLOBE PRATT

KELLEY, William Darrah (12 Apr. 1814–9 Jan. 1890), congressman, was born in Philadelphia, Pennsylvania, the son of David Kelley, a watchmaker and jeweler, and Hannah Darrah. William Kelley's father, who was financially ruined when William was still a boy, died in 1816. By the time he was thirteen, Kelley was apprenticed with a jeweler. When his indenture expired in 1834, he moved to Boston, where he became an enameler and spent his leisure hours studying, debating, and writing for local papers. In 1838 he returned to Philadelphia to read law and was admitted to the bar in 1841.

Kelley was appointed prosecutor of the pleas for Philadelphia in 1845 and rose to the position of judge of the court of common pleas two years later. In 1851, when the judgeship became an elective office, he was elected to a ten-year term.

Although Kelley had been a Democrat, the repeal of the Missouri Compromise in 1854 caused him to abandon the party and become one of the founders of the new Republican party in Pennsylvania. That year he made a famous speech in Philadelphia entitled "Slavery in the Territories," in which he proclaimed his antislavery views. He resigned his judgeship in 1856 to run for Congress in the Fourth Pennsylvania District. After losing that contest, he returned to private practice but ran again in 1860. Kelley was victorious this time, and he served in Washington for over twenty years. He was also a delegate to the 1860 Republican National Convention in Chicago that nominated Abraham Lincoln for the presidency.

In September 1862 Kelley joined an artillery company but never saw active service. Returning to his congressional seat, he was an avowed enemy of slavery and voted for every bill that supported the war effort and emancipation. He also advocated arming black troops, promoted equality and voting rights for the freed slaves, and voted for conscription. He was vocal in his criticism of General George B. McClellan's hesitant policies. He spoke in favor of military Reconstruction measures, such as the bill establishing the Freedman's Bureau. In a speech he gave in support of the bill in 1864, Kelley declared, "Humanity, the spirit of the nineteenth century, and Christian civilization demand its immediate passage."

Kelley was an outspoken champion of the freed slaves and of black suffrage. In 1865, arguing in response to a proposed Reconstruction bill, he introduced an amendment that would have extended suffrage to all male citizens, regardless of race, capable of reading the Constitution. The bill and the amendment were defeated. He also argued forcefully against segregation on Philadelphia's streetcars.

Although early in life Kelley had been an outspoken "free trader," the failure of the Walker Tariff in 1846, which eliminated the principle of protection, persuaded him to support protective tariffs. He was keenly aware of the crucial role iron and steel played in Pennsylvania's economy. Because one of his most frequent topics was the need for high protective duties on steel and pig iron, he earned the nickname "Pig Iron Kelley." He supported the Morrill Tariff of 1861, and he defended the "greenback," or paper currency, during and after the war. In fact, he was one of the few congressmen who supported both inflation and protective tariffs. Convinced that such tariffs kept precious metals, especially gold, from being drained from the economy, he therefore opposed the resumption of specie payments unless accompanied by a protective tariff.

Kelley also believed that an increased money supply would improve the economy of the financially ruined South and assist homesteaders in the West. Contraction, he felt, would inevitably lead the Treasury to bankruptcy. Among his more famous speeches were "Contraction the Road to Bankruptcy," delivered in the House on 18 January 1868, and "Farmers, Mechanics, and Laborers Need Protection—Capital Can Take Care of Itself," which he gave on 25 March 1870.

During his congressional career, Kelley served on the Committees on Agriculture, the Navy, and Indian Affairs. He served on the Committee on Ways and Means for twenty years and was its chairman from 1881 to 1883. He was briefly involved in the Crédit Mobilier scandal in 1872. Officers of the Crédit Mobilier holding company had been skimming substantial profits in construction of the Union Pacific Railroad, which was federally subsidized. The Crédit Mobilier began selling discounted stock to members of Congress in an effort to prevent a congressional investigation. Although evidence came to light that Kelley had purchased stock in the Union Pacific Railroad, he was never censured by Congress.

Kelley was married twice, first to Isabella Tennant, with whom he had one daughter. The year of their marriage is unknown. After his first marriage ended, in 1854 he married Caroline Bartram Bonsall, with whom he had eight children, three of whom survived to adulthood. One of his daughters, Florence Kelley, later became famous as a reformer, particularly in the movement to combat high infant mortality rates. He died in Philadelphia.

During his younger years, Kelley was considered one of the most electrifying and certainly one of the loudest orators in the House. Genial and unusually accessible, he carried on a voluminous correspondence while daily meeting dozens of officeseekers and lobbyists. While the Wood Tariff Bill was being argued in the House in 1878, as many as forty men would come crowding into Kelley's private rooms in Washington, exhorting his support. He was, perhaps, best known for his detailed knowledge of all matters pertaining to tariffs and protection and held a lifelong commitment to using tariffs to protect the wages of workingmen. Because of his long tenure as a congressman, Kelley became affectionately known as the "Father of the House."

• Kelley's papers are in the collections of the Historical Society of Pennsylvania. He published many of his speeches and writings, including *Speeches, Addresses, and Letters on Industrial and Financial Questions* (1872), *Lincoln and Stanton* (1885), and *The Old South and the New* (1880). For information on his congressional career, see Ira V. Brown, "William D. Kelley and Radical Reconstruction," *Pennsylvania Magazine of History and Biography* 85 (July 1961); and Floyd William Nicklas, "William Kelley: The Congressional Years, 1861–1890" (Ph.D. diss., Northern Illinois Univ., 1983). Frank G. Carpenter, *Carp's Washington* (1960), discusses Kelley's commitment to protective tariffs. A detailed description of Kelley's involvement in the Crédit Mobilier scandal is in Edward Winslow Martin, *Behind the Scenes in Washington* (1873). Kelley's obituaries are in the *Washington Evening Star*, 10 and 11 Jan. 1890, and the *New York Times*, 9 Jan. 1890. He was also memorialized in the House of Representatives on 12 Jan. 1890.

SILVANA SIDDALI

KELLOGG, Albert (6 Dec. 1813–31 Mar. 1887), botanist, was born in New Hartford, Connecticut, the son of Isaac Kellogg and Aurilla Barney, prosperous farmers. He took an early interest in plants, even gathering local herbs for use by his neighbors. He attended local schools until his parents concluded that he should go into the medical profession, so he began medical studies with "an eminent physician" in Middletown, Connecticut. He developed lung problems and returned to the family farm.

Advised to seek a milder climate for his health, Kellogg attended a medical college in Charleston, South Carolina. His health did not improve, so he moved to Mount Pleasant, Georgia, and then to Lexington, Kentucky. There he received the M.D. at Transylvania University in 1838 with a thesis titled "Narcotics." He practiced medicine in various places in Kentucky, Georgia, and Alabama. According to his biographer Edward Lee Greene, "It was the opinion of one who knew him in those days that he did not once, in all his career as a physician, request a payment. Naturally, he failed to obtain in medicine the means of subsistence, and abandoned the profession" (p. 146).

Kellogg met John James Audubon, already internationally known for his bird folios and publications and also widely traveled in the United States. He accompanied Audubon from the Southeast to San Antonio, Texas, which he reached in the fall of 1845. He returned to Connecticut and then spent some unspecified time in Ohio and the Mississippi River region.

Soon after news of the discovery of gold reached the East Coast in 1849, Kellogg was back in Connecticut, where, said Greene, "he found himself a man of some well earned local fame for travel, and was sought out and desired to join a small party of voyagers to California" (p. 147). The group bought a schooner and sailed by way of the Straits of Magellan. They stopped at Tierra del Fuego and at several points on both coasts of

South America, where Kellogg collected plants, and they reached Sacramento, California, in August 1849. Unfortunately, the plant collections were destroyed by flooding in that city shortly thereafter.

Kellogg stayed in Sacramento and the mining area for three or four years before moving to San Francisco. He was with the Connecticut Mining and Trading Company in Sacramento, and to a limited extent he practiced medicine in San Francisco. His primary interest then was botany, and he also wanted to see an organization formed for the advancement of science in that city. In 1852 (or before) he received branches and cones of the giant redwood (*Sequoiadendron giganteum*), and it is said that when he first saw the living trees, the tears rolled down his face, "so deeply was he moved by the sublime presence of these surviving monuments of a botanical age long dead." He began studying the tree and showed specimens to William Lobb, a collector for the London Horticultural Society. As a result, the English botanist John Lindley first described the tree in December 1853 as *Sequoia gigantea* before Kellogg had an opportunity to publish on it. With Hans Hermann Behr, he described it in detail in 1855 (California Academy of Natural Sciences, *Proceedings* 1 [7 May 1855]: 51–52).

Kellogg was one of seven men who established the California Academy of Sciences in San Francisco in April 1853. That institution became Kellogg's base of study. Apparently as a volunteer, he was one of its curators from 1853 to 1854, was curator of botany later, was its librarian from 1867 to 1869, and served on several of its committees over the years. He traveled to various parts of California to collect plants and to make drawings of them. He published a number of papers in the *Proceedings* of the academy and in some magazines in San Francisco. As described by Greene, his writing was "conscientiously exact in his descriptions" but tended to be "somewhat original" and "poetical." Deeply religious, he often derived his scientific names from biblical sources. He described many species of plants, but many of them later proved to have been previously named. He did not maintain extensive correspondence with botanists elsewhere in the United States, and he tended to recognize very small differences in plant specimens. Among his taxonomic descriptions that have survived are several California lilies, a small oak species, a California "lilac" or redroot (*Ceanothus cordulatus*), and others.

During the summer of 1867 Kellogg served as surgeon and botanist on the first government exploration of the coast and offshore islands of Alaska, under the direction of geodesist George Davidson of the U.S. Coast Survey. Kellogg collected several hundred species of plants, of which sets were placed in the herbarium of the California Academy of Sciences, the Smithsonian Institution, and the Academy of Natural Sciences of Philadelphia.

Kellogg's special interests were the trees and their environment. In 1882 he published *Forest Trees of California*, which was separately included that year as a supplement to the second report of the State Mineralogist of California. It is considered the first botanical account of the state's forests.

Although he was not technically trained, Kellogg has been described as the first professional botanist to settle in California. He helped to establish the California Academy of Sciences as a major scientific entity, the first on the West Coast.

Kellogg never married. An anonymous biographer said, "His childlike enthusiasm and unworldliness impressed all who met him" (*Zoe*, p. 2). For the last six years of his life he accepted a very nominal salary from the California Academy of Sciences, and he lived in Alameda, at the house of William G. W. Harford, a curator of the academy. Kellogg spent his days at the academy, continuing to make detailed ink drawings of the leaves, flowers, and seeds of native California trees until his death in Alameda. Some of his drawings were published later in the folio volume *Illustrations of West American Oaks* (1889–1890, in two parts), with text by botanist Edward Lee Greene and through funds from San Francisco banker James M. McDonald. The rest of his approximately 400 drawings have not survived.

• Information on Kellogg's M.D. degree is at Transylvania University. The California Academy of Sciences lost many early records in the earthquake and fire of Apr. 1906, some of which might have given more information on Kellogg's role there. Biographical accounts are [Edward Lee Greene], "Biographical Notice of Dr. Albert Kellogg," *Pittonia* 1 (1887): 145–51; and "Dr. Albert Kellogg," *Zoe* 4 (1893): 1–2. The account in *Dictionary of American Biography*, vol. 5, is helpful. An obituary is in the *San Francisco Chronicle*, 1 Apr. 1887.

ELIZABETH NOBLE SHOR

KELLOGG, Clara Louise (9 July 1842–13 May 1916), soprano and operatic impresario, was born in Sumterville (now Sumter), South Carolina, the daughter of George Kellogg and Jane Elizabeth Crosby, teachers. Both of her parents were from well-established Connecticut families, and shortly after her birth the family returned north, to Birmingham (now Derby), Connecticut. Clara Louise's father worked as an inventor and manufacturer, but his business failed around 1855; as a result the Kellogg family moved to New York City.

Kellogg first learned music from her parents, who were musical amateurs. She began studying the piano at the age of five. She attended the Ashland Seminary and Musical Institute in the Catskills and in the late 1850s studied with several New York voice teachers, including Achille Errani and Emanuele Muzio. After a modest concert tour in 1860 Kellogg made her New York debut as Gilda in Verdi's *Rigoletto* at the Academy of Music on 27 February 1861. She then accompanied the operatic company (managed by Maurice Grau) to Boston for a season, where she sang in Bellini's *La sonnambula* and Donizetti's *Linda di Chamounix* before the season was prematurely terminated because of the outbreak of the Civil War. During the war Kellogg continued to perform, appearing in some dozen roles in cities from Boston to Chicago; she also gave operatic concerts. Her first triumph occurred when she sang Marguerite in the New York premiere performance of Gounod's *Faust* at the Academy of Music on 25 November 1863. This was fortuitous, for over the next thirty years *Faust* (which was almost always sung in Italian) was one of the most popular operas in the United States, and for much of that time Kellogg was closely identified with Marguerite. Kellogg made her London debut, also as Marguerite, at Her Majesty's Theatre on 2 November 1867. Over the course of her career she sang more than forty roles in Italian, French, and English operas. She reportedly preferred playing Aida and Carmen, but it was as Marguerite that she was most successful. Her close public identification with this role is somewhat ironic, for Kellogg admitted in her memoirs that it was not a role she admired. "Musically, I loved the part of Marguerite," she wrote. "Dramatically, I confess to some impatience over the imbecility of the girl. From the first I summarily apostrophised her to myself as 'a little fool!'" (p. 80).

From 1868 through 1873 Kellogg sang regularly in concert and in operatic performances. She performed during the Handel Festival of 1868 in London and subsequently made concert tours of both Europe and the United States. In 1872 she sang with soprano Pauline Lucca in an opera company managed by Max Maretzek, and in 1873 she organized a troupe of her own, the Clara Kellogg English Opera Company, with which she hoped to popularize in the United States the performance of Italian and French opera sung in English. Kellogg hired C. D. Hess to serve as business manager; she reserved for herself not only the role of prima donna but also the position of artistic manager. In her latter role she selected the repertory, made decisions about costumes and stage settings, hired and coached both principal singers and chorus members, and oversaw rehearsals. During the first year Kellogg herself translated into English the foreign-language works used by the company and adapted them to the American stage. The repertory included many operas that were American favorites, including Balfe's *The Bohemian Girl*, Auber's *Fra Diavolo*, Verdi's *Il trovatore*, Mozart's *Le nozze di Figaro*, and Flotow's *Martha*. In addition, the company performed works relatively new to Americans, including Wagner's *Der fliegende Holländer*, Thomas's *Mignon*, Balfe's *Il talismano*, and Julius Benedict's *Lily of Killarney*. During the troupe's second season (1874–1875) Kellogg sang in no fewer than 125 performances; although this level of stamina is unthinkable today, it was not particularly extraordinary at the time. One of the goals of Kellogg's company was to firmly establish opera sung in English in the United States; the troupe frequently used the slogan "opera for the people" on its playbills and in its advertising. As such, the Kellogg English Opera Company represents a continuation of a movement that began in the United States in the late 1840s and early 1850s, when Italian opera first started to become identified as an "aristocratic" social endeavor. The company's attempt was also an extension of a similar "English opera" campaign in England. Kellogg's company, however, was only moderately successful, possibly because of competition from the Euphrosyne Parepa-Rosa, Caroline Richings, and other English opera companies; it disbanded after 1876.

During the late 1870s and early 1880s Kellogg resumed opera and concert appearances both in the United States and Europe (London, Paris, Vienna, and St. Petersburg); she also formed a number of short-lived concert troupes that traveled widely throughout the United States. In 1887 she married her manager, Carl Strakosch, the nephew of prominent operatic and concert impresarios Maurice and Max Strakosch (the latter had at one time been her manager). The couple adopted a child. After she was married Kellogg performed less frequently in public, and she eventually retired to the family estate "Elpstone" in New Hartford, Connecticut, where she died.

Kellogg had a pure, sweet soprano voice of large range and penetrating quality, and she was praised as a good actress. After her London debut, for example, a critic described her voice as "a soprano of pure and even quality, sufficiently brilliant in its upper portion, and intensely sympathetic in its middle and lower range." Kellogg, he continued, "has perfect command over a compass of two octaves. . . . her bravura-singing in florid ornamental passages has that distinctness and completeness of style so seldom realized; while her shake is irreproachable in closeness, evenness, and intonation." About her histrionic abilities the critic concluded, "Miss Kellogg is an excellent actress,—with an intelligent and expressive face, a graceful figure, and that propriety of gesture, action, and by-play, which denote that the study of acting, apart from singing, has occupied more of her attention than is usual with vocalists" (quoted in Winter, p. 466). Despite these abilities Kellogg never reached the status of contemporaries such as sopranos Adelina Patti and Lillian Nordica, perhaps because she lacked the undefinable charisma or stage presence typical of performers of the first rank. She was both ambitious and generous and had a deserved reputation as someone willing to encourage and assist struggling young artists (her generous pecuniary support to the impoverished young American soprano Emma Abbott, for example, was public knowledge during Kellogg's lifetime). Although she was not the first American-born prima donna, Kellogg was the first American singer to achieve a solid professional reputation in Europe. She was also indefatigable in her efforts to advance the cause of opera in English in the United States.

• There are several manuscript collections that contain materials related to Kellogg's life and career, but there is apparently no known collection of her papers. Scattered materials related to Kellogg are in the Bryant and Godwin papers in the Manuscripts and Archives Department of the New York Public Library and in the Albert Davis–Messmore Kendall Holographic File Collection of the Humanities Research Center of the University of Texas in Austin. Scrapbooks related to Kellogg are in the Metropolitan Opera Archives in New York, and correspondence is located in the Music Divi-sion of the New York Public Library. Kellogg's autobiography, *Memoirs of an American Prima Donna* (1913), remains the only book-length treatment of her life and career. It is, however, anecdotal and self-serving in nature and as such is of limited use to scholars. There is also useful but limited information in contemporary biographical compilations; particularly helpful are entries by Harriet Prescott Spofford in *Our Famous Women* (1884), William Winter in *Eminent Women of the Age* (1869), F. O. Jones in the *Handbook of American Music and Musicians* (1886), Phebe A. Hanaford in *Women of the Century* (1877), and Charles Lahee in *Famous Singers of Today and Yesterday* (1898). Timothy Hopkins, *The Kelloggs in the Old World and the New* (1903), is a good source for biographical material. An article titled "Miss Kellogg and English Opera" in the *New York Times*, 20 Feb. 1874, provides some insight into Kellogg's role as a proponent of English opera in the United States. Hobart H. Burr discusses Kellogg in the context of Americans' pride in women musicians in "American Women Musicians," *Cosmopolitan*, Aug. 1901. Obituaries are in *Musical America*, 20 May 1916, *Musical Courier*, 18 May 1916, and the *New York Times*, 17 May 1916.

KATHERINE K. PRESTON

KELLOGG, Frank Billings (22 Dec. 1856–21 Dec. 1937), lawyer and secretary of state, was born in Potsdam, St. Lawrence County, New York, the son of Asa F. Kellogg and Abigail Billings. When Kellogg was eight, his family, along with many neighbors, moved to Olmsted County in Minnesota. It was, he wrote, "the old, old story," a typical pioneering experience, the "far off and mysterious West, the railroad which I had never seen before, the steamship and the covered wagon on the prairies and the wilderness of the Northwest, the struggles in a wild and new land, the many disappointments, failures, and hardships." The family farm did not thrive. Kellogg went to a little country school from his ninth to fourteenth year, and that was all of his formal education. The farm work was very hard and at one point dangerous—caught out on the prairie in the blizzard of 1873, he nearly lost his life. At last he was admitted into the law office of a Rochester, Minnesota, lawyer, where he read law while supporting himself by working for a local farmer. He passed the bar in 1877, which was "a life line thrown to rescue me from a desperate struggle for a livelihood."

For a few years Kellogg accepted every case that came his way, but his luck turned when he entered a railroad litigation in 1884 and in the course of it consulted a cousin, Cushman Kellogg Davis, who was the leading lawyer of St. Paul. Two years later, when Davis won election to the U.S. Senate, his firm decided to add a partner and in 1887 selected Kellogg. The previous year Kellogg had married Clara M. Cook; they did not have children.

As a member of this prestigious St. Paul firm, Kellogg took on railroad and iron ore litigation connected with exploitation of the great Mesabi range. He came to know the titans of business organization, the Rockefellers and Andrew Carnegie, and he represented the railroad builder James J. Hill. During business trips to Washington he met Theodore Roosevelt (1858–1919), then a member of the Civil Service Commission. The two were about the same age and got along well, and when Roosevelt became president Kellogg had an easy entrée to the White House.

His friendship with Roosevelt led to several notable court cases against the most formidable industrial figures of the day, which Kellogg took for the federal government. Like his friend the president, he was alarmed by the sudden increase in corporate mergers, the formation of huge entities with the possibility of obtaining monopolies or near monopolies. Upon appointment as special assistant attorney general, he began by fighting the paper trust, known as the General Paper Company, and won. In 1906 he began prosecution of the Union Pacific Railroad, which under the direction of E. H. Harriman was eating up competitors at an alarming rate, and he took on the Southern Pacific when the government moved against it. These government victories led to the greatest case of the era—the prosecution of the Standard Oil Company for violating the Sherman Antitrust Act. After a favorable decision of the St. Louis circuit court, the case went to the Supreme Court. Kellogg won in 1911 with an interpretation of the Sherman Act that a combination was illegal if unreasonably in restraint of trade. Kellogg's name became well known; the newspaper press described him as "the trust buster." In 1912 he became president of the American Bar Association (ABA).

At this juncture politics beckoned. Kellogg had undergone a typical conversion from a conservative during the 1890s, who did not believe in government intervention in private enterprise, to a progressive a decade later. In his presidential address to the ABA he admonished his fellow lawyers to stand for "modern economic legislation," which, he explained, was "necessary to the development of the people." With perhaps undue faith in what they might achieve, he believed that lawyers could obtain such laws.

Elected as a Republican to the Senate in 1916, Kellogg served a single term during which he was a "mild reservationist," indicating he would accept the Treaty of Versailles if minor changes were made in its text. He did his best to oppose the "irreconcilables" and the antitreaty leadership of Henry Cabot Lodge. Lodge refused Kellogg a seat on the Foreign Relations Committee because Kellogg would not bind himself to support Lodge. Kellogg was put on the committee only in 1921. He was defeated for reelection in 1922 by Henrik Shipstead, the Farmer-Labor candidate.

President Calvin Coolidge liked Kellogg because they had the same points of view on domestic and foreign policy and perhaps also because Kellogg was one of the few senators who had been kind to Coolidge when the latter was only a vice president. To the bewilderment of many people, Coolidge appointed Kellogg ambassador to London in 1923 and, upon the resignation of Charles Evans Hughes, secretary of state on 4 March 1925. Duties of the former post largely concerned the settlement of German reparations and Allied war debts. Kellogg helped arrange a $110-million loan to Germany from the J. P. Morgan firm that helped ensure the Dawes Plan of 1924, which put German reparations on a revised schedule of payments to the Allies.

During his four years as head of the U.S. State Department, Kellogg presided over better relations with Mexico, largely through the agency of Ambassador Dwight W. Morrow. In Nicaragua Henry L. Stimson arranged the Peace of Tipitapa in 1927 between rival political factions and thereby eventually made it possible to pull out American marines, present since 1912. The two Latin American problems were closely allied. Kellogg had described Mexican leaders as "Bolshevist" because of their desire to nationalize oil deposits discovered before 1917, and the Mexicans returned Kellogg's bombast by intervening in the Nicaraguan civil war. The two special envoys allowed the secretary of state to extricate himself from these awkward situations.

In Asia Kellogg confronted the excessive demands of Chinese nationalism, encountering serious antiforeign incidents at Shanghai in 1925 and at Nanking in 1927. The Chinese persisted in seeking tariff autonomy and the abolition of extraterritoriality, and in January 1927 Kellogg announced the willingness of the United States to negotiate those issues, either together with the other foreign powers or unilaterally. He thus held firm to the traditional American policy of goodwill. During his secretaryship Kellogg hoped to extend the Washington Naval Conference limitations on battleships and aircraft carriers to all ship classes, but the Geneva Naval Conference of 1927 proved an abject failure, a head-on collision with Britain over limitations on cruiser tonnage.

Kellogg's principal diplomatic success was the Kellogg-Briand Pact of 1928, which the secretary at first envisioned as a way to avoid a bilateral treaty with France that would have been a negative military alliance (both countries promising not to go to war with each other). With a multilateral structure, he intended to make it worthless because of its impossibly broad membership. Instead, after permitting large reservations such as matters involving domestic jurisdiction, he came to believe that the treaty, in which the signing nations renounced war "as an instrument of national policy," really might prevent war. He was awarded the 1929 Nobel Peace Prize.

Kellogg's historical reputation has fared poorly in comparison with his predecessor Hughes, an intellectually impressive man, and his successor Stimson, a soldierly figure with an air of authority. Kellogg was nervous, hot-tempered, outspoken, perhaps undiplomatic. Lacking formal education, he pronounced the phrase "M. Briand" by reading the first capital letter as if it were Briand's initial rather than an abbreviation for monsieur. However, these were minor blemishes in a lawyer and secretary of state of intelligence and modesty. If in ideas and interests he did not reach beyond the preferences of his time, few people did during an era when the waves of prosperity appeared to be washing away the rancors of the world war of 1914–1918.

After leaving office in 1929, Kellogg returned to the practice of law in St. Paul. He served on the Permanent Court of International Justice at The Hague from 1930 until 1935. He died in St. Paul.

• Kellogg's papers are in the Minnesota Historical Society in St. Paul. The Department of State records in the National Archives constitute a rich source for his diplomatic actions, as does the detailed diary of Kellogg's assistant secretary for Western European affairs, William R. Castle, Jr., in the Houghton Library at Harvard University. The only biography, long out-of-date but containing reminiscences by its subject, is David Bryn-Jones, *Frank B. Kellogg: A Biography* (1937). For diplomacy see Nancy Harvison Hooker, ed., *The Moffat Papers: Selections from the Diplomatic Journals of Jay Pierrepont Moffat* (1956); Katherine E. Crane, *Mr. Carr of State: Forty-Seven Years in the Department of State* (1960); and Robert H. Ferrell, *Frank B. Kellogg and Henry L. Stimson* (1963). An obituary is in the *New York Times*, 22 Dec. 1937.

ROBERT H. FERRELL

KELLOGG, John Harvey (26 Feb. 1852–14 Dec. 1943), physician, surgeon, and health reformer, was born in rural Livingston County, Michigan, the son of John Preston Kellogg and Anne Stanley, farmers. In 1852 Kellogg's parents accepted the religious teachings that led to the organization of the Seventh-day Adventist church in 1863. This decision had a marked influence on their son's life. By 1856 the family had resettled in Battle Creek, Michigan. Part of the proceeds from the sale of their farm was used to relocate the infant Adventist publishing plant from Rochester, New York, to Battle Creek, where Kellogg's father now operated a small store and broom shop.

Kellogg's primary education was sporadic; work in the broom shop took precedence. At the age of twelve, he was invited by James White, a principal founder of Seventh-day Adventism and its initial publisher, to learn the printing trade. Ellen White, White's wife and the new denomination's prophetess and cofounder, had begun to write extensively on matters of health and hygiene. Kellogg set type for some of her early articles on health. An avid reader, he devoured the writings of earlier health reformers Sylvester Graham and Larkin B. Coles and became convinced of the superiority of the life style they advocated, which included temperance, vegetarianism, and the use of natural remedies.

Originally planning a teaching career, Kellogg taught for a year at the age of sixteen in a district school in Hastings, Michigan. Convinced by this of his need for more formal education, he enrolled in 1872 in a teacher training program at Michigan State Normal College in Ypsilanti. Later that year, Adventist leaders, who had become aware of their need for professionally trained physicians if they were to criticize conventional medical practices, sent some of their brightest youth to study at Russell Trall's reform Hygieo-Therapeutic College in Florence Heights, New Jersey. Kellogg was persuaded to be part of this group.

Five months at Trall's awakened Kellogg to his need for more conventional medical training. Encouraged by the Whites, he spent the next term at the University of Michigan Medical School. He then transferred to Bellevue Hospital Medical College in New York City, where he received an M.D. in 1875.

Kellogg intended to use his medical education only as a basis for teaching better health habits. In 1873 he became James White's chief editorial assistant in the production of the Adventist monthly, *Health Reformer*. The following year he was named editor, a position he held until his death. In 1879 Kellogg changed the name of the journal to *Good Health*.

Kellogg first demonstrated his interest in reforming American dietary habits with the publication in 1874 of a hygienic cookbook. That same year he authored *Proper Diet for Man*, which advocated vegetarianism, a key ingredient in the health regimen he later termed "biologic living." His system called for abstinence from alcoholic beverages, tobacco, tea, coffee, and condiments, and sparing use of eggs, dairy products, and refined sugars.

Kellogg advocated biologic living as a total way of life. He believed practitioners should follow a regular exercise program, get plenty of fresh air and sunshine, observe correct posture, and wear sensible clothing. He advocated drinking eight to ten glasses of water daily. Always suspicious of conventional drugs, Kellogg preferred to treat illnesses with hydrotherapy. His *Rational Hydrotherapy* (1901) was for several decades a standard text in the field.

In 1866 the Adventists established a small reform medical institution in Battle Creek. Ten years later this Western Health Reform Institute, with only twenty patients, seemed about to fold. Kellogg was persuaded to become its superintendent "for one year" but retained this position until his death. By the turn of the century, Kellogg had expanded the institute, which he renamed the Battle Creek Sanitarium in 1877, to accommodate 700 patients.

In 1879 Kellogg married Ella Eaton, a visitor to Battle Creek who had become interested in the sanitarium health program. The couple had no natural children but reared more than forty foster children, of whom they adopted several. A college graduate trained in domestic science, Ella Kellogg was a valuable collaborator in her husband's later food experiments. Her participation in the national Woman's Christian Temperance Union and the Young Women's Christian Association provided opportunities for her husband to share his ideas in these circles. Friends remembered that the Kelloggs gave little evidence of sentimental affection but demonstrated mutual respect for each other's abilities.

Kellogg's position at the sanitarium and a concern about mortality rates in abdominal surgery eventually convinced him to qualify as a surgeon. In 1883 he spent five months studying surgical procedures in London and Vienna. He returned for a similar period in 1889, spending part of the time as assistant to England's leading abdominal and gynecological surgeon,

Lawson Tait. Combining Tait's methods with his own "biologic" treatments, Kellogg later claimed a record of 165 abdominal surgeries without a fatality. He performed 22,000 surgical operations in a career that lasted until the age of eighty-eight.

Early in his career as sanitarium superintendent, Kellogg noted patient dissatisfaction with the institution's restricted, monotonous diet. Enlisting his wife's help, he set out to change this. Because he was convinced that the cereal grains basic to the diet he favored were more easily digested after prolonged baking, the Kelloggs developed a slow-baked, multigrain biscuit. These biscuits were then coarsely ground and named "Granola," which was based on the name of New York health reformer James C. Jackson's earlier creation, "Granula," which dated from the early 1860s.

Kellogg shared health reformer Horace Fletcher's enthusiasm for prolonged mastication of food. To encourage this, Kellogg requested patients to begin meals with a saucer of dry Granola or several slices of zwieback. Finding this unsatisfactory to patients, he began experiments with the assistance of his younger brother, Will Keith Kellogg, that led to the development of wheat flakes. The two men subsequently adapted the flaking process to corn and rice. John Kellogg patented his process in 1894, but he soon found that entrepreneurs rushed in to imitate his products. The most successful of these, Charles W. Post, patterned his "Grape Nuts" after Granola and his Postum after a cereal-based coffee substitute manufactured at the sanitarium. Kellogg maintained that he was "not after the business; I am after the reform; that is what I want to see."

Will Kellogg's attitude was different. As manager of the brothers' Sanitarium Food Company, he wished to increase their products' appeal and to begin extensive advertising. This was particularly important after the patent on the flaking process was declared invalid in 1903. In 1905 Will persuaded John to sell him the rights to the manufacture of corn flakes and established a new company to produce and market them. This led to a highly profitable business; unfortunately, however, it also led to hard feelings and repeated lawsuits between the brothers.

In addition to prepared breakfast cereals, John Kellogg developed a variety of imitation meats made from wheat gluten and nuts for use at the sanitarium. Some of these were marketed commercially with modest success. Peanut butter, also a John Kellogg idea, caught on widely but was not marketed successfully by either Kellogg. The same was true of an artificial milk developed by John Kellogg from soybeans in the 1930s.

Recognizing education's role in reform, Kellogg established schools of nursing, hygiene, physical education, and home economics at the sanitarium. In 1895, with Adventist support, he launched the American Medical Missionary College in Chicago to train doctors who would promote the concepts of biologic living. Kellogg served as its president until the loss of Adventist support led him to merge the college with

the University of Illinois Medical School in 1910. In 1923 Kellogg combined the various sanitarium schools with a liberal arts program to form Battle Creek College. He served as the college's president and chief financial supporter until 1938, when it became a casualty of the Great Depression and the declining income from his food creations.

For the first twenty years after becoming sanitarium superintendent, Kellogg enjoyed wide Adventist support and helped to develop a number of Adventist sanitariums in various parts of the United States and abroad. These relations grew increasingly tense after 1895 because Adventist leaders resented Kellogg's dominant personality and what they saw as his effort to divert church funds from evangelism to medical work. The situation worsened when the Battle Creek Sanitarium was destroyed by fire in 1902. Differences over the size of a rebuilt sanitarium and over theological interpretation led to Kellogg's expulsion from the Adventist church in 1907.

Kellogg retained control of *Good Health* and the Battle Creek Sanitarium. By the 1920s he had expanded the sanitarium to accommodate 1,200 patients. These included important personalities who ranged from manufacturers Edgar Welch and Joseph Patterson to political reformers Gifford Pinchot, William Jennings Bryan, and Ben Lindsey. Success led to unwise expansion of the sanitarium in 1927 and its decline during the subsequent depression. Kellogg shifted his major interest to a smaller institution near Miami, Florida, which had been the gift in 1930 of aviation magnate Glenn Curtiss, but which never attained the prominence of the Battle Creek institution.

Kellogg developed a wide variety of exercise equipment for use by his patients. He also became enamored with the eugenics movement and in 1914 established the Race Betterment Foundation, endowed with profits from his cereal creations, to publicize and promote eugenics. He promoted biologic living through numerous and varied speaking engagements and by writing nearly fifty books on aspects of health. He also served from 1878 to 1891 and from 1911 to 1917 on the Michigan State Board of Health.

Kellogg's cereal creations changed the average American breakfast. His extensive speaking and writing called attention to the importance of diet, exercise, and natural remedies in preserving and regaining health. Many of his ideas were accepted, at least in part, by physicians, nutritionists, and physical therapists. Some of his surgical techniques were widely imitated. After Kellogg's death in Battle Creek, Secretary of the Navy Frank Knox summarized the views of many when he wrote that Kellogg was one of the country's "greatest individualists and leaders in medicine," whose "contribution to national health and well-being was very great and will be long remembered."

• Collections of Kellogg's papers are at both the University of Michigan and Michigan State University. His widely sold subscription book, *Home Hand-book of Domestic Hygiene and Rational Medicine* (1900), provides an early overview of his efforts at health education. More mature presentations appear in *The New Dietetics* (1923) and *How to Have Good Health through Biologic Living* (1932). His Victorian views of sex are demonstrated in *Plain Facts for Old and Young* (1901). *Harmony of Science and the Bible on the Nature of the Soul and the Doctrine of the Resurrection* (1879) represents Kellogg's first venture into theology; his *The Living Temple* (1903) brought on a major confrontation with Adventist leaders. The monthly issues of *Good Health* (1879–1944), which all contain editorials or articles by Kellogg, show the development of his ideas and interests. His thirty-year correspondence with Ellen White is preserved by the Ellen G. White Estate of Silver Spring, Md. The most complete assessment of Kellogg's life and work is Richard W. Schwarz, "John Harvey Kellogg: American Health Reformer" (Ph.D. diss., Univ. of Michigan, 1964). Some of this material later appeared in the same author's *John Harvey Kellogg, M.D.* (1970). Kellogg's place within the health reform movement is treated in Ronald L. Numbers, *Prophetess of Health: A Study of Ellen G. White* (1976), and James C. Whorton, *Crusaders for Fitness: The History of American Health Reformers* (1982).

RICHARD W. SCHWARZ

KELLOGG, Laura Minnie Cornelius (10 Sept. 1880–c. 1949), Native American activist, was born on the Oneida reservation near Green Bay, Wisconsin, the daughter of Adam Poe Cornelius and Celicia Bread, farmers. A descendant of central New York State Oneida Indians who followed Indian missionary Reverend Eleazar Williams into the Wisconsin territory in 1822, she was a baptized member of the Episcopal Church of the Holy Apostles. Included in her prominent lineage were Daniel Bread, a major nineteenth-century Oneida chief in New York and Wisconsin who was known for his powerful oratorical skills, and Skenandore, the last of the New York chiefs, who had led the tribe's migration to Wisconsin.

Unlike many of her contemporaries, Kellogg managed to avoid attending distant Indian boarding schools. She was educated in the 1890s at Grafton Hall, an Episcopal boarding school largely for non-Indians located at Fond du Lac, Wisconsin. In the first decade of the twentieth century, she studied at Barnard College, Cornell University, the New York School of Philanthropy (later the Columbia University School of Social Work), Stanford University, and the University of Wisconsin, although she never received degrees from these institutions.

One of the best Indian linguists of her generation, with a superior command of Oneida and Mohawk as well as English, Kellogg had gained national attention by 1911 because of her spellbinding oratory before Indian and non-Indian audiences and her writing skills. As a public speaker, she told of the eighteenth-century League of the Iroquois, the lessons and wisdom of Indian elders, and the overriding concerns of Native Americans to win back their lands, which she insisted had been taken fraudulently by New York State and by land speculators. She was equally accomplished with a pen, devoting herself to writing on behalf of Progressive Era reform causes such as women's rights as well as writing political tracts on Indian issues, plays, and short stories. Her writings included *Our* *Democracy and the American Indian* (1920) and *Indian Reveries: Gehdos of the Lost Empire* (1921).

In 1911 Kellogg was one of the founders of the Society of American Indians, a national reform-minded organization largely composed of educated Indian professionals, and later she served variously as secretary of the organization's executive committee and vice president for education. Kellogg differed from the majority of the Society of American Indians, however, in her vehement opposition to the economic and educational policies of the Bureau of Indian Affairs. She was also more confident than other organization members that Native Americans could, without assistance, transform their reservations into self-sustaining communities. After her marriage on 22 April 1912 to Orrin Joseph Kellogg, a non-Indian attorney from Minneapolis, she became even more isolated from the Society of American Indians. Eventually, she broke with the organization, outlining her views in *Our Democracy and the American Indian*, which drew significant inspiration from the Mormon economic model of community development and survival.

Kellogg and her husband spent much of the time before, during, and after World War I organizing a massive Iroquois land-claims suit. For this legal effort, they made exorbitant promises and collected funds from poor Indians in Iroquois communities throughout the United States and Canada. Their collection methods led to their arrests in Oklahoma (1913) and Montreal (1925), although they were never convicted of fraud. In 1927 the U.S. District Court dismissed their Iroquois land-claims suit, *Deere v. St. Lawrence River Power Company*, because of a lack of jurisdiction.

Kellogg continued to exercise influence in Indian affairs into the 1930s, but her insistence on self-sufficiency became less appealing during the New Deal era when the government provided tribes with economic assistance and promoted Indian languages and cultural traditions. By the 1940s she was a forgotten woman who had outlived her time. According to Oneida tribal sources, she died in obscurity in the late 1940s. Her death certificate and burial record have not been located.

Acknowledged as a precursor of the contemporary land-claims movement and as a determined advocate of Indian education and economic development, Kellogg, nevertheless, has been accused by many Indian elders of fomenting divisions within Iroquois communities and swindling Indians of hundreds of thousands of dollars in her abortive efforts to litigate their land claims. Seeking to use her extraordinary abilities to help her people, she ended condemned by many of them as a common thief.

• Letters by Laura Cornelius Kellogg can be found in the central files of the Bureau of Indian Affairs in the National Archives and in the J. N. B. Hewitt Manuscripts, National Anthropological Archives, Smithsonian Institution. Other works by Kellogg not mentioned in the text include "Overalls and the Tenderfoot: A Story," *Barnard Bear* 2 (Mar. 1907):

5–18; "Industrial Organization for the Indian," in Society of American Indians, *Report of the Executive Council on the Proceedings of the First Annual Conference* (1912); and "Some Facts and Figures on Indian Education," *Society of American Indians Quarterly Journal* 1 (Apr. 1913): 36–46. Sources on Kellogg include Laurence M. Hauptman, "Designing Woman: Minnie Kellogg, Iroquois Leader," *Indian Lives: Essays on Nineteenth and Twentieth Century Native American Leaders*, ed. L. George Moses and Raymond Wilson (1985); Thelma Cornelius McLester, "Oneida Women Leaders," *The Oneida Indian Experience: Two Perspectives*, ed. Jack Campisi and Laurence M. Hauptman (1988); William A. DuPuy, "Looking for an Indian Booker T. Washington to Lead Their People," *New York Tribune*, 27 Aug. 1911; and Ramona Herdman, "A New Six Nations: Laura Cornelius Kellogg Sees the Old Confederacy Reestablished on a Modern Basis," *Syracuse Herald*, 6 Nov. 1927.

LAURENCE M. HAUPTMAN

KELLOGG, Louise Phelps (12 May 1862–11 July 1942), historian and documentary editor, was born in Milwaukee, Wisconsin, the daughter of Amherst Willoughby Kellogg and Mary Isabella Phelps. Her father, active in the Methodist church and in temperance societies, worked for several insurance companies. Educated at Dearborn Seminary and the Milwaukee College (later Milwaukee-Downer College), Kellogg received a B.L. in 1897 from the University of Wisconsin.

Before continuing her education, Kellogg taught at a private school in Wisconsin. After enrolling in the graduate program at the University of Wisconsin, she worked as a research assistant for Charles Haskins and Frederick Jackson Turner. She had received a fellowship from the Woman's Education Association of Boston, a precursor of the American Association of University Women, for study abroad and attended the University of Paris, the École des Hautes Études, and the London School of History and Economics in 1898–1899. Although Kellogg's early graduate work was in European and medieval history, she settled on American history as a specialization. Her dissertation, published as *The American Colonial Charter* (1903), was written under the direction of Frederick Jackson Turner and received the Justin Winsor Prize.

After receiving a Ph.D. in 1901 Kellogg was considered for a job assisting Charles Andrews and Frances Davenport in the compilation of a guide to records pertaining to colonial American history in the British Public Record Office. A year earlier, she was a finalist for a position at Northwestern University in Chicago, as dean of women. Deafness, from which she suffered throughout her life, may have been a factor that prevented her from obtaining these positions. In 1901 she began work at the State Historical Society of Wisconsin in Madison, where she would remain for the rest of her career. She served as a research historian and editor, assisting the director, Reuben Gold Thwaites. Although qualified to be the director, Kellogg remained in a lower level position, retiring as a senior research associate in 1941.

The State Historical Society had maintained rich collections documenting the revolutionary and early national periods in the Midwest and upper Ohio Valley, including the Lyman Copeland Draper manuscripts. For many years, Kellogg and Thwaites published volumes of the society's collections. After Thwaites's death in 1913, Kellogg continued the documentary publications, one of which, *Early Narratives of the Northwest, 1634–1699*, appeared as part of a series published in 1917. In addition to these documentary collections, Kellogg published two monographs, *The French Régime in Wisconsin and the Northwest* (1925) and *The British Régime in Wisconsin and the Northwest* (1935). She also wrote numerous scholarly articles and more than fifty biographical entries on French traders and pioneers in Wisconsin and the Old Northwest for the first edition of the *Dictionary of American Biography*.

Kellogg's scholarly accomplishments did not go unnoticed by her male colleagues in American history, and in 1930 she was elected as the first woman president of the Mississippi Valley Historical Association, the predecessor of the Organization of American Historians. The presidency was the highest form of scholarly recognition one could attain. More than forty years would pass before another woman would receive this honor. Kellogg was recognized as a role model and mentor for other women historians. Lucy Salmon of Vassar College sent many undergraduate history majors to the University of Wisconsin because she knew that Kellogg would take an interest in these young women. Kellogg also was active in the American Historical Association (AHA), serving as a member for more than forty years. In 1933 she was the only woman to serve on the AHA nominating committee and was part of the campaign orchestrated by women historians to get Nellie Neilson elected as the first woman president of the AHA.

As a member of numerous women's and civic associations, including the Daughters of the American Revolution, Kellogg served as a historical adviser to the Wisconsin Women's Christian Temperance Union, the Wisconsin Woman Suffrage Association, and the Wisconsin Federation of Women's Clubs. She helped them write histories of their organizations as well as stage plays and historical pageants that focused on American women.

In the mid-1930s Kellogg bought a car and hired a driver to take her across the country. In 1941 she traveled by car to the meeting of the Mississippi Valley Historical Association in Lexington, Kentucky. Her interest in automobile travel had been kindled by her colleague Harry Ellsworth Cole, president of the State Historical Society of Wisconsin, who traveled around the Old Northwest by car while researching the history of taverns for *Stagecoach and Tavern: Tales of the Old Northwest* (1930), which Kellogg completed after his death in 1929. Kellogg, who never married, died in Madison. She is buried with her parents in Milwaukee.

• The State Historical Society of Wisconsin in Madison has a large and rich collection of Kellogg's papers. The University of Wisconsin at Madison contains a record of her graduate work there and correspondence with Charles Haskins, Frederick Jackson Turner, and others. Turner's papers at the Huntington Library in San Marino, Calif., also contain correspondence with Kellogg. At the Library of Congress, Manuscript Division, Kellogg is represented in the papers of John Franklin Jameson and the records of the American Historical Association. She is mentioned in Jacqueline Goggin, "Challenging Sexual Discrimination in the Historical Profession: Women Historians and the American Historical Association, 1890–1940," *American Historical Review* 97 (June 1992): 769–802, and discussed in James L. Sellers, "Louise Phelps Kellogg," *Wisconsin Magazine of History* 37 (Summer 1954): 210, and Clifford L. Lord's column "Smoke Rings," *Wisconsin Magazine of History* 41 (Autumn 1957): 11–12. Obituaries are in the *Wisconsin Magazine of History* (Sept. 1942), *Wisconsin Archaeologist* (Sept. 1942), *American Historical Review* (Oct. 1942), and the *Wisconsin State Journal*, 14 July 1942.

JACQUELINE GOGGIN

KELLOGG, Minnie. *See* Kellogg, Laura Minnie Cornelius.

KELLOGG, Oliver Dimon (10 July 1878–26 Aug. 1932), mathematician, was born in Linwood, Pennsylvania, the son of Day Otis Kellogg, an Episcopalian minister, and Sarah Cornelia Hall. During Kellogg's youth his father left the ministry and became a professor of English literature at the University of Kansas and the American editor of the *Encyclopaedia Britannica*. Kellogg entered Princeton University in 1895, and he received his A.B. with high honors in 1899 and his M.A. in 1900. At Princeton he was influenced by Henry B. Fine and Edgar O. Lovett. A John. S. Kennedy Fellowship in 1899 enabled Kellogg to spend the academic years 1900–1901 in Berlin and 1901–1902 in Göttingen.

Kellogg wrote his doctoral dissertation, "Zur Theorie der Integralgleichungen und des Dirichletschen Prinzips," under the direction of David Hilbert in 1902 in Göttingen. At the time Hilbert was actively interested in Dirichlet's Principle, and Kellogg's dissertation was in the forefront of mathematical research as it represented a new approach to potential theory based on integral equations. Kellogg returned to Princeton as an instructor during the years 1902–1905, after which he became an assistant professor at the University of Missouri. In 1910 he was promoted to professor, and he remained in this capacity until 1919. In 1911 he married Edith Taylor, and the couple had one daughter. From June 1918 to June 1919 Kellogg served as a civilian consultant working on mathematical problems related to submarine detection devices at the U.S. Navy Experimental Station in New London, Connecticut. Upon the death of Maxime Bôcher he moved to Harvard University as a lecturer in 1919–1920. He subsequently rose through the ranks, serving as an associate professor (1920–1927) and as a professor from 1927 until his death. At the time of his death he had been designated to become the head of

the Harvard mathematics department in the fall of 1932. He was a member of the council of the American Mathematical Society (1908–1911 and 1921–1924) and a vice president of that organization (1927–1929).

Virtually all of Kellogg's mathematical research involved classical potential theory and its related mathematical disciplines of integral equations, real and complex function theory, and differential equations. At the time of his death he was acknowledged as the doyen of American potential theorists. Despite the recognition of his doctoral work and its extensions from 1902 to 1905—the renowned French mathematician Henri Poincaré had highlighted it in his Göttingen lectures of 1909—Kellogg came to regard it as unsatisfactory and made no subsequent use of it in his research. The reasons for this underscored both his modesty and the standards that led him to steadfastly underestimate the importance of his own work. First, he had not solved the problem as originally posed by Hilbert; second, it was impossible to separate his accomplishments from the greater work of his mentor; and finally, his analysis was incomplete and not always valid. It is instructive to note that some of the oversights and shortcomings that troubled Kellogg went unnoticed in the later work of both Poincaré and Hilbert!

Several of Kellogg's contributions, however, have had a lasting importance in classical potential theory. These include the Kellogg Theorem (1912) on harmonic and Green's functions, and the Birkhoff-Kellogg Theorem (1922) on invariant points in function space. The latter was a function-theoretical generalization of the famous Brouwer Fixed Point Theorem, and a decade later was to become the stimulus of the Schrauder-Leray theory. Kellogg employed Henri Lebesgue's theory of barrier functions to construct a solution of the Dirichlet problem (1923), and he established properties of his solution in 1926. In 1929 his book *Foundations of Potential Theory* became the first volume by an American author to be published by Springer-Verlag in their prestigious "Yellow Series" of mathematical monographs. A great success, it has remained one of the standard expositions of the subject. Accessible to both advanced undergraduates and beginning graduate students, it was noteworthy for its rigor and felicitous style. While not specifically mentioned, many of the proofs in the volume—even of well-known results—are original and due to Kellogg himself. This volume also includes the first statement of the celebrated Kellogg-Evans Lemma (proven in generality by Griffith C. Evans in 1933). At the time of his death Kellogg was preparing an advanced companion volume on potential theory, and this was eagerly awaited by researchers.

In addition to these contributions, Kellogg had an abiding interest in mechanics, as indicated by his textbook *Applications of the Calculus to Mechanics* (1909), coauthored with his fellow Göttingen student and University of Missouri colleague Earle R. Hedrick. In this book Kellogg and Hedrick attempted to incorporate the notions of mechanics into the mathematical curriculum (immediately following a year of calculus); although the book was well regarded, ultimately it was not widely adopted. Kellogg also wrote several pedagogical articles on the teaching of mechanics and a research paper on the mathematical theory of the gyroscope (1923).

By all accounts Kellogg was unfailingly generous in sharing his nascent ideas with his colleagues and students. His work was characterized by its originality and versatility. Moreover, apart from his pedagogical contributions, he generally chose to pursue challenging questions of a significant nature. Considered by many to be the obvious choice to succeed Bôcher at Harvard, Kellogg possessed unique abilities and talent that can appropriately only be compared to those of Bôcher. Kellogg died of a heart attack while mountain climbing near Greenville, Maine; his untimely death was a great shock to his Harvard colleagues and the mathematical community at large.

• Two of Kellogg's papers that are of historical value and give lucid examples of his style are "A Decade of American Mathematics," *Science* 53 (17 June 1921): 541–48, and "Recent Progress with the Dirichlet Problem," *Bulletin of the American Mathematical Society* 32 (Nov.–Dec. 1926): 601–25. A memorial tribute, containing a detailed discussion of his mathematical work and a complete list of his publications, is G. D. Birkhoff, "The Mathematical Work of Oliver Dimon Kellogg," *Bulletin of the American Mathematical Society* 39 (Mar. 1933): 173–77. An obituary is in the *Boston Evening Transcript*, 29 Aug. 1932.

JOSEPH D. ZUND

KELLOGG, Paul Underwood (30 Sept. 1879–1 Nov. 1958), editor and reformer, was born in Kalamazoo, Michigan, the son of Frank Israel Kellogg, a businessman, and Mary Foster Underwood. After graduating from high school in 1897, Kellogg worked for the *Kalamazoo Daily Telegraph*, where he acquired a taste for reporting and learned diverse journalistic skills. In 1901 he entered Columbia University. The following year, while attending the Summer School of Philanthropy, sponsored by the New York Charity Organization Society (COS), his talents were spotted by Edward T. Devine, editor of *Charities*, the society's publication, who added Kellogg to his editorial staff. For the next decade, the ambitious young journalist served an apprenticeship, attending to all aspects of reporting, editing, and publication. Promoted to positions of increasing responsibility, the young assistant editor was key in turning *Charities* into a journal of national circulation and influence.

On temporary reassignment in 1907 and 1908, Kellogg directed a research team that inquired into all aspects of life and labor in the city of Pittsburgh. Under his editorship, the findings were published in six substantial volumes. These monographs covered labor conditions in steel and related industries, the incidence and human consequences of industrial accidents, the varied roles of women and immigrant workers, family and domestic life, and civic activities. The *Pittsburgh Survey* (1910–1914), as the volumes came to be known, set a model for comprehensive sociological analysis that influenced journalism and academic scholarship for many years.

In 1909 Kellogg married Marion Sherwood from his home town of Kalamazoo; they had two children. That same year the COS journal, renamed the *Survey*, enlarged its mission to cover all aspects of human services, including charities, family and children's agencies, mental health, delinquency and crime, medical and school social work, community and neighborhood work. The journal also added to its agenda of social issues a wide range of public concerns then agitating American reformers—public health, workman's compensation, protective labor legislation, factory regulation, public assistance, and social insurance. Kellogg, named editor-in-chief of the *Survey* in 1912, was joined by his brother Arthur, for many years his professional partner and closest intimate, who became managing editor. They worked as a team until Arthur's death in 1934.

Under Kellogg's guidance and inspiration, the *Survey* became the country's preeminent serial publication on the developing profession of social work and social policy. The *Survey Midmonthly* (1921–1933) focused primarily on the training of social workers and the delivery of social services as well as research, education, scholarship, and administration. The *Survey Graphic* was lavishly illustrated and carried articles by noted public figures and experts. It informed a large audience of concerned citizens on issues extending well beyond social work itself, including war, famine relief, fiscal policy, public works, the environment, civil liberties, and civil rights, to name only a few.

Kellogg participated actively in a special committee of the National Conference of Charities and Correction that assembled a platform for welfare reform in 1912. He was a friend of Roger N. Baldwin, the director of the American Civil Liberties Union, and a passionate supporter of free speech. During World War I Kellogg played a major role in the founding of what became the Foreign Policy Association. He was also a leader in the crusade to save Nicola Sacco and Bartolomeo Vanzetti, two Italian-American anarchists found guilty of murder in the 1920s, from capital punishment. The Spanish civil war engaged his democratic sensibilities, and he was quick to recognize the plight of Jewish refugees from Central Europe in the 1930s. In the early New Deal years he served on the Advisory Council to the Committee on Economic Security, which was engaged in shaping the Social Security Act of 1935. His social and political philosophy drew nourishment from friends and associates in the settlement movement.

Kellogg's marriage to Marion Sherwood ended in divorce in 1934. In 1935 he married Helen Hall, head resident of the Henry Street Settlement on New York's Lower East Side; he made the settlement house his home until his death.

Kellogg's long and influential career was guided by two related principles. Through the *Survey* he hoped to elevate social work to higher standards of humane and efficient service; he also recognized that achievement of broad social reform was essential to the evolution of a more just society, in which the profession of social work could play a more creative and constructive role.

• Extensive personal and professional records are located in the papers of Paul U. Kellogg, Survey Associates, and Helen Hall, all on deposit at the Social Welfare History Archives, University of Minnesota, Minneapolis. These records include official correspondence, office memoranda, drafts of articles, and position papers; they also contain lengthy personal correspondence with many leaders in welfare and public policy. The standard biography is Clarke A. Chambers, Paul U. Kellogg and the Survey: Voices for Social Welfare and Social Justice (1971). An obituary is in the New York Times, 2 Nov. 1958.

CLARKE A. CHAMBERS

KELLOGG, Remington (5 Oct. 1892–8 May 1969), zoologist, was born Arthur Remington Kellogg in Davenport, Iowa, the son of Rolla Remington, a printer, and Clara Louise Martin, a schoolteacher prior to her marriage. He was one of three children. When he was six, the family moved to Kansas City, Missouri, where he later recalled having developed an interest in nature from the time he was in the fourth grade. He attended Westport High School, graduating in 1910, but had to work for a year in a dry goods store, in a packing plant, and on a construction crew to earn enough money to enter college.

Determined to continue his natural history studies, Kellogg entered the University of Kansas, where he concentrated at first on entomology and later turned his attention to mammals. He worked at various jobs during and between his years in college, several of which presented opportunities for permanent employment in his chosen field. During the years 1913–1916, for example, Kellogg served as a taxonomic assistant to the curator of birds and mammals at the university's natural history museum. He completed his A.B. in 1915 and his M.A. in 1916. Through his friend Alexander Wetmore, whom he met during his freshman year, Kellogg secured employment with the U.S. Biological Survey during the summers of 1915, 1916, and 1917, and following his graduation from the university in the winter of 1915–1916 he was a field assistant in southeastern Kansas.

During a trip to the East underwritten by the Biological Survey in 1915, Kellogg visited a number of museums, and he soon concluded that he wanted to focus his attention on marine mammals. Entering the University of California, Berkeley, as a doctoral student in the autumn of 1916, Kellogg soon became friendly with Joseph Grinnell, with John C. Merriam, who became his mentor at Berkeley, and with David Starr Jordan, the eminent ichthyologist who was then president of nearby Stanford University. Merriam facilitated a teaching fellowship, in the course of which Kellogg undertook the first of a number of paleontological studies of regional sea mammals. This was a study of fossil pinnipeds from the Tertiary along the Pacific coast, the results of which were published in

1921 and 1922. Kellogg did field work for the Biological Survey in the summer of 1917, first in Montana and then in California. His revision of a regional group of field mice was published in 1918.

For some eighteen months (Dec. 1917–June 1919) Kellogg interrupted his studies to enlist in the U.S. Army Corps of Engineers. From May 1918 until the end of his tour of duty in France, Kellogg worked under Major E. A. Goldman, in civilian life a senior biologist with the Biological Survey. Goldman's assignment was to control rat populations in the front-line trenches and some of the French coastal port facilities used by the military. Kellogg found some spare time for collecting bird and mammal specimens while in France; he sent some of these specimens to Berkeley, while others went to the University of Kansas.

Returning to Berkeley in the summer of 1919, Kellogg changed the focus of his doctoral studies from zoology to vertebrate paleontology, and in January 1920 he began his full-time career with the Biological Survey as an assistant biologist. That same year he married Marguerite Evangel Henrich, a fellow student at Berkeley; the couple had no children. His Ph.D. was awarded in 1928 for his dissertation, "The History of Whales—Their Adaptation to Life in the Water." This was subsequently published in two successive issues of the Quarterly Review of Biology. Kellogg's eight-year career with the Biological Survey—he was promoted to associate biologist in 1924—provided experience in several areas of zoology. While he spent a great deal of his time with the food habitats of birds of prey, he also did a similar study of diving ducks and alligators and examined the stomach contents of toads, primarily preserved specimens. Several important early studies included "The Habits and Economic Importance of Alligators" (1929) and Mexican Tailless Amphibians (1932); the latter was part of a projected larger project on North and Middle American Toads that was never finished.

Kellogg's doctoral mentor at Berkeley, John C. Merriam, also arrived in Washington in 1920 to take up new duties as president of the Carnegie Institution, and he arranged for Kellogg's appointment as a research associate in 1921. This post, which Kellogg held for twenty-two years, provided annual research grants that allowed him to continue working with marine mammals while maintaining his full-time association with the Biological Survey and, after 1928, with the U.S. National Museum. Following his transfer to the National Museum, where he served until 1941 as assistant curator of mammals, Kellogg was able to give much of his time to his marine mammal research. His early whale investigations focused on the Archaeoceti, the earliest fossil ancestors of present-day cetaceans. He subsequently turned his attention to the later Miocene and Oligocene forms. He was cautions about assigning fossils to specific higher taxa in the absence of adequate material, and focused to a great extent on developing evolutionary, zoogeographical, and ecological information about each species.

By 1930 Kellogg's reputation as a cetologist had been established, and he began to spend increasing amounts of time on issues relating to the international management of whale populations. He attended a League of Nations–sponsored conference in Berlin, Germany, in the spring of that year, the first of a number of international gatherings on the subject. He was U.S. delegate to the International Conference on Whaling held in London (1937), was instrumental in drafting two protocols (1937 and 1938) that placed limits on the hunting of certain species, and chaired the American delegations to the international conferences of 1944 and 1945. In 1946 he chaired the world meetings in Washington, and from 1949 to 1967 he served as U.S. commissioner on the International Whaling Commission, for which he was vice chairman (1949–1951) and chairman (1952–1954). He also led American delegations to sixteen gatherings of the International Whaling Commission, the last in 1964. Illness precluded any further participation, but his influence at these sessions had been considerable, even though the whaling industry in the United States had long been in decline.

During his tenure at the National Museum, Kellogg's work in mammalogy included the publication of annotated lists of the mammals of West Virginia (1937) and Tennessee (1939) and another of the Shenandoah National Park (1947), the latter completed with the cooperation of Alexander Wetmore of the Smithsonian. Other papers concerned fossil mammals found in various parts of the United States—some of which Kellogg had helped uncover—and, with E. A. Goldman, studies of new white-tailed deer species and of spider monkeys. Kellogg's administrative responsibilities increased with his appointment as curator of mammals in 1941. During World War II he was involved in several research projects involving disease transmission in Brazilian monkeys and South Pacific rodents. He also visited Brazil in 1943 as part of an effort to promote cultural relations among Latin-American scientists.

Kellogg became director of the U.S. National Museum in 1948 and assistant secretary for science of the Smithsonian Institution in 1958. Viewed by some colleagues as an often negative administrator, Kellogg was characterized as the "abominable no man." He retired in 1962 but continued working as a highly productive research associate at the Smithsonian for the remaining seven years of his life. He worked on fossil cetaceans throughout his career, and for a number of years he collaborated with G. S. Miller, Jr., on a third edition of the *List of North American Recent Mammals* (1955). Kellogg did not overlook the importance of sound popular works for the general public. He authored "Whales, Giants of the Sea," a major article for the *National Geographic Magazine* (1940), which was later revised and incorporated in the society's *Wild Animals of North America* (1960). His two other chapters in this volume were "The Rise of Modern Mammals" and "Mammals and How They Live." A member of many scientific organizations, Kellogg was president

of the Paleontological Society of Washington and served a three-year term as president of the American Society of Mammalogists (1946–1949). He was elected to the National Academy of Sciences in 1951. Kellogg died in Washington, D.C.

• Kellogg's papers are in the Smithsonian Institution Archives. Information on him is also in the Remington Kellogg Memorial Library of Marine Mammalogy, National Museum of Natural History, Washington, D.C. The most useful biographical sketch is Frank C. Whitmore, Jr., "Remington Kellogg, 1892–1969," in National Academy of Sciences, *Biographical Memoirs* 46 (1975), which includes a bibliography of Kellogg's articles and books by Jane Knapp. A shorter summary of Kellogg's career by Whitmore is in Keir B. Sterling et al., eds., *Biographical Dictionary of American and Canadian Naturalists and Environmentalists* (1997). See also the obituary by Henry W. Setzer in *Journal of Mammalogy* 77 (1977), and a biographical summary in Elmer C. Birney and Jerry R. Choate, eds., *Seventy-Five Years of Mammalogy (1919–1994)* (1994).

KEIR B. STERLING

KELLOGG, Samuel Henry (6 Sept. 1839–3 May 1899), missionary-linguist and pastor, was born in Quogue, Suffolk County, New York, the son of Samuel Kellogg, a Presbyterian minister, and Mary Pierce Henry. As a child he was precocious but frail, and he received his early education at home, except for about six months at Haverstraw (N.Y.) Mountain Institute. He attended Williams College briefly in 1856 but withdrew because of ill health. He matriculated at Princeton University in 1858 and graduated in 1861 as one of the top two graduates of the 100 members of his class. He then entered Princeton Seminary, from which he graduated in 1864. During his final seminary year, he was an instructor in mathematics at the college.

While a student at the seminary, Kellogg responded to an appeal for missionary service in India delivered by the Reverend Henry M. Scudder, son of a pioneer medical missionary to that country. He was ordained to service in India by the Hudson (N.Y.) Presbytery on 20 April 1864. Following his marriage in 1864 to Antoinette Whiting Hartwell, the couple left Boston for India in December of that year.

Kellogg spent most of the next eleven years in India, after 1872 at the Theological School of the India Synod at Allahabad. His greatest contribution was his monumental *Grammar of the Hindi Language* (1876; 2d ed. 1893), which became the standard work in the field. Among his services to the church was a translation of the larger catechism of the Presbyterian church into Hindi.

Following the death of his wife in 1876, Kellogg, with four children, returned to the United States and on 15 July 1877 was installed as pastor of the Third Presbyterian Church of Pittsburgh and soon thereafter as professor of didactic and polemic theology and lecturer in comparative religions at Western Seminary in Allegheny, Pennsylvania. In 1879 he married Sara Constance Macrum; they had four children. Kellogg amiably severed his ties with the Allegheny seminary in 1885 because of a disagreement over his premillennial views, that is, his belief that Jesus would return before the thousand-year reign spoken of in Revelation 20:1–5, which were not in favor at the seminary.

Kellogg was called as pastor of St. James Square Presbyterian Church in Toronto and served from 1886 to 1892. He served as professor of Hebrew and Old Testament exegesis at Knox College in Toronto in 1892.

Even while living in the United States and Canada, Kellogg retained a lively interest in missionary and linguistic work in India. He was a corresponding member of the American Oriental Society and published in its *Proceedings*. He was honored at the International Congress of Orientalists in Stockholm in 1889, and he attended the congress in London in 1891. He was a member of the Canadian Presbyterian Assembly's Foreign Mission Committee and a convenor of the Committee on the Palestinian Mission. His broad interests and his scholarship, particularly in linguistics, led to an associate membership in the Philosophical Society of Great Britain in 1885 and membership in the Victorian Institute of England.

In September 1892 Kellogg returned to India to assist in revising the Hindi Old Testament, a project sponsored jointly by the North India Bible Society and the British and Foreign Bible Society. He spent a good portion of each of the next six years in Landour, where the revision committee, composed of Kellogg, the Reverend W. Hooper of the Church Missionary Society, and the Reverend J. A. Lambert of the London Missionary Society, met to do its work. On the eve of the completion of the revision, Kellogg died in Landour as a result of a fall from a terrace on which he was riding his bicycle, an accident to which there were no witnesses.

Although he never held an important position in American Presbyterian circles, Kellogg was a scholar who wrote and lectured widely. His publications include nine books, numerous sermons and pamphlets, and scores of articles in popular as well as scholarly journals. *The Genesis and Growth of Religion* (1892) comprised the 1892 L. P. Stone Lectures at Princeton Seminary. His *Handbook of Comparative Religion* (1899) became a standard in the field for a number of years.

Kellogg held to the eschatological view known as premillennialism, concerning which he is called "a fair-minded critic of chiliasm" by Robert Whalen. He participated in the Niagara Conference, an annual meeting of evangelical ministers, evangelists, professors, and laymen who met at Niagara-on-the-Lake, Ontario, for refreshment and fellowship. Among the doctrines featured at Niagara was premillennialism. Kellogg read a paper, "Christ's Coming: Is It Premillennial?," at the first International Prophetic Conference held in New York's Church of the Holy Trinity in 1878 and served on the interim committee associated with the second conference in Chicago in 1886. These conferences advocated premillennial eschatology. Although a number of Presbyterian premillennialists

participated in these congresses, the ideas were not widely adopted by Presbyterian theologians and divines. Kellogg also wrote the entry on premillennialism for the *Schaff-Herzog Encyclopedia*, the most authoritative biblical encyclopedia of the period.

Kellogg enjoyed considerable respect among evangelicals in India, the United States, and Canada. Writing in 1906, James M. Thoburn said he "left an indelible impress upon the field of north India." All who were associated with the revision project acknowledged the leading role he played. Because of his learning, he offered stature to American evangelicals and especially to the cause of premillennial thought.

• Kellogg's writings include *The Jews: or, Prediction and Fulfillment* (1883); *The Light of Asia and the Light of the World* (1885) (a comparison of Christ with Buddha); *Are Premillennialists Right?* (1885); *From Death to Resurrection* (1885); *The Book of Leviticus* (in the Expositors' Bible series, 1891; repr. 1903); and *The Past a Prophecy of the Future and Other Sermons* (1904). His essays appeared in *Presbyterian Review*, *Presbyterian and Reformed Review*, *Princeton Review*, and *Bibliotheca Sacra*. A chapter in H. H. Holcomb, *Men of Might in India Missions* (1901), contains biographical information. His contribution to Presbyterian millennialism is briefly mentioned in Robert Whalen, "Calvinism and Chiliasm: The Sociology of Nineteenth-Century American Millenarianism," *American Presbyterians* 70 (1992): 168; and to American millennialism more broadly in Paul Wilt, "Premillennialism in America, 1865–1918" (Ph.D. diss., American Univ., 1970), and in Ernest Sandeen, *The Roots of Fundamentalism* (1970). Obituaries are in the *New York Tribune*, 5 May 1899, and in the *Missionary Review of the World*, Aug. 1899.

PAUL C. WILT

KELLOGG, Vernon Lyman (1 Dec. 1867–8 Aug. 1937), biologist and science administrator, was born in Emporia, Kansas, the son of Lyman Beecher Kellogg, a college professor, and Abigail Homer. Kellogg received his A.B. from the University of Kansas in 1889 and his M.S. in 1892. Following a year spent as a student at the University of Leipzig, he returned to Kansas as an associate professor. In 1894 he was lured to Stanford University where he remained on the faculty until 1920. He was married in 1908 to Charlotte Hoffman, with whom he had one child. During the First World War Kellogg was actively involved in Europe as the director of the Commission for Relief in Belgium. From 1917 to 1919 he worked for the U.S. Food Administration as head of the food mission to Poland. After the war Kellogg's activities focused on the National Research Council in Washington, D.C. He was a major organizing force of the NRC, initially acting as chair of the Divisions of Agriculture, Botany, and Zoology. He served as secretary of the NRC from 1919 until 1931, when he was made secretary emeritus, a post he filled until his death in Hartford, Connecticut.

Kellogg's work as a biologist reflected the influence of two important scientists: John Henry Comstock and David Starr Jordan. At the time Comstock was the leading American entomologist. While Comstock was associated with Cornell University for his entire career, Jordan (the first president of Stanford and an old fraternity brother from Cornell) persuaded Comstock to split his time between Stanford and Cornell in the early 1890s. Comstock helped recruit Kellogg to Stanford (initially as his assistant) and together they produced *The Elements of Insect Anatomy* (1895). At Stanford Kellogg increasingly was influenced by Jordan and moved away from some of his earlier, more taxonomically oriented, entomological work, chiefly on *Mellophaga* and *Lepidoptera*, toward general evolutionary concerns. Together they taught a course entitled "Bionomics," which attempted to use evolution as a unifying theme for all of biological science. They produced two popular textbooks, *Animal Life* (1900) and *Evolution and Animal Life* (1907). Kellogg spent more than fifteen years doing breeding experiments on silk worms, beetles, and honeybees (the latter with R. G. Bell). Two important things emerged from this research, each of which played a role in the more popular works he produced. First, he verified the ratios found by Mendel for a number of different traits. At the time many biologists saw Darwinism and Mendelism as mutually inconsistent. As a result of his research, the textbooks he and Jordan produced, although Darwinian, did not oppose Mendelism. This led them to recognize the genotype-phenotype distinction (the distinction between the discrete character of the hereditary material, the genes, and the sometimes discrete but sometimes continuous character of observed traits) long before most biologists. Second, and perhaps most important, Kellogg's experimental findings supported the claim that a number of traits distinguishing closely related species have no adaptive value. Combining this with Jordan's view that geographical isolation is a necessary first step in speciation, they were able to show that "subtle differences in the parent stock" in isolated groups are responsible for these nonadaptive traits.

Kellogg's influence on subsequent biology has not been fully appreciated. His most important popular work, *Darwinism Today* (1907), was the text that introduced Sewell Wright, arguably the chief founder of population genetics, to biology. Wright, in a series of papers published in the 1920s, formally combined Darwinism and Mendelism to explain nonadaptive traits in isolated populations, producing the concept of genetic drift. Thus Kellogg was an important precursor to the development of modern population genetics. He had an unusual combination of interests in traditional natural history and the newer experimental and quantitative methods becoming dominant in biology. "We are ignorant; terribly, immensely ignorant. And our work is to learn. To observe, to experiment, to tabulate, to induce, to deduce. . . . To question life by new methods, from new angles, on closer terms, under more precise conditions of control; this is the requirement and the opportunity of the biologist of today" (*Darwinism Today*, p. 387).

Kellogg's influence and interests went well beyond the scientific. He was a member of the eugenics commission of the American Breeders Association and like Jordan saw eugenics as a basis for pacifism (the fittest are sent to war and killed, decreasing the fitness of the population). His *Headquarters Nights* (1917), which recorded interviews with German officers recounting the thinking that led to the war, convinced William Jennings Bryan of the dangers of Darwinism, which were widely discussed by the officers. His activities on behalf of the U.S. Food Administration and the Commission for Relief in Belgium made him a leading expert on problems of food and its distribution. In 1917 he coauthored *The Food Problem*, which argued that in the future food and famine would determine the course of wars and which also developed proposals for how to avoid future food problems.

Kellogg is perhaps best remembered for his role on the National Research Council. In 1916 the National Academy of Sciences offered its services to President Woodrow Wilson for the purpose of providing scientific and technical assistance in the coming war effort. By the end of the war the usefulness of the NRC was established, so that in 1918 it became a permanent body aimed at increasing knowledge, strengthening defense, and generally contributing to the public welfare. During Kellogg's service as permanent secretary, the diverse activities of the NRC included a series of fellowships for young scientists at the beginning of their careers, support for research projects in various fields (with the expectation that these projects would eventually become independent of the NRC), a series of talks and bulletins that dealt with large issues or broad surveys of a field, and the general promotion and encouragement of cooperation in different scientific endeavors. The NRC was an excellent outlet for Kellogg's interests. As C. E. McClung put it in his biographical memoir of Kellogg for the National Academy of Sciences, "Practical applications of biology always interested him, but as the years passed and he saw the service which biology might render to social progress, this became the theme of his writings." The development of the NRC and its importance as an institutional force in science owes much to the efforts of its first permanent secretary.

• Some of Kellogg's papers are available at the Stanford University Archives, and some materials are available at the Smithsonian Institution Archives. The David Starr Jordan Collection at Stanford University also holds some of his correspondence and class notes. His most important taxonomic work is probably his "List of North American Species of Mallophaga," *Proceedings of the United States National Museum* 22 (1900): 39–100. Among his most significant evolutionary articles are "Is There Determinate Variation?" *Science* 24 (1906): 621–26, and (with R. G. Bell) "Studies of Variations in Insects," *Proceedings of the Washington Academy of Sciences* 6 (1904): 203–332. Important books include *American Insects* (1904), *Mind and Heredity* (1923), and *Evolution* (1924). The best biographical sources on Kellogg are C. E. McClung, "Biographical Memoir of Vernon Lyman Kellogg," National Academy of Sciences, *Biographical Memoirs* 20 (1938): 243–57, and C. C. Fisher, ed., *Vernon Kellogg, 1867–1937* (1939).

DAVID MAGNUS

KELLOGG, William Pitt (8 Dec. 1830–10 Aug. 1918), U.S. senator and governor of Louisiana, was born in Orwell, Vermont, the son of Sherman Kellogg, a minister, and Rebecca Eaton. He was educated at Norwich Military Institute in Northfield, Vermont. When his family moved to Peoria County, Illinois, in 1848, he taught at a local school while reading law. He was admitted to the bar in 1853 and opened a practice in Canton, Illinois. He became involved in the formation of the new Republican party in his state, attending its founding convention at Bloomington in 1856. In 1860 he was a delegate to the party's national convention in Chicago and was later selected as a presidential elector on the Lincoln ticket.

President Abraham Lincoln appointed Kellogg as chief justice of Nebraska Territory in March 1861, but when war broke out Kellogg returned to Illinois to recruit and lead the Seventh Illinois Volunteer Cavalry. He served in the Missouri campaign under General John Pope, but, despite winning promotion to brigadier general, he resigned after less than a year because of ill health. Briefly resuming his post in Nebraska, he left after appointment as U.S. collector of customs in New Orleans on 13 April 1865, the last patronage appointment that Lincoln was to make. Before moving to Louisiana, Kellogg married a Canton resident, Mary Emily Wills.

In Louisiana, Kellogg became a leading figure in Republican politics during Reconstruction. As collector, he used the substantial patronage and economic influence of the customhouse to build the party in the state. In 1868 the reconstructed legislature that was now controlled by the Republicans elected him to the U.S. Senate. He served only four years, resigning in 1872 to run for governor after breaking with the incumbent, Henry Clay Warmoth, who was pursuing a course that Kellogg felt was too conciliatory toward the former Confederates and insufficiently supportive of the interests and needs of the African Americans in the state. The election was critical for the Republicans, since Warmoth had led the bolt of the Liberal Republicans from the party and then endorsed the Democratic gubernatorial nominee, John D. McEnery. The ensuing campaign was bitterly fought, and its outcome was so unclear that two rival returning boards claimed victory. Meanwhile, two legislatures were assembled and two governors inaugurated. This impasse finally ended when, after an inconclusive congressional investigation, President Ulysses S. Grant recognized Kellogg as governor on 22 May 1873.

Kellogg's term as governor was engulfed in turmoil, most of which arose from the opposition party's anger at being denied control of the state. The legitimacy of his claim to govern was denied, and his administration was attacked and undermined by every means possible. The most extreme and violent measures that Democrats resorted to during Reconstruction were launched at the Kellogg regime in Louisiana. Kellogg tried to win confidence in his administration by proposing to settle the state's fiscal difficulties through funding the public debt and repudiating that portion of it that was thought to have been incurred illegally. He also proposed measures to reduce expenditures and lower taxes, and he tried to develop the state's economy by promoting railroad connections between New Orleans and Texas in the west and Shreveport in the north. Despite his tenuous control over the legislature, his funding plan was enacted, and he managed to reduce both spending and taxes by about a third in each case. Under the circumstances, this was a considerable achievement and should have earned him respect, even from the Democrats.

Kellogg's efforts at reform were, however, to be thwarted by the opposition's campaign of organized violence throughout the state. Three incidents in particular revealed how fragile was the hold of the Republicans outside the legislature. As early as April 1873, the courthouse at Colfax in Grant Parish was besieged. The Republican officials were driven off and between 50 and 100 of their supporters, mostly black, massacred. Although none were as bloody as Colfax, other attacks on local outposts of Republican control took place, the most notorious of which were the Coushatta massacre in Red River Parish in August 1874 and the battle of Liberty Place on 14 September 1874. The latter battle, outside the New Orleans customhouse, forced Kellogg himself to flee for his life, and he only regained control of the government with the aid of U.S. troops and presidential intervention. Under the ensuing Wheeler Compromise, worked out to settle the chaos in Louisiana, Congress provided for Kellogg to serve out the remainder of his term, but he could do little. The Democrats claimed unceasingly that the pervasiveness of lawlessness and violence proved he was unable to govern. Finally, the Democratic-controlled lower house of the state legislature voted to impeach him, though the Republican senate refused to convict.

In 1876 the Democrats gained control of the state after yet another disputed election that was settled by the Compromise of 1877. This election put Rutherford B. Hayes in the White House and gave the Democrats the three southern states, including Louisiana, that were still under Republican control. Kellogg himself was elected to the U.S. Senate, where his claim to the seat was contested but ultimately upheld, and he served a rather uneventful term. He was then elected to Congress from the sugar district of Bayou Teche, 1883–1885. He attended Republican National Conventions regularly until 1896, usually chairing the Louisiana delegation. He moved to Washington, D.C., where he owned sizable real estate investments and, at his death there, left an estate worth more than $300,000.

A major force in Louisiana Reconstruction, Kellogg was an able and courageous politician whose reputation has suffered, along with those of most of the northerners and others who worked to build and manage the Republican party in the South during Reconstruction.

• A small collection of Kellogg's papers is in the archives at Louisiana State University in Baton Rouge. John E. Gonzales, "William Pitt Kellogg: Reconstruction Governor of Louisiana, 1873–1877," *Louisiana Historical Quarterly* 29 (1946): 394–495, is a long article about Kellogg's administration. A brief biography can be found in Joseph G. Dawson III, ed., *The Louisiana Governors* (1990). See also Joe Gray Taylor, *Louisiana Reconstructed, 1863–1877* (1974); George C. Rable, *But There Was No Peace: The Role of Violence in the Politics of Reconstruction* (1984); and Ted Tunnell, *Crucible of Reconstruction: War, Radicalism and Race in Louisiana, 1862–1877* (1984). Obituaries are in the *Washington Post*, 11 Aug. 1918, and the Washington *Evening Star*, 10 Aug. 1918.

MICHAEL PERMAN

KELLOGG, W. K. (7 Apr. 1860–6 Oct. 1951), founder of the Kellogg Company and the W. K. Kellogg Foundation, was born Willie Keith Kellogg in Battle Creek, Michigan, the son of John Preston Kellogg, a broom-maker and a leader of the newly established Seventh-day Adventist church, and his second wife, Ann Janette Stanley. Believing that Christ's second coming was imminent, Kellogg's parents provided only a scant education for most of the seven of their eleven children who survived infancy. By the time he was in his early teens, Kellogg, who legally changed his name to Will Keith and who preferred to be called W. K., had begun working as a traveling salesman of brooms, and by age nineteen he was manager of a broom factory in Dallas, Texas. Returning to Michigan in 1880, Kellogg completed a three-month business course at Parson's Business College in Kalamazoo and went to work for his older brother, the flamboyant physician, author, and inventor Dr. John Harvey Kellogg. The elder Kellogg had begun operating what would become the Battle Creek Sanitarium on behalf of the Seventh-day Adventist church in 1876.

John Harvey Kellogg's interests were widespread; aside from his surgical practice, he presided over the ever-expanding sanitarium, founded numerous health food manufacturing firms, published several health magazines, and authored many books on the subjects of health and diet. While Dr. Kellogg's interests were varied, he paid little attention to day-to-day management concerns; although he never held a title, Kellogg was in fact the sanitarium's business manager for more than twenty-five years. Most significantly, he supervised his brother's food manufacturing operations, which made products primarily for sale by mail order to former guests of the "San."

Advancing the Seventh-day Adventists' promotion of a meatless diet, the Kelloggs established an experimental kitchen for nut and grain based foods shortly after arriving at the sanitarium. In the early 1890s the brothers began testing machinery that created flaked cereal products and developed a successful process for manufacturing wheat flakes in 1894 (it was patented the following year). Characteristically, Dr. Kellogg soon lost interest in the new food. Kellogg, recognizing flaked cereal's possibilities, added cornflakes to the product line and expanded manufacturing facilities to meet the ensuing demand.

Although they were the first, the Kelloggs were not the only manufacturers of ready-to-eat cereals in Battle Creek. C. W. Post, who had arrived in Battle Creek as a patient at the sanitarium, began his own cereal company in 1895. Many others soon followed, lured by the rapid success of several early ready-to-eat cereal manufacturers and attempting to capture some of the cachet of Battle Creek, which by the turn of the century had become known as the nation's breakfast cereal capital. Impatient with John Harvey's unwillingness to pursue the commercial possibilities of the cereal business and resentful of his brother's dominance over his career, Kellogg incorporated the Battle Creek Toasted Corn Flake Company in 1906. He enlisted a former sanitarium patient from St. Louis, Charles D. Bolin, to sell the initial stock subscription of $35,000. Under a series of complex contractual arrangements, John Harvey Kellogg maintained an interest in his brother's company until bought out for approximately $300,000 in 1911.

The antagonism between the two Kellogg brothers hardly abated after W. K. left his brother's employ. He filed suit against John Harvey in 1910; the settlement the following year gave W. K. exclusive use of the Kellogg name on cereal products in the United States. John Harvey sued his brother in 1916 to have him enjoined from using the Kellogg name in international markets. After protracted litigation and appeals, W. K. won exclusive use of the Kellogg name for cereal products in 1921.

W. K. Kellogg possessed a taciturn demeanor and a strong dislike for alcohol and tobacco. Despite his stern manner, he was a master salesman and undertook several nationwide tours to promote his product to grocery jobbers and merchants. His company became one of the nation's ten leading advertisers within the first decade of its founding. The firm also provided samples of its products to hundreds of thousands of homes. By 1940 the company had spent approximately $100 million on advertising. Kellogg stressed the complementary relationship between mass marketing and mass production, once commenting on the factory floor, "I don't like this hand packaging. I want products that run off conveyor belts into packages." Much of the success of his business was the result of Kellogg's attention to technological improvements in manufacturing equipment, as well as packaging innovations, such as the waxed paper liner common in cereal boxes today.

In 1922 the Toasted Corn Flake Company formally became the Kellogg Cereal Company, later shortened to the Kellogg Company. Although the company frequently introduced new products, it confined itself to the manufacture of breakfast cereal products during its founder's lifetime. Kellogg witnessed the demise of most entrants in the ready-to-eat cereal industry until there was only a handful of significant competitors in the early 1950s. The Kellogg Company enjoyed more than 40 percent of the domestic market for ready-to-eat cereal and an even larger share in many international markets during Kellogg's later years.

Always ashamed of his limited education and remembering the untimely deaths of many members of his family, Kellogg established the W. K. Kellogg Foundation in 1930. The foundation provides financial support for the advancement of health, agriculture, and education. After an initial bequest of $1 million, Kellogg gradually donated most of his 60 percent interest in the Kellogg Company to the foundation. The Kellogg Foundation, headquartered in Battle Creek, remains the largest shareholder of the Kellogg Company.

Kellogg married Ella Osborn Davis of Battle Creek in 1880. The couple had five children, three of whom lived to adulthood. Ella Kellogg died in 1912. Kellogg's second wife was Carrie Staines, a physician at the Battle Creek Sanitarium, whom he married in 1918; they had no children. By the mid-1920s the Kellogg Company had grown prosperous enough and its management structure had become well enough established that Kellogg was able to build a winter residence near Pomona, California, where he raised Arabian horses, and an estate in Dunedin, Florida. Kellogg enjoyed traveling, and he and his wife visited Europe, Asia, Australia, and South America.

Kellogg suffered from glaucoma and cataracts and was totally blind after 1941. He continued to serve on the board of directors of the Kellogg Company until 1946 and remained involved in the foundation's activities for several more years. Kellogg died in Battle Creek.

• Many details of the life of Kellogg are available for study in the collected papers of his brother John Harvey Kellogg, which can be found in the Michigan State University Archives and Historical Collections and at the Bentley Historical Library at the University of Michigan. A book-length biography of Kellogg, *The Original Has This Signature—W. K. Kellogg* (1956), was written by Horace B. Powell. Gerald Carson surveys the early history of Battle Creek's breakfast cereal industry in *Cornflake Crusade* (1957). An obituary is in the *Battle Creek Enquirer and News*, 7 Oct. 1951.

PEYTON PAXSON

KELLOR, Frances Alice (20 Oct. 1873–4 Jan. 1952), social reformer and arbitration specialist, was born in Columbus, Ohio, the daughter of Daniel Kellor and Mary Sprau. The family relocated to Coldwater, Michigan, in 1875. Engaging in the same housekeeping work as her mother, Frances Kellor paid for high school. However, after two years, she left school to become a reporter for the *Coldwater Republican*.

After graduating from Cornell Law School in 1897, Kellor enrolled as a part-time graduate student at the University of Chicago, which pioneered the emerging field of sociology. In *Experimental Sociology*, published in 1901, Kellor illustrated the link between the plight of female criminals and black migrants and environmental causes, which included the lack of employment and education. This connection proved fundamental to her career because it meant that the solutions to social problems rested beyond the realm of the individuals affected. Instead, these conditions, she argued,

must be addressed and remedied by the intervention of experts and their powerful institutions.

Kellor, in 1902, entered the New York Summer School of Philanthropy on a fellowship from the College Settlement Association, researching the corrupt practices of employment agencies in New York, Boston, Philadelphia, and Chicago. In 1903 Margaret Dreier of the New York's Woman's Municipal League persuaded the young reformer to concentrate her research efforts in New York.

Kellor and her research staff traveled to more than 700 employment agencies, posing both as prospective employers and employees, to observe firsthand the operations of these dubious institutions. Using her resulting 1904 book, *Out of Work*, as a guide for action, Kellor called for a program of both education and governmental intervention. She codrafted legislation to bring employment agencies under the control of a state commission. After the proposal's passage through the New York State Legislature, Kellor organized the Inter-Municipal Committee on Household Research to serve as the educational and informational center she strongly promoted. In 1906 Kellor co-formed the National League for the Protection of Colored Women, which attempted to educate southern migrant black women about the hindrances they faced during the employment process.

In 1908 the New York State Immigration Commission, developed by Governor Charles Evans Hughes with Kellor as secretary, recommended the creation of a Bureau of Industries and Immigration, which would function in a regulatory manner similar to the Inter-Municipal Committee. The state legislature enacted many of the committee's directives in 1910, with Hughes appointing Kellor as director of the bureau. The agency exerted great power, enforcing statutes that protected immigrants and addressed cases of employment manipulation and exploitation.

In an effort to gain greater control over reform, Kellor shifted her focus from the state to the national level. She wrote in a letter to her colleague Theodore Roosevelt about "how helpless New York State is to deal with international and interstate problems." When Roosevelt ran for the presidency in 1912 under the National Progressive party ticket, Kellor, Mary Dreier, and Jane Addams served as delegates to the convention. As national party director of publicity and research, Kellor concentrated on the woman suffrage cause, in the process scorning women who did not align themselves with the party.

Although Roosevelt lost the election of 1912, the party apparatus remained intact. The National Progressive Service, created by Kellor and associates, assembled experts from areas of government and the social research fields in an effort to reshape the affairs and purpose of political parties. The service enjoyed initial success, creating state bureaus, conducting social research, and working to institute Progressive reforms in various states. Despite these promising accomplishments, the service collapsed in 1914 because of Kellor's authoritarian manner of management and a clash with George Perkins, chairperson of the party's Executive Committee, over the contrasting aims of the service and of the party. While Kellor focused on the long-term reorganizing of political parties, Perkins wanted tangible results in the form of successful elections.

Always involved with the struggling immigrant in America, Kellor and others separated from the New York North American Civic League and formed a splinter group, the Committee for Immigrants in America. She drew the national government into the reform spotlight again by calling for the creation of the Division of Immigrant Education, which would assist in integration by offering English and civics classes, as well as adequate job training. As World War I progressed, Kellor capitalized on anxieties over the slow rate of immigrant assimilation by organizing a successful "National Americanization Day" on 4 July 1915, which promoted the common unity between citizens and immigrants. Controversy surrounds Kellor's wartime Americanization policy, with schools of thought debating about whether she encouraged the integration of immigrants into American society or urged a movement toward military preparedness with an emphasis on the dangers presented by the foreign born.

In 1916 Kellor campaigned for Charles Evans Hughes, the Republican candidate for president. She angrily lashed out against women who supported Woodrow Wilson, while also blaming the Republican party for not realizing the full potential of its women supporters. After the election and war, Kellor found herself again in the realm of immigration, designing the Inter-Racial Council in 1918 to continue the process of Americanization. The council then acquired the American Association of Foreign Language Newspapers, which controlled advertising in the immigrant press, and launched an anticommunism campaign.

Embarking on new endeavors during the last phase of her career, Kellor cofounded in 1926 the American Arbitration Association, which resolved industrial and international disputes. There she devised a code of ethics for arbitration that endured for many years. At the time of her death in New York City, Kellor was working on the board of the Pan American Union, attempting to foster better economic and legal ties between North America and South America.

In her self-confidence and self-righteousness, Kellor, who never married, typified one sort of pioneering social scientist. Applying the principles of social research to early twentieth-century American problems, she forged links among immigrants, industry, and the nation.

• Some of Kellor's correspondence and records is housed in the Manuscript Division of the Library of Congress. Kellor's other books include *Out of Work* (1915), *A Call to National Service* (1916), *Immigration and the Future* (1920), *The United States of America in Relation to the Permanent Court of International Justice of the League of Nations and in Relation to The Hague Tribunal* (1923), *Arbitration in the New Industrial Society* (1934), *Arbitration in Action: A Code for Civil, Commercial and Industrial Arbitration* (1941), and *American Arbitration:*

Its History, Functions, and Achievements (1948). With Antonia Hatvany she wrote *Security against War* (1924), *The United States and the International Court* (1925), and *Protocol for the Pacific Settlement of International Disputes in Relation to the Sanction of War* (1925). Kellor cowrote with others *Code of Arbitration, Practice and Procedure of the American Arbitration Tribunal* (1931) and *Arbitration in International Controversy* (1944). For more information on the controversy surrounding Frances Kellor's wartime activities, consult John Higham, *Strangers in the Land* (1963; rev. ed., 1988); Ellen Fitzpatrick, *Endless Crusade* (1990); and William Joseph Maxwell, "Frances Kellor in the Progressive Era: A Case Study in the Professionalization of Reform" (Ph.D. diss., Teachers College, Columbia Univ., 1968). An obituary is in the *New York Times*, 5 Jan. 1952.

CHRISTOPHER W. DIEMICKE

KELLY, Aloysius Oliver Joseph (13 June 1870–23 Feb. 1911), physician, medical educator, and writer, was born in Philadelphia, Pennsylvania, the son of Joseph Vincent Kelly, a physician and superintendent of St. Mary's Hospital, and Emma Jane Ferguson. Little is known about his childhood. He received his A.B. degree from LaSalle College, Philadelphia, in 1888 at the age of eighteen, and three years later the school awarded him a Master of Arts degree. After college he enrolled in the University of Pennsylvania Medical School, and he graduated with an M.D. in 1891. He was then appointed to a one-year residency at the St. Agnes Hospital in Philadelphia. From 1892 to 1894 he studied in Vienna, Heidelberg, Dublin, Prague, and London with such notable physicians as Franz Chvostek, Anton Weichselbaum, and Arnold Paltauf.

On his return to Philadelphia in 1894 Kelly began his multifaceted career, holding various professional positions, sometimes at several institutions simultaneously. From 1894 to 1897 he was the recorder of the hospital dispensary at the University of Pennsylvania Medical School. In 1894 he was appointed pathologist at St. Agnes Hospital, the following year physician at St. Mary's Hospital, and in 1897 physician at St. Agnes Hospital. He became director of the laboratories at the Philadelphia Polyclinic and College for Graduates in Medicine in 1895. Shortly thereafter he became chief of the pathology and bacteriology department at German Hospital and gave up his positions at Polyclinic and as pathologist at St. Agnes Hospital; in 1909 he was on the latter's medical staff.

At German Hospital Kelly worked closely with John B. Deaver, a surgeon. As pathologist there Kelly was able to collect a large number of specimens of diseases of the appendix, liver, and gall bladder. The samples were the basis for several lectures and articles: the 1905 Mutter Lecture of the College of Physicians of Philadelphia, "Infections of the Biliary Tract"; "Nature and Lesions of Cirrhosis of the Liver" (*American Journal of the Medical Sciences*, Dec. 1905); and a chapter on the liver, bile ducts, and gall bladder for Sir William Osler's *Modern Medicine* (1908).

In 1896 Kelly was named instructor of physical diagnosis at the University of Pennsylvania Medical School, and three years later he was appointed instructor of clinical medicine at the Medical School and assistant physician in the University Hospital. In his teaching position he became a close associate of John Herr Musser, who had been an assistant to Osler; Kelly served as chief of Musser's clinic. In 1903 Kelly rose to associate professor of medicine, and in 1906 to assistant professor, a position he held until his death.

In 1900 Kelly was asked to join the faculty of the medical school of the University of Vermont as professor of the theory and practice of medicine. He accepted with the understanding that the university would reform its curriculum and set higher standards for both faculty and students. During his ten-year part-time tenure at Vermont he initiated the reform of the curriculum and worked to raise the overall standards of the school. In 1906 Kelly accepted another teaching assignment, as professor of pathology at the Woman's Medical College of Pennsylvania and pathologist for the hospital attached to it.

Kelly had a flair for writing; his style was clear and pointed, and he expressed himself and his principles freely. In 1895 he wrote two articles on the opportunities and benefits of studying medicine in the countries where he had done his postgraduate studies. During his brief lifetime he wrote more than thirty major articles. He was editor of *International Clinics* (1903–1907) and of the *American Journal of the Medical Sciences* (1907–1911). In 1910, a few months before his death, Lea and Febiger published his textbook, *Practice of Medicine*. In 1911 Kelly, in association with Musser, completed two volumes of a planned four-volume treatise, *A Handbook of Practical Treatment*.

Kelly never desired a large private practice; his chief interests were in his clinic, laboratory and library. He was acknowledged as a fine medical writer and editor. He was a member of several national, state, and local professional organizations. Kelly was a devoted communicant of the Roman Catholic faith and close friends with many leading prelates of Philadelphia.

Kelly married Elizabeth Morrison McKnight on 30 October 1897; they had no children. Even during his last illness Kelly continued to perform his work and to aid others who asked for his help. He died at his Philadelphia residence of complications due to influenza.

• Kelly's career at various schools and hospitals is noted in Frederick P. Henry, ed., *Founder's Week Memorial Volume* (1909), pp. 317, 658, 709, 710; Martin Kaufman, *The University of Vermont, College of Medicine* (1979), pp. 84–85, 122–33, 138; and Burton A. Konkle, *A Standard History of the Medical Profession of Philadelphia* (1977), pp. 322, 365, 390, 411–12. Biographical sketches include James Tyson, "Memoir of Aloysius Oliver Joseph Kelly, M.D.," *Transactions of the College of Physicians of Philadelphia*, 3d ser., 34 (1912): lxii–lxviii; and "Obituary of A. O. J. Kelly," *American Journal of the Medical Sciences*, n.s., 141 (23 Feb. 1911). Newspaper obituaries are in the *Philadelphia Inquirer* and *Philadelphia Press*, both 24 Feb. 1911.

SAM ALEWITZ

KELLY, Colin Purdie (11 July 1915–10 Dec. 1941), army pilot, was born in Madison, Florida, the son of Colin Purdie Kelly, Sr., and Mary Mays. After attending high school in his hometown, Kelly spent a year at the Marion Military Institute in Florida before receiving an appointment to West Point in 1933. While there, he met Marion Wick, a stenographer, whom he wed in 1937, shortly after graduation; they had one son. Although commissioned as a second lieutenant in the infantry, Kelly requested to be assigned to the Army Air Corps, and in September he was sent to Randolph Field to receive his pilot's training. In October 1939 he went to Texas for advanced training. In January 1940 formal induction into the Army Air Corps followed and Kelly was assigned to the Nineteenth Bombing Group at March Field, California. Kelly made captain on 9 September 1940. His career would have been similar to that of most young officer graduates in World War II had it not been for circumstances surrounding his death.

When the Japanese fleet attacked Pearl Harbor, Kelly was based at Clark Field on Luzon in the Philippines commanding a B-17C Flying Fortress and acting as deputy squadron leader to the Nineteenth Bombing Group. On 10 December a Japanese convoy was reported in the vicinity of the Vigan region, and several U.S. bombers were ordered up to attack the convoy. Kelly's machine hastily took off with only three 600-pound bombs in bay (instead of eight) and made way for the Aparri region where the convoy was spotted. Kelly turned the Flying Fortress in a bomb run and released its ordnance, which reportedly struck one of the ships. Soon afterward, Japanese fighters attacked Kelly's plane, killing one of the gunners and damaging the machine to the point where Kelly ordered the crew to bail out while he kept the aircraft level. Soon after the surviving crew had bailed out, the plane exploded. Kelly's body was later found near the wreckage of his plane, which had crashed near Mount Arayat. His parachute had not opened.

Although one of the gunners had been killed, too, Kelly's death became the focus of the press reports, which stated that the ship Kelly had hit was the cruiser *Haruna*. The news quickly made its way to the United States, where Kelly was deemed the first U.S. Army hero of the war. In fact, historical evidence confirms that the *Haruna* was not in the Philippines, but in the Japanese home islands (it was sunk there on 28 July 1945). The heavy cruiser spotted by the B-17 crew may have been the *Ashigari*, but it wasn't sunk, and it isn't even clear that it was damaged. The facts, therefore, are reduced to confirming Kelly's act of bravery (ordering his men to bail out while he strove to control his damaged machine); also, his B-17 was the first U.S. bomber lost in aerial combat in World War II. The event, however, remains important in the mythical proportions it assumed.

Shortly after Kelly's death, conflicting reports circulated in the press; some said Kelly's bombs scored direct hits and some even suggested that Kelly had flown his crippled bomber straight into the *Haruna*. The discovery of the wreckage and of his body later proved otherwise, but the vision of selfless sacrifice touched the American nation. A country stunned by the Japanese surprise attack and hungering for bits of good news and inspiration reached out to Kelly's widow and their nineteen-month-old son. Toys, war bonds, and messages of support poured into the Kelly home that Christmas. Suggestions to award Kelly a posthumous Congressional Medal of Honor mounted fast, but instead Kelly received the Distinguished Service Medal.

As an Irish southerner, Kelly represented a particular slice of the average American who had come up through the ranks; his father was quoted as saying that "he was a fine specimen of manhood and, I guess, fairly bright. That's how he got his appointment to West Point." More telling, however, was a sentence from Reverend H. R. Latham's eulogy at Kelly's memorial service in Florida: "He died that Liberty and Christianity might live." The officer's background and sacrifice thus contributed to crystallizing the purpose of America's fight in the early days of World War II. More important, Kelly's wife, Marion, as the first war widow (once war was officially declared) also assumed an important role in the media coverage of the home front, as reports emphasized her pride in her husband's sacrifice and her diligent work as a stenographer for a California defense plant while raising her son.

The circumstances surrounding Kelly's death in combat illustrate the typically disorganized attempts at striking back at the Japanese fleet in December 1941: contingency plans hardly existed and elementary air war tactics were not applied, thus limiting any chances for an American success. The importance of Kelly's death therefore must be found in the impact it had on early American memories of World War II, encouraging a nation into combat and recording the young captain's name in military history.

• The National Air and Space Museum of the Smithsonian Institution has a biographical file that contains a series of clippings on Kelly. Thomas Collison, *Flying Fortress* (1943), and especially Edward Jablonski, *Flying Fortress* (1965), are valuable sources on both Kelly and the machine he flew. Reports in the *New York Times* between 13 and 25 Dec. reflect well the mood of the nation; see in particular Robert Nathan's poem in the *New York Times Sunday Magazine*, 21 Dec. 1941. On Kelly's family, see also *Liberty*, 6 June 1942, pp. 30–32; *Contact*, Oct. 1943, p. 8; *Life*, 6 July 1942, p. 70; *Official History of the United States Air Forces in World War II* (1983), pp. 206–7. An obituary is in the *New York Times*, 13 Dec. 1941.

GUILLAUME DE SYON

KELLY, Edward Joseph (1 May 1876–20 Oct. 1950), mayor of Chicago, Illinois, was born in Chicago, the son of Stephen Kelly, a policeman, and Helen Lang. One of nine children, he left school early to help support his family and later studied civil engineering in night classes at the Chicago Athenaeum. In 1910 he married Mary Edmunda Roche; they had one child. His first wife died in 1918, and Kelly married Margaret Ellen Kirk in 1922; they adopted three children.

In 1894 Kelly began working for the Metropolitan Sanitary District and rose through its ranks to become chief engineer in 1920. In 1924 he was appointed president of Chicago's South Park Board and presided over the transformation of the shabby lakefront into an attractive civic center adjacent to the central business district. Increasingly well known as one of Chicago's civic leaders, he became active in local Democratic politics but declined to run for elective office.

In 1933 Chicago mayor Anton J. Cermak was killed in an attempted assassination of president-elect Franklin D. Roosevelt, and local Democratic party chairman Patrick A. Nash, a wealthy contractor with extensive business dealings with the Sanitary District, arranged for the city council to select Kelly as Cermak's successor. After completing Cermak's term, Kelly was elected in 1935, overwhelming Republican Emil C. Wetten by a vote of 799,060 to 167,106. In 1939 he defeated Republican Dwight H. Green 822,469 to 638,068; and in 1943 he bested Republican George B. McKibbin 685,567 to 571,547.

In 1933, when Kelly became mayor, Chicago was suffering through the worst months of the Great Depression. The new chief executive faced a number of intractable problems—40 percent unemployment, a bankrupt city treasury, tax delinquency lists totaling 260 newspaper pages, and 14,000 public schoolteachers who had not received paychecks for months. Kelly acted swiftly and forcefully, dispensing checks to teachers and other municipal workers, securing state legislation to collect rent and taxes on delinquent properties, reducing a significant portion of the city debt, and attracting funds from the new Democratic administration in Washington, D.C. As conditions gradually improved, the new mayor received much of the credit. His popularity rose even more as he presided over Chicago's Century of Progress Exposition in 1933 and wisely extended the lucrative world's fair for a second year.

Along with his old friend Nash, Kelly also transformed the Cook County Democratic organization into one of the nation's most formidable big city political machines. The organization inherited from Cermak, a fragile ethnic coalition uniting Irish, Jewish, Polish, and German factions, grew more powerful at the very time when many political machines created in the nineteenth century were dissolving. The infamous Kelly-Nash machine retained the loyalty of a huge patronage army by rewarding the party faithful with a share of the spoils and offering ethnically balanced tickets at election time. Chicago's Republican business community supported Kelly because he kept the city solvent in perilous economic times, opposed personal property and state income taxes, and aided downtown merchants by constructing the multimillion-dollar State Street Subway that provided consumers with easier access to the city center. At the same time, Kelly maintained good relations with organized labor—despite the infamous 1937 Memorial Day Massacre at which Chicago policemen fired pistols into a crowd of fleeing Congress of Industrial Organizations (CIO) picketers, killing ten and wounding thirty more. After a U.S. Senate investigating committee condemned the city's role in the incident, Kelly met with CIO officials and promised future restraint by police.

Kelly added to the machine's electoral strength by attracting thousands of black voters who had traditionally supported Republican candidates. The mayor appointed blacks to a significant number of municipal posts, selected them as candidates for elective offices, and distributed government aid (federal as well as municipal and state) in unprecedented quantities to the South Side Black Belt. The Kelly-Nash machine successfully supported Arthur W. Mitchell for Illinois's First District seat in the U.S. House of Representatives, and Mitchell became the first black Democratic U.S. congressman. In 1942, with the machine's backing, William L. Dawson succeeded Mitchell and became the most powerful black congressman of his time. Kelly's capture of the black vote proved to be a significant factor in the Chicago Democratic machine's longevity, especially in the 1950s and 1960s when white flight and black population growth made the African-American vote a crucial commodity for white politicians seeking to maintain control of city hall.

Although the black community provided votes for the machine, its hazardous economic situation precluded the provision of financial resources. Accordingly, Kelly tapped the wealth of organized crime. His administration curtailed the gangland killings that occurred so often in the city during the Roaring Twenties but made no effort to eliminate gambling; the local newspapers estimated the annual tribute paid to the political machine by the vice lords to be $20 million. As a consequence, Chicago was known during the Kelly years as a wide-open town, where the politicians and police were on the take. Kelly boasted that his administration safeguarded the personal freedoms that the heavily ethnic, working-class population of Chicago demanded. More important, the Democrats profited from the revenue generated by crime syndicate-controlled gambling.

Roosevelt's New Deal also proved to be a generous benefactor of the Kelly-Nash machine. After the mayor's landslide victory in 1935, federal relief administrator Harry Hopkins went out of his way to direct great sums of federal money to the Works Progress Administration (WPA) office in Chicago. Convinced that Kelly was the most powerful politician in his state, Hopkins and other leading New Dealers dealt exclusively with the Chicago mayor—meanwhile ignoring Illinois governor Henry Horner and other Democratic reformers. In 1936 Roosevelt even supported Kelly's handpicked candidate for governor, Dr. Herman Bundesen, in an unsuccessful attempt to unseat the incumbent, Horner. Chicago's Democratic precincts turned out huge majorities for Roosevelt, and, as a result, Kelly became one of the president's political advisers and a noted power within the party nationally. Kelly emerged as one of Roosevelt's greatest champions and a consistent defender of the New Deal. At the 1940 Democratic National Convention in Chicago, the mayor packed the galleries with local government employees to support the president's nomination. In one of the most remarkable episodes in American political history, an unknown voice boomed forth from the convention hall's loudspeakers calling for Roosevelt's nomination and sparking a spontaneous demonstration by the delegates. The "Voice from the Sewers," which belonged to the city's superintendent of sewers, who acted on Kelly's orders, subsided after about an hour, and the president was overwhelmingly renominated. In 1944 Kelly was one of the influential big city bosses who prevailed upon Roosevelt to replace Vice President Henry A. Wallace on the Democratic ticket with Harry S. Truman.

A strong leader who ruled autocratically and—after Nash's death in 1943—unilaterally, Kelly turned the city council into a docile rubber stamp for his initiatives. After the end of the Second World War, however, ambitious Democrats began to chafe at the mayor's iron-handed rule. Public complaints increased about defalcations in the public schools, official tolerance of organized crime, corruption in the police department, and poor delivery of municipal services. Moreover, Kelly had taken the unpopular position of supporting open housing and the desegregation of public schools, which had damaged his standing among Irish, Polish, and German voters. Beset by a series of health problems and persuaded by party leaders that his nomination was doubtful, the septuagenarian mayor chose not to seek reelection in 1947. Thereafter, he maintained an engineering consulting firm and served as the Illinois Democratic national committeeman until his death in Chicago.

As boss of one of the nation's foremost political machines, Kelly dominated Chicago's politics and government and greatly expanded the organization's power. What came to be known in later decades as Mayor Richard J. Daley's machine was nurtured, shaped, and enlarged under Kelly's leadership. His fourteen-year mayoralty, spanning the Great Depression and World War II, resulted in significant changes for Chicago. The partnership between Kelly and the New Deal provided a major facelift for the city. As a result of an infusion of federal funds, the city's transportation network came to maturity with the completion of Lake Shore Drive, including the Outer Drive Bridge, and the opening of the State Street Subway. Funding from the Public Works Administration (PWA) resulted in the construction of thirty new schools and three public housing projects between 1933 and 1940; after 1937 the U.S. Housing Authority (USHA) provided the means for several more. WPA labor landscaped acres of parkland, provided road and sewerage repair, and enlarged the city's antiquated airport. Yet the vast improvements in Chicago's infrastructure notwithstanding, the city's reputation suffered because of its government by what U.S. Secretary of the Interior Harold L. Ickes called "the rottenest crowd in any section of the United States today" (Biles, *Big City Boss*, p. 36). For more than a decade, Mayor Kelly's political prowess made him a powerful force in national affairs and one of the key big city bosses who constituted an important part of Roosevelt's Democratic coalition.

• The lone biography of Kelly is Roger Biles, *Big City Boss in Depression and War: Mayor Edward J. Kelly of Chicago* (1984). For a brief synopsis, see Biles, "Edward J. Kelly: New Deal Machine Builder," in *The Mayors: The Chicago Political Tradition*, ed. Paul M. Green and Melvin G. Holli (1987). Also see the chapter on Kelly in Lyle W. Dorsett, *Franklin D. Roosevelt and the City Bosses* (1977). On Kelly's recruitment of black voters, see Biles, " 'Big Red in Bronzeville': Mayor Ed Kelly Reels in the Black Vote," *Chicago History* 10 (1981): 99–111. Obituaries are in the *New York Times* and the *Chicago Tribune*, 21 Oct. 1950.

ROGER BILES

KELLY, Emmett (9 Dec. 1898–28 Mar. 1979), clown, was born Emmett Leo Kelly in Sedan, Kansas, the son of Thomas Kelly, a railroad section foreman, and Mollie Schimick. His family bought a farm near Houston, Missouri, while he was still a little boy, and he received his entire formal education in that town's one-room schoolhouse. He dropped out of the eighth grade to help on the farm and, having been encouraged to make the most of his artistic abilities by both his mother and a former teacher, enrolled in a correspondence course offered by the Landon School of Cartooning in Cleveland, Ohio.

In 1917 Kelly left home for Kansas City, Missouri, in the hopes of becoming a newspaper cartoonist but quickly discovered that neither of its two papers required his services. Rather than return to the farm, he stayed in the big city and supported himself by working at a variety of jobs. He also began performing a comedic "chalk talk" at talent shows and local theaters, an act that led in 1919 to a gig as a clown-cartoonist with the Frisco Exposition Shows. Donning the garish suit and whiteface makeup of a clown, he drew caricatures on a large chalkboard while regaling the crowd with amusing stories. He also taught himself to do stunts on the trapeze and performed as an aerialist as well. In 1920 he finally landed a job as a cartoonist with the Adagram Film Company animating advertisements that were shown in Kansas City movie theaters. One of his creations was a hapless little hobo with a long, sad face and plenty of bad luck, the prototype for the clown character that one day he would play before circus-goers on two continents.

In 1921 Kelly gave up his old dream of being a cartoonist in favor of his new one of being a circus performer and joined Howe's Great London Circus as a trapeze artist and clown. However, his opening-night aerial performance was so disappointing that he was not allowed to return to the air for the rest of the tour. In 1922, having greatly improved his aerial technique by performing with the St. Louis (Mo.) Police Circus (a two-week charity fundraiser put on during the off-season), he signed on as a trapeze artist with John Robinson's Circus. In 1923 he married Eva Moore, one of his co-aerialists. For the next eight years he per-

formed with his wife on the double trapeze as the Aerial Kellys and doubled as a clown during the touring season, then spent the winter either in Indianapolis, Indiana, where he worked in a glove factory, or in Mulberry Grove, Illinois, where his parents had moved in 1922.

In 1929 the Aerial Kellys joined the Sells-Floto Circus but left it in 1931 when the nation's deteriorating financial situation forced it to stop touring. Unable to find work as a team, they joined the Hagenbeck-Wallace Circus the next year with her as part of an aerial ensemble act and him as just another resident of Clown Alley. Although he had always considered himself to be an aerialist first and a clown second, in 1932 he realized that his future as a circus performer dictated the wearing of greasepaint instead of spangled tights. Consequently, he set out to create a unique clown persona and in the process brought to life the hapless hobo that he had developed at Adagram. Clad in a tattered suit and a battered hat and sporting a five-day stubble, a pink nose, and an enormously sorrowful, white-lipped mouth, Weary Willie emerged as a surreal victim of the Great Depression. He convulsed his audiences simply by shuffling around the perimeter of the circus ring and staring balefully from time to time into the eyes of a nonplussed spectator, but he really brought down the house when he tried to crack a peanut with a sledgehammer or sweep up the spotlight with a frayed broom, two routines that became his trademark.

In 1934 Kelly joined the Cole Brothers and Clyde Beatty Combined Circus without his wife who, after having their second and last child that same year, divorced him in 1935. The breakup was a painful experience for him, and he compensated by throwing himself into the role of Weary Willie. As he did so, Willie's popularity increased with each new season until in 1937 he was invited to join Bertram Mills' Circus, an English troupe that was one of the best circuses in Europe. He toured primarily in England until 1939, when Great Britain entered World War II and he returned to the United States. He took his clown-cartoonist act into nightclubs and appeared in the 1940 Broadway musical comedy *Keep off the Grass* before rejoining the Cole-Beatty Circus. In 1942 he made his debut with the Ringling Brothers and Barnum & Bailey Circus, widely known as the Greatest Show on Earth. In 1944 he married and divorced Mildred Richey, an eighteen-year-old trapeze artist with whom he had no children. In 1950 he made his motion picture debut as a clown turned murderer in *The Fat Man* and in 1952 starred as Weary Willie in *The Greatest Show on Earth*. In 1954 he married Elvira Gebhardt, a circus acrobat, and they had two children.

Kelly retired from Ringling Brothers and Barnum & Bailey in 1956 and settled permanently in Sarasota, Florida, the off-season home of a number of circus performers. However, he continued to perform as Weary Willie in commercials, ice shows, operas, baseball games (he was the official spring training mascot of the 1957 Brooklyn Dodgers), European movies,

American television shows, and Nevada nightclubs. He died in Sarasota and was inducted posthumously into the Clown Hall of Fame in 1989.

Kelly's creation of Weary Willie revolutionized professional clowning and made him the country's most familiar clown. The sad-sack, shuffling antics of his unkempt, downtrodden hobo offered a complete contrast to the madcap cavorting of brightly colored, white-faced conventional clowns and has served as an alternate model for professional clowns ever since.

• Kelly's papers have not been located. An autobiography is Emmett Kelly, with F. Beverly Kelley, *Clown: My Life in Tatters and Smiles* (1954). For information on Kelly's career and on circus clowns in general, see John H. Towsen, *Clowns* (1976), and John Culhane, *The American Circus: An Illustrated History* (1990). Obituaries are in the *New York Times*, 29 Mar. 1979, and *Newsweek* and *Time*, both 9 Apr. 1979.

CHARLES W. CAREY, JR.

KELLY, Eugene (25 Nov. 1808–19 Dec. 1894), merchant, banker, and philanthropist, was born in County Tyrone, Ireland, the son of Thomas Boye Kelly. His mother's name and his parents' occupations are unknown. Little is known of his family background save that his father, heir to a formerly prominent and prosperous line, lost the balance of his fortune because of his participation in the rebellion of 1798. Following the rebellion, the elder Kelly changed his name from "O'Kelly" to the more common "Kelly" as a precaution against reprisals for his activities. Eugene received his education in a local hedge school, after which he became a draper's apprentice.

Kelly took active note of the flood of Irish citizens immigrating to America, his older brother John Kelly, later a noted figure in the Roman Catholic clergy, having joined their ranks in 1825. Some time around 1834 Kelly left for the United States himself, and upon his arrival in New York found employment with the firm of Donnelly & Company. His new position placed him solidly within the city's largest dry-goods concern, and after a few years with the firm, he relocated to Maysville, Kentucky. He married (date unknown) Sarah Donnelly, the sister of his employer; they had one daughter. Kelly soon prospered in his new location with his own firm. After about a year, he moved to St. Louis, Missouri, where he experienced continued success in the same business among a great number of his fellow Irish immigrants. Well established after a few years in that city, he returned to New York.

The death of his wife in 1848 and the publicity surrounding the discovery of gold in California in the following year provided sufficient motivation for Kelly to relocate once again, this time joining a mule train that eventually brought him to San Francisco. Delayed in his arrival until January 1850 by the need to settle old business affairs, Kelly assuaged his disappointment at falling short of true "forty-niner" status by founding the firm of Murphy, Grant & Co., a dry-goods business. A partnership with Daniel T. Murphy, Adam Grant, and Joseph A. Donohoe, the firm grew rapidly and was soon the largest concern of its type on the West Coast.

Kelly expanded his business interests into banking with the establishment of Eugene Kelly & Co. in New York in 1856. Although he established a branch of the bank in California under the name of Donohoe, Ralston & Company in 1861, Kelly concentrated his efforts on his New York operations after 1860. An additional inducement to remain in New York was his 1857 marriage to Margaret Hughes, the niece of New York Roman Catholic archbishop John Hughes. They had five sons.

With his efforts focused on New York and his finances more than secure, Kelly found time to devote himself to political and ecclesiastical activities as well as other business interests. He founded the Southern Bank of Georgia in Savannah during Reconstruction and held directorships at the Emigrant Savings Bank (which he also served as president), the National Park Bank, the Bank of New York, and the Equitable Life Assurance Society. A member of the New York Chamber of Commerce, Kelly also served as a trustee of the Metropolitan Museum of Art and the American Museum of Natural History. Active in the Democratic party, Kelly was a member of the New York City Board of Education for thirteen years and chairman of the Electoral Committee of the state of New York in 1884.

Extending his political activities to his native land, Kelly proved himself an ardent supporter of Irish nationalism. He served as treasurer of the Irish Parliamentary Fund and as president of the National Federation of America. During one appeal for $150,000, Kelly pledged $20,000 and quietly promised to supply the balance of funds if the need arose.

Kelly's most enduring legacy occurred with his church-related philanthropy. He donated heavily to a variety of Catholic charities and served as a trustee of St. Patrick's Cathedral in New York City. His greatest efforts, however, came in the service of Catholic higher education. He was a trustee of Seton Hall College in South Orange, New Jersey, and his role in the formation of the Catholic University of America in Washington, D.C., was particularly noteworthy. An original trustee and treasurer of the board of trustees in 1887, he endowed two professorial chairs, the Eugene Kelly Chair of Ecclesiastical History and the Margaret Hughes Kelly Chair of Holy Scripture, with a gift of $100,000 in 1889. He was rewarded for his many efforts on behalf of the church when his good friend and archbishop of New York Michael Corrigan obtained appointment for Kelly (subsequently accepted by his son Eugene Kelly, Jr., because of Kelly's poor health) as chamberlain of the cape and sword, a papal honor previously bestowed on only two other Americans.

Kelly spent his later years managing his affairs and slowly selling out his business interests. Eugene Kelly & Co. was dissolved in May 1894. He died at his residence in New York City.

Kelly's life and career typified the experience of many successful immigrants to the United States. He rose from poverty, arriving in the United States with

£100 in his pocket, to a position of wealth and prominence, which he used most conspicuously for the benefit of his church and its activities in higher education.

• No organized collection of Kelly's papers appears to have survived, although the New-York Historical Society holds a few scattered items. Kelly has been the subject of little scholarly attention; however, his career is discussed in C. Joseph Nuesse, *The Catholic University of America: A Centennial History* (1990), and John Tracy Ellis, *The Formative Years of the Catholic University of America* (1946). Obituaries are in the *New York Sun* and the *New York Herald*, 20 Dec. 1894.

EDWARD L. LACH, JR.

KELLY, Fanny Wiggins (15 Apr. 1845–15 Nov. 1904), captivity narrativist, was born near Orillia, Ontario, the daughter of James Wiggins, a farmer, and Margaret Barry. Although the father died en route, the family migrated in 1857 to Geneva in the Neosho Valley of Kansas, where they experienced the ravages of drought, grasshoppers, and the border conflict of the Civil War. Late in 1863, Fanny married Josiah Shawahan Kelly, a farmer and discharged Union veteran who had spent several years in California. Attracted to the new mining districts of what was then Idaho and would soon become Montana Territory, they began the long overland journey. Traveling at that time was dangerous for several reasons: the upper plains Indians were increasingly agitated in reaction to white encroachment, the bloody Minnesota Sioux rebellion of 1862 had only recently been put down, and many army troops had been withdrawn to fight against the South.

The Kellys were in a party of eleven, which included two women and two children, among them Mary J. Hurley, their niece, who was seven or eight years old. Plodding along slowly, with a small herd of livestock and five wagons loaded with a variety of trade goods, the group was at Little Box Elder Creek, some eighty miles west of Fort Laramie, on 12 July 1864 when it was attacked by a band of Oglala Sioux. Three men were killed on the spot, and one died later. Josiah Kelly escaped unscathed, but Fanny, Mary, Sara Larimer, and her small son were all captured by the Indians. The Larimers managed to escape after the first night. Mary also managed to slip away but was later found and killed.

For the next five months, Fanny Kelly was held captive, the personal slave of the elderly Chief Ottawa. The band moved through eastern Wyoming, up Powder River to the Tongue River, to the northern edge of the North Dakota Badlands, where Kelly witnessed the battle between General Alfred Sully and the Sioux at Killdeer Mountain. A few weeks later, she made contact with Captain James Liberty Fisk, then under attack while leading a train of Minnesotans to the Montana mines. His efforts to ransom her failed. To the public, Kelly later insisted in writing that she had been compelled to work as a menial and as a nurse for the injured and that she had not been sexually abused. In a memorial to Congress, however, she complained that she had been "forced to become the squaw of one

of the O-gal-lal-lah Chiefs, who treated her in a manner too horrible to mention, and during her captivity was passed from Chief to Chief, and treated in a similar manner."

Ultimately, after the army took a hard-nosed stance against the Indians, Kelly came into the hands of the Blackfeet Sioux, who escorted her to freedom at Fort Sully in Dakota Territory, either because they hoped to use her as a decoy to gain admission, as Kelly claimed, or because of increasing military pressure and the need of winter rations.

Reunited, the Kellys subsequently moved to Ellsworth, in western Kansas, where they built and operated a hotel until Josiah died of cholera in July 1867, just a week before the birth of the couple's only son. For a time, Fanny Kelly joined the Larimers at Sherman Station in Wyoming, where they ran a general store and a photography business and where she herself worked as a washerwoman while writing a manuscript of her captivity experience. Soon she broke with the Larimers and accused Sara of having stolen her manuscript and publishing it as her own. Larimer's volume, *The Capture and Escape; or, Life Among the Sioux*, appeared in 1870, but legal action by Kelly forced the destruction of the copies of a second book about Kelly before it could be distributed. Litigation between the two continued until the summer of 1876, when a private settlement was reached.

Meanwhile, Fanny had published her own account in 1871, *Narrative of My Captivity among the Sioux Indians*, a book sharing many similarities in sentences and paragraphs with Sara's work, and a book heavily embroidered with descriptive material and illustrations borrowed from other sources. Her book enthralled American readers, and by 1991 it had gone through eleven editions or printings, two of them in Canada.

Congress compensated Kelly $10,000 for property lost or destroyed and another $15,000 for a warning she managed to send to Fort Sully, although the fort was probably in no danger. She eventually settled in Washington, D.C., where in May 1880 she married William F. Gordon, a Kansas journalist who specialized in ghostwriting for prominent Americans. Probably she was a federal employee; certainly she had a successful career. She had extensive investments in real estate, including the Calvert Mansion in Riversdale, Maryland. She worked with private charities, especially those for women. She died in Washington.

Kelly's book—the story of her personal ordeal—was her main contribution to history. She provided graphic details of the attack, her life and travels in captivity among the Sioux, and her return to white society. To her own experiences, she added descriptions of geography, the Sully expedition, Indian customs, and the treatment of other prisoners taken without acknowledgement from other printed sources. In the tradition of captivity narratives going back to the seventeenth century, Kelly's account of her own trauma, suffering, and eventual triumph was typical of what generations of Americans had read. These narratives often helped shape public views of the western experience and American Indians.

• An important, carefully researched and documented account of the experiences of Fanny Kelly that is broader than its title is Randy Brown, "Attack on the Kelly-Larimer Wagon Train," *Overland Journal* 5 (Winter 1887): 16–40. Also illuminating is Clark and Mary Lee Spence, eds., "Prologue" and "Epilogue," in *Narrative of My Captivity among the Sioux Indians*, by Fanny Kelly (1990), pp. xxiii–lviii, 323–32. Fanny's handwritten, 23-page account of her ordeal, unembellished for publication, is found as Fanny Kelly Petition (1868), Exhibit "B," House Committee on Appropriations, 40th Cong., Record Group 233, National Archives. For the Kelly-Larimer litigation over publications, see Alan W. Farley, "An Indian Captivity and Its Legal Aftermath," *Kansas Historical Quarterly* 21 (Winter 1954): 247–56.

CLARK C. SPENCE

KELLY, Florence Finch (27 Mar. 1858–17 Dec. 1939), journalist and author, was born in Girard, Illinois, the daughter of James Gardner Finch and Mary Ann Purdom, farmers. Before she was seven years old, Kelly's eldest brother died in a Confederate prison camp, and her father was harassed for opposing slavery. Moving from farm to farm after her father renovated and resold each at a higher price, in 1869 the family settled in Kansas where farm life bred in Kelly "a spirit of co-operation," "individuality," and "sense of . . . kinship with the soil," while her father's habit of reading the newspaper aloud inspired an interest in public affairs and writing. Kelly read everything she could find, from an ancient medical handbook and the work of early women journalists Fanny Fern and Grace Greenwood to Milton's *Paradise Lost*. She published her first short story at fourteen in an eight-page Iowa paper.

In order to attend the only high school in the county, Kelly left home and worked for room and board. She received a teacher's certificate and taught in district schools until earning enough money for college. In 1877 she enrolled at the University of Kansas, joined the literary society and, later, was editor of the student magazine. Her first newspaper job was in the summer of her junior year with the state's leading daily paper, the *Topeka Commonwealth*. After graduating with her B.A. in 1881, she moved to San Francisco.

Dismayed by finding few positions open to women and reporting confined to news west of the Sierras, in May 1881 Kelly moved to Chicago. A letter of introduction to a successful newspaperwoman, Helen Ekin Starrett, helped her get hack work with city papers, then a more lucrative position at the publishing house of David Cook. By the autumn of 1881 she had enough money to move to Boston. Unable to find a permanent position, she made ends meet by writing articles on such topics as women's rights legislation and the repudiation of state debts as well as book reviews for *The Transcript*. She finally landed a permanent position with the *Boston Globe*, reporting on women's activities and writing art reviews and a weekly woman's column for the Sunday issue.

As the first woman on the *Globe*, Kelly challenged sexism by ignoring Victorian tenets that contradicted her role as journalist. After six months and a number of published editorials, she left the social page, permitted to devote herself to art, the women's movement, and the editorial page on which she worked with her future husband, Allen Kelly. Despite promotions, her small salary and lack of recognition led Kelly, in September 1884, to accept an offer as editorial writer for the *Troy (N.Y.) Morning Telegram*. She left Troy when Allen Kelly asked her to join him in Massachusetts as his wife and partner on his newspaper, the *Lowell Bell*. When the paper failed, they returned to Boston, married in December 1884, and in the early spring of 1885 moved to Fall River, Massachusetts, he as managing editor of the *Fall River Globe* and she as his editorial assistant. She resigned in the autumn in preparation for the birth of their son, who died of pneumonia before he was five.

In 1886 they moved to New York City where Kelly did freelance work for the Franklin Fyfe syndicate newspaper. When in 1887 her husband accepted a better job as city editor of Hearst's paper, the *San Francisco Examiner*, Kelly moved with him, writing, reporting, and interviewing for the *Examiner* and acting as correspondent for the *New York Sun*. Allen's poor health in the spring of 1893 precipitated their move to New Mexico, which she found "intriguing, delightful, . . . salubrious beyond any other region." In 1895 she had a second son. The following year they moved to Los Angeles, where Allen was city editor at the *Times*, to which Kelly contributed unsigned interviews, feature articles, sketches, and short stories based on her California and New Mexico experiences.

Kelly's success in writing a Sunday column, "The Woman of the Times," led to anonymous book reviewing and promotion to literary editor of the Sunday magazine book page. With this steady income, she began her first novel, *With Hoops of Steel* (1900), set in New Mexico. A move east to Philadelphia where her husband was chief editorial writer for the *North American* allowed Kelly to quit newspaper work and to concentrate on her family and writing fiction. In 1905 she accompanied her husband to New Zealand and Australia to study social and economic legislation. When they returned to the United States, Kelly wrote magazine articles and in 1906 began a thirty-year career writing for the *New York Times Book Review* in Adolph Ochs's famous style—"objectively, with no personal prejudice." While averaging 400 to 500 reviews a year, Kelly also wrote four more novels based on independent research and her experiences in the Southwest. She consistently received positive reviews, although the financial success of her books was hampered by poor marketing.

In 1916, inspired by Woodrow Wilson's devotion to democracy, Kelly took a leave of absence to campaign for the Democratic candidate in traditionally Republican Kansas, where she helped influence Wilson's reelection in a shocking turnabout of voter sentiment. That same year her husband died. Toward the end of

World War I, she wrote an account of America's war effort, *What America Did* (1919). After publishing her last novel, *The Dixons* (1921), she remained at the *New York Times Book Review* until 1936, when she became "tired of writing about other people's books" while "something within [her] was demanding individual expression." In *Flowing Stream*, her autobiography, she claims that her greatest achievement was her contribution to the development of the women's movement and the newspaper. Kelly believed that newspapers should fight sectionalism in the United States by expanding their areas of reporting. By also encouraging book reading, she argued, newspapers could help the nation "climb a little higher in knowledge and wisdom." Kelly died in Hartford, Connecticut.

• Kelly's correspondence with the University of Kansas is in the Alumni Association files. Her major publications not mentioned above include the novels *Rhoda of the Underground* (1909), *The Delafield Affair* (1909), and *Fate of Felix Brand* (1911), and a collection of short stories titled *Emerson's Wife and Other Western Stories* (1911). Kelly's autobiography, *Flowing Stream: The Story of Fifty-six Years in American Newspaper Life* (1939), provides the most detailed account of her life in addition to her views on women's rights, journalism, and the nation. A description of her campaigning for Wilson can be found in John D. Bright, ed., *Kansas: The First Century*, vol. 2 (1956). Obituaries are in the *Lawrence (Kans.) Journal World* and the *New York Times*, 18 Dec. 1939.

BARBARA L. CICCARELLI

KELLY, George Edward (16 Jan. 1887–18 June 1974), dramatist, was born in the Schuylkill Falls suburb of Philadelphia, Pennsylvania, the son of John Henry Kelly, an insurance executive, and Mary Costello. He belonged to a prominent Irish Catholic family whose most famous member, actress Grace Kelly, was the daughter of his brother John. Little is known about Kelly's childhood and early education; Kelly himself claimed that he was educated privately at home and in Europe. Although he expressed an early enthusiasm for mathematics and engineering, he never attended college. Kelly instead left home in 1911 to follow his brother Walter, an internationally famous mimic and monologist, into performing on the road.

Kelly enjoyed the acting life enough to stay with it, eventually finding his way along with his brother to the vaudeville circuit in 1915. At this time he began writing and directing his own one-act plays. He first turned to playwriting in order to provide himself with larger stage roles and fresh acting material. He wrote a number of parts for himself in plays such as *Finders Keepers* (1916) and *The Flattering Word* (1918), among others. In 1917 Kelly left acting and served for a year in the army before returning to the stage. At the end of the First World War Kelly began to tour the country as an actor, director, and vaudeville sketch writer.

In 1922 Kelly expanded one of his vaudeville efforts, *Mrs. Ritter Appears* (1917), into *The Torchbearers*, the first of ten full-length works he wrote in his career as a playwright and the first to be produced on Broadway. This play, an immediate success, was followed by two more Broadway hits: *The Show-Off* (1924) and *Craig's Wife* (1925). *The Show-Off*, Kelly's best-known work and the one on which his modern reputation rests, was so popular that several film versions were made of it, and it was also adapted as a novel. *Craig's Wife* won Kelly the 1926 Pulitzer Prize for drama. Because of the popular appeal of Kelly's plays, several of his characters from this period, such as Aubrey Piper, *The Show-Off*'s insufferable know-it-all, became full-blown cultural icons. Harriet Craig of *Craig's Wife* came to symbolize a distinctly feminine brand of middle-class materialism.

Perhaps because the remainder of the plays Kelly wrote in the latter half of the 1920s—*Daisy Mayme* (1926), *Behold the Bridegroom* (1927), and *Maggie the Magnificent* (1929)—failed to earn the popular and critical acclaim of his earlier efforts, he produced nothing between *Philip Goes Forth* in 1931 and *Reflected Glory* in 1936. In the years between those two plays, Kelly resided in Hollywood, working as a script consultant for Metro-Goldwyn-Mayer Studios. He also sought to parlay his abundant skills as a playwright into what he viewed to be the more promising career of screenwriting. Never particularly extroverted, Kelly grew dissatisfied with the collaborative nature of writing for the movies, and his only screenwriting credit was to be for his help on a 1935 gangster film, *Old Hutch*. "On the screen the method of working for a writer is different," he told the *New York Herald Tribune* (4 Oct. 1936) after returning to the theater, "since so many persons are responsible for the final result. . . . If you realize from the start that you can't work alone and creatively in the same way you do a play, you're safe." When *Reflected Glory* also suffered through a discouraging run, Kelly once again withdrew from the stage, only to return a decade later with *The Deep Mrs. Sykes* (1945) and *The Fatal Weakness* (1946), his last produced play.

Only in the first half of the 1920s did Kelly find an audience fully appreciative of his wit, style, and themes. While he continued throughout the remainder of his long life to tinker with scripts, he chose to spend most of his time away from the stage and with his family. On the whole, Kelly led a quiet, even reclusive, life. Though marriage was a key theme in many of his dramas, and though he was at one time romantically linked with actress Tallulah Bankhead, he remained a lifelong bachelor and even acquired a reputation as being something of a misogynist. Along with the 1926 Pulitzer, Kelly's awards included the Brandies University Creative Arts Award (1959), the Philadelphia Creative Arts Theater Award (1962), and the Theta Phi Drama Award of Distinction (1968). In 1957 Kelly moved to Sun City, a southern California retirement community, where he lived until shortly before his death in Bryn Mawr, Pennsylvania.

George Kelly was one of this country's most distinctive dramatic writers for two reasons. First, as he himself often noted, his art had very little to do with formal training: it grew entirely out of his years of hard experience acting on the road. And second, although Kelly's roots were firmly planted in vaudeville, he considered himself first and foremost a popular moralist. "The dramatist," he explained in an interview with the *New York Herald Tribune* (5 Feb. 1928), "is chiefly intent on putting life into focus—revealing a significant segment of human life in all fidelity and with a sense of its deepest values." Because of his strong belief in the didactic function of theater, Kelly turned to satirical drama as the best vehicle to communicate both his comic temperament and his more serious insights into human frailty. Kelly was, then, an unusual combination of droll vaudevillian and demanding schoolmaster. His finely crafted plays are notable for putting a unique comic perspective to the service of high moral purpose.

• Foster Hirsch, *George Kelly* (1975), is a complete assessment of Kelly's career and also contains useful biographical and bibliographical information. See Carl Carmer, "George Kelly," *Theatre Arts Monthly* 15 (1931): 322–30; Edward Maisel, "The Theatre of George Kelly," *Theatre Arts* 31 (1947): 39–43; Mary McCarthy, "George Kelly," in *Mary McCarthy's Theatre Chronicles, 1937–1962* (1963), pp. 97–104; and Arthur Wills, "The Kelly Play," *Modern Drama* 6 (1963): 245–55, for excellent, brief overviews of Kelly's style and themes. For the most complete bibliography of primary and secondary materials as well as a list of important play reviews, see Paul A. Doyle, "George Kelly: An Eclectic Bibliography," *Bulletin of Bibliography* 24 (1965): 173–74, 177. Obituaries are in the *New York Times*, 19 June 1974, the *Washington Post*, 21 June and 17 July 1974, and *Newsweek*, 1 July 1974.

KEVIN R. RAHIMZADEH

KELLY, Grace (12 Nov. 1929–14 Sept. 1982), actress, was born Grace Patricia Kelly in Philadelphia, Pennsylvania. Her mother, Margaret Majer, was a model and physical education instructor at the University of Pennsylvania, and her father, John Brendan Kelly, was a 1920 Olympic champion oarsman and wealthy contractor. Her brother, John Brendan Kelly, Jr., was also an Olympic-class oarsman. The product of a large, competitive Irish-American family, Grace Kelly, a shy, demure child, was educated at a Catholic school for girls and made her amateur debut at age ten on the Philadelphia stage.

Following her high school graduation in 1947, Kelly studied at the American Academy of Dramatic Arts in New York City while pursuing a successful career as a model in 1948–1950. Her uncle, George Kelly, an established playwright, was influential in her early career. She was a tall, athletic-looking, blue-eyed blond with strikingly beautiful looks, often described as the all-American girl next door. By 1949 Kelly appeared in summer stock theater and on Broadway in August Strindberg's drama *The Father*. Despite good notices, she was not cast in any other Broadway productions, but in 1949–1950 she appeared in more than sixty television shows, perfecting her craft as a pioneer in television dramas.

Kelly turned to Hollywood in 1950, and her first film was *Fourteen Hours* (1951). After more summer stock roles in Colorado, she won a small but significant role in *High Noon* (1952) opposite Gary Cooper. This low-budget adult western was Kelly's breakthrough role, setting a precedent for movies in which she was cast opposite older leading men with great success. *High Noon* was a box office and critical success, reviving Cooper's career and establishing Kelly as a talented newcomer.

Impressed by her screen test and role in *High Noon*, director John Ford persuaded Metro-Goldwyn-Mayer (MGM) to sign Kelly to a long-term contract. He recognized her cool ladylike demeanor as perfect for a leading role in his movie *Mogambo* (1953), for which she was nominated for an Academy Award as best supporting actress playing opposite Clark Gable. In recognition of her growing stature in Hollywood, *Look* magazine named Kelly the best actress in 1953 and *Life* magazine predicted that 1954 would be a "year of Grace."

Kelly won the New York Film Critics Award and an Academy Award as best actress for her performance in *The Country Girl* (1954). Her leading man, Bing Crosby, proposed marriage to her during the film but Kelly declined. Director Alfred Hitchcock, equally smitten by her wit, serene beauty, and aristocratic bearing, starred her in three films, *Dial M for Murder* (1954), with Ray Milland; *Rear Window* (1954), with James Stewart; and *To Catch a Thief* (1955), with Cary Grant. The director shrewdly continued the pattern of casting Kelly opposite older leading men with strong screen identities. Hitchcock appreciated Kelly's talent for romantic glamour, and in each film he emphasized her cool exterior and smoldering passion.

By 1954 Grace Kelly was the number one female movie star in the United States, but she was plagued by press reports about her romantic scandals with her leading men and Hollywood stars. In response, she became one of the first film stars to refuse MGM studio demands to cooperate with the press in exchange for favorable publicity. Her sudden rise to stardom and her popularity with the public made this possible. Stereotyped as aloof and cold, her appeal only increased in the somewhat conservative 1950s.

Teamed successfully once again with a ruggedly handsome older man, Kelly played opposite William Holden in *The Bridges at Toko-Ri* (1955). While filming *To Catch a Thief* in 1954 on the French Riviera, she met her future husband. In a spectacular televised ceremony, she married Prince Rainier III, the ruler of Monaco, on 19 April 1956. Kelly's brief but spectacular acting career ended after *High Society* (1956). She made only ten feature films and five documentaries. Princess Grace remained an international celebrity, active in civic affairs in the tiny principality of Monaco, in charity work, and as the mother of three children, Caroline, Stephanie, and Albert. Grace Kelly died in an automobile accident in Monaco.

• For information on Kelly, see Sarah Bradford, *Princess Grace* (1984); Arthur H. Lewis, *Those Philadelphia Kellys, with a Touch of Grace* (1977); and James Spada, *Grace: The Secret Life of a Princess* (1987). An obituary is in the *New York Times*, 15 Sept. 1982.

PETER C. HOLLORAN

KELLY, Howard Atwood (20 Feb. 1858–12 Jan. 1943), surgeon, gynecologist, and medical biographer, was born in Camden, New Jersey, the son of Henry Kuhl Kelly, a prosperous sugar broker, and Louise Warner Hard, the daughter of an Episcopal clergyman. During his youth, Kelly's mother instilled in him a love of the Bible and the natural sciences. He attended the University of Pennsylvania, receiving the A.B. in 1877. Kelly originally intended to become a naturalist, but his father persuaded him to study medicine so that he would have a more secure income. In 1882 he received his M.D. from the University of Pennsylvania. He then served sixteen months as resident physician at the Episcopal Hospital in Kensington, a Philadelphia suburb with many poor. In 1883, upon completion of his internship, Kelly established a two-room "hospital," which by 1887 evolved into the Kensington Hospital for Women and was supported by voluntary contributions. In 1888 Kelly performed the first caesarean section in Philadelphia in fifty years in which the mother survived. Among his colleagues this did much to enhance his reputation as a bold and skillful surgeon. During the year 1888–1889 he served as associate professor of obstetrics at the School of Medicine, University of Pennsylvania.

Kelly spent several months in Europe in 1886, 1888, and 1889. During this last visit he married Laetitia Bredow, the daughter of a prominent professor, Justus Bredow, whom he had met in Berlin; they had nine children. That same year, because of the esteem in which he was held by William Osler, who had moved from Philadelphia to Baltimore as chairman of medicine at the newly founded Johns Hopkins Hospital and School of Medicine, Kelly, "the Kensington colt," was chosen as Johns Hopkins's first professor of obstetrics and gynecology. In 1893, when the medical school opened, it became necessary to provide care for obstetrical patients. This section was developed by John Whitridge Williams. By 1899, wishing to devote himself wholly to gynecology, Kelly turned the instruction of obstetrics over to Williams, and that branch became an independent department. From that time onward Kelly devoted his efforts to gynecology and urology. In 1892 he took over a small sanitarium in Baltimore for his private cases. In 1912 this became the Howard A. Kelly Hospital ("Kelly Clinic"), at which until 1938 he served as physician in chief. During his tenure as chief of gynecology, Kelly fought against the idea of joining gynecology to general surgery and divorcing it from obstetrics. In 1919 the medical school adopted the "full-time" system, whereby professors were required to give up private practice and devote themselves solely to teaching and research. Unwilling to abandon his private patients, Kelly re-signed his professorship. From that time until his death, he was emeritus professor and honorary consultant in gynecology at the Johns Hopkins Hospital. Throughout his life Kelly pursued his interest in natural science, publishing works in ichthyology, herpetology, and anthropology. As a deeply religious Christian fundamentalist, he was a pillar of the Methodist Episcopal church, was active in preaching and evangelism, and lobbied against prostitution and, with the Anti-Saloon League, for prohibition.

During his years at Johns Hopkins, Kelly did much to develop the fields of gynecology, abdominal surgery, and urology. He gathered about him a group of able assistants, including Thomas Stephen Cullen, Hunter Robb, Hugh Hampton Young, and many others. He devised techniques for the diagnosis and treatment of diseases of the kidneys, ureters, and bladder, and he was one of the first to use cocaine for local anesthesia. His interest in cancer, radiation, and radium therapy resulted in many contributions. His name was eponymized in the Kelly pad for obstetrical and surgical tables, the Kelly cystoscope for visualization of the female bladder (he was the first to use air to inflate the bladder for examination and for catheterization of the ureters), the Kelly tubular vaginal and rectal speculae through which diagnostic and therapeutic procedures could be undertaken, and the Kelly operation for the correction of urinary incontinence in women. In 1898 his two-volume magnum opus *Operative Gynecology* appeared, containing a wealth of material. The illustrations were by Max Brödel, a prominent medical illustrator Kelly had attracted from Germany to join him in Baltimore, establishing a department of medical illustration. *Operative Gynecology* played a key role in establishing gynecology as a surgical specialty.

During the following two decades Kelly published a series of other important works, including *The Vermiform Appendix and Its Diseases*, with Elizabeth Hurdon (1905); *Gynecology and Abdominal Surgery*, with Charles P. Noble (2 vols., 1907–1908); *Medical Gynecology* (1908); and *Myomata of the Uterus*, with Thomas S. Cullen (1909). Kelly became interested in the value of photography as an adjunct to the teaching of surgery. To this end he developed a series of stereoscopic pictures, the *Stereo-Clinic* (84 sections, 1908–1915). In addition, he published *Diseases of the Kidney, Ureters, and Bladder*, with F. R. Burnham (1914). Brödel also illustrated most of these works. At a seventy-fifth birthday celebration in Kelly's honor, Brödel credited him with the development of medical illustration as a specialty.

A bibliophile, Kelly became interested in the history of medicine and medical biography, in part because of the influence of Osler. He viewed medical progress largely in terms of the dedicated individual physician and his personal achievements. He read Hebrew, Greek, and Latin, in addition to German and French, and was attracted to seminal works in the evolution of medical thinking. With Osler, William Henry Welch, and others of the Hopkins faculty, he founded the Johns Hopkins Hospital Historical Society. He published *Cyclopedia of American Medical Biography* (1912), which contained biographical essays on about 1,100 eminent deceased physicians and surgeons from 1610 to 1910; *Some American Medical Botanists* (1914); *American Medical Biographies*, with Walter L. Burrage (1920); and *Dictionary of American Medical Biography*, with Burrage (1928).

Among his honors, Kelly was an honorary member of many foreign medical societies. He received the LL.D. from the University of Aberdeen (1906), Washington and Lee University (1906), University of Pennsylvania (1907), Washington College (1933), and the Johns Hopkins University (1939). He was president of the Southern Surgical and Gynecological Society (1907) and the American Gynecological Society (1912). Kelly was made Commander, Order of Leopold of Belgium (1920), and was awarded the Order of the Cross of Mercy of Serbia (1922) and the Cross of Charity of the Kingdom of the Serbs, Croats, and Slovenes (1926). In 1928, on the 200th anniversary of the birth of John Hunter, Kelly delivered the oration to the Hunterian Society of London. In 1943 a U.S. Liberty ship was christened the *Howard A. Kelly*.

Throughout his life Kelly made numerous financial gifts to the Johns Hopkins Hospital and Medical School. He also donated a large collection of portraits of eminent physicians in the United States and abroad and bequeathed his library of over 4,000 rare books and manuscripts to that institution. Kelly died in Baltimore, Maryland.

• Kelly's papers are in the Alan Mason Chesney Medical Archives Division, Library of the Johns Hopkins Medical Institutions. A partial bibliography of his writings is M. W. Blogg, "Bibliography of Howard A. Kelly, M.D., LL.D., Hon. FRCS," *Bulletin of the Johns Hopkins Hospital* 30 (1919): 293–302. A biography is Audrey W. Davis, *Dr. Kelly of Hopkins: Surgeon, Scientist, Christian* (1959). Information on Kelly is in Thomas S. Cullen, "Dr. Howard A. Kelly, Professor of Gynecology in the Johns Hopkins University and Gynecologist-in-Chief to the Johns Hopkins Hospital," *Bulletin of the Johns Hopkins Hospital* 30 (1919): 287–93; "Howard Atwood Kelly, B.A., M.D., LL.D., F.A.C.S.," *American Gynecological Society Album of Fellows* (1930); "Howard Atwood Kelly," *Journal of the American Medical Association* 121 (1943): 277; George W. Corner, "Howard Atwood Kelly (1858–1943) as a Medical Historian," *Bulletin of the History of Medicine* 14 (1943): 191–200; and Willard E. Goodwin, "William Osler and Howard A. Kelly, 'physicians, medical historians, friends': As Revealed by Nineteen Letters from Osler to Kelly," *Bulletin of the History of Medicine* 20 (1946): 611–52.

LAWRENCE D. LONGO

KELLY, Jack. *See* Kelly, John Brendan.

KELLY, John (20 Apr. 1822–1 June 1886), politician, was born in New York City, the fourth of seven children of two Irish Catholic immigrants, Hugh Kelly, a grocer, and Sarah Donnelly. His first ambition was the priesthood, but his father's death, when Kelly was eight, forced him to quit parochial school. After working at a variety of low-paying jobs, Kelly formed a grate and soapstone firm by the time he was twenty-one. He finished his education in night school.

A bright, devout, physically imposing, and engaging person, Kelly became a popular figure in his ward as a volunteer fireman, captain of the Emmet Guards, a militia unit, an amateur actor, and a pugilist. He began his political career as a champion of Catholic and immigrant causes in response to the virulent nativism that infected New York City during the 1840s. In 1853, he joined the influential Tammany Society and was elected an alderman. The following year, he won the first of two successive congressional terms, but he resigned in 1857 to become sheriff of New York County. The office was unsalaried, but the sheriff shared a percentage of all fees. During his seven years as sheriff, Kelly earned the somewhat ironic title of "Honest John." He contributed large sums to Catholic charitable organizations and still managed to amass a fortune estimated at $800,000 by 1867 through both ethical and questionable means. Whatever his methods, money proved unimportant. In 1868, his wife (name unknown) died of consumption, and his three young children died shortly afterward. Kelly was consumed with grief, and he left the city for an extended trip overseas.

Out of the country for nearly three years, Kelly escaped the scandals that destroyed "Boss" William M. Tweed and the old Tammany leadership. To rebuild the shattered democracy, party reformers, led by Samuel J. Tilden, needed Kelly, a man allegedly untouched by corruption who had the support of immigrants, the city's largest bloc of voters. Kelly became the first Catholic leader of the city democracy; he reorganized and consolidated Tammany Hall and the Tammany Society along hierarchical lines, and he laid the foundations for Irish control of local politics, which lasted for nearly sixty years.

In 1876, Kelly started a second family when he married Teresa Mullen; they had two children. Kelly's political position also became more secure. He was city comptroller from 1876 to 1879 and helped reduce the municipal bonded debt. Even so, Kelly was never the undisputed leader of the city democracy. As adept at making enemies as he was at winning friends, he angered other Tammanyites because of his dictatorial methods, alienated reformers by assessing officeholders, and fought with state leaders, especially Tilden, over patronage. Although Kelly remained a power in the city, he lost stature when he lost the race for governor in 1879. Kelly's ill health and poor judgment, particularly in opposing Grover Cleveland's successful presidential campaign in 1884, marked the end of his career. Even before his death in New York City, real power in Tammany Hall had passed to Richard Croker.

• A few of Kelly's personal letters are scattered in a variety of sources, most notably the Samuel J. Tilden Papers in the New York Public Library, the Samuel L. M. Barlow Papers at the Henry E. Huntington Library, San Marino, Calif., and the Thomas F. Bayard Papers in the Library of Congress. Two biographies exist: J. Fairfax McLaughlin, *The Life and Times of John Kelly* (1885), is uncritical and must be treated with caution; Arthur Genen, "John Kelly: New York's First Irish Boss" (Ph.D. diss., NYU, 1971), presents a more balanced picture. See also Euphemia Blake, *History of the Tammany Society from Its Organization to the Present Time* (1901); Matthew P. Breen, *Thirty Years of New York Politics Up-to-Date* (1899); Alfred Constable and Edward Silberfarb, *Tigers of Tammany: Nine Men Who Ran New York* (1967); Alexander Flick, *Samuel Jones Tilden: A Study in Political Sagacity* (1939); Denis T. Lynch, *"Boss Tweed," The Story of a Grim Generation* (1927); Seymour J. Mandelbaum, *Boss Tweed's New York* (1965); Morris R. Werner, *Tammany Hall* (1928); and Gustavus Myers, *The History of Tammany Hall* (1901). A long and useful obituary is in the *New York Times*, 2 June 1886.

JEROME MUSHKAT

KELLY, John Brendan (4 Oct. 1889–20 June 1960), athlete and businessman, was born in Philadelphia, Pennsylvania, the son of John Henry Kelly, a woolen mill worker, and Mary Ann Costello. Both parents were Irish immigrants, and "Jack" Kelly was the youngest boy in a family of ten children. From modest beginnings, the Kellys of Philadelphia's East Falls, a working-class neighborhood near the Schuylkill River, went on to enjoy unusual success in business, entertainment, and sports. Among Kelly's brothers were Walter, a popular vaudevillian known as the "Virginia Judge," and George, an actor and Pulitzer Prize–winning playwright.

Kelly attended Philadelphia elementary schools, quitting after the eighth grade to follow his father and siblings into the neighborhood mill. He joined his brother Patrick's brick contracting firm, advancing from water boy to bricklayer to superintendent. While learning and practicing his trade, Kelly studied estimating and architectural drawing in night school. When time allowed, he devoted his considerable energy to sports.

A gifted athlete, Kelly won recognition in boxing, football, baseball, and basketball as well as in rowing. The Schuylkill River had been one of America's major rowing venues since the early nineteenth century. The young Kelly idolized the amateur champions who raced there and by his late teens was competing himself, winning his first race in 1909. As a member of the Vesper Boat Club, he rowed in single-, double-, four-, and eight-oared events, excelling in single and double sculls.

Both alone and paired with his cousin Paul Costello, Kelly won regularly in major regattas, becoming the nation's leading oarsman in the years just before World War I. He captured the American Henley in 1913 and the National Association of Amateur Oarsmen's singles the following year. Kelly won a record sixteen races in 1916 and over his career compiled a remarkable 126 consecutive victories.

Kelly's great strength and stamina were complemented by innate cunning and adroit strategy. His races were distinguished by explosive starts and superb pacing, by which he always seemed to win by exactly one length.

Kelly served with the U.S. Army in France in 1918, moving rapidly from private to lieutenant by war's end. He boxed to stay in condition, winning twelve heavyweight bouts in a service-sponsored tournament.

After returning to civilian life in 1919, Kelly plunged vigorously into brickwork and rowing. With a loan from his brothers he started John B. Kelly, Inc., and made it one of the country's largest brick construction firms. He also raced unbeaten to a string of rowing titles, including the NAAO singles in both 1919 and 1920.

In 1920 Kelly's application to race in England's Henley Regatta Diamond Sculls was rejected. Popular accounts blamed the rejection on Henley rules barring those who worked with their hands from competing with "gentlemen." However, a long-standing dispute between the Henley stewards and Kelly's club, Vesper, also may have influenced the decision. The former version was resurrected by sportswriters periodically throughout Kelly's life, adding immeasurably to his reputation and making him America's best known bricklayer.

At the 1920 Olympics in Antwerp, Belgium, Kelly scored a still unmatched triumph by winning both the single sculls and, with Costello, the double sculls on the same day. His feat was rendered more remarkable by his having just one hour's rest between events. He avenged the Henley snub by beating Diamond Sculls champion Jack Beresford in the singles final.

At the 1924 Olympics in Paris, Kelly and Costello successfully defended their double sculls title. Kelly earned his third Olympic gold medal, setting a rowing record shared with Costello and Beresford, among others.

Kelly married Margaret Katherine Majer, a magazine cover model and physical education instructor, in 1924. Their four children included son John B., Jr., twice victor in the Diamond Sculls and a four-time Olympian, and daughter Grace, an Academy Award–winning actress and princess of Monaco.

After retiring from competition in 1926, Kelly immersed himself in his family, his business, and his city. He remained close to rowing as a patron of the sport and as his son's coach. Kelly entered politics in the early 1930s, serving as Philadelphia's Democratic party chairman, losing a close and controversial mayoral race in 1935, and serving as Pennsylvania's secretary of revenue in 1936–1937. He then assumed a less active role in political affairs but remained a powerful force in Democratic circles into the 1950s.

Kelly's civic and charitable work, along with his financial, social, and athletic celebrity, made him Philadelphia's most popular and colorful citizen, a role he enjoyed thoroughly. A lifelong exponent of physical exercise, he served as chairman of the Federal Security Agency's Committee on Physical Fitness during World War II. In 1945 he established the John B. Kelly Award to honor those who do the most to promote youth sports.

Residing in a city where his ethnic background, religion, and politics could have held him down, Kelly rose from mill worker to millionaire. The same skill, aggressiveness, and determination he displayed in business carried him from sandlot heroics to international athletic acclaim. His place in rowing history and lore remains secure. During the 1920s, sport's "Golden Age," Kelly dominated his field as Babe Ruth, Red Grange, and Jack Dempsey did theirs. In recognition of his Olympic victories, he was elected to the National Rowing Foundation's Hall of Fame in 1956 as both a single and double sculler. Three years after his death in Philadelphia, a statue of Kelly in a racing shell was dedicated on the banks of the Schuylkill.

• An extensive clipping file on the Kelly family is in the Free Public Library of Philadelphia. There are several collective works on Kelly's family and biographies of his brothers and daughter. Sarah Bradford, *Princess Grace* (1984), provides some information on Kelly's life and personality. The anecdotal *Those Philadelphia Kellys, with a Touch of Grace* (1977), by Arthur H. Lewis, is more complete, if sensationalized. A fawning, sentimentalized account is John McCallum, *That Kelly Family* (1957). Walter C. Kelly, *Of Me I Sing: An Informal Autobiography* (1953), and Foster Hirsch, *George Kelly* (1975), afford a look at Kelly's early years. The less admirable aspects of Kelly's personal life are found in Steven Englund, *Grace of Monaco: An Interpretive Biography* (1984). Details of the 1920 and 1924 Olympic Games and Kelly's participation are found in Erich Kamper, *Encyclopedia of the Olympic Games* (1972); Lord Killanin and John Rodda, eds., *The Olympic Games: 80 Years of People, Events, and Records* (1976); Richard Schaap, *An Illustrated History of the Olympics*, 3d ed. (1975); and David Wallechinsky, *The Complete Book of the Olympics* (1984). Obituaries of Kelly are in the *New York Times* and the *Philadelphia Inquirer*, 21 June 1960.

JOSEPH LAWLER

KELLY, John Brendan, Jr. (24 May 1927–2 Mar. 1985), businessman and athlete, was born in Philadelphia, Pennsylvania, the son of John B. Kelly, Sr., a businessman, and Margaret Majer. The brother of actress Grace Kelly, he was the only son of parents who had distinguished themselves in sports prior to their marriage. His mother had been a competitive swimmer and had earned her college degree in physical education, while his father had won three gold medals in rowing at the 1920 Olympics in Antwerp, Belgium.

Born into a Catholic, Democratic family, Kelly knew affluence from an early age. His father owned a profitable brickwork company in Philadelphia. An early "inheritance" for the young Kelly, however, was unrelated to money. Instead, it was his father's unachieved goal of winning the Diamond Sculls event in London's Henley Royal Regatta. The pressure on Kelly was more than the obligation to win where his father had lost; in 1920 the English had flatly rejected the application of John Kelly, bricklayer.

Therefore, Kelly's early childhood afternoons were rarely spent with siblings or playmates. While other youngsters went from classrooms to traditional after-school activities, Kelly went to the Schuylkill River near the family's home. In a double scull, his father was the instructor; in a single scull, he was Kelly's competitor. Kelly's father eventually bought the Vesper Club, which sponsored swimming and rowing meets. The increased contact with other young athletes proved advantageous. Nevertheless, Kelly passed through childhood and adolescence in constant training for a physically demanding sport.

Kelly completed primary and secondary school at the William Penn Charter School in Philadelphia and the Pennsylvania Military Preparatory School. He then enlisted in the U.S. Navy and served for one year. He would complete another year of active duty in 1951, after which he was a reservist for fourteen years. In 1946 Kelly entered the University of Pennsylvania; by the time he received his degree in economics in 1950, he was better known as a sculler than as a student. After an unsuccessful attempt in 1946, Kelly won the Diamond Sculls event in 1947 and in 1949. With additional victories in the United States and Canadian rowing championships, he gained rowing's Triple Crown.

Several months after the first Diamond Sculls victory, Kelly received the James E. Sullivan Memorial Trophy, established in 1930 to recognize the outstanding amateur athlete in the United States. At twenty years of age Kelly had reached the goal his father had set for him and had joined "the most exclusive fraternity in American amateur sports."

Although Kelly won the single sculls events at the 1955 and 1959 Pan American games, he struggled in his four Olympic appearances. In London (1948) he was defeated in the semifinals. In Helsinki (1952) his success was more personal than athletic; he met Mary Freeman, a member of the swimming team, and married her in 1954. In Melbourne (1956) Kelly won a bronze medal. His Olympic career ended in Rome (1960) in the wake of younger scullers.

As a businessman and citizen of Philadelphia, Kelly seemed to earn the respect of his peers and the reputation of an important civic leader. He took charge of his father's company after his father's death in 1960. Active in Democratic politics, he won a councilman-at-large seat. He received a Philadelphia Zionist Award, and the Junior Chamber of Commerce twice selected him Outstanding Young Man of the Year. He chaired an Easter Seal campaign, and he served a term as president of the Philadelphia Athletic Club. He adjusted his role in athletics to include planning and decision-making, and he was elected president of the Amateur Athletic Union in 1970.

In those male-dominated areas of his life, Kelly had a playboy reputation that seemed to have little negative impact on him. Rationalizing his behavior was fairly easy; he was a handsome man who had been rowing while other teens had played out the issues of adolescence at the appropriate time. Furthermore, his father had enjoyed a similar community standing despite similar behavior.

Kelly's family was not as understanding as his peers. In 1968 his marriage ended after fourteen years and six children. His mother was less supportive of him than she had been of his father years earlier. Some saw Margaret Kelly's hand in Mary Kelly's eleven-year refusal to give Kelly the complete freedom of a divorce. His mother's displeasure with Kelly's personal life became blatantly obvious in 1975. In that year Kelly announced his interest in becoming mayor of Philadelphia. (His father had lost the 1935 mayoral election by a narrow margin.) He attended the appropriate Democratic party events and added to his existing political reputation. However, just prior to the nominating convention, Kelly's mother announced to the press that she would not support her son if the Democrats nominated him, and that she would support any Republican candidate. This action ended Democratic interest in Kelly, although it also ended the possibility that Kelly's alleged relationship with a transvestite would come into question during the campaign.

With politics no longer an option, Kelly continued his work in the family business and in amateur athletics. In 1981 he began his rise to the top of the International Olympic Committee (IOC) when he was elected fifth vice president. His personal life seemed smoother as he settled into his fifties; in 1981 he married Sandra Worley. He also made time for his ongoing commitment to personal fitness. From 1979 to 1983 he won the single sculls event in the Masters Rowing Championships, and he also swam and jogged.

In February 1985 Kelly was elected president of the IOC. His plans for the 1988 Winter and Summer Olympics in Calgary and Seoul, respectively, included more training sites for the athletes and more participation by women and minorities. One month after his election, however, Kelly collapsed and died while jogging near his Philadelphia home. Those who paid their respects in the days that followed demonstrated the diversity of Kelly's work and interests. Kelly's mother, debilitated by a stroke several years earlier, understood as little about his death as about the death of his sister Grace three years earlier.

• Biographies of Grace Kelly contain information about John B. Kelly, Jr. Among those are Robert Lacey, *Grace* (1994), and James Spada, *Grace: The Secret Lives of a Princess* (1987). Newspaper and magazine articles that document events in Kelly's life include *Life*, 28 July 1947, p. 69; *Sports Illustrated*, 10 May 1971, p. 32; and the *New York Times*, 23 Feb. 1948, 8 Aug. 1948, and 10 Feb. 1985. Obituaries are in the *Los Angeles Times*, 4 Mar. 1985, and the *New York Times*, 9 Mar. 1985.

SANDRA L. CLEMENTS

KELLY, King. *See* Kelly, Michael Joseph.

KELLY, Machine Gun (17 July 1895–17 July 1954), criminal, was born George Kelly Barnes, Jr., in Memphis, Tennessee. Little is known about his parents, his childhood, or his early adulthood. He was a student at Tennessee A&M College, where he met Geneva Mae Ramsey. They were married in Clarksdale, Mississippi, in 1919. They evidently had no children. She divorced him in 1926 for desertion and because he was

associating with persons of suspicious background and behavior. He is said to have been in Tennessee, New Mexico, and Texas. He served time in prison for bootlegging, vagrancy, and minor offenses. In 1929 Kelly married Kathryn Shannon Thorne, a 25-year-old "gun moll." They also evidently had no children. She had been married twice before, had been a prostitute, and had associated with known burglars. She bought a machine gun for $250 from a pawnbroker in Fort Worth, Texas, trained Kelly in its use, and nicknamed him "Machine Gun" Kelly after he allegedly wrote his name on a barn wall with bullets from it. The couple formed a criminal gang including friends from Texas and Minneapolis and St. Paul, Minnesota.

Already wanted on bank-robbery charges in four states in the Southwest, Kelly made himself even more notorious by especially vicious criminal activity in 1933. Among the crimes he was accused of that year were killing four police officers and a prisoner at the railroad station in Kansas City, Missouri, robbing the Federal Reserve bank in Chicago and killing a police officer there, and committing a murder in St. Paul. He was placed on the Most Wanted List of the Federal Bureau of Investigation. His most notorious crime occasioned his undoing. On 22 June 1933 Kelly, his wife (who was said to be the brains behind the plan), and Albert L. Bates kidnapped Charles F. Urschel, an oil millionaire and an influential political figure in Oklahoma City, Oklahoma. He was taken from his home by Kelly and Bates, both of whom were armed, was blindfolded and driven to a shack, and was held there for nine days. A ransom of $200,000 was demanded and was paid. Although Urschel heard a young woman arguing that he be killed, he was released unharmed.

Urschel gave details of a bumpy, fourteen-hour ride and of odors, weather conditions, the sound of two airplanes overhead daily with the exception of one day, and so on. These clues enabled FBI agents to locate the shack, which was on a farm in Paradise, Texas, owned by Robert G. Shannon, Kathryn Kelly's stepfather, and his wife Ora. Shannon was an influence peddler in local politics, had contacts with the underworld, and was suspected of providing hideouts at a price for wanted criminals. Shannon and Harvey Bailey, another member of the gang, were arrested with some of the ransom money in their possession. They were tried and sentenced—under the 1932 Lindbergh law making kidnapping a federal crime—to life in prison.

On 26 September 1933 Kelly and his wife were apprehended in a small bungalow in Memphis, Tennessee. The dapper Kelly had dyed his dark hair a lemon yellow, and the couple had "borrowed" Geraldine Arnold, the twelve-year-old daughter of an itinerant worker, so as to present themselves to the world as a harmless little family. Young Geraldine, who sent messages that led the FBI to Kelly, later received some of the reward money. A legend promoted by FBI director J. Edgar Hoover had it that, at the time of his capture, an armed but cowering Kelly shouted,

"Don't shoot, G-men, don't shoot!"—thus coining the term "G-men" for government agents. In truth, a Memphis detective, Sergeant W. J. Raney, entered the bungalow with a shotgun and caught Kelly, who was armed with an automatic. FBI agents remained outside as backup. In no time, G-men became heroes, however. In 1935 alone there were sixty-five movies featuring federal agents, the most famous being *G-Man*, starring James Cagney.

Machine Gun Kelly and his wife were tried, convicted, and sentenced to life imprisonment. Caught earlier in Denver, Bates was also tried, convicted, and given a life sentence; he died in Alcatraz. Later, FBI agents traced most of the ransom money to T. M. Coleman, Kathryn Kelly's grandfather, in Stratford, Oklahoma. It was determined that Coleman's ranch had been the Kelly gang's headquarters since the previous January. Kelly went to the federal prison in Leavenworth, Kansas (Oct. 1933), boasted that he would soon escape, and was transferred as a hardened criminal to Alcatraz (Sept. 1934). He was returned to Leavenworth (June 1951), where he made furniture until his death from a heart attack in the prison hospital. Having boasted that she would soon rendezvous with her husband, Kathryn Kelly was sent to a federal prison at Alderson, West Virginia. After a while she turned against Kelly and blamed him for "this terrible mess." She was later transferred to a workhouse in Cincinnati. She was granted a new trial in 1956 on a technicality and was released two years later without a second trial. She disappeared from recorded history.

• Details of Machine Gun Kelly's life are available in Carl Sifakis, *The Encyclopedia of American Crime* (1982); George C. Kohn, *Dictionary of Culprits and Criminals* (1986); Susan L. Stetler, *Almanac of Famous People* (1989); and Michael Kurland, *A Gallery of Rogues: Portraits in True Crime* (1994). Two books with especially revealing evidence concerning Hoover and the Kelly case are Jay Robert Nash, *Citizen Hoover: A Critical Study of the Life and Times of J. Edgar Hoover* (1972), and Anthony Summers, *Official and Confidential: The Secret Life of J. Edgar Hoover* (1993). An obituary that includes an early photograph of Kelly is in the *New York Times*, 18 July 1954.

ROBERT L. GALE

KELLY, Mervin Joseph (14 Feb. 1894–18 Mar. 1971), engineer and research director, was born in Princeton, Missouri, the son of Joseph Fenimore Kelly, a high school principal, and Mary Etta Evans. As a young child Kelly moved with his family to Gallatin, Missouri, where his father bought a hardware and farm implement store. In 1910 Kelly matriculated at the Missouri School of Mines and Metallurgy with the intention of becoming a mining engineer. He supported himself by working the first two years for the Missouri State Geological Survey as a mineral specimen cataloger and, during the summer after his sophomore year, in a Utah copper mine. This latter experience soured him on a career in mining, and he changed his field of study to general science. For the next two years he worked as an assistant in the chemistry department,

and by the time he received his B.S. in 1914, he had decided on a career in research. He spent the next year teaching physics and studying mathematics at the University of Kentucky, where he received an M.S. in 1915, the same year he married Katharine Milsted; they had two children. He then enrolled in the University of Chicago and studied physics under Robert Andrews Millikan, the first researcher to measure directly the electric charge of a single electron. Kelly received his Ph.D. in 1918.

That same year Kelly became a research physicist in Western Electric Company's Engineering Department, which in 1925 became part of Bell Telephone Laboratories (BTL), the research division of American Telephone and Telegraph Company (AT&T). His first assignment with BTL was to improve the reliability and service life of the vacuum tube, an electronic control device consisting of a heated filament and an electron collecting plate inside an evacuated glass bulb that was employed extensively throughout a telephone line to amplify and repeat a signal. In 1928 he was made the director of vacuum tube development; under his supervision the life span of the vacuum tube was increased by a factor of eighty and a special water-cooled vacuum tube for use in transoceanic submarine telephone cables was invented.

In 1934 Kelly became development director of transmission instruments and electronics at BTL, and in 1936 he was promoted to director of research. In this capacity he implemented an organized, analytical research program in solid-state physics in an effort to develop electronic control devices that did not rely on moving parts, heated filaments, or vacuums. The results of this program were shared with competitors via a patent-licensing symposium created by Kelly in order to stimulate solid-state research throughout the electronics industry. His endeavors in this regard bore fruit in 1947 when three BTL research engineers invented the transistor, an electronic control and amplification device that is smaller, lighter, more rugged, and more efficient and generates considerably less heat during operation than a vacuum tube.

Kelly contributed to the war effort during World War II by overseeing BTL's research for the U.S. government, including the development of microwave radar, gunsight control, and bombsights. He was promoted to executive vice president in 1944 and after the war devoted his attention to the development of peacetime applications of war-related developments, most notably the adaptation of the principles of radar to the development of microwave-relay radio transmission. He also encouraged the development of a call-accounting system that automatically charged telephone calls to the person placing the call, nationwide automatic dialing of long-distance calls, and electronic switchboards and equipment. In 1948 he played a major role in establishing a three-year Communications Development Training Program, known affectionately as "Kelly College," to provide specialized training in electronic technology as it applied to the communications industry for new BTL employees. In 1957 he oversaw the expansion of the CDTP program when New York University's College of Engineering opened a graduate center at BTL specifically designed to support BTL employees seeking graduate degrees.

Kelly became president of BTL in 1951 and chairman of the board in 1958. He retired the next year to become a research management consultant for International Business Machines Corporation. Although IBM retained him in large part to assess its programs and methods, he was particularly interested in and effective at identifying and achieving the promotion of the company's best technical minds. He also consulted for Bausch & Lomb Optical Company, Ingersoll-Rand Company, and Kennecott Copper Corporation and served as a special adviser to the National Aeronautics and Space Administration.

Kelly's achievements as a director of research stemmed partly from his philosophy concerning research and development. He firmly believed that every industrial firm should conduct a certain amount of pure research and that this research should take place along the same lines as academic research in that fundamental developments should proceed on an unscheduled basis and should be supervised by top management with a background in basic scientific research. To this end he advocated "organized creative technology," a three-step process whereby new principles, methods, and materials are discovered via basic research, engineered into new systems and projects, and developed for manufacture and application.

An equally important factor in Kelly's ability to successfully direct the width and breadth of research undertaken at BTL during his tenure was his personality. He was supremely confident in his ability to make the correct decision quickly, a confidence that was well-founded because of his intuitive understanding of the research process, and he implemented his decisions aggressively. His not-infrequent displays of temper earned him a reputation as a "fire-breather" and served to frighten a great many of his people; one of his colleagues refrained from socializing with Kelly "for fear of being struck by lightning" (Pierce, p. 191). On the other hand, he was always willing to listen to reason after he calmed down and admit to his mistakes on those rare occasions when he made them, and he refused to judge his people on any basis other than their ability to get the job done.

Kelly served as chairman of a number of government and professional committees, most notably the Defense Department's Committee on Continental Defense, the National Bureau of Standards' Statutory Visiting Committee, the Advisory Council of Princeton University's Department of Electrical Engineering, the Research Task Force of the Second Commission on Organization of the Executive Branch of the Government (known as the Hoover Commission), and the Science Advisory Board of the U.S. Air Force. He was elected to membership in the National Academy of Sciences and the American Academy of Arts and Sciences. He received the Presidential Certificate of Merit in 1947, the Medal of the Industrial Research

Institute in 1954, the Christopher Columbus International Communication Prize in 1955, the Air Force's Exceptional Service Award in 1957 and its Association Trophy Award in 1958, the National Security Industrial Association's James Forrestal Medal in 1958, the John Fritz Medal in 1959, the American Institute of Electrical Engineers / National Electrical Manufacturers Association's Golden Omega Award in 1960, the Joint Engineering Societies' Hoover Medal in 1961, and the University of Missouri's Centennial Medal of Honor in 1970. In 1960 he was given the AIEE's first Mervin J. Kelly Award in Telecommunications. He died in Port Saint Lucie, Florida.

Although Kelly was a talented researcher in his own right, his most important contribution was his ability to inspire and direct the research efforts of others. In addition to being able to recruit talented people, recognize their good ideas, and drive them aggressively if not relentlessly to develop those ideas into important technological innovations, he was also able to inspire AT&T's top management to allocate the necessary resources to BTL by convincing them of the importance of his people's work to the financial well-being of the company. In so doing, Kelly developed BTL into a complex yet well-run organization and the world's leading industrial research laboratory.

• Kelly's papers have not been located. A biography, which includes a bibliography, is John R. Pierce, "Mervin Joe Kelly," National Academy of Sciences, *Biographical Memoirs* 46 (1975): 191–219. Obituaries are in the *New York Times*, 20 Mar. 1971, and *Physics Today* (June 1971).

CHARLES W. CAREY, JR.

KELLY, Michael Joseph (31 Dec. 1857–8 Nov. 1894), baseball player, was born in Troy, New York, the son of Michael Kelly, an immigrant paper maker from Ireland, and Catherine (maiden name unknown). Kelly spent his formative years in Paterson, New Jersey, where his mother moved following his father's death. Young Mike dropped out of public school to take a position as a bobbin boy at a local textile mill. In 1873 he entered organized baseball with the Troy Haymakers. A two-year stint in his former hometown ended in 1875, when he played his first professional engagement with the Olympics of Paterson. His next stop was Columbus, Ohio, where he played for the Buckeye team for a portion of the 1878 season.

Kelly was recruited to play right field and catch for the Cincinnati Red Stockings of the National League that same year. Manager Cal McVey was not duly impressed with his young charge during Kelly's two years in Cincinnati, but according to Cap Anson, who scouted the young man for the Chicago club, there was more there than met the eye. Anson recalled that Kelly was "young, green, and . . . continually getting tangled in his own legs in an awkward boy fashion. I thought I saw a likely man in him on account of his hitting and base running. These always continued to be his strong points."

On the strength of Anson's recommendations, Kelly was signed by Chicago for the 1880 season. Gifted with a strong and accurate throwing arm, great speed, and an uncanny sixth sense as a hitter, Kelly came into prominence with the talented White Stockings, five-time National League pennant winners during the 1880s.

Kelly alternated between the outfield and catching, but he was also used by Anson at the other infield positions and even pitched in a dozen games. Versatile, flamboyant, and self-assured, he lacked good training habits and self-discipline; when it came to social drinking with the "boys," he was a disappointment to the teetotaling Anson.

Despite his drinking and carousing, Kelly was a hero to young and old, particularly among the Irish immigrants who fancied baseball. He is credited with introducing many innovations to the game. It is believed that he was the first catcher to flash hand signals to his pitchers and middle infielders; while playing the outfield one day and fielding a line drive on the first bounce, he demonstrated the possibility of throwing a runner out at first base.

While weighing Kelly's positive contributions to the national pastime, Bill James concluded in his *Historical Baseball Abstract* (1988) that "half of the National League's rules were written to keep King Kelly from cheating people." Indeed, Kelly never failed to exploit an opponent's weakness or an umpire's gullibility.

Kelly's exploits as a baserunner inspired vaudeville monologist and songwriter John W. Kelly to pen his immortal verse by borrowing from the popular ballpark chant, "Slide, Kelly, Slide!," which echoed across tiny Lakefront Park in Chicago every time the hometown hero came to bat:

Slide, Kelly, Slide!
Your running's a disgrace!
Slide, Kelly, Slide!
Stay there, hold your base!
If someone doesn't steal you!
And your batting doesn't fail you,
They'll take you to Australia!
Slide, Kelly, Slide!

The "Australia" reference had to do with Albert G. Spalding's celebrated 1888 baseball goodwill world tour. First performed in 1889, "Slide, Kelly, Slide!" became one of the most popular songs of its day after the invention of the Edison phonograph cylinder three years later. The song and the lyrics had staying power. In 1927, a Metro-Goldwyn-Mayer film of that name starred William Haines as Kelly.

In February 1887 Spalding, the president of the Chicago club, sold Kelly's contract to the Boston Beaneaters for the then-unheard-of sum of $10,000, the first sale of a "star" player in baseball's early history. It is commonly assumed that Kelly's raucous behavior had finally exhausted the patience of the Chicago management, but Anson said that urgency to maintain competitive balance in the league was an overriding concern. "We let him go to Boston because

a good price was offered at a time when the Chicago club had been too successful and when it was good policy to slightly weaken the club," Anson explained.

Thereafter, Kelly was known to his Boston admirers as the "$10,000 Beauty"—a moniker borrowed from a stage actress of the day. The Boston years marked the first noticeable decline in Kelly's ability. Alcoholism and lack of self-control began to exact a toll. In his four Boston seasons (including the 1890 Players League revolt), Kelly's fame and stature mounted. His image adorned billboards, sheet music, and handbills pasted to every back alley saloon from Charlestown to the North End. But after the 1890 season, when he spurned a $10,000 bribe offer from National League owners to prevent him from jumping to the Players League, his market value dropped precipitously.

The financially strapped New York Giants picked up his contract in 1893. However the ownership failed to keep Kelly sober, and his troubles with the bottle resulted in his playing just twenty games with a paltry .269 batting average. At the end of the season Anson tendered Kelly a conditional offer to return to Chicago in 1894, provided he would abstain from spirits. But Kelly knew it was impossible to meet that demand. Instead, he agreed to manage a veteran team from Allentown, Pennsylvania, and Yonkers, New York (those two teams merged midway through the season), known as the "Terrors," whose actual abilities belied their nickname.

Kelly bowed out of professional baseball in 1894, having completed sixteen seasons, with a composite average of .308, 1,813 hits, and 1,357 runs scored in 1,455 games. He won batting titles in 1884 (.354) and 1886 (.388). With his best days now far behind him, Kelly drifted into the vaudeville circuit, where he reprised the role of Ernest L. Thayer's "Casey at the Bat"; his normally supportive fans were not impressed. Next he opened a saloon with former umpire "Honest" John Kelly in New York, but the venture was short-lived.

On 5 November 1894 Kelly sailed from New York to Boston to complete a theatrical engagement at a local burlesque house. The weather was miserable, and he contracted pneumonia. Three days later he was moved to the Boston Emergency Hospital after his condition had taken a sudden, violent turn for the worse. "This is my last slide," he reportedly whispered to the ambulance attendant. He died later that evening. The next day a *Boston Globe* reporter wrote: "King Kelly heard the decision of the great umpire from which there is no appeal." More than five thousand Bostonians filed by his casket at the Elks Hall, a testament to his enduring popularity. In 1945 Kelly was elected to the National Baseball Hall of Fame.

• A file of clippings on Kelly is in the National Baseball Library, Cooperstown, N.Y. Michael Kelly's *"Play Ball": Stories of the Diamond Field* (1888) offers insights into forgotten nineteenth-century baseball. Kelly has received considerable coverage over the years. See James M. Long, "Long Live the King," *Baseball Magazine*, Nov. 1925; Byron Bancroft Johnson, "Slide, Kelly, Slide!" (ed. George Creel), *Saturday Evening Post*, 12 Apr. 1930; Harry Rayson, "'Slide, Kelly, Slide!' at the Old Ball Game," *Smithsonian*, Oct. 1982. Also see Lee Allen and Thomas Meany, *Kings of the Diamond* (1965); Valentine Davies, "The Great King Kelly," in *The Baseball Reader*, ed. Ralph S. Graber (1951); Robert M. Smith, *Heroes of Baseball* (1952); Roger Angell, ed., *A Baseball Century: The First 100 Years of the National League* (1976); Bill James, *Historical Baseball Abstract* (1988), for some rich anecdotes and critical assessment of Kelly and his teammates; and Arthur Ahrens and Edward Gold, *The Golden Era Cubs, 1876–1940* (1985), for some amusing anecdotes. For a good discussion of "Music of the Game," see Joel Zoss and John Bowman's *Diamonds in the Rough: The Untold History of Baseball* (1989). For Kelly's baseball statistics, see Macmillan's *Baseball Encyclopedia*, 9th ed. (1993); and John Thorn and Pete Palmer, eds., *Total Baseball*, 3d ed. (1993). Concise obituaries are in the *Chicago Inter-Ocean*, the *Chicago Tribune*, the *Chicago Daily News*, the *New York Times*, and the *Boston Globe*, all 9 Nov. 1894.

RICHARD C. LINDBERG

KELLY, Myra (26 Aug. 1875–30 Mar. 1910), educator and author, was born in Dublin, Ireland, the daughter of James Edward Kelly, a physician, and Annie Morrogh. After the family migrated to New York City when she was a child, Kelly's father developed a successful practice on Manhattan's East Side. She attended classes at St. Vincent Convent and Sacred Heart Convent and then was a student at the Horace Mann School (1891–1894) and Teachers College at Columbia University (1894–1899). With a diploma as a teacher of manual training, she taught primary grades at Public School No. 147, east of the Bowery, from 1899 to 1901, and then was a supervisory teacher at the Speyer School of Teachers College in 1902–1903.

Kelly had grown up observing poor families on the East Side, and with compassion, patience, and ingenuity she taught the children of immigrants, mostly Russian Jews, who often had difficulties adjusting socially and educationally. She was inspired by her experiences to write sketches about her pupils' difficulties. She had no difficulty publishing her stories, which were often amusing and fraught with pathos, in popular periodicals. She sent her first story, "A Christmas Present for a Lady," to two magazines and was discomfited when both accepted it, but it was published in December 1902 in *McClure's Magazine*. In this tale, a little Jewish boy gives Constance Bailey, his teacher, a rental receipt marked paid for their tenement hovel; he reasons that because his mother was ecstatically relieved to see it when his father gave it to her, the teacher will be similarly grateful.

Kelly's first book was a collection of ten such stories, *Little Citizens: The Humours of School Life* (1904). Revealing her powers of observation, the stories realistically depict the children's difficulties with language and their sometimes quirky behavior. In the tale "Love among the Blackboards" observant pupils fear that their beloved teacher will get married and leave them. Allan Macnaughtan, president of the Standard Coach Horse Company, read *Little Citizens* and, fascinated by it, sought Kelly's acquaintance. They were married in 1905; the couple had one child, who died in infancy. Their efforts to establish a literary colony near their home in Oldchester Village, Orange Mountains, New Jersey, resulted in Macnaughtan's bankruptcy in 1907.

Continuing to use her professional name, Kelly wrote and published steadily, but she wrote effectively only about her pupils. Thus, her *Wards of Liberty* (1907) is a collection of eight stories about East Side children who speak broken English, suffer in their tenement homes, and adore their teacher. *The Isle of Dreams* (1907) is a dreary novel about a painter who is saddened when she is invited to a country house as one of several weekend guests only to discover that her paintings, supposedly sought by many buyers, have all been purchased by the host. In anguish, she goes abroad in search of professional independence but finds that happiness lies back home. *Rosnah* (1908) features an Irish heiress who decides to impersonate the daughter of a crusty general when he returns from service in India and is a stranger to his own family. *The Golden Season* (1909), another novel, satirizes the antics of slightly unsavory coeds in a New York college; it also delivers a few special jabs at their mothers. With *Little Aliens: A Continuation of Little Citizens* (1910), a book of nine short stories, Kelly capitalized on the popularity of her first book. Its humor shades into deeper sadness as Kelly ever more forcefully depicts the deplorable living conditions and home life of ghetto families. *Her Little Young Ladyship*, a long novel published posthumously in 1911, clearly shows that Kelly's talent lay in shorter fiction.

Kelly wrote *The American Public School as a Factor in International Conciliation*, which was published as an eleven-page pamphlet in 1909 by the American Association for International Conciliation as a small part in an ongoing program to alleviate tensions allegedly caused by immigrants. Ill with tuberculosis from about 1908, she went with her husband to Torquay, in southwestern England, in 1910 in the hope of improving her health along the seacoast, but she soon died there.

In her best fiction, Kelly combines wit, situational humor, and pathos with endearing—if sometimes technically inaccurate—Yiddish-American speech patterns, to create an undercurrent of outrage at the pressures to which immigrants to New York's East Side were subjected as they tried to become Americans. In "In Loco Parentis" a little Jewish child relays his teacher's praise of his uncle thus: "She says all times how you is nice und fat." Kelly was often asked whether she was the model for the delightful teacher in her stories. In her introduction to *Wards of Liberty*, she gives this answer: "I admit regretfully that I was not. 'What I aspired to be and was not' Constance Bailey was. Only her mistakes are mine and her very earnest effort to set the feet of the First Reader Class in the path . . . to American Citizenship." This statement reveals both Kelly's admirable motive and her essential modesty.

• One letter from Kelly is in the Lilly Library, Indiana University; another is in the Lee Library, Brigham Young University. Elias Lieberman, *The American Short Story: A Study of the Influence of Locality in Its Development* (1912), touches not only on Kelly's making humor of her pupils' mangled English but also on her satirizing a stupid school official. Alter Brody, "Yiddish in American Fiction," *American Mercury* 7 (Feb. 1926): 205–7, attempts to demonstrate that the Yiddish-American talk of characters in Kelly's *Little Citizens* is gibberish. David M. Fine, *The City, the Immigrant and American Fiction, 1880–1920* (1977), stresses Kelly's sympathetic presentation of the ignorance, fears, and superstitions of her pupils. Steven L. Piott, "The Lesson of the Immigrant: Views of Immigrants in Muckraking Magazines 1900–1909," *American Studies* 19 (Spring 1978): 21–33, places Kelly's intention to show tenement life in the context of muckrakers, notably Lincoln Steffens. Obituaries are in the *New York Times* and the *New York Tribune*, 1 Apr. 1910.

ROBERT L. GALE

KELLY, Patsy (21 Jan. 1910–24 Sept. 1981), actress, was born Bridget Veronica Kelly, the daughter of John Kelly and Delia (maiden name unknown), who had emigrated from County Mayo, Ireland, and settled in a tough working-class Irish neighborhood in Brooklyn, New York. She began dancing as a child and by the age of thirteen was teaching dance in a New York school. However, it was as a deadpan, wisecracking comic that Kelly first made a mark on vaudeville stages and in musical comedy. She became known as a consummate ad-libber during the three years, beginning in 1926, that she toured in vaudeville as Frank Fay's partner. She made her Broadway debut in the revue *Harry Delmar's Revels* (1927), and her first notable successes came after she parted from Fay and had featured roles in *Earl Carroll's Vanities* (1930), *The Wonder Bar* (1931), which starred Al Jolson (then husband of dancer Ruby Keeler, one of her childhood friends), and *Flying Colors* (1932).

Producer Hal Roach, Jr., spotted Kelly on stage and signed her to a Hollywood contract in 1933 as the replacement for Zasu Pitts in a popular series of comedy short subjects costarring Thelma Todd. Following Todd's sudden and mysterious death in 1936 Roach unsuccessfully paired Kelly with Lyda Roberti. During this period Kelly also appeared in comic supporting roles (most often as a maid or best friend of the heroine) in feature films opposite stars such as Jolson, Bing Crosby, Gary Cooper, Judy Garland, Alice Faye, and Marion Davies. Her feature-length movies of the era include *Going Hollywood* (1933), *The Countess of Monte Cristo* (1934), *The Girl from Missouri* (1934), *Go into Your Dance* (1935), *Every Night at Eight* (1935), *Page Miss Glory* (1935), *Thanks a Million* (1935), *Private Number* (1936), *Sing Baby Sing* (1936), *Kelly the Second* (1936), *Pigskin Parade* (1936), *Wake Up and Live* (1937), *Nobody's Baby* (1937), *Pick a Star* (1937), *Ever Since Eve* (1937), *Merrily We Live* (1938), *There Goes My Heart* (1938), *The Cowboy and the Lady* (1938), *The Gorilla* (1939), *Hit Parade of 1941* (1940), *Road Show* (1941), *Topper Returns* (1941), *Broadway Limited* (1941), *Playmates* (1941), *Sing Your Worries*

Away (1942), *In Old California* (1942), and *Ladies' Day* (1943). Kelly's adeptness at broad physical comedy and the art of the wisecrack, coupled with her musical comedy expertise, gained her ranking among the outstanding popular performers of her time.

Kelly abruptly disappeared from movies in the early 1940s. Many reasons for her departure from the screen have been posited, but a combination of her struggles with alcoholism and the fact that she was a known lesbian in a less accepting era may have been significant factors in stalling her career. Kelly appeared only occasionally in straw hat summer stock theater tours during the 1940s and 1950s, often in productions starring her close friend, the celebrated stage actress Tallulah Bankhead. Kelly also turned up on radio and television sporadically beginning in the 1940s.

In the 1960s Kelly returned to movies in minor comic character roles in films such as *Please Don't Eat the Daisies* (1960), *The Crowded Sky* (1960), *The Naked Kiss* (1964), *The Ghost in the Invisible Bikini* (1966), *Rosemary's Baby* (1968), and in a cameo in *The Phynx* (1970). She also acted in an unsuccessful television series, "Valentine's Day" (1964). The year 1971 brought a significant triumph for Kelly when she returned to Broadway as the boisterous maid in a highly acclaimed revival of the 1924 musical comedy *No, No, Nanette*, starring Keeler (who had also been absent from the stage for many years). Critics rhapsodized about Kelly's rich comic gifts in her scene-stealing part, comparing her favorably with the great comics from the silent and early sound film eras. Kelly won a 1971 Tony Award as best supporting actress in a musical for *No, No, Nanette*. As a result, in 1973 she received costar billing opposite Debbie Reynolds in the successful revival of another old musical comedy, *Irene*, originally produced in 1919. Kelly's raucous performance as Reynolds's beer-guzzling Irish mother garnered her another Tony nomination, again in the supporting category. Jane Powell subsequently replaced Reynolds, but Kelly, basking in her newfound success, stayed with the show until it closed. Following her return to the theatrical limelight, Kelly went on to act in a short-lived television series called "The Cop and the Kid" (1976) and appeared in two films, *Freaky Friday* (1977) and *North Avenue Irregulars* (1979). She died in Woodland Hills, California.

• For information on Kelly, see Boze Hadleigh, *Hollywood Lesbians* (1994); Andy Edmonds, *Hot Toddy!* (1990); and Don Dunn, *The Making of No, No, Nanette* (1972). An obituary is in the *New York Times*, 26 Sept. 1981.

JAMES FISHER

KELLY, Robert Lincoln (22 Mar. 1865–12 Dec. 1954), educator, was born in Tuscola, Illinois, the son of Robert Kelly, a newspaper editor and Republican politician, and Anna Pearson. Both parents were members of prominent Quaker families in Ohio and Indiana, and Kelly grew up in a home steeped in Quaker influence. In 1866 the family moved to Mt. Vernon, Missouri; there Robert Kelly edited a Republican newspaper until 1874, when he moved his family to Bloomingdale, Indiana. Bloomingdale was a large and important Quaker community, and young Robert Kelly was educated in the Bloomingdale Academy, a Quaker secondary school that was regarded as one of the best in the Midwest. Immediately after graduating from the Bloomingdale Academy, he entered Earlham College, a Quaker school in Richmond, Indiana, where he graduated in 1888.

Kelly then became superintendent of schools in another Quaker community, Monrovia, Indiana, before going in 1890 to spend two years as principal of the Raisin Valley Academy, a Quaker school in Adrian, Michigan. In 1890 he also married Cecilia Rifner; they had three children. He spent the years 1893 to 1897 as head of yet another Quaker institution, the Central Academy in Plainfield, Indiana. He also became a recorded Quaker minister.

In 1898 Kelly entered the University of Chicago as a graduate student. He studied child psychology under the direction of John Dewey, specializing in testing procedures. In 1900 he became the acting president of Penn College, a Quaker school in Oskaloosa, Iowa. A year later he returned to Earlham as academic dean and professor of philosophy. He became acting president in 1902 and succeeded to the presidency of Earlham early in 1903.

Kelly served as president of Earlham until 1917. Under his leadership the college made considerable progress in funding and physical facilities. Kelly established important ties with philanthropists, winning money from Andrew Carnegie for a new library and endowment funds from the General Education Board. He focused on higher education by closing the college's preparatory department. The proportion of faculty with earned doctorates increased substantially. Earlham was in the first group of colleges to be accredited by the North Central Association in 1915.

Kelly, however, also presided over some of the most divisive controversies in Earlham's history. He supported religion professor Elbert Russell, an outspoken modernist, in his battles with fundamentalist-leaning Quakers who wanted Russell fired. By 1915, though, Kelly and Russell found themselves at odds over the direction of the college. Kelly saw progress in secularization, in the growth of a student campus culture like that of other colleges, and in downplaying Quaker connections; Russell wanted Earlham to maintain a strong Quaker identity. In the spring of 1915 Russell and his supporters among the faculty and alumni tried to force Kelly out through a board investigation of Kelly's administration. They accused Kelly of tolerating lax discipline in the boys' dormitory, tolerating smoking and drinking by faculty members, attempting to introduce dancing to campus, and financial mismanagement. They failed when the board absolved Kelly, but he was so chastened by his experience that he resigned early in 1917.

Kelly left Earlham to become the executive secretary of the Council of Church Boards of Education (CCBE). It was founded in 1911 to advance the inter-

ests of liberal arts colleges, most of which had denominational ties, and Kelly had been one of the leading spirits behind its organization. In January 1915 he also took a leading role in the founding of the Association of the American Colleges (AAC), in Chicago, being elected its first president. The dominant mood of the AAC in its early days was, as Hugh Hawkins has noted, "resistance to threat": its small colleges faced competition from state universities; groups like the Carnegie Foundation were criticizing the existence of an excessive number of church schools; and there was a widespread feeling that small colleges could not maintain the scholarly standards and quality of teaching found at research universities. Early in 1918, when the AAC established a central office in Chicago, Kelly became its executive secretary as well, although the Council of Church Boards continued to pay his salary until 1929.

Kelly was the critical figure in the early shaping of the AAC and generally in the shaping of cooperative associations in American higher education. While he headed it, the AAC grew from a membership of two hundred to five hundred institutions. He quickly recognized how central philanthropic foundations would become to higher education, and in 1922 he moved the joint CCBE-AAC office to New York City to maintain closer ties to the foundations. Kelly used his position partly to publicize and propagandize for small colleges but also to promote standardization and improvements in quality. That embraced everything from encouraging the use of standard statistical methods to make comparisons easier to setting standards for an "efficient college." Kelly and the AAC, however, resisted further movement toward becoming an accrediting agency. He also was a pioneer in lobbying efforts in Washington by American colleges, especially in the early days of the New Deal, when he was able to influence the provisions of the National Industrial Recovery Act relating to colleges.

Kelly retired from the AAC in 1937. He spent the rest of his life in Claremont, California, where he died.

• There is a small collection of Kelly papers, including an autobiography, in the Friends Collection at Earlham College. The AAC archives are at its headquarters in Washington, D.C. Kelly was the author of numerous articles in religious and educational journals from 1905 to 1940. His most influential books, written while he was with the AAC, include *Theological Education in America* (1924), *Tendencies in College Administration* (1925), and *The Effective College* (1928). For Kelly's early life and career at Earlham, see Opal Thornburg, *Earlham: The Story of the College* (1963). For his career with the AAC, see Hugh Hawkins, *Banding Together: The Rise of National Associations in American Higher Education, 1887–1950* (1992).

THOMAS D. HAMM

KELLY, Walt (25 Aug. 1913–18 Oct. 1973), cartoonist, was born Walter Crawford Kelly, Jr., in Philadelphia, Pennsylvania, the son of Walter Crawford Kelly, a theatrical scene painter, and Genevieve MacAnnula. Two years after Kelly's birth, family moved to Bridgeport, Connecticut, where young Kelly attended Warren Harding High School, publishing cartoons in the school newspaper and yearbook as well as in the *Bridgeport Post*, for which he also reported school news and sports. After graduating in 1930, he worked in a women's garment factory for three years and then joined the *Post* as a reporter. While there, he also produced his first regularly printed comic strip, an illustrated life of the city's most famous hometown boy, P. T. Barnum. Kelly was proud of his experiences as a working newspaperman, and throughout his life his closest friends were journalists.

In 1935 Kelly left Bridgeport to try freelancing his art in New York City, where, he said, he "starved quietly" but did some drawing for the embryonic comic book industry. Late in the year, he moved to Los Angeles because his inamorata in Bridgeport, Helen Delacy, had been transferred there. On 6 January 1936 Kelly joined the growing staff at Walt Disney Studios, working first in the story department, then in animation, on such features as *Fantasia, Dumbo, Pinocchio,* and *The Reluctant Dragon.* In September 1937 he married Delacy; they had three children. Kelly was not happy in the assembly-line work of animated cartooning, and so he seized the opportunity to leave that was afforded by the notorious labor dispute at the studio in the spring of 1941.

The Kellys returned to Connecticut, settling in Darien, from which Walt made frequent forays into New York City to find work. By late 1942 he had landed a regular assignment, drawing for Oskar Lebeck's *Animal Comics,* the first issue of which carried Kelly's feature about a voracious alligator named Albert, an opossum named Pogo, and some other animals in a southern swamp. Kelly worked in comic books for most of the decade, creating material for several Dell titles, and he illustrated some children's books. During World War II he was exempt from active military service because of childhood rheumatic fever, but as a civilian he illustrated dictionaries and language guidebooks for the Foreign Language Unit of the Army Service Forces.

In June 1948 Kelly was hired as art director for the *New York Star,* a short-lived revival of Ralph Ingersoll's crusading liberal journalistic experiment, *PM.* Kelly produced editorial cartoons (in which he represented Thomas E. Dewey as a mechanical man in the presidential race against Harry Truman) and all the other art in the paper, including, from 4 October on, a daily comic strip. For the strip, he resurrected the swampland characters he had created for *Animal Comics,* but now Pogo had the star billing. This incarnation of the feature lasted only until 28 January 1949, when the *Star* folded. Post-Hall Syndicate then began the national distribution of *Pogo* on 16 May 1949.

Pogo quickly transcended the "talking funny animal" tradition of its origins. At its core, the strip was a reincarnation of vaudeville, and its routines were often laced with humor that derived from pure slapstick. Kelly added the remarkably fanciful and inventive language of his characters—a "southern fried" dialect that

lent itself readily to his characters' propensity to take things literally and permitted an unblinking delight in puns. Adrift in misunderstood figures of speech, mistaken identities, and double entendres going off in all directions at once, Kelly's characters pursued various human endeavors without quite understanding their underlying purposes. And that was the trick of Kelly's satire: readers could not help but glimpse themselves in this menage, looking just as silly as they often were.

Kelly added overt political commentary to his social satire in 1952 when some of Pogo's well-meaning friends entered him in the presidential race, and the strip was never quite the same again. The double meaning of the puns took on political as well as social implications, and the vaudeville routines frequently looked suspiciously like animals imitating officials high in government. Kelly underscored his satirical intent with caricature: his animals had plastic features that seemed to change before the reader's eyes until they resembled those at whom the satire was directed. And the species suggested something about Kelly's opinions of his targets. Soviet boss Nikita Khrushchev showed up one time as a piratical pig; Cuba's Fidel Castro, as a goat; the implacable J. Edgar Hoover, as a bulldog. Kelly's first foray into the jungle of politics with caricature as his machete was in the summer of 1953, and his prey was Senator Joseph R. McCarthy, whose self-serving crusade to rout Communists from government yielded a new term for smear campaigning, "McCarthyism." Kelly ridiculed McCarthy in hundreds of newspapers nationwide nearly a year before Edward R. Murrow's celebrated unmasking of McCarthy on television.

One consequence of Kelly's satirical technique was that words and pictures were perfectly and inseparably wedded, the very emblem of excellence in the art of the comic strip: neither meant much when taken by itself, but when blended, the verbal and the visual achieved allegorical impact and a powerful satiric thrust, high art indeed.

In the last years of Kelly's stewardship of the feature, his political satire seemed sometimes a little strained, but his graphics matured into a dazzling display of decorative technique, and he reached for new allegorical heights in a curious long sequence set outside the swamp in "Pandemonia," a venue of the Australian outback that Kelly populated with prehistoric characters and features.

Kelly divorced his first wife in 1951, and later the same year he married Stephanie Waggony, with whom he had three children. She died of cancer in late 1969, and by then Kelly's diabetes and heart condition were creating fatal complications. He was virtually an invalid the last two years of his life; a gangrenous leg was amputated in October 1972, but he continued to produce the strip, even from a hospital room, and worked on an animated cartoon of his creation. He married his animation assistant Selby Daley (Margaret Selby) in 1971, and she supervised the production of the strip after Kelly's death in Hollywood, discontinuing the feature on 20 July 1975, after paying all the medical bills. At its best, *Pogo* was a masterpiece of comic strip art, an Aesopian tour de force—humor at each of two levels, one vaudevillian, the other satirical—and it opened to a greater extent than ever the possibilities for political and social satire in the medium of the newspaper comic strip.

• Kelly's papers and some original art are archived at the Ohio State University Cartoon, Graphic, and Photographic Arts Research Library in Columbus. Biographical information on Walt Kelly is in various volumes that reprint segments of *Pogo*. In *Ten Ever-Lovin' Blue-Eyed Years with Pogo* (1959), Kelly himself traces the history of the strip, annotating certain sequences with biographical background. A series of reprint books edited for Simon and Schuster's Fireside imprint by Selby Kelly and Bill Crouch, Jr., contain autobiographical and biographical articles and essays: *The Best of Pogo* (1982), *Pogo Even Better* (1984), *Outrageously Pogo* (1985), *Pluperfect Pogo* (1987), and *Phi Beta Pogo* (1989). A useful supplement to these materials is Selby Kelly and Steve Thompson, *Pogo Files for Pogophiles: A Retrospective on 50 Years of Walt Kelly's Classic Comic Strip* (1992). Much of the comic strip has been reprinted by Simon and Schuster in two dozen paperback books published during the run of the strip (beginning with *Pogo* [1951] and concluding with *Pogo's Bats and Belles Free* [1976]). Thompson, comp., *Walt Kelly and Pogo: A Bibliography and Checklist* (1987), attempts a complete listing of all Kelly's work and all published information about him. An obituary is in the *New York Times*, 19 Oct. 1973.

ROBERT C. HARVEY

KELLY, Walter C. (29 Oct. 1873–7 Jan. 1939), comedian and actor, was born in Mineville, New York, the son of John Kelly, an insurance broker, and Mary (maiden name unknown). Growing up in Mineville, Kelly became a machinist's apprentice, and while still in his teens he left his hometown to work in the shipyards of Newport News, Virginia.

During a brief layoff at the shipyards, in about 1895, Kelly went with friends to the courtroom of John Dudley Brown, a Newport News judge whose docket typically comprised violators from a variety of ethnic backgrounds—African Americans, Chinese, Japanese, and an assortment of immigrant Irish and Scotch laborers. The judge–a tall, gaunt Virginian who favored an outdated Prince Albert coat in lieu of judicial robes—made a lasting impression on Kelly, as did many of the humorous exchanges that occurred between the judge and those who appeared before him in his basement courtroom.

During a brief tour of duty in the navy during the Spanish-American War (1898), Kelly regaled his shipmates with his "Judge Brown stories," as he called them. Afterward he returned to Newport News and opened a small café, and he was soon persuaded by well-meaning friends and patrons to run for Congress. After an embarrassing defeat, Kelly left Newport News and moved to New York City, where his Judge Brown anecdotes soon earned him extra money as a speaker at Tammany Hall–sponsored rallies and fundraisers. These he parlayed into engagements at the Green Room Club in Manhattan, and it was there that

he was seen by theater producer A. L. Erlanger of the highly successful Klaw & Erlanger partnership. Erlanger offered Kelly a part in a musical adaptation of Mark Twain's *Huckleberry Finn* and also cast him in a minor role in a play called *The Office Boy* (1902–1903), but neither earned him much recognition.

Although the legitimate stage continued to elude him, Kelly was given a career break when the popular comedienne Marie Dressler hired him in the 1903–1904 season for a secondary part in a new vaudeville act she planned to introduce. When Dressler became ill before one of the performances, Kelly asked a wardrobe man to get him a swallowtail coat and a wide-brimmed hat. By curtain time he had transformed himself into a character much like John Dudley Brown in a new act Kelly billed as the "Virginia Judge." The act was an instant success, and from 1904 to 1912 he performed it in vaudeville theaters throughout the United States. He was also engaged for several performances in London.

Drawing upon the anecdotes and incidents he had witnessed in Judge Brown's courtroom, Kelly had a lode of material he could use for his act. When he wanted help polishing some of his routines he called upon his brother George Kelly, a fledgling writer who also aspired to a theatrical career. Walter Kelly built a small fortune with his Virginia Judge act on the Keith and Orpheum vaudeville circuits, yet he still wanted to pursue roles in the legitimate theater.

In 1914 Kelly was given a role in the play *The Whirl of the World* at the Winter Garden, but the production closed not long after its premiere. Thereafter he returned to the Keith circuit through the mid-1920s, at which time he accepted a long series of engagements in England. In the late 1920s he was still performing as the Virginia Judge in vaudeville, but he was also beginning to get character roles in such Broadway productions as *The Passing Show* (1927) and *The Great Day* (1929). During the 1920s his brother George was establishing himself as a playwright, commencing with *The Torchbearer* (1922) and *The Show-Off* (1924), which he had adapted from a well-known vaudeville sketch titled "Poor Aubrey." In 1925, while his brother was performing the Virginia Judge in England, George won a Pulitzer Prize for *Craig's Wife*, a play about feminine possessiveness.

In the early 1930s Kelly became interested in motion pictures, and he was given a small role in *Seas Beneath* in 1931. Two years later he returned to the stage and received rave reviews as the corrupt Congressman Solomon Fitzmaurice in the Maxwell Anderson hit, *Both Your Houses*. In 1935 he returned to Hollywood, where he appeared in two more films, *McFadden's Flats* and *The Virginia Judge*, the latter featuring material from his long-running vaudeville act. The following year he made his fourth and last film, *Laughing Irish Eyes*; he then returned briefly to the stage in a play called *Lend Me Your Ears*. His last performance took place in that production in October 1936, after which he retired.

Despite the well-documented popularity of the Virginia Judge, Kelly's comedy was something of an anachronism by the late 1920s, relying as it did on turn-of-the-century racial stereotypes that once pervaded vaudeville and music halls. Much of Kelly's Virginia Judge material was incorporated into a long-running series of phonograph recordings he made for the Victor Talking Machine Company after World War I. Like the "coon songs" and "darky comic specialties" that dotted the catalogs of the Edison and Columbia companies at that time, the Victor discs of the Virginia Judge featured characters and racial epithets that were increasingly frowned upon in polite society. Like his vaudeville act, however, Kelly's recordings had a loyal following, and they were still featured in the Victor catalogs in the early 1930s.

Kelly's 1936 retirement coincided, ironically, with the failure of *Reflected Glory*, his brother George's Broadway play. Another brother, Jack, parlayed a highly successful athletic career (including a winning Olympic performance in sculling) into a position of influence as a Democratic party leader in Philadelphia. Both Jack and George were at their brother's side when Kelly died in Philadelphia three weeks after he had been struck by an automobile in Hollywood. He had never married. Among the mourners at the funeral was Jack's young daughter, Grace, who was also destined for a show-business career, and whose life would eventually assume near-mythic proportions when she became Princess Grace of Monaco.

• Kelly is profiled in Abel Green and Joe Laurie, Jr., *Show Biz: From Vaude to Video* (1953); *Who Was Who in the Theatre, 1912–1976: A Biographical Dictionary of Actors, Actresses, Directors, Playwrights, and Producers of the English-Speaking Theatre* (1978); and Evelyn Mack Truitt, *Who Was Who on Screen* (1983). His stage performances as the Virginia Judge were reviewed regularly in *Variety* and *Billboard* throughout his vaudeville career. See, for example, "Walter Kelly's 'Judge'" *Variety*, 15 June 1918. For complete information about Kelly's recordings for the Victor Talking Machine Co., including unissued as well as issued performances, see Ted Fagan and William R. Moran, *The Encyclopedic Discography of Victor Recordings*, vol. 3 (1997).

JAMES A. DRAKE

KELLY, William (21 Aug. 1811–11 Feb. 1888), inventor in steel processing, was born in Pittsburgh, Pennsylvania, the son of John Kelly, a prosperous property owner, and Elizabeth Fitzsimons. The boy attended public schools in Pittsburgh. His biographer John Newton Boucher says that Kelly studied metallurgy but does not indicate where or how.

At the age of thirty-five, Kelly was engaged in a wholesale dry goods business in Pittsburgh and Philadelphia with his brother John and a brother-in-law named McShane. Among his duties was visiting customers in Pennsylvania, Ohio, Indiana, Kentucky, and Tennessee to collect on accounts and obtain new orders. On a trip to Nashville, Tennessee, in 1846, he met Mildred A. Gracy from Eddyville in southwestern Kentucky, and he went there to court her. In the vicinity he found a furnace and forge for iron, with satisfactory iron ore and considerable timber for making charcoal. He and his brother John transferred their business to McShane, and in 1846 or 1847 they bought the furnace and fourteen thousand acres of land along the Cumberland River. Kelly married Gracy at that time; they had several children.

The brothers worked the property for about a year, using ore found on the surface and producing iron kettles for boiling sugar. When they had exhausted the surface ore, they began shallow mining, but they were rapidly depleting the timber. At that time, iron ore was smelted into pig iron, then refined by alternating layers of charcoal and pig iron, firing the charcoal, and blasting the mass with air and more charcoal to increase the heat to vaporize the impurities and obtain malleable iron or steel. Kelly observed white-hot molten iron under the air blast and concluded that cold air introduced into the hot furnace would itself combine with carbon impurities and increase the heat. In 1847, to test this idea, he built a carefully designed furnace that he called a converter. When it failed to work satisfactorily, he built another. Creditors, including his father-in-law, believed that his cold-air process was ridiculous and insisted that he devote more time to managing the furnace and manufacturing iron products. His father-in-law even concluded that Kelly was of unsound mind and called a local physician to examine him, but the doctor, Alfred H. Champion, recognized the scientific basis for Kelly's work and became a strong supporter.

After completing a new blast furnace for his company in 1851, Kelly renewed his experiments. Over eighteen months he somewhat secretively built a series of converters, steadily improving them. He succeeded in making malleable iron, but the results were inconsistent, probably because of variations in the ore. He called his method the "pneumatic process" (from the Greek word for air), and it saved both fuel and time. With iron so produced he made large kettles and boiler plates for river steamboats. Not comfortable with using slave labor, he arranged to import ten Chinese workers, said to be the first brought to the United States (Boucher, p. 26).

Kelly hoped to improve his process for consistent results. When he learned that Henry Bessemer in England had applied for a U.S. patent on a similar process, granted on 11 November 1856, Kelly too applied for a patent, which was granted on 23 July 1857. Between these dates, a U.S. patent was granted to Robert F. Mushet of England on 26 May 1857 for adding specific amounts of iron, carbon, and manganese to cast iron to make steel. Mushet lost his significant patent in England through the neglect of his trustees, and there it became public property. In Kelly's claim it was noted that he had been making steel by his process for at least seven years before Bessemer applied for a patent in England. The U.S. acting commissioner of patents, S. T. Shugert, in April 1857 concluded that Kelly was the first inventor of the process. However, Bessemer was able to go into major production in England, where he held patents.

The panic of 1857 drove Kelly to bankruptcy. With support from the ironmaster Daniel J. Morrell of Johnstown, Pennsylvania, in 1857 Kelly built a new converter there and successfully demonstrated the production of steel from pig iron with cold air. About 1858 he and his family moved to Wellsville, Ohio. In 1861 Eben B. Ward of Detroit, Michigan, and Z. S. Durfee of New Bedford, Massachusetts, bought control of Kelly's patent. Operating as the Kelly Pneumatic Process Company, a firm in which Kelly retained some financial interest, they built a steel plant at Wyandotte, Michigan, where timber and iron ore were available. Kelly and his family moved to Louisville, Kentucky, in 1862, and he went into manufacturing axes.

In 1863 three others joined the Kelly Pneumatic Process Company and obtained patent rights from Mushet. This company in September 1864 produced the first steel by the Kelly method in the United States. Simultaneously, three men obtained control of Bessemer's U.S. patent on his machinery and began producing steel at Troy, New York, in 1865, but without Mushet's or Kelly's patents. To settle lawsuits, the two companies merged in 1866 as the Pneumatic Steel Association, but for unexplained reasons the agreement provided only 30 percent for the company that included Kelly, in spite of the importance of his patent. The consolidation required that the Bessemer name be used for the process, because it was associated in the United States with imported English steel, especially for railroad rails.

Kelly and Bessemer both applied for renewals of their U.S. patents that would expire in 1871. Iron manufacturers and railroad companies strongly protested the renewals, hoping to avoid paying royalties. Bessemer's application was refused in 1870 on the basis that he did not originate the process, while Kelly's patent was renewed for seven years. He considered that the renewal belonged to Ward, Durfee, and their associates as part of his original sale, and so he accepted very reduced royalties. As the production of steel increased greatly within a few years, Kelly's royalties amounted to about $450,000. He devoted his later years to real estate and investments and died in Louisville.

• James M. Swank, *History of the Manufacture of Iron in All Ages* (1892), describes the development of the process that came to be called Bessemer steel, including Kelly's role. John Newton Boucher, *William Kelly: A True History of the So-Called Bessemer Process* (1924), gives some details of Kelly's life and his various patents. Douglas Alan Fisher, *The Epic of Steel* (1963), pp. 114–22, also summarizes the sequence of inventions.

ELIZABETH NOBLE SHOR

KELLY, Wynton (2 Dec. 1931–12 Apr. 1971), jazz pianist, was born in Jamaica. Little is known of either his mother or father except that they were both of West Indian heritage. His family moved to Brooklyn when he was four and Kelly attended both Music and Art High School and Metropolitan Vocational. In an interview with Gene Lees for *Down Beat*, Kelly said he was unable to study piano at either institution, so he studied string bass and theory instead.

Kelly first worked professionally at thirteen. By the time he was fifteen, he was touring the Caribbean with bop tenor saxophonist Ray Abrams. Abrams's combo, which included Kelly, drummer Lee Abrams (Ray's brother), baritone saxophonist Cecil Payne, bassist Ahmad Abdul-Malik, and alto saxophonist Ernie Henry, also worked around Brooklyn. Kelly also played with Kansas City stylists tenor saxophonist Hal Singer and trumpeter Oran "Hot Lips" Page. He worked nearly a year with rhythm-and-blues tenor saxophonist Eddie "Lockjaw" Davis. Another experience mentioned by Kelly himself was a little-known group called The Three Blazes.

Kelly joined singer Dinah Washington as accompanist for three years around the time he first recorded for Blue Note; it is likely that this association is where he formed his penchant for popular song form. His first album as leader was a ten-inch trio recording for Blue Note that was never issued. By 1951 he was leading trio dates for Blue Note with swing bassists Oscar Pettiford and Franklin Skeete and former colleague Lee Abrams, a musical collaboration that resulted in the albums *New Faces, New Sounds* and *Piano Interpretations by Wynton Kelly*. Kelly joined Dizzy Gillespie in 1952 as pianist for Gillespie's big band, where he played until he was drafted into the army later that year. He also worked with tenor saxophonist Lester Young in 1952. Upon Kelly's discharge in June 1954, he rejoined Gillespie until late 1957. Kelly was featured on at least four recordings with Gillespie in 1957, most notably *The Big Band Sound of Dizzy Gillespie*.

He recorded and performed with J. J. Johnson in 1954 on *The Eminent J. J. Johnson I*, with bassist Charles Mingus and drummer Kenny Clarke. He was also featured on tenor saxophonist Sonny Rollins's *Sonny Rollins I* (1956) and *Newk's Time* (1958), which is a particularly strong Kelly feature with bassist Doug Watkins and drummer Philly Joe Jones. Some of Kelly's finest recorded playing may be found on a 1958 recording by trumpeter Blue Mitchell's sextet, which included Curtis Fuller on trombone, Johnny Griffin on tenor sax, Wilbur Ware on bass, and Philly Joe Jones on drums. Kelly also appeared on the main take of "Naima" on tenor saxophonist John Coltrane's milestone album *Giant Steps* (1959).

Trumpeter Miles Davis recruited Kelly in 1959 for his rhythm section. He liked Kelly's lyrical simplicity and uncomplicated touch. The transition from Bill Evans to Wynton Kelly in the Miles Davis quintet was documented by Kelly's sole performing contribution, the twelve-bar blues "Freddie Freeloader," to *Kind of Blue* (1959), the landmark album that defined the movement known as modal jazz. With the addition of bassist Paul Chambers and drummer Jimmy Cobb, one of jazz's legendary rhythm sections was created.

Miles Davis's recording *Someday My Prince Will Come* (1961) showed Kelly's diverse nature as a sideman—a florid, staccato, right-hand melodic style contrasted by a myriad of voicings and a richness of harmonic accompaniment, which remained on top of the beat with a wonderful sense of swing. Another notable recording was a 1960 session in Stockholm, which featured the rhythm section alongside Davis and Coltrane. In 1961 this quintet also performed a concert at Carnegie Hall. Kelly remained with Davis from 1959 until 1963, at which time Davis's entire rhythm section left to further their efforts as a trio.

Kelly had often performed and recorded in a trio setting. A notable recording in 1958, *Wynton Kelly I*, included Chambers, Cobb, and bass player Sam Jones. The trio recorded several albums together in the early 1960s, including *Kelly at Midnite* (1960), *Autumn Leaves* (1961), and *Wynton Kelly II* (1961). Albums that presented headliners that performed with the trio include *Kelly Blue* (1959), a classic album featuring Nat Adderley on trumpet, Benny Golson on tenor saxophone, and Bobby Jaspar on flute, and *Gettin' Together* (1960), which featured the trio with saxophonist Art Pepper. *Kelly Great!* (1959) was recorded with a quintet. A favorite addition to the trio was guitarist Wes Montgomery, as shown by the albums *Bags Meets Wes* (1961), with Montgomery and Modern Jazz Quartet vibraphonist Milt Jackson; the live album *Full House* (1962), with Montgomery and Johnny Griffin; and two recordings from 1965, *Smokin' at the Half Note* and *Wynton Kelly and Wes Montgomery*.

Throughout the late 1950s and early 1960s Kelly was considered the quintessential sideman, constantly in demand for recording and club dates. He possessed an uncanny ability to comp (accompany in a jazz setting) with a proper balance of background harmony and melodic material without interfering with the soloist. He recorded as sideman with Cannonball Adderley, John Coltrane, Art Farmer, Benny Golson, Dexter Gordon, Johnny Griffin, Jimmy Heath, Ernie Henry, Illinois Jacquet, Blue Mitchell, Steve Lacy, Art Pepper, Wayne Shorter, and Clark Terry.

Kelly worked and recorded frequently with several musicians whom he had met through Gillespie's big band. Tenor saxophonist Hank Mobley, who had worked with Gillespie initially in 1953, also performed at Miles Davis's 1961 Carnegie Hall concert with Kelly and bassist Paul Chambers. Kelly performed along with trumpeter Lee Morgan in Gillespie's big band throughout 1957. The combination of Mobley, Morgan, Kelly, and Chambers was particularly successful, and they recorded together on a number of occasions. Both Kelly and Chambers also served as sidemen with Hank Mobley on four noteworthy recordings for Blue Note during 1960 and 1961, *Soul Station, Roll Call, Workout,* and *Another Workout.*

Kelly remained active as a leader and sideman until his untimely death. He recorded two albums with Claus Ogermann and His Orchestra in 1963 and 1964, as well as the albums *Undiluted* (1965), *Blues on Purpose* (1965), and Kelly's last recording as leader, *Full View* (1967). If not the final recorded appearance of Kelly, the last recorded concert appearance by Kelly was *Wynton Kelly and George Coleman in Concert* (1968).

Kelly was a heavy drinker throughout his life. In 1971 he experienced an epileptic seizure in Toronto that killed him. He was only thirty-nine years old. It is believed that Kelly never married or had any children.

Kelly's style was influenced by pianists such as Erroll Garner, Bill Evans, Phineas Newborn, Jr., Oscar Peterson, Walter Bishop, Jr., and McCoy Tyner. He listened to Clyde Hart and Bud Powell as models for his comping style. Kelly truly loved to comp, which led to his ultimate success as a jazz pianist. Powerfully rhythmic with boundless energy, Kelly propelled the tempo easily with a light sound and a firm, clearly articulated touch that remained underneath the overall texture of the ensemble. Kelly attentively contributed exactly what was needed to enhance a soloist, from simple block harmonies to rhythmic vamps and extended chord clusters. In addition, he was one of the few great pianists whose reputation rested on a mastery of the 32-bar popular song form. Complacent yet intelligently calculated, Kelly's style wore the mark of a virtuoso.

A consistent and prudent musician, Kelly was admired by audiences and performers alike. His style influenced countless jazz musicians such as the entire Marsalis family, bassist and Kelly's cousin Marcus Miller, and several generations of pianists, including noted contemporaries Herbie Hancock and McCoy Tyner.

• David Rosenthal, *Hard Bop: Jazz and Black Music 1955–1965* (1992), offers outstanding insight into Kelly's style with a thorough analysis of Kelly's last album as leader, *Full View.* An excellent assessment of Kelly's recording career as leader and sideman is Tom Piazza, *The Guide to Classic Recorded Jazz* (1995). Gene Lees's interview in *Down Beat* 30, no. 1 (1963): 16, offers background regarding his playing career and style. See Michael Cuscuna's liner notes to *Wynton Kelly—New Faces New Sounds/Piano Interpretations* (Blue Note CDP 7 84456 2, 1991) and Richard Palmer, "Wynton Kelly," *Jazz Journal International* 39, no. 4 (1986): 15–16, for additional historical context. An obituary is in *Down Beat* 38, no. 11 (1971): 11.

DAVID E. SPIES

KELPIUS, Johannes (1673–1708), mystic and communitarian leader, was born in the Schässburg region of Transylvania-Saxony, the son of Georg Kelp, a Lutheran pastor (mother's identity unknown). Young Kelp (Latinized as Kelpius) studied at three universities (Tübingen, Leipzig, and Altdorf) and received a master's degree from Altdorf in 1689 with a treatise on natural theology. The scholarly world was also impressed by two more technical publications on ethics and theology, which he completed by the age of seventeen. He met the learned Johann Jakob Zimmermann, with whom he shared a deep interest in the theosophy of the shoemaker-mystic Jakob Boehme and the cabalistic speculations of the Rosicrucians. Kelpius accepted the calculations of Zimmermann, a noted mathematician, that the millennium would arrive in 1694, and he joined the pietist brotherhood of scholars (the Chapter of Perfection), who decided that the New World was the right place to await the Second Coming.

Zimmermann died shortly before the Chapter of Perfection was to embark at Rotterdam in August 1693, and the youthful Kelpius was elected as his successor. The trip to Pennsylvania was interrupted by a six-month stay in England, made necessary by the turbulence of King William's War. The group took advantage of the delay to draw close to the Philadelphian Society, led by Jane Lead(e), whose members were also followers of Boehme. These English "Behmenists" came to consider the Zimmermann/Kelpius initiative as part of their own mission.

Finally, the group left England in February 1694, undertaking the dangerous Atlantic crossing. They arrived on the Maryland shore in late June and made their way to the Philadelphia area. Germantown, north of the city, had become since 1683 the preferred destination for German settlers. It was on the "Ridge" along the Wissahickon Creek near Germantown that the newcomers established their cenobitic community. Members built a communal structure (the "Tabernacle") to house religious exercises and a school but lived in separate, primitive cells. Kelpius occupied a cave where he read and meditated. They called themselves the Contented of the God-Loving Soul, but outsiders often referred to them as the Society of the Woman in the Wilderness, after the esoteric passage in Revelation 12:6.

Kelpius and the others followed a semimonastic discipline of prayer, study, and astronomical observation. They also, however, taught the local children, held public worship services on the Ridge and in Germantown, and were known as good neighbors. They laid out a herbarium to raise medicinal herbs for use by the ill. Kelpius and his closest associate, Johann Gottfried Seelig, composed many hymns, some of which have been preserved. Kelpius's best-known writing was translated as *A Short, Easy, and Comprehensive Method of Prayer* (1761), which may have been first published in German in 1700. He never married.

With the delay of the anticipated millennium, some members drifted away into secular occupations, and some married. Several became active in the controversial religious life of colonial Pennsylvania, including Daniel Falckner and Justus Falckner (Lutherans) and Heinrich Bernhard Köster (Quaker, Anglican, and separatist), an associate of the controversialist George Keith. The saintlike Kelpius regretted religious strife and stayed true to his mystical beliefs. He corresponded avidly with Philadelphians in England, Pietists in Germany, and the religiously interested in America, including Seventh Day Baptists, Quakers, and Mennonites. He died of tuberculosis along the Wissahickon sometime before May 1708, still anticipating the end of the world. John Greenleaf Whittier immortalized him in his poem *The Pennsylvania Pilgrim* (1872) as "painful Kelpius from his hermit den / By Wissahickon, maddest of good men."

• Kelpius's devotional work was republished as E. Gordon Alderfer, ed., *A Method of Prayer* (1951), and contains a long biographical essay by the editor. A manuscript containing Kelpius's hymns, "Die klägliche Stimme der Verborgenen Liebe . . . " (c. 1705), was reproduced in *Church Music and Musical Life in Pennsylvania* (1926) by the Pennsylvania Society of the Colonial Dames of America. His diary was edited and published by Julius F. Sachse, "Diarium of Magister Johannes Kelpius," *Pennsylvania-German Society, Proceedings and Addresses* 25 (1914 [1917]), which also includes his known correspondence. The original diary is in the Historical Society of Pennsylvania in Philadelphia. Sachse gave extensive space to Kelpius in his monograph, *The German Pietists of Provincial Pennsylvania* (1895; repr. 1970). The most complete study is Willard M. Martin, "Johannes Kelpius and Johann Gottfried Seelig: Mystics and Hymnists on the Wissahickon" (Ph.D. diss., Pennsylvania State Univ., 1973). See also Elizabeth Fisher, "'Prophesies and Revelations': German Cabbalists in Early Pennsylvania," *Pennsylvania Magazine of History and Biography* 109 (1985): 299–333; Donald F. Durnbaugh, "Work and Hope: The Spirituality of the Radical Pietist Communitarians," *Church History* 39 (1970): 72–90; and Ernest L. Lashlee, "Johannes Kelpius and His Woman in the Wilderness," in *Glaube, Geist, Geschichte: Festschrift für Ernst Benz*, ed. G. Müller and W. Zeller (1967).

DONALD F. DURNBAUGH

KELSER, Raymond Alexander (2 Dec. 1892–16 Apr. 1952), bacteriologist and veterinarian, was born in Washington, D.C., the son of Charles Kelser, a mechanic, and Josie Mary Potter. The family, which was not well off, lived in Baltimore, Maryland, for a few years before returning to Washington. There Kelser attended public schools and decided during his elementary grades that he would enter medicine or law. His interest in law was the result of spending "countless hours" attending sessions of Congress and of various courts.

At the urging of his father, who could not afford the cost of higher education, Kelser attended the high school that offered a business course in spite of his own preference for academic preparation. At the age of seventeen, in order to earn money for college, he took and passed a civil-service examination for the position of "messenger" and was assigned to the Bureau of Animal Industry of the U.S. Department of Agriculture. There the chief of the Pathological Division, John R. Mohler, encouraged the young man and turned his interest to veterinary medicine. Kelser completed high school by means of evening classes.

Determined to attend college while still employed, Kelser enrolled in the School of Veterinary Medicine of George Washington University. Again through attending evening classes, he completed the degree of doctor in veterinary medicine in 1914. That same year he married Eveline Harriet Davison; they had one daughter.

Also in 1914 Kelser became a bacteriologist for the H. K. Mulford Company in Glenolden, Pennsylvania, but the position did not appeal to him. After a civil-service examination, he returned that same year to the Bureau of Animal Industry in Washington. There he was first assigned to fieldwork in Pennsylvania on an epidemic of foot-and-mouth disease in hoofed animals. With others in the bureau he began studies of treatments used for various diseases in animals. These projects included determining that the therapeutic activity of anthrax serum was the globulin. With colleague Adolph Eichhorn, Kelser developed a spore vaccine for anthrax that was an improvement over the bacterial vaccine that had been developed by Louis Pasteur in 1881. Kelser analyzed the techniques for immunizing animals against blackleg and determined the mechanisms of the disease. He also studied the causes of equine infectious abortion.

In 1918 Kelser became a lieutenant in the newly established Veterinary Corps of the U.S. Army, serving in veterinary laboratories in San Francisco and at the University of Pennsylvania. In 1920 he resigned his commission, went back to the Bureau of Animal Industry for a few months, and then returned to military service in the army, where he advanced in rank to brigadier general and in position to chief of the Veterinary Corps before his retirement in 1946.

From 1921 to 1925 Kelser was chief of the Veterinary Laboratory Division at the Army Medical School in Washington, D.C. He also enrolled as a graduate student at American University, from which he received an A.M. in 1922 and a Ph.D. in veterinary science in 1923. He began studies of filterable viruses, which can pass through filters that restrict bacteria and which were beginning to be recognized as causing a number of diseases in animals and humans. In 1921 and 1922 Kelser published on equine infectious anemia and equine influenza and their treatments in the *Journal of the American Veterinary Medicine Association*. He also developed an improved test for botulinum toxin in canned foods, a source of illness in humans.

From 1925 to 1928 Kelser was in the Philippine Islands as a member of the Army Department Research Board. His most significant accomplishment there was devising a vaccine for rinderpest (cattle plague), which affected cattle and the water buffalo used in agricultural fields in those islands. This was the first use of chloroform to inactivate a live virus for a vaccine. The vaccine eradicated rinderpest in the Philippines, and the disease has since been considerably reduced elsewhere by vaccination. Kelser also determined that the horse disease surra was transmitted by the horsefly *Tabanus striatus* and that the animal hosts were cattle and water buffalo, from which the fly acquired the protozoan parasite. He published the *Manual of Veterinary Bacteriology* in 1927, a widely used text that he revised four times; the fifth edition was coauthored with H. W. Schoening in 1948.

In 1928 Kelser returned to the Veterinary Laboratory Division at the Army Medical School. He created an improved vaccine for rabies, which used chloroform as the inactivating agent. In this project he found that infected tissue from the animal was a necessary in-

gredient along with the live virus. He also investigated equine encephalomyelitis, for which the means of transmission was then unknown. Through experiments with guinea pigs he found that the virus could be transmitted by a mosquito, and he then proved the point with horses. This important observation, said his biographer Richard E. Shope, "constituted the first demonstration of transmission of a neurotrop[h]ic virus by an insect" (p. 208). It led to discoveries by other scientists on transmission of certain viral infections by insects.

Kelser was a research fellow from 1933 to 1935 at the Harvard Medical School, where, working with bacteriologist Hans Zinsser, he devoted his time especially to perfecting laboratory techniques. In 1935 he was assigned by the army to Gorgas Hospital in the Panama Canal Zone. There he devised an improved technique for identifying the tropical American chagas disease in humans, which is caused by a protozoan.

From 1938 to 1946 Kelser was chief of the Veterinary Corps in Washington, D.C., serving through the wartime period that necessitated an increase in personnel from 126 to more than 2,200. He was considered very competent in handling the added duties of his post and in his interaction with other federal offices.

After his retirement from the army in 1946, Kelser became professor of bacteriology and dean of the School of Veterinary Medicine at the University of Pennsylvania until his death. There he increased the faculty, the research programs, and the buildings of the school. He served as a consultant to various federal offices.

Kelser was a pioneer in modern veterinary medicine, to which he introduced meticulous laboratory techniques. Some of his areas of research arose from his own intuition, and he solved several significant problems in diseases of animals. He was elected to the National Academy of Sciences in 1948. He died in Philadelphia, Pennsylvania.

• Significant papers by Kelser include "Identification of *Bacillus botulinus* and Its Toxin in Culture and in Canned Foodstuffs by Serological Methods," *American Journal of Public Health* 12 (1923): 366–76; "A Study of Rabies from the Standpoint of Etiology," *Journal of the American Veterinary Medicine Association* 46 (1924): 678–89; "An Improved Vaccine for Immunization against Rinderpest," *Philippine Journal of Science* 36 (1928): 373–93; and "Mosquitoes as Vector of the Virus of Equine Encephalomyelitis," *Journal of the American Veterinary Medicine Association* 82 (1933): 767–71. Two anonymous tributes to Kelser are in *Veterinary Medicine* 47 (1952): 250, and in *Journal of the American Veterinary Medicine Association* 120 (1952): 398–400. A biography by Richard E. Shope in National Academy of Sciences, *Biographical Memoirs* 28 (1954): 198–221, includes a bibliography. An obituary is in the *New York Times*, 17 Apr. 1952.

ELIZABETH NOBLE SHOR

KELSEY, Francis Willey (23 May 1853–14 May 1927), classicist and archaeologist, was born in Ogden, New York, the son of Henry Kelsey, a professor at Lake Forest College, and Olive Cornelia Trowbridge. He graduated from the University of Rochester in 1880 and for the next nine years taught Latin at Lake Forest University in Illinois, becoming a full professor in 1882. He studied in Europe from 1883 to 1885 and received an honorary Ph.D. from Rochester in 1886. That year he married Mary Isabelle Madger, with whom he had three children. He succeeded Henry S. Frieze in the chair of Latin language and literature at the University of Michigan in 1889, a position he held until his death. He studied for one year in Europe (1892–1893) and was director of the American School of Classical Studies in Rome (1900–1901).

By developing innovative and popular textbooks that stressed history and culture as much as language, Kelsey had a significant impact on the teaching of classics. Such books include Cicero's *De Senectute* and *De Amicitia* (1882), Lucretius's *De Rerum Natura* (1884), Caesar's *Gallic War* (1886), Xenophon's *Anabasis* (with A. C. Zenos, 1889), *Selections from Ovid* (1891), and *Select Orations and Letters of Cicero* (1892). His Caesar ran to twenty-one editions. However numerous his time-consuming projects, Kelsey taught a full load of classes until 1920.

Kelsey's energy in the service of major projects in classics was unrivaled, and he recognized early that classics needed the support of men of affairs. He was one of the classics profession's first and most effective fundraisers. He formed the Michigan Schoolmasters' Club, for whose Classical Conference he commissioned papers and testimonials supporting classical studies not only from classicists like Paul Shorey, William G. Hale, and Andrew Fleming West, but also from virtually every important political and business figure in the country, including President Woodrow Wilson, most of his cabinet, and three former presidents. Wealthy and influential men saw in Kelsey a man like themselves, a tireless, efficient, and sympathetic manager of large and worthwhile enterprises. Many of the Classical Conference contributions were collected in Kelsey's *Latin and Greek in American Education* (1911), which defined the value of classics in the American curriculum.

As an archaeologist Kelsey led expeditions to Pompeii and edited a series, Handbooks of Archaeology and Antiquities with Percy Gardner of Oxford, to which he contributed a translation of August Mau's *Pompeii, Its Life and Art* (1899). Between 1919 and 1921 he served as director of Near East research at the University of Michigan and raised funds for the university's first archaeological expedition to the Near East. He personally supervised the myriad details of each succeeding year's expedition and from 1924 to 1926 headed the excavations at Antioch of Pisidia, Karanis in Egypt, and Carthage. He and his students brought back enormous amounts of archaeological and papyrological remains, which have made the Michigan collection one of the finest in the world.

As a classicist Kelsey founded the University of Michigan Studies Humanistic Series with Henry A. Sanders in 1904 and published some twenty volumes on topics ranging from Greek and Latin to musical,

biblical, and Eastern studies. He spent countless hours editing the volumes of this wide-ranging series and was also able to contribute scholarly articles of his own to *Transactions of the American Philological Association* and *Classical Philology*. Just before he died he completed his translation of book 1 of Hugo Grotius's *De Jure Belli et Pacis* for the Carnegie Endowment for International Peace (1925). He also published *Excavations at Carthage, 1925: A Preliminary Report* (1926) and raised funds to save the German project known now as the *Thesaurus Linguae Latinae*, a multivolume lexical concordance of every word of classical Latin.

Kelsey was awarded a medal from the king of Belgium for his relief work in Michigan for refugee Belgian children, and for his excavation at Carthage he was awarded corresponding memberships in the Académie des Inscriptions et Belles-Lettres of France and the Deutsches Archäologisches Institut. He was president of the American Philological Association (1906–1907) and, having served as its secretary for a number of years, was also president of the Archaeological Institute of America (1907–1912).

Kelsey was a considerable scholar and a progressive educator but especially a skilled manager who could make great projects like the Michigan excavations work. All of his interests fed on others. His archaeological investigations enabled him to bring the ancient world to life in his classes and textbooks. He set the Michigan classics department in directions in which it still leads the nation: great support of scholarship, a world-class interest in papyrology and archaeology, a devotion to the development of innovative teaching materials, and the garnering of public support for the classics.

An opera enthusiast, Kelsey served for many years as president of the University Musical Society. He died in Ann Arbor. The Kelsey Museum of Archaeology, founded in 1928 in Ann Arbor, was named in his honor.

• There is a considerable archive of Kelsey's papers at the Bentley Historical Library, University of Michigan, but they shed little light on his personal life. His diary is unreflective, and he left no other memoirs or autobiographical writings. Obituaries include H. A. Sanders, *Classical Philology* 22 (July 1927): 308–10; John Garrett Winter, *Classical Journal* 23 (1927–1928): 4–6; and the *Rochester Alumni Review*, June–July 1927, p. 168.

WARD W. BRIGGS

KEMBLE, Edwin Crawford (28 Jan. 1889–12 Mar. 1984), physicist, was born in Delaware, Ohio, the son of Duston Kemble and Margaret Ann Day, Methodist missionaries. The young Kemble studied at Ohio Wesleyan University and originally had the intention of becoming a missionary. However, he early became convinced that he was not suited for such a calling, and he put himself through the Case School of Applied Science, where he obtained his B.S. in 1911. At Case he was closely associated with the experimental physicist D. C. Miller and wrote his senior thesis on acoustics under Miller's direction.

After graduating, Kemble was employed at the Carnegie Institute of Technology as an assistant instructor (1911–1912) and instructor of physics (1912–1913). On the recommendation of Miller he was awarded a fellowship to pursue graduate studies at Harvard. He entered there in 1913 and received his A.M. in 1914. Because of his unusually strong mathematical background, Kemble was given permission to do his doctoral research in theoretical physics. He received his Ph.D. in 1917 for his dissertation "Studies in the Application of the Quantum Hypothesis to the Kinetic Theory of Gases and to the Theory of Their Infra-red Absorption Bands," which was the first Ph.D. in theoretical physics to be given in the United States. This was nominally directed by Percy W. Bridgman; however, Kemble required minimal supervision.

During the war years 1917–1918 Kemble was employed as an engineering physicist at the Curtiss (Aeroplane) Motor Corporation in Buffalo, New York. He then taught for one semester in 1919 at Williams College before returning to Harvard. The remainder of his academic career was spent there as instructor (1919–1924), assistant professor (1924–1927), associate professor (1927–1930), and finally as professor (1930–1957). He was a Guggenheim fellow (Feb.–July 1927) in Göttingen and Munich and from 1940 to 1945 served as chair of the physics department at Harvard. During World War II Kemble directed the program for physics instruction of the army and navy officer programs at Harvard, did acoustic research for the Office of Scientific Research and Development (1944), and was deputy scientific director of the ALSOS Mission (Spring 1945). The latter mission was assigned the task of evaluating the status of the German atomic bomb program. After his formal retirement in 1957, Kemble served as director of the Harvard Academic Year Institute for High School Teachers funded by the National Science Foundation (1957–1960). He was elected a member of the National Academy of Sciences in 1931 and served as chair of its physics section (1945–1948).

Kemble was the first distinguished American quantum physicist, and through his research and teaching he did much to disseminate the new theory to an American audience. For more than four decades he was a major figure in the physics department at Harvard, and in this capacity he helped shape the development of American physics. His doctoral research explained the known second absorption band in the spectrum of carbon monoxide, and he predicted and experimentally discovered "harmonic" spectra in other gases. This work was cited by Niels Bohr in his early work, and starting in the 1919–1920 academic year Kemble gave regular courses on quantum theory at Harvard. He produced his first doctoral student, John H. Van Vleck (Nobel Prize in physics, 1977) in 1922, and he attracted many students, including Robert S. Mulliken, John C. Slater, and J. Robert Oppenheimer (as an undergraduate). Indeed, it has been estimated that between 1922 and 1935, over a third of the doctorates awarded in quantum theory in the United States were directed by Kemble or his students.

In 1926, as the chair of a National Research Council committee, he coauthored the report "Molecular Spectra in Gases." Following his return from study in Germany, he was invited to write a detailed review article on the new quantum theory for the inauguration of the new journal *Reviews of Modern Physics*. This article, "The General Principles of Quantum Mechanics: I and II" (1929, 1930), the second part being written with Edward L. Hill, was a significant contribution to the physics community. It marked the formal shift of Kemble's interest from molecular spectra to quantum theory, and soon he began to prepare a graduate level text on the subject that would be suitable for an American audience. This proved to be a monumental task, and the resulting volume, *The Fundamental Principles of Quantum Mechanics with Elementary Applications*, appeared only in 1937. It was an admirable book that eschewed many of the vagaries found in less careful presentations and notably gave a physicist's version of the von Neumann approach to the theory. However, it contained no significant breakthroughs in the theory and was perhaps too demanding and rigorous to achieve widespread popularity as a textbook. Nevertheless, for the dedicated reader, it was invaluable, and many physicists rate it as being Kemble's greatest contribution to theoretical physics.

During the period 1929–1939 Kemble was at the peak of his powers as a theoretician, and within ten days of the appearance of the famous Einstein-Podolsky-Rosen *Gedankenexperiment* (1935), he challenged their analysis. As the war years approached, Kemble felt himself unable keep up with current trends in physics, and at the war's end he switched his activities into designing science courses for nonspecialists as part of a general education program. This work ultimately led to his two-volume text *Physical Science: Its Structure and Development* (1966, 1970).

First and foremost, Kemble is remembered as a great expositor and teacher of quantum theory. In this, he felt an overriding compulsion to thoroughly *understand* the subject *before* attempting to explain it to his audience or seeking to apply it in a speculative manner. As he commented, he thought slowly and could only proceed in a step-by-step, methodical manner. This habit led to a precision and clarity in his writings that make them a noteworthy contribution to quantum theory.

In 1920 Kemble married Harriet Mary Tindle; they had two children. After his retirement, Kemble retained his interest in physics, and a few weeks before his death, which was probably in Cambridge, Massachusetts, he was still at work on revisions to his book on quantum theory.

• Kemble's papers are held by the Harvard University Archives. An autobiographical sketch is in *McGraw Hill Modern Scientists and Engineers*, vol. 2 (1980). Kemble's contributions are prominently featured in Katherine R. Sopka, *Quantum Physics in America: The Years through 1935* (1988).

His two essays, "Operational Reasoning, Reality, and Quantum Mechanics," *Journal of the Franklin Institute* 225 (Mar. 1938): 263–75, and "Reality, Measurement, and the State of the System in Quantum Mechanics," *Philosophy of Science* 18 (Oct. 1951): 273–99, provide valuable insight into his views on the interpretation and meaning of quantum mechanics. An obituary notice appears in *Physics Today*, Sept. 1987, pp. 97–99.

JOSEPH D. ZUND

KEMBLE, Fanny (27 Nov. 1809–15 Jan. 1893), author and actress, was born Frances Anne Kemble in London, England, the daughter of Charles Kemble, an actor and theatrical manager, and Marie-Thérèse de-Camp, a Swiss-French actress in Kemble's troupe. The niece of noted actress Sarah Siddons, Kemble became a member of what theater historian Mary M. Turner called "the most distinguished actor-family England has ever produced." As a child Kemble breakfasted with Walter Scott, sang duets with Thomas Moore, and posed for a portrait by Thomas Lawrence. Educated sporadically in English and Parisian schools, at which she acquired the reputation of a nonconformist, Kemble intended a writing career, but when financial ruin threatened her parents' theater in Covent Garden in 1829 she studied acting for three weeks and then made a sensational debut as Juliet in *Romeo and Juliet*.

The Kembles' theater was saved, and Kemble became the darling of the London stage. Her novel *Frances I*, begun when she was seventeen, became a popular play (produced in 1832). After a nationwide tour in 1831, Kemble crossed the Atlantic in 1832 with her father for a tour of the United States and Canada. Coinciding with the first wave of Shakespearean popularity in the United States, the tour quickly established Kemble as "the acknowledged Queen of Tragedy, from Boston to New Orleans" and as the first great actress to appear on the American stage. Of Charles and Fanny's New York debut Phillip Hone wrote, "I have never witnessed an audience so moved, astonished, and delighted." The young critic Walt Whitman subsequently referred to Kemble in his *Leaves of Grass*.

Kemble's art was spontaneous, depending on inspiration and brilliance. She remarked, "For aught I knew, I was Juliet; the passion I was uttering sending hot waves of blushes all over my neck and shoulders, while the poetry sounded like music to me as I spoke it, with no consciousness of anything before me, utterly transported into the imaginary existence of the play." Off the stage Kemble was not always admired in the United States. A critic in the *Germantown* (Pa.) *Telegraph* wrote in 1834, "He who weds her for an angel will discover . . . ere a fortnight, that she is nothing more or less than a woman, and perhaps one of the most troublesome kind in the bargain."

The Kembles' tour ended in 1834 with Fanny's marriage in Philadelphia to the slaveowning Pierce Butler, "a cultivated, courteous Southern gentleman . . . a young man of temperament and susceptability, accustomed to female adorations." Kemble may have married the well-to-do Butler partly so that her father could take the tour's earnings back to England, thus saving his theater. An unfettered soul, she had previously expressed doubts about her suitability as a wife, but it would have been in keeping with her character if she had just wanted to try the experience. The couple had two daughters.

Kemble had always intended to publish her thoughts about her first American visit. Appearing three years after countrywoman Frances Trollope's critical *The Domestic Manners of the Americans* (1832), Kemble's highly personal *Journal of Frances Anne Butler* (2 vols., 1835) seemed to some readers another condescension. Kemble complimented Americans ("the most extravagant people in the world") for giving huge bouquets of flowers and for being particularly "deferential to women." She found their "absolute and uncomplicated vulgarity . . . really not very objectionable" and commended William Cullen Bryant's poetry, the volunteer fire companies and hackney coaches, the Hudson River scenery, and steamboats. But she also pointed out uncivilized aspects—even New York had no running water—and expressed horror at "continual swallowing of mint julaps [sic], gin slings, brandy cocktails, and a thousand strong messes which they take *even before breakfast*." She also disliked the Americans' greasy dinners and the custom of separating the sexes following the meal: "When the gentlemen joined us they were all more or less 'How com'd you so indeed?'" she remarked. This statement displeased Edgar Allan Poe, who commented, "For a female to speak thus confidently is indelicate."

Kemble's *Journal*, which remains a useful primary source for social historians, appeared against the express wish of Butler, who believed that a gentleman's wife had no right to a public career. Butler first attempted to edit the *Journal* to his liking (Kemble refused, writing, "I consider it my duty not to submit my conduct to any other human being"). He then unsuccessfully offered Kemble's publisher $2,500 to suppress the book.

It was Kemble's thoughts on the rights of marriage partners that, according to biographer J. C. Furnas "identified her as one of the scatter of atoms likely to bond into the molecules making up feminism." Although she was never identified with a feminist movement, Kemble's ideas paralleled those of other "liberated" American women of her era, including Lucy Stone, Elizabeth Cady Stanton, and Angelina Grimké. As a married woman in the United States, Kemble had no right to her own money. She wrote to a friend in 1842, "Having *earned* money and therefore most legitimately *owned* it, I can never conceive that I have any right to the money of another person. . . . I cannot convince myself that that which I invent, *create*, in fact, can really belong to anyone but myself." In a second letter she commented, "A woman should be her husband's best . . . and dearest friend, as he should be hers. But friendship is a relation of equality, in which perfect respect for each other's liberty is exercised on both sides. That sort of marriage, if it exists at all anywhere, is, I suspect, very uncommon everywhere."

Conflict within Kemble's marriage informed much of her writing. In 1837 she began *An English Tragedy*, a play based on an English nobleman whose cheating at dice was thought unforgivable. Downplaying this aspect, Kemble focused on the consequences of his seduction of a friend's wife. Despite typically Victorian florid emotions and elaborate evasions, the play went unproduced because of its "grossness." Its ruined heroine, attacking her seducer in terms similar to those Kemble eventually laid before Butler ("the injury you have done in marrying me") is piously abjured, "Return to your right office, To make all men in love with Excellence." The self-justifying cuckold ironically commends marriage to his own sister because "a husband is a wall that builds itself between a woman and all other things." Perhaps speaking for Kemble, a minor character muses, "Oh! I have seen . . . the seamy, foul inside of what was held, *is* held, a prosperous wedlock."

By 1838, influenced by Unitarian minister William Ellery Channing's thoughts on slavery, Kemble had become a passionate abolitionist. She found her dependence on the profits of the family rice and cotton plantation intolerable. When Butler's father died and he was needed to take charge personally, she insisted on accompanying him and stayed for eighteen months. Inspired by the journal of Matthew Gregory Lewis, an Englishman who owned a West Indies sugar plantation, Kemble wrote *Residence of a Georgian Plantation in 1838–1839*. The work horrified Butler and remained unpublished until 1863.

Kemble returned to England in 1840; Butler followed, and for two-and-a-half years they appeared to have reconciled. They returned to the United States in 1843. Regarding their daughters as his possessions and threatening Kemble with their loss, Butler thwarted her attempts to return to the stage and to publish the plantation journal and articles on abolition. Once Butler sold Kemble's favorite horse, possibly because he knew that riding horseback gave her "a pleasurably unmarried feeling." Collecting and publishing ninety of her poems and securing the profits through her ingenuity, she bought the horse again. For a time Kemble and Butler lived apart within the same house, her access to the children limited to an hour daily. He wrote to her, "If you will govern your irritable temper, and if you can consent to submit your will to mine, we may be reconciled and may be happy." She returned, "Is it because you are better than myself? I am sure you would not say so, whatever I may think. Is it because you are more enlightened, more intellectual? You know that isn't so!"

Kemble left Butler and the children in 1845 and spent a recuperative year on the Continent. In 1847 she unsuccessfully attempted a stage comeback in England, criticized as "ignorant of the first rudiments of her art" and full of "American sentiments which she expressed too freely." When she returned to the United States in 1848 to answer Butler's divorce action, she began a successful career in dramatic readings, which, in fact, she much preferred to acting.

The Butlers' divorce inspired his self-justifying *Statement* (charging abandonment) and her eloquent *Answer*. When the decree came in 1849, she settled for $1,500 a year and two months with their daughters every summer; she agreed not to mention his unfaithfulnesses, duels, and financial mismanagement. Her readings were popular and remunerative, and Kemble bought the site of Tanglewood in the Berkshires. Turner writes, "She fished, she wore loose trousers, she rode alone, didn't water her punch and so got all the 'best' inhabitants quite drunk at tea one day, and she read unexpurgated versions of Shakespeare's bawdier plays at public performances." When the Civil War ended the demand for her readings, she returned to England in 1863. That same year both her collected *Plays* and *Residence of a Georgian Plantation in 1838–1839* were published.

The *Journal* vividly details Kemble's horror of the slaves' lot as well as her belief—later acknowledged as naive—that owners like Butler could free them if they wanted to. She grieved at the mutual degradation: "How honorable [Pierce] would have appeared to me begrimed with the sweat and toil of the coarsest manual labor to what he seemed, setting forth to these wretched, ignorant [pregnant] women, as a duty, their unpaid, exacted labour!" She complained of the influence on their daughter: "the universal eagerness in which they [the slaves] sprang to obey her little gestures of command. . . . Think of learning to rule despotically your fellow creature before the first lesson of self-government has been well spelled over!" Kemble reported that when she repeatedly interceded on the slaves' behalf, Butler charged her with making them more discontented and idle, thus bringing more punishment upon themselves.

Residence, with its firsthand record of cruelty and dehumanization and its unforgettable scenes of dead and dying in the plantation's infirmary, was published while Parliament was debating aiding the Confederacy; members quoted Kemble's words during proceedings. Perhaps only President Abraham Lincoln's Emancipation Proclamation, issued in January 1863, had greater influence in turning the English away from their self-interest as textile manufacturers.

Between 1863 and 1879 Kemble continued to shuttle between England and the United States, prospering as a writer and—until 1869—as a reader. She wrote several volumes of memoirs and may have been the first author to use a typewriter. She likened herself to the mannish novelist George Sand—"unamiable, very emphatic, very dictatorial." Stanton listed Kemble among women crucified by those fellow women who still observed man-made taboos.

In 1872 the American-English novelist Henry James met Kemble at a Rome dinner party given by her married daughter Sarah, who had become Kemble's companion. Kemble became the source for many of James's short stories as well as his novel *Washington Square*, based on her brother's jilting of an heiress after discovering that her father would disinherit her. Kemble's London home became a salon. To James she was "the first woman in London . . . a volcano . . . [who] wrote exactly as she talked, observing, asserting, complaining, confiding, contradicting, crying out and bounding off."

Kemble remained in Europe after 1879. In her adolescence she had imagined an ideal death: from a broken neck, having been swept off a horse at full gallop. In 1893 James recorded a very different end: "Mrs. Kemble, while being helped to bed by her maid, gave a little sigh and fell dead." She died in London. Kemble was brilliant and catalytic, the epitome of a vital human being.

• Few women's lives have been more fully written about than Kemble's. Among secondary sources are Leon Edel, *Henry James: A Life* (1985); J. C. Furnas, *Fanny Kemble: Leading Lady of the Nineteenth Century Stage* (1982); Henry Gibbs, *Affectionately Yours, Fanny: Fanny Kemble and the Theatre* (1946); Dame Una Pope-Hennessy, *Three English Women in America* (1929); Mary M. Turner, *Forgotten Leading Ladies of the American Theatre* (1990); and Constance Wright, *Fanny Kemble and The Lovely Land* (1972). Anthologies include Elizabeth Mavor, ed., *Fanny Kemble: The American Journals* (1990); and Eleanor Ransome, ed., *The Terrific Kemble: A Victorian Self-Portrait from the Writings of Fanny Kemble* (1978).

JAMES ROSS MOORE

KEMENY, John George (31 May 1926–26 Dec. 1992), computer scientist and mathematician, was born in Budapest, Hungary, the son of Tibor Kemeny, an import-export wholesaler, and Lucy Fried. Kemeny came to the United States in 1940, and his family settled in New York, where he attended the George Washington High School. In 1945 Kemeny became an American citizen and entered Princeton University. He interrupted his studies to serve on the Manhattan Project at the Los Alamos National Laboratory (1945–1946). Returning to Princeton after his service, he earned the B. A. in mathematics in 1947. During his undergraduate years he worked as research and teaching assistant and as instructor of mathematics at Princeton (1946–1948); he was also research assistant to Albert Einstein at the Institute for Advanced Study (1948–1949). He received the Ph.D. in mathematics from Princeton in 1949 with a dissertation written under the famous logician Alonzo Church. In 1949 the Office for Naval Research granted him a two-year postdoctoral fellowship. He married Jean Alexander in 1950; the couple had two children.

Kemeny's first full-time faculty appointment was in the philosophy department at Princeton in 1951. He left Princeton in 1953 to teach mathematics at Dartmouth College. Kemeny spent the rest of his career at Dartmouth, where he was chairman of mathematics from 1955 to 1967. As chairman Kemeny helped elevate the mathematics department to national prominence, notably in educational uses of computers: at Kemeny's initiative, the Kiewit Computation Center was inaugurated at Dartmouth as early as 1966; Ke-

meny also introduced finite mathematics as part of the curriculum in the social sciences. His teaching services earned him the Albert Bradley Third Century Professorship (1967–1972). He was elected thirteenth president of Dartmouth in March 1970 and became known for being the only university president to continue teaching two courses each year while in office (1970–1981). As president he helped change the all-male institution into a coeducational college and he renewed the college's founding commitment to educating Native Americans. He also initiated a program for continuing education in liberal studies aimed at business and professional people: this program became known as the Dartmouth Institute. Kemeny returned to full-time teaching in the mathematics department from 1982 until his retirement in 1991.

Kemeny's concern for mathematics education went beyond university teaching as he headed (1958–1960) the Commission on Mathematics Instruction that launched the "new math" in secondary education in the United States. His expertise was acknowledged outside academic circles when he became an adviser to the Rand Corporation in 1953, an assignment that he kept until 1969. In 1979 President Jimmy Carter appointed Kemeny chair of a commission to investigate a nuclear accident at an electric plant on Three Mile Island, Pennsylvania; the "Kemeny Commission," as it came to be called, criticized the nuclear power industry and its federal regulators.

Kemeny's contributions to mathematics cross the fields of logic, game theory, and probability theory. In his Ph.D. dissertation, "Type-Theory versus Set-Theory" (Princeton, 1949), Kemeny adapted to the construction of sets a formulation of the theory of types based on his previous determination of models that can apply to both formal and intuitionistic logical systems; he later (1956) gave novel definitions for two classes of semantic concepts that he applied to Kurt Gödel's formalization of set theory in order to carry out his own axiomatization. When Kemeny joined forces with economist Oskar Morgenstern and Dartmouth mathematician Gerald L. Thompson, they determined the largest technically possible expansion rate and the smallest interest rate that yields a profitless economy (1956). In "The Effect of Psychological Attitudes on the Outcomes of Games" (1957), Kemeny and Thompson modeled various psychological attitudes by attributing utility functions to the players; they showed how these functions influence the course of finite sequential games and secured theorems about the utility functions that produce winning behaviors. A monograph by Kemeny and his colleagues James Laurie Snell (from Dartmouth) and Anthony W. Knapp (from Cornell), *Denumerable Markov Chains* (1966), treats the probabilistic theory of Markov chains from the point of view of potential theory; it includes much of the coauthors' original work and was deemed rather unconventional when it was published.

Mathematical textbook publishing for the undergraduate market flourished during the 1950s. Like many contemporary texts, Kemeny's textbooks contained core chapters in logic, set theory, and algebra. They diverged from the approaches then current, however, by emphasizing finite mathematics, its role in various aspects of twentieth-century life, and its uses in the social and behavioral sciences. Written by Kemeny, Snell, and Thompson, *Introduction to Finite Mathematics* (1957) displayed all these features; with the cooperation of Arthur Schleifer, Jr., later versions of this classic text were adapted for social science students (1960) and then for business school students (1962). In the more theoretical *Finite Mathematical Structures* (1959), Kemeny, Snell, Thompson, and Hazleton Mirkil offered applications to electricity and engineering. Although narrower in scope, *Finite Markov Chains* (1960), by Kemeny and Snell, made the point that finite mathematics in general and the theory of Markov chains in particular should take a central place in the undergraduate curriculum. Most of these textbooks were often reprinted, sometimes with substantial revisions; some were translated into French, German, Czech, and Russian. They all promoted the view that Kemeny developed in his first book, *A Philosopher Looks at Science* (1959), which stemmed from his philosophy of science lectures at Princeton, namely that mathematics is the universal and exact language of the natural and the social sciences.

His important and varied mathematical accomplishments notwithstanding, Kemeny is even better known as the co-inventor of the computer language BASIC (the acronym for 'Beginners' All-purpose Symbolic Instruction Code). BASIC was a team effort: it was conceived, designed, and implemented by a small group of professors and undergraduate students who, starting in 1963, worked under the leadership of Kemeny and Thomas E. Kurtz—who was then director of the Computer Center at Dartmouth—to implement a computer time-sharing system at the college. Their goal was to make the computer readily available to the majority of students and faculty at a time when the higher-level language FORTRAN was inaccessible to users who had no formal training. BASIC was thus devised to be simple enough to enable untrained users to program the computer yet complex and flexible enough to suit various programming purposes. The venture received financial backing from the National Science Foundation and benefited from a close association with the General Electric (GE) company, from which came its machinery. In 1965 GE established a commercial time-sharing service that used the Dartmouth system. BASIC spread quickly: by the time the co-inventors published their book *BASIC Programming* (1967), several time-sharing systems offering BASIC had been implemented in the United States and major manufacturers were making BASIC available on their computer equipment. Personal computers and programmable calculators later used BASIC in their operating and programming methods and BASIC was adopted worldwide.

While involved with the implementation and promotion of BASIC, Kemeny pursued his mathematical investigations. His later work is mainly in the fields of probability theory and linear algebra.

The American Academy of Arts and Sciences elected Kemeny a member in 1967. For his innovations in computer science as well as for his mathematical work, Kemeny received several prestigious awards, such as the New York Academy of Sciences Award (1984), the Institute of Electrical and Electronics Engineers Computer Medal (1986), and the Louis Robinson Award (1990). Kemeny died in Etna, New Hampshire.

• In game theory Kemeny wrote with Morgenstern and Thompson "A Generalization of the von Neumann Model of Expanding Economy," *Econometrica* 24 (1956): 115–35. In the probabilistic theory of Markov chains he wrote with Snell "Semimartingales of Markov Chains," *Annals of Mathematical Statistics* 29 (1958): 143–54, and "Boundary Theory for Recurrent Markov chains," *Transactions of the American Mathematical Society* 106 (1963): 495–520. Kemeny's popular *Man and the Computer* (1972) is the outcome of a lecture series that Kemeny delivered at the American Museum of Natural History in New York City in 1971. He sang the praises of mathematics as a source of thinking models for administration in "What Every College President Should Know about Mathematics," *American Mathematical Monthly* 80 (1973): 889–901. Most of Kemeny's mathematical publications were reviewed in *Mathematical Reviews*. A history of BASIC is found in Thomas W. Hall, Jr., "'Basic' Computer Language," in the *Encyclopedia of Computer Science and Technology*, vol. 3 (1983), pp. 114–21, an article partly based on Kemeny and Kurtz's own account: "Dartmouth Time-Sharing," *Science* 162 (1968): 223–28. An interview of Kemeny conducted by Lynn A. Steen appeared in *Mathematical People: Profiles and Interviews*, ed. Donald J. Albers and G. L. Alexanderson (1985), pp. 153–65. A short obituary of Kemeny is in the *Notices of the American Mathematical Society*, Mar. 1993; p. 243.

LILIANE BEAULIEU

KEMEYS, Edward (31 Jan. 1843–11 May 1907), sculptor, was born in Savannah, Georgia, the son of William Kemeys and Abbie Brenton Greene. Around 1846, following his mother's death, he moved to his father's hometown of Scarborough, New York. Beginning his elementary education there, Kemeys subsequently attended public schools in New York City, where he completed high school and perhaps attended college. In 1856 he spent the first of four summer vacations with relatives in Dwight, Illinois, and quickly developed an appreciation for frontier life. On 31 March 1862 he joined the Union ranks, in Company C, Sixty-fifth New York Infantry. After four months he took a medical discharge but later rejoined, on 20 August 1863, as a captain, Company H, Fourth U.S. Colored Heavy Artillery, and served until 21 February 1866. Following the end of the Civil War, Kemeys undertook a two-year farming stint in Illinois. For eighteen months beginning in the fall of 1868, he was employed by an engineer corps in New York's Central Park. In that capacity he realized his true calling as an animal sculptor, and during visits to the park's zoo delighted in sketching and modeling the wild animals held there.

Once Kemeys had found his niche he attained success rapidly, an achievement that is all the more remarkable because he was essentially self-taught. In 1871 he exhibited a selection of plasters and bronzes at the American Institute of the City of New York. The following year his first public monument, the life-size bronze statue *Hudson Bay Wolves Quarreling over the Carcass of a Deer*, was erected in Philadelphia's Fairmount Park. (It was later installed in the zoological gardens.) In spring or summer 1873, using the income from this project, Kemeys journeyed west with a buffalo-hunting expedition. Traveling as a hunter-artist, he became familiar with anatomical and behavioral characteristics of frontier wildlife. American sculptor and author Lorado Taft aptly remarked in his *History of American Sculpture* (1903) that Kemeys "has studied them alive and dead, and has dissected every kind of four-footed creature" (p. 472).

Returning to New York by April 1874, Kemeys soon translated what he had learned into three dimensions and displayed three animal groups at the Centennial Exhibition held in Philadelphia in 1876: *Coyote and Raven, Playing Possum*, and *Panther and Deer*. In the autumn of the next year he traveled to London, where he had a successful gallery showing of his work. Kemeys then relocated to Paris and in 1878 exhibited *Bison and Wolves* to acclaim in the prestigious annual Salon. The sculptor's Parisian tenure was immensely influential, as he spent his time observing caged animals at the Jardin des Plantes and studying the work of the great French *animaliers*, most notably, Antoine Louis Barye. Because he was America's first sculptor to focus on native animal subjects, Kemeys was frequently called "the American Barye," an appellation that though flattering, was not entirely accurate. True, both artists delighted in sculpting the wild beast, but Kemeys's technique was less refined. His handling of form was loose and impressionistic; he created surface texture with broad hatchmarks, focusing on the animal's mood, whether it be fierce as in *A Grizzly Grave Digger* (1893 [modeled 1883]; Brookgreen Gardens, Murrells Inlet, S.C.) or capricious as in *The Jaguar Lovers* (1886; Corcoran Gallery of Art, Washington, D.C.). His friend Julian Hawthorne aptly noted in *Century Magazine* in June 1884 that Kemeys did not strive merely for "the accurate representation of the animal's external aspect" but rather for "the essential animal character or temperament which controls and actuates the animal's movements and behavior" (p. 214).

In the fall of 1878, feeling homesick, Kemeys returned to the United States. While in Paris, he had begun to shun modeling animals in captivity, and consequently, once back in his native land, he "plunged into the wilderness of the far west, lived with Indians, trappers and hunters, and studied the big game in action" (*Carter's Monthly*, Feb. 1898, p. 123). Aware that America's frontier was rapidly vanishing, he endeavored to document the physical and psychological traits of its wildlife. He was particularly drawn to feline subjects, often those engaged in tense encounter. *Still*

Hunt, a bronze representation of a ferocious crouching panther, was purchased by the City of New York and unveiled on a rocky outcropping in Central Park in June 1883. In May 1885 the Art Institute of Chicago gave Kemeys a one-artist show called Wild Animals and Indians, which featured sculptures as well as drawings and engravings. In 1888 his over-sized head of a bison (since destroyed) was installed on the Union Pacific Railroad bridge linking Omaha, Nebraska, and Council Bluffs, Iowa. Kemeys also exhibited small pieces at annual exhibitions held at the National Academy of Design and the Society of American Artists in New York City and the Pennsylvania Academy of the Fine Arts in Philadelphia.

In 1892 Kemeys moved to Chicago because of his involvement in preparations for the World's Columbian Exposition to be held there in 1893. His renditions of wild animals, among them six American panthers and pairs of buffalo and bears, decorated bridges of the fairgrounds. Twelve of his pieces, including the gold medal–winning *Panther and Cubs* (Art Institute of Chicago), were displayed in the Art Building. Kemeys remained in the Chicago area after the world's fair, making frequent forays west. In addition to garnering income from small bronze statuettes, he carried out three large projects in Illinois during the 1890s. He completed the pair of guardian lions that mark the entrance to the Art Institute of Chicago in 1894. In 1894–1895 he modeled relief panels of Indians and French explorers for the lobby of Chicago's Marquette Building. The last Illinois project as well as his last significant commission, *The Prayer for Rain*, portraying a Native American in ceremonial dress flanked by a panther and a deer, was dedicated in Champaign in 1899.

After the turn of the century, Kemeys began to be overshadowed by other younger animal sculptors, such as Solon H. Borglum (1868–1922) and Alexander Phimister Proctor (1862–1950). By 1902, having visited Texas, New Mexico, and Arizona, over a two-year period, Kemeys had moved to Washington, D.C. President Theodore Roosevelt, a friend whom he had met in 1886 when both were writing articles for the sporting magazine *Outing*, secured Kemeys's participation in the Louisiana Purchase Exposition to be held in St. Louis in 1904; for it Kemeys created bear figures that were situated at the side entrances to the Missouri State Building.

In 1906 Kemeys arranged for the United States National Museum in Washington to acquire a large body of his work; many of these pieces have since been moved to the National Museum of American Art, Smithsonian Institution. He was in declining health in the last years of his life, suffering from locomotor ataxia, and he died in Washington, D.C. Because of his military rank, Kemeys was buried in Arlington National Cemetery. His wife, Laura Sparkes Swing, an artist whom he had married in 1885 and with whom he had had one child, organized a memorial exhibition of more than one hundred plasters and bronzes at the Corcoran Gallery of Art in December 1907.

As the headmost American animal sculptor of the nineteenth century, Kemeys "was one of the first to see and appreciate the immediate world about him" and "to recognize the artistic possibilities of our own land and time" (*History of American Sculpture*, p. 473). His works, which combine the skills of a scientist, naturalist, hunter, and artist, are vital testaments to the enthusiasm and curiosity that Americans of his era felt about frontier life.

• Hamlin Garland, "Edward Kemeys: A Sculptor of Frontier Life and Wild Animals," *McClure's Magazine*, July 1895, pp. 120–31, and Leila Mechlin, "Edward Kemeys: An Appreciation," *International Studio* 26 (July 1905): 10–16, are two important contemporary appraisals of Kemeys's art. The authoritative scholarship on Kemeys has been conducted by Michael Richman and published in *Edward Kemeys, 1843–1907: America's First Animal Sculptor* (1972). Robin R. Salmon provides a useful biography of Kemeys in *Brookgreen Gardens Sculpture*, vol. 2 (1993), pp. 10–15. Obituaries are in the *New York Times* and the *Washington Post*, both 12 May 1907.

THAYER TOLLES

KEMP, Harry Hibbard (15 Dec. 1883–8 Aug. 1960), poet and writer, was born in Youngstown, Ohio, the son of Wilbert Elijah Kemp, a factory worker, and Ida Hibbard. Kemp first caught the public eye and warmed to its gaze when he returned home after tramping around the world at the age of seventeen. A vagabond with an intellectual bent and a talent for self-promotion, Kemp steeped himself in the English and American romantics, responded wholeheartedly to the radical idealism of the early 1900s, and studied the practiced showmanship of then-famous nonconformists such as Elbert Hubbard and Bernarr Macfadden.

While enrolled at the University of Kansas (1906–1911), Kemp garnered the sobriquet "The Tramp Poet." Newspapers picked up exaggerated reports of Kemp's dramatic arrival in Lawrence in a boxcar, and stories of the "studious hobo" and "boxcar bard" were widely copied. Kemp's poems began appearing in the *Independent* and the *American* magazines. Identifying himself as the poet of modern America, he criticized genteel poets for not writing about their own times. To gather materials for his poetry, Kemp worked ore boats, freights, threshing crews, lumber camps, rode the rails hobo style, and even went for a ride in a biplane. Although he anticipated Carl Sandburg, Edgar Lee Masters, Vachel Lindsay, and Robert Frost in his embrace of the common American scene, Kemp did not, like these poets, challenge genteel assumptions about proper poetic diction or verse form.

In 1907 Kemp's poetry came to the attention of Upton Sinclair, world-famous author of *The Jungle*, who decided that in Harry Kemp America had a new Walt Whitman. The Sinclair-Kemp friendship ended a few years later, however, when Kemp had an affair with Sinclair's wife, Meta. The triangle burst into a sensational front-page scandal in 1911 when, despite his reputation as an advocate of "free love," Sinclair sued for divorce.

Kemp settled in Greenwich Village in 1912 and soon became the quintessential bohemian in the new bohemia of 1912–1917. The bohemianism expressed in the fabled prewar Village was based on the conviction that life should be lived in the spirit of impertinent, idealistic, youthful rebellion. To demonstrate their belief in self-expression, bohemians dramatized themselves, as if they were allegorical figures in a pageant of life. Kemp acted out with unsurpassed flair his romanticized vision of himself as a great poet. The renaissance in American poetry and theater was stimulated by these bohemians, whose romance of the creative life begot an atmosphere that helped to nourish it.

Kemp's first book of poetry, *The Cry of Youth* (1914), was a testament to the idea of youth that loomed so large in the "Adolescence of the Twentieth Century," as Max Eastman characterized the prewar era. Although Kemp deplored the new modes of free verse and imagistic form, he was categorized as one of the "new poets" who were said to be inaugurating a poetry renaissance.

In his later collections—*The Passing God* (1919), *Chanteys and Ballads* (1920), *The Sea and the Dunes* (1926)—Kemp never altered his approach to poetry: unconventional subjects and attitudes expressed in a conventional style. Perhaps for this reason, Kemp achieved his greatest artistic (and commercial) success not in poetry, but in his bestselling prose work *Tramping on Life* (1922), an unconventional autobiographical narrative about an unconventional life. He wrote the book because he needed money to pay for his dying wife's treatment at the Saranac Lake Sanitarium. Kemp had married Mary Pyne in 1915. They were a celebrated couple in New York's version of La Bohème, but Rodolphe lost his Mimi in 1919.

In *Tramping on Life*, Kemp portrays his picaresque adventures as a literary tramp who believed that "wisdom was to be found more in the vagabond bye-ways of life than in the ordered and regulated highways." Dramatizing what Floyd Dell would later call "intellectual vagabondage," Kemp made his personal experiences representative of the restless, searching generation who rebelled against "the commercial, bourgeois practicality" of American society. Although *Tramping on Life* was popular when it appeared in the 1920s, it actually expressed the spirit of the "Innocent Rebellion" years (1900–1917). Harry Kemp had little in common with the Lost Generation writers who romanticized their disillusions; he preferred to romanticize his illusions. *Tramping on Life* captures an exuberant, post-Victorian, premodern era of optimistic idealism when the faith that life could be "tramped on" as if it were the stuff of one's dreams remained unshaken. In a 1926 sequel, *More Miles*, Kemp continued the spiritual autobiography of his bohemian generation.

Kemp remained a prominent player on the stage of the more commercialized Greenwich Village bohemia of the 1920s. Having participated in the formation of the Provincetown Players in 1916, Kemp sought to further the "little theater movement" rebellion against the commercial Broadway stage by organizing his own little theaters. Kemp directed and starred in plays he also wrote, some of which were published in *Boccaccio's Untold Tale* (1924). In *The Love-Rogue* (1923) Kemp adapted into English verse the original Don Juan play of Tirso de Molina. He also cultivated a persona as the "Don Juan of the radical world," though he did marry Frances McClernan in 1924. The couple separated in 1926 and divorced in 1930.

Like many of the New York bohemians, Kemp spent summers in Provincetown, Massachusetts, telling the tale of that Greenwich Village-by-the-sea community and of the genesis of the Provincetown Players in his novel *Love among the Cape Enders* (1931). He moved out to the dunes in 1927 or 1928 and lived there for the next thirty summers in a solitary shack by the ocean. Although his national reputation faded after the poor reception of his novel *Mabel Tarner* (1936), Kemp continued to be famous in smaller circles as the "Poet of the Dunes."

Kemp's fall from public notice can be explained by the anachronism of the "innocent rebellion" he continued to wage in a world no longer innocent and by the waning of his expressive powers brought on by the wear and tear of trying to turn a way of youth into a way of life. Unable to find a publisher, unwilling to give up his dream of immortal fame, Kemp published his own books and quixotically took to wearing a poet's cape and laurel wreath until his death in Provincetown.

Max Eastman said Harry Kemp "anticipated Ernest Hemingway in his . . . he-male bellicosity." Yet Kemp also wrote sonorous poetry. Here was a new image of the poet, not the dandyish aesthete of the 1890s but a poet who could box and had hopped freights. H. L. Mencken summed up the historical significance of Kemp's tramper-on-life posture: "He swam into public notice at a time when the literature of the land was suffering from a bad case of respectability. Into this sombre scene leaped Kemp not only with vineleaves in his hair, but also startling wisps of hay. . . . He taught the poets that respectability was dangerous to them."

Thinking of *Tramping on Life*, Frederick Hoffman called Kemp "a romantic predecessor of those whose life on the road in the thirties was dictated by grim economic facts." After the depression years, however, the figure of the intellectual vagabond reappears in Jack Kerouac and other beat generation writers who tramp the same literary road as their precursor Harry Kemp.

• Kemp manuscripts and other materials are widely dispersed in public, private and university collections. The major archives are at the University of Kansas and Indiana University. Kemp's other published works are *Judas* (1913), a play; *The Thresher's Wife* (1914), a long poem; *The Prodigal Son* (1919), a play; and *The Bronze Treasury* (1927), a poetry anthology. Kemp's privately printed works are as follows: *Don Juan's Notebook* (1929), *The Golden Word* (1930), *Where Now Green Gardens? (Harry Answers Omar)* (1945), *The*

Poet's Life of Christ (1946), *Poet of the Dunes* (1952), and *Rhyme of Provincetown Nicknames* (1954). *Poet of the Dunes* was reprinted in 1988, the only Kemp book still in print in the mid-1990s. A complete Kemp bibliography is found in the critical biography by William Brevda, *Harry Kemp: The Last Bohemian* (1986), the most complete modern assessment of Harry Kemp.

WILLIAM BREVDA

KEMPER, Jackson (24 Dec. 1789–24 May 1870), Episcopal bishop, was born in Pleasant Valley, Duchess County, New York, the son of Daniel Kemper, an army colonel, and Elizabeth Marius, his second wife. He attended the Episcopal Academy at Cheshire, Connecticut, and in 1805 entered Columbia College, New York, from which he graduated in 1809 as valedictorian of his class. He then studied theology with Benjamin Moore, bishop of New York, and John Henry Hobart, assistant minister of Trinity Church, New York City. William White, bishop of Pennsylvania, presiding bishop of the Episcopal church, and rector of the United Churches of Christ Church, St. Peter's, and St. James, Philadelphia, ordained Kemper deacon on 11 May 1811. On 14 May he became assistant minister of the United Churches, a position he held until 1 June 1831. He was ordained priest by Bishop White on 23 January 1814. His interest in missions on the western frontier manifested itself early. He was a leader in the formation of the Society for the Advancement of Christianity in Pennsylvania (18 Apr. 1812) and accepted assignment as its first missionary. In this capacity he made several journeys into frontier regions. In 1816 the Episcopal Missionary Society of Philadelphia was formed under his leadership. As a delegate to the general convention of 1820 he was instrumental in promoting the establishment of the Domestic and Foreign Missionary Society of the Protestant Episcopal Church in the United States of America and was named one of its managers.

In 1816 Kemper married Jerusha Lyman, who died in 1818. In 1821 he married Ann Relf, and they had three children over the next eight years; she died in 1832. On 1 June 1831 he resigned his position at the United Churches to become rector of St. Paul's Church, Norwalk, Connecticut.

The eighteenth general convention met at Philadelphia from 19 August to 1 September 1835. One of the main items on the agenda, and the issue that earned it the title the "Great Missionary Convention," was the inability of the Episcopal church to meet its missionary obligations and the demands of the West for bishops. The problem was partly financial and partly organizational. New dioceses could not afford to support a bishop, and under the canons of the church a diocese had to be organized and accepted by the general convention before it could elect a bishop. This put the western territories in an untenable position. The general convention of 1835 took action on the problem of bishops for the western territories by passing a canon, which provided that "the House of Clerical and Lay Deputies may, from time to time, on nomination of the House of Bishops, elect a suitable person or persons to be a Bishop or Bishops of this Church, to exercise Episcopal functions in States and Territories not organized as Dioceses." Under this new canon the House of Bishops nominated and the House of Deputies confirmed Kemper as the first missionary bishop with jurisdiction over Indiana and Missouri. On 25 September 1835 Kemper was consecrated at St. Peter's Church, Philadelphia, by Presiding Bishop William White (this was White's twenty-sixth and final consecration), assisted by Bishop Richard Channing Moore of Virginia and Bishop Philander Chase of Ohio.

Kemper was convinced that the only way to supply the West with clergy was to establish a school there. Kemper College, near St. Louis, was chartered on 13 January 1837 but closed in March 1845. In 1838 the general convention added Wisconsin, Iowa, and much of the Indian territories to Kemper's jurisdiction, and this earned him the title "Missionary Bishop of the Northwest." In May 1840 he visited General Theological Seminary, New York, and preached on the need for missionaries in the West. His sermon inspired three students to commit themselves to work for him, and on 30 August 1842 Nashotah House Seminary and semi-monastic community was founded at Nashotah, Wisconsin. He also participated in the founding of Racine College, Racine, Wisconsin, in 1852. In 1854 he became the bishop of Wisconsin, and on 8 October 1859 he resigned his missionary jurisdiction. One of his last official acts as missionary bishop was on 3 July 1859, when he ordained Enmegahbowh, a Chippewa Indian, to the diaconate.

Kemper has also been called the "Apostle of the Northwest," "Missionary of the West," and "Apostle of the Western Church." During his episcopate he traveled more than 300,000 miles, organized seven dioceses and hundreds of parishes, consecrated 100 church buildings, ordained more than 200 men to the ministry, confirmed an estimated 10,000 people, and baptized untold thousands. He died at Delafield, Wisconsin, and was buried at Nashotah House.

• The best collection of Kemper materials is in the archives of the Wisconsin State Historical Society, Madison. Some of this material has been published in *Wisconsin Historical Collections* 14 (1898): 394–449; *Nashotah Scholiast* 1 and 2 (Dec. 1883–June 1885): *passim*; *Wisconsin Magazine of History* 8 (June 1925): 423–45; and *Minnesota History* 7 (1926): 264–73. The earliest and still reliable study of Kemper is Greenough White, *An Apostle of the Western Church: Memoir of Jackson Kemper* (1900). A useful brief study is W. Norman Pittenger, *Jackson Kemper in the Northwest* (1957?). The Sept. 1935 issue of the *Historical Magazine of the Protestant Episcopal Church* is devoted to Kemper in honor of the centennial of his consecration as missionary bishop; it also includes the sermon preached by Bishop George Washington Doane of New Jersey at Kemper's consecration. George C. Tanner, *Fifty Years of Church Work in the Diocese of Minnesota, 1857–1907* (1909), treats Kemper's work in that diocese. See also four other articles in the *Historical Magazine*: E. Clowes Chorley, "The Missionary March of the Episcopal Church: Jackson Kemper and the Northwest," Mar. 1948, pp. 3–17; John M.

Weidman, "Incidents of Travel during Bishop Kemper's First Years in the West," Mar. 1944, pp. 36–43; James A. Muller, "Two Letters from Bishop Kemper," Dec. 1945, pp. 302–6; and Jack Richardson, "Kemper College of Missouri," June 1961, pp. 111–26. The 150th anniversary of Kemper's consecration was celebrated with a conference at Nashotah House and the publication of the papers presented; see Charles R. Henery, ed., *Beyond the Horizon: Frontiers for Mission* (1986).

DONALD S. ARMENTROUT

KEMPER, James Lawson (11 June 1823–7 Apr. 1895), Confederate general and governor of Virginia, was born in Madison County, Virginia, the son of William Kemper, a merchant and farmer, and Maria Elizabeth Allison. From 1840 to 1842 he was a student at Washington College in Lexington, Virginia, graduating from that institution with the equivalent of a modern-day B.A. During his student days in Lexington he also attended a civil engineering class at the Virginia Military Institute and, as a "Cincinnati cadet" volunteer, participated in a citizen-soldier training program as well.

Returning to his family's 1,300-acre farm, "Mountain Prospect," Kemper assisted in supervising the fifteen to twenty slaves that constituted the labor force, and he also taught in a local "old field" (primary) school. He then began law studies in Charleston, Virginia (now West Virginia), under the direction of Judge George W. Summers and was admitted to the bar in 1846. Volunteering for service in the Mexican War, Kemper was commissioned as a captain in the First Virginia Regiment early in 1847—the prelude to fifteen months of service with American occupation forces under the command of General Zachary Taylor.

Mustered out of the army in 1848, Kemper opened a law office in Madison Court House, Virginia. He achieved considerable success as an attorney and in 1853 married Cremora Conway "Belle" Cave. The couple would have seven children before Belle Kemper's death in 1870.

Meanwhile, the young attorney became increasingly involved in politics. Affiliating with the Democratic party, he was elected to the Virginia House of Delegates in 1853 and retained his seat as Madison County's representative for almost a decade. Although he played an active role in debates over banking policies and internal improvements, he gained particular distinction as an advocate of military preparedness—a concern accentuated by his fears of abolitionist agitation in the North. Indicative of his rapid rise to prominence, he became chairman of the house Committee on Military Affairs, secured the passage of a comprehensive militia reorganization act in 1858, and was appointed to head the Board of Visitors at the Virginia Military Institute. After Abraham Lincoln's victory in the 1860 presidential race, Kemper's devotion to southern rights took a more extremist turn: he spearheaded the legislative drive to summon the state convention that ultimately voted to secede from the Union.

With the outbreak of the Civil War, Kemper (already a brigadier general in the militia) was mustered into the Confederate army in May 1861 as colonel of the Seventh Virginia Infantry. Service at the battle of Bull Run (Manassas) was followed by a final stint in the house of delegates—this time as its Speaker—during the 1861–1862 session. Resuming his military duties, he was promoted to brigadier general in 1862 and fought bravely and effectively in the campaigns of the Army of Northern Virginia. At Gettysburg, while commanding a lead unit of General George E. Pickett's famous charge, Kemper was severely wounded and was captured by enemy troops. After three months as a prisoner of war, he was exchanged for a northern brigadier general in September 1863. Only partially recovered from his injuries (he walked with a pronounced limp for the rest of his life), Kemper was unfit for additional battlefield service. Instead he was promoted to major general in 1864, and he worked behind the lines as commander of his state's reserve forces and, subsequently, as an official in the Confederate Conscription Bureau.

During the immediate postwar years, Kemper struggled to rebuild his economic position in a devastated, impoverished Virginia. A variety of real estate, mining, railroad, and express mail ventures produced minimal returns, but revenues from a reviving law practice enabled him to build a new home at Madison Court House and to purchase sizable tracts of farmland in Madison and Cumberland counties.

Becoming active in politics once again, Kemper was appalled by the advent of Congressional Reconstruction and by the temporary ascendancy of the racially egalitarian, carpetbagger-dominated Republican party in Virginia. Anxious to thwart these developments, he helped to organize the state's white supremacy–oriented Conservative party in 1867, served as a delegate to the Democratic National Convention in 1868, and supported the coalition of Conservatives and moderate ("True") Republicans that defeated the Radical wing of the Virginia GOP in gubernatorial and legislative elections in 1869. Three years later he campaigned across the state as an at-large elector for the Liberal Republican–Democratic presidential ticket.

The Madison attorney's political activism, distinguished military record, and reputation for personal honesty brought him to the forefront in the contest for the Conservative gubernatorial nomination in 1873—a race in which he also benefited from the support of Petersburg railroad magnate William Mahone, an adept political organizer. Securing the endorsement of his party's state convention, Kemper went on to defeat Republican candidate Robert W. Hughes by more than 27,000 votes.

Inaugurated as governor in January 1874, Kemper pursued surprisingly moderate policies. Anxious to make Virginia prosperous once again, he endeavored to calm sectional antagonisms and to encourage immigration and investment from the North. Although committed to white rule, he espoused paternalistic attitudes toward blacks and insisted that he would pro-tect their civil rights. Transforming rhetoric into action, he defied powerful elements in his party by vetoing an 1874 bill that sought to replace popularly elected officials in black-majority Petersburg with a judge-appointed commission.

Increasingly, however, Virginia's $45 million public debt emerged as the central issue of Kemper's gubernatorial term. Contracted to finance antebellum internal improvements, this massive financial burden had been exacerbated by wartime property losses and by hardships stemming from the nationwide economic panic of 1873. Unfortunately, Kemper's 1874 drive to negotiate a one-third reduction in the interest rate on state bonds was blocked by legislative inertia and creditor intransigence. Unwilling to countenance repudiation, the governor then commenced a prolonged struggle to meet the annual interest payments while maintaining appropriations for public schools and other services. The results were disappointing. His efforts to discharge superfluous bureaucrats, reduce costs, and raise taxes aroused opposition or, at most, half-hearted support from lawmakers and the electorate. Opinionated and sometimes irascible, Kemper displayed little talent for patronage politics and the legislative coalition building that might have secured a more positive response to his programs.

Relinquishing the governorship to his successor in 1878, Kemper went home to practice law. He moved to "Walnut Hills" in Orange County, Virginia, early in the next decade. His death there ended the career of a courageous soldier and a resolute (though flawed) political leader.

• Extensive collections of Kemper's papers are available at the University of Virginia, the Virginia State Library, and the Virginia Historical Society. The published *Journals* of the Virginia House of Delegates and state senate (1874–1877) provide copies of official messages during his gubernatorial term.

Robert R. Jones analyzes various aspects of Kemper's activities in the following works: "Forgotten Virginian: The Early Life and Career of James Lawson Kemper, 1823–1865" (M.A. thesis, Univ. of Virginia, 1961); "Conservative Virginian: The Post-war Career of Governor James Lawson Kemper" (Ph.D. diss., Univ. of Virginia, 1964); "The Mexican War Diary of James Lawson Kemper," *Virginia Magazine of History and Biography* 74 (1966): 386–428; "James L. Kemper and the Virginia Redeemers Face the Race Question: A Reconsideration," *Journal of Southern History* 38 (1972): 393–414; and "James Lawson Kemper: Native-Son Redeemer," in *The Governors of Virginia, 1860–1978*, ed. Edward Younger and James Tice Moore (1982).

Although decidedly inferior to Jones's studies in terms of political analysis, Harold R. Woodward, *Major General James Lawson Kemper, C.S.A.: The Confederacy's Forgotten Son* (1993), does provide an informative account of the general's wartime experiences. For additional insights into Kemper's post–Civil War career, see Charles C. Pearson, *The Readjuster Movement in Virginia* (1917); Nelson M. Blake, *William Mahone of Virginia: Soldier and Political Insurgent* (1935); Allen W. Moger, *Virginia: Bourbonism to Byrd, 1870–1925* (1968); Jack P. Maddex, Jr., *The Virginia Conservatives, 1867–1879: A Study in Reconstruction Politics* (1970); and

Moore, *Two Paths to the New South: The Virginia Debt Controversy, 1870–1883* (1974). Obituaries are in the *Richmond Dispatch* and the *Richmond Times*, both 9 Apr. 1895.

JAMES TICE MOORE

KEMPER, James Scott (18 Nov. 1886–17 Sept. 1981), insurance executive and ambassador, was born in Van Wert, Ohio, the son of Hathaway Kemper, a prominent attorney, and Mary Jane Scott. After receiving his early education in the public schools of his hometown, he abandoned plans to attend Harvard and instead in 1905 became an office boy for a local insurance firm, the Central Manufacturers Insurance Company. Within two years he was named a special agent for Indiana and western Ohio, and in 1911 he moved to Chicago, Illinois, as the manager of the western department of the company. Leaving Central Manufacturers that same year, he joined Lumbermans & Manufacturers Insurance Company, where he also served as a manager.

Kemper entered the field of property and casualty insurance at a time when costs to insurers were rapidly rising as a result of a newly enacted Workman's Compensation Act in Illinois (1912), and the lumber industry eagerly sought methods of reversing the trend. After investigating a number of lumberyard fires, Kemper devised a "Safety First" program that significantly reduced insurance claims by emphasizing preventive measures and safety procedures. Kemper's work so impressed local insurance executives that he was offered the position of vice president and general manager of the newly organized Lumbermens Mutual Casualty Company of Chicago in 1912. Rapidly rising within the industry, Kemper married Mildred Estelle Hooper in 1913; they had three children.

Kemper rose to the position of president of Lumbermens Mutual in 1919. At that time, postwar increase in the number of vehicles on American roads gave rise to the need for automobile insurance. To meet the growing demand, Kemper organized the Kemper Insurance Group in 1920 (with himself as the firm's first president) and James S. Kemper and Co. (his own independent agency) in 1921.

Largely as a result of Kemper's aggressive leadership, his firms experienced rapid growth. Among the first mutual insurers to venture into the field of auto insurance, Kemper made a point of paying claims promptly, emphasizing that "if you can get a quick, fair settlement without long, expensive litigation, you are saving money in the long run and building good will at the same time." The Kemper Group was also among the first insurers to publish detailed financial statements, a practice that took on increasing importance after the onset of the Great Depression. Following the death of his first wife in 1927, Kemper married Gertrude Ziesing Stout in 1931; she had one son, whom Kemper adopted.

Kemper's rapid rise in the business world did not go unnoticed by his peers. He gained membership on the board of directors of the U.S. Chamber of Commerce in 1920 and also served as the first chairman of its insurance committee from 1920 to 1928. He later served the organization as its vice president (1937–1940) and as president (1940–1941). As his stature within the insurance industry grew, Kemper turned his efforts increasingly toward philanthropy. With his brother Hathaway he founded the Traffic Institute at Northwestern University in 1936 to provide valuable training in traffic management to law enforcement officials. In 1942 he founded the James S. Kemper Foundation, which provided scholarships to college students seeking careers in business or nursing, as well as financial assistance to myriad educational and charitable causes.

In the 1940s Kemper began to relinquish some of his many responsibilities; he left the presidency of Lumbermens Mutual in 1945 (but remained as its chairman until 1957) and also gave up the presidency of Kemper Insurance in 1941 (but retained the positions of chairman and chief executive officer until 1966). One aspect of his life's work remained undiminished: politics. An avid Republican who had witnessed his father's entertainment of party luminaries such as President William McKinley and Senator Mark Hanna, Kemper was a national convention delegate from 1936 to 1952 (and again in 1964), chaired the national finance committee from 1944 to 1946, and served as the national treasurer from 1946 to 1948. A heavy financial contributor to the party, he was also a personal friend of Presidents William Howard Taft, Herbert Hoover, and Dwight D. Eisenhower.

Kemper's long service to the Republican cause was rewarded in June 1953 when he was named as the U.S. ambassador to Brazil. A plainspoken man who never shied away from expressing controversial opinions on international relations—he was quoted in January 1941 (while the U.S. Chamber of Commerce president) as "doubting that the United States should trouble itself about anything except North America and the Panama Canal"—Kemper proved ill suited to the task. Although admired by the Brazilians for his financial acumen, he shocked the country when, during an October 1954 visit to Washington, he declared that coffee prices were likely to fall (which directly contradicted the recent assurances of Brazilian president Joao Cafe Filho). Further controversy ensued when he canceled a dinner invitation to a member of the U.S. House of Representatives the following month; the congressman, a Republican member of the Foreign Relations Committee, had criticized U.S. policies toward Latin America. Despite providing what Secretary of State John Foster Dulles termed "outstanding service," Kemper resigned his post in December 1954. He enjoyed being referred to as "Ambassador Kemper" for the rest of his life.

The recipient of numerous awards during his life, including the Chicago Medal of Merit (1962), the International Chicagoan of the Year (also 1962), the Order of the Southern Cross (from Brazil, 1967), and a membership in the Insurance Hall of Fame (1970), Kemper remained active in business until a few months before his death at his home in Chicago. His legacy was the organization that became known as the

Kemper Group, which by 1980 held $5 billion in assets and ranked as the fourteenth largest property and casualty insurance firm in the United States.

• Kemper's papers are at the Kemper National Insurance Company archives in Long Grove, Ill. Kemper's career received extensive coverage at its midpoint in *Current Biography* (1941) and in an article in the *New York Times*, 8 Oct. 1940. For coverage of his controversial tenure in Brazil, see the *New York Times*, 1 Dec., 4 Dec., and 29 Dec. 1954. His many informative obituaries include the *New York Times*, 19 Sept. 1981, the *Chicago Tribune*, 19 Sept. 1981, and the *National Underwriter*, 25 Sept. 1981.

EDWARD L. LACH, JR.

KEMPFER, Hannah Johnson (22 Dec. 1880–27 Sept. 1943), Minnesota legislator, was born Johanna Josefina on an English ship in the North Sea, the daughter of a ship stewardess and a sailor, names unknown. She was placed in a foundling home in Stavanger, Norway, and was adopted a few months later by Ole and Ingra Jensen or Jenson. She later used the name Hannah Johnson. In 1886 the family emigrated to the United States, finally settling in Erhard, Otter Tail County, in west-central Minnesota.

The family had a difficult time farming. Even as a small child, Hannah did home chores and also hired out for odd jobs to earn enough for school clothes and supplies. Her life was characterized by hardscrabble work to make ends meet. She attended school long enough to pass the state teachers' examination and at the age of seventeen began teaching in the district school at Friberg Township near her home. Kempfer was said by biographer Jon Wefald to be a "stern but compassionate" teacher, and newspaper accounts reported that she had prepared a hot meal for the students every noon. She was active, too, in the community, teaching Sunday school, attending quilting bees, and leading township meetings.

In May 1903 she married Charles Taylor Kempfer and moved to the nearby farm where Kempfer lived with his parents. She continued teaching and also helped the family finances by selling eggs, trapping animals and making fur coats, canning and selling produce, sewing, raising turkeys and pigs, and working in a country store in exchange for goods. Kempfer and her husband were childless, but they took in orphans or children needing a summer on the farm. Altogether, they reared eleven or twelve youngsters.

In Minnesota, women could vote in school elections beginning in 1875 and for library boards beginning in 1898. Women did not have full suffrage in the state, however, until the Nineteenth Amendment to the U.S. Constitution became law in 1920. The first election for the Minnesota legislature in which women were eligible to be candidates was in 1922.

Kempfer decided to run. Her husband was a little reluctant, but other family members and friends encouraged her. She covered her district in a Model T and campaigned as an independent, declining Nonpartisan League or other endorsement to avoid an obligation "to vote according to the dictation of any party

or individuals." She came in second among eight candidates for the four seats from District Fifty, Otter Tail County. In 1923 she was one of the first four women sworn in as members of the Minnesota House of Representatives. Sticking with her independent label, Kempfer served for eighteen of the next twenty years, failing to win reelection only in 1930. In those years, the legislature met only for a few weeks in odd-numbered years. During the sessions, she lived in an apartment in St. Paul and corresponded regularly with Charlie, who stayed on the farm. Apparently, this arrangement, although unusual in the 1920s and 1930s, was acceptable to them both.

Kempfer served on every house committee but one during her nine terms. She served continuously on the Game and Fish Committee and made a name for herself in that area, particularly in 1927 when she served as chair. The American Game Protection Association bulletin noted the "invasion" of women into fields previously the prerogative of men. However, it also reported that the committee had "never been more capably, sympathetically, or intelligently directed than under the administration of Mrs. Kempfer." This committee seemed to have passed legislation touching upon virtually every native species of fish or wild animal. Notably, it adopted legislation in 1925 and 1931 that ultimately brought all the state's natural resources management together in one big agency, the Department of Conservation. During Kempfer's stint as chair, a bill was enacted that for the first time required anglers to buy a fishing license. This was so controversial that Kempfer declined the chair in later years, and lingering complaints about the law may have contributed in 1930 to her single electoral defeat.

Kempfer explained her interest in wildlife by describing how she had befriended a partridge whose young had been shot and that later was killed by a weasel. That kind of personal incident was behind many of the issues she championed. She was an "illegitimate" child; she and her adoptive family had been poor and beset by illness and accident; she knew of tubercular teachers through her own teaching experience. She cosponsored a bill to extend to children born out of wedlock rights comparable to those of children born within marriage (enacted in 1927); she gave considerable effort to improving the lot of handicapped, sick, poor, and criminal persons in the state institutions; and in 1935 she introduced a successful bill to require tuberculin (Mantoux) tests of school employees. She served as a delegate to the White House Conference on Child Health and Protection in Washington, D.C., in 1930.

After the repeal of Prohibition in 1933, Kempfer voted to allow local option in determining whether or not liquor would be available. Kempfer was a "dry," but this vote tainted her as a "wet." She contended with angry constituents and temperance groups for the rest of her career.

Kempfer was in ill health for much of her life because of a kidney tumor caused by a blow received in a farm accident when she was eighteen years old. She chose to retire from public life after the 1941 session. She died in Fergus Falls, Minnesota.

Biographers called Kempfer "the first farm wife" to be elected to a state legislature, as well as noting her election as one of the first women legislators in Minnesota, other "firsts" in her career in the house, and the length of her tenure. Today she would be recognized as a farmer in her own right, as a teacher, and perhaps as an entrepreneurial woman. She did not have a national impact but was instrumental in many changes that have continued to influence life in Minnesota, and she was a forerunner of the multidimensional modern woman.

• The Hannah J. Kempfer Papers are in the possession of her niece, Margaret K. Miller, in Erhard, Minn. Microfilm copies of some of them are at the Minnesota Historical Society and at Moorhead (Minn.) State University. Notes on an interview with Miller (annotated by Miller) conducted by Sue E. Holbert on 30 and 31 Dec. 1974 are in papers entitled "Women Legislators in Minnesota: Notes Compiled by Ramona Burks, Joan Forester, Arvonne Fraser, and Sue Holbert" in the Minnesota Historical Society. Considerable information about Kempfer is found in the Elmer E. Adams Papers, Minnesota Historical Society. Published biographies include a brief sketch by Holbert and Fraser, "Women in the Minnesota Legislature," in *Women of Minnesota: Selected Biographical Essays*, ed. Barbara Stuhler and Gretchen Kreuter (1977), and C. N. Cornwall, comp., and Esther Stutheit, ed., *Who's Who in Minnesota* (1941).

SUE E. HOLBERT

KEMPFF, Louis (11 Oct. 1841–29 July 1920), naval officer, was born in Belleville, Illinois, the son of Friedrich Kempff and Henrietta (maiden name unknown). After attending the local schools in Belleville, Kempff entered the U.S. Naval Academy at Annapolis, Maryland, in September 1857. He completed the course of instruction in the spring of 1861, just as the U.S. Navy expanded during the first few months of the Civil War. Assigned to the sailing sloop *Vandalia* as an acting midshipman, he took part in the blockade off Charleston, South Carolina, and the capture of the Confederate blockade runner *Henry Middleton*. Appointed an acting master in October 1861, he participated in the battle of Port Royal, South Carolina, a month later. During the reduction of Confederate positions at Port Royal Ferry, Kempff was on board the flagship *Wabash* commanding a howitzer detachment. Following this action he remained with the Atlantic Squadron for the next fourteen months and participated in the captures of Fernandina, Florida; St. Mary's, Georgia; and Nassau Inlet, Jacksonville, and St. Augustine, Florida. Promoted to lieutenant in March 1863, Kempff reported to the commanding officer of the USS *Susquehanna* and took part in the bombardment of Servell's Point and the reoccupation of the former U.S. Navy Yard at Norfolk, Virginia.

In July 1863 Kempff reported aboard the USS *Sonoma*. He later transferred to the USS *Connecticut*, then on blockade duty off Wilmington, North Carolina, serving as the ship's executive officer until 1864. He

was reassigned to the USS *Suwanee*, part of the U.S. Pacific Squadron, in 1865, remaining there until 1867. Promoted to lieutenant commander in July 1866, Kempff transferred to the USS *Portsmouth*, then in 1867 to duty aboard the USS *Independence*. While attached to the Pacific Squadron, he participated in the scientific expedition that witnessed the total solar eclipse in 1871. He married Cornelia Reese in 1873; they had no children.

After brief tours of duty aboard the USS *Saranac* (1872) and the USS *California* (1873), Kempff reported ashore as inspector, Thirteenth Lighthouse District, in 1874. Advanced to the rank of commander, he remained there until March 1876, when he became an aide to the commandant, U.S. Navy Yard, Mare Island, California. In 1881 he became commanding officer of the steamer *Alert*. Beginning in January 1883, he successively served as inspector of ordnance at Mare Island and as commanding officer of the USS *Adams*, then in 1888, Kempff returned to Mare Island. In 1890 he became a member of the Board of Inspection, then located in San Francisco, California. Promoted to the rank of captain in May 1891, Kempff became general inspector of the USS *Monterey* in 1892 and later that year was a member of the navy's Court of Inquiry.

In February 1893 Kempff became a member of the navy's Examining and Retiring Board in Washington, D.C., before being appointed to several other boards of inquiry and court-martial tribunals. In May 1895 he entered the U.S. Naval War College, Newport, Rhode Island, where he completed the advanced course the following year. He then returned to the Examining and Retiring Board and was advanced to rear admiral in March 1899. He was posted to the Mare Island Navy Yard as commandant until 13 March 1900, when he became senior squadron commander, U.S. Naval Forces, of the Asiatic Squadron.

In May 1900, during the Boxer Rebellion, Kempff commanded the U.S. flotilla ordered to Chinese waters in support of allied ground operations and distinguished himself during the fighting in and around Taku, at the mouth of the Pai (Pei-ho) River. Upon his arrival, he ordered a combined landing force of navy bluejackets and marines ashore to protect the American legation in Peking (Beijing). The American landing force was joined by troops from Britain, Germany, other European countries, and Japan. The combined forces endured skirmishes and ambushes along the route to the Chinese capital, where they were attacked by large numbers of Boxers and turned back. When ships from the other allied countries were positioned at the mouth of the Pai River in order to bombard the fortresses there, Kempff refused to go along. He later explained that the "Chinese government had not committed, so far as I am aware, any act of open hostilities toward the foreign armed forces." Citing Kempff's refusal to fire on the fortresses, Secretary of the Navy John D. Long, in a telegram to the admiral, expressed "the satisfaction with his conduct which was felt by the Administration and the recognition of his discreet conduct in not joining in the fire on the forts." Relieved of command of the USS *Newark* in February 1901, Kempff transferred his flag to the USS *Kentucky* and proceeded to the United States, where the navy commended him for his successful tour while in the Far East and for his actions during the Boxer Rebellion.

After a brief period of convalescent leave, Kempff assumed command of the Twelfth Naval District, which at that time encompassed the entire Pacific Coast. Concluding forty-six years of continuous naval service, he retired on 11 October 1903. Despite his retirement, he accepted positions as inspector, Steamboat Boat Inspection Service, in 1904 and as a member of a naval board of inquiry in 1909. After completely retiring from active naval service in 1909, Kempff died in Santa Barbara, California.

Kempff's career as a naval officer followed the normal pattern of both sea and shore duty with special assignments, such as participation in tribunals and on examining and retirement boards. His skillful handling of the situation of Ta-ku, China, during the Boxer Rebellion demonstrated his solid professionalism as both a naval officer and a diplomat, skills not uncommon for naval officers during this era.

• The Naval Historical Center at the Washington Navy Yard has one folder of documents on Kempff's career, which sheds little light on him. Sources on Kempff are minimal; but for an account of the fighting during the Boxer Rebellion, see Dudley W. Knox, *A History of the United States Navy* (1936). The U.S. Naval Historical Division published a fact sheet on Kempff's career, *Rear Admiral Louis Kempff, United States Navy, Deceased.*

LEO J. DAUGHERTY III

KEMPSTER, Walter (25 May 1841–22 Aug. 1918), physician and professor of mental diseases, was born in London, England, the son of Christopher Kempster, a botanist and horticulturist, and Charlotte Treble. From an old English family of Norman extraction, Walter was seven years old when his father brought the family to the United States and settled in Syracuse, New York. He received his early education in public schools of that city. Introduced to social activism at a young age, Walter attended abolitionist meetings with his father, an ardent participant in the Abolitionist party and in prison reform.

The Civil War interrupted Kempster's preparations for college as he promptly enlisted in May 1861, becoming a private in the Twelfth New York Volunteers. At the end of his military service, Kempster, who was already studying medicine, was appointed hospital steward at Patterson Park General Hospital in Baltimore, Maryland. At his own request he returned in January 1863 to field service, during which he continued his medical studies informally, having chapters of medical books cut out and sent to him from home. In the spring he was promoted to first lieutenant, and he was present at all of his corps's engagements, including Gettysburg and General Robert E. Lee's retreat. Due to an incapacitating injury received in service, he resigned in December 1863. While convalescing he completed his medical education at Albany Medical

College and graduated from Long Island College Hospital in June 1864. He immediately returned to the army as acting assistant surgeon and shortly thereafter was promoted to executive officer. He remained a first lieutenant in active service until the close of the war.

Upon leaving military life Kempster began the study of nervous and mental diseases, the field in which he achieved national prominence. Throughout his otherwise varied professional life Kempster worked for nearly two decades in the medical administration of state institutions for the mentally ill. Leaving the Milwaukee medical practice he started in 1864, Kempster returned to Syracuse, where he was assistant superintendent of the New York State Asylum for Idiots from 1866 to 1867. In the latter year he was appointed assistant physician at the New York State Lunatic Asylum, Utica; he remained there for six years. At the Utica institution, Kempster trained under the direction of prominent superintendent John P. Gray. During this period (1867–1873) Kempster also served as assistant editor under Gray's editorship of the *American Journal of Insanity*. Kempster's work at the Utica institution secured for him in 1873 the superintendency of the Northern Hospital for the Insane in Oshkosh, Wisconsin, where he remained until 1884. Maintaining professional relations with Gray, Kempster served from 1874 to 1884 as assistant editor under Gray's editorship of the *American Journal of Insanity*.

While at the Utica state asylum, Kempster established in 1867 the first laboratory in any such U.S. institution for the study of the macroscopic and microscopic pathology of the brain. Credited as the first American physician to make systematic microscopic examinations of the brains of the mentally ill and to photograph pathological changes through the microscope, Kempster sought to determine whether a distinctive lesion was characteristic of each form of insanity. Gaining distinction for his work, Kempster was the first physician to be made an honorary member of the Chicago Pathological Society in 1875; in the same year he was requested to address the 1876 International Medical Congress, where his presentation of photomicrographs was well received. He aimed to demonstrate that insanity was a symptom of diseased brain tissue and not a disturbance of the mental faculties independent of disease; consequently, he was an advocate for the care of the insane in hospitals.

In addition to conducting microscopic investigations, Kempster often served as an expert witness in the jurisprudence of insanity, appearing in important cases in the United States and abroad. With former chief John P. Gray, he was a leading witness for the prosecution in the case against President James Garfield's assassin, Charles Guiteau. At a murder trial in Wales in 1891 his testimony caused the judge to conform for the first time in English courts to the American method of charging the jury, whereby a defendant's volition, rather than intellectual capabilities alone, was considered in the assessment of criminal responsibility.

In 1890 Kempster moved back to Milwaukee, but shortly thereafter he embarked on two trips abroad commissioned by the U.S. government. In 1891 he traveled throughout Russia investigating the causes of Jewish emigration, his findings being published by the U.S. government in two volumes in 1892. In December 1892 he married Frances S. Fraser of Milwaukee; the couple had no children. His second mission's objective was to ascertain how foreign governments dealt with contagious diseases, especially cholera, and to determine methods to prevent the introduction of such diseases into the United States. For this purpose he visited Turkey, Palestine, and Persia, mapping the route of former cholera epidemics from the Far East to Europe and publishing his report in 1894. This experience with cholera, rather than ties to Milwaukee, subsequently landed Kempster the post of that city's health commissioner.

In his tenure as health commissioner from May 1894 to 1898 Kempster was contentious but ultimately successful. His efforts to combat an epidemic of smallpox and to enforce quarantine during his first year in office roused the political enmity of a committee of aldermen who spearheaded opposition to his public health policies and fueled local riots against his attempts to isolate, sometimes forcibly, infected individuals. After Kempster was ejected from his office by police in February 1895, he brought suit to maintain his rights and was reinstated after one year with full compensation. During that year Kempster served as Professor of Mental Diseases at the Wisconsin College of Physicians and Surgeons, Milwaukee. Kempster resumed office and devoted considerable energy to general sanitation and hygiene measures, securing public health-related municipal legislation that ranged from the prevention of unnecessary noises to the daily analyses of water.

Kempster was a member of the Grand Army of the Republic, the Military Order of the Loyal Legion, and other military organizations. His numerous professional affiliations included membership in national, state, local, and special medical organizations, and in 1878 he served as chairman of the Section of Medical Jurisprudence, Chemistry, and Psychology of the American Medical Association. He was a member of the Masonic Fraternity and was involved with other benevolent and literary bodies. His first marriage having ended, in 1913 Kempster married J. L. J. Poessell; they had no children. He died in his Milwaukee home after a long illness, and he was buried in Arlington National Cemetery.

Successful in his diverse professional endeavors, Kempster achieved prominence in the fields of both public health and mental medicine. Viewed as a national authority on the question of insanity, he gained renown for his activities and studies as an asylum physician and superintendent. His prominence in public health circles followed from his federal government positions, due to the stature associated with those positions, as well as his experience with infectious diseases and public health measures that he gained through his government work.

• In addition to his contributions to medical journals, especially the *American Journal of Insanity*, Kempster prepared articles in pamphlet form, including *Reports of the Northern Hospital for the Insane* (1873–1884); *The Pathology of Insanity* (1875); *The Treatment of the Chronic Insane* (1875); *On the Jurisprudence of Insanity* (1878); *Mental Hygiene* (1879); *Some of the Preventable Causes of Insanity* (1879); and *Why Brains Wear Out* (1880). The most thorough biographical account is F. M. Sperry, *A Group of Distinguished Physicians and Surgeons of Milwaukee* (1904). See also Judith Walzer Leavitt, "Politics and Public Health: Smallpox in Milwaukee, 1894–1895" in *Sickness and Health in America* (1985) on Kempster's career as health commissioner of Milwaukee. For biographical material on Kempster, see J. A. Watrous, ed., *Memoirs of Milwaukee County* (1909). Obituaries are in the *Milwaukee Sentinel* and the *New York Times*, both 23 Aug. 1918, and the *Milwaukee Journal*, 22 Aug. 1918.

ELISA M. BECKER

KENDALL, Amos (16 Aug. 1789–12 Nov. 1869), journalist, postmaster general, and business agent, was born in Dunstable, Massachusetts, the son of Zebedee Kendall and Molly Dakin, farmers. Kendall spent his early years working on the family farm under the supervision of his father, a deacon in the Congregational church. After attending academies in New Ipswich, New Hampshire, and Groton, Massachusetts, he enrolled in 1807 at Dartmouth College. Frail and unaccustomed to independence, Kendall had difficulty adjusting to college life, especially because many of his classmates had moral standards much less strict than his own and because he had to drop out each winter to earn money by teaching school. But he adapted, made friends, and was so intelligent and hardworking that when he graduated in 1811 he ranked first in his class. Uncertain about his future, he spent the next few years in Groton studying law under Republican congressman William M. Richardson, who later became chief justice of the New Hampshire Superior Court.

Discouraged by the bleak New England economy during the War of 1812, Kendall decided to seek his fortune in the West. In February 1814 he went to Washington, D.C., to seek advice from members of Congress about opportunities in their states. He then traveled overland to Pittsburgh, down the Ohio River to Cincinnati, and on to Lexington, Kentucky. There he found a position as tutor in the home of Henry Clay and then worked as a lawyer, journalist, and postmaster before settling in 1816 in Frankfort, Kentucky, as editor and part owner of the *Argus of Western America*. A clear, incisive, sometimes caustic writer with a flair for combat, Kendall was an immediate success, equally adept at political give-and-take and serious expository writing.

During his twelve years as editor Kendall played a leading role in the political and economic struggles in Kentucky. His views on economic issues were generally moderate. He first supported the Bank of the United States as a means of bringing investment capital into the state but changed his mind after the bank began to tighten credit. Calling the bank unconstitutional, he published a series of articles in 1819 attacking the Supreme Court decision in *McCulloch v. Maryland*, which denied states the right to tax the bank. When the financial panic of 1819 began, he first resisted proposals by the Relief party in Kentucky, which sought to save debtors from losing their property. Only reluctantly did he accept measures restricting foreclosures and establishing a state bank to provide easy credit. But in 1823, after the court of appeals, the state's highest court, declared the foreclosure act unconstitutional, Kendall's restraint vanished. Believing that the will of the people had been thwarted by the decision of the court, he joined the New Court movement, which succeeded temporarily in reorganizing the court of appeals and appointing new judges.

In 1824 Kendall backed Clay for president even though Clay had not supported Relief policies. When Kendall's political friends flocked to Andrew Jackson after the election, Kendall hesitated and did not come out for Jackson until late in 1826. During the 1828 campaign Kendall and his assistant editor, Francis Preston Blair (1791–1876), spoke out vigorously for Jackson and helped him carry the state.

On taking office Jackson appointed Kendall fourth auditor of the Treasury. The two men were comfortable with each other because they both believed in the will of the majority and shared the common goals of wiping out corruption and resisting the power of the bank. Delighted when Kendall uncovered corruption in the Treasury Department, the president began to rely on him and others such as Martin Van Buren and William B. Lewis as unofficial advisers, a group that became known as the Kitchen Cabinet. Kendall strengthened his position in 1830 when he arranged to bring Blair to Washington as editor of a new Jacksonian party newspaper, the *Globe*.

Kendall became invaluable as a speech writer, having a hand in at least ten of Jackson's most important state papers, including his second inaugural address and five of his annual messages. Drawing on the antibank rhetoric of the Relief War, Kendall wrote Jackson's powerful message vetoing the bill to recharter the bank. In the election of 1832 Kendall prepared the Jacksonians' most important campaign statement, the Address from the Central Hickory Club, which defended the Jackson administration and called for a limited federal government. When South Carolina nullified the tariff in November 1832, Kendall wrote several articles for the *Globe* defending the Union. In 1833 he influenced Jackson's decision to remove the deposits from the bank and in August selected the banks to receive the funds. When the Senate passed resolutions censuring Jackson for his actions, Kendall helped write the president's "Protest."

Kendall showed his talent as an administrator in 1835 when he replaced the incompetent postmaster general William T. Barry. Within a year of taking office Kendall had ended abuses in the department, wiped out a large debt, and pushed a bill through Congress reforming the post office. He was less successful in dealing with the slavery question. When the American Anti-Slavery Society sent abolitionist pamphlets through the mails in 1835, he drew criticism in the North for advising southern postmasters not to forward them. He continued as postmaster general during the Van Buren administration, finally resigning in May 1840 to run the president's unsuccessful reelection campaign.

During his Washington years Kendall had become a mysterious legendary figure, supposedly controlling the presidency from behind the scenes. British traveler Harriet Martineau dubbed him "the moving spring" of Jackson's administration and said that he operated "all in the dark" (*Retrospect of Western Travel*, vol. 1 [1838], p. 257). She described the hush that came over the guests at a party when Kendall made one of his rare appearances. Some of the legend was justified, for Kendall had great influence and played a major role in building the Democratic party, but the opposition exaggerated his importance and often used him as a scapegoat.

After the election of 1840 Kendall suffered through a number of difficult years. Unsuccessful speculation in western land had left him deeply in debt, and his plight worsened when he borrowed money to buy 100 acres of farmland on the outskirts of Washington. He tried publishing a newspaper, *Kendall's Expositor* (1841–1843), and after it failed he started a claims agency; but nothing succeeded. Meanwhile he had lost a lawsuit to two mail contractors, Stockton and Stokes, whose claims he had disallowed when he was postmaster general. When he could not pay the damages, he was confined as a debtor to the boundaries of the District of Columbia for two years.

Poor health and family tragedies added to Kendall's woes. So thin and sallow that he was once compared to "Death on the pale horse," he had long endured head colds, lung disorders, and sick headaches (*Congressional Globe*, 25th Cong. 3d sess., p. 387). One observer described him on a hot June day, complaining of a headache, "buttoned up to the throat" with a "white linen handkerchief" bound about his head (John B. Derby, *Political Reminiscences* [1835], p. 58). Within a span of only fourteen months he was badly shaken when his two-year-old daughter Marion nearly died from illness, his son William was killed in a street encounter, and his mother-in-law and brother-in-law were burned to death. Bitter and despondent, he frequently called attention to his poor health and financial woes in his letters.

Just when Kendall's fortunes were at their lowest ebb, in 1845, he was approached by Samuel F. B. Morse, who was having difficulty handling his financial affairs after inventing the telegraph. Kendall agreed to become Morse's agent and plunged immediately into the telegraph business, forming companies, setting up telegraph lines, defending Morse's patent in court, and helping consolidate the companies into several large systems. By 1859 he was a millionaire.

In his later years Kendall devoted much of his time and fortune to charitable works. Ever since his days as editor in Kentucky he had been interested in the care of deaf-mutes. In 1857 he founded the Columbia Institution for the Deaf, Dumb, and Blind (now Gallaudet College). He donated land to the institution, enlisted the support of Congress, and served as the first president. Now a Baptist and a firm believer in the necessity of immersion, he became the principal benefactor of the Calvary Baptist Church in Washington.

During the Civil War Kendall returned to politics as a leading spokesman for the Unionist wing of the Democratic party. He published a series of articles in 1860 entitled *Secession Letters of Amos Kendall*, in which he condemned the South for threatening to secede and the North for giving the federal government excessive powers. In 1864 he wrote *Letters on Our Country's Crisis* and *Letters Exposing the Mismanagement of Public Affairs by President Lincoln*. His final effort was a letter in 1868 ridiculing Republican Reconstruction policies.

Kendall was married twice, first in 1818 to Mary B. Woolfolk, who died five years later, leaving him with three children, and then in 1826 to Jane Kyle, with whom he had eleven children. When she died in 1864, only four of Kendall's children were still living. Kendall himself died in Washington, D.C.

Throughout his long career Kendall showed rare skill in taking advantage of the opportunities offered by the changing society of antebellum America. A complex, driven man, he represented many of the central themes of the era, the rise of mass political parties, the triumph of individualism and liberal capitalism, and the development of widespread systems of communication through newspapers, the post office, and the telegraph.

• Small collections of Kendall papers are at the Library of Congress, Dartmouth College, the Massachusetts Historical Society, Gallaudet College, and the Filson Club in Louisville, Ky. Kendall letters can also be found in the Francis O. J. Smith Papers at the Maine Historical Society, in the Blair-Lee papers at the Princeton University Library, in the Ezra Cornell Papers at the Cornell University Library, and in many collections at the Library of Congress, including the papers of Andrew Jackson, Samuel F. B. Morse, and Martin Van Buren. See also the Postmaster General Letterbooks at the National Archives and the Alfred Vail Papers at the Smithsonian Archives. The *Autobiography of Amos Kendall* (1872) contains selections from Kendall's writings, with narrative by his son-in-law William Stickney. An invaluable source is the Frankfort, Ky., *Argus of Western America*, 1816–1829. See also the Washington *Globe*, 1830–1840 and the Washington *Kendall's Expositor*, 1841–1843. The best doctoral dissertations are Lynn L. Marshall, "The Early Career of Amos Kendall: The Making of a Jacksonian" (Univ. of California, Berkeley, 1962), and Terry L. Shoptaugh, "Amos Kendall: A Political Biography" (Univ. of New Hampshire, 1984). Kendall receives careful attention in Richard B. Latner, *The Presidency of Andrew Jackson: White House Politics 1829–1837* (1979); and Frank Maloy Anderson, *The Mystery of "A Public Man": A Historical Detective Story* (1948). Obituaries are in the Washington *Evening Star*, 12 Nov. 1869, and the *New York Times*, 13 Nov. 1869.

DONALD B. COLE

KENDALL, Edward Calvin (8 Mar. 1886–4 May 1972), biochemist, was born in South Norwalk, Connecticut, the son of George S. Kendall, a dentist, and Eva Frances Abbott. Edward Kendall became interested in chemistry in high school, an interest he continued at Columbia University, where he received a B.S. in 1908, an M.S. in 1909, and a Ph.D. in chemistry in 1910. Kendall's doctoral work investigated factors affecting the starch-reducing ability of the pancreatic enzyme amylase.

Kendall's first position after Columbia was in the chemical laboratory of Parke, Davis and Company in Detroit, where he remained only five months. In 1911 Kendall moved to St. Luke's Hospital in New York to establish a new biochemical laboratory. In 1914 he accepted a research position at the Mayo Clinic in Rochester, Minnesota. One year later he married Rebecca Kennedy, with whom he had four children. Kendall remained at the Mayo Clinic until 1951, when he moved to Princeton University to become a visiting professor of chemistry.

Kendall's contributions concerned the isolation and identification of naturally occurring compounds useful in the treatment of disease. This began with his short-lived assignment at Parke, Davis to isolate the hormone of the thyroid gland. He left the firm, unhappy with industrial research, but he continued his interest in the thyroid at St. Luke's and the Mayo Clinic. Proceeding from the results of Eugen Baumann of the University of Freiburg and of other workers who shed light on the physiology and biochemistry of the thyroid, in 1915 Kendall prepared thyroxine, a crystalline, iodine-based extract from the thyroid that reversed the effects of hypothyroidism. Eleven years later Charles Harington of University College in London elucidated the structure of thyroxine. Kendall's studies of the biochemistry of thyroxine also led him and his colleagues at the Mayo Clinic to help establish in 1929 the tripeptide chemical structure of glutathione, an important agent in physiological oxidations.

Kendall's most famous work, for which he was jointly awarded the Nobel Prize for medicine and physiology in 1950, with Philip Hench of the Mayo Clinic and Tadeus Reichstein in Switzerland, concerned the investigation of the adrenal cortex. Kendall's work in this area began in the late 1920s, a decade that witnessed increasing research by many on beef adrenal gland extracts and their value in treating Addison's disease in humans, a usually fatal disease linked to adrenal shutdown. Kendall set out to isolate and determine the chemical structure of the hormone of the adrenal cortex, the portion of the gland known to secrete the compound(s) in question. In 1933 he crystallized an extract assumed to be this hormone, but this extract did not exhibit any therapeutic activity in animals whose adrenals had been removed, and by the following year it became clear that the adrenal cortex yielded more than one hormone.

From 1934 to 1935 Kendall's team at the Mayo and two other laboratories, one at Columbia and Reichstein's group, independently isolated several adrenal compounds, four of which showed possible physiological activity; these were designated in Kendall's laboratory as A, B, E, and F. Over the next three years these groups established the chemical structure of the four compounds. In addition, biochemical and physiological models predicted some therapeutic promise for these compounds, particularly for Kendall's compound E, in traumas such as burns and in certain infections. Because hundreds of pounds of beef adrenals had to be processed to produce trace amounts of these compounds, once the structures were known, Kendall and others focused on synthesis.

After World War II began Kendall pursued his research on the chemistry of adrenal hormones under the institutional framework of the Committee on Medical Research (CMR) of the Office of Scientific Research and Development, which also supervised investigations of other therapeutic agents of wartime importance, such as penicillin and antimalarials. The CMR's interest was spurred by the possible application of adrenal hormones in shock and by rumors that Germany was employing adrenal gland extracts to counteract high-altitude oxygen deficiency in pilots. A major goal of the CMR program was to develop a practical synthesis of compound E, which showed the most promise therapeutically. Kendall developed a large-scale method to produce a precursor of compound E in 1944, and three years later workers at Merck and Company developed the means of converting this to compound E.

By this time compound E and the other adrenal hormones had not lived up to therapeutic expectations, and many workers abandoned this line of research. However, a completely different application, based on observations of patients with rheumatoid arthritis by Philip Hench, Kendall's colleague at the Mayo Clinic, had been planned by Kendall and Hench as early as 1941. They decided to try compound E in treating this disease as soon as enough of it could be manufactured. In September 1948 the first rheumatoid arthritis patient treated with the drug improved significantly, which convinced Kendall, Hench, and their supplier, Merck, to expand the study. Relief from the disease lasted as long as the drug was taken, although its long-term use had concomitant adverse reactions. Hench and Kendall named compound E "cortisone" in 1949. Kendall continued his work on the adrenal cortex after moving to Princeton, where he died.

Kendall thus played a pivotal role in the development of effective treatments for hypothyroidism and rheumatoid arthritis, and his work on the adrenal cortical hormones helped lead the way toward present understanding of steroid chemistry and the important therapeutic role of this class of pharmaceuticals. His numerous international honorary degrees, civic recognitions, and scientific awards, including the Nobel Prize, bear witness to the gravity of his achievements.

• Kendall's personal papers are housed at the Firestone Library, Princeton University, and Columbia University Library has a taped interview with Kendall. His account of the thyroid work is summarized in *Thyroxine* (1929). *Cortisone* (1971) is a useful autobiographical account. See also Dwight J. Ingle, "Edward C. Kendall," National Academy of Sciences, *Biographical Memoirs* 47 (1975): 249–90, which includes a bibliography of works by Kendall, and Robert E. Kohler, "Kendall, Edward Calvin," *Dictionary of Scientific Biography*, supp. 1. An obituary is in the *New York Times*, 5 May 1972.

JOHN P. SWANN

KENDALL, George Wilkins (22 Aug. 1809–21 Oct. 1867), editor and journalist, was born in Mount Vernon, New Hampshire, the son of Thaddeus Kendall, a store owner, and Abigail Wilkins. Kendall's family was poor, and the boy lived with his maternal grandparents for nearly ten years, receiving little formal education. After learning the printer's trade in Burlington, Vermont, Kendall was employed between 1825 and 1832 in printing jobs in Boston, Detroit, and Mobile, Alabama, in the latter city working for Thaddeus Sanford on the *Alabama Register*. In 1832 he settled briefly in New York City, where he became friendly with William T. Porter, the editor of the sporting and humorous weekly *Spirit of the Times*. Porter's influence would later inspire Kendall's newspaper contributions to the emerging field of American comic and sporting literature.

In 1833 Kendall left New York for Washington, D.C., where he worked for Duff Green on the *United States Telegraph* and was later employed at the *National Intelligencer*. In 1835 he moved to New Orleans, where he worked on the *True American* and then, with his friend Francis Asbury Lumsden, founded the city's first inexpensive daily newspaper, the *New Orleans Picayune*, the first issue of which appeared on 25 January 1837. (The paper's name derived from a small coin worth about six and a quarter cents.) Kendall and Lumsden made the *Picayune* a lively, attractive publication that became one of the important newspapers of the day because of its balanced reporting on current political news, its gossip column, its frequent reprinting of sporting and humorous material from the *Spirit of the Times*, and its comic, irreverent reports of events in New Orleans. Frederick Bullard in *Famous War Correspondents* remarks that the *Picayune* under Lumsden and Kendall's editorship was "a kaleidoscope in which all the hues of the many-colored life of the city were reflected" (p. 357). And John S. Kendall in "Kendall and the Founding of the New Orleans 'Picayune'" observes that the paper "won its position mainly by adopting the policies so satisfactorily pursued by the New York *Sun*, the Philadelphia *Ledger* and the Baltimore *Sun*," avoiding party conflicts while promoting state and local events (p. 272).

Four years after helping to found the *Picayune*, Kendall had perhaps the greatest adventure of his life when in 1841 he joined an expedition sponsored by President Mirabeau Buonaparte Lamar of Texas, then an independent republic, to Santa Fe in New Mexico, which was still under Mexican jurisdiction. Kendall's journey was prompted, as he later wrote in his *Narrative of the Texan Santa Fe Expedition* (2 vols., 1844), "by a strong desire to visit regions inhabited only by the roaming Indian, to find new subjects upon which to write, as well as to participate in the wild excitement of buffalo-hunting, and other sports of the border and prairie life" (vol. 1, pp. 13–14). What ensued were hunger, thirst, repeated attacks by Indians, capture of the party by Mexicans, imprisonment in Mexico City, and, for Kendall, smallpox and confinement in a leper hospital. Months of agitation by Kendall's American friends and negotiations by U.S. officials eventually resulted in his release after seven months in captivity, and he returned to New Orleans and to work on the *Picayune*.

Kendall, who supported the admission of Texas to the Union, was in Texas as a reporter when he heard the news of the Mexican War. Despite his earlier experiences, he accompanied the armies of Generals Zachary Taylor and Winfield Scott into Mexico as a war correspondent. While there, he captured a cavalry flag, was wounded in the knee, and earned widespread praise for devising, with Lumsden, methods for swift transmission of his war dispatches to the *Picayune*. The men fitted out a small steamer as a press ship; it met other ships bearing war news, readied the news for printing, and took it to New Orleans, where workers at the *Picayune* rushed it to the press. It was circulated in the city and transmitted by swift express riders to other newspapers in the country. Kendall's biographer Fayette Copeland says that his Mexican War journalism made him famous as "the first modern war correspondent and the most widely known reporter in America in his day" (p. 150).

Before leaving Mexico, Kendall had agreed to write a book about the war that a French artist, Carl Nebel, was to illustrate. In 1848 Kendall sailed to France to work on the book, which was published in New Orleans and New York in 1851 as *The War between the United States and Mexico Illustrated*. While in France, Kendall wrote frequent dispatches for the *Picayune* about the revolution of 1848. He also met and in 1849 married Adeline de Valcourt, a woman twenty-two years his junior, with whom he had four children. In 1852 he and his family moved to Texas near the present city of New Braunfels, where he became a sheep farmer at his ranch, "Post Oak."

After settling at Post Oak, Kendall began to withdraw from public affairs. He declined nomination as governor of Texas; and although he supported the South in the Civil War, as shown by his publications in the *Picayune*, he was unable to enlist in the conflict because of advancing age and infirmities. In the closing years of his life, he tended his ranching interests, continued to write for the *Picayune*, and traveled in the United States and France. He died suddenly of lung congestion at Post Oak. A talented author, Kendall is important for helping to establish, edit, and build the *Picayune*, for his achievements in journalism, and for his renown as a war correspondent.

• *Letters from a Texas Sheep Ranch, Written in the Years 1860 and 1867 by George Wilkins Kendall to Henry Stephens Randall*, ed. Harry James Brown (1959), gives an introduction with a biographical sketch. Further information about Kendall's life and writing may be found in Francis Brinley, *Life of William T. Porter* (1860); F. Lauriston Bullard, *Famous War Correspondents* (1914); Fayette Copeland, *Kendall of the Picayune* (1943); Frederic Hudson, *Journalism in the United States, from 1690 to 1872* (1873); John S. Kendall, "George Wilkins Kendall and the Founding of the New Orleans 'Picayune,'" *Louisiana Historical Quarterly* 11 (Apr. 1928): 261–85; Frank Luther Mott, *American Journalism: A History of Newspapers in the United States through 250 Years, 1690 to 1940* (1941); and Waddy Thompson, *Recollections of Mexico* (1846).

MARY ANN WIMSATT

KENDALL, Willmoore (5 Mar. 1909–30 June 1967), political scientist and journalist, was born in Konawa, Oklahoma, the son of Willmoore Kendall, a blind Methodist minister and author, and Pearl Anna Garlick. During his boyhood, spent in a succession of Methodist parsonages and small-town elementary schools, Kendall served as his father's eyes. The intense, ambivalent relationship with his father led to an intellectually precocious upbringing as well as changeable interests that would characterize his life. At thirteen he graduated from the Mangum, Oklahoma, high school. He attended Northwestern University and the University of Tulsa before transferring to the University of Oklahoma, where he received his B.A. in 1927. While still a teenager, Kendall ran away from home to New Orleans with the intention of going to South America. He reached New Orleans, but his plan failed. He then returned to Northwestern University, where in 1928 he received an M.A. degree in Romance languages. His thesis was a study of Spanish short-story writer and novelist Pío Baroja y Nessi.

In 1929, with Walter Lippmann as his journalistic idol, Kendall worked as a reporter for the *Chicago Herald and Examiner*. That same year, using the pseudonym Alan Monk, Kendall wrote his first short book, *Baseball: How to Play It and How to Watch It*, although he had never played the sport in college or professionally.

He returned to graduate school in September 1930 at the University of Illinois, where he spent two years teaching Spanish in the Department of Romance Languages as well as enrolling in courses in the Department of Philosophy.

In December 1931 he received a Cecil Rhodes Scholarship. During his Oxford years Kendall studied French, Spanish, and economics. By 1935, when he received a B.A. degree in the Honours School of Philosophy, Politics and Economics, he had became a Marxist. In 1935 he married Katherine Tuach. He spent 1936 in Madrid, Spain, working as a United Press reporter. His experience abroad broadened and changed his interests from literature to politics, while the Spanish Civil War converted him into an anti-Communist.

Kendall returned to the United States and enrolled as a doctoral student in the Department of Political Science at the University of Illinois. Charles Hyneman, a political scientist from the University of Illinois, left to become chairman of the School of Government and Public Affairs at Louisiana State University in Baton Rouge and offered Kendall an instructorship at Louisiana State University. While teaching at LSU from 1937 to 1940, Kendall's graduate students included Hubert Humphrey.

In 1938 he received an M.A. degree in economics from Oxford University and in 1940 earned a doctorate in political science from the University of Illinois.

Kendall's career as a political scientist was characterized by the same diversity that marked his formal education. His first teaching appointments following his doctorate were at Hobart College in Geneva, New York, and the University of Richmond in Richmond, Virginia.

Reflecting the chameleon-like quality for change in his professional life that had emerged during his Oklahoma boyhood, Kendall had quit teaching by the early 1940s to serve as a member of the Content Committee, Office of the Coordinator of Inter-American Affairs in Washington, D.C., and as a U.S. press representative in Bogota, Colombia. Kendall served in the U.S. Army during World War II and was assigned to the Inter-American Defense Board in Washington, D.C. Immediately after the war, he worked for the Central Intelligence Agency as chief of the Latin American Division in the Office of Reports and Estimates.

Returning to academia in 1947, he began a turbulent fourteen-year tenure at Yale University. He was on leave for much of this period, and his focus shifted between academic life and the military. From 1950 to 1954 he served as the project chair of POWOW (Military Psychological Warfare) in the Operations Research Office of Johns Hopkins University and the Department of the Army in Bethesda, Maryland. Holding the rank of major in the U.S. Air Force, he made frequent trips to the Far East. He and his wife divorced in 1951, and in 1952 he married Anne Brunsdale. They were divorced in 1956. He had no children in either marriage.

Returning to his interest in writing, Kendall, with two of his former Yale students, including William F. Buckley, founded the *National Review*, serving as book review editor and senior editor from 1955 to 1963. He severed his relationship with the *National Review* at the same time he let Yale buy out his university tenure.

As with his academic interests and ideological attachments, Kendall's professional and personal relationships lacked longevity. His academic journey from foreign language to economics to political science was a preamble to his careers, which showed even greater diversity: journalist, teacher, and government employee. Reared a Methodist, he became a skeptic and

then a Roman Catholic. Once a Trotskyite, his first trip to Spain during the Spanish Civil War transformed him into a fervent anti-Stalinist. He subsequently became an anti-Communist and anti–Franklin Roosevelt. Despite his ideological shifts, he remained a lifelong member of the Democratic party, although he was a conservative, or, more accurately, an authoritarian populist.

As the political science profession became increasingly empirical and quantitative after World War II, Kendall became increasingly isolated within it. Following his departure from Yale, he took several temporary teaching positions before he accepted the chair in the Department of Politics and Economics at the University of Dallas in Irving, Texas, in 1963.

Despite his reputation as an outspoken, articulate critic of liberal political thought in post–World War II America, Kendall's potential as a political theorist remained underdeveloped, reflecting his characteristic lack of sustained focus. Ever dissatisfied, Kendall thought about leaving the University of Dallas and working for the Lyndon Johnson administration.

He married his third wife, Nellie Cooper, in 1965, the year before he suffered his first heart attack. He subsequently suffered a second heart attack and died in Irving, Texas.

• The Willmoore Kendall Papers are at the University of Dallas Library in Irving, Tex. A number of his letters are in the Francis Wilson Papers, University of Illinois in Urbana, and in the William F. Buckley, Jr., Papers, Yale University Library. For a useful collection of letters between Willmoore Kendall and his father during his years on the Rhodes scholarship program, see *Oxford Years: The Letters of Willmoore Kendall to His Father*, ed. Yvona Kendall Mason (1993). His major book is *John Locke and the Doctrine of Majority Rule* (1941); his most significant journal articles are conveniently found in Nellie D. Kendall, ed., *Willmoore Kendall Contra Mundum* (1971). The most important evaluation of his professional career is by his former student George W. Carey, "Willmoore Kendall: Conservative Iconoclast," *Modern Age* 19 (1975): 127–35, and for important insights into his character, see Garry Wills, *Confessions of a Conservative* (1979). For a fascinating fictional version of his life, see the final short story in Saul Bellow, *Mosby's Memoirs and Other Short Stories* (1968).

WILLIAM D. PEDERSON

KENEDY, Patrick John (4 Sept. 1843–4 Jan. 1906), Catholic book publisher and real estate developer, was born in New York City, the son of John Kenedy, also a Catholic book publisher, and his second wife, Bridget Smith. John Kenedy emigrated from Ireland to the United States in 1815 and lived in various cities, including St. Louis, where he married Ellen Timon, with whom he had six children. They eventually settled in 1826 in Baltimore, where Kenedy opened a small book shop and publishing firm. After Ellen's premature death in 1835, John and his children moved to New York City, where he reestablished his bookselling and publishing firm. Because of the large number of publishing firms in the city and the growing

Irish and Catholic immigrant population, Kenedy decided to specialize in publishing Catholic books. His store soon became a meeting place for exiled Irishmen.

In 1842 John Kenedy married Bridget Smith, and the following year they had their only child, Patrick John. Patrick, or "P. J." as he was later known, received his formal education at the St. Vincent de Paul School operated by the French Christian brothers and entered his father's book publishing firm in 1860. He had a significant impact on the firm, particularly from 1859 to 1865 when the firm sold more than 275,000 Catholic catechisms, a firm specialty. In 1865 P. J. became a full partner in the firm, and upon his father's death the following year he became the sole proprietor.

In an effort to ensure the continued success of the firm, Kenedy expanded his line of catechisms and prayer books. By 1872 his catalog included ten different editions of such books available in twelve to eighteen different bindings. The success of this strategy allowed Kenedy to move the firm to larger quarters in 1873. Much of this success was the result of sales to parish missions.

Kenedy's new quarters were spacious and larger than he needed at the time. To share the cost of maintaining the building, Kenedy leased part of his space to Patrick Ford to serve as editorial offices for Ford's newspaper, the *Irish World*. Aware of the large numbers of Irish nationalists who were attracted to Ford and his paper, Kenedy added a list of Irish books to his list. During the 1870s Kenedy also began to buy the plates and stocks of other Catholic publishing firms that were going out of business. His success was, to a significant extent, built on the foundation of the poor business decisions of other Catholic publishing firms.

In 1895 Kenedy received the honorary title "Printer to the Apostolic See." Archbishop Michael Corrigan of New York had recommended the award to the Sacred Congregation of the Holy Faith, and the congregation issued the award in the name of Pope Leo XIII. Kenedy used this title on his catalog and on the title pages of many of his publications. He further validated his role as the "official" church publisher by issuing annual directories of the Catholic church in the United States.

Although Kenedy's principal interest was his publishing house, the majority of his income came from real estate development. He made a habit of attending sheriffs' auction sales in Manhattan, Brooklyn, and on Long Island. He had an extraordinary ability to predict which properties would increase in value. At the time of his death, Kenedy's real estate holdings were worth more than his publishing firm.

Kenedy married Elizabeth Teresa Weiser in 1873, a marriage that produced nine children, one of whom died in infancy. Two sons, Arthur and Louis, joined their father in the publishing firm, and the firm was finally incorporated in New York as P. J. Kenedy and Sons in 1904. Patrick John Kenedy died in New York City.

At his death, Kenedy's firm had become the foremost Catholic publishing company in the United States and annually produced up to 500 new titles a year. In his own quiet way, P. J. Kenedy epitomized the success of the second generation of Irish Catholics in the United States.

• Efforts to locate the papers of Patrick John Kenedy or the records of P. J. Kenedy and Sons have been unsuccessful. The firm was absorbed by Macmillan and Company in the mid-1960s. The best source of information on Kenedy is Robert C. Healey, *A Catholic Book Chronicle: The Story of P. J. Kenedy and Sons, 1826–1951* (1951), a booklet published by the firm. An obituary appears in the *New York Times*, 5 Jan. 1906.

TIMOTHY WALCH

KENEKUK (1790?–1852), religious and secular leader of the Vermillion Kickapoos, was born near the present-day Illinois-Indiana border at the confluence of the Wabash and Vermillion rivers. The identity of his parents is unknown. The name Kenekuk—also spelled Kanakuk, Kannakuk, Kanekuk, Kannekuk, Keeanakuk, Kenakuk, Kennekuk, Keuekuck—means "putting the foot upon a fallen object." Kenekuk's atypical religious views and charismatic leadership caused U.S. governmental officials and other whites to call him the Kickapoo Prophet.

Information on Kenekuk's early years is scant. He was identified as the "Drunkard's Son" in the 4 June 1816 peace treaty between the Vermillion Kickapoos and the U.S. government, one in a series of treaties designed to settle disputes between the tribes of the Old Northwest and the U.S. government dating from the War of 1812. Kenekuk first gained prominence in the years following this treaty.

According to tribal lore, as a young man Kenekuk was an alcoholic and a troublemaker, and he was banished from his village after murdering his uncle in a drunken rage. Forced to beg in nearby Illinois and Indiana settlements, he eventually found shelter with a "priest" (probably a Methodist minister). When Kenekuk expressed an interest in religion, the minister provided instruction to his Indian charge, who quickly grasped the fundamentals of the Bible and Christian ritual. Determined to atone for past transgressions, Kenekuk returned to his village proclaiming a new religion—a blend of Christianity and traditional Kickapoo belief.

Kenekuk preached a theology that was roughly similar to those of the Seneca mystic Handsome Lake and the Shawnee prophet Tenskwatawa. The doctrine differed radically from traditional American Indian religions and closely resembled the millennial preachings of the biblical prophets. Like other prophets, Kenekuk had "died" and gone to visit God—the Great Manitou—who told him that because the Kickapoos had abandoned traditional ways, they suffered defeat in battle and loss of tribal lands and that Kenekuk had been chosen as a messiah to guide the Indians to salvation and tribal revitalization.

Kenekuk's new religion combined aspects of Kickapoo ceremonialism, Protestant fundamentalism, and Catholic ritual. Approximately 400 Kickapoos and about 100 neighboring Potawatomis converted to the faith, venerating the Kickapoo Prophet while also worshiping Jesus, the Virgin, and the saints and believing in heaven, hell, and purgatory. They also attended formal services on Sundays and holy days. White observers noted that Kenekuk, like a Protestant fundamentalist, preached fire and brimstone, admonishing followers to eschew violence, alcoholism, and other evils. Sinners, who admitted their misdeeds at public confessions, readily submitted to whippings; white observers noted that Kenekuk himself bore visible scars from such lashings. To remember the commandments of the Great Manitou, each adherent possessed a prayer stick—a small wooden board on which were carved three sets of five traditional Algonquian figures. Kenekuk asserted that the prayer stick meant to Indians what the Bible meant to Christians.

The Kickapoo leader instructed followers to shun violence, remain at peace with whites, and to concentrate on farming to provide for their families. In a striking departure from Kickapoo tradition, men worked alongside women to plant and harvest the fields. Throughout the 1820s and early 1830s the Vermillion Kickapoos produced surpluses of corn and other crops to sell to white settlers. They were so successful that William Clark, the superintendent of Indian affairs at St. Louis, did not press them to abide by the 1819 land cession treaty that required them to move to a new Indian territory, west of the Mississippi River.

Kenekuk had not signed the 1819 treaty, for one of the primary tenets of his faith was a strict prohibition against parting with tribal lands. On several occasions Kenekuk apprised federal officials that Indian lands were not available for sale. In an 1827 council, for example, he informed Superintendent Clark: "The Great Spirit told me that no people owned the lands—that all was His, and not to forget to tell the white people that when we went into council."

Although Clark sympathized with the peaceful Kickapoos, the Black Hawk War that erupted in western Illinois in 1832 frightened white settlers, who called for firm measures against all Indians. Thus, that same year Clark induced Kenekuk to sign the Treaty of Castor Hill, which required the Vermillion Kickapoos to move to Kansas. Other Kickapoo bands also agreed to relocate in Kansas, and in 1833 Kenekuk and his followers joined their more traditional kinsfolk in villages on the Missouri River, a few miles north of Forth Leavenworth. Kenekuk and his devoted flock—now known as the Kansas Band—quickly reestablished themselves in the new land. Over the next two decades the band prospered, protecting their lands and maintaining their independence despite open hostility from the traditionalist Kickapoos and attempts by white traders, Indian agents, and missionaries to take their possessions and change their ways.

Kenekuk died of smallpox before the autumn of 1852; however, his followers endured. Unified by Kenekuk's teachings, they struggled mightily to preserve their customs and resisted efforts to take their lands. Their commitment to farming, abstention from alcohol and violence, and religious unity eventually made them acceptable neighbors to the flood of whites who migrated to Kansas after 1854. Despite difficult odds, they held onto a portion of their original holdings. A small number of Kenekuk's adherents has continued to live on the tiny Kickapoo reservation in northeastern Kansas.

• Important primary material on Kenekuk and his religion can be found in Louise Barry, *The Beginnings of the West: Annals of the Kansas Gateway to the American West, 1540–1854* (1972), and Barry, ed., "William Clark's Diary, May 1826–February 1831," *Kansas Historical Quarterly* 16 (Feb. 1948): 1–36, (May 1948): 136–74, (Aug. 1948): 274–305, (Nov. 1948): 384–410; Nicholas Point, *Wilderness Kingdom: Indian Life in the Rocky Mountains, 1840–1847: The Journals and Paintings of Nicholas Point, S.J.*, trans. and ed. Joseph P. Donnelly (1967); John Treat Irving, Jr., *Indian Sketches, Taken during an Expedition to the Pawnee Tribes (1833)* (2 vols., 1835; repr., ed. John Francis McDermott, 1955); Jerome C. Berryman, "A Circuit-Rider's Frontier Experiences," *Collections of the Kansas State Historical Society* 16 (1923–1925): 177–226; George Catlin, *Letters and Notes on the Manners, Customs, and Conditions of the North American Indians*, vol. 2 (1973); and Gilbert J. Garraghan, "The Kickapoo Mission," *St. Louis Catholic Historical Review* 4 (1922): 25–50. For a text of the 17 July 1831 sermon preached by Kenekuk to an audience of Indians and, through an interpreter, to white settlers in Illinois, see Gurdon S. Hubbard, "A Kickapoo Sermon," *Illinois Monthly Magazine* 1 (1831): 473–76.

The only full-length biography is Joseph B. Herring, *Kenekuk, the Kickapoo Prophet* (1988). For additional secondary material see Herring, *The Enduring Indians of Kansas: A Century and a Half of Acculturation* (1990); Arrell M. Gibson, *The Kickapoos: Lords of the Middle Border* (1963); Milo Custer, "Kannekuk or Keeanakuk: The Kickapoo Prophet," *Illinois State Historical Society Journal* 2 (1918): 48–56; James H. Howard, "The Kenakuk Religion: An Early Nineteenth Century Revitalization Movement 140 Years Later," *Museum News* 26, nos. 11–12 (1965): 1–49; and George A. Schultz, "Kennekuk, the Kickapoo Prophet," *Kansas History* 3 (1980): 38–46.

JOSEPH B. HERRING

KENNAN, George (16 Feb. 1845–10 May 1924), journalist and Russian specialist, was born in Norwalk, Ohio, the son of John Kennan, a lawyer and telegrapher, and Mary Ann Morse. His father's financial difficulties forced Kennan to leave school at age twelve to help support the family as a telegrapher.

Kennan's lifelong interest in Russia was the result of a connection made with Western Union during his Civil War service with the Military Telegraph Corps. In 1865 Western Union became the major partner in the Russian-American Telegraph Expedition, an effort to establish telegraph service between the United States and Russia by submarine cable across the Bering Strait. As a member of the expedition, Kennan spent over two years in northeastern Siberia, sometimes in Arctic terrain. When the project was abandoned in 1867 because of the completion of the Atlantic Cable, Kennan returned home through Siberia and

European Russia. He came away with a highly favorable view of all things Russian. In 1870 he published *Tent Life in Siberia: And Adventures among the Koraks and Other Tribes in Kamchatka and Northern Asia*, an adventure story with valuable ethnographic and geographic information. It earned Kennan the respect of both American and Russian scientists and geographers and was his most popular book.

Kennan returned to the Russian Empire in 1870 to explore the Caucasus, then spent the next decade in the United States attempting to establish a career as a lecturer and writer. He published in prominent periodicals and newspapers and gained a reputation as an expert on Arctic affairs and Russian matters. Despite his success, however, he struggled financially. The economic depression of the 1870s forced him to take other jobs, first in Medina, New York, then in New York City, and finally in Washington, D.C., where he worked for the Associated Press. In Medina he met Emiline Rathbone Weld, whom he married in 1879. They had no children.

In 1885–1886 Kennan returned to Russia, this time to study the Siberian exile system, often denounced by critics of the tsarist autocracy as barbaric. Kennan believed that an investigation at first hand would vindicate the Russian government and silence its opponents; instead, what he discovered caused him to join the opposition. Appearing first as a lengthy series in *Century* (1887–1891), then in book form as *Siberia and the Exile System* (1891), his exposé focused on the political exiles, many of whom fit Kennan's idea of noble, courageous fighters for freedom. His publisher called the *Century* series the "*Uncle Tom's Cabin* of Siberian exile." Kennan's advocacy surpassed the limits of American reform, however, for he justified the use of terror to bring down the tsar. His enchantingly told stories of oppression caused Americans to turn out in great numbers for his lectures; during the single season of 1889–1890 he actually lectured two hundred times in less than eight months.

Fame brought Kennan a measure of financial independence, allowing him to leave the Associated Press, but his circumstances still did not provide the freedom to concentrate solely on Russia. He served as a war correspondent for *Outlook* in Cuba during the Spanish-American War and in Japan and Manchuria during the Russo-Japanese War. Again for *Outlook*, during the early years of the century he defended American policy in Cuba and the Philippines and covered the powerful volcanic eruption in 1902 in Martinique. He exposed civic corruption in San Francisco and in the state of Delaware, as well as the mistreatment of Native Americans in the West, and for more than two decades he occasionally defended the Japanese against the era's Yellow Peril fears.

After a final trip to Russia in 1901, Kennan renewed his campaign for Russian democracy. Following the incomplete Revolution of 1905, writing in *Outlook* and *Century* he denounced the tsarist authorities' systematic violation of the promised reforms. His writings in the decade before World War I significantly influenced the final shift in American public opinion away from its traditionally favorable disposition toward the Russian government. The change had begun in the early 1880s with the influx of Russian Jewish immigrants carrying their stories of pogroms and government oppression and had gained momentum from Kennan's exposé of the Siberian exile system. Public opinion underpinned a concurrent shift in American foreign policy, which was a result of the first serious conflicts of interest between the two nations in more than half a century. Based on assessments like Kennan's, both policy and opinion were optimistically and mistakenly inclined to expect that a revolution would quickly replace the tsarist autocracy with liberal democracy.

Kennan worked for political change in Russia in other ways as well, raising money for political exiles and political prisoners and supporting causes favorable to the Russian freedom movement. In 1890 he helped to establish the Friends of Russian Freedom, which had branches in both the United States and England. That effort was part of a broader movement for Russian freedom led by Russian émigré propagandist Sergei M. Kravchinskii (Stepniak) in London, designed to create a surge of influential public opinion in Europe and America against the Russian government. The movement met with only limited success, but Kennan's role in it endeared him to the Russian opposition of all political stripes.

When the revolution finally came in 1917, Kennan at first rejoiced with his Russian friends. Then, after the Bolsheviks took power, he repeatedly denounced them in *Outlook* while privately urging the Wilson administration to intervene with major military force in Siberia in support of the anti-Bolshevik forces. Kennan had never described the Russian Marxists to his American readers, except to dismiss them as cranks, as he did all socialists. He thus was partially responsible for the ignorance with which Americans confronted the Bolshevik regime. To the end, which came in Medina, New York, he remained faithful to the belief that democracy would ultimately triumph.

Acquainted with many people in scientific, literary, and government circles, Kennan counted among his closest friends men like William Healey Dall, a paleontologist who had been with Kennan on his first Siberian adventure, and Alexander Graham Bell, near whom Kennan summered in Nova Scotia for thirty years. To such friends he was not only a talented journalist and devoted opponent of autocracy but a boon companion.

Kennan's historical significance lies in his influence on American-Russian relations, considered in the broader sense of cultural interaction and exchange rather than in just the narrower one of diplomatic relations, and his more limited influence on the Russian revolutionary movement. The most celebrated American interpreter of Russian life before the Revolution of 1917, his reach extended to Europe, where his writings were distributed in numerous translations.

• The major collection of Kennan's papers is in the Library of Congress. A smaller but important collection is in the New York Public Library. Major works not cited above include *Campaigning in Cuba* (1899; rep. 1971), *The Tragedy of Pelée: A Narrative of Personal Experience and Observation in Martinique* (1902; repr. 1969), *A Russian Comedy of Errors: With Other Stories and Sketches of Russian Life* (1915), and *E. H. Harriman: A Biography*, 2 vols. (1922). Kennan translated *Folktales of Napoleon: "Napoleonder," from the Russian; "The Napoleon of the People," from the French of Honoré de Balzac* (1902). The only full treatment, containing an extensive bibliography, is Frederick F. Travis, *George Kennan and the American-Russian Relationship, 1865–1924* (1990). See also George Frost Kennan, Introduction to *Siberia and the Exile System* (abr. ed., 1958), for a brief but perceptive biographical sketch; E. I. Melamed, *Dzhordzh Kennan protiv tsarizma* [George Kennan against tsarism] (1981), and Travis, "The Kennan-Russel Anti-Tsarist Propaganda Campaign among Russian Prisoners of War in Japan, 1904–1905," *Russian Review* 40 (1981): 263–77, on his campaign against the tsarist autocracy; Travis, "George Kennan and the Philippines," *Philippine Studies* 27 (1979): 527–36, on his support for American imperialism; and Taylor Stults, "George Kennan: Russian Specialist of the 1890s," *Russian Review* 29 (1970): 275–85, on his impact on American public opinion. An obituary is in the *New York Times*, 11 May 1924.

FREDERICK F. TRAVIS

KENNEDY, Archibald (1685–14 June 1763), New York colonial official and pamphleteer, was born in Craigoch, Ayrshire, Scotland, the son of Alexander Kennedy, a justice of the peace. His mother's name is unknown. He was a descendant of a younger branch of the earldom of Cassilis (the first earl was David Kennedy, 1509). Nothing is known of Kennedy's early life. He probably arrived in America in the entourage of a fellow Scotsman from Ayrshire, Governor Robert Hunter of New York, in June 1710. As a "lieutenant of Fuzileers" in the New York militia, Kennedy served in the abortive Canadian expedition of 1711. On 14 April 1712 he received a regular army commission as third lieutenant of the Independent Company of Foot at New York; he also functioned as adjutant of all four companies of British regulars in New York. In 1721 Governor Hunter sent Kennedy to England to petition for the strengthening of British garrisons on the frontier, a request that the Board of Trade rejected.

In 1722 Kennedy replaced Thomas Byerly, who had died, as receiver general and as collector for the port of New York, positions he held for thirty-nine years. In 1727 he became a member of the Council for New York. In this capacity he consented to the arrest of John Peter Zenger on 2 November 1734 for seditious libel, although he gave appearances of neutrality in the dispute between Zenger's supporters and Governor William Cosby. He also went along with the council in upholding the executions of persons condemned for the "Negro Conspiracy" of 1741.

In 1736 Kennedy married Mary Walter Schuyler, "a Gentlewoman of a Plentiful Fortune" and widow of Arent Schuyler. This was evidently Kennedy's second marriage since this Mrs. Kennedy, in her will shortly before her death in 1764, referred to Kennedy's son,

Archibald, as "son-in-law" (stepson). Kennedy had four children by his second marriage. His son Archibald Kennedy, with whom he is sometimes confused, became a captain in the royal navy and the eleventh earl of Cassilis in 1792.

As receiver general, Kennedy managed to increase collections of quit rents (2s. 6d. per hundred acres) from £400 when he first assumed office to about £800 annually by 1761. The amount was far short of an estimated £40,000 due annually. Efforts by Kennedy to bring enforcement through chancery proceedings failed. A 1742 act to improve rent collections on the "old patents" was disallowed by the Privy Council. Although a speculator himself, Kennedy believed that huge landholdings deterred needed immigration into the colony. The great landlords feared that expanded land revenue would free royal officials from dependence on assembly-fixed salaries.

Kennedy consistently supported the royal prerogative, thereby aligning himself with what has been dubbed the "Court party" in New York. He sided with Governor George Clinton versus the assembly over disputes regarding disbursements and also over removing control of Indian affairs from Albany officials. Unsuccessfully, however, from 1746 to 1749 he tried to bring peace between the political factions, one led by the governor and another led by James DeLancey, whose followers dominated the assembly. Among other duties, Kennedy was one of the commissioners to settle the boundary between Rhode Island and Massachusetts in 1740 and a member of the board of governors of King's College (later Columbia, chartered 31 Oct. 1754). He was a delegate to conferences with the Iroquois Indians during 1746, 1748, and 1753. Increasingly he became concerned that Great Britain was neglecting the northern colonies.

From 1750 to 1755 Kennedy published six pamphlets, bearing preponderantly on the themes of frontier defense and improved Indian relations, *Observations on the Importance of the Northern Colonies under Proper Regulations* (1750), *The Importance of Gaining and Preserving the Friendship of the Indians to the British Interest, Considered* (1751; repr. 1752), *An Essay on the Government of the Colonies* (1752), *Serious Considerations on the Present State of the Affairs of the Northern Colonies* (1754; repr. 1754), *Serious Advice to the Inhabitants of the Northern-Colonies on the Present Situation of Affairs* (1755), and *A Speech Said to Have Been Delivered Some Time before the Close of the Last Sessions, by a Member Dissenting from the Church* (1755).

Kennedy stressed fair dealings with the Indians, thereby making them good neighbors and retaining them as allies against the French. He believed that trade between Albany and Montreal should be entirely severed. If the French became "absolute Masters of the Indians," Kennedy wrote, "adieu to our *English* settlements." Kennedy proposed appointment of a superintendent of Indian affairs for each Indian nation, with assistants to teach Indian youths English, to distribute goods, and to regulate Indian trade. His ideas were implemented in the royal appointment of Sir

William Johnson as superintendent of the northern Indians (1756) and in the unsuccessful experiment known as the "Plan of 1764" (lasting only four years), which confined the Indian trade to small posts, one for each tribe, staffed by a commissary, blacksmith, and interpreter. Kennedy also called for the creation of barrier townships along the frontier, consisting of Scot Highlanders and German immigrants.

While always adhering to a British imperial perspective, Kennedy argued that the colonists should develop greater self-sufficiency and responsibility. He proposed intercolonial union, an idea which he imparted to Benjamin Franklin and which was influential in the formulation of the Albany Plan of Union of 1754. Kennedy proposed that commissioners from all the colonies meet annually at New York City or Albany to set quotas of contributions to the general defense (to be ratified by Parliament), to allot lands on the frontier, to erect forts, and to regulate the Indian trade. He had ideas about military command, as he outlined in a letter to Johnson, 24 May 1755, "Some Hints for a Commanding Officer" (*Papers of William Johnson*, vol. 1 [1921], pp. 539–40).

Owing largely to his own frustrations in failing to gain customs convictions in the admiralty court, Kennedy thought that Great Britain should eliminate most of the restrictions of the Acts of Trade and the requirement that enumerated commodities should be sent only to England—the latter he referred to as "a Solecism in Trade, and the bane of Industry." Like Franklin, Kennedy considered it in British interests to encourage colonial economic growth.

During his long life, Kennedy acquired extensive real estate holdings: in New York City, Ulster, Orange, and Albany Counties, and along the Mohawk as well as two farms in New Jersey. He owned Bedlow's Island (site of the Statue of Liberty), which he sold to the city for a handsome profit in 1758. He held lots, numbered one through three on Broadway, residing on the latter one. Several years after his death his son Archibald built a grand mansion on lot number one Broadway. The residence, which served as American and British headquarters during the Revolution, became a famous showpiece; it was torn down in 1882.

Kennedy resigned his posts as receiver general and collector of customs in 1761 because of infirmities of age; he also resigned his seat on the council in early 1763. He died in New York City after a brief illness. The *New-York Mercury* said of him that "he was a Gentleman who sustained a fair and amiable Character" (20 June 1763).

Few royal placemen were as capable and foresighted as Archibald Kennedy. While avoiding the local political fray and attempting to be a healer among factions, he was energetic in seeking British and colonial reassessment of Indian relations, imperial defense, and trade.

• A man of reticence, Kennedy apparently wrote very few letters. Some correspondence is found in *The Letters and Papers of Cadwallader Colden*, New-York Historical Society, *Collec-tions*, vols. 50–56 (1918–1923) and vols. 67–68 (1937). The *Calendar of Council Minutes, 1668–1783*, New York State Library, *Bulletin*, no. 58 (Mar. 1902), has entries regarding his public career. Also see E. B. O'Callaghan, ed., *Documents Relative to the History of the State of New-York*, vols. 6–7 (1855–1856). Kennedy's will and that of his second wife are found in New-York Historical Society, *Collections*, vol. 30 (1897), pp. 285–86 and 322. A fully researched and evaluative biography, though brief, is Milton M. Klein, "Archibald Kennedy: Imperial Pamphleteer," in *The Colonial Legacy*, vol. 2, *Some Eighteenth-Century Commentators*, ed. Lawrence H. Leder (1971), pp. 76–105. Lawrence C. Wroth, *An American Bookshelf 1755* (1934), comments on Kennedy's pamphlets and why three of them, which were published anonymously, are clearly attributed to him. Some of Kennedy's activities are recorded chronologically in I. N. Phelps Stokes, *The Iconography of Manhattan Island, 1498–1909*, vol. 4 (1922). The contemporary William Smith, Jr., *The History of the Province of New-York [to 1762]*, ed. Michael Kammen (1972 ed.), and the later Stanley N. Katz, *Newcastle's New York: Anglo-American Politics, 1732–1753* (1968), put Kennedy in a broad context of the political development of his time. A notice of Kennedy's death is in the *Scots Magazine*, July 1763.

HARRY M. WARD

KENNEDY, Charles Rann (14 Feb. 1871–16 Feb. 1950), playwright, actor, and producer, was born in Derby, England, the son of Edmund Hall Kennedy and Annie Leng Fawcett. He was the grandson and namesake of a famous Greek scholar and English barrister who was best known for his translations of Demosthenes' orations. Educated at College School in Saltley of Birmingham, Kennedy initially intended to enter the Anglican priesthood but at the age of thirteen changed his mind and entered business as a clerk. At sixteen he began to write short stories, poetry, articles, and drama, became a lecturer, and cultivated a talent and desire for acting.

Kennedy's first public stage appearance was in 1897 as a starving citizen in *The Seats of the Mighty* at His Majesty's Theatre, London. The following year he married Edith Wynne Matthison of Birmingham, Warwickshire, and also toured as Lord Drelincourt in *Jim the Penman*. At the conclusion of the tour he was made treasurer of the Metropole Theatre in Camberwell. Two years later he joined the theatrical company of Ben Greet, initially as business manager and later as an actor primarily performing Shakespeare. Kennedy's first appearance in the United States was in 1903 as the Doctor and Messenger in *Everyman* at Mendelssohn Hall in New York City. In 1905 he decided to devote the bulk of his time to writing plays, the role for which he is best remembered. In 1917 he and his wife became naturalized American citizens. (Their marriage was childless.)

The play that made Kennedy famous, *The Servant in the House*, was first produced at the Duke of York Theatre in London on 19 March 1907, followed a year later by its American debut at the Savoy Theater in New York on 23 March 1908. A witty, barbed satire of an increasingly elitist western Christian church, the play was Kennedy's only commercial success. The central character, a butler named Manson—apparently a play on "Son of Man," the expression that Jesus of the Gospels uses most often to describe himself—is a Christ figure, or "servant," who uses supernatural insight and personal charisma to bring redemption and spiritual renewal and hope to an old church. The plot, like that of many satires, works at two levels: one deals with the actual structural needs of a church in disrepair; the other involves a daughter's search for her forgotten father. Critical messages carry double meanings aimed at a self-seeking clerical authority that exploits and oppresses both the laboring classes and parish priests of integrity and at a church community that values vanity over humility. The second act proclaims a controversial but prophetic warning during a conversation between Manson and a worker named Robert Smith:

Robert. Fifteen years ago me an' my like adn't got a religion! By Gawd, we 'av one now! Like to ear wot it is?
Manson. Yes.
Robert. Socialism! Funny, ain't it?
Manson. *I* don't think so. It's mine, too!

Based on the success of *Servant*, the Savoy premiered Kennedy's *The Winterfeast*, as presented by the Henry Miller Associate Players, on 30 November 1908. A romance set in eleventh-century Icefirth, Iceland, *Winterfeast* examines the insidious results of hate while chronicling the destruction of the Thorkel family. Kennedy's next two plays, *The Flower of the Palace of Han* (1912) and *The Terrible Meek* (1912), all debuted at the Little Theater in New York. A daring one-act play that takes place entirely at the foot of the cross of Jesus, *The Terrible Meek* was hailed as an experiment in form for its interpretation of the crucifixion in terms of early twentieth-century pacifism. The action, as such, takes place on a darkened stage, which allows the audience only to hear the modern-sounding voices of three characters whose conversation gradually reveals them to be a captain and a soldier who have just executed a man and the mother of that man. At the end of the play the lights come up to reveal that the characters, costumed in first-century, Middle Eastern dress, are at the foot of a manned cross that stands between two others. The final lines, spoken by the captain, reveal the theme of the play as he says to the mother: "I tell you woman, this dead son of yours, disfigured, shamed, spat upon, has built a kingdom in this day that can never die. . . . The earth is *his* and he made it. He and his brothers have been moulding and making it through the long ages . . . The meek, the terrible meek, the fierce agonizing meek, are about to enter into their inheritance." Kennedy said he had been inspired to pacifism and to write the play while staring at warships in Hudson Bay. After *The Terrible Meek* was published by *Harper's*, he decided to further the cause of peace by sending a thousand copies of the magazine to a wide variety of world leaders. The play has since been performed thousands of times in churches and auditoriums. *The Necessary Evil*, which premiered on 19 March 1913 at the Fine Arts Theater

in Chicago, marked Kennedy's return to the stage, as the character John Heron.

In New York In January 1918, Kennedy performed in a production of *Everyman*. Later that same year, beginning on 9 April at the Théâtre du Vieux Colombier in New York, he produced his own play, *The Army with Banners*, a contemplative drama that tells the story of a morning in the early part of Christ's millennial reign. At about that time, he became professor of philosophy and joined with his wife as co-head of the department of drama at Bennett Junior College in Millbrook, New York. His theatrical acting from this time on was relegated to appearances in the annual Greek plays he produced in Millbrook and to parts in his own plays, but he would go on to have roles in three motion pictures: he played the part of Reilly in the 1923 film *Little Old New York*, he played Lieutenant Norton in the 1934 film *Crime without Passion*, and he had a bit part in the 1941 film *The Bride Came C.O.D.*

Between 1924 and 1926 the Kennedys traveled back and forth between the United States and England, and he spent most of the period producing and acting in his next four plays. *The Chastening* which depicts a time in the life of Christ as a young man, failed to get the Lord Chamberlain's license but was performed privately in London at St. Paul's Church and at the Mary Ward Hall in June 1924 with Kennedy in the title role. In July his play *The Admiral* was publicly produced, also at Mary Ward Hall. A satire on human frailties, the play depicts the relationship between Christopher Columbus and Queen Isabella of Spain. In August of that year the Kennedys traveled back to America to tour with the productions of *The Chastening*, *The Admiral*, and *Old Nobody*, and in 1926 he returned to London to present, at the St. Pancras People's Theatre, *The Salutation*, a romance that depicts the meeting of Dante and Beatrice in the presence of Francesca da Rimini and traces their spiritual experience.

In 1927 Kennedy compiled the first of three volumes of *A Repertory of Plays for a Company of Three Players*. The first volume includes *The Chastening*, *The Admiral*, and *The Salutation*; volume two (1933), *Old Nobody*, *Crumbs* (1931), and *Flaming Ministers* (1932); volume three (1940), *Face of God* (1935), *Beggar's Gift* (1935), and *Isles of the Blest* (1940). In 1930 he compiled six of his previously written plays into a volume titled *A Repertory of Plays for a Company of Seven Players and Two Short Plays for Smaller Casts*.

Kennedy's final play, *The Seventh Trumpet*, which debuted at the Mansfield Theatre in London on 21 November 1941, revived his fame in English and American theater; it also revealed an ideological turn away from pacifism as the increasingly evident wickedness of Hitler's Third Reich convinced him of the ethical necessity of World War II. Although it is an Arthurian drama, *The Seventh Trumpet* has been called the most contemporary of all of Kennedy's plays. It opens to find a London bobby named Percival, having been injured while trying to dispose of an explosive device, going to Glastonbury because the monastery of

St. Lazarus has been destroyed by aerial bombing. At Glastonbury he meets a Greek Orthodox monk in search of the Holy Grail as well as several pacifist Christians. They discuss the possible moral justification for the war and conclude—as most liberal thinkers had by then—that the evil of Nazism had to be checked, even if it required engaging in the evil of war.

In 1940 the Kennedys formally retired from Bennett Junior College and moved to Los Angeles. His last literary accomplishment was a series of poems titled "Sonnets for Armageddon," which were presented weekly in 1941 in *The Witness*, a publication of the Episcopal church. The poems were later collected by Margaret M. Gage into a volume published as *World Within: A Cycle of Sonnets* (1956). He died in Los Angeles.

Although he was often criticized for the overt Christian messages of his plays and for putting religion on stage, Kennedy never faltered in his commitment to using the medium as a political and ideological tool. In an interview that appeared on 29 March 1914, he explained why: "I say that Christ needs the play," Kennedy told writer Djuna Barnes. "He's made worse things than that His mediums: the ordinary grafter in the pulpit, the street corner orator, the humbler humbugs of every town. You get God and His Son clean on the stage, for there He is preached without hypocrisy. The person speaking the lines is an actor and is there for the art in the lines and not for the heft of the plate" (reprinted in *Interviews*, pp. 35–36).

• A manuscript of Kennedy's first play, *The Coming of Peace; or, The Old Order Changeth: An Allegory of the Changing Centuries, in One Scene* (1990), is available in microprint form in the collection *English and American Drama of the Nineteenth Century* (1967). Other of Kennedy's plays include *The Idol-Breaker* (1914), *The Rib of the Man* (1917), and *The Fool from the Hills* (1919). Interviews with Kennedy can be found in Djuna Barnes, *Interviews* (1985), and Joyce Kilmer, *Literature in the Making by Some of Its Makers* (1945). Two biographies are Donald R. Stoll, "The Dramaturgy of Propaganda: Charles Rann Kennedy (1871–1950)" (Ph.D. diss., Indiana Univ., 1982), and Mary Lou Steele (Sister Elizabeth Maureen, S.C.), "Charles Rann Kennedy, Playwright for Peace" (master's thesis, St. John's Univ., 1956). Commentary on Kennedy's career includes, A. C. Ward, *American Literature: 1880–1930* (1975); W. J. Meserve, *An Outline History of American Drama* (1965); and Arthur Hobson Quinn, *A History of the American Drama from the Civil War to the Present Day* (1943). Critical commentary on *The Servant in the House* includes G. K. Chesterton, *Miscellany of Men* (1912); O. W. Firkins, "The Supernatural in 'The Servant in the House,'" *Poet Lore*, Nov. 1909; and "'The Servant in the House' Its Author," *Independent*, July 1908. Critical commentary on *The Terrible Meek* includes Halford E. Luccock, *Contemporary American Literature and Religion* (1934; repr. 1970), and a production review in *Christian Century*, 14 June 1923. *The Seventh Trumpet* is briefly analyzed in Casper H. Nannes, *Politics in the American Drama* (1960), and a production of the play is reviewed in *Commonweal*, Dec. 1941. Obituaries are in the *New York Times*, 17 Feb. 1950, and the *Times* (London), 18 Feb. 1950.

CHRISTOPHER WIELGOS

KENNEDY, Jacqueline. *See* Onassis, Jacqueline Kennedy.

KENNEDY, John Alexander (9 Aug. 1803–20 June 1873), immigration official and police superintendent, was born in Baltimore, Maryland, the son of John Kennedy, a schoolmaster who, accompanied by his wife (name unknown), immigrated to the United States from the north of Ireland. After receiving a common school education, Kennedy learned the sign painter's trade. Residence in the slave state of Maryland bred in him a hostility to slavery that was to prove lifelong. In 1925 he became secretary of the newly formed Maryland Anti-Slavery Society, but the society was soon forced to disband by mob action. At about the same time he became Benjamin Lundy's partner in editing the *Genius of Universal Emancipation*, an abolitionist weekly then being published in Baltimore. After leaving Baltimore for New York City in 1828, Kennedy remained an avowed abolitionist and contributed many articles to William Lloyd Garrison's anti-slavery newspaper, the *Liberator*, founded in 1831.

In 1828, in partnership with an elder brother, William D. Kennedy, he opened a store in New York for the sale of painters' supplies. In 1832 he married Agnes Crawford; it not known whether they had children. John and William Kennedy's Scotch-Irish Protestant ancestry opened the way to membership in New York's Tammany Society, which in the early 1830s had not yet discovered the political importance of Catholic immigrants and which, indeed, still nominated only native-born Protestants for office. Thus, the two Kennedys soon rose to prominence as Democratic politicians. William became street commissioner before being elected Grand Sachem of Tammany Hall. John served three terms on the Common Council and was a delegate to the 1846 state constitutional convention. When the Mexican War revived controversy over slavery extension, John Kennedy identified himself with the Barnburners, the radical antislavery followers of Martin Van Buren. In 1848, when the Democratic National Convention failed to oppose slavery extension, he joined the movement to create the Free Soil party. Though he returned to the Democratic fold after the 1850 Compromise, the Kansas-Nebraska Act of 1854 led him to join the emerging Republican party.

In 1853 Kennedy was appointed a member of the New York State Emigration Commission, established in 1847 to guard New York against an influx of disease and pauperism and to protect arriving immigrants against fraud and exploitation. In 1855, when the commissioners opened an immigrant landing depot at Castle Garden at the southern tip of Manhattan to control more effectively the immigration process, he became its superintendent, a position he held until 1860. He owed his appointment to his friendship with Thurlow Weed, the Republican boss who had been largely responsible for creating the Emigration Commission and who effectively controlled it during the first twenty years of its existence. At Castle Garden, Kennedy had to contend with the hostility of booking agents, boardinghouse keepers, and others who preyed upon immigrants and who saw the landing depot, from which they were excluded, except in small numbers and under strict control, as a threat to their livelihood. Despite legal challenges, a succession of partisan legislative inquiries, and even physical violence, Kennedy largely succeeded in ending frauds and abuses and in establishing an orderly system for registering immigrants.

In 1860, after two years as a Republican member of the Board of Supervisors, Kennedy was named superintendent of the New York Metropolitan Police. His appointment followed the passage of the Metropolitan Police Act of 1857, a measure inspired by Weed that had transferred responsibility for policing New York City from local to state authorities and that had enabled the state legislature to change the composition of the police board so as to secure exclusive Republican control. Though Kennedy's appointment was politically motivated and he had had no previous experience of police work, the energy and executive ability he had shown at Castle Garden proved him to be well qualified for his new post. During his ten years as superintendent he improved police discipline and efficiency while resisting attempts by politicians to intercede in behalf of lawbreakers.

Kennedy's combativeness, high-handedness, and repeated infringements of civil rights often aroused great hostility. During the secession winter of 1860–1861 he arbitrarily seized shipments of arms intended for the South, only to be ordered by the courts to allow them to proceed. In late March 1861 he was again accused of exceeding his authority when he sent New York police officers to Baltimore to investigate rumors that president-elect Lincoln was in danger of assassination as he passed through the city en route to his inauguration. Whether or not Kennedy was instrumental, as he subsequently claimed, in uncovering the alleged assassination plot is unclear; the credit for doing so was also claimed by the celebrated detective Allan Pinkerton.

Kennedy won the confidence of the Lincoln administration and throughout the Civil War used his position to uphold the Union and the Republican party. He was among the New Yorkers who organized the Union League Club in 1863 in an effort to promote feelings of devotion to the Union and to make them politically effective. Appointed a federal provost marshal for New York City in August 1862, he apprehended a total of 4,000 deserters, as well as citizens he suspected of disloyalty. On election day in November 1862, he stationed policemen at polling places to record the names of would-be (Democratic) voters who had sworn themselves aliens in order to escape the draft. The following month he incurred fresh criticism from antiabolitionist New Yorkers when he mustered a large force of police to ensure a hearing for the antislavery orator Wendell Phillips. Kennedy came to embody Republicanism to the city's immigrant poor, which contributed to the near-fatal attack upon him during the New York City draft riots in July 1863.

Having learned that antidraft rioters were converging on the provost marshal's office at Third Avenue and Forty-sixth Street, where the draft lottery was taking place, Kennedy ordered reinforcements to the scene. He became separated from his men and, though out of uniform, was recognized by the rioters, who beat him savagely and left him for dead. His injuries incapacitated him for months and left him permanently lame. On hearing of the episode, William Lloyd Garrison wrote feelingly of how Kennedy had fallen "crushed and mangled under the blows of traitorous and proslavery ruffians . . . while doing manly service in the cause of liberty and order."

After the war Kennedy was less frequently in the public eye, but his strict enforcement of the 1866 Metropolitan Excise Act, which prohibited the sale of liquor on Sundays, enraged New York City's liquor dealers and its German community. The adoption of the Tweed charter for New York City in 1870 heralded the end of Kennedy's police career. All state commissions in the city having been abolished, the Metropolitan Police gave way to a municipal police department. After two years as president of a street railroad company, in 1872 he was appointed collector of assessments, an office he held until his death at his home in New York City.

Kennedy was a product of a political culture that looked on the police department primarily as a source of patronage and as a means of influencing elections. But despite his political involvement, his integrity and zeal were never questioned, even by those who likened him to Joseph Fouché, Napoleon's authoritarian minister of police. Despite the social disruption and accelerated growth of the Civil War decade, he brought stability and efficiency to police administration.

• Kennedy's papers do not appear to have survived, but there are letters from him in the papers of Thurlow Weed (University of Rochester Library), Abraham Lincoln (Library of Congress), and William Lloyd Garrison (Boston Public Library). No biography exists, but full obituaries appeared in the 21 June 1873 issues of the *New York Times*, the *New York Daily Tribune*, and the *New York Herald*. Kennedy's reports as superintendent of Castle Garden are in *Annual Reports of the Commissioners of Emigration of the State of New York from . . . 1847 to 1860 inclusive . . .* (1861). Further details of his work at the immigrant landing depot are in *Report of the Majority of the Committee appointed to investigate certain charges against the Commissioners of Emigration*, New York State Assembly Documents, 1859, no. 53. Kennedy's *Annual Reports of the Superintendent of the New York Metropolitan Police* are also printed in the New York State Assembly Documents, 1860–1870. For his work as Police Superintendent, see James F. Richardson, *The New York Police, Colonial Times to the Present* (1970). Kennedy's account of his role in thwarting the Baltimore plot appears in Benson J. Lossing, ed., *A History of the Civil War*, vol. 2 (1868), but its reliability is questioned in Norma B. Cuthbert, ed., *Lincoln and the Baltimore Plot, 1861* (1949). Kennedy's letters to the War Department are in *War of the Rebellion . . . Official Records of the Union and Confederate Armies*, (128 vols., 1880–1901). David M. Barnes, *The*

Draft Riots . . . (1863), is a contemporary account, but an excellent modern treatment is Iver Bernstein, *The New York City Draft Riots* (1990).

MALDWYN A. JONES

KENNEDY, John Arthur (17 Feb. 1914–5 Jan. 1990), actor, was born in Worcester, Massachusetts, the son of J. T. Kennedy, a dentist, and Helen Thompson. Educated in Worcester at South High School and Worcester Academy, Kennedy dreamed of being a jockey. Sprouting to a height of five feet eleven inches, which made him too tall to race horses, Kennedy turned his interest to the stage. He studied drama at Carnegie Institute of Technology in Pittsburgh and received his B.A. in 1934. In March 1938 Kennedy married actress Mary Cheffey; they had two children.

Upon graduation, Kennedy moved to New York and began his career with the Group Theatre, billing himself as John Kennedy. Then he performed with the Globe Theatre's touring classical repertory company. He made his Broadway debut in September 1937 at the St. James Theatre playing Bushy in Maurice Evans's *Richard II* and returned to that company in 1939 to play Sir Richard Vernon in Evans's *Henry IV, Part I*. Billing himself as J. Arthur Kennedy because another actor named John Kennedy was already a member of Actor's Equity, he played Jerry Dorgan in the Federal Theatre production of *Life and Death of an American* at the Maxine Elliott Theatre in May 1939. Dropping the initial J., Kennedy played Smithers in *International Incident* at the Ethel Barrymore Theatre opening in April 1940.

In 1940 James Cagney recruited Kennedy to play his younger brother in the Warner Bros. film *City for Conquest*. For the next six years Kennedy worked primarily in Hollywood, appearing in *Highway West* (1941), *High Sierra* (1941), *They Died with Their Boots On* (1941), *Strange Alibi* (1941), *Knockout* (1941), *Desperate Journey* (1942), *Air Force* (1943), *Devotion* (1946), *Boomerang* (1947), and *Cheyenne* (1947), among others. During these years Kennedy also served in World War II in the U.S. Air Force, First Motion Picture unit.

In 1947 Kennedy began juggling careers on both coasts—acting in movies and on the New York stage. In 1947 he starred as Chris Keller in Elia Kazan's production of Arthur Miller's *All My Sons* at the Coronet Theatre, for which Brooks Atkinson praised his "insight into the progress of the character" (*New York Times*, 30 Jan. 1947). Kennedy subsequently received an Antionette Perry (Tony) Award as best supporting actor for his portrayal of Biff in Miller's *Death of a Salesman* in 1949 at the Morosco Theatre. The critic for the *New York World Telegram* praised his performance, writing, "Only a rare young actor can sustain a role of hysterical intensity with any dignity but Arthur Kennedy does it with the utmost taste and strength" (11 Feb. 1949), and the *New York Sun* critic raved that Kennedy brought "tremendous force and drive to his playing of Biff . . . a vibrant young actor" (11 Feb. 1949).

During the next ten years Kennedy did his most acclaimed work, receiving five Academy Award nominations for roles in *Champion* (1949), *Bright Victory* (1951), *Trial* (1955), *Peyton Place* (1957), and *Some Came Running* (1959). He was named best actor by the New York Film Critics for *Bright Victory* and won a Golden Globe Award for best supporting actor for *Trial*. He also received a Film Daily Award and a Limelight Award for his role in *Elmer Gantry* (1960). Kennedy was also known for his roles in popular westerns—working with directors Nicholas Ray, Fritz Lang, and Anthony Mann in *The Lusty Men* (1952), *Rancho Notorious* (1952), *Bend of the River* (1952), and *The Man from Laramie* (1955), among others.

On Broadway, Kennedy continued his successful relationship with playwright Arthur Miller, starring as John Proctor in *The Crucible* (1953), and Walter Franz in *The Price* (1968). Many critics believed that in playing the role of Proctor, Kennedy had matured as an actor. In 1960 he scored a great success taking over the title role in Lucienne Hill's *Becket* when Anthony Quinn dropped out of the play, and Laurence Olivier switched roles to play Henry II. When the play toured to record houses in Boston, Washington, D.C., Detroit, Toronto, and New York, critics were pleased with the change. Richard Watts, Jr., said that Kennedy's performance made *Becket* "an even finer play . . . and Mr. Kennedy's sensitive characterization contributes importantly to its power" (*New York Post*, 21 May 1961).

During the late 1960s and throughout the 1970s Kennedy worked on made-for-television movies, low-budget westerns shot in Europe, and foreign films. During the 1980s he battled thyroid cancer and eye disease, rarely appearing on the stage or screen. He finished his last film, *Grandpa*, a few months before his death. He died in Branford, Connecticut.

Kennedy's success came as a supporting and character actor. Ephraim Katz claimed that Kennedy "demonstrated great versatility in a wide range of supporting roles and occasional leads, portraying with admirable subtlety a broad array of character shades ranging from benevolent to villainous, from dreamy idealist to cynical heel." One source claims Kennedy was "best at revealing the human sides of villainous characters and the dark streaks in admirable ones. This 'dimension' made him ideal for roles which highlighted or questioned the motives of the leading characters" (*Annual Obituary 1990*). Kennedy brooded and agonized over his roles in order to play them with great sincerity, sometimes isolating himself from his family during rehearsals to spare them from his intense preoccupation with a role.

• Significant information about Kennedy may be found in *Annual Obituary 1990*, which includes a complete listing of his appearances on stage and in film and television, and *Current Biography 1961*. Kennedy is also included in *Who's Who in the Theatre* (1981), David Thomson, *A Biographical Dictionary of Film* (1975, 1981), *International Motion Picture Almanac* (1991), Ephraim Katz, *Film Encyclopedia* (1979),

Cambridge Guide to World Theatre (1988), and David Ragan, Who's Who in Hollywood (1992). His obituary is in the New York Times, 7 Jan. 1990.

MELISSA VICKERY-BAREFORD

KENNEDY, John Fitzgerald (29 May 1917–22 Nov. 1963), thirty-fifth president of the United States, was born in Brookline, Massachusetts, the son of Joseph P. Kennedy, a millionaire businessman and public official, and Rose Fitzgerald, daughter of Boston mayor John F. Fitzgerald. John Kennedy's education stressed preparation for advancement of a Catholic in an Anglo-Saxon, generally anti-Catholic society. He entered Harvard College in 1936. Kennedy, known to his friends and family as Jack, was an indifferent student at first but became more interested in his studies following a European summer vacation after his freshman year. A longer stay in Europe in 1939 led to his senior honors paper, "Appeasement in Munich," which was published the following year as *Why England Slept*. Kennedy graduated from Harvard *cum laude* in 1940.

Kennedy enlisted in the U.S. Navy in September 1941. In 1943 a PT boat under his command in the South Pacific was sunk during a night attack by a Japanese destroyer. Kennedy and ten other survivors spent three days afloat in the ocean, during which Kennedy towed a wounded sailor for miles, gripping his life jacket in his teeth while swimming.

After his brother Joseph was killed in the war, Kennedy took on the responsibility of pursuing his family's political ambitions. In 1946 he won a hard-fought Democratic primary election in the Eleventh Congressional District of Massachusetts, a Democratic stronghold. He was easily elected in November and reelected in 1948 and 1950.

Kennedy's congressional record was undistinguished. He suffered from an assortment of physical difficulties, the most severe of which was diagnosed in 1947 as Addison's disease, an illness caused by an adrenal gland malfunction that weakens the body's immune system. His illnesses were partly responsible for his inattention to legislative duties, but his belief that public awareness of his condition would damage his prospects led him to conceal them. Congressional colleagues saw Kennedy's casual style as that of a playboy, the frivolous son of a rich man.

Kennedy's major legislative distinction was as a staunch supporter of federally funded housing, an issue of concern to the many war veterans in his urban district. He voted against the Taft-Hartley Labor Relations Act of 1947, which was bitterly opposed by organized labor. In 1952 Kennedy ran for the Senate and, in a classic contest of Irish-Catholic against Yankee, defeated incumbent Henry Cabot Lodge, Jr. The next year he married Jacqueline Bouvier; they had two children.

In the following years, Kennedy's life and career made a crucial turn for the better. The development of orally administered steroids that controlled his potentially lethal Addison's disease and two dangerous operations to correct back problems greatly improved his health. A scathing speech in 1954 on the French role in Indochina gained him generally favorable publicity. In 1956 his book *Profiles in Courage*, examining politicians who had retained their principles despite difficult circumstances, won a Pulitzer Prize, although after his death it was reported that the work had been ghostwritten by Theodore Sorensen and others.

By this time Kennedy's goal was the White House. Seeking to prove that neither his youth nor his religion was an insurmountable handicap in the pursuit of a political career, he set out to bolster his mediocre legislative record. In particular he sought to win over Democratic liberals, who were skeptical because of his father's reputation for being conservative and unscrupulous and because of his own failure to speak out against Senator Joseph McCarthy, whose irresponsible charges that many prominent leaders were pro-Communist were popular with many Massachusetts voters. Kennedy did support the St. Lawrence Seaway project despite its unpopularity in New England. He was nonetheless reelected in 1958 by a lopsided margin.

During the years leading up to the 1960 presidential election, Kennedy spoke frequently on issues related to national defense. He made much of the so-called "missile gap," alleging that the United States was losing its military advantage over the Soviet Union, although later he retracted the allegation. In the campaign for the 1960 Democratic presidential nomination, his principal rival was Senator Hubert Humphrey of Minnesota, a leader of the party's liberal wing. Senate majority leader Lyndon Johnson also entered the race, but his campaign was tentative and uncharacteristically feeble. Kennedy's primary victories over Humphrey in Wisconsin and West Virginia demonstrated to skeptics that a Roman Catholic candidate could win in a Protestant region. At the convention he secured the nomination on the first ballot and then improved his chances of carrying the crucial southern states by selecting Lyndon Johnson as his running mate.

The Republican presidential candidate was Dwight Eisenhower's vice president, Richard M. Nixon, who shared the ticket with Henry Cabot Lodge, Jr. The campaign featured the first televised debates between presidential candidates. In the first debate, Kennedy won decisively. Although the results of the other three debates were more even, Kennedy clearly benefited from the exchanges by overcoming apprehensions about his youth and inexperience and by strengthening his appeal to liberals.

Kennedy wooed the black vote effectively by speaking out in behalf of Martin Luther King, Jr., after the black leader was arrested and imprisoned in Georgia. He also continued to attack the Eisenhower administration's defense policies.

On Election Day, the Democratic ticket did particularly well in economically depressed areas, and Johnson demonstrated his value to the ticket by gaining votes in Texas and other southern states. Still, Kennedy's winning margin was paper thin. Although he carried the Electoral College handily, 303 to 219, his popular plurality was barely 100,000 out of some 69 million votes cast.

Members of Kennedy's staff and cabinet, largely youthful and energetic, projected an image of liberalism, activism, and sophistication that was in sharp contrast to that of Eisenhower's administration, which was made up of mostly conservative older men with business backgrounds. The young, articulate new president seemed to be an encouraging change from the fatherly but seemingly unimaginative Eisenhower. Kennedy was popular from the start. In his stirring inaugural address he sought to demonstrate his qualifications as a leader. The speech combined rhetorical appeals for patriotic dedication with stiff determination to resist Soviet expansionism. He stressed the need to assist the developing nations of what was becoming known as the Third World.

The narrowness of Kennedy's victory, however, combined with the lack of a liberal majority in Congress, called for presidential caution rather than boldness. Kennedy's expectations far exceeded his administration's ability to establish the New Frontier, the name of his domestic program. Kennedy hoped to increase federal aid to education, provide medical care for the elderly, and set up a cabinet-level office of urban affairs to oversee efforts to revitalize the nation's run-down inner-city slums. Later, he called upon Congress to reduce taxes in order to stimulate the lagging economy. However, substantial budget deficits prevented most of these proposals from getting anywhere.

Kennedy did persuade Congress to raise the national minimum wage from $1.00 to $1.25 an hour and to pass the Housing Act of 1961, which increased the construction of low-cost housing, and the Trade Expansion Act of 1962, which gave the president additional power to adjust tariff levels. However, his successes in domestic matters were few in number and mostly of minor significance.

Kennedy's record in dealing with civil rights issues also was mixed. His cautious approach disappointed civil rights activists. He argued that the situation in Congress made passage of new legislation unlikely and instead issued an executive order creating the Committee on Equal Employment Opportunity and outlawing racial discrimination in federal agencies. However, he did not sign the executive order banning discrimination in housing built with federal funds, a measure he had promised during the campaign, until November 1962. He also resisted pressure from Freedom Riders and other reformers that he take action to put an end to racial segregation in the southern states and to guarantee to southern blacks the right to vote.

However, events gradually forced Kennedy to take stronger action. On 30 September 1962, after Governor Ross Barnett denied the admission of black student James Meredith to the University of Mississippi, Kennedy dispatched federal marshals to insure Meredith's admission. When riots broke out, Kennedy sent troops to preserve order. The following spring, Martin Luther King, Jr., organized a march protesting segregation in Birmingham, Alabama. The local police unleashed dogs on the marchers, many of them women and children, and sprayed them with fire hoses. In June 1963, roused by these and similar events, Kennedy made a dramatic speech declaring his outrage at the denial of rights to black Americans in the South. The next month he called on Congress to enact sweeping civil rights reforms.

In foreign policy, the challenges posed by Communist Russia were Kennedy's major concerns as president. One particularly troubling issue was the ultimate fate of the divided city of Berlin, which Kennedy considered the most likely flash point for a third world war. Kennedy also became involved in the continuing American effort to strengthen the anti-Communist regime of Ngo Dinh Diem in South Vietnam.

In early 1961 the area of greatest concern was Cuba, where revolutionary leader Fidel Castro had declared himself a Marxist and was rapidly becoming an ally of the Soviet Union. The Eisenhower administration had supported the training of anti-Castro exiles who planned to invade Cuba and overthrow the new regime. Kennedy, after some hesitation, backed this scheme but he hoped to avoid actual American participation in the attack and to conceal American sponsorship of the invasion. The result was a disaster. The invaders landed in southern Cuba at the Bay of Pigs and within three days were all either killed or captured. This humiliation only intensified the president's determination to overthrow Castro and spurred the creation of a covert plan, Operation Mongoose, designed to overthrow the Cuban leader by sabotage and paramilitary means, including assassination.

Against this background, Kennedy met with Soviet Union premier Nikita Khrushchev in Vienna in June 1961. The shrewd, earthy Russian dominated the meeting, predicting that communism was destined to "bury" the capitalist system. He also threatened to enforce the "sovereign rights of the German Democratic Republic," meaning that he planned to drive the western nations out of Berlin.

After Kennedy returned to the United States, Khrushchev ordered the construction of a wall separating Communist East Berlin from the rest of the city in order to halt the flood of East Germans leaving their country in search of a better life in the West. Khrushchev also announced that the Soviet Union would resume the testing of nuclear weapons, and a number of huge hydrogen bombs were detonated in the atmosphere. Kennedy likewise ordered the resumption of such testing and an increase in American missile production, further escalating the Cold War arms race.

Khrushchev's threats also encouraged Kennedy to act more forcefully in Southeast Asia, where any sign of American weakness, Kennedy believed, would encourage the Russians to take over West Berlin. He agreed to neutralize Laos but sent Vice President Johnson to Vietnam to underscore his support of the Diem regime. On Johnson's recommendation he dispatched a mission headed by General Maxwell Taylor and Walt W. Rostow to assess the military situation. Taylor and Rostow persuaded him to send 8,000 combat troops to Vietnam; by November 1963 Kennedy had increased this force to nearly 17,000.

In the competition to win influence among the developing nations of Asia, Africa, and Latin America, Kennedy had more success, although it was still limited. In general, Kennedy sought to maintain a balance between supporting anticolonialism and keeping Third World countries out of the Communist bloc. His most significant innovation was the creation of the Peace Corps, an organization sponsoring American volunteers who worked as teachers and provided technical assistance at the grass-roots level, often in remote areas. Kennedy's Alliance for Progress, which had meager results, offered aid to Latin American nations in exchange for land reform and the establishment of more democratic policies. He also vigorously supported the United Nations' efforts to repress the rebellion of the province of Katanga from the Congo.

By far the most significant incident of the Kennedy administration involving foreign policy occurred in late 1962 in Cuba. That fall, U-2 aerial surveillance photos taken over Cuba showed that bases for missiles capable of carrying nuclear warheads were being built on the island by Soviet forces. After days of deliberation, on 22 October Kennedy appeared before a television audience to explain the situation to the American people and to demand that the launching sites be disbanded and the missiles withdrawn. He also imposed a "quarantine" on further shipments of offensive military equipment to Cuba and announced that the navy would prevent any vessel from carrying such material to the island. Never during the Cold War did the danger of nuclear war appear more imminent. Fortunately, Khrushchev backed down, and Soviet ships heading toward Cuba turned back. After delicate diplomatic maneuvering, Khrushchev agreed to remove the Russian missiles. The United States, in turn, implicitly agreed not to invade Cuba and to dismantle its Jupiter missile bases in Turkey.

The Cuban missile crisis was a major turning point in the Cold War. Speaking at American University in Washington, D.C., on 10 June 1963, Kennedy foreshadowed the future course of U.S.-Soviet relations by declaring that the United States did not want "a Pax Americana enforced on the world by American weapons of war" and reminded the Soviet Union that "we all inhabit this small planet. We all breathe the same air." His initiative was followed by a limited Nuclear Test-Ban Treaty, signed by the United States and the Soviet Union, together with Great Britain, in August 1963.

Meanwhile, fateful decisions were being made about American policy in Vietnam. President Diem's repression of Vietnamese Buddhists further undermined his popularity in the country, but he resisted American efforts to encourage him to reform his government. After months of hesitation, Kennedy finally decided to remove the American forces guarding

Diem. On 1 November 1963, Vietnamese Buddhist generals stormed the presidential palace and captured Diem, killing him the following day. The coup, however, only intensified political instability in Vietnam.

Barely three weeks after the assassination of Diem, Kennedy made a routine political trip, hoping to raise money from Democratic "fat cats" for his upcoming campaign for reelection and to heal a factional dispute that was weakening the Democratic party in the state. He never completed the trip. While Kennedy's motorcade was passing through Dealey Plaza in Dallas shortly after noon on 22 November, he was struck in the head and throat by bullets fired from a window on the sixth floor of the Texas Book Depository overlooking the plaza. Governor John Connally, who was accompanying him, also was wounded. The president was rushed to nearby Parkland Hospital, where he was pronounced dead. Shortly after the assassination, Lee Harvey Oswald, who reportedly had been seen at the Texas Book Depository, was arrested at a movie theater and accused of the crime. Two days later Oswald was shot and killed at a police station by Jack Ruby, a Dallas nightclub operator.

The bizarre circumstances of the assassination caused conspiracy theories to proliferate. A commission headed by U.S. Supreme Court chief justice Earl Warren, appointed by President Lyndon Johnson, concluded that Oswald was solely responsible for the assassination. Although many continue to suspect that the murder was a conspiracy planned by others, the weight of the evidence supports the original finding of the Warren Commission.

Kennedy's 1,037 days as president served as a bridge between the conservative consolidation of the Eisenhower administration and Lyndon Johnson's efforts to fulfill the promises of Franklin Roosevelt's New Deal, largely through initiatives begun by the New Frontier. It was a period of almost frenetic activity, highlighted by dramatic international confrontations and tense civil rights struggles at home. Kennedy's murder made him a martyr, and many Americans found it hard to cope with the sudden loss of this youthful, dynamic president whose eloquent expression of ideals had inspired great expectations.

The romantic image of Kennedy promoted by Jacqueline Kennedy and others after his death has not withstood the scrutiny of researchers and other critics. Close analysis of the Kennedy record and character has included revelations of extraordinary womanizing. As early as 1942, while serving with the Office of Naval Intelligence, Kennedy placed himself in a potentially compromising situation by being involved with Inga Avard, a Danish woman who was (wrongfully as it turned out) suspected of being a Nazi spy. Such exploits continued long after his marriage and during his presidency. Especially hazardous were affairs with Judith Campbell, known to be a friend of mobsters, and with Mary Pinchot Meyer, with whom he had a long-term relationship within the White House itself. Nevertheless, Kennedy became a model who attracted countless young people to government service, and many Americans continued to revere him long after his death.

• John F. Kennedy's papers are housed in the Kennedy Memorial Library at Columbia Point in Boston. The extensive collection, including staff and agency files from the presidential years, is bolstered by a vast number of oral history transcripts, which is fortunate given the relative paucity of personal material in the Kennedy papers. The Library of Congress houses the papers of Joseph P. Kennedy, Sr.

Two outstanding insider histories of the Kennedy presidency are Arthur M. Schlesinger, Jr., *A Thousand Days: John F. Kennedy in the White House* (1965), and Theodore C. Sorensen, *Kennedy* (1965). The standard biography is Herbert S. Parmet's two-volume work, *Jack: The Struggles of John F. Kennedy* (1980) and *JFK: The Presidency of John F. Kennedy* (1983). Written during Kennedy's campaign for the presidency but still useful is James MacGregor Burns, *John F. Kennedy: A Political Profile* (1961). For a highly laudatory account of Kennedy's political legacy, see Irving Bernstein, *Promises Kept: John F. Kennedy's New Frontier* (1991). David Burner, *John F. Kennedy and a New Generation* (1988), is a graceful, brief biography. Carl M. Brauer, *John F. Kennedy and the Second Reconstruction* (1977), is essential for an understanding of the New Frontier's contention with the civil rights movement. For Kennedy's diplomacy, especially his relations with Nikita Khrushchev, see Michael Beschloss's well-documented and detailed *The Crisis Years* (1991). On foreign policy, see the essays in Thomas G. Paterson, *Kennedy's Quest for Victory: American Foreign Policy, 1961–1963* (1989), as well as the scholarly analyses in James G. Blight and David A. Welch, *On the Brink: Americans and Soviets Reexamine the Cuban Missile Crisis* (1988). In *A Question of Character* (1991), Thomas C. Reeves discusses Kennedy's numerous personal indiscretions. Garry Wills, *The Kennedy Imprisonment* (1982), remains a provocative study of Kennedy's drive. Rich accounts of the remarkable Kennedy clan are in Peter Collier and David Horowitz, *The Kennedys: An American Drama* (1984), and Doris Goodwin Kearns, *The Fitzgeralds and the Kennedys* (1987).

HERBERT S. PARMET

KENNEDY, John Pendleton (25 Oct. 1795–18 Aug. 1870), politician and writer, was born in Baltimore, Maryland, the son of John Kennedy, an Irish immigrant and intermittently successful copper merchant, and Nancy Clayton Pendleton, who was descended from a distinguished tidewater Virginia family that included the well-known jurist Edmund Pendleton. The eldest of four boys, Kennedy grew up in Baltimore and spent his summers on his mother's family estate in western Virginia. In 1809 he entered the newly founded Baltimore College, and in 1812 he graduated with a B.A. degree. An avid reader, he continued his studies throughout his life by means of a conscientious reading program in philosophy, literature, and political economy. During the War of 1812 Kennedy joined the Fifth Regiment of the Maryland militia and fought against the British at the battles of Bladensburg and North Point.

After the war Kennedy read law, and he was admitted to the bar in 1816. For most of his life Kennedy practiced law sporadically; but he was always more attracted to a career in politics and writing, and eventu-

ally an inheritance from an uncle removed the necessity of his supporting himself through a legal practice. From 1820 to 1824 he served as a delegate from Baltimore in the Maryland Assembly, where he was a prominent supporter of internal improvements. Meanwhile he caught the attention of well-placed Baltimoreans who suggested him for a federal appointment. In 1823 President James Monroe appointed him secretary of legation to Chile, a position he at first accepted and then declined.

One reason for his change of mind was his involvement with Mary Tenant, the daughter of a wealthy Baltimore merchant, whom he married in 1824. She died in childbirth, and her son—and Kennedy's only child—died eleven months later. In 1829 Kennedy was remarried, to Elizabeth Gray, who remained childless throughout the couple's 41-year marriage.

During the 1820s Kennedy began his literary career as an essayist for a local magazine, the *Red Book*. In 1832, under the pseudonym Mark Littleton, he published *Swallow-Barn: A Sojourn in the Old Dominion*, his first novel and one of the earliest treatments of life on a southern plantation. In 1835 Kennedy finished a work of historical fiction set in the American Revolution entitled *Horse Shoe Robinson: A Tale of Tory Ascendancy*, which was followed three years later by *Rob of the Bowl*, a drama set in seventeenth-century Maryland. In 1840 he published a political satire, *Quodlibet*, and four years later his pamphlet *Defense of the Whigs* established his reputation as a political writer. During the 1840s Kennedy also completed *Memoirs of William Wirt*, a two-volume biography of one of his legal heroes.

Through his writing Kennedy hoped to create a national literature using historical sources as the basis for fiction. He grounded his plots in real events, such as the battle of Kings Mountain, and his popularity with both critics and readers made him one of the most influential American literary figures of his time. Heralded for his freshness of style and plot, Kennedy was considered by some to be the equal of such New England literary stars as Washington Irving and Nathaniel Hawthorne.

After thirteen years out of politics, in 1837 Kennedy was elected as the first Whig to represent his Baltimore district in Congress. He was defeated in the next election by the nominees of Baltimore's strong Jacksonian organization but then returned in the next two congresses to support the Whig's legislative program for an activist government of national banks, internal improvements, and high tariffs. Like most Whigs, he also opposed the annexation of Texas, on the grounds that the acquisition of any new territory would permit the expansion of slavery, an institution that he rejected on moral and economic grounds.

Elected to the Maryland Assembly in the early 1840s, Kennedy became the Speaker of the House in 1846. In 1853 President Millard Fillmore appointed him secretary of the navy, and during his tenure in that position Matthew Perry's expedition began its journey to Japan, and the Naval Academy in Annapolis was reorganized.

By the late 1850s Kennedy, who disliked both abolitionism and slavery, spoke out for sectional compromise. When the Whig party had collapsed during that decade, he opted out of party politics, enjoying the life of a country gentleman at his large estate on the Patapsco River. There he devoted himself to his commercial interests and to his writing. Concerned, as were many residents of the border states, by the growing divisiveness between North and South, in 1860 he completed several political pamphlets urging the creation of a border state confederation to serve as a buffer between the quarreling sections. Like many Marylanders, in 1860 he supported the Constitutional Union party of John Bell and Edward Everett, which he envisioned as a party "of the great body of friends of Union now so madly threatened by the exasperation of slavery." Remaining a stanch Unionist in the secession crisis, he was appointed to the Washington Peace Conference by Maryland's governor in 1861.

During the war Kennedy withdrew from politics and devoted himself to the civic activities that made him a respected local leader. He was active, for example, in the affairs of the University of Maryland, which he had earlier helped to organize. He also served as an officer of the Maryland Historical Society and drew up a plan for the Peabody Institute, a music school and library financed by his friend George Peabody. Along with shouldering these philanthropic responsibilities, Kennedy sat on the board of three railroad companies.

Toward the end of his life Kennedy traveled both in the United States and in Europe where he became friends with British writers, including William Thackeray. He died while on a visit to Newport, Rhode Island.

• The 130 volumes that make up Kennedy's papers are now available on twenty-seven reels as the John Pendleton Kennedy Papers, microfilm edition, National Historical Publications. See also John B. Boles, *Guide to the Microfilm Edition of the John Pendleton Kennedy Papers*. Other sources are Henry Tuckerman (Kennedy's literary executor), *The Collected Works of John Pendleton Kennedy* (1871), which includes Tuckerman's *Life*. Other biographies are Edward Gwathmey, *John Pendleton Kennedy* (1931); Charles H. Bohner, *John Pendleton Kennedy: Gentleman from Baltimore* (1961); and Joseph Ridgely, *John Pendleton Kennedy* (1966). Though dated, two of the best analyses of Kennedy's work appear in Vernon Louis Parrington, *Main Currents in American Thought* (1927), and William Taylor, *Cavalier and Yankee: The Old South and American National Character* (1961).

JEAN H. BAKER

KENNEDY, John Stewart (4 Jan. 1830–31 Oct. 1909), railroad commission merchant, private banker, and philanthropist, was born in Blantyre, Scotland (near Glasgow), the son of John Kennedy, probably a millhand, and Isabella Stewart. He attended school from age six to thirteen and received formal instruction outside of office hours for another four years.

He worked as an ironmonger for British iron firms, including a stint as a sales representative in the United States from 1850 to 1852. During that stay, he visited principal trade centers of both Canada and the United States, where he encountered Morris Ketchum Jesup, a New York railroad commission merchant and private banker. Kennedy resumed his career in Scotland from 1852 to 1856, after which he settled in New York when Jesup invited him to become a partner in M. K. Jesup & Co. (1857–1867). Revisiting Europe in 1867 and having garnered capital, contacts, and experience, Kennedy decided to go on his own at the expiration of the partnership agreement.

J. S. Kennedy & Co. opened in 1868 in New York City and successfully competed with already established firms. Kennedy was the senior partner in his own railroad commission merchant and private international banking house. Kennedy & Co. supplied and financed railroads, especially new and small ones; as a supplier it represented British and American iron manufacturers. As the railroads consolidated and internalized in the mid-nineteenth century many of the tasks previously performed by commission merchants, and as the manufacturers of railroad-related products did likewise, the commission merchant became obsolete. Like Jesup and his other competitors, Kennedy gradually specialized less in goods and more in money, credit, and banking. In this capacity he negotiated loans, sold securities, and performed other banking services.

Just as Jesup had dealt with emerging southern and western railroads, so did Kennedy, whose most profitable and enduring venture commenced in 1873. The St. Paul & Pacific defaulted, and the Dutch bondholders asked Kennedy to represent them. For five depression years he struggled to keep the railroad viable and other claimants at bay. In 1878 Kennedy negotiated the sale of this property to George Stephen Associates; James J. Hill emerged as the most famous of the associates, and Kennedy became Hill's financial intermediary and lifelong friend. In 1879 the new owners reorganized this property as the St. Paul, Minneapolis & Manitoba (later renamed the Great Northern). Personally worth about $500,000 in 1878, Kennedy's connection with this railroad and Hill, especially during the 1880s when he served as both vice president and director, vaulted Kennedy into the ranks of the wealthiest Americans. From about 1890 until his death his link to the Great Northern and Hill was primarily informal, although he did serve as a vice president and director of the short-lived Northern Securities Company, formed in 1901 to hold the securities of the Great Northern, the Northern Pacific, and the Chicago, Burlington & Quincy.

Like other Anglo-American private bankers, Kennedy & Co. channeled European capital to the United States, especially to railroads. In 1873 he became the New York agent of the Scottish American Investment Company of Edinburgh, holding that post until 1883. Kennedy remained an advisory board member of Scottish American for another fifteen years. Owing to his ability to recommend suitable railroad securities at the right price, Scottish American prospered as did Kennedy, both directly and indirectly.

In 1878 the City of Glasgow Bank collapsed through a fatal mixture of mismanagement, negligence, and fraud. The liquidators asked Kennedy to represent the shareholders. He realized on the bank's $5 million in American railroad securities, which reduced the shareholders' liability.

During his years as a commission merchant and private banker, Kennedy performed multiple functions, some of which entailed considerable risk, as evidenced by the number of railroads and mercantile houses that failed following the 1873 panic. Despite its profitability, Kennedy liquidated his firm in 1883 to lessen his nervous and physical strain.

Even prior to the liquidation, Kennedy had been associated with New York financial intermediaries, and afterward he expanded his scope as a financier. He served as a director of the Bank of the Manhattan Company from 1881 to 1909, as president pro tem during 1883–1884 and again in 1893, and as vice president during 1884–1888, until ill health compelled his resignation. Kennedy was a trustee of the Central Trust Company from 1882 to 1909 and occupied comparable posts with the National Bank of Commerce (1887–1909), the New York Life Insurance Company (1895–1909), and the United States Trust Company of New York (1896–1909).

In 1858 Kennedy had married Emma Baker, from an old New York commercial family; they had no children. By the 1870s he achieved a level of distinction as a philanthropist not only by virtue of his donations but also because of his active involvement in the organizations that received his gifts. An inconspicuous philanthropist despite his munificence, Kennedy decreed that no institution or structure bear his name, so deep were his Presbyterian religious convictions. Like others in his circle, he helped manage philanthropic institutions such as the New York Public Library, the Metropolitan Museum of Art, and the Presbyterian Hospital. Kennedy was a major benefactor of New York City and of national cultural, social, and civic institutions. Libraries and universities, hospitals and charities benefited from his money, his presence, and his managerial talent. Kennedy died in New York City as one of America's richest people. He built an estate of $60 million, mostly in securities of railroads; he willed about half to those institutions in which he had taken an active part.

A seminal figure in early railroad development, especially the Manitoba/Great Northern, Kennedy played a vital part in the history of American banking. He also figured significantly in the evolution of the joint charity movement, predecessor of the community chest, in New York and the United States.

• No Kennedy papers exist, but the James J. Hill Papers in the James J. Hill Reference Library contain several hundred Kennedy letters to Hill; also nonexistent are primary sources for the first half of Kennedy's life. Saul Engelbourg and Leonard Bushkoff, *The Man Who Found the Money: John Stewart Kennedy and the Financing of the Western Railroads* (1996), is a biography of Kennedy. Engelbourg, "John Stewart Kennedy and the City of Glasgow Bank," *Business and Economic History* 15 (1986): 69–82, details Kennedy's role in the liquidation of the American assets of this failed bank. In "John Stewart Kennedy and the Scottish American Investment Company," *Essays in Economic and Business History* 6 (1988): 37–54, Engelbourg studies Kennedy as agent of this major financial intermediary, and in "John Stewart Kennedy: Railroad Commission Merchant, Private Banker, and Philanthropist," *Essays in Economic and Business History* 4 (1986): 98–108, he furnishes an overview stressing selected facets of Kennedy's career. Ralph W. Hidy and Muriel E. Hidy et al., *The Great Northern Railway: A History* (1988), examine this most important of Kennedy's investments. Albro Martin, *James J. Hill and the Opening of the Northwest* (1976), explores the history of the Great Northern as well as the intimate relationship of Hill and Kennedy. An obituary is in the *New York Times*, 1 Nov. 1909.

SAUL ENGELBOURG

KENNEDY, Joseph Patrick (6 Sept. 1888–18 Nov. 1969), businessman and public official, was born in Boston, Massachusetts, the son of Patrick Joseph Kennedy, a saloonkeeper and politician, and Mary Hickey. Kennedy's perspective on life grew out of his origins in the Irish districts of Boston at the turn of the century. Grandson of an Irish immigrant and son of a prosperous ward leader of the Democratic party, his childhood swirled about friends and relatives, the culture of the Roman Catholic church, and politics. While he was proud of his Irish heritage and profited mightily from family and group associations, he came to understand that advancement to a higher level of power and status necessitated moving beyond an Irish identity.

Assisted by his father's influence and financial support, Kennedy attended the prestigious Boston Latin School and Harvard University, both strongholds of the Brahmin aristocracy. Failure to excel as a student or to breach long-established social barriers at either institution in no way slowed his pace. What he lacked in academic accomplishment he made up for in ambition, sociability, and sheer nerve. Graduating from Harvard in 1912, he worked for approximately one year as a state bank examiner. In January 1914, at age twenty-five, he maneuvered his selection as president of Columbia Trust Company, a bank his father had founded. In 1914 he married Rose Elizabeth Fitzgerald, belle of the Boston Irish and daughter of the mayor, John F. "Honey Fitz" Fitzgerald. They had nine children. In 1917 he became assistant general manager of the Fore River shipyard of the Bethlehem Steel Company. Two years later he joined Hayden, Stone and Company, an investment firm, through which he learned the intricacies of the stock market and how to use money to make money. By the start of the 1920s he had become a millionaire.

By 1927 Kennedy had shifted grounds, moving his growing family to New York City and plunging into the movie business. The moviemaking venture produced membership in the nation's most glamorous enterprise, but it neither noticeably expanded his fortune nor affected the industry, unless it was to lower the quality of films. The Hollywood years did reveal another aspect of Kennedy's storied reputation: that of a womanizer. His affair in 1927–1929 with starlet Gloria Swanson was to be only the most famous in a lifetime of extramarital flirtations and sexual escapades.

A full accounting of the sources of Kennedy's wealth remained impossible. Reports circulated about his involvement in bootlegging and other illegal trafficking in liquor during the era of Prohibition. While the stories did not lend themselves to solid documentation—the most specific reports came from gangster chieftains—they were too persistent to be dismissed. Clearly, Kennedy made huge sums of money from manipulation of the "bull" market of the late 1920s. One of the few major investors who sensed trouble in the economy, he pulled out of the market in time, thus avoiding the crash that began in 1929. By 1930 his fortune stood at an estimated $100 million.

Kennedy's association with politics stemmed more from tradition and appreciation of the sources of power than from ideology. A major contributor to the Democratic party and a strong supporter of Franklin D. Roosevelt, he was rewarded by the Roosevelt administration in 1934 with appointment to the Securities and Exchange Commission (SEC), a new agency entrusted with policing the stock exchanges. As chairman of the SEC, Kennedy became a true Washington insider. He entertained lavishly, courted powerful people, including the president, and seemed destined for higher things, even—assuming Roosevelt retired after two terms—a run at the presidency. Kennedy left the SEC in 1935, served briefly as chairman of the U.S. Maritime Commission, and at the end of 1937 persuaded Roosevelt to appoint him ambassador to Great Britain.

While the London post seemed a fitting step in the rise of Kennedy as a public official, in the end it produced his downfall. Starting his job in 1938, he exhibited a discomforting acceptance, if not approval, of the fascism that threatened to envelope Europe. In response to the aggressive moves on Adolf Hitler on the Continent, he repeatedly counseled appeasement. The start of the Second World War in September 1939 placed the ambassador out of step with leaders in London and his own government as well. As the Roosevelt administration aligned itself with the British cause, Kennedy, convinced that Germany would win, identified with the critics, the isolationists. Roosevelt's decision to run for a third term in 1940, a decision with which the ambassador disagreed, foretold no bright future in politics for Kennedy. He resigned the ambassadorship in November 1940, never again to be a candidate for high political office. He turned to what he knew best, making money. He earned an estimated $100 million through investments during the war and in 1945 made news with his purchase of the world's largest commercial building, the Merchandise Mart in Chicago. He also began the last great venture of his life: to use his wealth and connections to enhance the lives and professional careers of members of his family.

Kennedy's children established a collective identity rooted almost equally in individual triumph and in deepest tragedy. The tragedy came first, when in 1941 Rosemary Kennedy, who was born retarded, underwent an experimental neurosurgical procedure, a prefrontal lobotomy. The operation failed, leaving Rosemary severely retarded, destined to spend her life in a nursing convent in Wisconsin. A son, John F. Kennedy, escaped more than one scrape with death in military engagements in the Second World War. Near the end of that war, in August 1944, Joseph Kennedy, Jr., a naval officer, was killed when his bomber exploded. Only a few days later Kennedy's favorite daughter, Kathleen Kennedy, or "Kick," as she was called, who had married an English aristocrat, John Robert Cavendish, learned that her husband had been killed in France. Four years later Kick herself died in an airplane crash.

The triumphs usually were in line with Kennedy's self-admonition to be Irish and yet be more. While many of them would not have been possible without Kennedy's name recognition, money, and connections, his training in tough-minded competition helped prepare for the race. Taking up a role from his fallen brother, John Kennedy was elected to the U.S. House of Representatives in 1946 and in 1952 defeated Henry Cabot Lodge, Jr., for a seat in the U.S. Senate. The other sons, Robert "Bobby" Kennedy and Edward "Teddy" Kennedy, finished law school and set their sights on careers in government. The daughters married successful men who, aided by the Kennedy association, established national reputations. The crowning glory came in 1960 with John Kennedy's election to the presidency, a victory in which his father, who maneuvered vigorously behind the scenes, rightly could share. John's victory opened doors for other Kennedys. Bobby became attorney general, and Teddy filled John's Senate seat.

The 1960s, which started so promisingly, became an era of disaster. In 1961, less than a year after his son became president, Joseph Kennedy suffered a massive stroke, which left him an invalid, paralyzed on one side, and able to understand but not to speak. Then came John's assassination in November 1963, in the third year of his presidency, and the assassination of Robert, who was running for the presidency, in 1968. Edward's reputation was tarnished and his political career threatened in 1969 in a fatal incident at Chappaquiddick, Massachusetts. After a demoralizing eight-year illness, Joseph Kennedy died in Hyannis, Massachusetts.

Kennedy distinguished himself in three areas: as an aggressive and astute businessman, as an officeholder and mover in Democratic politics in the 1930s, and as the father of a large family of exceptional children. His role in the third category illuminated and magnified the first two and all aspects of his life and the memory that followed. His most important legacy was as a patriarch, founder of a dynasty in American life and politics, the reaches of which were yet to be determined.

• Information about Kennedy is at the same time open to public scrutiny and difficult to reach. The John F. Kennedy Library has huge stores of Joseph P. Kennedy Papers, but most are not open to researchers. Many people have contributed oral accounts about Kennedy, but the sources dry up the closer one gets to personal details. The studies have continued nonetheless. Joseph F. Dinneen, *The Kennedy Family* (1959), appeared at the time John Kennedy began a run for the presidency. A favorable biography is Richard J. Whalen, *The Founding Father: The Story of Joseph P. Kennedy* (1964). See also Rita Dallas, *The Kennedy Case* (1973), and Ronald Kessler, *The Sins of the Father: Joseph P. Kennedy and the Dynasty He Founded* (1996). Nancy G. Clinch, *The Kennedy Neurosis* (1973), is a harshly critical exercise in psychohistory. David E. Koskoff, *Joseph P. Kennedy: A Life and Times* (1974), is probably the most balanced biography; and Peter Collier and David Horowitz, *The Kennedys: An American Drama* (1984), a balanced, broader volume, explains the difficulty of research into the Kennedys. Specialized studies include Michael R. Beschloss, *Kennedy and Roosevelt: The Uneasy Alliance* (1980), and Doris Kearns Goodwin, *The Fitzgeralds and the Kennedys: An American Saga* (1987), by a semi-insider. An obituary is in the *New York Times*, 19 Nov. 1969.

ROSS GREGORY

KENNEDY, Kathleen Agnes (20 Feb. 1920–13 May 1948), sister of U.S. president John F. Kennedy and an English peer by marriage, was born in Brookline, Massachusetts, the daughter of Joseph Patrick Kennedy, a self-made millionaire, and Rose Fitzgerald, the daughter of John Francis "Honey Fitz" Fitzgerald, mayor of Boston. Kathleen, or "Kick," as family and friends called her because of her high spirits and sunny disposition, was the fourth of nine Kennedy children. The pet of the family and a special favorite of her father, the copper-haired, gray-blue eyed, energetic Kennedy was a delightful combination of dainty femininity and athleticism. Along with her brothers, Joseph, Jr., and John, she rounded out the Golden Trio—the ones on whom their father's ambitions rested.

Kennedy attended the Riverdale Country Day School until the age of thirteen when her mother transferred her to the Noroton Convent of the Sacred Heart in Connecticut because her social life began to eclipse her studies. In 1935 she spent a year of schooling abroad. In 1938, when President Franklin Roosevelt appointed her father as ambassador to England, Kathleen Kennedy became a British darling, suddenly surrounded by admirers and suitors. The Kennedys gave her the traditional coming-out party while in London, and she, along with her mother and sister Rosemary, was presented to the Royal Court at Buckingham Palace. She returned to the United States in 1940 and attended Finch College, a New York finishing school. When the family moved to Palm Beach, she enrolled in Florida Commercial College. She then procured a job as secretary to Frank Waldrop, an editor at the *Washington Times-Herald*. It was there that she met

and soon introduced Inga Arvad, a Danish-born journalist, to her naval ensign brother, John, with whom Arvad had a torrid affair. When Arvad left the *Times-Herald*, Kathleen Kennedy took over her column, "Did You Happen to See . . . ?"

Kennedy returned to England in 1943 to serve as a Red Cross volunteer and was assigned officer status (second lieutenant) in the U.S. Army to ensure privilege if captured by the enemy. In London she was program assistant at the Hans Crescent Club, where her chief duty was the maintenance of troop morale. When the *London Daily Mail* published a photograph of Kennedy bicycling to work in her Red Cross uniform, she became the quintessential symbol of the fresh-faced, all-American girl, volunteering for the war effort. Her father artfully arranged to have the picture run stateside.

In London, romance blossomed between Kennedy and William "Billy" Cavendish, the ninth marquess of Hartington, whom she had met during her father's ambassadorship to England. Because Cavendish was an Episcopalian, the Roman Catholic church refused to grant them a special dispensation for marriage. Despite her mother's vehement protest, they were married in a British civil ceremony on 6 May 1944. Cavendish, a member of the regular army reserve, was shot through the heart on 9 September 1944 during an attempt to secure the French village of Beverloo following the Allied invasion of France. After only five months of marriage, the marchioness of Hartington, as she was now called, was a widow at age twenty-four.

Drawn to the warmth of the Cavendish family and desiring to escape her mother's strict demands, Kennedy made England her permanent home. By 1946 she had fallen in love with another non-Catholic, Peter Fitzwilliam, who was seeking a divorce from Olive Plunkett, heiress to the Guinness fortune. Rose Kennedy threatened to disown her daughter if she carried out her plans for marriage. Consequently, Kennedy sought the approval of her father, who was to be in Paris on 15 May 1948 on a fact-finding mission for the Marshall Plan. Fitzwilliam and Kennedy planned a getaway to Cannes on the French Riviera for the weekend before the meeting with her father. On 13 May the couple boarded a De Havilland Dove plane, piloted by Peter Townshend and Arthur Freeman. The Cannes-bound plane crashed, having headed directly into a severe thunderstorm over the Rhône Valley; all four people on board perished. After gendarmes transported the bodies to town, Joseph Kennedy arrived to identify his daughter's body. Her brother John was devastated by his sister's death. He and Kathleen were the most alike in personality of all the Kennedy children. John had been a combination counselor, chaperone, and friend who cherished his role as big brother. In turn Kennedy always glowed with pride in John. Kathleen Kennedy was buried on 20 May. The duchess of Devonshire, her former mother-in-law, wrote her epitaph: Joy she gave / Joy she has found.

Interest in Kathleen Kennedy stems from her Kennedy connections, her independent spirit, and the continuing preoccupation with the tragedies that haunted the Kennedy family. Kennedy herself said to a friend that she "didn't know why she deserved such a wonderful life and she didn't know how it could possibly last" (Goodwin, p. 421).

• Kathleen Kennedy's letters are in the restricted Kennedy Family Papers, John Fitzgerald Kennedy Library, Boston, Mass. See the biography by Lynne McTaggart, *Kathleen Kennedy, Her Life and Times* (1983). Doris Kearns Goodwin, *The Fitzgeralds and the Kennedys* (1987), refers to Kathleen Kennedy's scrapbooks and personal correspondence. Nigel Hamilton, *JFK: Reckless Youth* (1992), also provides helpful anecdotal material. An obituary is in the *New York Times*, 14 May 1948.

CINDY SIGLER DAGNAN

KENNEDY, Robert Francis (20 Nov. 1925–6 June 1968), politician, was born in Brookline, Massachusetts, the son of Joseph Patrick Kennedy, a capitalist, and Rose Fitzgerald. His father Joseph made a fortune in the stock market and through other investments and served from 1938 to 1940 as U.S. ambassador to Great Britain. The seventh of nine children, Robert, known as "Bobby," graduated from Milton Academy in 1943. In March 1944 he enrolled in the Naval Reserve Officers' Training Corps, leaving it in February 1946 to become an apprentice seaman aboard the destroyer USS *Joseph P. Kennedy, Jr.*, which was named for his deceased brother, a naval pilot and war hero. After being discharged from the navy that May, he earned his A.B. in government from Harvard University in 1948. In 1950 he married Ethel Skakel; they had eleven children. In 1951 Kennedy graduated from the University of Virginia Law School.

Kennedy soon began working for the Department of Justice but left in 1952 to manage his brother John F. Kennedy's campaign for the U.S. Senate. He served briefly as an assistant counsel to Senator Joseph R. McCarthy's Permanent Subcommittee on Investigations of the Senate Government Operations Committee, resigning from it in July 1953. Kennedy soon returned to the McCarthy committee as minority counsel and then became chief counsel after the Democrats regained control of the Senate in 1955. Two years later he was named chief counsel of what became known as the Rackets Committee and made a name for himself by uncovering corrupt practices in the Teamsters' Union. In 1959 Kennedy left the committee to write *The Enemy Within* on his investigation, after which he managed John's successful campaign for the presidency.

In 1961 Kennedy was appointed attorney general of the United States. He continued his war against organized crime, involving seriously for the first time the Federal Bureau of Investigation. In May, after Freedom Riders seeking to integrate buses and bus terminals in Montgomery, Alabama, were harassed by local vigilantes, Kennedy sent 500 federal marshals to protect them. Kennedy also successfully petitioned the Interstate Commerce Commission to ban racial segregation in interstate bus terminals. Later he put an end to segregation in all forms of interstate transportation.

In the fall of 1962, when James Meredith, a black student, was admitted to the all-white University of Mississippi, Kennedy sent marshals to insure that he entered safely. When they proved inadequate in the face of mob violence, President Kennedy sent federal troops to restore order. "Ole Miss" was successfully integrated, as was the University of Alabama in June 1963, despite the resistance of Governor George Wallace. Kennedy went to Alabama to persuade Wallace to comply, but after Wallace proved unresponsive he left one of his chief aides behind, who, with the aid of marshals and the federalized Alabama National Guard, enforced the federal district court's desegregation order. Kennedy committed the FBI to the struggle for racial justice, though he compromised his principles by granting its chief, J. Edgar Hoover—who hated Martin Luther King, Jr.—as a quid pro quo, authorization to tap the telephones of King and other leaders of the Southern Christian Leadership Conference.

Kennedy served as his brother's closest adviser and participated in many of the important decisions made by the administration, notably during the Cuban Missile Crisis of 1962. As an ally of Cuba, the Soviet Union sent it 42 medium-range nuclear missiles, 42 heavy bombers, 24 antiaircraft missile sites (SAMs), and 22,000 troops and technicians, presumably to protect this small Communist state. On order were also 24 intermediate-range nuclear missiles, their obvious purpose being to reduce the United States' lead in the nuclear arms race by serving as a strategic deterrent against an American missile attack on the Soviet Union.

On 15 October 1962 an American U-2 spy plane first photographed the missile sites in Cuba. Insiders realized that the missiles had to be removed. There were important differences, however, in the lengths to which the president's advisers were willing to go. Robert Kennedy was a dove, arguing that bombing attacks on the missile sites, which the hawks favored, would kill thousands of civilians. Ultimately he and his allies carried the day, and a naval quarantine of Cuba was established as the first step in the campaign to force removal of the missiles. The president then sent Robert to meet with Soviet ambassador Anatoly Dobrynin on 23 October, beginning the negotiations that would avert a nuclear war. That same day the first Soviet ships bound for Cuba turned back from the quarantine line.

Events progressed rapidly thereafter. On 26 October Khrushchev replied to a message from the president, offering to remove the missiles in return for an American pledge not to invade Cuba. The next day, however, the Soviets unaccountably took a tougher line, demanding in addition the removal of the United States' obsolete Jupiter missiles from Turkey, which President Kennedy had ordered some months before but which had been delayed by bureaucratic inertia. Most of the president's advisers now agreed that the

United States could not withdraw the missiles under duress. Robert Kennedy then came up with the inspired idea to respond positively to Khrushchev's first letter and ignore the second. The president dispatched his brother to meet again with Dobrynin bearing a pledge not to invade Cuba if the Soviet missiles were withdrawn and promising in a verbal concession to remove the Jupiters from Turkey after a decent interval. The following day Khrushchev announced that Soviet missiles would be pulled out of Cuba. A combination of force, the threat of nuclear war, and secret diplomacy had paid off. That this crisis, the most perilous of the Cold War, did not get out of hand was Robert Kennedy's doing second only to that of the president himself.

The assassination of President Kennedy in Dallas on 22 November 1963 shattered Robert, who had been unusually close to his brother. For appearances' sake, he remained at his post, despite the animosity of President Lyndon B. Johnson. In 1964 he announced that he would run for the U.S. Senate from New York. He defeated the Republican incumbent Kenneth Keating by 719,693 votes, riding on the coattails of Johnson, who carried New York State by 2.7 million votes. In the Senate Robert joined his younger brother Edward, who had been sent to the upper chamber by Massachusetts voters in 1962. He was now a national figure and, as the Kennedy heir apparent, was looked to for leadership by Democrats unhappy with Johnson.

Increasingly their discontent turned on American policy toward Vietnam. Although John Kennedy had substantially increased the number of American "advisers" in South Vietnam, some of whom flew combat missions, by 1965 the issues had become less clear-cut. The strategic and political reasons for fighting in Vietnam appeared more and more insubstantial as American casualties rose. The government of South Vietnam was increasingly recognized as venal, incompetent, and lacking in popular support. The Communists always seemed able to match the American escalation of force. By 1968 millions of Americans either opposed the war altogether or had cooled toward it, Kennedy among them. He hesitated to express his doubts, however, because he supported President Johnson's Great Society program and did not wish to split the Democratic party.

Kennedy's support for social reform was not just a matter of expediency. It resulted from the deepening of his social conscience. At the start of his career Kennedy had been a middle-of-the-road Democrat who scorned liberals. He had been willing to promote reform only when it was not politically inconvenient. As attorney general he tried repeatedly to slow the pace of racial change in order to keep the South Democratic. In his Senate years, however, Kennedy came to identify with the downtrodden, especially those of minority races. He founded the Bedford-Stuyvesant Development and Services Corporation as a mechanism for rebuilding one of the worst ghettos in New York City. He developed personal relationships with civil rights leaders, including Cesar Chavez, head of the National Farm Workers Association. He was the only politician of his stature to champion the cause of Native Americans at the time.

Kennedy's reform efforts seem not to have been politically motivated. The poor tended not to vote, but even if they did, it was unlikely that they could furnish enough votes to send anyone to the White House. Nevertheless, Kennedy's drive and intensity, the qualities that made many regard him as ruthless, were more and more concentrated on the problems of racism and poverty. Kennedy inherited his brother's political following, but he made enemies on his own. He was mistrusted by business leaders, many labor leaders, and liberals who doubted his sincerity, and he was hated by many southerners and those on the far right, both because of his policies and because of his personality, which was seen as cold and calculating. His friends thought otherwise, admiring his passion, his energy, and his wit—which he often turned against himself. In 1965, after Canada renamed the tallest unclimbed mountain in North America after his brother John, Kennedy, who feared heights, arranged for two veteran climbers to guide him up it. When one asked what he had been doing to prepare for the climb, Kennedy replied: "Running up and down the stairs and hollering 'help.'" Inexperience notwithstanding, Kennedy made the ascent.

In 1967, as the war in Vietnam worsened, Allard Lowenstein, a political activist, began organizing a "dump Johnson" movement and asked Kennedy to be its standard-bearer. Kennedy refused, fearing that because of his bad relationship with Johnson he would be accused of splitting the Democratic party for personal reasons. Someone else would have to make the challenge. That man proved to be Senator Eugene McCarthy of Minnesota, a brilliant, sardonic, independent Democrat who in a long political career had never before displayed much in the way of leadership. His run was considered quixotic, as expert opinion held that a sitting president would not be denied renomination.

Tet changed everything. On 31 January 1968, the second day of Tet, the Vietnamese lunar new year, the Communist Vietcong attacked thirty-six provincial capitals, sixty-four district towns, many villages, and a dozen American bases in South Vietnam. Although they were defeated militarily after savage fighting, the Vietcong achieved a political triumph. President Johnson and his commanders had been insisting that victory was near at hand. After Tet, with General William Westmoreland asking for 206,000 troops in addition to the half million already engaged, McCarthy's sputtering campaign ignited, and students flocked to his side. Although he did not win a majority of votes in the New Hampshire primary, he came close. Moreover, owing to a complicated selection system, he actually gained a majority of the New Hampshire delegates to the Democratic National Convention.

McCarthy's successes forced Kennedy's hand. If he stayed out of the race his following would go to McCarthy by default, ending, possibly for good, his chances of becoming president. On the other hand, by entering, he would divide the antiwar vote, possibly ensuring Johnson's renomination. The latter seemed the lesser evil. On 16 March 1968 Kennedy announced his candidacy, infuriating the antiwar activists pledged to McCarthy. On 31 March, just before the Wisconsin primary, which he was expected to lose to McCarthy, President Johnson stunned the nation by announcing that he would not seek another term. Vice President Hubert Humphrey would run in his place.

The campaign that followed was unique. McCarthy, cool and ironic as ever, continued what he later called his "existential" race. Humphrey lined up the regular Democrats. Kennedy stormed the country, drawing huge crowds and firing them with purpose. His best address of the campaign was impromptu and elegiac. Soon after the assassination of Martin Luther King on 4 April in Memphis, Kennedy gave a scheduled speech in a black ghetto of Indianapolis where his audience had not yet heard the news. He told his listeners of the event and then spoke movingly of his own loss, of the importance of not giving way to rage, and of finding in tragedy meaning and strength. Kennedy concluded: "Let us dedicate ourselves to what the Greeks wrote so many years ago: to tame the savageness of man and to make gentle the life of this world. Let us . . . say a prayer for our country and for our people."

On 5 June, the date of the California primary, which he won, Robert Kennedy was fatally shot in Los Angeles by a deranged Palestinian, Sirhan Sirhan. The bullet destroyed the nation's most promising leader and put Richard Nixon in the White House.

Kennedy is best remembered for his thrilling presidential campaign in 1968 and its shocking conclusion. His place in history will probably turn on his role in helping save the human race from extinction during the Cuban Missile Crisis.

• The Robert Kennedy Papers are in the John F. Kennedy Library in Boston. Of Kennedy's own writings, the most engrossing is *Thirteen Days: A Memoir of the Cuban Missile Crisis* (1969). The longest and best biography is Arthur M. Schlesinger, Jr., *Robert Kennedy and His Times* (1978), a sympathetic memoir by a historian who was close to both John and Robert Kennedy. Ralph De Toledano, *RFK: The Man Who Would Be President* (1967), reveals the hatred Kennedy inspired among some of his contemporaries. David Halberstam, *The Unfinished Odyssey of Robert Kennedy* (1968), is a distinguished journalist's account of Kennedy's presidential campaign. Many books of reminiscence and oral history have been compiled by Kennedy's friends and admirers. William Vanden Heuvel and Milton Gwirtzman, *On His Own: RFK, 1964–1968* (1970), is an intimate history of Kennedy's last four years told by men who had served as his assistants. David Burner and Thomas R. West, *The Torch Is Passed: The Kennedy Brothers and American Liberalism* (1984), is a fair-minded analysis of the Kennedy influence on American politics. Garry Wills, *The Kennedy Imprisonment* (1982), is more critical. For a fuller discussion of sources on Kennedy, see the essay on him by Brooks D. Simpson in *Research Guide to American Historical Biography*, vol. 2, ed. Robert Muccigrosso (1988). Obituaries are in the *New York Times* and the *Washington Post*, 7 June 1968.

WILLIAM L. O'NEILL

KENNEDY, Rose Fitzgerald (22 July 1890–23 Jan. 1995), philanthropist and political matriarch, was born in Boston, Massachusetts, the daughter of John Francis Fitzgerald, a politician, and Mary Josephine Hannon. In 1904 the Fitzgeralds moved from Boston's immigrant North End to a fifteen-room house in the Boston suburb of Dorchester. While her mother nurtured her commitment to family and the Catholic church, her father introduced her to politics. Kennedy graduated with honors from Dorchester High School in May 1906, the same year her father, "Honey Fitz," was elected mayor. Because she was only fifteen, her parents prohibited her from attending Wellesley College. Instead, she enrolled at Sacred Heart Convent in Boston and the New England Conservatory of Music, where she became a skilled pianist. From 1908 to 1909 she attended Blumenthal Academy, a German convent finishing school in Valls, the Netherlands, attaining fluency in German and French. She completed her higher education at Manhattanville College of the Sacred Heart in Purchase, New York, and graduated in 1910.

Kennedy returned to Boston and took language classes at Boston University, joined the cultural associations *Alliance Française* and *Deutsche Gesselschaft*, taught catechism classes, and was active in settlement social work. As the youngest member of the Boston Public Library Investigating Committee, she recommended reading lists for children. When she was snubbed by the Brahmin-composed Junior League, she started her own women's club, the Ace of Clubs, which provided its women members with an opportunity to discuss international affairs, enlist guest speakers, and, in Kennedy's case, hone her public-speaking skills.

In October 1914 two prominent Irish immigrant families joined forces when Rose married Joseph Patrick Kennedy, who subsequently earned his fortune first as president of the Columbia Trust Company in Boston, then from lucrative investments in real estate, liquor, film production, and the stock market. In 1917 Joseph Kennedy turned over the bank to his father and became assistant general manager of Bethlehem Steel's shipyard at Quincy, Massachusetts. While breaking production records, he became acquainted with then Assistant Secretary of the Navy Franklin Delano Roosevelt. Meanwhile Rose Kennedy devoted herself to raising their family of nine children. In her autobiography *Times to Remember* (1974) she wrote, "I looked on child rearing not only as a work of love and duty but as a profession that was fully as interesting and challenging as any honorable profession in the world and one that demanded the best that I could bring to it" (p. 81). Because the Kennedys could afford domestic help, her household role was one of "planning, organizing, and supervising." Her penchant for orderliness was often exemplified in the press by references to her meticulous system of documenting each of her children's health problems on index cards. She shared with her children her knowledge of politics, history, foreign languages, etiquette, and fashion sense. She considered her greatest gift her determination to cope with life's vicissitudes through religious faith. In 1952 Pope Pius XII named her a papal countess in recognition of her exemplary Catholic life and her contribution to charities.

The Kennedys accrued enough wealth for homes in Hyannis Port, Massachusetts, and Palm Beach, Florida, and in 1926 they moved from Boston to New York, where her husband could monitor his Wall Street investments. (Their New York residency was later their son Robert's justification for running as the New York Democratic nominee for the U.S. Senate in 1964.) Rose Kennedy proved an asset to her husband when he turned to politics, having accompanied her father on many campaigns and socialized with foreign dignitaries. In September 1935 President Franklin D. Roosevelt appointed Joseph Kennedy to establish and chair the Securities and Exchange Commission and in 1937 to organize the U.S. Merchant Marine as head of the Maritime Commission. In 1938 Joseph Kennedy served as ambassador to Great Britain. The Kennedy family was welcomed by King George VI to the Court of St. James and presented to the queen. Rose Kennedy established a social setting, dignified yet informal, which befit a family with children and yet was appropriate for meetings of world leaders. When England announced war against Germany in September 1939, Rose Kennedy returned to the United States with her children and frequently spoke to women's groups about her experience as an ambassador's wife.

After the death of their oldest son in a World War II naval mission, the Kennedys founded the Joseph F. Kennedy Jr. Mental Retardation Foundation, to which the senior Joseph Kennedy willed the majority of his estate. The mental handicap of their oldest daughter, Rosemary, encouraged the entire family's pledge to contribute time to the foundation. Eventually it built schools for the mentally retarded in eighteen major cities of the United States. To support the work of the foundation, Kennedy promoted a collection of perfumes called Flame of Hope made by mentally retarded men and women.

When her sons entered the political arena, Rose Kennedy was instrumental in the success of their campaigns, adjusting her speeches to the class, ethnicity, and gender of her audience. In 1946 she contributed to her son John Fitzgerald Kennedy's run for Congress in Boston's Eleventh Congressional District, where the Fitzgerald name still carried weight. When John formally declared his candidacy for president in January 1960, Rose Kennedy joined the campaign with the rest of the family. She traveled to fourteen states and made forty-six appearances on behalf of her son. In *Times to Remember* she wrote, "I didn't miss a chance to ask anyone to vote for Jack. I talked with taxi drivers, elevator operators, waitresses, porters, manicur-

ists and anyone with whom I could strike up a conversation" (p. 371). To express his appreciation for her contribution, John presented her with a map of the United States on which he had marked the locations where she had campaigned for him. The Kennedy compound at Hyannis Port was firmly established by this time, with the houses of Robert and Ethel, John and Jackie, and Joseph and Rose Kennedy and houses owned by her other children nearby. "Joe and I by then were seventy-two and seventy. Both of us were healthy, active, enjoying life fully. We had suffered grievous losses but we rejoiced in our children who remained and in our grandchildren. And we had the excitement, the drama, the pride, the great thrill that our eldest surviving son was running for the presidency of the United States" (*Times*, p. 355–56). In 1960 John F. Kennedy became the thirty-fifth president of the United States. Rose Kennedy could not quite believe that "the almost impossible dream had come true" until she saw her son on television being escorted by President Dwight Eisenhower into the White House (*Times*, p. 378). She also campaigned for her youngest son, Edward Kennedy, in Massachusetts during his 1976 campaigned for reelection to the U.S. Senate.

Kennedy bore the assassinations of her sons John in 1963 and Robert in 1968 and the death of her husband in 1969 with dignified fortitude. She was publicly and privately recognized as matriarch of the Kennedy political dynasty, a champion of social service, a strict teacher, and a loving mother. The family's allegiance to and respect for Rose Kennedy was apparent when her four children—Edward, Jean, Eunice, and Patricia—praised their mother in the *New York Times* after she was portrayed as cold and unaffectionate in Nigel Hamilton's 1992 biography, *JFK: A Reckless Youth*. A series of debilitating strokes after 1984 left her partially paralyzed. She died at the Kennedys' Hyannis Port compound in Barnstable. Kennedy's birth date was officially named Rose Fitzgerald Kennedy Family Appreciation Day in 1990.

• The John F. Kennedy Library in Dorchester, Mass., holds 2,000 pages of Rose Kennedy's personal papers. Kennedy is the subject of several biographies that focus on her role as the devout matriarch of a political dynasty. See Gail Cameron, *Rose: A Biography of Rose Fitzgerald Kennedy* (1971), and Charles Higham, *Rose: The Life and Times of Rose Fitzgerald Kennedy* (1995). Florence King points out the failings of Higham's biography in "The Matriarch," *New York Times Book Review*, 23 Apr. 1995. Barbara Gibson, Rose Kennedy's secretary of ten years, weaves her memories of Kennedy in *Life with Rose Kennedy* (with Caroline Latham) (1986) and in *Rose Kennedy and Her Family* (with Ted Schwarz) (1995). See also David E. Koskoff's well-documented biography, *Joseph P. Kennedy: A Life and Times* (1974). In addition to recycling well-known Kennedy anecdotes and facts, Laurence Leamer secures new material through interviews with Kennedy family and friends for *The Kennedy Women: The Saga of an American Family* (1994). For an interview with Kennedy months after the assassination of her son Robert, see Laura Bergquist, "Rose Kennedy," in *Look*, 26 Nov. 1968. Coverage of Rose Kennedy's 100th birthday celebration is in the *New York Times*, 13 July 1990. Obituaries are in the *New*

York Times, 23 Jan. 1995, and the *Boston Globe*, 24 Jan. 1995. A number of tributes to Kennedy were published after her death in the *New York Times*, 24 and 25 Jan. 1995, and in the *Boston Globe*, 28 Jan. 1995.

BARBARA L. CICCARELLI

KENNEDY, William Sloane (26 Sept. 1850–4 Aug. 1929), biographer, poet, and anthologist, was born in Brecksville, Ohio, now a suburb of Cleveland, the son of the Reverend William Sloane Kennedy, a Presbyterian minister, and Sarah Eliza Woodruff. Kennedy attended Miami University of Ohio and Yale University, where he graduated in 1875. He then taught at Yale for the next two years. During 1877–1878 he attended the Meadville Theological Seminary (then a hotbed of Unitarian activity) in Pennsylvania, while also teaching locally. He studied at Harvard Divinity School between 1878 and 1880 but left without taking a degree. Rather than follow his father in the ministry, he embarked on a literary career and began working for the Philadelphia *American*. Two or three years later he became a proofreader for the Boston *Transcript*. In June 1883 he married Adeline Ella Lincoln, daughter of Cyrus and Abigail Lincoln of Cambridge, Massachusetts. The young couple, who remained childless, lived in Belmont, Massachusetts, where for the next few years he hoped (because of the low pay and long hours of his newspaper work) to secure a position in the Boston customhouse.

In addition to contributing articles to the New York *Critic*, the *Boston Herald*, the Boston *Index*, and the *Literary World*, Kennedy published short biographies of Henry Wadsworth Longfellow and John Greenleaf Whittier in 1882 and a life of Oliver Wendell Holmes in 1883. These were followed by *Wonders and Curiosities of the Railway* (1884), *Art and Life: A Ruskin Anthology* (1886), *The Poet as a Craftsman* (1886), *Breezes from the Field* (1886), *John G. Whittier, the Poet of Freedom* (1892), *In Portia's Gardens* (1897), *The Real John Burroughs* (1924), *Poems of the Weird and Mystical* (1926), and *An Autolycus Pack; or, What You Will* (1927). He also published translations of Camille Flammarion's *Psychic Mysterious Forces* (1907) and Cesare Lombroso's *After Death— What?* (1909).

Kennedy is best known now to students and specialists of Walt Whitman. He first met Whitman on 15 April 1880 in Philadelphia following the poet's lecture "The Death of Abraham Lincoln." Afterward, Kennedy went up to the poet and, as one witness later reported, Whitman "put his arms around my friend's neck and kissed him—a stripling he had never seen before that night." Although Kennedy was to become a fierce defender of *Leaves of Grass*, he initially expressed reservations about its "coarse indecencies of language" in an essay published in the *Californian* in 1881. He corresponded with Whitman until the poet's death and afterward became part of the Whitman Fellowship, a band of disciples that kept Whitman's reputation as a poet alive until it was recognized by scholars and critics in the 1930s. He wrote early essays on Whitman's Quaker and Dutch traits and composed in the mid-

1880s *Reminiscences of Walt Whitman*, which did not find a publisher until 1896. Like many books written about Whitman during his lifetime by friends, this one was influenced directly and perhaps altered by the poet. His other books on Whitman are *Walt Whitman's Diary in Canada* (1904) and the impassioned *Fight of a Book for the World* (1926), in effect the first "Walt Whitman handbook." A faithful disciple, Kennedy expressed his disapproval of biographers who were digging up trivia about the poet's life, especially before the publication of the first edition of *Leaves of Grass* in 1855. In *Reminiscences*, he also scoffed at emerging theories about Whitman's alleged homosexuality. Shortly before Whitman's death in 1892, Kennedy rhetorically asked the poet whether, after a thousand years, Whitman's birth would not be celebrated in the same manner as the birthday of Christ.

Following his wife's death in 1923, Kennedy moved to West Yarmouth, Massachusetts, spending his winters in Rome, Italy, and California. He drowned off of Cape Cod while swimming in Lewis Bay near his home. He is buried in Mt. Auburn Cemetery, Boston.

• A collection of Kennedy papers is at Rollins College, Winter Park, Fla. Unpublished letters of Kennedy to Whitman are in the Charles E. Feinberg Collection, Library of Congress. See also Gay Wilson Allen, *New Walt Whitman Handbook* (1975); Edwin Haviland Miller, ed., *Correspondence of Walt Whitman*, vols. 3–5 (1964, 1969); Charles T. Sempers, "Walt Whitman and His Philosophy," *Harvard Monthly*, Jan. 1888, pp. 149–56; and Charles B. Willard, *Whitman's American Fame* (1950). Obituaries are in the *New York Times* and the Boston *Transcript*, both 5 Aug. 1929.

JEROME LOVING

KENNEY, George Churchill (6 Aug. 1889–9 Aug. 1977), air commander, was born in Yarmouth, Nova Scotia, the son of Joseph Atwood Kenney and Louise Churchill. His parents were visiting Yarmouth at the time of his birth; the family lived in Brookline, Massachusetts, where he was reared. He attended the civil engineering program at Massachusetts Institute of Technology for three years but left without graduating in 1910 to take an engineering position with the Quebec Saguenay Railroad. He later worked as an engineer and construction manager with several companies, becoming president of Beaver Contracting and Engineering Corporation in 1916.

In 1917 Kenney joined the Aviation Section of the Army Signal Corps, earning his wings and becoming a first lieutenant. That fall he was transferred to France, where he became a fighter pilot in the Ninety-first Aero Squadron of the American Expeditionary Force's Air Service. By the end of World War I he had flown seventy-five missions, shot down two German planes, served as a flight commander, earned the rank of captain, and received a Distinguished Service Cross and a Silver Star. He had also developed what would become a lifelong commitment to military aviation. After the armistice he served in the Rhine occupation and returned to the United States in 1919.

In 1920 Kenney married Hazel D. Richardson; they had one child. Three years later he married Alice S. Macy, with whom he had one child. After the war there were few promotions in the army's air arm, called the Army Air Corps after 1925. Kenney remained a captain for seventeen years, serving across the nation as a squadron leader, instructor, production engineer, and inspector. He also graduated from the Air Corps's engineering and tactical schools, the Army Command and General Staff School, and the Army War College. After graduating from the latter in 1933, he was assigned to the Plans Division of the Chief of the Army Air Corps. Two years later he was promoted to major and made chief of operations and training of the General Headquarters Air Force, where he soon was promoted to lieutenant colonel. Following several command assignments, he was appointed chief of the Production Engineering Sections of the corps's Materiel Division in 1938. He was chosen for the post by Major General Henry H. "Hap" Arnold, the new chief of the Air Corps, who would become head of Army Air Forces in World War II. In January 1941 Kenney was promoted to brigadier general and appointed head of the Air Corps Experimental Depot, which was engaged in research, modification, and development of new aircraft and aerial weapons, fueling, and navigation systems. At the end of the year Arnold named him commander of the Fourth Air Force, on the West Coast, with the temporary rank of major general.

In July 1942 Army Chief of Staff George C. Marshall and Arnold met with Kenney to inform him of his appointment as commander of Allied Air Forces, Southwest Pacific Area, which was General Douglas MacArthur's theater of operations. For the next two years his main units were the Royal Australian Air Force and the United States Fifth Air Force; he commanded the latter for two years. In June 1944, while retaining command of Allied Air Forces, he turned over the Fifth to Major General Ennis C. Whitehead, his former deputy, and took command of the new United States Far East Air Forces. That command ultimately consisted of the Fifth, Seventh, and Thirteenth air forces. He was promoted to lieutenant general in October 1942 and to general in March 1945.

Kenney won MacArthur's confidence and friendship with his cocky, can-do attitude, bold and innovative tactics, and mastery of administration. He quickly transformed the theater's air organization from a passive, defense-minded outfit into a striking force that seized control of the skies from the Japanese. His command provided strategic and tactical air support for fifty-six amphibious invasions by MacArthur's Australian and American ground forces on New Guinea, New Britain, the Admiralties, the Moluccas, Borneo, and the Philippines. By early 1944 his Fifth Air Force had mounted more than 117,000 sorties, ranking second among the army's eleven combat air forces. In 1945 Kenney's planes supported ground operations from Borneo to Luzon and northward to Okinawa and Kyushu. His most notable achievements included transporting troops and supplies in the Papuan campaign of 1942–1943, the destruction of the enemy armada in the battle of the Bismarck Sea in early 1943, and daring airborne assaults in Northeast New Guinea in late 1943 and in the Philippines in early 1945. "Of all the brilliant air commanders of the war," MacArthur observed, "none surpassed him in those three great essentials of combat leadership: aggressive vision, mastery of air tactics and strategy, and the ability to exact the maximum in fighting qualities for both men and equipment."

After the war, Kenney led the Pacific Air Command from 1945 to 1946, the Strategic Air Command from 1946 to 1948, and the Air University from 1948 to 1951. After retiring in 1951, he maintained residences in New York City and Bay Harbor, Florida, and served for twelve years as president of the National Arthritis and Rheumatism Foundation. In 1955 he married Sarah Schermerhorn and, in 1971, Jeanette C. Stehlin; there were no offspring from either of these marriages. Kenney wrote four books on the war in the Southwest Pacific: *General Kenney Reports: A Personal History of the Pacific War* (1949), *The MacArthur I Know* (1951), *The Saga of Pappy Gunn* (1959), and *Dick Bong, Ace of Aces* (1960). He died in Bay Harbor.

Kenney, who was short and stocky, was nicknamed "Little George" and was known for his extremely colorful, fun-loving personality. Aggressive and decisive, he was also arrogant and very opinionated. His air superiors, including Arnold, regarded him in the first rank of highly professional, widely experienced air leaders. His cardinal flaw was the same as that of many top airmen: he was overly optimistic about what his air forces could accomplish.

• Kenney's papers and notebooks are in the Air Force Historical Research Center, Maxwell Air Force Base, Ala. In addition to his own books, see Herman S. Wolk, "George C. Kenney: MacArthur's Premier Airman," in *We Shall Return! MacArthur's Commanders and the Defeat of Japan, 1942–1945*, ed. William M. Leary (1988); Stanley L. Falk, "General Kenney, the Indirect Approach, and the B-29s," *Aerospace Historian* 27 (1981): 147–55; U.S. Strategic Bombing Survey, *The Fifth Air Force in the War against Japan* (1947); Wesley F. Craven and James L. Cate, eds., *The Army Air Forces in World War II*, vols. 4–5 (1950, 1953); and John L. Frisbee, ed., *Makers of the United States Air Force* (1987).
D. CLAYTON JAMES

KENNEY, Mary. *See* O'Sullivan, Mary Kenney.

KENNICOTT, Robert (13 Nov. 1835–13 May 1866), naturalist and explorer, was born in New Orleans, Louisiana, the son of John Albert Kennicott and Mary Shutts Ransom. The second of seven children, Kennicott was raised in a beautiful prairie grove eighteen miles northwest of Chicago. His father, a physician and educator as well as an enthusiastic amateur botanist, had moved the family to West Northfield (now Glenview), Illinois, in 1836. The Kennicott estate, known simply as "The Grove," was the perfect setting for a would-be naturalist, encompassing as it did a variety of rich and varied ecosystems. Robert was frail and often in ill health as a youth and as a consequence never attended school regularly. John Kennicott arranged for an Oxford-trained tutor to supplement his children's education, but he was their most important teacher. He encouraged frail Robert in particular to spend time outdoors studying nature, and by age fifteen Kennicott was experimenting with the effects of massasauga rattlesnake venom on a variety of animals. In addition to quite a menagerie of live animals, Kennicott had also begun to make collections of bird skins, eggs, insects, and snakes. In 1853 his father arranged for him to study with the leading naturalist of the Midwest, Jared P. Kirtland of Ohio. Over the next two years Kennicott learned many lessons in natural history from Kirtland and Philo R. Hoy of Wisconsin; the former taught him the fundamentals of entomology and how to properly skin birds and preserve specimens, while the latter emphasized keeping careful notes of all that he observed. In turn Kirtland and Hoy introduced Kennicott to several eastern naturalists, most notably Spencer F. Baird, assistant secretary of the Smithsonian Institution in charge of the natural history museum. Kennicott began corresponding with Baird, and before long he was sending sizable shipments of birds, mammals, reptiles, and amphibians to the Smithsonian. Baird responded with dozens of long, encouraging letters, and thus was formed a lifelong friendship.

Beginning in 1854, Kennicott wrote more than a dozen articles for the *Prairie Farmer* newspaper, one of the most respected agricultural journals in the nation. Kennicott revealed himself to be an ardent advocate of educating farmers and their children about the animals around them, in order to prevent the indiscriminate killing of snakes and other creatures. According to Kennicott, all of God's creations were adapted "to fill a certain place in Nature's magnificent System."

In 1855 Kennicott had his first opportunity to investigate southern Illinois, under the auspices of the Illinois Central Railroad and the State Agricultural Society. The result was his first major publication, a "Catalogue of Animals Observed in Cook County, Illinois," published in 1855 in the *Transactions of the Illinois State Agricultural Society*. This was the first attempt at documenting the fauna of Illinois. The following year, encouraged by Baird, Kennicott began publishing a three-part series dealing with the quadrupeds of Illinois, focusing particularly on small mammals injurious to farmers. These life histories were still being cited into the late twentieth century.

In 1857 Kennicott was one of the founders of the Chicago Academy of Sciences, and later that year he also helped establish the natural history museum at Northwestern University in Evanston. In the winter of 1857, at Baird's invitation, Kennicott traveled to the Smithsonian to study reptiles. Backed in part by the Smithsonian, in April 1859 Kennicott embarked on a three-year exploration of Canada and Russian America. His solitary travels took him above the Arctic Circle for a time, and he collected extensively, including large numbers of mammals, birds, eggs, and nests. Kennicott's collections were of immense value to naturalists; the animals and plants from these remote northern regions were then largely unknown to scientists, and Kennicott kept detailed notes on the habits of many of these birds and mammals. In addition, Kennicott's enthusiasm for collecting rubbed off on several employees of the Hudson's Bay Company, some of whom became avid collectors for the Smithsonian after Kennicott taught them how to collect, skin birds and mammals, and record locality data.

Kennicott returned to Illinois in 1862 after learning that the United States was engulfed in civil war. At first eager to enlist, Kennicott eventually hired a substitute, preferring to focus his energies on the Chicago Academy of Sciences. His dream was to create a major natural history museum in Chicago, a "young Smithsonian" for the western United States. Considerable impetus toward achieving this goal was realized in early 1864 when America's most famous naturalist, Louis Agassiz, visited Chicago. Agassiz testified to the value of Kennicott's Arctic collections, and his speech quickly convinced the wealthy men of Chicago to raise $50,000 for a new museum in Chicago. The Chicago Academy of Sciences was reorganized, and Kennicott was appointed director of the museum and to the board of trustees.

Throughout 1864 Kennicott worked diligently on behalf of the academy, but late in that year he was persuaded to return to the north country. The Western Union Telegraph Company planned an ambitious venture, which would link America and Europe via a telegraph line spanning the Bering Strait. Kennicott, one of the few white Americans to have explored extensively in the area, was appointed naturalist to Western Union's Russian-American Telegraph Expedition, with the stipulation that he be allowed to choose a small party of naturalists to accompany him. Kennicott and his party, which included the nineteen-year-old naturalist William H. Dall, departed New York in March 1865. After an eventful transit across Nicaragua, where Kennicott and several others apparently contracted malaria, the party arrived in San Francisco, only to be confronted with red tape and internal bickering. Kennicott's plans were contingent on taking full advantage of the short arctic summer to explore, but he and his party did not arrive at their base of operations, the island of St. Michael, until 8 September 1865.

Kennicott and his men were to explore the proposed telegraph route from the Seward peninsula to Fort Yukon, more than 700 miles. A steamer that was supposed to take them upriver failed, and as a result most of the winter was spent in hauling supplies to Nulato, a Russian post on the Yukon River. A shortage of food and sled dogs stranded Kennicott and his party at Nulato during an unusually severe winter, and they were eventually forced to wait for the spring thaw before they could canoe to Fort Yukon. Kennicott did not live to see it, as he died at the age of thirty at Nulato on 13 May 1866. The circumstances surrounding his death are uncertain, as some accounts mention heart disease, others suicide. In any event, thus was ended the career of one of nineteenth-century America's consummate explorer-naturalists.

A few days after Kennicott's death, the river became passable and his remains were shipped back to Illinois. With the successful laying of the transatlantic cable in mid-1866, the expedition was abandoned. However, the reports from this exploration documented the richness of the region's natural resources, and this information was used to help persuade Congress to purchase Russian America (Alaska) in 1867.

Kennicott was slightly built with dark eyes and long, wavy brown hair. Like others in his family, he was prone to melancholy and bouts of depression. One of Kennicott's colleagues characterized him as "a field naturalist of great power and accuracy of observation." As a descriptive naturalist, Kennicott is best known for his work on garter and rattlesnakes. He is credited with describing one genus, twelve species, and eighteen subspecies of North American serpents.

• The two best collections of Kennicott letters are at the Smithsonian Institution Archives and at the Grove, National Historic Landmark, Glenview, Ill. Works by Kennicott include a three-part study, "The Quadrupeds of Illinois Injurious and Beneficial to the Farmer," *Report of the Commissioner of Patents for the Year 1856: Agriculture*, 34th Cong., 3d sess., H. Doc. 65, 1857, pp. 52–110; *Report of the Commissioner of Patents for the Year 1857: Agriculture*, 35th Cong., 1st sess., S. Doc. 30, 1858, pp. 72–107; *Report of the Commissioner of Patents for the Year 1858: Agriculture*, 35th Cong., 2d sess., H. Doc. 105, 1859, pp. 241–56; and "Descriptions of New Species of North American Serpents in the Museum of the Smithsonian Institution," *Proceedings of the Academy of Natural Sciences of Philadelphia* 12 (1860): 328–38. The most complete biographical account of Kennicott's life to date is by a committee of the academy, "Biography of Robert Kennicott," *Transactions of the Chicago Academy of Sciences* 1, pt. 2 (1869): 133–226. Other articles include Donald Zochert, "Notes on a Young Naturalist," *Audubon* 82 (Mar. 1980): 35–47; James Alton James, "Robert Kennicott, Pioneer Illinois Natural Scientist and Arctic Explorer," *Transactions of the Illinois State Historical Society* 47 (1940): 22–39; Ronald S. Vasile, "The Early Career of Robert Kennicott, Illinois' Pioneer Naturalist," *Illinois Historical Journal* 87, no. 3 (1994): 150–70; and Debra Lindsay, *Science in the Subarctic: Trappers, Traders, and the Smithsonian Institution* (1993). Although somewhat biased, the obituary in the *Chicago Tribune*, 15 Nov. 1866, is a useful resource.

RONALD S. VASILE

KENNY, Elizabeth (20 Sept. 1880–30 Nov. 1952), nurse and developer of a treatment for poliomyelitis (infantile paralysis), was born in Warialda, New South Wales, Australia, the daughter of Michael Kenny and Mary Moore, homesteaders. Kenny's family moved frequently during her childhood, and her education was scattered and limited. At the age of eighteen she zealously taught herself the principles of anatomy and muscle function with the help of a surgeon friend, Aeneas John McDonnell, in order to help her brother William strengthen his frail frame through calisthenics.

A strong-willed young woman with no inclination toward domestic life, Kenny apprenticed herself to a local nurse and in 1911 began providing charity care to rural families, apparently without obtaining a formal nursing certificate. The same year she tended her first case of infantile paralysis in the bush. After receiving word from McDonnell that there was no known treatment for the condition, Kenny invented one, wrapping the child's contracted, painful muscles in strips of woolen blanket soaked in boiling water and wrung out. When the child's pain had been relieved, the affected limbs appeared paralyzed, but Kenny gently moved them and gradually trained the child to move them herself. Within the week she successfully treated five more poliomyelitis cases.

In 1915 Kenny gained an appointment in the Australian Army Nursing Service in World War I on the basis of a letter of recommendation from McDonnell. For three years she served mainly on ships bringing wounded soldiers home from battle. In December 1916 she was promoted from staff nurse to the rank of sister (equivalent to first lieutenant), a title she used for the rest of her life.

After her military discharge in 1919, Kenny returned to rural nursing. In 1926 she invented a rigid, wheeled stretcher, the Sylvia stretcher, to reduce jolting and prevent shock as patients traveled the rough bush roads to town hospitals. Kenny patented the stretcher and sold distribution rights throughout the world, ensuring adequate royalties to finance her travels and charity nursing for many years.

In 1931 Kenny began treating polio patients again. At that time the standard medical treatment for polio was to immobilize the patient's affected limbs in splints and plaster casts at the onset of the disease. This treatment was based on the theory that polio killed nerve cells, leaving the affected muscles paralyzed; if not immobilized, the flaccid muscles would be pulled out of place by opposing normal muscles, causing deformities. Kenny strongly disagreed and viewed immobilization as a form of torture. Based on her success with hot packs, as her woolen-blanket treatment came to be called, she gradually developed the concept that deformities resulted when muscles in "spasm" were not properly treated with hot packs in the acute stage of the disease. She also argued that the affected muscles were not paralyzed at all but that the patient experienced "mental alienation," the inability to move the muscles voluntarily. If the patient were not re-educated to move, "incoordination" or spasticity would result.

Word of Kenny's success with polio patients spread, and between 1932 and 1937 she established clinics in Townsville, Brisbane, Toowoomba, Sydney, and Newcastle, some of them government-sponsored. Her unorthodox ideas and treatment encountered full opposition from the medical establishment, which considered her a quack and refused to allow her to treat patients in the acute stage, fearing that abandonment of immobilization would result in deformities. In 1937 Kenny visited London and persuaded doctors to allow her to open a clinic in a wing of Queen Mary's Hospital for Children in Carshalton, Surrey. A royal commission in England evaluated her work in a 1938 report that concluded that abandoning immobilization was not harmful but that her method of early exercise and muscle retraining was of unproven value. The same year a royal commission of Australian physicians published a report denouncing her methods.

In 1940 Kenny decided to visit the United States in her crusade for acceptance of her treatment. That country was much more polio-conscious than Europe or Australia, having suffered major epidemics every summer since 1916; in addition, Franklin Delano Roosevelt, stricken with polio in 1921, had been elected president in 1932. In 1938 Roosevelt and Basil O'Connor had set up the National Foundation for Infantile Paralysis, whose "March of Dimes" fund drive was very successful.

Armed with letters of introduction from supportive Australian physicians, Kenny landed in San Francisco with Mary Stewart Kenny, whom she had adopted as an eight-year-old in 1926 and had later trained as a Kenny therapist. O'Connor received Kenny coolly in New York, as did physicians at the American Medical Association's headquarters in Chicago. She then traveled to the Mayo Clinic in Rochester, Minnesota, where she met Melvin Henderson and Frank Krusen; the latter was a pioneer in the new discipline of physical medicine. Intrigued but unconvinced, Krusen sent Kenny to Minneapolis, where a large number of polio patients were hospitalized. There she demonstrated reactivation of supposedly paralyzed muscles in patients for Wallace Cole and Miland Knapp of the University of Minnesota Medical School and John Pohl of Minneapolis General Hospital. These doctors were impressed enough to acquire funds from the National Foundation to keep Kenny in the city and to conduct a study of her treatment, which they assessed favorably in the *Journal of the American Medical Association* in 1941.

Following that evaluation and an endorsement from the National Foundation, a medical revolution ensued, and physicians all over the country abandoned splints in favor of hot packs and muscle re-education. Nine institutional training centers were set up nationwide to disseminate Kenny techniques. Kenny also became immensely popular with the general public. Between 1943 and 1951 she was named the second most admired woman (after Eleanor Roosevelt) by the Gallup Poll; in 1952 she was in the top spot. A Hollywood movie dramatizing her life was released in 1946; it starred Rosalind Russell, who also sat on the board of the Sister Kenny Institute, established (as the Elizabeth Kenny Institute) in Minneapolis in 1942.

Despite these triumphs, Kenny continued to antagonize the medical profession. She criticized any treatment different from her own and battled fiercely against the common use of respirators and muscle testing in polio patients. She also persisted in arguing that polio was primarily a disease of the muscles and skin and that the nerves were seldom involved, despite am-

ple scientific evidence to the contrary. Kenny's relations with the National Foundation became increasingly strained, and it stopped funding her work in Minneapolis in 1945, at which time private and Minneapolis city funding filled the gap. In 1951 Kenny returned to Toowoomba, Australia, where she died. She never married.

Kenny's treatment prevented many polio victims from being permanently crippled before the introduction of the Salk vaccine halted the disease's spread. Kenny overturned the damaging practice of immobilization and convinced the medical profession of the benefits of moist heat to relieve muscle pain and stiffness and the need for early muscle reactivation following neurological injury, principles that have been absorbed as fundamentals in modern rehabilitation therapy. The Sister Kenny Institute in Minneapolis became a major rehabilitation center for people afflicted by various crippling accidents and diseases.

• Victor Cohn published a meticulously researched biography and bibliography, *Sister Kenny: The Woman Who Challenged the Doctors* (1975). See also the chapter on Kenny in Tony Gould, *A Summer Plague: Polio and Its Survivors* (1995). Kenny's autobiography, *And They Shall Walk: The Life Story of Sister Elizabeth Kenny* (1943), written with Martha Ostenso, is not always reliable as a historical record, as Cohn discovered. Kenny also wrote three textbooks on her methods; the most articulate is *The Kenny Concept of Infantile Paralysis and Its Treatment* (1943), written with John F. Pohl. A good summary of the Kenny method is Wallace A. Cole et al., "The Kenny Method of Treatment for Infantile Paralysis," *Archives of Physical Therapy* 23 (1942): 399–418. An obituary is in the *New York Times*, 30 Nov. 1952.

DIANA KENNEY ANNIS

KENRICK, Francis Patrick (3 Dec. 1796–8 July 1863), Catholic prelate, was born in Dublin, Ireland, the son of Thomas Kenrick, a scrivener, and Jane Eustace. His younger brother, Peter Richard Kenrick, would serve as prelate of St. Louis, Missouri. The boys' uncle, the Reverend Richard Kenrick, supervised his nephews' education in local Irish schools and Francis Kenrick's seminary training at Rome's Urban College of the Propaganda from 1814 to 1821. Kenrick excelled academically in Scripture, patristic studies, and biblical and modern languages. After ordination in Rome on 7 April 1821, Kenrick accepted Bishop Benedict Flaget's invitation to teach theology at St. Thomas, a diocesan seminary in Bardstown, Kentucky, on the American frontier.

The immigrant cleric dealt firsthand with the principal challenges of the nascent U.S. Catholic church in a republic where a hostile Protestant majority dominated. To confront the culture's anti-Catholic bias, the newly ordained cleric accepted the apologist's role; that is, he used lectures and numerous newspaper articles to prove the truth of Catholic faith. *The Letters of Omega and Omicron on Transubstantiation*, based on a debate series, was published in 1829. Discourses on the sacraments of baptism and then confirmation followed. Kenrick's writings were distinctive in their knowledgeable use of both Scripture and patristic sources.

The priest's exceptional competence, despite only nine years of experience, and the dire shortage of American clergy explain his 1830 appointment as Philadelphia's coadjutor bishop with full administrative powers. In this post Kenrick faced one of the most volatile of the nineteenth-century conflicts between a Catholic bishop and a parish's republican-inspired lay trustees who wanted pastoral jurisdiction within their congregation. Like other American bishops, Kenrick adamantly refused to accept the claims of the trustees of Philadelphia's St. Mary's Parish to appoint and dismiss their pastor. Only after Kenrick imposed an interdict on the parish, thereby suspending the congregation's sacramental privileges, did the trustees eventually submit to the bishop's authority. Kenrick's decisive actions contributed to the U.S. episcopacy's united efforts against lay-controlled parishes. To ensure an end to trusteeism, Kenrick included in the decrees of the 1832 diocesan synod stipulations limiting trusteeism in accord with the U.S. Catholic hierarchy's decisions at the First Provincial Council in Baltimore (1829).

Kenrick faced more challenges in meeting the needs of a burgeoning Catholic immigrant population. Beginning in the 1830s the bishop supervised the building of a network of ecclesial institutions, schools as well as churches, in Philadelphia. He also tended the needs of Catholics scattered throughout his diocesan territory of Pennsylvania, Delaware, and western New Jersey.

Kenrick's concern extended to Catholic children attending public schools. He insisted that Catholics be permitted to use their own version of Scripture or at least be exempted from hearing the public schools' compulsory reading of the King James translation. The bishop's firm stance won some concessions from Philadelphia school officials in 1842 but raised anti-Catholic suspicions that Catholics desired a ban on school Bible reading. In 1844 the issue exploded into riots that resulted in thirteen deaths and the destruction of Catholic properties including St. Michael's and St. Augustine's churches. In fear for his life Kenrick fled the city only to return in three days after calm returned. While maintaining a charitable demeanor, he demanded just recompense for the damaged property. Three years after the riots, the parishes received partial compensation from the city. The incident, however, captured national attention, and Kenrick's irenic posture undermined anti-Catholicism's credibility.

Rome elevated Kenrick to archbishop of Baltimore on 3 August 1851 and appointed him apostolic delegate to preside at the First Plenary Council of Baltimore (1852). This council approved all the decrees promulgated at the seven previous provincial councils, all of which Kenrick had attended. His roles at these provincial councils had ranged from secretary to principal author of national pastoral letters. Through his participation in the councils, Kenrick actively supported and eventually led the U.S. episcopacy toward establishing itself as the American church's central administrative authority. As archbishop of Baltimore, Kenrick also served as liaison between the Holy See and the U.S. bishops who were supporting the declaration of the dogma of the Immaculate Conception. He witnessed the 1854 declaration of the dogma in Rome. The archbishop died in Baltimore in the midst of the Civil War.

Kenrick published numerous works during his lifetime. *The Primacy of the Holy See Vindicated*, first published in 1837, was a series of letters responding to Episcopal bishop John Henry Hopkins's *The Church of Rome in Her Primitive Purity Compared to the Church of Rome at the Present Day*. Six more editions followed with revisions made through the fourth edition (1855). The book received favorable notice in England's *The Rambler* and appeared in German translation. Kenrick perceived the book to be an American response to the Oxford Movement. The text argued for the primacy of the papacy in honor and jurisdiction by constructing a historical argument based on patristic sources, a method reminiscent of Newman's tracts.

He also produced two seminary manuals, reflecting the scholastic approach of his Roman training: *Theologia Dogmatica* and *Theologia Moralis*. His four-volume dogmatic theology appeared in 1840 with a second, three-volume revision completed in 1858. A three-volume moral theology manual addressing standard moral questions as well as those peculiar to the American situation appeared in 1843. His unfortunate defense of slavery as a U.S. social institution appears in this text. A revision of *Theologia Moralis* appeared in 1858. Both texts were used in U.S. seminaries through the mid-1870s.

Kenrick also attempted a revision of the Douay translation of the Vulgate, the official Catholic Bible since the sixteenth century. His efforts were partly inspired by the U.S. bishops' desire to equip Catholics with a more accurate translation of the Bible to mitigate Protestant criticism. The first translation published, *The Four Gospels* (1849), received critical notice both in the United States and Ireland. A complete New Testament translation with notes appeared in 1862. Kenrick also published a series of Old Testament translations with notes. He made limited use of modern biblical criticism as well as Hebrew and Greek manuscripts. Although the translation remained rooted in the Latin Vulgate, Kenrick's occasional inclusion of a nontraditional rendering of the text generated sharp criticism from a few in the U.S. hierarchy.

Archbishop Francis Patrick Kenrick contributed to the formation of a U.S. Catholic church marked by a powerful episcopacy who determined the limits to which church polity would accommodate the republican context. His scholarship, though limited to nineteenth-century concerns, influenced theological education and debate in the United States and to some extent in Europe. His work continues to be a valuable resource for the historian of U.S. Catholic religious thought.

• The Archdiocese of Baltimore Archives has a collection of Kenrick papers. His publications also include *A Letter on Christian Union* (1836), *The Catholic Doctrine of Justification* (1841), *A Treatise on Baptism* (1843), *Form of Consecration of a Bishop of the Roman Catholic Church* (1850), and *A Treatise on Baptism and Confirmation* (1852). A bibliography is in Patrick Carey, *The Roman Catholics* (1993), pp. 253–54. For examples of official episcopal documents that Kenrick authored see Hugh J. Nolan, ed., *Pastoral Letters of the American Hierarchy, 1792–1970* (1971). For personal writings, see Francis E. Tourscher's translation and editing of *Diary and Visitation Record of the Rt. Rev. Francis Patrick Kenrick, Administrator and Bishop of Philadelphia* (1916) and *Kenrick-Frenaye Correspondence* (1920). Standard sources concerning his life and work are Michael O'Connor, *Archbishop Kenrick and His Work* (1867); John J. O'Shea, *The Two Kenricks* (1904); Michael Moran, "The Writings of Francis Patrick Kenrick, Archbishop of Baltimore (1797–1863)," *Records of the American Catholic Historical Society of Philadelphia* 41 (1930): 230–62; and Hugh J. Nolan, *The Most Reverend Francis Patrick Kenrick, Third Bishop of Philadelphia, 1830–1851* (1948). For information on Kenrick's work as archbishop of Baltimore see Thomas W. Spalding, *The Premier See: A History of the Archdiocese of Baltimore, 1789–1989* (1989). For an assessment of his biblical translations see Gerald P. Fogarty, *American Catholic Biblical Scholarship: A History from the Early Republic to Vatican II* (1989).

SANDRA YOCUM MIZE

KENRICK, Peter Richard (17 Aug. 1806–4 Mar. 1896), the first Catholic archbishop of St. Louis, was born in Dublin, Ireland, the son of Jane Eustace and Thomas Kenrick, a scrivener. The Kenricks were a relatively prosperous middle-class family. Thomas's occupation indicates that he had acquired a literacy that many Irish Catholics of his generation did not possess because of penal legislation against Catholic education in Ireland. His sons, however, were born at a time when the penal legislation had lost most of its force, and Irish Catholics were beginning to move toward full emancipation. Peter Richard and his older brother Francis Patrick Kenrick, the sixth Catholic archbishop of Baltimore from 1851 to 1863, were sent to the best Latin schools of Dublin. Unlike Francis, who was educated for the priesthood in Rome, Peter Richard was educated totally in Ireland, entering St. Patrick's College at Maynooth in 1827 to study for the priesthood. After ordination in 1832 he was invited by his brother, then bishop of Philadelphia, to come to the United States and serve in the Diocese of Philadelphia, where, from 1833 to 1841, he became rector of the cathedral, president of St. Charles Borromeo Seminary, founding editor of the *Catholic Herald* (1833–1863), and vicar general of the diocese. From 1837 to 1838, moreover, he served as pastor of St. Paul's Church in Pittsburgh.

In 1841 he became coadjutor bishop of St. Louis, becoming bishop in 1843 and archbishop in 1847. During his long tenure as archbishop of St. Louis, he established various institutions to serve the growing number of German and Irish Catholic immigrants who rushed into the city and diocese. In the early 1840s his diocese embraced the states of Missouri, Arkansas, and the western portion of Illinois; the territories now constituting Kansas, Nebraska, and Oklahoma; and a number of Indian missions in the territory east of the Rocky Mountains. The diocese had about 100,000 Catholics, sixty-five churches, and seventy-four priests. Although the extent of his archdiocese was substantially reduced by the end of his episcopacy, the diocese itself had experienced dramatic growth: for example, the Catholic population had increased by 100,000, the number of churches by about 235, the number of priests by 200, and the number of parish schools by 130. As metropolitan, he was also instrumental in developing Catholic dioceses and institutions throughout the great Midwest, from Wisconsin on the north to Alabama on the south and Santa Fe on the west.

Kenrick was influenced in his early Irish education by a Gallican approach to ecclesiology, which emphasized the significance and quasi-autonomy of the national church. In the United States he favored those policies that demonstrated the American character of the Catholic church in this country and participated actively in the three national plenary episcopal councils of Baltimore in 1852, 1866, and 1884, which set the canonical standards and governing policies for the Catholic church in the United States. Despite his allegiance to his adopted country, however, he did not accept American policies that he believed were contrary to his people's interests. During the Civil War he refused to fly the United States flag above the cathedral for fear of alienating southern sympathizers, and after the war he refused to abide by the Drake Constitution, a Missouri law that required clergymen to swear a special oath of loyalty to the state.

Although he was not as prolific a writer and ecclesiastical controversialist as his older brother, Kenrick did become involved in the Catholic-Protestant theological battles of the antebellum period. In the midst of the Oxford Movement, for example, he wrote a major treatise against the validity of Anglican ordinations, arguing that the episcopal consecration of Matthew Parker (1504–1575), Anglican archbishop of Canterbury, was invalid because the proper form had not been followed. In 1896 Vatican officials used his 1841 arguments in preparing a case for the Vatican condemnation of Anglican ordinations as null and void.

In 1869 and 1870 Kenrick took an active role at the First Vatican Council, where he became the leading American opponent of the definition of papal infallibility, arguing in his pamphlet *Concio . . . in Concilio Vaticano habenda et non habita* (1870) that the teaching of papal infallibility was a theological opinion, not a definable doctrine, because evidence from Scripture and tradition was either silent on the issue or opposed to it. Although he eventually accepted the council's definition of papal infallibility, he never repudiated the arguments of his *Concio*, and he refused to make any public statements on his position after returning from the council.

Although Kenrick was an effective ecclesiastical leader, he irritated the German clergy within his own diocese with the favoritism he showed to the Irish clergy and their parishes. Some of his own fellow bishops, especially Baltimore's archbishop Martin John Spalding, also found him uncooperative at the national episcopal councils, and some were annoyed with his published objections to papal infallibility. Rome in particular had lost confidence in Kenrick and in 1872 appointed bishop John Patrick Ryan to be coadjutor archbishop of St. Louis with the right of succession. Kenrick did not give up all authority over his diocese, however, and when Ryan became archbishop of Philadelphia in 1884 Kenrick resumed full and sole control of the archdiocese until 1893 when bishop John J. Kain was appointed archbishop with right of succession. During the last years of his episcopacy, as he was nearing ninety, Kenrick's administrative behavior became erratic. For example, one day he would fix a parish's boundaries and then change them the next. Because of his unpredictable behavior, Rome appointed Kain archbishop in May of 1895. Kenrick was made titular archbishop of Marcianopolis, retired from all episcopal duties, and less than a year after retirement died in St. Louis.

• Kenrick's letters and unpublished works are located primarily in the archives of the archdioceses of St. Louis, Philadelphia, and Baltimore, and Propaganda Fide (Rome). Some of his published works include *The New Month of Mary* (1840), *The Validity of Anglican Ordinations* (1841; rev. ed. 1848), and *The Holy House of Loretto* (1842). At the present time there is no comprehensive and critical biography of Kenrick. Samuel J. Miller, "Peter Richard Kenrick: Bishop and Archbishop of St. Louis, 1808–1896," *Records of the American Catholic Historical Society of Philadelphia* 84 (Mar., June, Sept. 1973): 3–163, offers a brief informative biographical sketch, as does John J. O'Shea, *The Two Kenricks* (1904). John Rothensteiner, *History of the Archdiocese of St. Louis* (2 vols., 1928), is a well-documented but not well-written examination of Kenrick's work in the development of the archdiocese. Gerald Fogarty, "Archbishop Peter Kenrick's Submission to Papal Infallibility," *Archivum Historiae Pontificiae* 16 (1978): 205–23, is a critical assessment of Kenrick's activities after the First Vatican Council.

PATRICK W. CAREY

KENSETT, John Frederick (22 Mar. 1816–14 Dec. 1872), artist, was born in Cheshire, Connecticut, the son of Thomas Kensett, an engraver, painter, and publisher, and Elizabeth Daggett. His father was a well-established artisan who had learned his craft in his native England and had produced the first known engraved map of New Haven. His mother was the granddaughter of Naphtali Daggett, an eminent eighteenth-century Congregationalist cleric and author, a president of Yale College, and an influential supporter of the American Revolution. Kensett attended the Cheshire Episcopal Academy from 1820 to 1821 and began to study engraving with his father at an early age. He went on to study with his uncle, Alfred Daggett, also an engraver, in New Haven, and by 1828 was employed in his shop there. In 1829 he went to New York City to work for Peter Maverick, the best-known engraver in America; but in June of that year Kensett's father died, and he returned to New Haven to his uncle's firm, Daggett and Ely. He remained there and with the successor firm Daggett and Hinman, generally toiling at making maps, business cards, and labels, until 1835, although he applied unsuccessfully for a job with engraver Asher B. Durand in New York in 1832. After an argument with his uncle he went back to New York and worked with Nathaniel Jocelyn from 1835 to 1837. He returned to Daggett and Hinman for a time in 1837 and the following year took a place in Albany with Hall, Packard, Cushman & Co., engravers of bank notes, with whom he worked for two years.

During his long apprenticeship in engraving, Kensett privately pursued the study of painting. As his *New York Times* obituary reported, "Though delighting in the delicate manipulation required by the burin, [he] felt in his soul a capacity for color which painting alone could satisfy." In 1838 he exhibited a landscape painting at the National Academy of Design, praised by a New York newspaper as "a very fair production from a young engraver." In 1840, determined to develop his command of the brush by exposure to the old masters, he traveled to Europe with Durand and artists John Casilear and Thomas Rossiter. He visited his father's brother in London and haunted the Royal Academy, the British Museum, and the National Gallery. By 1841 he was settled in Paris, where he shared a studio with Boston landscape artist Benjamin Champney. While in Paris he often dined with prominent American artist John Vanderlyn and came to know painter Thomas Cole. In 1843 a legacy from his grandmother brought him back to London, where legal complications kept him for two years. Living with his uncle, who helped him financially, he contributed to his own support by sending engraved vignettes back to Hall, Packard, Cushman & Co. and other firms and also by painting. In 1844 two landscapes Kensett sent back to New York were sold, and after he returned to Paris in 1845, he embarked on an extensive tour of Germany, Switzerland, and Italy. In Rome he formed a close friendship with Thomas Hicks, later a successful New York portrait painter. In 1846 eight of his paintings were purchased by the American Art-Union, a prestigious fine arts association.

When Kensett returned to the United States in November 1847, his landscapes had already earned him some reputation. He took a studio in the New York University Building in Washington Square and worked diligently, selling enough canvases to the Art-Union during 1848 to pay all the debts he had incurred in Europe. That year he was elected an associate of the National Academy; the next year he was elected a full member and in 1850 became a member of its council. His paintings sold very well, and he was highly regarded by his colleagues, who often called on him for his services in professional organizations. He founded and was the first president of the Artists' Fund, dedicated to aiding indigent artists and their families. From 1859 to 1862 he was one of three appointed by President

James Buchanan to advise on the decoration of the national Capitol in Washington, D.C. In 1865 he was made the chairman of the Art Committee of the Sanitary Fair, which raised money for the Sanitary Commission to the Union army in the Civil War. In 1870 he became a founder, and later a trustee and member of the Executive Committee, of the Metropolitan Museum of Art in New York. Although a prolific artist who traveled widely, he was a leader in the cultural life of New York, enjoying close personal relations with many of the most successful artists of his time and associating with literary lights such as Ralph Waldo Emerson, Henry Wadsworth Longfellow, James Russell Lowell, and William Cullen Bryant. He never married.

Kensett did much to elevate the status of artists in the United States and was one of the most popular members of the Hudson River school, though not one of its most influential. His landscapes—including scenes of the Adirondack and Catskill mountains, the Connecticut coast, and the lakes and rivers of New York State—were characterized by a detailed observation of nature and expert craftsmanship that reflected the discipline acquired as a bank-note engraver. Kensett was appreciated, however, for the sensitivity and refinement of his handling of light and the classical purity of his compositions rather than for any great originality of treatment. Sometimes criticized for the sentimentality and excessive delicacy of his shimmering atmosphere, he never strove for the dramatic effects that contemporaries such as Durand, Albert Bierstadt, and Frederick Church gave to the same subjects.

Kensett's technique showed little development from the 1840s, though it became somewhat more impressionistic in his last years. His popularity grew steadily throughout his career, and after his death in New York City, the 600 paintings and drawings found in his studio were auctioned for $136,312, an enormous sum for the time. His posthumous reputation suffered with the arrival of modernism in American art, and for a time he was almost forgotten. A revival of interest in his period restored his prestige in the 1940s. Among Kensett's most famous paintings are "Along the Hudson" (Smithsonian Institution) and "Lake George" (Corcoran Gallery). His work, along with that of his contemporaries, was once again collected, with his painting "Eagle Cliff, Coast of Massachusetts" bringing $540,000 at auction in 1983. Kensett's paintings and drawings are included in the National Gallery of Art and the Corcoran Gallery in Washington, the Museum of Fine Arts in Boston, and New York's Metropolitan Museum.

• Documents, letters, and manuscripts relating to Kensett are in the Rossiter file and the American Art-Union Papers at the New-York Historical Society, the Edwin D. Morgan Collection at the New York State Library in Albany, the John Frederick Kensett Files at the Metropolitan Museum of Art and the National Academy of Design in New York, and the Royal Academy File at the Witt Art Reference Library in London. For contemporary accounts of the artist, see Benjamin Champney, *Sixty Years' Memory of Art and Artists* (1900),

and H. T. Tuckerman, *Book of the Artists* (1867). A complete biography is John Paul Driscoll and John K. Howat, *John Frederick Kensett: An American Master* (1985). Essays on Kensett are in many exhibition catalogs, including Joan C. Siegfried, "The Art of John Frederick Kensett," in *Frederick Kensett: A Retrospective Exhibit* (1967); John H. Howat, *John Frederick Kensett* (1968); and John Wilmerding et al., *American Lights: The Luminist Movement, 1850–1875* (1980). See also Ellen Johnson, "Kensett Revisited," *Art Quarterly* 20, no. 2 (1975): 71–92; W. M. S. Rasmussen, "A Journey into the American Paradise," *Arts in Virginia* 28, no. 1 (1988): 14–29; K. M. Bennewitz, "John Frederick Kensett at Newport," *American Art Journal* 21, no. 4 (1989): 46–65; M. W. Sullivan, "John Frederick Kensett at Newport: The Making of a Luminist Painter," *Magazine of Antiques*, Nov. 1990, pp. 1030–41; and Carol Troyen, "Retreat to Arcadia: American Landscape and the American Art Union," *American Art Journal* 23, no. 1 (1991): 21–37. Obituaries are in the *New York Times*, 15 Dec. 1872, and the *New York Tribune*, 16 Dec. 1872.

DENNIS WEPMAN

KENT, Aratus (17 Jan. 1794–8 Nov. 1869), clergyman and college founder, was born in Suffield, Connecticut, the son of Captain John Kent, a businessman and farmer, and Sarah Smith. At the age of nineteen Kent entered the sophomore class of Yale College under President Timothy Dwight. He may have been caught up in the revival that swept over the campus in 1815–1816, part of the national movement known as the Second Great Awakening, for he joined the Presbyterian church in 1816, the year of his graduation.

Kent studied for four years under eminent clergymen in New York City and in 1820 received a license to preach from the Presbytery of New York. Thereafter he served two one-year terms as a missionary in frontier Ohio, Massachusetts, and Connecticut. In 1822 he entered Princeton Theological Seminary and about two years later took a pastorate in Lockport, New York, where he received his ordination on 26 January 1825. He remained in Lockport until 1828, except when he was called home to care for his aged father, who died in 1827.

Thereafter Kent served briefly as a home missionary in New Hampshire, but according to later eulogists he had the strong conviction that God was calling him to labor in a more difficult field. He learned of an opportunity to serve in the American Home Missionary Society (AHMS), a newly established organization providing missionary services within the United States, supported primarily by Presbyterians and Congregationalists. In March 1829 he traveled to New York City to meet with the society's corresponding secretary, the Reverend Absalom Peters. Peters sent Kent to a northern tributary of the Mississippi River, where frontiersmen were mining approximately five million tons of lead ore each year. Kent traveled by steamboat to Galena, Illinois, a polyglot boomtown of some fifteen hundred people, with several thousand more living nearby. Arriving on a Sunday morning in April 1829, Kent set up benches in a half-constructed building and preached to about fifty people. There was neither an established church nor a minister within hundreds of miles. He was appalled by the community's swearing, drinking, gambling, and disregard of the Sabbath. Kent held services in a dining room, the barroom of a tavern, and the Galena courthouse, all of which were unsuitable. Consequently, he invested his salary in the purchase of a log cabin, where he conducted church services and taught school to some sixty children. In addition, he organized Bible, temperance, and antigambling societies. On 23 October 1831, with a nucleus of six members, Kent organized the First Presbyterian Church.

In 1832 the Black Hawk War interrupted Kent's missionizing, so he returned to the East. That same year he married Caroline Corning; within the year she returned with him to Galena. They had three children, all of whom died in infancy, but over the course of their marriage the Kents reared and educated twelve orphans. In addition, Kent recruited a number of young men into the ministry, nine of whose studies he helped to finance. The Kents' home became a way station for numerous traveling ministers and women teachers.

Kent's parish encompassed much of northern Illinois. He made his rounds on horseback, taking along a box of religious literature for distribution. On one 384-mile trip he preached more than twenty sermons, in addition to giving talks in Sunday schools and prayer meetings. His grammar was flawed, but his sermons rang with a deep religious conviction that attracted numerous converts, including 266 people who joined his church after a revival in the early 1840s. Kent was officially installed as the pastor of the First Presbyterian Church of Galena in 1841, but his parish duties did not diminish his influence on the entire region. He founded numerous Sunday schools as well as Presbyterian and Congregational churches in northern Illinois and southern Wisconsin.

Kent was convinced that the key to establishing a Christian society was to found schools for the education of Christian ministers, teachers, and mothers. So it was appropriate that when fifty-four "friends of Christian education in Northern Illinois, Wisconsin and Iowa" met in Beloit, Wisconsin, in 1844 to discuss the establishment of collegiate institutions, they turned to "Father Kent" for leadership. He led the group to charter a male institution, Beloit College in Beloit, Wisconsin (1846), and Rockford Female Seminary in Rockford, Illinois (1847). For the remainder of his life Kent served as vice president of the board of Beloit College and president of the board of Rockford Female Seminary. For both institutions, he dedicated the first buildings, helped to select administrators, raised funds, and recruited students.

In 1848 Kent was appointed by the AHMS to serve as agent for the northern Illinois region. Consequently, he resigned from his pastorate and assumed his new position, which included reporting on the moral and religious climate, overseeing the work of the churches, founding new churches and supplying them with pastors, raising financial support for missions,

and preaching. The AHMS hesitated to take a strong stand against slavery, but Kent abhorred the practice and often preached against it. He did not believe that slaveholders should be invited to preach in Presbyterian churches. Kent retired in 1861, after the commencement of the Civil War, but he continued to take assignments. Kent was deeply interested in the plight of the Santee Sioux. Most of the tribe's warriors were killed in the New Ulm Massacre of 1862 and the rest of the tribe were moved from Minnesota to the Santee Sioux Reservation in Knox County, Nebraska, the following year. Kent visited the Santee Agency in 1869. While there he became ill and died in Galena, Illinois, after returning home.

Kent is representative of a host of Calvinist missionaries who, fired by the zeal of the Second Great Awakening, migrated from New England to evangelize the frontier. These men cherished their memories of the society they left behind, with its well-established churches and schools, benevolent societies, and Puritan families. They believed that the future of the nation rested on their efforts to transform the western frontier into a stable Protestant region, complete with institutions modeled after those of New England. The imprint of their work survives in the numerous schools, churches, colleges, theological seminaries, and benevolent societies they established to foster and perpetuate their vision.

• Kent's missionary activities are described in numerous letters to the American Home Missionary Society, housed in the Amistad Research Center, New Orleans. See also the Aratus Kent Papers in the Beloit College Archives, Beloit, Wisc.; and the Aratus Kent Papers in the Rockford College Archives, Rockford, Ill. An informative article about Kent's early AHMS labors is Rev. Gordon Arthur Riegler, "Aratus Kent, First Presbyterian Minister in Northern Illinois," *Journal of the Presbyterian Historical Society* 13, no. 8 (1929): 363–80. A biographical article focusing primarily on Kent's educational activities is Lucy Forsyth Townsend, "Aratus Kent: Portrait of a College Founder," *Vitae Scholasticae* 7 (Fall 1988): 303–19. See also vital records of Suffield, Conn., and the tombstone legend of the Kents in Galena, Ill. Obituaries are in the *Galena Gazette*, 23 Nov. 1869, and *Beloit College Monthly*, vol. 16 (Mar. 1870).

LUCY FORSYTH TOWNSEND

KENT, Atwater (3 Dec. 1873–4 Mar. 1949), inventor and manufacturer, was born in Burlington, Vermont, the son of Prentiss J. Kent, a physician, and Mary Elizabeth Atwater. His first name was actually Arthur, but he used his middle name alone throughout his life. He attended Wooster Polytechnic Institute from 1895 to 1897 but left school to begin a manufacturing business and did not graduate.

Kent's initial business, created around 1895, was the Kent Electric Manufacturing Company, which made and advertised small motors and fans. The real beginning of his career, however, came with formation of the Atwater Kent Manufacturing Works in Philadelphia in 1902. The new firm made telephones, small voltmeters, and other small electrical devices. The product line expanded by 1905 into automobile devices, including the Kent-invented "Unisparker," an automobile ignition system that "integrated the usual series of weak sparks into a single hot spark for ignition" by combining "contact points, condenser, centrifugal advance mechanism, and distributor into one compact unit to be used with an ignition coil" (Douglas, p. 65). The device remained widely used into the 1970s. Kent married Mabel Lucas in Philadelphia in 1906; they had three children and adopted one child. During World War I, the Kent company manufactured military equipment, for example, a panoramic gun sight. By the end of his career, Kent would hold ninety-three patents.

Kent was best known for the popular radio receivers his firm made from 1922 to 1936. The firm began to sell radio receiver components in 1922, trading on its reputation and network of dealers. By early 1923, Atwater Kent radio advertisements offered fully assembled receivers in response to the growing radio mania. These were "breadboard" sets, so called because they lacked an external case and their components were mounted on wooden bases. The first enclosed Atwater Kents appeared in 1924. By late 1927, the company offered AC-powered receivers that plugged into a wall socket and dispensed with messy batteries. The market trend to bigger and fancier radios with more expensive consoles worked well until the depression, when other firms took over the market for small sets. The displacement was fairly sudden: while the company took six years to die, its market share plunged in just a year or so. Kent seems to have lost interest in the industry and his firm after that. The Atwater Kent company ceased operations in 1936 and Kent destroyed the firm's remaining records. An investment company of the same name still exists, controlled by the family, in Wilmington, Delaware.

The popular *Atwater Kent Hour* music program first aired in 1925 and was soon carried on many stations. The program broadcast popular orchestral music tending toward the semiclassical and featured only two sixty-second ads. As a key radio manufacturer, Kent was active in helping define policy for the new broadcasting business as a delegate to the 1924 and 1925 National Radio Conferences called by Secretary of Commerce Herbert Hoover.

After Kent closed his radio manufacturing operations, he retired to Hollywood, California, and lived in lavish retirement, until his death there. At the same time, he endowed (1938) the Atwater Kent Museum in Philadelphia, which focuses on social history and everyday life in that city. Through his foundation, he also purchased and refurbished the Betsy Ross home in the same city.

• The Atwater Kent Museum in Philadelphia maintains a clipping file on both the man and the firm, but holds no papers. Some family records are held by the Atwater Kent Manufacturing Company (an investment holding firm) in Wilmington, Delaware. The best review of the golden age of Atwater Kent radio manufacturing (1922–1932) is found in volume 1 of Alan Douglas, *Radio Manufacturers of the 1920s* (1988). Obituaries are in the *New York Times* and *New York Herald Tribune*, both 5 Mar. 1949.

CHRISTOPHER H. STERLING

KENT, Benjamin (? June 1708–22 Oct. 1788), lawyer, was the son of Joseph Kent, yeoman of Charlestown, and Rebecca Chittenden. The exact date and place of his birth are unknown, but he was baptized in Cambridge, Massachusetts, on 13 June 1708. He graduated from Harvard in 1727, taught school in Framingham, Massachusetts, for a while, and then returned to Harvard to study for the ministry. Briefly, in 1731, he was chaplain at Fort George in Maine and preached at nearby Brunswick. He later returned to Massachusetts, where he was soon accused of espousing a nonorthodox theology. Despite these concerns, the town of Marlborough called him as their minister in 1733, but his installation was delayed pending an unusual two-day meeting of the associated ministers of the region to test his theology. Although Kent passed this first test and was duly ordained on 31 October 1733, charges of Arminianism were leveled against him from the beginning of his tenure. An ecclesiastical council on the heresy charges was called in February 1735 to hear how far he had strayed from the tenets of Calvinism. As a result of the hearing, the council suspended him from office. When the council reconvened in June, it accepted Kent's resignation, but the town then refused to pay his back salary.

Kent's successful civil suit against the town of Marlborough for payment acted as a segue into his own practice of law. He became active as a lawyer in the Boston courts as early as 1739, picking up the dregs, which his more established colleagues disdained, thus earning himself the epithet of "Chimney sweeper of the Bar" (*Herald of Freedom*, 2 Feb. 1790). In 1740 he married Elizabeth Watts, daughter of Samuel Watts and Elizabeth Shute, of Chelsea. The couple had four children.

Kent continued practicing in the Boston courts, and in 1759 John Adams characterized him as being "for fun, Drollery, Humour, flouts, Jeers, Contempt. He has an irregular immethodical Head, but his Thoughts are often good and his Expressions happy." Adams, however, also noted that "it is the delight of this Kents Heart to teaze a Minister or Deacon with his wild Conceits, about Religion," perhaps a lighthearted retaliation for the treatment he had received at the hands of the church oligarchy (John Adams, *Diary*, vol. 1, p. 110, vol. 2, p. 50). In 1762 Kent advanced to the rank of barrister and began to practice in other counties as well. In 1770 he was one of the founding members of the Suffolk Bar, where he often presided as the senior barrister.

When sides were chosen on the eve of the Revolution, Kent came out firmly on the patriot side, aligned himself with the Committee of Correspondence, and became a member of the Sons of Liberty. An early advocate of independence, Kent wrote to Adams at Philadelphia in April 1776 that "the present time to make a final declaration of Independence is the best." He also spoke out for religious tolerance demanding that the Continental Congress "tollerate all Religions both Natural and reveal'd and establish none."

In April 1776 the Massachusetts state legislature appointed Kent as attorney general, a position he held until the following year when Robert Treat Paine succeeded him. Thereafter Kent acted as the attorney general for Suffolk County. One of Kent's duties as attorney general was to prosecute Loyalists, and at one point he was obliged to jail his own son-in-law, Sampson Salter Blowers. However, Blowers and his wife were soon able to remove to British-held Newport, where Kent's wife and elder daughter joined them. Soon afterwards they all moved to Nova Scotia. Kent remained in Boston and ensconced himself in the Blowers mansion. In 1777 he wrote to Edward Winslow, the exiled register of probate for Suffolk County, for the return of probate records from Halifax, Nova Scotia. The records, however, had passed into the hands of Foster Hutchinson, who claimed to still be judge of probate for the county and as such entitled to retain the records. Finally, in 1784 Governor John Hancock appointed Kent as agent for the state to go to Halifax and retrieve the records. It took four months to complete the deal, and Kent then wintered in Halifax before returning to Boston in April 1785. His return to Boston, however, was only to settle his affairs in Massachusetts, and in June of that year he again left for Nova Scotia, to spend his final days with his wife and daughters in Halifax, where he died.

Kent was an interesting transitional character, both in terms of the changing ministry and the developing role of lawyers as public leaders. However, his role in public affairs was always a minor one, and the choice to spend his final years back in a British colony was an ironic one.

• Kent's only published work was an early self-vindication about his theology, *A Sermon Preached at a Lecture in Marlborough . . . July 9, 1734. Upon the Divinity of Christ. Wherein it is Strongly Asserted, Proved and Vindicated against the Socinian & Arian Heresys, & c.* (1724). He also wrote a lengthy newspaper article for a supplement of the *Boston Evening Post*, 23 Apr. 1770, protesting accusations of perjury brought against him by a former client, Dr. Sylvanus Gardiner. The only substantial sketch of Kent's career is Clifford K. Shipton, *Sibley's Harvard Graduates*, vol. 8 (1951), pp. 220–30.

EDWARD W. HANSON

KENT, Charles Foster (13 Aug. 1867–2 May 1925), educator and author, was born in Palmyra, New York, the son of William Hotchkiss Kent and Helen Maria Foster, farmers. A good student, Kent received his early education at the Palmyra Union Classical School, after which, at the age of seventeen, he enrolled in the Sheffield Scientific School at Yale University. Kent decided to transfer to Yale College at the end of his freshman year. There he served as editor of the *Yale Daily News* in his senior year, participated in crew his junior and senior years, and was elected to Phi Beta Kappa.

Following his graduation in 1889 with a B.A., Kent became a Foote Scholar in Semitic languages at Yale's graduate school. In 1891 he was awarded a Ph.D. with a dissertation on "The Status Construtus in Assyrian." He spent the following academic year in postdoctoral work at the University of Berlin and then spent several months traveling in Egypt, Palestine, Turkey, and Greece. Returning to the United States in the fall of 1892, Kent assumed his first academic teaching appointment, instructor in biblical literature at the University of Chicago. He remained at Chicago until June 1895, when he became associate professor of biblical literature and history at Brown University in Providence, Rhode Island. In July of the same year he married Elizabeth Middleton Sherrill in Palmyra; they had two children.

The first of Kent's many publications on biblical topics, *Outline Study of Hebrew History* and *The Wise Men of Ancient Israel and Their Proverbs*, were published in 1895. The following year proved equally productive for Kent; *A History of the Hebrew People from the Settlement in Canaan to the Division of the Kingdom* was published, and in December he began a fruitful period of study with Professor Friedrich Delitzsch at the University of Breslau in Germany, which lasted until June of the following year. In 1897 Kent returned to the United States and published *A History of the Hebrew People from the Division of the Kingdom to the Fall of Jerusalem in 586 B.C.* Kent became a full professor in June 1898 and remained at Brown until 1901, when he accepted the Woolsey Professorship of Biblical Literature at Yale, which he retained until his death.

During these years Kent produced a continuous stream of publications, including *The Messages of the Earlier Prophets* (1898), with Frank Knight Sanders; *The Messages of the Later Prophets* (1899), with Sanders; *A History of the Jewish People during the Babylonian, Persian and Greek Periods* (1899); *The Messages of Israel's Lawgivers* (1902); *Origin and Permanent Value of the Old Testament* and *Historical and Topographical Maps for Bible Students* (both 1906); *The Work and Teachings of the Earlier Prophets* (1907); *The Heroes and Crises of Early Hebrew History* and *The Founders and Rulers of United Israel* (both 1908); *The Kings and Prophets of Israel and Judah* and *The Addresses, Epistles and Apocalypses of Israel's Prophets* (both 1909); *The Makers and Teachers of Judaism* and *The Great Teachers of Judaism and Christianity* (both 1911); *Biblical Geography and History* (1911) and *Making of a Nation* (1912), both with Jeremiah Whipple Jenks; *Life and Teachings of Jesus according to the Earliest Records* (1913); *The Work and Teachings of the Apostles* (1913); *The Testing of a Nation's Ideals* (1915), with Jenks; *The Social Teachings of the Prophets and Jesus* (1917); *A History of the Hebrew Commonwealth*, with Albert Edward Bailey, and *Jesus' Principles of Living*, with Jenks (both 1920); *The Children's Bible* (1922), with Henry

A. Sherman; and *The Growth and Contents of the Old Testament* (1925). From 1899 to 1930 he also edited, along with Sanders, the Historical Series for Bible Students and throughout his career contributed scholarly articles to a variety of magazines.

Kent is best remembered for his *The Student's Old Testament*, a carefully annotated scriptural translation that ran to six volumes: *Narratives of the Beginnings of Hebrew History* (1904), *Israel's Historical and Biographical Narratives* (1905), *Sermons, Epistles and Apocalypse of Israel's Prophets* (1910), *Israel's Laws and Legal Precedents* (1907), *The Songs, Hymns and Prayers of the Old Testament* (1914), and *Proverbs and Didactic Poems*, with Millar Burrows (posthumously published in 1927). He became involved in the controversy over Prohibition when his *The Shorter Bible* (2 vols., 1918–1921) was accused by the National Association against the Prohibition Amendment of editorial bias; critics claimed that all favorable references regarding alcoholic consumption had been deleted, while all negative statements had been retained. Kent denied any attempt to influence public opinion.

Kent used every means at his disposal to advance the cause of modern biblical scholarship. In addition to his prolific writing, he also lectured extensively at institutions such as the University of Pennsylvania, Lake Forest University, and Stanford University as well as at convocations such as those held by the Vermont Congregational churches (1918), the Fairfield (Conn.) Sunday School Workers (1919), and Chautauqua (1914 and 1924). His leadership was most evident in his efforts to found the Council of Schools of Religion (later the National Council on Religion in Higher Education), for which he served as a director from 1922 and as secretary of its board of trustees. Kent also served as secretary of the council's Commission on Courses of Study Preparatory to Religious Leadership and chaired the council's Commission on the Study of the Great Living Religions.

The ever-active Kent found time for civic activity, serving from 1907 to 1909 as the first president of the New Haven Civic Federation and as a third vice president of the New Haven Chamber of Commerce (1921). He was also active in clubs as varied as the American Oriental Society and the Society of Colonial Wars before his death from heart disease in Mount Carmel, Connecticut.

Kent served an important role in the late nineteenth-century movement to bring the standards of modern scholarship to bear on the study of biblical literature. In an age when theologians and clergy were struggling to come to grips with the impact of Darwinism, his writings attempted to place the Bible under scrutiny comparable to that being given to the natural sciences.

• The Bentley Historical Library at the University of Michigan, Ann Arbor, holds a small amount of Kent's correspondence among the Horace Lafayette Wilgus and Edward W. Blakeman papers. Additional correspondence can be found among the William Smith Culbertson Papers in the Manuscript Division, Library of Congress, and in the George Armstrong Wauchope Papers at the South Caroliniana Library, University of South Carolina, Columbia. Surprisingly little secondary work has been completed on his life and career; the best sources of information remain the *Obituary Record of Graduates Deceased during the Year Ending July 1, 1924* (1924), and Charles Hitchcock Sherrill, *Yale College, Yale University: Class of '89 Vicennial* (1910). An obituary is in the *New York Times*, 4 May 1925.

EDWARD L. LACH, JR.

KENT, Edward (8 Jan. 1802–19 May 1877), lawyer, politician, and judge, was born in Concord, New Hampshire, the son of William Austin Kent, a well-to-do merchant and politician, and Charlotte Mellen. After graduating with honors from Harvard University in 1821, Kent studied law briefly with Chancellor James Kent of New York and then with Benjamin Orr, a prominent Maine attorney. He opened his own practice in Bangor in 1825, and in 1827 he married Sarah Johnston of Hillsborough, New Hampshire; the couple had three children. Kent formed partnerships with Jonathan P. Rogers in 1828 and with future Maine Supreme Judicial Court justice Jonas Cutting in 1831.

A successful but not aggressive lawyer, Kent hated drudgery and discouraged litigation. A friend and legal colleague described him as "indolent" in the early stages of a case—at Harvard, Kent had presided over the Lazy Man's Club—but "earnest, forcible, [and] comprehensive" when "fairly engaged."

Kent took an early interest in politics, contributing occasional articles to newspapers and holding a variety of local offices in the 1820s and 1830s. He was, among other things, a member of the superintending school committee and presiding judge of the Penobscot County Court of Sessions. He also served three terms in the Maine House of Representatives as a National Republican and was elected as a Whig mayor of Bangor in 1836 and 1837, resigning during his second term to become governor of Maine.

Physically imposing, intelligent, affable, and unpretentious, Kent was widely popular. He was the Whig candidate in the annual elections for governor every year from 1836 through 1841. His victories in 1837 and 1840 made him the only non-Democrat to hold that office between 1831 and 1853. In 1840 the national Whigs, anticipating a presidential victory, sang that Maine had gone "hell bent for Kent" in its September election, although in fact no candidate had received a majority of the popular vote, and Kent had been elected by the legislature.

Kent generally adhered to standard Whig positions on the great issues of the day. For example, he favored a protective tariff, objected to the proliferation of small local banks, and opposed Maine's small-bills law and other Democratic attempts to drive paper money out of circulation. On social questions Kent exhibited the moralistic streak often associated with Whigs, excoriating the common practice of wagering on the outcome of political elections and advocating the prohibition of liquor, which he blamed for both poverty and crime.

Kent also opposed slavery and urged the legislature to provide procedural protections for blacks detained under the federal fugitive slave law.

In 1841 Kent was renominated for governor without his consent, lost, and returned to the full-time practice of law. However, he retained an active interest in public affairs. As governor, Kent had called on the federal government to end its apparent indifference to the long-standing northeastern boundary dispute between the United States and Great Britain and to support Maine's claim to the entire contested territory; after he left office, the Maine legislature appointed him to a commission to represent the state in the negotiations that resulted in the Webster-Ashburton Treaty of 1842.

A loyal Whig, Kent was an early and influential supporter of General Zachary Taylor in the presidential race of 1848. Although Taylor was a southern slaveholder, Kent saw him as the best hope of keeping both the Whig party and the nation from splitting along sectional lines. He nominated Taylor for president at the Whig National Convention and worked hard for his election. After his victory Taylor rewarded Kent with the consulate at Rio de Janeiro.

Kent lived in Brazil from late 1849 until 1853, when the Democrats regained the White House and replaced him. In addition to his normal consular duties—including reporting on American commerce in Rio de Janeiro and keeping records on American ships entering and leaving the port—Kent took a keen interest in the African slave trade. Appalled by the brutality of Brazilian slavery, he wrote long letters to officials in Washington, D.C., on the Brazilian government's efforts to halt the slave trade and the activities of Americans engaged in it. Kent also made recommendations to strengthen bills in Congress intended to curtail Americans' involvement in what he called the "unholy traffic."

Kent also reported to Washington on the yellow fever epidemics that regularly afflicted Brazil. While in Rio he lost two of his three children to the disease. Within a few years of returning home, his wife and third child also died.

From 1853 or 1854 until 1859 Kent practiced law in Bangor with his brother George. In 1855 he married Abby Anne Rockwood, with whom he had one child. Seeing no hope for the Whigs after the electoral debacle of 1852, he joined the Republican cause early on, corresponding with leading politicians and speaking at meetings around the state on its behalf. Despite his contributions to the success of the Republican party, however, his own quests for office proved fruitless, for he had been bypassed by "new men," including former Democrats who had not, Kent felt, demonstrated loyalty to the cause.

In 1859 Governor Lot Morrill appointed Kent to the Maine Supreme Judicial Court. Experienced and well read in the law, patient, impartial, and possessing a "commanding presence," Kent was well suited for a judicial post. He wrote several notable opinions in the 1860s dealing with war-related issues such as freedom

of the press and military bounties. In 1872, when the courts of Maine and other states were producing opinions that would later be viewed as landmarks of laissez-faire constitutionalism, Kent wrote a majority opinion rejecting a radical freedom-of-contract theory in favor of one that limited the power of quasi-public enterprises to set their own terms when dealing with the public (*True v. International Telegraph Company*).

Kent retired from the bench in 1873, took a European tour, and then practiced law in Bangor, where he died. In his last public position, he presided in 1875 over a commission to consider amendments to Maine's state constitution.

• Manuscript collections containing significant Kent correspondence include the William Pitt Fessenden Papers at the Western Reserve Historical Society; the Hamlin Family Papers at the University of Maine; the Washburn Family Papers at the Washburn-Norlands Library, Livermore Falls, Maine; and "Despatches from United States Consuls in Rio de Janeiro, 1811–1906," vols. 14 and 15, in the National Archives. Kent's judicial opinions can be found in vols. 46 through 61 of the *Maine Reports*. Biographical sketches of Kent include John E. Godfrey, "Memoir of Hon. Edward Kent, LL.D.," *Collections of the Maine Historical Society* 8 (1881): 449–80; Charles Hamlin, "The Supreme Court of Maine," pt. 5, *Green Bag* 8 (1896): 61–82; and the entry in *Biographical Encyclopedia of Maine of the Nineteenth Century* (1885). An obituary is in *Maine Reports* 66 (26 June 1877): 602–13.

DAVID M. GOLD

KENT, Jack (10 Mar. 1920–18 Oct. 1985), cartoonist and children's book writer, was born John Wellington Kent in Burlington, Iowa, the son of Ralph Arthur Kent, a salesman, and Marguerite Bruhl. Kent's father, whose work called for constant travel, took his family with him, and Kent lived in various places in the Midwest before beginning school in Chicago, Illinois. The family finally settled in Dallas, Texas, where he spent two years in high school before dropping out and began selling freelance advertising art to local newspapers and humorous cartoons to such national magazines as *Collier's*. A week after the United States declared war on Japan in 1941, he enlisted in the army and served until 1945. He saw action in Alaska and the South Pacific, attaining the rank of first lieutenant and learning Eskimo and Tagalog. Upon his discharge he returned to Texas, where he became a partner in a printing plant and learned all aspects of the business, but he continued to draw and submit cartoons.

In 1950 Kent created the comic strip *King Aroo*, a whimsical series about the diminutive, childlike monarch of the land of Myopia and his oddly assorted retinue of associates, human, animal, and undetermined. Launched as a daily and Sunday feature in November of that year by the McClure Newspaper Syndicate, it delighted a small but devoted following with its zany stories and exuberant wordplay, making Kent, as he later reported, "world famous for blocks around." A collection of the strips was published in 1952 with an introduction by popular-culture critic Gilbert Seldes, who praised Kent for "the sly grace that gives an uncommon sweetness to all his work" and noted that he "brings to the small company of fantasists the primary faculty of being able to create a compact universe that adheres strictly to a logic of its own."

Although *King Aroo* received considerable acclaim in literary circles, it never reached a distribution level of 100 newspapers—the syndicate break-even point—and was discontinued in 1960. So great was the devotion the strip inspired among its admirers, however, that one paper, the *San Francisco Chronicle*, sustained it alone for a time and even established a syndicate, Golden Gate Features, to distribute it. The market was not sufficient, however, and *King Aroo* abdicated for good on 14 June 1965.

Kent returned to the uncertain career of a freelancer, selling greeting-card designs to Hallmark Cards and advertising art and cartoons to a wide variety of publications, from *Humpty Dumpty*, the *Saturday Evening Post*, and *Collier's* to *Playboy*, and at times supplementing his meager earnings by driving trucks. In 1968 he discovered a market for his talents that the subtle and allusive wit of his comic strip had never brought him when he began to write fiction for the preschool to third-grade market. "I discovered," he later reported, "I have a natural empathy for my mental peers in the sandbox set." His first work of juvenile fiction, *Just Only John*, won an award from Chicago Graphics Associates and sold more than 400,000 copies. A prolific author, Kent wrote and illustrated forty-four children's books of his own and provided illustrations for twenty-one others. His books sold very well in Great Britain and were translated into fifteen languages. Many went into multiple editions and were selected by book clubs, and several were made into animated films, filmstrips, and phonograph records. The *New York Times* named *Jack Kent's Happy-Ever-After Book* one of the seven outstanding picture books of the year in 1976.

Informed by the same spirit of gentle irony and playful love of puns, asides, and skewed logic as his comic strip, Kent's children's books won praise for their harmony of text and illustration. His loose, free-flowing art, in pen and ink with occasional splashes of wash and tint, was as lively and spontaneous as his fanciful stories.

In 1954 Kent married June Kilstofte, a reporter who was sent to interview him for her San Antonio, Texas, newspaper when it subscribed to his comic strip. The couple had one child. Described as a modest and innocent gentleman much like his own creation King Aroo, Kent had far-ranging interests, including art, archaeology, language, architecture (he designed his own home), nature, and music. He and his wife were self-described "bibliomaniacs" and amassed a library of from 5,000 to 6,000 books on many subjects. Kent died in San Antonio.

• Articles on Kent are included in many biographical dictionaries of cartoonists and children's authors. Among the most extensive are Maurice Horn, ed., *World Encyclopedia of Comics* (1974); Lee Kingman et al., eds., *Illustrators of Children's Books, 1967–1976* (1978); Horn, ed., *Contemporary Graphic Artists*, vol. 1 (1984); Ron Goulart, ed., *The Encyclopedia of American Comics* (1990); and Horn, *100 Years of American Newspaper Comics* (1996). For critical studies, see Gilbert Seldes's introduction to Kent's *King Aroo* (1952); Rick Marschall, "God Save the King!" *Nemo*, Aug. 1986, pp. 5–6; and Ron Goulart, *The Funnies* (1995). Obituaries are in *Publishers Weekly*, 8 Nov. 1985, and *Contemporary Graphic Artists*, vol. 2 (1987).

DENNIS WEPMAN

KENT, James (31 July 1763–12 Dec. 1847), jurist, was born in Doanesburg, New York, the son of Moss Kent, Sr., a farmer and lawyer, and Hannah Rogers. Kent's mother died when he was seven years old, and his father remarried. From the age of five to nine he lived with his maternal grandparents in Norwalk, Connecticut, and at various boarding schools, most notably Ebenezer Baldwin's at Danbury. During Kent's years at Yale, 1777–1781 (graduating in 1781), the college was subject to war-caused interruptions, and during one British raid his grandparent's house was razed by the enemy. Nevertheless, Kent throughout his life remained the staunchest of Anglophiles (although he supported the patriot cause during the war). During one period that classes were suspended because of the war, Kent encountered Blackstone's *Commentaries on the Laws of England*, and "it inspired me at the age of 15 with awe, and I fondly determined to be a lawyer." In November 1781, shortly after graduating from Yale, Kent began preparation for the bar in the Poughkeepsie, New York, office of the state's attorney general, Egbert Benson. He was admitted in January 1785. Attempting solo practice at Fredericksburgh, near his birthplace, Kent could attract no clients and became the junior partner of Gilbert Livingston at Poughkeepsie in the following spring. Assured of financial security, in 1785 Kent was able to marry sixteen-year-old Elizabeth Bailey, with whose family Kent had roomed during his clerkship, and they had a model marriage for sixty-three years. The Kents had four children, three of whom lived to adulthood.

The wonders of the law that Kent had encountered were throughly challenged by the drudgery he underwent as Benson's clerk, yet he realized, as he began practicing in 1785, that "however crowded the Bar may be as to number, or however limited in their Fees, still the Study of the Law is so interwoven with Politics that it will always enable Gentlemen of active Geniusses to attain a decisive Superiority in Government." He made a sharp distinction between the need to earn a living and public policy making and advised prospective lawyers, including his brother Moss, accordingly, while rigorously dividing his own time between studying the mundane aspects of the law and studying its more philosophical parts. Indeed, he was a bibliophile throughout his life and pored over all sorts of learning, particularly the classics.

The small but rapidly growing town of Poughkeepsie shaped Kent's early career. Political differences among the revolutionary generation had been papered over during the war, but in the 1780s they were the basis for emerging political parties. Kent's penchant for order and his commercial orientation coincided with the values of New York's champions of the new federal constitution, such as John Jay, Benson, and Alexander Hamilton. The New York convention to ratify the Constitution met in Poughkeepsie during the summer of 1788, and Kent, an attentive spectator, was particularly impressed with Hamilton, whom he came to idolize, as indicated by a glowing tribute that Kent wrote on the latter's death. Similarly, he memorized the *Federalist* and wrote anonymous newspaper articles in support of the Constitution.

The earliest efforts Kent made to become a policy maker was as a successful assembly candidate in 1790 and 1792. As a vigorous Federalist, Kent was distraught by what he considered to be the theft of the governorship from John Jay by Antifederalist George Clinton in 1792, and that in addition to defeat at the hands of his brother-in-law in a 1793 race for the federal House of Representatives led him to conclude that the legislative branch did not suit him. The Antifederalist atmosphere of Poughkeepsie along with what he called his "unequal partnership" with Gilbert Livingston also prompted Kent's move to New York City in April 1793. At first the move was disastrous; his two-year-old daughter died of smallpox, he lacked business, and the cost of living was high. He was in despair, but Federalist connections came to his rescue. First, Columbia College's Federalist-dominated board of trustees selected him to fill a new law professorship in December 1793. After 1795, when the party got control of the state government, it supplied him with small but lucrative patronage appointments. He became master of chancery in 1796 and recorder of New York City (a part-time municipal judgeship) in 1797. The professorship lasted two years; lack of attendance in the second year led Kent to resign. He later called the lectures "slight & trashy," but Vice President John Adams, whose son was enrolled the first year, declared, "I am much pleased with the Lecture and esteem the talents and Character of the Professor."

An important new phase in Kent's life began in 1798, when the Federalist-controlled Council of Appointment (including Governor Jay) appointed him "to the grand object of my ambition," a seat on the New York supreme court. Kent was perhaps rash when he asserted that before he came to the bench "there was no law, and nobody knew what it was," Kent was responsible for two significant innovations: written opinions and published reports. While these practices would have occurred eventually, Kent was instrumental in getting his friend William Johnson appointed reporter in 1806, after three mediocre volumes by another reporter. Johnson's *Reports*, produced in close collaboration with Kent, became a model for such publications throughout the country. New York supreme court justices also performed executive or legislative duties, since they, along with the state's chancellor and governor, formed the Council of Revision, which held the veto power over all legislative bills, passing not only in respect to their constitutionality, but also in respect to whether they were "in the public good." This practice not only made the judiciary political policy makers, but caused them to be less inclined to exercise judicial review, since they had already considered a law's constitutionality. The individual justices also rode circuit trying cases throughout the state. Legal questions of any difficulty were postponed until the judges sat together in one place and, more important for Kent, had access to their books. The supreme court was not the state's highest court; its decisions, along with those of the chancellor, were subject to review by the Court for the Trial of Impeachments and the Correction of Errors (the official title for the court of errors), composed of the chancellor, supreme court justices, and the entire senate.

Kent served as associate or puisne justice on the state supreme court until 1804, when he became chief justice. While promotion to chief justice followed the policy of seniority practiced at the time, there is little doubt that Kent was the most committed of his colleagues to their profession. The one rival for applying learning to cases was Brockholst Livingston, who joined the court in 1802, but after Livingston was appointed to the U.S. Supreme Court in 1806, unanimity prevailed, often in the form of unsigned *per curium* opinions, which Kent maintained, probably correctly, were actually his. Kent claimed that this apparent domination was necessary because all his brethren were "democrats." This was not true, since a number of them were Federalists, and even those justices of the opposite party shared Kent's conservative social and economic views. The court's jurisprudence generally sought a system of social control with society's members performing their assigned functions, with Kent providing learned citations from English and European sources. The state was also in the vanguard of a "market revolution," which took off after the War of 1812, and then Kent was faced with adjusting the state's jurisprudence to rapidly changing social and economic conditions. His differences with Livingston had for the most part occurred because Kent was less inclined to break with precedents than Livingston was. Those differences that surfaced between Kent and his associates involved major issues like the War of 1812, which Kent vehemently opposed. These splits, moreover, often emerged on the Council of Revision rather than in the court system and cast Kent in the mistaken role of civil libertarian, as indicated in his unsuccessful opposition to "An Act to Aid in the Apprehension of Deserters" because it essentially violated the fundamental right that "no citizen of this State shall be taken or imprisoned but by due process of law." As the War of 1812 made Kent appear to be a protector of liberty, so too did the party battles of the era. In *People v. Croswell* (1803), the case of a Federalist printer accused of criminal libel, Kent accepted Hamilton's argument—an advanced position at the time—that truth could be used in defense and was to be determined by a jury. Since the supreme court was evenly divided, the rule did not become law until enacted by the legislature in 1805. It was finally inserted in the constitution of 1821. Perhaps more typical was Kent's opinion in the case of the blasphemer Ruggles. In affirming Ruggles's conviction, Kent held that, while no written law had been violated, the defendant's actions were covered by the common law, of which Christianity was part: "We stand . . . in need, of all that moral discipline, and of those principles of virtue, which help to bind society together" (*People v. Ruggles*, 8 *Johnson's Reports* 225, [1811], 227). Kent's views on freedom of religion and expression are summed up in his remarks at the 1821 constitutional convention that he "was in favour of rational freedom, not of licentiousness," and he acted accordingly.

Of the myriad questions to come before Kent, perhaps none surpassed the steamboat monopoly in importance. In exchange for developing an operating steamboat, the legislature had granted Robert Livingston and Robert Fulton a thirty-year monopoly for operating on New York waters. Competitors' suits quickly followed Livingston and Fulton's success, and in 1812, the court of errors was faced with the monopoly's appeal of Chancellor John Lansing's decree refusing to grant it an injunction as provided under the legislative grant. Of the several opinions, in *Livingston v. Van Ingen* (9 *Johnson's Reports* 507), Kent's is the most interesting, not only because of his reputation, but because it would frame the debate that would be continued by the Supreme Court under Chief Justice John Marshall in the 1824 case of *Gibbons v. Ogden*, after Kent had essentially iterated it in 1820 (*Ogden v. Gibbons*, 17 *Johnson's Reports* 488). Among the challenges to the monopoly grant was that it violated the clause of the U.S. Constitution that granted the federal government authority over interstate commerce. Kent's responded that the power to regulate commerce was concurrent—that until Congress enacted legislation that directly conflicted with a state law, the state law was valid. Undergirding Kent's legal reasoning, however, was his unfeigned enthusiasm for the steamboat's success: "Every lover of the arts, every patron of useful improvement, every friend to his country's honour, has beheld this success with pleasure and admiration." While the New York decisions were overturned by the Marshall Court's *Gibbons* decision, it was based on statutory interpretation—Marshall found that a congressional coasting act did indeed conflict with the monopoly grant. Kent's concurrent doctrine thus survived and became the basis for a commerce clause settlement by the Supreme Court in 1852. Instrumental in keeping Kent's concurrent doctrine afloat on the Supreme Court was Justice Smith Thompson, who had served as both Kent's law clerk and colleague on the New York supreme court. Similarly, Thompson was responsible for nurturing the doctrine of Native American sovereignty, which Kent had first enunciated in 1823 (*Goodell v. Jackson*, 20 *Johnson's Reports* 693) in ruling that, regardless of the military defeats they had suffered, the Oneida retained their sovereignty.

It was, however, Kent's elevation to chancellor in 1814 that was the apex of his judicial career, and he was always known as "the chancellor." In administering justice from the singular equity court, he was unencumbered by the need to work with the other court members, although perhaps his independence heightened the vexation of being reversed by the Court of Errors. Unlike other jurisdictions, Kent's rulings and opinions were published separately (edited of course by William Johnson), and since equity law was largely the product of England, its application coincided with Kent's objective of making English law applicable to the United States. In retirement, Kent noted that "I saw where justice lay, and the moral sense decided the court half the time; and I then sat down to search the authorities. . . . I always found principles suited to my views of the case." Kent reached the mandatory retirement age of sixty in 1823, the Constitutional Convention of 1821 not having fulfilled his unrealistic hope of extending his judicial career. Kent was a member of the convention, and his participation is best remembered for his opposition to change and prophecies of doom if universal suffrage were enacted. "We are destined to become a great manufacturing as well as commercial state, . . . and one master capitalist with his one hundred apprentices, and journeymen, and agents, and dependents, will bear down at the polls, an equal number of farmers, . . . who cannot safely unite for their common defense," contended Kent, and he later considered Andrew Jackson's reelection (in which he was a badly beaten presidential elector candidate) as vindication of his position. While Kent with his articulate conservatism did indeed project the image at the convention of defending the past, he was more often in the majority than in the minority.

And as much as Kent's friends might bewail the convention's unwillingness to keep him on the bench (there was no motion to that effect), his "enforced retirement," of close to a quarter century, may well have been the most productive part of his life. He was of course in demand as a consultant, for example, to the Cherokee Nation and New York City, but his major activity was preparing the *Commentaries on American Law*. This activity apparently began with his return to Columbia in January 1824, and the lectures for 1824–1825 composed the first two-volume edition. A subsequent edition was expanded to four volumes, and ultimately the work would go through fourteen editions in the nineteenth century, with all changes (both by Kent and his successors) occurring in the notes. In addition, countless abridgments, selected segments, and foreign editions appeared, demonstrating not only the *Commentaries*' pervasive influence, but also their universality. In short, Kent had succeeded in combining the practical and the theoretical in approaching the law in the manner he had long prescribed, and he had indeed demonstrated that it was the area for "Gentlemen of active Geniusses to attain a decisive Superiority in Government." The *Commentaries* continued his efforts as a judge to transplant the English common law to America, and its reliance on precedents had the two-prong effect of helping to maintain the primacy of judge-made law in contrast to codification by legislatures, while providing the legal profession with the degree and kind of certainty it craved. That a young Georgia lawyer a generation after Kent's death studied the *Commentaries* into the morning hours suggests their influence, as does the fact that young Tom Watson, in his agrarian radicalism, stood for everything that Kent had opposed. More than incidental was the handsome income that Kent derived from the *Commentaries*, helping to make his retirement most comfortable. Kent developed a physical regimen in his old age that complemented his mental activity, and he enjoyed remarkably good health until the last two months of his life. He died in New York City.

• While the majority of Kent's papers are at the Library of Congress, and are readily available on seven reels of microfilm, including one of travel narratives, there are other significant holdings. The Rare Book and Manuscript Library of Butler Library at Columbia University holds, in addition to manuscripts, a significant part of Kent's surviving library, of interest because of his habit of writing marginalia. The legal surviving parts of his library, complete with marginalia, are at the Law Library at Columbia University and at the New York State Library at Albany. John T. Horton, *James Kent: A Study in Conservatism, 1763–1847* (1939), is a worthwhile biography, but there is need for a new one. A splendid supplement is John H. Langbein, "Chancellor Kent and the History of Legal Literature," *Columbia Law Review* 93 (Apr. 1993): 547–94; the bibliography in Langbein's notes is quite complete. In addition, Kent's great-grandson, William, edited *Memoirs and Letters of James Kent* (1898). An obituary is in the *New York Daily Tribune*, 13 and 14 Dec. 1847.

DONALD M. ROPER

KENT, James Tyler (31 Mar. 1849–5 June 1916), homeopathic physician and educator, was born in Woodhull, New York, the son of Stephen Kent, a town clerk, and Carolyn Tyler. Evidence suggests that he was actually the illegitimate son of his brother Henry and sister Jane, since they were listed as "mother" and "father" on his death certificate. Kent earned a Ph.B. (1868) and A.M. (1870) at Madison College (now Colgate University) in Hamilton, New York. He studied medicine with a Dr. Brown in Woodhull and completed his medical degree in 1871 at the Eclectic Medical Institute in Cincinnati Ohio, one of the many "nontraditional" medical schools that flourished during the late 1880s. In 1874 Kent moved to St. Louis, Missouri, where he began a medical practice and taught as professor of anatomy in the American Medical College (Eclectic) in 1877–1878.

In 1878 Kent's wife fell ill, and, unable to help her, he called a local homeopathic physician, Richard Phelan, who cured her. Under Phelan's guidance, Kent began to study homeopathy—a system of medicine, codified in the early nineteenth century by Samuel Hahnemann in Germany, that uses minute doses of medicines (usually highly diluted) to cure illnesses whose symptoms are similar to the symptoms one would exhibit when ingesting larger quantities of the prescribed medicine. Often referred to by the Latin

phrase *similia similibus curentur* (let likes be cured by likes), this system stands in contrast to the conventional (or allopathic) method, which treats diseases with "contrary" substances (in a case of fever, for instance, a practitioner of allopathy would give a drug that will act on a physiologic level to reduce the fever, while a practitioner of homeopathy would give a drug that could, in a healthy person, cause a fever, in the belief that if the body is pushed in the direction it is already going, its internal mechanisms will reestablish homeostasis).

In 1881 Kent accepted a position as professor of anatomy at the Homeopathic Medical College of St. Louis. He became professor of materia medica in 1883. His mastery of homeopathy was quickly recognized by his peers. By 1884 homeopathic society transactions often carried the question, "Well, what would Dr. Kent say about this?"

In 1887 Kent was elected president of the International Hahnemannian Association. In 1888 he accepted an invitation from the Women's Homeopathic Hospital in Philadelphia to take over the practice of the recently deceased Adolph Lippe, one of the first homeopaths in Philadelphia, the founder of the International Hahnemannian Association in 1880, and a professor at the Homeopathic Medical College of Pennsylvania (now Hahnemann University).

In 1890 Kent founded the Post Graduate School of Homeotherapeutics in Philadelphia. Primarily funded by John Pitcairn, a homeopathic supporter and the founder of Pittsburgh Plate Glass, the school both offered homeopathic training and the services of a free clinic. By the time it ceased operation in 1900, the school had seen more than 40,000 patients and had trained twenty-five physicians, all of whom became leaders in the homeopathic movement through the first half of the twentieth century.

At the same time, Kent and his pupils were busy compiling what was to be his major work, the *Repertory of Homeopathic Materia Medica* (1897). This 1,380-page cross-referenced index of all the symptoms known to be caused by medicinal substances served as an index of the substances' possible uses based on the principle of "similia" (likes curing likes).

In 1900 Kent accepted an offer to relocate the postgraduate school to Chicago, where the school would be run under the auspices of the Dunham Homeopathic College. He became dean of the Dunham College, held a chair as professor of materia medica at the Hahnemann Medical College of Chicago, and taught at the Hering College in Chicago. He maintained a busy private practice and continued to edit his *Repertory*. He worked closely with Ehrhart and Karl, a homeopathic pharmacy, to design and build a machine to make high dilution homeopathic medicines. These "Kent Potencies" continued to be produced into the 1940s.

Kent served as editor for the *Medical Courier* in 1881–1882; *Journal of Homeopathics* from 1897 to 1899; and *The Homeopathician* from 1912 to 1916. At a time when homeopathic teaching was drifting closer to conventional medicine by suggesting that the medicines be used as "specifics" (i.e. *this* remedy for *that* disease) and that the medicines may be given in combination, these journals all espoused the traditional teachings of Hahnemann: the practice of selecting the remedy for the individual patient based on the symptoms presented and the giving of the single remedy.

Kent was a very private man and little is known about his personal life. His first wife, Ellen (maiden name unknown), died in 1872. He apparently met his second wife, Lucia "Lucy" H. (maiden name unknown), in St. Louis; she came with him to Philadelphia, where she died in 1895. The following year he married a physician, Clara Louise Toby, who helped him with the editing of his major work. He had no children.

Through his association with John Pitcairn, Kent became interested in the teaching of the Christian mystic Emanuel Swedenborg, and his major writings reflect the teachings of Swedenborg as they might be applied to homeopathy.

Kent's teaching was so effective that his students published two transcriptions of the lectures he had delivered in Philadelphia: *Lectures on Homeopathic Philosophy* (1900) and *Lectures on Materia Medica* (1905). They later published a collection of his essays, *Lesser Writings, Aphorisms, and Precepts* (1926), that had appeared in various homeopathic journals throughout his life. All of Kent's works are still in print and are considered by most practicing homeopaths to be among the best instruction in homeopathy that can be obtained.

In 1910 the Carnegie Foundation asked educator Abraham Flexner to evaluate all medical education in the United States. The *Flexner Report* (1910) recommended that medical schools employ a full-time faculty, set higher prerequisite education standards, keep their libraries up-to-date, and set minimum standards for pathology laboratories. The suggestions of the *Flexner Report* were adopted by the state medical boards and resulted in the closing of more than half the medical schools in the country at the time, including most of the small schools that admitted racial minorities and women. It also resulted in the closing of most of the homeopathic schools. Kent, reflecting on his struggle to keep homeopathy pure to the principles espoused by Hahnemann, and on his struggle against the mounting attacks on homeopathy by the conventional medical establishment, wrote to Margaret Tyler, a friend and fellow physician, "While I am only sixty-one years old, I am worn out. . . . I have been lecturing to classes on homeopathy and materia medica since 1883, and it has been a bitter fight continuously. Though I have enjoyed it, it has worn me out. For fifteen years I gained little but sneers; then, now and then, a pupil would try and do it. But not until I had put out the 'Repertory' twelve or thirteen years ago could I feel that I had made any impression." In the spring of 1916 he went to his vacation home in Stevensville, Montana, where he died and is buried.

Kent is generally acknowledged as the finest homeopathic thinker and physician at the turn of the century.

When the practice of homeopathy declined during the 1930s, Kent's pupils, who included the best homeopaths in India and Sir John Weir, physician to the English royal family, continued to instruct the next few generations of homeopathic physicians worldwide. The lessons Kent taught are still referenced as the most concise thinking on the subject. His *Repertory* is in constant use. It has recently been revised by two international teams of homeopaths and, in the late 1980s, was developed as a computer database by several companies.

• Little information is available on the life of Kent. The minutes of the Postgraduate School of Homeotherapeutics are in the Hahnemann University Archives in Philadelphia. The *Bradford Scrapbooks* (in the Hahnemann Archives) contain several letters from Kent and three short biographies. Several private homeopathic collections contain letters from Kent. A brief biography of him, written by Pierre Schmidt, appears in the introduction of the 1995 edition of Kent's *Repertory*. The "Memorial Edition" of *Lectures on Homeopathic Philosophy* (1920) contains many reminiscences of Kent by his pupils. Assorted details about his life and practice can be found in issues of the *Homeopathic Recorder* and the *Journal of Homeopathics*. Hela Michot-Dietrich published an article, "In Search of James Tyler Kent's Ancestors," in the *Zeitschrift für Klassische Homöopathie* (1985) and *Homeopathy Today* (1986), about Kent's lineage; and Klaus-Henning Gypser published several articles in the *Zeitschrift für Klassische Homöopathie* (1985).

JULIAN WINSTON

KENT, Joseph (14 Jan. 1779–24 Nov. 1837), physician and politician, was born in Calvert County, Maryland, the son of Daniel Kent and Anne Wheeler, farmers. Educated in Philadelphia, he returned to practice medicine in Lower Marlboro, Calvert County, in partnership with a Dr. Parran from 1799 to 1801, when he began practicing on his own. He married Eleanor Lee Wallace in 1804 and two years later moved to "Rosemount," a plantation near Bladensburg in Prince Georges County, where he farmed and continued to practice medicine. In the crisis that followed the attack of the British naval vessel *Leopard* upon the USS *Chesapeake* in the Chesapeake Bay in the summer of 1807, Kent joined the Thirty-fourth Regiment of the Maryland militia as a surgeon's mate and shortly became its regimental surgeon. Two years later he resigned to join the Second Maryland Militia Cavalry, was promoted to major, and quickly rose to become colonel of the unit.

In 1810 Kent was elected as a Federalist to his first public office, U.S. representative to the Twelfth Congress from Maryland's Second District. He was reelected in 1812. He served in the Maryland Senate in 1815 and as a Republican presidential elector for James Monroe in 1816. He was in 1818 returned to his seat in Congress, where he served until his resignation on 6 January 1826 to become governor of Maryland. During this first phase of his political career, Kent reflected the prewar nationalist sentiments of many southern Federalists, and when New England Federalists opposed the war, he, like many other southern Federalists, moved into the Republican party.

Kent's career also bespoke the link between local or state and national politics; domestic concerns about the reduced prices and demand for Maryland's commodities, such as tobacco and grain, in post-Napoleonic Europe; and the first effects of the new economic order that touted transportation and manufacturing improvements as effective ways to reduce costs and dependency on foreign markets. His National Republicanism under Monroe and John Quincy Adams was framed by Maryland's central position along the Atlantic seaboard and especially its border with what many in his generation regarded as a gateway to the western lands of the Ohio River valley, the Potomac River. He supported the construction of canals and turnpikes, which promised to increase the flow of agricultural commodities to markets. He additionally favored compromise during the Missouri debates to minimize state obstacles to the interstate common market promised by the federal Constitution of 1789. He opposed the efforts to raise tariff rates in 1820 and again in 1824, because they offered protection to manufacturers at the expense of his more numerous agricultural constituents.

The same impulses prevailed during Kent's terms as governor from 1826 to 1829, and he became enormously popular. He was reelected nearly unanimously in 1827 and again in 1828. His campaigns aligned Baltimore and the northern interests of the Western Shore involved in the Baltimore & Ohio Railroad with Annapolis and the Western Shore's southern interests in the Chesapeake & Ohio Canal, of which he himself was a director. Kent also favored prison reform, more aid to education, and the adoption of popular voting for the president through division of the state into geographic presidential districts. Aware that the Founding Fathers were passing away, he advocated preservation of state records generated during the revolutionary conflict. His first wife died in 1826, and in 1828 he married Alice Contee. He had a total of eleven children, ten of whom were born to his first wife.

In federal politics, Kent's selective support of the National Republicanism of John Quincy Adams and the American System of Henry Clay during the 1820s was channeled into Whiggery during the 1830s. In 1831 he served as vice president of the National Republican Convention in Baltimore that nominated Clay for the presidency. The following year Maryland's legislature elected Kent to the U.S. Senate, though an unknown illness prevented him from taking his seat until 2 December 1833. He supported Clay's Whig positions, including censuring President Andrew Jackson's removal of federal monies from the Second Bank of the United States and opposing the president's hostile attitude toward France. Kent specifically called for the president to negotiate with France to lower its taxes and reduce its restrictions on tobacco imports. He continued to press for aid to Maryland's two main internal improvement projects,

the Baltimore & Ohio Railroad and the Chesapeake & Ohio Canal, and perhaps surprising for a man who owned sixty-five slaves at his death, he opposed proposals to censor the mail because of the increasing numbers of abolitionist tracts sent south. He served in the U.S. Senate until a fall from his horse caused his death at "Rosemount." Clay delivered a eulogy at Kent's funeral.

• No corpus of Kent's papers exists but a small collection of his letters, seventeen items that date from 1821 to 1826, is in the Worthington papers, ms. 1466, at the Maryland Historical Society. Two sources that discuss Kent's life are Frank F. White, Jr., *The Governors of Maryland, 1777–1970* (1970); and Gerson G. Eisenberg, *Marylanders Who Served the Nation: A Biographical Dictionary of Federal Officials from Maryland* (1992). An obituary is in *Niles' Weekly Register*, 2 Dec. 1837.

GARY L. BROWNE

KENT, Robert Harrington (1 July 1886–3 Feb. 1961), ballistician, was born in Meriden, Connecticut, the son of Silas William Kent and Mary Elizabeth Chapman. He initially attended Columbia, intending to follow his family's intentions that he become a minister; but, after overcoming their objections, he transferred to Harvard to study physics and mathematics. There he was much influenced by the mathematical physicist Benjamin O. Peirce. He received his A.B. in 1910 and leisurely pursued his graduate studies during which he taught as an assistant in physics (1910–1916) and an instructor in mathematics (1914). He passed his doctoral examinations, but the Harvard physics department refused his proposal to write a theoretical dissertation on the determination of the laws of intermolecular repulsion from experimentally determined virial coefficients in the van de Waal's equation. This research was subsequently done by the noted British physicist John Edward Lennard-Jones (1924), who curiously was later to become—in a sense—Kent's opposite number in the British ballistics program during World War II. Kent then left Harvard and from 1916 to 1917 was an instructor in electrical engineering at the University of Pennsylvania.

Upon America's entry in World War I, Kent volunteered and became a first lieutenant in the Ordnance Department of the U.S. Army. He served in the Office of the Chief of Ordnance in Washington, D.C., together with Lieutenant James W. Alexander and later with the chief ordnance officer of the American Expeditionary Force in France. In these capacities, he was engaged in computing firing tables for a variety of Allied artillery pieces used by the American army. Kent rose to the rank of captain, was discharged in July 1919, and then rejoined the Office of the Chief of Ordnance as a civilian employee. In 1922 he transferred to the Ballistics Office at the Aberdeen Proving Ground in Maryland. This was reorganized into the Ballistics Research Division, which contained a staff of some thirty people under the leadership of Colonel Hermann H. Zorning in 1935. The division consisted of six sections, which respectively dealt with exterior, interior, and terminal ballistics; ballistic computations and measurements; and ammunition surveillance. In 1938 it was renamed the Ballistics Research Laboratory (BRL), with Colonel Zorning as director and Kent and Dr. Louis S. Dederick as associate directors in charge of the scientific work. Kent held this position from 1936 to 1948, and from 1948 to 1956 he was the associate technical director of the BRL. Upon his retirement in 1956, he remained a consultant to the BRL until his death.

In a literal sense, Kent's life was the BRL, and its scientific program was his career. He actively participated in virtually all of its technical research programs and projects, which included the design and motion of projectiles, the bores of cannons, heat transfer problems, ignition of propellants, armor piercing, ballistic instrumentation, piezoelectric gauges for ballistic measurements, supersonic fuses, recoil mechanisms, and other topics. If Kent did not know the required mathematics, physics, or chemistry, he learned it and then patiently taught it to his colleagues. Because of the nature of these subjects and the fact that much of the research was a collaborative endeavor, relatively little of this research was ever published in the open scientific literature. However, Kent's work on special solutions of powder gas (1938), solutions of the telegrapher's equation (1939), joint work with Alfred H. Hodge on piezoelectric gauges (1939), and a statistical paper with John von Neumann (1941) were formally published. He also contributed three chapters on the probability of hitting, exterior ballistics, and bombing from airplanes (the latter two written jointly with Dederick and Zorning, respectively), to the textbook *Elements of Ordnance* (1938), written by Lieutenant Colonel Thomas J. Hayes. Also, his BRL report on the applications of Siacci's methods to flat trajectories (1938), written with Henry P. Hitchcock, is frequently quoted in monographs on exterior ballistics.

However, Kent did not merely bring his scientific expertise to BRL projects, he also brought himself to their investigations. His leadership, warm friendship, and understanding of people were a unique asset to the BRL. He was a master of the art of gathering, and keeping, together groups of competent people, infusing them with the scientific method, and causing them to produce new and original work. This was also important in his handling of the various academics who willingly, or otherwise, found themselves attached to the BRL during wartime. In 1940 he was responsible for the formation of a BRL Scientific Advisory Committee that was intended to bring in eminent scientists to give advice on scientific and technical matters and aid in recruiting new personnel. The original committee consisted of Harold Urey, Isidor I. Rabi, Hugh Dryden, Bernard Lewis, Albert W. Hull, Henry N. Russell, Theodore von Kármán, and John von Neumann. Its membership was a testimony to Kent's gentle powers of persuasion, and gift of friendship, as many of its members served because their colleague and friend "Bob" asked them to serve. This committee acted as a bridge between the academic and military

worlds, and (with various changes in its membership) it remained an important adjunct to the BRL until 1977. Kent himself was also in no less demand: he was a member of the U.S. Air Force Scientific Advisory Board from 1946 to 1956, serving on its Guided Missile Panel (1946) and the Guidance and Control Panel 1947–1956 (as its chairman 1948–1954), and was a member of the Executive Committee 1948–1954. Altogether, Kent's service as the country's foremost expert in ballistics over a span of forty years was unique, and he was well deserving of his reputation of being America's only "complete ballistician."

Kent received a number of honors during his lifetime. He was awarded the Presidential Medal for Merit (1946), the Potts Medal of the Franklin Institute (1947), the Campbell Medal of the (Army) Ordnance Association (1955), as well as both the U.S. Army and Air Force Exceptional Service Medals. He was elected a member of the National Academy of Science (1951) and a fellow of the American Physical Society. The latter recognitions were quite unusual and based on his exceptional service to the nation in the field of ballistics rather than a traditional body of published scientific research.

Kent never married and died in his home at Havre de Grace, Maryland. On 24 September 1974 a new exterior ballistics laboratory at the BRL was officially named the R. H. Kent Building. His legacy lives on in the scientific expertise and professionalism that he brought to his work at the BRL.

• A collection of more than two hundred of Kent's BRL reports is held in the archives of the National Academy of Sciences, and his work is prominently featured in the first volume of the BRL official history, *Ballisticians in War and Peace: A History of the United States Army Ballistics Research Laboratories, 1914–1956* (1956). The second volume of this history, dealing with the period 1957–1976, was dedicated to Kent's memory. As noted previously, Kent wrote little that was published in the open literature; however, three of his expository papers (which were obviously intended to interest scientists in military problems) deserve special notice: "The Flight of the Projectile," *Journal of the Franklin Institute* 226 (July 1938): 19–33; "Some Hydrodynamical Problems Related to Ballistics," *American Mathematical Monthly* 48 (Jan. 1941): 8–14; and "Explosives and Their Military Applications," *Journal of Applied Physics* 13 (July 1942): 348–54. These not only shed light on the scientific problems considered by the BRL, but also reveal Kent's felicitous style and taste. For a brief biographical synopsis, see Leslie E. Simon et al., National Academy of Sciences, 42 (1971): 94–117. An obituary notice is in the *New York Times*, 4 Feb. 1961.

JOSEPH D. ZUND

KENT, Rockwell (21 June 1882–13 Mar. 1971), artist, was born in Tarrytown Heights, New York, the son of Rockwell Kent, an attorney and mining engineer, and Sara Ann Holgate. Kent spent his infancy and early childhood in privileged circumstances, at family homes in Tarrytown, New York City, and on Long Island. When he was five his father died, and henceforth family resources were limited. Kent was not told of his father's death and had to infer the news himself; when his suspicions were confirmed he reacted angrily and began misbehaving. To improve his behavior, his mother sent him to a military boarding school when he was ten, with the help of scholarships and financial assistance from an aunt who noticed his nascent artistic talent.

In the summer of 1895 Kent accompanied his mother to Dresden, Germany, where she studied ceramics. She returned to New York that fall and started a china-making business to support the family. Kent helped paint his mother's wares, and the activity seemed to have a settling effect on his behavior. He also enrolled at the Horace Mann School in New York City and graduated in 1900. That fall he entered Columbia University on a scholarship to study architecture, but during his two years there he was not an especially good student. He preferred campus activities—fraternity membership, the college drama club, the staff of the humor magazine—and also enjoyed off-campus art lessons at the New York School of Art with realist painters William Merritt Chase and Robert Henri. In 1902 he dropped out of Columbia to study full time at the School of Art.

Kent's increasingly unconventional lifestyle, which embraced both vegetarianism and leftist politics, put him at odds with his family. In 1905, determined to become a painter, he abruptly moved to Maine. There, with skills he had learned as an architecture student, he built his own house and supported himself by doing various odd jobs while he painted seascapes. He reconciled with his family in 1907 when he returned to Tarrytown to hold his first show, an exhibition of fourteen paintings.

For the next several years, Kent lived in Maine, New York City, and on Caritas Island, Connecticut. In Connecticut he made friends with several prominent American socialists, including Mother Jones and W. E. B. Du Bois. He married his first wife, Kathleen Whiting, a niece of the painter Abbott Thayer, in 1909; the couple had five children. During this marriage Kent also had an extended relationship with a woman publicly identified only as "Janet," by whom he also had a child. Supporting this second family depleted his resources, much of which came from his wife, and the marriage finally ended in divorce in 1926.

Long before the divorce, however, Kent had begun spending extended periods away from home to paint rugged coastal sites, first in Newfoundland and later in Alaska and Tierra del Fuego. He supported his trips by holding exhibitions periodically back in the United States and also by publishing accounts of his adventures. His first book, *Wilderness: A Journal of Quiet Adventure in Alaska*, was published in 1920. This was followed by *Voyaging: Southward from the Strait of Magellan* (1924) and *Salamina* (1935), an account of two voyages he made to Greenland in 1931 and 1934. Kent also earned money for his painting expeditions by selling shares in his personal corporation, Rockwell Kent, Inc., which he established in 1916.

Shortly after his divorce in 1926, Kent married his second wife, Frances Lee, a young divorcée with a son. The following year they settled on a farm in the Adirondacks near the village of Au Sable Forks, New York. Kent rebuilt the house and barn, named the property Asgaard Farm, and established a dairy business there; it remained his home for the rest of his life. This marriage did not last either, however, and in 1940, following a second divorce, Kent married Sally Johnstone, an Englishwoman who was his secretary. That year he also published his first autobiography, *This Is My Own* (1940).

Kent enjoyed a reputation as a noted painter during the period between the two world wars, turning out not only seascapes but also figure drawings, paintings, etchings, and lithographs. His works were bought by private collectors and major American institutions, including the Metropolitan Museum of Art and the Frick Collection in New York City. His popularity, especially during the 1930s, was probably aided by his socialist sympathies. Kent's openly expressed admiration for Communism and the Soviet Union was reflected in some of his etchings and lithographs, which included idealized depictions of industrial workers in a manner reminiscent of the socialist realism then flourishing in the Soviet Union; some of this artwork was done without charge to illustrate leftist publications.

However, art with a political message was only one part of Kent's large output. Apparently seeing no contradiction of his personal convictions, he also turned out advertising illustrations for luxury products, including Rolls-Royces. Among Kent's best-known work was a series of woodcuts and lithographs illustrating new editions of Shakespeare plays and other literary classics, such as *Moby Dick*, which he created in the decade prior to World War II. Under the pseudonym Hogarth, Jr., he also contributed satirical and humorous drawings to the magazine *Vanity Fair*.

Kent was active in several left-wing organizations, including the American Artists' Congress, the League of American Writers, the Soviet-American Friendship Society, and the International Workers Order. His political activities often gained him national attention, as they did in 1937 when he added a message supporting Puerto Rican independence to a post office mural he painted in Washington, D.C., and four years later, when he championed the rights of Earl Browder, a prominent U.S. Communist.

Kent was again in the news in 1949, when the House Un-American Activities Committee named him as a leading U.S. subversive. Kent had never denied his affiliations or sympathies, but in the Cold War climate of the late 1940s an affinity for leftist politics was no longer appealing or even publicly acceptable. Denied a passport during the 1950s because he refused to sign an affidavit swearing that he was not a Communist party member, Kent took the case to the U.S. Supreme Court and eventually won (*Kent v. Dulles*, 1958).

Meanwhile, Kent's artistic career floundered. Artistic taste had passed him by: realism was out of favor, having been supplanted by abstract expressionism, and his work was no longer in demand. His politics also made American museums wary of acquiring his work, although the Soviet government bought a number of his paintings for the Hermitage and Pushkin museums. Kent, however, continued to paint and in 1960 he began distributing his artwork to friends.

Kent, who had published a second autobiography, *It's Me, O Lord*, in 1955, continued to espouse his political views. He was an early supporter of the Communist cause in Vietnam, and in 1967, when he was awarded the Lenin Peace Prize by the Soviet Union, he donated more than a third of the $28,000 stipend to the National Liberation Front in South Vietnam for medical supplies. He died at his Farm in upstate New York.

A controversial figure during his lifetime, Kent is remembered for his paintings and graphics rather than for his politics. His stark, vigorous landscapes, painted in a style sometimes characterized as "romantic realist," are considered important contributions to American painting in the early twentieth century.

• The major portion of Kent's papers is in the Archives of American Art at the Smithsonian Institution; the Butler Library of Columbia University includes a smaller collection. In addition to Kent's autobiographies, see David Traxel, *An American Saga: The Life and Times of Rockwell Kent* (1980). See also Fridolf Johnson, *Rockwell Kent: An Anthology of His Works* (1982), and Richard V. West, *"An Enkindled Eye": The Paintings of Rockwell Kent* (1985). An obituary is in the *New York Times*, 14 Mar. 1971.

ANN T. KEENE

KENTON, Simon (3 Apr. 1755–29 Apr. 1836), frontiersman, was born near Hopewell village in Fauquier County, Virginia, the son of Mark Kenton, an emigrant from Ireland, and Mary Miller, of Scotch-Welsh descent. His parents were farmers. Kenton was unschooled and never learned to read or write. As a youngster he avoided as much farm work as he could.

At age fifteen Kenton fell in love with Ellen Cummins, who, however, decided to marry a young farmer, William Leachman. In April 1771 Kenton, bared to the waist, greeted the newlyweds as they exited the church and challenged Leachman to a fight. Kenton was thoroughly thrashed. Several months later Kenton again provoked a fight with Leachman; managing to tie Leachman's long hair to a sapling, Kenton had the advantage and knocked his opponent unconscious. Believing he had killed Leachman and would be punished accordingly, Kenton fled to the western frontier of Virginia, along the Ohio River valley. Living off roots and greens in the forest, he became a master of survival techniques. Kenton changed his last name to Butler to avoid detection. Eventually he earned enough money from assisting pioneer farmers to purchase a gun and powder, and he made his way to Pittsburgh. During the winter of 1771–1772 and 1773 Kenton and several companions hunted along the Cheat, Ohio, and the Great and Little Kanawha rivers. They were attacked by Indians along the Ohio and barely made their escape.

Kenton's first military experience was as a scout for Colonel Angus McDonald's unsuccessful campaign of June 1774 against Indians in the Muskingum Valley of Ohio. He served in the same capacity for Governor John Murray, earl of Dunmore's militia army of Virginia in its Indian expedition down the Ohio River in the fall of 1774. Kenton carried dispatches between Dunmore and Colonel Andrew Lewis, who commanded a wing of the army. Kenton was not present at the battle of Point Pleasant, 10 October 1774.

In spring 1775 Kenton explored north central Kentucky and made his campsite at Limestone (now Maysville), Kentucky, on the Ohio River, where he built a cabin and planted corn. He became a greeter and guide for newcomers and surveyors entering the Kentucky bluegrass country. He spent much of his time at Boonesborough and Logan's Fort. An event of 24 April 1777 brought fame to Kenton as a preeminent Indian fighter as well as a frontiersman. One hundred Shawnees led by Blackfish surprised the settlers at Boonesborough. Daniel Boone and a small party, outside the fort at the time, were set upon by warriors. Kenton rushed out of the gate and shot an Indian about to tomahawk Boone, whose leg had been broken by a gunshot. Hoisting Boone on his shoulders, he darted through a number of Indians to the safety of the fort. Variations of the story include Kenton himself tomahawking an Indian, knocking another down with the barrel of his rifle, and throwing Boone's body against two of the Indians.

From May to July 1778 Kenton served as a captain on George Rogers Clark's western expedition. From Kaskaskia, on the Mississippi River, Kenton went as a spy to the British post at Vincennes on the Wabash River. Kenton's report on the inadequate defenses of this post was sent to Kaskaskia by another scout, while Kenton returned to Kentucky, bearing news of Clark's capture of Kaskaskia.

Two months later Kenton accompanied Boone and a raiding party across the Ohio River. On 13 September 1778, while Kenton was attempting to get recovered horses across the river, he was captured by Shawnees. Kenton's capture was the beginning of an ordeal of many months—one of the most renowned episodes of American frontier history. Because the Indians had a score to settle with Kenton, he was sentenced to be burned at the stake, not as a local event but as an intertribal ceremony to be held at Sandusky. Kenton gained a short reprieve by being adopted by a squaw but was subsequently variously tortured, including being forced to run the gauntlet nine times. He was twice saved from burning, first by the intervention of the renegade Simon Girty and then by both Chief Logan of the Mingo Indians and Pierre Druillard, an Indian trader and interpreter for the British. Eventually Kenton was turned over to the British garrison at Detroit. Escaping in June 1779, Kenton made his way to join Clark's troops at Vincennes.

Kenton is credited with many exploits, not the least of which being the sinking of a boat carrying a British cannon in the Ohio River as an Indian raiding force led by British captain Henry Bird was returning from a devastating incursion into Kentucky in the summer of 1780. Kenton served as a scout in the expeditions against Shawnee towns led by Clark in 1780 (he fought at the battle of Piqua, 8 Aug.) and in November 1782 and by Benjamin Logan in 1786.

About 1780 Kenton, learning that his boyhood victim Leachman had lived, resumed using the name Kenton instead of Butler. Returning to Virginia in late 1783, Kenton brought his family to settle at Kenton's Station, near Limestone. His father died on the trip. From 1786 to 1794, with the rank of major, Kenton had charge of 100 Kentucky spies and scouts, known as "Kenton's boys." In this capacity Kenton served with Kentucky militia assigned to General Anthony Wayne's army during 1793–1794. Kenton, however, was not present at the battle of Fallen Timbers on 20 August 1794.

Kenton married Martha "Patsey" Dowden in 1787. A fire at the Kenton house near Limestone in 1796 left his wife badly burned and caused her to have a miscarriage; she died a few days afterward. Kenton married Elizabeth Jarboe, a cousin of his first wife, in 1798. In all, Kenton had twelve children: four with his first wife, seven with his second, and an illegitimate son with Ruth Calvin. At the end of 1798 the Kenton family moved across the Ohio River to a 1000-acre farm four miles north of Springfield, Ohio.

Always searching for new lands to claim, Kenton, on his own hook, in 1802 signed a treaty with the "Wabash" Indians for lands between the Miami and Wabash rivers—an action that had no legal standing. Kenton declined an appointment as brigadier general of the Ohio militia in 1804 because he and his son were about to leave for Missouri to visit Boone and to attend to land and business affairs there. In all, Kenton made four trips to Missouri. In 1810 Kenton joined the Methodist church, and the family moved to near Urbana, Ohio. During the War of 1812 Kenton joined Isaac Shelby's Kentucky troops; he was present but had no major role at the battle of the Thames, 5 October 1813.

Kenton invested in several frontier stores. His land speculation was enormous. Because of his illiteracy he had to rely on other persons for his record keeping. Kenton at one time claimed some 400,000 acres in Kentucky, Ohio, Indiana, and Missouri. When he moved to Ohio he assigned in trust 145,000 acres in Kentucky to his son John. Because of unpaid taxes and court losses over disputed claims, Kenton forfeited most of his lands and in later life existed on the verge of poverty. He was imprisoned for debt in Urbana in 1810 for about a year and again, briefly, in 1812. Tricked into testifying in a land case in Kentucky in 1820, he wound up in the Mason County jail for debt, being released only after Kentucky abolished all imprisonment for debt in December 1821.

In 1820 Kenton settled in Zanesfield, Ohio, and in 1827 the state of Ohio provided him with a $20 monthly pension. In 1832 Kenton gave his Zanesfield property to his newlywed son, William, and then resided in a cabin four miles north of the town, where he died. He was buried near Zanesfield but later was reinterred at Urbana. Kenton County, Kentucky, established 1840, is named for him. Kenton's life was a grand adventure. He seemed to be everywhere on the early trans-Appalachian frontier. As an Indian fighter and scout, he had no peer.

• The Kenton papers, in the Lyman C. Draper Collections at the State Historical Society of Wisconsin, contain materials that Draper gathered for a biography of Kenton, including biographical sketches, depositions, notes by Kenton's comrades, and a few original documents, such as those relating to land surveys. Allan W. Eckert, *The Frontiersmen* (1967), is a thoroughly researched, lively narrative of Kenton's life, if at times with some poetic license; it interweaves Kenton's activities with those of his associates. Also a sound, dramatic narrative of lesser scale is Patricia Jahns, *The Violent Years; Simon Kenton and the Ohio-Kentucky Frontier* (1962). An older straightforward biography is Edna Kenton, *Simon Kenton: His Life and Period, 1755–1836* (1930). For Kenton's relationship with Daniel Boone, see John M. Faragher, *Daniel Boone: The Life and Legend of an American Pioneer* (1992). Sketches of Kenton include Lewis Collins, revised by Richard H. Collins, *Collins' Historical Sketches of Kentucky: History of Kentucky*, vol. 2 (1966), pp. 442–54; R. W. McFarland, "Simon Kenton," *Ohio Archaeological and Historical Publications* 13 (1904): 1–39; and John McDonald, *Biographical Sketches* (1838), pp. 197–267. A brief tribute to Kenton is in the *Western Christian Advocate*, 24 June 1836.

HARRY M. WARD

KENTON, Stan (15 Dec. 1911–25 Aug. 1979), jazz musician, was born Stanley Newcomb Kenton in Wichita, Kansas, the son of Thomas Floyd Kenton, a salesman and entrepreneur, and Stella Emily Newcomb, a piano teacher. At age five, Kenton moved with his family to Los Angeles. As a child he studied piano with his mother and in later years with Frank Hurst, a theater organist, and Earl "Fatha" Hines. During his sophomore year in high school, Kenton formed his first musical group, the Bell Tones. "From the time I was fourteen years old, I was all music," he recalled. "Nothing else even entered my mind." He began writing his own music and, after graduating from high school, worked full time as a pianist with several musical groups. In 1935 Kenton married Viola Peters; they had one child, and the marriage ended in divorce.

In 1933 Kenton began his professional career as pianist and arranger for the Everett Hoagland band, playing at the Rendezvous Ballroom in Balboa Beach, California. In this period of his career he was influenced by Claude Thornhill's piano style and Benny Carter's arrangements. During the 1930s he also studied classical music with Charles Dalmores, played piano in the NBC house band and the dance bands of Vido Musso and Gus Arnheim, played and arranged for the Gil Evans band, arranged scores for Russ

Plummer, and served as assistant musical director for Earl Carroll's theater-restaurant.

In 1940 Kenton was ready to start his own organization. The first test recordings for his new band were made in November at the Music City Record Shop in Hollywood, and the fledgling group made its debuts at the Pavilion in Huntington Beach and the Diana Ballroom in Los Angeles. On Memorial Day in 1941 his fourteen-piece group, known as the Artistry in Rhythm Orchestra (named after the theme song he had written for it), began a summer-long engagement at the Balboa Beach Rendezvous Ballroom. Later that year Maurie Cohen, owner of the prestigious Hollywood Palladium, signed the band to a five-year contract.

Stan Kenton's band began its first nationwide tour in January 1942, ending at New York's Roseland Ballroom. Overall, the band received an enthusiastic response at Roseland and attracted many admirers, although the syncopated rhythms and staccato, brassy sound presented a challenge to some of the dancers. In 1943 the band joined comedian Bob Hope's network radio show, but Kenton soon became resentful that his orchestra was being used as nothing more than "accompaniment." The response to his first recordings, on the Decca label, was also disappointing. Leaving Decca, he signed on with Capitol Records and continued to record, successfully, for the Capitol label until 1968. "Eager Beaver" was one of his first hits with Capitol. During the war years, 1941–1945, soloists with the band included Art Pepper, Stan Getz, Boots Mussulli, and singer Anita O'Day.

An important year in the evolution of Artistry in Rhythm was 1946: Pete Rugolo took over much of the arranging. Rugolo understood and was able to interpret through his arrangements the sound and style that Kenton wanted for his band. The group also had a new vocalist, June Christy, whose renditions contributed greatly to the instant popularity of "Tampico" and "Across the Alley from the Alamo." The band, now numbering eighteen members, was chosen by *Look* magazine as "Band of the Year"; Kenton-affiliated musicians dominated the *Down Beat*, *Metronome*, and *Variety* jazz polls. In 1947, having spent six months off the road, Kenton's band went through something of a metamorphosis: he changed the name to the Progressive Jazz Orchestra, expanded the brass section, added guitar, and increased the number of trombones, saxophones, and percussion instruments. Concerts were well attended and well received; the orchestra won first place in the annual *Down Beat* readers' poll and performed at Carnegie Hall. Their concert at the Hollywood Bowl in 1948 attracted 15,000 people, and *Variety* declared that the Progressive Jazz Orchestra was "the hottest box office attraction in the country."

In 1949–1950 Kenton again expanded the group working for him: his Innovations in Modern Music orchestra included strings, woodwinds, and two French horns. Musicians included Maynard Ferguson, Laurindo Almeida, Shelly Manne, and many other notable jazz artists, as well as singer June Christy. This ambitious venture was short lived; by 1952 Kenton had reduced the size of the orchestra to a more manageable and commercially viable nineteen pieces. In 1951 Kenton married Ann Richards, a vocalist in his band; this second marriage produced two children and was to end in divorce as well.

For the next few years Kenton's musical signature continued to evolve in collaboration with such gifted composers and performers as Shorty Rogers, Gerry Mulligan, Marty Paich, Bill Holman, Bill Russo, Lee Konitz, Zoot Sims, and Bill Perkins. In 1953 Kenton took the orchestra on its first European tour, playing to capacity crowds, and continued to receive recognition and popular acclaim in the United States. In 1954 he joined Louis Armstrong and Duke Ellington as the third member of *Down Beat's* Jazz Hall of Fame.

Under a reciprocal agreement with Ted Heath, in 1956 the Kenton orchestra became the first American "big band" to tour England since 1937, while Heath's British band toured the United States. Kenton was commissioned to write scores for two ballets, one commemorating the marriage of Grace Kelly and Prince Rainier of Monaco and the other in honor of the birthday of Queen Wilhelmina of the Netherlands. Returning to the United States, he purchased the Rendezvous Ballroom in Balboa Beach in 1957 to provide a home base for his orchestra. He was also given the first *Playboy* magazine jazz award, an honor he received annually for the next seven years.

In 1959 Kenton established the Kenton Clinics for young musicians at Indiana and Michigan State Universities, marking the beginning of a new venture to promote jazz study and performance on college campuses. (In later years this model would be emulated on college and even high school campuses throughout the world.) As Kenton's influence in jazz music education widened, he became a principal motivator for establishing the National Association of Jazz Educators (now the International Association of Jazz Educators). Many of the organization's founders were Kenton's colleagues in his summer collegiate jazz camps. During the 1960s and 1970s he received a number of honorary degrees in recognition of his interest in and contributions to musical education, including Villanova University, Drury College in Springfield, Missouri, and the University of Redlands.

In 1961 Kenton added four mellophoniums, which he helped to design, and introduced his Mellophonium Orchestra in Las Vegas. In 1962 the orchestra was awarded a jazz album Grammy by the National Academy of Recording Arts and Sciences for its recorded performance of Leonard Bernstein's Broadway musical *West Side Story*, and in 1963 the *Adventures in Jazz* album was a Grammy winner as well. In 1964 Kenton recorded a "Wagneresque" album—his own compositions arranged "as if [Richard] Wagner were writing for the Stan Kenton orchestra." In 1965 he premiered another large orchestral ensemble, the Neophonic Orchestra, which he referred to as "the world's only orchestra devoted to contemporary music."

In 1967, after lecturing extensively at universities and colleges in the Southwest, Kenton wrote a new library for the orchestra and made his final recording for Capitol Records. The next year he made his first film, *The Substance of Jazz*. By 1970 he had formed his own recording and publishing companies, Creative World Records and Creative World Music Publications. He toured extensively during the next few years and produced a second jazz film, *Bound to Be Heard*. Kenton toured with his band in Japan in 1974 and Europe in 1976, while continuing with his Kenton Clinic schedule. In 1977 he suffered severe injuries from a fall, but he returned to the road, still in a weakened condition, the following year. He recorded his last albums on his Creative World label in 1976 but continued touring until disbanding his orchestra in 1978. Stan Kenton died in Los Angeles.

For Kenton aficionados, many of his own musical compositions were enduring triumphs, some of which he continued to play during his last tour. "Artistry in Rhythm," his signature theme, was a blend of classical motifs, jazz riffs, and Latin rhythms, usually with Kenton playing a piano introduction followed by the full band unleashed. "Concerto to End All Concertos," a composition named in jest, demonstrated Kenton's ability to write in combined classical and jazz modes; the arrangement singled out each section of the orchestra to give individual musicians a chance to improvise. "Collaboration" was written by Kenton along with his alter ego Pete Rugolo and was a significant event in their individual careers as composers. "Capitol Punishment" was a pyrotechnical up-tempo progressive-jazz composition. "Etude for Saxophones," "Reed Rapture," and Opus in Pastels" were components of a saxophone suite; they stand as examples of the lyrical qualities of Kenton's writing. "Southern Scandal" and "Painted Rhythm" were among his most popular tunes; a step beyond swing, they foreshadowed his "Progressive" and "Innovations" eras. "Theme for Sunday" was regularly requested and performed during Kenton's U.S. "Innovations in Modern Music" tours in the early fifties. "Sunset Tower," named after the Capitol Records Tower in Hollywood, evoked a West Coast ambiance. "Artistry in Silhouette" with its chromatic simplicity recalled Kenton's earlier writings; it was written as a ballad but performed as an up-tempo piece.

Stan Kenton's music has been described as "the headiest combination of love, emotion, intellect, form, freedom, boldness and fire ever known." Kenton contributed uniquely to the evolution of jazz in America. He was an innovator in his field who relentlessly explored the possibilities of jazz music, pursuing his artistic vision not only to achieve his own goals but also to motivate and assist young musicians whom he hoped would follow in his footsteps. He constantly challenged his musicians and his audiences to accept and embrace new ideas in sound and style.

• All of the Stan Kenton orchestras' music is archived, as cataloged by Leon Breedon, longtime Kenton colleague, at the University of North Texas at Denton. Kenton's papers, awards, and mementos, including many personal items, are in the Stan Kenton Collection at the California State University, Los Angeles, Special Collections Library. Pete Venudor and Michael Sparke, *The Standard Kenton Directory* (1968), includes a complete listing of Kenton's commercially produced off-air and on-site 1937–1949 recordings. Michael Sparke with Pete Venudor and Jack Hartley, *Kenton on Capitol and Creative World* (1994), is a discography of Kenton recordings on those two record labels. Michael Spark with Pete Venudor and Jack Hartley, *Stan Kenton: The Studio Sessions* (1998), documents Kenton's studio sessions that had as their primary purpose the production of sound recordings.

Carol Easton, *Straight Ahead: The Story of Stan Kenton* (1973), is a biography originally authorized but later discounted by Kenton. William F. Lee, *Kenton: Artistry in Rhythm* (1980), edited by Audree Coke, Kenton's personal manager and companion in the last years of his life, is an authorized biography. Lillian Arganian, *Stan Kenton: The Man and His Music* (1989), is a series of interviews with Kenton colleagues. Anthony J. Agostinelli, *Stan Kenton: The Many Musical Moods of His Orchestras* (1985), reviews Kenton's wide-ranging musical experiments and expressions. Edward F. Gabel, *Stan Kenton: The Early Years* (1993), is a personal recollection by an assistant manager for the band in the early years. Christopher A. Pirie and Dr. Siegfried Mueller, *Artistry in Kenton: The Bio-discography of Stan Kenton and His Music* (2 vols., 1969–1973), covers Kenton's 1937–1956 compositions. Chris Pirie, *Artistry in Kenton: Book One, Primary* and *Artistry in Kenton: Book One, Orchestral Historiography* (1995), is a two-volume updated and revised bio-discography covering the period 1937–1953. Michael Sparke, *Jazz Discographics Presents: The Great Kenton Arrangers* (1968), focuses on Bill Holman, Gene Roland, Johnny Richards, Pete Rugolo, and William Russo, principal composers and arrangers who worked with Kenton during his professional career.

ANTHONY J. AGOSTINELLI

KENWORTHY, Marion Edwena (17 Aug. 1891–26 June 1980), psychiatrist and educator, was born in Hampden, Massachusetts, the daughter of John Kenworthy, a textile manufacturer, and Ida Miller, a teacher. Kenworthy's determination to become a doctor grew out of the emotional impact of her mother's long-term illness and death when Marion was nine years old. As no preliminary undergraduate degree was required for application to medical school, Kenworthy entered Tufts University School of Medicine at age seventeen. Of the 144 students in her class, twelve were women. By the end of the first year, only seven women remained. She graduated cum laude in 1913.

Following graduation, Kenworthy had accepted an internship and residency at the Women's Hospital in Worcester, Massachusetts, which probably would have led to a specialty in obstetrics and gynecology. At the last minute, however, she interviewed at Gardner State Hospital and in May 1913 became their first woman physician. At that time Gardner State had 2,400 patients in cottages spanning 200 acres. Kenworthy was in charge of about 300 women on the hospital's chronic ward. She began the first boarding-out program at Gardner State Hospital by arranging to release patients to live with families in the community, whom she then visited once a month. During her three and a half years at Gardner State, Kenworthy spent free weekends and vacations working at the Boston Psychopathic Hospital, where she became professionally associated with Elmer Southard, a pioneer in social psychiatry, who became one of the greatest influences on her life. Her colleagues in training at Boston Psychopathic included Karl Menninger, Karl Bowman, Harry Solomon, Mary Jarrett, Frankwood Williams, Herman Adler, and Lawson Lowrey, who all went on to make significant contributions in various fields of human service.

Kenworthy moved to Foxboro State Hospital in Foxboro, Massachusetts, a more acute care service, as a senior psychiatrist in 1917. Knowing that her professional career had reached its pinnacle for a woman within the state hospital system, she left Foxboro in July 1919 when a friend and former teacher offered her the opportunity to teach mental hygiene in New York City. For the next two and a half years she taught courses in mental health to future physical education teachers at the Central School of Hygiene, run by the Young Women's Christian Association. During this time she also conducted research on children with glandular problems at the Vanderbilt Clinic at the New York State Neurological Institute, where she met psychiatrist Bernard Glueck. Glueck invited Kenworthy to lecture at the New York School of Social Work in 1920. In order to practice medicine in the state of New York, she took medical exams in the winter of 1919–1920.

Kenworthy began practicing psychoanalysis in 1921 after undergoing her own analysis by Otto Rank during his first visit to the United States and before his break with Sigmund Freud. She credited this experience with inspiring her to bring dynamically oriented aspects of psychiatry to bear throughout her life's work. Among the first psychiatrists with a private practice in child psychiatry in New York City, Kenworthy maintained a thriving private practice, which included patients of all ages, for most of her professional career and long into retirement.

In 1921 Kenworthy also began teaching at the New York School of Social Work (now the Columbia University School of Social Work), where she developed an analytically oriented assessment tool she called the ego-libido method. A structured conceptual system designed to help students assess personality and improve their understanding of human behavior, the ego-libido method, although it eventually proved obsolete, provided a basic understanding of psychoanalytic principles to a generation of social work students. As an instructor in the Department of Mental Hygiene from 1921 to 1924, its director from 1924 to 1940, and professor of psychiatry from 1940 to 1956, Kenworthy taught more than 10,000 students.

In 1922 Kenworthy began work as assistant director of the Bureau of Childrens' Guidance, a psychiatric treatment facility for children and one of five demonstration clinics established by the Commonwealth Fund. A model project designed to provide field training for social work students, the bureau emphasized interdisciplinary collaboration in a teamwork approach to mental health and treated close to 600 children over the course of five years. When Glueck left the bureau in 1924, Kenworthy replaced him as its medical director and retained the position until the bureau's close in 1927. In 1929 she coauthored with Porter Lee, dean of the New York School of Social Work, *Mental Hygiene and Social Work*, which summarized the child guidance work done at the bureau.

Kenworthy worked to further the professionalization of social work and to establish a role for social workers within major social institutions, including the military and the juvenile justice system. During World War II she was instrumental in establishing the first mental health unit within a basic training camp, a model that was duplicated throughout the United States and subsequently led to the development of an occupational classification for social workers in the military. She continued her service to the military through her appointment in 1944 by General George C. Marshall to the National Civilian Advisory Committee to the Women's Army Corps. Her role on the advisory committee, which included worldwide travel, led to a report recommending improved selection and assignments for women in the service. Beginning in 1932 Kenworthy also worked for several decades with Judge Justine Wise Polier in New York City to integrate mental health concepts and services into the juvenile court system and into adoption services.

Kenworthy's contemporaries remembered her as distinguished and gracious and as having a regal bearing as well as the ability to "swear like a trooper when her sense of righteous indignation was aroused" (Bernard, *Psychiatric Annals* 9 [June 1979]). Her tall and angular appearance produced a dominating presence and reinforced the authority she brought to her many endeavors.

During the course of her professional career, Kenworthy was vice president of the American Psychiatric Association (1965–1966), president of the American Psychoanalytic Association (1958–1959), and president of the Group for the Advancement of Psychiatry (1959–1961), the first woman to hold each position.

When Kenworthy retired from Columbia University in 1956, a chair in psychiatry was established in her name, and she received acclamations from notables such as President Dwight Eisenhower, Drs. Karl and William Menninger, and Eugene Meyer, the publisher of the *Washington Post*. At the same time she was made professor emeritus in psychiatry and a member of the Board of Trustees of Columbia University.

For over fifty years Kenworthy lived with Sarah Swift, a social worker, until Swift's death in 1975. Kenworthy died in New York City.

Called the "mother" and "patron saint" of psychiatry in social work (Deutch, p. 10), Kenworthy is recognized as being among the first psychiatrists to introduce psychoanalytic ideas systematically into social work education and practice, and she is credited with fostering child psychiatry and the child guidance movement. She catalyzed interdisciplinary coordination across mental health settings and mental health organizations in a lifelong effort to provide and refine quality mental health services.

• Kenworthy's papers, including records from the Bureau of Child Guidance, course lecture notes, participation in social work professional organizations and events, and World War II documentation, are in the Columbia University Rare Books Library. Papers having to do with her participation in psychiatric associations and issues can be found in the historical archives at Payne Whitney Hospital in New York City. Some of her most noteworthy publications include "Training for Psychiatric Social Work," *Hospital Social Service* 7 (1923): 33–37; "Mental Health in Childhood," *Mental Hygiene* 10, no. 2 (1926): 242–52; and "Psychoanalytic Concepts in Mental Hygiene," *Family* 7 (Nov. 1926): 213–23.

For biographical information see transcribed interviews with Kenworthy by Albert Deutch (22 Feb. 1956) and by Spafford Ackerly (29 June 1971) in the Columbia and Payne Whitney holdings. Also noteworthy are Henry Brosin, "Marion Edwena Kenworthy, M.D.: An Appreciation," *Group for the Advancement of Psychiatry's Circular Letter* (Spring 1981); Viola Bernard, "Profiles of Famous American Psychiatrists: Marion E. Kenworthy, M.D.," *Psychiatric Annals* 9 (June 1979); "Marion E. Kenworthy, M.D.," *Journal of the American Academy of Child Psychiatry* (1981); Charlotte Towle, "Marion E. Kenworthy: A Social Worker's Reflections," *Social Service Review* 30, no. 4 (Dec. 1956); and Albert Deutch, "Dr. Marion E. Kenworthy—A Commemorative," New York School of Social Work (1956). An obituary is in the *New York Times*, 27 June 1980.

REBECCA SPERLING

KENYON, Dorothy (17 Feb. 1888–11 Feb. 1972), attorney, political activist, and judge, was born in New York City, the daughter of William Houston Kenyon, an attorney, and Maria Wellington Stanwood. In 1904 Kenyon graduated from Horace Mann High School in New York City. She then attended Smith College, graduating in 1908 with a bachelor of arts degree in economics and history.

After college Kenyon visited Mexico, where the plight of the Indians provoked in her a sense of social obligation. She then enrolled in the New York University School of Law, one of the few law schools in the United States that then admitted women, and received a doctor of jurisprudence degree in 1917. Declining an offer to work with her brothers at her father's law firm, she instead conducted research for the federal government on wartime labor and prepared studies for the delegates to the Paris peace conference in 1919.

Through the 1920s Kenyon practiced law in private firms in New York. In 1930 she and Dorothy Straus established their own firm, Straus and Kenyon, which lasted until 1939. Throughout the depression years Kenyon served on a wide range of social reform commissions in New York City. In 1936 she chaired New York City's committee to investigate women's courts and called for more lenient treatment of prostitutes and for more aggressive prosecution of pimps. As deputy commissioner of licenses in 1936 and 1937 she opposed Mayor Fiorello LaGuardia's decision to revoke the licenses of the city's burlesque theaters, arguing

that they provided "the only beauty in the lives of icemen and messenger boys" (*New York Times*, 14 Feb. 1972). In 1937 Kenyon became one of the first women to gain admittance to the New York City bar association, and in 1939 she was appointed by Mayor LaGuardia to the Municipal Court. The following year she lost in the election for the judgeship to a fellow Democrat and resumed her private law practice.

Outside of her legal work, Kenyon was an increasingly prominent figure in New York and national left-liberal politics. She served as legal counsel to the Cooperative League of the United States and was a vigorous proponent of the cooperative movement. Having become a member of the national board of directors of the American Civil Liberties Union (ACLU) in 1930, Kenyon argued unsuccessfully against the expulsion from the ACLU of Elizabeth Gurley Flynn in 1940 because Flynn was a member of the Communist party. From 1938 she was also a member of the League of Nations Committee on the Status of Women. In New York politics Kenyon worked with the anti-Tammany fusion movement, which elected LaGuardia in 1933, and with the American Labor party in the late 1930s.

In the 1940s Kenyon continued to practice law and remained active in a variety of feminist and social reform efforts. In 1946 she was hired by the State Department to serve as the U.S. delegate to the United Nations (UN) Commission on the Status of Women. In that position, which she held until 1950, Kenyon advocated a more significant role for women in the UN and its agencies, particularly the World Health Organization. She also directed a campaign to establish international treaties that would guarantee equal rights for women, particularly with regard to pay, property rights, and political privileges.

Kenyon's years of service in organizations affiliated with the Communist party invited the wrath of Senator Joseph R. McCarthy in 1950. McCarthy charged that while serving in government appointments she had been affiliated with twenty-eight "Communist-front organizations," including the National Council of American-Soviet Friendship and the American-Russian Institute. That year she was the first person called before the Senate Foreign Relations Subcommittee, which investigated McCarthy's charges that various government officials were disloyal because of their ties to the Communist party. Kenyon admitted that she had been affiliated with many of the organizations listed but denied "any connection of any kind or character with communism or its adherents" and called McCarthy "an unmitigated liar" and "a coward" (*New York Times*, 14 Feb. 1972). Before the subcommittee she offered an explanation of her political history:

With all the mistakes and errors of judgment which the best of us can and do commit only too frequently, I submit that the record proves without a question that I am a lover of democracy, of individual freedom, and of human rights for everybody, a battler, perhaps a little too much of a battler sometimes, for the rights of the little fellow who gets forgotten or frightened or shunned because of unpopular views . . . The converse of these things: dictatorship, cruelty, oppression and slavery, are to me intolerable. I cannot live in their air, I must fight back. This is not perhaps a very wise or prudent way to live, but it is my way. . . . There is not a Communist bone in my body. (quoted in Buckley and Bozell, p. 79)

Kenyon fared well compared to many who were called before the Senate subcommittee, but she received no more public appointments after her appearance. Writing four years after her testimony before the subcommittee, conservative authors William F. Buckley and L. Brent Bozell concluded that Kenyon was "a loyal American" and probably not a member of the Communist party (p. 84).

Kenyon continued her law practice and remained active in left-liberal movements through the 1950s and 1960s. She helped establish legal services for the poor in the Chelsea neighborhood in Manhattan, donated legal services to various organizations in the civil rights movement, and advocated integration of the New York City schools. Kenyon was also active in the anti–Vietnam War movement and in a host of feminist organizations in New York City.

Kenyon died in New York City. As one of the first successful female attorneys and judges in the United States, she was a pioneer for women in the legal profession. She also made her mark as a prominent activist in many of the most important social reform movements of the twentieth century.

• Kenyon's papers, including speech and clipping files, correspondence, various records of her governmental work, and an oral history interview, are deposited in the Sophia Smith Collection at Smith College. Useful sections on Kenyon can be found in Isabella Taves, *Successful Women* (1943), and William F. Buckley and L. Brent Bozell, *McCarthy and His Enemies* (1954). An obituary is in the *New York Times*, 14 Feb. 1972.

THADDEUS RUSSELL

KENYON, Josephine Hemenway (10 May 1880–10 Jan. 1965), pediatrician and health educator, was born in Auburn, New York, the daughter of Charles Carroll Hemenway, a Presbyterian minister, and Ida Eliza Shackelford. When Kenyon was eleven, the family moved to Glasgow, Missouri, where her father accepted a position as president of Pritchett College. Later she studied at Pritchett, receiving a bachelor's degree in 1898 and a master's degree the following year.

Kenyon moved in 1899 to Philadelphia, where she studied biology under Hunt Morgan at Bryn Mawr College in preparation for a career in medicine. In 1900 she entered the School of Medicine at Johns Hopkins University in Baltimore, where she acquired an exceptional education under noteworthy physicians such as William Henry Welch, Sir William Osler, William Stewart Halsted, and Howard Atwood Kelly. In 1904 she was one of three women to graduate in a class of forty-five and among the earliest women to

graduate from the medical school as a whole. She won a highly competitive house medical officer internship at the Johns Hopkins University Hospital, a position she held for a year.

In 1905 Kenyon began a six-year residency at the Babies' Hospital of New York City, among the first U.S. institutions devoted exclusively to the care of infants under age three. She worked in the clinical laboratory of the hospital's chief physician, Luther Emmett Holt, a founding father of pediatrics as a medical specialty in the United States and well known for his excellence in teaching. During her residency she conducted research on influenza and meningitis diseases of children with Holt and Martha Wollstein, another resident who later became a noteworthy medical researcher at the Rockefeller Institute. Following her residency, Kenyon opened a private pediatric practice in New York City. In 1911 she married James Henry Kenyon, a neurosurgeon who was also on staff at Babies' Hospital. The couple later had two daughters.

While establishing her medical practice, Kenyon also began a career as an educator in child care, social hygiene, and sex education. As early as 1909 she delivered special lectures at Teachers College, Columbia University, and in 1913 won an appointment there as lecturer, a position that she held for twenty-four years. During her appointment, Kenyon initiated a course in child care, a task for which Holt had recommended her, stating that she was "the best man I ever had on my staff." She also lectured on health education and social hygiene—instruction in the proper sexual conduct of women intended to deter prostitution and venereal disease. Like many women physicians of the period, Kenyon became involved in the public health works of social reform organizations. She worked for the Presbyterian Church in the U.S.A. Board of National Missions; the New York Diet Kitchen, which helped in the campaign to improve the quality of the city's milk supply by providing uncontaminated milk to nursing mothers; and the national board of the Young Women's Christian Associations (YWCA), on which she served as associate director of the Bureau of Social Education, supervisor of lectures of the Social Morality Committee, and chair of the Bureau of Health.

In her work for the YWCA, Kenyon organized a nationwide lecture series on sex education and social hygiene delivered by women physicians and aimed at audiences of young women throughout the nation. During World War I she organized another lecture series that focused on the proper sexual conduct of women among soldiers, and she became the acting director of the Women's Work Section of the Social Hygiene Division, Commission on Training Camp Activities of the U.S. War Department. With director Katherine Bement Davis, an important social worker who directed the Bedford Hills Reformatory in New York, Kenyon oversaw lecture programs, pamphlet distributions, and the showing of *The End of the Road*, a harshly moralistic film that admonished women against sexual relations with men outside of marriage.

Following these wartime projects, she and the other members of the Social Morality Committee organized an International Conference of Women Physicians that took place in the autumn of 1919. The conference lasted for a month and featured discussions on women's and children's health issues. One outcome of the conference in which Kenyon participated was the founding of the Women's Foundation of Health, for which she served as executive secretary. The foundation sponsored laboratory research on women's health issues and the publication of health education pamphlets, such as the Positive Health series.

Kenyon's work on the board of the YWCA ended in 1921, and the following year she assumed a new role in public health education that established her as a popular scientific authority in child care. A growing concern about infant mortality during the first two decades of the century promoted popular women's magazines to provide regular advice columns for mothers on prenatal and infant care. In 1922, the year in which the *Delineator* contracted Holt as a columnist, Kenyon accepted a position with *Good Housekeeping* to direct the Health and Happiness Club. This club began as a correspondence service that provided expectant mothers with a series of eight letters on prenatal care for the cost of postage. Within months, the club expanded its service to include a second series, the Baby's First Year. The following year, she began writing monthly columns that focused on problems of infant care raised in the letters of the mothers who belonged to the club. During World War II her position at *Good Housekeeping* expanded to director of the Baby Center, which provided child care resources and advice to mothers at the magazine's headquarters in New York City. Throughout her career, she also wrote feature articles on topics such as child and adolescent behavior for *Parents' Magazine* and the American Medical Association's health education magazine, *Hygeia*, and served on the editorial board of the *Journal of the American Medical Women's Association*.

After a decade as a columnist, Kenyon wrote *Healthy Babies Are Happy Babies: A Complete Handbook for Modern Mothers* (1934), contributing to a genre of child care manuals that her teacher Holt had pioneered in 1894 with *The Care and Feeding of Children*. Her book's popularity, paralleled only by that of Holt's manual, arose from her appeal as both mother and physician. During the course of the book's five revisions (the final two authored jointly by Kenyon and her daughter Ruth Kenyon Russell, also a practicing physician), her trend in pediatric advice shifted from an emphasis on following rigid schedules to attending to a child's "on-demand" schedule, as in feeding. Parallel to this shift, she increasingly emphasized the healthy emotional development of the child as well as the health of the mother before and after pregnancy. Hazel Corbin, the longtime general director of the Maternity Center Association, instructed new mothers that "the soundest advice I can give you on baby care is to get a copy of that book" (Carolyn Conant Van Blarcom, *Getting Ready to Be a Mother* [1922; rev. ed.,

1940], p. 188). The book underwent nineteen printings in the United States and five translations abroad.

Kenyon practiced medicine throughout her career, maintaining affiliations with hospitals in New York, including the Neurological Institute, the New York Infirmary for Women and Children, and Bellevue Hospital. She was a member of several professional medical societies, including the American Medical Association, and a fellow of the New York Academy of Medicine. Kenyon continued to live in New York until 1950, when she moved to Boulder, Colorado, to live near her daughters' families (her husband had died in 1939). Before moving, she closed her pediatric practice but continued to write for *Good Housekeeping* until 1952. She remained in Boulder, where she died.

Kenyon won widespread recognition primarily as a child health educator through her many popular writings. In this role she became one of the most visible women authorities to participate in the U.S. movement for a scientific motherhood, which was characterized by the promotion of expert scientific advice for raising children and which appealed to women of a new, educated middle class in the early decades of the twentieth century.

• Kenyon's research articles are indexed in the *Index Medicus*. In addition to her book and magazine articles, she also wrote a foreword to Ethel S. Beer, *The Day Nursery* (1942), and a memorial on William Worthington Herrick, president of the New York Academy of Medicine and the father-in-law of her daughter Ruth, in *Bulletin of the New York Academy of Medicine* 21, no. 9 (1945): 499–501. Dr. Ruth Kenyon Russell provided helpful comments and source materials. Kenyon's role as an organizer of lectures on sex education is recorded in the YWCA's *Report of the Social Morality Committee* (1919) and in the YWCA national archives. Elizabeth O. Toombs highlights the proceedings of the 1919 International Conference of Women Physicians and includes Kenyon's portrait in "In the Hands of Women," *Good Housekeeping*, May 1919, p. 40. Historical overviews include Regina Morantz-Sanchez, *Sympathy and Science: Women Physicians in American Medicine* (1985); Allan M. Brandt, *No Magic Bullet: A Social History of Venereal Disease in the United States since 1880* (1985); and Rima Apple, *Mothers and Medicine: A Social History of Infant Feeding, 1890–1950* (1987). *Good Housekeeping* announced the establishment of the Health and Happiness Club and later the Baby Center in "The Health and Happiness Club: A Service for the Mother-to-Be and the Baby-to-Come," *Good Housekeeping*, Nov. 1922, p. 74; "Good Housekeeping Opens a Baby Center," *Good Housekeeping*, May 1943, pp. 134–35, 223. Background to the explosion of prenatal and infant care manuals and advice columns in U.S. popular magazines at the time Kenyon began her writing career may be found in Richard A. Meckel, *Save the Babies: American Public Health Reform and the Prevention of Infant Mortality, 1850–1929* (1990). Christopher Brooks highlighted Kenyon's career in "She's Helped to Raise a Million Babies (More or Less)," *Good Housekeeping*, May 1940, p. 17. Obituaries appear in the *New York Times*, 11 Jan. 1965, and the *Journal of the American Medical Association* 192, no. 1 (5 Apr. 1965): 75.

DONALD L. OPITZ

KENYON, William Squire (10 June 1869–9 Sept. 1933), senator and jurist, was born in Elyria, Ohio, the son of Fergus Lafayette Kenyon, a Congregational minister, and Harriet Anna Squire. In 1878 the family moved to Iowa City, Iowa. Although his father hoped he would enter the ministry, William took an early interest in the law. Since his family's financial resources were limited, he worked his way through two years at Iowa (later Grinnell) College before transferring to the University of Iowa, where he completed the law course in 1890. The next year he passed the Iowa bar exam, moved to Fort Dodge, Iowa, and set up practice. In 1893 he married Mary J. Duncombe, daughter of a prominent and well-regarded lawyer in the area. They had no children.

Following his appointment as prosecuting attorney for Webster County in 1892, Kenyon quickly earned a reputation as a skilled trial lawyer. He returned to private practice in 1897, but three years later, at the age of thirty-one, he was elevated to the bench as judge of the Eleventh Judicial District of Iowa. His salary, however, was inadequate to support his family, and he resigned and joined his father-in-law's legal practice. From 1907 to 1910 Kenyon served as general counsel for the Illinois Central Railroad. Between March 1910 and April 1911 he changed sides and worked for the federal government as special assistant to Attorney General George W. Wickersham in charge of enforcing the Hepburn Rate Act and the Sherman Antitrust Act, which often put him at odds with his former benefactors.

Kenyon probably would have stayed in Washington, D.C., but politics in Iowa brought him back home. Senator Jonathan P. Dolliver's sudden death in October 1910 led to a bitter struggle between the conservative standpatter and the Progressive wings of the Iowa Republican party. Since Iowa was staunchly Republican in its politics, the two factions often skirmished for voters. Kenyon, boosted by the Progressives, triumphed on the sixty-seventh ballot of the Iowa legislature in 1911. He was elected for a full term by the legislature in 1912 and was reelected without opposition by the general populace in 1918.

As one of the youngest people ever elected to the U.S. Senate, Kenyon showed himself an able student of the Senate's workings, and within a short time he was introducing legislation on a variety of fronts. Faithful to his progressive inclinations, Kenyon favored direct election of senators, downward tariff revision, taxes on both personal incomes and corporate profits, and higher veterans' pensions. He vigorously sought to abolish child labor and sponsored legislation making it illegal to transport liquor into "dry" territories. He believed firmly in the rights of the laboring person, and in 1919 he chaired the Senate committee investigating the nationwide steel strike and the West Virginia coal dispute. Kenyon was a charter member and leader of the "farm bloc," a group of southern and midwestern senators who sought federal assistance for agricultural relief. A staunch opponent to U.S. involvement in World War I, he was one of the handful of senators who blocked President Woodrow Wilson's plan to arm merchant ships. When the United States entered the war in April 1917, Kenyon reversed his stance, believing that the nation should not be divided during the crisis, and supported the war effort. During the war he advocated the conscription of wealth as well as manpower. Kenyon believed that the United States should recognize France's enormous contribution to the war and, after hostilities ceased, cancel any debts owed the United States. At the conclusion of the war, his interest in internationalism still lukewarm, Kenyon joined the mild reservationists regarding U.S. participation in the League of Nations.

Despite his years in the contentious political arena, Kenyon was never entirely comfortable with political life. He tired of deal making and constituency stroking and longed to return to the quieter, more reflective life of a judge. In January 1922, to the dismay of his colleagues in the Senate, he eagerly accepted President Warren G. Harding's offer to become a judge of the U.S. Court of Appeals, Eighth Circuit, and served in this position until his death. His most famous opinion was his well-reasoned decision canceling the Teapot Dome oil leases, which reversed a lower court ruling. (In 1921 Secretary of the Interior Albert B. Fall had convinced Secretary of the Navy Edwin Denby to transfer control over U.S. naval oil reserves at Teapot Dome, Wyoming. Fall then secretly leased the reserves to oilman Harry F. Sinclair, for which he received a "loan" of $25,000. A Senate investigation subsequently uncovered Fall's questionable transactions, and he spent a year in jail. Kenyon's reversal of the lower court ruling was upheld by the Supreme Court.)

Happy as a judge, Kenyon turned down cabinet positions offered by President Calvin Coolidge, although he did accept appointment by President Herbert Hoover in 1929 as a member of the National Commission on Law Observance and Enforcement, chaired by his former boss Wickersham.

Kenyon had a sharp legal mind and enjoyed the intricacies and challenges of the law. As a politician, he worked well with all factions in the Senate and remained committed to progressive ideals throughout his professional career. He died at his summer estate near Bath, Maine.

• Small quantities of Kenyon's papers are located in the Herbert Hoover Presidential Library, West Branch, Iowa, and the Iowa State Historical Department and the University of Iowa, Iowa City. Two lengthy treatments are Howard Eldred Kershner, *William Squire Kenyon and the Kenyon-Duncombe Williams-Squire Family Histories* (1935), and Elizabeth Putnam, "An Investigation of the Judicial Appointment of Senator William Squire Kenyon" (master's thesis, Drake Univ. 1968). Other sources useful for supplementary biographical information include *In Memoriam: William S. Kenyon, 1869–1933* (1934); Daniel Potts, "William Squire Kenyon and the Iowa Senatorial Election of 1911," *Annals of Iowa* 38 (Winter 1966): 206–22; and Herbert F. Margulies, "The Moderates in the League of Nations Battle: The Case of William S. Kenyon," *Midwest Review* 12 (1990): 16–33. His obituary is in the *New York Times*, 10 Sept. 1933.

EDWARD A. GOEDEKEN

KEOKUK (c. 1790–1848), Sauk (Sac) chief, was born at Saukenuk, his tribe's village near the mouth of the Rock River in present-day Illinois, a member of the Fox clan. His mother, Lalotte, was part French. An imposing figure and an eloquent speaker, Keokuk (Watchful Fox) rose to prominence during the War of 1812 when, despite his lack of fighting experience, he took advantage of a perceived U.S. threat to Saukenuk to gain the rank of Sauk war chief. Although there is no evidence of Keokuk's participation in battles with the Americans, he was a tribal leader of consequence by the end of the war.

By the early 1820s Keokuk had gained a reputation among U.S. officials as someone with whom they could negotiate, one official remarking: "If things are well managed in two or three years more his word among the Sauks and foxes [sic] will be their law." In the mid-1820s the United States pressured the Sauk and Fox to move west into what would become Iowa, based on the Treaty of 1804, by which they had agreed to give up their land in northern Illinois and southern Wisconsin when the government determined that it was needed for white settlers. Keokuk, who had visited several eastern cities as part of an Indian delegation to Washington in 1821, recognized the futility of armed resistance against such a force. Black Hawk, a fellow Sauk who was courageous but relatively unsophisticated, did not.

Demonstrating that he was not simply a dupe of the Americans, Keokuk refused a government bid in 1829 to purchase mineral lands west of the Mississippi River, declaring that the Indians had been cheated by the Treaty of 1804. As the pressure for removal intensified, however, the Sauk and Fox split into factions, Black Hawk promoting resistance and Keokuk counseling submission. Most of the Sauk sided with Keokuk, abandoned Saukenuk in 1831, and moved across the Mississippi. Black Hawk, however, led his followers back to the village twice, each time triggering a military response; the second confrontation led to the Black Hawk War of 1832.

Keokuk worked to keep as many Indians neutral as possible and was even influential with some of the more militant because he had been a forceful spokesman for their right to wage war against traditional foes, such as the Sioux and Menomonees. As the war subsided, Keokuk surrendered to the Americans several of the late combatants who had taken refuge among the neutrals.

In the treaty concluding the war in 1832, the United States punished the Sauk and Fox by requiring the cession of nearly six million acres in Iowa. They rewarded Keokuk's collaboration by excluding from the cession the area encompassing Keokuk's village. To solidify his position of leadership, the officials also proclaimed Keokuk civil chief, a hereditary rank that was not in their power to grant.

In the next decade Keokuk maintained his political connections with U.S. officials despite vociferous opposition from his people. Officials made certain that payments to the tribe were made not to individuals, but to the chiefs, which permitted Keokuk to reward his friends and punish his enemies. The Fox, who had never accepted the government's linkage of them with the Sauk, denounced him as a mixed blood who used his pretended chieftainship to acquire luxuries for himself while others went hungry. On some counts, however, Keokuk won grudging approval from his critics. He continued to uphold the right of the Sauk and Fox to wage war against the Sioux, and he steadfastly opposed the government's introduction of teachers and missionaries into Indian communities.

Keokuk was the principal tribal spokesman at negotiations in 1836, 1837, and 1842 that resulted in the sale to the United States of the approximately twelve million acres of land they held in Iowa. Given the determination of the government to expel them from Iowa, it was inevitable that they would leave; the question was whether they would go north or south. In 1841 Keokuk helped block initial pressures to move north. A year later he accepted a government proposal that the Sauk and Fox sell their Iowa holdings and move south to what would become Kansas. Some chiefs dissented, but Keokuk's oratory and his judicious distribution of gifts and favors undercut the opposition. They were given three years to relocate.

In the fall of 1845, after exploring the site, Keokuk led his following to their new home in east-central Kansas. During his last three years he saw conditions deteriorate rapidly for his people. Their new home was not as suitable for agriculture, and they hunted at the risk of clashing with tribes native to the area. As in Iowa, white intruders harassed them, and liquor vendors plied their trade. The political divisions among the tribes worsened, and most of the Fox either refused to leave Iowa or returned. Keokuk continued to cooperate with the government, further alienating members of the tribes.

Keokuk's death in Kansas was first attributed to poison and later to dysentery "brought on by a drunken frolic."

• For Keokuk's career prior to 1820, see *Black Hawk (Ma-Ka-Tai-Me-She-Kia-Kiak): An Autobiography*, ed. Donald Jackson (1955). William T. Hagan, *The Sac and Fox Indians* (1958), deals with Keokuk's role as tribal leader. Alvin M. Josephy, Jr., *The Patriot Chiefs: A Chronicle of American Indian Leadership* (1961), praises Black Hawk at the expense of Keokuk; Don Fixico, "The Black Hawk–Keokuk Controversy," in *Indian Leaders: Oklahoma's First Statesmen*, ed. H. Glenn Jordan and Thomas M. Holm (1979), sides with Keokuk. P. Richard Metcalf, "Who Should Rule at Home?: Native American Politics and Indian-White Relations," *Journal of American History* 61, no. 3 (1974): 651–65, emphasizes the importance of clan affiliation. Michael D. Green is also revisionist with his "'We Dance in Opposite Directions': Mesquakie (Fox) Separatism from the Sac and Fox Tribe," *Ethnohistory* 30 (1983): 129–40.

WILLIAM T. HAGAN

KEPHART, Ezekiel Boring (6 Nov. 1834–24 Jan. 1906), clergyman and college president, was born in Decatur Township, Clearfield County, Pennsylvania, the son of Henry Kephart and Sarah Goss, pioneer farmers. Kephart was raised in a log cabin on a mountain farm. His early education consisted of the daily lessons of pioneer living as well as several months each winter in a schoolhouse two miles from his home. When Kephart was fourteen, he and his elder brother began their own lumber business. They cut trees and constructed large timber rafts, which they navigated on adventurous journeys down the Susquehanna River. At the age of seventeen Kephart made a religious commitment to the Christian faith that prompted his ministerial interests.

A desire for further education led to Kephart's enrollment in Dickenson Seminary (Williamsport, Pa.) in the summer of 1856. In need of additional money, Kephart soon left Dickenson and returned to his home to raft timber. In the fall of 1857, along with his elder brother, Kephart entered Mount Pleasant College (Mount Pleasant, Pa.). This same year the college was merged with Otterbein College in Westerville, Ohio, and Kephart matriculated into Otterbein. Once again in financial need, he left Otterbein in 1858, returning to the lumber business and teaching in his childhood school. In January 1859 he was licensed to preach in the United Brethren denomination. Kephart was assigned to an itinerant preaching circuit in Troutville, Pennsylvania, and during the next three years he pastored churches in Johnstown, Altoona, and Greensburg. In 1860 he married Susan J. Trefts; they had four children, two of whom died in infancy.

In 1864 Kephart returned to Otterbein and received a B.S. degree in 1865. Upon graduation he spent one year as president of Collegiate Institute, a United Brethren college in Leoni, Michigan. He left this position as the school was unable to draw a sufficient number of students. In 1867 he pastored in the Mount Pleasant circuit of churches until receiving an appointment to the presidency of Western College (Western, Iowa). He remained the head of this United Brethren college from 1868 until 1881. A student of Kephart's remarked, "I was sometimes rude, he was always patient; discouraged, he would bear me up; and when I did wrong, he forgot it. As time goes on, I realize more and more how his influence in the earlier years has entered into the shaping of my life in these later years" (John, p. 142). While at Western College, Kephart earned from Otterbein College an A.B. in 1870, an A.M. in 1873, and a D.D. in 1881.

In addition to his duties as college president, Kephart served as an Iowa state senator from 1872 to 1876. He was the chairman of both the Committee on Temperance and the Committee to Investigate the Iowa State Agricultural College. His main interest and success as a senator was in sponsoring legislation for the improvement of public schools. In 1875–1876 the republican party asked him to accept their nomination for the Iowa governorship with a reasonably assured election, but he declined, stating that he had devoted his life to the Christian church. He also declined the nomination for the presidency of the Iowa State Agricultural College in 1877.

Kephart's most significant work was as a bishop of the United Brethren church. Initially elected in 1881, Kephart was reelected six times until he retired in 1905 with the status of bishop emeritus. As one of five presiding bishops, Kephart oversaw numerous districts, visiting churches and pastors regularly. He diligently worked to advance the educational interests of the church, vigorously supporting higher education. During the years of 1890 to 1893 he was selected to visit the denomination's overseas missions and made extensive and repeated trips to missionaries in Europe, Africa, and Palestine. While bishop, Kephart published four larger works, *Authenticity and Interpretation of the Holy Scriptures* (1889), *A Manual of Church Discipline* (1895), *Apologetics; or, A Treatise on Christian Evidences* (1901), and *A Brief Treatise on the Atonement* (1902). With these works he sought to elucidate central doctrines of the Christian faith as well as specific practices of the United Brethren denomination. He also earned an LL.D. from Lebanon Valley College. Upon his retirement he continued to reside in Annville, Pennsylvania.

Kephart was known as a man of deep character and was well liked because of his inner strength and friendliness. Nicholas Castle, who served with Kephart as bishop, wrote in remembrance of him: "He has left his mark on the whole denomination, as an educator, legislator, author, and bishop. He traveled widely, read and studied much and carefully, and stored a good memory with the richest treasures of thought, all of which gave him great brilliancy and force in the pulpit" (John, p. 18).

Kephart's influence in American history was primarily in his enthusiastic support of both private and public education and his leadership in the United Brethren church. Whether working as a college president, bishop, or state senator, he maintained a keen devotion to his Lord as well as the people he was called to serve. Kephart died unexpectedly while assisting in the promotion of the opening of Indiana Central College in Indianapolis.

• A complete biography of Kephart's life is L. F. John, *The Life of Ezekiel Boring Kephart* (1907). See also A. W. Drury, *History of the Church of the United Brethren in Christ* (1924). Obituaries are in *Religious Telescope*, 31 Jan. 1906; *Watchword*, 6 Feb. 1906; and the *Indianapolis News*, 25 Jan. 1906.

STEVEN L. PORTER

KEPLEY, Ada Harriet Miser (11 Feb. 1847–13 June 1925), lawyer and social reformer, was born in Somerset, Ohio, to Henry Miser and Ann Knowles. The family moved to St. Louis, Missouri, in 1860 and then to the pioneer village of Effingham, Illinois, in 1866. Her parents operated a hotel, and her father served as constable in the county until he died in 1872. Her mother ran the first book store and news depot in Effingham and was the proprietor of its second circulating library until she died in 1878.

Shortly after the family's move to Effingham, Ada met Henry B. Kepley, a solo law practitioner. They married in 1867. With her husband's encouragement, Kepley began to study law, first under his direction and then in a more formal setting, a one-year course at Union College of Law (Northwestern) in Chicago in 1869. When Ada Kepley received the LL.B. degree in June 1870, she became the first woman to graduate from a law school in the United States. Despite Kepley's educational achievement, Illinois state law denied her admission to the state bar because she was a woman. In response, Kepley's husband drafted a bill banning sex discrimination in professional occupations. The bill became state law in 1872, but Kepley, who was more interested in social reform than legal practice, did not apply for admission to the bar in Illinois until 1881, when she gained easy admission.

During the 1870s and 1880s, Kepley directed her reform efforts to suffrage, equal rights for women, and temperance. In 1881 she ran for state attorney general of Illinois on the Prohibition party ticket and used the campaign-generated publicity to promote temperance as well as to educate the populace about women's right to vote and to hold public office. As much as she was involved in the temperance work of the Prohibition party, she believed so strongly in the importance of women's suffrage that she left the party "when they threw the woman's ballot plank out."

Kepley, nevertheless, remained strongly committed to the cause of temperance. As a member of the Woman's Christian Temperance Union, she corresponded with national leaders and served in a few elected WCTU positions, but she did her most important work in her hometown of Effingham. In 1884, when Effingham's elected male officials denied the local branch of the WCTU access to town buildings for its meetings, Kepley, with her husband's assistance, purchased the Southern Methodist Church, converted it into a public meeting house, and made it the headquarters for the local WCTU. From 1885 to 1896 Kepley edited Effingham County's temperance paper, the *Friends of Home*, provoking rather than avoiding controversy in its pages. For the eleven years of her editorship, she endured ridicule from saloon keepers and many townspeople for publishing the names of men whom she witnessed frequenting saloons in town, persisting even after a liquor dealer's son tried to kill her in 1897. In 1892 Kepley became the minister of the socially progressive Unitarian Society and used her new position to publicize her temperance message.

One of Kepley's most ingenious contributions to temperance was the incorporation of children into her activism. Though she never had children of her own, she believed that they were the key to the success of the temperance movement. She organized local youths into study groups she called the "Band of Hope," where they learned about the dangers of alcohol. The Band of Hope accompanied Kepley to public temperance events, including WCTU-sponsored parades and picnics. Carrying dolls, toys, and pets as they marched, they were a poignant reminder to bystanders of the importance of temperance to America's future generations.

Kepley was tightly connected to a range of women's organizations. She was a member of the Equity Club, which was a national correspondence club of women lawyers, and of the Daughters of the American Revolution, the Eastern Star, and a local reading circle, the "High Cult Emerson Club." In 1895 she represented Effingham at the annual meeting of the Illinois Federation of Women's Clubs.

Following her husband's death in 1906, Kepley secluded herself on Kepley Spring Farm, a 200-acre livestock farm outside of Effingham. With the help of a foreman, she managed the farm but made poor business decisions. To save the farm and pay off her debts, she sold some of her property and she wrote an autobiography, *A Farm Philosopher: A Love Story* (1912). Despite her efforts, she could not raise enough money to pay off her debts; she ultimately sold the farm and moved to a small house in town.

In her later years, Kepley wandered around town in outdated and tattered dresses of velvet and brocade, carrying candy for children and food for dogs. When she became ill, her friends tried to help her, but she was too proud to accept their charity. She was eventually hospitalized as a charity patient and died a pauper in Effingham.

• Kepley's Equity Club letters and a biographical essay are in Virginia G. Drachman, ed., *Women Lawyers and the Origins of Professional Identity in America* (1993). Additional information is in Peggy Pulliam, "Effingham's Fighting Female," in *Effingham County, Illinois—Past and Present*, ed. Hilda Engbring Feldhake (1968); and Frances Willard and Mary Livermore, eds., *A Woman of the Century: Leading American Women* (1893). A description of Kepley's efforts to open the Illinois bar to women can be found in Lydia Hoyt Farmer, *The National Exposition Souvenir: What America Owes to Women* (1983).

VIRGINIA G. DRACHMAN

KEPPARD, Freddie (27 Feb. 1890–15 July 1933), cornetist, was born in New Orleans, Louisiana. His father was a cook; his parents' names are unknown. His older brother, guitarist and tuba player Louis Keppard, claimed that Freddie was born in 1889 and first played violin, then mandolin and accordion, though he is known to have played guitar. He took up cornet at the age of sixteen. According to Alphonse Picou, he first played cornet in public at a picnic when Manuel Perez became ill. Picking up Perez's cornet, he played blues. It was well received, and thereafter he put aside the guitar. Keppard studied cornet with Adolphe Alexander, Sr.

Details of his activities are confusing: accounts are casual and conflicting; bands shifted personnel to suit the circumstances of day-to-day life; and musicians and historians have tried to give contributions an enhanced significance by moving the chronology forward. Early on he played with Pops Foster and trombonist Willie Cornish. Substituting for Perez at Leonard Bechet's twenty-first birthday party in April 1907, he played with a young Sidney Bechet. Around this time he started and led the Olympia Orchestra, with either Picou, George Baquet, Bechet, or Jimmie Noone on clarinet. The flexibility of personnel was such that Freddie himself was sometimes replaced by Joe Oliver (not yet "King" Oliver). An engagement at the Tuxedo dance hall happened to anticipate the instrumentation of the Original Dixieland Jazz Band: cornet, clarinet, trombone, piano, and drums. Jelly Roll Morton places this event in 1908 (in Lomax), but the hall did not open until 1909.

Handing over leadership of the Olympia to violinist A. J. Piron, Keppard traveled to California to join bassist Bill Johnson in the Original Creole Orchestra (also known as the Creole Band, and similar titles) in the spring of 1914. From 1914 to 1918 the band toured on several vaudeville circuits and thereby disseminated an early jazz style nationwide before the first recordings by the Original Dixieland Jazz Band (1917). Initially its instrumentation was violin, cornet, clarinet, trombone, guitar, string bass, and drums. Violinist Jimmy Palao is sometimes called its leader, rather than Johnson, who is named as its manager. After a temporary breakup in 1917, the band resumed playing under Keppard's leadership in Chicago and then again on tour. During an engagement in New York (perhaps Dec. 1915 or Apr. 1917, or later still), Keppard declined an offer to record for the Victor label. Among the reasons given for this seemingly colossal mistake, including a fear that other musicians would copy his style, the most likely was a dispute over money (Chilton, *Bechet*, p. 31). These may all be excuses to hide a late and for some reason unacceptable effort: "Tack 'em Down," recorded by the unidentified Creole Jazz Band for Victor in New York on 2 December 1918, was never issued.

In 1918 Keppard settled in Chicago, where details of his activities continue to be confusing. The Original Creole Band disbanded in the spring, but Keppard worked briefly at the Royal Gardens with Johnson. He joined clarinetist Lawrence Duhé's band at the Dreamland Cafe. By the end of 1918 he was the leader at the De Luxe Gardens, billed as King Keppard to rival King Oliver, though on occasion he also played second trumpet in Oliver's own band at the Royal Gardens. At the De Luxe he was joined by Bechet, who temporarily left Duhé's band after an argument over wages. He worked at the Lorraine Club with Noone and concurrently with Mae Brady's band at Dreamland.

Keppard joined Doc Cooke's theater orchestra for two years beginning in the fall of 1922, except for a period with Erskine Tate's Vendome Orchestra, and in June 1923 he recorded two titles with a group drawn from Tate's orchestra. He worked occasionally with pianist Tony Jackson and was a member of Johnny Dodds's group at Burt Kelly's Stable intermittently for six years starting in 1924. He rejoined Cooke from late 1925 to early 1926 before recording four titles, including "Here Comes the Hot Tamale Man," with Noone and Johnny St. Cyr in a small group under Cooke's name, but without Cooke, in June 1926. Tracks from that same period by pianist Jimmy Blythe, "Messin Around" [*sic*] and "Adams Apple" [*sic*], have been cited as evidence of Keppard's declining abilities, but it is now believed that the unidentified and incompetent cornetist is not Keppard. After leading his own band and making his only recordings as a leader in September 1926, he rejoined Cooke from spring 1927 until September of that year. He was again briefly with Tate in early 1928. He led a band in spring 1928, worked with reed player Jerome Don Pasquall late that year, and toured Illinois and Indiana with his own band. Returning to Chicago, he joined Charlie Elgar at the Savoy Ballroom. Keppard died in Chicago of tuberculosis. He was survived by his wife; details of this marriage are unknown.

According to Morton, Keppard was "about my colour [Morton was light-skinned], Creole accent, a good spender, wore plenty nice clothes, had women hanging around all day long, liked to drink a lot" (Lomax, p. 154). Singer Lizzie Miles reported that he was clannish and always spoke to her in patois to prevent others from eavesdropping (Chilton, *Bechet*, p. 30). Acclaimed for his powerful playing, he "could play any kind of song good. Technique, attack, tone, and ideas were all there" (cornetist Thomas "Mutt" Carey, quoted in Shapiro and Hentoff, p. 45). In addition to improvisatory skills, he had the aural equivalent of a photographic memory, and in an attempt to hide his inability to read music, he would make excuses for not playing a piece the first time through, only to play it perfectly the next time.

With Keppard having recorded only infrequently and late in his career, there is no surviving aural evidence of his contributions as one of the first "kings" of the jazz cornet. Nevertheless his brief session as a leader in 1926 has sometimes been underappreciated in the literature. For recordings made at a time when the genius of Louis Armstrong was already well documented, one cannot get carried away with praise, but certainly Keppard's impressive playing requires no apology. At the opening of "Stockyard Strut" he presents a dignified, polished, relaxed, in-tune, and rhythmically foursquare melody suggesting classic ragtime. Later he loosens the reins to incorporate moments of creative improvisation, sliding "blue notes," and a gentle swing. This contrast is carried further on two versions of "Salty Dog," where Keppard shows himself to be fully in control of the blues idiom and additionally shows sensitivity to instrumental balance by complementing rather than dominating solos by clarinetist Johnny Dodds and singer Papa Charlie Jackson.

• Nat Shapiro and Nat Hentoff, eds., *Hear Me Talkin' to Ya: The Story of Jazz as Told by the Men Who Made It* (1955), collects remembrances (some previously published) from several musicians with whom Keppard played. A documentary account of the Creole Band is Samuel B. Charters and Leonard Kunstadt, *Jazz: A History of the New York Scene* (1962). Andy Ridley, "The Keppard Brothers," *Footnote* 19, no. 3 (Feb.–Mar. 1988): 4–9, supplies an overview, with all the attendant and difficult problems regarding chronology and affiliations. The most accurate overview is in John Chilton, *Who's Who of Jazz: Storyville to Swing Street* (1985).

Two taped interviews with Louis Keppard (4 Aug. 1957; 19 Jan. 1961) are in the archives of Tulane University; for a transcript of the latter, see the microform *New York Times Oral History Program: New Orleans Jazz Oral History Collection* (1979), no. 6, chap. 89. Bocage's Memories of Keppard, taped 29 Jan. 1959, also are at Tulane; for a transcript, see the microform *New York Times Oral History Program: New Orleans Jazz Oral History Collection* (1978), no. 8. Keppard's years in New Orleans are remembered in Alan Lomax, *Mister Jelly Roll: The Fortunes of Jelly Roll Morton, New Orleans Creole and "Inventor of Jazz"* (1950), pp. 126, 153–55; Johnny St. Cyr's unfinished biography, "Jazz as I Remember It, Part One: Early Days," *Jazz Journal* 19, no. 9 (Sept. 1966): 6–8, 10; and Donald M. Marquis's documentary study, *In Search of Buddy Bolden: First Man of Jazz* (1978). Details of Keppard's personality and of his associations with Bechet appear in the first four chapters of John Chilton, *Sidney Bechet: The Wizard of Jazz* (1987). Lawrence Gushee investigates the murky history of "How the Creole Band Came to Be" in *Black Music Research Journal* 8, no. 1 (1988): 83–100. Details of Keppard's later years appear in Albert McCarthy, *Big Band Jazz* (1974), pp. 21–25, and in St. Cyr, "Jazz as I Remember It, Part Four: Chicago Days," *Jazz Journal* 20, no. 1 (Jan. 1967): 14–16.

BARRY KERNFELD

KEPPEL, Francis C. (16 Apr. 1916–19 Feb. 1990), educational administrator, was born in New York City, the son of Frederick Paul Keppel and Helen Tracy Brown. His father was dean of Columbia College and in 1923 became president of the Carnegie Corporation of New York.

Francis Keppel was brought up in New York City in an intellectual atmosphere characterized by concern for educational reform. He attended the Groton School in Massachusetts and in 1934 entered Harvard, where he received a B.A. Despite his positions as a graduate dean and then as a U.S. commissioner of education, the B.A. was his highest earned degree. During his undergraduate years he studied sculpture privately, and after graduation he moved to Rome, where he continued this pursuit at the American Academy. He returned home after a year, having decided his talent was not of the highest caliber, and took a position at Harvard as assistant dean of freshmen, a position he held from 1939 to 1941. Keppel married Edith Moulton Sawin in 1941. They had two children.

During World War II Keppel was secretary of the Joint Army-Navy Committee on Welfare and Recreation in Washington, D.C.; later, with the rank of private, he entered the U.S. Army's Information and Education Division, from which he was discharged in 1946 as a first lieutenant. He then returned to Harvard as assistant to the provost. Two years later he became dean of the Graduate School of Education, continuing in that position until he was selected by President John F. Kennedy to be U.S. commissioner of education in 1962. While at Harvard, he was appointed by President Harry Truman to the Committee on Religion and Welfare. In 1956 he was named to the executive committee of the National Council of Administrative

Leadership, followed in 1957 by his appointment as chairman of the Council of Cooperation in Teacher Education. In 1960 he was invited to serve on President Kennedy's Taskforce on Education.

During Keppel's tenure at Harvard University, student enrollment quadrupled, as did the size of the faculty, while the endowment more than doubled. Keppel is given credit for having revitalized the master of arts in teaching (MAT) degree. The underlying idea of the MAT was to attract promising liberal-arts graduates to prepare for careers in teaching. He also sponsored innovative programs in team teaching, programmed learning, and the use of television in education.

As U.S. commissioner of education, Keppel led the drive for passage of the Elementary and Secondary Education Act of 1965; he was known throughout his life as a strong proponent of programs designed to improve the learning opportunities of poor children. He is also credited with having facilitated the passage of the Higher Education Facilities Act, the Manpower Training and Development Act, and the Library Services Act. While at the head of the U.S. Office of Education, Keppel vigorously enforced the provisions for equal educational opportunity contained in the 1964 Civil Rights Act by threatening to withhold federal aid from racially-segregated school systems. With the establishment of a cabinet-level office for health, education, and welfare, he was named assistant secretary for education in 1965.

Keppel left government in 1966 to become chairman and chief executive officer of the General Learning Corporation, a joint venture of General Electric and Time, Inc. He held this position until 1974, when he became director of the Aspen Institute for Humanistic Studies for a Changing Society. He also served as a member of the Harvard University board of overseers from 1967 to 1973.

In 1977 Keppel took up duties as a senior lecturer at Harvard University. He continued active teaching until his death in Cambridge, Massachusetts.

• Keppel authored *Necessary Revolution in American Education* (1966) and *Personnel Policies for Public Education* (1961). Contemporary assessments of his role in the John Kennedy and Lyndon Johnson administrations may be found in Eugene Eidenberg and Roy D. Morey, eds., *Act of Congress: The Legislative Process and the Making of Educational Policy* (1969), and Nelsen Lichtenstein, *Political Profiles: The Kennedy Years* (1965). Information concerning Keppel's professional life after he left government and the Office of Education is in Nancy Hoffman and Robert Schwartz, "Remembrance of Things Past: An Interview with Francis Keppel and Harold Howe II," *Change* 22 (Mar.–Apr. 1990): 52–57. An obituary is in the *New York Times*, 20 Feb. 1990.

WILMA S. LONGSTREET

KEPPEL, Frederick Paul (2 July 1875–8 Feb. 1943), educator and foundation executive, was born on Staten Island, New York, the elder son of Frederick Keppel and Frances Matilda Vickery, both natives of Ireland. His father was a successful art dealer. Keppel grew up in a genteel Protestant family of comfortable means. After a short stint working in the stockroom of his father's business, he entered Columbia College, where he edited the college newspaper, helped start a poetry magazine, rowed on the Columbia crew, and was also an excellent student. After receiving the A.B. in 1898, he worked briefly for the publishers Harper & Brothers and then, in 1900, returned to Columbia.

Keppel served as assistant secretary (1900–1902), secretary (1902–1910), and then as dean of Columbia College (1910–1917). His greatest accomplishments as dean had to do with establishing procedures to ensure that students received the necessary advice and assistance. In 1906 he married Helen Tracey Brown, a niece of J. P. Morgan (1837–1913). The couple had five children. They lived on a large estate in Montrose, New York, surrounded by friends. Keppel enjoyed country living, especially planting trees or creating vistas through the woods.

Keppel left Columbia in 1918 to assist Secretary of War Newton D. Baker in Washington, D.C., rising within a year to the newly created position of third assistant secretary of war. He worked closely with Raymond Fosdick, later president of the Rockefeller Foundation, in developing recreation and educational programs for the troops. After the war, he was employed briefly by the American Red Cross and then the International Chamber of Commerce in Paris. Finally, in December 1922, he was appointed president of the Carnegie Corporation of New York. He remained in the post until 1941.

The Carnegie Corporation, established in 1911 as the last and largest of the philanthropic trusts created by the steel magnate Andrew Carnegie, had an original endowment of $125 million (to which $10 million was added after Carnegie's death in 1919). Its mandate was broad: "to promote the advancement and diffusion of knowledge and understanding." Keppel, its fourth president, immediately transformed the foundation's character, turning what had been an austere, formal institution into one that an associate described as "the most informal and friendly in the business" (John M. Russell, "Inside FPK," in *Appreciations of Frederick Paul Keppel by Some of His Friends* [1951], p. 74). Owing to financial constraints and in order to pursue his own interests, he also changed the pattern of grant making. Large, institution-building grants were replaced by more numerous small grants, and the corporation's initial interest in developing science and professional expertise was replaced by a new interest in promoting adult education and disseminating high culture.

Under Keppel's leadership, the corporation sought to develop professional standards for librarianship, as part of the effort endowing the Graduate Library School at the University of Chicago. Following interests Keppel had developed during the First World War, it also organized the American Association for Adult Education to administer a wide-ranging program of grants that supported activities ranging from lectures at the People's Institute in New York City to summer workshops for world leaders in Williamstown, Massachusetts. Another area of central concern was the arts, which the corporation assisted through grants to individuals, through the distribution of educational materials to schools and colleges, and through assistance to organizations like the American Federation of the Arts and the American Association of Museums.

Although Keppel tried to focus the corporation's grants into clearly defined programs, his inclination toward generosity resulted in what associates called "scatteration"—many small grants to a great variety of individuals and causes. The wide distribution of funds combined with Keppel's open personality and his many speeches and published essays, which appeared in Carnegie Corporation *Annual Reports* and several books—notably *The Foundation: Its Place in American Life* (1930) and *Philanthropy and Learning* (1936)—all contributed to public acceptance of "the foundation" as an important institution of American philanthropy. Although Keppel was widely recognized in his day, his reputation was not long lived. As is often the case with foundation executives, his accomplishments as president of the Carnegie Corporation are remembered in connection with Andrew Carnegie's name.

Keppel, who was widely known as "FPK," was genial, urbane, and fun-loving. As a result of his generosity, friendliness, and charm, he was held in great affection by a wide circle of acquaintances. He was a member of many clubs and organizations and especially enjoyed the Century Association in New York City, where he usually met friends for lunch. But despite his "love of people and his gaiety," a lifelong friend observed, he "had a high, stern Scotch-Irish covenanting spirit" (R. C. Leffingwell, "Postscript," in *Appreciations*, p. 123).

This aspect of Keppel's personality played an important role in the most famous project undertaken by the Carnegie Corporation during his presidency. This was the classic study of race relations in the United States, *An American Dilemma: The Negro Problem and Modern Democracy*, by the Swedish economist Gunnar Myrdal (1944). The study originated in Carnegie Corporation trustee interest in the possibilities of developing adult education programs for black Americans. Its focus changed dramatically after Myrdal was selected to conduct the inquiry and redefined the scope and focus of the investigation. Often overwhelmed by what he observed as he traveled through the South, Myrdal sometimes despaired of finishing the book and worried about the consequences of reporting what he had seen. "If I was afraid, Keppel was not," he wrote later. "The facts were before me. My job was . . . to discover the truth for myself, without side glances toward what might be politically desirable or possible" (Gunnar Myrdal, "Author's Preface to the Twentieth Anniversary Dedication," *An American Dilemma* [1962], pp. xxv–xxvi).

In October 1942 Keppel left the Carnegie Corporation to join the President's Committee on War Relief Agencies and then to work for the State Department's

Board of Appeals on Visa Cases. He died in New York City. He had suffered a heart attack during one of his many trips between Washington, D.C., and New York and died almost immediately.

• There is a collection of Keppel papers in the Rare Book and Manuscript Library of Butler Library at Columbia University, which also houses the records of the Carnegie Corporation of New York, including Keppel memoranda and correspondence. In addition to books cited in the text, biographical information is available in David Keppel, *FPK* (privately printed, 1950). Along with the *Annual Reports* and the two books cited, Keppel wrote *The Arts in American Life* (with R. L. Duffus) (1933) and *Education for Adults and Other Essays* (1926). On the Carnegie Corporation and Keppel's role in it, see Ellen Condliffe Lagemann, *The Politics of Knowledge: The Carnegie Corporation, Philanthropy, and Public Policy* (1989).

ELLEN CONDLIFFE LAGEMANN

KEPPLER, Joseph (1 Feb. 1838–19 Feb. 1894), political cartoonist, was born in Vienna, Austria, the son of Johann Keppler, a confectioner, and Josepha Pellwein. The modest circumstances of Keppler's family forced him to earn money for his art studies by joining several traveling theatrical companies in the Austro-Hungarian empire. Keppler was not only a promising artist but a talented actor as well. In 1856 he enrolled in the Akademie der Bildenden Künste in Vienna, where he gained a strong education in the German style of cartoon art. He later worked briefly as a staff artist on the Viennese humor magazine *Kikeriki* (Cock-a-doodle-do). During this period Keppler traveled throughout Europe, gaining recognition as an actor. In 1864 he married a 23-year-old Viennese actress, Minna Rubens. The Kepplers had twins in 1867, but both died shortly after birth, and Keppler's father urged them to make a fresh start in the United States. Johann Keppler had emigrated after the revolution of 1848 to New Frankfort, Salina County, Missouri, where he ran a general store and farmed. Keppler followed his father to America in 1867 and settled in St. Louis, Missouri, which had a large German colony. Sadly, Minna Keppler died of tuberculosis in December 1870, but in 1871 Keppler married Pauline Pfau of St. Louis, and they later had three children.

Keppler had planned to attend medical school but instead found work first as an actor and later as a theater manager. He also wanted to publish his own humor magazine. His first attempts, *Die Vehme* (The star chamber) in 1869 and *Puck* in 1871, were published in German in St. Louis. Both magazines lasted less than a year but brought him to the attention of Frank Leslie, and English engraver who had emigrated to the United States and become the publisher of many periodicals, among them *Frank Leslie's Illustrated Newspaper*, a popular weekly. Leslie offered Keppler a position in New York, after the failure of *Puck*, in 1872.

Keppler moved to New York, and by 1875 he was in charge of drawing most of the cover cartoons for *Frank Leslie's Illustrated Newspaper*. Keppler specialized in cartoons that attacked President Ulysses S. Grant and

political graft. Despite his success, he still wanted a magazine of his own, and in 1876 he founded a second *Puck*. Adolph Schwarzmann, a printer and the publisher of *Muzik Zeitung*, a weekly devoted to New York music and opera, supplied the capital while Keppler had complete editorial control. Initially a German-language publication, *Puck* was so popular that Keppler published an English edition in 1877. It lasted until 1918, twenty-two years longer than the German version.

Keppler's fresh style, which combined German caricature with beauty of line and a keen sense of satire, set his work apart from that of his main rival, Thomas Nast. Grant was Nast's hero, while Keppler lost no opportunity to criticize the president. He was also a master of lithography, first in black and white and later in color, while Nast used the tighter lines of woodblocks.

The success of *Puck* attracted contributions from well-known American artists including Eugene Zimmerman and Bernard Gilliam, and Keppler hired the young, talented Henry Cuyler Bunner as assistant editor for *Puck*. Bunner, a scion of a prominent New England family fallen on hard times, had a talent for directing *Puck* toward the popular social issues of the day, such as woman suffrage, machine politics, and school conditions. Critics said that Keppler took his ideas from others and merely drew the cartoons, but Keppler always had the last word on *Puck*'s content. His large cartoons featured many recognizable figures drawn in a sweeping, romantic style. Between 1878 and 1879 *Puck* jibed at the Mormons, Henry Ward Beecher, the Catholic church, and certain immigrant groups, especially the Chinese and Irish. The journal alternately supported and ridiculed American reformers and mocked Thomas Edison for his unscrupulous business practices.

The election of 1880 consolidated *Puck*'s position as the premier interpreter of the American scene. The campaign inspired one of Keppler's most popular cartoons, "Forbidding the Banns," an indictment of James Garfield's participation in the Crédit Mobilier scandal. In the 1884 presidential campaign, *Puck* supported Grover Cleveland. James Blaine, the Republican candidate, was constantly ridiculed by *Puck*'s cartoonists. The magazine ran a cartoon of Blaine clad only in undershorts, his body tattooed with his political sins. Probably *Puck*'s most effective cartoon, it was gleefully distributed by the Democrats. Later, President Cleveland acknowledged the importance of the journal to his election. *Puck*'s circulation increased 10,000 copies per week during this race.

In 1885 Keppler built the *Puck* building in lower Manhattan, featuring two large statues, six and ten feet tall, of Keppler's trademark, the Shakespearean cupid Puck. Both held a banner with the motto "What fools these mortals be!" The building became a New York City landmark.

Puck continued as a relatively nonpartisan champion of social and political reform until the late 1890s. In 1893 Keppler brought *Puck* to the World's Columbian

Exposition in Chicago. *Puck*'s World's Fair Edition was published in a crowded, poorly ventilated building on the Chicago fairgrounds during the length of the exposition. Stress and exhaustion from this experience damaged Keppler's health, and he died at home in New York City. The magazine declined steadily after his death and that of Bunner, two years later. He left an estate estimated at $500,000.

Thomas Nast, Keppler's greatest rival, saw the world in black and white. He believed passionately in his causes, and he viewed life as a constant struggle against good and evil; however, Nast's values were formed during the idealistic Civil War years. Keppler came to the United States during the Gilded Age, a period noted for its corruption. He was a skeptical and cynical man who lacked the powerful convictions of Nast and used his pen to satirize all sides. His style was less harsh than Nast's and seldom without humor, serving as a model for modern cartoonists such as Jeff McNelly and Mike Lukovich.

• Keppler's death mask, family papers, memorabilia, and a few original cartoons are at the New-York Historical Society; other collections are at the New York Public Library and in private hands. Bibliographical information can be found in H. C. Bunner, *A Selection of Cartoons from Puck by Jos. Keppler* (1893); A. B. Maurice and F. T. Cooper, *The History of the Nineteenth Century in Caricature* (1904); Frank Weitenkampf, *American Graphic Art* (1912); Richard S. West, *Satire on Stone: The Political Cartoons of Joseph Keppler* (1988); Richard Marschall, "A History of the Comic Strip," pt. 1, "*Puck* Magazine and the Ascendance of the Cartoon," *Comics Journal*, Sept. 1980, pp. 132–39, and Marschall, "The Stage Is Set: The History of the Comic Strip," pt. 2, "The Decline and Death of *Puck* Magazine," *Comics Journal*, Oct. 1980, pp. 84–87. Obituaries are in the *New York Times*, the *New York Herald*, the *New York Tribune*, and the *New York World*, all 20 Feb. 1894.

ELSA A. NYSTROM

KERBY, William Joseph (20 Feb. 1870–27 July 1936), Catholic priest and promoter of professional social work, was born in Lawler, Iowa, the son of Irish immigrants Daniel P. Kerby, a prosperous banker, and Ellen Rockford. One of ten children, he attended St. Joseph's (now Loras) College in Dubuque. After graduating in 1889, he entered St. Francis de Sales Seminary in Milwaukee and was ordained a priest for the Diocese of Dubuque on 21 December 1892. He then continued the study of theology at the recently opened Catholic University of America in Washington, D.C., where the relatively liberal Belgian professor Thomas J. Bouquillon impressed on him the importance of the social sciences for the moral theologian; he received the S.T.L. degree in 1894. In 1902, when the Diocese of Sioux City, Iowa, was established, Kerby was attached to it.

Invited to prepare himself for a teaching career at the Catholic University, he studied sociology in Louvain, Berlin, and Bonn and was awarded a doctorate in social and political sciences by the Catholic University of Louvain in 1897; his published dissertation was titled *Le Socialisme aux États-Unis* (Socialism in the United States [1897]). He was then appointed an associate professor of sociology at the Catholic University of America and head of the department; he was promoted to the rank of ordinary professor in 1906. He remained department head until 1933 and continued to teach until he died. He also taught courses and exerted a strong influence at Trinity College in Washington, D.C., for three decades following its opening in November 1900, thus promoting the higher education of women.

Kerby became widely known as a lecturer and writer. His thinking was both original and progressive, combining advocacy of social justice and reform with orthodoxy in faith and tradition in devotion. In numerous articles he contributed to the development of Catholic social theory and practice. From the standpoint of the gospel teaching that those who are strong have a moral obligation to help those who are weak, he argued in favor of social reform. His best-known book, *The Social Mission of Charity* (1921), has been called a milestone in American Catholic social work. From 1911 to 1917 he was editor of the *St. Vincent de Paul Quarterly*, the information bulletin of the eponymous society of which he had been a member since his youth.

Early on, Kerby became involved in efforts to organize Catholic charity work and to make social work not simply a profession, but also a movement for social reform. At the same time, he tried to move his co-religionists from their traditional preference for private, local charitable or relief activities to an acceptance of a scientific approach to curing the ills of society as a whole. He pursued this goal through three major initiatives.

First, he played the principal role in founding the National Conference of Catholic Charities in 1910. Kerby was elected secretary of the executive committee and held that office for ten years. In addition to managing the biennial meetings, he worked to bring structure and professionalism to Catholic social work and to overcome conservative attitudes and the general apathy of American Catholics toward social problems. He made the conference a sounding board and a clearinghouse for the exchange of ideas and mutual aid and a channel of Catholic views to the federal government. As a means of publishing scholarly studies and statistical research he launched the *Catholic Charities Review* in 1916.

Second, after the United States entered World War I, Kerby met with two other priests and a layman in order to consolidate the activities of scattered Catholic bodies under a central direction. The result was the founding in 1917 of the National Catholic War Council under the auspices of the American hierarchy. Kerby was a member of the council's Committee on Special War Activities and chairman of the Subcommittee on Women's Activities. In the latter position he strove first to identify and register the 4,470 organizations of Catholic women and then to coordinate their activities and to foster communication among them.

The subcommittee opened and administered visitors' houses (for relatives and friends of servicemen) and community houses and girls' clubs (for young women employed in war industries or reconstruction); it arranged for the overseas work of Catholic women, and it operated a personnel bureau for trained social workers, whom Kerby appointed to positions as needed. When the subcommittee was dissolved in August 1920, the National Council of Catholic Women was founded, and Kerby became its moderator.

Third, after the war he was instrumental in founding, under the aegis of the National Council of Catholic Women, the National Catholic School of Social Service in Washington, D.C., as a permanent institution for training social welfare workers; opened in 1918, it was the first residential professional school of social work for women. Kerby taught sociology at the school until 1933 and, beginning in February 1924, was acting director for five and a half years, increasing enrollment and raising standards. When a board of trustees was established in 1925, he became its vice president and retained that office until his death.

Kerby was also engaged in related work outside the Catholic church. In 1919 he became a member of the White House Conference on Standards of Child Welfare. In 1920 President Woodrow Wilson appointed him to the Board of Charities for Washington, D.C., and Presidents Warren G. Harding in 1923 and Calvin Coolidge in 1926 renewed the three-year appointment. In 1934 he was asked by aides of Franklin D. Roosevelt to support the National Recovery Administration publicly; complying, he delivered a radio address on a nationwide hook-up, explaining the difference in approach to social justice between the New Deal and the previous economic programs. He also encouraged Catholics to cooperate with their fellow citizens in charitable undertakings.

During the Great Depression Kerby came to admit the necessity of greater state intervention for the achievement of social reform. He no longer thought that state action should be a last resort, infrequent and minimal in extent, that private charity should be preferred, and that the state should not initiate or administer programs but rather should merely protect the rights of those in need. After 1929 he advocated government intervention to alleviate the widespread and chronic misery. His recommendation of social legislation provoked the criticism of some Catholics, but he vigorously defended his position. He also changed his opinion regarding the causes of poverty. Previously he had held that poor people were in part to blame for their condition because of sin, especially sloth and intemperance; now he recognized that many people were indigent not because they lacked virtue or industriousness but because they could not secure employment and earn their livelihood.

After World War I Kerby had begun to write more on spiritual topics, especially for priests. Two collections of his previously published articles for priests, *Prophets of the Better Hope* (1922) and *The Considerate Priest* (1937), became popular books, and he became one of the most sought-after preachers of retreats for priests in the country. In 1927 he assumed the editorship of the *Ecclesiastical Review*, a monthly for priests, and held it for the rest of his life.

In 1934 Kerby was awarded the honorary rank of Domestic Prelate of His Holiness with the title of Right Reverend Monsignor. He died in Washington, D.C., and was buried in Sioux City. Six years later the William J. Kerby Foundation was established to further appreciation of the essential relationship between democratic belief in human dignity and the basic teachings of Christianity. The foundation pursued this aim through publications and by supplying scholarship funds for lay students of social work.

Kerby was noted for his gentleness and humility, his loyalty to friends, helpfulness to students, and kindness to all, his preference for simplicity and solitude, and his fidelity to priestly ideals. Throughout his life he strove to unite charity and science (or, as he used to say, to foster "scientific charity"), theology and sociology, Christianity and philanthropy, religion and scholarship. He emphasized the value of education in the pursuit of social reform, proclaimed the rights and duties of the laity in the church and in society, and especially extolled the role of women in modern life. Finally, he stimulated the clergy to a keener awareness of their responsibility for leadership in the social movement. He was a pioneer in the arousing of the American Catholic social conscience.

• Kerby's papers are deposited at the Catholic University of America. He has been the subject of two M.A. theses written at the same university: Sister Mary Klein, "A Bio-Bibliography of William J. Kerby" (1955), and Timothy M. Dolan, "Prophet of a Better Hope: The Life and Work of Monsignor William Joseph Kerby" (1981), and of one S.T.L. thesis, Robert E. Harahan, "The Social Ethics of William J. Kerby" (1980). He and one of his students are the subject of a Ph.D. dissertation by Bruce H. Lescher, "The Spiritual Life and Social Action in American Catholic Spirituality: William J. Kerby and Paul Hanley Furfey" (Graduate Theological Union, 1991). Some of his main accomplishments are treated by Loretto R. Lawler, *Full Circle: The Story of the National Catholic School of Social Service* (1951), and Donald P. Gavin, *The National Conference of Catholic Charities, 1910–1960* (1962). His educational work is evaluated in several books written about his institution, most notably C. Joseph Nuesse, *The Catholic University of America: A Centennial History* (1990). See also, John J. Burke, C.S.P., "An Appreciation," *American Ecclesiastical Review* 95 (Sept. 1936): 225–33. An obituary is in the *New York Times*, 28 July 1936.

ROBERT TRISCO

KERN, Edward Meyer (26 Oct. 1823–23 Nov. 1863), **Richard Hovendon Kern** (11 Apr. 1821–26 Oct. 1853), and **Benjamin Jordan Kern** (3 Aug. 1818–14 Mar. 1849), artists and explorers, were born in Philadelphia, Pennsylvania, the sons of John Kern III, a customs house collector for the Port of Philadelphia, and Mary Elizabeth Bignell. The Kerns' eight children were well educated and trained in the arts and sciences. Three of the boys (John IV, Edward, and Richard) were artists, and Benjamin earned an M.D. from the Pennsylvania Medical College.

Edward and Richard taught drawing from their house on Filbert Street and in schools such as the Franklin Institute. It was Edward who first broke away, joining John Charles Frémont on his third western expedition in 1845. The party left Westport (Kansas City) in June, amid expansionist tensions concerning the future of the northern Mexican provinces. The scientific expedition was thus large (sixty men) and well armed. In the field Edward sketched Indians, campsites, flora, and fauna, aided Frémont with the cartography, and collected specimens of plants and animals, which he sent to eastern scientists by way of his brothers in Philadelphia.

East of the Sierras the expedition split. Frémont led one group directly across the mountains. He gave Kern the chief responsibility for the other, and with Old Joe Walker as their guide they crossed the Sierras at what became known as Walker Pass and followed a river that flows into Tulare Lake. Not realizing there were two such rivers (the King's and the Kern), the parties did not meet as planned, but the unmapped river on which Kern camped was named by Frémont in his honor. Thus the Kern River, Kern County, and all their derivatives became memorials to Edward.

Once in California with the Mexican War imminent, the scientific expedition was transformed into an instrument of conquest. During the Bear Flag Revolt of 1846 Frémont placed Kern in command of Fort Sutter, where captives, including General Mariano Vallejo, were imprisoned. As commander of the fort, Kern dealt with Indians, raised recruits for the fighting, and organized relief for the ill-fated Donner Party.

After the war Edward returned home by sea. He and his brothers, Richard, the artist, and Benjamin, the medical doctor, had been elected to the Philadelphia Academy of Natural Sciences. With such credentials the three offered themselves for positions as artists-scientists and doctor for Frémont's fourth expedition. This venture was a privately financed attempt to prove the feasibility of a winter railroad across the southern Rockies. Thirty-three men, including the Kern brothers, assaulted the wintry mountains west of Pueblo, Colorado, along the thirty-eighth parallel. In the San Juan Range they encountered the most severe storms in memory. Frémont doggedly refused advice to retreat or change their course until toward the end of December the men and animals began to give out. Eventually almost one-third of the expedition perished. The remaining ragged groups, struggling down the mountains without their leader (Frémont had traveled ahead), were finally rescued in late January. The experience left the Kerns bitterly resentful of Frémont's judgment and behavior.

Stranded in Taos, the brothers were anxious to return home, but they needed their possessions, which had been cached in the snows. With the first thawing, Ben Kern and Bill Williams, the guide, returned to the Rockies, found their belongings, and were ready to return. But on 14 March 1849 a band of Ute, incensed by a recent army atrocity committed on their tribe, came across the two men and in a fit of vengeance murdered them.

Edward and Richard were now stranded in New Mexico. By a happy coincidence, Lieutenant James Harvey Simpson had just arrived, desperately needing draftsmen to complete the report on his route from Fort Smith. Completing that task, the Kerns were commissioned as cartographers and artists by Colonel John M. Washington for a major punitive expedition into the heart of the Navajo country. They recorded ethnographic details, made some of the earliest drawings of ancient pueblo ruins in Chaco Canyon and Canyon de Chelly, and sketched the Zuñi pueblo and Morro Rock.

During 1850 the two Kerns were employed by successive army expeditions passing through New Mexico. Singly or together they worked for Lieutenant Simpson, Lieutenant John Parke, Lieutenant John Pope, and Captain Henry Judd. In August 1851 they finally left Santa Fe on separate expeditions. Edward joined Lieutenant John Pope on a reconnaissance from Santa Fe to Fort Leavenworth. Dick moved west with Lieutenant Lorenzo Sitgreaves exploring the Little Colorado River.

Back home in Philadelphia the field skills of Edward and Richard made them logical choices for further exploring expeditions. Dick went west on one of the Pacific Railroad surveys of 1853, that of Captain John W. Gunnison along the thirty-eighth parallel. On this expedition he and Gunnison were together killed by Ute not far from the continental divide, where Ben had been struck down.

In June 1853 Edward sailed aboard the USS *Vincennes* on the North Pacific Exploring Expedition under Commander Cadwalader Ringgold and, later, Lieutenant John Rodgers. Edward added taxidermy and photography to his scientific and artistic pursuits. The expedition surveyed coasts from Hong Kong, the Bonins, Okinawa, and Japan to the mainland of Siberia. Their purpose was to make possible an increasing trade with the Far East implied by Matthew Perry's concurrent opening of Japan. It was two years before the *Vincennes* returned to San Francisco.

In 1858 Edward signed on the USS *Fenimore Cooper* as cartographer and artist for Lieutenant John Brooke in the first extensive surveys of the route from San Francisco to China. Stranded in Japan by an accident to their ship, they returned aboard the first Japanese naval vessel to visit the United States, the *Kanrin Maru*.

In the Civil War Edward was irregularly commissioned as captain of topographical engineers and enlisted in the Army of the West under his idol and erstwhile antagonist, John Charles Frémont. Edward served in St. Louis for four months until Frémont was recalled by President Abraham Lincoln in November 1861. Returning discouraged to Philadelphia, he set up as a teacher of drawing, resuming the role he had played when he first left for the West. Only forty years old, he died two years later of epileptic convulsions at his home in Philadelphia.

The three brothers, all short-lived, made their mark on the science and art of the American West. Their maps and lithographs contributed significantly to the work of Frémont, Pope, Washington, Simpson, Sitgreaves, Rodgers, and Brooke, and their collections in the field enhanced the studies of eastern scientists such as Joseph Leidy and Henry Schoolcraft.

• The most extensive Kern papers, including the Fort Sutter Papers and other journals and letters, are in the Huntington Library, San Marino, Calif. Edward and Richard both have modern biographies, Robert V. Hine, *In the Shadow of Frémont: Edward Kern and the Art of American Exploration, 1845–1860* (1982), and David J. Weber, *Richard H. Kern: Expeditionary Artist in the Far Southwest, 1848–1853* (1985). Compare the earlier William J. Heffernan, *Edward M. Kern: The Travels of an Artist-Explorer* (1953).

ROBERT V. HINE

KERN, Jerome (27 Jan. 1885–11 Nov. 1945), composer, was born Jerome David Kern in New York City, the son of Henry Kern, a merchant, and Fannie Kakeles, both from immigrant German Jewish families. The family moved to Newark in 1897, and, after graduating from Thirteenth Avenue School in 1899, Kern entered Newark High School, where his early attempts at composition were performed. Anxious to become a songwriter, in 1902 he gained an introduction to the publisher Edward B. Marks, who gave him a job making out bills and invoices and also issued Kern's first published compositions. Under his mother's guidance, he had become a highly proficient pianist, and in 1902–1903 he studied harmony, theory, and composition at the New York College of Music. He apparently also studied music theory and composition briefly near Heidelberg. Around 1903–1904 Kern came into an inheritance and sought to buy a junior partnership in Marks's firm but was refused. In 1904, therefore, Kern joined the firm of T. B. Harms, which remained his publisher for the rest of his career.

Kern worked as a song plugger, demonstrating new songs, for Harms and as a rehearsal pianist in Broadway theaters. With these connections he began providing additional songs for American adaptations of European musical shows. His first major success came in 1905 with "How'd You Like to Spoon with Me?" (lyric by Edward Laska) for *The Earl and the Girl*. His success in songwriting was furthered by visits to England, where in 1906 several of his songs were interpolated into London shows, notably two with words by P. G. Wodehouse for the musical play *The Beauty of Bath*. His London visits enabled him to see European works prior to their American productions and gained him a commission from the impresario Charles Frohman to compose songs for the American adaptations. While in London he met Eva Leale, whom he married at Walton-on-Thames in 1910. They had one daughter who was for a time married to band leader Artie Shaw.

By World War I over one hundred of Kern's songs had been interpolated into about thirty shows, among which the most noteworthy was "They Didn't Believe Me" (lyric by Herbert Reynolds) for the 1914 New York version of the British musical *The Girl from Utah*. It was this song in particular that set the pattern for twentieth-century American popular song, in which everyday speech was presented in a natural way. Kern's style greatly influenced George Gershwin and Richard Rodgers, among others.

The first scores entirely of Kern's composition achieved little success. However, between 1915 and 1918 four musicals were performed at the Princess Theatre in New York that provided sharp contrasts with the large-scale European imports then in vogue. The theater seated only about three hundred, and the shows called for an orchestra of about twelve players, a small cast, limited sets, and an intimate style of production. With librettist Guy Bolton, Kern took the 1905 London musical *Mr. Popple (of Ippleton)*, which was already on a more intimate scale than the currently popular operettas, and adapted it with a new score as *Nobody Home* (1915). It was followed by *Very Good, Eddie* (1915), which became Kern's first internationally produced show, and *Oh Boy!* (1917), which introduced the song "Till the Clouds Roll By." Though *Leave It to Jane* (1917) and *Oh Lady! Lady!* (1918) were not so popular, the former was successfully revived in 1959, and the latter remains significant as the show for which the song "Bill" was originally written. The last three of these shows had lyrics by Wodehouse.

Thereafter Kern produced several song-and-dance musical comedies that introduced various songs that have become classics, such as "Look for the Silver Lining" (lyric by B. G. DeSylva) from *Sally* (1920), and "Who?" (lyric by Oscar Hammerstein II) from *Sunny* (1925). Both of these shows were also big successes in London, helping to establish the American musical's international vogue. Then, in 1927, came his most important work, *Show Boat*, a musical play with lyrics by Hammerstein, perhaps the most influential Broadway musical ever written. At least six songs became standard favorites, including "Ol' Man River," "Can't Help Lovin' Dat Man," and "Why Do I Love You?" as well as "Bill," taken over from *Oh Lady! Lady!* More important was the degree to which the show used an American subject and integrated music, speech, drama, and characterization to a hitherto unprecedented degree.

Hammerstein was also lyricist for *Sweet Adeline* (1929), which was distinguished by the songs "Why Was I Born?" and "Don't Ever Leave Me." Then came two scores for works with European settings and parts for operatic voices: *The Cat and the Fiddle* (1931), with the song "She Didn't Say Yes" (lyric by Otto Harbach), and *Music in the Air* (1932), with "I've Told Every Little Star" (lyric by Hammerstein). *Roberta* (1933) provided a more up-to-date American story and the classic song "Smoke Gets in Your Eyes" (lyric by Harbach). The latter show went on to be filmed in 1935 with the added songs "I Won't Dance" and

"Lovely to Look At," establishing Kern's new career as a composer of songs for Hollywood musicals. (*Roberta* was remade in 1952.) Subsequent films included *Swing Time* (1936), featuring Fred Astaire and Ginger Rogers and the songs "A Fine Romance" and "The Way You Look Tonight" (lyrics by Dorothy Fields); *High, Wide and Handsome* (1937), with Hammerstein's "The Folks Who Live on the Hill" and "Can I Forget You?"; and *Joy of Living* (1939), with Fields's "You Couldn't Be Cuter." In 1939, Kern's final stage show, *Very Warm for May* (lyrics by Hammerstein), was a failure on Broadway, despite the song "All the Things You Are," one of his most beguiling and harmonically most adventurous.

Thereafter Kern lived in Hollywood, writing almost exclusively for films and producing some of his most sophisticated songs. These included "The Last Time I Saw Paris" (1940), which was written with Hammerstein on the fall of Paris and won an Academy Award when interpolated into the film *Lady Be Good*. Others were "Dearly Beloved" (lyric by Johnny Mercer), sung by Fred Astaire in *You Were Never Lovelier* (1942), and "Long Ago and Far Away" (lyric by Ira Gershwin), sung by Gene Kelly in *Cover Girl* (1944). Kern's career was cut short by his sudden death at Doctors' Hospital in Manhattan, after he collapsed in a street in Manhattan due to a cerebral hemorrhage. He had gone to New York for a revival of *Show Boat*. At the time of his death he was planning to compose the score for a new stage musical, eventually set by Irving Berlin as *Annie, Get Your Gun!*

Although it is for his individual songs that Kern's name remains most widely celebrated, the importance of *Show Boat* for the American musical theater has never been questioned. For decades the show was revived with updated orchestrations and with its substantial orchestral underscoring of the dialogue reduced. However, during the 1980s, the rediscovery of the original performing material, with orchestrations by Robert Russell Bennett (Kern's regular orchestrator from 1923 on), led to a large-scale recording and opera house productions in both America and Europe. Other shows, too, have been performed and recorded in their original scoring, reinforcing the significance of Kern's work in providing a bridge between the older European operetta tradition and that of the American musical. He was, in the words of fellow composer Arthur Schwartz, "the daddy of modern musical comedy."

Kern avoided larger, symphonic musical forms, except in *Scenario* (1941), based on themes from *Show Boat*, and his *Mark Twain Suite* (1942). Possessing a less startlingly original talent than Gershwin, he used his native shrewdness and his natural melodic gift to develop the distinctive attributes of incisive but varied rhythm and conversational phrasing that distinguish classic American popular song. His earliest songs had few pretensions to more than vaudeville effectiveness, but his final film songs were notable for the compactness of their musical structures and their increasing range of emotional expression. His shrewdness extended beyond purely musical creativity to a strong business sense, exemplified not only by his early investment in the music publishing firm of T. B. Harms (whose flagging fortunes he soon began to revive) but also by his success as a book collector, a hobby that dated back to his youthful visits to London. In 1929 his book collection, which was especially strong in English literature, was sold for $1.75 million.

An enjoyable companion in his earlier days, with an impish charm and sense of humor, Kern later became somewhat remote and at times difficult to work with. It was doubtless partly for this reason that he never came to be thought of as part of a songwriting partnership in the way Gershwin and Rodgers were. However, it was also a recognition of his individual stature. Although in his later years he changed lyricists frequently, he never had the slightest difficulty attracting the best.

• Kern's contribution to the Broadway musical theater may be seen in context in Stanley Green, *The World of Musical Comedy* (1960; 4th ed., 1980), and Gerald Bordman, *American Musical Theatre* (1978; 2d ed., 1986). The definitive Kern biography is Gerald Bordman, *Jerome Kern: His Life and Music* (1980), which is supplemented by various books on specific aspects of his career. P. G. Wodehouse and Guy Bolton, *Bring on the Girls* (1953), offer hilarious firsthand accounts of Kern's early theatrical successes, while the history of his theatrical masterpiece is lovingly explored in Miles B. Kreuger, *Show Boat: The Story of a Classic American Musical* (1977). Andrew Lamb, *Jerome Kern in Edwardian London* (1981; 2d ed., 1985), fills in details of Kern's apprentice years in London, while Alex Wilder, *American Popular Song* (1972), provides critical analysis of some of his songs. Personal reminiscences of Kern are included in Max Wilks, *They're Playing Our Song: From Jerome Kern to Stephen Sondheim* (1973).

ANDREW LAMB

KERN, Richard H. *See* Kern, Edward Meyer.

KERNER, Otto (15 Aug. 1908–9 May 1976), federal judge and governor of Illinois, was born in Chicago, Illinois, the son of Otto Kerner, a prominent Democratic political leader, attorney general of Illinois, and U.S. Appeals Court judge, and Rose Chmelik. Educated in public schools in Oak Park, Illinois, and at Chicago Latin School, Kerner graduated from Brown University in 1930, attended Trinity College of Cambridge University in England from 1930 to 1931, and received a law degree from Northwestern University in 1934. That same year he was admitted to the Illinois bar, and the following year he joined his father's law firm, Kerner, Jaros and Tittle, as a partner. In 1934 Kerner married Helena Cermak Kenlay, the daughter of Chicago mayor Anton Cermak. The marriage solidified two of Chicago's leading Democratic families, each having powerful ties to the city's Eastern European ethnic communities. The couple had no children, but in 1954 they adopted the two children of Helena's daughter (from a previous marriage) following that daughter's death in an automobile accident.

In 1934 Kerner joined the Black Horse Troop of the Illinois National Guard. On active duty during World

War II he saw action as a field artillery officer with the Ninth Infantry Division in Europe and the Thirty-second Infantry Division in the Pacific. He retired from the National Guard in 1954 with the rank of major general. In 1947 Jacob M. Arvey, the boss of the Chicago Democratic machine, recommended Kerner to President Harry S. Truman for appointment as U.S. district attorney for the Northern District of Illinois. Kerner's record in this capacity was solid but unremarkable: he prosecuted no cases with significant political consequence and was not vigorous in attacking organized crime. He once stated: "There is no such thing as organized or syndicated crime or gambling. It's only newspaper talk" (Howard, *Good and Competent Men*, p. 294).

Proud, dignified, and handsome, Kerner's erect, military bearing caused him to appear taller than he actually was. His sophisticated demeanor, cordial manner, agreeable campaign style, and unique ability to appear above mundane Chicago party politics all made him extraordinarily popular with voters in Chicago and throughout the state. His public image was enhanced by his renown as an outdoorsman and his strong association with the leadership of the Boy Scouts. Kerner's reputation for personal integrity, combined with his party loyalty, led to his election to a Cook County circuit judgeship in 1954 and to his reelection in 1958. Closely allied with Chicago mayor Richard J. Daley and the Chicago political machine, Kerner won the Democratic nomination for governor in 1960. He defeated two-term incumbent William G. Stratton by a stunning margin of more than 500,000 votes. In that same election, Democratic presidential candidate John F. Kennedy narrowly defeated the Republican nominee Richard M. Nixon by fewer than 9,000 votes in Illinois, thereby securing the crucial electoral votes needed to win the presidency. Although some Republican leaders subsequently accused the Democrats of fraud in Chicago and Cook County, Kerner's enormous coattails probably had far more to do with Kennedy's narrow victory than any voter irregularities.

During Kerner's first term as governor, Illinois enjoyed unparalleled economic growth, enabling him to win reelection in 1964 over business executive Charles Percy. Kerner won despite scandals surrounding his campaign manager and head of the state department of revenue, Theodore Isaacs, a longtime friend, law partner, and financial adviser. Throughout his two terms, Kerner confronted a hostile Republican majority in the Illinois Senate, which attacked him for being too liberal and too friendly with the Daley forces. Kerner nevertheless succeeded in obtaining legislation that approved sales tax increases, an increase in the corporate tax to pay for government operations, additional state aid to education at all levels, and the creation of the state Board of Higher Education and a statewide system of junior colleges. He also successfully pushed for a fair employment practices law, consumer credit reforms, a revised criminal code, and a state mental health program that became nationally recognized. In 1966 Kerner appointed a Business Management Study Commission to assist in modernizing state government—a feat Kerner viewed as his greatest accomplishment. He failed, however, to persuade the conservative and Republican-dominated general assembly to enact fair housing laws and lamented, "Civil disorders will still be the order of the day unless we create a society of equal justice" (*Chicago Daily News*, 16 Aug. 1968). During his terms in office Kerner called out the Illinois National Guard four times to quell civil disturbances in Chicago.

Following a summer of riots in cities across the country during 1967, President Lyndon B. Johnson appointed Kerner to head the National Advisory Commission on Civil Disorders. The commission's work led to the publication of *The Report of the National Advisory Commission on Civil Disorders* (1968), popularly known as the "Kerner Report," which blamed the nation's urban riots on prejudice, bigotry, and racial injustices. The report warned that the nation was moving toward two separate and unequal societies, and it urged local and national action in the areas of education, employment, open housing, and welfare reform. The report brought Kerner national attention, and within a week of its publication Johnson nominated him for the U.S. Court of Appeals for the Seventh Circuit. Kerner resigned as governor on 22 May 1968.

Kerner's career and reputation were shattered in 1973, when he became the first sitting U.S. Appeals Court judge convicted in a criminal trial. He was charged with involvement in a scheme directed by Isaacs to secure stock in racetracks owned by Marjorie "Marje" Everett, known as the "Queen of Illinois Racing," in return for political favors. Kerner was vigorously prosecuted by an aggressive, young U.S. district attorney named James R. Thompson, a Republican who harbored gubernatorial ambitions. Along with Isaacs, Kerner was found guilty of seventeen counts of tax evasion, bribery, fraud, and perjury. Kerner maintained that the indictment and trial were politically motivated, claiming that he was the victim of an attempt by the Nixon administration to avenge Nixon's loss in the 1960 presidential election. Following his conviction, Kerner resigned as a federal judge in July 1974 and served seven months of his twenty-month sentence in the federal penitentiary in Lexington, Kentucky. He was given an early release in March 1975 to undergo treatment for lung cancer. Kerner spent his final months campaigning for prison reform and trying to rehabilitate his reputation. Meanwhile, his political allies and personal friends sought unsuccessfully to secure a presidential pardon from President Gerald R. Ford. Kerner died in Chicago.

• The Illinois State Historical Library in Springfield holds an extensive collection of Kerner's papers relating to his public career. Relevant publications include Robert P. Howard, *Illinois: A History of the Prairie State* (1972); Howard, *Mostly Good and Competent Men: Illinois Governors 1818–1988* (1988); M. W. Newman, "Governor Kerner's Own Story," a series of articles in the *Chicago Daily News*, Aug. 1968, reprinted in many downstate newspapers; and Fred R. Harris and Roy W. Wilkins, eds., *Quiet Riots, Race and Poverty in the United States: The Kerner Commission Twenty Years Later* (1988). For information about the racetrack scandal and trial, see Robert E. Hartley, *Big Jim Thompson of Illinois* (1979); and Hank Messick, *The Politics of Persecution: Jim Thompson, Marje Everett, Richard Nixon, and the Trial of Otto Kerner* (1978). An obituary and related articles are in the *Chicago Tribune*, 10, 11, and 12 May 1976.

MICHAEL J. DEVINE

KEROUAC, Jack (12 Mar. 1922–21 Oct. 1969), novelist and poet, was born Jean-Louis Lebris Kerouac in Lowell, Massachusetts, the son of Leo Kerouac, a printer, and Gabrielle Levesque, a laborer in shoe factories. Kerouac's "first tongue was the Franco-American *joual*," an "Anglicized, abbreviated and musical form of French spoken by the Quebecois of the Saint Lawrence Valley and by the waves of their descendants who came down to New England mill towns and built a separate culture" (Clark, p. 3). In 1926 Kerouac's older brother Gerard died at age nine from rheumatic fever. An "extraordinary child" who was "both gentle and outgoing" (Nicosia, p. 25), Gerard's spiritual resignation to his suffering convinced both his mother and the nuns who taught him at the St. Louis de France parish school that he was destined for sainthood. Kerouac began to learn English under the tutelage of the same nuns; he would remain forever haunted by the memory of Gerard and the mystery of death.

Kerouac quickly became a voracious reader who constructed in solitude an array of imaginative worlds inspired by the popular culture he fervently embraced, from horse racing newspapers he composed by hand to carefully wrought comic strips inspired by the heroes of pulp magazines and radio serials. From 1936 to 1939 he attended Lowell High School, where he was an outstanding athlete as well as a highly gifted student. In 1938 Kerouac scored the winning touchdown in Lowell's annual Thanksgiving Day game with Lawrence High, on a dazzling run that enshrined his name in the annals of local folklore and vindicated his father, who had loudly protested the alleged misuse of his son's talents by Lowell's football coach.

Kerouac's parents hoped that Jack might become an attorney or an insurance executive; recognizing in his athletic abilities a vehicle for upward social mobility, his mother encouraged him to accept a scholarship to Columbia University in 1939. Since that Ivy League institution looked askance at Kerouac's public school preparation, he was required to complete a postgraduate year of high school work at the Horace Mann school in Riverdale, New York, before enrolling at Columbia in the autumn of 1940. He became a star running back with the Columbia freshman team, but a broken leg suffered at the end of a long kickoff return effectively ended his athletic career. An erratic student who preferred exploring the city to attending class, he read widely and with great passion in American and European literature. In the autumn of 1941 Kerouac left Columbia and worked at various jobs between New York and Lowell before signing on as a merchant

seaman with the SS *Dorchester*. He later enlisted in the U.S. Navy, but shortly after convincing a naval psychiatrist that he was "too much of a nut, and a man of letters" (Charters, p. 37), he was discharged from the service as an "indifferent character." He shipped out on another merchant vessel before returning in 1944 to New York, where he reenrolled at Columbia and struggled with the disapproval of his parents, who had moved to nearby Ozone Park, Queens, in search of work in war industries.

Kerouac's halfhearted return to college (and football) proved short lived, but in 1944 he met fellow Columbia students and aspiring writers Allen Ginsberg and Lucien Carr, who in turn introduced him to William S. Burroughs, a thirty-year-old Harvard graduate and scion of a wealthy St. Louis family with an extensive knowledge of drugs, literature, and the demimonde surrounding New York's Times Square. Kerouac, who had already written a book of short stories and a novel, "The Sea Is My Brother" (neither work was ever published), collaborated with Burroughs on another unpublished work, "And the Hippos Were Boiled in Their Tanks," an account of Lucien Carr's slaying, in August 1944, of an older man who had been pursuing a romantic interest with Carr for some time. After rolling the body into the Hudson River, Carr had asked Kerouac for help in disposing of the weapon, which led to Kerouac's arrest and imprisonment as a material witness to the crime. When his father refused to bail him out, he called his girlfriend, Edie Parker, and after borrowing bail money from her family suggested they marry. Although the killing was treated as an "honor slaying" and the charges against him were later dropped, the incident seemed to confirm Kerouac's desire for a literary career freed from expectations of respectability, though he continued to depend on his mother as a source of financial support for years to come.

Kerouac and Parker moved into her family's home in Michigan, but after working off his debt he returned to New York in October 1944 to launch another round of wandering, brooding, and writing. (His marriage to Parker was annulled in 1949.) Shortly after his father's death from stomach cancer in 1946, Kerouac began work on a sprawling family saga, heavily influenced by the novels of Thomas Wolfe. *The Town and the City* (1950) was set in a New England mill town modeled after the Lowell of his childhood. Though overwritten and overwrought, the novel demonstrated Kerouac's lyrical, even musical sensibility and prodigious literary energy as well as his essentially sacramental imagination. As Ginsberg later explained, all of Kerouac's works concerned "mortal souls wandering earth in time that is vanishing under our feet" (Charters, p. 65). Kerouac coined the term "Beat Generation" primarily as a spiritual commentary on his world-weary New York companions, who were oriented toward a kind of post-apocalyptic mysticism. "They kept talking about the same things I liked," he explained of his Beat friends in 1959, "long outlines of personal experience and vision, night-long confessions full of hope that had become illicit and repressed by War, stirrings, rumblings of a new soul (that same old human soul)."

In 1946 Kerouac met Neal Cassady, a frenetic 21-year-old drifter from Denver, Colorado, who lent a dose of western ruggedness to the milieu of New York "hipsters" that had become the focus of Kerouac's literary attention. Between 1947 and 1950 Kerouac and Cassady shared several transcontinental journeys that became the basis for *On the Road*, the celebrated novel that would not be published until 1957. Frustrated by the conventional prose style of *The Town and the City*, Kerouac experienced a breakthrough in 1951 after talking with a New York friend, architecture student Ed White, who suggested that he try "sketching" his prose in a spontaneous, impressionistic fashion. Kerouac had grown obsessed with bebop, the highly improvisational jazz form pioneered by Charlie Parker, Dizzy Gillespie, Max Roach, and others in New York during the Second World War. The sketching technique, which Kerouac later termed "spontaneous prose," was designed to adapt the highly vocal, rhythmically complex idiom of bebop into narrative form. In the essay "Essentials of Spontaneous Prose" (1958), Kerouac explained, "Sketching language is undisturbed flow from the mind of personal secret idea-words, *blowing* (as per jazz musician) on subject of image."

Kerouac's literary art bore no resemblance to the undisciplined "beatnik" writing of the late 1950s. His extraordinary attention to detail, astonishing memory, and encyclopedic grasp of European and American literature, popular culture, and world religions enabled him to create densely textured narratives that, when read aloud as they were meant to be, achieved an incantatory dimension rarely experienced in modern literature. Between 1951 and 1956 he wrote numerous unpublished novels, poems, spiritual tracts, and sketches, including a manuscript for "On the Road" he considered the "authentic" version, though it would be published in 1973 as *Visions of Cody*. Considered by many his masterwork, it represents without question his fullest exploration in spontaneous prose.

Kerouac was decidedly *not* a novelist in the conventional sense. As Norman Mailer observed in 1959, "His sense of character is nil." Yet Mailer went on to suggest that "it is better to forget about him as a novelist and see him instead as an action painter or bard" (*Advertisements for Myself*, p. 427). Kerouac insisted in 1962 that his books were "just chapters in the whole work which I call *The Duluoz Legend*. . . . The whole thing forms one enormous comedy, seen through the eyes of poor Ti Jean (me), otherwise known as Jack Duluoz, the world of raging action and folly and also of gentle sweetness seen through the keyhole of his eye" (*Big Sur*). In eschewing conventional plot structure for a discursive, expansive, participatory mode, Kerouac anticipated the emergence of the nonfiction novel and the new journalism of the 1960s. Some of his very best work, such as the rhapsodic sketch "The Railroad Earth" (repr. in *Lonesome Traveler* [1960]),

defied classification by literary standards of the era. Kerouac's example inspired numerous writers toward experimentation in literary form. In the mid-1950s he was a familiar figure at poetry readings on both coasts, where his influence was deeply felt in the work of Gregory Corso, Robert Creeley, and Allen Ginsberg. In Tangier, Morocco, in 1957 he typed the manuscript and ultimately supplied the title of the best-known "novel" from William S. Burroughs, *Naked Lunch*.

When *On the Road* was finally published by Viking in September 1957, it created an instant literary sensation. Though it was hailed by Gilbert Milstein in the Sunday *New York Times Book Review* as a "major novel" whose publication was a "historic occasion," it was more commonly dismissed as a self-indulgent, irresponsible, or dangerous book. Kerouac himself, an "overnight" literary celebrity at age thirty-five, had grown beyond the seemingly aimless wanderings celebrated in *On the Road*. A serious, theologically sophisticated Roman Catholic, he had also become deeply interested in Buddhism by the mid-1950s. In *The Dharma Bums* (1958), Kerouac described his experiences with Gary Synder and other devotees of Eastern mysticism in the San Francisco Bay area, which had become the center of Beat life. Now that he was a certified literary commodity, publishers rushed into print the works he had written during his highly productive decade of obscurity, from *The Subterraneans* (1958), an account of his brief relationship with an African-American woman, written over three days and nights in 1953, to *Dr. Sax* (1959), a lush meditation on the spirits and phantoms of his Lowell boyhood. He also produced a volume of poetry, *Mexico City Blues* (1959).

In 1958 *San Francisco Chronicle* columnist Herb Caen coined the term "beatnik" as a play on the name of a recently launched Soviet satellite. Americans soon became familiar with a lifestyle featuring cheap wine, marijuana, cool jazz, black leotards, and terrible poetry declaimed before maudlin audiences at subterranean coffeeshops. None of this was even remotely linked to Kerouac or his literary vocation, but at the height of the beatnik craze his appearances on television programs such as the "Tonight Show" (then hosted by Steve Allen) only furthered his identification with the new bohemians. Kerouac's increasing problem with alcohol was fatally linked with the burdens of a fame he never wholly resisted. By drinking more heavily than usual before his public appearances, he only encouraged the disdainful treatment his work received at the hands of numerous pundits. Although Kerouac had experimented with illegal drugs—especially benzedrine—in the 1940s, caricatures of Beat authors as drug-crazed barbarians found in critiques by Norman Podhoretz and others were woefully deficient. Nor was he an advocate of the sexual licentiousness associated with Beat literature. His permanent address throughout most of his adult life was his mother's home. "It's a monastery," he once told a friend, "and I'm a monk and she's a reverend mother." Kerouac did fail to take responsibility for a child he fathered in

1951 during a brief marriage to Joan Haverty, but his obvious shortcomings as an adult were sources of embarrassment rather than platforms from a literary manifesto.

In *Big Sur*, his 1962 "comeback" novel, Kerouac starkly depicted the self-destructive trajectory of his life since the publication of *On the Road*. Craving both solitude and genuine companionship, Jack Duluoz careens from the retreat of a cabin at Big Sur to San Francisco's North Beach and back. The novel offers one of the most arresting treatments of alcoholism in modern literature, and although it ends with the narrator experiencing the vision of the Cross of Christian redemption, Kerouac himself was unable to recover from the depths he plumbed in his writing. He wrote several more novels in the mid-1960s, but his incandescent gifts had been spent if not squandered. He made occasional humiliating public appearances but was mostly confined to the home in St. Petersburg, Florida, he shared with his mother and his third wife, Stella Sampas, the sister of a boyhood friend from Lowell, whom he married in 1966. Critics reported that he had become a right-wing Catholic, but he had always been both essentially conservative and indifferent to politics. Kerouac collapsed in the bathroom of his home and was rushed into surgery, where he died of an abdominal hemorrhage, the result of his alcoholism.

Jack Kerouac's writings became extremely popular with young people throughout the world. It was often said that the message of freedom he conveyed was especially appealing to those unwilling to conform to society's expectations. Yet readers of all ages—as well as those who never read Kerouac at all but felt they "knew" his work just the same—who viewed him primarily as a social critic or as a bohemian icon overlooked his true vocation as a writer. His work clearly reflected many critical themes from postwar American life, but Kerouac's focus never wavered from the herculean task he had shouldered: to invent a literary form that most truly conveyed the array of sounds, visions, and memories that haunted and then consumed him. A complex and deeply troubled individual, his body of work stands as a remarkable legacy of his commitment.

• Collections of Jack Kerouac's papers may be found in numerous research libraries, including Columbia University, the University of Texas at Austin, and the New York Public Library. In addition to works cited in the text, other important works by Kerouac include *The Scripture of the Golden Eternity* (1960), *Visions of Gerard* (1963), *Desolation Angels* (1965), and *Vanity of Duluoz* (1968). The most prominent biographies are Ann Charters, *Kerouac: A Biography* (1973); Dennis McNally, *Desolate Angel: Jack Kerouac, the Beat Generation, and America* (1979); Gerard Nicosia, *Memory Babe: A Critical Biography of Jack Kerouac* (1983); and Tom Clark, *Jack Kerouac, a Biography* (1984). Barry Gifford and Lawrence Lee, *Jack's Book: An Oral Biography of Jack Kerouac* (1978), is informative and revealing, as is "The Art of Fiction XLI," a *Paris Review* interview with Kerouac (Summer 1968): 60–105. An obituary is in the *New York Times*, 22 Oct.

1969. An account of Kerouac's final days is Jack McClintock, "This Is How the Ride Ends," *Esquire*, Mar. 1970, pp. 138–39, 188–89.

JAMES T. FISHER

KERR, Robert Samuel (11 Sept. 1896–1 Jan. 1963), oil executive and politician, was born in Indian territory, near present-day Ada, Oklahoma, the son of William Samuel Kerr, a farmer, clerk, and politician, and Margaret Eloda Wright. Kerr's upbringing as a Southern Baptist had a profound influence on his life. Not only did his religious beliefs lead him to teach Sunday school and to shun alcohol throughout his adulthood, it also aided his political aspirations in a conservative state where Baptists were the single largest denomination.

After graduating from high school, Kerr taught while he earned a two-year degree from East Central State Normal School in Ada. He briefly studied law at the University of Oklahoma until poverty forced him to drop out in 1916. When the United States entered the world war in 1917, Kerr was commissioned as a second lieutenant in the army. He never saw combat, but he used his active involvement in the Oklahoma National Guard and the American Legion to forward his business and political careers.

During the early 1920s Kerr struggled in both his personal and professional lives. He passed the Oklahoma bar exam in 1922, but a business failure the previous year had left him deeply in debt. In 1924 his wife of more than four years, Reba Shelton, died in childbirth. The next year he married Grayce Breene, the youngest daughter of a wealthy Tulsa family. They had four children.

Kerr used his new family connections to enter the oil business with his brother-in-law, James L. Anderson, as his partner. By 1929 the Anderson-Kerr Drilling Company had become so prosperous that Kerr abandoned his law practice to focus on oil. Anderson retired in 1936, and Dean A. McGee, former chief geologist for Phillips Petroleum, joined the firm, which changed its name in 1946 to Kerr-McGee Oil Industries, Incorporated. Kerr-McGee diversified into global drilling for petroleum and processed other fuels and minerals, including uranium and helium.

Kerr's growing wealth and business ties made him a power in state Democratic politics during the 1930s. In 1942 he ran for the Democratic nomination for governor as a supporter both of the New Deal and of a vigorous U.S. role in World War II. Oklahoma's Democrats were divided over President Franklin Roosevelt's policies, leading to a bitter campaign. Kerr narrowly won the primary and went on to triumph by a small margin in the general election.

His four-year term as governor served as a turning point for Oklahoma's politics and economy. For the first time in the state's history, executive-legislative relations remained cordial, largely due to Kerr's patient leadership. When not cultivating legislators the governor prepared his state to weather postwar economic storms. Kerr traveled more than 400,000 miles to sell

Oklahoma's products and potential throughout the nation. Not coincidentally, Kerr's boosterism also promoted his own political fortunes. In 1944 he was chosen to deliver the keynote address at the National Democratic Convention, where he played a back-room role in the selection of Harry S. Truman as vice president.

Kerr used his success as governor to catapult himself into the U.S. Senate in 1948. Although he had national ambitions, he always put what he perceived to be the interests of his state first. Unlike many of his peers he generally neglected headline-grabbing issues, including anticommunism, foreign affairs, and civil rights, in favor of more mundane topics such as oil policies and public works. He believed Oklahomans would benefit most, and support him strongly, if he concentrated on concrete economic matters.

In the Senate Kerr's activism on natural gas regulation quickly won him a reputation for being a staunch defender of his region and its special interests, including his own petroleum company. His personality reinforced these first impressions. Kerr's colleagues widely considered him a brilliant debater who overwhelmed his opponents with his passion and his mastery of policy detail. Journalist Marquis Childs, writing in the *Saturday Evening Post* (9 Apr. 1949), nicknamed Kerr "the big boom from Oklahoma: the richest—and loudest—man in the United States Senate." His parochialism, compounded by regional stereotyping in the press, torpedoed his effort to win the Democratic nomination for the presidency in 1952.

A disappointed Kerr then threw himself completely into his legislative work. He built alliances with the powerful southern and western Democrats who dominated the Senate, including Richard Russell of Georgia and Lyndon Johnson of Texas. Kerr relied on these friends and on careful committee preparation to pursue regional economic development. The Arkansas River Navigation System became his defining goal through his three terms in the Senate. The $1.2 billion federal project, centered in northeastern Oklahoma, fostered more than $3 billion in commercial and industrial development in the Arkansas River basin during the two years after its completion in 1971. A once stagnant portion of his state quickly emerged as a regional economic hub.

In the early 1960s Kerr became "the uncrowned King of the Senate," according to one of his colleagues. His legislative acumen combined with changes in congressional leadership to make his allegiance pivotal to President John F. Kennedy's programs on Capitol Hill. On issues of common interest, such as space and taxes, Kerr cooperated with Kennedy to guarantee mutual success. On areas of disagreement, including Medicare, Kerr stymied the president. The *Wall Street Journal* (3 Jan. 1963) summarized the relationship with only some exaggeration: "Mr. Kennedy asked; Mr. Kerr decided."

At the peak of his power Kerr fell ill and died at Bethesda Naval Hospital outside of Washington, D.C. Kerr's death contributed to Kennedy's legislative difficulties in 1963, marked the end of the Democratic party's dominance in Oklahoma politics, and signaled the passing of a major figure in the oil industry, but in addition to an estate estimated to be worth at least $35 million, he left a legacy that extended beyond partisan or business affairs. His forceful use of the federal government to spur regional development, an approach shared by contemporaries, including Johnson, helped integrate the South and Southwest into the national economy. The rise of the "Sunbelt" ultimately transformed all aspects of American life. Robert Kerr played a significant role in that transformation.

• Kerr's personal papers are in the Carl Albert Center at the University of Oklahoma in Norman. Some of the papers from his gubernatorial administration are in the Oklahoma Department of Libraries, Archives and Records Division, in Oklahoma City. Kerr authored a book on natural resources policy, *Land, Wood and Water*, ed. Malvina Stephenson and Tris Coffin (1960). Anne Hodges Morgan, *Robert S. Kerr: The Senate Years* (1977), focuses on his political career but also covers briefly his personal and business affairs. For analysis of his term as governor, see William P. Corbett, "Robert Samuel Kerr, Governor of Oklahoma, 1943–1947," in *Oklahoma's Governors, 1929–1955: Depression to Prosperity*, ed. LeRoy H. Fischer (1983), pp. 124–49. John S. Ezell, *Innovations in Energy: The Story of Kerr-McGee* (1979), summarizes his business ventures. To understand Kerr's impact on his state's political development, examine James R. Scales and Danney Goble, *Oklahoma Politics: A History* (1982). An obituary is in the *New York Times*, 2 Jan. 1963.

PETER G. FELTEN

KERR, Sophie (23 Aug. 1880–6 Feb. 1965), author and editor, was born in Denton, Maryland, the daughter of Jonathan Williams Kerr, a nurseryman, and Amanda Catherine Sisk. Little is known about her childhood and education. She graduated from Hood College in Frederick, Maryland, in 1898 and received an M.A. from the University of Vermont in 1901. In 1904 she married civil engineer John D. Underwood. Their marriage lasted four years and produced no children. Although she was divorced in 1908, Kerr continued to publish under her married name until about 1915.

Kerr had an early career as a newspaper and magazine editor. She moved to Pittsburgh, Pennsylvania, where she was the women's page editor at the *Pittsburgh Chronicle-Telegraph*, then editor of the women's Sunday supplement at the *Pittsburgh Gazette-Times*. She also served on the staff of the *Woman's Home Companion* and eventually became managing editor of the magazine. Although primarily a writer of fiction, Kerr occasionally wrote about social issues, particularly those concerning her female readers. For example, she published "Married Women and the Job" in the March 1927 issue of the *Woman's Home Companion*.

Although Kerr's prolific literary career began in 1899 with the sale of a short story to *Country Gentleman* magazine, she was known primarily as a writer for women's magazines. The greatest number of her stories appeared in the *Woman's Home Companion*. The *Saturday Evening Post* published more than one hundred of her stories and serialized several of her novels.

Other stories appeared in *Woman's Day, Vogue, Collier's, Ladies' Home Journal, Cosmopolitan,* and *McCall's.*

Kerr's stories and novels are light and humorous. Many are set on Maryland's Eastern Shore, capturing the rural and maritime character of the region where she spent her childhood. *The Sound of Petticoats* (1948), a collection of short stories set on the Eastern Shore, concludes with an essay on local culture and cuisine. Her first novel, *The Blue Envelope* (1917), is the story of an innocent but pragmatic young heroine who is pursued by foreign spies determined to capture the chemical formula she has unwittingly agreed to carry. In the end, her pluck and ingenuity win her both safe passage and romance. In *The See-Saw* (1919) an unfaithful husband discovers the error of his ways and returns to his forgiving wife. *Mareea-Maria* (1929) concerns a Maryland farmer who defies his mother to marry an Italian woman. Rachael Vincent of *There's Only One* (1936) finds love and romance when she takes a job as a maid in the home of the mother who gave her up for adoption. *Wife's Eye View* (1947) tells the tale of a woman who finds success but not happiness as a writer. In 1934 Kerr and Anna Steese Richardson wrote *Big-Hearted Herbert*, a play based on one of Kerr's stories in the *Saturday Evening Post*. Kerr also wrote *So Women Can't Take It*, a play celebrating feminine courage, which was used as a recruiting tool by the Women's Army Corps beginning in 1944.

Critics praised Kerr for her clever humor, her likable characters, her polished prose, and her ability to capture local color. Her works rarely strayed beyond the lightest of themes but were suspenseful, entertaining, and skillfully written. *Miss J. Looks On* (1935), a novel, centers on the fate of a wealthy family ruined by the 1929 stock market crash. A reviewer called it a "well-written narrative that without false sentiment or heroics . . . holds the interest all the way through without insulting the intelligence" (*New York Times*, 26 May 1935). Such measured praise was typical of critical response to Kerr's writing.

Kerr's novels were bestsellers, particularly in the 1930s and 1940s. For most of her adult life, she lived in New York City, where her literary success allowed her an active and prominent social life. An enthusiastic gourmet, she collaborated with Jane Platt on a cookbook, *The Best I Ever Ate* (1953). She died in New York City.

Kerr was an exceptionally prolific writer who intended to entertain and amuse. The popularity of her work testifies to her ability to consistently meet the expectations of her readers. Her stories and novels remain useful sources of local color and are reflections of the popular taste of their times.

• Washington College in Chestertown, Md., is the repository of Kerr's personal library, a complete collection of her novels, and a small collection of her possessions. Several of Kerr's short stories are collected in *Love at Large* (1916) and *Confetti* (1927). Her novels, besides those mentioned above, include *The Golden Block* (1918), *Painted Meadows* (1920),

One Thing Is Certain (1922), *Tigers Is Only Cats* (1929), *In for a Penny* (1931), *Stay Out of My Life* (1933), *Fine to Look At* (1937), *Adventure with Women* (1938), *Curtain Going Up* (1940), *The Beautiful Woman* (1940), *Michael's Girl* (1942), *Jenny Devlin* (1943), *Love Story Incidental* (1946), and *Tall as Pride* (1949). Biographical information about Kerr appears in H. R. Warfel, *American Novelists of Today* (1947). An interview is in *Ladies' Home Journal*, May 1928. Her obituary is in the *New York Times*, 8 Feb. 1965.

KATHLEEN FEENEY

KERSEY, Kenny (3 Apr. 1916–1 Apr. 1983), jazz pianist, was born Kenneth Lyons Kersey in Harrow, Ontario, Canada. His parents' names are unknown, but Kersey's father was a cellist and Kersey studied with his mother, who taught piano. During further studies at the Detroit Institute of Musical Art, he took up the trumpet.

Kersey went to New York to work as a trumpeter and pianist in 1936, but physical problems made him give up the brass instrument. He replaced pianist Billy Kyle in Lucky Millinder's big band in February 1938; later that year he was a member of Billy Hicks and his Sizzling Six. By the year's end he had left Hicks for a brief stay with singer Billie Holiday for the opening of a second Café Society in Greenwich Village. While continuing to work there with trumpeter Frankie Newton's band in 1939, he made recordings with Holiday and Newton. Kersey was a member of trumpeter Roy Eldridge's band at the café in mid-1940 and for recordings from that year. He replaced Count Basie at clarinetist Benny Goodman's sextet session in December 1940 and had brief solos on "Breakfast Feud" and "I Can't Give You Anything But Love."

Still at Café Society, Kersey joined trumpeter Henry "Red" Allen in mid-November 1940. A review of the band in *Swing* (Jan. 1941) stated:

Pianist Kersey was fine with Frankie Newton's band when Cafe Society opened, better with Roy Eldridge's great little band of six months ago, and is magnificent with Red Allen. The kid's a virtuoso. He trills and glisses with monumental ease, but never sacrifices good taste to his fluent technique. . . . Ken's got a wonderful feeling for the rhythm, and really gets the proper percussive flavor out of his instrument.

Allen's band broadcast on Henry "Hot Lips" Levine's NBC radio show "The Chamber Society of Lower Basin Street" in February 1941. He recorded "K. K. Boogie" with Allen's band in April, and later that month they gave a concert at Carnegie Hall, "The Art of Boogie Woogie."

While with Allen, Kersey also participated in jam sessions at Minton's Playhouse in Harlem along with swing musicians and practitioners of the incipient bop style. There he recorded "Stardust II" and "Kerouac" as a member of trumpeter Dizzy Gillespie's quartet, including drummer Kenny Clarke. Kersey left Allen's band in October 1941. He was the pianist in trumpeter Cootie Williams's big band from late 1941 to early 1942, and he recorded a solo on Williams's version of pianist Thelonious Monk's composition "Epistrophy." Kersey's performance was later described by writer Gunther Schuller as florid in manner and ill-suited to Monk's piece.

In May 1942 he replaced Mary Lou Williams in Andy Kirk's big band, and he immediately presented Kirk with a big hit in his rendition of his own composition, "Boogie Woogie Cocktail." Drafted into the U.S. Army soon thereafter, he was stationed at Camp Kilmer, near New Brunswick, New Jersey, in Special Services, playing in a band that included trumpeter Buck Clayton. During the mid-1940s he made guest appearances with Kirk, who recalled, "whenever I'd play the Apollo Theatre he'd come up to New York and I'd bring him on stage in his uniform and the place would go wild." While in the army Kersey also recorded with alto saxophonist Pete Brown in July 1944 and with trombonist Trummy Young in May 1945.

Discharged in January 1946, he joined tenor saxophonist Teddy McRae's band, and in February he recorded with singer Cousin Joe, accompanied by Pete Brown's band. From April 1946 through May 1947 he toured the country with the all-star package show, "Jazz at the Philharmonic," initially as a member of a rhythm section accompanying Clayton, tenor saxophonists Coleman Hawkins and Lester Young, and singer Helen Humes. Among their recorded performances are versions of "JATP Blues" and "I Can't Get Started."

Kersey's association with "Jazz at the Philharmonic" is said to have extended to early 1949, but during this period, he was clearly active elsewhere. He returned to the downtown location of Café Society with Clayton's quintet (soon expanded to a sextet) from May to July 1947. Later that year into 1948, he was again back at the café with clarinetist Edmond Hall's band, and he rejoined Eldridge late in 1948.

In April 1949 Hall brought a new band that included Kersey into the Savoy Cafe in Boston. They broadcast from the club, and in December they were recorded there "live," with Kersey's sprightly swing piano melodies and delicate chording featured in solos on "Careless Love" and "Please Don't Talk about Me When I'm Gone." He left Hall early in 1950 and during the spring worked in reed player Sidney Bechet's band in New York City. Kersey rejoined Hall in San Francisco in August; later that month he returned to New York City with Hall to participate in a jam session at the Stuyvesant Casino.

Kersey was with Allen again from 1951 to 1952 and joined clarinetist Sol Yaged's trio from 1952 to 1954. Around this time he also worked with Clayton, Yaged, and trombonist Herb Flemming in a band in New York City. He recorded a rhythm-and-blues session with trombonist Clyde Bernhardt, leading under the pseudonym of Ed Barron in 1953, and he was in jazz sessions with trumpeter Charlie Shavers in October 1954, trombonist Jack Teagarden in November, and trumpeter Jonah Jones in December. During 1955 he worked with Shaver's band and recorded with trumpeter Ruby Braff.

In March 1956 he participated in the last of Clayton's acclaimed studio jam sessions for the Columbia label. The relaxed and extended versions of "All the Cats Join In," "After Hours," and "Don't You Miss Your Baby" gave him ample opportunity to perform his swing, blues, and boogie-woogie soloing. He rejoined Yaged's group from 1956 to 1957, and toward the end of the decade he worked at the Metropole with Clayton and at Central Plaza, both in New York City. When a stroke eventually prevented his playing, his daughter took care of him. Details of his marriage or of other children are unknown. He died in New York City.

• Considerable details and fine photos appear in Manfred Selchow, *Profoundly Blues: A Bio-Discographical Scrapbook on Edmond Hall* (1988). See also Frank Driggs, "My Story, by Andy Kirk," *Jazz Review* 2 (Feb. 1959): 12–17; repr. in *Jazz Panorama* (1962; repr. 1979), pp. 119–31; John Chilton, *Sidney Bechet: The Wizard of Jazz* (1987); Buck Clayton assisted by Nancy Miller Elliott, *Buck Clayton's Jazz World* (1987); and Gunther Schuller, *The Swing Era: the Development of Jazz, 1930–1945* (1989), pp. 361, 403.

BARRY KERNFELD

KERSHAW, Joseph Brevard (5 Jan. 1822–13 Apr. 1894), lawyer, soldier, and politician, was born in Camden, South Carolina, the son of John Kershaw, a judge, and Harriette Du Bose. The Kershaws were a distinguished South Carolina family. Joseph was named for his paternal grandfather, who had immigrated to America from England in 1748 and was prominent in the American Revolution. Joseph's father was mayor of Camden for several years and served one term in the U.S. Congress. Joseph studied for a career in law in the offices of the distinguished South Carolina lawyer John M. De Saussure and passed the South Carolina bar at age twenty-one. In 1844 he married Lucretia Douglas; the couple had one son and four daughters. After practicing for several years, beginning in June 1844, he participated in the Mexican War as a volunteer, serving as a lieutenant in South Carolina's Palmetto Regiment. In Mexico, he saw action in several battles but became ill and was evacuated back to the United States in June 1847. Kershaw was elected to the South Carolina state legislature in 1852 and 1854, and he was a member of the state's 1860 secession convention that met in Charleston, South Carolina.

Kershaw saw the first shot of the American Civil War and fought in increasingly important Confederate army leadership positions until the last days of the conflict. In early 1861 he recruited the Second South Carolina Volunteer Infantry Regiment and served as its colonel. The unit occupied Morris Island in Charleston Harbor and defended that position during the bombardment of Fort Sumter, 12–14 April 1861. The regiment was brigaded under Brigadier General Luke M. Bonham at the first battle of Bull Run (Manassas) in July 1861. On 13 February 1862 Kershaw was promoted to brigadier general and placed in command of a brigade normally assigned to the division of Major General Lafayette McLaws. This division usually fought under the control of General James Longstreet's corps headquarters. Kershaw fought with distinction during the Peninsula campaign of the spring and summer of 1862. He also fought at the battle of Second Bull Run (Second Manassas), and in the fall of 1862 he led his brigade at the costly battle of Antietam. In December of that same year his brigade was in the famed sunken road below Marye's Heights during the battle of Fredericksburg.

In 1863 Kershaw attained his greatest eminence, mostly in offensive operations directed by General Longstreet. In the spring Kershaw fought at the battle of Chancellorsville, and in early July he led his brigade in a desperate attack on the second day of the battle of Gettysburg. In this costly, failed attempt to break the Union center on Cemetery Ridge, Kershaw lost half his brigade. Along with McLaws and Longstreet, Kershaw and his troops then proceeded west to Tennessee and participated in the battle of Chickamauga, where he was involved in the defeat of the Union right wing.

In 1864 Kershaw returned to the Army of Northern Virginia, was promoted to major general on 18 May, and began the long battle to defeat the advances of Union general U. S. Grant toward the Confederate capital, Richmond. Now commanding a division, Kershaw operated in Longstreet's corps at the battles of the Wilderness, Spotslyvania, Cold Harbor, and Petersburg.

Kershaw survived the war, living through a succession of difficult events. In March 1865, when Confederate forces failed to hold the defensive perimeter around Richmond, he and his skeletonized division followed Robert E. Lee's badly depleted Army of Northern Virginia westward. At Sayler's Creek, he made a stand along with the rest of General Richard Ewell's corps. Trapped by a growing number of Federal units, the Confederate corps surrendered on 6 April 1865. Kershaw was imprisoned at Fort Warren, Boston, Massachusetts, for a few weeks, then he was released in July.

Returning to Camden, Kershaw resumed his pursuit of the law and politics. He was briefly a member of the state senate and for one year was president of that body until the more stringent Reconstruction measures were enacted. In 1870 he became a member of the Union Reform party convention, preparing and supporting resolutions that recognized the Reconstruction Acts as legitimate.

At the end of Reconstruction in 1877, Kershaw resumed his public service. Elected to South Carolina's Fifth Circuit judgeship, he served as a judge for sixteen years. During the 1880s he wrote two articles about his Civil War experience, "Kershaw's Brigade at Fredericksburg" and "Kershaw's Brigade at Gettysburg," that were published in *Battles and Leaders of the Civil War*, volume 3, edited by Robert U. Johnson and Clarence C. Buel (1887–1888). In bad health, he left the bench in 1893 and was appointed Camden's post-master, serving in that position until his death in Camden.

Kershaw's imprint on American history was as a competent citizen soldier. Despite his lack of formal military training, he quickly developed excellent battle instincts and a marked talent for steady leadership under trying conditions.

• References to the Kershaw family are in *South Carolina History and Genealogical Magazine*, Jan. 1924. Kershaw's Civil War battle record is detailed in *The War of the Rebellion: A Compilation of the Official Records of the Union and Confederate Armies* (128 vols., 1880–1901). He is mentioned in U. R. Brooks, *South Carolina Bench and Bar*, vol. 1 (1908); Yates Snowden, *History of South Carolina*, vol. 2 (1920); James Longstreet, *From Manassas to Appomattox* (1896); and Jefferson Davis, *The Rise and Fall of the Confederate Government* (1881). An obituary is in the Charleston, S.C., *News and Courier*, 14 Apr. 1894.

ROD PASCHALL

KERTÉSZ, André (2 July 1894–28 Sept. 1985), photographer, was born Andor Kertész in Budapest, Hungary, the son of Lipót Kertész, a bookseller, and Ernesztin Hoffman. As a child he was an indifferent student and an accomplished truant. His father died of tuberculosis in 1908, and an uncle who was a member of the Budapest Stock Exchange became his guardian. Through this uncle, Kertész found a position as a clerk at the bourse after receiving his baccalaureate from Budapest's Academy of Commerce in 1912. That year he bought his first camera and began photographing street scenes. Kertész was recruited into the Austro-Hungarian army in 1914 and traveled through much of Central Europe. He brought his camera along and took pictures, not of conflict and violence, but of life in the trenches and behind the lines. In 1915 he was shot within an inch of his heart and was partially paralyzed for a year; when he returned to the front, he found that his regiment had been captured by the Russians.

Kertész returned from the army and went back to work at the stock exchange in 1918, but he was more interested in photography than business and continued to take pictures of his family, friends, and the Hungarian countryside in his spare time. From 1917 on, his work was published occasionally in Hungarian magazines. In 1925 he convinced his mother to let him go to Paris. There Kertész lived in Montparnasse, began to call himself André, and became a regular in avant-garde literary and artistic circles. He eventually became friends with Piet Mondrian, Fernan Léger, Mare Chagall, Alexander Calder, Alberto Giacometti, and other important artists of the day. Kertész had had no formal art training, and only in Paris did he become aware of work by contemporaries Alfred Stieglitz, Paul Strand, Man Ray, and Laslo Moholy-Nagy. However, he was already developing his own style, which focused on trivial but telling details and showed a taste for spatial ambiguity and the slightly strange. Kertész was not particularly interested in achieving optimal sharpness in his pictures but aimed instead to capture the essence of a moment or mood. He often waited hours for passing figures to assume the composition he wanted. A contemporary commented, "While other cameramen bunched together, Kertész loitered on the sidelines filming the significant background of world-shaking events."

In Paris, Kertész photographed his Hungarian friends, artists' studios, street and café scenes, and the public gardens. In March 1927 he had his first show, at Jan Slivinsky's avant-garde gallery Au Sacre du Printemps. In 1928 he was included in the First Independent Salon of Photography, alongside Berenice Abbott, Eugène Atget, Nadar, and Man Ray. That year he bought his first Leica camera (the brand he used for the rest of his life), although he had been working in the spontaneous style associated with that compact, portable camera for many years. In the late 1920s and early 1930s Kertész published work in the surrealist magazines *Bifur*, *Variétés*, and *Minotaure*. The influence of this movement was seen in his series of "distortion nudes," made with parabolic mirrors, begun in 1933. With the rise of photography as illustration in magazines in this period, Kertész's photo-essays were widely published in French and German magazines, such as *Vu*, *Cahiers d'art*, *Art et Médécine*, *Mode und Kultur*, and *Frankfurter Illustrierte*. He became one of the most influential photographers in Europe, and both Brassaï and Henri Cartier-Bresson later acknowledged the impact of his example. His work was shown in Film und Foto, an important show in Stuttgart in 1929, and museums began to buy his photographs. In 1928 Kertész married photographer Rósza-Josephine Klein. They had no children, and the marriage ended in divorce in 1930.

In Paris in the 1930s Kertész was successful, relatively prosperous, and widely admired. His photographs were shown in the United States for the first time in 1932, at the Julien Levy gallery in New York City. He published two books, *Enfants* (1933) and *Paris vu par André Kertész* (1934). In 1933 he married Elizabeth Saly, his girlfriend from Budapest. They had no children. The increasingly nationalistic tendencies of the 1930s began to make Kertész's work appear too neutral and insufficiently topical. In 1936 he went to the United States for what he expected to be a one-or two-year stay on a contract with the Keystone Agency, where he worked for a year. While Kertész missed Paris and the acclaim he had received there, he found it difficult to make enough money to return to Europe, and the rise of fascism meant that, as a Hungarian Jew, he might have trouble finding work. Although he never fully acclimated to the United States and did not speak English well, Kertész lived in New York City for the rest of his life, becoming a U.S. citizen in 1944. During World War II he was labeled an enemy alien by law and was barred from taking pictures on the street, his favored subject. He was given solo shows at the PM Gallery in New York in 1937 and at the Art Institute of Chicago in 1946; the Museum of Modern Art in New York bought one of his photos in 1941. Kertész had to wait another twenty years for widespread attention, however. The lack of fame in America made him bitter and increased his sense of isolation.

Although Kertész's work had been in demand by magazines in Europe, it was not suited to the American market. *Life* declined to print pictures it had commissioned from him, saying that his photographs "talked too much." Kertész, who described himself as a sentimentalist, disdained American photography, which he described as "perfect technique but expressing nothing." However, in order to make a living he worked for *Vogue*, *Town and Country*, *House and Garden*, and similar magazines. In 1949 he signed an exclusive contract with Condé Nast, for whom he mostly photographed interior architecture. His commercial work in New York was merely workmanlike, partly because he refused to adhere to the limits of photography practiced in that milieu.

During the 1940s and 1950s Kertész continued to take pictures for himself, but around 1950 he was forced to stop printing his own negatives, having developed an allergy to photographic chemicals. He and Elizabeth moved to an apartment above Washington Square in 1952, and André began a series of photos of the square that he worked on for the rest of his life. While his photographs had often employed disorienting angles and distortion, in New York they had an air of greater distance from the subject, perhaps a reflection of his relationship to his adopted country.

In 1962 Kertész canceled his contract with Condé Nast and devoted himself to his own work. His international reputation quickly revived. In 1963 he recovered and reprinted (with some changes) negatives he had taken in Paris that had been lost since World War II. Kertész was given shows in Paris (1963) and New York (1964), and for the rest of his life his work was exhibited in museums and galleries around the world. He was also awarded honors in the United States. He was invited to a White House reception in 1965 and received a Guggenheim Fellowship in 1974. Elizabeth's death in 1977 was devastating to Kertész. She had known him throughout his life as a photographer and had constituted a link to Hungary. In the mid-1970s he began to travel to France regularly, where he received the Grand Prix in photography in 1982. In 1985 André Kertész of Paris and New York, a show at the Art Institute of Chicago and at the Metropolitan Museum of Art in New York, brought together his early and late work. He died at home in New York City.

When Kertész began working, photographers often tried to imitate painting, with large-plate pictures and special printing techniques. Kertész always rejected these effects, instead exploring the idiom of purely photographic description and working with portable cameras and small negatives. During his youth and early career, black-and-white photography became portable. This led to a new realism, of which Kertész was a leading proponent, and played an important part in the development of photographic reportage in the 1930s. Like other realist photographers, Kertész strove to record the world reduced to its legible essence, almost as pictograms. He valued reserve, sincerity, modesty, and discretion in photography, not the search for effects. He never altered his photos other than cropping them. He described photography as "being at the window," aptly reflecting the sense of distance and separation often found in his pictures.

• Books by Kertész not mentioned above include *Nos amies les bêtes* (1936), *Day of Paris* (1945), *Americana* (1979), *From My Window* (1981), *André Kertész: A Lifetime of Perception* (1982), and *Hungarian Memories* (1982). His negatives and papers are held by the French Ministry of Culture. Exhibition catalogs include *André Kertész, Photographer* (1964), *Kertész on Kertész: A Self Portrait* (1985), and *André Kertész: His Life and Work* (1994), which includes a chronology and bibliography. Obituaries are in the *New York Times*, 29 and 30 Sept. 1985.

BETHANY NEUBAUER

KESSLER, David (1860–14 May 1920), actor, was born in Kishinev, Russia, the son of a poor, religious innkeeper father, who sent his son out on the streets to peddle. Kessler's mother's name is unknown. He received almost no formal education. As a teenager he supposedly decided to become an actor after seeing a troupe of Yiddish actors, despite his father's opposition. At the age of twenty Kessler joined a Jewish-language theater, first as a stagehand and then as an actor. He toured southern Russia with this company, which was run by Judel Goldfaden, the brother of Avram Goldfaden, the playwright considered to be the founder of the Yiddish-language theater. When the czarist government banned Jewish-language performances in 1883, Kessler and a company of actors that included Sigmund Mogulesco and Bertha Kalish went to Rumania, touring throughout that country. Three years later Kessler went to London.

Arriving in the United States in about 1890, Kessler quickly became one of the leading actors in the thriving Yiddish-speaking world of New York City's Lower East Side, competing with other such luminaries as Jacob Adler, with whom he acted when he first arrived in New York, and Boris Thomashevsky, with whom he would also on occasion act. The competition between Kessler and Adler was so intense that Kessler sued Adler over the lease of the Grand Theatre in 1906.

Kessler was a successful actor and actor-manager at several downtown Yiddish theaters, including the Thalia, Windsor, and Peoples theaters, eventually managing the stock company at the David Kessler Second Avenue Theatre, which he co-owned with Max R. Wilner and which was dedicated on 14 September 1911. The dedication was so celebrated an event that even Mayor William Gaynor attended. The location of Kessler's playhouse was significant because, until the opening of his theater, the center of the New York Yiddish-language theater had been the Bowery. Eventually, other major Yiddish companies and performers followed Kessler to Second Avenue, which would be nicknamed the Jewish Broadway. Kessler also toured his Yiddish productions throughout the United States.

Among the cities he performed in during the first two decades of the twentieth century were Hartford, Syracuse, Scranton, Pittsburgh, Indianapolis, Chicago, Milwaukee, Minneapolis, St. Louis, and Los Angeles.

Kessler's repertoire was extensive. He appeared in Yiddish versions of contemporary American, French, and German plays, such as Sudermann's *Heimat*, in which he played an aristocratic Prussian father, as well as in translations of dramas by Shakespeare, including *Othello*. However, Kessler was best known for his performances in the plays of Jacob Gordin, a playwright who attempted to create a more refined Yiddish theater, and whose dramas downplayed the comic, melodramatic traditions of the popular Jewish theater. Kessler first appeared in Gordin's play *Siberia* in 1891 with Adler's company. Among the other plays by Gordin in which Kessler starred were *The Kreutzer Sonata* (adapted from Tolstoy), *Sappho*, *God, Man, and Devil*, *Shloimke Charlatan*, and *The Slaughter*. Kessler also performed in many other notable Yiddish dramas, including Sholem Asch's *God of Vengeance*, David Pinski's *Yankel the Smith*, and Leon Kobrin's *Yankel Boile*.

Kessler appeared once on Broadway in English in Samuel Shipman's melodrama *The Spell*, which opened on 19 September 1907 at the Majestic Theatre. Playing an immigrant banker whose wife is in love with an evil bank employee, Kessler's character saves both his marriage and the bank in Shipman's melodrama, which was not well received critically and which ran for only two weeks.

During a performance in Brooklyn of Gordin's adaptation of *The Kreutzer Sonata*, Kessler was taken ill with a severe intestinal ailment. Contemporary newspaper accounts reported that the Yiddish star died in New York City while recovering from an emergency operation. According to the *New York Times*, there was "one of the greatest crowds ever gathered for a ceremony of mourning on the east side. More than 100 patrolmen were needed" for Kessler's funeral. Among those who delivered the eulogies were leading stars and playwrights in the New York Yiddish theater, including Jacob Adler, Sholom Asch, and Bertha Kalish, the popular actress whom Kessler had brought over from Europe.

Kessler, who was married twice, had a daughter, Ida, by his first marriage, who also acted in the Yiddish theater. Kessler's second marriage was to the mother of Max R. Wilner, his business partner in the David Kessler Second Avenue Theatre.

Kessler dedicated much of his career to improving the quality of the Yiddish theater. His goal was to move Yiddish theater from *shund*, nonliterary popular entertainment, to artistic, literary drama. When he opened Kessler's Second Avenue Theatre, the *New York Times* announced that he was to "lead a stock company in the production of particularly Yiddish plays by such playwrights as Jacob Gordin, Sholom Asch, Joseph Lateiner, and Isidor Zolataroffsky." In addition, Kessler strove to improve the quality of performance in the Yiddish theater, again trying to convert the popular, audience-conscious style into a more emotionally realistic representation. Kessler, a tall, broad man, who was often described as "peasant necked," excelled at high-pitched emotional performances as well as more subtle characterizations. A contemporary English-language critic remarked about Kessler's theater that "the acting is forceful, realistic—and often inspired." Apocryphal tales glorify Kessler's berating late-arriving audience members and talkative spectators, as well as criticizing the melodramatic plays that the Lower East Side audience adored even while he was performing in them. Kessler's attention to performance detail and his exacting managerial style resulted in his being nicknamed "the Henry Irving of the east side" by the *New York Times*.

• Additional information on Kessler is in the Billy Rose Theatre Collection at the New York Public Library for the Performing Arts, Lincoln Center. Mendel Osherowitch's *David Kessler* (1930) is a short biography in Yiddish. A description of Kessler's performance in *The Spell* is in Gerald Bordman, *American Theatre: A Chronicle of Comedy and Drama, 1869–1914* (1994). An article on the opening of Kessler's Second Avenue Theatre is in the *New York Times*, 15 Sept. 1911. General information can also be found in David S. Lifson, *The Yiddish Theatre in America* (1965), and Nahma Sandrow, *Vagabond Stars: A World History of Yiddish Theater* (1977). Irving Howe's *World of Our Fathers* (1976) contains an extended description of the Yiddish theater and Kessler. Obituaries are in *Variety Obituaries* (1988) and the *New York Times*, 15 May 1920.

ALVIN GOLDFARB

KETCHEL, Stanley (14 Sept. 1886–15 Oct. 1910), professional boxer, was born Stanislaus Kiecal in Grand Rapids, Michigan, the son of Thomas Kiecal and Julia Oblinsky, both of Polish descent. The family name was changed to Ketchel and young Ketchel's name was changed from "Stanislaus" to "Stanley" before he left home at fifteen. He went to Butte, Montana, where he worked as a hotel bellboy and a bouncer in a saloon. A brawler and street fighter, he began fighting all comers at Butte's Casino Theater for $20 a week, showing much natural ability. He was tutored by an ex-fighter, Freddie Bogan, and served as a sparring partner to the area's outstanding fighter, Maurice Thompson. In 1904 he began to appear in professional fights.

From 1904 to 1906 Ketchel frequently boxed in Montana rings, winning nearly all of his bouts. Possessed of great punching power, he knocked out thirty-five opponents in forty fights and gained local fame. In late 1906 he went to Nevada, working odd jobs at Tonopah and Goldfield. At first he had difficulty finding fights but attracted attention by knocking out George Brown in Sacramento, California, in May 1907.

Ketchel and Joe Thomas, a highly rated middleweight, fought a series of three sensational fights in northern California, the first a draw, Ketchel winning by a knockout in the second and by a decision in the third. He followed with a one-round knockout of the then famous Mike Sullivan of Boston. On 9 May 1908 Ketchel fought Sullivan's twin brother, Jack, for the vacant middleweight championship; the match took place in Colma (outside San Francisco), and Ketchel won the title on a knockout in the twentieth round.

Ketchel's sudden rise to prominence, coupled with his style, personality, and appearance, immediately made him the most popular man in boxing. Known to his friends as "Steve," he was affable and generous. Sportswriters labeled him as the "Michigan Assassin" because of his potent punching ability. Strikingly handsome, he was a two-fisted, impetuously aggressive, extremely quick fighter who was willing to take his opponents' punches to land his own. Sportswriter Robert Edgren wrote of Ketchel, "He doesn't extend his left hand and foot and fight along lines taught in boxing schools. Right and left sides are exactly alike to him. He shifts constantly and naturally. He gets in close and punches. . . . As the right lands the left whips over like a flash against the same mark. Or is it the left and then the right? Ketchel leans over and sends hooks and uppercuts to the body. And shoulder and body swing in with every blow."

Managed by Willus Britt, Ketchel lost no time in putting his title on the line. He made successful defenses in June, July, and August 1908 against Billy Papke, Hugo Kelly, and Joe Thomas, then met Papke in a return fight in September at Vernon (then a small town surrounded by and later absorbed into Los Angeles). At the start of the first round Papke struck Ketchel a hard blow just as Ketchel reached out to touch gloves for the traditional beginning "handshake." Papke then launched a devastating attack. Ketchel failed to recover and suffered severe punishment before being knocked out in the twelfth round, losing the middleweight title.

In November at Colma he and Papke met again and Ketchel regained the title after giving his opponent a terrible beating. In 1909 Ketchel won four fights on the East Coast, two of them over the legendary Philadelphia Jack O'Brien. This match was followed by his last fight with Papke, at Colma, which Ketchel won by decision after another vicious battle.

On 16 October 1909 Ketchel fought Jack Johnson for the world heavyweight title at Colma in one of the most famous fights in boxing history. Johnson was 6'1" tall and weighed 205 pounds, and Ketchel was 5'9" and weighed 170 pounds. With these natural advantages and much superior defensive skills, Johnson dominated the fight for ten rounds. In the eleventh, Ketchel began a desperate attack and succeeded in punishing Johnson. At the start of the twelfth round Ketchel rushed across the ring and knocked Johnson down, badly hurting the champion. When Johnson arose, Ketchel repeated the assault but ran into a sudden counterattack that knocked him out. Although the loser, he was now more popular than ever.

Willus Britt died soon after the Johnson fight, and Ketchel fell under the influence of the famous humorist and bon vivant, Wilson Mizner. Without a manager's guidance, Ketchel lived in high style, driving recklessly, spending freely, soon losing most of his money. In 1910 he had five fights in the East, including a newspapermen's decision over the great Sam Langford. In October, realizing that he had to change his life-style if he was to remain in the ring, Ketchel went to Missouri, where he had bought property, and lived on a friend's adjoining ranch. However, he became involved in a quarrel with a ranch hand, Walter Dipley, and Dipley's former common-law wife, Goldie Smith. Dipley shot him while he was eating breakfast, and Ketchel died soon afterward.

Ketchel is often ranked by boxing experts as among the greatest middleweights of all time, despite his comparatively brief career. His punching power and great quickness, together with remarkable endurance and recuperative power and an indomitable fighting spirit, made him a formidable opponent even for much heavier men. His likable but reckless personality, his handsome features, and his sensational fights made him one of the most popular fighters in boxing history. He won fifty-five of his sixty-four fights, scoring forty-nine knockouts. He was an inaugural inductee into the International Boxing Hall of Fame.

• Ketchel's record most recently appeared in the 1986–1987 edition of *The Ring Record Book and Boxing Encyclopedia*, ed. Herbert G. Goldman. A good biographical sketch appears in John D. McCallum's *The Encyclopedia of World Boxing Champions* (1975). A flawed biography by Nat Fleischer, *The Michigan Assassin*, was published in 1946. Several good articles on Ketchel have appeared in *The Ring*, including Ed Smith, "The Ketchel I Knew," Feb. 1934; Webb Kyle, "Stanley Ketchel, the Michigan Assassin," Mar. 1937; Hype Igoe, "Ketchel Many Sided," Jan. 1939; Harvey McClellan, "The Cowboy Crushed," Dec. 1941; Dan Daniel, "Ketchel versus Papke—Socking Series Saga," Dec. 1946; and John Lardner, "Stanley Ketchel: The First Middleweight Great," Apr. 1983. "My Brother, Stanley Ketchel," by Arthur Ketchel, Jr., appeared in *Boxing Illustrated*, Sept. 1961. An account of Ketchel's early career is given by Frank Bell in *Gladiators of the Glittering Gulches* (1985). The most thorough obituary is in the (Grand Rapids, Mich.) *Sunday Herald*, 16 Oct. 1910. Accounts of Ketchel's major fights can be found in many contemporary newspapers.

LUCKETT DAVIS

KETTERING, Charles Franklin (29 Aug. 1876–25 Nov. 1958), inventor and automotive engineer, was born in Loudonville, Ohio, the son of Jacob Kettering and Martha Hunter, farmers. He attended public schools and graduated at the top of his high school class. He spent two years teaching and then enrolled in the engineering program at the Ohio State University. Forced by chronic eye inflammation to withdraw at the beginning of his sophomore year, he took a job with a local telephone company line crew. Two years later he returned to Ohio State and graduated in 1904.

After graduation Kettering took a job as an electrical inventor with the National Cash Register Company (NCR) in Dayton, Ohio. There, under the tutelage of president and marketing genius John Patterson (whose other "graduates" included future IBM founder Thomas Watson), Kettering mastered the art of

translating good ideas into salable products. "I didn't hang around much with the other inventors or the executive fellows," Kettering recalled. "I lived with the sales gang. They had some real notion of what people wanted." What he learned from the marketing people helped him transform the cash register from a money box into a powerful tool of management planning. He invented the first commercially successful electric cash register and then figured out ways of incorporating it into automated accounting and banking machine systems. Some of these innovations clearly anticipated computerized inventory control.

Kettering left NCR in 1909 to go into business for himself. With the technical assistance of several moonlighting NCR engineers, he developed a battery ignition for automobiles and sold it to Cadillac. He and NCR executive Edward Deeds then incorporated the Dayton Engineering Laboratories Company, or Delco, to manufacture and market the ignition system. Delco ignitions became standard equipment on several major cars within two years.

Kettering next hit upon the idea that would earn him automotive immortality: the electric self starter. Other inventors had experimented with various kinds of self starters, including electrical ones. What distinguished Kettering's was his insistence that it be part of an integrated system of starting, lighting, and ignition. Drawing on his earlier experiences with electric cash register motors, Kettering put together a motor small and powerful enough to do the job and then designed the storage battery, voltage regulator, generator, and other components around it. Cadillac ordered 12,000 units for its 1912 models, followed by Oakland, Oldsmobile, Auburn, and Jackson. By 1914 Delco boasted one-quarter of the automotive starting, lighting, and ignition market; 2,370 employees; and annual profits of $1.5 million. Without question, the electric self starter was a milestone in automotive history. If the claims of contemporary journalists that the self starter did more for women's emancipation than universal suffrage were clearly exaggerated, Kettering's invention certainly put more women (and older people) behind the wheel than ever before.

Delco's financial success, along with Kettering's lack of interest in management, made it an attractive target for a corporate takeover. In 1916 it caught the eye of William Crapo Durant, the aggressive entrepreneur who had founded General Motors in 1908. In 1916 Durant acquired five independent automotive accessory manufacturers, including Delco, as part of United Motors. Kettering received $2.5 million in cash and $1.5 million in stock for his share of Delco. Three years later, when Durant merged United Motors into General Motors, those shares made Kettering one of the corporation's largest single shareholders and eventually one of the nation's wealthiest men.

Meanwhile, Kettering spent World War I trying to apply some of the lessons of automotive production to the military. Along with Deeds, Orville Wright, and other local inventors and businessmen, he incorporated the Dayton Wright Airplane Company. Under army contract Kettering and a team of engineers designed and built a self-guided aerial torpedo, which was actually a small biplane with a high explosive warhead and automatic controls. This top secret project was decades ahead of its time—a direct ancestor of the cruise missile. Kettering could never get it to work reliably, however, and so it never saw action. Delco did contribute to the war effort by manufacturing thousands of aircraft ignition systems and by developing a synthetic aircraft fuel.

A postwar reorganization at General Motors, masterminded by Pierre du Pont and his protégé Alfred Sloan, put Kettering in charge of a new corporate research laboratory. That gave him responsibility for looking beyond the immediate needs of Chevrolet, Buick, and the other operating divisions and for planning a technical strategy for the entire corporation. For his debut, Kettering proposed a novel air-cooled engine (called the copper-cooled for its cooling fins), which he thought would challenge Ford in the low-price market and pull General Motors out of a postwar automotive recession. Instead, the project nearly bankrupted General Motors and forced corporate executives to rethink the place of Kettering's laboratory within the organization.

What Kettering seemed to forget was that his laboratory could only develop the car. The operating divisions would have to manufacture and sell it. Research and production engineers largely worked at cross purposes, and the tension gradually escalated. Things got so bad at one point that Kettering threatened to quit and take the project with him. After three years of losing money, momentum, and managerial control, du Pont and Sloan scrapped the venture. To turn the laboratory from a corporate liability into an asset, Sloan, who became General Motors president in 1923, organized a special technical committee charged with integrating research, production, and marketing.

Sloan also concluded that Kettering had been aiming at the wrong end of the market. General Motors, he decided, had no real chance against Ford at the entry level. Rather than compete directly with the Model T, General Motors would offer a car for every purse and purpose, as Sloan liked to say. To help customers take the first step, he introduced consumer credit, and to keep them moving, if only in the same place, he introduced the annual model change.

Of course Sloan's strategy depended in large measure on Kettering's ability to deliver the right kind of automobile. For only when this year's model was significantly more appealing than last year's could General Motors entice buyers into falling for the annual model change and the full model line. Kettering called it "keeping the customer dissatisfied," and his laboratory mastered it. He once explained the strategy in one of his typically homespun but insightful stories. Select the best example of contemporary automotive art and seal it in a glass case, he said. Then put the price in gold letters on the front. Check back each year to see if the posted price still seemed fair. "And what do you think you can get for that car at the end of fifteen years?" he asked. "It will be just as good as it was when we put it in the case, but the only man who will buy it is the junk dealer."

Keeping the customer dissatisfied became General Motors' not-so-secret weapon in the fight with Ford; the results were dramatic. In 1920, when Kettering became research director, Ford was selling more than half the automobiles in the country, and General Motors less than a quarter. By the end of the decade those figures were reversed.

Perhaps Kettering's most visible improvement was Duco, a fast-drying, durable, colored lacquer. Henry Ford liked to say he would give his customers any color they wanted, so long as it was black, because only black baking enamel was cheap and quick-drying. Duco, by cutting finishing time for colored paints from weeks to hours, gave customers a rainbow of choices, and gave General Motors a big edge in the low-price market. So did Kettering's innovations in crankcase ventilation, crankshaft vibration damping, bearings, brakes, and dozens of other incremental improvements. Ford designed a car suited for the mass market and then figured out how to manufacture it cheaply. In a similar way, Kettering democratized automotive luxury.

Kettering often defined industrial research as a kind of corporate insurance policy—as a way, he said, of finding out what you are going to do when you can no longer do what you are doing now. To that end, he tried not only to keep pace with the market, but to stay a step or two ahead. Long before other engineers were worrying about petroleum shortages and mileage per gallon, Kettering was improving automotive fuel economy and efficiency. He had begun studying combustion back at Delco, initially in response to complaints that his battery ignitions somehow caused knock, a common malfunction of gasoline engines in those days, and later as part of his research on aviation fuels.

An anticipated postwar fuel crisis convinced Kettering to make fuel economy a top research priority at General Motors. A team led by Thomas Midgley, Jr., reinterpreted knock as a failing of the fuel, rather than of the engine, and then identified a number of antiknock additives, culminating in the discovery of tetraethyl lead (TEL) in 1921. Even at extreme dilutions, TEL suppressed knock completely. Kettering introduced "Ethyl" gasoline, a name he coined himself, at a Dayton filling station in 1923.

While the commercial potential of TEL looked staggering—Americans were then using some four billion gallons of gasoline a year and increasing their consumption by 20 percent annually—General Motors was in no position to exploit its discovery directly. Instead it joined Standard Oil of New Jersey in forming Ethyl Corporation, with Kettering as the first president. A national health scare in 1924 almost wiped out a promising start. Following a well-publicized accident at a TEL blending plant in New Jersey, in which dozens of workers were killed or injured, the sale of leaded gasoline was temporarily suspended. Kettering and other Ethyl officials argued strenuously that TEL was only dangerous in the chemical plant, not in the gas tank, and convinced the surgeon general to recommend only more rigorous industrial safety standards. Within a year leaded gasoline was back on the market. Although in fact relatively safe as a consumer product, its manufacturers paid little attention to the long-term environmental implications of TEL, despite exponential increases in American gasoline consumption.

Kettering kept a team of General Motors chemists busy studying combustion fundamentals throughout the 1920s and 1930s. They developed octane rating and also learned how to make nonleaded gasolines as knock resistant as leaded ones, without the polluting additives. Because these gasolines cost more to manufacture, gasoline without the lead paradoxically cost more than gasoline with it. Long after new oil strikes and improved refining techniques made the oil crisis of the 1920s a distant memory, Kettering kept after the fuel question. After World War II he introduced the high compression V-8 (or Kettering Engine).

Sloan once said that General Motors was in the business of making money, not making cars, and over the years Kettering's inventions helped the company diversify into new markets as well as strengthen its hold on traditional ones. Kettering's laboratory developed Freon, the first truly safe refrigerant, which shored up the sagging fortunes of General Motors's Frigidaire subsidiary. He also put General Motors in the railroad business with an improved diesel engine with solid fuel injection, a two-stroke cycle, better scavenging, and alloy construction, giving it far less weight per horsepower than anyone had previously imagined. Backed by the tremendous resources of General Motors, Kettering's diesel gave the Electromotive Division a commanding position in the diesel locomotive market. Ironically enough, Kettering was also responsible for General Motors's failure in the automotive diesel market. Completely committed to his two-stroke design, Kettering consistently killed off four-stroke diesel programs at General Motors. Consequently General Motors later found itself at a considerable disadvantage when four-stroke automotive diesels proved to be the better bet.

Kettering directed General Motors research from 1920 until his retirement in 1947 but served as a consultant thereafter. Over those years he probably contributed as much to the technical development of the automobile as any other American engineer and more to making the automobile a convenient necessity of everyday life.

Although General Motors transferred the research laboratory to Detroit in 1924, Kettering and his wife, Olive Williams, whom he had married in 1905, continued to live in Dayton, where they raised one child. Kettering kept one suite of rooms at a luxurious Detroit hotel and another at the Waldorf-Astoria in New York. He always told friends that his home was in Dayton, but since he could not find a job there, he had to work in Detroit!

In his later years Kettering increasingly devoted himself to research questions outside the automotive field. He and Sloan founded the Sloan-Kettering Institute for cancer research in New York. He established the Kettering Foundation for the support of photosynthesis and solar energy research. And he set up a series of private laboratories for fundamental studies of magnetism. Despite a well-deserved reputation for downplaying the value of a textbook education, he gave generously to a variety of educational institutions, particularly Antioch College, which he admired for its co-operative education programs. He also became a popular and widely quoted speaker and something of a cheerleader for the American Way. Like Henry Ford, Kettering had little use for history, saying that you never get anywhere looking in your rearview mirror. Instead, he looked to the future because, as he often explained, "we will have to spend the rest of our lives there." He died at home in Dayton.

• Some of Kettering's papers are held by the General Motors Institute Alumni Collection of Industrial History in Flint, Mich., which also holds an extensive collection of oral histories of former associates and an excellent photographic archive. The rest of Kettering's General Motors papers are held by the General Motors Research Laboratories in Warren, Mich. Wright Patterson Air Force Base in Dayton, Ohio, has some important holdings on Kettering's aviation interests. NCR Corporation has Kettering's papers from his days as an electrical inventor there. Thomas Boyd, ed., *Prophet of Progress: Selections from the Speeches of Charles F. Kettering* (1961), offers a good sample of the Kettering philosophy, along with a comprehensive list of publications. Boyd's biography, *Professional Amateur: The Biography of Charles Franklin Kettering* (1957), provides an appreciation by a long-time friend and collaborator. Zay Jeffries, "Charles Franklin Kettering," *National Academy of Sciences, Biographical Memoirs* 34 (1960): 106–22, has an incomplete list of publications and patents but does include some personal reflections from an associate. Alfred P. Sloan, Jr., *My Years with General Motors* (1964), gives a curiously impersonal though invaluable perspective on Kettering's career with General Motors from the president's office. Stuart W. Leslie, *Boss Kettering: Wizard of General Motors* (1983), is the only scholarly biography. John B. Rae, *The American Automobile Industry* (1984), and James J. Flink, *The Automobile Age* (1988), place Kettering's career in the larger context of American automotive history.

STUART W. LESLIE

KEY, David McKendree (27 Jan. 1824–3 Feb. 1900), federal judge and postmaster general of the United States, was born in Greene County, Tennessee, the son of John Key, a Methodist minister, and Margaret Armitage. In 1826 his father moved the family to Monroe County, Tennessee, where he became one of the founders and first trustees of Hiwassee College. David Key graduated in the first class of Hiwassee in 1850, serving as both a tutor for younger students and vice president of the college while completing his undergraduate degree. Having also read law in college, Key was admitted in 1850 to the bar in Monroe County; subsequently he began practicing law in Kingston, Tennessee, before moving in 1853 to Chattanooga, where he would remain, except for his years in the military and in Washington, D.C., until his death. In

1857 he married Elizabeth Lenoir, a member of an aristocratic family originally from North Carolina. They would have eight children.

Immediately successful as a lawyer in Chattanooga, Key was an active Democrat, becoming a close friend and protégé of Andrew Johnson and serving as a presidential elector on the James Buchanan ticket in 1856 and on the John C. Breckinridge ticket in 1860. At the outbreak of the secession crisis in 1861, however, he ignored the warning of Johnson and fell under the spell of Isham Harris, Tennessee's firebrand secessionist governor. Although Key served the Confederacy loyally, becoming lieutenant colonel of the Forty-third Regiment, Tennessee Infantry, he was appalled by the arrest of many old friends in East Tennessee, whose imprisonment without trial and subsequent deaths seemed to make a mockery of what he had believed was the raison d'être of the Confederacy—individual liberty. Wounded and captured at Vicksburg, Key swallowed his pride and wrote to his old friend, now President Andrew Johnson, at the end of the war, asking for a pardon. Johnson responded magnanimously, and Key returned to Chattanooga with his family to recommence the practice of law.

In an 1867 visit to the White House, Key was warmly received by Johnson, who confided to his old friend many of his own difficulties with the Radical Republicans in Congress. Again active in Democratic circles, Key in 1870 was among those chosen to rewrite Tennessee's constitution and in the same year was elected chancellor of the third district of Tennessee. In 1875 he was appointed U.S. senator to temporarily succeed Johnson, who had died in that office, but when the Tennessee legislature met in 1877 to select a permanent choice for the unexpired term Key was defeated by James E. Bailey. His defeat was due to a number of speeches Key had made in the Senate, urging sectional reconciliation and backing some Republican measures he believed would bring economic prosperity to the South. Although Key's farsighted speeches of reconciliation earned him the lasting enmity of many southerners and Tennessee Democrats, these efforts ultimately assisted the move toward national reconciliation in the Compromise of 1877.

Appointed postmaster general by Rutherford B. Hayes in May 1877, Key used this office to increase badly needed postal routes in the South and West. As the only Democrat in Hayes's cabinet, however, he was denounced by southerners as a traitor and attacked by northern Republicans for appointing too many Democrats to postal jobs. Unable to resolve the dilemma between political patronage and civil service reform, Key resigned in 1880 to accept the office of U.S. district judge for the eastern and middle districts of Tennessee.

As a federal district judge until his retirement in 1894, Key displayed more interest in seeking justice for the downtrodden and dispossessed than in following legal precedents or winning political popularity. Sympathetic to the plight of small farmers in East Tennessee, Judge Key horrified many by allowing convicted moonshiners to delay beginning their sentences until they had finished making a crop for their families. Although sharing the racial prejudices of his age, he also bitterly denounced the inherent injustices of segregation, insisting time and again to hostile audiences that justice was color-blind and that the federal Constitution mandated political equality for all. Key died in Chattanooga.

Much of Key's political career involved taking extremely unpopular positions for conscience's sake. A large, jovial man of magnetic personality, he was often able to maintain personal friendships with those who otherwise abhorred his political positions. His biographer, David M. Abshire, views as Key's greatest tragedy his inability to apply all of his personal force and will to fulfilling his own vision for a progressive, prosperous South, free of racial antagonisms. Yet in the context of his own time and place, even speaking out publicly about equal justice under the law for blacks and the necessity of reconciliation between North and South after the Civil War places Key in bold relief when contrasted to most of his contemporaries in Tennessee and the South.

• The most complete source of primary materials on Key's life is the D. M. Key Papers, Chattanooga Public Library; this collection contains a scrapbook of newspaper articles about Key not available from any other source. The best biography of Key is David M. Abshire, *The South Rejects a Prophet: The Life of Senator D. M. Key, 1824–1900* (1967). For Key's career at Hiwassee College, see Robert L. Hilten, *The Hiwassee Story: From Pioneer Days to the Space Age* (1970). Other biographical and family material is contained in Joshua W. Caldwell, *Sketches of the Bench and Bar of Tennessee* (1898), and Mrs. Julian C. Lane, *Key and Allied Families* (1931). For Key's role in the Compromise of 1877, see C. Vann Woodward, *Reunion and Reaction: The Compromise of 1877 and the End of Reconstruction* (1951), and Keith I. Polakoff, *The Politics of Inertia: The Election of 1876 and the End of Reconstruction* (1973). An obituary is in the *Chattanooga Sunday Times*, 4 Feb. 1900.

DURWOOD DUNN

KEY, Francis Scott (1 Aug. 1779–11 Jan. 1843), author and lawyer, was born in Frederick (now Carroll) County, Maryland, the son of John Ross Key, an army officer in the revolutionary war, and Ann Phoebe Charlton. After graduating from St. John's College in Annapolis, he studied law and in 1801 opened his law practice in Fredericktown with Roger B. Taney, who married his sister and would later serve as chief justice of the U.S. Supreme Court. In 1802 Key married Mary Tayloe Lloyd; they had eleven children. Soon after his marriage, he moved to Georgetown, D.C., and began legal practice there in association with his uncle Philip Barton Key.

During the War of 1812 British troops occupied Washington, burned stores and public buildings, including the Capitol, and advanced on Baltimore. In the fall of 1814 Francis Scott Key was asked to negotiate the release from British forces of a Washington physician, William Beanes, who had been taken prisoner and confined aboard a ship in the British fleet. Key secured the release of Dr. Beanes, but he was detained on the HMS *Surprise* by the British as preparations were being made to land British troops. Under guard, Key, Beanes, and others were released to their ship, the *Minden*, and on 13–14 September 1814, during the naval bombardment of Fort McHenry in Baltimore, Key observed the fight from the American vessel. Key remained on deck during the night, and when morning came he was excited to see the American flag still flying over the fort. According to an account of the incident given by Chief Justice Taney, Key composed "The Star-Spangled Banner," wrote it out on his way to shore, and revised the notes in his hotel that night.

Key is remembered and revered by the American public as the composer of the national anthem. The melody of "The Star-Spangled Banner" came from the popular British work "To Anacreon in Heaven," a well-known drinking song. The lyrics were printed in the *Baltimore American* on 21 September 1814, and although the song became moderately popular, it was not widely accepted as a national song until the time of the Civil War. The idea that the United States should have an official national song came somewhat later in the nineteenth century. In 1861 Congress formed a committee to select a national hymn by public competition, but no award was made. John Philip Sousa arranged an official version of "The Star-Spangled Banner" for the U.S. armed forces that was played by military and naval bands in the 1890s. But it was not until 3 March 1931 that Congress officially accepted the song as "the national anthem of the United States of America."

Although Key had composed verses before "The Star-Spangled Banner" for his own pleasure, he did not seem to regard himself as a poet or as a serious writer of songs. He made little effort to write verse for publication but rather composed pieces for his own enjoyment and that of his friends. These pieces, written mostly on plain slips of scrap paper without revision, were collected and published posthumously in *Poems of the Late Francis S. Key, Esq.* in 1857. Some of the verses in the book are hymns; Key was deeply religious and had considered the clergy as a profession. Other pieces in the collection are occasional verses, likewise of scant merit; nevertheless, Key had a continuing interest in literature and published in 1834 a volume titled *The Power of Literature and Its Connection with Religion.*

"The Star-Spangled Banner" has been in recent times censured for its awkward melodic line, but its lyrics are now so much a part of the popular patriotic imagination that any attempt at literary analysis would perhaps seem unusual. (The second and third stanzas of the original song are often omitted in public ceremonies as a gesture of courtesy to the British; the words "hireling and slave" of stanza three refer to the common British practice of using mercenary soldiers.) It is interesting that the critic Charles F. Richardson, writing in *American Literature*, mentions the "bald, rude rhymes" in the work. He goes on to say that the

song, along with "Adams and Liberty" and "Hail Columbia," is "so closely enshrined in the patriotic heart . . . that no one stops to think of . . . [its] literary poverty" (vol. 2 [1889] p. 26). Richardson's comments seem a just assessment of a work that had not yet become a national symbol.

In addition to being the writer of a song that was to become the national anthem, Key was a talented and effective public speaker and served as a delegate to the general conventions of the Episcopal church for a number of years (1814–1826). He was also a lay reader for St. John's Church in Georgetown. Around 1830 he left Georgetown for permanent residence in Washington. An attorney with a large, successful practice in the federal courts, Key served as the U.S. attorney for the District of Columbia between 1833 and 1841. Perhaps his most significant achievement as an attorney was his negotiation of a settlement in 1833 between the Alabama state government and the federal government over the Creek Indian lands at the behest of President Andrew Jackson (T. C. McCorvey, "The Mission of Francis Scott Key to Alabama in 1833," *Alabama Historical Society Transactions* 4 [1904]: 141–65).

Key died in Baltimore at his daughter's home, and his body was put temporarily in his daughter's family vault; in 1866 it was moved to Mount Olivet Cemetery in Frederick. Monuments to Key are located there, at Fort McHenry National Monument, in the city of Baltimore, and in Golden Gate Park in San Francisco.

• Key's manuscript of "The Star-Spangled Banner" is now in the Maryland Historical Society, Baltimore. A biography is Francis Scott Key-Smith's *Francis Scott Key, Author of the Star-Spangled Banner* (1911); other biographical material may be found in Anne Key Barstow, "Recollections of Francis Scott Key," *Modern Culture* 12 (Nov. 1900): 204–13, and Mrs. Julian C. Lane, *Key and Allied Families* (1931). For additional material on "The Star-Spangled Banner," see Francis Scott Key-Smith, "The Story of the Star-Spangled Banner," *Current History* 32 (May 1930): 267–72; P. H. Magruder, "The Original Manuscript of the Final Text of the 'Star-Spangled Banner,'" *Proceedings of the U.S. Naval Institute* 53 (June 1927): 647–51; and O. G. T. Sonneck, *Report on the Star-Spangled Banner* (1909). For an interesting historical perspective concerning the national anthem, see *The Cambridge History of American Literature*, vol. 3 (1917); a published copy of the song along with two additional verses by Key is in the *Cyclopaedia of American Literature* (1875).

RICHARD E. MEZO

KEY, Philip Barton (12 Apr. 1757–28 July 1815), lawyer and politician, was born in Cecil County, Maryland, the son of Francis Key, a clerk of the county court, and Anne Arnold Ross, the daughter of John Ross, a prominent attorney in Annapolis. Descending from Philip Key, who emigrated to St. Marys County from London, England, about 1720, the Keys grew into a large and prominent family who intermarried with several others on Maryland's Western Shore during the first half of the eighteenth century. They included lawyers, planters, physicians, millers, and public officers such as sheriffs and clerks of county courts. One of Philip's uncles, Edmund, served as Maryland's attorney general from 1764 to 1766. Key was most likely named after his uncle Philip Barton Key, who died in 1756.

The American Revolution was a civil war for Key and his only brother John Ross Key, who married Ann Charlton in 1775 and fathered, in 1779, Francis Scott Key, later the author of "The Star Spangled Banner." John Ross Key identified early and strongly with the patriot cause, and went off as a lieutenant with Thomas Price's Maryland Rifle Company to the siege of Boston. Philip Barton Key remained in Annapolis and studied law. In December 1777, following Sir William Howe's impressive invasion up the Chesapeake Bay and capture of Philadelphia, Key joined the British forces and in April 1778 accepted a captaincy in James Chalmers's regiment known as the Maryland Loyalists. He accompanied them to New York, and in 1779 the regiment was then sent to Florida. Besieged in Pensacola by Spanish troops, the regiment surrendered in 1781 and was taken to Havana, Cuba, where Key was paroled. He then went to London, completed his legal studies at the Middle Temple, and returned to Maryland in 1785. There he studied law under Gabriel Duvall, one of the state's preeminent lawyers. Key was admitted to the bar in St. Marys County in 1787 and in Annapolis in 1790. On 4 July 1790 Key, still drawing his half-pay as a retired British officer, married Ann Plater, the daughter of George Plater, a wealthy planter of St. Marys County and a prominent patriot who would be elected governor in 1791. The rift the Revolution had caused between Key and his brother had apparently mended over time, because in 1792 Key was named one of two trustees of his brother's estate.

Key's legal abilities and connections centered his work in Annapolis, from which he was elected annually as a Federalist to Maryland's House of Delegates from 1794 to 1799. His staunch support of President George Washington's policies and his attacks on the Republican opposition caused his defeat in 1800; but with the passage of the Judiciary Act of 1801 by the outgoing Federalists, President John Adams appointed Key chief justice of the fourth United States circuit court, and Key moved near Georgetown, D.C. When the Republican administration of president Thomas Jefferson abolished this office the next year, Key widened his legal practice from Georgetown into Montgomery County, Maryland. About the same time, his nephew Francis Scott Key joined him in his Georgetown practice.

Key's most famous case was his defense of the Supreme Court justice and fellow Federalist Samuel Chase, who was impeached and tried before the U.S. Senate in 1805. Key established his residence near the village of Norbeck in Montgomery County the following year, and he also relinquished his half-pay allowance from Great Britain. This enabled him to run for and be elected as a Federalist representative of Maryland's third congressional district and to serve in the Tenth, Eleventh, and Twelfth Congresses from 1807 until 1813.

Key's Federalism cast him into a predictable opposition to the proposals and proceedings of the Republican administrations of Jefferson and James Madison. With respect to foreign policy, he opposed the Embargo Act of 1807, interdicting commerce with foreign nations; the nonintercourse bill proposed in 1809 as a substitute for the Embargo Act; the invasion and annexation of West Florida in 1810; and Madison's asking Congress to declare war in 1812. On the other hand, he supported the bill in 1811 to recharter the first Bank of the United States, and he promoted the status of the District of Columbia by helping to establish a standing District committee in the House of Representatives. He continued to practice law after his congressional career ended in 1813. He died in Georgetown.

• Several collections at the Maryland Historical Society contain Key's papers or information about Key: the Philip Barton Key Commonplace Book (mss. 510); the Harper Letters (mss. 1304); the Aldine Collection (mss. 7); the Robert Goodloe Harper Papers (mss. 1884); the Shriver Family Papers (mss. 2085); the Francis Scott Key Papers (mss. 2199); the Dr. Upton Scott Papers (mss. 1722); the Frederick County Historical Society Collection (mss. 2417); the Key Family Papers (mss. 909); the Howard Papers (mss. 469); and an oral history, Edith Claude Jarvis (OH. 8255). Some of Key's service in James Chalmers's Maryland Loyalist regiment is traced in Captain Caleb Jones, *Orderly Book of the "Maryland Loyalists Regiment," June 18th, 1778 to October 12th, 1778*, ed. P. L. Ford (1891). Key is also listed in the *Biographical Directory of the American Congress, 1774–1961* (1961).

GARY L. BROWNE

KEY, V. O. (13 Mar. 1908–4 Oct. 1963), political scientist, was born Valdimer Orlando Key, Jr., in Austin, Texas, to Valdimer Orlando Key, a lawyer and farmer, and Olive Terry. Key spent his early years in Lamesa in West Texas, where his father was active in local politics. Later Key claimed that time spent hanging around the courthouse square had helped shape his political sensitivities and ability to comprehend politics. From 1925 to 1927 he attended MacMurry College in Abilene and finished his undergraduate studies at the University of Texas, where he also started his graduate work (A.B., 1929; M.A., 1930). Key earned his Ph.D. at the University of Chicago (1934), having written his dissertation under Charles Merriam, the pioneer of behavioral studies in political science; "The Techniques of Political Graft in the United States" examines graft as a means of social control and influence. Key married a fellow political science graduate student, Luella Gettys, in 1934; they had no children.

Key's teaching career began in 1934 at UCLA. After stints on the Social Science Research Council (1936–1937) and the National Resources Planning Board (1937–1938), he took a position at Johns Hopkins (1938–1949) but during World War II went on leave to serve with the Bureau of the Budget (1942–1945). From Hopkins, Key moved to Yale (1949–1951); his last appointment was at Harvard (1951–1963).

Even before the war interrupted his scholarly work, Key was a productive author. *The Administration of Federal Grants to States* appeared in 1937; *The Initiative and Referendum in California*, written with W. W. Crouch, in 1939; *The Problem of Local Legislation in Maryland* in 1940; and the textbook *Politics, Parties, and Pressure Groups* in 1942 (5th and final edition, 1964).

Key initially hesitated to involve himself in the research that was to win him lasting fame in the world of political science. In 1946 a former teacher of his at the University of Texas, Roscoe Martin, secured Rockefeller Foundation funding that enabled the Bureau of Public Administration at the University of Alabama to study the electoral process in the South. Only after considerable persuasion on Martin's part did Key accept the directorship of the project. The resulting *Southern Politics in State and Nation* (1949) was a scholarly masterpiece, comprehensively covering the politics of the eleven southern states. It raised fundamental questions about the role of race and the consequences for the solidly Democratic South of the adherence to one-party politics. Key wrote, "In its grand outlines the politics of the South revolves around the position of the Negro. . . . Whatever phase of the southern political process one seeks to understand, sooner or later the trail of inquiry leads to the Negro." Whites in the predominantly black areas, desiring to prevent Republican meddling in southern race relations, had successfully imposed their will on their states. Yet by yielding to the desires of these whites for solidarity in national politics, southern states had to forgo competitive political parties, saddling themselves internally with the chaos of factional politics.

Key relied on Alexander Heard and Donald Strong for 538 interviews that averaged seventy minutes each, creatively blending the resulting insights with aggregate data analysis into a 675-page work written in a clear and lively style. *Southern Politics in State and Nation* won the Woodrow Wilson Foundation Award for the best book about government and democracy to appear in 1949. Key overtly stated the values undergirding his research: a belief in democracy as professed in the United States, a belief that southerners had the same capacity for self-government as other U.S. citizens, and "the conviction that the best government results when there is free and vigorous competition at the ballot box in contests in which genuine issues are defined and candidates take a stand." These core beliefs motivated much of his scholarly writing.

Key's later work often elaborated on and extended concerns addressed in *Southern Politics*. In *A Primer of Statistics for Political Scientists* (1954), he sought to train others in "the considerable utility of simple quantitative techniques"; his *American State Politics: An Introduction* (1956) was focused on barriers to two-party politics in nonsouthern states; in *Public Opinion and American Democracy* (1961), he attempted to place new survey knowledge within a political rather than a sociological or psychological context; and in *The Responsible Electorate: Rationality in Presidential Voting, 1936–*

1960 (posthumously published, 1966), Key argued that "voters are not fools," that opinions about policies and judgments of governmental performance strongly influence the voting decision.

The most influential of Key's several articles, "A Theory of Critical Elections" (*Journal of Politics* 17 [Feb. 1955]: 3–18) offered an analysis of abrupt and lasting changes in the political party system. Key took up the question of partisan changes that were not such sharp, immediate breaks with the past in "Secular Realignment and the Party System" (*Journal of Politics* 21 [May 1959]: 198–210); over the years, he argued, gradual but cumulative alterations in partisan affiliations could produce sizable changes in the party system. These articles launched an extensive literature on partisan realignments.

When Samuel Eliot Morison retired from Harvard in 1955, Key was appointed to succeed him as holder of the Jonathan Trumbull chair. In 1958 Key was elected president of the American Political Science Association. After a long bout with a chronic illness that was not fully diagnosed, Key died at age fifty-five in Beth Israel Hospital in Brookline, Massachusetts.

As Milton Cummings noted, Key stressed the importance of three principles in the academic study of politics: that empirical inquiry be tied to political theory, that methodology be used imaginatively, and that one do rigorous scholarly work with wider relevance to the society at large. He is generally regarded as one of the leaders of the postwar "behavioral revolution" in American political science and contributed substantially to a more quantitative orientation in political science. According to Alexander Heard, Key "was the leading student of American politics in his generation." Or as William Havard has it: "I regard V. O. Key as the most astute and comprehensive professional student of American politics over the past fifty years. Furthermore, I think *Southern Politics . . .* remains the most impressive book published in the general area of American politics since World War II. Largely because of *Southern Politics*, Key probably had a greater impact on American political science than any other individual of his time or since."

• Key's correspondence is in the Harvard University Library; papers related to *Southern Politics in State and Nation* are in the Vanderbilt University Library; and papers related to his other books are in the John F. Kennedy Presidential Library in Boston. See *V. O. Key, Jr. and the Study of American Politics*, ed. Milton C. Cummings, Jr. (1988). Alexander Heard's "Introduction to the New Edition" and William C. Havard's "V. O. Key, Jr.: A Brief Profile" in the 1977 reissue of *Southern Politics in State and Nation* are insightful sources. Havard's piece is a reprint from *South Atlantic Urban Studies* 3 (1979): 279–88. For the making of *Southern Politics in State and Nation*, see Alexander P. Lamis and Nathan C. Goldman, "V. O. Key's Southern Politics: The Writing of a Classic," *Georgia Historical Quarterly* 71 (1987): 261–85. An obituary is in the *New York Times*, 5 Oct. 1963.

HAROLD W. STANLEY

KEYES, Charles Rollin (26 Dec. 1864–18 May 1942), geologist, mining engineer, and publisher, was born in Des Moines, Iowa, the son of Calvin Webb Keyes, a wealthy merchant and entrepreneur, and Julia Baird Davis. Keyes entered the State University of Iowa in 1883, securing his bachelor's degree in 1887 and, after leaving the campus, his A.M. in 1890.

While Keyes was an undergraduate student he was an assistant in the museum at the State University of Iowa, where he began assembling an important collection of fossil crinoids (a group of marine invertebrates related to starfish). In 1887 and 1889 he was employed by Charles Wachsmuth and Frank Springer, freelance specialists on fossil crinoids, as a paleontologist and an artist. While a graduate student at Iowa he was also employed as an assistant geologist in the U.S. Geological Survey. From 1889 to 1892 he attended the Johns Hopkins University as a University Scholar and Fellow, receiving his Ph.D. in 1892. In 1890 Keyes became chief geologist and paleontologist in the Missouri Geological Survey, remaining in that position until 1892, when he became the assistant state geologist of Iowa.

In 1894 Keyes left the Iowa Geological Survey and was appointed director of the Missouri Bureau of Geology and Mines. In 1897 Keyes resigned and went to Europe, Africa, and Asia to study geological formations, and from 1898 through 1902 he wrote extensively. Some of Keyes's important work included an outline of the succession of Late Carboniferous (coal-bearing) strata of Iowa and Missouri and the definition of their major subdivisions. North American geologists adopted his classification for rocks of this age, and his scheme was later incorporated into a global classification advanced in the late twentieth century.

Keyes was president of the New Mexico School of Mines from 1902 through 1906. In 1906–1907 he spent another year traveling and studying. In 1907 Keyes's career shifted from survey and academic work to mining geology and engineering, and he became president and general manager of various mining companies, including president and managing geologist of the American Mines Exploration Company. He made a credible contribution through his work with midcontinent and New Mexican lead, zinc, and silver deposits.

In 1922 Keyes initiated the publication of the journal the *Pan-American Geologist*, purportedly as a revival of the *American Geologist*, which had been published from 1888 through 1905 by a group of midwestern geologists and paleontologists in a spirit of "populist" opposition to expanding dominance of the U.S. Geological Survey and the eastern universities. Keyes opened the pages of his journal to "wholesome speculative discussion, constructive criticism, and creative productivity" (*Pan-American Geologist* 37 [1922]). Initially he was able to publish works by a diversity of professional peers. His autocratic editing and controversial style, however, soon drove away many contributors. This, and the flood of very short papers written by Keyes to further his rejected theoretical ideas and to "correct"

what he saw as mistakes in the publications of others, brought the *Pan-American Geologist* professional disrespect. Keyes authored 1,340 papers in his journal between 1922 and 1942.

Keyes entered politics as a Democrat in Iowa and was the Democratic candidate for the Senate in 1918. He was defeated along with all Iowa democratic candidates for Congress and for the governorship. He was a Fellow of the Geological Society of America and a member of the American Institute of Mining Engineers, the American Association for the Advancement of Science, the Mining and Metallurgical Society of America, the Iowa Academy of Science, the St. Louis Academy of Science, and other scientific organizations.

Among Keyes's notable publications, *Geological Formations of Iowa* (1893), *Coal Deposits of Iowa* (1894), and *Paleontology of Missouri* (1894) monographically summarize the stratigraphy, paleontology, and coal resources of the region and define the bipartite subdivision of the Pennsylvanian system. *Origin and Classification of Ore Deposits* (1900) introduces a classification of ore deposits based on their geological relationships rather than according to their chemical origins. *Ozark Lead and Zinc Deposits: Their Genesis, Localization, and Migration* (1909) is a comprehensive explanation for stratiform ore deposits that may form.

In 1927 Keyes married Julia Ferguson; they had no children. His speculative publications on eolian erosion, such as "Deflation and the Relative Efficiencies of Erosional Processes Under Conditions of Aridity" (1910), asserted that the topography of the Basin Ranges and the Great Plains resulted almost entirely from wind erosion. This paper and "Midcontinental Eolation" (1911), although published in the *Geological Society of America Bulletin*, brought him into conflict with "establishment" geologists, and further papers on the topic were refused by the *Bulletin*'s editors. His later papers on the effect of changes in the earth's speed of rotation on deformation ("Orogenic Consequences of a Diminished Rate of Earth's Rotation" [1922]) and on astronomical causes of glaciation ("Astronomical Theory of Glaciation; and Newcombian Criticism" [1925]), which were even more speculative, also were rejected for publication in the *Bulletin*, and they appeared in the *Pan American Geologist*. Keyes expressed his frustration in "Judicial Attitudes in Geological Criticism" (1922).

After 1922, excepting abstracts of papers read before the Geological Society of America, Keyes's scientific writing was essentially confined to the *Pan-American Geologist*, which he continued to edit until his death in Tucson, Arizona.

• A brief account of Keyes's life and work is "Dr. Charles Rollin Keyes," *Pan-American Geologist* 77, no. 5 (June 1942): 321–22. William Lee Stokes, "Geology of the Eastern Great Basin—Past Successes and Future Problems," *Utah Geological Association Publications* 16 (1987): 91–104, briefly comments on Keyes's influence on ideas about the origin of the Basin Ranges. An obituary is in the *New York Times*, 20 May 1942.

RALPH L. LANGENHEIM, JR.

KEYES, Erasmus Darwin (29 May 1810–14 Oct. 1895), soldier and businessman, was born at Brimfield, Massachusetts, the son of Justus Keyes, a physician, and Elizabeth Corey. His family moved to Kennebec County, Maine, when he was still young, and it was from that state that he gained an appointment to West Point in 1828. He graduated four years later and was commissioned brevet second lieutenant. His posts during the early years of his service included Fort Monroe, Virginia, and Charleston, South Carolina (during the nullification crisis). In 1833 he was commissioned a regular second lieutenant in the Third Artillery. In 1837 he married Caroline M. Clarke. They had five children.

During most of the time from 1837 to 1841, Keyes served as aide-de-camp to the army's top general, Winfield Scott. In 1841 he was promoted to captain in the Third Artillery, and thereafter his posts included New Orleans, Louisiana, Fort Moultrie, South Carolina, and West Point, where he served as an instructor in artillery and cavalry. His duties at the academy kept him out of the Mexican War. Most of the 1850s he spent in the Pacific Northwest, often in combat with the American Indians there, and on at least one occasion he won official commendation for his conduct in battle. In 1853 his wife died. On 12 October 1858 he was promoted to major in the First Artillery, and on 1 January 1860 he returned to his old duties on Scott's staff, promoted for this service to the grade of lieutenant colonel.

As it did to other officers of the old army, the Civil War brought Keyes rapid advancement. On 19 April 1861 he left Scott's staff and took up duties in forwarding New York volunteer troops to the front. On 14 May he became colonel of the Eleventh U.S. Infantry. By July of that year he commanded a brigade in General Daniel Tyler's division, and in this capacity he participated in the first battle of Bull Run (First Manassas). Though the battle was a debacle for the North, Keyes won commendation for his own conduct in it. When in November of that year General Don Carlos Buell was transferred to Kentucky, Keyes was moved up to command Buell's old division in the Army of the Potomac.

By March 1862 Keyes was one of the four most senior of the Army of the Potomac's twelve division commanders. These four also happened to be the only Republicans among the twelve, the others being Democrats and creatures of Democratic Army of the Potomac commander George B. McClellan. In that month's strategic disagreements, Keyes was the only one of the Republican generals who favored McClellan's plan for a roundabout approach to Richmond by way of the peninsula between the York and James rivers rather than Abraham Lincoln's proposal for a more direct advance on the Confederate capital. Acquiesc-

ing to McClellan and the majority of his Democratic generals, Lincoln nevertheless determined at once both to improve the organization of the army and to provide a check on McClellan's leadership by creating corps organizations and assigning the four senior generals to command them. He assigned Keyes to command the IV Corps. On the peninsula that May, Keyes received promotion to major general of volunteers. On the last day of that month, his corps received the brunt of the Confederate attack at Fair Oaks, and for his courageous performance there, Keyes was promoted to brevet brigadier general in the regular army. He served through the army's retreat down the peninsula during the Seven Days' battles, though McClellan, who did not trust his competence, attempted to keep him out of the fighting as much as possible.

When the army was withdrawn from the peninsula that summer, the IV Corps was left behind to form the nucleus of a permanent Federal presence at the lower end of the peninsula, thus pinning down Confederate troops to cover Richmond. Keyes continued to command it, but during the months that followed the IV Corps became essentially a dummy headquarters unit, with most of its combat troops transferred to other fronts. To complicate matters further, beginning in December 1862 Keyes simultaneously held assignments under the authority of VII Corps headquarters. Until April 1863 he commanded the post of Yorktown under VII Corps auspices, and from then until August he commanded a division of the VII Corps posted at Suffolk. In all of these commands he was subordinate to the overall Federal commander on the peninsula, General John A. Dix. Meanwhile, in 1862 Keyes had married Mary Loughborough Bissell, with whom he subsequently had five more children.

When Robert E. Lee's Confederate Army of Northern Virginia moved into Maryland and Pennsylvania in June 1863, Dix wanted to threaten Richmond to prevent reinforcements from going to Lee. The Federal peninsula commander accused Keyes of lack of aggressiveness in this endeavor and further taxed him with other failures over recent months. Keyes demanded a court of inquiry but to no avail. On 1 August 1863 the IV Corps was officially abolished, and two weeks later Keyes was transferred to administrative duties on the army retiring board. On 6 May 1864 he resigned his commissions and returned to civilian life after thirty-six years in uniform.

Keyes settled in San Francisco, California, and became successful in grape culture, mining, and banking. He was vice president of the California Vine-Culture Society for Napa County. From 1867 to 1869 he was president of the Maxwell Gold Mining Company, and from 1868 to 1870 he was president of the Humboldt Savings and Loan Society. While traveling in Europe with his wife, he died in Nice, France.

• Keyes published *Fifty Years' Observation of Men and Events* in 1884. See also Robert U. Johnson and Clarence C. Buel, eds., *Battles and Leaders of the Civil War* (4 vols., 1884–1887); Stephen W. Sears, *To the Gates of Richmond: The Pen-*

insula Campaign (1992); U.S. War Department, *The War of the Rebellion: A Compilation of the Official Records of the Union and Confederate Armies* (128 vols., 1880–1901); and Ezra J. Warner, *Generals in Blue: The Lives of the Union Commanders* (1964).

STEVEN E. WOODWORTH

KEYES, Frances Parkinson (21 July 1885–3 July 1970), writer, editor, and traveler, was born in Charlottesville, Virginia, in James Monroe's house, the daughter of John Henry Wheeler, a scholar and head of the Greek department at the University of Virginia, and Louise Fuller Johnson Underhill. When John Wheeler died in 1887, Louise Wheeler moved to "The Oxbow," a family home near Newbury, Vermont, where Frances spent the summer months. In the winter months they relocated to Boston so Frances could attend school. Although she did graduate from Miss Winsor's school in Boston, she described her formal education as "sketchy."

Her paternal grandmother, for whom Frances Parkinson was named, was a scholar who matriculated at Mount Holyoke Seminary. She taught her granddaughter how to read and provided lessons in Latin, French, and mathematics. When she was nine, Frances was taken to Europe by her mother, who was leaving her third husband, Albert E. Pillsbury of Boston. This year abroad, as she states in her autobiography *Roses in December* (1960), was "probably the most valuable one of my entire education." Often left on her own, the child visited museums and developed her "natural proclivity for wandering." As she traveled with her mother through Germany, France, and Switzerland, she also learned German. After she returned to Boston, her mother enrolled her at Miss Winsor's. Superior in languages and deficient in mathematics, her lack of a formal education caused her some problems as the teachers did not know where to place her. But, characteristically, Frances worked extremely hard and rose to the top of her class. Although she did pass the qualifying examination for Bryn Mawr, she did not attend because she married Henry Wilder Keyes (rhymes with eyes) in 1904.

They had met when Frances was just a child. When she married, she was eighteen, twenty-two years younger than Henry. They lived in his family home of "Pine Grove Farm," near Haverhill, New Hampshire, with their three children. Henry Keyes was elected governor of New Hampshire in 1917 and to the U.S. Senate for three terms, from 1919 to 1937. The family moved to Alexandria, Virginia, and Frances Keyes became an active Washington hostess. She was often a guest at the White House as well as on Embassy Row. Her facility with five languages and her social background were assets.

But Frances Parkinson Keyes was not a typical society hostess, focusing only on receptions and galas. Sensing that there were many women who would love to learn about the Washington scene from a female perspective, she began a series of monthly "Letters from a Senator's Wife," which ran for fourteen years in *Good Housekeeping* and increased the magazine's circulation by more than 100,000.

Keyes had wanted to be a writer since she was seven years old. She had no encouragement from her mother, who, in fact, ripped up some of her work; her husband, as she states in her autobiography, "regarded my predilection for scribbling with an eye as unfriendly and disparaging as my mother's." Money had been a problem with Frances before her marriage, and Henry Keyes had no great fortune. She hoped to supplement their income by her writing, "a source of modest revenue, which would help pay the butcher, the baker, and the candlestick maker." Like many women during that time, she had to write secretly, and her first novel, *The Old Gray Homestead* (1919), was written in longhand when she was nursing her third child. It was only in the 1930s that she started writing steadily.

During her lifetime Keyes wrote novels, letters, short stories, poems, biographies, autobiographies, and a cookbook. She was an associate editor at *Good Housekeeping* from 1923 to 1935, and from 1937 to 1939 she edited the *Daughters of the American Revolution Magazine*, which she renamed the *National Historical Magazine*. In addition she wrote articles for other magazines, and her 1923 interview of the elusive Rachele Mussolini (wife of the Italian dictator Benito Mussolini) was considered a "scoop."

It is as a novelist, however, that she is best known. Although she published her first novel in 1919, not until the publication of *Honor Bright* in 1936 did she hit the weekly bestseller list in the United States. She had become a bestselling author in England the previous year with *Senator Marlowe's Daughter*. The critics did not think highly of her, but the public did. Seven novels, including *Dinner at Antoine's* (1948), *Joy Street* (1950), *Steamboat Gothic* (1952), and *Blue Camellia* (1957), made the annual bestseller list. Her novels sold more than 20 million copies. Reviewers pointed out failures in plotting and an almost pedantic attention to detail, and they criticized the informative foreword or author's note that traditionally prefaced her novels as tedious or superfluous. But when she omitted the note, the public demanded it be restored. Her reading audience wanted education along with recreation, and her novels supplied both.

To read Keyes today is to read social history. Her novels are characterized by a wealth of detail that may have struck some contemporary critics as tedious but today can be seen as evocative of places and manners. Like Jane Austen, Keyes puts a magnifying glass to a particular segment of society. Cities such as New Orleans, Boston, and London are brought to life. Detailed descriptions of how people behaved in social situations, customs and dress at celebrations, and even what was then everyday etiquette are a window to the past. This attention to minutia in creating her settings and characters was so precise that a bridal party was outfitted based on descriptive detail in a Keyes novel.

After her husband died in 1938, her "scribbling" was no longer an avocation but a vocation, and she worked hard at it. She traveled extensively to the settings of her books and stated that she would not write about a place where she had not "shopped and cooked and kept house." In all, she traveled to Western Europe twenty-five times; she also went to South America, Mexico, and the Middle East.

Confirmed in the Episcopal church, Keyes became a Roman Catholic in 1939 and was selected as the outstanding Catholic woman of the year in 1946. She received the Medal of Honor of the General Council of the Seine in 1950 for her work as a novelist and journalist, and a Silver Medal of French Recognition in 1951 for her work in the reconstruction of the Abbey of the Benedictines at Lisieux. She was awarded the Order of Isabella the Catholic in 1959 in recognition of work in Spain and the French Legion of Honor in 1962.

Keyes died at the historic "Beauregard House" in the French Quarter of New Orleans. Built by the grandfather of chess genius Paul Morphy and formerly owned by Confederate general P. T. G. Beauregard, the house became her winter writing headquarters. Both Morphy and Beauregard are leading characters in two of her novels, *The Chess Players* (1960) and *Madame Castel's Lodger* (1962). In 1948 she established the Keyes Foundation to aid young writers and restore historic houses. Today the Keyes Foundation maintains Beauregard House, which is open to the public.

• An extensive collection of Keyes's manuscripts is at the University of Virginia. The Beauregard House has Keyes memorabilia as does The Oxbow and Pine Grove Farm. A complete list of her writings, including her four autobiographies, can be found in *Contemporary Authors*, new rev. ser., vol. 7 (1982). An interview is in *The Book of Catholic Authors*, 5th ser. (n.d.). Secondary sources include Robert Wernick, "The Queens of Fiction," *Life*, 6 Apr. 1959, pp. 139–52; *American Women Writers* (1980); *Twentieth-century Romance and Historical Writers*, 2d ed. (1990); Leigh A. Ehlers, "An Environment Remembered," *Southern Quarterly* 20 (Spring 1982): 54–65; and Jane F. Bonin, "Frances Parkinson Keyes: Mining the Mother Lode," *Louisiana Literature* 5 (Spring 1988): 71–77. An obituary is in the *New York Times*, 4 July 1970.

MARCIA B. DINNEEN

KEYS, Clement Melville (7 Apr. 1876–12 Jan. 1952), financier and aviation entrepreneur, was born in Chatsworth, Ontario, Canada, the son of George Keys, a minister, and Jessie Margaret Evans. Keys graduated with an A.B. degree from the University of Toronto in 1897 and taught history and classics at Ridley College in St. Catherines, Ontario, for three years. He moved to New York City in 1901 and joined the staff of the *Wall Street Journal*, becoming railroad editor two years later. On 15 June 1905 Keys married Florence E. Hayes; they had two daughters. In 1906 he left the *Journal* to become financial editor of the magazine *World's Work*. He left that magazine in 1911 and set up C. M. Keys & Co., and investor's service, which was later expanded into an investment banking house. During his early years in New York, Keys became widely known as a consultant on finance and management. He developed a reputation as a strong proponent of unfettered capitalism and an adversary of governmental regulation.

Keys's career in aviation began in 1916 when he became vice president of the Curtiss Aeroplane and Motor Company. With his help the company was able to manufacture airplanes for Great Britain; it was the only U.S. company producing airplanes for Europe at that time. In 1917 businessman John N. Willys acquired control of Curtiss Aeroplane and hired Keys as chief of the financial committee. Keys successfully landed millions of dollars of government contracts for Curtiss Aeroplane during World War I. Willys suffered financially from the economic depression of 1920–1921, giving Keys the opportunity to buy a controlling interest in the company for less than $4 a share. In 1924 Keys became an American citizen and also remarried. Indiola Arnold Reilly, his second wife, survived him. They had no children.

Keys's aviation empire grew rapidly in the 1920s. He maintained the Curtiss research facilities for the development of better airplanes but concentrated his efforts on organizing and financing aviation companies and airlines. In 1928 he created North American Aviation as a holding company to consolidate his aviation interests. Included in North American was Transcontinental Air Transport (TAT). TAT began as a combined air and rail service designed to avoid night flights, which were considered dangerous, but the system was too cumbersome and expensive and was abandoned. TAT was then combined with Western Air Express as Transcontinental and Western Air and began all-air service between New York and Los Angeles in 1930. TAT would become the main component of Trans World Airlines.

In 1929 Keys accomplished the historic merger of two aviation giants: Curtiss Aeroplane and Motor, and the Wright Aeronautical Corporation. The new firm, Curtiss-Wright Corporation, owned twenty-nine subsidiaries and was affiliated with eighteen other aviation companies. With assets of $70 million, it was the largest aviation holding company in the country. Keys now controlled a fleet of 500 airplanes averaging a million miles per month in flight.

Keys's success was due to his notable financial skill, a growing interest in commercial aviation due in part to Charles Lindbergh's flight across the Atlantic, and the airmail transportation business fostered by the Kelly Air Mail Act of 1925. Keys, however, apparently failed to appreciate the future prospects of passenger airlines—as his involvement with the National Air Transport (NAT) company demonstrates. North American Aviation controlled NAT, and it was through this link that Keys could direct the NAT's policies. NAT controlled the lucrative mail route between New York and Chicago, but Keys refused to develop a passenger service along this route. United Air Lines saw the possibilities of such a route and bid for control of NAT. NAT's stockholders decided to join United rather than fight it, and NAT was absorbed by United in 1930. Meanwhile, the value of North American stock fell rapidly after the onset of the Great Depression. Originally offered at $12.50 a share, the stock fell to $1 a share by 1932. That year Keys decided to withdraw from all his aviation interests.

Keys remained in semiretirement until 1942, when he established the C. M. Keys Aircraft Service, Inc., in New York City, a finance company that specialized in securing military contracts for the aircraft industry. Keys was also chairman of a number of other companies, including Mackenzie Muffler Company of Youngstown, Ohio; the Buffalo Pressed Steel Company (a Mackenzie subsidiary); the Carl G. Fisher Corporation, makers of automobile lights; and the Montauk Beach Company, an association of property owners to protect private beach property. Keys died at his home in New York City.

• A good source for Keys's life and career is Henry L. Smith, *Airways* (1942). Other information can be obtained from *The National Cyclopaedia of American Biography*, vol. A (1930), and C. J. Kelly, Jr., *The Sky's the Limit* (1963). An obituary is in the *New York Times*, 13 Jan. 1952.

AARON GILLETTE

KEYSERLING, Leon (22 Jan. 1908–9 Aug. 1987), chairman of the Council of Economic Advisers, was born in Beaufort, South Carolina, the son of William Keyserling and Jennie Hyman, owners of varied agricultural and mercantile enterprises. Keyserling, a bright student, finished public school in Beaufort, South Carolina at the age of sixteen. Entering Columbia University, he studied with Rexford Tugwell, an institutional economist and later a prominent New Dealer. Keyserling graduated in 1928 with a B.A. in economics. After earning a law degree from Harvard in 1931, he returned to Columbia as a Ph.D. student in economics. He did not finish his dissertation but instead joined the U.S. Department of Agriculture when the Democrats came to power in 1933.

Within a very short time, Keyserling became New York senator Robert F. Wagner's major assistant. Wagner was the leading congressional Democrat, a liberal who wrote much of the New Deal's reform legislation. Keyserling's contributions were significant. In the 1933 National Industrial Recovery Act, Keyserling was the main draftsman of the famous Section 7A, which provided governmental encouragement for workers to organize unions. This Section 7A was placed in the National Labor Relations Act of 1935 (the Wagner Act) when the Supreme Court declared the National Industrial Recovery Act unconstitutional. By preparing studies, writing speeches, and giving congressional testimony, he was deeply involved with the National Labor Relations Act, the Social Security Act (1935), and the U.S. Housing Act (1937). In 1940 Keyserling married Mary Dublin; they were childless. At one time a professor of economics at Sarah Lawrence, Mary was active in a number of reform and consumer groups.

From 1937 to 1946 Keyserling worked in various housing agencies. He was acting administrator of gov-ernment-financed housing for war workers from 1942 to 1946 and general counsel of the National Housing Authority. In addition, he contributed to the creation of the Department of Housing and Urban Development. Author of the National Housing Act of 1949, he played a key role in guiding that legislation through Congress.

At a time when national political conventions did not include the drafting of a platform via hearings and subcommittees, Keyserling wrote the platform for the Democratic party's presidential campaigns in 1936, 1940, and 1944. He wrote these documents at the request of Senator Wagner, who was chairman of the Platform Committee. On occasion Keyserling wrote campaign speeches for Franklin D. Roosevelt. Thus in 1936 he provided the presidential response to the Republican presidential candidate, Alf Landon, who charged that the new Social Security system was a fraud that would never pay a cent in benefits. Similarly, in the 1940 campaign Keyserling prepared the president's public reaction to a former ally of the New Deal, John L. Lewis, president of the United Mine Workers, who supported Wendell L. Willkie, the Republican presidential nominee.

In an essay contest sponsored by the Pabst Beer Company in 1944, Keyserling won second place, writing on the future of the American economy. Significantly, parts of the essay later appeared in the Employment Act of 1946, particularly the idea of a governmental council of economists. The Employment Act addressed the public's apprehensions regarding a mature economy. During the New Deal, many policy makers and politicians feared that the American economy could not expand, and a similar concern, that major postwar depression was possible, emerged during World War II. This stagnation thesis of a high level of unemployment and underemployment was a chief worry of the New Deal and of postwar liberalism for the next half-century. The issue was the relationship between "guns," the maintenance of a strong military presence on the global scene as required by the emerging Cold War, and "butter," money for increased domestic programs that former New Dealers desired. Keyserling believed that the American economy could support both a strong interventionist foreign policy and increased domestic programs. Indicative of Keyserling's commitment to "guns and butter" were his contributions, advice, and writings that led to National Security Council Directive 68, the cornerstone of the containment policy.

Keyserling's last significant contribution to Democratic party politics was as a member of Clark Clifford's Monday night supper group. The Democratic party lost control of Congress in 1946, and in response these advisers met regularly for the next two years, shaping the strategy and tactics that elected Harry Truman president in 1948.

Appointed vice chairman of the Council of Economic Advisers (CEA) in 1946, Keyserling became chairman three years later. He supported a policy of economic growth sustained by joint planning and cooperation between private business and the federal government. Although he urged increased governmental spending on the demand side, he was not a Keynesian economist. Intellectually, Keyserling's thought was grounded in the institutionalism of Tugwell and his mentor Simon Patten. Politically, Keyserling was sensitive to the partisan rhetoric that Keynesianism and liberal reform were just "tax, tax and spend, spend."

Because Keyserling was an effective chairman of the CEA, Truman sought his advice. Keyserling regularly attended cabinet meetings, and he competently represented the administration before Congress and the public. Apparently Keyserling's advice was sound. During the Korean War, when the possibility of inflation posed many political problems, the federal government had an average surplus of $1.7 billion for the years 1947 to 1953, a small inflation rate, and nearly full employment. During the height of McCarthyism, Senator Joe McCarthy charged Keyserling and his wife with being Communists. In 1951 they successfully defended themselves against his baseless charges.

Keyserling retired in 1953 and founded the Conference on Economic Progress, a tax-exempt nonprofit foundation concerned with public policy, which he directed until 1972. From that year until his death he lobbied for a broad range of liberal causes and organizations. Among his many honors, he was named Man of the Year by both the New York and Washington, D.C., chapters of the American Jewish Congress.

Keyserling died in a Washington, D.C., hospital. An intellectual in governmental service, his political and rhetorical skills contributed to both the New Deal and the Fair Deal. He also lobbied for liberal policies in the days of the New Frontier and the Great Society, contributing to the Full Employment and Balanced Growth Act of 1977 (the Humphrey-Hawkins Act). Throughout his life he followed his institutional vision for equity in the United States.

• Keyserling's papers are at Georgetown University as part of the Senator Robert F. Wagner Papers. Keyserling's own collection is at the Harry S. Truman Presidential Library. For Keyserling's rejection of Keynesianism see his oral history interview in David C. Colander and Harry Landreth, eds., *The Coming of Keynesianism to America* (1996). Keyserling's career is discussed in Donald K. Pickens, "Truman's Council of Economic Advisers and the Legacy of the New Deal," in *Harry S. Truman: The Man from Independence*, ed. William F. Levantrosser (1986). Insightful views of Keyserling's liberalism are in Alonzo L. Hamby, *Beyond the New Deal: Harry S. Truman and American Liberalism* (1973) and *Man of the People, A Life of Harry S. Truman* (1995). Ernest R. May, ed., *American Cold War Strategy, Interpreting NSC 68* (1993), contains a copy of the document and helpful commentaries. Keyserling's obituary is in the *New York Times*, 11 Aug. 1987.

DONALD K. PICKENS

KHAN, Fazlur Rahman (3 Apr. 1929–27 Mar. 1982), structural engineer, was born in Dacca, Bangladesh, the son of Abdur Rahman, a scholar and mathemati-

cian, and Khadija Khanum. Khan studied engineering at the Bengal Engineering College in Calcutta, but political uprisings forced him to return to Dacca in 1950 shortly before graduation. He persuaded the University of Dacca to grant him a bachelor of engineering degree based on his previous course work. For the next two years he lectured at Dacca and worked as an assistant engineer for the highway department. In 1952 Fulbright and Pakistani fellowships brought him to the University of Illinois at Champaign-Urbana. He studied at the school for three years and earned a master of science degree in structural engineering (1952), a master of science in theoretical and applied mechanics (1955), and a doctor of philosophy in structural engineering (1955).

After receiving his degrees, Khan worked for two years as a project engineer with the firm of Skidmore, Owings, and Merrill (SOM) in Chicago, Illinois. In 1957 a stipulation of his scholarships required that he return to East Pakistan, where he worked as an executive engineer with the Karachi Development Authority. Although his job had great status, Khan felt that the administrative tasks prevented him from pursuing design work. He wrote to SOM to secure a more challenging position and returned to Chicago in 1960. Accompanying him was his new wife, Liselotte A. Turba, whom he had married in 1959; they had one daughter.

In the United States, Khan rose to the top of his profession. Within his first year at SOM, he became a senior designer. Over the next decade he advanced to senior project engineer, associate partner, head of the Structural/Civil Division, and finally partner (in charge of structural engineering) in 1970, a position he held until his death. In his twenty-five years with SOM, Khan was responsible for the engineering design of many major architectural projects. He gained recognition for his development of a number of new structural systems for tall buildings. Foremost among these were his innovations in tubular structures, both for reinforced concrete and for structural steel. He pioneered the concept in 1963 when he devised a support system capable of withstanding the gravity and wind loads of tall buildings using beam-columns or diagonal bracing on a building's exterior. The concept, radically different from the predominant system of skeletal construction, rendered tall buildings economically feasible by reducing the amount of steel or concrete needed.

Although Khan first experimented with tubular design in the 43-story DeWitt-Chestnut Apartment Building (1964) in Chicago, his most famous applications were in the 100-story John Hancock Center (1970) and the 110-story Sears Tower (1974), both in Chicago. The structures were created in collaboration with SOM design partner Bruce Graham. When built, the John Hancock Center was the tallest mixed-use building in the world, combining apartments and offices in one structure. A diagonal framed tube system, the building has huge external X-braces that provide structural support as well as aesthetic detail. The cross-bracing greatly reduced cost premiums for resisting wind loads so that the actual cost of construction was equivalent to that of a more traditional 35-story building.

For the Sears Tower, the expression of structure was again used as a design element. Khan brought together nine slender towers of different heights to create an efficient and rigid overall structure. The sharing of the individual towers' interior columns greatly reduced construction costs. With its distinctive profile of "bundled tubes," the Sears Tower, 1,454 feet high, reigned as the world's tallest building for more than twenty years, bringing Khan and Graham much recognition.

A noteworthy variation of Khan's tubular concept is the "tube within a tube" system. Another economical approach, this concept utilizes an exterior wall of closely spaced piers and a rigid interior core for overall support against gravity and wind loads. Khan successfully applied the system to Houston's One Shell Plaza (1971), the tallest reinforced concrete building in the world when built. He later developed a composite system in which the advantages of reinforced concrete and steel construction are combined in one building.

Not limited to high-rise construction, Khan developed an award-winning roof design for the Haj Terminal of the King Abdul Aziz International Airport (1980) in Jeddah (Jidda), Saudi Arabia. The 105-acre facility has a tentlike roof of 210 retracting umbrellas. Travelers are able to escape from the intense heat of the sun without the use of costly air conditioning. Khan's other innovative roof designs include the cable-supported roof of the Baxter Travenol Laboratories, Inc. (1975) in Deerfield, Illinois, and the immense suspended dome of the Hubert H. Humphrey Metrodome (1982) in Minneapolis, Minnesota.

Part of Khan's success is attributed to his personality. Colleagues described him as affable, urbane, well-spoken, and philosophical. He was said to have a manner of "overwhelming casualness." These qualities, along with a keen sense of aesthetics, allowed him to work easily with architects. This ability facilitated the successful marriage of structural engineering and architectural design that is the essence of his work. To Khan this collaboration represented a significant advancement in the building art. In an interview with *Engineering News-Record* (10 Feb. 1972), he said, "The greatest step the building team has made in the past decade is that the engineer, as part of that team, is finally looking at the whole structure with architecture integrated as part of the whole. This group thinking results in a systems building that satisfies all requirements."

Khan's humanitarianism was expressed in a variety of ways. In his personal life, he was a devout Moslem who aided refugees from his politically restless homeland. In his professional life, he taught at the Illinois Institute of Technology as an adjunct professor from the 1960s until 1982. Additionally, he published more than seventy-five technical papers in engineering and architectural journals on topics relating to the analysis, design, and construction of complex structures. He lectured before civic and educational audiences around the world. He served as chair of the International Council on Tall Buildings and Urban Habitat and was a member of many professional organizations, including the National Academy of Engineering.

Khan's efforts were recognized throughout his career. He was an elected fellow of the American Society of Civil Engineers and the American Concrete Institute. The recipient of numerous awards from national and international professional organizations, he was named Construction Man of the Year by *Engineering News-Record* in 1972. On a more personal level, the Structural Stability Research Council wrote of him in a memorial resolution (30 Mar. 1982): "The generosity with which he gave of his time beyond technical matters serves as a beacon and an example to all of us. It was more than interest that he showed. He genuinely cared about individuals."

Khan was traveling in Asia and the Middle East when he suffered a fatal heart attack in Saudi Arabia. During his productive career, he had become a leader in his profession and achieved international distinction for his innovative and cost-saving designs. He was acknowledged by his peers for the key role he played in shaping the design of high-rise buildings. In a tribute written after his death, *Engineering News-Record* (1 Apr. 1982) proclaimed, "His structures will stand for years and his ideas will never die."

• A collection of Khan's technical papers is in the Skidmore, Owings, and Merrill Technical Library, Chicago. An archive containing press releases, Khan's curriculum vitae, and testimonials written by colleagues and friends at the time of his death is in the Marketing Department of SOM. Important mid-career assessments are Richard M. Kielar, "Construction's Man of the Year: Fazlur R. Khan," *Engineering News-Record* (10 Feb. 1972), pp. 20–23, and "Fazlur Khan: Avant Garde Designer of High-rises," *Engineering News-Record* (26 Aug. 1971), pp. 16–18. An explanation of his technical innovations is Kielar, "Building Design Reduces Steel with Concrete-Tube Wind Bracing," *Engineering News-Record* (3 June 1971), pp. 18–19. A collection of obituaries and memorial resolutions is published in the *Times* 13 (Aug. 1982): 2–3, a publication of the International Council on Tall Buildings and Urban Habitat.

LISA A. TORRANCE

KHARASCH, Morris Selig (24 Aug. 1895–9 Oct. 1957), organic chemist, was born in Kremenets, Ukraine, Russia, the son of Selig Kharasch, a tobacco grower and merchant, and Louise Kneller. Although the family lived a comfortable existence, Kharasch came to the United States in 1907 because of its greater educational opportunities. He settled in Chicago in the care of an older brother and gained a reputation for brilliance in Chicago public schools. The University of Chicago awarded him a bachelor's degree in 1917 and a doctorate in chemistry in 1919. He was a National Research Council fellow at Chicago for three years. From 1922 to 1928 he was a faculty member of the University of Maryland. In 1923 he married Ethel May Nelson; they had two children.

Kharasch's dissertation was on organomercurial compounds and their chemotherapeutic uses. He continued this research at Maryland by synthesizing organic mercury compounds and investigating their therapeutic and agricultural applications. Kharasch's most important contribution to chemotherapy was his 1928 synthesis of Merthiolate, an ethyl mercury salicylic acid derivative. It was widely used as a germicide in treating nose and throat infections, for bladder irrigation, and for disinfecting instruments.

While at Maryland Kharasch also worked with several organomercurials that were effective fungicides. These became commercial products available to farmers worldwide. They controlled seed-borne plant diseases and thereby increased the yields of food and fiber crops such as cotton, corn, and wheat. In 1949 Kharasch received the John Scott Medal of the Franklin Institute for the discovery of these fungicides and their importance to American agriculture.

In 1928 Kharasch returned to the University of Chicago as an associate professor. He became professor in 1930, Carl Eisendrath Professor of organic chemistry in 1935, and Gustavus and Ann Swift Distinguished Service Professor in 1953. In 1956 the university honored him by creating the Institute of Organic Chemistry with Kharasch as director.

In one of his first investigations at Chicago, Kharasch isolated ergonovine and other extracts of ergot in the 1930s. Crude extracts of ergot were used to induce childbirth. Ergonovine replaced the extracts, and Kharasch received in 1935 the Gold Medal of the American Medical Association.

Kharasch's major contribution to science was the creation of free radical organic chemistry. Moses Gomberg of the University of Michigan discovered the first organic free radicals in 1900. His substances, however, were rare and seemed to contain a trivalent carbon atom, contrary to structural theory with its assumption of the tetravalence of carbon atoms. Most organic chemists rejected Gomberg's claims and did not believe in the existence of free radicals.

What led Kharasch into this area in the 1930s was his study of a reaction between hydrogen bromide and allyl bromide. Different laboratories reported different reaction products, and the explanations offered did not impress Kharasch. His investigation revealed that older samples of allyl bromide gave a different reaction product than did fresh samples. He concluded that allyl bromide must react with oxygen in the air to form peroxides that then yield a different product than fresh, oxygen-free allyl bromide. Kharasch published his study in 1933, and the phenomenon came to be known as the "peroxide effect." To explain this effect, in 1937 he introduced the concept of free radical intermediates and a mechanism of a free radical chain reaction.

From this seemingly narrow investigation, Kharasch created a new field by discovering, inventing, and explaining many organic reactions in terms of free radical intermediates. Over the years he revealed whole families of free radical reactions, including old reactions never before comprehended and new ones never before imagined. Unlike Gomberg, he changed chemists' thinking, converting them to the concept of highly reactive free radicals containing an unpaired electron.

Free radicals proved relevant to polymer chemistry. Chemists believed that the addition reaction of two monomers to form a polymer was a chain reaction. Kharasch illuminated the subject with his concept of the free radical chain reaction, and he demonstrated the presence of free radicals in a variety of polymerizations. During World War II this research became essential to the war effort. With the shortage of natural rubber due to the loss of South Pacific sources to Japan, the government had to quickly create a synthetic rubber industry. The task was to produce buna rubber by polymerization of butadiene and styrene. Kharasch participated in the buna rubber project, most importantly in overcoming a bottleneck in its production. During the polymerization reaction a gel formed that grew rapidly into masses of "popcorn" polymer that interrupted the formation of buna rubber. Kharasch discovered how to inhibit the formation of popcorn by adding oxides of nitrogen to the process. He continued to contribute to the government synthetic rubber program until his death, making important studies on the initiation, inhibition, mechanism, and control of polymerization reactions.

Kharasch also founded vehicles for the publication of original research in organic chemistry. He was the most important figure in the founding of the *Journal of Organic Chemistry* (1936), the primary source for organic chemistry. Near the end of his life he helped establish the international journal *Tetrahedron* (1957) and was its first American editor. For his achievements in chemistry he was elected to the National Academy of Sciences in 1946. For his wartime services President Harry S. Truman conferred on him the Presidential Medal of Merit in 1947.

Kharasch was a masterful teacher and director of graduate students. He was unfailingly generous and purchased clothing for impoverished students, sent them food parcels, and helped them financially if they fell on hard times. He inspired tremendous respect because of his humility and wisdom. He also delighted people with his humor, wit, and storytelling ability.

Kharasch's characteristics as a scientist were brilliance, originality, a great imagination, and irreverence for the conventional. He was so devoted to research that for many years he did not take a vacation, and when he did he became restless and usually returned to Chicago ahead of schedule. For relaxation he played bridge, poker, chess, and billiards and did so with zest and daring. His death following a heart attack came in Copenhagen, Denmark, while on government assignment.

Kharasch was essential to reinvigorating a science by his questioning of current assumptions, in this instance the universal tetravalency of carbon in organic chemistry. He proposed the existence of trivalent free radicals and demonstrated that these entities were relatively stable structures essential to the study of organic reactions. Because of Kharasch, free radicals became a fundamental part of organic and polymer chemistry.

• There is no collection of Kharasch papers. Kharasch wrote with Otto Reinmuth his only book, *Grignard Reactions of Nonmetallic Substances* (1954), a monograph on the most important type of organometallic compounds. Frank H. Westheimer wrote the most important study of Kharasch's life in National Academy of Sciences, *Biographical Memoirs* 34 (1960): 123–52, which includes a bibliography of his publications. William A. Waters, ed., *Vistas in Free-Radical Chemistry* (1959), is a memorial volume that includes interpretive essays, reprints of his most significant articles, and a bibliography of publications. A lucid exposition of his discovery of free radicals is R. D. Ballinger and K. Thomas Finley, "Morris Selig Kharasch: A Great American Chemist," *Chemistry* 38 (June 1965): 19–20. Kharasch's studies of organic mercury compounds and their application to agriculture and medicine are summarized in *Chemical and Engineering News* 27 (7 Feb. 1949): 342–43. Obituaries are in the *New York Times*, 11 Oct. 1957; *Journal of Organic Chemistry* 23 (1958): 1239–40; and *Proceedings of the Chemical Society* (1958): 361–62.

ALBERT B. COSTA

KICKING BEAR (1852?–1904), Native American religious leader, was the son of Black Fox, chief of the Oyukpe band, and Iron Cedar Woman. He was born a member of the Oglala Lakota tribe, which ranged across present-day Nebraska, South Dakota, and Wyoming. He was related to Crazy Horse, the famed Sioux warrior and a later colleague. Kicking Bear married Woodpecker, a Minneconjou Lakota, another of the seven western Sioux polities whose lands encompassed a large portion of the northern Plains. They had at least three children.

Kicking Bear's early role among his tribe was that of a medicine man, possibly that of a mystic, albeit one of lower status. Later accounts charge him as the 1874 assassin of a clerk of the Red Cloud Agency, the U.S. government's Indian agency for Red Cloud's followers. The assassination precipitated the establishment of Camp Robinson in the White River country. He also served as a warrior during the Great Sioux War of 1876–1877 and fought at the battles of Rosebud, Little Bighorn, and Slim Buttes, though these achievements likewise gained him little notoriety outside his own circle. It was not until the time of the Ghost Dance troubles on Pine Ridge Reservation in 1890–1891 that Kicking Bear became a national figure.

Confined to reservations in the Dakotas after their military and political setbacks of the 1870s and 1880s, the disillusioned Lakotas proved to be ready recipients of a new religion sweeping the West. The Ghost Dance, as espoused by the Paiute prophet Wovoka, promised a return of the buffalo, of one's ancestors, and of the old ways of life and the corresponding disappearance of the white people. In 1889–1890 Kicking Bear joined a delegation of Sioux emissaries sent to Wovoka's Nevada home to

learn more about the Ghost Dance. Kicking Bear returned to the Minneconjou reservation at Cheyenne River a confirmed believer of the eminent return of an Indian messiah and became, with the Brulé Lakota man Short Bull, one of the two most passionate proselytizers of the new movement.

The year 1890 found Kicking Bear crisscrossing reservations, laying out the tenets of the Ghost Dance religion and gathering new converts, especially from the Oglalas of Pine Ridge Reservation. In September Kicking Bear returned to Cheyenne River, by which time he and his religious following had drawn the attention—and concern—of the government authorities. At least one-third of the approximately 5,500 Oglalas were considered fervent followers.

Sitting Bull, the Hunkpapa Lakota leader, invited Kicking Bear to his Standing Rock home in October 1890 to teach the Ghost Dance. The government agent, seeking to restrict its spread, forcibly expelled him from the reservation. After the U.S. Army takeover of the Sioux agencies at Pine Ridge and Rosebud in mid-November, Kicking Bear and his followers fled to the northern edge of the Pine Ridge Reservation. There at an isolated tableland near the Badlands of South Dakota, called "the Stronghold," over 3,000 danced undisturbed by the soldiers.

Negotiations between the government and the Ghost Dancers consumed late November and December, and, as the troubles on the Sioux reservations garnered the nation's attention, the name of Kicking Bear rose to prominence. Military officials, though, impugned Kicking Bear's motives by suggesting he was using the Ghost Dance merely to obtain a following.

Suspecting a degree of belligerence among the Ghost Dancers (which did not exist) and fearing their outbreak against exposed white settlements, the army demanded the surrender of the up-to-now passive Ghost Dancers. Kicking Bear and Short Bull, whose roles as Lakota leaders were minimal before the troubles, now were considered the keys to a peaceful settlement, equivalent in stature to longtime political figures Red Cloud, Young Man Afraid of His Horses, and American Horse.

Inadvertently, invitations by Kicking Bear and Short Bull to Sitting Bull and Big Foot, a Minneconjou leader, to come to the Stronghold and dance may have led to the latter's deaths. Fearing his departure from Standing Rock, the government arrested Sitting Bull; he was killed during the resultant melee. Big Foot and his followers avoided arrest at Cheyenne River and made their way south to Pine Ridge, where the band was captured by the Seventh Cavalry and brought to camp at Wounded Knee.

Kicking Bear and his fellow Ghost Dance leaders, succumbing to the government's promises and threats during December negotiations, had abandoned the Stronghold and begun their fifty-mile trek to Pine Ridge Agency. After word of the massacre of Big Foot's band on December 29, Kicking Bear and his immediate followers fled again to the safety of the

Stronghold, their numbers grown to include refugees from Pine Ridge Agency and earlier defectors.

After a flurry of inconclusive skirmishes between warriors and soldiers, peace talks, now directed by Major General Nelson A. Miles, began again in early January 1891. The talks with Kicking Bear and other Lakota leaders soon bore fruit. Surrendering Sioux, first in small groups, then whole villages, came to Pine Ridge Agency and turned in their firearms. Kicking Bear, one of the last holdouts, gave his rifle to General Miles on 15 January, an act that the nation's readers saw as the formal end of the "Ghost Dance War."

Fearing a revival in the spring, Miles sent Kicking Bear, Short Bull, and about twenty fellow Ghost Dancers to Fort Sheridan, Illinois, as federal prisoners. Buffalo Bill Cody, a close friend of Miles, saw an opportunity for a public relations coup and used his government connections to secure the prisoners to his care—as members of his Wild West Show. Kicking Bear agreed to the arrangement and found himself on tour, performing reenactments of the recently concluded events before European audiences.

In his absence, Kicking Bear's religion withered away. Practice of the Ghost Dance was suppressed on the Sioux reservations, though the passing of the spring 1891 deadline for the millennium may have cost it far more followers. By the time of Kicking Bear's return, government authorities had confidently pronounced the religion's demise as a major force.

Little is known of Kicking Bear's later years, though in 1896 he served as an Oglala tribal delegate to Washington, D.C. Shortly before his death he began to teach the Ghost Dance again, but these later efforts never garnered him the notoriety or influence of the dangerous winter of 1890–1891. His actions as the principal leader of the Ghost Dance religion among the Lakota were seen as desperate responses, ultimately failures, to intolerable conditions. Now they carry the veneration of an honorable opposition to distasteful assimilation policies and to onerous restrictions on Native American freedoms.

• Two manuscript collections that address Kicking Bear, the Ghost Dance, and Wounded Knee are *Reports and Correspondence Relating to the Army Investigations of the Battle of Wounded Knee and to the Sioux Campaign of 1890–91*, National Archives microfilm publication M983; and Special Case 188, "The Ghost Dance," Record Group 75, Records of the Bureau of Indian Affairs, National Archives. The best overview of the Ghost Dance troubles of 1890–1891 and Kicking Bear's role in it remains Robert M. Utley, *The Last Days of the Sioux Nation* (1963). A more recent examination is Richard E. Jensen et al., *Eyewitness at Wounded Knee* (1991). See also a classic in anthropological literature, James Mooney, *The Ghost-Dance Religion and the Sioux Outbreak of 1890* (1991).

R. ELI PAUL

KIDD, William (c. 1645–23 May 1701), pirate, was apparently born in Greenock, Scotland, the son of a Protestant minister. Little else is known of his early years except that he went to sea as a young man. He does not appear in the records until 1689, when he was the captain of a ship commissioned as a privateer by Governor Christopher Codrington of Nevis. During King William's War many ships, some of them buccaneers, were enrolled to fight the French. Kidd's men did not savor serving in Codrington's little navy and one night abandoned Kidd when he was ashore, leaving with the ship and Kidd's fortune. Kidd was fortunate in his friends, for Governor Codrington gave him a ship with which to pursue his men and retrieve his fortune.

Kidd's men left the Caribbean, where the war was making the life of pirates too difficult. In the spring of 1690 they sailed to New York City with Kidd in pursuit. When he arrived, his old crew had already moved on, but Kidd found opportunity in New York in the final stages of Leisler's rebellion. Kidd sided with the forces sent from England to reassert royal authority by putting his ship and men at their service. He would be rewarded with honors and money, and for these reasons he gave up his life at sea and settled in New York City.

In 1691 Kidd made an advantageous marriage with Sarah Cox Oort, who brought a modest fortune to the marriage. They had two daughters. The only trade that Kidd knew was that of a mariner, and so he dabbled in privateering and advertised his willingness to capture pirates who were raiding local commerce. In conjunction with his fellow Scot Robert Livingston, an ambitious politician, he devised the scheme of seeking a royal commission as a privateer/pirate hunter. The two of them journeyed in 1695 to England, where Livingston made contact with Richard Coote, the earl of Bellomont, the newly appointed governor of New England and New York. With his help they not only managed to get the commission but also the financial support of Bellomont's patrons, the Whig Junto who were the king's chief ministers at this time. Kidd's commission allowed him to seek out and destroy the pirates who were ravaging trade, especially in the Indian Ocean.

Kidd acquired a new ship, the *Adventure Galley*, and returned to New York in 1696 to sort out his affairs and complete his crew. He then sailed to the Indian Ocean. In 1697, after brief stops to revictual his ship, he appeared at the mouth of the Babs-al-Mandab straits and attacked the famously wealthy Moslem pilgrim fleet on its way home to India. He was driven off by the fleet escort, the English East India Company ship *Sceptre*. He later hovered near the west coast of India and he tried further unsuccessful attacks. These failures caused his men to question his leadership, and in 1697, during an argument with one of the chief malcontents, his gunner William Moore, Kidd killed him with a wooden bucket. This kept his crew quiet for a while and allowed Kidd the time to finally start capturing ships. These were local trading vessels, none of which carried the great wealth necessary to justify the later claims of a vast fortune.

After these successes, in 1698 Kidd went to the island of Saint Marie near the east coast of Madagascar, where the *Adventure Galley* was beached and then burned for the iron work. He then prepared one of his captives, the *Quedah Merchant*, for the voyage home. While on the island of Saint Marie, Kidd consorted with known pirates such as Robert Culliford, an act against the spirit if not the letter of his mission. Before he departed the island, his men deserted him in droves to remain in the Indian Ocean in hopes of making their fortunes.

With a depleted crew Kidd started home in 1698 to what would be a harsh welcome, for while he rested in Madagascar the East India company used him as the scapegoat for all the pirates bedeviling their trade in the East. Unfortunately for Kidd, his sponsors were out of office by 1700 and the government was made up of men in alliance with the East India Company, all of whom wanted to defame the Junto. Colonial governors were warned to watch for Kidd and to arrest him.

He arrived at the Danish island of Saint Thomas, where he received a cool welcome. By that time he knew with certainty the danger that awaited him. He soon made contact with other traders from Curaçao and exchanged a great deal of his goods for more portable forms of wealth, such as money or bills of exchange, in the river Higuey on the island of Hispaniola. He then sailed north, where he hovered near New York City while contacting family and friends before sailing on and off the eastern tip of Long Island seeking more intelligence of his situation. By this time Bellomont was in Boston, and after desultory negotiations at long range, Kidd sailed into Boston, where he was arrested by Bellomont, who probably sought to pacify his political enemies in England and keep alive the possibility of getting part of Kidd's fortunes as a reward for his actions.

Kidd was sent to prison in England. He probably had hopes that he could count on his sponsors for help and that his privateering commission and the French documents he had seized from captured ships would allow him to avoid trial and punishment. In England he was kept under close guard, and whenever he was questioned he denied everything. The government may have offered him a deal wherein if he testified against his sponsors the government would seek a lesser sentence, but he refused and kept his peace. Needless to say, his sponsors encouraged him in this behavior.

Kidd and a few of his men were tried for piracy and Kidd also for the murder of William Moore. Kidd was denied his evidence in the form of the French documents, and he finally was convicted and condemned to death. The rope broke on the first attempt; he was hanged on the second attempt in Wapping, London, England.

Kidd has been portrayed as the unwitting tool of great men who used him and abandoned him when it suited their interests. He certainly was denied evidence in the form of the French documents, but the fact is that Kidd did commit piracy and kill a member of his crew, not crimes that could easily be explained away. Nonetheless he was unfortunate in having great men as his friends who were perfectly capable of allowing his death to ease their own situation. While there are many reports that his treasure is buried anywhere from the South China Sea to Nova Scotia, there is no evidence that it exists.

• Records relating to Kidd's career can be found in the Public Record Office, especially in the High Court of Admiralty and the Colonial Office. E. B. O'Callaghan, ed., *Documentary History of the State of New York* (4 vols., 1849–1851), and Berthold Fernow, *Documents Relative to the Colonial History of the State of New York* (15 vols., 1856–1887), contain extensive treatments of portions of Kidd's career.

For biographies see Robert C. Ritchie, *Captain Kidd and the War against the Pirates* (1986); Dunbar M. Hinrichs, *The Fateful Voyage of Captain Kidd* (1955); and Harold T. Wilkins, *Captain Kidd and His Skeleton Island* (1935).

ROBERT C. RITCHIE

KIDDER, Alfred Vincent (29 Oct. 1885–11 June 1963), archaeologist, was born in Marquette, Michigan, the son of Alfred Kidder, a mining engineer, and Katherine Dalliba. During his boyhood Kidder developed a great interest in ornithology. At the age of fifteen he published a paper on his interest, "A Bittern at Close Range" (*Bird-Lore* 3 [1901]: 173). He acquired his interest in archaeology both from his father and his brother Homer. The former provided copies of Peabody Museum (Harvard University) archaeological reports, and the latter guided him on trips to various archaeological sites in Europe. His education was well rounded. He attended Buckingham School and Browne and Nichols School in Cambridge, Massachusetts, La Villa School at Ouchy, Switzerland, and finally the Noble and Greenough School in Boston before going onto Harvard University to train as a medical doctor.

During the summer of 1907 Kidder changed his mind about becoming a medical doctor. This change in career choice was mainly due to his archaeological field experience under Edgar Lee Hewett of the School of American Archaeology in Santa Fe. Hewett's "field school in archaeology" gave Kidder his initial acquaintance with the American Southwest. He worked under Hewett's tutelage during both the summers of 1907 and 1908. At this field school he met Sylvanus Morley, who became a lifelong friend and accomplished Mayanist. Frederic Ward Putnam, the second director of the Peabody Museum of Archaeology and Ethnology, was also instrumental in guiding Kidder into archaeology. While at Harvard University, Kidder took various classes in anthropology under Roland B. Dixon, Franz Boas, and Alfred Marsten Tozzer. He completed his bachelor's degree in 1908 and his Ph.D. in 1914 with a dissertation that put forward a new methodology for the study of prehistoric southwestern pottery. In 1910 Kidder married Madeleine Appleton; they had five children.

From 1914 to 1915 Kidder collaborated with Samuel J. Guernsey to formulate the archaeological chronology of the southwestern United States. From 1915 through 1925 Kidder carried out one of the longest field archaeological projects in the history of southwestern archaeology: the investigations at Pecos Pueblo, New Mexico. The principle of geologic stratigraphy was practiced there, and Kidder used this principle to tie other archaeological sites of the area to Pecos Pueblo both in time and space. Kidder asked the physical anthropologist at Pecos, Earnest Albert Hooten, for the first time to analyze human skeletal material in situ. Out of this experience Hooten created the criteria for obtaining age and sex determinations of human skeletal material in prehistoric populations. During his years at Pecos Pueblo, Kidder utilized a multidisciplinary approach to field archaeological studies by involving many practitioners from other sciences in the resolution of archaeological problems. Some of the contributing sciences to Kidder's work were chemistry, astronomy, agronomy, public health medicine, and engineering. While at Pecos, Kidder was to provide two other important services to the developing science of Americanist archaeology. For one, Pecos Pueblo was a field method training ground for students. Well-known American archaeologists who received their first field training from Kidder included George C. Vaillant, Carl Guthe, and Robert Wauchope, among others. Secondly, Kidder began the Pecos Conferences, which became a forum for archaeologists to identify common field problems and develop the means of their resolution. The Pecos Classification, which was based on differences in ceramics and their depth of deposit in archaeological sites, was born during one of the conferences. This was the first attempt to organize and describe what was then known about southwestern prehistoric cultures.

In 1929 Kidder began the second half of his archaeological career by becoming the chairman of the Carnegie Institution of Washington's Division of Historical Research. Although his attention had turned for the most part to the Maya, he continued work on his Pecos Pueblo materials through the year 1958. As the new director for the Carnegie's archaeological effort in Mayan archaeology, he introduced his "pan-scientific"/multidisciplinary approach to the explanation of Mayan archaeology. Aerial archaeology began as a method during this time. Kidder and Charles A. Lindbergh (1902–1974) worked jointly on the discovery of Mayan sites throughout the Yucatan and in other locations. The airplane became a valuable tool in the location of new Mayan sites as well as possible transportation routes between various Mayan cities. He also employed his friend Sylvanus G. Morley, who became well known for his work in deciphering Mayan hieroglyphs. Kidder's best-known Mayan investigations were of the Kaminaljuyu mounds in Guatemala, which he conducted at the request of the Guatemalan government. Kidder was instrumental in nurturing the careers of the archaeologists Anna O. Shepard and Tatiana Proskouriakoff. The former was extensively involved in the analysis of Mayan ceramics and the latter in the architecture of the Maya.

In 1950 Kidder retired from the Carnegie Institution. Although he might have continued his service for a few more years, the Carnegie Institution was beginning to change its focus of support away from the social sciences and humanities to the "hard sciences." Interest in nuclear technology channeled funding away from archaeology, and the Carnegie's program of Mayan research closed its doors in 1958. From 1950 until his death Kidder lived on Holden Street in Cambridge, Massachusetts, where both students and colleagues at Harvard sought his counsel. There was a constant parade of archaeologists going through the Kidder home. While in retirement Kidder taught a graduate course in archaeology at the University of California at Berkeley. He died at his home in Cambridge.

Conducting fieldwork without methodological precedent, Kidder created many of the field methodologies now in use in Americanist archaeology. In addition to these accomplishments, he is best remembered for the first synthesis of knowledge about southwestern archaeologic, *Introduction to Southwestern Archaeology with a Preliminary Account of the Excavations at Pecos* (1924; rev. ed., 1962), and for his administration of the Carnegie Institution of Washington's program of Mayan archaeology.

• The Alfred Vincent Kidder Papers, on deposit in the Harvard University Archives, are primary resource materials for charting the development of southwestern and Mesoamerican archaeology. Biographies of Kidder include Richard Woodbury, *Alfred V. Kidder* (1973), and Douglas R. Givens, *Alfred Vincent Kidder and the Development of Americanist Archaeology* (1992). Robert Wauchope, Alfred Vincent Kidder 1885–1963," *American Antiquity* 31, no. 2, pt. 1 (1965): 149–71, and Gordon R. Willey, "Alfred Vincent Kidder," *National Academy of Sciences, Biographical Memoirs* 39 (1967): 292–322 and *Portraits in American Archaeology: Remembrances of Some Distinguished Americanists* (1988), provide excellent biographical sketches. Earnest Albert Hooten, "The Indians of Pecos Pueblo, a Study of Their Skeletal Remains," *Papers of the Phillips Academy, Southwestern Expedition, Number 4*, (1930) provides excellent evidence of the early physical anthropology being practiced on location at an archaeological site and continues the analysis of Pecos Pueblo that Kidder asked Hooten to undertake and complete. Kidder's "Southwestern Ceramics: Their Value in Reconstructing the History of Ancient Cliff Dwelling and Pueblo Tribes: An Exposition from the Point of View of Type Distinction" (Ph.D. diss., Harvard Univ., 1914), contains his discussion of stratigraphy and pottery as the keys to understanding time and space of an archaeological culture. His work with the Carnegie Institution is discussed in "The Impact of A. V. Kidder on the Carnegie Institution of Washington and American Archaeology," *Athenaeum Society Review* 5, no. 1 (1989):5–11.

DOUGLAS R. GIVENS

KIDDER, Daniel Parish (18 Oct. 1815–29 July 1891), Methodist missionary, minister, and educator, was born at South Pembroke (later Darien), Genesee County, New York, the son of Selvey Kidder, a businessman, and Mehetabel Parish. His mother died when he was ten months old, after which his father took him to live with an aunt and uncle in Randolph, Vermont. When Daniel was thirteen his father (now remarried) took him back to live in Darien. An unusually mature young man, Kidder took sole administrative and instructional charge of the district school, and then of a school at Darien Center, soon after arriving at his father's home.

In 1832 Kidder enrolled in the Genesee Wesleyan Seminary, and while there he experienced a religious conversion. Undeterred by his father's opposition—which years later turned to pride—Kidder launched himself into a life of rigorous self-discipline and devotion to Christ and to Methodism. By 1836, having graduated from Wesleyan University in Middletown, Connecticut, he had received first his license to "exhort" and then to preach. Before his ordination he taught briefly in the Amenia (N.Y.) Seminary. Also in 1836 he married Cynthia Harriet Russell.

After serving briefly as a minister in the Rochester district of the Genesee Conference of the Methodist Episcopal church, Kidder became convinced that he needed to obey the biblical injunction to go abroad and preach the gospel, and late in 1837 he was called as his church's second missionary to Brazil. Arriving in Rio de Janeiro with his wife early in 1838, he began to distribute Portuguese Bibles, travel the country, and preach. His attempts to spread Protestantism in this predominantly Roman Catholic country were cut short in 1840 when his wife died; grieving and unable to continue his mission work while caring for his two young children (one an infant), he returned with his family to the United States. In 1841 he was stationed as minister at Paterson, New Jersey. He later published two books based on his Brazilian experience: *Sketches of Residence and Travels in Brazil* (2 vols., 1845) and, coauthored with Reverend James C. Fletcher, *Brazil and the Brazilians* (1857).

During his two years in and around Paterson, in addition to bringing converts into the fold, Kidder addressed himself to various social and religious issues, such as temperance and the claims of the Millerites and the Mormons, believing it was his duty to oppose what he considered to be social evil and doctrinal error with direct argument. His influential anti-Mormon book, *Mormonism and the Mormons: A Historical View of the Rise and Progress of the Sect Self-Styled Latter-Day Saints*, was published in 1842. Two years later he published a translation of, and added a preface and appendix to, a Portuguese book condemning celibacy as a condition of the priesthood in Roman Catholicism. In March 1842 Kidder married Harriette Smith, the principal of the Worthington (Ohio) Female Seminary; they would have three children, two daughters and a son. Later that year he was assigned to a preaching circuit in the Trenton, New Jersey, area.

Kidder harbored strong opinions about education, especially theological education, and he worked to improve the Sunday schools in his circuits. In 1844 the General Conference elected him editor of Sunday school publications and tracts and corresponding secretary of the Sunday School Union, positions he held for the next twelve years. During this period, because of his untiring efforts, Kidder became known throughout the rapidly expanding Methodist Episcopal church both in America and to some degree, in Europe. He reorganized the church's Tract Society and its Sunday School Union; he vastly improved many church publications, most notably the *Sunday School Advocate*; he promoted training for Sunday school teachers and made Sunday school a central pillar of church life; he prepared standard catechisms; he nurtured the growth of the Sunday School Fund; and he built up church libraries.

With the Sunday school and the Tract Society prospering, Kidder turned his attention to higher education. He became a founder of the Garrett Biblical Institute in Evanston, Illinois, a graduate school of theological education that opened in September 1856. Kidder accepted the position of chair of practical theology and for the next fifteen years taught theology, church history, and most notably, homiletics, the science of composing and delivering sermons. While at Garrett he wrote the first textbook to be issued from a Methodist theological school, a book that many critics of his day called the best treatise on homiletics to come out of an American seminary: *A Treatise on Homiletics, Designed to Illustrate the True Theory and Practice of Preaching the Gospel* (1864). Contrary to many other treatises, which tend to view homiletics as an aspect of rhetoric (the art of effective communication) and thus significantly dependent on classical and other secular rhetorical theories, Kidder based his treatment on the conviction that homiletics is "not a branch or species of rhetoric" but rather "a higher science to which rhetoric, logic, and other systems of human knowledge are tributary."

In 1871, because Garrett planned to merge with Northwestern University, an institution that was not subject to the control of his church, Kidder resigned his position and became professor of practical theology at Drew Theological Seminary in Madison, New Jersey. Over the following decade, he taught homiletics, among other subjects, and published *The Christian Pastorate* (1871) and *Helps to Prayer* (1874). In 1881, learning that the trustees of the seminary were about to displace him in order to bring in a new professor, he resigned. The church leadership, valuing his ability and reputation as an educator, immediately made him secretary of the board of education, a post that enabled him to continue to influence Christian education. Always arguing—against the prevailing tradition in nineteenth-century American Methodism—that ministers should complete a thorough course of liberal arts and graduate theological training before entering the ministry, Kidder worked to bring in funds necessary to help needy students complete such training. Kidder was quite successful in this regard; the education fund increased from about $3,000 to $50,000 annually during his tenure as secretary. Failing health caused him to resign in 1887. He then returned to Evanston, where he died four years later.

Although Kidder was able to teach others to speak well, he was not a charismatic speaker. A reporter covering a preaching conference heard Kidder speak between two powerful orators and later described him as "a mill pond between two cataracts." However, as that same reporter also reflected, a mill pond provides "safer swimming, broader sailing, and deeper fishing" than does a cataract and thus is an apt image of Kidder as a man of many talents and sound orthodoxy. Kidder helped to raise the standards of intellectual preparation for the Christian ministry in the nineteenth century. The foundations he laid have supported the health and growth of Christian education at every level in both the Methodist tradition as well as in other denominations that have looked to its model. These labors, along with his devotional books and articles, his accounts of missionary experiences and travels, his books designed to train ministers, and the sheer volume of writings—including more than 800 books—that passed under his editorial eye and hand, make Kidder a significant figure in American church history, most importantly as a shaper of religious education.

• Diaries belonging to Kidder and his second wife are in the Special Collections Department of the Rutgers University Libraries; the library at Garrett Theological Seminary in Evanston, Ill., has Kidder's diaries as well as his correspondence, sermons, lectures, speeches, notebooks, and other papers. For his criticisms of celibacy see *Demonstration of the Necessity of Abolishing a Constrained Clerical Celibacy, Exhibiting the Evils of That Institution and the Remedy* (1844), a translation from Portuguese of a book by Diego A. Feijo. In addition to his other published works, Kidder wrote articles for the *Christian Advocate and Journal*, the *Sunday School Advocate*, and *Golden Days*, a Sunday school periodical for youth, and contributed numerous entries to John McClintock and James Strong, eds., *Cyclopedia of Biblical, Theological, and Ecclesiastical Literature* (1885), and to Henry Kiddle and Alexander Schem, eds., *The Cyclopedia of Education: A Dictionary of Information for the Use of Teachers, School Officers, Parents, and Others* (1876). The readiest source of information is the biography by his son-in-law, G. E. Strobridge, *Biography of the Rev. Daniel Parish Kidder, D.D., LL.D.* (1894). Critical reactions to Kidder's major works can be found in various publications; for example, *Sketches of Residence and Travels in Brazil* (1845) was reviewed in vol. 17 of the *Princeton Review*, vol. 427 of the *Methodist Quarterly Review*, and vol. 68 of the *North American Review*. Obituaries are in the *Chicago Tribune*, 30 July 1891, and the *Christian Advocate*, 6 Aug. 1891.

RUSSEL HIRST

KIEFFER, Aldine Silliman (1 Aug. 1840–30 Nov. 1904), music publisher, composer, and founder of a singing school system that for generations defined southern gospel music, was born in Saline County, Missouri, the son of Mary Funk and John Kieffer, a singing-school teacher. After his father's death, Kieffer's mother took her young son and moved back to the family's ancestral home in the Shenandoah Valley of Virginia, to a location called Singer's Glen. There young Kieffer was raised under the influence of his grandfather Joseph Funk, a leading nineteenth-century song publisher. Kieffer grew up in the singing-school tradition, learning his first song when he was but a boy. As a teenager, he worked in his grandfa-

ther's printing plant, where Funk had published the *Harmonia Sacra*, one of the most popular and influential of pre–Civil War religious songbooks.

Kieffer fought for the South during the Civil War and wound up in a Union prison at the end of the conflict. There he met a guard named Ephraim Ruebush, a fellow singing-school teacher, and it was Ruebush who helped get him released from prison. The two returned to Singer's Glen, where they found the old Funk printing shop in a sad state of disrepair. Ruebush soon began courting and eventually married Kieffer's sister Lucilla, and the new brothers-in-law determined to resurrect the press. They first resumed publication of a religious-music periodical that Funk had started, the *Southern Musical Advocate and Singer's Friend*, which gave way in 1870 to the new and even more successful *Musical Million*. That periodical was to run for some forty years and, in the words of George Pullen Jackson, "was of inestimable value in instilling in the growing legions of rural music-teachers—and that meant singing-school teachers only—a sense of solidarity and professional self-respect."

Ruebush and Kieffer's new publishing company was soon publishing songbooks, though in a radically new format. Whereas the old prewar religious songbooks were big, heavy, oblong omnibus volumes, the newer ones were thin, often paperbacked, and usually contained only 100 songs, many of which were new numbers written expressly for the volume at hand. The first Ruebush-Kieffer book was the *Christian Harp*, which sold some 168,000 copies; later collections included *Song-Crowned King* (1869), *Glad Hosannas* (1871), and *The Day-School Singer* (1876). The firm also published instruction books, patriotic books, and even a collection of Kieffer's collected poems, *Hours of Fancy; or, Vigil and Vision* (1881). Many of these poems were in fact song lyrics that had appeared in earlier songbooks.

As Kieffer gained power and influence in the southern singing community, he used his position and his *Musical Million* to promote the seven-shape musical notation system that he used in his books. In this system a note's shape, not its position on the staff, determined its sound. It was a notation system that had already been abandoned in the North in favor of the familiar round notes used today. Kieffer, however, saw the difference between the systems in terms of class struggle: the country versus the city, the South versus the North; democracy versus elite; congregational singing versus paid professional choirs; even the plain, everyday Protestants against the "monkish roundheads." Though his detractors referred to Kieffer as "the Don Quixote of Buck-Wheat Notes," he did succeed in spreading his methods throughout the South and Southwest. To promote his ideas even further, in 1874 he helped found the Virginia Normal Music School at New Market, Virginia; this is generally recognized as the first real singing school in the South. Over the next three decades the school produced dozens of song leaders, song writers, and even publishers like James D. Vaughan. Kieffer died in Dayton, Virginia.

In later years, the sons of Ruebush and Kieffer carried on the tradition of the press, and it still existed into the 1990s as the Shenandoah Press. Singing schools are still held at Singer's Glen, and the old *Christian Harmony* book is still used by some rural congregations in the area. Though he eventually lost his battle against the use of round notes, Kieffer played a major role in the democratization and decentralization of the gospel-music publishing industry, and in doing so helped give to the music many of its unique characteristics.

• A good general account of Kieffer and his times is in George Pullen Jackson, *White Spirituals in the Southern Uplands* (1933). Also useful, though less accessible, is O. F. Morton, "The Ruebush-Kieffer Company," *Musical Millions* 42 (Aug. 1911): 84. A more detailed account of the whole Shenandoah Valley school of publishing is found in Harry Eskew, "Shape-Note Hymnody in the Shenandoah Valley, 1816–1860" (Ph.D. diss., Tulane Univ., 1966). Bibliographical data about Kieffer's company is in Grace I. Showalter, *The Music Books of Ruebush Kieffer 1866–1942: A Bibliography* (1975). The author has also relied on personal interviews with Stella Vaughan Walbert, James D. Walbert, Connor Hall, Harlan Daniel, and William B. Davidson.

CHARLES K. WOLFE

KIEFT, Willem (Sept. 1597–27 Sept. 1647), director of New Netherland, was born in Amsterdam, the Netherlands, the son of Gerrit Willemszoon Kieft, a merchant, and Machteld Huydecoper. Kieft's maternal grandfather was Jan Jacobszonn Bal, a well-known magistrate of Amsterdam. Kieft entered the merchant trade in La Rochelle, France, apparently failed in business there, and then went to the Ottoman Empire in order to ransom Christians who were held as prisoners by the Turks. It was later claimed that Kieft embezzled part of the ransom money, but this inauspicious start to his career did not stand in his way.

Kieft returned to the Netherlands and, probably because of the influence of his relatives, was sworn in on 2 September 1637 as the new director general of New Netherland. Kieft sailed on the *Harinck* and arrived at New Amsterdam on 28 March 1638. He found the colony in a sorry state: the fort was dilapidated, the streets were made of mud, and the colonists were drinking, fighting with each other, and carrying on illicit trade with the Indians. Determined to set matters straight, Kieft set himself up as a virtual dictator. He named a council of only two members, himself, with two votes, and Johannes Montaigne, a doctor, with one vote. Kieft imposed strict rules on the populace in an effort to increase the strength and organization of the colony.

Kieft encountered enormous problems during his tenure as director (28 Mar. 1638–11 May 1647). First, he faced the growing problem of encroachment on the boundaries of New Netherland by Swedish and English settlers. Some of these incursions were fairly innocuous; Anne Hutchinson, Lady Deborah Moody, and others settled within New Netherland on terms advantageous to both sides. But the Swedish colony on the Delaware River and the English settlements at Hartford, New Haven, and Southampton, Long Island, were all seen as direct threats to the survival of New Netherland, which always had a much smaller population than its English counterparts. During his ten years as director, Kieft alternately threatened, cajoled, and pleaded with the English to respect the boundaries of the Dutch colony. In all of this, Kieft was a loyal and conscientious employee of the Dutch West India Company.

Kieft was less diplomatic in his relations with his own colonists and with the Indians who lived around Manhattan Island. Kieft allowed the colonists to select the Council of Twelve Men (1641), but, after the councillors made a formal petition for greater civil liberties, Kieft abruptly dismissed them (8 Feb. 1642) and went back to ruling by decree. In 1639 Kieft had initiated a policy of levying taxes of maize and furs on the local Indian tribes. Taxes and misunderstandings eventually led to a full-scale, though sporadic, Dutch-Indian war, which raged on and off from 1640 to 1645. Kieft overrode the objections of his colonists and authorized a brutal massacre of Weckquaskee Indians at Pavonia (25–26 Feb. 1643). This short-term victory made the Indian war more intense; in response nearly all the Indian tribes joined together and fought against the Dutch. When a peace was finally concluded (30 Aug. 1645), the Indians had suffered 1,600 casualties, and New Amsterdam had shrunk to a population of only 250 persons. At the height of the Indian conflict, Kieft was denounced from the pulpit by Everardus Bogardus and was nearly assassinated by an irate colonist. The Eight Select Men, a new representative body, wrote a long memorial to the lords of the West India Company on 28 October 1644 asking for a new governor. In response to this and to numerous other complaints, the West India Company replaced Kieft with Petrus Stuyvesant, who arrived at New Amsterdam in May 1647.

Kieft surrendered his office to Stuyvesant and departed aboard the *Princess*, sharing the voyage with Bogardus, the leader of the Eight Select Men, Cornelis Melyn, and other members of the anti-Kieft coalition. Kieft and his foes alike intended to present their versions of events before the lords of the West India Company. The anticipated showdown was averted when the *Princess* sank off the coast of Wales. Kieft and Bogardus were both lost; Melyn was among the twenty passengers who survived. Apparently, Kieft had never married.

Even a sympathetic historian cannot rehabilitate the reputation of Kieft. He was arrogant, shortsighted, and bigoted, especially against the Native Americans. He thwarted the Dutch colonists' attempts to develop a representative government, and his dictatorial rule was anything but benevolent. The massacre of the Weckquaskee Indians at Pavonia was one of the most atrocious in the colonial history of North America, and the Indian war greatly retarded the development of

New Netherland. The most favorable thing that can be said for Kieft is that he was vigilant in his defense of New Netherland against English and Swedish incursions. One might add that Kieft played an interesting role in intercolonial relations; he corresponded with John Winthrop, Sr., and entertained individuals as diverse as Father Isaac Jogues and Roger Williams at the fort on Manhattan. In sum, Kieft was a vigorous but intemperate and misguided director who left matters in New Netherland as bad as—and possibly worse than—he had found them when he first arrived. Although his tenure as director coincided with the Golden Age of the Netherlands, that golden age was not duplicated in the Dutch experience in North America.

• Kieft's defense against the charges laid against him is "Journal of New Netherland, 1647," in *Narratives of New Netherland, 1609–1664*, ed. J. Franklin Jameson (1909), pp. 267–84. Primary sources relating to Kieft, the council, the Council of Twelve, and the Eight Select Men are all to be found in E. B. O'Callaghan, ed., *Documents Relative to the Colonial History of the State of New York* (1856). An up-to-date and thorough account of New Netherland, and Kieft in particular, is Henri van der Zee and Barbara van der Zee, *A Sweet and Alien Land: The Story of Dutch New York* (1978). Further information is in Michael Kammen, *Colonial New York: A History* (1975); Alexander C. Flick, ed., *History of the State of New York*, vol. 1 (1962); Ellis Lawrence Raesly, *Portrait of New Netherland* (1965); William R. Shepherd, *The Story of New Amsterdam* (1926); and John Brodhead, *History of the State of New York*, vol. 1 (1853). Finally one can examine Kieft as "William the Testy," in Washington Irving's humorous *A History of New York* (1809; repr. 1902).

SAMUEL WILLARD CROMPTON

KIERAN, John Francis (2 Aug. 1892–10 Dec. 1981), sports writer, radio personality, and naturalist, was born in the Bronx, New York City, the son of James Michael Kieran, an educator, and Kate Donahue. He grew up in a book-oriented home. His father was a public school principal who later became a professor of education at Hunter College and then president of that institution. His mother was a school teacher before her marriage who, said Kieran, "quoted the classics on the slightest provocation."

Kieran, who played on the school's baseball team, graduated cum laude from Fordham College in 1912. His family owned a farm in Dutchess County, and after graduation Kieran lived there for a year trying to earn a living as a poultry farmer, while supplementing his income teaching in a one-room district schoolhouse. But as he explained in his autobiography, although he "loved the life on the farm," and it "quickened" his "youthful love of the outdoors into a growing interest in natural history," he "couldn't make a living there."

Determined not "to sponge" further on his father, Kieran returned to New York in the autumn of 1913 and became a general handyman for a sewer construction project. However, he tired of the long subway ride to and from work six days a week and in 1915 convinced an editor at the *New York Times*, who was also a family friend, to give him a position in the sports department. Kieran was soon the paper's regular golf reporter, although he was also dispatched to cover other sports.

World War I interrupted Kieran's newspaper career. One month after the United States declared war on Germany, Kieran enlisted in an engineering outfit and, in August 1917, landed in France. His unit suffered some casualties, and Kieran "remembered months of mud and misery, moments of stark terror, and hopeless hours where there seemed no way out." Still, he came home physically unscathed. In 1919 Kieran married Alma Boldtmann; the couple had three children.

After being discharged from the service in May 1919, Kieran resumed his career with the *Times*. But in 1922 he shifted to the *New York Tribune* when he was offered a job as a baseball writer with a byline (at the *Times*, all the sports writers were anonymous, as generally were the news columnists). He switched briefly to the *New York American* in 1925 but returned to the *Times* in January 1927 to begin a regular signed column he called "Sports of the Times." It was the first daily bylined column of any kind to appear in that newspaper, though other signed columns soon after appeared elsewhere in the *Times*.

Kieran's assignment was to produce a sports column of about 1,100 words seven days a week (annual vacations excepted). The result was a rather unusual column that revealed both his broad learning and sense of humor. He covered an array of sports, including boxing, baseball, football, hockey, track, horse racing (in 1935 he went to England to report on the Grand National Steeplechase), tennis, rugby, and golf. But at various times his column touched on subjects such as ancient history, modern art, organic and inorganic chemistry, and astronomy. Occasionally it contained quotes from Virgil, Plato, St. Augustine, Keats, and Browning or featured even Kieran's own light verse. Thus on one occasion he wrote the following couplet concerning golf etiquette: "Of cutting words that blight and pall, / The worst are these: 'You played my ball.'"

Although he continued to do his "Sports of the Times" column, in 1938 Kieran accepted an invitation to become a regular panelist, along with Clifton Fadiman, Oscar Levant and Franklin P. Adams, on a new radio quiz show called "Information Please." The regulars, who were joined by guest panelists, answered questions sent in by members of the listening audience. If the panel was stumped by a question, the sender received as his reward a 24-volume set of the *Encyclopedia Britannica*. The show, broadcast weekly on NBC, established Kieran's reputation as "Mr. Encyclopedia." A keen reader who possessed a retentive memory, Kieran successfully answered questions not only about sports but also on such subjects as mythology, art, science, and literature.

"Information Please" made Kieran a nationally known figure. But he found it increasingly burdensome to do the show, write his column, and fulfill the obligations he assumed after the Japanese attack on

Pearl Harbor (such as working for the Red Cross and preparing broadcasts for the Office of War Information). So, regretfully, in December 1941 Kieran left the *Times* and accepted an offer from the *New York Sun* to write a 500-word general interest column called "One Small World." In December 1944, however, heart trouble caused him to resign from the *Sun*, ending his career as a journalist. That same year his wife died, and in 1947 he married Margaret Ford.

Since the year he had lived on a farm and developed an interest in nature, Kieran had steadily deepened his appreciation of the natural world. Through regular morning strolls in the woods near his home in the Riverdale section of the city, he extended his knowledge of the local flora and fauna. When the opportunity arose while covering an outdoor sporting event, he did some birdwatching. In 1928 he had begun to write nature stories for the *Times* Sunday Magazine.

After retiring from the *Sun*, Kieran was able to spend much more of his waking hours tracking the comings and going of birds and learning about native trees, shrubs, and flowers. Although he continued with "Information Please" until the show left the air in 1948 and subsequently did several short-lived television programs, writing about nature became his principal occupation after 1945. That Kieran was successful in this endeavor is clear from the strongly positive response of reviewers to his nature books. These included *Footnotes on Nature* (1947); *Introduction to Birds* (1950); *Introduction to Trees* (1954); *John James Audubon*, coauthored with his wife Margaret Kieran (1957); and *Treasury of Great Nature Writing* (1957).

His magnum opus, however, was *A Natural History of New York City* (1959). The naturalist Edwin Way Teate declared it "in many ways the best treatment the natural history of a great city has ever received" (*New York Times*, 27 Sept. 1959). In 1960 Kieran won the John Burroughs Medal in recognition of his achievement. The following year he was awarded a special certificate for his book by the Park Association of New York. His sports writing also continued to receive acclaim; in 1973 the National Baseball Hall of Fame presented Kieran with its J. G. Taylor Spink Award for excellence in baseball writing.

In 1952 Kieran decided to exchange the canyons of Manhattan for a rustic setting. After some searching, he settled on Rockport, Massachusetts, where he spent the remainder of his life and where he died.

• Several references to Kieran are in the Columbia University Oral History Collection, Columbia University. The most satisfactory account of Kieran's life and career is his autobiography, *Not Under Oath: Recollections and Reflections* (1964). To supplement his autobiography, consult *Current Biography* (1940), pp. 454–57; Arthur Bartlett, "John Kieran: Expert on Everything," *Coronet*, Mar. 1949, pp. 41–46; and an interview with Kieran when he was about eighty years old in Jerome Holtzman, *No Cheering in the Press Box* (1973), pp. 34–45. An obituary is in the *New York Times*, 11 Dec. 1981.

RICHARD HARMOND

KILBANE, Johnny (18 Apr. 1889–31 May 1957), boxer, was born John Patrick Kilbane in Cleveland, Ohio, the son of John T. Kilbane and Laura Gravette. When his father became blind, Kilbane had to leave school after the primary grades to help support the family. While working as a switch tender in a railroad yard he decided to become a boxer. In 1907 he was discovered by lightweight boxer Jimmy Dunn, who taught him and managed him throughout Kilbane's career.

Kilbane began fighting professionally in December 1907. Undefeated in his first twenty-eight fights, he boxed in the Cleveland-Pittsburgh area until 1910, when he visited Boston and won two fights there. Later that same year he challenged Abe Attell, the featherweight champion, for the title, but he lost decisively by being overly cautious. A nontitle rematch with Attell in January 1911 ended inconclusively when both fighters fell to the floor and Attell, who was leading on points, suffered a broken arm and could not continue. In May 1911 Kilbane lost a disputed decision to highly regarded Joe Rivers in Los Angeles, but he followed with six consecutive victories, including a knockout of Rivers in a rematch.

These successes brought Kilbane another featherweight title fight with Attell on 22 February 1912 in Los Angeles. His accurate left jab and right-hand punches produced a decisive victory by decision over the fading champion. By then, Kilbane had perfected the orthodox style, clever boxing tactics, and boxing ability that kept him on top for many years. Veteran boxing manager Jimmy Dime described his style:

Kilbane was a veritable "streak of lightning" in action. . . . He seemed to withdraw or sidestep out of danger without any effort . . . catching blows on his gloves . . . parrying and hitting with practically one motion. . . . As an attacking marksman Kilbane excelled them all. His blows were as clean and sharp as a rifle shot. . . . He had the faculty of picking out the slightest opening and driving through a telling punch, and his beautiful feinting made most of his openings. . . . He wasted very few blows. (*Boxing* [Great Britain], 29 Mar. 1922, p. 105)

Kilbane scored few knockouts, usually preferring to box cautiously, but he showed a good punch in knocking out Benny Chavez, Patsy Cline, Willie Jackson, George Chaney, and Alvie Miller, among others.

Kilbane defended his title against Johnny Dundee on 29 April 1913 in Los Angeles; he barely escaped with a draw. Always highly protective of his championship, he avoided the unorthodox Dundee thereafter, even though Dundee continued to be the most deserving contender for many years. Kilbane did make successful defenses against Jimmy Walsh in Boston in 1912 and 1913, Jimmy Fox in Oakland, California, in 1913, Chaney in Cedar Point, Ohio, in 1916, Eddie Wallace in Bridgeport, Connecticut, in 1917, Miller in Lorain, Ohio, in 1920, and Danny Frush in Cleveland in 1921, although the first Walsh fight and the Wallace defense were judged to be draws.

During his years as champion, Kilbane frequently fought in states in which official decisions were not allowed by law. Contemporary newspaper accounts show that Kilbane usually won his fights easily, seldom extending himself. Often he was content to outbox his opponents, without seriously attempting to knock them out. In nontitle fights, he outpointed Kid Williams, Benny Leonard, Freddie Welsh, and many other highly regarded featherweights and lightweights. His only serious misjudgment was in taking a rematch with Leonard, who knocked him out in three rounds of a nontitle fight in Philadelphia in 1917.

After military service during World War I, Kilbane returned to action but with his skills diminished. He showed little inclination to defend his title, and he went into virtual retirement in 1922. However, he was induced to defend once more, against Eugene Criqui in New York City on 2 June 1923. Criqui, a French war hero whose jaw had been surgically reconstructed after a gunshot wound, was outboxed for five rounds, but he connected with a powerful right to the jaw in the sixth. Kilbane, victim of a one-punch knockout, was at last dethroned. It was his final fight and only the second time he had been knocked out in 142 fights.

Kilbane married Irene McDonnell in 1911, and they had two children. He was a charming and gregarious man with many friends, but his failure to give the popular Dundee a rematch brought him heavy public criticism. After his retirement, he remained on the fringes of boxing and, at different times, operated a gymnasium, ran a health farm, refereed, and was a boxing instructor in Cleveland public schools. He entered politics, failing to win elections for the Cleveland city council and for sheriff, but he served a two-year term as an Ohio state senator in 1941–1942, and he was a state representative in 1952. He worked in the county engineer's office and finally was appointed municipal court clerk, serving in that post until his death in Cleveland.

Kilbane had the longest uninterrupted reign as a boxing champion at any weight level until surpassed by Joe Louis. He was elected to the International Boxing Hall of Fame in 1995.

• Kilbane's complete record is available in Herbert G. Goldman, ed., *The Ring Record Book and Boxing Encyclopedia, 1986–1987*. A good article on his early life and career is J. P. Garvey, "Kilbane, New Champion, Has Had a Brief Career," *Philadelphia Item*, 23 July 1912. Other, more derivative sources, are Jerry Fitch, *Cleveland's Greatest Fighters of All Time* (published privately, 1980), and John D. McCallum, *The Encyclopedia of World Boxing Champions* (1975). A factually accurate obituary written by Jersey Jones is in *The Ring*, Aug. 1957, pp. 40–41.

LUCKETT V. DAVIS

KILBY, Christopher (25 May 1705–Oct. 1771), merchant, was born in Boston, Massachusetts, the son of John Kilby and Rebecca Simpkins, heirs of New England merchant families. Early in life he was apprenticed to a Boston merchant, William Clark, and in 1726 became his junior partner. The same year he married Clark's daughter, Sarah Clark. William Clark, a distinguished and wealthy merchant, and his brother, John Clark, a legislator, carried on an extensive trade with England and the West Indies, a trade in which Kilby often served as their agent abroad, contracting for products. About 1735 Kilby formed a partnership with Benjamin Clark, the youngest son of William Clark, and they were very successful for a few years. Blending commercial affairs with politics, in May 1739 Kilby became a Boston member of the Massachusetts House of Representatives. His prominence in legislating was impressive but ended abruptly in December 1739 when the house sent him as a special agent to England as it prepared to battle Governor Jonathan Belcher on a variety of business and political issues, which apparently included support of a plot to remove the governor from office.

In London Kilby soon replaced the resident agent and served into the early 1750s. His major business as Massachusetts agent was to handle trade matters, which he did extraordinarily well, winning the backing of merchants on both sides of the Atlantic. Soon he joined the English firm of Sedgewick and Barnard, which was engaged in wartime provisioning of British troops in the American colonies. Kilby, in handling official and private business, appeared regularly before the Board of Trade and often conferred with members of the ministry. He helped get Belcher recalled from and William Shirley appointed to the Massachusetts governorship in 1741. Many of the new governor's tasks in dealing with the home government were transacted by Kilby. When war with France broke out in 1744, Kilby brought special information on Louisbourg's possible capture and the defense of Nova Scotia to ministerial attention. His activities mounted when Britain organized campaigns against Quebec in 1746 to 1748. With his own provisioning business growing, he gradually relinquished the government agency to William Bollan, the son-in-law of Shirley, and in the 1750s he and his Boston friends (e.g., Thomas Hancock) became the suppliers of British troops in Nova Scotia and the frontier in America. His superiors included generals of the British army such as Lord Loudoun, James Abercromby, and Jeffrey Amherst.

As the Seven Years' War broke out, Kilby and his English merchant associates won a major provisioning contract, and he journeyed to New York to serve as "agent-victualler" for the British army in North America. Until 1763 his headquarters were in New York as the resident partner of his London firm, and there he managed much of the provisioning of the troops, which included local purchases in New York and New Jersey and the warehousing of a vast amount of imported English merchandise.

Kilby's return to England in 1763 brought a change in activities. He used his wealth from the agency to buy an extensive estate and other property in the parish of Dorking, County Surrey, which he improved until his death there. As he withdrew gradually from his merchant business in London, he enjoyed revenue from his lands in Surrey and, perhaps, the pleasures of a country gentleman. His first wife had died in 1739, leaving him with two young daughters, who joined him in England in 1747. Sometime after his first wife's death, Kilby married Martha Neaves, probably in England. Kilby represented the merchant interests in London and the colonies that enjoyed until 1763 the advantages of wartime commerce and membership in the empire.

• Most research libraries with prerevolutionary collections will have much Kilby personal and business correspondence. The Hancock papers at the Harvard Business School are full of references to commercial dealings with Thomas Hancock. The Loudoun papers at the Huntington Library, San Marino, Calif., have letters on the provisioning business. Kilby's activities are discussed in Winifred Lovering Holman, "Kilby Notes," *American Genealogist* 28 (1952): 37–40; Charles W. Tuttle, "Christopher Kilby, of Boston," *New England Historical and Genealogical Register* 26 (1872): 43–48; George Arthur Wood, *William Shirley: Governor of Massachusetts 1741–1756* (1920); and John A. Schutz, *William Shirley: King's Governor of Massachusetts* (1961).

JOHN A. SCHUTZ

KILDAHL, John Nathan (4 Jan. 1857–25 Sept. 1920), Lutheran clergyman and educator, was born in Namdalseidet, Indherred, Norway, near Trondhjem, the son of Johan Kildahl and Nikoline Buvarp. In 1866 he migrated with his family to Goodhue County, Minnesota, where his father was employed as a parochial school teacher in the parish of Rev. Bernt J. Muus for a few years until his health failed. Through the encouragement of his pastor Kildahl attended Luther College, Decorah, Iowa, from which he graduated in 1879, followed by study at Luther Theological Seminary, Madison, Wisconsin, where he received a candidate in theology degree in 1882. Both schools were operated by the conservative Norwegian Synod. While a seminary student, Kildahl went through a spiritual crisis of profound significance. Through his study of the Bible, the counsel of an older seminarian, and the impact of his introduction to the writings of Carl Olof Rosenius, the influential Swedish lay theologian, he gained certainty of his salvation. He married Bertha Søine in 1882; they had five children.

In the summer of 1882 Kildahl was ordained a minister and served as pastor of the Vang and Urland congregations in Goodhue County for seven years. During the school year 1885–1886 he was granted a leave of absence by his parish to serve as president of nearby Red Wing Seminary, the theological school of Hauge's Synod. Throughout his career he enjoyed the confidence of the pietistic Haugeans. During the 1880s the Norwegian Synod, to which he and his congregations belonged, was rent by controversy over the doctrine of predestination (election). Kildahl played a prominent role on the side of the so-called Anti-Missourians, whose leaders included neighboring pastors Bernt J. Muus and Marcus O. Bøckman. His position was that God's gracious choosing of a sinner for salvation is in view of his foreseen faith (intuitu fidei) in Christ; the

emphasis is on faith. The opposing position was that God by grace in view of the merits of Christ chooses one for faith and salvation; the emphasis is on grace. The unusual name, Anti-Missourian, derived from opposition to what they regarded as undue theological influence of the Missouri Synod upon the Norwegian Synod. After the withdrawal of the Anti-Missourians from the Norwegian Synod during 1887–1888, Kildahl was among those who worked diligently on behalf of the merger movement that resulted in the formation of the United Norwegian Lutheran Church in America (commonly referred to as the United Church) in 1890. The uniting groups were the Anti-Missourian Brotherhood, the Norwegian-Danish Conference, and the Norwegian-Danish Augustana Synod.

In 1889 Kildahl became pastor of Bethlehem Lutheran Church in Chicago, where he served for ten years. His strenuous and fruitful ministry in Chicago was notable for the effectiveness and popularity of his preaching; the occurrence of a spiritual awakening in the congregation, during which many were brought to faith in Christ and/or gained assurance of faith; and the large number of ministerial acts (baptisms, marriages, funerals) that he performed annually. He had developed into one of the most effective preachers in the United Church, widely known for his gospel-centered sermons.

In 1899 the United Church chose Kildahl to be president of St. Olaf College, Northfield, Minnesota. He assumed the presidency at a crucial time for the college. In the wake of the 1890 merger a controversy over the ownership of St. Olaf developed, in the course of which the college for several years was without any synodical connection. The turbulence ended in 1899 when St. Olaf became the college of the United Church. Under his leadership firm ties with the United Church were nurtured. Its character as a coeducational Lutheran liberal arts college was reaffirmed. While many of its graduates continued to enter the ministry and other full-time religious vocations, Kildahl emphasized that its aim was to prepare young men and women to make significant contributions to American society in all walks of life. When he assumed the presidency in 1899, the student body numbered 184. By the end of his tenure in 1914 the student enrollment had increased to 518. He also expanded and modernized the curriculum through increased course offerings and provision for electives. In the course of his tenure the physical plant of the campus was enlarged. One of Kildahl's most important contributions was the recruiting of a group of outstanding teachers for the faculty, among them F. Melius Christiansen, composer of choral music and director of the college choir, and Ole E. Rølvaag, professor of Norwegian language and literature and author of immigrant novels. Their reputations reached for beyond the campus.

Kildahl made a deep spiritual impact on the college, identifying it firmly with the United Church and its mission. Moreover, he exemplified a vibrant religious life and encouraged students to have an interest in world missions. He retired as president in 1914 and became professor of systematic theology at the United Church Seminary in St. Paul (1914–1917) and its successor, Luther Theological Seminary (1917–1920). He also taught homiletics, for which he was eminently qualified. Kildahl's theology was traditional Lutheran orthodoxy. The center of his teaching and preaching was the gospel, the message of salvation by God's grace through faith in Christ. He died in Minneapolis.

Kildahl served in many positions and on many committees and boards of the church. In the United Church he was general secretary (1890–1895), mission secretary (1895–1899), vice president (1912–1917), and member of the union committee (1906–1910, 1912–1917). In 1917 the Norwegian Lutheran Church in America (NLCA) was formed through a merger, and he served the new church body as vice president until his death. One of the most respected Norwegian-American Lutheran leaders of his generation, he was also a representative figure in that he combined both the piotistic and orthodox emphases of his Norwegian Lutheran tradition. His writings were chiefly of a devotional and doctrinal nature, including articles in church periodicals, booklets, and tracts. The most highly regarded of his writings is a collection of sermons on biblical texts for the entire church year, *Synd og Naade* (1912), which was translated into English and published under the title *Concerning Sin and Grace* (1954).

• Kildahl's papers are located in the St. Olaf College Archives, Northfield, Minn., and the archives at Luther Seminary, St. Paul, Minn. The primary source about Kildahl is Rasmus Malmin, ed., *Dr. John Nathan Kildahl. En Mindebok* (1921). Three histories of St. Olaf College contain discussions of his presidency: C. A. Mellby, *Saint Olaf College through Fifty Years 1874–1924* (1925); William C. Benson, *High on Manitou: A History of St. Olaf College, 1874–1949* (1949); Joseph M. Shaw, *History of St. Olaf College, 1874–1974* (1974). Shaw's work is particularly insightful. Biographical data are found in O. M. Norlie, ed., *Norsk lutherske prester i Amerika, 1843–1913* (1914), which was translated and revised by Malmin, Norlie, and O. A. Tingelstad as *Who's Who among Pastors in all the Norwegian Lutheran Synods of America, 1843–1927* (1928). Obituaries are in *Lutheran Church Herald,* 5 and 12 Oct. 1920.

EUGENE L. FEVOLD

KILGALLEN, Dorothy (3 July 1913–8 Nov. 1965), journalist and radio and television personality, was born Dorothy Mae Kilgallen in Chicago, Illinois, the daughter of James Lawrence Kilgallen, a journalist, and Mae Jane Ahern, a singer. Her father's work took the family to Laramie, Wyoming, then to Indianapolis, Indiana, and back to Chicago, where he began a long association with the Hearst newspaper syndicate. Dorothy attended grade schools in Indianapolis and Chicago. When the family moved to Brooklyn, New York, she continued school there and graduated from high school in 1930. After her freshman year at the College of New Rochelle, she accepted a summer job in 1931 as a cub reporter for the *New York Evening Journal.* She never returned to college.

A career in journalism was difficult for women at this time. Although between 1920, when women gained the right to vote, and 1930 the number of female reporters had roughly doubled, most were relegated to women's and society pages, some were still labeled "stunt girls" and "sob sisters," and their male supervisors exploited them, played favorites, excluded them from male-only conferences and professional organizations, and denied them front-page and byline celebrity by rewriting their work. Nonetheless, Kilgallen soon earned bylines for clever sentimental stories of hospitalized children. She was assigned the morgue beat and reported a ferryboat explosion, a marriage mill, murders, trials, and executions. Indefatigible, she wrote 250,000 words of copy during a five-week murder trial in 1933, in Salem, Massachusetts, and covered the 1935 trial in Flemington, New Jersey, of Bruno Hauptmann, convicted in the Lindbergh kidnapping case.

In a stunt that was characteristic of Hearst newspapers, the *Journal* entered Kilgallen in a contest with two rival reporters in a race around the world using commercial means. Although her time of twenty-four days, twelve hours, and fifty-two minutes lost by almost six days, her rapid-fire reports cabled along the way intrigued her readers and became her popular book *Girl around the World* (1937). In Calcutta she described her taxi as it "wheezed and coughed" on its way to the "so-called airport." Flying over Indo-Chinese jungles, she expressed the fear that "tigers and great constrictor snakes lie in wait for little girls." Late in 1936 she reported show-business gossip from Hollywood in her own column; collaborated on *Fly Away Baby,* a 1937 movie based on her globe-girdling; and took a bit part as a reporter in the film *Sinner Take All* (also 1937). She covered high-society news back in New York, reported the 1937 coronation of George VI in London, and in 1938 took over the syndicated "Voice of Broadway" column for her *Journal* (called the *Journal-American* since 1937). In it she combined gossip, malice, and trivia about politicians, celebrities, and entertainers, including jazz musicians. She happily led a frenzied life attending lavish theatrical events, choosing dining locales by a game called "Restaurant Roulette," mingling with the glittering and the tawdry alike, and taking notes on nightclub matchbooks.

In 1940 Kilgallen married Richard Tompkins Kollmar, a radio and stage actor. The wedding ceremony, at St. Vincent's Catholic Church in New York City, drew an elite from the entertainment and political worlds. The couple had three children but were often troubled, owing to her superior professional status, their—especially his—alcoholism, their money woes, and their extramarital affairs. In 1941 Kilgallen became a radio personality, with "Voice of Broadway," produced at first by CBS. In 1947 it became NBC's "Dorothy Kilgallen Show." In 1945 she and her husband initiated "Breakfast with Dorothy and Dick," broadcast from their swank Park Avenue apartment by the Mutual Broadcasting System (MBS) until 1963 and offering theater and personal gossip, conservative political opinions, and praise of sponsors' products. Kilgallen also starred on "Leave It to the Girls" (MBS, 1945–1949), a thirty-minute panel discussion by four career women responding with humor to problems and questions sent in by listeners. Panelists included Lucille Ball, Binnie Barnes, and Constance Bennett. This became a TV show (NBC, 1949–1951; ABC, 1953–1954).

In 1950 CBS hired Kilgallen to be one of the original panelists on "What's My Line?" Within two years the half-hour TV program had a nightly audience of almost 10 million, became the longest-running prime-time TV game show, and helped Kilgallen double to 146 the number of newspapers carrying her "Voice of Broadway," thus making it one of the most popular and influential columns. Original *What's My Line?* panelists, hosted by newsman John Daly, were New Jersey governor Harold Hoffman, psychiatrist Richard H. Hoffman, and poet-critic Louis Untermeyer. Among many guest panelists were comics Fred Allen and Steve Allen, and actress Faye Emerson. By the late 1950s the regular cast was Daly, TV personality Arlene Francis, and publisher Bennett Cerf. Kilgallen's acerbic, often tactless wit on the show became legendary. A mild example was her barking out of turn to help a rival contestant identify a veterinarian and thus call attention to herself. Kilgallen also appeared on at least seven other TV shows, including CBS's "To Tell the Truth" (from 1956) and "I've Got a Secret" (from 1961).

Often photographed in beautiful attire—with white gloves as her signature—Kilgallen was named one of the world's ten best-dressed women four times and was as famous as many of the celebrities on whom she reported. She counted her subjects either as admirable—for example, Grace Kelly; Queen Elizabeth II, whose 1957 New York cavalcade Kilgallen crashed in her own Rolls-Royce; Ava Gardner; Ernest Hemingway, who praised her style; Sophia Loren, whom she adored; Marilyn Monroe; Johnnie Ray, one of her lovers; and Dr. Samuel Holmes Sheppard, whose innocence she proclaimed—or as inimical—Fidel Castro; Sheilah Graham; Nikita Khrushchev, comparing Mrs. Khrushchev's dress to a homemade sofa slipcover; Ernie Kovacs, at whose cigars she grimaced; and Frank Sinatra, calling him conceited and moody and being labeled by him "the chinless wonder."

By 1960 Kilgallen's credits included at least 6,000 columns. Owing to liquor, barbiturates, and anemia, she fell ill covering John F. Kennedy's inaugural parties in 1961. By 1962 she and her husband were often too hung over to do their "Dorothy and Dick" show live from their five-story townhouse on East Sixty-eighth Street. To add to their woes, a New York restaurant her husband opened in 1957 failed within six years and left him unemployed and morose. In 1963 Kilgallen went to London and covered the John Profumo–Christine Keeler scandal. In January 1964 she was unsuccessfully sued for libel by Elaine Shepard, a rival journalist. Kilgallen's testimony and that of her husband at the trial were undoubtedly perjured. February found her in Dallas, Texas, covering the trial of Jack L. Ruby, who killed Lee Harvey Oswald, President Kennedy's alleged assassin. She interviewed Ruby privately but published nothing about what he said.

Conservative though she remained, Kilgallen testified on behalf of Lenny Bruce, the comedian sued in 1964 by New York State for obscenity. Bruce lost that trial but won on appeal. Later in 1964 she went to Austria, Italy, and London on 20th Century–Fox press junkets and met and began an intense affair with an unnamed young newspaperman and songwriter. The two were together in New York and elsewhere later. In August she and the *Dallas Times–Herald* scooped other papers in publishing Ruby's testimony before the Warren Commission, a month before the official release. She tried so desperately to ferret out evidence concerning Kennedy's death, contrary to the official version, that the Federal Bureau of Investigation and perhaps other governmental agencies became alarmed.

After appearing on "What's My Line?" the evening of 7 November 1965, Kilgallen had a few drinks in public and retired. The next day she was found dead in bed. After sloppy work by the police, the medical examiner, and toxicologists, it was ruled that she had died of an accidental combination of alcohol and barbiturates. It has been inconclusively, and perhaps irresponsibly, speculated that she may have committed suicide or been murdered. Her widowed husband committed suicide in 1971.

• The Billy Rose Theatre Collection at the New York Public Library for the Performing Arts, Lincoln Center, contains more than seventy scrapbooks Kilgallen assembled, with her columns, photographs, personal memorabilia, and articles by her and about her. Her Ruby notes have disappeared. The best source of information about her is Lee Israel, *Kilgallen* (1979). Ishbel Ross, *Ladies of the Press* (1936), and John Jakes, *Great Women Reporters* (1969), contain brief treatments. Ernest Lehman, "24 Glittering Hours with Dorothy Kilgallen," *Cosmopolitan*, Sept. 1950, pp. 66–69, 151–54, is a flattering personality sketch. Kilgallen's posthumously published *Murder One* (1967) collects her coverage of six sensational 1934–1959 indicted murderers and their trials, including that of Dr. Sheppard. Gilbert Fates, *"What's My Line?" The Inside History of TV's Most Popular Panel Show* (1978), discusses Kilgallen's central part. Detailed information on women in the history of journalism is in Ishbel Ross, *Ladies of the Press: The Story of Women in Journalism by an Insider* (1936), and Maurine H. Beasley and Sheila J. Gibbons, *Taking Their Place: A Documentary History of Women and Journalism* (1993). Inaccurate obituaries are in the *Journal-American*, 8 Nov. 1965, and the *New York Times*, 9 Nov. 1965.

ROBERT L. GALE

KILGORE, Carrie Sylvester Burnham (20 Jan. 1838–29 June 1909), lawyer and suffragist, was born in Craftsbury, Vermont, the daughter of James Elisah Burnham, a prosperous woolen manufacturer, and Eliza Annis Arnold, a schoolteacher and artist. Her mother died before Carrie was three, and her father died when she was twelve. Their deaths left her in the custody of guardians who believed she had received enough education for a woman and required her to work long hours in the family factory and kitchen. She took a position as a schoolteacher at fifteen, and she was able to continue her education with earnings from various jobs. She began her studies at Craftsbury Academy in Vermont and later studied in Newbury, Vermont (later Wesleyan Seminary), where she studied classics. The combined demands of work and schooling took their toll. Overworked and undernourished, she developed typhoid fever. After recovering, she went to live with her older sister in Sun Prairie, Wisconsin, where she taught classics and mathematics for the next five years. She also taught physiology and drawing at Evansville Seminary.

In 1863 Burnham moved to New York City and enrolled in the Hygeio-Therapeutic College of Bellevue Hospital to increase her knowledge of physiology and anatomy. She was in the first class of women admitted to that institution. Enrolled concurrently at the Boston Normal Institute for Physical Education, also in New York, Burnham received her medical degree from that institution in 1864. After working a summer there, she moved to Philadelphia, where she took over a "French School for Young Ladies" and introduced gymnastics to local schools.

Burnham began reading law in Philadelphia with Damon Young Kilgore, a lawyer and former Methodist minister, whom she had known in Wisconsin. After several years of informal study under his direction, she decided to register formally as a law student at the University of Pennsylvania Law School in 1870 but was denied admission on the grounds that she was a woman. Her several petitions to be allowed to sit for the bar exam were denied by the Board of Examiners. After ten years of intensive and prolonged struggle, Burnham was admitted to the University of Pennsylvania and in 1883 became the law school's first woman graduate. She was allowed to practice before the Orphan's Court in Philadelphia that same year and was admitted to the court of Common Pleas in 1884. On 11 May 1886, aided by legislation passed the previous year, Burnham gained admission to the Supreme Court of Pennsylvania, and in 1890 she was admitted to the U.S. Supreme Court.

Burnham's career as a suffragist began in 1871 when her ballot was rejected on election day, although she had fulfilled the formal requirements to vote in Philadelphia. She then began legal proceedings against canvassers of the Fourteenth Ward. In 1873 she was finally able to make an extensive statement to the Pennsylvania Supreme Court. Before the court she maintained that the common meaning of terms such as "freeman," "citizen," and "people" in both the state and federal constitutions includes women and that as a citizen she should enjoy the right to vote. Although she lost the case, she was praised by the chief justice for her "able and exhaustive argument" before the court. During this time, she also wrote on the legal status of women for the Citizen's Suffrage Association.

In 1876 Burnham married her former tutor, Damon Kilgore. The two entered into an "ante-nuptial contract," which stipulated that Mrs. Kilgore would not be subject to the legal disadvantages imposed upon married women at the time. The couple had two children. After his death in 1888, Carrie Kilgore took over her husband's private practice and was retained by all but one of his former clients.

In 1886 Kilgore was the first woman master in the chancery in Pennsylvania and served as the solicitor of a corporation. Late in life she pursued her interests in ballooning, becoming the sole female passenger on board during the first ascension of the Philadelphia Aeronautical Recreation Society. She died in Swarthmore, Pennsylvania.

A pioneer in woman suffrage, Carrie Burnham Kilgore was one of the first women admitted to practice law in the United States. She won recognition in the suffrage movement through her clearly reasoned arguments, but she was unable to appreciate the public's reluctance for reform and consequently never became an effective public advocate for the cause.

• Papers in the Hoadley Collection of the late Francis Hoadley of Swarthmore, Pa., contain valuable information about Kilgore, including an interview with her daughter Fanny Kilgore Hoadley (Mrs. George Hoadley). *Woman Suffrage: The Argument of Carrie S. Burnham* (1873) and *The Address of Carrie Burnham Kilgore before the Legislature of Pa.* (1881) are included in the Radcliffe Collection of Women's History of the Schlesinger Library. There is very little published material about Carrie Burnham Kilgore's life. Among the most extensive and accurate accounts are Lelia J. Robinson's article, "Women Lawyers in the United States," *The Green Bag* 2 (1890): 28–29; Ellen A. Martin's "Admission of Women to the Bar," *Chicago Law Times*, Nov. 1886; and the entry under Kilgore's name in *Mothers of Achievement* (1976). Shorter portraits of her life are in Joseph Adelman, *Famous Women* (1926), and *The National Cyclopaedia of American Biography* (1893), although the latter contains inaccuracies. Kilgore is also mentioned in Elizabeth Cady Stanton, *History of Woman Suffrage*, vol. 3 (1887; repr. 1969), and Inez Haynes Irwin, *Angels and Amazons* (1933). An obituary is in the *New York Times*, 30 June 1909.

MICHAEL GRADY PARKER

KILGORE, Harley Martin (11 Jan. 1893–28 Feb. 1956), lawyer and politician, was born in Brown, West Virginia, the son of Quimby H. Kilgore and Laura Jo Martin. He grew up in Mannington, where his father operated a small oil drilling business, and graduated from the local high school. He received a law degree from the University of West Virginia in 1914 and spent two years as a teacher, coach, and principal in the public schools. In 1916 he established a law practice in Beckley, but with the outbreak of World War I he entered the U.S. Army in May 1917 and rose to the rank of captain before his discharge in March 1920. Thereafter he served in the West Virginia National Guard until 1953, achieving the rank of colonel. He returned to his law practice in 1920 and the following year married Lois Elaine Lilly of Bluefield. They had two children.

During the next twenty years Kilgore established himself as a prominent member of the state bar association. In 1932 he won election as judge of the Raleigh County criminal court and helped reform the state's juvenile justice system with an emphasis on rehabilitation and prevention rather than punishment. A lifelong Democrat, he actively participated in the lengthy process of rebuilding the state party organization. In 1940 Kilgore won a narrow primary election victory over two opponents for the U.S. Senate and easily defeated Republican Thomas Sweeney in the general election.

In the Senate Kilgore closely aligned himself with the liberal wing of his party. He became an active member of the Senate Special Committee to Investigate the National Defense Program chaired by then-senator Harry S. Truman. Kilgore chaired the Special Subcommittee on War Mobilization, an endeavor that led to his call for an emergency mobilization process. Kilgore's efforts contributed significantly to President Franklin D. Roosevelt's executive order creating the Office of War Mobilization in 1943. This experience influenced Kilgore's advocacy of federal policy to encourage scientific and technological research.

Despite his impressive first-term record Kilgore confronted serious opposition to his bid for reelection in 1946. He confronted a powerful national Republican tide as well as unexpected opposition from John L. Lewis and other leaders of the United Mine Workers. Labor leaders were opposed to his confusing position on the wartime Smith-Connolly Anti-Strike Bill of 1941 (he had been absent from crucial votes due to Truman Committee investigation trips). He also voted for several federal hydroelectric dam projects in West Virginia and Pennsylvania that mine union leaders feared would reduce the demand for coal. Only an exhaustive campaign enabled him to win reelection by a scant 3,534 votes over Sweeney. Crucial to his razor-thin margin, however, were sympathetic mine workers who refused to follow their union leaders' recommendations.

During his second term Kilgore continued his liberal course. He led a determined but unsuccessful opposition to the Taft-Hartley Act in 1947, which sought to curb the power of organized labor, and he consistently supported President Truman's ambitious Fair Deal agenda—expansion of social security benefits, public housing, urban redevelopment, increases in the minimum wage, full employment, national health insurance, reclamation, federal aid to education, and rural electrification. In 1950 Kilgore sponsored legislation establishing the National Science Foundation—a program that grew out of his advocacy of wartime mobilization. Kilgore's liberalism extended to foreign policy as well. He supported Truman's containment policy in 1947–1949 by voting for the European Recovery Program, military aid to Greece and Turkey, and membership in the North Atlantic Treaty Organization. Also in 1950 he supported armed intervention in Korea, vigorously opposed the McCarran Internal Security Act, and succeeded in promoting passage of a liberalized version of the Displaced Persons Act.

In 1952 Kilgore once again had to seek reelection under adverse circumstances. The popular Dwight D. Eisenhower led a strong Republican ticket at a time when widespread public dissatisfaction with Truman policies threatened to overwhelm Democratic incumbents. Although his opponent, Chapman Revercomb, accused Kilgore of having "appeased and sympathized with communists," he won decisively by campaigning proudly on his liberal voting record.

As a member of the Senate Judiciary Committee, in 1953 and 1954 Kilgore opposed the constitutional amendment proposed by Senator John Bricker, a conservative Republican from Ohio. Since 1952 the Bricker Amendment had commanded enthusiastic support among conservatives of both political parties who believed that by requiring Senate ratification of all executive agreements it would abolish Yalta-type secret diplomacy. The amendment also would have prohibited treaties from being used to effect domestic law. Ultimately on 26 February 1954 Kilgore cast the deciding vote against a modified Bricker Amendment in the form of a substitute amendment introduced by Senator Walter George (D-Ga.). He did so in dramatic fashion, rising from a sickbed to appear in the Senate chambers following an initial vote approving the amendment by precisely the two-thirds majority required (60–30). It was the most important vote he cast in his sixteen years in the Senate. Two years and two days later he died at the Bethesda (Md.) Naval Hospital.

Kilgore's legacy was that of an honest, hardworking, and well-informed liberal legislator who consistently promoted the interests of the working men and women of his state. He was known for his rumpled appearance and his kindly and unassuming demeanor. A man of few hobbies—"my main hobby is trying to go fishing"—the workaholic Kilgore did find time for extensive reading, priding himself on his knowledge of American history. He was a member of the Masonic Order, the American Legion, the Loyal Order of Moose, the Benevolent and Protective Order of Elks, and Sons of the American Revolution.

• The papers of Harley Kilgore are located in the West Virginia Collection at the University of West Virginia Library in Morgantown. There is no biography, but his senatorial career is surveyed in Robert F. Maddox, *The Senatorial Career of Harley M. Kilgore* (1981). David McCullough, *Truman* (1992), places Kilgore's important role in defense and mobilization policy within a larger perspective. His pivotal role in defeating the Bricker Amendment is recounted in Richard O. Davies, *Defender of the Old Guard: John Bricker and American Politics* (1993), and Duane Tananbaum, *The Bricker Amendment Controversy: A Test of Eisenhower's Political Leadership* (1988). See also the *Congressional Directory* (1955), pp. 150–51; *Time*, 8 Mar. 1954, p. 27, and 12 Mar. 1956, p. 110; and *Newsweek*, 12 Mar. 1956, p. 74. See the *New York Times*, 29 Feb. 1956, for a detailed obituary. The *Congressional Record*, 9 July 1956, pp. 12091–112, contains a number of eulogies and reprints of obituaries from West Virginia newspapers.

RICHARD O. DAVIES

KILLENS, John Oliver (14 Jan. 1916–27 Oct. 1987), author, was born in Macon, Georgia, the son of Charles Myles Killens, Sr., a restaurant manager, and Willie Lee Coleman, an insurance company clerk. Killens attended the local public school for African Americans, Pleasant Hill School, through grade seven, after which he attended Ballard Normal School, a private institution that provided education for African Americans through the twelfth grade, one year longer than the public high schools. Following his graduation in 1933, Killens attended Edward Waters College in Jacksonville, Florida, for one year, after which he transferred to Morris Brown College in Atlanta, Georgia. Killens left Morris Brown during his sophomore year for employment with the National Labor Relations Board (NLRB) in Washington, D.C., where (according to Killens) he was the only black employee at the time. He continued his college education as an evening student at Howard University and Robert H. Terrell Law School.

During World War II Killens served from 1942 to 1945 in a U.S. Army amphibious unit with duty in the South Pacific for twenty-seven months. He eventually rose to the rank of master sergeant. In 1943 Killens married Grace Ward Jones, with whom he had two children. Following the war Killens, electing to pursue a writing career, abandoned his law studies, even though he was only six months from graduation. To support his family, he returned to the NLRB, working there until 1948, when he became a union organizer.

During the summer of 1948 Killens enrolled in Columbia University to study creative writing under Dorothy Brewster. He took up residence in New York City and continued to study at Columbia on the GI Bill. Persisting with creative writing, union organizing, and "soaking up life in Harlem" ("The Half," p. 287), he was associated with Langston Hughes, Paul Robeson, and W. E. B. Du Bois. Finally, in the late 1940s or early 1950s Killens joined three of his friends to form the Harlem Writers' Guild. Shortly thereafter he read the first chapter of his first novel, *Youngblood*, to the group; eventually *Youngblood* became the first work of fiction to come from the guild, which nurtured, among others, Louise Meriwether, Rosa Guy, Maya Angelou, and playwright-actor Ossie Davis. Meanwhile, Killens continued to study writing in seminars taught by Saul Bellow at New York University (NYU), Helen Hull at Columbia, and others. Viola Brother Shore of NYU assisted Killens in contacting editors and publishers.

The publication in 1954 of *Youngblood*, which ranks as Killen's major work, was a success, and he became something of a celebrity. Harry Belafonte bought the screen rights to *Youngblood*, and through book promotion tours, which Langston Hughes helped Killens plan, he met pianist and singer Nat King Cole and John Johnson, publisher of the *Negro Digest*, *Ebony*, and *Jet* magazines. *Youngblood*, which was reprinted in 1982, is regarded as a classic African-American protest novel.

Killens followed this success with *And Then We Heard the Thunder* (1964), based on his World War II experiences as an African American serving in a segregated army. *Thunder* was nominated for a Pulitzer Prize in 1964, but the committee awarded no prize for that year. He suffered the same fate in 1971, the year of the publication of *Cotillion; or, One Good Bull Is Half the Herd*, which was also nominated for a Pulitzer Prize. In all, Killens wrote six novels for adults.

When Killens was not writing, he was fighting injustice and racism. He was active in the Brooklyn National Association for the Advancement of Colored People (NAACP), where he organized a "Night of Stars" as a fund raiser in 1957. A gentle, soft-spoken man, he was nevertheless unsympathetic with nonviolence and eventually became a follower of Malcolm X, whom Killens asserted "did not teach non-violence, but he did advocate self-defense" ("Speaking Out," p. 11). And while he admired Martin Luther King, Jr., Killens rejected "turning the other cheek" because he was convinced that "people don't respect you unless you fight" (*Macon Courier*, 4 Jan. 1979). Killens also observed that "moral suasion alone has never brought about a revolution" ("Speaking Out," p. 10).

Killens's writing was an extension of his conviction that he should be of service to his people. As one who used his pen to try to change society, Killens's literary productions, based on the black experience, included the themes of black self-esteem, black manhood, black unity, and even black folklore. To Killens, "All art is social, all art is propaganda, notwithstanding all propaganda is not art" (*Dictionary of Literary Biography*, vol. 33, p. 145). Like Richard Wright, whom he greatly admired, he believed that the main goal of art is to attack and thus alter society.

Killens exerted considerable influence on African-American writers, whom he always encouraged and assisted. During his service as writer-in-residence at Fisk University (1965–1968), he established one of the first Black Writers' Conferences in the United States. He continued to initiate writers' conferences at Howard University as writer-in-residence from 1971 to 1976 and at Medgar Evers College, where he served as a distinguished professor from 1981 until his death. He also was an adjunct professor at Columbia University from 1970 to 1973. In 1986 he conducted one of his last writing seminars in his hometown of Macon, where his students included Tina Ansa, a bestselling author in the 1990s.

Killens was the recipient of many honors in his lifetime. He served as vice president of the Black Academy of Arts and Letters and as chairman of the Harlem Writers' Guild. Other awards included the Howard University Creative Writers Workshop Award (1974), election to the Black Film Makers Hall of Fame (1976), a National Endowment for the Arts Fellowship (1980), and the Distinguished Writer Award of the Middle Atlantic Writers' Association (1984).

Killens died in Brooklyn, New York. With his writing, his political activities, and his teaching, Killens, like James Baldwin and Ralph Ellison, provided a spark for a more vigorous African-American literary movement in the United States, which flourished during the 1960s.

• Additional book-length works by Killens include *Black Man's Burden* (1965), *'Sippi* (1967), and *Slaves* (1969). He also wrote a biography of the poet Alexander Pushkin, titled *Great Black Russian: The Life and Times of Alexander Pushkin* (1988), and two books for children, *Great Gittin' up Morning: A Biography of Denmark Vesey* (1972) and *A Man Ain't Nothin' but a Man: The Adventures of John Henry* (1975). Killens also authored three plays, two screenplays, and numerous articles and short stories, which appeared in such diverse publications as the *Saturday Evening Post*, the *New York Times Magazine*, *Ebony*, *Redbook*, *TV Guide*, and *Black Scholar*. Killens's works have been published in fifteen countries, including Russia, Japan, and the People's Republic of China. According to his wife, Killens also wrote a novel, titled "The Minister Primarily," and a text on writing, "Write On!," which remain unpublished. Killens also edited (with Jerry W. Ward, Jr.) *Black Southern Voices: An Anthology of Fiction, Poetry, Drama, Nonfiction, and Critical Essays* (1992).

The best source of information on Killens is his memoir, "The Half Ain't Never Been Told," which he wrote for *Contemporary Authors Autobiography Series*, vol. 2 (1985). Sources of information about his writing include the *Dictionary of Literary Biography*, vol. 33 (1979); *Contemporary Literary Criticism*, vol. 10 (1979); and *Modern Black Writers* (1978). Also important are Killens's article, "Speaking Out: Negroes Have a Right to Fight Back," *Saturday Evening Post*, 2 July 1966, pp. 10–11, and an interview, "Noted Author Returns—Meets with Community Leaders," *Macon Courier*, 24 Jan. 1979. A lengthy obituary with photograph is in the *New York Times*, 30 Oct. 1987.

JOAN B. HUFFMAN

KILLPATRICK, James (c. 1692–1770), physician and poet, was born in Carrickfergus, Ireland, into a commercial family. (Later in his life he used the name "Kirkpatrick.") He matriculated at the University of Edinburgh in 1708 but returned to Ireland before earning a degree to set up as a medical practitioner. He had scant success. To improve his fortune he immigrated in 1717 to South Carolina, where an uncle, David Killpatrick, resided. The voyage to America was troubled by pirates, who relieved Killpatrick of his small stock of valuables. He established a practice in Charleston with a clientele in the merchant and official classes. In 1727 he married Elizabeth Hepworth, the daughter of the colony's secretary. He was hired as attending physician to the St. Philip's Hospital, where his principal task was treating the poor. Early in the 1730s he established a pharmacy, which was the principal local source for medicines until Dr. Thomas Dale established his laboratory in 1735.

Killpatrick's abilities as a physician came most conspicuously to public attention during the smallpox epidemic of 1738. The disease entered Carolina on the *London Frigate*, a slave vessel, and spread explosively through the countryside. Nearly every household in Charleston harbored a victim. Inland its effects on the Cherokees were even harsher, killing half the population by some estimates. In the face of such high mortality, local physicians embraced the controversial treatment of inoculation, following the example of Mr. Mowbry, the surgeon of the British man-of-war in Charleston Harbor. Killpatrick became the most energetic inoculator in the city, his enthusiasm perhaps fired by the death of his son from the disease. When the *South Carolina Gazette* editorialized against inoculation, Killpatrick wrote in its defense, explaining the errors committed by the physician in the most notorious local inoculation incident in *The Case of Miss Mary Roche* (1738). Dale, the physician concerned, attacked Killpatrick's criticism of his treatment and commenced a pamphlet war about the proper method of inoculation. Because of the literary skills of Killpatrick and Dale, the battle became the local sensation until the Carolina Assembly intervened by prohibiting the practice of inoculation.

The imperial administration of the colony clearly did not share the legislature's benighted view of medicine, for Killpatrick was appointed surgeon on James Edward Oglethorpe's expedition against St. Augustine in 1739. His abilities attracted the notice of Charles Townshend, admiral of the British West Indian Fleet, who convinced Killpatrick that his future lay in London. In 1742 Killpatrick left Carolina for England. There he changed his name to Kirkpatrick (perhaps because of the onus arising from the newspaper controversy in Carolina), became fully credentialed as a doctor, published *An Essay on Inoculation Occasioned by the Smallpox Being Brought into South Carolina in 1738* (1743), and became a European medical celebrity for his treatise *The Analysis of Inoculation* (1754). He inoculated the French royal family and much of the British aristocracy. His later years were spent translating the works of S. A. Tissot, culminating in a heavily annotated version of *An Essay on the Disorders of People of Fashion; and a Treatise on the Diseases Incident to Literary Persons* (1772).

Killpatrick's interest in the afflictions of literary artists may have arisen from his own literary ambitions. During his residence in Carolina, he reworked a long "narrative philosophical and descriptive poem in five Cantos," *The Sea-Piece*, intended as the great poetic testament to Britain's *imperium pelagi* (empire of the seas). Inspired by the paeans to mercantilism penned by Edward Young, Killpatrick's work, which was published in London in 1750, was a belletristic meditation on commercial imperialism. While Killpatrick admired Young's politics, he proclaimed Alexander Pope to be the regent in the empire of letters. In *An Epistle (in Verse) to Alex, Pope Esq. from South Carolina* (1737) Killpatrick pledged his allegiance to Pope's reign as the metropolitan arbiter of taste and manners. Upon Pope's death in 1744, Killpatrick in London memorialized the archpoet in *Eligia Popi in memoriam infelis nymphae in Latinum versum reddita* (1744). Killpatrick died in London, forgotten as a poet but immensely respected as a pioneer in the development of inoculation as a medical treatment.

• Killpatrick's medical writings, in addition to those mentioned, *A Full and Clear Reply to Doctor T. Dale* (1739), *A*

Letter to the Real and Genuine Pierce Dod by Dod Pierce (1746), and *Some Reflections on the Causes and Circumstances That May Retard or Prevent the Putrefaction of Dead Bodies* (1751). His other poetical works include *Celeberrimi Popii tentamen de modis criticis. Scripta digudicanda. Latine tentatum* (1745) and, as James Kirkpatrick, *A Popii excerpta quaedam—Latine redidit* (1749). For his medical career see Joseph Ioor Waring, "James Killpatrick and Smallpox Inoculation in Charleston," *Annals of Medical History*, n.s., 10 (1938): 301–8. On Killpatrick's verse epistle to Alexander Pope, see Austin Warren, "To Mr. Pope: Epistles from America," *Publications of the Modern Language Association* 49 (1933): 61–73. Killpatrick's work, under the name Kirkpatrick, as a laureate of mercantilism is discussed in David S. Shields, *Oracles of Empire* (1990).

DAVID S. SHIELDS

KILMER, Joyce (6 Dec. 1886–30 July 1918), poet and soldier, was born Alfred Joyce Kilmer in New Brunswick, New Jersey, the son of Frederick Barnett Kilmer, a professional chemist, and Annie Ellene Kilburn, a writer and composer. Joyce Kilmer studied at Rutgers College from 1904 to 1906 and then at Columbia University. Two weeks after graduating from Columbia with an A.B. in June 1908, he married Aline Murray, a competent poet and the stepdaughter of Henry Mills Alden, editor of *Harper's Monthly Magazine*. The couple had five children, one of whom died in infancy. Kilmer taught Latin in a high school in Morristown, New Jersey, in 1908 and 1909, after which he and his wife moved to New York City.

Kilmer worked briefly as editor of a journal for male horseback riders and as a salesman in a bookstore. Then, for three years beginning in 1909, he worked as a lexicographer for publishers of the *Standard Dictionary*. Kilmer, an avowed socialist, wrote for the socialist newspaper *Call* and began to meet fellow intellectuals. Outgrowing his political radicalism, he began enjoying lunches with emerging writers such as Richard Le Gallienne and Bliss Carman. Even before moving to New York, he had written some verse. In 1911 Kilmer published *Summer of Love*, his first book. It contains embarrassingly juvenile efforts. In "Ballade of My Lady's Beauty," for example, the poet claims that his love is a more "goodly sight" than Eve, Lilith, and Venus. Even Sainte Marie falls short, though "[i]n cerule napery bedight." Nor will the poet "rhymes . . . indite" or "garlands . . . twine" for Helen, who "caused a grievous fray." His refrain explains why: "No lady is so fair as mine."

Kilmer was literary editor of the *Churchman*, an Episcopalian magazine, in 1912 and 1913 and then was employed by the *New York Times* as a contributor to its Sunday book review and magazine sections. When "Trees," his most famous poem, was published in *Poetry: A Magazine of Verse* (Aug. 1913), Kilmer gained immediate fame. This immensely popular poem begins, "I think that I shall never see / A poem lovely as a tree," and ends, "Poems are made by fools like me / But only God can make a tree." In between, however, is a strained metaphor: the tree is suckled by the earth, lifts its leafy arms to pray, wears a robin's nest in its hair, and has a snow-covered bosom.

During the next four years Kilmer was busy and successful. When his daughter was stricken with infantile paralysis, he and his wife found spiritual comfort by joining the Roman Catholic church in 1913. He edited the poetry sections of the *Literary Digest* and *Current Literature*. He lectured widely and wrote critical essays, first published in popular magazines such as *America*, *Bookman*, *Bellman*, *Catholic World*, *Munsey's Magazine*, *Puck*, and *Smart Set*. Collections of his poetry are *Trees and Other Poems* (1914) and *Main Street, and Other Poems* (1917). His prose works were gathered in *The Circus, and Other Essays* (1916). *Literature in the Making, by Some of Its Makers* (1917) is a collection of interviews he conducted with William Dean Howells, Amy Lowell, and Edwin Arlington Robinson (his favorite poet), among other writers. Kilmer also published *The Courage of Enlightenment: An Address* (1917) and edited *Dreams and Images: An Anthology of Catholic Poets* (1917).

When the *Lusitania* was sunk by a German submarine on 7 May 1915, Kilmer discarded his neutrality, published a poem about the sinking titled "The White Ships and the Red" (*New York Times*, 16 May 1915), and began to sympathize with the Allied cause. Seventeen days after the United States entered World War I in 1917, he enlisted in the Seventh Regiment of the New York National Guard as a private. When the regiment was federalized, Kilmer obtained permission to transfer to the 165th Infantry—formerly the "Fighting Sixty-ninth" (part of the famous Rainbow Division). His motive was probably twofold—to get into combat faster and to associate with Irish soldiers in this unit because he claimed some Irish ancestry, liked the Irish, and loved Irish literature. He was assigned duty as a statistician in regimental headquarters. He shipped to France, did intelligence and patrol work, and was promoted to sergeant. His unit was involved in the second battle of the Marne. While scouting German machine-gun nests near the Ourcq River south of the village of Seringes, he was killed by a bullet through his head. The war poems he wrote in France were collected by his friend Robert Cortes Holliday as part of *Joyce Kilmer* (2 vols., 1918). Kilmer's incomplete history of his regiment was published as part of his friend Francis P. Duffy's *Father Duffy's Story* (1919).

Kilmer was much influenced by seventeenth-century English religious poets such as Richard Crashaw, George Herbert, and Henry Vaughan. He also imitated verses by three writers of the late nineteenth and early twentieth centuries—A. E. Housman, Coventry Patmore (whom he deliberately mirrored), and especially E. A. Robinson. Kilmer's poem "Martin" reads much like a character study by Robinson. Kilmer's poetry is ultra-traditional in technique, never innovative, never forward-looking. When his mother set his "Trees" to music and published it in her *Whimsical Whimsies* in 1927, Kilmer and his best-loved poem became even more popular.

• Most of Kilmer's widely scattered papers are in the Houghton Library at Harvard University, the Manuscripts Division of the Library of Congress, the University of Notre Dame Archives, and the Alderman Library at the University of Virginia. Robert Cortes Holliday, ed., *Joyce Kilmer*, has a long biographical memoir. Biographical information is also in Annie Kilburn Kilmer, *Memories of My Son, Sergeant Joyce Kilmer* (1920), and Kenton Kilmer, *Memories of My Father, Joyce Kilmer* (1993). Alfred Kreymborg, *Our Singing Strength: An Outline of American Poetry (1620–1930)* (1929), gently identifies Kilmer's limitations. Critical commentary on Kilmer is in Katherine M. C. Brégy, *Poets and Pilgrims, from Geoffrey Chaucer to Paul Claudel* (1925), and James J. Daly, *A Cheerful Ascetic and Other Essays* (1931). Cleanth Brooks and Robert Penn Warren, *Understanding Poetry* (1938), ridicules Kilmer's "Trees." An obituary is in the *New York Times*, 18 Aug. 1918.

Robert L. Gale

KILPATRICK, Hugh Judson (14 Jan. 1836–2 Dec. 1881), army officer and diplomat, was born near Deckertown (now Sussex), New Jersey, the son of Simon Kilpatrick, a farmer and colonel in the state militia, and Julia Wickham. Kilpatrick attended the U.S. Military Academy at West Point and was two years behind Joseph Wheeler. On 6 May 1861 Kilpatrick graduated seventeenth out of forty-five and joined the First U.S. Artillery. On the same day he married Alice Shailer; they had no children.

On 9 May 1861 Kilpatrick became a captain, Company H, Fifth New York Infantry, and at Big Bethel, Virginia, on 10 June 1861 he was wounded. He became lieutenant colonel of the Second New York Cavalry (25 Sept. 1861) and colonel (6 Dec. 1862). He commanded a brigade in General George Stoneman's raid toward Richmond (29 Apr.–8 May 1863), where he distinguished himself for destruction of railroads, and at Brandy Station (9 June 1863). The aggressive Kilpatrick was appointed brigadier general of volunteers on 13 June 1863, leading a brigade at Aldie (17 June) and Upperville (21 June), Virginia, and after 28 June the Third Cavalry Division. His fight with Jeb Stuart on 30 June at Hanover, Pennsylvania, contributed to the Confederate cavalry's late arrival at Gettysburg. On 3 July Kilpatrick's Second Brigade, commanded by George A. Custer, distinguished itself against Stuart, but Kilpatrick was criticized for ordering another brigadier, Elon J. Farnsworth, to charge the infantry, an attack in which Farnsworth was killed.

Charles Francis Adams, Jr., of the First Massachusetts Cavalry, remarked on 12 July 1863, "Kilpatrick is a brave injudicious boy . . . who will surely come to grief" (*A Cycle of Adams Letters, 1861–1865*, vol. 2 [1920], pp. 44–45). Until March 1864 Kilpatrick took part in all major cavalry actions of the Army of the Potomac, and near the end of the New York draft riots, on 17 July 1863, he was given command of the few cavalry in that city. He was an aggressive, even reckless, commander, but when he led the Kilpatrick-Dahlgren raid (28 Feb.–3 Mar. 1864) on Richmond, he hesitated in front of the city even though he outnumbered the home guards, thus contributing to the expedition's disastrous failure.

From 25 April to 13 May 1864 Kilpatrick commanded the Third Cavalry Division of the Army of the Cumberland in the invasion of Georgia. He was badly wounded at Resaca in May but returned in July to fight Confederate cavalry commanded by General Wheeler. James Harrison Wilson reported that Sherman said, "I know that Kilpatrick is a hell of a damned fool, but I want just that sort of a man to command my cavalry on this expedition" (*Under the Old Flag* [1912], p. 372). Sherman made use of Kilpatrick's ruthlessness and flair for destruction.

Kilpatrick got the sobriquet "Kil-Cavalry" for wearing out his horses and men. One of the more controversial Civil War generals, he had a reputation for confusing fact and fiction and was severely criticized by contemporaries and historians. In Colonel Theodore Lyman's *Meade's Headquarters*, Kilpatrick was called "a frothy braggart, without brains . . . he gets all his reputation by newspapers and political influence" ([1922], p. 79). Albert E. Castel spoke of Kilpatrick's "serious deficiencies of both intellect and character" (*Decision in the West* [1992], p. 116).

Yet after the March to the Sea, Sherman wrote in a letter from Savannah on 29 December 1864 to Kilpatrick, "The fact that to you, in a great measure, we owe the march of four strong infantry columns, with heavy trains and wagons, over 300 miles, through an enemy's country, without the loss of a single wagon and without the annoyance of cavalry dashes on our flanks, is honor enough for any cavalry commander" (*Official Records*, ser. 1, vol. 44, p. 368). Only once after Atlanta, at Phillips Crossroads, North Carolina (3 Mar. 1865), did Confederate cavalry penetrate to the Federal infantry. Although he was unpredictable and tactically unsophisticated, Kilpatrick's bravery, dramatic personality, and ability to communicate his enthusiasm inspired loyalty in many of his men. He also had a shrewd appreciation of the power of the press. He was brevetted major general, U.S. Army, in March 1865 and became major general of volunteers in June 1865.

After the war, President Andrew Johnson appointed Kilpatrick minister to Chile (1865–1868). Kilpatrick's first wife had died in 1863. In 1866 he married Louisa Valdivoso; they had two children. He edited *Our Magazine*, a literary monthly, in 1871, and in 1872 he supported the Democrat Horace Greeley against President Ulysses S. Grant. He was popular on the lecture circuit and corresponded with literary figures. Kilpatrick and J. Owen Moore wrote a five-act play, *Allatoona: An Historical and Military Drama* (1875), about West Point cadets in the Civil War. Revised in 1930 as *The Blue and the Gray* by Christopher Morley, who said, "Naive and vivid as a Currier and Ives print, it has seemed to us worthy of preservation" (p. vii), it played for fifty-two performances at the Old Rialto in Hoboken, New Jersey. Kilpatrick gave one of the best lines to an African-American character, "Ben," who says before dying, "bondman—must—be—free."

A Republican again, Kilpatrick was an unsuccessful candidate for Congress in 1880 and that same year was a delegate to the Republican National Convention. He was also a director of the Union Pacific Railroad. In 1881 President James A. Garfield appointed him minister to Chile again. Kilpatrick quarreled with the American minister to Peru, General Stephen A. Hurlbut, over the war between Peru and Chile, Kilpatrick supporting his wife's country, Chile. Kilpatrick had a reputation as a ladies' man. His granddaughter Lady Thelma Furness would introduce the prince of Wales (Edward VIII) to Wallis Warfield Simpson. Kilpatrick died in Santiago de Chile of Bright's disease and is buried at West Point.

• The National Archives has Kilpatrick material. His reports are in *The War of the Rebellion: A Compilation of the Official Records of the Union and Confederate Armies* (128 vols., 1880–1901). Kilpatrick's "Lee at Gettysburg," *Our Magazine*, May 1871, pp. 81–86, is very critical of Lee. For Kilpatrick on Wilson and Sherman, see the *New York Times*, 8 Apr. 1876. Kilpatrick appears in Herman Melville's poem "The March to the Sea," *Battle-Pieces* (1866); and in a book by his great-granddaughter, Gloria Vanderbilt, *Black Knight, White Knight* (1987). Biographical sketches of Kilpatrick are in Christopher Morley, ed., *The Blue and the Gray; or, War Is Hell* (1930); and Mary Elizabeth Sergent, *They Lie Forgotten* (1986). Ph.D. dissertations on Kilpatrick are George Wayne King, "The Civil War Career of Hugh Judson Kilpatrick" (Univ. of South Carolina, 1969); and John Edward Pierce, "General Hugh Judson Kilpatrick in the American Civil War" (Pennsylvania State Univ., 1983). William A. Tidwell et al., *Come Retribution: The Confederate Secret Service and the Assassination of Lincoln* (1988), and Tidwell, *April '65: Confederate Covert Action in the American Civil War* (1995), claim the Kilpatrick-Dahlgren raid gave Confederate leaders motivation to retaliate against Abraham Lincoln. An obituary by J. H. Wilson is in George W. Cullum, *Biographical Register of the Officers and Graduates of the U.S. Military Academy*, vol. 2 (1891), pp. 786–90.

RALPH KIRSHNER

KILPATRICK, William Heard (20 Nov. 1871–13 Feb. 1965), professor of educational philosophy, was born in White Plains, Georgia, the son of James Hines Kilpatrick, a teacher and Baptist minister, and Edna Perrin Heard. The stern Baptist ministerial tradition of Kilpatrick's childhood held a profound influence on him throughout his career. In 1888 Kilpatrick entered Mercer University (Macon, Ga.), a Baptist denominational school, and was graduated in 1891 with an A.B. After graduation he attended Johns Hopkins University for one year and then returned to Mercer, where he was awarded in 1892 an M.A. in mathematics, in part on the basis of his graduate work at Johns Hopkins. For the next five years Kilpatrick taught and served as principal of various public schools in Georgia as well as returning to Johns Hopkins for one additional year of study. In 1897 he accepted a professorship of mathematics at Mercer until 1906, during which time he also served as acting president of the institution from 1902 to 1905. While Kilpatrick never aspired to the presidency of the institution, he left Mercer after the appointment of a most unsympathetic president and after certain members of the board of trustees charged him with "heresy" for not believing in the Virgin Birth. (Ironically, Kilpatrick's theological position during this time was in accord with the Social Gospel Movement, then quite rare in the Southern Baptist tradition.)

Kilpatrick returned to teaching in the public schools of Georgia for one year before proceeding to Teachers College at Columbia University in 1907 to enroll in graduate studies and, in 1909, to become a part-time instructor of the philosophy of education. Kilpatrick completed the Ph.D. in 1912 with a dissertation titled "The Dutch Schools of New Netherlands and Colonial New York" and accepted an appointment at Teachers College, where he became a full professor in 1918. Kilpatrick remained at Teachers College until his mandatory retirement in 1937 and thereafter continued an active and prolific writing career in New York City until his death.

The professional watershed for Kilpatrick was the publication of his 1918 *Teachers College Record* essay, "The Project Method: The Use of the Purposeful Act in the Educative Process." Kilpatrick did not invent this concept since the "project method" was then popular in agricultural education, architecture, and vocational education and can be traced back to sixteenth-century France. He did, however, extend the project method to all subjects of the school curriculum, a somewhat notable innovation. The main criterion for the selection of a project was "wholehearted purposeful activity proceeding in a social environment," this being quite a contrast to curriculum development as proposed by Franklin Bobbitt and others who determined the curriculum for children by tabulating the activities of adults.

A basic premise of Kilpatrick's project method, certainly influenced by the work of John Dewey, maintained that the child must come before the curriculum. While teachers play a crucial role in providing "wise guidance" in directing the child to projects and activities, Kilpatrick preferred that children engage in four specific steps of any given project: "purposing, planning, executing, and judging." Unfortunately, misapplications of the project method led Kilpatrick to underscore that education was not "to turn children loose to make their own decisions." Blending the importance of student needs and interests with the direction and leadership of the teacher, Kilpatrick came to be known as a spokesperson for progressive education and the child-centered school.

From his vantage point as a faculty member at Teachers College and with the philosophical underpinnings and endorsement of Dewey, Kilpatrick made his greatest contributions as a teacher and public figure. The leading position of Teachers College in national educational debates at the time was unsurpassed. *Saturday Review* editor Norman Cousins recalled that Teachers College "in the mid-thirties was a forcing-house of intellectual and political activity. Classrooms were more than a site for instruction; they were arenas for ideological combat. Within the faculty itself were fascinating ideological and philosophical divisions" (*Teaching Education* 1 [1987]: 23). Kilpatrick was the acknowledged leader of the faculty and the "master of the classroom." The *New York Post*, in an interview on 6 March 1937, dubbed him the "million dollar professor" from the totaling of fees paid by his students during one summer session at Teachers College. It was not uncommon for Kilpatrick to coordinate a class numbering in the hundreds—on occasion 650—through a combination of lecture and group discussion.

Kilpatrick used his national influence to initiate many educational and social projects, including the formation of the John Dewey Society; the founding of Bennington College in Vermont (a leading institution of progressive education at the postsecondary level); and the founding of the *Social Frontier*, the most profound journal of educational criticism and reconstruction of the twentieth century (which he edited from 1937 to 1943). Kilpatrick served as president of the New York Urban League from 1941 to 1951, as chair of the Bureau of Intercultural Education from 1940 to 1951 and of the American Youth for World Youth from 1946 to 1951, and as a member of the Board of Directors of the League for Industrial Democracy. His influence from the 1930s through the 1950s became international, and he is still widely recognized in Germany where the project method remains one of the more popular methods of teaching.

Kilpatrick, forever cast as John Dewey's disciple, served to popularize the project method, progressive education, and the child-centered school during the early to mid-twentieth century. While Kilpatrick's reputation will always suffer from charges of the misapplications of Deweyian and progressive ideals, he did fulfill the important role of a teacher and popularizer of progressive education. Moreover, as late as 1951 Dewey stated that "Kilpatrick had never fallen victim to the one-sidedness of identifying progressive education with child-centered education. . . . he has always balanced regard for the psychological conditions and processes of those who are learning with consideration of the social and cultural conditions in which as human beings the pupils are living" (Tenenbaum, p. viii). The presence of an eloquent spokesperson with a near-religious belief in the power of education and the striking yet youthful appearance of the "white haired gentleman from Georgia" with a distinct Southern accent combined to create a powerful image. While Kilpatrick's originality and importance in the history of education will always be in dispute, his role as speaker and teacher of progressive education must not be overlooked.

Kilpatrick was married three times. In 1898 he married Marie Beman Guyton, with whom he had his only three children; she died in 1907. In 1908 he wed Margaret Manigault Pinckney, who died in 1938. In 1940 Kilpatrick married his former secretary, Marion Y. Ostrander. Kilpatrick died in New York City.

• An extensive collection of William Heard Kilpatrick's papers is housed at Mercer University. An even larger collection of scrapbooks, diaries, and other materials is located at Special Collections, Milbank Memorial Library, Teachers College, Columbia University. A complete bibliography of Kilpatrick's works appears in the Nov. 1961 issue of *Studies in Philosophy and Education*. In addition to the project method monograph, Kilpatrick's best-known textbooks include *Foundations of Method* (1925), *Education for a Changing Civilization* (1926), *Education and the Social Crisis* (1932), *Remaking the Curriculum* (1936), *Group Education for a Democracy* (1940), and *Philosophy of Education* (1951). Kilpatrick contributed to two legendary collections, *The Foundations and Technique of Curriculum-Construction* (1926; the Twenty-seventh Yearbook of the National Society for the Study of Education) and *The Educational Frontier*, which he edited in 1933. Biographies include Samuel Tenenbaum, *William Heard Kilpatrick: Trail Blazer in Education* (1951), and William Van Til, "William Heard Kilpatrick: Respecter of Individuals and Ideas," in *Teachers and Mentors* ed. Craig Kridel et al. (1996), chap. 18. See also Boyd H. Bode, *Modern Education Theory* (1927), chap. 7, and Lawrence Cremin, *The Transformation of the School* (1961). *Educational Theory* dedicated its Jan. 1966 issue to the career of Kilpatrick, and an obituary is in the *New York Times*, 14 Feb. 1965.

CRAIG KRIDEL

KILTY, William (1757–10 Oct. 1821), jurist and army surgeon, was born in London, England, the son of Captain John Kilty, a merchant seaman, and Ellen Ahearn. Raised in London, Kilty was educated at the College of St. Omer in France. He accompanied his family to Maryland around 1774, settling in Annapolis, where he studied medicine under Dr. Edward Johnson.

Upon completion of his apprenticeship, Kilty pledged himself to the American war effort, serving in Maryland's Fourth Regiment as a surgeon's mate from April 1778 to 1780 and as a surgeon from 1781 to 1783. On 16 August 1780 he was taken prisoner at the Battle of Camden in South Carolina. During his captivity, Kilty returned to Annapolis, where he was forced to stay for the duration of the war. A strident patriot, he remained in the army for nearly two years beyond Britain's surrender, and in May 1783 he became a founding member of the Maryland Society of the Cincinnati.

Following his discharge from the army, Kilty appears to have abandoned his medical career, devoting himself instead to the study of law. He also took an interest in government, although he never held office, and in August 1786 he published *History of a Session of the General Assembly of the State of Maryland, Held at the City of Annapolis, Commenced November 1785*. Kilty established himself at the bar and in April 1789 was appointed by the Maryland House of Delegates to act as an agent of the state in the purchase and sale of British property seized during and after the war. The following year he married Elizabeth Middleton of Calvert County, Maryland. At the time of Elizabeth's death in 1807, they had no children.

Kilty continued to practice law in Annapolis through the 1790s. In 1798 he was appointed by the

General Assembly to compile the statutes of the state, and in 1799 and 1800 he published in two volumes his best-known work, *The Laws of Maryland*, popularly known as *Kilty's Laws*. In 1800 Kilty settled in Washington, D.C. After John Adams enlarged the court system through the Judiciary Act of 1801, Kilty, by default, became one of the president's "midnight appointments." In accordance with the act, Adams created the Circuit Court for the District of Columbia, staffing the court with Federalist jurists and appointing former Supreme Court justice Thomas Johnson to the chief justiceship. Johnson declined the appointment, but by the time Adams learned of his nominee's refusal, it was too late for the former president to appoint another. In Johnson's place, Thomas Jefferson appointed Kilty on 6 January 1802, a position he held until 25 January 1806, when he accepted an appointment as chancellor of Maryland. He held this office until his death.

In June 1807, during a public meeting held in Annapolis denouncing the attack of the U.S.S. *Chesapeake* by the H.M.S. *Leopard*, President Jefferson appointed Kilty to a committee of prominent residents determined to support Jefferson's action and to ensure the curtailment of all commercial intercourse with Britain. The following year Kilty published his third work, *The Landholder's Assistant*, which included state regulations regarding the confiscation and sale of British property. Kilty's next work, *A Report on All Such English Statutes as Existed at the Time of the First Emigration of the People of Maryland, and Which by Experience Have Been Found Applicable to Their Local and Other Circumstances*, followed in 1811. In 1818 Kilty collaborated with Thomas Harris and John N. Watkins to produce his final work, a revised edition of his *Laws of Maryland*, to which were added four volumes.

The chancellor's literary endeavors, however, were not confined to legal topics. He also authored *A Burlesque Translation of Homer's Iliad, with Notes, the Second Part*, an unpublished sequel to Thomas Bridges's 1764 work of the same title. Additionally, he is believed to have written *The Vision of Don Crocker*, a satirical poem published in 1813.

Kilty devoted his remaining years solely to matters of chancery. As a federal judge, he enjoyed a reputation as an erudite, industrious, and astute jurist, and he was equally esteemed in his office as chancellor. From the bench in Annapolis, he appears to have been as accessible as he had been during his years of practice, responding to regular requests from acquaintances for legal advice.

Kilty made his name as a legal scholar, most notably for his *Laws of Maryland*, but his principal contribution to society in general, and jurisprudence in particular, was a lifetime of service at the bar. Considered honest, upright, and enlightened by his contemporaries, he labored in defense of American liberties from the Revolution through the War of 1812. A broadly educated, capable, and fair-minded jurist, Kilty was a man highly respected both in his professional and personal lives. His death, lamented one eulogist, "has de-

prived Maryland of the only person that exactly knew what is the constitution of the state!" He died in Annapolis.

• Select correspondence of William Kilty, including his commission as state land agent, is in the *Kilty Papers* (MS 1217) at the Maryland Historical Society. A record of Kilty's military service appears in *Archives of Maryland*, "Muster Rolls" (1900); *Archives of Maryland*, vol. 45 (1927) and vol. 48 (1931); and W. T. R. Saffell, ed., *Records of the Revolutionary War* (1858). Kilty's appointment to the Circuit Court of the District of Columbia is in *Journal of the Executive Proceedings of the Senate of the United States of America*, vol. 1 (1828). His appointment and tenure as a federal judge is briefly addressed in W. B. Bryan, *A History of the National Capital*, vol. 1 (1914), and his years as chancellor of Maryland are discussed in W. L. Marbury's "The High Court of Chancery and the Chancellors of Maryland," *Proceedings of the Tenth Annual Meeting of the Maryland Bar Association* (1905). Other sources include Elihu S. Riley, *The Ancient City: A History of Annapolis in Maryland* (1887), and J. Thomas Scharf, *History of Maryland*, vol. 2 (1879). Also useful is Howard A. Kelly and Walter L. Burrage, *American Medical Biographies* (1920), although this source erroneously credits John Adams with Kilty's circuit court appointment. Obituaries are in the *National Intelligencer*, the *Niles' Weekly Register*, and the *Maryland Republican*, all 13 Oct. 1821.

KEVIN R. CHANEY

KIMBALL, Dan Able (1 Mar. 1896–30 July 1970), businessman and secretary of the navy, was born in St. Louis, Missouri, the son of John Harney Kimball, occupation unknown, and Mary Able. He received his early education in the public schools of St. Louis, although accounts differ as to whether he graduated from Soldan High School or dropped out to take a job as a mechanic in a local garage that specialized in the repair of electrically powered automobiles. All sources agree, however, that he took correspondence courses in engineering to further his education.

With the American entrance into World War I, Kimball enlisted in 1917 in the aviation section of the U.S. Army's Signal Corps. Receiving his initial instruction at the Berkeley, California, ground school (where he was a classmate of future general James H. Doolittle), he then completed flight school at Rockwell Field, San Diego. Commissioned as a second lieutenant in the Army Air Corps on 1 March 1918, Kimball spent the balance of the war flying pursuit craft in France. He left the service after the end of the war as a first lieutenant but retained a love of flying for the rest of his life.

Upon returning to the United States, Kimball took a sales position in the Los Angeles office of the General Tire and Rubber Company in early 1919. Rising steadily through the ranks, he became area manager and later the manager of an eleven-state western region. He took time in 1925 to marry Dorothy Ames; the couple had no children.

In 1941 Kimball moved to the Washington, D.C., office of General Tire. With the threat of World War II looming, General Tire obtained numerous defense contracts, which included the production of items such as life rafts for the government. On Kimball's recommendation the company also acquired the Aerojet Engineering Company of Azusa, California. The firm, a pioneer in the production of jet-assisted takeoff (JATO) apparatus (used in assisting aircraft in takeoffs from short runways), benefited greatly from the infusion of General Tire capital, and General Tire gained substantial profits from the additional product line.

Kimball served as executive vice president and general manager of Aerojet and was also named as a vice president of the parent company. In addition, he headed the development program at Aerojet that, in cooperation with Douglas Aircraft Company and other manufacturers, helped to develop the Aerobee rocket, which proved useful in conducting weather research in the early years of the U.S. space program.

Although Kimball had risen to the board of Directors of General Tire by 1948, another career beckoned. A lifelong Democrat, Kimball was rewarded for his fundraising efforts on behalf of Harry Truman in the 1948 elections (he was one of only a handful of business executives to support the president's reelection bid) with an appointment in February 1949 as assistant secretary of the navy for air.

Taking a leave of absence from his positions at General Tire, Kimball soon had to deal with the uproar that ensued when Secretary of Defense Louis A. Johnson canceled plans for a "supercarrier" (the *United States*) in favor of building additional B-36 bombers for the air force. While both Navy Secretary John Sullivan and Under Secretary W. John Kenny resigned in protest, Johnson managed to persuade Kimball to remain at his post. Kimball received a promotion to under secretary of the navy after only six weeks on the job but proved more than able in his new position. In the wake of the so-called Admiral's Revolt, Kimball's ability to get along with almost everyone proved invaluable, as did his long familiarity with the defense industry and government agencies.

As under secretary Kimball implemented a new policy that allowed civilian employee supervisors not only to join unions but also to participate actively in union meetings. He also received praise from members of the House Civil Service Committee for his administration of the navy's loyalty-security program. Ever loyal to Truman, he spoke out repeatedly on behalf of the president's defense program, arguing that the balance that Truman was attempting to achieve between profligate spending and an undermanned military represented the only sound course of action.

After the appointment of Naval Secretary Francis Matthews as ambassador to Ireland, Kimball assumed the position of secretary of the navy on 31 July 1951. While his immediate task was the replacement of the chief of naval operations, Admiral Forrest Sherman, who had died of a heart attack just nine days before, his overall responsibilities were demanding as well. The Korean War was in progress, and Kimball had not only to support naval operation in that conflict but also was charged with maintaining naval readiness as a deterrent against Communist aggression elsewhere. He also faced the challenge of raising morale in the navy, which faced a potentially reduced role in the nation's overall defense. All this had to be achieved in the face of relative budget austerity.

On all accounts Kimball proved successful. The Korean conflict, as well as Kimball's political skills, served to loosen congressional pursestrings. With greater access to funds, plans were advanced to produce a new series of Forrestal-class carriers, which, because of their ability to carry planes with the capacity to deliver nuclear warheads, recaptured the offensive role in national defense that the navy had seemingly lost to the air force. A strong advocate of nuclear-powered vessels, Kimball's administration coincided with the laying of the keel of the *Nautilus*, the world's first nuclear-powered submarine. Kimball also urged the modernization of naval weapons systems, most notably in the replacement of conventional weapons with guided missiles in shipboard antiaircraft batteries. Sensing that one of the greatest threats to national security came from Soviet submarines, Kimball commissioned a pioneering Helicopter Antisubmarine Squadron (HS-1) to counter the potential danger.

Leaving office at the end of the Truman administration, Kimball returned to General Tire and in July 1953 became president of a renamed Aerojet-General Corporation. He later served as chairman of the board, retiring in 1969. His first marriage ended in divorce in 1957, and in August of the next year he married syndicated political columnist Doris Fleeson; this marriage also produced no children.

Kimball remained active in his chosen community. His proudest efforts came after the Watts riots in the summer of 1965. In the aftermath of that civil disorder Kimball attempted to establish a factory in the neighborhood, with priority in hiring being given to youths with troubled backgrounds. After he retired, Kimball maintained homes in both Palm Springs, California, and Washington, D.C., where he died.

Kimball used hard work, business savvy, and political skills to build a successful career in both civil service and private enterprise. The tenure of the first army man to head the navy was regarded as more than successful by friends and observers alike.

• The papers of Dan Able Kimball are held at the Harry S. Truman Library in Independence, Mo. The best source of information on his career at General Tire is Dennis J. O'Neill, *Whale of a Territory* (1966), while his stint as secretary of the navy receives extensive coverage in Paolo E. Coletta, ed., *American Secretaries of the Navy*, vol. 2 (1980). An obituary is in the *New York Times*, 31 July 1970.

EDWARD L. LACH, JR.

KIMBALL, Dexter Simpson (21 Oct. 1865–1 Nov. 1952), mechanical and industrial engineer, was born in New River, New Brunswick, Canada, the son of William Henry Kimball, a millwright, and Jane Patterson. In 1881 Kimball moved with his family to Port Gamble in the Puget Sound area of Washington State, where his father obtained employment in the local lumber industry and Kimball received an excellent grade-school education that included Latin, Greek, algebra, and elementary physics.

At the age of sixteen Kimball began his apprenticeship as a machinist. He first learned how to operate planing machines in his uncle's shop in Port Madison, but continued at the Puget Mill Company's shop in Port Gamble, where he acquired a wide range of skills including steam-engine operation, emergency repair work, and basic tool-making activities. By the age of twenty he had served as the chief engineer and machinist at his company's Port Ludlow mill. To expand his technical horizons, Kimball left the lumber industry in 1887. He soon became a machinist at the Union Iron Works in San Francisco, which was then constructing the *Charleston* for the U.S. Navy. He later helped construct the *Olympia* as well. In 1893 Kimball began his scientific engineering education at Stanford University, an experience that proved to be quite appealing. After graduating with an A.B. in 1896, he returned to the engineering design department of the Union Iron Works. There he put his new mathematical engineering knowledge to good use, especially in the design of a 500-ton hydraulic press and a large hoisting engine for the Anaconda Mining Company. The success of the latter resulted in that company hiring Kimball to supervise the operation and construction of heavy machinery at their mining operations in Butte, Montana. Before leaving, Kimball married in 1898 Clara Evelyn Woolner; they had three children.

At the end of 1898, Kimball received an offer to teach machine design at Cornell University. Albert W. Smith, his advisor at Stanford, had recommended him. In this pioneering engineering program, Kimball's colleagues included William Durand, Robert Thurston, Rolla Carpenter, Harris J. Ryan, and John H. Barr. Kimball introduced a new course in heavy-machine design and took over a course on mechanism design. Together with Barr, he developed a senior-level course in production engineering. Although he enjoyed Cornell, Kimball left after his three-year contract expired in 1901 to become the works manager of the Stanley Electric and Manufacturing Company in Pittsfield, Massachusetts, which manufactured electrical generators. In addition to plant construction and equipment purchasing, Kimball worked increasingly on production problems. In 1902 General Electric purchased Stanley and acquired Kimball in the process. He then supervised the production of transformers at the Stanley plant. In general, this work gave Kimball hands-on experience at incorporating Taylor's scientific management and rational economic principles into production management.

In 1904 Kimball returned to Cornell as professor of machine design and construction. He initially modernized the machine shop and industrial arts program, but was soon teaching machine-design courses as well. This motivated Kimball to complete the textbook that John Barr had started. *Elements of Machine Design* (1909) was a success. It provided algebraic design equations of such elements as springs, bearings, rivets, beams, plates, axles, belt transmissions, flywheels, gears, and frames. The focus was on using the equations, rather than deriving them. Nevertheless, the book helped promote a mathematical orientation to mechanical design practice in the United States.

Kimball's greatest accomplishment was his leadership in the creation and legitimization of the discipline of industrial engineering, especially through his innovative course on production management at Cornell. It is believed to be the first American engineering course that formally incorporated the economics of industrial production. Such concepts as Taylor's management principles, the laws of diminishing returns, division of labor, and cost-benefit analysis were addressed. Kimball's landmark book, *Principles of Industrial Organization* (1913), was based on this course. Especially noteworthy is its broad historical overview, its sensitivity to labor's perspective, and its emphasis on the importance of coordinating production, design, and marketing efforts. Much to his credit, Kimball also discussed both the benefits and liabilities of the major components of mass production. He wrote in the 1947 edition of *Principles of Industrial Organization*, for example, that "America stands in danger of losing her manufacturing supremacy because of the extreme to which mass production has been pushed in this country (p. 81). Kimball's background in the construction and design of production machinery and in production management is reflected in this work. His principal concern was with obtaining optimum production rates and costs. Kimball's other books include *Industrial Education* (1911), *Elements of Cost Finding* (1914), *Plant Management* (1919), *Industrial Economics* (1929), and his autobiography *I Remember* (1953). He also edited *The Book of Popular Science*.

Kimball received a mechanical engineer degree from Stanford in 1913. Following a temporary appointment as Cornell's president at the end of World War I, he was appointed dean of Cornell's newly formed College of Engineering in 1920, a position he held until his retirement in 1936. During that period, Kimball held other administrative positions: president of the American Society of Mechanical Engineers (1921–1922), vice president of the Federated American Engineering Societies (1920–1922), chairman of the second Pan-American Conference on Standardization (1927), president of the American Engineering Council (1926–1928), and president of the American Society for the Promotion of Engineering Education (1929). During World War II, he served as chief of the priority section, Machine Tools Division, War Production Board (1942–1943). In spite of such responsibilities, Kimball continued to teach. In addition to his industrial engineering class at Cornell, he was the Brackett lecturer at Princeton University (1929) and lectured at Stanford's Graduate School of Business (1930) and at the U.S. Naval Academy's Graduate School (1943–1952). Kimball died in Ithaca, New York.

• Kimball's autobiography, *I Remember* (1953), is the most important source. It contains a complete list of his publications. An obituary is in the *New York Times*, 2 Nov. 1952.

BRETT D. STEELE

KIMBALL, Fiske (8 Dec. 1888–14 Aug. 1955), architectural historian, architect, and museum director, was born Sidney Fiske Kimball in Newton, Massachusetts, the son of Edwin Fiske Kimball, an educator, and Ellen Leora Ripley. Kimball received a B.A. and a master's degree in architecture from Harvard University in 1909 and 1912, respectively. According to Kimball, the education he and his colleagues received at Harvard caused them to pursue "teaching, writing and editing rather than practice." Kimball began his career as an architectural educator at the University of Illinois at Urbana, where he was hired as an instructor for the 1912–1913 academic year. During the year Kimball met and married Marie Goebel, the daughter of a professor of German philology at the university. The couple had no children. The university's nepotism rule prohibited Kimball's reappointment, so he began the following fall semester as an assistant professor of architecture at the University of Michigan. In addition to his teaching responsibilities, Kimball designed resort cottages in Michigan (1913–1915) and a residential tract in Ann Arbor (1914–1917). During this period the Kimballs began their research on the architectural works of Thomas Jefferson. One aspect of Kimball's study, Thomas Jefferson's design for the Virginia Capitol, became his dissertation topic; his doctorate was awarded by the University of Michigan in 1915. Receipt of Harvard University's Sachs Fellowship in the Fine Arts (1916–1917) allowed him to examine architectural drawings and other primary documents related to American architecture from 1776 to 1830.

In 1917 Kimball returned to the University of Michigan, where he taught for another year in the School of Architecture. In 1918, Kimball's final year in Ann Arbor, he held the positions of temporary head of the Department of Fine Arts and acting curator of the university's fine arts collections. Kimball was appointed professor of art and architecture and head of the new McIntire School of Fine Arts at the University of Virginia in 1919. His expertise on Jefferson's architecture, recognized since the publication of *Thomas Jefferson, Architect* (1916), was applied when, as university architect, a position he held concurrently, he was involved with the expansion of Jefferson's campus. Kimball designed or supervised a number of large-scale campus projects, including the McIntire Amphitheatre (1920–1921), and the Memorial Gymnasium (1920–1923). In 1923 Kimball assumed the position of Samuel F. B. Morse Professor of the Literature of the Arts of Design at New York University. He was again appointed university architect, with the New York firms of McKim, Mead & White and, later, Eggers & Higgins functioning as associated architects. Beginning in 1924 Kimball supervised projects at the university's University Heights campus on Fordham Heights in the Bronx and at its Washington Square location in Manhattan.

By the mid-1920s Kimball was considered the leading authority on American architecture of the republican or federal period. Kimball rebelled against the structural determinism and moral authority of the medievalism that characterized the scholarship of the previous generation. He devised an analytical method that used architectural documents and material remains as evidence for the interpretation of a building's development. These data were then assessed within the wider context of the major trends affecting the historic period. His *History of Architecture* (1918), coauthored with George H. Edgell, remained the standard architectural handbook until the 1940s. Through his numerous publications on American art, architecture, decorative art, and landscape design, including *Domestic Architecture of the American Colonies and of the Early Republic* (1922), which is a landmark in American architectural history, and *Mr. Samuel McIntire, Carver, the Architect of Salem* (1940), Kimball methodically documented the artistic development of the United States. His architectural criticism, including contemporary sections of *American Architecture* (1928), reflected the view that the legacy of the "classic unity of form" of Jefferson and other figures of the federal period formed a national tradition that freed the late nineteenth-century works of McKim, Mead & White from contemporary "realistic movements" (of art and architecture) in favor of "a purely abstract art of form and color."

Kimball's scholarly interests had begun to shift to eighteenth-century Europe early in the 1920s. France became the primary focus of his studies, which culminated in his definitive volume *The Creation of the Rococo* (1943). Kimball's interest in the interior character of the rococo style was intensified by his responsibilities as director of the Pennsylvania Museum (now Philadelphia Museum of Art), a position he held beginning in 1925. In that capacity, Kimball's first responsibility was to fill the architectural shell of the newly constructed Greek revival museum building designed by the Philadelphia firm of Borie, Trumbauer, and Zantzinger. He designed the lower floor of the museum to house its study collections. The upper floor was filled with a series of galleries that were flanked by period rooms, where contemporary works of painting, sculpture, and decorative arts were arranged according to "evolutionary sequence." Kimball worked closely with the museum's architects to design the installations for the galleries and period rooms. Among Kimball's best-known acquisitions for the museum were the John G. Johnson collection of Flemish paintings, the Foule collection of medieval and Renaissance art, the Gallatin collection of twentieth-century art, and the Louise and Walter Arensberg collection of pre-Columbian and modern art. His achievements at the museum were recognized in 1951, when Kimball received the Philadelphia Award, established by Edward Bok, founder of the *Ladies' Home Journal*.

Another aspect of Kimball's work at the museum was the restoration of eighteenth- and early nineteenth-century houses located in Fairmount Park, west of the museum. Kimball undertook the project, known as the "Chain of Colonial Houses," with the Philadelphia architect Erling H. Pedersen. Most of the houses were open to the public, and several of them were furnished with objects from the museum's collections. By the mid-1920s Kimball was considered a leader in the emerging field of American historic preservation. He viewed preservation as an obvious outcome of scholarly research on historic American buildings. He chaired the American Institute of Architects' Committee on Historic Monuments and Scenic Beauties (1923) and the Restoration Committee for Monticello (1924), Thomas Jefferson's home. In 1928 Kimball became a member of the Advisory Committee of Architects for the restoration of Colonial Williamsburg. This experience, coupled with his own academic reputation, placed Kimball in an influential position when the federal government implemented newly promulgated preservation legislation in the 1930s and early 1940s. Outstanding among Kimball's architectural projects was the house he designed for Marie and himself, known as "Shack Mountain" (1935–1937). Built on a site just west of the University of Virginia, this contemporary house reflects Kimball's belief in the enduring character of the Jeffersonian works that he synthesized in the conception of his own residence.

Kimball died in Munich, Germany, five months after his wife's death. He had been in Europe gathering material for a new volume on the baroque period. The historical method that Kimball devised and eloquently demonstrated, first through his publications on American architecture and later in his European works, produced studies of lasting scholarly value. Through his architectural and administrative skills, Kimball was able to make tangible the results of his scholarship in the form of architectural works and restoration projects. The public culmination of Kimball's talent was his design and installation of the Philadelphia Museum of Art.

• Kimball's papers are in the Philadelphia Museum of Art Archives, the Fogg Museum, Harvard University, and the Manuscript Division, Alderman Library, University of Virginia. In addition to the works cited in the text, see his "The American County House," *Architectural Record* 46 (1919): 291–400; "The Development of American Architecture," *Architectural Forum* 28 (1918): 1–5, 81–86, and 29 (1918): 21–25; "Gunston Hall," *Journal of the Society of Architectural Historians* 13 (1954): 3–8; "A Harmonious Residential Development at Ann Arbor, Michigan," *Architecture* 38 (1918): 273–80; *Jefferson's Grounds and Gardens at Monticello* (1927); "The Modern Museum of Art," *Architectural Record* 66 (1929): 559–80; "Regional Types in Early American Architecture," in *Great Georgian Houses of America*, vol. 2 (1933); and "Romantic Classicism in Architecture," *Gazette des Beaux-Arts*, 6th ser., no. 25 (1944): 95–112. Collaborative works include "The Creators of the Chippendale Style," with Edna Donnell, *Metropolitan Museum Studies* 1 (May 1929): 115–54, and 2 (Nov. 1929): 40–59; and *Great Paintings in America*, with Lionello Venturi (1948). Mary Kane has covered all his works in *A Bibliography of the Works of Fiske Kimball* (1959). On Kimball and his career, see Lauren Weiss Bricker, "The Contributions of Fiske Kimball and Talbot Faulkner Hamlin to the Study of American Architectural History" (Ph.D. diss., Univ. of California, Santa Barbara, 1992), and Bricker, "The Writings of Fiske Kimball: A Synthesis of Architectural History and Practice," in *The Architectural Historian in America*, ed. Elisabeth Blair MacDougall (1990). See also George Roberts and Mary Roberts, *Triumph on Fairmount: Fiske Kimball and the Philadelphia Museum of Art* (1959); and Bricker, "American Backgrounds: Fiske Kimball's Study of Architecture in the United States," in *The Early Years of Art History in the United States*, ed. Craig Hugh Smyth and Peter M. Lukehart (1993). An obituary is in the *New York Times*, 16 Aug. 1955.

LAUREN WEISS BRICKER

KIMBALL, George Elbert (12 July 1906–6 Dec. 1967), physical chemist and operations research specialist, was born in Chicago, Illinois, the son of Arthur Gooch Kimball, a cutlery salesman, and Effie Gertrude Smallen, a former elementary school teacher. His family moved to New Britain, Connecticut, when he was three years old after his father was promoted and reassigned to corporate headquarters. He attended the local public schools and completed one year at Phillips Exeter Academy in New Hampshire before matriculating at Princeton University in 1924. Although technically a chemistry major, he also took a number of courses in physics and mathematics and received his B.S. in 1928, his A.M. in 1929, and his Ph.D. in quantum chemistry in 1932.

Kimball remained at Princeton for a year as an instructor of chemistry and then in 1933 went to the Massachusetts Institute of Technology as a two-year National Research Fellow. By employing the principles of quantum mechanics, which had coalesced into a consistent body of physical law only seven years earlier and which proved to be particularly useful for calculating the dynamics and energy levels of valence or shared electrons in molecules, he hoped to arrive at a better understanding of the chemical properties of solids. He also lectured on quantum chemistry and laid the groundwork for a new course in theoretical physics. After teaching physics at Hunter College for a year, in 1936 he married Alice Thurston Hunter, with whom he had four children, and took a position as an assistant professor of chemistry at Columbia University, where he continued his investigations into the physics of chemistry in general and the quantum mechanics of chemical bonds and reaction rates in particular. In 1944 he, Henry Eyring, and John Walter published *Quantum Chemistry*, a systematic exposition of the principles of physical chemistry in textbook form and a work that was identified more than forty years later as one of the seven best accounts of that discipline's main themes.

In 1942, when the United States entered World War II, Kimball joined the U.S. Navy's Operations Research Group (ORG), a task force that used mathematical algorithms to analyze and formulate the tactics employed by American destroyers against German submarines. Specifically, ORG developed sophisticated search plans for finding enemy submarines as well as geometric patterns for the optimal placement of depth charges when attacking them. In 1943 he became ORG's deputy director; shortly thereafter the group expanded its scope of operations by developing tactics for convoy protection, American submarine attacks on Japanese shipping, and countermeasures against kamikaze suicide attacks. After the U.S. nuclear attack on Hiroshima, he and Philip M. Morse, ORG's director, briefed the secretary of the navy and the Joint Senate-House Naval Affairs Committee on the naval implications of the atomic bomb. He received the Presidential Citation of Merit for his contributions to the war effort and recorded the results of much of ORG's activity in *Methods of Operations Research*, written with Morse and published in 1951 after it was declassified by the U.S. government.

After the war Kimball returned to Columbia and was promoted to associate professor in 1946 and full professor in 1947. Although he continued to experiment with chemical physics, he also maintained his interest in operations research, which he defined as "a scientific method of providing executive departments with a quantitative basis for decisions regarding the operations under their control" (1951, p. 1), and furthered his relationship with the Department of Defense. From 1945 to 1951 he served on an advisory panel on underwater ordnance. In 1946 he became a consultant to the Office of the Chief of Naval Operations and worked closely with the Operations Evaluation Group, the peacetime equivalent of ORG. In 1949 he became a consultant to the Weapons Systems Evaluation Group and analyzed operations for the Joint Chiefs of Staff and the secretary of defense. He also served on the U.S. Army Science Advisory Panel and played an important role in establishing the North Atlantic Treaty Organization (NATO) Advisory Panel on Operations Research.

In 1950 Kimball began to do part-time work for Arthur D. Little, Inc., a research and management consultant to industry and government. This affiliation convinced him of the applicability of the principles of operations research to the peacetime management challenges faced by both the public and private sectors, and in 1952 he helped to organize the Operations Research Society of America as a way to publicize its benefits. He was a member of the society's first governing council and in 1964–1965 served as its president. In 1956 he left academia and moved to Winchester, Massachusetts, to become Little's science adviser; he was promoted to corporate vice president in 1961. As a consultant to Little's clients, he studied a wide range of topics such as decision theory for management, model testing, dynamic programming and project scheduling, inventory control, reliability analysis, reconciliation of profit and public welfare, and the discovery and application of knowledge.

Kimball was elected to the National Academy of Sciences in 1954. He was a fellow of the American Physical Society and the New York Academy of Science, chairman of the Northeastern Section of the American Chemical Society, and an associate editor of the *Journal of Chemical Physics*. He was a member of the Statistical Advisory Committee of the U.S. Census and served his community as a consultant to the Winchester School Committee, a trustee and president of the Hackensack Unitarian Church in New Jersey, and a committeeman for various Boy Scout troops. He died in Pittsburgh, Pennsylvania, while attending a meeting of the Visiting Committee of Carnegie-Mellon University's chemistry department.

Kimball made two important contributions to American society. His first book and his scholarly articles applied the principles of quantum mechanics to the study of chemistry, thereby broadening the knowledge of scientists and students alike. He made the principles of operations research accessible and understandable to managers in the military, industry, and government, thereby allowing them to develop simple, effective solutions to their immediate problems.

• Kimball's papers have not been located. A good biography of Kimball, including a complete bibliography of his publications, appears in Philip M. Morse, National Academy of Sciences, *Biographical Memoirs* 43 (1973): 129–46. The importance of his book on quantum chemistry is assessed in Philip S. C. Matthews, *Quantum Chemistry of Atoms and Molecules* (1986). His obituary is in the *New York Times*, 7 Dec. 1967.

CHARLES W. CAREY, JR.

KIMBALL, Heber Chase (14 June 1801–22 June 1868), religious leader and businessman, was born near Sheldon Village, Franklin County, Vermont, the son of Solomon F. Kimball, a blacksmith and farmer, and Anna Spaulding. Poorly educated, he farmed, herded sheep, blacksmithed, and manufactured potash during his youth. Crushed by the Jeffersonian embargo and the War of 1812, Kimball's father resettled the family in West Bloomfield, New York. In 1820 Kimball moved to nearby Mendon to work in his older brother's pottery business. In November 1822 he married Vilate Murray; they had ten children. Revivalism in Western New York led Kimball and his wife to join the Baptists in 1831.

A friendship with Brigham Young and a series of religious experiences preceded Kimball's conversion and baptism into the Church of Jesus Christ of Latter-day Saints/Mormon (LDS) in January 1832. Kimball devoted the remainder of his life to service in the LDS church. In the summer of 1832 he left for a proselyting mission in western New York, the first of eight missions he filled during the next twelve years. In late 1832 Kimball moved his family to Kirtland, Ohio, where Joseph Smith had established the church's headquarters. He joined Zion's Camp, an expedition sent to redeem Mormon settlers from persecution in Missouri. Along with a number of other Zion's Camp participants, Kimball was called to the original "Council of the Twelve Apostles" in February 1835. Eventually the council achieved a position in the church leadership second only to Smith and his two counselors.

In 1837 Kimball led six other missionaries on a proselyting mission to England. This mission began the massive conversions that sent a flood of Mormons from the rapidly industrializing British Isles to the United States. Returning to the United States in 1838, Kimball moved his family to Far West, Missouri. Civil war in Missouri led Governor Lilburn W. Boggs to issue his infamous extermination order, and the state expelled the Mormon people and imprisoned a number of its leaders, including Smith. During the winter of 1838–1839, Young, Kimball, and others helped to resettle the Mormons in Quincy, Illinois. After Smith escaped from jail he established the LDS in the city of Nauvoo in western Illinois. In 1840 Kimball returned to England with a majority of the council to resume their successful missionary labors. By mid-1841, when Kimball returned to the United States, the small cadre of missionaries had converted approximately 7,500 Britons.

Returning to Nauvoo, Kimball constructed an impressive brick home, and he engaged in religious, business, and public affairs. He was among the first to participate in the temple rituals that Smith introduced in 1842. Shortly thereafter, under Smith's direction, Kimball entered into plural marriage with Sarah Peak Noon, an English convert whose husband had abandoned her. Unlike most polygamists who married one additional wife, Kimball eventually married at least forty-three women. Seventeen of Kimball's plural wives bore him sixty-five children, forty-three of whom lived to maturity. Sixteen of his marriages ended in divorce or separation, though his first marriage did not.

The assassination of Smith in June 1844 found Kimball and other leaders campaigning in the East on behalf of Smith's candidacy for president of the United States. Learning of the murder in early July, Kimball and the others returned to Nauvoo. After a mass meeting, the council, under Brigham Young, assumed leadership of the church. Continued civil war and violence in Hancock County led the majority of the Mormons to abandon Nauvoo, to establish temporary settlements on the Missouri, and eventually to resettle in Utah. Kimball entered the Salt Lake valley with the pioneering party in July 1847. In the fall of 1847 he and most of the members of the council returned to the temporary settlements on the Missouri. There, the church members sustained Young as the new church president and Kimball as his first counselor.

After returning to Utah in 1848, Kimball never again left the region, and he devoted the remainder of his life to building the community and the LDS church. Establishing his primary residence on the block northeast of Temple Square in Salt Lake City, Kimball built homes, farms, and businesses in other towns as well. In 1849 Kimball and his associates applied for admission to the Union as the state of "Deseret." In spite of his lack of legal training or formal education, Kimball's high church position led to his nomination as chief justice of the proposed state's supreme court. Congress refused to admit the state of Deseret into the Union and instead organized the Utah Territory in 1850. Kimball then served in the territorial legislature.

In addition to these political activities, Kimball presided over the church's temple rituals, helped to supervise missionary activities, and promoted the establishment of towns, businesses, and farms throughout the Mountain West. He also helped develop such enterprises as a freighting company to carry goods between the United States and the Utah Territory.

Although Kimball attended the theater, dances, and musical performances and provided education for his children, he seemed antagonistic to those things he perceived as an excessive devotion to high culture. He tried to discourage participation in the local Elocution Society, and his opposition to the Polysophical Society, a local cultural association, helped to bring about its dissolution. He died in Salt Lake City.

Passionately devoted to Mormonism, Kimball contributed significantly to the success and growth of his church and to the development of the Mormon empire in the West. His leadership in opening and expanding the British mission added new blood to Mormon society. As a member of the Council of the Twelve and the First Presidency he assisted in shepherding the Mormon community through some of the most trying times in its history.

• Most of Kimball's papers and journals are in the Archives of the Church of Jesus Christ of Latter-day Saints in Salt Lake City. Some are in private hands, and others are located in repositories such as the Manuscripts Department at the Brigham Young Univ. Library. Several of his journals have been published, but the best compilation is *On the Potter's Wheel: The Diaries of Heber C. Kimball*, ed. Stanley B. Kimball (1987). Many of Kimball's sermons are published in Brigham Young et al., *Journal of Discourses* (26 vols., 1854–1886). The best complete biography is Stanley B. Kimball, *Heber C. Kimball: Mormon Patriarch and Pioneer* (1981). Orson F. Whitney, *Life of Heber C. Kimball*, 2d ed. (1945), also contains valuable information.

THOMAS G. ALEXANDER

KIMBALL, Nathan (22 Nov. 1823?–21 Jan. 1898), Union general, was born in the hamlet of Fredericksburg, Washington County, Indiana, the son of Nathaniel Kimball, a small merchant who shipped produce and other farm products to New Orleans for sale and shipment to other countries, and Nancy Furgeson. Orphaned in 1829, he was raised by his mother's father in Fredericksburg. He attended Indiana Asbury College (now DePauw University) from 1839 until 1841 but did not graduate. He then traveled to Independence, Missouri, where he taught school and later worked as a store clerk, farmer, and stage driver. He finally returned to Fredericksburg and in 1843 began the study of medicine under the tutelage of Alexander McPheeters, whose sister, Martha Ann McPheeters, Kimball married in 1845. The couple had one child.

Kimball practiced medicine until the outbreak of the Mexican War, when he raised a company of volunteers and on 20 June 1846 was appointed captain in the

Second Indiana Regiment. At the battle of Buena Vista (22–23 Feb. 1847), the regiment fled from the field in disorder as a result of the cowardly actions of its colonel. Kimball, however, rallied his own company and continued fighting. Mustered out on 23 June 1847 at New Orleans, he returned to Fredericksburg and ran an unsuccessful campaign for Indiana state senator as a Whig. In April 1850 his wife died, and Kimball moved to Livonia, Indiana, where in July of that same year he married Martha's sister, Emily McPheeters. They had five children.

When the Civil War erupted, Kimball was practicing medicine at Loogootee in Martin County. Commissioned captain by Governor Oliver Perry Morton, he helped to recruit a regiment and was mustered into Federal service as colonel of the Fourteenth Indiana on 7 June 1861. Later that year Colonel Kimball and his regiment saw action at Cheat Mountain (Sept.) and along the Greenbrier River (Oct.) in present-day West Virginia.

Sent to the Shenandoah Valley, Kimball commanded the First Brigade of General James Shields's division, V Corps, Army of the Potomac. In the spring of 1862 Confederate general Thomas "Stonewall" Jackson was charged with holding Federal troops in the Shenandoah Valley and marched to strike Shields at Winchester. On 22 March Shields was wounded in a skirmish near Kernstown, south of Winchester, and Kimball assumed command of the division, which bivouacked in line of battle. Although outnumbered two-to-one, Jackson attacked the Federal right flank on 23 March and was driving it back when Kimball's own brigade moved from its concealed position north of Kernstown and checked the advance. Pushing ahead, Kimball's force drove Jackson from the field, inflicting more than 700 casualties on the enemy. Kimball's performance earned the praise of Shields, who wrote, "Special thanks are due to Colonel Kimball, commanding First Brigade, and senior officer in the field. His conduct was brave, judicious, and efficient. He executed my orders in every instance with vigor and fidelity, and exhibited judgment and sagacity in the various movements that were necessarily intrusted to his discretion" (*Official Records*, vol. 12, pt. 1, p. 342). His actions at Kernstown earned Kimball promotion to brigadier general of volunteers to rank from 15 April 1862.

On 17 September 1862 his brigade, now part of the II Corps, fought with grim determination at Antietam in action along the Sunken Road, and again he earned the praise of his superiors. William H. French, the division commander, wrote of Kimball, "to whom the division is indebted for a brilliant display of courage never surpassed." Continuing in brigade command, Kimball next participated in the failed assaults on Marye's Heights at Fredericksburg, Virginia (13 Dec. 1862), in which his brigade again distinguished itself. Kimball was badly wounded in the thigh "while gallantly leading his troops to charge the first line" of the enemy. His loss was "severely felt by myself and the division," wrote General French.

After his recovery the following spring, Kimball led the Provisional Division, XVI Corps, Army of the Tennessee, in the siege of Vicksburg. After the capture of Vicksburg on 4 July 1863, he served for a time in the District of Eastern Arkansas against Sterling Price. Entrusted with important dispatches relative to the political climate in Arkansas, he traveled to Washington and presented his views to the authorities concerning the reentry of Arkansas to the Union. He then returned to Arkansas with instructions from President Abraham Lincoln to assist in the reorganization of the state government by superintending the process through which loyal citizens took the prescribed oath of allegiance.

In the spring of 1864 Kimball commanded a brigade attached to the First Division of the IV Corps, Army of the Cumberland, which joined General William T. Sherman's army group in its advance on Atlanta. On 20 July Kimball directed his men with consummate skill in the battle of Peachtree Creek, for which service he was given command of a division. After the fall of Atlanta, Kimball was ordered to southern Indiana to assist in suppressing the activities of the Knights of the Golden Circle, a secret order of southern sympathizers. Offered the Republican nomination for lieutenant governor of Indiana in 1864, he declined, as his duty was with the army. He returned to the front in time to participate in the battles of Franklin (30 Nov.) and Nashville (15–16 Dec.), earning the "highest commendation" from his superiors for the skillful manner in which he handled his command and for his "personal gallantry displayed in trying positions." Brevetted major general on 1 February 1865 for services rendered during the war, he was mustered out of the service on 24 August.

Kimball devoted the remainder of his life to civil and political service. He was active in veterans' affairs and helped to organize the Grand Army of the Republic in Indiana, becoming its state commander. He also wrote of his war experiences and contributed the article "Fighting Jackson at Kernstown" to *Battles and Leaders of the Civil War*, vol. 2 (1884). In 1866 he was elected state treasurer as a Republican and served two terms. He was then elected to the state legislature in 1872 and served on the Committee of Ways and Means. In 1873 President Ulysses S. Grant appointed him surveyor general of Utah. Settling in Ogden, Kimball later became postmaster under President Rutherford B. Hayes and served in that capacity until his death in Ogden.

Kimball was a solid and reliable soldier in two wars. Personally brave, he maintained his composure in the heat of battle, and his actions inspired those around him. His conduct earned the respect and confidence of both his superiors and the men under his command. Although Kernstown was the only major engagement in which he exercised overall command, Kimball's performance at all levels of command created an exemplary record. In March 1915, in recognition of his service to the country, the federal government erected a monument to Kimball on the grounds of Vicksburg National Military Park in Vicksburg, Mississippi.

• The English Collection (M98, Box 60, Folder 8), Indiana Historical Society, contains manuscripts concerning Kimball. For more information see *The War of the Rebellion: A Compilation of the Official Records of the Union and Confederate Armies*, ser. 1, vols. 5, 12, 19, 21, 22, 24, 38, and 45 (128 vols., 1880–1891); Ezra J. Warner, *Generals in Blue* (1964); and Stewart Sifakis, *Who Was Who in the Union* (1988). See also Leonard A. Morrison and Stephen P. Sharples, *History of the Kimball Family in America*, vol. 2 (1897).

TERRENCE J. WINSCHEL

KIMBALL, Spencer Woolley (28 Mar. 1895–5 Nov. 1985), Mormon apostle and president of the Church of Jesus Christ of Latter-day Saints (LDS church), was born in Salt Lake City, Utah, the son of Andrew Kimball, a carpenter, farmer, and salesman, and Olive Woolley. His father presided over an LDS "stake" (similar to diocese) in Arizona. Until he was forty-eight, Kimball lived in Thatcher, Arizona, the periphery of what geographers call the Mormon Cultural Region centering on Salt Lake City. He completed one semester at the University of Arizona in 1917 and during that same year married Camilla Eyring; they had four children.

As a typical Mormon, Kimball combined secular occupations with service as a local church leader. As a bank teller, then insurance salesman and real estate agent, he served successively as stake clerk, counselor to the stake president, and stake president. Few Mormons expected the central leadership to look in the Arizona backwater for a new general authority (full-time leader of the entire LDS church), and in 1943 Kimball was devastated to learn of his appointment to the central hierarchy. "How could *you* be an Apostle of the Lord? You are not worthy. You are *insignificant*," he told himself, and actually considered suicide. Instead, Kimball accepted the church president's reassurance that his appointment was the result of divine inspiration. He moved with his family to Salt Lake City, where he was ordained an apostle on 7 October 1943.

For thirty years, Apostle Kimball was best known for five things. First, his unpretentious demeanor as one of the church's highest administrators. Second, his publicly hugging and kissing persons from all walks of life. Third, his special assignment to promote the interests of American Indians in the LDS church from 1945 onward. Fourth, his many physical afflictions, including throat cancer, which left him with a deep, husky voice after the surgical removal of most of his vocal cords in 1957. Fifth, his rigorous attack on sexual misconduct among the Latter-day Saints.

Kimball's ascension as LDS church president in 1973 was an even greater shock than his appointment as an apostle had been. Harold B. Lee, the youngest LDS president in nearly fifty years, had served barely sixteen months when he died of a heart attack. Chosen to succeed him as president, Kimball was ordained by the Quorum of the Twelve Apostles on 30 December 1973. During his twelve-year presidency, Kimball introduced stunning changes in LDS administration, doctrine, and practice.

An early innovation occurred in April 1974, when Kimball appointed David M. Kennedy as "special representative" to conduct international diplomacy in the interest of the LDS church and its missionary program. Kennedy had served as U.S. treasury secretary, ambassador-at-large, and ambassador to the North Atlantic Treaty Organization (NATO). Later, faced with the massive growth of Mormon populations throughout the world, Kimball introduced totally new administrative structures to the LDS church. He also allowed local leaders to perform ecclesiastical acts previously restricted to general authorities. In October 1975 the First Quorum of Seventy became a new quorum of general authorities. He allowed stake presidents to ordain seventies in 1974, to ordain bishops in 1975, and six years later to ordain patriarchs. Also, fifty-four years after the last such appointment, Kimball began selecting LDS general authorities whose native language was not English. In 1975 he appointed a native Belgian, followed by Dutch, German, Japanese, Argentine, and Swiss general authorities. In addition, President Kimball advanced ethnic Americans such as a Nisei and a Navajo to the Mormon hierarchy.

Kimball stunned many Mormons by dissolving some general authority offices. In October 1976 the First Council of Seventy and the Assistants to the Twelve ceased to exist administratively and were merged into the recently formed First Quorum of Seventy. Three years later, he eliminated the office of patriarch to the church, previously defined as one of the church's "prophets, seers, and revelators." Kimball also changed the tradition of lifetime tenure for all LDS general authorities. In September 1978 the First Presidency (made up of Kimball and his two counselors) announced an emeritus status for general authorities due to age or physical infirmity. Later, in April 1984, his administration began appointing some general authorities for five-year tenures only. The LDS church's central hierarchy had not experienced such sweeping changes since the days of Mormonism's founder, Joseph Smith.

Rivaling the impact of these structural changes within the Mormon hierarchy were changes in LDS scripture. In April 1976 two previously published visions (of Joseph Smith and of Joseph F. Smith) were adopted as additions to the Standard Works. This was the first addition of revelations to the church's official canon in a century and the first addition of any new document since 1914. Then, in 1981, a new edition of the Book of Mormon changed the prophecy that the "Lamanites" (American Indians) would "become white and delightsome." In the new edition, the meaning was changed from skin color to spirituality: "become pure and delightsome." This was the first doctrinal change in the words of the Mormon scripture since 1837, and it reflected the fact that generations of Native-American Mormons had not become light-skinned.

Kimball also ended some of Mormonism's most traditional practices. In 1978 he discontinued stake quarterly conferences and ended all local prayer circle meetings. In December 1979 he no longer required persons "endowed" in LDS temples to wear a one-piece undergarment frequently mocked by non-Mormons. Instead, Mormons could wear a two-piece temple "garment" similar to conventional American underwear. The next year, a Consolidated Meeting Schedule of three hours on Sundays eliminated weekday meetings for women, teenagers, and children as well as the traditional twice-daily Sunday meetings.

Kimball received international attention for his most dramatic change in traditional LDS policy. In June 1978 he announced a revelation ending the LDS church policy of prohibiting priesthood to persons of black African ancestry. The upcoming completion of a Mormon temple in São Paulo had augured nightmarish complications in maintaining the priesthood restriction among the mixed-race Brazilians and their ancestors, for whom vicarious ordinances would be performed in the new temple. Both Mormons and non-Mormons heralded this as the most stunning Mormon event since the LDS church officially abandoned polygamy in 1890.

Only seventeen temples had been dedicated in the 143 years of Mormonism before Kimball's presidency, but during his administration, twenty-one new temples were dedicated in the United States and fourteen other countries. In addition, a dozen temples that were dedicated after his death had been publicly announced during his presidency. Although Mormonism had a significant non-U.S. population since the late 1830s, no other LDS president had so thoroughly internationalized the church's sacred privileges and structures.

Given the extraordinary pattern of change during the Kimball administration, it is not surprising that some innovations failed and that some announcements had to be reversed. For example, in the hope of increasing the number of full-time missionaries, Kimball reduced the time of service for male missionaries from twenty-four months to eighteen months in 1982. Total missionary numbers actually declined, however, and the First Presidency reversed the policy two years later. Also, reflecting Kimball's preoccupation with Mormon sexual behavior, the First Presidency announced in January 1982 that it "interpreted oral sex as constituting an unnatural, impure, or unholy practice." This announcement instructed local leaders to make sure that both single and married persons were not granted temple recommends if participating in oral sex. Reactions to this new policy were so negative and widespread that ten months later the First Presidency instructed local leaders that "you should never inquire into personal, intimate matters involving marital relations between a man and his wife."

In addition, during the Kimball administration the LDS church developed a reputation for being hostile toward women's rights. In October 1976 the First Presidency released a statement against ratification of the Equal Rights Amendment to the U.S. Constitution, saying, "We fear it will even stifle many God-given feminine instincts." Then, in December 1979, Virginia's local church leaders (in consultation with headquarters in Salt Lake City) excommunicated Sonia Johnson, president of Mormons for the ERA. The proposed Equal Rights Amendment failed to be ratified in 1982, after being defeated in key states under heavy lobbying by Mormon anti-ERA activists directed by delegated emissaries from LDS headquarters. The impression of antifemale bias in the Kimball presidency was heightened by a February 1985 letter of the First Presidency to all church officers "on the subject of rape." Instructions in the letter indicated that each raped Mormon woman needed to convince the male LDS officers that she had not "willingly consented" to the sexual encounter or else face ecclesiastical discipline.

Media coverage of the controversies and missteps of the Kimball presidency paled, however, beside his administration's triumph in enhancing the public image of Mormonism. In April 1978 the *Reader's Digest* published the first installment of advertising inserts by the LDS church, an unprecedented event. Then, in December 1980, "Mr. Krueger's Christmas," a dramatic production starring James Stewart and produced by the LDS church with a proselytizing message at the end, was broadcast on national television. It was rebroadcast a year later on stations in all major U.S. markets and in several foreign nations. The Kimball presidency also directed the production of "Home Front" public interest spots for television. These spots, which prominently identified the LDS church as sponsor, eventually received Emmy awards.

Incapacitated during the last three years of his presidency by subdural hematomas and surgeries, President Kimball remained the focus of Mormon devotion. In January 1985 LDS church members in the United States and Canada held a special fast and donated more than $6.5 million to aid famine victims in Africa. This campaign, invoked in Kimball's name, was a charitable expression of his earlier revelation to grant LDS priesthood to black Africans and to all peoples of color. Kimball's death in Salt Lake City ended his endeavors to teach Mormons to accept fundamental change in the LDS church as normative.

• Biographies include Edward L. Kimball and Andrew E. Kimball, Jr., *Spencer W. Kimball* (1977); Edward L. Kimball, *The Story of Spencer W. Kimball* (1985); and Francis M. Gibbons, *Spencer W. Kimball* (1995). For Kimball's counseling on sexuality, see his *The Miracle of Forgiveness* (1969), his controversial *New Horizons for Homosexuals* (1971), and *Teachings of Spencer W. Kimball* (1982). For evaluations of his moral crusade, see Eugene England, "A Small and Piercing Voice: The Sermons of Spencer W. Kimball," *Brigham Young University Studies* 25 (Fall 1985): 79–80; and Ron Schow et al., *Peculiar People: Mormons and Same Sex Orientation* (1991), pp. xxv–xxvi. For Kimball's reversal of the priesthood ban on blacks, see Lester Bush, Jr., and Armand Mauss, eds., *Neither White Nor Black: Mormon Scholars Confront the Race Issue in a Universal Church* (1984); and Mark L.

Grover, "The Mormon Priesthood Revelation and the São Paulo Temple," *Dialogue: A Journal of Mormon Thought* 23 (Spring 1990): 11–53. For the Kimball presidency and the ERA, see the LDS church publication *The Church and the Proposed Equal Rights Amendment: A Moral Issue* (1980); O. Kendall White, Jr., "Mormonism and the Equal Rights Amendment," *Journal of Church and State* 31 (Spring 1989): 249–67; and D. Michael Quinn, "The LDS Church's Campaign against the Equal Rights Amendment," *Journal of Mormon History* 20 (Fall 1994): 85–155. For administrative developments, see Dennis L. Lythgoe, "Lengthening Our Stride: The Remarkable Administration of Spencer W. Kimball," *Brigham Young University Studies* 25 (Fall 1985): 5–17; Edward L. Kimball, "The Administration of Spencer W. Kimball," *Sunstone* 11 (Mar. 1987): 8–14; and James B. Allen and Glen M. Leonard, *Story of the Latter-day Saints*, rev. ed. (1992). Obituaries are in the *Deseret News*, 6 Nov. 1985; the *New York Times*, 7 Nov. 1985; the *Christian Science Monitor*, 7 Nov. 1985; and the *Los Angeles Times*, 10 Nov. 1985.

D. MICHAEL QUINN

KIMBALL, William Wirt (9 Jan. 1848–26 Jan. 1930), naval officer, was born in Paris, Maine, the son of William King Kimball, an army officer, and Frances Freeland Rawson. Kimball graduated from the U.S. Naval Academy in 1869 into a post–Civil War navy of obsolete warships, outdated organization, and few opportunities for officer promotion. Promoted in 1874 to lieutenant, a rank he retained for twenty-three years, he served on the first torpedo boats in the navy between 1875 and 1879. He tied his career to development of torpedoes, torpedo boats, and eventually the submarine. Kimball was among the first group of officers assigned in 1870 to the Navy Torpedo Station in Newport, Rhode Island. In 1882 he married Esther Smith Spencer. The couple did not have children.

During the 1880s Kimball developed machine guns and magazine guns for torpedo boats. While at the Brooklyn Navy Yard in 1885, he met John P. Holland, the inventor of a new submarine boat. They formed an immediate friendship, and Kimball promoted Holland's submarine boats in the Navy Department and in testimony before congressional committees. Kimball was the first officer to dive in and test the underwater reliability of the Holland submarine. Although he helped Holland secure navy contracts for the submarine, Kimball's primary contribution lay in development of the torpedo boat (a small, swift warship used primarily to protect coastal waters and harbors against larger men-of-war) and torpedo-boat destroyer (a forerunner of the destroyer-class warship). He commanded the first torpedo-boat flotilla in the navy in 1897.

Assistant Secretary of the Navy Theodore Roosevelt (1858–1919) helped Kimball develop the torpedo-boat flotilla in time for duty during the Spanish-American War of 1898. Roosevelt also used Kimball and a group of officers that formed an inner circle around the assistant secretary as an informal naval general staff to prepare the navy for war against Spain. Kimball contributed his intelligence-gathering and war-planning experience to the group. He had made an extended intelligence-gathering trip through the Isthmus of Panama in 1885, preparing a special intelligence report on a canal route. Between 1894 and 1897 Kimball served in the Office of Naval Intelligence, where he assembled information for his plan "War with Spain, 1896," which called for a simultaneous blockade of Cuba and strike against Spanish forces in the Philippines. He provided Roosevelt with regular summaries about foreign naval developments, naval technology, and war-making potential; after war broke out in 1898, he commanded an auxiliary cruiser during the battle of Santiago.

After the Spanish-American War, Kimball commanded the torpedo boat *Alert* (1901–1903), served as a district lighthouse inspector, and in 1905 received command of the battleship *New Jersey*. He took command of the Nicaragua Expeditionary Squadron in 1909 with the rank of acting rear admiral. He assumed a major diplomatic role in this revolution, bypassing regular State Department channels in an attempt to settle differences between warring factions. Kimball blamed American business interests and consular agents for stirring up an antigovernment movement, and he supported the Nicaraguan dictator, José Zelaya. Kimball retired from duty in 1910 but returned to active service during the First World War as the president of a naval examining board. In later years Kimball promoted naval expansion through the Navy League, further development of the submarine, and naval aviation. He died at home in Washington, D.C.

Kimball promoted two new types of warships during the late-nineteenth century—the torpedo boat and the submarine. Both soon became integral parts of the fleet and of fleet operations. He also helped to improve the naval intelligence and war-planning mechanisms, and between 1870 and 1910 he remained an outspoken advocate of technological innovation, naval growth, and expansive foreign policies.

• There is no Kimball biography or collection of personal papers. Peter Karsten, *The Naval Aristocracy: The Golden Age of Annapolis and the Emergence of Modern American Navalism* (1972), includes Kimball as one of the more aggressive navalists during the era of American emergence as a world naval power. Richard D. Challener, *Admirals, Generals, and American Foreign Policy, 1898–1914* (1973), reveals the extensive interventionist role that Kimball assumed during the Nicaraguan revolution of 1908. Elting E. Morison, ed., *The Letters of Theodore Roosevelt*, vol. 1 (1951), documents the Kimball-Roosevelt relationship, while the Kimball-Holland friendship is discussed in Richard Knowles Morris, *John P. Holland, 1841–1914: Inventor of the Modern Submarine* (1966). Kimball's intelligence and war-planning activities can be followed in John A. S. Grenville and George B. Young, *Politics, Strategy, and American Diplomacy* (1966); Ronald Spector, *Professors of War: The Naval War College and the Development of the Naval Profession* (1977); and Jeffery M. Dorwart, *The Office of Naval Intelligence: The Birth of America's First Intelligence Agency, 1865–1918* (1979).

JEFFERY M. DORWART

KIMMEL, Husband Edward (26 Feb. 1882–14 May 1968), U.S. Navy admiral, was born in Henderson, Kentucky, the son of Marius Manning Kimmel, a businessman, engineer, and Civil War veteran, and Sibbella Lambert. Kimmel graduated from the U.S. Naval Academy in 1904 and subsequently studied at the Naval War College. He served as a junior officer in battleships and destroyers and on the staffs of fleet commands afloat and ashore, specializing in gunnery. In 1912 he married Dorothy Kinkaid, a daughter and sister of admirals. Two of their three children became U.S. Navy submariners. During the First World War Kimmel was posted to England, serving as staff gunnery officer of Battle Squadron Six, and afterward to the Naval Gun Factory (1920–1923). He then commanded destroyer divisions in the Asiatic Fleet and was destroyer squadron commander with the Battle Fleet between 1928 and 1930. He rose to the rank of captain in 1926 and rear admiral in 1937. In the early 1930s he commanded the battleship *New York* and thereafter all battleships of the Battle Force, U.S. Fleet (1934–1935). Following three years as budget officer of the Navy Department, in which position he won the respect of Congress, he returned to sea in 1938 in command of Cruiser Division Seven and in 1939 of all the fleet's cruisers. He had built a career reputation as a big gun expert and a meticulous staff officer, but he knew little about aviation.

In May 1940 President Franklin Roosevelt sent the fleet to Pearl Harbor, Hawaii, in hopes that it would have a restraining effect on Japan, which was at war with China and coveted the colonies of Southeast Asia. On 1 February 1941 the navy was subdivided into Pacific and Atlantic Fleets to fight a two-ocean war. To his astonishment, Kimmel was catapulted over forty-six senior officers and named commander in chief, U.S. Pacific Fleet (CinCPac), with the rank of admiral. The appointment reflected his solid record and the esteem of his fellow admirals. According to navy legend, however, Roosevelt wanted "the two toughest sons-of-bitches" to run the new fleets. Chief of Naval Operations Harold Stark recommended Kimmel and Rear Admiral Ernest J. King. As Kimmel was already commanding in the Pacific and King in the Atlantic, convenience was apparently a factor in the decision. The fact that he had briefly served as aide to Roosevelt when the latter was assistant secretary of the navy apparently played no part in the decision.

For nine months Kimmel strove to train and equip the Pacific Fleet. He felt that it was inadequate for its task under War Plan Rainbow Five (derived from War Plan Orange, a blueprint to defeat Japan that had been studied by the navy for decades). The fleet would ultimately operate offensively, but initially it was to distract the Japanese from attacking Singapore until the Royal Navy could reinforce its base there. Kimmel's own war plan hinted strongly at a more aggressive mission—enticing the enemy to a battleship fight in the Central Pacific as soon as war broke out.

During 1941 Washington did not fully inform Kimmel of the extent of Japan's rising belligerency, which had been detected by breaking its diplomatic code. Kimmel did receive a warning from Washington on 27 November that war was imminent. By then Admiral Isoroku Yamamoto had secretly dispatched six aircraft carriers to destroy the fleet in Hawaii. Kimmel made offensive preparations, such as training for carrier raids on enemy bases and maneuvering for a fleet engagement, but did little to improve the defenses of Pearl Harbor, for example by installing antitorpedo nets. When Japanese aircraft struck without warning on the morning of 7 December 1941, Kimmel could do nothing. The Japanese sunk or damaged 8 battleships, destroyed 108 aircraft on the ground, and killed over 2,400 Americans. It remains the greatest defeat ever suffered by the U.S. Navy to date. When a spent bullet crashed through his office window, Kimmel murmured, "It would have been more merciful had it killed me" (Prange, p. 516).

Kimmel was removed from command on 17 December 1941 and demoted. His last act before Admiral Chester W. Nimitz succeeded him was an aborted attempt to relieve the siege of an American base at Wake Island. He retired from the navy on 1 March 1942 and subsequently worked for an engineering outfit that did naval work in New York.

U.S. government agencies conducted eight investigations to fix the blame for the disaster. Kimmel testified prominently before a joint committee of Congress in January 1946, after the war was over. Two strong elements of his personality emerged. He was a man obsessed with details who insisted that he had followed regulations, and he refused to accept an iota of blame. His self-justification was somewhat plausible, because he had not been privy to all intelligence, although decoded intercepts never suggested Pearl Harbor might be a target. (In the 1990s the National Security Agency disclosed that lower-level Japanese radio traffic hinting at an attack had been intercepted but not decoded until after the war, because in 1941 there were barely enough codebreakers to handle top-level intercepts.)

The committee's Democratic majority concluded that Kimmel committed lapses of judgment. He kept his ships in port on weekends while spies observed, he failed to glean the worst danger from his own intelligence experts, and he did not coordinate defenses with the army. Most damning was the lack of aerial reconnaissance. His fleet had forty-nine flying boats on Oahu capable of patrolling eight hundred miles to sea, and some army planes were available. (The Japanese launched planes two hundred miles from Pearl Harbor.) Kimmel unconvincingly argued that he held back because he could not conduct a perfect 360° search. Republican members also criticized him despite their desire to discredit the by then deceased Roosevelt.

Mainstream historians, such as Gordon Prange, have agreed with the committee and especially have noted Kimmel's blindness to Yamamoto's striking power. A 1991 study argued that, desiring to be "the American Nelson," Kimmel was so aggressive in fighting intentions as to overlook the need for defense (Miller, p. 312). All historians note, however, that higher commanders were also guilty of lapses but were not fired in disgrace. Clinging to Kimmel and his army counterpart, Lieutenant General Walter Short, is the aura of having been made political scapegoats. Revisionists have even claimed that American leaders learned in advance of the attack but, because of their negligence or private desire for war, did not inform Kimmel and save the fleet. Such arguments, however, are hardly credible.

Admiral Kimmel died at his home in Groton, Connecticut. Efforts by retired officers and sympathetic historians to restore posthumously his rank and reputation continued into the 1990s without success.

• Kimmel's papers (1907–1968, 20 cu. ft.) at the University of Wyoming Library, Laramie, Wyo., have not been widely cited. An outline of Kimmel's career is in the Naval History Division, Washington, D.C., Navy Yard. His slim autobiography, *Admiral Kimmel's Story* (1955), is an angry self-defense and tells little of the man. Kimmel figures prominently in most works about Pearl Harbor. For the military prelude, the fountainhead is the forty-volume joint congressional committee investigation (15 Nov. 1945–15 July 1946), which includes documents and the wartime hearings: U.S. Congress, *Hearings before the Joint Committee on the Investigation of the Pearl Harbor Attack (PHA)*, 79th Cong., 1st and 2d sess., 1946. The most comprehensive books appeared in the 1980s. A stunning tour de force is Gordon W. Prange, *At Dawn We Slept* (1981), completed after his death by Donald M. Goldstein and Katherine V. Dillon. Prange conducted hundreds of interviews. Goldstein and Dillon, *Pearl Harbor: The Verdict of History* (1986), devotes three chapters to Kimmel and agrees he was culpable. Roberta Wohlstetter, *Pearl Harbor: Warning and Decision* (1962), the most insightful book on readiness and blame, offers the widely accepted idea that the "noise" of irrelevant data obscured the "signal" of useful intelligence. Kimmel's own war plan is analyzed in Edward S. Miller, *War Plan Orange* (1991). A stridently partisan effort to resuscitate Kimmel's reputation is Captain Edward L. Beach, *Scapegoats* (1995). Pearl Harbor ranks with the Kennedy assassination in attracting conspiracy theorists. The best-known revisionist work is John Toland, *Infamy* (1982), which alleges a cover-up by Roosevelt.

EDWARD S. MILLER

KINCAID, Bradley (13 July 1895–23 Sept. 1989), country singer and composer, was born in Garrard County, Kentucky, the son of William Plummer Kincaid and Elizabeth Hurt, farm laborers. The Kincaid homestead in Garrard County was near the Point Leavell community, eighteen miles from the present-day town of Berea. The area was rich in Scotch settlers and the old ballads they had brought with them; these songs were generally sung unaccompanied, in a high, keening style that later formed the basis for bluegrass and country singing styles. Both of Kincaid's parents sang, though his father, a devout Campbellite, was deeply interested in church songs and shape note singing; his mother sang old British ballads like "Fair Ellender" and "Barbara Allen." When he was still a boy, Bradley received as a present an old guitar for which his father had traded a fox hound; guitars were unusual in the mountains then, and Kincaid at once began learning how to use it to accompany the old ballads. This technique eventually allowed him to forge the singing style

that would win him fame; he also dubbed the guitar his "hound dog" guitar, a phrase he would later popularize in his professional career.

As a teenager Kincaid tried farming, but one fall he realized that he had made only $40 for a year's work and decided to try to improve his lot. He enrolled in 1914 in Berea College, a school devoted to educating mountain children, and worked toward his high school degree. While there he met pioneer folk song collector John F. Smith and began to get some sense of the complex history of the old ballads he was singing. After a three-year interruption, during which he enrolled in the army and served in France during World War I, he returned to Berea; he began formally studying music as well and fell in love with his teacher, Irma Foreman, a native of Brooklyn, New York; they were married in 1922 and had four children.

Two years later the young couple decided to try their luck in Chicago and moved there, where Kincaid attended a Young Men's Christian Association College at night. He also began singing with a formal YMCA barbershop quartet and through them got an audition at WLS radio. Though located in the heart of Chicago, WLS was owned by Sears Roebuck (the initials WLS stood for "World's Largest Store"), and the station had a mission to service the kind of rural midwestern and southern audience that formed so much of its mail-order customers. Thus in 1924 they had started a novelty-country music program called "The National Barn Dance." The manager of the show, Don Malin, invited Kincaid to come down on Saturday night and sing a few "old folk songs." Needing the money ($15 a night), Kincaid agreed, borrowed a guitar, and worked up his arrangement of "Barbara Allen." Mail poured in—big laundry baskets full—and he found himself not only a regular on the show, but the leading entertainer on the show.

Establishing a routine that would be the blueprint for several generations of country radio singers to come, Kincaid continued to play on the air for a modest salary, but by 1927 he made his serious income from doing personal appearances in the region around the station. Kincaid also began to print songbooks with some of his favorite songs in them; he could sell these by mail or in theaters while making personal appearances for fifty cents. The first of these, published in 1928, sold more than 100,000 copies. He became the first country singer to use this method of promotion.

"Barbara Allen" was so requested that Kincaid sang it virtually every Saturday night for four years over the powerful WLS station. His other favorites included pieces like "Pearl Bryan," "Methodist Pie," and "The Fatal Derby Day." He also developed a repertoire of cute, sentimental songs that included pieces like "The Little Shirt My Mother Made for Me," "Gooseberry Pie," and "Liza up a Simmon Tree." In 1928 he began recording some of his radio favorites, at first for the Starr Piano Company (Gennett) in Richmond, Indiana. Many of these discs were released through Sears's own labels, such as Silvertone and Challenge, and sold through the catalog; soon the catalogs contained a special section listing records by "The Kentucky Mountain Boy," as well as Kincaid songbooks and copies of his "hound dog" guitar. By the end of 1930 he had recorded some sixty-two songs on various labels—he continued to record well into the 1970s. By 1934 Kincaid was one of the nation's favorite singers, outpointing singers like Al Jolson and Gene Austin.

Kincaid soon left WLS for greener pastures and throughout the 1930s traveled on a dizzying round to various stations, including WKDA (Pittsburgh, Pa.), WGY (Schenectady, N.Y.), WEAF (New York City), and finally WBZ in Boston, Massachusetts. In Boston he worked with a young apprentice, Marshall "Grandpa" Jones, later to win fame on the Grand Ole Opry. Another member of his troupe was Harmonica Joe Troyan, a Cleveland musician who also specialized in comedy. The trio found that rural New Englanders liked the old songs as well as the midwesterners.

Though Kincaid steadfastly stuck to the older, simpler, acoustic style of music, he managed to remain popular through the 1940s. He did a successful stint at WLW Cincinnati and was a major star during the mid-1940s on WSM's Grand Ole Opry in Nashville. He himself wrote a number of "modern" songs, such as "The Legend of the Robin Red Breast" and "Brush the Dust off That Old Bible," about the atomic bomb.

In 1950 Kincaid chose to retire to open a music store in Springfield, Ohio. He recorded a series of LPs for the Texas-based Bluebonnet Company, a sort of "collected works" for posterity, in 1963. He also often returned to his alma mater at Berea to visit with students and folklorists. In the late 1970s he collaborated with Berea professor Loyal Jones to create a full-length biography and list of the songs in his repertoire. After being seriously injured in an automobile accident, he died in Springfield.

• A useful source on Kincaid is Loyal Jones, *Radio's "Kentucky Mountain Boy" Bradley Kincaid* (1980).

CHARLES K. WOLFE

KINCH, Myra (6 Dec. 1903–20 Nov. 1981), modern dancer and choreographer, was born in Los Angeles, California, the daughter of Henry S. Kinch and Marguerite L. Cody, occupations unknown. She began her formal study of dance as a high school student, exploring a wide variety of dance forms, including ballet, under the tutelage of Dorothy S. Lyndall and her associate Bertha Wardell. Kinch's entrance into the theatrical profession was delayed, however, by her mother's insistence that she complete her education. Graduating from the University of California at Los Angeles with a B.S. in 1925, she taught dancing at the local Nature Music School until 1926. Kinch then joined a Prolog troupe, the live revues designed to accompany film showings, touring West Coast movie houses for the next two-and-a-half years as an exotic dancer.

The stock market crash of October 1929, with its withering effect on theatrical production, denied Kinch her expected Broadway debut. For the next three depression years she worked as a specialty dancer in a variety of local venues, including hotel floor shows, night clubs, revues (*Temptations of 1930*), and stage plays (*They Had to See Paris; Marco Millions*, both 1930). During this period she also prepared solo recital material, presenting a successful debut program on 24 March 1930 at the Beaux Arts Auditorium in Los Angeles. Described by the *Los Angeles Evening Express* as "a born dancer," Kinch was perceived by the *Los Angeles Record* as highly individual. "She follows no definite school or style. Her dances are beautifully her own" (25 Mar. 1930). In a second recital on 14 April 1931 at the Wilshire-Ebell Theatre in Los Angeles, Kinch continued her custom of performing to the music of serious composers such as Claude Debussy, Maurice Ravel, and George Gershwin, also experimenting with percussion accompaniment. Mary Mayer reported in the *Los Angeles Times* that "she has the gift of drawing vivid pictures for her audience. Her sense of line and color, her sense of the dramatic in setting and gesture, seem to know no bounds" (16 Apr. 1931).

Winifred Aydelotte, a critic for the *Los Angeles Record*, recognized in Kinch a special talent for comedy, for which she came to be well known: "The most popular number on her entire program was 'Revue', in which Miss Kinch manages to be a complete stage show. She is, in turn, the soprano, the chorus, the specialty dancer, the show girl, and then—a miracle—a finale" (15 Apr. 1931). With this critical encouragement, Kinch hazarded a European debut at Max Reinhardt's Komödie theater in Berlin on 8 May 1932 to mixed critical reviews. The Berlin correspondent of London's *Dancing Times* appreciated her "glowing youth and physical beauty" but deemed her choreography "superficial," although "her good taste and culture were gladly acknowledged" (June 1932). She then returned home, where she continued to perform as a recitalist and with a small group. Kinch also toured California and the Southwest, appearing at Mexico City's Teatro Politeama in 1934 and in the film *The Lives of a Bengal Lancer* (1935).

In 1937 Kinch was appointed director of the Los Angeles Dance Project's Western Sector, a branch of the Federal Theatre Project funded through the Works Progress Administration. Until the dissolution of the Federal Theatre by Congress in 1939, Kinch toured under its aegis with a modern dance group featuring her *An American Exodus* (1937) and *Let My People Go* (1938), choreographed opera ballets (*Aida*; Felix Borowski's comic *Fernando del Nonsentsico*, both 1937) and musical revue numbers (*Revue of Reviews; Ready! Aim! Fire!*, both 1937), and provided dance direction for the Federal Theatre's Treasure Island presentations at San Francisco's Golden Gate International Exposition in 1939. Also in 1939 she married composer-pianist Manuel Galea, who had long served as Kinch's artistic partner, writing and arranging music for her dance works and accompanying her performances; he continued in that capacity throughout her career. The couple had no children.

For most of the World War II years Kinch taught on the UCLA faculty as an assistant dance instructor (1940–1944). In the mid-1940s she and her husband moved permanently to the East Coast. Her activities at this time included choreography for Broadway musicals (*Love in the Snow*, 1946; *Romance*, 1947) and participation in the New York–based nonprofit performing cooperative the Choreographers' Workshop.

In 1948 Kinch was appointed head of the modern dance department of the school of the Jacob's Pillow Dance Festival in Lee, Massachusetts, by its founder and director Ted Shawn. She continued in the post through the 1966 summer season. The stability and continuity of the position enabled Kinch to enjoy more than a decade of sustained creativity. During this time she produced both serious and comic works, among them a series inspired by Greek myths (*Of Dreadful Magic*, 1949; *Along Appointed Sands*, 1951; *The Tower of Rage*, 1952) and a version of Shakespeare's *King Lear* (*Sundered Majesty*, 1955), with Shawn as the demented monarch and Kinch as his wronged daughter Cordelia. She also created her comic masterpiece *Giselle's Revenge* (1953), a hilarious spoof of the romantic ballet that owes much to the macabre cartoons of Charles Addams; and *Tomb for Two* (1957), a send-up of inane opera ballets with Verdi's *Aida* as its target. Kinch also served as dance director for a number of pageants and large-scale arena productions, including Paul Green's symphonic drama *The Common Glory* (1949), his *Faith of Our Fathers* (1951), his *The Founders* (1957), and the mammoth Chicago *Festival of Faith* (1954). During the 1950s Kinch appeared on television programs such as "Camera Three" and "Frontiers of Faith."

In the early 1960s Kinch led a small company on two North American tours in a program of her comic works, publicized as *The Light Fantastic*. Retiring as a performer in 1967, she continued to choreograph and teach master classes until she and her husband settled in Bonita Springs, Florida, in 1976. Among her last activities was the staging of her *Folk Songs* and the now-classic *Giselle's Revenge* for the Florida Ballet Theatre of Tampa in 1979. She died at home in Bonita Springs.

Kinch was a true American independent, both in attitude and accomplishment. Resisting domination by either of the rival schools established by Martha Graham and by Doris Humphrey and Charles Weidman, she forged an individual style distinguished by free-ranging but precisely defined movement allied with emotionally expressive gesture suitable to the character of the work, whether lyric, comic, or dramatic. Kinch's combination of qualities as performer and choreographer were summed up in the *American Dancer* of October 1937: "She has background, both technical and intellectual, choreographic skill, imagination, tolerance, an American viewpoint, and a magnificent sense of humor." Among modern dancers Kinch is perhaps unique in her antic and irreverent commentaries on the forms, figures, and pretensions of a profession not particularly noted for being amused by itself.

• The principal sources for material concerning Kinch are the microfilmed scrapbooks (1926–1965) of clippings and programs housed in the Dance Collection, the New York Public Library for the Performing Arts, Lincoln Center, a gift from Kinch. The library collection also includes clipping files, photographs, videos of Kinch performing and teaching, and a taped interview with critic Walter Terry, in which Kinch discusses the principles and techniques of modern dance as contrasted with those of classical ballet. Access to individually indexed and cataloged items is through the *Dictionary Catalog of the Dance Collection* (1974) and its annual supplements, *Bibliographic Guide to the Dance*, published through 1991. Another useful source for reviews is S. Yancey Belknap, comp., *Guide to Dance Periodicals* (10 vols., 1959–1963), covering the period from 1931 to 1962. Biographical entries for Kinch are included in *The Dance Encyclopedia*, ed. Anatole Chujoy and P. W. Manchester (1967), and *Biographical Dictionary of Dance*, ed. Barbara Naomi Cohen-Stratyner (1982). The updated paperback edition of Don McDonagh, *Complete Guide to Modern Dance*, rev. ed. (1977) contains a short biographical entry about Kinch and a "choreochronicle" of her work as well as a thorough description of her best-known dance, *Giselle's Revenge*. An obituary is in the *New York Times*, 24 Nov. 1981.

JACQUELINE A. MASKEY

KING, Carol Weiss (24 Aug. 1895–22 Jan. 1952), attorney and civil rights activist, was born in New York City, the daughter of Samuel W. Weiss, a prominent attorney, and Carrie Stix, a member of a well-known mercantile family. King graduated from the Horace Mann School (1912) and Barnard College (1916) before receiving her law degree from New York University in 1920. In 1917, while attending law school, she married Gordon Congdon King, a writer, who died of pneumonia in 1930. Their one child, Jonathan, became a publisher of books for G. P. Putnam's Sons. In 1921 King joined the law firm of Hale, Nelles & Shorr and in 1925 became a founding partner of its successor, Shorr, Brodsky & King.

King was among the leaders of the radical left in support of the African-American civil rights movement. After an altercation with whites on a freight train in Alabama in 1931, nine frightened black youths were swept through the state courts on rape charges and eight of them were sentenced to death. King joined in writing the brief on appeal for the young men, who had become known as the "Scottsboro Boys." Her advocacy contributed to the famous 1935 Supreme Court decision in *Norris v. Alabama* forbidding the exclusion of blacks from juries.

King's interest in labor issues developed when she worked as a research fellow for the American Association for Labor Legislation after she graduated from college. However, her involvement in the protection of labor rights first made headlines in 1933, when she initiated a false arrest action against the state of New York after her advocacy in a textile workers strike representing the American Civil Liberties Union. She later would be central to the establishment and support of two organizations on the left wing of the American labor movement, the International Juridical Association (IJA) and the International Labor Defense (ILD).

Combining her civil rights and labor interests, King defended Harry Bridges, CIO leader of the International Longshoremen's and Warehousemen's Union on the West Coast. In 1938 the secretary of labor obtained an arrest warrant, and Bridges was charged with membership in the Communist party and faced deportation to Australia. King demanded an independent judge and a public proceeding, and as a result James M. Landis, dean of the Harvard Law School, was appointed as a special officer. The press and the public were admitted for the first time to a deportation hearing. Apart from King's talent for obtaining substantial press coverage, her defense was notable for establishing counsel's right to purchase a copy of the trial transcript and to subpoena witnesses. Ultimately, Landis accepted none of the government's charges and found that, indeed, a conspiracy against Bridges existed. Numerous other efforts by the government to deport Bridges also failed, in part because of King's legal skills.

King's staunchly militant, procommunist views and her association with left-wing organizations prompted investigations into her views and activities by several congressional committees. In 1939 a House investigatory committee, headed by Representative Howard Smith of Virginia, questioned her as part of its efforts to demonstrate that the IJA was the driving force behind the National Labor Relations Board's (NLRB) opposition to proposed amendments to the Wagner Act. The committee asserted that the constitutional scheme that provided for the separation of powers prohibited an administrative agency from influencing legislation. King also was questioned, as secretary of the IJA, about the conduct of several NLRB aides who were charged with unlawfully assisting strikers in their labor dispute with a Pennsylvania hosiery mill.

King played an important role in several civil rights organizations, including the Joint Anti-Fascist Refugee Commission, the American Committee for the Protection of the Foreign Born, and the Civil Rights Congress.

Acknowledged more as a writer of briefs than for her oral arguments, several of King's cases reached the Supreme Court. Arguing a contempt-of-court charge against Bridges in 1941, she persuaded the Court that the right to freedom of speech guaranteed in the First Amendment applied to aliens as well as to citizens. In 1950 she challenged the authority of immigration inspectors to act in lieu of judges in deportation hearings. Her challenge ultimately succeeded, and that year a ruling by the Supreme Court (*Wang Yang Sung v. McGrath*) led to the retrial of hundreds of would-be deportees.

Politics and the law were closely intertwined in King's pursuit of social justice. In 1949 she testified in opposition to the confirmation of Tom C. Clark for Supreme Court justice. She accused the former attorney general of improper conduct in dealing with the foreign-born, particularly Gerhart Eisler, an Austrian-born refugee of World War II, whom in 1947 she had defended against charges that he was an enemy alien.

In the postwar period, when political activity on behalf of liberal or Communist causes generated public hostility, King demonstrated courage and skill by intervening on behalf of many unpopular clients. She provided her clients with vigorous legal representation, often overcoming bias against women in her male-dominated profession. Personally, she endured the early death of her husband and the burdens of a single working mother. She died in New York City.

During a period of intense social and political conflict, King exposed many troubling aspects of the anti-Communist hysteria, maintained legal limits on the conservative reaction to the growth of organized labor, and confronted hostility toward the civil rights movement. Although best known for her defense of several controversial figures associated with the Communist party, King also handled thousands of immigration and naturalization cases for less prominent individuals. Throughout her career, she fought vehemently against what she considered the unconstitutional persecution of members of the Communist party and the misapplication of the deportation laws.

• The Carol Weiss King Collection at the Meiklejohn Civil Liberties Institute, Berkeley, Calif., contains many of King's papers and correspondence. For additional information, see Ann Ginger, *Carol Weiss King: Human Rights Lawyer, 1895–1952* (1993), and the obituary in the *New York Times*, 23 Jan. 1952.

NORMAN SILBER

KING, Charles (16 Mar. 1789–27 Sept. 1867), editor, merchant, and college president, was born in New York, New York, the son of Rufus King, a diplomat, and Mary Alsop. His father, having succeeded Thomas Pinckney as minister plenipotentiary to the Court of St. James, moved with his family to London, England, in 1796. After a few years at a local school, Charles and his older brother John Alsop King were sent in December 1799 to Harrow, a private secondary school in Middlesex, where they had Lord Byron and Robert Peel as classmates. Leaving Harrow in December 1804, King and his brother then attended a branch of the École Polytechnique in Paris, France, for a few months, after which Charles King took a clerking position with Hope & Company, a banking firm in Amsterdam, the Netherlands.

Returning to New York in 1806, King continued his business career in the mercantile firm of Archibald Gracie. In 1810 he was made a partner in the firm, and he married Eliza Gracie, his employer's oldest daughter; they would have seven children. Although he did not hide his Federalist distaste for the War of 1812, King nevertheless served as a captain of the militia in New York. He also successfully ran for election to the New York State Assembly in 1813, where he served one term. The following year King began an extended business sojourn in England; while there, he agreed to join a commission investigating the 6 April 1815 massacre of American prisoners at Dartmoor, England. Serving at the behest of Henry Clay and Albert Gallatin, he issued a report (along with his English counterpart, Francis Seymour Larpent) on 26 April that the American public interpreted as being too lenient toward the British. The report was held against King and his father for years.

The year 1823 was one of marked change for King, as the Gracie firm went out of business and his wife died. That year he purchased the *New York American,* an evening newspaper in the fiercely competitive New York City market, and assumed control of its business and editorial operations. During this period, in October 1826, he married Henrietta Liston Low; they had six children. For twenty-two years King endeavored to improve the financial fortunes of the *American,* without success. In 1845 he merged the paper with the *Morning Courier and New-York Enquirer,* operated by James Watson Webb and Henry J. Raymond, and he remained with the publication as an associate editor.

King retired to his estate, "Cherry Lawn," in Elizabethtown (now Elizabeth), New Jersey, in 1848. He remained active in business-related affairs, holding important positions with the Bank of New York and the New York Chamber of Commerce; his younger brother, James Gore King, served as president of the latter organization. King also wrote the "History of the New York Chamber of Commerce," which was published in *Collections of the New York Historical Society,* 2d. ser., 2 (1849). King was also in great demand as a public speaker, and he established a reputation in New York society as a forceful, yet dignified and sympathetic figure.

King's prominence in society, as well as his business experience, undoubtedly contributed to his selection as president of Columbia College in November 1849. At the time of his inauguration, Columbia was a small school with a local student body, a small faculty, an inadequate physical plant, and a burdensome debt load. Nevertheless, there was reason for optimism; the college held tracts of land in Manhattan that were increasing in value as the city grew northward from Battery Point.

The King administration at Columbia was noted for several initiatives, not all of which came to fruition. In September 1850 King recommended the establishment of a chair in American history, which was not adopted. In October 1852 he urged the appointment of a committee to explore the possibility of abolishing tuition; the same committee was also charged with studying the ramifications of establishing "University," or graduate-level, studies. Neither of these proposals came to pass, either. King took time from his duties—which included examining students for entrance, teaching, and keeping college minutes and tardiness reports—to contribute to *Outline of a Course of English Reading, Based on That Prepared . . . by the Late Chancellor Kent, with Additions by Charles King . . . Edited with Further Additions and Notes by Henry A. Oakley*

(1853). In 1857, however, major changes occurred. The College relocated uptown, leaving its Park Place location for the facilities of the former Deaf and Dumb Asylum; the entire block bordered by Forty-ninth and Fiftieth Streets and Madison and Fourth Avenues was subsequently acquired. The location was far from ideal; a stockyard faced the college, and nearby Potter's Field cemetery—through which a street had recently been placed—featured disinterred coffins that were not removed for about a year. Nevertheless, the move provided for a badly needed upgrade in facilities.

The move was soon followed by curriculum changes. The standard course of study was revised; optional courses—Department of Letters, Department of Science, and Department of Jurisprudence—were now a matter of students' choice in their senior year. While the change was short-lived, it did attract more students to Columbia. Under King's leadership, Columbia established the School of Law in 1858 and the School of Mines and Metallurgy in 1863, and it merged with the College of Physicians and Surgeons in 1859. Other innovations occurred as well. The beginning of athletics at Columbia took place at King's instigation. While he outraged the trustees by suggesting the establishment of a college billiards hall, he managed to provide (out of his own pocket) for a teacher of boxing and fencing.

The Civil War years were stressful for King. In addition to the loss of students and rental income suffered by the college, one of his sons was wounded at the Battle of the Wilderness, another died of malaria in camp, and yet another, General Rufus King, was accused of drunkenness while on duty. Advancing age also took its toll, and King resigned as president in March 1864. He spent a year in a rental house in Oyster Bay, Long Island, New York, after which he relocated with his family to Rome, Italy, to join his son Rufus, then serving as the last U.S. minister to the Papal States. Taken ill with gout in the spring of 1867, King died at Frascati, near Rome.

King represented a transitional figure in the history of Columbia University. A nonprofessional aristocrat placed in command of an underfunded college, handicapped by the onset of war and age, he nevertheless presided over the first stirrings of growth that would turn Columbia into a world-renowned educational institution.

• King's papers do not appear to have survived; however, several of his manuscripts are held at Columbia University and the New-York Historical Society. His career at Columbia can be traced in John Howard Van Amringe, "President Charles King, 1849–1864," in *A History of Columbia University, 1754–1904* (1904); Horace Coon, *Columbia: Colossus on the Hudson* (1947); and Frederick Paul Keppel, *Columbia* (1914). His daughter Gertrude King Schuyler provided an intimate portrait of his life in "A Gentleman of the Old School," *Scribner's Magazine,* May 1914, pp. 611–19. An obituary is in the *New York Times,* 30 Sept. 1867.

EDWARD L. LACH, JR.

KING, Charles Bird (26 Sept. 1785–18 Mar. 1862), artist, was born in Newport, Rhode Island, the only child of Captain Zebulon King and Deborah Bird. When

King was four his father, a revolutionary war veteran, was killed by Indians while tilling land in Ohio awarded to him for his military service. King was left a sizable estate that made him financially independent throughout his life. He was raised by his mother in the Moravian church whose traditions of honesty, industry, austerity, and universal Christian brotherhood made a deep impression on him. Both his childhood friends and those of his later years remarked on his generous, unselfish nature and pleasant disposition. He was educated in Newport, and his schoolmates included the future artist Washington Allston. King made frequent visits to the Redwood Library and Athenaeum, where he nurtured his taste for literature and art.

His grandfather, Newport merchant Nathaniel Bird, evidently was an amateur painter of sea pieces and appears to have encouraged his grandson to pursue a career in the arts. He may also have given King some lessons in painting, but the *Newport Daily News* of 20 March 1862 reported that King received his first lessons in drawing and painting from Newport artist Samuel King (no relation). King did study with Edward Savage in New York City from 1800 to 1805. Upon the completion of his apprenticeship he returned to Newport.

In 1806 King went to London for further study. He attended the Royal Academy and also took lessons from Benjamin West. During his six years in England he became friends with several other American artists working or studying in London, including John Trumbull, Samuel F. B. Morse, Charles Robert Leslie, Samuel Lovett Waldo (with whom he roomed from 1806 to 1808), and Thomas Sully, who became his closest friend. He also was friendly with some of the leading British artists, among them William Beechey and David Wilkie. King's earliest surviving work, a painting titled *Still-Life, Game* was painted in 1806, the year of his arrival in London. His other English work has not been traced, but he is known to have painted religious subjects, scenes from Shakespeare, genre pictures, copies of portraits by Sir Joshua Reynolds, copies after mythological scenes by Benjamin West, portraits of his landlord's family, and a self-portrait.

King returned to the United States in the summer of 1812. He visited his home town and presented twenty-seven books to the Redwood Library, including volumes on the arts, history, and science. By the end of the year he had settled in Philadelphia, Pennsylvania, then the art capital of the United States and the home of his friend Sully, who had returned from England two years earlier. However, he seems to have received few commissions and departed after only about a year for Richmond, Virginia. By the end of 1814 he was in Washington, D.C. After a visit to Philadelphia, and possibly to Newport, he settled in Baltimore, Maryland, in late 1815. During his three years there he painted some of his best pictures. *Poor Artist's Cupboard* (c. 1815, Corcoran Gallery of Art) is both a well-executed illusionistic painting and a sharp commentary on the lack of support for the fine arts in America. He also painted portraits of prominent lawyer William Pinkney and War of 1812 hero John Stricker. They were the first of many national figures he would portray.

Early in 1817 King again visited Washington where he painted portraits of President James Monroe and Daniel Webster. The portrait of Monroe is a seated full-length depiction measuring 42½ by 27½ inches. An engraving by Charles Goodman and Robert Piggot, published by W. H. Morgan on 15 December 1817, accurately reproduced the portrait and was widely circulated. It was the first work of King's to be engraved, and Rembrandt Peale based his own portrait of Monroe on it. The portrait of Webster is a simpler bust-length and a more direct characterization and is one of the earliest likenesses of a man who was one of the most depicted Americans of the nineteenth century.

King returned to Baltimore after a few months and painted portraits of Charles Carroll of Carrollton and Carroll's son-in-law Robert Goodloe Harper. By the autumn of 1818, however, he had returned to the nation's capital, where he lived for the rest of his life, spending summers in Newport. He painted many likenesses of national leaders, prominent Washingtonians, and distinguished visitors. Among the best known of his sitters—and the best of his portraits—are Henry Clay (1821, Corcoran Gallery of Art), John C. Calhoun (c. 1822, Corcoran Gallery of Art), and Louisa Catherine Adams (1821, National Museum of American Art).

King's best-known portraits, however, are not of Washington's elite but of the many American Indians who visited the nation's capital during the early nineteenth century. Beginning in the winter of 1821–1822 and for the next twenty years, he painted members of the Indian delegations invited by the U.S. government to visit Washington and other eastern cities. He received this commission from the War Department, then headed by John C. Calhoun; the portraits were destined to become part of a collection of memorabilia known as the Indian Gallery and administered by the department's Bureau of Indian Affairs. The Indian Gallery, which eventually included more than one hundred portraits by King, was transferred in 1858 to the Smithsonian Institution where, tragically, it was destroyed by fire in January 1865. However, a few originals survive, as do replicas and other life portraits kept by King for his own collection, and the entire Indian Gallery was copied by Henry Inman around 1834. King, whose father had been killed by Indians, might have seemed an ironic choice to paint portraits of Indians, but he always did so with sympathy and understanding. Among the finest of these works are the portraits of the Pawnee Loup chief Petalesharro (Generous Chief), the Oto Shaumonekusse (Prairie Wolf), and his wife, Hayne Hudjihini (Eagle of Delight) (all 1822, White House Collection), and the Sauk and Fox chiefs Black Hawk (c. 1833) and Keokuk (1827). King's most impressive painting of an Indian subject is the group portrait of five warriors, *Young Omaha, War Eagle, Little Missouri, and Pawnees* (1822, National Museum of American Art). It is a well-designed composition that effectively uses light and color as well as a searching depiction of Indian character.

In addition to his work in portraiture King continued to paint subject pictures throughout his career and also an occasional landscape. Fifteen years after *Poor Artist's Cupboard* he painted a similar still life, *The Vanity of the Artist's Dream* (1830, Fogg Art Museum, Harvard). *Itinerant Artist* (c. 1830, New York State Historical Association, Cooperstown) shows an artist painting a portrait under the most trying conditions, perhaps recalling King's own early days on the road. *Interior of a Ropewalk* (c. 1845, Bayly Art Museum, Univ. of Virginia, Charlottesville) is, as King's biographer Andrew Cosentino has written, "a tour de force of perspective drawing and . . . one of the earliest representations of an industrial scene" (p. 95). *Grandfather's Hobby* (c. 1824, Henry Francis du Pont Winterthur Museum) depicts a small boy wearing his grandfather's hat and spectacles and reading a newspaper. A rare foray into literary painting, *Rip Van Winkle Returning from a Morning Lounge* (c. 1825, Museum of Fine Arts, Boston), was inspired both by Washington Irving's *The Legend of Sleepy Hollow* and the genre paintings of Sir David Wilkie. King even dabbled in architecture, in 1830 designing a home for his friend Joseph Gales, Jr., in Washington.

King was a prominent figure in Washington society and counted many national figures among his friends, including Presidents James Monroe and John Quincy Adams. He also was on good terms with most of his fellow American artists. In addition to Thomas Sully, his artist friends included Rembrandt Peale, John Vanderlyn, and John Gadsby Chapman; to Chapman, King bequeathed $300 and two small mannequins. He was well liked, forthright in his dealings with others, and had a keen sense of humor. He died in Washington, D.C., and was buried in the Newport Island Cemetery in his native town. Unmarried, he left a sizable estate resulting not only from his successful career but also from several inheritances and shrewd investments in Washington real estate.

Much of King's surviving work is competent but uninspired. However, a number of his portraits and genre pieces are among the best produced in America up to that time. The fact that he depicted so many American Indians is particularly noteworthy, both artistically and culturally. Except for George Catlin, no other American painted as many Indians as he, and King portrayed them with sympathy and understanding.

• Most of King's papers are in the Redwood Library and Athenaeum and at the Newport Historical Society. His last will and testament is at the Federal Records Center in Suitland, Md. Two self-portraits—one painted in 1815, the other in 1858—belong to the Redwood Library. King gave the library about 140 paintings during his lifetime and bequeathed to them another 75. Most, however, were deaccessioned between 1885 and 1970 (including all of the Indian portraits), but some forty paintings—still the largest single collection of his work—remain at the Redwood. Other institutions holding his work include the National Museum of American Art, the Corcoran Gallery of Art, the White House Collection, and the Museum of Fine Arts, Boston. The best study of King's life and career is Andrew J. Cosentino, *The Paintings of Charles Bird King (1785–1862)*, the catalog of an exhibition held at the National Collection of Fine Arts (now the National Museum of American Art), Smithsonian Institution, from 4 November 1977 through 22 January 1978. A brief account of King's life and career is in William Dunlap, *History of the Rise and Progress of the Arts of Design in the United States* (1834). Herman J. Viola's *The Indian Legacy of Charles Bird King* (1976) is a detailed account of the portraits King painted for the Bureau of Indian Affairs.

DAVID MESCHUTT

KING, Charles Glen (22 Oct. 1896–23 Jan. 1988), biochemist, was born in Entiat, Washington, the son of Charles Clement King, a merchant and fruit grower, and Mary Bookwalter. In 1918 he earned the B.S. in the State College of Washington. In 1919 he married Hilda Bainton, a college classmate; they had three children. After a short period in army service King undertook graduate studies at the University of Pittsburgh, where he received the M.S. in 1920 and the Ph.D. in 1923. He later took postdoctoral work in biochemistry at Columbia University (1926–1927) and at Cambridge University in England (1929–1930).

King was a chemistry instructor at Pittsburgh from 1920 to 1926, an assistant professor from 1926 to 1930, and a professor from 1930 to 1943. In 1942 he returned to Columbia as a visiting professor of chemistry and in 1946 was retained as a full professor, a position King held until 1962 when he became emeritus.

At the time King was starting his career, a deep interest in trace materials in nutrition was emerging. Several investigators were gaining insights into the role of trace amounts of a few substances having remarkable effects on health. These substances became characterized as vital amines, soon referred to as vitamins because not all of them are amines. Productive research on these compounds began to emerge early in the twentieth century.

King became interested in the foods that have a curative role on the disease known as scurvy, the scourge of seafaring men and of armies far from their home base. The disease had been recognized by James Lind, a Scottish ship surgeon who, around 1770, had supplied a ship's crew with lemons, whose juice prevented scurvy on long voyages. His treatment was successful, but many naval officers and captains of commercial ships avoided the treatment and failed to carry lemons as an antiscorbutic agent, so the disease remained endemic for another century.

Before the end of the third decade of the twentieth century King was exploring scurvy as a food deficiency, now generally recognized as a lack of a certain vitamin or necessary food ingredient. Before 1930 the term vitamin C was assigned to the deficiencies related to the absence of a water-soluble chemical present in juices of citrus fruits and in a variety of fruits and vegetables. By 1932 King and his academic associate W. A. Waugh reported the isolation of a crystalline substance in lemon juice that was curative of scurvy in guinea pigs. Shortly thereafter the Hungarian biochemist Albert Szent-Györgyi and his American associate Joseph L. Svirbely reported that a similar substance isolated from adrenal glands, as well as from oranges, lemons, and cabbage, had curative properties toward guinea pigs suffering from scurvy.

From 1921 to 1941 King was an active investigator in the laboratory, but after that time he became very active in encouraging and promoting the scientific research of others through fundraising efforts. He became involved in the Nutrition Foundation, an agency that sought funds for scientific research in the nutritional sciences, serving as scientific director (1942–1955), executive director (1955–1961), president (1961–1963), and trustee (1963 onward). His work with the Nutrition Foundation was essentially hardcore fundraising for subsequent distribution among research chemists and medical research leaders. King proved to be unusually effective in these efforts. By keeping abreast of new directions in nutritional science he was able to use foundation money with great vision.

King also served on the U.S. Department of Agriculture Research Policy Committee (1946–1957), was a member of the Food and Nutrition Board (1941–1970) and the Food Law Institute (1950–1962), and was a trustee of the Boyce Thompson Institute (1957–1975), a councilor of the Rockefeller Foundation (1963–1966), and a member of the executive board of the Robert Welch Foundation (1954–1963). In 1960 he served as president of the Fifth International Council on Nutrition. King was a councilor to the Office of the Surgeon General (1940–1966) and was U.S. Commissioner to the United Nations International Children's Emergency Fund (UNICEF) (1968–1969) and to the United Nations Food and Agricultural Organization.

King also received numerous prizes and awards, including the Pennsylvania Award of Merit (1938), Pennsylvania Public Health Association Award (1939), Pittsburgh Award (1943), John Scott Award (1949), Nicholas Appert Award of the Institute of Food Technologists, Chicago Section (1955), Charles Spenser Award of the American Chemical Society (1963), and the Conrad Elvehjem Award, American Institute of Nutrition (1966). His research and his activity in scientific and government projects resulted in more than 200 scientific papers, besides his numerous lectures to public organizations.

King's principal diversion from chemistry was cultivation of prize rose bushes at his home in Kennett Square, Pennsylvania.

• Charles King published only one book, *A Good Idea: The History of the Nutrition Foundation* (1976). He expressed himself extensively in scientific journals and frequent public addresses involving his scientific results. A particularly useful publication is his "Vitamin C, Ascorbic Acid," *Physiological Reviews* 16 (1936): 238–62, which presents a comprehensive review of the vitamin C story through 1935, with 169 literature references. His and Waugh's reports on the discovery of vitamin C appear in *Science* 75 (1932): 357, 630, and *Journal of Biological Chemistry* 97 (1932): 325.

AARON J. IHDE

KING, Clarence Rivers (6 Jan. 1842–24 Dec. 1901), geologist and first director of the U.S. Geological Survey (USGS), was born in Newport, Rhode Island, the son of James Rivers King, a China trader, and Caroline Florence Little. The King family enjoyed comfortable circumstances until the bankruptcy of King & Company in 1857, after which Mrs. King, her husband having died in Amoy, China, in 1848, solved her financial problem through marriage to George S. Howland, the owner of a white lead factory in Brooklyn, New York.

King entered Yale's Sheffield Scientific School in fall 1860 and completed its chemistry program within two years, receiving the Ph.B. with honors in 1862. Thereafter he read intensively in geology in New York City, taking time out to attend Louis Agassiz's lectures in glaciology at Harvard. In hope of gaining practical training in geology as a member of Josiah D. Whitney's Geological Survey of California, he rode horseback across the continent during the summer of 1863. He was readily accepted as a volunteer on the Whitney survey, a position he retained until fall 1866, receiving thorough training in the science of geological surveying.

King's trip across the continent had sown in his mind the idea of a cross-country geological survey, an ambition that work with Whitney fostered. On returning to the East, King sold the concept of the U.S. Geological Exploration of the Fortieth Parallel to Congress in early 1867, and the survey was assigned to the command of the U.S. Army Engineers, with King reporting directly to General A. A. Humphreys, chief of engineers. It was King's mission to map the topography and to survey the geology and natural resources of the area that flanked the transcontinental railroad between the Sierra Nevada and the Great Plains. His able corps sailed to California via Panama in summer 1867, crossed the Sierra, and began its fieldwork in western Nevada.

The fieldwork lasted until late in 1872, climaxing with King's exposure of the Great Diamond Hoax in northwest Colorado, a sensational event that glamorized his personality and earned him a reputation for impeccable integrity. A mesa not far from Browns Park had been salted with diamonds and other gemstones; its "discovery" touched off a "diamond craze" that led to the incorporation of some twenty-five companies capitalized at a total of a quarter-billion dollars for the purpose of working the false diamond field. King investigated the mesa and found it salted, deflating one of the most disastrous swindles ever perpetrated. This exposure alone, according to the *Nation* (12 Dec. 1872, p. 380), "more than paid for the cost of the [entire] survey" and was the most dramatic incident in the history of all the great western surveys, except Major John Wesley Powell's epic descents of the Green and Colorado rivers. King's corps was the first of the four western surveys to complete its fieldwork; partly for that reason its successful methods in the field, its exacting standards, and its distinguished publications served as models for the three other surveys—those of Powell, Ferdinand Hayden, and George M. Wheeler.

King's *Systematic Geology* (1878) brought to a climax the seven-volume *Report of the Fortieth Parallel Survey*, which synthesized the paleontology, stratigraphy, tectonics, and geological history of all the areas that King's corps had explored. But the book that brought King the greatest literary credit was *Mountaineering in the Sierra Nevada* (1872), a volume of fourteen sketches inspired by his adventures with the Whitney survey. Concerning it, the writer William Dean Howells remarked to President Hayes in 1879 that his sole complaint against King was "that a man who can give us such literature should be content to be merely a great scientist."

Howells's remark came at the time King was assisting the campaign of the National Academy of Sciences to spur Congress to authorize the U.S. Geological Survey, to supersede and consolidate on a national basis the work of the several western surveys. He worked closely with Abram Hewitt, who was the most active advocate in Congress of the projected USGS. King wrote a crucial clause for Hewitt's bill—the one that created the office of geological director and defined its duties. After Congress authorized the USGS on 3 March 1879, King competed with Hayden for the directorship, winning it a month later.

As director of the USGS, King appointed excellent personnel and adopted policies that would put the Survey on much of its future track. His program emphasized economic geology, making the USGS the ally of the mining industry. At the same time King projected a wide-ranging scientific classification of the national domain. He also participated personally in the work of the Public Lands Commission of 1879 and in the survey of precious metals for the Tenth U.S. Census. An additional accomplishment of significance was his organization of an extensive publications program for the USGS, which projected at least a dozen volumes on subjects of both theoretical and practical geology, including monographs on the mining districts of Leadville and Eureka, Nevada, as well as the Comstock Lode, treatments of the prehistoric Lake Bonneville and the Grand Canyon region, and O. C. Marsh's monograph on the extinct *Dinocerata*. By 1881 King concluded that he had achieved his objective of establishing the USGS on a firm foundation, so he tendered his resignation and left office at the end of the Hayes administration. His choice of successor was Powell, then chief of the Bureau of Ethnology at the Smithsonian.

King's later life was dominated by a futile pursuit of wealth, at first in the promotion of gold and silver mines in Mexico. His promotion of one such mine took him in 1882 to Europe, where he toured the Continent and bought an art collection with most of the money he had earned from investments in three cattle ranches in the western United States. (Two of the ranches were taken over by King's ranching partner, Hewitt, and the third was bought by Richard Frewen, an Englishman who ran cattle in Montana.) In England he hobnobbed for two years with the aristocracy, including Baron Ferdinand de Rothschild and the Prince of Wales. After King's return to the United States, however, all of his Mexican mines failed, and he spent most of his time thereafter as a consultant for other mine owners and as an expert witness in some of the most spectacular mining litigation of the day. But even during his most depressed days he was an active clubman, belonging to several fashionable clubs in New York such as the Century Association, where he was held in high esteem as a raconteur and good fellow by his associates, including such celebrities as Theodore Roosevelt, John Hay, and Henry Adams. Adams idolized King and called him "the most remarkable man of our time."

In the midst of this most public life King (always attracted to dark-skinned women) entered into a common-law marriage in 1888 with a black nursemaid, Ada Copeland. King assumed the name James Todd for the purpose of this marriage, which he kept secret even from close friends. The couple had five children, one of whom died in infancy. King provided for his family until his death from tuberculosis in Phoenix, Arizona. He was buried in Newport, renowned as a writer, raconteur, and one of the foremost geologists of the nineteenth century.

• King's personal papers are at the Huntington Library in San Marino, Calif., part of the James D. Hague Collection. King's correspondence as chief of the Fortieth Parallel Survey and as director of the U.S. Geological Survey is held in Record Groups 57 and 77 at the National Archives. Thurman Wilkins, *Clarence King: A Biography* (1958; rev. ed., 1988), contains a detailed account of King's life, with a bibliography that lists all of King's writings and the whereabouts of many of his scattered letters. Henry Adams, *The Education of Henry Adams* (1918), contains glowing passages about King and has been a principal means of keeping his name alive. Richard A. Bartlett, *Great Surveys of the American West* (1962), is an excellent source on the King survey. Van Wyck Brooks, *New England: Indian Summer, 1865–1915* (1940), contains a vivid literary assessment of King. See also S. F. Emmons, "Biographical Memoir of Clarence King, 1842–1901," National Academy of Sciences, *Biographical Memoirs* 6 (1909): 25–55, for an early treatment of King's career by a professional colleague. William H. Goetzmann, *Exploration and Empire: The Explorer and the Scientist in the Winning of the American West* (1966), considers the full sweep of King's services as a government geologist. James D. Hague, ed., *Clarence King Memoirs: The Helmet of Mambrino* (1904), offers intriguing reminiscences of King by twelve close friends as well as an autobiographical sketch by King. Patricia O'Toole, *The Five of Hearts: An Intimate Portrait of Henry Adams and His Friends, 1880–1918* (1990), places King gracefully in the center of the Hay-Adams milieu. Mary C. Rabbitt, *Minerals, Lands, and Geology for the Common Defense and General Welfare*, vol. 1, *Before 1879* (1979), and vol. 2, *1879–1904* (1980), presents a history of both the antecedents of the USGS and its first twenty-five years. Michael L. Smith, *Pacific Visions: California Scientists and the Environment, 1850–1915* (1987), discusses the work of the California Geological Survey, including the period of King's membership.

THURMAN WILKINS

KING, Edward Smith (8 Sept. 1848–27 Mar. 1896), journalist and author, was born in Middlefield, Massachusetts, the son of Edward King, a Methodist minister, and Lorinda Smith. When King was three years old his father disappeared during an ocean voyage. His mother became a schoolteacher, and subsequently married Samuel W. Fisher, a clergyman, in 1860 in Huntington, Massachusetts. King's stepfather later abandoned the ministry, became a teacher and mill worker, and provided his stepson's basic education.

King's journalism career began in 1864 when he left home to become a reporter for the *Springfield (Mass.) Daily Union*. In 1866 he joined the staff of the *Springfield (Mass.) Republican*, and two years later *My Paris* was published. Davis's first book is an idealistic tale of Parisian life based on his impressions of the city while covering the Paris exposition of 1867.

In 1870 King became a reporter for the *Boston Morning Journal*. His first major assignment was as a correspondent during the Franco-Prussian War; he also investigated the activities of the Commune of 1871. King enthusiastically thrust himself into the thick of the conflict, assisting with the wounded and twice getting arrested by the Germans as a spy. Two novels came from this experience: *Kentucky's Love* (1873), which is an adventure tale about war correspondents, and *Under the Red Flag* (1895), which is set in Paris and deals directly with the events of the Commune shortly before its bitter and bloody end.

King published a series of articles about the post–Civil War South, which were collected as *The Great South* (1875). During King's travels through the southern states to gather material for these articles, he met George Washington Cable. The two men became great friends, and King helped Cable get his early stories published in *Scribner's Monthly*.

King lived in Europe from 1875 to 1888, but he continued to work as a correspondent for the *Boston Morning Journal*. Throughout this period, he covered the Carlist Wars in Spain and the Russo-Turkish War of 1877–1878 in the Balkans. It was during this time that King's two volumes of poetry appeared: *Echoes from the Orient* (1880) and *A Venetian Lover* (1887). Two novels were also published during his European residence. *The Gentle Savage* (1883) dramatizes the difficulties experienced by an Oklahoma Indian when he is brought up amid European manners. *The Golden Spike* (1886) depicts the opening of the Northern Pacific Railroad, which King had reported on during one of his rare jaunts to America. Other books to appear during this time were *French Political Leaders* (1876) and *Europe in Storm and Calm* (1885), the latter being a compilation of newspaper articles describing European life. He also contributed several travel sketches to a

travel book, *On the Rhine* (1881), and wrote a critical introduction to M. French Sheldon's *Salammbô of Gustave Flaubert* (1885).

King returned to America in 1888 and wrote columns for the *New York Morning Journal* and for *Collier's Once a Week*. In 1893 he published his finest novel, *Joseph Zalmonah*, an exposé of the sweatshops and social abyss of New York. He continued to produce fiction and poetry that frequently appeared in the newspapers for which he wrote. Other projects in his later years were ostensibly intended to take advantage of his vast knowledge of Europe, especially *Cassell's Complete Pocket Guide to Europe* (1891), which he compiled and updated for subsequent editions. King never married, and at the time of his death he lived in Brooklyn with his half-sister and her husband. He died in Brooklyn of an undisclosed illness.

Though he thought of himself as a serious artist and had aspirations to be an important poet, King may best be remembered as a hard-working journalist who distinguished himself as a war correspondent and chronicler of some of the late nineteenth century's most important events. His background as a journalist in search of the unvarnished truth led to the writing of his fine novel, *Joseph Zalmonah*. With its publication, King, along with many other American journalist-authors of the 1890s, struck a blow in the fight for literary realism by demonstrating that poverty and the problems of the cities could be compelling subject matter for social observation.

• Additional information is in Stanley Kunitz and Howard Haycraft, *American Authors, 1600–1900* (1938), and the *Dictionary of American Biography*. Obituaries are in the *New York Evening Post*, 28 Mar. 1896, and the *Springfield (Mass.) Republican*, 29 Mar. 1896.

THOMAS NEWHOUSE

KING, Emma Belle (5 June 1873–1 July 1966), Shaker eldress, was born in Providence, Rhode Island, the daughter of Daniel Sylvester King, a carpenter and horsecar conductor, and Nancy Ellen Rowley. Emma and her sister Mary Ellen King were placed with the Shakers (United Society of Believers in Christ's Second Appearing) in Canterbury, New Hampshire, in 1878. There is some indication that a brother, Daniel S. King, arrived several years later in 1881. Although there is little record of Emma's parents or how she came to be placed in Canterbury, it is clear that her mother lodged with the Shakers at one point. Of her father's whereabouts the records say nothing. King does refer, however, in a memorial written for Sister Lizzie Horton, to a period in her childhood in which she was "in grief over the demise of a much loved father."

Unlike their sister, both Mary Ellen and Daniel left the Shakers, in 1893 and 1891, respectively. Emma, however, decided to stay, despite offers of adoption and inheritance from relatives in Rhode Island, and in 1894 she signed the Covenant of the United Society of Believers.

King had a predisposition to ill health, though her constitution seemed to improve somewhat after living with the Shakers. She learned all the domestic skills that were taught to the young women of the community and was known as an exceptionally good dressmaker, supplying many of the children and sisters with dresses over the years. King also sang first alto with a quartet of sisters. She was especially noted, however, as a studious child and became an assistant teacher in the Shaker school at the age of eighteen.

King attended, along with several other sisters, courses at Plymouth State College and received a teacher's diploma. She taught with Jessie Evans and Lillian Phelps from 1891 through 1912. Bertha Lindsay described her as "a very exacting person . . . she demanded the best of herself and those she taught." King's philosophy of education is evident in an essay written for the teacher's institute in which she states, "To cultivate self-reliance in any branch of education, the teacher must be guided by the rule—'Never do for a pupil what he can possibly do for himself' . . . never answer a question which the pupil by deliberate thought or patient research, is able, himself, to answer."

In 1913 King was appointed associate eldress and given responsibility for the young people of the community. She became the eldress at Canterbury in 1920 upon the death of Jennie Fish, though she had been acting eldress since 1918 during Fish's illness, with Phelps as her associate. In 1947 King assumed the additional responsibilities of the Central Ministry, joining Frances Hall of Pittsfield, Massachusetts, and later Gertrude Soule of Sabbathday Lake, Maine. King was also instrumental in the closure of Mount Lebanon, New York, in 1947, presiding over the move of the Central Ministry to Hancock, Massachusetts, and then to Canterbury, New Hampshire, in 1957. Mount Lebanon had been struggling since the Great Depression, and members there were aware of it. Large portions of the property had been sold, and furniture and farm equipment was being dispersed regularly to pay bills almost a decade before the decision was made to move the Mount Lebanon sisters to Hancock village. King had been advised that consolidation could only strengthen the position of the remaining members by better using fewer resources. While many viewed the closing of Mount Lebanon, the seat of Shaker leadership for almost two centuries, as a sign of the failure of Shakerism, King did not. King's fine mind and direct style of leadership, honed by thirty years of service as eldress to the Canterbury community, was helpful as she was called on to help guide the dwindling number of members of the United Society of Believers.

King sold and donated many documents and objects to John S. Williams during the 1950s, a personal collection that later became the Shaker Museum at Old Chatham, New York. Such an exchange served two driving purposes for King: to preserve Shaker history and to gain financial aid during what were trying times for the Shakers. Documents are still available to researchers in the Emma B. King Library at the museum.

In 1956 King wrote *A Shaker's Viewpoint* in an attempt to address public sentiment that Shakerism had failed and to remind people of the principles of Shakerism, which she believed had been proven and would continue to influence individuals in all walks of life. True to the Shaker notion of the "gifts of the season," King reminded the reader that the world moves forward. When Hall died in 1957, Emma moved to first position in the ministry. In 1959 she established the Shaker Central Trust Fund to be administered by a board of trustees made up of representatives from each remaining village and their legal advisers. The trust consolidated existing financial assets and was the repository of funds derived from the sale of properties and assets at villages that closed. The intent was to provide for the future of the remaining members, preserve Shaker history, and educate the world's people about Shakerism. King continued in the lead ministry position until 1964, at which time failing health required that she resign. After the closing of Hancock village in 1960 and the demise of the last male member, Delmer Wilson, at Sabbathday Lake in 1961, King and Gertrude Soule, in consultation with members of both villages, decided to close the society to new members in 1965. Much speculation surrounds this decision, but little can be stated with certainty. Some historians suggest that King and Soule were concerned that the young people of the time who might be attracted to communal living were not necessarily inclined to the celibacy and routine required by the Shakers. Others suggest that there were concerns that some new members might be attracted by reports of a substantial trust fund. Finally, there was no living Shaker elder to serve as minister and teacher to new male members, so no men could have signed the covenant. King died in Canterbury, New Hampshire.

• Information on King and some of her papers are located in the archives at Canterbury Shaker Village, Canterbury, N.H., and at the Shaker Museum and Library, Old Chatham, N.Y. Stephen J. Stein, *The Shaker Experience in America* (1992), is an excellent source. See also Elmer R. Pearson and Julia Neal, *The Shaker Image*, 2d ed. (1994), which includes photos of King and her contemporaries; and Bertha Lindsay, *Seasoned with Grace* (1986), which contains relevant reminiscences. An obituary is in the *Shaker Quarterly* 6, no. 3 (Fall 1966).

ERIKA M. BUTLER

KING, Ernest Joseph (23 Nov. 1878–25 June 1956), naval officer, was born in Lorain, Ohio, the son of James Clydesdale King, a railroad shop foreman, and Elizabeth Keam. King earned an appointment through competitive examination to the U.S. Naval Academy in 1897. After brief duty on the cruiser *San Francisco* in Cuban waters during the Spanish-American War in 1898, King graduated fourth in the class of 1901. He served between 1901 and 1906 on a variety of warships, including the cruiser *Cincinnati* in Asiatic waters during the Russo-Japanese War of 1904–1905 and the battleships *Illinois* and *Alabama*. King became a drill master at the Naval Academy in 1906. In 1905 he married Martha Egerton; they had seven children.

Extremely ambitious and impatient with the rate of promotion, in 1909 King accepted the patronage of a rising young admiral, Hugo Osterhaus, commander of the Battleship Division, Atlantic Fleet. As Osterhaus's flag secretary, King met other important senior officers and learned how to organize a flag officer's duties. After a short tour as engineer officer on the battleship *New Hampshire* in 1910, King rejoined Osterhaus as flag secretary in 1911, when the admiral assumed command of the Atlantic Fleet. King returned to the U.S. Naval Academy in 1912 as executive officer of the Naval Engineering Experiment Station, where he also edited professional papers for the Naval Institute *Proceedings*.

King received his first command in 1914, the aging destroyer *Terry*, and then commanded the new 1,000-ton destroyer *Cassin* as part of the Atlantic Fleet Destroyer Flotilla. Though stimulated by the demands of seamanship and innovative tactics that accompanied the destroyer command, King's career ambitions led him once again to accept the patronage of an influential admiral when in 1915 he joined Vice Admiral Henry T. Mayo's staff. As chief of staff for the commander in chief of the Atlantic Fleet, King learned the art of command, participated in operational planning, and continued to make important career contacts. King accompanied Mayo to Europe during the First World War to inspect U.S. naval forces in Britain and to confer with wartime civilian and military leaders. King visited the battlefields and observed British fleet operations. His role as Mayo's chief assistant during the war earned King the Navy Cross.

Career opportunities diminished after the war as the navy cut back on manpower and scrapped warships under the terms of the Washington Naval Arms Limitation Treaty. King had to settle for command of the Naval Postgraduate School in Annapolis in 1919, where he was frustrated in attempts at curriculum reform. When Admiral Henry B. Wilson, whom King thought incompetent, became superintendent of the naval academy, King asked for a transfer in 1921 to command a supply ship. He searched anxiously for a better assignment, finding two fields for professional advancement in the postwar navy, the submarine service and naval aviation. He commanded a submarine flotilla and the submarine base at New London, Connecticut, between 1922 and 1926. King earned national publicity when in late 1925 he directed the recovery of the sunken submarine *S-51*. Next King took flight training at Pensacola Naval Air Station (an unusual step for an older officer), commanded a seaplane tender, and in 1928 became an assistant to Chief of the Bureau of Aeronautics William Moffett.

King struggled with shore billets, hated bureaucrats, and feuded with his superior officer Moffett. He escaped from the stifling Washington bureaucracy finally in June 1930 to take command of the aircraft carrier *Lexington*. When Moffett died in the crash of the airship *Akron*, King returned to Washington and became the second chief of the Bureau of Aeronautics in April 1933. It was not a happy assignment. King fought continually with naval aviation pioneer Captain John H. Towers, who thought that he should have replaced Moffett as the bureau chief. King's problem with Towers stemmed not only from personal animosity but also from fundamental differences over the role of naval aviation in future wars. King continued to express impatience as well with bureaucrats and superior officers, whom he found overly conservative in adopting innovations in naval tactics, weapons, and engineering and more concerned with protecting their jobs than in improving the naval service.

King welcomed the chance to leave Washington in June 1936 to command a force of seaplanes. In 1938 he took command of the aircraft carrier battle force comprised of the *Saratoga*, *Lexington*, and *Ranger*. In 1938 King's battle force brilliantly executed a surprise carrier aircraft strike against Pearl Harbor as part of War Game Problem XIX. He later felt that the navy had failed to learn anything from his demonstration. Now past sixty, King's naval career seemed about to conclude in 1939 without fulfilling his dream of becoming the chief of naval operations (CNO), the navy's top command. President Franklin Roosevelt had appointed Rear Admiral Harold Stark instead, and King went to the Navy General Board, an advisory committee of senior naval officers established in 1900 that was by 1939 little more than a place for older officers to sit until retirement. Nevertheless King used this time to reflect on strategy and organization and to make recommendations later tested in actual warfare between 1941 and 1945. King advised that, in the event of a war in the Pacific against Japan, the United States needed to pursue an offensive war in the Central Pacific rather than hold a defensive line from Pearl Harbor to Midway. He recommended the better integration of small, fast warships, aircraft, and submarines into the fleet to operate with battleships and aircraft carriers. He also criticized the lack of preparation for war.

King's criticisms of the navy while on the General Board probably convinced Chief of Naval Operations Stark, Secretary of the Navy Frank Knox, and President Roosevelt to give King command in December 1940 of the Patrol Forces, U.S. Fleet, in the Atlantic. German U-boat activities there threatened to undermine American neutrality in the war that had broken out in Europe in September 1939. Roosevelt re-created the defunct Atlantic Fleet, and in February 1941 King became its commander in chief, vigorously prosecuting antisubmarine warfare and convoy operations against Germany in an undeclared (and illegal) Atlantic war. The Japanese surprise air attack on American bases at Pearl Harbor ended the ambiguity of neutrality and propelled King, a constant critic of the lack of naval preparedness and planning, to the position of commander in chief of the U.S. Fleet (COMINCH) on 30 December 1941. As COMINCH King had full authority over all operational planning and fleet operations, reporting directly to the president. For the moment, Stark remained the CNO with vague authority over long-range planning and procurement and supply functions.

King immediately initiated a strategy of a two-front war. He accepted American commitment to defeat Germany first in the Atlantic war but insisted that the navy hold the Hawaii-Midway defensive line as the base for an offensive against Japan in the Pacific. He recognized at once that, in order to pursue this strategy, he needed more authority over the allocation and distribution of material and manpower—authority then held by the CNO and civilian secretaries. Realizing that the divided lines of responsibility could hinder the war effort, Stark voluntarily resigned as CNO in March 1942 and urged the president to appoint King combined COMINCH and CNO. Roosevelt agreed, apparently with some reluctance, to make King the most powerful naval officer in American history.

Combining COMINCH and CNO gave King the means to guide naval operations more aggressively during the Second World War but initiated a bitter struggle for power with Secretary Knox and Undersecretary of the Navy James Forrestal (who became secretary in 1944). Knox, Forrestal, and their allies in the navy, such as Vice Chief of Naval Operations Frederick Horne, intrigued throughout the war to take the CNO office away from King and to maintain more civilian authority over personnel and resource procurement policies, most notably control over the shipyards and shipbuilding. King's fight with Forrestal became especially bitter and personal as the COMINCH sought to organize the navy along the lines of a modern business corporation, decentralizing authority by preserving some of the old bureau system.

Throughout the war King conducted strategic planning through his position on the Joint Chiefs of Staff (JCS), created by Roosevelt in February 1942, and to a lesser extent with British strategists on the Combined Chiefs of Staff (CCS). King's relationship to both bodies defined his contribution to the conduct (and outcome) of the Second World War. He usually placed naval interests ahead of all others during deliberations in these strategic planning organizations. He maintained that the U.S. Navy was the best force with which to protect the U.S. coastal frontiers and to carry the offensive against the Japanese in the Pacific. This parochialism brought him into conflict with his Allied counterparts over the choice of operational theaters, timetables, and command decisions and into rivalries with U.S. military leaders such as General Douglas MacArthur, commander of U.S. forces in the southwest Pacific, and General Henry H. Arnold, chief of the Army Air Force and fellow JCS member. Fortunately, King developed a good working relationship with Army Chief of Staff George C. Marshall on the JCS despite his deep disagreement with Marshall's call for unified theater commanders to control all air, ground, and sea forces. King and Marshall cooperated in pressing for a cross-channel strategy against Germany while keeping the offensive against Japan in the Pacific.

King was a major architect of strategy during the Second World War, at least General Marshall's equal in laying out steps for a two-front war and in selecting areas for operations and the distribution of forces. Though he listened to the advice of his commanders, particularly that of Admiral Chester Nimitz, whom King selected to command the Pacific Fleet, King determined the pace and shape of the Pacific war more than any other person. Soon after Pearl Harbor he pursued a relentless offensive against Japan that resulted in the critical battles of the Coral Sea and Midway. He concentrated on blocking Japanese advances into the South Pacific by pressing the Guadalcanal operation and launched a southwest Pacific offensive against Japanese naval forces in the Solomons. King's main Pacific strategy, based partly on War Plan ORANGE (a study of possible war against Japan begun years before at the Naval War College), called for an American advance against Japan through the Central Pacific. This strategy led to the American attack on Tarawa in the Gilbert Islands to establish an advanced base from which to bomb Japanese forces in the Marshall Islands.

King's Central Pacific strategy confronted opposition. Planners on the JCS and CCS complained that King's plans drained resources, particularly landing craft, from Mediterranean and European operations. U.S. Army planners preferred to attack Japan from the southwest Pacific theater through the Philippines and Formosa, a strategy that put General MacArthur in command of the American offensive in the Pacific. Even Admiral Nimitz told King that a shortage of ships and men made it difficult to seize Japanese strongholds in the Marshall, Carolina, and Mariana islands. In response King modified his Central Pacific strategy, bypassing some Japanese-held islands and accepting a second offensive against Japan through the Philippine-Formosa route, which resulted in the American naval victory at the battle of the Philippine Sea.

The world war gave King the power to determine strategy, run an organization, and get the job done his way, a task that he could never have handled in peacetime. When Japan surrendered in August 1945, King seemed lost, uncertain what his job would be now that the fighting had ended. To avoid criticism of the navy, he quickly abolished the COMINCH position in October 1945 and recommended that Pacific Fleet commander Nimitz become CNO. King never retired from the navy, maintaining a postwar office in the Pentagon, but he had no role in Cold War naval organization, strategies, or policies. A stroke incapacitated him in 1949, and he died seven years later at the Portsmouth Naval Hospital.

King was a professional naval officer comfortable with duty at sea and ill suited temperamentally for shore duty or dealing with bureaucracy of any kind. A student of tactical and technological innovation, King displayed impatience with conservative bureaucrats or naval officers who opposed experimentation and change. His intense, sometimes mean-spirited and abusive personality fit the wartime demands of the U.S. Navy, which needed a leader to crush incompetence, barrel through obstacles, and do what was necessary to get the fleet and department organization to fight and win the war at sea. In the end, the Second World War made King one of the greatest naval leaders in American history.

• A large collection of King's papers are in the Manuscript Division of the Library of Congress. Collections of papers by and about King are also on deposit in the Operational Archives, Naval History Division, Washington Navy Yard, and in the Naval Historical Collection, Naval War College, Newport, R.I. Autobiographical material can be found in Ernest J. King and Walter Muir Whitehill, *Fleet Admiral King: A Naval Record* (1952). The best biography of King is Thomas B. Buell, *Master of Sea Power: A Biography of Fleet Admiral Ernest J. King* (1980). King's role in the Second World War can be traced in Robert William Love, Jr., "Ernest Joseph King," in *The Chiefs of Naval Operations* (1980).

JEFFERY M. DORWART

KING, Grace Elizabeth (29 Nov. 1852?–14 Jan. 1932), author, was born in New Orleans, Louisiana, the daughter of William Woodson King, a prominent lawyer, and Sarah Ann Miller. In the spring of 1862, during the Federal occupation of New Orleans, the family fled to L'Embarras Plantation in south central Louisiana. Over the next three years, Grace King was tutored in history, French and English literature, handwriting, and the Presbyterian catechism by her parents and her maternal grandmother. Financially ruined by their loyalty to the Confederacy, the family returned to New Orleans after the Civil War, and William King slowly rebuilt his legal career.

Grace King enrolled as a day student at the Institut St. Louis, a school for girls, where she excelled in French. After graduating in 1868, she studied modern languages and English composition at the Sylvester-Larned Institut and the Institut Cénas. An early influence on King's love of history and French culture was Charles Gayarré, a family friend and noted Creole historian. After her parents died, King moved with two of her sisters to a Greek Revival house on Coliseum Street, where she frequently entertained local and visiting intellectuals at her "Friday afternoons." She never married.

In her *Memories of a Southern Woman of Letters* (1932), King says she began to write seriously in 1885 after a "rankling taunt" from Richard Watson Gilder, editor of the *Century Magazine*. When King complained that New Orleans author George Washington Cable insulted his city by favoring "colored people over white" and "the quadroons over the Creoles," Gilder asked, "If Cable is so false to you, why do not some of you write better?" On the recommendation of Charles Dudley Warner, the resulting story, "Monsieur Motte," appeared in the first issue of the *New Princeton Review* in January 1886. This sentimental account of an impoverished young white girl at a Creole school based on the Institut St. Louis appealed to readers of local-color fiction. In contrast to many re-

gionalist writers, however, King made limited use of dialect, even in her portrayal of the faithful quadroon Marcélite. Warner, an editor for *Harper's*, invited King to Hartford, Connecticut, and introduced her to his neighbors, Samuel (Mark Twain) and Olivia Clemens. The Clemenses became close friends of King, who visited them at their rented villa in Florence in 1892 on her first trip to Europe.

King's first novel, *Monsieur Motte* (1888), incorporates her earliest short story into a four-part structure of contrasting units that Robert Bush compares to a sonata. According to Robert Bush, "*Monsieur Motte* as much as any work of fiction reflects the social history of Reconstruction New Orleans" (*Grace King: A Southern Destiny*, p. 97). Realistic in many of her details, King was nevertheless biased by her devotion to the "Lost Cause." Although she often portrays a mutual devotion between black and white women, she also reveals her bitterness toward African Americans who abandoned their former masters. King was equally bitter toward whites of any social class who profited from the fall of the South.

In 1892 five of King's long Louisiana stories were collected in *Tales of a Time and Place*. The opening selection, "Bayou L'Ombre, an Incident of the War," describes the shock of two adolescent sisters when their slaves abruptly answer the call to freedom: "This, this they had not thought of, this they had never read about, this their imagination in wildest flights had not ventured upon. This was not a superficial conflict to sweep the earth with cannons and mow it with sabres; this was an earthquake which had rent it asunder, exposing the quivering organs of hidden life." The thirteen stories in King's second collection, *Balcony Stories* (1893), are generally short and subtle, perhaps an effect of her reading of Guy de Maupassant's short fiction. The saddest of King's tragic quadroons is the title character of "The Little Convent Girl," who drowns silently at the story's conclusion.

During the 1890s King also wrote many historical and biographical works. Encouraged by editor Hamilton Wright Mabie, she undertook her first serious archival research for *Jean Baptiste Le Moyne, Sieur de Bienville* (1892), the earliest biography on the founder of New Orleans. King collaborated with Tulane University professor John R. Ficklen, a fellow officer of the Louisiana Historical Society, on the textbook *A History of Louisiana* (1893). Her *New Orleans, the Place and the People* (1895), praised by William Dean Howells and Edmund Wilson, was long considered the best work on the city for a general audience. Two biographical sketches for *Harper's*, "Madame la Baronne Blaze de Bury" (1893) and "Theo. Bentzon—Madame Th. Blanc" (1896), praise the influential Frenchwomen who welcomed King to their Paris salons.

King's later works include an episodic, largely autobiographical novel of the Reconstruction years, *The Pleasant Ways of St. Médard* (1916), and *La Dame de Sainte Hermine* (1924), a historical romance set in New Orleans in the second quarter of the eighteenth century, Bienville's era. Both books depict various levels of society at critical moments in Louisiana's history. Similarly, the Civil War and Reconstruction dominate the autobiography, which was published posthumously the year King died in New Orleans. A late episode in *Memories of a Southern Woman of Letters* is her 1926 visit to Robert E. Lee's tomb: "We felt as Moses did before the burning bush, 'the place whereon thou standest is holy ground.'"

King was elected a fellow of the Royal Society of England in 1913, and in 1918 the French government awarded her the Palmes d'Officier de l'Instruction Publique. In her memoirs, however, King is most moved by the elaborate tribute of the Louisiana Historical Society in 1923—"and the band played 'Dixie.'" During her life King was well known as a champion of New Orleans, particularly its aristocratic Creole heritage. Upon King's death, writer Dorothy Dix said, "She has done more than any one woman for Southern literature." Subsequently, however, King's work received little attention until the 1970s. In the final quarter of the twentieth century, she benefited from a new attention to women writers, gender issues, ethnic groups, and genres (such as history, autobiography, and local-color fiction) that had formerly been slighted. Helen Taylor concludes that King, like Ruth McEnery Stuart and Kate Chopin, is "to a modern sensibility—deeply racist" (p. xiii); yet, these three Louisiana authors were among "the first group of women to be accepted by northern editors and publishers as professional writers" (p. xii).

• The Grace King Papers in the Department of Archives and Manuscripts, Louisiana State University, Baton Rouge, contain thousands of letters and documents, along with photographs and other memorabilia and many journals and manuscripts. Works by King not mentioned in the text include *De Soto and His Men in the Land of Florida* (1898), the children's book *Stories from Louisiana History* (with John R. Ficklen [1905]), *Creole Families of New Orleans* (1921), *Mount Vernon on the Potomac: History of the Mount Vernon Ladies' Association of the Union* (1929), several uncollected stories, and several uncollected biographical sketches written for magazines. Some of these stories and sketches, with other representative works, are gathered by Robert Bush in *Grace King of New Orleans: A Selection of Her Writings* (1973), prefaced by Bush's long introduction. Bush made extensive use of the Grace King Papers in his biography *Grace King: A Southern Destiny* (1983). David Kirby takes a psychoanalytic approach to King's works in *Grace King* (1980). The most complete bibliography is Bess Vaughan, "A Bio-Bibliography of Grace Elizabeth King," *Louisiana Historical Quarterly* 17 (1934): 752–70. Chapters on King appear in Anne Goodwyn Jones, *Tomorrow Is Another Day: The Woman Writer in the South, 1859–1936* (1981), and Helen Taylor, *Gender, Race, and Region in the Writings of Grace King, Ruth McEnery Stuart, and Kate Chopin* (1989). An obituary is on the front page of the *New Orleans Times-Picayune*, 15 Jan. 1932.

JOAN WYLIE HALL

KING, Henry (11 May 1842–15 Mar. 1915), journalist and author, was born in Salem, Ohio, the son of Selah Williams King and Eliza Aleshire. King developed an affinity for the Republican party early in life when he went with his father, who was a delegate, to hear Abraham Lincoln at the Bloomington convention in 1856. The family had moved to Illinois several years earlier. There he received a common school education and learned the printer's trade. He returned later as a reporter to cover the Lincoln-Douglas debates. When the Civil War broke out, he became known as "the boy orator" for his frequent exhortations in the state. Calling for volunteers to serve the North, King himself served four years, becoming a captain.

Following the Civil War, King held various newspaper positions in the Midwest. He edited the *Quincy (Ill.) Whig* and a series of publications in Kansas: the *Kansas State Record*, the *Weekly Commonwealth*, and the *Topeka Daily Capital*. He also briefly edited the *Kansas Magazine*, a literary publication. King also contributed historical and literary articles to national magazines, such as the *Century*. These were often based on his reminiscences of the Lincoln campaign. He was described by *St. Louis Globe-Democrat* correspondent Walter B. Stevens as "one of the most polished, forceful writers of his generation."

King made his lasting reputation with the *Globe-Democrat*, which was Republican in its political philosophy despite its name. He started as a political and editorial writer in 1883, along with working on special assignments. By 1897 King had become the editor, taking over from Joseph B. McCullagh, renowned in newspaper circles as a great managing editor and for his close relationship to President Andrew Johnson. King had assumed many of McCullagh's duties several years before the editor's suicide in late 1896.

King earned his national reputation as a muckraking editor. The *Globe-Democrat* joined papers around the country in denouncing graft and bribery in local government. On one occasion, King himself examined the St. Louis "auditor's books for several hours to see whether there was collusion in the granting of contracts" by city hall officials. He criticized corruption and inefficiency in city services, claiming, for example, that the police were "so deeply occupied assessing the force and making presents to the police board that reports of burglaries" annoyed them. He claimed to defend the "greatest good for the greatest number," an editorial principle gauged to appeal to the waves of immigrants, mostly German, arriving in that prosperous and expanding city.

To appeal further to this new, mass audience, King adopted many of the techniques of "yellow journals" so prominent in the East. He first began using large pictures and heavy black headlines around the time of the Spanish-American War. King later added three-column cartoons on the front page, more cartoons on the sports pages, a prominent society section with "descriptions of the food served and the clothes worn by the women," a real estate listing, and a page for bicyclists. King also inaugurated a table of contents on page one, an unusual procedure at the turn of the century. During the national political conventions, King would send at least four artists to record the activities.

The *Globe-Democrat*'s Sunday edition was the most popular, with its colored comics and light, interesting articles. King's conservative nature, however, prevented his *Globe-Democrat* from equaling the reckless news making of William Randolph Hearst's *New York Journal*.

King was a strong proponent of journalism education and active in Missouri newspaper organizations. At the invitation of his friend Walter Williams, the founder of the world's first professional journalism school at the University of Missouri, King presented a series of lectures to students in anticipation of the opening of the school. At the *Globe-Democrat* King encouraged many young journalists-to-be to follow their inspirations to become reporters. As early as 1880 King had addressed the Missouri Press Association, noting, "A town without a newspaper is a town ready to fence in and whitewash; a settlement that lacks a printing office must get one or be sold for taxes." He was the first president of the Missouri Republican Editorial Association and worked with Williams at the World's Press Parliament at the Louisiana Purchase Centennial Exposition in 1904. King contributed to the history of journalism with *American Journalism* (1871), which was his address before the Editors' and Publishers' Association of Kansas, and with "The Story of Kansas and Kansas Newspapers" for the *History of Kansas Newspapers* (1916).

Evincing his love for newspapering and his confidence in the power of the press in the lives of the people, King refused two appointments to the U.S. Senate. He was never a candidate for office. He believed his newspaper offered him more independence of thought than a political position, even if, as he admitted, "newspapers are influenced in a measure by the business interests of the community." His newspaper, moreover, benefited from the influence of St. Louis businessmen, since he had "learned that their success is indispensable in promoting welfare and progress." His editorials, which were "a marked and distinguishing feature of the paper," reflected his devotion to the Republican business ideology of the late nineteenth century.

Henry King, with a common school education, led the *Globe-Democrat* "into the front rank of metropolitan journalism," according to Jim Hart, who wrote a history about the newspaper in 1961. Once, when asked for biographical material, King wrote, "Life generally uneventful, simply a story of trying to do my best wherever placed." He believed that "news is history, not opinion" and "the interests of the community are the interests of the newspapers." He was married in 1861 to Maria Louise Lane; they had two children. King died in St. Louis.

• There are no manuscript collections of Henry King. For information on his career, see Jim Hart, *The History of the St. Louis Globe-Democrat* (1961); William Taft, *Missouri Newspapers* (1964); Charles C. Clayton, *Little Mack: Joseph B. Mc-Cullagh of the St. Louis Globe-Democrat* (1969). For biographical information, see J. W. Leonard, *The Book of St. Louisans* (1906); Walter B. Stevens, *St. Louis, History of the Fourth City*, vol. 3 (1909); and King's obituaries on 16 Mar. 1915 in the following papers: *St. Louis Globe-Democrat*, *St. Louis Republic*, *St. Louis Post Dispatch*, *Kansas City Times*, and *Kansas City Journal*.

WILLIAM H. TAFT

KING, Henry (24 Jan. 1886–29 June 1982), film director, was born in Christiansburg, Virginia, the son of Isaac Green King and Martha Ellen Sumner, farmers. When King was twelve his father died, and he went to work for the Norfolk and Western railroad. Attracted to the stage since childhood, King left the railroad to work as an actor in touring stock companies. In 1912 he began acting in films for the Lubin Company in California. As he had in the theater, he made suggestions for staging scenes, which led to his directing films beginning in 1916. His 1919 film *23½ Hours Leave* for producer Thomas Ince was one of the most successful pictures of the year.

King's first major artistic success, and one of the films on which his reputation as a director stands, was the 1921 film *Tol'able David*, a nostalgic look at nineteenth-century rural America produced for his own company, Inspiration Pictures. King shot the film in his native Virginia, and his direction provides not only realistic detail but a sensitivity to the lives of the farm people. King's command of the narrative style of filmmaking was ahead of his contemporaries and was acclaimed not only by critics in America but by Russian filmmaker and theorist V. I. Pudovkin, who used examples of King's direction of this film in his 1929 book *Film Technique*.

King went even farther to find locations for two films in the early 1920s. While American filmmaking was becoming concentrated in Hollywood, King's *The White Sister* (1922), which was a triumph for Lillian Gish and created a new star in Ronald Colman, and *Romola* (1924) both take great advantage of Italian locations and sets. King returned to Hollywood to direct for producer Samuel Goldwyn, for whom his two biggest hits were the delicately handled melodrama *Stella Dallas* (1925) and the outdoor romance *The Winning of Barbara Worth* (1926). In the latter, King cast in a small role a cowboy extra named Gary Cooper, beginning Cooper's long career.

Like many silent-film directors, King made the transition to sound films relatively easily, with only a few fights with the sound engineers. King's emphasis on storytelling in film was well suited to sound films. In 1930 King began his 32-year career for Fox Studios (which became 20th Century-Fox in 1935). He directed two films with Will Rogers, and the second, *State Fair* (1933), was not only the best of the three films made from the story but such a success that it temporarily saved Fox from receivership in the middle of the depression.

Producer Darryl Zanuck, whose screenwriters provided the kind of narrative scripts King did so well, allowed him to become the studio's most popular and commercially successful director. King's experience enabled him to handle such big historical pictures as *Lloyds of London* (1936), which made Tyrone Power a star, and *In Old Chicago* (1937), whose fire sequence King shot against a setting sun to emphasize the brightness and heat of the flames. King could also do big musical films, such as *Alexander's Ragtime Band* (1938), based on the songs and career of Irving Berlin.

King's *Jesse James* (1939), from a Nunnally Johnson screenplay, was one of the most entertaining westerns of the 1930s. King's insistence on shooting in James's native Missouri added to the realistic visual detail of the film. *The Black Swan* (1942) is not only witty (the script is by Ben Hecht) but is one of the most visually gorgeous of all the Technicolor pirate films. King's 1943 religious film *The Song of Bernadette* shows King's restraint at its best, especially in comparison with other religious films. Jennifer Jones won an Academy Award for her performance in the film.

King's direction of Zanuck's 1944 biography *Wilson* is vivid and detailed, but the script, by Lamar Trotti, is never completely compelling. Although the film received five Oscar nominations, including one for King and one for Best Picture, as writer Deems Taylor noted in the 1950 edition of *A Pictorial History of the Movies*, "The public was more interested in seeing films of World War II than the story of the man who tried to prevent it." King's 1945 film *A Bell for Adano* contains one of his finest sequences, in which the women of an Italian village (built on the Fox backlot) come into the town square to greet returning soldiers. King's camera movements following the different people and his decision to shoot the final meeting as a long shot from above against the harsh shadows of the square add to the emotion of the moment.

In 1949 King returned to the real Italy for an entertaining swashbuckler, *Prince of Foxes*, although Zanuck insisted that the film be shot in black and white rather than in color, since King's previous color swashbuckler, *Captain from Castile* (1947), was one of his few films to both go over budget and lose money.

Twelve O'Clock High (1949) is a powerful drama of the pressures of command, with Gregory Peck as a commander of a bomber group in World War II. The visual details of the huts, the offices, and the planes show King's attention to detail and make the film better than MGM's glossier film on the same subject the same year, *Command Decision*. The following year King and Peck collaborated again, this time on the classic western *The Gunfighter*, one of the first "adult" westerns of the 1950s. The story told of an aging gunfighter who wants to retire but cannot escape his past. Although studio head Spyros Skouras hated the realistic moustache King had Peck wear, the critics loved the film (more than audiences, for whom the film was ahead of its time). In 1951 King returned to the rural South, this time to Georgia for *I'd Climb the Highest Mountain*. Lamar Trotti's excellent script gave King a chance to capture the turn-of-the-century rural America of picnics and Sunday-go-to-meetings. There is warmth without excess sentimentality.

In the early 1950s Fox introduced the wide-screen process CinemaScope, which King used very effectively in *Untamed* and *Love Is a Many-Splendored Thing* (both 1955). The former film was shot in South Africa; the latter, in Hong Kong (although the hill the two lovers meet on was in Malibu, Calif.). Zanuck's production of Ernest Hemingway's *The Sun Also Rises* (1957), like his earlier King-directed *The Snows of Kilimanjaro* (1952), is filled with the physical detail typical of King, which is somewhat incongruous with Hemingway's leaner prose style. The same was true of King's last two films, *Beloved Infidel* (1959) and *Tender Is the Night* (1961), the first about F. Scott Fitzgerald and the latter an adaptation of Fitzgerald's novel. King's work is less stylized and more physical than Fitzgerald's.

King was married in 1914 to Gypsy Abbott, with whom he had three children. She died in 1952, and in 1958 King married Ida Davis, with whom he had no children. King died in Toluca Lake, California.

While King was praised early in his career for *Tol'able David* and late in his career for *The Gunfighter*, his more commercial films did not receive as much critical approval. Although King had more financially successful films than either D. W. Griffith or John Ford, his critical reputation has suffered in comparison with both. King has not been seen by historians as the innovator Griffith was, and his direction is not as dramatically intense as Ford's. On the other hand, King is not afflicted with Griffith's Victorianism, nor with Ford's sentimentality. King presented his stories in a straightforward style, putting his cinematic skills at the service of the story. His most representative films give a nostalgic view of rural and small-town America that few other directors caught on film.

• Two collections of King's papers exist. One, which includes documents and scrapbooks, is in the American Heritage Center at the University of Wyoming in Laramie. The other, which includes King's annotated scripts and his studio contracts, is in the Margaret Herrick Library of the Academy of Motion Picture Arts and Sciences in Beverly Hills, Calif. Frank Thompson, ed., *Henry King, Director: From Silents to 'Scope* (1995), pulls together extensive oral history interviews conducted over several years by David Shepard and Ted Perry. Walter Coppedge, *Henry King's America* (1986), contains considerable biographical material, in addition to detailed analyses of five of King's most important films. Kevin Brownlow includes a long interview with King about his silent films in *The Parade's Gone By . . .* (1968).

TOM STEMPEL

KING, Henry Churchill (18 Sept. 1858–27 Feb. 1934), theologian and educator, was born in Hillsdale, Michigan, the son of Henry Jarvis King, a college administrator, and Sarah Lee. He grew up in Hillsdale and attended Hillsdale College for over a year.

In 1877 King transferred to Oberlin College, from which he graduated in June 1879. He then began his theological studies at Oberlin Theological Seminary. While he was a seminary student King became a Latin and mathematics tutor in Oberlin's preparatory department and served as summer school administrator. He received his bachelor of divinity degree in June 1882 and the following month married Julia Marana Coates in a ceremony performed by James Harris Fairchild, Oberlin's president and King's mentor, whose irenic evangelical theology based on the principle of benevolence deeply influenced King's thought. The Kings would have four children.

King received a master of arts degree in philosophy and religion from Harvard Divinity School in 1884 and then returned to Oberlin College as an associate professor of mathematics and teacher of the freshman Bible course. Interested in social reform, he ran unsuccessfully in 1887 and 1889 for the Ohio State Senate on the Prohibition ticket. His 1888 survey and report on Ohio's secondary and higher educational institutions led to statewide agreement on the coursework to be offered at each level and a standardization of collegiate admissions. He then was elected to serve on the national Committee of Ten chaired by Charles W. Eliot, president of Harvard, whose 1893 report was a landmark in establishing national curricular guidelines.

By 1890 King had begun to teach philosophy and theology, taking a year with his family in 1893–1894 to study at the University of Berlin, where he pursued his interests in philosopher Hermann Lotze and theologian Albrecht Ritschl, later translating works of both scholars into English. In 1897 King became professor of systematic theology, succeeding Fairchild. He soon published his most systematic statements of a new theology, *Reconstruction in Theology* (1901) and *Theology and the Social Consciousness* (1902).

King belonged to a generation of theological progressives who rejected the old Calvinist orthodoxy based on absolute decrees of God and adherence to creedal doctrines. Yet he also shared with his Common Sense predecessors in theology and education a belief in the universality and dependability of both natural and moral law in their respective spheres. This enabled him to accept the theory of evolution of species and to endorse the scientific spirit while also maintaining the autonomy of a personal God and the freedom and responsibility of the moral person. King's theology was distinctive for its focus on the value and sacredness of the person, which led him to interpret the relationship of God and humanity as a developing friendship between persons, characterized by mutual respect, self-surrender and community of interests. He held a moderate Social Gospel position, insisting on social reform but only in order to enhance the freedom of persons to attain the highest moral life.

In 1902 King became Oberlin's sixth president. The following twenty-five years of his administration were notable for college growth, curricular reform to include the natural and human sciences, and continued concern for morally rigorous but enjoyable student life, as well as for King's extensive activities in national and international affairs. The predominant theme of King's presidential writings, in keeping with the Progressive Era, was the building of character. He taught the senior Bible course for many years, basing it on his text *Rational Living* (1905), in which he argued that all the principles of modern psychology joined with the insights of Scripture in showing the way to the highest moral character and happiness as exemplified in the supreme person of history, Jesus Christ. King was a serious, even severe man, not without humor but holding himself to exacting standards and expecting no less of others.

King was a much sought after preacher and lecturer. A board member of the Carnegie Foundation for the Advancement of Teaching from 1906 to 1927 and president of the Religious Education Association and the Association of American Colleges, he also served on the American Board of Commissioners for Foreign Missions. In 1919 President Woodrow Wilson appointed him to serve on the Inter-Allied Commission on Mandates in Turkey, an arm of the Commission to Negotiate Peace, following World War I. In collaboration with Chicago businessman Charles R. Crane (later U.S. ambassador to China), King issued a report on the postwar situation in the Middle East, recommending that no Jewish state be established in Palestine and that every effort be made to stabilize autonomous Arab states in the area.

In 1927, weakened by a muscular disease, King retired from the presidency of Oberlin, one of the last generation of clergy presidents in American colleges and universities. He died in Oberlin.

• King's collected papers may be found in the archives of the Oberlin College Library. Among his seventeen published books, the most notable in addition to those described above are *The Laws of Friendship, Human and Divine* (1909), *The Ethics of Jesus* (1910), *The Moral and Religious Challenge of Our Times* (1911), *A New Mind for a New Age* (1920), and *Seeing Life Whole: A Christian Philosophy of Life* (1923). The major biography of King is by Donald M. Love, *Henry Churchill King of Oberlin* (1956). For interpretations of King's thought and influence see also John Barnard, *From Evangelicalism to Progressivism at Oberlin College, 1866–1917* (1969), and Frank Hugh Foster, *The Modern Movement in American Theology* (1939). A substantial obituary is in the *New York Times*, 28 Feb. 1934.

THOMAS E. FRANK

KING, John (1 Jan. 1813–19 June 1893), physician and pharmacologist, was born in New York City, the son of Harman King, a custom house official, and Marguerite La Porte. He completed his undergraduate education (it is not known which college he attended) mostly to placate his parents' desire that he enter some sort of commercial pursuit; however, he was more interested in a scientific career and while in school read extensively about physics, chemistry, and botany. In 1833 he married Charlotte Armington, with whom he had eight children. In 1835 he delivered a series of lectures on topics related to the earth's magnetism at the Mechanic's Institute of New York and the New Bedford (Mass.) Lyceum.

King's lifelong interest, however, involved the relationship between botany and pharmacology. This interest was probably inspired by King's reading of two of the day's popular texts: Constantine Rafinesque's *Medical Flora; or Manual of Medical Botany of the United States of North America* (1828–1832), which advanced an early eighteenth-century English contention that any disease encountered within the geographic limits of a particular country could be treated with the derivative of a plant native to that country; and Wooster Beach's *The American Practice of Medicine* (1833), which carried this idea one step further by rejecting the use of all therapeutics except those derived entirely from vegetable sources. These two texts attained the status of Holy Writ among the so-called "botanic physicians" who made up the Reformed School of American medicine. King had always been interested in botany as a hobby, and these books probably inspired him because they showed that botanic knowledge could be put to medical use.

Whatever his inspiration may have been, in the early 1830s King began studying many "folk remedies," whose active ingredients were derived primarily from plants, and set out to discover new vegetative sources for therapeutic drugs. His first success came in 1835 when he produced podophyllin from the dried underground stems and roots of the mayapple, a herbaceous plant native to eastern North America, and showed that this drug could be used effectively and safely to remove warts and other benign skin tumors. Podophyllin also proved to be an effective and palatable purgative and was eventually adopted by a number of physicians as a substitute for calomel. The most important of his other discoveries include oleoresin of iris, the first drug to be produced from the resin of a plant, and the medicinal alkaloids hydrastine and sanguinarine, which he derived from the herbs goldenseal and bloodroot, respectively.

King's interest in botanical pharmacology led him to enroll sometime during the latter half of the 1830s in the Reformed Medical College of the City of New York, which had been founded by Beach in the early 1830s. Because this institution rejected the accepted methods of medical practice and consequently did not enjoy the sanction of the New York state legislature, when King graduated in 1838 he did not receive an M.D. He remained at the college as a teacher for several years before moving to New Bedford, Massachusetts, where he opened a medical practice. In 1846 he relocated to Sharpsburg, Kentucky, and for the next two years practiced medicine there and in neighboring Owingsville.

In 1848 three factions of botanical practitioners—the Reformed Physicians (the faction to which King belonged), the Medico-Physicists, and the Botanics—joined forces in their common struggle against the regular medical profession. Meeting together in Cincinnati, Ohio, at a convention at which King served as secretary, they formed the American (changed to "National" in 1849) Eclectic Medical Association. This name was chosen because its members adhered to no one school of medical thought but instead utilized a number of different methods for the treatment of disease. In time "eclecticism" evolved into a system of medicine that not only espoused the use of botanically derived therapeutics but also treated disease as a condition totally unrelated to any other aspect of the patient's overall health, thus placing it in sharp contrast to the holistic approach. King continued to participate in the association's activities and in 1878 served as its president.

In 1848 King moved his practice to Cincinnati but closed it the next year to accept a position as professor of materia medica (pharmacology) and therapeutics at Memphis (Tenn.) Institute, an early eclectic school of medicine. In 1851 he became professor of obstetrics at Cincinnati's Eclectic Medical Institute, the first incorporated eclectic school of medicine in the United States. He authored a number of texts, including three concerning medical conditions peculiar to women, but the most important of his works was *The American Dispensatory* (1852). This book, which went through eighteen editions in the next forty years, offered a compendium of virtually everything known about the therapeutic properties of native American plants and became eclecticism's handbook on pharmaceuticals. In 1853, six years after the death of his first wife, he married Phebe Rodman Platt, with whom he had no children. In 1891 he retired from teaching to his home in North Bend, Ohio, where he died.

King made two important contributions to the development of American medicine. He furthered the advance of American pharmacology by discovering the therapeutic uses of a number of botanical sources. He also played an important role in the development of eclecticism by helping to organize the movement into a unified organization, teaching for a number of years at one of its foremost institutions, and writing one of its most important handbooks.

• King's papers have not been located. His other book-length writings include *American Obstetrics* (1853); *Women: Their Diseases and Treatment* (1858); *The Microscopist's Companion* (1859); *The American Family Physician* (1860); *Chronic Diseases* (1866); *The Urological Dictionary* (1878); and *The Coming Freeman* (1886), a nonmedical text espousing the cause of the working class. King's contributions are discussed in William G. Rothstein, *American Physicians in the Nineteenth Century* (1972). An obituary is in the *Cincinnati Times-Star*, 23 June 1893.

CHARLES W. CAREY, JR.

KING, Louisa Boyd Yeomans. *See* King, Mrs. Francis.

KING, Martin Luther (19 Dec. 1897–11 Nov. 1984), Baptist pastor and civil rights activist, was born Michael King in Stockbridge, Georgia, the son of James Albert King, an impoverished sharecropper, and Delia Linsey, a cleaning woman and laundress. As a boy King attended school from three to five months a year in an old frame building, where Mrs. Lowe, the wife of the pastor of Floyd's Chapel Baptist Church, taught 234 children in all grades. At Floyd's Chapel, King gained confidence as a singer and had a growing sense of a call to preach. At fifteen, when he delivered a trial sermon at Floyd's Chapel and was licensed to preach, King had learned to read but could not yet write. As a young country preacher he occasionally visited Atlanta. At twenty he left Stockbridge and settled there. He lived in a rooming house and worked at various jobs, including making tires in a rubber plant, loading bales of cotton, and driving a barber-supply truck.

As a young Baptist preacher seeking a start in life, King acquired a Model T Ford to get to small preaching appointments in middle Georgia. In 1919 he met the Reverend Adam Daniel Williams of Atlanta's Ebenezer Baptist Church and began courting his daughter, Alberta Christine Williams. Three years later, at twenty-five, King became the pastor of Travelers Rest Baptist Church in East Point, Georgia; entered Atlanta's Peter James Bryant Preparatory School at the fifth grade level; and began assisting A. D. Williams at Ebenezer Baptist Church. After graduating from the preparatory school, he entered Morehouse College in 1926. On Thanksgiving Day King married Alberta Williams and moved into her parents' house on Auburn Avenue. They had three children. In 1930 King received his degree in theology from Morehouse.

When his father-in-law died in 1931, King was called to the pulpit of Ebenezer Baptist Church. Steadily, he built it from a congregation of a few hundred people in deep financial trouble into a prospering congregation of 4,000. In 1934 King attended the World's Baptist Convention in Berlin, Germany, and toured Europe and the Holy Land. After the European trip, King changed his name to Martin Luther King. His ministry occasionally drew criticism, as when he allowed the Ebenezer Church choir, led by his wife, to sing for a gala ball in celebration of the premiere of *Gone with the Wind*. The Baptist choir's appearance was controversial both for its association with social dancing and for its performance in the livery of slaves before an exclusively white audience. As an officer of Atlanta's branch of the National Association for the Advancement of Colored People, the Atlanta Civic and Political League, and the Atlanta Baptist Ministers Association between 1935 and 1945, however, King was better known as a leader in the struggle for black voting rights and pay equity for African-American public school teachers in the city.

By the late 1940s two of King's children, Willie Christine King at Columbia University and Martin Luther King, Jr., at Crozer Theological Seminary and, later, Boston University, were doing graduate work at northern schools; son Alfred Daniel Williams "A. D." King was working on his degree at Morehouse, where the elder King was on the board of trustees. Young Martin returned to Atlanta each summer to help with the demands at Ebenezer. King would have preferred for his older son to return to Ebenezer full time, but he accepted his decision to earn a doctorate at Boston and then take another pastorate at Dexter Avenue Baptist Church in Montgomery, Alabama. King's confidence in his older son grew as he led the Montgomery bus boycott and founded the Southern

Christian Leadership Conference (SCLC) to spearhead the civil rights movement in the South. The elder King joined the board of directors of the SCLC in 1957 and welcomed his son as co-pastor at Ebenezer Baptist Church in 1960. When Robert F. Kennedy interceded to win the release of Martin Luther King, Jr., from the Reidsville, Georgia, state prison later that year, Martin Luther King, Sr., endorsed John F. Kennedy in a closely contested presidential race with Richard M. Nixon, which may have influenced the result in several key states. Both supportive of their common cause and concerned for his son's safety, King commonly offered advice on the side of caution, but he respected his son's independent judgment.

King's life was marked by deep tragedy from 1968 to 1976. After his older son was assassinated on 4 April 1968, his younger son, A. D., became co-pastor with him of Ebenezer Baptist Church. A. D. King drowned in a swimming accident on 21 July 1969. A deranged gunman, Marcus Wayne Chenault, shot and killed Alberta Williams King on 30 June 1974 as she played the organ for services at Ebenezer Baptist Church. Two years later a granddaughter, Esther Darlene King, died of a heart attack while she was jogging. King retired from the Ebenezer pulpit in 1975. In retirement he relished his status as an elder statesman of the civil rights movement, playing a significant role in the nomination and election of Jimmy Carter as president in 1976 and supporting the work of his daughter and daughter-in-law Coretta Scott King in building Atlanta's Martin Luther King, Jr., Center for Nonviolent Social Change. Martin Luther King, Sr., died in Atlanta.

• The papers of Martin Luther King, Sr., are in two collections: the Ebenezer Baptist Church Papers and the King Family Papers, both of which are in private hands. The King Family Papers include transcripts of his recollections and preliminary drafts of his autobiography; Martin Luther King, Sr., with Clayton Riley, *Daddy King: An Autobiography* (1980). See also David R. Collins, *Not Only Dreamers: The Story of Martin Luther King, Sr., and Martin Luther King, Jr.* (1986). The autobiography should be read critically, however. The introduction to Clayborne Carson and Ralph E. Luker et al., eds., *The Papers of Martin Luther King, Jr.*, vol. 1 (1992); esp. pp. 18–35, interprets King's recollections in comparison with a wide range of public and private documents. Important obituaries are in the *Atlanta Constitution*, 12 Nov. 1984; the *Atlanta Daily World*, 15 Nov. 1984; and the *Atlanta Journal*, 12 nov. 1984.

RALPH E. LUKER

KING, Martin Luther, Jr. (15 Jan. 1929–4 Apr. 1968), Baptist minister and civil rights leader, was born Michael King, Jr., in Atlanta, Georgia, the son of the Reverend Michael King and Alberta Williams. Born to a family with deep roots in the African-American Baptist church and in the Atlanta black community, the younger King spent his first twelve years in the home on Auburn Avenue that his parents shared with his maternal grandparents. A block away, also on Auburn, was Ebenezer Baptist Church, where his grandfather, the Reverend Adam Daniel Williams, had served as pastor since 1894. Under Williams's leadership, Ebenezer had grown from a small congregation without a building to become one of Atlanta's prominent African-American churches. After Williams's death in 1931, his son-in-law became Ebenezer's new pastor and gradually established himself as a major figure in state and national Baptist groups. In 1934 the elder King, following the request of his own dying father, changed his name and that of his son to Martin Luther King.

King's formative experiences not only immersed him in the affairs of Ebenezer but also introduced him to the African-American social gospel tradition exemplified by his father and grandfather, both of whom were leaders of the Atlanta branch of the National Association for the Advancement of Colored People. Depression-era breadlines heightened his awareness of economic inequities, and his father's leadership of campaigns against racial discrimination in voting and teachers' salaries provided a model for the younger King's own politically engaged ministry. He resisted religious emotionalism and as a teenager questioned some facets of Baptist doctrine, such as the bodily resurrection of Jesus.

During his undergraduate years at Atlanta's Morehouse College from 1944 to 1948, King gradually overcame his initial reluctance to accept his inherited calling. Morehouse president Benjamin E. Mays influenced King's spiritual development, encouraging him to view Christianity as a potential force for progressive social change. Religion professor George Kelsey exposed him to biblical criticism and, according to King's autobiographical sketch, taught him "that behind the legends and myths of the Book were many profound truths which one could not escape." King admired both educators as deeply religious yet also learned men. By the end of his junior year, such academic role models and the example of his father led King to enter the ministry. He described his decision as a response to an "inner urge" calling him to "serve God and humanity." He was ordained during his final semester at Morehouse. By this time King had also taken his first steps toward political activism. He had responded to the postwar wave of antiblack violence by proclaiming in a letter to the editor of the *Atlanta Constitution* that African Americans were "entitled to the basic rights and opportunities of American citizens." During his senior year King joined the Intercollegiate Council, an interracial student discussion group that met monthly at Atlanta's Emory University.

After leaving Morehouse, King increased his understanding of liberal Christian thought while attending Crozer Theological Seminary in Pennsylvania from 1948 to 1951. Initially uncritical of liberal theology, he gradually moved toward Reinhold Niebuhr's neoorthodoxy, which emphasized the intractability of social evil. He reacted skeptically to a presentation on pacifism by Fellowship of Reconciliation leader A. J. Muste. Moreover, by the end of his seminary studies King had become increasingly dissatisfied with the abstract conceptions of God held by some modern theologians and identified himself instead with theologians who affirmed the personality of God. Even as he continued to question and modify his own religious beliefs, he compiled an outstanding academic record and graduated at the top of his class.

In 1951 King began doctoral studies in systematic theology at Boston University's School of Theology, which was dominated by personalist theologians. The papers (including his dissertation) that King wrote during his years at Boston displayed little originality, and some contained extensive plagiarism; but his readings enabled him to formulate an eclectic yet coherent theological perspective. By the time he completed his doctoral studies in 1955, King had refined his exceptional ability to draw upon a wide range of theological and philosophical texts to express his views with force and precision. His ability to infuse his oratory with borrowed theological insights became evident in his expanding preaching activities in Boston-area churches and at Ebenezer, where he assisted his father during school vacations.

During his stay at Boston, King also met and courted Coretta Scott, an Alabama-born Antioch College graduate who was then a student at the New England Conservatory of Music. On 18 June 1953 the two students were married in Marion, Alabama, where Scott's family lived. During the following academic year King began work on his dissertation, which he completed during the spring of 1955.

Although he considered pursuing an academic career, King decided in 1954 to accept an offer to become the pastor of Dexter Avenue Baptist Church in Montgomery, Alabama. In December 1955, when Montgomery black leaders formed the Montgomery Improvement Association to protest the arrest of NAACP official Rosa Parks for refusing to give up her bus seat to a white man, they selected King to head the new group. In his role as the primary spokesman of the yearlong boycott movement, King utilized the leadership abilities he had gained from his religious background and academic training and gradually forged a distinctive protest strategy that involved the mobilization of black churches and skillful appeals for white support. As King encountered increasingly fierce white opposition, he continued his movement away from theological abstractions toward more reassuring conceptions, rooted in African-American religious culture, of God as a constant source of support. He later wrote in his book of sermons, *Strength to Love* (1963), that the travails of movement leadership caused him to abandon the notion of God as a "theological and philosophically satisfying metaphysical category" and caused him to view God as "a living reality that has been validated in the experiences of everyday life." With the encouragement of Bayard Rustin and other veteran pacifists, King also became a firm advocate of Mohandas Gandhi's precepts of nonviolence, which he combined with Christian principles.

After the Supreme Court outlawed Alabama bus segregation laws in late 1956, King sought to expand the nonviolent civil rights movement throughout the South. In 1957 he became the founding president of the Southern Christian Leadership Conference (SCLC), formed to coordinate civil rights activities throughout the region. Publication of *Stride toward Freedom: The Montgomery Story* (1958) further contributed to King's rapid emergence as a national civil rights leader. Even as he expanded his influence, however, King acted cautiously. Rather than immediately seeking to stimulate mass desegregation protests in the South, King stressed the goal of achieving black voting rights when he addressed an audience at the 1957 Prayer Pilgrimage for Freedom. During 1959 he increased his understanding of Gandhian ideas during a monthlong visit to India as the guest of Prime Minister Jawaharlal Nehru. Early the following year he moved his family, which now included two children, to Atlanta in order to be nearer SCLC headquarters in that city and to become co-pastor, with his father, of Ebenezer Baptist Church. (The Kings' third child was born in 1961; their fourth was born in 1963.)

Soon after King's arrival in Atlanta, the southern civil rights movement gained new impetus from the student-led lunch counter sit-in movement that spread throughout the region during 1960. The sit-ins brought into existence a new protest group, the Student Nonviolent Coordinating Committee (SNCC), which would often push King toward greater militancy. In October 1960 King's arrest during a student-initiated protest in Atlanta became an issue in the national presidential campaign when Democratic candidate John F. Kennedy called Coretta King to express his concern. The successful efforts of Kennedy supporters to secure King's release contributed to the Democratic candidate's narrow victory.

As the southern protest movement expanded during the early 1960s, King was often torn between the increasingly militant student activists and more cautious national civil rights leaders. During 1961 and 1962 his tactical differences with SNCC activists surfaced during a sustained protest movement in Albany, Georgia. King was arrested twice during demonstrations organized by the Albany Movement, but when he left jail and ultimately left Albany without achieving a victory, some movement activists began to question his militancy and his dominant role within the southern protest movement.

During 1963, however, King reasserted his preeminence within the African-American freedom struggle through his leadership of the Birmingham campaign. Initiated by SCLC in January, the Birmingham demonstrations were the most massive civil rights protest that had yet occurred. With the assistance of Fred Shuttlesworth and other local black leaders and with little competition from SNCC and other civil rights groups, SCLC officials were able to orchestrate the Birmingham protests to achieve maximum national impact. King's decision to intentionally allow himself to be arrested for leading a demonstration on 12 April prodded the Kennedy administration to intervene in the escalating protests. A widely quoted letter that King wrote while jailed displayed his distinctive ability to influence public opinion by appropriating ideas from the Bible, the Constitution, and other canonical texts. During May, televised pictures of police using dogs and fire hoses against demonstrators generated a national outcry against white segregationist officials in Birmingham. The brutality of Birmingham officials and the refusal of Alabama governor George C. Wallace to allow the admission of black students at the University of Alabama prompted President Kennedy to introduce major civil rights legislation.

King's speech at the 28 August 1963 March on Washington, attended by more than 200,000 people, was the culmination of a wave of civil rights protest activity that extended even to northern cities. In King's prepared remarks he announced that African Americans wished to cash the "promissory note" signified in the egalitarian rhetoric of the Constitution and the Declaration of Independence. Closing his address with extemporaneous remarks, he insisted that he had not lost hope: "So I say to you, my friends, that even though we must face the difficulties of today and tomorrow, I still have a dream. It is a dream deeply rooted in the American dream that one day this nation will rise up and live out the true meaning of its creed—we hold these truths to be self-evident, that all men are created equal." He appropriated the familiar words of "My Country 'Tis of Thee" before concluding, "And when we allow freedom to ring, when we let it ring from every village and hamlet, from every state and city, we will be able to speed up that day when all of God's children—black men and white men, Jews and Gentiles, Catholics and Protestants—will be able to join hands and to sing in the words of the old Negro spiritual, 'Free at last, free at last, thank God Almighty, we are free at last.'"

King's ability to focus national attention on orchestrated confrontations with racist authorities, combined with his oration at the 1963 March on Washington, made him the most influential African-American spokesperson of the first half of the 1960s. Named *Time* magazine's man of the year at the end of 1963, he was awarded the Nobel Peace Prize in December 1964. The acclaim King received strengthened his stature among civil rights leaders but also prompted Federal Bureau of Investigation director J. Edgar Hoover to step up his effort to damage King's reputation. Hoover, with the approval of President Kennedy and Attorney General Robert Kennedy, established phone taps and bugs. Hoover and many other observers of the southern struggle saw King as controlling events, but he was actually a moderating force within an increasingly diverse black militancy of the mid-1960s. As the African-American struggle expanded from desegregation protests to mass movements seeking economic and political gains in the North as well as the South, King's active involvement was limited to a few highly publicized civil rights campaigns, particularly the major series of voting rights protests that began in Selma, Alabama, early in 1965, which secured popular support for the passage of national civil rights legislation, particularly the Civil Rights Act of 1964.

The Alabama protests reached a turning point on 7 March when state police attacked a group of demonstrators at the start of a march from Selma to the state capitol in Montgomery. Carrying out Governor Wallace's orders, the police used tear gas and clubs to turn back the marchers soon after they crossed the Edmund Pettus Bridge on the outskirts of Selma. Unprepared for the violent confrontation, King was in Atlanta to deliver a sermon when the incident occurred but returned to Selma to mobilize nationwide support for the voting rights campaign. King alienated some activists when he decided to postpone the continuation of the Selma-to-Montgomery march until he had received court approval, but the march, which finally secured federal court approval, attracted several thousand civil rights sympathizers, black and white, from all regions of the nation. On 25 March King addressed the arriving marchers from the steps of the capitol in Montgomery. The march and the subsequent killing of a white participant, Viola Liuzzo, dramatized the denial of black voting rights and spurred passage during the following summer of the Voting Rights Act of 1965.

After the successful voting rights march in Alabama, King was unable to garner similar support for his effort to confront the problems of northern urban blacks. Early in 1966 he launched a major campaign against poverty and other urban problems, moving into an apartment in the black ghetto of Chicago. As King shifted the focus of his activities to the North, however, he discovered that the tactics used in the South were not as effective elsewhere. He encountered formidable opposition from Mayor Richard Daley and was unable to mobilize Chicago's economically and ideologically diverse black community. King was stoned by angry whites in the Chicago suburb of Cicero when he led a march against racial discrimination in housing. Despite numerous mass protests, the Chicago campaign resulted in no significant gains and undermined King's reputation as an effective civil rights leader.

King's influence was further undermined by the increasingly caustic tone of black militancy of the period after 1965. Black militants increasingly turned away from the Gandhian precepts of King toward the black nationalism of Malcolm X, whose posthumously published autobiography and speeches reached large audiences after his assassination in February 1965. Unable to influence the black insurgencies that occurred in many urban areas, King refused to abandon his firmly rooted beliefs about racial integration and nonviolence. He was nevertheless unpersuaded by black nationalist calls for racial uplift and institutional development in black communities. In his last book, *Where Do We Go from Here: Chaos or Community?* (1967), King dismissed the claim of Black Power advocates "to be the most revolutionary wing of the social revolution taking place in the United States," but he acknowl-

edged that they responded to a psychological need among African Americans he had not previously addressed. "Psychological freedom, a firm sense of self-esteem, is the most powerful weapon against the long night of physical slavery," King wrote. "The Negro will only be truly free when he reaches down to the inner depths of his own being and signs with the pen and ink of assertive selfhood his own emancipation proclamation."

Indeed, even as his popularity declined, King spoke out strongly against American involvement in the Vietnam War, making his position public in an address on 4 April 1967 at New York's Riverside Church. King's involvement in the antiwar movement reduced his ability to influence national racial policies and made him a target of further FBI investigations. Nevertheless, he became ever more insistent that his version of Gandhian nonviolence and social gospel Christianity was the most appropriate response to the problems of black Americans.

In November 1967 King announced the formation of the Poor People's Campaign, designed to prod the federal government to strengthen its antipoverty efforts. King and other SCLC workers began to recruit poor people and antipoverty activists to come to Washington, D.C., to lobby on behalf of improved antipoverty programs. This effort was in its early stages when King became involved in a sanitation workers' strike in Memphis, Tennessee. On 28 March 1968, as King led thousands of sanitation workers and sympathizers on a march through downtown Memphis, black youngsters began throwing rocks and looting stores. This outbreak of violence led to extensive press criticisms of King's entire antipoverty strategy. King returned to Memphis for the last time in early April. Addressing an audience at Bishop Charles J. Mason Temple on 3 April, King affirmed his optimism despite the "difficult days" that lay ahead. "But it doesn't matter with me now," he declared, "because I've been to the mountaintop [and] I've seen the promised land." He continued, "I may not get there with you. But I want you to know tonight, that we, as a people, will get to the promised land." The following evening King was assassinated as he stood on a balcony of the Lorraine Motel in Memphis. A white segregationist, James Earl Ray, was later convicted of the crime. The Poor People's Campaign continued for a few months after his death but did not achieve its objectives.

Until his death King remained steadfast in his commitment to the radical transformation of American society through nonviolent activism. In his posthumously published essay, "A Testament of Hope" (1986), he urged African Americans to refrain from violence but also warned, "White America must recognize that justice for black people cannot be achieved without radical changes in the structure of our society." The "black revolution" was more than a civil rights movement, he insisted. "It is forcing America to face all its interrelated flaws—racism, poverty, militarism and materialism."

After her husband's death, Coretta Scott King established the Atlanta-based Martin Luther King, Jr., Center for Nonviolent Social Change to promote Gandhian-Kingian concepts of nonviolent struggle. She led the successful effort to honor King with a federal holiday on the anniversary of his birthday, which was first celebrated in 1986.

• Collections of King's papers are at the Martin Luther King, Jr., Center for Nonviolent Social Change in Atlanta and the Mugar Memorial Library at Boston University. King's writings are collected in James Melvin Washington, ed., *A Testament of Hope: The Essential Writings of Martin Luther King, Jr.* (1986). Biographies include David Levering Lewis, *King: A Biography*, 2d ed. (1978); Stephen B. Oates, *Let the Trumpet Sound: The Life of Martin Luther King, Jr.* (1982); and David J. Garrow, *Bearing the Cross: Martin Luther King, Jr., and the Southern Christian Leadership Conference, 1955–1968* (1986). See also two works by Taylor Branch, *Parting the Waters: America in the King Years, 1954–63* (1988) and *Pillar of Fire: America in the King Years, 1963–65* (1998). An obituary is in the *New York Times*, 5 Apr. 1968.

CLAYBORNE CARSON

KING, Mrs. Francis (17 Oct. 1863–16 Jan. 1948), garden designer and writer, was born Louisa Boyd Yeomans in Washington, New Jersey, the daughter of Alfred Yeomans, a Presbyterian minister, and Elizabeth Blythe Ramsay. Educated in private schools, in 1890 she married Francis King, a Chicago mercantilist. They established a home, "Orchard House," in the central Michigan town of Alma, located about forty miles west of Saginaw. The couple had three children.

King created her first garden at Alma. Her approach to garden construction was architectural. It involved the creation of spaces, or rooms, designed for different uses and separated in order to provide a sense of privacy in the garden. She thought of the gardener as artist, planner, and creator but not as grubber. That role, as she often noted, was filled by hired workmen who followed her plans.

King's first book was *The Well-Considered Garden* (1915). Introduced by Gertrude Jekyll, with whom King had corresponded for years, it focused on color and color harmony in the garden and advocated the development of a verbal standard for colors in order to correct the confusion created by the indiscriminate use of color words. She was influenced by Jekyll in this regard and often discussed the problem in her writing. Because her books and articles had to be illustrated with black-and-white photographs and thus could not show the reader what color harmonies were being described, King had to rely on the careful use of terminology; her concern was that other writers were not as rigorous in their use of words, to the detriment of their readers. King's work followed in the tradition of an earlier garden writer, Helena Rutherfurd Ely. Her book, *A Woman's Hardy Garden*, published in 1903, was the first of its type in the United States and it soon became a bestseller. Ely's work also drew on the garden-writing tradition of Gertrude Jekyll.

In the conclusion of *Chronicles of the Garden* (1925), which she dedicated to Gertrude Jekyll, King wrote, "Each one has his own best thing. Mine is the garden." This "best thing" provided the basis for her writing and speaking career. A prolific writer, King published many articles for popular magazines, and these formed parts of the nine books she published. Much of her writing centered on specific varieties of plants, all carefully noted by common as well as botanical names. Little of what she wrote revealed her personal experience, although she was free with her opinions, often writing in a direct second-person style addressed to the reader. Her overriding concern was the beauty and pleasure that ordinary middle-class women could create for themselves and their families.

Perhaps it was Alma's proximity to farm country that led to King's interest in the role of women in agriculture. In 1913 she became the first president of the Women's National Farm and Garden Association, which was organized to introduce women to outdoor work. In a speech called "Vocations for Women in Agriculture," which King delivered at the opening of a dormitory for women students at Massachusetts Agriculture College (now the University of Massachusetts), she described the range of physical work that women can do in raising livestock, poultry, seed, and bees. This speech later appeared as a chapter in her *Pages of a Garden Note-book* (1921). By 1917 when the United States entered World War I, members of the association were ready to fill in for the men who left the farm to join the armed services.

The Garden Club movement started slowly in the first years of the twentieth century, and King was publicly identified with the movement from the beginning. In 1915, when she was serving as president of the Michigan club, one of the earliest garden clubs, King realized that forty-nine like groups were operating around the country. She helped to form the national Garden Club of America in 1913 and served as one of its vice presidents. By the 1940s the movement comprised thousands of clubs with hundreds of thousands of members.

King was honored many times for her work. In 1921 the Massachusetts Horticultural Society awarded her the George Robert White Medal, a national honor considered the highest award bestowed for gardening. The Garden Club of America honored her with its medal of honor in 1923. She also received a distinguished service award from the National Home Planting Bureau and served as vice president of the Garden Club of London as well as an honorary member and officer of many local and state garden clubs. She was received by the Dutch court when she attended a bulb show in the Netherlands, and she was active in the American Dahlia Society, the American Rose Society, the American Gladiolus Society, the Royal Horticultural Society of Great Britain, and the Royal National Tulip Society of England.

After her husband's death in 1927, King moved to "Kingstree" in South Hartford, New York, in 1928. The garden she created there is described in her book

From a New Garden (1930). She died at the home of her daughter in Milton, Massachusetts, eight years after Louise S. B. Saunders dubbed her the "Dean of American Gardening" (*House and Garden*, Mar. 1940).

• King's personal memorabilia is housed in the library of the Massachusetts Horticultural Society in Boston. The records of the Women's National Farm and Garden Association housed in Schlesinger Library at Radcliffe College, includes the "King Memorial Scrapbook." King's other books include *The Little Garden* (1921), *Variety in the Little Garden* (1923), *The Beginner's Garden* (1927), *The Flower Garden Day by Day* (1927), and *The Gardeners Colour Book* (1929). One of her last published articles is "Potpourri of Gardening," *House and Garden*, Apr. 1945. See also Buckner Hollingsworth, *Her Garden Was Her Delight* (1962). An obituary is in the *New York Times*, 18 Jan. 1948.

LINDA H. ELEGANT

KING, Preston (14 Oct. 1806–13 Nov. 1865), politician and leading opponent of slavery extension, was born in Ogdensburgh, New York, the illegitimate son of John King, a local landowner, and Margaret Galloway. He graduated from Union College in 1827 and studied law in the offices of the rising Democratic leader, Silas Wright. Heavily set and physically unprepossessing, King never married and devoted his considerable energies to the political arts, particularly party organization and policy advocacy. He remained close to Wright and, through him, to the Democracy's national leader, Martin Van Buren. In addition to practicing law, King edited the Jacksonian newspaper the *Saint Lawrence Republican* beginning in 1830 and was active in the state party, rising during the next decade and a half to become an important spokesman of the Van Buren–Wright faction. Like other Democrats he rigidly advocated the cause of limited government and republican nationalism, both as an editor and in a succession of political offices beginning with his appointment in 1833 as postmaster at Ogdensburgh, a key position for advancing the Democracy's organization and campaign activities. He served in the New York State Assembly from 1835 to 1838, rising to become leader of the minority, and then was elected to Congress in 1842, serving two terms as a Democrat.

King became involved in efforts along New York's border in 1838 in support of the Canadian rebellion against Great Britain, actively encouraging local armed involvement by New Yorkers against the British. He led an effort to rescue Americans captured during the revolt, and, afterward, overwhelmed by his failure to bring them back and the human costs of that failure, he broke down and spent some months in early 1839 in a mental hospital. He quickly returned to his editorship and political activities, however.

A member of the more radical wing of the New York Democracy, King was particularly hostile to banking and, from the mid-1840s on, the spread of slavery. He strongly reacted against the Polk administration's aggressive willingness to expand slave territory and joined with other northern congressmen in framing and pushing the anti–slavery extension Wilmot Proviso in 1846. King precipitated a major battle over the expansion of slavery into any territory acquired from Mexico by reintroducing the proviso in January 1847, after Congress reassembled. In 1848 he and other Van Burenites, now called Barnburners, joined Whigs in creating the Free Soil party in protest against the continuing control of the Democracy by its expansionist southern wing. King served two terms as a Free Soil congressman from the Ogdensburgh area between 1849 and 1853. No egalitarian, he was committed, as were many Free Soilers, to keeping western lands open for white yeomen, accepting state-established limits on black freedoms and the colonizing of free blacks. At first strongly opposed to those parts of the compromise measures of 1850 that benefited slavery, he ultimately came to support the legislation as a means of ending the crisis over expansion and reestablishing the unity of the Democratic party.

King rejoined the Democracy in 1852 and supported Franklin Pierce for president but pulled away again because of the party leadership's renewed acquiescence in slavery's expansion with the Kansas-Nebraska Act in 1854. An early organizer of the Republican party in New York and closely allied with William H. Seward and Thurlow Weed in state politics thereafter, he unsuccessfully ran for New York secretary of state in 1855, but he was elected to the U.S. Senate by his new party the next year, serving one term to 1863.

King remained active in Republican politics during the Civil War, chaired the party's fundraising and campaign coordinating National Congressional Committee from 1860 to 1864, and was a delegate to the Republican National Convention in 1864 and a presidential elector that year. King supported Andrew Johnson's nomination as vice president in 1864. The latter appointed him collector of customs in New York City in 1865. The mental stress that had affected King in 1839 reappeared at the time of this appointment and culminated in his suicide by jumping from a ferry boat in New York Harbor, apparently because of the pressures of his post. He was buried in Ogdensburgh alongside his parents.

• No large body of King papers has survived, although very small collections exist in a number of New York state depositories. There are also important letters from and about King in the extensive collection of Martin Van Buren Papers in the Library of Congress. A full-length biography is Ernest Muller, "Preston King: A Political Biography" (Ph.D. diss., Columbia Univ., 1957). There is much about King's public activities in such books as John Garraty, *Silas Wright* (1949); Herbert Donovan, *The Barnburners* (1925); Frederick J. Blue, *The Free Soilers: Third Party Politics, 1848–1854* (1973); Chaplain W. Morrison, *The Wilmot Proviso and the Democratic Party, 1846–1848* (1963); and Hendrik Booraem, *The Formation of the Republican Party in New York* (1983).

JOEL H. SILBEY

KING, Richard (10 July 1825–14 Apr. 1885), rancher, the son of unknown Irish immigrants, was born in New York City. Poor relatives apprenticed him at age eight or nine to a jeweler, who abused him. At age eleven King fled, stowing away on a ship bound for Mobile, Alabama, but he was discovered when four days at sea. The captain took pity on the lad, putting him ashore at Mobile, where King found work as a cabin boy on steamers plying the Alabama River. One ship's master taught him to read and sent him to Connecticut to live with his sisters, where he received eight months' schooling, all the education he ever acquired.

At term's end, sixteen-year-old King enlisted with Captain Henry Penny for service in the Seminole War in Florida. Afterward, King worked on steamboats on the Apalachicola and Chattahoochee rivers, earning a pilot's license by 1843 when he met Mifflin Kenedy, seven years King's senior and master of the itinerant steamboat *Champion*. In 1846 Kenedy wrote King from Texas, inviting King to join him in working for the army, ferrying men and matériel along the Rio Grande for General Zachary Taylor, then fighting the Mexican War. King arrived in 1847 and briefly served Kenedy as pilot aboard the government-owned riverboat *Corvette*, which steamed upriver as far as Camargo, 220 miles inland. Before the year's end, King captained *Colonel Cross*, which made the same run.

Released from service, in 1849 King successfully bid $750 to buy his ship, which had cost the U.S. government $14,000 three years earlier, and he commenced hauling cutlery, hardware, machinery, liquor, tobacco, tools, wines, and other goods from Brownsville, Texas, up the Rio Grande, mostly to Matamoros, Mexico, where many commodities were contraband, and carrying beef hides, live animals, pig lead, specie, and bullion back downstream. In 1850, King joined Kenedy and two associates in Brownsville to form M. Kenedy & Co. to build and operate steamboats on the Rio Grande. By the end of the Civil War, when the firm was renamed King, Kenedy & Co., it ran twenty-six steamers and virtually monopolized river traffic along the Texas-Mexican border, profiting handsomely in circumventing the Union blockade by ferrying Confederate cotton to Mexico for European buyers. The partners remained in business until 1872, when, no longer able to control shipping because of competition from railroads, they disbanded.

Meanwhile, in association with Captain Gideon K. "Legs" Lewis, a Texas Ranger, about 1852 King had commenced raising cattle as a sideline on grassy coastal plains between Brownsville and Corpus Christi, a semitropical expanse then called "Wild Horse Desert." In 1853 he paid residents who had fled the area during the Mexican War $300 for rights to 15,500 acres of land, originally part of the Rincón Santa Gertrudis Spanish land grant, and sold Lewis an undivided half interest for $2,000. The next year, the partners bought an adjacent 53,000-acre tract (the de la Garza Santa Gertrudis grant) for $1,800. Lewis, who left the rangers in 1853, managed the spread, hiring hands and buying cattle, while King attended to shipping interests. The profitable King-Lewis association ended abruptly in 1855 when Lewis was shot to death in Corpus Christi by an irate husband. Through a friend, King purchased Lewis's interest from his estate at auction for about $1,600 and, for another $200, exercised an option on Lewis's 12,000 acres on Padre Island, bringing King's land holdings to about 80,000 acres.

Needing capital, in 1856 King sold an undivided interest in the de la Garza grant to James Walworth, a riverboater and an associate in M. Kenedy & Co., and in 1860 enlarged the ranching enterprise to include Kenedy. As R. King & Co., they bought more land and livestock, including horses, mules, hogs, sheep, and goats, but the partners found so little market for cattle that beeves were slaughtered for their hides and tallow, and hogs were fattened on the renderings. Despite limited markets for their animals, the disruption of the Civil War, and incessant raids of Mexican border bandits, by 1865 the operation had more than doubled, to about 200,000 acres. When Walworth died in 1865, King and Kenedy purchased his widow's shares of both firms for $50,000. Convinced by complications caused by the deaths of partners that their affairs were too entwined, King and Kenedy amicably ended their business association in 1867 by dividing the land and livestock between them. Neither man advocated open-range ranching, and well before the advent of barbed wire both fenced their respective properties, each of them enclosing more than 100,000 acres with creosoted cypress posts and hard pine planks hauled at considerable expense from Brownsville, in large measure to keep rustlers at bay.

Owning more than 40,000 head of cattle at the outset of the post–Civil War boom in cattle raising, King profited substantially on trail drives northward to Kansas, Longhorns worth merely $2 locally bringing $40 or more in Abilene. He invested profits in more land and cattle, increasing his holdings in South Texas to 614,140 acres on which he grazed 60,000 animals at the time of his death. By then he had also commenced crossbreeding Durham cattle with Longhorns to produce meatier animals than the bony beasts that thrived on the coastal plains, and eventually King Ranch experiments produced the Santa Gertrudis breed. Also with Mifflin Kenedy, King organized and built the San Diego, Corpus Christi, & Rio Grande Railroad (1876–1880), which was eventually sold to the Mexican National Railway Company.

King married Henrietta Chamberlain in 1854, and they had two sons and three daughters. He died of cancer in San Antonio and was buried in Kingsville, Texas, the community nearest his ranch, which had been named for him. Inheriting all of his estate, valued in excess of $1 million, Henrietta King entrusted the ranch's management to her son-in-law, Corpus Christi attorney Robert J. Kleberg, Sr., who followed Richard King's admonition, "Buy land. Never sell!" as well as continued his cattle-breeding experiments. By the time of Kleberg's death in 1932, the King Ranch aggregated more than one million acres and was the largest enterprise of its kind in the world. Its holdings have since grown to include more than eleven million acres in Texas, Africa, Australia, and South America.

In the 1980s its Texas holdings alone contained more producing oil and gas wells than in all of Saudi Arabia.

• No biography of Richard King exists, but Tom Lea, *The King Ranch* (2 vols., 1957), authorized by the Kleberg family, which now controls the King Ranch, provides much information about the founder. Also helpful are sketches of King contained in James Cox, *Historical and Biographical Record of the Cattle Industry and Cattlemen of Texas and Adjacent Territory* (2 vols., 1894); James W. Freeman, ed., *Prose and Poetry of the Live Stock Industry of the United States* (1904); J. Marvin Hunter, comp. and ed., *The Trail Drivers of Texas* (1925); and Walter Prescott Webb and H. Bailey Carroll, eds., *The Handbook of Texas* (2 vols., 1952). William Broyles, Jr., "The Last Empire," *Texas Monthly*, Oct. 1980, pp. 150–73, 234–78; Dick Frost, *The King Ranch Papers: An Unauthorized and Irreverent History of the World's Largest Landholders, the Kleberg Family* (1985); and "The World's Biggest Ranch," *Fortune*, Dec. 1933, pp. 48–61, 89–98, 103–9, contain much additional information.

JIMMY M. SKAGGS

KING, Roswell (3 May 1765–15 Feb. 1844), builder, overseer, and manufacturer, was born in Windsor, Connecticut, the son of Timothy King and Sarah Anne Fitch, weavers. King's parents were poor at his birth but prospered thereafter. The extent of his education is unknown, but some is presumed on account of his birth in New England, where schools were generally available, and to his writing ability. Like many New Englanders in the postrevolutionary period, he moved to the South. He settled in Darien, Georgia, in 1789 and married Catherine Barrington in 1792. The couple had nine children. In Darien, King became county surveyor, justice of the peace, justice of the county inferior court, and a member of the Georgia House of Representatives (1794–1795). Two brothers, Reuben and Thomas, also came to Darien after King. King and his brother Reuben entered into a partnership to tan leather and make shoes, with his brother doing the work and King apparently supplying the capital. Early in his stay at Darien, King was the builder of Thomas Spalding's South End House on Sapelo Island, built of tabby.

In 1802 King became manager of Major Pierce Butler's rice and sugar plantations near Darien and his sea island cotton plantations on St. Simons Island, some ten miles by water from Darien. The Butlers lived in Philadelphia, so King ran the plantations. His responsibilities included general oversight of the planting operations, sale of produce, and management of the slaves. However, Butler knew the plantations and many of his slaves well and kept in close touch with King by letter. King was an efficient manager who made a profit every year for Butler. King and his family lived at Hampton Plantation on St. Simons Island, but he was frequently at Butler Island Plantation, just across the river from Darien. In 1819 he resigned his position and was succeeded by his son Roswell King, Jr.

When Fanny Kemble, an English actress, and her husband, Pierce Butler (the major's grandson), came to visit the Georgia plantations during the winter of 1838–1839, Kemble talked with a number of residents of the area who had known King and were familiar with how he ran the plantations. They all agreed that he was an excellent manager, but they differed as to his treatment of the Butler slaves. A number of slave women gave unfavorable accounts of King in this regard. The only specific that Kemble passed on was that King was "cruel and unscrupulous," separating men and women who lived together as man and wife if he heard of any disagreement between them. After separations King bestowed the men and women on other partners of his choosing.

King owned town property in Darien, a rice plantation with his own slaves, and an interest in a sawmill and in the Bank of Darien, a leading Georgia bank. In the early 1830s the Bank of Darien sent King to Dahlonega, in the heart of the area in north Georgia where gold had been discovered, to look after its interest there.

King was impressed with north Georgia and about 1837 secured a large tract of land in Cobb (now Fulton) County, about twenty miles north of the future site of Atlanta. He founded a town on his land and named it Roswell. He gave out ten-acre lots to friends from the Georgia and South Carolina coast if they would move to Roswell and build respectable houses there. His sons Barrington and Roswell, Jr., joined him in the Roswell Manufacturing Company, a cotton textile mill that they established there in 1839. King brought an architect from Connecticut, an English gardener, and about forty slaves from the Darien area to get the town established. A number of fine houses and a Presbyterian church were soon built. Roswell eventually became a bedroom community for Atlanta, with a population of 47,923 in 1990.

King had unbounded energy, was a hard worker, and possessed considerable vision. By the time of his death he was a member of the social and economic elite. He believed that the South's future lay in both agriculture and industry, as his work on the coast and in Roswell shows. He died in Roswell about six years after the founding of the town, sufficient time for him to see its growth and the prosperity to come.

King was a representative example of a plantation manager for an absentee owner, but he is undoubtedly best remembered as the founder of Roswell, Georgia, where a number of fine antebellum homes (at least one of which was built by a King) and the church still survive, and as the founder of the Roswell Manufacturing Company, one of the earliest cotton mills in Georgia.

• A number of Butler collections at the Historical Society of Pennsylvania can be identified from the bibliography and notes of Malcolm Bell, Jr., *Major Butler's Legacy: Five Generations of a Slaveholding Family* (1987), the most complete treatment of the Butler plantations and King's place there. A collection of his son Barrington's papers is in the Georgia State Archives. See also Frances Anne Kemble, *Journal of a Residence on a Georgian Plantation in 1838–1839* (1863), Margaret Davis Cate, *Our Todays and Yesterdays: A Story of Brunswick and the Coastal Islands*, rev. ed. (1930), Bessie

Lewis, *Hampton Plantation at Butler's Point on St. Simons Island, Ga.* (1978), Sarah Blackwell Gober Temple, *The First Hundred Years: A Short History of Cobb County in Georgia* (1935), and Burnette Vanstory, *Georgia's Land of the Golden Isles* (1956).

THE EDITORS

KING, Rufus (24 Mar. 1755–29 Apr. 1827), U.S. senator and diplomat, was born in Scarborough, Maine, the son of Richard King, a merchant, and Isabella Bragdon. King entered Harvard in the summer of 1773. Soon he began a lifelong membership in the Episcopal church and with his fellow students shared the excitement kindled by the Coercive Acts and the movement toward independence. Though the son of a Tory, he denounced the arrival of British troops in June 1775. "America spurns the production of the petty tyrant," asserted King, "and treating it with deserved contempt, stands firm upon the pillars of liberty, immovable as Heaven and determined as fate. One kindred spirit catches from man to man" (King, vol. 1, pp. 7–8). He graduated in 1777 at the head of his class.

Immediately after graduation, King began to study law under Theophilus Parsons at Newburyport, Massachusetts. But in August 1778 King sought an opportunity to serve in the army as the war again spread northward. Volunteering for militia service, King was given the rank of major and served as an aide to General John Glover during the brief expedition aimed at recapturing Newport, Rhode Island. In July 1780 King ended his three-year apprenticeship with Parsons. At the end of its session in Salem that month, the Court of Common Pleas in Essex County admitted King to practice law. For three years he argued cases of trespass or small debts. By October 1781 he was a justice of the peace and for a few years presided over minor local disputes and cases of assault and battery. In June 1783 he was admitted to practice before the Supreme Judicial Court of Massachusetts. By the middle of 1784 King seemed assured of success as a lawyer. He displayed a persuasive power in court, and his reputation was growing.

King served as a delegate to the Massachusetts General Assembly in 1783, 1784, and 1785. Believing that France was becoming too influential in the national government, King at first opposed a federal tariff in order to limit the power of Congress. But his experience as a delegate to Congress during the period 1784–1786 convinced him that he had been wrong. Indeed, as chairman of a committee on finances in 1786, he urged all the states to assist in payment of federal expenses. The Congress subsequently sent him and James Monroe on an unsuccessful mission to persuade the Pennsylvania legislature to follow Massachusetts's example of granting Congress a five percent impost.

As a child King had witnessed slavery in his father's household; after Massachusetts ended the institution he did not strongly oppose its existence in other states since he viewed it as a local matter. But slavery in federal territory was a very different issue, and King consistently denounced it, beginning in 1785, for political and moral reasons. In March 1785 he called for neither "slavery nor involuntary servitude" in the area to be known as the Northwest Territory. This phrase would later be incorporated in the Ordinance of 1787, which King partially drafted, and Nathan Dane introduced into Congress while King was serving in the Constitutional Convention at Philadelphia. Although concerned about the development of the West, King was willing to sacrifice western interests to ensure the prosperity of the East, as seen in his support of John Jay's fruitless efforts to obtain a commercial treaty with Spain by dropping the demand for free navigation of the Mississippi River.

In March 1786 King married Mary Alsop, the only daughter of a wealthy New York merchant. They had seven children. The three oldest sons, John, Charles, and James, especially distinguished themselves in public and business careers. In 1787 the Massachusetts legislature selected King as one of the state's delegates to the Philadelphia convention. Earlier King had asserted that only the Confederation Congress had the authority to amend the Articles of Confederation, but by January 1787 he was certain that the Confederation had reached a crisis and that the Congress would not act to institute needed changes. Therefore he contended that the convention held an equal right to amend the Articles of Confederation. Moreover, he supported a much stronger national government, where power would reside in the hands of the most populated states.

As a member of the Committee of Style, King did not greatly influence the wording of the Constitution. But he may have inserted the clause prohibiting states from impairing the obligation of contracts. His support for this clause primarily resulted from his closeness to merchants and creditors in New York. Before signing the Constitution, King suggested that the official records of the convention be either destroyed or left in the custody of the president since this would prevent opponents of the Constitution from using the proceedings to bolster their position. The convention subsequently agreed to turn over its journal and other papers to George Washington. Four months later King served as a delegate to the Massachusetts convention that ratified the Constitution.

The following year King moved with his family to New York City. He abandoned his law practice when he was elected to the state assembly, which in July 1789 selected him as a U.S. senator. A strong supporter of Alexander Hamilton's economic policies, King helped create the first Bank of the United States and served on its board of directors. He staunchly supported Washington's proclamation of neutrality and denounced the provocative statements by Edmond Genet, the French minister. Moreover, King led the attack against Albert Gallatin's right to be a senator, asserting that Gallatin, a Swiss immigrant, had not been a citizen of the United States for the nine years required by the Constitution. But King, like other Federalist leaders, was also suspicious of the influence of continental Europeans on American life and recognized Gallatin's strong ties to Hamilton's opponents.

Months after his reelection by a small majority of the New York legislature in early 1795, King co-authored, with Alexander Hamilton and John Jay, the "Camillus" papers, the most important essays published in defense of the Jay Treaty. When Thomas Pinckney resigned as minister to the Court of St. James, Hamilton and others supported King's appointment. President Washington, however, initially doubted the political wisdom of selecting King since he was known to favor England over France. Nevertheless, King received the appointment, and he proved to be an able and effective diplomat who helped to prevent a break in severely strained Anglo-American relations.

To block additional Irish support for the Jeffersonian Republicans in the United States, King successfully intervened to prevent the emigration of rebel leaders to the United States after the failure of the Irish rebellion in 1798. Though unable to get the British government to accept any limit to the practice of impressing American sailors, King convinced the British government in 1802 to accept a payment of £600,000 from the United States for the full satisfaction of all claims recoverable at the end of the revolutionary war that could not be recovered through ordinary legal procedure. Furthermore, U.S. courts would be open in the future to British creditors, and the London seizure commission would reconvene at once.

In August 1803 King tendered his resignation, a result of his length of service and the refusal of the Jefferson administration to revise the Jay Treaty's commercial provision, which was soon to expire. In February 1804 the Federalists named Charles Cotesworth Pinckney and King as candidates for the presidency and vice presidency. In the election the Republican candidates, Thomas Jefferson and George Clinton, swept to an easy victory.

With no immediate prospect of public office, King moved his family to Jamaica, New York, twelve miles from New York City. King also became involved in civic, church, and educational projects, including participation in the founding of the New-York Historical Society. In 1808 the Federalists again nominated Pinckney and King as their presidential and vice presidential candidates; once more they were decisively defeated by the Republican candidates.

Several months after the declaration of war in 1812, the New York legislature selected King as a U.S. senator. During the war he often led the Senate opposition against what he considered the Madison administration's inept actions. King particularly believed that James Madison's dependence on privateers failed to provide sufficient strength to America's naval defenses. He thus blamed Madison for inadequate protection of the Empire State, especially New York harbor. Moreover, King, like other commerce-conscious senators, opposed the president's plan for a new embargo. But King refused to participate in the Hartford Convention at the end of 1814. Opposed to disunionism, he hoped that moderates at the convention would triumph. In 1816 King became the Federalist standard-bearer in the presidential election, but the Federalists offered electoral tickets in only three states, Massachusetts, Connecticut, and Delaware. The last Federalist candidate for president, King received only 34 electoral votes against James Monroe's 183.

Remaining in the Senate, King voted against the bill creating the second Bank of the United States in 1816, primarily because he believed that the new bank would increase the patronage power of the Republican-controlled presidency. He later sponsored a navigation act that closed U.S. ports to British vessels coming from ports closed to U.S. vessels. He proposed that public lands be sold at a lower price and for cash, and he supported pensions for revolutionary war veterans. King also backed an amendment to the Constitution, dividing each state into electoral districts for the choice of presidential and vice presidential electors, which was meant to end southern control of the presidency by undermining the unity of electoral votes in the slave states.

In 1820 King was reelected to the Senate. He strongly opposed the admission of Missouri as a slave state since he wanted to prevent an increase in the South's political power and because he believed slavery went against natural law. But King continued to assert that the Constitution protected slavery where it already existed. Moreover, the New Yorker refused to support a proposal for the gradual abolition of slavery in the national capital and advocated the colonization of freed slaves outside of the United States.

In 1821 he served as a delegate at the New York Constitutional Convention. It adopted a new state constitution, which King believed was in some ways better than the original. He was especially pleased that it abolished the inefficient Council of Appointment and Council of Revision and required a two-thirds majority of the legislature to override the governor's veto.

Suffering from gout, King retired from the Senate in March 1825. But the next month he reluctantly agreed to serve one more term as minister to Great Britain. King, however, became ill in England, which forced his return to the United States in August 1826. He died less than a year later in New York City.

King served as a diplomat and as a politician during the first thirty-five years after the adoption of the Constitution. But by the time he reached a position of great leadership, the Federalist party was in decline. Indeed, except for John Marshall, King was the only original member of the Federalist party who refused to join the Republicans and yet remained an important national leader during the first decades of the nineteenth century. As a Federalist patriarch, he sought to protect and to advance the United States' prosperity and liberty by using history as the guide for developing public policy. Near the end of his career, King asserted: "The great secret of Life is to know when and where we are to cease our Efforts to mend or improve our Condition. . . . Experience and its lessons are safer Guides than the deductions of our Reason, which . . . are much influenced by the prevailing course of things, and the success of measures undertaken without prudence" (Rufus King to Edward King, 13 June 1820, in Ernst, p. 408).

• Most of Rufus King's manuscripts are in the New-York Historical Society. Additional correspondence is in the Henry E. Huntington Library, San Marino, Calif.; the Cincinnati Historical Society; the Lilly Library of Indiana University; the Library of the University of Texas; and the Columbia University Libraries. The best biography is Robert Ernst, *Rufus King: American Federalist* (1968). Also useful is Charles R. King, ed., *The Life and Correspondence of Rufus King*, (6 vols., 1894–1900).

STEVEN E. SIRY

KING, Rufus (26 Jan. 1814–13 Oct. 1876), soldier, editor, and diplomat, was born in New York City, the son of Charles King, a merchant and the ninth president of Columbia College, and Eliza Gracie. After attending the preparatory academy of Columbia, Rufus entered the U.S. Military Academy at West Point in 1829. After graduating fourth in the class of 1833, he was commissioned into the elite corps of engineers but resigned three years later to accept a position as a civil engineer with the New York & Erie Railroad. In 1839 he began a career as a newspaper editor. After two years with the *Albany Daily Advertiser*, he spent three years working with the prominent Whig editor Thurlow Weed on the *Albany Evening Journal*. In 1839 King was appointed adjutant general of New York's militia by Weed's close political ally Governor William H. Seward; he held this post for four years. In 1836 he married Ellen Eliot, who died in 1838; the couple had no children. Five years later, King married her sister Susan Eliot, with whom he had two children.

In 1845 King left New York to settle in the Wisconsin Territory. There he became editor and part-owner of the *Milwaukee Sentinel and Gazette*, which under his leadership became a powerful voice in Wisconsin politics. Embracing the Whig ideology of social improvement through government action, King advocated federal assistance for internal improvements, promoted the development of public libraries, and endorsed Prohibition. In 1846 he played a leadership role in the defeat of the first proposed Wisconsin constitution, which he opposed for its provisions proscribing banks. Two years later he was a member of the constitutional convention that framed the charter under which Wisconsin was admitted to the Union. In 1847 and 1850 he made unsuccessful bids for the mayoralty of Milwaukee. An especially enthusiastic promoter of education, King was a member of the University of Wisconsin's board of regents from 1848 to 1854, served on the board of visitors at West Point in 1849, and from 1859 to 1860 was a highly successful superintendent of the Milwaukee schools.

When the Lincoln administration took office, King was offered by his old ally Secretary of State Seward the post of minister to the Papal States, which he accepted on 22 March 1861. After the fall of Fort Sumter, he secured a leave of absence from this post and was commissioned a brigadier general of volunteers on 17 May 1861. On 5 August 1861 he reported for duty in Washington and assumed command of a brigade that eventually consisted of the Second, Fifth, Sixth, and Seventh Wisconsin, and Nineteenth Indiana volunteers. King's command, the only unit of its size to serve in the eastern theater composed entirely of troops from west of the Appalachians, over the next year and a half of service earned the nickname the "Iron Brigade."

In October 1861 King's brigade was attached to a division commanded by Irvin McDowell. When McDowell was promoted to corps command on 13 March 1862, King replaced him as division commander. In June McDowell's corps, which had spent most of May and June in the vicinity of Fredericksburg, was combined with Union forces in the Shenandoah Valley into a single army under the command of John Pope and ordered to make an overland campaign against Richmond. In July King was offered promotion to corps command in Pope's army but turned it down.

On 27 August 1862 his division was ordered to march to Manassas Junction and attack Confederate forces that had raided Union stores there. The orders were canceled the next day, and King was instead ordered to move toward Centreville, Virginia, along the Warrenton Turnpike. On the evening of the twenty-eighth, King's division was attacked by Confederate forces under the command of Thomas J. "Stonewall" Jackson. Just before the fighting began, King suffered an epileptic fit. Although the fit was less severe than one he had suffered several days before that had compelled him to ride in an ambulance, it nonetheless incapacitated him and compelled his units to fight the battle of Groveton (or Brawner's Farm) without any overall direction.

After the fighting had ended, a still unsteady King met with his brigade commanders, who objected to his plan to maintain the division's position along the Warrenton Turnpike. Their protestations, and information that indicated he faced Jackson's entire command, convinced King that his best course of action would be to retreat toward Manassas Junction. After reaching Manassas on the morning of the twenty-ninth King, still debilitated by the seizure and worn down by the evening's retreat to Manassas, turned his command over to his senior brigade commander. King's retreat stunned Pope, who had issued orders—that King never received—to hold his position. King's decision, and rumors that his unsteady disposition was due to drunkenness, made him a convenient target in Pope's post-battle search for scapegoats. A court of inquiry eventually reprimanded King for disobedience of orders and dereliction of duty.

King never again held a combat post. After the second battle of Manassas, he saw garrison duty at Fort Monroe, Virginia, sat on the court-martial of Fitz John Porter, and served as military governor of Norfolk. On 20 October 1863 he resigned his commission to accept reappointment as minister to the Papal States. He served in Rome until 1 January 1868, when Congress cut off funds to that post. The high point of his service in Rome was his arrest of John H. Surratt, who had fled the United States after being implicated in the Lincoln assassination plot. King served as deputy collector of customs for the port of New York until ill health compelled his resignation in 1869. He spent his remaining years in quiet retirement in New York City, where he died.

King's reputation was irrevocably scarred by the events of 28–29 August 1862. Yet on the evening of the twenty-eighth his battered, isolated division faced an enemy that outnumbered them three to one. Reinforcements could not have arrived in sufficient numbers to prevent the effective destruction of his command had Jackson chosen to attack on the morning of the twenty-ninth. Rufus King did not cost the Union army the second battle of Manassas. Indeed, the men his decision saved would, over the next three years, prove themselves among the finest in the Union army.

• There is no extant collection of King's personal papers. Various materials are scattered, however, among the collections of the State Historical Society of Wisconsin. Short biographical sketches are provided by his son Charles King, "Rufus King: Soldier, Editor, and Statesman," *Wisconsin Magazine of History* 4 (June 1921): 371–81, and by Ezra J. Warner, *Generals in Blue* (1964), and George W. Cullum, *Biographical Register of Officers and Graduates, U.S. Military Academy* (1891). Also see Alice E. Smith, *The History of Wisconsin*, vol. 1, *From Exploration to Statehood* (1973); Richard N. Current, *The History of Wisconsin*, vol. 2, *The Civil War Era, 1848–1873* (1976); Bayard Still, *Milwaukee: The History of A City* (1948); and Milo Quaife, ed., *The Attainment of Statehood* (1928), which are informative on his prewar career. Good sources on King's Civil War service include U.S. War Department, *War of the Rebellion: A Compilation of the Official Records of the Union and Confederate Armies* (70 vols. in 128 parts, 1880–1901), and Alan T. Nolan, *The Iron Brigade: A Military History* (1961). Alan D. Gaff, *Brave Men's Tears: The Iron Brigade at Brawner Farm* (1988), is harshly critical of King's performance at that battle. John J. Hennessy, *Return to Bull Run: The Campaign and Battle of Second Manassas* (1993), is more sympathetic. King's service in Rome can be traced in Leo Francis Stock, ed., *United States Ministers to the Papal States: Instructions and Despatches, 1848–1868* (1933), pp. 278–440.

ETHAN S. RAFUSE

KING, Samuel Archer (9 Apr. 1828–3 Nov. 1914), balloonist, was born in Tinicum, Pennsylvania, the son of Isaac B. King, a physician; his mother's name is unknown. In 1859 he married Margaret Roberts; they had two children.

Little is known of his early life except that he began his aeronautical career inauspiciously in 1851 with a near-fatal balloon ascent in Philadelphia. Undaunted, King tried again the next day, this time with more success. Eventually he totaled more than 450 flights as he thrilled thousands at Fourth of July exhibitions and state fairs. But King was more than a showman; he was an innovator widely credited with being the top aeronaut (balloonist) in the days before Samuel P. Langley and Wilbur and Orville Wright grabbed the spotlight with gliders and powered flying machines. In 1860 he hovered his balloon over Boston while photog-

rapher William Black took several pictures—among the first, if not the first, aerial photos.

King also introduced the soon-to-be indispensable drag rope to America. A famous English aeronaut named Charles Green had discovered the use of the drag rope several years before King first tried it in 1858. The rope acted as an altitude stabilizer, allowing the aeronaut to keep a given distance from the ground without constantly throwing out ballast to rise or eliminating gas to descend. If the balloon dropped suddenly, its weight would be reduced by the extra rope dragging on the ground, checking the descent; but if air currents should push the balloon up suddenly, its total weight would increase by that section of rope usually lying on the ground. The rope also was claimed to reduce rotary motion in the air.

Overland, the drag rope had its limits on anything but a flat, treeless landscape. Over a large body of water, however, its appeal was obvious. King was a cautious man, but he was convinced, as were many aeronauts of his day, that a transatlantic balloon voyage was possible. Judging the trip at anywhere from 3,000 miles and a week's duration to 10,000 miles and a month, King said it could be a precursor to a trip around the world.

Seeing the growing interest in airplanes, King wrote a magazine article called "How to Cross the Atlantic in a Balloon" (*Century*, Oct. 1901). In an introduction to the article, Cleveland Abbe, professor of meteorology for the U.S. Weather Bureau, said King "relies upon his management, and not upon aeroplanes, electric motors, whirling-fans, or any of the other complicated mechanisms that are but as toys in comparison with the power of the wind. We have no doubt that if he stays up long enough he will pass from America to Europe." King tried to finance the flight, which he thought would cost about $14,000, by taking long overland voyages with members of the press and representatives of the U.S. Signal Service, a branch of the army. But he never convinced the general public or the government to back him, despite his arguments, in the *Century* article, that the proposed balloon crossing would be comparable to the "first Atlantic cable, or the first steamship, or the first voyage of Columbus." He hoped to demonstrate "the latent possibilities of navigation by balloons instead of the impossible flying-machine for which the world has been waiting so long."

A technical highlight of the *Century* article is King's thinking on the lack of a light, pliable skin to retain enough hydrogen gas for a long trip. The oiled silk or cotton then in use was sufficient for short excursions because the inevitable slow gas leak was inconsequential. For a long trip, though, King suggested varnishing several thicknesses of silk after they had been sewn together. He also planned on a crew consisting of a captain, a first assistant expert in ocean navigation, and a second assistant who could pilot or navigate. For a voyage that under the worst of contrary wind conditions could last up to two months, the three were to divide their time between three "basket-cars": the command car fitted with beds; a "safety-car" where heating, lighting, and cooking could be done without danger of igniting the balloon's gas; and a car devoted solely to astronomical observations. An aluminum lifeboat, equipped with food and emergency equipment, would complete the assemblage. Rope ladders would allow the crew to move between the cars.

King continued to make short overland balloon flights. When he died in Philadelphia, King was the world's oldest aeronaut and the best known of the late nineteenth-century balloonists who scoffed at early airplane experiments. Though he did as much as anyone to popularize his avocation and add to its safety, ballooning has remained little more than an expensive sport. As one aviation historian put it, King and his contemporaries, "despite their hundreds of flights and their earnest belief in the future of aeronautics, made no significant contributions in the way of technical improvements" (Milbank, p. 164). Balloon enthusiasts would argue with that assessment, citing King's American popularization of the brilliantly simple drag rope and his imaginative, yet carefully thought out, additions to the literature on transoceanic flight.

• The balloonist himself wrote *The Balloon: Noteworthy Aerial Voyages from the Discovery of the Balloon to the Present Time, with a Narrative of the Aeronautic Experiences of Mr. Samuel A. King* (1879). One of the most complete assessments of King is in Jeremiah Milbank, Jr., *The First Century of Flight in America, an Introductory Survey* (1943). He gets a brief, laudatory mention in John P. V. Heinmuller, *Man's Fight to Fly: Famous World-Record Flights and a Chronology of Aviation* (1944). A detailed account of his earlier and mid-career flights, with little mention of technical innovations, can be found in *Appleton's Cyclopedia of American Biography* (1888). An obituary is in the *New York Times*, 4 Nov. 1914.

DAVID R. GRIFFITHS

KING, Stanley (11 May 1883–28 Apr. 1951), businessman and college president, was born in Troy, New York, the son of Henry Amasa King, a lawyer and judge, and Maria Lyon Flynt. His family's roots were in the Connecticut Valley, and in 1893 King moved with his family to Springfield, Massachusetts, where he attended the public schools. Enrolling in 1900 in Amherst College, his father's alma mater, King completed the course in only three years, obtaining an A.B. summa cum laude. After reading law with his father's firm, he entered Harvard Law School in 1904 as a second-year student, graduating in 1906 with an A.M. (having had only two years in residence at Harvard, he was deemed ineligible for an LL.B.).

Admitted to the bar in 1906, King found the prospective salaries offered by Boston law firms discouraging. As he wished to marry, he took a classmate's advice and applied to the W. H. McElwain Shoe Company, which was a major manufacturer of shoes in the Boston area. In December 1906 he married Gertrude Louisa Besse of Springfield; they had three children.

The McElwain company was profitable and progressively managed, and as legal adviser to the firm, King's income increased rapidly. He also found in McElwain personally a positive role model and mentor. Upon McElwain's death in early 1908, the firm's management was split among King, three of McElwain's sons, and another partner. With the advent of war in 1914, United States trade with belligerent countries was curtailed; this caused shoe orders overall to drop 50 percent. King, who had already made a few business trips to Europe, was again sent abroad with the goal of increasing direct sales to allied and non-allied countries in need of military footware. He spent fifteen months in war-ravaged Europe, including a long stint in a Russia that was on the brink of revolution.

After returning from Europe, King found that his law school classmate, Felix Frankfurter, had recommended him for a position with the newly formed Council of National Defense. Initially serving on the Committee on Supplies, his performance was such that in September 1917 he was appointed confidential clerk to Secretary of War Newton D. Baker. On 20 July 1918 he was promoted to become Baker's private secretary; in this post King served as a troubleshooter, dealing with several tough labor negotiations. He also accompanied Baker on his third and final inspection tour of postwar Europe. Resigning in May 1919, King returned to the McElwain Company and was promptly elected vice president.

Disaster soon struck. Wartime inflation had driven commodity prices sky-high. The company had ordered a huge supply of animal hides from India at market peak, only to see prices collapse shortly thereafter. Forced into payment with deflating dollars, the company was soon awash in red ink. King managed to negotiate a successful merger with the St. Louis-based International Shoe Company in 1921. Although the factory workers' jobs were saved, almost all of King's (and the other directors') equity was liquidated. King was soon asked to serve as eastern manager of the merged firm. Cutting his own salary in half, he was soon named as a director of the company. Using borrowed money to purchase company stock, he met his stated goal of reviving the eastern business within five years; he retired in April 1927 with his fortune restored.

In the meantime, King had reestablished himself in Boston civic circles. He served as a director of the Boston Chamber of Commerce. In 1919–1920 he became re-involved with Amherst, serving as vice chairman of a capital campaign that raised more than $3 million for the college. His performance was so conspicuous that he was elected to the board of trustees of Amherst College in June 1921. Joining the board with fellow Amherst graduate Calvin Coolidge, it was an organization that had changed almost completely from its makeup of clerics in the early days of the college to one that was largely secular in its membership. A major task faced by the board was the removal from office of college president Alexander Meiklejohn, a brilliant scholar but an erratic administrator who had lost nearly all of his support among the faculty and trustees. King was a leading figure in the efforts of the trustees, which ultimately resulted in Meiklejohn's resignation. He impressed fellow board members with his grasp of the issues involved, and the incident also served to focus King's attention on the multitude of duties and obligations faced by a college president.

King was additionally burdened during this period by the sudden death of his wife on 10 April 1923. On a happier note, he was instrumental during his term on the board in establishing the Folger Shakespeare Library in Washington, D.C., which was established in 1931 by a gift from the estate of oilman and Amherst graduate Henry C. Folger. The library was administered by the Amherst trustees, and King handled all legal negotiations connected with the transfer of materials from the estate. He later wrote a book about the experience titled *Recollections of the Folger Shakespeare Library* (1950). King was reelected to the Amherst board of trustees in 1926. After his second five-year term had expired he was elected a life member of the trustees. He was ultimately elected president of the college and installed on 1 July 1932.

As the first president of Amherst to come to the position with a background in business, King needed all the acumen he could muster as the Great Depression was at its deepest point, and academia had not been spared its effects. King had help, however; he had married Margaret Pinckney Jackson Allen in 1927, following her divorce.

The King administration was both progressive and pragmatic. Sound financial management was evident in the fact that no layoffs or salary reductions were required of faculty or staff. College enrollment actually increased, as did the size of the physical plant. The administration was streamlined with the creation of the Committee of Six, which superseded a multitude of faculty committees with overlapping responsibilities. Admission requirements were modernized; in particular, an onerous Latin language requirement was dropped. A comprehensive master plan that covered all aspects of student life at postwar Amherst was adopted, which enabled the college to adjust to the huge influx of returning veteran students. Most colleges faced the same challenge; the plan allowed Amherst to survive the period with a minimum of problems.

King surprised many by stepping down as president in 1946. He then served as president emeritus until his sudden death at his summer home in Martha's Vineyard, Massachusetts; an hour earlier he had agreed to speak at the following year's commencement.

Stanley King found success in both business and higher education; his career as an educator provides a good example of the benefits that can be derived from individuals with nonacademic backgrounds in positions of authority within academia.

• The papers of Stanley King are held at the Amherst College Archives, Amherst, Mass. King also wrote *A History of the Endowment of Amherst College* (1950), which traced the financial management of the college during the depression. The standard biography, Claude Moore Fuess, *Stanley King of Amherst* (1955), is factual but laudatory to a fault. An obituary is in the *New York Times*, 29 Apr. 1951.

EDWARD L. LACH, JR.

KING, Susan Petigru (23 or 25 Oct. 1824–11 Dec. 1875), writer, was born Susan Dupont Petigru in Charleston, South Carolina, the daughter of James Louis Petigru, a lawyer and attorney general of South Carolina, and Jane Amelia Postell, the daughter of a modest planter. After attending private day schools, she studied at Mme Ann Talvande's academy in Charleston and completed her education at Mme Guillon's finishing school in Philadelphia in 1839. On her return home she embarked upon the life of a belle, although her father suffered major financial losses from 1837 to 1842.

Impetuous, flirtatious, and quick-tempered, Sue, as she was always called, was pressed by her mother to marry soon and well. In 1843 she married Henry Campbell King; they had one child. The son of a wealthy Charleston attorney, Henry had been trained for the law in Germany but had not developed a significant practice. The marriage, never emotionally satisfying for Sue, got on better after 1850 when Henry became the junior partner in his father-in-law's law firm.

From 1845 until 1861, Sue King entertained frequently, met visiting dignitaries—lecturers, writers, politicians—at her own or her father's home, and was part of the fashionable Charleston society that prescribed a domestically oriented role for married women. Rebellious at any restriction on her behavior she began to write and, although her travels to New York and Saratoga in 1849 and 1850 furnished settings for several of her stories, the principal characters were Carolinians. In 1854 Appleton published her first collection, *Busy Moments of an Idle Woman*. The opening work, "Edith," is a traditional romance, but the short stories published with it develop themes that are central to nearly all her subsequent writing: a bitingly realistic critique of loveless marriages and various explorations of flirtations and courtships in which one character, generally but not always male, exploits the naïveté of the other protagonist. Despite its anonymity, King's authorship was quickly guessed in Charleston and the characters were matched with their putative originals, thus making King's aunt Louise Porcher fear that her writing would "make her more unpopular than ever."

Despite a largely southern readership, King's next and most highly praised novel, *Lily*, was also published in the North, but by Harper, in 1855. It is the story of a beautiful, blonde, rich orphan wooed by a man interested only in her fortune who not only is emotionally attracted to Lily's darker and poorer cousin but has a mulatto mistress as well. While developing this main story line, King lambastes older women who fail to warn younger ones of the snares men lay and explores jealousy between women. If at this distance the characters cannot be traced to their Carolina originals, King's cousin J. Johnston Pettigrew alleged that in fact all King's characters were "copies of what has actually existed." The settings are similarly drawn from real life: the plantation of an uncle, her Philadelphia boarding school, and familiar Charleston mansions.

Neither *Sylvia's World* nor *Crimes Which the Law Does Not Reach*, published respectively as serials in *Knickerbocker Magazine* and *Russell's Magazine* and then collected in a single volume published by Derby and Jackson in 1859, veers from this pattern. Much of *Sylvia's World* unfolds on Sullivan's Island, where the Kings spent long periods, and develops the character of Bertha St. Clair, who projected King's self-image as a worldly and experienced woman and became a major character in her last book. Similarly, the first stories in *Crimes* are autobiographical accounts of a young girl whose reputation is ruined by scandal-mongering gossip and of a young woman forced by her mother to marry a wealthy man physically unattractive to her. *Gerald Gray's Wife*, whose character models are openly discussed in Mary Boykin Chesnut's Civil War diary, was completed in 1863 and published as a *Southern Field and Fireside Novelette* in 1864. In it King launched her most extended and incisive critique of marriage, "from which there is no withdrawal, to which no bounds are assigned, never to be honorably dissolved," yet an institution in which many a woman finds that the man "she swore to honor and obey, was not capable of inspiring either sentiment. . . . She will learn to 'manage' him . . . or they will fight for supremacy, or she will be sullenly 'conquered,' or ingloriously conquer him, and so live, 'till death do them part!'"

King's own unhappy marriage ended when Henry was fatally wounded at the battle of Secessionville in June 1862. Apparently inheriting little from his debt-burdened estate, she tried with scant success to live by writing and, at war's end, by giving readings in northern cities. But by 1867 she was in Washington working as a government clerk. Her last published story, "My Debut," appeared the next year in *Harper's Magazine*. While it does address the marginal position of a working woman, it is largely a romantic story and ends happily with the heroine's marriage.

In 1870, King married Christopher Columbus Bowen, the Radical Republican boss of Charleston County and a South Carolina congressman. A pariah to Sue's family and former associates, Bowen had been court-martialed, stripped of his rank, and dismissed from the Confederate army for forgery and for being absent without leave. He had then been arrested by the civil authorities, but never tried, for planning the murder of his commanding officer. In addition, he was convicted of bigamy in 1871, though he was soon pardoned by President Ulysses S. Grant. Sue, notwithstanding, continued to live with Bowen in a physical comfort rare in postwar Charleston but in almost complete social isolation. She wrote no more. Although her tough-minded portrayal of Charleston society was confined to the prewar years, and her commentary on politics and slavery to an occasional page or two, she differed from her contemporary "literary domestics"

in her searing commentaries on sexual politics. In so doing, she went well beyond mere description of a localized, parochial society. At the time she died in Charleston, the bitterness of Reconstruction had made her yet more of a pariah than had her chastisement of marital tyranny and deceit.

• There is no collection of King's papers. In addition to the works mentioned in the text, the novel *Actress in High Life: An Episode in Winter Quarters* (1863) is sometimes attributed to King, although for no discernible reason. Steven M. Stowe, "Country, City, and the Feminine Voice," in *Intellectual Life in Antebellum Charleston*, ed. Michael O'Brien and David Moltke-Hansen (1986), treats her fiction, as does J. P. Scafidel, "Susan Petigru King: An Early South Carolina Realist," in *South Carolina Women Writers . . .* , ed. J. B. Meriwether (1979).

JANE H. PEASE
WILLIAM H. PEASE

KING, Thomas Butler (27 Aug. 1800–10 May 1864), congressman and diplomat, was born in Palmer, Massachusetts, the son of Daniel King, a captain in the revolutionary war, and Hannah Lord. King attended Westfield Academy until both his parents died. In 1816 he was placed under the care of his uncle, Zebulon Butler, who arranged for King to study law under both Garrick Mallory, a lawyer and jurist in Wilkes Barre, Pennsylvania, and Henry King, Thomas's brother. King was admitted to the bar in 1822.

After visiting his brother in Waynesville, Georgia, in 1823, King decided to begin his law practice there and became a member of the aristocratic planter society of Glynn County. On 2 December 1824 he married Matilda Page, daughter of William Page, a large landowner; they would have ten children. With his marriage, King assumed control of Page's estate at Retreat Plantation on Saint Simons Island, Georgia.

In the 1830s and 1840s King emerged as a prominent local, sectional, and national leader supporting cotton interests and commercial expansion. Elected to the Georgia state senate in 1832, 1834, 1835, and 1837, he began his political career as a Jacksonian Democrat. He soon became a staunch Whig, however, promoting government-financed internal improvements and economic expansion. He participated in commercial conventions in Augusta, Georgia, Charleston, South Carolina, and Macon, Georgia, between 1837 and 1839, and he led an unsuccessful attempt to develop the port of Brunswick, Georgia. Following a failed campaign for governor in 1837, King won election to the U.S. House of Representatives from Georgia's First District in 1838, 1840, 1844, 1846, and 1848. As chair of the House Committee on Naval Affairs, he sought to maintain, modernize, and expand the U.S. Navy by promoting the establishment of a Home Squadron and the adoption of the Naval Reorganization Act of 1842. His interest in expanding overseas commerce led him to advocate mail subsidies for American shipping, enlargement of the merchant marine, the construction of a transcontinental railroad and the Panama railway, and the development of steamship lines to China.

Despite his strong support for Zachary Taylor in 1848 and his role as a distinguished voice among "Commerce Whigs," King's hopes for an appointment as secretary of the navy were dashed by the opposition of his Georgia rivals Alexander Hamilton Stephens and Robert Toombs. Nonetheless, Taylor called on King to gather intelligence on California's political future under the guise of sending him west to study the need for mail steamship lines and survey routes for the Panama railway. In accordance with Taylor's wishes, King urged Californians to seek immediate statehood. Because of his support for Pacific mail steamship service, King received consideration for a California senatorship in 1849, but he lost to John C. Frémont and William Gwin. Despite this political setback, King continued to hope for a cabinet position because of his service in California and a scandal concerning a land claims settlement involving legal clients of Secretary of War George W. Crawford. Such ambition quickly vaporized, however, with the president's death and the Democratic-controlled Georgia legislature's partisan censure of King's activities in California.

King returned to California to establish business ties and again seek election to the Senate. In October 1850 President Millard Fillmore boosted King's political aspirations by appointing him collector of the Port of San Francisco, the most powerful federal office on the Pacific Coast. Controversies arose over his enforcement of the Customs House regulations, and the Fillmore administration was criticized for its slow confirmation of land titles in California and disregard for patronage recommendations from state officials; thus King failed to organize an effective Whig party in California. He lost his 1851 Senate race to John Weller by a strict party vote.

Between 1853 and 1859, King focused much of his attention on the declining fortunes of his cotton plantation at Retreat. His efforts to promote and finance the construction of a transcontinental railroad along the thirty-second parallel fell victim to the panic of 1857. Reentering Georgia politics in 1859 as a Democrat, he continued to promote internal improvements and sought to establish direct commercial links between southern ports and Europe to expand the cotton trade.

Though a moderate secessionist at the Democratic party convention in Charleston in 1860, King supported the Confederacy. When Georgia seceded from the Union, Governor Joseph E. Brown appointed King as a commissioner to England, France, and Belgium to gain recognition of the state's independence prior to the formation of the Confederacy and to establish direct steamship lines between Savannah and European ports. King's success in negotiating a steamship contract with the Liverpool firm of Frederick Sabel and Company, however, was in vain because of the Union blockade. After returning home to his new plantation in Ware County, in 1862 King narrowly failed to unseat Julian Hartridge from the Confederate Congress

in an election riddled with election fraud. While contesting the election results, King died of pneumonia in Ware County. An ardent champion of planter interests and the maritime concerns of his nation, King's economic concerns provided a foundation for American commercial expansion during the second half of the nineteenth century.

• King's papers are in the Southern Historical Collection at the University of North Carolina, Chapel Hill. Edward M. Steel, Jr., *T. Butler King of Georgia* (1964); Paul Murray, *The Whig Party in Georgia, 1825–1853* (1948); and Bruce A. Ragsdale, Kathryn Allamong Jacob, and Duane Nystrom, eds., *Biographical Directory of the United States Congress, 1774–1989* (1989), examine King's career as lawyer, planter, congressman, diplomat, and advocate of economic expansion.

DEAN FAFOUTIS

KING, Thomas Starr (17 Dec. 1824–4 Mar. 1864), Universalist minister and lecturer, was born in New York City, the son of Thomas Farrington King, a Universalist minister, and Susan Starr. Since his father moved from one pastorate to another, young King spent most of his formative years in Portsmouth, New Hampshire, and Charlestown, Massachusetts. He had little formal schooling and even that was terminated when he was fifteen years old because his father died. Forced to work in support of the family, he was at times a clerk, a bookkeeper in a dry-goods store, an assistant teacher in a grammar school (1840), a principal at another (1842), and in 1843 a bookkeeper at Charlestown Naval Yard. Throughout this time King actively pursued intellectual maturation. A voracious reader, he absorbed information at a remarkable pace and took advantage of lectures offered in Cambridge or Boston. His vigorous mind and thirst for knowledge drew the attention of Unitarian clergy and social reformer Theodore Parker, and through him King flourished among Boston's intelligentsia. At some point he began a serious program of theological study under the tutelage of local Universalist orator Hosea Ballou, and in 1845 he preached his first sermon. The following year he was ordained and assumed his father's old pulpit, the Universalist Church of Charlestown, where he served as pastor for two years.

In 1848 King became minister of the Hollis Street Unitarian Church in Boston. Unitarians and Universalists had separate origins and different sociological characteristics, but their common interests brought them into increasing agreement, as witnessed by King's easy transition from one denomination to the other. Also in 1848 he married Julia Wiggin; they had no children. Large crowds came to hear King speak, and it is difficult to say whether they attended because of his oratorical skills or his ideas. Both factors made him immensely popular. Possessed of a rich voice and sparkling personality, he could express himself clearly with both humor and deep moral earnestness. Not only was he acknowledged to be one of Boston's leading preachers, he also traveled widely as a speaker on the lyceum circuit, where his blend of charm and zeal impressed additional thousands.

By 1860 King had decided to take his ministry to California. Lecture tours throughout the eastern United States had acquainted him with conditions beyond the Bay State, and he regarded his move to a Unitarian church in San Francisco as something of a missionary enterprise. There he met continued success, drawing large audiences, achieving solvency in a struggling church, and completing its new construction plans. His lectures on Goethe, Socrates, Daniel Webster, and George Washington riveted his listeners, as did those on patriotism and the Constitution. Collections of his sermons found wide and constant readership, with several editions being reprinted and sold into the 1890s. Always a nature lover and avid hiker, King explored the California mountains and wrote of their beauty. He was instrumental in publicizing the Yosemite Valley and other natural wonders of the Pacific slope. His ability to accomplish that feat was confirmed much earlier in his poetic descriptions of nature in New England—for instance, this portrait of a sunset in *The White Hills* (p. 271): "The west was drenched in peach bloom; and over the whole mass of the towering fleece that mimicked Mont Blanc, was spread a golden flush just ready to flicker into rose-color, . . . which faded away to leave a death pallor as mournful as the upheaved snows of Switzerland can show, after the soul of sunshine has mounted from their crests."

King was a key figure in establishing Unitarianism on the West Coast, but his contribution in another sphere was equally significant. When the American Civil War began in 1861, there was some sympathy for California to remain neutral or even to set itself up as a separate republic. Stung by what he regarded as disastrous possibilities, King penned probably his best and certainly his most crucial address. He canvassed the state repeatedly with "Peace, What It Would Cost Us," arguing with forceful eloquence that neutrality was moral cowardice and secession a physical threat to Union success. His powerful appeals to federalist principles were pivotal in maintaining a spirit of loyalty to the national government. During the war King was also instrumental in raising large sums of money for the U.S. Sanitary Commission, an agency that distributed medicines and hygienic items to field hospitals in the Union army. King contracted diphtheria, which led to pneumonia and death at his residence in San Francisco. It is said the whole state mourned when its popular young minister died. Mountain peaks were named for him, and statuary were erected, notably in San Francisco's Golden Gate Park. Another indication of his continuing renown occurred in 1931 when the state of California placed King's statue in the U.S. Capitol as its representative citizen.

• Some materials related to King are in the California Historical Society Library, San Francisco, but the bulk of his lectures and journals are housed in the Bancroft Library at the University of California, Berkeley. The publication for which King is best known is *The White Hills: Their Legend, Landscape, and Poetry* (1859). Other works are *Patriotism and Other Papers by Thos. Starr King. With a Biographical Sketch, by Hon. Richard Frothingham* (1864); *Christianity and Humanity: A Series of Sermons*, ed. Edwin P. Whipple (1877); and *Substance and Show, and Other Lectures*, ed. Whipple (1877). Biographical information is in Charles W. Wendte, *Thomas Starr King: Patriot and Preacher* (1921); Richard Frothingham, *A Tribute to Thomas Starr King* (1921); and Arnold Compton, *Apostle of Liberty: Starr King in California* (1950). An obituary is in the *New York Times*, 5 Mar. 1864.

HENRY WARNER BOWDEN

KING, William (9 Feb. 1768–17 June 1852), merchant shipper, army officer, and governor of Maine, was born in Scarborough, Maine, the son of Richard King, a merchant and shipowner, and Mary Black. He was educated at home, but he spent one term at Phillips Academy in Andover, Massachusetts.

In 1791 King moved to Topsham, Maine, where he became partners with his brother-in-law, Dr. Benjamin Porter, in a store, lumbermill, and shipyard. King oversaw the construction of five vessels by 1796 that he operated in the West India trade. King relocated to nearby Bath, Maine, in 1800 and soon became the leading citizen both of that community and of Maine, then a part of Massachusetts. He married Ann M. Frazier of Boston in 1802, and the couple had two children. During this time King built a home and a shipyard and quickly became a successful merchant capitalist. He pioneered the New Orleans cotton trade with Liverpool, England, and established two banks, a marine insurance company, a toll road, and a small cotton and woolen mill. He also invested in real estate, purchasing land in Franklin County and naming it Kingfield.

At the same time, King quickly became the most influential politician in Maine. In 1795 he was elected to the Massachusetts General Court as a Federalist. In 1803 he switched from the Federalist party to the Democratic-Republican party of Thomas Jefferson, and he was narrowly elected to the Massachusetts General Court in 1805. There he became a spokesman for average citizens of the district of Maine and the acknowledged leader of the movement to separate Maine from Massachusetts. King led a successful effort to pass a law in 1808 giving rights to the thousands of settlers who had moved to Maine after the Revolution and "squatted" on former Loyalist lands. He was also instrumental in the passage of an 1811 act doing away with a compulsory tax to support the Congregational church.

In 1808 King was commissioned a major general and placed in command of the Eleventh Division of militia composed of Maine residents. This involved him in military duties during the War of 1812. King called the militia to arms in June 1814, when the British invaded and occupied eastern Maine as they had during the Revolution. When Massachusetts refused to provide aid to oust the enemy, King made a concerted effort to win separation after the war; but he and his supporters failed to win sufficient votes in an 1816 referendum because of opposition in coastal towns.

In 1818 King was elected to the Massachusetts State Senate and began a methodical effort to win separation. He worked to elect separationists and published broadsides and articles in the *Eastern Argus*, a Portland, Maine, newspaper he supported financially. King went to Washington and met with his half-brother, Senator Rufus King of New York, and Secretary of the Treasury William H. Crawford to lobby for passage of a revised federal navigation law to win the support of maritime communities. When the new law passed, King promised Maine Federalists one-third of appointments in a new state government. As a result of King's work, in addition to Massachusetts's refusal to aid Maine in 1814, the separation referendum was approved overwhelmingly in July 1819, and in October King was elected president of the constitutional convention. When Maine statehood was linked to the slavery issue and the admission of Missouri to the Union, King first opposed, then later agreed to support, the Missouri Compromise, which brought statehood to Maine in March 1820. King was named acting governor and then elected to the office unopposed in April. Reelected to a second one-year term in 1821, he proposed legislation to encourage manufacturing and to purchase the half of Maine public lands held by Massachusetts, but both initiatives failed.

King resigned as governor in June 1821 to become a commissioner to settle Spanish claims under the Adams-Onís Treaty. When he returned to Maine in 1824, he was appointed commissioner of public buildings in 1828 and oversaw the construction of the first state house in Augusta. In 1830 King was appointed collector of customs in Bath.

With the rise of the Jacksonian Democrats, King's U.S. Bank charter was not renewed in 1832 and government deposits were withdrawn, creating a shortage of funds. When King's term as collector of customs ended in 1834, a Jackson supporter was appointed. Having switched to the Whig party, he was defeated in a run for governor in 1835. King's business career also suffered a decline. He left shipbuilding and shipping, and he was forced to sell off his real estate holdings. King became forgetful and confused after 1847, and his affairs were put into the hands of a guardian. His home in Bath and farm in Kingfield were sold at auction, and he died penniless in Bath.

From 1807 until 1821 King was the most influential citizen of the district of Maine and the acknowledged leader of the separation movement because of his remarkable leadership skills. In recognition of his contributions, the Maine legislature appropriated funds in 1853 to erect a monument on his grave, and he was selected as one of two Maine representatives in the hall of heroes in the Capitol building in Washington, D.C.

• King's papers are in the collections of the Maine Historical Society, Portland. A biography is Marion Jaques Smith, *General William King: Merchant, Shipbuilder, and Maine's First Governor* (1980). King is the most prominent personality described in Ronald F. Banks, *Maine Becomes a State: The Movement to Separate Maine from Massachusetts* (1970).

JOEL WEBB EASTMAN

KING, William Rufus Devane (7 Apr. 1786–18 Apr. 1853), U.S. senator and vice president, was born in Sampson County, North Carolina, the son of William King, a well-to-do planter and North Carolina state legislator, and Margaret Devane. After attending the University of North Carolina (1801–1804), William R. King left school to read law. Admitted to the bar at the end of 1805, he commenced practice in Clinton, the county seat of Sampson County. He was elected to the lower house of the North Carolina legislature in 1808, was chosen a circuit solicitor in 1809, and was elected to Congress in 1810. There he allied himself with the young nationalists later known as the War Hawks. King's first speech supported using tariffs to encourage domestic manufactures and proposed a protective duty on salt. He voted for the declaration of the War of 1812 and supported its vigorous prosecution.

King resigned from Congress in April 1816 to accept appointment as the secretary to the legation headed by William Pinkney, who had been appointed minister both to Russia and to the Kingdom of the Two Sicilies. After a year abroad King returned to the United States in the summer of 1817, and in 1818 he removed to the Alabama Territory, settling in Dallas County, in the Black Belt. He began planting on an extensive scale; the eighty slaves he owned in 1820 made him Dallas County's second-largest slaveholder.

King played a leading role in the founding of the city of Selma, located near his plantation. He was active in the constitutional convention of 1819, serving as a member of the Committee of Fifteen that actually drafted the new state constitution. He was elected as one of Alabama's first two U.S. senators in the fall of 1819, drawing the short term. Elected, despite strong opposition, to a full term in 1822, he was reelected without opposition in 1828 and 1834 and then on a party-line vote over the Whig nominee in 1840.

During his first twenty-five years in the Senate, King focused his attention particularly on public land questions. He sought lower prices, preemption rights, and easier terms for purchasers, and he led the Jacksonian opposition to Henry Clay's bill to distribute the proceeds of public land sales to the states. By this time a moderate opponent of protective tariffs, he voted against the tariffs of 1816, 1824, and 1828. In the nullification crisis, he opposed both nullification and the Force Bill, denounced John C. Calhoun for advocating nullificationist doctrines, but reluctantly accepted the tariff of 1832 and cooperated actively with Henry Clay in securing the passage of the compromise tariff of 1833. He supported all of Andrew Jackson's actions during the Bank War and Martin Van Buren's independent treasury bill. But he did not favor a wholly specie currency; instead he sought to limit bank notes to large denominations so that the daily business of ordinary citizens would be in specie, with paper money available only for substantial commercial transactions.

During these years King formed a close and affectionate relationship with James Buchanan of Pennsylvania. The two lifelong bachelors shared the same views on most public questions and in private life held each other in the highest regard. It is not clear whether the friendship had a sexual component, although contemporaries sometimes implied that it did. The relationship was never overtly a political issue. It certainly much influenced each man's attitude toward the emerging sectional conflict, however, leading Buchanan to defend southern interests from the attacks of abolitionists and convincing King that, despite those attacks, most northerners were not in fact inimical to his region. King's strong desire for sectional compromise was a significant element in his devotion to the Democratic party. To ensure the party's intersectional character, King at the Democratic national convention of 1832 sponsored the requirement of a two-thirds vote to nominate a candidate. This rule was intended to guarantee that no one could be nominated without support from both northern and southern delegations.

In April 1844 King resigned his Senate seat in order to accept John Tyler's (1790–1862) appointment as minister to France. King strongly favored Tyler's proposal to annex Texas, and he shared with the administration the fear that France might support Mexico in resisting the action. He succeeded, however, in securing French promises of neutrality both on the Texas question and on the United States' dispute with Britain over Oregon. During his time in Paris, too, King, with the cooperation of Secretary of State John C. Calhoun, undertook to bribe French newspaper editors to obtain the insertion of articles favorable to American slavery.

King returned to the United States in the fall of 1846 and almost at once began maneuvering to regain his Senate seat. In 1847 King's successor, Dixon H. Lewis, sought election to a full term, and King became a candidate against him. A deadlock ensued; Whig legislators remained loyal to a third candidate, while King's orthodox Jacksonian supporters found Lewis, the leader of the Democracy's small Calhounite faction, unacceptable. The bitter contest continued through eighteen ballots until King withdrew his name and Lewis was chosen. In June of 1848 Alabama's other senator, Arthur P. Bagby, resigned to become minister to Russia, and Governor Reuben Chapman appointed King to succeed him. In 1849 King was elected to a full term, defeating Chapman and a Whig after three ballots.

The sectional controversy dominated King's last years in the Senate. King served as a member of the select committee of thirteen that drafted the Compromise of 1850, and he vigorously defended the measures from the attacks of Southern Rights members. He refused to vote for the Omnibus Bill, however, because the Senate would not agree to his amendment to divide California and leave its southern half in territorial status under popular sovereignty. During this

same session King and Stephen A. Douglas obtained the enactment of a bill to grant alternate sections of public lands along their routes to the Illinois Central and Mobile and Ohio Railroads, to aid their construction. This act was probably the most important legislative achievement of King's congressional career because it served as a model for the many railroad land grants passed by Congress over the next quarter-century. In his role as chairman of the Senate Foreign Relations Committee, he also led the effort to secure the ratification of the Clayton-Bulwer Treaty.

King was an authority on the Senate's rules and had served as the body's president pro tempore from 1836 to 1841. On the death of Zachary Taylor in July 1850, King again was chosen president pro tempore, and he presided over the Senate for the next two and a half years. In the summer of 1852, the Democratic national convention nominated King for the vice presidency on the ticket with Franklin Pierce—in part to placate the disappointed followers of James Buchanan. Although he was elected in November, King had contracted tuberculosis, and his health was rapidly failing. On the advice of his doctor, he resigned from Congress on 20 December 1852 and went to Havana, Cuba.

A special act authorized U.S. Consul William L. Sharkey to administer King the oath as vice president in Cuba, and he was sworn in on 24 March 1853, the only president or vice president in American history to be inaugurated on foreign soil. Wishing to die in Alabama, however, King returned to the United States in April. He died the day after arriving at his plantation in Dallas County, Alabama.

• Few of King's papers have survived, but there are small collections at the Alabama Department of Archives and History, Montgomery, and in the Southern Historical Collection of the University of North Carolina, Chapel Hill; his letters to James Buchanan are in the Buchanan papers at the Historical Society of Pennsylvania, Philadelphia. On King's career, see John M. Martin, "William Rufus King, Southern Moderate" (Ph.D. diss., Univ. of North Carolina, Chapel Hill, 1956); three articles by Martin: "William R. King and the Compromise of 1850," *North Carolina Historical Review* 39 (Autumn 1962): 500–518, "William R. King: Jacksonian Senator," *Alabama Review* 18 (Oct. 1965): 243–67, and "William R. King and the Vice-Presidency," *Alabama Review* 16 (Jan. 1963): 35–54; and Martin's sketch of King in the *Dictionary of North Carolina Biography* vol. 3 (1988).

J. MILLS THORNTON III

KING PHILIP. *See* Philip.

KINGSBURY, Albert (23 Dec. 1862–28 July 1943), inventor, mechanical engineer, and professor of engineering, was born at Goose Lake near Morris, Illinois, the son of Lester Wayne Kingsbury, the superintendent of a stoneware factory, and Eliza Emeline Fosdick. After graduating from high school in 1880, Kingsbury acquired his advanced education in fits and starts. He studied one year at Buchtel College (later University of Akron) in Ohio in the Latin-scientific course but dropped out in 1881 and took a job as a machinist's apprentice with the Turner, Vaughn and Taylor Company of Cuyahoga Falls, Ohio. In September 1884 Kingsbury reentered school at Ohio State University in Columbus, Ohio, where he studied mechanical engineering. At the end of his sophomore year, because of a lack of funds, he again dropped out of school. Later in 1886, at the arrangement of Professor S. W. Robinson of Ohio State University, he went to work at the Carver Cotton Gin Company, East Bridgewater, Massachusetts. He then became a machinist at Warner and Swasey Company in Cleveland, Ohio. In the fall of 1887 Kingsbury reentered school at Sibley College, Cornell University. While at Cornell he studied under R. H. Thurston and was assigned problems in lubrication, a field that would become his life's work. After graduating from Cornell in 1889, he took a teaching position at the New Hampshire College of Agriculture and the Mechanic Arts at Hanover, New Hampshire (later the University of New Hampshire at Durham). In 1890 he returned to private industry and worked for his cousin Hoarace B. Camp in Cuyahoga Falls as superintendent of a brickmaking-machine factory. From 1891 to 1899 he taught as a full professor at New Hampshire College. In 1893 he married Alison Mason of Stamford, Connecticut; they had five children.

While performing basic research in the field of friction of screws and nuts ("Experiments on the Friction of Screws," *Transactions of the American Society of Mechanical Engineers* 17 [1896]: 96–116), Kingsbury became aware of the possibility of using air as a lubricant. In late 1896 Kingsbury was directed to the theoretical work on lubrication of engineering professor Osborne Reynolds, and the following year Kingsbury published an article on air-lubricated bearings ("Experiments with an Air-lubricated Bearing," *Journal of the American Society of Naval Engineers* 9 [1897]). Kingsbury's academic work saw little direct application; he sought instead to answer basic questions that would further the science of lubrication and to teach students who would eventually utilize their knowledge in practical applications.

In 1898 Kingsbury began what was probably the most important part of his research when he moved from the study of air lubrication to experiments with tilting, segmented, oil-thrust bearings. Thrust bearings counteract the forces of a turning shaft parallel to the axis of rotation (as opposed to journal bearings, which counteract the forces perpendicular to the rotation of a shaft). The need for thrust bearings increased as machinery became larger and heavier and turned faster. In 1898 and 1899 Kingsbury had students apply his concept of a tilting-pad oil-thrust bearing in experimental installations in an electric generator and a vertical steam engine. While this student work had little immediate effect on the industry, it proved essential to Kingsbury's later patent claims.

In 1899 Kingsbury took a new teaching position at Worcester Polytechnic Institute in Worcester, Massachusetts, where he continued his research in lubrication. At Worcester, his students Walter S. Graffam

and William S. Traill continued research on the oil-thrust bearing in 1900. In 1903 Kingsbury returned to private industry as a general engineer for Westinghouse Electric and Manufacturing Company in Pittsburgh, Pennsylvania. There he designed a tilting-pad oil-thrust bearing for Westinghouse in 1904, but it was discarded after an unsuccessful shop test. In 1906 Westinghouse began a patent application for the oil-thrust bearing, but the president, E. M. Herr, did not approve, and Kingsbury had to personally pay for the expense of obtaining the patent. The initial patent application was denied because of British engineer Anthony Michell's existing patent of 1904, but it was granted after the filing of affidavits of priority by Kingsbury's students Frank L. Baker, Harry Nelson Putney, Graffam, and Traill. (The business ramifications of the independent development of the bearing by Kingsbury and Michell, and their separate ownership of American and British patents, appears to have been initially solved by the splitting of the market. Kingsbury and Michell initially, and informally, divided the American and European markets for bearings and avoided patent litigation. In subsequent years both the Michell and Kingsbury companies competed head to head.) In 1909 Kingsbury was able to convince H. P. Davis, the vice president and manager of engineering at Westinghouse, to allow the installation of the experimental bearing on a large vertical motor only after the inventor himself agreed to bear the cost of its production. Although it worked in shop tests, Westinghouse rejected the revolutionary bearing, and the motor was shipped to the customer with a common roller bearing. A conservative attitude toward engineering innovation was not unusual; the Westinghouse corporate reaction to dramatic engineering change was typified, according to Kingsbury, by the statement "there ain't no such animal." When in 1910–1911 Westinghouse finally became interested in the bearing, Kingsbury sold them a limited license to use the design.

In 1912 Kingsbury received his first opportunity to install his new bearing design. The contract from the Pennsylvania Water and Power Company called for him to replace the existing roller bearing on the McCall's Ferry (now Holtwood) 10,000-horsepower hydroelectric generator with a bearing of his own design. Kingsbury supervised the installation of an oil-thrust bearing built by Westinghouse, which almost immediately failed but, after being remachined to tighter specifications, operated faultlessly.

The Kingsbury bearing differed substantially from the roller-thrust bearing that it largely replaced. The Kingsbury bearing has an enclosed, flat running plate on which tilting, flat, loose-fitting shoes (metal plates that balance on pivots) ride on a thin wedge of oil. The oil actually supports the load or thrust of the turning shaft. If properly maintained, the bearing exhibits little actual wear. In addition to having maintenance advantages, Kingsbury bearings also significantly decreased the amount of energy lost to friction as compared to roller bearings.

After their success at Holtwood, Kingsbury's bearings became popular for large hydroelectric stations and pumping installations. In 1917 the U.S. Navy began using Kingsbury bearings on propeller shafts (the British Navy had begun using Michell bearings in 1914). This application of the bearing to maritime use firmly secured Kingsbury's reputation and fortune. In 1921 Kingsbury set up his own manufacturing operation, Kingsbury Machine Works, Inc., in Philadelphia, Pennsylvania, but continued to contract out much of his work. He died in Greenwich, Connecticut.

Kingsbury's early academic career exemplified the turn-of-the-century change in engineering style and education. Where traditional engineers once made choices based on shop floor experience and intuition, the new wave of engineers, like Kingsbury, made decisions based on mathematics, scientific experimentation, and theoretical understanding. Whether assigned to Kingsbury or to Michell, the invention of the tilting-pad oil-thrust bearing remains an important contribution to heavy machinery design. Its adoption and use in hydroelectric stations, large pumps, and maritime engines increased efficiency and greatly decreased maintenance and downtime.

• As with many engineers, no great archive of papers exists for Kingsbury. The Cornell University Department of Manuscripts and University Archives has an interesting group of papers that document the tax case of *Albert Kingsbury v. the United States* in 1925. Additional information on Kingsbury's patent and tax battles can be found in Ewart Hobbs, reporter, *Cases Decided in the Court of Claims of the United States, June 1, 1929–January 31, 1930*, vol. 68 (1930), pp. 680–93. Insight on Kingsbury's invention can be found in his article "Development of the Kingsbury Thrust Bearing," *Mechanical Engineering* 72 (Dec. 1950): 957–62. See also J. E. L. Simmons and S. D. Advani, "Michell and the Development of Tilting Pad Bearings," undated and unpublished in the collection of the Division of Engineering and Industry, National Museum of American History, Washington, D.C.; A. G. M. Michell, "Progress of Fluid-Film Lubrication," *Transactions of the American Society of Mechanical Engineers* 51, pt. 2 (1929): 153–63; and Diedre Watters, "Kingsbury's Famed Bearing," *Economy Magazine*, Mar. 1984. An obituary is in the *New York Times*, 29 July 1943.

PETER LIEBHOLD

KINGSLEY, Clarence Darwin (12 July 1874–31 Dec. 1926), education reformer, was born in Syracuse, New York, the son of Edwin Abijah Kingsley, a lawyer and Phi Beta Kappa graduate of Union College, and Emma Howell Garnsey, a Vassar College graduate and high school teacher of German. When Kingsley was eight years old his father died, and he spent most of his youth as part of an extended family in the Garnsey homestead. Graduating first in his class at Syracuse High School, he entered Colgate University where he majored in science and mathematics and was elected to Phi Beta Kappa. Upon graduation in 1897 he enrolled in Colgate Theological Seminary and supported himself as an instructor of mathematics in the college. While there he assisted in the preparation of the second edition of James Taylor's textbook in the calculus.

In 1902, before completing his preparation for the Baptist ministry, Kingsley left Colgate, renounced his ambition to become a missionary to China, and became a social worker in Edward T. Devine's Charity Organization Society of New York. He was assigned to work among the city's growing population of derelict men and alcoholics. He also enrolled in Teachers College, Columbia University, where Devine taught as an adjunct professor, to take courses in sociology, education, and ethics. His master's essay, submitted to the faculty of political science in 1904, was titled "The Treatment of Homeless Men in New York City." The high rate of recidivism among homeless men proved disheartening to Kingsley, however, and that year he left social work to become a teacher of mathematics in Brooklyn's Manual Training High School. He was also assigned the duty of preparing the semester schedule for students and faculty.

Kingsley soon discovered the problems inherent in trying to fit a large student body with diverse vocational needs into a schedule that could also meet a wide variety of college entrance requirements. He addressed this dilemma in three reports published in the *Bulletin of the New York High School Teachers Association*. They were instrumental in bringing him to national attention. The first report (1907–1908) tabulated the widely varied college entrance requirements. The second (1909–1910) addressed the problem of Brooklyn's rapidly growing high school population and the need for additional construction. Kingsley argued that new space should be provided on the present sites to expand the variety of specialized offerings at existing high schools. He called the projected new space the "university high school." He buttressed his argument with data that showed the high cost in time and money being paid by Brooklyn's current 11,667 students to travel to the high school of their choice. This report was prepared with the assistance of Elizabeth Seelman, a teacher of English at Girl's Commercial High School who in 1914 became Kingsley's wife; they had no children. The final report (1910–1911) proposed a remedy to the varied college entrance requirements, a plan for articulating the work of the high school and the college; in it Kingsley argued that a high school course that prepared for life was also good preparation for college.

Kingsley took his final report, along with favorable comments from one hundred college presidents, teachers' associations, and school superintendents, to the annual convention of the National Education Association (NEA) in Boston in July 1910. He contended that there was a wide discrepancy between what the colleges were demanding for admission and what the New York schools considered the best preparation for life. He called for the colleges to accept all standard subjects taught in the high schools, urged that the language requirement be reduced to one language, which could be a "modern" language, and advocated the acceptance of the "new" subjects of the household and practical arts, the commercial subjects, economics, civics, music, and art. His plan rejected dualism and sought to bring the student body together so that the best preparation for life would also be considered good preparation for college.

Kingsley's views met with the favorable response of three NEA departments, and one of them, the Department of Secondary Education, created a blue ribbon committee with Kingsley as its chairman to investigate the problem further. The *Report of the Committee of Nine on the Articulation of High School and College*, which was published by the NEA in 1911, was little more than a refinement of Kingsley's New York report, but he considered it a starting point. He continued his personal study of college entrance requirements and, appointed as "special agent" of the U.S. Bureau of Education, a nonpaying position, had his study published as *Bulletin No. 7* of the bureau for the year 1913. He had found that only about one-fourth of the 204 liberal arts colleges studied would accept four units of practical work for admission as recommended by the NEA report. Clearly if high school programs were going to meet the needs of the community the colleges would need to be more flexible. In 1912, at Kingsley's request, the NEA expanded his committee by adding twelve subcommittees to determine how each of the several subjects could serve a dual function. In 1913, again at Kingsley's request, the NEA added a reviewing committee, the NEA Commission on the Reorganization of Secondary Education, charged with providing a set of aims and evaluating the work of the twelve committees reorganizing the subjects. This committee produced the famous *Cardinal Principles of Secondary Education* with its "seven aims" for education. Stated in broad terms the seven aims referred to health, command of fundamental processes, worthy home membership, vocation, citizenship, worthy use of leisure time, and ethical character. The report was published as *Bulletin No. 35* of the U.S. Bureau of Education for 1918. It became probably the single most important force in shaping American secondary education in the twentieth century.

In 1912 the position of high school agent in Massachusetts opened, and Kingsley's appointment to that post gave him the time to work on the NEA-sponsored reorganization. There William Orr, a member of Kingsley's Committee on the Articulation of High School and College, was deputy commissioner for high schools, and David Snedden was the commissioner of education. Snedden urged a quite different and more extreme form of reorganization. In 1911 he had endorsed the report of the committee, guardedly noting that it represented "a distinct step in advance in the solution of the high school problem." After that, however, Kingsley and Snedden went separate ways. Snedden called for course reorganization based on precisely defined objectives that were job related and a different set of objectives for each vocational destination. As early as 1910 Kingsley's objectives were stated

in terms of life activities broad enough in scope to provide common experiences for students headed for different roles in life. Snedden wanted each subject to contribute to the student's maximum vocational efficiency, while Kingsley advocated common backgrounds and vocational flexibility.

Cardinal Principles of Secondary Education opened the way for the rise of the large comprehensive high school not unlike the "university high school" Kingsley envisioned in 1907. In 1922 the NEA Commission on the Reorganization of Secondary Education published as *Bulletin No. 23* of the U.S. Bureau of Education its report titled "High School Buildings and Grounds" to meet the needs of the schools. In 1923 Kingsley left Massachusetts to become a private consultant in school-building construction. He died shortly after collapsing from an internal hemorrhage on the steps of the Cincinnati Union Station as he was returning from an assignment.

Through his careful study of existing institutions, dedication, and vision Clarence Kingsley worked a significant change in schooling at the secondary level. Though primarily a high school teacher, his reforms became national in scope.

• Kingsley's many reports for the New York High School Teachers Association are in the annual yearbooks of the association in the New York Public Library. Much material relating to the NEA Commission on the Reorganization of Secondary Education (CRSE) and Kingsley's central role in that work is in Record Group 12 of the files of the U.S. Commissioner of Education in the National Archives. Perhaps Kingsley's most significant comment on the work of the CRSE is in "Discussion and Correspondence," *School and Society*, 5 July 1919. See also "Certain Features in the Report on Cardinal Principles of Secondary Education," *Third Yearbook of the National Association of Secondary School Principles* (1919). For Kingsley's efforts to make the more modern and practical subjects available to all students, see "How Can We Best Secure a Working Agreement between Colleges and High Schools?," *Proceedings of the Association of Schools and Colleges of the Middle States and Maryland* 27 (1913): 61–68. See also his "Meetings of the CRSE," *High School Quarterly* 3 (Apr. 1915): 174–75; "Meetings of the CRSE," *Educational Administration and Supervision* 1 (May 1915): 330–37; "The Reorganization of Secondary Education," *Journal of Education* 77 (15 May 1913): 543; "The Reorganization of Secondary Education—New Aims of the Modern High School," *Journal of Education* 79 (23 Apr. 1914): 458; and "Report of the Progress of the Reviewing Committee of the NEA Commission on the Reorganization of Secondary Education," *High School Quarterly* 4 (July 1916): 287–90. Walter H. Drost, "Clarence Kingsley—the New York Years," *History of Education Quarterly* 6 (Fall 1966): 18–34, is a somewhat more detailed account of Kingsley's efforts for secondary reorganization. Obituaries are in the *Cincinnati Inquirer*, 31 Dec. 1926, and the *Syracuse Post Standard*, 1 Jan. 1927.

WALTER H. DROST

KINGSLEY, Darwin Pearl (5 May 1857–6 Oct. 1932), insurance executive, was born near Alburg, Vermont, the son of Hiram Pearl Kingsley, a farmer and state legislator, and Celia LaDue. After attending local common schools and the Barre (Vt.) Academy, Kingsley entered the University of Vermont at Burlington in the fall of 1877. Forced by modest finances to walk to the campus, he worked his way through the university by doing a variety of jobs, including a stint as the college bell ringer, and graduated with an A.B. in 1881.

Seeking greater opportunity in the West, Kingsley visited his sister's Wyoming ranch following graduation, but, finding employment prospects there slim, he drifted to Denver, Colorado, where he taught school for a year. Still restless, he then moved to the frontier town of Grand Junction, Colorado, where, after several abortive attempts at finding employment, he purchased the local Republican newspaper, the *Grand Junction News*, with borrowed funds. The new newspaper publisher soon channeled an active dislike of the local government into a political crusade against graft; this crusade soon turned so bitter that he was forced to employ an armed bodyguard. Kingsley's efforts did not go unnoticed; the plain-spoken Vermonter earned enough approbation from the citizens of his adopted state to be named in 1884 as an alternate delegate to the Republican National Convention. That same year he married Mary M. Mitchell of Grand Junction; they had one child.

Nominated and elected in 1886 as state auditor and commissioner of insurance of Colorado, Kingsley once again attracted positive attention, this time from several major insurance companies. Having taken due notice of Kingsley's relentless prosecution of fraudulent insurance firms as well as his thoughtful industry studies, the companies competed with each other for his services. Following the expiration of his term, Kingsley returned to New England in the service of the New York Life Insurance Company. Working out of a Boston office, he served from 1889 as inspector of agencies for the New England region. His performance was such that in 1893 he was promoted to superintendent of agencies and moved to New York in the process. His first wife having died in 1890, Kingsley married Josephine I. McCall, the daughter of New York Life president John McCall, in December 1895; they had four children. Rising rapidly within the company, Kingsley was promoted to third vice president and a member of the board of directors in 1898. In 1903 he was named vice president, and on 17 June 1907, on the recommendation of interim president Alexander E. Orr, Kingsley became president of New York Life.

Kingsley's rise to the upper management of the company occurred during one of the most controversial periods of its history. Although the company had enjoyed steady growth since its founding in 1845, dark clouds now hovered on the horizon. At the height of the Progressive Era, an internal controversy at nearby business rival Equitable Insurance precipitated a public outcry against company officers of the major life insurers receiving huge salaries and low-interest loans from each other's companies while policyholders' dividends were being reduced. This controversy, fanned by the local press, resulted in 1905 in an investigation initiated by the New York legislature by what came to be known as the Armstrong Committee (after the lead

investigator). Following a series of hearings, the New York state legislative body enacted laws in 1906 that limited the underwriting of new business as well as the amount of "surplus" (reserve funds held by insurance companies against claims) that a company was allowed to maintain. The distribution of accumulated policy dividends, one of the major points in the controversy, was also subjected to increased state regulation. While New York Life had emerged from the investigation relatively unscathed, the stress created by the controversy contributed to former president McCall's death shortly after his resignation at the end of 1905.

Assuming his presidential duties, Kingsley sought to regain the trust of both the legislature and the public. Follow-up inspections of New York Life revealed full compliance with the laws, and Kingsley eventually succeeded in getting the more onerous provisions of the Armstrong legislation revised. Business volume, which was actually in decline when Kingsley took office and which bottomed out in 1908, was increased so dramatically that after ten years in office Kingsley could point with pride to a near doubling of company assets and receipts to a sum that almost matched the total received in the company's previous sixty years of existence.

Kingsley directed this growth in the face of the most troubled of times. The Armstrong Committee furor was followed shortly by the panic of 1907; greater trouble yet awaited with the advent of World War I. Following the outbreak of war, Kingsley moved to build up the company's cash reserves as a hedge against a surge in claims (although the United States was not directly involved in the conflict, Kingsley's predecessors had expanded the company's business worldwide, covering a healthy portion of the market in the war-stricken nations). While claims resulting from the war proved surprisingly small in number—about 4 percent of the total for the period from 1914 to 1918—the influenza epidemic of 1918 proved far more costly, with claims almost doubling the total received as a result of the war. Nevertheless, blessed by sound actuarial theory and underwriting policies, as well as by increased efficiencies in internal operations and wise investments, the company emerged from the war years in a secure financial condition.

Two major developments dominated the latter years of Kingsley's administration. New York Life withdrew from its overseas markets, gradually transferring most of its policyholders to local companies by 1925. Although forced out of the Soviet Union by the new government, the contraction from its former global scope enabled the company to focus on its efforts in the United States and Canada. A new home office, dreamed of by Kingsley for nearly ten years, opened in late 1928 at 51 Madison Avenue with great fanfare.

Kingsley diverted time from his activities at New York Life to serve as president of the New York State Chamber of Commerce in 1920–1921. He also served on the board of directors of Chemical Bank & Trust Company and New York Trust Company. A longtime trustee of the University of Vermont, Kingsley was a literate man whose views found expression in his own writings—*The First Business of the World* (1903), *Militant Life Insurance* (1911), *Let Us Have Peace* (1919), and *Life Insurance Is Light* (1927)—and whose tastes were expressed in his large collection of Shakespearean folios and quartos. Forced by declining health to retire as company president in 1930, he retained the title of chairman of the board until his death at his home in New York City.

Kingsley rose from early poverty to assume the leadership of one of the world's largest life insurance firms. His administration presided over some of the most tumultuous periods in American history, and the continued prominence of New York Life is his primary legacy.

• Kingsley's papers are in the New York Life Insurance Company archives in New York City. The best source of information on his life and career continues to be Lawrence F. Abbott, *The Story of NYLIC: A History of the Origin and Development of the New York Life Insurance Company from 1845 to 1929* (1930). A good overview of both the insurance industry and the Armstrong Committee is provided by R. Carlyle Buley, *The American Life Convention, 1906–1952* (1953). An extensive obituary is in the *New York Times*, 7 Oct. 1932.

EDWARD L. LACH, JR.

KINGSLEY, Norman William (26 Oct. 1829–20 Feb. 1913), dental surgeon and sculptor, was born in Stockholm, New York, the son of Nathaniel Kingsley and Eliza Williams, farmers. At age four he moved with his family to Poultney, Vermont, and about five years later to Bradford County, Pennsylvania, where he helped with the farm during growing season and attended an academy in Troy, New York, during the winter. At age fifteen he moved to Elmira, New York, and worked as a clerk and bookkeeper in several business establishments. He also began developing his considerable ability as an artist by dabbling in the engraving of copper and wood, and in the process earned a considerable local reputation. In 1847 he returned to Troy, where he clerked in a general store for a year before moving to Elizabeth, New Jersey, to study dentistry with his uncle A. W. Kingsley. Although the elder Kingsley refused to teach him how to make false teeth from porcelain, a secret that the dental profession guarded jealously, he soon learned to do so on his own by carefully observing his uncle and then conducting experiments in the laboratory and kiln while his mentor was on holiday.

In 1850 Kingsley married Alma W. Shepard, with whom he would have two children, and moved to Oswego, New York, where he worked briefly as the assistant of B. C. Leffler, a local dentist. Later that year he opened a dental practice of his own but closed it in 1852 to move to New York City. After practicing with Solyman Brown and Samuel Lockwood for a year, he opened his own dental practice and quickly gained a wide reputation for the quality of his gold plates and carved porcelain teeth, particularly after specimens of his work won several gold and silver medals at world's fairs in New York in 1853 and in Paris two years later.

In 1859 Kingsley became interested in helping patients born with a cleft palate by developing a satisfactory way to close the congenital fissure in the roof of the mouth. Although his method of filling the gap by inserting a custom-shaped plate of gold worked well enough, he soon developed a way to make a plaster model of the oral cavity from which he molded an artificial palate made from soft vulcanized India rubber. This latter device worked so well that it won for him the gold medals of the American Dental Convention in 1863 and the Odontographic Society of Pennsylvania in 1864 and quickly gained for him an international clientele; while touring Europe in 1864 and 1865 he was feted as a benefactor of mankind by the London Medical and Surgical Society and the French Academy of Medicine.

Kingsley also invented a number of devices for surgically repairing abnormal conditions occurring in the oral cavity, the most important ones being the first portable gas blowpipe for use in dental surgery and the Kingsley splint, an oral device made of vulcanized rubber used to set a fractured jaw. This splint, still in use more than a century later, is molded to fit the patient's jawbone and then secured to the jaw by wires extending outside the mouth to a headband. He also developed several innovative procedures, the most important one being the use of the occipital bone at the base of the skull as a support for bridgework and dentures.

In 1866 Kingsley founded the New York College of Dentistry and for the next three years served as its first dean and professor of dental art and mechanism. In the 1870s he set out to compile the widely dispersed bits of information concerning the surgical correction of teeth that are out of position or misaligned as well as of other abnormalities of the oral cavity. He published the results in *A Treatise on Oral Deformities as a Branch of Mechanical Surgery* (1880; Gr. ed., 1881), which served for several decades as the only textbook treatment of orthodontic surgery. He also authored a number of articles on decayed and misshapen teeth, adenoid growths, the deleterious effects on the development of the incisors of thumbsucking, and the surgical correction of cleft palates.

Kingsley achieved a considerable degree of renown as a sculptor and artist. Although he did not achieve critical acclaim, his many busts and statues in clay, marble, and bronze earned the approbation of a considerable number of unsophisticated art enthusiasts. His most famous works are *Evening Star*, a clay model of his conception of the perfect female head; a heroic marble bust of Jesus Christ from which an engraving was made and used in 1871 as the frontispiece of a book about the life of Christ; and a portrait bust of Whitelaw Reid, who succeeded Horace Greeley as publisher of the *New York Tribune*. He also adapted his gas blowpipe for use in "flame-painting" and used this device to reproduce on wood monochromatic copies of a dozen portraits by the famous Dutch painter Rembrandt. These copies attracted considerable contemporary attention because of the novelty of the technique used to create them but have since come to be regarded as mere curiosities.

Kingsley was a delegate to the international medical congress in London in 1881 and served as president of the Dental Society of the State of New York in 1886–1887. He also presided over the New York State Board of Censors for sixteen years. In 1904 he retired to Warren Point, New Jersey, where he died.

Kingsley contributed to the advance of dentistry in two ways. His inventions relieved the suffering of cleft palate patients and continue to permit the treatment of a number of oral conditions. His textbook on orthodontic surgery earned for him the sobriquet "father of modern orthodontia" (Thorpe, p. 548).

• Kingsley's papers have not been located. A biography is in Burton Lee Thorpe, *History of Dental Surgery*, vol. 3: *Biographies of Pioneer American Dentists and Their Successors*, ed. Charles R. E. Koch (1910), pp. 542–59.

CHARLES W. CAREY, JR.

KINKAID, Thomas Cassin (3 Apr. 1888–17 Nov. 1972), naval officer, was born in Hanover, New Hampshire, the son of Thomas Wright Kinkaid, a naval officer, and Virginia Lee Cassin. Born into a navy family, Kinkaid spent his early years in a variety of locations dictated by his father's career. Following graduation from a high school in Washington, D.C., Kinkaid entered the U.S. Naval Academy in Annapolis, Maryland, in 1904. Graduating in 1908 as a passed midshipman, he joined the battleship *Nebraska* in San Francisco and participated in the cruise of the "Great White Fleet" around the world (1907–1909). Commissioned as an ensign in 1910, he served from then until 1919 mostly in battleships and received postgraduate training in ordnance at the Naval Academy and at various industrial sites. While assigned to the battleship *Minnesota* in 1911, he married Helen Sherbourne Ross of Philadelphia, with whom he had no children.

America's declaration of war on Germany in April 1917 found Kinkaid serving as a gunnery officer in the battleship *Pennsylvania*. The ship spent its time with most of the Atlantic Fleet on the East Coast preparing for battles that never occurred. After World War I Kinkaid alternated between assignments ashore and on shipboard. During 1929–1930 he attended the Naval War College. Promoted to captain in 1937, he commanded the heavy cruiser *Indianapolis* and then in 1938 was detailed to Rome, Italy, as the naval attaché. Following further sea duty in 1941, Kinkaid was promoted to rear admiral just before the December 1941 Japanese attack on Pearl Harbor.

After assuming command of Cruiser Division Six, Kinkaid participated in the battle of the Coral Sea (May 1942) and the battle of Midway (June 1942). In August 1942 he transferred his flag to the aircraft carrier *Enterprise* and served as a carrier task force commander. His ships covered the August invasion of Guadalcanal and then defended the lodgment in the battle of the Eastern Solomons (Aug. 1942) and the battle of the Santa Cruz Islands (Oct. 1942). There

was some unhappiness with Kinkaid after the latter battle, but his superior officers recognized that the loss of the carrier *Hornet* was unavoidable. For his service as a cruiser division and carrier task force commander in combat, Kinkaid earned two Distinguished Service Medals. He was also recognized at Admiral Chester Nimitz's Pacific Fleet headquarters as a "fighting admiral." When Kinkaid was detached from his *Enterprise* task force command, his immediate superior was Vice Admiral William F. Halsey. In Kinkaid's detachment orders, Halsey recognized his achievements: "For a period of many months you have commanded carrier forces operating in this area with skill and effectiveness. You have inflicted great damage upon the enemy in repeated engagements. . . . I desire to pay full tribute to your superb work in the past" (23 Nov. 1942).

In early January 1943 Kinkaid journeyed from the South Pacific to Kodiak, Alaska, to take charge of the North Pacific Force, a joint navy, army, and army air corps command. His orders from Admiral Nimitz were to stop any further Japanese encroachments and to expel them from Kiska and Attu in the Aleutians, islands they had occupied in June 1942. In January Kinkaid's forces quickly captured Amchitka Island. Four months later, after a very difficult campaign, an army-navy expedition recaptured Attu. For his success at Attu, Kinkaid was promoted to vice admiral. After Attu, Kinkaid and Major General Simon B. Buckner laid plans to retake Kiska. On 15 August 1943 army and Canadian troops splashed ashore only to find that the Japanese had already evacuated the island. Kinkaid had fulfilled his assignment; the enemy had been expelled from the Aleutians. His successes were recognized in Washington, D.C., and at Pearl Harbor with his promotion and the award of a third Distinguished Service Medal.

In November 1943 Kinkaid reported to the Brisbane, Australia, headquarters of General Douglas MacArthur. There he became commander of the Seventh Fleet; his superior was Admiral Ernest J. King, the chief of naval operations in Washington. He also became commander of the Allied Naval Forces, Southwest Pacific Area (SWPA), under MacArthur's direct command. Kinkaid's predecessors had failed to please two difficult commanders, but he had the critical joint operations experience they had lacked. Kinkaid's principal mission, and that of his Seventh Fleet, was to provide amphibious lift and beachhead protection to SWPA forces as they moved against Japanese garrisons on the road back to the Philippines. Before the October 1944 Leyte assault, the largest operation under Kinkaid's command was his three-pronged attack in April aimed at Hollandia, New Guinea.

In returning MacArthur's forces to the Philippines at Leyte, Kinkaid's Seventh Fleet, in collaboration with Admiral Halsey's Third Fleet, fought four major battles in defense of the Leyte Gulf beachhead. The Seventh Fleet's battleship–cruiser force, in a night action on 24–25 October, completely destroyed a Japanese force approaching Leyte Gulf from the south by way of the Surigao Strait. A few hours later a group of sixteen lightly armored escort carriers repulsed the main Japanese force under Admiral Takeo Kurita, which had approached Leyte Gulf by way of the San Bernardino Strait to the north. This Japanese fleet had been badly mauled by Halsey's carriers the previous day. The final action in the battle for Leyte Gulf came when Third Fleet carriers and cruisers decimated a decoy Japanese carrier force approaching from the north. This great four-part battle ended the threat of the Japanese fleet to MacArthur's campaign. The victory at Leyte Gulf was Kinkaid's greatest military achievement.

After Leyte, the Seventh Fleet invaded Mindoro in December 1944 and in January 1945 led the invasion of Luzon at Lingayen Gulf. For his accomplishments under MacArthur's command, Kinkaid was advanced to the rank of full admiral and received the Army Distinguished Service Medal. MacArthur lauded him as a "master of naval warfare." Kinkaid concluded his Seventh Fleet command by taking the surrender of Japanese forces in Korea during September and October 1945.

Between January 1946 and his retirement in May 1950, Kinkaid was the commander of the Eastern Sea Frontier, with his headquarters in New York City. During his retirement years in Washington, D.C., he served for six years as a member of the National Security Training Commission, which made plans for universal military training. In 1953 Kinkaid began fifteen years as a member of the American Battle Monuments Commission (AMBC). In those years the ABMC created military cemeteries and monuments in Europe, Africa, the Pacific, and on both coasts of the United States. Kinkaid died in Bethesda, Maryland, and was buried with full military honors in the Arlington National Cemetery.

Kinkaid's fame is based on his achievements as a "fighting admiral" during World War II. Success as a carrier task force commander in the South Pacific, followed by his achievements in the Aleutians, led to his assignment as General MacArthur's naval commander, which in turn enabled Kinkaid to earn his place in history.

• The personal and official manuscripts of Kinkaid are at the Naval Historical Center, Washington, D.C. The center also holds other important papers concerning his career, namely those of Fleet Admiral Ernest J. King and Fleet Admiral Chester W. Nimitz. An oral history taken by John T. Mason covers a good deal of Kinkaid's naval career; it was published by the Columbia University Oral History Projects Office: *The Reminiscences of Thomas Cassin Kinkaid* (1961). An analysis of his accomplishments during World War II is in Gerald E. Wheeler, "Admiral Thomas C. Kinkaid, United States Navy," in *Men of War: Great Naval Leaders of World War II*, ed. Stephen Howarth (1993); and Wheeler, "Thomas C. Kinkaid: MacArthur's Master of Naval Warfare," in *We Shall Return! MacArthur's Commanders and the Defeat of Japan 1942–1945*, ed. William M. Leary (1988). Seventh Fleet amphibious operations are detailed in Daniel E. Barbey, *MacArthur's Amphibious Navy: Seventh Amphibious Force Operations, 1943–1945* (1969). The history of the *Enterprise* task force operations is related in Edward P. Stafford, *The Big E* (1962); and Eric Hammel, *Guadalcanal: The Carrier Battles* (1987). For Kinkaid's role in the battle for Leyte Gulf, consult C. Vann Woodward, *The Battle for Leyte Gulf* (1947); Hanson W. Baldwin, "The Sho Plan: The Battle for Leyte Gulf, 1944," in *Sea Fights and Shipwrecks* (1955); Samuel Eliot Morison, *Leyte, June 1944–January 1945*, Vol. 12 of *History of United States Naval Operations in World War II* (1958); and Edwin B. Hoyt, *The Battle for Leyte Gulf: The Death Knell of the Japanese Fleet* (1972). An accurate obituary is in the *Washington Post*, 18 Nov. 1972.

GERALD E. WHEELER

KINLOCH, Cleland (1760–12 Sept. 1823), planter and legislator, was born in Charleston, South Carolina, the son of Francis Kinloch, a planter, and Anna Isabella Cleland, both of Scottish descent. His father's death left Kinloch a ward of Governor Thomas Boone at age seven. The governor sent him abroad for schooling (which was very rare for South Carolina youths). He studied at Eton College in England and in Rotterdam, Holland, where, intending to be a merchant, he pursued commercial studies. The revolutionary war prevented his returning to the United States until after the South Carolina Confiscation Act of 1782, which fined his estate at 12 percent of its value. He planned to return to England, but the inheritance of his father's Weehaw Plantation in 1784 led to his choosing the life of a rice planter instead. Subsequently Kinloch expanded Weehaw to 5,000 acres and made a number of major improvements. Apparently he was relieved of the fines, but his factor, John White, was trustee of his 300 slaves as late as 1790. On 15 April 1786 Kinloch married Harriet Simmons, the daughter of Ebenezer Simmons, Jr., and Jane Stanyarne. This union produced one child.

Kinloch was a scientific agriculturist of the first order. He decided early on to adopt Gideon Dupont's system of taking full advantage of tidal flows in rice cultivation (developed about 1783 by Dupont at Goose Creek on the Cooper River in the Charleston District), using canals, trunks, and floodgates of the variety that he had observed in Holland. The first use of irrigation waters for rice culture was begun in the 1720s, using water from ponds or dammed up streams to flood inland swamps to provide moisture for the rice plants. This system of flowing, however, had two serious shortcomings: it was too subject to flooding (heavy rains could lead to the breaking of the upper dam, thus allowing too much water on the field), and it did not provide enough water to kill grass and weeds. In the late 1750s planters in the Georgetown area began using tidal waters from the rivers for irrigation. While this would limit rice growing to the river valleys (only ten to twenty miles along the rivers were generally suitable for tidal flows), it provided a much more stable supply of water, not subject normally to flooding and ample to kill most of the grass and weeds in the four or five floodings of the growing season. Dupont's advanced form of tidal flowing immediately began to replace inland swamp flooding. A major factor in this was Kinloch's popularizing of the system at Weehaw. Too, he recruited Jonathan Lucas (inventor of the rice mill in South Carolina) to construct at Weehaw an advanced design rice mill, which operated with the tides and was so efficient that it threshed, husked, and barreled the rice in one operation.

Not only did Kinloch expand the acreage of the plantation, he also beautified the grounds with lush gardens, hiring a Scottish gardener to add ornamentation to his property. He also developed new rice fields along the Wateree. Now possessing considerable wealth, Kinloch sojourned in Europe in 1804 and spent a number of summers in Newport, Rhode Island. However, not fully content with his Weehaw surroundings, he decided to purchase a 600-acre tract in the high hills of Santee in 1807, where he built a three-story mansion with a sizable rotunda, which he named "Acton." With extensive gardens and a library of 745 volumes, Acton provided a summer retreat from the malarial conditions existing in the low land.

Far more than a man of commerce or applied science, Kinloch's initial governmental experience was as a delegate for Prince George Winyah Parish to the 1788 ratifying convention for the U.S. Constitution, where he voted in the affirmative. He was subsequently elected by the same parish to the Eighth, Ninth, Tenth, and Thirteenth General Assemblies (1789–1794, 1799–1800). Along the way he served as a charter member of the Georgetown Library Society and, after his move to Acton, on the vestry for St. Mark Parish, and he represented the church at the Episcopal state conventions.

Kinloch's careful and skilled management in rice planting led to continuous prosperity and success on his plantations until the great storm of 1822, which inflicted damages of $30,000. A year later he died at Acton, with burial in the Episcopal churchyard at Stateburg, South Carolina. Kinloch was a major figure among the rice planters, for he did perhaps as much as anyone to demonstrate the merits of tidal flowing and improved milling.

• A manuscript sketch of Kinloch (prepared by Langdon Cheves III) and some Kinloch family papers are in the Cheves family collection in the South Carolina Historical Society in Charleston. See George C. Rogers, *The History of Georgetown County, South Carolina* (1970; repr. 1990); David Ramsay, *The History of South Carolina*, vol. 2 (1809); and James M. Clifton, ed., *Life and Labor on Argyle Island: Letters and Documents of a Savannah River Rice Plantation, 1833–1867* (1978). Obituaries are in the *Charleston Courier* and the *Charleston Southern Patriot and Advertiser*, both 17 Sept. 1823.

JAMES M. CLIFTON

KINNERSLEY, Ebenezer (30 Nov. 1711–4 July 1778), scientific lecturer and teacher, was born in Gloucester, England, the son of William Kinnersley and Sarah Turner. The family emigrated to America in 1714, and William Kinnersley became assistant minister to the Pennepeck Baptist Church, Lower Dublin, near Philadelphia. Nothing is known of Ebenezer Kinnersley's education. He was baptized on 6 September 1735,

married Sarah Duffield in 1739, and moved to Philadelphia about that time, working as a shopkeeper and occasionally preaching at the Philadelphia Baptist Church.

He found the emotional preaching of George Whitefield and other revivalists distasteful, and on Sunday 6 July 1740, during the height of the Great Awakening, he attacked their "horrid Harangues" and "Enthusiastick Ravings." The following Saturday, he was tried at a church meeting and condemned. He angrily justified himself and took the apologia to his friend Benjamin Franklin, who printed it as a postscript to the *Pennsylvania Gazette* of 24 July 1740. Consequently, the church appointed a nine-person committee to investigate Kinnersley, and seven of the committee signed a judgment against him. Kinnersley replied with a *Second Letter from Ebenezer Kinnersley to His Friend in the Country* (1740), but Franklin would not print it. Kinnersley then paid Andrew Bradford and William Bradford to do so. The underlying reason for the quarrel was Kinnersley's belief in a "rational religion" and in an Enlightenment "God of Order." His position blended Newtonianism with the scientific deism common among eighteenth-century intellectuals. Though he was ordained a Baptist minister in 1743, he retained his independence of thought and in 1747 published *A Letter to the Reverend the Ministers of the Baptist Congregations, in Pennsylvania and the New Jerseys*, maintaining that "the *Right* of *Private Judgment*" was the "very Basis of the *Protestant Reformation*." Kinnersley's independence may explain why no congregation ever chose him as its minister.

By 1747 Franklin was immersed in electrical experiments, and Kinnersley and other friends were constantly at his home, helping Franklin conduct the experiments and occasionally making suggestions. Franklin advised Kinnersley to tour the country giving lectures on electricity and, as he later wrote in the *Autobiography*, drew up two lectures for him, "in which the Experiments were rang'd in such Order and accompanied with Explanations, in such Method, as that the foregoing should assist in Comprehending the following." Kinnersley left Philadelphia for a southern tour in April 1749. He advertised in the Annapolis *Maryland Gazette* on 10, 17, and 24 May 1749. The advertisements first published both the Franklinian system of electricity ("That it is a real *Element*, intimately united with all other Matter, from whence it is *collected* by the Tube, or Sphere, and not *created* by the Friction") and Franklin's suggestion that lightning is electrical in nature ("Various Representations of Lightning, the Cause and Effects of which will be explained by a more probable Hypothesis than has hitherto appeared; and some useful Instructions given how to avoid the Danger of it"). Kinnersley's brief advertisement attracted international attention, appearing in both the *Gentleman's* and the *Scots* magazines for January 1751, and the lectures were likewise resoundingly successful.

By the time that Kinnersley advertised in the *Pennsylvania Gazette* on 11 April 1751, Franklin had theorized that a metal rod affixed to the top part of a building would carry a lightning stroke down the rod. Kinnersley's 1751 advertisement now added: "How to secure Houses Ships, &c. from being hurt by its destructive Violence." Kinnersley, therefore, first publicly announced and published the effectiveness of the lightning rod. He toured the northern colonies from September 1751 to July 1752, attracting large crowds and privately performing experiments with natural philosophers in Boston, Newport, and New York. He effectually combatted religious prejudice against the use of lightning rods. After lecturing in Philadelphia in the fall of 1752, he toured the West Indies in the winter of 1752–1753 but returned when Franklin asked if he would be interested in being master of the Philadelphia Academy's English School.

Kinnersley became master of the English School in 1753 and professor of the English Tongue and Oratory when the Philadelphia College was established in 1755. At the college's first commencement (1757), he received a master of arts degree. His contemporaries celebrated him as a teacher, and former students remembered him with pleasure. He resigned in the fall of 1772 because of ill health.

Throughout the latter part of his life, he continued experimenting with electricity and giving lectures. In 1758 William Smith, provost of the college and an enemy of Franklin, charged that Franklin had stolen Kinnersley's theories. Kinnersley replied to Smith (who was his immediate superior) in the *Pennsylvania Gazette* for 30 November 1758, claiming that Franklin had "an undoubted right, preferable to the united merit of all the electricians in America, and, perhaps, in all the World" to the recognition he had received. In their publications on electricity, Franklin and James Bowdoin credited Kinnersley with a number of minor discoveries, but Kinnersley reported his major investigation in a 12 March 1761 letter to Franklin. He had invented an electrical air thermometer and proved by it that electricity melted by heat, rather than by a cold fusion, as Franklin and all predecessors had supposed. He concluded the letter with the wish that "the name of FRANKLIN, like that of NEWTON," be made immortal. On 20 March 1767 Kinnersley was elected a member of the American Society for Promoting Useful Knowledge, and on 26 January 1768 he was chosen a member of the American Philosophical Society. He occasionally lectured on electricity at the Philadelphia Academy until 1775, when he retired to Lower Merion, where he died. Though Sir Charles Blagden wrote to Sir Joseph Banks from Philadelphia on 26 March 1778 that Kinnersley had just died, his tombstone at the Pennepeck graveyard records his death as 4 July 1778.

• Kinnersley's few manuscripts are mainly at the Historical Society of Pennsylvania. I. Bernard Cohen printed the most significant, a full version of the "First Part" of "A Course of Experiments on the Newly Discovered Electrical Fire," in *Benjamin Franklin's Experiments: A New Edition of Franklin's Experiments and Observations on Electricity* (1941), pp. 409–21. Kinnersley's letters to Franklin are in Leonard W. Labaree et al., eds., *The Papers of Benjamin Franklin* (1957–), of

which thirty vols. had appeared up to 1995. Morgan Edwards sets forth a number of facts concerning his religious history in *Materials towards a History of the Baptists in America* (2 vols., 1770–1792). Joseph Priestley praised his electrical experiments in *History and Present State of Electricity* (1767). For Kinnersley's teaching career, see Thomas Harrison Montgomery, *A History of the University of Pennsylvania from Its Foundation to A.D. 1770* (1900), and Edward Potts Cheyney, *History of the University of Pennsylvania* (1940). For a biography, together with a primary and secondary bibliography, see J. A. Leo Lemay, *Ebenezer Kinnersley, Franklin's Friend* (1964).

J. A. LEO LEMAY

KINNICK, Nile Clarke, Jr. (9 July 1918–2 June 1943), college football player, was born in Adel, Iowa, the son of Nile Kinnick and Frances Clarke, farmers. In 1934 the family moved to Des Moines, where Kinnick's father took a job with the Federal Land Bank. Kinnick was a standout athlete in baseball, basketball, and football at Benson High School in Des Moines, and he made all-state in football and basketball. A high school "A" student, he entered the University of Iowa in 1936.

In college, Kinnick was both an outstanding student and athlete. Although he was a basketball starter as a sophomore and junior and the team's second-highest scorer in 1938, he gave up the sport to spend more time on his studies. He was elected to Phi Beta Kappa in 1939 and graduated magna cum laude in 1940.

When Kinnick joined the varsity football team in 1937, Iowa had won only six games in the Western Conference (now the Big Ten) since 1930. Under first-year coach Irl Tubbs, the 1937 Iowa squad failed to make any improvement, winning one game and losing seven. The 5'9", 170-pound Kinnick, however, had an outstanding season, making the all-Western Conference team at quarterback. An all-around player, he could run, pass, punt, and drop-kick field goals with facility. During 1938 he was hobbled for most of the season by an ankle injury as Iowa posted a dismal 1–6–1 won-loss-tied record.

The following season, Kinnick played for a new head coach, Edward "Eddie" Anderson, a former Notre Dame player. Kinnick had his finest season and one of the best by a back in college football history. He recalled that "we lost so many games my first two years we just sort of got used to it. We didn't mind losing, and that's bad. . . . Dr. Anderson gave us that intense desire we needed to win." Kinnick became known as the "Ironman" in 1939. After sitting on the bench for part of Iowa's opening win over South Dakota (41–0), he played full sixty-minute games on successive Saturdays against Indiana, Michigan, Wisconsin, Purdue, Notre Dame, and Minnesota.

Kinnick led Iowa to a 6–1–1 record, its best since 1924 and an exact reversal of 1938. Starting at halfback, he was personally involved in 107 of the Hawkeyes' 135 points. He threw three touchdown passes against both Indiana and Wisconsin, scored three touchdowns against South Dakota, passed for two fourth-quarter touchdowns to beat Minnesota, and scored the winning touchdown and drop-kicked the extra point to upset Notre Dame, 7–6. In all, it was a storybook year, highlighted by his leading the nation in kickoff returns and pass interceptions for the nationally ninth-ranked Hawkeyes. As a result of a final game tie with Northwestern in which he was injured, Iowa finished second in the Big Ten. Kinnick still holds four Iowa interception, kickoff return, and punting records. "Nile was the leader, the inspiration," coach Anderson recalled. "Because of his spirit, we had as many as eight players who would go the full 60 minutes with him in a tough game."

After the season, Kinnick won the Heisman Trophy as well as the Maxwell and Walter Camp trophies as the leading college football player in the country. He was unanimously selected as an All-America halfback, and he beat out Joe DiMaggio as the Associated Press "No. 1 Athlete of the Year," the first football player so honored. At the December 1939 Heisman Award banquet, Kinnick remarked that "I thank God that I was born to the gridirons of the Middle West and not to the battlefields of Europe. I can speak confidently and positively that the football players of this country would rather fight for the Heisman Trophy than for the *Croix de Guerre.*"

The following year Kinnick played in the College All-Star game and threw a touchdown pass, but he turned down a relatively lucrative offer to play professional football. In September 1940 he entered law school at Iowa and coached freshman football. Just before the Japanese attack on Pearl Harbor, he left law school when his naval reserve unit was called to duty. He became a navy pilot, training in Florida and the Caribbean.

On 2 June 1943 Kinnick was lost at sea on a training mission when his fighter plane crashed in the Gulf of Paria off the Venezuelan coast, four miles from his aircraft carrier, the U.S.S. *Lexington.* A crash boat arrived at the scene within minutes, but the crew was unable to find Kinnick, who had been seen to fall free of the plane. University of Iowa president Virgil Hancher remarked that "those who knew Nile felt certain his character and ability guaranteed him a high place in the state and nation. It is a great tragedy that a life so promising should be cut short." The university established a scholarship in Kinnick's memory and named the football stadium after him. Kinnick was elected to the College Football Hall of Fame in 1951.

• The University of Iowa has published *A Hero Perished: The Diary and Selected Writings of Nile Kinnick* (1991). Materials relating to Kinnick's career are in the College Football Hall of Fame. A biography is D. W. Stump's *Kinnick: The Man and the Legend* (1975). See also John T. Brady, *The Heisman: A Symbol of Excellence* (1984); Scott M. Fisher, *The Ironmen: 1939 Iowa* (1989); Ron Fimrite, "Nile Kinnick," *Sports Illustrated,* 31 Aug. 1987; Al Hirshberg, *The Glory Runners* (1968); Mervin D. Hyman and Gordon S. White, Jr., *Big Ten Football: Its Life and Times, Great Coaches, Players and Games* (1977); John D. McCallum, *Big Ten Football, Since 1895* (1976); and Richard Whittingham, *Saturday Afternoon: College Football and the Men Who Made the Day* (1985). An obituary is in the *New York Times,* 5 June 1943.

JOHN M. CARROLL

KINO, Eusebio Francisco (10 Aug. 1645–15 Mar. 1711), Jesuit missionary, explorer, and cartographer, was born in Segno (Tirol), near Trent in northern Italy, the son of Francisco Chini and Margarita (maiden name unknown). Later in his life, as a missionary in the New World, he was to alter the spelling of the surname, Chini or Chino, so that it would be pronounced as it is in Italian.

Kino studied in the Jesuit colleges in Trent and later at Hall (Austria) near Innsbruck, where he vowed to enter the Society of Jesus. On 20 November 1665 he entered the novitiate of Landsberg, near Augsburg (Bavaria), and subsequently studied at Freiburg. His theological, philosophical, mathematical, geographical, and cosmographical studies were carried out at the University of Ingolstadt, where he had as mentors cartographers Adam Aigenler and Heinrich Scherer, and at the University of Munich. He taught at the Jesuit college in Hall from 1670 to 1673, and following ordination in 1676 terminated his theological training at Oettingen.

In 1678 Kino requested service in the foreign missions and soon set out for Seville with other Jesuits bound for the Americas. Following a lengthy wait for a secure sailing of the fleet, he departed from Cádiz on 27 January 1681 and, arriving in Veracruz in May, proceeded to Mexico City, where he served in the principal Jesuit residence, the Casa Profesa, until 1683. He was then assigned as missionary and cosmographer to the expedition of Admiral Isidro de Atondo y Antillón, who had been designated to found a Jesuit mission on the peninsula of California. In April 1683 Atondo attempted settlement at the bay of La Paz, but because of conflict with local Indian groups he abandoned the area and continued northward some 250 miles along the coast of the Gulf of California with Kino. On 5 October 1683, at a site named San Bruno, twenty kilometers north of present-day Loreto, Kino founded the first mission in the Californias. After clearing fields and constructing a church and outbuildings between December 1684 and January 1685, Kino and Atondo led the first expedition across the peninsula to the Pacific coast. In February and March they explored the gulf coast south to Ligüí. Because of problems of supply, San Bruno was abandoned in May 1685, and Kino returned to Mexico City, where he sought additional funds to continue his work, while Atondo conducted a brief exploration of the Gulf of California.

In 1686 Kino was assigned to expand the Sonora mission field in northwestern New Spain and in 1687 founded Nuestra Señora de los Dolores on the San Miguel River. During the following decade he undertook fourteen expeditions, founding missions at Caburica, Tubutama, Caborca, Guevavi, and Cocóspera as well as discovering numerous other potential mission sites in Sonora and introducing agriculture and livestock raising to the region. The Pima revolt of 1695 interrupted his labors but did not halt his plans. In 1697–1698, with Captain Juan Mateo Manje, he explored to the delta of the Colorado River and confirmed the peninsularity of California, which for almost a century had been depicted by cartographers as an island. In 1700 he founded San Xavier del Bac near modern Tucson, Arizona. The following year, with Father Juan María Salvatierra, S. J., he sought to establish an overland supply route from Sonora to California; when this proved impractical he established maritime supply from Guaymas to Loreto in 1703. In 1708 he was appointed superior of the missions of Pimería Alta (southern Arizona and northern Sonora) with headquarters in Santa María Magdalena, Sonora.

In addition to charting the definitive relation of California to the continent, during a quarter century Kino explored and accurately mapped over 50,000 square miles of northwestern New Spain, through some of the most rugged, dry, hot, and inhospitable territory of North America. As a friend of the Indians, he baptized some 4,500 neophytes, the descendants of whom continue to practice Catholicism. As a builder of missions and some nineteen cattle ranches, Kino formed the nuclei of modern towns and introduced animal husbandry, their modern economic base, in the region. His writings provide a basis for the ethnic and natural history of the regions in which he labored. He died in Santa María Magdalena, Sonora. His statue, representing the state of Arizona, is in the National Hall of Statuary in the Capitol, Washington, D.C.

• Major depositories for Kino manuscript diaries, correspondence, and treatises are the Archivum Romanum Societatis Jesu, Rome; Archivo General de la Nación, Mexico, ramo Misiones; Archivo General de Indias, Sevilla, sección Audiencia de Guadalajara; and The Bancroft Library, University of California, Berkeley. In his lifetime, apart from five major maps of Sonora-California, he published the *Exposición astronómica de el cometa . . .* (1681), a treatise based upon medieval concepts on the origin of comets soundly refuted by Carlos de Sigüenza y Góngora in his *Libra Astronómica y Philosófica* (1690). Many of his manuscript reports, diaries, and letters as well as studies based upon them have been published in the twentieth century. They include two by Kino, *Crónica de la Pimería Alta. Favores Celestiales* (1985) and *Las Misiones de Sonora y Arizona,* ed. Francisco Fernández del Castillo (1922); two by Herbert E. Bolton, *Kino's Historical Memoir of Pimería Alta* (1919; repr. 1948) and *Rim of Christendom: A Biography of Eusebio Francisco Kino, Pacific Coast Pioneer* (1936; repr. 1984); six by Ernest J. Burrus, *Correspondencia del P. Kino con los Generales de la Compañía de Jesús, 1682–1707* (1961), *Kino and the Cartography of Northwestern New Spain* (1965), *Kino and Manje, Explorers of Sonora and Arizona* (1971), *Kino escribe a la Duquesa: Correspondencia del P. Eusebio Francisco Kino con la Duquesa de Aveiro* (1964), *Kino's Plan for the Development of Pimería Alta, Arizona and Upper California* (1961), and *Kino Reports to Headquarters* (1954); two by Charles W. Polzer, *Eusebio Kino, padre de la Pimería Alta* (1984) and *Kino Guide II: His Missions—His Monuments* (1982); and Fay Jackson Smith, John L. Kessell, and Francis J. Fox, *Father Kino in Arizona* (1966).

W. MICHAEL MATHES

KINSEY, Alfred Charles (23 June 1894–25 Aug. 1956), entomologist and sex researcher, was born in Hoboken, New Jersey, the son of Alfred Seguine Kinsey, instructor of mechanical arts at Stevens Institute of Technology, and Sarah Ann Charles. His father, a domineering and relentlessly pious patriarch, intimidated Sarah and the children. Alfred was a frail boy who contracted rheumatic and typhoid fever. Perhaps as compensation for his early confinement to the home, in adolescence Alfred acquired a passionate interest in nature and resolved to become a biologist. He was valedictorian of the Columbia High School class of 1912.

His plans to continue with biology were dashed by his father, who insisted that Alfred study engineering at Stevens; he also pressured Alfred to continue teaching Sunday school. Alfred enrolled at Stevens that fall, but his lack of interest was evident in his lackluster academic performance. After he had completed his sophomore year, he summoned the nerve to inform his father that he had withdrawn from Stevens and had decided to attend Bowdoin, a rural college in Maine noted for its biology program. His father exploded in rage, and the two never reconciled. Alfred thrived academically at Bowdoin and was almost immediately named an assistant in zoology, one of the department's highest honors. In 1916 he graduated magna cum laude and delivered one of the commencement addresses. His parents did not attend.

Kinsey spent the following summer, as he had so many others, indulging his love of the outdoors by working as a counselor in a camp for boys. That fall he enrolled in the graduate program in applied biology at the Bussey Institute of Harvard University. There he came under the spell of William Morton Wheeler, an eminent zoologist who served as something of a surrogate father to Kinsey, albeit of a very different sort from the titanic pillar of probity who loomed over his early life. A confidant of H. L. Mencken, Wheeler was urbane and irreverent. As a biologist, he was less interested in the new genetics, which emphasized laboratory work, and instead called on students to emulate Darwin by going into the field to refine taxonomy, the categorization of species. Wheeler's prescription perfectly suited Kinsey, who shed his religious upbringing, and eventually came to repudiate it with an abiding vengeance. Next, in 1917 Kinsey began studying the classification of the gall wasp, an ant-sized insect that lives in parasitic relation to various shrubs and trees, especially oak. For his dissertation he collected and examined thousands of gall wasps, identifying sixteen new species. He received his Ph.D. in September 1919 and took advantage of a traveling fellowship to spend the next year collecting gall wasps in stands of oak from New England to Appalachia and from Texas to California.

In 1920 Kinsey accepted a teaching appointment in zoology at Indiana University. There he met Clara McMillen, a graduate student in chemistry. Two months later, he proposed to her, and they were married in June 1921. They had three children who survived to adulthood.

At Indiana University, Kinsey proved an able lecturer but often an arrogant and overbearing colleague; once he was nearly dismissed for intemperate criticisms of Carl H. Eigenmann, an esteemed zoologist and former dean. As a scholar, Kinsey continued with his research on gall wasps. During the 1920s and 1930s, he collected and cataloged some 35,000 of them. He found time as well to write a high school text; his *Introduction to Biology* and its later editions sold half a million copies. The royalties helped fund Kinsey's innumerable field trips. In 1930 he published *The Gall Wasp Genus Cynips: A Study of the Origin of Species*, in which he identified forty-eight new species of gall wasp. This book and its subsequent volume, *The Origin of Higher Categories in Cynips* (1936), were well received by specialists but failed to attract the broader attention Kinsey felt his extraordinary efforts warranted. In particular, he was not offered a professorship at any of the nation's most prestigious universities.

Though he resolved to undertake intensive study of another genus of gall wasp, he became involved in a campus dispute in the spring of 1937 that changed his life. The student newspaper launched a crusade against the university's antediluvian sex education instruction, offered under the Victorian euphemism of health and hygiene. In early 1938 Kinsey volunteered to develop a team-taught and thoroughly scientific course on marriage and the family. Kinsey found support in this matter, and a host of others over the next two decades, from the university's new president, Herman B. Wells, who was eager to push Indiana to the forefront of intellectual trends. At Wells's prodding, the trustees approved of Kinsey's noncredit course.

In June 1938 seventy women and twenty-eight men enrolled in the course. Kinsey's lectures were the main attraction, and he featured candid descriptions, supplemented by slides, of the biology of erotic stimulation, the mechanics of sexual intercourse, the methods of contraception, and, in a final lecture, the limitless diversity of nature. After briefly outlining his work on gall wasps, he described a similarly wide variation in human sexual apparatus. The most significant fact of biology, Kinsey declared, is that "no two individuals are alike." Although his tone was clinical and his manner that of an amiable if disinterested scientist, he raised his voice to a powerful denunciation of sexually repressive attitudes and laws. If Americans were not so "inhibited," Kinsey bristled, "a twelve-year-old would know most of the biology which I will have to give you in formal lectures as seniors and graduate students" (Jones, p. 328). The course won the praise of students and many others on campus. Enrollment doubled that fall and by 1940 approached 400.

Kinsey was not satisfied with teaching the immense variety of human sexuality: he resolved to prove it as well. To this end, he transferred his obsession (and some of his methodology) from gall wasps to the study of human sexuality. He included in the marriage course obligatory private conferences whose ostensible purpose was to allow students to raise questions they were too shy to pose in class. While Kinsey indisputably provided them with useful information, he also made use of these conferences to encourage students to provide their sexual histories. He did this through an ingeniously designed, fluidly structured questionnaire covering scores of topics; to preserve anonymity, he recorded responses in his own private code. (The final version of the survey consisted of from 300 to 521 separate items, depending on the number and variety of the respondent's sexual behaviors.) Kinsey administered the first survey in July 1938 and managed to interview more than half of the class before the end of the year. He now resolved to undertake thousands of these interviews. Much as he formerly used weekends and vacations to plunge into some stand of oaks to gather gall wasps, he now made his way to the big cities, especially Chicago, where he hoped to fathom the rich diversity of human sexuality by interviewing legions of prostitutes, homosexuals, and others.

In 1940, as Kinsey pressed forward with his classes and interviews, formidable opposition began to take shape in Indiana. Physicians complained that Kinsey's lectures and private conferences were stirring up his students' sexual passions; sexual education was best left to those—i.e., physicians—who understood the particular needs of their patients. Local ministers, too, denounced Kinsey for stressing the physiological basis for marriage at the expense of its religious and moral dimensions. Under pressure from the trustees, President Wells issued an ultimatum: that Kinsey either withdraw from the marriage course or discontinue the private conferences. Kinsey gave up the course and continued with the interviews.

His goal was to create the most complete and most scientific data bank on human sexuality ever compiled. To hire additional interviewers and tabulators, he sought funding from the Committee for Research in Problems with Sex (CRPS), a standing unit of the National Research Council that received most of its funds from the Rockefeller Foundation. In July 1961 the CRPS, headed by Robert Yerkes, awarded Kinsey an initial grant of $1,600; to this Indiana University added another $1,200, which enabled Kinsey to interview African Americans in Gary, Indiana, and prison inmates in the region as well. In subsequent years, the CRPS sharply increased its support, and in 1947 the Rockefeller Foundation, at Kinsey's urging, directly channeled funds into Kinsey's new Institute for Sex Research, which was affiliated with Indiana University but nominally separate from it.

In 1948 Kinsey published *Sexual Behavior in the Human Male*. Based on over 5,300 case histories, the book offered a succession of revelations: that about half of American men engaged in homosexual activities before adolescence; that 90 percent had masturbated; that between 30 and 45 percent had adulterous sexual relations; that 70 percent had patronized prostitutes; and that 17 percent of farm boys had had sexual relations with animals. The overwhelming point was that males had powerful sexual urges that society pointlessly sought to suppress. Kinsey singled out religion, especially the Catholic church, for inducing guilt. Though filled with tables and graphs and issued by W. B. Saunders, a medical publishing firm, *Sexual Behavior in the Human Male* was an instant popular success, selling 200,000 hardback copies in two months. Kinsey was lionized in the popular press as a second Galileo or Darwin. Not everyone agreed, with the sharpest dissent coming from religious leaders. The Right Reverend Monsignor Maurice Sheehy, for example, denounced the volume as "the most antireligious book of our times" (Jones, p. 576).

The book royalties were plowed back into the Institute, which also received regular increases in funding from the Rockefeller Foundation. Kinsey hired and carefully trained a team of interviewers to gather more case histories—he aimed for a total of 100,000—and he also collected a staggering cache of books, "how to" manuals, primitive artifacts, and implements of an erotic or sexual nature; these were housed at the Institute's library.

Kinsey's *Sexual Behavior in the Human Female* (1953) reinforced the main conclusion of its predecessor volume: that human sexual practices bore little relation to social attitudes about them; and the chasm between the two was filled with guilt. Of his large sample of women, 62 percent had masturbated, half had engaged in sexual intercourse before marriage, and 26 percent had committed adultery. More troubling to conservatives was Kinsey's assertion that women with "orgasmic experience" early in life tended to have greater sexual satisfaction in marriage. As had its predecessor, the book rocked the nation. In August, Kinsey made the cover of *Time*; in November, *U.S. News and World Report* identified him as the "most widely noticed man in the United States" after President Dwight D. Eisenhower. Critics were equally visible and vociferous. "It is impossible to estimate the damage this book will do to the already deteriorating morals of America," evangelist Billy Graham thundered. In 1954 a congressional committee decided to investigate Kinsey's financial backers, which meant the Rockefeller Foundation.

By this time, however, Kinsey was trying to fend off criticism from another quarter. Many in the scientific community had from the start been troubled by Kinsey's evident assumption that a huge sample was an acceptably representative one. In 1951 the Rockefeller Foundation assigned a team of prominent statisticians to assess Kinsey's data and recommend improvements in sampling technique. The statisticians' final report was generally supportive; but it nevertheless insisted that Kinsey undertake significant revision of his sampling methodology. Kinsey balked at their recommendations, arguing that random sampling was impossible when asking such intimate questions. But by the time *Sexual Behavior in the Human Female* appeared in print, the Rockefeller Foundation had decided to cease funding the Institute.

Though slowed by heart trouble, Kinsey in his last years worked feverishly on a volume on homosexuality, sought alternative funding sources, and continued to take sexual histories. He conducted his 7,985th—and final—interview on 24 May 1956. He died in Bloomington, Indiana.

In 1997 historian James H. Jones, after interviewing many of Kinsey's friends, former students, and colleagues, published a revelatory biography of Kinsey. Jones found that from his adolescent years nearly to his death, Kinsey engaged in savagely painful sadomasochistic acts and was repeatedly involved in unusual and inventive sexual practices. During field trips to gather gall wasps, he often went naked and pressured the male students who accompanied him to engage in sexual relations. He became less cautious over time and at the Institute organized, participated in, and even filmed all manner of voyeuristic, homosexual, and other sexual activities involving interview subjects, prostitutes, colleagues, and spouses. Jones showed that Kinsey was not a dispassionate, numbers-crunching scientist, but a zealous reformer who sought to exorcise his own sexual demons, and the repressive society he believed gave rise to them, with an invincible army of hard facts.

But his facts were not as solid as he imagined, and in any case they failed to sustain his analytical suppositions. As a theoretical scientist, Kinsey was second-rate. Biologist Stephen Jay Gould derided Kinsey's gall wasp taxonomy as "bloated," for Kinsey had over-emphasized the significance of "transient and minor local variants" (Gould p. 230, n. 148). Similarly, Kinsey's dogged pursuit of additional sexual histories, disproportionately taken from people whose behaviors most interested him, vitiated the broader relevance of his data. A greater weakness still, as anthropologist Margaret Mead and theologian Reinhold Niebuhr pointed out, was Kinsey's neglect of the emotional and social aspects of human sexuality. Yet Kinsey was indisputably a tireless researcher who opened up new fields of scientific investigation and transformed the way Americans discussed sex and sexuality. His data and the publicity surrounding them weakened the hold of traditional religious and moral values and did much to prepare the way for the "sexual revolution" of the 1960s.

• Kinsey's papers and letters—some 50,000 of them—are located at the Kinsey Institute for Research in Sex, Gender, and Reproduction Archive at Indiana University, Bloomington. Other materials can be found in the Indiana University Archives, the Indiana University Oral History Project, the Committee for Research in Problems in Sex at the National Research Council Archives in Washington, D.C., and the Rockefeller Archives Center, Pocantico Hills, Sleepy Hollow, N.Y. The essential biography is James H. Jones, *Alfred C. Kinsey: A Public/Private Life* (1997). For an earlier, less revealing biography, by a former member of Kinsey's staff, see Cornelia V. Christenson, *Kinsey: A Biography* (1971). See also Paul Robinson, *The Modernization of Sex: Havelock, Alfred Kinsey, and William Masters and Virginia Johnson* (1976); Sidney Ditzion, *Marriage, Morals, and Sex in America: A His-

tory of Ideas (1953); and Vern L. Bullough, *Science in the Bedroom: A History of Sex Research* (1994). On Kinsey's reputation as a taxonomist, see Stephen Jay Gould, "Of Wasps and WASPs," *Natural History*, Dec. 1982.

MARK C. CARNES

KINSEY, John (c. 1693–11 May 1750), Quaker politician and lawyer, was born in Philadelphia, the son of John Kinsey, a carpenter, politician, and Quaker minister, and Sarah Stevens. The younger John Kinsey likely attended the Friends Public School until the family moved to Woodbridge, New Jersey, sometime between 1702 and 1704. The older Kinsey placed him with a joiner in New York as an apprentice, but as a friend wrote after Kinsey's death, "having an Inquisitive disposition, and a Genius for something above his then employ, he left his master before his time was out, & applied himself to the Study of the Law." He probably studied in Philadelphia with David Lloyd, for he was admitted to the bar in that city in 1724.

He settled in Woodbridge to practice law and in 1725 married Mary Kearney of Philadelphia; they had at least two children. Their son James became prominent in New Jersey politics, serving as a member of the First Continental Congress and as chief justice of the state supreme court.

John Kinsey was elected to the New Jersey assembly in 1727 and in 1730 was named Speaker, a position formerly held by the elder John Kinsey. A modern historian gave Kinsey credit for many reforms in New Jersey, writing that "the ninth assembly had been intoxicated by the generous supply of liberal ideas served up by its favorite, Kinsey," but the governor of the province at that time called him a "man of sense and honesty, [who] had a great regard for His Majesties Service, and the prosperity of the Province. . . . " Kinsey continued to sit in the New Jersey assembly for a time after he moved to Philadelphia early in 1731.

There were more opportunities to practice law in Philadelphia, and almost immediately Kinsey was elected to the Pennsylvania assembly where he was soon active on several committees. In 1739 he became Speaker of the assembly and held that office, except for a brief interval, until his death. He was also attorney general of the province from 1738 to 1741 and was named acting trustee of the General Loan Office in 1738, a position he held for the remainder of his life.

Kinsey, a Quaker active in Pennsylvania, New Jersey, and Delaware, was chosen in 1731 as presiding clerk of the Philadelphia Yearly Meeting, the most important position in the denomination. Of Kinsey's tenure as Speaker, historian Thomas Wendel has written that "by virtue of his leadership in Quaker affairs and his position of attorney general and afterwards as chief justice, [he] had a near monopoly on the reins of power until his death."

In 1739 Pennsylvania governor George Thomas, acting on directives from London, asked the assembly to recruit and supply a militia to join forces attacking Spain in the War of Jenkins' Ear. When the hostilities broadened to include France in King George's War (1740–1748), the governor made similar requests for men and money. Quakers, or the Society of Friends, had opposed wars for several generations, beginning with their founder, George Fox, who issued a statement to Charles II in 1661 denying "all outward wars and strife and fightings. . . . " William Penn had emphasized this principle in Pennsylvania, and Quakers in government since had sought to avoid involvement in wars. John Kinsey, as the acknowledged leader among the Quakers and also Speaker, ably enunciated these beliefs for the overwhelmingly Quaker assembly, which already had a tradition of opposing new taxes. The assembly was further outraged when the governor allowed indentured servants to enlist in the militia, depriving their masters of their service. During the resulting impasse the assembly refused to appropriate money to pay Governor Thomas's salary; the governor, in turn, removed Kinsey from the post of attorney general.

Kinsey negotiated a compromise with the governor in 1743 after several years of confrontation. Thomas agreed to sign legislation he had rejected in the past, and the assembly agreed to pay his salary. As a reward for breaking the political logjam Kinsey was named chief justice of the Pennsylvania supreme court, a post he held until his death. He also headed a commission that met with the Six Nations in Albany in 1745 to assure the Indians of the support of the Pennsylvania government and to urge them not to attack the French as some other colonies wished. He also served on a commission named in 1737 to negotiate with Maryland on the boundary between the two provinces.

While trying a case in Burlington before the New Jersey supreme court, Kinsey suddenly became ill, presumably with a stroke, and died that evening. When his affairs were settled, it was found that his estate owed the General Loan Office £3,000, a sum fifteen times greater than his salary as chief justice, for he had taken that much money for his own use. The Quakers had issued a statement in 1746 warning members to be careful in their dealings lest the Friends be dishonored "by any imprudence of its members in their worldly engagements." It went on to warn against "hazardous enterprises" and called on members to "content themselves with such a plain and moderate way of living" as was consistent with the Quaker way of life. News of Kinsey's misuse of public funds was a crushing blow to the Friends, and for two centuries Quaker historians largely ignored Kinsey. More recently, his financial irregularities have been considered along with his influence as one of the most important Quaker political figures in the colonial era since William Penn.

• There is no collection of Kinsey papers, and information about him is scattered in various published and unpublished sources. The most complete biographical sketch is Edwin B. Bronner, "The Disgrace of John Kinsey, Quaker Politician, 1739–1750," *Pennsylvania Magazine of History and Biography* 75 (1951): 400–15. Thomas Wendel, "The Speaker of the House, Pennsylvania, 1701–1776," *Pennsylvania Magazine of History and Biography* 97 (1973): 3–21, evaluates Kinsey along with other Speakers. Alan Tully, *William Penn's Legacy: Politics and Social Structure in Provincial Pennsylvania, 1726–1755* (1977) and "Quaker Party and Proprietary Policies: The Dynamics of Politics in Pre-Revolutionary Pennsylvania, 1730–1775," in *Power and Status: Officeholding in Colonial America,* ed. Bruce C. Daniels (1986), pp. 75–105, discusses Kinsey along with other politicians. In the same volume, Richard Alan Ryerson, "Portrait of a Colonial Oligarchy: The Quaker Elite in the Pennsylvania Assembly, 1729–1776," pp. 106–35, also discusses Kinsey. Jean R. Soderlund, *Quakers & Slavery: A Divided Spirit* (1985), discusses Kinsey in New Jersey and Pennsylvania, and John E. Pomfret, *Colonial New Jersey* (1973), is useful for the early period.

EDWIN B. BRONNER

KINYOUN, Joseph James (25 Nov. 1860–14 Feb. 1919), pathologist, was born in East Bend, North Carolina, the son of John Hendricks Kinyoun, a physician, and Elizabeth Conrad. Reared in Centre View, Missouri, Kinyoun first studied medicine as an apprentice to his father. In 1880 he enrolled for a year's course of lectures in St. Louis Medical College, after which he attended Bellevue Hospital Medical College of New York University, where he received the M.D. in 1882.

Kinyoun returned to Missouri to practice with his father and took special instruction in surgery and gynecology. In 1883, after his attention was drawn to a report of Louis Pasteur's pioneering research in microbiology, Kinyoun began studying microscopy, examining not only microorganisms but also diseased tissues. Two years later he took a course of instruction in bacteriology from Herman M. Biggs at the Carnegie Laboratory at New York's Bellevue Hospital. In 1884 Kinyoun married Elizabeth Perry, who was from Centre View; they would have four children.

In 1886 Kinyoun joined the U.S. Marine Hospital Service. The following year service leaders decided to incorporate the new bacteriological techniques into their quarantine work in New York and chose Kinyoun to establish such a laboratory. He styled the one-room facility in the Staten Island Marine Hospital a "laboratory of hygiene," after the laboratories of the Germans, who were leaders in the new science. Within a month Kinyoun provided bacteriological confirmation of his colleagues' clinical diagnosis of cholera among passengers on an arriving ship. This work is often cited as the first bacteriological diagnosis of cholera in the western hemisphere. He also studied yellow fever, whose viral etiology was then unknown. From this small beginning grew the National Institutes of Health, the agency that provides most federal support for biomedical research in the United States.

In 1891 the laboratory, whose name gradually was transformed into the "Hygienic Laboratory," was moved to Washington, D.C., near service headquarters. Kinyoun advocated research as a fundamental role of the service, but for another decade the laboratory was viewed simply as a useful adjunct to the agency's mission to prevent the introduction of epidemic disease into the United States. To this end, Kinyoun designed the Kinyoun-Francis sterilizer, a disinfecting device for ships, and he demonstrated the superiority of sulfur dioxide as a fumigating gas. He was also asked to test water wells in the District of Columbia for bacterial contamination and to report on the ventilation of the U.S. House of Representatives.

To promote interest in research and expand the bacteriological knowledge of his colleagues, Kinyoun inaugurated a course of instruction in bacteriological techniques for junior service officers. He also continued his own studies in bacteriology at Johns Hopkins and Georgetown University schools of medicine, receiving a Ph.D. in 1896 from Georgetown. Concomitantly, from 1890 to 1899 he served as professor of hygiene, bacteriology, and pathology at Georgetown. Beginning in 1890 Kinyoun traveled to Europe several times to study emerging laboratory techniques with many pioneers in bacteriology, including Robert Koch and Elie Metchnikoff. On an 1894 trip he learned the method for preparing diphtheria antitoxin. Horses were inoculated with increasingly large doses of diphtheria bacilli and, when they had built up massive amounts of antibodies against the toxin produced by the microbes, they were bled and their immune sera used to treat patients. On his return Kinyoun launched production of diphtheria antitoxin at the Hygienic Laboratory, making it one of the earliest sites of antitoxin manufacture in the United States.

In 1899, for reasons that remain unknown, Surgeon General Walter Wyman removed Kinyoun as director of the Hygienic Laboratory and ordered him to assume command of the service's San Francisco quarantine station. Two years later Kinyoun became embroiled in a controversy about the nature and extent of an outbreak of bubonic plague in San Francisco. Although his laboratory diagnosis of plague was confirmed by an outside commission, and his recommendations for prevention were in line with standard service policy, Kinyoun became a symbol of unwelcome federal intervention in state health matters and was transferred out of San Francisco by Surgeon General Wyman. He then represented the service in Japan, where he conducted research on tropical diseases, and was later stationed in Hong Kong and in British Columbia. On 19 April 1902 he resigned from the service, reportedly with bitter feelings about a lack of service support for his actions in San Francisco.

In 1903 Kinyoun was named director of the H. K. Mulford Company laboratories in Glenolden, Pennsylvania. Mulford commercially produced biologicals such as diphtheria antitoxin and smallpox vaccine. Kinyoun held this post until 1907 when he returned to Washington, D.C. From 1907 to 1909 he served as professor of pathology and bacteriology at George Washington University School of Medicine, and from 1909 to 1919 he directed the bacteriological laboratory for the District of Columbia. In the latter capacity, he served as mentor to a future surgeon general, Thomas Parran, and he developed a technique for detecting tubercle bacilli in sputum samples that is still used and known as the "Kinyoun method."

In 1917, when the United States entered World War I, Kinyoun was given leave of absence by the District of Columbia to serve as an expert epidemiologist in the army. He served in North and South Carolina until 6 December 1918 when he was ordered back to Washington and appointed pathologist at the Armed Forces Medical Museum. He held this position until his death in Washington of lymphosarcoma of the neck.

Although he made no outstanding bacteriological discoveries himself, Kinyoun's leadership as founder of the laboratory that became the National Institutes of Health earned him a place among the pioneers of medical research in the United States. He understood the potential of bacteriological techniques and their implication for medicine, and he strove to incorporate them as useful techniques into federal public health responsibilities. In 1895 or possibly 1897 (sources differ about the date), Kinyoun was awarded the Order of Bolivar from Venezuela for "eminent sanitary services" rendered, and in 1906 he was starred by *American Men of Science* as one of the leading pathologists in the United States. He also served as president of the Society of Bacteriologists and was a member of many medical organizations.

• The bulk of primary materials about Kinyoun—seventy-five boxes of correspondence—was destroyed. A small collection of Kinyoun's papers and photographs, primarily relating to his experiences in San Francisco, are held by the National Library of Medicine in Bethesda, Md. Many books from his personal library were donated by his daughter to the Clendenning Medical Library in Kansas City. Some relevant materials may be found in the National Archives, Records of the Public Health Service, RG 90, and his service personnel file is available from the Federal Records Center in St. Louis, Mo.

Details of Kinyoun's life and career vary in the standard biographical sources, including obituaries. In particular, his death date is given as 14 Feb. in some sources, 15 Feb. in others. The correct date of 14 Feb. was established by consulting the *Washington Star* obituary published in the city of his death and noting that he died "on Friday" (14 Feb.). Other dates given above have been verified by primary sources whenever a discrepancy appeared.

Biographical material is also available in Paul F. Clark, *Pioneer Microbiologists of America* (1961), pp. 206–7. Kinyoun's work is placed in the context of Public Health Service history in Ralph C. Williams, *The United States Public Health Service, 1798–1950* (1951), pp. 249–50, and in Bess Furman, *A Profile of the United States Public Health Service, 1798–1948* (1973), pp. 202–3. It is examined in the context of the history of the National Institutes of Health in Victoria A. Harden, *Inventing the NIH: Federal Biomedical Research Policy, 1887–1937* (1986), pp. 13–15. For more information on Kinyoun's role in the 1901 San Francisco plague outbreak, see Charles McClain, "Of Medicine, Race, and American Law" *Law and Social Inquiry* 13 (1988): 447–513. Obituaries appear in the *Washington Star*, 16 Apr. 1919; *Washington Medical Annals* 18 (1919): 51–52; and *Journal of the American Medical Association* 72 (1919): 668.

VICTORIA A. HARDEN

KINZEL, Augustus Braun (26 July 1900–23 Oct. 1987), metallurgist and research director, was born in New York City, the son of Otto Kinzel, a professional pianist, and Josephine Braun, a college teacher of mathematics. In 1919 Kinzel, who was known as "Gus," received an A.B. cum laude in mathematics from Columbia University. As a youth he had become fluent in German and French, acquired a love for history and literature, and learned to play the piano. He once said, "Early in my career I learned two behavioral guides. First, choose a field of endeavor that you enjoy. If you enjoy your work you will be successful. Second, any transaction must benefit all parties therein. Otherwise, it just isn't worthwhile" (*Who's Who in America 1984–85*). He followed this philosophy all of his life.

Kinzel began his professional career in 1919 as a metallurgist at the General Electric Company in Pittsfield, Massachusetts. He soon took leave, however, to attend the Massachusetts Institute of Technology and in 1921 received a B.S. in general engineering. Shortly after his graduation he won an American-endowed fellowship to study at the University of Nancy in France and in 1922 was awarded a D.Met.Ing., *au titre étrangère*. He then rejoined the General Electric Company but soon left to work as a metallurgist at the Henry Disston and Sons steel plant near Philadelphia. His new position allowed him the opportunity to be a lecturer and instructor in advanced metallurgy at Temple University.

In 1926 Kinzel was hired as a research metallurgist at the then Union Carbide and Carbon Research Laboratories, Inc. The corporation at the time had a reputation for maintaining aggressive and well-directed programs of fundamental research, development, and engineering, which were recognized and rewarded by its management. One of his early assignments was to analyze the explosive failure of all-welded pressure vessels under high working pressures. He concluded that the units met the published specifications for materials and construction and that it was the steel that had failed at ultimate strength. His further analysis showed, however, that the existing boiler code, which dated back to the 1890s, was inadequate for stress concentrations at the head corners, thus causing the failures. He then went on to design an elliptical head that eliminated the corner stress, a design that is still used today in pressure vessels. In 1927 he married Doris Plishker; they had three children.

By 1931 Kinzel became chief metallurgist at the laboratories. He then went back to the University of Nancy for further study on welding processes and in 1933 was awarded an Sc.D. Returning to America he continued his climb up the research/administration ladder at the Union Carbide and Carbon Research Laboratories. On the way up he coauthored the two-volume *The Alloys of Iron and Chromium*, published by the Engineering Foundation. Volume one, *Low-Chromium Alloys*, appeared in 1937, and the second volume, *High-Chromium Alloys*, was published in 1940. His research evolved into the creation of "Cromansil," considered to be the first widely used "low-alloy, high-strength steel." This led to the development of other high-strength steels containing zirconium and titanium. He was also author or coauthor of more than 100 technical papers on metallurgy and obtained more than forty patents. He delivered numerous memorial lectures for the American Institute of Mining, Metallurgical, and Petroleum Engineers (AIME), American Welding Society, and the American Society for Metals, as well as giving lectures in Great Britain, Italy, and Russia on welding and related topics. His greatest expertise was in the fields of welding and alloy steels. Other research accomplishments were his design of a portable testing machine, exploring the nondestructive testing of welds by sonic and X-ray methods, and developing what is known as the "Kinzel bend test" to assess the ductility of various metal alloys. His studies on alloy steels included deoxidizing and alloy elements, powder cutting, scarfing of stainless steel, and solving numerous difficulties of steel welding.

The World War II years were very active for Kinzel. In addition to serving as a consultant for the Manhattan Project at the Los Alamos, Oak Ridge, Argonne, Knolls, and Brookhaven laboratories, he was in charge of the metals branch of the Technical Industrial Intelligence Committee in Europe. In 1945 he was made a brigadier general for TIIC and served several months in England, France, and Germany on a secret mission. After the dropping of the atomic bombs, he was a member of the initial Manhattan District Committee for the World Control of Atomic Energy and helped draft the classified report that became the basis for the Lilienthal and Baruch plans. With the end of the war Kinzel continued to serve on the Defense Science Board and the Naval Research Advisory Committee, becoming chair of the latter in 1953–1954.

Kinzel became vice president of the then Union Carbide subsidiary Electro Metallurgical Company in 1945 and its president in 1948. This was a billion-dollar industrial group whose products became the raw materials for most of the processing industry in the United States and Canada. Its Marietta, Ohio, plant produced a new variety of low-carbon ferrochromium, developed by him, for use in expediting manufacture of stainless steels. In 1954 he was appointed director of research for the Union Carbide Corporation and in 1955 vice president of research. During this period he contributed much to the development of a new process for making titanium metal. He retired from Union Carbide in 1965.

With his retirement, Kinzel became president and chief executive officer of the Salk Institute for Biological Studies in San Diego, California, a position that he held until 1967. His principal responsibility was to promote more vigorous fundraising for its pioneering programs. In 1965 he was also appointed to the board of directors of the Sprague Electric Company.

During his active career, Kinzel was very involved in the affairs of numerous engineering and science societies and councils. He was elected into the Metals Progress Hall of Fame in 1953. In 1958 he was elected president of the AIME and in 1960 was awarded its James Douglas Gold Medal. He was also president of the Engineers Joint Council and chair of the Division of Engineering and Industrial Research of the Nation-

al Research Council in 1960. He was the recipient of numerous honorary degrees and a member of the National Academy of Sciences and the American Philosophical Society. In addition he served as a board member or trustee of many organizations, including the MIT Corporation, California Institute of Technology, the Jet Propulsion Laboratory, Salk Research Institute, Systems Development Corporation, American Optical Company, and Beckman Instrument Company. In 1964 he was appointed by Governor Nelson Rockefeller as vice chair of the newly formed New York State Science and Technology Foundation.

One of Kinzel's greatest achievements was serving as a founding member and first president of the National Academy of Engineers. In this position he was instrumental in the formulation of many of its policies and philosophies. Kinzel published numerous scientific and technical papers, but he is best known for his two-volume *The Alloys of Iron and Chromium*, which became the standard in this field.

Kinzel's hobbies included flying, sailing, and designing and building contemporary furniture. After his first marriage ended in divorce, he married in 1945 Marie MacClymont, who had two children by a previous marriage; he also adopted another daughter, who was a classmate of his daughters. He died in his home in La Jolla, California.

Kinzel himself best summed up and followed his own philosophy: "The scientist is a man of the laboratory, the library, and the land of logic. The engineer is, and should be, a man of affairs in a world of both changing fashions and economic realities. The more he knows about the present, the better engineer he'll be" (Cisler and Wagner).

• Several biographical sketches of Kinzel have appeared as memorial tributes. The best of these are Walker L. Cisler and Harvey A. Wagner, "Augustus B. Kinzel, 1900–1987," National Academy of Engineering of the United States of America, *Memorial Tributes*, vol. 6 (1993), pp. 110–13, and William T. Golden, "Augustus B. Kinzel (26 July 1900–23 October 1987)," *Proceedings of the American Philosophical Society* 138, no. 1 (Mar. 1994): 165–68. Other informal biographies appeared in technical journals over the years, especially in 1958 when he was elected president of AIME. An obituary is in the *New York Times*, 29 Oct. 1987.

ROBERT J. HAVLIK

KINZIE, Juliette Augusta Magill (11 Sept. 1806–15 Sept. 1870), historian, writer, and early Illinois settler, was born in Middletown, Connecticut, the daughter of Arthur William Magill, a banker, and Frances Wolcott. She received a richer and more complete education than that usually available to young women. She attended a boarding school in New Haven, Connecticut; was tutored by her uncle, Alexander Wolcott, in Latin and other languages while he was a student at Yale; and spent time at Emma Willard's school in Troy, New York. She studied a variety of subjects, including music and "natural history," and later claimed to have been fascinated from her youngest days by stories of the American frontier. She met John Harris

Kinzie, the son of the famous Indian trader John Kinzie, through Alexander Wolcott, who had married John Kinzie's sister. Juliette Magill married John H. Kinzie in 1830, and they immediately moved to the Northwest, spending the first three years of their marriage at Fort Winnebago, now in Wisconsin. It was there that Juliette Kinzie first heard stories of the 1812 Massacre at Chicago from her mother-in-law and her husband. In 1834 the Kinzies moved to Chicago, where in 1844 Juliette Kinzie published an account based on what she had heard, *Narrative of the Massacre at Chicago, August 15, 1812, and of Some Preceding Events*. In a note at the beginning of the narrative, Kinzie protests that "this little record, taken, many years since, from the lips of those who had been eyewitnesses . . . was not designed for publication" but that "at the solicitation of many friends, and to avoid the possibility of its unauthorized appearance in print, the writer has consented to its publication in its original form." Perhaps this is a reference to or an attempt to forestall the incorporation of the material in Henry Brown's early *History of Illinois* (1844), where her work did appear, "without right or authority" (Joseph Kirkland, *Story of Chicago*, 1892). Although the narrative was published anonymously, and at first some supposed that John H. Kinzie (in whose name the manuscript was entered for copyright) was the writer, Kinzie soon acknowledged authorship.

Kinzie included a reworking of this slight account in *Wau-Bun: The "Early Day" in the North West*, which was published by Derby and Jackson in 1856. The first edition was published in New York and Cincinnati, and a second edition came out in 1857 from Derby, with a Chicago edition the same year published by D. B. Cook and Co. *Wau-Bun* is a mixture of autobiography and history. It recounted Juliette Kinzie's own experiences as an early settler of Wisconsin and Illinois amid a general description of the lives of local Native Americans, the history of white settlement in Chicago, and the activities of her father-in-law. As Kinzie noted in her preface, "It never entered the anticipations of the most sanguine that the march of improvement and prosperity would, in less than a quarter of a century [that is, since the time when she had arrived at what was a frontier outpost], have so obliterated the traces of 'the first beginning,' that a vast and intelligent multitude would be crying out for information in regard to the early settlement of this portion of our country." *Wau-Bun* attempted to fill this gap and was well received, perhaps because its historical narrative is combined with what Milo Quaife called Kinzie's "fondness for romance and for dramatic effect" (*Chicago and the Old Northwest*, 1913).

Kinzie was aware that her descriptions of relationships between the white settlers and the Native Americans were out of keeping with the majority cultural opinion. She noted in her preface, "Some who read the following sketches may be inclined to believe that a residence among our native brethren and an attachment growing out of our peculiar relation to them, have exaggerated our sympathies, and our sense of the

wrong they have received at the hands of the whites." And despite the centrality in her account of the "massacre," Native Americans were presented as fully rounded characters, and their cultures, customs, and language were discussed with respect.

The Kinzie family was involved in every aspect of Chicago's civic and social life throughout the nineteenth century. Kinzie herself, a devout Episcopalian, was active in her church (built on land the Kinzies donated) and, as one contemporary commented, was "the pioneer of art and literature in Chicago" (Rufus Blanchard, *Discovery and Conquests of the Northwest*, 1900). Among their other civic activities, the Kinzies participated in the founding of the Chicago Historical Society, including the donation of a collection of manuscripts. In 1869 a novel by Kinzie, *Walter Ogilby*, was published by Lippincott (the title page included the words "by the Authoress of *Wau-Bun*") and in 1871 another, posthumous, novel, *Mark Logan, the Bourgeois*, was also published by Lippincott. *Mark Logan* was another reworking of the materials she first used in the 1844 *Narrative* and in *Wau-Bun*, experiences and memories that had colored her entire life. She had six sons, several of whom served in the Civil War, and one daughter; her granddaughter and namesake Juliette Gordon Low founded the Girl Scouts of America. Kinzie died while summering in Amagansett, Long Island.

• The State Historical Society of Wisconsin has some papers and letters of Juliette Kinzie and other family members, as do the Chicago Historical Society, the Southern Collection of the University of North Carolina, and the Gordon Family Papers at the Georgia Historical Society. Almost every history of Illinois or Chicago devotes some space to the Kinzie family, and *Wau-Bun* has remained of interest to historians and literary critics. Although he took pains to show the ways in which *Wau-Bun* fails as traditional history, Milo Quaife acknowledged the importance of the book as cultural artifact and provided a comprehensive account of Kinzie's life in his 1932 introduction to an edition of the text, which he also discussed in several other books and articles during his long career of exploring the history of the old Northwest. Nina Baym's 1992 introduction to yet another reprinting of *Wau-Bun* provides another reading of the text as history, as does her discussion of the text and Kinzie in *American Women Writers and the Work of History, 1790–1860* (1995). Hugh D. Duncan, *The Rise of Chicago as a Literary Center* (1964), and Kenny J. Williams, *In the City of Men* (1974), discuss *Wau-Bun* as a text and Juliette Kinzie as an author that together provided models for the women writers of "dynasty novels" of Chicago (perhaps following the lead of Lennox Bouton Grey's unpublished University of Chicago doctoral dissertation, "Chicago and 'the Great American Novel'" [1935]).

JOANN E. CASTAGNA

KIP, William Ingraham (3 Oct. 1811–7 Apr. 1893), first bishop of the Episcopal church in California, was born in New York City, the son of Leonard Kip, a banker, and Maria Ingraham. Born to wealth, he received an excellent education, starting his studies at Rutgers and completing them at Yale College, receiving his B.A. from Yale in 1831. He began his preparation for the ordained ministry at the Protestant Episcopal Theological Seminary in Alexandria, Virginia, and then moved to the General Theological Seminary in New York City, receiving his B.Div. in 1835. That year he also married Maria Elizabeth Lawrence; they had one child.

Ordained after graduation, Kip served as an assistant both at St. Peter's Church in Morristown, New Jersey (1835–1836), and at Grace Church in New York City (1836–1837) before being called as a rector to St. Paul's Church in Albany, New York, in 1838. In Albany Kip quickly rose to prominence as an apologist for the Anglican catholic tradition (advocating the view that the Anglican church is catholic in nature rather than, as some argued, protestant or evangelical) and as a writer of historical books. In 1853 he was elected by the general convention to be a missionary bishop in order to develop the Episcopal church's ministry in California.

Kip was an unlikely candidate for missionary work on the frontier. Born to privilege and status in a wealthy Dutch family that traced its ancestry back to New Amsterdam, he was patrician in both outlook and manner. He was a scholar, a collector of valuable paintings, and did not move with ease outside of his social environment. His wife came from a similar background, a member of a banking family. Kip seems to have considered the appointment to California as a divine call for self-sacrifice, not unlike the martyrdom of the early Christians in the Roman imperial age.

After a hazardous sea trip Kip and his family arrived in California in 1854. They settled in San Francisco where he assumed the duties of rector of Grace Church along with the duties of his episcopal office. At this time only two full-time Episcopal priests were active in the state. The transient population that had rushed headlong to California hoping to find quick riches in the gold fields proved to be an unpromising base for building an orderly church life in the state. Kip dutifully made the rounds of the scattered communities in the state, at times with military escort through hazardous country, but he was more in his element in the study, while traveling in Europe, or developing the cultural resources of San Francisco. He contributed large sums of money to promote the cultural life of San Francisco and used his personal fortune to support the work of the church.

Kip's ideal of the church was inspired by the churches of Europe. He was among the pioneers in the Episcopal church in the cathedral building movement, but he did not live to see one constructed in California. He was unsuccessful in his attempt to found a college but succeeded in establishing a hospital, St. Luke's in San Francisco (1871). He also tried to develop a ministry to the state's native peoples and to Chinese immigrants, whom he considered a part of his pastoral responsibility, but a lack of resources and qualified personnel frustrated his efforts.

Kip continued his scholarly activities in the midst of his heavy clerical duties, writing on historical and theological subjects, for example, *The Christmas Holidays in Rome* (1857), *The Unnoticed Things of the Scripture* (1869), and *The Early Days of My Episcopate* (1860). His theological views were best expressed in *The Double Witness of the Church*, published in 1843. In it Kip argued that the Episcopal church had maintained the apostolic tradition while the Roman Catholic church had distorted it, and the Protestant churches had abandoned it altogether. Kip presented biblical and historical evidence for the claim that the primitive and normative organization of the church was focused on and propagated by the episcopate. Protestants denied this. Rome distorted it by claiming universal jurisdiction for the Bishop of Rome.

Kip continued his episcopal labors almost to the end of his long life. He received some relief from his heavy burden when the northern part of the state was formed into a separate diocese in 1874. In 1890 an assistant bishop was elected and assumed almost all episcopal responsibilities. Kip died in San Francisco.

• Kip's papers are in the diocesan archives in California. The principal study of his life, and the best source of information, is John E. Rawlinson, "William Ingraham Kip: Tradition, Conflict and Transition" (Ph.D. diss., Graduate Theological Union, 1982). See also George Barrett, "William Ingraham Kip of California," in *Pioneer Builders for Christ*, vol. 2, ed. P. M. Dawley (n.d.), pp. 1–18, and Edward L. Parsons, "William Ingraham Kip: First Bishop of California," *Historical Magazine of the Protestant Episcopal Church* 11 (June 1942): 103–25.

FRANK SUGENO

KIPHUTH, Robert John Herman (17 Nov. 1890–7 Jan. 1967), swimming coach and athletic director, was born in Tonawanda, New York, the son of John Kiphuth, a mill hand, and Mary Benin. After graduating from Tonawanda High School in 1909, he became physical education director at the Tonawanda Young Men's Christian Association. He studied physical education at Harvard in the summer of 1912.

The head of Yale's athletic department, William Gilbert Anderson, hired Kiphuth as an instructor in 1914. Kiphuth married Louise Delaney in 1917; they had one son. That same year Professor Anderson asked Kiphuth to supervise the Carnegie swimming pool. In 1917 Richard Mayer, captain of the swimming team, asked Kiphuth to coach them. Becoming varsity coach in 1918, Kiphuth stressed conditioning and especially dry-land exercises, defying prevailing wisdom. He often used pulley weights, a medicine ball, and calisthenics, which he systematized. Kiphuth's work in bodybuilding proved so successful that he was asked to give special work to the Yale crews and the football and hockey teams. From 1918 to 1924 Yale swimmers won sixty-five consecutive dual meets. From 1923 to 1926 Kiphuth spent the summers studying in Europe. He eventually would exert an international influence on swimming, as noted by a British publication: "This remarkable man's prolific writings on land conditioning, which he pioneered, and water training techniques have had a tremendous influence on world competition swimming" (*Swimming Times*, Mar. 1967).

In Amsterdam in 1928 Kiphuth coached the U.S. Olympic women's swimming team to five titles. He coauthored with Winthrop M. Phelps of Yale Medical School *The Diagnosis and Treatment of Postural Defects* (1932) and was promoted to assistant professor of physical education that year. He served as head coach of the 1932 U.S. Olympic swimming team; at Los Angeles, he guided the American women to six titles and the men to three. From 1933 to 1935 he chaired the swimming commission of the Amateur Athletic Union. Kiphuth coached the American swimming teams that competed in Japan in 1931, 1934, and 1935. In Berlin in 1936, Kiphuth coached the U.S. men's Olympic swimming team, which won two gold medals and included 1938 Yale graduate John Macionis.

Yale swimming teams won 175 straight dual meets from 1924 to 1937. With undergraduates, Kiphuth emphasized the carryover sports—"the type of athletics that a graduate can carry on with after he is thrown into the daily grind of his profession or business" (*Yale Alumni Weekly*, 27 Apr. 1934). Kiphuth was admired by alumni and faculty families. His exercise programs included professors' spouses and children, whom he often taught to swim. He was appointed a fellow of Timothy Dwight College in 1936 and associate professor and director of the Payne Whitney Gymnasium in 1940. His wife died in 1941.

During World War II Kiphuth wrote *Swimming* and *How to Be Fit* (both 1942). He advised young men to exercise before enlisting or being drafted because the "Army's thirteen weeks' basic training is too short a time to toughen up a man if he is soft. But it's long enough to make him miserable" (*Collier's*, 16 Jan. 1943). Kiphuth suggested schools and colleges form competitive combat teams for the "physically ambitious . . . modeled on the Olympic Pentathlon, but adapted to training for war victories, not athletic ones." Wartime swimming even included the ability "to zigzag in the water and submerge quietly to avoid gunfire" (*Collier's*, 16 Jan. 1943). Yale resembled a military base; Kiphuth administered physical training for army and navy officer-training schools located on campus. Kiphuth's contribution to the war effort helped servicemen and servicewomen across the entire range of physical ability.

After victories in sixty-three straight dual meets, Yale's streak, begun in 1940, was stopped in 1945 by the U.S. Military Academy at West Point. Kiphuth was appointed Yale athletic director in 1946. At the 1948 London Olympics at the Empire Pool, Wembley, the U.S. men's swimming team, coached by Kiphuth, became the first in Olympic history to win every event. Four Yale swimmers won seven medals in London: James McLane, Allan Stack, John Marshall, and Alan Ford (who had been featured in *Life*, 5 Mar. 1945).

In 1949, Kiphuth suffered a heart attack. His son Delaney, a varsity football player from Yale's class of 1941, became athletic director. Kiphuth, continuing

to coach and teach, became full professor in 1950 and editor of the new periodical *Swimming World* in 1951. He also conducted swimming clinics at U.S. Army bases in Europe in 1951, 1952, and 1953. At the 1952 Olympics in Helsinki, Kiphuth did not coach. Six Yale swimmers, however, competed for the United States: James McLane (gold medal), Wayne Moore (gold), Allan Stack (gold), Frank Chamberlain, John Marshall, and Donald Sheff. Rex Aubrey, a 1957 Yale graduate, competed for Australia. Recruiting swimmers was one of Kiphuth's greatest strengths. At the Melbourne Olympics in 1956, Perry Jecko of Yale performed for the U.S. swimming team. In 1959 Kiphuth retired after winning 182 straight dual meets. From 1918 to 1959 his teams won 528 dual meets and lost twelve. Fourteen National Collegiate Athletic Association championships and thirty-eight Eastern Intercollegiate championships were won by Yale.

After retirement, Kiphuth worked with U.S. Navy swimmers at Yale. Jeffery Farrell, one of his students, won two gold medals at the 1960 Olympics in Rome. Kiphuth advocated physical fitness for all, stating, "It will enable you to lead when your turn comes" (*Collier's*, 16 Jan. 1943). The press called Kiphuth the greatest swimming coach in the world, but he did not like to swim. The *Yale Daily News* (9 Jan. 1967) wrote, "There was always talk that he himself could not swim, but he destroyed the rumors in 1948 when he jumped into the pool at a Yale carnival and swam 15 yards across the tank as the crowd cheered."

Kiphuth's influence reached beyond athletics. Yale President Kingman Brewster, Jr., noted, "To Bob Kiphuth . . . all learning was an exercise in self-fulfillment and self-discipline. Generations of students and colleagues at Yale and throughout the world have outdone themselves because of the values he inspired and the standards he set" (*Yale Daily News*, 9 Jan. 1967). Gerald R. Ford, thirty-eighth president of the United States and a 1941 graduate of Yale Law School, knew Kiphuth while working as an assistant varsity football coach and head junior varsity football coach from 1935 to 1940. President Ford lauded his colleague: "Bob Kiphuth epitomized the highest principles of leadership in the coaching profession. He inspired young people to achieve their best by the example he set as a person and a coach" (letter to the author, 1 Dec. 1993). Kiphuth died in New Haven.

• Kiphuth's papers are at the Payne Whitney Gymnasium, Yale University. Kiphuth manuscripts also are located at the Henning Library, International Swimming Hall of Fame, Fort Lauderdale, Fla. Kiphuth's articles include "Speed and Skill in Swimming," *Scholastic Coach*, Nov. 1932; "The Payne Whitney Gymnasium of Yale University," *Research Quarterly*, Mar. 1933; "'Keeping Fit' After College Days," *Yale Alumni Weekly*, 27 Apr. and 8 June 1934; "Japan Challenges America in the Water," *Literary Digest*, 12 May 1934; and "You Can't Sink," *American Magazine*, Aug. 1936. Interviews are in the *New York Times*, 16 Mar. 1931 and 22 Jan. 1955, and Charles R. Walker, "Muscles for Victory," *Collier's*, 16 Jan. 1943. Yale Department of Athletics, *Yale and the Olympics, 1896–1980* (1981), contains material on the

Kiphuth Fellowship program and Kiphuth's career. Jean M. Henning, *Six Days to Swim: A Biography of Jeff Farrell* (1970), describes Kiphuth's coaching of Farrell; see also Arthur Daley, "Mind Over Matter," *New York Times*, 22 Aug. 1960. Obituaries are in the *New York Times*, 9 Jan. 1967; *Yale Daily News*, 9 and 10 Jan. 1967; Philip F. Hersh, "The Grand Old Man of Swimming," *Yale Alumni Magazine*, Feb. 1967; and *Swimming Times*, Mar. 1967.

RALPH KIRSHNER

KIPNIS, Alexander (13 Feb. 1891–14 May 1978), bass singer, was born in Zhitomir, Ukraine, the son of Isaiah Kipnis, a fabric merchant, and Machli (maiden name unknown), Russian Jews living in humble circumstances. Though his parents were not musically accomplished, he learned to love Russian peasant songs by the age of four or five. When he was about twelve years old, he ran off with a light opera troupe that visited his home village; he earned some money as a boy soprano but then returned home. His father wanted him to work in the family cloth business, but Alexander was determined to follow a musical career. He joined a vagabond troupe of players and took up study of the trombone and the double bass. Later he attended the Warsaw Conservatory, where he studied conducting. He graduated in 1912 with honors.

Kipnis sang in the school chorus at the Warsaw Conservatory. An impresario who heard his voice after it had broken was much impressed and urged him to take up singing as a career. Accordingly, he took lessons from an Italian teacher at the Conservatory, attended the opera regularly to absorb different singing styles, and was also influenced by hearing the great Italian Mattia Battistini sing. Kipnis became a military bandmaster in the Russian army to avoid being conscripted as a private soldier, but he never returned to Russia.

After leaving military service, Kipnis moved to Berlin, where he studied voice with Ernst Grenzebach at the Klindworth-Scharwenka Conservatory. He also took singing lessons from the heldentenors Lauritz Melchior and Max Lorenz. After appearing in operettas in Berlin in 1913 and 1914, he was interned as an enemy alien in Germany at the start of World War I. Though soon released, he was kept under police surveillance for the rest of the war.

These restrictions did not prevent Kipnis from embarking on a distinguished career as a bass singer. He made his operatic debut as the hermit in Carl Maria von Weber's *Der Freischütz* at the Hamburg Opera in 1915 and was a member of the Wiesbaden Opera from 1917 until 1922. There he built up his operatic roles, including Kezal in Bedřich Smetana's *The Bartered Bride*, Ramfis in Giuseppe Verdi's *Aida*, Bartolo in Wolfgang Amadeus Mozart's *The Marriage of Figaro*, and Titurel and Gurnemanz in Richard Wagner's *Parsifal*. His European operatic career was extensive between the two world wars. Kipnis became a leading basso at the Charlottenburg Opera, Berlin (1919–1930), at the Berlin State Opera (1932–1935), and at the Vienna State Opera (1935–1938). He performed at the Bayreuth Festival between 1927 and 1933 and sang at most of Europe's leading opera houses, including Covent Garden, the Munich Opera, the Paris Opera, and La Scala, Milan. Between 1932 and 1937 he appeared annually at the Salzburg Festival. In 1936 he sang at the Glyndebourne Festival in England.

Kipnis's American career was equally prestigious. He went to the United States for the first time in 1923 and became a member of the Chicago Civic Opera for nine seasons. For a decade beginning in 1926, he was a principal guest singer at South America's leading opera house, the Teatro Colón, Buenos Aires. In 1925 he married Mildred Levy, the daughter of an American concert pianist, Heniot Levy. They had one child, Igor, who became an internationally renowned harpsichordist. Alexander Kipnis became an American citizen in 1931. He decided to make the United States his permanent residence after Austria was annexed to Nazi Germany in 1938.

Kipnis made his belated debut at the Metropolitan Opera in New York in 1940. He stayed there for seven seasons, singing seventy-four performances of thirteen roles in a variety of languages. He was acclaimed for his performances of Sarastro in Mozart's *The Magic Flute*, Arckel in Claude Debussy's *Pelléas et Mélisande*, Baron Ochs in Richard Strauss's *Der Rosenkavalier*, and for a series of Wagnerian roles—Hagen in *Götterdämmerung*, Hunding in *Die Walküre*, and King Marke in *Tristan und Isolde*. His most celebrated role, however, was Boris Godunov in Modest Mussorgsky's opera of that name, with his interpretation of King Philip in Verdi's *Don Carlos* falling a close second. Kipnis retired from a stage singing career in 1946.

Alexander Kipnis was the most celebrated Russian bass singer to succeed Feodor Chaliapin in an international career. He mastered his craft at the beginning of his career and maintained high musical standards in a remarkably consistent fashion. Though he never sang on stage in his native Russia, he appeared in most of the world's major opera houses in the French, Italian, German, and Russian repertoire. He was renowned for the ease, nobility, sonority, and security of his voice in all registers throughout a two-octave compass, and for his vivid and versatile characterization of the major bass operatic roles. He was also a polished and widely admired soloist in the lieder literature—a somewhat rare achievement for a deep-timbred bass singer—and he gave many art song recitals. Especially praised for his interpretations of lieder by Franz Schubert, Johannes Brahms, Hugo Wolf, and Debussy, he made many recordings of this repertoire and of his operatic roles for the German Odeon and Columbia record companies. Perhaps his finest recordings were made at the Berlin State Opera in 1930–1931. In later years, Kipnis gave master classes in singing at the New York College of Music, the Juilliard School of Music, and the Berkshire Music Center in Tanglewood. He lived for many years in rustic seclusion near Westport, Connecticut, where he died.

• Some Kipnis papers are in the Department of Special Collections, Mugar Memorial Library, Boston University. Taped reminiscences by Kipnis are available in Yale University's Historical Sound Recordings Division. His career is discussed in J. B. Steane, *The Grand Tradition: Seventy Years of Singing on Record* (1974); David Ewen, *Musicians since 1900: Performers in Concert and Opera* (1978); and Nigel Douglas, *Legendary Voices* (1992). Frequent references to Kipnis's recordings are found in Alan Blyth, ed., *Opera on Record* (1979), and *Song on Record*, vol. 1, *Lieder* (1986). Informative articles and a discography by Alfred Frankenstein, Eduardo Arnosi, and J. Dennis appeared in *The Record Collector* 22, nos. 3 and 4 (1974): 53–79, with some addenda in the same magazine, 23, nos. 7 and 8 (1976): 166–71. An obituary is in the *New York Times*, 16 May 1978.

KENNETH MORGAN

KIRALFY, Imre (1 Jan. 1845–27 Apr. 1919), and **Bolossy Kiralfy** (1 Jan. 1848–Mar. 1932), dancers and producers of realistic-pictorial theater, were born in Pest, Hungary, the sons of Jacob Königsbaum, a cloth manufacturer, and Anna (maiden name unknown). The brothers were born shortly before the unsuccessful Hungarian Revolution of 1848. When Königsbaum, a nationalist, lost his fortune during the revolution, the young boys supported the family as child performers. First Imre, at age five, joined two years later by Bolossy, earned a living for the family by performing traditional folk dances in theaters and at private performances throughout the Austrian Empire. By virtue of their youth the children escaped official censure against public shows of nationalism for performing dances of the Hussars, Hungarian cavalry, and Cossacks. They changed their name from Königsbaum (king's tree) to Kiralfy, a shortening of *kiralyfy*, meaning prince (or king's son).

In 1859 the family moved to Berlin so that the boys and their younger sister Haniola could study with the noted ballet master Paul Taglioni at the Ballet Academy of the Royal Opera House. In 1860 they went to Paris to continue their training at the Paris Opéra while performing in the evenings at the Boulevard Theatres. These popular Parisian theaters produced enormous spectacles, productions that relied for their success on large numbers of dancers, elaborate changing scenery, and lavish costumes. Both brothers wanted to become producers and were deeply impressed with the theaters' sophisticated backstage equipment, efficient management, and principles of organization. Their first opportunity to produce came in 1865 when, while performing in England with Haniola, they were asked to take charge of *The Pearl of Tokay* at the Alhambra Theatre. In 1868 they were given an even larger assignment by the Belgian government, a five-day public fete in Brussels that included operas, ballets, pantomimes, sports, and a pageant of four thousand soldiers.

In 1869 the Kiralfy troupe of Hungarian dancers, with Haniola, Imre, and Bolossy as soloists, their younger sisters Katie and Emilie as seconds, and six other dancers recruited in London, made its New York debut performing a Magyar czardas (a Hungarian national dance) in George L. Fox's *Hiccory Diccory Dock* at the Olympic Theater. Critics hailed the troupe for its exuberance and dazzling technical feats. Imre and Bolossy, however, continued to pursue their dreams of producing. They believed that the United States was an ideal environment for European-style extravaganzas.

The Kiralfy brothers began their career as producers in the United States with no capital but with experience in a variety of European theaters as performers, choreographers, and directors, their own good business sense, and tireless energy. By October 1870 their eleven-member troupe had grown to a company of sixty; in 1871 it was even larger. The brothers, much in demand as choreographers and directors, demonstrated their flair for novelty and a particular skill in maneuvering masses of dancers in complicated patterns. In an 1871 revival of *Humpty Dumpty*, for instance, they devised a dance for the Amazon warriors in which the male warriors locked their shields above their heads while the female Amazons climbed up the stairs formed by the shields.

In 1873 the brothers gathered their entire family for the "Ballet of Nations" in *The Black Crook*, at Niblo's Garden Theater in New York City. They then purchased the touring rights for this popular melodrama and later used the profits to finance their own work. Shortly after the family's final appearance together as performers, on 6 April 1874 in St. Louis, they retired from performing to devote themselves to their growing theatrical empire. Haniola took charge of the dancers hired by her brothers, and the two younger sisters married and withdrew from the theater. This left only the youngest Kiralfy brother, Arnold, who pursued a career as a leading dancer in many of his brothers' productions. Although Arnold turned to producing later in life, he never achieved the stature of his two elder brothers.

Between 1873 and 1887 the brothers remained in the United States, where they imported and produced proven European spectacles. In 1875, for example, they produced Jules Verne's *Around the World in Eighty Days* at the New York Academy of Music, featuring the largest ballet New York had ever seen and realistic stage effects that included the sinking of a steamer at sea, a balloon ascension, a railway engine pulling cars across the stage, and a live elephant tramping through a jungle. Their name became synonymous with productions of epic proportions using large contingents of dancers and elaborate special effects. Often they had several productions running simultaneously, some on the road, others in New York City. In addition to European theatrical properties, the brothers occasionally choreographed and directed their own original spectacles. They branched out into real estate, financing and building the Alhambra Palace in Philadelphia in conjunction with the Centennial celebration in 1876.

By 1882 the name Kiralfy had come to mean lavish productions. According to the 7 October *Music and Drama*:

They are artists in everything pertaining to color and stage effects; they are experts in dancing and everything connected with it; they are admirable musicians, practiced stage carpenters, thorough mechanics, and they can handle a calcium [light] as readily as a Spanish woman can manipulate a fan. Every improvement made in stage mounting of heavy pieces within the past fifteen years has either been invented or improved or made practicable by them. Indefatigable workers, they are always intent on new devices.

After a disagreement in 1886 Imre and Bolossy severed their partnership. In doing so, they inaugurated a fierce competition that lasted the rest of their lives. Their individual productions grew steadily larger until finally they outgrew the interiors of even the roomiest theaters. They then moved to outdoor amphitheaters, where they could mount epic productions with casts often numbering in the hundreds. In 1885 Imre had produced *The Fall of Babylon* at an outdoor theater on Staten Island, New York, and followed this in 1890 with *Nero; or, the Fall of Rome*. Not to be outdone, Bolossy built the Palisades Amusement Park in New Jersey, where he produced *King Solomon; or, the Destruction of Jerusalem* in 1891. Unlike the earlier imported spectacles, these outdoor extravaganzas were written, directed, designed, and, in many cases, choreographed by the brothers. Stage movement was worked out on giant graphs with rubber stamps indicating groups of dancers. Intricate footwork for the ensemble was abandoned in favor of simple steps to connect the formations. Although European ballerinas filled the majority of the featured dance roles, the necessity for star performances was diminished by the immense size of the cast.

Each brother in turn worked for the Barnum and Bailey Greatest Show on Earth. In 1892 and 1893 Imre produced a circus "spec" (a spectacular production that ended the circus performance each evening), *Columbus; or, the Discovery of America*. He later moved this production to the Chicago Auditorium Theater in conjunction with the World's Columbian Exposition, the Chicago fair of 1893, and retitled it *America*. Bolossy created spectacles for the 1901 Pan-American Exposition in Buffalo and the 1904 St. Louis World's Fair.

Both brothers married members of their company while in New York. In 1872 Imre married Marie Graham, and shortly thereafter Bolossy married Elise Marie Walden, a German woman he had met in London. In the 1890s Bolossy divorced, later to marry Helen Dawnay. He had three children by his first marriage and five by his second marriage. Imre had nine children.

Worsening economic conditions in the United States in the early 1890s made the production of large-scale entertainments less practical, so the brothers moved their separate businesses to London. There Imre mounted *Venice in London* (1892) at the Olympia, an exhibition hall. For this entertainment he created scaled-down, architecturally accurate versions of the major tourist attractions in Venice, Italy. Complete with waterways and gondolas, *Venice in London* allowed audiences to enjoy the sights and sounds of a warm summer day on the Grand Canal in the midst of a dismal London winter. Twice a day audiences could attend Imre's production *Venice, Bride of the Sea*, a combination of Shakespeare's *Merchant of Venice*, naval sea battles on the manmade lake within the Olympia, and dances, including cancans. The following year, with an even greater expenditure, Bolossy produced at the Olympia *Constantinople*, with harems, camels, cancan dancers, and warring Arab chieftains astride their horses.

Imre gathered backers to assist him in the creation of new exposition centers and became the lessee and director general of exhibitions, first at the Earl's Court and later when he built White City, a 140-acre amusement center specially equipped to house his spectacles and expositions. From 1900 until his death in London, Imre produced a series of successful international expositions of his own devising: "Empire of India," "The Victorian Era," "The Universal Exhibition," and "The Franco-British Exhibition." In a sense Imre became the British Empire's public relations agent, glorifying imperialism.

Bolossy, preferring the creative work behind the footlights to financial speculation and empire-building, divided his time between New York and the Continent and continued his work as a director and choreographer throughout the 1890s and the first decade of the twentieth century. As his children grew older, he coached and trained them in their own act. His daughter Verona and son Calvin became the Kiralfy Kiddies, touring vaudeville circuits accompanied by their parents. Bolossy also died in London.

Although audiences and scholars have largely forgotten the work of the Kiralfy brothers, they were very influential, inspiring the next generation of showmen. Their dissolving and re-forming masses of dancers, transforming scenery, and mechanical special effects pointed the way for early filmmakers, and their pageants and processionals lived on in American circus specs. Imre and Bolossy Kiralfy brought lavish European entertainments to the American stage, popularizing the spectacle as a legitimate form of theater. Over the last two decades of the nineteenth century they expanded their indoor productions, eventually filling outdoor amphitheaters with epics involving casts of hundreds for vast audiences. Their work prepared early twentieth-century audiences for the filmed epics of Cecil B. de Mille and the massive stage works of Max Reinhardt.

• The Billy Rose Theatre Collection and the Dance Collection at the New York Public Library for the Performing Arts, Lincoln Center, and the Museum of the City of London have information on the Kiralfy brothers in the form of programs, clippings, and photographs. The best source for information on the Kiralfy brothers comes from Bolossy Kiralfy's autobiography, *Bolossy Kiralfy: Creator of Great Musical Spectacles, an Autobiography* (1988). For information on Imre Kiralfy, see "My Reminiscences," *The Strand*, July 1909, and *My Life's Ambition* (1888). The brothers' best-known works include *Naiad Queen* (1873), *The Deluge* (1874), *A Trip to the Moon* (1877), *Azurine: Voyage to the Earth* (1876), *Enchantment* (1879), *Black Venus* (1881), *Michael Strogoff* (1881), *Excelsior* (1883), *Seiba and the Seven Ravens* (1884), and *The Ratcatcher* (1885).

Productions mounted by Bolossy Kiralfy include *Siege of Troy* (1885), *Patrie (Dolores)* (1888), *Mathias Sandorf* (1888), *The Water Queen* (1889), *Antiope* (1889), *The Orient* (1895, 1896, 1897, 1900), *Tribute to Balkis* (with Barnum and Bailey, 1901), *Louisiana Purchase Spectacle* (1904), *Dunbar at Delhi* (with Barnum and Bailey, 1904), *Peace* (with Barnum and Bailey, 1906), *Pocahontas* (1907), *Tomorrow: A Christmas Pantomime* (1907–1908), and *In the Land of Miracles* (1910).

Productions mounted by Imre Kiralfy include *Grand Naval Spectacle* (1898), *India and Ceylon* (1896), *Victorian Era* (1897), *Universal* (1898), *Greater Britain* (1899), *Woman's International* (1900), *Military* (1901), *Paris in London* (1902), *Japanese-British* (1901), *London Coronation* (1911), and *Latin-British* (1912).

Also see Edward Bennet Marks, *They All Had Glamour: From the Swedish Nightingale to the Naked Lady* (1944). Harold Hartley, *Eighty-Eight— Not Out: A Record of Happy Memories* (1939), discusses Imre's early work at London's Olympia. An obituary of Imre Kiralfy is in the *New York Dramatic Mirror*, 13 May 1919; one of Bolossy Kiralfy is in the *New York Times*, 9 Mar. 1932.

BARBARA BARKER

KIRBY, Ephraim (23 Feb. 1757–20 Oct. 1804), law reporter and Connecticut Jeffersonian, was born near Washington in Litchfield County, Connecticut, the son of Abraham Kirby and Eunice Starkweather, farmers. In December 1775, after five months in the Connecticut militia, three months of which were spent investing British-occupied Boston, Kirby returned to his Litchfield home to begin the study of law with attorney Reynold Marvin. In December 1776 he enlisted as a trooper in the Second Continental Dragoons. He fought at Brandywine and Germantown.

In 1779, having recovered from a wound-induced coma, Kirby read law and argued local cases for absent lawyers. Attributing the difficulties that he encountered in obtaining clients to "a partial Education, & a Want of Connections," he sought the status accorded by an officer's rank. From August 1782 until December 1783 he served as an ensign in Colonel Jeremiah Olney's Rhode Island Battalion. According to family legend, Kirby participated in nineteen revolutionary battles or skirmishes and received thirteen wounds. Few patriots had served as he had both in the opening campaign at Boston and in the war's final, abortive February 1783 expedition against Fort Oswego in western New York. In 1784 he married Ruth Marvin; they had eight children, two of whom died in childhood. Confederate general Edmund Kirby Smith was his grandson.

Lacking family connections and labeled a troublemaker by Litchfield society for having aroused the enmity of his neighbor Oliver Wolcott (1726–1797), a signer of the Declaration of Independence, Kirby was solely dependent on his own ability and initiative to achieve legal prominence. He thus determined to produce the first volume of state law reports to be published in the United States, which would provide a needed ready access to American as well as English common law. In spite of the work's importance, only 227 subscribers could initially be found. The commitment of the state's general assembly to purchase 350 copies made possible the publication of his *Reports of Cases Adjudged in the Superior Court of the State of Connecticut from the Year 1785 to May 1788 with Some Determinations in the Supreme Court of Errors* (1789).

By traveling the legal circuit, Kirby developed a wide range of contacts throughout his native state. He was active in the state militia, in which he rose in 1800 to the rank of lieutenant colonel, as well as in the Society of the Cincinnati and the Masons. In 1789 he organized a businessman's temperance society, which is said to have been the first of its kind in America. In 1798 he was elected the first general grand high priest of the Royal Arch Masons.

Although Kirby continued to practice law, his energies after 1791 increasingly were devoted to land speculation and politics. He became one of the principal organizers of the Connecticut Land Company purchase of the Ohio Western Reserve. In 1791, using the pen name "Brutus," he inaugurated a newspaper war in the *Litchfield Monitor* against leading Federalist Oliver Wolcott. Kirby emerged as the vocal and visible spokesman around whom critics of Connecticut's "Standing Order" rallied. Within three years he became the propagandist and leader of the legislative faction that sought to divert the proceeds from the sale of the Connecticut Western Reserve from the state's Congregational clergy to its schools.

In the 1790s, when Connecticut Federalists routinely vilified critics of government policy as enemies to society, Kirby helped found an opposition political organization, which in the latter years of the decade merged into the national Jeffersonian movement. Kirby's 1794 "Cassius" letters, which attacked the concentration of power and privilege in the state senate and condemned the interference of the established Congregational church in politics, were widely debated and served as a catalyst for the creation of the Democratic-Republican party in Connecticut.

During Kirby's lifetime, he and his Democratic-Republican associates were defeated in almost every statewide election and legislative vote; but the party he was instrumental in creating would in 1817 end a quarter century of Federalist dominance. Kirby's political contribution lay in the fact that, in the face of insurmountable odds and despite the financial hardship it caused him, he persisted in his effort to persuade the citizens of Connecticut about the dangers of allowing a few families to dominate their government, generation after generation, virtually unchecked by the democratic processes of free enquiry and fair elections.

Between 1791 and 1801 Kirby represented Litchfield fourteen times in the state legislature. In recognition of his efforts in the Jeffersonian cause, Kirby was appointed supervisor of internal revenue for Connecticut by President Thomas Jefferson in July 1801. Discovering that Jefferson's patronage appointments had left the Democratic-Republicans almost leaderless in the Connecticut Assembly, Kirby resigned his federal post in September 1802 and resumed his legislative role.

In 1801, 1802, and 1803 the Republicans ran Kirby as their candidate for governor. Although he had no expectation of winning, his candidacy posed the first organized threat to Federalist dominance of that office. Having suffered financial reverses from investing over $30,000, much of it borrowed, in lands from Vermont to Virginia, he again sought a patronage income. In 1803 President Jefferson appointed him one of three commissioners responsible for resolving conflicting land claims in the Mississippi Territory above Spanish Mobile. After an arduous four-month journey, Kirby convened the land board at Fort Stoddert in February 1804. Between February and July the commission adjudicated 269 land claims, which had been filed by 146 residents of the Tombigbee-Tensaw settlements. At Jefferson's behest, he assumed additional responsibilities in 1804 as a federal judge for the Mississippi Territory and became the first federal judge to reside in what would become the state of Alabama. In this position, Kirby regularly communicated his assessments of local conditions to the president. Jefferson was sufficiently impressed by Kirby's work to offer him in a letter written in December 1804 the governorship of the Mississippi Territory. Unfortunately, while concluding the land commission's business at Fort Stoddert, Kirby had died six weeks earlier of yellow fever.

• The Ephraim Kirby Manuscripts Collection at Duke University Library contains letters received, and a few written, by Kirby. The General Edmund Kirby-Smith Manuscripts Collection of the Southern Historical Collection, University of North Carolina at Chapel Hill, holds several personal letters from Ephraim Kirby to his wife. Kirby's activities in the Mississippi Territory, including his reports to President Jefferson, can be found in Clarence E. Carter, ed., *Territorial Papers of the United States: Mississippi*, vol. 5 (1937). Useful biographical sketches of Kirby include Theodatus Garlick, "Biography of Ephraim Kirby," *Transactions of the Western Reserve Historical Society* 2 (Jan. 1883): 183–86, and Thomas McAdory Owen, "Ephraim Kirby, First Superior Court Judge in What Is Now Alabama," *New York Genealogical and Biographical Record* 33 (July 1902): 129–34. On Kirby's law reports, see Alan V. Briceland, "Ephraim Kirby: Pioneer of American Law Reporting, 1789," *American Journal of Legal History* 16 (Oct. 1972): 297–319. For Kirby's activities in the Mississippi Territory, see three articles by Briceland in the *Alabama Review*: "Ephraim Kirby: Mr. Jefferson's Emissary on the Tombigbee-Mobile Frontier in 1804," 24 (Apr. 1971): 83–113; "The Mississippi Territorial Land Board East of the Pearl River, 1804," 32 (Jan. 1979): 38–68; and "Land, Law, and Politics on the Tombigbee Frontier, 1804," 33 (Apr. 1980): 92–124.

ALAN V. BRICELAND

KIRBY, John (31 Dec. 1908–14 June 1952), jazz bassist and bandleader, was born in Baltimore. Details about his parents are unknown. Abandoned, Kirby had a horrible childhood in an orphanage; it "left him without social graces, and he lacked formal education." He sold newspapers, shined shoes, and groomed horses before securing a job as a Pullman porter on the Pennsylvania Railroad. In 1924 he came to New York with a trombone, which was immediately stolen. He worked in restaurants to buy a tuba and then performed in Harlem, returning to the railroad when opportunities to play were scarce. He was a member of Bill Brown and his Brownies briefly in 1928 and again from 1929 into early 1930. Having begun to play string bass as well as tuba, he switched between both on Brown's recording "What Kind of Rhythm Is This?" (1929).

In April 1930 Kirby joined Fletcher Henderson's big band. "John was a lonely, bewildered kid, who tried hard to be accepted by his peers," trumpeter Rex Stewart wrote. "He finally succeeded because of his hail-fellow-well-met act, but when he was caught off guard, it was plain to see that Kirby really was introspective and a thinker." Having begun to take lessons on string bass from Wellman Braud, Kirby continued regularly playing both instruments until 1933, when he settled on the string bass and thereafter rarely used the tuba. Not a soloist, he filled the instrument's traditional role of providing a firm rhythmic and harmonic foundation, as on such recordings as "Chinatown, My Chinatown" (1930) and "New King Porter Stomp" (1932), both on string bass, and "I'm Crazy 'bout My Baby" (1931), on tuba. He also recorded late in 1930 with the Chocolate Dandies, a group of Henderson's men under Benny Carter's direction.

After leaving Henderson in March 1934, Kirby joined Chick Webb's orchestra, with which he recorded "Stompin' at the Savoy" and "Don't Be That Way." The following year he briefly led a group before returning to Henderson's orchestra from October 1935 until April 1936. He rejoined Webb in the summer of 1936 and became a member that autumn of the Mills Blue Rhythm Band under Lucky Millinder. From 1935 and extending into 1938, he frequently accompanied Billie Holiday on recordings under Teddy Wilson's name and her own.

Kirby's greatest fame came when he began leading a sextet with colleagues from his past big bands. It took shape at the Onyx Club in New York from May to August 1937, during which time its leadership was credited to trumpeter Frankie Newton, singer Leo Watson (who was attempting to play drums), and Kirby. Meanwhile, Marietta Williams, singing under the stage name Maxine Williams, had secured a job at the Onyx and a recording date with Claude Thornhill in a septet that included Newton and Kirby, but not Watson, who by August had been replaced by O'Neill Spencer. For swing versions of two Scottish tunes, the singer was, by a twist of show business logic, given the Irish surname by which she became famous: Maxine Sullivan. "Loch Lomond" was a hit, and by the fall, with Newton having left, Sullivan was starring at the Onyx Club with Kirby's sextet. Comprising trumpeter Charlie Shavers, clarinetist Buster Bailey, alto saxophonist Russell Procope, pianist Billy Kyle, Kirby, and Spencer, the group carved out its own identity, separate from Sullivan's Scot-Irish jazz, but linked to her gentle, subdued swing style.

The sextet memorized (and later wrote out, to accommodate changes in personnel) sprightly arrangements in which coordinated passages for muted trumpet, low- to mid-register clarinet, and sweet-toned alto saxophone, alternated with or accompanied brief solos, as on such recordings as "Rehearsin' for a Nervous Breakdown," "Undecided" (both 1938), and "Front and Center" (1939). Its repertory consisted of popular tunes of the swing era, new themes based on these tunes, and swing-oriented arrangements of classical and light classical material; a piece such as "Beethoven Riffs On" (recorded in 1941), with improvisations and melodic statements based on the slow movement of the Seventh Symphony, was, if less bombastic than many examples of big bands "swingin' the classics," aesthetically equally unsuccessful. Shavers and Kyle were the best soloists; both Bailey and Procope delivered their finest improvisations elsewhere, but given the sextet's orientation toward arrangement, this was not a serious flaw. Kirby as usual concentrated on underpinnings, and Spencer mainly used brushes (rather than sticks) for softness. Exceptions to these stylistic tendencies may be heard on "Royal Garden Blues" (1939), which includes "open" (i.e., unmuted) trumpet, a bass solo, and a flamboyant snare drum solo.

By the time of these recordings Sullivan and Kirby were married and had enjoyed a long stand at the Onyx, with the privilege of being the first African Americans to secure a sponsored network radio show, "Flow Gently, Sweet Rhythm." The quiet polish of Kirby's sextet appealed to affluent audiences, and after leaving the Onyx the group was popular at jazz clubs, including the Famous Door in New York, and posh venues, such as the Pump Room of the Hotel Ambassador East in Chicago. The year 1942 marked a turning point in Kirby's life. His marriage ended (they had no children), Sullivan's independent popularity having carried her in another direction, and the sextet was decimated by Spencer's illness (he died in 1944) and the military draft, which took Kyle and, early the next year, Procope. Personnel changed with increasing rapidity, and interest in the sextet's idiosyncratic style declined. By 1947 Kirby was without work, and he had contracted diabetes. He reconstituted the original sextet (with Sid Catlett replacing Spencer on drums) for an unsuccessful concert at Carnegie Hall in December 1950. After working briefly with Henry "Red" Allen and in the spring of 1951 with Buck Clayton, he moved to the Los Angeles area, where he worked occasionally with Benny Carter. Unhappy and often unemployed, Kirby died in Hollywood from diabetes, its effects compounded by a fondness for alcohol and sweets. He was survived by his second wife, Margaret; her maiden name is unknown.

Having had little impact on the music's history, Kirby's sextet has only a modest stature in jazz. He is remembered mainly as a bassist in the first decade of big band jazz and in ad hoc small groups of the swing era.

• Rex Stewart surveys Kirby's career and remembers his friendship with Kirby in *Jazz Masters of the Thirties* (1972), pp. 151–59. Walter C. Allen, *Hendersonia: The Music of Fletcher Henderson and His Musicians: A Bio-Discography* (1974), documents Kirby's years with the Henderson band. Gunther Schuller gives a brief, glowing assessment of Kirby's work with Henderson and Webb in *Early Jazz: Its Roots and Musical Development* (1968) and *The Swing Era: The Development of Jazz, 1930–1945* (1989). *The Swing Era* also offers (pp. 812–16) a detailed, damning assessment of Kirby's sextet. This viewpoint is counterbalanced in surveys by the sextet's saxophonist, Russell Procope, *Jazz Journal*, May 1967, pp. 6–7, and its trumpeter, Charlie Shavers, *Jazz Journal*, May 1970, pp. 8–9. Ian Crosbie, *Jazz Journal*, Mar. 1972, pp. 26–28, offers the most detailed study, and Arnold Shaw, *52nd Street: The Street of Jazz* (1977), includes an interview with Maxine Sullivan. Another useful account is Chip Deffaa, "Still Gently Swinging," *Mississippi Rag* 12 (Aug. 1985): 10–11. A catalog of his recordings as a leader is by Charles Garrod, *John Kirby and His Orchestra / Andy Kirk and His Orchestra* (two distinct studies, published together) (1991). Obituaries include two in *Down Beat*, 16 July and 30 July 1952.

BARRY KERNFELD

KIRBY, Rollin (4 Sept. 1875–9 May 1952), cartoonist and illustrator, was born in Galva, Illinois, the son of George Washington Kirby, a shoe merchant, and Elizabeth Maddox. When Kirby was still a small child, his family moved to Hastings, Nebraska, where he was educated in the public schools. At the age of nineteen he went to New York City, where he studied art with John H. Twachtman and Hugh H. Breckenridge at the Art Students League. He next went to Paris to study at the École Nationale des Beaux-Arts and the Atelier Julien with an aging James A. McNeill Whistler, who seemed more interested in being admired by his students than in teaching them. Kirby's interest in politics was heightened in France, where he attended the second trial of Alfred Dreyfus, a Jewish army officer whose 1894 conviction of treason based on forged papers was later overturned. Upon his return to the United States in 1900, Kirby's work was shown at the National Academy, but he abandoned painting when he could not make a living from it. In 1901 he began to illustrate magazines, including *American*, *Century*, *Collier's*, *Harper's*, *McClure's*, *Life*, and *Scribner's*. In 1903 he married Estelle Carter, an actress; they had one child.

Dismissing illustrations as "chain stuff" (*Quill*, p. 6), Kirby in 1911 turned to cartoon drawing. That year he worked for the *New York Evening Mail*, the next year for the *New York Sun*, and the following one for Joseph Pulitzer's *New York World*, where he remained until 1939 (staying with it even after it became the *World-Telegram* in 1931). During his first year with the *World* his social cartoon series "Sights of the Town" was an immediate hit. His drawing style was influenced by a contemporary cartoonist, Boardman Robinson, whose crayon took on a "palpitating effect," which captured the "lithographic power" of the French artist Honoré Daumier (Hess and Kaplan, p. 142). In 1914 Kirby's timely cartoons began appearing daily on the *World*'s editorial page, with never more than ten hours elapsing between their conception and publication. Each day except Sunday, before drawing these political cartoons, he met with the *World*'s editorial board. During these meetings exchanges with his editor Frank Irving Cobb sharpened and focused Kirby's ideas, which he expressed in "articulate" grease-pencil lines (*American Artist*, p. 5). With Kirby thinking of his cartoons as editorials, they became the focal point of the "fighting" *World*, the nation's most influential paper. By 1920 his Mr. Dry—a "tall, sour, weedy," comical, and rather clerical figure with a stove-pipe hat—was almost as universally recognized as was Uncle Sam, whom Kirby called "the most overworked" cartoon figure in America (*American Artist*, p. 6). By creating a puppet who expressed what Kirby called "the canting hypocrisy" many felt in "the quasi-ecclesiastical overtones" of the Prohibition movement, Kirby helped bring down the Eighteenth Amendment (*American Artist*, p. 6). With repeal, Mr. Dry's usefulness was over, and Kirby—who was articulate with words as well as with lines, writing articles, short plays, and verse—buried him in "The Death of a Puppet" (*Vanity Fair*).

Kirby seldom used labels, kept his cartoons simple, made their ideas "explode in the reader's face" (Kirby quoted in *Quill*, p. 7), and became the most famous political artist of his era. He received the first Pulitzer Prize given for cartoons for his "On the Road to Moscow," published in 1921. He won a second Pulitzer Prize for his "News from the Outside World," published in 1924 and picturing Uncle Sam as a hobo accompanied by hoboes from two other nations that had also failed to join the League of Nations. His third Pulitzer Prize was for a cartoon published in 1928. It featured Kirby's overfed GOP puppet standing aghast at the word "Tammany!" while surrounded by an angelic choir of sixteen Republicans—three in prison garb—besmirched by scandal. Walter Lippmann, one of the greatest newspaper columnists of his time, who worked with Kirby on the *World*, called him "the biggest gun" in that newspaper's attack on "the pillars of Republicanism"—an attack that eventually drove their party from power (*Highlights*, p. xiii). Even though Kirby's cartoons were "meant to hurt and to confound," Lippmann insisted that their complete lack of self-righteousness kept them from being venomous (*Highlights*, p. xv). Kirby called cartoonists "the victims of an outworn tradition." To be understood they must use stock figures—like Uncle Sam and his own Mr. Dry—and draw their puppets according to regulations: "to be fat is to be predatory," thinness "is the symbol of distress" and an open bid "for sympathy," the "larger the cigar the more . . . insolent becomes the smoker," and "whiskers and merit seldom go hand in hand" (*Current Opinion*, pp. 532, 533, 535).

When the *World-Telegram* began opposing many New Deal projects, Kirby left the paper for the *New York Post*, where he worked from 1939 to 1942. After that date he continued "to fight the rise of hate" by contributing to *Look*, the *New Yorker*, *Vanity Fair*, the Sunday *New York Times*, and other journals (*Quill*, p. 14).

Back in early 1917 Kirby had joined the newspaper barrage against Senator Robert La Follette of Wisconsin, which by 1940 he had come to regret. La Follette had opposed President Woodrow Wilson's arming of merchant ships. The most powerful of Kirby's many cartoons on the subject, "The Only Adequate Reward," pictured La Follette as the leader of the "willful twelve" who had voted against the president, receiving a huge iron cross from a mailed fist, representing Germany. In a 1940 letter to La Follette's family Kirby, who shared the antiwar attitudes of many who were left of center at the time, stated that the years had "brought a better sense of values" to him, that he now saw La Follette's stand as "a brave fight against an overwhelming tide of chauvinism and war hysteria" and regretted adding his "tiny bit" to La Follette's "burden" (La Follette and La Follette, p. 632).

Although Kirby insisted that "the idea is seventy-five per cent of a cartoon" (*American Artist*, p. 5), he was a master in drawing the human figure and kept a six-foot mirror in his office to pose for action drawings and to check out body details. In 1944 a hundred of his cartoons were shown at the Museum of the City of New York. Titled New York between Two Wars, the exhibition was a brilliant, broad-sweeping review of social and political life in the United States during those years. When Kirby died in New York City, collections of his cartoons were already prized by the Metropolitan Museum of Art, the Library of Congress, the New York Public Library, and other great institutions.

• The New York Public Library's collection of 1,029 of Kirby's original cartoons, mostly from the 1930s, are available on two reels of microfilm. Kirby wrote about his drawings and those of his colleagues in "Cartoon: United States," *Encyclopaedia Britannica*, 14th ed., vol. 4, p. 950, and in his *Highlights: A Cartoon History of the Nineteen Twenties* (1931). See also his "Death of a Puppet," *Vanity Fair*, Dec. 1933. For articles that quote him extensively, see "Rollin Kirby," *The Quill*, Apr. 1939, pp. 6–7, 13–14; "Cartoonist Criticizes Our Cartoonists," *Current Opinion*, Apr. 1920, pp. 532–35; "Rollin Kirby: A Great American Political Cartoonist," *American Artist*, June 1940, pp. 5–7; and "Cartoonists as They See Themselves: Rollin Kirby," *Literary Digest*, 16 Sept. 1933, p. 9. For Kirby's place in the history of American cartoons, see Stephen Hess and Milton Kaplan, *The Ungentlemanly Art: A History of American Political Cartoons*, rev. ed. (1975); William Murrell, *A History of American Graphic Humor, 1865–1938* (2 vols., 1933–1938); Everette E. Dennis and Melvin L. Dennis, "100 Years of Political Cartooning," *Journalism History* 1 (Spring 1974): 6–10; and Gerald W. Johnson, *The Lines Are Drawn* (1958), pp. 60–65. For a description of Kirby's La Follette cartoons and his apology to the senator's family, see Belle Case La Follette and Fola La Follette, *Robert M. La Follette 1855–1925* (2 vols., 1953), and for more about

Kirby and the *World*, see James Wyman Barrett, *Joseph Pulitzer and His World* (1941). An obituary is in the *New York Times*, 10 May 1952.

OLIVE HOOGENBOOM

KIRCHWEY, Freda (26 Sept. 1893–3 Jan. 1976), editor and publisher of the *Nation*, was born Mary Frederika Kirchwey in Lake Placid, New York, the daughter of George Washington Kirchwey, a prominent reform-minded lawyer, and Dora Wendell, a schoolteacher. Kirchwey had an older sister and two brothers, one of whom died as a child. Kirchwey attended the Horace Mann School and then Barnard College. At Barnard she wrote editorials against fraternities of women (later known as sororities) because of their discrimination against certain groups. She was especially troubled by the exclusion of Jews. While in college she also wrote in support of woman suffrage and continued to do so while employed as a society commentator for a sporting newspaper, the *Morning Telegraph* (1915–1916). She graduated from Barnard in 1915 and married Evans Clark later that year, keeping her maiden name. She and Evans had three sons, Brewster, Michael, and Jeffrey. Brewster died within his first year, and Jeffrey died at age seven.

In 1918 Kirchwey worked as an editorial assistant for the literary magazine *Every Week* and for the *New York Tribune* before beginning her lifelong work on the *Nation* in August 1918. Oswald Garrison Villard had just reorganized the crusading journal, one of the country's oldest political journals. Kirchwey's rise to prominence at the *Nation* began with work in the journal's International Relations Section (IRS). She collected articles to be used for this section, and soon contributed pieces herself. Within seven months she became the editor of the IRS. The knowledge she acquired from both published sources and international figures with whom she came into contact influenced her for years to come.

Kirchwey shaped the policies of the *Nation* as she served in various roles over the years. In 1922 she became managing editor and then was literary editor from 1928 to 1929. She advanced to executive editor of a board of four editors in 1933; within four years she had overall control. To help finance the journal during difficult times, Kirchwey created a nonprofit company, *Nation* Associates, that became the owner of the journal. From then on, she was head of management as well as editor and publisher of the *Nation*.

Kirchwey's writings spanned the twentieth century and touched on many important themes in social, political, and diplomatic history. As a new woman of the 1920s, she explored issues of changing mores in her own life as well as in the pages of the journal. She published a series on changing morality and another one about modern women, their careers, and their relationships with men and families. The first series, "New Morals for Old," was published as *Our Changing Morality* (1924), with Kirchwey as editor. She believed that major changes in women's lives and the economy created changing social mores. Yet Kirchwey reflected

here own dilemma of struggling to develop a personal value system amidst these changes when she concluded that the modern woman was still searching for "a new sort of certainty." Kirchwey continued her search in a second series, "These Modern Women," published between 1926 and 1927. This series showed Kirchwey's fascination with psychology, as she had the life stories of anonymous prominent women analyzed in the *Nation* by a Jungian psychoanalyst, a behaviorist psychologist, and a neurologist.

Kirchwey may well have been using these articles to help her find answers for some marital difficulties she and Evans were experiencing at this time. Early in 1930 she left her work on the *Nation* to take her ill son Jeffrey to Florida in hopes of helping him recuperate from extensive tuberculosis and spinal meningitis. Jeffrey did not recover. After his death Freda Kirchwey became depressed and could not work for quite some time. When she did resume her work on the journal in 1933, she shifted her focus from women's issues to domestic economic issues and international affairs. The world she returned to was coping with the Great Depression and the growth of international fascism.

A "militant liberal," Kirchwey moved the journal from its former pacifist stand to advocacy of collective security and, eventually, war. Throughout World War II she included in the journal exposés of fascism in Germany, Italy, and Spain. The *Nation* was one of the few American publications that reported Hitler's mass murders of the Jews and other Nazi atrocities. Kirchwey wrote in support of refugees, fleeing from fascism, and she endorsed Israel as a homeland for the Jews. During World War II Kirchwey also created a "Political War" section to publish views of foreign leaders who had been ousted from their homelands by fascist forces. Kirchwey was horrified by the United States's use of the atom bomb at Hiroshima and Nagasaki to end the war. She organized a public forum to discuss nonmilitary uses of nuclear power and the necessity for restraints on this new force and edited pieces from that forum for *The Atomic Era: Can It Bring Peace and Abundance?* (1950).

Kirchwey will be remembered as a significant voice in political journalism and particularly as a voice of conscience during World War II. Kirchwey's retirement from the *Nation* in 1955 found her writing occasional pieces for the *York (Penn.) Gazette and Daily*. She also served as the Women's International League for Peace and Freedom's delegate to the United Nations. During her last years, she devoted most of her professional energy to the Committee for a Democratic Spain, working to restore a democratic government in Spain. While she tried for years to write it, she was unable to complete a manuscript about her life at the *Nation*. She died in St. Petersburg, Florida.

• The Schlesinger Library of Radcliffe College houses the Freda Kirchway Papers, in which can be found numerous writings, letters, and public addresses. Information can also be found in private collections, especially in the collection of her son, Michael Clark. While data about Kirchwey exists in the archives of many other figures of her day, the Papers of Oswald Garrison Villard, Houghton Library, Harvard University, and those of Dorothy Kirchwey Brown, Schlesinger Library, Radcliffe College, are most helpful. In addition to books that she edited, Freda Kirchwey published scores of signed *Nation* articles. Her many other unsigned editorials are found in a set of fragile annotated copies of the *Nation* at New York Public Library. For works about her, see Sara Alpern, *Freda Kirchwey: A Woman of the Nation* (1987), and an essay titled, "In Search of Freda Kirchwey: From Identification to Separation" also by Sara Alpern in *The Challenge of Feminist Biography: Writing the Lives of Modern American Women*, eds. Sara Alpern et al. (1992). The following magazine article about her is particularly noteworthy: "Oh, Stop That Freda!" *Saturday Evening Post*, 9 Feb. 1946, pp. 21–22. See also *Independent Woman*, 1 Nov. 1937. Obituaries are in the *Barnard Bulletin* 80 (26 Jan. 1976): 3; Carey McWilliams, "The Freda Kirchwey I Knew," *Nation*, 17 Jan. 1976, p. 38; the *New York Times*, 4 Jan. 1976; and the *Washington Post*, 10 Jan. 1976.

SARA ALPERN

KIRCHWEY, George Washington (3 July 1855–3 Mar. 1942), lawyer, criminologist, and professor, was born in Detroit, Michigan, the son of Michael Kirchwey, a livestock and wholesale meat dealer, and Maria Anna Lutz. His father had actively participated in the German revolution of 1848. Educated in various private and public schools in both Chicago and Albany, Kirchwey graduated in 1875 as class valedictorian and enrolled at Yale University. Four years later he received his B.A. with honors, and after studying at Yale Law School and later at Albany Law School, he was admitted to the state bar in New York in 1882. In 1883 he married Dora Child Wendell; they had four children. Freda Kirchwey, their youngest daughter, became editor and publisher of the liberal weekly the *Nation*.

Kirchwey originally set up practice in Albany and remained there for almost ten years. However, he found the daily workings of his firm, which centered mostly around civil cases, less than challenging. From 1887 to 1889 he supplemented his successful legal career by acting as editor of historical documents for New York State. In 1889 he accepted a post as dean of the Albany Law School, where he also taught classes on contract law and jurisprudence. By 1891 he accepted a post at Columbia Law School, where he remained until 1916.

At Columbia, Kirchwey used an intense and Socratic focus on individual cases, as opposed to teaching legal rules, to force aspiring lawyers to consider not only a case's outcome but also the legal reasoning behind each ruling. He published two volumes of case studies (1899–1902) and edited a collection of texts on real property law (1900). Well liked by his colleagues and students, he in 1901 became dean at Columbia, serving in this position until 1910, during which time he was also Kent Professor of Law.

Combining his knowledge of theory with his concern for ethical application of the law, Kirchwey quickly became interested in social issues, particularly

prison reform. Elected to serve on the Executive Committee of the New York Prison Association in 1907, he cast his lot with Thomas Mott Osborne, then warden of Sing Sing. Osborne, an untiring opponent of the Auburn system, believed that the customary practice of suppressing prisoners' individuality through harsh treatment ultimately destroyed the very fiber of inmates that might have led to reform. After "serving" a week's term in the Auburn prison as inmate "Tom Brown," Osborne took the suggestion of a prisoner and formed the Mutual Welfare League, a forum by which prisoners were able to govern themselves. Eventually instituted under Osborne at Sing Sing, the plan was a success and seemingly disproved the notion of the atavistic criminal, a concept devised by Italian criminologist Cesare Lombroso that both Kirchwey and Osborne refused to accept.

Kirchwey's interests in social reform prompted him to relinquish his position as dean in 1910. From 1913 to 1914 he was a member of the New York State Commission on Prison Reform. A year later he succeeded Osborne as warden of Sing Sing when Osborne was indicted by the Westchester County grand jury for immorality and mismanagement of the prison. Osborne was accustomed to such partisan accusations, and the case never went to trial. Kirchwey continued Osborne's practice of self-government for the prisoners, but his stint as warden was short-lived. In 1916 Osborne was reinstated.

In 1916 Kirchwey also left Columbia permanently. A year later he became a member of the faculty at the New York School of Philanthropy, and in 1918, after the institution changed its name to the New York School of Social Work, he was named head of the Department of Criminology, a position he retained until his retirement in 1932. As department head, Kirchwey openly denounced the death penalty, a punishment he regarded as a "demoralizing spectacle." One of the first presidents of the American League for the Abolition of Capital Punishment, he wrote in his entry "Capital Punishment" in *The Encyclopedia of the Social Sciences* (1933): "Capital punishment maintains its hold as a human institution because of the fear and resentment which murder excites and because of a persistent faith in its necessity either as a deterrent influence or as the only conclusive means of protecting the community against a convicted malefactor. For this faith there is not the slightest evidential support" (vol. 3, p. 195).

Kirchwey also continued his crusade for prison reform, critically examining the penal systems of both Pennsylvania (1918–1919) and New Jersey (1917), presiding over a survey of the daily functions of Chicago's Cook County Jail, and serving as director of the National Society of Penal Information, an organization that eventually joined forces with the Welfare League Association to become the Osborne Association. In 1929 the society published the *Handbook of American Prisons and Reformatories* (edited by Paul W. Garrett and Austin H. MacCormick). As director Kirchwey edited numerous reports and all the comments in the handbook, which sought "not only to inform the citizens of each state about their own institutions, but also to furnish to state and federal officials a basis for comparison with other institutions" (p. ix).

Kirchwey ventured into the political arena only once. In 1912 he was nominated by the state Progressive party for judge of the New York Court of Appeals after helping to draft the party platform that same year. Among other offices, he served as president of the New York Society of Criminal Law and Criminology, as vice president of the American Society of International Law, and from 1933 to 1940 as chairman of the National Board of Review of Motion Pictures, where he worked to ensure the use of movies as a vehicle for public education. Neither his intellectual nor his humanitarian interests were domestically bound. In 1912 he was a delegate to the International Peace Congress in Geneva, and from 1915 to 1917 he was president of the American Peace Society. When the First World War erupted, he quickly sided with the Allies, urging the United States to protest the invasion of Belgium, a neutral nation. After World War I ended, he served as New York director of U.S. Employment Services, helping locate jobs for thousands of overseas veterans who were returning to the states. Kirchwey estimated at one time that 100,000 unemployed veterans lived in New York. Undaunted by this statistic, however, he aided 3,000 of the 22,000 soldiers of the Seventy-seventh Division who had come back from France jobless. Kirchwey died at his home in New York.

Always conscious of what it meant to be human, of individual circumstances, and of the way life could sometimes place a person in direct conflict with society, Kirchwey championed the true American sentiment of liberty and justice for all, including the accused, the guilty, and the disenfranchised. Although he used both legal and academic artillery, for Kirchwey a social problem was never "merely intellectual." He was aware of the human faces and dilemmas behind every law, every theory, every social ill, and every social solution.

• Freda Kirchwey manuscripts and correspondence are in the Schlesinger Library at Radcliffe College. Samples of George W. Kirchwey's views concerning behavior and corrections are in "Criminology," in *Encyclopedia Britannica*, 14th ed. (1929). For his opinions concerning the death penalty see "The Death Penalty," Annual Congress of the American Prison Association, *Proceedings* 52 (1922): 363–77; and "The Administration of Criminal Justice," Annual Congress of the American Prison Association, *Proceedings* 53 (1923): 256–62. For more information on Osborne and the history of American criminology, see J. J. Chapman, "Osborne's Place in Historical Criminology, "*Harvard Graduates' Magazine*, Mar.–June 1927. A short memorial to Kirchwey is Rustem Vambery, "George W. Kirchwey (1855–1942)," *Nation*, 14 Mar. 1942. An obituary is in the *New York Times*, 5 Mar. 1942.

DONNA GREAR PARKER

KIRK, Alan Goodrich (30 Oct. 1888–15 Oct. 1963), naval officer, was born in Philadelphia, Pennsylvania, the son of William Thomson Kirk, a wholesale grocer, and Harriet Goodrich. He graduated from the U.S. Naval Academy in 1909, served in the Asiatic Fleet, and during the First World War was an ordnance specialist at the Naval Proving Ground in Dahlgren, Virginia. He married Lydia Selden Chapin, daughter of a naval officer, in 1918; the couple had three children. During the 1920s he was executive officer of the presidential yacht *Mayflower*, served at the Bureau of Ordnance, and was gunnery officer of the battleship *Maryland*. After studying and teaching at the Naval War College in Newport, Rhode Island, Kirk received his first command, the destroyer *Schenck*, in 1931. He went on to serve as executive officer of the battleship *West Virginia*, captain of the cruiser *Milwaukee*, and operations officer to Admiral Claude Bloch, commander in chief of the U.S. Fleet.

In 1939 Kirk became naval attaché in London. His urgent pleas for greater Anglo-American cooperation, along with his emphatic warnings of Britain's peril in 1940, played an important role in convincing the Franklin D. Roosevelt administration to become more closely involved in the war. Kirk also gained a thorough knowledge of Royal Navy methods and an abiding respect for that service, both of which served him well in subsequent joint operations. Although his forceful personality sometimes chafed under paternalistic Royal Navy officers, Kirk learned readily from the British and was able to work with them smoothly and successfully.

Appointed director of Naval Intelligence in March 1941, Kirk struggled to meet the navy's intelligence needs while fiercely resisting the efforts of Rear Admiral Richmond Kelly Turner's War Plans Division to assume responsibility for estimating enemy intentions. Kirk's organization produced a variety of clues warning of the impending Japanese attack but was unable to turn those clues into clear and specific warnings, thanks in part to the debilitating conflict with the War Plans Division. Sea duty in command of a destroyer squadron escorting Atlantic convoys came as a welcome relief in October.

In March 1942 Kirk returned to London as chief of staff to Admiral Harold Stark, commander of U.S. naval forces in Europe, in which capacity he was intimately involved in Allied strategic planning. In February 1943 he became commander of the Atlantic Fleet's amphibious force, in charge of training American naval forces for the Sicily landings the following July. He led one of the amphibious task forces in those landings and accomplished his mission despite unexpectedly difficult beach conditions and enemy armored counterattacks, which his naval gunfire helped to defeat. In June 1944 Kirk commanded all the American naval forces in the Normandy landings, the largest amphibious operation in history. Soon after, Kirk became commander of all American naval forces in France. He retired with the rank of admiral in 1946 and was appointed ambassador to Belgium. He then served as ambassador to the Soviet Union from 1949 to late 1951 and ambassador to the Republic of (Nationalist) China in 1962. He died in New York City.

• Most of Alan Kirk's papers from 1937 to 1945 are in the Operational Archives at the Naval Historical Center, Washington Navy Yard, Washington D.C. Some additional papers, ranging from 1919 to 1961, are in the Naval Historical Foundation Collection, Manuscript Division, Library of Congress. In the absence of an autobiography or biography, the best sources regarding Kirk's life are his oral history (1961) in the Columbia University Oral History Collection, Columbia University, and Clark G. Reynolds, *Famous American Admirals* (1978). Secondary works bearing on his career include Jeffery M. Dorwart, *Conflict of Duty: The U.S. Navy's Intelligence Dilemma, 1919–1945* (1983); James R. Leutze, *Bargaining for Supremacy: Anglo-American Naval Collaboration, 1937–1941* (1977); and Samuel Eliot Morison, *History of United States Naval Operations in World War II*, vol. 9, *Sicily-Salerno-Anzio* (1954), and vol. 11, *The Invasion of France and Germany* (1957). Obituaries are in the *New York Times* and the *Washington Post*, 16 Oct. 1963.

DAVID MACGREGOR

KIRK, Andy (28 May 1898–11 Dec. 1992), jazz and popular bandleader and bassist, was born Andrew Dewey Kirk, the son of Charles Kirk and Dellah (maiden name unknown). The family lived in Cincinnati, Ohio, but Kirk may have been born just across the river in Newport, Kentucky; he was unsure. His mother died around 1901, his father disappeared, and he was raised by his mother's half sister, Mary Banion, a domestic who moved her family to Denver in 1904.

In his youth Kirk sang and studied piano, but took neither activity seriously. At age sixteen he quit high school. About three years later, while working as a porter and shoe shiner in Sterling, Colorado, he bought a tenor saxophone and taught himself to play. He returned to Denver and, while working as a mailman, became a musician. He acquired other instruments, including a tuba and a string bass, which he played under bandleader and violinist George Morrison. While with Morrison, Kirk performed in New York (1920), worked alongside visiting pianist Jelly Roll Morton (spring 1921), and toured widely (1922 and 1924). On 22 July 1925 Kirk married pianist Mary Colston, a childhood friend and musical colleague; they had one child.

After less significant affiliations, including an unsuccessful attempt to break into the Chicago jazz scene, Kirk joined trumpeter Terrence Holder's ten-piece band, the Dark Clouds of Joy, in Dallas around 1927. The band played mainly in Tulsa and Oklahoma City. In January 1929 Holder left the group, and Kirk was elected leader. Saxophonist John Williams, violinist Claude "Fiddler" Williams, and drummer Edward "Crackshot" McNeil were among the members of Holder's band who stayed with Kirk and the band, renamed the Twelve Clouds of Joy.

The band's first success came at a whites-only venue in Kansas City, Missouri, in June 1929. "Our band didn't stress jazz, though we played it. We emphasized dance music—romantic ballads and pop tunes

and waltzes," Kirk explained in his autobiography (p. 62). After that the Clouds of Joy began touring extensively. At an audition for a record date in Kirk's new home base, Kansas City, pianist Marion Jackson failed to show up, and Williams's wife, Mary Lou Williams, sat in with the band. She returned to the studio for the band's first recordings in November 1929, for which she also supplied several pieces, including "Mess-A-Stomp," "Corky Stomp," and "Lotta Sax Appeal." This last title was released under John Williams's name.

In January 1930 the Twelve Clouds of Joy went to New York City to entertain at the Roseland and Savoy Ballrooms. In Chicago, at rehearsals for a recording session in April 1930, producer Jack Kapp noticed Jackson at the piano and insisted on having Mary Lou Williams instead. She thus continued to serve as the band's only pianist on record, including a session in October 1930 that produced "Dallas Blues." The next year, having already participated in some performances, Williams replaced Jackson permanently.

During the early 1930s Kirk's Twelve Clouds of Joy toured the Midwest and Northeast extensively, returning when convenient to Kansas City, where nightlife flourished under a corrupt administration scarcely touched by the depression. March 1931 brought recordings for the Victor label that were released under singer Blanche Calloway's name because Kirk was contracted to Brunswick, and the band toured with Calloway in the role of director before Kirk successfully defeated this attempt to wrest the Clouds from his direction.

In these early years Kirk carried the bass line: a photo from 1929 or 1930 shows him holding a conductor's baton and standing near his tuba, tuba mutes, and bass saxophone. By 1934 at the latest, when tubaist and string bassist Booker Collins joined the band—if not two or three years earlier—Kirk had given up this essential instrumental role and functioned solely as conductor.

Important new sidemen included trumpeter Irving "Mouse" Randolph (1931 to spring 1934) and a succession of tenor saxophonists: Ben Webster (1933–July 1934), Lester Young (briefly in summer 1934), and Buddy Tate (late 1934 to summer 1935). Unfortunately the band did not record in this period. Tate's successor, Dick Wilson (1936–1941), who became the Clouds' greatest soloist on record, exhibiting a style considerably more original than Kirk's featured soloist and writer, Mary Lou Williams. Wilson and Williams figure prominently on such studio recordings as "Walkin' and Swingin'," "Moten Swing," "Bearcat Shuffle," "Christopher Columbus," and "Corky" (all from Mar. 1936); "Wednesday Night Hop" and "In the Groove" (Feb. 1937); and "Ring Dem Bells" (Jan. 1941), and on live recordings from the Trianon Ballroom in Cleveland in 1937.

The other crucial hiring was singer Pha Terrell, who joined the band in 1933. The version of his romantic ballad, "Until the Real Thing Comes Along," recorded in April 1936 became a huge hit. Further ballads followed, including Terrell's rendition of "Dedicated to You" (Dec. 1936). With the Twelve Clouds now numbering fifteen, including the leader and Terrell, Kirk embarked on his first southern tour in 1937 on the strength of the popularity of "Until the Real Thing Comes Along." From that year through the 1940s the Clouds of Joy toured about 50,000 miles annually throughout the nation and in Canada, while also alternating with the big bands of Fletcher Henderson, Louis Armstrong, and Earl Hines for residencies at the Grand Terrace in Chicago from 1936 to 1939. Having earlier expressed disappointment that record companies were not interested in having an African-American band record its stylistically white dance repertory (as he described it), Kirk changed his mind after the success of Terrell's vocals and instead expressed regret that there were now fewer opportunities to play jazz.

In 1939 Kirk moved his home to New York City. Important new bandmembers included tenor saxophonist Don Byas (1940), singer June Richmond (1939–1943), and guitarist Floyd "Wonderful" Smith (1939–1942), whose brilliantly original and eccentric "Floyd's Guitar Blues" featured electric steel guitar playing (Mar. 1939). Tenor saxophonist Al Sears (1941–1942) was replaced by Jimmy Forrest (1942–1948), who at one point played alongside tenor saxophonist Eddie "Lockjaw" Davis (1944). Williams and her second husband, trumpeter Shorty Baker, left Kirk in 1942. Trumpeter Howard McGhee, featured on "McGhee Special," joined in 1941, and pianist Kenny Kersey, featured on "Boogie Woogie Cocktail," was drafted in 1943. Richmond's singing on "Hey Lawdy Mama" was another highlight from this July 1942 recording session.

At some point saxophonist Charlie Parker joined Kirk briefly. Trumpeter Fats Navarro played alongside McGhee in 1944, pianist Hank Jones joined after Kersey was drafted, and Joe Williams sang with the band briefly in 1946. Kirk's band had a central role in the movie *Killer Diller* (1948), but his great musicians were gone by this point. The performances are unremarkable, the improvising tenor saxophonists in particular inviting harsh comparisons to soloists who had previously passed through the band. The Clouds of Joy ceased touring in 1949, but Kirk continued to lead bands intermittently into the early 1950s.

In 1952 Kirk went into the real estate business in New York City. The following year he became a Jehovah's Witness, and he subsequently played in Witnesses' orchestras for mass meetings at Yankee Stadium. In the late 1960s he managed the Hotel Theresa in Harlem. During the 1980s he worked for the musicians union in New York City, where he died.

Without leaving a truly remarkable legacy, apart from Wilson's improvisations and Smith's bizarre experiment in amplified sound, Kirk's Clouds of Joy were among the best of the many big bands (whether African-American or white) that were comfortable playing in a wide array of jazz and pop styles, from a slow foxtrot to a polka, from the lindy hop to a waltz.

During the war years, as the Clouds of Joy diminished in importance, Kirk's band provided a training group for trumpeters and saxophonists who would become prominent in modern jazz.

• His autobiography is Andy Kirk and Amy Lee, *Twenty Years on Wheels* (1989); it includes Howard Rye's catalog of Kirk's recordings. An extensive interview is in the oral history collection of the Institute of Jazz Studies, Newark, N.J. Published surveys and interviews are by Frank Driggs, "My Story, by Andy Kirk," *Jazz Review* 2 (Feb. 1959): 12–17, repr. in *Jazz Panorama*, ed. Martin Williams (1962; repr. 1979); Gene Fernett, *Swing Out: Great Negro Jazz Bands* (1970); Albert McCarthy, "Andy Kirk and His Clouds of Joy," *Jazz and Blues* 1 (Dec. 1971): 18–19, 22–23; Ross Russell, *Jazz Style in Kansas City and the Southwest* (1971); Albert McCarthy, *Big Band Jazz* (1974); Mary Lou Hester, *Going to Kansas City* (1980); George T. Simon, *The Big Bands*, 4th ed. (1981); and Lowell D. Holmes and John W. Thomson, eds., *Jazz Greats: Getting Better with Age* (1986). For interviews with Kirk's sidemen, see Max Jones, *Talking Jazz* (1987), and Nathan W. Pearson, Jr., *Goin' to Kansas City* (1987). A catalog of recordings is by Charles Garrod, *John Kirby and His Orchestra; Plus Andy Kirk and His Orchestra* (1991). For musical assessment, see Gunther Schuller, *The Swing Era: The Development of Jazz, 1930–1945* (1989). See also "Andy Kirk and the Witnesses," *Down Beat* 28 (12 Oct. 1961): 14, and Walter C. Allen, *Hendersonia: The Music of Fletcher Henderson and His Musicians: A Bio-discography* (1973). An obituary is in the *New York Times*, 15 Dec. 1992.

BARRY KERNFELD

KIRK, Edward Norris (14 Aug. 1802–27 March 1874), Presbyterian and Congregationalist clergyman, was born in New York City, the son of George Kirk, a dry goods storekeeper and Presbyterian elder who had emigrated from Scotland in 1778, and Mary Norris. At ten years of age Kirk moved to Princeton, New Jersey, to live with his uncle Robert Voorhees, a prosperous merchant. In 1816 Kirk entered the College of New Jersey (later Princeton University), receiving the B.A. in 1820. He worked in a law office and studied law in New York City until a religious conversion in 1822 led him to enroll in Princeton Theological Seminary in November 1822; he graduated in 1825 but remained for a further year of study. He was licensed to preach by the Presbytery of New York in 1826. In 1855 he was awarded a doctor of divinity degree by Amherst College. He never married.

From 1826 to 1828 Kirk was an agent for the American Board of Commissioners for Foreign Missions, preaching on behalf of missions in the south and mid-Atlantic states. The missionary cause remained important to him, and he frequently addressed meetings of missionary associations.

In 1828 Kirk was invited to the Second Presbyterian Church of Albany, New York (a congregation that included Martin van Buren) as associate to the ailing Dr. John Chester and ordained to the ministry. Kirk's revivalistic preaching, however, soon gave offense, and in 1829 he was dismissed. His supporters at Second Church founded the Fourth Presbyterian Church of Albany and chose him as their pastor that same year.

Kirk now identified himself with "New School" Calvinism, objecting to what he considered an exaggerated emphasis upon human depravity and helplessness. He invited the evangelist Charles G. Finney to preach from his pulpit when other Albany churches were closed to him, and, in order to train ministers sympathetic to revivals, he joined with Nathan Beman of First Presbyterian Church in Troy in establishing the short-lived Troy and Albany Theological School. While at Albany he was involved in reform causes, advocating public schools, total abstinence from alcoholic beverages, and the abolition of slavery. The abolitionist Gerrit Smith spoke from his pulpit. Kirk also supported education and equal rights for African Americans and came to favor racial integration. In a sermon of 1856, "Our Duty in Perilous Times," he lamented the mistreatment of Indians, Negroes, and Mexicans as a national sin.

In 1837 Kirk resigned from his pastorate for health reasons and traveled abroad, where he preached at revivals in Britain and established contacts with evangelical Protestants in France and Geneva. He translated a work on the inspiration and infallibility of Scripture by the Genevan free church theologian Louis Gaussen (*Theopneusty*, 1842) and later abridged and translated Gaussen's *The Canon of the Holy Scriptures* (1862); he was eventually able to preach in French. He returned to the United States in 1839, and from then until 1842 he was secretary of the Foreign Evangelical Society, a Protestant organization dedicated to missions in Roman Catholic countries.

During 1839–1842 Kirk also traveled widely as a revivalist, preaching in New York City, Philadelphia, Pennsylvania, New Haven and Hartford, Connecticut, and Boston, Massachusetts. In 1842 he became pastor of the Mount Vernon Congregational Church in Boston, a congregation organized for him (the future evangelist Dwight Moody was converted in 1855 while attending there). Movement between the allied Presbyterian and Congregationalist denominations was common at the time, but Kirk also came to be convinced that the separatist and congregational polity derived from the Pilgrim Fathers was more consonant with Christian and American freedom than Presbyterian polity. Before coming to Boston and repeatedly afterwards, Kirk maintained that the best of what was truly American went back to the New England Puritans (whom he contrasted with unprogressive southern "Cavaliers").

Although he settled in Boston, he continued his international involvements. In August 1846 he attended the organizing meeting of the Evangelical Alliance in London, England. In 1857 he took leave from his congregation in order to help establish the American Church in Paris, France, preaching there for some months before taking a tour of the Holy Land. Defending Protestant foreign missions in 1865, he declared that they would abet such reforms abroad as the improvement of the status of women and the growth of democracy (*Rev. Dr. Kirk's Sermon before the American Board*).

Kirk was deeply involved in the crisis over slavery. In 1860 he traveled through the southern states in the company of the Princeton geologist Arnold Guyot, viewing slavery at first hand. After war began, he declared the Northern cause a righteous one and excoriated rebels. He preached to troops gathered in Boston and visited the Army of the Potomac. In the 1864 presidential campaign he gave speeches on behalf of Abraham Lincoln and the Republicans. In 1865, as the American Missionary Association focused its efforts on the spiritual and educational needs of the freed slaves Kirk, in recognition of his contributions to this cause, was elected to its presidency, a largely honorary post. A supporter of Radical Reconstruction, Kirk advocated the use of federal troops to guarantee voting rights and full citizenship for Southern blacks and to reconstitute the state governments of the defeated Confederacy.

Kirk's health declined after the war, although he delivered a series of lectures at Andover Theological Seminary in 1868, published in 1875 as *Lectures on Revivals*, and was appointed chaplain to the Senate of Massachusetts in 1869. That same year he withdrew from full pastoral labors at the Mount Vernon Church, where he had come to be a beloved patriarch. He died in Boston.

Many of Kirk's sermons were published individually as well as in collections, and he also wrote several brief works for the American Tract Society: *The Waiting Saviour* (1865) and *Behold the Lamb of God!* (1865). *Lectures on the Parables of our Saviour* (1857) is a work of biblical exposition.

A representative of the moderate and evangelical Calvinism of many Congregationalists and of the "New School" Presbyterians, the urbane and scholarly Kirk was important in establishing revivalism in northeastern cities and was an appealing example of American revivalism abroad. A leader in many of those mission and reform causes that have been dubbed the "benevolent empire," Kirk believed that the success of the American republic depended upon a virtuous citizenry, and that the churches should promote the revivals and take the lead in the reforms necessary to shape that virtuous citizenry and to purge the nation of slavery, drunkenness, and other evils, so that it could be an example to the world.

• Manuscript sermons are in the Library of the American Congregational Association, Boston, Mass. Correspondence involving Kirk is in the Evarts Family Papers, 1753–1960, in the Yale University Library; and in the Aaron Hobart Papers, 1767–1929, in the New England Historic Genealogical Society in Boston, which also has some of the records of the Mount Vernon Congregational Church. Many of Kirk's important early sermons are included in *Sermons on Different Subjects* (1840); later sermons appear in *Discourses Doctrinal and Practical* (1857); sermons that express his views on public matters include *Oration, July 4, 1836* (1836), *Oration on the Occasion of the National Fast, May 14, 1841* (1841), *The Church Essential to the Republic* (1848), *Great Men are God's Gift: A Discourse on the Death of Daniel Webster* (1852), *Addresses of the Rev. Drs. Wm. Hague and E. N. Kirk at the An-*

nual Meetings of the Educational Commission for Freedmen (1863), *Sermons Preached in Boston on the Death of Abraham Lincoln* (1865), and *Only One Human Race, A Sermon Preached before the American Association . . . October 25, 1865.*

David O. Mears's *Life of Edward Norris Kirk, D.D.* (1877) contains letters and autobiographical reminiscences of Kirk and also a list of his publications. William G. McLoughlin, Jr., *Modern Revivalism: Charles Grandison Finney to Billy Graham* (1959), discusses Kirk's relation to Finney; Owen Peterson, *A Divine Discontent: The Life of Nathan S. S. Beman* (1986), discusses Kirk's relation to Nathan Beman. Richard Carwardine in *Trans-atlantic Revivalism* (1978) and *Evangelicals and Politics in Antebellum America* (1993) describes Kirk's revival activities in Britain and his views on slavery. His role in founding the American Church in Paris is recounted in Ruth Dixon, *A Church on the Seine: The American Church in Paris, 1814–1981* (1981). Obituaries are in the *Boston Transcript, Boston Daily Advertiser,* and *New York Times,* all 28 Mar. 1874.

DEWEY D. WALLACE, JR.

KIRK, Rahsaan Roland (7 Aug. 1935–5 Dec. 1977), jazz musician, was born Ronald Theodore Kirk in Columbus, Ohio, the son of Theodore Kirk and Gertrude Broadus. Kirk was blind from infancy. He first demonstrated an interest in music when he was a small boy. Anxious to become the bugler at summer camp, he began blowing the notes of the overtone series on a water hose. Soon his parents gave him a bugle, which he played for a few years before switching to trumpet. He gave up that instrument, however, when his eye doctor decided that the continuous force required to blow the instrument was hard on Kirk's eyes. When Kirk was about twelve he began playing clarinet in the band at Columbus's Ohio State School for the Blind, learning by listening to the teacher play his parts on the piano. At home he began practicing on the C-melody saxophone; he picked up a few pointers from a friend, but mostly he learned on his own. By age fifteen he was playing tenor saxophone in clubs with a local rhythm-and-blues band led by Boyd Moore.

At sixteen, Kirk had a dream in which he played two instruments at once. In a local music store he found an unusual instrument called the manzello—basically a soprano saxophone with a slightly curved neck and a forward-facing bell. He bought it and began playing it in simultaneous tandem with his tenor saxophone. A year or two later he acquired a stritch, which is basically a straight alto saxophone. After making a few modifications to his instruments, he was able to play all of them at once, using carefully worked out three-part harmonies. He also used each of them for solo improvisations.

Kirk made his first recording, on the King label, in 1956, but the album was poorly distributed and is little known. (He used the name Roland from at least the time of this recording, but why he used it is unknown. He added the honorific Rahsaan, a name that came to him in a dream, in 1970.) His second album, *Introducing Roland Kirk* (7 June 1960), made after he moved to Chicago, was better distributed and marked his entry onto the national jazz scene. Soon after recording it he

played with some world-famous jazz musicians during a short concert tour of Germany. On a subsequent stay in New York City he made another album, *Kirk's Work* (11 July 1961), and he worked a three-month engagement with Charles Mingus's group (he appears on Mingus's albums *Oh Yeah* and *Tonight at Noon,* 6 Nov. 1961).

From 1962 until the end of his life Kirk led various jazz combos, often using the title the Vibration Society. He appeared frequently at jazz festivals and in jazz clubs worldwide. Along the way, he added flute and a variety of unorthodox woodwinds to some forty-five other instruments, many of them homemade. In the fall of 1975 a stroke paralyzed his right side. Despite the disability, he resumed performing within a few months. Although he no longer could play two or three instruments at once, his modifications to his tenor saxophone and the unusual techniques he had developed early in his career enabled him to play one-handed. He also continued playing flute, with the aid of a neck-supported holder. He suffered a second stroke in 1976. For a few months in 1977 he and saxophonist Frank Foster operated the Vibration School of Music in East Orange, New Jersey. Kirk also resumed playing, but with greatly reduced strength and facility. He died in Bloomington shortly after giving two concerts at Indiana University. He was survived by his wife, Dorthann.

Kirk's earliest recording shows that by age twenty-one he had a firm grasp of the bebop musical language, an excellent tone, and a sure command of the supposedly unwieldy manzello and stritch. He also used his two-instrument technique in a thoroughly musical way to state theme choruses and interludes that contrasted effectively with his one-horn improvised solos. Subsequent recordings document an evolving and maturing solo style and the development of his three-horn ensemble technique.

During his prestroke years his playing was filled with energy and rhythmic drive. His emotions seemed to burst the bounds of his instruments, as he ended saxophone phrases with audible groans, sang in a frenzied manner while playing flute, and punctuated choruses with blasts on a siren or a whistle (all heard on the album *Three for the Festival,* 7 July 1968). On stage, his appearance was unusual, with some instruments hanging from neck straps and others sticking from his pockets or from the bell of his tenor saxophone, all within easy reach. Sometimes he kept his melodic ideas flowing without interruption by means of circular breathing (inflating his cheeks with pockets of air that he used while inhaling through his nostrils); his recording of *Saxophone Concerto* (1972) without break extends for twenty-one minutes.

Kirk had a passionate interest in all jazz styles, and he paid tribute to Sidney Bechet, Duke Ellington, Billie Holiday, Lester Young, Charlie Parker, Charles Mingus, John Coltrane, Horace Silver, and other jazz greats in his compositions. He also was interested in European classical music of the twentieth century (recording an album titled *Variation on a Theme of Hinde-*

mith, 11 June 1963), African music, and music of the Middle East and India. Although his fundamental style was in the bebop idiom, he played New Orleans–style (Dixieland) jazz and free jazz with great facility. A staunch believer in the musical traditions that he represented, he preferred to call his music black classical music rather than jazz.

• An early article on Kirk by Don DeMicheal (*Down Beat*, 23 May 1963) contains useful biographical information, as do articles by Eric Levin in *Jazz*, Spring 1977; Joachim-Ernst Berendt in *Jazz Forum*, Mar. 1978; and Michael Ullman in *Jazz Lives* (1980). Kirk speaks his mind on a variety of subjects in Todd Barkan's article in *Down Beat*, 15 Aug. 1974. *Swing Journal* published a discography in Oct. 1976. Barry Kernfeld's article in *The New Grove Dictionary of Jazz* (1988) concludes with a helpful bibliography. An obituary, written by jazz critic John S. Wilson, is in the *New York Times*, 6 Dec. 1977.

THOMAS OWENS

KIRK, Samuel Child (15 Feb. 1793–6 July 1872), silversmith, was born in Doylestown, Pennsylvania, the son of Joseph Kirk and Grace Child. Many of his ancestors had been English silversmiths. Kirk attended a Quaker Friends' school and in 1810 was apprenticed to James Howell, a Philadelphia silversmith. Howell died before Kirk completed the standard seven-year apprenticeship. Kirk then took charge of Howell's shop until he turned twenty-one, when he decided to move to Baltimore, Maryland, to pursue his own business. His move coincided with the Maryland legislature's introduction of a new law that regulated the silver standard and established the Baltimore Assay Office. Unique to the city, the law took effect on 1 August 1814, and it required silver objects made or sold in Baltimore to contain no less than eleven ounces Troy (equal to 91.7 percent pure silver alloy). A smith paid an appointed assayer to test, weigh, and then mark his silver with the approved marks of quality: a dominical letter specific to a particular year and the head of Mercury, the Roman god of commerce.

As a result of the Assay Law, Baltimore silver became more expensive than that made or sold elsewhere. Within this context, in 1815 Kirk entered into a partnership with John Smith, a Philadelphia-based businessman with ties to silversmiths and retailers. This connection seems to have allowed Kirk and Smith to thrive at a time when other silversmiths were failing. By 1818 22 percent of the silver assayed in Baltimore came from their shop. Around that time Kirk had also made a change in his personal life. In 1817 he had married Albina Powell; they had eight children.

Kirk ended his relationship with Smith, and his shop's name changed to Samuel Kirk in 1821. In 1828 his shop accounted for 93 percent of all assayed silver. By 1830 Kirk and other Baltimore silversmiths succeeded in having the Assay Law modified; instead of paying an assayer to identify the quality of silver, the smith himself was allowed to do so. The assay office, however, still existed for some years, and Kirk continued to have his products marked there. By continuing to have his wares marked, Kirk ensured that his products retained a symbol that the public associated with quality. Between 1830 and 1843 99 percent of the silver assayed came from Kirk's shop.

Kirk's success also came through his revival of an old design technique known as repoussé, which means "raised in high relief." The process involves "bumping out" a design from the inside of an object, thus giving a sculptural quality to the silver. Although sometimes credited with reintroducing the process to nineteenth-century America, Kirk was not the only silversmith to use the technique. However, his firm did appear to produce more examples of repoussé than any other firm in the country. As a result, his designs of flowers, foliage, and landscape vignettes on hollow ware became known as "Baltimore Repoussé," or "Kirk Silver." The style, with its showy, overflowing designs, fit well with Victorian tastes. However, it was also expensive, for the process required many hours of handwork.

The firm's name became Samuel Kirk and Son in 1846, when Kirk's oldest son, Henry Child Kirk, began to work with him. In 1861 his other two sons, Charles Douglas and Clarence Edwin, joined, and the name changed to Samuel Kirk and Sons. Seven years later Charles and Clarence left the business, and the name reverted to Samuel Kirk and Son. Kirk ran the company until his death, at which time his oldest son took over and was joined by his son, Henry Child Kirk, Jr. From 1896 to 1924 the business was known as Samuel Kirk & Son, Co.; in 1924 it changed to Samuel Kirk and Son, Inc. It remained with that name until 1979, when it became Kirk-Stieff Inc.

Part of Samuel Kirk's success lay in his talent as a marketer of his own product. He secured an 1824 commission from the marquis de Lafayette, who purchased two silver presentation goblets as a thank you to his Washington, D.C., host. Four years later, at the parade to celebrate the opening of the Baltimore and Ohio Railroad, Kirk was credited with supplying all of the silver on the silversmith's float.

Kirk possessed exceptional talent as a silversmith. His reintroduction of repoussé, strong craftsmanship skills, and canny promotional abilities made Baltimore silver world renowned. With a career that spanned nearly sixty years, Kirk was the founder of the oldest continuously operating silver shop in the United States.

• Samuel Kirk's papers, including account books, company histories, and a copy of an English design book in which Kirk sketched designs, are in the archives of the Maryland Historical Society. Extant Kirk objects can be found in private collections and in numerous museums, including the Maryland Historical Society, Baltimore Museum of Art, Winterthur Museum, and the Metropolitan Museum of Art. Documents regarding the establishment and terms of the Baltimore Assay Office are located in the Baltimore City Archives. For an example of a company-produced history, see Samuel Kirk & Son, Co., *The Story of the House of Kirk the Oldest Silversmiths in the United States Established 1817* (1914). For the most comprehensive studies of Kirk see Jennifer Faulds Goldsborough, *Eighteenth and Nineteenth Century Maryland Silver in the Collection of the Baltimore Museum of Art* (1975) and *Silver in Maryland* (1983), and Gregory R. Weidman et al., *Classical Maryland, 1815–1845: Fine and Decorative Arts from the Golden Age* (1993).

KRISTIN HERRON

KIRKBRIDE, Thomas Story (31 July 1809–16 Dec. 1883), psychiatrist, was born on a farm in eastern Bucks County, Pennsylvania, the son of John Kirkbride and Elizabeth Story, farmers, who were active members of the Bucks County Society of Friends.

Thomas Kirkbride was a delicate child thought to be ill suited to farming. His father, after suffering a painful illness, encouraged him to become a doctor, a profession highly respected among the Quakers. Kirkbride recalled in his "Autobiographical Sketch" (1882) that while still a boy, he "began to regard medicine as his path in life."

To prepare his son for a medical career, the elder Kirkbride made sure Thomas got a good education. He attended two excellent local academies, then was apprenticed to a prominent New Jersey physician, the French émigré Nicholas Belleville. Belleville taught his pupil the basics of bedside medicine: how to diagnose common illnesses, make up prescriptions, and treat injuries. The majority of early nineteenth-century doctors got the sum of their medical training in this fashion; but for Kirkbride, the preceptorial served only as preparation for a more ambitious goal: to attend medical school. In the fall of 1828 he entered the University of Pennsylvania Medical School, the oldest and one of the most prestigious medical schools in the United States.

The revolution in clinical observation and pathological research taking place in the hospitals of Paris had yet to influence American medical schools. Instead, Kirkbride learned by rote a system for explaining and treating disease that had changed little since the time of Benjamin Rush, Philadelphia's most prominent eighteenth-century physician. Kirkbride found himself more interested in the practical art of surgery than the theoretical speculations about disease emphasized in his professors' lectures.

After finishing his M.D. in 1832, Kirkbride applied for a residency at the Pennsylvania Hospital, but lost out in the fierce competition for the post. To gain experience that would improve his chances for the next year, he accepted a residency at the Friends Asylum, a small Quaker-run mental hospital in nearby Frankford, Pennsylvania. There he supervised the medical care of the patients and learned the elements of "moral treatment," a new approach to treating insanity pioneered by Quakers at the York Retreat in England. The proponents of moral treatment believed that the insane could be benefited, and in many cases cured, by following an ordered, daily routine. The staff rewarded cooperative patients with praise and privileges, and subjected unruly ones to constant surveillance and restrictions. The asylum milieu was designed to bring out the "inner light" of reason Quakers believed to remain in even the most hopeless of cases.

Kirkbride left the asylum after a year to begin his residency at the Pennsylvania Hospital. In 1836 he finished his residency and started a private practice in Philadelphia. Kirkbride determined to get as much surgical experience as he could, hoping ultimately to return to the Pennsylvania Hospital as attending surgeon.

In 1840 Kirkbride received a job offer that dramatically changed the course of his medical career. The managers of the Pennsylvania Hospital had decided to build a separate asylum for the institution's mental patients, which was to be located across the Schuylkill River, near the rural village of Blockley. They approached Kirkbride to assume the duties of chief superintendent. Despite his love of surgery, Kirkbride found himself tempted by the job; he had begun to wonder if an extensive surgical practice might be too taxing for his health, which was never robust. He was probably also attracted by the unusual degree of administrative authority he would enjoy at the new hospital; as chief superintendent of the asylum, he would have far more power than an attending surgeon in the general hospital. Thus Kirkbride decided to switch specialties and devote his career to asylum medicine, as psychiatry was then termed.

Under his management the Pennsylvania Hospital for the Insane, which opened in 1841, soon became recognized as one of the best mental hospitals in the country. Following the principles of moral treatment he had learned at the Friends Asylum, Kirkbride dispensed with the routine use of physical restraints and provided the patients a full schedule of amusements including lectures, parties, and exercise. Although simple in style, the asylum was comfortable and meticulously maintained. Kirkbride created varied landscapes around the hospital to form the backdrop for the patients' walks and rides. By these measures he made "Kirkbride's", as the asylum came to be known, attractive to middle- and upper-class families looking for relief from the care of insane relatives.

In 1844 Kirkbride helped to found the Association of Medical Superintendents of American Institutions for the Insane (now known as the American Psychiatric Association), the first medical specialty organization in the United States. He published articles on asylum construction and management in the *American Journal of Insanity*, which were subsequently published in 1854 as a book, *On the Construction, Organization, and General Arrangements of Hospitals for the Insane*. In 1851 and 1853 the association adopted a set of propositions on hospital design written by Kirkbride, which remained its official policy for over thirty years. According to Henry Hurd's 1916 survey, *Institutional Care of the Insane*, mental hospitals in twenty-seven states and the District of Columbia were built according to the so-called linear or Kirkbride plan. Kirkbride's advice on asylum design was also sought by state legislators, governors, and even presidents.

Kirkbride's architectural plans showed his skill at balancing the need for control and surveillance with the need to attend to small details, which had an influence on patients but were "not readily appreciated by a careless observer," as he wrote in *On the Construction*. He stressed that whether a window was left locked or opened could make the difference between life and death for a suicidal patient. To ensure the safety and well-being of patients, Kirkbride believed it was essential to have the asylum ruled by one all powerful, ever vigilant medical authority.

As a clinician Kirkbride was distinguished by his gentle manner and fervent devotion to moral treatment. Although he refused to rule out the use of physical restraints, he employed them rarely. Kirkbride also gained fame for the elaborate program of patient education and entertainment offered at the hospital. He early recognized the value of photography and was the first to introduce the lantern slide program as a therapeutic diversion for mental patients, an innovation that was widely copied at other asylums.

But even at the midcentury highpoint of enthusiasm about moral treatment, Kirkbride's job as an asylum superintendent was a difficult one. His daily work involved constant attention to a myriad of details, overseeing patient care, answering inquiries from their families, supervising a large and sometimes unruly staff, and maintaining the heavily used buildings and grounds. Kirkbride experienced firsthand the anxieties, even physical dangers, of mid-nineteenth-century asylum life. In 1849 a former patient shot him in the head; fortunately his old-fashioned Quaker hat deflected the bullet. In the late 1860s he became embroiled in several lawsuits instituted by patients who challenged the commitment laws of the era, which made it very easy for families to commit relatives.

In a broader sense, Kirkbride's conception of moral treatment suffered from the internal contradictions common to nineteenth-century humanitarian reforms. On the one hand, moral treatment brought about a more humane standard of care for the mentally ill, as compared to their often subhuman treatment in eighteenth-century institutions. On the other hand, the regimen subjected patients to a greater degree of surveillance and control, which many of them resented and resisted. Inmates themselves often found institutional life far from humane. And despite Kirkbride's efforts to maintain perfect order in the wards, the fundamental character of mental disorder created an undertow of violence and chaos that belied his benign characterization of moral treatment.

Still, the most serious challenge to Kirkbride's authority came from outside, not inside, his asylum. In the 1870s younger asylum superintendents and members of the new medical speciality of neurology began to question the older generation's insistence on small, cure-oriented mental hospitals. As the number of chronic cases piled up in state mental hospitals and local almshouses, critics complained that Kirkbride's asylum design was too expensive and inflexible to meet the needs of all of the insane. Instead, they urged public authorities to build more inexpensive cottage-style facilities for chronic cases. Kirkbride's response was invariably the same: large institutions for incurable patients would inevitably deteriorate into custodial warehouses.

In states such as New York and Massachusetts, welfare authorities ignored his warning and built larger and larger hospitals in the 1860s and 1870s. But such was Kirkbride's prestige in the profession that the resolutions he drafted in the early 1850s insisting on small "mixed" asylums providing acute and chronic care were not repealed until 1888. Even then, they were made nonbinding rather than repudiated outright.

In retrospect, Kirkbride's insistence on small, expensive-to-maintain mental hospitals seems quite unrealistic. As head of an elite private hospital, he was relatively insulated from the political and economic problems their care posed for state officials. Yet his prediction that large state hospitals for incurable patients would degenerate into custodial facilities soon proved correct.

Kirkbride's own institution offered probably the highest standard of care for the mentally ill available in nineteenth-century America. Because he maintained control over admissions, Kirkbride was able to prevent the accumulation of chronic cases. During his tenure the asylum's cure rates remained cause for modest optimism about the value of moral treatment; although the number cured dropped, from 53 percent of patients discharged in the 1840s to 41 percent in the 1870s, the return of even a modest number of patients to a productive life seemed an accomplishment in light of the formerly grim prognosis for insanity.

In the 1880s and 1890s, the psychiatric profession abandoned moral treatment as a formal therapeutic rationale and turned to more somatic approaches to mental illness. But many of the basic elements of moral treatment developed in Kirkbride's time, including the twentieth-century methods known as occupational therapy and milieu management, have remained essential to institutional psychiatry.

In 1839 Kirkbride had married Ann Jenks; they had two children. Four years after her death in 1862, he married Eliza Ogden Butler, a woman he had earlier treated as a patient; they had four children. Although such a relationship between doctor and former patient would now be considered an ethical violation, the Butler-Kirkbride marriage was not regarded as improper by the standards of their own times, which embodied a very paternalistic conception of doctor/patient and male/female relationships. After their marriage, Eliza Butler Kirkbride took an active role in asylum life, paying special attention to the women patients, and helped her husband prepare his widely read *Annual Reports*. Her continued mental health was regarded as testimony to his ability as a healer and to the value of asylum treatment in general. Thomas Kirkbride died in Philadelphia.

• Kirkbride's papers, including his journals, correspondence, and casebooks, are in the Institute of the Pennsylvania

Hospital Archives, Philadelphia. The collection includes a copy of his "Autobiographical Sketch . . . Dictated in 1882," privately printed in Philadelphia that same year. The *Annual Reports of the Pennsylvania Hospital for the Insane*, published during his years as superintendent, are a valuable source of information about his hospital career. The standard secondary account of Kirkbride's career is Nancy Tomes, *A Generous Confidence: Thomas Story Kirkbride and the Art of Asylum Keeping* (1984). Other useful accounts of Kirkbride's place in American psychiatry are contained in Gerald Grob, *Mental Institutions in America: Social Policy to 1875* (1972), and Constance McGovern, *Masters of Madness: Social Origins of the American Psychiatric Profession* (1985). Obituaries include a memorial by his wife, Eliza Butler Kirkbride, "Memorial of Thomas Story Kirkbride," *Annual Report of the Pennsylvania Hospital for the Insane* (1883), pp. 26–163, which is the longest and best of the published contemporary accounts of his life; and the Philadelphia *Evening Star*, 20 Dec. 1883.

NANCY TOMES

KIRKLAND, Caroline Matilda (11 Jan. 1801–6 April 1864), writer and editor, was born in New York City, the daughter of Samuel Stansbury, a businessman, and Eliza Alexander. While the family's financial situation fluctuated with her father's various business ventures, Caroline, by virtue of the Stansburys' high social standing, received an above-average education for a female in the early nineteenth century, chiefly in schools run by a Quaker aunt. She spent her early adulthood as a teacher, both before and after her marriage to William Kirkland, also an educator, in 1828. Together they founded a girls' school in Geneva, New York, shortly after their marriage.

In 1835 the Kirklands and their four children moved to Michigan Territory, where William Kirkland became involved in land speculation and in planning and building the new village of Pinckney. The family's experiences in the wilderness were the source for Caroline Kirkland's first book, *A New Home—Who'll Follow? Or, Glimpses of Western Life*, published in 1839 under the pseudonym "Mrs. Mary Clavers, An Actual Settler." An immediate popular and critical success, *A New Home*, was a satirical look at life on the prairie, praised both then and now as the first honest portrait of the isolation, grime, greed, and competition facing an early American settler. Contemporary literary critics, including Edgar Allan Poe, admired Kirkland's writing for its realistic account of westward settlement, at a time when East Coast emigrants, including the Kirklands, were often seduced into the wilderness by the romanticized narratives of authors such as Washington Irving and James Fenimore Cooper. One reviewer called *A New Home* "a work of striking merit; such as we do not often meet with in these days of repetition and imitation . . . [and] one of the most spirited and original works which have yet been produced in this country" (Osborne, pp. 54–55). Poe wrote, "Unquestionably [Kirkland] is one of our best writers, has a province of her own, and in that province has few equals" (Osborne, p. 55). However, the Kirklands' Michigan neighbors were less enthusiastic, offended by the Easterner's descriptions of the "petticoated denizens" of "wretched log-huts" as gossipmongering rustics, far removed from "the civilized world" she had left behind, despite Kirkland's use of fictitious names throughout the book and her inclusion of herself as an object of satire, as in an encounter with a muddy Michigan road: "For a few steps I made out tolerably, but then I began to sink most inconveniently. Silly thin shoes again. Nobody should ever go one mile from home in thin shoes in this country, but old Broadway habits are *so* hard to forget" (*A New Home—Who'll Follow*, chapter 19).

Kirkland published a second Western memoir, *Forest Life* (1842), before, faced with financial setbacks and their neighbors' continuing negative reaction to *A New Life*, the Kirklands returned to New York City in 1843. There they opened another school and both wrote magazine articles. A third collection of Kirkland's wilderness sketches, *Western Clearings*, was published in 1846.

Following the accidental drowning death of her husband in October 1846, Kirkland, needing extra money to care for her children, added to her teaching salary by becoming editor of *The Union Magazine of Literature and Art*. She sought to manage the publication both to attract established writers from her New York circle of friends, such as William Cullen Bryant and Nathaniel Park Willis, and to provide an outlet for worthy new talent. She also continued her prolific contributions of miscellaneous essays, reviews, and short stories to her own and other magazines. Stung by her neighbors' umbrage over *A New Home*, Kirkland's subsequent writing style softened. Her increasingly moralistic, sentimental writings remained popular with the general public and were frequently compiled in ladies' gift books, but never again did Kirkland achieve the critical acclaim garnered by her first literary effort.

Kirkland died in New York City while actively involved in fundraising for food and supplies for the Union cause during the Civil War. Her oldest son, Joseph, became a prominent author in the late 1800s, carrying on his mother's tradition of literary realism.

Kirkland was a well-known literary figure to the average reader during her lifetime but is little remembered today. Her three books on the settlement experience in the Midwest, especially the first, *A New Home—Who'll Follow?*, are her only writings that have retained any literary esteem. They are still accessible to the modern reader and the source of her continued reputation as one of the pioneers of the American realist literary movement, or, as Annette Kolodny has stated, "the direct progenitor of that bold new direction in American letters" (p. 155). Kirkland's later works are now considered dated, ephemeral, and lacking in the fresh, witty style that made *A New Home* so popular with critics and the public. She has been "rediscovered" in the late twentieth century due to the feminist movement's interest in early American women writers.

• Kirkland's extant papers are housed in scattered libraries across the United States. William S. Osborne, *Caroline M. Kirkland* (1972), is the most comprehensive critical study of Kirkland's career and includes an extensive bibliography of her books and magazine articles, as well as notable secondary sources to that time. Henry Nash Smith, *Virgin Land: The American West as Symbol and Myth* (1950), is a classic treatise on popular representations of the westward expansion that includes an evaluation of Kirkland's writings in their historical and literary context. For more recent extended discussions of Kirkland's most influential work, see Lori Merish, "'The Hand of Refined Taste' in the Frontier Landscape: Caroline Kirkland's *A New Home, Who'll Follow?* and the Feminization of American Consumerism," *American Quarterly* 45 (1993): 485–523; Annette Kolodny, "The Literary Legacy of Caroline Kirkland: Emigrants' Guide to a Failed Eden," in *The Land Before Her: Fantasy and Experience of the American Frontiers, 1630–1860* (1984); and Sandra A. Zagarell, "'America' as Community in Three Antebellum Village Sketches," in Joyce W. Warren, ed., *The (Other) American Traditions: Nineteenth-Century Women Writers* (1993).

JULIE A. THOMAS

KIRKLAND, James Hampton (9 Sept. 1859–5 Aug. 1939), educator and university president, was born in Spartanburg, South Carolina, the son of William Clarke Kirkland, an itinerant Methodist preacher, and Virginia Lawson Galluchat. Kirkland's father died when Kirkland was five and his mother raised her children in as cultured an atmosphere as their genteel poverty allowed. She sent four sons to the local southern Methodist college, Wofford. Having enrolled at age fourteen, he received his A.B. in 1877 and an A.M. in Greek and Latin in 1878. He remained at Wofford as an instructor for five years.

With the small savings of five years of teaching, he departed in 1883 for the University of Leipzig. After two years of spartan living and the absorption of as much material, and as much of the scientific method of imparting it, as he could, he obtained a Ph.D. in 1885, with a thesis on Anglo-Saxon poetry. Before leaving Europe Kirkland was able to spend a semester at the University of Berlin and to tour Italy. He was much impressed with the high and classical culture of the Old World, particularly of Rome. He had also realized that there was a better way to teach and to learn than what was then current in the United States. "It is not sufficient to know what one man has said on a certain point; we must know what all men have said, and on this basis form our own judgments," he wrote (Mims, p. 47).

Returning to South Carolina in 1886 a learned and sophisticated scholar, Kirkland found employment at Vanderbilt University as professor of Latin. The university was then thirteen years old and completely Methodist in tone and makeup. It was dominated by its bishop founder, Holland N. McTyeire, tyrannical, but bound neither by the sectarian views of his church nor by the ideological constraints of a South emerging from Reconstruction. He wanted the best scholars available. Kirkland was representative of the young faculty ready to reorganize the curriculum, abolish

preparatory classes, raise admission standards, and inaugurate a true graduate program.

Kirkland taught Latin to undergraduates and a few graduate students, publishing in 1893 his major work, *Satires and Epistles of Horace*, as well as a moderate number of both scholarly and popular (for religious periodicals) articles. His energies were principally directed, however, toward committee work and the myriad concerns of administering what was then emerging as the leading university of the South. Thus, when Chancellor Landon Cabell Garland retired in 1893 with no obvious successor, the elevation of the 34-year-old Kirkland to the office can be attributed to the faculty's appreciation of what they were getting: "when a clear head . . . [was] needed" (Mims, p. 96).

Kirkland seldom lost his clear head during the ensuing forty-four years of building Vanderbilt into a significant American institution, one of the two or three best in the South. He was the acknowledged leader of southern educational reform on the secondary as well as university levels. In 1895 the Southern Association of Colleges and Secondary Schools (originally called the Association of Colleges and Preparatory Schools of the Southern States) was formed to upgrade admission standards and graduation requirements, and Kirkland became its secretary. Under his continuing leadership the association, not at first popular, became sought after as an accrediting agency. Kirkland served as its president in 1911–1912 and 1920–1921, and on its executive committee for forty years.

In 1895 Kirkland married Mary Henderson, a well-to-do and accomplished young woman with social ties to Tennessee families; they had one child. Despite his wife, daughter, and fine house on campus, the 1890s were a hard apprenticeship for Kirkland. The new chancellor was armed only with "his own ambition, his willingness to work and to endure unending frustrations." Vanderbilt needed a reorganized medical school (with a new building in 1895), a dental school, a new building for the law school, and an "annex" for women. These were hindered by inadequate support from the founding family, the Vanderbilts, from Nashville, but most noticeably from the southern Methodist church (the Methodist Episcopal Church, South) in whose care the university supposedly resided. Kirkland now began what was to be a lifetime of letter writing, traveling, speech giving, and the endless building up of networks of friendships and acquaintanceships in order to establish Vanderbilt University on secure financial ground and to enable it to grow as he saw opportunities arise.

During the 1890s the student body increased in numbers and in quality to be the best in the South as entrance and grading levels rose. Nonetheless, the violence at football games and the rude behavior of fraternity boys caused Kirkland to tighten rules but not forbid the activities, a decision characteristic of his administration.

Beginning in 1901, however, conservative Methodists who disliked the lenient policies of the chancellor led to a demand to have the Board of Trust (trustees) appoint more Methodists to the faculty. In 1904, when the board refused to back Kirkland's choice of a highly qualified Baptist for dean of the Academic Department (Arts and Sciences), Kirkland threatened to resign. He was won back by the board's pledge to maintain "Christian scholarship," and to allow the chancellor to make all nominations to university posts. For ten more years the "War of the Bishops" raged, with Kirkland pitting his calculated advances to moderate Methodists against Bishop Elijah E. Hoss's pulpit-launched accusations. Marked by increasing reliance on legal maneuvers, the essential issue became who was going to own Vanderbilt, the southern Methodist church or its own Board of Trust? On appeal to the Tennessee Supreme Court in 1914 the court case was won by Vanderbilt and Kirkland led a victory parade of students.

From then on the chancellor was free to openly cement his ties to northern philanthropists: the Rockefeller-backed General Education Board (GEB), the various Carnegie charities (he was a member of the Carnegie Foundation board from 1917 and chairman in 1922 and 1923), and the George Peabody Fund. Kirkland, aiming to shore up Vanderbilt's always precarious financial underpinnings, and to enlarge its influence in the South, made close personal ties with Abraham Flexner, Wallace Buttrick, Frederick Gates, and even Vanderbilt and Rockefeller family members.

Although Kirkland worked to arrange an affiliation with the local George Peabody College for Teachers, questions of financing, control, and, ultimately, land use never were satisfactorily settled and he called the affair "one of the real disappointments of my life." However, the Vanderbilt medical school, begun in 1914 with a grant of $1 million from Andrew Carnegie and in 1919 one of $4 million from the GEB, opened in 1925 with a new hospital attached; the medical school was deemed the best in the South.

By the 1920s, divorced from the Methodists, Kirkland had his own Board of Trust and from then on "he molded a university more and more to his own taste" (Conkin, p. 228). Now, with the aid of his northern allies, he began the task of raising the quality of the College of Arts and Sciences to the level of the well-endowed medical school. The former had become more regional, even more local, in makeup and in sentiment than it had been in the 1890s. A result of this conservative, insular climate was the increasing narrowness of the student population and the decline in faculty quality—professors to the left or to the far right were not welcome, and mediocrity was preferred over critical thinking and creativity. For example, although the chancellor's closest faculty ally (and later his biographer), Edwin Mims, had hired John Crowe Ransom in 1914 for the English department, in 1936 the same Ransom, now internationally famous, was allowed to leave Vanderbilt for Kenyon College after he had led a faculty revolt.

In 1925, reacting to the verdict in the Scopes trial (concerning the teaching of evolution), Kirkland said: "The answer . . . is the building of new laboratories on the Vanderbilt campus for the teaching of science. The remedy for a narrow sectarianism and a belligerent fundamentalism is the establishment on this campus of a School of Religion." These words were cheered at home and quoted approvingly across the nation. Kirkland had become the source of the authority and prestige of Vanderbilt for the faculty and students and it was difficult to see the future without him. So although he attempted to retire in 1933, recognizing his own failing powers, he stayed on until 1937. Two years later he died at Ahmic Lake, Ontario, his vacation home. The main building on the Vanderbilt campus was, appropriately, renamed after him.

Kirkland, as he aged, exhibited the weaknesses of his strengths: earlier he examplified the "new," moderate but energetic, South emerging from Reconstruction, but in the 1930s he could not envision a newer and desegregated South. In religion, too, he could deal with the old-line Methodists, but could not sympathize with the social gospel of his younger, or more radical, colleagues. He presided over the shift from a literate and classical, southern, Vanderbilt to a modern university with strong professional schools and specialized training. He hired good faculty but not extremists; he treated them fairly but not always equally. He was not interested in mass education or new teaching methods.

As a leader and manager Kirkland knew to a fault how to manage people and to inspire their loyalty, but fear of the loss of certain loyalties led him to less than admirable compromises, such as the unjust firing in 1934 of Joseph K. Hart, a distinguished professor of education whom the chancellor had recently hired with some fanfare, because Hart turned out to be too radical in his views and too persuasive to students. Kirkland was finally forced to buy him off. He kept the university's finances in his own hands (he was de facto treasurer until 1933); clear headed and adroit, he was able to look beyond the current budget.

Kirkland had enormous energy and powers of concentration on the job and the ability to restore them with hunting and fishing trips and the breeding of prize-winning irises. Austere and sometimes forbidding in public, he was known to have had a very happy marriage and a capacity for warm friendships.

• Kirkland's papers, personal and administrative, are in the collections of Vanderbilt University (see Conkin, below, for locations). Edwin Mims, faculty member and close friend of Kirkland's, wrote the standard biography, *Chancellor Kirkland of Vanderbilt* (1940), and additional material can be found in Mims's *History of Vanderbilt University* (1946). For a more distanced history of Kirkland and his career and for an overview of sources, see Paul K. Conkin, *Gone with the Ivy, a Biography of Vanderbilt University* (1985). Abraham Flexner's *I Remember* (1940) gives a professional and personal view of Kirkland. See also the *New York Times* obituary, 6 Aug. 1939, and editorial, 7 Aug. 1939.

CARROLL WINSLOW BRENTANO

KIRKLAND, Joseph (7 Jan. 1830–28 Apr. 1894), lawyer and author, was born in Geneva, New York, the son of William Kirkland, a one-time professor at

Hamilton College, and Caroline M. Stansbury, who became a prominent editor and writer (first under a pseudonym and then under her married name, Caroline Stansbury Kirkland). The family moved to the Michigan peninsula to homestead in 1835, though the experiment was a financial failure, and they returned to New York eight years later. Largely educated at home, Joseph Kirkland traveled to Europe in 1847–1848 and clerked briefly in the editorial offices of the original New York *Putnam's* in 1852 before moving to Illinois in 1856 to enter private business, first as a traveling auditor for the Illinois Central Railroad, later as supervisor of mining operations for the Carbon Coal Company of Tilton, Illinois. During the Civil War he served as an aide-de-camp on the staffs of Generals George McClellan and Fitz-John Porter and, while participating in the battles of Malvern Hill, Antietam, and Fredericksburg, he rose to the rank of major. In 1863 he resigned his commission, returned to Illinois, and married Theodosia Burr Wilkinson of Syracuse, New York. Four children were born to them between 1865 and 1874. After the coal-mining business that he founded in 1865 failed in 1871, Kirkland worked for the U.S. Internal Revenue Service, and in 1880 he was admitted to the Illinois bar. He practiced law until 1890 with Patrick Mark Bangs.

Meanwhile, Kirkland nurtured his avocational interest in literature. He helped to organize the Literary Club of Chicago in 1871 and in 1876 joined the Saracen Club, another literary club whose members included Henry Blake Fuller and Samuel Willard. Kirkland's adaptation of Alphonse Daudet's play *Sidonie* was produced under the title *The Married Flirt* by the McVicker Theatre Company in Chicago during a two-week run in December 1877 and became something of a local cause célèbre. Kirkland also began to review books for the Chicago *Dial* in 1880.

A pioneering realist, Kirkland earned a modest literary reputation with his first novel, *Zury: the Meanest Man in Spring County* (1887), a tale of the midwestern settlements based in part upon his own adolescence in Michigan. *Zury* was hailed as a minor masterpiece for its truthful treatment of native materials. As William Dean Howells noted in a review, Kirkland caught the "look and speech" of the "gaunt, sallow, weary, world-worn women" and the "tireless, rude, independent and mutually helpful men" with "a certainty that can come only of personal knowledge." Hamlin Garland added that the novel "is absolutely unconventional—not a trace of old-world literature or society—and every character is new and native."

Kirkland's episodic and virtually plotless second novel, *The McVeys* (1888), contains material he had deleted in revision from *Zury*. His third novel, *The Captain of Company K* (1891), a potboiler based on his Civil War experiences, took first prize in a fiction contest sponsored by the *Detroit Free Press*, where it was first published serially. Widely regarded as a model for Stephen Crane's *The Red Badge of Courage*, it depicted the misery of battle from the point of view of an army private. Neither of these later novels was as criti-

cally successful as *Zury*, and Kirkland later remarked to Garland, his friend and protégé, that he had begun to write fiction "too late and lost the ability to emotionalize what I remembered." On his part, Garland later credited Kirkland with discovering the midwestern farm as a field for fiction.

In 1889 Kirkland became literary editor of the *Chicago Tribune*, which two years later printed his series of letters from Nicaragua, where he had traveled as a special correspondent with an official party charged with inspecting sites for a canal across the isthmus. He also published stories and articles in the *Century, America, Scribner's*, and the *Atlantic*. Kirkland's last years were devoted to a series of local histories, including his two-volume *The Story of Chicago* (1891) and his meticulously researched *The Chicago Massacre of 1812* (1893). Upon his death of an apparent heart attack at his home in the city, he was engaged in editing the official *History of Chicago* (2 vols., 1895), later completed by his daughter Caroline.

Though he was only incidentally a man of letters, Kirkland deserves to be remembered both for extending the frontiers of western fiction and for inspiring by example such writers as Garland and Crane. His friend Lucy Monroe later reminisced, in fact, that he had been a "ready and interesting talker" who was "more at home with the young than the old," a "warm hearted" man whose "raillery was never bitter." Yet he was more than a minor talent who caught reflected light, whose only significant triumphs were vicarious ones. No less than Howells's *The Rise of Silas Lapham* and *A Hazard of New Fortunes* depicted the new, urban nouveaux riches, Kirkland's *Zury* epitomized a moment and milieu in American literary history, with its realistic portrayal of the midwestern farmer.

• Most of Kirkland's papers are deposited in the Newberry Library, Chicago. Small collections of his letters are located at the University of Southern California, Princeton University, Columbia University, Johns Hopkins University, and the Library of Congress. A facsimile edition of *Zury*, with a valuable introduction by John T. Flanagan, appeared in 1956. The only book-length biography is Clyde E. Henson, *Joseph Kirkland* (1962). Obituaries are in the *Chicago Tribune* and *Boston Transcript*, 30 Apr. 1894, and Lucy Monroe published her brief memoir of Kirkland in the *Critic*, 5 May 1894.

GARY SCHARNHORST

KIRKLAND, Samuel (1 Dec. 1741–28 Feb. 1808), missionary, was born in Norwich, Connecticut, the son of the Reverend Daniel Kirtland and Mary Perkins. Samuel Kirkland (it is uncertain as to when he changed his last name) grew up in a household that was emotionally and financially unstable. He decided to follow his father into the ministry, and in 1760 he became the first white pupil to enter More's Indian Charity School in Lebanon, Connecticut. Coming under the influence and direction of his father's friend Eleazar Wheelock (the future founder of Dartmouth College), Kirkland soon chose to become a missionary. He studied at the College of New Jersey (1762–1764) and received his degree in absentia in 1765 because he had left the college for his first missionary endeavor, to the Seneca Indians, one of the six tribes of the Iroquois nation in upstate New York.

Adopted into the family of the leading Seneca sachem in Kanadasegea (present-day Geneva, N.Y.), Kirkland showed great promise in his early work; he was diligent, courageous, and faithful. He returned to Lebanon, Connecticut, in May 1766 and was ordained by Wheelock on 19 June 1766. Instead of returning to the land of the Senecas, Kirkland moved to a new mission in Kanowaroghare, the chief village of the Oneida Indians, another tribe of the Iroquois nation. In 1769 Kirkland married Jerusha Bingham, a niece of Wheelock; they had six children. The couple soon made their home in the Oneida country, where they were often overwhelmed by the demands made on their energies by the Indian concept of hospitality. Despite his new familial closeness with Wheelock, Kirkland soon had a falling out with his mentor, and by 1770 Kirkland had changed sponsors; he became responsible to the Society for the Propagation of Christian Knowledge in Scotland rather than to his father-in-law.

The start of the American Revolution brought a temporary end to Kirkland's ministry. During the revolutionary war, he served as an unofficial diplomat between the Continental Congress in Philadelphia and the Oneida and Tuscarora tribes (the majority of which maintained neutrality due to Kirkland's efforts). He also directed a group of Oneida scouts and served as chaplain of Fort Schuyler (later renamed Fort Stanwix) and was also chaplain for General John Sullivan's expedition against the Iroquois tribes that had sided with Great Britain during the war.

Kirkland faced a daunting challenge in 1783 when he considered how to rebuild his ministry. His Oneida charges had been made destitute and thoroughly demoralized during the war, and he declared in a letter to his wife that they had become "filthy dirty, nasty creatures, a few families excepted" (Pilkington, p. 121). This outburst of negative emotion was by no means typical of Kirkland; he worked tirelessly on the behalf of the Oneida people, and by 1786 he had largely succeeded in bringing his ministry back to where it had been in 1774, prior to the Revolution.

Kirkland was a witness to the Treaty of Fort Stanwix (1784), and in the early 1790s he was influential in dissuading the Iroquois from joining the Indian tribes of Ohio in a general war against the whites. In 1792 he brought a deputation of Iroquois chiefs to Philadelphia, where they pledged friendship to the United States.

Kirkland made a thorough census of the Iroquois lands in 1789, and he received a grant of 4,000 acres of land, deeded to him both by the Oneida nation and the government of New York. His first wife died in 1788, and in 1796 he married Mary Donnally, with whom he had no children. In spite of the generous gift of land he had received, Kirkland stumbled into financial and personal difficulties in his later years. He succeeded in having the Hamilton-Oneida Academy chartered by New York State (31 Jan. 1793), but the school never became the place for biracial learning that he had intended. Few Indian students ever attended the school, and in 1812 it became Hamilton College. One of Kirkland's sons went bankrupt in 1799 and virtually pulled his father down with him; Kirkland was only able to retain a small farmstead in Clinton, New York. His Oneida charges became increasingly desperate during the last years of his life; his valiant efforts, conducted over forty years, had been insufficient to protect them from the clash between Indian culture and the white man's ways. These disappointments weighed heavily on Kirkland. He died in Clinton following an attack of pleurisy.

Kirkland was one of the most remarkable missionaries of the revolutionary era. His long presence among the Oneida Indians (1766–1808), his ceaseless efforts to preserve a peaceful neutrality during the revolution and the upheavals of the early 1790s, and his perseverance in the face of numerous personal trials made him stand out in his own time period. Completely committed to his lifelong mission, he suffered from the misfortune of having his work coincide with the decline of the Iroquois nations. Had he been born earlier and been able to commence his work ten or twenty years sooner, he might have stood a fair chance of bringing some of the Iroquois to Christianity without the complications of revolution and war. As it was, the events of the American Revolution and the encroachment of white settlers on the lands of the Iroquois were disastrous for his flock. Little known today outside the community of Hamilton College, Kirkland remains a striking example of the idealistic and humanitarian values that were exemplified by a handful of missionaries in colonial and revolutionary America.

• Kirkland's papers are at Hamilton College, Dartmouth College, and the Massachusetts Historical Society. The most valuable sources are *The Journals of Samuel Kirkland*, ed. Walter Pilkington (1980), and Barbara Graymont, *The Iroquois in the American Revolution* (1972). There are also Stephen Valone, "Samuel Kirkland, Iroquois Missions and the Land, 1764–1774," *American Presbyterians* 65 (1987): 187–94, Annette D. Trepp, "The Churchmen and the Indians: The Role of the Missionaries in the Indian War," *Queen City Heritage* 48, no. 1 (1990): 20–31, and Willard Thorp, "Samuel Kirkland, Missionary to the Six Nations; Founder of Hamilton College," in *The Lives of Eighteen from Princeton*, ed. Willard Thorp (1946).

SAMUEL WILLARD CROMPTON

KIRKPATRICK, Andrew (17 Feb. 1756–6 Jan. 1831), lawyer and judge, was born in Minebrook, New Jersey, the son of David Kirkpatrick and Mary McEowen, farmers. Kirkpatrick spent his early years on the farm, where his father brought him up in a strict manner, with the intent that Kirkpatrick would become a Presbyterian minister. After graduating from the College of New Jersey at Princeton in 1775, he began studying theology under Rev. Samuel Kennedy but soon left Kennedy's tutelage to study law. Kirkpatrick's father was so unhappy about this decision that he expelled his son from the family. Kirkpatrick supported himself by tutoring for families in Virginia and New York, and then by teaching classics at Queens College Grammar School (later called Rutgers). From 1783 to 1785 he studied law with William Paterson, a well-known lawyer who later became governor of New Jersey and a Supreme Court justice of the United States.

Kirkpatrick was admitted to the bar of New Jersey in 1785. He resided for a time at his sister's home in Morristown, New Jersey, but two years later, after his library was destroyed by a fire, he moved to New Brunswick, New Jersey, which was his home for the rest of his life.

In 1787 Kirkpatrick established a legal practice and became a leading member of the bar. He married Jane Bayard in 1792; they had seven children. In 1797 he was elected to the general assembly of New Jersey and later that year was appointed an associate justice of the New Jersey Supreme Court, which began his long judicial career. In 1799 Kirkpatrick ran for governor of New Jersey and lost a close election to Richard Howell, a Federalist. Although Kirkpatrick himself was described as a "moderate Federalist," the Republican party, which had been divided in the 1798 election, united to support Kirkpatrick in 1799.

In 1803 the state legislature elected him chief justice. Both supporters and detractors found him an imposing chief justice, with his good looks and impressive head of white hair. In addition to the duties of his position, he served as one of the original trustees of the Princeton Theological Seminary and was elected chairman of its board. He was a trustee of the college as well from 1809 until his death.

Kirkpatrick was a conservative thinker on the criminal law who opposed confining criminals in state prisons and supported capital punishment and the whipping post for many offenses. He was a scholar of the common law of England as it developed before 1776, but he did not accept the authority of English cases and innovations after that time. In 1799 the New Jersey legislature passed a controversial law, of which Kirkpatrick was reputedly the author, that barred the use in New Jersey courts of any law book, reported legal decision, or digest published in Great Britain after 1776. The law was repealed in 1818. Despite the fact that his association with the law eroded some of his support in the legislature, he was reelected chief justice twice.

One of Kirkpatrick's most noteworthy decisions, *Arnold v. Mundy*, 6 *New Jersey Laws* 1 (Supreme Court 1821), is a case of lasting importance, forming the basis of decisions on public access to private lands in cases as recent as 1984. He concluded in his decision that lands washed by the tides are common to all citizens, and that every citizen has a right to use those lands. This principle came to be known as the public trust doctrine and has been applied by the New Jersey Supreme Court in upholding the public's right of access even to privately owned beaches. Kirkpatrick's opinion in *Arnold v. Mundy* is quite lengthy, and the antecedents cited are both extensive and diverse. They include civil texts, the grant by Charles II of the land comprising New Jersey, English common law cases, and the Magna Carta. In short, the opinion reveals Kirkpatrick's scholarly side.

Another Kirkpatrick decision of note, *Den v. Morris*, 7 *New Jersey Laws* 6 (Supreme Court 1822), contains a learned discussion of the doctrine of adverse possession that has frequently been cited as a leading decision. In *Den v. Morris*, Kirkpatrick's scholarly approach is again revealed. The opinion does not establish any novel legal doctrine. Rather, it presents a learned discussion of the law of adverse possession as it developed by 1822. The decision has been cited and relied upon numerous times in New Jersey cases for its exposition of the basic principles of the doctrine. This is the opinion's lasting influence. Kirkpatrick was also instrumental in creating the office of reporter of the decisions of the New Jersey Supreme Court. In 1820 he was elected a member of the legislative council.

In 1824 Kirkpatrick failed to win reelection as chief justice. According to Lucius Q. C. Elmer, the speaker of the state assembly, although Kirkpatrick "had some very high qualifications for his office, he had some very grave defects." Elmer cited his failure to "keep pace with the changes of the law, in his time very great, especially in cases involving the law of personal property and negotiable instruments." Elmer also cited complaints by younger members of the bar that Kirkpatrick "failed to listen patiently to their arguments, and sometimes checked them with 'caustic severity.'" In support of Kirkpatrick, the historian Joseph G. Wilson called him "a man of a singularly social turn of mind, full of anecdote, with remarkable power of narration, fond of discussion and argument, and often carrying his ingenuity to the verge of paradox." Wilson nevertheless admitted that Kirkpatrick's wit was "keen and biting at times," but asserted that it was "only severe when directed against ignorance and pompous pretenses" (James Grant Wilson, pp. 43–44).

After Kirkpatrick left the bench, he retired to his New Brunswick home, where he died.

• A summary of the life of Andrew Kirkpatrick is in Edward Quinton Keasbey, *The Courts and Lawyers of New Jersey*, vol. 2 (1912), pp. 688–94. The more personal opinions of Lucius Q. C. Elmer are in Elmer's book, *The Constitution and Government of the Province and State of New Jersey* (1872), pp. 301–11. Other biographical summaries are in John Whitehead, *The Judicial and Civil History of New Jersey* (1897), pp. 407–11; and the address of Joseph G. Wilson in *Proceedings of the New Jersey Historical Society*, 2d ser., 2 (1872): 79–97, also published as James Grant Wilson, *Memorials of Andrew Kirkpatrick and his Wife Jane Bayard* (1870). A discussion of the public trust doctrine in *Arnold v. Mundy* and its place in New Jersey law is in "State Citizen Rights Respecting Greatwater Resource Allocation: From Rome to New Jersey," *Rutgers Law Review* 25 (1971): 571–710; and for the extension of the doctrine to the public right of access to oceanfront property, see *Borough of Neptune City v. Borough of Avon-by-the-Sea*, *New Jersey Reports* 61 (1972): 296, 303–11.

ANDREW T. FEDE

KIRKPATRICK, James. *See* Killpatrick, James.

KIRKPATRICK, Ralph Leonard (10 June 1911–13 Apr. 1984), harpsichordist and musicologist, was born in Leominster, Massachusetts, the son of Edwin Ashbury Kirkpatrick, a psychologist and Florence May Clifford. He began to study piano at age six and first had an opportunity to play the harpsichord in 1929 while an undergraduate at Harvard. In May 1930 he made his first public appearance as a harpsichordist. After receiving the A.B. degree in 1931, in fine arts rather than music, he was awarded a Paine Travelling Fellowship for music study in Europe in recognition of his performances on the harpsichord of J. S. Bach's *Goldberg Variations* and Concerto in D Minor. Once Kirkpatrick arrived in Paris in the fall of 1931, he studied music theory with Nadia Boulanger and harpsichord with Wanda Landowska. He also attended courses at Landowska's École de Musique Ancienne in Saint-Leu-La-Forêt. He acknowledged having gained technically from his work with Landowska, although they were temperamentally incompatible. His letters of the period attest to his dislike of her pretensions and of her loyalty to a type of modern harpsichord that had little in common with the historical instrument. After some time, he began to study harpsichord secretly with Paul Brunold, who owned a fine antique harpsichord. He also continued to research seventeenth- and eighteenth-century performance practice at the Bibliothèque Nationale.

In July 1932 Kirkpatrick went to England to study in Haslemere with Arnold Dolmetsch, mainly on the clavichord. There he acquired a Dolmetsch clavichord, which he treasured to the end of his life and which he bequeathed to the Yale Collection of Musical Instruments. In England he continued his performance practice research at the British Museum. In October he moved to Berlin briefly and made a successful debut in January 1933, performing Bach's *Goldberg Variations*. In May he left for Italy, where he gave his first paid concert at Bernard Berenson's Villa i Tàtti near Florence. The summer of 1933 found Kirkpatrick teaching at the Salzburg Mozarteum, where he added the fortepiano to the instruments at his command.

On his return to the United States, Kirkpatrick began his concert career, playing harpsichord at recitals as well as continuo and obbligato harpsichord in chamber, orchestral, and choral concerts. In 1936 he made his first recordings in New York for the Musicraft label. In 1938 he published an edition of Bach's *Goldberg Variations*, with a valuable introduction dealing with performance practice. In the summer of that year Kirkpatrick taught briefly at Bennington College in Vermont. Also in 1938 he became director of the festivals of eighteenth-century music at the Governor's Palace in Williamsburg, Virginia, a post he held until 1946.

In 1940 Kirkpatrick was appointed to the music faculty of Yale University and was elected a fellow of Jonathan Edwards College. He took an active part in the college's musical life, organizing and performing in many concerts. He continued to teach there as professor of music until his retirement in 1976. His pupils numbered many distinguished American harpsichordists, including William Christie, Albert Fuller, Mark Kroll, and Fernando Valenti. The growing demand for his solo recitals forced Kirkpatrick to give up all but the most important engagements as continuo harpsichordist, notably the annual performances of Bach's *Saint Matthew Passion* by the New York Philharmonic under Bruno Walter. He also concertized extensively during the mid-1940s with violinist Alexander Schneider, presenting programs of sonatas by Bach, Handel, and Mozart, which were recorded for CBS Masterworks.

During World War II, Kirkpatrick was commissioned by a New York publisher (who ultimately declined the manuscript) to write a study of the life and works of Domenico Scarlatti. With the end of the war, he resumed his concert career in Europe and was able to continue his research there into musical and biographical source materials on Scarlatti. During two summers at the American Academy in Rome, he outlined *Domenico Scarlatti*, which became a classic musical biography, published in 1953. It was often reprinted with revisions and since has been translated into French, German, Italian, and Japanese. By way of further musical illustration, Kirkpatrick edited sixty Scarlatti sonatas, the first modern urtext edition in modern times. He performed these sonatas as a cycle in three recitals during the concert season of 1952–1953 and recorded them for CBS Masterworks. Renowned younger keyboardists, such as Alfred Brendel and Gustav Leonhardt, have gratefully recalled the deep impression made by Kirkpatrick's Scarlatti performances in the 1950s and 1960s. Although he never undertook a complete modern edition of Scarlatti's sonatas, he edited an eighteen-volume complete edition of facsimiles of authentic manuscripts and early printings, which was published in 1972.

Despite Kirkpatrick's preference for the sound of the classic harpsichord, which he experienced in his work with Brunold and occasional encounters with playable historical examples, he was obliged to perform for most of his career on instruments whose principal virtue was their availability. In the United States he was heard most often on harpsichords made under Dolmetsch's direction at the Chickering piano factory in Boston during 1906–1910; these were closer to his ideal than were those of distinctly modern type. Later he made considerable use of harpsichords made by Dolmetsch's American disciple, John Challis. Finally, in the 1950s, instruments based on historical examples began to emerge from the Boston workshop of Frank Hubbard and William Dowd. Kirkpatrick encouraged them enthusiastically and performed publicly thereafter in the United States on their instruments. During the late 1940s he had recorded works of Mozart and Haydn on a Challis fortepiano of modern design, but gave up performing on it in 1956, "in honor of the Mozart bicentenary," as he put it.

His recordings of Bach's complete keyboard music for Deutsche Grammophon, begun in 1956, were mainly played on the harpsichord but included a number of disks on the clavichord that many critics feel represent his finest playing. Kirkpatrick's vast repertoire encompassed sixteenth-century works by Antonio de Cabezón and William Byrd; seventeenth-century music by later virginalists, Henry Purcell, Louis Couperin, and their contemporaries; all the works of Bach; dozens of Scarlatti sonatas; the keyboard music of Handel, Jean-Philippe Rameau, and François Couperin; and important twentieth-century music for harpsichord by Elliot Carter, Henry Cowell, and Quincy Porter. His playing was marked by technical mastery, a true virtuoso temperament, and unerring musicality. These qualities were still evident even after he was afflicted by total blindness in 1976. Kirkpatrick died in Guilford, Connecticut.

• Kirkpatrick's papers were bequeathed to the Library of the School of Music at Yale University. In addition to *Domenico Scarlatti*, his writings include an autobiography, *Early Years* (1985), with an epilogue by Frederick Hammond, and *Interpreting Bach's Well-Tempered Clavier: A Performer's Discourse on Method* (1984). Larry Palmer, *Harpsichord in America* (1989), has an important chapter on Kirkpatrick. An obituary is in the *New York Times*, 16 Apr. 1984.

HOWARD SCHOTT

KIRKUS, Virginia (7 Dec. 1893–10 Sept. 1980), editor, book reviewer, and author, was born in Meadville, Pennsylvania, the daughter of Frederick Maurice Kirkus, a clergyman, and Isabella Clark. When Kirkus was eight years old, she told her father that when she grew up, she wanted to "make books." The world of books became part of who she was.

Kirkus grew up in Wilmington, Delaware, where her father was rector of Trinity Episcopal Church. She attended private schools: the Misses Hebbs School in Wilmington and later the Hannah More Academy in Reistertown, Maryland. In 1916 she graduated from Vassar College with an A.B. in English. She continued her education at Teachers College, Columbia University, in New York City.

By 1917 she had started a career teaching English and history at the Greenhill School in Wilmington. After three years, Kirkus returned to New York City for a job as assistant fashion editor for *Pictorial Review*. She never returned to teaching, but the education of children was always important to her, particularly through her interest in books for children.

Kirkus later took a job as "back of the book" editor at *McCall's* and did some freelance writing for Doubleday, including her first book, *Everywoman's Guide to Health and Personal Beauty* (1922). She also edited *Micah Clarke* (1922), by Sir Arthur Conan Doyle, and *Robert Bacon, Life and Letters* (1923), by James Brown Scott.

At this point in her life Kirkus was looking for a change in employment and learned that Harper Brothers was considering the publication of a new magazine for women. Kirkus was invited to submit a prospectus for a magazine that would serve the needs of post–World War I women. The publisher sought a proposal that was a complete departure from the currently familiar home/food/fashion magazines. Kirkus's prospectus would have pleased the women of the 1990s with its focus on intellectually and politically active women and its features on social issues, the arts, and consumer-tested household goods.

Harper, however, decided that the start-up costs for such a magazine were too high and, instead, offered Kirkus another position in the newly created department for publishing books for children. In 1925 Kirkus became head of the children's book department at Harpers, working with children's books in "the days when children's books were coming into their own." As Kirkus wrote in *The Horn Book* (Dec. 1953), she felt like a trail blazer "in a field that had long been fairly static."

One author Kirkus secured for Harper Brothers was Laura Ingalls Wilder. At first Kirkus was not interested in reading a manuscript written by an elderly lady about her pioneer childhood. However, she agreed to read the manuscript and took it to pass the time on a train bound for Westport, Connecticut. Kirkus became so absorbed in the story of the little house in the woods that she missed her train stop. She promptly signed Wilder, recognizing the worth of the book that would be published as *Little House in the Big Woods* (1932). Harper Brothers proceeded to publish the series of Wilder books, known as Little House on the Prairie, which would become classics of children's literature and be recreated in an extremely popular television show, which aired from 1974 to 1983.

Unfortunately, the Great Depression forced Harper to discontinue its children's department in 1932. Although Kirkus was offered another position at Harper, she opted for an extended vacation. Returning from visiting her family in Munich, Kirkus developed the idea for a prepublication book review service. In January 1933, at her request, twenty publishers submitted galley proofs of books for review. And with ten subscribers, Virginia Kirkus Bookshop Service was born.

The Kirkus Service (as it became known) was a success from the beginning; eventually nearly every publishing firm would submit advance galley proofs of their books to be reviewed by Kirkus and her four assistants in the bimonthly bulletin. Written in an informal, readable style, the reviews were informative but not pretentious, and they were unbiased. The reviews gave book buyers direction, and Kirkus's critiques were accurate in assessing reader appeal 85 percent of the time. She admitted that she made some mistakes, such as her negative assessment of *Anthony Adverse* as "too long," but she also discovered "dark horses" such as *Cry the Beloved Country* and *The Caine Mutiny*. A regular part of the Kirkus Service remains reviewing children's books.

In 1936 Kirkus married Frank Glick, a personnel director of a New York City department store. They had no children.

Along with running her business, Kirkus continued to write and edit. With Frank Scully she wrote two books of games: *Fun in Bed for Children: First Aid in Getting Well Cheerfully* and *Junior Fun in Bed: Making a Holiday of Convalescence* (both in 1935). She wrote *A House for the Week Ends* (1940), about the restoration of the country house in Redding Ridge, Connecticut, where she and her husband spent their weekends. Her children's book, *The First Book of Gardening* (1956), was also inspired by her experiences in the country. Kirkus wrote articles for *Saturday Review*, *Horn Book*, *Library Journal*, and other book-oriented publications. She served on the Governor's Commission on Rural Libraries in Connecticut from 1961 to 1964 and was in demand on the lecture circuit.

When she retired from business in 1962, Kirkus and her longtime partner Ruth Basham sold the Kirkus Service to a third partner Alice Wolff. At that point the business had grown to eight full-time reviewers and freelance reviewers as needed. Since then, the business changed hands several times, but kept her name and continued to evaluate thousands of books annually.

Kirkus edited books, wrote books, and reviewed books, reading more than 700 books a year. Her innovative book reviewing service provided unbiased, "no nonsense" critiques of forthcoming books to a variety of buyers, including book stores, libraries, radio and television stations. As a former Kirkus reviewer once noted, "Kirkus moved fast and talked fast." And what Kirkus did for bookselling and libraries was to "ma[k]e everything move a little faster" (Gerhardt, p. 77). She also provided buyers, with her honest, down-to-earth reviews, "a check on the natural enthusiasm of publishers' blurbs." She died in Danbury, Connecticut.

• For a full article on Kirkus's life and the Kirkus Bookshop Service, see *Current Biography* (1954). F. Peter Model's article, "Eye on Publishing," *Wilson Library Bulletin*, Jan. 1988, pp. 63–64, has information on the Kirkus service, including how it was founded and subsequent changes in ownership. Kirkus's own article, "The Discovery of Laura Ingalls Wilder," *The Horn Book* 29 (Dec. 1953): 428–30, provides background on publishing books for children. A tribute to Kirkus is editor L. N. Gerhardt's "Virginia Kirkus, 1893–1980," *School Library Journal*, Oct. 1980, p. 7. Obituaries are in the *School Library Journal*, Oct. 1980, p. 100; the *New York Times*, 11 Sept. 1980; *Newsweek*, 22 Sept. 1980; and *Publishers Weekly*, 26 Sept. 1980.

MARCIA B. DINNEEN

KIRKWOOD, Daniel (27 Sept. 1814–11 June 1895), astronomer, was born in Harford County, Maryland, the son of John Kirkwood and Agnes Hope, farmers of Scotch-Irish ancestry. After studying at a local country school, Kirkwood, at age nineteen, decided to try his hand at teaching in Hopewell, Pennsylvania. When in 1833 or 1834 one of his students expressed an interest in learning algebra, the mathematically illiterate Kirkwood suggested that teacher and student learn the subject together. In doing so, Kirkwood discovered his aptitude for the mathematical sciences. In 1834 he enrolled as a student in the York County Academy in Pennsylvania. After completing his studies four years later, he became an instructor in mathematics at the academy. In 1845, while serving as principal of the Lancaster High School, he married Sarah A. McNair of Bucks County, Pennsylvania; they had at least one child.

In 1851 Kirkwood left Pottsville Academy (Pa.), after serving two years as its principal, for a professorship in mathematics at Delaware College. He remained in Newark, Delaware, until 1856, spending his last two years there unhappily as president of the college. In 1856 he took a position as professor of mathematics at Indiana University, where he remained until his retirement in 1886, with an interlude from 1865 to 1867 as professor at Washington and Jefferson College in Pennsylvania. Although a shy, retiring man, he apparently performed satisfactorily in the classroom.

In the late 1830s Kirkwood had begun a decade-long search for a mathematical law governing the axial rotations of the planets in the same way that German astronomer Johannes Kepler's third law regulated their orbital revolutions around the sun. Inspired by the nebular hypothesis of Pierre Simon Laplace, according to which the planets had evolved from rings abandoned by a contracting solar nebula, Kirkwood in 1833–1834 discovered a simple mathematical formula. Later known as Kirkwood's analogy, it related the number of rotations performed by a planet during its orbit around the sun to the width of the original zone of nebulous rings from which the planet had developed. When the American astronomer Sears Cook Walker presented this discovery to the 1849 meeting of the American Association for the Advancement of Science, he described it as "the most important harmony in the Solar System discovered since the time of Kepler, which, in after times, may place their names, side by side, in honorable association" (Numbers, p. 46). Many American scientists, though fewer European counterparts, saw Kirkwood's analogy as providing crucial confirmation of Laplace's nebular hypothesis, and patriotic writers hailed the backwoods astronomer as the American Kepler.

Kirkwood went on from this early success to become one of the country's leading authorities on the origin and structure of the solar system. In three books—*Meteoric Astronomy* (1867), *Comets and Meteors* (1873), and *The Asteroids* (1888)—and nearly 200 articles he showed how a modified nebular hypothesis accounted for a wide range of heavenly phenomena, including comets, asteroids, and meteors. By 1880 he had concluded that the planets had originated not from rings abandoned by the sun but from matter ejected from ruptures in the sun's primitive equatorial belt. His most lasting contribution was his explanation of the so-called gaps in the asteroid zone, where a number of planetoids revolve around the sun between Mars and Jupiter. These gaps, he explained in 1866, had resulted from the powerful disturbing force of Jupiter. He attributed the divisions of Saturn's rings to similar forces.

Throughout his life Kirkwood remained a devout Christian and loyal Presbyterian. For years he taught a Sunday school class of adolescent boys, and he never hesitated to witness for his faith. At Indiana University he once described a particular demonstration as being "as true as that there is a God in heaven." When asked how he would explain this to an atheist, he straightened "up to his full height," reported a colleague, "and with glittering eye he said, 'I would try to keep my temper and get away as quickly as possible'" (Swain, p. 143). Despite the worrisome skepticism of some of his scientific colleagues, Kirkwood denied that science and religion were in conflict. And although the nebular hypothesis at first glance seemed to diminish God's role in creating the world, Kirkwood assured the faithful that divinely ordained natural laws demonstrated God's power as effectively as miracles.

Following his retirement from Indiana University, Kirkwood moved to a seven-acre orange grove in Riverside, California. After settling in the West, he accepted an appointment as a nonresident lecturer in astronomy at the newly opened Stanford University. He died in Riverside. A street in Bloomington, Indiana, an observatory at Indiana University, and an asteroid, number 1,578, are named in his honor.

• There is no surviving collection of Kirkwood's manuscripts or correspondence. Two of his contemporaries left short biographical sketches: William W. Payne, "Daniel Kirkwood," *Popular Astronomy* 1 (1893): 167–69; and Joseph Swain, "Daniel Kirkwood," Astronomical Society of the Pacific, *Publications* 13 (1901): 140–47. On Kirkwood and the nebular hypothesis, see Ronald L. Numbers, "The American Kepler: Daniel Kirkwood and His Analogy," *Journal for the History of Astronomy* 4 (1973): 13–21, and Numbers, *Creation by Natural Law: Laplace's Nebular Hypothesis in American Thought* (1977).

RONALD L. NUMBERS

KIRKWOOD, James Pugh (27 Mar. 1807–22 Apr. 1877), sanitary engineer, was born in Edinburgh, Scotland. His father, a merchant, sent him to an academy at Galashiels at the age of eight and in 1818 sent him abroad for a year of schooling in Rotterdam, where he became proficient in Dutch and French. He returned home to work in his father's store. James Kirkwood, however, left the world of commerce at the age of fourteen to apprentice with a surveyor, Thomas Granger. After completing the required term of his apprenticeship, Kirkwood remained with Granger until 1832. Then, knowing that more opportunities for engineers existed in the United States than in Scotland, he emigrated to America.

Kirkwood's subsequent career in the United States is a good example of the growth of civil engineering in the nineteenth century and its evolution from a profession of generalists to one of specialists. Over forty years, as Kirkwood practiced engineering, he moved gradually from being a generalist willing to tackle any project to a specialist in an emerging field, waterworks engineering.

When Kirkwood arrived in the United States, railroad construction was booming. Having been provided with a letter of introduction to a noted railroad engineer, William Gibbs McNeil, Kirkwood began working on railroads in New England. His engineering competence was recognized quickly, and he took on positions of greater responsibility. During the early 1840s he oversaw projects ranging from the establishment of a naval depot in Pensacola, Florida, to general construction in Albany, New York. In December 1848 he was named general superintendent of the Erie Railroad. Kirkwood resigned this position in 1850 to become chief engineer of the Missouri Pacific Railroad, a position he held for five years. The town of Kirkwood, Missouri, is named for him.

In 1855 Kirkwood resigned as chief engineer and returned to New York City, where he undertook his first work involving public water supplies. A water main had to be moved without interruption of service to the city. Kirkwood successfully supervised this project and shortly afterward became chief engineer of the Nassau Water Works in Brooklyn. As a consulting engineer, he continued to work on a variety of projects throughout the Northeast and elsewhere. He undertook numerous studies of all aspects of waterworks engineering, from reservoirs and pumping systems to the material used for pipes. Kirkwood was among the first American civil engineers to speak out on the dangers of using lead pipe in water distribution systems.

In 1865 the St. Louis Water Commission in Missouri hired Kirkwood to make recommendations for a water supply for that city. Slow sand water filtration, first introduced in 1827 in London, England, was becoming common practice in European cities. The commissioners paid Kirkwood to travel to Europe to make a thorough study of these filtration processes. Kirkwood undertook an exhaustive study and published his findings in a comprehensive illustrated report titled *A Report on Slow Sand Water Filtration* following his return from Europe. The St. Louis water commissioners, however, were reluctant to invest the funds required to implement Kirkwood's recommendations. At the time, little was known about the role contaminated water played in the transmission of diseases such as typhoid and cholera. Although St. Louis decided against following Kirkwood's advice, numerous other cities, including Poughkeepsie, New York, did commission him to design slow sand water filtration plants. In addition, for several decades following its publication, waterworks engineers around the world relied on the information provided by Kirkwood's St. Louis report to design and build water filtration plants.

Kirkwood was in poor health for many years and spent his final decades as an invalid. He never married. Despite his frailty, however, he maintained an active engineering consulting practice, as well as taking a strong interest in professional organizations and publications. He helped found the American Society of Civil Engineers (ASCE) and served as its second president. During his lifetime the ASCE grew from a local club with a handful of founding members to a national organization of more than a thousand engineers. Shortly after his seventieth birthday, Kirkwood traveled to Lynn, Massachusetts, to consult on a waterworks project and became very ill; he returned to New York City, where he died.

• Biographical sketches are found in tributes published shortly after Kirkwood's death, notably in *Proceedings of the American Society of Civil Engineers* 4 (1878). Kirkwood is also mentioned in passing in the chapters "Community Water Supply" and "Sewers and Wastewater Treatment" in Ellis L. Armstrong et al., eds., *History of Public Works in the United States 1776–1976* (1976), and in Raymond H. Merritt, *Engineering in American Society 1850–1875*.

NANCY FARM MANNIKKO

KIRKWOOD, John Gamble (30 May 1907–9 Aug. 1959), physical chemist, was born in Gotebo in the Oklahoma Territory, the son of John Millard Kirkwood, later president of Kansas Motor Car Company, and Lillian Gamble. Kirkwood attended the College Hill Elementary School in Wichita, Kansas, and entered Wichita High School at age thirteen. Three years later he enrolled in the fledgling California Institute of Technology (Caltech) with 160 other young men. Strong preparation in mathematics enabled him to take advanced calculus and differential equations. He studied freshman chemistry with James Edgar Bell; junior organic chemistry with Howard J. Lucas (one of the nation's first physical-organic chemists); junior physical chemistry with Stuart Jeffrey Bates, using a new textbook (*An Advanced Course of Instruction in Chemical Principles*) by department head Arthur Amos Noyes; and physics. These subjects were the foci of Kirkwood's career. Two years later he transferred to the University of Chicago, graduating with an S.B. degree in 1926.

Kirkwood entered the Massachusetts Institute of Technology (MIT) in February 1927 and received his Ph.D. in 1929. His thesis research ("An Experimental Study of the Dielectric Constant of Carbon Dioxide as a Function of Its Density") was directed by physical chemist Frederick G. Keyes, with whom Kirkwood published six papers during postdoctoral appointments at MIT between 1930 and 1934.

Kirkwood broadened his experience in physics and chemistry during postdoctoral fellowships at Harvard (1929–1930) with John Slater. In 1930 he married Lillian Gladys Danielson; they had one child. He traveled to Europe in 1931 to study for a year with Peter Debye at Leipzig, Arnold Sommerfeld at Munich, and Fritz London at Berlin. At Leipzig (together with George Scatchard, on leave from MIT), Kirkwood extended the pioneering theories of Debye on the electrical forces between ions in water solutions, investigating models for solutions of simple salts and for solutions of amino acids and proteins. Characteristically, Kirkwood described each model clearly, developed the consequences in impressive mathematical detail, and interpreted the results for chemists who had

comparatively little mathematical sophistication. His paper on a statistical theory of intermolecular forces appeared in the *Journal of Chemical Physics* (1933) together with contributions from most American leaders of physical chemistry; Kirkwood was to publish at least one paper annually in this journal for more than a decade.

In 1934 Kirkwood was appointed assistant professor at Cornell University in Ithaca, New York. He received the American Chemical Society Award in Pure Chemistry in 1936, presenting the paper "Statistical Mechanics of Liquid Solutions" (*Chemical Reviews* 19 [1936]: 275–307). Kirkwood was visiting associate professor of chemistry in 1937–1938 at the University of Chicago and returned to Cornell as Todd Professor of Chemistry. In 1941 he suggested in the *Journal of Chemical Physics*, a new method of fractionating proteins by electrophoresis convection, which he and coworkers developed into an instrument commercialized by Caltech's Arnold O. Beckman.

During World War II Kirkwood worked on theories of shock waves and explosives for the Navy Office of Scientific Research and Development, for the Naval Ordnance Laboratory and Ballistics Research Laboratory at Aberdeen Proving Ground (Maryland), and for the Los Alamos (New Mexico) Scientific Laboratory. He developed a polyelectrolyte battery and was a consultant for the Atomic Energy Commission.

In May 1947 the Noyes professorship was established in Linus Pauling's molecular biology program at Caltech, and Kirkwood was appointed to that chair. He taught courses in statistical mechanics, advanced chemical thermodynamics, and quantum chemistry. He received the Theodore William Richards Medal in 1950.

Yale appointed Kirkwood Sterling Professor of Chemistry, director of the Sterling Chemistry Laboratories, and chairman of the chemistry department in 1951. He joined a department already exceptionally strong in the physical chemistry of solutions; the faculty included Raymond Fuoss (with whom he had collaborated since 1941), Herbert Harned, Philip Lyons, Louis Meites, Lars Onsager, Benton Owens, Andrew Patterson, and Julian Sturtevant. Sturtevant was pioneering in biophysical chemistry research, and Kirkwood hired protein physical chemist Seymour Jonathan Singer from Caltech. It was a stimulating group of colleagues for Kirkwood. He was elected to the National Academy of Sciences (1942), the American Philosophical Society (1943), the American Academy of Arts and Sciences (1948), and the American Association for the Advancement of Science (1948). In 1952 he and his wife divorced.

In 1953 Kirkwood was awarded the Gilbert Newton Lewis Medal, recognizing him as "a scientist's scientist." University of Wisconsin's Joseph O. Hirschfelder wrote that he regarded Kirkwood "as one of the greatest scientists of our generation." Kirkwood undertook extensive lecture tours throughout the world in this period. He was on the editorial boards of *Archives of Biochemistry and Biophysics*, *The Physics and*

Chemistry of Solids, *Journal of Chemical Physics*, and *Molecular Physics*.

In 1956 Kirkwood was appointed director of the Division of Sciences at Yale, in part because of his leadership in obtaining computer resources for the graduate school. Two years later he was diagnosed with inoperable colon cancer, but he continued his demanding schedule of teaching, administration, and writing. Also in 1958 he married Platonia Kaldes. On leave from Yale for the spring semester 1959, he spent two months at the University of Chicago before going to Europe for four months. He was Lorentz Professor at the University of Leiden in the Netherlands during May. He lectured at a June course on thermodynamics of irreversible processes in Varenna, Italy. He returned to New Haven, Connecticut, on 6 August and died at Grace–New Haven Hospital.

Kirkwood, in the tradition of Willard Gibbs and Peter Debye, used mathematics confidently and freely as a language to expose quantitatively the consequences of chemical models. He was an able experimentalist, an exceptionally creative and productive theoretician, an effective mentor, and a trusted leader in the scientific community. The Kirkwood medal, recognizing outstanding contributions in chemistry, is awarded annually in his honor by the Yale chemistry department and the New Haven Section of the American Chemical Society.

• Lecture notes from Kirkwood's graduate course in advanced chemical thermodynamics were compiled by Irwin Oppenheim, Alexander Rich, and Martin Karplus into a mimeographed edition. Oppenheim published a revised version as a textbook, *Chemical Thermodynamics* (1961). Kirkwood's 147 pages of mimeographed notes from his statistical mechanics lectures at Princeton (spring 1947) also circulated widely. Both sets of notes are in the Manuscripts and Archives Department, Sterling Memorial Library, Yale University, as is a collection of his scientific correspondence for the years 1951–1959 and a list of his 130 publications from 1930 to 1954. Kirkwood's research papers were reprinted in eight volumes together with commentaries: *Quantum Statistics and Cooperative Phenomena*, ed. Frank H. Stillinger, Jr. (1965); *Dielectrics, Intermolecular Forces, Optical Rotation*, ed. Robert H. Cole (1965); *Macromolecules*, ed. Peter L. Auer (1967); *Proteins*, ed. George Scatchard (1967); *Shock and Detonation Waves*, ed. William W. Wood (1967), including summaries or reprints of his reports to the Office of Scientific Research and Development from the 1940s; *Selected Topics in Statistical Mechanics*, ed. Robert W. Zwanzig (1967); *Theory of Liquids*, ed. Berni J. Alder (1968); and *Theory of Solutions*, ed. Zevi W. Salsburg, with commentary by Jacques C. Poirier (1968). References are not consistently given to the original sources. For research publications from 1953 to 1959, see the biennial *Directory of Graduate Research* (1955, 1957, 1959). An obituary is in the *New York Times*, 11 Aug. 1959.

GEORGE FLECK

KIRKWOOD, Samuel Jordan (20 Dec. 1813–1 Sept. 1894), politician and businessman, was born in Harford County, Maryland, the youngest child of Jabez Kirkwood, a farmer and blacksmith, and Mary Alexander Wallace, the second wife of Jabez. Kirkwood

was educated at a school situated on a corner of the Kirkwood farm and, later, at his uncle's private school in Washington, D.C. He taught school briefly in York County, Pennsylvania, and then clerked in his brother's Washington, D.C., drug store. In 1835 economic considerations motivated the Kirkwoods to move to Richland County, Ohio, near Mansfield, to farm eighty acres. During the next several winters Kirkwood also taught school in the district.

In 1840 Kirkwood was appointed deputy assessor of Richland County, and he also clerked in a store owned by the county assessor. A year later he moved to Mansfield, the county seat of Richland County, to read law with Thomas W. Bartley, a future governor and supreme court justice of Ohio. Admitted to the bar in 1843, Kirkwood went into partnership with Bartley. Later that year Kirkwood married Jane Clark, a teacher. He was elected county prosecutor in 1845 and remained in office until 1849. In April 1850 he was elected a delegate to the Ohio Constitutional Convention, charged with the task of revising the state's governance document, and served from May 1850 to March 1851. During 1851 he went into partnership with Barnabas Burns, following Bartley's election to Ohio's supreme court. In 1855 the Kirkwoods moved to Iowa to be near Jane's family. There Kirkwood joined Jane's brother, Ezekiel Clark, in a milling and farm operation, while the childless Jane cared for her brother's children.

Originally a conservative, antislavery Democrat, Kirkwood helped found the Iowa Republican party in 1856 largely because of his antipathy to the Kansas-Nebraska Act, which allowed territories to decide whether they would be "slave" or "free." In 1856, too, he was elected to the Iowa senate where he helped enact legislation to create the State Historical Society. Motivated by both personal ambition and a strong sense of public service and responsibility, Kirkwood held important elective and appointive offices for the next twenty-five years. In 1857 he was elected chairman of the Republican State Central Committee, and in 1859 he became his party's nominee for governor. Running largely on an antislavery platform and adopting a deliberate casualness of attire, Kirkwood defeated his Democratic opponent, former U.S. senator Augustus C. Dodge.

Kirkwood performed the finest service of his long political career during his two terms as governor of Iowa, 1860–1864. After supporting Abraham Lincoln's nomination and electoral campaign, he became one of the president's stalwart supporters during the critical early years of the Civil War. "I supported the administration in conducting the war, before it struck at slavery," he wrote. "I support it now when it strikes at slavery and I shall continue to support it if it ceases to strike at slavery." Though formerly a political moderate, Kirkwood was compelled by the demands of office to espouse and voice the more radical positions of his party during the war, including his view of secession as treason, his determination to prosecute the war to its fullest regardless of fiscal costs, his call for the use of black troops, and his support of conscription, which was unnecessary while he occupied the governor's office. He also had to contend with, and ultimately suppress, the antiwar activities of secret societies within Iowa. Called Copperheads by the Republicans, such groups as the Knights of the Golden Circle engaged in various subversive plots to end the war.

Refusing to seek a third consecutive term as governor and also declining to become ambassador to Denmark, Kirkwood returned to the practice of law in 1864. However, he could not resist an opportunity to become U.S. senator when James Harlan (1820–1899) resigned his Senate seat to become secretary of the interior that same year. Governor William M. Stone permitted the Iowa legislature to fill Harlan's unexpired term, and that body elected Kirkwood in January 1866. He served until 4 March 1867 and did not participate in the impeachment trial of President Andrew Johnson. Harlan returned as Kirkwood's successor for the full term then.

From 1867 to 1875 Kirkwood engaged in the practice of law. He became the compromise Republican candidate for governor in 1875 when the frontrunner, James B. Weaver, fell short of the needed votes for nomination. Despite his opposition to the growing Prohibition movement in the Iowa Republican party, Kirkwood was elected as Iowa's governor for the third time. His persistent ambition to be U.S. senator prompted him to resign as governor when the Iowa legislature selected him to be U.S. senator for a full term beginning on 4 March 1877. In 1881 he resigned to accept appointment as secretary of the interior under President James A. Garfield. As senator he supported the Republican positions favoring protective tariffs and a sound, specie-based currency. As interior secretary, he sought to improve the educations and living conditions of Native Americans. When President Chester A. Arthur replaced him in the cabinet with another appointee, Kirkwood returned to Iowa to assume the presidency of the Iowa City National Bank. Except for an unsuccessful race for Congress in 1886, he remained a private citizen for the rest of his life. He died at his home in Iowa City.

Kirkwood never acquired the national renown of several of his contemporaries in the U.S. Senate or cabinet. He was a dedicated, moderately conservative, journeyman Republican who devoted himself to public service throughout his life whenever the opportunity arose. His career as teacher, prosecutor, state legislator, governor, senator, and cabinet member strongly outweighed his activities in business and law. In public office and out he followed the mainstream of his party on the various issues of the day. His significance for posterity rests upon his activities as governor of Iowa during most of the Civil War years.

• Kirkwood's public and private papers and letterbooks are in the State Historical Society of Iowa, in Des Moines and Iowa City. Benjamin F. Shambaugh included Kirkwood's official papers as governor in *The Messages and Proclamations of the Governors of Iowa*, vols. 2 and 4 (1903). Dan E. Clark wrote Kirkwood's biography, *Samuel Jordan Kirkwood* (1917). See also William B. Hesseltine, *Lincoln and the War Governors* (1948), and Leland Sage, *William Boyd Allison* (1956). Hubert H. Wubben, *Civil War Iowa and the Copperhead Movement* (1980), is a fine study of Kirkwood's wartime leadership.

MORTON M. ROSENBERG

KIRLIN, Florence Katharine (6 Oct. 1903–25 July 1987), government official, was born in Kendallville, Indiana, the daughter of Edmond S. Kirlin, a factory foreman, and Nellie Vesta Latson, a former schoolteacher. She entered Indiana University in 1920 as a business major and received her bachelor's degree in 1924. In 1926 she received an M.A. in psychology from the same institution.

Also in 1926 Kirlin became executive secretary of the Indiana League of Women Voters in Indianapolis, where she played an active role in promoting the League's legislative program, which supported reforms such as child labor and school attendance laws, a state public welfare system, and permanent registration of voters. During her seven years with the Indiana League, Kirlin developed skills in dealing with the state legislature and the press that would prove extremely valuable in her later career.

In 1933 Kirlin took a leave of absence to join the Federal Emergency Relief Administration (a predecessor of the Works Progress Administration), which was set up to provide jobs and work relief during the depression. She was put in charge of women's and professional projects for the state of Indiana. By the time she left in 1934, 10,000 women were employed on public work projects in the state.

In 1934 Kirlin moved to Washington, D.C., to become congressional secretary (later congressional and principal secretary) for the National League of Women Voters. During her ten years with the National League, she became an expert on the legislative process and got to know many members of Congress personally. She continued to battle for reforms such as the Food, Drug, and Cosmetic Act of 1938, which considerably improved the consumer protection provisions of the 1906 Food and Drug Act. At the national Republican and Democratic political conventions every four years, Kirlin presented the League's position on issues to the platform committees. During each congressional election she also distributed questionnaires to determine where the candidates stood on the issues and the voting record of each incumbent.

In August 1944 Kirlin left the League to become director of personnel research for the United Nations Relief and Rehabilitation Administration (UNRRA), a new international organization created to provide relief for countries liberated from the Axis powers. In March 1945, at a time when few women were in professional nonclerical positions in the Department of State, she joined the department as special assistant to Dean Acheson, who was then assistant secretary of state for congressional relations and international conferences. Her League of Women Voters experience made her familiar with the background, committee assignments, and attitudes of most congressmen and senators, and Acheson assigned her to research and to keep track of all legislation affecting the Department of State. After Acheson became under secretary of state in August 1945, Kirlin served as his executive assistant until he left in June 1947.

In August 1947 the congressional relations function was transferred to the new Department of State counselor, Charles "Chip" Bohlen. Kirlin became Bohlen's special assistant and essentially acted as his deputy. Shortly after Acheson became secretary of state in January 1949, in response to a letter from Eleanor Roosevelt asking that the Truman administration put women in positions where they had a say on policy, the new secretary mentioned Kirlin as one of several women already in "highly responsible positions" in the Department of State (Homer L. Calkin, *Women in the Department of State: Their Role in American Foreign Affairs* [1978]).

The position of assistant secretary for congressional relations was restored after Acheson became secretary, and Kirlin returned to the Bureau for Congressional Relations. During the next thirteen years she served six assistant secretaries, functioning as senior congressional relations specialist for the bureau.

Kirlin became responsible for following through the entire legislative process all legislation dealing with economic matters, particularly foreign aid and trade, that affected the Department of State. She helped the Bureau of Economic Affairs to develop its yearly legislative program and advised the legal adviser's office, which usually drafted department legislation, on what Congress's point of view was likely to be toward proposed legislation. She helped to plan the department's presentations before Congress and briefed department officials scheduled to appear before congressional committees on the issues and the positions of the committee members. She also acted as liaison with the Senate Foreign Relations Committee and the House Foreign Affairs Committee.

As a representative of the Bureau of Congressional Affairs, Kirlin attended a session convened in Geneva from 28 October 1954 to 7 March 1955 by the contracting parties of the General Agreement on Tariffs and Trade (GATT) to modify the 1947 GATT agreement and to draw up a charter for an international organization for trade cooperation. (The latter was never approved by Congress.) Later in 1955 she served as acting assistant secretary of state for congressional relations for three and a half months while Assistant Secretary Thruston Morton was in Geneva—the first woman ever to hold such a position.

In 1962 Kirlin served briefly as the Department of State liaison with the newly formed Peace Corps and helped to plan the Peace Corps's first international conference in Puerto Rico. She then became United Nations adviser to the department's Bureau of Economic Affairs. In this position she worked with the Bureau of International Affairs to coordinate U.S. policy on international economic and trade issues raised in the United Nations and other international organizations. She also attended the annual U.N. Economic and Social Council (ECOSOC) meetings in Geneva as adviser to the U.S. delegation.

During her twenty years at the Department of State, Kirlin served as one of a handful of women pioneers who filled senior positions with exceptional competence and skill and who helped to pave the way for the much larger number of professional women who joined the department after she retired in 1965. As former Assistant Secretary for Congressional Relations William Macomber said at her memorial service, Kirlin was a "tremendous inspiration" to him and to her colleagues and had been an effective liaison with Congress during the postwar period when good relations between the Department of State and Congress were of critical importance.

Soon after her death in Washington, D.C., Kirlin was chosen by Radcliffe College's Arthur and Elizabeth Schlesinger Library on the History of Women in America as one of thirty-eight women federal employees honored for their contributions to American life. She never married.

• Kirlin left no papers or autobiography. The primary source of information regarding her career is a Women in Federal Government Project oral history interview dated 17, 18, and 19 November 1981, which was part of a project begun by the Arthur and Elizabeth Schlesinger Library on the History of Women in America at Radcliffe College to record the careers and contributions of women who began their federal government careers during the first half of the twentieth century. An obituary is in the *Washington Post*, 28 July 1987.

NINA DAVIS HOWLAND

KIRSTEIN, Louis Edward (9 July 1867–10 Dec. 1942), retailing executive and civic leader, was born in Rochester, New York, the son of Edward Kirstein, an eyeglass manufacturer, and Jeanette Leiter. After completing grammar school, Kirstein engaged in a number of business occupations. He managed the business affairs of minor league baseball teams in the South and later owned the American Association team in Rochester. Early in his career, he experienced a series of financial mishaps and reportedly turned down an offer from George Eastman to become an early investor in the Kodak camera. In 1896 Kirstein married Rose Stein, whose father was a wealthy merchant of men's clothing. Kirstein joined his father-in-law's firm in 1901.

Business had taken Kirstein to Boston on numerous occasions; there he made the acquaintance of Edward A. Filene and Lincoln Filene, proprietors of the William Filene's Sons Company, a successful retailer of women's clothing. After protracted negotiations, begun in 1909, Kirstein agreed to invest $250,000 and joined the Filene firm in 1911. The Filene brothers had courted Kirstein primarily for his expertise in the merchandising of men's wear, and added that line when Kirstein joined the firm. Kirstein joined as one of four vice presidents of the firm. Negotiations among the Filene brothers and the vice presidents resulted in an arrangement whereby Edward and Lincoln Filene each held twenty-six percent of the voting common stock of the firm, and each of the vice presidents held twelve percent. The 1913 agreement also called for control of the firm to pass from the Filene brothers to the vice presidents by 1 March 1928. After the resignation of one vice president at the beginning of World War I and the death of another in 1925, Kirstein and the other remaining vice president, Edward J. Frost, acquired increasing influence within the firm. Kirstein assumed authority for all store publicity and most merchandising and became known for such industry adages as, "retailing needs less figuring, more fingering."

As Kirstein's power grew, his relationship with Edward Filene steadily deteriorated. Although a generous philanthropist and supporter of labor's right to organize, Kirstein was decidedly profit-oriented in his business practices, and directed most of his attention to day-to-day operation of the store. Filene, while jealously viewing himself as Kirstein's equal in merchandising expertise, demonstrated more interest in idealistic social experimentation. Filene organized one of the first employee credit unions in the nation, and, rather than simply cede control to the company's vice presidents under the 1913 agreement, he later proposed a plan to allow all store employees to purchase an interest in the firm. Kirstein found an ally in Lincoln Filene, and by 1928 Edward, although still president of the firm, unhappily found himself little more than a figurehead. In direct contradiction with Edward's wishes to have Filene's become employee-owned, the firm joined with F. & R. Lazarus of Columbus, Ohio, and Brooklyn's Abraham & Straus to form the widely held Federated Department Stores in 1929. Shares of Lazarus and Abraham & Straus stock were traded for fractional shares of Federated stock; Filene's shares were traded evenly.

Lincoln Filene and Kirstein actively sought cooperative efforts with other department stores to share sales data and acquire mass buying power. Kirstein was active in the Retail Research Association, a consortium of nineteen department stores organized in 1917 to exchange data regarding sales and operating expenses, and the Associated Merchandising Corporation, founded the following year, which operated buying offices throughout the world. In 1939 Kirstein served as chairman of the American Retail Federation, established during the depression as a lobbying and publicity organization for retailers.

In his travels for business and pleasure, Kirstein made nearly a hundred trips to Europe and visited Australia. Never owning a home in Boston, Kirstein resided with his wife and three children in luxurious Back Bay apartments.

In an article in the *Atlantic Monthly*, "Mind Your Own Business" (Oct. 1932), Kirstein urged business executives to focus on their own firms' affairs rather than answer recurring calls to lead charitable organizations. Despite this directive, Kirstein maintained a strong presence in civic and religious affairs. A long-time member of the Board of Trustees of the Boston Public Library, Kirstein was one of the library's most generous benefactors and provided both a building and operating capital for a business research branch, named for his father, that opened a few blocks away from Filene's main store in 1928. Kirstein also gave time and money to hospitals, the Boy Scouts, and various Jewish organizations, including the American Jewish Committee, which he served as vice president. A supporter of Franklin Roosevelt's New Deal, Kirstein was chairman of the National Recovery Administration's Industrial Advisory Board in 1933. He also chaired the Boston Port Authority and served on state and local public safety commissions.

Although quick to point out that he had little formal schooling, Kirstein supported higher education, and served on the Harvard Graduate School of Business's Board of Visitors. A frequent speaker before business and charitable organizations, Kirstein offered two distinct themes. Among retailers, he emphasized that careful attention to the needs and desires of consumers was the key to generating profits (which in turn created jobs); before social welfare and civic groups, he championed efforts to reduce human suffering. Kirstein combined these themes in a talk before Harvard faculty and students in the 1920s, where he declared that "business ought to contribute to three large ends in the social development of this country. First, it ought to contribute toward efficiency in the production of wealth. Second, it ought to contribute toward justice in the distribution of wealth. Third, it ought to contribute toward wisdom in the consumption of wealth."

Kirstein died in Boston. His will provided significant sums to charitable organizations.

• Kirstein's papers are in the Historical Collections of the Baker Library, Harvard University. The collection includes copies of Kirstein's speeches and extensive correspondence regarding business matters and civic activities. Kirstein published a second essay in the *Atlantic Monthly*, "Full Value Received," Jan. 1939, pp. 88–95. See also Tom Mahoney and Leonard Sloane, *The Great Merchants* (1974). An obituary is in the *New York Times*, 11 Dec. 1942.

PEYTON PAXSON

KIRTLAND, Jared Potter (10 Nov. 1793–10 Dec. 1877), naturalist and physician, was born in Wallingford, Connecticut, the son of Turhand Kirtland, a land agent, and Mary Potter. Kirtland's father moved from Connecticut to Poland, Ohio, in 1803, leaving Kirtland behind in the care of his maternal grandfather, Jared Potter, who was a physician and naturalist. Kirtland attended the Wallingford and Cheshire Academies and, under the tutelage of his grandfather, had an extensive education in natural history and particularly in horticulture. When his father became ill in 1810, Kirtland traveled to Poland, Ohio, frequently stopping along the way to study natural history and to visit gardens and orchards. Upon arriving in Poland, he began teaching in the village school and may have intended to stay for a prolonged period, but the death of his grandfather in 1811 caused Kirtland to return to Wallingford. He inherited Potter's library and enough money to enable him to study medicine, first with preceptors in Wallingford and Hartford, and then, beginning in 1813, at the new medical school at Yale. In 1814 he attended medical school at the University of Pennsylvania but returned to Yale, from which he received a medical degree in March 1815. Continuing his studies in natural history, he studied geology and mineralogy at Yale with Benjamin Silliman and botany with Eli Ives, and at the University of Pennsylvania he studied botany with Benjamin Smith Barton. In May 1815 he married Caroline Atwater; they had three children.

Kirtland opened a medical practice that same year in Wallingford, where he also served as village postmaster and in 1818 was elected judge of probate court. From 1818 to 1823 he practiced medicine in Durham, Connecticut. Throughout this period, his interest in natural history and horticulture grew. He developed gardens and orchards and experimented with growing various plants from seeds and with the budding and grafting of fruit and ornamental trees. In 1822 his youngest daughter died, and a year later his wife died. Shortly thereafter he returned to Poland with his surviving children. He brought with him a small stock of his fruit and ornamental trees, forming a nucleus around which he developed elaborate orchards and plantings at his new home. Although he had intended to establish a mercantile business in Ohio as his chief means of income, a need there for physicians persuaded him to continue his medical practice. In 1825 he married Hannah Fitch Tousey of Newton, Connecticut; they had no children. In the summer of 1829 his only son died. His second wife died in 1857.

From the time he arrived in Poland, Kirtland devoted himself to his medical practice and to studies in natural history and horticulture, but he found time for political service as well. In 1828 he was elected to the Ohio State Legislature, where he served three terms. He worked for reform in prisons, particularly advocating the substitution of industrial work for idleness. He also served on legislative committees for canals and medical colleges, in the former case helping to secure a charter for the Ohio and Pennsylvania Canal.

Kirtland made his most significant discovery in natural history in 1829 when he observed that the naides, or fresh-water mollusks, believed to be hermaphroditic, were in fact bisexual and that innumerable species described in the literature were simple sexual variations on this mollusk. This work was published in "Observations on the Sexual Characters of the Animals Belonging to Lamarck's Family of Naïdes" (*American Journal of Science and the Arts* 26 [July 1834]: 117–20).

In 1837 Kirtland joined the faculty of the Ohio Medical College in Cincinnati. Shortly afterward he also accepted a position with the Ohio Geological Survey. Like some other states, such as New York, Ohio included a natural history survey in the geological survey, and Kirtland was hired as naturalist. Giving up private practice at this time, he confined his medical activities to teaching and consulting so that he would have enough time to devote to the survey. He never again had a private practice. His report for the survey, published in the *Second Annual Report of the Geological Survey of the State of Ohio* ([1838], pp. 157–200), was the most comprehensive catalog of the animals of the state that had yet been published. Further work for the survey was precluded by the survey's demise in 1838, when the state legislature failed to allocate additional money for the project.

In 1842 Kirtland left the Cincinnati school to join the faculty at the Willoughby Medical College, east of Cleveland. At Willoughby, however, Kirtland was among several faculty members who became unhappy with educational standards there and decided to form another medical school. As a result, Kirtland became a founder in 1843 of the Medical Department of Western Reserve University (now Case Western Reserve University) in Cleveland, where he was professor of the theory and practice of medicine until 1863 and, for several months in 1846, served as dean of the school. He retired in 1864 and was named emeritus professor of the theory and practice of medicine.

Kirtland was active in the medical affairs of Cleveland and of the state. He encouraged the building of a new school of medicine, often with personal donations of cash, and argued for fair compensation of physicians and standardized fees. In 1839 he was elected president of the Third Ohio Medical Convention, and in 1848 he was elected president of its successor, the Ohio State Medical Society. At the beginning of the Civil War he offered to examine recruits at Cleveland and Columbus and donated his pay from these services to the Soldiers Aid Society of Northern Ohio. He made no major contributions to theoretical medicine, but, in contrast to general medical opinion, he believed that typhoid fever was spread through drinking water from wells and cisterns. He therefore encouraged the use of water from Lake Erie, provided it was taken from a place in the lake that was free of contaminants. The city subsequently adopted his idea.

Throughout this period in Cincinnati and in Willoughby, Kirtland had continued to maintain his farm in Poland. In 1838 or 1839, however, he acquired a farm on Detroit Road, five miles west of Cleveland in what was then called East Rockport (now the city of Lakewood). He wanted to create a model farm and orchard where he could experiment with improved varieties of flowers and fruits. He was especially interested in cherries and developed twenty-six varieties, which earned him the local name "cherry king."

Always interested in organizing people of like interests and in disseminating information, Kirtland worked to establish a school of agriculture in the state and was a leading member of the Ohio Agricultural Society. In 1845 he organized the Cleveland Academy of Natural Sciences, which met in his lecture room at the medical school. That same year he established a museum of specimens at the medical school and gave public lectures on natural history. To encourage still more interest in natural history, Kirtland established a magazine called the *Family Visitor*, published in Cleveland from 1850 to 1853, which contained many of his own observations on plants and animals. In 1860 he helped organize the North American Beekeeper's Society and served as its first president. In 1869 the Cleveland Academy of Natural Sciences was reorganized as the Kirtland Society of Natural Sciences, of which he was president until 1875.

Kirtland's activities and comments suggest that he leaned toward broad social, political, and religious reform. He opposed slavery, was a member of the Free Soil party, refused to be affiliated with any particular church, and favored coeducation. He admitted women to his medical lectures and sometimes held special classes in taxidermy for women at his home.

Kirtland had a library of more than 6,000 volumes and published over 200 articles during his lifetime, mostly on natural history and horticulture. He carried on a lively correspondence with naturalists, botanists, zoologists, and horticulturalists but rarely attended scientific meetings that were not held in his immediate vicinity. His work on the Naides was widely known and recognized, as was his work with plants. His name and work are immortalized in the names of several species, such as the Kirtland Warbler, discovered in Ohio and named in his honor by his friend Spencer F. Baird, and in such diverse other ways as the Kirtland Pump Station, through which water from Lake Erie is brought to the city of Cleveland, and the Kirtland Hall of the Cleveland Museum of Natural History. Known locally as the "Sage of Rockport," Kirtland was characterized as enthusiastic, wise, animated, impressive, and single-handedly responsible for early knowledge of the natural history of the Mississippi Valley. Kirtland thought of himself as indecisive and cautious in all his actions but successful primarily because of his desire to please others and to excel. He died at his farm in Rockport, Ohio.

Kirtland's work in natural history and medicine shows him to have been a keen observer and hard worker. The area in which he may have had the most far-reaching influence is horticulture, but an extensive evaluation of his influence in this area has yet to be attempted.

• A collection of Kirtland's papers at the Western Reserve Historical Society in Cleveland contains a sketch of Kirtland that is possibly autobiographical. A collection at the Cleveland Museum of Natural History contains many articles about Kirtland, copies of correspondence from other collections, and extensive correspondence concerning efforts to research Kirtland's life and contributions. A large collection of letters addressed to his friend Samuel P. Hildreth is in the Hildreth papers at the Marietta (Ohio) College Library. A few of Kirtland's books are in the Special Collections Department of the Case Western Reserve University Library. The rest of his library in medicine, natural history, and horticulture is at the Historical Division of the Cleveland Health Sciences Library. Two of his bound letterbooks covering the period 8 Feb. 1850 to 27 June 1853 and 12 Apr. 1854 to 1 Aug.

1856 are in the Historical Division of the Cleveland Health Sciences Library. The most useful general articles on Kirtland are John S. Newberry, "The Ohio Naturalist," *Cleveland Herald*, 24 May 1879, the source from which most later sketches are taken; Charles Whittlesey, "Personnel of the First Geological Survey of Ohio," *Magazine of Western History* 2 (1885): 76–81; and Agnes Robbins Gehr, "Jared Potter Kirtland," Cleveland Museum of Natural History, *Explorer* 2, no. 7 (1952): 1–32. Newberry's sketch was read before the National Academy of Sciences in 1879 and published in National Academy of Sciences, *Biographical Memoirs* 2 (1886): 129–38.

PATSY GERSTNER

KISS, Max (9 Nov. 1882–22 June 1967), pharmacist and businessman, was born in Kisvárda, Hungary, the son of Illes Kiss, a lumber merchant, and Regina Schwartz. In 1897, after finishing high school, Kiss left home and came to the United States via Hamburg, Germany. In later years he would recount that he had heard from a cousin that "everyone in America shoveled gold right from the streets," and Kiss wanted to shovel.

Kiss arrived in New York City penniless. He wandered the streets for sixteen hours before being directed to the Baron de Hirsch Home, a shelter for immigrants. Within days he got a job nailing skins for a furrier at $2.50 a week. About a month later, he became an apprentice druggist and in 1902 entered the Columbia University College of Pharmacy. He graduated with a Ph.G. in 1904 and became a citizen of the United States that same year.

In 1906, at age twenty-four, Kiss returned to Hungary to visit his family. On the voyage to Europe, Kiss met a physician who told him about phenolphthalein ($C_{20}H_{14}O_4$), an odorless and tasteless white crystalline synthetic organic compound that had been developed a few years before by the German chemist Karl Joseph Bayer, the inventor of aspirin. Initially, phenolphthalein was used as an analytical reagent in acid-based titration. Once in Hungary, Kiss learned that a Hungarian professor, Zoltan von Vamossy, had accidentally discovered phenolphthalein's laxative properties while testing it for harmlessness for use in detecting adulterants in wine. Knowing from his experience working in a drugstore that there was a sizable market for laxatives, Kiss saw an opportunity.

For the next year, Kiss experimented (mostly on himself) to find the right dosage and to check the reliability of phenolphthalein as a laxative. His innovation was the combining of the powder with a pleasant-tasting chocolate base. Kiss knew that children, especially, fought against taking castor oil, then the most common laxative. Kiss's new, pleasant-tasting laxative won wide acceptance.

In 1906 Kiss quit his job as a pharmacist to concentrate on the manufacturing, packaging, and marketing of his laxative, which he originally named Bo-Bo (from bonbon). However, that name had a prior claimant. Kiss later recalled that he came up with a new name when his brother, Adolf, while reading a Hungarian newspaper, commented, "They have ex lax in Hungary." Ex lax was a legal term for an extraordinary condition of stalemate in the Hungarian Parliament; in short, it was when all legislative and governmental functions were blocked. The name Ex-Lax could also be construed as a contraction for excellent laxative.

The Ex-Lax company grew rapidly, but Kiss discovered that he lacked the capital to expand fast enough to keep up with the demand. Undercapitalized in its early years, the firm incorporated in 1906, with Israel Matz, a drug wholesaler, supplying most of the additional funding. Under Kiss's management, Ex-Lax became the world's largest selling laxative. In 1910, he married Mina Cohen; they had two children.

Kiss's real genius lay in sales and advertising. He used point-of-purchase displays and free consumer samples to introduce his product. Also one of the first to exploit the new media of motion pictures to promote his product, Kiss produced a movie commercial for showing in local theaters. Millions of Americans saw young children climbing a tree to eat apples and then running home to mom with a stomachache. Of course, the movie mom reached for the Ex-Lax. Kiss later recounted that when he made the commercial "there were no apples on the tree so I bought some and tied them on. I found out later it was an oak tree."

Kiss realized that many customers asked their druggists to recommend a laxative, so he offered store owners shares of Ex-Lax stock at one share per $10 order. Later these shares would be purchased for $500 per share by the General Cigar Company. As a result of Kiss's extensive and innovative marketing, the Ex-Lax logo, stenciled on the corner drugstore's window, became a part of Americana. (For example, an Ex-Lax logo is a prominent part of Edward Hopper's painting *Drugstore*.)

Kiss served as secretary of the firm from 1908 to 1928 and as treasurer and chairman of the board from 1908 until his death. Although Kiss's personal genius was primarily in marketing, it was under his leadership that the Ex-Lax company moved into product development and became a diversified pharmaceutical company with plants in Canada and England in addition to the United States. In 1966, the year before his death, Ex-Lax, Inc., had sales of over $10 million.

Kiss was active in philanthropy and civic affairs. He was honorary president of the Convalescent Home of New York in Brooklyn. He was president of the Brooklyn College Hillel Building Corporation when it built a center at the school. He was active in the Federation of Jewish Philanthropies, B'nai B'rith, the American Pharmaceutical Association, and the Boy Scouts. Kiss died in Atlantic Beach, Long Island, New York.

• The Pharmacy Library of the University of Wisconsin School of Pharmacy in Madison has a biographical file on Kiss as part of their Kremers Reference Files collection. See also the article in *Drug Trade News*, 5 Aug. 1963. Obituaries are in the *New York Times*, 23 June 1967, and *Time*, 30 June 1967.

JAMES D. NORRIS

KISTIAKOWSKY, George Bogdan (18 Nov. 1900–7 Dec. 1982), chemist and government adviser, was born in Kiev, Russia, the son of Bogdan Kistiakowsky, a professor of legal philosophy at the University of Kiev, and Marie Berenstam. Kistiakowsky attended private schools in Moscow and Kiev. Concluding during the revolution of 1917 that the Bolsheviks were completely authoritarian, he sympathized with the anti-Bolshevik cause and joined the White Russian army during World War I as a soldier in the infantry and the tank corps. After enduring a bout of typhus, he fled from the Red Army on a commandeered ship and spent a year in the Balkans and Turkey.

Choosing not to return to the Union of Soviet Socialist Republics, Kistiakowsky entered the University of Berlin in 1920, with financial support from an uncle. He completed his undergraduate work quickly and earned a Ph.D. in chemistry in 1925, with a dissertation on the decomposition of chlorine monoxide from light or by added chlorine. For a short time he was assistant to his adviser Max Ernst August Bodenstein. On a fellowship from the International Education Board, from 1926 to 1928 Kistiakowsky was at Princeton University, where he was associated with chemist Hugh Stott Taylor. During his first year there he married Hildegard Moebius from Sweden; they had one child. In 1927 he published as a monograph of the American Chemical Society *Photochemical Processes*, which was well received by other scientists. In 1928 he became an assistant professor at Princeton, and soon thereafter, with W. T. Richards, published "An Attempt to Measure the Velocity of Dissociation of Nitrogen Tetroxide by the Method of Sound Waves (*Journal of American Chemical Society* 52 [1930]: 4661–71), which first demonstrated the earlier prediction by Albert Einstein that the velocity of sound could be used to measure rates of chemical reactions.

In 1930 Kistiakowsky became an assistant professor of chemistry at Harvard University, at the invitation of James Bryant Conant, chairman of the chemistry department. In 1933 he became a U.S. citizen and advanced to associate professor at Harvard, then to the position of Abbott and James Lawrence Professor of Chemistry in 1937.

Kistiakowsky was a lively teacher, noted for a sense of humor that included practical jokes, and encouraged students to question and to solve problems themselves. At times he livened his lectures with pyrotechnics. He was a capable laboratory researcher, who, according to colleague Edgar Bright Wilson, Jr., believed "that a good physical chemist should be personally skilled in the manual arts of the plumber, carpenter, glass-blower, mechanician and electrician, with a bit of electronics and optics thrown in and a good command of methods of solving differential equations" (Dainton, p. 381).

In the field known as chemical kinetics, concerned with the detailed steps by which chemicals react, Kistiakowsky's researches included various aspects of photochemistry and reactions of gases. He also investigated atomic reactions, which were of keen interest to scientists in Germany, which was a major center in all aspects of physical chemistry in the 1930s. In photochemistry he created new intense light sources to ensure his results. One of his early papers, "The Ionization Potentials of Nitrogen and Hydrogen on Iron and Other Metals" (*Journal of Physical Chemistry* 30 [1926]: 1356–63), was a detailed effort to determine chemical effects at the fine surface of metals. His study with E. O. Wiig, "Photochemical Decomposition of Ammonia" (*Journal of the American Chemical Society* 54 [1932]: 1806–20), was a pioneering paper in the field. With James B. Conant, he published a summary, "Energy Changes Involved in Addition Reactions of Unsaturated Hydrocarbons" (*Chemical Reviews* 20 [1937]: 181–94). Several papers, coauthored chiefly with W. E. Vaughan in the 1930s, were on thermodynamic measurements based on heat of hydrogenation in molecules, which provided greater accuracy in determining chemical reactions. Papers in another series in the 1930s, with coauthors, were measurements of the rates at which changes occur in the geometry of organic compounds ("cis-trans" isomerization).

With colleagues Kistiakowsky published a long series under the title "Heats of Organic Reactions" in the *Journal of the American Chemical Society* in the 1930s and 1940s. He developed new equipment for many of his chemical studies, especially in calibration techniques, and his work in the field showed considerable experimental ingenuity. His paper "Some Aspects of Investigations of Molecular Structure of Organic Compounds" (*Journal of Physical Chemistry* 41 [1937]: 175–83) was a summary of physical methods that could be used to determine the structure of organic compounds.

As involvement in World War II by the United States approached, civilian scientists and President Franklin Delano Roosevelt in 1940 established the National Defense Research Committee, directed by Vannevar Bush, to provide scientific information to the military leaders. Conant, who was then president of Harvard, headed the chemistry division, and Kistiakowsky was appointed to it as chief of its explosives unit. From 1941 he was also a member of the National Academy of Sciences Committee on Atomic Energy. During visits to England in 1941 and 1942 he learned that the British had conducted more advanced research in explosives and propellants than was the case in the United States. For example, explosives mixed with various forms of fine dust were being provided to saboteurs in occupied countries. In 1942 Kistiakowsky established a laboratory at Bruceton, Pennsylvania, for further researches. His version, made with flour by a new process and known as "Aunt Jemima" (for a well-known brand of pancake mix) could actually be baked into food substances, and it was a safer material against accidents than the British products. He oversaw its testing in air and then in water at a research laboratory in Woods Hole, Massachusetts. Among other uses, it was provided to Chinese guerrilla forces against Japanese invaders.

In 1944 Kistiakowsky became leader of the explosives division of the Manhattan Project at Los Alamos, New Mexico, which developed the triggering device of conventional explosives to detonate the first atomic bomb. He observed the first test at Alamogordo, New Mexico, on 16 July 1945. He was awarded the Medal for Merit in 1946 and the British Medal for Service to the Cause of Freedom in 1948.

After World War II, Kistiakowsky resumed his teaching and research at Harvard. In addition to providing some undergraduate teaching, he advised many graduate students. Busy with his many projects, he sometimes failed to observe students' technical dilemmas promptly, according to his Harvard colleagues, but when he became aware of the problem, he provided logical analysis. "When he brought his help [to bear], everyone around knew that a major action was taking place" (Galbraith et al., p. 2). As a leader in his department, which he served as chairman from 1947 to 1950, he instigated an effort to revise admissions procedures at Harvard College, to increase the appeal for students interested in science.

Kistiakowsky published a number of papers with colleagues during the 1950s on gaseous detonations. Another field of chemistry, represented in "Structural Investigations by Means of Nuclear Magnetism: Rigid Crystal Lattices" (with H. S. Gutowsky, G. E. Pake, and E. M. Purcell, *Journal of Chemical Physics* 17 [1949]: 972–81), was the first to apply nuclear magnetic resonance to chemistry, opening up a new field in medical diagnostic techniques. With Robert Gomer in 1951 ("Rate Constant of Ethane Formation from Methyl Radicals," *Journal of Chemical Physics* 19 [1951]: 85–91), he developed a new method for determining the absolute rate of recombination of two methyl radicals, a technique that became standard. His publications in chemistry totaled more than 200, and much of his work was considered pioneering by his colleagues.

Having developed great concern over the possibility of nuclear attack, Kistiakowsky served on government advisory committees, especially for the Department of Defense on nuclear weapons, their delivery systems, and national security matters. In 1954 he urged that the development of the intercontinental ballistic missile be given high priority. In 1957 he was appointed by President Dwight D. Eisenhower a member of the President's Science Advisory Committee. After participating in 1958 in a conference in Geneva, Switzerland, with representatives of the U.S.S.R. on reducing the dangers of surprise attack, he devoted his efforts to reducing the international arms race and urging an agreement to reduce stockpiles of nuclear weapons.

When James B. Killian, Jr., resigned as the presidential science adviser in 1959, Kistiakowsky was appointed by President Eisenhower to the position, for which he took a leave of absence from Harvard. In this role he advised the president on new military weapons programs, on nuclear arms control, and on proposals for agreements to stop the testing of nuclear weapons. Kistiakowsky's diary of this time, *A Scientist at the*

White House (1976), describes the meetings of panels and councils, comments on distinguished foreign and domestic visitors to the White House, and, from an insider's viewpoint, describes the complexity of policy making at the highest level.

After his resignation as presidential science adviser in 1961, Kistiakowsky returned to Harvard and devoted his efforts to more research in chemistry, to some advisory committees, and to the National Academy of Sciences. His collaborations in the 1960s and 1970s included many analyses of shock waves and additional papers on the nature of gaseous detonations. From 1962 to 1969 he served on the advisory board to the U.S. Arms Control and Disarmament Agency. His judgment, expressed during hearings on the Nuclear Test Ban Treaty of 1963, was that "only a Pyrrhic victory could be achieved in a nuclear war" (quoted in Rathjens, p. 2).

Kistiakowsky served the National Academy of Sciences as the first chairman of its Science and Public Policy and Report Review committees. From 1965 to 1972, as vice president of the academy for two terms, he set up a study group on world population problems. He advised the military on efforts to scale down the war in Vietnam but was dissatisfied with the military policies. In 1967, concerned about that war, he severed all his advisory positions to U.S. military officials. He participated in the several Pugwash conferences on science and world affairs that began in 1958, and in 1977 he became chairman of the Council for a Livable World, which was an effort by scientists and other concerned citizens to advise the U.S. Senate on a rational arms policy and to prevent nuclear war. In public forums he criticized the allocation of federal resources to defense and to the space program instead of to civilian technological programs, and he strongly opposed any escalation of nuclear weapons. His publications on these subjects included "The Limitations of Strategic Arms" (with G. W. Rathjens, *Scientific American* 222 [1970]: 19–29), "Strategic Armsrace Slowdown through Test Limitations" (with Herbert F. York, *Science* 185 [1974]: 403–5), "The Arms Race: Is Paranoia Necessary for Security?" (*New York Times Magazine*, 27 Nov. 1977), and "A Chemist Speaks Out on the Neutron Bomb" (*Chemical Engineering News* 56 [24 Apr. 1978]).

Kistiakowsky was divorced in 1942 and married Irma E. Shuler in 1945; they had no children and were later divorced. He married Elaine Mahoney in 1962; they had no children. He became emeritus professor at Harvard in 1971.

Kistiakowsky's accomplishments in chemistry were recognized by seven medals from the American Chemical Society and its sections, the Lehman Award of the New York Academy of Sciences, the Franklin Medal of the Franklin Institute, and other honors. He was elected to the National Academy of Sciences in 1939. For his service to the federal government, in addition to the awards cited earlier, he received the Medal of Freedom in 1961 from President Eisenhower, the National Medal of Science from President Lyndon B. Johnson in 1967, and the Exceptional Service Award of the U.S. Air Force in 1967. He died in Cambridge, Massachusetts.

• Kistiakowsky's correspondence and other papers are at Harvard University Archives. A biographical account is Frederick Dainton, "George Bogdan Kistiakowsky, 1900–1982," *Biographical Memoirs of Fellows of the Royal Society* 31 (1985): 377–408, which includes a bibliography of his scientific publications. Memorials include those by George W. Rathjens, "George B. Kistiakowsky, 1900–1982," *Bulletin of the Atomic Scientists* 39 (1983): 2–3; by Jerome B. Wiesner, "George Kistiakowsky," *Physics Today* 36 (1983): 70–72; and by J. Kenneth Galbraith et al., "George Bogdan Kistiakowsky," *Harvard University Gazette*, 21 Dec. 1984. Obituaries are in the *New York Times* and the *Washington Post*, 9 Dec. 1982.

ELIZABETH NOBLE SHOR

KITCHIN, Claude (24 Mar. 1869–31 May 1923), congressman and majority leader, was born in Scotland Neck, North Carolina, the son of William Hodge Kitchin, a former congressman and Populist party official, and Maria F. Arrington. Kitchin graduated from Wake Forest College and married Katherine Mills, daughter of one of his professors, in 1888; they had nine children. Two years later he won admission to the bar and then traveled the state as a bank examiner. He later became president of his home town's small bank. He was elected to Congress in 1900 by supporting the Democratic party's white supremacy campaign, which was particularly virulent in the eastern part of the state. He took the seat of a black lawyer, Republican George H. White, who had served two terms. In only one future race, after challenging the preparedness policies of President Woodrow Wilson in 1916, did he face significant opposition, and then he won handily. In all he served twelve terms.

Kitchin's early career in Congress was similar to that of most other Democratic representatives from the South. He voted against tariffs, gibed at Republican foibles, and loyally supported his party's leadership. Named to the Ways and Means Committee in 1911, he helped shape the Underwood-Simmons tariff of 1913. The workings of the seniority system brought him to the post of majority leader in February 1915, after the election of Oscar W. Underwood of Alabama to the Senate. On only a few issues—such as his consistent and long-standing opposition to a large navy—did he demonstrate much independence of either the Democratic platform or, after 1913, the Democratic president.

Kitchin became majority leader of the Democratic House just as the country began to experience the effects of the Great War and President Wilson was moving to a position of what he termed "a wise preparedness." Although Kitchin supported the president's stand on the torpedoing of the *Lusitania* by the Germans, he came out publicly against Wilson's plan to enlarge the army and increase the navy, both of which he insisted were unnecessary to ensure the nation's defense. Unable to block the president and defeat his preparedness program, he was in an excellent position as chairman of the Ways and Means Committee to determine how to finance the plan. While the administration devised excise taxes to pay for preparedness appropriations, Kitchin successfully piloted increased income and inheritance taxes and a special tax on munition makers through the House to pay for all but $8 million of the $274 million defense budget.

In response to Wilson's request for a declaration of war, Kitchin took the floor in April 1917, to oppose American involvement. Dramatically defying his party and president on a major issue, the majority leader insisted that "nothing in that cause [of the Allies], nothing in that quarrel, has or does involve a moral or equitable or material interest in or obligation of our Government or our people." His stance, a result of his small-town southern heritage and his irritation with wealthy munitions manufacturers, swelled the antiwar vote in the lower chamber from probably a dozen to fifty, but it tarred him as a renegade. After war was declared, Kitchin returned to a position of supporting the administration, even on the issue of conscription, about which he had serious reservations. On the issue of taxation, however, he became determined to force those who profited from the conflict to pay for it. In the Revenue Act of 1918, which Kitchin intended as a permanent part of the internal revenue code, he included a graduated excess profits tax on corporations that, an opposing administration spokesman wrote, "goes to the very root of the social and economic problem." He shepherded the tax successfully through the House, watched the Senate mangle it, and then patched it up in conference committee; it remained a major achievement for progressives during World War I. Not surprisingly, it fell victim to the Republican administration of Warren G. Harding, which brought about its prompt repeal. Kitchin suffered a stroke in April 1920. He died in Wilson, North Carolina.

• Kitchin's papers are located in the Southern Historical Collection at the University of North Carolina at Chapel Hill. Useful secondary sources include Alex M. Arnett, *Claude Kitchin and the Wilson War Policies* (1937); H. Larry Ingle, "Pilgrimage to Reform: A Life of Claude Kitchin" (Ph.D. diss., Univ. of Wisconsin, 1967); H. Larry Ingle, "The Dangers of Reaction: Repeal of the Revenue Act of 1918," *North Carolina Historical Review* 44 (Jan. 1967): 72–88.

H. LARRY INGLE

KITCHIN, William Hodge (22 Dec. 1837–2 Feb. 1901), lawyer and politician, was born in Lauderdale County, Alabama, the son of Boas Kitchin and Arabella Smith, planters. Kitchin grew up in his parents' hometown of Scotland Neck in Halifax County, North Carolina, in the heart of the state's black belt, after they moved back from Alabama in 1841. The family struggled during the recession in the 1840s but retained their slaves. At twenty-two Kitchin matriculated at Emory and Henry, a Methodist college in southwestern Virginia, but he did not graduate because the Civil War intervened. He promptly enlisted, rising to captain, a rank

"Cap'n Buck" prized all his life. On furlough in 1863 he married Maria Figus Arrington of a prominent local family; they had eleven children, including two congressmen (one also a governor), a college president (Thurman D. Kitchin of Wake Forest College), and a state senator. Returning to the Army of Northern Virginia, the newlywed was wounded and captured at Spotsylvania Courthouse in May 1864. Always determined and strong-willed, he refused to take the oath of allegiance at the war's end and remained in federal custody until mid-June 1865. Physically domineering, fast-tempered, and combatant, Kitchin modestly described himself as a military Baptist, a convenient stance in a region where Baptists outnumbered other denominations. In politics, he cultivated his seemingly instinctive knack for bombast and hurled religion and race, sometimes both together, at enemies.

Kitchin was admitted to the bar in 1869 and soon thereafter journeyed to California to settle a large land claim, earning $20,000. He speculated in mortgages, timber, and real estate, loaned money to poorer neighbors, and on occasion served as an agent for northern lending firms. In 1872, more by default than because of aptitude, he got the Democratic nod against a white Republican for the Second District congressional seat but could not overcome the solid black majority. Six years later, two black Republicans split the vote in a race for the same seat, and Kitchin's support of Greenback-tinged economic reforms won him 45 percent and the coveted spot. Despite championing greenbacks over national bank notes and endorsing an income tax, his single term produced little save verbal spats with another member, Daniel Russell, a Republican later to be North Carolina's governor and requisite attacks on proposals to enforce black voting rights. "Let no man call me a leveler," he vociferated. Renominated in 1880, this time he faced a Republican party united under a white carpetbagger and carried only three of the district's ten counties.

By the mid-1880s Kitchin had gained notoriety as one of the state's most outspoken white supremacists; he was also a determined critic of national Democrats, particularly President Grover Cleveland, whose support of the gold standard smacked too much of Wall Street and his Republican predecessors. Josephus Daniels, editor of the Raleigh *News and Observer*, denominated him "the original advocate of white supremacy and the father of the expression." Editing his hometown weekly, the *Democrat*, Kitchin had a ready platform to draw the color line and oppose tariffs, national banks, and lengthy pension lists. He firmly decided by 1888 that issues of revenue, fraud, and corruption won no votes, so he counseled other partisans that "when you talk of negro equality, negro supremacy, negro domination to our people, every man's blood rises to boiling heat at once." By 1892 Kitchin was disgruntled enough by Cleveland's ascendancy in the Democratic party to counsel that his nomination would be a "plausible, if not a solid, reason for a third party," but he could not bring himself to join the recently organized Populists, even if they shared his disgust for the gold standard; indeed, to counter them, he garnered a state legislature seat for the Democrats. After the legislature adjourned, he secured a federal appointment, going to New Orleans to enforce Chinese exclusion, but he quit in disgust after six weeks because of the low pay.

A year later, in May 1894, in a surprising turnabout, a fed up Kitchin announced his conversion to the Populist party and brought his special brand of oratorical vitriol to the cause of defeating Cleveland's policies. Though he opposed Populist platform planks for a federal subtreasury system and public ownership of railroads, the party touted him as evidence of a Democratic surge into their ranks and named him to the state executive committee. His efforts did help boost Republican-Populist fusionists to their massive victory in 1894. However, aghast at the results of racial power sharing in the reform-minded legislature—not to mention its failure to reward him with the post of state prison superintendent—Kitchin opted again for the white man's party and white metal in 1896, all the while passing himself off as a Populist. This strategy failed, with fused Populists and Republicans sweeping the state from governor on down. Like other prominent white leaders, Kitchin, proclaiming that he had never been off the Democratic platform, threw himself into the effort to disfranchise black voters. In the midst of this white supremacy campaign two years later, the state was electrified at the audacity of a black Halifax official who swore an affidavit before the Supreme Court that Kitchin and other armed men had invaded his home in the dark of night to frighten him into resigning. His black eyes flashing, Cap'n Buck mounted an airtight alibi, in court and out, and got the warrant for his arrest dismissed. His son William Walton Kitchin won the Fifth District congressional seat in 1896 and the governorship in 1909, and his son Claude Kitchin won his old position in 1900, both beneficiaries of the antiblack tide their father had done so much to propel. Kitchin's death in Scotland Neck ended the career of one of the state's most race-conscious figures, a southern Democrat at large, even as a Populist.

• Letters from, to, and about Kitchin are scattered in various manuscript collections in the Southern Historical Collection at the University of North Carolina at Chapel Hill, but no collection of his correspondence has been found. For a contemporary's published assessments, see Josephus Daniels's memoirs, *Tar Heel Editor* (1939) and *Editor in Politics* (1941). A picture of Kitchin in his Civil War uniform is opposite p. 605 in vol. 1 of Walter Clark, ed., *Histories of the Several Regiments and Battalions from North Carolina* (1901). Eric Anderson, *Race and Politics in North Carolina, 1872–1901: The Black Second* (1981), includes background on Kitchin's congressional district and valuable information about him. H. Larry Ingle, "A Southern Democrat at Large: William Hodge Kitchin and the Populist Party," *North Carolina Historical Review* 45 (1968): 178–94, is the only published study, although a sketch by Eric Anderson appears in *Dictionary of North Carolina Biography*, vol. 3 (1988). An obituary is in the Scotland Neck *Commonwealth*, 7 Feb. 1901.

H. LARRY INGLE

KITCHIN, William Walton (9 Oct. 1866–9 Nov. 1924), congressman and governor, was born near Scotland Neck, Halifax County, North Carolina, the son of William Hodges Kitchin, a lawyer and congressman, and Maria Arrington. The youth attended the local Vine Hill Academy before enrolling at Wake Forest College, from which he graduated in 1884. At first Kitchin embarked upon a career in teaching and journalism, teaching at a local school and working part-time as editor of the *Scotland Neck Democrat* in 1885–1886. He also read law with his father and with John Manning at the University of North Carolina at Chapel Hill, and he was admitted to the bar in 1887. In January 1888 Kitchin moved to Roxboro, North Carolina, to practice law, but he quickly developed an interest in local politics. In 1890 he became chairman of the county executive committee of the Democratic party.

Kitchin's political career accelerated in the 1890s. He was the unsuccessful Democratic nominee for the state senate in 1892. That year he married Musette Satterfield, with whom he had six children. In 1893 he served as a state legislator and spent time on bills and proposals dealing with schools, eleemosynary concerns, budgetary matters, and local constituent requests. Three years later, in 1896, he won election as a Democrat from the Fifth Congressional District to the U.S. House of Representatives. This victory gave him the distinction of being the only Democrat elected to Congress from North Carolina that year, a time of local Republican-Populist ascendancy and national Democratic divisions. The Democrats split over the presidential candidacy of William Jennings Bryan and the vexatious currency issue of the gold standard versus the free coinage of silver.

Kitchin represented his constituency in the House from 1897 to 1909 and served on the Committee on Naval Affairs and the Committee on Manufacturers, among others. Espousing Bryan's political philosophy, he delivered speeches in the House in support of silver coinage (24 Mar. 1898) and in opposition to President William McKinley's foreign policy and imperialism (17 May 1900). On 31 May 1900, in a forceful presentation, Kitchin attacked the trusts and urged more stringent enforcement of antitrust measures.

By 1908 Kitchin decided to leave Congress to seek the governorship of his state. Running on an antitrust, reform platform against the candidate of the machine wing of his party, Asheville attorney Locke Craig, Kitchin secured the Democratic gubernatorial nomination and was elected governor by a majority of some 37,000 votes. Serving from 1909 to 1913, he increased public expenditures for education, public works, and health care. He signed legislation for the protection of forests, regulation of foodstuffs, regulation of packing and sale of fish, appointment of inspectors of utility meters, free treatment of indigent people afflicted with diphtheria, and prohibition of blacklisting. He also supported improvements in factory conditions, Prohibition, child labor laws, direct primaries, regulation of corporations, balanced budgets, and new road construction. His was a reform-minded administration in tune with the Progressive movement of the era, but his many successes also earned him political enemies. Kitchin lost a bid for renomination in 1912, overpowered by the machine of U.S. senator Furnifold M. Simmons, who backed Craig for the governorship.

Upon the expiration of his gubernatorial term in 1913, Kitchin returned to private practice and never again entered public life. He practiced law for five years in Raleigh, North Carolina, with the firm of Manning and Kitchin. When his health began to decline, he retired to his home in Scotland Neck, where he died.

An impressive political figure who antagonized some Democratic stalwarts, Kitchin was a competent congressman and governor in an era of change. A brother of Claude Kitchin, one of the most brilliant orators in Congress, he was an outstanding speaker who sought reforms and voiced the concerns of the common people of his state.

• The Kitchin papers are in the Southern Historical Collection at the University of North Carolina at Chapel Hill. The papers consist of approximately 2,000 items and include personal, professional, and political correspondence, speeches, letterbooks, clippings, and photographs. Other letters are in the manuscript collections of his contemporaries, including the Woodrow Wilson Papers in the Manuscripts Division of the Library of Congress. Kitchin's speeches are in the *Congressional Record* from 1897 to 1909. Obituaries are in the *New York Times* and the *Raleigh News and Observer*, 10 Nov. 1924.

LEONARD SCHLUP

KITTREDGE, George Lyman (28 Feb. 1860–23 July 1941), professor of English, was born in Boston, the son of Edward Lyman Kittredge, a storekeeper, and the widowed Deborah Lewis Benson. Kittredge went to Roxbury Latin School in 1875 and to Harvard to study classics in 1878, supported by money from friends. At Harvard he came under the influence of Francis James Child, the first professor of English at Harvard and a pioneering scholar in ballad literature. After graduating Kittredge became in 1883 a Latin teacher at the Phillips Exeter School in Exeter, New Hampshire. There he met Frances Gordon, daughter of another teacher at the school; they married in 1886 and had three children.

Kittredge, who had been working privately under the direction of Child and had spent a year of study in Germany (1886–1887), began teaching in the English department at Harvard in 1888 and was appointed full professor in 1895. He taught principally Shakespeare, Chaucer, English and Germanic philology, and Old English. His classes were famous, and he became a legendary figure in undergraduate mythology (his graduate classes were notably more relaxed and informal). He lectured on texts line by line, answering appropriate questions from students in minute philological detail, and kept his classes in awe with a mixture of genuine erudition and pedagogic trickery (he always brought his remarks to a close walking down the aisle and out of the lecture hall as the hour bell tolled). He

cut an imposing figure, white-haired and white-bearded from the age of 40, handsomely patriarchal, an inveterate cigar smoker; he always dressed in a pale-gray suit and carried a cane, with which he would remove offending undergraduate headgear; he was ever conscious of his dignity and lived in a barely suppressed fury at any slight that might be offered to his favorite authors, himself, or the English language.

He was never chairman of the English department, nor did he ever take a Ph.D. "Who would have examined me?," he is reputed to have replied when asked why he lacked a doctorate, but honors and honorary degrees were showered on him throughout his life. In 1913 he was presented with the *Kittredge Anniversary Papers* and in 1917 was named first Gurney Professor of English Literature. Two high points in his career were the address on Shakespeare that he gave on 23 April 1916 in the Sanders Theatre at Harvard at the request of the president and Fellows of Harvard College, and the Northcliffe lectures on Shakespeare that he gave at University College, London, in 1932. The latter were followed by a triumphal tour throughout England, as the foremost American literary scholar of his day, and the award of an Honorary Litt.D. at Oxford. His retirement in 1936 was a public event, announced in the Boston newspapers; he toured the United States in 1937, lecturing on Shakespeare, a kind of royal progress.

Kittredge's first published work was the revision, with James Bradstreet Greenough, of Joseph H. Allen and Greenough's *Latin Grammar* (1888), but he soon began to emulate F. J. Child, his great teacher. His *Observations on the Language of Chaucer's Troilus* (1894) was modeled directly on Child's study of Chaucer's language, and *Words and Their Ways in English Speech* (1901), a nontechnical account of English word formation, etymology, and semantic change that he wrote with Greenough, was dedicated to Child's memory. His edition of Child's *English and Scottish Popular Ballads* (1904) is a work of the first importance in making Child's formidable scholarship more accessible to the general reader. Meanwhile, he was doing other editorial work (the Latin *Arthur and Gorlagon*, 1903) and much occasional work as a writer of reviews, encyclopedia articles, and school textbooks, such as *The Mother Tongue* (1900), a primer that he wrote with Sarah Louise Arnold, and *An Advanced English Grammar* (1913).

Another area of activity, again pioneered by Child, was in the study of folklore and folk history. *The Old Farmer and His Almanack* (1904) is a popular collection of New England folklore, but *Witchcraft in Old and New England* (1929) is a lavishly annotated compendium consisting of three long and substantially researched chapters (on medieval witchcraft, English witchcraft and James I, and the New England background to the Salem witch trials of 1692, the last two published separately some years before) filled out with chapters of a more anecdotal kind on broader topics. The book is written, as always, in a lively and engaging way, and the tone is wise, benevolent, paternal, authoritative: "common misapprehensions" were meat and drink to Kittredge. But, though "historical understanding" is constantly invoked, there is little sense of historical contingency or change: like folklore, witchcraft for Kittredge is universal and identical whether found among our forefathers, "uneducated folk today," or "contemporary savages" (p. 23).

Kittredge's greatest importance, however, is as a literary scholar and critic. *A Study of "Sir Gawain and the Green Knight"* (1916) is a classic of its kind, a study of the relationships of the sources and analogues of the great fourteenth-century English poem, based on a division of the poem into plot elements that are then traced back to their different origins. The technique is that of historical phonology, textual stemmatics, or folktale motif analysis, all of them quasi-scientific forms of investigation that have remained influential throughout the twentieth century. Kittredge concludes by arguing that *Gawain* is derived directly from a lost French original in which the major plot elements were already combined.

Kittredge's work on Chaucer has been of much more far-reaching and long-lasting importance. It began early, with his brilliant essays, "Chaucer's Pardoner" (1893), "Chaucer and Some of His Friends" (1903), and "Chaucer's Discussion of Marriage" (1912), and the best of it is enshrined in the six lectures that he gave at Johns Hopkins in 1914 and published in 1915 as *Chaucer and His Poetry*. Here, in a wide-ranging survey of Chaucer's principal poems, Kittredge propounds his belief in Chaucer as a great dramatic poet and a master of psychological realism: as Bradley was to Shakespeare, so is Kittredge to Chaucer. *Troilus and Criseyde* is a "masterpiece of psychological fiction" and "the first novel, in the modern sense, that ever was written in the world, and one of the best" (p. 109). *The Canterbury Tales* is a "Human Comedy," principally interesting for its dramatic revelation of the character of the pilgrims: "the Pilgrims do not exist for the sake of the stories, but *vice versa*. Structurally regarded, the stories are merely long speeches expressing, directly or indirectly, the characters of the several persons" (p. 155). This view of Chaucer's two major poems has been enormously influential, and Kittredge's book is still widely read. Kittredge's technique is to present himself as an authoritative guide to the poems, serenely confident of all the eternal verities of the human condition, warm, optimistic and reassuring in his humanity, and genially dismissive of other views or of the possibility of conflict or disturbance within the poems (the salacious comic tales, or fabliaux, are never mentioned). The reading is characterized by Kittredge's inimitable grace and ease of style, dazzling simplicity, and fatherly certainty. Even when no one is left who believes what he says, everyone will want to read what he writes.

Kittredge's lectures on Shakespeare, for which he was perhaps most famous in his day, found their way into print only through a series of annotated editions of single plays, culminating in his one-volume annotated Shakespeare (1936). But he will be chiefly remembered as a critic of Chaucer, as a legendary Harvard cult figure, and as the teacher of generations of American medieval scholars, including John Matthews Manly, Karl Young, Carleton Brown, and John Livingston Lowes.

• A large Kittredge archive is in the Widener Library at Harvard University, including college prize papers, lecture notes, class readings, and notes by eminent students (including those of F. N. Robinson, 1891–1892) from his Chaucer lectures. All of Kittredge's major full-length publications are mentioned above. His most important independently published essays are as follows: "Chaucer's Pardoner," *Atlantic Monthly*, Dec. 1893, pp. 829–33; "Chaucer and Some of His Friends," *Modern Philology* 1 (1903–1904): 1–18; "The Date of Chaucer's Troilus," *Chaucer Society*, 2d ser. 42 (1909); "Chaucer's Discussion of Marriage," *Modern Philology* 9 (1911–1912): 435–67; "Chaucer's Lollius," *Harvard Studies in Classical Philology* 28 (1917): 47–133. Clyde Kenneth Hyder, *George Lyman Kittredge: Teacher and Scholar* (1962), is a full-length biography. A briefer notice is in Rollo Walter Brown, "King of the Anglo-Saxons," chap. 4 of his *Harvard Yard in the Golden Age* (1948). See also James Thorpe, *Bibliography of the Writings of George Lyman Kittredge* (1948), and a valuable brief biographical introduction by Bartlett Jere Whiting to the 1970 reissue of Kittredge's *Chaucer and His Poetry*. An obituary by J. L. Lowes is reprinted in *Harvard Scholars in English*, ed. W. J. Bate (1992).

DEREK PEARSALL

KITTREDGE, Mabel Hyde (19 Sept. 1867–8 May 1955), civic and social worker, was born in Boston Massachusetts, the daughter of Rev. Abbott Eliott Kittredge, a pastor of New York's Central Presbyterian Church, and Margaret Ann Hyde. Kittredge attended private schools, finishing her formal education at Miss Porter's School in Farmington, Connecticut, but she never "translated these privileges into any sense of social exclusiveness or superiority; and . . . never regarded her education as 'finished'" (Gilkey, sect. 3).

Wanting "to make a more abundant life possible for all those who had been denied her privileges" (Gilkey, sect. 3), Kittredge joined social worker Lillian Wald at the Henry Street Settlement House in New York City's Lower East Side. Ideally, the settlement house provided a place for local immigrants to interact through organized activities and to learn necessary skills or knowledge to adjust to American life. Convinced that the greatest hindrance to immigrants was poor housing conditions, in 1901 Kittredge founded and was president of the Association of Practical Housekeeping Centers in New York.

Emphasizing hands-on learning, the association created a model flat in the Russian Jewish quarter of the tenements and provided daily lessons to the foreign population and poor on cleaning, hygiene, cooking, child rearing, personal health, and budgeting within limited means. Kittredge explained in her 1905 article, "Homemaking in a Model Flat," that the "home-making center stands for the right of every child to have a healthy start in life, by giving him intelligent care during the first years of childhood" (*Charities and the Commons*, pp. 180–81). The second model flat was established in an Italian neighborhood with trained Italian-speaking teachers. While laws were passed to guarantee certain standards of housing (such as indoor plumbing), Kittredge found that housing conditions did not improve because newcomers, who were expected to "build our subways and our skyscrapers," were not instructed on the use of the modern day conveniences. In her article "The Need of the Immigrant" (*Journal of Home Economics* 2 [Oct. 1913]), she wrote, "I believe sometimes these people must long just to see once how it ought to be done when one lives on the sixth floor instead of in a cottage; how it ought to be done to please the housekeeper, the tenement house inspector, and the street cleaning department" (p. 308). Kittredge recognized, however, that providing immigrants with a model home and instruction was not sufficient. In order to help immigrants take advantage of domestic advancements, one had to know and understand the immigrant. "It seems as though we hand out improvements to the immigrant, but we do not, so to speak, make him one of the committee. We do not even take the trouble to meet him and know him and understand how to obtain his cooperation" (p. 310).

In 1913 Kittredge arranged for the construction of two model flats on Ellis Island to ensure that the immigrant's first impression of home management in the United States was positive. By 1915 her successful program convinced the New York public school system to adopt a housekeeping program as part of its curriculum. Each participating public school either aligned itself with a nearby housekeeping center or built a model flat of its own with the Board of Education paying for the instructor.

In addition to her active social work, Kittredge published three books providing instructions on economizing, furnishing, and keeping the home sanitary: *Housekeeping Notes: How to Furnish and Keep House in a Tenement Flat* (1911), *Practical Homemaking: A Textbook for Young Housekeepers* (1914), and *A Second Course in Homemaking, with Two Hundred Inexpensive Cooking Receipts* (1915). In 1917 Kittredge answered President Wilson's wartime call to women to practice strict economy with *The Home and Its Management: A Handbook in Homemaking with Three Hundred Inexpensive Cooking Receipts*, in which Kittredge argued that "there is a close relation between the homes of a nation and the health of a nation, and an intimate relation between the homes of a people and the character of a people" (p. 3).

Kittredge believed that adequate daily nourishment was integral to a successful education system. In 1908 she organized a lunch system for New York elementary schools and in November of that year the first lunch was served. The School Lunch Inquiry Committee, founded by Kittredge, supervised the diet, concessionaires, costs, and solicitation of outside help for students unable to pay. In her 1910 article, "Experiments with School Lunches in New York City," Kittredge

concluded, "if the State is to educate children . . . it is mere waste of money to try to educate a half starved child" (*Journal of Home Economics*, p. 174).

At the close of World War I in 1919, Kittredge assisted Herbert Hoover by working with the Committee for the Relief of Belgium in raising funds for the impoverished women and children in war-stricken Belgium and northern France. She was honored by the city of Lille, France, for her contribution with a beautiful emblem woven of the finest lace with the arms of Great Britain, France, and America intertwined around those of Belgium. In 1920 she was appointed a member of the Belgian American Educational Foundation in New York. That same year she traveled with fellow social workers Jane Addams and Alice Hamilton to the newly organized Soviet Union to study the effect the Russian Revolution had on women and children. In 1935 Columbia University awarded Kittredge a bronze medal for giving "years of an active life to improving the living and housekeeping conditions of tens of thousands of dwellers on Manhattan Island" (Gilkey, sect. 3).

Kittredge, who had never married, spent the final years of her life in the cottage she had constructed for a summer home in Bass River, Cape Cod, Massachusetts. She was known locally for her resourcefulness, self-sufficiency, warmth, and sense of humor. She died in Bass River after an extended illness and was memorialized in a printed address by Rev. Charles Gilkey of South Yarmouth Methodist Church "so our countrymen may know how one of their own New Englanders became one of America's 'Immortals' and a 'First Citizen' of Cape Cod."

• The Mabel Hyde Kittredge Papers at the Schlesinger Library, Radcliffe College, include Rev. Charles W. Gilkey's memorial address (privately printed on 10 June 1956). In addition to her works mentioned above and several articles that she published in the *New Republic*, 31 July and 18 Dec. 1915, 3 June 1916, and 11 Aug. 1917, on domestic economizing and housing, see Kittredge's "The Housekeeping Centers of New York," *Journal of Home Economics* 7 (Feb. 1915): 63–65. Obituaries are in the *New York Times*, 9 May 1955, and the *Journal of Home Economics* 47 (Dec. 1955): 753.

BARBARA L. CICCARELLI

KLAUSER, Julius (1854–22 Apr. 1907), music theorist and teacher, was born in New York City, the son of Karl Klauser, a music educator and well-known music editor, and Karolina Strasser. Trained in music by his father, who was employed as music director at Miss Porter's School for girls, Julius enjoyed the benefits of a concert series established by his father at the school. He also became acquainted with his father's many friends in the music profession, including Theodore Thomas, the first famous American symphony conductor, and composer John Knowles Paine. In 1871 Julius was sent to Germany for music studies with Salomon Jadassohn at the Leipzig Conservatory.

Returning in 1874 Klauser settled in Milwaukee, Wisconsin, where he taught music and conducted experiments in music psychology (by testing his students) that were related to his pedagogical and theoretical ideas. Believing that music is rooted in innate human perception, he gathered information about what tone-related phenomena are recognized simply and directly, how the gifted hear, and the potential for training average and ungifted students. Klauser's theoretical conclusions culminated in a book-length study, *The Septonate and the Centralization of the Tonal System: A New View of the Fundamental Relations of Tones* (1890). The work is a significant, original contribution in the history of Western music theory at the end of the nineteenth century, a period during which it became apparent that existing music theory could not reasonably accommodate innovations in the works by late nineteenth-century composers. The theories underlying current pedagogy and analysis were inadequate for explaining the chromatic language that appeared in musical compositions. Klauser's work examines some of the most fundamental issues concerning theorists at the end of the nineteenth century: the acoustical basis of music; the structure of tonal relationships; notation; and tuning. He attempted to develop a comprehensive theoretical system that could account for the new chromaticism directly, in order to eliminate the prevailing cumbersome contemporary theoretical practices.

The primary feature of Klauser's theory is the placement of the tonic or key note literally at the center of the tonal system. This is an idiosyncratic notion that was never adopted but is nevertheless logical on a rudimentary level. Whereas conventional studies claim that the simplest level of tonal relationships (i.e., those existing in the white keys of a piano) is represented by the scale of C major—C, D, E, F, G, A, B, C—Klauser asserted that the simplest level of tonal relationships is represented by what he called the Septonate, consisting of G, A, B ascending to C and F, E, D descending to C.

Klauser's work seems to have emerged in isolation from the professional field of music theory. This is symptomatic of creative work in the field in the United States at that time, when no centers for such studies existed. Therefore his work had little impact. Nevertheless Klauser's ideas are particularly noteworthy because of the strong similarities between his views and those emanating from the Austrian tradition, which later evolved in the paradigmatic work of Heinrich Schenker, probably the most influential theorist of the twentieth century, particularly in American academies. Klauser and Schenker's work developed independently but arose from the same need to explain contemporary developments in composition. Klauser was a well-trained student of the German school of music theory, but (although he never directly mentions any members of the Austrian theoretical establishment) he may have been influenced by ideas being developed in Austria that contradicted those he was being taught in Leipzig. Among the ideas Klauser shared with the forward-thinking Austrians are a contrapuntal orientation (i.e., thinking in terms of coexisting horizontal lines instead of vertical simultaneities

or chords), the ascribing of melodic origins to dissonance (in the form of melodic elaborations that conceptually replace piling-up notes in tertian formations), the possibility of interpreting chord inversion contrapuntally (rather than as an independent configuration), the interpretation of dissonant chords contextually (whereby their analysis is not determined by a dissociated, absolute label), concern with the idea of an underlying "tonality" (instead of simply local key centers at different points in a composition), and the differentiation between modulation and transitory shifts (i.e., between those tonal movements to other keys that last for a sustained period of time and momentary shifts that are simply chromatic, local elaborations). Nevertheless, there are some important differences between Klauser's system and those developed by the Austrians, such as Klauser's rejection of the significance of acoustics to music.

Klauser's work aspired to being a science of music and turned to the newly developing science of tone psychology to find music's natural, scientific basis, instead of the commonly held sources in acoustics (concern with the overtone system as the natural source of music) and physiology (concern with the structure of the ear). Klauser's vision of music was rooted in innate music perception: what people are capable of hearing. Taking issue with the harmonic orientations in existing theory pedagogy, Klauser maintained that music study should begin with counterpoint. He theorized that the genesis of a musical composition is found in its melody or "prominent voice," citing the sketchbooks of Beethoven for evidence that melody is the point of departure in the compositional process and that "the development and elaboration of thought into harmony and form is [sic] a later process." Klauser's specific formulation of the prominent voice marks a fundamental change in the history of music-theoretical ideas preceding the Schenkerian "revolution," because it identified a series of single tones that contains inherent suggestions for its harmonic elaboration as a new analytical category. Klauser's theory received a devastating review by theorist Bernhard Ziehn—known for his biting reviews—whose theoretical orientation was antithetical to Klauser's. "Their differences were derived from their aesthetic judgments, which determined . . . how they interpreted the compositional techniques used in nineteenth-century repertory." Klauser, who favored neoclassical composers like Brahms, attempted to penetrate the nature of the relationships between harmony and melody, chromaticism and diatonicism; he sought the diatonic frameworks underlying the chromatic thematic material of nineteenth-century music. Ziehn, the advocate of Liszt and Bruckner, focused on the local chromatic verticalities, "seeing music from the perspective of its newest, most innovative features" (Baron, pp. 232–34).

Klauser's second book is a largely derivative study. Never completed, it was published posthumously in 1909 as *The Nature of Music: Original Harmony in One Voice*, having been assembled from his notes by his wife, Elizabeth Eldred Klauser, whom he had married in 1883; the number of their children, if any, is unknown. Klauser had intended to devote the final chapter of the study to chromaticism and modulation. Another study, called "Birds of Idlewild, 1903," a collection of bird songs that Klauser recorded mainly near Sturgeon Bay and Silver Lake, Wisconsin, was included at the end of the posthumously published book. The location and cause of his death are unknown.

• Other than Bernhard Ziehn, "Julius Klauser's Septonat," in *Jahrbuch der Deutsch-Amerikanische Historischen Gesellschaft von Illinois*, ed. Julius Goebel, vols. 26–27 (1927), the only known discussion of Klauser's work is Carol K. Baron, "At the Cutting Edge: Three American Theorists at the End of the Nineteenth Century," *International Journal of Musicology* 2 (1993): 193–247, which is an extensive treatment of Klauser's system, placed in a historical context.

CAROL K. BARON

KLAW, Marc Alonzo (29 May 1858–14 June 1936), theatrical entrepreneur and producer, was born in Paducah, Kentucky, the son of Leopold Klaw and Caroline K. Blumgart. He moved with his widowed mother to Louisville when he was five. There he attended both elementary and public high school, after which he received his law degree from Louisville Law School in 1879. Although he practiced law for a while, his primary interest was in theater; he was for a time the dramatic editor of the Louisville *Commercial*, where he also served as press agent. It was in the latter capacity that he attracted the attention of Gus Frohman, the brother of the theatrical producers Charles Frohman and Daniel Frohman. Gus Frohman assigned Klaw his first big legal case—that of hunting down the pirates who were producing various plays without paying the required royalties. As it turned out this was also Klaw's last case, for he had become completely enamored of the theater. His legal investigations had made abundantly clear to him the chaotic and disordered condition of theatrical road shows, and he at once perceived the need for reform. To pursue his theatrical ambitions further, he abandoned the practice of law and moved to New York City around 1887.

Shortly thereafter Klaw met Abraham L. Erlanger, a leading figure among theatrical entrepreneurs. In 1888 the two men formed a partnership that lasted thirty years, during which time they gained virtual control of the American theatrical business. Although Klaw's name appeared first, Erlanger was the real power figure in the partnership. The contrast between the two men could not have been greater. Klaw was quiet and reflective, Erlanger crass and aggressive: together they were a most effective team. In their first joint venture they bought out the old Taylor Theatrical Exchange and renamed it the Klaw and Erlanger Exchange. Though their assets were meager—about $500, a few pieces of office furniture, and the contract of one leading actress, Fanny Davenport—their success was immediate. Within seven years Klaw and Erlanger's business had become the second largest agency in the country. They represented many of the theater's leading performers and controlled nearly all bookings in the legitimate theaters of the South.

In 1895 Klaw and Erlanger met secretly with a group of leading theatrical entrepreneurs, including Charles Frohman and Al Hayman. Their ostensible purpose was to bring order to the unruly business practices of the theater, especially the disorganized booking system. The result was the creation of the Theatrical Syndicate (or Trust as it was also known). Under the forceful leadership of Klaw and Erlanger, the group succeeded within a very short time in monopolizing almost every major American theater and in controlling producers, directors, and actors and actresses, to streamline economic aspects of the business and hence maximize profits. Few performers had the courage to buck the syndicate but some did resist, namely Sarah Bernhardt and Minnie Maddern Fiske, although they were often forced to perform in tents. During this time Klaw and Erlanger successfully produced a number of their own shows. For a time in 1907 they even dabbled in producing vaudeville.

The power of the syndicate was threatened by the advent of the Shubert brothers during the first decade of the twentieth century. A bitter competition between the Shuberts and the syndicate ensued, with the Shuberts emerging triumphant. They replaced the syndicate as the ruling power in America's theatrical business. Klaw and Erlanger continued to function as joint entrepreneurs until 1919, when they abruptly dissolved their partnership as a result of a personal disagreement; the two went their separate ways for the remainder of their careers. In 1920 Klaw formed his own company, which produced a number of successful plays during the 1920s. In 1921 he built the Klaw Theater on West 45th Street, which was used as a theater until the mid-1930s, when it became a radio studio for the Columbia Broadcasting System; it was demolished in 1954. Klaw's first wife, Antoinette M. Morris of Boston (marriage date unknown), died in the early 1920s (they had two children). In 1925 Klaw married Blanche Violet Day Harris, a young English woman whom Klaw had known since her childhood. They were married in Sussex, England, and the news was kept from the public for two weeks; they had no children. In 1927 Klaw withdrew from the theater business entirely, and two years later moved to Bracken Fell, Hassocks, Sussex, England, where he lived in retirement until his death.

• There is no biography of Marc Klaw. Two magazine articles he wrote contain information on the Theatrical Syndicate: "The Theatrical Syndicate," *Cosmopolitan*, Dec. 1904, and "The Theatrical Syndicate from Inside," *Saturday Evening Post*, 3 Apr. 1909. Bits and pieces of information on Klaw can be obtained from Brooks Atkinson, *Broadway* (rev. ed., 1974); Robert Grau, *Forty Years Observation of Music and the Drama* (1909), *The Businessman in the Amusement World* (1910), and *The Stage in the Twentieth Century* (1912); Arthur Hornblow, *A History of the Theatre in America*, vol. 2 (1919); Glenn Hughes, *A History of the American Theatre: 1700–1950* (1951); Brooks McNamara, *The Shuberts of*

Broadway (1990); Jerry Stagg, *The Brothers Shubert* (1968); and Garff B. Wilson, *Three Hundred Years of American Drama and Theatre* (1973). Especially valuable are the obituaries in the *New York Times*, 15 June 1936, and *Variety*, 21 June 1936.

CHARLES W. STEIN

KLEIN, Anne (3 Aug. 1923–19 Mar. 1974), fashion designer, was born Hannah Golofski in Brooklyn, New York, the daughter of Morris Golofski and Esther (maiden name unknown). (Like many Jewish Americans of her generation, Klein adopted a less Jewish-sounding variant of her name, "Anne," early in her professional career.) Hannah Golofski went to the Girls' Commercial High School in Brooklyn, where she discovered her natural gift for design. By the age of fifteen she had already obtained work as a freelancer preparing sketches for a wholesale fashion house. Upon graduation from high school, she declined a scholarship to the Traphagen School of Fashion Design in order to work full time in the garment industry. After only a year out of school she accepted a position at Varden Petites, where she redesigned the firm's entire line, replacing its dresses for short, plump figures with a line of junior dresses based on a lean silhouette. In so doing, she virtually invented a whole new set of sizes in women's ready-to-wear clothing, a category of sophisticated clothes for young women later known as Junior Miss.

The designer's precocious talent brought her to the attention of many in the New York fashion world, including Ben Klein, a prominent manufacturer of women's wear. They married in 1948, and in the same year Ben founded Junior Sophisticates with Anne as the company's principal designer. A small woman herself, Anne well understood the sartorial needs and frustrations of shorter women. Prior to her innovations, clothing in petite sizes tended to have more in common with children's wear than with adult clothes. Klein abandoned buttons, bows, and frills in favor of sleek, elegant styles that had long been the privilege of average-size and tall women, permanently transforming the design of petites' fashions. Klein was also the first American designer to follow Coco Chanel's lead in adapting men's clothes—suits, jackets, trousers, even shirts—for women.

Klein responded presciently to emerging changes in the lives of urban American women in the 1950s—the entry of increasing numbers of women into the business world, the expansion of the middle class, an increasingly informal lifestyle—by introducing the concept of separates, which allowed women to buy a flexible array of jackets, blouses, skirts, and slacks designed for mixing and matching. Klein's influence on both American and European designers was especially strong in this period of her career.

The Kleins' working relationship grew strained toward the end of the decade, and by 1960 Anne had left Junior Sophisticates and divorced Ben. She married Matthew "Chip" Rubinstein in 1963 and established that year her own freelance design studio, which was incorporated as the Anne Klein Studio two years later. Klein's business thrived; she was especially adept at the wholesale redesign of faltering lines on short notice. Among her clients were Charles Revson, who paid her an unprecedented six-figure fee for salvaging his Evan-Piccone and Dynasty lines, and Sandy Smith and Gunther Oppenheim, owners of the Pierre Cardin license for coats. So successful were Klein's designs for Smith and Oppenheim that they offered to provide the capital for her to found an independent sportswear company. Anne Klein and Company began operation in 1968, with Klein as director and half-owner. By the early 1970s Klein's clothes were carried by more than 800 American department stores and specialty shops. When the Takihyo Company of Japan purchased half interests in both the studio and the company in 1973, they acquired one of the most successful labels in women's fashion.

The simplicity and elegance of Klein's work, and her sense of line and proportion, were admired throughout her career. Her inventiveness also never diminished: in the late 1960s Klein patented a special girdle for wearing under mini-skirts; she later developed an "inside-out" women's raincoat that, with all its pockets and zippers on the inside, kept personal items dry and still easy of access; noting the difficulty small children had with buttons, she pioneered the use of snaps on doll clothes; and she designed interiors for both an aircraft and a car. Even when hospitalized and near death from cancer in 1974, Klein continued to work, drawing designs for an improved hospital room and hospital bed. She was a fashion innovator also in her use of unexpected materials (as in her jeans made of satin), and in borrowing ideas from casual or business clothes for evening wear, and vice versa (in one celebrated line of formal evening outfits, for example, she combined gray flannel and white satin). Some have credited Klein with essentially inventing sportswear, a distinctively American contribution to the world of fashion.

Klein won the prestigious Coty Fashion Award in both 1955 and 1969 and was elected to the Coty Fashion Hall of Fame in 1971. She was the first fashion designer to win the Neiman Marcus Award for Fashion Leadership more than once, receiving the award in 1959 and again in 1969. In 1973 Klein was invited as the only woman and as one of five American designers to share the runway with five leading French designers in a special fashion show to raise money for the renovation of the royal palace at Versailles. The metropolitan Museum of Art in New York City restaged the American component of the show in 1993.

One of Klein's strengths was her instinct for recognizing design talent. Bill Blass, later a major designer in his own right, was taken on by Klein early in her career to do sketches. Her own company succeeded in part because of its outstanding team of younger designers, especially Donna Karan, Louis Dell'Olio, and Maurice Antaya. (Karan went on to found her own highly profitable company in 1985; Dell'Olio, who had been co–head designer with Klein for several years before her death, assumed full responsibility for the Anne Klein line until 1993, while Antaya took over the lower-priced, youth-oriented Anne Klein II line at the same time.)

Klein died at Mount Sinai Hospital in New York City. Hundreds of leading figures in the fashion industry crowded her funeral two days later to pay tribute to a woman who was, in the words of the innovative designer Rudi Gernreich, "one of the great forces of fashion, fashion with a real American look." The Anne Klein Collection continued until 1996, when Takihyo, which had latterly become sole owners of both of Klein's companies, finally terminated the line, twenty-two years after its founder's death.

• No collection of Klein papers is known to exist. Sources of information about her career are difficult to locate; the account of her life provided above was based to a considerable extent on interviews with contemporaries of Klein. Caroline Rennolds Milbank, *New York Fashion: The Evolution of American Style* (1988), pp. 191, 226, 257, 285–86, offers few details. *Fifty Years of American Women in Fashion*, the catalog accompanying the Fashion Group's retrospective show at the Galleries at the Fashion Institute of Technology (18 Sept.–24 Oct. 1981), is more informative. The obituary and related article appearing in the *New York Times*, 20 and 22 Mar. 1974, are a useful starting-point for further research.

FRED CARSTENSEN

KLEIN, Charles (7 Jan. 1867–7 May 1915), librettist and playwright, was born in London, England, the son of Hermann Klein, a Russian immigrant, and Adelaide Soman. Although little is known of his childhood, he was a member of a family well versed in English art and culture. His brothers, Hermann, Manuel, and Alfred, were prominent as music critic, composer, and actor, respectively. Klein began his theatrical career after his arrival in the United States in 1883 when he played the title role in *Little Lord Fauntleroy* and juvenile parts in *The Messenger from Jarvis Section* and *The Romany Rye*. He married Lillian Gottlieb in 1888.

Klein first wrote for the theater in 1890, when he was commissioned to revise *The Schatchen*, in which he was then appearing. This was followed by a collaboration with Charles Coote on *A Mile a Minute* (1890), written for actress Minnie Palmer. He came into prominence as a dramatist in 1897 with the Charles Frohman production of *Heartsease*.

From the mid-1890s through the early 1900s Klein served as librettist for a number of American musicals, including *El Capitan* (1896), with lyrics by Tom Frost and John Philip Sousa; *The Charlatan* (1898), designed for De Wolf Hopper with lyrics by Sousa; *A Royal Rogue* (1900), with a score by W. T. Francis; *Mr. Pickwick* (1903), a Hopper vehicle with music by Klein's brother Manuel; *The Red Feather* (1903), a Florenz Ziegfeld production with music by Reginald de Koven; and *Cousin Lucy* (1915), with musical numbers by Jerome Kern.

Klein's immense success, however, arrived with *The Auctioneer* (1901) and *The Music Master* (1904), both written for and produced by David Belasco, in

which David Warfield became famous in the title roles. Klein's melodramas were among the most successful of the first decade of the twentieth century, primarily because of their focus on themes of contemporary life in the United States. His *The Lion and the Mouse* (1905) was prompted by a visit to the U.S. Senate. Although written on contract with Frohman, it was rejected by the manager-producer as being totally unworthy of a production. The play was eventually produced by Henry B. Harris with Klein sharing in the enormous success of the venture. Other plays of note include *The Daughters of Men* (1906), *The Third Degree* (1909), *The Next of Kin* (1909), *The Gamblers* (1910), and *Maggie Pepper* (1911). In 1913 he collaborated with Montague Glass in dramatizing some Jewish short stories that, as *Potash and Perlmutter*, were successful both in New York and in London a year later. Klein also worked for Frohman as a play reader and censor. Frohman and Klein were aboard the *Lusitania* when it sank in 1915, claiming the lives of both men.

Klein's theory of playwriting seems to have been loftier than his practice. In an Ada Patterson interview in *Theatre Magazine* (June 1906, pp. 157, 159), he was asked "Should a playwright be a man of many activities or a scholar?" He replied, "He must, primarily, be a playwright. You cannot make a musician unless the primordial germ is there. A playwright, born to his craft, builds dramas instinctively, as a beaver builds dams." In the writing of melodrama, Klein's formula was "to write the big act first and make everything else subservient," as opposed to the natural order of serious drama or tragedy where the central idea is followed by the evolution of its characters. The exposition of the theme grapples with the conflict of the characters and their personalities, and the sequence of events ultimately results in the unfolding of the plot. In Klein's melodramas, "Mechanics receive the first consideration and the characters are mere puppets bobbing about at the will of the monarch Mechanics." Klein's plays were theatrically effective in their day, and so, even if Klein's material was no match for his dedication, his work deserves a place in the annals of the American theater.

• Arthur Hobson Quinn, *A History of American Drama from the Civil War to the Present Day*, vol. 2 (1927); *Oxford Companion to the Theatre*, 4th ed. (1983); and Robert L. Sherman, *Actors and Authors, with Composers and Managers Who Helped Make Them Famous* (1951), are important sources. See also Montrose J. Moses, *The American Dramatist*, 3d ed. (1925); David Ewen, *New Complete Book of the American Musical Theater* (1970); and Gerald Bordman, *American Musical Theatre* (1978). Numerous articles appear in *Theatre Magazine* (1902–1917), as well as *Harper's Weekly*, 8 Dec. 1906; the *New York Dramatic Mirror*, 12 Dec. 1896, 2 Nov. 1910, and 12 May 1915; and the *New York Times*, 8 and 9 May 1915.

LOUIS A. RACHOW

KLEIN, Chuck (7 Oct. 1904–28 Mar. 1958), baseball player, was born Charles Herbert Klein near Southport, Indiana, the son of Frank Klein and Margaret

Vacker, farmers. Klein was a star athlete at Southport High School, from which he graduated in 1923. He worked briefly on a construction road gang and in a steel mill, where he developed his 6′, 185-pound frame by hurling 200-pound ingots.

After playing semiprofessional baseball, Klein signed a minor league contract with Evansville of the Three I League in 1927. The next year, while he was hitting .331 at Fort Wayne of the Central League, his contract was purchased for $7,500 by the Philadelphia Phillies, which outbid the New York Yankees. In 64 games with the Phillies in 1928 Klein showed signs of greatness by hitting .360.

Over the next five seasons Klein's offensive statistics were among the most outstanding in baseball history. He led the National League in eighteen offensive categories. During that span he averaged .359, along with 36 home runs per year, 139 runs batted in, 132 runs scored, 224 hits, and a slugging percentage of .636. Among National League records he established during those years were most runs scored (158) and most extra base hits (107). His 445 total bases in 1930 remained the most by any National League left-handed hitter almost seven decades later. Klein won one batting title (.368 in 1933) and the Triple Crown (first in batting average, runs batted in, and home runs), captured four home run titles (1929, 1931–1933), and was twice named the National League's Most Valuable Player by the *Sporting News* (1931, 1932).

Klein was also a superb defensive player who mastered the tricky dimensions of Baker Bowl, the Phillies' home field. With the ballpark's high tin fence only 280 feet from home plate in right field, he learned to play rebounds and caroms off the wall so effectively that he established a single-season record (1930) for assists, 44, that has not been challenged.

The financially straitened Phillies traded Klein to the Chicago Cubs in November 1933 for three journeymen players and $65,000, a huge sum at the time. In Chicago, Klein never duplicated his high quality of play with the Phillies, although he still hit .301 and .293 in his two full seasons as a Cub. In the 1935 World Series, which the Cubs lost in six games to the Detroit Tigers, he hit .333 with one home run.

With the Cubs, Klein began to experience a series of minor injuries, probably muscle pulls then called charley horses. It is believed by many that Klein's drinking began to affect his performance from the mid-1930s. He returned to the Phillies in 1936 and experienced his last strong season, scoring and driving in more than 100 runs for the sixth and final time. That July in Pittsburgh, Klein joined an exclusive group of sluggers—including Lou Gehrig, Willie Mays, and Mike Schmidt—to hit four home runs in a single game. That same year he married Marie Torpey; they had no children and divorced in 1956.

Klein's career dragged to a close after a short tour with Pittsburgh in 1939 before he returned to the Phillies; he retired following the wartime season of 1944. He also coached for the Phillies from 1942 through 1945.

Klein played seventeen years in the major leagues, producing some impressive career statistics, among them 2,076 hits, a lifetime batting average of .320, plus 300 home runs, 1,168 runs scored, and 1,201 runs batted in. His lifetime slugging average of .543 remained fifteenth among all hitters a half-century after his final game. At his death Klein held many National League hitting records, the most impressive probably being the single-season marks of most extra base hits (107) and most runs scored (158), both in 1930.

Following his playing days, Klein ran a bar in the working-class neighborhood of Kensington in Philadelphia. Heavy drinking had impaired his health, and beginning in 1948 he suffered from cancer and a disease of the central nervous system that left him a semi-invalid. He moved to Indianapolis in 1947 to live with close relatives. He died there of a cerebral hemorrhage.

Klein was elected to baseball's Hall of Fame in 1980, finally gaining the recognition he had longed for throughout his retirement years.

• Information on Klein's career is in Frank Bilovsky and Rich Wescott, *The Phillies Encyclopedia* (1993), and Lowell Reidenbaugh, *Cooperstown: Where Baseball's Legends Live Forever* (1983). Lengthy obituaries are in the *Philadelphia Bulletin* and *Philadelphia Inquirer*, both 29 Mar. 1958.

JOHN P. ROSSI

KLEM, Bill (22 Feb. 1874–16 Sept. 1951), baseball umpire, was born William Joseph Klem in Rochester, New York, the son of Michael Klimm, a German immigrant wagonmaker, and Elizabeth (maiden name unknown). Klem debuted in professional baseball in 1896 as a catcher for Hamilton, Ontario, in the Canadian League, but he developed a sore arm and was released the following year. He traveled throughout the Northeast working for a bridge construction company and playing semipro ball as a first baseman.

In 1902, while working in Berwick, Pennsylvania, he offered to umpire a game. He enjoyed the experience, and with the assistance of American League umpire Francis "Silk" O'Loughlin he signed in August 1902 to umpire in the Class D Connecticut State League. The next year he moved up to the Class B New York State League, and, following the lead of an uncle, he changed the spelling of his surname to Klem, thinking it had "a firmer sound and was a fitter name for an arbiter." In 1904 he advanced to the Class A American Association, and in 1905 he joined the National League. In 1910 he married Marie Kranz; they had no children.

During thirty-eight seasons in the major leagues, Klem became the most famous and most highly respected umpire in baseball history. Every part of his performance—his booming voice, encyclopedic knowledge of the rules, emphatic gestures when making calls, uncanny accuracy in judgment, and unquestioned control of the game—was unrivaled. The acknowledged master at calling balls and strikes, he often volunteered to umpire home plate instead of the bases after the advent of two-man crews in 1910. (The frequent claim that he called balls and strikes exclusively until 1921 is untrue.)

Despite being shorter (5′7″) than most umpires, Klem was tough-talking and stern, a disciplinarian who would not tolerate the questioning of his calls. His verbal battles with such scrappy managers and players as John McGraw and Frankie Frisch were legendary, and over his career he reputedly ejected more players and managers than any major league umpire. His trademark method for ending an argument, first used in the American Association, was to draw a line on the ground with his shoe, forbid his antagonist to cross it on threat of banishment, and smartly walk away from the argument. Klem's autocratic style resulted partly from an inflated ego, but primarily it came from a sincere belief in the correctness of his calls. Although several of his decisions were overturned by league presidents, he repeatedly issued such declarations as "I never missed one in my life" and "I never called one wrong." Only after retirement did he admit the possibility of fallibility by saying, "I never missed one in my heart." He gloried in the deferential nickname "The Old Arbitrator" given him by sportswriters, but he despised the moniker "Catfish," a derogatory reference to his supposedly piscine facial characteristics coined in the American Association.

Klem had a profound impact on the umpiring profession. The arm gestures to signal fair or foul balls that he initiated in the American Association carried over into the majors and soon became common practice throughout professional baseball. Similarly, after temporarily losing his voice in 1906, he developed the system of hand signals still used today to designate balls and strikes as well as safe and out calls. He popularized use of the padded chest protector worn inside the jacket, and he began the practice of calling pitches from a low crouch to the left of the catcher for right-handed batters and to the right for left-handed hitters, allowing the umpire a clearer view of the ball.

Perhaps most importantly, Klem helped raise the stature of umpires by demanding and commanding respect. He shunned familiarity, addressed players and managers as "Mister," and was accorded the same formality. His authoritarian style did much to curb the rowdyism that afflicted baseball in the early twentieth century, and his unquestioned personal integrity did much to establish the reputation of umpires as being scrupulously honest at a time when gambling, and even game-fixing, was common. As his personal reputation grew, he used his influence to help umpires secure better pay and working conditions, including dressing rooms at the ballpark.

Just as Tommy Connolly became the prototype for American League umpires, Klem used his personality and preferences to shape the National League staff. Because of his influence, National League umpires were shorter but more flamboyant and combative than their American League counterparts, who, while physically larger, were more diplomatic and low-key.

At Klem's insistence, National League umpires when working the plate with few exceptions wore inside chest protectors, crouched in the "slot" between the catcher and batter, and called "low" strikes, while American League umpires continued to wear the inflated "balloon" outside protector, look directly over the catcher's head, and call "high" strikes. On Klem's directive, National League umpires stood in foul territory along the foul lines and in the infield behind the pitcher with a runner on first, while American Leaguers in the same situations straddled the foul lines and stood in the outfield just behind second base.

As of the late 1990s, Klem held the record for the most World Series assignments (18) and games (108) umpired, far more than runner-up Cy Rigler's ten Series and sixty-two games. From his first postseason assignment in 1908 through 1918, he missed working only two World Series (1910 and 1916), and in one stretch he was assigned to five consecutive Series (1911–1915). His pattern after 1920 of working the Series every other year came to an end after the 1934 Series when he got into an argument with baseball commissioner Kenesaw Mountain Landis for publicly berating a player for calling him "Catfish" and betting on horse races. Landis thereafter refused to sanction Klem for the World Series, relenting only when National League president Ford Frick persuaded him to allow Klem to umpire the 1940 Series as a farewell tribute.

Except for working five games at the end of the 1941 season, Klem retired as an active umpire in 1940 to become the league's first chief of umpires in the twentieth century, a position he held until his death. During the season he supervised the league staff and scouted minor league umpires, spending the off-season in Miami Beach, his home since the 1920s, fishing from his boat *The Old Arbitrator*. He died in nearby Coral Gables.

Klem received many honors and accolades throughout his career. He and Jack Sheridan of the American League were chosen to umpire the New York Giants–Chicago White Sox world tour during the winter of 1913–1914. He represented the National League in the first All-Star game in 1933, and he was selected to umpire the 1938 contest. In 1939 he became the first umpire to receive the "meritorious service" award from the New York chapter of the Baseball Writers Association. When feted by the New York Giants on "Bill Klem Night" at the Polo Grounds on 2 September 1949, he voiced his passion for the game: "Baseball to me is not a game; it is a religion." In 1953, Klem and Tommy Connolly, his contemporary in the American League, became the first umpires elected to the National Baseball Hall of Fame.

• A clippings file on Klem is in the National Baseball Library, Cooperstown, N.Y. With the assistance of William J. Slocum, Klem wrote a brief but informative autobiography serialized in 1951 in *Collier's* as "'I Never Missed One in My Heart,'" 13 Mar.; "Jousting with McGraw," 7 Apr.; "Diamond Rhubarbs," 14 Apr.; and "My Last Big-League

Game," 21 Apr. James M. Kahn, *The Umpire Story* (1953), provides context for Klem's career, as do F. C. Lane, "The Dean of All World's Series Umpires," *Baseball Magazine*, Oct. 1933; John B. Kennedy, "Always Right," *Collier's*, 22 Apr. 1933; and Bob Considine, "Foghorn," *Collier's* 13 Apr. 1940. Important obituaries are in the *New York Times*, 17 Sept. 1951, the *Miami Herald*, 17–20 Sept. 1951, and the *Sporting News*, 26 Sept. 1951.

LARRY R. GERLACH

KLEMPERER, Otto (14 May 1885–6 July 1973), conductor, was born in Breslau, Germany (now Wrocław, Poland), the son of Nathan Klemperer, a businessman, and Ida Nathan. Both parents were musical, and Otto's mother began giving him piano lessons when he was four years old. That same year, 1889, the family moved to Hamburg, where Gustav Mahler was director of the opera company.

Klemperer graduated from the Johanneum, Hamburg's prestigious Gymnasium, in 1901, and shortly thereafter enrolled at the Hoch Conservatory in Frankfurt. After a year there he moved to Berlin, where he studied at the Klindworth Scharwenka Conservatory until 1905, and then at the Stern Conservatory for two years. His musical training included the study of piano, violin, and composition. In the following decades he wrote and published a number of musical works, including a mass, a violin concerto, and several operas and symphonies, but as early as 1905 he may have decided to pursue a conducting career.

In that year, as a student in Berlin, he conducted a performance of Gustav Mahler's Symphony No. 2 in C minor (the "Resurrection"); the composer was present and came backstage afterward to congratulate Klemperer. Mahler would soon play a definitive role in the development of Klemperer's career.

In 1906 Klemperer made his formal conducting debut in Max Reinhardt's production of *Orpheus in the Underworld* at the Neues Theater in Berlin, substituting at the last minute for the well-known conductor Oskar Fried. A year later, Mahler recommended Klemperer for his first official appointment, as chorus master and later conductor of the Deutsches Landestheater in Prague. During the next decade Mahler was responsible for the appointment of Klemperer as the conductor of opera orchestras in Hamburg, Bremen, and Strasbourg as well.

In 1917 Klemperer moved to Cologne, where he conducted both symphony and opera orchestras for the next seven years. He married Johanna Geissler, an opera singer, in 1919 after converting from Judaism to his fiancée's Roman Catholic faith. In 1924 he returned to Berlin to conduct the Volksoper. His American debut occurred two years later, when he joined the New York Symphony Orchestra as guest conductor for eight weeks, beginning on 15 January 1926. During this time he gave Mahler's Ninth Symphony and Leoš Janáček's Sinfonietta their first performances in the United States.

In 1927 Klemperer received a much sought after appointment as head of Berlin's state-sponsored Kroll Opera. The newly created Kroll became one of three opera houses in Berlin, along with the State Opera, conducted by Erich Kleiber, and the Municipal Opera, led by Bruno Walter. The Kroll had been founded to present new and experimental works, and during the next four years Klemperer made it one of the leading avant-garde companies in the world. Under his tenure, the Kroll presented the first staged performances of several major works, including Igor Stravinsky's *Oedipus Rex* and Arnold Schoenberg's *Erwartung*. He also created new productions of such standards as *Madama Butterfly* and *Don Giovanni*.

In 1931 the Prussian government dropped its support of the Kroll for financial reasons, and with the folding of the company Klemperer went on to become a part-time conductor at the State Opera. That same year he was awarded the German government's Goethe Medal by President Paul von Hindenburg for his contributions to German culture. However, when Adolf Hitler came to power in 1933, Klemperer was dismissed from his post at the State Opera, was personally attacked in German newspapers, and was fined for allegedly owing back taxes. This harassment led him to flee to Austria and then to Switzerland.

In 1935 Klemperer came to the United States at the invitation of William Andrews Clark, Jr., an American copper magnate and the founder and a major supporter of the Los Angeles Philharmonic, who offered Klemperer a guest conductorship with the orchestra. During the next four years, Klemperer also appeared as a conductor with the New York Philharmonic and the Pittsburgh Symphony. As a prominent member of the expatriate music community in Los Angeles, he became especially friendly with two of its members, Schoenberg and Ernst Toch. He also developed a strong interest in American jazz.

Klemperer's career received another setback in 1939, when he was diagnosed with a brain tumor. Following emergency surgery in Boston, he was left with a partial paralysis on his right side. During 1940, as he underwent intensive physical therapy, Klemperer was reduced to conducting minor ensembles in New York City. Early in 1941 he voluntarily entered a private sanatorium in Rye, New York, for treatment of an undisclosed ailment. When he left the grounds without permission, an all-points bulletin was issued for his arrest on charges that he was "dangerous and insane." He was finally located in Morristown, New Jersey, and forced to spend a night in jail before he was judged mentally competent and released.

Soon afterward, in order to restore his musical reputation, Klemperer spent most of his savings to assemble an orchestra of seventy musicians and rent Carnegie Hall, where he gave a sympathetically reviewed performance of works by Bach, Mozart, and Hindemith. Despite this effort, he received no major conducting appointments, and during the war years he was forced to conduct minor ensembles throughout the United States.

Klemperer returned to Europe in 1946 and settled in Switzerland. That year he conducted a well-received performance of Bach's *St. Matthew Passion* in Rome. Other conducting assignments followed in Sweden, Switzerland, and France. In 1947 Klemperer was appointed head of the Budapest Opera and held that post for three years. In 1950 he presented acclaimed performances of Mahler's Resurrection Symphony in Sydney, Australia, and his career again appeared to be on the ascent. However, in 1951 he suffered still another setback when he was seriously injured in a fall at the Montreal airport. For four years he was forced to conduct from a wheelchair before finally being able to stand unaided in 1955.

Klemperer continued to conduct European orchestras for the next few years until the fall of 1958, when another disaster threatened to end not only his career but his life: he was severely burned when the pipe he was smoking set his bed on fire, and he was hospitalized for many months. He returned to the podium in September 1959 to conduct the Philharmonia Orchestra of London at the Lucerne Festival, and his success there led to his appointment as the Philharmonia's conductor for life.

As the leader of the Philharmonia, Klemperer achieved worldwide eminence. On tour and through numerous long-playing recordings, the orchestra under Klemperer's direction became celebrated for its powerful presentations of classics by German composers from Bach through Mahler and Bruckner, and he was widely proclaimed as a worthy heir to Toscanini. At 6'5", Klemperer was a commanding presence on the podium despite the mishaps that had left him with a shuffling gate and a permanent grimace. Harold Schoenberg, the principal music critic for the *New York Times* during Klemperer's heyday, later recalled that at public performances the conductor "commanded awe, pity and terror" as he forcefully beat time with his fists.

Although the Philharmonia was based in London, Klemperer continued to live in Switzerland. After the death of his wife in 1956, he was looked after by his daughter at their home in Zurich. Klemperer also had a son, Werner, who became a noted actor. After several weeks of failing health, Otto Klemperer died in Zurich.

• Annotated musical scores used by Klemperer are in the collections of the John F. Kennedy Library at the California State University, Los Angeles. For biographical information on Klemperer, see his memoir, *Minor Recollections* (1964); Walter Legge, "Otto Klemperer: Pages from an Unwritten Autobiography," *Gramophone* 51 (Dec. 1973): 1169ff, and (Jan. 1974): 1351–54; and Peter Heyworth, *Otto Klemperer: His Life and Times* (2 vols., 1983, 1996). See also Martin Anderson, ed., *Klemperer on Music: Shavings from a Musician's Workbench* (1986), which includes a bibliography of Klemperer's own compositions; Heyworth, ed., *Conversations with Klemperer* (1973; rev. ed., 1985), a collection of the editor's interviews with the conductor; and Klemperer, *Erinnerungen an Gustav Mahler* (1960), the conductor's account of his association with Mahler. For a comprehensive collection of Klemperer's writings, see Stephen Stomper, ed., *Über Musik und Theater: Erinnerungen, Gespräche, Skizzen* (1982). An obituary, together with an appreciative essay by Harold Schoenberg, appears in the *New York Times*, 8 July 1973.

ANN T. KEENE

KLINE, Franz (23 May 1910–13 May 1962), painter, was born in Wilkes-Barre, Pennsylvania, the son of Anthony Kline and Anne Rowe. After his father committed suicide in 1917, Kline was sent to Girard College in Philadelphia, a free boarding school for orphaned boys. When his mother remarried in 1925 Kline joined his family in Lehighton, a railroad town in eastern Pennsylvania. He studied at Boston University from 1931 to 1935 and then at Heatherly's School of Fine Art in 1937 and 1938. In 1938 he married Elizabeth Vincent Parsons, a British dancer, and they settled permanently in New York City. At various times during his career he taught at Black Mountain College, Pratt Institute, and the Philadelphia Museum School of Art.

Kline did not set out to be a painter. A gifted draftsman, he decided on a career as a commercial artist, working as an illustrator, a cartoonist, and a department store designer before establishing himself as an artist. His experience as a draftsman stayed with him after he began painting abstractly in 1950. His figurative work is characterized by a boldly simplified pictorial organization. A preference for chiaroscuro was established early; he favored strong value contrasts rather than subtle modeling of form. By 1948 he was using dark craggy lines to delineate his figures, as in *Nijinsky as Petrouchka* (private collection).

Chiaroscuro effects would shape Kline's mature work. His best-known paintings, like *Monitor* (1956, private collection), were executed in black and white and are characterized by wide slashing strokes of paint colliding and diffusing across a large canvas. The tremendous energy manifest in his brushwork places Kline among the action painters, one type of abstract expressionists. These painters favored a gestural style of pigment application. The act of painting for them was a vigorous physical process that could be followed by tracing the movement of the brushwork. At the other end of the spectrum were the color field painters such as Mark Rothko and Barnett Newman, who favored large unbroken expanses of color spreading slowly across the picture plane. Color field painting is more subdued when compared to the fractured surfaces and frenetic pitch of action painting. Kline, however, shared one attribute with the color field painters. Typically the work of such action painters as Willem de Kooning and Jackson Pollock maintains a separation between figure and ground, with abstract strokes hovering distinctly on the surface of the canvas. It is harder to separate figure from ground in Kline's work. Black and white elements bleed and feather, making their boundaries less precise. The resulting image is a series of interlocking planes of equal emphasis, rather than separate foreground and background entities.

Despite their appearance of nonobjectivity, Kline's images are firmly rooted in the literal. Kline reportedly arrived at his signature style after using a Bell-Opticon projector in de Kooning's studio to enlarge his own realistic, albeit vigorously brushed drawings. According to de Kooning's wife, the painter Elaine de Kooning: "A four by five inch brush drawing of the rocking chair . . . loomed in gigantic black strokes which eradicated any images, the strokes expanding as entities in themselves, unrelated to any reality but that of their own existence . . . From that day, Franz Kline's style of painting changed completely" (E. de Kooning, p. 14).

Kline's use of black and white created striking contrasts, but it was not governed solely by formal considerations. Rather, this combination ultimately reinforced his ties to reality. Although Kline made his home in Manhattan, his paintings always remained steeped in the industrial Pennsylvania landscape of his youth. He gave his abstractions titles such as *Monitor* and *Mahoning* (1956, Whitney Museum of American Art, N.Y.), the former the name of a train line, and the latter of a Pennsylvania town. In light of these titles, it becomes apparent that Kline's paintings are reminiscent of the cold, snowy, industrial Pennsylvania landscape. Black and white mingle on the canvas, creating trellised patterns recalling the train yards, soot-stained snow, and thick, cold winter air.

Although he made his mark as a monochromatic painter, Kline reintroduced color into his work in the late 1950s. The new images retained the thick, slashing, gestural style of his black and white paintings, yet they were less austere. Kline traded melodrama for stability in works like *King Oliver* (1958, private collection). The addition of color slows the pace, making for a more measured rhythm. Whereas the color abstractions lack the drama of Kline's black and white images, they signal an inevitable development in his oeuvre. Having apparently exhausted the possibilities of monochrome, Kline needed to return to the multiplicity that only color could provide. But the color images are not more complex or more carefully considered than the black and whites, given that Kline achieved an astonishing number of effects using just these limited means. The color marks are simply calmer and less aggressive.

Kline did not see the development of his reintroduction of color to its fruition. He died of heart failure in New York City at the height of his career; just two years earlier he had been awarded the prize at the Thirtieth Venice Biennale. Although he was not the only abstract expressionist painter who worked in monochrome, Kline's name is virtually synonymous with black and white painting. The economy of gesture and forcefulness of his black and white paintings transcend their limited palette, ensuring that he will continue to be best known for these stark, dramatic works.

• On Kline's black and white paintings see David Anfam, *Franz Kline: Black and White* (1994). Harry Gaugh has written extensively on Kline, including the exhibition catalogs *The Vital Gesture: Franz Kline* (Cincinnati Art Museum,

1985) and *Franz Kline: The Color Abstractions* (Phillips Collection, Washington, D.C., 1979). See also Stephen C. Foster's catalog from an exhibition at the Tàpies Foundation, *Franz Kline: Art and the Structure of Identity* (1994). Elaine de Kooning's catalog of a memorial exhibition, *Franz Kline* (Washington Gallery of Modern Art, Washington, D.C., 1962), p. 14, is also a good resource. An obituary is in the *New York Times*, 15 May 1962.

PAMELA A. COHEN

KLINEBERG, Otto (2 Nov. 1899–6 Mar. 1992), psychologist, was born in Québec City and raised in Montréal, Québec, Canada, the son of Louis Klineberg, an insurance salesman, and Jenny Scheffer. As a young man Otto was an outstanding student, first at Montréal High School and then at McGill University (B.A., 1919), where he won first class honors in philosophy and psychology. With the encouragement of his teacher J. W. A. Hickson, he obtained a scholarship for graduate study in philosophy at Harvard University, where he earned an M.A. in 1920.

Because of the uncertain employment prospects for an academic, Klineberg began to prepare for a career in medicine and psychiatry at McGill Medical School. He found medicine uninteresting, however, and after receiving his M.D. (1925) he obtained a Ph.D. in psychology from Columbia University (1927). There he also took classes in anthropology from Edward Sapir and Franz Boas and underwent what he characterized as an almost religious conversion to a cross-cultural perspective. "How could [Western] psychologists speak of *human* attributes and *human* behavior," he asked, "when they knew only one kind of human being?"

From 1926 to 1935 Klineberg's research on cultural influences on intelligence played a major role in social scientists' adoption of an environmentalist view of the behavior of racial and ethnic minorities. First, he administered performance tests to Yakima Indian children in Washington State and found that their low scores were due to a refusal to rush on timed problems. When judged by the number of errors made, the Indians' responses were superior. This finding, that apparent racial differences in performance were cultural in origin, fit well with the cultural relativism of Boas and became the basis of Klineberg's dissertation (*Archives of Psychology*, no. 93 [1928]).

From 1927 to 1929 a National Research Council grant allowed Klineberg to test children in Germany, France, and Italy who fit the physiognomic criteria for what were considered the Nordic, Alpine, and Mediterranean races. When these groups of children lived in the same geographical area, Klineberg showed, their test performances did not differ significantly. Returning to Columbia as a research associate in anthropology, Klineberg challenged the nativist idea that the higher test scores of African-American children in schools in the northern United States were due to the selective migration of the more intelligent to the North, rather than to the increased educational opportunity there. When Klineberg checked southern school records, he found that the grades of students who later moved to the north were no better than those of their nonemigrating peers. And when Klineberg and his students tested New York City children, they found that the longer a southern-born student had lived in New York City the higher his IQ was likely to be (Klineberg, *Negro Intelligence and Selective Migration* [1935]).

In 1931 Klineberg became an instructor in the psychology department at Columbia, where he stayed for thirty years, rising to the rank of professor and helping administer an interdisciplinary program in social psychology. Together with his wife and collaborator Selma Gintzler (they married in 1933 and had three children), Klineberg traveled widely and lived in Mexico (1933), China (1935–1936), and Brazil (1945–1947), where he held visiting appointments and demonstrated his gift of acquiring new languages. He moved in 1962 to Paris, where he taught at the University of Paris and École des Hautes Études until 1982, when he returned to New York and taught part-time at the City University of New York. He died in Bethesda, Maryland.

Throughout his career Klineberg was active in organizations and agencies that applied psychological research to social problems, including the Society for the Psychological Study of Social Issues, which he helped lead and served as president in 1941–1942. During World War II he worked as a propagandist in the Office of War Information, as an analyst in the Foreign Broadcast Monitoring Service, and as an interviewer for the U.S. Strategic Bombing Survey. He also consulted for the Carnegie Corporation's Study of the American Negro, writing background reports for Gunnar Myrdal's *An American Dilemma* and editing the companion volume *Characteristics of the American Negro* (1944). Most significantly, he contributed to the *Brown v. Board of Education* Supreme Court case by consulting for the National Association for the Advancement of Colored People Legal Defense Fund, testifying in an earlier desegregation suit, and signing the plaintiffs' social science brief. He also supervised the dissertation research of Kenneth B. Clark, which he then encouraged the NAACP to use as evidence of the harmful effects of school segregation.

Beginning in the late 1940s, Klineberg contributed his talents as a researcher, administrator, and publicist to organizations applying social science to international relations. He directed the United Nations Educational, Scientific, and Cultural Organization's International Tensions Project in 1948–1949 and surveyed the relevant research in his influential *Tensions Affecting International Understanding* (1950). At the same time, he served on the committee that founded the World Federation for Mental Health (WFMH), dedicated to analyzing the psychological and psychiatric aspects of international conflicts. Returning to UNESCO from 1953 to 1955, he served as head of the Division of Applied Social Sciences, and director of the Department of Social Sciences. In demeanor he was dignified, gentle, and direct; to his writing he applied these qualities as well as his personal optimism and good humor.

Although some criticized Klineberg's writing on culture as unduly vague and relativistic, his research on race and intelligence was widely regarded as "sober and scientifically objective" (Willard Z. Park, *Annals of the American Academy of Political and Social Sciences* 184 [Mar. 1936]: 246), leading to "fair and just" conclusions (Thomas R. Garth, *Annals* 180 [July 1935]: 244), that Klineberg conveyed with "restraint" and in a "dispassionate" manner (Melville J. Herskovits, *New Republic*, 4 Mar. 1936, p. 118). He also won praise for not ruling out the possibility that future researchers would find biological explanations for some racial differences. Liberal activists celebrated the timing and effectiveness of Klineberg's early work, characterizing his *Negro Intelligence* as a "swift, cleverly placed *solar plexus* for the broad paunch of one of the social golems of our day—the ogre of Nordicism in education" (Alain Locke, "A Swift Solar Plexus," *Survey* 71 [1935]: 346). Conservatives were more critical; they included the Columbia psychologists Henry Garrett and Carl Warden, who viewed their junior colleague Klineberg as a subversive who falsified his data to suit his political goals. Klineberg's later writing on international relations was generally well received, although it was open to criticism for the "psychologism" inherent in the philosophy of UNESCO and the WFMH, that is, an emphasis on the barriers to peace that exist "in the minds of men" (Rosenberg, p. 338). Historians of psychology generally agree with Carl Degler's assessment that no psychologist between the world wars was "more tireless or ingenious" than Klineberg in casting doubt on hereditarian views of racial differences (Degler, *In Search of Human Nature* [1991], p. 179).

• Klineberg left no personal papers, but some correspondence exists in the Franz Boas Papers at the American Philosophical Society and in the Kenneth B. Clark Papers (box 57) at the Library of Congress. In *Annals of the New York Academy of Sciences* 602 (1990): 35–50, Klineberg acknowledges his wife as coauthor of two of his most notable books, *Race Differences* (1935) and *Social Psychology* (1940). His work for UNESCO is represented by the pamphlets *Race and Psychology* (1951) and *Social Implications of the Peaceful Uses of Nuclear Energy* (1963); see also his *Human Dimension in International Relations* (1964). The best biographical sources are Klineberg's essay in Gardner Lindzey, ed., *History of Psychology in Autobiography*, vol. 6 (1974), and an oral history, *The Reminiscences of Otto Klineberg* (1985). For Klineberg's role in *Brown v. Board of Education*, see Richard Kluger, *Simple Justice* (1976). Conservative editorial criticism of Klineberg is exemplified in "Back to the Barnyard," in the *New York Herald Tribune*, 9 Aug. 1931. For a critical appreciation of his writing on international relations, see Milton J. Rosenberg, "Psychology of Peace," *Contemporary Psychology* 10 (1965): 337–39. A partial bibliography of Klineberg's work and a photograph can be found in *American Psychologist* 35 (1980): 76–81. Obituaries are in the *New York Times*, 10 Mar. 1992, and *American Psychologist* 48 (1993): 909–10.

BENJAMIN HARRIS

KLINGELSMITH, Margaret Center (27 Nov. 1859–19 Jan. 1931), law librarian and author, was born in Portland, Maine, the daughter of Isaac Henry Center and Carolina How Evans, both of whom were members of prominent New England families. Margaret's early education was in private schools in Newton, Massachusetts, and Portland, Maine. In 1884 she married Joseph M. Klingelsmith in Atlanta, Georgia.

In 1896 Margaret Klingelsmith began the study of law at the University of Pennsylvania, where she was an outstanding student; she graduated with honors in 1898, earning a bachelor of laws degree. Klingelsmith, one of the first women admitted to the law school at the University of Pennsylvania, was also one of the first women admitted to the Philadelphia bar (1898).

The Biddle Law Library of Klingelsmith's alma mater was established in 1886, and she became its third librarian in 1899. A year later she published a history of the law school in the university's *Proceedings at the Dedication of the New Building of the Department of Law* (1900). At the time of Klingelsmith's appointment, the library had only 4,000 volumes, but during her tenure it became a leading law library, eventually containing 82,000 volumes. During her thirty-two years as librarian, she developed a knack for finding rare and valuable books for the library's collection. Her search for these books led her abroad. One productive venture was made in 1910 when she traveled to England on a trip arranged by William Draper Lewis, then dean of the law school. On this trip Klingelsmith purchased more than 600 items from English dealers. When she returned, she submitted to the law faculty a report of her trip and a list of her more interesting purchases. This report was later published as *Report of the Librarian on Her Trip to England and the Continent* (1910).

Klingelsmith became an authority on paleography and early English year books. She put this knowledge to use in 1915, when she published an English translation of a massive fifteenth-century work in Norman French, *Stafham's Abridgement of the Law* (2 vols., 1915). The following year, in recognition of her scholarly achievements, especially this translation, the University of Pennsylvania awarded her an honorary master of laws degree, the first such award by the institution to a woman.

Klingelsmith was known for her erudition and wit, characteristics that came across in her writings. She wrote many essays and biographies for scholarly publications, mostly of legal figures, and frequently contributed to legal periodicals. She assisted with the preparation of material for the *Digest of Decisions and Encyclopaedia of Pennsylvania Law 1754–1898* (23 vols., 1898–1906), edited by William Draper Lewis and George Wharton Pepper, and for the second edition of *Pepper and Lewis's Digest of Laws* (1910).

Klingelsmith, a founder of the American Association of Law Libraries, served as the organization's vice president in 1912 and 1913. She was also a member of the Woman's Suffrage Association and, at one time, a Democratic candidate for justice of the Superior Court of Pennsylvania. She was generally regarded as supportive to both law students and members of the Philadelphia bar and was considered a superb librarian by her colleagues.

Klingelsmith was a member of the first generation of female lawyers to benefit from the earlier struggles of women to be admitted to law schools and to the full practice of law in the state of Pennsylvania. An important predecessor was Carrie Burnham Kilgore, who spent eleven years fighting to be admitted to classes at the law school of the University of Pennsylvania (she matriculated in 1883), and sixteen years to be admitted to full practice in the courts of Philadelphia and Pennsylvania. Kilgore became a sort of role model to Klingelsmith. Klingelsmith died in Pennsylvania, and following her death a tablet was erected to her memory in the Biddle Law Library.

• There is no full-length account of Klingelsmith's life. Obituaries appear in the *Pennsylvania Gazette*, 4 Feb. 1931, the *University of Pennsylvania Law Review* (Nov. 1931), the *Evening Public Ledger*, 20 Jan. 1931, and the *Philadelphia Inquirer*, 21 Jan. 1931.

BETHANY K. DUMAS

KLOPFER, Donald Simon (23 Jan. 1902–30 May 1986), publisher, was born in New York City, the son of Simon Klopfer, an unsuccessful shirtwaist maker, and Stella Danziger. Following his father's death in 1912, Klopfer's mother married Emanuel Jacobsen, a partner in his family diamond-cutting business, the United Diamond Works, in Newark, New Jersey. After graduating from DeWitt Clinton High School at age fourteen, Klopfer went to Phillips Academy in Andover, Massachusetts, before entering Columbia University in 1918; the following year he transferred to Williams College.

In 1920, at the end of Klopfer's sophomore year, he responded to his stepfather's insistence and joined the family diamond business. On his stepfather's death, he received a one-sixth share of the enterprise. Seeing no future there, he readily sold his interest in 1925 to raise his half of the $200,000 needed to buy with Bennett Cerf the Modern Library division from Boni & Liveright.

The Modern Library, with its backlist of inexpensive reprints of literary classics, prospered under the care of Cerf and Klopfer; in just two years they recovered their entire investment plus $50,000 they had borrowed for operating expenses. They paid themselves modest salaries and put the rest of their earnings back into the business. From the start, Cerf looked after promotion, advertising, publicity, and editorial matters, while Klopfer took care of the office, sales, and production. Klopfer's common sense, wry humor, and cheerful skepticism provided the perfect counterbalance for Cerf's flamboyant personality.

With the Modern Library doing well, Cerf and Klopfer branched out to distribute Nonesuch Press titles and other limited editions in the United States and to publish their own luxury editions "at random."

They established Random House in 1927, only to have the demand for more expensive volumes disappear with the stock market crash and the depression. Hard economic times, however, did not seriously affect the Modern Library's steady sales. Thus the partners used the Random House imprint for a modest venture into trade publishing. This part of the business grew in importance through a series of acquisition and publishing coups.

When the Horace Liveright firm failed in 1933, Random House signed Eugene O'Neill and his editor, Saxe Commins. In 1934 Cerf and Klopfer instigated and won a court test of obscenity in favor of James Joyce's *Ulysses*; as a result, Random House became Joyce's American publisher. The 1936 absorption of the Smith and Haas publishing enterprise brought Robert Haas into Random House as a partner along with several notable authors including William Faulkner, Edgar Snow, and Robert Graves. By 1937 Klopfer's fair treatment of editors and his generous friendship with authors such as Faulkner prompted editors from other publishers to gravitate to Random House, bringing with them over the next decade writers of stature or great promise, such as Sinclair Lewis, Robert Penn Warren, James Michener, John O'Hara, Truman Capote, and Irwin Shaw.

World War II, in which Klopfer served as a major in U.S. Army Air Corps intelligence in England, interrupted Random House's steady growth. After the war, and before the Modern Library's business was challenged by paperback books, the firm published a profitable collegiate dictionary and ventured into juvenile titles. The Dr. Seuss series and Beginner Books caught the surge of the baby boom market. Cerf's activities as author, syndicated humorist, and television personality brought Random House broad public attention. By the time Haas sold his share of the firm to Klopfer's stepson, Charles A. Wimpfheimer, and left the partnership in 1956, offers to buy the company began to come from larger publishers.

Thirty percent of company stock was sold publicly in 1959 to establish a market value for Random House and to solve potential inheritance problems. By coincidence, the next year the new ability to exchange stock aided in the acquisition of Alfred A. Knopf, Inc., which became an autonomous, wholly owned subsidiary and which almost doubled the Random House business. That acquisition brought a strong backlist of acknowledged masterpieces by Willa Cather, Thomas Mann, and H. L. Mencken, among others, as well as critical and popular successes by contemporary authors like John Hersey, John Updike, and Hammond Innes. Other acquisitions followed, and in 1961 Random House stock was listed on the New York Stock Exchange. Klopfer and Cerf, realizing that their company had become highly attractive to the emerging communications conglomerates, were ready with their main condition of sale—publishing independence. This condition was accepted and subsequently honored by RCA, which purchased Random House for $38 million in 1966. Klopfer succeeded Cerf as

chairman of the board of directors in 1970 and retired in 1975.

Klopfer made many contributions to the art of book production through his long association with the American Institute of the Graphic Arts (president, 1949–1950), and he served as president of the American Book Publishers Council (1954–1956). He married three times. His marriage to Marian Ansbacher in 1927 ended in divorce (1933); they had one child. His 1937 marriage to Florence Selwyn Wimpfheimer ended with her death in 1979. When Klopfer died in New York City, he was survived by Kathleen Loucheim, whom he had married in 1980.

During his fifty years as a publisher, Klopfer quietly and consistently nurtured authors' creativity while strongly resisting corporate and government restraint on an author's freedom of utterance. Publishing to him was always much more than a business.

• The best short account of Klopfer's role in Random House can be found in John F. Baker, "Fifty Years of Publishing at Random," *Publishers Weekly*, 4 Aug. 1975. Klopfer's contribution to the enterprise is also described in *At Random: The Reminiscences of Bennett Cerf* (1977), edited from oral history interviews at the Columbia University Oral History Collection by Phyllis Cerf Wagner and Albert Erskine. Klopfer contributed two interviews to the Columbia Oral History Collection—one on the funeral of Faulkner, which he attended, the other on his life and association with Random House authors. A privately printed volume, *Donald S. Klopfer, an Appreciation*, appeared in 1987. An obituary is in the *New York Times*, 31 May 1986.

RICHMOND D. WILLIAMS

KLUCKHOHN, Clyde Kay Maben (11 Jan. 1905–29 July 1960), anthropologist, was born in LeMars, Iowa, the adopted son of George Wesley Kluckhohn and Katherine Swanzey, occupations unknown. Kluckhohn matriculated at Princeton University but, due to illness resulting from a childhood bout with rheumatic fever, was forced to abandon Princeton and was sent in 1923 to the Vogt family ranch (home of future anthropologist Evon Z. Vogt) at Ramah, New Mexico. It was here that Kluckhohn encountered the Navaho (Navajo), a people he would study for the remainder of his life. In 1927 he published his first book, *To the Foot of the Rainbow*, an account of his travels on horseback through Navaho country.

Kluckhohn was awarded the A.B. in 1928 from the University of Wisconsin, where he majored in the classics. The breadth of his scholarship in this area is evident in the Brown University Colver Lectures, which he gave in the last year of his life. These lectures, published posthumously as *Anthropology and the Classics* (1961), are an excellent introduction to Kluckhohn's primary theoretical concerns and an illustration of how they can be applied to a body of cultural and historic data from a particular society.

Kluckhohn spent the early 1930s in Europe. He was psychoanalyzed in Vienna, studied at the university in that city, and became acquainted with the Anthropos group, who were working on an evolutionary typology/geography of culture, led by Father Wilhelm Schmidt. In 1931–1932 Kluckhohn was a Rhodes Scholar at Oxford University, where he studied anthropology with R. R. Marrett, Beatrice Blackwood, and T. K. Penniman. In 1932 Kluckhohn returned to the United States and married Florence Rockwood, a sociologist, with whom he would have one child. Also in 1932 he began a two-year stint as assistant professor of anthropology at the University of New Mexico. In 1933 he published his second book, *Beyond the Rainbow*, which describes additional pack trips into previously unexplored Navaho territory.

Appointed to an instructorship at Harvard University in 1935, Kluckhohn was awarded the Ph.D. in anthropology from that institution in 1936. As a student at Harvard, Kluckhohn studied with Alfred M. Tozzer, Roland B. Dixon, Lauriston Ward, and E. A. Hooton. His dissertation, "Some Aspects of Contemporary Theory in Cultural Anthropology," was a defense of the German-Austrian *Kulturkreislehre*, or culture evolution theory. Kluckhohn remained at Harvard (except for the World War II years when he served as a government consultant) for the duration of his career. He served as chair of the Department of Anthropology and was certainly its most distinguished and well-known member. Along with Talcott Parsons, Henry Murray, and Gordon Allport, Kluckhohn founded the Department of Social Relations for the purpose of creating a dynamic, all-encompassing, generic social science. He also served as the curator of southwestern ethnology for the Peabody Museum and as the first director of Harvard's Russian Research Center.

Throughout his career Kluckhohn served as a consultant to or officer of many government agencies and private foundations, including the Office of Indian Affairs, the War Department, General Douglas MacArthur's Tokyo headquarters, the Central Intelligence Agency, and the Department of State. He was elected to the National Academy of Sciences, served as chair of the Division of Anthropology and Psychology of the National Research Council, chair of the Section of Anthropology of the National Academy of Sciences, and president of the American Anthropological Association (1947). He was an honorary member of the American Philosophical Society, the American Academy of Arts and Sciences, and the Royal Anthropological Institute. He received the Viking Fund Medal in 1950, awarded by the American Anthropological Association.

Kluckhohn was an accomplished field ethnographer as his many publications on the Navaho attest. He made a continuous study of their culture for nearly forty years. A number of monographs and many influential articles as well as Kluckhohn's classic ethnography *Navaho Witchcraft* (1944) were based on his extensive field data. *Navaho Witchcraft* was innovative in its synthesis of psychological, psychoanalytical, sociological, and anthropological theory in a brilliant demonstration of the functioning of social control in Navaho society. Talcott Parsons hailed it in the *American Journal of*

Sociology as a "conspicuous example of a new and promising type in the study of social phenomena" where "the effect of [Kluckhohn's] use of 'psychology' is to transform ethnography into the dynamic analysis of a social system" (50, no. 6 [1946]: 566–57).

Important as it is, Kluckhohn's contribution to Navaho studies did not lie solely in his own ethnography but also in the sponsorship of other researchers. From 1936 to 1948 he served as director of the Ramah Project research on the Ramah Navaho in which many of his students and colleagues participated. In 1949 he became a founder and advisory board member of the Comparative Study of Values in Five Cultures Project, which made individual studies of five cultural/ethnic groups (Navaho, Zuñi, Hispanic-American, Mormon, white Texan) in the Ramah vicinity.

In an influential series of articles, Kluckhohn explored the tension between cultural relativity and cultural universals. In "Universal Categories of Culture," published in Alfred Kroeber's *Anthropology Today*, he concluded that "there is a generalized framework that underlies the more apparent and striking facts of cultural relativity. . . . Cultural concepts are human artifacts, but the conceptualization of nature is enough bound by stubborn and irreducible fact so that organisms having the same kind of nervous system will at the very least understand one another, relatively free from arbitrary convention" (1953, pp. 520–21).

Anthropologist and Africanist Melville J. Herskovits recalled that Kluckhohn "consistently followed both microethnographic and macroethnographic lines of anthropological interest. . . . The work of Kluckhohn, when taken in its totality, can be best envisaged as a canon on these two themes. Constantly deepening his understanding of Navaho culture by repeated field trips, aided by his command of the language, he used his insights into this particular culture to sharpen the questions he raised concerning the nature and significance of human behavior in general" (pp. 129–30). Kluckhohn's later theoretical pursuits were especially influenced by the work of anthropologist Franz Boas and his students Edward Sapir, Alfred Kroeber, and Ruth Benedict and by anthropologist Ralph Linton.

Kluckhohn was a pioneer in the area of psychological anthropology and edited, with psychologist Henry Murray, the famous volume *Personality in Nature, Society and Culture* (1948). He wrote a number of articles on the individual, on the relationship of psychology to anthropology, and on the use of personal documents in anthropology. Especially noteworthy is his *The Personal Document in Anthropology* (1945).

From his early paper "Patterning as Exemplified in Navaho Culture" (in *Language, Culture and Personality*, ed. Leslie Spier [1941]) to "Navaho Categories" (in *Culture in History: Essays in Honor of Paul Radin*, ed. Stanley Diamond [1960]), published in his last year of life, Kluckhohn continued to refine a theoretical framework in which to discuss cultural patterns. In many of his publications he emphasized the need for dealing with both "implicit" (that part of culture of which members of the group are either unaware or only partially aware) as well as "explicit" culture. He also called for a standardization of terminology and suggested the use of a three-level hierarchy of pattern, configuration, and ethos ("Covert Culture and Administrative Problems," *American Anthropologist* 45 [1943]: 221). Patterns could be either "sanctioned" (ideal) or "behavioral" (based on actual observed behavior). The value system was composed of the sanctioned patterns and some but not all of the configurations ("unconscious assumptions"). Ethos was the central integrating principle. Kluckhohn's interest in creating a systematic science of values was still under development at the time of his death, but he had already introduced the concept of binary opposition— derived from the linguistics of Roman Jakobson—for describing a grammar of values for particular societies. These writings were part of Kluckhohn's efforts to develop a theory that would be amenable to the comparative study of cultures. This same goal is evident in his contributions to Talcott Parsons and Edward Shils, eds., *Toward a General Theory of Action* (1951), and in his collaboration with Alfred Kroeber, *Culture: A Critical Review of Concepts and Definitions* (1952), a compendium and typology of various definitions of the term *culture*.

Kluckhohn was a vocal critic of anthropology as a discipline. The archaeologist Richard Woodbury referred to him as a "sympathetic but merciless critic" of American archaeology (*American Antiquity* 25, no. 3 [1961]: 407). Kluckhohn was especially blunt in his article "The Conceptual Structure in Middle American Studies," in which he accused archaeologists of being "but slightly reformed antiquarians" who specialized in a "great deal of obsessive wallowing in detail of and for itself" (in C. L. Hay et al., *The Maya and Their Neighbors* [1940], p. 42). He accused American anthropology of being "unusually parochial" and intellectually "moribund" ("The Place of Theory in Anthropological Studies," *Philosophy of Science* 6 [1939]: 340, 344) and anthropologists in general of being "notorious among social scientists for their neglect of library research" (*The Personal Document in Anthropology* [1945], p. 83).

These criticisms cannot be applied to Kluckhohn himself; he was among the most innovative and erudite of anthropologists. He was, as anthropologist George Peter Murdock eulogized in 1961, "probably the most intellectually sophisticated anthropologist of his generation. . . . If Margaret Mead typifies anthropology to the general public, Clyde Kluckhohn represented the subject to his professional colleagues" (p. 4). Nor did Kluckhohn neglect the general public. He wrote popular articles, encyclopedia entries, and high school textbook materials. He summarized many of his theories in his bestselling introduction to anthropology, *Mirror for Man: The Relation of Anthropology to Modern Life* (1949), which won the McGraw-Hill Prize for the best popular work on science and has continued to be a valuable resource. Kluckhohn died in Santa Fe.

• The Kluckhohn Papers (1930–1960) are held by the Harvard University Archives. Kluckhohn's most important publications in Navaho ethnography include two monographs coauthored with his friend Leland C. Wyman, *Navaho Classification of Their Song Ceremonials* (1938) and *An Introduction to Navaho Chant Practice* (1940), and two general works cowritten with Dorothea Leighton, *The Navaho* (1940) and *Children of the People* (1947). With Evon Vogt and Leonard McCombe, Kluckhohn produced a picture book, *Navaho Means People* (1951). Two monographs were published posthumously, *The Ramah Navaho* (1966) and, with W. W. Hill and Lucy Wales Kluckhohn, *Navaho Material Culture* (1971). The first theoretical piece published by Kluckhohn was "Some Reflections on the Method and Theory of the *Kulturkreislehre*," *American Anthropologist* 38 (1936): 157–96. His "Recurrent Themes in Myths and Mythmaking" (*Daedalus* 88 [1959]: 268–79) has been reprinted in several anthologies.

Kluckhohn also published important papers in physical anthropology, linguistics, psychology, and Russian studies, including the monograph, coauthored by Raymond Bauer and Alex Inkeles, *How the Soviet System Works* (1956). Kluckhohn's son, anthropologist Richard Kluckhohn, edited *Culture and Behavior: The Collected Essays of Clyde Kluckhohn* (1962). Walter Taylor et al. edited a festschrift volume, *Culture and Life: Essays in Memory of Clyde Kluckhohn* (1973).

For biographical information, see Fred J. Hay's entry in the *International Dictionary of Anthropologists* (1991); Melville J. Herskovits in National Academy of Sciences, *Biographical Memoirs* 37 (1964): 129–59; George Peter Murdock's obituary in *Behavioral Science* 6, no. 1 (1961): 1–4; and Talcott Parsons and Evon Z. Vogt's obituary (with Lucy Wales's complete bibliography of Kluckhohn's work) in *American Anthropologist* 64, no. 1 (1962): 140–61.

FRED J. HAY

KNAPP, Hermann Jakob (17 Mar. 1832–30 Apr. 1911), ophthalmologist, was born in Dauborn, Prussia, the son of Johann Knapp. (His mother's name is unknown.) He received the usual preliminary training in the humanities and aspired to become a poet. His father convinced him to turn to medicine and sent him to study at the universities in Munich, Würzberg, Berlin, Leipzig, and Giessen. Knapp received a medical degree from Geissen in 1854. The emerging field of ophthalmology fascinated Knapp. He made extended visits to Berlin, where he was an assistant to German ophthalmologist Albrecht von Graefe. He also studied in Utrecht, Holland, where Dutch ophthalmologist Franz C. Donders had begun to systematize the anomalies of accommodation and refraction. In London, he observed the ophthalmic surgery of Sir William Bowman and George Critchett, and in Paris he studied at the Sorbonne and visited the clinic of Louis August Desmarres.

In 1859 Knapp was admitted to the teaching faculty at Heidelberg and in 1865 was appointed associate professor. He married Adolfine Becker in 1864; they had two children. In 1867 Knapp first visited the United States, where opportunities for physicians impressed him, and the following year he relinquished his position in Heidelberg and moved with his wife and young daughter to New York City.

In an age when the major American ophthalmologists journeyed to Europe in an attempt to absorb in a few years some of the knowledge and traditions that existed abroad, Knapp became the first Old World professor in the field to resign a coveted position and settle permanently in the United States. An outstanding surgeon and teacher, he is best remembered for the founding of the *Archives of Ophthalmology and Otology* in 1869. Originally written in both German and English and published simultaneously in Germany and the United States, the journal evolved into the *Archives of Ophthalmology* and became affiliated with the American Medical Association in 1928. Knapp remained editor from 1869 until his death in 1911, when he was succeeded by his son, Arnold Knapp. A prolific writer, Hermann Knapp contributed approximately 150 articles to the *Archives* and more than fifty important articles to the *Transactions of the American Ophthalmological Society* and *Transactions of the American Otologic Society*. His complete bibliography contains more than 300 items.

On his arrival in New York in 1868, Knapp founded a private clinic for diseases of the eye and ear. This clinic was shortly incorporated as the Ophthalmic and Aural Institute, initially located at 46 East Twelfth Street, a building bought and equipped by Knapp himself. Following Knapp's death, the institute was moved to the southwest corner of Fifty-seventh Street and Tenth Avenue and its name changed to the Knapp Memorial Eye Hospital. This facility subsequently merged with the Columbia College of Physicians and Surgeons in 1940.

In addition to lecturing and teaching in his own institution, Knapp became lecturer in diseases of the eye and ear at University of the City of New York (later New York University) in 1875 and four years later was listed as instructor in physical examination of the eye. He served as professor of ophthalmology at New York University from 1882 to 1888, when he became professor of ophthalmology at the College of Physicians and Surgeons, the medical department of Columbia University, where he remained for fourteen years, becoming professor emeritus in 1903. After the death of his wife in 1874, he had married Hedwig Sachsowsky in 1878; they had one daughter.

Knapp was an outstanding surgeon who popularized a method of cataract extraction involving von Graefe's "peripheric-linear" excision with extracapsular extraction (surgical removal of the opaque lens cortex and nucleus leaving the capsule of the lens in place). Also a highly regarded pathologist, Knapp had a particular interest in ophthalmic tumors. His *Treatise on Intraocular Tumors*, published in both English (1868) and German (1869), stands as one of the most important nineteenth-century works on that subject. It shaped ophthalmologists' understanding of the pathology and treatment of eye tumors through much of the early twentieth century.

Knapp was also a successful inventor of ophthalmic instruments. Of particular importance during the late nineteenth and early twentieth centuries were his improved lid forceps; Knapp's roller forceps for the treatment of trachoma; Knapp's knife needle for the discission (cutting into) of secondary cataract and the division of incarcerated capsule; Knapp's headrest for the Helmholtz ophthalmometer; Knapp's ophthalmotrope; Knapp's ophthalmoscope; Knapp's apparatus for demonstrating the course of rays in astigmatism; Knapp's ocular speculum; Knapp's cystotome; and Knapp's operating chair.

Knapp served as the first chairman of the American Medical Association's Section of Ophthalmology and was a member of the American Ophthalmological Society and American Otological Society. He was president of the New York Ophthalmological Society and the New York Pathological Society and served as a member of numerous foreign medical societies.

Knapp died in Mamaroneck, New York.

• A bibliography of Knapp's writings appears in J. Hirschberg, *The History of Ophthalmology*, vol. 9, trans. F. A. Blodi (1990). A biography of Knapp, with particular attention to his contributions to ophthalmology appears in Daniel M. Albert, *Men of Vision* (1994), and in Burton Chance, *Clio Medica Ophthalmology* (1962). His contributions were also reviewed by Charles Snyder in the *Archives of Ophthalmology* 66 (1961): 595. A contemporary tribute by Charles Bramman Meding is in the *Archives of Ophthalmology* 40 (1911): 511. Obituaries are in the *Archives of Ophthalmology* 40 (1911): 357; the "Proceedings of the Forty-seventh Annual Meeting," *Transactions of the American Ophthalmological Society* (1911): 687–93; and the *New York Tribune*, 2 May 1911.

DANIEL MYRON ALBERT

KNAPP, Samuel Lorenzo (19 Jan. 1783–8 July 1838), writer, was born in Newburyport, Massachusetts, the son of Isaac Knapp and Susanna Newman. The sixth of nine children, he grew up in a matriarchal home, the result of his sea captain father's long absences. After attending Dartmouth College (1800–1804) and working in the Boston law office of Theophilus Parsons, Knapp tried repeatedly to make a living as a lawyer, beginning in 1809 when he opened his office in Newburyport. In 1812 he was elected to the Massachusetts legislature, and, in 1814, he became a regimental colonel of the state militia. That same year he married Mary Ann Davis, the daughter of General Amasa Davis, quarter master general of Massachusetts. They had two children.

In the meantime, he became a familiar figure at local functions, gaining a reputation as an orator and an enthusiast of Freemasonry. Knapp was imprisoned for debts in 1816 after the birth of the first of his two daughters. Thus restricted, he turned to writing as a means of livelihood, producing a pseudo-journal describing a tour of New England by a "Frenchman," *Extracts from the Journal of Marshal Soult* (1817). Following his release, he was associated for a time with Daniel Webster, an early college friend, in his law work in Boston.

While continuing to practice law, Knapp engaged in a variety of literary pursuits. These included his contributions to J. T. Buckingham's *New England Galaxy and Masonic Magazine* (1817) and his own *Biographical Sketches of Eminent Lawyers, Statesmen, and*

Men of Letters (1821), a volume devoted to prominent individuals familiar to him. Knapp began newspaper writing in 1824, becoming the editor of the Boston *Commercial Gazette*, which he continued to edit after founding the *Boston Monthly Magazine* in 1825, a publication with an Americana focus.

In 1826 Knapp and Daniel Webster were selected to deliver the official Boston eulogies for John Adams (1735–1826) and Thomas Jefferson at a service attended by President John Quincy Adams. Late that year, leaving his financially unsuccessful ventures behind, Knapp settled with his family in Washington, apparently at the suggestion of the president. When Andrew Jackson became president in 1829, the Knapps moved again, this time to New York City. There he completed his *Lectures on American Literature* (1829). The first full history of American literature, it sounded clearly his nationalistic call for the teaching of what would later be known as American studies.

While *Lectures* deals primarily with the American past, Knapp focuses more directly on his contemporaries in his next book. *Sketches of Public Character . . . with Notices of Other Matters* (1830) includes discussions of William Wirt, Edward Everett, Lydia Sigourney, Sarah J. Hale, and John Vanderlyn, whose portrait of Knapp hangs in the Baker Library at Dartmouth College. This book covers numerous topics, ranging from comments on the American mind and the Library of Congress to challenges to the government to create a national university and to support the arts.

During his last years, having finally abandoned law, Knapp experimented with new literary ideas and wrote quickly in order to support his family. *Advice on the Pursuits of Literature* (1832), a textbook on pioneer literature, went through four editions by 1841. *American Biography* (1833), Knapp's most comprehensive collective biography, was published separately and as part of *The Treasury of Knowledge, and Library of Reference* (1833, 1850, 1855). *Female Biography* (1834), which strongly supports women's education, went through five editions by 1846 and was a source for many subsequent sketches of Sarah J. Hale and Rufus W. Griswold. *Library of American History: A Reprint of Standard Works . . . with Copious Notes . . . Intended to Give the Reader a Full View of American History*, one of his most ambitious undertakings, was first published in weekly installments, then brought out in two impressive volumes in 1835. Perhaps Knapp's weakest work—presenting lifeless characterizations in vaguely historical situations—was his fiction: a novel, *Polish Chiefs* (1832), dealing with the American Revolution, and two volumes of tales based on American themes (1834, 1836).

In addition to the hundreds of short biographical pieces Knapp wrote, he used his personal recollections to produce several longer individual studies. He enhanced *Memoirs of General Lafayette* (1824, 1826) with his personal accounts of the French general's visit to Boston in 1824. Knapp's preface to Susanna Rowson's posthumously published *Charlotte's Daughter* (1828), on which all modern studies of that early American novelist are based, grew out of their long friendship. Knapp's *A Memoir of the Life of Daniel Webster* (1831) was the first authorized biography of that statesman; Knapp's collection on Thomas Eddy (1834) remains the only extensive study of the prison reformer; *The Life of Aaron Burr* (1835) was the first book-length treatment of Burr. Knapp's last work, *The Life of Lord Timothy Dexter* (1838), reflecting the author's Newburyport childhood memories of the eccentric merchant, is the primary source on Timothy Dexter.

Usually written in haste and in a scrawl that left much interpretation for the typesetters, Knapp's writing exhibits the popular effusive style of his time and the "generous nature" he considered necessary for a biographer. His emphasis was not on the great historic figures; he wished instead to preserve the contributions of ordinary citizens who had made life in America a little better. In the process, he often presented his characters in the context of American culture, a concept never more fully visualized than in his work.

In declining health, in 1835 Knapp moved to Hopkinton, Massachusetts, where he continued to write voluminously until shortly before his death.

• For background, see A. M. Knapp, *The Knapp Family in America* (1909). The first detailed review of Knapp's life's work, including an incomplete 48-item bibliography, was Fred Lewis Pattee, "A Record of Forgotten Fame: Samuel Lorenzo Knapp . . . Perhaps Dartmouth's Greatest Literary Light," *Dartmouth Alumni Magazine*, Dec. 1936, pp. 7–9, 72. A facsimile edition of *Lectures on American Literature* (1961) has an introduction by Richard Beale Davis and Ben Harris McClary that locates this work in its historical context. Ben Harris McClary, "Samuel Lorenzo Knapp and Early American Biography," *Proceedings of the American Antiquarian Society* 95 (Apr. 1985): 39–67, corrects many biographical and bibliographical errors that had been passed through traditional reference sources. Obituaries are in the *Boston Evening Transcript*, 9 July 1838, and the *Knickerbocker*, July 1838.

BEN HARRIS MCCLARY

KNAPP, Seaman Asahel (10 Dec. 1833–1 Apr. 1911), college president and advocate for the improvement of southern agriculture, was born in Schroon Lake, Essex County, New York, the son of Bradford Knapp, a physician, and Rhonda Seaman. Following preparatory work at Troy Conference Academy, Poultney, Vermont, he enrolled at Union College, Schenectady, New York, in 1852 and graduated with honors in 1856. Three weeks later he married Maria Elizabeth Hotchkiss of Hampton, New York; the couple had five children. Knapp taught initially at Fort Edward Institute, Fort Edward, New York, where he soon became a junior partner in the administration of the institute. Then in 1863 he purchased half-interest in his alma mater, the Troy Conference Academy, known subsequently as Ripley Female College. In 1864 Knapp joined with eight other men to incorporate a business school specifically for young men, named Poultney Normal Institute.

A serious accident in 1866 virtually crippled Knapp for several years, forcing him to give up teaching. Upon his doctor's advice to seek outdoor activities, he bought a farm at Big Grove in Benton County, Iowa. After his relocation to the Midwest, Knapp began a lifelong study of agriculture. By 1872 he was publishing a journal, *The Western Stock Journal and Farmer.* On his farm Knapp used improved varieties of seed and livestock. Before long he helped organize and became the first president of the Iowa Improved Stock Breeders' Association. Knapp's fame as a farmer brought him a professorship of agriculture—the newly established chair of Practical and Experimental Agriculture—and the position of manager of the farm at Iowa State Agricultural College in 1879. While there he drafted the first experiment-station bill for Congress, by which experimental farms would be established to demonstrate better farming techniques. His bill eventually became the Hatch Act of 1887. In 1884 he was chosen president of Iowa State.

Before long Knapp was involved in farming in Louisiana. In 1883 the North American Land and Timber Company, organized by a group of English and American speculators, purchased approximately 1.5 million acres of state and federal land in southern Louisiana, about two-thirds of which were coastal marshland. The object was to drain the marshes for conversion into rice fields. Rice had been grown in Louisiana almost as early as in South Carolina; however, it had never achieved any great commercial importance there, being grown only in small amounts on the bottomlands bordering the Mississippi River. The North American Land and Timber Company undertook to enlarge the rice-growing area of Louisiana by developing large-scale commercial rice production in the coastal marshlands. "Plow boats"—floating barges stationed in canals half a mile apart to pull plows, cultivators, or reapers on cables back and forth across the fields—would be used for the plowing, cultivating, and harvesting. This scheme was hazardous because it depended upon a technique that had not yet been proven, but as many as seventy acres a day were being worked per plow boat. Eventually, however, this reclamation project was abandoned, partially because of engineering difficulties but principally because of competition from an unexpected quarter.

A surprising turn of events in rice planting in Louisiana was to come in the development of the Land and Timber Company's remaining 500,000 acres, upland prairies. Knapp was chosen to lead in this undertaking in 1885. His strategy was to set up experimental farms, manned by midwesterners, where a wide diversification of crops could be displayed to encourage migration to the area. The farmers soon discovered that rice could be grown on the upland prairies. It was only natural for these transplanted midwesterners to apply their small-grain techniques and equipment to the culture of rice, a development which would effect the greatest single change in the history of rice planting. The prairie uplands had sufficient elevation to enable the farmer to drain off the water (here supplied by pumps from streams and wells, creating almost limitless available acreage) when the grain was ripe. This technique dried out the land, which became firm enough to support the heavy harvesting machines, something the soggy soil of the river bottoms or coastal marshes could not do. Thus, within a few years this revolution in rice planting increased the yield per man ten- to twenty-fold. One man and four mules could plant and harvest 100 acres of rice. The Knapp revolution, further enhanced by the importation of Japanese Kiushu rice seed, which produced about 25 percent greater yields, catapulted Louisiana into first place among the rice-producing states in 1889, and by 1900 Louisiana was producing approximately 70 percent of the total American crop.

The Knapp revolution and a series of devastating hurricanes around the turn of the century led to the quick demise of the Old Rice Kingdom of the Carolinas and Georgia, and by the early 1900s there was virtually no rice production in that region. A Rice Growers' Association was established in Louisiana, which Knapp led as president for several years. He also was appointed a special agent of the Department of Agriculture in 1898 to promote agriculture in the southern states. In this capacity he made trips to the Orient in 1898 and 1901 to investigate rice production, including milling and varieties of seed (such as the Kiushu seed that he brought back from Japan). In 1902 he studied agriculture in Puerto Rico.

Knapp's greatest opportunity for improving southern agriculture came in 1903, when the boll weevil crossed over into Texas from Mexico. Through a farm demonstration he was able to convince the Texas farmers that the best way to fight the boll weevil was to practice general principles of good farming, which would include crop rotation, deeper plowing, improved seed selection, and fertilizers. The Department of Agriculture was so impressed that it appropriated $40,000 in November 1903 to enable Knapp's men to conduct similar demonstrations over a large area; eventually 7,000 to 8,000 farmers joined the program. This gave birth to the Farmer's Cooperative Demonstration Work (1903) in the department, where careful object lessons were carried out in the southern states. While the boll weevil remained, crop yields using Knapp's methods increased 50 to 100 percent over yields on farms using older techniques. The General Education Board (established by John D. Rockefeller to improve education in the South) even contributed to the effort, feeling that when the economic status of rural taxpayers increased, southern schools would improve. Boys' and girls' clubs, forerunners of the 4-H clubs, were organized in which the new farming techniques were taught, and eventually hundreds of agents from Virginia to Texas were directing farmers in the use of Knapp's new methods.

Knapp wrote a number of Department of Agriculture bulletins and articles for periodicals; he also made many addresses in the South, a number of which were published in the proceedings of various organizations and conferences. Knapp died in Washington, D.C.

From the year of his death until 1914 the Farmer's Co-operative Demonstration Work was continued by Bradford Knapp, his son; then it was absorbed by the Smith-Lever Act into the extension work of the Department of Agriculture. A fitting memorial for Knapp's great work has been the Seaman A. Knapp School of Country Life, associated with the George Peabody College for Teachers in Nashville, Tennessee.

• The best biography of Knapp is Joseph Cannon Bailey, *Seaman A. Knapp, Schoolmaster of American Agriculture* (1945). See Rodney Cline, *The Life and Work of Seaman A. Knapp* (1936), and H. C. Saunders, "Seaman A. Knapp, Father of Agricultural Extension," *McNeese Review*, 5 (1953): 15–24. See also O. B. Martin, *Demonstration Work, Dr. Seaman A. Knapp's Contribution to Civilization* (1921); and A. C. True, *A History of Agricultural Extension in the United States* (1928) and *A History of Agricultural Education in the United States* (1929). An obituary is in the *(Washington, D.C.) Sunday Star*, 2 Apr. 1911.

JAMES M. CLIFTON

KNEASS, Strickland (29 July 1821–14 Jan. 1884), civil engineer and railroad official, was born in Philadelphia, Pennsylvania, the son of William Kneass, an artist and engraver, and Mary Turner Honeyman. Named in honor of architect and family friend William Strickland, Strickland Kneass completed his early education at Dr. James Espy's classical academy before becoming an assistant to his brother Samuel Honeyman Kneass, an architect and engineer, on the construction of the Delaware & Schuylkill Canal and the railroad line between Philadelphia and Wilmington, Delaware. In 1836 he entered Rensselaer Polytechnic Institute in Troy, New York, graduating in 1839 with an honors degree in civil engineering. After working briefly as a surveyor for the Commonwealth of Pennsylvania's projected railroad between Harrisburg and Pittsburgh, he moved to Washington to become a draftsman in the navy department's Bureau of Engineering. Subsequently, he was employed by the special British commission preparing maps of the boundary between the New England states and Canada's eastern provinces, and by the federal government on the general maps of the border survey.

In 1847 Kneass left government service to become an assistant to J. Edgar Thomson, the chief engineer for the Pennsylvania Railroad, which had succeeded to the task of completing the rail link from Harrisburg to Pittsburgh. By 1850 Kneass had supervised construction of the line over the Allegheny Mountains to Hollidaysburg, where it connected with the Commonwealth's New Portage Road to Pittsburgh. Promoted to the post of first assistant engineer, he then oversaw construction of the PRR's repair shops and engine house at Altoona and the rebuilding of the New Portage line to eliminate the steep grades at the summit of the Alleghenies through the construction of tunnels, viaducts, and infills, most notably, the famed Horseshoe Curve west of Altoona and the 3,670-foot tunnel at Gallitzin.

In 1853 Kneass returned to Philadelphia to wed Margaretta Sybilla Bryan (they would have five children) and to accept the position of associate engineer with the projected North Pennsylvania Railroad, but two years later he resigned this post to accept an appointment by the Philadelphia Select and Common Councils as chief engineer and surveyor for the newly consolidated city and county of Philadelphia. Subsequently reelected to this position for three five-year terms, he organized the city's Department of Surveys & Registry Bureau and oversaw the design and construction of a new drainage system for the expanded city, including the channeling in large sewers of the flood-prone Cohocksink and Mill creeks. He encouraged and directed the expansion of the city's street railway system from two to eighteen lines, many laid out to his specifications. He served as engineer and surveyor in the establishment of Fairmount Park in 1867 and its expansion in 1868, ensuring the city of Philadelphia of a supply of pure and safe drinking water by preserving the Schuylkill River and Wissahickon Creek from industrial development. He was the designer and builder of the iron and granite Chestnut Street Bridge, completed in 1866, and the associated regrading of Chestnut Street to span the Schuylkill and railroad right-of-ways on both banks, and also of the double-decked Fairmount (Callowhill Street) Bridge, completed in 1875, crossing both the Schuylkill and the adjacent Pennsylvania railyard to service the increased vehicle and streetcar traffic that would be generated by the impending Centennial Exposition. Both bridges have since been demolished and replaced. During the Civil War, in preparation for the feared invasion of Pennsylvania by the Army of Virginia under Robert E. Lee, he prepared defense and navigational surveys of the Lower Susquehanna River Valley and, assisting Alexander Dallas Bache, produced maps of proposed fortification sites around the perimeter of the city of Philadelphia.

In 1872 Kneass resigned his municipal post to return to the employ of the Pennsylvania Railroad as assistant to President J. Edgar Thomson. Continuing in this capacity under PRR presidents Thomas A. Scott and George B. Roberts, in 1880 he was also appointed president of numerous Pennsylvania subsidiaries, among them the Pennsylvania & Delaware Railroad, the Trenton Railroad, and the Columbia, Port Deposit & Western Railroad, and made director of the Pittsburgh, Cincinnati, & St. Louis Railroad (Panhandle Route). In 1878 he was elected president of the Eastern Railroad Association, which he transformed into an influential trade organization. Kneass was also a prominent member of the American Philosophical Society, the Franklin Institute, and the American Society of Civil Engineers and was a charter member and early president of the Engineers' Club of Philadelphia. Kneass died in Philadelphia.

In both the public and the private sectors, Kneass's engineering achievements were significant factors in the nation's economic development. For the city of Philadelphia, enlarged in 1854 from the colonial limits established by William Penn, Kneass oversaw the creation of a municipal infrastructure worthy of the nation's second largest city and serving as a foundation for its role as a late nineteenth-century industrial center. For the Pennsylvania Railroad, Kneass's plans for the road over the difficult barrier of the Alleghenies achieved the long-sought aim of a direct rail link between Philadelphia and Pittsburgh, providing the region with a means to compete for western trade with New York's Erie Canal and the South's Baltimore & Ohio line. In later years, as assistant to three of the Pennsylvania's chief executives, Kneass oversaw the expansions and consolidations that transformed the PRR into the nation's largest rail system, stretching from New York City west to Chicago and the Mississippi Valley.

• For more information on Strickland Kneass, see J. Thomas Scharf and Thompson Westcott, "Surveys and Surveyors" in *History of Philadelphia* (1884). Kneass's work for the Pennsylvania Railroad is detailed and illustrated in Edwin P. Alexander, *On the Main Line: The Pennsylvania Railroad in the Nineteenth Century* (1971), and for the city of Philadelphia in Robert F. Looney, *Old Philadelphia in Early Photographs, 1839–1914* (1976), and Russell Weigley et al., *Philadelphia: A 300-Year History* (1985).

WILLIAM ALAN MORRISON

KNEELAND, Abner (6 Apr. 1774–27 Aug. 1844), freethinker and Universalist clergyman, was born in Gardner, Massachusetts, the son of Timothy Kneeland, a soldier in the revolutionary war, and Moriah Stone. After attending common schools, Kneeland studied for a short time at the Chesterfield Academy in New Hampshire and worked as a carpenter. In 1797 he married Waitstill Ormsbee; three of their four children reached adulthood. Although Kneeland joined the Baptist church, which licensed him to preach in 1801, he became a Universalist two years later and in 1804 was licensed to preach by that denomination. In addition to preaching, Kneeland taught school and published several popular spelling books.

In 1805 Kneeland was appointed town minister in Langdon, New Hampshire, which he later represented in the state legislature (1810–1811). His first wife having died, he married Lucinda Mason in 1806; before she also died, they had five children, three of whom reached adulthood. Beginning in 1811, Kneeland was the minister of a Universalist church in Charlestown, Massachusetts, but coming to doubt the divine origin of the Bible, he left the ministry in 1814. The year before he had married Eliza Osborn, a widow; after they were married (it would be a childless union), he helped to manage her retail hat business. Beginning in 1817, after that business failed and his theological doubts had lessened, he began to preach at Whitestown, New York, and continued there until the fall of 1818, when he settled at the Lombard Street Universalist Church in Philadelphia.

In 1822 Kneeland published his translation of the New Testament, which left in Greek "all references to future punishment, hell, and damnation" (Miller, vol. 1, p. 187). From 1819 to 1823 he edited the *Christian Messenger*, which he renamed the *Philadelphia Universalist Magazine and Christian Messenger*. For a year after that periodical's demise, Kneeland edited the secular *Gazetteer*. During these Philadelphia years, he was especially influenced by the writings of Joseph Priestley, an early Unitarian and a scientist, and by Robert Dale Owen, a Welsh utopian socialist with whom he became acquainted.

In 1825 Kneeland moved to New York City as the minister of the Prince Street Church. The congregants—members of the Second Society of United Christian Friends—found him to be increasingly controversial, and early in 1827 he and some of the congregation broke away to establish a new group, which met at Tammany Hall and other places. During that year he also began to edit the *Olive Branch* (soon to be the *Olive Branch and Christian Inquirer*). Kneeland's group splintered again in 1828, after he invited Fanny Wright, a controversial social reformer from Scotland, to lecture to it.

Kneeland broke with Universalists and explained why in six lectures delivered in August 1829. That same year he published the lectures as *A Review of the Evidences of Christianity*, which went through six editions in ten years. Those who remained his followers began in 1830 to call themselves "Moral Philanthropists," published the *Free Inquirer*, and became the "nucleus for the largest and most durable of all the free-thought societies formed in New York during this epoch of radicalism" (French, p. 203).

As the 1830s began, Kneeland was immensely popular. He influenced those Americans for whom religious dogma was no longer sacred, and he was in step with those who were concerned that the social and political promises of 1776 remained unfulfilled for many citizens. In 1831 he moved to Boston, where he was paid $500 a year to lecture and travel for the First Society of Free Enquirers, a nonsectarian forum of opinion that had been formed the year before (following Fanny Wright's summer lecture series) and that would continue for a decade. Regretting that much of his life had been spent promoting religious institutions and ideas in which he no longer believed, Kneeland felt a sense of urgency in spreading his new message. Almost immediately he founded and edited the *Boston Investigator* (published from 1831 to 1904). This weekly social-reform journal of the free-thought movement advocated public schools, women's rights, a better life for working people, and the abolition of slavery and imprisonment for debt.

In the second issue of his paper Kneeland printed a "Marriage Catechism," which insisted that a marriage was not binding if it did not produce happiness for the parties immediately concerned. Not surprisingly, its many critics complained that Kneelands "catechism" threatened the bonds of society itself. Besides radical books and pamphlets, Kneeland offered for sale the first birth-control manual published in the United States, Robert Dale Owen's *Moral Physiology; or, A Brief and Plain Treatise on the Population Question*

(1830), which went through five editions in six months. In 1833, after physician Charles Knowlton had served a jail term for publishing a marriage manual that he had written, he presented it orally to Kneeland's congregation, and Kneeland printed and distributed it as a lecture.

Kneeland constantly linked the freedoms gained in the American Revolution with the goals of worldwide progressive movements. In the *Boston Investigator* he pushed for equality regardless of sex and race. His opponents, who considered him a moral and social menace, feared both the subject matter of his paper and his popularity. His society was growing rapidly; as many as 2,000 people (a third of them women) attended his lectures and social evenings, and his paper's circulation reached 2,500 copies a week.

Glorying in animated dialogue, Kneeland regularly published, in the *Boston Investigator*, the critical letters he received and his replies to them. In one of his replies published in December 1833, Kneeland—who considered himself a pantheist rather than an atheist—quoted an earlier letter of his own, which stated that he did not "believe in god" and called the Universalists' "god . . . a chimera of their own imagination" (Miller, vol. 1, p. 192). Indicted for blasphemy, under a statute originally enacted in 1782, Kneeland was accused by Massachusetts Attorney General James T. Austin of committing treason against the interests of society. Over the course of four years of litigation, which resulted in three hung juries, Kneeland argued in his own defense, and a "Persecution Fund" kept him financially solvent. Throughout he was sustained by Dolly L. Rice, a widow whom he married in 1834, his third wife also having predeceased him; he and Dolly would have four children, three of whom reached adulthood.

Ultimately Kneeland was found guilty of blasphemy. When his conviction was upheld by Chief Justice Lemuel Shaw—in a decision called one of the worst of his career—150 of the most influential residents of the state petitioned the Massachusetts governor to pardon him. (Among the petitioners were Ralph Waldo Emerson, William Ellery Channing, Theodore Parker, William Lloyd Garrison, George Ripley, and Bronson Alcott.) Nevertheless, Kneeland, as Parker phrased it, "was jugged for sixty days" (Miller, vol. 1, p. 193).

On 17 August 1838, when Kneeland emerged from jail, he appeared to be, as Parker had predicted, "all foaming," like "beer from a bottle" (Miller, vol. 1, p. 193). He admonished his celebrating followers to "remember this when you go to the polls" (French, p. 220), but he was tired of bucking persecution. In March 1839 he left for the Iowa Territory, becoming part of what has been called the first plan for colonizing Iowa—a two-year-old plan worked out by the First Society of Free Enquirers. With eight other families, Kneeland and his family formed a frontier community they called Salubria, in Van Buren County, two miles south of Farmingham. Their hope to make their cluster of farmhouses the center of free thought in the West did not materialize, but Kneeland wrote eigh-

een letters to the *Boston Investigator* to keep its readers in touch with the settlement. When Kneeland, who remained notorious, dabbled in Iowa politics as a Democrat in 1840 and 1842, "church" Democrats combined with Whigs to defeat what they called the "infidel ticket." Except for a few months when he taught school in Helena, Arkansas, Kneeland remained in Salubria, where he died.

Admiring Kneeland's "gentle courage," Boston physician and poet Oliver Wendell Holmes noted that "his temperate statement of opinions . . . threatened to shake the existing order of thought like an earthquake" (Stillman F. Kneeland, p. 222). He was early America's best-known and most influential freethinker.

• Printed material pertinent to Kneeland, including sermons and tracts, can be found at the Andover-Harvard Library of the Harvard Divinity School, Cambridge, Mass., and at the Massachusetts Historical Society, Boston. See *A Series of Letters in Defence of Divine Revelation* (1816) for Kneeland's discussion of the divine origin of the Bible with Hosea Ballou, a leading Universalist clergyman. Besides writing numerous hymns himself, Kneeland compiled the *Philadelphia Hymn Book* (1819) and *National Hymns* (1832). He also wrote *A Brief Sketch of a New System of Orthography* (1807) and the *American Pronouncing Spelling Book* (1824), which detailed a phonetic system of spelling. For Kneeland's printing of the first marriage manual, see *Two Remarkable Lectures Delivered in Boston by Dr. C. Knowlton on the Day of His leaving the Jail at East Cambridge, March 31, 1833, Where He Had Been Imprisoned for Publishing a Book* (1833). For Kneeland's story with a Universalist slant, see Russell E. Miller, *The Larger Hope: The First Century of the Universalist Church in America, 1770–1870* (2 vols., 1979–1985). Especially helpful is Roderick S. French, "Liberation from Man and God in Boston: Abner Kneeland's Free-Thought Campaign, 1830–1839," *American Quarterly* 32 (1980): 202–21. Also of interest are Henry Steele Commager, "The Blasphemy of Abner Kneeland," *New England Quarterly*, Mar. 1935, pp. 29–41; Ruth A. Gallaher, "Abner Kneeland: Pioneer Pantheist," *Palimpsest* 20 (1939): 209–25; Mary R. Whitcomb, "Abner Kneeland: His Relations to Early Iowa History, *Annals of Iowa*, 3 ser., 6 (1904): 340–63; Stillman Foster Kneeland, *Seven Centuries in the Kneeland Family* (1897); and Samuel Gridley Howe, "Atheism in New England," *New England Magazine* 7 (1834): 500–9, 8 (1835): 53–62. An obituary is in the *Boston Investigator*, 25 Sept. 1844.

OLIVE HOOGENBOOM

KNEELAND, Samuel (31 Jan. 1697–14 Dec. 1769), printer and publisher, was born in Boston, Massachusetts, the son of John Kneeland and Mary Green, granddaughter of colonial printer Samuel Green. After serving an apprenticeship with his uncle Bartholomew Green, Kneeland established his own printing business and began impressively. In 1717 he advertised for subscribers and printed Cotton Mather's *Psalterium Americanum* the following year. Kneeland would publish many Mather works during the next decade. Besides Mather, several New England divines, most notably Thomas Foxcroft and Benjamin Colman, would provide a steady stream of business for the ambitious young printer. Kneeland's 1721 marriage to Mary Alden, great-granddaughter of John

Alden and Priscilla Alden, reinforced his New England heritage. In 1724 Kneeland revealed his interest in early New England literary and religious history with the second edition of New England's first printed sermon, Robert Cushman's 1622 *Sin and Danger of Self-Love*. With Bartholomew Green, Kneeland became printer to the Massachusetts House of Representatives from 1723 to 1728. Kneeland, again in conjunction with Green, printed Samuel Willard's (1640–1707) posthumous *Compleat Body of Divinity* (1726), the largest publication project to that date undertaken in America. The title page of the folio work was printed in black and red, the earliest example of rubrication in an American book.

In 1727 Kneeland entered a partnership with his cousin Timothy Green II. Together, they became printers to the Massachusetts House of Representatives after the death of Bartholomew Green in 1732. Kneeland remained printer for the lower house of the legislature until 1761. With his new partner, Kneeland continued to publish religious books, including reprints of popular English devotional works such as Richard Baxter's *Call to the Unconverted* (1731) and John Bunyan's *Grace Abounding* (1732). They also printed many works by the most important religious thinkers and writers of early eighteenth-century New England, including sermons by Charles Chauncy (1705–1787) and Mather Byles. Thomas Prince was a special favorite. They printed Prince's *Vade Mecum for America* (1731), his edition of John Mason's (1600–1672) *Brief History of the Pequot War* (1736), *The Chronological History of New-England* (1736), and Prince's *Christian History* (1743–1745), the earliest American religious periodical. Starting in the late 1730s, the Great Awakening provided additional printing jobs. Kneeland and Green printed works by George Whitefield and Gilbert Tennent, and, with Whitefield's encouragement, they printed the third edition of Cotton Mather's conduct book for women, *Ornaments for the Daughters of Zion* (1741). They also printed Jonathan Edwards's (1703–1758) first published work, *God Glorified in the Work of Redemption* (1731); *Sinners in the Hands of an Angry God* (1741); and *A Treatise concerning Religious Affections* (1746), which was so popular that, as Kneeland noted in the first edition, "near thirteen hundred books [were] subscribed for, and more subscriptions sent in than books printed." In 1752 Kneeland and Green produced the first Bible in the English language printed in America. As Isaiah Thomas remembered, "It was carried through the press as privately as possible, and had the London imprint of the copy from which it was reprinted, viz: 'London: Printed by Mark Baskett, Printer to the King's Most Excellent Majesty,' in order to prevent a prosecution from those in England and Scotland, who published the Bible by a patent from the crown." The work did not sell quickly, however, and Kneeland would later reissue it with a new title page.

Besides such ambitious printing projects, Kneeland also ran a newspaper. In August 1720 he had taken over printing the *Boston Gazette* from James Franklin.

When Bartholomew Green became the printer of the *Boston Gazette* in 1727, Kneeland established the *New-England Weekly Journal* with the encouragement of Mather Byles, announcing that "regular Schemes for the Entertainment of the ingenious Reader, and the Encouragement of Wit & Politeness" were forthcoming (quoted in Granger, p. 26). The paper included much poetry by Byles, Matthew Adams, and the Reverend John Adams (1704–1740). In 1727 Kneeland started publishing the "Proteus Echo" essays in the *Boston Gazette*, which would gain a reputation as one of colonial America's best essay series. Fifty-two numbers appeared from 10 April 1727 to 1 April 1728. In 1736 Kneeland and Green took over the *Boston Gazette* from Bartholomew Green, Jr., who had been printing the paper since his father's death. When the publisher of the *Boston Gazette* died in October 1741, Kneeland and Green became the proprietors. On 20 October 1741 they combined the two papers, changing the title to the *Boston Gazette, or New England Weekly Journal*, which was altered on 27 October 1741 to the *Boston Gazette, or, Weekly Journal*.

In late 1752 Green left the firm, and Kneeland carried on alone. Kneeland continued the newspaper, altering its title to the *Boston Gazette, or, Weekly Advertiser* (3 Jan. 1753). In April 1755 Kneeland sold the paper to Benjamin Edes and John Gill and spent the remainder of his career printing items for the house of representatives as well as religious works. Kneeland's government jobs included two Indian treaties in 1753 and 1754. He also continued to print some of the most important religious treatises in America, including Jonathan Edwards's *A Careful and Strict Enquiry into the . . . Freedom of the Will* (1754) and *The Great Christian Doctrine of Original Sin* (1758). Among Kneeland's last efforts were Samuel Hopkins's (1721–1803) *Life of . . . Jonathan Edwards* (1765) and two volumes of Edwards's posthumous works that same year. With these final works, Kneeland retired, perhaps recognizing that with the death of Edwards, New England's golden era of religious publishing had ended. Overall, Kneeland's religious convictions, his printing skill, and his ambition helped make him one of Boston's most prominent printers during the mid-eighteenth century. He died in Boston.

• Some Kneeland letters survive among the Joseph Bellamy Papers at the Hartford Seminary Foundation Library. Kneeland's imprints are listed in Charles Evans, *American Bibliography* (1903–1934). Information concerning Kneeland within Evans is easily accessible using Roger Pattrell Bristol, *Index of Printers, Publishers, and Booksellers Indicated by Charles Evans in His American Bibliography* (1961). See also Bristol's *Supplement to Charles Evans' American Bibliography* (1970). Kneeland's newspapers are discussed in Clarence S. Brigham, *History and Bibliography of American Newspapers 1690–1820* (1947). Other sources include Isaiah Thomas, *The History of Printing in America*, ed. Marcus A. McCorison (1970); Lawrence C. Wroth, *The Colonial Printer* (1938; repr. 1964); Harry Miller Lydenberg, "The Problem of the Pre-1776 American Bible," *Papers of the Bibliographical Society of America* 48 (1954): 183–94; Rollo G. Silver, "Government

Printing in Massachusetts, 1751–1801," *Studies in Bibliography* 16 (1963): 161–200; Bruce Granger, *American Essay Serials from Franklin to Irving* (1978); and Benjamin Franklin V, ed., *Boston Printers, Publishers, and Booksellers: 1640–1800* (1980).

KEVIN J. HAYES

KNERR, Harold Hering (4 Sept. 1882–7 or 8 July 1949), cartoonist, was born in Bryn Mawr, Pennsylvania, the son of Calvin Knerr, a physician, and Melitta Hering. At an early age he showed a talent for drawing, and while attending art school in Philadelphia he drew cartoons and comics for several area newspapers (his first recorded contribution to the field appeared in 1901). Working in a clearly delineated, exaggerated style reminiscent of cartoonists Rudolph Dirks and James Swinnerton (1875–1974), Knerr soon became so fluent in the nascent idiom of the comics that he was able to sell comic series of his own creation to the *Philadelphia Inquirer* while still in his teens and twenties, notable among them *Hard Luck Willie* (1903) and *Mr. George and Wifey* (1904).

Knerr's best-known and longest-lasting creation of the period, however, was *Die Fineheimer Twins*, which he started in February 1903. Starring a set of mischievous twins at war with the adult world, it was, like so many other comics of its time, an imitation of Dirks's extraordinarily successful *Katzenjammer Kids*. Although clearly derivative, it displayed a quality of style and wit and a sheer comic verve that made it more than a simple exercise in mimicry. At the same time Knerr kept on pouring out more original creations, such as *Zoo-Illogical Snapshots* (1911) and *That Irresistible Rag* (1913), but *Die Fineheimer Twins* remains his early masterpiece.

Knerr's skill and reputation attracted the attention of newspaper magnate William Randolph Hearst after Hearst's bitter legal battle with Dirks over ownership of the *Katzenjammer Kids*. The federal courts had ruled in appeal that Hearst had title to the strip but that Dirks could go on drawing the characters for the competition. In November 1914 Knerr took over the comic strip (trumpeted as "The Original" Katzenjammer Kids) for Hearst, while Dirks drew his version of the strip for Joseph Pulitzer's rival *New York World* under the title *Hans and Fritz* (later changed to the *Captain and the Kids*).

Of course the court's novel arrangement resulted in fierce competition between the two artists. Their contest was as heated and colorful in its own way as the legendary rivalry between Hearst and Pulitzer. In their attempts to outdo each other, Knerr and Dirks, each in his own inimitable style, set the tone, pace, and flavor of the whole period. They outrageously stole characters, ideas, and entire situations from each other. Exuberantly escalating the antics of their unedifying heroes, they let the action run wild, pulling out all stops—both of them encapsulating at once the vibrant spirit of the comics in the sublime effrontery of it all.

Having inherited a cast of already legendary characters from Dirks, Knerr set out to elevate the basic situation to quasi-mythological proportions. During the first twenty years of his tenure he dispatched the Katzenjammer tribe—made up of the terrible twins Hans and Fritz, their mother "Die Mama," "Der Captain," and "Der Inspector"—on a worldwide path of destruction extending from the Arctic to the African jungles and from Hollywood to the Amazon forests. They even briefly claimed to be Dutch citizens during the anti-German hysteria of World War I, when the strip's title was changed to the *Shenanigan Kids* (after the war it reverted to its original name).

The Katzenjammers' cataclysmic voyages ended in 1935 when they all landed on an island off the coast of Africa ruled by benevolent King Bongo. After settling there they were soon joined by Miss Twiddle, a martinet of a tutor brought in for the thankless task of teaching the kids civilized manners, and her niece Lena. Knerr rounded out his cast of characters with the introduction of the foppish Rollo Rhubarb, Miss Twiddle's star pupil, whose underhanded schemes often proved more than a match for the kids' devilish tricks. In addition there were literally thousands of extras: royal guards, tax collectors, and traveling salesmen, not to mention visiting royalty, lost explorers, and hosts of wild animals, each delineated and individualized with a sure hand and a fine comic touch. On this broad canvas Knerr painted countless variations of his basic theme of all against all, until his death in his New York City hotel room.

Knerr's last comic-page creation of any consequence was *Dinglehoofer und His Dog Adolph* (later *Dinglehoofer und His Dog*), started in 1926 as a companion strip to the *Katzenjammer Kids*. In a tone of quiet humor contrasting with the hectic farce of the Katzenjammers, it told of the low-key adventures of a dumpy, middle-aged, middle-class German American named Dinglehoofer ("Mr. Dingy"), his young ward Tad, and his feisty bulldog Adolph, later replaced by a basset hound called Schnappsy. A tender and funny strip, *Dinglehoofer* survived its creator by several years. Knerr also drew occasional illustrations, notably for "This Dumb World," a series of articles by Bruno Lessing (the pen name of Rudolph Block, Knerr's syndicate editor).

Harold Knerr and Rudolph Dirks apparently never met; it is ironic that their names should forever be linked in any discussion of the comics. Knerr has been praised for his brilliant continuation of Dirks's original concept, but his contribution did not stop there. He brought to the strip a better organization, a sharper focus, and a sense of composition and motion much admired by Picasso and the surrealists. When people speak about the Katzenjammer Kids, Knerr's is the version to which they most often refer. His single-minded devotion to his characters shines through in his minute attention to detail, his accomplished draftsmanship, and his flair for comic effect. A shy, bald, bespectacled man, Knerr never married. In the Katzenjammers he found his true family.

• All standard reference works on the comics contain information about Knerr and his work. See especially Martin Sheridan, *Comics and Their Creators* (1942), Coulton Waugh, *The Comics* (1947), Stephen Becker, *Comic Art in America* (1959), Pierre Couperie and Maurice Horn, *A History of the Comic Strip* (1968), Jerry Robinson, *The Comics: An Illustrated History* (1974), Horn, ed., *The World Encyclopedia of Comics* (1976), and Ron Goulart, ed., *The Encyclopedia of American Comics* (1990). An obituary is in the *New York Times*, 9 July 1949.

MAURICE HORN

KNIGHT, Austin Melvin (16 Dec. 1854–26 Feb. 1927), naval officer, was born in Ware, Massachusetts, the son of Charles Sanford Knight and Cordelia Cutter. Appointed to the U.S. Naval Academy in June 1869 from Florida, Knight graduated in May 1873. Soon after graduation, Knight reported to the screw sloop *Tuscarora*, which carried out deep-sea soundings in the Pacific. Promoted to ensign in July 1874, he returned to the Naval Academy in January 1876 to teach English, history, and international law. In 1878 he married Alice Phinney Tobey of Milwaukee, Wisconsin. She died the next year.

Ordered in September 1878 to the screw steamer *Quinnebaug*, which operated on the Mediterranean station, Knight received promotion to master (a rank that later became lieutenant, junior grade) in October 1879. Joining the new screw steamer *Galena* in August 1880, Knight participated in relief efforts at earthquake-ravaged Chios, Greece, on the Aegean Sea, in April 1881, and helped protect the U.S. consulate in Alexandria, Egypt, in June 1882, when a British naval landing force seized the port after an uprising of Egyptian troops.

Detached from *Galena* in January 1884, Knight commanded the "experimental battery" (a facility later designated as the naval ordnance proving ground) at Annapolis, overseeing important developmental work on guns, gun mounts, ammunition, ballistics, range finding, and new types of powder. Promoted to lieutenant in December 1885, he married Elizabeth Harwood Welsh of Annapolis in April 1886. They had two daughters and one son.

Knight took his practical experience gained at the proving grounds to sea in March 1889, as ordnance officer of the cruiser *Chicago*, but he returned to the Naval Academy in September 1892 to teach physics and chemistry. After service in the frigate *Lancaster* (Sept. 1895–Mar. 1896) and the gunboat *Castine* (Mar. 1896–Dec. 1896), Knight joined the monitor *Puritan* and served as the navigator. The ship operated on the Cuban blockade during the war with Spain in 1898.

Returning to the Naval Academy in September 1898, Knight headed its department of seamanship until May 1900, when he assumed command of the training ship *Newport*. The paucity of texts on seamanship for a navy that was making increasing use of steam rather than sail as a motive power, had compelled Knight to write his own text on the subject, *Modern Seamanship* (1901), which became a standard work in the field.

Knight remained at the academy until June 1901, when he journeyed to Newport, Rhode Island, to attend the Naval War College. After instruction there, Knight served briefly as executive officer of the cruiser *Olympia* in October 1901 before he assumed command later that same month of the converted yacht *Yankton*, which operated principally in the waters off Cuba and Puerto Rico on survey duty. He received promotion to commander during that time.

Given command of the gunboat *Castine* in November 1903, Knight was detached in April 1904 to report to the Navy Department for special duty in the Bureau of Ordnance. Promoted to captain in July 1907, he assumed command of the armored cruiser *Washington* in October of the same year. He returned to the Navy Department in June 1909, resuming his work as a member of the special board that directed the Bureau of Ordnance's experimental work on explosives, projectiles, fuses, and ballistics. Promoted to flag rank in May 1911, he eventually became president of the special board on ordnance before his tour in the bureau ended in April 1912.

After the creation of reserve fleets on both the Atlantic and Pacific coasts of the United States, Knight was given command of the Atlantic Reserve Fleet at Philadelphia. On 1 May 1912 he hoisted his flag in the armored cruiser *Tennessee*. The fleet consisted of six old battleships, two armored cruisers, two scout cruisers, and a collier. After the outbreak of the First Balkan War in late 1912, Knight was made commander in chief of a special service squadron to stand ready to protect American lives and property in the region. *Tennessee* sailed from Philadelphia in November 1912 for the Near East, but no occasion arose for military action, and the squadron returned to the United States early the following year.

Knight returned to his duty as commander in chief of the Atlantic Reserve Fleet in March 1913, breaking his flag in the battleship *Wisconsin*. He later shifted his flag back to *Tennessee* in October 1913, shortly before he was detached to become commandant of the Naval Station at Narragansett Bay, Rhode Island, and of the Second Naval District, with additional responsibilities as president of the Naval War College.

From December 1913 to February 1917 Knight, an advocate of naval preparedness, broadened the curriculum of the War College, instituting a one-year course that included requirements to write theses concerning the principles and practice of strategy and the relation of policy to war and the preparation for war, as well as the study of logistics, tactics, and strategy for the Pacific Ocean. He also increased the size of the student body of officers and of the physical plant of the institution, and, as he said in his opening address of 1917, saw the War College "vitalized by a new comprehension of its mission and a new consciousness of its power."

In April 1917 Knight became commander in chief, Asiatic Fleet, with the rank of admiral, and subsequently distinguished himself during the crisis in Siberia occasioned by the Russian civil war. After the overthrow of the Bolshevik regime in Vladivostok in July 1918 by Czech troops stranded in the Far East port, Allied forces, including marines under Knight's command, intervened. Amid a complex international situation, Knight cooperated fully with foreign commanders in protecting Vladivostok and supporting the operations of anti-Bolshevik Czech troops in Siberia with medical aid and supplies. The Woodrow Wilson administration, however, did not heed his call for a more aggressive American intervention against the Soviets. For his "services in connection with Allied operations carried on, at, and near Vladivostok," Knight received the Distinguished Service Medal. In recognition of his impassioned support of its cause, the Czechoslovak Republic accorded him its Cross of War; the government of Japan, with whose naval forces Knight had so "punctiliously and effectively" cooperated in Siberia, awarded him the Grand Cordon of the Rising Sun.

Retiring from the navy on 16 December 1918, Knight was recalled to active duty in March 1919 to chair the board charged with reviewing recommendations for awards of the Medal of Honor, the Distinguished Service Medal, and the Navy Cross. The board was dissolved in October 1919 but reconvened in January 1920 to revisit the issue as the result of dissatisfaction in the naval service over the matter of awards. After the dissolution of the board in June 1920, Knight was relieved of all active duty. He died in Washington, D.C.

• Biographical material on Knight is contained in the Ship Name and Sponsor File, in the Ships' Histories Branch of the Naval Historical Center, Washington, D.C., for the destroyer *Knight* (DD-633), named in the admiral's honor in 1941. On Knight's role in revitalizing the Naval War College, see John B. Hattendorf et al., *Sailors and Scholars: A Centennial History of the Naval War College* (1984); Knight also coauthored (with his aide Lieutenant William D. Puleston) *History of the United States Naval War College* (1916). William R. Braisted, *The United States Navy in the Pacific: 1909–1922* (1971), discusses Knight's strategic views and his tour as commander in chief, Asiatic Fleet. Books that specifically deal with U.S. involvement in Siberia include Betty Miller Unterberger, *America's Siberian Expedition, 1918–1920: A Study of National Policy* (1956), and James William Morley, *The Japanese Thrust into Siberia, 1918* (1957). A discussion of the work of the Knight board and the controversy over the awarding of medals in the wake of World War I is contained in Elting E. Morison, *Admiral Sims and the Modern American Navy* (1942), and Tracy B. Kittredge, *Naval Lessons of the Great War* (1921), as well as in the published hearings, U.S. Congress, *Hearings before a Subcommittee on Naval Affairs*, 66th Cong., 2d sess., 1920. An obituary is in the *Army and Navy Register*, 5 Mar. 1927.

ROBERT JAMES CRESSMAN

KNIGHT, Daniel Ridgway (15 Mar. 1839–9 Mar. 1924), painter, was born in Philadelphia, Pennsylvania. His early life in no way prepared him for his life's work. His parents were devout Quakers, and according to the strictures of that sect, he grew up in a home where the display of pictures was forbidden. After completing his schooling in Philadelphia, he was apprenticed to a local, Quaker-owned hardware store. At night he would draw, copying illustrations from books that he borrowed from the library of the Franklin Institute. His grandfather was impressed by the quality of the drawings and showed them to persons in the Philadelphia art world. Consequently Knight was encouraged to study art, and in 1858 he enrolled in the Pennsylvania Academy of the Fine Arts, which he attended for nearly three years. In 1861 he went to Paris, where on 9 October he registered in the atelier of the Swiss-born painter Marc-Charles-Gabriel Gleyre, who specialized in religious subjects and themes from ancient and modern history. When Knight successfully passed the entrance exam to the École des Beaux-Arts, he studied as well with history painter Alexandre Cabanel. Both masters emphasized the human figure, correctly proportioned and heroically posed in the classical tradition. Canvases were to be highly finished and to abound with finely rendered detail. These qualities are apparent in Knight's paintings throughout his career.

When Confederate forces threatened Philadelphia in 1863, Knight returned home and enlisted in a Chambersburg, Pennsylvania, regiment. His wartime experience provided the inspiration for a number of canvases, including *The Burning of Chambersburg, Pennsylvania* (1867, Washington County Museum of Fine Arts, Hagerstown, Md.).

After the war Knight opened a studio in Philadelphia where he taught and painted for seven years. One of his students was Rebecca Morris Webster, whom he married in 1871. Knight returned to Paris with his bride in late 1871 or 1872. The first of their three children, Louis Aston Knight, who would also be a painter, was born in Paris in 1873. Within a year of his return to France Knight met battle painter Jean-Louis-Ernest Meissonier. So great was the professional attraction between this French master and the American painter that Knight was inspired to move to Poissy, a small town on the River Seine, where Meissonier lived. He purchased a sixteenth-century chateau, which would remain his primary residence for the remainder of his life. In the garden he constructed a studio entirely of glass, a hothouse really, where he could paint in natural light the year round.

At Poissy Knight began to paint his signature theme, pictures of the local peasant people, predominantly female, engaged in day-to-day chores or idly posed amidst the flowery fields and gardens for which Poissy was famous. His first great success, *Les laveuses (The Washer Women)*, executed under Meissonier's guidance, shows a group of peasant women of varying ages ranged along a river's edge with large baskets of clothing to wash. The canvas was exhibited in the Paris Salon of 1875 and was purchased from the salon by F. O. Matthiesen of New York. Other examples of the theme of peasant women outdoors include *Hailing the Ferry* (1888, Pennsylvania Academy of the Fine Arts,

Philadelphia) and *The Shepherdess* (1896, Brooklyn Museum).

Awards came rapidly to Knight beginning in the early 1880s. He received honorable mention at the salon of 1882 for his painting *Un deuil*. He took the third-class gold medal at the salon of 1888 and a gold medal in Munich the same year. In 1889 he was awarded the silver medal at the Universal Exposition held in Paris, and in 1892 he received the cross of the Legion of Honor of France; he was subsequently made a knight and an officer of that organization.

Knight earned comparable recognition in his native country. His paintings were frequently shown at the National Academy of Design and the Pennsylvania Academy of the Fine Arts, which bestowed on him the Grand Medal of Honor in 1893. He received the Columbian Medal at the World's Columbian Exposition at Chicago in the same year.

Wishing to add variety to his landscape settings, in 1896 Knight purchased a primitive old house at Rolleboise, a tiny hillside village on the Seine below Poissy, where he lived a hermitlike existence with his son Louis Aston, the two of them painting, hunting, and sailing. Until his death he kept the chateau at Poissy, which his wife preferred, as well as a small apartment in Paris.

Knight did his patriotic duty to France during the First World War by providing the original art for *Bas de Laine*, a print that was distributed throughout France to push the third French war loan.

In 1901 art critic Harold T. Lawrence observed, "Few American painters have attained wider or more substantial popularity than Daniel Ridgway Knight." He cited the winsome qualities of Knight's paintings as responsible for their enduring appeal. Knight's aim was not realism like that of his contemporary, French artist Jules Breton, who focused on the poverty and debilitating labor of peasant life; rather, Knight strove to portray rural life's more bucolic aspects. Knight died in the American Hospital in Paris.

Though contemporary writers described Knight's subjects as his peasant neighbors at Poissy and Rolleboise, this was true only in part. Actually Knight hired models whom he clothed in garments that he bought from the local peasants. His subjects, described by George W. Sheldon in 1888 as "contented and prosperous children of the soil" (*Recent Ideals of American Art*), have in the late twentieth century been ironically dubbed "genteel peasants" by H. Barbara Weinberg in *The Lure of Paris* (1990).

• A brief but comprehensive biography is included in the exhibition catalog by Pamela Beecher, *A Pastoral Legacy: Paintings and Drawings by the American Artists Ridgway Knight and Aston Knight* (1989). This catalog also includes a very useful selected bibliography. Obituaries are in *Art News* 22 (15 Mar. 1924): 6, and the *New York Times*, 10 Mar. 1924.

CYNTHIA SEIBELS

KNIGHT, Etheridge (19 Apr. 1931–10 Mar. 1991), poet, was born in Corinth, Mississippi, the son of Etheridge "Bushie" Knight and Belzora Cozart.

Knight grew up in Paducah, Kentucky, quit school after the eighth grade, and later ran away from home. During his teenage years he learned various toasts from the older African-American men with whom he frequented bars and poolrooms. Toast-telling, or reciting long narrative poems, usually in rhyming couplets, was a social activity Knight enjoyed and later perfected in his prison years.

At age seventeen Knight joined the U.S. Army, serving as a medical technician from 1947 to 1951. He was wounded in Korea and became addicted to morphine, the drug used to treat him. Before his enlistment, however, he had already begun using drugs to escape the pain and disillusionment of growing up in poverty. He continued to abuse narcotics after his discharge and in 1960 was given a 10- to 25-year sentence for armed robbery, committed to support his habit. He served most of his sentence at the Indiana State Prison and was paroled in November 1968. Upon his release from prison, Knight married poet Sonia Sanchez, with whom he had corresponded while incarcerated.

Knight had found among his fellow inmates a receptive audience for the toasts he recited. "The ability to talk is power," he said. "I learned that very young, that the people who could rap and write, you didn't have to fight as much" (*MELUS*, p. 9). He soon applied his understanding of the components of a successful toast—interesting subjects, identifiable characters, and specific language—to written poetry. By 1963 he was writing and submitting poetry for publication. He established contacts with black poets, writers, and publishers such as Sanchez, Gwendolyn Brooks, and Dudley Randall. Randall's Detroit-based small press, Broadside, meant as an outlet for black writing, published Knight's first book of poetry, *Poems from Prison*, in 1968.

Knight's emergence as a poet coincided with the rise of the Black Arts movement, which began in the early 1960s and continued through the mid-1970s. Not since the Harlem Renaissance of the 1920s and early 1930s had such an outpouring of literature and art come from the African-American community. Black Aestheticians (as those involved in the movement were called) used their art to encourage racial pride and political involvement, specifically on the part of the working class and the poor. Knight, who certainly wrote on these themes, expressed his reason for writing by saying that he and other poets are naturally meddlers: "The result of a poet's meddling emerges in different ways. Sometimes it's a howl or a scream; sometimes it's a love song or a jubilee; sometimes it's 'arty' intellectual masturbation. But always the main motivation must be loving concern" (*Born of a Woman*, p. xiii).

Knight's concern for his audience, primarily the African-American community, is apparent in poems such as "A Watts Mother Mourns While Boiling Beans" and "For Black Poets Who Think of Suicide" (1973). In the former work, a mother laments the fate of her young son, who has taken to the streets and caused her to endure constant fear for his life. In the latter, Knight urges fellow black poets to "live—not leap from steel bridges (like the white boys do)" (repr. in *Born of a Woman*, p. 70). Knight said early in his career that the black artist should be accountable only to black people, but he later acknowledged that his poetry evokes feelings of a universal nature and could therefore extend to a wider readership. He was comfortable with the evolution of his work and considered his later poems less narrow instead of less black.

Knight's next book after *Poems from Prison*, *Black Voices from Prison* (1970), contains selections of his poems, letters, and essays as well as work from other prison inmates. In the early 1970s he was writer-in-residence at the University of Pittsburgh, the University of Hartford, and Lincoln University, respectively. He received a grant from the National Endowment for the Arts in 1972, and a year later he published *Belly Songs and Other Poems*, which was nominated for both the National Book Award and the Pulitzer Prize. A Guggenheim Fellowship followed in 1974.

Despite his professional success, Knight's personal life continued to be in turmoil. Sanchez divorced him, and his second marriage, to Mary Ellen McAnally in 1973, also ended in divorce, after two children were born. He could not shake his drinking and drug problems. Then, in the late 1970s, he moved to Memphis, Tennessee, and married Charlene Blackburn, with whom he had a son.

Knight continued to conduct poetry readings and workshops into the 1980s. He received a second grant from the National Endowment for the Arts in 1980, the same year his fourth collection of poetry, *Born of a Woman*, was published. In the preface to this book, Knight admits to making "slight changes in some of the 'older' poems" in order not to offend potential readers. For instance, from the poem "Hard Rock Returns to Prison from the Hospital for the Criminal Insane" (1968), he changed a line containing the phrase "like indians at a corral" to "like a herd of sheep." He did not want to perpetuate racism or sexism in his poems because he felt that to do so was "an evil" that could lead to "artistic and/or actual suicide."

Dorothy Abbott, the editor of *Mississippi Writers, Reflections of Childhood and Youth*, vol. 3, *Poetry* (1988), which includes four of Knight's poems, said of his work that it "reflected the prison, the male experience, and the aesthetic of the 1960s" but with the power of forming "a passionate, loving connection with black and white readers." Knight's most often anthologized poem is "The Idea of Ancestry" (1968), which has been praised as one of the best poems about the African-American conception of family history. The poem begins with the narrator describing the pictures of forty-seven family members taped to his cell wall. "I know their dark eyes," Knight comments, "they know mine. . . . I am all of them, they are all of me" (*Mississippi Writers*, vol. 3, p. 165). In this poem as well as many of his others, Knight's use of punctuation and his spacing of words assist the reader in determining how the voice should sound saying the lines. Knight relied strongly on his toast-telling expertise to fill his written poetry with rhythm and a sense of oral speech patterns.

His final collection of poetry, *The Essential Etheridge Knight*, was published in 1986. He died in Indianapolis, Indiana. In his belief that the art of poetry involves a trinity—the poem, the poet, and the people—Knight remained committed to his audience throughout his career. Though some critics did not consider him a major figure in poetry because of the slight number of poems he produced, most agreed that his language was vital and his subject matter vast.

• Interviews with Knight appear in *MELUS* 12, no. 2 (1985): 7–23; *Black American Literature Forum* 18, no. 1 (1984): 11–14; and *New Letters* 52, no. 2–3 (1986): 167–76. For articles concerning and analyzing Knight's poetry, see Myles Raymond Hurd, "The Corinth Connection in Etheridge Knight's 'The Idea of Ancestry,'" *Notes on Mississippi Writers* 25, no. 1 (1993): 1–9; Craig Werner, "The Poet, the Poem, the People: Etheridge Knight's Aesthetic," *Obsidian* 7, no. 2–3 (1981): 7–17; Ashby Bland Crowder, "Etheridge Knight: Two Fields of Combat," *Concerning Poetry* 16, no. 2 (1983): 23–25; and Patricia Liggins Hill, "'Blues for a Mississippi Black Boy': Etheridge Knight's Craft in the Black Oral Tradition," *Mississippi Quarterly* 36, no. 1 (1982–1983): 21–33. An obituary is in the *New York Times*, 14 Mar. 1991.

STACY KLEIN
LISABETH G. SVENDSGAARD

KNIGHT, Frank Hyneman (7 Nov. 1885–15 Apr. 1972), economist and philosopher, was born in White Oak Township, McLean County, Illinois, the son of Winton Cyrus Knight and Julia Ann Hyneman, farmers. He completed two years at Lexington High School, though census returns indicate that he was frequently absent, presumably for work on the farm. A younger brother, Melvin, who became a distinguished historian at Berkeley, left school at age thirteen. Melvin recalled that his mother had taught him Greek at an early age. He also remembered that the home was well supplied with books.

Shortly before his twentieth birthday, Knight enrolled in the short-lived (1893–1908) American University at Harriman, Tennessee, where he remained for two years. American had no entrance requirements to speak of and sought to provide instruction to entrants with a wide range of preparations, abilities, and interests. He also attended the summer session of the University of Chicago in 1906, taking one math and two upper-level physics courses. In Harriman Knight met and impressed the Reverend Frederick Kershner, a conservative Disciples of Christ minister, who had received an M.A. from Princeton and studied with Woodrow Wilson. Kershner became the head of the Christian Theological Seminary at Butler University. Despite Knight's later open hostility toward religion, the friendship between Kershner and Knight was lifelong.

Following the demise of American University in 1908, Kershner went as president to tiny and struggling Milligan College, also in east Tennessee, and arranged for Knight to enroll and serve as college secretary and teach secretarial subjects. Knight spent 1907–1908 working as a secretary at the Jamestown Exposition. After taking a wide range of courses, including three in religion with Kershner in his senior year, and receiving his bachelor of philosophy degree in 1911, Knight moved on to the University of Tennessee. On graduation day he married a fellow student, Minerva Shelburne, from Pennington Gap, Virginia. Four children were born to the marriage before the couple divorced in 1928.

In 1913 Knight received both a bachelor and a master's degree from Tennessee with many honors. While his main interest seems to have been philosophy (one teacher later recalled Knight as "too pessimistic, too much influenced by Schopenhauer"), he again took a wide range of subjects and even served as a teaching assistant in chemistry. His master's thesis was on the German literary figure, Gerhart Hauptmann, an early exponent of social realism. Knight received a fellowship to study for the doctorate in philosophy at Cornell University. His iconoclastic attitude toward his subject troubled the Cornell philosophers and threatened to terminate his graduate career. Fortunately, Knight had taken two courses in economics with Alvin Johnson, who spotted his outstanding talent for economic theory and arranged for his transfer to the economics department.

Johnson directed Knight's attention to a frontier problem in economics—the nature of profit and entrepreneurship. After Johnson's departure from Cornell, Knight worked with Allyn Young, later to be the first American to hold a professorship at the London School of Economics. Knight received the doctorate in 1916. His dissertation eventually became the classic *Risk, Uncertainty and Profit* (1921). It helped him get an appointment for two years (1917–1919) at the University of Chicago, where he revised his doctoral effort for publication with critical help from John Maurice Clark and Jacob Viner.

In 1919 Knight went to the University of Iowa, where he produced a number of his most influential essays, including "The Limitations of Scientific Method in Economics" (1924) and "The Ethics of Competition" (1923). The first attacked the view that the "scientific" study of economics can make human behavior ever more predictable. The second reflected on the incompatibility of the culture of commerce with most people's ideal of the good society. While at Iowa Knight also found time to translate Max Weber's *General Economic History* (1927). He studied history for its own sake and not because he believed that it would make him a better economic theorist. For Knight, economic theory had the important but limited function of explaining the operation of markets. Since buyers and sellers were largely motivated by self-interest, he argued, an economic theory incorporating this assumption had universal validity. He profoundly distrusted the work of institutional economists and economic historians who, in emphasizing the influence of

law and custom in economic life, either questioned this assumption or failed to trace out its implications.

In 1928 Knight moved to the University of Chicago, bringing with him a young colleague, Henry Simons, through whom many of Knight's views were to reach a wider audience. Knight remained at Chicago for the rest of his life, notwithstanding his disdain for the Thomistic educational philosophy of its president, Robert Maynard Hutchins. In 1929 he married Ethel Verry, a social worker who for many years was head of the Chicago Child Care Society. They had two children.

As an economic theorist Knight's contributions were few but of great importance. *Risk, Uncertainty and Profit* offered a reasoned justification of formal economic theory that ultimately became the dominant methodology of American economics. (Admittedly many of the arguments used by Knight had earlier been advanced by John Neville Keynes in Britain and Carl Menger in Austria.) Knight also emphasized, for the first time, the necessity of viewing economic life as a matter of decision making under conditions of uncertainty. For, as he was fond of repeating, decision making under conditions of perfect certainty—a much used assumption of economic theorists—is only automatic response to stimuli and hence not even "human."

In *Risk, Uncertainty and Profit* Knight advanced a theory that made profit the reward, often negative, of entrepreneurs who accept the responsibility for organizing production in the face of uncertainty. This theory of profit was later repudiated by Knight as depending on a "period of production" (during which entrepreneurs incur costs but have to wait for a reward until the finished product is sold) in which he no longer believed. Knight pointed out that in a world of organized capital markets, a change in expected income resulting from investment is capitalized, and so "realized," as soon as it is perceived. His recantation has gone largely unnoticed and was really excessive. In fact, Knight's theory of profit still finds a place in practically all introductory textbooks. The theory's survival can be explained because it works well for small owner-manager businesses if not for large corporations where the functions of decision making and uncertainty bearing are divorced.

Knight's other important contribution to economic theory was his article, "Some Fallacies in the Interpretation of Social Cost" in the *Quarterly Journal of Economics* (1924). Here Knight revealed a major error in the foundations of the then dominant Pigouvian school of welfare economics and so paved the way for the later work of Ronald Coase that completely changed the way economists viewed market failure. Knight showed that what A. C. Pigou had treated as market failure was, in fact, failure to use a market. During the last third of his career Knight's interests strayed far from formal economic theory, though he did write a number of rambling articles and book reviews on capital and interest theory.

Knight first made his professional reputation as an economic theorist, yet economic theory was never his main interest after Cornell. All through his life he read prodigiously in history, philosophy, religion, and all of the social sciences. From Iowa City he wrote to Kershner that he was spending more time preparing to teach a Sunday school class than he was giving to his university classes in economics. Even while supporting Knight's appointment at Chicago, Jacob Viner lamented that Knight was "wasting himself in metaphysical speculation."

Knight's major works outside technical economics are *The Economic Order and Religion* (1945), written in the form of a dialogue with the theologian Thornton Merriam, and *Intelligence and Democratic Action* (1960). In both books he is totally contemptuous of social engineering. It probably cannot be done, he argues, and discussion of it distracts attention from the central problem of democratic politics—how to achieve and maintain consensus on ends. As Knight saw it, we are all pretty much prisoners of our past, and all efforts to effect change through politics are constrained by this fact. Revolutionary change is to be rejected (when choice is possible) because it usually weakens the consensus on means and ends necessary for any decent society, which, by his definition, is one that functions with a minimum use of force.

It was as a teacher of economic theory and the history of economics that Knight had his greatest impact. By conventional standards he could be judged a bad teacher, often arriving in class with no apparent preparation and given to rambling digressions and intemperate remarks. (His denunciations of John Maynard Keynes could be especially violent.) Nor did he have a good track record as an adviser of doctoral candidates in need of guidance. Still, the force of Knight's personality and intellect was powerful. For many who studied with him, and especially for the highly talented few, he was an influence that changed their lives. One of Knight's outstanding qualities was his preoccupation with ethical issues. For most of his adult life he savagely denounced organized religion, especially Catholicism, for its authoritarian doctrine, yet he always felt the need for a connection and communication with theologians. He left the Disciples of Christ for the Unitarians while in Iowa City.

Knight, especially in the 1930s, was deeply pessimistic about the human condition. Nevertheless, he never gave up the good fight, which for him was trying to understand. He did no outside consulting, wrote no textbooks, and took no leaves for government service or political campaigns. He believed that such diversions would interfere with his dedication to "getting it right." In the depths of the Great Depression, Knight wrote "The Case for Communism: From the Standpoint of an Ex-Liberal" (1932). It was a despairing and bitter commentary on the follies of political democracy rather than an endorsement of communism. Knight had second thoughts about publication and sought to call back all copies circulating in manuscript. He failed.

Knight is often cited with Jacob Viner as the founder of the "Chicago School" of economics with its emphasis on rigorous economic theory and a preference for market over political solutions. In the hands of these two teachers formal economic theory came to be the core of the graduate training of an economist for the first time in an American university. Academic economics in the United States had developed under the pervasive influence of the German Historical School and its antitheory bias. Knight was fond of saying that economics is not nearly as important as most people believe and that "rationality" is constrained by tribal loyalties, religious passions, and the drive for power and prestige. He had little sympathy for the efforts of his colleagues Gary Becker and George Stigler to apply economic theory to politics.

Nor was Knight inclined to enthuse over the merits of free markets whose workings he had helped to make clear. He did not doubt that over a wide spectrum of problems, market solutions were preferable to political solutions both because they were more efficient and because they involved less coercion. He also believed that the skills needed for success in politics were even more unequally distributed than were those needed for success in the market. But he also believed that markets produce and perpetuate inequalities of income, wealth, and power and an impersonality in personal relations that is cause for regret. Knight had little interest in encouraging empirical work in economics and often seemed impervious to its results. George Stigler recorded that no amount of evidence to the contrary could convince Knight that under capitalism the distribution of income was not becoming increasingly unequal.

From the 1920s onward, Knight questioned the increasing use of mathematics in economics. This skepticism was based partly on his belief that, notwithstanding its elegance and importance, economic theory is really a simple subject that mathematical treatments serve to obscure. One of his favorite observations was that economic theory consists mainly of telling people truths that would be virtually self-evident, "even insultingly obvious," if they did not have a vested interest in not seeing them. Another was that in economic theory it is necessary to change the terminology every few years; otherwise economists would die of boredom.

There is hardly any consensus on the place of Knight in twentieth-century social science beyond agreement that *Risk, Uncertainty and Profit* is a classic, and that he was one of the most influential teachers of his time. His disdain for elaborate methodology and its nomenclature makes him seem hopelessly archaic to most present-day scholars. His heavy irony and often brutal humor are not in accord with modern tastes. A case can be made that Knight was too much of a philosopher for economists and too much of an economist for philosophers. Still, by virtue of his courage, originality, and irascibility, both the man and his work retain the power to fascinate. Although he was often a lonely voice in an increasingly mathematical and empirical profession, Knight did not lack for recognition. He received many honorary degrees and awards and served as president of the American Economic Association in 1950. He died in Chicago.

• Frank Knight's papers are in the University of Chicago Library. Thirty-five years of correspondence between Knight and Kershner is in the Frederick Kershner Papers, Christian Theological Seminary, Indianapolis. Much information on the Knight family is in the archives of the McLean County Historical Society, Bloomington, Ill. Knight's early life is traced in Donald Dewey, "Frank Knight before Cornell: Some Light on the Dark Years," *Research in the History of Economic Thought and Methodology* 8 (1990): 1–37. Knight's work in the history of economics is assessed in Richard Howey, "Frank Hyneman Knight and the History of Economic Thought," *Research in the History of Economic Thought and Methodology* 1 (1983): 163–85. The force of Knight's personality can be glimpsed in Edward Shils, "Some Academics, Mainly Chicago," *American Scholar* (1981), and James Buchanan, "Frank H. Knight," in *Remembering the University of Chicago*, ed. Edward Shils (1991). Knight's place in twentieth-century social science is considered in Dorothy Ross, *The Origins of American Social Science* (1991). An excellent overview of Knight's life and most important work is Ross Emmett, "The Economist as Philosopher: Frank H. Knight and American Social Science during the Twenties and Early Thirties" (Ph.D. diss., St. John's College, Manitoba, 1990). A comprehensive assessment of Knight's work by one of his closest associates is George Stigler, "Frank Hyneman Knight," in *The New Palgrave: A Dictionary of Economics*, ed. John Eatwell et al. (1987). An obituary is in the *Journal of Political Economy* 81 (1973).

DONALD DEWEY

KNIGHT, Goodwin Jess (9 Dec. 1896–22 May 1970), governor of California, was born in Provo, Utah, the son of Jesse Knight, an attorney and mining engineer, and Lillie Milner. Knight's family moved to Los Angeles, California, when he was a young child. To help cover his expenses, "Goodie" Knight worked as a hard-rock miner while attending Stanford University, where he served as editor of the school yearbook, the *Quad*. He soon withdrew from the university to join the U.S. Navy, where he served as an apprentice seaman during World War I. Upon his discharge from the service, Knight returned to Stanford and subsequently received his B.A. in 1919. He then studied political science at Cornell University from 1919 to 1920. In 1921 Knight, who had also served as a reporter on the *Los Angeles News*, was admitted to the California bar.

In 1925 Knight formed a law partnership with Thomas Reynolds that lasted for some ten years and became one of the leading firms in the state. Nevertheless, he actually made more money as president and general manager of the Elephant Mining Company, based in Mojave, California, which operated profitable gold mines in Kern County. In 1935, in return for political favors, Knight, a Republican, was appointed by Governor Frank Merriam to the Los Angeles Superior Court, where he served until 1946. He acquired somewhat of a reputation as "the actors' judge," for the manner in which he handled divorce cases. Twice, he

went before the voters, and both times he was returned to his seat on the superior court. All the while his political ambitions grew. Beginning in 1941 he hosted "The Open Forum," a radio talk show in Los Angeles, and later "The Round Table," a radio program based in San Francisco. In 1944 Knight was defeated in a bid for the Republican nomination to the U.S. Senate by Lieutenant Governor Frederick N. Houser. In a well-publicized 1946 campaign in which he called for fiscal restraint and development of California's water resources, Knight was elected lieutenant governor, resoundingly defeating State Senator John F. Shelley.

Knight sought diligently to be more than simply a figurehead as the state's second-in-command; he chaired the Interstate Cooperation Commission and served on the Toll Bridge Authority, the Lands Commission, and the Disaster Council. He acquired a reputation as California's finest political orator and was said to have delivered as many as 250 speeches in a single year. By 1950 Knight's political base throughout the state was such that the Republican nomination for the U.S. Senate seat, eventually garnered by Congressman Richard M. Nixon, could have been his for the asking. But by this point Knight had no desire to leave the state.

All was not smooth at the top rungs of the Republican party, however, perhaps in part because of the clashing ambitions of Lieutenant Governor Knight and Governor Earl Warren. For his part, Warren might well have been displeased with Knight's more conservative stance regarding state health insurance policy, loyalty oaths, investigations of alleged subversion, and government spending. On the other hand the lieutenant governor and his staff saw Warren as cold and aloof, unlike the gregarious, lively, warm, and at times eloquent Knight. The Warren-Knight rift threatened to rupture, with many analysts terming their relationship an "annoyance." But the antagonisms subsided when Earl Warren was appointed to the U.S. Supreme Court, and Knight became governor of California on 5 October 1953.

Previously viewed as a conservative, Knight who appeared to grow in the job, proved to be a progressive governor, much in the vein of fellow Republican Warren and his own immediate successor, Edmund Brown, Sr. Knight proceeded to increase state aid for the disabled, higher education, mental health, medical care for the elderly, and unemployment insurance compensation, and he created the state's Department of Water Resources, completed the Feather River project involving the construction of the immense Oroville Dam, fought a proposed right-to-work law, and was no friend of prayer in the schools. He forthrightly urged that racial and religious "bitterness, bigotry, and fear" be replaced by "understanding, mutual appreciation, and respect for the rights of others." He sang the praises of the Bill of Rights, including the First Amendment rights of religion, speech, press, and assemblage, and the Fourth Amendment right to be free from illegal searches and seizures. To the dismay of many members of his own party, he deemed "the union label" to be a significant force "in our democratic way of life." But as was characteristic of many politicians of this era, Knight genuflected to anti-Communist mania, issuing a series of executive proclamations decrying the "terrible tyranny" of "Communistic imperialism" and commending "the All-American Conference to Combat Communism," a right-wing patriotic organization.

Initially, Knight's efforts to placate all sides of the political spectrum appeared to bear considerable fruit. In 1954 Knight won election to a full term as governor, with a margin of more than 550,000 votes, and flirted briefly with a bid for the Republican party vice presidential nomination in 1956. But Knight's pro-labor stance had antagonized many in the ranks of his own party, who had come to view him as "another Earl Warren." Consequently, California Republicans stood sorely divided among the supporters of Knight, Vice President Richard M. Nixon, and the archconservative U.S. senator William F. Knowland, who had his eye on the governorship. In what was known as "The Big Switch," Knight, pressured by Nixon and other party leaders, reluctantly agreed in 1958 to run for the U.S. Senate, while Knowland attempted to replace him in Sacramento. Both, however, went down to resounding defeats, with Knight—who felt he had been "sandbagged" by Nixon and Knowland—bested by Democratic congressman Clair Engle. As Nixon evidently feared, the division within Republican ranks enabled the Democrats to sweep to victory.

Knight served as a television news commentator in Los Angeles after his tenure as governor came to an end and made an aborted bid for a return to the governor's mansion in 1962. A bout with hepatitis compelled him to withdraw from that race, which eventually pitted Nixon against the incumbent Democratic governor Pat Brown. Rumor was afoot that Nixon had implored Knight not to run, with an aide of the vice president purportedly dangling before him "any job Goodie wanted," including chief justice of the California Supreme Court. Later chairman of the board of the Imperial Bank in Los Angeles, Knight fleetingly considered throwing his hat in the ring in 1966 once again, much to the chagrin of friends and allies.

Adjudged by his friends "a great family man," Knight was married twice, to Arvilla Pearl Cooley in 1925, the mother of his two daughters, and then following her death in 1952, to Virginia Carlson in 1954. He died in Inglewood, California.

• Knight's official papers are housed at the California State Archives, Rosedale; his private papers are at Stanford University. Additional correspondence and oral histories relating to Knight are held by the Bancroft Library at the University of California at Berkeley. Detailed biographical sketches appear in Ralph Friedman, "The Gay Beaver," *Frontier Magazine*, June 1958, pp. 10–19; H. Brett Melendy and Benjamin F. Gilbert, *The Governors of California* (1965); and the *California Blue Book* (1958). Important political campaigns involving Knight are covered in Thomas Barclay, "The 1954 Election in California," *Western Political Quarterly* 7 (1954):

597–604, and Trotton J. Anderson, "The 1958 Election in California," *Western Political Quarterly* 11 (1959): 276–300. An obituary is in the *New York Times*, 23 May 1970.

ROBERT C. COTTRELL

KNIGHT, John Shively (26 Oct. 1894–16 June 1981), newspaper publisher, was born in Bluefield, West Virginia, the son of Charles Landon Knight, a lawyer and newspaper publisher, and Clara Scheifley. His father had moved to Bluefield to practice law in 1893 and later started an ill-fated newspaper in Winston-Salem, North Carolina, before moving to Akron, Ohio, where he became co-owner of the *Akron Beacon-Journal* in 1903.

Knight was educated at public schools in Akron and a private boarding school in Maryland. He enrolled at Cornell University in 1914 but left without graduating three years later. He was commissioned a second lieutenant in the infantry and served in France during the later stages of World War I. Knight began work in 1920 as a reporter for Charles Landon Knight's *Beacon-Journal*. After his father was elected to Congress in 1920, Knight became managing editor of the paper in 1921. In 1921 he married Katherine McLain, daughter of a wealthy wholesale grocer; they had his only three children before her death in 1929.

When his father bought the *Springfield (Ohio) Sun* in 1922, Knight became editor and proceeded to attack the powerful Ku Klux Klan. The prolabor *Akron Press*, owned by the Scripps-Howard chain, bought the probusiness *Akron Times* in 1925 to create the *Times-Press*, which promised to wage a fierce subscription battle with the politically moderate *Beacon-Journal*. Age and illness forced his father to make Knight publisher of the *Beacon-Journal*. Because Scripps-Howard owned United Press, the *Times-Press* dropped its Associated Press franchise, which Knight quickly acquired in 1925. The *Beacon-Journal*'s circulation increased steadily under Knight's guidance.

Upon the sale of the *Springfield Sun* to James M. Cox in 1928, the Knights purchased the *Massillon (Ohio) Independent*. Knight married a wealthy divorcée, Beryl Zoller, in 1932 and assumed the leadership of the family business when his father died in 1933. Struggling to survive the Great Depression, Knight resisted offers from Scripps-Howard to buy the *Beacon-Journal* and instead acquired the rival *Times-Press* in 1938, paid for with 30 percent of the *Beacon-Journal*'s stock. The *Beacon-Journal* remained a supporter of the Republican party in the 1930s, although it also backed John L. Lewis's new Congress of Industrial Organization, which brought into its membership the rubber workers' union at the Goodyear plant in Akron.

Breaking away from his provincial beginnings in Ohio, Knight purchased the faltering *Miami Herald* from Frank B. Shutts in 1937 for $2.5 million. It was the start of a significant expansion for Knight Newspapers, which developed into the largest U.S. newspaper chain over the next thirty-five years. In 1938 Knight bought and discontinued the competing tabloid *Miami Tribune* from Moses Annenberg for $600,000 and the transfer of ownership of the *Massillon Independent*. The Knight newspaper empire expanded further in 1940 with the purchase of the morning *Detroit Free Press* from E. D. Stair for $100,000 in cash and $3.1 million in promissory notes, followed by the acquisition of the afternoon *Chicago Daily News* in 1944 from Frank Knox's heirs for $2.1 million. Knight was elected president of the American Society of Newspaper Editors in 1944 and a director of the Associated Press in 1946.

By the early 1950s each of Knight's big city dailies was netting about $1 million in profits. Knight's brother James had a vacation home in North Carolina and knew publisher Curtis Johnson of the *Charlotte Observer*. Following Johnson's death, James urged John to purchase the *Observer*, which he did in late 1954 for $7 million. Because of his brother's interest in the paper, John Knight left management in Charlotte to James. In 1959 the Knights added the failing afternoon *Charlotte News* to their newspaper holdings. When Marshall Field IV offered in 1959 to pay $24 million, three times the stock value, for the *Chicago Daily News*, Knight accepted the profitable deal, which netted him personally $18 million. Knight acquired the *Tallahassee Democrat* in 1965. Knight won a Pulitzer Prize for commentary in 1968 for a series of editorials opposing the Vietnam War that appeared in all Knight papers. The following year Knight Newspapers became publicly owned with the sale of 950,000 shares. The Knights retained control of about 59 percent of the stock.

Also in 1969 Knight bought the Annenbergs' morning *Philadelphia Inquirer* and afternoon *Daily News* for $55 million. Knight also acquired reputable papers in two Georgia cities: the *Macon Telegraph* (morning) and the *Macon News* (afternoon) in 1969 and the *Columbus Ledger-Enquirer* in 1973. Knight Newspapers merged in 1974 with the Ridder Group, a chain of nineteen newspapers owned by a German-American family, to form Knight-Ridder Newspapers, Inc., composed of 35 dailies with 4 million subscribers. By 1980 the company had revenues exceeding $1 billion with a circulation of 25 million. After Beryl Knight's death in 1974, Knight married a third time, in 1976, to Frances Elizabeth Augustus. He died in Akron, Ohio, leaving the newspaper fortunes to his only surviving son, Charles Landon Knight II.

Knight was able to build a major newspaper empire by examining closely the financial numbers and choosing independent, competent managers to run the papers. More than once in his career, despite his personal support of Republicans, Knight had stressed that newspapers and politics did not mix. He believed that local editors would know their readers better than corporate officials. In the 1940s Knight wrote a famous memorandum to an editor at the *Chicago Daily News* stating the Knight Newspapers' commitment to "inform rather than instruct" and to "be scrupulously fair to all sides in the presentation of our editorial policies." Knight stressed to all his employees the importance of retaining a newspaper's integrity, a quality

that begins with its personnel. He embraced new technology and always expanded his holdings cautiously yet determinedly. The communities where Knight papers existed trusted their papers to provide complete coverage of news and sound editorial advice.

• Knight's corporate and personal papers are housed at the University of Akron. A comprehensive biographical work is Charles Whited, *Knight: A Publisher in the Tumultuous Century* (1988), which contains a complete bibliography. Nixon Smiley, *Knights of the Fourth Estate* (1974), Frank Angelo, *On Guard: A History of the Detroit Free Press* (1981), and Jack Claiborne, *The Charlotte Observer: Its Time and Place, 1869–1986* (1986), focus on Knight's role with his papers in Miami, Detroit, and Charlotte. Obituaries are in the *Washington Post* and the *New York Times*, both 17 June 1981, and *Time*, 29 June 1981.

DANIEL WEBSTER HOLLIS III

KNIGHT, Lucian Lamar (9 Feb. 1868–19 Nov. 1933), editor, archivist, and historian, was born in Atlanta, Georgia, the son of Confederate general George Walton Knight, a lawyer and cotton merchant, and his second wife, Clara Corinne Daniel, a teacher. Named for Lucius Quintus Cincinnatus Lamar, Jr., an American statesman and relative on his mother's side, young Lucian Knight lost his father in 1869 and, with financial support from his uncle John Benning Daniel, grew up in Atlanta under the influence of his mother's strong spirit. Before entering the University of Georgia in 1885, he had been introduced by his cousin Henry W. Grady to Joel Chandler Harris and other writers at the *Atlanta Constitution*. After graduating from the university with honors in 1888, Knight entered law school at Georgia. He discontinued his studies, however, after gaining early admission to the bar in April 1889. He set up a law practice in Macon, only to move to Atlanta in 1890.

In 1892, having tired of the law profession, Knight joined the *Constitution* staff, first as a reporter and later as the literary editor. In 1895 he married Edith Marie Nelson of Atlanta. They had Knight's only children, two daughters. During Knight's ten years at the *Constitution*, he became a noted writer, poet, historian, speaker, and master of ceremonies. Also during these years, he developed two passionate pursuits—the study of Georgia history and lay preaching in Atlanta's Presbyterian churches.

Knight played a major role in the 1901 establishment of the Westminster Presbyterian Church. In 1902 he began graduate studies both at Princeton University and Princeton Theological Seminary. He received an A.M. from the university in 1904 and a certificate of graduation (later a B.D.) from the seminary in 1905. On 13 November 1905 he was ordained to the ministry and soon afterward was installed as associate pastor of the Central Presbyterian Church in Washington, D.C. A failing marriage and subsequent ill health, however, forced him to give up his ministry. In early 1906 Knight traveled alone to Europe to recover his health. Later that year he moved to Catalina Island in southern California. He joined the law firm of Harris and Harris in Los Angeles but spent most of his time studying and writing. In 1907 he compiled his first major historical work, *Reminiscences of Famous Georgians*. Upset by his divorce of that same year, he found strength in the completion of a second volume of *Reminiscences*, published in 1908. He then returned to Atlanta, where he worked for a short period on the staff of Agnes Scott Institute before becoming associate editor of the *Atlanta Georgian* from 1908 to 1910 and managing editor for the *Library of Southern Literature* series from 1908 to 1913.

In 1913 Knight accepted an appointment as the compiler of Georgia state records, a position begun by former governor William J. Northen. Over the next three years Knight completed the editing of four volumes of *The Colonial Records of the State of Georgia* (vols. 22–26). He then edited *Georgia's Landmarks, Memorials, and Legends* (2 vols., 1913–1914), and six volumes of *A Standard History of Georgia and Georgians* (1917). These works remain definitive popular histories. Also in 1917 Knight married Rosa Talbot Reid of Eatonton. That same year the University of Georgia awarded Knight an honorary LL.D. By then Knight had become one of Georgia's leading and most influential citizens. His love for his state and its history led him to help found the Georgia Historical Association in 1917. He served as the organization's first president until 1919, when it amalgamated with the Georgia Historical Society.

During World War I Knight collected records on Georgia's service persons. Seeing the need for an official department of archives, he persuaded the legislature in 1918 to establish the Department of Archives and History. In that same year he was named director of this department and made Georgia's first state historian, a position he retained until 1925. In spite of attempts in 1919, 1921, and 1922 to abolish the department, Knight and his supporters prevailed. As an avid promoter of Georgia's history, Knight worked hard to collect, store, and index the records of the state. In 1923 he published the first state *Statistical Register*. Also in 1923, motivated by the movement to carve on the side of a mountain a Confederate memorial, he produced his chief poetic work, "Stone Mountain, or The Lay of the Gray Minstrel." After his retirement at the end of 1924, he continued to write and speak. Between 1924 and 1931 he wrote and edited numerous historical works, among which are *Woodrow Wilson* (1924), *Tracking the Sunset* (1925), *Alexander H. Stephens* (1930), and *Encyclopedia of Georgia Biography* (1931).

In 1931, having suffered great financial losses during the depression, Knight and his wife moved to Safety Harbor, Florida, and the next year to St. Simons Island, Georgia. He died in Clearwater, Florida, and was buried at Christ Church, Frederica, on St. Simons Island. Knight was a product of the ideals of the Old South that prevailed after the Civil War, and yet he was an innovative contributor to the evolving New South at the turn of the century. As orator, amateur historian, and founder of his state's archive department, his was a pioneering contribution.

• Many of Knight's personal papers are in the Henry W. Grady Collection and the Joel Chandler Harris Collection at Emory University, Atlanta. Other works by Knight include *Memorials of Dixie-land* (1919), *Georgia's Roster of the Revolution* (1920), *Annual Reports of State Historian and Director of the Department of Archives and History* (1920–1924), *Biographical Dictionary of Southern Authors* (1929), *How the Sunday Lady Won the Mountains* (n.d.), and *A Sketch of the Work of John Wesley in Georgia* (n.d.). For a full biography see Evelyn Ward Guy, *Lucian Lamar Knight* (1967), which contains a bibliography and a complete list of writings, and "Lucian Lamar Knight," biographical file, Office of Statistical Register, Georgia Department of Archives and History, Atlanta. For Knight's contributions to the Presbyterian church, see *Biographical Catalogue of the Princeton Theological Seminary, 1815–1932* (1933). An obituary is in the *Atlanta Constitution*, 20 and 22 Nov. 1933.

CHARLES A. RISHER

KNIGHT, Margaret E. (14 Feb. 1838–12 Oct. 1914), inventor, was born in York, Maine, the daughter of James Knight and Hannah Teal. When Knight was a young child, her family moved to Manchester, New Hampshire. She apparently had very little formal education beyond secondary school, and yet it was at a very young age that Margaret Knight created her first invention. At twelve years old she designed a stop motion device to protect workers in the cotton textile mills from injury. She had witnessed an accident one day while visiting her brothers at work at a local mill. A shuttle slipped out of a loom, piercing an employee with its steel tip. The new device invented by Knight was designed to prevent such an accident from occurring. Margaret also worked in the cotton textile mills until her late teens.

An introspective glance into Knight's childhood appeared in the 21 December 1872 edition of the *Woman's Journal* and sheds light on the personality of this female inventor:

As a child I never cared for things that girls usually do; dolls never possessed any charms for me. I couldn't see the sense of coddling bits of porcelain with senseless faces; the only things I wanted were a jack knife, a gimlet and pieces of wood. My friends were horrified. I was called a tom-boy, but that made very little impression on me. I sighed sometimes because I was not like the other girls, but wisely concluded that I couldn't help it, and sought further consolation from my tools. I was always making things for my brothers; did they want anything in the line of playthings they always said, "Mattie will make them for us." I was famous for my kites, and my sleds were the envy and admiration of all the boys in town. I'm not surprised at what I've done. I'm only sorry I couldn't have had as good a chance as a boy, and been put to my trade regularly.

Throughout her twenties and early thirties, Knight worked various short term jobs; she worked in the upholstery industry, did home repairs, learned daguerreotype, ambrotype, and photography, as well as engraving on silver. In 1867 Knight went to work for the Columbia Paper Bag Company in Springfield, Massachusetts. While working at Columbia, she began experimenting with various models of machines that could cut, fold, and paste flat-bottomed paper bags. After numerous wooden and iron models, Knight perfected the machine and sought a patent, only to discover that Charles F. Annan had taken her idea and already petitioned a patent for a device very similar to her own. Knight pursued the matter legally, spending $100 per day, plus expenses, for sixteen days to fight Annan. After a lengthy, costly, and frustrating dispute, Knight was awarded the patent. She was thirty-two years old. It was her first patent, but by no means her last. It was erroneously reported in Knight's obituaries in both the *Framingham Evening News* and the *New York Times* that Knight received eighty-seven patents throughout her illustrious career. She actually received twenty-seven patents for her many notable inventions.

In addition to inventing a machine to cut, fold, and paste flat-bottomed paper bags, Knight invented household devices, a "tin can contrivance," as well as a window frame and sash. Near the end of the nineteenth century Knight moved to Framingham, Massachusetts, where she concentrated her efforts on machinery for shoe cutting devices. Between 1890 and 1894 she was awarded approximately six patents for such inventions.

At the turn of the century Knight devoted her inventive labor toward automobile machinery. Her *Framingham Evening News* obituary states that she "has had the satisfaction of seeing many of her ideas adopted throughout the world. Miss Knight's characteristic Yankee ingenuity reached a climax when she perfected her sleeve valve motor. Her latest invention, the silent Knight motor, is being heralded all over the world as the latest refinement in automobile motors."

Knight lived the last twenty-five years of her life in Framingham, where she continued to invent up until her death there. Independent, economically self-sufficient, and apparently never married, Knight transgressed traditional gender roles for women of the Victorian era and by using her mechanical mind for practical purposes defied all expectations for a member of her sex.

• Knight's obituary in the *Framingham Evening News*, 13 Oct. 1914, and Edith J. Griswold's article, "A Famous Woman Inventor," in the *Woman Lawyer's Journal*, Dec. 1914, are perhaps the most interesting sources relating to Knight, in part because they were written shortly after her death. The most comprehensive account of her life and inventions is in Anne Macdonald's *Feminine Ingenuity: Women and Invention in America* (1992). Ethlie Ann Vare and Greg Ptacek, *Mothers of Invention: From the Bra to the Bomb, Forgotten Women and Their Unforgettable Ideas* (1987), includes a brief description of Knight's accomplishments, highlighting her paper bag machine.

STACEY L. ALLEN

KNIGHT, M. M. (29 Apr. 1887–23 June 1981), economist and historian, was born Melvin Moses Knight near Bloomington, Illinois, the son of Winton Knight and Julia Hyneman, farmers. One of nine children, at age thirteen Knight was helping cultivate the fields, hiring the help, keeping the books for the family farm, and being tutored in Greek by his mother. In 1910, without a high school education, he followed his elder brother Frank to Milligan College in Tennessee. After two years at Milligan and a brief period at the University of Tennessee, he received a B. A. in English in 1913 and an M. A. in history in 1914 at Texas Christian University. He studied history for an additional year at the University of Chicago and received a Ph.D. in sociology from Clark University in 1917. The title of his dissertation was "Taboo and Genetics."

Knight spent the next three years as an ambulance driver for the French and, later, the American forces during World War I. He spent 1919 working in a Rumanian field hospital, primarily in Transylvania and Hungary.

In 1920 Knight became a faculty member in the history department at Hunter College. He held subsequent brief appointments at Utah and Berkeley before joining Columbia University's history faculty from 1923 to 1926. An Amherst Memorial Fellowship allowed him to spend 1926-1928 traveling and studying the French colonial system. While in Paris in 1926 he married Eleanor Gehmann, a scholar in her own right; they had no children. In 1928 he joined the economics faculty of the University of California, Berkeley, where he remained until he retired in 1954. M. M., as he was known, together with his brothers, Frank at the University of Chicago, and Bruce at Dartmouth College, constituted the outstanding family of the economics profession from the 1920s to the 1940s.

M. M.'s and Frank's views of economics differed deeply. Referring to Frank's preeminent position as an economic theorist, M. M. once said, "every profession needs at least one or two good metaphysicians." Though also a theorist, M. M. rooted his theories about the process of economic growth and expansion in empirical observation, rather than specializing in abstract logical deduction. His focus was on the discipline of geography, the role of technology in economic change, the impact of the environment (what we today call ecology) on countries and cultures and primarily on how things get done in human affairs. As he said in a letter dated 17 May 1927 to Dr. Frederick D. Kershner in Paris, "Other aspects of the Roman traces (across North Africa) were the ones that attracted my attention—for example the farm ruins, with irrigation wells, etc., showing how it was cultivated." He was especially interested in such key historical linkages as the relationship among watch-making, the design of machine tools, and labor productivity.

Knight's interest in geography and the environment is best illustrated by his seminal piece, "Water and the Course of Empire in North Africa" (*Quarterly Journal of Economics* 43 [1928]), and his interest in mechanics by his first important work, the two-volume *Diction-naire practique d'aéronautique française-anglaise* (1918).

Late-twentieth-century economists tend to place their policy recommendations within a rigorous but narrow analytical framework, so that schools of thought about the economic process are distinguished primarily by the degree to which they regard economic markets as efficient or partially flawed and by the short time horizons of economic analysis. Other economists who deviate from the analytical mainstream, such as Thorstein Veblen and more recently John Kenneth Galbraith, tend to focus on the institutional framework of the economy, the interaction of interest groups, and especially the role of finance within the institutional framework. By contrast, Knight's time horizon was long, and the richness and complexity of his view of economic change fit neither the equilibrium nor the institutional category. From today's perspective, his model of economic development resembles the approach used by contemporary evolutionary biologists. The original version of evolutionary theory that followed Charles Darwin involved a steady process from a lower order of organisms to a higher order. A modern view of evolution as a series of punctuated equilibria, with its denial of any teleology in evolution and its emphasis on catastrophic extinctions and on the creation of niches or opportunities for the rapid spread of species, is close to Knight's view of how economic development and colonization have occurred in human history.

Knight saw human history, especially the development of North Europe after the fall of Rome and the subsequent drive by Europeans for colonization, as essentially a process that was driven by investment opportunities. These opportunities were provided by the existence of open space, resources, and the available technology. In his voluminous writings and in his teaching, he emphasized the tendency of students of history to underestimate the importance of technology and the environment in economic development. He sketched the essence of his theoretical model in a brief passage in *Introduction to Modern Economic History* (1940):

Back of all the detailed problems loomed the general fact that the North Atlantic world could not be merely reconstructed—it must be redesigned to a considerable extent. During four centuries at least it had absorbed surplus capital and consumption goods and contributed to the produce of underpopulated spaces in vast amounts. Frontiers of settlement of trade and of empire were largely used up. An Occidental form of society steeped in the habit and philosophy of acceleration must now learn to decelerate—"to drive in traffic," so to speak (p. 189).

Knight's analysis of economic change and development centered on the role of large-scale investment opportunities. To each such opportunity there were limits, and the nature of the environment and density of population affected the ability of a society to exploit them. In this system, technology played a key role in creating and sustaining what development could take place over an extended period of time. Knight's view of this process was pessimistic. In time, each investment opportunity gets used up. Therefore, economic growth in any particular society has finite horizons. As he continually reiterated, "no economy is in itself a perpetual motion machine." He used his theory of economic growth against finite margins to explain the expansion of the Phoenicians, the development of the economy of North Europe, and the expansion of Europe into the modern world. A simple illustration: Imagine a valley with scattered agricultural villages, a river that provides continuous irrigation and fertilization, and an elementary agricultural system of plowing, sowing, and reaping. This combination of rich agriculture and low population density produces a social surplus. This surplus leads to some improvements in technology, metallurgy, geometry, and architecture, but also to more rapid increases in population. Population growth with this given technology set leads to dissipation of some of the surplus in wars and the construction of tombs and pyramids. Ultimately the increase in population plus the failure to continuously improve and enlarge the underlying technology set leads to diminishing returns, and the society stagnates, economic growth ceases, i.e., the space available has been used up by population increases and no new technology has been developed to increase labor productivity.

Knight's major publications include *Economic History of Europe to the End of the Middle Ages* (1926), *The Americans in Santo Domingo* (1928), *Morocco as a French Economic Venture* (1937), and *Introduction to Modern Economic History* (1940). Knight also contributed numerous entries to the original edition of the *International Encyclopedia of the Social Sciences* (1968), including "Backward Countries," "Chartered Companies," "Commercial Routes," "Colonies," "Companionate Marriage," "Handcrafts," "Morocco Question," "Plantation Wares," "Precious Stones," "Serfdom," and "Slavery (Medieval)." In Knight's introduction to his translation of Henry E. Sée's *The Economic Interpretation of History* (1929), he reveals his close intellectual connection with the leading French historians of the period. Equally important in revealing Knight's view of history is his review "The Geohistory of Fernand Braudel" in the *Journal of Economic History* 10 (1950).

Knight led a rich personal and academic life. His house in Berkeley was open for spirited discussion by students and others, which were always conducted in a cloud of cigarette smoke. In the classroom he presented the image of an intellectual giant who was sympathetic and would listen carefully to students of all ability, although many could only partially understand the richness and complexity of his vision of history.

Of the numerous students whom he influenced at Berkeley, perhaps the best known is Douglas North, cowinner of the 1993 Nobel Prize in economic science.

Knight died in Berkeley. His influence continues through his writings, his students, and particularly his clear recognition of and emphasis on the central role of technology and environmental change on economic development.

• Knight's principal publications that have not already been mentioned include "Conditions within Roumania and Turkey," *Journal of International Relations* 10 (1920); *Taboo and Genetics: A Study of the Biological, Sociological and Psychological Foundation of the Family*, with I. L. Peters and P. Blanchard (1922); "Liquidating Our War Illusions," *Journal of International Relations* 12 (1923); "The Companionate and the Family: The Unobserved Division of an Historical Institution," *Journal of Social Hygiene* 10 (1925); "The Moroccan War with France and Spain," *Current History* 23 (1926); "Recent Literature on the Origins of Modern Capitalism," *Quarterly Journal of Economics* 41 (1927); "Economic History in France," *American Economic Review* 18 (1928); "Karl Marx's Interpretation of History," *Political Science Quarterly* 43 (1928); "Economic History," *American Economic Review* 19 (1929); "The Conquest of Algeria: A Case of Historical Inertia," in *Essays in Intellectual History* (1932); "French Colonial Policy: The Decline of 'Association,'" *Journal of Modern History* 5 (1937); "The Role of Indo-China in Asia," in *The Renaissance of Asia* (1941); and "Economic Space for Europeans in French North Africa," *Economic Development and Cultural Change* 1 (1956). For a more detailed biographical account and a partial bibliography, see G. Pontecorvo and C. Stewart, "Memoir: Melvin Moses Knight," *Explorations in Economic History* 16 (1979): 240–45.

GIULIO PONTECORVO

KNIGHT, Sarah Kemble (19 Apr. 1666–25 Sept. 1727), diarist and businesswoman, was born in Boston, Massachusetts, the daughter of Thomas Kemble, a merchant, and Elizabeth Trerice. She married Richard Knight of Boston, of whom little is known, and had one child.

The Boston census in 1707 recorded that Sarah Knight, then a widow, headed her deceased father's Moon Street household and shop. She kept boarders and may also have taught school. Knowledgeable about law, she served as a copier of legal documents and witness to one hundred or more deeds. In 1704, she traveled to New York to settle a family estate, keeping a diary of her journey that was first published in 1825 in *The Journals of Madam Knight, and Rev. Mr. Buckingham*. The diary remains an important source on social conditions in the early eighteenth century. Her trip was made on horseback, accompanying the post rider in stages, or with a local person who could direct her along the way. She crossed rivers in tippy canoes or over tottering bridges, and she stopped at inns usually memorable for unappetizing food, uncomfortable beds, and uncouth people. She also stayed at times with relatives or friends, such as the minister in New London, Connecticut, Gurdon Saltonstall, who treated her "very handsomely."

When her daughter Elizabeth married John Livingston in 1713 and moved to New London, Sarah Knight followed. She soon was operating a shop, a tavern, and an inn, and she engaged extensively in land speculation. She acquired Livingston lands, originally purchased from the Mohegan Indians, that her son-in-

law had sold off and bought other property in partnership with Joseph Bradford, an eminent landholder. Joshua Hempstead, a versatile New Londoner, recorded in his diary that he surveyed her land, determined its boundaries, and wrote leases for her tenants. Her business activities got her into trouble on at least one occasion: in 1718 she was indicted and fined for selling alcohol to the Indians. Nevertheless, Knight was a respected member of the community and a pewholder in the Norwich Congregational church. After her death at her inn on the Norwich road, she was brought for burial to New London, where her gravestone still stands. Probate records valued her lands in Norwich at £210, and her farm, household goods, and personal effects in New London at £1850, an estate of considerable wealth.

Sarah Knight is best known today for her forty-page diary, which Theodore Dwight (1796–1866) published without revealing the name of the author. Soon after, the manuscript was accidentally destroyed. Readers at the time believed the journal was fictitious, or, if factual, the work of a man. Not until William R. Deane, in the June 1858 issue of *Littel's Living Age*, named Knight as the author did the diarist's true identity become known. Deane based his attribution on information forwarded to him by the historian Frances M. Caulkins, who had interviewed a descendent of the administratrix of Elizabeth Livingston's estate.

Some commentators have treated the diary primarily as a historical record and have identified locations that Knight described but left unnamed. For example, it was Haven's tavern, near North Kingston, Rhode Island, where revelers kept her awake by loudly debating the origins of the word "Narragansett"; it was Fisher's tavern, in Dedham, where frequenters ignored her questions because they were "tyed by the Lipps to a pewter engine" (drinking cup). Other scholars view the journal as an account of the frontier, calling it "a realistic picture of rural manners" or a description of "lubberland . . . the abode of rude leveling."

Recent analysis has been of the diary's literary merits, which are regarded as extraordinary. Critics have placed her journal in the picaresque tradition, characterized by episodes of travel, comments on morals and manners, and the use of comedy. Knight's figurative language has been compared positively with the humor of Mark Twain. One commentator argued that Sarah Knight wrote with Homer's *Odyssey* in mind; by treating her own journey in mock heroic fashion and portraying herself as an urbane Bostonian in rural Connecticut she represents the Greek among the barbarians. Another view emphasized the range of Knight's reading; the poetic portions of the journal indicate acquaintance with Dryden and his contemporaries, while other passages show familiarity with the Elizabethan romances of *Parismus* and the *Knight of the Oracle*. Also, Knight's satiric tone, tolerant amusement with herself and others, and reference to God as her "Great Benefactor" suggest that she was acquainted with works of the early Enlightenment. In general, commentators have noted that the journal reveals a mind characterized by wit, intelligence, and refreshing independence.

• The original manuscript of the journal and the copy made of it by Theodore Dwight, Jr., for the 1825 edition are no longer extant. No other writings by Knight have yet been found. A manuscript collection of newspaper clippings, archival research notes, and genealogical data relating to Sarah Knight, prepared by William R. Deane, is held by the New England Historic Genealogical Society in Boston. There is no biography. Alan Margolies gives a history of the manuscript and its nineteenth-century editions in "The Editing and Publication of 'The Journal of Madam Knight,'" *The Papers of The Bibliographical Society of America* 58 (1964): 25–32. Commentary on the journal has been made by George Parker Winship, in *The Journal of Madam Knight* (1920), and Malcolm Freiberg, in *The Journal of Madam Knight* (1972). Literary criticism of the journal is found in the introduction to the annotated edition by Sargent Bush, Jr., in *Journeys in New Worlds: Early American Women's Narratives*, ed. William L. Andrews (1990); Ann Stanford, "Images of Women in Early American Literature," in *What Manner of Woman: Essays on English and American Life and Literature*, ed. Marlene Springer (1977), pp. 184–210, and "Three Puritan Women: Anne Bradstreet, Mary Rowlandson, and Sarah Kemble Knight," in *American Women Writers: Bibliographical Essays*, ed. Maurice Duke et al. (1983), pp. 3–20.

BARBARA E. LACEY

KNOPF, Adolph (2 Dec. 1882–23 Nov. 1966), professor of geology, was born in San Francisco, California, the son of German immigrants George Tobias Knopf, a building contractor, and Anna Geisel. The family owned a ranch in open country south of San Francisco (near the San Andreas fault, movement along which caused the San Francisco earthquake of 1906), and Knopf's early years were divided between country and city. He entered the University of California at Berkeley in 1900, earning a bachelor's degree in 1904 and a master's degree in geology in 1906; he pursued graduate work in geology for an additional year. His primary professor there, whom he always admired and revered, was Andrew C. Lawson, an outstanding geologist and the author of definitive monographs on the geology of the San Francisco area and on the 1906 earthquake.

In 1906, on the advice of Lawson, who had worked for the U.S. Geological Survey, Knopf went to work for the survey, which assigned him first to field projects on ore deposits in Alaska. Among other work in his six Alaskan field seasons, he completed a report on the tin deposits on the western end of the Seward Peninsula. In 1909 the report was accepted at Berkeley as a dissertation for his Ph.D. During the winter seasons, he lived and worked in Washington, D.C., where in 1908 he married Agnes Burchard Dillon; they had four children. In his fourteen years with the geological survey, his field assignments were shifted from Alaska to Montana, Nevada, and California. The survey published nine of his reports on the geology of ore deposits in Alaska and these states, as well as reports by Knopf for twelve years thereafter.

In 1920 Knopf was called by Yale University to the position of professor of petrology vacated by the death of Louis V. Pirsson. Knopf's first wife had died in 1918, and in 1920 he married Eleanora Frances Bliss, a well-known geologist in her own right, who left her position with the geological survey to move with him to New Haven, Connecticut. The couple had no children. Although he never lost his interest in the geology of ore deposits, Knopf turned more and more to general problems of petrology, and it is as a petrologist and an outstanding teacher of petrology that he is best remembered. His research on both ore deposits and petrology is characterized by meticulous accuracy and (often sharply) critical evaluation of ideas and hypotheses. He is not known as the initiator of major concepts but rather as the critic who forced others to modify or even abandon popular but not securely founded ideas. An outstanding example was his steady and reasoned opposition to the broad concept of "granitization"— that all granite is produced by metasomatic alteration in the solid state of other, preexisting rocks. This concept became quite widespread in the 1930s and 1940s but has since been largely abandoned, at least in its all inclusive form. Knopf's critical attitude contributed largely to its rejection.

At Yale, Knopf became acquainted with B. B. Boltwood, who had shown that radioactivity results from the decay of uranium and thorium to different isotopes of lead and that decay provides a method of determining the age in millions of years of appropriate minerals and rock samples; hitherto only the relative age of rocks could be determined (except for estimates based on insecure assumptions). Knopf took up the challenge of evaluating the new method geologically, helping to demonstrate its great value as well as its pitfalls. Thus he became a recognized authority in the new and rapidly developing field of determining the age of the Earth and major events in its history.

After he retired from Yale in 1951, Knopf and his wife moved to the San Francisco region, after what had been for him a sort of Babylonian exile from his native California. Stanford gave him the title of visiting professor, and he taught there, on a somewhat less strenuous schedule, for the rest of his life. In those years, assisted by his wife, he began a new field project on the Boulder bathylith in Montana, which he had first studied forty years earlier; his last published report and article present some of the results. He died in Palo Alto, California.

Knopf received many honors for his scientific work. He was appointed Sterling Professor at Yale in 1938 and was elected to the National Academy of Sciences in 1931 and to the American Academy of Arts and Sciences in 1948. He was president of the Geological Society of America in 1944 and was awarded its Penrose Medal, the highest honor in North American geology, in 1959. In many of these honors he was proud to have followed his mentor Lawson.

Tall and handsome, with aquiline features, Knopf gave the impression of being austere and abrupt; apparently he was rather shy, being quite short-sighted (a distinct advantage in microscopic petrology). He expected from himself and others, especially students, unflagging industry and meticulous accuracy and could be quite caustic when these traits were not forthcoming. He was the sort of teacher about whom there are innumerable stories. When in class he asked a student a question, he would sometimes whip off his pince-nez and appear to glare ferociously at the student; it took some students considerable time to recover from fright and gather their wits to answer the question. But no one who took his courses ever forgot him or was not a better scientist for the experience. Once his expectations were met, he was a wise counselor and warm friend.

• The Adolph Knopf Papers in Manuscripts and Archives at Yale University is a small and incomplete collection; no other collection of papers is reported. Useful summaries of his life and work are given by Donald Blackstone in his presentation of the Penrose Medal to Knopf, Geological Society of America, *Proceedings for 1959* (1960), pp. 87–89; by Charles Park in a memorial, Geological Society of America, *Proceedings for 1966* (1968), pp. 261–66; and by Chester Longwell in National Academy of Sciences, *Biographical Memoirs* 41 (1970): 235–49.

JOHN RODGERS

KNOPF, Alfred A. (12 Sept. 1892–11 Aug. 1984), publisher, was born Alfred Abraham Knopf in New York City, the son of Samuel Knopf, an advertising executive and financial consultant, and Ida Japhe. His mother died when he was four years old, and, although his father remarried, his father remained the primary influence in his life as he grew up. Knopf attended public schools in New York City until his college preparatory training at the MacKenzie School in Westchester County, from which he graduated in 1908.

Knopf enrolled in Columbia College in 1908, planning to go on to Harvard Law School and become a lawyer. Although Knopf said that his years at Columbia were like serving time at Sing Sing prison, he was inspired there to make an important career goal change. In his senior year he became the advertising manager of the *Columbia Monthly*, an undergraduate magazine. His work on the magazine and the influence of some of his literature professors led to his interest in publishing. He was further encouraged by his acquaintance with John Galsworthy, the British novelist, with whom he began corresponding while working on a paper for a literature class. Knopf visited Galsworthy during the summer of 1912 on a trip to Europe immediately after he graduated from Columbia. During that trip he met other authors and discovered the high quality of materials and typography used in books published in England. He returned home determined to become a publisher.

His father helped Knopf in 1912 to obtain his first job after college at Doubleday, Page and Co., where he worked for a year and a half, first as a clerk in the firm's accounting department and then in several other departments, including sales and advertising. It was at this company that Knopf said he learned how to publish books. He started his second job in 1914 as an assistant at Mitchell Kennerly, another New York publishing firm, where Knopf decided to start his own publishing business. His boss hurried him along toward this goal by firing him after learning of his plans. Knopf's third job, begun in 1915, just three years after leaving Columbia College, was as founder and president of Alfred A. Knopf, Inc. His company opened in a small room in the same Manhattan building where his father had his offices. He had $5,000 to invest in his effort and the assistance of Blanche Wolf, whom he had met while at Columbia College. The two soon married on 4 April 1916; they would have one son. Knopf was also helped by his father, who worked with the firm until his death in 1932.

The Borzoi, or Russian wolfhound, became the firm's colophon and years later continued to be recognized as a symbol of excellent bookmaking. Knopf's plan was to bring good literature in translation from Europe to America and to sell attractive books made of high-quality materials. The first book published by his firm in 1915 was a translation of *Four Plays* by Émile Augier, a French playwright. The book did not generate strong sales, but from the beginning Knopf placed more importance on the quality of the writing of his books than on making immediate profits. He soon learned that there was no copyright in America for W. H. Hudson's *Green Mansions*, a romance set in South America, so he obtained permission to publish it in 1916 with an introduction by his friend John Galsworthy. This book sold well enough to provide the new publisher some financial security.

In 1917 Knopf published more American works, though he continued to produce European books in translation. Carefully choosing writers who seemed of enduring quality, he gradually included works by such exceptionally gifted writers as Sigmund Freud, D. H. Lawrence, E. M. Forster, Albert Camus, Franz Kafka, Jean-Paul Sartre, W. Somerset Maugham, Dashiell Hammett, Conrad Aiken, James Baldwin, Langston Hughes, André Gide, and H. L. Mencken. In addition to fiction and poetry, Knopf published books about music, wine, food, photography, nature, and important works by such historians as Samuel Eliot Morison, Kenneth Stamp, Arthur Schlesinger, Sr., and Oswald Spengler. By the 1940s, Knopf began to publish translations of works by South American authors, such as the Brazilians Jorge Amado and Gilberto Freyre. Twenty-six authors published by Knopf were awarded Pulitzer Prizes, including Willa Cather, John Updike, John Cheever, Wallace Stevens, and Richard Hofstadter, and sixteen were Nobel laureates, including Thomas Mann and T. S. Eliot.

The firm's success was not due to bestsellers—Knopf once said that he believed bestseller lists should be banned by law—but because Knopf selected books that were good enough to maintain less spectacular sales over a long period of time. Knopf published one magazine, the *American Mercury*, a monthly literary magazine begun in 1924 and edited by H. L. Mencken, whom Knopf first met while working for Doubleday, Page and Co. A mutual admiration for the works of Joseph Conrad led to their meeting and becoming good friends. The *American Mercury* was quite highly regarded, and Knopf continued as publisher until 1934 when the magazine became independent. Mencken greatly admired Knopf and once described him as the perfect publisher.

In spite of continued success, Knopf felt uncertain about the firm's future when in 1959 his son, Alfred, Jr., left the company to start up his own venture, Atheneum Publishers, so in 1960 Alfred A. Knopf, Inc., was merged with Random House, owned by Knopf's good friends Donald Klopfer and Bennett Cerf. The arrangement allowed Knopf to remain as chairman of the board and his wife Blanche to serve as president. Knopf also retained editorial control for several years. On 4 June 1966 Knopf's wife and business partner for half a century died. In the following spring he married Helen Norcross Hedrick, a widow and author whose book he had published more than twenty-five years earlier. Soon after Blanche's death, Knopf gave up independent control of his company, which then became a subsidiary of Random House. In 1980 S. I. Newhouse and Sons purchased both Random House and Alfred A. Knopf, Inc., though Knopf has been described as an influence on the firm until his death.

Despite the many distinguished authors that Knopf published, his firm's bestselling book was Kahlil Gibran's *The Prophet* (1923), which had sold more than two million copies before Knopf's death. Knopf was said to have been embarrassed by the success of *The Prophet*, in part because in his later years he believed that the publishing industry was beginning to decline largely because of the pursuit of bestsellers and an emphasis on profits over literary quality. In fact, he said in an interview with the *New York Times* a few years before his death that he believed that the beginning of the end of Western civilization had arrived and that the cause was greed.

In addition to his passion for publishing, Knopf's interests included photography, good wine and food, and the preservation of national parks and historic sites. From 1950 to 1956 he was a member and for a time chairman of the federal government's advisory board on national parks, historic sites, buildings, and monuments. In 1960 he was presented with the Cornelius Amroy Pugsley Gold Medal for Conservation and Preservation. His publishing awards included the Gold Medal of the American Institute of Graphic Arts (1950), a distinguished service award from the Association of American University Presses (1975), and a distinguished achievement award from the National Book Awards Committee (1975). Knopf was the author of a few books himself, including *Some Random Recollections* (1949), *Publishing Then and Now* (1964), *Blanche W. Knopf, July 30, 1894–June 4, 1966* (1966), and *Sixty Photographs* (1975).

Knopf maintained an apartment in Manhattan but since 1928 lived primarily in his country house in Pur-chase, New York, where he died of congestive heart failure. A few months before his death, John Updike presented him with an award on behalf of the Mac-Dowell Colony, a distinguished writers' colony in Peterboro, New Hampshire, for his many years of promoting literary careers. Updike said on this occasion that "for something like seventy years, Alfred Knopf and the publishing firm he created have brightened the world of American books. In a field prone to false excitements, he has kept his eye on the matter of quality—quality in printing, quality in writing." After his death, the *New York Times* described him as "one of America's outstanding publishers, whose imprint bore his own name and whose books symbolized quality for more than half a century."

• *Portrait of a Publisher, 1915–1965* (1965) is a set of two chapbooks published to celebrate the fiftieth anniversary of the founding of Alfred A. Knopf, Inc. The first one includes material from writings and speeches by Knopf himself, and the second includes essays in which forty-four authors discuss Knopf. Clifton Fadiman, ed., *Fifty Years: Borzoi Books 1915–1965: A Retrospective Collection*, contains sample passages from books published by Knopf. John Tebbel, *A History of Book Publishing in the United States*, vols. 2 and 3 (1975, 1978), puts Knopf's career in the context of American publishing. Bennett Cerf's autobiography, *At Random* (1977), contains information about Knopf, Cerf's friend and fellow publisher. Obituaries are in the *New York Times* and the *Los Angeles Times*, both 12 Aug. 1984; in *Newsweek* and *Time*, both 20 Aug. 1984; and in the *Chicago Tribune*, 13 Aug. 1984.

ALAN KELLY

KNOPF, Blanche Wolf (30 July 1894–4 June 1966), publisher, was born in New York City, the daughter of Julius W. Wolf, a wealthy jeweler, and Bertha Samuels. The younger of two children and the only daughter, she was raised in a prosperous Jewish household in New York City. She was taught by French and German governesses and attended the Gardner School. In 1911, while her family was spending the summer on Long Island near the Knopf residence, she met Alfred A. Knopf, then a student at Columbia University, and they soon became engaged. Blanche encouraged Alfred to become a publisher, and in 1915, after he had worked briefly in other firms, they founded their own publishing house under the corporate name Alfred A. Knopf, Inc. Blanche and Alfred married on 4 April 1916. Shortly after the birth of their only child, Alfred, Jr., in 1918 they entrusted their son's care to a nurse so that Blanche could work full-time in the business. Both she and Alfred essentially spent the remainder of their lives developing the company and were responsible for its financial success and prestige.

The Knopf firm early became solidly established. During the first few years the Knopfs created and solidified a high standing as publishers of quality books by important writers. In 1916 Blanche had devised the Borzoi imprint on Knopf books. At the time, she was fond of the looks of borzois (Russian wolfhounds) and proposed that a drawing of one be used as a colophon. Later she owned two borzois but found them unlikable: "They were cowardly, stupid, disloyal, and full of self-pity, and they kept running away." She turned to Yorkshire terriers as pets and said she wished she had chosen a better dog for the imprint. The Borzoi books attracted literary attention and helped make the Knopf reputation. In *The Borzoi 1920* (1920), commemorating the first five years of the firm, the Knopfs listed 236 books by 167 authors that they had published.

Blanche Knopf was important in all aspects of the firm's operations. She became expert in technical matters, including typography, paper, ink, and printing. She edited works and wrote advertising copy. She had a keen interest in business and management, serving first as office manager and then in 1921 as vice president and director of the firm, a position she held until 1957 when she became president and director.

But it was her ability to attract authors that made Blanche Knopf such an asset. She was knowledgeable about contemporary literature and had good intuition about changing trends in belles lettres. During the first years the firm had made its reputation by publishing European authors in well-designed American editions. Blanche Knopf was fluent in French, spoke Spanish and Italian, and was of Viennese extraction on her father's side. She arranged for expert English translations for those authors who wrote in other languages. She was charming, persuasive, and helpful to her writers in numerous ways—including with their personal problems—and she established loyal relationships with many of them.

Beginning in the 1920s and continuing throughout the 1930s, Blanche traveled annually to Europe to acquire manuscripts from both prominent writers and newcomers. In the 1940s, when World War II cut off travel to Europe, she turned her attention to South America. She arranged for the publication of books by Eduardo Mallea, Jorge Amado, Germán Arciniega, Gilberto Freyre, and others who were little known in the United States and took charge of Knopf's entire Latin American field of business.

After World War II she directed the firm's efforts in the British and Continental fields and continued to add writers. Among the British writers she garnered over the years were Hammond Innes, Elizabeth Bowen, Ivy Compton-Burnett, Muriel Spark, Angela Thirkell, and Alan Sillitoe. Among the French writers she signed up were André Gide, Jules Romains, Jean-Paul Sartre, Simone de Beauvoir, and Albert Camus. Other of her authors included William Shirer, Sigmund Freud, Ilya Ehrenburg, and Mikhail A. Sholokhov. Although her foreign authors tended to be intellectuals, in the United States she worked most notably with mystery writers, in particular the authors of hardboiled detective novels like Dashiell Hammett, James M. Cain, and Raymond Chandler. Bestsellers were rare, but the firm continued to publish belles lettres, music, and history and to carry a backlist of books that sold steadily throughout the years.

Blanche and Alfred Knopf sometimes worked together in publishing writers, but for the most part they worked independently. Although their offices were separated only by a secretary's room, they were both possessive of their "finds." This attitude was evident in their private lives as well. Although they occasionally hosted weekend dinner parties, they largely went their separate ways. Geoffrey Hellman in an article in the *New Yorker* (4 Dec. 1948) refers to this "divergence" as "an amicable one." In 1928 Alfred bought a house in the country, at Purchase, New York; Blanche preferred the city and moved to an apartment on West 55th Street in Manhattan, only a short walk from the offices at 501 Madison Avenue, where she lived for the rest of her life. She insisted on being known as Blanche W. Knopf rather than Mrs. Alfred A. Knopf.

She was annoyed by the male-only rules of the Publishers' Lunch Club, the Book Table, and other trade organizations to which Alfred belonged. She periodically started clubs for women in book publishing and allied businesses, but they were short-lived. Not one of the other women was even close to her own rank within the business world, and, as Blanche complained, the talk was largely social. She asserted that there was no difference between male and female publishers, other than the lack of the latter: once when invited to a women's college to talk on the future of women in publishing, she declined, saying there seemed to be little future for them.

Knopf was widely known for her cocktail parties, dinner parties, and literary teas. She was a brilliant and cosmopolitan woman, often noted for her fashionable clothing and jewelry. She cared for her authors and worked hard to promote them. Among her own articles is "An American Publisher Tours South America" (*Saturday Review*, 10 Apr. 1943), in which she praised the sense "of newness, of aliveness, of something being created virtually from the ground up by people who find joy and excitement in that creation, and a great hope for the future." In "Albert Camus in the Sun" (*Atlantic Monthly*, Feb. 1961), she gives a moving and sympathetic portrait of Camus, calling him "the conscience of the post-war era." Blanche had attended the Nobel Prize ceremonies in Stockholm in 1957 to see Camus honored, and in detailing her relationship with him over the years, she does not fail to mention—both the Knopfs were good at self-promotion—that "Camus was the eleventh Nobel Prize winner to be published by us." She was attached to other writers as well, particularly to Robert Nathan and to H. L. Mencken; the Knopfs published much of their work and sponsored for a decade Mencken's editorship of *The American Mercury*.

In recognition of her work in discovering, encouraging, and publishing writers, the French government named Knopf a chevalier of the Legion of Honor in 1949 and in 1960 made her an officer, an honor seldom given to a woman. For her interest in Brazilian writers she was made a cavaleiro of the Brazilian Order of the Southern Cross in 1950 and two years later was given the rank of officer. She was awarded honorary degrees by Franklin and Marshall College (1962), Western College for Women (1966), and Adelphi University (1966).

Alfred A. Knopf, Jr., whom his parents called Pat, had initially joined the family firm but left it in 1959 to form his own company, Antheneum Press, a move that further strained family connections. The Knopfs sold their firm to Random House in 1960 but retained control of their own division for the remainder of their lifetimes. Harding Lemay, who worked as their top assistant for a decade during this time, describes the aging Blanche Knopf as suffering from illnesses and failing eyesight but remaining indefatigable, fiercely competitive, and alert. She died in her sleep in New York.

Blanche Knopf was unique in her field, the first woman to be a major book publisher. Alden Whitman, chief obituary writer of the *New York Times,* claimed "she made the firm and graciously permitted Alfred to take the bows" (*The Obituary Book,* p. 69). Her keen sense of literary trends in securing authors not only gave the firm profits and status, but often made the reputation of the authors and clearly helped shape the course of twentieth-century literature. For many years she was a celebrity in her own right, and she deserves her own place in the history of business and the arts.

• Knopf's papers, mainly various letters and editorial files, are in the Humanities Research Center of the University of Texas library at Austin. Carl Bode, *Mencken* (1969) and *The New Mencken Letters* (1977); Frank MacShane, *Selected Letters of Raymond Chandler* (1981); and Sara Mayfield, *The Constant Circle* (1968), contain selected letters to or from Knopf and other scattered references to her. Photographs of Knopf appear in "Golden Anniversary of Excellence," *Life,* 23 July 1965, p. 37, and Alfred A. Knopf, *Sixty Photographs* (1975). Alden Whitman, *The Obituary Book* (1971), provides a biographical sketch. Another source is pt. 3 of Geoffrey T. Hellman's article on Alfred Knopf in the *New Yorker,* 4 Dec. 1948, pp. 40–53. Additional references are in Harding Lemay, *Inside, Looking Out* (1971); Clifton Fadiman, ed., *Fifty Years: Borzoi Books* (1965); and Charles A. Madison, *Book Publishing in America* (1966), all of which deal with the Knopf publishing firm. Obituaries are in the *New York Times,* 5 June 1966, *Publishers Weekly,* 13 June 1966, and *Newsweek,* 20 June 1966.

LOIS MARCHINO

KNOPF, Eleanora Frances Bliss (15 July 1883–21 Jan. 1974), geologist, was born in Rosemont, Pennsylvania, the daughter of General Tasker Howard Bliss, a chief of staff of the U.S. Army, and Eleanora Anderson. During her childhood her father was usually stationed in Washington, D.C., but in the period before, during, and after World War I, when he was a principal representative of the United States in the Allied councils and treaty negotiations, his family could be with him only occasionally. She always remembered the two years, from 1905 to 1907, that they spent together in the southern Philippines, after her graduation from Bryn Mawr College in 1904.

At Bryn Mawr Eleanora Bliss became a geologist under the tutelage of Florence Bascom, who specialized in the study of rocks, especially complex metamorphic rocks. Bascom founded the geology depart-

ment at the college and served as a geologist with the U.S. Geological Survey (USGS). Bliss did both her undergraduate and graduate work under Bascom, at one critical point leaving her mother, who was extremely deaf, in the Philippines in order to do so. She received her Ph.D. from Bryn Mawr in 1912. Her dissertation was prepared jointly with a close friend, another of Bascom's students who became a geologist, Anna Jonas. The dissertation, which was published by the USGS in 1916, dealt with a region of complex metamorphic rocks in the Doe Run–Avondale region of Pennsylvania. Bliss and Jonas subsequently collaborated on several papers, most notably one on the structure and origin of a group of metamorphic rocks called schists in Pennsylvania and Maryland (1923) and another on the geology of the McCalls Ferry–Quarryville district of Pennsylvania (1929). In those and other publications, the two women broke with their mentor in a controversy over the age and interpretation of the so-called Wissahickon schist and surrounding rocks of southeastern Pennsylvania. The argument, which peaked in the mid-1930s, eventually involved everyone concerned with Appalachian geology.

Described as charming, kind, and considerate, Eleanora Bliss's intellectual style was not one of personal confrontation. Considerably before the appearance of her own paper on metamorphic terranes in 1935, she had become an inactive participant in the Wissahickon controversy and shifted her field work from the Pennsylvania-Maryland Piedmont to the similar and equally complex Taconic region of New York and New England. In part this shift was the result of a different set of associations and a different milieu. In 1920, at the age of thirty-six, she had married a widower with children, Adolf Knopf, also a USGS geologist, and moved with him to New Haven, Connecticut, where he had been appointed a professor at Yale. It was an exceptional marriage of like minds, although they did not coauthor any works.

Eleanora Bliss Knopf was never allowed to hold any kind of academic appointment or to teach any formal courses at Yale, but she maintained a working space, introduced students informally to geological problems and field methods, and remained active in the USGS (she had become a full geologist with the USGS in 1928). Despite her treatment at Yale, in later life Knopf maintained that if a woman did as good work—or preferably a little better work—as a man in the same job, she would "have no trouble."

One of Knopf's greatest contributions was introducing to American geologists pioneering techniques for studying rock structure that had been developed by the Austrian petrologist Bruno Sander. Fluent in three languages and able to read others, Knopf had read Sander's difficult work in German. She had become interested in it when she realized that she "had practically reached a blank wall after struggling for thirty years with the structural intricacies of metamorphic rocks in the Appalachian mountains and the Piedmont Province." Field observations and the microscopic study of rocks alone did not afford a key to the interpretation of geologic structure in those areas. After visiting Sander in Innsbruck, she mastered the new analytical methods and introduced them in a series of professional papers and in *Structural Petrology* (1938, coauthored with Earl Ingerson), her best-known work. She also contributed related work on the experimental deformation of rocks in the laboratory. She then applied these techniques, along with those of mapping from aerial photographs, to interpret the Taconic region centering around the Stissing Mountain area of New York that she had first begun to study in 1925.

Having served the U.S. Geological Survey from 1912 and the Maryland Geological Survey from 1917 to 1926, Knopf officially resigned her position as geologist with the USGS in 1938, although she continued to accept assignments for several years thereafter. In 1951 the Knopfs retired to California, where she became a research associate and lectured in the geology department at Stanford University. Her culminating publication on the Stissing Mountain area was published by Stanford in 1962. She was a fellow of the Geological Society of America, serving on its board of editors from 1937 to 1939, and she served as chairperson of the Committee on Experimental Deformation of Rocks of the National Research Council from 1944 to 1949. She also served as president of the Peninsula Geological Society of California. In 1960 Bryn Mawr presented her with a citation for distinguished service at its seventy-fifth anniversary convocation. Following the death of her husband in 1966, Knopf devoted herself to completing research they had done together in Montana. She died in Menlo Park, California.

Eleanora Bliss Knopf is best known for her fieldwork and publications on the rock structure of major areas in the northeastern United States. At a time when few women pursued careers in geology, especially field geology, she gained national respect and recognition for her careful research, both alone and in collaboration with others, and for her ability to apply new analytical methods to complex structural problems.

• A collection of Knopf's correspondence and other papers are in the Tasker Howard Bliss Papers at the Library of Congress. The Bryn Mawr College archives contain a few letters and documents from an alumna biofile, including two forms filled out by Knopf in 1953 and 1970. The USGS Field Records Library in Denver, Colo., has her field records for the Stissing Mountain studies from 1925 to 1954. The fullest biographical treatment, which includes a selected bibliography, is John Rodgers, "Memorial to Eleanora Bliss Knopf," *GSA Memorials* 6 (1977). See also Charles F. Park, Jr., "Memorial to Adolf Knopf (1882–1966)," *GSA Proceedings* (1966): 261–66; and Richard V. Dietrich, "Memorial to Anna I. Jonas Stose," *GSA Memorials* 6 (1977). Useful background is provided by Margaret W. Rossiter, *Women Scientists in America: Struggles and Strategies to 1940* (1982), and by Michele L. Aldrich, "Women in Geology," in *Women of Science: Righting the Record*, ed. G. Kass-Simon and Patricia Farnes (1990), pp. 52–57. An obituary is in the *Redwood City (Calif.) Tribune*, 23 Jan. 1974.

LOIS B. ARNOLD

KNORR, Nathan Homer (23 Apr. 1905–7 June 1977), third president of the Watch Tower Society (1942–1977), was born in Bethlehem, Pennsylvania, the son of Donel Ellsworth Knorr and Estella Bloss. At age sixteen he came in contact with followers of Charles Taze Russell, known as "International Bible Students," "Russellites," or "Millennial Dawnists." He soon left the Dutch Reformed church in which he had been reared to join the movement. Upon his graduation from high school in Allentown, Pennsylvania, in 1923, he entered the full-time colporteur ministry of his newfound faith.

Later in 1923 Knorr joined the "working family" at "Bethel," the world headquarters and chief printing plant of the Bible Students, located in Brooklyn, New York, where the organization was incorporated as the People's Pulpit Association of New York. After first working in the shipping department, he advanced to coordinator of all printing activities. In 1932 he became general manager of the publishing office and printing plant.

In 1931 the movement had adopted the name "Jehovah's Witnesses." Knorr quickly advanced in the hierarchy; in 1934 he was elected a director of the People's Pulpit Association, becoming vice president the following year. In 1940 he was chosen vice president of the Watch Tower Bible and Tract Society of Pennsylvania, the parent corporation of the movement. Upon the death of President "Judge" Joseph F. Rutherford in 1942, Knorr became president of both American corporations and of the International Bible Students Association of England, all of which were lifetime offices. (In 1956 the People's Pulpit Association changed its name to Watchtower Bible and Tract Society, Inc. of New York.)

As president Knorr had responsibility for direction of overall policy, supervision of editorial work, oversight of the missionary branches, and management of the food farm (which fed the employees at Bethel) and of the radio station WBBR. He gained a reputation as both an organization man and an autocrat.

One major characteristic of his presidency was his establishment of what has been described as a "collective oligarchy." In 1942 he began publishing all literature anonymously. At the same time he also stamped all correspondence with the corporation's name rather than a personal signature.

A second important feature was his effort to better train the Witnesses as "publishers" of their message. He established the Gilead Watchtower Bible School in South Lansing, New York, in 1943 to train both domestic leaders and missionaries. About the same time he created a "Theocratic Ministry School" in each Witness congregation in order to train members to be better door-to-door preachers and public speakers. To support these educational endeavors, Knorr oversaw the production of several textbooks, including *Theocratic Aid to Kingdom Publishers* (1945), *Equipped for Every Good Work* (1946), and *Qualified to Be Ministers* (1955). This training enabled Witnesses to replace their portable phonographs, which had carried Judge

Rutherford's voice into homes, with personal sermons based on outlines supplied by headquarters.

Knorr also sought to develop the consciousness of Jehovah's Witnesses as participating in a larger international organization. He traveled to Central and South America three times before the end of World War II. Beginning in 1945 he went frequently to Europe, Asia, and Africa. In 1946 he created semiannual circuit conventions and in 1948 and 1949 held annual district conventions. These regional meetings were supplemented by large international assemblies, held in Cleveland in 1946 and in New York in 1950, 1953, and 1958. In 1963 more than 500 members joined Knorr and other Witness leaders in an "Around the World Convention," which traveled by airplane eastward from Milwaukee, Wisconsin, to Pasadena, California. The 115,240 "peak publishers" in 1942 had grown to 2,223,538 worldwide by the time of Knorr's death.

Other changes in practice and emphasis also took place during Knorr's presidency. The society began stressing integrity in both individual and business matters and since 1962 obedience to secular as well as spiritual authority. Knorr's marriage in 1953 to Audrey Irene Mock, a Bethel housekeeper, was one of the first in the community, and it symbolized the move from discouraging marriage because it was a distraction from the "preaching work," as the society had previously done, to encouraging it. The society began teaching that the family was the basic unit of the theocratic society of Jehovah's Witnesses; it also began to insist that marriages be legally recognized, whereas previously the society had argued that Jehovah did not authorize the state to perform marriages.

Although not particularly concerned with doctrine or trained in biblical languages, Knorr served on the New World Translation Committee, which sought to develop a correct translation of the Bible. Vice president Frederick Franz probably played the major role in the project, with Knorr presenting the New Testament portion to the New York convention in 1950. The translation was completed in 1960 and published the following year. A series of doctrinal books also appeared, including *The Truth Shall Make You Free* (1943), *Let God Be True* (1946), *Make Sure of All Things* (1953), and *From Paradise Lost to Paradise Regained* (1958). These works replaced those by Russell and Rutherford as authoritative statements of Witness belief.

In 1966 Frederick Franz predicted that Armageddon would occur in 1975, a prediction that increased adherents to the faith in the early 1970s and lost many of them after it failed to come true. Also in the mid-1960s, Knorr gave an editorial committee of three researchers, led by Raymond Franz, Frederick's nephew, a free hand to consult non-Watchtower sources in preparation of an *Aid to Bible Understanding* (1971). In the course of their research, this committee began questioning aspects of Witness biblical and historical chronology. Coupled with the failure of the Armaged-

don prediction, this questioning ultimately led to a purge of at least nine individuals at Bethel in 1980.

Meanwhile, widespread dissatisfaction among the Witnesses and criticism of Knorr's autocratic style during the previous decade led in 1971 to establishment of the Governing Body, which made the president, at least theoretically, only first among equals. The Governing Body attained greater power in 1975, about the time that Knorr was diagnosed as having a cancerous tumor. He died at the society's complex in Wallkill, New York, and was succeeded to the presidency by Frederick Franz.

• Biographical information regarding N. H. Knorr may be found in books dealing with Jehovah's Witnesses. Marley Cole, *Jehovah's Witnesses: The New World Society* (1955), and Timothy White, *A People for His Name: A History of Jehovah's Witnesses and an Evaluation* (1968), provide a Jehovah's Witness perspective. A Roman Catholic viewpoint appears in William J. Whalen, *Armageddon around the Corner: A Report on Jehovah's Witnesses* (1962). Barbara Grizzuti Harrison, *Visions of Glory: A History and a Memoir of Jehovah's Witnesses* (1978), and Heather and Gary Botting, *The Orwellian World of Jehovah's Witnesses* (1984), give personal impressions of Knorr. The most scholarly evaluations of Knorr's presidency are Alan Rogerson, *Millions Now Living Will Never Die: A Study of Jehovah's Witnesses* (1969); James A. Beckford, *The Trumpet of Prophecy: A Sociological Study of Jehovah's Witnesses* (1975); and M. James Penton, *Apocalypse Delayed: The Story of Jehovah's Witnesses* (1985). An obituary is in the *New York Times*, 12 June 1977.

GARY LAND

KNOTT, James Proctor (29 Aug. 1830–18 June 1911), U.S. congressman and governor of Kentucky, was born in the Cherry Run community of Washington (now Marion) County, Kentucky, the son of Joseph Percy Knott, a civil engineer and teacher, and Maria Irvine McElroy. He received a common school education, but lacking funds for further studies, Knott read borrowed law books and attended local trials while assisting at his father's school. Looking for greater opportunities than his home area offered, in 1850 Knott moved to Memphis, Missouri, and found employment as deputy circuit clerk for Scotland County. A year later he was admitted to the bar.

In 1852 Knott married Mary E. "Mollie" Foreman, who died during childbirth a year later. Knott then immersed himself in work and rapidly became the area's leading attorney. During a visit to Kentucky in 1858, he married his first cousin, Sarah Rosanna "Sallie" McElroy; they had no children. The newlyweds moved to Jefferson City, and that November Knott was elected to the Missouri legislature, where he pushed for better roads and improved schools. As chairman of the Judiciary Committee, Knott represented the state in the impeachment trial of circuit judge Albert Jackson and conducted the proceedings. Impressed with Knott's legal knowledge and courtroom deportment, in 1859 the governor appointed him to fill the vacant office of attorney general; a year later the people confirmed Knott's position by a majority of 20,000 votes. When the Civil War started in

1861, Knott, a moderate who believed the South had the right to secede but personally opposed separation, refused to take a loyalty oath to the Union. Subsequently he was briefly imprisoned, and he resigned his position as attorney general. When a similar oath was required of lawyers and jurors, he left the state and returned to Kentucky in March 1862 to practice law in Lebanon.

In the post–Civil War years, Kentuckians elected Knott to six terms in the U.S. House of Representatives (1867–1871, 1875–1883). Perhaps reflecting Kentucky's agricultural economy and the postwar bitterness of its residents, which resulted from real and imagined mistreatment by the Union army and government, Knott opposed Reconstruction and the high protective tariff. He also served as chairman of the Judiciary Committee and served as one of the managers of the impeachment proceedings against former Secretary of War William Belknap. Knott also opposed the use of federal funds for projects that profited only a few. He spoke eloquently against spending $180,000 to pave Washington's Pennsylvania Avenue, and his famed Duluth Speech of 1871 ridiculed the proposed subsidy of a railroad through the wilds of Minnesota. Widely distributed, the latter earned praise for Knott and the publicity helped spur remote Duluth's growth. The city later hailed Knott as its hero. The Kentuckian apparently regretted making the satirical speech, for although it brought him fame, he feared that it eroded his credibility.

In 1883 Knott announced his candidacy for the Democratic nomination for governor of Kentucky. Delegates to the gubernatorial convention that May battled through seven ballots before nominating Knott. Throughout the summer campaign, he and Republican Thomas Z. Morrow of Somerset debated the issues of the day. Both spoke of the need to reform the prison, educational, and tax systems. Each man also blamed his opponent's political party for the state's problems. In the August election, Knott easily won, 133,615 to 89,181.

In his messages to the legislature, Knott continued to advocate the changes he espoused during the campaign, reiterating the pleas of his predecessor Luke P. Blackburn for a new prison to relieve brutally overcrowded conditions at the penitentiary at Frankfort. The legislature appropriated funds to construct the branch facility at Eddyville, which opened in 1886. Nevertheless, to address the immediate need—and in the absence of a parole board—Knott employed his executive pardon with greater frequency than many friends and foes deemed wise.

Knott wanted a complete reform of the state's tax system. To correct the disparity between the market and assessed values of taxable property, the governor suggested the creation of a state agency to equalize tax assessments and eliminate corporate exemptions. The legislature created the Board of Equalization but ignored his call to revoke tax immunities. The assembly also failed to grant the governor's request for a uniform pay scale for local public officials and to transfer certain expenses to local governments.

Echoing decades of requests for educational reform and with the aid of a committee of prominent citizens, Knott pushed the legislature to create a stronger and more uniform public school system; the lawmakers assented. The new law defined the school year, regulated the course of study, listed the duties of state and local school boards, replaced county commissioners with popularly elected superintendents, authorized a state teachers' association, and created a state board of education and a normal school for blacks at Frankfort.

Knott's unsuccessful efforts to calm civil disturbance in Rowan County marred his tenure as governor. One of the Commonwealth's bloodiest, the Martin-Tolliver feud saw twenty men killed and sixteen wounded during a three-year period. Although he sent a special prosecutor, truce negotiators, and the state guard, Knott failed to end the eastern Kentucky bloodbath. A gun battle on the streets of Morehead followed by vigilante action prompted his successor to dispatch state troops to finally settle the disorder.

On leaving the executive office in early September 1887, Knott returned to the practice of law and served as special assistant to the state's new attorney general, successfully arguing in 1889 before the Supreme Court in the Green River Island Case regarding the disputed Kentucky-Indiana border. He also served as a delegate to the 1890 constitutional convention (which produced the document under which Kentucky continues to labor) and helped draft its Bill of Rights. In 1892 Knott accepted a position teaching civics and economics at Centre College in Danville. In 1894 he helped create the institution's law school and became its first dean and professor, a position he held until ill health following a stroke forced his retirement in 1902. Knott spent his remaining years in Lebanon, where he died.

• Knott's gubernatorial papers are in the Kentucky Department of Libraries and Archives, Frankfort, and much about his career as the state's executive appears in era newspapers, in the *Journals* of the state house and senate, and in *Kentucky Documents* (biennial reports of state officials and institutions). Five boxes of Knott's private papers, housed in the Department of Library Special Collections at Western Kentucky University, Bowling Green, include Knott's speeches, family correspondence, a diary kept by his mother, photographs, floral watercolors by Knott, and a number of witty poems and delightful cartoons about his congressional colleagues. "Report of Capt. Ernest MacPherson to Adj. Gen. Sam Hill," in *Kentucky Documents, 1887* (1887), concerns the Rowan County feud. For published materials on Knott, see Edwin W. Mills, "The Career of James Proctor Knott in Missouri," *Missouri Historical Review* 31 (Apr. 1937): 288–94; Helen Bartter Crocker, "J. Proctor Knott's Education in Missouri Politics, 1850–1862," *Bulletin of the Missouri Historical Society* 30 (Jan. 1974): 101–16; Hambleton Tapp, "James Proctor Knott and the Duluth Speech," *Register of the Kentucky Historical Society* 70 (Apr. 1972): 77–93; and Robert M. Ireland, "Proctor Knott," in *Kentucky's Governors, 1792–1985*, ed. Lowell H. Harrison (1985).

NANCY DISHER BAIRD
MATTHEW LUNSFORD

KNOWLAND, William Fife (26 June 1908–23 Feb. 1974), U.S. senator and newspaper publisher, was born in Alameda, California, the son of Joseph Russell Knowland, a congressman and newspaper publisher, and Ella Fife. Beginning his political life early, Knowland made his first speech at the age of twelve for presidential candidate Warren Harding. The elder Knowland groomed William for a political career and occasionally had his teenage son substitute for him as chair at meetings of the Republican Committee of California. Knowland entered the University of California at Berkeley in 1925. One year later he married Helen Herrick. The couple raised three children. After receiving his bachelor's degree in political science in 1929, Knowland joined the staff of his father's newspaper, the Oakland, California, *Tribune*. In 1933 he became both assistant publisher of the *Tribune* and an assemblyman in the California state legislature.

Knowland was elected to the California Senate in 1934. Already rising in California Republican politics, he became a member of the Republican National Committee in 1938 and was chosen as chair of the body's executive committee in 1941. Drafted into the army in 1942, Knowland entered Officers' Candidate School at Fort Benning, Georgia. In the army he served as a staff writer and eventually rose to the rank of major.

In 1945, while serving in Europe, Knowland received news that he had been appointed by California governor Earl Warren to replace the recently deceased Senator Hiram Johnson. Knowland's father had been a major supporter of Warren's political ambitions. Knowland subsequently was discharged from the army and returned to the United States to take his seat in the Senate. He was elected to the Senate in his own right the following year, defeating Democratic congressman Will Rogers, Jr. During his first few years in the Senate, Knowland served on the Special Committee to Investigate the National Defense Program and the War Investigation Committee. The latter committee investigated and reported alleged abuses on the part of U.S. occupation forces in Europe, for which the members received sharp criticism. Knowland also served on the Senate Appropriations Committee, the Rules and Administration Committee, and the Joint Congressional Committee on Atomic Energy.

During the Harry S. Truman years Knowland disagreed with many of the administration's policies. While the administration was generally favorable to organized labor, Knowland called for greater legislative restrictions on the power of unions. He supported the 1947 Taft-Hartley Bill, which made the closed shop illegal and placed other restrictions on unions, helping to pass the legislation over a presidential veto. Knowland also supported the Tidelands Oil Bill of 1946, which would have given control of offshore oil deposits to the individual states. Truman vetoed the measure, but it was passed in a modified form in 1953. Knowland did, however, support Truman's plan to give aid to Communist-threatened Greece and Turkey in 1947, parting company with some of his more isolationist colleagues.

California voters reelected Knowland to a second term in 1952. Initially he supported the moderate policies of the Dwight D. Eisenhower administration, but he gradually began to drift toward the conservative wing of the Republican party. After the Communist victory in China in 1949, Knowland had become a stanch opponent of the Beijing (Peking) regime. Along with a group of like-minded politicians known as the "China Lobby," he supported the return of Nationalist leader Chiang Kai-shek. Knowland increasingly became disenchanted with the administration's foreign policy in regard to China and Asia, which he believed to be overly lenient toward Communism.

When Chinese membership in the United Nations was being considered in 1954, Knowland pressured the Eisenhower administration to oppose the measure. On several occasions Knowland proposed legislation to forbid Communist Chinese entry into the United Nations, eventually threatening to resign his leadership over the matter. Knowland's preoccupation with China gained him the pejorative nickname of the "Senator from Formosa."

Upon the death of Senate Republican majority leader Robert Taft of Ohio in 1953, Knowland became the Senate majority leader at the unprecedented young age of forty-five. He held this position for only two years, becoming minority leader after Democratic gains in 1955. Although as majority leader Knowland supported most of Eisenhower's domestic policies, he was, in the words of one historian, "neither an effective spokesman for administration policy nor a strong party leader." In accordance with White House wishes, Knowland successfully halted a Democratic filibuster of the 1954 Atomic Energy Bill. He parted company with the administration in his unsuccessful support of the Bricker Amendment, a measure to reassert the authority of Congress in treaty making.

Knowland further alienated himself from the administration and Eisenhower Republicans in the Senate by his steadfast support of Senator Joseph McCarthy. Hoping to diffuse growing Senate discontent with McCarthy, Knowland called for a special bipartisan committee to investigate censuring McCarthy. Knowland, supporting McCarthy until the end, voted against the committee's recommendation to censure.

Knowland began maneuvering for the 1956 Republican presidential nomination against political rival and fellow Californian Richard Nixon. When President Eisenhower chose to seek a second term, Knowland announced he would not seek the nomination. In 1958 Knowland announced his candidacy for the governorship of California in a move designed to position himself for the 1960 Republican presidential nomination. Unfortunately for Knowland, he lost the gubernatorial election to Democratic candidate Edmund Brown.

Knowland returned to the *Tribune* in 1958, becoming president and publisher of the newspaper upon the death of his father in 1966. He unsuccessfully opposed the American Newspaper Guild's effort to unionize the newspaper. Knowland served on Barry Goldwater's presidential campaign staff in 1964 and backed Ronald Reagan for the Republican presidential nomination in 1968. Knowland and Helen divorced in 1972. He married Ann Dickson later that year but again filed for divorce in 1973. In 1974 Knowland's body was found at his Monte Rio, California, summer home with a single gunshot to his head. The death was ruled a suicide. The final years of Knowland's life were in marked contrast to his seemingly overnight rise to national prominence. Seriously considered to be a presidential contender in the 1956 election, Knowland slipped into relative political obscurity after his defeat for governor in 1958.

• Knowland's papers are collected at the Bancroft Library, University of California, Berkeley. For a brief, if biased, account of Knowland's political philosophy see William S. White, "What Bill Knowland Stands For," *New Republic* 134 (27 Feb. 1956): 7–10. For contemporary views of Knowland's presidential prospects in 1956 see Patrick McMahon, "Knowland and Johnson in 1956," *American Mercury* 79 (Oct. 1954): 39–44, and "'56 Nears, Nixon-Knowland Rivalry Grows," *U.S. News and World Report*, 16 July 1954, pp. 60–62. An obituary is in the *New York Times*, 25 Feb. 1974.

SCOTT C. ZEMAN

KNOWLES, John Hilton (23 May 1926–6 Mar. 1979), physician, cardiopulmonary physiologist, and hospital and foundation administrator, was born in Chicago, Illinois, the son of James Knowles, a former World War I flying ace and vice president of Rexall Drug Company, and Jean Laurence Turnbull, an artist. Knowles spent his early childhood years in Normandy, Missouri; when he was twelve, he and his family moved to Belmont, Massachusetts. After graduating from Belmont High School in 1944, Knowles enrolled at Harvard, majoring in biochemistry. Sports and jazz music were his chief interests in college. With classmate Jack Lemmon, the future Academy Award–winning actor, Knowles played four-handed piano for the Harvard radio station and duets for the Imperial Hotel in addition to composing theater music. These extracurricular activities came at the expense of Knowles's grades; he was rejected by eleven medical schools. After graduating from Harvard in 1947, he enrolled at Washington University School of Medicine in St. Louis, where he became serious about his studies. He was elected to Alpha Omega Alpha, the national medical honor society, and in 1951 received his medical degree cum laude.

Knowles began his medical internship in Boston at Massachusetts General Hospital (MGH), where he met Edith Morris LaCroix, a cytology technician. They were married in 1953 and were to have six children. In 1952–1953 Knowles continued his residency at Harvard Medical School, where he also was a teaching fellow. From 1953 to 1955 Knowles served as a lieutenant at Portsmouth Naval Hospital in Virginia in charge of the cardiopulmonary laboratory. From 1956 to 1957 he studied physiology at the University of Rochester Medical School and at the University of Buffalo and then returned to MGH in 1958 as chief resident in internal medicine. He also joined the faculty at Harvard Medical School, where he would rise through the ranks to become, in 1969, a professor of medicine. In 1959 Knowles was appointed chief of the pulmonary diseases unit at MGH. He found medical specialization unfulfilling, because he was concerned with the broad socioeconomic problems of medicine. He believed that his calling lay in administrative work, and in 1961 he became assistant physician and director of medical affairs at MGH. In 1962, at the age of thirty-five, he was appointed general director of the hospital.

In one of his first moves as director of MGH, Knowles disposed of the long, hard wooden benches in the emergency ward and outpatient department—which he scored as symbols of "the cattle-car concept of medicine"—and replaced them with comfortable chairs. At the time he was director, U.S. hospitals were beginning to establish coronary care and other specialized-care units, and Knowles helped to introduce nine such intensive care units at MGH. During his tenure, MGH also increased its services to the Boston community: the hospital assigned psychiatrists to work with schools, courts, and social agencies; it established a neighborhood clinic in the depressed Charlestown area of Boston; and it opened a medical station at Logan International Airport for airport employees and passengers. Commenting on the changes at MGH that he helped to implement, Knowles said, "The purpose of all this is to change the hospital from a center for acute care to a center for preventive medicine" (*Newsweek*, 9 June 1969, p. 68).

With his pungent language, Knowles used his position as director of MGH as a rostrum to reproach the medical profession's inattention to economic and social concerns. While a champion of the private enterprise system, he was critical of private medicine's failure to provide adequate care for the young, the elderly, and the poor, and he spoke out against exorbitant medical fees and unnecessary surgical operations. In 1968 he testified before a Senate subcommittee on the need for comprehensive prepaid health insurance for all Americans, and in a 1969 appearance before a congressional joint economics subcommittee on fiscal policy, Knowles stated: "Our health statistics in certain areas are frankly embarrassing. The health of some 30 million poor people is abysmally bad and almost totally neglected." These concerns reflected Knowles's belief that unless the medical profession increased its public responsibility, the government would be forced to assume greater control of the profession.

Knowles preached preventive medicine, which was more beneficial to patients and less costly than acute, curative medicine, although more difficult to administer and less lucrative for physicians. He bemoaned the erosion of individual responsibility in the United States and urged massive public education on health issues. Knowles's view was that the individual had the power and moral responsibility to maintain his or her health by following proper guidelines regarding sleep, exercise, diet and weight, alcohol, and smoking; and individuals also depended on social policies designed to improve education and develop accessible health care.

Eminent as both an administrator and a physician, Knowles was favored to win a nomination from President Richard Nixon's new administration as assistant secretary for health and scientific affairs in the Department of Health, Education, and Welfare (HEW). Knowles, although a political independent, had helped to raise funds for Nixon's 1960 and 1968 presidential campaigns and had the backing of Nixon's designated HEW secretary, Robert Finch, as well as the support of several powerful medical organizations, including the American Hospital Association. However, Knowles's strident views alienated conservatives, who thought his ideas resembled socialized medicine. That opposition prevented his nomination.

Knowles's blunt views drew more fire from colleagues in 1972, when he was quoted in an interview as saying that 30 to 40 percent of doctors were "making a killing" in medicine by performing unnecessary surgery. The Massachusetts Medical Society's Committee on Ethics and Discipline censured Knowles for these remarks.

Knowles continued as director of MGH until 1972, when he became president of the Rockefeller Foundation in New York. In that role, Knowles helped to create the International Agricultural Development Service, an autonomous private agency designed to support rural development, and he also established international programs concerned with issues such as energy conservation and world peace. In 1974, as a member of Nelson Rockefeller's Commission for Critical Choices, Knowles organized a group to study health care issues and edited their work as a book, *Doing Better and Feeling Worse: Health Care in the United States* (1977). Knowles was also a professor at New York University Medical Center. He served in this capacity and as president of the Rockefeller Foundation until his death from pancreatic cancer at MGH.

One of the most visible and outspoken physicians of his time, Knowles foresaw the need for basic changes in American health care. Although a prolific writer and active medical researcher, he stressed patient care above teaching and research while director of MGH and increased the hospital's communication with city and state agencies, moving it closer to the model of preventive care that he advocated. His ultimate aim was to increase the social conscience of the medical community.

• The Rockefeller Archive Center of Pocantico Hills in North Tarrytown, N.Y., has the papers of John Knowles. These holdings cover his career at Massachusetts General Hospital and the Rockefeller Foundation (1960–1979) and include personal correspondence, speeches, newspaper clippings, films and tape recordings, photographs, and an unpublished manuscript, "Dr. Knowles's Journal." Knowles was the author of *Respiratory Physiology and Its Clinical Applications*

(1959), considered a classic textbook in its field, and of "The Struggle to Stay Healthy," a bicentennial essay for *Time*, 9 Aug. 1976, pp. 60–62. He also wrote numerous articles and book reviews. Many of Knowles's lectures at various hospitals and universities have been published as pamphlets. Knowles was the editor of *Hospitals, Doctors and the Public Interest* (1965); *The Teaching Hospital; Evolution and Contemporary Issues* (1966); *Views of Medical Education and Medical Care* (1968); and *China Diary* (1976). Profiles include J. Kronenberger, "Rockefeller Foundation Gets a Medical Renegade," *Life*, 30 June 1972, p. 73; and "Doctor for All Ills," *Time*, 17 July 1972, pp. 71ff. An interview with Knowles is in *Intellectual Digest*, Feb. 1972. Obituaries are in the *New York Times* and the *Boston Globe*, 7 Mar. 1979; and *Forum on Medicine*, Aug. 1979.

YANEK MIECZKOWSKI

KNOWLTON, Charles (10 May 1800–20 Feb. 1850), physician, was born in Templeton, Worcester County, Massachusetts, the son of Stephen Knowlton and Comfort White, farmers. Knowlton spent much of his boyhood engaged in manual labor, with the tedium broken by two-month school sessions in summer and winter. At the age of seventeen he began to be disturbed by gonorrhoea dormientium (involuntary seminal emissions while sleeping), which was then regarded by medical authorities as a grave threat to health and sanity. For three years Knowlton sought help from ten different physicians, and survived heroic regimens of drugs and blisters, but he became deeply depressed and incapable of work. In 1821 Knowlton moved into the home of a local mechanic, who offered electrical therapy for his ailment (a common approach to treatment during this era). The mechanic (whose surname was Stuart) also provided the pleasant company of six vivacious daughters, one of whom, Tabitha, Knowlton married in 1821. They were to have four children. He spent the rest of his life pursuing medical knowledge and criticizing conventional Christian beliefs.

Knowlton began the study of medicine as an apprentice to Dr. Charles Wilder of Templeton, Massachusetts, but, characteristically, became dissatisfied with the instruction that his mentor offered and stole a corpse so that he could learn anatomy firsthand. He partially financed his first course of study at New Hampshire Medical Institution (now Dartmouth Medical School) through another "resurrection," and although he was initially mocked by the more affluent students as a country bumpkin of eccentric appearance, he attained academic and social acceptance and completed his M.D. in 1824 with a thesis on the necessity of public support for dissection if medical education was to improve. While a student he was indicted for corpse stealing and, after beginning private practice, was convicted of illegal dissection and imprisoned for two months in Worcester, Massachusetts. While jailed, Knowlton wrote *Elements of Modern Materialism* (1829), a defense of agnosticism and an attempt to demonstrate that human thought and behavior could best be understood as the result of environmental conditioning and physical laws. The book did not sell, and the cost of its publication left Knowlton heavily in debt. Robert Dale Owen invited him, nevertheless, to address other freethinkers in Manhattan, and it was probably through Owen that Knowlton conceived the work that would gain him international fame, *Fruits of Philosophy, or the Private Companion of Adult People* (1832), the first popular manual on contraception by an American physician.

Owen had made a case for planned parenthood in *Moral Physiology* (1831), but Knowlton thought that the contraceptive method Owen advocated, coitus interruptus, required too much sacrifice of pleasure on the part of the male. Accordingly, he began research for *Fruits of Philosophy*, which provided a survey of human sexual anatomy and physiology, a philosophical defense of contraceptive practice upon utilitarian grounds, and formulas for spermicidal douches, Knowlton's recommended method. Shortly after he published *Fruits*, Knowlton settled in the Berkshire village of Ashfield, Massachusetts, where his practice prospered in spite of conflicts with local clergy over his "immoral works." Knowlton's birth control manual sold well, and he was prosecuted three times under the state common law obscenity statute for selling it. First, he was fined fifty dollars in Taunton; then a prosecution in Lowell led to three months of hard labor in the East Cambridge jail; and finally, a charge in Greenfield was dropped after two juries failed to reach a verdict. Claiming that these legal actions were inspired by his freethinking rather than by his advocacy of birth control, Knowlton won his struggle for acceptance by his Ashfield neighbors. He became an outspoken critic of quackery and a prominent member of the Massachusetts Medical Society. His writings appeared frequently in free thought journals and in the *Boston Medical and Surgical Journal* (now *New England Journal of Medicine*). He died of heart disease while visiting relatives in Winchendon, Massachusetts.

Knowlton was the first of many nineteenth-century physicians to publish sexual advice manuals that included descriptions of contraceptive methods. His *Fruits* sold well throughout the century in both authorized and pirated editions. When the English freethinkers Charles Bradlaugh and Annie Besant were prosecuted for reprinting *Fruits* in 1877, their highly publicized trial did more than any other event in the nineteenth century to spread the news that sex and procreation could be separated. Knowlton's career illustrates the fact that the beginning of the dramatic decline in the birth rate of native-born whites in the United States preceded urbanization, the decline in infant mortality, and other social phenomena that some social scientists have assumed to be the determinants of demographic transitions. While Knowlton's anticlericalism was out of fashion by the mid-nineteenth century, his practical advice to married couples found an eager audience, and his vision of a science of human behavior proved prophetic.

• Knowlton's autobiography, which ends in 1829, and an obituary by his son-in-law, were published in the *Boston Medical and Surgical Journal* 45 (10 Sept. 1851): 111–20 and (24 Sept. 1851): 149–57. Knowlton's career is discussed in the context of social and medical history by James Reed, *From Private Vice to Public Virtue: The Birth Control Movement and American Society since 1830* (1978), pp. 3–33. For other reviews of Knowlton's career and influence, see Norman Himes, "Charles Knowlton's Revolutionary Influence on the English Birth Rate," *New England Journal of Medicine* 199 (6 Sept. 1928): 461–65, and Robert E. Riegel, "The American Father of Birth Control," *New England Quarterly* 6 (Sept. 1933): 470–90.

JAMES REED

KNOX, Dudley Wright (21 June 1877–11 June 1960), naval officer and historian, was born in Fort Walla Walla, Washington Territory, the son of Thomas Taylor Knox, a U.S. Army colonel, and Cornelia Manigault Grayson. After graduating from the U.S. Naval Academy in 1896, Knox spent the next two years at sea assigned to the battleship *Massachusetts* and received his ensign commission on 6 May 1898. During the Spanish-American War, he served on ships operating in Cuban and Philippine waters and later commanded two small gunboats, the USS *Albay* and the USS *Iris*, during the Philippine insurrection. After participating in the Boxer Rebellion campaign, he was an inspector of ordnance in Brooklyn, New York, and the commander of the First Torpedo Flotilla, which comprised the first destroyers in the navy. Subsequently, he was ordnance officer of the USS *Nebraska* during the Atlantic Fleet's cruise around the world from 1907 to 1909. In 1908 Knox married Lily Hazard McCalla; they had one child.

After serving as aide to the commandant of the Mare Island Navy Yard, California, in 1908–1909 and as fleet ordnance officer of the Atlantic Fleet and then the Pacific Fleet from 1909 to 1911, Knox studied and served at the Naval War College in Newport, Rhode Island, from 1912 to 1913. While at the War College, he developed a close association with then captain William S. Sims, and from 1913 to 1914 Knox served as his staff aide when Sims commanded the Atlantic Torpedo Flotilla. After a two-year stint in the Office of Naval Intelligence, Washington, D.C., Knox was commandant of the U.S. Naval Station, Guantánamo Bay, Cuba, in 1916–1917. Soon after America's entry into World War I, Admiral Sims, commander, U.S. Naval Forces operating in European waters, ordered Knox to London. Knox first worked in Sims's Planning Section, which dealt with the strategic employment of the Allied naval forces, and later in his Historical Section, where he was charged with collecting documents relating to the navy's participation in the war, with publication as the intended goal.

Knox's postwar assignments were at the Naval War College and as commander of the cruisers *Brooklyn* and *Charleston*, and he was passed over for promotion twice for health reasons. He requested shore duty that "accords with my special training—something which will spur me to my best endeavors (in spite of impaired morale!) and give the government the best there is left in an old has-been" (Knox papers, ZB Files, Naval

Historical Center). The navy's stringent rules in 1921 dictating a requisite amount of sea duty for promotion purposes forced Knox, because of ill health, to resign from active duty and accept an assignment on the retired list. His second career began in 1921 as officer in charge of the Historical Section and the Office of Naval History and Records, one of his choices, and proved the most rewarding for himself and the navy.

Knox's naval career spanned fifty-four years. He spent the first twenty-nine years moving frequently between ship or shore duty. His second career lasted twenty-five years and was the more gratifying for Knox, because he was able to devote himself to two cherished pursuits: writing articles on historical and contemporary naval themes and collecting and organizing the navy's operational records. This constituted the most important work of Knox's career.

Knox was a prolific writer for forty years. As a frequent contributor to the *U.S. Naval Institute Proceedings* and several newspapers, he addressed such topics as naval doctrine, disarmament and preparedness, neutrality, and Japan's militarism. His award-winning essay, "The Role of Doctrine in Naval Warfare" (*U.S. Naval Institute Proceedings*, Mar.–Apr. 1915), earned him a reputation in the navy as a profound thinker on professional subjects. The Naval War College reprinted this essay twenty years later for use in its classes. Knox's historical interests were far ranging, as evidenced by articles on the American Revolution, the naval war with France in 1798, the American Civil War, and Theodore Roosevelt's Great White Fleet.

Knox made his most enduring contribution to naval history as head of the Office of Naval Records and Library. In a January 1926 *Proceedings* article entitled "Our Vanishing History and Traditions," he noted that the paucity of naval histories was largely because of the "inaccessibility of authentic sources." Knox attempted to rectify this problem by transforming the office from a custodian of unorganized documents into a nationally known repository of manuscript and pictorial collections that were systematically acquired, arranged, and preserved and by publishing significant naval documents.

While safeguarding naval documents was one of Knox's goals, he also endeavored to make them more accessible through publication. Despite congressional budget cuts in the 1920s that reduced his personnel by a third and stopped printing funds, Knox's staff continued to assemble documents for eventual publication. The election of Franklin D. Roosevelt in 1932 was fortuitous for the office, because it meant presidential support for its mission. Knox noted in a 1948 memoir, "Association with Franklin D. Roosevelt" (Knox papers, Library of Congress), that Roosevelt summoned him to the White House early in his first administration to express his interest in publishing naval documents. They discussed printing documentary editions on the Quasi-War with France, the Barbary War, the War of 1812, and the Mexican War. Although the editions originally were to be paid for through their sales, Roosevelt obtained the requisite

congressional funding, and from 1935 to 1938 the office published seven volumes of *Naval Documents Related to the Quasi-War between the United States and France*. Six volumes of *Naval Documents Related to the United States Wars with the Barbary Powers* (1939–1945) and a supplementary register of officers and ships (1945) came out during World War II. The war, however, ended any further appropriations for documentary publications.

The Navy Department during World War I did not order the creation of a historical section to collect wartime documents until the war was almost over. Knox had headed that effort then, and he recognized the need to have a collection process in place early in World War II so that information would be more readily attainable for current use as well as for writing operational histories after the war. He succeeded in assembling a group of academics to collect and archive the operational history of the navy in the war, and naval historians have used this documentation extensively.

Knox oversaw the navy's historical offices until his final retirement in 1946, attaining the rank of commodore in 1945. After World War II he established the Naval Historical Foundation's collection of private documents relating to the history of the U.S. Navy, Marine Corps, Coast Guard, and Merchant Marine; it is an invaluable resource. He died at Bethesda (Md.) Naval Hospital.

• The predominant focus of Knox's papers in the Naval Historical Foundation Collection at the Library of Congress is correspondence from 1921 to 1949 and copies of his articles and speeches. The National Archives holds Knox's journal as commander of the gunboat *Albay*. The Early Naval Records Collection (ZB Files) at the Naval Historical Center contains biographical summaries and correspondence relating to his naval career before 1922. His *History of the United States Navy* (1936; repr. 1948), is notable for its integration of economic, political, social, and military history. In *The Eclipse of American Sea Power* (1922), Knox reviewed the consequences of the 1922 treaties of naval limitation. In a collaborative venture with Franklin D. Roosevelt, Knox wrote the narrative text for *Naval Sketches of the War in California* (1939), a pictorial account of the naval seizure of Calif. during the Mexican War. Obituaries are in the *U.S. Naval Institute Proceedings* 86 (Nov. 1960): 103–5, and the *New York Times*, 12 June 1960.

CHRISTINE F. HUGHES

KNOX, Frank (1 Jan. 1874–28 Apr. 1944), newspaper publisher and secretary of the navy, was born in Boston, Massachusetts, the son of William E. Knox, an oyster dealer, and Sarah Collins. Although christened William Franklin, Knox was usually called Frank and had dropped his first name entirely by 1900. Knox attended high school in Grand Rapids, Michigan, but did not graduate, completing his preparatory work at Alma College in Alma, Michigan, which he entered in 1893. After leaving Alma in 1898 Knox, an ardent supporter of the war with Spain, joined the First Volunteer United States Calvary, popularly known as the Rough Riders. Its leader, Lieutenant Colonel Theodore Roosevelt, became Knox's model in politics and, to some extent, in life. After brief service Knox contracted malaria in Cuba and was mustered out, returning to Michigan in August 1898. Later that year he married Annie Reid; they had no children.

Beginning as a reporter in Grand Rapids, Knox became publisher of a paper in Sault Ste. Marie, Michigan, in 1902 with his partner John A. Muehling. Knox and Muehling sold the paper in 1912 and that same year founded the *Manchester Leader* in New Hampshire. They soon took control of its rival and renamed and reorganized the papers, with the *Manchester Union* offering statewide coverage while the *Leader* continued to serve Manchester. Knox was publisher and co-owner of the newspapers, which Muehling ran in his absence. An active supporter of entry into World War I, Knox severely criticized President Woodrow Wilson for maintaining American neutrality. He also served as president of the Military Training Camps Association in New Hampshire, which sought to prepare young men to become officers in the U.S. Army. Despite his age and his opposition to many of Wilson's policies, Knox saw action in World War I, rising to become a major of artillery after enlisting as a private.

In 1927 Knox accepted William Randolph Hearst's offer to become publisher of his newspapers in Boston. The next year he was named general manager of Hearst's newspaper empire. Knox resigned from the Hearst organization in 1930 and the following year became publisher and part owner of the financially strapped Chicago *Daily News*, one of the nation's largest papers with a circulation of some 400,000, which he returned to profitability in the midst of the Great Depression. Knox was both a good businessman and a crusading editor, using his papers to fight saloons, Democrats, and waste and corruption in government.

During these years Knox was active in party politics as a Theodore Roosevelt Republican. Like many others, however, Knox's loyalty was more to the man than to his ideas. TR believed that government should aggressively address national problems while seeking to establish harmonious relations among government, business, and the general public. He also supported a wide variety of social reforms, particularly in his 1912 campaign. Knox, on the other hand, was uninterested in reforms except as they promoted efficiency and economy in government. His strongest link to Roosevelt, beyond the personal, was their common opposition to the stand-pat Republican old guard. In 1911 Knox managed TR's preconvention Midwest campaign. In 1912 he became a leader of the short-lived Progressive party, which nominated TR for president after he failed to win the Republican nomination. In 1920 Knox was the floor manager for Leonard Wood—who had been the Rough Riders' colonel and nominal commander—during Wood's presidential bid at the Republican National Convention. Four years later Knox ran for office himself but failed to gain the Republican nomination for governor of New Hampshire.

Like many formerly progressive Republicans Knox was against the New Deal, which he believed imposed too many regulations on business while also promoting social reforms that either verged on socialism or were best left to private charities. Knox hoped to win the Republican presidential nomination in 1936, but Governor Alfred M. Landon of Kansas could not be stopped. Knox had to settle for second place on the ticket and was buried under a landslide of Roosevelt votes.

As the Second World War neared, Knox argued for a strong defense, and when fighting broke out in Europe he favored full aid to the Allies short of outright intervention. In the summer of 1940 he was nominated to be secretary of the navy by President Franklin D. Roosevelt, joining the cabinet in August. His appointment coincided with that of another leading Republican, Henry L. Stimson—by coincidence another former artillery officer—who became secretary of war. Together their nominations strengthened Roosevelt's cabinet and gave it a bipartisan flavor in time for the presidential election of 1940.

As civilian head of the navy Knox presided over the greatest expansion in the service's history, seeing it rise from a force of scarcely more than 200,000 (including marines) in 1940 to one numbering some 3.5 million troops at the time of his death. No figurehead, Knox provided the navy with important leadership. After only a month in office he negotiated many of the details concerning the exchange of U.S. destroyers for British bases in the Western Hemisphere. He called for U.S. escorts of lend-lease convoys in the summer of 1941, leading isolationists to demand his impeachment. He was never more decisive than in the dark days that followed 7 December 1941. As its secretary Knox had boasted that the U.S. Navy was "second to none"; he was therefore one of many who endured great embarrassment after the Japanese attack on Pearl Harbor. The day after the attack Knox left Washington for Hawaii. On returning to Washington, D.C., he told reporters that both the army and navy had been caught napping. He then relieved Admiral Husband E. Kimmel as commander of the Pacific fleet, replacing him with a man who was to become one of the navy's greatest leaders, Admiral Chester W. Nimitz. He also made Admiral Ernest J. King, a brilliant if ruthless officer, commander in chief of the U.S. fleet and chief of naval operations. Among Knox's best civilian appointees were Adlai E. Stevenson as special assistant to Knox and Under-Secretary James V. Forrestal, who succeeded Knox. Both were able managers and noted for their integrity and character.

In addition to being an effective administrator the outspoken Knox championed a number of controversial wartime proposals. The most important of these was a national service bill that would have provided the federal government with something along the lines of a civilian labor draft. In 1944, when President Roosevelt asked for it, this bill would have eliminated manpower shortages that existed both in some war industries and in the military. Congress's failure to enact it, despite the efforts of Knox, Stimson, and others, did considerable harm to the war effort. A bluff, vigorous, profane man, Knox died in Washington, D.C., after a series of heart attacks that had begun less than a week earlier when he attended the funeral of his long-time partner John Muehling.

As a newspaper owner and publisher Knox differed from other businessmen of his era only in being more successful than most. As a candidate for office he failed to give people any compelling reason to support him because his ideas were conventional, and he never developed the personal following that would have compensated for his lack of campaign skills. Knox made his mark all the same and deserves to be remembered for helping to revitalize the navy after its defeat at Pearl Harbor and for his role as a highly partisan individual who put country above politics at a time when many did not. President Roosevelt addressed this point in his tribute to Knox, saying, "I like to think of his bigness and his loyalty. Truly he put his country first." There could be no better epitaph.

• Knox's papers are in the Library of Congress and the Correspondence File of the Secretary of the Navy, National Archives. A biography has yet to be published; however, his career is discussed at length by George H. Lobdell, Jr., in "Frank Knox 11 July 1940–28 April 1944," in *American Secretaries of the Navy*, vol. 2, ed. Paolo Coletta (1982). See also Lobdell, "A Biography of Frank Knox" (Ph.D. diss., Univ. of Illinois, 1954), and Robert Albion, *Makers of Naval Policy, 1798–1947* (1980). An obituary is in the *New York Times*, 29 Apr. 1944.

WILLIAM L. O'NEILL

KNOX, Henry (25 July 1750–25 Oct. 1806), revolutionary war general and Secretary of the Department of War, was born in Boston, Massachusetts, the son of William Knox, a shipmaster, and Mary Campbell. Henry Knox attended Boston Public Latin Grammar School until the death of his father in 1762, whereupon he was apprenticed to a bookseller. In 1771 he became the proprietor of the London Book-Store in Boston, and kept a large inventory of military works for his British officer clientele; reading many of the books himself he mastered knowledge of military engineering and artillery. At age eighteen Knox joined the local artillery company, and in 1772 was second in command of the Boston Grenadier Corps. In July 1773 he lost two fingers on his left hand in a hunting accident.

Knox married Lucy Flucker, daughter of the royal provincial secretary, Thomas Flucker, in 1774. A recurrent tragedy for the Knoxes was the loss of nine of their twelve children in infancy or before adulthood.

After escaping, along with his wife, through the British lines at Boston in summer 1775, Knox met George Washington, the commander in chief of the new Continental army; this was the beginning of a close friendship of twenty years. Knox became attached to the army as a civilian consultant, not being commissioned until 17 November 1775 as colonel and head of the artillery regiment of twelve companies. He

thereafter became chief of artillery for the Continental army.

The hefty, 25-year-old Knox performed a remarkable feat in bringing the captured arsenal at Fort Ticonderoga to Washington's camp at Cambridge. The 300-mile trek involved crossing frozen rivers and the steep hills of the Berkshires in western Massachusetts. By the end of January 1776, Knox had hauled 43 cannon, two howitzers, 14 mortars and coehorns, 7,000 rounds of cannon shot, 2,000 muskets, and 31 tons of musket shot to Washington's headquarters. The cannon and munitions, along with the military cargo of the captured British brigantine, the *Nancy*, enabled Washington to install heavy fire power on Dorchester Heights, overlooking the harbor, thus causing the British to evacuate Boston. Knox's artillery continued to be important to Washington's army, from the New York–New Jersey campaign of 1776–1777, to the battle of Yorktown in 1781. Knox from time to time advised manufacturers of artillery. Not only did Washington prize Knox's expertise and ability, but also he found relaxation in the company of the jovial Knox.

Congress appointed Knox brigadier general in December 1776 and in March 1782 made him the youngest major general in the Continental army. He established his headquarters at West Point, and on 23 December 1783 he was designated by Washington to succeed him as commander in chief. Knox presided over the continuing demobilization of the army, and by the end of 1783 he had only some eighty men under his command at West Point.

Knox was much concerned with the military preparedness of the new republic. In the 1780s he proposed establishment of both an army and a naval academy. His "Plan for the General Arrangement of the Militia of the United States" recommended universal military service, suggesting a militia to be on call by the national government, with the ranks to be filled by local drafts, if necessary. The militia would be sectioned into three "corps": advanced, ages 18–20; main, 20–45; and reserve, 46–60—with days of training ranging from two per year for the reserve to forty-six for the advanced corps. Congress rejected Knox's plan for a select militia under federal control, and the Uniform Militia Act of 1797 left to the states the responsibility for militia enrollment (ages 18–45) and training.

On 8 March 1785 the Confederation Congress named Knox Secretary at War, succeeding Benjamin Lincoln. Knox's duties, as an agent of Congress rather than head of an independent executive department, were mainly clerical, reporting to Congress. He had charge of Indian affairs, even when Congress in 1787 named a northern and a southern Indian superintendent. Indian treaties were made with the Iroquois and the Ohio Valley Indians, opening up lands, but the treaties with the latter tribe were regarded as fraudulent by a majority of the Indians. Except for military excursions by Kentuckians, there were no Indian wars during the Confederation period. The 700-man American regiment, at a half dozen posts, served more to check on squatters crossing the Ohio than to guard against the Indians.

Knox was a strong advocate of strengthening the national government. At his urging Congress in 1787 voted for 2,040 men for a new army, ostensibly to offer protection from the Indians but actually to be used in quelling Shays's Rebellion. Only several hundred troops were raised, and then too late to be of service in western Massachusetts. Knox persuaded state militia at the federal arsenal at Springfield, Massachusetts, to resist an attack—an important factor in crushing the insurgency.

As the new government under the Constitution was formed, Knox was appointed Secretary of War on 12 September 1789, the only high Confederation official continued in the same post. In the formative years of the cabinet Knox took the side of Alexander Hamilton against Thomas Jefferson and Edmund Randolph, over such issues as the national bank, though the relationship between Knox and Hamilton became quite strained. The ever-meddling Hamilton was able to have the procurement of army supplies transferred from the war office to the Treasury. During the Whiskey Rebellion Washington approved a leave for Knox to look into his business affairs in Maine; actually Knox was miffed at Hamilton's role in designing the government's response to the rebellion. Knox, who also had naval responsibilities, was instrumental in Congress's decision to begin construction of six frigates, intended for use against the Barbary pirates in the Mediterranean.

Much of the War Department's work focused on Indian affairs. Knox brought about the first treaty concluded under the new government, the Treaty of New York in 1790, with the Creeks. The treaty was ratified by both sides while the Indian delegation, headed by Alexander McGillivray, was in the Senate chamber.

The Indian wars in the Ohio country brought fewer successes. General Josiah Harmar met a humiliating defeat in October 1780, and the next year, on 4 November, General Arthur St. Clair lost almost half his army. Washington held St. Clair responsible for the 1791 disaster, though St. Clair was exonerated by Congress despite his negligence and bad judgment; Knox himself became somewhat a scapegoat for the delay in army supply. Knox oversaw the unsuccessful Indian negotiations of 1792–1794 and the support for General Anthony Wayne's legionary force that finally prevailed over the Indians at Fallen Timbers on 20 August 1794. Washington seems to have resented Knox's overstaying his leave in 1794, and on Knox's return there was an evident coolness between the two men. This appears to have been one reason for Knox's resignation, effective 31 December 1794.

The Knoxes resided at their splendid mansion, "Montpelier," in Thomaston, Maine. During the quasi-war with France, 1798–1800, Knox was embittered that President John Adams (1735–1826), in nominating general officers for a provisional army, placed in order of rank: Washington, as lieutenant general, and Hamilton, Charles Cotesworth Pinckney, and Knox as

major generals. Knox refused to serve under Hamilton.

Much of Knox's time at Montpelier was spent managing his varied enterprises—lime quarrying, brick making, fishing, farming, sawmilling, and shipbuilding. Knox had a huge domain of land, part of the Samuel Waldo tract that had come into the possession of Lucy Knox and some two million acres that he and William Duer had arranged to purchase from the state of Massachusetts for ten cents an acre; William Bingham bought out Duer's interest. Squatters overran much of Knox's Maine lands. He became nearly bankrupt.

The Knoxes entertained lavishly during the government years and at Montpelier. They were an imposing couple: he, at 280 pounds, she at 250. Mrs. Knox saw herself as a leader in fashion and society, occasionally meriting ridicule for her efforts. Thomas Jefferson was one who took neither of the Knoxes seriously. Unquestionably, however, Knox, from the sum of his military and governmental service, rendered to Washington the most valuable assistance of any of the general officers of the revolutionary war. Knox died at Montpelier after suffering from an infection caused by swallowing a fragment of a chicken bone.

• The Henry Knox Papers at the Massachusetts Historical Society are an extraordinary collection of private and public correspondence and other documents (in microfilm edition, 55 reels). Many Knox letters and documents are found in the War Department material and the Papers of the Continental Congress in the National Archives and the Washington papers at the Library of Congress. Two of three biographies have merit but give short shrift to Knox's governmental career: Noah Brooks, *Henry Knox: A Soldier of the Revolution* (1900; repr. 1974), and North Callahan, *General Washington's General* (1958). See also Harry M. Ward, *The Department of War, 1781–1795* (1962). Richard C. Knopf, *Anthony Wayne: A Name in Arms—The Wayne-Knox-Pickering-McHenry Correspondence* (1960), allows close inspection of Knox's war administration for 1792–1794. Frederick S. Allis, *William Bingham's Maine Lands, 1790–1820* (2 vols., 1954), concerns Knox's landholdings.

HARRY M. WARD

KNOX, John (14 Dec. 1900–25 June 1990), New Testament scholar and theologian, preacher, and editor, was born in Frankfort, Kentucky, the son of Absalom Knox and Emma Mann. Knox's father had served as secretary of local chapters of the Young Men's Christian Association and by 1906 was ordained in the Southern Methodist church. Methodist itinerancy required the family to move often between parishes in Pennsylvania, Virginia, West Virginia, and Maryland. His father's "irresistibly contagious" Christian commitment convicted Knox, and when he was thirteen years old he determined to serve the church. His father had little schooling, but from him Knox absorbed a love of reading and learning and his first lessons in the art of writing.

In 1916, without completing high school, Knox qualified to enter Randolph-Macon College in Ashland, Virginia, where he pursued a major in classical languages. There he first encountered the "historical method in Bible study," to which he found himself "absolutely unyielding in my opposition." Thirty-five years later Knox would dedicate a book, *Criticism and Faith* (1952), to his college Bible teacher Frank Leighton Day, but at first he could not accept Day's critical study of the Bible on theological grounds. The future scholar was uniquely and ironically, excused from the required Bible course.

Completing his bachelor of arts with honors in 1919, Knox immediately began serving six small Methodist congregations in eastern West Virginia, a "happy and rewarding" rural ministry. By 1920, posted to a parish in suburban Baltimore, Knox "began to feel a very keen desire for further training" that led him in 1921 to the theological school of Emory University in Atlanta, Georgia. There he began to focus on New Testament studies and found lifelong friendship with the New Testament scholar Ernest Cadman Colwell. Their teacher, Andrew Sledd, persuaded Knox at last to accept historical-critical study of the Bible. He came to understand biblical "inerrancy" as "not only unnecessary, but really alien."

During his struggle to accept the critical study of the Bible, walking late one spring night, Knox found himself overwhelmed by "the awful beauty and sheer immediacy of God." In the "indescribable ecstasy" and "incredible peace" of that mystical moment, all of his doubts about God vanished, and the universe became to him "one vast delicious music." Never again would Knox's faith be threatened by his studies.

The challenges of life and death were, however, another matter. Knox's father died in January 1924 after an illness of many months that had interrupted his son's formal theological studies. Preaching in his father's stead through his decline and death, Knox now confronted questions of human immortality and devastating loss. His faith remained firmly established, but its corollary, hope, was almost extinguished. The ensuing five years would be for Knox a time of ferment and crisis that would form definitively his faith and life's work.

Knox returned to Emory in the fall of 1924 to complete his seminary education and to begin teaching in the religion department of Emory College. In conversation with Colwell, Knox determined to make "the ethical ideas and example of Jesus" the norm for his life. He would give himself entirely to the service of God, "which was the service of others," and "those in greatest need" would have "first claim" on his time and his money. For several months Knox pursued this "radically new way of life," and it gave him "great spiritual joy." Relatives and friends were troubled by his new behavior, but to Knox it "seemed theoretically sound," and his "experience was confirming its validity." Yet ultimately he abandoned "the entirely selfless life"—not because he desired or decided to leave it, but because he "could not stand the strain of so unremitting a moral demand, or . . . so exalted a moral elation." Failure led to disillusion: How could the young

theologian preach what he could not practice? Only after an attempt to join the life of Jane Addams's Hull-House in Chicago during the summer of 1927 did Knox conclude that he had mistakenly tried "by sheer force of will, to live a redemptive life." He later came to understand that "we act creatively, and therefore redemptively, only by grace." Knox reflected on these experiences in *The Ethic of Jesus in the Teaching of the Church* (1961) and in the book that he regarded as his "most important," *Life in Christ Jesus* (1961).

As Knox pondered how better to prepare for his teaching after this spiritual experiment, he was drawn to the study of Christian social ethics, although his academic preparation and interests had been focused on the New Testament. In 1926 he was invited to join a summer seminar of travel and study in Europe conducted by the missionary and social critic Sherwood Eddy. This tour introduced Knox to several influential American adherents of the social gospel and took him to the principal cities of Europe, where he interviewed high officials and heads of state. On his return Knox soon found that his usefulness to Emory College was ending. Some parents and alumni had already complained of Knox's "biblical views," but it was his letter to an Atlanta newspaper about working conditions and wages in local cotton mills that caused the college to terminate his contract. Necessity dictated a decision, and in the summer of 1927 Knox entered the University of Chicago on a fellowship to study the New Testament.

Having not yet clearly discerned or accepted the final direction that his call to follow Jesus would take, Knox left Chicago at the end of 1927 for an appointment as a Methodist minister in Bethesda, Maryland. In the fall of 1929 he moved to Nashville, Tennessee, where he became minister of the chapel and professor of religion at Fisk University. In 1930 he married Lois Adelaide Bolles; they had two sons. Fisk was then one of the few truly interracial college communities in the South, and Knox and his wife entered fully into its life. Both were more than willing to accept rejection from outsiders in exchange for the friendship and community of African-American students, colleagues, and neighbors.

After five years at Fisk, Knox took a leave of absence to complete his doctoral studies at the University of Chicago; he earned his Ph.D. in 1935. William Faulkner, an African-American friend from Atlanta, served the Fisk chapel in Knox's absence. Early in 1935 the president of Fisk, Thomas Elsa Jones, announced that Faulkner would serve the chapel permanently while Knox continued as professor of religion. Knox was dismayed. He and Jones, both white, had differed strongly about the degree of commitment required of whites who would serve Fisk. Jones declared that whites should come to Fisk as they would join "any other college"; Knox countered that any white person who came to Fisk should come not in spite of its ethnic identity but because of it, to "identify" completely with that community. Knox was not disposed only to teach religion in any college; his offer to share in the work of the chapel was rebuffed. Returning from their sabbatical, the Knoxes sadly realized that their most useful contribution to the community they loved had now ended. They left Fisk reluctantly in 1936, never again to live in such a predominantly black world. Forty years later Knox still regarded his service in the Fisk chapel as "the most significant period in my career."

Doctoral study in Chicago had once again immersed Knox in the historical-critical method of Bible study. Henry Nelson Wieman introduced him to the work of Alfred North Whitehead, and Edgar Johnson Goodspeed's investigations of the development and collection of the letters of Paul captured Knox's imagination and inspired his works *Philemon among the Letters of Paul* (1936), *Marcion and the New Testament* (1942), and *Chapters in a Life of Paul* (1950). Shirley Jackson Case's exposition of the role of historical process in human life helped shape Knox's own thinking on Christ and the Christian life. Knox later recalled with some irony that Case had "helped make me much more of a Catholic than I was in those days."

Another influential mentor, Charles Clayton Morrison, brought Knox in 1936 back to Chicago to edit *Christendom*, a new quarterly journal of scholarly ecclesiology and ecumenism, and to assist in editing Morrison's influential pan-Protestant *Christian Century*. Knox also edited theological books for Willett, Clark, and Company. Editing became, with his own writing, a great part of Knox's vocation. For Morrison he also composed the first of his works in Christology, *The Man Christ Jesus* (1941), following it with *Christ the Lord* (1945). The life and letters of St. Paul continued to occupy his attention in scholarly articles, along with the maelstrom of editorial commentary on contemporary American religion and society in the *Christian Century*.

Early in 1938 Knox was asked to become associate professor of New Testament at Hartford Theological Seminary, and Morrison offered *Christendom* to the committee planning the nascent World Council of Churches. But no sooner was Knox installed in Connecticut than he was called back to Chicago by his old friend Colwell, now dean of the University of Chicago Divinity School. Colwell invited Knox to become associate professor of preaching and editor of the *Journal of Religion* and he was soon appointed professor of preaching and New Testament. The University of Chicago Press offered him the post of editor in chief, but Knox declined. In 1943 Knox left Chicago, accepting a position as Baldwin Professor of Sacred Literature at Union Theological Seminary in New York City.

During the next twenty-three years Knox fully matured as a scholar, an author, and an editor. Fifteen of his twenty-two books were written during his years at Union, along with fifty articles, essays, pamphlets, and editorial introductions. Knox served as associate editor of *The Interpreter's Bible* (12 vols., 1951–1957), producing two of its commentaries (on St. Paul's letters to the Romans [1954] and Philemon [1955]), and

The Interpreter's Dictionary of the Bible (4 vols., 1962). Beginning in 1960 Knox was a member of the Standard Bible Committee, which maintained and revised the Revised Standard Version, and in 1964 he was asked to join the translation committee that would produce the New American Bible under Roman Catholic auspices.

Knox wrote as a teacher and preacher; to him, students continued to command the center of gravity. In 1945 he became the director of studies at Union (effectively the academic dean for Union seminarians) until a heart ailment forced him to curtail his activities after 1957. In 1957 Anglican students at Union asked Knox, still a Methodist, to sponsor their organization. They did not know that Knox had for some time been in discussions with members of the clergy of the Episcopal church, and their request accelerated his transition to the Anglican Communion. After his wife and younger son had been confirmed with him, and it became clear that he would not have to renounce his forty-three years of ministry as a Methodist, Knox sought and was granted ordination in the Episcopal church in 1962.

After Knox's retirement from Union in 1966, nineteen leading scholars—colleagues and former students—offered tribute to him and dialogue with his work in *Christian History and Interpretation* (1967). He immediately joined the faculty of the Episcopal Theological Seminary of the Southwest, remaining in Austin, Texas, until 1972. Even after deteriorating health brought an end to his regime of writing and teaching, Knox still grappled with intellectual and moral challenges presented by former students—some of them women struggling to realize their callings in church and academe. In his last book, *A Glory in It All* (1985), Knox continued to confront social issues of the day with an ethic centered in Christ and the church, just as he had done in Atlanta sixty years earlier. He died in Medford, New Jersey.

• Knox's compelling and sometimes critical memoir is *Never Far from Home* (1975); it remains the primary source for understanding his life and work. Several assessments of his theological and exegetical work appear in W. R. Farmer et al., eds., *Christian History and Interpretation* (1967), including a bibliography edited by John Coolidge Hurd. Discussions of his work on the Acts of the Apostles appears in Mikeal C. Parsons and Joseph B. Tyson, eds., *Cadbury, Knox, and Talbert: American Contributions to the Study of Acts* (1992). In this volume Parsons completes the bibliography published by Hurd twenty-five years earlier.

DON HAYMES

KNOX, John Jay (19 Mar. 1828–9 Feb. 1892), banker and regulator of national banks, was born in Augusta, New York, the son of John J. Knox and Sarah Ann Curtiss. His father established the Bank of Vernon in 1839, and Knox became a teller there after graduating from Hamilton College in 1849. He was a teller in the Burnet Bank in Syracuse from 1852 to 1856, when he joined the Susquehanna Valley Bank in Binghamton as cashier. Knox had been involved in organizing both of these upstate New York banks. Together with a younger brother he conducted a private banking business in St. Paul, Minnesota, from 1857 to 1862.

An article Knox wrote supporting the establishment of a national banking system brought him to the attention of Secretary of the Treasury Salmon P. Chase, who hired him as a clerk under the treasurer of the United States in 1862. Chase soon moved him to his own office, where he became disbursing clerk. Knox served in that position until early April 1865, when he accepted the cashiership of the newly opened Exchange National Bank of Norfolk, Virginia. Unable to find a way to reduce the bank's expenses, however, he resigned after a few months. Secretary of the Treasury Hugh McCulloch immediately offered him back his clerkship. From 1866 to February 1873 Knox was in charge of the Treasury's mint and coinage correspondence. McCulloch promoted him to deputy comptroller of the currency on 12 March 1867.

Knox drafted a proposed bill to revise the laws governing the U.S. Mint in April 1870 at the request of Secretary of the Treasury George Boutwell. The Coinage Act of 12 February 1873 substantially embodied his recommendations, including the omission of the silver dollar from the list of coins to be minted. This last stipulation Knox mentioned in three places in his transmission of the bill. Nevertheless, advocates of the free coinage of silver later denounced demonetization as the "Crime of 1873," claiming that financial interests had conspired to establish a gold standard clandestinely. Knox carefully documented the falsehood of this charge in 1876 and again in 1891 in presentations before the Committee on Coinage of the House of Representatives.

In April 1872 President Ulysses S. Grant appointed Knox comptroller of the currency, charged with overseeing and regulating the national banking system established in 1863–1864. Knox was reappointed by Presidents Rutherford B. Hayes and Chester A. Arthur, serving twelve years in the post. During his tenure his staff grew to more than ninety (including forty-two women), and he supervised more than 2,500 national banks. Though formally under the control of the secretary of the treasury, by the end of his administration Knox had become relatively independent, enjoying substantial discretion in carrying out the National Bank Act and in recommending changes in the law. Each year Knox notified hundreds of banks of violations of the Bank Act and brought them under "the discipline of the law." Knox confessed to the 1883 bankers' convention that "it has sometimes seemed as though the title of 'the scolding Comptroller' would be appropriate." Thanks to his "wisdom and firmness," many troubled banks were restored to a sound condition, *Bankers Magazine* stated in 1892.

Supervisory on-site examinations and mandatory reports of condition contributed to the low failure rate of national banks. Of the seventy-three closed during Knox's tenure, forty had capital of less than $100,000. Disgruntled shareholders of Pacific National Bank of Boston, closed on 22 May 1882, accused Knox of malfeasance, but on 22 April 1884 the House Banking Committee found nothing to indicate that Knox "was activated by an improper motive or was guilty of any intentional violation of the law."

Knox resigned on 30 April 1884, having completed only two years of his third five-year term. "The intelligence which he has brought to the complicated duties of his office has never been surpassed in any similar station," stated the *Nation*.

Knox arrived in New York City in May 1884 to assume the more lucrative position of president of the National Bank of the Republic. He regularly sent out his own bank's statement of condition to all banks but never directly solicited business already handled by another bank. In seeking correspondent bank business, Knox would never promise what he could not deliver. His first concern as a banker was safety, though Knox "would extend every legitimate assistance to anyone in distress who deserved it and [was] worth saving," his cashier Eugene H. Pullen noted. His bank's share of total assets of all forty-eight national banks in New York City was a modest 1.82 percent in the fall of 1883, soared to 3.41 percent in 1889, but retreated to 2.85 percent in October 1891.

Both as government official and as prominent banker, Knox participated in the fierce national debate on the "money question." He spoke out frequently for "real money," also known as "honest money." Greenback proposals to substitute Treasury notes for national bank notes would mean, he warned, that "the volume of the currency will be controlled, not by the demands of business and the wants of the country, but by the views and action of political parties and of Congress" (*Annual Report of the Comptroller of the Currency* [1878], p. xxii). Knox applauded Secretary of the Treasury Charles Foster's "purpose to maintain gold payments," to redeem Treasury notes "at all times in gold coin," in his last appearance before an American Bankers Association convention in November 1891.

Though a voluminous writer on financial subjects, Knox published only one book in his lifetime, *United States Notes* (1884). Regarding the book, Samuel J. Tilden wrote, "Every good citizen, friendly to an honest circulating medium . . . is indebted to you." Knox's series of essays, "A History of Banking in the United States," in *Rhodes' Journal of Banking* (1892), 218 closely printed pages, provided the nucleus of the posthumous 1900 volume bearing the same title.

In 1871 Knox had married Caroline E. Todd, daughter of William B. Todd, a large property holder in the District of Columbia. Seven children were born of this marriage. He died in New York City, having presided over the growth of the National Bank of the Republic "to the full stature of the great banks of the city" (*Bankers Magazine*, Mar. 1892, p. 694). London's *Bankers Magazine* remembered Knox as "one of the soundest authorities on currency and banking in America."

• Archives of the Knox family consisting of "The Circular Letter" (8 vols.), a letter forwarded to family members in turn, are in the collection of the New-York Historical Society. Knox's first appearance in print was as the anonymous author of "A National Authenticated Currency" and "A National Currency and Banking System," *Hunts Merchant Magazine*, Feb. 1862, pp. 113–18, 119–28. He set forth his ideas on currency and banking in his *Annual Report of the Comptroller of the Currency* for the years 1872 through 1883. The library of the Office of the Comptroller of the Currency in Washington has a bound set in twenty-four volumes of *Reports and Addresses of Comptroller Knox*. He contributed a comprehensive essay entitled "Banking in the United States" to *Lalor's Cyclopedia of Political Science, Political Economy and Political History of the United States*, vol. 1 (1881), pp. 204–22. *A History of Banking in the United States* (1900) is a careful revision of Knox's manuscript updated by Bradford Rhodes, editor of *Bankers Magazine*, and associate editor Elmer Youngman, who enlisted a corps of writers for the chapters dealing with individual states not covered by Knox. A longtime official in the comptroller's office, Thomas P. Kane, provides valuable background to Knox's career in *The Romance and Tragedy of Banking* (1922). See also Edwin Leland Harper, "The Policy-Making Role of Federal Political Executives: The Case of the Comptroller of the Currency" (Ph.D. diss., Univ. of Virginia, 1968). An obituary is in *Rhodes' Journal of Banking* 19 (Mar. 1892): 237–44.

BENJAMIN J. KLEBANER

KNOX, Philander Chase (6 May 1853–12 Oct. 1921), attorney general, U.S. senator, and secretary of state, was born in Brownsville, Pennsylvania, the son of David S. Knox, a banker, and Rebecca Page. He attended Mount Union College in Ohio and graduated with an A.B. degree in 1872. While in Ohio he became friends with William McKinley, then the district attorney of Stark County. Following graduation he read law in Pittsburgh and was admitted to the bar of Allegheny County, Pennsylvania, in 1875. He was an assistant U.S. district attorney for western Pennsylvania from 1876 to 1877, when he formed a partnership with James H. Reed that lasted until Knox entered public service in 1901. In 1880 Knox married Lillie Smith; they had four children.

Knox built a reputation as a corporation lawyer and was instrumental in the formation of the Carnegie Steel Company in 1900. In 1899 President McKinley asked him to become attorney general. Knox declined because of his corporate obligations, but when McKinley invited him again two years later he accepted, becoming attorney general on 9 April 1901. After McKinley's death, Theodore Roosevelt (1858–1919) directed Knox to initiate a suit against the Northern Securities Company, a railroad holding company formed by James J. Hill, J. P. Morgan (1837–1913), and others to control railroad lines in the Northwest. Despite his business background, Knox believed that the company presented a danger to competition, and he personally took charge of the litigation. The case became a test of whether the Sherman Antitrust Act (1890) could be enforced and upheld as constitutional. He argued the case for the United States before the Supreme Court, which upheld the government in 1904. Knox was also a close adviser to Roosevelt on the acquisition of the Panama Canal Zone in 1903–1904, and

he drafted legislation that led to the establishment of the Department of Commerce and Labor in 1903.

Knox was "a dapper bit of a man, a tiny figure charged with life, quick-stepping, alert and nervous" (Coolidge, p. 471). Theodore Roosevelt called him "little Phil" (Scholes, 1961, p. 60). He played golf and maintained a stable of trotting horses. In June 1904 the governor of Pennsylvania appointed him to fill out the unexpired term of the late U.S. senator Matthew S. Quay, and the state legislature elected him to a full term in January 1905. Knox attained a leadership position in the Senate, including the chairmanship of the Rules Committee. He became less favorable to Roosevelt's domestic policies, such as the Hepburn Act, to regulate the railroads. Nevertheless, in 1906 the president offered him an appointment to the Supreme Court, which Knox declined. He also made an abortive campaign for the presidential nomination in 1908 as a conservative. One newspaper said Knox was "being used as a stool-pigeon by the men who have conspired to efface every policy for which President Roosevelt stands" ("Sizing up the Knox Boom," p. 1014).

Upon his election as president in 1908, William Howard Taft asked Knox to serve as his secretary of state. Knox soon gained a great deal of influence within the Taft administration, allowing his aides to carry out the broad lines of policy that he established. Knox reorganized the department to emphasize geographical divisions, and he stressed the merit system in the operation of the diplomatic service. Despite these changes, foreign envoys complained that the department remained inefficient and plagued with press leaks.

Knox was primarily identified with the policy of "dollar diplomacy." Taft and his secretary of state argued that the best way to promote stability in Latin America and Asia was to encourage U.S. corporations to invest in these regions. That approach would, they contended, reduce the need for direct intervention by the U.S. government. Knox believed that "the borrower is the servant of the lender" (Scholes, 1961, p. 62) and that a nation with American investments on its territory would be inclined to follow Washington's lead. The policy proved easier to state in theory than to execute in practice. Knox proposed to oversee the finances of Honduras and Nicaragua through U.S. management of their custom revenues and debts. The two Latin American countries gave in to U.S. pressure. The Senate, however, failed to approve the treaties that embodied these policies, and in 1912 the United States sent troops to Nicaragua to keep a friendly government in power.

In China the fate of "dollar diplomacy" was equally unfortunate. Knox endeavored to secure loans from U.S. bankers to enable China to build railroads in Manchuria. The initiative encountered resistance from Japan and Russia and did not succeed. However, Knox did obtain loans from U.S. bankers to support China's railroads and currency.

Knox settled some long-standing disputes with Canada and Great Britain. The agreement that he and Taft negotiated with the Canadians for expanded reciprocal trade received approval from the Congress, but Canadian voters defeated the government that favored the pact, and the Parliament rejected it. The secretary and the president also tried unsuccessfully to obtain Senate approval of arbitration treaties with Great Britain and France. In 1911 Taft offered Knox a Supreme Court appointment, but again Knox said no.

Following Taft's defeat in 1912, Knox practiced law in Pittsburgh. In 1916 he won election to the Senate and resumed a leadership role among Republicans there. A principal opponent of the Treaty of Versailles in 1919, his resolution to separate consideration of the League of Nations from the treaty became a major challenge to Woodrow Wilson. He drafted the "round-robin" against the league that thirty-seven Republicans signed in March 1919, and he also prepared reservations for inclusion in the pact when it was debated in the Senate later that year. Knox voted against the treaty in the end because he believed it imposed greater foreign policy obligations on the United States than were proper under the treaty-making power. He offered resolutions rescinding the declarations of war against Austria and Germany, which Wilson vetoed. Once Wilson left office in 1921, Knox again offered his resolution, and it was adopted and signed. A peace treaty with Germany was submitted to the Senate in September 1921. Knox died in Washington.

Prominent as attorney general for his support of Roosevelt's trust policies and as secretary of state for applying "dollar diplomacy," Knox proved to be a dedicated and effective senatorial foe of Wilson. Overall, Knox was a significant force in the conservative wing of the Republican party during the first two decades of the twentieth century.

• Knox's personal papers are at the Library of Congress; other aspects of his public life are covered in the Theodore Roosevelt and William Howard Taft papers, also at the Library of Congress. The records of the Department of Justice and the Department of State during Knox's tenure are in the National Archives. The public statements and records of Knox's cabinet offices can be found in his reports as attorney general and in U.S., *Papers Relating to the Foreign Relations of the United States, 1909–1913* (1910–1914). There is as yet no biography of Knox. Herbert F. Wright, "Philander Chase Knox, Secretary of State," in *The American Secretaries of State and Their Diplomacy*, vol. 9, ed. Samuel F. Bemis (1929), is an older account. Walter Scholes, "Philander C. Knox," in *An Uncertain Tradition: American Secretaries of State in the Twentieth Century*, ed. Norman Graebner (1961), is critical. For contemporary comments, see L. A. Coolidge, "Knox, Attorney General, Lawyer," *McClure's Magazine*, 19 (1902): 471–73, and [no author] "Sizing Up the Knox Boom," *Literary Digest* 34 (29 June 1907): 1013–14. For balanced assessments, see Anita Torres Eitler, "Philander C. Knox, First Attorney-General of Theodore Roosevelt, 1901–1904" (Ph.D diss., Catholic Univ., 1959); Paige Mulhollan, "Philander C. Knox and Dollar Diplomacy" (Ph.D diss., Univ. of Texas, 1966); and W. V. Scholes and Marie V. Scholes, *The Foreign Policies of the Taft Administration* (1970). A lengthy obituary appears in the *New York Times*, 13 Oct. 1921.

LEWIS L. GOULD

KNOX, Rose Markward (18 Nov. 1857–27 Sept. 1950), food manufacturer, was born in Mansfield, Ohio, the daughter of David Markward, a druggist, and Amanda Foreman, and christened Helen Rosetta. She attended public schools in Mansfield and in her early twenties moved with her parents to Gloversville, New York. There she took a job sewing gloves, a job that introduced her to a glove salesman, Charles Briggs Knox, whom she married in February 1883; they had three children. He continued in sales, switching to knit goods, while the family lived in New York City and Newark, New Jersey.

In 1890 the Knoxes decided jointly to invest their savings of $5,000 in a gelatin business located in Johnstown, New York. Local tanneries assured a supply of animal skin, sinew, and bones from which to extract the gelatin. The first challenge that they faced was to generate stronger demand for their product. Gelatin, a protein substance that was not widely used then, was considered primarily a food for invalids or a delicacy, because of the difficulty of extracting it at home. Knox both developed gelatin recipes in her own kitchen and participated with her husband on sales trips.

Recognizing the need for housewives to know how to use gelatin in new ways, in 1896 Knox published *Dainty Desserts*, a recipe booklet; the company was soon distributing a million copies a year. Her husband relied on more theatrical and masculine approaches to promotion, including using a dirigible—perhaps the first time one was used for advertising—and keeping a stable of race horses he called the Gelatin String. He also involved himself in other businesses: a newspaper in Gloversville, a hardware store in Johnstown, a power company in Versailles, Kentucky, and a line of medicated ointments. He died in 1908. Knox sold these ventures and focused on the gelatin business. She declaimed she intended to run the business herself only until her two sons came of age (a daughter had died in infancy), but her elder son, Charles, soon died; by 1913, when James joined the business, she had no intention of retiring.

Knox decided that she would run her business in "a woman's way." She dropped her husband's flamboyant approaches and emphasized advertising to women, added a second recipe booklet, *Food Economy*, in 1917, gave demonstrations to show how to use gelatin, put recipes on the gelatin boxes, and ran ads as a column titled "Mrs. Knox Says." She established an experimental kitchen and created fellowships at the Mellon Institute to develop new uses for gelatin; in aggregate she authorized more than $500,000 for such work. This helped develop new industrial—mostly photographic—and medical markets. She learned how to use her sales force to gather critical market information, becoming herself a shrewd buyer. She was strikingly successful: in 1911 she moved the company to a larger plant; by 1915 the value of Knox Gelatin had tripled, and she incorporated it with a capital of $300,000. In 1925 that capitalization rose to $1 million. In 1916 the company acquired a half interest in a former supplier, Kind and Landesmann, of Camden, New Jersey, which was renamed Kind and Knox; in 1930 Rose Knox became vice president. In 1936 all gelatin operations were put in a new Camden plant while Knox and Company in Johnstown handled packaging and distribution. Knox was then America's largest producer of unflavored gelatin, with 60 percent of sales from food products, 40 percent from nonfood applications.

Knox was an innovator in labor relations. She closed the rear door of the plant, asking all employees—"ladies and gentlemen working together"—to come in "through the front door." In 1913 she instituted a five-day work week—but asked workers to produce as much as they had working five and a half days—and gave workers a two-week annual vacation and sick leave. She had no time clocks in the plant. During the depression, rather than lay off workers, she expanded, developing a line of flavored gelatin manufactured in the new Camden plant. Although a demanding boss, she maintained a workplace that generated remarkable loyalty: in 1940, 85 percent of her employees had been with the firm for at least twenty-five years. In 1937, when she celebrated her eightieth birthday with the help of her staff, she promoted her son James to the vice presidency of the company. She herself continued to work regularly for another eight years, when arthritis forced her to conduct business from home. Finally, on her ninetieth birthday, in 1947, she agreed to make her son—now fifty-five—president of the company, while she remained as chairman of the board.

In 1929 the American Grocery Manufacturers' Association elected her to the board of directors; she had been the first woman to attend its meetings and was the first elected to any of its offices. In 1949 an article in *Collier's* declared her "America's foremost woman industrialist." She contributed regularly to various institutions in Johnstown. She gave $200,000 for the fully equipped Knox Athletic Field and founded both the Willing Helpers Home for Women and, in 1920, the Federation of Women's Clubs for Civic Improvement of Johnstown, of which she served as the first president. In 1949 a radio drama, "Lady of Johnstown," was broadcast nationally in recognition of her business and civic achievements. Her favorite hobby was raising orchids, which she made into a profitable sideline. She died in Johnstown.

The Knox firm continues today as two separate entities. T. J. Lipton, a unit of Unilever, bought Knox in the early 1970s. Then in 1994 R. J. R. Nabisco acquired the American rights to Knox gelatin to add to its Royal Desserts line; Kind & Knox, with headquarters in Sergeant's Bluff, Iowa, became a wholly owned subsidiary of DGF Stoess AG, a German-based global gelatin producer. Kind & Knox now operates the largest gelatin factory in the world, supplying gelatin for industrial applications, principally in pharmaceuticals and photographic supplies.

• Neither Knox nor the firm has apparently left any records. There are several newspaper or journal articles about her; see "Happiness Headquarters," *Time*, 29 Nov. 1937, p. 55; Edith Asbury, "Grand Old Lady of Johnstown," *Collier's*, 1 Jan. 1949, p. 20. An obituary is in the *New York Times*, 29 Sept. 1950.

FRED CARSTENSEN

KNOX, Samuel (1756–31 Aug. 1832), Presbyterian minister and educator. Although little is known of his early years, Knox was the son of a poor farm family in County Armagh, Ireland. By 1786 he had emigrated to Bladensburg, Maryland, where he taught in the grammar school (1788–1789). He returned to Europe in 1789, and received an M.A. from the University of Glasgow in 1792. After the Presbytery of Belfast licensed him for the ministry, he returned to the United States and was assigned by the Baltimore Presbytery to the Bladensburg pastorate (1795–1797). Thereafter he continued in the dual capacities, common then for rural Presbyterian ministers, of schoolteacher and supply pastor of Frederick (1797–1803) and Soldier's Delight (1804–1809), both in Maryland. He served again as principal of the Frederick Academy from 1823 to 1827, but his main teaching post was as principal of a private academy in Baltimore which merged with Baltimore College (1808–1820). Following a dispute with the trustees of Frederick Academy over retention of the Lancastrian method of instruction, which he had been using, Knox retired in 1827 and lived in Frederick until his death.

He was married first, in Ireland, to Grace Gilmour, his cousin, with whom he had four daughters; she died in 1812. He was then married to Zeruiah McCleery of Frederick, Maryland, in 1822; they had no children. Like many clergymen in the new nation, Knox was outspoken on public affairs, often engaging in political quarrels. By polemical sermon and pamphlet he supported Thomas Jefferson's position on a strict separation of church and state. Yet his theology did not permit a Jeffersonian sympathy for the unitarian views of Joseph Priestley, whom he assailed.

Knox is memorably identified as one of the first designers of national schooling. In 1797 he shared with Samuel Harrison Smith a prize of $100 offered by the American Philosophical Society for the best "system of liberal education and literary instruction" submitted to the society. Knox had the essay printed in Baltimore in 1799 as *An Essay on the Best System of Liberal Education, Adapted to the Genius of the Government of the United States. Comprehending also, an Uniform General Plan for Instituting and Conducting Public Schools, in This Country, on Principles of the Most Extensive Utility. To Which Is Prefixed, an Address to the Legislature of Maryland on That Subject.* Knox outlined here a comprehensive federal system or ladder of schooling from coeducational parish schools to county academies for boys, to state colleges; then to a national university under the direction of a national board of education with representatives in each state, to whom county supervisors, or rectors, would report. Both instruction and instructors would be secular. Higher learning would be pursued in a rural setting; colleges would be designed as three related, concentric, rectangular buildings of graduated size in order to foster a community of learning. The plan stressed uniformity of instruction and reading at each level and regularized standards of promotion. College admission would be open to all who demonstrated classical and mathematical proficiency (and who could pay the uniform expenses of room and board). Throughout, Knox was advocating schooling for the attainment of an American identity, or cultural nationalism, in a republic of fledgling states. In keeping with the republican faith of his enlightened age, a faith that transcended party disagreements, he held that an educated people promotes virtue and public happiness.

• Knox's *Essay* is reprinted in Frederick Rudolph, ed., *Essays on Education in the Early Republic* (1965). See also Ashley Foster, "Samuel Knox: Maryland Educator," *Maryland Historical Magazine* 50 (1955): 173–94; Bernard C. Steiner, "Reverend Samuel Knox," in *Report of the Commissioner of Education for the Year 1898–99*, vol. 1 (1900), pp. 557–604; Roy J. Honeywell, *The Educational Work of Thomas Jefferson* (1931; repr. 1964); and Lawrence A. Cremin, *American Education: The National Experience, 1783–1876* (1980). Knox's death is recorded in the *Daily National Intelligencer*, 4 Sept. 1832.

WILSON SMITH

KNOX, William (1732–25 Aug. 1810), Anglo-American government official and pamphleteer, was born at Monaghan, Ireland, the son of Thomas Knox, a physician, and Nicola King. Although William's paternal family was descended from Scots Presbyterian settlers in northern Ireland, his father converted to the Anglican Church of Ireland. Consequently, William spent his childhood and early manhood within the privileged ranks of the Anglo-Irish establishment. His mature personality—as well as his ideas about secular and religious affairs—were heavily influenced by the Anglicized form of Calvinism that Thomas Knox, by example as well as instruction, systematically impressed upon his son. After receiving his early education in the local Anglican schools of Monaghan, William attended Trinity College, Dublin. Here in the Irish capital he also served his political apprenticeship under the tutelage of Sir Richard Cox, a prominent leader of the Irish parliamentary opposition during the Anglo-Irish political crisis of 1753–1756.

In 1756 Knox was appointed provost marshal of the fledgling colony of Georgia, where he resided from 1756 to 1762, acquiring plantation properties near Savannah. By the outbreak of the American Revolution, he had acquired over, 2,500 acres worked by 122 black slaves. During his stay in Georgia, Knox also served on the provincial Council and was instrumental in promoting the authority of the colonial governor and the council vis-à-vis that of the general assembly, particularly in establishing the independent role of the executive and the upper house in the fiscal affairs of the colony.

Knox returned to Great Britain in 1762 to serve as Georgia's agent in London; at the same time he was seeking office in the imperial capital. The closing phase of the Seven Years' War provided an opportune moment for individuals with any experience in colonial matters, and Knox was quickly engaged in an unofficial capacity to provide advice to Lords Egremont and Shelburne, who as southern secretary and president of the Board of Trade, respectively, had primary responsibility for the imperial aspects of the proposed treaties of peace and for the development of new policies for the expanded empire. In particular, several of Knox's recommendations were incorporated in the creation of the new colony of East Florida. For three years he also continued to serve as Georgia's agent before the imperial government, being singularly successful in defending Georgia's claims to the lands between the Altamaha and St. John rivers against the rival claims of South Carolina. On another occasion Knox joined with the agent for South Carolina in persuading the Board of Trade and Parliament to allow the two colonies to export rice directly to South America. In 1765, however, the Georgia assembly dismissed him when he published a pamphlet, *The Claim of the Colonies . . .* , which defended Parliament's theoretical right—though not the practicality—of levying the Stamp Act upon the colonies.

Subsequently, Knox was able to attach himself to the political faction headed by George Grenville. With Grenville's patronage and personal assistance he published two more pamphlets, which established his reputation both as a significant imperial thinker and as a political polemicist to be reckoned with. The first, *Present State of the Nation* (1768), placed the controversy over colonial policy within the broad contexts of Anglo-French rivalry, mercantilistic economics, and imperial constitutional reform. In this work Knox provided the best articulation of his ideal of the empire as an integrated system wherein all of the constituents (British as well as colonial) reciprocally bore responsibilities and restrictions for the purpose of securing economic and military advantages that were otherwise unattainable. Although Knox defended the constitutional principle of parliamentary supremacy, as well as colonial conformity to imperial trade regulations, he also advocated concessions to American views on various constitutional and economic issues. He argued that the colonists should be given representation in the imperial Parliament; he recommended that in place of parliamentary taxation a system of quotas and requisitions be created whereby colonies would be allowed to determine the means of raising contributions for imperial purposes, and he insisted that the colonists be granted greater freedom to carry their products directly to foreign markets. The pamphlet also directly impeached the policies of the Rockingham Whigs, particularly their repeal of the Stamp Act and passage of the Declaratory Act, which he regarded as simultaneously ineffectual and provocative to the Americans. Consequently, he drew a pointed rejoinder in Edmund Burke's *Observations on a Late State of the Na-*

tion (1769). Contemporary critics acknowledged that these two works, taken together, represented the best statement of the major competing views of British public affairs in the aftermath of the Seven Years' War. By contrast Knox's subsequent *Controversy Between Great Britain and Her Colonies* (1769) was essentially a polemical tract-of-the-moment, a focused rebuttal of the various colonial claims to exemptions from parliamentary taxation, particularly those recently advanced in John Dickinson's (1732–1808) *Letters from a Farmer in Pennsylvania* (1767–1768). Increasingly convinced of American intransigence, Knox argued in *Controversy* for an uncompromising assertion of parliamentary sovereignty that admitted no room for those concessions to American constitutional views that had characterized his earlier pamphlets.

Appointment to government office became a financial imperative for Knox, whose meager resources, significantly reduced by the loss of the Georgia agency, had been increasingly strained by expanded family responsibilities. In 1765 he had married Letitia Ford, also of Ireland, and in 1768 the first of their seven children was born. Even as Knox became aware that his attachment to Grenville seemed unlikely to lead directly to office, his established reputation as a colonial expert and political pamphleteer served to promote his public and private fortunes. In 1770 Knox obtained an appointment as an undersecretary in the newly created American Department of the imperial government. Although he claimed that in his official capacity he regularly advised the government to pursue a moderate course in America, he simultaneously contributed to the growing breach that led to the American Revolution by publishing two pamphlets, *The Justice and Policy of the Late Act of Parliament for . . . Quebec* (1774) and *The Interests of the Merchants and the Manufacturers of Great Britain . . .* (1774), which defended the American policies of the North administration. During the American War of Independence Knox carried out a wide range of administrative duties, playing a particularly prominent role in promoting the use of Loyalist and Indian forces in America. Ironically, as an undersecretary for America he was even more instrumental in recommending and carrying into effect trade concessions for Ireland during the years 1778–1780.

For Knox, Britain's defeat in the revolutionary war was a personal disaster. With the withdrawal of British forces from America Knox lost his plantations in Georgia, and after the fall of North's government he became a focus of attacks by Burke and other enemies among the Whigs, who finally forced his dismissal from office in 1782. For almost a decade he attempted unsuccessfully to restore his public and private fortunes by attaching himself to various political factions. Yet even out of office he helped to influence Anglo-American affairs when, as an adviser to the Fox-North coalition (1783), he instigated the policy that virtually cut off trade between the United States and Britain's West Indian colonies—a measure that was to trouble relations between the two countries for many decades.

Knox eventually gave up the pursuit of office in 1790 after being awarded compensation from the British Loyalist Claims Commission for the loss of his Georgia properties. Although his last two decades were mainly devoted to the activities of a country gentleman at various rural retreats in England and Wales, he never lost his zeal for politics. He served as agent for the Loyalist provinces of New Brunswick and Prince Edward Island, and on several occasions he employed his ever-prolific pen in political controversies. Particularly noteworthy was his campaign in 1789–1790 against William Wilberforce's parliamentary efforts to abolish the British slave trade, for which cause Knox republished an earlier pamphlet, *Three Tracts Respecting the Conversion and Instruction of the Free Indians and Negro Slaves* (1768; repr. 1789), and wrote a new tract, *A Letter from W. K., Esq., to W. Wilberforce* (1790). In these two works Knox provided a defense of slavery based on the doctrines of evangelical Christianity—an approach that anticipated by more than half a century a major theme of the apologia developed by proslavery advocates in the American antebellum South. Knox spent the last years of his life in the company of his children at Ealing, Middlesex, where he occupied his time writing tracts on religious subjects.

William Knox has been recognized as a major contributor to the evolution of British imperial thought prior to the American Revolution. The nature and significance of that contribution is nonetheless historically paradoxical and historiographically controversial. Originally Knox, both as a pamphleteer and a colonial official, sought to reconcile British and American interests within an integrated imperial system. However, as differences over economic policies and political relationships escalated into a comprehensive conflict over the constitutional principles of sovereignty and liberty, Knox in his publications increasingly proclaimed that the empire could be preserved only by an active assertion of parliamentary supremacy over the colonies. Privately he acknowledged that war with America could mean disaster for his personal fortunes, and he even took part in official and unofficial efforts at reconciliation. Nevertheless, Knox in the final analysis contributed most effectually to the development of, and apologia for, the British policy of coercion that led to the American Revolution.

• The bulk of William Knox's papers are collected at the William L. Clements Library, Ann Arbor, Mich., which also houses important Knox manuscripts in the Germain and the Shelburne papers. Other sizable collections of Knox manuscripts are in the Public Record Office (London), the British Library, and the Staffordshire Record Office, Stafford. The Historical Manuscripts Commission provides extensive excerpts from Knox's manuscripts in its *Report on Manuscripts in Various Collections*, vol. 6 (1909). In addition to those works cited in the text, the most significant of Knox's publications are *Considerations on the State of Ireland* (1778) and *Extra Official State Papers* (2 vols., 1789). The most comprehensive study of Knox's life and thought is Leland J. Bellot, *William Knox* (1977). Bellot examines particular aspects of

Knox's contributions to colonial policy in Howard H. Peckham, ed., *Sources of American Independence*, vol. 2 (1978) and to proslavery thought in "Evangelicals and the Defense of Slavery in Britain's Old Colonial Empire," *Journal of Southern History* (Feb. 1971): 19–40. For a different perspective on particular aspects of Knox's earlier writing on colonial policy see Thomas C. Barrow, ed., "A Project for Imperial Reform: 'Hints Respecting the Settlement for our American Provinces,' 1763," *William and Mary Quarterly* (Jan. 1967): 108–26. Richard Koebner, *Empire* (1961), depicted Knox as one of the earliest modern exponents of true "imperialist" thinking, while Knox's official career is a significant feature of two studies of colonial administration: Margaret Marian Spector, *The American Department of the British Government* (1940), and Franklin B. Wickwire, *British Subministers and Colonial America* (1966).

LELAND J. BELLOT

KNUDSEN, William Signius (25 Mar. 1879–27 Apr. 1948), automobile executive, was born Signius Wilhelm Poul Knudsen in Copenhagen, Denmark, the son of Knud Peter Knudsen, a customs inspector, and Augusta Zollner. Knud Peter had four children by a previous marriage, and with the six children by his second wife the large family struggled to survive on his meager salary. At age six Signius Wilhelm was put to work afternoons pushing a cart of window glass for a glazier. He received an above-average education for his time—nine years of public school followed by two years of night school at the Danish Government Technical School, from which he graduated with honors and a silver watch for his high grades in mathematics.

At fifteen Knudsen was apprenticed for four years to a wholesale firm dealing in hardware, crockery, and toys. He then worked for the importing firm Christian Achen as a junior clerk and bicycle assembler and was soon placed in charge of the warehouse. With Axel Klingenberg, a salesman, Knudsen built one of the first tandem bicycles in Denmark, and they became professional pacemakers in long-distance bicycle races in Denmark, Sweden, and northern Germany.

In 1900 Knudsen landed in New York with $30 in his pocket. He found lodging at a Lutheran mission in the Battery and lived on the free lunches provided with a nickel beer at the saloons on lower Broadway until he found a job reaming holes in steel plate for torpedo boats for seventeen-and-a-half cents an hour at the Seabury Shipyards in Morris Heights, New York. The Seabury timekeeper reported his name as "William Knudsen." Soon he was promoted to "bucker-up," the worker who held an iron bar against the hot rivets while they were hammered into place. After the shipyards closed in the fall, Knudsen found a job repairing locomotive boilers.

Shortly after returning from a brief visit home to Denmark in 1902, Knudsen took a job with the John R. Keim Mills, a Buffalo, New York, bicycle manufacturer. His first job at Keim was producing engines for an English steam car, the Foster Wagon, his first experience with an automobile engine. Hard times came to the Keim mills with the saturation of the market for bicycles. To replace the lost bicycle business, Keim made a variety of stamped steel products.

To learn to make steel components stronger and lighter, Knudsen took a course in steelmaking at the Lackawanna Steel Company plant. He and William H. Smith, the Keim plant superintendent, then developed a method for forming and drawing steel that they thought could be applied to automobile parts. (Knudsen also helped to establish the first U.S. acetylene welding plant at Keim in 1906.) On hearing that Henry Ford was in the market for axle housings, he and Smith traveled to Detroit to see him. They returned to Buffalo with a $75,000 order, the largest in Keim's history. This was the beginning of an increasingly close relationship between Keim and Ford that resulted in the purchase of Keim by the Ford Motor Company in 1911.

Ford was moving rapidly away from being an assembler of jobbed-out components toward integrated manufacturing. A visit to the Briggs Manufacturing Company, which was supplying Ford bodies, convinced Knudsen that Keim also could make bodies and assemble cars; this resulted in a contract with Ford to do so in Buffalo. In 1912 the Keim workers struck to protest the piecework rates on some outside contracts. "That suits me," declared Henry Ford. "If the men don't want to work, get some flat cars and move the flatcars and machinery to Highland Park [Mich.]." Three days later the move had been accomplished; then in late 1913 Knudsen supervised the move to Detroit of key Keim personnel and their families.

In 1911 Knudsen had married Clara Elizabeth Euler, with whom he had four children. Knudsen's first job at Ford was setting up branch assembly plants throughout the country because cars could be shipped cheaper by rail in knocked-down form and assembled locally. By 1916 he was in charge of twenty-eight Ford branch assembly plants.

The outbreak of World War I in Europe resulted in a steel shortage that threatened to halt production of the Model T. Ford gave Knudsen the job of obtaining adequate supplies of sheet steel. He did that so effectively that Ford invited him to "come upstairs and start handling the shop" at a salary of $25,000 a year plus a 15 percent bonus.

Ford's war production was the most diversified of any American manufacturer. Knudsen was made superintendent over all war production at Ford in addition to his other duties. He developed a way to mass-produce cylinders for the Liberty aircraft engine by closing the end of a piece of vanadium steel tubing to form the head of the cylinder. He also worked out a way to mass-produce the *Eagle Boat* submarine chasers without experienced shipyard workers by numbering each of the *Eagle Boat*'s parts, punching the boat's plates on machinery, and supervising the construction of a special assembly plant with three production lines, each capable of carrying seven boats.

In 1918 Knudsen was named Ford production manager under Charles E. Sorensen and P. E. "Pete" Martin. Knudsen supervised the conversion of the Ford plant back to civilian production of the Model T, but the callous treatment of employees by Sorensen and Martin appalled him. The only Ford executive he admired was Edsel Ford. He worked with Edsel on a number of ideas to upgrade the Model T that ended up being vetoed by Henry Ford, who began telling other employees to ignore Knudsen and countermanding his orders. Knudsen resigned in 1921. At the time his salary was $50,000 plus a 15 percent bonus.

After a ten-month stint as general manager of Ireland & Mathews, a Detroit manufacturer of stove trimmings, plumbers' supplies, and automobile parts, Knudsen was employed by General Motors to improve the GM operating units. After only three weeks he was appointed vice president of operations at Chevrolet by GM president Pierre S. du Pont. In May 1923 Alfred P. Sloan, Jr., replaced du Pont as GM president, and in January 1924, Knudsen was named president and general manager of the Chevrolet Division and a vice president and director of GM.

The Chevrolet car was not competitive in quality or price with the Model T, and resources had been wasted trying to get into production an experimental "revolutionary car" with an air-cooled engine developed by Charles E. Kettering. Knudsen initially had informed du Pont that the so-called copper-cooled Chevrolet should be put into production at once; but after working with Kettering for eighteen months, he persuaded Sloan to abandon the project. Knudsen's attention then focused on correcting the main defect of the water-cooled Chevrolet car—a bad rear axle—and on improving it both mechanically and in appearance. This was largely accomplished by the 1926 model year, when the 13 to 1 ratio by which the Model T had outsold Chevrolet in 1921 was cut to 2 to 1, forcing Ford to withdraw the Model T from production. Further improvements were capped by the move from a four- to a six-cylinder engine in 1929. Chevrolet outsold Ford in every year from 1931 through 1986 except 1935 and 1945.

At Chevrolet, Knudsen innovated modern "flexible" mass-production techniques. Machinery at the Ford Highland Park plant was so specialized that even small changes bottlenecked production, and the switchover to Model A production at the River Rouge plant involved closing down production at Ford for some seven months at an estimated then-exorbitant cost of some $250 million. Such a disruption of production was irreconcilable with bringing out a new model every three years that the Sloanist marketing strategy envisioned. Knudsen resolved this problem at GM by replacing single-purpose machine tools with standard general-purpose ones, by decentralizing assembly operations, and by buying more components from outside suppliers. These innovations made the accommodation of change possible and were soon copied by both Ford and Chrysler.

On 16 October 1933 Knudsen became GM executive vice president in charge of coordinating production for all of the corporation's car manufacturing divi-

sions. Then when Sloan replaced Lammot du Pont as chairman of the GM board in 1937, Knudsen moved up to the GM presidency.

Knudsen left GM in May 1940 to serve as chairman of the National Defense Advisory Council. In September he resigned his $459,000-a-year position at GM to work for the government at no salary. At a secret meeting in New York he called on American automobile manufacturers to give their full cooperation to U.S. defense plans and began to mobilize the production of tanks, aircraft engines, and 35,000 aircraft. In January 1941 Knudsen was made codirector—with Sidney Hillman, president of the Amalgamated Clothing Workers—of the Office of Production Management (OPM). When the functions of the OPM were taken over in 1942 by the War Production Board, chaired by Donald M. Nelson, Knudsen was "demoted" to director of war production in the War Department. He served in this capacity for the duration of the war. For his contribution to the war effort, Knudsen was awarded two Distinguished Service medals.

After his separation from the army in 1945, Knudsen returned to GM as a member of the board of directors and as a consultant. But he was angered and hurt that there no longer seemed a place for him in the corporation. He died in Detroit.

Henry Ford called Knudsen "the best production man in the United States." Despite his fame and high position, Knudsen had remained a simple, decent man, whose door was always open to subordinates, and a "soft touch" who gave unstintingly and almost always anonymously to numerous charitable causes.

• Despite his importance, Knudson has received very little attention by scholars. A full-length account of his life was published a year before his death: Norman Beasley, *Knudsen: A Biography* (1947). An informative chapter on Knudsen is in Christy Borth, *Masters of Mass Production* (1945), and Knudsen's contribution to "flexible" mass production is most fully explained in David A. Hounshell, *From the American System to Mass Production: The Development of Manufacturing Technology in the United States* (1984). The most comprehensive biographic article on Knudsen, based in part on a 9 June 1987 interview with his son Semon, is James J. Flink, "William Signius Knudsen," in *The Automobile Industry, 1920–1980*, ed. George S. May (1989). An obituary is in the *New York Times*, 28 Apr. 1948.

JAMES J. FLINK

KNUDSON, Albert Cornelius (23 Jan. 1873–28 Aug. 1953), Methodist theologian and educator, was born in Grandmeadow, Minnesota, the son of Asle Knudson, a Methodist minister, and Susan Fosse. The fourth of nine children of Norwegian immigrants, Albert Knudson grew to maturity in Iowa and Minnesota, where his father was one of the founders and leaders of the Norwegian-Danish Methodist Conference. During his senior year in high school, young Knudson experienced a "conversion to Christ" in an evangelical Wesleyan sense and joined the Grace Methodist Church, St. Paul, Minnesota. The valedictorian of the senior class of St. Paul High School in 1889, he earned a B.A. in classics with highest honors from the University of Minnesota in 1893.

Influenced by local Methodist ministers with ties to the Boston University School of Theology (the theological college of the university), Knudson decided to go there to train for the Methodist ministry. At Boston, he came under the influence of church historian Henry C. Sheldon, theologian Olin A. Curtis, Old Testament scholar Hinckley G. Mitchell, and especially philosopher Borden Parker Bowne. Awarded an S.T.B. in 1896, he remained for doctoral study with Bowne and was named Jacob Sleeper Fellow of Boston University for study at the Universities of Jena and Berlin in Germany in 1897–1898. While in Germany, he attended the lectures of some of the most noted scholars of the day, including the church historian Adolf von Harnack.

From 1898 to 1900 Knudson taught church history at Illiff School of Theology, Denver, Colorado. While there, he was ordained to the Methodist ministry and, in 1899, married Mathilde Johnson, the daughter of a Norwegian Methodist minister. They had no children. In 1900 Knudson completed his Ph.D. in philosophy from Boston University and moved to Baker University, Baldwin, Kansas, to serve as professor of philosophy and English Bible from 1900 to 1902. He accepted a similar position at Allegheny College, Meadville, Pennsylvania, where he remained from 1902 to 1906.

In 1906 Knudson began his remarkable 37-year career at Boston University. He was invited to return as professor of Hebrew and Old Testament exegesis, which he taught until 1921, when he was named professor of systematic theology, a position he held until his retirement in 1943. He also served concurrently as dean of the School of Theology from 1926 to 1938.

Knudson contributed regularly to Methodist publications and was an active member of the New England Southern Conference. Twice, in 1932 and 1936, his conference elected him a delegate to the General Conference of the Methodist Episcopal Church. He also represented Methodists at the ecumenical Edinburgh Conference on Faith and Order in 1937, and he was a member of the Uniting Conference of the Methodist Church, which, in 1939, brought together the Methodist Episcopal church, the Methodist Episcopal Church (South), and the Methodist Protestant church to constitute the Methodist church. Professional recognition included membership in the American Philosophical Association, Phi Beta Kappa, and Delta Upsilon and election as a fellow of the American Academy of Arts and Sciences.

The occasion of Knudson's return to Boston University was the dismissal of his former Old Testament teacher Mitchell on heresy charges brought on by Mitchell's introduction of biblical criticism (especially what was then called higher criticism) into his classroom. The Methodist Episcopal church, which had established Boston University in 1839, was locked in a bitter struggle over control of its theological training schools between those who defended a historic Wesleyan view of the Bible, based on verbal plenary inspiration and traditional evangelical theology (mostly the bishops and lay leaders), and those who advocated a new approach to the study of the Scriptures, based on current scientific understanding and the tools of literary criticism (mostly professors in the theological seminaries), which, according to its critics, produced a less orthodox and more liberal theology. The new theological liberalism in the United States reflected increasing contacts between American universities and their German counterparts, where the new theology flourished. Knudson, one of a generation of American theological students who traveled to Germany to imbibe the new scholarship firsthand, quickly incorporated higher criticism (later more commonly known as literary or source criticism) into his teachings. Operating in the context of current scientific assumptions and using philological methods and an evolutionary hypothesis, biblical scholars of the new school applied rational methods of inquiry to the text of the Bible. Higher/literary critics put to biblical texts a new set of questions that usually concerned three things: the literary development of texts; the preliterary, oral developments that lie behind the texts; and the final process of editing or redaction, by which the texts have reached their present form. Many traditional Methodists believed that this approach was irreverent and led to skepticism.

It was in this milieu that Knudson tried to create a theological system that, on the one hand, preserved historic Methodist evangelical piety but, on the other, allowed his coreligionists to adjust to a more modern theology. In so doing, he escaped Mitchell's fate by capitalizing on his own genial personality (he was a great baseball fan) and keen sense of humor, his considerable persuasive powers, the merits of his case, and the increasing battle-weariness of most Methodist leaders of the period. Historically speaking, Knudson can be regarded as a liberal-evangelical, part of a generation of Protestant intellectuals who tried to bridge the gap between the old and new theologies.

In this quest, Knudson was guided by his mentor and friend Bowne, the chief American proponent of philosophical personalism. Bowne and others developed this philosophy in reaction to pantheism, materialism, the social Darwinism of Herbert Spencer, and Hegelian absolutism on the one hand and fundamentalism and dogmatic supernaturalism on the other. In so doing, they combined idealism with theism and created a philosophical system in which person is the ontological ultimate and for which personality is thus the fundamental explanatory principle. To them, the personality, be it divine or human or other, was the supreme value of and key to understanding reality— hence, the term "personalism." Bowne taught that the infinite person, God, creates finite persons, endowing them with real but somewhat attenuated free will. God's ethical purpose is that persons may become cocreators of a moral society governed by mutual respect and loyalty to God. Moreover, God is in nature, and nature expresses God, but God's being and purpose transcend the natural order. Persons do not overlap with each other or with God, and they can fulfill their natures only when they control sense and appetite in accordance with reason and love. Bowne's approach appealed to Knudson because, in a period of thought dominated by scientific rationalism, it undergirded the independence of religion and made it possible to preserve the traditional Methodist emphasis on religious experience and ethical obligations.

Knudson, therefore, set out to formulate a system of theology grounded in Bowne's personalism. In so doing, he emphasized a religious apriorism, pointing out that certain necessary religious assumptions were as valid as certain necessary assumptions of the natural sciences. In his view, religion stood in its own right as an "autonomous validity," much as does humankind's cognitive nature. Thus, he maintained, there is a religious apriority, as there are theoretical, moral, and aesthetic apriorities. Further, he attempted to make personalism acceptable in Methodist circles not only by correlating it with Christian thought but also by providing an abundant historical background as he argued for its acceptance. At the same time, he tried to insure its scholarly acceptance by appealing to Kantian epistemology for philosophical support. Knudson's thought also reflected his own years of scholarly study of the Bible and the devotional habits of Christian piety that saturated his mind as a result of his upbringing in a Methodist parsonage. He developed his argument for a personalistic Christian theology most fully in his book *The Validity of Religious Experience* (1937).

One of the most influential Protestant theologians in the United States in the first half of the twentieth century, Knudson spread his "Boston personalism" by means of his lectures, his students, and especially, his many books, the most important of which were *The Philosophy of Personalism* (1927), *The Doctrine of God* (1930), and *The Doctrine of Redemption* (1933). On the scholarly level, it was Knudson who first placed Bowne's philosophy in historical perspective, elaborated its relationship to important rival systems, and classified it among the various types of personalistic philosophy. On the practical level, he enabled a generation of Methodist ministers to continue to preach what sounded like the old-fashioned gospel while adjusting their theology to modern modes of thought. In doing this, Knudson believed that he had preserved the core of the gospel, namely, the offer of divine grace, and refuted the secular humanism of his day.

Knudson is best understood as a transitional figure in the history of American Christianity. His influence lasted for more than a generation, from about 1920 to 1960, during the period of the full vigor of theological liberalism in American Protestantism, after which it largely disappeared in the wake of neo-orthodoxy and the evangelical revival. Predeceased by his wife in 1948, Knudson died at Cambridge, Massachusetts.

• Knudson's papers are in the library of the Boston University School of Theology. His books, other than those mentioned, include *The Old Testament Problem* (1905), *The Bea-* con Lights of Prophecy (1914), *The Religious Teaching of the Old Testament* (1918), *The Prophetic Movement in Israel* (1921), *Present Tendencies in Religious Thought* (1924), *The Principles of Christian Ethics* (1943), *The Philosophy of War and Peace* (1947), and *Basic Issues in Religious Thought* (1950). Edgar S. Brightman, ed., *Personalism in Theology: A Symposium in Honor of Albert Cornelius Knudson* (1943), contains a tribute to Knudson by his former student and longtime friend and colleague Elmer A. Leslie, a bibliography of Knudson's books and articles up to 1943, and numerous essays on various aspects of philosophic personalism. See also Leslie, "Albert Cornelius Knudson: An Intimate View," *The Personalist* 35 (Oct. 1954): 357–63; and L. Harold DeWolf, "Albert Cornelius Knudson as Philosopher," *The Personalist* 35 (Oct. 1954): 364–68. The historical and theological context of Knudson's work is best set forth in Robert E. Chiles, *Theological Transition in American Methodism, 1790–1935* (1965); and Paul Deats and Carol Robb, eds., *The Boston Personalist Tradition in Philosophy, Social Ethics, and Theology* (1986). An obituary is in the *New York Times*, 30 Aug. 1953.

ROBERT D. LINDER

KOBER, Arthur (25 Aug. 1900–12 June 1975), author and journalist, was born in Brody, Austria-Hungary, a center of Yiddish culture, the son of Adolph Mayer, a bushelman, and Tillie Ballison. The family came to the United States in 1904, settling first in Harlem, a part of New York City then populated by many Jewish immigrants, and moving soon thereafter to the Bronx. Kober left the High School of Commerce after only one semester, which caused him to comment later, "That's why I write in the first person and don't worry about grammar." He went to work at fourteen as a stock clerk for Gimbel's department store. Between 1915 and 1922 one odd job followed another. He became a stenographer for the Maxwell Automobile Company, then for the author Grenville Kleiser. He also sailed as a bellboy on a ship bound from New York to San Francisco via the Panama Canal.

In 1922 Kober was hired as an assistant to Claude Greneker, one of Lee Shubert and J. J. Shubert's theatrical press agents. Soon thereafter, he went to work for another Shubert press agent, Jed Harris. Between 1923 and 1930 Kober was press representative for such Broadway shows as *Artists and Models* (1923), *Broadway* (1926), *Spread Eagle* (1927), *Cock Robin* (1929), *Ruth Draper* (1929), *The Green Pastures* (1930), and *Strike Up the Band* (1930). In 1925 Kober produced *Me*, a play by Henry Myers, at New York's Princess Theatre. On 25 December 1925 he married author and playwright Lillian Hellman; though they were divorced seven years later, they remained friends. A prolific journalist during the 1920s, Kober wrote newspaper columns for the *New York World* and the *Evening Sun* and the Hollywood and New York columns for the *Morning Telegraph*. Toward the end of the decade, he also edited the *Paris Comet*, an English-language magazine.

In 1930 Kober moved to Hollywood as a screenwriter, working on screenplays for *It Pays to Advertise* (1931), *The Secret Call* (1931), *Up Pops the Devil* (1931), *Make Me a Star* (1932), *Guilty as Hell* (1932),

Meet the Baron (1933), *Mama Loves Papa* (1933), *Ginger* (1935), *It's Great to Be Alive* (1933), *Headline Shooter* (1933), *Hollywood Party* (1934), *Great Hotel Murder* (1935), *Calm Yourself* (1935), *Early to Bed* (1936), and *The Big Broadcast of 1937* (1936). Although hardly brilliant, Kober's work on these screenplays was professional, revealing his ability to deal with disparate subject matter.

Kober's best work appeared in the short stories he wrote about young stenographers and clerks with whom he had worked and the first-generation Jewish immigrants he remembered from his formative years in the Bronx. Revealing a keen ear for distinctive speech patterns, he not only depicted these people with warmth and humor, but he made their style of English famous. "Mr. Kober was to the Bronx," the *New York Times* said, "what Erskine Caldwell was to Georgia, William Faulkner to Yoknapatawpha County in Mississippi, and James Joyce to the unconscious."

Utilizing Jewish dialect and a Bronx setting, Kober began publishing his Ma and Pa Gross stories in the *New Yorker* during the depression (he contributed to the *New Yorker* from 1926 to 1958). Twenty-five of Kober's stories about the Grosses were collected in *Thunder over the Bronx* (1935) with an introduction by Dorothy Parker. For the Grosses, who represented something new in Jewish-American literature, nothing is trivial. Everything is seen in exaggerated terms, and almost everything is terrible. Yet Kober does not treat the Grosses or their fellow Jewish immigrants as persecuted victims. The reader does not have to feel sorry for the Grosses, who are learning how to make their way. Kober's stories focusing on their unmarried daughter Bella and her tireless search for a husband were collected in *My Dear Bella* (1941) and *Bella, Bella Kissed a Fella* (1951).

In 1937 Kober's play, *Having Wonderful Time*, which was staged at New York's Lyceum Theatre, won the Roi Cooper Megrue prize as the best comedy of the year. A romantic comedy, it is about the summer romances that blossomed at the resort hotels in the Catskill Mountains. Characters of every social class speak the same fractured English, and many camp guests are having a wonderful time only when loudly complaining. Kober wrote the screenplay for the film version of *Having Wonderful Time*, which was released in 1938. His collection of stories entitled *Pardon Me for Pointing* was published the following year. On 11 January 1941 Kober married Margaret Frohnknecht, who died in 1951. The Kobers had one child.

In 1941 Kober returned to Hollywood, where he worked on screenplays for *The Little Foxes* (1941), *Wintertime* (1943), *In the Meantime, Darling* (1944), *Don Juan Quilligan* (1945), and *My Own True Love* (1948). In the mid-1940s Kober also published two volumes of stories, *Parm Me* (1945) and *That Man Is Here Again* (1946). In the introduction to *That Man Is Here Again* Kober reflected on Hollywood, describing a studio system run by authoritarian studio bosses and producers while agents and a variety of hangers-on spent much of their time hustling easy money. Kober insisted that he liked some of these Hollywood types, but the stories in the volume indicate the contrary. In fact, what he saw as the system's corruption had made him bitter about Hollywood.

With Joshua Logan and Harold Rome, Kober wrote *Wish You Were Here*. Based on Kober's play *Having Wonderful Time*, this musical opened at New York City's Majestic Theatre on 25 June 1952. *A Mighty Man Is He*, a comedy written by Kober and George Oppenheimer, was produced at several playhouses in Massachusetts and Maine during the summer of 1954. *Ooooh, What You Said!*, Kober's last collection of stories, appeared in 1958. During the 1960s, Kober wrote for such television series as "Leave It to Beaver," "Harrigan and Son," and "My Three Sons," as well as for "GE Theatre."

Kober had begun an autobiography during the 1950s, but it was unfinished at the time of his death in New York City. Kober's popularity declined as descendants of the Grosses found it increasingly difficult to recognize themselves in his work, a fact that should not obscure Kober's important contributions to the development of modern urban humor in the United States.

• Material regarding Kober and his work can be found in the *New York Times Book Review*, 28 Oct. 1951; Dale Kramer, *Ross and the New Yorker* (1951); Lillian Hellman, *An Unfinished Woman: A Memoir* (1969); Walter Blair and Hamlin Hill, *America's Humor: From Poor Richard to Doonesbury* (1978); E. J. Kahn, Jr., *About The New Yorker & Me* (1979); William Wright, *Lillian Hellman: The Image, the Woman* (1986); and Carl Rollyson, *Lillian Hellman: Her Legend and Her Legacy* (1988). Obituaries are in the *New York Times*, 13 June 1975, and the *Washington Post*, 15 June 1975.

L. MOODY SIMMS, JR.

KOCH, Adrienne (10 Sept. 1912–21 Aug. 1971), historian and educator, was born in New York City, the daughter of John Desider Koch, a manufacturer, and Helen Karman. Professionally, Koch retained her maiden name throughout her career, which began in philosophy. She earned a B.A. from New York University in 1933 and an M.A. and a Ph.D. from Columbia University in 1934 and 1942, respectively. Her dissertation, "The Philosophy of Thomas Jefferson," revealed her interest in American intellectual history, particularly in the political thought of the Founding Fathers. This topic would remain the central focus of her scholarly work.

Despite a distinguished academic record, Koch initially experienced difficulty in finding a faculty post. In 1942 she received the prestigious Woodbridge Prize for writing the best dissertation in Columbia's philosophy department, and a year later the university's press published her thesis. *The Philosophy of Thomas Jefferson* (1943) earned favorable notices. Nevertheless, Koch, even with five years experience as a philosophy instructor at New York University, could not obtain a professorship. This failure can be partially attributed to gender bias. Years later philosopher Sidney Hook, one of Koch's mentors, unwittingly revealed the mind set of male academics of his generation when he characterized his protégé in her younger days as "a budding, eager-eyed scholar, incongruously embodied in a lovely frame that made all eyes turn as she passed by." Not surprisingly, Koch became a tenacious advocate of equal rights for women.

Failing to receive a teaching position, Koch, taking advantage of growth in the federal bureaucracy during World War II, commenced a period of government service. She worked as a researcher with the Office of War Information (1941–1943) and as a senior analyst with the Foreign Economic Administration (1943) and the National Planning Association (1944).

During the 1940s Koch increased her reputation as an authority on the Founding Fathers. She co-edited compact editions of the most important writings of Thomas Jefferson (1944) and of John Adams and John Quincy Adams (1946) for the Modern Library series of inexpensive classics. The Jefferson volume, Koch's best-selling work, was widely adopted for college courses and remained in print for more than fifty years. In 1947 Koch married Lawrence Robert Kegan, an economist. They had twins, a daughter and a son.

Buoyed by her publications and benefited by the postwar expansion of American higher education, Koch at last obtained a professorship at Tulane University in 1946. In a peripatetic career she also taught at the universities of California, at Berkeley (1956–1964), and Maryland, at College Park (1966–1971), as well as holding several visiting chairs and doing much guest lecturing. Her interdisciplinary approach to scholarship found her at various times listed as a member of departments of philosophy, history, political science, and American studies.

From the late 1940s through the early 1970s Koch published a considerable body of work on the political thought of America's founding generation. In *Jefferson and Madison: The Great Collaboration* (1950), her most famous monograph, Koch maintained that James Madison's contributions to both political philosophy and party politics equaled if not exceeded those of Jefferson, thereby helping to revive scholarly interest in the lesser-known Virginian. The philosopher-turned-historian also strongly influenced early American historiography through cogently argued essays contributed to the *William and Mary Quarterly* and through a volume of lectures, *Power, Morals, and the Founding Fathers: Essays in the Interpretation of the American Enlightenment* (1961). In her substantial introduction to a hefty anthology of writings by the framers, *The American Enlightenment: The Shaping of the American Experiment and a Free Society* (1965), Koch emphasized her principal theme that George Washington, Jefferson, Madison, and their contemporaries were "philosopher-statesmen and not merely political leaders brought to power in a time of revolutionary upheaval."

By the late 1950s Koch had emerged as a social critic striving to reach beyond academe. Her 1959 volume *Philosophy for a Time of Crisis* culled selections from noted thinkers she believed relevant in an era haunted by nightmares of communist domination and nuclear annihilation. Throughout the 1960s Koch contributed book reviews and op-ed pieces to the *New York Times*, the *Washington Post*, the *Nation*, and other mass market publications. In these essays she forcefully advocated greater opportunities for women. Koch took a dim view, however, of "infantile," "obscenity-shouting radicals" who denounced the Founding Fathers while enjoying the rights for which the revolution had been fought. "Utopian idealism accompanying violent revolution," she opined, "leads to total control." Koch concluded, "The avoidance of this syndrome by the American Revolution is perhaps its most precious lesson" (*New York Times*, 4 July 1970, p. 20).

Koch's burgeoning career as both historian and public intellectual ended prematurely, as she succumbed to cancer in a New York City hospital. At her death, Koch left unfinished a study of the Grimké sisters, the celebrated nineteenth-century reformers, on which she had long labored. Fragments of this final work were published in a volume of the *Maryland Historian* that was dedicated to her memory.

Koch, along with contemporaries such as Perry Miller and Douglass Adair, treated early American thinkers and schools of thought with seriousness, rescuing them from the debunking of the Progressive Era and the 1920s. In the process, she contributed to a "consensus" view of American history that more radical scholars have accused of dismissing dissident, nonelite viewpoints. As a social critic, Koch zealously advocated women's rights while criticizing what she regarded as the extremism of the 1960s. Above all, despite discrimination due to her gender, Koch, through her writings, successfully bridged the widening gap between the academy and the general public.

• Koch's personal papers have remained in private hands. In addition to the works cited in the text, Koch's published writings include scholarly editions of James Madison's *Notes of Debates in the Federal Convention of 1787* and his *Advice to My Country* (both 1966). Charles F. Madden, ed., *Talks with Social Scientists* (1968), contains an interview with Koch. A special issue of the *Maryland Historian* 3 (1972): 1–85, features memorial tributes and a bibliography of Koch's writings. J. P. McCabe, "The Declaration of Independence and the Frailties of Historical Method," *Historian* 57 (1995): 859–72, critiques Koch as a "consensus" historian. Obituaries are in the *American Historical Review* 77 (1972): 246–47; the *Journal of American History* 58 (1972): 1086; and the *New York Times*, 23 Aug. 1971.

RICKY EARL NEWPORT

KOCH, Fred Conrad (16 May 1876–26 Jan. 1948), biochemist, was born in Chicago, Illinois, the son of Louise Henrietta Fischer and Frederick Koch (occupations unknown). Koch studied chemistry at the University of Illinois, receiving the B.S. in 1899 and the M.S. in 1900. Koch remained there, serving as an instructor in chemistry, for two years. He married Bertha Ethel Zink in 1901. A year later, he began working as a research chemist for the Armour Packing Company, a position he held until 1909. At that time he entered the University of Chicago, where he earned a Ph.D. in physiological chemistry in 1912 under Albert P. Mathews, working on the digestive hormone gastrin and on "the iodine-containing complex in thyreoglobulin." He also studied under Julius Stieglitz. After his wife's death in 1918, he married the biochemist Elizabeth Miller in 1922. He had no children.

Although some Chicago faculty members had originally expressed reservations about awarding a fellowship to a 33-year-old graduate student, Koch rewarded their trust and defied stereotypes by producing his most significant work after the age of fifty. In the laboratory, Koch was known for his "skill in devising equipment and analytic methods" and for his contributions on a wide range of biochemical topics, including the enzymes of the gastric tract, the hormones influencing pancreatic function, and the thyroid hormones. His work on vitamins—conducted in collaboration with his second wife—included the discovery that ultraviolet light converts cholesterol into a precursor of vitamin D. His innovations included the "Koch pipette," a stopcock pipette with a reservoir; a modified form of the volumetric amino nitrogen apparatus; and the micro-Kjeldahl method for total nitrogen estimation.

Koch was a dedicated teacher, devoting a great deal of effort to the development of a general course in biochemistry. His laboratory manual, *Practical Methods in Biochemistry* (1934), went through many editions. Perhaps his most significant contribution to biochemistry, however, was the guidance he provided to the forty doctoral students and twenty master's degree recipients in his laboratory, many of whom went on to become leaders in educational and research institutions across the country.

Koch's unselfishness and his commitment to encouraging independence among his students was nowhere better illustrated than in the work produced by his laboratory on testicular extracts. His student Lemuel C. McGee produced an important doctoral dissertation in 1927 on the biological activity of these substances. Previous studies—beginning with those of Charles-Edouard Brown-Sequard in 1889—had been flawed by the lack of reliable methods of isolation and assay. Working under Koch's direction, McGee and T. F. Gallagher developed workable techniques. This research was facilitated by the accessibility of Chicago slaughterhouses, including Armour and Company, which provided the laboratory with seventy pounds of frozen bull testicles each week.

Koch obtained funds for this research from the pharmaceutical company Squibb and Sons in 1926, and (with the help of zoologist and scientific administrator Frank R. Lillie) he received more sustained support from the National Research Council Committee for Research on Problems of Sex. Also with Lillie's help, he arranged for his students to collaborate with Carl R. Moore and his associates (including Mary Juhn, Lincoln V. Domm, Dorothy Price, and Winifred Hughes) in Chicago's Department of Zoology. The resulting series of papers appeared in the *American Journal of Physiology* (Dec. 1928) and the *American Journal of Anatomy* (Jan. 1930). Although Koch's own name appeared only as second author to Gallagher on one report, he was acknowledged in the text of the others as a valued mentor. This research became popularized by Paul de Kruif in *The Male Hormone* (1945).

Koch became acting chair of his department in 1919, was promoted to full professor in 1923, and became the chair of the Department of Biochemistry when it was organized in 1936. His efforts to expand the facilities and the work of the department were frustrated on occasion by competition from other departments and the indifference of key university administrators. Koch retired in 1941 as Frank P. Hixon Distinguished Service Professor Emeritus of Biochemistry. He then accepted the post of director of biochemical research at Armour and Company, where he remained for the rest of his life.

Koch represented the United States as a delegate to the League of Nations Conference on Standardization of Sex Hormones in 1935 and at the Pan-American Congress on Endocrinology in 1941. He served on the council and as secretary of the American Society of Biological Chemists and was a leading member of the Association for the Study of Internal Secretions, serving on its council, as its president in 1937 and 1938, and receiving its Squibb Award. Koch also held office, at various times, in the Chicago section of the American Chemical Society and the Institute of Medicine of Chicago. He was a member of the American Association for the Advancement of Science.

In addition to professional interests, Koch shared with his second wife a passion for symphonic music, cross-country automobile and trailer travel, and photography. He was conservative in his social and political views and orderly and punctual in his personal habits. Koch curtailed his activities somewhat after a heart attack in 1946 and died in Chicago two years later.

• Among Koch's more important papers are, with T. F. Gallagher, "Testicular Hormone," *Journal of Biological Chemistry* 84 (1929): 495–500, and a review essay, "The Male Sex Hormones," *Physiological Review* 17 (1937): 153–238. The outlines of Koch's career can be found in Thomas L. McMeekin, "Obituary. Fred Conrad Koch, 1876–1948," *Archives of Biochemistry* 17 (1948): 207–9; and Martin Hanke, "Fred Conrad Koch, 1876–1948," *Science* 107 (1948): 671–72. The significance of Koch's work is discussed in Robert E. Kohler, *From Medical Chemistry to Biochemistry: The Making of a Biomedical Discipline* (1982). The hormone work of his laboratory is treated in Adele E. Clarke, "Money, Sex, and Legitimacy at Chicago, circa 1892–1940: Lillie's Center of Reproductive Biology," *Perspectives on Science* 1 (1993): 367–415. Obituaries are in the *New York Times*, 27 Jan. 1948, and *Chemical Engineering News*, 9 Feb. 1948.

BONNIE ELLEN BLUSTEIN

KOCH, Frederick Henry (12 Sept. 1877–16 Aug. 1944), drama educator and author, was born in Covington, Kentucky, the son of August William Koch, a cashier for the Aetna Life Insurance Company, and Rebecca

Cornelia Julian. Following Frederick's birth the family returned to Peoria, Illinois, where Koch's grandfather operated a store. Frederick graduated from Peoria High School at age seventeen, went on to Caterals Methodist College in Cincinnati, and then earned his bachelor's degree in English from Ohio Wesleyan University in 1900. In March 1901 Koch entered a theater arts program at the Emerson School of Oratory in Boston, graduating in 1903. After he accepted a position in the Department of English at the University of North Dakota, Koch's career as an educator began to take shape.

Koch's first production at North Dakota, Sheridan's *The Rivals*, also toured the state, after which other well-known plays from Europe and America were performed. Achieving the rank of assistant professor in 1907, Koch took leave to attend Harvard, receiving his Master's degree in English, with a concentration in dramatic literature in 1909. At Harvard Koch was inspired by George Pierce Baker, who stimulated Koch's interest in creating drama of a uniquely American quality. Before returning to North Dakota, Koch toured North Africa, the Middle East, and Greece, studying art and architecture. In Athens Koch met Loretta Jean Hanigan; the two were married in Hanigan's home town of Denver in March 1910. They had four sons.

Returning to the University of North Dakota, Koch began encouraging a creative spirit similar to that of his Harvard mentor. The first of Koch's playwriting experiences produced two collaborative student dramas, *A Pageant of the North West* (1914) and *Shakespeare, the Playmaker* (1916). He next turned to the development of a drama distinctly born of the North Dakota landscape. In "Drama In The South" Koch would later write of these early Dakota experiments as: "Simple folk plays, near to the good, strong, windswept soil. . . . plays of the travail and the achievement of a pioneer people!" On 19 December 1916, the recently formed Sock and Buskin Society produced the first in a series of original plays based on the personal experiences of individual student authors, among them Maxwell Anderson. By the time the group presented their fifth series in December 1917, the name The Dakota Playmakers was taken to indicate an emphasis on the making rather than the interpretation of drama. The group continued to tour the state with their productions of student one-acts, often performing for audiences who had never before attended a play. When in Grand Forks, the group performed their pageants and folk dramas at the Bankside Theatre, an open-air theater situated along the curve of a stream that separated the performance space from the audience space while simultaneously enhancing acoustics.

Koch's success with playmaking at North Dakota, led to an invitation in 1918 by Dr. Edwin Greenlaw, then head of the Department of English, to bring his developing folk play enterprise to the University of North Carolina at Chapel Hill. Koch's initial impact on the university curriculum was the creation of English 31, Dramatic Composition: "A practical course in the writing of original plays," with the "Emphasis placed on the materials of tradition and folk-lore, and of present-day life" (Selden, p. 12). The course, followed shortly by the organization of the Carolina Playmakers, provided the initial bill of experimental one-act plays, performed on a temporary stage in the Chapel Hill High School. Presentations included *The Return of Buck Gavin* by Thomas Wolfe, who also played the title character, and performances were given at the school until 1925 when The Playmakers Theatre was dedicated. The playbill announced "Carolina Folk Plays," which, according to "Proff" Koch as he came to be known, was the first use in the American theater of the term "folk plays," defined by Koch in "Drama In The South" as "that form of drama which is earth-rooted in the life of our common humanity."

Later in 1919 the Playmakers first performed in the Forest Theatre in Chapel Hill, a natural amphitheater seating approximately one-thousand people. That same year Koch also established the Bureau of Community Drama within the University Extension Division, through which the Playmakers assisted in the organization and productions of drama groups throughout the state, which led to Koch's creation of The Carolina Dramatic Association in 1922–1923, a statewide organization governing the rapidly multiplying community groups. In 1920 the Playmakers gave their first tour of the state with a program that included *The Last of the Lowries* by Paul Green. The year 1922 saw the publication of the first series of *Carolina Folk Plays* with an introduction by Koch. He also continued cultivating the pageant drama form, and his own, *Raleigh, The Shepherd of the Ocean*, first produced in 1920, provided the direction for such successful outdoor dramas as those of Playmaker alumni Paul Green (*The Lost Colony*) and Kermit Hunter (*Unto These Hills*). Finally, in 1936 a new Department of Dramatic Art, headed by Koch, was established along with a full graduate program; however, Koch's chief interest remained his student authors and the development of American folk drama. Koch died while surf bathing at Miami Beach, Florida, where he was visiting family. His body was cremated and returned to Chapel Hill. On 22 May 1953 the University dedicated their open-air performance space The Koch Memorial Forest Theatre.

Through twenty-five years at the University of North Carolina, Koch encouraged students in the writing of over four hundred original one-act folk plays. While nearly universally acclaimed for his work in developing the beginnings of an American folk drama, Koch did have detractors, some of whom came from within the Playmaker family. Norris Houghton's account of the Playmaker's history in *Advance From Broadway* (1941), acknowledges Koch's "pervasive and indomitable" enthusiasm, but notes "a joyous disregard for any kind of standard" (pp. 265–66). Houghton furthers his position by quoting former Playmaker William Peery's 1939 essay "Carolina Playmaking." Peery maintains that, "recent student authors do not know at first hand, and they are not a part of, the life with which Playmaker plays most commonly deal. They will have to face problems typical of today or lose that creative power of native materials which largely accounts for the success of folk movements in the past" (p. 267).

Despite such criticism, Koch's reputation as a leader in the field of American folk drama obtains validity through the numerous young authors he fostered through the Carolina Playmakers, among them Paul Green, Josephina Niggli, Kermit Hunter, Loretto Carroll Bailey, and Thomas Wolfe, many of whom returned to take staff positions. This encouragement and the establishment of a people's theater, what Koch preferred to call folk theater, exist as a vital and genuine contribution to the development of a distinctly American dramaturgy.

• The University of North Carolina at Chapel Hill Library Manuscripts Department holds the collected papers of Professor Koch, as well as the records of the Department of Dramatic Art from 1922–1980, which may offer information regarding Koch's handling of departmental affairs. The most complete description of Koch's life and work remains Samuel Selden's *Frederick Henry Koch: Pioneer Playmaker* (1954). Walter Spearman, with the assistance of Selden, provides some new material in *The Carolina Playmakers: The First Fifty Years* (1970), though the second half of the book is devoted to the group's development after Koch's death. A Memorial Issue of *The Carolina Play-Book* (1944) edited by Archibald Henderson, again makes use of Selden's firsthand accounts but also offers the perspectives of other Playmakers, including Kai Heiberg-Jurgensen and Paul Green. One of Koch's major formal addresses, "Drama in the South," is reprinted in this volume, as well as a list of all Playmaker productions. Norris Houghton's *Advance From Broadway* contains brief information on Koch's activities, as does Arthur Hobson Quinn's *A History of The American Drama*, vol. 2 (1927). Nancy Pennington, "A people's theatre?: folk-playmaking at the University of North Carolina, Chapel Hill, 1918–1944" (M.A. thesis, Univ. of North Carolina, 1992), also examines the functioning of the Playmakers. Of those materials written by Koch, *Making a Regional Drama* (1932) and the numerous introductions he provided for the various series of *Carolina Folk-Plays* offer some insight into Koch's feeling for his students and the work they produced. An obituary is in the *New York Times*, 18 Aug. 1944.

MATTHEW D. BLISS

KOCH, Vivienne (1914–29 Nov. 1961), educator and literary critic, was born in New York City, the daughter of John D. Koch, a manufacturer, and Helen Karman. As children, Vivienne and her brother and sister were often cared for by their Hungarian immigrant grandparents and by a German nurse, so they grew up trilingual. Vivienne's early education was at public schools in New York City. She later attended Washington Square College, a division of New York University. Her initial interest as an undergraduate was in theater, but during her sophomore year she felt unsatisfied with the intellectual challenges it offered, and her interest switched to literature and philosophy. She

received her B.A. in 1932 and went on to Columbia University, where she received her M.A. with the completion of her thesis on Anton Chekhov in 1933.

Although Koch's first career preference was teaching, she was unable to find an academic job after completing graduate work. She chose instead to enter social work. For three years she was a field worker in Harlem, investigating applicants for government relief. In 1935 she married Norman MacLeod, a writer connected politically with the communist movement and poetically with the Imagists. They had no children and divorced in 1946.

In 1937 Koch began her teaching career at Mount Holyoke College, but she did not enjoy the all-female atmosphere and visited New York City frequently to escape what she called the "plethora of women." After her first year of teaching she returned to New York City and social work. She then spent two years in a supervisory position training field workers, but she became unhappy with "the inadequacies both of the 'philosophy' of case work . . . and the undemocratic political pressures" of the profession. Finally she left social work permanently, and after a year's hiatus as a housewife (which she points out was "the only year of my adult life in which I hadn't a paying 'job'"), she fully devoted herself to her career of teaching and writing (Kunitz, p. 531).

Koch cited 1944 as the start of her mature writing career, at which time she began the regular publication of articles and book reviews that continued throughout her career. At this time she also embarked on a varied teaching career, teaching English for two years at the Bread Loaf School of English and three years at Columbia University, appointments that sometimes overlapped with each other or with her appointment at New York University. She spent the majority of her teaching career at New York University's Division of General Studies (a division intended for adult education), where she taught until her death. Over her seventeen-year career, Koch taught a wide range of classes, including public speaking, great figures in American literature, the Bible and literature, and reading for pleasure. Her choice of courses indicates a concern with both the literary and the practical education of her students, spheres that seemed to Koch to be intimately connected. Koch's teaching career was of great importance to her, although she felt that, especially at the university level, teachers received insufficient pay for work that required a great deal of dedication.

Koch's main academic interest was literary modernism, especially James Joyce, W. B. Yeats, and William Carlos Williams. In 1949 she traveled to England on a Rockefeller Fellowship, doing research that would contribute to her second book. Her first major publication was a work of criticism, *William Carlos Williams* (1950), in which she gave a New Critical reading of Williams's entire body of work. The book received only lukewarm praise; critics lauded its scope but criticized its lack of original or illuminating analysis. In 1951 Koch published *W. B. Yeats: The Tragic Phase,* an analysis of the poems written between 1934 and 1939. Perhaps in response to criticism of her first book, in *The Tragic Phase* she more sharply focused her critical view, asserting that the poems constructed a "field of meaning" from "the paradox of sex" (sexual conduct) and that in his later years Yeats's sexual suffering was the primary motivation for his poetry. This book too received only moderate praise. Koch was complimented for her perceptive reading but criticized for expounding New Critical theory while being inconsistent in its application—she occasionally used biographical material rather than restricting her interpretation to the text itself. In the introduction she espoused a critical approach that dictated that "the best way to read a poem is as poetry, and not as a number of other things like 'philosophy,' 'history,' 'sociology,' 'ideas,' or anything else which poems are sometimes taken to be"; she admitted, however, the limited relevance of biography, a concession her critics perhaps ignored. In the introduction to *William Carlos Williams* she summed up her philosophy of literary criticism: "Criticism is not written as a signature for eternity, but as a discipline in extending the limits of that receptivity with which the reader approaches the work criticized." She also published widely in little magazines and academic journals.

In 1953 Koch was an instructor at the Salzburg Seminar of American Studies in Austria, an experience that inspired her only novel, *Change of Love* (1960). This book went unnoticed by critics. She was also a founding member of the James Joyce Society. She conducted a series of poetry readings (1953) through New York University in an attempt to establish a wider audience for her favored poets and to introduce poetry to an audience that might not otherwise have access to it. In 1955 Koch married John F. Day, a television industry executive. They had no children.

Although she published no other books, Koch continued to teach and publish book reviews and articles through 1961. She died in New York City. Koch's belief in the immediacy of poetry, and her broad approach to the reading and teaching of literature, set her firmly in the tradition of egalitarian education.

• Koch provided an autobiographical sketch for Stanley J. Kunitz, ed., *Twentieth Century Authors* (1955). A bibliography of works by and about her is in Marion Sader, ed., *Little Magazine Index*, vol. 4 (1976). An obituary is in the *New York Times*, 30 Nov. 1961.

AMY VONDRAK

KOCH, William Frederick (6 Apr. 1885–9 Dec. 1967), physician and discoverer and promoter of new medications alleged to cure cancer and other diseases, was born in Detroit, Michigan, the son of German immigrants Martin Koch and Christina Faulstich. Koch attended the University of Michigan, receiving an A.B. in premedical studies (1909), an M.A. (1910), and a Ph.D. in biochemistry (1916). He served from 1910 to 1913 as assistant in physiology and instructor in histology at the Michigan Medical School and from 1914 to

1919 as professor of physiology at the Detroit College of Medicine and Surgery (later part of Wayne State University), from which he received an M.D. in 1918. Koch married Luella Schmidt in 1916; the couple had four children.

In 1919 Koch announced that he had discovered a cure for cancer. He abandoned teaching to devote himself full time to research, development, distribution, and treating patients with his "synthetic antitoxins." Initially Koch claimed to extract his curative serums from the heart and brain of cows but soon asserted that he was preparing his medications chemically. He injected them singly or combined, giving them various names until in 1936 he settled on commercial names: Glyoxylide and Malonide, preferable for combating cancer and other degenerative diseases, and Benzoquinone, more effective for treating allergies, diabetes, and acute infections. In 1926 Koch Laboratories, Inc., and the Koch Cancer Foundation were established in Detroit. For his medicines, Koch secured an English patent in 1939, American patents in 1941 and 1945, and American trademarks in 1948.

The serums, Koch stated, did not directly kill disease-causing germs and viruses but instead revived the body's waning immune system so that it might combat invading microorganisms. With respect to cancer, during which the oxidation phase of carbohydrate metabolism had become inadequate, Koch claimed that Glyoxylide, acting as a catalyst, restored this deficiency by counteracting the poison that had diminished the normal oxidation power of cells. Koch posited also that what others saw as symptoms of worsening disease, like increased fever and pain, were really signals that his injected remedy was working. Further, adopting a key principle of homeopathy learned from the homeopathic medical department at Michigan, Koch asserted that his catalytic agents gained immensely in efficacy by reason of repeated dilution. The original "mother liquid" of Glyoxylide, as finally distributed in its two-cubic-centimeter ampules for injection, had been diluted with water by a factor of 10^{12}, that is, one part of the active ingredient to a trillion parts of water.

Trained extensively in bioscience, Koch could write and speak its vocabulary fluently. In a steady stream of pamphlets and books, including *The Prevention of Cancer* (1926), *Cancer and Its Allied Diseases* (1929), *Natural Immunity* (1936), *The Chemistry of Natural Immunity* (1938), and *The Survival Factor in Neoplastic and Viral Diseases* (1961), he explained, elaborated, and modified his doctrines. Koch persuaded some 3,000 practitioners to use his medicines and more thousands of patients to accept the message underlying his complex jargon, that his medications could cure all diseases in most people and that Glyoxylide could cure cancer in at least eight out of ten cases deemed hopeless by the regular medical profession. Koch's publications were filled with testimonials from users of his serums who rejoiced at having been cured and whose doctors backed up their claims. Included among these patients was one of Koch's sons, whose life was said to have been saved from polio. Koch's expositions of his theories, one critic wrote, were "among the best counterfeits of sound medical writing in the entire annals of pseudo-science" (Gardner, p. 213). Leaders of scientific medicine and government regulatory officials became persuaded that Koch was a shrewd and knowing charlatan.

Criticism of Koch's claims began in 1920 (and continued in 1924), when the Wayne County Medical Society in Detroit investigated Koch's own patients and found no case in which Glyoxylide alone had produced a cure or even a decided benefit. Trials of Koch's treatment at Yale University in the 1930s and by the Cancer Commission of the Province of Ontario, reported in 1943, failed to find evidence supporting Koch's claims. The American Medical Association repeatedly condemned Koch's "cure" for "awakening false hopes" when it was "not in any sense established as either scientific or reliable" (*Cancer "Cures" and "Treatments"*). In the late 1920s and early 1930s four federal agencies—the Food and Drug Administration, the Federal Trade Commission, the National Institutes of Health, and the Post Office Department—considered regulatory actions against Koch but decided his methods of distributing his unlabeled wares directly to physicians were not assailable under existing laws.

In 1938 both the FDA and the FTC secured new and stronger laws and took Koch to court. The FDA charged him with misbranding his medicines because none was an antitoxin and none would perform the cures claimed for it. In the longest trial in FDA history up to that time (12 Jan.–28 May 1943), the government sought to show by all possible tests that Koch's medications did not differ from distilled water. The Glyoxylide in dilution was so infinitesimal, a government attorney remarked, "that it would be like dumping a cocktail in the Detroit River and expecting to get a kick out of the water going over Niagara Falls" (*Time*, 20 Apr. 1942, p. 66). Medical experts testified to the medications' lack of value, while Koch's believing patients and practitioners presented their testimonials from the witness stand. The jury could not agree on a verdict. A second and longer trial (20 Feb.–23 July 1946) came to the same result. During deadlocked jury consideration, one member got too sick to continue. The defense opposed a government motion to continue deliberations with eleven jurors. In August 1948, seeing no sure resolution from a third trial with the same evidence, the government moved for an order of nolle prosequi, which was granted by the court.

The FTC fared better in modifying Koch's promotional claims. In 1942 the commission secured from a U.S. district court an injunction forbidding Koch and the Koch Laboratories, pending a hearing before the commission, from disseminating false advertising. After extensive hearings, the FTC strengthened its restraints by issuing a cease and desist order in September 1951 that forbade Koch to use any advertisement intended to induce purchasers to use his products. Koch petitioned for review of the order to the Court of Appeals for the Sixth Circuit, which in July 1953 confirmed the commission's ruling and ordered the distributors of Koch's medication to obey it.

Midway through the FTC's extended action, Koch, who was also aware that the FDA was developing new evidence in anticipation of a third trial, took steps to lessen his legal jeopardy. He had been badly shaken when, before the first trial, he had been arrested at his Florida seaside home and had spent a night in jail. In August 1948 Koch Laboratories, Inc., was dissolved and in November was replaced by a new creation, the Christian Medical Research League, as distributors of Koch's medications. The league, whose chief officers were conservative religious evangelists, sought to obey FTC taboos, organizing regional conventions of practitioners as a way of spreading the word and conferring with FDA officials to seek approval of a prescription mode of distributing the medications. The league also paid religious and political ultraconservatives Lawrence Reilly, publisher of the *Eleventh Hour*, and Gerald B. Winrod, publisher of *The Defender*, to publicize Koch's products. Both men also boosted Koch's message with broadcasts over a Mexican radio station. A *Defender* article was read on the floor of the Senate by Senator William Langer of North Dakota shortly after Langer and Koch met in 1948, and the doctor sent a crew of young women to Washington, D.C., to mail copies of the pertinent *Congressional Record* pages (7 June 1948) under Langer's frank to every physician in the country.

For several years the league's new modes of promotion boosted sales of Koch's medications beyond the levels the doctor had achieved. But in the 1950s controversy among league officials, charges of scandal, and the rise of competing quackeries, especially the clinic set up in Dallas by the layman Harry Hoxsey, led to a waning market for Koch's wares. Koch had no official role within the league, though he did influence its policies through correspondence with Winrod and received 15 percent of the league's gross income paid into a family trust fund. In December 1948, within a month after the league's incorporation, Koch had moved to Brazil, which he had visited seven years earlier, becoming acquainted with important governmental officials. His wife had died in 1937, and Koch married a Hungarian woman, Yutta, the widow of a Brazilian physician. In a laboratory near Rio, Koch conducted research in cooperation with the Brazilian agriculture and health ministries, administering his medications to both people and cattle. He continued defending in print his theories of the universal efficacy of Glyoxylide, now renamed SSR (Synthetic Survival Reagent), although Brazilian medical authorities became increasingly skeptical of his claims. Koch never abandoned interest in use of his medicines in the United States. Four years before his death in Rio de Janeiro, he wrote the FDA protesting the use of his Glyoxylide by a Texas chiropractor.

• The extensive administrative files and case jackets in the Food and Drug Administration Records in the National Archives provide full manuscript coverage of Koch's activities, especially from the late 1920s onward. The *Journal of the American Medical Association* kept up a running critique of Koch and his medications, a summary of which appeared in the AMA pamphlet, *Cancer "Cures" and "Treatments"* (1927). Koch's work is discussed favorably in Albert L. Wahl, *The Birth of a Science* (1949); Gerald B. Winrod, *The New Science in the Treatment of Disease* (1971); and Frederick L. Compton, *Extensive Index Covering Dr. William Frederick Koch's Medical System* (1986). Criticisms of Koch appear in Martin Gardner, *Fads and Fallacies in the Name of Science* (1957); Wallace F. Janssen, "Cancer Quackery: Past and Present," *FDA Consumer* (July–Aug. 1977); and an unpublished paper in the author's possession by Richard E. McFadyen, "Cancer Quackery, Medical Freedom of Choice, and the Radical Right: The William Koch Case" (1978).

JAMES HARVEY YOUNG

KOCHER, A. Lawrence (24 July 1885–6 June 1969), architect, editor, and scholar of American colonial architecture, was born Alfred Lawrence Kocher in San Jose, California, the son of Rudolph Kocher, a Swiss-born jeweler and watchmaker, and Anna (maiden name unknown). He received his B.A. from Stanford University in 1909 and his M.A. from Pennsylvania State University in 1916. He studied architecture at the Massachusetts Institute of Technology from 1909 to 1912. In 1910 he married Amy Agnes Morder. She died of cancer prior to 1932, the year of his marriage to Margaret Taylor. He had two children.

Kocher's professional life was rich and varied. He began his career as an instructor in architectural history and design at Penn State in 1912. In 1918 he was promoted to full professor and served as head of the Department of Architecture until 1926. A licensed architect, he designed the University Club at Penn State and the Joseph Priestley Memorial Museum in Northumberland, Pennsylvania.

Kocher left Penn State in the fall of 1926 to become head of the School of Art and Architecture at the University of Virginia. While in Virginia, he pursued his interest in design as architect of Christ Church Parish House in Charlottesville, as well as fraternity houses, schoolhouses, and private residences. During this period he also made measured drawings of the colonial buildings in the United States, publishing an important series of articles on the American country house in *Architectural Record*: "The American Country House" (59 [Nov. 1925]: 401–512), "The Country House: Are We Developing an American Style" (60 [Nov. 1926]: 385–502), and "The Country House: An Analysis of the Architect's Method of Approach" (62 [Nov. 1927]: 337–45, 446–48).

In 1926 Kocher turned his attention to architectural journalism, serving first as contributing editor and in the summer of 1928 as associate editor of *Architectural Record*. By 1928 he had left the University of Virginia, taking on greater responsibility as managing editor and then editor of the journal, where he remained until 1938. Owing to his wide-ranging interests and progressive editorship, Kocher successfully revitalized what was then considered to be this country's leading professional journal. To *Architectural Record* he attracted such important contributors as Henry-Russell Hitchcock and Douglas Haskell. Kocher cast the journal into a vehicle for introducing American readers to the modern movement in Europe and America while serving as a forum on modernist discourse. During the late 1920s Hitchcock published a groundbreaking article on the "new pioneers" (Oud, Le Corbusier, and Gropius), and Frank Lloyd Wright published another of his episodic series of articles, "In the Cause of Architecture." With the contributions of the Danish-born architect Knud Lonberg-Holm and others, Kocher published a number of articles on technical developments that helped to inform modernist practitioners. *Architectural Record* also published important surveys of historical buildings in the United States. Through his initiatives Kocher assisted many European modernists to acquire a following in America. In 1929, for example, Kocher published Le Corbusier's first article in an American publication and provided the title: "Architecture as an Expression of Materials and Methods of Our Times." Also largely through Kocher's efforts, Le Corbusier was able to obtain sponsorship in 1935 for his first American lecture tour.

Aside from his seminal role as editor, Kocher also advanced the cause of modernism in the United States as a practicing architect. In 1929 he entered into partnership with Gerhard Ziegler. Their most significant work was a project for a skyscraper apartment house called Sunlight Towers (published in versions for the city and the country) that reflected the ideals of European modernism and, more specifically, Le Corbusier's visionary schemes of the early 1920s. Suggesting new systems of construction, Kocher and Ziegler raised their apartment tower on a platform to separate it from traffic and stores, while providing for recreation areas. Corner casement windows, horizontal bands of windows ("sun chambers" on the roof), and porches for gardens combined the amenities of the favored low-rise garden apartment with the advantages of better light and air offered by the tower. However, both public and private sectors were unresponsive to the Sunlight Towers project. Housing specialist Henry Wright opposed Sunlight Towers because it would have required a change in private land ownership and unprecedented integrations of housing and transportation infrastructures. The project was never built. Kocher and Ziegler also designed a modernist house in concrete for the popular novelist Rex Stout in Fairfield County, Connecticut (1933).

From 1930 to 1935 Kocher worked in partnership with the Swiss émigré architect Albert Frey, who had been a member of Le Corbusier's Paris atelier. Together Kocher and Frey cast themselves as Le Corbusier's followers in the United States. For the annual exhibition of the Architectural League of New York in 1931, they constructed a prototypical house intended for mass production, later known as the Aluminaire, "A House for Contemporary Life" (located on the Wallace Harrison estate, Syosset, N.Y., until 1986; now located at the New York Institute of

Technology, Central Islip, N.Y.). This metal and glass house was one of the few examples of American architecture included in the landmark "Modern Architecture: International Exhibition," better known as the International Style exhibition, held at the Museum of Modern Art in 1932. In their subsequent book *The International Style*, Henry-Russell Hitchcock and Philip Johnson called it "an experimental house with a skeleton of aluminum and with walls thinner than are permitted by urban building laws." They also designed the Ralph-Barbarin House, near Stamford, Connecticut (1932), and the "Kocher Canvas Weekend House," Northport, Long Island, New York (1934, demolished). In 1938 Kocher renewed his collaboration with Frey to design a project for the Swiss pavilion at the 1939 New York World's Fair (the commission was given to William Lescaze instead). On his own Kocher designed a modernist "House of Plywood," which was constructed at the World's Fair.

Kocher served as a visiting professor at the Carnegie Institute of Technology from 1938 until 1940, when he left to take on what the historian Lawrence Wodehouse has called "an innovative educational experiment" at Black Mountain College in North Carolina. There he was responsible for the campus design, serving as a professor of architecture from 1940 to 1943. In 1944 he joined both the Colonial Williamsburg Foundation, where he served as architectural records editor until 1954, and the College of William and Mary in Williamsburg, where he held the post of lecturer in fine arts until 1959. As early as 1928 Kocher was appointed to the first Advisory Committee of Architects at Colonial Williamsburg, where he helped to establish policy governing its restoration work. He was the author of numerous reports on colonial Williamsburg buildings as well as a glossary of eighteenth-century architectural terms. He also served as chairman of the Committee on Preservation of Historic Monuments and Natural Resources of the American Institute of Architects. He died in Williamsburg. As both modernist and preservationist, Kocher maintained a paradoxical position within the historiography of the modern movement in America.

• The principal archive of information on Kocher is the A. Lawrence Kocher Collection at the Colonial Williamsburg Foundation in Williamsburg, Va. Kocher is the coauthor with Howard Dearstyne of *Colonial Williamsburg: Its Buildings and Gardens 1850–1900* (1949) and *Shadows in Silver: A Record of Virginia* (1954). Kocher's most significant articles, all in *Architectural Record*, include "Early Architecture of Pennsylvania," 48 (1920–1922); "The Library of the Architect," 56, pt. 1 (Aug. 1924): 123–28, pt. 2 (Sept. 1924): 218–24, pt. 3 (Oct. 1924): 316–20, pt. 4 (Dec. 1924): 517–20; 57, pt. 5 (Jan. 1925): 29–32, pt. 6 (Feb. 1925): 125–28, and pt. 7 (Mar. 1925): 221–24ff. Kocher also published numerous articles in *Architectural Record* with Albert Frey, among them "Real Estate Subdivisions for Low-Cost Housing," 69 (Apr. 1931): 323–27; "New Materials and Improved Construction Methods," 73 (Apr. 1933): 281–93; and "Subsistence Farmsteads," 75 (Apr. 1934): 349–56. For bibliographies of both Kocher's extensive collection of books and his writings as well as a biographical essay on Kocher by Lawrence Wode-

house, see Cynthia Zignego Stiverson, *Architecture and the Decorative Arts: The A. Lawrence Kocher Collection of Books at the Colonial Williamsburg Foundation* (1989). See also Wodehouse, "Kocher at Black Mountain," *Journal of the Society of Architectural Historians* 41 (Dec. 1982): 328–32. On the work of Kocher and Gerhard Ziegler, see "Sunlight Towers," *Architectural Record* 65 (Mar. 1929): 307–10; "Sunlight Towers," *Architectural Record* 67 (Mar. 1930): 286–88; and Kocher and Ziegler, "House of Rex Stout, Fairfield County, Connecticut," *Architectural Record* 74 (July 1933): 45–51. On the work of Kocher and Frey, see Frey, *In Search of a Living Architecture* (1939); Joseph Rosa, *Albert Frey, Architect* (1990); Douglas Haskell, "The Architectural League and the Rejected Architects," *Parnassus* 3 (May 1931): 12–13; Kocher and Frey, "Aluminaire: A House for Contemporary Life," *Shelter* 2 (May 1932): 54–56; *Modern Architecture: International Exhibition* (1932); and Henry-Russell Hitchcock, Jr., and Philip Johnson, *International Style: Architecture since 1922* (1932). An obituary is in the *New York Times*, 8 June 1969.

MARDGES BACON

KOCHERTHAL, Josua von (1669–27 Dec. 1719), Lutheran clergyman, was born Josua Harrsch in Fachsenfeld, near Aalen, Württemberg, sixty kilometers east of Stuttgart in the Kocher Valley—hence his later pseudonymn. His mother was Katharina Adelmann, and his father was Hans Jörg Harrsch, a schoolmaster at Neubronn, whose three successive wives had twenty-three children. Despite the expenses so many siblings entailed, Kocherthal enjoyed a superior education. He began his Gymnasium studies at Schwäbisch Hall in 1676 and matriculated at the university at Jena in 1695. His doctoral dissertation was published after he took his degree in 1696 at Tübingen; in the work, he examined and answered controversial questions regarding the true nature of the Lutheran pastoral ministry. Kocherthal, probably in 1696, married Sibylla Charlotta Winchenbach, with whom he had four children. He served from 1696 to 1708 as Evangelical (Lutheran) pastor in Eschelbronn, a village that lies in the Kraichgau, the area southeast of Heidelberg. Kocherthal succeeded Anthony Jacob Henckel as pastor in Eschelbronn. Henckel later emigrated to Pennsylvania and served as pastor in Germantown. It is for his role in leading a small, initial 1708 migration of some forty-one persons to New York; for leading a second, even greater migration to that colony; and for writing to encourage migration to North America that Kocherthal is known to history under his adopted name.

Migration in and out of the southwest territories of the old Holy Roman Empire was no novelty, and the migrations to North America are best seen within this broader tradition of movements within Europe. Yet the French Wars that devastated the economy of this region beginning in the 1690s probably motivated Kocherthal's first trip to London in 1704 to investigate what chances for economic advancement might lie within the colonial world of Great Britain. The pietist Francke Foundations at Halle had already established connections at the Court of St. James at the German Lutheran Royal Chapel established in the late 1690s by Prince George of Denmark, consort to Princess Anne. The reputations of other German speakers interested in North America—especially the mystic Johann Kelpius and the Erfurt pietist Daniel Falckner, who had joined Kelpius at Wissahickon, Pennsylvania, and in 1698 published an account of North America for Halle—would have been known to Kocherthal during his conversations in London.

Almost simultaneous with Kocherthal's interest in America, the Bernese promoter of emigration schemes Franz Ludwig Michel traveled to Virginia in 1701–1702 and began laying plans for a mining venture in Carolina. Many residents of the Kraichgau had come from Switzerland and still maintained family and business ties there. Thus, the Bernese venture was also the topic of conversation and interest in the region where Kocherthal was pastor.

Kocherthal identified Carolina as a promising destination for emigrants in his famous pamphlet published in 1706, *Außführlich und Umständlicher Bericht von der Berühmten Landschafft Carolina in dem Engelländischen America Gelegen* (Comprehensive and circumstantial report of the famous province Carolina located in English America). By 1709 the work already enjoyed a fourth edition. Kocherthal's recruiting efforts for emigrants initially garnered fifty-three followers. Traveling in February 1708 to Frankfurt, he managed to find passage for these first persons, who arrived in London in April with him and his wife, both identified as thirty-nine years of age by English authorities. The Halle pietists supported these arrivals at first but became alarmed that British authorities, with whom they worked closely through the Society for the Promoting of Christian Knowledge, might take offense at German speakers among the clergy who promoted emigration to Carolina without British permission. They had good grounds for anxiety.

By October 1708 Kocherthal had taken forty-one members of this first, small group to the colony of New York and settled fifteen families at Newburgh. By May 1709 he was back in London, where he found that in the previous month 800 "Palatines" had arrived in London, the vanguard of what eventually developed into a mass exodus of somewhere between 10,000 and 13,000 persons who flooded the city of 600,000 between the summer of 1709 and early 1710. These Palatines were actually German speakers from various parts of the German Southwest. Playing on British outrage at the destruction of German Reformed centers, such as Heidelberg, in the French Wars of the 1690s, Kocherthal had claimed to be leading victims of French brutality at Landau in the Electoral Palatinate. Given the ignorance among the British of exact geographic knowledge of the splintered, confusing map of the German Southwest in the early eighteenth century, German speakers did not find it hard to continue to exploit sympathy for the "distressed Palatines." In fact, neither Kocherthal nor most of the emigrants came from Landau or, strictly speaking, from the Palatinate proper, as can be proved from the church

record Kocherthal kept in New York noting the origins of his congregants.

To counter Kocherthal's pamphlet and to discourage prospective emigrants from contemplating a journey to the New World, the Halle fathers ordered their lay preacher in London, Anton Wilhelm Böhme, to refute Kocherthal's work. Böhme's denunciatory *Das verlangte, nicht erlangte Canaan . . .* (The desired, not attained, Canaan; 1709) failed, however, to dampen enthusiasm. While British public opinion turned against the deluge of immigrants camped in London, other English agents and promoters in Frankfurt and elsewhere in the German states continued to circulate Kocherthal's writing and other fulsome descriptions of the New World. Bound together with a title page in golden lettering, the writings became known as the "little golden book" of fantastic promises about life across the Atlantic. Kocherthal returned to New York in the summer of 1710 as a much larger Palatine group of 2,344 arrived in the colony in a scheme whereby they were to produce tar and pitch on the estate of Robert Livingston (1654–1728). Kocherthal settled across the river from Quassaic (now Newburgh) at Newton, ministering to German-speaking Protestants at East Camp, Newburgh, and to those Palatines who fled enforced labor on Livingston's manor for settlements on the Schoharie and Mohawk rivers.

After the death of his wife in 1713, Kocherthal spent the last six years of his life in declining health. He died at West Camp. The German Reformed among the settlers failed to obtain pastors for themselves, and German Lutherans only in 1725 secured Wilhelm Christoph Berkenmeyer through the Lutheran Consistory at Hamburg's London connection. Berkenmeyer married Benigna Sybilla Kocherthal, Kocherthal's eldest daughter, who with her siblings erected a headstone for their father that was later misread to indicate his birthplace as "Bretten," a town under the lordship of the archbishopric of Speyer, further obscuring the origins of this clever Swabian pastor's manipulation of British sympathy for the "poor distressed Palatines." He had, perhaps unwittingly, helped set in motion what became the largest voluntary non–English-speaking eighteenth-century migration to British North America.

• Older accounts of Kocherthal should be disregarded in favor of Heinz Schuchmann, "Der Eschelbronner Pfarrer Josua 'Kocherthal' und die pfälzische Massenauswanderung nach Nordamerika 1708/09," in *Kraichgau: Heimatforschung im Landkreis Sinsheim unter Berücksichtigung seiner unmittelbaren Nachbargebiete*, ed. Adam Schlitt (1968; repr. 1970); Frederick S. Weiser, trans., "Notes on the Origins of Joshua Kocherthal," *Concordia Historical Institute Quarterly* 41 (1968): 147–53; Arno Sames, *Anton Wilhelm Böhme 1673–1722: Studien zum ökumenischen Denken und Handeln eines halleschen Pietisten* (1990); Walter Allen Knittle, *Early Eighteenth Century Palatine Emigration* (1937; repr. 1970); Harry J. Kreider, *Lutheranism in Colonial New York* (1942); Lawrence J. Leder, *Robert Livingston, 1654–1728, and the Politics of Colonial New York* (1961); A. G. Roeber, *Palatines, Liberty, and Property: German Lutherans in Colonial British America*

(1993); and Lowell Colton Bennion, "Flight from the Reich: A Geographic Exposition of Southwest German Emigration, 1683–1815" (Ph.D. diss., Syracuse Univ., 1971).

A. G. ROEBER

KOEHLER, Robert (28 Nov. 1850–23 Apr. 1917), painter and art educator, was born in Hamburg, Germany, the son of Theodor Alexander Ernst Koehler, a machinist, and Louise Carolina Christiane Bueter, a fine needlework instructor. In 1854 the family moved to the United States. They stayed briefly in New York City before moving to Milwaukee, Wisconsin, where they joined family and where Robert's parents continued working at their respective professions. It was in this German-American community that Koehler's ties to Germany were reinforced.

Koehler attended the German and English Academy, where classes conducted in German as well as English ensured his early command of his native tongue. After graduating in 1865, Koehler continued lessons with his school's drawing master, who had trained at the highly respected Royal Academy of Fine Arts in Munich. That same year he apprenticed in commercial printing at the Milwaukee firm of Seiffert and Lawton; it was not long, however, before his interest in drawing superseded his interest in commercial printing and he turned to lithography. With a lithographic career in mind, he worked toward a new objective: European study. In preparation he took additional private lessons from Heinrich Roese, a portrait painter. Both artists encouraged further study in Europe; however, without the financial backing he needed, Koehler realized his ambitions would have to be supported by his printing skills. Thus, in 1871 he moved to Pittsburgh, Pennsylvania, to work as a lithographer. Suffering unspecified eye trouble and fearing blindness, he went to New York for eye surgery and remained there, finding work at the Arthur Brown printing company. From 1871 to 1873 he attended the National Academy of Design at night. In the autumn of 1873 he left for Munich.

In October 1873 Koehler was admitted to the Royal Academy of Fine Arts. He studied with Professors Carl von Piloty, an acclaimed artist-teacher, and Ludwig Thiersch and became socially involved with them as well, attending their Sunday teas, where he met an interesting array of academics and professionals. Years later Koehler wrote in the *Minneapolis Society of Fine Arts Bulletin* (2, no. 1 [Jan. 1907]: 7) that living economically did "not mean to frequent the very cheapest restaurants, wear your clothes to shred and shun good company."

Koehler returned to the United States after two years in Munich owing to the depletion of his funds. Back in New York, he enrolled at the newly organized Art Students' League and returned to the National Academy of Design, exhibiting there from 1878 until 1893. He met George Ehret, a German immigrant and prosperous brewery owner who became a patron and, learning of Koehler's desire to pursue his studies in Germany, contributed the necessary capital.

Back in Munich in 1879, Koehler reenrolled at the Royal Academy, studying with Ludwig von Loefftz, a genre and landscape painter, and Franz von Defregger, a genre and history painter. He also participated in the artistic life of the city by joining the Munich Artists' Association, the Etchers' Society, and the American Artists' Club, of which he was four times president. There he made lifelong friendships with William Merritt Chase and Frank Duveneck. He also enjoyed his first success as a portrait painter.

By the mid-1880s Koehler was organizing major exhibitions as well as teaching. Asked to coordinate the American section of the international exhibitions held in Munich in 1883 and 1888, he returned to New York on both occasions to solicit entries from established artists. In 1887, unable to remain in the United States long enough to complete preparations, he delegated the work to a committee. When their efforts foundered, he reoriented the presentation to one he could supervise: American artists studying in Europe. For his efforts Koehler was awarded the Cross of the Order of St. Michael by the prince regent of Bavaria. Koehler also directed a private art school beginning in 1885; by 1888 he had established his own academy.

In 1889 he was awarded an honorable mention at the Exposition universelle in Paris for *The Strike*. Painted in 1886, it was exhibited at the National Academy of Design that same year. This six-by-nine-foot painting, his most famous, recalls an 1877 railroad workers' strike in Pittsburgh. It is thought to be the first artistic representation of such a subject and was especially noteworthy for its sympathetic viewpoint.

By December 1892 Koehler was back in New York City. He reestablished himself as a portraitist, finding space at the Van Dyke Studios. Shortly thereafter Douglas Volk, director of the Minneapolis School of Fine Arts, persuaded Koehler to succeed him. Although he continued to paint throughout his directorship, Koehler focused on art education and appreciation, not only for the school but for the community at large. He founded the Art League, an assemblage of artists, academics, and professionals, which organized exhibitions and held fortnightly discussions on art. He lectured and wrote articles. He contributed heavily to the *Minneapolis Society of Fine Arts Bulletin*, founded in 1905. In 1895 he married Marie Franziska Fischer in New York; they had one son.

By now the Minneapolis School of Fine Arts was financially viable and gaining in reputation. Attendance was up. For some years a scholarship was awarded by Koehler's friend William Merritt Chase (presumably for further study at the Chase School of Art) to the best student. In 1898 Koehler, still serving as director, became the financial administrator as well. In 1899 he added the Department of Decorative Design, thereby offering classes in various handicrafts and simultaneously realizing the original goals of the directors of the Minneapolis Society of Fine Arts (the school's parent organization) to include the "industrial" with the "fine" arts courses. In the summer of 1909 he again expanded the school's curriculum to include the Normal Department for the training of school art teachers.

Koehler believed wholeheartedly in the educational value of exhibitions. In 1900 he organized the society's first annual exhibition of American artists, selecting established names and a range of styles. For seven years he directed the Minnesota State Arts Society/ Council, founded in 1903 to promote the arts both in the schools and in manufacturers' designs.

Koehler retired from the directorship of the Minneapolis School of Fine Arts in 1914. That same year he was honored by the Art League as the first recipient of their $200 honor fund, which he used that summer to visit East Coast art centers and to paint with Frank Duveneck in Gloucester, Massachusetts. He became a docent in 1915 at the Minneapolis Institute of Arts, the Society of Fine Arts' newly opened museum. In 1916 he was appointed a lecturer at the University of Minnesota. He died in Minneapolis.

Because his energies were directed more to the cause than the execution of art, Koehler is recognized primarily as an art educator and arbiter of taste. The Minneapolis College of Art and Design, the Minneapolis Institute of Arts, and the Minnesota State Art Board are manifestations of his early efforts to establish local institutions of national reputation and significance.

• The Minneapolis Public Library, the Minneapolis College of Art and Design, and the Minnesota Historical Society all maintain archives of varying depth and import on Koehler. The most extensive is in the Minneapolis Collection of the Minneapolis Public Library. Of note in the Research Center at the Minnesota Historical Society are the *History of the Koehler Family* and some correspondence that deals primarily with *The Strike*. A lucid and interesting essay that gives context to Koehler's Minnesota years is Thomas O'Sullivan, "Robert Koehler and Painting in Minnesota, 1890–1915," in the exhibition catalog *Minnesota 1900: Art and Life on the Upper Mississippi, 1890–1915*, ed. Michael Conforti (1994). Peter C. Merrill, "Robert Koehler, German-American Artist in Minneapolis," *Hennepin County History* 47, no. 3 (Summer 1988): 20–27, focuses entirely on Koehler, giving his family background as well as the details of his career. An obituary is in the *Minneapolis Journal*, 24 Apr. 1917.

COLLES BAXTER LARKIN

KOENIGSBERG, Moses (16 Apr. 1878–21 Sept. 1945), journalist, was born in New Orleans, Louisiana, the son of Harris Wolf Koenigsberg, a tailor and businessman, and Julia Foreman. Both parents were Jewish immigrants from Poland. Precocious and big for a child, Koenigsberg moved swiftly into the adult world. At age twelve he was unjustly accused of plagiarism and punished, causing him to leave school. Afterward he briefly attached himself to a revolutionary army in Mexico, clerked in a law firm, and became a reporter on the *San Antonio (Tex.) Times*—at the age, he claimed, of thirteen. After exposing a corrupt fee system among prosecuting attorneys he was indicted for criminal libel and left town. The charge was eventually dropped.

For the next twelve years Koenigsberg was a nomad, working at various newspapers in the Southwest and Midwest and moving on, his size and self-confidence serving as an entrée in the rough journalistic world of that time and region. He worked briefly in Houston and New Orleans before returning to San Antonio, where before the age of fifteen he became the publisher of the *Evening Star*, only to quit when he discovered that the owner was blackmailing businessmen. He went to work for the *Forth Worth (Tex.) Mail*, unsuccessfully attempted to capture a gang of train robbers, then peddled the story of his stunt to several newspapers—his first step in the syndication business. He moved on to big-city journalism via brief stops in Kansas City, St. Louis, Chicago, Pittsburgh, and New York. Eventually he drifted back to St. Louis and was based there for five years.

At the start of the Spanish-American War in 1898, Koenigsberg sought to reach the insurgents in Cuba but got only as far as Florida. There he enlisted as a private in an Alabama regiment, with correspondent's credentials from the *Mobile Register*. After his division was devastated by illness, he wrote an exposé-history, titled *Southern Martyrs* (1898). It was published over stiff opposition from the army.

After the war Koenigsberg alighted in Chicago, where he made his first contact with the organization of America's leading journalistic impresario, William Randolph Hearst, and was hired by Hearst's *Chicago American* in 1901. That job did not last long, but after a muckraking sojourn in Minneapolis he returned to Chicago and became city editor of Hearst's *Evening American*. There Koenigsberg presided over a strenuously sensational newsroom known in that era as the "Madison Street madhouse." He supervised coverage of the fire at the Iroquois Theatre, in which six hundred people died.

Soon mired in office politics at the *Evening American*, Koenigsberg was relieved to receive a summons from Hearst in 1907 to come to New York, where he signed a "personal service contract," a legal device designed to stop defections. He was then shipped on to a thankless post as business manager at the feeble *Boston American*. Two years later he was permitted to return to work at headquarters in New York. By his own account, he alienated all of Hearst's major lieutenants, and fell into corporate limbo. For several years he served as a newspaper scout for Hearst, assessing properties and often running them for a time after they were bought.

In 1913 Koenigsberg tried to set out on his own. Backed by a Cuban publisher, he organized an independent feature syndicate. But the Hearst organization persuaded a state court that Koenigsberg was still bound by his contract. To mollify him Hearst set him up in a separately incorporated syndicate, the Newspaper Feature Service. Recruiting such stars as Richard Outcault, who had created the important comic strip "The Yellow Kid," Koenigsberg was soon distributing to a weekday circulation of 18 million.

From this point Koenigsberg's responsibilities proliferated. His most important step was the incorporation in 1915 of King Features Syndicate as a Hearst subsidiary. The name was not "a claim to sovereignty" but from a translation of his name. King Features soon rose to the top of its field on the strength of articles by celebrities and regular features such as the comic strip "Bringing up Father."

At the end of World War I Koenigsberg was handed Hearst's International News Service (INS), which had discredited itself with stolen, fake, and pro-German stories. Koenigsberg gradually restored the INS to respectability and profitability, meanwhile carrying on a prolonged dispute with the rival Associated Press over the latter's effort to establish exclusive property rights in news. In 1927 Koenigsberg, representing the INS at a conference sponsored by the League of Nations, won his point in a resolution that stated: "No one may acquire the right of suppressing news of public interest" (Hudson, p. 388). This principle was eventually affirmed, in a different context, in a Supreme Court decision in 1945 (*Associated Press v. U.S.*).

In 1923 Koenigsberg married Vivian Carter; they had one daughter. By 1928 Koenigsberg appeared to have settled into a lifetime career with Hearst. The King Features Syndicate had prospered; more than two thousand newspapers used its features and it had a gross income in 1927 of more than $6 million a year. But again Hearst proved to be a difficult boss. After the League of Nations conference Koenigsberg accepted an award from the French government, only to have Hearst denounce such decorations in a public letter. In February 1928, when he received the decoration, Koenigsberg resigned from the Hearst organization. (He returned the decoration in 1933 when the French defaulted on a war debt payment.)

Now on his own, Koenigsberg engaged in a string of enterprises. He sought to organize a chain of newspapers and tried to buy the *Denver Post*—a plan ruined by the stock market crash of 1929. He aided in the creation of a new Sunday magazine for the *Philadelphia Inquirer* and other new publications. He died in New York City.

Koenigsberg was an energetic entrepreneur with sometimes surprising devotion to journalistic principle who had the misfortune of devoting most of his career to an unprincipled organization. He is remembered chiefly in the continued existence of the King Features Syndicate, but his more important legacy was the groundwork he laid for ending monopolistic practices in news distribution.

• The chief source of information concerning Koenigsberg is his autobiography *King News* (1941). Supplementary information is in W. A. Swanberg, *Citizen Hearst* (1961), and in *Editor & Publisher*, 25 Feb. 1928, p. 5. On the syndicate business, see Alfred McClung Lee, *The Daily Newspaper in America* (1937), and Silas Bent, *Ballyhoo* (1927). On the controversy about ownership of news, see Kent Cooper, *Barriers Down* (1942); Manley O. Hudson, "International Protection of Property in News," *American Journal of International Law* 20 (Apr. 1928): 385–89; and *Editor & Publisher*, 13 and 27 Aug. and 3 and 10 Sept. 1927. Obituaries are in the *New York Times*, 22 Sept. 1945; the *New York Journal-American*, 21 Sept. 1945; and *Editor & Publisher*, 29 Sept. 1945.

JAMES BOYLAN

KOENIGSWARTER, Pannonica de (10 Dec. 1913–30 Nov. 1988), patron of jazz musicians, was born Kathleen Annie Pannonica Rothschild in London, England, the daughter of Nathaniel Charles Rothschild, an English banker and son of the first Lord Rothschild, and Rozsika Wertheimstein, a Hungarian sportswoman. Kathleen Rothschild experienced an affluent, overly protected, isolated, and heavily regimented childhood. She was sent to a finishing school in Paris at age sixteen, by which time she was becoming enamored of American jazz, a taste acquired via her brother, a pianist who collected jazz recordings and was acquainted with jazz musician Teddy Wilson.

After traveling through Germany, Austria, and Italy, Pannonica received a coming-out ball in London and was presented to the king and queen of England. Her life revolved around parties, automobiles, and, from age twenty-one, airplanes. Shortly after learning to fly, she met French baron and mining engineer Jules de Koenigswarter, also a flyer. When he proposed marriage and she hesitated, coming to the United States instead, he followed. Married in 1935, she entered into a relationship that would prove to be as stifling as her upbringing. Her resulting disdain for order, propriety, and schedules would later make her perfectly suited to the jazz life.

The Koenigswarters resided in Paris and from late 1938 in a château near Dreux. When Jules became involved in the war as a colonel d'artillerie in the French army in 1939, the baroness took over management of the household and brought their two children and her stepson first to London and then to a family on Long Island. Leaving them behind for six years, she joined the antifascist France Forever organization and followed her husband to French Equatorial Africa, where she broadcast into Vichy African territories and worked on decoding and translating. She drove for the War Graves Commission and participated in the fights for Italy and Germany, becoming a private second class in the Free French Army, her work as a driver taking her into combat zones. With the war's end and the reunion with her family, her life became tedious again. Her husband, now a celebrated colonel, chose to become a diplomat. Residing in Norway (1946–1949) and then in Mexico City, they had two more children.

In the early 1950s Pannonica de Koenigswarter increasingly spent time in the company of jazz musicians in New York City. Already acquainted with Wilson, she met Lionel Hampton, Art Blakey (who credited her with teaching him how to behave as a bandleader), and Thelonious Monk, who would become her closest friend. By 1953 she was settled in New York and separated from her husband. She became known as a passionate and discerning fan of modern jazz and a friend of its finest African-American practitioners, who could count on her for monetary assistance and a place to sleep if needed. From time to time her contributions became more specifically focused, as in 1954, when she managed Blakey's newly formed Jazz Messengers.

For all her good works, Koenigswarter won a degree of notoriety after the greatest bop musician, Charlie Parker, died in her apartment at the Hotel Stanhope in March 1955. By her own account, he was seriously ill when he arrived on 9 March, but he refused to go to the hospital. He died three days later, but she did not report the death for nearly another three days in an effort to notify his wife first. The resulting sensationalized publicity hastened her divorce, formalized a year later when the baron remarried.

Also in 1956 Monk, his wife Nellie, and their two children stayed with the baroness at her new apartment in the Hotel Bolivar after their apartment was destroyed by fire. Her most important achievement came in 1957, when her assistance in collecting character references for Monk led to his reacquiring a New York City cabaret card, without which (in an onerous and happily now-defunct tradition) an "undesirable" musician could not work in the city. His resulting engagement at the Five Spot revitalized his career and, in a not insignificant way, jazz.

The baroness moved to Weehawken, New Jersey, in January 1958 after tiring of the controversies involved in having jazz musicians disembark from her Bentley to enter a fancy New York hotel apartment. She kept the car and over the years eventually acquired as many as seventy cats, who contributed to the chaos at home. By October 1958 Monk was holding frequent late night to early morning rehearsals with tenor saxophonist Charlie Rouse in the Weehawken house, with its Steinway piano and spacious facilities. More unwanted publicity came the baroness's way in October 1958 when Monk got into a scuffle with police in Wilmington, Delaware, while the three were riding together. Koenigswarter was arrested for marijuana possession, sentenced to a three-year term, and acquitted only after a similar period of legal maneuvering; Monk lost his cabaret card for another two years. In 1959 she was again working as an occasional manager, this time for pianist Sir Charles Thompson and tenor saxophonist Hank Mobley.

In the jazz community Koenigswarter was mainly known as Nica, a name commemorated in "Nica's Tempo" by Gigi Gryce, "Blues for Nica" by Kenny Drew, "Tonica" by Kenny Dorham, "Nica" by Sonny Clark, "Nica Steps Out" by Freddie Redd, and "Nica's Dream" by Horace Silver. Monk composed the ballad "Pannonica" for her. He lived with Koenigswarter from 1970, when he began to withdraw from public performance, until his death in 1982. During some portion of this period bop pianist Barry Harris also resided with them, and the baroness helped support Harris's Jazz Cultural Center in New York City. The spirit of her relationship with Monk is captured in the documentary film *Thelonious Monk: Straight, No Chaser* (1989), for which she was interviewed a few months before her death in New York City.

• The finest account of Koenigswarter is by Nat Hentoff, "The Jazz Baroness," *Esquire*, Oct. 1960, pp. 98–100, 102. Further details of the circumstances of Parker's death appear in interviews with Koenigswarter and Robert Freymann, the attending physician, in Robert Reisner, ed., *Bird: The Legend of Charlie Parker* (1962; repr. 1975), pp. 131–35. See also the anonymous essay "The Loneliest Monk," *Time*, 28 Feb. 1964, pp. 84–88. Obituaries are in the *New York Times*, 2 Dec. 1988, and *Down Beat*, Apr. 1989.

BARRY KERNFELD

KOERNER, Gustave Philipp (20 Nov. 1809–9 Apr. 1896), lawyer, German-American political leader, and diplomat, was born at Frankfort on the Main, Germany, the son of Bernhard Koerner, a book dealer, and Maria Magdalene Kaempfe. In 1828 he completed studies at the Gymnasium at Frankfort and enrolled at the University of Jena, where he became active in the *Burschenschaft*, a liberal nationalist movement of students. In 1830 he moved to Munich to study law but in December 1830 was imprisoned for four months after being involved in a student disturbance. He then left Munich, the university having been closed, and enrolled in 1831 at Heidelberg, where he was granted a doctorate in law in 1832. The next year he was admitted to practice in Frankfort. He soon became involved in the revolutionary movements that led to an uprising (Frankfurt *Attentat*, 3 Apr. 1833). When the uprising failed, he was obliged to flee to France. There he joined with the family of Theodore Engelmann, a close friend from his university days; they and others were planning to emigrate to Missouri. They arrived in New York in June 1833, traveled to St. Louis, and eventually settled in nearby St. Clair County, Illinois, which was developing as a center for educated and professional German émigrés known as the "Latin Farmers."

Koerner determined to adapt to the practice of law in the United States. With that objective, he learned the English language, read widely in U.S. law and politics, and in 1834 enrolled at the law school of Transylvania University in Kentucky. In February 1835 he was admitted to the Illinois bar and opened a law office in the St. Clair county seat, Belleville. In 1836 he married Sophie Engelmann, the sister of his friend Theodore; the Koerners had eight children.

Koerner was naturalized in 1838 and quickly entered into U.S. politics, becoming, like most Germans of the time, a member of the Democratic party. He advocated full participation of the German immigrants in politics and in 1838 translated and edited a German edition of the Illinois constitution and major laws. In 1842 he was elected to the Illinois House of Representatives. Three years later he was appointed to the Illinois Supreme Court and served until 1848, when a new state constitution lowered the salaries of justices and made the post elective by popular vote. Declining to run for a new term, Koerner returned to his law practice.

The failure of the European revolutions of 1848 led to the migration of many former German revolutionaries to the United States, where they began to assume leadership roles in the German-American community. Some outspoken newcomers became critical of earlier German leaders as being too moderate and politically compromising. In 1850–1851 Koerner wrote a series of newspaper articles in defense of the "Grays," the earlier leaders, against the "Greens," the refugees of 1848. While thus recognized as a leader of the Grays, Koerner frequently found himself cooperating with the newer generation in the political turmoil of the late 1850s.

In 1852 Koerner was elected lieutenant governor of Illinois on the Democratic ticket, serving from January 1853 to January 1857. When Illinois's powerful Democratic senator Stephen A. Douglas introduced the Kansas-Nebraska Act in 1854, which repealed the previous prohibition on slavery in some of the western territories, Koerner was strongly opposed to the measure but hesitated to voice public opposition while still a member of the Democratic state administration. For two years he hoped in vain to turn away the Democratic party from support of Douglas's measure. Only after the national Republican party convention of 1856 did he actively change political allegiance to support the new opposition party and advocate alignment of Germans with it. He chaired the Republican State Convention of 1858, which nominated Abraham Lincoln to oppose Douglas for the U.S. Senate. At the 1860 Republican National Convention, Koerner actively supported Lincoln for the presidential nomination and served on the Platform Committee, which drafted a plank disavowing legislation against the foreign-born.

When the Civil War broke out, Koerner served as an aide with the rank of colonel to General John C. Frémont in Missouri. In June 1862 President Lincoln appointed him to be minister to Spain, replacing his fellow German-American Carl Schurz in that position. His ministry was greatly concerned with the threat of Spanish influence in Santo Domingo and with discouraging trade between Spanish-held Cuba and the Confederacy. Taking a leave of absence to campaign for Lincoln in the 1864 election, he never returned to Spain and submitted his resignation in December 1864.

With the end of the Civil War, Koerner returned to the practice of law and to state affairs in Illinois. He served on the board of the Illinois Soldiers' Orphans Home (1865–1873) and from 1871 to 1873 on the state Railroad and Warehouse Commission. Although he was a presidential elector for Ulysses S. Grant in 1868, he became increasingly critical of the corruption of the Grant administration and of the harsh Reconstruction policy of the congressional Republicans. Koerner, therefore, joined the Liberal Republican movement in 1872 and supported the joint ticket of the Liberal Republicans and the Democrats, despite his disillusionment with Horace Greeley as a presidential candidate. In 1876 Koerner supported the presidential candidacy of the Democrat Samuel J. Tilden and thereafter remained a Democrat, convinced that the Republican

party had lost sight of its principles of the 1850s and had become characterized by corruption and the domination of business interests.

From the 1870s until his death Koerner continued an active law practice in partnership with his son, Gustave A. Koerner. He also wrote widely and published articles on law, foreign affairs, politics, and history. His *Das Deutsche Element in den Vereinigten Staaten von Nordamerika, 1818–1848* (1880) sought to illuminate the role of those German Americans who arrived before the "Forty-eighters." He died at Belleville, Illinois.

Koerner's greatest significance was as one of the earliest nineteenth-century German leaders to give political direction to his fellow immigrants and bring them into the mainstream of American politics. His erudition and judicial aloofness lessened his popular appeal, but he represented the German element well to other American political leaders, who respected him for his high principles and his knowledge of law and politics. By leading a substantial portion of the Illinois Germans into the Republican party between 1856 and 1860, he helped create a political revolution within German America.

• A small collection of material on Koerner is in the Illinois State Historical Library. The same library holds files of the *Belleviller Zeitung*, a newspaper he wrote for anonymously in pre–Civil War years. Important political correspondence is in the Lyman Trumbull Papers and the Robert Todd Lincoln Collection, both in the Library of Congress. Koerner's two-volume *Memoirs of Gustave Koerner, 1809–1896*, ed. Thomas J. McCormack (1909), is one of the classic political memoirs of the nineteenth century. Koerner also published a memoir of his experiences in Spain, *Aus Spanien* (1867). Heinrich A. Rattermann, *Gustav Körner* (1902), draws on Koerner's manuscript memoir but adds excerpts from his literary works.

JAMES M. BERGQUIST

KOFFKA, Kurt (18 Mar. 1886–22 Nov. 1941), experimental psychologist and one of the early leaders of Gestalt psychology, was born in Berlin, Germany, the son of Emil Koffka, a lawyer and *Justizrat* (royal councilor of law), and Luise Levi (or Levy). Kurt Koffka came from a long line of prominent Prussian lawyers. Among the many advantages of his comfortable bourgeois family life was the tutelage of an English-speaking governess. Although Luise Koffka was Jewish, the family belonged to the Evangelical church. Koffka's maternal uncle, a biologist, stimulated the boy's interest in science and philosophy. Koffka attended the Wilhelms Gymnasium in Berlin and passed his *Abitur* (graduation examinations) in 1903. He then matriculated at the University of Berlin, where he studied with Alois Riehl, a neo-Kantian philosopher. Koffka spent 1904–1905 at the University of Edinburgh, mainly for the sake of improving his English; while there he became closely acquainted with prominent British scholars and scientists. Koffka's international outlook, his devout Anglophilia, his fluency in English (both written and spoken), and his comfort in English-speaking milieus, all of which would eventually lead him to the United States, owed much to his year in Scotland.

On his return to Berlin in 1905, Koffka transferred from philosophy to psychology, convinced that he was at heart an empiricist. He based his first published paper, "Untersuchungen an einem protanomalen System," a study of his own colorblindness, on research he conducted in the physiological laboratory directed by Wilibald Nagel. In 1908, under the supervision of Carl Stumpf, at the time Berlin's leading experimental psychologist, Koffka completed his doctoral dissertation "Experimental-Untersuchungen zur Lehre vom Rhythmus," which examined parallel auditory and visual rhythms.

In 1909 Koffka married Mira Klein, who had been a devoted research subject during his dissertation experiments, but he divorced her in 1923 to marry Elisabeth Ahlgrimm, not long after she had earned her Ph.D. at the University of Giessen. Koffka's second marriage also ended in divorce in 1923, when he remarried his first wife. In 1928 Koffka divorced yet again and remarried Ahlgrimm. None of Koffka's four marriages yielded children.

Koffka left Berlin in 1909 for the University of Freiburg, where his old mentor Riehl had previously taught and where he assisted Johannes von Kries, professor of physiology in the medical faculty. Koffka next worked as an assistant to Oswald Külpe and Karl Marbe at the University of Würzburg, which was still at this time a major center for experimental research in psychology. In 1910 Koffka moved to Frankfurt as one of two assistants to the newly appointed Friedrich Schumann. Schumann's other assistant was Wolfgang Köhler; Max Wertheimer was working on the perception of motion at the time in a laboratory shared with Schumann. In the year of intense collaboration that followed, Koffka, Köhler, and Wertheimer (the intellectual leader of the group) laid the experimental and theoretical groundwork for an innovative approach to human psychology: the Gestalt theory.

"Form," "configuration," "pattern," and "shape" are rough equivalents of the German word *Gestalt*. The term evokes a fundamental principle of Gestalt theory, that any whole is always more than the sum of its parts, which derive their significance from their relations to that whole. Accordingly, people perceive complex entities holistically and are only then able to analyze their constituent parts, rather than building up a sensory impression of the whole from a disjunctive assembly of individual sensations. Koffka and his colleagues were motivated at first by their shared rejection of the piecemeal reduction of experience into its atomistic components (or "sensations"), a method common to late-nineteenth-century theories of perception in Europe and the United States. Gestalt psychology relied instead on phenomenological insights developed by Christian von Ehrenfels, with whom Wertheimer had studied, and allied them with experimental methods. In part, Gestalt psychology constituted an attempt to reclaim the scientific study of the mind as a humanistic enterprise and to address problems of meaning, value, and experience that mechanistic psychology had neglected. While Koffka is considered neither the most original experimentalist nor the most original theorist of the three Gestalt pioneers, he was to become the new theory's most effective spokesman and its chief evangelist in the United States.

In 1911 Koffka accepted an appointment under August Messer at the University of Giessen. The proximity of Giessen to Frankfurt allowed Koffka to remain in close contact with Wertheimer and Köhler. With the coming of war in 1914, Koffka began a research project on the treatment of brain-injured patients, especially aphasics, working with Robert Sommer, professor of psychiatry and director of the Psychiatric Clinic at Giessen. Later Koffka worked for the army and navy on problems of sound localization. In 1918 he was promoted to *außerordentlicher Professor* in experimental psychology (including experimental educational psychology), a position that significantly increased his teaching responsibilities, without, however, a commensurate rise in salary. A stream of experimental reports flowed from his laboratory, authored by both Koffka and his students, including eighteen papers published in *Psychologische Forschung*, the journal of the Gestalt group, edited by Wertheimer, Köhler, and Koffka. In 1921 Koffka was also named director of the Psychology Institute at Giessen; when the Hesse-Darmstadt government failed to appropriate startup funds for the laboratory, he successfully organized an association of friends to subsidize the venture.

In 1921 Koffka published *Die Grundlagen der Psychischen Entwicklung*, in which he applied Gestalt theory to developmental psychology, albeit without the thorough experimental underpinnings that supported the Gestalt theory of sense perception. He argued that infants respond at first to organized wholes, which they perceive in an almost undifferentiated environment, and are able only later to distinguish among the separate sensory impressions that contribute to these wholes. Also in the early 1920s, Koffka began to receive invitations to lecture in the United States; given his modest means and Germany's hyperinflation, it is hardly surprising that he accepted. Encouraged by his reception in the United States, Koffka published an important paper on Gestalt approaches to perception in the *Psychological Bulletin* (then edited by Robert Ogden) in 1922; Ogden translated Koffka's book on child psychology, published as *The Growth of the Mind* in 1925. With its emphasis on the important role intuition plays in learning, the book influenced educational theory in the United States and helped encourage a shift away from the reliance on rote learning.

In Germany, however, Gestalt theory made headway only against the concerted opposition of traditional psychologists entrenched in the university system's bureaucracy. Koffka, identified as the movement's public advocate, drew the ire of the old guard, who—it seemed—could confine his career to the provincial backwater of Giessen forever. Koffka hoped to secure a post in England, but no offer was forthcoming. Instead, the United States beckoned again. Koffka spent the academic year 1924–1925 as a visiting professor at Cornell University; in 1926–1927 he had a similar position at the University of Wisconsin. In 1927 an extraordinary offer came his way: the post of William Allan Neilson Research Professor at Smith College, with the promise of his own fully equipped, fully funded laboratory staffed with assistants, and freedom from any teaching or publication requirements. He accepted immediately. As before in Germany, most of Koffka's research at Smith focused on problems in visual perception. The results of his laboratory's experiments appeared in *Psychologische Forschung* and were also published as the *Smith College Studies in Psychology* (4 vols., 1930–1933). Among Koffka's assistants was the young Molly Harrower, with whom he pursued a collegial correspondence that lasted until his death; she became his scientific executor. At the end of his five-year appointment, Koffka accepted a professorship in psychology at Smith, a post that he held for the rest of his life. In 1932 he went on a research expedition to Uzbekistan sponsored by the Soviet Union but contracted relapsing fever (a spirochetal infection borne by lice and ticks).

On his return from the aborted trip to Uzbekistan, Koffka began work on his mammoth *Principles of Gestalt Psychology* (1935), which drew on twenty-five years of experimentation and demonstrated the application of Gestalt principles to a wide range of psychological topics, including learning and memory. While acknowledging flaws in the Gestalt system, he pointed toward fruitful directions for research and theory. Koffka also extended the established Gestalt critique of J. B. Watson's stimulus-and-response psychology, rejecting its reductive positivism.

With his life's greatest task behind him, Koffka, like Wertheimer in his later work, turned to explore a range of social, ethical, and aesthetic questions from a Gestalt point of view. Koffka's dialogue-essay "The Ontological Status of Value" (1935), his article "Problems in the Psychology of Art" (1940), and his lectures on such topics in political philosophy as tolerance and freedom exemplified and encouraged the broad extension of the Gestalt approach, as in later work by social psychologist Kurt Lewin, art historian and theorist Rudolf Arnheim, and art critic John Berger.

While at Oxford for a year as a visiting professor in 1939, Koffka worked with patients suffering from brain lesions at the Nuffield Institute and at the Military Hospital for Head Injuries. The tests that he devised at the Military Hospital to evaluate judgment and comprehension in brain-injured patients were soon widely adopted.

Although Koffka was compelled in his last years to restrict his activities because of a heart condition, he continued to teach until only a few days before his death from coronary thrombosis at his home in Northampton, Massachusetts.

• Koffka's scientific papers are held by the Archives of the History of American Psychology in Akron, Ohio. Molly Harrower provides details of Koffka's life after 1922 in her *Kurt Koffka: An Unwitting Self-Portrait* (1983), a eulogy to a long-time friend based largely on her correspondence with Koffka. W. Metzger's "Kurt Koffka, Professor der Psychologie," in *Neue deutsche Biographie*, vol. 12 (1980), pp. 417–18, is an appreciation by an important German Gestalt psychologist and has become the standard German biographical source. Metzger is stronger on Koffka's science than on his life. Mitchell G. Ash, *Gestalt Psychology in German Culture, 1890–1967: Holism and the Quest for Objectivity* (1995), includes an extensive discussion of Koffka's role in the Gestalt movement. However, Ash acknowledges in only a cursory manner the background of experimental psychology in Germany that underlay the work of Koffka and his colleagues.

THE EDITORS

KOFOID, Charles Atwood (11 Oct. 1865–30 May 1947), zoologist, was born in Granville, Illinois, the son of Nelson Kofoid and Janette Blake, farmers. Kofoid entered Oberlin College in 1885, working his way through school by waiting on tables and chopping wood. His interest in natural history was inspired by an undergraduate professor, Albert Wright. Kofoid's first experience in teaching came in his junior year, when he worked as an assistant in zoology. During this time he also became engaged to his classmate, Carrie Prudence Winter. He earned his B.A. in 1890 and continued as a teaching fellow at Oberlin for an additional year before moving on to Harvard to complete his education. He received his M.A. in 1892 and his Ph.D. in 1894, writing his dissertation on the cell lineage in the land slug *Limax*, under the guidance of the zoologist Edward L. Mark. Kofoid and Winter were married that same year; they had no children.

Soon after receiving his degree, Kofoid became an instructor of vertebrate morphology at the University of Michigan. Then, in 1895, he moved to Urbana, Illinois, to teach zoology at the University of Illinois. He was also superintendent of a natural history survey of the Illinois River and spent six years studying freshwater microorganisms, particularly planktonic and protozoan groups, which became the focus of his later work. In 1901, at the invitation of his Harvard friend and associate William Emerson Ritter, Kofoid moved to Berkeley to teach at the University of California. He spent the remainder of his career there, retiring in 1936 as professor of zoology and chairman of the department.

Kofoid's work in zoology focused on several areas. His chief research concern was study of aquatic microorganisms. He did extensive work on the morphology and distribution of marine plankton, especially the tintinoids and the dinoflagellates, and was an avid collector of specimens. He accompanied Alexander Agassiz on a collecting voyage in the South Seas (1904–1905) and developed two collecting devices that bear his name: the Kofoid self-closing bucket (1905) and the Kofoid horizontal net (1911). His most notable contribution to this area was a book on the morphology of protozoans, *The Free-Living Unarmored Dinoflagellata*

(1921), which he cowrote with his student Olive Swezy. Kofoid also helped to establish the Marine Biological Station of San Diego at La Jolla—now Scripps Institution of Oceanography—a facility that from 1903 to 1912 was the site of summer marine research for Berkeley students. In addition to his university research, Kofoid was active in public health and public service. He was commissioned as a major in the Sanitary Corps of the U.S. Army during World War I, studying human parasites such as hookworm and tapeworm. After the war he became director of the parasitological work at the Parasitological Division of the California State Board of Health and helped to organize a laboratory for training medical technicians. He also studied damage by shipworms and termites in harbor buildings in San Francisco Bay.

Kofoid was a prolific writer and editor. He produced more than 240 articles and books and served as editor for *Biological Abstracts* and *University of California Publications in Zoology* (1908–1933), which dedicated a volume to him on his retirement. Among his monographs are *The Biological Stations of Europe* (1910), *Marine Borers of the San Francisco Bay Region* (1921), and *Amoeba and Man* (1923). His academic and scientific affiliations included the American Society of Zoologists, American Society of Naturalists, American Association of Anatomists, Ecological Society of America, American Association for the Advancement of Science (fellow), National Academy of Sciences (elected to membership in 1922), American Public Health Association, American Microscopical Society, and California Academy of Sciences. He was also awarded gold medals at the St. Louis (1904) and San Francisco (1915) world's fairs for his work with plankton, especially dinoflagellates, from 1896 to 1903.

Kofoid enjoyed a long and meaningful home life with his wife. They were both members of the Congregational church and deeply interested in missionary work. They also enjoyed traveling and collecting books. They amassed a library of more than 40,000 volumes, including 11,000 rare books on the history of science and a complete set of all the editions of Charles Darwin's works. Kofoid bequeathed his library to the University of California a few months before his death in Berkeley.

• Kofoid's former personal library is in the University of California Libraries and bears his name. The most detailed biographical information on Kofoid is Richard B. Goldschmidt, "Charles Atwood Kofoid: 1865–1947," National Academy of Sciences, *Biographical Memoirs* 26 (1952): 121–51. An obituary is Harold Kirby, "Charles Atwood Kofoid," *Science* 106 (1947): 462–63.

BRYONY ANGELL
KEITH R. BENSON

KOHLBERG, Alfred (27 Jan. 1887–7 Apr. 1960), international businessman and proponent of McCarthyism, was born in San Francisco, California, the son of Manfred Kohlberg, a dry goods shopkeeper descended from German-Jewish immigrants, and Marianne "Mary" Wurtenberg, a teacher. Kohlberg matriculated at the University of California in 1904 but never graduated, choosing instead to pursue business interests in printing and subsequently join the family business. His travels as a dry goods salesman took him to Texas, where he met Selma Bachrach. They married in 1911 and had one son.

After seeing some particularly impressive textiles from China at the Panama Pacific Expo in 1915, Kohlberg embarked on the first of many business visits to the Far East, where he established a network of associations with dry goods producers that would make him a prosperous man. He developed an international production system, wherein he purchased Irish linen kerchiefs; exported them to China, where female piece laborers embroidered them at minimal cost; and sold them in the United States. In later years he became identified in the press by the flashy "Kohlkerchiefs" that graced the pockets of his suit jackets. Personal tragedy struck Kohlberg in 1919, when his wife and son contracted nephritis, an infectious condition of the kidneys. Both succumbed to the illness. In 1921 Kohlberg married Charlotte Albrecht. They had four children before divorcing. In 1933 Kohlberg married Jane Myers Rossen. The couple resided outside of New York City while he maintained his import business in Manhattan. They had no children, and Jane Kohlberg died in 1951. The following year Kohlberg married for the fourth time to Ida Jolles, a Viennese refugee from the Nazi occupation and the owner of a successful needlepoint business. They had no children.

It fit the character of this energetic and well-connected entrepreneur that he was not a passive spectator to the political instability sweeping across Europe and Asia in the 1930s. In 1939 Kohlberg began contributing his energies as a fundraiser to the fledgling United Jewish Appeal. He remained active in Jewish philanthropic organizations throughout his life, but his most zealous cause was in support of Nationalist China, first in its struggles against Japan and later against Communists led by Mao Tse-tung. Even though Kohlberg lacked academic training, his extensive business connections in Asia won him the job of chairman of the Executive Committee of the American Bureau for Medical Aid to China (ABMAC). He shuttled between Washington, New York, and China, reporting on the effectiveness of operations related to United China Relief (UCR) during World War II. He came to question the level of corruption and mismanagement attributed by U.S. officials and China policy makers to Chiang Kai-shek's government, and he bridled at the pessimism he discerned among American officials toward the Nationalist cause. Kohlberg became convinced that the stoic acceptance of Chiang Kai-shek's imminent downfall among some officials betrayed hidden sympathies or outright support of Communist ascension in the region. He voiced his accusations within the UCR, and when he failed to unseat his opponents, he left the organization in 1943. Kohlberg subsequently joined the Institute of Pacific

Relations (IPR), a private think tank with influential ties to the State Department. There, too, he detected evidence of what he believed to be Communist sympathies in the organization. He accused the IPR of serving as a conduit for Communist propaganda and a possible front for disloyal activities. When his complaints generated an unsatisfying response within the IPR, he took his concerns to Washington, where he appeared before the Senate Subcommittee on Internal Security.

In 1946 Kohlberg discovered the American China Policy Association (ACPA), a conservative lobby organization devoted to winning increased aid for Nationalist China and attacking contrarian dissent. The anti-Communist tenor of the organization suited Kohlberg's brand of Republican politics, and he discovered he was a natural lobbyist. From his office in Manhattan, he generated hundreds of press releases, wrote scores of letters to Congress and news organizations, and compiled exhaustive reports detailing alleged pro-Communist sympathies in the Far East Bureau of the U.S. State Department. He made frequent contributions to *China Monthly*, an English-language paper distributed in China, in which he questioned U.S. commitments to Nationalist China and virulently attacked distinguished skeptics, such as Owen Lattimore. He also published *Plain Talk*, a journal devoted to attacking the quiescence of U.S. policy toward China.

Kohlberg rose in the ACPA from vice president to chairman of the board, and his passion to influence investigations of internal loyalty after 1946 made his name synonymous with the "China Lobby," an informal collective of individuals and institutions highly critical of the "loss" of China to communism. The China Lobby sought support for the government in exile in Taiwan and political accountability at home. Kohlberg sprang to national prominence following the 1949 release of a State Department White Paper detailing the failed American policy to unite Communist and Nationalist factions in China. Kohlberg decried the "great conspiracy" in U.S. foreign policy, in which the country continued to fight communism in Europe while opting to "throw away Asia." Conservative Republican members of Congress, known collectively as the "China Bloc," echoed the sentiments of Kohlberg and the China Lobby, attacking supposed Communist sympathies within the government and calling for investigations.

By 1950 Kohlberg and the activities of the China Lobby won the attention of Senator Joseph McCarthy (R.-Wis.), who became a willing ally and political pipeline for Kohlberg's efforts to trace and unmask Communist sympathy and infiltration among Americans stationed in China prior to 1949. McCarthy informally teamed with the ACPA, which supplied files to support McCarthy's domestic anti-Communist crusade. McCarthy pushed for congressional exploration of the loyalty problem Kohlberg perceived among the State Department's China officers. Investigations by the Internal Security Subcommittee of the Committee on the Judiciary under Senator Pat McCarran (the McCarran commission) resulted in a purging of the Far East Branch of the State Department, prematurely ending the careers of numerous State Department diplomats, including John Carter Vincent, John Service, John Paton Davies, and O. Edmund Clubb. The China Lobby was less successful in changing U.S. attitudes toward China, but Kohlberg was ebullient over the outcome of the hearings and grateful to McCarthy for vindicating him in his long-running battles with leading China policy makers. Kohlberg declared that his only regret about the senator was that he was "too cautious about using his information."

On domestic loyalty issues, Kohlberg continued as an influential and vigilant presence in anti-Communist efforts throughout the 1950s. He served as a member of the Special Committee on Radio and Television of the Joint Committee against Communism in New York. This organization investigated and publicly discredited and blacklisted many radio and television actors, writers, producers, and directors through the publication of a pamphlet entitled *Red Channels* (1950). He also served as national chairman of the American Jewish League against Communism and became its honorary president in 1955.

While Kohlberg's efforts to swing U.S. support behind Chiang Kai-shek and the Nationalist government could not overcome a popular revolution nor redirect U.S. Cold War policy abroad, he succeeded in generating publicity on behalf of inconsistencies he saw in American foreign policy. His significant historical impact was in fueling American prejudices toward subversives and fears of Communist infiltration at home and abroad. His information campaigns and lobbying efforts supplied a willing Congress with accusations that briefly fueled McCarthy's rise to national prominence and contributed to the decimation of the professional ranks of the State Department's East Asian experts. Kohlberg is remembered as an exemplary McCarthyite. His work in New York played on national fears of dissent and subversion and succeeded in discrediting and disrupting the lives and careers of many Americans in the entertainment field. The *New York Times* reported that some spoke of Kohlberg as "the Jewish Joe McCarthy." He died in Manhattan.

• Kohlberg's papers are at the Hoover Institution on War, Revolution, and Peace at Stanford University. A sympathetic biographical account of Kohlberg's life is Joseph Keeley, *The China Lobby Man: The Story of Alfred Kohlberg* (1969). A critical but still useful historical account of the activities of Kohlberg and the China Lobby is Ross Y. Koen, *The China Lobby in American Politics* (1960; rev. ed. 1974), which includes a partial bibliography of articles written by Kohlberg. Two academic studies that examine the historical context within which Kohlberg and the China Lobby operated are Stanley Bachrack, *The Committee of One Million* (1976), and Foster Rhea Dulles, *American Policy toward Communist China 1949–1969* (1972). Information about Kohlberg is in Gary May, *China Scapegoat: The Diplomatic Ordeal of John Carter Vincent* (1979). See also Robert Garson, *The United States and China since 1949: A Troubled Affair* (1994); Phillip Horton, "The China Lobby—Part Two," *Reporter*, 29 Apr. 1952; and

Charles Waartenbaker, "The China Lobby," *Reporter*, 15 Apr. 1952. An obituary is in the *New York Times*, 8 Apr. 1960.

DEREK W. VAILLANT

KOHLER, Elmer Peter (6 Nov. 1865–24 May 1938), organic chemist, was born in Egypt, Pennsylvania, the son of Lewis A. Kohler and Elizabeth Newhardt, farmers. In 1886 he graduated from Muhlenberg College, where he took only one chemistry course. After graduation he worked for the Santa Fe Railroad. Desiring to become a mineral assayer, he went to Johns Hopkins to study chemistry where Ira Remsen accepted him because of his thorough knowledge of German. A fascination with organic chemistry, which was to be lifelong, soon replaced his interest in minerals.

After earning his Ph.D. in 1892, he taught general and organic chemistry at Bryn Mawr until 1912, eventually becoming department chairman. During this time he published thirty-two papers on research mostly conducted with his own hands, though gifted students, including Marie Reimer, Gertrude Heritage, and Margaret MacDonald, assisted with some. In 1912 he moved to Harvard, where he stayed until his death, except for nearly two years in Washington, D.C., during World War I, when he headed the offense section for research for the Chemical Warfare Service. The mission was to prepare new toxic chemical agents, and Kohler's group was responsible for preparing the arsenic compounds known as adamsite and lewisite.

Kohler never married, went to almost no scientific meetings, and never gave public lectures. This withdrawn life was due to shyness, not indifference; he was, however, a superb lecturer in his advanced organic chemistry course and in freshman chemistry. He was an outstanding mentor to his many research students, of whom twenty became professors and some became department heads in colleges and universities. Some, including Henry Gilman (Iowa State), James B. Conant and F. H. Westheimer (Harvard), L. I. Smith and C. F. Koelsch (Minnesota), and R. C. Fuson (Illinois), developed outstanding academic research careers. J. B. Conant and Max Tishler became eminent outside of academic chemistry.

Kohler was among the first organic chemists of significant attainment to have been schooled entirely in the United States. Together with others of his generation, Kohler helped establish in America strong traditions of teaching and research in the subject. His interest in reaction mechanisms inspired a number of students to work in this field, and through them his influence on the development of physical organic chemistry was especially great. Kohler kept up with developments, such as new ideas of chemical bonding, and utilized them in his research and lectures.

His research dealt with fundamental problems, such as addition to conjugated systems, organic sulfur compounds, and steric hindrance. With Joseph T. Walker and Max Tishler, he verified Jacobus Henricus vant Hoff's sixty-year-old prediction that substituted al-

lenes could be obtained in an optically active state because of molecular asymmetry. This work settled an important question about the three-dimensional arrangement of organic compounds. In his last years he attempted to isolate the antipernicious factor from liver, but adequate methods of separation and assay were not yet available.

Kohler's research increased the knowledge of how reactions proceed—reaction mechanisms. Verifiable information about the behavior of simple organic compounds contributes to the understanding of fundamental life processes (biochemistry and molecular biology). The work of Kohler and his students furnished valuable insights and, hence, influenced the development of the life sciences.

Kohler had a very direct, shrewd mind, which he expressed frankly and sometimes bluntly. He gave wise answers to nonchemical as well as chemical questions. For instance, he contributed to matters of academic policy and advised students about jobs. He spent his summers at his ancestral home in Pennsylvania and in travel, including hiking trips in mountains here and overseas. He accepted almost no honors, although he was a member of the National Academy of Sciences, and took few administrative positions, being seldom absent from his laboratory during the school term. He served very effectively as chairman of the Harvard department in the 1930s. He died in Boston.

• The Harvard archives contain Kohler correspondence. The best sources are J. B. Conant's article in *National Academy of Sciences, Biographical Memoirs* 27 (1952): 264–91, with a complete list of Kohler's publications, and Conant, *My Several Lives* (1970). The present account is based partly on personal recollection of Kohler.

D. STANLEY TARBELL

KOHLER, Kaufmann (10 May 1843–28 Jan. 1926), rabbi, was born in Fürth, Bavaria, the son of Moritz Kohler, the director of a Jewish orphan asylum, and Babette Löwenmayer. He received a Talmudic education at various yeshivot around Germany. At age twenty he went to Frankfurt am Main to study with Samson Raphael Hirsch, an orthodox rabbi who championed living a strictly observant religious life while remaining part of the secular world.

Kohler obtained a university education in addition to his rabbinical training, and his studies at the universities of Munich (1864–1865), Berlin (1865–1867), and Erlangen (Ph.D., 1867) in comparative history and philology undermined his faith that the rigid code of behavior governing Jewish observance came directly from God. Rather, like other reform-minded Jewish intellectuals and rabbis in Germany, he held that the particular strictures of Jewish law reflected the values and needs of the times for which they had been formulated. The rest of his career was devoted to adapting Jewish tradition to the demands of modernity.

Kohler's doctoral thesis, "Der Segen Jakobs," utilized the methodology of higher criticism to examine the biblical story of Jacob. By arguing that the Pentateuch was not of divine origin and thus subject to historical criticism and analysis, Kohler effectively disqualified himself from any rabbinical post in Germany. After two years of postgraduate study at the University of Leipzig, he accepted an invitation from Temple Beth-El in Detroit, Michigan, arriving in the United States in 1869.

Two years later Kohler was hired by the Sinai Congregation in Chicago, Illinois. There he guided a congregation eager to reconcile Jewish ritual with their needs as acculturated Americans living in a Christian society. In 1874 Kohler introduced the first successful Jewish Sunday morning worship service in the United States. He recognized that this move broke radically with Jewish tradition and blurred the lines that distinguished Judaism from Christianity. Yet he argued that meeting the needs of Jews who had to work on Saturdays was the only way to preserve the still vital and essential idea of the Jewish Sabbath.

Kohler's marriage to Johanna Einhorn in 1870 (they would have four children) cemented his relationship with her father, David Einhorn, one of the most respected and radical German-born rabbis in the United States. Kohler replaced Einhorn when he retired from the rabbinate of New York's Temple Beth-El in 1879. Through frequent contributions to the national Jewish press, Kohler had already established himself as one of the best educated, most serious, and most radical rabbis in the land. In New York, where he was caught between the traditionalism of Eastern European Jews and the religious indifference of acculturated German Jews, he championed the cause of reform. In 1885 Kohler delivered a widely publicized defense of Reform Jewish principles in a series of lectures titled *Backwards or Forwards*. That same year, he organized the Pittsburgh Rabbinical Conference and was chief author of the radical Pittsburgh Platform that crystallized Reform as a distinct movement and remained the central expression of Reform principles until 1937.

In 1903 Kohler was appointed president of Hebrew Union College, the movement's rabbinical seminary in Cincinnati. His fervent anti-Zionist stance brought him into conflict with several faculty members. Despite this tension, he succeeded in tightening academic standards, introducing the critical study of the Bible, and overseeing the school's move to an expanded campus.

In addition to his extensive pedagogical and theological writings, Kohler participated in the creation of the *Union Prayer Book* (1894), which provided a uniform liturgy for the Reform movement. He also edited the theology and philosophy entries in the *Jewish Encyclopedia* (1901–1906), and he helped prepare the Jewish Publications Society's 1917 English translation of the Bible.

Although he was one of the foremost exponents of classical Reform Judaism, he was troubled by the empty, symbolic Judaism that seemed to accompany the acceptance of his theoretical beliefs. Kohler never abandoned his call for new, relevant forms of observance, but increasingly he advocated forms that were distinctly Jewish, reflecting an emotional allegiance to the all-embracing religious culture of his youth. In 1891, for example, he rescinded his claim that any day other than Saturday could serve as the Jewish Sabbath.

Kohler's career embodied a sincere spiritual and scholarly struggle to understand the place of tradition and ritual in a world of science and reason. Kohler retired in 1921 from Hebrew Union College and returned to New York, where he lived until his death there.

• The Kaufmann Kohler Collection at the American Jewish Archives in Cincinnati, Ohio, contains Kohler's correspondence files as well as a large collection of his sermons. Kohler's most important work was *Jewish Theology Systematically and Historically Considered* (1918), originally published in Leipzig as *Grundriss einer Systematischen Theologie des Judentums auf Geschichtlicher Grundlage* (1910); a posthumous collection of his sermons and papers was published in 1931 as *Studies, Addresses, and Personal Papers*. Accounts of his life can be found in Samuel S. Cohon, "Kaufmann Kohler the Reformer," in *Mordecai M. Kaplan: Jubilee Volume on the Occasion of His Seventieth Birthday*, ed. Moshe Davis (1953), and in *Studies in Jewish Literature, Issued in Honor of Professor Kaufmann Kohler* (Kohler Festchrift, 1913). Articles about Kohler include Ellen Messer, "Franz Boas and Kaufmann Kohler: Anthropology and Reform Judaism," *Jewish Social Studies* 48 (1986): 127–40; Karla Goldman, "The Ambivalence of Reform Judaism: Kaufmann Kohler and the Ideal Jewish Woman," *American Jewish History* 79 (1990): 477–99; and Yaakov Ariel, "Kaufmann Kohler and His Attitude toward Zionism: A Reexamination," *American Jewish Archives* 43 (1991): 207–23. Important obituaries include David Philipson, *Central Conference of American Rabbis Yearbook* (1926): 170–77, and Adolph S. Oko, *Menorah Journal* 12 (1926): 513–21.

KARLA GOLDMAN

KOHLER, Max James (22 May 1871–24 July 1934), jurist, historian, and Jewish communal worker, was born in Detroit, Michigan, the son of Kaufmann Kohler and Johanna Einhorn. His parents were Jewish immigrants from Germany, and both his father and grandfather, David Einhorn, were leading rabbis of the Reform Movement in American Judaism. Upon the death of Kohler's grandfather in 1879, his father assumed Einhorn's pulpit at New York's Congregation Beth El, and the family moved to that city. There he grew up in an atmosphere infused with a devotion to both religious values and scholarly pursuits. After completing high school, Kohler attended the College of the City of New York, where he won several important literary prizes. Following his graduation in 1890, he entered Columbia University, from which he received both M.A. (1891) and LL.B. (1893) degrees. He was admitted to the New York State bar in 1893 and became an assistant U.S. attorney for the Southern District of New York, resigning after four years to start a private law practice. In 1906 he married Winifred Lichtenauer, who died in 1922. No children resulted from the marriage.

While working in the U.S. attorney's office, Kohler found himself charged with prosecuting a number of individuals under the country's Chinese exclusion laws. During these proceedings, he became deeply concerned for the plight of immigrants, and when he began his own legal practice in 1898, he made their defense his specialty. He soon became one of the leading immigration lawyers in the country, developing his expertise arguing cases on behalf of the Chinese but later also defending the rights of Japanese, Armenian, Syrian, Indian, and Jewish immigrants. Central to Kohler's legal philosophy was a vision of America as an asylum for the oppressed of foreign lands. His approach entailed a strong insistence on the extension of due process to the immigrant, holding that the government was not permitted to submit new arrivals to arbitrary procedures that abridged their basic right to settlement. Kohler advocated judicial safeguards for immigrants and fought to limit the sometimes onerous requirements for entry, which he felt resulted from the biases of the immigration officials. Kohler personally led a campaign against William Williams, the commissioner of immigration in New York, whom he accused of anti-Semitism and instituting unfair policies at Ellis Island, the country's main immigrant depot. Kohler most notably distinguished himself as a critic of the Dillingham Immigration Commission, whose report to Congress in 1911 he decried as the dawn of a new "Know-Nothing Era." In response to its findings that unrestricted immigration posed a threat to the American way of life, Kohler attacked the commission as a secretive body driven more by prejudice than concern for the law. Following his work against the commission, he began to offer his legal services free of charge to organizations involved in immigrant defense. He subsequently played a major role in moderating the literacy test imposed in 1917, arguing successfully that those fleeing religious persecution should be exempt from its provisions. Ultimately, Kohler's efforts could not stem the tide of anti-immigrant sentiment that led to the passage of the Johnson-Reed Act of 1924, restricting immigration to its lowest level in decades. His contribution to the development of national immigration policy, however, was recognized in 1933, when the secretary of labor appointed him to the Committee on Ellis Island and Immigrant Relief. Many of Kohler's briefs and articles concerning immigration law were published posthumously under the title *Immigration and Aliens in the United States* (1936).

During the period in which the Dillingham Commission was active, Kohler became increasingly involved in the defense of Jewish rights. Between 1909 and 1911, he and Simon Wolf, representing a number of American Jewish organizations, argued before the commission against the racial classification of Jewish immigrants as "Hebrews," a designation they felt questioned the potential of Jews for citizenship. Kohler served as a member of the Board of Delegates of American Israelites, an early Jewish defense agency, and sat on the executive board of the American Jewish Committee, an organization concerned with Jewish rights in the United States and abroad. On behalf of the committee, Kohler contributed to a legal brief opposing an alien registration law adopted by the state of Michigan in 1931 and during the same year authored a brief against the proposal of Rutgers University to limit the enrollment of Jews. Kohler's interest in international Jewish affairs began during World War I, when he studied the legal background of Jewish rights at diplomatic conferences, hoping to provide some precedent for the treatment of Jewish claims after hostilities ceased. In the 1930s, he became concerned over the increasingly tenuous legal position of German Jewry and suggested methods by which the United States might intervene on its behalf.

Kohler's extensive knowledge of history and sociology was frequently apparent in his legal briefs and revealed his devotion to scholarly pursuits. He was particularly interested in the history of American Jews and was a pioneer in research and writing on the topic. He was a founding member of the American Jewish Historical Society (AJHS), founded in 1892, and edited one of the first monographs in American Jewish history, Charles P. Daly's *The Settlement of the Jews in North America* (1895). He also wrote dozens of articles for the AJHS's annual *Publications*. Kohler's writings explored the civil status of Jews during the colonial period, chronicled the history of religious liberty in America, and argued that Jews had played an important role in American social, political, and economic life. Despite a focus on Jewish patriotism, however, Kohler avoided the one-sided apologetics characteristic of some early ethnic historians, sometimes opposing what he considered exaggerated claims about the importance of certain Jewish historical figures. And while most leaders of the AJHS followed a policy of cautiously defending the record of Jewish contributions, Kohler was less restrained in directly rebutting the claims of anti-Semites with historical data.

After his death in Long Lake, New York, Kohler was widely remembered as one of the most significant advocates for the immigrant during the period of mass immigration to the United States. In both his legal work and scholarship, Kohler defended immigrant groups by arguing that basic legal principles and historical precedent guaranteed their place in American society. Armed with this premise, he felt comfortable contesting the claims of high governmental officials in his legal actions and patrician anti-Semites in his writings. "If he felt that he was in the right," wrote Leon Huhner, a friend and colleague of Kohler's, "no man or group stood so high, nor was any writer so eminent, whom he would not challenge" (Huhner, p. 300).

• Kohler's papers are held by the American Jewish Historical Society. A complete bibliography of his writings was published by Edward Coleman in the *Publications of the American Jewish Historical Society* 34 (1937): 165–263. Coleman's bibliography also contains a listing of biographical articles about Kohler. The most helpful of these are Leon Huhner, "Necrology: Max James Kohler," *Publications of the American Jewish Historical Society* 34 (1937): 295–301, and Irving Lehman, "Max J. Kohler," *American Jewish Yearbook* 37 (1935–

1936): 21–25. The best account of Kohler's career can be found in Naomi W. Cohen, *Encounter with Emancipation: The German Jews in the United States, 1830–1914* (1984). On the origins of American Jewish historical writing and Kohler's role, see Jeffrey Gurock, "Cautious Defenders," *American Jewish History* 81 (Winter 1993–1994): 169–70. An obituary is in the *New York Times*, 25 July 1934.

ERIC L. GOLDSTEIN

KOHLER, Walter Jodok (3 Mar. 1875–21 Apr. 1940), manufacturer and politician, was born in Sheboygan, Wisconsin, the son of John Michael Kohler, Jr., a manufacturer and businessman, and Lillie Vollrath. His father came to the United States from his native Austria at the age of ten in 1854. In 1871 his father moved to Sheboygan and two years later started a foundry and machine shop to make agricultural implements. He added the manufacture of enamelware and after a few years dropped the production of implements. In 1888 the original company was incorporated as Kohler, Hayssen and Stehn Manufacturing Company and was devoted to the manufacture of enamel bathroom fixtures and kitchenware. In 1898 the old Sheboygan plant was sold and new production facilities built on open farmland west of Sheboygan. In 1912 the firm became the Kohler Company.

Walter J. Kohler attended the Sheboygan public schools but did not attend college. In 1890, at the age of fifteen, he went to work as a laborer in his father's company. Three years later he was a foreman. In 1900 he married Charlotte H. Schroeder of Kenosha, Wisconsin; they had four children. That same year, Kohler's father died, and his older brother Robert became president of the company while he was named plant superintendent. When Robert died unexpectedly in 1905, at age thirty-one, Walter assumed the presidency of the Kohler Company, a position he would hold until 1937, when he was elected chairman of the board of directors and his brother Herbert V. Kohler became president. During Walter Kohler's administration, the manufacturing facilities were greatly expanded and the range of products vastly enlarged. Best known for premium quality bathroom and kitchen fixtures, Kohler also produced gasoline engines, gasoline-powered electric-generating plants, brass plumbing fixtures, boilers, and radiators.

Concerned that an unattractive industrial town might develop around the new plant west of Sheboygan, Kohler dreamed of building an attractive model village where workers and managers could live together in harmony. Toward that end, in 1912 he visited Europe, touring various industrial garden cities. After his return, Kohler hired various experts who developed a comprehensive plan for the village of Kohler, Wisconsin (incorporated in 1912). In recognition of Kohler's successful efforts in creating the village, Lake Forest University awarded him an honorary doctorate in 1929, and the Society of Arts and Sciences awarded him its National Service Fellowship Medal in 1934.

Like many Wisconsin industrialists of the time, Kohler was active in the Wisconsin Republican party.

In 1900 the dominant Republicans split into the Progressives, led by the La Follettes, and the Stalwarts, to which Kohler belonged. In 1928 a fight broke out over the election of delegates to the Republican National Convention. Kohler was elected delegate-at-large by such a decisive majority that his colleagues urged him to run for governor. Taking advantage of a split in the Progressives, Kohler won the Republican primary and the governorship.

As governor, Kohler tried to bring his business experience to bear in the political arena by streamlining government operations and reducing expenditures. Under his leadership, the legislature enacted a modern budgeting procedure, a single employee trust fund that replaced several scattered funds, an extension of the state civil service system, a comprehensive children's code, and a revised and strengthened workmen's compensation law. The Department of Agriculture and Marketing was created out of several departments, a full-time highway commission was established, and the bureaus of purchasing and personnel were set up.

About halfway through Kohler's term, the stock market crashed and the Great Depression began. Like President Herbert Hoover, Governor Kohler at first tried to minimize the seriousness of the situation. Despite Kohler's popularity, Progressive Philip La Follette announced his candidacy in 1930 for the Republican gubernatorial nomination and launched a wide-ranging campaign. Kohler, confident of victory, spent little time campaigning. In the September primary, La Follette decisively beat Kohler and in November overwhelmed his Democratic rival. Determined to regain the governorship, Kohler defeated La Follette in the 1932 primary but lost to his Democratic opponent in the landslide that elected Franklin D. Roosevelt president.

The coming of the depression and the New Deal brought challenges to Kohler and the Kohler Company. Coming from a conservative, paternalistic background, Kohler took pride in treating his employees with respect and demonstrating concern for their welfare. Not surprisingly, he was opposed to collective bargaining and was firmly committed to the concept of the open shop. The Kohler Company had prospered during the 1920s. Jobs had been secure; wages had been high. Although the onset of the depression curtailed construction, the company continued full-time production. It was not until 1932 that Kohler had to order wage and hour reductions and finally layoffs.

After passage of the National Industrial Recovery Act (1933) opened the way for union membership drives, American Federation of Labor (AFL) organizers arrived in Kohler determined to take advantage of the situation and to defeat Kohler's open-shop practices. On 16 July 1934, after Kohler had rejected the AFL's demand to bargain collectively for all Kohler workers, AFL members struck the company. Although the strike was peaceful at first, violence later broke out; two strikers were killed, and more than forty were injured, events that shattered Kohler's idyllic vision of labor-management harmony. In September 1934 the Kohler Worker's Association, a company union, defeated the AFL union in an election conducted by the National Labor Relations Board. Despite the defeat, picketing continued until 1941, when the strike ended without Kohler recognizing the union, thus preserving his commitment to the open shop. Kohler, however, had died during the previous year at his country estate, "Riverbend," just outside of Kohler.

A prominent Wisconsin manufacturer, Walter J. Kohler built the Kohler Company into the leading American producer of high-quality bathroom and kitchen fixtures. He also led the development of a still-recognized model village and served his state well in his single term as governor.

• No collection of Walter J. Kohler papers is available to the public. The Kohler Company has published several historical brochures that contain material on the family. In addition, the *Sheboygan Press* library has source materials on the Kohlers and the Kohler Company. Also useful is vol. 2 of F. L. Holmes, ed., *Wisconsin: Stability, Progress, Beauty* (5 vols., 1946). The best general accounts of Kohler's political career appear in Paul W. Glad, *History of Wisconsin*, vol. 5, *War, a New Era, and Depression, 1914–1940* (1990). See also Robert C. Nesbit and William F. Thompson, *Wisconsin: A History*, 2d ed. (1989). Walter H. Uphoff, *Kohler on Strike: Thirty Years of Conflict* (1966), is the best overall look at the two labor strikes that played a crucial role in the history of the Kohler Company. Obituaries are in the *Milwaukee Journal* and the *New York Times*, both 22 Apr. 1940.

STEVEN B. KARGES

KÖHLER, Wolfgang (21 Jan. 1887–11 June 1967), psychologist, was born in Reval, Estonia, the son of German parents, Franz Köhler, a Gymnasium director, and Wilhelmine Girgensohn. When Köhler was six, the family returned to Germany. He attended the Universities of Tübingen in 1905–1906, Bonn in 1906–1907, and Berlin from 1907 to 1909. In Berlin, where he earned the Ph.D. in 1909, he studied psychology with Carl Stumpf and, equally important for his intellectual development, field physics with Max Planck. In 1912 Köhler married Thekla (maiden name unknown); they had four children. The marriage ended in divorce. A second marriage to Lili Harleman in 1927 produced one child.

After Berlin, Köhler became assistant to Friedrich Schumann at the Psychological Institute in Frankfurt am Main. Here he met psychologists Max Wertheimer and Kurt Koffka. The three of them began the collaboration that was to become Gestalt psychology.

Gestalt psychology was put forth as a protest against the prevailing psychologies, which were both atomistic and mechanistic, in conformity with psychologists' conceptions of the physical sciences. Taking as their model a different conception of science—field theory in physics—the Gestalt psychologists took their field in new directions. The movement was launched by a 1912 paper by Wertheimer. This article was followed in 1913 by an incisive critique of the assumptions of the traditional psychologies by Köhler, "Über un-

bemerkte Empfindungen und Urteilstäuschungen." Over the years, Köhler's many critical articles and reviews, in addition to a great deal of empirical work by him and his students, advanced the new nonatomistic psychology.

In 1912 the Prussian Academy of Sciences founded an anthropoid station on Tenerife in the Canary Islands; the next year Köhler became its director. He had intended to stay for a year, but the outbreak of World War I made it impossible for him to return to Germany until 1920. During this period he studied the problem-solving capabilities and other intelligent behavior of apes. His *Mentality of Apes* (in German, 1917; English trans., 1924) quickly became, and has remained, a classic. It recounts experiments that differed from most of the previous research on animals, which had used problems beyond the comprehension of the subjects or had concealed relevant aspects of the problem situation, thus forcing the animals to learn mechanically by trial and error or by association. When given the opportunity to behave intelligently, with insight, Köhler's apes did so, and a new direction was opened for empirical work and for theory in the psychology of thinking. His future writings continued to clarify the concept of insight.

In addition to his work on problem solving, Köhler performed important experiments on perceptual functions in chimpanzees and, for comparison, in hens; new methods for experimentation on learning also were devised, methods that produced learning far more quickly than the tedious procedures of the time.

Köhler wrote another major book during his stay in Tenerife, *Die physischen Gestalten in Ruhe und im stationären Zustand* (1920), in which he begins to work out the relations between Gestalt psychology and physics. It is thus central to Köhler's thinking, since psychology depends on physiology and ultimately on physics for its explanations. The concept of Gestalt was found not to be exclusive to psychology, but to apply to physics as well. Thus, according to Köhler, there are physical systems that have specific properties as wholes, not derivable from their constituent parts, and they are transposable—the characteristics of Gestalten as described by philosopher Christian von Ehrenfels in 1890, long before Gestalt psychology was conceived.

The line of thinking begun in *Die physischen Gestalten* was developed by Köhler throughout his life. If physics possesses Gestalt phenomena, it is reasonable to hypothesize, as Wertheimer had done, that there are structural identities between psychological phenomena and the corresponding physical processes in the brain (a physical system within the physical organism). This hypothesis, psychophysical isomorphism, led Köhler to much research, for example, to the discovery of figural aftereffects (see *Dynamics in Psychology* [1940]). His method was to go from psychological phenomena to physiological hypotheses, from which were derived new consequences for perception, and so on, back and forth between psychology and physiology. "Trespassing," Köhler once said, "is one of the most successful techniques in science." This line of experimentation led him to begin investigation of possible correlates of perceptual processes, steady electric currents in the cerebral cortex.

Another aspect of Köhler's concern with the relations of psychology and physics is seen in his analysis of evolutionary theory. What can evolution do and what can it not do? Evolution provides constraints on physical processes in the nervous system (and elsewhere in the organism), as learning also introduces constraints. But neither can produce the natural processes that are shared by the organism with the rest of nature. As Köhler puts it, "Why so much talk about inheritance, and so much about learning—but hardly ever a word about invariant dynamics? It is this invariant dynamics, however constrained by histological devices, which keeps organisms and their nervous systems going" (*The Task of Gestalt Psychology* [1969], p. 90). Thus Köhler breaks out of the nativism-empiricism dichotomy, emphasizes a factor usually at best only implicit in discussions of evolution, and again shows the organism in its place in nature.

In 1920 Köhler was able to return to Germany, where he became acting director of the Psychological Institute of the University of Berlin. In 1921 he along with Wertheimer, Koffka, and others founded and edited the *Psychologische Forschung*, a journal that contained much of the work of Gestalt psychology until 1938. As the pages of this journal testify, the new approach penetrated one field of psychology after another during this period.

Called to Göttingen in 1921, Köhler became professor of experimental psychology and philosophy and director of the psychological institute. In 1922 he returned to Berlin, where he became professor of philosophy and director of the university's psychological institute. Under his leadership, the institute thrived. With Wertheimer also at the institute until 1929, and Kurt Lewin until 1932, Berlin became the center for Gestalt psychology and drew students from many countries, including the United States.

On 30 January 1933 Hitler came to power in Germany. The universities were among the early targets of the Nazis, who interfered with the administration and activities of the psychological institute; assistants were dismissed or appointed without Köhler's consent. Köhler repeatedly protested against these intrusions; promises of noninterference were repeatedly broken by the Nazi officials. In April 1933 Köhler broadened his protest, taking a public stand against the Nazis' dismissal of Jewish professors in "Gespräche in Deutschland," which appeared in *Die Deutsche Allgemeine Zeitung*. He stressed the contributions of Jews and praised those Germans who had not joined the Nazi party: "Never have I seen finer patriotism than theirs." By 1935 it was clear that his courageous struggle could not succeed, and Köhler emigrated to the United States, where he continued his teaching and research at Swarthmore College.

Already well known to American psychologists and much respected by them, Köhler had been visiting professor at Clark University in 1925–1926, William James Lecturer at Harvard in 1934–1935, and visiting professor at the University of Chicago in 1935. Well acquainted with American psychology, he had written *Gestalt Psychology* (1929) in English, he said, "for America." His William James Lectures, published as *The Place of Value in a World of Facts* (1938), opens up the problem of value to a scientific approach; values had been neglected, indeed excluded, by American psychologists who prided themselves on a value-free science.

Köhler's experimental work was elegant and produced much new research. An impressive lecturer, he was sought after both in America and in Europe. During the 1950s and 1960s he maintained a close relationship with the Free University of Berlin, which bestowed on him the unusual honor of Ehrenbürger. He was a member of the Institute for Advanced Study in Princeton from 1954 to 1956. In 1958 he delivered the Gifford Lectures in Edinburgh. In that same year he retired from Swarthmore and continued his work as a visiting research professor at Dartmouth College. In 1967 he delivered the Herbert S. Langfeld Memorial Lectures at Princeton. Published posthumously as *The Task of Gestalt Psychology*, they provide an excellent introduction to Gestalt psychology as well as an authoritative text for psychologists.

Köhler was the recipient of many honors. The American Psychological Association awarded him its Distinguished Scientific Contributions Award in 1956 and was to have presented him its gold medal in 1967; he was president of the association in 1958–1959. He was a member of the National Academy of Sciences, the American Academy of Arts and Sciences, and the American Philosophical Society. Die Deutsche Gesellschaft für Psychologie awarded him its Wundt Medal and made him its honorary president on his eightieth birthday. Köhler died in Enfield, Massachusetts.

Everywhere respected, Köhler's work led to research by psychologists throughout the world. His books were translated into German, French, Italian, Spanish, Japanese, and other languages. Gestalt psychology transformed the fields of perception and of thinking, and Gestalt problems continue to reemerge. Köhler's impact on psychology has been profound and lasting.

Köhler was no less impressive as a personality than as a scientist. His theoretical opponents, no less than those who shared his views, admired him. He appreciated good scientific criticism of his work; if he had made a mistake or overlooked something, he acknowledged his error with quiet enjoyment and went to work to try to settle the issue by new experimentation. On the other hand, if an opponent was in error, he patiently went over the evidence, raised pertinent questions, and dealt objectively with the central issue. He always had time for his younger colleagues, his assistants, and his students, whom he helped in many ways. When he was leaving Germany, he wrote to Donald K. Adams, a friend and professor of psychology at Duke University, "My deepest anxiety refers to the assistants. I am not yet sure whether I shall be able to place them somewhere." In human relations, he was generous and courageous, as is illustrated by his lonely struggle against the Nazis. A man of wide culture and lively interests, his quiet sense of humor and his unusual sensitivity to persons made him a fascinating colleague and friend. He is memorialized in the words of Hans Hörmann, a friend and professor of psychology: "We are grateful to him for showing us what a man could be."

• The major collection of Köhler's letters and manuscripts is in the Library of the American Philosophical Society in Philadelphia. Among the other archives in which his letters can be found are the Archives of the History of American Psychology at the University of Akron and the archives of Harvard University. A bibliography of his published writings, compiled by Edwin B. Newman, is in Mary Henle, ed., *The Selected Papers of Wolfgang Köhler* (1971), which, in addition to papers that he wrote in English, includes a number of translations of articles that first appeared in German and French. Abbreviated translations of papers by Köhler, Wertheimer, Koffka, and their students are in Willis D. Ellis, *A Source Book of Gestalt Psychology* (1938). Among many appreciations of Köhler are S. E. Asch, *American Journal of Psychology* 81 (1968): 110–19; R. Bergius et al. *Psychologische Forschung* 31 (1967): I–XVII; and Mary Henle, *Year Book of the American Philosophical Society* (1968), pp. 139–45. The story of Köhler's struggle against the Nazis is related in Henle, "One Man against the Nazis—Wolfgang Köhler," *American Psychologist* 33 (1978): 939–44. An obituary is in the *New York Times*, 12 June 1967.

MARY HENLE

KOHUT, Alexander (22 Apr. 1842–25 May 1894), rabbi and Judaic scholar, the son of Jacob Kohut and Cecelia Hoffman, was born in Félegyháza, Hungary, and was raised in the town of Kecskemét. Kohut attended the local public school and received a private Judaic education. After attending high school in Budapest, he entered the Jewish Theological Seminary of Breslau, Germany, which was headed by Rabbi Zacharias Frankel and included on its faculty the great historian, Heinrich Graetz. At the same time, Kohut studied Oriental philology and Semitics at the local university. Under the direction of Frankel, Kohut wrote a thesis on the Parsic influence on ancient Jewish angelology and demonology, for which he was awarded a doctorate from the University of Leipzig in 1864. The dissertation was later published by the German Oriental Society. In 1865, while still in rabbinical school, Kohut served as a preacher in the community of Tarnowitz in Upper Silesia.

Receiving his ordination in 1867, Kohut embarked upon a rabbinical and scholarly career that was to bring him great prestige in Hungary over the next two decades. In 1867 he became rabbi in Stuhlweissenburg, Hungary, and was later appointed county superintendent of schools, becoming the first Jew to hold such a position in that country. The author of numerous scholarly articles, often dealing with Persian influences on Judaism, Kohut was recognized by the Congress of Jewish Notables, which met in Budapest in

1868 and made him its secretary. In 1872 Kohut became chief rabbi at Fünfkirchen, and in 1880 he accepted a position at Grosswardein, where he attracted the attention of Koloman von Tisza, the Hungarian prime minister. Tisza selected him as the Jewish representative to the Hungarian Parliament, a position that he never filled because of his immigration to the United States.

Accepting a position at New York's Congregation Ahavath Chesed (now Central Synagogue), Kohut arrived in the United States on 31 May 1885. Although Ahavath Chesed was a moderate Reform synagogue, Kohut saw himself as a traditionalist whose religious standpoint was similar to that of twentieth-century Conservative Judaism. Within a short time of his arrival Kohut became involved in a spirited pulpit debate with Reform Rabbi Kaufmann Kohler of New York's Temple Beth El. In a series of sermons Kohut passionately supported the cause of traditional Judaism, while Kohler defended the ideology of Reform. The Kohut-Kohler controversy, as it is known, established Kohut's national reputation as an outspoken defender of the Jewish tradition, and it also helped to galvanize the position of the Reform movement, which found expression in the Pittsburgh Platform of November 1885. The product of a conference of nineteen rabbis, the Pittsburgh Platform summarized the essential philosophy of Reform Judaism in the late nineteenth century, negating such traditional concepts as ceremonial law, the dietary laws, and the belief in a personal messiah.

In 1886 Kohut joined with Rev. Sabato Morais of Philadelphia and Rev. Henry Pereira Mendes of New York to found in New York City the Jewish Theological Seminary of America to train traditional rabbis and teachers for the American Jewish community. In founding the seminary, Kohut and his associates were seeking to counteract the spread of American Reform Judaism, whose most prominent leader was Rabbi Isaac Mayer Wise of Cincinnati. They were also seeking to provide a traditional alternative to Wise's Hebrew Union College, the only rabbinical school in the United States at the time. At the seminary, where he was a member of the advisory board, Kohut taught Talmud and Midrash. He continued his scholarly career by writing many articles, including some pioneering studies of Yemenite Hebrew literature and translating the Jewish prayerbook, and he served as a trustee and a member of the publication committee of the Jewish Publication Society. In 1891 Kohut was appointed examiner in rabbinics at Columbia College.

As a scholar, Kohut's magnum opus, which took twenty-four years to complete, was the *Aruch Completum* (in Hebrew, the *Arukh Ha-Shalem*), a vast Talmudical dictionary consisting of eight enormous folio volumes with more than 4,000 double-column pages. The work was based upon the *Arukh* of Rabbi Nathan ben Yehiel of Rome, which was compiled around the year 1100. Starting in 1878 Kohut published four volumes in Hungary. The remaining four were published in Vienna after he came to the United States, the last volume appearing in 1892, and a supplement was published in New York in the same year. In the United States, Kohut was assisted in publishing the *Arukh* by a generous stipend from the great philanthropist Jacob Schiff.

On a personal level, Kohut was known for his brilliant oratory, his personal kindness, and his devotion to his students, among whom were Stephen S. Wise and Joseph H. Hertz, who went on to distinguished rabbinical careers. Upon the passing of his wife, Julia Weissbrunn Kohut, in 1886, Kohut was left to raise eight children. The following year he married Rebekah Bettelheim, the daughter of Rabbi Albert Bettelheim. Rebekah Bettelheim Kohut pursued a long and successful career in social welfare and education and was the author of several books of memoirs. Alexander Kohut died of cancer in New York. Kohut's brother, Adolph, was a well-known journalist and author in Germany. Alexander Kohut's son George Alexander Kohut was a rabbi and educator who also served for a time as the assistant librarian of the Jewish Theological Seminary of America.

• Archival material relating to Alexander Kohut is found in the Library of the Jewish Theological Seminary of America. For a bibliography of Kohut's writings, see George Alexander Kohut, "A Memoir of Dr. Alexander Kohut's Literary Activity," in *Proceedings*, Jewish Theological Seminary Association (1894). For a limited autobiographical sketch, see "A Chapter from My Life, The Origin of the *Aruch Completum*," *American Hebrew*, 2 Dec. 1892, pp. 147–48. For an introduction to Kohut's theology, see his commentary on *The Ethics of the Fathers* (1885; repr. 1920). Also see Rebekah Kohut, *My Portion* (1925); Moshe Davis, *The Emergence of Conservative Judaism: The Historical School in 19th Century America* (1965); Ismar Elbogen, "Alexander Kohut, 1842–1942," in *American Jewish Year Book 5703* (1942–1943); Naomi W. Cohen, *Encounter with Emancipation: The German Jews in the United States 1830–1914* (1984); Pamela S. Nadell, *Conservative Judaism in America: A Biographical Dictionary and Sourcebook* (1988); and Robert E. Fierstien, *A Different Spirit: The Jewish Theological Seminary of America, 1886–1902* (1990).

ROBERT E. FIERSTIEN

KOHUT, Heinz (3 May 1913–8 Oct. 1981), psychoanalyst, was born in Vienna, Austria, the son of Felix Kohut, a pianist who went into the paper business after World War I, and Else Lampl. His strong-willed mother played the major role in the life of her adored only son. She kept him from school for four years and hired tutors; later, however, he attended one year of elementary school and the Döblinger Gymnasium before studying medicine at the University of Vienna. Growing up in a prosperous Jewish family, Kohut was exposed to the best of Viennese culture, attending the opera as often as three times a week and becoming acquainted with trends in literature and the arts. When he was eleven to thirteen years of age, Else Kohut hired a tutor, Ernst Morawetz, probably a university student, to spend most afternoons with Heinz and take him to the opera and museums. This tutor, about whom Kohut always spoke with great fondness, gave much meaning to a childhood otherwise lonely.

As a child and young man, Kohut was interested in all the cultural leaders of Vienna, including Sigmund Freud. Kohut first sought psychotherapy in 1937 from a psychologist named Walter Marseilles, who was an expert in the Rorschach test (a means of eliciting imaginative responses to abstract graphic images). The next year Kohut went into analysis with a renowned psychoanalyst and friend of Freud, August Aichhorn. In early 1939 Kohut left Vienna for England, where he stayed awhile in a camp for immigrants before acquiring his visa for the United States. He arrived there in 1940; with $25 in his pocket, he took a bus to Chicago to join his childhood friend, Siegmund Levarie, who had previously arrived and obtained a position at the University of Chicago.

Further training in medicine took Kohut through residencies in neurology and psychiatry at the University of Chicago, but he ended, as he probably expected all along, in psychoanalysis. He went through a second "didactic" (and for him painstaking) analysis with Ruth Eissler in the early and mid-1940s and began course work at the Chicago Institute for Psychoanalysis in 1947, while he was still working in neurology and psychiatry at the University of Chicago. He graduated from the institute in 1950 and immediately joined its faculty. Although he maintained a connection with the university as a lecturer in psychiatry, he worked full time for the rest of his life as a clinical psychoanalyst. In two other milestones around this time, Kohut married Elizabeth Meyer in 1948 and had his only child, Thomas, in 1951.

Kohut's star quickly rose during the 1950s in the Chicago psychoanalytic community, where he was widely—though sometimes reluctantly—recognized as the reigning genius. He published a number of important articles in these years on applied psychoanalysis, but his greatest contribution was an essay on empathy, first presented in 1956 and published as "Introspection, Empathy, and Psychoanalysis: An Examination of the Relationship between Mode of Observation and Theory" (*Journal of the American Psychoanalytic Association* 7 [1959]: 459–83). In it Kohut argued that the essential way of knowing in psychoanalysis was through empathy, which he defined as "vicarious introspection." Anything else was quixotic and false to the tradition. He never wavered from this position, and empathy would become the centerpiece of what he later called "self psychology."

In 1964 and 1965 Kohut served one term as president of the American Psychoanalytic Association, but in general his aspirations were not toward administrative leadership of the profession but rather toward his own writing and scholarship. The first result was the 1971 monograph *The Analysis of the Self: A Systematic Approach to the Psychoanalytic Treatment of the Narcissistic Personality Disorders*. It had a significant impact on the field by extending Freud's theory of narcissism and introducing what Kohut called the "self-object transferences" of mirroring and idealization. Kohut followed that book with *The Restoration of the Self* (1977), which moved from a focus on narcissism to a discussion of the self, its development and vicissitudes, and the "tension gradient," or dynamic relationship, of what he then called the "bipolar self," the twin axes of grandiosity and idealization, an idea that has not generally endured. In 1978 the first two volumes of his papers, *Search for the Self*, appeared. His renown and fame were assured.

Kohut had contracted lymphatic cancer in 1971, though it went into remission. In 1979 he had bypass surgery, from which there were some complications and a lengthy recovery. In the next few years he suffered inner-ear troubles and pneumonia, and by 1981 he was in a state of general decline; he died in Chicago. Despite his illnesses, however, he had continued to work. By the time of his death his book *How Does Analysis Cure?* was largely complete, though it did not appear until 1984, edited by a colleague, Arnold Goldberg, with the assistance of Paul Stepansky. Posthumous publications also included a volume of new and republished essays, *Self Psychology and the Humanities* (1985); volumes three and four of *Search for the Self* (1990, 1991); and a volume of Kohut's correspondence edited by Geoffrey Cocks, *The Curve of Life* (1994).

The essence of Kohut's contribution is that he found a way to abandon drive theory, the classical Freudian theory of the instincts, while still retaining a view of the self that includes conscious and unconscious motivations and places new emphasis on empathy and the symbolic construction of the world in the self (what he called "selfobjects," those others whom we experience psychologically as carrying out our own self functions). Because of his relative obscurity and difficult prose, in some respects Kohut's greatest influence has been indirect, filtered through his impact on the writings of others interested in holistic ideas of the self. Many theologians, philosophers, historians, critics, and humanists have incorporated Kohut's ideas into their writings, often without really knowing their source. Recent feminist writing of a psychological bent, as well, has found in Kohut a perspective on the self that avoids the insidious sexism in much of psychoanalysis. Finally, one might say that much of the public discourse in a society obsessed with psychological meanings has been profoundly influenced by Kohut. The American perception of dissociation, for example, from multiple personalities to the ravages of trauma in sexual abuse and war, owes some of its deeper elements to his work. Kohut transformed the way many psychoanalysts think about narcissism, about "objects," about sexuality and sexualization, about aggression and rage, about dreams, about the relationship between psychoanalysis and the humanities in general, about many ethical values, and about the very meaning of the self in human experience.

• A collection of Kohut's papers is in the Kohut Archives, Chicago Institute for Psychoanalysis. Besides the books and collections of papers mentioned in this essay, two edited collections of his lectures have appeared: Miriam Elson, *The Kohut Seminars on Self Psychology and Psychotherapy with Adoles-*

cents and Young Adults (1987); and Paul Tolpin and Marian Tolpin, *The Chicago Institute Lectures* (1996). Note also *The Psychology of the Self: A Casebook*, ed. Arnold Goldberg (1976), on which Kohut collaborated. An annual in the field is published under the editorship of Goldberg, *Progress in Self Psychology*; as of 1996 twelve volumes had appeared. An obituary is in the *New York Times*, 10 Oct. 1981.

CHARLES STROZIER

KOHUT, Rebekah Bettelheim (9 Sept. 1864–11 Aug. 1951), social welfare activist and educator, was born in Kaschau, Hungary, the daughter of Albert Siegfried Bettelheim, a rabbi and physician, and Henrietta Weintraub, a schoolteacher. The Bettelheim family, including Rebekah and her four siblings, came to the United States in 1867 and lived in Philadelphia, in Richmond, Virginia (1868–1869), and in San Francisco (1875).

Rebekah took several courses at the University of California at Berkeley. Her pursuit of higher education apparently aroused "considerable objection" from the board of the synagogue her father served. But Rabbi Bettelheim, whose late wife had broken with tradition and entered the male preserve of schoolteaching in the Old World, championed his daughter's cause. Rebekah's religious faith was challenged at Berkeley, but ultimately, she wrote, "I became spiritually stronger than I had expected." She took pride in her people and "glory in [her] religion." And she dedicated herself to fulfilling the obligations of *tsedakah* (righteousness), to "a compassionate working for the betterment of the general Jewish lot" and for a "humane civilization."

As a woman of many talents, and inspired by her mother "to seek out all kinds of less sheltered activities," Rebekah aspired to "a career of service" and useful "significant work," rather than "a life limited to housewifely duties." But on a trip to New York City in 1886 she met Alexander Kohut, a distinguished rabbi and scholar of Hungarian origin, twenty-two years older than Rebekah, and a widower with eight children. In less than a year they were married. Rebekah's energies and aspirations, as she wrote to her sister, were channeled into being "the wife of a great man" and a "mother to the motherless." Besides running a household of ten people, Rebekah Kohut took over her husband's correspondence and translated his Sabbath service sermons for publication. She also instituted and ran the sisterhood of her husband's synagogue, did volunteer work for the Women's Health Protective Association, and directed a kindergarten on the Lower East Side of New York.

Alexander Kohut was, in Rebekah's words, "dubious of the wisdom of a public career for me." While implied resentment of her husband surfaced sporadically in her memoirs, she was consistent in her admiration for him. When he became ill in 1893, she nursed him for fourteen months. She never left his side, not even to read a paper at the first Congress of Jewish Women, held in 1893, as part of the Chicago World's Fair. "Afterward," Rebekah Kohut reminisced, "when I heard about the gathering of Jewish women, and of the splendid material for social service brought together by Hannah Solomon and Sadie American . . . I was sorrier than ever that I had not been present."

Her husband's death in 1894 and the prospect of gradual impoverishment moved Kohut to pursue a more active public life and a career. She became a well-known speaker on cultural and literary topics and taught confirmation classes at the flagship Reform synagogue Temple Emanuel. In 1899, with the aid of Jacob Schiff, the New York banker and philanthropist, she opened the Kohut College Preparatory School for Girls, a day and boarding institution that enrolled more than 100 students per year.

Throughout, Kohut remained an advocate of Jewish causes and reform. In 1896, when the national General Federation of Women's Clubs welcomed the National Council of Jewish Women to join, but not as a "religious group," Kohut insisted that the council forgo membership in the larger American organization. "This is a Council of Jewish Women," she insisted. "Let us put it into our Constitution, and into our preamble and everywhere." As president of the New York Council of Jewish Women (1897–1901), she promoted Jewish women's activism and spoke for woman suffrage. She was also committed to religious "suffrage" for Jewish women. Raised by a father who believed women should "face the world 'like men,'" Kohut resented the unequal treatment of women in the synagogue: "My participation in America in many campaigns for women suffrage made me a self-conscious champion of equal rights. In being obliged to mount the gallery where women sat by themselves behind curtains shutting them away from the eyes of the males below, I underwent an internal rebellion."

Kohut's rebellion did not prevent her from fulfilling the traditional roles of wife and mother, but she interpreted these broadly and was critical of a culture "that renders young women useless for anything but . . . dispensing tea and small talk." She continued to campaign for better education and broader social opportunities than were usually accorded Jewish women in the early twentieth century, and she continued, in the Hebrew tradition of *tikkun olam* (the obligation to repair or improve the world), to be a model of the productive Jewish woman involved in constructive social purpose. Beginning in 1914 Kohut headed the Young Women's Hebrew Association employment bureau, and during World War I she chaired the Employment Committee of the Women's Committee for National Defense. Recognized for special competence in the problems of the unemployed, she was appointed to the Federal Employment Clearing House in 1917. After the war, under Kohut's direction the National Council of Jewish Women began its relief work for Jewish refugees. Kohut made many trips to war-torn Europe to determine the extent of aid required. In 1923 in Vienna she was elected president of the World Congress of Jewish Women (also known as the International Council of Jewish Women).

Kohut's interests and activities in the area of unemployment intensified during the Great Depression. In 1931 she was appointed to the New York State Advisory Council on Employment, and in 1932 she served on the Joint Legislative Commission on Unemployment. During World War II she played a leading role in the American Women's Association, the Vocational Service for Juniors, and the Bureau of Jewish Social Research. In 1942 she was again elected president of the World Congress of Jewish Women. Until her death in New York City, Kohut, true to the prophetic injunctions of the Hebrew scriptures, and still asking herself, "Won't anybody do anything about the world, make it a better place for the children growing up?" remained active and effective in philanthropic and social welfare organizations.

• Kohut's papers and correspondence are at the American Jewish Historical Society in Waltham, Mass., and the American Jewish Archives in Cincinnati. Her autobiographies, *My Portion* (1925) and *More Yesterdays* (1950), are indispensable. Additional information about her life and ideas can be gleaned from her other writings, including *As I Know Them: Some Jews and a Few Gentiles* (1929) and *His Father's House: The Story of George Alexander Kohut* (1938). Useful secondary sources include Charlotte Baum et al., *The Jewish Woman in America* (1976); Jacob Rader Marcus, *The American Jewish Woman, 1654–1980* (1981); June Sochen, *Consecrate Every Day: The Public Lives of Jewish American Women, 1880–1980* (1981); and Faith Rogow, *"Gone to Another Meeting": The National Council of Jewish Women, 1893–1993* (1993). An obituary is in the *New York Times*, 12 Aug. 1951.

GERALD SORIN

KOLB, Lawrence (20 Feb. 1881–17 Nov. 1972), mental health administrator and expert on narcotic addiction, was born in Galesville, Maryland, the son of John Joseph Kolb and Caroline Kirchner. Kolb received an M.D. from the University of Maryland in 1908. In 1909, after completing his internship, he was commissioned as an assistant surgeon in the U.S. Public Health Service, to which he dedicated the next thirty-six years of his professional life.

Kolb was assigned to the Reedy Island Quarantine Station from 1909 to 1913 and to the Ellis Island Immigration Station from 1913 to 1919. In 1915 he received advanced training in psychiatry at the New York State Psychiatric Institute and in 1919 became the medical officer in charge of the hospital for psychoneurotic veterans at Waukesha, Wisconsin. From 1923 to 1928 he worked at the Hygienic Laboratory in Washington, D.C. (forerunner of the National Institutes of Health). It was there that he did his most important clinical, laboratory, and epidemiological research on narcotic addiction.

After studying the cases of 230 drug addicts, Kolb concluded that most had abnormal personalities. Relatively few had become addicted through medication. The majority, Kolb maintained, were either psychopaths, neurotics, or inebriates who had switched from alcohol to opiates, exchanging one addiction for another. The abnormal or psychopathic users, Kolb argued, felt heightened pleasure when they used narcotic drugs, while normal persons experienced only the relief of pain.

These views were contested by Charles Terry, Ernest Bishop, and other physicians, who argued that addiction was a drug-induced pathology that could afflict anyone rather than evidence of an underlying mental disorder. Although the etiological debate was revived in the 1960s, Kolb's position that addiction was rooted in personality disorder remained dominant between the 1930s and the 1950s and still had many proponents decades later.

Kolb also found himself at odds with propagandists like Richmond Hobson, who described addicts as dangerous criminals and addiction as a widespread and worsening social problem. Kolb denied that opiates, which are powerful tranquilizers, triggered violent behavior and was able to document, in a 1924 study co-authored with Andrew DuMez, that per capita consumption of opiates had been declining in the United States for some time.

In 1928 Kolb was sent to Europe, charged with investigating procedures for the mental examination of emigrants who wished to come to the United States. In 1933 he was named director of the U.S. Justice Department's Medical Center at Springfield, Missouri, where he pioneered in developing ways of treating and rehabilitating physically and mentally ill offenders. Because of his expertise in addiction, he was named in 1934 director of the first federal narcotic hospital, then under construction in Lexington, Kentucky.

Kolb was disappointed to learn that the structure of the Lexington facility had been patterned on prison architecture. When the facility began receiving patients in 1935, Kolb, who regarded addicts as more deserving of medical care than of punishment as common criminals, housed as many of them as possible outside of cell blocks. Under Kolb's leadership, the Lexington Hospital embarked on four decades as the preeminent addiction treatment and research facility in the United States.

In 1938 Kolb became chief of the Mental Hygiene Division of the Public Health Service in Washington, D.C., where he initiated several innovative programs, including psychiatric treatment centers for merchant seamen and public health training for mental health personnel. He also helped plan and lobbied for the National Institute of Mental Health, the successor agency of the Mental Hygiene Division, which was established by the National Mental Health Act of 1946.

A quietly determined man with wide interests and great organizational skill, Kolb was no believer in passive old age. In 1945, having retired with the rank of assistant surgeon general, he accepted a position as medical consultant to the California Bureau of Prisons and later served as deputy medical director of the California Department of Mental Hygiene. In 1951 he retired from his California post, only to become the assistant superintendent of the Norristown State Hospital in Pennsylvania, where he also assisted with a comprehensive survey of the mental health needs of Philadelphia. He finished at Norristown in 1952 but continued to do a few private consultations until 1954.

Throughout his career Kolb was critical of the national tendency to treat alcoholism and addiction as police matters. He was particularly outspoken about the demonization of narcotic addiction. In 1962 he published *Drug Addiction: A Medical Problem*, which included a plea to treat addicts as mentally disturbed patients and to avoid harsh, mandatory sentences. "In approaching the problem," Kolb warned, "we should keep in mind that this country suffers less from the disease than from the misguided frenzy of suppressing it."

Kolb, who had married Lillian Hess Coleman of Baltimore in 1910, had three children. His oldest son, Lawrence Coleman, also had a distinguished career in psychiatry and was the author of *Modern Clinical Psychiatry*, a standard text on the subject. Kolb died at the U.S. Naval Hospital in Bethesda, Maryland.

• Kolb's papers are in the History of Medicine Division of the National Library of Medicine, Bethesda, Md. The preface to Kolb's *Drug Addiction: A Medical Problem* briefly recounts his career. The book includes most of his key articles on addiction, except for two coauthored with Andrew G. DuMez, "The Prevalence and Trend of Drug Addiction in the United States and Factors Influencing It," *Public Health Reports* 39 (1924): 1179–1204, and "Absence of Trans Immunizing Substances in the Blood of Morphine and Heroin Addicts," *Public Health Reports* 40 (1925): 548–58. The most thorough and perceptive obituary, by Robert Felix, appeared in the *American Journal of Psychiatry* 130 (1973): 718–19.

DAVID COURTWRIGHT

KOLB, Reuben Francis (16 Apr. 1839–23 Mar. 1918), scientific farmer and leader in the Populist movement, was born in Eufaula, Alabama, the son of Davis Cameron Kolb, a merchant and cotton factor, and Emily Frances Shorter. Both of Kolb's parents died within two years of his birth, and his maternal grandfather, General Reuben C. Shorter, and his uncle, John Gill Shorter, who served as governor during the Civil War, reared him. The public service of his ancestors impressed Reuben Francis. He attended Howard (Samford) College and the University of North Carolina, where he graduated in 1859. In 1860 he married Mary Caledonia Cargile; they had three children.

After the election of Republican Abraham Lincoln in 1860, Kolb became active politically. The youngest delegate to the state convention, he voted for secession. He joined the Confederate army and served one year in Pensacola. Then in March 1862 he raised an artillery company known as "Kolb's Battery," which won renown at Chickamauga. Kolb was wounded during the battle for Atlanta. After the war he returned to a ruined plantation and, as a Redeemer, opposed Federal Reconstruction. The panic of 1873 again ruined him financially.

By the late 1870s Kolb had become a leading scientific agriculturalist, diversifying his farming. He practiced crop rotation, experimented with fruits and vegetables, and used hired labor. His hybridized "Kolb

Gem" variety of watermelon, with a sweet taste and thick rind that allowed longer storage, became a national favorite. In 1889 Kolb harvested from two acres 200,000 of these, on which he netted ten cents apiece. Watermelon and other seeds sold to packing houses helped restore his fortune.

As word of Kolb's agricultural experiments spread, his reputation as a scientific farmer increased. During the 1870s he joined others in the nonpolitical Grange to promote agricultural reforms, such as crop diversification, wage labor, and cooperatives. The Grange declined in importance by the 1884 incorporation of the Alabama State Agricultural Society. Kolb was a founding member of the society and promoted truck farming at the state fair, which it sponsored and he directed in 1886. He was named a trustee to the Agricultural and Mechanical College at Auburn in 1886, and following his appointment as commissioner of agriculture in 1887, he managed the state's experiment station located there. That year the National Farmers' Congress elected Kolb president and reelected him to the position in 1889. With the organization of the Farmers' Alliance in Alabama in 1887, Kolb's interests turned to politics. He joined the Alliance and attended the national convention in St. Louis in 1890. Borrowing a Grange tactic, Kolb established traveling farmers' institutes, where lecturers from Auburn and the Farmers' Alliance preached improved agricultural methods at barbecue socials that resembled political rallies. Immensely popular with the farmers, Kolb had erected a grass-roots base from which he challenged the conservative Bourbon Democrats in 1890.

Planters and Bourbon newspapers, such as the Montgomery *Advertiser* and Mobile *Register*, viciously attacked Kolb and the Alliance. Four candidates opposed Kolb for the Democratic party nomination for governor in 1890, and while in convention balloting he led on thirty-three roll calls, on the thirty-fourth a combination defeated him in favor of Bourbon Thomas Goode Jones. Kolb accepted the convention verdict, though supporters and many others denounced it as corrupt. Responding to Kolb's challenge, Jones refused to reappoint him agriculture commissioner, which served to further strengthen the political resolve of the Farmers' Alliance. Bourbon newspapers vigorously condemned the Ocala platform of 1890, denouncing as socialism the subtreasury plan for government-backed farm loans that promised economic relief to farmers. Using the "Bloody Shirt" tactic, they accused the agrarian movement of undermining white supremacy in Alabama.

Kolb and the ever more popular Alliance politicized both white and black farmers in a class struggle against corporations, railroads, and the developing iron industry. Again Jones thwarted Kolb's effort to receive the Democratic party nomination for governor in 1892, forcing Kolb to run as a Jeffersonian Democrat, the de facto People's party in Alabama, in a contest marred by corruption in plantation counties that secured Jones's reelection. Denied office—for no state law or constitutional clause permitted him to contest

the election—Kolb claimed victory by 45,000 votes nonetheless. The state legislature countered with the Sayre Law, which placed serious restrictions on voting. Two years later 50,000 fewer people voted in the gubernatorial election that pitted an independent Kolb against the Bourbon Democrat William Calvin Oates. The panic of 1893 had worsened the plight of the state's farmers, and most Kolb supporters favored Populist measures such as the subtreasury plan. Kolb hammered at the previous corrupt elections and demanded an honest vote count. The Bourbons used nonissues and alarmist tactics, claiming that a Kolb victory would lead to the restoration of "Negro rule" and end all law and order. Despite successful attempts at fusion among Jeffersonian Democrats, Republicans, Greenbacks, and Populists, the August 1894 general election returns clearly demonstrated that Kolb lost because planters stuffed ballot boxes with the votes of "dead negroes and faithful hounds" (Moore, p. 723).

Kolb symbolized Populism in Alabama. Through his newspaper, the *People's Tribune*, published in Birmingham (1894–1896), he promoted a reform agenda and class-based politics in a biracial third-party effort to overthrow Bourbon Democracy. During the gubernatorial election of 1896, Kolb supported the fusion candidate, Albert T. Goodwyn, yet by the presidential election later that year, Kolb had followed the silver issue back into the fold of the Democratic party and endorsed William Jennings Bryan. He continued to decry political corruption and in 1900 supported the constitutional movement to disfranchise black voters manipulated by planters as the only way to assure honest elections. Like Georgia's Thomas E. Watson, Kolb's return to one-party politics was marked by frustration. In 1910 Kolb was elected commissioner of agriculture. Again he ran for governor in 1914, earning the sobriquet "Run Forever Kolb," but dropped out of the race after a poor showing in the primary. The reformer and battler for farmers had become an anachronism. He spent his final years as a businessman in Montgomery, where he died.

• The manuscript sources on Kolb are scattered. Some may be found in the Kolb-Hume Collection at Auburn University and others in the Reuben F. Kolb File and Papers of the state commissioners of agriculture at the Alabama Department of Archives and History in Montgomery. Kolb's newspaper is available on microfilm at the Birmingham Public Library. Biographical materials can be located in Albert Burton Moore, *History of Alabama*, vol. 1 (1927), pp. 696–753; Thomas McAdory Owen, *History of Alabama and Dictionary of Alabama Biography*, vol. 3 (1921), pp. 992–95; and Joel C. DuBose, *Notable Men of Alabama*, vol. 1 (1904), pp. 78–79. On the Populist movement see John B. Clark, *Populism in Alabama* (1927); Sheldon Hackney, *Populism to Progressivism in Alabama* (1969); and especially William Warren Rogers, *The One-Gallused Rebellion* (1970). See also Rogers's essay, "Reuben F. Kolb: Agricultural Leader of the New South," *Agricultural History* 32 (1958): 109–19. Articles of note include Karl Louis Rodabaugh, "Fusion, Confusion, Defeat and Disfranchisement: The 'Fadeout of Populism' in Alabama," *Alabama Historical Quarterly* 34 (Summer 1972):

131–53; Leah R. Atkins, "Populism in Alabama: Reuben F. Kolb and the Appeals to Minority Groups," *Alabama Historical Quarterly* 32 (Fall and Winter 1970): 167–80; and Charles Grayson Summersell, "The Alabama Governor's Race in 1892," *Alabama Review* 8 (Jan. 1955): 5–35. An obituary is in the Montgomery *Advertiser*, 24 Mar. 1918.

GLENN T. ESKEW

KOMPFNER, Rudolf (16 May 1909–3 Dec. 1977), physicist and radio engineer, was born in Vienna, Austria, the son of Bernhardt Kompfner, an accountant and musician, and Paula Grotte. His middle-class Jewish family fully participated in turn-of-the-century Viennese social life, including its musical culture. He was educated in public school (1915–1920), the Gymnasium (1920–1924), and Realschule (1924–1927) in the twentieth district of Vienna. Influenced by an uncle, Fritz Keller, to take up architecture, he was admitted to the Technische Hochschule in Vienna in 1927 and acquired an engineering degree (Diplom-Ingenieur) from the Faculty of Architecture in 1933.

The ascension of Adolf Hitler to political power in Germany was a warning signal to Austrian Jews. Roy Franey, an Englishman who had married Kompfner's cousin, arranged for Kompfner to emigrate to England in 1934. Four years later his sister and parents followed, again with Franey's sponsorship. Kompfner began his architectural career in England with the firm of P. D. Hepworth in London. In 1936 he became the managing director of the construction firm Almond Franey & Son, for whom he directed several successful projects that were largely concentrated in the Bermondsey district of London. During this time he also took up a side career as a graphic artist and book illustrator.

Around 1935 Kompfner returned to a childhood interest in physics. As a hobby he regularly spent his evenings in the Patent Office Library on Chancery Lane, reading scientific books and journals. His occasional companion during these library visits was Peggy Mason, whom he married in 1939; they had two children. He kept a notebook of research interests, which in time carried original ideas inspired by his reading of recent publications in television and microwave electronics. His first patent, related to television, was accepted in December 1937, and his interest in microwave tubes led to the submission of a paper to the journal *Wireless World* in 1939. Soon thereafter, in June 1940, Kompfner was interned as an enemy alien on the Isle of Man but was released in December through the intervention of friends and family and by declaring himself stateless. While in internment, however, he roomed with the mathematician Wolfgang H. J. Fuchs, with whom he published a paper on the physics of electron beams in 1942.

The increasing depth of his self-designed studies in physics and the interruption of his architectural career by the internment redirected Kompfner's career at the age of thirty-two. While Kompfner was still on the Isle of Man, his "hobby" had attracted attention. The editor of *Wireless World*, Hugh Pocock, had directed the attention of the British Admiralty to Kompfner's 1939 paper, which could not be published in wartime because of the sensitivity of developments in microwave electronics. In September 1941 F. E. Brundrett of the Royal Naval Scientific Service of the Admiralty hired Kompfner as a temporary experimental officer and assigned him to the physics laboratory of Professor M. L. Oliphant at Birmingham University. Although he had not previously set foot in a physics laboratory, he immediately went to work on the development of high-powered magnetrons and klystron amplifiers for the improvement of radar transmission. While in Birmingham, he invented the traveling-wave tube in 1943; this was a new device for sharply amplifying the output of radar transmitters at high microwave frequencies by coordinating the acceleration of electron beams with the motion of electromagnetic waves. Kompfner was promptly promoted to principal scientific officer by the Admiralty. In 1944 he transferred to the Clarendon Physics Laboratory at Oxford University, which was headed by Frederick A. Lindemann, Viscount Cherwell. He also worked in close collaboration with F. N. H. Robinson at the Services Electronic Research Laboratory (SERL) in Baldock on the design and construction of more powerful traveling-wave tubes. In 1947 he enrolled in the physics department at Oxford, where he obtained his doctorate in 1951.

Years before completing his studies at Oxford, Kompfner had been recruited by John R. Pierce of the Bell Telephone Laboratories. Pierce had become familiar with Kompfner's wartime reports, discovered their shared research interests, and quickly worked out a wave analysis of the traveling-wave tube. Kompfner enthusiastically accepted Pierce's offer and applied for a visa for the United States shortly after World War II ended, but he did not receive it until 1951. In December of that year he joined the technical staff of the Bell Laboratories, located in Murray Hill, New Jersey. As a researcher in Pierce's group, Kompfner was hired principally to continue his work on tunable traveling-wave oscillations and tubes. In 1952 he and Neal Williams began work that led to the invention of the Backward Wave Oscillator, an important variation of the traveling-wave tube. His responsibilities expanded to include administrative tasks. In 1955 Kompfner was appointed the director of electronics research, in 1957 the director of electronics and radio research, and in 1962 the associate executive director of research of the Communication Sciences Division of the Bell Laboratories.

In 1958 Kompfner began a fruitful series of collaborations with Pierce in the new area of satellite-based telecommunications. Pierce had speculated on the use of artificial satellites for telecommunications in an article published in 1955, but the launch of Sputnik in 1957 gave new urgency to his "science fiction," as Kompfner later called it. In 1958 Kompfner realized that the invention of the solid-state maser offered new means for the amplification of radio signals, and together Pierce and Kompfner published a pathbreaking paper on "transoceanic communication by means of satellites" in *Proceedings of the IRE* (47 [1959]: 372–80). This work led to the Echo Satellite Project, conducted jointly by the Bell Laboratories, the Jet Propulsion Laboratory of the California Institute of Technology, and the National Aeronautics and Space Administration under Kompfner's general direction. The Echo I satellite was launched on 12 August 1960. In 1962 AT&T launched the Telstar satellite to carry live television transmissions across the Atlantic Ocean; this experiment was also the first application of a traveling-wave tube for telecommunications, some twenty years after Kompfner's original invention. Having helped make satellite broadcasting possible, Kompfner also participated in or influenced fundamental work on masers, superconductivity, antenna design, and optical communications at Bell Laboratories.

In 1973 Kompfner retired from the Bell Laboratories. He accepted concurrent appointments as a professor of applied physics at Stanford University and as a professor of engineering at Oxford University. His work focused on scanning optical microscopes at Oxford and, with the support of Joint Services Electronics Program funding, on the construction of the first acoustical microscopes at Stanford. Awards recognizing Kompfner's contributions were numerous and included the Duddell Medal of the Physical Society of London, the David Sarnoff Award of the Institute of Electrical and Electronics Engineers, and the Stuart Ballantine Medal of the Franklin Institute. He was a member of the National Academy of Engineering and the National Academy of Sciences. Kompfner died in Stanford, California.

• Kompfner's personal and professional papers, including laboratory notebooks on loan from the Bell Telephone Laboratories, are held in the Department of Special Collections at Stanford University. Kompfner published two accounts of the invention of the traveling-wave tube: "The Invention of Traveling Wave Tubes," *IEEE Transactions on Electronic Devices* ED-23 (July 1976): 730–38, and *The Invention of the Traveling-Wave Tube* (1964). The most useful biographical sources are J. R. Pierce, National Academy of Sciences, *Biographical Memoirs* 54 (1983): 156–80; and Pierce, "Winning Ways: Kompfner's Career—The Rudolf Kompfner Memorial Lecture," *International Journal of Electronics* 48 (1980): 375–88. W. A. Atherton, "Rudolph [*sic*] Kompfner (1909–1977)," *Electronics World and Wireless World* 97 (Jan. 1991): 66–68, derives largely from Pierce's articles.

HENRY LOWOOD

KOOPMANS, Tjalling Charles (28 Aug. 1910–26 Feb. 1985), econometrician and mathematical economist, was born in 's Graveland, the Netherlands, the son of Sjoerd Koopmans and Wijtske van der Zee, schoolteachers. The grammar school Koopmans and his two brothers attended was that at which their father was headmaster.

Koopmans's particular contributions to economics are perhaps best understood in the context of his extensive undergraduate work in mathematics and theoretical physics. He entered the University of Utrecht on a scholarship in 1927, and after a half decade of studies that included the publication of two papers on quantum mechanics, Koopmans received his M.A. equivalent in mathematics. He had become interested in economics well before this, however, and under the initial guidance of Jan Tinbergen in Amsterdam (1934) and Ragnar Frisch (1935) in Oslo, who would themselves later share the first Nobel Prize in economic sciences (1969) for their foundational contributions to econometrics, he wrote *Linear Regression Analysis of Economic Time Series*, for which the University of Leiden awarded him a Ph.D. in 1936. That year he married Truus Wanningen; they had three children.

Together with Tinbergen; Frisch; Trygve Haavelmo, another Nobel Prize (1989) laureate; and Jacob Marschak, Koopmans was in large measure responsible for the introduction of modern methods of statistical inference into economics, and for the demise of "measurement without theory" that had been often associated with the National Bureau of Economic Research (NBER) in the United States. The mathematical principles that inform the identification and "maximum likelihood" estimation of behavioral parameters in small (single equation) and large (multiple equation) econometric models, for example, are those outlined in *Statistical Inference in Dynamic Economic Models* (1950) and *Studies in Econometric Method* (1953), the landmark Cowles Commission monographs for which he served as coeditor and contributor.

He spent brief periods as a lecturer at the Netherlands School of Economics (1936–1938) and the League of Nations (1938–1940) in Geneva. After the Nazi occupations of France and the Netherlands, Koopmans fled Europe for the United States, where he remained, with brief interludes, until his death in New Haven, Connecticut. It was in his role as a statistician for the Combined Shipping Board (1942–1944) at the British Consulate in Washington, D.C., that he would embark on a new line of research, for which he was awarded the Nobel Prize in 1975, an honor he shared with Leonid Kantorovich of the Soviet Union. Koopmans's long association with the Cowles Commission, then affiliated with the University of Chicago, began in 1944, and when the commission moved to New Haven (where it became the Cowles Foundation for Research in Economics) in 1955, he became the Alfred Cowles Professor of Economics at Yale, a position he held until his retirement in 1980.

It was in a 1944 Shipping Board memorandum, "Exchange Ratios between Cargoes on Various Routes," published for the first time in his *Scientific Papers* (1970), that Koopmans established the first foundations for that branch of mathematical economics/operations research familiar to all economists as "activity analysis." In simple terms, activity analysis reduces a substantial number of static allocation problems into the maximization of some "objective function" subject to various "constraints" on "inputs." One could, for example, calculate what combination of methods of production would maximize net national income in model economies given the "endowments" of labor and capital or, as in the Shipping Board memorandum, what routes would maximize the value of delivered cargo given constraints on the number of ships, number and location of ports, and time. His solution algorithm for such problems generated "implicit values" or "shadow prices" for each of the inputs, values that were identical (under special conditions) to their prices on competitive markets. This established a connection between competition and efficient resource use. It was also a method, however, that (in principle, if not in practice) allowed central planners to set "rational" prices for plant managers, and this was the natural focus of Kantorovich's research, itself an extension of his studies of Soviet railroads. The first of Koopmans's *Three Essays on the State of Economic Science* (1957) is a masterful introduction to the welfare properties of competitive allocation mechanisms in terms of activity analysis.

From the mid-1950s onward, Koopmans's principal research interest concerned the optimal allocation of economic resources *over time*. One of the best introductions to this work is his "On the Concept of Optimal Economic Growth" in *The Economic Approach to Development Planning* (1965).

Koopmans was known to friends as a modest scholar, one committed to precise answers for narrow, well-defined questions, and as an accomplished amateur musician and chess enthusiast. In addition to the Nobel Prize, he was elected a member of the National Academy of Sciences and the American Academy of Arts and Sciences and served as president of both the American Economics Association and the Econometric Society.

• Archival material is available, some in the form of Cowles Foundation discussion papers, at Yale. Much of Koopmans's most important published and unpublished research is available in *The Scientific Papers of Tjalling C. Koopmans* (1970). He was also a coeditor (with Armen Alchian) and contributor to *Activity Analysis of Production and Allocation* (1951) and one of the coauthors of *Energy Modelling for an Uncertain Future* (1978). Herbert Scarf, a longtime colleague at the Cowles Foundation, also wrote an eloquent tribute, "Tjalling Charles Koopmans," *Cowles Foundation Discussion Paper Number 1029* (1992). An obituary is in the *New York Times*, 2 Mar. 1985.

PETER HANS MATTHEWS

KOPLIK, Henry (28 Oct. 1858–30 Apr. 1927), pediatrician, educator, and microbiologist, was born in New York City, the son of Abraham S. Koplik and Rosalie K. Prager. Koplik received his undergraduate education at the City College of New York, where he obtained his bachelor of arts degree in 1878. In 1881 Koplik completed his medical school studies at the Columbia College of Physicians and Surgeons in the City of New York. The following year, 1882, he served his internship at the Bellevue Hospital of New York City.

Koplik, like many young, aspiring physicians-to-be in the United States during the turn of the century, spent the years after his internship (1883–1887) learning medicine in the medical clinics of Vienna, Munich, Berlin, and Prague, studying with some of the most prominent physicians and medical scientists then in practice. These included the public health expert, Max von Pettenkoffer of Munich; the world-renowned bacteriologist and developer of the germ theory of disease, Robert Koch of Berlin; and Alois Epstein, director of the Foundling Hospital in Prague. Koplik's decision to blend clinical medicine, pediatrics, and bacteriology defined his career as a specialist in childhood diseases. His particular interest became preventive medicine. Koplik returned to New York City in 1887, armed with an arsenal of specialized training and ready to assault the diseases of childhood.

Koplik joined the ranks of most American physicians of this period with an interest in childhood diseases who combined their pediatric practice with adult care in order to make ends meet financially. Indeed, in 1889, more than two-thirds of the 100 founding members of the American Pediatrics Society spent at least half of their time in adult or general medical practice.

Koplik began his professional career in New York City by applying for and receiving the coveted position of attending physician in the diseases of women and children at the Good Samaritan Dispensary on the Lower East Side. Medical dispensaries were a nineteenth-century institution that provided medical care for the urban poor, neighborhood clinics where medical examinations and minor operations were available and medicines were dispensed. The wide and varied clinical experience gained by the practitioner led many dispensary physicians into far superior positions in the world of clinical medicine. Koplik's practice at the Good Samaritan was almost entirely devoted to care for impoverished East European Jewish and southern Italian immigrant children and their mothers.

During his years at the Good Samaritan Dispensary, Koplik published prodigiously, focusing on his researches into bacteriology, general pediatrics, and infant feeding issues. In 1902, Koplik published the first edition of his magnum opus, *The Diseases of Infancy and Childhood Designed for the Use of Students and Practitioners of Medicine*. The book went through four successive editions.

Koplik was also instrumental in setting up the first goutte de lait in the United States at the Good Samaritan Dispensary in 1889. These institutions—first developed in France—were milk depots that provided free, clean, fresh milk modified for needy infants, in concert with well-baby pediatric examinations. The pediatrician complained that by the time he examined many of his young patients, they were already too ill to help. Since gastrointestinal illnesses related to the consumption of improperly handled or stored milk were a major source of infant mortality and morbidity in urban New York at the turn of the century, Koplik hoped that his goutte de lait would ameliorate the diarrhea and subsequent dehydration and death of infants with gastrointestinal infections. By directly connecting the distribution of clean milk for babies with anticipatory medical examinations, Koplik instituted a new approach to pediatric medical care that continues to be practiced to the present. He remained involved with the goutte de lait until 1914.

Koplik is best known for his 1896 description of the pathognomonic sign of measles—"minute bluish-white specks" on the inner surface of the mouth—which are still referred to by pediatricians as "Koplik's spots." Measles was a common contagious disease in turn-of-the-century New York, and good nursing care, parental love, and strict isolation (or quarantine) were the only available treatments for this infection. Unlike other contagious diseases of childhood, measles tended to make small children quite ill and susceptible to secondary infections and complications. It was also difficult for physicians to diagnose measles before the appearance of the well-known red, maculopapular rash. The problem with this method of diagnosis, however, is that the child with full-blown measles has already been contagious to others for at least three days, which only contributes to its further spread among susceptible children. By noticing the mouth lesions, which tend to appear a few days before the full-blown skin rash of measles, it became possible to isolate and treat a budding case of measles before that child had a chance to interact and play with other susceptible children.

In 1900, in recognition of his brilliant medical career, Henry Koplik was offered the position of attending pediatrician at the Mount Sinai Hospital of New York City, where he practiced for the next twenty-five years. He also maintained a private consultation practice on the Upper East Side of New York. In 1925 Koplik retired from active practice. He died in New York City. Koplik, who developed the first free pediatric milk dispensary in the United States, wrote numerous clinical papers and an influential textbook of pediatrics, and described the pathognomonic sign of measles, was one of the most prominent pediatricians in the United States during the early twentieth century.

• Koplik published broadly on his findings, including "The Diagnosis of the Invasion of Measles from a Study of the Exanthmema as It Appears on the Buccal Mucous Membrane," *Archives of Pediatrics* 13 (1896): 918–22; "A New Diagnostic Sign of Measles," *Medical Record* 53 (1898): 505–7; and "The History of the First Milk Depot or Goutte de Lait with Consultations in America," *Journal of the American Medical Association* 63 (1914): 1574–75. Biographical articles include Murray Bass, "Henry Koplik," in *Pediatric Profiles*, ed. Bordon Veeder (1957), and Howard Markel, "Henry Koplik, M.D., the Good Samaritan Dispensary of New York City, and the Description of Koplik's Spots," *Archives of Pediatrics and Adolescent Medicine* 150 (May 1996). See also James J. Walsh, *History of Medicine in New York: Three Centuries of Medical Progress*, vol. 4 (1919), pp. 173–74. Koplik's position in the history of pediatrics can be found in Fielding Garrison, "The History of Pediatrics," in *Garrison's History of Medicine*, 3d ed. (1924). An obituary is in the *New York Times*, 1 May 1927.

HOWARD MARKEL

KORESH, David (17 Aug. 1959–19 Apr. 1993), religious leader, was born Vernon Wayne Howell in Houston, Texas, the son of Bobby Howell, a student, and Bonnie Clark. His mother, fourteen years old at the time of his birth, dropped out of school and married Joe Golden, a nightclub owner, after ending her relationship with Howell. She soon divorced the allegedly abusive Golden, left her two-year-old son with her mother, Earline Clark, and moved to Dallas.

Koresh was first exposed to biblical teachings through his grandmother, who was a member of the Seventh-day Adventist (SDA) church, a sect founded in the mid-nineteenth century by American Ellen G. White that stresses contemporary prophecy and the purification of its members in anticipation of Christ's imminent return. After Koresh's fifth birthday, his mother took him to the Dallas suburb of Richardson, where he experienced early failure in school as a result of dyslexia. He found a measure of solace in learning to play the guitar, but religion remained his great concern as he memorized extended passages from the Bible, immersed himself in SDA teaching, and participated in Christian exhortation both in and out of church.

After completing the ninth grade, Koresh dropped out of Garland High School and began working as a carpenter. In 1977 his relationship with a sixteen-year-old girl ended when she became pregnant, causing him to sink into a long depression. He settled in Tyler, Texas, where he was expelled from an SDA congregation for aggressively questioning the authority of church leaders and exclaiming his belief that the church was in need of a new prophet. His friend Harriet Phelps told him about the Branch Davidians, a Christian sect situated outside Waco, Texas, whose leader, Lois Roden, claimed to be such a prophet. Koresh joined the Branch Davidians at their Mount Carmel commune in 1981.

The Branch Davidians were the theological descendants of SDA leader Victor Houteff, who in 1929 had broken from the church and formed a community he claimed to represent the "servants of God" mentioned in the book of Revelation whose "sealing" would mark the beginning of the end of the world. The group settled at Mount Carmel in 1955 after Houteff's death, remaining intact despite the constantly changing teachings of a series of leaders.

Koresh entered the world of Roden and the Davidians already immersed in Christian apocalyptic mysteries. He immediately energized the somewhat lethargic community—particulary Roden, whom Koresh courted on both religious and romantic terms. Her son George, who believed himself to be the next rightful prophet of the Davidians, became threatened by Koresh's growing power and began wearing a gun to Bible studies.

In January 1984 Koresh married fourteen-year-old Rachel Jones; they had two children. The following year Koresh and his wife traveled to Israel, where he claimed to have received a monumental vision from God. Returning with this "Cyrus message" (named for the biblical king who freed the Hebrews from their Babylonian captivity), he discovered that George Roden had taken control of Mount Carmel, changed its name to Rodenville, and ousted Koresh's sympathizers. Koresh led a group of approximately forty people to a compound near Palestine, Texas, where they endured the poorest of living conditions to live as his disciples.

Koresh's personal charm, earthy humor, and encyclopedic knowledge of the Bible made him a convincing orator, even to the most well-educated listener. Like Davidian leaders before him, he claimed that he had been chosen to fulfill a messianic role in God's plan to save humankind. He and his followers came to see him as the personification of "the Lamb" who opens the sealed scrolls in the book of Revelation, a figure traditionally interpreted as Christ.

As Koresh's authority over his continually increasing flock grew, he introduced what he called a "new light" doctrine, the main component of which was that his special role required him to marry and have children with more than one woman. By doing so he claimed he would create a new divine lineage and take on the sexual burdens of the male Davidians, who would find their true mates in heaven. Koresh's first nonlegal marriage is believed to have been to fourteen-year-old Karen Doyle in the spring of 1986. He then began a relationship with Michelle Jones, who was twelve years old and the sister of his legal wife, Rachel; she had three daughters by Koresh. Eventually Koresh fathered approximately fifteen children by numerous women in the group and "annulled" all marriages but his own.

In 1987 Koresh was charged with attempted murder after a victimless gun battle with George Roden. Koresh was acquitted; Roden, however, soon murdered another man and was imprisoned. Koresh and his followers immediately returned to Mount Carmel. In May 1990 he changed his legal name to David Koresh ("Koresh" is Hebrew for "Cyrus") and claimed that all Davidians shared his last name.

Koresh continued to recruit new members through trips to SDA congregations around the United States and the world, particularly Britain and Australia. The number of Davidians living inside Mount Carmel eventually grew to 130 men, women, and children, with many others offering their financial support of Koresh's ministry from afar.

In 1990 Marc Breault, a former resident of Mount Carmel, began publicizing Koresh's activities in an attempt to undermine his role as a prophet within Davidian circles in Australia. A series of investigations into the Davidians began as a result of his and others' testimony, bringing to light stories of Koresh's illicit marriages and equally troubling reports of alleged physical abuse of children within the commune. Koresh's theology had also turned increasingly militaristic. Davidians had begun a regimen of physical and mental training in preparation for a final apocalyptic battle with an enemy that Koresh came to identify as the U.S. government. Agents from the Bureau of Alcohol, Tobacco, and Firearms (BATF) also discovered that the group had been building an arsenal of weapons and explosives, spending nearly $200,000 over the previous six years.

In the spring of 1992 the *Waco Tribune-Herald* began an investigation of Koresh and the Davidians. Koresh, aware that the world's spotlight was on him, convinced his followers that the inevitable confrontation would be a fulfillment of his divine role. On 27 February 1993 the *Tribune-Herald* ran the first part of a seven-part series called "The Sinful Messiah," which portrayed Koresh as a dangerous cult leader. The next day 100 BATF agents surrounded Mount Carmel in an attempt to raid the compound for illegal weapons. The Davidians were ready for the agents, who were caught in a barrage of gunfire; when the shooting stopped nearly an hour later, four federal agents and six Davidians lay dead.

The Federal Bureau of Investigation (FBI) immediately took over the government's operations and began negotiating with Koresh, who considered the raid an unprovoked attack. From the start, communication between Koresh and the FBI was thwarted by the two sides' irreconcilable interpretation of the events. Koresh and his followers believed themselves faithful martyrs; FBI officials saw the Davidians' activities as rooted in criminal rather than religious motivations. Koresh eventually allowed thirty-seven individuals, including twenty-one children, to leave, but the majority of his followers remained with him and never considered the apostasy of surrender.

The FBI eventually adopted a strategy aimed at wearing down the Davidians' resolve by making conditions inside the compound unbearable. However, the length of the siege, the belief that Koresh would never peaceably surrender, and the concern for the welfare of the Davidian children—later voiced poignantly by Attorney General Janet Reno and President William Clinton—convinced the FBI that waiting was futile. While Koresh was writing what he claimed to be the ultimate explanation of the seven apocalyptic seals of the book of Revelation, FBI leaders planned a more aggressive strategy.

Before dawn on 19 April 1993, FBI officials informed Koresh and the Davidians that they were preparing to inject nonlethal tear gas into the compound, stressing that the action was not an assault. Koresh furiously instructed his followers to put on gas masks and move to locations farther inside the fort-like structure. FBI tanks blasted holes in the walls and engulfed the buildings with gas, but not one Davidian was forced out. Just past noon, FBI agents spotted small fires at three different locations within the compound. The high wind and the low quality of the buildings caused the fires to spread rapidly, and the entire compound was quickly consumed. Nine Davidians survived the fire; seventy-four others, including Koresh, perished.

Later reports by FBI sharpshooters and some survivors stated that the Davidians had started the fires and mercifully killed most of the children by gunfire; other members of the group denied this charge, claiming that FBI tanks had knocked over oil lamps and inadvertently blocked escape routes. BATF and FBI leaders were also severely criticized for mistakes in judgment that may have worsened or even caused the tragedy. In any case, Koresh's life and the conflagration at Mount Carmel exemplify the sometimes volatile nature of revelatory religion in the midst of secular American culture.

• Sensationalistic but informative accounts of Koresh's life are given in Brad Bailey and Bob Darden, *Mad Man in Waco: The Complete Story of the Davidian Cult, David Koresh, and the Waco Massacre* (1993), and Kenneth Samples et al., *Prophets of the Apocalypse: David Koresh and Other American Messiahs* (1994). Works that examine Koresh and the Mount Carmel tragedy in the context of American political, theological, and legal issues are Dick J. Reavis, *The Ashes of Waco* (1995); Stuart A. Wright, ed., *Armageddon in Waco: Critical Perspectives on the Branch Davidian Conflict* (1995); James R. Lewis, ed., *From the Ashes: Making Sense of Waco* (1994); and James D. Tabor and Eugene V. Gallagher, *Why Waco?: Cults and the Battle for Religious Freedom in America* (1995). The seven-part series chronicling Koresh and the Branch Davidians published at the start of the Mount Carmel siege is Mark England and Darlene McCormick, "The Sinful Messiah," *Waco Tribune-Herald*, 27–28 Feb., 1 Mar. 1993. Articles that appeared during and after the siege include Richard Lacayo, "Cult of Death," *Time*, 15 Mar. 1993, pp. 36–39; Harrison Rainie et al., "The Final Days of David Koresh," *U.S. News & World Report*, 3 May 1993; and Gordon Witkin, "How David Koresh Got All Those Guns," *U.S. News & World Report*, 7 June 1993, pp. 43–44.

JAY MAZZOCCHI

KORNGOLD, Erich Wolfgang (29 May 1897–29 Nov. 1957), composer, was born in Brünn in the Austrian crown land of Moravia (now Brno, Czech Republic), the son of Dr. Julius Korngold, a noted Austrian music critic, and Josephine Witrofsky. Exhibiting remarkable musical precocity, Korngold initially studied with his father but later was sent to composer-teacher Robert Fuchs. At age ten, he played his compositions for Gustav Mahler, who pronounced him "*ein Genie! ein Genie!*" (a Genius!). Upon Mahler's recommendation, Korngold studied with Alexander Zemlinsky, who orchestrated the eleven-year-old composer's first major work, the ballet *Der Schneemann* (The Snowman, 1908–1909). Before Korngold had reached the age of nineteen, Arthur Nikisch had conducted his *Schauspiel Ouverture* with the Leipzig Gewandhaus Orchestra (1911), Felix Weingartner had conducted his *Sinfonietta* with the Vienna Philharmonic (1913), and his two one-act operas, *Violanta* and *Der Ring des Polykrates*, had been produced in Munich (1916). In addition, Korngold had composed two piano sonatas (1908, 1910) and a piano trio (1909–1910) and spent two uneventful years in the Austrian army (1916–1918). On 4 December 1920 his most famous and critically acclaimed work, the three-act opera *Die tote Stadt* (The Dead City), was simultaneously premiered in Hamburg and Cologne. It has sustained worldwide success since that time.

During the 1920s, Korngold continued to compose and was greatly responsible for the Johann Strauss revival with his reorchestrations of *A Night in Venice* (1923) and *Cagliostro in Vienna* (1926). In 1929, he began his long collaboration with director Max Reinhardt in a new version of Strauss's *Die Fledermaus*. Korngold reworked the entire score; it ultimately became the operetta *Rosalinda* (1942, rev. 1947). Between 1930 and 1934 Korngold taught composition at the Vienna Academy of Music and in 1932 was named along with Arnold Schoenberg in a poll conducted by the *Neue Wiener Tagblatt* as one of the two greatest living composers.

In 1934 the 37-year-old Korngold arrived in Hollywood at the invitation of Max Reinhardt to adapt Mendelssohn's music for the Reinhardt film *A Midsummer's Night Dream* (1935). The score was received with great enthusiasm because of the original manner in which Korngold arranged the music to fit just behind the action and dialogue. Unlike other film composers, Korngold did not use mechanical devices such as cue sheets, click tracks, or a stopwatch to fit music to film. Instead, Warner Brothers provided him with a private projection room and piano, and Korngold had the projectionist run the film continuously while he composed to the running picture. (He had already worked out themes for each principal character based on the shooting script.) Finalizing his sketches at home, he returned to the projection room and played the score, making only minor adjustments, while the projectionist "punched" or marked on the film the beginning of each musical sequence to be recorded. Relying only on his innate sense of timing to fit the music to the film, Korngold then entered a musical soundstage and conducted the orchestra while the film was projected on a large screen. He maintained complete control of the final product; no studio chief, producer, or director heard the music before the sneak preview.

From 1934 to 1938, Korngold balanced his time between Hollywood and Vienna, but by the late 1930s the Nazis had totally restricted performances of his operas, and with the *Anschluss* in 1938, Korngold was most grateful to have a picture-to-picture contract and a long-term working relationship with Warner Brothers. That year, he permanently moved to Hollywood with Luzi, his wife of fourteen years, and their two sons; he became a naturalized U.S. citizen in 1943. While in Hollywood he wrote the music for many films, including *Give Us This Night* (1936), *Captain Blood* (1936), *The Green Pastures* (1936), *Anthony Adverse* (1936), *Another Dawn* (1937), *The Prince and the Pauper* (1937), *The Adventures of Robin Hood* (1938), *Juarez* (1939), *The Private Lives of Elizabeth and Essex* (1939), *The Sea Hawk* (1940), *The Sea Wolf* (1941), *Kings Row* (1942), *The Constant Nymph* (1942), *Devotion* (1943), *Between Two Worlds* (1944), *Of Human Bondage* (1946), *Escape Me Never* (1947), and *Deception* (1946).

Although Korngold wrote only eighteen original film scores during his thirteen-year career at Warner Brothers, his influence on the medium was assured. His phenomenal gift for melodic invention, brilliant orchestral textures, and impeccable taste in creating grand symphonic scores that perfectly supported the dramatic action established standards that have been rarely surpassed to this day. Korngold received two Academy Awards for his film scores (*Anthony Adverse* and *The Adventures of Robin Hood*); he was the highest-paid film composer of his era and the first major composer with an international reputation to work on a regular basis in Hollywood. As a renowned composer, he brought great prestige to the Warner Brothers studio. His unique contract allowed him to maintain the rights to reuse the music from his films as long as it was not synchronized to a film score; Korngold often reused his film themes in his concert works, reasoning that after their theatrical release they would never be heard again. Ironically, his film work in Hollywood was disdained by much of the serious music community, even though Korngold considered it as important as his concert works and recognized film to be a new art form.

After 1947, Korngold retired from film music, other than arranging Richard Wagner's music for the film *Magic Fire* (1954), and devoted the final decade of his life to resurrecting his concert music career both in the United States and abroad. Works from this period included the Violin Concerto in D (1945, premiered by Heifetz), the Cello Concerto in C (1946), the *Symphonic Serenade for Strings* (1947), and the Symphony in F-sharp (1951–1952).

Because Korngold remained true to the Romantic tradition throughout his career regardless of the changing trends in twentieth-century music, critics often judged his compositions most severely. Since his death, however, both his film music and his concert works have enjoyed an enthusiastic reevaluation, with numerous recordings and concert performances, while contemporary film composers continue to pay homage to the symphonic style he painstakingly developed. An amiable and humorous man, Korngold died of a heart seizure in North Hollywood, California.

• Korngold's music manuscripts (including the film scores), letters, and memorabilia are located at the Library of Congress. The University of Southern California has additional copies of the film scores and parts in its Warner Brothers collection. The Leo Baeck Institute in New York City has a small collection of letters from his earlier career (1902–1928). There is no major biography of Korngold in English. The most important book on Korngold's life is by his wife, Luzi Korngold, *Erich Wolfgang Korngold: Ein Lebenbild* (1967). *The Korngolds in Vienna* (1991) is a collection of memoirs and essays written by Julius Korngold (1860–1945), the composer's father, and traces much of the early career of his son Erich. It also contains the most authoritative list of the composer's works, with premiere dates and an excellent bibliography and discography. Tony Thomas's section on Korngold in his *Music For the Movies* (1973) continues to be the most engaging article about the composer in English.

LANCE C. BOWLING

KOŚCIUSZKO, Tadeusz Andrzej Bonawentura (12 Feb. 1746–15 Oct. 1817), revolutionary war officer and leader for Polish independence, was born at one of his family's estates, either "Mereczowszczyna" or "Siechnowicze," both near Kosów, Poland, the son of Ludwig Tadeusz Kościuszko, an army colonel and member of the minor gentry, and Thecla Ratomska. As the youngest of four sons, Kościuszko could share in inheritance but not control of the family estates. Thus he chose an army career. His father died in 1758, and his mother ten years later. After being tutored by an uncle and briefly attending a Jesuit school in Brześć, Kościuszko, from 1755 to 1760, studied at a school of the Piarist Fathers in Lubieszów, near Pinsk. Sponsored by Prince Casimir Czartoryski, Kościuszko entered the Royal Corps of Cadets at the Royal Military School in Warsaw in December 1765. After one year he was an ensign and an instructor of students; in 1768 he was promoted to captain, graduating the following year.

Kościuszko received a royal scholarship and borrowed money from his brother to enroll at the École Militaire in Paris in 1769. He subsequently studied artillery and engineering in Mézières, France, and for about a year he attended the Académie Royale de Peinture et de Sculpture in Paris. Kościuszko became a skilled artist and draftsman, and many of his sketchings have been preserved.

Kościuszko returned to Poland in 1774. Poland had experienced its first partition, and the army was almost nonexistent. His brother's mismanagement had left the family estates on the verge of bankruptcy. Kościuszko fell passionately in love with Ludwika Sosnowska, whose father, a wealthy nobleman, put an end to the relationship. Kościuszko would never marry. Brokenhearted and with no possibility of career advancement in Poland, Kościuszko decided to seek his fortune abroad. He probably was acquainted with Charles Lee (1731–1782), who served in the Polish army from 1765 to 1770 as an honorary major general and subsequently held a high military command in America. With a loan from his brother-in-law, Kościuszko went to America to obtain an officer's commission from Congress. Awaiting Congress's decision after arriving at Philadelphia on 30 August 1776, he was employed by the Pennsylvania Committee of Defense to lend his engineering talents in the construction of American forts on the Delaware River. On 18 October 1776 Congress appointed Kościuszko a colonel of engineers.

Kościuszko joined the northern army at Ticonderoga, where he sought to establish a wide range of fortifications on the hills surrounding the fort and especially to make Mount Defiance a main line of defense. His advice went unheeded, and a British army under General John Burgoyne, by emplacing big guns on Mount Defiance, was able to capture Fort Ticonderoga on 5 July 1777. As engineer to the northern army under General Horatio Gates, Kościuszko selected the battlefield and supervised fortifications that contributed to the American victory at Saratoga on 17 October 1777.

From March 1778 to June 1780 Kościuszko was responsible for building the defenses at West Point. He cultivated a garden that is still maintained at the U.S. Military Academy as "Kościuszko's Garden." When

Gates assumed the command of the southern army, he invited Kościuszko to be chief of engineers for the Southern Department. Kościuszko arrived in the South after Gates's disastrous defeat at Camden, South Carolina. Gates was replaced by General Nathanael Greene, with whom Kościuszko served during the remainder of the war. During the winter of 1780–1781 Kościuszko had charge of reconnaissance of the Catawba River and supervised transportation of Greene's army as it raced to and crossed the Dan River. One of Kościuszko's feats was the building of wagons, with detachable wheels, that could also serve as boats. At the unsuccessful siege of Ninety-Six, South Carolina, 22 May–19 June 1781, he was criticized for convincing Greene to concentrate the attack on the enemy's strongest position and for erecting siege works too close to the enemy's fortifications. During 1782, near Charleston, South Carolina, Kościuszko acted primarily as a cavalry officer. At war's end he was brevetted a brigadier general (13 Oct. 1783). He helped found the Society of the Cincinnati in 1783.

In summer 1784 Kościuszko returned to Poland and settled at Siechnowicze in the role of a small landlord. In October 1789 he received a commission as major general in the Polish army. He led a radical reform of the Polish army, recruiting peasants as regular soldiers. Leading Polish forces in the war with Russia that began in 1792, he managed to save the Polish army from annihilation at Dubienka, 18 July 1792. King Stanislaw Augustus made him a lieutenant general and conferred upon him the citation of *Virtuti Militari*, Poland's highest military honor. With the defeat of the Polish army, Kościuszko went into exile at Leipzig, Saxony. Returning to Poland in 1794, he assumed military and political leadership for Polish independence. He wrote and promulgated the "Act of Insurrection," similar to America's Declaration of Independence, and also the "Manifesto of Polanliec," which called for freeing the serfs. He was victorious at the battle of Raclawice, 4 April 1794, and turned back the Prussians at the siege of Warsaw, but Kościuszko's army was defeated at Szczekociny, when Prussian troops arrived to assist the Russians. Kościuszko suffered a decisive defeat by the Russians at Maciejowice, 10 October 1794, where he was severely wounded from a lance through a thigh and a sword blow to the head. Captured, he spent two years in Russian prisons. Poland ceased to exist after the third partition in 1795. Upon Catherine II's death, Kościuszko won favor from the new tsar, Paul I, who treated him as a war hero.

Leaving Russia in 1797, Kościuszko visited England, where the king's doctors attended to his wounds, and then the United States, arriving at Philadelphia on 18 August 1797. He received a hero's welcome. Congress provided him pay for his war services in the amount of $18,912.03, $2,947.33 for four years of interest on the debt, and 500 acres of land in Ohio.

In May 1798 Kościuszko left the United States for Paris, where he lived for the next three years. In 1800 he wrote, in French, a manual, *Manoeuvres of Horse Artillery*, published in English in the United States in 1808. The handbook became widely used by the American army, and Kościuszko has been regarded as the father of American artillery tactics.

Kościuszko preferred exile from his native land because of the foreign oppression. From 1801 to 1815 he lived with the family of Peter Joseph Zeltner, first minister of the Helvetian Republic, at Berville, Switzerland. From 1815 until his death Kościuszko resided with the family of Franz Xavier Zeltner at Solothurn, Switzerland. Tsar Alexander I invited Kościuszko to the Congress of Vienna in 1814; Kościuszko attended but was disappointed that nothing was done to liberate Poland. Thomas Jefferson and Kościuszko were frequent correspondents from 1798 until Kościuszko's death. In a letter to Jefferson dated 5 November 1805, Kościuszko wrote, "It is pusillanimity and indecision which destroy Nations, but never their valor and order." Kościuszko donated the proceeds from the sale of his Ohio lands to establish the Colored School at Newark, New Jersey. Before he died at Solothurn, he emancipated his serfs. In 1818 his body was transferred from Switzerland to a crypt in the cathedral at Cracow; his heart was preserved in an urn for museum display, and his intestines were interred at Zuchwil, Poland.

Kościuszko was a hero in the cause of liberty on two continents, exemplifying republican virtue by his public service and defense of liberty. He was self-effacing to the point of refusing to seek promotion in the American army, and he looked after the welfare of the common soldier. Jefferson said of Kościuszko in a letter to Gates, 21 February 1798, "He is as pure a son of liberty as I have ever known, and of liberty which is to go to all, and not to the few and rich alone."

• Kościuszko's papers are in the Archives and Museum of the Polish Catholic Union of America, Chicago. His correspondence is scattered in collections of Continental army officers, including the George Washington Papers, Library of Congress. Some of the military material is published in Metchie J. E. Budka, ed., *Autograph Letters of Thaddeus Kosciuszko in the American Revolution* (1977). Kościuszko's role in the southern campaigns can be traced in Richard K. Showman, ed., *The Papers of General Nathanael Greene*, vols. 4–7 (1986–1994), and successive volumes. For a bibliography, see Janina W. Hoskins, comp., *Tadeusz Kosciuszko 1746–1817, A Selective List of Reading Materials in English* (1980). The definitive biography, in two parts, is Miecislaus Haiman, *Kosciuszko in the American Revolution* (1943) and *Kosciuszko: Leader and Exile* (1946). The latter contains Kościuszko-Jefferson correspondence, 1798–1817, in full or summarized. A good, popular biography is Monica M. Gardner, *Kosciuszko: A Biography*, rev. ed. (1942).

HARRY M. WARD

KOSINSKI, Jerzy Nikodem (14 June 1933–3 May 1991), novelist, was born Jerzy Nikodem Lewinkopf in Lodz, Poland, the son of Mieczyslaw Lewinkopf, a textile entrepreneur, and Elzbieta Wanda Weinreich. Jerzy's early years were scarred by the Nazi threat. A Jewish family of solid financial means, the Lewinkopfs survived the war largely as a result of the father's shrewdness. When the family moved from Lodz to Sandomierz in 1939 Jerzy's father began the process of changing the family's name from Lewinkopf to Kosinski to disguise their Jewish identity. On several occasions the family narrowly escaped capture by the Germans as they moved from place to place just months before all Jewish citizens were relocated to concentration camps. Kosinski would later alter the story of his early years, falsely asserting that he was separated from his parents at the age of six and wandered from village to village, allegedly undergoing a series of horrible abuses—one of which left him mute until his adolescent years.

Before entering the University of Lodz in 1950, Kosinski became a respected photographic artist; his background in photography would remain an influence on his writing. After receiving a master's degree in social sciences in 1954 and a second master's degree in history in 1955, Kosinski enrolled as a doctoral student at the Polish Academy of Sciences in Warsaw. In 1957 he spent part of the year in Moscow as a visiting graduate student. His observations of the totalitarian systems in Eastern Europe would leave him with a lasting anticommunist sentiment. Later that year, Kosinski went to New York City to study at Columbia University. He became a U.S. citizen in 1965.

Before coming to the United States, Kosinski had little interest in writing as a vocation because of the high degree of censorship in the Soviet bloc. However, the challenge of experimenting with a new language, English, and the prospect of writing without restrictions intrigued him. Kosinski arrived in America with marginal English skills, and he often told stories of soliciting editorial help from telephone operators.

Despite receiving a Ford Foundation Fellowship in 1957–1958, Kosinski's early years in the United States were plagued with financial problems, and he took various odd jobs to support himself. In the summer of 1960 Kosinski found a part-time job cataloging the library of Mary Emma Hayward Weir, the widow of industrialist Ernest T. Weir. Kosinski and Mary Weir, eighteen years his senior, were married in 1962; they had no children. This marriage gave him the financial security that he desperately wanted, and he soon became known in New York social circles. Mary's health problems, coupled with her severe alcoholism, led to their divorce in 1966; she died two years later. In 1965 Kosinski met Katherina "Kiki" von Fraunhofer, who became his lifelong companion. They were married in 1987; they had no children.

As early as 1961 Kosinski had begun work on a loosely autobiographical novel detailing the experiences of an orphaned boy wandering through Eastern Europe during World War II. The novel, *The Painted Bird* (1965), is generally regarded as Kosinski's masterpiece. The novel's episodic form, coupled with its lack of plot and the seeming futility of existence that it reflected, epitomized widespread sentiments in the mid-1960s. It received a strong critical reception in the United States, but it was even more successful in Europe, winning the Prix du Meilleur Livre Étranger in France for the best foreign book of the year. It also introduced several themes for which Kosinski's work and persona would be known: the power of the individual to manipulate reality both of the self and of others, and the power to invent the self. Kosinski recognized the enormous potential of power in its various forms, and he explored this potential in much of his work. In *Passing By: Selected Essays, 1962–1991* (1992), he described his literary role: "I see myself as an adversary novelist whose role is to confront—not to escape from—life's threatening encounters. There is nothing in my novels that couldn't take place in these United States in the very city block in which so many of us live" (p. 42). Many readers have found the graphic violence and sex in Kosinski's "threatening encounters" excessive. With the exception of *Being There* (1971), the other novels are loosely autobiographical and episodic; they often involve bizarre scenarios in which the lives of others are heavily affected by the elaborate covert actions of the Kosinski persona.

Kosinski's second novel, *Steps* (1968), also received a strong reception, winning the National Book Award in 1969. He successfully adapted *Being There* into a screenplay; the film, produced in 1980 and starring Peter Sellers, earned Kosinski the best screenplay award from the Writers Guild of America.

Kosinski's career and reputation continued to flourish until 1982. That year the *Village Voice* published a damning exposé of Kosinski based on contradictions in his account of his childhood in Poland, allegations that he was covertly involved with the CIA, and evidence that his novels had received unethical amounts of collaborative help. There was speculation that while writing *Being There* Kosinski had heavily borrowed from or perhaps even plagiarized an obscure Polish spy novel, and that he had written *The Painted Bird* in Polish and given no credit to a series of translators and collaborators. His reputation was irreparably tarnished. Hoping to restore his reputation, Kosinski labored over his final novel until he committed suicide in his New York City apartment.

Despite the inconsistencies in his background, Kosinski will be remembered as an important voice for Polish-American culture and as a writer who explored the power and complexities of the self. In critiquing Kosinski's most important work, *The Painted Bird*, James Park Sloan noted that the novel is "odd in every respect—its expansion of experience into a surreal inner theater, its construction with help from editors and translators, its lack of dialogue, and its existence at the shadowy border between fiction and personal statement—it remains a major aesthetic response to the Holocaust and a provocative documentation of the complex and reverberative consequences of violence and evil" (p. 450). The novel marks Kosinski as an important American author of the late twentieth century.

• Kosinski's papers are at Spertus College of Judaica in Chicago. Other fictional works by Kosinski include *The Devil Tree* (1973), *Cockpit* (1975), *Blind Date* (1977), *Passion Play* (1979), *Pinball* (1982), and *The Hermit of 69th Street* (1988).

Significant nonfiction works include *The Future Is Ours, Comrade* (Joseph Novak, pseud., 1960), *No Third Path* (Joseph Novak, pseud. 1962), and *Notes of the Author on "The Painted Bird"* (1965). See Tom Teicholz, ed., *Conversations with Jerzy Kosinski* (1993), for a collection of interviews. The definitive biography, which includes a complete bibliography, is James Park Sloan, *Jerzy Kosinski: A Biography* (1996). For other book-length studies, see Welch D. Everman, *Jerzy Kosinski: The Literature of Violation* (1991); Norman Lavers, *Jerzy Kosinski* (1982); Paul R. Lilly, Jr., *Words in Search of Victims: The Achievement of Jerzy Kosinski* (1988); Byron L. Sherwin, *Jerzy Kosinski: Literary Alarm Clock* (1981); and Sepp L. Tiefenthaler, *Jerzy Kosinski* (1980). An obituary is in the *New York Times*, 4 May 1991.

ANDREW STUART MCCLURE

KOSLOFF, Theodore (22 Jan. 1882–22 Nov. 1956), dancer and film actor, was born Fedor Mikhailovich Kozlov in Moscow, Russia, the son of Mikhail Fedorovich Koslov, a violinist in the Bolshoi Theater, and Maria Ivanovna Lebedeva. His parents married in 1883, and the following year the elder Kozlov legally adopted Fedor.

Kozlov studied at the Bolshoi Theater School in Moscow, developing into a dancer of prodigious technical virtuosity and powerful dramatic skill. He joined the Bolshoi Ballet in 1900 but transferred to Maryinsky in Saint Petersburg the following year, where, in his debut performance, he partnered Tamara Karsavina, who described him as a "dancer of impeccable and noble style." Before long, he became the chosen partner of the Maryinsky's *prima ballerina assoluta*, Matilda Kshessinska. Kozlov returned to Moscow in 1904, followed in 1905 by his future wife, the Saint Petersburg–trained dancer Alexandra Baldina, whose meteoric rise within the Bolshoi paralleled Kozlov's own.

In 1909, Kozlov, his younger brother Aleksei, and Baldina joined Serge Diaghilev's Ballets Russes for its first Paris season. Kozlov (now known as Kosloff, or Koslov) won acclaim in the *Polovtsian Dances* from *Prince Igor* and successfully took over from an ailing Vaslav Nijinsky as the Poet in Michel Fokine's *Les Sylphides*. At the season's end, Kosloff joined Karsavina and a small company at the London Coliseum, the first of the much-heralded Russian dancers to be seen in England. During an equally successful return engagement the following year, Kosloff accepted a lucrative contract to appear in the United States on the Orpheum vaudeville circuit. However, his request for an extension of leave from the Bolshoi was denied, resulting in his official dismissal from the Imperial Theaters on 16 August 1910. Severed from the institution in which he had been reared from the age of seven, Kosloff became his own impresario with a mission to democratize the aristocratic art of ballet. "I am very glad that vaudeville has taken up the Russian ballet," he told the *New York Times* on 4 June 1916. "[Ballet] should be for the people and vaudeville will bring it to them."

While Kosloff still performed occasionally in Europe, the United States became the focus of his ambi-

tion. In 1911, with vaudeville star Gertrude Hoffman, Kosloff presented his reconstructions of Fokine's *Schéhérazade*, *Cléopâtre*, and *Les Sylphides* to audiences from New York to California, to largely favorable reviews. During the tour, Kosloff and Baldina were married on 26 October 1911 in San Francisco. Their only child, Irena (sometimes Irene or Irina), born in Moscow the following year, became permanently incapacitated as a result of meningitis. Although performing remained a priority for Kosloff, this new responsibility apparently precipitated a desire for a level of financial stability touring alone could not provide. He turned to teaching.

He immigrated to the United States in December 1912, one of the first in a wave of twentieth-century immigrants from the imperial Russian ballets to influence the development of dance in America. The Kosloff brothers opened a studio in New York City, and Theodore consolidated his position by wooing the wealthy and influential, a task for which he was well suited. Radiating confidence, Kosloff was characterized as having "that indefinable and unaccountable gift of the gods which gives power over other human beings" (Wardell, p. 55). The New York studio was left in Alexis's hands when Kosloff settled in Los Angeles in 1917, opening a studio there followed by another in San Francisco in 1923 or 1925. Kosloff was a gifted teacher who stressed the importance of a total artistic education. Among the first generation of American dancers he trained were Agnes de Mille, Flower Hujer, Nana Gollner, Paul Petroff, Dimitri Romanov, and Broadway stars Marilyn Miller and Mary Eaton.

Meanwhile, Kosloff choreographed and performed from Broadway to Hollywood, while his "Imperial Russian Ballet" made three tours on the Keith-Orpheum circuit between 1916 and 1919. In pursuit of performing outlets for his students, who danced regularly in movie prologues (the dance performances that preceded movie showings), Kosloff accepted an appointment as ballet master to the California Opera Company in 1925. The following year he directed the San Francisco Opera Ballet, but his largest audiences were found at the Hollywood Bowl. Many of the ballets he presented there were restagings of Fokine works: *Schéhérazade* (1926); Kosloff's version of *Les Sylphides*, renamed *Chopin Memories* (1932); *Petrouchka* (1937); and *Le Spectre de la Rose* (1938), which was given with *Shingandi*, an original work set in Africa to music by David Guion, first presented in Dallas, Texas, in 1933.

Kosloff's film career began in 1917 when Cecil B. De Mille cast him as an Aztec prince in *The Woman God Forgot*. His exotically dramatic style proved ideal for the silent screen. In a period of ten years, he appeared in starring and supporting roles in over twenty films, winning increasing critical acclaim. With the introduction of sound, acting roles became sporadic for the man whose English remained heavily accented. Nonetheless, Kosloff bowed out in illustrious company: he played the dancing instructor in *Stage Door* (1937), starring Katharine Hepburn, Ginger Rogers, and Lucille Ball. Kosloff's choreographic film credits include a notable collaboration with LeRoy Prinz in the arrangement of a *ballet mécanique* for *Madame Satan* (1930), in which Kosloff danced the Spirit of Electricity. He became a U.S. citizen on 27 January 1928.

Kosloff was a well-known figure in Los Angeles society, but it was in Dallas between 1929 and 1934, aided by the English ballerina Vera Fredova (Winifred Edwards), that he almost attained his dream of forming a permanent American ballet company. Heavily supported by the city's business leaders, the Kosloff Ballet played to capacity houses. That the enterprise ultimately failed was owing in part to financial problems exacerbated by the depression and by Baldina's divorce suit in 1934. Kosloff returned to Los Angeles, where he was teaching the day he died.

Because Kosloff left no immediate tangible legacies to the dance—no company or choreography survived—only later was his influence recognized. On his arrival in the United States, ballet was not considered an American art form. Through not only his teaching but also his willingness to perform in any venue, to take the dance to the greatest number of people, Kosloff played a significant role in reversing that perception.

• Major collections of archival material are in the Dance Collection of the New York Public Library for the Performing Arts and the Mary Bywaters Collection in the Dallas Public Library. The most extensive information on Kosloff's American dance and film career is in Suzanne Carbonneau Levy, "The Russians Are Coming: Russian Dancers in the United States, 1910–1933" (Ph.D. diss., New York Univ., 1990). Naima Prevots, *Dancing in the Sun: Hollywood Choreographers 1915–1937* (1987), focuses on Kosloff's influence on dance in California and his productions at the Hollywood Bowl. See also Michael Morris, *Madam Valentino* (1991), pp. 40–63. Frances Bruce, "The Kosloff Ballet and the City of Dallas, 1929–1934: An Interpretive Study of Reciprocal Meaning" (M.A. thesis, Texas Woman's Univ., 1992), analyzes the attempt to form a permanent ballet company. Kosloff discusses the development of ballet in the United States in "Where Are We Dancing? To Circus Not to Terpsichore's Shrine," *Dallas Morning News*, 8 Sept. 1929. On Kosloff's teaching philosophy see Bertha Wardell, "Ballet Teaching Is a Man's Job," *Dance Magazine*, Oct. 1928, pp. 22, 55; and Agnes de Mille, *Dance to the Piper* 1952, (repr. 1987), pp. 51–62. Obituaries are in *Dance News* and *Dancing Times*, both Jan. 1957.

FRANCES M. BRUCE

KOSTELANETZ, André (22 Dec. 1901–13 Jan. 1980), orchestra conductor and popularizer of classical music, was the son of Nachman Kostelanetz and Rosalie Dimscha. Born in St. Petersburg, Russia, into a wealthy Russian-Jewish family of amateur musicians, the young André began to study the piano at a very early age and performed in his first recital at the age of five. He was, at first, a less than eager student who hid from his teachers, although he continued his studies, both privately and at the St. Petersburg Conservatory, through 1922.

Kostelanetz began his operatic conducting career in Petrograd (formerly St. Petersburg) in 1920 as assistant conductor at the Grand Opera House. Although his family had emigrated to the United States in 1917, he stayed behind to maintain a claim on the family's considerable land holdings. This proved an unsuccessful effort, however, and in 1922 Kostelanetz left for the United States with virtually no material possessions. He became a naturalized citizen in 1928. Once in New York City, Kostelanetz went to work for Andreas Dippel's Opera Company. He accompanied many opera singers in recital and served as a rehearsal pianist at the Metropolitan and Chicago Grand Opera Companies. His conducting career blossomed when he began to work for the Atlantic Broadcasting Company (later CBS) in 1930.

In 1931 Kostelanetz became the conductor of the CBS Symphony Orchestra on the "Chesterfield Hour," a popular radio program. His combination of symphonic music, popular music, and jazz delighted his audiences, even if critics often scorned his work. In his career, Kostelanetz made more than 200 recordings with Columbia Records, achieving lifetime sales of more than fifty-two million copies. He received *Radio Guide's* Medal of Merit in 1936 for his broadcast, which brought "light classical" music to millions of listeners throughout the United States. He performed works that audiences recognized and enjoyed, eschewing modern or experimental works.

Kostelanetz married operatic diva Lily Pons in 1938 (they were divorced in 1958 and did not have children). *Life* magazine described them as "the biggest draw in the music business today" when they appeared together in a series of summer outdoor concerts throughout the country in 1939. The Chicago concert in this series was reported to have attracted an audience of 250,000, a record for the time. In 1942 Kostelanetz commissioned four new orchestral works that were intended to make a musical statement in support of American democracy during World War II. These included Virgil Thomson's *The Mayor LaGuardia Waltzes* and *Canons for Dorothy Thompson*, Jerome Kern's *Portrait for Orchestra (Mark Twain)*, and *A Lincoln Portrait*, by Aaron Copland. He premiered Paul Creston's *Frontiers*, an evocation of the travails and triumphs of nineteenth-century migrants to the American west, with the Toronto Symphony the following year. The Copland piece has remained popular in the orchestral and recording repertoire.

Kostelanetz was eager to learn what his audiences thought of his radio concerts, and, during World War II, he conducted audience surveys, discovering that the "Beer Barrel Polka" was more popular than any other song with soldiers, who also preferred marches to patriotic songs by Tin Pan Alley composers. He was awarded an Asiatic-Pacific ribbon by the U.S. Army for his overseas service to the troops during World War II. This included training and conducting orchestras of soldiers in North Africa, the Persian Gulf, and Italy during the summer of 1944 and in the European Theater of War in the winter of 1944–1945. In 1960 Kostelanetz married Sara Gene Orcutt, a marriage that also ended in divorce.

For the rest of his career, Kostelanetz continued to enjoy public acclaim. He was a guest conductor with most of the major orchestras in the United States, performing standard symphonic works and new orchestral pieces as well as popular "light classics." He was the principal conductor of the New York Philharmonic's Promenade Concerts. In addition to his wartime commissions, Kostelanetz also encouraged and supported the composing efforts of Ferde Grofé, Paul Creston, William Schuman, and Alan Hovhaness. In June 1967 he conducted the first performance of Ezra Laderman's *Magic Prison* with the New York Philharmonic. The work is scored for two narrators and orchestra and was inspired by the poetry of Emily Dickinson. William Walton dedicated his *Capriccio burlesco* to Kostelanetz, who conducted the New York premiere with the New York Philharmonic in 1968. Kostelanetz died of a heart attack while on vacation in Port-au-Prince, Haiti.

• *Echoes: Memoirs of André Kostelanetz* was published in 1981. The early portion of Kostelanetz's life is chronicled in *Current Biography* (1942). Articles include *American Magazine* (May 1938), *Etude* (July 1939), and *Time* (4 Oct. 1937, 3 Oct. 1938, and 11 May 1942). See also Bernard Jacobson, "André Kostelanetz," in *The New Grove Dictionary of American Music*, ed. Stanley Sadie and H. Wiley Hitchcock (1986), and obituaries in the *New York Times*, 15 Jan. 1980; *Time*, 28 Jan. 1980; and *Newsweek*, 28 Jan. 1980.

BARBARA L. TISCHLER

KOTLER, Aaron (18 Feb. 1892–29 Nov. 1962), Talmud scholar, was born in Sislowitz, Russia, the son of Shneur Zalman Kotler, the communal rabbi of Sislowitz, and Sarah Pesha. A descendant of a long line of prominent rabbis, Kotler received his early education from his father and private tutors. In 1903, at the age of eleven, Kotler was sent to Krinik to study with Rabbi Zalman Sender Shapiro, communal rabbi of Krinik. A prodigious student of Jewish religious literature, Kotler enrolled in the Slobodka yeshiva, one of the leading institutions of Talmud study at that time. From 1906 to 1912 Kotler distinguished himself as an outstanding Talmud scholar. Before World War I Kotler transferred to the Slutsk yeshiva to join the eminent Rabbi Isser Zalman Meltzer, who headed a branch of the Slobodka school in Slutsk, Lithuania.

In 1914, following his marriage to Chana Pearl, the daughter of his mentor, Rabbi Meltzer, Kotler was appointed Talmud lecturer at the Slutsk yeshiva. (Kotler and his wife eventually had two children.) During World War I the school remained intact despite disruptions caused by the hostilities. Serious hardship arose only in 1917 with the outbreak of the Bolshevik revolution. Accordingly, in 1920 Meltzer and Kotler moved the yeshiva to Kletsk, a town across the border in Poland. Following the departure of his father-in-law to Palestine, Kotler became the head of the Kletsk yeshiva, which for the next two decades flourished under Kotler's administration. By 1930 he was widely regarded as one the great Talmud scholars of Eastern Europe.

With the outbreak of World War II, Kotler was forced to flee Poland, first making his way to Vilnius, Lithuania, and from there traveling to the Far East, where he secured an entry visa for the United States. Arriving in San Francisco in 1940, Kotler immediately went to New York City, where like many other rabbis who had succeeded in escaping wartorn Europe, devoted much of his energy to the Vaad Hatzalah, an organization established by the Agudath ha-Rabbonim, a rabbinic union, to rescue European Jews and assist war refugees.

In 1944 Kotler established the Beth Midrash Gevoha, a Talmud academy in Lakewood, New Jersey. In forming this institution, Kotler sought to attract outstanding students of Talmud in the United States in an effort to establish an American yeshiva with the lofty standards of prewar European scholarship. Kotler discouraged his students from acquiring a university education so that they could devote themselves exclusively to the study of Talmud and religious literature. By contrast, the Rabbi Isaac Elchanan Theological Seminary in New York City and the Hebrew Theological College in Chicago encouraged their students to be university educated in an effort to accommodate to the challenges of modern, American life. By educating a generation of Talmud scholars and inspiring his students to establish new Talmudic academies throughout the United States and Canada, Kotler's Lakewood yeshiva came to have a significant influence on the vitality of American Orthodox Jewish life. Graduates of Beth Midrash Gevoha established yeshiva high schools and rabbinical schools throughout the United States, and their alumni have made contributions to the professional rabbinate as well.

Kotler emerged as one of the most significant Orthodox rabbinic leaders of his time, not only in the United States, where he was chairman of Agudath Israel's Moetzet Gedolai ha-Torah (Council of Torah Sages), but throughout the Orthodox Jewish world, where Kotler's opinion on matters of Jewish affairs was highly regarded. Kotler's concerns about a secular government in the state of Israel and his opposition to cooperation with Reform and Conservative rabbinic and lay groups has remained the perspective of some Orthodox Jews. Following the creation of the state of Israel in 1948, Kotler's support of various religious institutions in Israel, particularly Chinuch Atzmahi, an independent religious school system, was crucial for the development of religious life in Israel.

Tens of thousands of admirers attended Kotler's funeral in New York City, where he was eulogized by many prominent American rabbis. Additional eulogies were offered in Israel, where Kotler was taken for burial near his father-in-law.

• Kotler published little during his lifetime. Most of his writings were prepared by students and published posthumously. See *Ha-Pardes* 48, no. 8 (May 1974): 26–27; *Mishnat Rabbi Aharon: Chidushim u'Biurim al ha-Rambam* (1975); *Kuntres Keter Torah im Hosaphot* (1976); *Oseph Chidushei Torah* (1983); Moshe Weissman, ed., *Sefer Yetziat ha-Shabbat*

(1981); *Mishnat Rabbi Aharon: Reshit Chochma, Sechel Tov u'Tochachot Maamarim v'Sichot Musar* (1982); *Mishnat Rabbi Aharon: She'elot u'Teshuvot, Chidushim u'Biurim b'Omek ha-Sugyot* (1985); *Mishnat Rabbi Aharon: Chidushim u'Biurim b'Omek ha-Sugyot v'divrei ha-Rishonim v'ha-Rambam b'Inyanei Zeraim, Taharot* (1986); and *Mishnat Rabbi Aharon: Chidushim u'Biurim b'Omek ha-Sugyot v'Divrei Rishonim* (1990).

Brief articles on Kotler's life and career can be found in Asher Rand, *Toldoth Anshe Shem* (1950), p. 109; Jacob D. Kamson, ed., *Yahadut Lita* (1959), p. 235; Aaron Ben Zion Shurin, *Keshet Gibborim* (1964), pp. 244–48; Alex J. Goldman, *Giants of Faith: Great American Rabbis* (1964), pp. 257–73; Oscar Feuchtwanger, *Righteous Lives* (1965); *Jewish Observer*, May 1973, p. 7; and Alter Pekier, *From Kletzk to Siberia: A Yeshiva Bachur's Wanderings during the Holocaust* (1985).

MOSHE SHERMAN

KOUSSEVITZKY, Serge (26 July 1874–4 June 1951), double-bass virtuoso and conductor, was born Sergei Aleksandrovich Kusevitskii in Vishny-Volotchok, Tver (now Kalinin), Russia, the son of Alexander Koussevitzkii and Anna Barabeitchik. Both of his parents were musical; his mother was a pianist and his father, a *klezmir* violinist, playing for small plays, operas, weddings, and parties. Koussevitzky displayed musical talent at an early age, learned to play several instruments, and won a scholarship to study the double bass at the Moscow Philharmonic Music School at age fourteen. He became a virtuoso double bass player and joined the Bolshoi Theatre Orchestra in 1894, where he remained for eleven years. In 1896 Koussevitzky began giving solo recitals. He also composed and arranged a number of works for the double bass. Sometime before 1902 he married Nadezhda Galat, a member of the Bolshoi Corps de Ballet. A few years later he met Natalya Uskov, daughter of a wealthy tea merchant, and married her in 1905 after divorcing his first wife. He had no children with either wife.

Koussevitzky's second marriage made him a multimillionaire. He continued an illustrious solo career as a double-bass player but became increasingly interested in conducting and in promoting and publishing new music. The Koussevitkzys settled in Berlin, where Serge observed many leading conductors of the day, including Richard Strauss, Artur Nikisch, and Felix Weingartner. He made his public conducting debut with the Berlin Philharmonic Orchestra in 1908. He founded his own orchestra in 1909 and programmed works that he particularly admired. He gave regular concerts with the orchestra and also undertook guest conducting engagements up to the First World War, appearing in London, Berlin, and throughout Russia. His wife's money helped him to establish a publishing house, Editions Russes de Musique, which presented compositions by various Russian composers, including Prokofiev, Medtner, Stravinsky, and Scriabin.

After the collapse of the tsarist regime in Russia in 1917, Koussevitzky lost much of his wealth and property but was offered the post of director of the State Symphony Orchestra in St. Petersburg. He remained in Russia for three years but became worried by the country's political situation and left with his wife for Paris in 1920, transferring with him the headquarters of Editions Russes de Musique. From 1921 until 1929 Koussevitzky conducted the "Concerts Koussevitzky" at the Paris Opera and received great acclaim for performances of music by late romantic and impressionist French and Russian composers. He gave premieres of works that he had commissioned, including Honegger's *Pacific 231* and Ravel's orchestration of Moussorgsky's *Pictures at an Exhibition*. Attracting the attention of visiting concertgoers from Boston, he was invited to succeed Pierre Monteux as chief conductor of the Boston Symphony, the most French-sounding of major American orchestras, in 1924. From that time onward, his musical career was based mainly in the United States.

Koussevitzky improved the already fine standard of the Boston Symphony Orchestra and gave it prestige by championing much new music by European composers such as Ravel, Roussel, Stravinsky, and Hindemith and by American composers such as Howard Hanson, Copland, Roy Harris, Walter Piston, William Schuman, and Roger Sessions. Each concert season brought a flood of new performances; the only conductor in the United States to have similarly enterprising programs at the time was Leopold Stokowski. To mark the fiftieth anniversary of the Boston Symphony in 1931, Koussevitzky commissioned and conducted Ravel's Piano Concerto in G Major, Hindemith's Concert Music for Brass and Strings, Stravinsky's Symphony of Psalms, and works by Prokofiev, Roussel, Gershwin, Hanson, and Copland. Between 1924 and 1941, Koussevitzky gave the world premieres of ninety-nine works, seventy-five of which were American or American oriented.

Koussevitzky and the Boston Symphony Orchestra participated in the Berkshire Music Festival, based at Tanglewood, near Lenox in western Massachusetts, from 1936 onward. Two years later they began to play there under the newly constructed wedge-shaped concert hall known as "the Shed." In 1940 Koussevitzky transformed the summer school at Tanglewood into the Berkshire Music Center, to which he attracted gifted students from all over the world who studied performance, composition, and conducting with distinguished guest faculty. The most renowned pupil during Koussevitzky's association with the center was Leonard Bernstein.

While in Boston, Koussevitzky toured occasionally in Europe, appearing in Britain with both the BBC Symphony and London Philharmonic orchestras. He regularly returned to Paris. But the center of his musical activities remained Boston. In 1941 he became an American citizen. His second wife died the following year. As a memorial to her, he set up the Koussevitzky Music Foundation to provide funds to commission works from composers of all nationalities. Among the foundation's commissions was Britten's opera *Peter Grimes* (1945). In 1947 Koussevitzky married his second wife's niece, Olga Naumoff, who had lived with the couple since 1924. In 1949 he retired from his position with the Boston Symphony after a tenure of twenty-five years. In the same year, he established the Serge Koussevitzky Music Foundation at the Library of Congress as a permanent endowment to commission new compositions and to assist with their performance. Koussevitzky died in Boston.

Proud, vain, and emotional by temperament, Koussevitzky was a colorful, magnetic, cosmopolitan personality who did more for the performance of contemporary music in the first half of the twentieth century than any other conductor. He was also the first Russian conductor to rise to international fame. Though unable to speak idiomatic English and beset with an imprecise beat with the baton, he was able by sheer willpower and conviction to schedule and conduct progressive, challenging, and memorable programs. His conducting of classical music by Haydn, Mozart, and Beethoven was often idiosyncratic and willful yet never dull. He was in his element in conducting Russian and French music of the nineteenth and early twentieth centuries, playing even Tchaikovsky's best-known symphonies with a spontaneity each time he conducted them. His commitment to contemporary music was such that if audiences failed to applaud, he turned around on the podium and told them that the piece would be played again.

Koussevitzky fashioned the Boston Symphony Orchestra into an ensemble almost unrivaled in its day in terms of tonal splendor and dramatic power, something that can still be heard on his many recordings for RCA Victor and EMI. His wealth and generosity left important, ongoing legacies via his music foundations, the Tanglewood Festival, and the Berkshire Music Center. Koussevitzky was awarded many honorary degrees. He received the Finnish Order of the White Rose for championing the music of Sibelius, and France appointed him a Chevalier of the Legion d'honneur.

• An extensive collection of Koussevitzky's manuscripts is housed in the Music Division of the Library of Congress. Substantial original material on his American career can be found in the Boston Symphony Orchestra's Archives, deposited at the Mugar Memorial Library, Boston University. There is also a Serge Koussevitzky Archive at the Boston Public Library. A chronological list of completed works commissioned by the Koussevitzky Foundations is given in H. Wiley Hitchcock and Stanley Sadie, eds., *The New Grove Dictionary of American Music*, vol. 2 (1986). Among many books dealing with Koussevitzky's career are Arthur Lourie, *S. A. Koussevitzky and His Epoch* (1931); Mark A. De Wolfe Howe, *The Boston Symphony Orchestra, 1881–1931* (1931); Howe, *The Tale of Tanglewood* (1946); Hugo Leichtentritt, *Serge Koussevitzky: The Boston Symphony Orchestra and the New American Music* (1946); Moses Smith, *Koussevitzky* (1947); Charles O'Connell, *The Other Side of the Record* (1947); Harold C. Schonberg, *The Great Conductors* (1968); David Wooldridge, *A Conductor's World* (1970); Herbert Kupferberg, *Tanglewood* (1976); Janet Baker-Carr, *Evening at Symphony: A Portrait of the Boston Symphony Orchestra* (1977); David Ewen, *Musicians since 1900: Performers in Con-*

cert and Opera (1978); Boris Goldovsky, *My Road to Opera* (1979); and Humphrey Burton, *Leonard Bernstein* (1995). The book by Moses Smith is particularly useful for its appendices listing world premieres by the Boston Symphony Orchestra during Koussevitzky's tenure and for its list of compositions by American composers conducted by Koussevitzky in Boston. Koussevitzky's recordings are discussed in John Holmes, *Conductors on Record* (1982). An obituary of Koussevitzky is in the *New York Times*, 5 June 1951.

KENNETH MORGAN

KOVACS, Ernie (23 Jan. 1919–13 Jan. 1962), television comedian and actor, was born Ernest Edward Kovacs in Trenton, New Jersey, the son of Andrew John Kovacs (András János Kovács), a policeman, and Mary Chebonick (Maria Csebenyák). His parents' Hungarian heritage was an essential part of Kovacs's upbringing; he grew up bilingual in an ethnic working-class neighborhood near the Trenton riverfront. The family's financial situation improved when Kovacs's father left the police department to become a bootlegger. Kovacs's parents were ostentatious spenders who doted on him. They dressed him in velvet and allowed him to have a pony, an unlikely pet for an urban family. When Prohibition ended, the family opened a restaurant, where Kovacs would treat his playmates to desserts.

Except for a year at the private Bowen School, Kovacs attended public schools in Trenton. He was bright, but undisciplined. He read widely, wrote for his own amusement, and loved the music classes. But bad grades and truancy, probably related to the failure of the family business, delayed his graduation from high school by a year (1937).

Trenton Central High School had a strong drama program guided by Harold Van Kirk, who recognized and disciplined Kovacs's innate theatricality. Van Kirk cast him as the Pirate King in *The Pirates of Penzance*, then invited Kovacs to work with him during the summer of 1937 at the John Drew Theatre in East Hampton, Long Island. The director also helped Kovacs secure a scholarship to the New York School of the Theatre.

Kovacs went to New York City in 1938 with little money; he soon was impoverished. He worked long hours at odd jobs, ate badly and infrequently, smoked too much, and could not resist all-night card games. In 1939 he came down with pleurisy and pneumonia while working at a Brattleboro, Vermont, summer theater, and he was hospitalized for eighteen months. Van Kirk visited the ill Kovacs and later reported that the patient never complained: "We'd go to the hospital to cheer him up; but he'd cheer us up. Not only us, but all the other patients, too. Those poor, tired, sick old people, they never laughed so hard in their lives."

In 1941 Kovacs returned to Trenton. He tried to launch a career in local theater, even starting his own troupe, but his efforts failed. He worked briefly as a drugstore counterman until a friend pointed him toward a job as staff announcer at WTTM, a Trenton radio station. Kovacs soon developed several programs for himself, most of them marked by zany stunts and offbeat concepts. He parodied the station's advertisements and hawked nonexistent products. He even added comic sound effects to his live broadcasts of professional wrestling matches. He also wrote restaurant reviews and a column of gossip and humorous commentary for the *Trentonian*.

He married dancer Bette Lee Wilcox in 1945. She deserted Kovacs and their two daughters in 1949 but reappeared in 1951, not long after the comedian's network television debut, seeking a divorce and custody of the children. The court awarded custody of the children to Kovacs, but in 1953 his ex-wife abducted them. A distraught Kovacs devoted nearly all of his free time to recovering his daughters. The girls were restored to their father in June 1953. Kovacs married singer Edie Adams, a regular on his television programs, in 1954. They had one child.

In 1950 Kovacs broke into television as host of a daytime cooking program on Philadelphia's WPTZ. His task was to interview local chefs as they demonstrated how to prepare their favorite recipes, but Kovacs turned "Deadline for Dinner" (or "Dead Lion For Dinner," as he dubbed it) into a vehicle for comedy. The program ran for two years, during which time he maintained a hectic schedule. He was still on radio at WTTM, headed the local radio employees' union, continued his newspaper column, and added a short-lived game show to his duties at WPTZ. In November 1950 he launched an early-morning variety program. Ubiquitous and original, the stylish, mustachioed comedian with the ever-present cigar had become the phenomenon of Philadelphia television.

He attracted the attention of WPTZ's parent company, NBC, which put him on the network in a variety of formats in 1951 and 1952. "Time for Ernie" was a one-man daytime comedy show, "Ernie in Kovacs-land" a summer prime-time variety show, and "Kovacs on the Korner" a daytime comedy variety program. All originated from Philadelphia; all were short-lived.

In 1952 Kovacs moved to WCBS-TV, the CBS affiliate in New York City, to do another daytime variety program. He took the same cast and format to prime time on the network from December 1952 to April 1953. Unlike most other successful television performers, Kovacs never settled into a single programming formula. Although he had a devoted following, his idiosyncratic style could not sustain high ratings, nor was it well suited to conventional formats. As a consequence, it was rare for a Kovacs program to survive for more than a few months, though the comedian maintained a presence on national television, in one format or another, season after season, until his death. He did variety shows, hosted a quiz program, appeared on game show panels, briefly inherited "The Tonight Show" from Steve Allen, wrote and produced an irreverent program about classical music, introduced silent film classics, covered Macy's Thanksgiving parade, acted on drama anthology programs, created a series of highly original comic commercials for Dutch Mas-

ters cigars, and, at the end, was doing monthly prime-time comedy specials on ABC.

Kovacs was widely regarded as the most innovative artist yet to appear on the emerging medium. His best work broke away from the conventions of vaudeville, and even radio comedy. He exploited the technical possibilities of television to give full expression to a unique comic sensibility marked by incongruities, visual puns, and creative sound effects. His Nairobi Trio (which evolved into the Simian Orchestra) consisted of a conductor, a pianist, and a timpanist dressed as apes wearing overcoats and bowler hats. They would mime, like mechanical toy monkeys, a musical performance, but always things went awry. A commentator called the skit "nihilistic opera." In another Kovacs piece the comedian is perched on the limb of a tree. He saws off the limb, but it remains stationary while the tree topples over. In the widely hailed "Eugene" program, done entirely without dialogue, Kovacs wanders into a library, opens a copy of "Camille," and a sickly cough is heard.

His humor was irreverent, but not satirical; he mocked television, but not society. His comedy, by design, lacked verbal wit and rapid-fire comic timing. Often it was loose, baggy, and slow-paced, qualities that gave it the appearance of being improvised (as it sometimes was). Much of it (the Nairobi Trio skit, for instance) was inspired by some piece of music Kovacs had heard.

He also wrote a behind-the-scenes novel about television (*Zoomar*, 1957), did a Las Vegas nightclub act (with Edie Adams), and appeared in ten feature films (1957 through 1962). Kovacs was proud of his novel (which he claimed to have written in just thirteen days), but it received mixed reviews. There was a certain unwitting irony in its portrayal of television as a creative dead end, for it was in that medium that the comedian did his most original work. Indeed, his cabaret act suffered because Kovacs's comedy had come to depend so heavily on the kind of technical tricks that were available to him only in the television studio. His Las Vegas appearances did not enhance his reputation; they merely fed his appetite for gambling. Nor did Kovacs have great success in Hollywood, where he was not so free to shape his material as he had been in early television. Nevertheless, Richard Quine, who directed him in four films, called Kovacs "an intuitive actor" who "required very little direction" and who "was always quick to find that extra little schtick." Kovacs typically played supporting roles but left his comic imprint on popular but otherwise undistinguished films such as *Operation Mad Ball*, *North to Alaska*, and *It Happened to Jane*. He also starred in two very marginal, low-budget pictures, *Wake Me When It's Over* and *Five Golden Hours*.

Behind the camera the comedian was flamboyant yet soft-spoken, volatile but considerate. He was quick to credit his coworkers but, according to a biographer, "liked to project the illusion that he wrote all of his own material or just made it up as he went along." He was a profligate spender and compulsive gambler, habits that led to heavy debts and tax problems.

Kovacs died in an automobile accident in Beverly Hills, California. "Nothing in Moderation" was his epitaph.

• The television archive at the University of California at Los Angeles holds Kovacs's papers, scripts, and visual recordings of the comedian's television programs. Some of the visual material has been reissued in compilations for home video, including *The Best of Ernie Kovacs*. Most of his ten films have been released on video cassette, as has *Ernie Kovacs: Between the Laughter*, the TV dramatization of his divorce and custody battles, and *Ernie Kovacs: Television's Original Genius*, a compilation of program excerpts and reminiscences by family, friends, and coworkers. The full range of Kovacs videos is described in the *Philadelphia Inquirer*, 25 July 1991. *Sing a Pretty Song* (1990) is a memoir by Kovacs's second wife, Edie Adams (with Robert Windeler). *The Ernie Kovacs Phile (1987)*, by David G. Walley, is a reprint of *Nothing in Moderation: A Biography of Ernie Kovacs* (1975); a fan's tribute that emphasizes Kovacs's performances rather than his private life, it effectively captures the spirit of the comedian's off-center perspective. The essential biography is Diane Rico, *Kovacsland* (1990). It is thoroughly researched and supplies credits for virtually all television and movie appearances by the comedian. Rico contends that Kovacs influenced such later TV programs as "Laugh In," "Saturday Night Live," and "Late Night with David Letterman." David Marc, *Demographic Vistas: Television in American Culture* (1984), situates Kovacs in the context of popular culture, while Robert Rosen, "Ernie Kovacs: Video Artist," in Peter D'Agostino, ed., *Transmission: Theory and Practice for a New Television Aesthetics* (1985), places him among the avant-garde.

WILLIAM HUGHES

KRACAUER, Siegfried (8 Feb. 1889–26 Nov. 1966), social scientist and author, was born in Frankfurt am Main, Germany, the son of Adolph Kracauer, a businessman, and Rosette Oppenheimer. After the early death of his father, he was brought up by his uncle Isidor Kracauer, a prominent historian of the Frankfurt Jewish community. Siegfried studied architecture, philosophy, and sociology at various polytechnic schools and universities in Munich and Berlin from 1908 to 1914. In 1915 he earned his doctorate in engineering from Berlin Polytechnic Institute.

Kracauer began his professional career as an architect, but soon after the successful publication in several German periodicals of his essays on cultural, philosophical, and sociological issues he forsook architecture for the craft of writing. In 1920 he joined the staff of the *Frankfurter Zeitung*, becoming the newspaper's cultural affairs editor. His reporting for the prestigious paper additionally served as the basis for two of his books: *Solziologie als Wissenschaft* (Sociology as a science) (1922), a critically acclaimed sociological study; and *Die Angestellten* (The employees) (1930), a treatise on German white-collar workers. During this period Kracauer also found literary success with the publication in 1928 of his semiautobiographical antiwar novel, *Ginster*. Two years later he married Elizabeth Ehrenreich; they had no children.

In March 1933 Kracauer and his wife left Germany to escape the Nazis and sought refuge in Paris. While in France, Kracauer had a difficult time financially, struggling to earn a living writing articles for French and Swiss newspapers and journals. He continued to write other things, completing a second novel in 1934, although the book did not find a publisher until 1977. In 1937 he wrote *Orpheus in Paris: Jacques Offenbach and the Paris of His Time*, a biography of the famous nineteenth-century French composer.

Kracauer immigrated to the United States in April 1941 and became a naturalized American citizen in 1946. Upon his arrival he secured a position as a special assistant to the curator of the Museum of Modern Art Film Library in New York City, where he studied the Nazi war propaganda contained in German newsreels. Kracauer worked there until 1943, at which time he was awarded a Guggenheim Fellowship. With the support of this grant, he continued his analysis of German nationalism, this time focusing on the German cinema from 1919 to 1933. In 1947 he published one of his best-known books, *From Caligari to Hitler*, a sociological study detailing the earliest manifestations of Nazism on film. In addition, he contributed articles on the effect of motion pictures to professional journals such as *Public Opinion Quarterly* and magazines such as *Harper's*.

In the early 1950s Kracauer began to do research and analysis for the Evaluation Branch of the Voice of America. He served at that post from 1950 until 1952, at which time he became a senior staff member on Columbia University's Bureau of Applied Social Research. In 1956 he collaborated with Paul Berkman on *Satellite Mentality*, a profile of Eastern European refugees. The book was not as well-received as many of his earlier efforts.

Despite forays into other areas of research, Kracauer's greatest work was done in the area of film, and, according to the *New York Times*, he was "best known [in America] for his studies of the motion picture as a powerful chronicle of the social scene and a medium of symbolic imagery symptomatic of the ideas and attitudes of the time" (28 Nov. 1966). In 1960 he published *Theory of Film*, in which he delves into the deepest psychological underpinnings of the film medium. He emphasizes his belief in substance over style, arguing that the subject of what is filmed is more important than the manner in which it is filmed and edited together. In the book he states, "What is the essence in film no less than photography is the intervention of the filmmaker's formative energies in all the dimensions which the medium has come to cover. Everything depends on the 'right' balance between the realistic tendency and the formative tendency; and the two tendencies are well balanced if the latter does not try to overwhelm the former but eventually follows its lead."

Late in his life Kracauer began to receive newfound attention in his native Germany with the release in 1963 of a collection of his essays, *Das Ornament der Masse*, and the re-release of his first novel, *Ginster*. Kracauer remained in the United States though, moving away from the study of film in order to begin to focus on the philosophy of history. At the time of his death in New York City, he had compiled a nearly completed manuscript on the subject. The manuscript, titled *History: The Last Things before the Last*, was published three years after his death. In the autobiographical statement that accompanied the book, Kracauer states that he viewed his total life's work as attempts "to bring out the significance of areas whose claim to be acknowledged in their own right has not yet been recognised."

• Kracauer's papers are in the Schiller National Museum in Marbach am Neckar, Baden-Württemberg, Germany. For more information, see "The Extraterritorial Life of Siegfried Kracauer," in Martin Jay's *Permanent Exiles: Essays on the Intellectual Migration from Germany to America* (1985); *Text-Kritik*, Oct. 1980, which was dedicated to him; and Theodor W. Adorno, in the *Frankfurter Allgemeine Zeitung*, 1 Dec. 1966. An obituary is in the *New York Times*, 28 Nov. 1966.

FRANCESCO L. NEPA

KRAEMER, Henry (22 July 1868–9 Sept. 1924), pharmacognosist and teacher, was born in Philadelphia, Pennsylvania, the son of John Henry Kraemer, a merchant, and Caroline Fuchs. Orphaned at an early age, he attended Girard College from 1877 to 1883 and then spent five years as an apprentice in the pharmacy of Clement B. Lowe. In 1889 he received the graduate in pharmacy degree (Ph.G.) from the Philadelphia College of Pharmacy. During his senior year at the college and the year thereafter, he was assistant in general chemistry to Professor Samuel P. Sadtler at the University of Pennsylvania.

He began his teaching career at the College of Pharmacy of the City of New York as instructor in materia medica in 1890. While in New York he took a special course in botany at Barnard College, and in 1891 he enrolled in the School of Mines of Columbia University, from which he obtained a bachelor of philosophy degree in 1895. He then accepted a professorship in botany and pharmacognosy at the School of Pharmacy of Northwestern University and was granted an immediate leave of absence to study in Germany. In 1896 he received his Ph.D. from the University of Marburg and returned to take up his teaching position at Northwestern. However, a year later he accepted the position of professor of botany and pharmacognosy at the Philadelphia College of Pharmacy, where he remained until 1917. He was the curator of the college herbarium and served also as director of the microscopical laboratory at the college and taught courses in microscopic examination and bacteriology as well. In 1917 he accepted the position of professor of pharmacognosy at the College of Pharmacy at the University of Michigan. He held that post for two years and then served as dean of the college for another year. At Michigan he directed studies in pharmacognosy in cooperation with the Botanical Gardens, reporting, in 1918, that more than 25,000 plants representing over fifty species were grown. Kraemer resigned from the University of Michigan in 1920 to do research and

consulting. In 1921 he became director of the respected correspondence courses in pharmacy run by the *Pharmaceutical Era*.

Kraemer edited the *American Journal of Pharmacy* from 1898 to 1917 and contributed some sixty articles to that journal himself. He published widely in many other journals as well, largely in the field of pharmacognosy. His investigations went beyond taxonomy to include chemical and microscopic analyses. He had demonstrated this interest as early as his senior year at the Philadelphia College of Pharmacy in his prizewinning thesis on "a microscopical and chemical study of white oak bark." Pharmacognosy, he believed, included the study of the plants themselves as well as the study of systemic botany and phytochemistry.

Kraemer's scientific interests, however, went beyond the scope of pharmacognosy. At the Woods Hole Marine Biological Laboratory he was one of a group interested in metals, and he published articles (1905) on the action of copper foil on intestinal organisms and on the use of copper in water purification. After his retirement from the University of Michigan and until his death, he and his wife operated the Kraemer Research Laboratory in Mount Clemens, Michigan, where they did "a great deal of work in human pathology and bacteriology" and routine analyses for physicians. He was also active in litigation relative to drug adulteration.

Kraemer was a member of the revision committee of the *United States Pharmacopoeia* and served as chairman of the subcommittee on botany and pharmacognosy for the 1900, 1910, and 1920 revisions. He served on the council on pharmacy and chemistry of the American Medical Association from 1911 to 1921. He served as botanical editor of the twentieth edition (1918) of the *Dispensatory of the United States*.

In 1917 Kraemer was president of both the American Conference of Pharmaceutical Faculties and the Philadelphia Botanical Club. An active member of the American Pharmaceutical Association, Kraemer annually presented the report of the progress of pharmacy to the association from 1893 to 1895. He was a member, as well, of the Botanical Society of America, the Torrey Botanical Club, the American Association for the Advancement of Science, and the American Philosophical Society, among other organizations, and was an honorary member of the Pharmaceutical Society of Great Britain and of the Société de Pharmacie de Paris.

One of the foremost American pharmacognosists of the early twentieth century, Kraemer put his stamp on the teaching of pharmacognosy in U.S. pharmaceutical and medical schools. His *A Course in Botany and Pharmacognosy* appeared in 1902, and, as *A Text-book of Botany and Pharmacognosy*, it went through three further editions until 1910. In 1912 he published *Outline of a Course in Botany, Microscopy, and Pharmacognosy, with Question Sets for the Use of Teachers and Students in Pharmacy*. Intending to reach beyond pharmaceutical and medical circles, he published his *Applied and Economic Botany*, in two editions, in 1914 and 1916. His *Scientific and Applied Pharmacognosy, Intended for the Use of Students in Pharmacy and Practicing Pharmacists, Food and Drug Analysts and Pharmacologists* appeared in 1915. It was published in a second edition in 1920 and in a third edition, posthumously, under the aegis of an "editorial committee" in 1928. Indeed, the textbook in pharmacognosy by Edmund N. Gathercoal and Elmer H. Wirth that appeared in 1936 and 1947 was "based on the third edition of Kraemer's *Pharmacognosy*." The illustrations and photographic reproductions in Kraemer's books were largely his own handiwork. Kraemer was an early champion of the use of photography, including color photography, in pharmacognosy.

In 1894 he married Theodosia Rich, with whom he had two children. The marriage ended in divorce, and in 1922 he married Minnie Behm, with whom he had a daughter. He died in Detroit, Michigan.

• The chief biographical sources are E. G. Eberle, "Henry Kraemer," *Journal of the American Pharmaceutical Association* 7 (1918): 581–83; Kraemer's obituary, also in the *Journal* 13 (1924): 980–82; and J. W. England, *The First Century of the Philadelphia College of Pharmacy 1821–1921* (1922), pp. 174, 415–16. A brief "Lebenslauf" can be found in his Ph.D. dissertation, "Viola tricolor L. in morphologischer, anatomischer und biologischer Beziehung" (Univ. of Marburg, 1897).

DAVID L. COWEN

KRAENZLEIN, Alvin Christian (12 Dec. 1876–6 Jan. 1928), track and field athlete, was born in Milwaukee, Wisconsin, the son of John G. Kraenzlein, a brewer, and Augusta (maiden name unknown). Kraenzlein's track and field career began in 1895, during his senior year at East Side High School in Milwaukee. An all-around performer, he won the 100- and 220-yard dashes, 120-yard high hurdles, 220-yard low hurdles, high jump, long jump, and shot put in a meet against crosstown rival West Side High School. In the 1895 Wisconsin Interscholastic championships he nearly duplicated that performance, capturing first place in the 100-yard dash (10.4 seconds), 120-yard high hurdles (17.4 seconds), 220-yard low hurdles (27.5 seconds), high jump (5′6″), and shot put (38′10″).

In 1895 Kraenzlein entered the University of Wisconsin to study engineering. The multitalented trackman dominated the university's 1896 freshman-sophomore track and field meet, winning the 220-yard low hurdles and the high jump, placing second in the 100-yard dash, and finishing third in shot put. In 1897 he established an indoor world record of 36.6 seconds in the 300-yard low hurdles. He also won the 220-yard low hurdles and the high jump in the 1897 Western Intercollegiate Conference championship, leading Wisconsin to the team title. As a member of the Chicago Athletic Club, he captured the 1897 Amateur Athletic Union's national title in the 220-yard low hurdles.

That same year Kraenzlein left Wisconsin for the University of Pennsylvania, where he came under the tutelage of Michael Murphy, then the nation's leading track and field coach. At Penn, Kraenzlein dominated the hurdling events and the long jump. In 1898 he set an indoor world record of 6.0 seconds for the 50-yard high hurdles. He captured both the 120-yard high hurdles and 220-yard low hurdles at the AAU championships in 1898 and 1899 and at the Intercollegiate American Amateur Athletic Association (IC4A) championships in 1898, 1899, and 1900. His 1898 AAU victory in the 120-yard high hurdles resulted in a world record of 15.2 seconds, and his IC4A win in the 220-yard low hurdles that year produced a world record of 23.6 seconds. The 220 low-hurdle mark stood as a world standard for a quarter-century. At the 1899 Penn Relays Kraenzlein established a world record of 24′3½″ in the long jump. Later that year, he captured the same event in both the AAU and IC4A championships, improving the world record by one inch in the long jump. Moreover, Kraenzlein sprinted to AAU and IC4A titles in the 100-yard dash in 1899 and 1900. Captain of the Penn track and field team in 1900, he scored a record eighteen points in the IC4A championship, leading Penn to its fourth consecutive title.

In 1900 Penn's championship track and field team was one of several college teams that represented the United States in the Olympic Games at Paris. Penn first competed in the British Amateur Athletic Association championships in London where Kraenzlein captured BAAA titles in the 120-yard high hurdles and the long jump. His winning time in the hurdles of 15.4 seconds marked a world record for grass tracks. At the Olympic Games, which were held in conjunction with the Paris Exposition, Kraenzlein won an unprecedented four individual gold medals in the 60-meter dash (7.0 seconds), 110-meter high hurdles (15.4 seconds), 200-meter low hurdles (25.4 seconds), and the long jump (23′6¾″). Each winning performance set a new Olympic record.

After the 1900 Games, Kraenzlein retired from competition. Having graduated with a degree in dentistry in 1901, he returned to Milwaukee and established a small practice. He also managed the Milwaukee Athletic Association. He returned east to Belmar, New Jersey, in 1902 to marry Claudine Gilman; they had no children. He moved his dentistry practice to Philadelphia, where he stayed until 1906 when he became the track and field coach at Mercersburg Academy. In 1910 he became an assistant professor of physical training and track and field coach at the University of Michigan. Among the athletes he coached at Michigan, the most notable was Ralph Craig, who won Olympic titles in both the 100 and 200 meters in 1912.

In 1913 the German government signed Kraenzlein to a five-year, $50,000 contract to prepare the German Olympic team for the 1916 Games, scheduled to be held in Berlin. However, the event was canceled with the outbreak of war. Kraenzlein returned to the United States and served in the army as a physical training specialist. After the war he worked as an assistant track and field coach at Penn. In 1922 he divorced and moved to Cleveland, Ohio, where a sister lived. His final years were spent coaching young boys at various summer camps and club trackmen in Havana, Cuba, during the winter. In late 1927 he suffered from pleurisy and died from endocarditis.

Kraenzlein is a pivotal figure in the development of track and field. Historians of the sport regard him as the father of straight lead-leg hurdling. Hurdlers continue to employ this technique, which permits the athlete to clear the barriers without breaking stride. Track and field authority Roberto L. Quercetani points out that although Arthur C. M. Croome of Great Britain first attempted the style in 1886, Kraenzlein perfected the technique. The style probably came naturally to him because of his sprinting and long-jumping skills. Kraenzlein remains the only track and field performer to have won gold medals in four individual events in a single Olympiad. While Jesse Owens, in 1936, and Carl Lewis, in 1984, also collected four gold medals, each of them won one medal in a relay event. A member of the National Track and Field Hall of Fame, Kraenzlein also was elected to the U.S. Olympic Committee Hall of Fame, the only athlete competing before 1956 to hold both honors.

• The archives of the University of Pennsylvania and the University of Wisconsin and the University of Michigan's sports information office contain biographical files on Kraenzlein. For details of his career, see Bill Mallon and Ian Buchanan, *Quest for Gold: Encyclopedia of American Olympians* (1984). Statistical information on his performances is found in Frank G. Menke, *The Encyclopedia of Sports*, 4th rev. ed. (1969), and David Wallechinsky, *The Complete Book of the Olympic Games*, rev. ed. (1988). For Kraenzlein's place in the history of athletics, see Roberto L. Quercetani, *A World History of Track and Field Athletics* (1964). Obituaries appear in the *Pennsylvania Gazette*, 13 Jan. 1928, and the *Philadelphia Inquirer* and *Philadelphia Ledger*, both 7 Jan. 1928.

ADAM R. HORNBUCKLE

KRAFT, James Lewis (11 Nov. 1874–16 Feb. 1953), businessman and inventor, was born in Fort Erie, Ontario, Canada, the son of George Franklin Krafft and Minerva Alice Tripp, farmers. It is unknown when the change in the spelling of his last name occurred. Kraft was raised in a strict Mennonite environment characterized by hard work and strict discipline. After graduation from high school he left the farm to become a clerk in a Fort Erie general store. In 1903 he moved to Buffalo, New York, where he attended a business college while working as a janitor and selling eggs, cheese, and ice. The following year he moved to Chicago, where he remained for the rest of his life. He became a naturalized citizen in 1911.

Kraft entered the cheese business in Chicago by purchasing it in bulk from wholesalers and delivering it in small quantities to local grocers packaged in tinfoil and glass jars. He thus spared grocers the daily loss incurred by slicing and discarding dried cheese from the large cheese wheels that were exposed to the air. After an initial setback the business began to prosper, and four of his brothers joined him in forming J. L. Kraft and Brothers in 1909.

Kraft pursued an aggressive program of expansion and innovation that characterized his career. He mailed circulars to retail grocers and advertised on billboards and on elevated trains. Anticipating growth beyond Chicago he opened an office in New York City in 1912, looking toward overseas business. He expanded his line of cheeses to thirty-one varieties and opened his own cheese factory.

Although packaging extended the shelf life of cheese, spoilage remained a problem during hot summer months, especially in the South. Kraft solved this problem in 1916, after extensive experimentation, by patenting a method that ground, blended, and pasteurized cheese, which he then sold in four-ounce tin packages. The U.S. armed forces bought six million pounds of his canned cheese during World War I, contributing to the firm's $6 million in sales in 1917—the year he incorporated the business.

After the war Kraft continued to expand and innovate. He first utilized color advertisements in national magazines in 1919. The following year he purchased a Canadian cheese company, and by the end of the decade he had opened sales offices in Britain and Germany. His ongoing focus on research resulted by 1922 in several additional patents for cheese processing. Although he was subsequently forced to share certain rights with rival Phenix Cheese Company, the terms of the patents were generally quite favorable to him. By mid-decade Kraft had established the world's largest laboratory devoted solely to cheese research. A product of this research was the famous five-pound cheese loaf, wrapped in foil and inserted into a wooden box. In 1924—the year the firm's name changed to Kraft Cheese Company—James Kraft hired a home economist to set up a test kitchen to originate recipes and experiment with new products.

Kraft also expanded in the 1920s by purchasing more than fifty dairies. In 1928 Kraft merged with Phenix Cheese Company to form the Kraft-Phenix Cheese Company. Phenix contributed the famous Philadelphia Cream Cheese to the product line. The merged firm employed 10,000 people in thirty states and four foreign countries and accounted for about a third of all domestically sold cheese. Three years later Kraft-Phenix was purchased by National Dairy Products Company, a holding company formed in 1923 that within ten years had directly acquired 194 dairies. Thus within a decade the dairy industry became an oligopoly. National Dairy's largest competitors were the Bordon Company and Beatrice Creamery (Meadow Gold Butter). Kraft-Phenix remained a fairly autonomous subsidiary of National Dairy, leaving James Kraft in charge.

The depression failed to thwart Kraft's policies. He continued aggressive advertising in 1933 by announcing the largest advertising budget in the firm's history. Part of that budget went to launching the "Kraft Musical Review" on radio, later renamed "Kraft Music Hall" and hosted by crooner Bing Crosby. A stream of new products well suited to depressed household budgets emerged from research, beginning with Velveeta in 1928 and followed by Miracle Whip (1933), Kraft Macaroni and Cheese Dinner (1936), and Parkay Margarine (1937). Furthermore, the firm had expanded its products to include salad dressing, caramels, marshmallows, and ice cream toppings. The company changed its name in 1945 to Kraft Foods to reflect this product mix.

The federal government, which unsuccessfully sought on several occasions in the 1930s to prove Kraft-Phenix and other large dairies guilty of pricefixing, once again became a major purchaser of Kraft cheese for field rations during World War II. Following the war Kraft presided over the firm's ongoing growth and development. In 1947 he sponsored "Kraft Television Theater," one of the medium's first major programs. New Kraft products came to market, such as processed cheese slices in 1949 and a processed cheese spread called Cheez Whiz in 1952. A year earlier Kraft had retired as chairman of the board and was succeeded by his brother John.

James Kraft remained devoutly religious throughout his life, ascribing his business success to God's help. He joined North Shore Baptist Church in Chicago, where he served as Sunday school superintendent for forty years. A trustee of Northern Baptist Theological Seminary, he underwrote many a clergyman's education. His employee communications were interspersed with religious texts. Although he sponsored radio and later television programs, he was skeptical of their humor.

Kraft's major hobby was the collection of jade. He set up a lapidary workshop in his home, where he made rings for meritorious employees until the number of such employees forced him to turn to professional jewelers. His interest and expertise as a collector led him to write *Adventures in Jade* in 1947. Kraft received numerous honors, including several honorary doctorates and the Gutenberg Award of the Chicago Bible Society in 1952. He married Pauline Elizabeth Platt of Chicago in 1910; they had one daughter. He died in Chicago.

James L. Kraft helped revolutionize the manufacture and distribution of cheese and cheese products. Innovations in processing, aided by refrigeration in the 1920s, made cheese available year-round. Packaging cheese extended its shelf life, improved its handling hygienically, and allowed Kraft to use brand names in advertising in print and on radio and television. Ongoing research and development led to new products and product lines. Per capita consumption of cheese increased 50 percent between 1918 and 1945, due in part to Kraft's efforts. His career mirrored many of the major business trends of that period.

• Kraft is included in Joseph T. Fucini and Suzi Fucini, *Entrepreneurs* (1985); Milton Moscowitz et al., *Everybody's Business: A Field Guide to the 400 Leading Companies in America* (1990); and John N. Ingham, ed., *Biographical Dictionary of American Business Leaders* (1983). Arthur L. Baum, "Man with a Horse and Wagon," *Saturday Evening Post*, 17 Feb. 1945, provides a personal look at Kraft. For information about the company after Kraft's death, see Thomas Derdak, ed., *International Directory of Company Histories* (1990), and the company-sponsored *Kraft through the Years* (1988). Obituaries are in the *Chicago Tribune* and *New York Times*, both 17 Feb. 1953.

LLOYD L. SPONHOLTZ

KRAFT, Joseph (4 Sept. 1924–10 Jan. 1986), journalist, was born in South Orange, New Jersey, the son of David Harry Kraft, a businessman, and Sophie Surasky. His early education was at the Fieldston School in New York City. He began his distinguished career in journalism while still in high school, reporting on school sports for the *New York World Telegram*. He then entered Columbia College, but his education there was interrupted by three years of service, during World War II, in the U.S. Army Signal Corps as a translator of Japanese. The reverence for hard fact visible in his writings was undoubtedly inculcated in his service in the war years as he learned to deal with military intelligence of the highest order. Kraft finished college at Columbia as a member of Phi Beta Kappa and the valedictorian of the class of 1947. From 1948 to 1951 he was a history fellow at the Institute of Advanced Studies at Princeton University and also studied at the Sorbonne in Paris.

After finishing his education in 1951, Kraft worked for a year or so as an editorial writer for the *Washington Post* and then in 1953 joined the staff of the Sunday issue of the *New York Times*, where he remained until 1957. He married Polly Winton, an artist, in 1960; he became stepfather to her two sons. After working for a time as a freelance writer, he became the Washington correspondent for *Harper's* from 1962 to 1965. In 1963 he began publishing columns with the Field Newspapers Syndicate. With this syndicate association and his association with the *Los Angeles Times* and its syndicate after 1980, Kraft's columns would be seen by readers of over 200 newspapers with a circulation in the millions.

Kraft's worldwide travels and interviews with world leaders won him the Overseas Press Club's award for distinguished reporting in 1958, 1973, and 1980, along with Columbia University's John Jay Award for Distinguished Professional Achievement in 1983. In that same year the French government made him a chevalier in the Legion of Honor. His work as a speechwriter for John F. Kennedy during the 1960 campaign brought him into the fringe of politics, which he entered again during the 1976 presidential election when he served on a panel of questioners during a debate between candidates Jimmy Carter and Gerald R. Ford.

Kraft published widely in magazines besides those of his primary employment, in particular the *New Yorker*, *Foreign Affairs*, the *Saturday Evening Post*, *Esquire*, the *Observer* of London, and *L'express* of Paris. Admirers of Kraft have often compared him to Walter Lippmann, a comparison that is unfortunate because the concerns of the two journalists were so different. Kraft was without peer as a reporter. The articles he prepared for the *New Yorker* between 1978 and 1983, for instance, show astonishing range, originating from sites in and around the Middle East: Egypt, Israel, Turkey, Syria, Saudi Arabia, Iraq, Pakistan, and the Soviet Union. They feature countless interviews with leaders and lesser figures of the various nations he visited and are full of history lessons revealing the background to many current affairs.

An excellent example of Kraft's work is "Letter from Saudi Arabia," published in the 4 July 1983 issue of the *New Yorker*. At the time oil prices, elevated so greatly by the development of the Organization of Petroleum Exporting Countries (OPEC) in the 1970s, had dropped significantly, and OPEC, and Saudi Arabia in particular, had only recently recovered some muscle in world affairs. Kraft's graphic descriptions of the scene in Jidda, Saudi Arabia's principal city, his analyses of the city's ruling class and his naming of its members, and his interviews of the leaders of the nation offer information that remains of value despite all the seemingly new information made available to the West since the article's publication.

Kraft's greatest work, however, may well be his writings on Algeria, which he published between 1958 and 1961 and which culminated in the book *The Struggle for Algeria* (1961). The articles appeared in the *New York Times Magazine*, the *New Republic*, and the *Saturday Evening Post* with evocative titles such as "Algeria, Not Tunisia," "Big 3 of Algeria's Rebels," "De Gaulle Remains the Mystery," "I Saw the Algerian Rebels in Action," and "We Are All Victims in Algeria." The book is a profound study, with chapter titles that are a precise encapsulation of its contents: "Native Grounds," "The Rebels," "The Army," "The Politics," "The Ides of May," "De Gaulle," "Peace of the Brave," and "The Lesson." These writings show so keen an understanding of the events and the pain felt on all sides that the logic behind his being named a chevalier de France is readily apparent.

Kraft's involvement with the Kennedy administration resulted in little publication under his own name, except for the book *The Grand Design: from Common Market to Atlantic Partnership* (1962), which presented the Kennedy plan of "Atlantic Partnership." His work as a syndicated columnist began shortly before Kennedy's assassination in 1963 and continued with essays for the Los Angeles Times syndicate, appearing three times a week in the *Los Angeles Times* and the *Washington Post*.

Kraft is remembered as one of the first nationally published newspaper columnists to come out strongly against the Vietnam War. His predisposition to this stand may be seen throughout *The Struggle for Algeria*, particularly in the final chapter, in which he writes: "Thus, for the foreseeable future, the convulsions of Africa and Asia are a fixture which not even the Big Two can control." He is also credited with having coined the term "Middle America" before it was adopted by the Nixon administration.

One of the aspects of Kraft's career that brought him a great deal of attention was his harsh criticism of President Jimmy Carter, visible in the *Washington Post* column of 19 July 1979 titled "A Genuine Outsider": "For one thing, he is a genuine outsider. As a rural Southerner he is not at home in what I have called Big America—the world of the main corporations, unions, cities and universities. Not only did he come to power by challenging the established structure in the country, but he stays in power by renewing the challenge." After a few paragraphs Kraft goes on to say that Carter "trades in enmities, in part because he lacks the natural attributes of leadership. He has neither the heroic stature of an Eisenhower nor the glamour of a Kennedy. Not even the governing skills of a Nixon or Johnson."

Judging by the book *The Other Side of the Story* (1984) by Jody Powell, Carter's press secretary, Kraft's criticisms of Carter were not taken kindly. Powell takes at least three opportunities to speak disparagingly of Kraft in his book, singling him out as a White House reporter who was hostile to everything the Carter administration attempted to do, "one of the strangest sorts of a peculiar breed" (p. 55).

Kraft's criticisms of President Ronald Reagan were almost as harsh. An example may be seen in the *Washington Post* column of 10 April 1984, titled "Sleaze": "The President's claim that 'I believe the halls of government are as sacred as our temples of worship' . . . does not square with the record. Could it be that Reagan is just an actor mouthing phrases to dupe the public? Elmer Gantry in the White House? Probably not. More likely is the proposition that he doesn't know the record, that he is an aging leader, out of touch with what is happening all around him."

In one of the many obituaries written at the time of Kraft's relatively early death, James Reston, the chief political columnist for the *New York Times*, is quoted as saying: "The main thing about Joe Kraft is that he tried to deal with the causes of human suffering rather than the results. . . . With the possible exception of I. F. Stone, no journalist of his time in Washington studied the official documents more carefully, questioned officials more precisely or worked so hard knowing he had so little time, to fight for the facts against the television pretenses of contemporary politicians." Kraft died in Washington, D.C.

• Kraft's other books are *Profiles in Power: A Washington Insight* (1966) and *The Chinese Difference* (1973). Michael Massing, "Great Man Will Travel," *Nation*, 23 May 1981, pp. 633–4, is filled with general information on Kraft, even though the principal intent is to bemoan what the writer considers to be Kraft's defeat by the rigors of writing thrice-weekly columns. Also see "Kraftsmanship," *Newsweek*, 4 July 1966, p. 54; and C. Clifford and R. Lemon, "While Joe Kraft Humbles the Elevated in Print, Wife Polly Elevates the Humble on Canvas," *People Weekly*, 15 Feb. 1982, pp. 119–20. Obituaries are in the *New York Times* and the *Washington Post*, 11 Jan. 1986; the *Chicago Tribune*, 12 Jan. 1986; and *Newsweek*, 20 Jan. 1986.

ALFRED H. MARKS

KRAMER, Frank Louis (21 Nov. 1880–8 Oct. 1958), bicycle racer, was born in Evansville, Indiana, the son of Louis H. Kramer, a lumber merchant and amateur athlete, and Helen Euler. During the early 1890s the parents believed Frank exhibited symptoms of tuberculosis. They bought him a high-wheeled "safety" bicycle for exercise and sent him to the supposedly healthier atmosphere of East Orange, New Jersey, to live with Dillon and Lillian Bennett, who became his foster parents. In his first bicycle sprint race, held during May 1896 at Weequahic Park in Newark, New Jersey, he finished last. When "ordinary" bikes, equipped with equally sized wheels and pneumatic tires, supplanted safeties in public favor, Kramer switched to the newer type. He gained notice in 1897 when, during one day's competition in White Plains, New York, he won two cups and six medals. In 1898 and 1899 he captured the national amateur sprint championships.

From an undersized, frail youngster, Kramer grew into a robust athlete. He was fractionally under six feet tall, big-boned, barrel-chested, muscular, golden-haired, and called "Chisel Chin" because of his jutting jaw and pronounced underbite. Noting the huge cash the famous black cyclist Major Taylor was accumulating in prize money, Kramer turned professional in 1900. After Kramer defeated former U.S. sprint champion Tom Cooper, the Pierce-Arrow company, which manufactured automobiles and bicycles, signed him to race their custom-made, nickel-plated bikes. That summer Taylor vanquished him in several meets in the East and the Middle West and in the final of the U.S. professional sprint championship at the banked wooden velodrome in Newark. Kramer never again lost a championship event to Taylor and proceeded to dominate sprint races, winning the U.S. titles from 1901 through 1916.

Floyd McFarland, a rider turned promoter, managed Kramer and Jackie Clark, the "Australian Rocket," in 1906, and publicly nicknamed them "Big Steve" and "Little Steve." Throughout his career, Kramer remained "Big Steve" to the sport's public. Kramer usually defeated Clark, despite the latter's explosive sprints. In the 1908 U.S. championship at Madison Square Garden, New York City, Kramer won the half-mile and one-mile events by coming from behind to nip Clark at the finishes.

Although universally regarded as the world's best cyclist, Kramer competed in the world championship only once, when it was held at Newark; he won the event. He did undergo European tours in 1905, 1906, 1913, and 1914, drawing record crowds in Paris, Berlin, Brussels, Copenhagen, and other western European capitals and defeating all rivals more frequently than not. During his first two tours, he won the Grand Prix of Paris, each time earning purses of $2,500 for those sprint races.

Kramer obsessively sought racing perfection. Quiet and reserved, he made few friendships and did not fraternize with other riders away from the tracks. He raised roses and chickens in East Orange and lived a temperate, Spartan existence. Always physically fit, he employed a trainer, Jack Neville, to guide his training and apply daily massages. He went to bed punctu-

ally at nine o'clock every evening, practiced long hours at the track regularly, studied racing techniques and tactics thoroughly, and periodically spent days at the Pierce-Arrow factory in Buffalo, New York, scrutinizing bicycle construction. He also meticulously kept books recording his receipts and expenditures.

In 1911 "Colonel" John M. Chapman, the "czar of bike racing," constructed a new velodrome in the Vailsburg section of Newark, enclosing a six-laps-to-the-mile banked track, and signed Kramer to a ten-year contract to ride exclusively under his control. Repeatedly Kramer beat the greatest world talent Chapman could bring to Newark, mostly at sprint distances but occasionally at longer races. He rode in six-day bike races, with different partners, in 1911, 1912, and 1918, winning none of them. He became so uniformly dominant in sprint races that eventually other riders, including his chief rival, Alf Goullett, combined against him, by "teaming," a practice of three opponents alternately challenging him in sprints while the others conserved energy, tiring him, beating him, and sharing prize monies coequally. These tactics almost lost Kramer the 1915 championship to Goullett and caused him to consider retirement. Such incidents prompted the National Cycling Association to reduce the number of racers in championship semifinals and finals from four to two.

After losing his sprint title to Arthur Spencer in 1917, Kramer installed a larger gear on his shiny silver bike, regained the U.S. championship in 1918, and won it again in 1921. He closed out his career on 25 and 26 July 1922 with attempts to better his own best time of 15⅘ seconds for one-sixth of a mile and the world record of 15⅖ seconds, set in 1911 by Albert Krebs. At the New York Velodrome on 25 July his time was only 16 seconds, but at the Newark Velodrome on the next evening he equalled the world record, a remarkable performance by a 41-year-old veteran after a five-minute ovation rendered him by 20,000 spectators. At retirement he also held world records for one-quarter-, one-third-, one-half-, and three-quarter-mile sprints. The bicycle racing historian Walter Bardgett named Kramer the greatest all-time bike racer over Goullett, Taylor, and all others. Chapman never found a star to replace Kramer; and the sport, whose attendance marks surpassed baseball's at times, virtually disappeared after a 1930 fire destroyed the New York Velodrome; it resumed later on a lesser scale.

Kramer married Helen Malcolmson Hay of East Orange on 24 November 1924; they had no children. During their honeymoon he took her to the bike races in Paris, at the Velodrome d'Hiver, a site of his earlier triumphs. Unacquainted with his heroic status among racing fans throughout the world, she was astonished when he was recognized immediately and hoisted on a bike to pedal a slow lap to the accompaniment of tumultuous cheering in memory of his accomplishments there. He cherished the recollection of that incident more than those of his most impressive victories. For many years he performed as an official and a meet referee for the National Cycling Association, participated in civic affairs, served on the East Orange police commission, and, principally, managed Record Ambulance, a nonprofit, partly charitable ambulance transportation service for the hospitals and people of the Orange communities. He died in East Orange.

• Two feature articles describe Kramer's victories and personality: David Chaumier, "Yesterday: Back in the Early 1900s, Bicycling Was Big and Frank Kramer Was King," *Sports Illustrated*, 11 Feb. 1985, pp. 192–98; and Al Laney, "Boy Cyclists Don't Know 'Big Steve' but All East Orange Knows Him," *New York Herald Tribune*, 24 Dec. 1946. Peter Nye, *Hearts of Lions: The History of American Bicycle Racing* (1988), details events during Kramer's time. The *New York Times* provides coverage of Kramer's accomplishments in its issues of 10 Aug. 1915 and 26 and 27 July 1922. Andrew Ritchie, *Major Taylor: The Extraordinary Style of a Champion Bicycle Racer* (1988), describes the Kramer-Taylor rivalry. Other useful materials are in Frank G. Menke with revisions by Suzanne Treat, *The Encyclopedia of Sports*, 6th rev. ed. (1977), pp. 199–211; Arthur Judson Palmer, *Riding High* (1956), pp. 175–76; and Ralph Hickok, *A Who's Who of Sports Champions* (1995), p. 448. An obituary is in the *New York Times*, 9 Oct. 1958.

FRANK V. PHELPS

KRAMER, Samuel Noah (28 Sept. 1897–26 Nov. 1990), Sumerologist and historian, was born in Zashkov (Ukraine), a Jewish ghetto near Kiev in tsarist Russia, the son of Benjamin Kramer, a teacher of the Talmud, and Yetta (maiden name unknown). He grew up in a family that was immersed in the study of the Hebrew Bible. Benjamin Kramer decided to emigrate to the United States out of fear of anti-Semitic pogroms, and in 1905 the family settled in Philadelphia, where the young Kramer's name, originally Simcha Noach, was anglicized to Samuel Nathan. Only as an adult did Kramer resume using his original middle name in the slightly altered version, Noah.

While receiving a secular education he continued to study the Talmud in the yeshiva run by his father. After high school he enrolled in the Philadelphia School of Pedagogy and after graduation in 1917 started to teach in his father's school. He then enrolled at Temple University, where he obtained a B.S. in education in two years (exact year unknown). After some failed experiments in business, law, and philosophy, Kramer enrolled at Dropsie College of Philadelphia in 1925. There he became interested in Egyptology, but after a falling out with his teacher he moved to the University of Pennsylvania where he was introduced to the study of ancient Mesopotamia by Ephraim Avigdor Speiser. He completed his doctoral dissertation, "The Verb in The Kirkuk Tablets," in 1929. In 1930 he received a grant from the American Council of Learned Societies that enabled him to travel to Iraq. There, by chance, he became responsible for the publication of cuneiform tablets written in Sumerian that were excavated by the German expedition at Fara. Theophile Meek, the man originally contacted for the work, was unable to join the German excavators, and

Kramer, as the only other epigraphist in Iraq at that moment, was sent in his place.

After returning to the United States in June 1931 he remained unemployed because of limited job opportunities in his field. In 1932 the Oriental Institute of the University of Chicago invited him to collaborate in its Assyrian Dictionary project until 1936. At Chicago he became heavily involved with Sumerian, the non-Semitic language used throughout Mesopotamian history alongside the Semitic Akkadian language. He was introduced to the principles of Sumerian grammar by Arno Poebel and was asked to edit two volumes of Sumerian literary texts left by the late Edward Chiera. This project introduced him to Sumerian literature, the subject that would occupy the rest of his life. In 1933 he married Mildred Tokarsky; they had two children.

The Rockefeller board cut most of its support for the Oriental Institute as a result of the depression, and a few weeks before the end of the 1935–1936 academic year Kramer was informed of his immediate dismissal. After the chairman of the local chapter of the American Association of University Professors argued that the notification of the dismissal was too late, Kramer was reinstated for one year. This enabled him to apply successfully for a grant from the Guggenheim Foundation. With this grant, which was renewed for the 1938–1939 academic year, he traveled to Istanbul, where he started to copy the Sumerian literary texts excavated at Nippur in modern Iraq and stored in the Archaeological Museum of Istanbul. When he returned to Philadelphia he obtained permission to study similar material in the University Museum of the University of Pennsylvania, a research project supported for four years by the American Philosophical Society. In that period he was asked to treat Sumerian mythology at an interdisciplinary seminar in the Department of Oriental Studies of the University of Pennsylvania, and after a well-received lecture to the American Philosophical Society on the myth of the descent of Inanna into the netherworld, he was offered the position of associate curator of the Babylonian Section at the University Museum in 1943. In 1948 he obtained the position of Clark Research Professor of Assyriology and curator of the tablet collection at the University of Pennsylvania, a secure academic post that enabled him to continue his work on the Sumerians and their literature.

His publications treated this subject in two different ways. On the one hand he continued his scholarly editions of texts, work based at first on his copies of tablets stored in Istanbul and Philadelphia and later also on those from the Hilprecht Collection in Jena, the Pushkin Museum in Moscow, the British Museum in London, and the Ashmolean in Oxford. He also used this material as the basis of a series of books intended for the general public: *Sumerian Mythology* (1944), *History Begins at Sumer* (1959), *The Sumerians* (1963), and *The Sacred Marriage Rite* (1969). Both types of publications revolutionized his field of scholarship. His scholarly editions presented numerous previously unknown or badly understood texts for the first time. His popular books introduced Sumerian history and culture to a public unaware of this ancient people. These books as well as numerous lectures made him the best-known and most popular scholar in his discipline. He officially retired from the University of Pennsylvania in 1968 but remained active as a visiting professor in various European countries and in Israel, publishing several articles and books in subsequent years. Active to the end of his life, he died in Philadelphia.

Kramer was generally admired and liked by his colleagues in the field. He had a good sense of humor and a pleasant personality and was eager to talk with younger scholars and students. He was not very good at lecturing undergraduate students, but his close interaction with doctoral students made him an excellent adviser. Although his family background was steeped in the Jewish religion and he supported the existence of the modern state of Israel, he traveled extensively in the Arab world, had close relationships with Iraqi scholars, and hoped "to revive the spiritual and familial bond between Arab and Jew."

• An autobiography, *In the World of Sumer* (1986), lists Kramer's publications up to that date. With Jean Bottéro he wrote *Lorsque les dieux faisaient l'homme* (1989), his last major work. An obituary is in the *New York Times*, 27 Nov. 1990.

MARC VAN DE MIEROOP

KRAPP, George Philip (1 Sept. 1872–21 Apr. 1934), philologist and man of letters, was born in Cincinnati, Ohio, the second son of Martin Krapp and Louisa Addams. His father, a veteran of the Union armies, had been captured at Gettysburg and was mustered out by President Lincoln. George Philip was raised in Springfield, Ohio, where his father had opened a grocery store. The family was strongly Germanic; George Philip attended Wittenberg College in Springfield and after graduation went to Johns Hopkins to pursue his doctorate. At Baltimore George Philip remained in residence for just three years (1894–1897); his doctoral thesis was published in 1900 as *The Legend of Saint Patrick's Purgatory: Its Later Literary History*. Meanwhile, in 1897, he had accepted a position as instructor in English at Teacher's College, a division of Columbia University. An offer from the University of Cincinnati brought him back to Ohio for the years 1908–1910; but then Columbia, realizing that his talents would be better displayed in the Graduate School than in Teacher's College, lured him back to Morningside Heights. In December 1911 he married Elisabeth, daughter of Carl Fredrick von Saltza, and settled into the life of the metropolis. In due course they produced three children who lived to maturity.

Though he quickly became, and for most of his life remained, a New York City apartment dweller, there was a side of George Philip that the city never fully absorbed. Even when a boy in Springfield, he botanized methodically along the forest trails and river bottoms of the district. Wilderness and solitude were always important parts of his life. At Columbia he met a Latinist of similar tastes named Charles Baker; they shared frequent backwoods summers with a canoe, a sack of flour, a flitch of bacon, a frying pan, and a fly rod as their total equipment. They were not, except incidentally, hunters or fishermen; they were outdoorsmen. George Philip's nomadic streak ran deep and lasted long. One summer, well after he was married and thoroughly domesticated in the New York area, he cut loose and went rambling alone out west. Sometimes he hiked, sometimes he hitched; whether he had a roof over his head did not seem to matter. He jawboned with unemployed miners and shared the cowboys' favorite delicacy (canned peaches) in the shade of the bunkhouse. His new friends must have thought him a curious tramp; likely he was more interested in their phonemes and morphemes than in their critters and cayuses.

Another year he arranged to summer with his older son in some remote Mormon settlements high in the mountain valleys of Mexico. It was rough country, infested with cougars, diamondback rattlers, and the last resentful, trigger-happy remnants of some exiled Apache tribes. The complexities of language did not attract him so much as the sheer wildness of the land, the roughness of the people, the sense of adventure. He was not like any other philologist his wife (safe in Connecticut) could have married.

The scholarly work of George Philip Krapp took from the beginning two contrasting directions. He was interested in, and soon became one of the world's authorities on, Old English (often called Anglo-Saxon). The poetry of this seminal but long-since-obliterated culture survived mainly in bits and pieces; assembling and interpreting it occupied George Philip for many years, and teaching Old English to graduate students was a major part of his academic commitment. This work culminated in the six-volume edition of *Anglo-Saxon Poetic Records*, on which he was at work (with the help of his graduate assistant E. V. K. Dobbie) at the time of his death. The set appeared between 1931 and 1953.

Alongside his work on Old English, George Krapp was attracted to the history of the English language, particularly the shapes it assumed in the New World of America. Belying his own ironic formula that "a man owes it to his students to teach badly," he was an outstanding instructor. It was not unheard-of for a particularly bright student to realize that there was more in his course than he or she had been able to carry away, and so to take it again. His work was not simply for graduate students or for his fellow professors, it reached a popular audience far outside the academy. An early book, *Modern English, Its Growth and Present Use* (1909), argued strongly that "good English" was not and never had been determined by recourse to grammatical laws and logical formulas, but by the common usage of cultured and intelligent speakers. The book was successful enough in its argument to reduce its own thesis to something like a truism; yet it was so forceful in its quiet presentation that sixty years after its first publication it was reissued in an edition only slightly revised and modernized by Professor Albert Marckwardt. Popular handbooks like *A Comprehensive Guide to Good English* (1927) were also widely influential in conveying a steady sense of language as a mutable, mutual set of rules rather than a hedge of elitist forbiddings. In the same vein, *The Rise of English Literary Prose* (1915) combined a sense of historical weight with a vision of the language's long-term growth through a sequence of immediate applications.

The English Language in America (2 vols., 1925) profited in part from previous work done on the subject by that vigorous publicist H. L. Mencken (1919). But it also had a special fascination of its own. Finding out how words were pronounced a hundred or two hundred years ago, long before the invention of any recording devices, was a compelling long-range puzzle. Especially successful was George Krapp's exploration of eighteenth- and nineteenth-century town registers, where the clerks, typically not highly educated men, often spelled words about the same way they pronounced them. Rural archives thus provided an unexpected lode of linguistic history; and his penchant for living in the country gave the scholar a strong lead toward important historic materials.

George Philip Krapp did not appear a restless or feverishly busy man. He never drove a car, worked a typewriter, or accepted an administrative post; he belonged to an absolute minimum of professional organizations and never attended a conference. But he used his spare minutes scrupulously. A full-fledged national history for young people appeared in 1924 under the title *America the Great Adventure*; three years later he adapted the story of his father's adventures in the Civil War into a children's book, *Sixty Years Ago*. *In Oldest England* (1912) and *Tales of True Knights* (1921) made medieval materials available to the young. Other such children's books—about eight or ten—appeared at intervals. Meanwhile he regularly wrote for the editorial page of the *New York Times* brief, quiet observations on the changing natural scene, such as feathered visitors and the fringed gentians lining up along a swamp trail.

While on sabbatical leave with his family in southern France (1930–1931), he carried along a well-thumbed Chaucer with which he used to stroll out mornings by the Mediterranean and take shelter behind a rock from the *mistral*. Not until the family had moved back to chilly, depression-racked New York did anyone know he had been translating—or, better, re-Englishing—Chaucer's romantic novel in verse, *Troilus and Criseyde*. The book was published in 1932 by Random House with exotic woodblock prints by Eric Gill. It was adopted by the Literary Guild and is one of his most genial publications—a deft and witty work of poetry, surprising only to those who had not appreciated earlier his urbane and cosmopolitan spirit.

After a brief illness, George Philip Krapp died in New York. He did not "revolutionize" English studies, or try to do so, but he recalled them to a humane and civilized rationalism which seems to be an enduring part of the heritage.

• A bibliography of the writings of George Philip Krapp was published by E. V. K. Dobbie in *American Speech*, Dec. 1934 and Apr. 1935. An obituary appears in the *New York Times*, 22 Apr. 1934.

ROBERT MARTIN ADAMS

KRASNER, Lee (27 Oct. 1908–20 June 1984), abstract expressionist artist, was born Lena Krassner in Brooklyn, New York, the daughter of Joseph Krassner, a fruit and vegetable dealer and fishmonger, and Anna Weiss. (Krasner changed her first name in childhood; she dropped the second *s* in her original surname around 1943.) Her father immigrated to the United States in 1905, during the Russo-Japanese War, from the village of Shpikov, near Odessa, Russia. Krasner's mother, three older sisters, and a brother arrived at Ellis Island on the Dutch liner *Ryndam* in 1908. Krasner (called Lenore) was born nine months and two weeks after her parents' reunion and was followed in America by a younger sister.

The household in which Krasner was raised was female-dominated, European, and strict, with little time for, or interest in, cultural enrichment. Russian, Yiddish, and Hebrew were spoken more often than English. Childhood memories of Russian fairy tales and Hebrew calligraphy in prayer books would have later reverberations in Krasner's art. Krasner considered herself religious until her preteen years when she entered a rebellious stage, and the discovery of Nietzsche and Schopenhauer radically altered her acceptance of the tenets of Orthodox Judaism.

After graduating from elementary school in Brooklyn, Krasner attended Washington Irving High School in Manhattan, the only public school where a girl could major in art. Despite poor grades even in her art classes, Krasner gained entrance in 1926 to the Cooper Union for the Advancement of Science and Art in Greenwich Village. The conservative curriculum and approach there were not consistent with Krasner's nonconformist temperament, so in 1928 she transferred to the National Academy of Design (NAD), where, once again, she was considered "a nuisance and impossible" by her teachers. Ilya Bolotowsky, at the NAD concurrently, later characterized Krasner as "a very bold muscular painter" who did not fit in with the school's prescribed style. Her contrary approach was in large part due to her discovery in these years of the Museum of Modern Art, the impact of which she later described as "like a bomb that exploded."

When the depression depleted her finances, Krasner left the NAD in 1932 to waitress and attend City College of New York education courses at night, while continuing to draw at the Greenwich Village Settlement House. There, in the class of one of his protégés, Krasner encountered the famous "hollow and bump" figure-articulation method of regionalist painter Thomas Hart Benton. This method would enable her, later on, to more fully understand the artistic background of Jackson Pollock, often ranked as the most important abstract expressionist. Pollock, who moved to New York in 1930 from California to study with Benton, became Krasner's husband in a ceremony at the Marble Collegiate Church on 25 October 1945.

During the depression, however, Krasner had a long-term live-in relationship with Russian-born portrait painter Igor O. Pantuhoff, a Prix de Rome winner she had met at the NAD. She attempted to paint social realist cityscapes, but her attention was diverted to more avant-garde European trends represented by such artists as de Chirico, Mondrian, Miro, and Matisse. In 1937, when Krasner entered the Hans Hofmann School of Fine Arts, she at last found a teacher sympathetic to her interests and talents. Hofmann, a German emigré, had studied in Paris from 1904 to 1914, learning cubism and fauvism firsthand. He taught in Munich and Berkeley before opening his school in New York. In 1958 Hofmann was quoted in *Time* magazine as saying that Lee Krasner was "one of the best students I ever had." Frequently asked if Pollock had attended his school, Hofmann always replied, "No, but he was a student of my student, Lee Krasner."

Krasner's ability to assimilate Hofmann's synthesis of the formal innovations of Picasso and the color of Matisse is seen in the extraordinary series of charcoal nudes and oil still-life studies she produced at the Hofmann School from 1937 to 1940. During this period, she moved from semi-abstract works to advanced compositions in which she summarized diagrammatically the tensions in space created by the subject. As noted by Barbara Rose, Krasner at this time seemed to have a more radical understanding of the implications of French modernist art than did her teacher. Her work was also more sophisticated than Pollock's at that point, and she was to play an important role in his artistic education after their meeting in late 1941.

While at the Hofmann School, Krasner exhibited with the American Abstract Artists group, was active politically in the Artists Union, and joined the Public Works of Art Project, becoming a supervisor in the Mural Division of the Fine Arts Project of the Works Progress Administration (WPA) by 1939. She was put in charge of such major projects as Leonard Seweryn Jenkins's *The History of Navigation* painted for the Brooklyn Public Library in Brownsville. Finally allowed in late 1941 to design her own mural, Krasner created an innovative still life–based abstraction for radio station WNYC, which was never executed because of Franklin Roosevelt's conversion of the WPA to a war services organization in March 1942.

Krasner's selection in 1941 for a special exhibition, "French and American Painting," organized by artist/connoisseur/entrepreneur John Graham for the design firm of McMillen Inc., precipitated her meeting with Pollock, the most decisive event of her personal and artistic life. Krasner recognized immediately—and with more conviction than anyone else—that Pollock, a laconic westerner of Scotch-Irish extraction and an alcoholic with mental instabilities, was also an extraor-dinarily original artist. She was to devote the next fourteen years (and, in some ways, the rest of her life) mostly to furthering his, not her own, career. Krasner later described her reaction to Pollock's work as "a force, a living force—the same kind of thing I responded to in Matisse, Picasso and Mondrian." Realizing that her own work was not metamorphic or expressive enough, she later recalled, "The transition I went through from the Academy to Cubism, I once more had to go through from Cubism to Pollock. . . . If Hofmann broke up the Academy, then Pollock broke up Hofmann."

By all accounts, Krasner may have done as much for Pollock as he did for her. John Bernard Myers, editor of the avant-garde publication *View*, once characterized their relationship as "truly symbiotic—a two-way street." Krasner's "eye and her support" have been credited by art critic Clement Greenberg as being absolutely catalytic for Pollock's development. After their marriage, Krasner and Pollock moved from Manhattan to The Springs, near East Hampton, on the south fork of Long Island. They had no children. Her first attempts to divest herself of a cubist framework and reach inside herself for imagery—as Pollock had—resulted in several years of failed canvases Krasner dubbed "Grey Slabs." Her husband's association with Peggy Guggenheim's Art of This Century Gallery exposed Krasner more directly to surrealist automatic methods, which she first successfully applied not to painting but to a pair of mosaic tables in 1946–1947.

While Pollock developed his signature large, all-over, poured, and dripped works in the barn studio, Krasner finally moved on to an important series: the *Little Images* (c. 1947). These smaller-scale canvases were covered edge to edge with rhythmically accentuated touches, swirls, or rows of runelike hieroglyphs. Like Pollock, Krasner focused on an exploration of the possibilities of drawing in paint, but she retained a traditional wrist control in contradistinction to his more improvisational whole body movement. In the hieroglyphic *Little Images*, in particular, surrealist automatic methods seem to become infused with Krasner's memories of Hebrew writing to produce enigmatically suggestive proto-alphabetic compositions merging the abstract and organic.

Actually, in Krasner's *Little Images*, she synthesized numerous early influences, evidence that she had finally come to terms with her own experience, a lesson she credited to Pollock. Simultaneously, these tiny works presaged important aspects of her subsequent artistic career. In her first solo exhibition, at the Betty Parsons Gallery in 1951, Krasner distilled the concerns of the hieroglyphs to minimally articulated, thinly brushed grids, in which chromatic sensitivity replaced automatic gesture. (Many consider these the two poles of abstract expressionism.) The complex counterpointing of space seen in many of the *Little Images* returned during 1953–1955 when Krasner collaged over the Parsons paintings, pasting onto them large dramatic Matissean nature configurations culled from her own and Pollock's other discarded works, resulting in such works as *Bald Eagle* (1955; private collection).

After the tragedy of her husband's fatal automobile accident in 1956, Krasner returned to the allover dripped technique both had begun to use in the late 1940s. Moving into Pollock's barn studio, she painted huge umber and white canvases, such as *The Eye Is the First Circle* (1960; private collection), whose ferocity of rhythm contrasts sharply with the more lyrical interweavings of the *Little Images* she had more tentatively poured from a tiny can. Just as she had done with the hieroglyphs, Krasner engendered these forms with a vigorous backward stroke reminiscent of Hebraic calligraphy. In other gestural works of the 1960s, Krasner reprised different aspects of her preoccupation with ancient forms of writing, suspending signs and symbols in blurred space, or creating more sharply focused emblematic enlargements of shapes she had earlier multiplied in miniature. In her final major collage series, exhibited at the Pace Gallery in 1977, including *Past Continuous* (1976; Guggenheim Museum), Krasner combined with painted panels sharply sheared sections of charcoal figure drawings from the Hofmann School years, as well as their own rubbed-off "ghost" images, to work out another variation on the ongoing dialogue in her work between gesture and grid. In effect, she once again redistilled an imagistic focus out of the allover composition by recontextualizing her past.

Without a doubt, Lee Krasner and Jackson Pollock were radically altered as both artists and human beings by the emotional subtext of their relationship. In various ways, and at different times in their union, the interpersonal dynamic that governed it both expanded and limited the aesthetic as well as the personal choices of these two talented, volatile personalities. Overshadowed by Pollock at every turn, it was not until 1978, when a major exhibition of the formative years of abstract expressionism was held at the Whitney Museum of American Art in New York, that Krasner's role as the sole female pioneer of the movement became widely acknowledged. As a result, Krasner began to be revered as a feminist heroine by many younger women artists. Certainly, the complexity of what is often characterized as her "working relationship" with Pollock is a defining feature of Lee Krasner's importance to the history of postwar American art. On her death in New York City, her will established the Pollock-Krasner Foundation whose multimillion dollar endowment helps support needy and neglected artists.

• Lee Krasner's papers are in the Archives of American Art, Smithsonian Institution. Important catalogs and monographs include Barbara Rose, *Lee Krasner and Jackson Pollock: A Working Relationship* (1982) and *Lee Krasner: A Retrospective* (1983); Sandor Kuthy and Ellen G. Landau, *Lee Krasner— Jackson Pollock: Künstlerpaare—Künstlerfreunde; Dialogue d'artistes—résonances* (1989); Robert Hobbs, *Lee Krasner* (1993); and Ellen G. Landau, *Lee Krasner: A Catalogue Raisonné* (1995). See also Landau, "Lee Krasner's Early Career, Parts One and Two," *Arts Magazine* 56 (Oct. 1981): 110–22 (Nov. 1981): 80–89. Major permanent collections of Kras-

ner's work are at the Museum of Modern Art, the Metropolitan Museum of Art, and the Whitney Museum of American Art, New York; the Museum of Fine Arts, Houston, Tx.; and the National Museum of Women in the Arts, Washington, D.C. An obituary is in the *New York Times*, 21 June 1984.

ELLEN G. LANDAU

KRAUS, Charles August (15 Aug. 1875–27 June 1967), chemist, was born in Knightsville, Indiana, the son of John Henry Kraus and Elizabeth Schaefer, farmers. Kraus entered the University of Kansas in 1893 with the intention of becoming an electrical engineer. However, as Kraus stated, "I became more interested in physics than in engineering, and by the beginning of the Junior year, was spending more time reading literature relating to physics than to engineering." Of particular interest to Kraus was the fundamental question of how electricity was conducted through metals. This line of research, conceived during his undergraduate years, was to form the basis of his major contributions to physical chemistry over the next seven decades.

During Kraus's undergraduate years at Kansas, pioneering work using liquid ammonia as a solvent for conductance studies was done by H. P. Cady, an undergraduate, and E. C. Franklin, a professor of physical chemistry. Cady had shown that liquid ammonia itself was not a conductor but that when a salt such as potassium iodide was added the solution became an excellent conductor. At the cathode the solution turned blue, which was shown to be a characteristic of all the alkali metals. Further experiments showed that various metals were not converted into any compound by reaction with the ammonia. A solution of sodium in liquid ammonia was shown to be a powerful reducing agent. These results could only be rationalized by assuming that the process of dissolving an alkali metal in liquid ammonia produces solvated electrons.

Kraus continued the work initiated by Cady with Franklin and shifted his interest now to chemistry. He had taken only one undergraduate course, yet he published with Franklin in 1898 a qualitative and partial quantitative study of the solubility of more than 500 substances in liquid ammonia. After his graduation in 1898, Kraus pursued graduate work at Kansas for one year, which was followed by a year at the Johns Hopkins University, and an additional year at Kansas that led to an instructorship in physics at the University of California. Kraus continued his conductivity studies and in 1904 joined the physical chemistry research group of A. A. Noyes at the Massachusetts Institute of Technology. In the course of his research work he obtained his Ph.D. in 1908. By 1912 he was an assistant professor of physical chemistry and a very successful researcher. Among his achievements of this era was the preparation of the first intermetallic compound, Na_2Pb, using a liquid ammonia system. Kraus also produced a detailed explanation of the behavior of solutions of metals in liquid ammonia. He conclusively showed that in such a solution the metal forms a cation that is balanced by the solvated electron produced by the ionization of the metal. Thus, when metals dissolve in liquid ammonia, they produce electrons that are surrounded by an envelope of ammonia molecules and thus behave like a conventional anion.

While at MIT Kraus began to investigate the preparation and properties of organometallic compounds in which the bond between the metal and carbon is covalent in nature. Among the first of these compounds produced was methyl mercury (I), which was shown to have metallic properties.

In 1914 Kraus was appointed professor of physical chemistry at Clark University in Worcester, Massachusetts, a position he held for ten years until his final move to Brown University. While at Clark Kraus and his colleague G. F. White started preliminary work on the use of the metal-ammonia system as a tool in organic synthesis, because the solvated electron is the most potent reducing agent possible in nature. In these reductions the electronegative substituent accepts an electron producing an anion while the rest of the molecule is transformed into a radical. The radical can react in several different ways, such as forming an anion, abstracting a hydrogen atom, or reacting with the ammonia solvent. Thus the sodium in ammonia reduction of triphenylmethyl chloride produces sodium chloride and the triphenylmethide ion. Kraus and his students began significant work on the synthesis of organometallic compounds in which the anion is a metal covalently bonded to carbon. Compounds of tin were studied and trimethyltin hydride was produced. This led to Kraus being hired as a consultant to develop a method for industrial-scale synthesis of tetraethyl lead in 1922. Because lead and tin are in the same family, Kraus used his knowledge of tin chemistry and quickly solved the problem. The reaction of ethyl chloride with an equiolar alloy of lead and sodium led to an economical synthesis that was used by the newly founded Ethyl Corporation in 1924.

Kraus's work from 1924 when he came to Brown until his retirement, which only occurred because of ill health in his mid-eighties, was a continuation of the work begun at MIT and Clark. Pioneering work on organometallic analogues of carbon, such as silicon, germanium, tin, and lead, was carried out and led to forty publications. Among the important discoveries was the demonstration that carbon was not alone in catenation ability but that tin could form a chain of five atoms.

A very important area of investigation by Kraus was the behavior of electrolytic solution in which the solvent was not water. Kraus maintained that water, which had been extensively used, was an exceptional solvent. A general theory of electrolytes had to be formulated by studies in a range of nonaqueous solvents from nonpolar to polar and aprotic versus protic. By use of the concepts of long-range ionic interactions presented by P. Debye and E. Hückel as well as the ion-pair formation hypothesis of N. Bjerrum, Kraus and coworkers presented a general theory of electrolytic solutions.

Kraus was elected president of the American Chemical Society in 1939 and received the Nichols (1923), Gibbs (1935), Richards (1936), and Priestly (1950) medals from this society for his achievements. He was married to Frederica Feitshans and they had three children. Kraus died in Providence, Rhode Island.

• No archival materials or book-length biographies on Kraus are available. A complete list of all publications by Kraus may be found in National Academy of Sciences, *Biographical Memoirs* 42 (1971): 141–59. An obituary is in the *New York Times*, 28 June 1967.

MARTIN D. SALTZMAN

KRAUS, Lili (4 Mar. 1903?–6 Nov. 1986), concert pianist, was born in Budapest, Hungary, the daughter of a Czech father, Victor Kraus, a stone grinder, and a Hungarian mother, Irene Bak. Both 1903 and 1905 are listed in reputable sources as the year of her birth. Kraus began piano study when she was six years old. Two years later she was accepted at the Budapest Academy of Music, where Zoltán Kodály and Béla Bartók were her teachers. When she was only thirteen years old, she began her teaching career with private piano students in Vienna. She graduated from the academy in 1922, receiving the school's highest honor. Continuing study at the Vienna Conservatory of Music, she was the pupil of Edward Steuermann and Artur Schnable. In 1925 she was given full faculty status at the Vienna Conservatory.

Kraus taught at the conservatory for approximately six years. During this time she established herself as a highly respected concert pianist. She became one of the most popular recitalists and symphony orchestra soloists in England and in continental Europe during the 1930s. She toured in many countries, even annually in China, Japan, Australia, New Zealand, and South Africa. In addition to her live performances, she began recording the solo and chamber works of Mozart, Haydn, and Beethoven. These recordings demonstrated her extraordinary ability to interpret these works. She also joined violinist Szymon Goldberg in what became known as the Kraus-Goldberg Duo. Not only did the duo travel to many cities of Europe, but they also recorded the ten Beethoven violin and piano sonatas. One of Kraus's earliest recordings was of the Mozart Fantasy and the Sonata in C Minor (K. 475 and K. 457). As a result of the attention this recording brought to Mozart's works, a Mozart Society was founded in London. Continuing to record Mozart's works, Kraus and members of the Vienna Octet recorded the seven Piano Trios, which won the Grand Prix du Disque.

In 1930 Kraus married Otto Mandl, a noted philosopher. With a young daughter and son, she and her husband moved to London and became naturalized British subjects. Beginning a world tour in the Dutch East Indies in 1942, Kraus and her husband were taken prisoners by the Japanese in Java. They were in captivity for three years, during which time Kraus was allowed to play the piano one time a month. When they were released, Kraus resumed touring, beginning in Australia and New Zealand. She was granted New Zealand citizenship for her "unrelenting efforts in the aid of countries in need as well as for educational achievements." From 1948 Kraus had a full schedule on the international concert circuit; her tours included solo and chamber recitals and performances with leading orchestras all over the world.

Kraus's first visit to the United States in 1949 created a new outlet for her musical skills. Not only was she recognized for her outstanding performing ability, but she was much in demand as a teacher. She appeared frequently on television, lectured at many leading universities, presented master classes for students and teachers, and served as an adjudicator for many festivals and competitions. She played a Schubert recital in Carnegie Hall and appeared frequently at the Mostly Mozart and Tanglewood festivals. During 1949–1951 she served as head of the piano department at the University of Cape Town. She moved in 1953 to San Francisco, where she held a position at the Music and Arts Institute. Her lecturing opportunities increased with her sponsorship from EDUCO records, for which she presented seminars, master classes, and concerts.

Kraus was invited to play a royal command performance at the wedding banquet of the shah of Iran, a concert in England's Canterbury Cathedral, and the first concert given in the new city of Brasilia. She was an adjudicator at the Van Cliburn International Piano Competition in Fort Worth, Texas, and she made a visit to Albert Schweitzer in Lambaréné, Gabon, where she played solo selections and some four-hand selections with Schweitzer. She presented the first American performance of Schubert's "Grazer" Fantasie on 2 November 1969 for the Columbia Broadcasting System's "Camera Three" television series. From 1967 to 1983 Kraus was artist in residence at Texas Christian University in Fort Worth. In that position she led master classes, played with the university orchestra, and coached many students.

Kraus seemed to be at ease on stage, and she had immediate rapport with her audience. As a teacher, she demanded much of her students. She possessed remarkable pedagogical skills, which were enhanced by her encouraging spirit, and was known as a pianist of considerable virtuosity and stamina. In New York during the 1966–1967 series, she played twenty-five Mozart concertos; the next year she performed the complete Mozart sonatas. Commenting on her affection for Mozart on the record jacket of *Mozart Sonatas, K. 279–330*, she stated, "Since Mozart is the purest essence of music, it can only be that he fills my heart to the utmost. . . . I think Mozart's mind had the same melancholy trend as mine, with a mischievous exuberance that allows one to bear the sorrows of life. . . . Intense virility [is] always apparent beneath the chaste and graceful form. . . . Self-pity never asserts itself and passion is always tempered with modesty."

Kraus was regarded as one of the foremost interpreters of piano works of the classical period, particularly of Mozart concerti and sonatas. Yet her performing repertoire also included works by Chopin, Beethoven, Bartók, and many others. She recorded for English Parlophone, Discophile Français, Vox, Decca, RCA, and EDUCO records. She received many awards and honors, including the Cross of Honor for Science and Art, given to her by Austria on 4 March 1978.

During the last decade of her life, Lili Kraus spent time with her family near Asheville, North Carolina. Active in musical activities in that area, she was responsible for the establishment of the Music in the Mountains Festival in 1969. Through her involvement with other festivals and educational projects, her influence continues to spread to younger generations. Her dedication to performing, teaching, and recording substantiated her worldwide recognition as one of the great twentieth-century musicians. She died in Asheville, North Carolina.

• The Texas Christian University Library in Fort Worth has some of Kraus's programs and publicity notices. The Toe River Arts Council in Asheville, N.C., and Kraus's daughter have preserved materials about her. For further information see Dean Elder, "Lili Kraus: Regal Lady of the Keyboard," *Clavier* 19 (Sept. 1980): 21–27; Frans Schreuder, "Remembering Lili Kraus: A Vanishing Tradition," *Piano Journal* (London) 23 (June 1987): 11–12; and an interview in *Piano Quarterly* 110 (Summer 1980): 48. Obituaries appear in the *New York Times*, 7 Nov. 1986, and the *Los Angeles Times*, 8 Nov. 1986.

LINDA P. SHIPLEY

KRAUS-BOELTÉ, Maria (8 Nov. 1836–1 Nov. 1918), educational reformer, was born in the town of Hagenow in the North German province of Mecklenburg-Schwerin, the daughter of Johann Ludwig Ernst Boelte, a lawyer, judge, and local magistrate, and Louise Ehlers, also a member of a family with a tradition of public service. The household was rich, prominent, and cultivated. Maria's interest in progressive educational methods was probably stimulated in part by the unusually egalitarian atmosphere of her home, which acquaintances called the "little republic." Boelté (the accent was probably added to facilitate English-speakers with the pronunciation) was first educated at home by a local clergyman and also learned music from her mother. Later she attended two private girls' schools. At eighteen she was confirmed and presented to society. Her favorite free-time occupation was charitable work with the local village children.

An aunt who was active in women's organizations urged Boelté to take up the profession of kindergarten teacher, one of the few professions then open to women. Boelté studied in Hamburg at a school run by Luise Levin, the widow of Friedrich Froebel, the German educator who had developed a method of early childhood education—the kindergarten or "child garden"—that rejected the conventional emphasis on religious training and rote memorization in favor of educational games and nature study. Kindergarten methods were strongly advocated by many revolutionaries and reformers of 1848 and were subsequently prohibited by the conservative regimes that took power in Prussia and many other German states after the repression of the revolution in 1851. When Boelté completed her training in the 1850s, therefore, she had no opportunity to put her skills into practice, yet she retained a strong commitment to the ideals of the movement, which sought to regenerate both education and society as a whole.

Like many kindergarten teachers and founders, Boelté had to search abroad to find an outlet for her talents. She traveled to England, where in 1859 she took charge of a kindergarten founded in London by an exiled German revolutionary, Bertha Ronge (or, as she sometimes spelled her name, Rongé). After Ronge returned to Germany and the kindergarten closed, Boelté took a job as a governess in a wealthy household. In 1862, along with other British kindergartners, she exhibited samples of kindergarten work at the London International Exhibition.

In 1867, the kindergarten ban having been rescinded in 1860, Boelté returned to Germany. For a while she worked with Johanna Goldschmidt, a Jewish reformer who ran a kindergarten training school in Hamburg. She later tried to set up a kindergarten in Schwerin but encountered strong opposition from the local clergy and teachers who still associated the kindergarten method with revolution and unorthodox religious beliefs. She then moved to the more liberal, port city of Lübeck, where the local educational authorities allowed her to set up a preschool institution on the condition that it not be called a kindergarten.

In 1870 Boelté read an article by German exile John Kraus, who was then active in kindergarten work in Washington, D.C., and subsequently began a correspondence with him. By this time the kindergarten movement, which had been brought to the United States by exiled German revolutionaries, had gained many American adherents. In 1871 she closed her kindergarten in Lübeck and returned to England, where she later accepted a teaching position in a school in New York City headed by Henrietta B. Haines. Boelté arrived in New York in 1872 and married Kraus in 1873; they would adopt one child, a daughter. In 1873 the couple set up a training institution for kindergarten teachers, the New York Normal Training School for Kindergarten Teachers, Kindergarten and Adjoining Classes. The trainees worked in an affiliated kindergarten and elementary school program that enrolled children from three to ten years of age. The school also offered an evening class for mothers, and in 1890 a training program for private children's nurses was added. After 1890 the kindergarten and the elementary classes were discontinued.

Like Froebel, Kraus-Boelté viewed the kindergarten teacher's profession as an extension of motherly nurture from the family into the public sphere. Qualifications for entrance into the kindergarten training program included "a quick and responsive sympathy with children," a "motherly heart, something which . . . gives a clear insight into child nature," as well as "an exact knowledge and spiritual comprehension united with dextrous handling of the Kindergarten material" (Boelté in Barnard, ed., p. 557). This "material," also referred to as "gifts," consisted of simple objects, such as balls, blocks of different shapes, sticks, yarn, and colored paper. The teacher directed the child in a series of "occupations" or tasks that involved using these objects to construct various forms and patterns. Froebel, a philosopher, believed that such activity provided insight into the structure of the universe, in which many parts combined to form a harmonious whole. Although she was a strict and orthodox believer in Froebel's methods, Kraus-Boelté warned against routinized applications, insisting that the gifts and occupations were intended to develop the child's individuality and creativity. Along with John Kraus, Kraus-Boelté described these methods in the *Kindergarten Guide* (1877).

Kraus-Boelté served as president of the Kindergarten Department of the National Education Association in 1899–1900 and also taught the first college-level courses on kindergarten methods at New York University from 1903 to 1907. During her later years she was involved in many controversies within the kindergarten teachers' organization, the International Kindergarten Union, regarding the revision of Froebel's methods to conform to more modern educational theories and the conditions of American life. Kraus-Boelté retired from full-time work to write and lecture in 1913. She died five years later in Atlantic City, New Jersey.

Kraus Boelté was one of a remarkable group of German immigrants who played a major role in creating both the kindergarten and the profession of kindergarten teaching in the United States. Among the graduates of the New York Normal Training School were Susan Elizabeth Blow, who helped to found the first public-school kindergarten in St. Louis in 1873 and went on to teach at Columbia Teachers' College, and Elizabeth Harrison, who founded a major professional school, Chicago Kindergarten College, in 1893. The Froebelian kindergarten provided the basis for the subsequent institutional and theoretical development of early childhood education, and the women and men of the kindergarten movement were some of the earliest advocates of the reform and development of local, state, and national child welfare programs.

• A few archival materials are in the Maria Kraus-Boelté Collection, Manuscript Division, Library of Congress. Information on Kraus-Boelté's life can be found in her "Reminiscences of Kindergarten Work, Addressed to Dr. Henry Barnard" and "The New York Normal Kindergarten and Associated Model Classes," both in *Papers on Froebel's Kindergarten*, ed. Henry Barnard (1881); Rachel L. Rogers, "Prof. John Kraus and Mrs. Maria Kraus-Boelté and Their United Work," *Kindergarten News* 7 (Sept. 1896): 1–9; and *Annual Report of the Kraus Alumni Kindergarten Association* (1915–1916). Agnes Snyder, *Dauntless Women in Early Childhood Education* (1972), gives information on Kraus-Boelté's role in the education of Susan Blow and Elizabeth Harrison. An obituary is in the *New York Times*, 3 Nov. 1918.

ANN TAYLOR ALLEN

KRAUSE, Herbert Arthur (25 May 1905–22 Sept. 1976), novelist, English professor, poet, and naturalist, was born near Friberg, Minnesota, the son of Arthur Krause, a farmer and blacksmith, and Bertha Peters. Krause's parents were first-generation descendants of devout German immigrants who settled as farmers in the hill country north of Fergus Falls, Minnesota. Their folkways and fundamentalist Lutheran religion were important concerns in his first two novels.

Krause attended a one-room school in Friberg Township, staying for four years in the ninth grade because there was no high school nearby, and the authorities required students to remain in school until age sixteen. Krause earned enough money to enter Park Region Luther Academy in 1926 by working on the nearby Otter Tail dam, but his father's early death in 1927 placed the family in straitened financial circumstances for many years to follow. As the eldest of four sons, Krause struggled for years to assist the family while pursuing his plans to become a teacher and a writer.

Krause completed high school at the academy in 1929. He first enrolled in the Missouri Synod–supported Concordia Teachers College in River Forest, Illinois, and a few days later in the Concordia Theological Seminary in Springfield, Illinois, but he found the atmosphere unappealing at both places. Consequently, he returned to the Norwegian Lutheran–supported Park Region Academy. There he completed two years of college, finishing in 1931. Krause's graduation from St. Olaf College in Northfield, Minnesota, in 1933 and his later employment at Augustana College in Sioux Falls, South Dakota, both Norwegian Synod colleges, led him to declare that he had "defected to the Norwegians."

For Krause, such ethnic and religious matters were of great concern as he contemplated a career. As a youth he had been encouraged by his parents and a pastor to prepare for the Missouri Synod ministry or for a career as a teacher in one of the synod's parochial schools. In 1937, however, Krause wrote of his growing disillusionment with the narrowness of his church: "I was brought up in the Lutheran persuasion, of the German Missouri group, the ideals of which I hold still to be important in my life but the rigors of which I find have been mellowed by valued contacts with other denominations" (letter to Presbyterian College, 13 July 1937). In his first novel, *Wind without Rain* (1939), Krause explored in detail the deleterious effect of the spiritual environment of his German community on a sensitive and artistic spirit.

At St. Olaf College, Krause had begun to develop in poetry and drama the themes central to his three later novels: the beauty of nature, the pain of poverty and late-blooming talent, and the sorrow of lost love. When he entered the University of Iowa, where he earned an M.A. in 1935, he took with him the first outline of a novel about farm life in the Friberg area, the area he called "Pockerbrush." Encouraged by a summer in Vermont at the Bread Loaf School of English in 1935 under the tutelage of writers such as Doro-thy Canfield Fisher, Theodore Morrison, Robert Frost, and Stephen Vincent Benét, Krause submitted the first chapters of *Wind without Rain* to several publishers. The novel was published by Bobbs-Merrill in early 1939. Reviews were strongly favorable, stressing the work's rich poetry and gloomy atmosphere, and by mid-March it was listed as a bestseller in New York and Chicago. The most perceptive of the reviewers, novelist Wallace Stegner, who had known Krause at Iowa, called *Wind without Rain* "one of the best first novels in a good many years" and a beautiful, if not comforting, book (*Saturday Review of Literature*, 11 Feb. 1939). On 16 March Krause received the $1,000 Friends of American Writers Award in Chicago, a prize then as monetarily valuable as the Pulitzer.

In the meantime, Krause had begun his long-awaited career as a college professor, accepting a position in the fall of 1938 as chairman of the English department at Augustana College. He remained there for the rest of his life, becoming writer-in-residence in later years and in 1970 founding the Center for Western Studies, an expression of his career-long commitment to writing about the northern prairies and plains of the American West. The center remains an important regional resource for the study of the area.

During the eight years that passed before his next novel appeared in 1947, Krause published *Neighbor Boy* (1939), a book of poems reminiscent of Frost's lyrics but with Pockerbrush names and settings. He also began the study of ornithology, an interest that grew in importance and led him increasingly toward environmental concerns.

As early as September 1940 Krause had begun writing to farm equipment manufacturers in order to collect information for his next novel, *The Thresher*. As a child of seven, Krause recalled, he had seen his first steam threshing machine, "the funnel of the smokestack pushing up, and then the gripping wonder of sparks and white steam rushing and hoarse grunts and the sudden terrifying scream of the whistle tearing into my ears." In the spring of 1944 he was awarded a University of Minnesota Fellowship in Regional Writing in order to complete the novel, and it was published in early 1947, quickly becoming a bestseller. The novel also appeared in special editions for the armed forces and book clubs, selling almost 400,000 copies, a sales record for a resident of South Dakota. The reviews were favorable: the *Saturday Review* (8 Feb. 1947) praised the "strong, poetic writing," and a *Chicago Sun* critic hailed the novel as an authentic document that chronicled "the evolution of threshing machines and newer methods of harvesting and handling grain" (19 Jan. 1947). The novel's success brought Krause an offer in 1948 from Stegner to teach at Stanford University, but he politely declined, preferring to remain in the Midwest.

In 1954 Krause's third and last novel, *The Oxcart Trail*, was published. The work tells the story of Shawnie Dark's flight from the law, his journey through Sioux and Chippewa country from St. Paul toward the Red River Valley of the North, and his requited love for the frontier schoolteacher Debbie Wells. *The Oxcart Trail* was virtually ignored by national magazines, although it sold better than most other novels published by Bobbs-Merrill that year. It won no bestseller rankings or prizes, and Krause considered it a failure.

For the next two decades Krause continued his teaching at Augustana College; he also tried his hand at more poetry, wrote many essays and short pieces about nature study, and took on two projects that capped his writing career. The first of these, a powerful and sympathetic dramatic treatment of the life of Crazy Horse, remains unpublished and unperformed. The second, *Prelude to Glory* (1974), a collection of newspaper reports of George Custer's incursion into the Black Hills in 1874, won a wide readership and was favorably reviewed. It was a fitting climax to Krause's long love affair with the American West and its versatile and fascinating people. He never married. He died in Sioux Falls.

• Krause's papers, letters, manuscripts, galley proofs, photos, notes, class lectures, and the Krause Collection of Western Americana are in the Center for Western Studies, Augustana College, Sioux Falls, S. Dak. The most recent assessments of his work are Arthur R. Huseboe, *Herbert Krause* (1985), which includes a bibliography; and Huseboe's lengthy introduction to *Poems and Essays of Herbert Krause* (1990). Huseboe and William Geyer, eds., *Where the West Begins* (1978), contains an introduction about Krause and essays by Robert C. Steensma on *Wind without Rain* and by Kristoffer F. Paulson on *The Thresher*. Four useful theses about Krause's work include Vi Ann Sattre Christensen, "The German Immigrant as Portrayed in the Novels of Herbert Krause" (M.A. thesis, Mankato State College, Minn., 1968); Leslie M. Baylor, "The Functions of Nature in Herbert Krause's Pockerbrush Novels" (M.A. thesis, Idaho State Univ., 1965); Valborg Berge Solovskoy, "The World of Nature in the Writings of Herbert Krause" (M.S. thesis, Mankato State College, 1973); and Barbara Roberts Upton, "A Study of the Works of Herbert Krause with Special Emphasis on *The Thresher*" (M.S. thesis, Mankato State College, 1963).

ARTHUR R. HUSEBOE

KRAUTH, Charles Philip (7 May 1797–30 May 1867), Lutheran pastor and educator, was born in New Goshenhoppen, Pennsylvania, the son of Charles James Krauth, a German-born church organist and schoolteacher, and Katherine Doll. During his childhood the family moved frequently, residing for a time in Philadelphia and York, Pennsylvania; Baltimore, Maryland; and Winchester and Norfolk, Virginia. As a student in the schools where his father taught, young Charles showed early promise in mathematics and language study.

Krauth began training in medicine with a private teacher, William Boswell Selden of Norfolk, and then at the University of Maryland. The family's financial situation was always precarious, however, and lack of funds brought his medical studies to an end. While en route to borrow money from a relative, he met with the Reverend David Frederick Schaeffer, of Frederick, Maryland, who later suggested he become a clergyman

and personally supervised Krauth's training, as was the practice at the time. When a call came in 1818 from the Reverend Abraham Reck of Winchester, Virginia, for a pastoral assistant, Krauth was sent there to combine his studies with practical experience.

The following year, after the Ministerium of Pennsylvania licensed Krauth to preach, he took up pastoral responsibilities at Martinsburg and Shepherdstown (in what is now West Virginia), and he was ordained in 1821. In late 1820, he married Catherine Susan Heiskell of Staunton, Virginia. The couple had two children before Catherine's death in 1824. Krauth's activities at this time included assisting Schaeffer in editing the *Lutheran Intelligencer* and founding the Synod of Maryland and Pennsylvania in 1820. The synod elected him president in 1826.

Krauth, Benjamin Kurtz, and Samuel Simon Schmucker met in 1825 to discuss the state of ministerial training in the United States; they pledged to seek support from the Ministerium of Pennsylvania to establish a seminary to prepare pastors for Lutheran congregations. They also gathered about five dollars toward the expenses of such an institution. For the remainder of their lives, though not always in theological accord, Krauth, Kurtz, and Schmucker were colleagues united by their connections with Gettysburg Theological Seminary, which was established in 1825, and by their leadership in the maturing American Lutheran church. Krauth's first official position was as secretary of the seminary's board.

Krauth moved to St. Matthew's of Philadelphia in 1827. The resources of new colleagues and access to libraries and books fostered his development as a preacher and a scholar. Despite his weak voice, Krauth's reputation grew as a preacher who was capable of explaining Scripture and touching human hearts in both English and German. His commitment to using English was further demonstrated by the aid he gave to the preparation of Schmucker's English hymnbook of 1829.

In 1833 Krauth left St. Matthew's to join Schmucker on the faculty of Gettysburg Theological Seminary and teach Hebrew and theology, providing instruction in German. Pennsylvania College (now Gettysburg College) was founded to provide preseminary training; Krauth also taught there and served as its president from 1834 to 1850. He then limited his teaching to the seminary, serving for the remaining seventeen years of his life as professor of biblical and Oriental literature. During the battle of Gettysburg, Krauth's house was used as a Confederate hospital. While in Gettysburg, Krauth married Harriet Brown, with whom he had two children.

In 1848, after three terms as treasurer, he was elected president of the General Synod, a cooperative, advisory federation of regional synods. Throughout his career, even during the midcentury controversy over adaptation of distinctive Lutheran teachings to American evangelical Protestantism, Krauth maintained harmonious relations with the faculties and boards of both the Gettysburg Theological Seminary and Pennsylvania College. He helped found and edit (1850–1861) the *Evangelical Review*, which took a more moderate position than the view held by neo-Lutherans such as Schmucker. Krauth's son, Charles Porterfield Krauth, took a stronger stand in opposition to Schmucker and helped found Mount Airy (Philadelphia) Seminary. The elder Krauth's irenic spirit made him avoid open conflict. In most disputes, both sides were able to claim his support. A leader among the early generation of North American–born and trained Lutheran clergymen, Krauth contributed to the development and consolidation of Lutheranism in the United States, advocating a moderate evangelical confessional position.

• A few of Krauth's letters and lectures are housed in Wentz Memorial Library, Lutheran Theological Seminary, Gettysburg, Pa. A chapter-length biography begins Adolph Spaeth, *Charles Porterfield Krauth*, vol. 1 (1898), and a biographical sketch is in J. C. Jensson, *American Lutheran Biographies* (1890). For additional information, see A. R. Wentz, *Gettysburg Lutheran Theological Seminary*, vol. 1 (1964); Charles H. Glatfelter, *A Salutary Influence: Gettysburg College, 1832–1985*, vol. 1 (1987); and "Reminiscences of Deceased Lutheran Ministers: Charles Philip Krauth," *Evangelical Quarterly Review* (Jan. 1868): 89–120.

L. DeAne Lagerquist

KRAUTH, Charles Porterfield (17 Mar. 1823–2 Jan. 1883), theologian and educator, was born in Martinsburg, Virginia (now W.Va.), the son of Charles Philip Krauth, a Lutheran minister, and Catherine Susan Heiskeii. Between his mother's death before his first birthday and his father's peripatetic career, Krauth was raised at several sites in his first ten years before being settled in 1833 at Gettysburg, Pennsylvania, where his father was president of Pennsylvania College, a Lutheran institution. Krauth matriculated at that college in 1834, graduated in 1839, then attended the affiliated Gettysburg Seminary from 1839 to 1841 to earn his credentials for the Lutheran ministry. He pastored churches in Baltimore, Maryland, from 1841 to 1847; in the upper Shenandoah Valley, principally Winchester, Virginia, from 1847 to 1855; and in Pittsburgh (1855–1859) and Philadelphia (1859–1861), Pennsylvania. Krauth was married twice: in 1844 to Susan Reynolds of Baltimore (she died in 1853) and in 1855 to Virginia Baker of Winchester, Virginia. He had five children, of whom two survived him.

During his twenty years in the pastorate, Krauth pursued a rigorous course of reading in biblical studies, the church fathers, and classic Lutheran theology. In the process he began amassing a personal library that at his death would number 15,000 volumes and qualify as one of the finest private collections in the country. At the same time he became the most sophisticated and best-read Lutheran theologian in the United States and a growing opponent of the American Lutheran movement associated with Samuel S. Schmucker and Benjamin Kurtz, who down-played the distinctiveness of the tradition in the hope of cooperating with the Reformed- (or Calvinistic-) descend-

ed evangelicalism that was characterized in the antebellum era by intense revival services and moral crusades. Against this Krauth championed the confessional approach, which stressed renewed commitment to the foundational documents of Lutheranism, especially the Augsburg Confession. The riches of the Lutheran past, Krauth argued, promised a deeper, more stable faith than did overwrought revivalism, and it provided a healthy social counterpoint to the restlessness and splintering that revivalism bred. Krauth also anticipated, correctly, that the traditionalist path would gain favor and power among the massive number of German immigrants who were pouring into the nation.

In 1861 Krauth resigned his pastorate to devote himself full time to the confessionalist cause as editor, until 1867, of the *Lutheran and Missionary* magazine. He was also named the first professor of systematic theology at the confessionalist Lutheran Theological Seminary founded at Philadelphia in 1864. The internal church conflict peaked in 1867 with the formation of the General Council, a union of confessionalist organizations to rival the more Americanized General Synod; Krauth served as the General Council's chief theologian, wrote its founding document and permanent constitution, helped shape its liturgy, and presided over its national meetings until 1877. He steered the council in a conservative direction in the hope of winning the allegiance of the immigrant Lutheran masses in the Midwest. Although that strategy succeeded only in part, Krauth's reputation as an intellectual and institutional leader remained secure. His magnum opus, *The Conservative Reformation and Its Theology* (1871), epitomized Lutheranism's confessional renewal and remains a landmark in the history of American Protestant theology as a whole.

In addition to his denominational and seminary labors, Krauth taught philosophy at the University of Pennsylvania from 1868 until his death, concentrating on ethics and epistemology. He tried to synthesize the realist and idealist strains in the academic philosophy of the era and gave much of his energy in the 1870s to revising and amplifying British philosophy textbooks, by means of his knowledge of German sources, for the American academic market. He also served the university as vice provost from 1873 through 1882 and participated on the Old Testament panel of the American Revision Committee, which produced a modernized edition of the King James Bible in 1881. He was working on a biography of Luther at his death in Philadelphia.

Although overwork doubtless hastened Krauth's premature death, it also testified to his wide range of talents and interests and to the religious commitment that animated them all. As his friend, the eminent church historian Philip Schaff, said of Krauth: "His learning did not smother his genius, nor did his philosophical attainments impair the simplicity of his faith. . . . Our country has produced few men who united in their persons so many excellences."

• Krauth's papers are in the Krauth Memorial Library, Lutheran Theological Seminary, Philadelphia. The only biography is by his son-in-law, Adolph Spaeth, *Charles Porterfield Krauth* (2 vols., 1898, 1909), and includes much primary material and a complete bibliography. Two interpretive anthologies shed complementary light on some key Krauth texts, Sydney E. Ahlstrom, ed., *Theology in America: Major Protestant Voices* (1967), and Theodore G. Tappert, ed., *Lutheran Confessional Theology in America, 1840–1880* (1972).

JAMES D. BRATT

KRAYER, Otto Hermann (22 Oct. 1899–18 Mar. 1982), pharmacologist, was born in Köndringen, Baden, Germany, the son of Hermann Krayer, an innkeeper, and Frieda Berta Wolfsperger. Early in his life Krayer's intellectual gifts attracted the attention of the schoolmaster, who persuaded his parents to continue his education at the six-year middle school in Emmendengen. Since World War I was in progress, Krayer entered the army and was sent to the western front; shortly before the armistice, he was wounded. While recovering, he completed the university entrance requirements, and in 1919 he enrolled in the University of Freiburg medical school. In 1920 he transferred to the medical school at the University of Munich. In 1922 he returned to the University of Freiburg for clinical studies. Bored with the didactic lectures, Krayer sought intellectual stimulation and undertook a project on the comparative anatomy of the amphibian kidney under Wilhelm von Möllendorf. The lectures in pharmacology from Paul Trendelenberg impressed Krayer, and after completing his formal course he spent part of 1925 working in Trendelenberg's department. In 1926 he received his M.D. degree for his dissertation on apocodeine. He then began a career in pharmacology as Trendelenberg's assistant. When Trendelenberg moved to Berlin, Krayer followed and rapidly advanced through the ranks from Oberassistant to Privatdocent. When Trendelenberg became seriously ill, Krayer assumed full responsibility for the department, and upon his chief's death in 1931 he was made acting head and the following year professor extraordinarius of pharmacology and toxicology. Because of the heavy teaching and administrative loads, there was no time for research. Krayer was also left with the task of completing and publishing the third edition of Trendelenberg's textbook of pharmacology as well as the second volume of his *Die Hormone*. The appointment of Wolfgang Heubner to fill the department chair allowed Krayer to finish *Die Hormone* and return to research. In 1933 Krayer was granted a leave of absence for one year to join Herman Rein in Göttingen for experiments with Starling's heart lung preparation (HLP). While in Göttingen, Krayer was offered the professorship of pharmacology at Düsseldorf to replace Philipp Ellinger, who was removed from the chair by the Nazis because he was a Jew. Krayer, not a Jew, refused the appointment with the statement that he could not accept the chair of pharmacology at Düsseldorf whose incumbent had been removed because he was of Jewish ancestry. This act resulted in the barring of Krayer by the Nazi government from entering any government academic institution and from using any state library or scientific facility. In 1933 Krayer was granted a one-year leave of absence to study in Verney's laboratory in London, supported by a Rockefeller Foundation grant. Here he continued his work with Verney using the HLP.

Because of the unsettled conditions in Germany, Krayer accepted the directorship of the pharmacology department at the American University at Beirut, and his friend Dr. Erna Ruth Philipp joined him as literary assistant. In the three years at the American University in Beirut, Krayer spent little time with research. Most of his effort was devoted to teaching and revising the fourth edition of Trendelenberg's textbook of pharmacology. In 1937 Krayer received the invitation to succeed Reid Hunt, who was retiring as professor of pharmacology at the Harvard Medical School. Krayer accepted the position and on arriving in Boston found the department poorly equipped for research and possessing an inadequate budget. Disappointed, Krayer considered taking the chair of pharmacology at Peping School in China. When the pharmacology classes of 1940 and 1941 heard he was considering leaving Harvard, they petitioned Krayer to stay and delivered a copy of their petition to Dean C. Sidney Burwell. In 1940 Krayer married Erna Ruth Philipp; they had no children. Krayer remained at Harvard, and during World War II developed one of the best departments of pharmacology in America at Harvard. Despite Krayer's success in building a fine pharmacology department, just as he reached retirement age the administration began to question the importance of pharmacology in the curriculum and were attempting to destroy what Krayer had built. When Krayer retired in 1966 he was somewhat disgusted with the administration of the Harvard Medical School, and for five years after he left the department he did not once return.

Krayer's early studies on the cardiac toxicity of neosalvasan using the dog heart-lung preparation (HLP) initiated his lifelong interest in studying the effects of drugs on the circulation. Nearly all Krayer's experiments on the heart employed the HLP, a difficult technique he mastered early in his career. In 1942 Krayer began his studies on the pharmacological action of the tertiary and secondary amine veratrum alkaloids. He found that the tertiary amine veratrum alkaloids produced hypotension (reduced blood pressure) and bradycardia (slowed heart rate) through a reflex stimulation of chemoreceptor reflexes in the heart and lung—the Bezold-Jarisch reflex.

The secondary amine veratrum alkaloids, in addition to their reflex hypotensive action, had a decelerative action on the cardiac pacemaker that was not blocked by atropine. Of particular importance was that the epinephrine acceleration of the heart of the HLP was abolished by small doses of the secondary amine veratrum alkaloid while the positive inotropic action (effect on the speed of muscle action) of epinephrine was not affected. Thus the secondary amine veratrum alkaloids separated the chronotropic (heart rate) effects from the ionotropic (muscle strength) effects of catecholamines.

In 1955 Krayer investigated reserpine, a pure alkaloid from Rauwolfia. Administration of reserpine accelerated the heart in the same way as norepinephrine infusion. When Matti Paasonen, a Finnish scientist, measured the catecholamine levels in blood and cardiac tissue, he found low norepinephrine concentration: reserpine had depleted the catecholamine of cardiac tissue. In the HLP of dogs pretreated with reserpine, administration of norepinephrine produced no cardiac acceleration and serotonin had no effect. These studies of Krayer demonstrated that reserpine had a general direct action depleting amine transmitters from both peripheral and central stores. A retiring person who did not blow his own horn and who became disgusted with fights over priority, Krayer never was given the proper recognition for this important work.

After Krayer retired he and his wife moved to Tucson, Arizona, in September 1971. He died in Tucson.

• Ten boxes of Krayer's personal and departmental papers are in the Harvard University Archives. Krayer's life and work are chronicled in Avram Goldstein, National Academy of Sciences, *Biographical Memoirs* 57 (1987): 151–225; Ulrich Trendelenburg, "Remembrances," *Life Sciences* 22 (1978): 1113–14; M. Reiter and Ulrich Trendelenburg, *Naunyn-Schmiedeberg's Archives of Pharmacology* 320 (1982): 1–2; and P. B. Dews, *Trends in Pharmacological Sciences* 4 (1983): 143–46.

DAVID Y. COOPER

KRECH, David (27 Mar. 1909–14 July 1977), professor of psychology, was born Yitzhok-Eizik Krechevsky in a small village in Russia, the son of Joseph Krechevsky, a salesman, and Sarah Rabinowitz. At the age of four Krech accompanied his family to the United States, where they settled in New London, Connecticut. Krech took to schooling, was a good student, and, according to his autobiography, soon became the "most educated American" in his family. In addition to the regular fare, he spent an hour a day in Hebrew School, where he learned some Hebrew and learned to read and write in Yiddish. His love of the Hebrew language and its literature endured throughout his life and remained long after he had rejected all formal religion.

After graduating from high school, Krech, going by the more anglicized Isadore Krechevsky, went to the Washington Square College of New York University (NYU), where, in the course of prelaw studies, he discovered psychology and realized for the first time, as he put it, that "man himself could be examined objectively and scientifically. This revolutionary (for me) idea made it a science more noble than all the rest." Following graduation in 1930, Krech continued his studies at NYU, during which time he read Karl Lashley's *Brain Mechanisms and Intelligence* (1929), one of the first major attempts to understand how the rat's brain controls its ability to solve problems. Krech was struck particularly by Lashley's observation that the

rats in some tasks appeared to attempt solutions to discrimination problems that might involve position responses, alternation, and so forth, before finally coming to the correct solution. Krech devised a way of observing these attempted solutions and, after gaining a master's degree, transferred to the University of California at Berkeley for his doctoral studies.

At Berkeley Krech worked with Edward C. Tolman, a major contributor to the study of animal cognition. Tolman reportedly described Krech's research as "hypotheses in rats," and the name stuck. Krech gained rapid notoriety for his research because it supplied the first evidence that animals associate only those environmental cues to which they are attending at the time. It was a radical notion and a sharp departure from the dominant antimentalistic behaviorism of the day. Krech's discoveries resulted in an opportunity, after he received a Ph.D. in 1933, to work with Lashley in investigating the neural bases of hypotheses behavior at the University of Chicago.

While in Chicago, Krech became active in politics. In this context, he participated in a symbolic strike on Memorial Day 1937 at the Republic Steel Corporation in Gary, Indiana, where, in Krech's words, the strikers "were met by point blank fire from a force of Chicago police." Krech and other witnesses signed a statement condemning the action, an event that led to his departure from the University of Chicago. Krech then spent a year on a fellowship at Swarthmore College followed by a year as a half-time assistant professor at the University of Colorado. When the University of Colorado learned of his activities in Chicago, the appointment was downgraded to a half-time instructorship. These circumstances ultimately led to his departure from the University of Colorado in June 1939. Krech spent the next two years as managing editor of a social action newsletter in New York.

From 1941 until 1945, both as a sergeant in the army and as a civilian, Krech worked for the U.S. government and, in the course, became a social psychologist concerned with the measurement of attitudes and, ultimately, the evaluation of candidates for spies going into enemy-occupied territory. In 1943 Krech married Hilda Gruenberg, with whom he had one child. Following the war and a year at Swarthmore College (during which he began to publish under the name David Krech), in 1947 he returned to Berkeley as an associate professor of psychology and spent the rest of his academic career there. Soon after joining the Berkeley faculty, Krech collaborated with social psychologist Richard Crutchfield in writing what was then a revolutionary book in social psychology. Published in 1948, *Theory and Problems of Social Psychology* gave social psychology for the first time a theoretical base in the psychology of perception and, most notably, in Gestalt psychology. The book was widely adopted as a text and established Krech's eminence in a field of psychology disparate from that in which he had been trained.

After a number of years during which Krech was an active participant in social and personality psychology, Krech returned in the early 1950s to biological psychology and collaborated with several individuals, including Mark R. Rosenzweig, then a recent addition to the Berkeley faculty in physiological psychology; Edward L. Bennett, a neurochemist; and Marian C. Diamond, a neuroanatomist. This team and its associated students and fellows, with the active support of the noted chemist Melvin Calvin, set out to investigate how differences in the experience of animals might affect chemical activity of the brain and in turn how these changes in the chemical activity of the brain might affect behavior. Their experiments brought the unexpected finding that both formal training and informal experience lead in rats to changes in the level of activity of the brain enzyme cholinesterase. Measurement of enzymatic activity per unit of tissue weight led to the even more surprising finding that training or enriched environmental experience causes increases in the weight of regions of the cerebral cortex as well as changes in the anatomy of neurons in the cerebral cortex.

For his varied contributions, Krech received many honors, including the Distinguished Scientific Contribution Award of the American Psychological Association, an honorary doctorate from the University of Oslo, and two Fulbright fellowships. He died at his home in Berkeley.

• Two of Krech's important articles are I. Krechevsky, "'Hypotheses' in Rats," *Psychological Review* 39 (1932): 516–32, and David Krech et al., "Enzyme Concentrations in the Brain and Adjustive Behavior-Patterns," *Science* 120 (10 Dec. 1954): 994–96. His entertaining and informative autobiography is in G. Lindzey, ed., *A History of Psychology in Autobiography*, vol. 6 (1974), pp. 219–50. A complete bibliography through 1970 is in *American Psychologist* 26 (1971): 82–86.

DONALD A. RILEY
MARK R. ROSENZWEIG

KREHBIEL, Henry Edward (10 Mar. 1854–20 Mar. 1923), music critic and historian, was born in Ann Arbor, Michigan, the son of Jacob Krehbiel, an itinerant Methodist minister, and Anna Marie E. Haacke. Henry, the third of nine children, attended public schools in Michigan and after 1864 in Cincinnati, where the Central German Methodist Conference assigned his father to a position. In Cincinnati, Krehbiel studied violin with Gelsselbecht and harmony with Baetens and directed the choir at his father's church. He had no university education, although he studied law briefly from 1872 to 1874. Krehbiel secured a position at the Cincinnati *Gazette*, where he developed reporting skills by writing on various subjects, including crime and sports. He continued self-instruction in musical subjects and was music editor from 1874 to 1880.

In 1880 Krehbiel went to New York, expecting to edit the *Musical Review*, a recently founded weekly. Instead, Whitelaw Reid invited him to replace the *New York Tribune*'s aging senior music and literary critic, John R. G. Hassard. Hassard, however, doubted Krehbiel's qualifications, so Krehbiel was assigned other tasks at the *Tribune*, during which time he embarked on a systematic course of musical self-study. When Hassard retired in 1884, Krehbiel assumed full responsibility as the paper's music critic, a position that he held until his death.

Krehbiel was married twice. In 1880 he married Helen Osborne, an organist and children's writer; they had one child. After the death of his first wife, Krehbiel was remarried, in 1896, to Marie Van of Cincinnati, a well-known professional soprano of French descent; the second marriage did not produce children.

To his position at the *Tribune* Krehbiel brought a broad range of intellectual interests, a sensitive ear, and a zeal for high aesthetic and moral values, the latter of which he sometimes expressed in reviews. He helped to create the distinctly American variety of music criticism that emerged from Boston and New York in the 1880s, journalistic in style but erudite in content. Krehbiel's peers included the leading American music critics of the time: William Foster Apthorp and Philip Hale of Boston; Henry T. Finck, William J. Henderson, and Richard Aldrich (1863–1937) of New York; and, later, James Gibbons Huneker. Of these only Krehbiel, the midwesterner, was not formally trained in music. Apthorp, Finck, and Aldrich had studied at Harvard; Hale at Yale; Henderson at Princeton; and Huneker at the National Conservatory in New York. Several had studied abroad as well. It is notable that Krehbiel was succeeded at the *Tribune* by another self-taught music critic, Lawrence Gilman.

Krehbiel annotated programs for the New York Philharmonic Society for twenty years and wrote the first history of the society for its fiftieth anniversary in 1892. He published more than twenty-five books, including histories of choral music and opera in New York; edited scores for publication; translated opera libretti; offered an annual lecture series at the Institute of Musical Art; and wrote his regular critical essays and reviews. Krehbiel served as the American adviser for the second edition of the Grove *Dictionary of Music and Musicians*. His research on folk music was presented at the World's Columbian Exposition in Chicago in 1893, and in 1900 he served as a member of the international music jury at the Paris Exposition. In 1901 he received the cross of the French Legion of Honor.

Krehbiel's contributions to intelligent public discourse on musical subjects, whether for the scholar or the generalist, were both informative and exhortative. He attempted through reasoned discourse to refute those who assumed that music was too transcendent for commentary and also to admonish those who indulged in what he considered emotional excess: "Many persons speak about music in an extravagantly sentimental manner; many more affect not to be able to speak about it at all. Which of these two affectations is the less objectionable I do not know; but this I do know, neither is amiable, and neither reflects credit on the civilization of which this century makes frequent boasts" (*Harper's New Monthly Magazine*, Mar. 1890).

Krehbiel tended toward a conservative posture, especially in later years, rejecting the music of Arnold Schoenberg and Igor Stravinsky; his writings, however, were instrumental in increasing widespread public awareness and understanding of new works of Tchaikovsky, Brahms, and Wagner. Krehbiel's advocacy helped to cultivate in New York audiences an interest in the late romantic repertoire that was sometimes ahead of European acceptance of the same works. He commended Dvořák, newly arrived in New York as director of the National Conservatory, to the American public in a *Century* essay in September 1892. "There is measureless comfort," he wrote, "in the prospect which the example of Dvořák has opened up. It promises freshness and forcefulness of melodic, harmonic, and rhythmic contents, and newness and variety in the vehicles of utterance. It drives away the bugaboo of formlessness, which for so long a time has frightened the souls of fearful conservatives, by pointing the way to a multifarious development of forms."

In addition to energetic contributions to the musical education of his general readership and to the critical successes of new works including Tchaikovsky's Sixth Symphony and Dvořák's ninth symphony (*New World*), Krehbiel made his mark in musical scholarship. He undertook the first English-language version of Alexander Thayer's three-volume *Ludwig van Beethovens Leben*. The Thayer-Krehbiel *Life of Ludwig van Beethoven* was published in 1921 through the efforts of the Beethoven Association of New York. Krehbiel's aim was to complete and augment the original, using the vast body of Thayer's papers. Krehbiel's erratic scholarly methods, however, caused subsequent scholars difficulty in distinguishing Thayer's intentions from Krehbiel's intrusions in some passages.

Although Krehbiel's lack of formal training may have led to unevenness in his scholarship, it also contributed to his adventurous, eclectic taste as a listener. He is notable for his serious attention to vernacular musics and non-Western musics, far removed from the cultivated art music tradition of his readership. In a *Century* essay examining Chinese music theory (Jan. 1891), he began, "The musical art of a people who represent one-fifth of the earth's population ought to be studied; if not for the sake of esthetic pleasure, at least in the interest of scientific knowledge." He analyzed 500 collected African-American spirituals and published his findings in *Afro-American Folksongs: A Study in Racial and National Music* (1914). Although subsequent ethnomusicologists rejected his conclusions as to the solely black origins of this music, Krehbiel's pioneering book stimulated much response and early interest in the field.

Krehbiel died in New York City. The *New York Times* obituary noted that his colleagues knew him as "the Dean" of music critics, and a tribute by Aldrich claims that "he was the leading musical critic of America." About Krehbiel's New York circle, Edward Olin Downes wrote, "These five . . . dominated the critical scene not only in New York but to a large extent throughout the country for a span of over forty years,

and they exercised their power with a sense of responsibility and idealism."

• Krehbiel's principal books are *Notes on the Cultivation of Choral Music and the Oratorio Society of New York* (1884), *Review of the New York Musical Season* (5 vols., 1885–1890), *Studies in Wagnerian Drama* (1891), *The Philharmonic Society of New York: A Memorial Published on the Occasion of the 50th Anniversary of the Founding of the Philharmonic Society* (1892), *How to Listen to Music* (1897), *Music and Manners in the Classical Period* (1898), *Chapters of Opera* (1908; 2d ed., 1909, 3d ed., 1911), *The Pianoforte and Its Music* (1911); *More Chapters of Opera* (1919), and *English Version of Wagner's Parsifal* (1920). In addition to regular features and reviews for the *New York Tribune* from 1880 to 1923, he contributed to *Century Illustrated Monthly Magazine*, *Harper's New Monthly Magazine*, *Scribner's Magazine*, and the *Atlantic Monthly*. Also noteworthy is his article "Alexander Thayer and his *Life of Beethoven*," *Musical Quarterly* 3 (1917): 628–40.

Krehbiel's work is treated in Michael Sherwin, "The Classical Age of New York Musical Criticism, 1880–1920" (M.A. thesis, CUNY, 1972), and Edward Downes, "The Taste Makers; Critics and Criticism," in *One Hundred Years of Music in America*, ed. P. H. Lang (1961). A contemporary account of Krehbiel's role appears in the chapter "Literary Factors in Musical Progress" in W. S. B. Mathews, *A Hundred Years of Music in America: An Account of Musical Effort in America* (1889). Joseph A. Mussulman, *Music in the Cultured Generation: A Social History of Music in America, 1870–1900* (1971), treats Krehbiel's writing for the monthly literary magazines. An obituary is in the *New York Times*, 21 Mar. 1923, and an extended tribute by Richard Aldrich is in *Music and Letters* 4 (1923): 266–68.

LINDA C. FERGUSON

KREISLER, Fritz (2 Feb. 1875–29 Jan. 1962), violinist and composer, was born Friedrich Kreisler in Vienna, Austria, the son of Samuel Severin Kreisler, a general medical practitioner and amateur violinist, and Anna (maiden name unknown). Fritz's father and musical friends devoted Saturday afternoons to string quartet playing. Young Fritz listened, and at age four, having successfully played the national anthem on a toy violin for the Saturday group, he received a genuine small violin from his father. Jacques Auber, concertmaster at the Ring Theater and a friend of Dr. Kreisler, agreed to teach Fritz, who made rapid progress. In 1882 Kreisler was admitted to the Vienna Conservatory. He studied violin with Joseph Hellmesberger, Jr., and studied harmony and theory with Anton Bruckner. Kreisler's piano skills, much lauded by colleagues in later years, were self-taught while he was at the conservatory. Kreisler gave his first public violin performance in 1884 in a conservatory concert, and in 1885 he won first prize for violinists, the conservatory's gold medal, which was an unprecedented accomplishment for a ten-year-old.

Kreisler qualified for a scholarship to the Paris Conservatory, and there, beginning in 1885, he studied composition with Leo Delibes and violin with Joseph Lambert Massart, a pupil of Rudolf Kreutzer. Massart emphasized emotive playing and, under his influence, Kreisler developed a notable ingredient of his own expressive style—a sustained vibrato with variable intensity. In 1887 Kreisler competed for the Premier Prix at the conservatory and was declared first among the five violinists and two pianists who received the prize. Massart wrote to Kreisler's father several years later and declared: "I have been the teacher of Wieniawski and many others; but little Fritz will be the greatest of them all."

Kreisler made his American debut in Boston on 9 November 1888, having been invited to appear in fifty concerts with pianist Moriz Rosenthal, a pupil of Franz Liszt. After his return to Vienna late in 1889, Kreisler studied Greek, Latin, and physics with his father. He then commenced general course work at the Piaristen Gymnasium, a high school conducted by Catholic lay brethren of the Piarist order. Within two years he had passed his *Abitur* (equivalent to qualifying for one's junior year in college), and he entered medical school in 1893. Kreisler completed two of the five required years before beginning a two-year training program in the imperial Austrian army in 1895. Kreisler's diverse educational background contributed to his lifelong intellectual curiosity and keen interest in science, philosophy, and rare books.

During this time Kreisler had neglected the violin, but around 1897, on renewing practice during an eight-week period of seclusion, he recovered his manual dexterity. His first public appearance in Vienna did not occur, however, until 23 January 1898; between 1896 and 1899 Kreisler spent much time mingling in Vienna coffeehouses with music critic Eduard Hanslick, composers Johannes Brahms, Hugo Wolf, and Richard Heuberger, and members of Vienna's literati. These interactions were reflected in Kreisler's playing, which was described as being imbued with unsurpassed elegance and tenderness, the congenial spirit and *Gemütlichkeit* of old Vienna.

Recognition as a world-class violinist came to Kreisler on 1 December 1899 in Berlin, where he performed the Mendelssohn Concerto with the Berlin Philharmonic Society conducted by Artur Nikisch. Eugène Ysaÿe, the reigning king of violinists, stood up and applauded, a gesture that confirmed Kreisler's exceptional merit. From then until his permanent retirement in 1950, Kreisler's reputation continued to grow. He supplanted Ysaÿe and withstood competition from Jan Kubelik, Jacques Thibaud, Mischa Elman, and Jascha Heifetz, whose technical perfection surpassed, but whose reputation did not eclipse, that of Kreisler. Early in the twentieth century Kreisler toured first with pianist Harold Bauer and later with Bauer and cellist Pablo Casals as a piano trio. During the 1901–1902 season he performed with cellist Jean Gerardy and pianist Josef Hofmann. Kreisler toured throughout continental Europe, the British Isles, Scandinavia, and the United States. He also performed in the Orient (Japan, China, Korea, 1923), Australia (1925), South America (Argentina, Brazil, Uruguay, 1935), and Eastern Europe (Greece, Bulgaria, Yugoslavia, 1936).

As a reserve officer in the Austrian army, Kreisler was called to service on 31 July 1914 after the outbreak of World War I. He was sent to the Russian front, was seriously wounded on 9 September, and was consequently honorably discharged in November. After he had recovered, but still visibly limping, Kreisler returned to the concert stage in a performance at New York's Carnegie Hall on 12 December 1914, for which he received enthusiastic plaudits. Many of Kreisler's subsequent performances were benefits for war orphans and artists trapped in war zones. As the conflict escalated and the United States entered the war, Kreisler maintained that art and politics were separate. But he had served his homeland, and general war hysteria in the United States forced Kreisler to retire temporarily from the stage.

Distressed by the war, Kreisler sought solace in composition. He completed the somber String Quartet in A Minor (1919) and the operetta *Apple Blossoms* (1921), with Victor Jacobi. At his postwar return at Carnegie Hall on 27 October 1919, the audience gave him a five-minute ovation when he entered the stage. The British gave Kreisler an overwhelming reception in London in May 1921, and wherever he performed audiences were enthralled. In 1924 Kreisler returned to perform in France, his spiritual musical home.

Also in 1924, the peripatetic Kreisler bought a wooded property in Grünewald, a quiet, residential section of western Berlin. The location proved an idyllic retreat, a place to house the treasured books and art works he had acquired while on concert tours. When he moved to the United States in 1939, Kreisler transferred his book collection to England for safekeeping. This fortuitous move (the Berlin house was bombed during World War II) greatly benefited the Golden Rule Foundation and the Lenox Hill Hospital of New York when Kreisler agreed in 1949 to sell his library of incunabula for charitable purposes. Kreisler's humane spirit is also evident in the time and money that he and his wife, Harriet Lies, whom he married in 1902, generously devoted to various causes. The couple had no children. Kreisler became a U.S. citizen in 1943.

Authors, critics, and friends portrayed Kreisler as modest and friendly, with persuasive charm. With attention to nuance and subtlety of phrasing, he projected his genuine affection for the music and the listeners. Kreisler was endowed with a phenomenal musical memory; the celerity with which he learned musical scores is legendary. His lack of practice as an adult convinced him that he would provide a poor example as a violin teacher, a role he adopted just once. Kreisler remained an excellent pianist and was able to accompany colleagues, demonstrate interpretive ideas for accompanists, and facilitate his own composing process. As a composer, he was most recognized for the melodious vignettes he contributed to the standard violin repertoire: *Caprice Viennois, Liebesleid* (1910), *Liebesfreund* (1910), *Schön Rosmarin* (1910), and *Tambourin Chinois*. The cadenzas Kreisler wrote for the Beethoven Concerto when he was nineteen are highly regarded, as are his numerous transcriptions and the compositions that he claimed were reworkings of old masters' compositions but were in fact his own. When in 1935 this "deception" came to light, Ernest Newman, chief music critic of *The Times* (London), questioned Kreisler's ethics. The articles and retorts surrounding the matter make lively reading.

Kreisler began recording regularly in 1910, and his records were bestsellers on every continent. His renewal contract with the Victor Talking Machine Company in 1925 guaranteed him huge royalty earnings. In 1935 Kreisler recorded the ten Beethoven sonatas for violin and piano with Franz Rupp for the Beethoven Society of London. Other notable recording collaborations include those with Irish tenor John McCormack, pianist and close friend Sergei Rachmaninoff, violinist Efrem Zimbalist, soprano Geraldine Farrar, and his brother, cellist Hugo Kreisler.

Kreisler's artistry, compositional expertise, and lack of pretense ensured the respect and friendship of fellow musicians and colleagues, among them violinists Zimbalist, Elman, Joseph Szigeti, Nathan Milstein, and Heifetz. In 1975 violin professor Joseph Gingold stated, "Kreisler's legacy is not the technical wizardry of Heifetz or the sumptuous tone of Elman, but the embodiment of all that was attractive, humane, and endearing among the musicians of his time." He died in New York City.

• The Library of Congress Music Division—Composers' Holograph Collections—houses Kreisler music manuscripts, programs, clippings, photographs, and memorabilia. For reflections on his war experience, see Kreisler, *Four Weeks in the Trenches* (1915; 3d rev. ed., 1981). Louis P. Lochner, *Fritz Kreisler* (1950; 3d rev. ed., 1981), blends factual details with quotes from Kreisler and colleagues and includes a list of Kreisler compositions, transcriptions, and arrangements (the Schott catalog, complete with themes from thirty-eight Kreisler works), along with a discography, a bibliography that lists numerous magazine and newspaper articles, and a detailed index. Charles Foley, "One of Nature's Noblemen," and Irving Kolodin, "Kreisler—A Category of His Own," both in the written material included with *Fritz Kreisler in Immortal Performances*, RCA Victor Red Seal LM-6099 (1962), provide an overview of Kreisler's life and artistry. Historical reissues of Kreisler recordings are available on compact disc from RCA (Red Seal), Biddulph, and Pearl. See also Samuel Applebaum and Sada Applebaum, *With the Artists* (1955) and *The Way They Play*, vol. 1 (1972), for information based on personal interviews with Kreisler; Harold C. Schonberg, *The Glorious Ones: Classical Music's Legendary Performers* (1985); Boris Schwarz, *Great Masters of the Violin* (1983); Henry Roth, *Great Violinists in Performance* (1987); Margaret Campbell, *The Great Violinists* (1981); James Creighton, *Discopaedia of the Violin, 1889–1971* (1974); Allan Kozinn, *Mischa Elman and the Romantic Style* (1990); Artur Weschler-Vered, *Jascha Heifetz* (1986); Marc Pincherle, *The World of the Virtuoso* (1963); and Richard Schickel and Michael Walsh, *Carnegie Hall: The First One Hundred Years* (1987). An obituary is in the *New York Times*, 30 Jan. 1962.

JOANNE SWENSON-ELDRIDGE

KREMERS, Edward (23 Feb. 1865–9 July 1941), pharmaceutical educator and phytochemist, was born in Milwaukee, Wisconsin, the son of Gerhard Kremers, a secretary-treasurer of the Milwaukee Gas & Light Company, and Elise Kamper. German culture and education were dominant influences that shaped Kre-

mers's life and career. To escape the events in Germany in 1848 his family immigrated to one of the most Germanic parts of the United States. In elementary school, all but two or three of Edward's peers were studying German. His high school, operated by the German Reformed church, was modeled after a German secondary school. After graduation in 1882, Kremers apprenticed in Milwaukee with an immigrant German pharmacist, Louis Lotz. After a two-year apprenticeship Kremers studied at the Philadelphia College of Pharmacy for a year (1884–1885); he then enrolled in the University of Wisconsin to earn a Ph.G. certificate (1886) and a B.S. degree (1888).

Also in 1888 Kremers sailed for Germany to earn a Ph.D. degree (1890) under the renowned phytochemist Otto Wallach at Bonn and Göttingen. His dissertation, titled "The Isomerism within the Terpene Group," opened a research path that he followed throughout a productive career, namely, the chemistry of medicinal plants and especially of the volatile oils contained in plants. As a German American, Kremers had been able to absorb a deep understanding of German culture and education while abroad; he returned to Wisconsin with a missionary zeal for reforming American pharmaceutical education and practice.

Two years after Kremers accepted an instructorship in the Department of Pharmacy of the University of Wisconsin at Madison, his distinguished chairman and mentor, Frederick B. Power, resigned to accept a research post in the pharmaceutical industry. Although only twenty-seven years old, Kremers was selected to succeed him (1892) as head of the department, a position he would hold for the rest of his career (forty-three years). Also in 1892 Kremers married Laura Haase of Milwaukee; they had four children.

During the 1890s he became the leading exponent of university education for prospective pharmacists on the same level as other science-based curricula, a field previously dominated by schools offering shorter programs of study and often emphasizing a memorization of drug lore rather than an understanding of the science underlying pharmacy. The same year that Kremers became director, the university announced a pharmacy curriculum of four years' study (albeit optional) leading to a B.S. degree. This was the first such program in the United States, and when the apprehensive university president asked how many students he expected in the proposed curriculum, Kremers replied, characteristically, "Mr. President, I am not concerned with numbers but with an ideal." Ahead of its time and although at first ignored by most American schools, Kremers's innovation was emulated within three years by four other universities. Eventually it became the national standard, thus upgrading pharmacy services for citizens everywhere.

Through the B.S. program Kremers not only offered graduates the advantage of a broad-based university education but the basis for earning higher research degrees. Kremers himself had undertaken laboratory investigations while still an undergraduate; and in

Germany, then a world center for scientific research, Kremers observed the potential for societal contributions that Ph.D. degrees in specialized fields of pharmacy could generate. Accordingly, he moved decisively to make Wisconsin a leader in research. In 1902 the university awarded under Kremers's supervision the first Ph.D. degree in pharmaceutical chemistry, a further innovation soon adopted at other American universities. More than fifty Ph.D. degrees eventually were earned under Kremers's personal guidance by students who went on to positions in government, industry, and academia. At least seventeen of his former graduate students eventually became deans of pharmacy at other universities. Kremers expanded his scientific influence further in 1913 by attaining legislation that authorized the establishment at Wisconsin of the first state-supported Pharmaceutical Experiment Station on American soil, to disseminate information on the basis of research and to cooperate with the U.S. Department of Agriculture (because of Kremers's emphasis on medicinal plants).

Kremers wrote several hundred phytochemical and pharmaco-historical papers and notes, and he continued to influence his field as an editor and translator. For example, Kremers was coeditor, then editor, of *The Pharmaceutical Review* (1896–1909). In 1898 he founded and edited *Pharmaceutical Archives*, the first journal in American pharmacy devoted entirely to original scientific articles. He founded and edited *The Badger Pharmacist*, the first American periodical devoted mainly to pharmaceutical history, which appeared irregularly from 1930 to 1941. An enduring contribution to Kremers's field of science was his translation of a classic German work by E. Gildemeister and Frederick Hoffmann, published in the United States as *The Volatile Oils* (1900; rev. ed., 3 vols., 1913–1922).

Although Kremers may be best remembered as a contentious reformer of pharmaceutical education and as a medicinal-plant chemist, his Germanic background imbued him with a deeply held belief in the value of a balance between the sciences and humanities in a well-educated professional. He invested a generous share of his efforts in the pursuit of this conviction, and became the most scholarly American historian of the pharmaceutical field up to his time. It was largely on Kremers's initiative that a Section on Historical Pharmacy was established (1904) in the American Pharmaceutical Association. He was an early exponent of a place for the history of sciences in American universities, and at Wisconsin he announced (1907–1908) pioneering courses in the history of pharmacy and the history of chemistry. In 1940 he coauthored with George Urdang the first book to offer a systematic historical account of how pharmacy developed in the United States, which remains in print (much modified) as *Kremers and Urdang's History of Pharmacy*. In addition, he built several outstanding historical collections of pharmaceutical books, ephemera, and artifacts.

Kremers died in Madison, which had served as the base for his entire professional career. He had been "an inspiring and even impetuous initiator," as Urdang put it, "rather than a man finishing meticulously one job after the other." Kremers's blunt attacks on the status quo sometimes alienated those whose support he sought; but his followers, inspired by his principles and personality, helped to achieve a more hospitable climate for his objectives. The leadership posts and honors that came to Kremers late in his career testified to a growing appreciation of the role he had been fulfilling as a bold agent of change in the pharmaceutical field—a reformer who left an enduring mark on one facet of health care in the United States.

• Kremers's papers, in the Archives Division of the State Historical Society of Wisconsin, include fragments of an unpublished memoir, correspondence, reminiscences, notes and essays, trip diaries, and family memorabilia. Other resources are personal papers in the Kremers reference files at the F. B. Power Pharmaceutical Library, University of Wisconsin-Madison; a manuscript bibliography of Kremers's writings in the office of the American Institute of the History of Pharmacy, Madison, Wis.; and administrative records of the School of Pharmacy during Kremers's directorship in the University Archive. A full-scale biography has yet to be published. The most valuable article about Kremers is George Urdang's "Edward Kremers (1865–1941): Reformer of American Pharmaceutical Education," *Transactions of the Wisconsin Academy of Sciences, Arts and Letters* 37 (1945): 111–35, repr. in *American Journal of Pharmaceutical Education* 11 (1947): 631–58. An especially informative obituary is in *Science*, 26 Sept. 1941, pp. 293–94.

GLENN SONNEDECKER

KRESGE, Sebastian Spering (31 July 1867–18 Oct. 1966), founder of the retail store chain named for him, was born in Bald Mount, Pennsylvania, the son of Sebastian Kresge and Catherine Kunkle, poor farmers. Extremely frugal and religiously devout, his parents encouraged hard work and money-making activities. In childhood Sebastian earned money keeping bees, and he continued that activity as an adult hobby.

Eager to escape the hardships of farm life, Kresge persuaded his parents to finance his education in return for his entire income until he reached the age of twenty-one. The arrangement enabled him to attend the Fairview Academy in Brodheadsville and the Gilbert Polytechnic Institute. In 1886 he taught at Gower's School in Monroe County, Pennsylvania. He then settled in Scranton, where he worked as a deliveryman and clerk for a grocer. After completing a four-month course in 1889 at Eastman's Business College in Poughkeepsie, New York, he returned to Scranton and worked as a bookkeeper, an insurance salesman, and half owner of a bakery that failed.

Beginning in 1892 Kresge was a traveling salesman for a company in Wilkes-Barre that specialized in tinware and hardware. Among his customers who prospered despite a widespread depression were Frank W. Woolworth, and John G. McCrorey, founders of the two earliest dime store chains. Impressed by the potential of their business, he tried to buy his way into the F. W. Woolworth Company, but Frank Woolworth rebuffed him. He then struck a deal in 1897 with McCrorey: in return for $8,000 Kresge had frugally saved, McCrorey would train him and take him as a partner in new stores.

His partnership with McCrorey lasted long enough for Kresge to learn about display, merchandising, management, and store location. Training began with two weeks at the store in Jamestown, New York, owned by McCrorey and managed by his cousin George C. Murphy. As equal partners, Kresge and McCrorey then opened a store in Memphis, which Kresge managed, and later one in Detroit, which Murphy managed. After sixteen months in Memphis, he worked for a few more months as an assistant buyer at McCrorey's headquarters in Johnstown, Pennsylvania. In November 1898 Kresge moved to Detroit, taking over from Murphy as manager five months later. In the fall of 1899 Kresge ended his partnership with McCrorey, giving McCrorey $3,000 and his share in the Memphis store in return for sole ownership of the store in Detroit. McCrorey (later changed to McCrory) and Murphy each went on to build successful chains.

Kresge, establishing his headquarters in Detroit, built a much larger and more profitable organization. Between 1900 and 1907 he operated in partnership with his brother-in-law, Charles J. Wilson, also a former partner of McCrorey. Their company, Kresge and Wilson, owned eight stores in the Midwest when Kresge bought out Wilson and changed the firm's name to the S. S. Kresge Company. Incorporated in 1912 with capitalization of $7 million, it had eighty-five stores and annual sales of $10 million, ranking in the dime store business behind only F. W. Woolworth. It expanded into cities in the Midwest and the Northeast but avoided the Southeast by Kresge's personal agreement with Samuel H. Kress, founder of a rival chain. Before the Great Depression the company operated almost 600 stores, including some in Canada, with annual sales over $156 million.

Kresge's success in mass marketing stemmed from a combination of skills and efforts. To a degree unusual even among those who built the dime store chains, he applied rigorous work habits, attention to detail, and strict economy of operations. He was a fearless financial plunger, with sound judgment and daring enterprise. The strength of his corporate culture rested on strict morality and progressive personnel policies. He recruited and retained talented subordinates who shared his outlook, and he was proud that many of them became wealthy working for him. Although the business depended on low operating costs, including low wages for the female sales staffs, he paid more than the prevailing wages. Before the practices were common, Kresge provided employees with sick leave, paid holidays, profit-sharing bonuses, and retirement pensions. When falling stock prices in 1932 threatened the investments of many employees, he tried unsuccessfully to protect them by using his own money to maintain a standing "buy" order for the company's stock.

Company president until 1925 and chairman until four months before his death, Kresge was always closely involved with the company's key personnel and policy decisions. He attended every board meeting and studied every report. He followed both the buying and the selling ends of the business, frequently visiting the company's stores and those of competitors. In 1920 he acquired as a subsidiary the chain's dinnerware supplier, the Mt. Clemens (Michi.) Pottery Company. In 1911 he decided that the 10¢ price limit at "Red Front" stores was too restrictive, and the company started selling items from 25¢ to $1 in a few "Dollar Stores," models for the "Green Front" stores it launched during the 1920s. After World War II it abandoned that price limit too and sold a wider range of goods. Like other variety store chains during the 1950s, it also introduced self-service and opened stores in suburban areas.

By the late 1950s, however, all the variety store chains faced formidable competition from other kinds of mass retailers. Some of the chains, such as S. H. Kress, went out of business, and others tried to continue without sufficiently adapting. S. S. Kresge, long the second largest chain in the field, briefly fell behind the W. T. Grant Company, then pursuing overly aggressive expansion. Unlike the other variety store chains, Kresge overcame adversity by bold innovation. The company adopted a strategy mapped out by Harry B. Cunningham, promoted to president in 1959. It converted some unprofitable stores with long leases in deteriorating neighborhoods into Jupiter stores that stocked discount merchandise as well as variety items. More importantly, it invested $80 million in a new chain of free-standing discount department stores built with large parking lots. The first of those suburban K-Mart stores opened in 1962 in Garden City, near Detroit. When Kresge died, his company's sales topped $1 billion, mostly due to the 150 K-Mart stores.

Although the variety store chain provided the basis of his fortune, Kresge did pursue other business interests. During the 1920s he became president of Kresge Realty Company and owner of several department stores: The Fair in Chicago; Palais Royale in Washington; Stern Brothers in New York; and stores in New Jersey renamed Kresge-Newark and Steinbach-Kresge. His personal fortune, by the end of the decade, exceeded $200 million, and his stock brokerage account was worth about $30 million.

For other reasons besides his business success, during the 1920s Kresge attracted wide public attention. For one thing, he made no effort to conceal the eccentric frugality that made him a notorious penny pincher. He wore clothes and shoes and drove cars until they fell apart. He often shopped for bargains in his own stores and boasted that he never spent more than thirty cents for lunch, regularly eating at the stores' restaurant counters. A devout Methodist and a staunch Republican, he never used tobacco or alcohol and disapproved of gambling. That strict morality led him to prominently support the YMCA and the Anti-

Saloon League and to organize the National Vigilance Committee for Prohibition Enforcement.

Ironically for this embodiment of traditional values, he also attracted public attention when his first two marriages broke up and he married women twenty-five years younger. His first wife, Anna Emma Harvey, whom he married in 1897, complaining about his stinginess, divorced him in 1924. That year, after reportedly giving his former spouse and their five children $10 million in the settlement, he married Doris Mercer. Four years later, after a scandalous divorce case in which he reportedly gave his second wife $3 million, he married Clara Katherine Zitz Swaine. He had no children by his second or third wives.

Personal frugality notwithstanding, Kresge believed that with great wealth came the obligation to make the world a better place. His support for the Rotary, the YMCA, various Methodist organizations, and Prohibition fit that goal. More important, with an initial gift of $1.3 million, he created in 1924 the Kresge Foundation "to help human progress." Treasurer of the foundation until his death, he eventually gave it most of his personal fortune, including Kresge stock worth about $100 million. By then the foundation's net worth was $175 million, and it had made grants totaling $70 million for charitable, educational, and philanthropic purposes. At the dedication of Kresge Hall at the Harvard Graduate School of Business Administration in 1953, his speech consisted of only six words: "I never made a dime talking!" He died at his home in East Stroudsburg, Pennsylvania.

• The papers of Sebastian Kresge, his son Stanley Kresge, and the S. S. Kresge Company are all on deposit at the Michigan Historical Collection, Bentley Library, University of Michigan, Ann Arbor. Stanley S. Kresge, as told to Steve Spilos, *The S. S. Kresge Story* (1979), is an authorized history. An obituary is in the *New York Times*, 19 Oct. 1966.

ALAN R. RAUCHER

KRESS, Samuel Henry (23 July 1863–22 Sept. 1955), retail store chain founder, was born in Cherryville, Pennsylvania, the son of John Franklin Kress and Margaret Dodson Connor. After the family moved to Slatington, Pennsylvania, his father operated a drugstore and later two commissary stores at the mines. Kress attended and may have graduated from high school. At age seventeen Kress started teaching at an elementary school three miles from his family home. In 1887, then twenty-four years old, he used his savings to buy a stationery and novelty store in Nanticoke, Pennsylvania. About that time he also took on the responsibility of rearing his six siblings after both of his parents had died. In 1890 he bought out his wholesaler in nearby Wilkes-Barre, Pennsylvania. Three years later his brother Claude Washington Kress, then only seventeen years old, joined the business. While in Wilkes-Barre, Kress became friendly with Fred W. Kirby, who operated a small dime-store chain, one of many partnerships of Frank W. Woolworth, founder of the dime-store chain business. Impressed by Kirby's success, Kress decided that he too could operate a chain of stores selling low-priced merchandise.

In 1896 Kress launched what became the basis of his fortune by opening a large dime store in Memphis, Tennessee. The store proved highly successful in its first year, and the next year he opened a second store in Nashville, Tennessee, and installed Claude as its manager. By 1900 he was operating a chain of eleven stores, mainly in the South, with sales reaching nearly $500,000. Deciding to broaden his merchandise line, he raised the price limit to twenty-five cents, and cutting loose from his Pennsylvania roots he sold the stores there and moved his headquarters from Wilkes-Barre to New York City, where he could maintain closer contacts with suppliers. Incorporated in 1907, that year S. H. Kress & Company operated fifty-one stores with sales of more than $3 million.

The firm followed policies of strict frugality, petty discipline, and shrewd merchandising. During its early years employees removed and saved nails from crates, reused cartons and twine, and wrapped packages in old newspapers. Executive offices were quite spartan. His ruthlessly centralized authoritarian management, including close surveillance of executives, exceeded even the rigid norm within the variety chain business. According to cost-conscious competitors, Kress was especially "hardboiled" about employee pay.

Besides hairsplitting control over operating expenses, Kress built his success by selling relatively good quality but inexpensive merchandise at low markups. Rather than buying cheap merchandise available from jobbers, he went directly to manufacturers. By offering to buy in big lots and sometimes providing capital for their expansion, he convinced manufacturers to supply his stores with special merchandise, such as the first five-cent cup and saucer, that could be sold quickly. Compared with competitors' stores, Kress offered customers a narrower range of items but more genuine bargains.

Conservatively financing expansion from its own earnings, S. H. Kress built one of the country's largest and most successful variety store chains. Kress aimed to operate not the greatest number of stores but the most attractive and most profitable stores. After World War I the company consistently achieved higher sales per store and per linear foot of counters than the largest variety chains. Unlike competitors that usually leased their stores, Kress bought land and built most of his own distinctive stores, which after 1930 used art deco designs. Moving outside of its base in the South, it also expanded to the West Coast but seldom opened in the Midwest and Northeast, reportedly to avoid confusing customers with the similarity of his stores' names and those of the rival S. S. Kresge chain. One notable exception to that regional concentration was New York City, where in 1936 the company opened a spectacular superstore at Thirty-ninth Street and Fifth Avenue. Besides Kress's own success, the company also trained John Josiah Newberry and

William W. McLellan, two executives who each left to launch his own successful variety store chain.

Kress served as company president until 1924 and then as chair until his death. In 1929, when the firm operated more than 200 stores and had sales of nearly $70 million, he established the Samuel H. Kress Foundation to promote the welfare and progress of the human race, giving it more than 40 percent of the company's voting stock. Soon afterward he started turning over active management to his brother Claude, who had become president in 1924. While he operated the company, Claude combated both the Great Depression and the political campaigns against chain stores. Instrumental in establishing the Kress Library of Business and Economics at Harvard University, Claude retired from the presidency in 1939 and died the following year. Samuel, then seventy-seven, returned as chief executive officer, but in 1941 he suffered a paralytic stroke. Although he remained as chair, thereafter he left management to his brother Rush Harrison Kress, fourteen years his junior.

Under Rush Kress, who assumed the presidency in 1941 and later became vice chair and chief executive officer, the company did not adapt well to the postwar market. It was slow to upgrade merchandise lines or to move stores into rapidly growing suburban shopping centers. When Samuel Kress died, the chain was still at near peak, with 264 stores, annual sales of nearly $168 million, and 24,000 employees, but minority stockholders were complaining loudly about declining profits, dividends, and stock prices. By 1958 even other trustees of the Kress Foundation started to challenge Rush's leadership. Subsequent changes in the company's top management, however, failed to halt the downward slide. The Genesco Corporation bought the controlling interest in 1963 and later liquidated the company.

Modest, parsimonious, and ever watchful against those who would take advantage of him or his fortune, Samuel Kress never married, and apart from business he had only one great passion; he was a great collector and patron of fine art. He started collecting in 1910 and, under the tutelage of Bernard Berenson, during the 1920s became a genuine connoisseur and a shrewd appraiser of Old Masters. Often driving hard bargains with art dealers such as Joseph Duveen and Daniel Wildenstein, he sometimes bought at discount huge lots that included second- and third-rate works to obtain a few real prizes. Eventually, he amassed the largest and most encyclopedic private collection of Old Masters ever assembled in the Western hemisphere.

Deciding against building his own museum, Kress found other ways to share his art with the public. During the early 1930s he pioneered the concept of the traveling exhibition by sending many prize Italian paintings on a tour of municipal museums across the country; afterward, he donated some of them to the museums' permanent collections. During the 1938 Christmas shopping season he put on display at the store on Fifth Avenue a recent acquisition, Giorgione's *The Adoration of the Shepherds*. The National Gallery of Art became the principal beneficiary of Kress's gifts; in 1939 he donated 375 paintings and other art valued at $25 million to the fledgling collection. And from 1945 until his death he served as the gallery's president and gave it three-quarters of all its Old Masters. His other art donations enriched many regional museums, universities, libraries, and religious institutions.

A Lutheran whose German ancestors came to America in 1752, Samuel Kress belonged to the Sons of the American Revolution, the Masonic Order, and the Republican party. He died in New York City, bequeathing most of his $17.5 million estate to the Kress Foundation. Thus, even after the disappearance of the company Kress had started, the foundation continued to support his legacy through art.

• Samuel H. Kress did not deposit personal or business papers in any repository. Ben Gordon, "50 Years of the Kress Idea," *Chain Store Age*, Nov. 1946, pp. 2–8, provides biographical information supplied by the company. Each of the Kress brothers is portrayed in *National Cyclopaedia of American Biography*, vol. 31 (1944), vol. 41 (1956), and vol. 47 (1965). "Great Kress Giveaway," *Life*, 16 Nov. 1953, pp. 148–60, tells the story of Kress's art collection. "S. H. Kress: Who's in Charge?" *Fortune*, Nov. 1957, pp. 170–71, explains how the company declined under Rush Kress. An obituary is in the *New York Times*, 23 Sept. 1955.

ALAN R. RAUCHER

KREYMBORG, Alfred Francis (10 Dec. 1883–14 Aug. 1966), poet and editor, was born in New York City, the son of Herrmann Kreymborg, a store owner, and Louise Nascher. The youngest of five children, "Ollie," as he was called, was raised a Roman Catholic and educated in the public schools on Manhattan's East Side. A prodigy, Kreymborg was self-taught at chess, at one point tying with world champion José Capablanca. It was Kreymborg's boyhood interest in the mandolin, however, that led to his lifelong literary career. Unable to compose music, the eighteen-year-old Kreymborg wrote a "prose symphony"; thereafter he devoted himself to perfecting his own brand of *vers libre*.

Actively involved with the Manhattan art scene by 1913, the year of the renowned Armory Show, Kreymborg was a regular at Alfred Stieglitz's famous "291" gallery on Fifth Avenue. In 1915 Kreymborg married Gertrude Lord; in 1918, after his first marriage ended in divorce, he married Dorothy Bloom. During the same period, Eugene O'Neill's Provincetown Players staged one of Kreymborg's verse plays, *Lima Beans*. In 1920 Kreymborg and his wife traveled the country with their popular puppet theater.

In the spring of 1921, the Kreymborgs left on an extended tour of Europe, first joining the American expatriate scene in Paris. From there, they journeyed to Italy and then to Munich and London in time to be on hand for the publication of T. S. Eliot's *The Waste Land*. Back in the United States, the Kreymborgs repeated their puppet theater tour around the country while he wrote his autobiography, *Troubadour* (1925). Except for another European trip in the early 1930s, they lived in lower Manhattan for the rest of their lives, making summer excursions to Cape Cod.

As a periodicals editor, Kreymborg was an important force on the American literary scene during the formative years of modernism from 1910 to 1940. His first venture, a New York "little magazine" called the *Glebe* published Ezra Pound's *Des Imagistes, An Anthology* in 1914, with work by James Joyce, Pound, H.D., Amy Lowell, and William Carlos Williams.

Glebe folded after only one year. In 1915 Kreymborg founded another magazine, *Others*, which—before it suspended publication in 1919—published works by Carl Sandburg, Wallace Stevens, T. S. Eliot, and Conrad Aiken. In Rome in 1921 Kreymborg and Harold Loeb started *Broom*, but Kreymborg's involvement only lasted one year. In 1927 he launched with Van Wyck Brooks, Paul Rosenfeld, and Lewis Mumford the influential literary annual *American Caravan*. Kreymborg remained with that showcase journal through its last volume in 1936.

Kreymborg's own considerable body of poetry offers a telling road map of formal trends and thematic focuses in American poetry from 1910 to 1945. His first published volume, *Love and Life and Other Studies* (1910), was followed by two chapbooks collected in *Mushrooms* in 1916. This early poetry mixed *vers libre* forms, Imagist description, and a Whitmanesque fervor for the common lot. In his next volume, *Blood of Things* (1920), Kreymborg continued to experiment with modernist themes and verse forms. But beginning with the volume *Less Lonely* (1923), Kreymborg became more and more a traditionalist, with more formal rhyming couplets, sonnets, and blank verse lines.

During the latter half of the 1920s, besides two more volumes of poetry—*The Lost Sail* (1928) and *Manhattan Men* (1929)—Kreymborg published *Our Singing Strength* (1929), a 630-page history of American poetry. As the United States struggled under the Great Depression, Kreymborg's poetry began to record a growing awareness of society's distresses and of the poet's obligation to speak out.

In *Arms and Armageddon*, a volume composed between 1939 to 1944, Kreymborg continued to grapple with the increasingly complex socioeconomic and political developments of the day on both the domestic and international scenes. *Man and Shadow: An Allegory*, a book-length poem composed during World War II and published in 1946, pointedly addressed an America arriving at its preeminent place in world history as a result of the victorious conclusion of the war.

Kreymborg published his last volume, *No More War and Other Poems*, in 1950, but other poems appeared in such outlets as *Poetry* and the *Saturday Review of Literature* into the late 1950s. In his later years, he became president of the Poetry Society of America and was elected to the National Institute of Arts and Letters. He also sat regularly as a judge for the Pulitzer Prize in poetry. Kreymborg died in Milford, Connecticut.

Despite his considerable contributions and influence as an editor, Kreymborg as a poet never achieved the widespread popular appeal of a Frost, Sandburg, or Edgar Lee Masters. By the same token, his midcareer shift to formalism cost him the continued academic scrutiny accorded to more avant-garde modernists such as Pound and Eliot that would have made for a substantial body of critical assessments. As a result, Kreymborg is little anthologized. He has become a minor but important figure in a major literary movement.

• Kreymborg's papers are distributed among a number of holdings, including: the American Academy of Arts and Letters; the Shields Library, Univ. of California, Davis; the Baker Library, Dartmouth College; the Houghton Library, Harvard Univ.; the Univ. of Illinois Archives, Urbana; the Lockwood Memorial Library, SUNY/Buffalo; the Fred Lewis Pattee Library, Pennsylvania State Univ.; the Charles Patterson Van Pelt Library, Univ. of Pennsylvania; the Humanities Research Center, Univ. of Texas, Austin; and the Beinecke Library, Yale Univ. Other works by Kreymborg not mentioned above include *Edna, the Girl of the Street* (1915), *To My Mother* (1915), *Plays for Poem-Mimes* (1918), *Plays for Merry Andrews* (1920), *Scarlet and Mellow* (1926), *Funnybone Alley* (1927), *Prologue in Hell* (1930), *I'm No Hero* (1933), *The Planets: A Modern Allegory* (1938), and *The Selected Poems, 1912–1944* (1945). For material regarding Kreymborg's life and works, see Allen Tate, *Sixty American Poets*, rev. ed. (1954), and Russell Murphy, "Alfred Kreymborg," in *Dictionary of Literary Biography*, vol. 54, pp. 192–201, as well as Kreymborg's autobiography, *Troubadour*. An obituary is in the *New York Times*, 15 Aug. 1966.

RUSSELL ELLIOTT MURPHY

KRIMMEL, John Lewis (30 May 1786–15 July 1821), painter, was born Johann Ludwig Krimmel in Ebingen, in the duchy of Württemberg, now Germany, the son of Johann Jacob Krimmel and Elisabetha Catharina Nördliner, confectioners. The Krimmel family was among the most prosperous and prominent in Ebingen, a village among rocky hills overlooking the plains of central Europe. Krimmel's father died in 1796, and after his mother died in 1803, he became the ward of his sister Christiane Elisabetha and his brother George Frederick. The village school was available to John through the age of fourteen. Studies elsewhere are unrecorded until an American contemporary, William Dunlap, credibly reports training about 1806 in Stuttgart from the court painter to the duke of Württemberg, Johann Baptist Seele. In 1809 Krimmel sailed to Philadelphia to work with his brother, a merchant; he anglicized his name at that time.

Krimmel left his brother's business to pursue a career as an artist on 6 July 1810. From the beginning, he specialized in painting scenes from daily life, a subject only occasionally treated by his contemporaries. Nine of his eleven pictures known to survive as of 1987 and most of the fifty-five recorded works are genre subjects. They range in date from 1812 to 1820 and include those his contemporaries considered his most ambitious. Significant among them are two pictures that Krimmel exhibited together at the Pennsylvania Academy in 1813 and that publicly revealed his goal of an American genre school inspired by that of England.

One was a copy of his print of Sir David Wilkie's English scene of 1806 entitled *The Blind Fiddler*. The other was an American scene entitled *Quilting Frolic* (1813, Winterthur Museum). While he derived inspiration from Wilkie's work, Krimmel did not copy elements from it; similarly, Krimmel's successors were equally reticent to adapt specifics from Krimmel's pictures or prints. But Krimmel's influence on other artists validated his belief, widely publicized in the *Portfolio* and *Analectic* magazines, that contemporary American life was an appropriate subject for American art.

Krimmel never married, though an engagement to a Miss Miller is reported. The obscure Swiss or German artist Alexander Rider probably lived with him during most of his years in Philadelphia. Krimmel's sketchbooks reveal that he often made short trips away from Philadelphia and that he traveled widely in Europe for about two years, beginning late in 1816, after settling his sister's estate in Ebingen. Krimmel's active participation in the artistic life of Philadelphia is revealed by his membership in the Society of Artists of the United States, the Columbian Society of Artists, and the Association of American Artists, which elected him president in 1821. Krimmel regularly exhibited at the local Pennsylvania Academy of the Fine Arts and in New York City at the American Academy of the Fine Arts. He accidentally drowned in Germantown, Pennsylvania.

Krimmel earned a place in Philadelphia and in the history of American painting as the first artist basing his reputation on contemporary genre subjects. Krimmel did not become an American citizen, but he placed the energy of his wiry build and the blunt humor of his cheerful temperament into creating pictorial satires of American life.

• Most of Krimmel's rare works are in public collections. Among them are his paintings *Portrait of the Reverend John Gottlieb Ernestus Heckewelder* (1820, American Philosophical Society, Philadelphia), *The Conflagration of the Masonic Hall, Chestnut Street, Philadelphia* (1819, Art Institute of Chicago), *Blindman's Buff* (1814, Terra Museum of American Art, Chicago), *Village Tavern* (1814, Toledo Museum of Art), *View of Centre Square on the Fourth of July* and *The Country Wedding* (1812 and 1820, respectively, Pennsylvania Academy of the Fine Arts), and *Election Scene, State House in Philadelphia* (1815, Winterthur Museum, Delaware). Seven sketchbooks are at the Winterthur; watercolors are at the Historical Society of Pennsylvania, the Library of Congress, and the Springfield Art Museum in Springfield, Mo. Prints based on paintings and drawings are at the Academy of Natural Sciences Library in Philadelphia, the Historical Society of Pennsylvania, the Library Company of Philadelphia, and the Winterthur. The only two letters by Krimmel known are in the Archives of American Art in Washington, D.C., and the Historical Society of Pennsylvania. They are published, along with references to Krimmel by his contemporaries, in the biography, critical analysis, and catalogue raisonné by Milo M. Naeve, *John Lewis Krimmel: An Artist in Federal America* (1987).

MILO M. NAEVE

KRISHNAMURTI, Jiddu (11 May 1895–17 Feb. 1986), celebrated spiritual teacher, was born in the southern Indian town of Madanapalle in what is now the state of Andhra Pradesh, the son of a brahmin, Jiddu Naraniah, and Sanjeevamma Jiddu. His father was a civil servant and dedicated Theosophist, who after his retirement moved his family to the headquarters estate of the Theosophical Society at Adyar, near Madras. The Theosophical Society, established by Helena Blavatsky and Henry Steel Olcott in 1875, was concerned with recovering an ancient wisdom believed to underlie all religion and was especially sympathetic to the religious traditions of India. There, Krishnamurti was "discovered" in 1909 by the Theosophical writer and reputed seer C. W. Leadbeater, who believed that the boy had the potential to become the "vehicle" of a coming World Teacher, a manifestation of Maitreya, the future Buddha. He and Annie Besant, world president of the Theosophical Society, determined to educate the young Krishnamurti and prepare him for this extraordinary vocation. They persuaded Naraniah to entrust him and his brother Nityananda (who was to serve as Krishnamurti's companion) to their care. He was raised by Theosophists at Adyar, in England, and in Ojai, California. Although attempts to enter him in an English university were unsuccessful, he became a poised and articulate young man. In 1910 he published *At the Feet of the Master*. This slim volume, written under the pseudonym Alcyone, was said to be instructions received during his sleep by Krishnamurti from a spiritual Master; it became a Theosophical classic. In 1911 the Order of the Star in the East was formed under his nominal headship, with sections in many countries, to hold rallies and publish literature preparing the world for his messianic mission. In 1912 Krishnamurti's father, Naraniah, brought legal action to recover his two sons from the Theosophists. Although successful in the lower courts, his suit was eventually dismissed on a technicality by the Privy Council in London.

In the 1920s considerable excitement over Krishnamurti and his proclaimed role as the future World Teacher built up in Theosophical circles. He was wildly adulated, and his every public word was scrutinized for evidence that the Coming was imminent. His life alternated between organized speaking tours and life in semiretreat, generally in Ojai. From 1922 to 1924, in Ojai, he is said by some accounts to have undergone a mysterious inward, spiritual "process" that, like a powerful initiation, reportedly changed him profoundly, leaving him extremely sensitive both physically and spiritually. In 1925 his brother, Nityananda, perhaps his only truly intimate companion, died. Both events appear to have shaken Krishnamurti free of any complacent acceptance of the role planned for him by his Theosophical mentors and convinced him that he must find his own way and determine his own life. In August 1929, at an Order of the Star camp in Ommen, the Netherlands, Krishnamurti astonished and disconcerted an audience of some three thousand by dramatically dissolving the order, dissociating himself from formal Theosophy, and rejecting for himself all organized spirituality. In his speech he declared, "I maintain that truth is a pathless land, and you cannot approach it by any path whatsoever, by any religion, by any sect."

Henceforth until his death, Krishnamurti pursued an independent vocation as a distinguished lecturer and teacher of nameless truth and "choiceless awareness." His 1929 statement threw institutional Theosophy into considerable disarray. But it should be noted that some Theosophists saw his later pronouncements as no more than taking the bent of all Theosophy toward mysticism to its ultimate point and that his separation from his Theosophical friends and patrons was gradual. Krishnamurti did not establish an entirely separate pattern of life and work until the middle thirties. As late as the 1990s the Theosophical Publishing House continued to keep his books in print.

During the years after 1929 Krishnamurti largely traveled about the world, except for the World War II years, which he spent in retirement in Ojai. (Ojai became Krishnamurti's regular home, and he attained permanent resident status in the United States in 1977.) During these tours he gave public lectures and engaged in dialogues with audiences in which he tried to communicate his vision of truth as an attitude and a knowing beyond words, located in the present. He also began founding schools, in India, Europe, Canada, and the United States. He particularly enjoyed dialogues with small groups. The lecture tours and the schools were supported by a roster of patrons, some quite wealthy, in India, Europe, and North and South America; in the late 1960s Krishnamurti foundations in England, the United States, and elsewhere were formed to further his work. After his death, these foundations maintained communication among his followers and handled distribution of the large number of Krishnamurti books, audiotapes, and videotapes.

Krishnamurti's teaching, in brief, was that truth is not found in verbal or intellectual formulation but in the "choiceless awareness" of daily existence and mental activity. We construct symbols and beliefs, even what we call knowledge, in the hope of securing the universe with them, but they become chains that bind the mind far more than they control infinite reality. True freedom, therefore, is "freedom from the known" (in the title of one of his books). It lies in simple observation without past or future, simple doing without knowing, without agonizing over choices on the basis of our always imperfect knowledge.

Krishnamurti's appeal comes from his simple yet far-reaching message of the possibility of uncomplicated truth and life and in his extraordinary personal air of spirituality. George Bernard Shaw once called him "the most beautiful human being I ever saw." Whatever his lasting importance, few people have had so unusual a life and few have so gracefully renounced one highly exalted spiritual opportunity and embraced another.

• Mary Lutyens's *Krishnamurti: The Years of Awakening* (1975) and *Krishnamurti: The Years of Fulfillment* (1983) are a standard biography; they are summarized, with additional material, in her *The Life and Death of Krishnamurti* (1990). The important perspective of an Indian associate can be found in Pupul Jayakar, *Krishnamurti: A Biography* (1986). Sidney Field, *Krishnamurti: The Reluctant Messiah* (1989), is an informal memoir of a long friendship. A more controversial memoir that brings out some alleged very human characteristics of the teacher is Radha Rajagopal Sloss, *Lives in the Shadow with J. Krishnamurti* (1991).

Krishnamurti's own books, some twenty-five, largely collections of lectures, include *The First and Last Freedom* (1954), *Commentaries on Living* (3 series: 1956, 1958, 1960), *Freedom from the Known* (1969), *Exploration into Insight* (1980), and two interesting autobiographical fragments from journals, *Krishnamurti's Notebook* (1976) and *Krishnamurti's Journal* (1982).

ROBERT S. ELLWOOD

KRIZA, John (15 Jan. 1919–18 Aug. 1975), ballet dancer, was born in Berwyn, Illinois, the son of John Kriza, who ran a meat market, and Marie Billy. Kriza's parents came to America from Czechoslovakia. His mother introduced him to dance, enrolling her underweight seven-year-old son in a ballet class to strengthen him. Upon graduation from Morton Junior College, Kriza continued his dance studies with Mildred Parchal in Berwyn, Illinois, and then with Bentley Stone in Chicago. In 1938 and 1939 he gained performance experience with the Chicago Dance Project of the WPA Federal Theatre Project and the Chicago Civic Opera Ballet under Ruth Page's directorship, and in 1940 he toured South America with the first American ballet company to do so, the Page-Stone company.

A turning point came when Kriza decided to explore career possibilities in New York. He is reported to have auditioned three times on the same day for Ballet Russe de Monte Carlo, for a musical comedy on Broadway, and for Ballet Theatre. Kriza was successful at all of these auditions, but he decided to accept Ballet Theatre's offer, joining them for their inaugural 1940–1941 season. He then danced with Lincoln Kirstein's American Ballet Caravan, touring South America in 1941. His roles included a marine in Antony Tudor's *Time Table*, the Hermit in the Lew Christensen-José Fernandez *Pastorela*, and Polka: Couple in Black and White in George Balanchine's *Divertimento*. Upon his return he rejoined Ballet Theatre, appearing on short notice in *Gala Performance* and *The Beloved*. In succeeding seasons Kriza created roles in virtually every important ballet in Ballet Theatre's increasingly varied repertory. His career also ventured into films as he appeared in *Yo Bailé Con Don Porfro* (1942), *Yolanda* (1943), and *The Three Musketeers* (1943).

In Tudor's *Dim Lustre* (1943), Kriza was given one of the most challenging variations ever choreographed by Tudor, with rapid turns and leaps. He danced it superbly, without sacrificing the romantic atmosphere of the piece. During the 1944 season Johnny (as he was affectionately known) took over Anton Dolin's role of the evil prince in Agnes de Mille's *Tally-Ho!* and received praise for his Drummer Variation in David Lichine's *Graduation Ball* (1944).

The same year saw the creation of one of the most significant roles of Kriza's repertory—the Second Sailor in *Fancy Free*. It provided an opportunity to display his proficient technique, exuberant personality, and gift for characterization. Furthermore, he exemplified an American-born dancer performing a quintessentially American role. As American-made ballet continued to assert its independence from European forbears, Kriza's dancing contributed to its rising status.

The lead role of the antagonist Pat Garrett in the 1944 revival of Eugene Loring's *Billy the Kid* again formed an important element of Kriza's repertory, and he was later to perform the lead for over two decades, skillfully portraying the transformation of a young boy into a ruthless frontier killer. His association with Robbins was renewed with the creation of two roles created for Kriza: the Blues Duet in *Interplay* (1945), and Another Man in *Facsimile* (1946). The teamwork of the trio in *Facsimile*, comprising Kriza, Nora Kaye, and Robbins, was commended for "conveying complete artistic justification to every move and gesture" (Amberg, p. 139).

Kriza was increasingly recognized as a highly talented dancer with a genial personality that made him popular among colleagues and audiences. In 1948 he was guest artist with the New York City Ballet; he also guested with the Chicago Opera Ballet and Sociedad Pro-Arte, Havana.

In 1951 Ballet Theatre and Britain's Royal Ballet were on the same touring circuit, with Kriza's and Nora Kaye's version of the Black Swan pas de deux from *Swan Lake* reviewed more favorably than Margot Fonteyn's and Robert Helpmann's rendition. Kriza had proved himself an adept partner, and Roland Petit came to New York especially to stage *Les Demoiselles de la Nuit* (1951), bringing with him Colette Marchand to dance the leading role with Kriza.

A brief venture into musical comedy followed with Kriza's appearance in *Kiss Me Kate* and *Brigadoon* as well as some nightclub, vaudeville, TV spots and summer stock in Cohasset, Massachusetts (1952). Kriza had earlier performed in summer stock, but his first love remained classical dance, and in 1953 he joined Ballet Theatre's tour of the Soviet Union, receiving ovations at the Bolshoi.

When a *Dance Magazine* interviewer asked Kriza in 1954 to name his favorite role, he replied "I haven't got one—it's always fun to try something new" (Lansdale, p. 34). This penchant to explore new horizons was also evident in Kriza's life away from theater. In his mid-thirties the dancer took on a 75-acre dairy farm, about an hour from Chicago's Loop. A tenant managed the herd of twenty Holstein cows and grew corn and oats. The home was equipped with a darkroom for Kriza to develop his photographs, and it provided a retreat where he could relax between Ballet Theatre engagements.

Throughout the 1950s and 1960s Kriza's dancing career flourished. He was complimented for performances as Colin in *La Fille Mal Gardée* (1955), making the lover come alive as a believable character and dancing with elegant finish. Kriza was equally comfortable in classical romantic and dramatic roles. Further roles included His Imperial Excellency in Tudor's *Offenbach in the Underworld* (1956), Stanley in Valerie Bettis's *A Streetcar Named Desire* (1956), Leonardo in Alfred Rodrigues's *Blood Wedding* (1957), principal dancer in Herbert Ross's *Concerto* (1958), principal dancer in Job Sanders's *The Taming* (pas de deux, 1962), and First Intruder in Bentley Stone's *L'Inconnue* (1963).

Kriza's career took on a more administrative cast in 1966, when he became assistant director of American Ballet Theatre, overseeing stage revivals. He also taught classes and became known as "Mr. Ballet Theatre." Company trustee Charles Payne declared that he occupied a unique and very special position within the company, similar to that later filled by Mikhail Baryshnikov; both were "understanding, cooperative, generous of their time and talent, blessed with humor sometimes sly but always good, and, above all, totally dedicated to the integrity of their art" (Payne, p. 345).

Both Baryshnikov and Kriza participated in the company's thirty-fifth anniversary celebrations in January 1975. It was one of the last major dance events that Kriza attended. He died the same year near Naples, Florida, drowning in the Gulf of Mexico while visiting his sister. He never married.

• Further resources are available at the Dance Collection, The New York Public Library for the Performing Arts, Lincoln Center. Contemporary accounts of Kriza's dancing and popularity are in George Amberg, *Ballet—The Emergence of an American Art* (1949); Nelson Lansdale, "Versatile John Kriza," *Dance Magazine*, July 1954, pp. 33–34; Walter Owen, "Meet John Kriza," *Dance Magazine*, Dec. 1945, p. 15; and Rosalyn Krokover, *The New Borzoi Book of Ballets* (1956). Secondary sources include Martha Bremser, ed., *International Dictionary of Ballet* (1993), and Charles Payne, *American Ballet Theatre* (1977).

MELANIE TRIFONA CHRISTOUDIA

KROC, Ray (5 Oct. 1902–14 Jan. 1984), franchise industry pioneer and baseball team owner, was born Raymond Albert Kroc in Oak Park, Illinois, the son of Louis Kroc, a Western Union employee, and Rose Hrach. Baseball was his greatest childhood passion. He became an avid Chicago Cubs fan at an early age and attended games frequently. Thanks to his mother, he also became an accomplished pianist early in life.

Kroc dropped out of high school after his sophomore year to join the Red Cross as an ambulance driver. The United States had just entered World War I and the fifteen-year-old Kroc was anxious to be at the center of things. After some discussion, his parents allowed him to lie about his age and enlist. Kroc was sent to New Jersey and assigned to the same company as the sixteen-year-old Walt Disney. The war ended before their training was completed.

Kroc returned to school but dropped out after one semester. His main interests were music and making money. A good jazz pianist, he eventually worked for several popular local bands. He met his first wife, Ethyl Fleming, while playing at a resort in Michigan. They were married in 1922 and had one child.

Kroc had become a salesman for the Lily-Tulip company shortly before his marriage. To supplement his wages he played piano at radio station WGES. One of his incidental duties was finding talent to fill air time. One of his hires was a song-and-comedy team called "Sam and Henry." They later changed their name to "Amos and Andy" and went on to become the most famous radio comedy duo of the 1920s.

Driven by the fear of ending up like his father, who he felt was always scrambling to make ends meet, Kroc was continually looking for the chance to make more money. In 1926 the Chicago papers were filled with stories of fortunes being made in the Florida land boom. Proud of his abilities as a salesman, Kroc arranged a five-month leave of absence from Lily and moved to Florida to try his hand at real estate, but the boom collapsed shortly after the Krocs arrived. Nearly destitute, Kroc took a job playing piano in a nightclub to earn the money to send his wife and daughter back to Chicago. He followed along later in the couple's Model T.

Kroc later recalled the trip back to Chicago as one of the lowest points in his life. It was late September 1926, and he was too poor to buy an overcoat or gloves for the trip home. He arrived late on a cold, windy night. As he later told an interviewer for *Nation's Business*, he was "frozen stiff, disillusioned and broke." He was also determined to stop moonlighting and focus all of his efforts on doing one job, but doing it very well. He returned to Lily-Tulip and stayed for the next ten years, ending as the midwestern sales manager.

Kroc prospered during the Great Depression; he liked selling and traveling and understood the restaurant business, but he eventually became restless for his big opportunity. He thought he found it in the multimixer, a multispindled milkshake maker. He left Lily-Tulip in 1937 to set up a company to sell the machine, invented by one of his customers, and in 1939, after a rocky two-year partnership with his former supervisor at Lily-Tulip, Kroc became sole owner of Prince Castle. Sales improved substantially under Kroc's ownership, but the outbreak of World War II and accompanying restrictions on the use of copper for civilian goods ended production of the multimixer for the war's duration.

Kroc's decision to quit Lily-Tulip began the deterioration of his first marriage. The depression was still on, and his wife was incredulous that he would give up a well-paying job to start an unknown business selling an untried product. Kroc, who was critically short of money in the early years at Prince Castle, felt betrayed when his wife refused to work for the new firm.

The multimixer business boomed in the years immediately after World War II, but by the mid-1950s the decline of the soda fountain threatened Prince Cas-

tle's future. Accordingly, Kroc began to look for new outlets for the multimixer. One place that drew his notice was McDonald's, a little drive-in operated by Maurice and Richard McDonald in San Bernardino, California. McDonald's was using eight multimixers, far more than any other restaurant in the United States. In April 1954 Kroc decided to visit the place that needed the ability to make forty milkshakes at one time. To his amazement, it was a little octagonal building with no indoor seating. It served only burgers (fifteen cents), fries (a dime), and drinks. Meals were produced assembly-line fashion, and it typically took less than a minute for a customer to place his order and receive his meal.

Kroc was fascinated with the system's potential. As he watched the quickly moving line of customers wrap around a corner of the building, Kroc became fairly certain he had found what he needed to revive multimixer sales. After the lunch rush he introduced himself to the McDonalds and toured their stand. He returned the next day to see if they had any plans for expansion. They didn't. They had already sold fourteen licenses for McDonald's outlets to operators in California and Arizona and had been disappointed with the results.

Kroc offered to oversee the marketing of their name and system. He promised to deal with all problems and to scrupulously protect the McDonald's reputation by rigidly maintaining standards of quality, cleanliness, and service. Although initially somewhat skeptical, the brothers were quickly won over by Kroc's obvious enthusiasm, experience with the restaurant business, and sales ability. He returned to Chicago with a 99-year contract allowing him to serve as their exclusive agent. In exchange Kroc would receive 1.9 percent of every licensee's gross sales. The McDonalds were to receive .5 percent of all sales—this to come from Kroc's 1.9 percent. Kroc was required to copy the design of the McDonald's new restaurant, including its distinctive golden arches, and follow all their methods exactly. He opened the first store, with himself as part owner, in April 1955. By the end of the year he had sold seven additional franchises.

Kroc began McDonald's with the hope of selling more multimixers. As he became more involved with the business, however, he came to realize that his greatest profit lay in selling restaurants rather than mixers. Thus, in 1960, when he needed money to finance his divorce, he sold Prince Castle rather than his rights to McDonald's. By that time McDonald's had 238 units with total sales of $37 million.

Kroc bought out the McDonald brothers for $2.7 million in 1961. In 1965, when the company had nearly 700 units operating and needed money for further expansion, Kroc took the company public. By the end of the decade nearly 1,500 McDonald's were open worldwide. At the time of Kroc's death a new McDonald's was opening on average every seventeen hours.

Once, when asked to explain his company's remarkable success to an interviewer for the *New York Times Magazine*, Kroc claimed it was because "McDonald's people take the hamburger business just a little more seriously than anybody else." An idea of just how seriously can be gained by looking at the specifications for a McDonald's regular hamburger. Each patty was 3.875 inches wide and .221 inches thick, weighed 1.6 ounces, and was made of beef containing not more than 18.9 percent fat. Similar exacting standards existed for every other product sold.

An even more important reason for McDonald's success was the corporation's ability to produce hamburger stands with the same efficiency and uniformity as its franchisees produced hamburgers. The corporation's most important product was restaurants—not hamburgers. Beginning in the early 1960s McDonald's pioneered in developing a corporate infrastructure capable of producing and supporting small firms at high volume and relatively low cost. By the mid-1960s, when franchisees purchased the right to open a McDonald's restaurant, they received a professionally located site holding a distinctive, well designed, and fully equipped outlet selling a well established and heavily advertised product. Franchise holders received intensive training in every phase of operations and management and close, continuing support from the corporate office. Most small firms fail within five years; in contrast, during McDonald's first thirty years only one franchisee failed. During the mid-1960s, when a typical outlet cost between $110,000 and $125,000, the company charged a $10,000 franchise fee and collected a bit over 10 percent of gross monthly sales in rent and royalties.

Although McDonald's was the axis around which his world revolved, Kroc's private life changed greatly after 1956, when he met Joan Smith. He divorced his first wife in 1961 in an unsuccessful attempt to woo the also unhappily married Smith. Shortly after Smith's rejection Kroc married Jane Dobbins Green in 1962 but remained smitten with Smith. When they next met in late 1968 Kroc convinced her they should marry. Kroc divorced Green in 1968 and married Smith in early 1969. He had no children with Green or Smith.

His union with Smith was happy and perhaps as a result Kroc, who had just retired from the presidency of McDonald's, but remained chairman of the board, began to spend a bit more time on noncompany matters. Among the most significant of these were his charitable contributions. Kroc focused his giving on three areas, medical research, substance-abuse programs, and child welfare. Because of his lifelong interest in the Chicago Cubs, Kroc tried to buy the team. The owner was unwilling to sell, however, so in 1974 Kroc bought the only team then available, the San Diego Padres, for $10 million. He quickly gained a reputation as an active and colorful figure. After the first, and poorly played, home game of the 1974 season, for example, Kroc stormed into the press box and used the ballpark's public address system to apologize to the fans and to scold the team for its poor performance.

Kroc had a major impact on American society and American business. McDonald's and its imitators changed what, where, and how Americans eat. By 1990 roughly 160,000 fast-food outlets blanketed the United States and, according to a National Restaurant Association survey, only 4 percent of Americans never ate fast food.

One of the chief reasons fast food became ubiquitous in American culture was the development of business-format franchising, a system that allows big firms, with their greater resources and efficiencies, to actually manufacture small firms. McDonald's set the standards in both these industries. Much of McDonald's success can be traced directly to Kroc's almost fanatical devotion to the company. Others were more important in developing the systems that allowed McDonald's to cover the globe with restaurants, but it was Kroc whose focus on quality, uniformity, and cleanliness allowed McDonald's to separate itself from the competition. Kroc died in San Diego.

• Kroc's personal papers are held by the McDonald's Archives, located in Elk Grove, Ill.; however, they are not open to the public. The two best sources of Kroc's life are Ray Kroc (with Robert Anderson), *Grinding It Out: The Making of McDonald's* (1978), and John Love, *Behind the Arches* (1986). For a good brief treatment, see Ted C. Hinckley and Roderick C. Johnson, "Ray Kroc, Embodiment of Mid-Twentieth Century America," *Journal of the West* 25 (Jan. 1986): 94–102, and "For Ray Kroc, Life Began at 50. Or Was It 60?" *Forbes*, Jan. 1973, pp. 24–30. For an interesting, wide-ranging interview with Kroc, see "Appealing to a Mass Market," *Nation's Business*, July 1968, pp. 71–74. An obituary is in the *New York Times*, 15 Jan. 1984.

THOMAS S. DICKE

KROEBER, Alfred Louis (11 June 1876–5 Oct. 1960), anthropologist, was born in Hoboken, New Jersey, the son of Florence Martin Kroeber, an importer of European clocks, and Johanna Muller. The family soon returned to New York City, where Alfred's younger brother and two sisters were born. Both parents were of upper-middle-class German-American Protestant stock, respectful of learning and the arts. German was the household language. Young Alfred was educated first by a tutor and then in private schools. He entered Columbia College in 1892, earning an A.B. in literature in 1896 and an A.M. in 1897.

At the start of his graduate studies Kroeber enrolled in a course in American Indian languages offered by anthropologist Franz Boas, who had joined the Columbia faculty that year. Boas had his students analyze narratives in the Chinook language, which he had transcribed during fieldwork in Oregon, so that they could discover the underlying structure of the language. Intrigued, Kroeber again enrolled in Boas's course the next year and had the opportunity to do firsthand research in language and culture with six Eskimo people whom explorer Robert Peary had brought from the central Arctic. He also took Boas's other two course offerings, in physical anthropology and statistical theory, and several courses in psychology with other faculty members. In 1899 he made his first field trip, to study the Arapaho Indians living in

Oklahoma, and the following year he visited the Wyoming branch of the Arapaho and other Plains tribes. By this time he was firmly committed to the new discipline of anthropology.

From August to December 1900 Kroeber worked as curator of anthropological collections for the small California Academy of Sciences in San Francisco. Finishing the basic work on the collections, he asked for funds for a brief field trip to northwestern California, where he visited the Yurok tribe along the lower Klamath River and the adjacent coast. He returned to San Francisco, requested additional field funds, and visited the Yokuts in the southern San Joaquin Valley and the Mohave in the southeastern California desert. Back in San Francisco at year's end, he was told that the academy board could not afford to provide curators with funds for fieldwork and that he was being dismissed. Kroeber returned to New York, where in 1901 he completed his dissertation on symbolism in Arapaho art and received the first doctorate in anthropology to be awarded by Columbia University.

Having glimpsed the diversity of California Indian languages and cultures, Kroeber sought to return to the state. His opportunity came from Phoebe Apperson Hearst, a regent of the University of California and widow of mining magnate George Hearst, who hoped to collect artifacts for a proposed, but never completed, university museum. Between 1899 and 1905 she sponsored archaeological fieldwork, most notably by German-born Max Uhle in Peru and by Harvard-trained George A. Reisner in the Nile Valley of Egypt.

By 1901 Hearst was also considering establishing at the University of California at Berkeley a center for anthropological research in California Indian culture. On the advice of Zelia Nuttall, an archaeologist and Hearst's personal friend, Hearst and Berkeley president Benjamin Ide Wheeler decided to employ Kroeber immediately. When Kroeber arrived back in California in late August 1901, there was, as yet, no official department of anthropology at Berkeley, but on 10 September the other university regents approved Hearst's offer to fund for five years a department that would have a museum component and a publishing and public lecture program, and would eventually offer classroom instruction. Frederic Ward Putnam, curator of Harvard's Peabody Museum of American Archaeology, was to head an advisory committee; Kroeber was to be the department's instructor; and Pliny Earle Goddard, a graduate student of linguistics with Wheeler, was to be the assistant. Two years later Putnam was named professor of anthropology and chairman of the Berkeley department, with the plan that he would continue his work at the Peabody and spend his summers in Berkeley. Because of Putnam's increasingly poor health, however, Kroeber was, in effect, the day-to-day administrator of the department almost from its beginnings, and certainly after December 1902, when Hearst's secretary, Gerald d'Aquin, relinquished his duties as executive officer of the advisory committee to Kroeber.

In the spring of 1902, at Wheeler's behest, Kroeber taught the department's first course, in North American ethnology. Concentrating on Eskimo and Pueblo and Plains Indian cultures, the course attracted six students. Kroeber then spent nearly six months in linguistic fieldwork, collaborating with Roland B. Dixon of Harvard on an initial survey of the many Indian languages spoken in California. Concentrating on the Yurok and the Karok of the Klamath, on the Yuki of the north central coast, and the Mohave of the southeastern desert, he also made a survey of the central coastal area between Santa Barbara and San Francisco. There, among the scattered survivors of the Spanish mission system, he took down short vocabularies in the Chumash, Salinan, and Costanoan languages. In November he reported to Putnam and Hearst that the the "linguistic map of the state, hitherto a chaos, is now reduced to the beginnings of a system" (Phoebe A. Hearst Papers, 3 Nov. 1902).

Following these six months, the most intensive period of fieldwork in Kroeber's long career, Kroeber and Dixon continued intermittently to collaborate on the survey project until 1919, when they produced their principal paper, "Linguistic Families of California" published in the Berkeley department's monograph series, *Univ. of Calif. Publications in Am. Archaeology and Ethnology* 16:47–118. By that time, with the help of linguists Edward Sapir and John P. Harrington, they had established interrelationships between languages and thus were able to reduce the number of language stocks in California from John Wesley Powell's earlier estimate of twenty-two to six.

In 1903 Hearst's museum collections were moved from a corrugated iron storage structure on the Berkeley campus into a four-story building at the Affiliated Colleges in San Francisco, where they remained until 1931. The storehouse in Berkeley, with some minor remodeling, thereupon became headquarters for the anthropology department for the next fifty years. This physical setting, which, according to Kroeber's biographer Julian Steward, "verged on the ludicrous" (*Am. Anthropologist* 63:1045) did not diminish the department's academic standards. By the fall of 1903 Kroeber and his colleague Goddard had arranged to offer four years of undergraduate coursework at Berkeley. Kroeber again taught North American ethnology and added courses in North American languages and in the Indians of California. Goddard in the spring semester offered a course that concentrated on the Athabascan speakers of northern California, particularly the Hupa, and another in laboratory phonetics. In 1908 the department awarded its first doctorate to Samuel A. Barrett, whose dissertation was on Pomo basketry.

The future of the department appeared uncertain between 1904 and 1908, when Hearst's income was greatly reduced because of capital expenditures needed at her mine holdings. In 1905 she pledged, nevertheless, to support the anthropology department on a smaller scale for another three years. Although in 1908 the regents took on the responsibility for Kroeber and Goddard's salaries and allocated a small sum for general expenses, there was no longer enough money for field research.

Edward Sapir, a brilliant student of Boas's, had spent the 1907–1908 academic year as a research assistant at Berkeley, working with a few Northern and Central Yana speakers in the upper Sacramento Valley. The year marked the start of a steady correspondence between Kroeber and Sapir on linguistic issues and on the personalities in the coterie of American anthropologists.

In 1909 Goddard, seeing an uncertain future in California, accepted an offer from the American Museum of Natural History in New York. With Putnam's retirement that year, Kroeber became head of the Berkeley department, but, unable to find a suitable replacement for Goddard, he taught all four undergraduate and three graduate courses himself. Adding to this strain was worry over the health of his wife, Henriette Rothschild of San Francisco, whom he had married in 1906. Diagnosed as tuberculous, she died in 1913.

Thomas T. Waterman and Nels C. Nelson became instructors in Kroeber's department in 1910. Nelson took over the archaeology courses but stayed only two years before he too was lured to the American Museum. Waterman, a colorful personality, became Kroeber's somewhat erratic mainstay from 1910 to 1917 and again in 1920–1921. Waterman's popularity as a teacher caused undergraduate enrollments to soar; as a consequence, graduate courses suffered, and no doctorates were granted at Berkeley between 1911 and 1926.

In 1912 Kroeber hired Edward W. Gifford as assistant curator of the museum in San Francisco. With only a high school education, Gifford gradually assumed most of the supervision at the museum, undertook ethnological fieldwork, and became a part-time instructor of anthropology.

When Kroeber and Waterman learned in 1911 that a "wild" American Indian had been found at Oroville in the upper Sacramento Valley, they conjectured that he was a member of a Yana group. Kroeber sent Waterman to Oroville to secure the Yana's release from jail. In San Francisco the Yana was given shelter at the museum, and Kroeber gave him the name Ishi, which meant "man" in the Yahi dialect of Yana, a dialect not previously known to linguists. Sam Batwi, a speaker of the related Central Yana dialect, was returned to his home after the two anthropologists adjudged him to be personally uncongenial to Ishi. Thereafter Ishi had to be his own interpreter.

In the summer of 1915 Kroeber was finally able to arrange for Sapir to come to Berkeley from Ottawa, Canada, to work on Yahi linguistics with Ishi. Their two months' work, although difficult, was fruitful because of Sapir's "brute memory" of elements from other Yana dialects (Kroeber papers, Additions, 23 Sept. 1915). Ishi, who had had previous bouts of illness, became seriously ill that August and died of tuberculosis in March 1916. His death, which occurred while Kroeber was in New York on his first sabbatical, seems to have affected Kroeber deeply, coming less

than three years after his wife's death. In the spring of 1918 Kroeber requested a leave of absence and returned to New York, where he underwent a brief psychoanalysis. Besides the difficulties of his inward life he was also suffering periodic physical pain as a result of a serious illness, which he later discovered was Ménière's disease and which destroyed his hearing in one ear. Back in California, he spent much of his time between 1920 and 1923 practicing as a lay analyst in San Francisco before returning wholeheartedly to anthropology.

By 1917 Kroeber had already completed his massive *Handbook of the Indians of California* (1925), a compilation of the available information on the Californian tribes, most of it Kroeber's own data but also drawing on material collected by Goddard, Sapir, Gifford, Barrett, Waterman, and Nelson. Kroeber's next major undertaking, *Anthropology* (1923), was the first textbook in the new discipline and one that attracted a sizable general audience because of its readability. In this work Kroeber argued that there was no objective evidence of the inferiority of any racial group, especially that of blacks. The book was widely used until it was superseded by a larger and more sophisticated version in 1948.

In 1921, after Waterman's second departure from Berkeley, Kroeber invited Robert H. Lowie, formerly with the American Museum, to join him on the Berkeley faculty. Like Kroeber, Lowie had been a student of Boas, and he had taught at Berkeley for a time during the previous decade. A close colleague until Kroeber's retirement in 1946, Lowie chaired the department for eleven of the twenty-five years that the two men worked together. Kroeber credited him with developing a systematic program of graduate studies. As an element of this program, Kroeber strongly recommended that doctoral students write ethnological reports on traditional western North American cultures while information could still be gleaned from tribal elders. Of the thirty-four dissertations written in the Berkeley department between 1926 and 1946, all but six were works that salvaged ethnographical traditions. In the 1930s two younger faculty members joined the department: Ronald L. Olson (in 1931), whose primary responsibility was to teach the introductory classes in physical and cultural anthropology; and Theodore D. McCown (in 1938), who taught advanced classes in physical anthropology and Old World archaeology.

In 1924, while on a brief trip to the Valley of Mexico, Kroeber made his first archaeological excavations. During the next two years he undertook two longer archaeological expeditions, these to Peru. The 1925 trip was inspired by studies that he and his student W. D. Strong had made of Max Uhle's collections of pottery from sites at Chincha and Ica. At Cañete, working at a site that Uhle had not explored, Kroeber found two previously unknown pottery styles. The following year he found and sketched the now famous desert markings at Nazca, and excavated burials in prehistoric cemeteries along the periphery of the Nazca Valley.

Archaeologist John H. Rowe regarded these finds as Kroeber's major archaeological discoveries. The five monographs Kroeber published on his Peruvian field-work set a new standard of reporting in Peruvian archaeology, although his chronology was later superseded.

In 1926, between his two trips to Peru, Kroeber married Theodora Kracaw Brown, a beginning graduate student in anthropology at Berkeley; she was the widowed mother of two young sons, whom Kroeber adopted. The marriage resulted in two children of their own. Their daughter, Ursula K. Le Guin, became a noted writer of fiction.

From 1934 to 1938 Kroeber conducted "culture element" surveys of western Indians. Under his direction, thirteen investigators gathered yes-or-no responses to hundreds of questions about ethnographic traits from one or two representatives of 254 tribes or bands. The aim, according to Kroeber's *The Nature of Culture* (1952), was to ensure "greater comparability of cultural information" than existed in published ethnographies (p. 263). He acknowledged, however, that contemporary ethnologists and social anthropologists had paid little attention to the twenty-five survey reports because they were then more interested in studies of tribal acculturation or were averse to quantitative treatments. Kroeber's important *Cultural and Natural Areas of Native North America* (1939) was actually written in 1931, before the first culture element surveys were begun. This work dealt with culture wholes and with culture centers, or locales of greatest cultural productivity. Here he expressed his unchanging view that "cultures occur in nature as wholes; and these wholes can never be entirely formulated through consideration of their elements" (p. 4).

Starting in the early 1920s Kroeber had regularly taught an advanced undergraduate course called "Outlines of Culture Growth," which had examined human origins, the beginnings of culture, and Old World civilizations. The lengthy manuscript that evolved from the course, *Configurations of Culture Growth*, was written between 1931 and 1938 but not published until 1944 because the sheer bulk of Kroeber's evidence met with resistance from publishers. In this work Kroeber examined the wavelike character of culture growth and the clustering of recognized geniuses in certain periods and particular countries. Although anthropologists were respectful of the effort that went into the writing of *Configurations*, it has probably been the least influential of Kroeber's major works.

During World War II Kroeber was asked to coordinate an Army Specialized Training Program at Berkeley to teach the Chinese, Japanese, Thai, and Vietnamese languages to selected trainees who, it was planned, would accompany American invasion forces landing in Asia. Kroeber, under great pressure, had a heart attack in September 1943. He was a semi-invalid for months and resumed his ASTP work only as an adviser.

Kroeber retired in 1946 and thereafter accepted guest lectureships at several American universities: Harvard (1947–1948), Columbia (1948–1952), Brandeis (1954), and Yale (1958). He continued to write, completing a number of linguistic and ethnographic studies he had begun in the first decade of the century. In March 1960 a new anthropology building was dedicated at Berkeley, with space for the museum of anthropology. The building was named for Kroeber, who was present at the dedication. In September 1960 he traveled to Burg Wartenstein, Austria, to chair an international symposium on "anthropological horizons," sponsored by the Wenner-Gren Foundation for Anthropological Research. After the conference he and his wife vacationed in Paris, where he died suddenly in their hotel room.

Kroeber is regarded as the successor to Franz Boas for his fieldwork and his writings on American Indian—especially Californian—linguistics and ethnology. He directed a leading academic department of anthropology for over forty years, and his students led the profession for a generation after him. Among the honors that he received were membership in the National Academy of Sciences, honorary degrees from several of the most prominent universities in the United States, and—in 1946—the Huxley Medal from the Royal Anthropological Institute in London, the highest honor in British anthropology. Regarded as the last of the great generalists in his academic discipline, he made notable contributions to archaeology and cultural anthropology, and in fact to all fields of anthropology except physical anthropology.

• Kroeber's papers are in three collections at the Bancroft Library, University of California, Berkeley: the A. L. Kroeber Papers, the Department and Museum of Anthropology Archives, and the Phoebe A. Hearst Papers. Some reminiscences about his own boyhood appear in Kroeber's contribution to the collective memoir *Carl Alsberg, Scientist at Large*, ed. Joseph S. Davis (1948). Theodora Kroeber provided an evocative biography of her husband in *Alfred Kroeber: A Personal Configuration* (1970); the book is not, however, generally reliable on dates. See also her classic account, *Ishi in Two Worlds* (1961), on the relationship of Kroeber and Ishi. For Kroeber's and Sapir's discoveries of the relationships between California Indian languages, see *The Sapir-Kroeber Correspondence: Letters between Edward Sapir and A. L. Kroeber, 1905–1925*, ed. Victor Golla (1984).

Ralph Beals's entry on Kroeber in David L. Sills, ed., *International Encyclopedia of the Social Sciences* (1968–1979), vol. 8, concerns Kroeber's theoretical views. Julian Steward, *Alfred Kroeber* (1973), is a brief biography with some selected writings by the subject. For later commentaries see Timothy H. H. Thoresen, "Kroeber and the Yurok, 1900–1908," an introduction to Kroeber's important *Yurok Myths* (1976); Eric R. Wolf, "Alfred L. Kroeber," *Totems and Teachers: Perspectives on the History of Anthropology*, ed. Sydel Silverman (1981); and Thomas Buckley, "Kroeber's Theory of Culture Areas and the Ethnology of Northwestern California," *Anthropological Quarterly* 62 (1989): 15–26.

Obituaries and memoirs by former students or colleagues include Steward, "Alfred Louis Kroeber, 1876–1960," *American Anthropologist* 63 (1961): 1038–60, which is followed by Kroeber's bibliography to 1961, compiled by Ann J. Gibson and John H. Rowe; Dell Hymes, "Alfred Louis Kroeber," *Language* 37 (1961): 1–28, on Kroeber's contributions to linguistics; and John H. Rowe, "Alfred Louis Kroeber, 1876–1960," *American Antiquity* 27 (1962): 395–415, on his contributions to archaeology.

GRACE WILSON BUZALJKO

KROEGER, Alice Bertha (2 May 1864–31 Oct. 1909), librarian and administrator, was born in St. Louis, Missouri, the daughter of Adolph Ernst Kroeger, a journalist, philosopher, and translator, and Eliza Bertha Curren. Kroeger's father participated in a philosophical organization in St. Louis headed by William Torrey Harris, who was known among librarians for devising a classification scheme antedating Melvil Dewey's. Adolph Kroeger served as a municipal treasurer and became involved in a misunderstanding that resulted in his conviction for forgery in 1870. Although he was subsequently exonerated, his two-year prison term deeply embarrassed his family and may have contributed to Alice Kroeger's lifelong shyness.

Kroeger attended the public schools of St. Louis, earning a high school diploma in 1881 at age seventeen. She could not attend college at that time because of the financial needs of her family and instead took a job as a clerk in the St. Louis Public Library. While working there from 1882 to 1889, she developed her library expertise and experience from practice rather than formal education. The library's administrator, Frederick M. Crunden, affirmed her special ability for the profession and her literary background. In 1889 at the American Library Association's annual meeting in St. Louis, Kroeger was recognized by noted librarian Charles A. Cutter. Because she was too shy to speak, he summarized her suggestions about cataloging work and its relation to public service, with its emphasis on catalogers knowing what the public needs. Kroeger felt that this rapport could best be accomplished by having catalogers work at the reference desk for part of the time so that they would know how to handle cataloging problems more effectively.

In 1889 Kroeger enrolled in the New York State Library School at Albany, where Melvil Dewey was the guiding spirit, but she stayed only until April 1890, when she accepted a cataloging position at the St. Louis Public Library. In 1891 she returned to the library school at Albany to continue her schooling and graduated with highest honors. She felt that even while she learned librarianship from practice, she had also developed specialized knowledge from formal schooling. Librarianship had attracted several future leaders in this growing profession, including Kroeger, Katharine L. Sharp, Mary E. Robbins, Salome Cutler Fairchild, and Mary Wright Plummer, all of whom were Dewey's protégés.

In the fall of 1891 Kroeger became librarian of the Drexel Institute of Art, Science and Industry when it opened in Philadelphia. A year later (Nov. 1892) she launched the library school at Drexel, which was modeled after the New York State Library School at Albany. Dewey, the leading library educator of the day, recommended to the institute's president, James McAlister, that Kroeger be made director of the Drexel library school. Only the third library school after Albany to open in the United States, Drexel responded to the need for trained librarians at a time when the public library system was rapidly expanding, a response that added impetus to the development of librarianship as a profession. Initially technical in nature, the program focused on the core subjects of library economy and cataloging but included other subjects like bibliography, the history of books and printing, and English literature. Students competed by rigorous examination for admission to the eight-month program. From the beginning Kroeger headed a growing faculty that included McAlister, who taught a course on the history of books and printing.

Library schools in other areas of the country had preceded Drexel. Pratt Institute in Brooklyn opened in 1890, and the Armour Institute in Chicago opened in 1892. While these schools dealt with the vocational aspect of librarianship, their curricula included the application of arts and sciences, the goal to prepare library directors and leaders modeled closely on the program at Albany. Kroeger formally announced the new, enriched curriculum at Drexel and how it would be established in 1892.

In addition to her job as a library educator, Kroeger was also a scholar. Her *Guide to the Study and Use of Reference Books* appeared in 1902. It has come out in numerous editions since then and has been the standard source for library professionals for almost 100 years. Originally published to assist students and library workers in the study of reference books and their selection, the *Guide* included 800 reference titles, and was the first compendium to bring together information on reference sources from diverse fields. A contemporary review noted that this book met a real need by helping to familiarize users with the better-known reference literature.

Kroeger participated actively in academic and professional circles. She was a lecturer at the University of Pennsylvania on the subject of bibliography, a fellow of the American Library Institute, a member of the American Library Association's Council, and a member of the ALA Committee on Library Training. The Committee on Library Training, under the aegis of the American Library Association, was established because of the profession's need to have an organized forum through which to assert its interests in the preparation of library workers. In 1903 this committee consisted of five women trained and encouraged by Dewey: Robbins, Plummer, Fairchild, Sharp, and Kroeger.

Kroeger's contemporaries regarded her as circumspect in dress and behavior. She was physically attractive but her personality was reticent and rigid. Some of her students later recalled being afraid of her. She devoted herself entirely to the library school and the profession, perhaps even to the detriment of her health. Kroeger died after a summer trip to Europe failed to improve her health. The cause was listed as heart failure, probably caused by neurasthenia or pernicious anemia.

Kroeger came into the nascent profession of librarianship at a period in history when women were beginning to articulate their right to full enfranchisement as citizens. As a spokeswoman for these ideals, and as a leading library educator, she instilled high standards of practice in the first women students. Recognizing that theory gained through education can improve practice, she focused on the significance of librarianship as a profession, and on the training of women who would become administrators in the growing system of public libraries in the United States. Her students regarded her educational method as one of "splendid systematic training." In addition to educating future librarians, Kroeger contributed frequently to library literature. Coming as it did in these early stages of librarianship, her *Guide to the Study and use of Reference Books* defined the genre of reference works as distinctive to librarianship's particular mission of information provision and systematic reading guidance. After her early death, her zeal for the profession was keenly missed at Drexel and in the library world.

• Kroeger details the Drexel curriculum in a report to the Minnetonka Conference *Bulletin of the American Library Association* (Sept. 1908). She is described by Laurel A. Grotzinger in "Dewey's Splendid Women and Their Impact on Library Education," *Milestones to the Present* (1978), pp. 125–52; by Doris Mariani in "Some Reminiscences of Alice B. Kroeger," *Graduate School of Library Science Newsletter* (Spring 1974); and by a former student in "Tribute to Alice Bertha Kroeger," *Library Journal* 34 (Dec. 1909): 551. Sarah K. Vann also writes of her in *Training for Librarianship before 1923* (1961). Kroeger's work is detailed in M. E. Nehlig, "The History and Development of the Drexel Institute Library School" (master's thesis, Drexel Institute School of Library Science, 1952); Edward D. McDonald and Edward M. Hinton, *Drexel Institute of Technology, 1891–1941: A Memorial History* (1942); and Guy Garrison, "Drexel University: Graduate School of Library Science," *Encyclopedia of Library and Information Science*, vol. 7 (1972), pp. 302–5. Her *Guide to the Study and Use Reference Books* is noted by Carl M. White in his *Historical Introduction to Library Education: Problems and Progress to 1951* (1976), and in Constance M. Winchell's preface to her *Guide to Reference Books* (1967). Patricia Archibald Burke also discusses it extensively in "Development of the *Guide to Reference Books* from Alice B. Kroeger to Constance M. Winchell" (Ph.D. diss., Univ. of N.C. at Chapel Hill, 1989).

MARY ELLEN COLLINS

KROEGER, Ernest Richard (10 Aug. 1862–7 Apr. 1934), organist, pianist, composer, and teacher, was born in St. Louis, Missouri, the son of Adolph Ernst Kroeger, a journalist, and Eliza B. A. Curren. He began studying piano with his father and later studied with Egmont Froelich, Waldemar Malmene, and Charles Kunkel. He studied music theory with Wilhelm Golder and Peter G. Anton, violin with Ernst Spiering, and instrumentation with Louis Mayer. He served as organist at several churches in St. Louis, including Trinity Episcopal (1878–1885), Grace Episcopal (1887), and Church of the Messiah (1885–1921). In 1879 he gave his first organ recital; then from 1893

to 1923 he performed an organ recital annually. He was also one of the founders of the American Guild of Organists in 1896. From 1893 to 1903 he served as the conductor of the Morning Choral Club and from 1910 to 1912 he directed the Amphion Club and was associated with other music societies. He was music director of Forest Park University from 1887 and head of his own Kroeger School of Music from 1904. He held both positions until his death. He served as president of the Music Teachers National Association in 1896 and then was president of the Missouri Music Teachers Association for two years (1897–1899). Kroeger was the master of musical programs for the Louisiana Purchase Exposition in 1904 (also known as the St. Louis World's Fair). He was a member of the French Academy from 1904 and was elected to the National Institute of Arts and Letters in 1915.

Kroeger taught and lectured at schools in St. Louis and elsewhere. He performed piano recitals in St. Louis and throughout the United States, being especially successful in lecture-recitals. His repertoire included more than 700 works. He played organ recitals at the Panama-Pacific Exposition in 1915. He taught instrumental courses at the University of California, Beckeley, in 1915 and at Cornell University from 1916 to 1923. He was musical director of the John Burroughs School and the extension division of Washington University (St. Louis). He contributed criticism to St. Louis newspapers at various times and also contributed articles to various music journals, including *Kunkel's Musical Review*, two volumes of the *Musical News* (Sept. 1897–Nov. 1898), the *Musical Bulletin*, and *Bulletin of the St. Louis Art League*. He married Laura A. Clark of Lebanon, Missouri, in 1891; they had four children. He died in St. Louis.

Among Kroeger's numerous compositions are *Hiawatha*, a symphonic overture that premiered in July 1898 by the Theodore Thomas Orchestra for the Omaha Exposition, and two pieces that premiered at the 1904 Louisiana Purchase Exposition, *March of the Indian Phantoms* and *Lalla Rookh*, a symphonic suite that was Kroeger's most successful orchestral composition and was performed many times by numerous orchestras. His *Festival Overture*, composed to commemorate the 100th anniversary of Missouri joining the Union, was first performed on 6 November 1921 by the Saint Louis Symphony Orchestra, and his symphonic poem *Mississippi, Father of Waters* premiered on 19 February 1926. He composed a symphony in B flat and wrote many organ works, including *March Pittoresque*, *Festal March*, and *Oriental Scenes*. He also composed and published six string quartets, several sonatas for solo instruments with piano, and several chamber works with piano, as well as some 175 piano pieces and more than 100 songs.

• In addition to the journals listed in the text, Kroeger also contributed the following articles to the *Proceedings of the Music Teachers' National Association*: "Methods versus Method," 4th ser., 31 (1909): 173–78, and "The Passing of a Virtuoso," 15th ser., 42 (1920): 152–57. Kroeger and his works are discussed in William Francis Collins, *Laurel Winners: Portraits and Silhouettes of American Composers* (1899); Rupert Hughes and Arthur Elson, *American Composers* (1900; repr. 1973); and Ernest C. Krohn, *A Century of American Music* (1924), repr. in *Missouri Music* (1971). Obituaries are in the *St. Louis Post-Dispatch* and the *St. Louis Globe Democrat*, both 8 Apr. 1934.

JAMES M. BURK

KROGER, Bernard Henry (24 Jan. 1860–21 July 1938), grocery store chain founder, was born in Cincinnati, Ohio, the son of John Henry Kroger and Mary Gertrude Schlebbe, dry-goods vendors. Both parents were immigrants from Germany, who met and married in the Cincinnati area. The Kroger family lived in rooms above their store, where the ten children worked alongside their parents. Under Mary's direction the family store thrived until the depression of 1873, when the business was lost. John Kroger died soon thereafter, and "Barney," as the young Kroger was known, and his siblings had to leave school in order to secure full-time employment. At age thirteen Barney found a job as a clerk in Rheum's drugstore in downtown Cincinnati. He enjoyed the work but stayed for only nine months. Later in life he explained that his reason for leaving Rheum's was because his work schedule prevented him from attending church on Sundays. Finding it difficult to locate another job in the city, he was hired on a farm near Pleasant Plain, Ohio, about thirty miles outside of Cincinnati. Work on the farm was hard, living conditions were sparse and unhealthy, and he was only paid $6 a month. After eighteen months in this situation, he contracted malaria and had to return home to Cincinnati. On the cold walk back to the city, Kroger later claimed, he vowed never to do farm work again and to prove himself in business, choosing Cincinnati as the place to do it.

Once back in the city, Kroger looked for a job that could begin the successful career that he envisioned. Still wearing his farm clothes, he was frequently heckled as he walked the streets looking for work. Soon, however, he found employment with the Great Northern and Pacific Tea Company, selling its products door-to-door. Kroger was hired despite the proprietor's reluctance to entrust his samples to a sixteen-year-old salesman. After learning from the proprietor how to demonstrate and sell coffee and tea, Kroger set off to find customers. His first stop was a bakery, where he promptly sold the baker a pound of coffee and a quarter pound of tea. He sold four pounds of coffee to his next customer. He totaled $35 in sales that first day, earning eighty-five cents in commission for his day's work and $7 by the end of the week. He immediately realized his natural skill at selling food, and he continued to expand his customer list and profits. Kroger enjoyed great success on his tea and coffee route until the company changed management and began selling products of inferior quality. Many of his regular customers were soon buying elsewhere. Kroger grew frustrated by the company's direction and soon left, but he later explained that the experience

there had taught him two valuable lessons: he could make good money by selling food, and "people, even those with little income, are willing to pay for good food, but they will not have inferior merchandise at any price" (*Barney Builds a Business*, p. 7).

After his departure from Great Northern, Kroger remained in Cincinnati and joined the newly formed tea firm of William White & Company, once again selling coffees and teas from a wagon throughout the city. This company, however, soon folded due to mismanagement, and Kroger once again changed jobs. His next position was selling tea and coffees from a wagon for the Imperial Tea Company. He pessimistically believed that he had little opportunity for advancement within this company, and he decided to accept a job with a large tea wholesaler in New York City. Before he could leave, however, the owners of Imperial Tea approached him with an offer to manage their entire business. Kroger signed a contract that gave him 10 percent of the company's profits, $12 per week, and complete control over all operations. He immediately fired everyone except the delivery boy. Next he bought a new cash register, hired a cashier, and proceeded to run the business with just himself and the two employees, often working seventeen hours a day. Insisting on the highest quality, his goal was to maintain higher standards in his product line than would be expected by his most meticulous customer. As Kroger's reputation became known, wholesalers selling inferior merchandise quickly learned not to call on him. His customers also noticed his higher standards and eagerly bought. Under his direction the Imperial Tea Company posted an unprecedented profit of $3,100 for that year, giving Kroger a $310 bonus. He approached the owners with a request to use his bonus to buy a larger share of the business. They declined, so Kroger withdrew his money and quit, with the idea in mind of starting his own business.

Kroger was once again without a job, but this time his goal was to open his own store. Although he had a considerable sum of money for 1883, it was still not enough to begin the grocery and tea business that he envisioned. In order to realize his dream, Kroger formed a partnership with B. A. Branagan, and together they rented market space, painted the exterior red, and opened a small grocery store in downtown Cincinnati. Kroger chose the name Great Western Tea Company for their new business and bought a shiny red wagon, a gilded harness, and a handsome horse to make deliveries. From the beginning he wanted his operation to stand out above his competitors. Unfortunately, two weeks later their new wagon collided with a train and was wrecked. Then one month later the Ohio River flooded and destroyed all of the store's stock. Despite these misfortunes, Kroger and Branagan made a substantial profit in 1883. With his share of the year's profits, Kroger then bought out Branagan's half of the partnership and finally had a store that was completely his own. From that point on he channeled nearly all of his profits into further expanding his business, living frugally in one room and working each day from before dawn to midnight.

Kroger's profits continued to grow as more customers frequented his store. Some walked many extra blocks to his Great Western Tea Company, often past other competing and more convenient grocers. Known for superior quality, Kroger's market soon developed a citywide reputation. After scarcely more than a year in business, he opened a second market in another area of the city and then opened a third three months later in another district. By June 1885 Kroger opened his fourth store in Cincinnati. After less than two years in his own grocery business, Kroger had built a small yet impressive chain of markets. He would later claim that his secret to success was maintaining overhead expenses, such as rent, labor, and fuel, as 4 percent of the overall gross profits. In addition to keeping to such a slim overhead, Kroger also employed immediate relatives in his initial expansion. In 1886 Kroger married Mary Emily Jansen, with whom he had seven children.

Using the already extensive A&P chain as a model, Kroger set out to build a grocery empire. Although it greatly increased overhead costs, his was one of the first chains to buy full-page advertising space to promote products and attract customers. In these ads he frequently offered prices lower than any of his competitors. Despite his continued emphasis on the highest standards of quality, Kroger also consistently offered the best prices. To achieve both goals, he bought far greater quantities than anyone else. When his competitors bought a case of a certain grocery item, Kroger bought a carload, an approach to purchasing that allowed him great latitude in setting sale prices.

By 1893 Kroger owned seventeen stores, and at age thirty-three he was one of the wealthiest men in Cincinnati. By 1902 he had forty stores and was manufacturing and marketing store-brand products. That same year he incorporated, changing the company name to the Kroger Grocery and Baking Company and expanding to other Ohio cities such as Hamilton, Dayton, and Columbus. Along with expansion came innovation. During this same period Kroger bought a meat company chain and included butchering operations in each of his stores, becoming the first grocer in the country to do so. He also was among the first grocers to develop an extensive fleet of trucks to provide for his own transportation needs. Next he continued to geographically and numerically expand at a rapid rate by purchasing entire grocery chains in financial distress and converting them into Kroger stores. Kroger's grocery operation was soon one of the country's largest, covering the Midwest from St. Louis to Cleveland. (By the end of the twentieth century the Kroger Company was the largest grocery chain in the country and the fifth largest retailer in the world.) By 1928 Kroger had reached his business goals and was tiring of the day-to-day management of the chain. That year he sold his majority interest. He also married Alice Farrington Maher, his first wife having died in 1899. Kroger spent the next decade in banking in Ohio and then in retirement in Florida and on Cape Cod, where he died.

Kroger built an enormous grocery chain and in the process introduced advertising strategies, wholesale-buying approaches, and retailing innovations that became norms in the grocery industry, setting the stage for the modern supermarket, which appeared after World War II.

• The location of Kroger's papers, if still in existence, is not known. Kroger's business achievements are freqently mentioned in books concerning food and more specifically in histories of the grocery industry. The only dedicated biographies have a proprietary interest, having been commissioned, printed, and distributed by the Kroger Company. These include George Laycock, *The Kroger Story: A Century of Innovation* (1983), and a brief, 24-page booklet, *Barney Builds a Business: The Story of the Founding of the Kroger Company* (1983). Neither of these publications are widely available in libraries, but both are available from the company's headquarters in Cincinnati. An obituary is in the *Cincinnati Times-Star*, 22 July 1938.

DAVID GERARD HOGAN

KROL, Bastiaen Janszen (1595–1674), representative of the Dutch Reformed church (first colonial "comforter of the sick") and colonial administrator in New Netherland, was born in Harlingen in the province of Friesland, the Netherlands, the son of Jans Krol and Annetjen Egberts. Bastiaen Krol had little formal education. He was employed in the fabric industry as a plush or velours worker when in 1615 he married Annetjen Stoffelsdocter, with whom he had three children. Krol signed his marriage certificate with a cross, suggesting he was unable to write his name at this time.

In 1623 Krol applied to the consistory of the Reformed church in Amsterdam for appointment as a "comforter of the sick" in one of the Dutch colonies. For this post, literacy was a prerequisite, so Krol must have developed these skills during the early years of his marriage. After several examinations of his qualifications, character, and spiritual state, he was approved to serve in the fledgling colony of New Netherland and departed Holland in January 1624 for Fort Orange.

The duties of a comforter of the sick were carefully spelled out in the so-called *Ziekentroost*, or *Den Siecken Troost; Twelk is een onderwysinge inden gheloove, ende den wech der salicheyt; om ghewillichlick te sterven* (The consolation of the sick; which is an instruction in the faith and the way of salvation to prepare believers to die willingly), first published in 1571. In the Netherlands, comforters of the sick assisted an ordained minister in his pastoral work by visiting, comforting, and encouraging the sick, poor, and sorrowing members of the congregation. In New Netherland in 1624, where there was no ordained minister, Krol, in addition to his visiting role, was instructed by the Amsterdam classis to conduct religious services and read the scriptures, set prayers, and sermons from certain approved texts. He was not permitted to serve communion, to baptize, or to perform marriages.

On his first visit to New Netherland, Krol stayed for only a few months, returning to the Netherlands to apprise the consistory of Amsterdam in November 1624 of the need for an ordained minister in the colony to marry couples, to baptize, and to minister to the inhabitants in general. The consistory could not see its way to supplying a minister to so tiny a community, but it authorized Krol to perform baptisms and marriages, though cautioning him to use only the approved texts for these sacraments and not his own wording. Krol was also charged with instructing the Indians "in the Christian religion out of God's Holy Word." He was later described as well acquainted with the Indian language.

Krol returned to New Netherland in January 1625, probably now to New Amsterdam, which was beginning to replace Fort Orange in importance. He remained for about eighteen months, accepting in August 1626 the position of commissary or agent at Fort Orange for the West India Company. In 1628 Jonas Michaelius, an ordained minister, arrived in the colony to organize the first church, and Krol became a member of Michaelius's consistory in New Amsterdam.

In 1629 Krol returned again to the Netherlands but the following year accepted appointment as commander at Fort Orange, also playing an additional role as representative of Kiliaen van Rensselaer, the patron of Rensselaerswyck. Early in 1632, on van Rensselaer's recommendation, he became temporary director general of New Netherland, succeeding Pieter Minuit. Krol remained in this post for a year, until the arrival of Wouter van Twiller in April 1633. From 1638 to 1643 he again commanded Fort Orange, where his good relations with the Indians enabled him to play an active role in securing the release from them of a number of French captives.

Krol's first wife died in January 1645 and in October of that year he married the widow Engeltie Baerents Valentijn. It is not known whether they had children together. He died in Amsterdam at about eighty years of age and was buried on 14 March 1674 in the churchyard of the Noorderkerk.

His ambition in service of church and country and his rise from lowly plush worker to director general, even though temporary, of New Netherland mark Krol as a man of good character and substantial capability. It has been noted that his influence with the Indians around Fort Orange, and his ability to speak their language, accounted largely for the friendly relations between the Dutch and the Indians during his tenure in New Netherland.

• Primary records concerning Krol are found in Edward T. Corwin, ed., *Ecclesiastical Records of the State of New York*, vol. 1 (7 vols., 1901–1916); A. J. F. van Laer, ed., *Van Rensselaer Bowier Manuscripts* (1908); and Van Laer, trans. and ed., *Documents Relating to New Netherland, 1624–1626, in the Henry E. Huntington Library* (1924). Secondary works include Albert Eekhof, *Bastiaen Jansz. Krol: Krankenbezoeker, Kommies en Kommandeur van Nieuw-Nederland, 1595–1645* (1910); Eekhof, *Jonas Michaelius, Founder of the Church in New Netherland* (1926), chap. 1; and Gerald F. De Jong, "The *Ziekentroosters* or Comforters of the Sick in New Netherland," *New-York Historical Society Quarterly* 54 (1970): 339–59.

FIRTH HARING FABEND

KRONENBERGER, Louis (9 Dec. 1904–30 Apr. 1980), writer and critic, was born in Cincinnati, Ohio, the son of Louis Kronenberger, Sr., a merchant, and Mabel Newwitter. From 1921 to 1924 he attended the University of Cincinnati, but he left without completing a degree; instead, he moved to New York City to become a writer. He took a clerical job at the *New York Times* and reviewed books for the *Times* and *Saturday Review*. By 1926 Kronenberger was an editor at Boni and Liveright, a position he held until 1933. In 1929 he published his first book, *The Grand Manner*, a novel praised by critics for its sophistication and assurance.

Kronenberger continued as an editor, working for Alfred A. Knopf from 1933 to 1935, then for *Fortune* magazine from 1936 to 1938. He also edited and introduced *An Anthology of Light Verse* (1935) for Modern Library—the first of his many anthologies. He made his primary reputation, however, as a drama critic for *Time* magazine (1938–1961) and for the New York City magazine *PM* (1940–1948). Kronenberger's praise was a near guarantee of box-office success. Although he particularly appreciated such dramatists as Congreve and Chekhov, Kronenberger was attuned to contemporary work: he championed the innovative Rodgers and Hart musical *Pal Joey*. Kronenberger married Emily L. "Emmy" Plaut in 1940; they had two children.

Even while serving as drama critic for both *Time* and *PM*, Kronenberger found time for other writing. His *Kings and Desperate Men: Life in Eighteenth-Century England* (1942), he said, "attempts a big canvas, deals seriously with human ideas and emotions, and seeks to portray human beings as truthfully as possible." *New York Times* reviewer Robert van Gelder wrote of it, "The emphasis always is on men and women—the soldiers, the writers, the politicians, the fops and artists and rakes, on the best things they said, on the most characteristic things they did, on what they intended and what they achieved. The pace never lets down, nor does the style, which is animated, colorful and never strained." *Marlborough's Duchess* (1958) was another critically praised biography.

Kronenberger's expertise on court intrigue did not reflect a penchant to practice it. His critical integrity led him to write a lukewarm review of *Kiss the Boys Goodbye* (1938) by Clare Booth Luce, wife of his employer, Henry R. Luce. Kronenberger, then newly hired at *Time*, must have felt that his job was on the line; nevertheless, Henry Luce ran the review without ill will, although Clare Luce later snubbed Kronenberger socially.

Kronenberger also achieved recognition in an academic career. During 1950–1951 he was a visiting lecturer at Columbia University, and he was an adjunct professor there in 1961. From 1951 to 1970 he lectured on theater arts at Brandeis University. He served as a visiting professor at City College of New York (1953–1954), Stanford University (1954 and 1963), New York University (1958), Harvard University (1959), and the University of California, Berkeley (1968). He also held a visiting lectureship at Oxford University (1959) and was the Christian Gauss Seminar lecturer at Princeton University (1961).

Throughout these years Kronenberger was also connected with organizations supporting artists and promoting the arts: Yaddo (beginning in 1948), the Lincoln Center Library-Museum (1964), the Rockefeller Report on the Performing Arts (1965), the National Institute of Arts and Letters (secretary, 1953–1956), and the American Academy of Arts and Sciences. He belonged to the Century Association in New York, St. Botolph Club in Boston, and the Athenaeum in London. His achievements and service were recognized with a Guggenheim fellowship (1969–1970).

During his teaching years Kronenberger remained active as an editor and writer. He edited and introduced several anthologies, notably *Cavalcade of Comedy* (1953), *George Bernard Shaw: A Critical Survey* (1953), *Six Plays by Richard Brinsley Butler Sheridan* (1957), *Novelists on Novelists: An Anthology* (1962), and *The Viking Book of Aphorisms* (1962). *Atlantic Brief Lives* (1971), a collection of biographical essays by prominent writers and scholars, is of lasting interest. He wrote *The Thread of Laughter: Chapters on English Stage Comedy from Jonson to Maugham* (1952), based on the courses he taught at Columbia and Brandeis; *Company Manners: A Cultural Inquiry into American Life* (1954), an attempt to capture the spirit of the "Age of Anxiety"; *The Republic of Letters: Essays on Various Writers* (1955); *A Month of Sundays* (1961), a novel; *The Polished Surface: Essays in the Literature of Worldliness* (1969), essays ranging from La Rochefoucauld to Edith Wharton; and *No Whippings, No Gold Watches: The Saga of a Writer and His Jobs* (1970), in which Kronenberger cast himself as "a kind of jack of all trades" in a "series of very subjective memoirs." He also wrote for the stage: he translated Jean Anouilh's *Mademoiselle Colombe* in 1954; and his *The Heavenly Twins*, based on Albert Husson's *Les pavés du ciel*, was produced on Broadway in 1955.

Kronenberger spent his later years writing biographies. *The Extraordinary Mr. Wilkes: His Life and Times* (1974) and *Oscar Wilde* (1976) were praised for being balanced and very readable. He died in Brookline, Massachusetts.

• In addition to works cited in the text, Kronenberger wrote *Grand Right and Left* (1952), a novel, and the nonfiction works *The Cart and the Horse* (1964), *The Last Word: Portraits of Fourteen Master Aphorists* (1972), and *A Mania for Magnificence* (1972). A complete list of Kronenberger's writings, including volumes he translated, edited, or contributed to, is in *Contemporary Authors*, new rev. ser. vol. 2 (1989), pp. 393–94.

JUDITH E. FUNSTON

KRUEGER, Walter (26 Jan. 1881–20 Aug. 1967), army officer, was born in Flatow, West Prussia (now Zlotow, Poland), the son of Julius Krüger, an army officer and prominent landowner, and Anna Hasse. In 1889, after the death of Krueger's father, the family emigrated to Ohio. In 1898 he left high school to join the army during the Spanish-American War. He served with the Second Volunteer Infantry in Cuba and was promoted to sergeant. He then enlisted in the regular army. Commissioned as a second lieutenant of infantry in 1901, he saw duty in the Philippines during the Philippine insurrection. Upon his return he married Grace Aileen Norvell in 1904; they had three children.

Krueger's early military career included assignments at the Infantry and Cavalry School, from which he graduated in 1906, and the Staff College, from which he graduated in 1907. He taught German at the Army Service School in Fort Leavenworth from 1909 to 1912 and saw service on the Mexican border in 1916. He also translated German military works for the army.

Krueger was a staff officer with the Eighty-fourth and Twenty-sixth Divisions during World War I. He served as chief of staff of the Tank Corps in France and assistant chief of staff of the Sixth and Fourth Corps in occupied Germany. After the war he studied military strategy and tactics at the Army War College, from which he graduated in 1921, remaining there as an instructor in 1921–1922. He also attended the Naval War College, graduating in 1926, and taught there from 1928 to 1932. He was on the War Department general staff from 1922 to 1925 and served as assistant chief of staff from 1936 to 1938. From 1936 to 1938 he was also a member of the Joint Army and Navy Board. In addition to these staff positions, he commanded the Sixth Infantry and Jefferson Barracks (1932–1934), the Sixteenth Infantry Brigade and Fort Meade (1938–1939), the Second Division and Fort Houston (1939–1940), the Eighth Corps (1940–1941), and during World War II, the Third Army and Southern Defense Command (1941–1943). He later remarked that his command of the Third Army's 300,000 men during the 1941 maneuvers in Louisiana was an invaluable experience for World War II.

After Pearl Harbor, Krueger was considered by many to be too old for overseas duty. He continued training the Third Army, emphasizing preparation of junior combat officers. In January 1943 General Douglas MacArthur requested that Krueger supervise training of the Sixth Army in Australia. Assuming command in February, Krueger then took the Sixth Army, called "the most seagoing Army in American history," through twenty-one major engagements against the Japanese, from New Guinea to the Philippines. After the Japanese surrendered, he commanded the Sixth Army during the occupation of Japan. He retired in San Antonio, Texas, in 1946 and died in Valley Forge, Pennsylvania.

Krueger, who held every army rank from private to full general, was known as a "soldier's general." He was a strict disciplinarian but demonstrated sincere concern for the men under his command. Realizing the importance of initiative at all levels, he encouraged his subordinates to use their own judgment. In World War II he was both a leading specialist in training combat forces and a combat commander who led the largest American land campaign (Luzon) in the Pacific. He neither sought nor received much public acclaim. General MacArthur, though impatient with Krueger's cautious leadership in the Philippines, nevertheless praised his abilities. Krueger's many distinctions included the Distinguished Service Cross, Distinguished Service Medal (army and navy), and Legion of Merit.

• Krueger's personal papers, including correspondence, maps, speeches, photographs, and other documents from 1899 to 1963, are at the U.S. Military Academy Library at West Point. The Henry Decker Papers at the U.S. Army Military History Institute in Carlisle Barracks, Pa., contain correspondence of Krueger's Sixth Army headquarters from 1943 to 1946. Other correspondence is in the Hanson Weightman Baldwin Papers at the George C. Marshall Research Foundation Library in Lexington, Ky. Krueger's World War II memoirs are published as *From Down Under to Nippon: The Story of Sixth Army in World War II* (1953). Two of his translations of German military works were published commercially: Friedrich Immanuel, *The Regimental War Game* (1907), and General Julius K. L. Mertens, *Tactics and Technique of River Crossings* (1918). There is still no book-length biography of Krueger, but his Pacific campaigns are covered widely in the literature of World War II, including Ronald H. Spector, *Eagle against the Sun: The American War with Japan* (1985); D. Clayton James, *The Years of MacArthur*, vol. 2 (1975); and Robert Ross Smith, *Triumph in the Philippines* (1963). Obituaries are in the *New York Times*, 21 Aug. 1967, and *Newsweek*, 4 Sept. 1967.

FRANCIS C. STECKEL

KRUESI, John (15 May 1843–22 Feb. 1899), master machinist and assistant to Thomas A. Edison, was born Johann Heinrich Krusi in Heiden, Switzerland. Little is known of his parents, who died when he was still an infant. He was placed in an orphanage. He began an apprenticeship as a locksmith in St. Gall, and when he completed it he moved to Zurich and worked as a journeyman machinist. There he met August Weber and formed a friendship that would influence his career. The two young men traveled to Paris to view the exhibits of the great international exposition in 1867 and then on to Holland and Belgium to gain some practical experience. After three years they moved to London, where they took in the latest developments in machine tools and power transmission.

Weber soon left London to seek employment in the United States, and his letters convinced Kruesi to follow him. Kruesi arrived in 1870 and entered the great Singer sewing machine works in Elizabeth, New Jersey, as a machinist. It was probably in the German-

speaking community in Newark that he heard of the young Thomas Edison and the machine shop he had established in Ward Street, Newark. Edison was rapidly making his name as an inventor: stock tickers, automatic telegraphs, electric pens, and telegraph transmitters were made in this shop. Kruesi entered Edison's employ in 1871 and played a significant part in the inventor's work. Also in 1871 Kruesi married Emily Zwinger. Several of their eight children continued their father's association with Edison and the electrical industry. Paul Kruesi worked for a time at Edison's West Orange laboratory, and Walter Kruesi was an employee of General Electric.

Edison was an industrialist and inventor, but he was no craftsman. He relied on others to turn his ideas into working models, and it was in this role that John Kruesi made up some of the most significant inventions of the nineteenth century. There is a famous drawing of the tinfoil phonograph dated 29 November 1877—the first complete rendering of the machine—on which Edison scrawled "Kruesi—make this." In his long association with the great inventor, Kruesi transformed hundreds of Edison's rough sketches into working machines and made important contributions to the many inventions credited to Edison.

When Edison moved his operation from Newark to Menlo Park in 1876, creating his famous "invention factory," Kruesi took on new responsibilities. He remained Edison's right-hand man—the master machinist who was entrusted with the most important inventions—but he also took over the job as foreman of the machine shops that made models of inventions and manufactured the products emerging from the laboratories. Kruesi distinguished himself as a tireless worker and demanding manager of a highly skilled but unruly work force. Kruesi played an important part in the experiments that led to Edison's famous electric light—one of Kruesi's hairs was used as a test filament in an incandescent lamp—and it was Kruesi who built the dynamos that were to power the first electric lighting system. Kruesi led the team of men who established the factory to make incandescent lights, designing and making the machine tools, laying out the factory, and installing all of the machinery. It was in this role that he was most valuable to Thomas Edison.

Once the main elements of the electric lighting system had been perfected at the Menlo Park laboratory, Edison moved his laboratory to New York City, where he intended to establish the first power station and lighting network. In 1881 Kruesi followed Edison to New York and was given charge of the Edison Underground Electric Tube factory, which was responsible for all the underground cables used in the network. Here Kruesi became an inventor in his own right, designing the cables, connectors, junction boxes, and safety cutouts. He was granted several patents for this work, and the conduit that carried the cables was known as the "Kruesi tube."

Edison established several factories to manufacture the component parts of his lighting system, and the largest and most important facility was the Edison Machine Works. The first works were in New York City, but, as the demand for equipment was so great, a new and much larger factory was built in Schenectady, New York, in 1886. Kruesi was appointed general manager and chief mechanical engineer. As Edison's electric lighting empire grew even larger, new business organizations had to be created to operate and supply a national system of electric lighting ventures. The General Electric Company absorbed many of the old Edison organizations when it was created in 1892, including the Edison Machine Works, and Kruesi retained his post as manager of the great factories at Schenectady.

At Schenectady, Kruesi had to manage a very large manufacturing operation while still retaining his position as a designing engineer. His services were sorely missed during the 1890s by Edison, who tried to tempt his old associate back to the laboratory bench, but to no avail. Kruesi had become a company man.

In 1894 Kruesi's assistant George Emmons was made manager of the Schenectady works. Kruesi retained his position as chief engineer. When General Electric and the Thomson-Houston Electric Company were merged in 1895, Kruesi became a consulting engineer, a position he held until his death.

The amount of attention given to Edison and his inventions has obscured the great contributions made by his craftsmen. Master mechanics like Kruesi made Edison's inventions work and in doing so added their own innovations to the devices sketched out by the great inventor. As a factory manager, Kruesi was a major figure in the electrification of the United States. His long tenure as manager of the Edison Machine Works covered the pioneering work of creating the electric lighting system and then the mass production of its perfected parts. Kruesi was called "Honest John" by his workmates at the Edison laboratory. It was a testament to his integrity and the respect he gained as a foreman. Edison referred to him as a faithful associate and collaborator, never as his subordinate.

• Kruesi's papers have not been located or printed. Several of his laboratory notes and his letters to Thomas Edison have been published in the *Thomas A. Edison Papers*, ed. Reese V. Jenkins et al. (1989–). All the biographies of Edison give some information on Kruesi. See Matthew Josephson, *Edison: A Biography* (1959), or Robert Conot, *A Streak of Luck* (1979). The most detailed account of his work in the development of the electric light is in Robert Friedel and Paul Israel, *Edison's Electric Light: Biography of an Invention* (1986). See also Francis Jehl, *Menlo Park Reminiscences* (1937), which was written by one of Kruesi's coworkers at the Edison laboratory.

ANDRE MILLARD

KRUPA, Gene (15 Jan. 1909–16 Oct. 1973), jazz drummer and bandleader, was born Eugene Bertram Krupa in Chicago, Illinois, the son of Bartley Krupa, an alderman, and Ann Oslowska, a milliner. Krupa attended St. Bridget's and Immaculate Conception parochial schools. He studied alto saxophone (or by another account, piano) from about age nine but soon switched

to drums. From about age eleven he helped his older brother at the Brown Music Company and demonstrated a fine memory for the recordings that he heard there.

Krupa's own accounts of the years 1924 to 1928 are inconsistent, with events conflated and substantial discrepancies in dating; hence it may be impossible precisely to trace his early participation in the jazz scene in Chicago, which in principle would throw greater light on his stylistic development. After he dropped out of Immaculate Conception, his mother sent him to St. Joseph's College in Indiana to study for the priesthood (1924–1925, or perhaps one year later), with the understanding that if he gave a sincere effort and it did not work out, he could turn to music. This he did, going to Chicago in fall 1925 (or 1926). He began to play with such musicians as cornetist Jimmy McPartland, trombonist Floyd O'Brien, clarinetists Frank Teschemacher and Mezz Mezzrow, and pianist Joe Sullivan, who were developing a spin-off of New Orleans jazz that would come to be known as Chicago jazz. Most significantly, he was deeply impressed by the drumming skills of their colleague, Dave Tough, and Tough in turn introduced him to African-American New Orleans jazz musicians resident in Chicago, especially drummer Baby Dodds, who influenced Krupa's technique and showmanship. Krupa replaced Tough in the Blue Friars in 1925 (or 1926), and, Tough having gone to Europe, Krupa played on the definitive recordings of Chicago jazz made by Red McKenzie and Eddie Condon's Chicagoans in December 1927: "Sugar," "China Boy," "Nobody's Sweetheart," and "Liza." He returned to the studio with a similar group, the Chicago Rhythm Kings, headed by trumpeter Muggsy Spanier, in April 1928, but the drums were not as well recorded. During this period, 1927 to 1928, Krupa played with Joe Kayser's dance orchestra while also participating in after-midnight Chicago jazz sessions at the Three Deuces.

Moving to New York, Krupa recorded "Shim-me-sha-wabble" with Red Nichols's group under Miff Mole's nominal leadership and "Oh! Baby" and "Indiana" with Condon's quartet (including Teschemacher and Sullivan) in July 1928; on the latter session Krupa's drums are overbearing, but at least this recording imbalance affords a convenient opportunity to study his technique at an early stage in his career. After his mother became terminally ill (or, by another account, died), Krupa went back home and worked with Thelma Terry and her Playboys, including tenor saxophonist Bud Freeman, under whom Krupa recorded "Craze-o-logy" in December. In 1929 he returned to New York and joined Nichols's band, with which he recorded in April.

While in New York Krupa began studies with Stanford "Gus" Moeller, who taught him to read percussion notation and to play in a visually exaggerated manner. Like many aspiring white musicians, Krupa frequented Harlem clubs, and he was deeply influenced by drummer Chick Webb; unlike many, he participated in racially integrated recording sessions with pianist Fats Waller (Sept. 1929) and with tenor saxophonist Coleman Hawkins under the name of the Mound City Blue Blowers (Nov. 1929). Krupa played alongside Condon, Benny Goodman, and Glenn Miller under Nichols's direction in the pit orchestra of George Gershwin's musicals *Strike Up the Band* (19 Jan. to midyear 1930) and *Girl Crazy* (Sept. 1930 into 1931). He recorded with Nichols throughout this period, including "After You've Gone" (Feb. 1930). He also recorded with Bix Beiderbecke and with Hoagy Carmichael's band (both in Sept. 1930).

Krupa then played in dance orchestras, initially returning to Chicago to work with Irving Aaronson (1931–1932) and then joining Russ Columbo, Horace Heidt, and, in Atlantic City, Mal Hallet (1933). During the run of *Girl Crazy* Krupa had been awakened daily by a call from hotel telephone operator Ethel May Fawcett, whom he married in 1933; they had no children. He returned to Chicago to join the novelty orchestra of multi-instrumentalist Buddy Rogers (1933–1934). Having recorded under Goodman's leadership in 1933 and 1934, Krupa joined Goodman's new big band in mid-December 1934, and his movie-star looks and aggressively athletic drumming style were crucial in making this the band that launched the swing era. Characteristic recordings with Goodman's orchestra include "King Porter Stomp" (1935), "Walk, Jennie, Walk," "Swingtime in the Rockies," and "Bugle Call Rag" (all from 1936), but he is best known for his extended solo on "Sing, Sing, Sing" in a collaborative arrangement developed in 1936 and recorded the following year. Krupa was also a member of Goodman's racially integrated small group—initially a trio with pianist Teddy Wilson on record from 1935 and in concert from 1936 and then a quartet when Goodman began to use vibraphonist Lionel Hampton in mid-1936. For many jazz fans Krupa's greatest artistic contributions are his brushed snare drum accompaniments and solos in this delicate setting, as preserved on such recordings as "After You've Gone" and "Who?" (1935), "China Boy" and "Tiger Rag" (1936), and "Runnin' Wild" and "Avalon" (1937). He also began recording as a leader in November 1935 and February 1936, the latter session involving Goodman, trumpeter Roy Eldridge, and tenor saxophonist Chu Berry.

As Krupa's popularity grew and his big-band drumming became bombastic, Goodman's irritation increased, although he never forgot the debt he owed Krupa for helping to catapult the band to fame. They argued publicly in the weeks following an acclaimed concert at Carnegie Hall on 16 January 1938. Krupa quit and formed his own big band that debuted in Atlantic City on 16 April. Apart from presenting the eccentric scat singer Leo Watson for a few months in summer or fall 1938, Krupa's orchestra was unremarkable in its first years, and the drum solo was overworked. From this time onward, the importance of his drumming declined and highlights came from others, most notably singer Anita O'Day and trumpeter Eldridge, whom Krupa hired in 1941. Krupa supported

and defended Eldridge as much as he could through Eldridge's traumatic experience touring as the only African American in the big band. Their recordings together include "Let Me Off Uptown," "After You've Gone," and "Rockin' Chair," all from 1941, and they appeared in the film *Ball of Fire* (1942).

In 1942 Krupa divorced. In 1943 he disbanded his orchestra, after having been arrested for marijuana possession and sentenced to three months in prison. The story is intricate and somewhat contradictory, but there is no doubt that in the public eye Krupa was branded as a drug addict (wrongfully), and his career was hampered permanently. He rejoined Goodman's orchestra on 21 September 1943 and Tommy Dorsey's in mid-December 1943 before reforming his own in summer 1944. Following a then-current fashion for sugary popular music, Krupa added a string section that not surprisingly contributes nothing to the reformed big band's best recording from this period, "Leave Us Leap" (Jan. 1945). At midyear he dropped the strings from the band.

Krupa remarried Ethel in 1946, and in that year he began hiring young musicians who turned the band toward bop, although the leader was never comfortable with bop percussion patterns. His most important sidemen in this vein were baritone saxophonist Gerry Mulligan, who arranged "Disc Jockey Jump" (recorded in 1947); trumpeter Red Rodney; and, at decade's end, trombonists Frank Rosolino, Frank Rehak, and Urbie Green. Krupa disbanded this orchestra in 1951.

Over the next two decades Krupa toured the world, initially as a member of Jazz at the Philharmonic, for which he played in all-star groups and led his own small group (1951–1953), and from 1954 as the leader of a quartet. He performed in the films *The Glenn Miller Story* (1954) and *The Benny Goodman Story* (1955). Ethel died in 1955 or 1956, and in 1959 he married Patricia Bowler; they subsequently adopted two children. He toured again with Jazz at the Philharmonic in 1959 and that same year was the subject of an absurdly fictionalized film biography, *The Gene Krupa Story*, which among other faults cruelly reinforced the mistaken public perception of Krupa as a drug addict.

After a heart attack in 1960 he reduced the quartet's activities somewhat. From 1963 until his death he also participated in reunions of Goodman's quartet. In this final decade he suffered from leukemia, emphysema, and ruptured spinal discs. He was divorced in 1968. Although his ability to play declined badly, he nonetheless performed into his final year. He died in Yonkers, New York. As had been done previously for other famous leaders of the swing era, a Gene Krupa "ghost band" formed in 1986 under the direction of trombonist Rex Allen.

Albeit at a cost of considerable tastelessness, Krupa enlarged the audience for jazz and perhaps single-handedly established the drums as an instrument for star soloists via his flamboyant playing with Goodman's big band and especially his sweat-soaked frenzy of tom-tom drumming on "Sing, Sing, Sing." This famous booming tom-tom solo was not typical of his playing, which instead relied heavily on crisp snare drumming in which he adapted ragtime- and parade-based techniques to the rhythmic flow of Chicago jazz and swing. Although eventually his fundamental conception, based on an "oom-pah" drum rhythm, sounded old-fashioned by comparison to the shimmering cymbal sounds that better suited swing rhythm, Krupa's playing was innovative and widely influential in its time.

• The fullest biographies are Rudi Blesh, *Combo: USA: Eight Lives in Jazz* (1971); Bruce Crowther, *Gene Krupa: His Life & Times* (1987); and Burt Korall, *Drummin' Men: The Heartbeat of Jazz: The Swing Years* (1990). Additionally much detailed information on Krupa appears in D. Russell Connor's chronology of Goodman's life, *Benny Goodman: Listen to His Legacy* (1988). Bruce H. Klauber collects published material and new interviews of Krupa's colleagues in *World of Gene Krupa: That Legendary Drummin' Man* (c. 1990). See also "'Band Business Is on Way Up Again,' Says Krupa," *Down Beat* 17 (25 Aug. 1950): 3; Jim Burns, "Lesser Known Bands of the Forties: Gene Krupa and Georgie Auld," *Jazz Monthly*, no. 160 (June 1968): 8–10; Albert McCarthy, *Big Band Jazz* (1974); Karen Larcombe, "Gene Krupa, 1909–1973," *Modern Drummer* 3/5 (Oct./Nov. 1979): 12–15, 53, 60; Anita O'Day and George Eells, *High Times, Hard Times* (1981; repr. 1989); Mary Lee Hester, "The Exciting Gene Krupa," *Mississippi Rag* 13 (Aug. 1986): 1–4; and James Lincoln Collier, *Benny Goodman and the Swing Era* (1989). Theodore Dennis Brown supplies a detailed and enthusiastic assessment of Krupa's drumming in "A History and Analysis of Jazz Drumming to 1942" (Ph.D. diss., Univ. of Michigan, 1976). Gunther Schuller offers a much harsher assessment in *The Swing Era: The Development of Jazz, 1930–1945* (1989). An exhaustive list of his recordings as a leader is by Charles Garrod and Bill Korst, *Gene Krupa and His Orchestra*, vol. 1, 1935–1946 (1984); *Gene Krupa and His Orchestra*, vol. 2, 1947–1973 (1984). See also Klaus Stratemann, *Buddy Rich and Gene Krupa: A Filmo-discography* (1980), and Ernest Ronowski, *Gene Krupa: LP- und FS-Liste* (LP and TV list), vol. 1 (1987). An obituary is in the *New York Times*, 17 Oct. 1973.

BARRY KERNFELD

KRUTCH, Joseph Wood (25 Nov. 1893–22 May 1970), writer, was born in Knoxville, Tennessee, the son of Edward Waldemore Krutch, a businessman, and Adelaine Wood. From 1911 to 1915 he attended the University of Tennessee, where his initial interests were science and mathematics. However, after becoming a habitual theatergoer and the editor of the university's student magazine, he decided to major in English. He continued his studies at Columbia University, where he received his master's degree in 1916 and his Ph.D. in 1924. The Van Dorens were important influences on Krutch's scholarly life. Carl Van Doren directed his thesis, and Mark Van Doren offered friendly criticism of his work. In 1923 Krutch married Marcelle Leguia, a nurse. They had no children.

In the early 1920s Krutch tried his hand at both teaching and essay writing. After an unfulfilling tenure as a composition instructor at Brooklyn Polytechnic, he resigned. He was much more successful in his writing career, which he began as a book and drama reviewer for both the *Saturday Review of Literature* and *The Nation*. In 1924 Krutch became a permanent staff member of *The Nation*. His responsibilities included theater reviews and general commentary on American culture.

During this decade Krutch also authored three books: *Comedy and Conscience after the Restoration* (1924), *Edgar Allan Poe* (1926), and *The Modern Temper* (1929). The first work, a publication of his dissertation on post-restoration theater, received perfunctory reviews. The book on Poe caused some controversy since Krutch, using the latest in Freudian analysis, focused on Poe's neurotic sexuality as the basis for his creativity. However, it was publication of *The Modern Temper* that put Krutch in the center of the intellectual ferment of his times.

Many of the leading contemporary thinkers, including Bertrand Russell and Granville Hicks, hailed the work as a thoroughgoing, thoughtful analysis of the modernist mood. Krutch discussed what he believed to be the main elements of twentieth-century life: alienation, loss of meaning, and separation from nature. His summation included a sentence that he would recant in his later life: "Ours is a lost cause and there is no place for us in the natural universe." While Krutch was intellectually capable of authoring a most articulate critique of modernism, he proved temperamentally unsuited to living comfortably with its conclusions. Ultimately he would reject modernism for its negation of the value of the individual and its lack of concern for nature.

Krutch's career during the 1930s was marked by both success and conflict. His reputation as a scholar grew with the publication of *Five Masters: A Study in the Mutations of the Novel* (1930) and *Experience and Art: Some Aspects of the Esthetics of Literature* (1932). These books demonstrated Krutch's concern with the diminishing role of humanism in literature and the arts in general. His 1934 work *Was Europe a Success?* voiced his appreciation of European culture despite its flaws and his alarm at those who were prepared to dismantle it. A number of his essays in *The Nation* elaborating on his disillusionment with socialism and other radical movements caused some of the leftist American intellectuals to dismiss his writing as reactionary humanism. His lack of sympathy for communism and his traditional liberal belief in the individual left him out of step with many of his colleagues. In 1937 Krutch relinquished most of his duties at *The Nation* in order to accept a full-time teaching position at Columbia.

In 1932 Krutch had purchased a home in rural Connecticut and found his fascination with the world of nature grew as his interest in New York's cultural life slowly waned. He remained a drama critic, but he found less and less of value in contemporary theater. His teaching career was rewarding, but he was nonetheless sometimes ill at ease with the social demands and political struggles of the university.

His major publications during the 1940s demonstrate the gradual shift of his interests. In 1944 he finished a lengthy biography of Samuel Johnson. Krutch found a kindred spirit in Johnson; they shared deep moral convictions, a distaste of extremism, and a belief in the primacy of reason and common sense. The positive reception of *Samuel Johnson* served as the impetus for Krutch's undertaking of another biography, that of Henry David Thoreau, which was published in 1948. Krutch found many of his own concerns reflected in those of Thoreau: the importance of the individual, the need for values, the deadening influence of materialism, and nature as a pathway to spiritual fulfillment. He applauded Thoreau's desire for a familiarity with his environment and his hatred of conformity. These two facets of Thoreau's philosophy had become increasingly important in Krutch's own life.

In 1949 Krutch published his first book of nature writing, *The Twelve Seasons*. In this work Krutch demonstrated to himself and to an appreciative audience that he could be a successful practitioner of the familiar essay about nature. It was followed in 1950 by *Great American Nature Writing*, his selection of outstanding essays by other writers in this genre, and in 1952 by *The Desert Year*, his reflections on a sabbatical year in the Arizona desert. This work, considered a classic of the Southwest, revealed a side of Krutch that was diametrically opposed to that of *The Modern Temper*. Krutch now focused on the necessity of a joyful life within the context of nature rather than alienation from it.

In 1952 Krutch decided to give up teaching, his position as drama critic, and even the East Coast in favor of a new life in the desert near Tucson. Here he continued both his observations of the arid environment he had come to appreciate and his writing on nature, society, and American culture. Two of his works completed in Arizona amounted to a rejection of the modernist outlook: *"Modernism" in Modern Drama* (1953) and *The Measure of Man: On Freedom, Human Values, Survival and the Modern Temper* (1954), for which he received the 1954 National Book Award for nonfiction. In the latter work Krutch posited that traditional human values had been eroded by modern doctrines such as Marxism, Freudianism, and behaviorism. He saw totalitarianism and uniformity as the outcome of many of the political and psychological movements of the twentieth century. Moreover, he was deeply troubled by the same "quiet desperation" in contemporary society that Thoreau had noted in the nineteenth century.

From 1955 to 1961 Krutch authored five more books that demonstrated his interest in the ecology of the Southwest and his belief in the need for a wholistic worldview. In *The Voice of the Desert* (1955), *Grand Canyon* (1958), and *The Forgotten Peninsula: A Naturalist in Baja California* (1961) he reflected on geological, biological, and anthropological topics that captured his interest during his explorations of the Sonoran Desert and the canyon country of northern Arizona. The Baja book was the result of ten trips into the Mexican wilderness, many with his industrialist friend Kenneth Bechtel, who shared Krutch's enthusiasm for the desert. The other two works from this peri-

od, *The Great Chain of Life* (1956) and *Human Nature and the Human Condition* (1959), are philosophical considerations of a wide range of topics: humanity's role in the larger scheme of nature, determinism, education, consumerism, dehumanization, freedom, and morality. In general Krutch emphasized the need for a sense of human value but cautioned against a solely anthropocentric perspective on life.

During the last eight years of his life Krutch published, among other works, an autobiography, *More Lives than One* (1962), and two collections of essays, *If You Don't Mind My Saying So: Essays on Man and Nature* (1964) and *And Even if You Do: Essays on Man, Manners and Machines* (1967). He also continued to write occasional columns for the *American Scholar* and the *Saturday Review*. In 1967 he collaborated with photographer Eliot Porter on one of his last books, *Baja California and the Geography of Hope*. In the introduction he stated his belief, which had evolved over forty years, in "the sense that nature is the most beautiful of all spectacles and something of which man is a part; that she is a source of health and joy which inevitably dries up when man is alienated from her."

Joseph Wood Krutch died at his home in Tucson. Over the course of his lifetime he had written hundreds of essays and reviews; scholarly works on literature, philosophy and society; and books reflecting his enthusiasm for nature. While Krutch's *The Modern Temper* became an essential document of early twentieth-century American intellectual history, equally important was his influence on later nature writers such as Edward Abbey. After his death Krutch's reputation as a literate naturalist grew as interest in the environment, especially that of the Southwest, continued to develop.

• The majority of Krutch's papers are in the Manuscript Division of the Library of Congress. His correspondence with Mark Van Doren is at the Columbia University Library, and his early correspondence while at *The Nation* is available at the Houghton Library of Harvard University. A number of his manuscripts are also in the special collections of the University of Arizona and the University of Tennessee, Knoxville. Works of Krutch's not cited above are *The Comedies of William Congreve* (ed.) (1927), *The American Drama since 1918* (1939), *Selected Letters of Thomas Gray* (ed.) (1952), *The Best of Two Worlds* (1953), *The Gardener's World* (ed.) (1959), *The World of Animals: A Treasury of Lore, Legend and Literature by Great Writers and Naturalists from 5th Century B.C. to the Present* (ed.) (1961), *Modern Literature and the Image of Man* (1962), *Thoreau: Walden and Other Writings* (ed.) (1962), *A Treasury of Birdlore* (ed. with Paul S. Eriksson) (1962), *Herbal* (1965), *Eighteenth Century English Drama* (ed.) (1967), *The Best Nature Writing of Joseph Wood Krutch* (1969), *The Most Wonderful Animals That Never Were* (1969), and *A Krutch Omnibus: Forty Years of Social and Literary Criticism* (1970). John D. Margolis, *Joseph Wood Krutch: A Writer's Life* (1980), is the most complete analysis of the man and his work. A helpful overview of his writing is Anthony L. Lehman, "Joseph Wood Krutch: A Selected Annotated Bibliography of Primary Sources," *Bulletin of Bibliography* 41

(June 1984): 74–80. An obituary is in the *New York Times*, 23 May 1970. A tribute, "The Many Worlds of Joseph Wood Krutch," appeared in *Saturday Review*, 25 July 1970.

PAUL N. PAVICH

KUBIK, Gail Thompson (5 Sept. 1914–20 July 1984), composer, was born in South Coffeyville, Oklahoma, the son of Henry Kubik, a lumberyard owner, and Evalyn Thompson, a singer and aesthete. Soon after his birth, the family moved to Coffeyville, Kansas, where his mother established an extraordinary artistic environment in their home and community. Kubik recalled,

She was a remarkable woman. She created an atmosphere in which music was one of the values that you just did not question. And I suppose it was inevitable that my older brother and I became professional musicians. . . . Mother looked around and observed that Coffeyville didn't have much music; so nothing would do but that she would organize concerts. And single-handedly, she and my father did just that, bringing to our little town world-famous artists like Amelita Galli-Curci, Ernestine Schumann-Heink, John McCormick, and Tandy McKenzie. She had this marvelous American characteristic of having an idea, and against all skepticism and lack of encouragement, just pushed it through.

Kubik decided at an early age that music was the focal point of this life; he was extraordinarily precocious and a musical prodigy. He played the piano, but his principal instrument was the violin, which he studied with Alexander Baird of Independence, Kansas. At age fifteen, Kubik became the youngest person offered a scholarship by the prestigious Eastman School of Music, Rochester, New York. He attended East Evening High School by night and university courses by day, graduating in 1932 and 1934, respectively. Kubik was the youngest graduate of the Eastman School to complete degree requirements in both violin and composition and graduated "with distinction." While there, his principal teachers were Samuel Belov (violin), Irving McHose (theory), and Edward Royce and Bernard Rogers (composition). In 1930 the Kubik Ensemble was formed, a quartet that concertized successfully in New York and throughout the Midwest. Gail's brothers Howard and Henry Jr. played piano and cello; Gail, the violin; and Evalyn was soprano soloist.

At age nineteen Kubik joined the music faculty of Monmouth College, Monmouth, Illinois. Concurrently, he studied composition with Leo Sowerby at the American Conservatory of Music, Chicago, from which he earned a master of music degree, cum laude, in 1935. The following year, he composed *American Caprice* (orchestra and solo piano) for his Monmouth students; his first large-scale composition to attract national attention, it was performed subsequently by the Syracuse Orchestra and the Chicago Civic Orchestra. The same year, Kubik left Monmouth College for South Dakota Wesleyan University, Mitchell, South Dakota, where one of his precollege students was

George McGovern, the future Democratic presidential nominee.

In 1937 Kubik received a fellowship at the Mac-Dowell Colony (a retreat for artists in Peterborough, New Hampshire), the youngest person so honored, and left Wesleyan to pursue graduate work at Harvard University—at twenty-two, the youngest person ever accepted into their doctoral program in music. His principal teachers there were Walter Piston and Nadia Boulanger, a visiting professor from France. Both influenced his compositional style strongly, and Boulanger, especially, was taken by the young composer and his music. She became an ardent supporter of his music and remained so always. She premiered his choral piece, "Daniel Drew," to critical acclaim in a concert at the Library of Congress, as well as in Paris. Its subsequent publication made it one of the first of Kubik's extensive catalog of published works. In 1938 Boulanger and Piston recommended Kubik for a position at Teachers College, Columbia University, New York City, which he accepted and held until 1940, when he left to become staff arranger-composer for the NBC radio network. On 5 April 1939, while at Teachers College, Kubik married his student, Jessie Maver Dunn, the former wife of a prominent physician.

In 1941 Kubik left NBC to became a successful freelance composer. He won the Jascha Heifetz–Carl Fischer Prize for his Concerto for Violin, securing commissions for the orchestral pieces "Whoopee-ti-yi-yo" and "Variations on a 13th-Century Troubadour Song" for the CBS and NBC orchestras, respectively. Also that year he composed his first film score for *Men and Ships*, wrote incidental music for Max Catto's play *They Walk Alone*, and completed his Sonatina for Piano. Additionally, he taught at several New York City area music schools, part-time. The following year Kubik wrote the critically acclaimed score for the film *The World at War* and assumed duties as musical consultant for the Bureau of Motion Pictures of the Office of War Information. There, he scored several other motion pictures before entering military service in 1943, during which he served as a composer in Culver City, California, for the Army Air Corps's First Motion Picture Unit. In that capacity, he cemented his position as the foremost composer of wartime documentary films, scoring William Wyler's *The Memphis Belle* and *Thunderbolt*, plus numerous other movies, in addition to composing music for radio shows. In 1943 violinist Louis Kaufman premiered Kubik's Sonatina for Violin and Piano in Los Angeles and New York City.

While in California, Kubik wrote a number of articles for periodicals and lectured eloquently about composing for film and radio as well as the demands and responsibilities facing contemporary composers. In 1944 he was awarded the first of two Guggenheim fellowships; meanwhile, his marriage to Jessie disintegrated, and they agreed to divorce in January 1946. When the war ended, Kubik returned to New York City with a new romantic interest, Joyce Scott-Paine, the daughter of a wealthy British industrialist, whom he wed in December 1946.

That same year, he composed music for Jessamyn West's *A Mirror for the Sky*, a folk opera intended for the Broadway stage but never produced there. It is a superb score, and portions of it were published later as two choral suites. Subsequently, in 1947, he completed the orchestral work "Bachata" (drawn from his *Men and Ships* film score) and in 1948, a series of fifty-six compositions for the Robert Shaw Chorale. These represent some of Kubik's best work and are marvelously original and captivating. In 1949 he finished Symphony in E-flat, his first of three works in that genre. The same year he scored Joseph Lerner's film *C-Man*, garnering excellent reviews. Subsequently, the film score served as the basis for his Pulitzer Prize–winning orchestral composition, Symphony Concertante (1952). The year 1949 also saw the premiere of Kubik's Sonata for Piano, with Frank Glazer as pianist, in Carnegie Hall and his return to Hollywood in search of film work. Early in 1950 Kubik scored two cartoons for Columbia Pictures, *Gerald McBoing Boing* and *The Miner's Daughter*. Both scores are delightful and witty; the former cartoon, based on a story by Dr. Seuss, won the Academy Award and British Film Institute Award for best animated film. His adaptation of the *McBoing Boing* music for percussion soloist and orchestra has become a staple of the symphonic repertoire. From *The Miner's Daughter*, Kubik drew music for his chamber piece, "Boston Baked Beans: An Opera Piccola" (1952). Kubik received the Prix de Rome the same year and worked at the American Academy in Rome, beginning a prolonged period during which he lived abroad. In 1951 he divorced his second wife, and in April 1952 he married Mary Tyler, the daughter of a prominent American clergyman, whom he met in Rome. In 1952 Kubik scored a second film, *Two Gals and a Guy*, for Laurel Productions, the company that released *C-Man*, and the following year he became friends with poet Theodore Roethke, whose *The Monotony Song* he set to music. Kubik also wrote a remarkable cartoon score, *Transatlantic: A Short Cut Through History* (1952), for Philip Stapp and a French production company. This score served as the basis for his critically acclaimed chamber piece, Divertimento I (1959).

Kubik remained abroad until 1955, pursuing an active career as a composer and conductor—working with the Orchestra Sinfonica della Radio Italiana, the London Philharmonic, the orchestra of the British Broadcasting Corporation, and the Orchestre Symphonique de Paris—when he returned to Hollywood to score William Wyler's *The Desperate Hours*. His music for this chilling drama was shockingly modern and strident by Hollywood standards, and the head of Paramount Studios pulled most of the music from the film. Later, as a conciliatory gesture, Paramount returned the music rights to Kubik—an unheard-of gesture—and published, at their expense, a suite that Kubik drew from the film, "Scenario for Orchestra" (1957). His second symphony was commissioned by the Louisville Orchestra and premiered in 1956. Symphony No. 3, the result of a commission by Dimitri Mitropoulos and the New York Philharmonic, was presented the next year. In 1958 Kubik composed his first music for television, an episode for *The Twentieth-Century* titled "Hiroshima," as well as the chamber pieces Divertimento II (1958) and Sonatina for Clarinet and Piano. Early in 1959 he scored a second episode for *The Twentieth-Century*, titled "The Silent Sentinel."

In the summer of 1959 Kubik returned to Europe, where he remained until 1967. There he scored another animated film, *Down to Earth* (1959); delivered a lecture at the Venice Film Festival; and wrote a scathing attack of the musical avant-garde in an article for *Saturday Review*. In 1962 Kubik scored a film for MGM (Europe), *I Thank a Fool*, although his music was eventually removed from the film because he refused to give the studio rights to the music. Later, he drew the composition "Scenes for Orchestra" from the film score. In 1965 he received a second Guggenheim award and resided at the Cité Internationale des Arts in Paris. The following year he lectured throughout the United States and Europe and did a series of programs on American music for Radio Eireann (Ireland).

Kubik returned to the United States in late 1967 and composed steadily. In the summer of 1969 he met novelist Joan Allred Sanders at the MacDowell Colony, and they became involved romantically. In September 1970 Kubik divorced his wife and married Sanders. That year saw the premiere of a large-scale work for orchestra, chorus, and narrator, *A Record of Our Time*, which Kubik wrote for Kansas State University, where he had held a one-year appointment as composer in residence. While there he also scored a cartoon, *Leopold the See-through Crumb Picker*, and wrote music for *The Eisenhower Years*, a production of the National Educational Radio Network. Later, this music was transformed into "Five Theatrical Sketches (Divertimento III)" (1971). In 1970 Kubik accepted an offer to become composer in residence at Scripps College, Claremont, California, where he remained for a decade. His fourth marriage did not have the same longevity; he was divorced in 1972. While at Scripps he composed and published a number of pieces, including "Scholastica" (1972), "A New Texas Grimorium," and "Magic, Magic, Magic" (1976). In 1980 he was forced to retire because of a mandatory age limit (sixty-five) imposed by the state of California. He sued the state unsuccessfully with the help of the American Civil Liberties Union in an attempt to overthrow the law. Upon retiring, Kubik traveled abroad extensively and spent a considerable period of time in France, where he maintained a Paris apartment and a home in Vensaque. His death in West Covina, California, was the result of a parasitic infection, kala-azar (leishmaniasis), which he probably acquired in Africa and which was misdiagnosed until it was too late to combat.

Throughout most of his career, Kubik was considered a modernist. His rhythmically active, virtuosically conceived, tonally centered music was related stylistically to that of Aaron Copland, but it became passé with the advent of serial music. Despite this, Kubik steadfastly refused to change his style. In the last years of his life, he became somewhat bitter, thinking that the musical world had passed him by. Ironically, had he lived a short time longer he would have witnessed a resurgence of interest in his music and those of his generation, corresponding to the decline in popularity of the dodecaphonists. Kubik left no progeny, save for an extensive catalog of musical compositions. He excelled in composing for the media and in drawing concert pieces from these works; his vocal music is of consistently high quality, and his instrumental work is articulate and challenging.

He tended to be litigious, and many individuals found his personality brusque and egocentric; others cherished his gregariousness, warmth, and stimulating qualities. He was dedicated completely to his craft and said, "For me, music is as close to a miracle as I'll ever come to believing in. My belief in music, and the power of music, and the magic of music is absolute."

• Kubik's papers and original manuscripts are in the Farrell Library, Special Collections, Kansas State University, Manhattan, Kans., and the Library of Congress, Washington, D.C. Kubik's writing on music is represented by "The Composer's Place in Radio," *Hollywood Quarterly* 1, no. 1 (Oct. 1945): 60–68; "Film Music and Public Taste," *Film Music Notes* 3, no. 9 (June 1944); "Music in the Documentary Film," *Writers Congress: The Proceedings of the Conference Held in October 1943 under the Sponsorship of the Hollywood Writers' Mobilization and the University of California* (1944; repr. in *Music Publishers' Journal* [Sept.–Oct. 1945]: 13, 54–56); "Movie Audiences: Musically Mature or Adolescent?," *Film Music Notes*, Apr. 1946; "Composing for Government Films," *Modern Music* 23, no. 3 (1946); and "An American in Paris—and Elsewhere," *Opera News*, 4 Nov. 1967, pp. 8–13. He is the subject of Max Lyall, "The Piano Music of Gail Kubik" (D.M.A. diss., Peabody Conserv. of Music, Johns Hopkins Univ., 1980). Articles about Kubik include Frederick W. Sternfeld's "Current Chronicle," *Musical Quarterly* 36, no. 2 (Apr. 1950): 274–76; "Gail Kubik's Score for C-Man," *Hollywood Quarterly* 4, no. 4: 360–69; "Kubik's McBoing Score," *Film Music Notes* 10, no. 2 (Nov.–Dec. 1950): 1–9; Everett Helm's "Gail Kubik's Score for C-Man: The Sequel," *Quarterly of Film, Radio, and Television* 9, no. 3 (Spring 1955); "Sounding the Artist's Dilemma: Even Composers Seek Meaning in the Pressures of Traditional and Modern Society," *Res Publica* 1, no. 2 (1973); and Richard D. Haines's "Music: A Form of Protest," *Instrumentalist* 25 (Feb. 1971): 26–27. Obituaries are in the *New York Times*, 25 July 1984, and *Variety*, 8 Aug. 1984.

ALFRED W. COCHRAN

KUHIO (26 Mar. 1871–7 Jan. 1922), prince of Hawaii and the islands' second territorial delegate to the U.S. Congress, was born Jonah Kuhio Kalanianaole Piikoi at Kola, Kauai, to Princess Kekaulike Kinoike II and high chief David Kahalepouli Piikoi. His mother was related to the ancient kings of Maui and Hawaii, and her grandfather was King Kaumualii of Kauai.

Known as Kuhio throughout his life, he attended St. Albans School, a private academy in Honolulu conducted by Alatau T. Atkinson, where he received the nickname Prince Cupid. He and his two brothers lived in the Atkinson home while being tutored. Kuhio enjoyed playing marbles, pio (a Hawaiian game), and fist fighting, learning early to defend himself and others. In 1880, when Kuhio was nine, his father died, and King Kalakaua appointed Kuhio's mother governess of the island of Hawaii. The boys remained in Honolulu attending school at St. Albans and, later, Punahou, where Kuhio excelled in football, wrestling, boxing, track, baseball, and rowing.

In 1883 King Kalakaua gave the three boys the title of prince. Later the constitution of 1887 confirmed their position, and their mother was renamed a princess of the Kalakaua dynasty. The formal coronation of King Kalakaua and Queen Kapiolani was held at the same time and proved to be an international event. Kuhio carried the crown of Queen Kapiolani, his aunt, in the procession. That evening all of Honolulu rejoiced in the new electric lights that lighted the throne room for the coronation ball. Kuhio was brought up at court as a member of the royal family.

After completing his education in Honolulu, Kuhio attended St. Matthew's Military Academy in San Mateo, California. He returned to the islands each summer. In March 1888 Kalakaua sent Kuhio to Japan, where he spent a year building new diplomatic relationships. The king hoped he would marry into the Japanese royal house, but Kuhio had other ideas. Upon his return to Hawaii, he served in the Ministry of Interior and Customs, where he proved efficient and industrious. The king hoped to train him for high offices and possibly to inherit the throne, although the king's immediate heir was his sister Liliuokalani. Kuhio soon joined his brother David for further education in England, where they both studied business. While in England, Kuhio often visited Princess Kaiulani, his cousin and the daughter of Liliuokalani's sister Likelike.

King Kalakaua died in 1891, and Kuhio returned from England to become active in the court of the new queen Liliuokalani, who made him and David heirs presumptive in case of the death of her heir apparent, Princess Kaiulani. In local Hawaiian politics, the princes now dropped their surname Piikoi, with David using Kawananakoa and Kuhio using Kalanianaole as their last names. Thus the public could distinguish between the brothers as they entered political public life.

In January 1893 Queen Liliuokalani attempted to introduce a reform constitution that would have strengthened the monarchy. A Committee of Safety was organized against her, however, and she was deposed. A provisional government was established with Sanford B. Dole as its head, and later, on 4 July 1894, the Republic of Hawaii was launched. The displacement of the queen and the monarchy infuriated Kuhio, and he determined to reestablish the throne. While on a hunting trip to Molokai, Kuhio and a friend, John Wise, planned an insurrection to overthrow the provisional government and restore the queen. The plot was discovered, and Kuhio was found guilty of misprision of treason in February 1895; he was sent to Oahu prison and fined $1,000. Chiefess Elizabeth Kahanu Kaleiwohi Kaauwai, who was in love with Kuhio, visited him every day in prison. They were married in October 1895 after his release and lived quietly in Honolulu.

Shortly after Hawaii was annexed by the United States as a territory in 1898, Princess Kaiulani died, leaving David and Kuhio as claimants to the former throne. Dissatisfied with annexation, Kuhio and Elizabeth went on a belated honeymoon around the world in 1899. Upon their return, Kuhio accepted the new state of political affairs in Hawaii and became involved with the Home Rule party composed of Hawaiians and former royalists.

In the election of 1900, Home Rulers won nine of thirteen seats in the Hawaiian senate and fourteen of twenty-seven seats in the lower house of the legislature. The Republicans, however, in power nationally, convinced Kuhio to break with the Home Rulers and join their party in 1902. He ran for territorial delegate to the U.S. Congress, despite the fact that his brother David led Hawaii's Democratic party, and defeated the incumbent Robert Wilcox (1855–1903). In Congress Kuhio devoted his energies to securing legislative appropriations for the territory and converting the Hawaiians to Americanism. He served on House committees on agriculture, coinage, weights and measures, military affairs, and territories. Over poker tables, on golf courses, and in committee rooms, Kuhio worked behind the scenes, while his wife entertained in lavish Hawaiian style. Congressmen who visited Kuhio in Hawaii became aware of the island's special needs. Kuhio was reelected in 1904 and rented an extra apartment in Washington, D.C., wherein he created a men's club called the Bird's Nest decorated with hunting trophies from Africa and plied his politics. Kuhio secured monies for Hawaiian lighthouses and new public buildings and for dredging Honolulu harbor. He repeatedly won reelection to Congress, where he obtained numerous benefits for the island. In Congress he voiced a growing fear of Oriental influence in Hawaii.

The passage of the Hawaiian Homes Commission Act in 1921 reflected Kuhio's desire to preserve the Hawaiian race from extinction by rehabilitating native Hawaiians through a homesteading program. Land would be granted to Hawaiians who desired to return to farming or ranching, and the parcels would be large enough for commercial production as well as for family sustenance. After passage of the act, approximately 200,000 acres of land were set aside for Hawaiian homesteads on the islands of Oahu, Kauai, Maui, Hawaii, and Molokai. Claimants had to be twenty-one years old and have 50 percent or more Hawaiian blood to qualify for 99-year leases that were inheritable by heirs with the same qualifications. Loans could be obtained from the commission to build homes and purchase livestock or farming equipment.

Kuhio's other political policies focused on lobbying for price supports on Hawaiian sugar, appropriations for the leper colony at Kalaupapa, and increased aid for public schools. Kuhio was a strong advocate of prohibition. In 1919 the secretary of the navy, Josephus Daniels, visited Hawaii at Kuhio's invitation, and the naval board subsequently approved $27 million to carry out Kuhio's suggested improvements. Kuhio also introduced the first statehood bill for Hawaii, but it did not pass. He also endorsed the territory's bill for woman suffrage in 1919, and his wife spoke for it before the combined Hawaiian legislature.

Kuhio died at home in Honolulu after suffering a heart attack. He was given a state funeral in Hawaii with full military honors.

• Kuhio's legislation is well documented in the *Congressional Record*, and his papers may be found in the State Archives of Hawaii. For a full account of his life, see Lori Kamae, *The Empty Throne: A Biography of Hawaii's Prince Cupid* (1980). Information on Elizabeth Kalanianaole can be found in Barbara Bennett Peterson, ed., *Notable Women of Hawaii* (1984).

BARBARA BENNETT PETERSON

KUHN, Joseph Ernst (14 June 1864–12 Nov. 1935), U.S. Army officer, was born in Leavenworth, Kansas, the son of Gottlieb Victor Kuhn and Anna Maria Kempel. After graduating from high school, Kuhn received an appointment to the U.S. Military Academy at West Point, New York, in 1881. He graduated in 1885 and received a commission in the U.S. Army Corps of Engineers. Kuhn's first assignment with the Corps of Engineers took him to Detroit, Michigan, where he served as an assistant supervisor for maintaining rivers, harbors, and fortifications. Kuhn returned to West Point as an instructor in the engineering department from 1889 to 1894. In 1900, after two intervening Corps of Engineers assignments—first as a supervisor at the Presidio in San Francisco, California, and then as assistant to the chief of engineers in Washington, D.C., receiving a promotion to major in 1896—he became supervisor of facilities at West Point.

Kuhn's first overseas assignments included the Philippine Islands, Japan, and China, where in addition to his engineering duties he observed the Japanese armies in the field during the Russo-Japanese War (1904–1905) and assisted in the building of fortifications in the Philippines. He returned to the United States in 1906, reporting to the commander of the Corps of Engineers in Norfolk, Virginia, where as chief engineer he was charged with the maintenance of rivers and harbors. From 1909 to 1915 he served as director of instruction at the U.S. Army Command and General Staff College, Fort Leavenworth, Kansas; head of the Corps of Engineers office in Philadelphia, Pennsylvania; and commanding officer at the army's depot and School of Engineering in Washington, D.C.

In 1915, the same year that he was promoted to colonel, Kuhn was sent to the U.S. Embassy in Berlin,

Germany, where he served as military attaché and military observer. This assignment proved to be as fortuitous for the army as it was for Kuhn: he was in a position to make observations that would be of great value two years later when the United States entered World War I. In 1916 he married Caroline Waugh Parker; they had two children. On his return home—to head the army's War College—the insights he had gained in Germany helped him to prepare his students for the battlefields on the Western Front. His knowledge of German military capabilities also caused him to be concerned about the state of America's preparedness for war; when he queried supply bureau chiefs as to how long it would take to equip an army of one million men, he received answers ranging from nine months to two and a half years. Kuhn had a deep respect for the professionalism of the German army even as he focused on engaging it in battle.

On 6 April 1917 the United States declared war on Germany, and the army quickly began mobilizing for service overseas. When the War Department ordered the formation of the Seventy-ninth Division, it selected Kuhn as its commanding officer, a post he would hold until the Armistice with the rank of brigadier general. Kuhn assumed command in August, and with the prospect of trench warfare in mind, he immediately set out to prepare the division for service in France with the American Expeditionary Force (AEF). In June advance detachments of the division embarked for France, arriving at the port of Brest. The division eventually occupied the Avorcourt sector in preparation for the Meuse-Argonne operation (Sept. 1918). Attacking toward Montfaucon, Kuhn's division captured Haucourt as well as Malancourt after bitter fighting and for three straight days remained on the attack, eventually pushing north toward St.-Mihiel. Kuhn's division went on to fight at Troyon, in Lorraine, and joined with French troops to clear this sector as the Germans fought a bitter rearguard action. Participating in the final offensive of the war, the division captured Crepion, Wavrille, Gibercy, and Ville-devant-Chaumont.

After the Armistice in November 1918, the Seventy-ninth Division took part in enforcing the surrender agreement, assisted with battlefield reclamation, and guarded enemy prisoners and material captured in the war. Kuhn remained with the division until its deactivation at Camp Dix, New Jersey, in May 1919 and went on to assume commands at Camp Kearney, California (1919–1920), Schofield Barracks, Hawaii (1920–1923), and Vancouver Barracks, Washington (1923–1925). He was promoted to major general in 1925. For a time it appeared that he might succeed General John J. Pershing as the army's chief of staff, but this appointment never materialized.

Kuhn retired from the army in 1925 and took a position as technical adviser to the Copley Press. He was a member of the advisory board to the San Diego branch of the Pacific States Building and Loan Association, and he served as chairman of the San Diego Chapter of the American Red Cross. In 1932, his first wife having

died, he married Helen Spires. He remained active in the San Diego area until his death there.

Kuhn distinguished himself throughout his military career as a military professional who understood the complexities of modern war. His leadership and skill in handling large numbers of troops earned him the distinguished French Croix de Guerre as well as the U.S. Army's Legion of Merit award.

• The U.S. Military Academy holds in its papers collection eleven boxes of Kuhn's material, CU 3058 (1934). Biographical information appears in Edward M. Coffman, *The War to End All Wars*, 2d ed. (1986) and William A. Stofft et al., *Order of Battle of United States Land Forces in the World War: American Expeditionary Forces: Divisions*, vol. 2 (1988); the latter can be found at the Center for Military History in Washington, D.C. "Joseph Ernst Kuhn, Class of 1885," *USMA, Annual Report* 3058 (1937) is a biographical memorial; an obituary is in the *New York Times*, 13 Nov. 1935.

LEO J. DAUGHERTY

KUHN, Walt (27 Oct. 1877–13 July 1949), painter, was born Walter Francis Kuhn in Brooklyn, New York, the son of Francis Kuhn and Amalia Hergenhan, who had emigrated from Bavaria in 1861 and established a food supply business. During Kuhn's childhood his mother, the granddaughter of a Spanish diplomat, took him to the theater and also encouraged his interest in drawing and painting. He attended local schools but left high school in 1893 after selling a drawing to a magazine. He then enrolled at the Brooklyn Polytechnic Institute and attended art classes there for several years. During the late 1890s Kuhn supported his artistic ambitions by working in a sporting goods store and running a bicycle shop. In 1899 he moved to San Francisco and became a cartoonist for a local newspaper, *The Wasp*.

Kuhn aspired to become a serious artist, however, and his father agreed to sponsor his training abroad. Kuhn returned to New York and in early 1901 sailed for Europe. He enrolled at the Académie Colarossi in Paris but did not like the city, and after only a brief stay he traveled on to Germany. During the summer of 1901 he studied with Hans von Hayek in Dachau, and that fall he enrolled at the Royal Academy in Munich as a pupil of Heinrich von Zügel, an animal painter. After two years Kuhn returned to New York City, where he painted neoimpressionist canvases in the evenings while working days as a cartoonist for the magazines *Punch*, *Judge*, and *Life*. He also contributed cartoons to several newspapers, including the *New York World*, where he soon became a full-time cartoonist. Kuhn married Vera Spier, a jewelry designer from Washington, D.C., early in 1909; the couple later had one child. In April of that year Kuhn quit his job at the *World* to devote more time to painting.

Kuhn had become increasingly familiar with the New York art world, in part by attending weekly studio receptions of the painter Robert Henri, whose style was a major influence on his work. He also made connections as a faculty member at the New York School of Art during the winter of 1908–1909. In 1910 he began what was to become an important friendship with another New York painter, Arthur B. Davies.

Kuhn had his first one-man show at the Madison Gallery during the winter of 1910–1911; the response was generally favorable. In December 1911 he and three other painters—Henry Fitch Taylor, Jerome Myers, and Elmer Livingston MacRae—met at the gallery to organize a society for the exhibition of works by themselves and other progressive painters, both European and American. The resulting organization was the Association of American Painters and Sculptors, established in 1912. Arthur B. Davies became its president and Kuhn the executive secretary.

In the fall of 1912 Kuhn traveled to Europe to collect paintings for a show sponsored by the association and planned for the coming year. He gathered the most avant-garde canvases he could find in Cologne, The Hague, Munich, and Berlin and then joined Davies and expatriate painter Walter Pach in Paris, where the three men acquired more paintings on loan for the show. The resulting exhibition was held at the sixty-ninth Regiment Armory on Twenty-fifth Street in New York City, where it opened on 17 February 1913. The Armory Show, as it was called, introduced the American public to works by Vincent Van Gogh, Pablo Picasso, Henri Matisse, Marcel Duchamp, Raoul Dufy, and Paul Signac and also showed paintings by neglected American modernists, including Albert Pinkham Ryder, John Sloan, Charles Sheeler, William Glackens, and George Bellows.

The Armory Show was a sensation. Though it sparked enormous controversy among traditionalists—Duchamp's *Nude Descending a Staircase* was particularly singled out for scorn—it proved to be a turning point in American art. Progressive painting in the United States had most recently been concerned with scenic realism, but the varied experiments of European modernism signaled to both American painters and their audience that a new benchmark had been created abroad.

As a consequence of the Armory Show, Kuhn, like Davies and many of their contemporaries, changed his style in the following decade to reflect cubist and other modernist influences. Kuhn did not realize much financial success at this time, however, and in addition to his paintings he supplemented his income by designing theater and circus costumes. His early love of the theater also led him to create vaudeville routines as a means of support. During this time he acted as an adviser to several wealthy art collectors, including the prominent patron John Quinn.

During the 1920s Kuhn struggled for recognition as he tried to find a mature style uniquely his own. Beginning in the spring of 1925 he spent a year abroad, leaving his family at home while he systematically studied Old Master paintings in the Louvre and the Prado, especially the works of Goya and Rembrandt. He was also drawn to Greek and Egyptian art and borrowed from those styles in creating his own. Upon his return to New York City in 1926 he began teaching at the Art Students League. His mature style was in evidence by 1929, when he painted one of his best-known canvases, *The White Clown*.

In the 1930s Kuhn finally achieved the recognition he had sought for so long. First the Whitney Museum in New York City bought a major painting, *The Blue Clown*; then Kuhn began exhibiting regularly at the city's Marie Harriman Gallery, and critics praised him for his work. He became best known for his depictions of circus performers and clowns, which expressed pathos without sentimentality, although he continued to paint landscapes and still lifes as well. During the 1930s Kuhn also designed club car interiors for several streamliners, including the *City of Denver* and the *City of Los Angeles*; he later provided decorative panels for the *City of Los Angeles*. In 1939 he wrote and produced *Walt Kuhn's Adventures in Art*, a motion picture about his work. Reproductions of his major paintings to date were published in book form a year later (*Fifty Paintings by Walt Kuhn* [1940]).

Kuhn painted regularly at his studio on East Eighteenth Street in New York City until the fall of 1948, when he suffered a nervous breakdown following his last one-man show and had to be hospitalized. His health continued to deteriorate, and he died in White Plains, New York.

Today Kuhn's work can be found in major public and private collections of American painting in the United States and abroad. Although he did not attain the stature of a Thomas Eakins, Winslow Homer, or Edward Hopper, most knowledgeable critics would rank him as a notable American artist. His greatest contribution was not his painting, however, but his creation of the Armory Show of 1913, and for this he is considered a major figure in American cultural history.

• Biographical information on Walt Kuhn can be found in the exhibition catalog *Walt Kuhn, 1877–1949* (1960; Cincinnati Art Museum); Philip R. Adams, *Walt Kuhn, Painter: His Life and Work* (1978); and *Who Was Who in America*, vol. 2 (1950). See also Milton Brown, *The Story of the Armory Show* (1963; 2d ed., 1988); Brown, *American Painting: From the Armory Show to the Depression* (1955); and the fiftieth-anniversary issue of *Art in America* 51, no. 1 (1963), which is devoted entirely to the Armory Show of 1913. In addition, see Kuhn's pamphlet, *The Story of the Armory Show* (1938). An obituary is in the *New York Times*, 14 July 1949; see also the obituary notice in *ArtNews*, Sept. 1949.

ANN T. KEENE

KUIPER, Gerard Peter (7 Dec. 1905–24 Dec. 1973), astronomer, was born Gerrit Pieter Kuiper in Harenkarspel, The Netherlands, the son of Gerrit Kuiper, a tailor, and Antje de Vries. Local schools failed to provide Kuiper with the credentials required by the Dutch university system, but he passed a special examination to enter the astronomy program at the University of Leiden. Kuiper began his studies in September 1924, earning the B.Sc. in 1927 and the Ph.D. in 1933. During his years at Leiden he studied with theoretical physicist Paul Ehrenfest and astronomers Ejnar Hertzsprung, Willem de Sitter, and Jan Oort. Kuiper became an assistant at the university observatory in 1928 and served as a member of the Dutch solar eclipse expedition to Sumatra in 1929.

Following completion of his Ph.D., Kuiper accepted a research fellowship at the Lick Observatory in California. He worked with the noted astronomer Robert G. Aitken for the next two years, expanding the statistical survey of double stars that had served as his doctoral research at Leiden. He also determined more accurately the mass-luminosity relationship of main-sequence stars and showed that white dwarfs were stars of high mass that did not follow this relationship. Kuiper joined the Harvard College Observatory staff in August 1935 but soon accepted a position at the Yerkes Observatory of the University of Chicago. Before moving to Chicago, Kuiper married Sarah Parker Fuller in 1936; two children were born to the couple. Appointed assistant professor of astronomy at the university, he was promoted to associate professor in 1937, the same year he became a naturalized citizen, and professor in 1943. While continuing his stellar research, Kuiper participated in the design and construction of the 82-inch reflecting telescope for the McDonald Observatory near Fort Davis, Texas. Jointly operated by Yerkes and the University of Texas, the facility was completed in March 1939. Kuiper remained at the University of Chicago until 1960, serving as Yerkes director from 1947 to 1949 and again from 1957 to 1960.

In 1943 Kuiper took a leave of absence from Yerkes to work on radar countermeasures at Harvard's Radio Research Laboratory. He joined Eighth Air Force headquarters in England the following year as an operations analyst to continue his investigations under field conditions. He participated in the ALSOS mission to assess the state of German science and, in early 1945, was instrumental in rescuing the eminent scientist Max Planck from eastern Germany. During the war years as well Kuiper had refocused his research interests toward planetary astronomy. Returning to the McDonald Observatory during the winter of 1943–1944, he found spectrographic evidence of methane on Saturn's moon Titan, the first discovery of an atmosphere on a satellite.

Kuiper expanded his planetary research after the war, discovering the fifth satellite of Uranus (Miranda) in February 1948 and the second moon of Neptune (Nereid) the following May. Kuiper also addressed the question of solar system formation, suggesting that a small amount of the solar system's primeval material remained as comet nuclei in the region beyond the orbit of Uranus. Although this concept had little impact when Kuiper proposed it in the early 1950s, theoretical and observational work forty years later confirmed the "Kuiper belt" as the source of many short-period comets and as the location of primeval solar system material.

The 1950s also witnessed Kuiper's increasing interest in the study of the Moon. In an attempt to codify existing information, Kuiper suggested the production of a photographic lunar atlas that would include high-resolution photographs from various observatories. With support from the National Science Foundation beginning in 1957, he coordinated the preparation of the *Photographic Lunar Atlas* and oversaw its publication in 1960.

The lunar atlas project failed to compensate for Kuiper's growing dissatisfaction with his position at Yerkes Observatory. Increasingly burdened by administrative duties, he also recognized that his lunar studies were not highly regarded by his colleagues, most of whom pursued stellar and galactic research. Kuiper thus began to consider the establishment of a separate institute in the American Southwest to further the lunar research he had initiated. The recent selection of Kitt Peak as the national observatory site indicated the superiority of southern Arizona for visual astronomy and convinced Kuiper that the astronomy program at the University of Arizona in Tucson would experience significant growth. In early 1960 the university announced that it would house the institute. During the summer Kuiper and his Yerkes staff moved to Tucson and established the Lunar and Planetary Laboratory.

While coordinating the move to Tucson, Kuiper began his long association with the National Aeronautics and Space Administration (NASA). Invited to serve on the agency's Planetary and Interplanetary Sciences Subcommittee in May 1960, Kuiper soon began to receive significant NASA support for the expansion of his laboratory. Major funding from NASA during the 1960s included $1.2 million for the Space Sciences Building on the university campus and various grants to erect large telescopes on the Santa Catalina Mountains north of Tucson. Kuiper also contributed to the development of various NASA space probes. Following the failure of the first five Ranger probes to the Moon, the program was reorganized under Kuiper in 1963; the redesigned spacecraft were much more successful. The Lunar and Planetary Laboratory remained actively involved with NASA space probes throughout the next four decades. Kuiper retired as laboratory director in 1973 but retained his teaching and research positions at the University of Arizona.

Beginning in the late 1950s Kuiper was also actively involved in site surveys for new observatories. He conducted early examinations of Cerro Tololo in Chile and Mauna Kea in Hawaii, both of which emerged as major observatory locations in the 1970s. In mid-December 1973, despite a heart attack earlier in the year, Kuiper traveled to Mexico to coordinate an aerial survey of possible observatory sites in the Guadalajara area and to record two television programs on astronomy. He suffered a fatal heart attack in Mexico City.

Described by colleagues as a very private individual who was often polite to the point of deference, Kuiper was also a person to drive himself and others to complete tasks quickly and effectively. He received many awards during his lifetime, including election to the National Academy of Sciences and the Janssen Medal of the French Astronomical Society. His native country honored him with the rank of commander, Order of Orange-Nassau, in 1947. Craters have been named after Kuiper on the Moon, Mars, and Mercury.

• The principal collection of Kuiper manuscript material is housed in the Special Collections Department of the University of Arizona Library in Tucson. Other relevant archival material may be found in the Mary Lea Shane Archives of Lick Observatory at the University of California, Santa Cruz, and in the Yerkes Archives of the University of Chicago. Important articles authored by Kuiper include "The Empirical Mass-Luminosity Relation," *Astrophysical Journal* 88 (1938): 472–507; "Titan: A Satellite with an Atmosphere," *Astrophysical Journal* 100 (1944): 378–83; and "On the Origin of the Solar System," in *Astrophysics*, ed. J. A. Hynek (1951), pp. 357–424. Kuiper edited *The Atmospheres of the Earth and Planets* (1949), *The Solar System* (4 vols., 1953–1963), and *Telescopes* (1960). A comprehensive survey of his career with a complete list of publications is Dale P. Cruikshank, "Gerard Peter Kuiper," National Academy of Sciences, *Biographical Memoirs* 62 (1993): 258–95. Also see Ewen A. Whitaker, *The University of Arizona's Lunar and Planetary Laboratory: Its Founding and Early Years* (1985); Joseph N. Tatarewicz, *Space Technology and Planetary Astronomy* (1990); and Ronald E. Doel, *Solar System Astronomy: Communities, Patronage, and Interdisciplinary Research, 1920–1960* (1996). An obituary is in the *New York Times*, 25 Dec. 1973.

GEORGE E. WEBB

KUMMER, Clare Rodman Beecher (9 Jan. 1873–22 Apr. 1958), playwright and songwriter, was born in Brooklyn, New York, the daughter of Eugene Francis Beecher. Her father, a nephew of Henry Ward Beecher, was a man of comfortable means and an amateur tunesmith, and he encouraged his daughter's interest in the arts. The young girl's mother (whose name cannot be ascertained) was equally dedicated to the arts and frequently entertained guests at gatherings for the performance of music and the reading of plays. In 1885 at the age of twelve Clare Beecher was enrolled in the Packer Collegiate Institute in Brooklyn. Leaving after three years, she went on to study music privately. In 1895 she married Frederic Arnold Kummer, a civil engineer at the time, but better known in later years as a playwright and novelist. The couple had one child, a daughter, Marjorie, who in adulthood acted in her mother's plays. The marriage ended in divorce, but the genteel theatrical press of the day omitted all mention of the divorce in interviews and almost invariably referred to Clare Kummer as "Miss Kummer." Having gained a measure of fame under that surname, she retained it professionally for the rest of her life. In 1910 she married again, to Arthur Henry, also a playwright.

Although it was as a comic dramatist that she achieved her most memorable work, Kummer initially won attention as a songwriter. This occurred in 1903, when two of her first songs, "Egypt" and "Sufficiency," were chosen to amplify the score of a Broadway musical, *The Girl from Kay's*. In 1905 she contributed the song "Dearie" to another musical, *Sergeant Brue*. "Dearie" soon became one of the most popular numbers of the era; the sheet music sales ran to over a million copies, making her too much money, Kummer later observed, to think quite yet of turning playwright. It was not until 1912 that she received an introduction to the art of creating stage dialogue, when she collaborated with Sydney Rosenfeld, a seasoned writer of musical-comedy librettos, on the adaptation of a Viennese operetta, *The Opera Ball*.

Some four years later while motoring on Long Island, Kummer was shown an estate whose owners were often absent and left it in charge of their twenty servants. It occurred to her that in such circumstances the servants would be tempted to live as luxuriously as their employers, and in this she saw the makings of a comedy. The result, *Good Gracious Annabelle*, which opened in 1916 to popular and critical acclaim, was her first independent work to reach Broadway. In this comedy and those that followed, she demonstrated a subtlety and slyness of wit seldom found on the popular stage in her time.

In addition to her initial hit, among her best plays are *A Successful Calamity* (1917; written for the popular actor-playwright William Gillette, a relation by marriage), *Be Calm, Camilla* (1918), *Rollo's Wild Oat* (1920), and *Her Master's Voice* (1933)—each a lightly satiric portrait of the well-to-do. Frequently appearing in her casts was her son-in-law, the English-born comic actor Roland Young. His droll underacting matched perfectly her delicate, understated comic style. "May I sit down?" says his character in *A Successful Calamity*. "It doesn't take me long to get up."

During the 1920s Kummer developed scenarios for the Fox Film Corporation. Later, the success of *Her Master's Voice* brought her a contract to write screenplays for Metro-Goldwyn-Mayer; no films, however, resulted from the contract. Meanwhile, Broadway continued to attract her; neither the passing of the years, the death of Arthur Henry in 1934, nor the declining popularity of her work lessened her enthusiasm for the stage. Her last play, *Many Happy Returns*, was produced in 1945. She died in Carmel, California.

Published interviews with Kummer suggest an attractive social manner, a sure sense of her own talent, and a reluctance to discuss her personal life. She took greater pleasure in talking about her characters. Of them she once remarked, "The rich make beautiful comedies. They are so irrepressible; they are so unrestrained. . . . They make comedies of themselves, I assure you."

• Information on the life of Clare Kummer is regrettably sparse. No detailed, accurate obituary has come to light. Of only limited value are the miscellaneous press clippings on her life and career in the files and scrapbooks of the New York Public Library for the Performing Arts at Lincoln Center. The same collection also has files on Frederic Arnold Kummer and Arthur Henry. For a detailed, extended interview, see "Clare Kummer's Story," *New York Times*, 11 Feb. 1917. For a shrewd analysis of Kummer's dramatic technique, see P. L., "Clare Kummer," *New Republic*, 20 Apr. 1921.

MALCOLM GOLDSTEIN

KUNITZ, Moses (19 Dec. 1887–20 Apr. 1978), biochemist, was born in Slonim, Russia, the son of David Kunitz and Celia Resnik. He immigrated to the United States in 1909. Shortly after his arrival in America, Kunitz worked in a factory that manufactured straw hats; in 1910 he attended the Cooper Union Evening School of Chemistry. Kunitz married Sarah Blum in 1912, and they had two children. He became a U.S. citizen in 1915. In 1913 he obtained a job as a technical assistant in the laboratory of Jacques Loeb, an experimental physiologist and head of the laboratory of General Physiology at the Rockefeller Institute for Medical Research (now the Rockefeller University), remaining in that position until 1923. Encouraged by Loeb, Kunitz continued his education for two years at the Electrical Engineering School of Cooper Union, earning a B.S. in 1916, and one year at the Extension School of Columbia University. Kunitz studied two more years at Columbia's School of Mines, Engineering, and Chemistry. In 1922 he enrolled in Columbia University as a graduate student in biochemistry, earning a Ph.D. in biochemistry in 1924. At the Rockefeller Institute for Medical Research (RIMR), he was an assistant in general physiology from 1923 to 1925 and an associate in general physiology from 1926 to 1940. He was appointed an associate member in 1940, a member in 1950, and member emeritus in 1953. When the RIMR became a degree-granting institution, he was named professor.

Kunitz's early work in the laboratory of Jacques Loeb explored the properties of gelatins in salt solutions. These experiments illustrated the behavior of proteins and the importance of pH in determining the binding ions of proteins and led to the development of scientific instruments used to measure osmotic pressure and cataphoresis. Subsequent research cannot be discussed without the mention of fellow RIMR colleague John H. Northrop. Kunitz began his association with Northrop in 1924, the year of Loeb's death. From 1924 to 1931, with Northrop, Kunitz continued his investigation of topics related to the properties of gelatin and proteins. In 1928 his wife died.

In 1930 Northrop and Kunitz isolated pure crystalline pepsin, a digestive enzyme, in order to determine whether pepsin was composed of one or several proteins. By 1931, using the phase rule solubility method, which tests for the purity of proteins, Kunitz and Northrop demonstrated that pepsin crystals were composed of one protein. Kunitz, however, faced difficulties in isolating the pancreatic enzyme trypsin. He was able to purify and crystallize the precursor of trypsin and chymotrypsin from the beef pancreas, then activating the enzymes and recrystallizing them in active form. They applied the phase rule method to crystalline trypsin and chymotrypsin, thereby determining that these enzymes were also pure proteins. In 1932 he fully described the molecular properties and range of activity of crystalline trypsin. In 1936 Kunitz and Northrop clarified the mechanism of digestive enzymes by illustrating why these enzymes do not destroy human tissue by identifying and isolating, in pure form, a trypsin isolator. The research of this period was presented in the book *Crystalline Enzymes*, 2d ed. (1948), by Northrop, Kunitz, and Roger Herriott. In addition, Kunitz, Northrop, and M. L. Anson established methods of determining the molecular weight and volume and the hydration of various proteins.

In 1939 Kunitz married Rebecca Shamaskin. From 1939 to 1952 he successfully isolated pure crystalline ribonuclease (RNase) (1940) and deoxyribonuclease (1948). Through Kunitz's scientific work, these enzymes—which are important to the fields of genetics and virology—were purified, commercially produced, and made available to other researchers, thus enabling further biochemical studies. In the 1940s scientists used these products in research that ultimately proved that DNA was a carrier of genetic or inheritable material, and later in the 1950s experiments illustrated the infectious nature of viral RNA and DNA. Kunitz also isolated and crystallized many other important enzymes including chymotrypsinogen, trypsinogen, and pyrophosphatase.

With the advent of World War II, Kunitz was called on as one of several scientists to become involved with government research at the RIMR. In 1941 the RIMR and the U.S. Office of Scientific Research and Development (OSRD) initiated the investigation of lethal gases used in battle. Kunitz, with Northrop, studied the physiological action of mustard gas once released into the environment. Also at this time and into the early 1950s Kunitz worked on the isolation and characterization of hexokinase and inorganic pyrophosphate from baker's yeast.

Between 1926 and 1949 Kunitz and Northrop conducted all research at the RIMR's branch of Animal and Plant Pathology in Princeton, New Jersey. With the closing of the Princeton branch in 1950, Northrop moved to the University of California at Berkeley while Kunitz returned to the RIMR's New York City site in 1949 and was promoted to full member. During the last productive years of his life, he studied the alkaline phosphatase of the chicken intestine and an invertase of yeast. However, Kunitz was unsuccessful in isolating the pure crystalline forms of these materials.

Kunitz was named Carl Neuberg Medalist by the American Society of European Chemists and Pharmacists in 1957 and elected a member of the National Academy of Sciences in 1967. He was a member of the Society of Experimental Biology, the American Society of Biological Chemists, the Society of General Physiologists, and the American Association for the Advancement of Science. He left Rockefeller for good in 1972 and lived with his daughter in Lasdale, Pennsylvania. He died in a Philadelphia nursing home.

• The papers of Moses Kunitz are in the Rockefeller University Archives at the Rockefeller Archive Center, Tarrytown, New York, and comprise laboratory notes and records, laboratory photographs, memorabilia, and reprints. For a comprehensive summary of Kunitz's scientific career, see George W. Corner, *A History of the Rockefeller Institute, 1901–1953: Origins and Growth* (1965); and National Academy of Sciences, *Biographical Memoirs* 58 (1989): 305–17. See also the obituary written by Roger M. Herriott in *Nature*, 28 Sept. 1978, pp. 351–52, and the obituary in the *New York Times*, 25 Apr. 1978.

RENEE D. MASTROCCO

KUNKEL, Louis Otto (7 May. 1884–20 Mar. 1960), plant virologist, was born in Audrain County near Mexico, Missouri, the son of Henry Kunkel and Katie Price Spencer, homestead farmers. At age sixteen he left school to harvest wheat in the Midwest before moving on to budding peaches in a nursery, where he gained a lifelong interest in peach trees and their diseases. he returned to high school in 1903 and in 1906 entered the University of Missouri at Columbia; he received his first exposure to botany a year later at a lecture by a visiting Cornell University scientist and well-known mycologist, Benjamin Minge Duggar. Kunkel obtained a B.S. in education in 1909, an A.B. in 1910, and an M.A. in 1911, having served as assistant in botany from 1909 to 1911. After spending the following academic year in the Henry Shaw School of Botany of Washington University at the Missouri Botanical Garden in St. Louis, he went to Columbia University, where his scientific outlook was influenced by his association with Robert A. Harper, head of the botany department. Kunkel completed his dissertation on factors affecting the toxicity of inorganic salts to the fungus *Neurospora sitophila* and received his Ph.D. in Botany in 1914. He married Johanna Caroline Wortman in 1915; they had four children.

Immediately following graduate school Kunkel became a pathologist with the Bureau of Plant Industry of the U.S. Department of Agriculture (USDA) in Washington, D.C., conducting studies on powdery scab and wart diseases of potato and on clubroot of cabbage. He received a fellowship for 1915 and 1916 to study in Germany, Holland, and Sweden, kindling an interest in virus diseases of potatoes. A desire to work in the tropics led Kunkel to request leave from the USDA in 1920 to take a position as associate pathologist with the hawaiian Sugar Planters' Association. The mysteries of the virus diseases of sugar cane enthralled him. Within four months he had solved the puzzle of the transmission of the virus that caused sugar cane mosaic. The virus was transmitted, Kunkel demonstrated, not by aphids living on sugar cane, as others had suggested, but by an aphid that attempted to feed on sugar cane in the absence of its customary weed hosts. Thus Kunkel took the first major steps along a research path in virology that he would follow the rest of his life.

Returning to the U.S. mainland in 1923, Kunkel accepted a position as pathologist at the new Boyce Thompson Institute for Plant Research in Yonkers, New York. As a researcher and administrator from 1924 to 1932, he guided the nascent science of plant virology in the United States. His research concentrated on characterizing the nature of plant viruses, determining whether they were microorganisms or non-living chemicals, and elucidating the relationships among viruses, insect vectors, and host plants. From diseased asters, Kunkel demonstrated that one species (*Macrosteles fascifrons*) of the small, plant-feeding insects called leafhoppers transmitted the aster yellows virus (now known to be a phytoplasma). He found the virus infecting and overwintering in more than forty different plant families and reproducing in both the plant and the leafhopper. He also solved a perplexing mystery of pathogen transmission when he found that a leafhopper (*Macropsis trimaculata*) was the insect vector of peach yellows. As director of research in plant pathology Kunkel assembled a brilliant research team, including Francis O. Holmes, the originator of the local lesion assay for plant viruses, Helen Purdy Beale, the first scientist to use serology for plant virus identification, and Wendell M. Stanley, a future Nobel laureate in chemistry for his crystallization of tobacco mosaic virus and for the first isolation of a self-reproducing, mutable pathogen on the borderline between living and nonliving matter.

Early in the 1939s plans to add a division of plant pathology to the program of comparative pathology at the Princeton branch of the Rockefeller Institute for Medical Research led to the successful recruitment of Kunkel to head this new division. After visiting many American and European laboratories of plant pathology, he brought many innovations to the new laboratory and assembled a group of outstanding young scientists, including eight from the Boyce Thompson Institute, to continue groundbreaking studies on plant viruses. The next seventeen years of research at the Princeton laboratories coincided with an era of unparalleled growth in plant virology worldwide, Kunkel continued his emphasis on yellows diseases and found that many of them could be cured through heat treatments tolerated by the host plants. As a control technique, heat treatment proved to be a tremendous benefit to commercial plant growers.

In 1949, when the plant pathology laboratories of the Rockefeller Institute at Princeton were integrated into the parent institute in New York City, Kunkel supervised the construction of the new laboratory and greenhouse facilities. In July 1949 he became an emeritus member of the Rockefeller Institute, but he remained as head of the plant pathology group until 1955, when he returned to his own research full time. During the later part of his career Kunkel demonstrated the phenomenon of cross-protection, in which infection of a plant by one strain of the aster yellows virus protected against another, more virulent strain of the virus. His last major discovery was the demonstration of a similar cross-protection phenomenon in the insect vectors of aster yellows.

Kunkel continued to unravel the mysteries of plant viruses, phytoplasmas, and their insect vectors until his death in Newtown, Pennsylvania. He influenced the science of plant virology, which developed largely during the time of his active research, at all stages. The Nobel laureate Wendell Stanley (1965) wrote of Kunkel, "He tended to be very practical and had a flair for devising experiments that always seemed to yield results that provided decisive answers to problems of importance."

Kunkel was elected to the National Academy of Sciences (1932) and the American Philosophical Society (1942). He received the Certificate of Merit from the Botanical Society of America in 1956 and the Distinguished Service Award of the New York Botanical Garden in 1959. He was a member of the Botanical Society of America, the American Phytopathological Society, the American Society of Naturalists, Phi Beta Kappa, and Sigma Xi. Kunkel's scientific insight, administrative prowess, and ability to recruit and retain the best scientists for his programs placed the developing area of plant virology on a firm scientific foundation and nurtured it from relative infancy to maturity as a discipline within plant pathology and the biological sciences.

• Kunkel's papers (1930–1959) are in the Rockefeller University Archives, Rockefeller Archive Center, North Tarrytown, N.Y. For biographical and bibliographical information see Wendell M. Stanley, *Louis Otto Kunkel, May 7, 1844–March 20, 1960*, National Academy of Sciences, *Biographical Memoirs* 38 (1965): 145–60. See also F. O. Holmes, "Louis Otto Kunkel, 1884–1960," *Phytopathology* 50 (1960): 777–78; and K. Maramorosch, "Louis Otto Kunkel (1884–1960)," *Review of Tropical Plant Pathology* 7 (1992): 101–12. An obituary is in the *New York Times*, 22 Mar. 1960.

C. LEE CAMPBELL

KUNSTLER, William Moses (7 July 1919–4 Sept. 1995), attorney and political activist, was born in New York City, the son of Monroe Bradford Kunstler, a prosperous physician, and Frances Mandelbaum. A French major and varsity swimmer, he graduated Phi Beta Kappa from Yale University in 1941. Kunstler volunteered for the signal corps in World War II and rose to the rank of major, winning the Bronze Star for his service in the Pacific. After the war he attended Columbia Law School, graduating in 1948. While in law school he wrote book reviews for the *New York Times*, *New York Herald Tribune*, *Life Magazine*, *Atlantic Monthly*, and various other papers in New York, Boston, Chicago, and San Francisco, often writing under the pen name David Tilden. He also taught a writing class at Columbia University and read books for Paramount Pictures, recommending titles for movies. Kunstler later said he "was a student at Columbia for all the wrong reasons; because it offered status, prestige and the promise of a reasonably high income" (*The Independent*, 6 Sept. 1995).

After law school Kunstler opened a small practice with his brother and taught part time at New York Law School. He recommended his Columbia classmate, Roy Cohn, for a part-time teaching position, and Cohn returned the favor by bringing him an early client, Senator Joseph McCarthy, whose will Kunstler prepared. Kunstler later wrote he recommended Cohn "because I had no inkling then of what a total snake he was" and that when he drafted McCarthy's will "I was not at all political then and felt privileged to draw up

the will of a U.S. Senator" (*My Life as a Radical Lawyer*, p. 89).

In the 1950s Kunstler wrote radio scripts for one station and did interview shows for another. He also began representing civil rights clients in New York, including the black journalist William Worthy, who had lost his passport for traveling to China and was later convicted for going to Cuba without a passport and then returning to the United States. In 1961, in his first successful constitutional appeal, Kunstler persuaded the Fifth Circuit Court of Appeals that the law under which Worthy was convicted was unconstitutional.

Kunstler published *Beyond a Reasonable Doubt?* (1961), which protested, on the grounds that the trial was unfair, the recent execution in California of Caryl Chessman. That June the American Civil Liberties Union (ACLU) asked Kunstler to serve as a pro bono counsel to the freedom riders in Jackson, Mississippi, who were challenging segregated facilities in the South by riding on buses in integrated groups. By the end of that year he had become what he called "a special trial counsel" for the Reverend Martin Luther King, Jr. For the next few years Kunstler spent increasingly large amounts of time in the South representing civil rights workers. Comparing his new career to his earlier law practice, he later wrote, "In the South, I was reborn into a man I liked better, one who contributed to society and tried to make a difference" (*My Life*, p. 105).

During this period Kunstler was deeply involved in the civil rights movement. In addition to representing King and other black leaders, Kunstler represented Nathan Schwerner, the father of Michael Schwerner, one of three civil rights workers who was murdered near Philadelphia, Mississippi, in 1964. He also represented the Congress of Racial Equality (CORE) and King's Southern Christian Leadership Conference (SCLC). In 1962 he won his first case in the U.S. Supreme Court, *In re Shuttlesworth* (1962). Kunstler did not personally get to argue the case because the court, without hearing any oral argument, ordered the release of the Reverend Fred L. Shuttlesworth, who had been arrested for violating a Birmingham, Alabama, segregation statute. Kunstler's tactic, a direct application to the court for a writ of habeas corpus, was a novel strategy that has since been used in many civil rights and death penalty cases.

Throughout the 1960s Kunstler continued to represent civil rights plaintiffs, but he also broadened his celebrity client base. He represented the comedian Lenny Bruce, who was often prosecuted for obscenity, and Congressman Adam Clayton Powell, Jr., when the Congress refused to seat him. In November 1963 Kunstler agreed to represent Lee Harvey Oswald, the alleged assassin of President John F. Kennedy. However, Jack Ruby assassinated Oswald before Kunstler left for Dallas. In 1966 Kunstler represented Ruby, who was then appealing his conviction for killing Oswald. Kunstler also began to represent various cultural and political radicals, including opponents of the Vietnam War, such as Jerry Rubin, Abbie Hoffman, Father Daniel Berrigan, the Black Panther party, and Student Non-violent Coordinating Committee (SNCC) leaders Stokely Carmichael (later known as Kwame Toure) and H. Rap Brown.

By 1968 the raspy-voiced, disheveled Kunstler, with his trademark wild hair, was well known in civil rights and radical circles and among legal academics. In 1969 he gained national and international fame as the lead defense attorney in the conspiracy trial of the Chicago Seven (originally the Chicago Eight before Black Panther leader Bobby Seale was tried separately). The defendants (including his existing clients Rubin and Hoffman) had been charged with conspiring to cause riots at the National Democratic Convention in Chicago in 1968. Kunstler helped turn the trial into political theater, persistently challenging and goading Federal District judge Julius Hoffman, who responded in ways that made the judge appear intolerant, clumsy, bigoted, and tyrannical. At the end of the trial Hoffman charged Kunstler with 160 counts of contempt and sentenced him to jail for four years and thirteen days. However, Kunstler served no time in jail; an appeals court overturned the convictions of the defendants and virtually all of the contempt citations. After the Chicago trial Kunstler remained famous, continuing to represent radicals, civil rights figures, and various outcasts.

As the civil rights and antiwar movements withered away, Kunstler was something of a radical lawyer in search of a cause. Although he continued to represent radicals and rebels, increasingly his clients included less savory figures whose crimes were either nonpolitical or outside the tradition of American politics. Thus, he represented mafia dons Raymond Patriarca, Joe Bonnano, and John Gotti; Sheik Omar Abdel-Rahman and his followers, who were accused of masterminding bombings in New York City; El Sayyid Nosair, who was charged with murdering the militant founder of the Jewish Defense League, Rabbi Meir Kahane; Yusef Salaam, who was convicted of a brutal rape in what was known as the Central Park Jogger case; Colin Ferguson, the Jamaican immigrant who shot up a crowded commuter train in 1993, killing a number of passengers; and members of the Hell's Angels motorcycle club.

In 1989 Kunstler made a lasting contribution to U.S. constitutional law in *Texas v. Johnson*. Here Kunstler successfully argued against the constitutionality of a Texas law punishing flag burning. Over the course of his career Kunstler was involved in more than sixty other Supreme Court cases, although rarely on the winning side. Indeed, the court refused to hear more than half the cases Kunstler appealed.

Over his lifetime Kunstler's clients read like a "who's who" of radical causes. He represented Malcolm X, the Reverend Benny Walls (leader of the Albany, Ga., civil rights marches), Seale of the Black Panthers, and Native-American activist Leonard Peltier. He represented federal judge Alcee Hastings in an attempt to overturn his impeachment and removal from office and Washington, D.C., mayor Marion Barry, who was convicted on cocaine charges. In addition to representing actors Joey Heatherton and Marlon Brando, Kunstler played a vengeful judge in Spike Lee's movie *Malcolm X* (1992) and played himself in Oliver Stone's movie *The Doors* (1991). He also had parts in *Mean Streets* (1973), *Carlito's Way* (1993), and *The Paper* (1994).

Kunstler married Lotte Rosenberger in 1943, and they had two daughters before divorcing. In 1975 he married Margaret Ratner, with whom he also had two daughters. Kunstler died in New York City.

• The best sources for Kunstler are his autobiography, *My Life as a Radical Lawyer* (1994), his many articles, contemporary newspaper articles, and the many books written about the events in which he participated, especially the 1969 Chicago conspiracy trial. Among his writings not mentioned above are *First Degree* (1960), . . . *And Justice for All* (1963), *The Minister and the Choir Singer* (1964), and *Deep in My Heart* (1966). Obituaries are in the *Washington Post* and the *New York Times*, both 5 Sept. 1995.

PAUL FINKELMAN

KUNZ, George Frederick (29 Sept. 1856–29 June 1932), gem expert, was born in New York City, the son of J. Gottlieb Kunz, an immigrant German baker, and Marie Ida Widmer, a native of Switzerland. When Kunz was eleven years of age he moved with his family to Hoboken, New Jersey, and attended public schools there. Unable to afford college, Kunz taught himself mineralogy after work at Cooper Union in New York. In 1879 Kunz married Sophia Handforth, with whom he had two children; she died in 1912. In 1923 he married Opal Logan Giberson; their marriage was annulled in 1930.

Kunz began working for Tiffany & Company in 1879, an association that lasted until his death. His first position was, simply, gem expert, but most of his duties involved making acquisitions, at which he was most successful. His rise was rapid, and he was made a vice president; finally he became a trustee. The contacts he gained through Tiffany & Company made Kunz a socially prominent person. His clients included important people of commerce and letters who were mineral and gem collectors: J. Pierpont Morgan, Thomas A. Edison, Irénée du Pont, Heber Reginald Bishop, Washington A. Roebling, Isaac Lea, Clarence S. Bement, and Stanley Field. Kunz also assembled and sold large collections of gems and minerals to many museums in the United States and abroad.

Kunz was special agent of precious stones, an honorary position, for the United States Geological Survey from 1883 to 1909. He was also founder and president of the New York Mineralogical Club; honorary curator of precious stones for the American Museum of Natural History; president of the American Metric Society; president of the American Scenic and Historic Preservation Society; president of the American Folklore Society; curator of the New York Academy of Sciences; secretary of the American Society of Arts and Science; corresponding secretary of the Philadelphia

Academy of Sciences; and councilor of the Grolier Club of New York. He became an officer of both the Legion of Honor of France and of the Imperial Rising Sun of Japan as well as a knight of the Order of St. Olaf of Norway. He was honored with a master's degree and two doctoral degrees. In 1903 a new pink gem variety of the mineral species *spodumene* was discovered in California, and it was named kunzite in his honor.

Kunz wrote several books about minerals and gems, including *Gems and Precious Stones of North America* (1890); *Gems, Jewelers' Materials and Ornamental Stones of California* (1905); *History of the Gems Found in North Carolina* (1907); *The Book of the Pearl*, with Charles H. Stevenson (1908), still considered to be the best work ever published on pearls; *The Curious Lore of Precious Stones* (1913); *Magic of Jewels and Charms* (1915); *Ivory and the Elephant* (1916); *Shakespeare and Precious Stones* (1916); and *Rings for the Finger* (1917). *Rings for the Finger*, all about the ring from antiquity to modern times, is dedicated to Peter Cooper and "The Cooper Union of Arts and Sciences, in the laboratories, lecture rooms and library of which the author spent useful, profitable evening hours for several years, at a time when there were no other opportunities of a similar nature in the city of New York."

Perhaps more important than Kunz's enduring published works were the many hundreds of gem- and mineral-oriented articles, scientific and popular, that he wrote for the various journals of his day and the many topical and timely newspaper interviews he granted on these subjects. Through these publications, with the prestige of Tiffany & Company behind him, he gained more attention than anyone in his field had previously received. He made the world of gems, jewelry, and minerals exciting and interesting to the public (especially those gems known today as semiprecious, which were virtually ignored before his efforts on their behalf), a legacy that survives to this day.

It was the marketing of these so-called semiprecious stones that Kunz considered to be his revolutionary theory. At that time the best jewelers, his employers included, as well as private collectors were not interested in such stones. Jewelers' stocks consisted almost exclusively of diamonds, rubies, sapphires, and pearls. Kunz spoke once of showing his avant-garde treasures to Oscar Wilde, who was a collector of traditional gemstones. Wilde remarked, "But my dear Kunz, these are exquisite, charming! I believe I admire them even more than the precious stones. My dear fellow, I see a renaissance of art, a new vogue of jewelry in this idea of yours!"

Kunz died in New York City. His personal gem and mineral library, considered to be the finest in his day, was presented by his heirs to the United States Geological Survey in Reston, Virginia.

• The largest portions of Kunz's surviving correspondence are held by the American Museum of Natural History, the New-York Historical Society, and Richard Hauck of Franklin, N.J. Additional information about Kunz can be found in Herbert P. Whitlock, "Memorial to George Frederick Kunz," *Bulletin of the Geological Society of America* 44 (1933): 377–94; in Lawrence H. Conklin, *Notes and Commentaries on Letters to George F. Kunz* (1987); and in autobiographical reminiscences of Kunz "as told to Marie Beynon Ray," *Saturday Evening Post*, 26 Nov. and 10 Dec. 1927; and 21 Jan., 31 Mar., and 5 May 1928. Obituaries are in the *New York Times* and *New York Tribune*, both 30 June 1932; articles on Kunz's will and bequests are in the *New York Times*, 9 July 1932 and 7 Nov. 1933.

LAWRENCE H. CONKLIN

KUNZE, John Christopher (5 Aug. 1744–24 July 1807), Lutheran minister, was born in Mansfield, Artern-on-the-Unstrut, in Saxony, Germany, the son of Jahn Godfried Kunze, a farmer and innkeeper. Both his parents died in 1758. He studied at the Glauchau Orphan School and later at the Marburg Gymnasium. In 1763 he entered the Academy of Leipzig (later the University), where he studied history, theology, and philosophy. He taught for three years at Kloster Bergen near Madgeburg and in 1769–1770 served as an orphanage inspector at Greiz. Kunze's autobiography reveals an experiential, biblically oriented soul-searcher typical of the German Pietist tradition of the era.

Kunze was ordained a Lutheran minister in Wernigerode, Germany. He accepted an invitation to work with Henry M. Muhlenburg in Philadelphia, Pennsylvania, and arrived in New York in September 1770. Subsequently, he married Muhlenburg's twenty-year-old daughter, Margaretta Henrietta in July 1771. They had five children. He later succeeded Muhlenburg as pastor of Zion Lutheran Church in Philadelphia in 1779.

Kunze was a leading educator and organizer in the new nation. He had a working knowledge of five languages and studied medicine, astronomy, and numismatics. Although his own English-speaking ability was limited, he recognized the future of English in the United States and made a life work of educating Lutheran ministers in English. To that end, he began in 1773 a Seminarium in Philadelphia, which became a pre-theological school. The chief impetus behind the establishment of the Seminarium was funding from the Grundregeln der Gesellschaft zur Beforderung des Christenthums und aller nutzlichen Erkenntnisz unter den Teutschen in America (the Society for the Propagation of Christianity and Useful Knowledge among the Germans in America). This voluntary society became a vehicle for Christian education of youths, similar to the Charity School movement in England. One of Kunze's stated objectives was to teach English to the children of the Pennsylvania German community. The society was to be supported by wealthy patrons and church congregations.

However, during the British occupation of Philadelphia in 1776, Kunze's school closed for want of students and teachers, and he became a librarian at the colonial statehouse. In 1779 he was appointed professor of philology (later Hebrew and philosophy) at the University of Pennsylvania, where he also earned his M.A. and organized an expanded German studies program called the "Institute" that essentially folded his earlier enterprise into the University's new charter. It was Kunze's stated desire to have a distinct theological faculty in the University of Pennsylvania, based on the University of Halle model, but the trustees tabled the suggestion.

In 1784 Kunze responded to a call from a combined congregation of Trinity and Christ Churches, a Lutheran and Reformed merger in New York City. Concurrent with his pastoral labors, he was also named professor of oriental languages and literature at Columbia College. Inspired by the American Philosophical Society in Philadelphia, he helped form the Society for Useful Knowledge and served on its executive committee. He also worked with Baron von Steuben to found the German Society of New York. He was not able, however, to realize his major educational purposes in New York City and settled for a position in a new free-standing school in upstate New York.

From 1797 to 1807 Kunze served as professor of theology at the Hartwick Seminary Foundation in Otsego County, New York, earning $500 a year. His students became the first English-language-trained Lutheran ministers in the United States. He also worked hard to unite the scattered Lutheran pastors in the colonies and succeeded in 1786. Nine pastors from eighteen congregations in the New York and New Jersey region formed the Ministerium of New York at Ebenezer Church in Albany, New York, on 23 October 1786. Kunze was elected president and remained in that position until his death.

Kunze was widely respected for his scholarship and linguistic capabilities. His knowledge of Hebrew and Arabic brought rabbis and others to his circle. He produced sermons, astronomical observations and predictions, and educational proposals. In 1795 he prepared the first Lutheran hymn and prayer book in English in the United States and an edition in English of Luther's *Shorter Catechism*. He prepared a Hebrew grammar that was not published, owing to lack of Hebrew type. The U.S. Congress under the Articles of Confederation named Kunze an official translator in 1785. He was elected a member of the American Philosophical Society and served as one of its secretaries. For his efforts, the University of Pennsylvania awarded him a doctor of divinity degree at the same commencement it awarded George Washington the doctor of laws degree. Kunze was the first Lutheran clergyman to receive the degree in America. In 1986 the Lutheran Ministerium republished his *Autobiography* in recognition of his pioneering role in the Lutheran church in America.

• Kunze's works in German include *Einige Gedichte und Lieder* (1778), *Von den Absichten und dem bisherigen Fortgang der privilegirten Deutschen Gesellschaft zu Philadelphia in Pennsylvanien* (1782), and *Ein Wort für den Verstand und das Herz vom Rechten und Gebanten Lebenswege* (1781). Kunze's *Autobiography* covers the German portion of his career and was translated and edited by Donald H. Mills. The diary of his transatlantic voyage is reprinted in *Halle Reports*, vol. 2, pp. 657–71. A most informative work is Carl F. Haussmann,

Kunze's Seminarium and the Society for the Propagation of Christianity and Useful Knowledge among the Germans in America (1917), which contains transcripts of Kunze's Minute Book and details of the Seminarium. An obituary is in the *New York Herald*, 29 July 1807.

WILLIAM H. BRACKNEY

KURTZ, Benjamin (28 Feb. 1795–29 Dec. 1865), Lutheran pastor, editor, and church leader, was born in Harrisburg, Pennsylvania, the son of Benjamin Kurtz and Elizabeth Gardner. Kurtz studied theology with John George Lochman and in 1815 was licensed to preach by the Ministerium of Pennsylvania, joining his uncle, John Daniel Kurtz, in his congregation as assistant pastor for a short term. He then served as a pastor in Hagerstown, Maryland, from 1815 to 1831, and in Chambersburg, Pennsylvania, from 1831 to 1833. In 1820 he helped to form the Synod of Maryland and Virginia and later that year helped Simon Schmucker and others establish the General Synod, the first national organization of Lutheran synods in America. He joined with Schmucker in 1825 to found the Gettysburg Theological Seminary and the following year went to Europe to solicit funds and books for the fledgling institution. During his two-year tour of Europe, he managed to secure funding of $10,000 as well as five thousand books for the seminary. Through this effort, he made a name for himself both in Europe and the United States.

Kurtz was a strong advocate of many of the new trends and methods that characterized American evangelical Protestantism. In his Hagerstown congregation he introduced English-language services, prayer meetings and revivals, temperance and benevolent societies, and Sunday schools, all of which were quite new and controversial among Lutherans in America. Kurtz also suggested that some elements of historical Lutheran theology, liturgy, and practice were not suitable for American Lutherans and advocated changes to bring his church closer to the majority of American Protestants.

In 1833 Kurtz's health failed, and he was forced to leave his parish position. He accepted the invitation of John Gottlieb Morris to take over as editor of a struggling church newspaper, the *Lutheran Observer*, a position that he held in Baltimore, Maryland, until 1861. He was a very successful editor, expanding the paper to weekly publication and increasing its circulation to many thousands of copies. The *Lutheran Observer* became a major publication among American Lutherans, and Kurtz used his position as editor to increase his power and prestige within the General Synod. Through the pages of the *Observer*, he advocated and furthered the reforms he had introduced in his congregations, especially revivalism, temperance and benevolent societies, and the theological modification of American Lutheranism. His book *Why Are You a Lutheran?* (first published in 1843, with several subsequent editions) outlined his chief theological positions. He also gained attention outside of Lutheran circles. In 1846 he returned to Europe as a delegate to the meeting of the Evangelical Alliance in London, England, and during the 1850s he dueled in print with John W. Nevin, a Reformed theologian at Mercersburg Seminary. Kurtz strongly defended the so-called "new measures" in revivalism, including protracted revival meetings, emotional preaching and testimonies, and the "anxious bench," where prayers were said for those who were about to convert.

In 1855 Schmucker, Kurtz's friend and theological ally, introduced a theological document titled the *Definite Synodical Platform*, a proposal advocating an "American Lutheranism" addressed to the pastors of the General Synod that sought to reform Lutheranism. Key to this effort was the "American Recension" of the Augsburg Confession (1530), the most authoritative of the Lutheran confessions. The attempt was made to move American Lutherans theologically closer to other American Protestants by cleansing the Augsburg Confession of five "errors": approval of the ceremonies of the Mass, approval of private confession and absolution, denial of the divine obligation of the Sabbath, affirmation of baptismal regeneration, and affirmation of the real presence of the body and blood of Christ in Holy Communion. Although Kurtz strongly supported the *Platform* in the pages of the *Observer*, the proposal was soundly rejected by the majority of Lutheran synods. In 1857 Kurtz and a few friends, alarmed by the conservative Lutheran trend in the Maryland Synod, left and formed a new body, the Melanchthon Synod, which embodied the theology of the *Platform*.

In 1858 Kurtz founded the Missionary Institute (later Susquehanna University) in Selinsgrove, Pennsylvania, to meet the shortage of ministers. Although not officially in competition with Gettysburg Seminary, the new institute, with Kurtz as superintendent, sought a shortened ministerial course in practical theology and piety, as against Gettysburg's classical theological curriculum. Although the institute was intended to produce pastors in accordance with Kurtz's theological position, the effort was not generally successful, and Kurtz's declining health limited his involvement with the new institution.

Kurtz was married three times, first to Ann Barnett, who died about 1833, then to Mary Catherine Baker, who died about 1836, and then to Mary Calhoun. He died in Baltimore. Five children survived him.

Through his position as church leader and editor, Kurtz made friends who supported him strongly and enemies who detested him. Not as theologically astute and nuanced as his close friend Schmucker, he had a firm personal piety and a strong theological position. Yet for all his influence and exertions, Kurtz could not move Lutherans in America to an acceptance of the new understanding of Lutheranism that he himself embraced so fervently.

• Kurtz's papers are in the Archives of the Lutheran Theological Seminary, Gettysburg, Pa. The greatest part of his writing is in the *Lutheran Observer* (1833–1861). Charles A. Hay, *Memoirs of Rev. Jacob Goehring, Rev. George Lochmann, D.D., and Rev. Benj. Kurtz, D.D., LL.D.* (1888), is a short biography with a list of publications. John G. Morris, *Fifty Years in the Lutheran Ministry* (1878), is a personal remembrance by a close associate, as is Martin Luther Stoever, "Benjamin Kurtz, D.D., LL.D.," *Evangelical Quarterly Review* 18 (1867). Abdel R. Wentz, *History of the Evangelical Lutheran Synod of Maryland* (1920), and Wentz, *History of Gettysburg Theological Seminary* (1927), are important for historical background, as is William Clark and Arthur Wilson, *The Story of Susquehanna University* (1958). Vergilius Ferm, *The Crisis in American Lutheran Theology* (1927), studies the theological debate over "American Lutheranism," including Kurtz's role. John Groh, "Revivalism among Lutherans in America in the 1840s," *Concordia Historical Institute Quarterly* 43 (1970), examines Kurtz on revivalism and his debate with Nevin.

MARK GRANQUIST